RAND McNALLY
WORLD ATLAS
PREMIER EDITION

RAND McNALLY

WORLD ATLAS

PREMIER EDITION

ENGRAVED, PRINTED AND PUBLISHED BY

RAND McNALLY & COMPANY

NEW YORK   CHICAGO   SAN FRANCISCO

Printed in U.S.A.

EXPLANATION OF INDEX

The key letters and figures following the names of cities and towns, in the Index, refer to that point on the map at which lines, if drawn between corresponding letters at the sides and between corresponding numbers at the top and bottom of the map, will intersect. For example, locate "Chicago, B-10". If the diagram below represents the map, Chicago will be found near the intersection of lines B-B and 10-10.

Chicago..........B-10
Chicago Heights...B-10
Clinton..........H-5
Collinsville.......F-8
Danville..........J-5
Decatur..........H-6
DeKalb..........H-2
Dundee, E. & W....I-2
Duquoin.........G-10
East St. Louis.....E-9

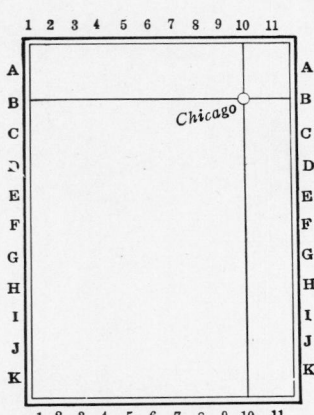

The figures placed before the names of cities and towns in the indexes on the margins of maps, denote the population in thousands or hundreds, according to the headings. Exact population figures are given in the complete indexes which follow the map section.

Reference marks on maps: State Capitals and County Seats are indicated thus on the U. S. State maps: State Capital, ◉; County Seat, ⊙.

1947?

H

Recent Changes
in the Map of the World

*A review in special maps of the territorial and political changes
resulting from World War II and other recent international events.*

Although at first glance an atlas of today's world may not appear greatly
different from one of prewar date, further examination and analysis will reveal
that war, diplomacy, nationalism and revolution have brought about many
significant alterations in the political face of the earth during the last ten years.

All of these recent changes have been incorporated into the basic maps of this
World Atlas, which show the political divisions and boundaries of the world as
they exist today. In order, however, that readers may visualize these changes
more readily, a special Map Supplement has been prepared which illustrates in
full color both the new postwar political map of the world today and the major
transfers of territory and political changes in Europe and Asia.

WHAT THIS SPECIAL MAP SUPPLEMENT
SHOWS ABOUT THE WORLD OF TODAY

1. **The latest complete political map of the World** in full
color, showing peace treaty boundaries and other recent
territorial and political map changes in Europe, Asia, Africa
and the Pacific.

2. **A political problems map of present-day Europe,**
showing all the transfers of territory resulting from World
War II, the zones of allied occupation in Germany and the
present division of Europe over the Marshall Plan for
Economic Recovery.

3. **A map of the de facto partition of Palestine,** showing the
areas included in the new Jewish state of Israel and the
areas designated for Arab rule, with Jerusalem as an international neutral zone.

4. **A map of the division of India,** showing the two new
nations of Pakistan and the Union of India, the disputed
areas of Kashmir and Junagadh, the new Dominion of Ceylon
and other neighboring independent states.

5. **A postwar map of Eastern Asia** showing the dismember-
ment of the former Japanese Empire following its surrender
to the Allied Powers, the areas regained by China, the territories acquired by the Soviet Union and the Russian and
American Zones of Occupation in Korea.

6. **The flags of the 57 members of the United Nations;**
including the new flags of Pakistan, Yemen, the Union of
India, the Republic of Lebanon, the Peoples Republic of
Yugoslavia and other member nations.

MAJOR CHANGES IN AREAS AND POPULATIONS
RESULTING FROM WORLD WAR II

Country		1938	1948	Country		1938	1948
Bulgaria	Area	39,814	42,814	Italy	Area	119,703	116,533
	Population	6,319,232	7,022,206		Population	43,691,000	44,636,775
China	Area	2,903,475	3,422,000	Japan	Area	263,357	147,889
	Population	424,795,000	469,257,000		Population	105,226,100	73,114,308
Czechoslovakia	Area	54,192	49,373	Poland	Area	149,915	119,800
	Population	15,215,000	12,035,000		Population	34,220,000	23,911,172
Finland	Area	149,954	130,159	Romania	Area	114,000	91,600
	Population	3,834,662	3,947,702		Population	19,319,330	16,409,367
Germany	Area	181,683	137,674	Soviet Union	Area	8,173,000	8,436,000
	Population	66,616,000	65,910,000		Population	170,000,000	193,500,000
Greece	Area	50,147	51,145	Yugoslavia	Area	95,551	98,436
	Population	7,020,000	7,485,700		Population	15,630,129	16,743,000

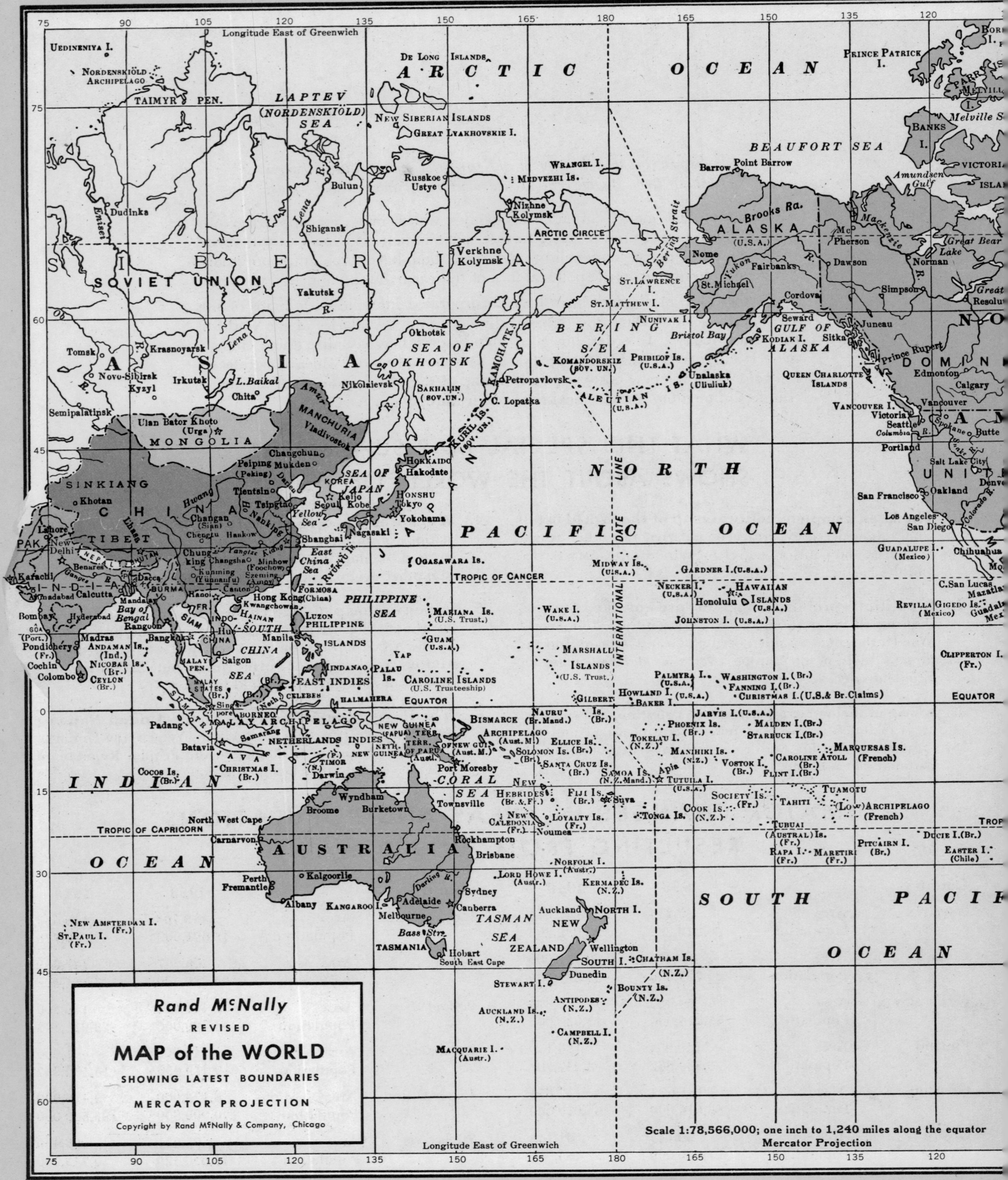

Rand McNally

REVISED

MAP of the WORLD

SHOWING LATEST BOUNDARIES

MERCATOR PROJECTION

Copyright by Rand McNally & Company, Chicago

Scale 1:78,566,000; one inch to 1,240 miles along the equator
Mercator Projection

Longitude East of Greenwich

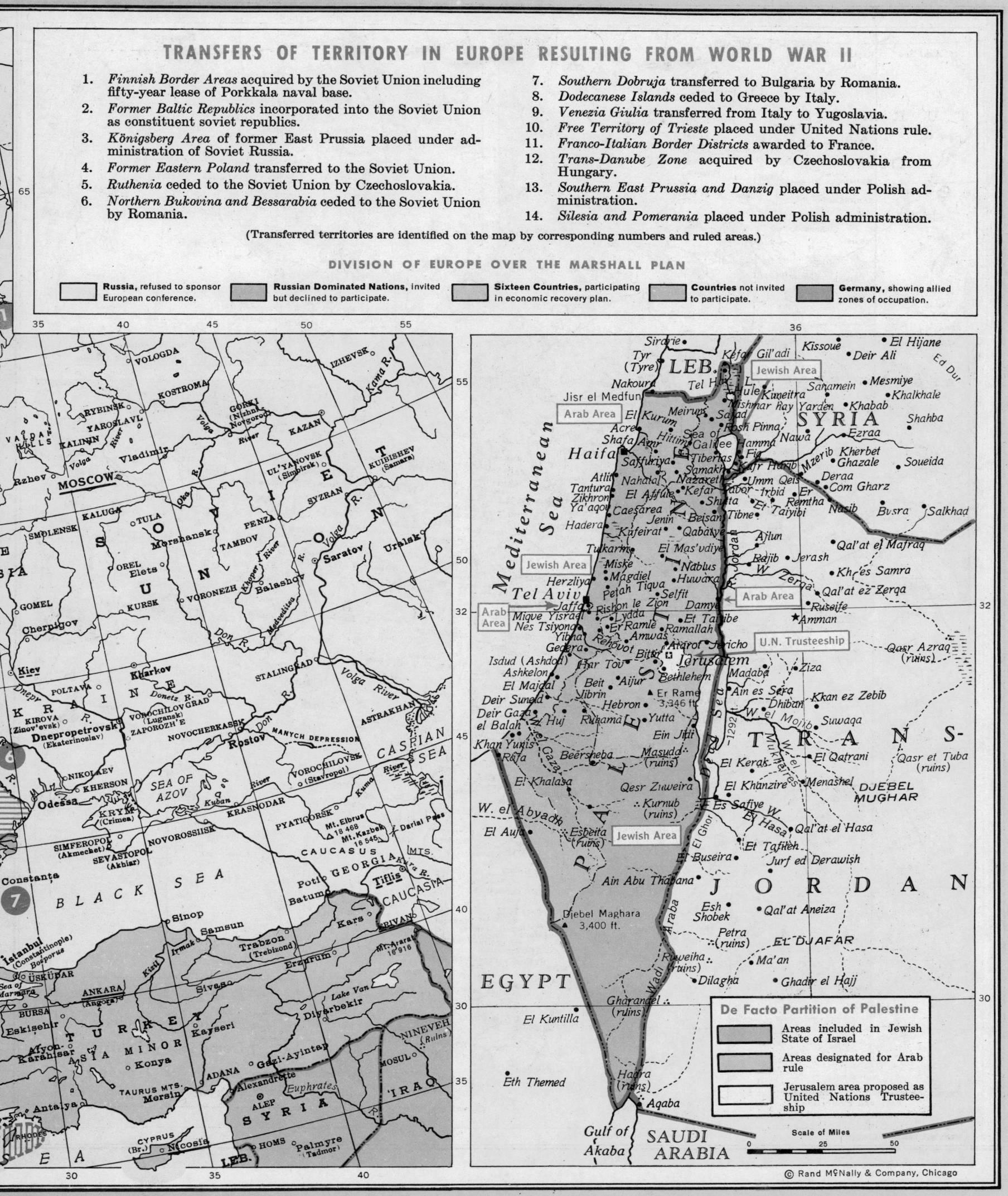

TRANSFERS OF TERRITORY IN EUROPE RESULTING FROM WORLD WAR II

1. *Finnish Border Areas* acquired by the Soviet Union including fifty-year lease of Porkkala naval base.
2. *Former Baltic Republics* incorporated into the Soviet Union as constituent soviet republics.
3. *Königsberg Area* of former East Prussia placed under administration of Soviet Russia.
4. *Former Eastern Poland* transferred to the Soviet Union.
5. *Ruthenia* ceded to the Soviet Union by Czechoslovakia.
6. *Northern Bukovina and Bessarabia* ceded to the Soviet Union by Romania.

7. *Southern Dobruja* transferred to Bulgaria by Romania.
8. *Dodecanese Islands* ceded to Greece by Italy.
9. *Venezia Giulia* transferred from Italy to Yugoslavia.
10. *Free Territory of Trieste* placed under United Nations rule.
11. *Franco-Italian Border Districts* awarded to France.
12. *Trans-Danube Zone* acquired by Czechoslovakia from Hungary.
13. *Southern East Prussia and Danzig* placed under Polish administration.
14. *Silesia and Pomerania* placed under Polish administration.

(Transferred territories are identified on the map by corresponding numbers and ruled areas.)

DIVISION OF EUROPE OVER THE MARSHALL PLAN

Russia, refused to sponsor European conference.	**Russian Dominated Nations**, invited but declined to participate.	**Sixteen Countries**, participating in economic recovery plan.	**Countries** not invited to participate.	**Germany**, showing allied zones of occupation.

De Facto Partition of Palestine

Areas included in Jewish State of Israel

Areas designated for Arab rule

Jerusalem area proposed as United Nations Trusteeship

Scale of Miles
0   25   50

© Rand McNally & Company, Chicago

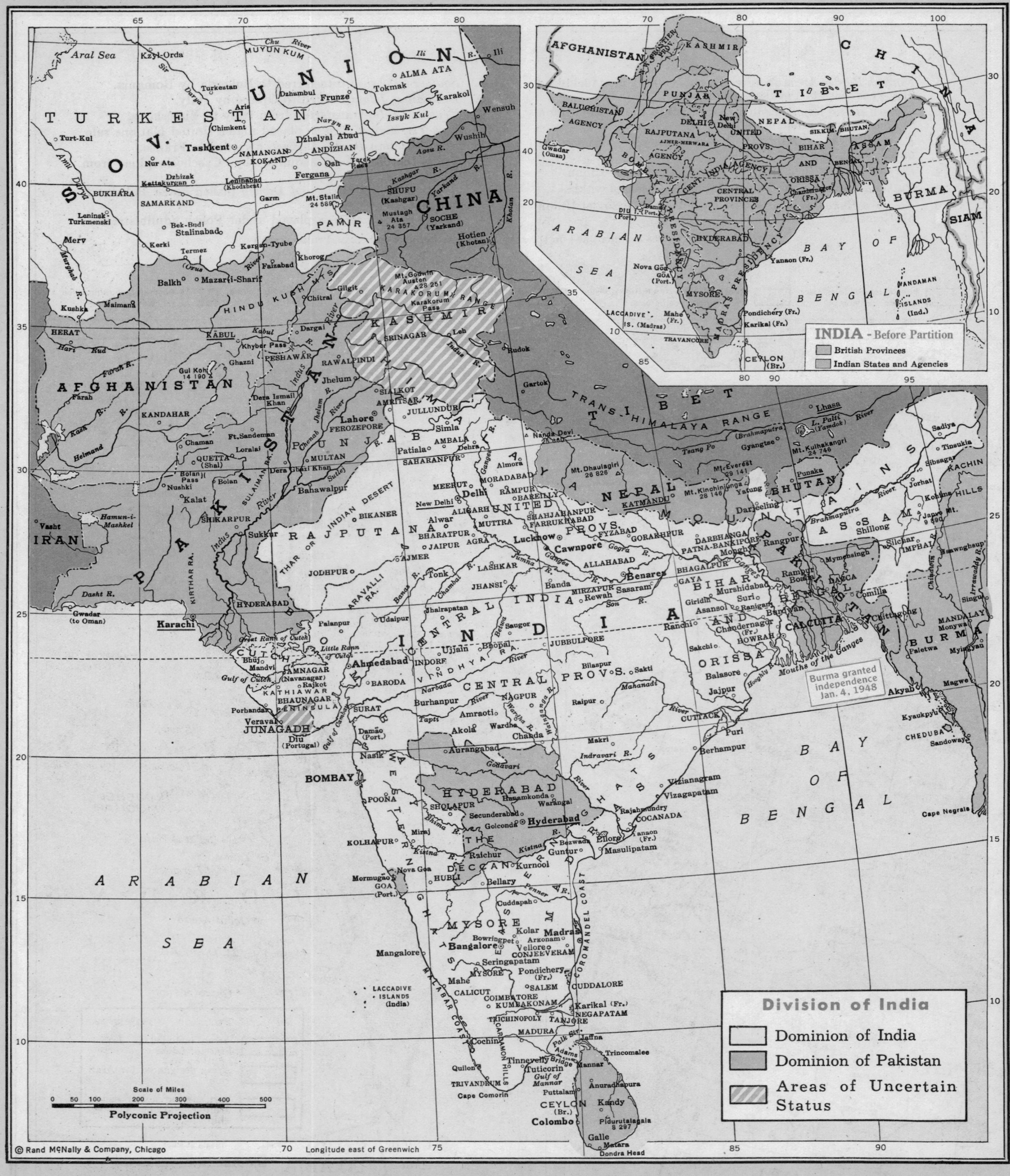

Division of India

☐ Dominion of India
▨ Dominion of Pakistan
▧ Areas of Uncertain Status

INDIA – Before Partition
☐ British Provinces
▨ Indian States and Agencies

Burma granted independence Jan. 4, 1948

Scale of Miles
0 50 100 200 300 400 500
Polyconic Projection

© Rand McNally & Company, Chicago

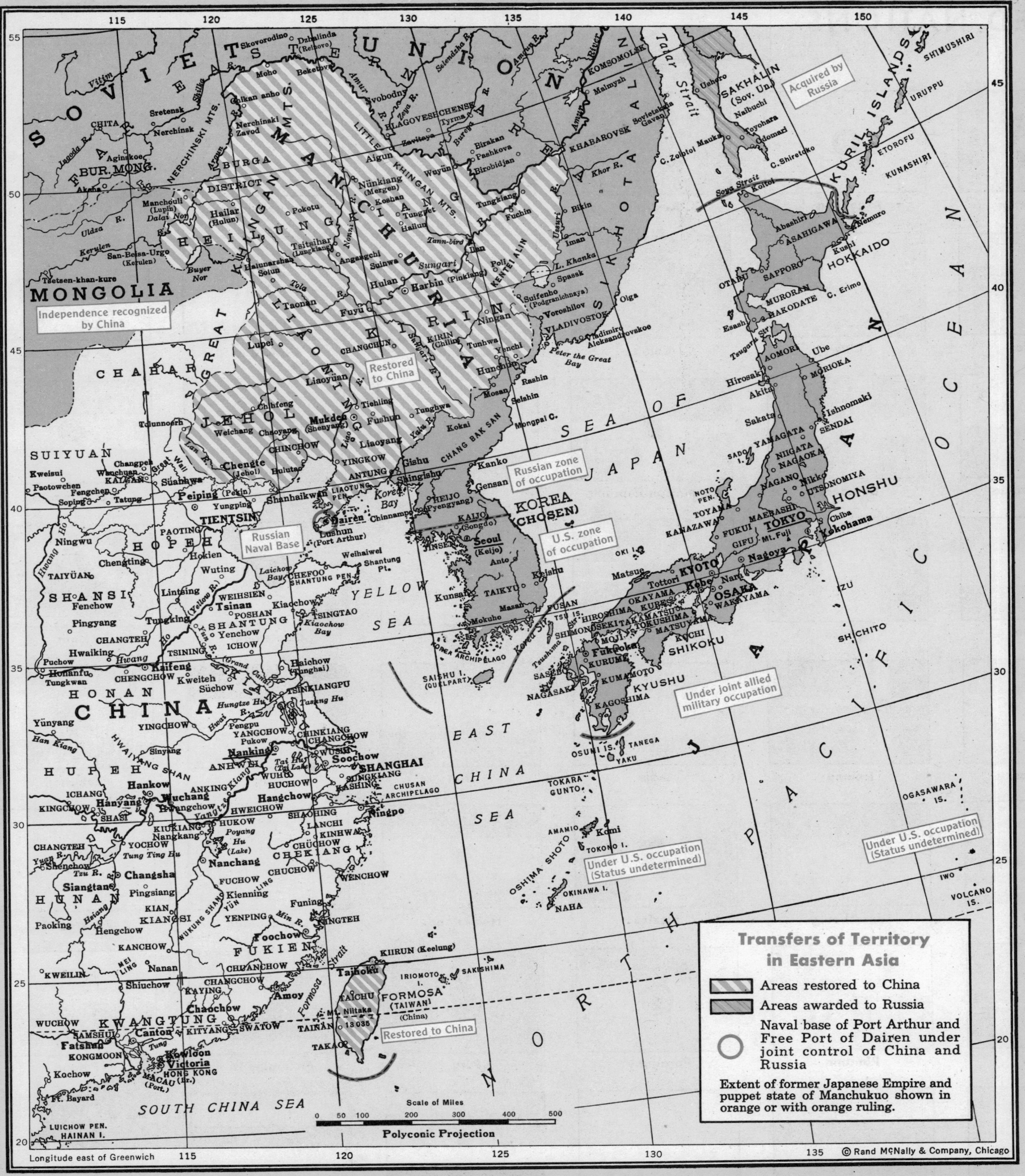

Transfers of Territory in Eastern Asia

Areas restored to China

Areas awarded to Russia

○ Naval base of Port Arthur and Free Port of Dairen under joint control of China and Russia

Extent of former Japanese Empire and puppet state of Manchukuo shown in orange or with orange ruling.

Scale of Miles

0 50 100   200   300   400   500

Polyconic Projection

Longitude east of Greenwich

© Rand McNally & Company, Chicago

MEMBERS of the UNITED NATIONS

United States

Burma

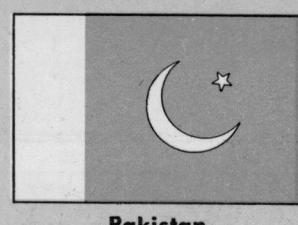
Pakistan

Yemen

Afghanistan

Argentina

Australia

Belgium

Bolivia

Brazil

Canada

Chile

China

Colombia

Costa Rica

Cuba

Czechoslovakia

Denmark

Dominican Republic

Ecuador

Egypt

El Salvador

Ethiopia

France

Great Britain

Greece

Guatemala

Haiti

Honduras

Iceland

India

Iran

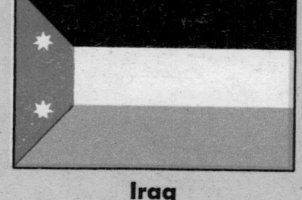
Iraq

Lebanon

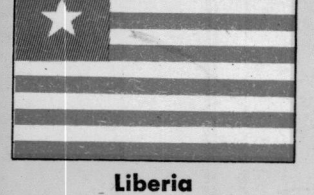
Liberia

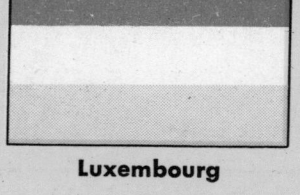
Luxembourg

Mexico

Netherlands

New Zealand

Nicaragua

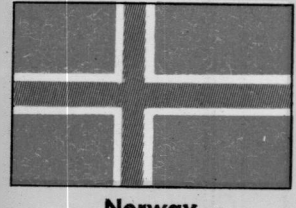
Norway

Panama

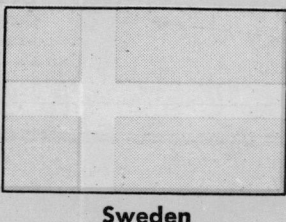
Paraguay

Peru

Philippine Is.

Poland

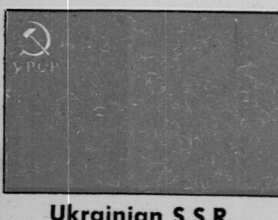
Saudi Arabia

Soviet Union

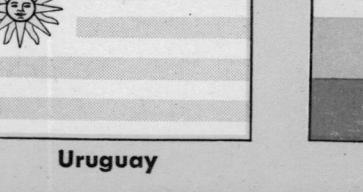
Sweden

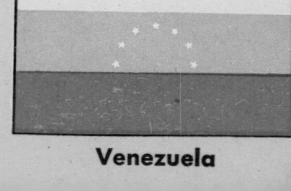
Syria

Siam

Turkey

Ukrainian S.S.R.

Union of South Africa

Uruguay

Venezuela

White Russian S.S.R.

Yugoslavia

THE CONTENTS

PART I. MAPS OF THE WORLD

(NOTE: The *de facto* boundaries shown on various world maps represent conditions existing at the date of revision. These do not always agree with the *de jure* boundaries which the Federal Government must recognize for reasons of state.)

PART II. MISCELLANEOUS REFERENCE MATERIAL

ALPHABETICAL INDEX

To Principal Political Divisions of the World

Map Page	Map Key	Political Division	Form of Govt. or Ruling Power	Capital	Area in sq. miles	Population	Pop. per sq. m.
121	O-4	Aden Colony & Prot.	Great Britain	Aden	112,000	600,000	5.4
126	H-20	Afghanistan	Emirate, Indep.	Kabul	245,000	12,000,000	48.9
128	......	Africa			11,529,480	157,759,000	13.7
23	.....	**Alabama**	United States	Montgomery	51,609	2,832,961	55.0
74	.....	**Alaska**	United States	Juneau	586,400	72,524	0.1
119	M-13	Albania	Republic	Tiranë	10,629	1,135,000	107.0
80	I-19	Alberta	Canada (Br.)	Edmonton	255,285	796,169	3.1
129	C-17	Algeria	France	Alger	847,818	7,234,684	8.5
123	Q-20	Andaman Is.	India (Br.)	Port Blair	2,508	19,223	7.6
116	E-19	Andorra	Principality	Andorra la Vieja	191	6,000	31.4
128	H-17	Anglo-Egyptian Sudan	Great Britain	Khartoum	969,600	6,000,000	6.2
128	N-13	Angola	Portugal	Luanda	484,729	3,738,010	7.4
122	O-10	Annam	France	Hué	57,939	5,656,000	97.8
94	K-23	Antigua, with Barbuda	Leeward Is. (Br.)	St. John	171	41,024	239.9
121	L-5	Arabia			1,000,000	7,000,000	7.0
97	M-12	Argentina	Republic	Buenos Aires	1,072,745	13,906,694	13.0
24	.....	**Arizona**	United States	Phoenix	113,909	499.261	4.4
25	.....	**Arkansas**	United States	Little Rock	53,102	1,949,387	36.7
120	R-17	Armenia	Soviet Union	Yerevan	11,580	1,281,599	110.7
94	P-16	Aruba	Curaçao (Neth.)		69	37,337	541.0
128	M-2	Ascension I.	Great Britain	Georgetown	34	159	4.7
121	.....	Asia			16,188,200	1,151,939,000	71.2
134	......	Australia	Br. Com'w'lth	Canberra	2,974,581	7,137,221	2.4
118	H-6	Austria	Republic	Wien	32,360	6,760,233	208.6
120	Q-19	Azerbaidzhan	Soviet Union	Baku	33,196	3,209,727	96.7
10	H-19	Azores Is.	Portugal	Angra do Heroismo	990	284,755	286.6
94	E-10	Bahama Is.	Great Britain	Nassau	4,404	68,846	15.6
126	Q-5	Bahrein Is.	Sheikhdom (Br.)	Manama	250	120,000	480.0
116	J-21	Balearic Is.	Spain	Palma	1,935	423,000	218.6
94	O-25	Barbados	Great Britain	Bridgetown	166	203,411	1225.4
132	K-18	Basutoland	Great Britain	Maseru	11,716	562,311	47.9
128	P-15	Bechuanaland	Great Britain	Mafeking	275,000	265,756	0.9
128	L-15	Belgian Congo (incl. Ruanda)	Belgium	Leopoldville	941,809	14,159,264	15.0
114	M-12	Belgium	Kingdom	Bruxelles	11,752	8,361,220	711.5
15	Q-15	Bermuda Is.	Great Britain	Hamilton	19	33,428	1759.4
123	E-23	Bhutan	Kingdom	Punaka	18,000	300,000	16.7
133	I-11	Bismarck Arch.	New Guinea (Br.)	Lae	19,660	247,780	12.5
98	......	Bolivia	Republic	Sucre and La Paz	416,040	3,533,090	8.5
133	H-5	Borneo, Netherlands	Neth. Indies	Bandjermasin	206,810	2,306,000	11.1
99	J-13	Brazil	Republic	Rio de Janeiro	3,286,169	45,300,000	13.8
80	I-11	British Columbia	Canada (Br.)	Victoria	366,255	817,861	2.2
93	B-8	British Honduras	Great Britain	Belize	8,598	61,723	7.1
133	G-5	British North Borneo	Great Britain	Sandakan	31,106	299,311	9.6
133	H-5	Brunei	Great Britain	Brunei	2,500	37,868	15.1
119	L-19	Bulgaria*	Republic	Sofija	42,814	6,734,232	157.3
119	L-19	Bulgaria (1939)	Republic	Sofija	39,814	6,319,232	159.2
123	M-22	Burma	Republic	Rangoon	233,492	14,667,146	62.8
26	.....	**California**	United States	Sacramento	158,693	6,907,387	43.7
122	Q-7	Cambodia	France	Pnom-Penh	53,820	3,046,000	56.6
128	J-11	Cameroons, French	France	Yaoundé	166,489	2,609,508	15.6
79	......	Canada	Br. Dominion	Ottawa	3,694,863	11,506,655	3.1
75	.....	**Canal Zone**	United States	Balboa Heights	553	51.827	93.6
128	F-2	Canary Is.	Spain	Sta.Cruz de Tenerife	2,807	731,000	260.4
132	N-12	Cape of Good Hope	Un. of S. Afr. (Br.)	Capetown	277,169	3,684,027	13.2
11	J-19	Cape Verde Is.	Portugal	Praia	1,516	181,286	119.5
133	G-12	Caroline Is.	U. S. Trust		380	38,433	101.1
94	H-5	Cayman Is.	Jamaica (Br.)	Georgetown	93	6,670	71.7
133	I-6	Celebes	Neth. Indies	Makasser	72,966	4,231,906	58.0
93	......	Central America			.....	....	.....
118	......	Central Europe			.....	....	.....
123	R-14	Ceylon	Br. Dominion	Colombo	25,332	5,712,000	225.5
107	Q-12	Channel Is.	Great Britain		75	93.061	1240.8
97	J-3	Chile	Republic	Santiago	286.322	5,341,317	18.7
122	H-12	China*	Republic	Nanking	3,422,000	469,257,000	137.1
122	H-12	China (1935)	Republic	Nanking	2,903,475	424,795,000	149.7
122	D-24	Chosen, see Korea					
133	J-3	Christmas Island	Singapore (Br.)		60	1,313	21.9
122	R-7	Cochin China	Fr. Indochina	Saigon	24,705	4,616,000	186.9
10	L-2	Cocos Is.	Singapore (Br.)		1	1,142	1142.0
100	......	Colombia	Republic	Bogotá	439,825	9,905,748	22.5
28	.....	**Colorado**	United States	Denver	104,247	1,123,296	10.8
128	N-23	Comoro Is.	Madagascar (Fr.)	Dzaoudzi	836	128,608	153.8
29	.....	**Connecticut**	United States	Hartford	5,009	1,709,242	341.2
133	L-22	Cook Is.	New Zealand (Br.)	Awarua-Awatlu	280	16,350	58.4
111	Q-3	Corsica	France		3,367	322,854	96.0
93	N-14	Costa Rica	Republic	San José	19,238	706,596	36.7
119	R-20	Crete	Greece	Erakleion	3,330	441,687	132.7
95	......	Cuba	Republic	Habana	44,217	4,778,583	108.1
94	P-16	Curaçao	Netherlands	Willemstad	403	122,540	304.1
127	K-7	Cyprus	Great Britain	Nicosia	3,584	377,000	105.2
118	G-10	Czechoslovakia*	Republic	Praha	49,399	14,004,179	288.1
118	G-10	Czechoslovakia (1937)	Republic	Praha	54,192	15,215,000	280.7
128	J-7	Dahomey	Fr. W. Africa	Porto Novo	43,232	1,424,220	33.0
128	H-1	Dakar	Fr. W. Africa	Dakar	68	165,188	2429.2
40	H-22	**Delaware**	United States	Dover	2,057	266,505	124.7
110	H-8	Denmark	Kingdom	Kõbenhavn	16,571	3,776,328	227.8
40	I-11	**District of Columbia**	United States	Washington	69	663,091	9611.4
94	D-23	Dominica	Windward Is. (Br.)	Roseau	305	53,202	174.4
94	I-15	Dominican Republic	Republic	Ciudad Trujillo	19,129	1,969,773	103.0
133	I-5	Dutch East Indies	See Netherlands Indies		.....	....	.....
10	N-13	Easter I.	Chile		46	228	4.8
120	..	Eastern Europe			.....	....	.....
102	C-5	Ecuador	Republic	Quito	101,481	3,170,796	31.2
130	......	Egypt	Kingdom	Cairo	383,000	15,951,800	41.6
107	......	England	Great Britain	London	50,874	38,173,950	750.4
131	D-13	Eritrea	(Provisional)	Asmara	45,783	596,944	13.0
120	G-4	Estonia	Soviet Union	Tallinn	18,300	1,122,000	61.3
131	L-13	Ethiopia	Empire	Addis Ababa	350,000	7,500,000	21.4
104	......	Europe			3,771,000	532,600,000	141.2
110	E-24	Faeroes, The	Denmark	Thorshavn	540	25,744	47.7
136	......	Falkland Dependency	Falkland Is. (Br.)		.....	....	.....
96	Q-12	Falkland Is.	Great Britain	Stanley	4,618	2,440	0.5
128	K-10	Fernando Po	Sp. Guinea	Santa Isabel	795	20,873	26.3
135	P-18	Fiji Is.	Great Britain	Suva	7,083	227,280	32.0
120	E-5	Finland*	Republic	Helsinki	130,159	3,947,702	30.3
120	E-5	Finland (1939)	Republic	Helsinki	149,954	3,834,662	25.6
30	......	**Florida**	United States	Tallahassee	58,560	1,897,414	32.4
122	K-21	Formosa	China	Taihoku	13,836	5,872,000	424.0
111	......	France	Republic	Paris	212,421	41,980,000	197.4
128	L-12	French Equatorial Africa	France	Brazzaville	912,049	3,422,815	3.8
122	O-10	French Indochina	France	Hanoi	284,522	23,250,000	71.2
133	L-24	French Oceania	France	Papeete	1,544	44,000	29.0
128	H-5	French Sudan	Fr. W. Africa	Bamako	591,064	3,794,270	6.4
128	H-6	French West Africa	France	Dakar	1,814,810	15,582,535	8.6
102	Q-3	Galapagos Is.	Ecuador	Progreso	3,029	661	0.22
128	I-1	Gambia	Great Britain	Bathurst	4,068	199,520	49.0
120	Q-15	Georgia	Soviet Union	Tbilisi	26,866	3,542,289	131.9
31	......	**Georgia**	United States	Atlanta	58,876	3,123,723	53.1
112	......	Germany*	(Provisional)		137,674	59,595,000	432.8
112	......	Germany (1937)	Republic	Berlin	181,683	66,616,000	363.5
116	Q-19	Gibraltar	Great Britain	Gibraltar	2	21,372	10686.0
133	H-16	Gilbert Is. & Ellice Is.	Great Britain	Ocean I.	473	34,359	72.6
123	M-7	Gôa (Port. India)	Portugal	Nova Gôa	1,516	579,969	382.5
128	J-6	Gold Coast	Great Britain	Accra	91,843	3,786,659	41.2
11	R-16	Graham Island	Falkland Is. (Br.)		.....	....	.....
106	H-16	Great Britain & N. Ireland	Kingdom	London	94,278	46,688,814	495.2
119	P-16	Greece*	Kingdom	Athēnai	51,145	7,485,700	146.3
119	P-16	Greece (1939)	Kingdom	Athēnai	50,147	7,020,000	140.0
14	O-4	Greenland	Denmark	Godhavn	837,620	18,163	0.02
94	P-24	Grenada	Windward Is. (Br.)	St. George	133	87,805	660.2
94	A-23	Guadeloupe and Dep.	France	Basse-Terre	688	308,000	447.7
133	F-11	**Guam**	United States	Agana	206	22,077	107.2
93	E-5	Guatemala	Republic	Guatemala	42,044	3,452,328	81.5
99	B-6	Guiana, British	Great Britain	Georgetown	89,480	364,694	4.1
99	C-8	Guiana, Netherlands	Netherlands	Paramaribo	54,291	189,436	3.5
99	C-11	Guiana, French & Inini	France	Cayenne	34,354	36,975	1.1
128	I-2	Guinea, French	Fr. W. Africa	Conakry	96,886	2,117,705	21.8
128	I-1	Guinea, Portuguese	Portugal	Bissau	13,944	351,089	25.2
128	K-10	Guinea, Spanish	Spain	Santa Isabel	10,860	167,500	15.4
94	I-12	Haiti	Republic	Port au Prince	11,069	3,000,000	271.0
121	L-6	Hasa	See Saudi Arabia		.....	....	.....
76	......	**Hawaii**	United States	Honolulu	6,433	423,330	67.5
121	K-4	Hejaz	See Saudi Arabia		.....	....	.....
114	F-20	Holland	See Netherlands		.....	....	.....
93	F-11	Honduras	Republic	Tegucigalpa	59,160	1,173,032	19.8
122	L-15	Hong Kong	Great Britain	Victoria	391	1,007,000	2575.4
118	I-12	Hungary	Republic	Budapest	35,849	9,034,815	250.4
110	B-21	Iceland	Republic	Reykjavik	39,709	126,000	3.2
32	......	**Idaho**	United States	Boise	83,557	524,873	6.3
128	F-4	Ifni	Spain	Ifni	741	35,000	47.2
33	......	**Illinois**	United States	Springfield	56,400	7,897,241	140.0
123	......	India	Br. Dominion	New Delhi	1,228,267	330,000,000	268.7
34	......	**Indiana**	United States	Indianapolis	36,291	3,427,796	94.4
99	C-11	Inini	French Guiana	Cayenne	30,301	6,099	0.20
35	......	**Iowa**	United States	Des Moines	56,280	2,538,268	45.2
126	K-10	Iran (Persia)	Kingdom	Tehran	628,000	15,055,115	23.9
127	L-20	Iraq	Kingdom	Baghdad	143,240	4,412,959	30.8
109	......	Ireland	Republic	Baile Atha Cliath	26,592	2,944,000	110.7
108	E-6	Isle of Man	Great Britain	Douglas	221	50,000	226.2
113	......	Italy*	Republic	Roma	116,793	44,530,000	383.0
113	......	Italy (1939)	Kingdom	Roma	119,703	43,691,000	365.0
128	J-4	Ivory Coast	Fr. W. Africa	Abidjan	184,174	4,047,041	21.9
94	J-8	Jamaica	Great Britain	Kingston	4,470	1,237,063	277.0
124	......	Japan*	(Provisional)	Tokyo	147,889	72,222,000	488.4
124	K-15	Japanese Empire (1937)	Empire	Tokyo	263,357	105,226,100	399.5
133	J-4	Java and Madeira	Neth. Indies	Batavia	51,029	47,800,000	936.7
36	......	**Kansas**	United States	Topeka	82,276	1,801,028	21.9
120	F-9	Karelia	Soviet Union	Petrozavodsk	63,300	470,000	7.4
123	P-13	Karikal	France	Karikal	52	62,453	1138.9
121	H-11	Kazakh	Soviet Union	Alma-Ata	1,059,377	6,145,937	5.8
37	......	**Kentucky**	United States	Frankfort	40,395	2,845,627	70.4
128	K-21	Kenya	Great Britain	Nairobi	224,960	3,698,400	16.4
11	P-24	Kerguelen Is.	France		1,318	....	.....
121	J-11	Kirghiz	Soviet Union	Frunze	75,926	1,459,301	19.1
122	D-24	Korea	(Provisional)	Kyŏngsŏng (Seoul)	85,206	24,326,327	285.6
121	K-6	Kuwait	Sheikhdom (Br.)	Kuwait	1,930	80,000	41.5
79	J-21	Labrador	Newfoundland (Br.)		112,400	4,850	0.04
121	Q-19	Labuan	North Borneo (Br)	Victoria	35	8,644	247.0
123	P-5	Laccadive Is.	India (Br.)	Kavaratti	744	16,050	21.6
122	O-8	Laos	Fr. Indochina	Vientiane	78,349	1,012,000	12.9
120	H-3	Latvia	Soviet Union	Riga	25,400	1,951,000	77.0
127	M-10	Lebanon	Republic	Beyrouth	3,474	848,833	241.4
94	L-23	Leeward Is.	Great Britain	St. John	410	100,847	246.0
128	J-2	Liberia	Republic	Monrovia	43,000	1,500,000	34.9
128	F-13	Libya	(Provisional)	Tripoli	633,040	888,401	1.4
117	F-20	Liechtenstein	Principality	Vaduz	65	11,218	172.4
120	H-1	Lithuania	Soviet Union	Vilnyus	28,000	4,047,000	144.5
38	.....	**Louisiana**	United States	Baton Rouge	48,523	2,363,880	48.7
114	Q-20	Luxembourg	Grand Duchy	Luxembourg	998	296,913	297.0
22	L-14	Macau	Portugal	Macau	4	374,737	93684.3

*Figures shown are estimates based on postwar boundaries.

6

Premier Edition.

*Figures shown are estimates based on postwar boundaries.

Premier Edition.

	Apia, Samoa	Azores Islands	Berlin, Germany	Bombay, India	Buenos Aires, Argentina	Calcutta, India	Capetown, U. of S. Africa	Cape Verde Islands	Chicago, U.S.A.	Darwin, Australia	Denver, U.S.A.	Gibraltar, Gibraltar	Hong Kong, China	Honolulu, Hawaii	Istanbul (Constantinople), Turkey	Juneau, Alaska	London, England	Los Angeles, U.S.A.	Manila, Phil. Is.	Melbourne, Australia	Mexico, D. F., Mexico	Moskva (Moscow), Soviet Union
Apia		9644	9743	8154	6931	7183	9064	10246	6557	3843	5653	10676	5591	2604	10175	5415	9789	4828	4993	3113	5449	9116
Azores Islands	9644		2185	5967	5417	6549	5854	1499	3093	10209	3991	1249	7572	7180	2975	4526	1527	4794	8250	12101	4385	3165
Berlin	9743	2185		3910	7376	4376	5977	3194	4402	8036	5077	1453	5500	7305	1078	4560	574	5782	6128	9919	6037	996
Bombay	8154	5967	3910		9273	1041	5134	6297	8054	4503	8383	4814	2673	8020	2991	6866	4462	8701	3148	6097	9722	3131
Buenos Aires	6931	5417	7376	9273		10242	4270	4208	5596	9127	5928	5963	11463	7558	7568	7759	6918	6118	11042	7234	4633	8375
Calcutta	7183	6549	4376	1041	10242		6026	7148	7981	3744	8050	5521	1534	7037	3646	6326	4954	8148	2189	5547	9495	3447
Capetown	9064	5854	5977	5134	4270	6026		4509	8449	6947	9327	5076	7372	11532	5219	10330	6005	9969	7525	6412	8511	6294
Cape Verde Islands	10246	1499	3194	6297	4208	7148	4509		4066	10664	4975	1762	8539	8311	3507	5911	2731	5772	9221	10856	4857	3982
Chicago	6557	3093	4402	8054	5596	7981	8449	4066		9346	918	4258	7790	4244	5476	2305	3950	1741	8128	9668	1673	4984
Darwin	3843	10209	8036	4503	9127	3744	6947	10664	9346		8557	9265	2642	5355	7390	7105	8598	7835	1979	1964	9081	7046
Denver	5653	3991	5077	8383	5928	8050	9327	4975	918	8557		5122	7465	3338	6154	1831	4688	828	7661	8759	1434	5485
Gibraltar	10676	1249	1453	4814	5963	5521	5076	1762	4258	9265	5122		6828	8075	1874	5273	1094	5936	7483	10798	5629	2413
Hong Kong	5591	7572	5500	2673	11463	1534	7372	8539	7790	2642	7465	6828		5537	4980	5634	5981	7240	693	4607	8776	4439
Honolulu	2604	7180	7305	8020	7558	7037	11532	8311	4244	5355	3338	8075	5537		8104	2815	7226	2557	5296	5513	3781	7033
Istanbul	10175	2975	1078	2991	7568	3646	5219	3507	5476	7390	6154	1874	4980	8104		5498	1551	6843	5659	9088	7102	1088
Juneau	5415	4526	4560	6866	7759	6326	10330	5911	2305	7105	1831	5273	5634	2815	5498		4418	1842	5869	8035	3219	4534
London	9789	1527	574	4462	6918	4954	6005	2731	3950	8598	4688	1094	5981	7226	1551	4418		5439	6667	10501	5541	1549
Los Angeles	4828	4794	5782	8701	6118	8148	9969	5772	1741	7835	828	5936	7240	2557	6843	1842	5439		7269	7931	1542	6068
Manila	4993	8250	6128	3148	11042	2189	7525	9221	8128	1979	7661	7483	693	5296	5659	5869	6667	7269		3941	8829	5130
Melbourne	3113	12101	9919	6097	7234	5547	6412	10856	9668	1964	8759	10798	4607	5513	9088	8035	10501	7931	3941		8422	8963
Mexico, D. F.	5449	4385	6037	9722	4633	9495	8511	4857	1673	9081	1434	5629	8776	3781	7102	3219	5541	1542	8829	8422		6688
Moskva	9116	3165	996	3131	8375	3447	6294	3982	4984	7046	5485	2413	4439	7033	1088	4534	1549	6068	5130	8963	6688	
New Orleans	6085	3524	5116	8865	4916	8803	8316	4194	831	9545	1079	4757	8480	4207	6171	2905	4627	1675	8724	9275	934	5756
New York	7242	2422	3961	7794	5297	7921	7801	3355	711	9959	1628	3627	8051	4959	5009	2854	3459	2446	8493	10355	2085	4662
Nome	5438	4954	4342	5901	8848	5271	10107	6438	3314	6235	2925	5398	4547	3004	5101	1094	4381	2876	4817	7558	4309	4036
Oslo	9247	2234	515	4130	7613	4459	6494	3444	4040	8022	4653	1791	5337	6784	1518	4045	714	5325	6016	9926	5706	1016
Panama	6514	3778	5849	9742	3381	10114	7014	3734	2325	10352	2636	4926	10084	5245	6750	4460	5278	3001	10283	9022	1495	6711
Paris	9990	1659	542	4359	6877	4889	5841	2666	4133	8575	4885	964	5956	7434	1401	4628	213	5601	6673	10396	5706	1541
Peiping (Peking)	5903	6565	4567	2964	11974	2024	8045	7763	6592	3728	6348	6009	1226	5067	4379	4522	5054	6250	1770	5667	7733	3597
Port Said	10485	3391	1747	2659	7362	3506	4590	3672	6103	7159	6819	2179	4975	8738	693	6215	2154	7528	5619	8658	7671	1710
Quebec	7406	2240	3583	7371	5680	7481	7857	3355	878	9724	1752	3383	7650	5000	4644	2660	3101	2579	8124	10497	2454	4242
Reykjavik	8678	1777	1479	5191	7099	5409	7111	3248	2954	8631	3596	2047	6031	6084	2558	3268	1171	4306	6651	10544	4622	2056
Rio de Janeiro	8120	4428	6144	8257	1218	9376	3769	3040	5296	9960	5871	4775	10995	8190	6395	7598	5772	6296	11254	8186	4770	7179
Roma	10475	2125	734	3843	6929	4496	5249	2772	4808	8190	5561	1034	5768	8022	854	5247	887	6326	6457	9934	6353	1474
San Francisco	4786	4872	5657	8392	6474	7809	10241	5921	1855	7637	946	5936	6894	2392	6700	1525	5355	345	6963	7854	1885	5868
Seattle	5222	4501	5041	7741	6913	7224	10199	5714	1743	7619	1020	5462	6471	2678	6063	899	4782	956	6641	8186	2337	5199
Shanghai	5399	7229	5215	3133	12197	2112	8059	8443	7053	3142	6698	6646	772	4934	4959	4869	5710	6477	1152	5005	8039	4235
Singapore	5850	8326	6166	2429	9864	1791	6016	8700	9365	2075	9063	7231	1652	6710	5373	7235	6744	8767	1479	3761	10307	5238
Tokyo	4656	7247	5538	4188	11400	3186	9071	8589	6303	3367	5795	6988	1796	3850	5556	4011	5938	5470	1863	5089	7035	4650
Valparaiso	6267	5678	7795	10037	761	10993	4998	4649	5268	8961	5452	6408	11607	6793	8172	7271	7263	5527	10930	6998	4053	8792
Washington, D. C.	7066	2667	4167	7988	5216	8088	7894	3486	594	9923	1490	3822	8148	4829	5216	2834	3665	2295	8560	10173	1878	4883
Wellington	2062	11269	11265	7677	6260	7042	7019	10363	8349	3310	7516	12060	5853	4708	10663	7475	11682	6714	5162	1595	6899	10279
Wien	10010	2291	328	3718	7368	4259	5671	3147	4694	7974	5383	1386	5429	7626	783	4895	772	6108	6120	9792	6306	1044
Winnipeg	6283	3389	4286	7644	6297	7424	9054	4556	714	8684	798	4435	7096	3806	5361	1597	3918	1525	7414	9319	2097	4687
Zanzibar	9892	5323	4309	2855	6421	3859	2346	4635	8358	6409	9221	4103	5414	10869	3312	8795	4604	10021	5763	6802	9484	4270

	Bombay, India	Buenos Aires, Arg.	Capetown, Un. of S. Afr.	Colombo, Ceylon	Gibraltar, Gib.	Halifax, Can.	Hamburg, Ger.	Honolulu, Hawaii	Istanbul, Tur.	Le Havre, France	Lisboa, Port.	Liverpool, Eng.	Manila, P. I.	Melbourne, Austl.	New Orleans, U.S.	New York, U.S.	Panama Roads, C.Z.	Port Said, Egypt	Rio de Janeiro, Brazil	San Francisco, U.S.	Shanghai, China	Singapore, Malay Sts.	Valparaiso, Chile	Wellington, N.Z.	Yokohama, Japan
Bombay		9601	5469	1042	5639	8760	7552	9631	4412	7024	6036	7156	4361	6365	10927	9413	14921	3511	8998	11247	5328	2824	11356	7961	6155
Buenos Aires	9601		4345	9415	6074	6600	7622	8744	8488	7074	6148	7178	12128	8477	7233	6761	6311	8259	1325	10062	13087	10782	3181	6956	13921
Capetown	5469	4345		5070	5982	7386	7388	11948	7058	6861	5912	7001	7821	6998	9382	7814	7417	6148	3769	11154	8787	6511	6977	7531	9614
Colombo	1042	9415	5070		6227	9278	8090	8594	4920	7563	6577	7717	3399	5380	11489	9941	13919	4010	8839	10289	4370	1825	11073	7058	5151
Gibraltar	5639	6074	5982	6227		3051	1863	10433	2099	1336	350	1490	9641	11257	5271	3714	5038	2217	4816	8775	10553	8008	9006	12847	11353
Halifax	8760	6600	7386	9278	3051		3480	8152	5147	3082	2792	2891	12591	11876	2517	686	2718	5257	5332	6456	12792	10961	10196	11592
Hamburg	7552	7622	7388	8090	1863	3480		11283	3939	573	1543	1083	16678	13066	5935	4166	5888	4058	6354	9625	12349	9838	8900	13758	14734
Honolulu	9631	8744	11948	8594	10433	8152	11283		12510	10757	10363	10682	5571	5691	7046	7718	5395	12604	9875	2408	4986	6772	6816	4736	3908
Istanbul	4412	8488	7058	4920	2099	5147	3939	12510		3421	2430	3543	8245	9928	7384	5788	7115	910	6897	10884	9210	6700	11540	10037
Le Havre	7024	7074	6861	7563	1336	3082	573	10757	3421		1017	578	10856	12540	5315	3640	5363	3521	5820	9095	11822	9312	8347	12801	12649
Lisboa	6036	6148	5912	6577	350	2792	1543	10363	2430	1017		1148	9867	11551	5377	3403	4968	2532	4858	8737	10833	8323	7975	12459	11660
Liverpool	7156	7178	7001	7717	1490	2891	1083	10682	3543	578	1148		11111	12764	5266	3539	5287	3652	5932	9024	12201	9490	8299	12778	13399
Manila	4361	12128	7821	3399	9641	12591	16678	5571	8245	10856	9867	11111		5214	12414	13086	10764	7335	11524	7164	1338	1578	11967	5647	2023

8

FORTY-FIVE WORLD CITIES
Statute Miles

	New Orleans, U.S.A.	New York, U.S.A.	Nome, Alaska	Oslo, Norway	Panama, Panama	Paris, France	Peiping (Peking), China	Port Said, Egypt	Quebec, Canada	Reykjavik, Iceland	Rio de Janeiro, Brazil	Roma (Rome), Italy	San Francisco, U.S.A.	Seattle, U.S.A.	Shanghai, China	Singapore, Malay States	Tokyo, Japan	Valparaiso, Chile	Washington, D.C. U.S.A.	Wellington, New Zealand	Wien (Vienna), Germany	Winnipeg, Canada	Zanzibar, Africa
Apia	6085	7242	5438	9247	6514	9990	5903	10485	7406	8678	8120	10475	4786	5222	5399	5850	4656	6267	7066	2062	10010	6283	9892
Azores Is.	3524	2422	4954	2234	3778	1659	6565	3391	2240	1777	4428	2125	4872	4501	7229	8326	7247	5678	2667	11269	2291	3389	5323
Berlin	5116	3961	4342	515	5849	542	4567	1747	3583	1479	6114	734	5657	5041	5215	6166	5538	7795	4167	11265	328	4286	4309
Bombay	8865	7794	5901	4130	9742	4359	2964	2659	7371	5191	8257	3843	8392	7741	3133	2429	4188	10037	7988	7677	3718	7644	2855
Buenos Aires	4916	5297	8848	7613	3381	6877	11974	7362	5680	7099	1218	6929	6474	6913	12197	9864	11400	761	5216	6260	7368	6297	6421
Calcutta	8803	7921	5271	4459	10114	4889	2024	3506	7481	5409	9376	4496	7809	7224	2112	1791	3186	10993	8088	7042	4259	7424	3859
Capetown	8316	7801	10107	6494	7014	5841	8045	4590	7857	7111	3769	5249	10241	10199	8059	6016	9071	4998	7894	7019	5671	9054	2346
C. Verde Is.	4194	3355	6438	3444	3734	2666	7763	3672	3355	3248	3040	2772	5921	5714	8700	8589	8589	4649	3486	10363	3147	4556	4635
Chicago	831	711	3314	4040	2325	4133	6592	6103	878	2954	5296	4808	1855	1743	7053	9365	6303	5268	594	8349	4694	714	8358
Darwin	9545	9959	6235	8022	10352	8575	3728	7159	9724	8631	9960	8190	7637	7619	3142	2075	3367	8961	9923	3310	7974	8684	6409
Denver	1079	1628	2925	4653	2636	4885	6348	6819	1752	3596	5871	5561	946	1020	6698	9063	5795	5452	1490	7516	5383	798	9221
Gibraltar	4627	3459	5398	1791	4926	964	6009	2179	3383	2047	4775	1034	5936	5462	6646	7231	6988	6408	3822	12060	1386	4435	4103
Hong Kong	8480	8051	4547	5337	10084	5956	1226	4975	7650	6031	10995	6894	6471	5709	772	1652	1796	11607	8148	5853	5429	7096	5414
Honolulu	4207	4959	3004	6784	5245	7434	5067	8738	5000	6084	8190	8022	2392	2678	4934	6710	3850	6793	4829	4708	7626	3806	10869
Istanbul	6171	5009	5101	1518	6750	1401	4379	693	4644	2558	6395	854	6700	6063	4959	5373	5556	8172	5216	10663	783	5361	3312
Juneau	2905	2854	1094	4045	4460	4628	4522	6215	2660	3268	7598	5247	1525	899	4869	7235	4011	7271	2834	7475	4895	1597	8795
London	4627	3459	4381	213	5278	213	5054	2154	3101	1171	5772	887	5355	4782	5710	6744	5938	7263	3665	11682	772	3918	4604
Los Angeles	1675	2446	2876	5325	3001	5601	6250	7528	2579	4306	6296	6326	345	956	6477	8767	5470	5527	2295	6714	6108	1525	10021
Manila	8724	8493	4817	6016	10283	6673	1770	5619	8124	6651	11254	6457	6963	6641	1152	1479	1863	10930	8560	5162	6120	7414	5763
Melbourne	9275	10355	7558	9926	9022	10396	5667	8658	10497	10544	8186	9934	7854	8186	5005	3792	5089	6998	10173	1595	9792	9319	6802
Mexico, D.F.	934	2085	4309	5706	1495	5706	7733	7671	2454	4622	4770	6353	1885	2337	8039	10307	7035	4053	1878	6899	6306	2097	9484
Moskva	5756	4662	4036	1016	6711	1541	3597	1710	4242	2056	7179	1474	5868	5199	4235	5238	4650	8792	4883	10279	1044	4687	4270
New Orleans		1173	3937	4795	1603	4788	7314	6756	1534	3711	4796	5439	1923	2098	7720	10082	6858	4514	968	7794	5385	1418	8754
New York	1173		3769	3672	2231	3622	6823	5590	439	2576	4820	4273	2568	2419	7357	9630	6735	5094	204	8946	4224	1281	7698
Nome	3937	3769		3836	5541	4574	3428	5745	3489	3366	8586	5082	2547	1976	3784	6148	2983	8360	3792	7383	4657	2599	8209
Oslo	4795	3672	3836		5691	832	4360	2211	3263	1083	6482	1243	5181	4591	5020	6246	5221	7914	3870	10974	850	3854	4803
Panama	1603	2231	5541	5691		5382	8906	7146	2659	4706	3294	5703	3322	3651	9324	11687	8423	2943	2080	7433	6026	2998	8245
Paris	4788	3622	4574	832	5382		5101	1975	3235	1380	5703	682	5441	4993	5752	6671	6033	7251	3828	11791	644	4118	4396
Peiping (Peking)	7314	6823	3428	4360	8906	5101		4584	6423	4903	10768	5047	5902	5396	662	2774	1307	11774	6922	6698	4639	5907	5803
Port Said	6756	5590	5745	2211	7146	1975	4584		5250	3227	6244	1317	7394	6759	5132	5088	5842	8088	5796	10249	1429	6032	2729
Quebec	1534	439	3489	3263	2659	3235	6423	5250		2189	5125	3943	2642	2353	6981	9097	6417	5504	610	9228	3858	1199	7443
Reykjavik	3711	2576	3366	1083	4706	1380	4903	3227	2189		6118	2044	4199	3614	5559	7160	5472	7225	2800	10724	1805	2804	5757
Rio de Jan.	4796	4820	8586	6482	3294	5703	10768	6244	5125	6118		5684	6619	6891	11340	9774	11535	6124	4797	7349	6136	6010	5589
Roma	5439	4273	5082	1243	5703	682	5047	1317	3943	2044	5684		6240	5659	5677	6232	6124	7420	4435	11524	463	4803	3712
San Francisco	1923	2568	2547	5181	3322	5441	5902	7394	2642	4199	6619	6240		680	6132	8479	5131	5876	2437	6739	5988	1504	9958
Seattle	2098	2419	1976	4591	3651	4993	5396	6759	2353	3614	6891	5659	680		5703	8057	4777	6230	2335	7242	5376	1150	9359
Shanghai	7720	7357	3784	5020	5752	6671	662	5132	6981	5559	11340	5677	6132	5703		2377	1094	11650	7442	6054	6036	6350	5971
Singapore	10082	9630	6148	6246	11687	6671	2774	5088	9097	7160	9774	6232	8479	8057	2377		3304	10226	9834	5292	6036	8685	4480
Tokyo	6858	6735	2983	5221	8423	6033	1307	5842	6417	5472	11535	6124	5131	4777	1094	3304		10635	6769	5760	5679	5575	7040
Valparaiso	4514	5094	8360	7914	2943	7251	11774	8088	5504	7225	6124	7420	5876	6230	11650	10226	10635		4977	5785	7783	5931	7184
Wash., D.C.	968	204	3792	3870	2080	3828	6922	5796	610	2800	4797	4435	2437	2335	7442	9834	6769	4977		8745	4429	1243	7884
Wellington	7794	8946	7383	10974	7433	11791	6698	10249	9228	10724	7349	11524	6739	7242	6054	5292	5760	5785	8745		11278	8230	8122
Wien	5385	4224	4657	850	6026	644	4639	1429	3858	1805	6136	463	5988	5376	6036	6036	5679	7783	4429	11278		4604	3983
Winnipeg	1418	1281	2599	3854	2998	4118	5907	6032	1199	2804	6010	4803	1504	1150	6350	8685	5575	5931	1243	8230	4604		8416
Zanzibar	8754	7698	8209	4803	8245	4396	5803	2729	7443	5757	5589	3712	9958	9359	5971	4480	7040	7184	7884	8122	3983	8416	

TWENTY-FIVE WORLD PORTS
Statute Miles

	Bombay, India	Buenos Aires, Arg.	Capetown, Un. of S. Afr.	Colombo, Ceylon	Gibraltar, Gib.	Halifax, Can.	Hamburg, Ger.	Honolulu, Hawaii	Istanbul, Tur.	Le Havre, France	Lisboa, Port.	Liverpool, Eng.	Manila, P. I.	Melbourne, Austl.	New Orleans, U.S.	New York, U.S.	Panama Roads, C. Z.	Port Said, Egypt	Rio de Janeiro, Brazil	San Francisco, U.S.	Shanghai, China	Singapore, Malay Sts.	Valparaiso, Chile	Wellington, N.Z.	Yokohama, Japan
Melbourne	6365	8477	6998	5380	11257	11876	13066	5691	9928	12540	11551	12764	5214		10780	11452	9130	9040	9416	8011	6012	4396	7222	1737	5606
New Orleans	10927	7233	9382	11489	5271	2517	5935	7046	7384	5315	5377	5266	12414	10780		1970	1650	7498	5965	5287	11495	13207	5335	4663	11169
New York	9413	6761	7814	9941	3714	686	4166	7718	5788	3640	3403	3539	13086	11452	1970		2323	5895	5493	6059	12176	11693	5335	9814	8846
Panama Roads	14921	6311	7417	13919	5038	2718	5888	5395	7115	5363	4968	5287	10764	9130	1650	2323		7217	5058	3737	9853	12097	3013	7491	8846
Port Said	3511	8259	6148	4010	2217	5257	4058	12604	910	3521	2532	3652	7335	9040	7498	5895	7217		7006	10986	8301	5791	10225	10630	9128
Rio de Janeiro	8998	1325	3769	8839	4816	5332	6354	9875	6897	5820	4858	5932	11524	9416	5965	5493	5058	7006		8794	12490	10179	4191	7915	13317
San Francisco	11247	10062	11154	10289	8775	6456	9625	2408	10884	9095	8737	9024	7164	8011	5287	6059	3737	10986	8794		6339	8467	5919	6800	5223
Shanghai	5328	13087	8787	4370	10553	12707	12349	4986	9210	11822	10833	12201	1338	6012	11495	12176	9853	8301	12490	6339		2545	11806	6184	1199
Singapore	2824	10782	6511	1825	8008	11047	9838	6772	6700	9312	8323	9490	1578	4396	13207	11693	12097	5791	10179	8467	2545		12534	5992	3345
Valparaiso	11356	3181	6977	11073	9006	5731	8900	6816	11020	8347	7975	8299	11967	7222	4663	5335	3013	10225	4191	5919	11806	12534		5799	10740
Wellington	7961	6956	7531	7058	12847	10196	13758	4736	11540	12801	12459	12778	5647	1737	9133	9814	7491	10630	7915	6800	6184	5992	5799		5736
Yokohama	6155	13921	9614	5151	11353	11592	14734	3908	10037	12649	11660	13399	2023	5606	10489	11169	8846	9128	13317	5223	1199	3345	10740	5736	

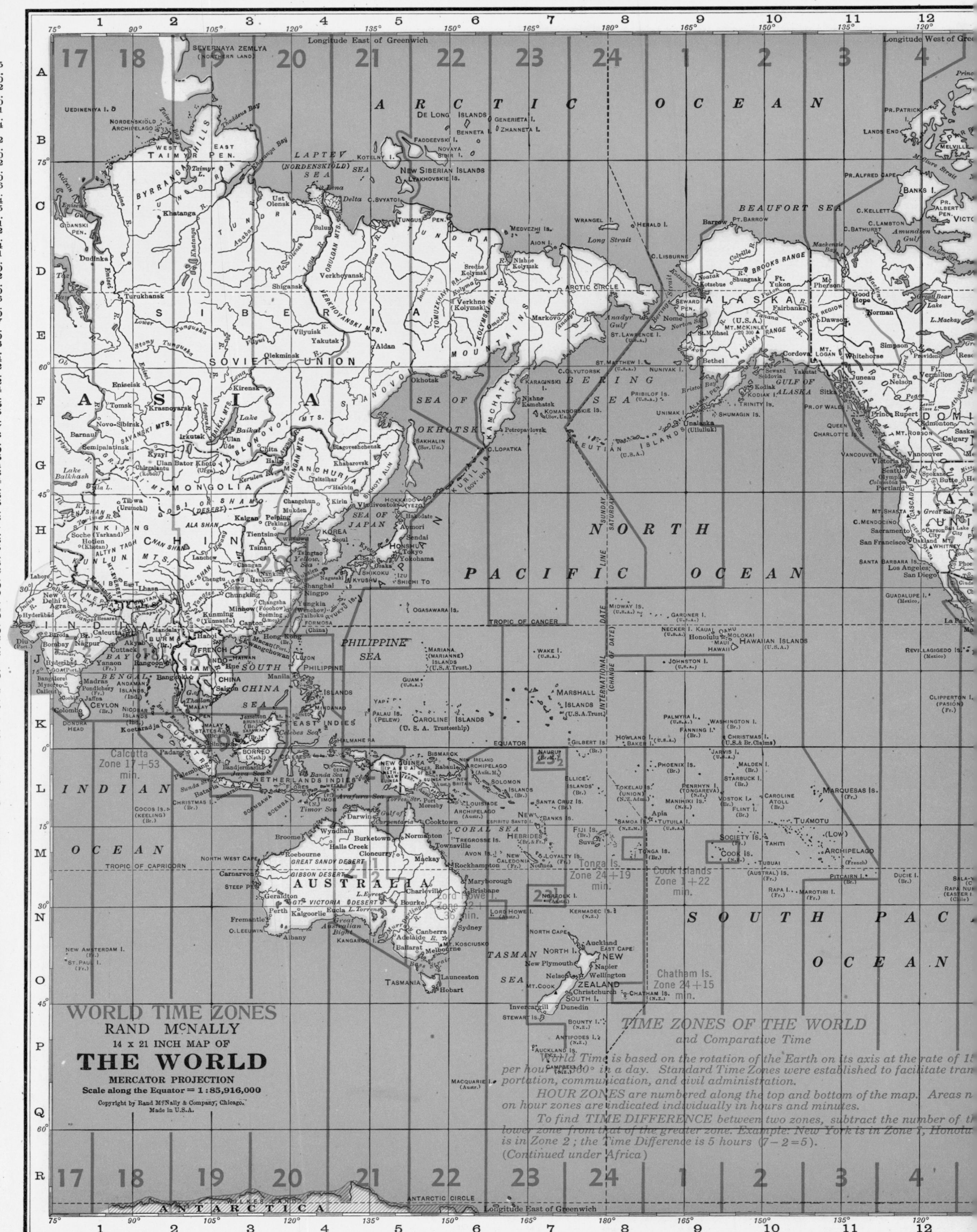

THE WORLD

WORLD TIME ZONES

RAND McNALLY
14 x 21 INCH MAP OF
THE WORLD
MERCATOR PROJECTION
Scale along the Equator = 1:85,916,000
Copyright by Rand McNally & Company, Chicago.
Made in U.S.A.

TIME ZONES OF THE WORLD
and Comparative Time

World Time is based on the rotation of the Earth on its axis at the rate of 15° per hour (360° in a day. Standard Time Zones were established to facilitate transportation, communication, and civil administration.

HOUR ZONES are numbered along the top and bottom of the map. Areas not on hour zones are indicated individually in hours and minutes.

To find TIME DIFFERENCE between two zones, subtract the number of the lower zone from that of the greater zone. Example: New York is in Zone 1, Honolulu is in Zone 2; the Time Difference is 5 hours (7 − 2 = 5).
(Continued under Africa)

Calcutta Zone 17 +53 min.

New Guinea Zone 22 +32 min.

Australia Zone 21 +36 min.

Tonga Is. Zone 24 +19 min.

Cook Islands Zone 1 +22 min.

Chatham Is. Zone 24 +15 min.

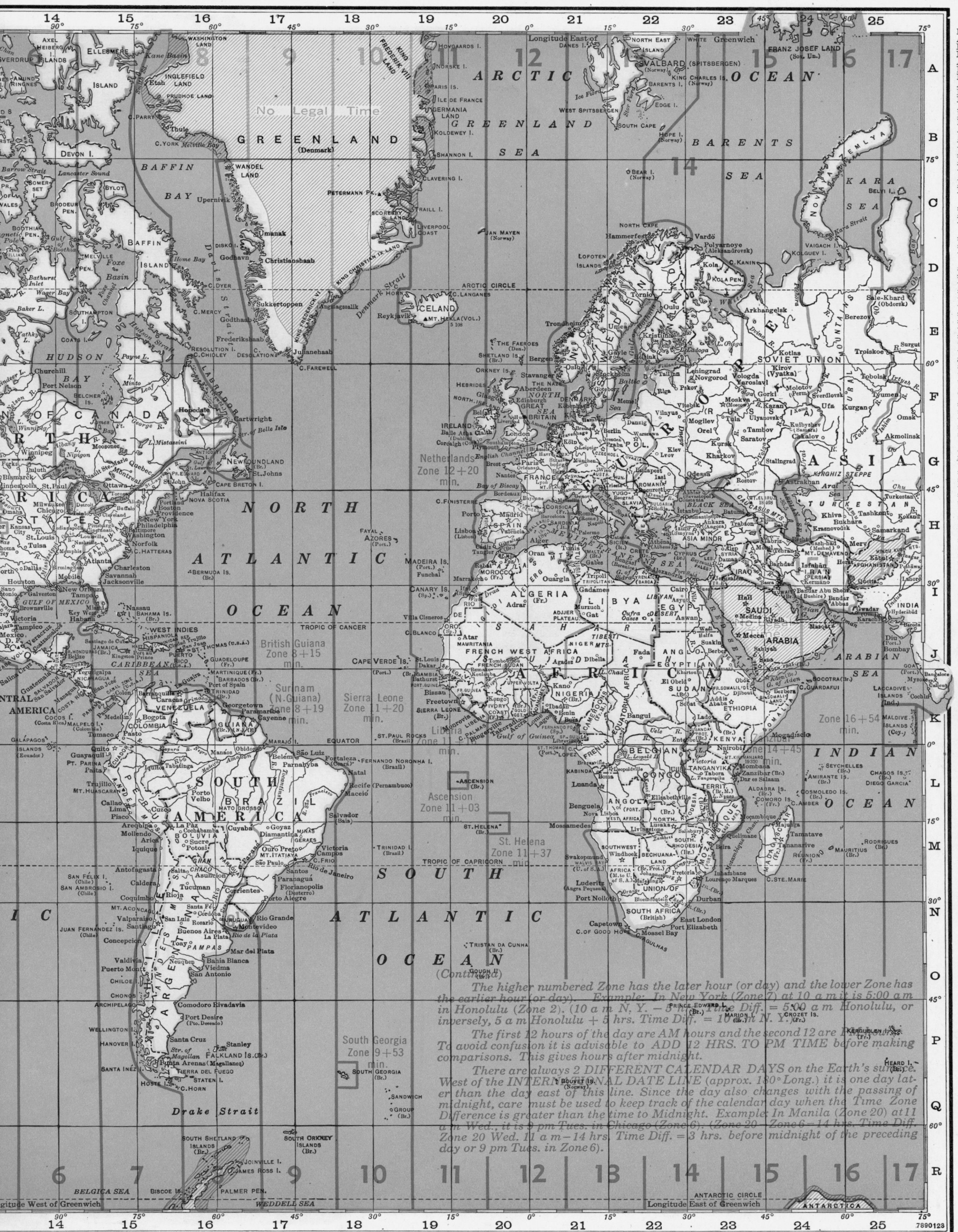

The higher numbered Zone has the later hour (or day) and the lower Zone has the earlier hour (or day). Example: In New York (Zone 7) at 10 a m it is 5:00 a m in Honolulu (Zone 2). (10 a m N.Y. — 5 hrs Time Diff. = 5:00 a m Honolulu, or inversely, 5 a m Honolulu + 5 hrs. Time Diff. = 10 a m N.Y.)

The first 12 hours of the day are AM hours and the second 12 are PM. To avoid confusion it is advisable to ADD 12 HRS. TO PM TIME before making comparisons. This gives hours after midnight.

There are always 2 DIFFERENT CALENDAR DAYS on the Earth's surface. West of the INTERNATIONAL DATE LINE (approx. 180° Long.) it is one day later than the day east of this line. Since the day also changes with the passing of midnight, care must be used to keep track of the calendar day when the Time Difference is greater than the time to Midnight. Example: In Manila (Zone 20) at 11 a m Wed., it is 9 pm Tues. in Chicago (Zone 6). (Zone 20 - Zone 6 = 14 hrs. Time Diff. Zone 20 Wed. 11 a m — 14 hrs. Time Diff. = 3 hrs. before midnight of the preceding day or 9 pm Tues. in Zone 6).

RAND McNALLY

POLAR MAP OF THE WORLD

The new approach to modern warfare and future air travel

THE late Global War has forced us to revise many of our pat, smug concepts inherited from the past and unconsciously accepted as fixed and final. Whether we know it or not, when we see something new, we judge it and limit it by the unconscious content of our minds, collected throughout our life from past patterns, experiences, and the accumulated experience of our forefathers. From time to time radically new elements are thrust upon us that require the uprooting and changing of old concepts. Among these ideas destined for the scrap pile is that of a predominantly east and west world, with Europe essentially east of the United States and Asia to the westward, etc.

Our old approach to and thoughts of the earth have been controlled and molded by the graphic picture of the earth most frequently presented to us. This has been in the form of Mercator World Maps spread out

predominantly east and west. This projection was designed several hundred years ago as a technical instrument to meet the needs of the marine navigators who followed Columbus in inter-continental marine commerce and then world commerce via the open ocean routes. Polar cold and ice blocked commerce across the Arctic wastes. Since that time practically all world maps have been made on Mercator's projection, spread out predominantly east and west.

With this image before us for generations, the east and west world became a more or less fixed concept. This is further emphasized by the fact that all globes of the earth have heretofore been mounted on a polar axis to rotate east and west.

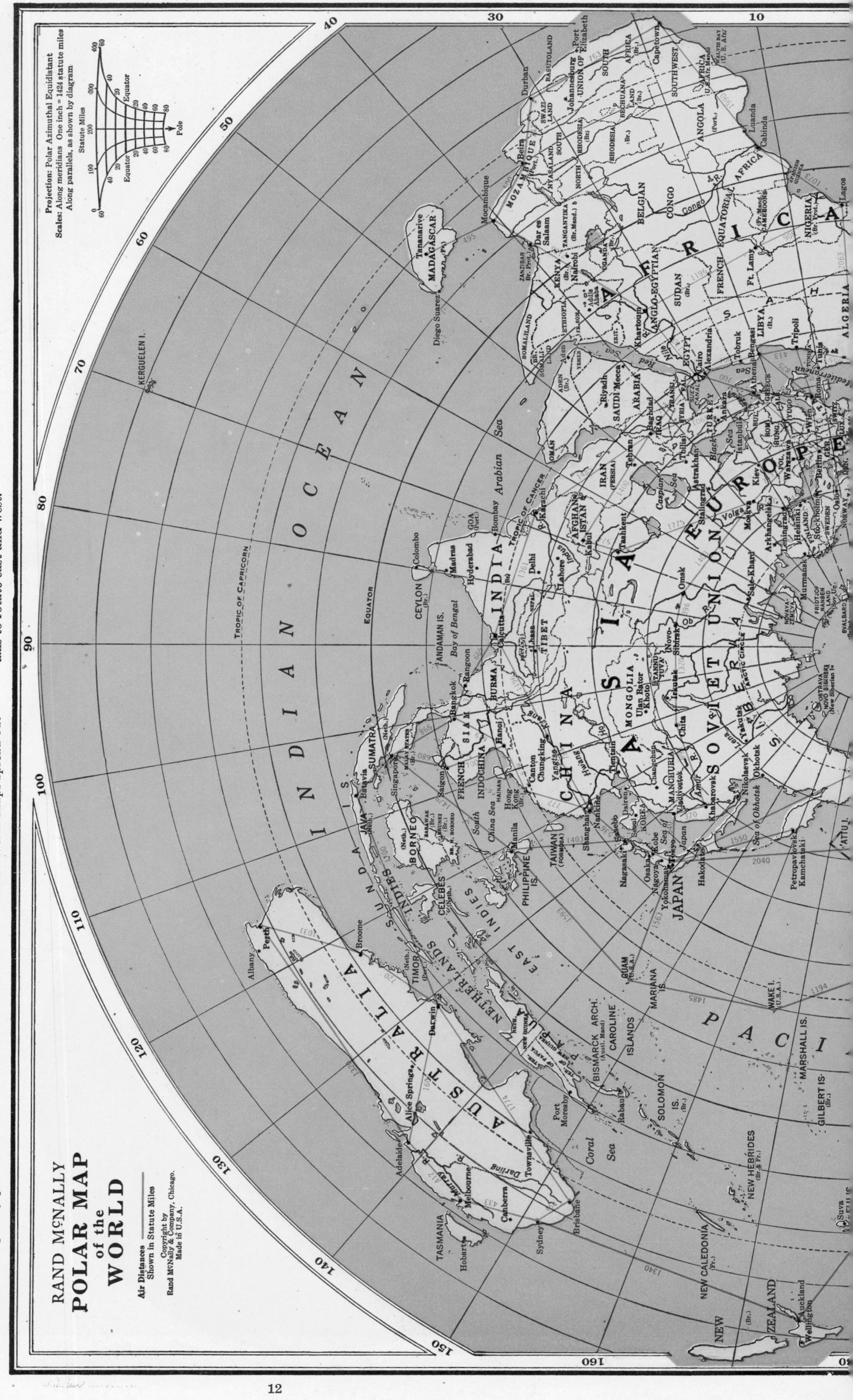

Projection: Polar Azimuthal Equidistant
Scales: Along meridians One inch = 1424 statute miles
Along parallels, as shown by diagram

12

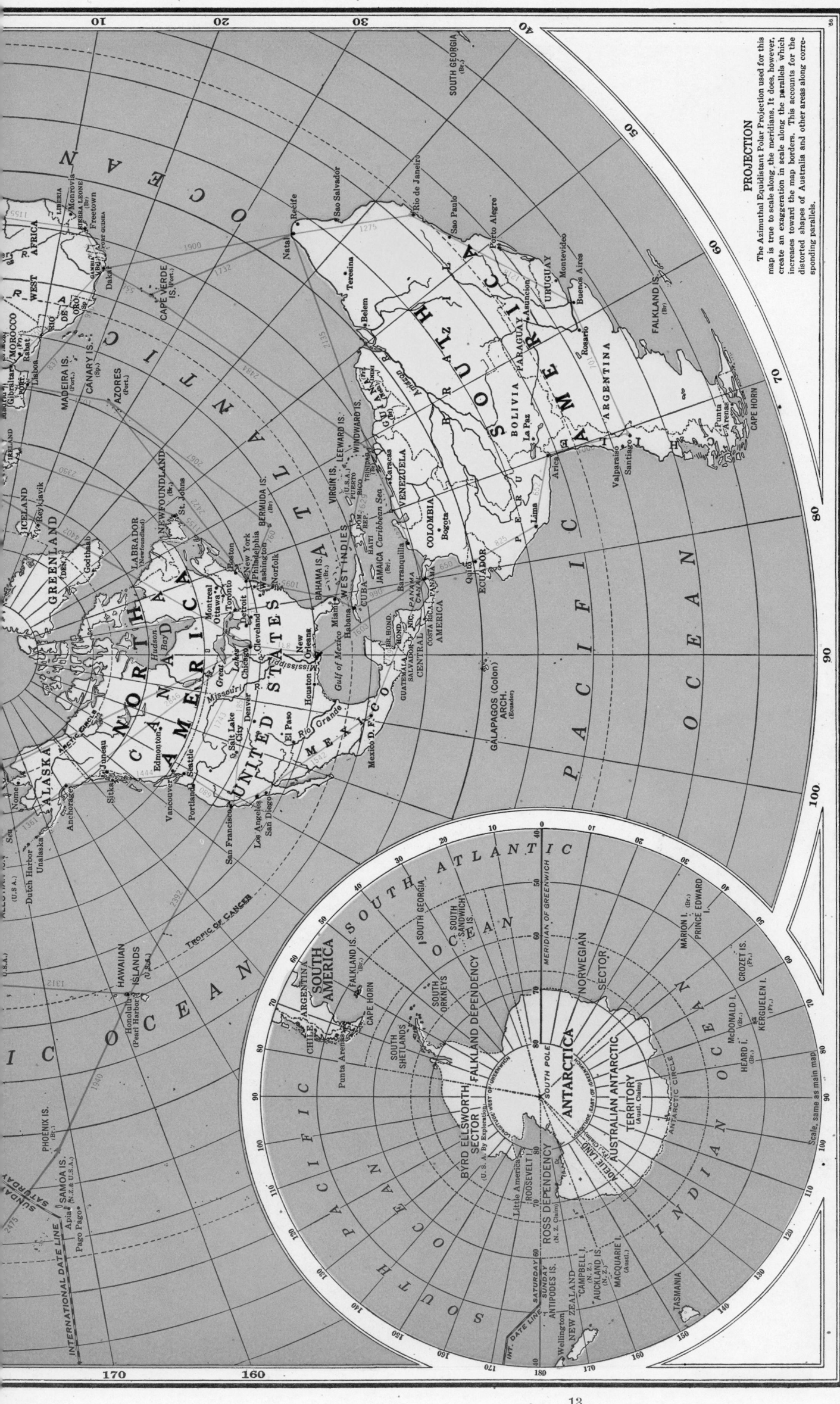

The Azimuthal Equidistant Polar Projection used for this map is true to scale along the meridians. It does, however, create an exaggeration in scale along the parallels which increases toward the map borders. This accounts for the distorted shapes of Australia and other areas along corresponding parallels.

The advent of the airplane and radio requires a new approach to the earth, one based on the shortest world distance and direction between points in question. This means great circle relationships in distance, path, and direction. The concept has been gradually spreading among technicians. As a result of World War II, there has been new emphasis on the need of presenting this revised conception of the world to the public. This has now been done in the form of a new World Map, centered on the North Pole and radiating therefrom in true distance and direction.

The new Rand McNally Polar World Map was designed with this in mind. A comparative glance between this and a Mercator World will make one wonder why we remained bound by the old world image so long. A glance at the Polar Map shows that the major part of the land masses of the world clusters around the North Pole, and the shortest, or great circle, routes between North America and Europe or Asia lie near or across the Arctic region.

To the airplane the cold of the Arctic offers no barrier. In fact the best and calmest flying weather is in that area, where there are very few storms such as we know in the temperate latitudes. To aircraft, up, not north, is cold. The temperatures of the upper air, especially of the stratosphere, are no colder over the Pole than elsewhere. Furthermore, stratosphere flying offers calm weather, changeless temperatures, less resistance, and greater possible speed; and the stratosphere is much closer to the earth's surface over the Arctic region than it is in warm latitudes.

Thus, for air commerce we eliminate the old Arctic barrier and find rather an inviting avenue of world travel. A glance at the Polar World Map will show how much closer the population centers of the world are by this new centralized and short highway.

Our concepts of basic directions must also be revised. You can see on this map that Asia is closer to the United States by a northerly route than by any other and that Europe lies decidedly northeast of the United States, rather than toward the east, as is usually thought. You can also see that the Aleutian Islands of Alaska are the most direct route and the natural stepping stones from Japan to continental United States, etc., etc.

No one flat map, however, can give an entirely true concept of the earth. An orange peel cannot be spread out flat without having it split and break in several places. When we spread out the earth's surface for a flat map, we fill in these breaks by mathematical adjustments which produce exaggerations of one kind or another. On the New Polar Map the southern continents and oceans are exaggerated in an east-and-west direction. The Mercator Map exaggerates the Polar Regions in both directions and in fact cannot show the actual poles because of its mathematical limitations.

The only way the earth can be truly represented is on a globe, and this has the disadvantage of not being spread out so that we can take it all in at a glance. To meet the demands of current times in understanding relationships in the world of the airplane, we must consult the globe and several world maps of different design. The most important of these maps today is the new Polar presentation of the world.

13

14

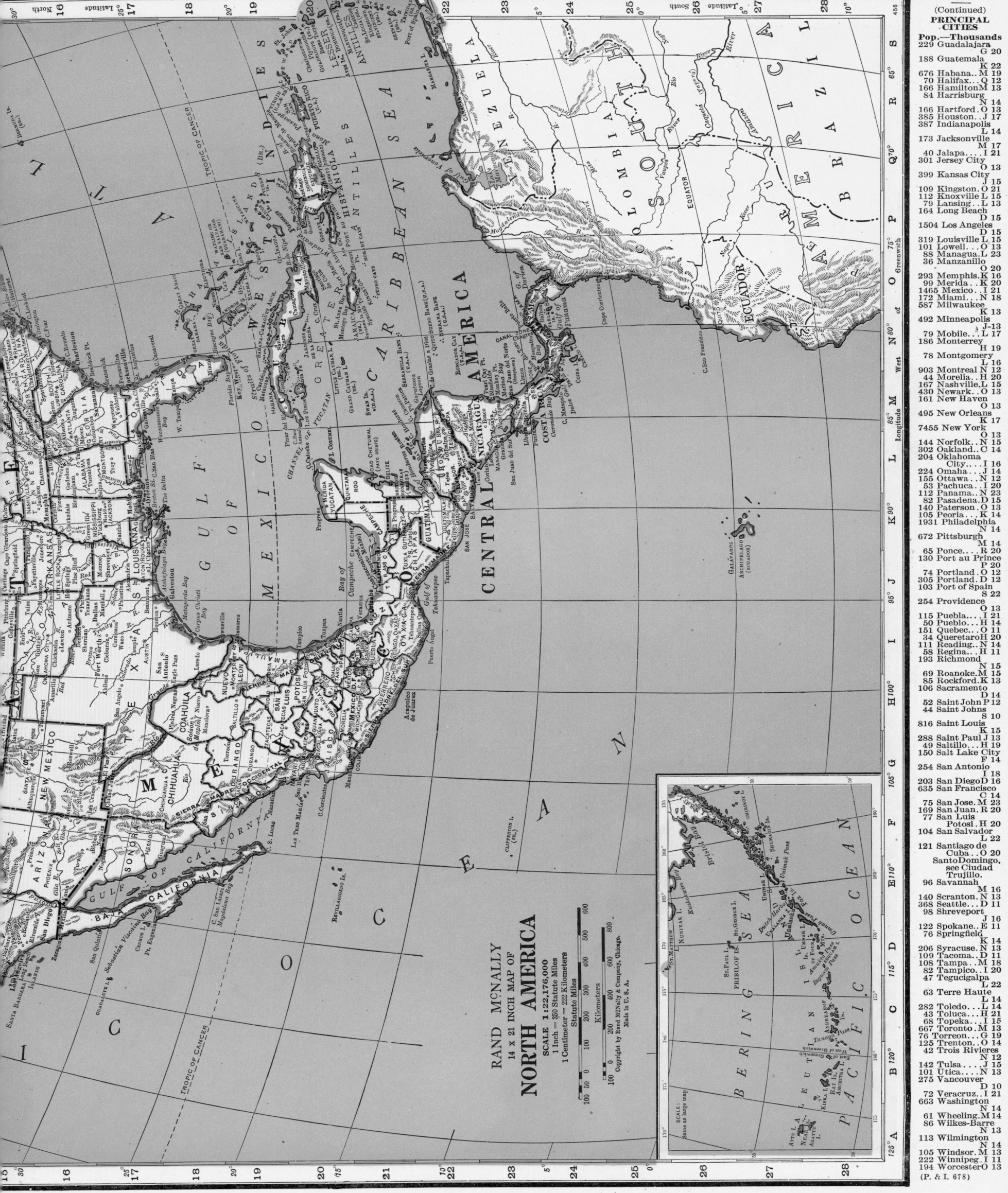

RAND McNALLY
14 x 21 INCH MAP OF
NORTH AMERICA

SCALE 1:22,176,000
1 Inch = 350 Statute Miles
1 Centimeter = 222 Kilometers

Copyright by Rand McNally & Company, Chicago.
Made in U.S.A.

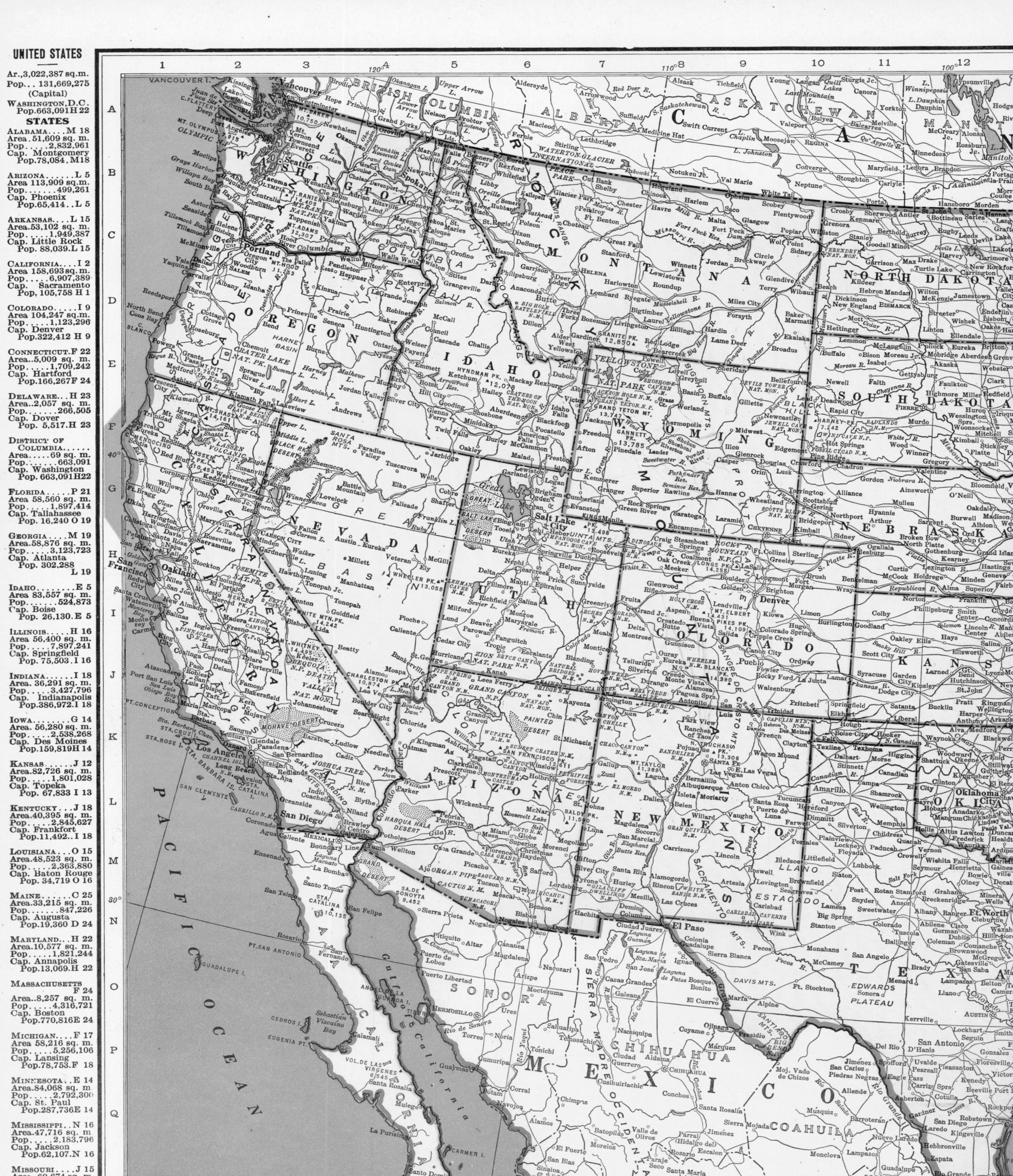

16

RAND McNALLY
14 x 21 INCH MAP OF
UNITED STATES
SCALE 1:9,757,000
1 Inch = 154 Statute Miles
1 Centimeter = 97 Kilometers
Statute Miles
Kilometers
Copyright by Rand McNally & Company, Chicago.
Made in U.S.A.

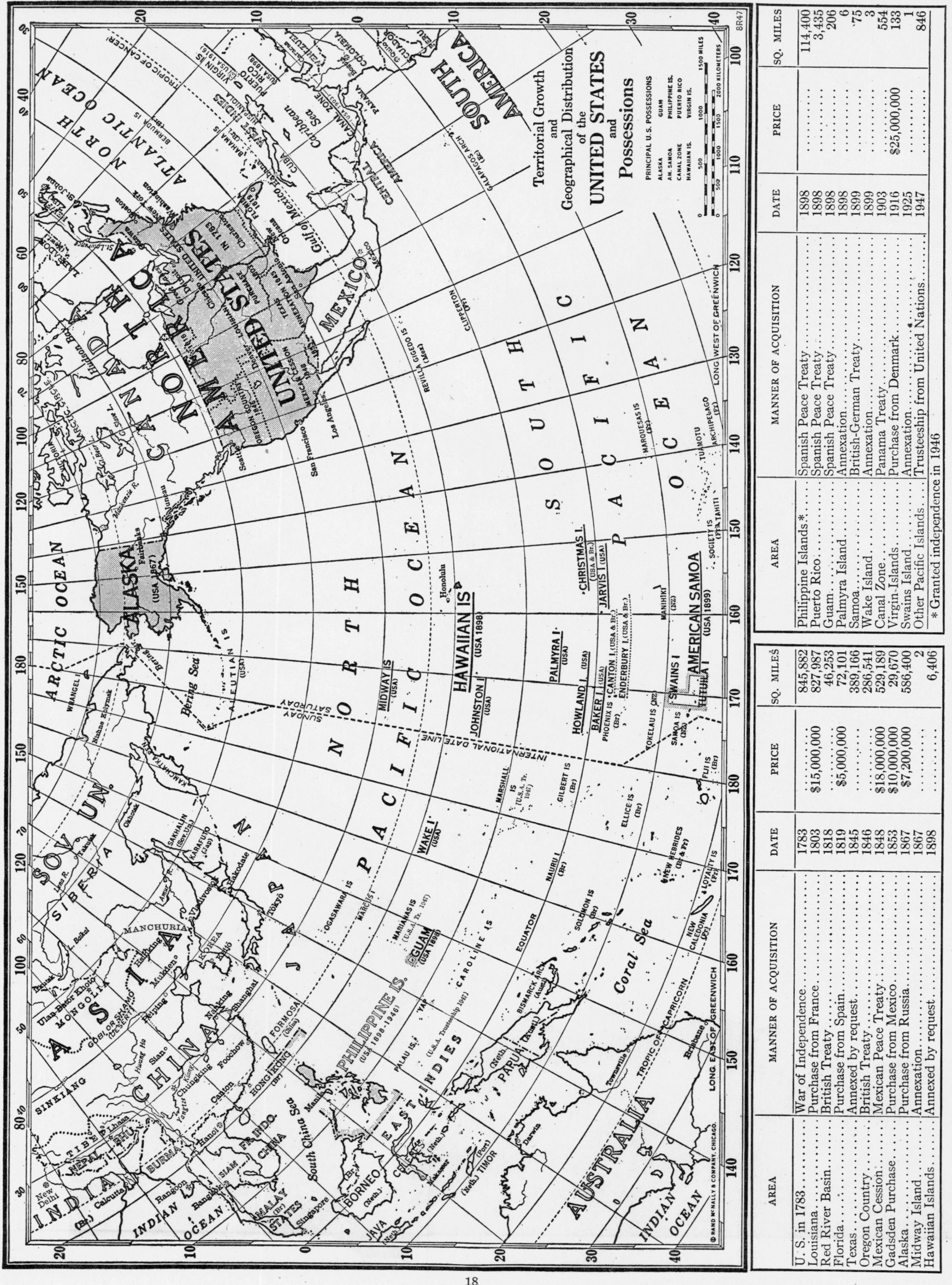

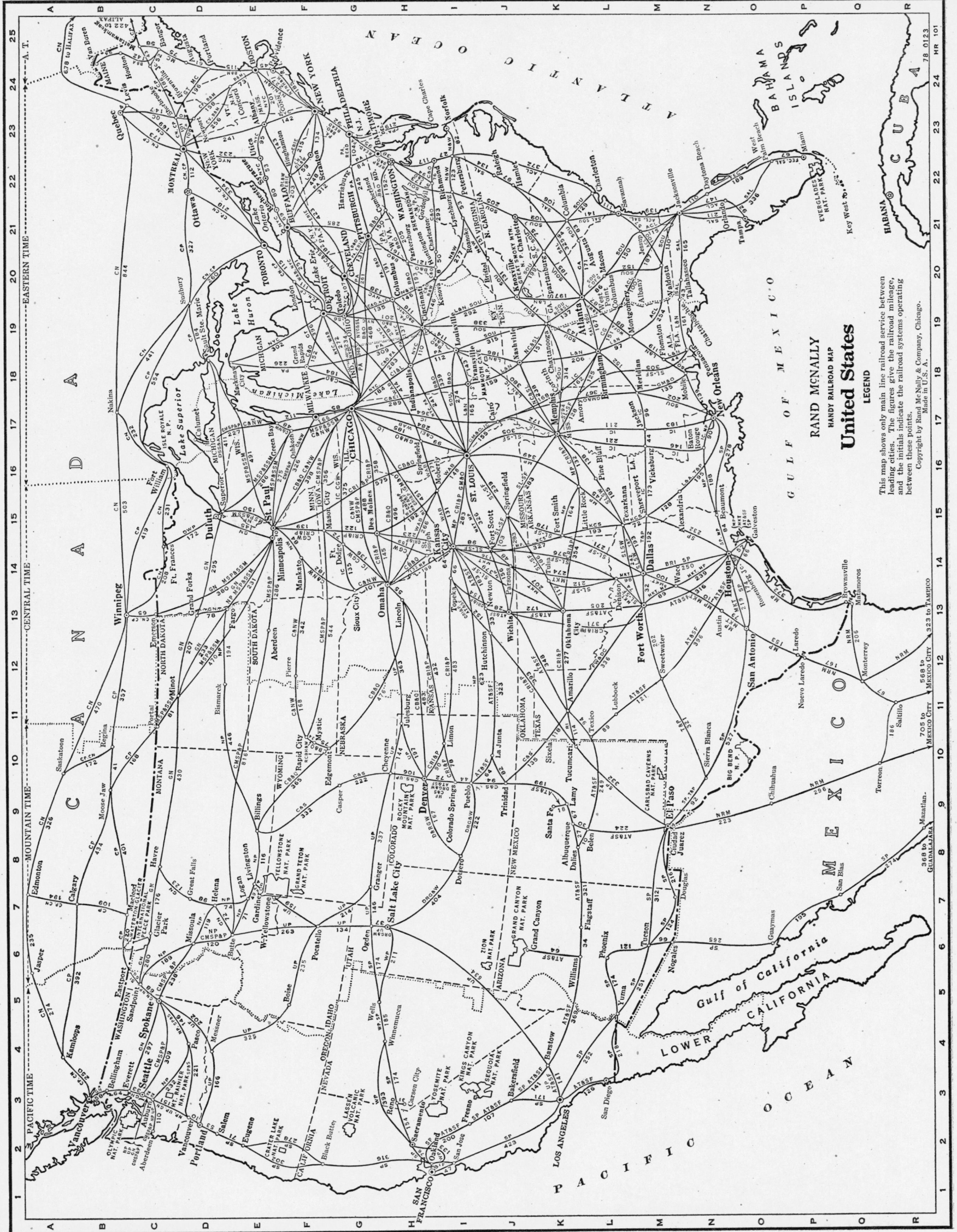

RAND McNALLY
HANDY RAILROAD MAP
United States
LEGEND

This map shows only main line railroad service between
leading cities. The figures give the railroad mileage,
and the initials indicate the railroad systems operating
between these points.

Copyright by Rand McNally & Company, Chicago.
Made in U.S.A.

19

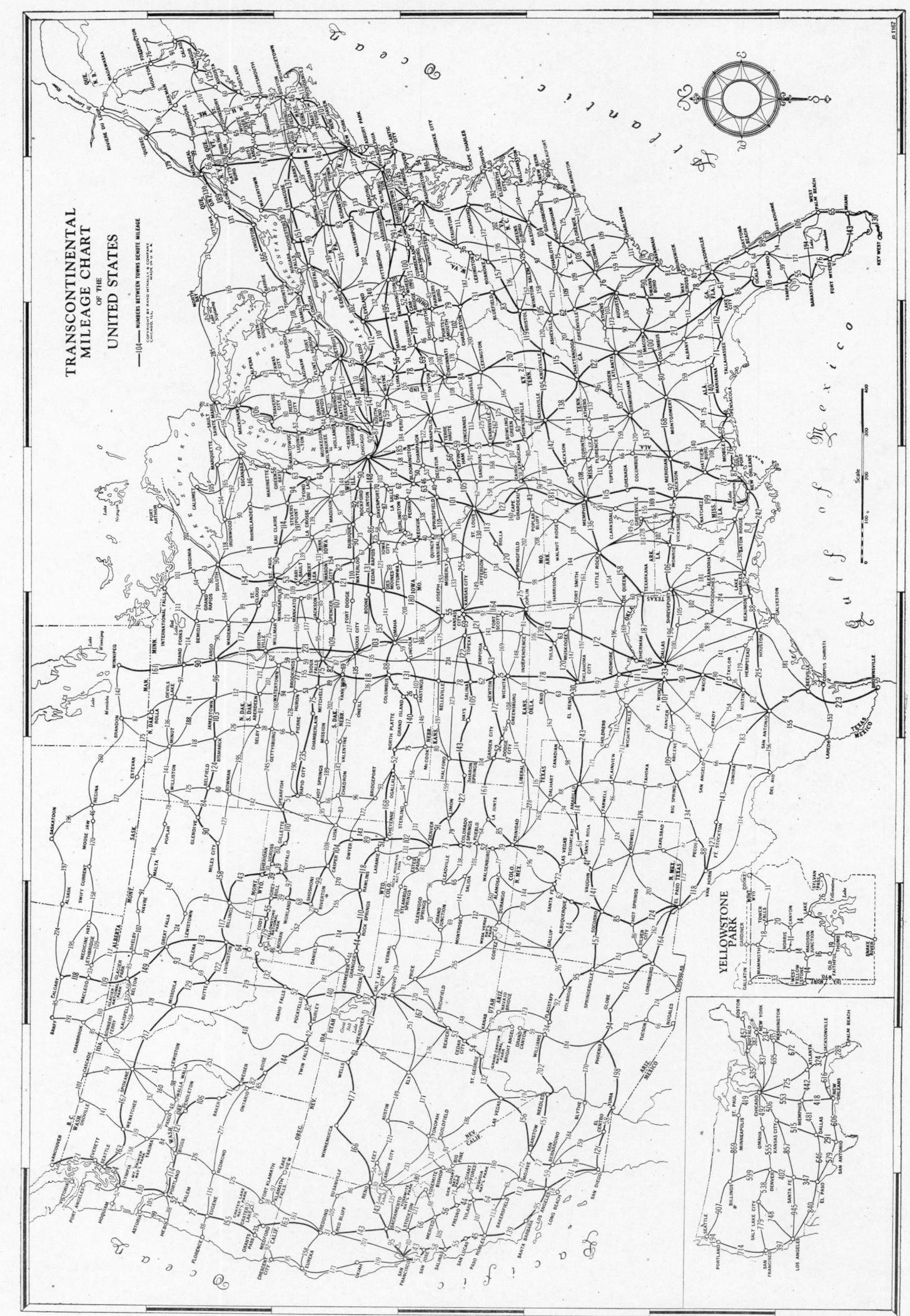

TRANSCONTINENTAL
MILEAGE CHART
OF THE
UNITED STATES

YELLOWSTONE
PARK

20

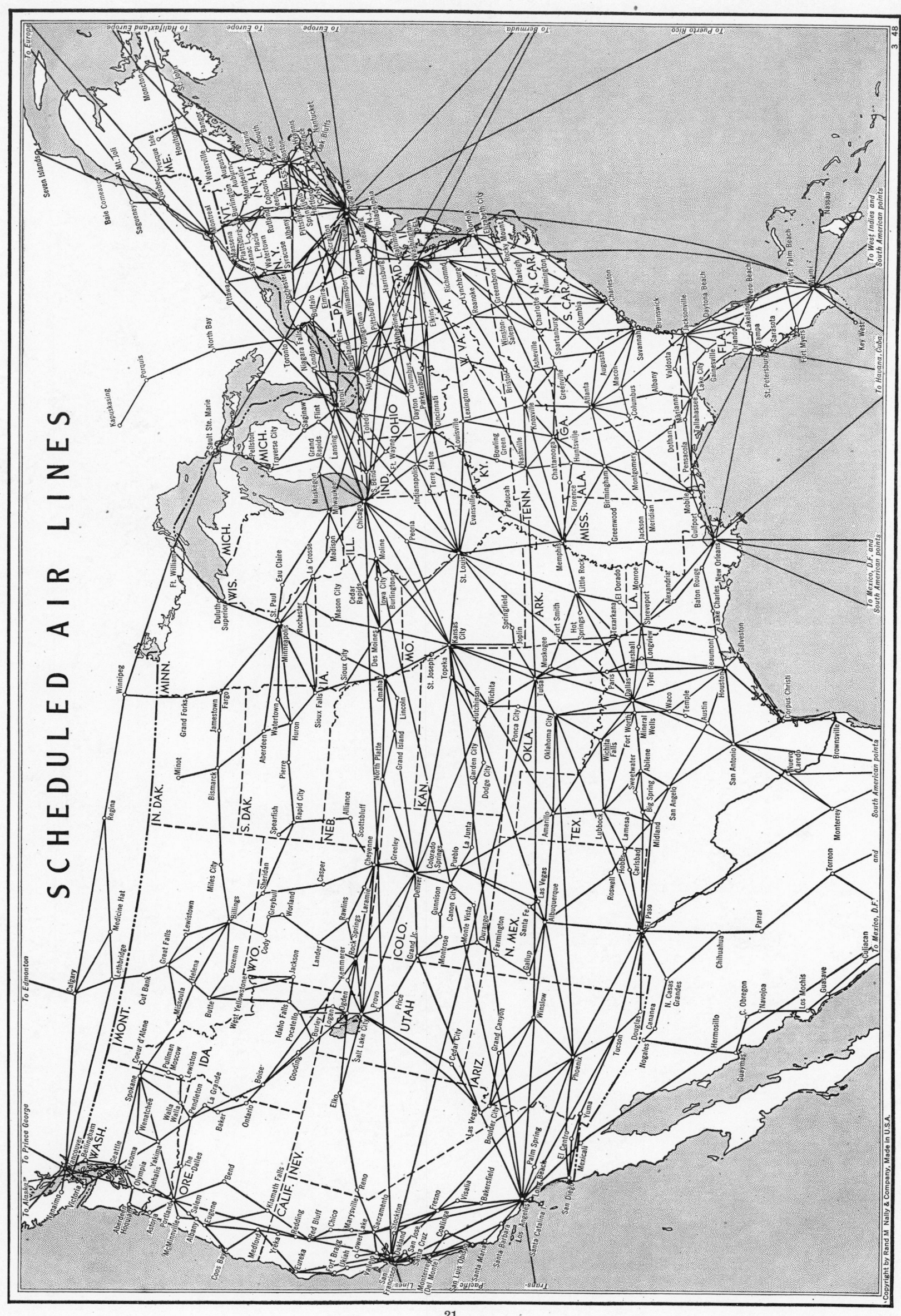

SCHEDULED AIR LINES

Air-Line Distances Between Fifty U. S. Cities
Given in Statute Miles

	Washington, D.C.	Vermilion, S. Dak.	Springfield, Mass.	Spokane, Wash.	Shreveport, La.	Seattle, Wash.	Schenectady, N.Y.	San Francisco, Calif.	Salt Lake City, Utah	St. Louis, Mo.	Richmond, Va.	Portland, Ore.	Portland, Me.	Pittsburgh, Pa.	Phoenix, Ariz.	Philadelphia, Pa.	Omaha, Nebr.	Oklahoma City, Okla.	Norfolk, Va.	New York, N.Y.	New Orleans, La.	Nashville, Tenn.	Missoula, Mont.	Minneapolis, Minn.	Miami, Fla.	Memphis, Tenn.	Louisville, Ky.	Los Angeles, Calif.	Kansas City, Mo.	Jacksonville, Fla.	Houghton, Mich.	Hot Springs, Ark.	Hastings, Nebr.	Galveston, Tex.	Fort Worth, Tex.	Fargo, N. Dak.	El Paso, Tex.	Detroit, Mich.	Des Moines, Iowa	Denver, Colo.	Cleveland, Ohio	Cincinnati, Ohio	Chicago, Ill.	Buffalo, N.Y.	Brownsville, Tex.	Boston, Mass.	Boise, Idaho	Baltimore, Md.	Atlanta, Ga.	Albuquerque, N. Mex.
Albuquerque, N. Mex.	1648	742	1889	1028	704	1178	1823	893	483	938	1628	1107	2015	1498	330	1748	718	518	1696	1810	1030	1117	895	980	1710	938	1174	663	675	1492	1252	773	588	803	561	968	228	1360	833	332	1417	1248	1126	1577	838	1881	774	1670	1273	

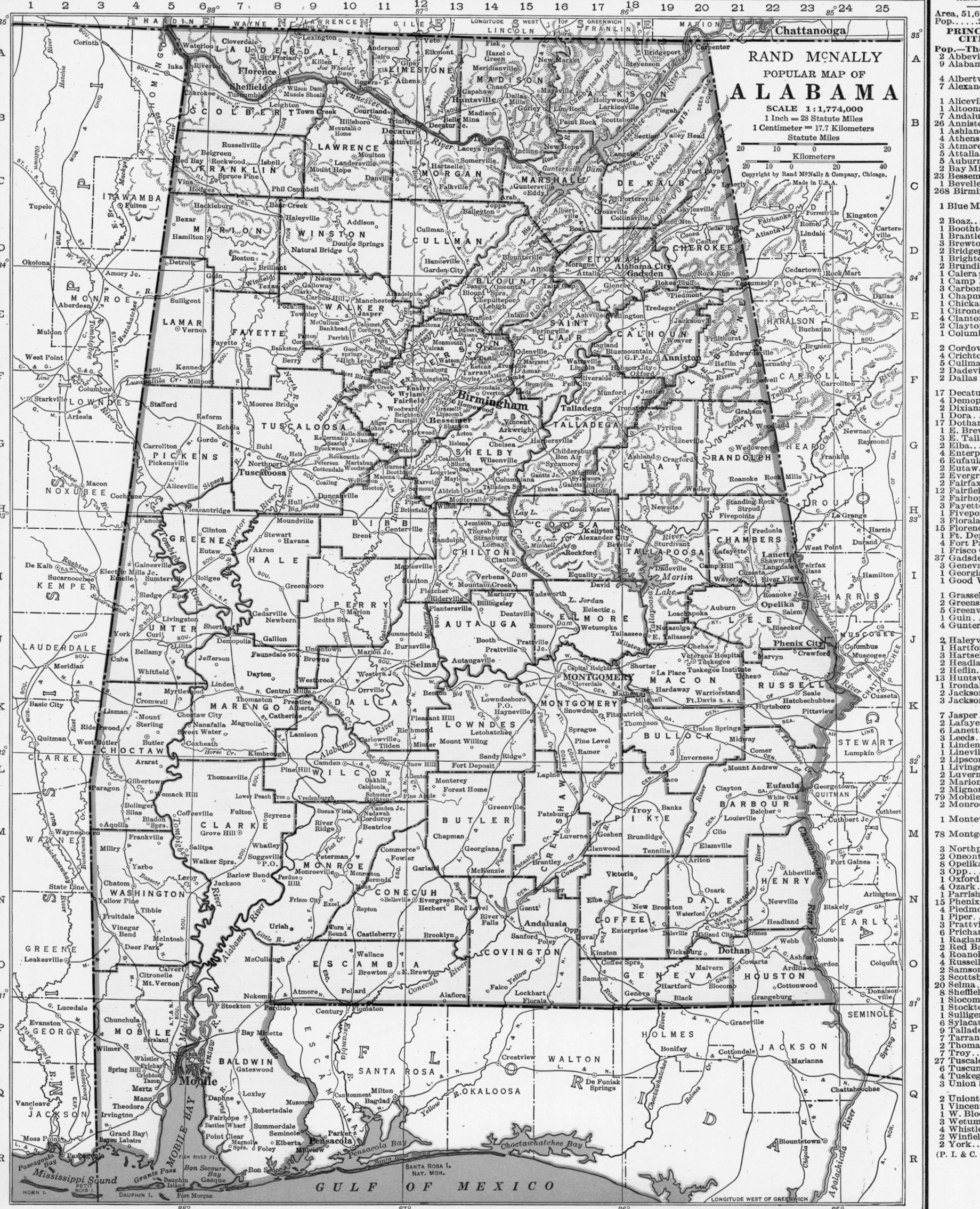

RAND McNALLY POPULAR MAP OF ALABAMA

SCALE 1:1,774,000
1 Inch = 28 Statute Miles
1 Centimeter = 17.7 Kilometers

Copyright by Rand McNally & Company, Chicago. Made in U.S.A.

ALABAMA

Area, 51,609 sq. m.
Pop.....2,832,961

PRINCIPAL CITIES

Pop.—Thousands

2	Abbeville..M 22
9	Alabama City D 17
4	Albertville..O 16
7	Alexander City H 18
1	Aliceville...H 5
1	Altoona...D 16
1	Andalusia..N 15
26	Anniston...F 19
2	Ashland...E 19
1	Athens....A 12
3	Atmore...O 8
2	Attalla....D 17
5	Auburn...J 21
2	Bay Minette P 7
23	Bessemer..G 12
1	Beville....L 18
268	Birmingham F 13
1	Blue Mountain F 19
2	Boaz...D 17
1	Boothton..G 12
2	Brantley...M 16
2	Brewton...O 11
1	Brighton...G 12
1	Brundidge M 19
1	Calera...H 13
1	Camp Hill..I 19
1	Carbon Hill E 9
1	Chapman..M 13
1	Chickasaw..P 5
1	Citronelle...O 4
4	Clanton...I 14
1	Clayton...L 21
1	Columbiana G 14
2	Cordova...E 11
2	Crichton..Q 5
5	Cullman..D 13
2	Dadeville..I 19
1	Dallas Mills B 14
17	Decatur..B 12
2	Demopolis..J 6
2	Dixiana..E 14
17	Dothan...O 21
1	E. Brewton O 11
3	E. Tallassee J 19
2	Elba...N 17
4	Enterprise N 18
5	Eufaula...L 23
1	Eutaw....I 6
2	Evergreen N 12
1	Fairfax....I 23
2	Fairfield...F 12
2	Fairhope..Q 5
2	Fayette....F 11
3	Fivepoints H 22
2	Florala...P 16
15	Florence...B 8
1	Ft. Deposit L 14
1	Fort Payne C 19
1	Frisco City N 9
4	Gadsden..D 18
3	Geneva...O 21
1	Georgiana M 13
1	Good Water H 17
1	Grasselli...F 12
1	Greensboro. I 8
5	Greenville..L 14
2	Guin....E 10
4	Guntersville C 16
2	Haleyville..D 8
1	Hartford...O 19
1	Hartselle..C 12
1	Headland..N 22
1	Heflin...F 20
13	Huntsville..B 14
1	Irondale...F 14
2	Jackson...N 6
2	Jacksonville E 19
7	Jasper....E 10
1	Lafayette..I 21
6	Lanett...I 22
2	Leeds....F 14
1	Linden...K 7
1	Lineville..G 19
2	Lipscomb..G 12
1	Livingston..J 5
2	Luverne...M 16
2	Marion...J 10
1	Mignon..H 16
79	Mobile...Q 5
2	Monroeville M 10
1	Montevallo H 13
78	Montgomery J 16
3	Northport..G 8
1	Oneonta..E 15
3	Opelika...I 21
1	Opp....N 16
1	Oxford...F 19
1	Ozark...N 20
1	Parrish..E 10
5	Phenix City J 24
4	Piedmont..E 20
1	Piper...H 11
3	Prattville..J 16
1	Prichard..Q 5
1	Ragland...E 17
1	Red Bay..C 5
4	Roanoke..F 21
4	Russellville B 8
1	Samson..O 17
20	Selma...J 12
8	Sheffield..B 8
1	Slocomb O 20
1	Stockton..P 6
1	Sulligent..E 5
2	Sylacauga..G 16
6	Talladega..F 17
7	Tarrant...F 13
2	Thomasville L 7
7	Troy...M 18
27	Tuscaloosa..G 8
6	Tuscumbia..B 8
1	Tuskegee..J 20
3	Union Springs K 20
2	Uniontown..J 9
1	Vincent...G 15
1	W. Blocton H 11
3	Wetumpka..J 16
2	Whistler...P 5
2	Winfield...F 10
2	York....J 4

(P. I. & C. 789)

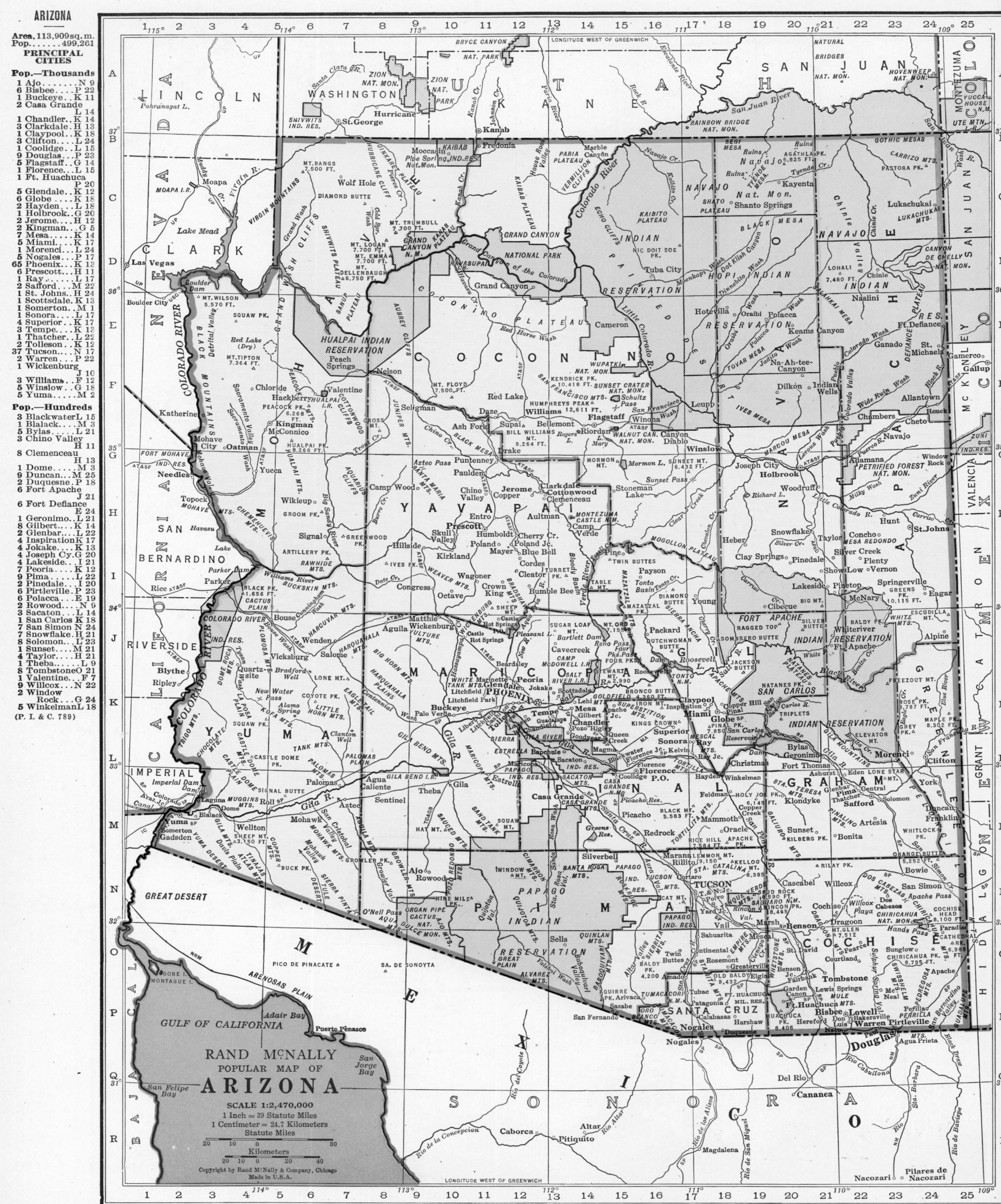

ARIZONA

Area, 113,909 sq. m.
Pop......499,261

PRINCIPAL CITIES

Pop.—Thousands
1 Ajo.......N 9
6 Bisbee....P 22
1 Buckeye..K 11
2 Casa Grande L 14
1 Chandler..K 14
1 Clarkdale.H 13
1 Claypool..K 18
3 Clifton....L 24
2 Coolidge..L 15
9 Douglas...P 23
1 Flagstaff..G 14
1 Florence...L 15
1 Ft. Huachuca P 20
5 Glendale..K 12
6 Globe.....K 18
2 Hayden....L 18
1 Holbrook..G 20
2 Jerome....H 12
1 Kingman...G 5
7 Mesa......K 14
5 Miami.....K 17
1 Morenci...L 24
2 Nogales...P 17
65 Phoenix...K 12
6 Prescott...H 11
1 Ray.......L 17
5 Safford...M 22
1 St. Johns..H 24
1 Scottsdale.K 13
1 Somerton..M 1
3 Sonora....K 17
4 Superior...K 17
3 Tempe.....K 13
2 Thatcher..K 22
2 Tolleson..K 12
37 Tucson....N 17
2 Warren....P 22
1 Wickenburg J 10
3 Williams...F 12
5 Winslow...G 18
5 Yuma......M 2

Pop.—Hundreds
3 Blackwater L 15
1 Blalack....M 3
5 Bylas......L 21
2 Chino Valley H 11
8 Clemenceau H 13
1 Dome......M 3
1 Duncan....M 25
2 Duquesne..P 18
4 Fort Apache J 21
6 Fort Defiance E 24
1 Geronimo..L 21
1 Gilbert....K 14
2 Glenbar...L 22
4 Inspiration K 17
4 Jokake....K 13
4 Joseph Cy..G 20
1 Lakeside...I 21
7 Peoria....K 12
5 Pima......L 21
2 Pinedale...I 20
1 Pirtleville P 23
4 Polacca....E 19
2 Rowood....N 9
2 Sacaton...L 14
1 San Carlos L 18
7 San Simon N 24
7 Snowflake.H 21
8 Solomon...L 23
1 Sunset....M 21
4 Taylor....H 21
1 Theba.....L 9
1 Tombstone O 21
1 Valentine..N 7
1 Willcox....N 22
2 Window
   Rock....G 24
5 WinkelmanL 18
(P. I. & C. 789)

RAND McNALLY
POPULAR MAP OF
ARIZONA

SCALE 1:2,470,000
1 Inch = 39 Statute Miles
1 Centimeter = 24.7 Kilometers
Statute Miles
Kilometers

Copyright by Rand McNally & Company, Chicago
Made in U.S.A.

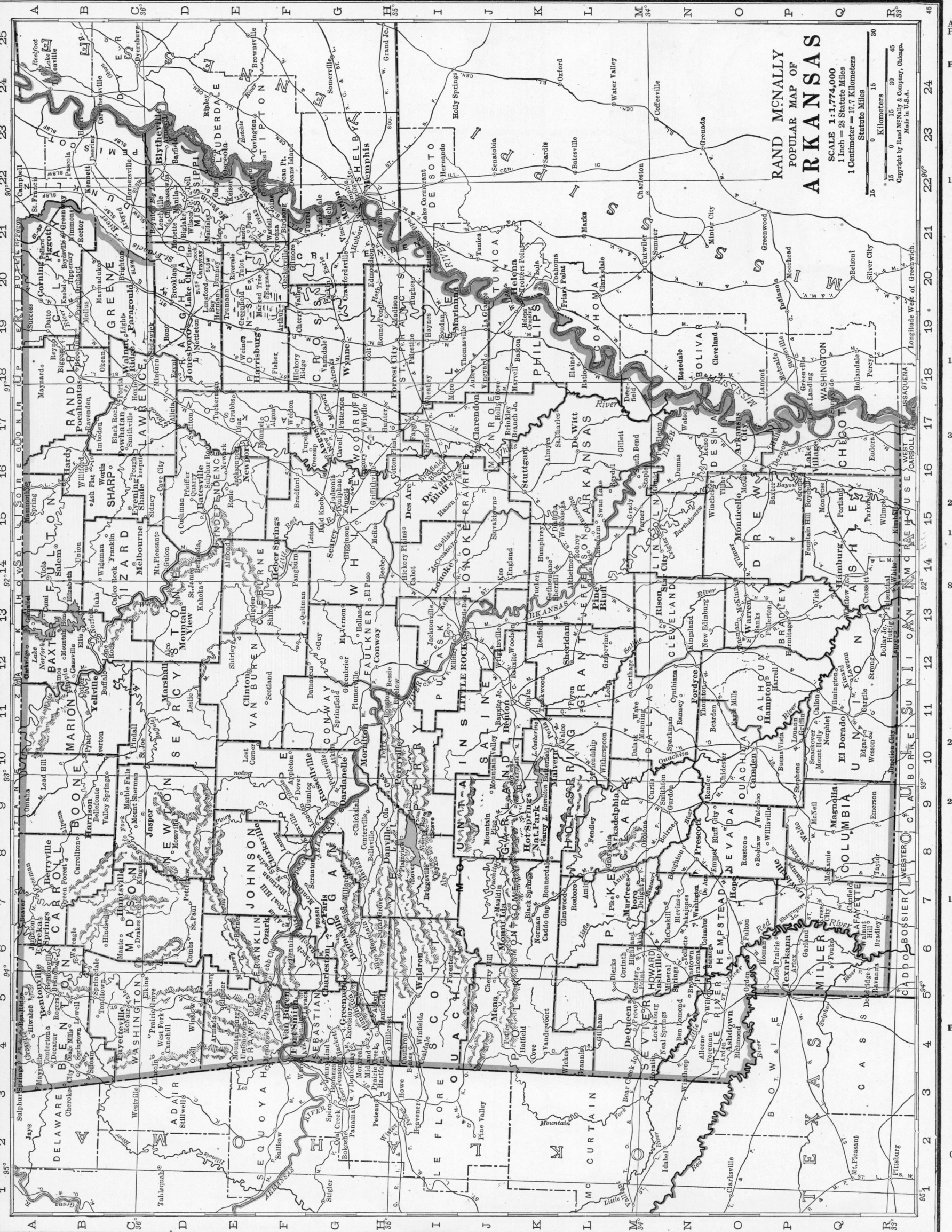

RAND McNALLY
POPULAR MAP OF
ARKANSAS
SCALE 1:1,774,000
1 Inch = 28 Statute Miles
1 Centimeter = 17.7 Kilometers
Statute Miles
Kilometers
Copyright by Rand McNally & Company, Chicago.
Made in U.S.A.

ARKANSAS

Area, 53,102 sq. m.
Pop.....1,949,387

PRINCIPAL CITIES

Pop.—Thousands

(P. I. & C. 789)

CALIFORNIA

Area, 158,693 sq. m.
Pop.....6,907,387

PRINCIPAL CITIES

Pop.—Thousands

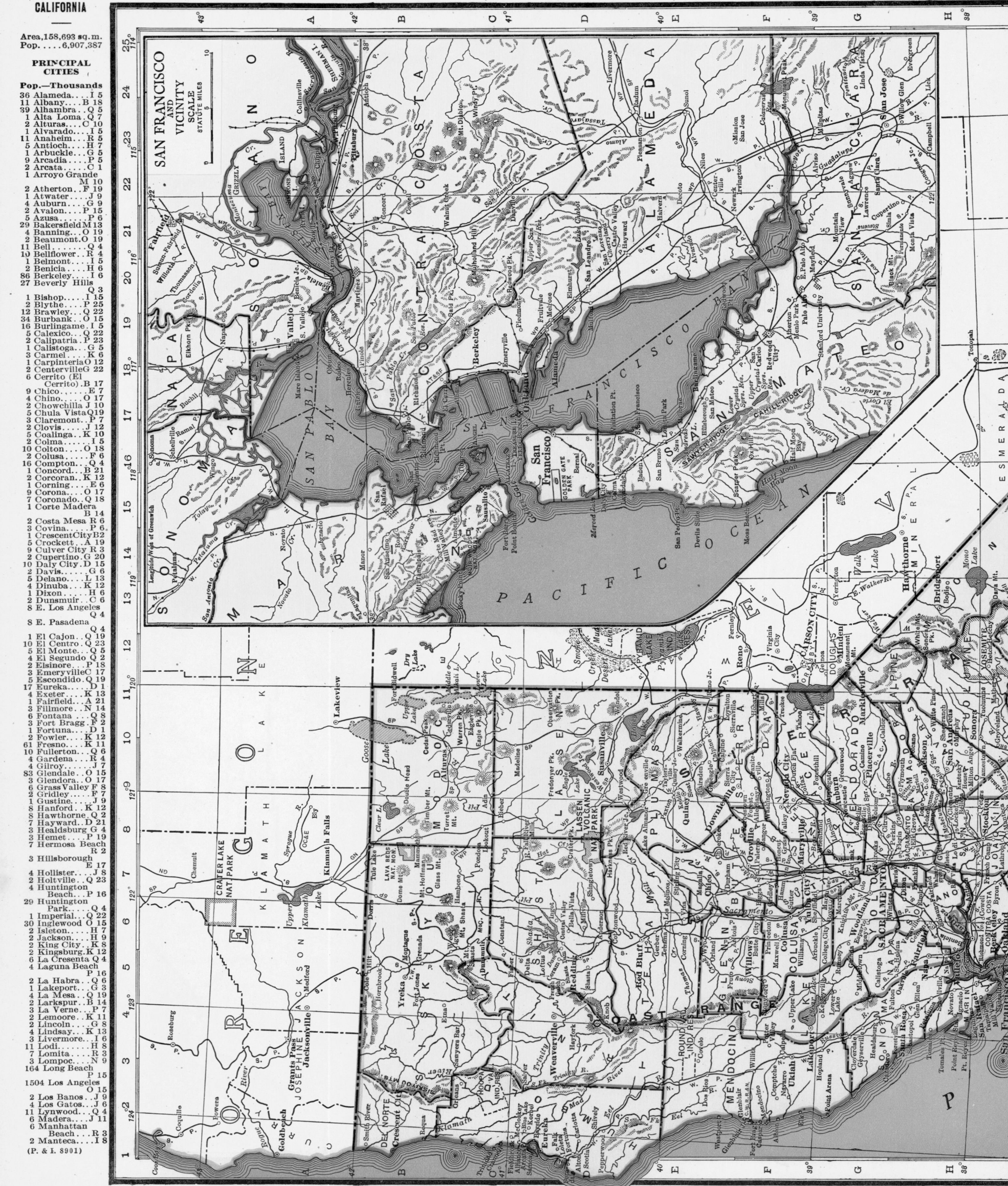

RAND MCNALLY
14 x 21 INCH MAP OF
CALIFORNIA
SCALE 1:2,820,000
1 Inch = 44.5 Statute Miles
1 Centimeter = 28.2 Kilometers

Statute Miles

Kilometers

Railroads ——— Electric Lines ———

Copyright by Rand McNally & Company, Chicago.
Made in U.S.A.

27

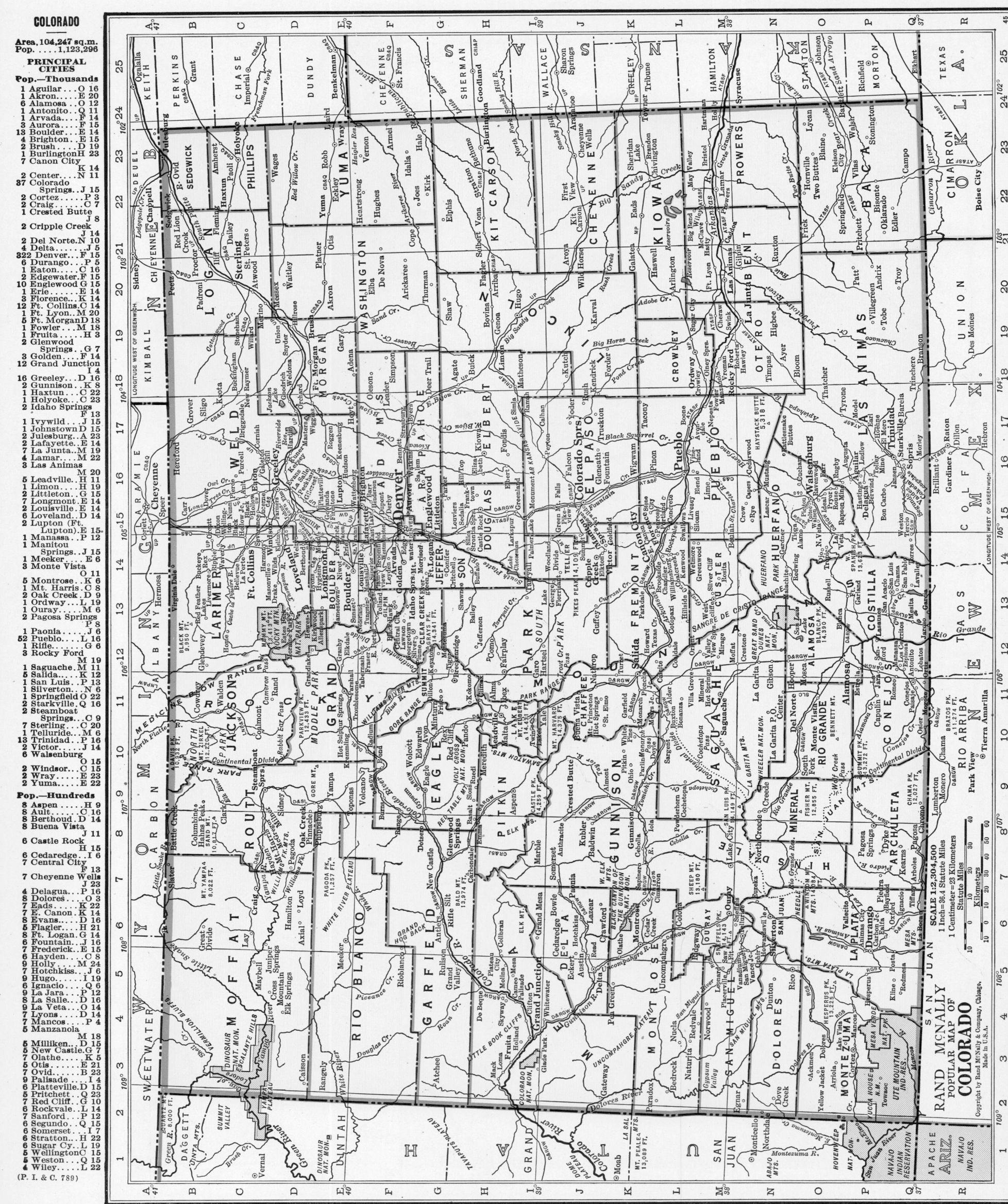

COLORADO

Area, 104,247 sq.m.
Pop. 1,123,296

PRINCIPAL CITIES

Pop.—Thousands

1 Aguilar . . . . O 16
1 Akron . . . . E 20
6 Alamosa . . O 12
2 Antonito . . Q 11
4 Arvada . . . . F 15
3 Aurora . . . . F 15
13 Boulder . . . . E 14
4 Brighton . . E 15
2 Brush . . . . . D 19
1 Burlington H 23
7 Canon City
K 14
2 Center . . . . N 11
37 Colorado
Springs . J 15
2 Cortez . . . . P 3
2 Craig . . . . . C 7
1 Crested Butte
J 8
2 Cripple Creek
J 14
2 Del Norte . N 10
2 Delta . . . . . J 5
322 Denver . . F 15
5 Durango . . P 5
2 Eaton . . . . E 14
1 Edgewater . F 15
10 Englewood G 15
1 Erie . . . . . E 14
2 Florence . . K 14
12 Ft. Collins . D 14
5 Ft. Lyon . . M 20
5 Ft. Morgan D 18
1 Fowler . . . M 18
1 Fruita . . . . H 3
2 Glenwood
Springs . G 7
3 Golden . . . F 14
12 Grand Junction
I 4
16 Greeley . . . D 15
2 Gunnison . . K 8
1 Haxtun . . . C 22
1 Holyoke . . C 23
2 Idaho Springs
F 13
1 Ivywild . . . J 15
1 Johnstown D 15
2 Julesburg . A 23
1 Lafayette. E 14
4 La Junta . . M 19
3 Lamar . . . M 22
3 Las Animas
M 20
5 Leadville . . H 11
1 Limon . . . H 19
7 Littleton . . E 14
2 Longmont. E 14
2 Louisville . E 14
6 Loveland . D 14
2 Lupton (Ft.
Lupton) E. 15
1 Manassa . . P 12
1 Manitou
Springs. J 15
1 Meeker . . . E 6
3 Monte Vista
O 11
5 Montrose . . K 6
1 Mt. Harris . C 8
2 Oak Creek . D 9
1 Ordway . . L 19
2 Ouray . . . . K 6
2 Pagosa Springs
P 8
2 Paonia . . . J 6
52 Pueblo . . . L 16
2 Rifle . . . . . G 6
7 Rocky Ford
M 19
1 Saguache . . K 10
5 Salida . . . . K 12
1 San Luis . . P 13
2 Silverton . N 6
1 Springfield O 22
2 Starkville . Q 16
9 Steamboat
Springs . . C 9
7 Sterling . . C 20
1 Telluride . . N 6
13 Trinidad . . P 16
2 Victor . . . . J 14
6 Walsenburg
O 15
2 Windsor . . . D 15
2 Wray . . . . E 23
5 Yuma . . . . E 22

Pop.—Hundreds

8 Aspen . . . . H 9
8 Ault . . . . . D 14
8 Berthoud . D 14
8 Buena Vista
J 11
6 Castle Rock
H 15
4 Cedaredge . J 6
7 Central City
F 13
7 Cheyenne Wells
J 23
4 Delagua . . P 16
8 Dolores . . O 3
7 Eads . . . . K 22
7 E. Canon . K 14
3 Evans . . . . D 15
8 Flagler . . . H 21
8 Ft. Logan G 14
6 Fountain . . K 15
5 Frederick . E 15
4 Hayden . . . C 8
9 Holly . . . . M 24
7 Hotchkiss. . J 6
7 Hugo . . . . Q 6
1 Ignacio . . . Q 6
6 La Jara . . P 12
5 La Salle . . D 16
6 La Veta . . O 14
7 Lyons . . . . D 14
2 Mancos . . P 4
5 Manzanola
M 18
5 Milliken . . D 15
5 New Castle. G 7
7 Olathe . . . K 5
6 Otis . . . . . B 21
8 Ovid . . . . B 23
9 Palisade . . I 4
5 Platteville . D 15
6 Pritchett . Q 23
5 Red Cliff . G 10
7 Rockvale . K 14
7 Sanford . . P 12
8 Segundo . . Q 15
6 Somerset . . I 7
6 Stratton . . H 22
5 Sugar City . L 19
5 Wellington C 14
9 Weston . . . Q 15
4 Wiley . . . . L 22

(P. I. & C. 789)

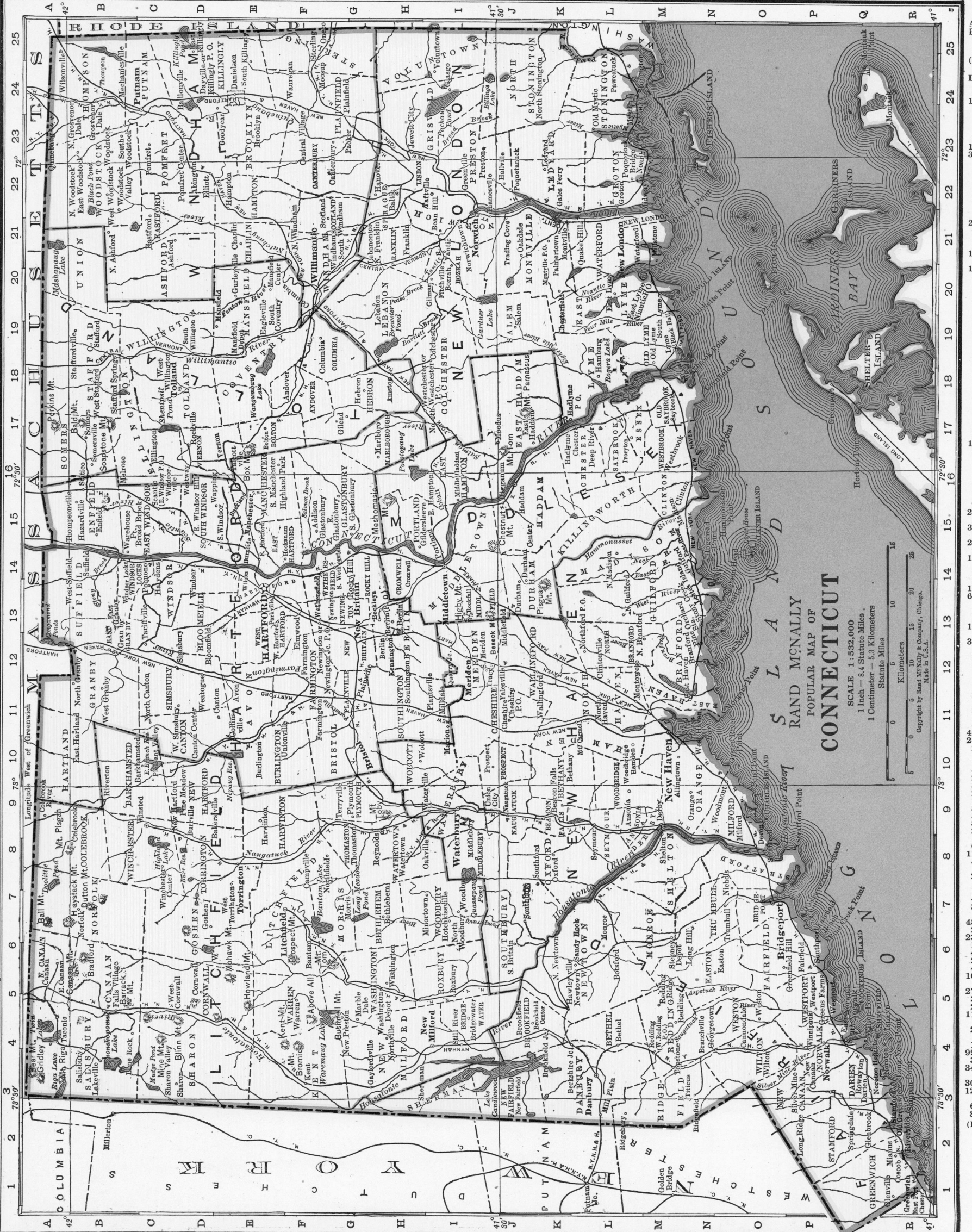

Area, 5,009 sq. m.
Pop......1,709,242

PRINCIPAL CITIES
(■Township Classi-
fied as Urban)

Pop.—Thousands
5	Allingtown	M 10
19	Ansonia	L 9
2	Baltic	H 22
1	Beacon Falls	K 9
3	Bethel	L 4
2	Branford	N 12
147	Bridgeport	O 7
30	Bristol	G 10
1	Broad Brook	B 15
2	Burnside	E 15
1	Canaan	A 5
1	Chester	I 17
1	Clinton	N 16
1	Collinsville	E 11
3	Cromwell	H 14
22	Danbury	L 3
5	Danielson	E 24
3	Darien	Q 3
1	Deep River	L17
10	Derby	M 8
1	E. Haddam	J 17
19	East Hartford	E 14
6	E. Haven	E 11
1	East Lyme (Niantic)	L 20
5	E. Norwalk	Q 4
5	E. Port Chester	R 1
1	Elmwood	R 13
9	Enfield	B 15
3	Essex	L 18
5	Fairfield	P 6
1	Farmington	F 12
1	Gildersleeve	I 15
4	Glastonbury	F 15
2	Glenbrook	Q 3
17	Greenwich	R 1
5	Groton	L 22
1	Guilford	N 14
166	Hartford	E 14
4	Jewett City	H 23
1	Kensington	H 12
2	Lakeville	B 4
1	Litchfield	F 7
1	Long Hill	N 7
1	Madison	M 15
23	Manchester	E 16
39	Meriden	I 12
1	Middlebury	I 8
26	Middletown	I 14
11	Milford	L 11
1	Milldale	I 11
2	Moosup	F 24
3	Mystic	L 23
15	Naugatuck	J 9
69	New Britain	G 13
2	New Canaan	P 3
161	New Haven	L 11
30	New London	L 21
3	New Milford	I 4
1	Niantic (E. Lyme)	L 20
1	Noank	M 23
2	Norfolk	D 6
2	Noroton Heights	R 3
1	North Grosvenor Dale	A 24
11	N. Haven	L 11
40	Norwalk	P 4
24	Norwich	L 21
1	Old Greenwich	R 2
1	Orange	N 9
4	Pawcatuck	L 25
2	Plainfield	G 24
3	Plantsville	I 11
2	Portland	I 14
1	Preston	I 23
8	Putnam	C 24
2	Riverside	R 2
8	Rockville	D 17
2	Sandy Hook	K 6
2	Seymour	L 8
11	Shelton	M 8
2	Southington	I 11
2	South Manchester	E 16
1	Southport	P 6
4	Springdale	Q 3
3	Stafford Springs	B 18
48	Stamford	K 2
23	Stonington	M 24
23	Stratford	O 3
1	Suffield	B 14
4	Taftville	H 22
2	Terryville	G 9
4	Thomaston	G 8
5	Thompsonville	A 15
27	Torrington	E 7
3	Union City	J 9
2	Unionville	F 11
11	Wallingford	K 12
2	Warehouse Point	B 15
1	Washington	H 5
99	Waterbury	I 9
4	Watertown	H 8
34	W. Hartford	E 13
30	W. Haven	N 10
12	Willimantic	F 20
6	Windsor	D 14
8	Winsted	C 9

(P. I. & C. 789)

29

FLORIDA

Area, 58,560 sq. m.
Pop.... 1,897,414

PRINCIPAL CITIES

Pop.—Thousands

4 Apalachicola	D 2
1 Apopka	G 17
4 Arcadia	K 16
4 Auburndale	H 16
3 Avon Park	J 18
5 Bartow	I 16
4 Belle Glade	L 21
2 Blountstown	B 1, N 12
2 Bonifay	M 9
2 Boynton	M 24
7 Bradenton	J 13
2 Brooksville	G 13
1 Cedar Keys	F 10
7 Chattahoochee	B 2
2 Chipley	M 10
10 Clearwater	I 12
2 Clermont	G 16
1 Clewiston	L 20
3 Cocoa	H 21
8 Coral Gables	N 23
1 Crescent City	E 17
2 Cross City	D 10
3 Dade City	H 14
3 Dania	N 24
23 Daytona Beach	E 19
2 Deerfield	M 24
3 De Funiak Springs	M 7
7 De Land	F 18
4 Delray Beach	M 24
2 Dunedin	I 12
2 Dunnellon	F 13
3 Eustis	F 16
3 Fernandina	B 17
18 Fort Lauderdale	M 24
2 Fort Meade	I 16
11 Fort Myers	L 16
8 Fort Pierce	J 23
2 Frostproof	I 17
14 Gainesville	D 13
2 Graceville	M 10
1 Green Cove Springs	C 16
1 Greenville	B 8
2 Haines City	H 17
2 Hallandale	N 24
1 Hastings	D 17
1 Havana	B 4
2 Hialeah	N 23
2 High Springs	D 12
1 Holly Hill	E 19
6 Hollywood	N 24
1 Homestead	O 22
1 Inverness	F 14
173 Jacksonville	B 15
2 Jasper	B 11
13 Key West	N 16
3 Kissimmee	H 18
6 Lake City	C 12
22 Lakeland	I 15
5 Lake Wales	I 17
7 Lake Worth	L 24
1 Largo	I 12
5 Leesburg	F 16
3 Live Oak	C 11
3 Madison	B 9
4 Manatee	J 13
3 Marianna	M 11
3 Melbourne	H 21
172 Miami	N 24
28 Miami Beach	O 24
2 Miami Shores	N 24
2 Milton	M 3
2 Monticello	B 7
2 Mount Dora	F 17
2 Mulberry	I 15
4 New Smyrna Beach	F 20
9 Ocala	E 14
2 Okeechobee	J 20
37 Orlando	G 18
1 Ormond	E 19
1 Oviedo	G 19
5 Pahokee	L 22
2 Palatka	D 17
2 Palm Beach	L 24
3 Palmetto	J 13
12 Panama City	O9
37 Pensacola	N 3
2 Perry	C 8
1 Plant City	I 15
2 Pompano	M 24
2 Port St. Joe	P 11
1 Port Tampa City	I 13
2 Punta Gorda	L 15
4 Quincy	B 4
12 Saint Augustine	D 18
2 Saint Cloud	H 18
61 Saint Petersburg	I 12
10 Sanford	G 18
11 Sarasota	J 13
3 Sebring	J 18
2 S. Miami	O 22
1 Starke	D 14
2 Stuart	K 23
16 Tallahassee	B 5
108 Tampa	I 13
3 Tarpon Springs	H 12
1 Tavares	F 16
2 Titusville	G 20
3 Vero Beach	J 22
3 Wauchula	J 16
34 West Palm Beach	L 24
1 Wildwood	F 15
2 Winter Garden	G 17
6 Winter Haven	I 16
5 Winter Park	G 18
1 Zephyrhills	H 14

(P. I. & C. 789)

RAND McNALLY
POPULAR MAP OF
FLORIDA

SCALE 1 : 2,471,000
1 Inch = 39 Statute Miles
1 Centimeter = 24.7 Kilometers

Statute Miles

Kilometers

Copyright by Rand McNally & Company, Chicago.
Made in U.S.A.

4567

RAND McNALLY
POPULAR MAP OF
GEORGIA

SCALE 1:1,964,000
1 Inch = 31 Statute Miles
1 Centimeter = 19.6 Kilometers
Statute Miles

Copyright by Rand McNally & Company, Chicago.
Made in U.S.A.

Area, 58,876 sq. m.
Pop. 3,123,723

PRINCIPAL CITIES

Pop.—Thousands

1	Acworth	E 5
2	Adel	O 12
19	Albany	M 7
2	Alma	M 17
4	Americus	L 8
1	Arlington	N 4
2	Ashburn	M 10
21	Athens	E 13
302	Atlanta	F 6
66	Augusta	G 20
6	Bainbridge	O 6
4	Barnesville	H 8
3	Baxley	M 18
3	Bibb City	J 3
1	Blackshear	N 19
3	Blakely	N 4
1	Blue Ridge	B 8
1	Boston	P 10
1	Bowdon	G 2
15	Brunswick	O 22
4	Buford	E 8
5	Cairo	O 8
3	Calhoun	C 4
2	Camilla	N 7
3	Canton	D 7
6	Carrollton	G 2
6	Cartersville	E 5
9	Cedartown	E 1
2	Chickamauga	B 3
2	Claxton	K 20
2	Cochran	J 12
8	College Park	F 6
53	Columbus	J 4
3	Commerce	D 12
2	Conyers	F 7
2	Cordele	L 10
2	Cornelia	C 11
4	Covington	F 10
2	Cuthbert	L 4
7	Dallas	F 3
10	Dalton	C 3
4	Dawson	M 6
17	Decatur	F 8
2	Donalsonville	O 5
5	Douglas	N 14
2	Douglasville	F 4
8	Dublin	J 14
3	Eastman	K 13
12	East Point	F 7
4	E. Thomaston	I 8
2	Eatonton	G 13
1	Edison	M 4
6	Elberton	E 16
2	Fairburn	F 5
2	Fitzgerald	M 13
1	Forsyth	H 9
1	Fort Gaines	M 2
2	Fort Valley	I 9
10	Gainesville	D 9
1	Glennville	L 20
2	Gordon	I 12
1	Grantville	H 5
2	Greensboro	G 13
13	Griffin	H 7
5	Hapeville	F 6
2	Hartwell	D 15
2	Hawkinsville	K 12
2	Hazlehurst	L 17
4	Hogansville	H 3
2	Jackson	H 8
2	Jefferson	E 12
2	Jesup	M 20
4	La Fayette	C 3
22	La Grange	H 3
2	Lavonia	D 14
2	Lawrenceville	E 8
2	Lithonia	F 8
5	Louisville	H 18
1	Lumpkin	L 4
2	Lyons	K 18
2	McCaysville	B 7
2	McRae	L 15
58	Macon	I 10
2	Madison	F 12
1	Manchester	I 6
5	Marietta	E 6
2	Metter	J 20
7	Milledgeville	H 12
3	Millen	I 20
2	Monroe	E 10
2	Montezuma	K 9
2	Monticello	H 11
10	Moultrie	N 9
4	Nashville	O 14
7	Newnan	G 5
2	Ocilla	M 13
2	Pelham	O 7
2	Perry	J 11
4	Porterdale	F 9
4	Quitman	P 11
1	Richland	K 5
1	Rockmart	F 2
26	Rome	D 3
2	Rossville	B 2
2	Roswell	D 7
2	Royston	D 13
4	Sandersville	H 14
96	Savannah	K 23
2	Shellman	L 5
2	Silvertown	I 6
1	Smyrna	E 6
2	Social Cir.	F 11
2	Sparta	G 14
3	Statesboro	J 20
4	Stone Mt.	F 8
2	Swainsboro	J 17
4	Sylvania	I 22
2	Sylvester	M 10
2	Tallapoosa	F 1
2	Tennille	I 15
10	Thomaston	I 8
13	Thomasville	P 9
3	Thomson	G 18
5	Tifton	N 11
4	Toccoa	C 12
2	Trion	C 3
1	Unadilla	K 10
2	Union Point	F 14
16	Valdosta	P 12
3	Vidalia	K 18
2	Vienna	L 10
1	Villa Rica	F 3
4	Warrenton	G 15
2	Washington	F 15
17	Waycross	O 17
4	Waynesboro	H 20
4	West Point	J 2
4	Winder	E 11
2	Wrightsville	I 16

(P. I. & C. 789.)

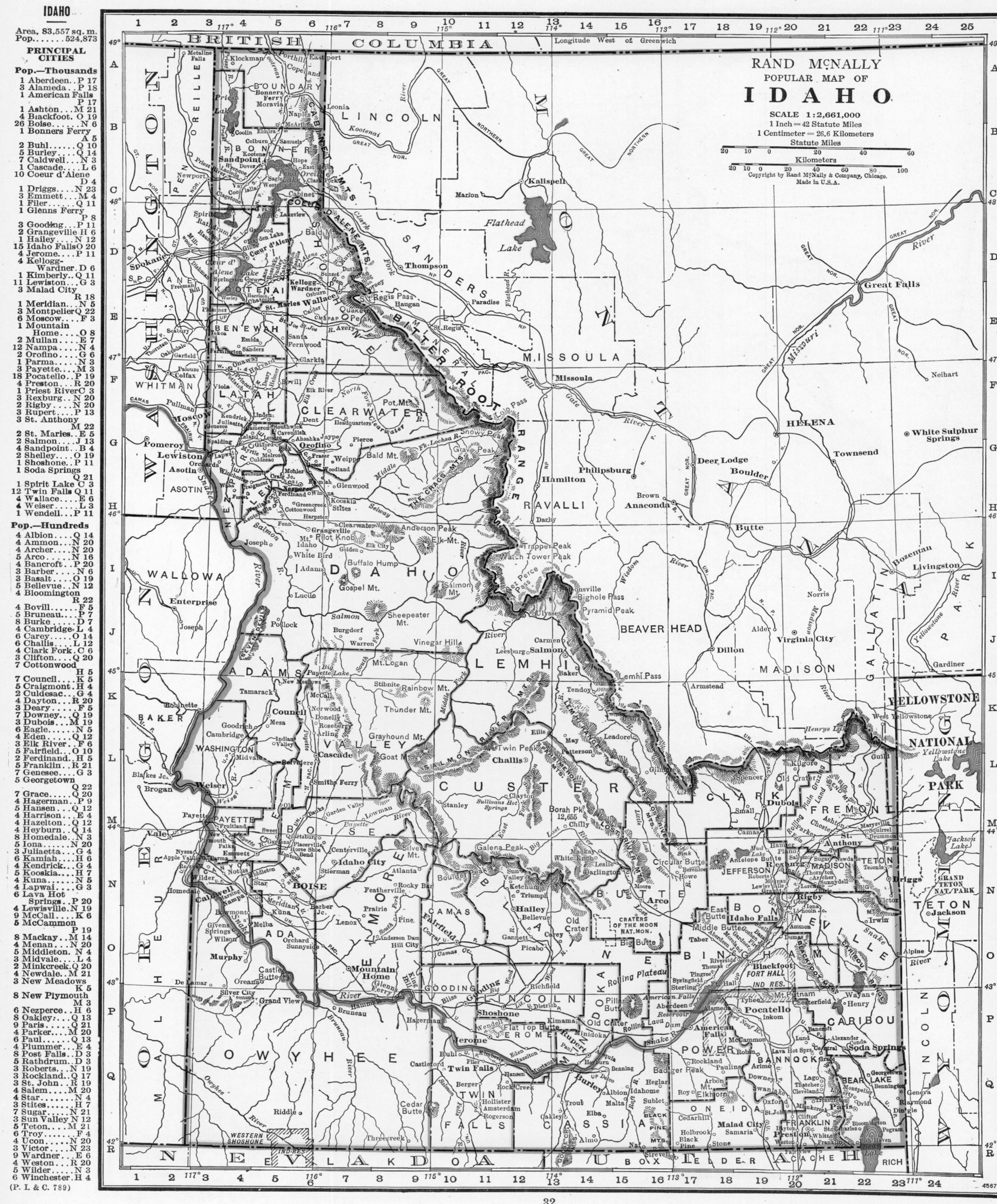

IDAHO

Area, 83,557 sq. m.
Pop......524,873

PRINCIPAL CITIES

Pop.—Thousands

1 Aberdeen...P 17
3 Alameda...P 18
1 American Falls
    P 17
1 Ashton...M 21
4 Blackfoot..O 19
26 Boise.....N 6
1 Bonners Ferry
    A 5
2 Buhl.....Q 10
5 Burley...Q 14
7 Caldwell...N 3
1 Cascade...L 6
10 Coeur d'Alene
    D 4
1 Driggs...N 23
3 Emmett...M 4
1 Filer....Q 11
1 Glenns Ferry
    P 8
3 Gooding...P 11
2 Grangeville H 6
1 Hailey...N 12
15 Idaho FallsO 20
4 Jerome...P 11
5 Kellogg...
    Wardner. D 6
1 Kimberly..Q 11
11 Lewiston...G 3
3 Malad City
    R 18
1 Meridian...N 5
3 Montpelier Q 22
6 Moscow...F 3
1 Mountain
    Home...O 8
2 Mullan...E 7
12 Nampa...N 4
2 Orofino...G 6
1 Parma...N 3
1 Payette..M 3
18 Pocatello P 19
1 Preston...R 20
1 Priest RiverC 3
1 Rexburg..N 20
2 Rigby...N 20
3 Rupert...P 13
3 St. Anthony
    M 22
2 St. Maries...E 5
2 Salmon...J 13
4 Sandpoint..B 4
3 Shelley...O 19
1 Shoshone..P 11
1 Soda Springs
    Q 21
1 Spirit Lake Q 3
12 Twin Falls Q 11
4 Wallace...E 6
1 Weiser...L 3
1 Wendell..P 11

Pop.—Hundreds

4 Albion...Q 14
4 Ammon...N 20
4 Archer...N 20
4 Arco...N 16
4 Bancroft..P 20
3 Barber...N 6
1 Basalt...O 19
2 Bellevue..N 12
1 Bloomington
    R 22
4 Bovill...F 5
3 Bruneau..P 7
8 Burke...D 7
4 Cambridge L 4
6 Carey...O 14
3 Challis...L 12
4 Clark Fork..C 6
3 Clifton...Q 20
7 Cottonwood
    H 5
7 Council...K 5
5 Craigmont..H 4
5 Culdesac..G 4
3 Dayton...R 20
4 Deary...F 5
7 Downey...Q 19
3 Dubois...M 19
8 Eagle...N 5
4 Eden...Q 12
4 Elk River..F 6
5 Fairfield...O 10
5 Ferdinand..H 5
4 Franklin...R 21
7 Genesee...G 3
7 Georgetown
    Q 22
7 Grace...Q 20
7 Hagerman..P 9
4 Hansen...Q 12
4 Harrison...E 4
4 Hazelton..Q 12
4 Heyburn...P 13
8 Homedale..N 3
1 Iona...N 20
4 Juliaetta..G 4
6 Kamiah...H 6
4 Kendrick..G 4
5 Kooskia...H 7
4 Kuna...N 5
4 Lapwai...G 3
4 Lava Hot
    Springs...P 20
4 Lewisville.N 19
7 McCall...K 6
5 McCammon
    P 19
8 Mackay...M 14
4 Menan...N 20
4 Middleton..N 4
3 Midvale...L 4
2 Minkcreek Q 20
4 Newdale..O 20
3 New Meadows
    K 5
8 New Plymouth
    M 3
6 Nezperce..H 6
6 Oakley...Q 13
9 Paris...Q 21
4 Parker...M 20
4 Paul...Q 13
4 Plummer...E 4
8 Post Falls..D 3
5 Rathdrum..D 3
3 Roberts...N 19
6 Rockland..Q 17
8 St. John...R 19
4 Salem...N 20
4 Star...N 4
3 Stites...H 7
7 Sugar...N 21
4 Sun Valley N 12
5 Teton...M 21
6 Troy...F 4
3 Ucon...N 20
3 Victor...N 23
9 Wardner...E 6
4 Weston...R 20
5 Wilder...N 3
6 Winchester H 4

(P. I. & C. 789)

RAND McNALLY
POPULAR MAP OF
IDAHO

SCALE 1:2,661,000
1 Inch = 42 Statute Miles
1 Centimeter = 26.6 Kilometers
Statute Miles
Kilometers
Copyright by Rand McNally & Company, Chicago.
Made in U.S.A.

4567

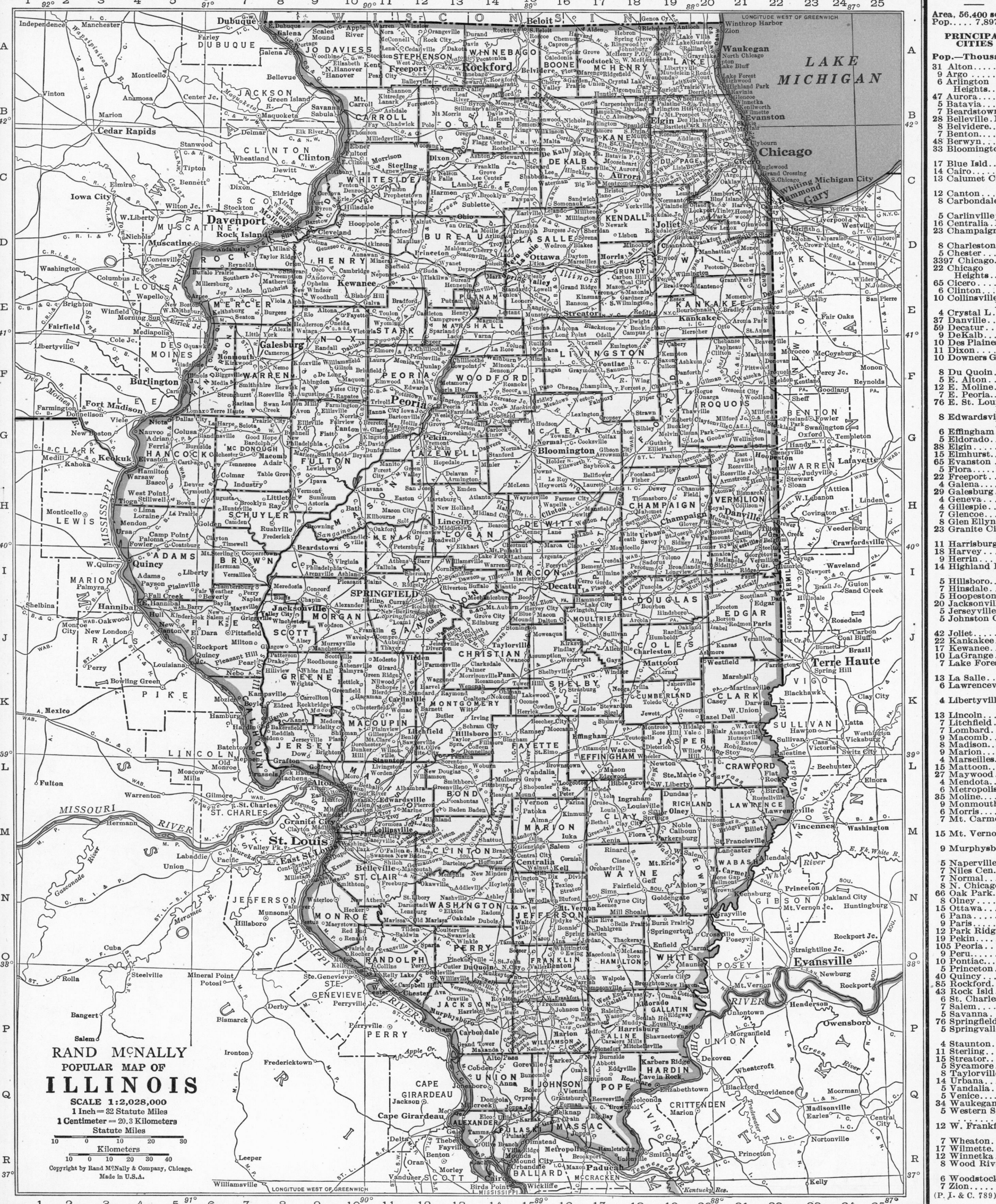

RAND McNALLY
POPULAR MAP OF
ILLINOIS

SCALE 1:2,028,000
1 Inch = 32 Statute Miles
1 Centimeter = 20.3 Kilometers
Statute Miles

Kilometers

Copyright by Rand McNally & Company, Chicago.
Made in U.S.A.

ILLINOIS
Area, 56,400 sq. m.
Pop.... 7,897,241

PRINCIPAL
CITIES

Pop.—Thousands

31 Alton.....L 10
9 Argo.....C 21
6 Arlington
Heights..B 20
47 Aurora...C 18
5 Batavia..C 18
7 Beardstown.I 8
28 Belleville.M 11
8 Belvidere..A 16
7 Benton...O 16
48 Berwyn...C 21
33 Bloomington
G 15
17 Blue Isld..C 21
14 Cairo....R 14
13 Calumet City
C 22
12 Canton...G 10
8 Carbondale
P 14
5 Carlinville.K 11
16 Centralia.N 15
19 Champaign
H 19
8 Charleston.J 19
5 Chester...O 11
3397 Chicago.C 21
22 Chicago
Heights..D 21
65 Cicero...C 21
10 Clinton...H 15
10 Collinsville
M 11
6 Crystal L..A 18
37 Danville..H 22
59 Decatur..I 15
5 DeKalb..B 16
10 Des Plaines.B 20
11 Dixon....C 13
10 Downers Gr.
C 20
9 Du Quoin..O 14
5 E. Alton..L 10
12 E. Moline..D 8
7 E. Peoria..G 12
76 E. St. Louis
M 10
8 Edwardsville
M 11
6 Effingham.L 16
5 Eldorado..P 18
38 Elgin....B 18
15 Elmhurst..C 20
8 Evanston..B 21
7 Flora....M 18
22 Freeport..A 12
5 Galena....A 9
29 Galesburg..F 9
5 Geneva...C 18
5 Gillespie..K 11
8 Glencoe..B 21
5 Glen Ellyn.C 19
23 Granite City
M 10
11 Harrisburg.P 17
9 Harvey...C 21
5 Herrin...P 15
14 Highland Park
B 21
5 Hillsboro..K 13
7 Hinsdale..C 20
5 Hoopeston.G 21
20 Jacksonville J 9
5 Jerseyville..L 9
5 Johnston City
P 16
42 Joliet....D 19
6 Kankakee..E 20
17 Kewanee..E 11
10 LaGrange..C 20
7 Lake Forest
A 20
13 La Salle..D 15
6 Lawrenceville
M 22
6 Libertyville
A 20
13 Lincoln...H 14
7 Litchfield..K 12
5 Lombard..C 20
3 Macomb...G 7
5 Madison..M 10
4 Marion...P 16
5 Marseilles.D 16
15 Mattoon..J 17
27 Maywood..C 20
3 Mendota..D 15
3 Metropolis.R 17
35 Moline...D 8
7 Monmouth..F 7
3 Morris...D 18
7 Mt. Carmel
N 21
15 Mt. Vernon
N 16
9 Murphysboro
P 14
5 Naperville..C 19
5 Niles Cen..B 21
6 Normal....G 15
8 N. Chicago.A 20
66 Oak Park..C 21
9 Olney....M 20
15 Ottawa....D 16
6 Pana.....K 15
3 Paris....J 21
5 Park Ridge.B 20
19 Pekin....G 12
105 Peoria....F 12
9 Peru.....D 15
10 Pontiac...F 17
3 Princeton..D 13
40 Quincy...I 4
85 Rockford..A 15
43 Rock Isld..D 8
6 St. Charles.B 18
5 Salem....M 16
5 Savanna...B 10
34 Waukegan.A 20
5 Western Spgs.
C 20
12 W. Frankfort
O 16
4 Staunton..K 11
5 Sterling..C 12
15 Streator..E 16
8 Sycamore..B 17
7 Taylorville.J 14
14 Urbana...H 19
5 Vandalia..L 15
5 Venice...M 10
34 Waukegan.A 20
5 Western Spgs.
C 20
12 W. Frankfort
O 16
6 Wheaton..C 19
17 Wilmette..B 21
12 Winnetka..B 21
8 Wood River
L 10
6 Woodstock.A 17
7 Zion.....A 21

(P. I. & C. 789)

33

4567

INDIANA

Area, 36,291 sq. m.
Pop. 3,427,796

PRINCIPAL CITIES
Pop.—Thousands

RAND McNALLY
POPULAR MAP OF
INDIANA

SCALE 1:1,521,000
1 Inch = 24 Statute Miles
1 Centimeter = 15.2 Kilometers
Statute Miles

Copyright by Rand McNally & Company, Chicago.
Made in U.S.A.

34

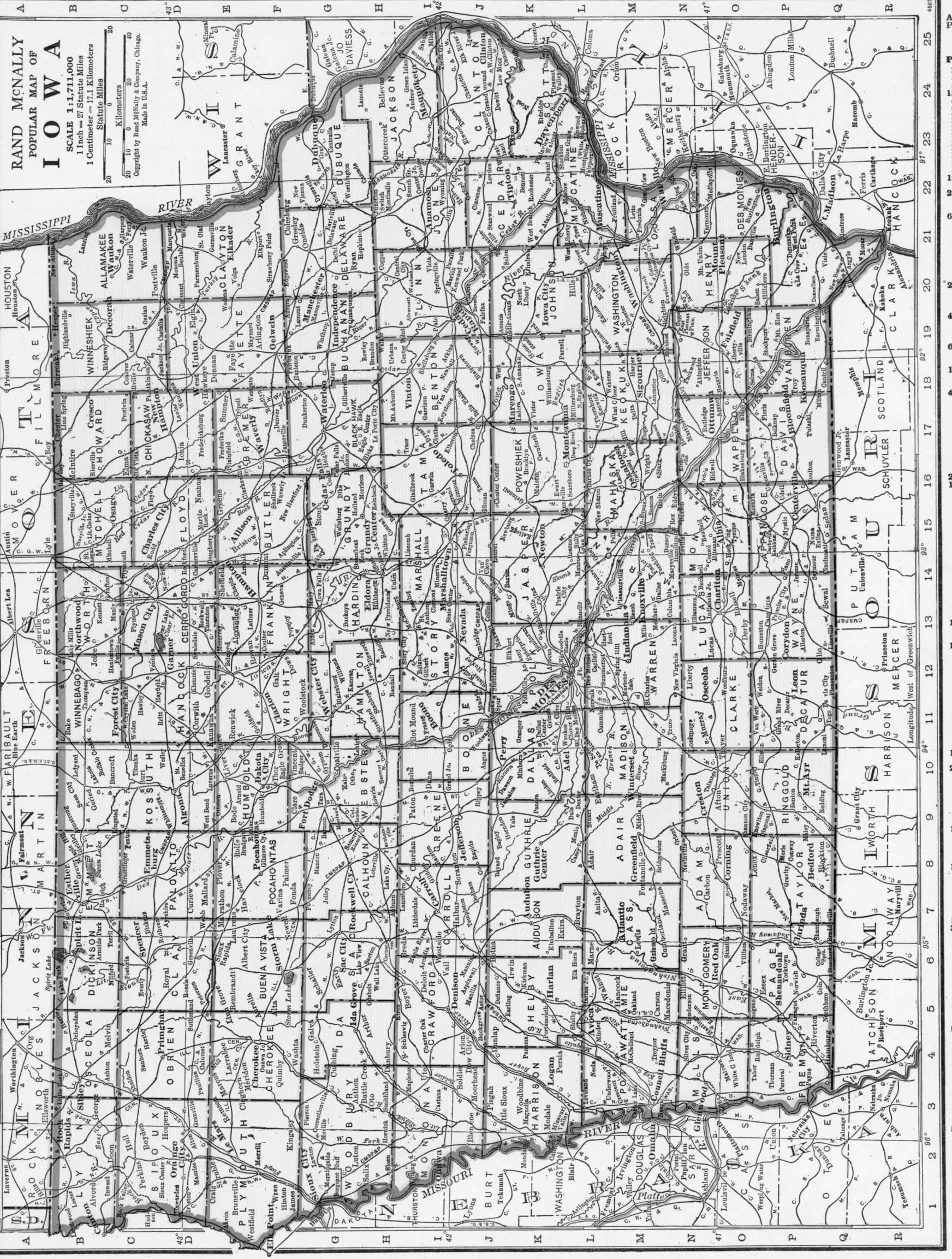

RAND McNALLY
POPULAR MAP OF
IOWA

SCALE 1:1,711,000
1 Inch = 27 Statute Miles
1 Centimeter = 17.1 Kilometers

Copyright by Rand McNally & Company, Chicago.
Made in U.S.A.

35

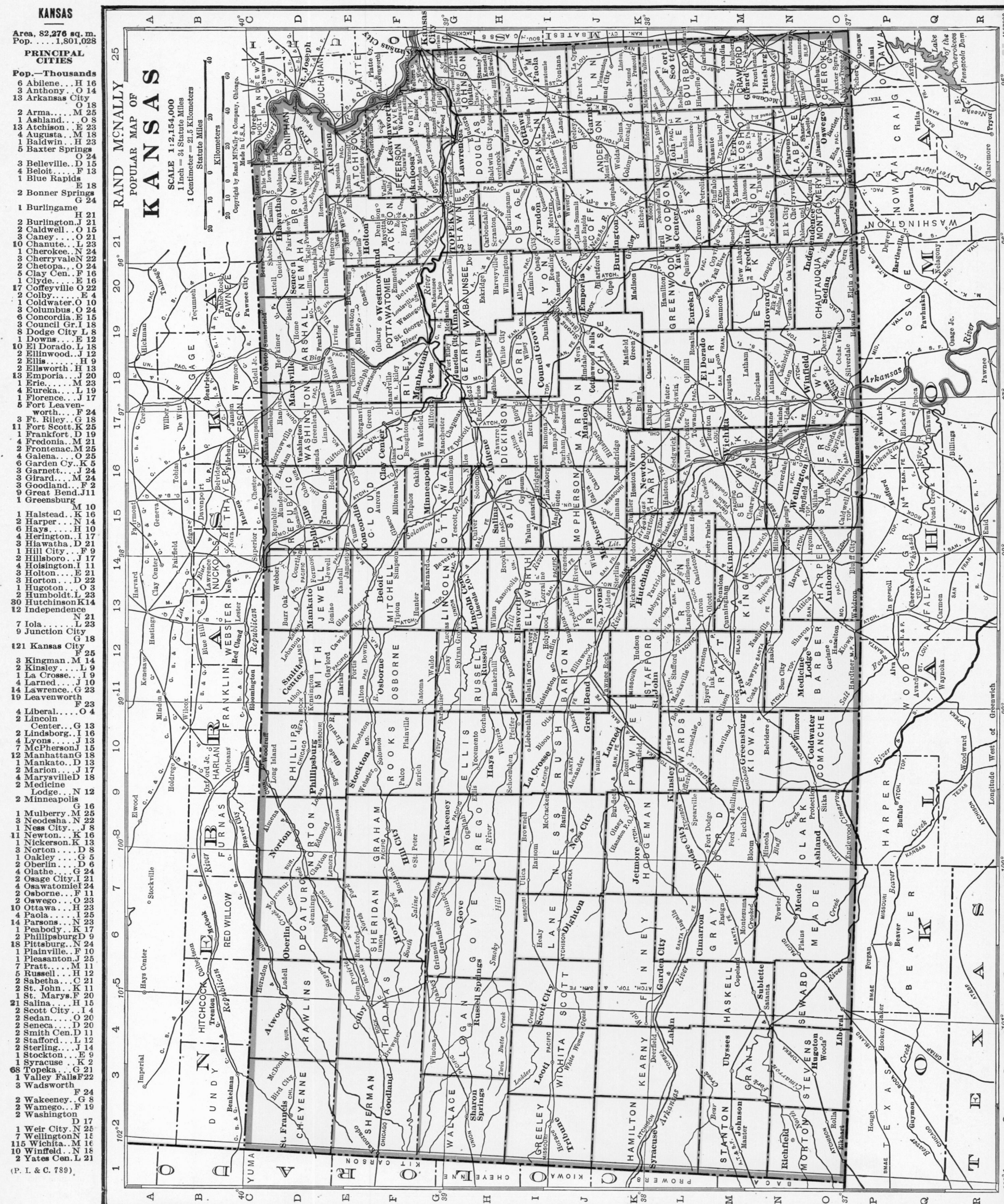

KANSAS

Area, 82,276 sq. m.
Pop.....1,801,028

PRINCIPAL CITIES

Pop.—Thousands

City	Ref
6 Abilene	H 16
3 Anthony	O 14
13 Arkansas City	O 18
2 Arma	M 25
4 Ashland	O 8
13 Atchison	E 23
4 Augusta	M 18
1 Baldwin	H 23
5 Baxter Springs	O 25
3 Belleville	D 15
4 Beloit	F 13
1 Blue Rapids	E 18
2 Bonner Springs	G 24
1 Burlingame	H 21
2 Burlington	J 21
2 Caldwell	O 15
2 Caney	O 21
10 Chanute	L 23
2 Cherokee	N 24
2 Cherryvale	N 22
2 Chetopa	O 24
4 Clay Cen.	F 17
1 Clyde	E 16
17 Coffeyville	O 22
1 Colby	E 4
1 Coldwater	O 10
6 Columbus	O 24
6 Concordia	E 15
1 Council Gr.	I 18
8 Dodge City	L 8
1 Downs	E 12
10 El Dorado	L 18
2 Ellinwood	J 12
2 Ellis	J 10
2 Ellsworth	H 13
13 Emporia	J 20
1 Erie	M 23
4 Eureka	L 19
1 Florence	J 17
5 Fort Leavenworth	F 24
3 Ft. Riley	G 18
11 Fort Scott	K 25
2 Frankfort	D 19
4 Fredonia	M 21
4 Frontenac	M 25
4 Galena	O 25
5 Garden Cy.	K 5
3 Garnett	J 24
3 Girard	M 24
3 Goodland	F 2
11 Great Bend	J 11
1 Greensburg	M 10
1 Halstead	K 16
2 Harper	N 14
6 Hays	N 10
1 Herington	I 17
3 Hiawatha	D 21
1 Hill City	F 9
2 Hillsboro	J 17
1 Hoisington	J 11
2 Holton	E 21
2 Horton	D 22
1 Hugoton	O 3
2 Humboldt	L 23
30 Hutchinson	K 14
12 Independence	N 21
2 Iola	L 23
9 Junction City	G 18
121 Kansas City	F 25
3 Kingman	N 14
2 Kinsley	L 9
1 La Crosse	J 10
4 Larned	J 10
19 Lawrence	G 23
19 Leavenworth	F 23
4 Liberal	O 4
2 Lincoln Center	G 13
2 Lindsborg	I 16
2 Lyons	J 13
2 McPherson	I 15
12 Manhattan	G 18
1 Mankato	D 14
2 Marion	J 17
2 Marysville	D 18
2 Medicine Lodge	N 12
2 Minneapolis	G 16
1 Mulberry	M 25
3 Neodesha	N 22
2 Ness City	F 8
11 Newton	K 16
3 Nickerson	K 13
3 Norton	D 8
2 Oakley	G 5
2 Oberlin	D 6
4 Olathe	G 24
4 Osage City	I 21
4 Osawatomie	I 24
2 Osborne	F 11
2 Oswego	O 23
10 Ottawa	H 23
4 Paola	I 25
14 Parsons	N 23
1 Peabody	K 17
2 Phillipsburg	D 9
18 Pittsburg	N 24
1 Plainville	F 10
1 Pleasanton	J 25
7 Pratt	M 12
5 Russell	M 11
2 Sabetha	C 21
1 St. John	K 11
1 St. Marys	F 20
21 Salina	H 15
2 Scott City	J 5
2 Sedan	O 20
2 Seneca	D 20
2 Smith Cen.	D 11
2 Stafford	L 12
2 Sterling	J 14
1 Stockton	E 9
2 Syracuse	K 2
68 Topeka	G 21
1 Valley Falls	F 22
3 Wadsworth	F 24
2 Wakeeney	G 8
2 Wamego	F 19
2 Washington	D 17
1 Weir City	N 25
7 Wellington	N 16
115 Wichita	N 16
10 Winfield	N 18
2 Yates Cen.	L 21

(P. I. & C. 789)

RAND McNALLY POPULAR MAP OF KANSAS

SCALE 1:2,154,000
1 Inch = 34 Statute Miles
1 Centimeter = 21.5 Kilometers
Statute Miles

Copyright by Rand McNally & Company, Chicago
Made in U.S.A.

36

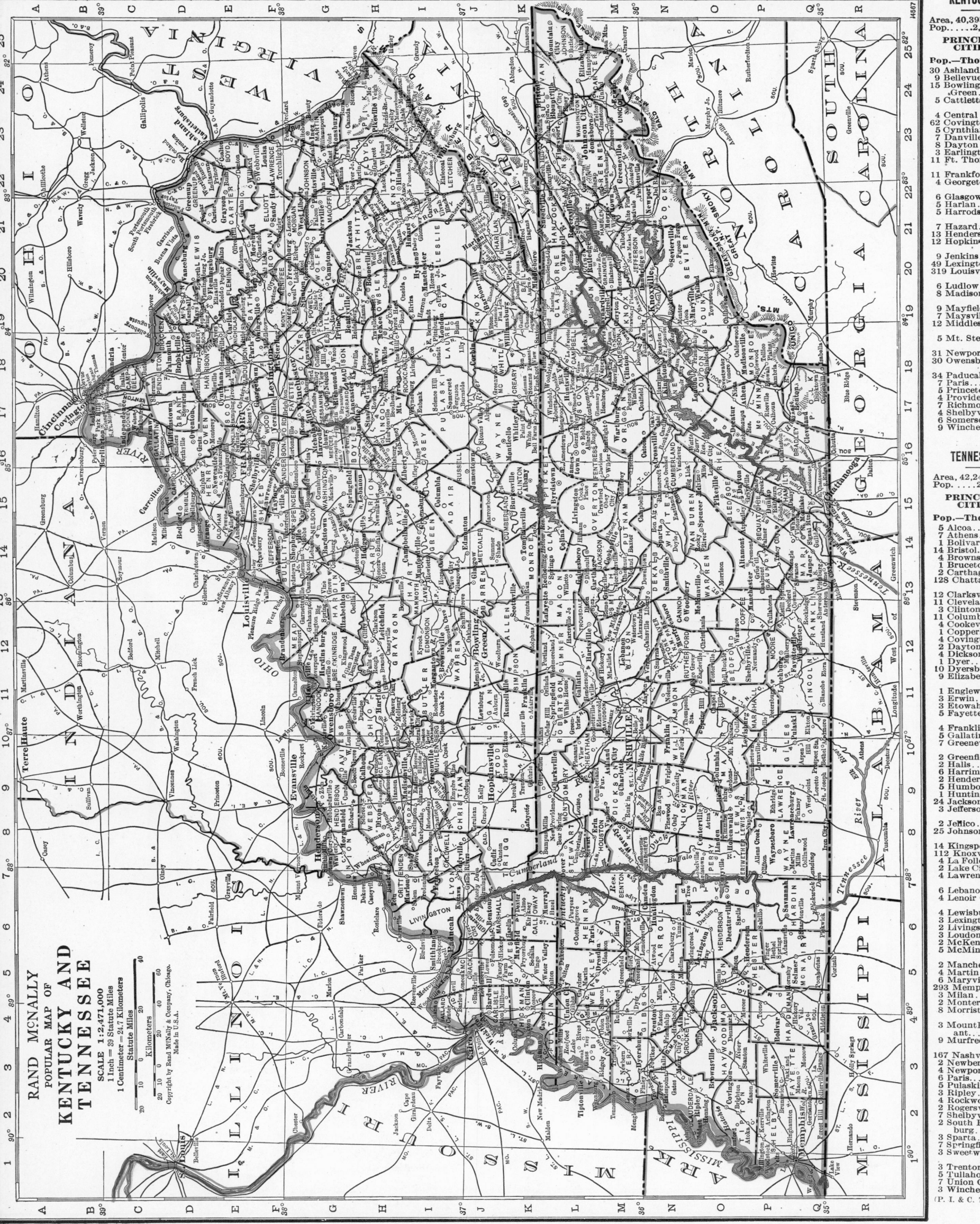

37

LOUISIANA

Area, 48,523 sq. m.
Pop....2,363,880

PRINCIPAL CITIES

Pop.—Thousands

7 Abbeville..N 11
27 Alexandria..H 9
2 Amite....K 17
2 Arcadia....C 8
7 Bastrop...B 12
35 Baton Rouge
....L 14
1 Bayou Goula
....M 14
1 Bernice...A 9
2 Berwick...O 14
15 Bogalusa..J 19
6 Bossier...C 5
2 Breaux Bridge
....M 12
4 Bunkie....J 11
1 Campti...E 7
2 Church Point
....L 10
1 Colfax....G 9
1 Cottonport J 11
1 Cotton Valley
....A 6
1 Coushatta..L 7
4 Covington..L 18
10 Crowley...M 10
1 Delhi....C 13
1 Denham Spgs.
....L 15
3 De Quincy..L 6
4 De Ridder..J 6
4 Donaldsonville
....M 15
3 Elizabeth...J 8
5 Eunice....L 9
1 Farmerville B10
3 Ferriday..G 13
1 Franklin...O 13
2 Franklinton J 18
2 Garyville..M 17
1 Gibsland...C 7
1 Glenmora..J 9
2 Gramercy..N 16
11 Gretna....N 19
1 Gueydan...N 9
6 Hammond..L 17
1 Harvey....N 18
1 Haynesville.A 7
1 Hodge.....D 8
1 Homer.....B 7
9 Houma....P 16
1 Independence
....K 17
5 Jackson...J 14
5 Jeanerette.N 12
7 Jennings...M 8
3 Jonesboro..D 8
2 Jonesville.G 12
2 Kaplan...N 10
2 Kenner...N 18
2 Kentwood..J 17
1 Kinder....L 8
19 Lafayette..M 11
5 L. Arthur..N 8
21 L. Charles..M 6
4 Lake Providence..B 14
1 Lecompte..I 10
1 Leesville..I 6
1 Logansport.E 4
2 Lutcher...N 16
2 Mandeville.L 19
4 Mansfield..E 5
1 Mansura...I 11
1 Many....G 5
2 Marksville.I 11
1 Merryville..K 5
7 Minden...C 11
28 Monroe...C 11
7 Morgan City
....O 14
1 Napoleonville
....N 15
7 Natchitoches
....F 7
14 New Iberia N 12
495 New Orleans
....N 18
2 New Roads K 13
4 Oakdale....J 9
2 Oak Grove..B 14
1 Oil City...B 4
5 Opelousas..K 11
2 Patterson..O 14
2 Pineville..H 10
1 Plain Dealing
....A 5
5 Plaquemine
....M 14
4 Ponchatoula
....L 17
2 Port Allen L 14
2 Rayne....M 10
2 Rayville...C 12
2 Reserve...M 17
7 Ruston....C 9
2 St. Martinville
....M 12
98 Shreveport C 5
3 Slidell....M 20
3 Springhill..A 6
1 Sulphur....M 6
6 Tallulah...C 14
3 Thibodaux O 16
1 Vidalia...G 13
4 Ville Platte
....K 10
2 Vinton....M 5
2 Vivian....A 4
1 Washington
....K 11
2 Welsh....M 8
9 W. Monroe C 11
5 Westwego.N 18
2 White Castle
....M 14
5 Winnfield..F 9
3 Winnsboro E 12
1 Zwolle....G 5

(P. I. & C. 789)

RAND McNALLY
POPULAR MAP OF
LOUISIANA

SCALE 1:2,091,000
1 Inch = 33 Statute Miles
1 Centimeter = 20.9 Kilometers

Copyright by Rand McNally & Company, Chicago. Made in U.S.A.

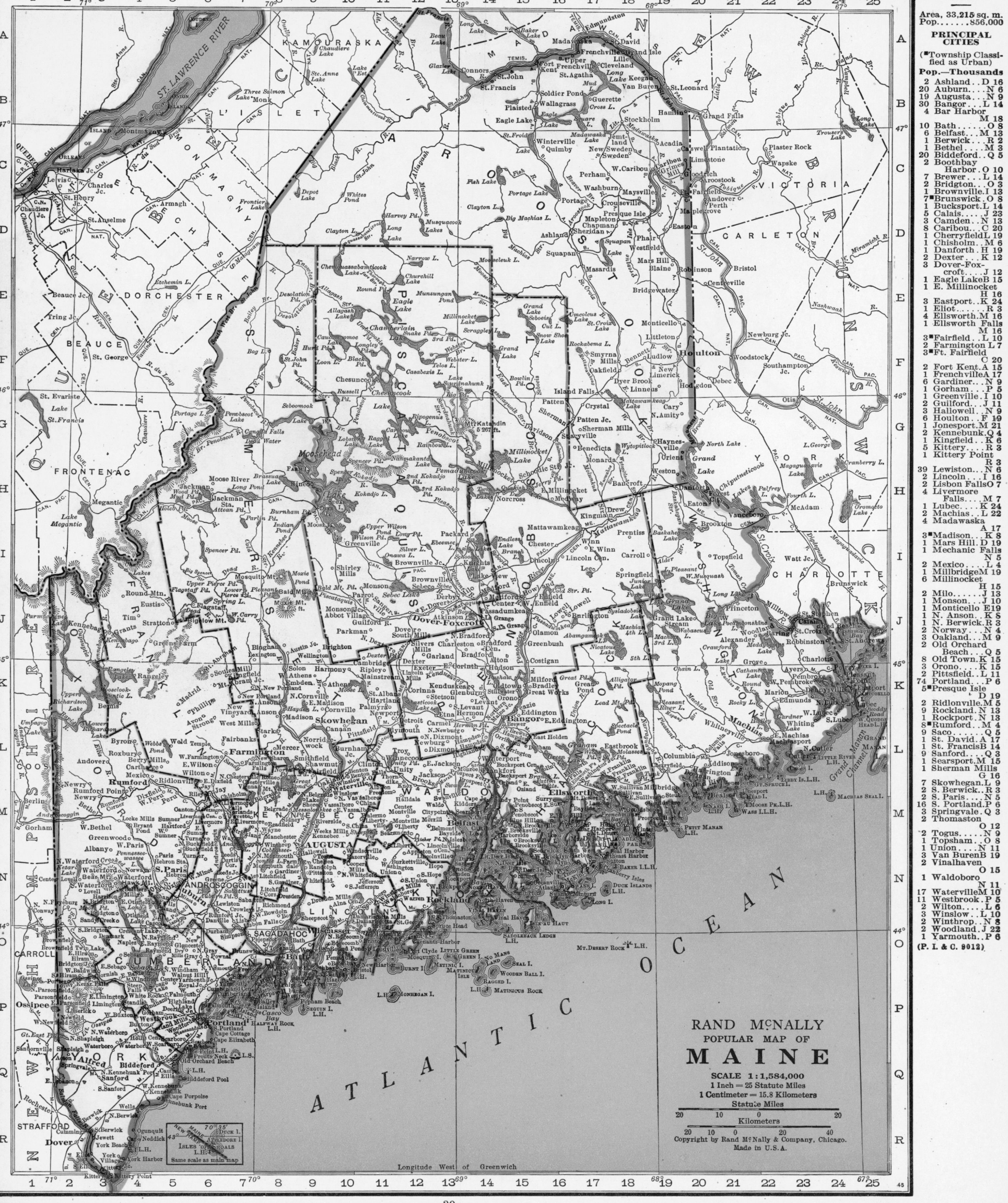

Area, 33,215 sq. m.
Pop......856,000

PRINCIPAL CITIES

(*Township Classified as Urban)

Pop.—Thousands

2	Ashland....D 16
20	Auburn....N 6
19	Augusta....N 9
30	Bangor...L 14
4	Bar Harbor
	....M 18
10	Bath....O 8
6	Belfast..M 13
1	Berwick...R 2
1	Bethel....M 3
20	Biddeford..Q 5
2	Boothbay
	Harbor..O 10
7	Brewer...L 14
2	Bridgton...O 3
1	Brownville..J 11
7*	Brunswick..O 8
5	Bucksport..L 14
5	Calais..J 23
2	Camden..N 13
8	Caribou...C 20
1	Cherryfield L 19
1	Chisholm..M 6
1	Danforth..H 19
2	Dexter...K 12
3	Dover-Fox-
	croft..J 12
1	Eagle Lake B 15
1	E. Millinocket
	H 16
3	Eastport..K 24
1	Eliot....R 3
4	Ellsworth..M 16
1	Ellsworth Falls
	M 16
3*	Fairfield...L 10
2	Farmington L 7
3*	Ft. Fairfield
	C 20
2	Fort Kent..A 15
1	Frenchville A 17
6	Gardiner...N 9
1	Gorham....P 5
2	Greenville. I 10
2	Guilford...J 11
3	Hallowell..N 9
6	Houlton...F 21
1	Jonesport..M 21
2	Kennebunk Q 4
1	Kingfield...K 6
1	Kittery....R 3
1	Kittery Point
	R 3
39	Lewiston...N 6
2	Lincoln....I 16
5	Lisbon Falls O 7
4	Livermore
	Falls....M 7
1	Lubec....K 24
2	Machias..L 22
4	Madawaska
	A 17
3*	Madison....K 8
1	Mars Hill. D 19
1	Mechanic Falls
	N 5
2	Mexico....L 4
3	Millbridge M 19
6	Millinocket
	H 15
2	Milo.....J 12
1	Monson...I 10
1	Monticello E 19
1	N. Anson..K 8
1	N. Berwick. R 3
2	Norway...N 4
2	Oakland...M 9
2	Old Orchard
	Beach..Q 5
5	Old Town. K 15
4	Orono....K 15
2	Pittsfield..L 11
74	Portland...P 6
5*	Presque Isle
	D 19
2	Ridlonville. M 5
9	Rockland..N 13
1	Rockport..N 13
6	Rumford...M 4
4	Saco.....Q 5
1	St. David. A 17
1	St. Francis B 14
6	Sanford...Q 3
1	Searsport..M 13
1	Sherman Mills
	G 16
7	Skowhegan. K 8
3	So. Berwick. R 3
2	S. Paris...N 5
16	So. Portland. P 6
3	Springvale..Q 3
2	Thomaston
	O 12
2	Togus....N 9
3	Topsham...O 8
1	Union....N 12
3	Van Buren B 19
2	Vinalhaven
	O 15
1	Waldoboro
	N 11
17	Waterville M 10
11	Westbrook..P 5
1	Wilton....N 6
3	Winslow..L 10
2	Winthrop..N 8
3	Woodland..J 22
1	Yarmouth..P 6

(P. I. & C. 9012)

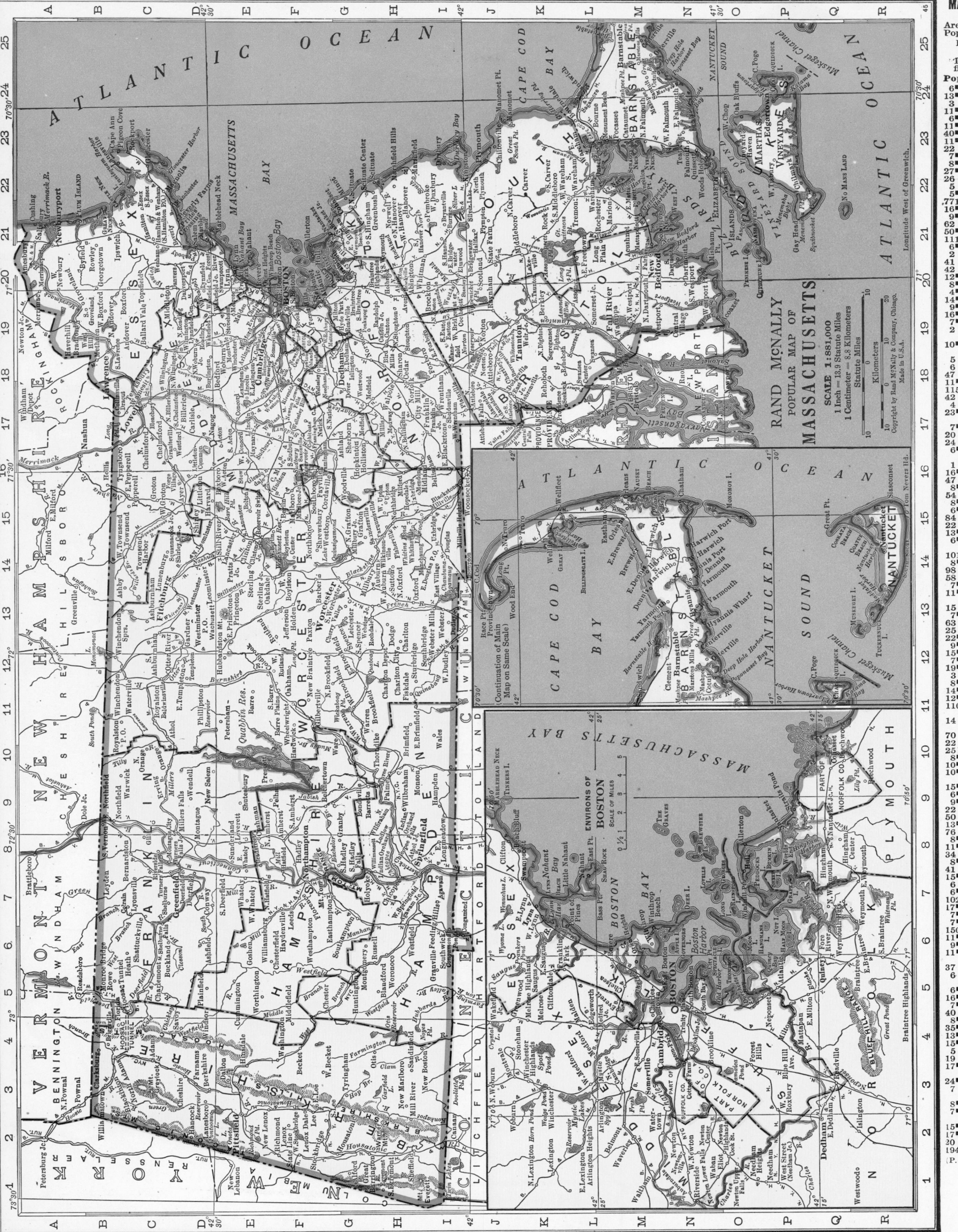

RAND McNALLY
POPULAR MAP OF
MASSACHUSETTS

SCALE 1:881,000
1 Inch = 13.9 Statute Miles
1 Centimeter = 8.8 Kilometers
Statute Miles
Kilometers
Copyright by Rand McNally & Company, Chicago.
Made in U.S.A.

Continuation of Main
Map on Same Scale)

ENVIRONS OF
BOSTON
Scale of Miles

Area, 8,257 sq. m.
Pop.......4,316,721
PRINCIPAL CITIES
Township Classi-
fied as Urban
Pop.—Thousands

6	Abington	H 20
13	Adams	C 4
3	Agawam	J 7
11	Amesbury	A 20
6	Amherst	F 8
11	Andover	C 19
40	Arlington	C 18
11	Athol	C 10
22	Attleboro	J 17
7	Auburn	H 14
8	Barnstable	M 25
27	Belmont	E 18
26	Beverly	C 21
5	Billerica	D 17
6	Blackstone	I 15
77	Boston	F 20
16	Braintree	G 20
8	Bridgewater	I 20
62	Brockton	I 20
50	Brookline	E 19
111	Cambridge	E18
6	Canton	H 18
2	Chelmsford	C17
41	Chelsea	E 19
42	Chicopee	H 7
12	Clinton	E 14
8	Concord	E 17
3	Dalton	D 3
14	Danvers	C 20
7	Dartmouth	N20
16	Dedham	G 18
7	Dracut	C 17
2	E. Bridgewater	I 20
10	Easthampton	G 6
5	E. Milton	P 5
6	Edgeworth	L 4
47	Everett	E 19
7	Fairhaven	M 20
115	Fall River	M19
42	Fitchburg	D 13
4	Foxboro	I 18
23	Framingham	G 16
7	Franklin	I 17
20	Gardner	D 13
24	Gloucester	C 23
6	Gt. Barrington	G 1
2	Grafton	G 15
16	Greenfield	C 7
47	Haverhill	A 19
8	Hingham	G 21
54	Holyoke	G 7
8	Hudson	F 16
5	Ipswich	B 21
24	Lawrence	B 18
22	Leominster	D 14
13	Lexington	E 18
6	Longmeadow	I 7
101	Lowell	C 17
8	Ludlow	H 8
98	Lynn	E 19
58	Malden	E 19
7	Mansfield	I 18
11	Marblehead	D 21
7	Marlboro	F 15
5	Maynard	E 17
63	Medford	E 19
25	Melrose	E 20
22	Methuen	B 19
15	Middleboro	J 21
15	Milford	H 16
9	Millbury	G 14
3	Milton	G 19
3	Monson	H 9
8	Montague	D 8
14	Natick	F 17
6	Needham	F 18
110	New Bedford	M 20
14	Newburyport	A 21
70	Newton	F 18
22	N. Adams	B 3
15	Northampton	F8
8	N. Andover	B19
8	N. Attleboro	I 18
10	Northbridge	H 15
15	Norwood	G 19
6	Orange	C 10
22	Palmer	H 9
50	Peabody	D 20
50	Pittsfield	E 2
13	Plymouth	J 23
76	Quincy	G 20
8	Randolph	H 19
8	Reading	E 20
34	Revere	E 20
41	Rockland	H 21
41	Salem	D 21
15	Saugus	K 5
6	Shrewsbury	F15
9	Somerset	I 8
102	Somerville	F19
7	Southbridge	I 12
7	S. Hadley	G 8
7	Spencer	H 13
150	Springfield	H 7
11	Stoneham	E 19
9	Stoughton	H 19
11	Swampscott	D 20
37	Taunton	K 19
6	Turners Falls	C 8
6	Uxbridge	I 15
16	Wakefield	E 19
14	Walpole	H 18
40	Waltham	E 18
9	Ware	G 10
35	Watertown	M 2
13	Webster	H 13
6	Wellesley	F 17
5	Westboro	H 15
19	Westfield	H 6
17	West Spring-	
	field	H 7
24	Weymouth	G 20
7	Whitinsville	H 14
15	Winchester	E 18
17	Winthrop	M 6
20	Woburn	D 18
194	Worcester	G 13

(P. I. & C. 789)

MICHIGAN

Area, 58,216 sq. m.
Pop.....5,256,106

RAND McNALLY
POPULAR MAP OF
MICHIGAN

SCALE 1:2,408,000

1 Inch = 38 Statute Miles
1 Centimeter = 24 Kilometers
Statute Miles

Kilometers

Copyright by Rand McNally & Company, Chicago.
Made in U.S.A.

43

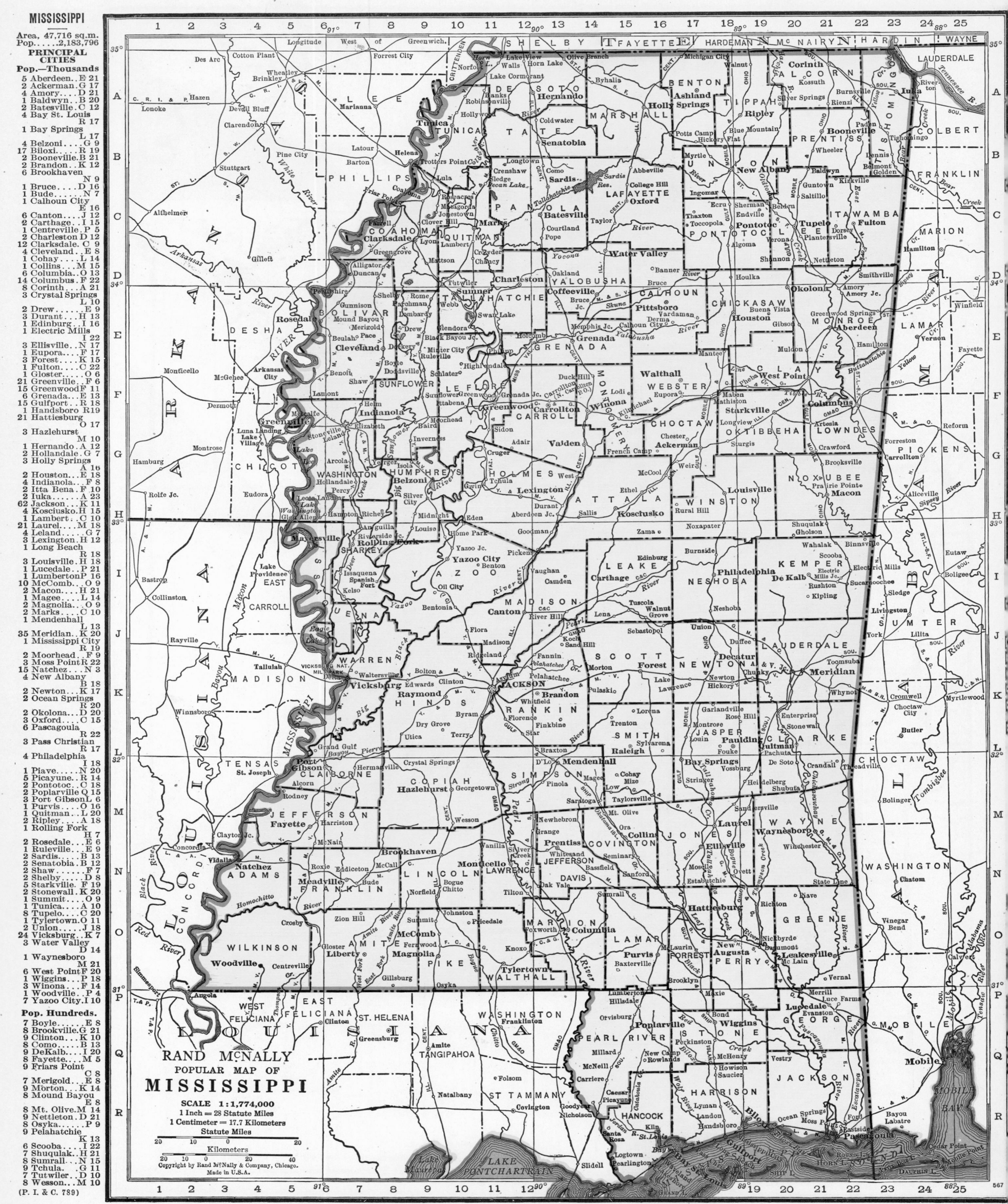

MISSISSIPPI

Area, 47,716 sq.m.
Pop....2,183,796

PRINCIPAL CITIES
Pop.—Thousands

5 Aberdeen..E 21
2 Ackerman..G 17
4 Amory....D 21
4 Baldwyn..B 20
2 Batesville..C 12
4 Bay St. Louis
       R 17
1 Bay Springs
       L 17
4 Belzoni....G 9
17 Biloxi....R 19
2 Booneville.B 21
2 Brandon..K 12
6 Brookhaven
       N 9
1 Bruce....D 16
1 Bude.....N 7
1 Calhoun City
       E 16
6 Canton...J 12
2 Carthage..I 15
2 Centreville.P 5
2 Charleston D 12
12 Clarksdale..C 9
6 Cleveland..E 8
1 Cohay....L 14
1 Collins...M 15
6 Columbia..O 13
14 Columbus..F 22
3 Corinth..A 21
3 Crystal Springs
       L 10
2 Drew.....E 9
1 Durant....H 13
1 Edinburg..I 16
1 Electric Mills
       I 22
3 Ellisville..N 17
2 Eupora...F 17
3 Forest....K 15
1 Fulton....C 22
1 Gloster...O 6
21 Greenville..F 6
15 Greenwood.F 11
6 Grenada..E 13
15 Gulfport..R 18
1 Handsboro R 19
21 Hattiesburg
       O 17
3 Hazlehurst
       M 10
1 Hernando..A 12
3 Hollandale.G 7
3 Holly Springs
       A 16
1 Houston...E 18
4 Indianola..F 8
2 Itta Bena..F 10
2 Iuka....A 23
62 Jackson...K 11
4 Kosciusko.H 15
1 Lambert...C 10
21 Laurel...M 18
4 Leland....G 7
1 Lexington.H 12
1 Long Beach
       R 18
1 Louisville..H 18
1 Lucedale..P 21
1 Lumberton P 17
10 McComb..O 9
2 Macon....H 21
1 Magee....L 14
1 Magnolia..O 9
2 Marks....C 10
1 Mendenhall
       L 13
35 Meridian..K 20
1 Mississippi City
       R 19
2 Moorhead..F 9
2 Moss Point R 22
15 Natchez...N 3
4 New Albany
       B 18
2 Newton...K 17
2 Ocean Springs
       R 20
2 Okolona..D 20
3 Oxford....C 15
2 Pascagoula R 22
3 Pass Christian
       R 17
4 Philadelphia
       I 18
1 Piave....N 20
2 Picayune..R 14
2 Pontotoc..C 18
2 Poplarville Q 15
2 Port Gibson L 6
1 Purvis....O 16
1 Quitman..L 20
2 Ripley....A 18
5 Rolling Fork
       H 7
2 Rosedale..E 6
2 Ruleville..E 9
2 Sardis....B 13
2 Senatobia.B 12
2 Shaw....D 8
2 Shelby...D 8
5 Starkville..F 20
2 Stonewall.K 20
2 Summit...O 9
1 Tunica...A 11
2 Tupelo...C 20
2 Tylertown.O 11
2 Union....J 18
24 Vicksburg.K 7
3 Water Valley
       D 14
1 Waynesboro
       M 21
6 West Point F 20
1 Wiggins..P 18
1 Winona...F 14
1 Woodville.P 4
7 Yazoo City.I 10

Pop. Hundreds.

7 Boyle....E 8
8 Brookville.G 21
8 Clinton...K 10
8 Como....B 13
8 DeKalb..I 20
8 Fayette...M 5
7 Friars Point
       C 8
7 Merigold..E 8
7 Morton...K 14
8 Mound Bayou
       E 8
8 Mt. Olive.M 14
9 Nettleton.D 21
8 Osyka....P 9
9 Pelahatchie
       K 13
6 Scooba...I 22
7 Shuqualak.H 21
8 Sumrall..N 15
9 Tchula...G 11
7 Tutwiler..D 11
8 Wesson...M 10

(P. I. & C. 789)

RAND McNALLY
POPULAR MAP OF
MISSISSIPPI

SCALE 1:1,774,000
1 Inch = 28 Statute Miles
1 Centimeter = 17.7 Kilometers
Statute Miles

Copyright by Rand McNally & Company, Chicago.
Made in U.S.A.

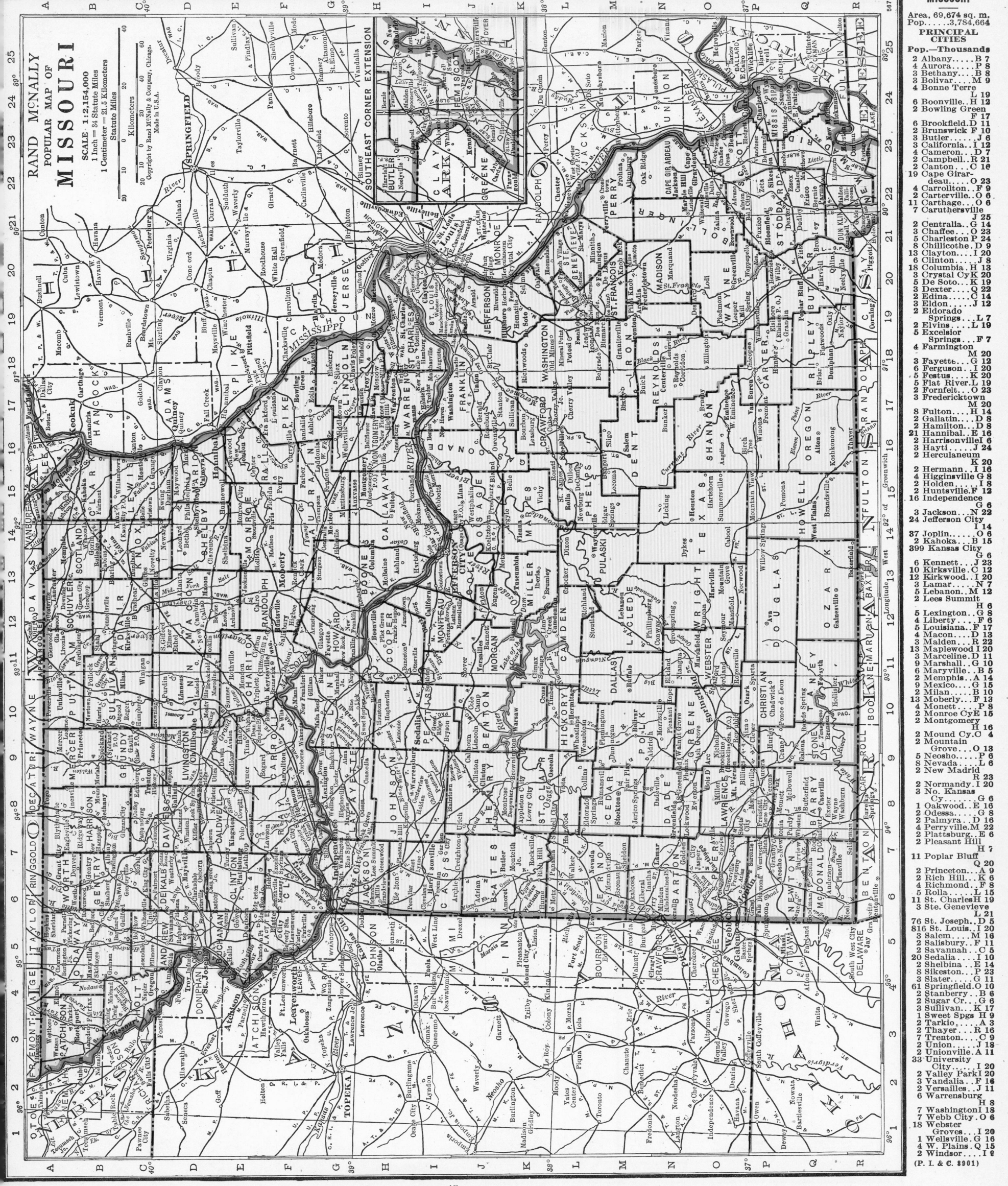

RAND McNALLY
POPULAR MAP OF
MISSOURI

SCALE 1:2,154,000
1 Inch = 34 Statute Miles
1 Centimeter = 21.5 Kilometers
Statute Miles

Copyright by Rand McNally & Company, Chicago
Made in U.S.A.

SOUTHEAST CORNER EXTENSION

45

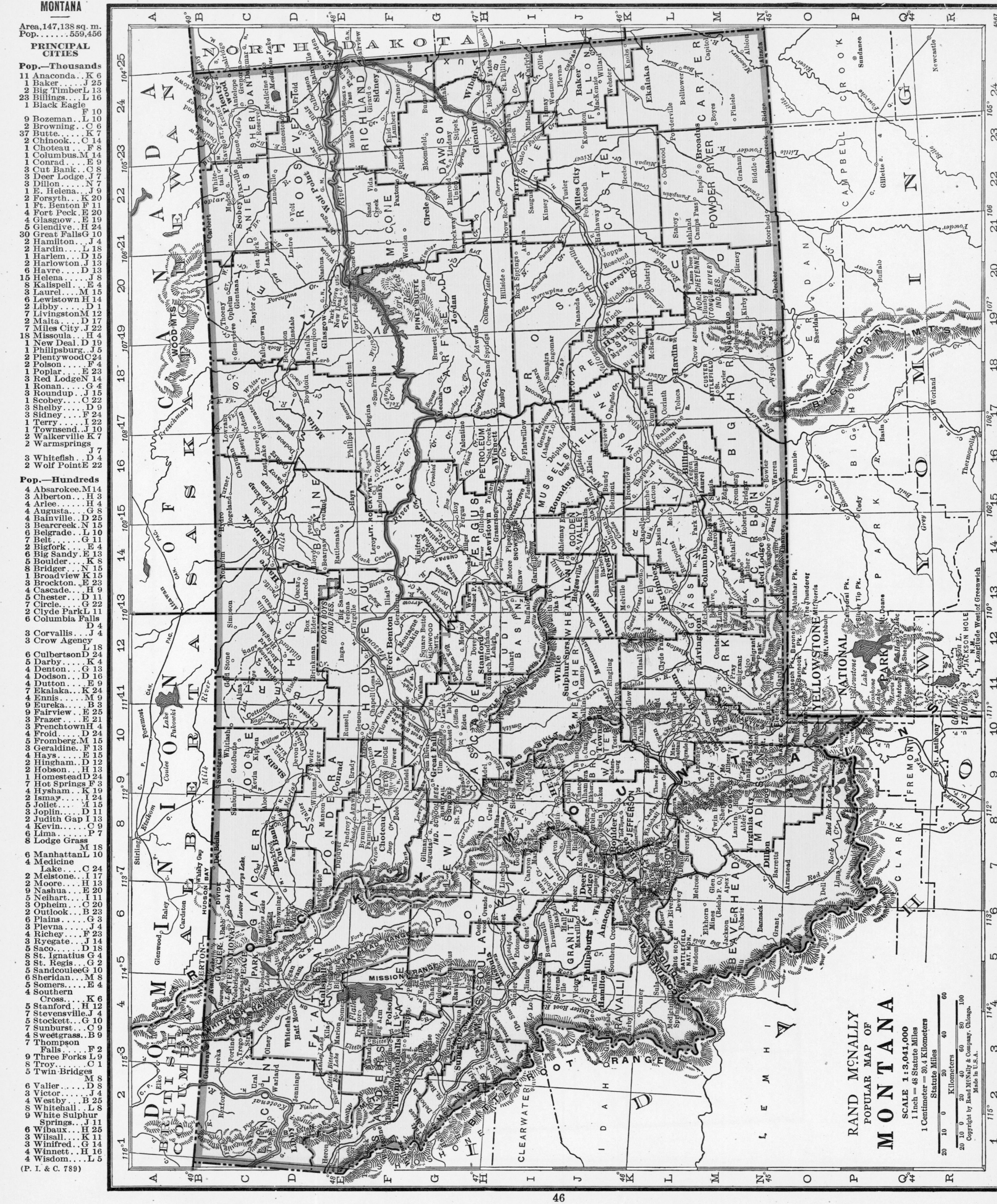

MONTANA

Area, 147,138 sq. m.
Pop...... 559,456

PRINCIPAL CITIES

Pop.—Thousands

11	Anaconda..	K 6
1	Baker......	J 25
2	Big Timber	L 13
23	Billings...	L 16
1	Black Eagle	
		F 10
9	Bozeman..	J 10
2	Browning..	C 6
37	Butte......	K 7
2	Chinook...	C 14
1	Choteau...	F 8
1	Columbus.M	14
1	Conrad....	E 9
1	Cut Bank.	C 8
3	Deer Lodge	J 7
3	Dillon....	N 7
1	E. Helena..	J 9
2	Forsyth...	K 20
1	Ft. Benton	F 11
1	Fort Peck.	E 20
2	Glasgow...	E 19
5	Glendive..	H 24
30	Great Falls	G 10
2	Hamilton..	J 4
2	Hardin...	D 18
1	Harlem...	D 15
1	Harlowton	J 13
6	Havre....	D 13
15	Helena...	J 8
8	Kalispell..	E 4
2	Laurel...	M 15
6	Lewistown	H 14
1	Libby....	D 1
2	Livingston	M 12
2	Malta....	D 17
7	Miles City.	J 22
18	Missoula..	H 4
1	New Deal.	D 19
2	Philipsburg	J 5
1	Plentywood	C 24
1	Polson....	F 4
1	Poplar....	E 23
1	Red Lodge	N 14
1	Ronan...	G 4
2	Roundup..	J 15
1	Scobey...	C 22
1	Shelby...	D 9
2	Sidney...	F 25
1	Terry....	I 22
1	Townsend..	J 10
2	Walkerville	K 7
2	Warmsprings	
		J 7
3	Whitefish.	D 4
2	Wolf Point	E 22

Pop.—Hundreds

4	Absarokee.M	14
5	Alberton..	H 3
4	Arlee.....	H 4
4	Augusta...	G 8
3	Bainville..	D 25
3	Bearcreek.	N 15
6	Belgrade...	L 10
7	Belt......	G 11
2	Bigfork...	E 4
8	Big Sandy..	E 13
5	Boulder...	K 8
3	Bridger...	N 15
1	Broadview	K 15
5	Brockton..	E 23
4	Cascade...	H 9
3	Chester...	D 11
2	Circle....	G 22
2	Clyde Park.L	11
2	Columbia Falls	
		D 4
3	Corvallis...	J 4
3	Crow Agency	
		L 18
6	Culbertson.D	24
5	Darby....	K 4
4	Denton...	G 13
4	Dodson...	D 16
4	Dutton...	E 9
3	Ekalaka...	K 24
3	Ennis....	M 9
8	Eureka...	B 3
9	Fairview...	E 25
3	Frazer....	E 21
3	Frenchtown	H 4
5	Froid....	D 24
3	Fromberg.M	15
3	Geraldine..	F 13
2	Hays.....	E 15
2	Hingham..	D 12
2	Hobson...	H 13
3	Homestead.D	24
3	Hot Springs	F 3
2	Hysham...	K 19
2	Ismay....	I 24
5	Joliet....	M 15
3	Joplin....	D 11
2	Judith Gap	H 13
6	Kevin....	C 9
6	Lima.....	P 7
8	Lodge Grass	
		M 18
6	Manhattan.L	10
4	Medicine	
	Lake...	C 24
2	Melstone..	I 17
2	Moore....	H 13
2	Nashua...	E 20
5	Neihart...	I 11
2	Opheim...	C 20
2	Outlook...	B 23
5	Plains....	G 3
4	Plevna...	J 4
4	Richey...	F 23
3	Ryegate...	J 14
5	Saco.....	D 18
4	St. Ignatius	G 4
5	St. Regis..	G 2
3	Sandcoulee.G	10
8	Sheridan..	M 8
5	Somers....	E 4
5	Southern	
	Cross....	K 6
5	Stanford..	H 12
5	Stevensville	J 4
5	Stockett..	G 10
5	Sunburst..	C 9
4	Sweetgrass.	B 9
7	Thompson	
	Falls...	F 2
9	Three Forks	L 9
3	Troy.....	C 1
5	Twin Bridges	
		M 8
6	Valier....	D 8
3	Victor....	J 4
4	Westby...	B 25
5	Whitehall.	L 8
9	White Sulphur	
	Springs..	J 11
6	Wibaux...	H 25
3	Wilsall...	K 11
9	Winifred..	G 14
4	Winnett..	H 16
4	Wisdom...	L 5

(P. I. & C. 789)

RAND McNALLY
POPULAR MAP OF
MONTANA

SCALE 1:3,041,000
1 Inch = 48 Statute Miles
1 Centimeter = 30.4 Kilometers

Copyright by Rand McNally & Company, Chicago.
Made in U.S.A.

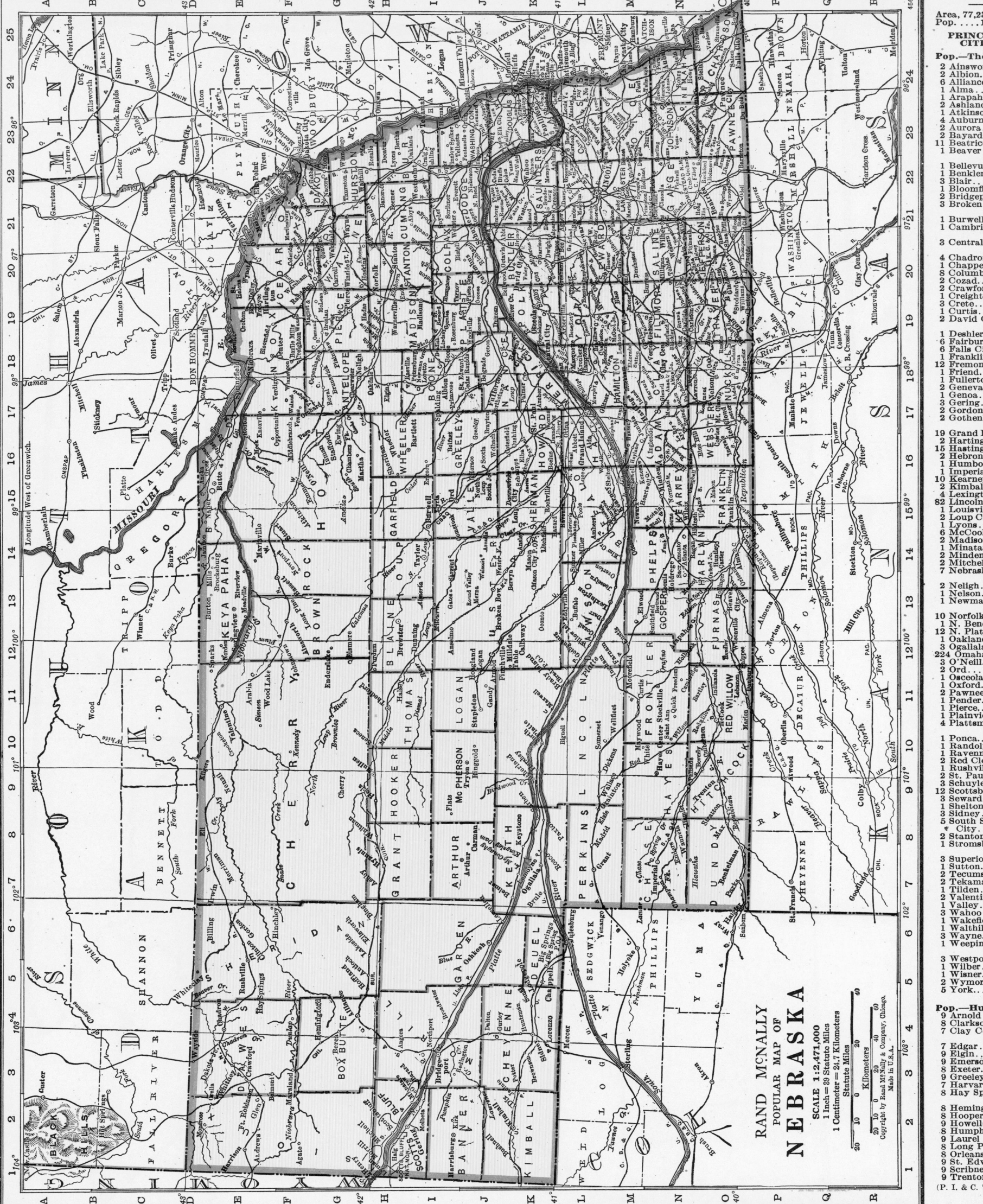

RAND McNALLY
POPULAR MAP OF
NEBRASKA

SCALE 1:2,471,000
1 Inch = 39 Statute Miles
1 Centimeter = 24.7 Kilometers

Copyright by Rand McNally & Company, Chicago.
Made in U.S.A.

(P. I. & C. 789)

47

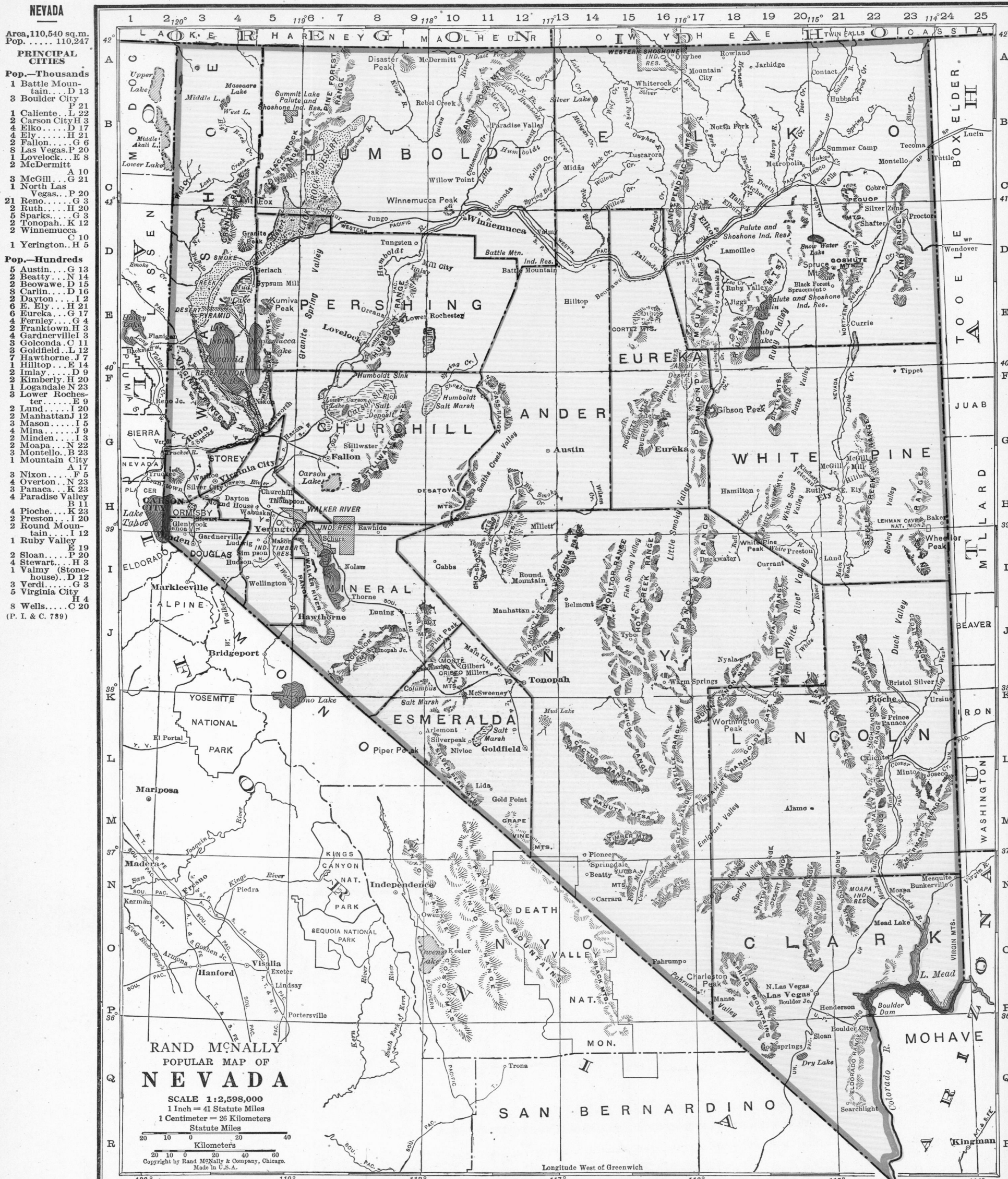

NEVADA

Area, 110,540 sq.m.
Pop... 110,247

PRINCIPAL CITIES

Pop.—Thousands

1	Battle Mountain	D 13
3	Boulder City	P 21
1	Caliente	L 22
2	Carson City	H 3
2	Elko	D 17
4	Ely	H 21
2	Fallon	G 6
8	Las Vegas	P 20
1	Lovelock	E 8
2	McDermitt	A 10
3	McGill	G 21
1	North Las Vegas	P 20
21	Reno	G 3
1	Ruth	H 20
2	Sparks	G 3
2	Tonopah	K 12
2	Winnemucca	C 10
1	Yerington	H 5

Pop.—Hundreds

5	Austin	G 13
2	Beatty	N 14
5	Beowawe	D 15
2	Carlin	D 16
2	Dayton	I 2
6	E. Ely	H 21
6	Eureka	G 17
4	Fernley	G 4
1	Franktown	H 3
1	Gardnerville	I 3
3	Golconda	C 11
3	Goldfield	L 12
7	Hawthorne	J 7
1	Hilltop	E 14
2	Imlay	D 9
2	Kimberly	H 20
2	Logandale	N 23
3	Lower Rochester	E 9
2	Lund	I 20
2	Manhattan	J 12
3	Mason	I 5
3	Mina	J 9
3	Minden	I 3
2	Moapa	N 22
2	Montello	B 23
1	Mountain City	A 17
3	Nixon	F 5
2	Overton	N 23
3	Panaca	K 23
4	Paradise Valley	B 11
4	Pioche	K 23
2	Preston	I 20
4	Round Mountain	I 12
1	Ruby Valley	E 19
2	Sloan	P 20
4	Stewart	H 3
1	Valmy (Stonehouse)	D 12
3	Verdi	G 3
5	Virginia City	H 4
8	Wells	C 20

(P. I. & C. 789)

RAND McNALLY
POPULAR MAP OF
NEVADA

SCALE 1:2,598,000
1 Inch = 41 Statute Miles
1 Centimeter = 26 Kilometers

Statute Miles

Kilometers

Copyright by Rand McNally & Company, Chicago.
Made in U.S.A.

Longitude West of Greenwich

48

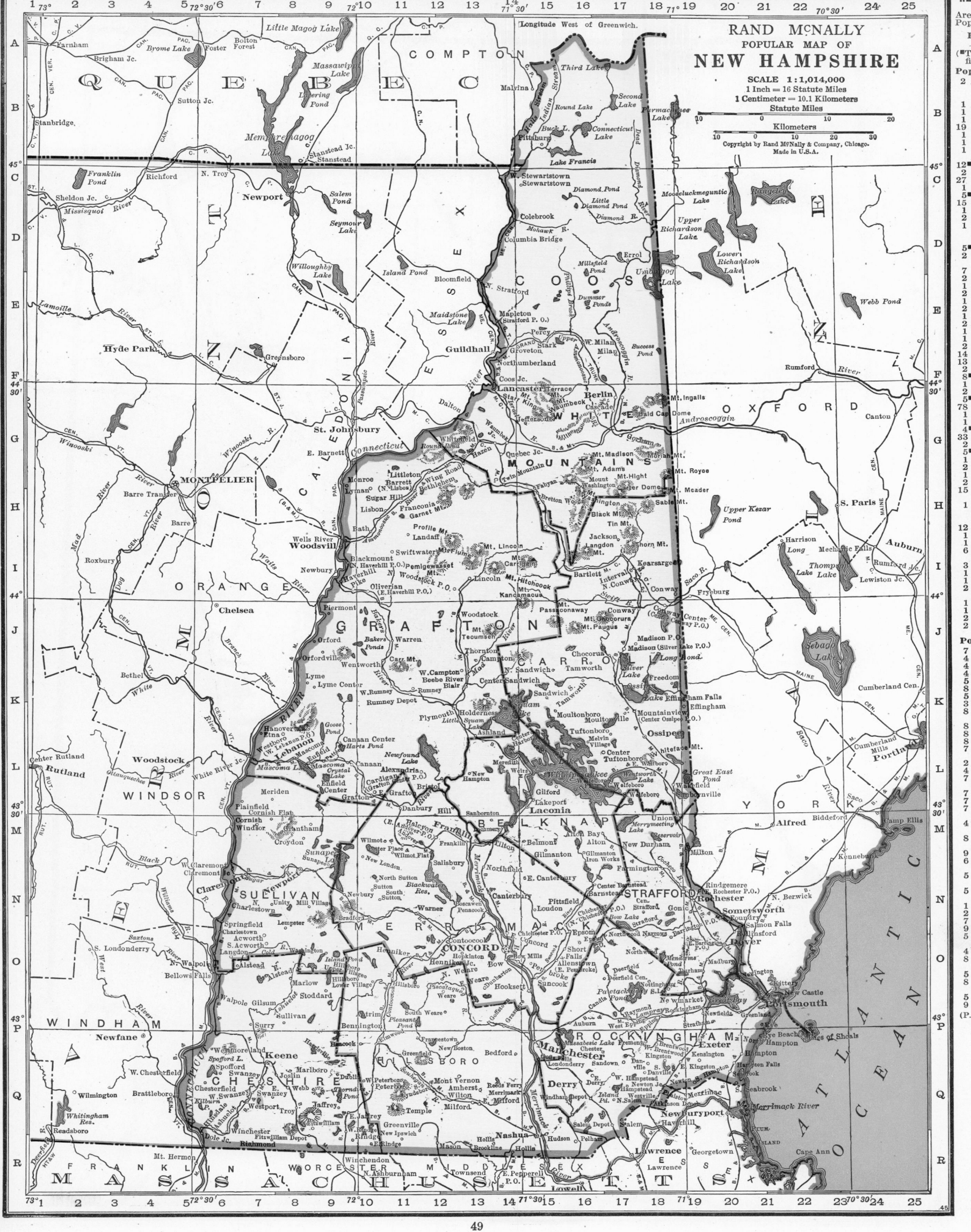

RAND McNALLY
POPULAR MAP OF
NEW HAMPSHIRE

SCALE 1:1,014,000
1 Inch = 16 Statute Miles
1 Centimeter = 10.1 Kilometers
Statute Miles

Kilometers

Copyright by Rand McNally & Company, Chicago.
Made in U.S.A.

Longitude West of Greenwich.

NEW HAMPSHIRE

Area, 9,304 sq. m.
Pop......491,524

PRINCIPAL CITIES
("Township Classified as Urban")

Pop.—Thousands

2	Allenstown (East Pembroke)..O 15	
1	Antrim....P 11	
1	Ashland...K 12	
1	Bedford....P 14	
19	Berlin....F 17	
1	Bristol....L 12	
1	Cascade..F 17	
1	Charlestown O N 6	
12	Claremont.N 7	
2	Colebrook D 14	
27	Concord...O 14	
1	Conway...J 18	
1	Derry....Q 16	
15	Dover....O 20	
1	Durham...O 19	
2	E. Jaffrey.Q 10	
1	E. Rochester (Ringemere) N 19	
2	Exeter....P 19	
2	Farmington N 18	
7	Franklin..M 13	
2	Gorham...G 17	
1	Greenville.R 12	
2	Groveton..F 14	
1	Hampton..P 20	
2	Hanover...K 7	
1	Henniker.O 11	
1	Hillsboro..O 11	
1	Hinsdale..Q 5	
1	Hooksett..O 14	
2	Hudson...R 15	
14	Keene....P 7	
13	Laconia..M 15	
2	Lancaster.F 14	
8	Lebanon...L 8	
1	Lincoln...I 13	
1	Lisbon...H 11	
5	Littleton..G 12	
78	Manchester P 15	
1	Marlboro..Q 8	
1	Meredith..L 14	
4	Milford...Q 13	
33	Nashua...R 15	
2	Newmarket P 19	
5	Newport..N 8	
1	N. Walpole O 6	
2	Peterboro Q 10	
1	Pittsfield .N 16	
2	Plymouth.K 12	
15	Portsmouth O 21	
1	Ringemere (E. Rochester)....N 19	
12	Rochester.N 19	
3	Salem.....O 17	
1	Seabrook..S 20	
6	Somersworth N 20	
3	Suncook..O 15	
1	Tilton....M 13	
1	Troy.....Q 8	
2	Westboro (W. Lebanon).L 7	
1	Whitefield G 13	
1	Wilton....Q 12	
2	Wolfeboro.L 17	
15	Woodsville I 10	

Pop.—Hundreds

7	Alton....M 17	
3	Andover..M 11	
4	Bath.....H 10	
4	Belmont..M 14	
5	Bethlehem H 12	
8	Bow......O 14	
5	Canaan...L 10	
3	Candia...P 17	
5	Contoocook O 12	
8	Enfield....L 8	
8	Epping...P 18	
8	Goffstown.P 13	
5	Hampstead Q 17	
2	Hopkinton O 13	
4	Kingston..P 17	
7	Londonderry G 15	
5	Loudon...M 15	
5	Milton...M 19	
7	New Boston P 12	
4	New Ipswich R 11	
8	New London M 10	
9	N. Conway I 18	
2	North Haverhill.....I 10	
5	N. Stratford E 13	
5	N. Woodstock I 12	
1	Pelham...R 16	
2	Pittsburg.B 15	
7	Plaistow..P 18	
3	Raymond..P 17	
5	Rollinsford N 20	
4	Rumney...K 11	
8	Salem Depot P 17	
5	Salmon Fs N 20	
8	Sanbornville L 19	
5	Walpole..P 6	
9	Winchester R 6	

(P. I. & C. 789)

NEW JERSEY

Area, 7,836 sq. m.
Pop.....4,160,165

PRINCIPAL CITIES
(*Township Classified as Urban)

Pop.—Thousands

15 Asbury Pk.I 21
64 AtlanticCy.P 16
9 Audubon..K 9
79 Bayonne..F 19
28 Belleville..E 19
10 BergenfieldD 21
42 Bloomfield E 18
7 Bogota...D 20
7 Boonton..D 16
8 Bound Brook F 15
16 Bridgeton..O 7
11 Burlington.J 12
5 Caldwell...D 17
118 Camden...M 9
6 Carlstadt..D 20
12 Carteret...F 18
17 *CliffsidePk.D 21
49 Clifton...D 19
10 Collingswood K 9
13 *Cranford..F 18
10 Dover....D 15
5 Dumont...C 21
5 Dunnellen.F 16
69 E. Orange .E 18
4 EdgewaterD 21
110 Elizabeth.F 18
19 EnglewoodD 21
9 Fair Lawn.D 20
5 Fairview..D 20
9 Fort Lee..D 21
7 Franklin..B 15
7 *Freehold..I 18
25 Garfield...D 20
5 Glassboro..M 9
8 Glen RidgeE 18
5 Glen Rock C 19
14 Gloucester..K 9
6 GuttenbergE 21
26 Hackensack D 20
10 Haddonfield K 10
6 Haddon HtsL 9
8 Haledon...C 18
8 Hammonton M 12
14 Harrison..E 19
6 Hasbrouck Hts.....D 20
13 HawthorneD 19
6 Highland Park G 16
50 Hoboken..E 20
55 Irvington..E 18
301 Jersey Cy.E 20
39 Kearny...E 19
5 Keyport...G 19
5 Lakewood .J 18
4 Lambertville H 11
6 Leonia...D 21
24 Linden....F 18
5 Lodi....D 20
17 Long Branch I 21
17 *Lyndhurst E 19
8 Madison..E 16
5 Manville..G 14
6 Maple Shade K 10
23 *Maplewood E 18
7 Metuchen.G 17
15 Millville..O 10
40 Montclair.D 18
6 Moorestown K 11
15 MorristownE 15
7 Mt. Holly.K 12
430 Newark...E 19
33 New Brunswick..G 16
11 N. Plainfield F 16
22 Nutley....E 19
9 Ocean CityP 15
36 Orange...E 18
5 Palisades Pk....D 21
5 Palmyra..K 10
61 Passaic..D 19
140 Paterson.D 19
7 Paulsboro..L 7
6 Penns Gr..M 5
41 Perth Amboy G 18
18 Phillipsburg E 8
6 Pitman...M 8
37 Plainfield..F 16
11 Pleasantville O 15
6 Princeton.H 13
6 Prospect Pk.D 19
17 Rahway...F 17
5 Raritan...F 14
11 Red Bank.H 20
11 Ridgefield Park D 20
15 RidgewoodC 19
14 Roselle...F 18
10 Roselle Pk.F 18
15 RutherfordE 19
9 *Salem....N 5
8 Sayreville.G 17
12 Secaucus..E 20
10 Somerville.F 14
8 S. Amboy.G 18
8 S. Orange.E 18
5 S. PlainfieldF 16
11 S. River...E 17
16 Summit...E 17
7 Tenafly...C 20
7 Totowa...D 18
125 Trenton..I 13
56 Union CityE 20
8 Ventnor..P 16
5 Verona...D 18
8 Vineland..O 10
5 WallingtonD 19
5 Washington E 10
14 *Weehawken E 20
18 Westfield..F 17
39 W. New York E 21
26 W. Orange E 18
5 Westwood.C 20
5 Wildwood.R 12
27 *Woodbridge F 18
8 Woodbury.L 8

(P. I. & C. 789)

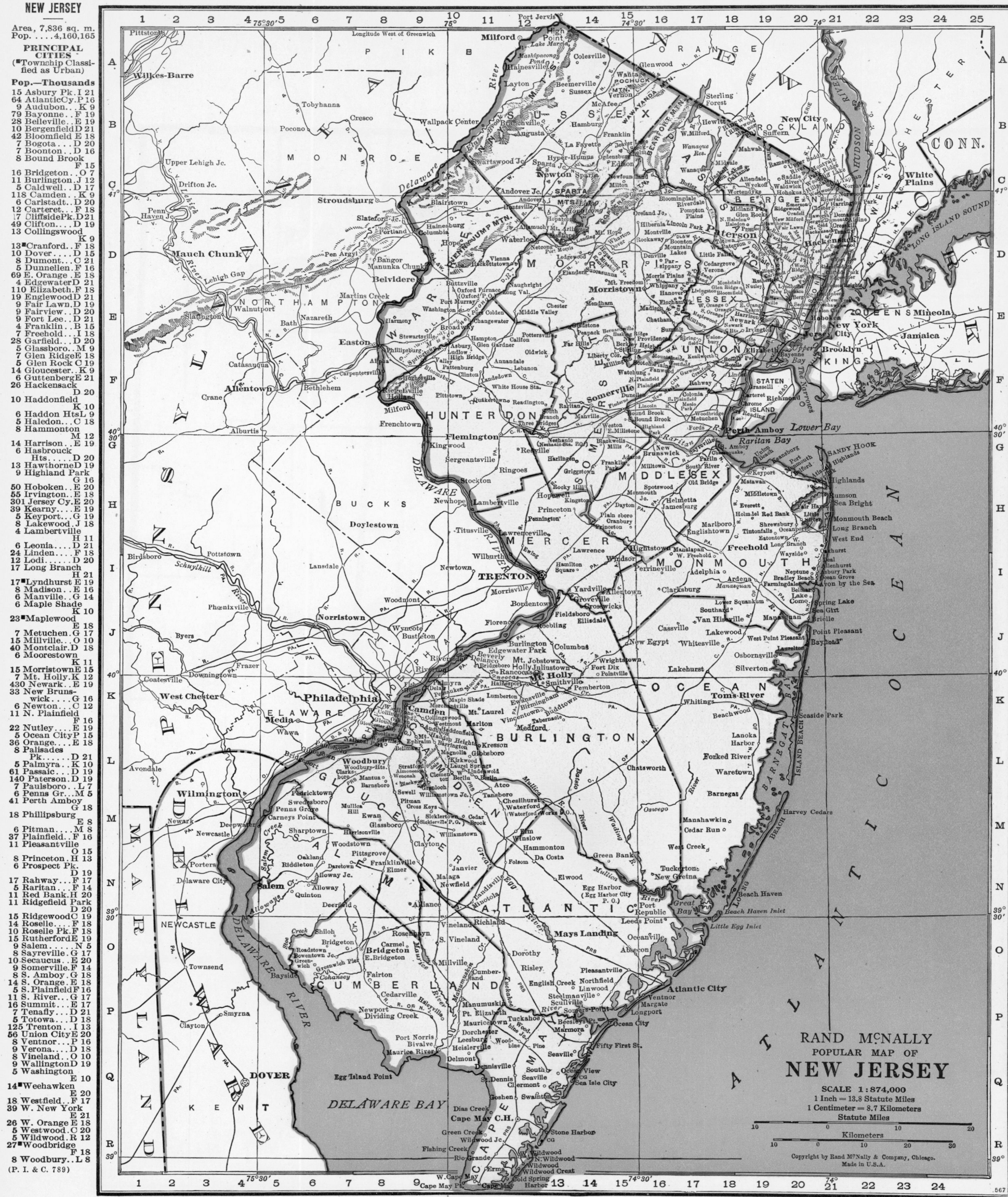

RAND McNALLY
POPULAR MAP OF
NEW JERSEY

SCALE 1:874,000
1 Inch = 13.8 Statute Miles
1 Centimeter = 8.7 Kilometers
Statute Miles

Kilometers

Copyright by Rand McNally & Company, Chicago.
Made in U.S.A.

50

Area, 121,666 sq.m.
Pop......531,818

PRINCIPAL CITIES

Pop.—Thousands

4	Alamogordo...M 12
35	Albuquerque...G 11
4	Artesia...M 20
3	Belen...H 10
2	Bernalillo...G 10
7	Carlsbad...N 20
1	Carrizozo...K 14
3	Clayton...D 24
10	Clovis...I 25
1	Conchas Dam...F 21
2	Dawson...C 18
4	Deming...O 6
4	East Las Vegas (Las Vegas town)...F 17
2	Farmington...C 4
1	Ft. Bayard...M 4
2	Ft. Sumner...I 21
7	Gallup...F 2
11	Hobbs...M 25
3	Hot Springs...L 7
1	Hurley...M 4
1	Isleta...H 11
1	Jal...O 25
8	Las Cruces...N 10
6	Las Vegas...F 16
1	Lordsburg...N 2
2	Lovington...M 23
2	Magdalena...J 8
2	Mesa Rica...F 20
2	Mesilla...N 9
1	Mora...I 16
1	Mountainair...I 13
2	Old Albuquerque...G 9
1	Portales...J 25
5	Raton...B 19
13	Roswell...L 19
1	Roy...E 20
20	Santa Fe...F 13
2	Santa Rosa...H 19
5	Silver City...M 3
4	Socorro...J 10
1	Springer...D 18
1	Tererro...E 15
1	Tucumcari...G 22
1	Tularosa...M 13
1	Vaughn...H 17
1	Wagon Mound...E 18

Pop.—Hundreds

4	Adelino...H 11
5	Alameda...G 10
5	Allison...F 1
4	Anton Chico...G 16
8	Aztec...C 5
5	Cebola...C 11
4	Central...M 4
7	Chama...B 11
5	Cimarron...C 17
7	Cleveland...E 16
5	Columbus...P 6
5	Cordova...E 14
7	Cuba...E 9
2	Derry...M 8
3	Des Moines...C 22
7	Dexter...L 20
8	Dixon...D 14
5	Dona Ana...N 10
3	Elida...J 22
4	Ensenada...C 12
5	Espanola...D 14
7	Estancia...H 13
5	Ft. Stanton...K 15
7	Glencoe...L 15
9	Hagerman...L 21
5	Hatch...N 8
5	Hope...M 19
7	Jarales...H 10
2	Jemez...F 11
3	Lake Arthur...M 19
7	Los Lunas...H 11
5	Maxwell...C 19
9	Melrose...I 23
2	Mosquero...E 21
4	Questa...C 15
4	San Jose...F 15
3	San Marcial...K 9
5	Santa Cruz...E 14
5	Sugarite...B 20
5	Texico...I 25
8	Truchas...E 14
4	Willard...H 13

(P. I. & C. 789)

SCALE 1:2,534,000
1 Inch = 40 Statute Miles
1 Centimeter = 25.3 Kilometers
Statute Miles
20 10 0   40
Kilometers
20 10 0   20   40   60
Copyright by Rand McNally & Company, Chicago.
Made in U.S.A.

RAND McNALLY
POPULAR MAP OF
NEW MEXICO

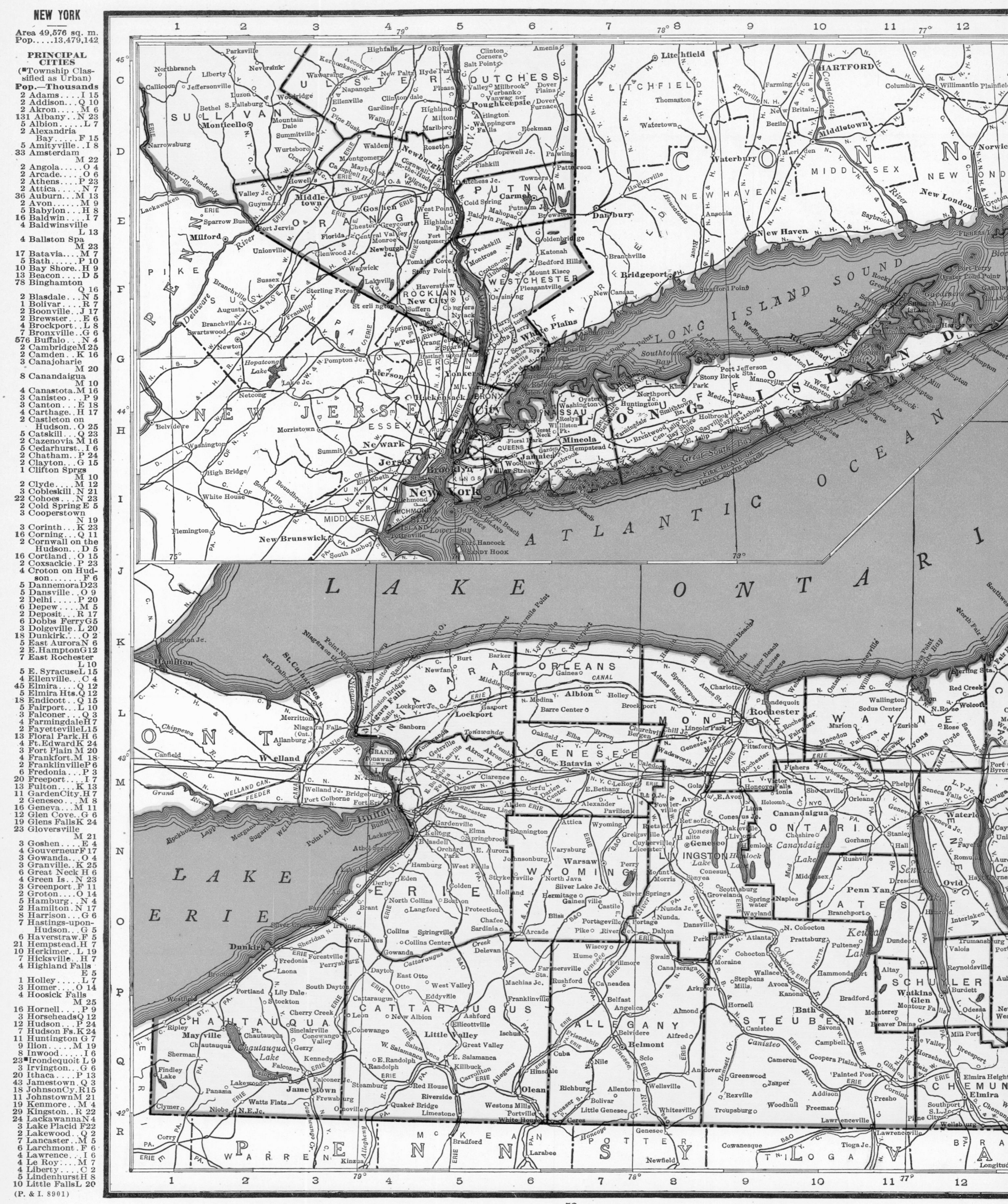

53

NORTH CAROLINA

Area, 52,712 sq. m.
Pop.....3,571,623

PRINCIPAL CITIES

Pop.—Thousands

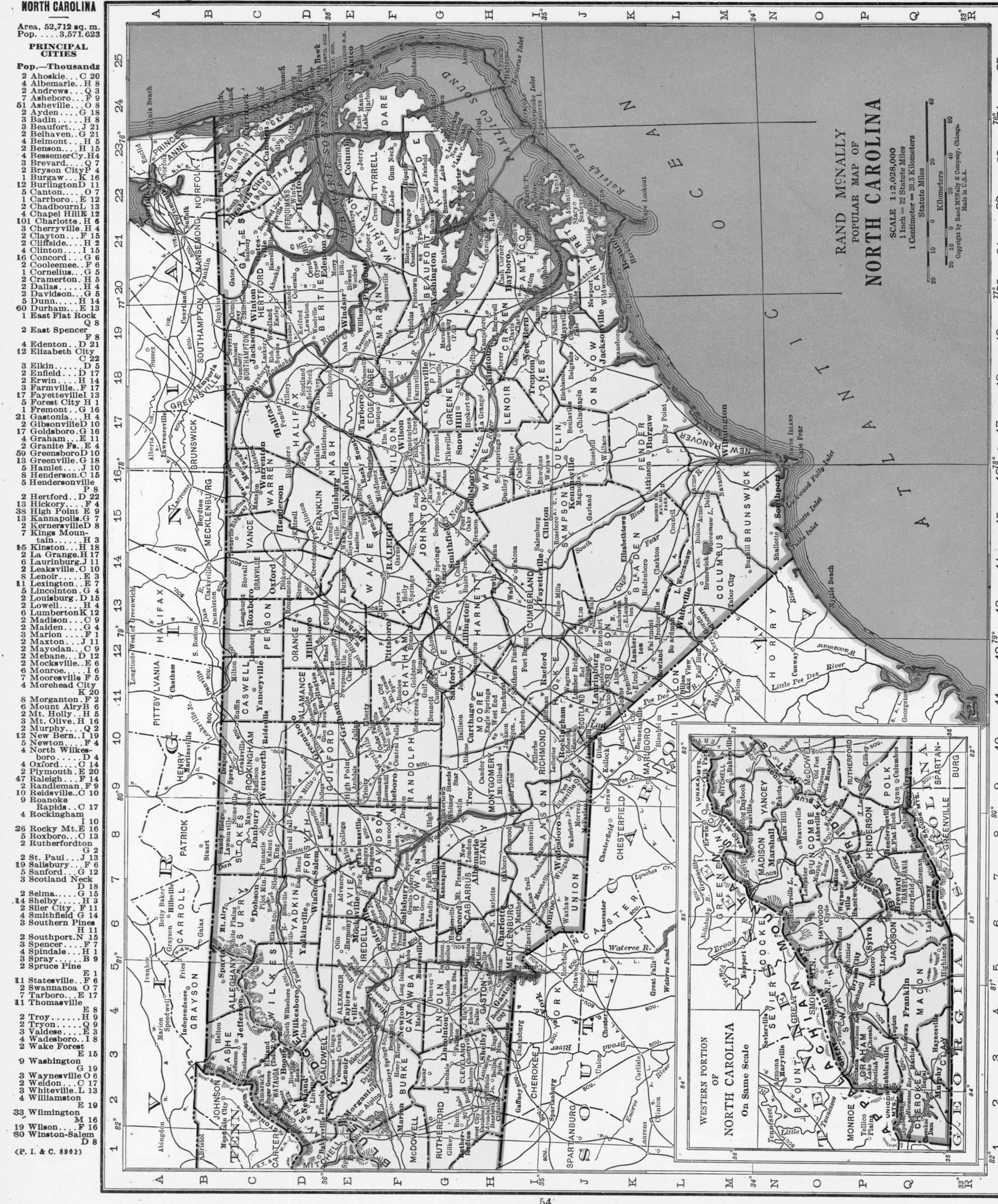

RAND McNALLY
POPULAR MAP OF
NORTH CAROLINA

SCALE 1:2,028,000
1 Inch = 32 Statute Miles
1 Centimeter = 20.3 Kilometers
Statute Miles

Copyright by Rand McNally & Company, Chicago.
Made in U.S.A.

WESTERN PORTION OF
NORTH CAROLINA
On Same Scale

55

OHIO

PRINCIPAL CITIES

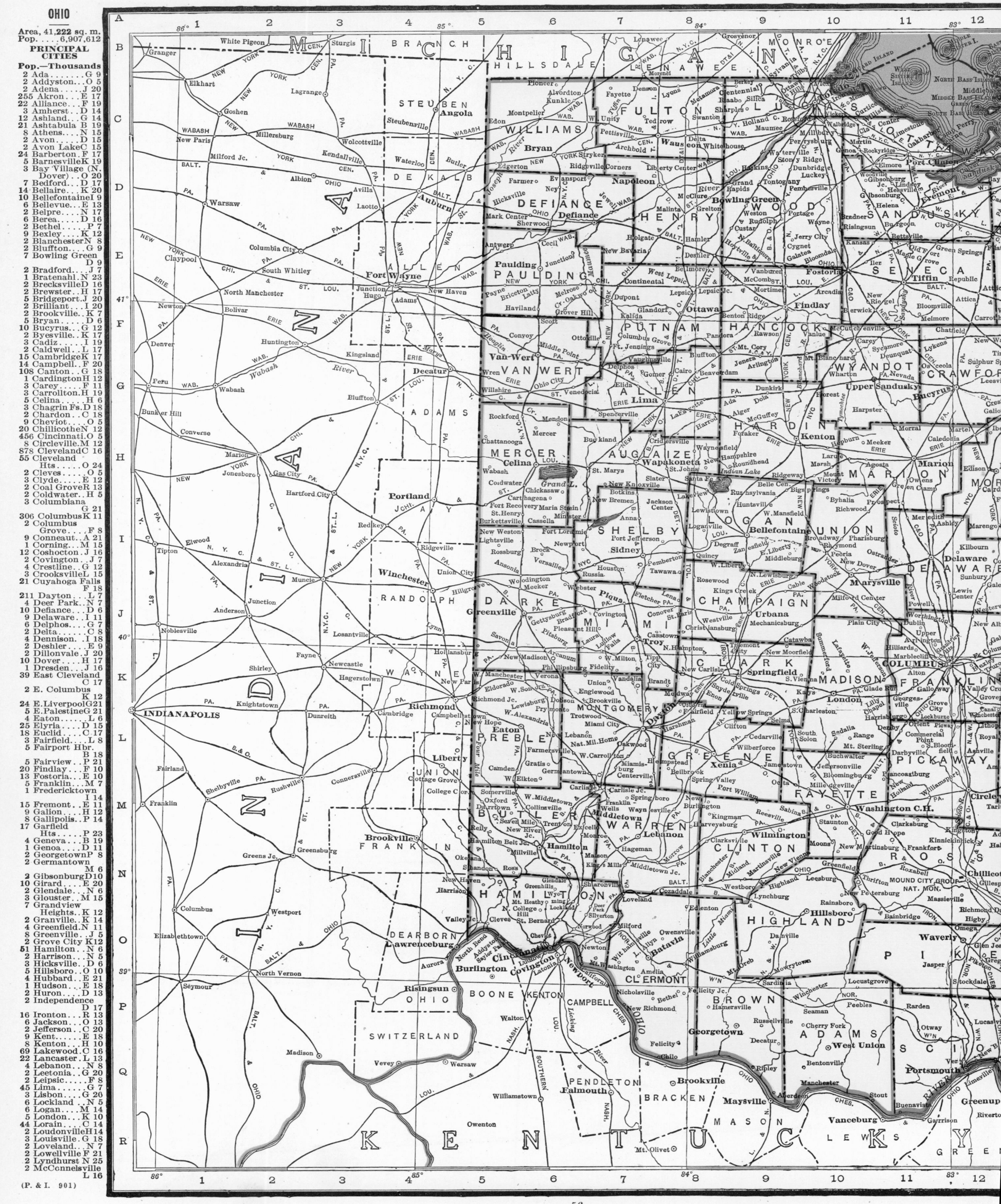

(P. & I. 901)

RAND McNALLY
14 x 21 INCH MAP OF
OHIO
SCALE 1 : 1,255,000
1 Inch = 19.8 Statute Miles
1 Centimeter = 12.5 Kilometers
Statute Miles

Kilometers

Railroads ——— Electric Lines ——

Copyright by Rand McNally & Company, Chicago.
Made in U.S.A.

CLEVELAND
AND VICINITY
SCALE 1 : 456,200
1 Inch = 7.2 Statute Miles

6   57

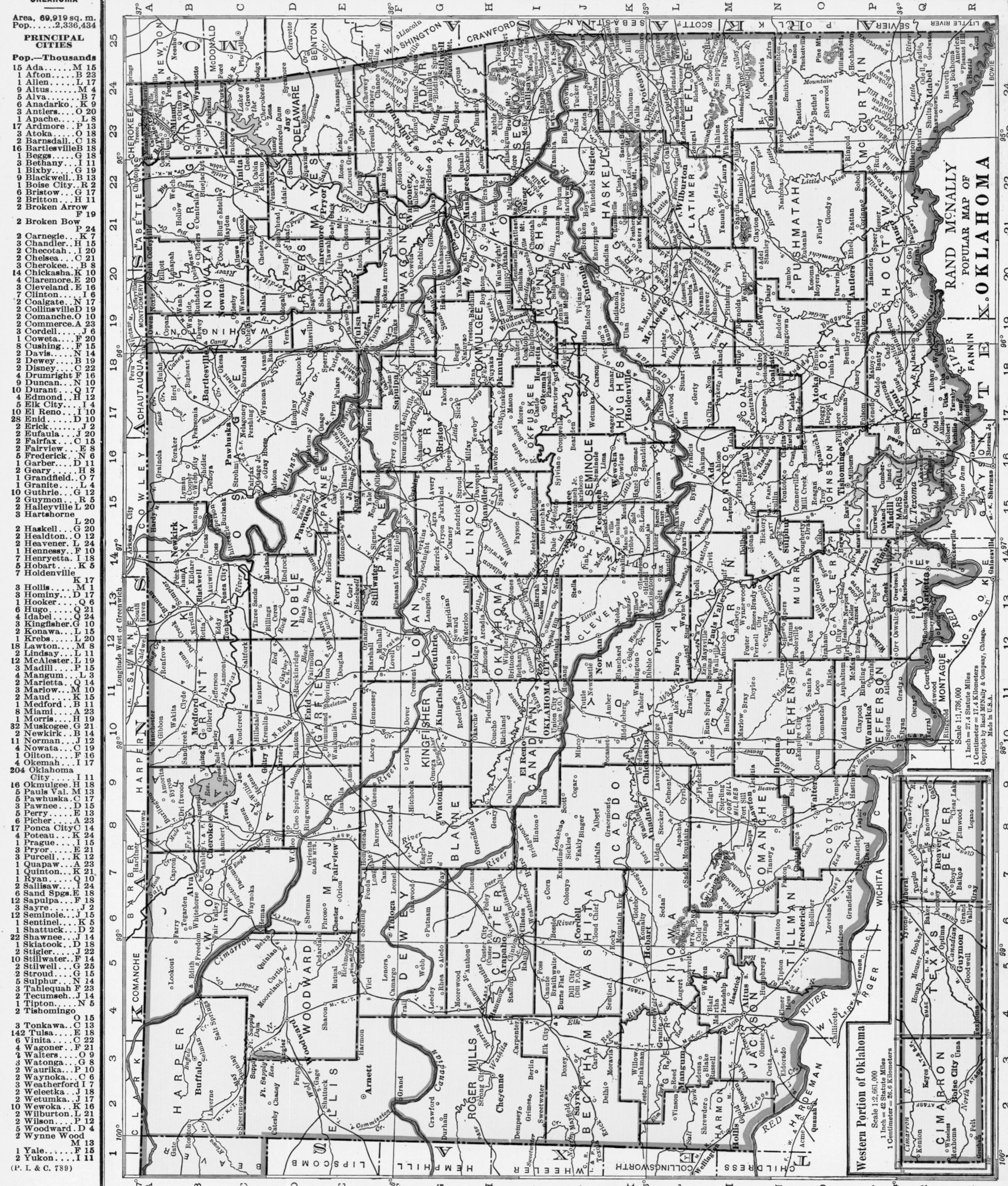

OKLAHOMA

Area, 69,919 sq. m.
Pop..... 2,336,434

RAND McNALLY POPULAR MAP OF OKLAHOMA

Scale 1:1,795,000
1 Inch = 27.4 Statute Miles
1 Centimeter = 17.4 Kilometers
Rand McNally & Company, Chicago

Western Portion of Oklahoma

Scale 12,661,000

Cimarron

RAND McNALLY

POPULAR MAP OF OREGON

SCALE 1:2,186,000
1 Inch = 34.5 Statute Miles
1 Centimeter = 21.9 Kilometers
Statute Miles

Copyright by Rand McNally & Company, Chicago.
Made in U.S.A.

59

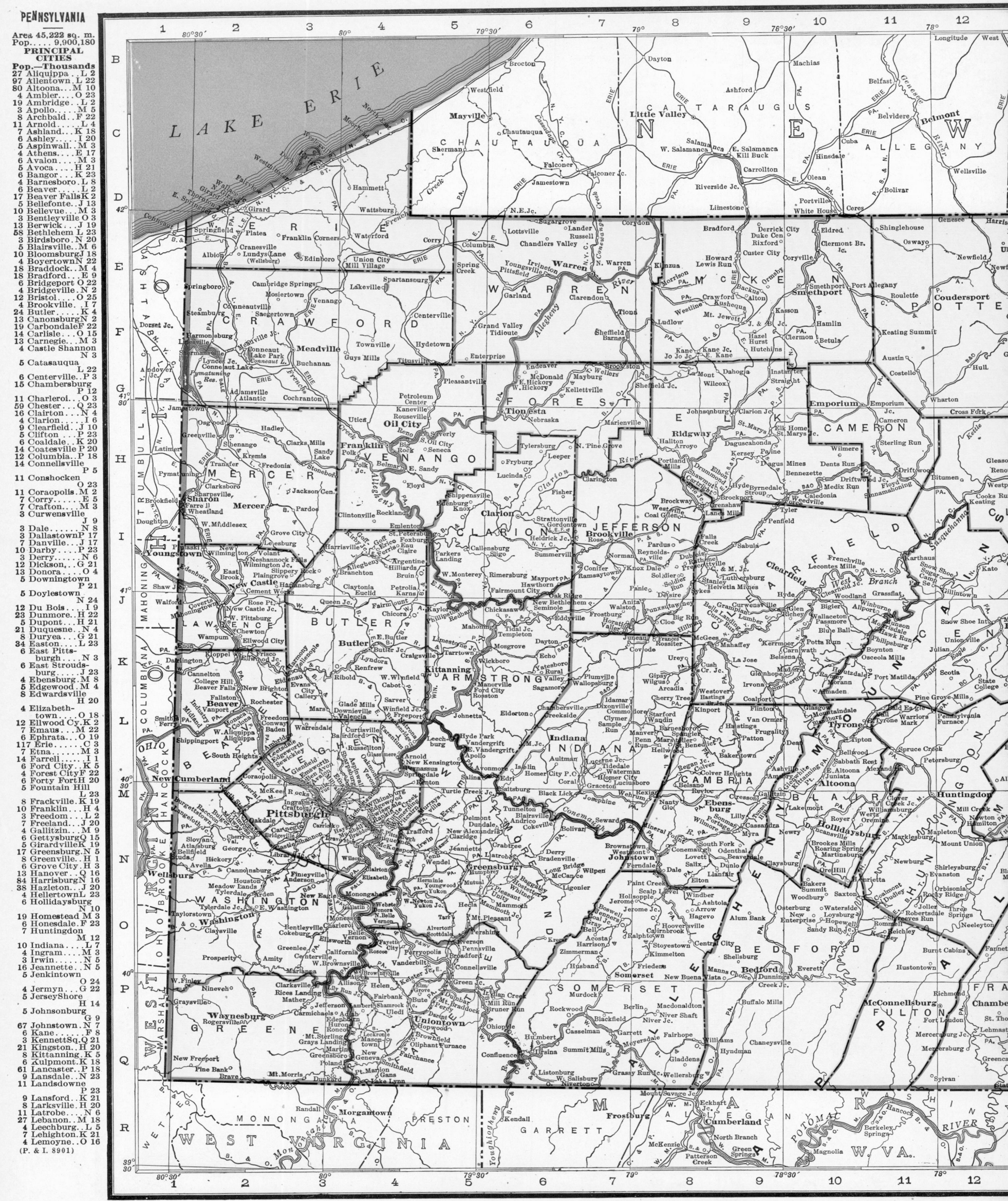

PENNSYLVANIA

Area 45,222 sq. m.
Pop.... 9,900,180

PRINCIPAL CITIES

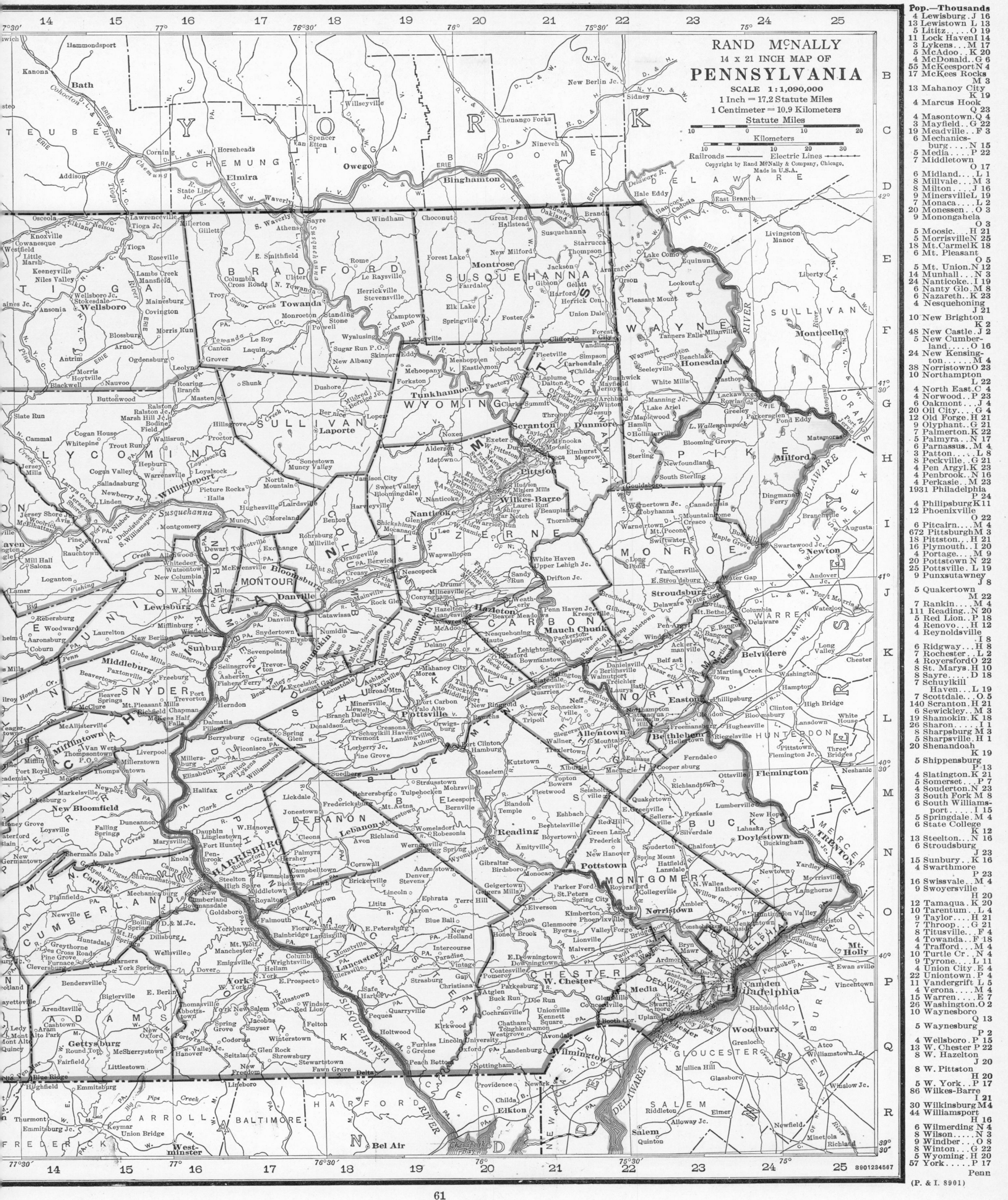

RAND McNALLY
14 x 21 INCH MAP OF
PENNSYLVANIA
SCALE 1:1,090,000
1 Inch = 17.2 Statute Miles
1 Centimeter = 10.9 Kilometers
Statute Miles
Kilometers
Railroads   Electric Lines
Copyright by Rand McNally & Company, Chicago.
Made in U.S.A.

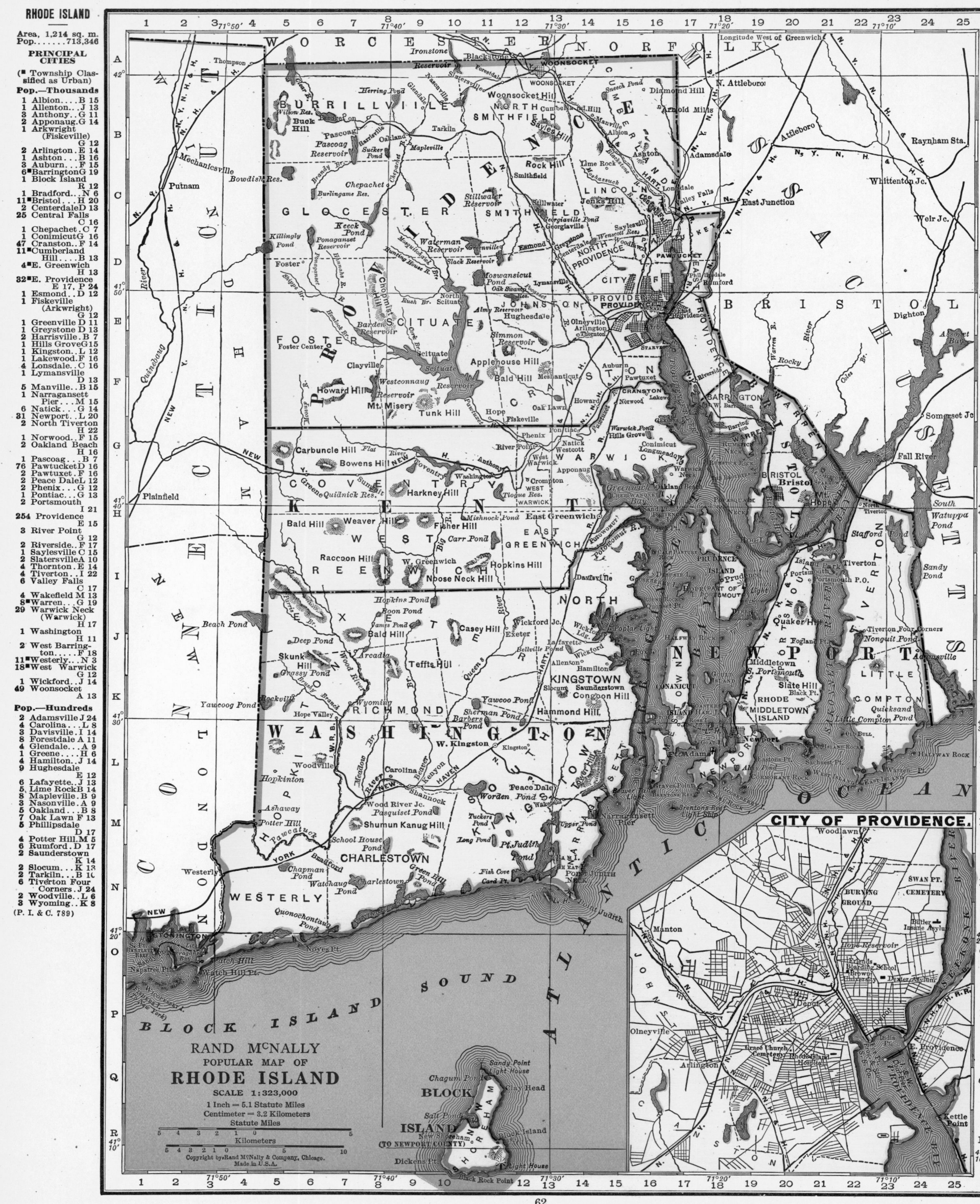

RHODE ISLAND

Area, 1,214 sq. m.
Pop......713,346

PRINCIPAL CITIES

(■ Township Classified as Urban)

Pop.—Thousands

1 Albion....B 15
1 Allenton..J 13
3 Anthony..G 11
2 Apponaug.G 14
1 Arkwright
   (Fiskeville)
       G 12
2 Arlington..E 14
1 Ashton...B 16
3 Auburn...F 15
6 ■Barrington G 19
1 Block Island
       R 12
1 Bradford..N 6
11 ■Bristol..H 20
2 Centerdale D 13
25 Central Falls
       C 16
1 Chepachet..C 7
1 Conimicut G 16
47 Cranston..F 14
11 ■Cumberland
   Hill...B 13
4 ■E. Greenwich
       H 13
32 ■E. Providence
   E 17, P 24
1 Esmond...D 12
1 Fiskeville
   (Arkwright)
       G 12
1 Greenville D 11
1 Greystone D 13
2 Harrisville..B 7
1 Hills Grove G15
1 Kingston..L 12
4 Lakewood.F 16
4 Lonsdale..C 16
1 Lymansville
       D 13
5 Manville..B 15
1 Narragansett
   Pier..M 15
6 Natick...G 14
31 Newport..L 20
2 North Tiverton
       H 22
1 Norwood..F 15
2 Oakland Beach
       H 16
1 Pascoag..B 7
76 Pawtucket D 16
3 Pawtuxet..F 16
2 Peace Dale L 12
2 Phenix...G 12
2 Pontiac...G 13
2 Portsmouth
       I 21
254 Providence
       E 15
3 River Point
       G 12
2 Riverside..F 17
2 Saylesville C 15
2 Slatersville A 10
4 Thornton..E 14
4 Tiverton..I 22
1 Valley Falls
       C 17
4 Wakefield M 13
8 ■Warren...G 19
29 Warwick Neck
   (Warwick)
       H 17
1 Washington
       H 11
2 West Barring-
   ton...F 18
11 ■Westerly..N 3
18 ■West Warwick
       G 12
1 Wickford..J 14
49 Woonsocket
       A 13

Pop.—Hundreds

2 Adamsville J 24
4 Carolina...L 8
2 Davisville.I 14
4 Forestdale A 11
4 Glendale...A 9
1 Greene...H 6
4 Hamilton..J 14
9 Hughesdale
       E 12
6 Lafayette..J 13
5 Lime Rock B 14
8 Mapleville..B 9
3 Nasonville..A 9
5 Oakland...B 8
2 Oak Lawn F 13
5 Phillipsdale
       D 17
4 Potter Hill.M 5
6 Rumford..D 17
2 Saunderstown
       K 14
2 Slocum...K 13
2 Tarkiln...B 10
6 Tiverton Four
   Corners J 24
1 Woodville..L 6
3 Wyoming..K 8

(P. I. & C. 789)

RAND McNALLY
POPULAR MAP OF
RHODE ISLAND

SCALE 1:323,000

1 Inch = 5.1 Statute Miles
Centimeter = 3.2 Kilometers
Statute Miles

Copyright by Rand McNally & Company, Chicago.
Made in U.S.A.

CITY OF PROVIDENCE.

RAND McNALLY
POPULAR MAP OF
SOUTH CAROLINA

SCALE 1:1,565,000
1 Inch = 24.7 Statute Miles
1 Centimeter = 15.6 Kilometers

Statute Miles

Kilometers

Copyright by Rand McNally & Company, Chicago.
Made in U.S.A.

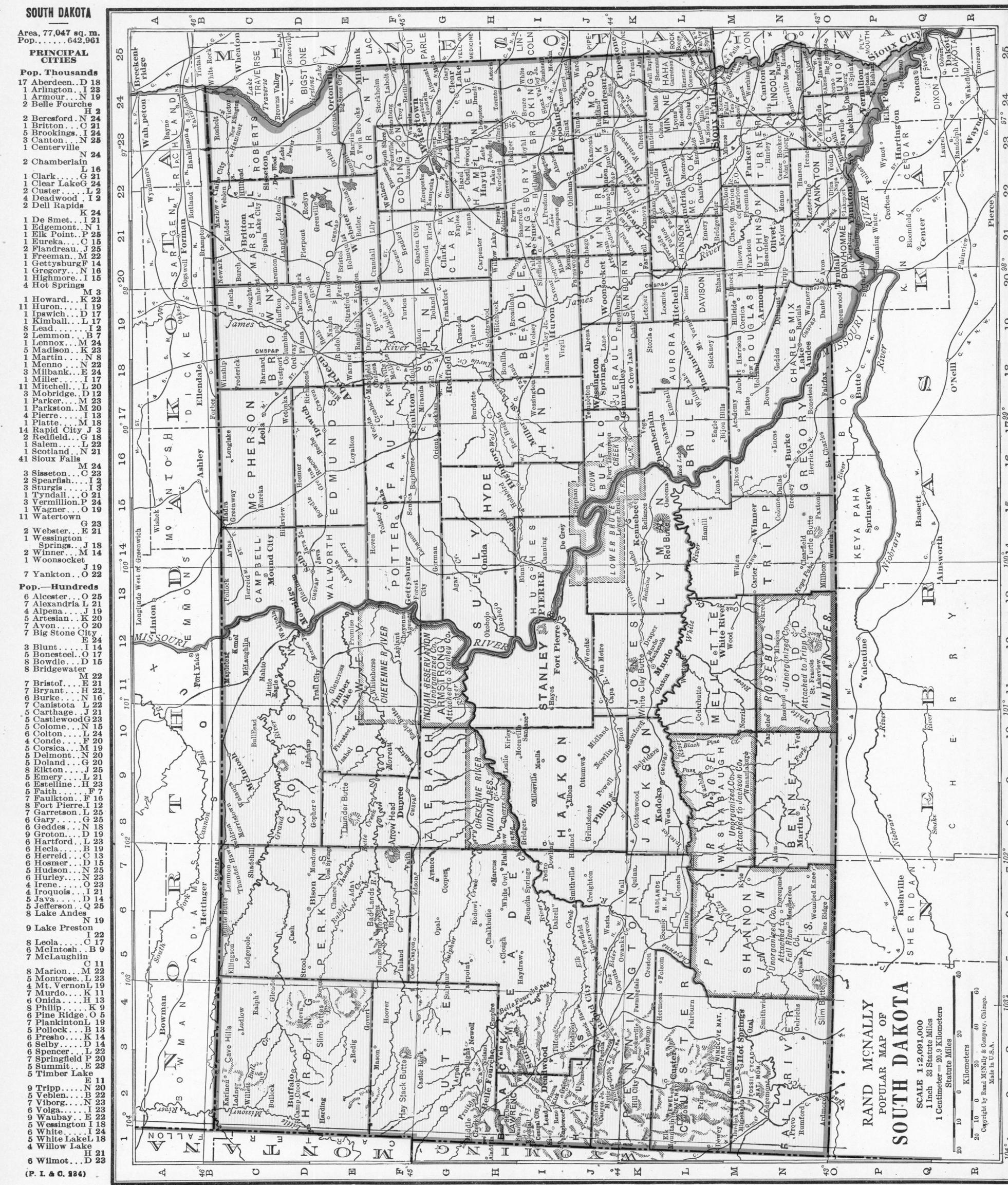

SOUTH DAKOTA

Area, 77,047 sq. m.
Pop......642,961

PRINCIPAL CITIES

Pop. Thousands

17 Aberdeen...D 18
1 Arlington...I 23
1 Armour....N 19
2 Belle Fourche
........H 2
2 Beresford..N 24
1 Britton....O 21
5 Brookings.J 24
1 Canton....N 25
1 Centerville
........N 24
2 Chamberlain
........L 16
1 Clark......G 21
1 Clear Lake.G 24
1 Custer.....L 2
4 Deadwood..I 2
1 Dell Rapids
........K 24
1 De Smet...I 21
1 Edgemont..N 1
1 Elk Point..P 25
1 Eureka....O 15
1 Flandreau.J 25
1 Freeman...M 22
1 Gettysburg.F 14
1 Gregory...N 16
1 Highmore..I 15
4 Hot Springs
........M 3
11 Howard....K 22
11 Huron.....I 19
1 Ipswich...D 17
1 Kimball...L 17
1 Lead.......I 2
2 Lemmon...B 7
2 Lennox....M 24
1 Madison...K 23
1 Martin....N 8
2 Menno.....N 22
3 Milbank...E 24
1 Miller.....I 17
11 Mitchell..L 20
1 Mobridge..D 12
1 Parker....M 23
1 Parkston..M 20
1 Pierre.....I 13
1 Platte.....M 18
14 Rapid City.J 3
8 Redfield...G 18
1 Salem.....L 22
1 Scotland..N 21
41 Sioux Falls
........M 24
3 Sisseton...C 23
2 Spearfish..I 2
2 Sturgis....I 3
1 Tyndall...O 21
1 Vermillion.P 24
1 Wagner....O 19
11 Watertown
........G 23
2 Webster...E 21
1 Wessington
Springs..J 18
1 Winner...M 14
1 Woonsocket
........J 19
7 Yankton...O 22

Pop.—Hundreds

6 Alcester....O 25
7 Alexandria.L 21
4 Alpena....J 19
6 Artesian..K 20
7 Avon......O 20
7 Big Stone City
........E 24
3 Blunt......I 14
6 Bonesteel..O 17
8 Bowdle....D 15
6 Bridgewater
........M 22
7 Bristol....E 21
7 Bryant....H 22
6 Burke.....N 16
7 Canistota.L 23
5 Carthage..J 21
6 Castlewood.G 23
5 Colome....N 15
6 Colton....L 24
6 Conde.....F 20
5 Corsica...N 19
6 Delmont...M 20
5 Doland....G 20
8 Elkton....J 25
6 Emery.....L 21
6 Estelline..H 23
7 Faith.....F 7
7 Faulkton..F 16
1 Fort Pierre.I 12
7 Garretson..L 25
5 Gary......G 25
6 Geddes....N 18
9 Groton....D 19
6 Hartford..L 23
6 Hecla.....B 19
5 Herreid...C 13
5 Hosmer....D 15
5 Hudson....N 25
6 Hurley....N 23
4 Irene......O 23
5 Iroquois..I 21
5 Java......D 14
5 Jefferson..Q 25
6 Lake Andes
........N 19
9 Lake Preston
........I 22
8 Leola.....C 17
6 McIntosh..B 9
7 McLaughlin
........C 11
6 Marion....M 22
5 Montrose..L 23
6 Mt. Vernon.L 19
7 Murdo.....K 11
6 Onida.....H 13
8 Philip....K 9
6 Pine Ridge.O 5
7 Plankinton.L 19
5 Pollock...B 13
6 Presho....K 14
6 Selby.....D 14
5 Spencer...L 22
7 Springfield.P 20
5 Summit....E 23
5 Timber Lake
........E 11
9 Tripp.....N 20
5 Veblen....B 22
5 Viborg....N 23
5 Volga.....J 22
9 Waubay...E 22
5 Wessington.I 18
6 White.....I 24
5 White Lake.L 18
4 Willow Lake
........H 21
6 Wilmot...D 23

(P. I. & C. 284)

RAND McNALLY POPULAR MAP OF SOUTH DAKOTA

SCALE 1:2,091,000
1 Inch 33 Statute Miles
1 Centimeter 20.9 Kilometers

Copyright by Rand McNally & Company, Chicago.
Made in U.S.A.

RAND McNALLY
POPULAR MAP OF
UTAH

SCALE 1:2,028,000
1 Inch = 32 Statute Miles
1 Centimeter = 20.3 Kilometers
Statute Miles

Copyright by Rand McNally & Company, Chicago.
Made in U.S.A.

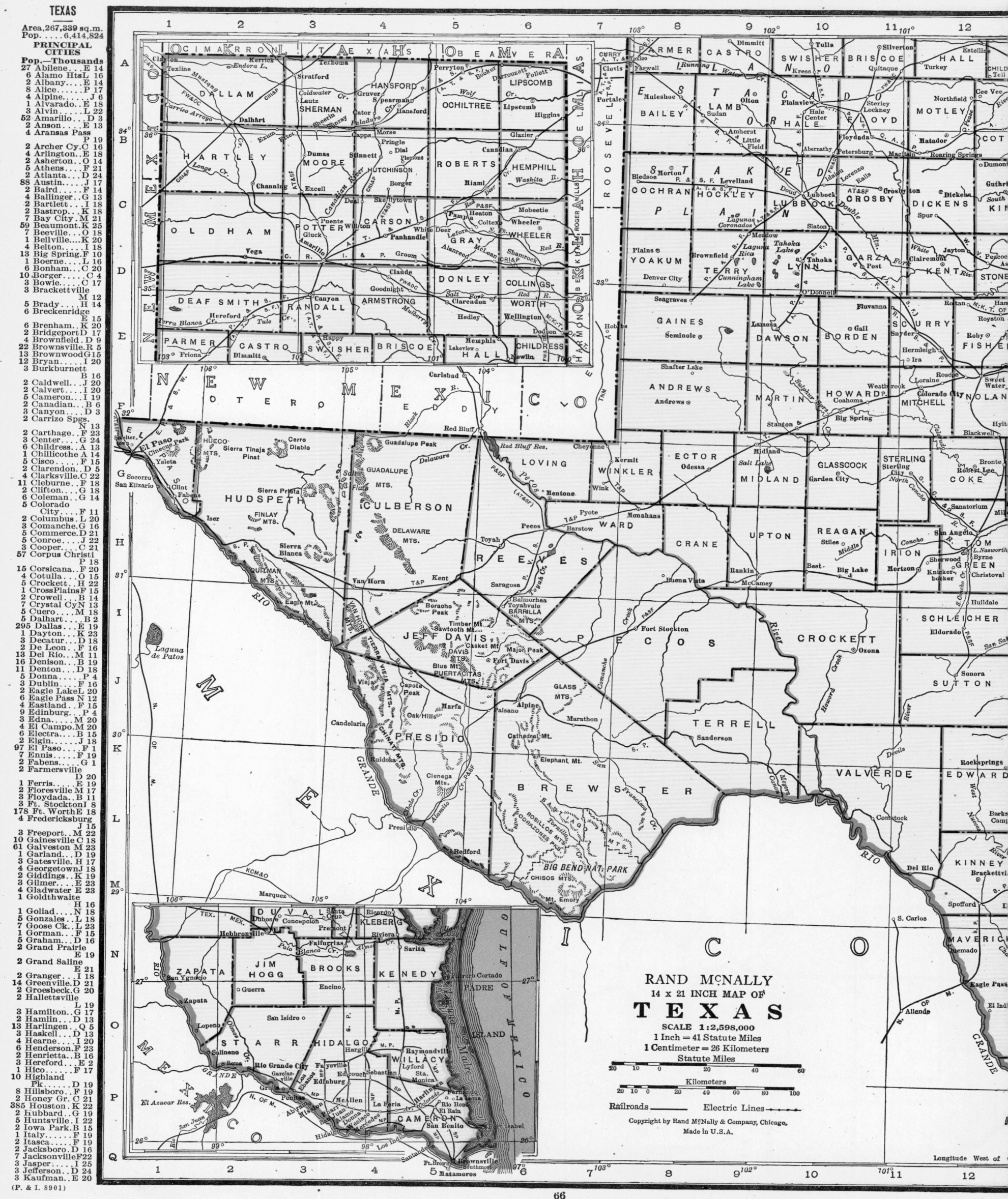

TEXAS

Area, 267,339 sq.m.
Pop.....6,414,824

PRINCIPAL CITIES
Pop.—Thousands

27 Abilene.....E 14
6 Alamo Hts.L 16
8 Albany.....E 14
8 Alice.....P 17
4 Alpine.....J 6
4 Alvarado.E 18
3 Alvin.....L 22
52 Amarillo..D 3
2 Anson.....E 13
4 Aransas Pass
P 19
2 Archer Cy.C 16
4 Arlington..E 18
8 Asherton..O 14
5 Athens.....F 21
88 Atlanta.....D 24
88 Austin.....J 17
4 Baird.....F 14
2 Ballinger..G 13
2 Bartlett.....I 18
5 Bastrop...K 18
7 Bay City..M 21
59 Beaumont.K 24
7 Beeville.....O 18
6 Bellville....K 20
8 Belton.....I 18
13 Big Spring.F 10
2 Boerne....L 16
6 Bonham..L 20
10 Borger.....C 4
2 Bowie.....C 17
2 Brackettville
P 12
5 Brady.....H 14
6 Breckenridge
E 15
6 Brenham..K 20
2 Bridgeport.D 17
3 Floydada.M 11
9 Brownfield.D 9
22 Brownsville.R 5
29 Brownwood.G 15
12 Bryan.....I 20
2 Burkburnett
B 16
2 Caldwell...J 20
2 Calvert.....I 20
3 Cameron..I 19
2 Canadian..B 6
2 Canyon....D 3
2 Carrizo Spgs.
N 13
2 Carthage...F 23
6 Center.....G 24
3 Childress...A 13
1 Chillicothe A 14
2 Cisco.....F 15
2 Clarendon..D 5
4 Clarksville.C 22
11 Cleburne...E 18
2 Clifton.....G 18
4 Coleman...G 14
5 Colorado
City.....F 11
2 Columbus..L 20
4 Comanche.G 16
5 Commerce.D 21
5 Conroe.....J 22
2 Cooper.....C 21
57 Corpus Christi
P 18
15 Corsicana..F 20
2 Cotulla.....O 15
5 Crockett...I 22
1 CrossPlainsF 15
2 Crowell.....B 14
7 Crystal CyN 13
5 Cuero.....M 18
5 Dalhart.....B 2
295 Dallas.....E 19
1 Dayton....K 23
3 Decatur...D 18
2 De Leon...F 16
13 Del Rio....M 11
18 Denison...B 19
11 Denton....D 18
5 Donna.....P 4
3 Dublin.....F 16
2 Eagle LakeL 20
6 Eagle Pass N 12
9 Eastland...F 15
4 Edinburg...P 4
4 Edna.....M 20
4 El Campo.M 20
6 Electra.....B 15
2 Elgin.....J 18
97 El Paso....F 1
7 Ennis.....F 19
2 Fabens.....G 1
2 Farmersville
D 20
1 Ferris.....E 19
1 Floresville M 17
3 Floydada.M 11
3 Ft. StocktonI 8
178 Ft. WorthE 18
4 Fredericksburg
J 15
3 Freeport...M 22
10 Gainesville C 18
61 Galveston M 23
1 Garland...D 19
3 Gatesville. H 17
4 GeorgetownJ 18
2 Giddings..K 19
2 Gilmer.....E 23
6 Gladewater E 23
1 Goldthwaite
H 16
1 Goliad.....N 18
5 Gonzales..L 18
7 Goose Ck..L 23
2 Gorman....F 15
2 Graham....D 16
2 Grand Prairie
E 18
2 Grand Saline
E 21
2 Granger....I 18
14 Greenville. D 21
2 Groesbeck.G 20
2 Hallettsville
L 19
3 Hamilton..G 17
2 Hamlin.....D 13
13 Harlingen..D 5
3 Haskell.....D 13
4 Hearne.....I 20
6 Henderson.F 23
2 Henrietta..B 16
3 Hereford...E 2
3 Hico.....F 17
10 Highland
Pk.....D 19
8 Hillsboro...F 18
2 Honey Gr..C 21
385 Houston..K 22
2 Hubbard...G 19
5 Huntsville..I 22
2 Iowa Park.B 15
2 Italy.....F 19
2 Itasca.....F 19
2 Jacksboro.D 16
7 Jacksonville F22
3 Jasper.....J 25
3 Jefferson..D 24
3 Kaufman..E 20

(P. & I. 8901)

66

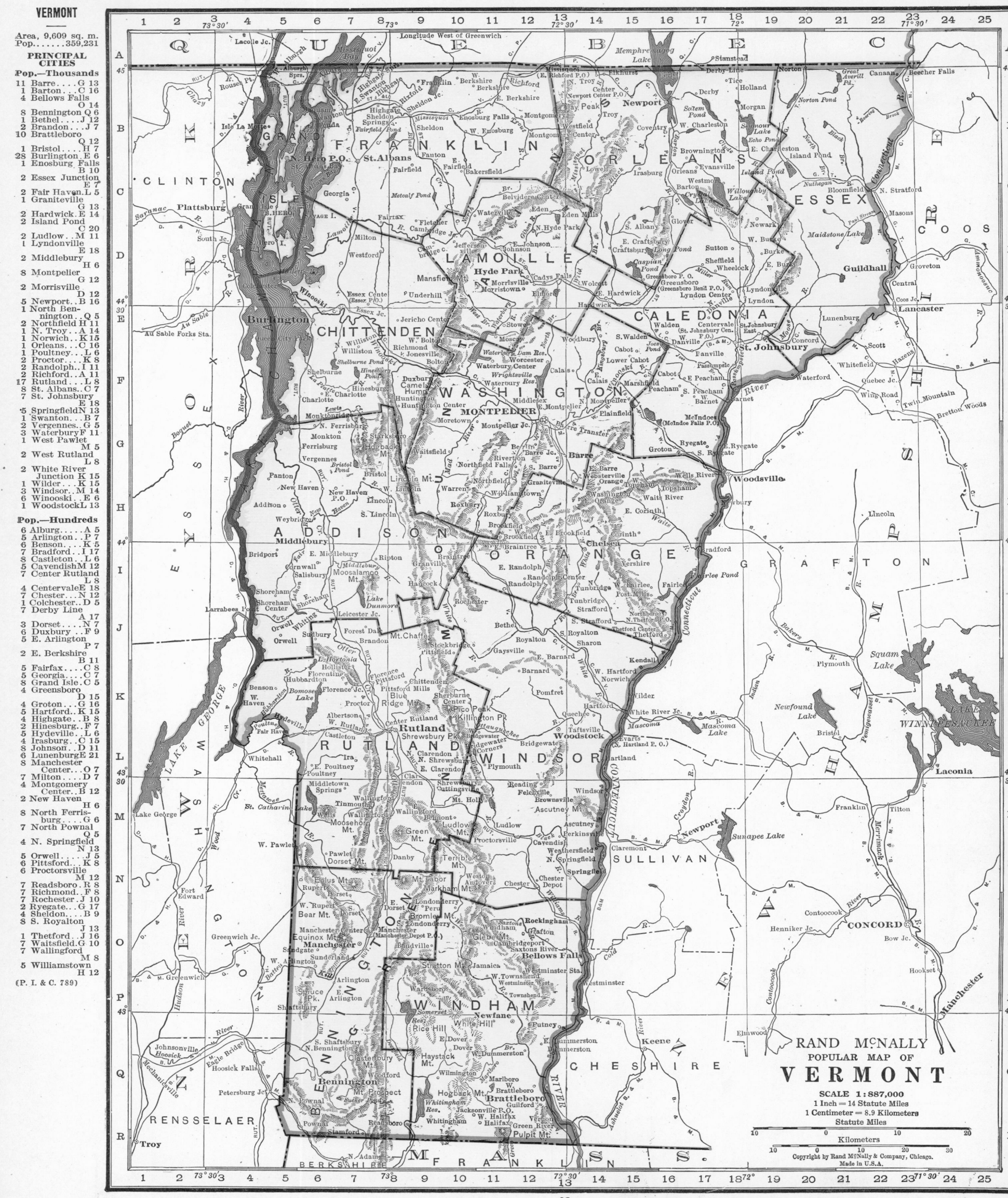

VERMONT

Area, 9,609 sq. m.
Pop......359,231

PRINCIPAL CITIES

Pop.—Thousands

11 Barre.....G 13
1 Barton...C 16
4 Bellows Falls
    O 14
8 Bennington Q 6
1 Bethel....J 12
4 Brandon...J 7
10 Brattleboro
    Q 12
1 Bristol....H 7
28 Burlington.E 6
1 Enosburg Falls
    B 10
2 Essex Junction
    E 7
2 Fair Haven.L 5
1 Graniteville
    G 13
2 Hardwick.E 14
2 Island Pond
    C 20
4 Ludlow..M 11
2 Lyndonville
    E 18
2 Middlebury
    H 6
8 Montpelier
    G 12
2 Morrisville
    D 12
2 Newport..B 16
1 North Bennington...Q 5
2 Northfield H 11
2 N. Troy...A 14
1 Norwich..K 15
1 Orleans...C 16
2 Poultney...L 6
2 Proctor....K 8
1 Randolph..I 11
2 Richford..B 11
17 Rutland...L 8
8 St. Albans..C 7
7 St. Johnsbury
    E 18
5 Springfield N 13
1 Swanton...B 7
2 Vergennes..G 5
3 Waterbury F 11
1 West Pawlet
    M 5
2 West Rutland
    L 8
2 White River
    Junction K 15
1 Wilder....K 15
2 Windsor..M 14
6 Winooski..E 6
1 Woodstock L 13

Pop.—Hundreds

6 Alburg.....A 5
5 Arlington..P 7
2 Benson....K 5
7 Bradford..I 17
2 Castleton..L 6
5 Cavendish M 12
7 Center Rutland
    L 8
4 Centervale E 18
2 Chester...N 12
1 Colchester..D 5
7 Derby Line
    A 17
3 Dorset....N 7
9 Duxbury ..F 9
5 E. Arlington
    P 7
2 E. Berkshire
    B 11
5 Fairfax....C 8
5 Georgia...C 7
4 Grand Isle.C 5
4 Greensboro
    D 15
6 Groton....G 16
5 Hartford..K 15
8 Highgate...B 8
2 Hinesburg..F 7
5 Hydeville..L 6
4 Irasburg..C 15
2 Johnson...D 11
6 Lunenburg E 21
7 Manchester
    Center...O 7
7 Milton....D 7
1 Montgomery
    Center..B 12
2 New Haven
    H 6
8 North Ferrisburg...G 6
7 North Pownal
    Q 5
4 N. Springfield
    N 13
5 Orwell....J 5
6 Pittsford..K 8
1 Proctorsville
    M 12
7 Readsboro. R 8
7 Richmond..F 8
7 Rochester.J 10
2 Ryegate...G 17
4 Sheldon...B 9
8 S. Royalton
    J 13
1 Thetford..J 16
7 Waitsfield.G 10
7 Wallingford
    M 8
5 Williamstown
    H 12

(P. I. & C. 789)

RAND McNALLY
POPULAR MAP OF
VERMONT

SCALE 1:887,000

1 Inch = 14 Statute Miles
1 Centimeter = 8.9 Kilometers
Statute Miles

Kilometers

Copyright by Rand McNally & Company, Chicago.
Made in U.S.A.

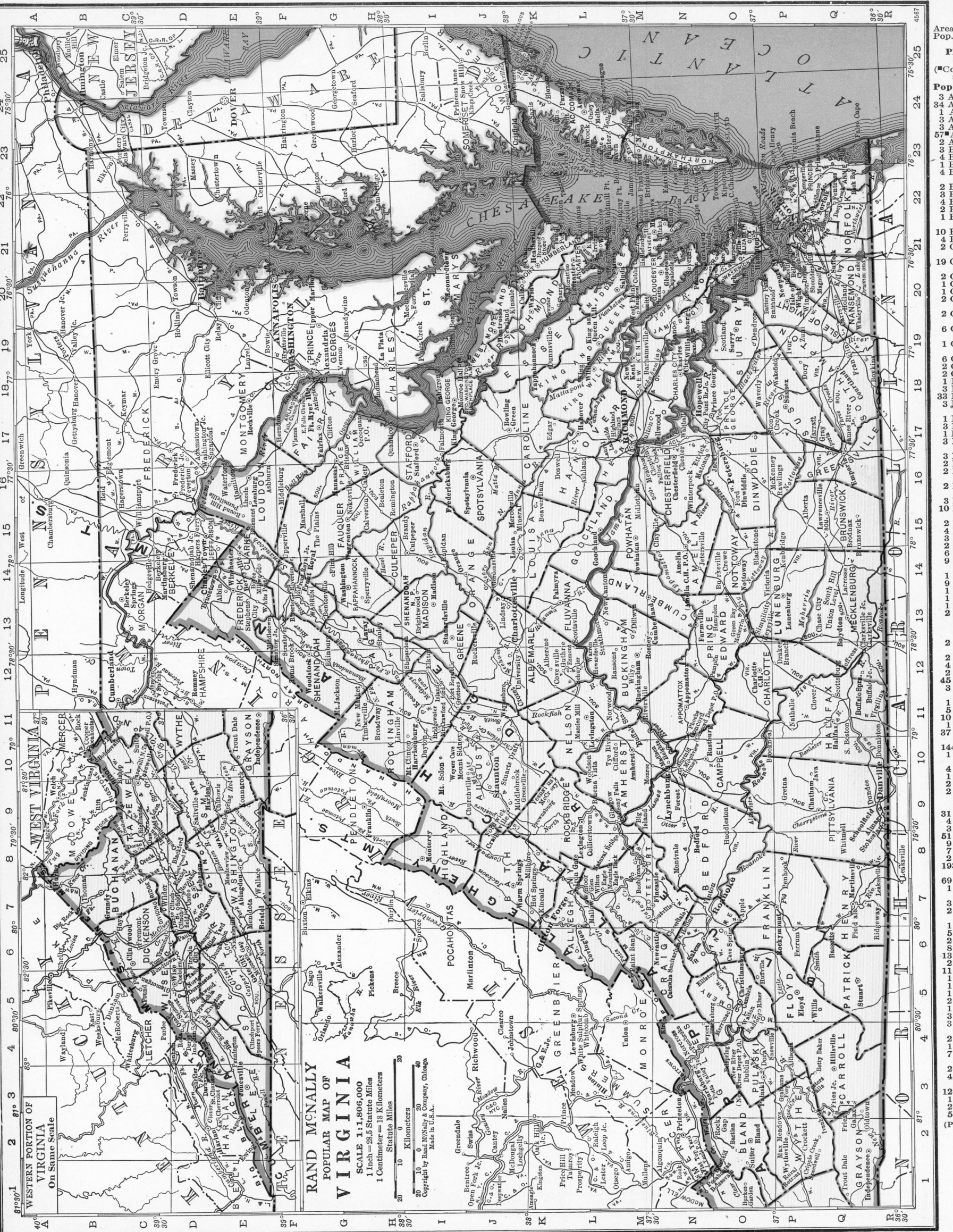

Area, 40,815 sq. m.
Pop....2,677,773.

PRINCIPAL CITIES

(■County Classified
as Urban).

Pop.—Thousands

3 Abingdon...E 8
34 Alexandria G 18
1 Almagro...R 9
3 Altavista...O 9
3 Appalachia.D 4
57■Arlington.G 18
3 Ashland...L 18
2 Ashland...Q 6
4 Bassetts...P 7
6 Bedford...N 8
1 Berryville.E 14
4 Big Stone Gap.
..........D 4
2 Blacksburg O 5
3 Blackstone O 14
4 Bluefield...N 1
2 Boissevain.B 10
1 Bridgewater
..........I 11
10 Bristol....E 7
4 Buena Vista.L 9
2 Cape Charles.
..........N 22
19 Charlottesville
..........K 12
2 Chase City Q 13
1 Chatham...Q 9
1 Chester...N 17
2 Chincoteague
Island...K 23
2 Christiansburg
..........O 6
6 Clifton Forge
..........L 7
1 Colonial Beach
..........I 19
6 Covington...L 6
2 Crewe....O 14
2 Culpeper..H 14
1 Damascus..E 8
1 Dante....D 6
33 Danville...N 10
3 East Falls
Church...F 18
1 Elkton....I 12
6 Emporia..Q 16
1 Ettrick...N 17
2 Falls Church
..........F 18
3 Farmville..N 13
2 Fieldale...Q 7
2 Fort Myer
Heights..F 18
2 Fortress
Monroe..P 21
3 Franklin..Q 19
10 Fredericksburg
..........I 17
2 Fries....K 3
2 Front RoyalF 14
3 Galax....K 3
2 Gate City..E 5
6 Hampton..P 21
9 Harrisonburg
..........F 11
1 Herndon..F 17
1 Hopewell..N 17
1 Hot SpringsK 7
1 Ivanhoe...Q 3
1 Jewell....C 8
2 Kecoughtan
(Veterans
Administration
Home)...O 21
2 Lawrenceville
..........Q 15
2 Leesburg..E 16
4 Lexington..L 9
2 Luray....G 13
45 Lynchburg N 10
2 Madison
Heights..N 10
1 Manassas G 16
2 Marion...D 10
10 Martinsville Q 7
2 Narrows...N 3
37 Newport News
..........P 21
144 Norfolk..P 21
1 N. Emporia
..........Q 16
4 Norton....D 5
1 Onancock..L 23
2 Orange....J 14
2 Pennington
(Pennington
Gap)....E 4
31 Petersburg O 17
4 Phoebus..O 21
1 Pocahontas B 1
51 Portsmouth P 21
1 Pulaski...O 3
8 Radford...N 4
2 Richlands..C 8
193 Richmond
..........M 17
69 Roanoke..N 7
1 Rockymount
..........P 7
2 Saltville..D 9
2 Shenandoah
..........H 12
1 Smithfield..P 20
5 So. Boston Q 11
4 South Hill Q 14
13 So. Norfolk Q 22
18 Staunton..J 10
2 Strasburg..F 13
11 Suffolk...Q 20
2 Tangier...K 22
2 Tazewell..C 10
5 Toms Creek D 6
2 Victoria...P 14
1 Vienna....F 17
5 Vinton...N 7
Virginia Beach
..........P 23
2 Warrenton G 15
2 Waverly..P 18
Waynesboro
..........J 11
4 West Point M 19
4 Williamsburg
..........N 20
12 Winchester E 14
1 Wise....D 5
2 Woodstock F 12
5 Wytheville P 2

(P. I. & C. 789)

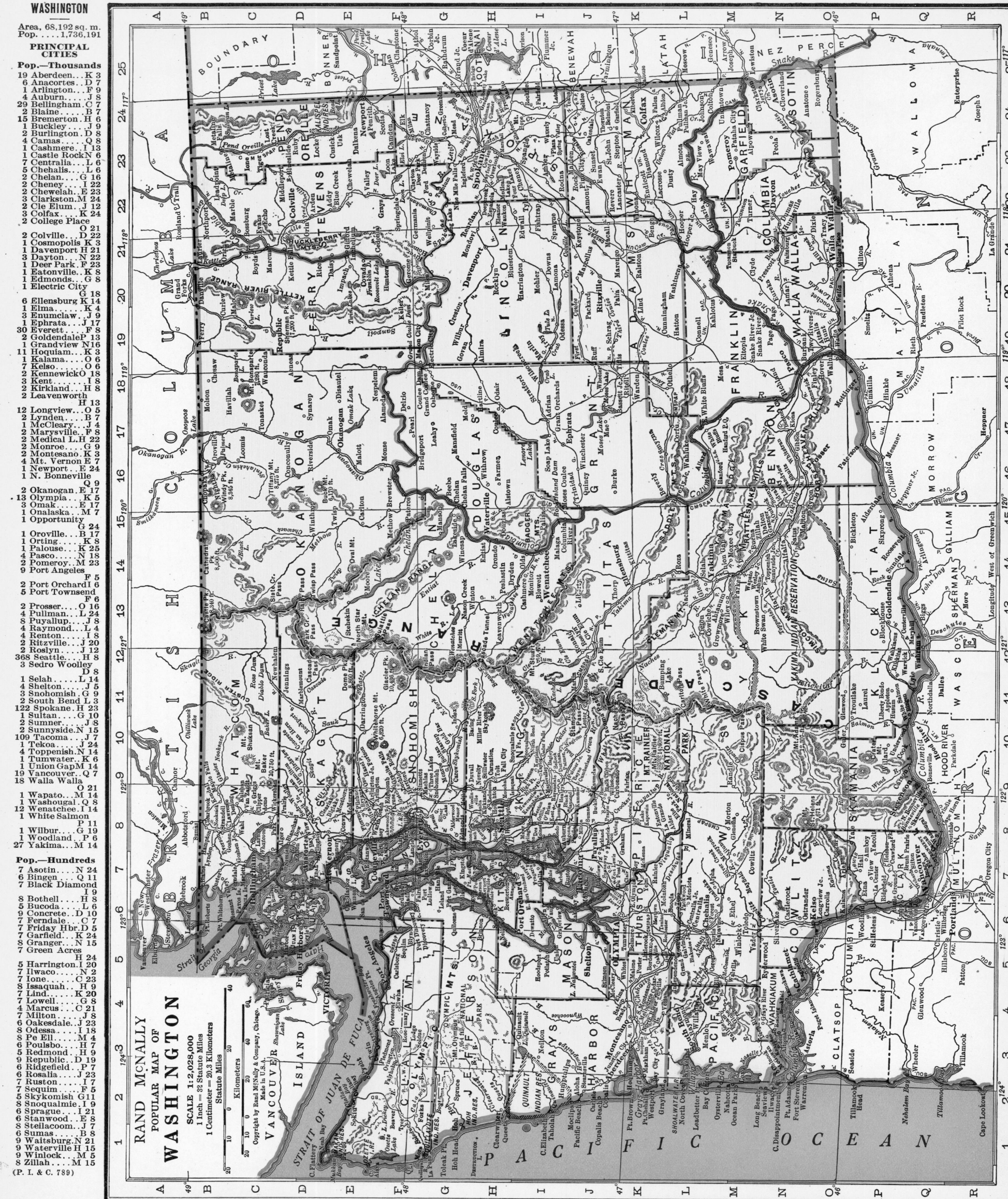

WASHINGTON

Area, 68,192 sq. m.
Pop. ... 1,736,191

PRINCIPAL CITIES

Pop.—Thousands

19	Aberdeen...K 3
6	Anacortes..D 7
1	Arlington...F 9
4	Auburn.....J 8
29	Bellingham.C 7
3	Blaine.....B 7
15	Bremerton..H 6
1	Buckley....J 9
2	Burlington.D 8
2	Camas.....Q 8
1	Cashmere...I 13
1	Castle Rock.N 6
1	Centralia..L 6
2	Chehalis...L 6
2	Chelan....G 16
2	Cheney....I 22
2	Chewelah..E 23
5	Clarkston..M 24
2	Cle Elum...J 12
2	Colfax.....K 24
2	College Place
	O 21
2	Colville...D 22
1	Cosmopolis.K 3
2	Davenport.H 21
3	Dayton....N 22
1	Deer Park..F 23
1	Eatonville.K 8
1	Edmonds...G 8
1	Electric City
	G 18
6	Ellensburg.K 14
1	Elma......K 4
1	Enumclaw..J 9
1	Ephrata...J 17
30	Everett....F 8
2	Goldendale.P 13
1	Grandview.N 16
11	Hoquiam...K 3
1	Kalama....O 6
1	Kelso.....O 6
2	Kennewick.O 18
2	Kent.......I 8
2	Kirkland...H 8
2	Leavenworth
	H 13
12	Longview...O 5
1	Lynden....B 7
1	McCleary..J 4
1	Marysville..F 8
2	Medical L.H 22
2	Monroe....G 9
2	Montesano.K 3
4	Mt. Vernon.E 7
1	Newport...E 24
1	N. Bonneville
	Q 9
	Okanogan..E 17
13	Olympia...K 5
1	Omak.....E 17
1	Onalaska..M 7
1	Opportunity
	G 24
1	Oroville...B 17
1	Orting....K 8
1	Palouse...K 25
4	Pasco.....N 18
1	Pomeroy...M 23
9	Port Angeles
	F 5
2	Port Orchard.I 6
2	Port Townsend
	F 6
2	Prosser...O 16
4	Pullman...L 24
8	Puyallup..J 8
4	Raymond...L 4
4	Renton....I 8
2	Ritzville..J 20
1	Roslyn....J 12
368	Seattle...H 8
3	Sedro Woolley
	D 8
1	Selah.....L 14
4	Shelton...J 5
1	Snohomish.G 9
2	South Bend.L 3
122	Spokane..H 23
1	Sultan....G 10
2	Sumner....J 8
2	Sunnyside.N 15
109	Tacoma....J 7
1	Tekoa.....J 24
1	Toppenish.N 14
1	Tumwater..K 6
1	Union Gap.M 14
19	Vancouver.Q 7
18	Walla Walla
	O 21
1	Wapato....M 14
1	Washougal.Q 8
12	Wenatchee.I 14
1	White Salmon
	P 11
1	Wilbur....G 19
1	Woodland..P 6
27	Yakima....M 14

Pop.—Hundreds

7	Asotin....N 24
6	Bingen....Q 11
7	Black Diamond
	I 9
8	Bothell....H 8
3	Bucoda....L 6
5	Concrete...D 10
7	Ferndale...C 7
7	Friday Hbr..D 5
7	Garfield...K 24
2	Granger...N 15
9	Green Acres
	H 24
5	Harrington.I 20
4	Ilwaco....N 2
7	Ione.....C 23
8	Issaquah..H 9
7	Lind.....K 20
7	Lowell....G 8
7	Marcus....C 21
7	Milton....J 8
6	Oakesdale..J 23
8	Odessa....I 19
5	Pe Ell....M 4
6	Poulsbo...H 7
8	Redmond...H 9
5	Republic...D 19
6	Ridgefield..P 7
8	Rosalia...J 23
7	Ruston....J 7
5	Sequim....F 5
8	Skykomish.G11
8	Snoqualmie.I 9
5	Sprague...I 21
8	Stanwood..E 8
6	Stellacoom.J 7
8	Sumas....B 8
9	Waitsburg.N 21
8	Waterville.H 15
9	Winlock...M 5
8	Zillah....M 15

(P. I. & C. 789)

RAND McNALLY
POPULAR MAP OF
WASHINGTON

SCALE 1:2,028,000
1 Inch = 32 Statute Miles
1 Centimeter = 20.3 Kilometers

Statute Miles

Kilometers

Copyright by Rand McNally & Company, Chicago.
Made in U.S.A.

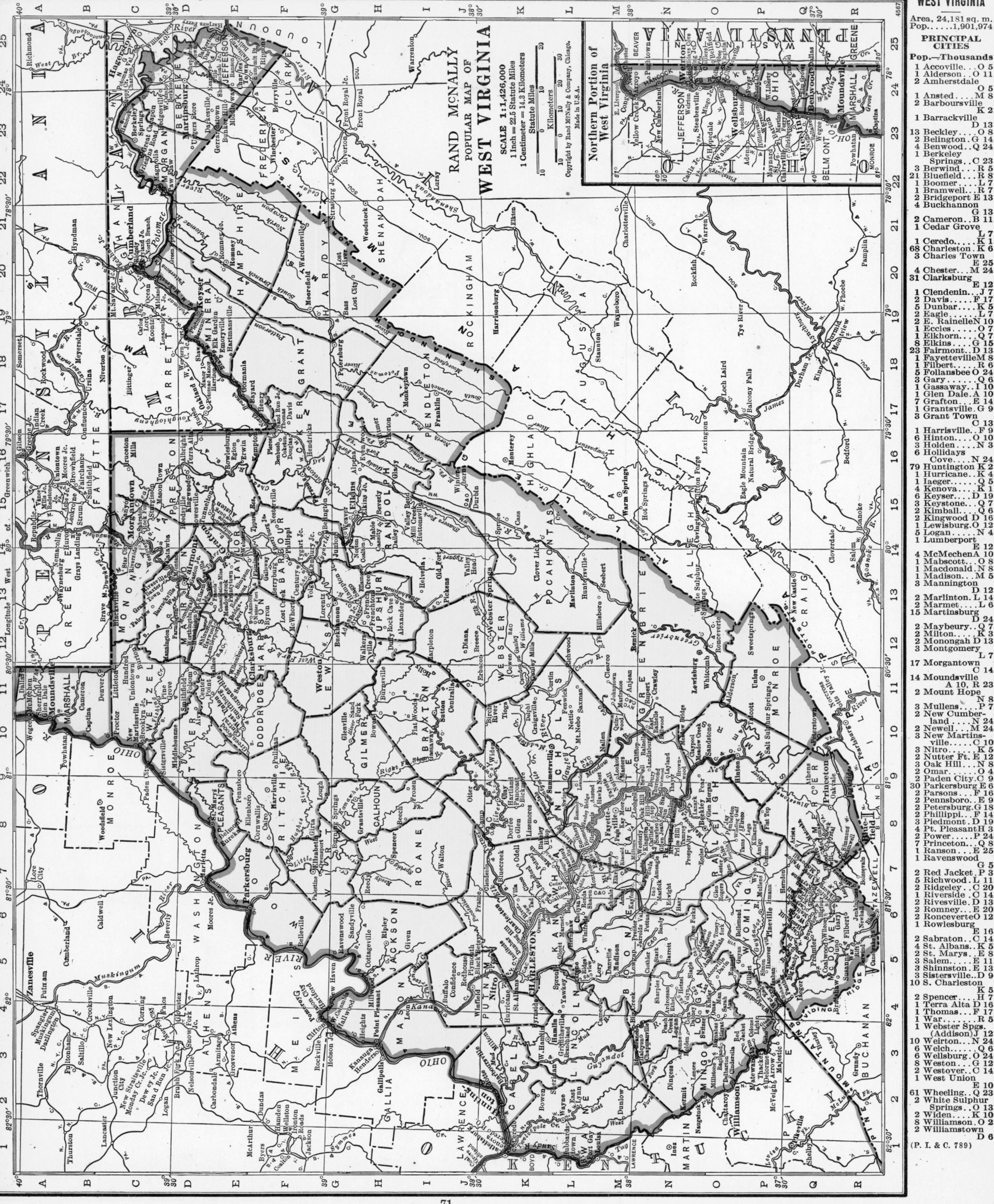

Area, 24,181 sq. m.
Pop.....1,901,974

RAND McNALLY
POPULAR MAP OF
WEST VIRGINIA

SCALE 1:1,426,000
1 Inch = 22.5 Statute Miles
1 Centimeter = 14.3 Kilometers
Statute Miles

Copyright by Rand McNally & Company, Chicago.
Made in U.S.A.

Northern Portion of West Virginia

WISCONSIN

Area, 56,154 sq. m.
Pop.....3,137,587

PRINCIPAL CITIES

Pop.—Thousands

RAND McNALLY
POPULAR MAP OF
WISCONSIN

SCALE 1:2,154,000
1 Inch = 34 Statute Miles
1 Centimeter = 21.5 Kilometers

Statute Miles

Kilometers

Copyright by Rand McNally & Company, Chicago.
Made in U.S.A.

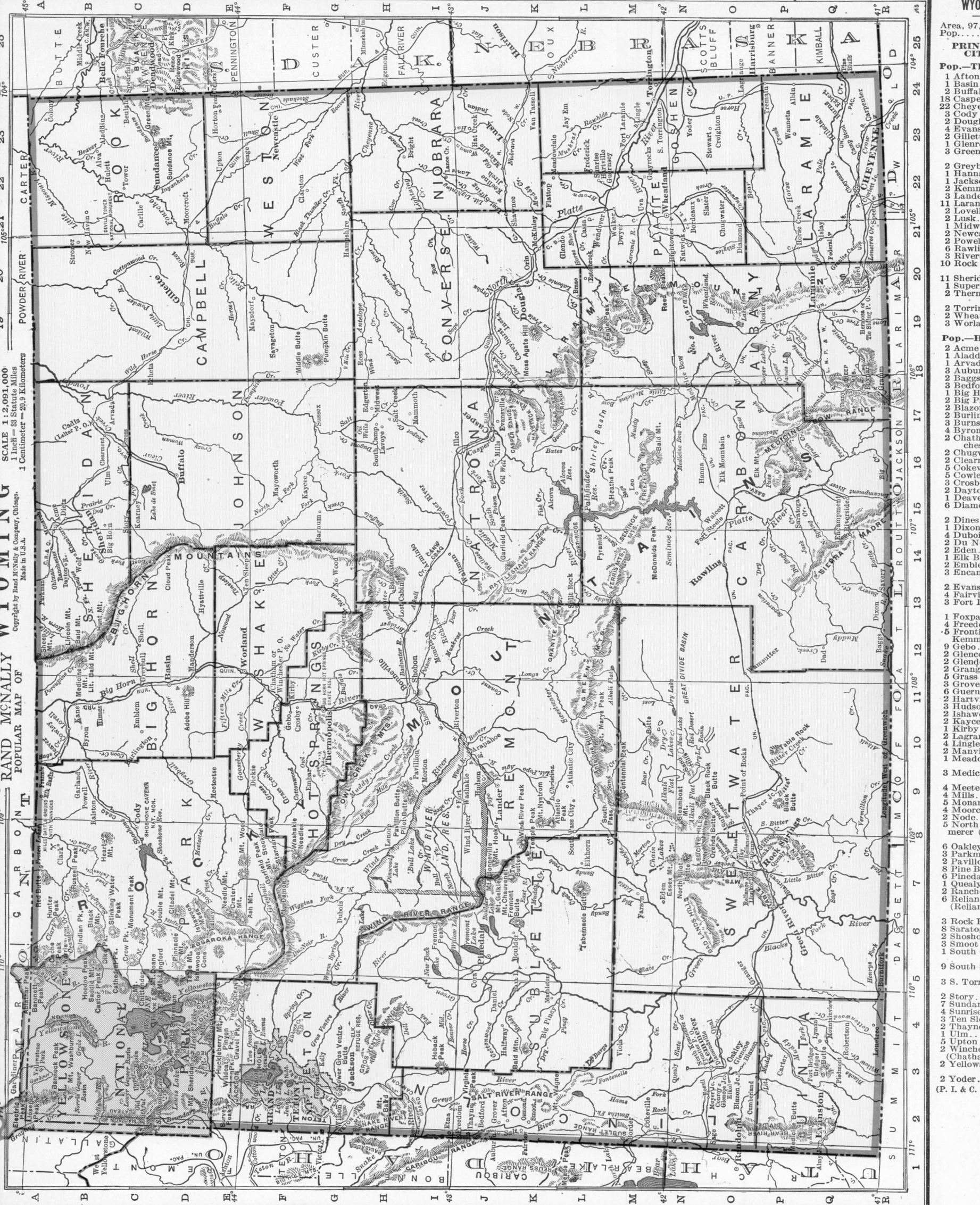

Area, 97,914 sq. m.
Pop......250,742

PRINCIPAL CITIES

Pop.—Thousands

1	Afton	J 2
1	Basin	D 12
2	Buffalo	D 16
2	Casper	J 17
22	Cheyenne	R 22
3	Cody	C 8
2	Douglas	K 19
4	Evanston	Q 2
2	Gillette	D 20
1	Glenrock	J 18
3	Green River	P 6
2	Greybull	C 12
1	Hanna	N 16
1	Jackson	G 3
2	Kemmerer	N 4
1	Lander	J 9
11	Laramie	O 20
2	Lovell	A 11
1	Lusk	J 23
1	Midwest	H 17
2	Newcastle	F 23
2	Powell	B 9
6	Rawlins	N 14
3	Riverton	I 11
10	Rock Springs	P 8
11	Sheridan	B 14
1	Superior	O 8
2	Thermopolis	G 10
2	Torrington	M 24
2	Wheatland	N 21
3	Worland	E 12

Pop.—Hundreds

2	Acme	A 15
1	Aladdin	B 23
1	Arvada	B 17
2	Auburn	J 1
2	Baggs	R 12
3	Bedford	J 2
1	Big Horn	B 14
2	Big Piney	K 4
6	Blazon	Q 3
2	Burlington	C 10
4	Burns	Q 24
2	Byron	B 10
2	Chatham (Winchester)	F 11
2	Chugwater	O 21
3	Clearmont	B 16
5	Cokeville	M 2
2	Cowley	A 10
2	Crosby	F 10
2	Dayton	B 14
2	Deaver	A 10
6	Diamondville	O 3
2	Dines	O 3
1	Dixon	R 13
2	Dubois	F 6
4	Du Noir	F 7
2	Eden	N 7
1	Elk Basin	A 9
2	Emblem	C 11
2	Encampment	O 15
2	Evansville	J 17
4	Fairview	K 2
3	Fort Laramie	M 23
1	Foxpark	R 18
4	Freedom	I 2
5	Frontier (North Kemmerer)	N 3
9	Gebo	F 10
2	Glencoe	O 3
2	Glendo	K 21
2	Granger	O 5
2	Grass Creek	F 9
2	Grover	J 2
6	Guernsey	M 22
3	Hartville	L 22
2	Hudson	J 9
2	Ishawooa	D 7
2	Kaycee	F 15
2	Kirby	F 11
2	Lagrange	O 24
4	Lingle	M 23
2	Manville	J 23
1	Meadowdale	K 22
3	Medicine Bow	N 18
4	Meeteetse	E 9
4	Mills	J 16
5	Monarch	A 15
2	Moorcroft	D 21
2	Node	K 23
5	North Kemmerer (Frontier)	N 3
6	Oakley	O 3
2	Parkman	A 15
2	Pavillon	I 10
8	Pine Bluffs	Q 25
6	Pinedale	J 6
1	Quealy	N 3
2	Ranchester	A 14
6	Reliance (Reliance Mine)	O 7
3	Rock River	O 18
3	Saratoga	P 15
2	Shoshoni	I 11
3	Smoot	K 2
1	South Camp	H 17
9	South Superior	O 9
3	S. Torrington	M 24
2	Story	C 15
3	Sundance	C 22
4	Sunrise	L 22
4	Ten Sleep	E 14
2	Thayne	J 2
3	Ulm	B 16
5	Upton	E 22
2	Winchester (Chatham)	F 11
2	Yellowstone Pk.	A 2
2	Yoder	N 23

(P. I. & C. 789)

ALASKA

Area, 586,400 sq.m.
Pop....... 72,524

PRINCIPAL CITIES

Pop.—Thousands

Pop.—Hundreds

(P. I. & C. 9012)

RAND McNALLY
POPULAR MAP OF
ALASKA

SCALE 1:8,364,000
1 Inch = 132 Statute Miles
1 Centimeter = 83.6 Kilometers
Statute Miles

Copyright by Rand McNally & Company, Chicago.
Made in U.S.A.

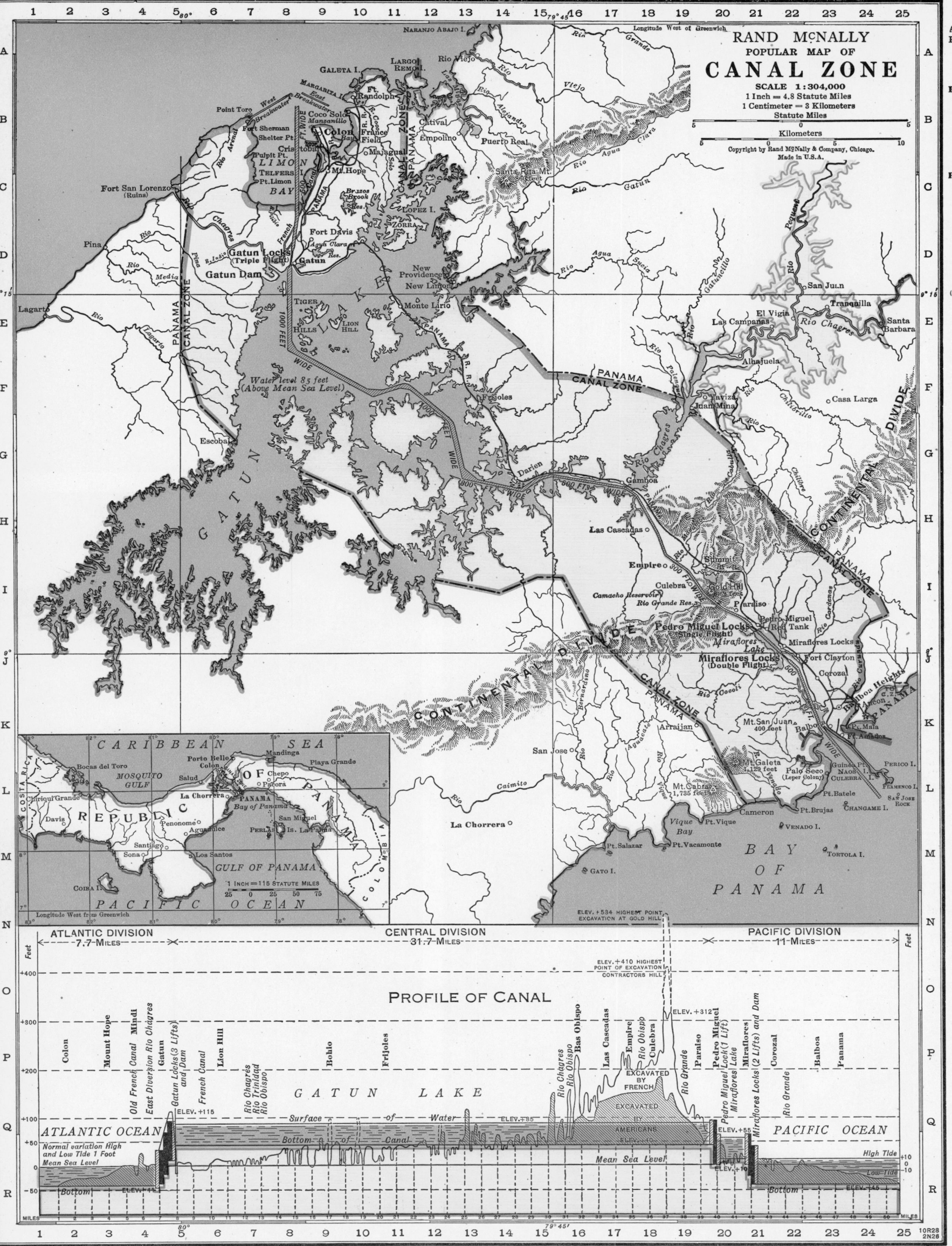

RAND McNALLY
POPULAR MAP OF
CANAL ZONE
SCALE 1:304,000
1 Inch = 4.8 Statute Miles
1 Centimeter = 3 Kilometers
Statute Miles

Kilometers

Copyright by Rand McNally & Company, Chicago.
Made in U.S.A.

CANAL ZONE

Area....553 sq. m.
Pop........51,827

PROFILE OF CANAL

ATLANTIC DIVISION
7.7 Miles

CENTRAL DIVISION
31.7 Miles

PACIFIC DIVISION
11 Miles

ATLANTIC OCEAN

GATUN LAKE

PACIFIC OCEAN

Mean Sea Level

75

10R28
2N28

HAWAII

Area..6,433 sq. m.
Pop. 423,330

PRINCIPAL CITIES

Pop.—Thousands

4	Aiea	F 11
1	Eleele	C 4
4	Ewa	F 11
1	Hakalau	L 23
2	Haleiwa	E 10
1	Hana	H 20
1	Hanapepe	C 4
1	Hawi	K 20
23	Hilo	M 23
1	Honokaa	L 22
179	Honolulu	F 11
2	Kahuku	D 11
2	Kahului	H 17
3	Kapaa	B 5
3	Kekaha	C 4
1	Kohala	K 20
2	Koloa	C-5
5	Lahaina	H 17
4	Lanai City	H 15
4	Lihue	C 5
1	Makaweli	C 4
1	Mountainview	N 23
1	Naalehu	P 21
2	Pahala	O 22
1	Pahoa	N 24
4	Paia	H 18
2	Papaikou	M 23
2	Pearl City	E 11
4	Puunene	H 18
5	Wahiawa	E 11
3	Waialua	E 10
1	Waianae	E 10
7	Wailuku	H 17
1	Waimanalo	F 12
1	Waimea	C 4
7	Waipahu	F 11

Pop.—Hundreds

4	Anahola	B 5
4	Haiku	H 18
1	Halawa	K 20
3	Hanalei	B 4
1	Hanamaulu	C 5
1	Hauula	E 11
1	Holualoa	N 20
9	Honomu	L 23
1	Honouliuli	F 11
1	Hookena	O 20
1	Hoopuloa	O 20
2	Kaanapali	H 16
4	Kailua	M 20
8	Kalaheo	C 4
2	Kalapana	O 24
5	Kapoho	N 25
7	Kaunakakai	G 15
1	Kawaihae	L 20
4	Kealia	N 20
8	Kealia	B 5
2	Keanae	H 19
5	Keokea	H 17
5	Kilauea	B 5
4	Kukuihaele	K 21
5	Laupahoehoe	L 23
9	Makawao	H 18
1	Mana	C 3
1	Napoopoo	N 20
1	Ninole	L 23
1	Papaaloa	L 23
5	Pauwela	H 18
7	Waiakea	H 18
2	Waiohinu	P 21
2	Waipio	K 21

(P. I. & C. 567)

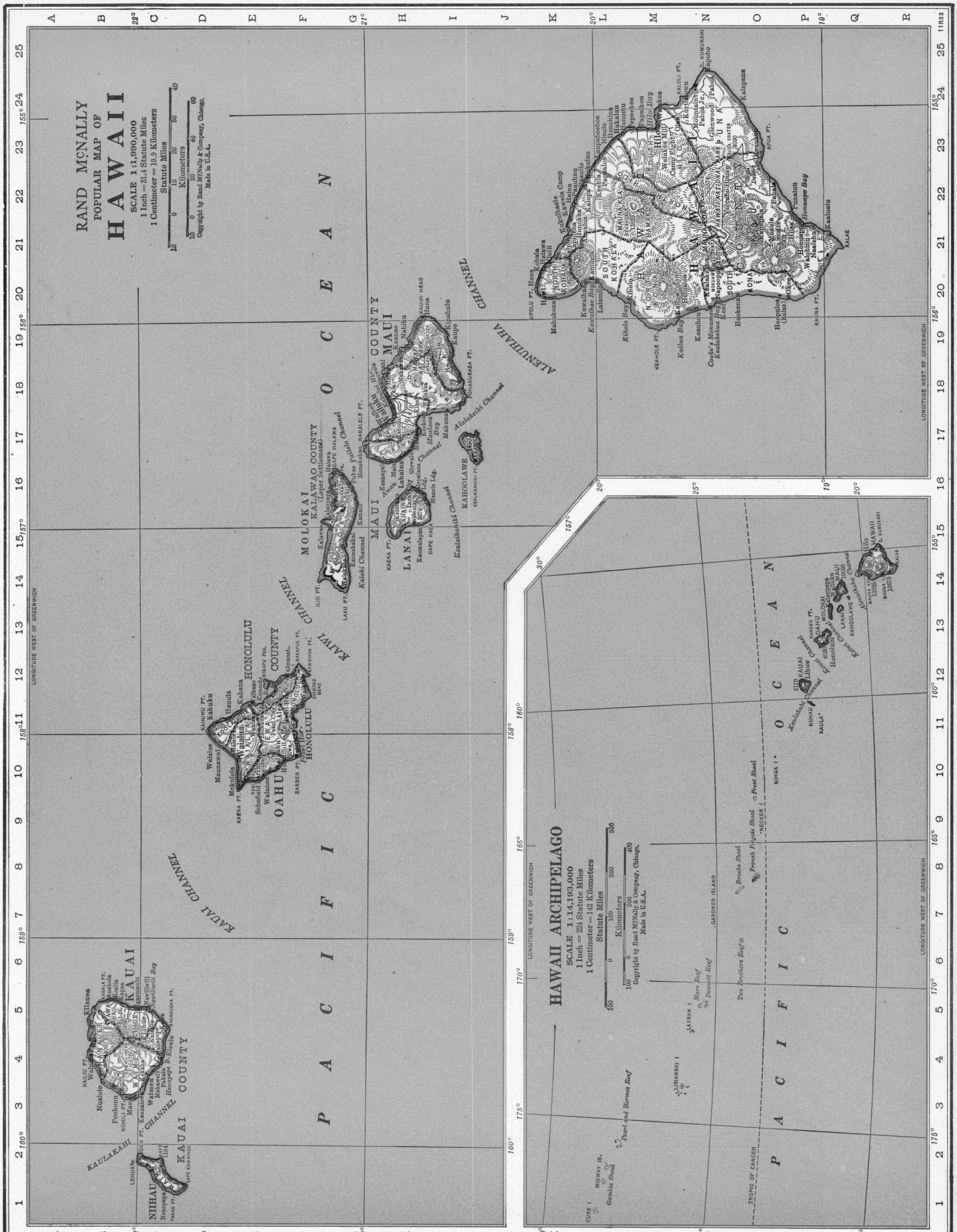

RAND McNALLY
POPULAR MAP OF
HAWAII

SCALE 1:1,990,000
1 Inch = 31.4 Statute Miles
1 Centimeter = 19.9 Kilometers
Copyright by Rand McNally & Company, Chicago.
Made in U.S.A.

Statute Miles

Kilometers

HAWAII ARCHIPELAGO

SCALE 1:14,193,000
1 Inch = 224 Statute Miles
1 Centimeter = 142 Kilometers
Copyright by Rand McNally & Company, Chicago.
Made in U.S.A.

Statute Miles

Kilometers

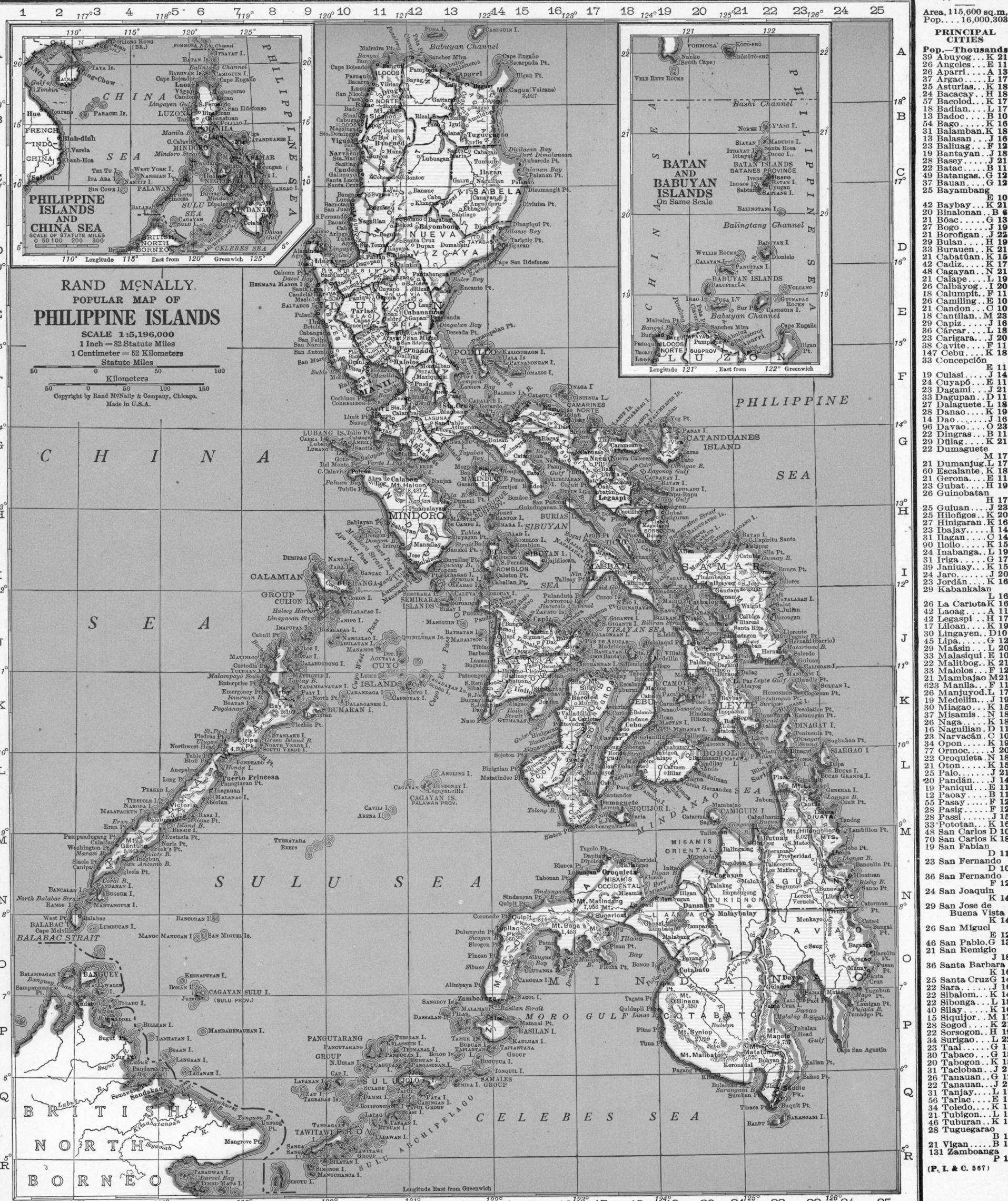

Area, 115,600 sq.m.
Pop.... 16,000,303

PRINCIPAL CITIES
Pop.—Thousands

(P. I. & C. 567)

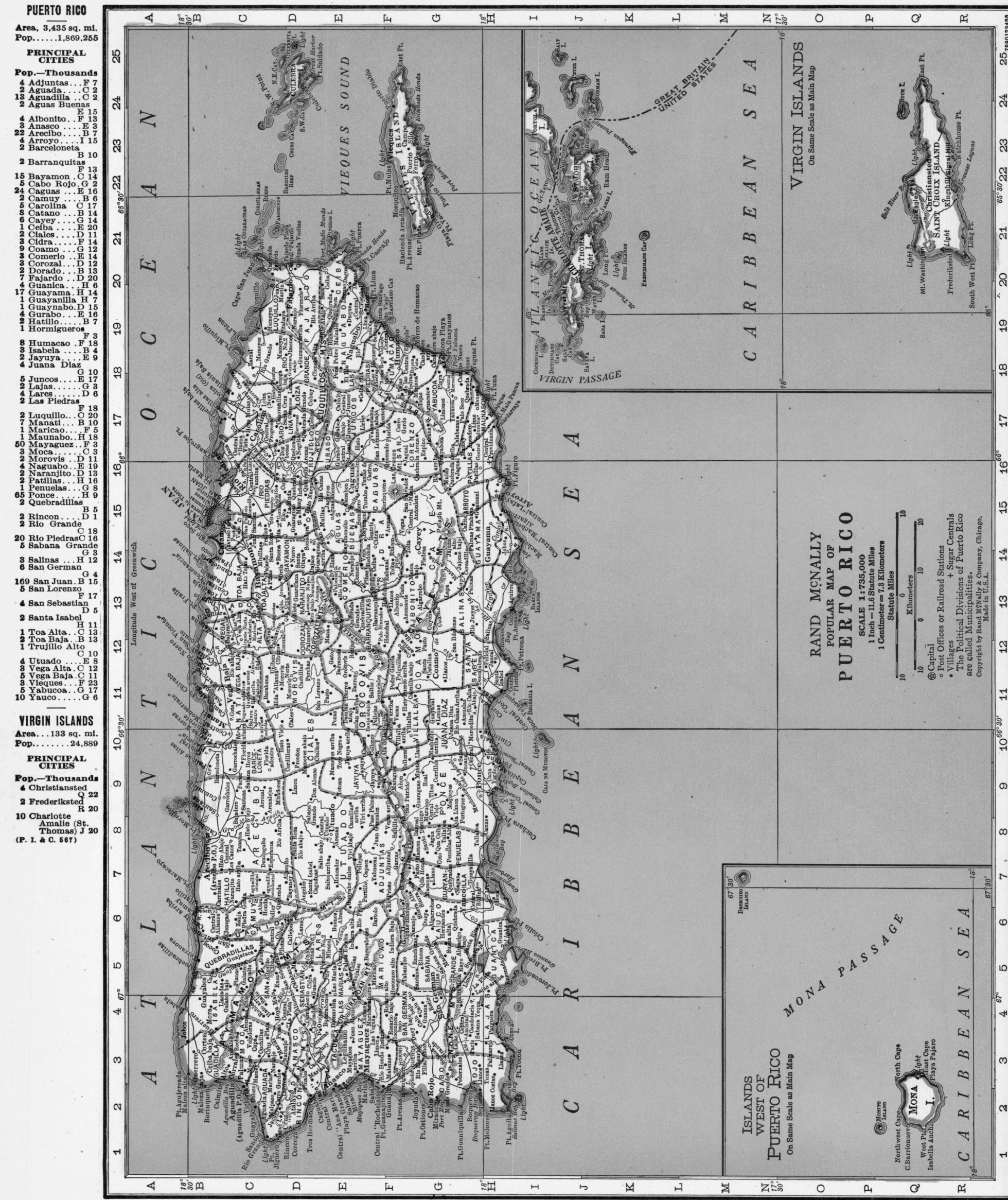

PUERTO RICO

Area, 3,435 sq. mi.
Pop......1,869,255

PRINCIPAL CITIES

Pop.—Thousands

4	Adjuntas	F 7
2	Aguada	C 2
13	Aguadilla	C 2
2	Aguas Buenas	E 15
4	Aibonito	F 13
3	Anasco	E 3
22	Arecibo	B 7
2	Arroyo	I 15
2	Barceloneta	B 10
2	Barranquitas	F 13
15	Bayamon	C 14
5	Cabo Rojo	G 2
24	Caguas	E 16
2	Camuy	B 6
5	Carolina	C 17
8	Catano	B 14
2	Cayey	G 14
1	Ceiba	E 20
2	Ciales	D 11
2	Cidra	F 14
9	Coamo	G 12
3	Comerio	E 14
3	Corozal	D 12
2	Dorado	B 13
3	Fajardo	E 20
4	Guanica	H 6
17	Guayama	H 14
1	Guayanilla	H 7
5	Guaynabo	D 15
2	Gurabo	E 16
2	Hatillo	B 7
1	Hormigueros	F 3
8	Humacao	F 18
3	Isabela	B 4
3	Jayuya	E 9
4	Juana Diaz	G 10
5	Juncos	E 17
5	Lajas	G 3
2	Lares	D 6
2	Las Piedras	F 18
2	Luquillo	D 20
7	Manati	B 10
1	Maricao	F 5
1	Maunabo	H 18
50	Mayaguez	F 3
2	Moca	C 3
2	Morovis	D 11
2	Naguabo	E 19
2	Naranjito	D 13
2	Patillas	H 16
1	Penuelas	G 8
65	Ponce	H 9
2	Quebradillas	B 5
2	Rincon	D 1
2	Rio Grande	C 18
20	Rio Piedras	C 16
5	Sabana Grande	G 3
3	Salinas	H 12
6	San German	G 3
169	San Juan	B 15
5	San Lorenzo	F 17
4	San Sebastian	D 5
2	Santa Isabel	H 11
1	Toa Alta	C 13
1	Toa Baja	B 13
1	Trujillo Alto	C 10
4	Utuado	E 8
3	Vega Alta	C 12
5	Vega Baja	B 11
3	Vieques	F 23
9	Yabucoa	G 17
10	Yauco	G 6

VIRGIN ISLANDS

Area...133 sq. mi.
Pop.......24,889

PRINCIPAL CITIES

Pop.—Thousands

4 Christiansted
         Q 22
2 Frederiksted
         R 20
10 Charlotte
    Amalie (St.
    Thomas) J 20
(P. I. & C. 567)

RAND McNALLY
POPULAR MAP OF
PUERTO RICO
SCALE 1:735,000
1 Inch = 11.6 Statute Miles
1 Centimeter = 7.3 Kilometers
Statute Miles

Kilometers

⊕ Capital
○ Post Offices or Railroad Stations
• Villages
+ Sugar Centrals
The Political Divisions of Puerto Rico
are called Municipalities.
Copyright by Rand McNally & Company, Chicago.
Made in U.S.A.

VIRGIN ISLANDS
On Same Scale as Main Map

ISLANDS
WEST OF
PUERTO RICO
On Same Scale as Main Map

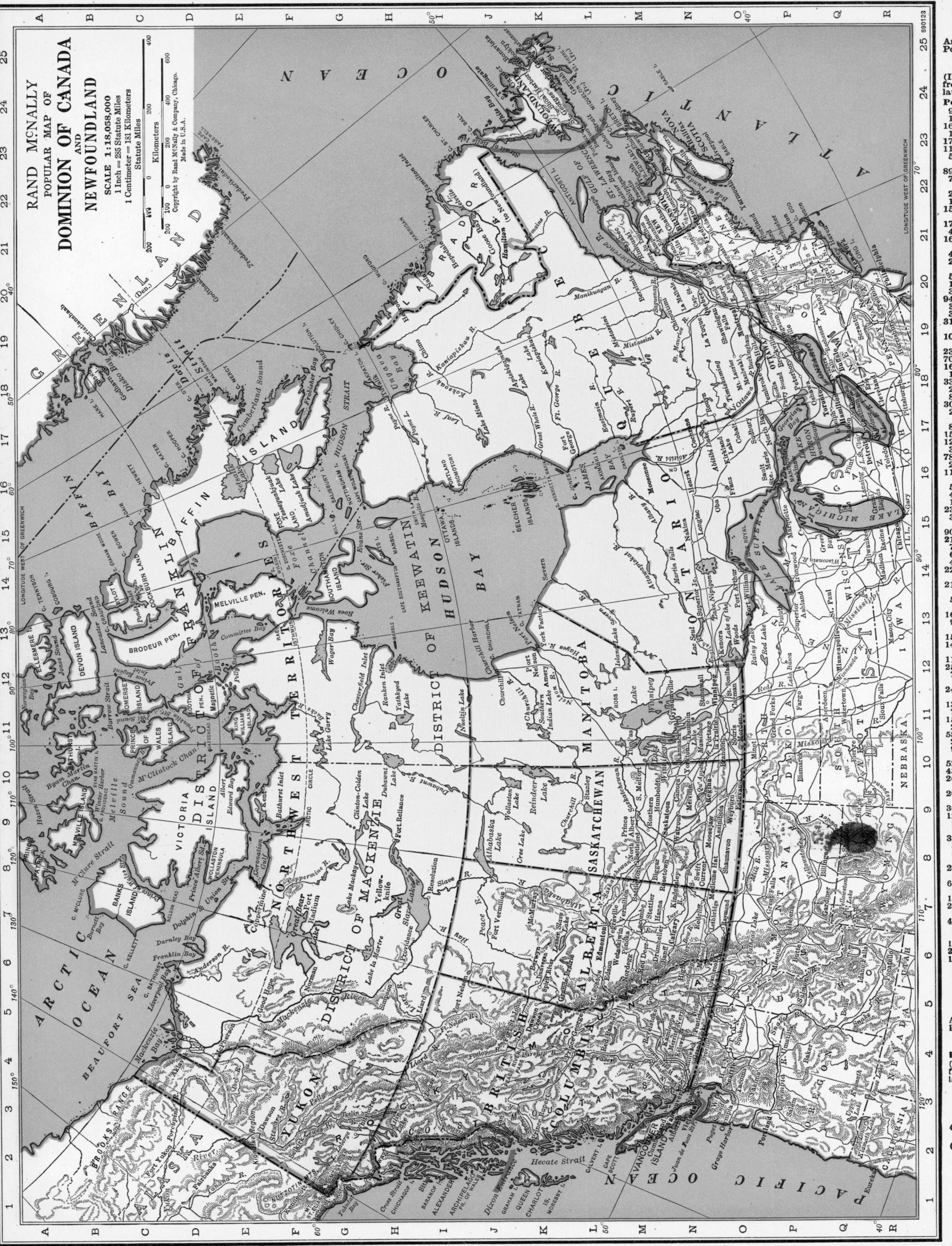

RAND McNALLY
POPULAR MAP OF
DOMINION OF CANADA
AND
NEWFOUNDLAND

SCALE 1:18,058,000
1 Inch = 285 Statute Miles
1 Centimeter = 181 Kilometers
Statute Miles

Copyright by Rand McNally & Company, Chicago.
Made in U.S.A.

DOMINION OF CANADA

Ar. 3,694,863 sq. m.
Pop. . . . 11,506,655
PRINCIPAL CITIES
(Including Figures from Latest Population Estimates)

Pop.—Thousands

9 Amherst. . . N 22
1 Assiniboia. . . O 9
16 Belleville. . . P 19
1 Battleford . M 8
17 Brandon. . . O 11
11 Brockville. . P 19
5 Buckingham
O 19
89 Calgary. . . . N 6
7 Campbelltown
M 21
2 Cardston . . O 6
1 Carman. . O 11
15 Charlottetown
M 23
17 Chatham. . R 17
4 Chatham. . M 22
16 Chicoutimi
M 20
4 Cochrane. . N 17
2 Cumberland
M 3
5 Dauphin. . N 11
1 Dawson. . . E 2
3 East AngusO 20
94 Edmonton. . L 7
3 Estevan. . O 10
3 Fernie. . . . N 6
31 Ft. William
O 14
10 Fredericton
N 22
23 Guelph . . . Q 17
70 Halifax. . N 23
166 Hamilton Q 18
1 Hanna. . . . M 7
13 Hull . . . . O 19
2 Humbolt. . M 9
8 Kenora. . O 12
30 Kingston. . P 19
2 La Malbaie
N 20
8 La Tuque. N 19
15 Lethbridge. N 7
12 Levis. . . . O 20
3 Liverpool. . O 23
78 London. . . Q 17
2 Macleod . . N 6
11 Medicine Hat
N 7
5 Megantic. . O 20
4 Melville . M 10
1 Merritt. . . N 4
23 Moncton. . N 22
3 Mont Laurier
N 19
903 Montreal.O 19
21 Moose Jaw. N 9
7 Nanaimo. . N 3
6 Nelson. . . N 5
4 Newcastle.M 22
4 New West-
minster. . N 3
21 Niagara Falls
Q 18
5 North Battle-
ford . . . . M 8
16 North Bay O 17
9 North Van-
couver. . M 4
155 Ottawa. . O 19
14 Owen Sound
P 17
11 Pembroke. O 18
25 Peterboro. P 18
7 Portage la
Prairie. N 11
24 Port Arthur
O 14
13 Pr. Albert. M 9
7 Pr. Rupert. K 2
151 Quebec. . O 20
58 Regina. . . N 9
2 Revelstoke.M 5
2 Riviere du
Loup. . . N 20
52 Saint John N 22
43 Saskatoon. M 8
26 Sault Ste.
Marie. . P 16
20 Shawinigan
Falls . . . O 20
36 SherbrookeO 20
12 Sorel . . . O 20
2 Souris . . . O 11
1 Stettler. . M 7
32 Sudbury. O 17
3 Sussex. . . N 22
6 Swift Current
N 8
28 Sydney. . . M 23
3 The Pas. . M 11
667 Toronto. . Q 18
9 Trail . . . . N 5
10 Truro. . . . M 23
275 Vancouver N 3
44 Victoria. . N 3
2 Vegreville. L 7
2 WetaskiwinM 7
2 Weyburn. . O 9
105 Windsor. . R 17
222 Winnipeg.O 11
12 WoodstockN 21
6 Yarmouth.O 22
6 Yorkton. . N 10

NEWFOUNDLAND AND LABRADOR

Area 155,134 sq.m.
Pop. 304,850
PRINCIPAL CITIES
Pop.—Thousands
(Including Figures from Latest Population Estimates)

4 Bonavista. J 25
4 Carbonear.K 25
2 Harbor Grace
K 25
1 St. GeorgesL 23
44 St. John's.K 25
3 Twillingate J 24

(P. L. & C. 345)

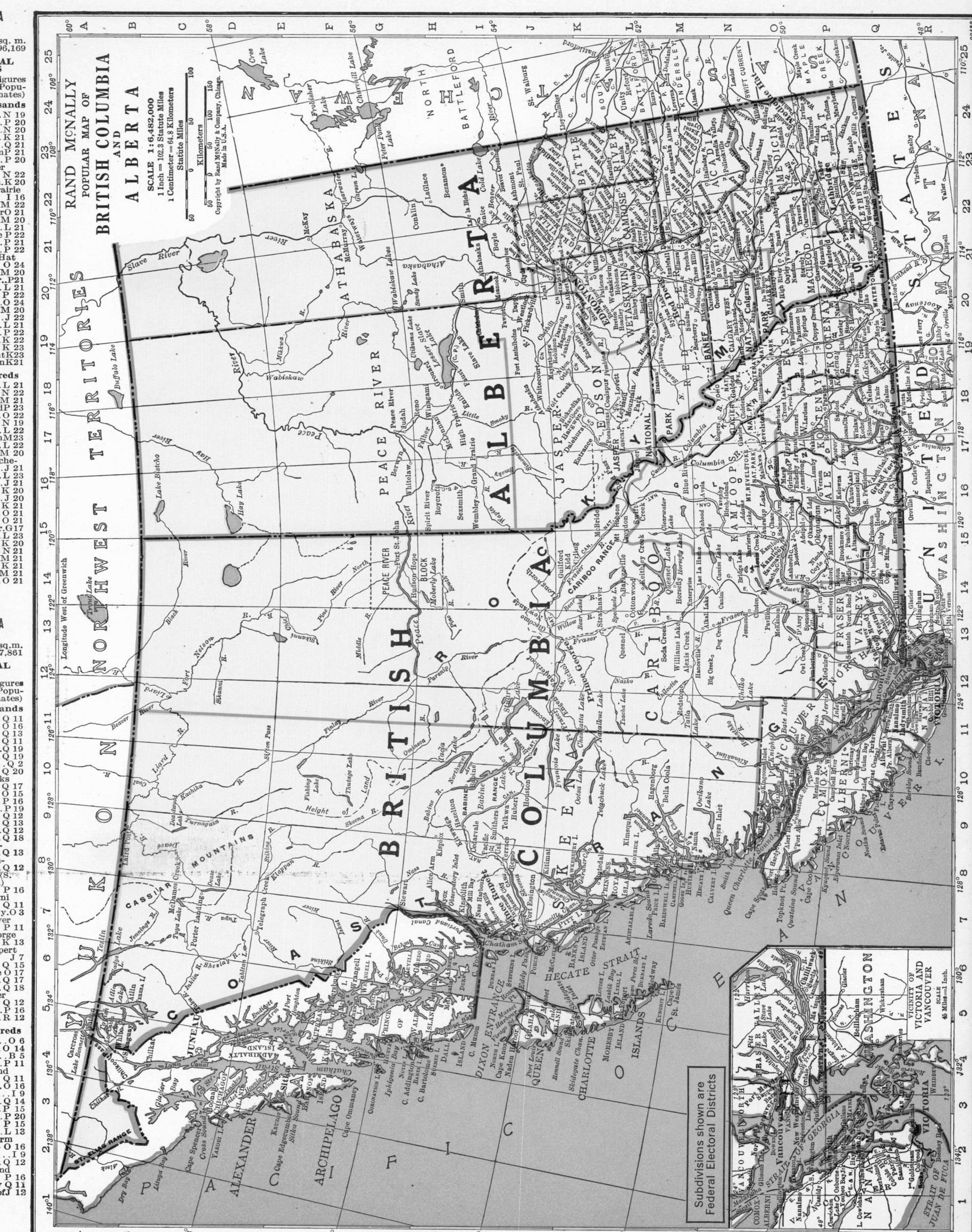

RAND McNALLY
POPULAR MAP OF
BRITISH COLUMBIA
AND
ALBERTA

SCALE 1:6,482,000
1 Inch = 102.3 Statute Miles
1 Centimeter = 64.8 Kilometers
Statute Miles
Kilometers

Copyright by Rand McNally & Company, Chicago.
Made in U.S.A.

Subdivisions shown are Federal Electoral Districts

VICINITY OF VICTORIA AND VANCOUVER

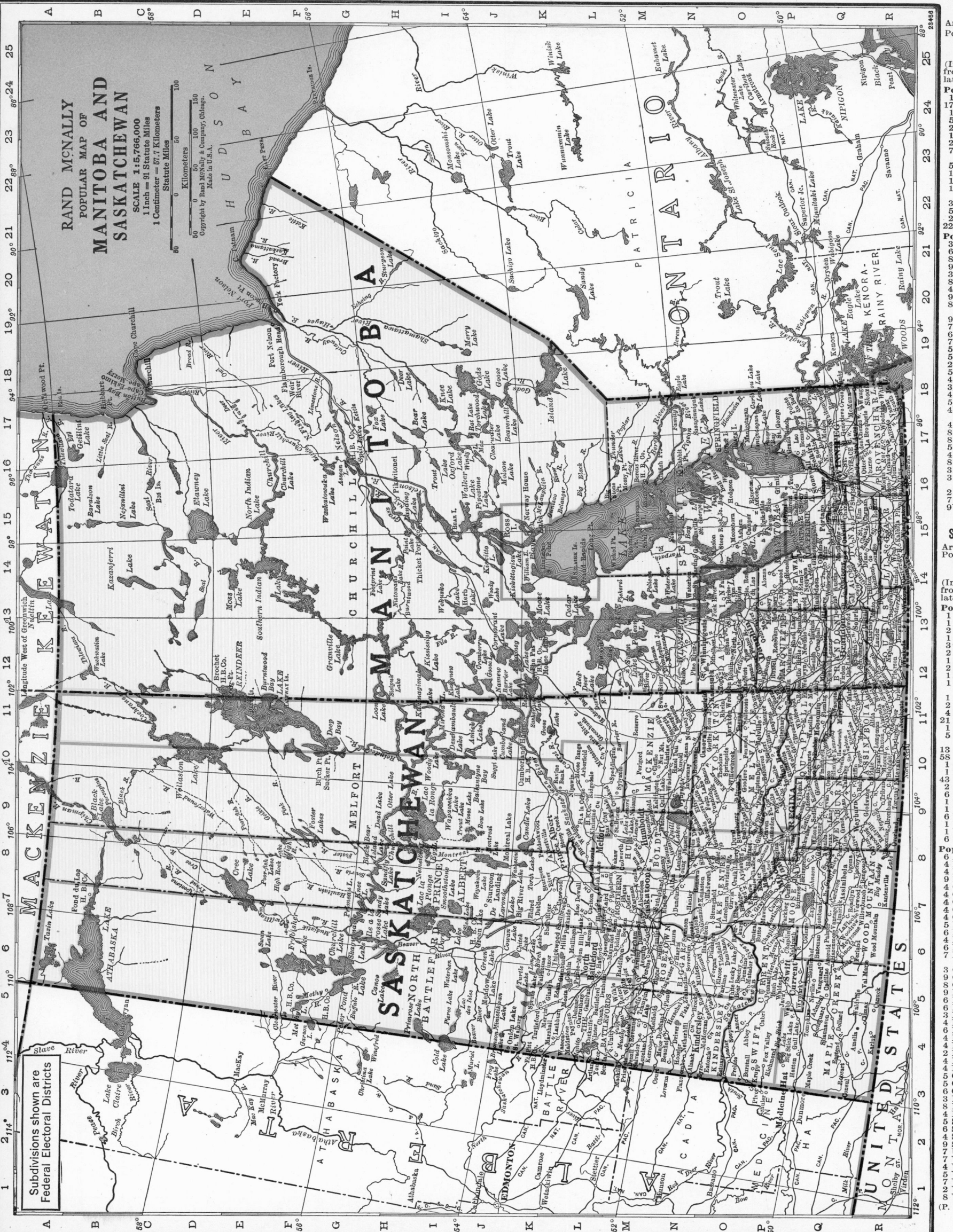

MACKENZIE

Area 527,490 sq.m.

Pop. of Northwest Territories, which includes Keewatin, Franklin and Mackenzie **12,028**

PRINCIPAL CITIES

Arctic Red River E 2
Coronation . . . E 13
Fort Smith . . . Q 16
Good Hope . . . G 5
Hay River . . . P 13
Kittigazuit . . . B 4
Liard . . . . Q 7
McPherson . . . D 2
Norman . . . . I 7
Port Epworth F 15
Providence . . . O 12
Rae . . . . M 13
Resolution . . . O 15
Simpson . . . . . N 9
Sinnak . . . . C 2
Wrigley . . . . . . L 7

(P. & I. 7 R 26)

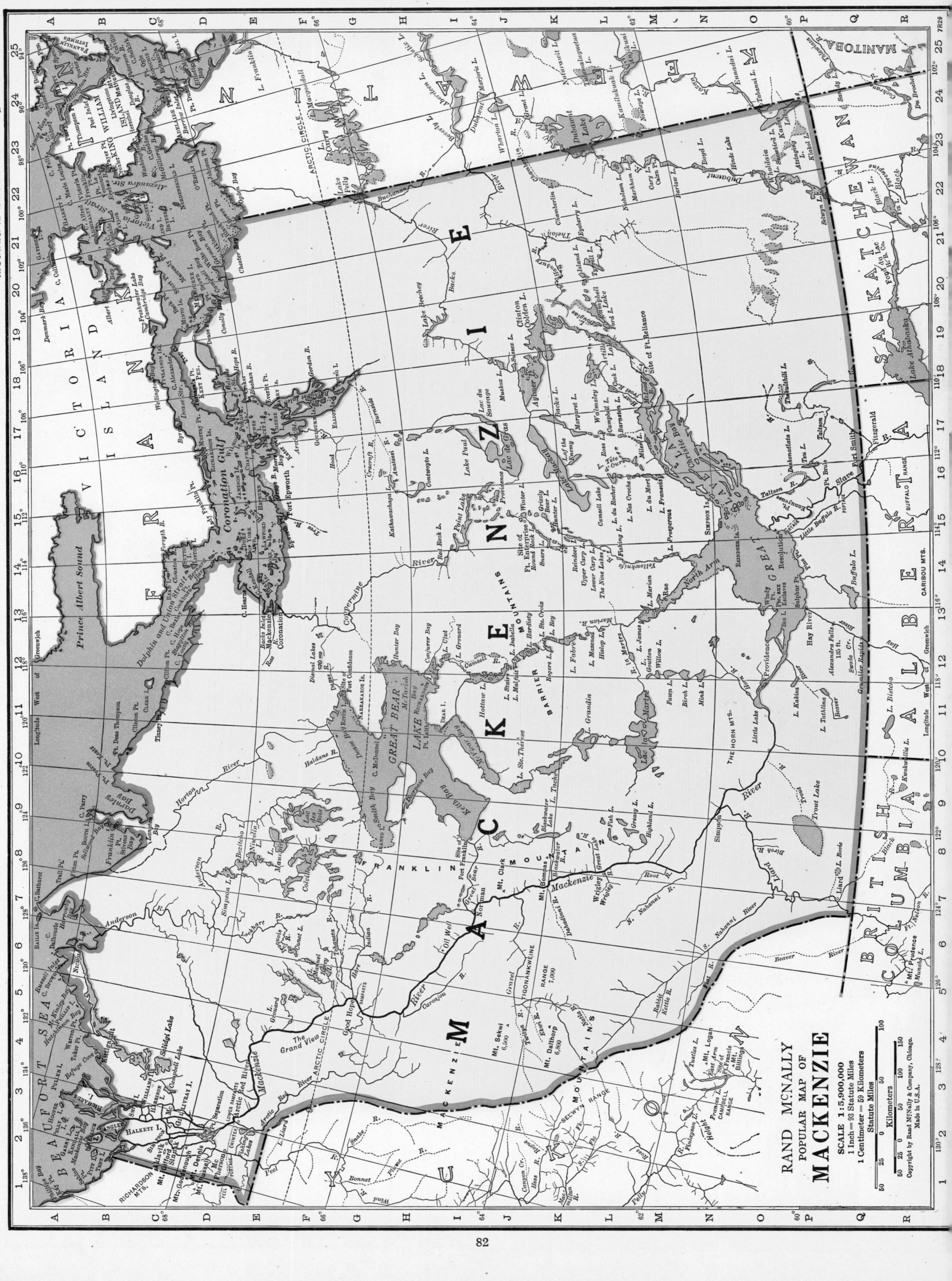
RAND McNALLY
POPULAR MAP OF
MACKENZIE
SCALE 1:5,900,000
1 Inch = 93 Statute Miles
1 Centimeter = 59 Kilometers
Statute Miles
Kilometers
Copyright by Rand McNally & Company, Chicago.
Made in U.S.A.

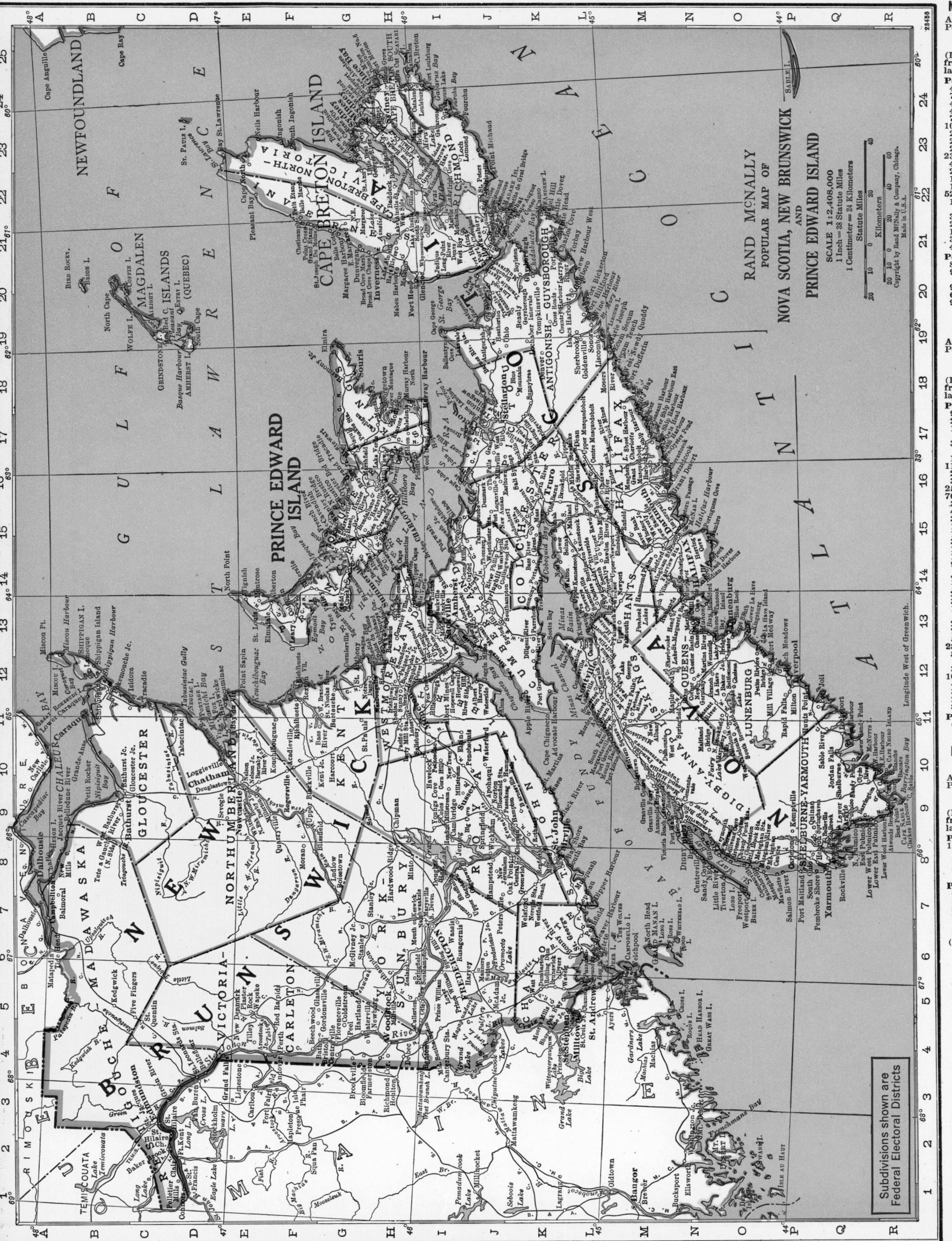

NEW BRUNSWICK

Area..27,985 sq. m.
Pop......457,401

PRINCIPAL CITIES
(Including Figures
from Latest Popu-
lation Estimates)

Pop.—Thousands
4 Bathurst...C 9
7 Campbellton A7
4 Chatham...E 10
4 Dalhousie...A 8
8 Edmundston C3
10 Fredericton. I 7
2 Grand Falls E 4
2 Marysville . I 7
2 Milltown...L 5
23 Moncton...H 12
4 New Castle. E 9
1 Sackville..I 13
1 St. Andrews L 5
1 St. George. L 6
52 St. John... H 8
1 St. Leonards
Station.. D 4
3 St. Stephen L 5
2 Shediac...H 12
1 S. Devon...I 7
3 Sussex.....J 10
4 Woodstock .H 4

Pop.—Hundreds
8 Hartland..G 4
9 Hillsborough
H 12
9 Petitcodiac. I 11
6 Shippigan .B 12
9 Tracadie..C 11

NOVA SCOTIA

Area..21,068 sq. m.
Pop......577,962

PRINCIPAL CITIES
(Including Figures
from Latest Popu-
lation Estimates)

Pop.—Thousands
9 Amherst...I 13
2 Antigonish. J 19
1 Bridgetown
M 10
3 Bridgewater
O 12
1 Canso....K 22
11 Dartmouth N15
2 Digby.....N 9
1 Dominion H 24
25 Glace Bay. H 24
70 Halifax...N 15
4 Inverness . H 21
4 Kentville. L 12
1 Liverpool. P 12
1 Lockeport. Q 11
1 Louisburg. J 24
1 Lunenburg O 13
1 Middleton M 11
1 Mulgrave . J 20
9 New Glasgow
I 17
7 N. Sydney G 24
1 Oxford . . J 14
2 Parrsboro . J 13
2 Pictou...J 17
1 Port Hawkes-
bury.. J 21
2 Shelburne. Q 10
7 Springhill . J 13
2 Stellarton. J 17
28 Sydney . . H 24
8 Sydney Mines
G 24
3 Trenton...J 17
10 Truro...K 16
4 Westville.. J 17
3 Windsor . . M 13
2 Wolfville.. L 13
8 Yarmouth .Q 8

Pop.—Hundreds
6 Port Hood. I 20

PRINCE EDWARD ISLAND

Area..2,184 sq. m.
Pop......95,047

PRINCIPAL CITIES
(Including Figures
from Latest Popu-
lation Estimates)

Pop.—Thousands
15 Charlottetown
H 16
1 Souris.... G 18
5 Summerside
G 14

Pop.—Hundreds
6 Alberton. F 14
5 Cardigan . H 17
8 Georgetown H18
8 Kensington
G 15
8 Montague H 17

(P. & I. 678)

RAND McNALLY
POPULAR MAP OF
NOVA SCOTIA, NEW BRUNSWICK
AND
PRINCE EDWARD ISLAND

SCALE 1:2,408,000
1 Inch = 38 Statute Miles
1 Centimeter = 24 Kilometers

Subdivisions shown are
Federal Electoral Districts

ONTARIO

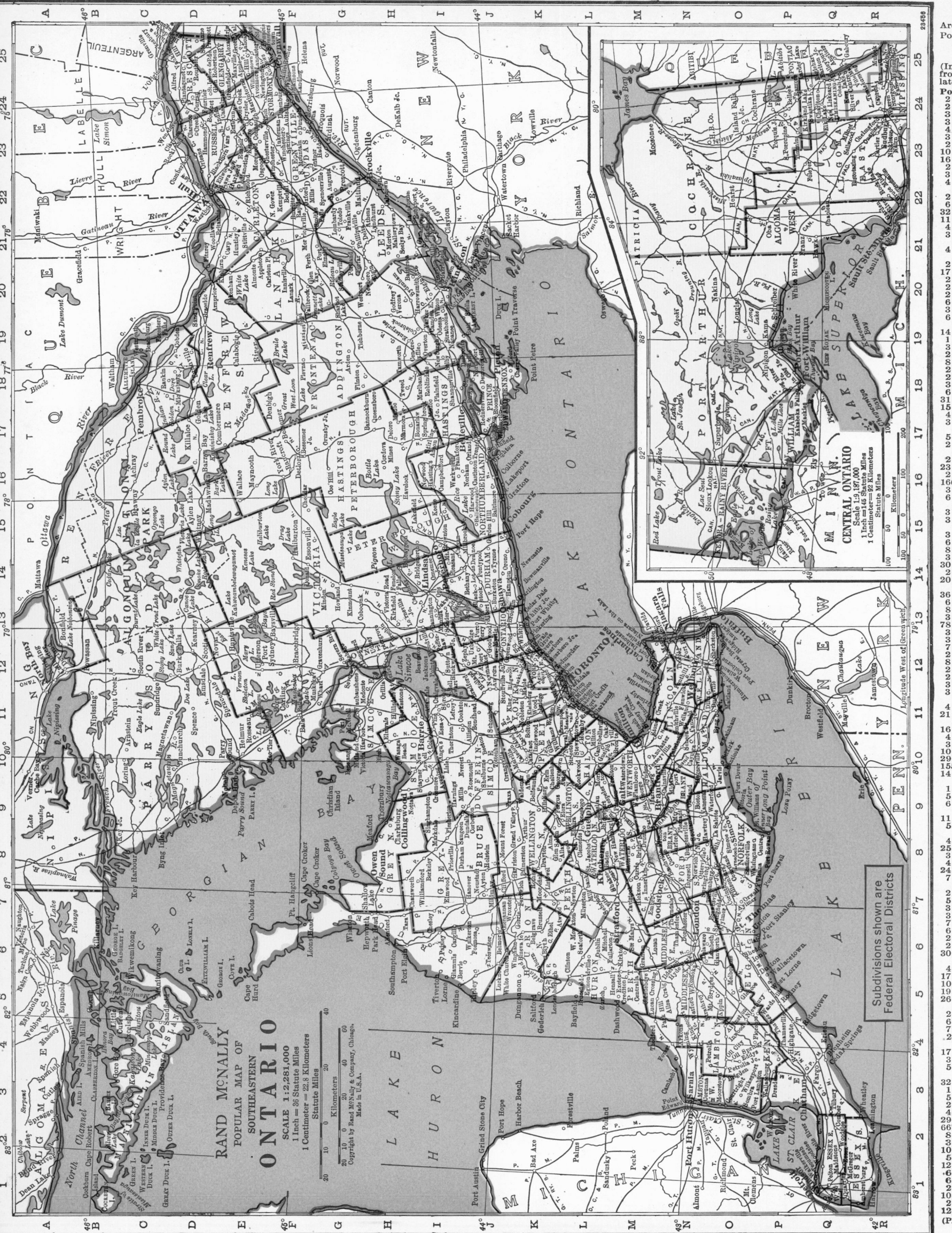

ONTARIO

Area 412,582 sq.m.
Pop.....3,787,655

PRINCIPAL CITIES

(Including Figures from Latest Population Estimates)

Pop.—Thousands

Pop.	City	Ref
2	Acton	L 10
2	Alexandria	E 25
3	Almonte	E 20
2	Amherstburg	R 1
4	Arnprior	D 20
3	Aurora	J 12
2	Aylmer	O 7
10	Barrie	I 11
16	Belleville	I 17
2	Blenheim	Q 4
3	Blind River	A 2
4	Bowmanville	K 14
2	Bracebridge	F 12
6	Brampton	K 11
32	Brantford	N 9
11	Brockville	H 22
4	Burlington	M 10
3	Campbellford	I 16
4	Carleton Place	F 21
2	Chapleau	Q 22
17	Chatham	P 3
2	Chesley	I 7
2	Clinton	L 6
2	Cobalt	Q 25
2	Cobourg	J 15
3	Cochrane	O 24
6	Collingwood	H 9
14	Cornwall	F 25
1	Deseronto	I 18
3	Dunnville	O 11
2	Durham	I 8
2	Eastview	D 22
2	Elmira	L 8
3	Essex	Q 2
3	Fergus	K 9
2	Ft. Frances	P 15
31	Ft. William	P 18
15	Galt	L 9
4	Gananoque	I 21
2	Georgetown	K 10
5	Goderich	G 12
2	Gravenhurst	K 5
2	Grimsby	M 11
23	Guelph	L 9
2	Haileybury	Q 24
166	Hamilton	M 10
3	Hanover	J 7
4	Hawkesbury	C 25
3	Hespeler	L 9
2	Humberstone	O 12
3	Huntsville	E 12
3	Ingersoll	N 7
6	Kenora	O 15
3	Kincardine	I 5
30	Kingston	I 20
2	Kingsville	R 2
20	Kirkland Lake	Q 24
36	Kitchener	L 8
6	Leamington	R 2
3	Lindsay	I 14
3	Listowel	K 7
78	London	N 6
3	Meaford	H 8
3	Merritton	N 12
7	Midland	G 10
2	Milton	L 10
8	Mimico	L 11
3	Mitchell	L 6
2	Mt. Forest	J 8
3	Napanee	I 19
3	New Liskeard	Q 24
4	Newmarket	J 12
21	Niagara Falls	N 13
16	North Bay	A 12
4	Oakville	M 11
2	Orangeville	J 10
10	Orillia	H 12
29	Oshawa	J 13
155	Ottawa	D 22
14	Owen Sound	H 7
1	Palmerston	K 8
5	Paris	M 9
6	Parry Sound	E 10
11	Pembroke	C 18
5	Penetanguishene	G 10
4	Perth	F 21
25	Peterboro	I 15
3	Petrolia	N 3
4	Picton	J 18
24	Port Arthur	P 18
7	Port Colborne	O 12
2	Port Dover	O 9
3	Port Hope	J 15
2	Portsmouth	I 20
2	Prescott	C 23
7	Preston	M 9
6	Renfrew	D 19
2	Ridgetown	Q 5
2	Rockland	D 23
30	St. Catharines	M 12
4	St. Marys	M 6
17	St. Thomas	O 6
10	Sandwich	Q 1
19	Sarnia	N 3
26	Sault Ste. Marie	R 21
2	Seaforth	L 6
6	Simcoe	O 9
7	Smiths Fs.	G 21
2	Southampton	H 6
17	Stratford	M 7
3	Strathroy	N 5
	Sturgeon Falls	R 24
32	Sudbury	R 23
1	Thessalon	R 22
5	Thorold	N 12
2	Tilbury	Q 3
3	Tillsonburg	O 8
29	Timmins	P 23
667	Toronto	L 12
3	Trenton	J 17
3	Walkerton	J 8
10	Walkerville	Q 1
5	Wallaceburg	P 3
12	Welland	N 12
6	Weston	K 11
6	Whitby	K 13
2	Wiarton	G 7
105	Windsor	Q 1
2	Wingham	K 6
12	Woodstock	N 7

(P. & I. 678)

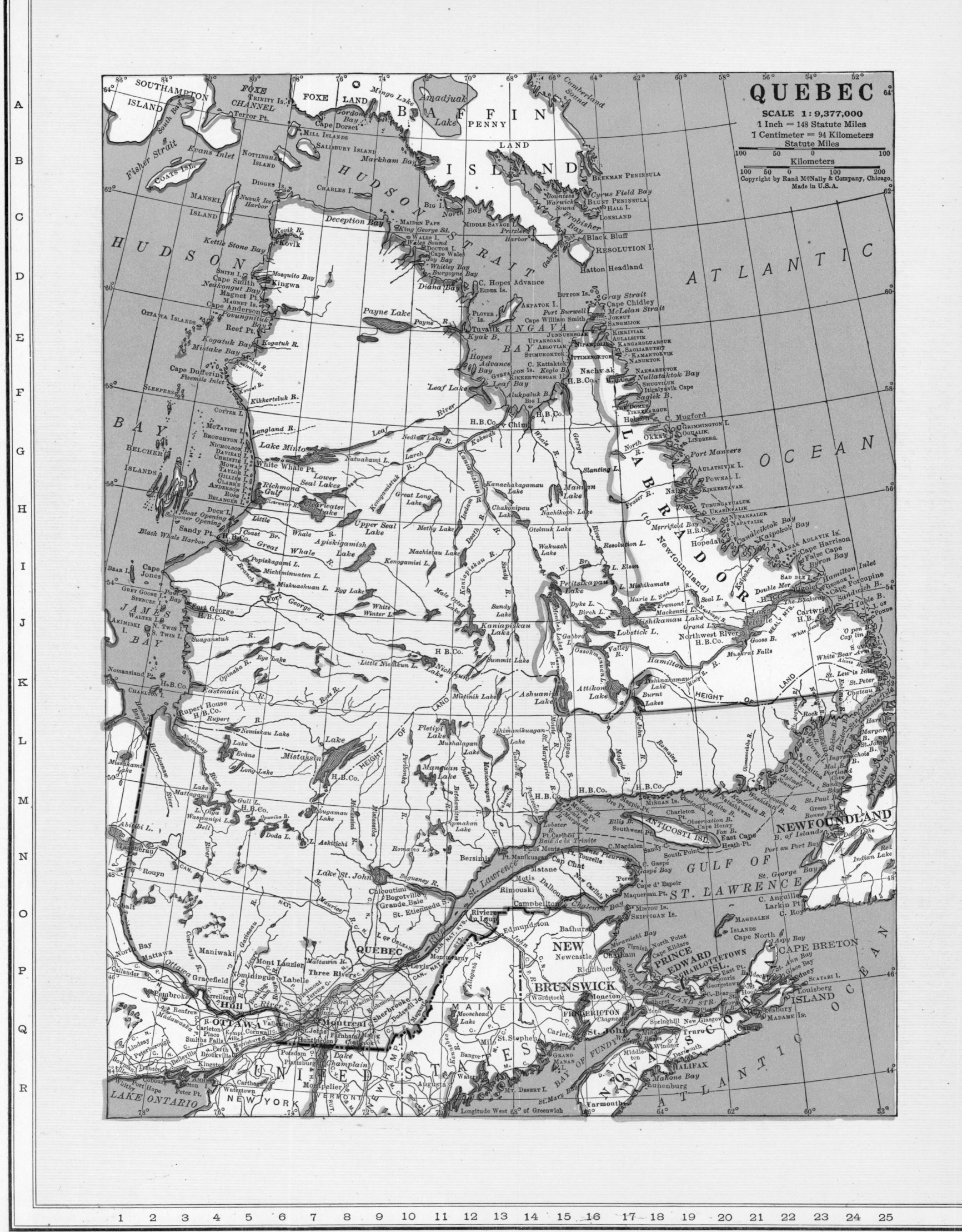

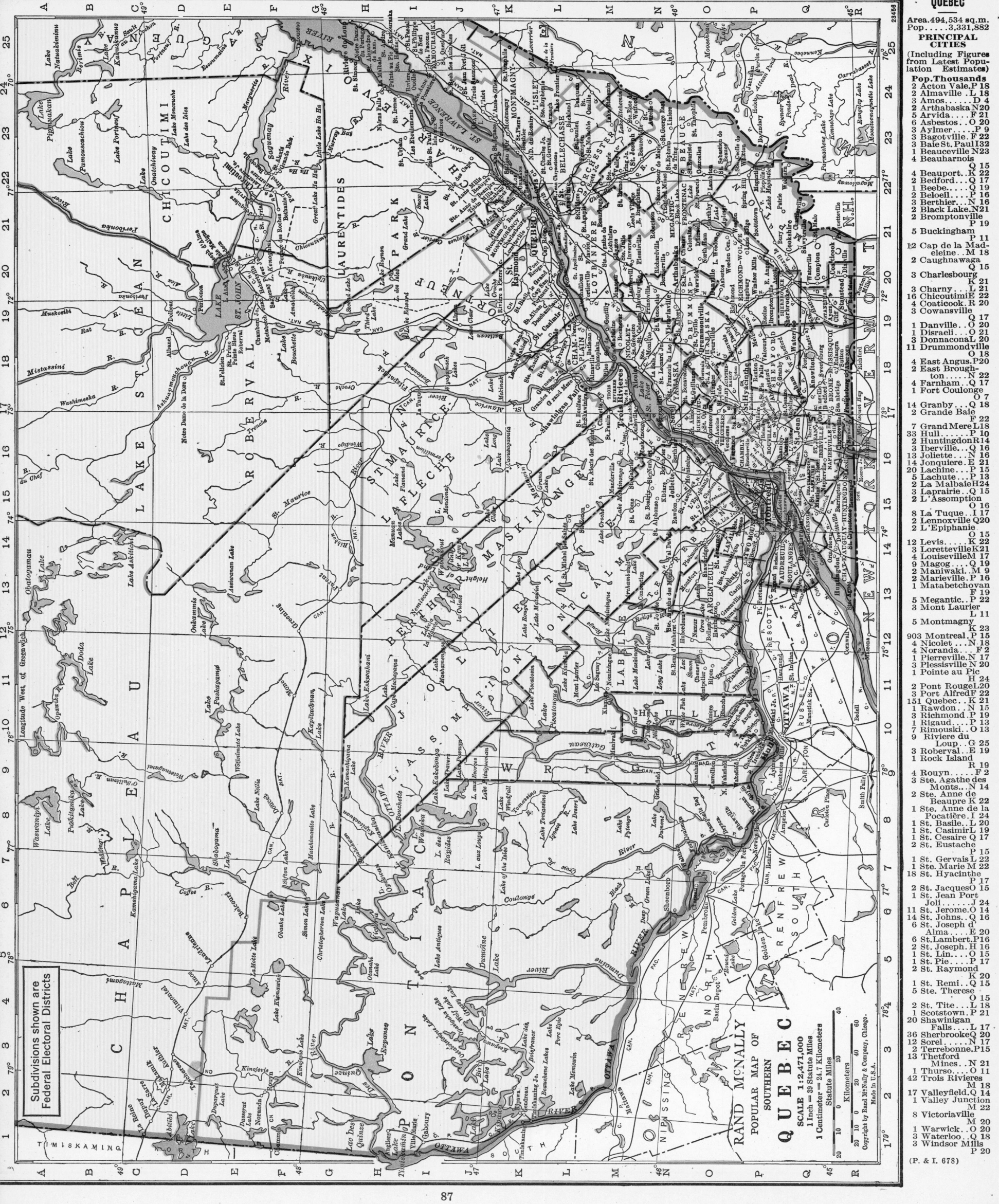

RAND McNALLY
POPULAR MAP OF
SOUTHERN
QUEBEC
SCALE 1:2,471,000
1 Inch = 39 Statute Miles
1 Centimeter = 24.7 Kilometers
Statute Miles
Kilometers
Copyright by Rand McNally & Company, Chicago.
Made in U.S.A.

Subdivisions shown are
Federal Electoral Districts

QUEBEC

Area..494,534 sq.m.
Pop.....3,331,882

**PRINCIPAL
CITIES**
(Including Figures
from Latest Popu-
lation Estimates)

Pop.Thousands
2 Acton Vale.P 18
2 Almaville .L 18
2 Amos......D 4
2 Arthabaska N20
5 Arvida...P 21
6 Asbestos..O 20
3 Aylmer....P 9
2 Bagotville. F 22
3 Baie St. Paul I 32
1 Beauceville N23
4 Beauharnois
                Q 15
4 Beauport..K 22
1 Bedford...Q 17
1 Beebe.....Q 19
2 Beloeil...P 16
3 Berthier..N 16
2 Black Lake N21
2 Bromptonville
                P 19
5 Buckingham
                P 11
12 Cap de la Mad-
   eleine..M 18
2 Caughnawaga
                Q 15
3 Charlesbourg
                K 21
1 Charny...L 21
16 Chicoutimi E 22
4 Coaticook..R 20
3 Cowansville
                Q 17
1 Danville..O 20
1 Disraeli..O 21
3 Donnacona L 20
11 Drummondville
                O 18
4 East Angus.P 20
2 East Brough-
   ton......N 22
4 Farnham ..Q 17
1 Fort Coulonge
                O 7
14 Granby...Q 18
2 Grande Baie
                F 22
7 Grand Mere L18
33 Hull.....P 10
7 Huntingdon R14
1 Iberville..Q 16
13 Joliette..N 16
14 Jonquiere. E 21
20 Lachine...P 15
5 Lachute...P 13
2 La Malbaie I 24
2 Laprairie.Q 15
1 L'Assomption
                O 16
8 La Tuque..I 17
2 Lennoxville Q20
1 L'Epiphanie
                O 15
12 Levis.....K 22
1 Loretteville K21
4 Louiseville M 17
2 Magog....Q 19
2 Maniwaki.M 9
2 Marieville.P 16
1 Matabetchovan
                F 19
5 Megantic..P 22
3 Mont Laurier
                L 11
5 Montmagny
                K 23
903 Montreal.P 15
4 Nicolet...N 18
1 Noranda...F 2
1 Pierreville.N 17
3 Plessisville P 20
1 Pointe au Pic
                H 24
2 Pont Rouge L20
3 Port Alfred F 22
151 Quebec..K 21
1 Rawdon...N 15
3 Richmond.P 19
1 Rigaud....P 13
7 Rimouski..O 13
9 Riviere du
   Loup...G 25
3 Roberval..E 19
1 Rock Island
                R 19
4 Rouyn....F 2
3 Ste. Agathe des
   Monts...N 14
2 Ste. Anne de
   Beaupre K 22
1 Ste. Anne de la
   Pocatiere. I 24
1 St. Basile. L 20
1 St. Casimir L 19
1 St. Cesaire Q 17
2 St. Eustache
                P 15
1 Ste. Gervais L 20
1 Ste. Marie M 22
18 St. Hyacinthe
                P 17
2 St. Jacques O 15
1 St. Jean Port
   Joli......J 24
11 St. Jerome.O 14
14 St. Johns. Q 16
6 St. Joseph d
   Alma....E 20
6 St.Lambert.P16
1 St. Joseph. H 16
1 St. Lin...O 15
1 St. Pie...P 17
2 St. Raymond
                K 20
1 St. Remi. Q 15
1 Ste. Therese
                P 15
2 St. Tite...L 18
1 Scotstown. P 21
20 Shawinigan
   Falls...L 17
36 Sherbrooke Q 20
12 Sorel.....N 17
2 Terrebonne.P15
13 Thetford
   Mines.. N 21
1 Thurso...O 11
42 Trois Rivieres
                M 18
17 Valleyfield.Q 14
1 Valley Junction
                M 22
8 Victoriaville
                M 20
1 Warwick..O 20
1 Waterloo..Q 18
3 Windsor Mills
                P 20

(P. & I. 678)

YUKON

Area 207,076 sq.m.
Pop........4,914

PRINCIPAL CITIES

(Including Figures from Latest Population Estimates)

Pop.

.. Black Hills . L 5
.. Bonanza (Grand Forks) . . . K 4
.. Carcross . . . Q 10
.. Carmacks . . . N 8
.. Champagne . P 8
1043 Dawson . K 4
.. Fortymile . . . J 3
.. Glacier Creek K 2
.. Granville . . . K 5
.. Hunker . . . . K 5
.. Kluane . . . . P 5
.. Last Chance K 4
.. Mayo Landing L 9
.. Minto Bridge L 9
.. Paris . . . . . K 5
.. Pelly . . . . . M 6
.. Radford . . . K 4
.. Scroggie Creek L 4
.. Stewart River L 4
.. Sulphur . . . K 4
.. Teslin . . . . Q 13
.. Thistle Creek L 4
754 Whitehorse P 9

(P. & I. 9 R 28)

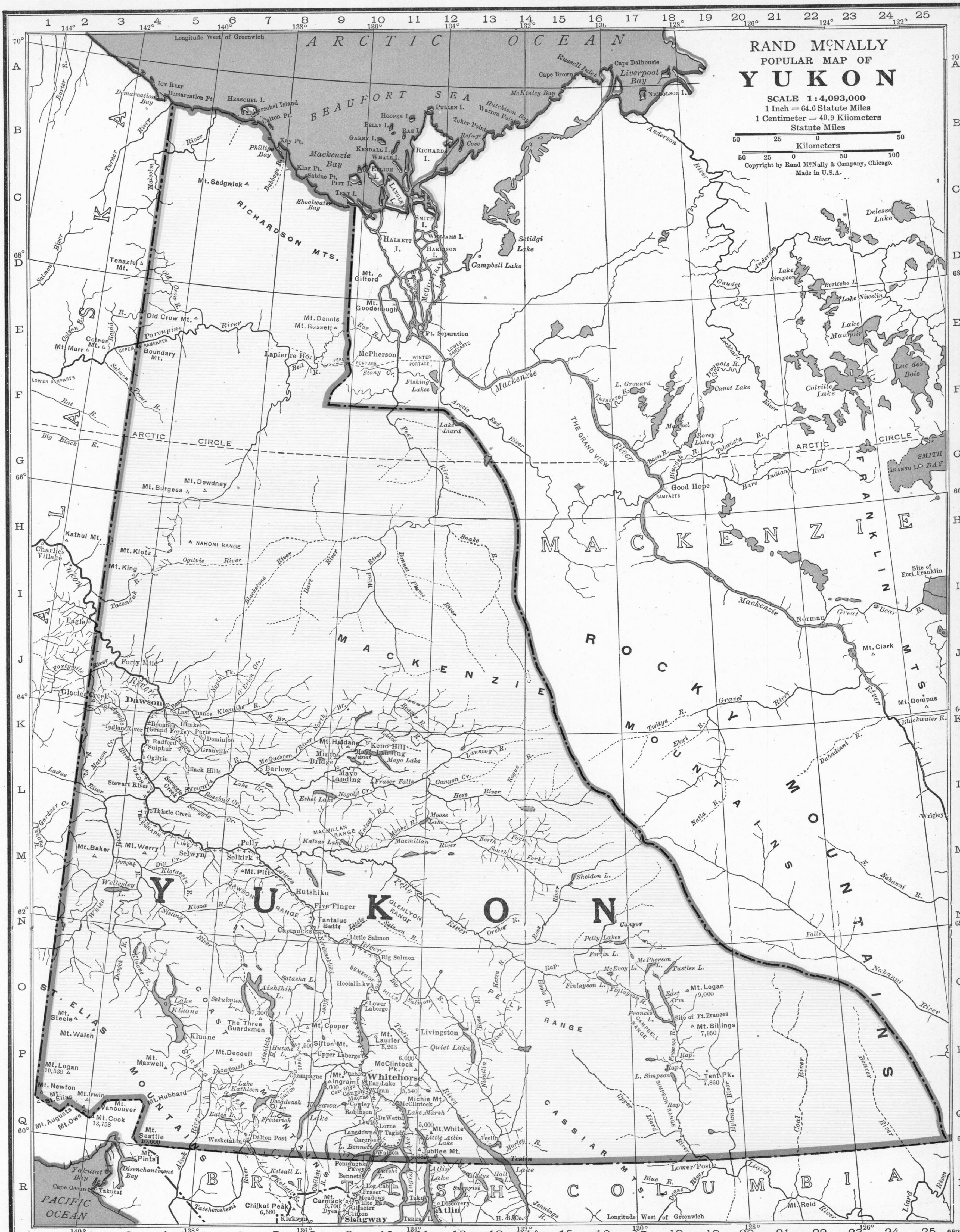

RAND McNALLY
POPULAR MAP OF
YUKON

SCALE 1:4,093,000
1 Inch = 64.6 Statute Miles
1 Centimeter = 40.9 Kilometers
Statute Miles

Copyright by Rand McNally & Company, Chicago.
Made in U.S.A.

88

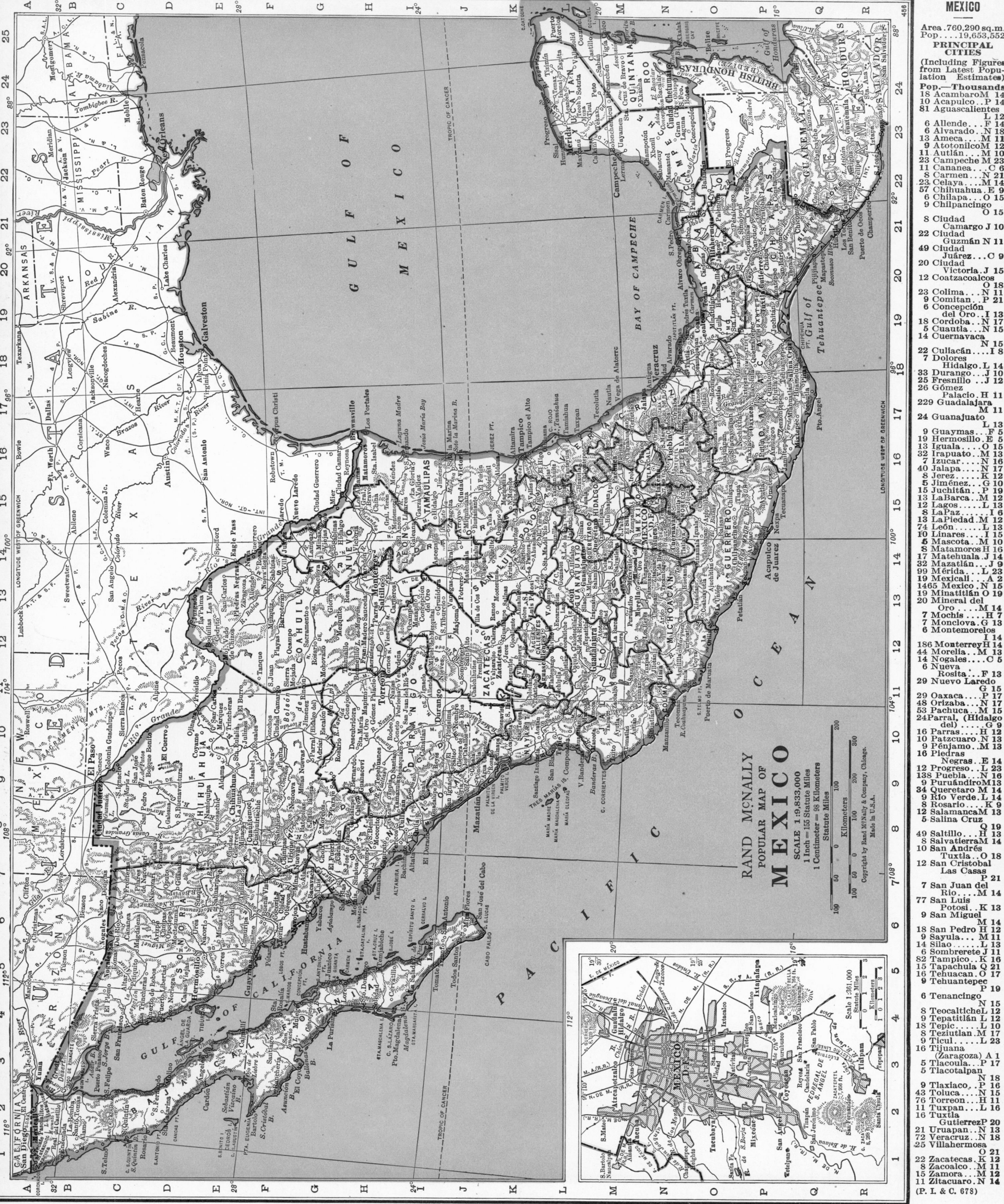

RAND McNALLY
POPULAR MAP OF
MEXICO

SCALE 1:9,833,000
1 Inch = 155 Statute Miles
1 Centimeter = 98 Kilometers

Copyright by Rand McNally & Company, Chicago.
Made in U.S.A.

MEXICO

Area..760,290 sq.m.
Pop....19,653,552

**PRINCIPAL
CITIES**

(Including Figures
from Latest Popu-
lation Estimates)

Pop.—Thousands

18	Acambaro	M	14
10	Acapulco	P	14
81	Aguascalientes		
		L	12
6	Allende	F	14
6	Alvarado	N	18
13	Ameca	M	11
9	AtotonilcoM		12
11	Autlán	M	10
23	Campeche	M	23
11	Cananea	C	6
7	Carmen	N	21
23	Celaya	M	14
57	Chihuahua	E	9
9	Chilapa	O	15
9	Chilpancingo		
		O	15
8	Ciudad Camargo	J	10
22	Ciudad Guzmán	N	11
49	Ciudad Juárez	C	9
20	Ciudad Victoria	J	15
12	Coatzacoalcos		
		O	18
23	Colima	N	11
9	Comitan	P	21
6	Concepción del Oro	I	13
18	Cordoba	N	17
5	Cuautla	N	15
14	Cuernavaca		
		N	15
22	Cullacán	I	8
7	Dolores Hidalgo	L	14
33	Durango	J	10
25	Fresnillo	J	12
26	Gómez Palacio	H	11
229	Guadalajara	M	11
24	Guanajuato		
		L	13
9	Guaymas	F	5
19	Hermosillo	E	5
13	Iguala	O	15
32	Irapuato	M	13
7	Izucar	N	16
40	Jalapa	N	17
8	Jerez	E	12
5	Jiménez	G	10
15	Juchitán	P	19
12	LaBarca	M	12
12	Lagos	L	13
8	LaPaz	I	6
13	LaPiedad	M	12
74	León	L	13
10	Linares	I	14
5	Mascota	M	10
16	Matamoros	H	16
17	Matehuala	I	13
32	Mazatlán	J	9
99	Mérida	L	23
19	Mexicali	A	2
1465	Mexico	N	15
19	Minatitlán	O	19
20	Mineral del Oro	M	14
7	Mochis	H	7
7	Monclova	G	13
6	Montemorelos		
		I	14
186	Monterrey	H	14
44	Morelia	M	13
14	Nogales	C	5
6	Nueva Rosita	I	13
29	Nuevo Laredo		
		G	15
29	Oaxaca	P	17
48	Orizaba	N	17
53	Pachuca	M	15
24	Parral, (Hidalgo del)	G	9
16	Parras	H	12
13	Patzcuaro	N	13
8	Pénjamo	M	13
16	Piedras Negras	E	14
12	Progreso	L	23
138	Puebla	N	16
4	Puruándiro	M	13
34	Queretaro	M	14
9	Rio Verde	L	14
8	Rosario	K	9
12	SalamancaM		13
5	Salina Cruz		
		Q	19
49	Saltillo	H	13
8	SalvatierraM		14
10	San Andrés Tuxtla	O	18
12	San Cristobal Las Casas	P	21
7	San Juan del Rio	M	14
77	San Luis Potosi	K	13
9	San Miguel	M	14
18	San Pedro	H	12
5	Sayula	M	11
14	Silao	L	13
6	Sombrerete	J	11
82	Tampico	K	16
15	Tapachula	Q	21
12	Tehuacan	O	17
9	Tehuantepec		
		P	19
6	Tenancingo		
9	TeocalticheL		12
8	Tepatitlán	L	12
18	Tepic	M	10
4	Teziutlan	M	17
7	Ticul	L	23
16	Tijuana (Zaragoza)	A	1
5	Tlacoula	P	17
5	Tlacotalpan		
		N	18
9	Tlaxiaco	P	18
43	Toluca	N	15
76	Torreon	H	11
11	Tuxpan	N	16
16	Tuxtla GutierrezP		20
21	Uruapan	N	13
72	Veracruz	N	18
25	Villahermosa		
		O	21
22	Zacatecas	K	12
8	Zacoalco	M	11
15	Zamora	M	12
11	Zitacuaro	N	14

(P. I. & C. 678)

8

89

MEXICO
Western Part
PRINCIPAL CITIES
(Including Figures From Latest Population Estimates)

Pop.—Thousands

2 Aguascaliente ... J 9
3 Alamos ... K 14
3 Aldama ... G 19
1 Arizpe ... E 12
2 Batopilas ... K 16
2 Bermejillo ... L 23
1 Buena Vista ... I 12
1 Caborca ... D 9
2 Cacalotan ... R 19
11 Cananea (La Cananea) ... O 12
1 Canatlan ... O 21
1 Carichic ... H 16
2 Casas Grandes ... D 15
57 Chihuahua ... H 18
8 Ciudad Camargo (Santa Rosalia) ... I 20
2 Ciudad Guerrero ... H 16
49 Ciudad Juarez ... E 18
1 Colonia Guadalupe ... C 18
2 Concordia ... Q 19
2 Coneto ... N 21
2 Cosala ... O 18
22 Culiacan ... O 17
3 Cumpas ... E 13
1 Cusihuiriachic ... H 17
33 Durango ... P 21
5 Eldorado ... O 17
3 El Fuerte ... L 15
1 El Verde ... Q 19
4 Empalme ... I 11
1 Ensenada ... B 2
2 Escuinapa ... R 19
26 Gomez Palacio ... M 23
2 Guadalupe de los Reyes P 18
2 Guanacevi ... M 21
1 Guasabas ... F 14
2 Guaymas ... I 11
19 Hermosillo ... G 11
6 Huatabampo ... K 13
2 Ignacio Allende ... O 22
2 Jimenez ... J 20
2 Julines ... H 20
1 La Ojuela ... M 22
1 La Parrilla ... P 22
10 La Paz ... P 12
9 Lerdo ... M 23
4 Magdalena ... D 11
4 Mapimi ... M 22
32 Mazatlan ... R 18
2 Meoqui ... H 20
19 Mexicali ... A 4
2 Mineral Ocampo ... H 15
2 Mocorito ... M 16
2 Moctezuma ... F 13
1 Mulege ... K 9
3 Muleros ... P 22
5 Nacozari ... D 13
2 Namiquipa ... G 16
11 Navojoa ... J 13
14 Nogales ... C 11
2 Nombre de Dios ... P 22
1 Noria La ... Q 18
2 Oputo ... E 13
6 Panuco ... Q 19
24 Parral (Hidalgo del) ... K 19
16 Parras ... M 25
1 Pedricena ... N 22
2 Pericos ... N 16
7 Pilares de Nacozari ... D 13
1 Pitiquito ... D 9
1 Potam ... J 11
1 Rosales (Santa Cruz Rosales) ... H 19
8 Rosario ... R 19
1 Sacramento ... M 23
3 Sahuaripa ... G 14
2 San Andres ... H 18
2 San Blas ... L 14
3 San Buenaventura ... E 16
1 San Fernando ... E 4
2 San Ignacio ... P 18
3 San Jose del Cabo ... R 13
3 San Juan de Guadalupe ... O 24
7 San Juan del Rio ... N 22
2 San Juanico ... L 10
14 Santa Bárbara ... K 19
6 Santa Eulalia ... H 19
1 Santa Isabel ... H 18
2 Santa Maria de Ocotlan ... R 21
1 Santa Marie del Oro ... L 20
6 Santa Rosalia ... J 9
3 Santiago Papasquiaro ... N 20
2 Saucillo ... I 20
3 Sinaloa ... M 15
1 Siqueros ... Q 18
2 Suaqui ... G 13
2 Temosachic ... G 16
2 Tepehuanes ... N 19
16 Tijuana (Zaragoza) ... A 1
1 Todos Santos ... Q 12
2 Torin ... J 12
76 Torreon ... M 23
3 Ures ... F 12
2 Velardena ... N 23
3 Villa Escobedo ... J 19
2 Villa Lopez ... K 20
3 Villa Union ... Q 19
22 Zacatecas ... R 25

(P. & I. 678)

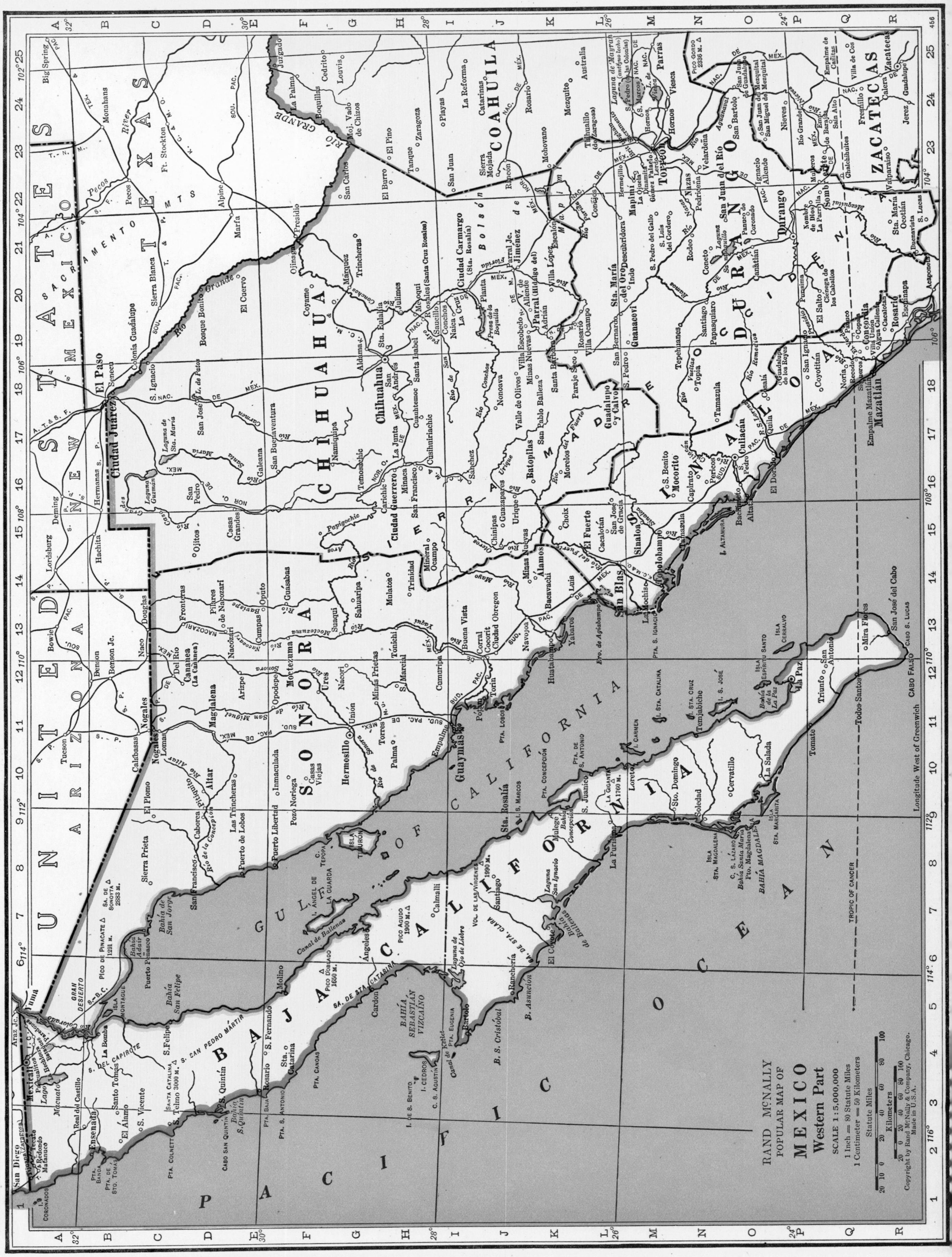

RAND McNALLY
POPULAR MAP OF
MEXICO
Western Part

SCALE 1:5,000,000
1 Inch = 80 Statute Miles
1 Centimeter = 50 Kilometers

Statute Miles
Kilometers

Copyright by Rand McNally & Company, Chicago
Made in U.S.A.

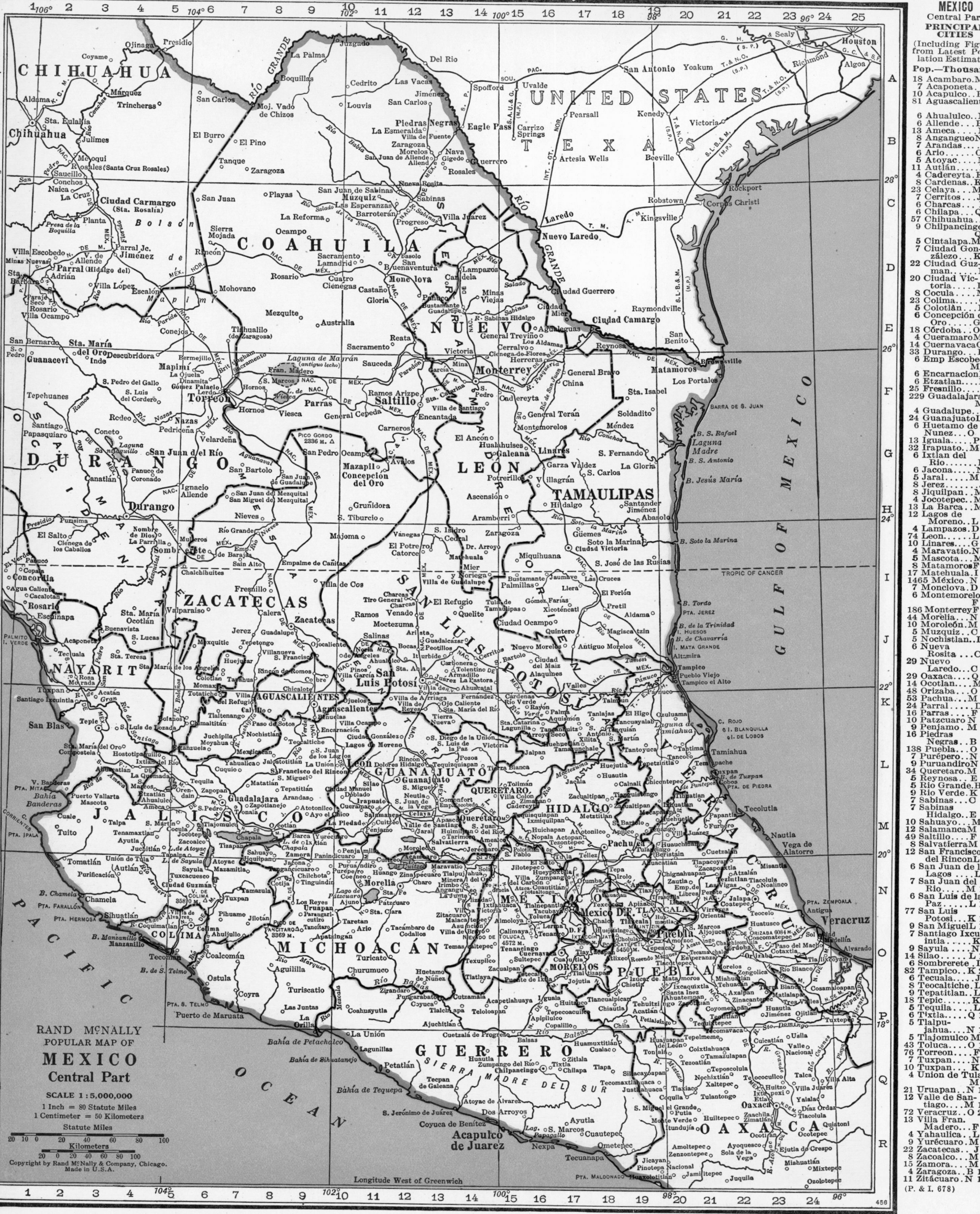

MEXICO
Central Part
PRINCIPAL
CITIES
(Including Figures
from Latest Popu-
lation Estimates
Pop.—Thousands

18 Acambaro.M 13
6 Ahualulco..M 5
6 Allende...B 13
13 Ameca....M 5
8 AnganguenN 14
4 Aranda...L 9
5 Ario.....O 10
6 Atoyac...M 6
11 Autlán...N 4
4 Cadereyta.F 15
5 Cárdenas.K 15
23 Celaya...M 13
7 Cerritos..J 14
6 Charcas...I 12
6 Chilapa...Q 17
57 Chihuahua.B 1
9 Chilpancingo
.....Q 15
5 Cintalapa.M 14
7 Cocula....M 5
22 Ciudad Gon-
zález....K 12
22 Ciudad Guz-
man.....N 5
20 Ciudad Vic-
toria....I 17
8 Cocula....M 5
23 Colima...O 6
8 Colotlán...K 7
6 Concepción del
Oro.....G 11
18 Córdoba..O 22
6 CueramaroM 11
14 Cuernavaca O17
33 Durango..H 4
6 Emp Escobedo
.....M 13
6 Encarnación K 9
8 Etzatlan...L 5
25 Fresnillo..I 12
229 Guadalajara
.....M 7
4 Guadalupe..J 9
24 GuanajuatoL 12
6 Huetamo de
Nunez...O 13
13 Iguala....N 16
32 Irapuato..M 11
6 Ixtlan del
Río......L 4
6 Jacona...N 9
6 Jaral....M 12
8 Jerez.....J 7
13 Jiquilpan..M 8
4 Jocotepec.M 6
13 La Barca..M 8
12 Lagos de
Moreno..L 10
4 Lampazos.D 12
74 Leon.....L 10
10 Linares...G 16
4 Maravatio.N 13
4 Mascota...M 3
8 MatamorosF 20
17 Matehuala.I 13
1465 México..N 17
7 Monclova.D 11
6 Montemorelos
.....G 15
186 MonterreyF 14
44 Morelia...N 12
10 Moroleón.M 12
5 Muzquiz..C 11
5 Nochistlan.L 8
6 Nueva
Rosita...C12
29 Nuevo
Laredo...C 16
29 Oaxaca...Q 23
14 Ocotlan...M 8
22 Orizaba...O 20
53 Pachuca..M 8
24 Parral...D 2
16 Parras...F 10
10 Patzcuaro N 11
9 Penjamo..M 11
16 Piedras
Negras...C 13
138 Puebla...O 19
9 Purépero..N 10
9 PuruandiroN 10
34 Queretaro.M 14
5 Reynosa...F 15
8 Río Grande.H 7
9 Río Verde.K 15
5 Sabinas...C 12
5 Sabinas
Hidalgo..E 14
10 Sahuayo..M 8
14 SalamancaM 12
49 Saltillo...F 12
8 SalvatierraM 13
12 San Francisco
del RinconL10
6 San Juan de los
Lagos...L 9
7 San Juan del
Río......M 15
6 San Luis de la
Paz.....L 13
77 San Luis
Potosí...K 12
9 San MiguelL 13
7 Santiago Ixcu-
intla...K 2
9 Sayula...N 6
14 Silao....L 11
6 Sombrerete.I 2
82 Tampico..K 20
6 Tecuala...J 2
8 Teocaltiche.L 8
9 Tepatitlan.L 8
18 Tepic....K 3
5 Tequila...L 6
9 Tixtla...Q 16
5 Tlalpu-
jahua...N 14
5 Tlajomulco M 6
43 Toluca...N 16
76 Torreon...F 7
7 Tuxpan...N 7
9 Tuxpan...K 2
4 Union de Tula
.....M 4
21 Uruapan..N 10
12 Valle de San-
tiago....M 12
72 Veracruz..O 24
13 Villa Fran.
Madero..F 8
4 Yahualica.L 8
9 Yurécuaro.M 9
22 Zacatecas..J 9
2 Zacoalco..M 6
15 Zamora...M 9
4 Zaragoza..B 12
11 Zitácuaro.N 14

(P. & I. 678)

456

91

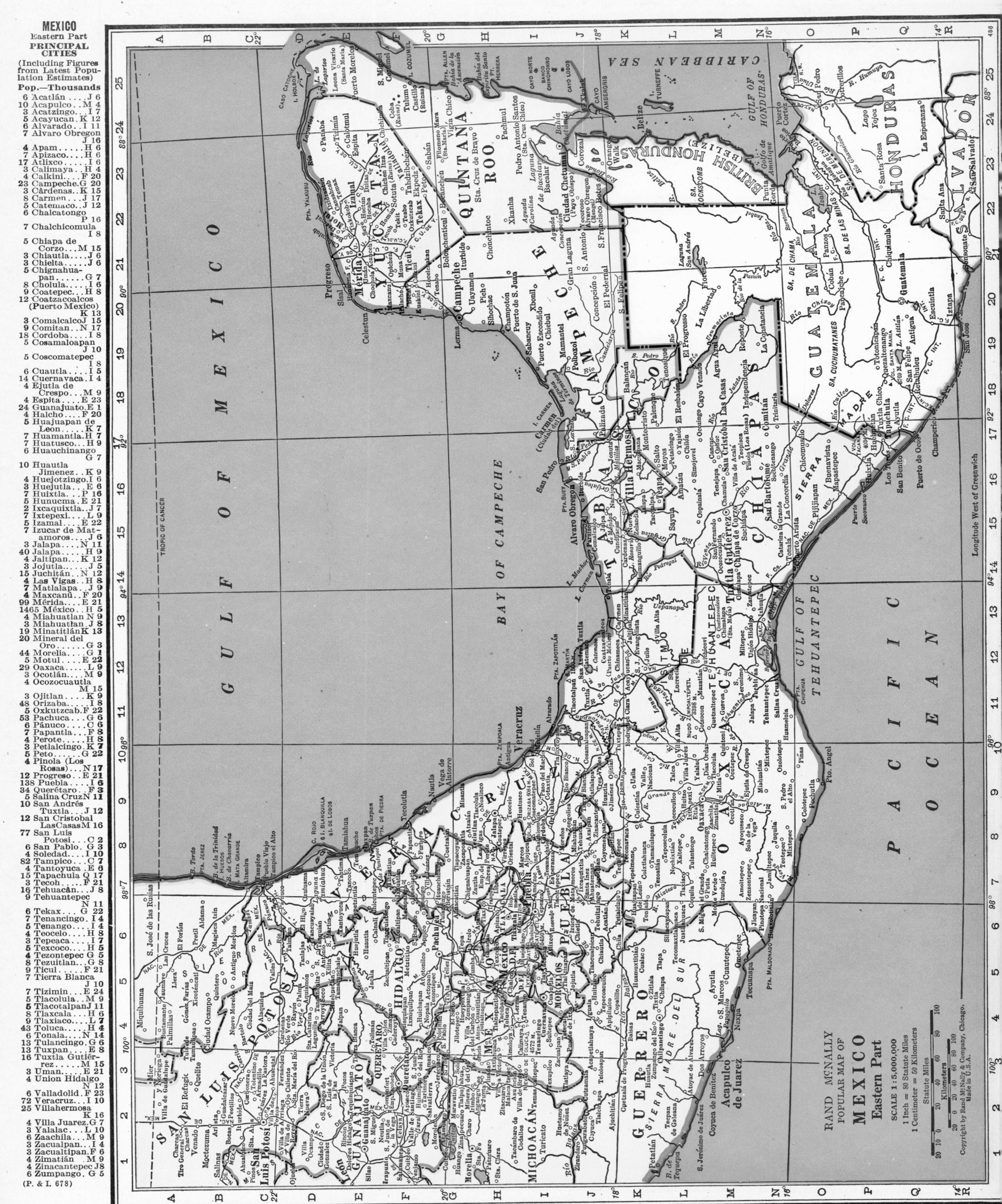

RAND McNALLY POPULAR MAP OF
MEXICO
Eastern Part
SCALE 1:5,000,000
1 Inch = 80 Statute Miles
1 Centimeter = 50 Kilometers
Copyright by Rand McNally & Company, Chicago.
Made in U.S.A.

RAND MCNALLY
POPULAR MAP OF
CENTRAL AMERICA

SCALE 1:5,576,000
1 Inch = 88 Statute Miles
1 Centimeter = 55.8 Kilometers
Made in U.S.A.

Statute Miles

Kilometers

Copyright by Rand McNally & Company, Chicago.

Longitude West of Greenwich

PRINCIPAL ISLANDS

Antigua, with
Barbuda ...K 23
Area..171 sq. m.
Pop.......41,024

Bahama Is...E 11
Area..4,404 sq. m.
Pop.......68,846

Barbados....O 25
Area..166 sq. m.
Pop.......203,411

Cuba.........F 6
Area 44,164 sq. m.
Pop.....4,777,284

Curaçao.....P 16
(Colony)
Area......403 sq. m.
Pop......122,540

Dominica...M 24
Area......305 sq. m.
Pop.......53,202

Dominican Republic.....I 14
Area.19,332 sq. m.
Pop.....1,768,163

Grenada.....P 24
Area..133 sq. m.
Pop.......87,805

Guadeloupe and
Dependencies L 24
Area...688 sq. m.
Pop......308,000

Haiti........I 13
Area.11,069 sq. m.
Pop......3,000,000

Jamaica....J 8
Area..4,470 sq. m.
Pop.....1,237,063

Martinique..M 25
Area...385 sq. m.
Pop......248,116

Montserrat..K 23
Area...32 sq. m.
Pop.......14,600

Puerto Rico..J 18
Area..3,435 sq. m.
Pop.....1,869,255

St. Kitts.....K 22
with Nevis
Area....150 sq. m.
Pop.......37,694

St. Lucia....N 24
Area...233 sq. m.
Pop.......74,699

Tobago.....Q 25
Area..114 sq. m.
Pop.......25,358

Trinidad....R 25
Area..1,862 sq. m.
Pop......510,141

Virgin Is....J 20
(British)
Area...58 sq. m.
Pop.......7,129

Virgin Is...J 20
(U. S.)
Area...133 sq. m.
Pop.......24,889

PRINCIPAL CITIES

Pop.—Thousands

22 Arecibo...J 18
15 Aux Cayes J 11
14 Basse TerreB 22
19 Bridgetown
        O 25
78 Camaguey..G 7
20 Cap Haitien
        H 13
37 Cardenas...E 4
24 Castries...N 23
29 Ciego de Avila
        F 6
49 Cienfuegos..F 5
120 Ciudad Trujillo
   (Santo Domingo)
        J 15
61 Fort de France
        M 24
22 GuanabacoaE 3
42 Guantanamo
        H 10
676 Habana
   (Havana) E 3
36 Holguin....G 9
109 Kingston..J 8
16 Lamentin. G 24
36 Manzanillo H 8
115 Mariano..E 3
50 Matanzas..E 4
50 Mayaguez. J 18
29 Nassau....O 8
26 Pinar del Rio
        E 2
44 Pointe à Pitre
        L 24
65 Ponce...J 18
130 Port au Prince
        J 13
17 Port du Moule
        L 24
103 Port of Spain
        R 24
10 Roseau...D 23
16 Sagua la Grande
        E 5
19 St. George P 24
19 San Fernando
        R 24
10 St. Johns. K 23
14 Sancti-Spiritus
        F 6
169 San Juan. J 19
28 Santa Clara E 5
53 Santiago...I 14
121 Santiago de
   Cuba....H 9
   Santo Domingo,
   see Ciudad
   Trujillo.
15 Trinidad...F 5
26 Willemstad P 16

(P. I. & C. 67)

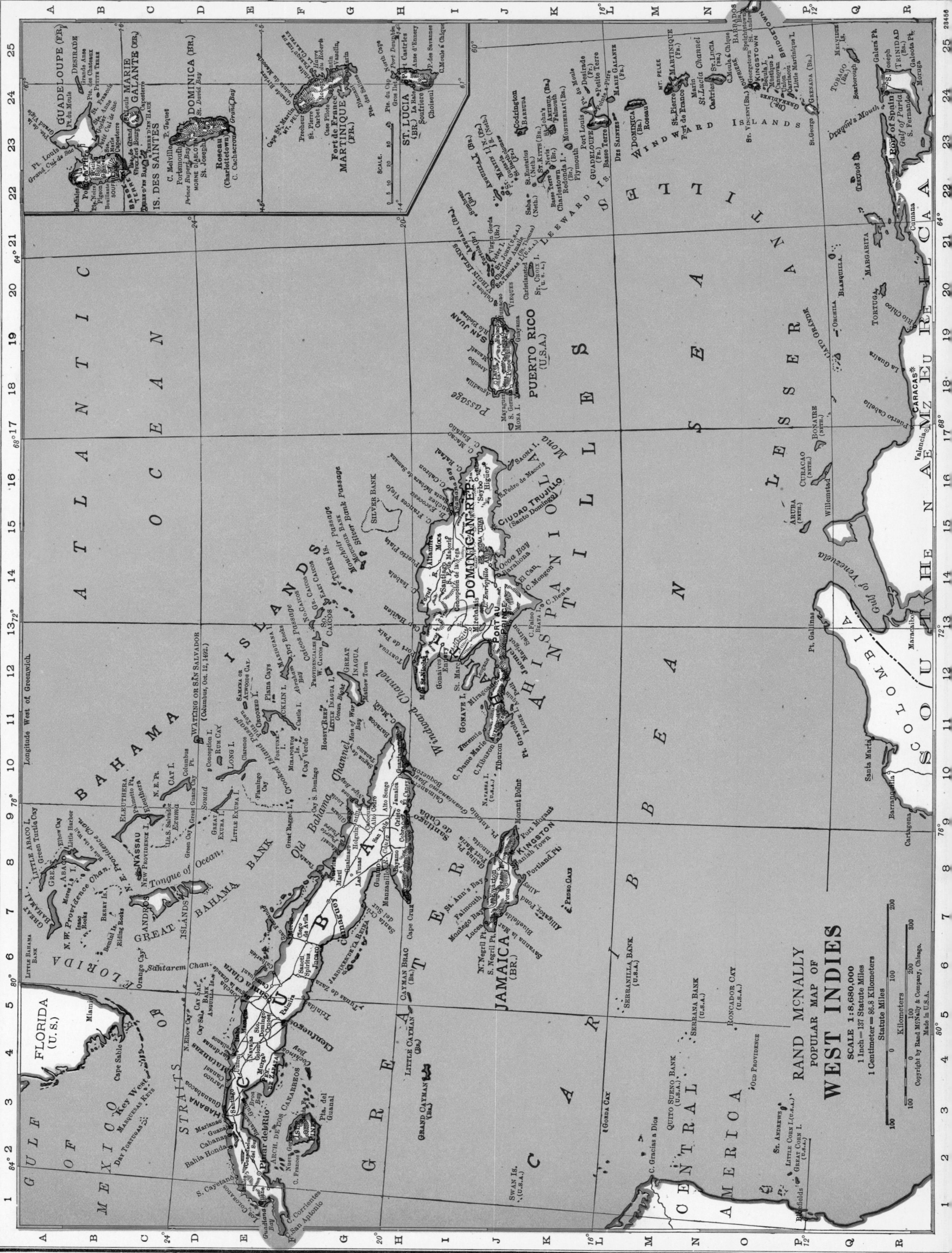

RAND McNALLY
POPULAR MAP OF
WEST INDIES

SCALE 1:8,680,000
1 Inch = 137 Statute Miles
1 Centimeter = 86.8 Kilometers

Copyright by Rand McNally & Company, Chicago.
Made in U. S. A.

RAND McNALLY
POPULAR MAP OF
CUBA
SCALE 1:3,738,000
1 Inch = 59 Statute Miles
1 Centimeter = 37.4 Kilometers
Statute Miles
Kilometers
Copyright by Rand McNally & Company, Chicago.
Made in U.S.A.
ATLANTIC OCEAN
GULF OF MEXICO
CARIBBEAN SEA
BAHAMA ISLANDS (BR.)
GREAT BAHAMA BANK
STRAITS OF FLORIDA
OLD BAHAMA CHANNEL
FLORIDA (U.S.)
TROPIC OF CANCER
Longitude West of Greenwich

CUBA

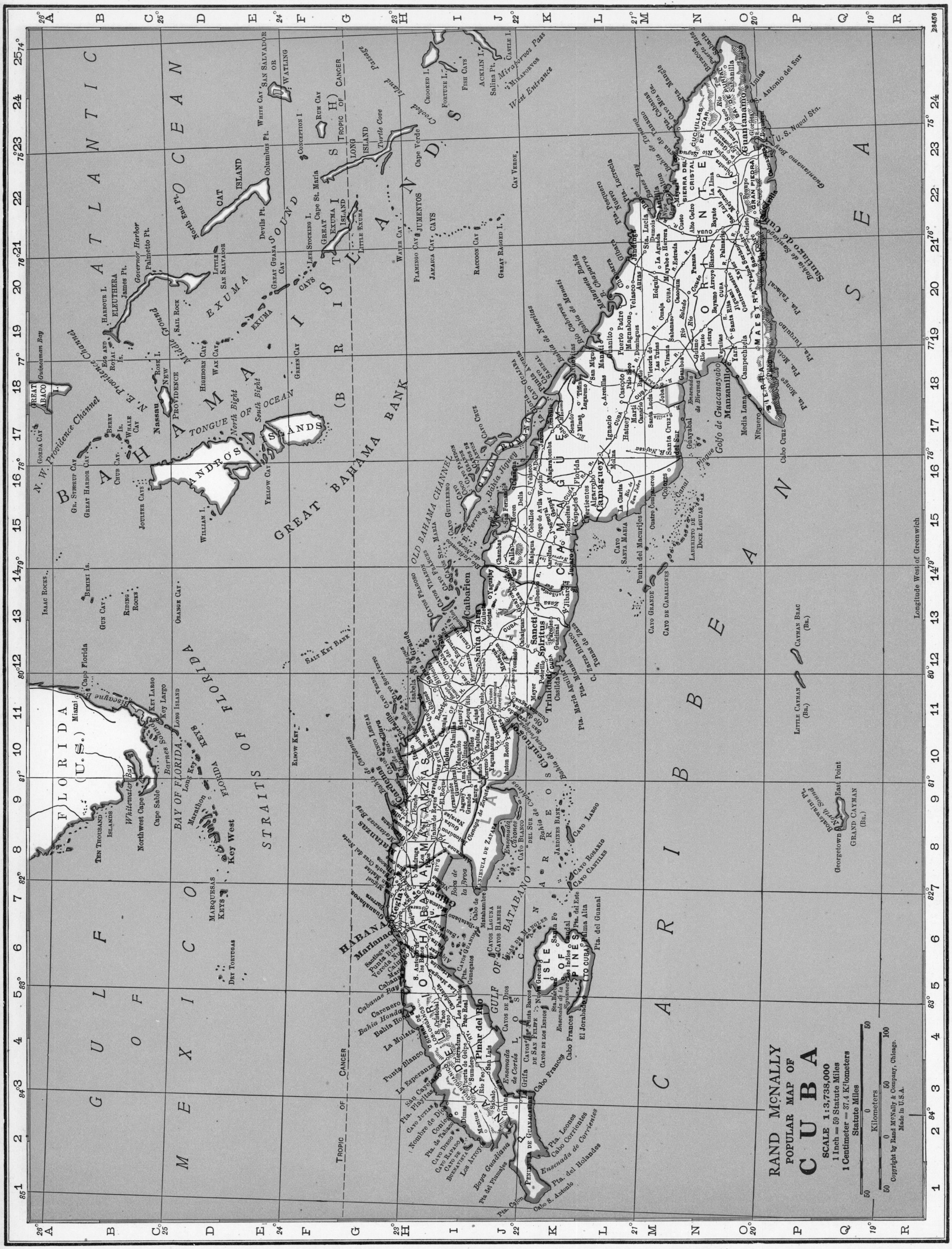

Area. 44,217 sq. m.
Pop. 4,778,583

PRINCIPAL CITIES

(Including Figures from Latest Population Estimates)

Pop.—Thousands		
3	Agramonte	I 9
3	Aguacate	H 7
4	Aguada	I 10
6	Alacranes	I 8
6	Alquizar	H 6
5	Alto Cedro	N 21
13	Artemisa	H 5
2	Banaguises	I 10
16	Banes	M 22
10	Baracoa	N 25
5	Batabanó	I 7
16	Bayamo	N 19
8	Bejucal	H 6
4	Bolondron	I 8
16	Cabaiguan	J 13
2	Cabañas	H 5
4	Cacocum	N 20
20	Caibarién	I 13
2	Caimito	H 6
2	Calimete	I 10
78	Camaguey	L 16
12	Camajuani	I 12
6	Campechuela	O 18
2	Candelaria	I 5
37	Cardeñas	H 9
3	Carreno	J 10
2	Cascajal	I 10
2	Ceballos	K 15
29	Ciego de Avila	K 15
49	Cienfuegos	J 11
2	Cifuentes	I 12
12	Colon	I 10
2	Cristo	O 21
9	Cruces	J 11
3	Cumanayagua	J 11
8	Encrucijada	I 12
4	Esperanza	I 12
2	Florida	L 16
17	Fomento	J 12
8	Gibara	M 21
22	Guanabacóa	H 7
3	Guanabana	H 8
42	Guantánamo	O 23
2	Guareiras	I 10
23	Güines	H 7
676	Habana (Havana)	H 6
36	Holguin	M 20
3	Isabela	H 12
3	Jagueyal	K 15
3	Jaguey Grande	I 9
7	Jatibonico	K 14
14	Jiguani	O 20
2	Jobabo	M 18
13	Jovellanos	H 9
5	Lajas	J 11
2	Limonar	H 8
3	Los Palacios	I 4
3	Lugareño	L 18
3	Madruga	H 7
3	Majagua	K 14
6	Manguito	I 10
36	Manzanillo	O 18
115	Marianao	H 6
5	Martí	M 18
50	Matanzas	H 8
5	Maximo Gomez	H 9
3	Mayari	N 22
3	Melena	H 7
2	Minas	L 17
17	Moron	J 15
3	Niquero	O 17
12	Nuevitas	K 18
2	Ojo de Agua	J 11
2	Palmarito	O 21
16	Palma Soriano	O 21
6	Palmira	J 11
26	Pinar del Rio	I 3
20	Placetas	J 13
2	Potrerillo	J 11
8	Puerto Padre	L 20
3	Punta Brava	H 6
8	Quemados de Guines	I 11
2	Quivican	H 6
2	Rancho Veloz	H 11
4	Ranchuelo	J 11
23	Regla	H 6
10	Remedios	I 13
2	Rio Feo	J 3
3	Rodas	J 10
2	Rodrigo	I 11
2	Sabalo	J 3
2	Sabanilla	O 25
16	Sagua la Grande	I 12
14	San Antonio de los Baños	H 6
14	Sancti Spiritus	K 13
2	San Felipe	I 7
2	San Fernando	J 11
8	San Jose	H 7
11	San Luis	O 21
5	San Miguel	H 7
3	San Nicolas	I 7
28	Santa Clara	I 12
6	Santa Cruz del Norte	H 7
2	Santa Cruz del Sur	N 16
2	Santa Fe	K 6
121	Santiago de Cuba	O 21
9	Santiago de las Vegas	H 6
3	Santo Domingo	I 11
4	Senado	K 17
3	Sitiecito	H 11
3	Taco Taco	I 5
15	Trinidad	K 12
7	Union de Reyes	H 8
12	Victoria de las Tunas	M 19
9	Yaguajay	J 13
6	Zulueta	J 13

(P. & I. 678)

SOUTH AMERICA
(Including Figures from Latest Population Estimates)

Ar. 6,845,000 sq. m.
Pop....96,527,000

ARGENTINA
Ar. 1,072,745 sq. m.
Pop..13,906,694
PRINCIPAL CITIES
Pop.—Thousands
72 Bahia Blanca ....N 11
2568 Buenos Aires ...M 13
339 Cordoba...L 10
126 La Plata..M 13
513 Rosario...L 12
148 Santa Fe.L 12

BOLIVIA
Area. 416,040 sq.m.
Pop....3,533,090
PRINCIPAL CITIES
Pop.—Thousands
301 La Paz....H 8
30 Sucre.....I 10

BRAZIL
Ar. 3,286,169 sq. m.
Pop....45,300,000
PRINCIPAL CITIES
Pop.—Thousands
167 Belém....D 18
142 Fortaleza.F 22
263 Porto Alegre ....L 16
328 Recife (Pernambuco.F 24
1564 Rio de Janeiro.....J 20
293 Salvador (Bahia)..G 22
160 Santos. J 18
1254 São Paulo J18

CHILE
Area 286,322 sq.m.
Pop.....5,341,317
PRINCIPAL CITIES
Pop.—Thousands
993 Santiago...M 8
210 Valparaiso.L 7

COLOMBIA
Area. 439,825 sq.m.
Pop.....9,905,748
PRINCIPAL CITY
Pop.—Thousands
326 Bogotá....C 5

ECUADOR
Area. 101,481 sq.m.
Pop.....3,170,796
PRINCIPAL CITIES
Pop.—Thousands
173 Guayaquil.D 2
166 Quito.....D 3

GUIANA
(British)
Area. 89,480 sq. m.
Pop.......364,694
PRINCIPAL CITY
Pop.—Thousands
73 Georgetown..B 13

GUIANA
(Neth.)
Area. 54,291 sq. m.
Pop.......189,436
PRINCIPAL CITY
Pop.—Thousands
61 Paramaribo..B 14

GUIANA & ININI
(French)
Area. 34,354 sq. m.
Pop.......36,975
PRINCIPAL CITY
Pop.—Thousands
12 Cayenne...C 16

PARAGUAY
Area. 150,516 sq.m.
Pop.....1,040,420
PRINCIPAL CITY
Pop.—Thousands
100 Asuncion.J 13

PERU
Area. 482,257 sq.m.
Pop.....7,023,111
PRINCIPAL CITY
Pop.—Thousands
534 Lima.....G 4

URUGUAY
Area. 72,172 sq. m.
Pop.....2,202,936
PRINCIPAL CITY
Pop.—Thousands
708 Montevideo..M 14

VENEZUELA
Area. 352,141 sq.m.
Pop.....3,850,771
PRINCIPAL CITY
Pop.—Thousands
267 Carácas...A 9
(P. I. & C. 67)

RAND McNALLY
POPULAR MAP OF
SOUTH AMERICA
SCALE 1:25,724,000
1 Inch = 406 Statute Miles
1 Centimeter = 257 Kilometers
Statute Miles
Kilometers
Copyright by Rand McNally & Company, Chicago.
Made In U.S.A.

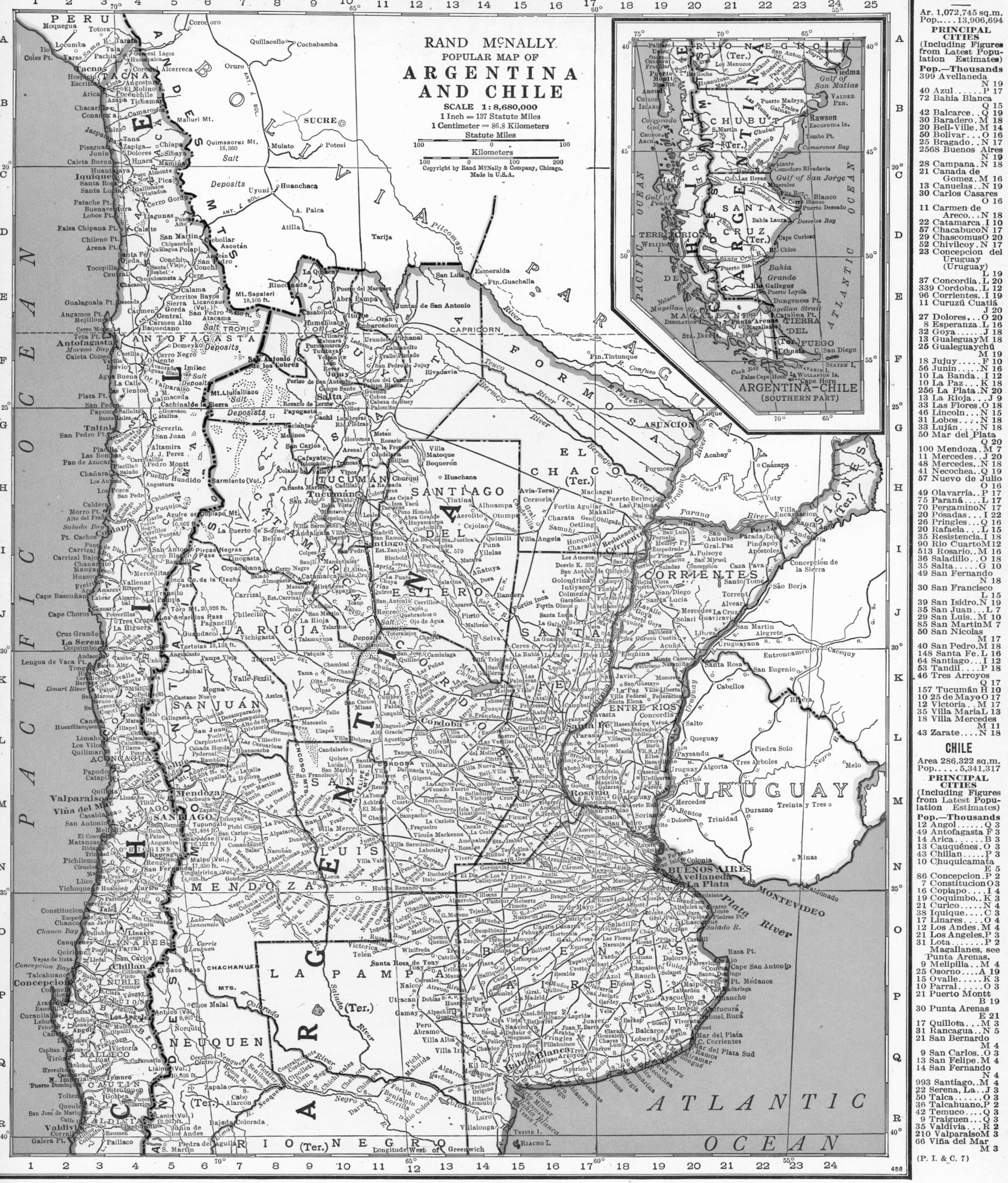

RAND McNALLY
POPULAR MAP OF
**ARGENTINA
AND CHILE**

SCALE 1 : 8,680,000
1 Inch = 137 Statute Miles
1 Centimeter = 86.8 Kilometers
Statute Miles

Copyright by Rand McNally & Company, Chicago.
Made in U.S.A.

ARGENTINA-CHILE
(SOUTHERN PART)

ARGENTINA

Ar. 1,072,745 sq.m.
Pop..... 13,906,694

**PRINCIPAL
CITIES**
(Including Figures
from Latest Popu-
lation Estimates)
Pop.—Thousands
399 Avellaneda
.........N 19
40 Azul......P 17
72 Bahia Blanca
.........Q 15
42 Balcarce..Q 19
30 Baradero..Q 19
20 Bell-Ville.M 14
50 Bolivar...O 16
25 Bragado..N 17
2568 Buenos Aires
.........N 19
28 Campana..N 18
21 Canada de
Gomez..M 16
13 Canuelas..N 19
30 Carlos Casares
.........O 16
11 Carmen de
Areco....N 18
22 Catamarca.I 10
57 ChacabucoN 17
29 ChascomusO 19
52 Chivilcoy.N 17
23 Concepcion del
Uruguay
(Uruguay)
.........L 19
37 Concordia.L 20
339 Cordoba..L 12
96 Corrientes.I 19
11 Curuzu Cuatia
.........J 20
27 Dolores...O 20
8 Esperanza.L 16
32 Goya......J 18
13 GualeguayM 18
25 Gualeguaychú
.........M 19
18 Jujuy....F 10
56 Junin....N 16
10 La Banda..H 9
10 La Paz....K 18
266 La Plata..N 20
33 La Rioja...J 8
33 Las Flores.O 18
46 Lincoln...N 15
31 Lobos....N 18
33 Lujan....N 18
50 Mar del Plata
.........Q 20
100 Mendoza..M 7
11 Mercedes..J 20
48 Mercedes..N 18
41 Necochea..Q 19
57 Nuevo de Julio
.........O 17
49 Olavarria..P 17
75 Parana....L 17
70 PergaminoN 17
20 Posadas...I 22
26 Pringles..Q 16
62 Rafaela...L 15
85 Resistencia.I 18
90 Rio CuartoM12
513 Rosario..M 16
36 Saladillo..O 18
35 Salta.....G 10
49 San Fernando
.........N 18
30 San Francisco
.........L 15
39 San Isidro.N 19
35 San Juan..L 7
29 San Luis..M 10
85 San MartinM 7
50 San Nicolas
.........M 17
40 San Pedro.M 18
148 Santa Fe.L 16
64 Santiago..I 12
53 Tandil...P 18
46 Tres Arroyos
.........Q 17
157 Tucuman.H 10
10 25 de MayoO 17
12 Victoria..M 17
35 Villa MariaL 13
18 Villa Mercedes
.........M 11
43 Zarate....N 18

CHILE

Area 286,322 sq.m.
Pop.....5,341,317

**PRINCIPAL
CITIES**
(Including Figures
from Latest Popu-
lation Estimates)
Pop.—Thousands
12 Angol....N 3
43 Antofagata F 3
14 Arica....B 3
13 Cauquénes.O 3
43 Chillan...P 3
10 Chuquicamata
.........E 5
86 Concepcion.P 2
7 Constitucion.O 3
16 Copiapo...I 4
19 Coquimbo..K 3
21 Curico....N 4
38 Iquique...C 3
12 Linares...N 4
10 Los Andes.M 4
21 Los Angeles.P 3
31 Lota.....P 2
Magallanes, see
Punta Arenas
9 Melipilla..M 4
25 Osorno....A 19
15 Ovalle....K 3
10 Parral....N 4
21 Puerto Montt
.........B 19
30 Punta Arenas
.........E 21
17 Quillota...M 3
31 Rancagua..N 5
21 San Bernardo
.........M 4
9 San Carlos.O 3
13 San Felipe.M 4
14 San Fernando
.........N 4
993 Santiago..M 4
22 Serena, La..J 3
50 Talca....O 3
42 Talcahuano.P 2
9 Traiguen..Q 3
9 Temuco...Q 3
93 Valdivia..R 2
210 ValparaisoM 3
66 Viña del Mar
.........M 3

(P. I. & C. 7)

456

BOLIVIA

Area 416,040 sq.m.
Pop.....3,533,090

PRINCIPAL CITIES

(Including Figures from Latest Population Estimates)

Pop.—Thousands

6 Acacio	J 8
9 Achacachi	H 3
5 Achiri	I 3
3 Achocalla	H 4
7 Aigachi	H 3
4 Aiquile	J 9
5 Alcalá	K 11
9 Ancoraimes	G 2
11 Anzaldo	I 8
4 Araca	I 5
5 Arani	I 8
6 Aroma ó Sicasica	I 5
5 Ascención	G 14
6 Ayata	G 3
5 Ayoayo	I 4
3 Azurduy	L 12
5 Betanzos	K 9
3 Bolivar	J 7
4 Caiza	L 9
4 Calacoto	I 3
3 Calamarca	H 4
4 Calcha	L 10
3 Callapa	I 4
3 Camata	G 3
6 Capinota	I 7
4 Caquiaviri	I 3
5 Caracollo	I 6
4 Cavari	I 6
4 Challacollo	I 6
5 Challapata	K 6
4 Charagua	K 13
5 Charazani	G 2
4 Chayanta	J 7
4 Chuma	G 3
5 Cliza	J 8
60 Cochabamba	I 7
5 Colomi	I 8
6 Colquechaca	J 8
6 Comarapa	J 11
5 Concepcion	H 16
8 Copacabana	H 2
5 Corque	J 5
8 Cotagaita	M 9
5 Cotoca	I 14
5 Escoma	G 2
4 General Saavedra	I 13
5 Huanchaca	L 7
3 Huaqui	H 3
6 Huarina	H 3
2 Independencia	I 7
6 Italaque	G 2
5 Izozog	K 14
4 Junchara	N 10
5 Lagunillas	K 13
7 Laja	H 4
301 La Paz	H 4
4 Livilivi	M 10
5 Macha	J 8
3 Machaca	J 7
6 Mocomoco	G 2
3 Molinero	J 9
4 Monteagudo	K 12
5 Morachata	I 7
3 Moromoro	J 12
50 Oruro	J 6
4 Padilla	K 11
4 Parapiti Grande	
5 Pária	L 8
5 Peñas	H 3
5 Pescado	K 11
5 Pitantora	J 9
3 Pocpo	J 9
7 Pojo	I 10
3 Poopo	J 6
4 Portachuelo	I 13
40 Potosi	K 8
3 Presto	K 11
4 Pucará	J 12
4 Pucarani	H 3
4 Pulacayo	L 7
4 Punata	I 8
14 Quillacollo	I 7
5 Riberalta	B 7
18 Sacaba	I 8
11 Sacaca	J 7
5 Salinas	K 5
7 Salinas de Yocalla	I 7
5 Samaipata	J 12
8 San Benito	I 8
3 San Ignacio	I 12
4 San José	I 17
11 San Lucas	L 10
7 Sta. Ana de Calacala	I 7
33 Sta. Cruz	I 13
8 Santiago de Hauta	H 3
4 Santiago de Machaca	I 2
8 Santibanez	I 7
4 Sipesipe	I 7
30 Sucre	K 9
5 Talabera ó Puna	K 9
8 Talina	M 8
4 Tapacari	I 7
9 Tarabuco	K 10
4 Tarata	I 8
27 Tarija	M 11
4 Tarvita	L 11
10 Tinguipaya	K 8
7 Tintin	J 9
7 Tiraque	I 8
7 Toco	I 8
6 Tomahe	L 9
4 Toropalca	L 9
7 Totora	I 9
7 Trinidad	F 10
7 Tupiza	M 8
4 Turuchipa	K 10
5 Uioma	I 3
5 Umala	I 4
5 Uyuni	L 7
6 Vacas	I 8
6 Vallegrande	J 12
3 Ventila	I 7
4 Vilavila	I 7
3 Villar	K 11
3 Vitichi	L 10
7 Warnes	I 13
5 Yamparaez	K 10
4 Yura	L 8

(P. I. & C. 78)

RAND McNALLY
POPULAR MAP OF
BRAZIL
AND GUIANAS
SCALE 1:15,840,000
1 Inch = 250 Statute Miles
1 Centimeter = 158 Kilometers
Statute Miles
Kilometers
Copyright by Rand McNally & Company, Chicago.
Made in U.S.A.

BRAZIL
Ar. 3,286,169 sq. m.
Pop....45,300,000
PRINCIPAL
CITIES
(Including Figures
from Latest Popu-
lation Estimates)
Pop.—Thousands
13 Alagoinhas.I 22
51 Aracajú....I 23
16 Araguary...L 14
32 Bagé.....Q 10
Baía, see
Salvador.
19 Barbacena..
M 17
17 Barretos..M 14
33 Baurú....N 13
167 Belém...E 14
180 Belo Hori-
zonte..M 17
14 Blumenau.P 13
17 Cachoeira.Q 10
19 Cachoeira do
Itapemirim
M 19
34 Campina
Grande..G 24
79 Campinas..
N 15
23 Campo
Grande..F 21
53 Campos...N 19
17 Caxias....P 12
Ceara, see
Fortaleza.
13 Corumbá...L 7
16 Cruz Alta..P 10
19 Cuiabá....K 8
101 Curitiba..O 13
14 Feira de Sant'
Anna...I 21
25 Florianopolis
P 14
142 Fortaleza.F 22
16 Garanhuns H 24
15 Goiânia...K 14
16 Guaratinguetá
N 16
16 Ilheos....J 21
14 Itabuna..J 21
14 Itajahy..P 14
15 Itajuba..N 16
13 Itapetininga
N 14
13 Jequié...J 21
73 João Pessoa
(Parahiba)
G 25
17 Joinville..O 13
52 Juiz de Fora
M 17
30 Jundiahy..N 15
86 Maceio...I 23
68 Manaus
(Manáos)..E 5
14 Montes Claros
K 18
14 Mossoró..F 23
52 Natal....G 25
13 Nazareth..J 21
126 Niteroi
(Nictheroy)
N 18
16 Nova Friburgo
N 18
23 Parnahyba.F 20
18 Passo Fundo
P 11
63 Pelotas..Q 11
30 Ponta Grossa
O 12
263 Porto Alegre
Q 12
328 Recife..M 14
48 Ribeirão Preto
N 15
1564 Rio de
Janeiro.N 18
50 Rio Grande
Q 11
293 Salvador
(Baía)..J 22
27 Sant' Anna do
Livramento
Q 9
160 Santos..N 15
25 São Carlos do
Pinhal..M 14
23 São João d'el
Rey..M 17
14 São Leopoldo
Q 12
59 São Luiz
(Maranhao) E 18
1254 São Paulo
N 15
14 Sobral..F 21
12 Theophilo-
Ottoni..L 19
35 Teresina..F 19
34 Uberaba..L 14
22 Urusyayana Q 8
43 Vitória...M 20
30 Volta Redonda
N 16

GUIANA
(British)
Area..89,480 sq. m.
Pop......364,694
PRINCIPAL
CITIES
(Including Figures
from Latest Popu-
lation Estimates)
Pop.—Thousands
73 Georgetown A 7
11 New Amster-
dam....B 7
GUIANA
(Neth.)
Area..54,291 sq. m.
Pop......189,436
PRINCIPAL
CITY
(Including Figures
from Latest Popu-
lation Estimates)
Pop.—Thousands
61 Paramaribo.B 9
GUIANA & ININI
(French)
Area..34,354 sq. m.
Pop......36,975
PRINCIPAL
CITY
(Including Figures
from Latest Popu-
lation Estimates)
Pop.—Thousands
12 Cayenne..B 11
(P. I. & C. 67)

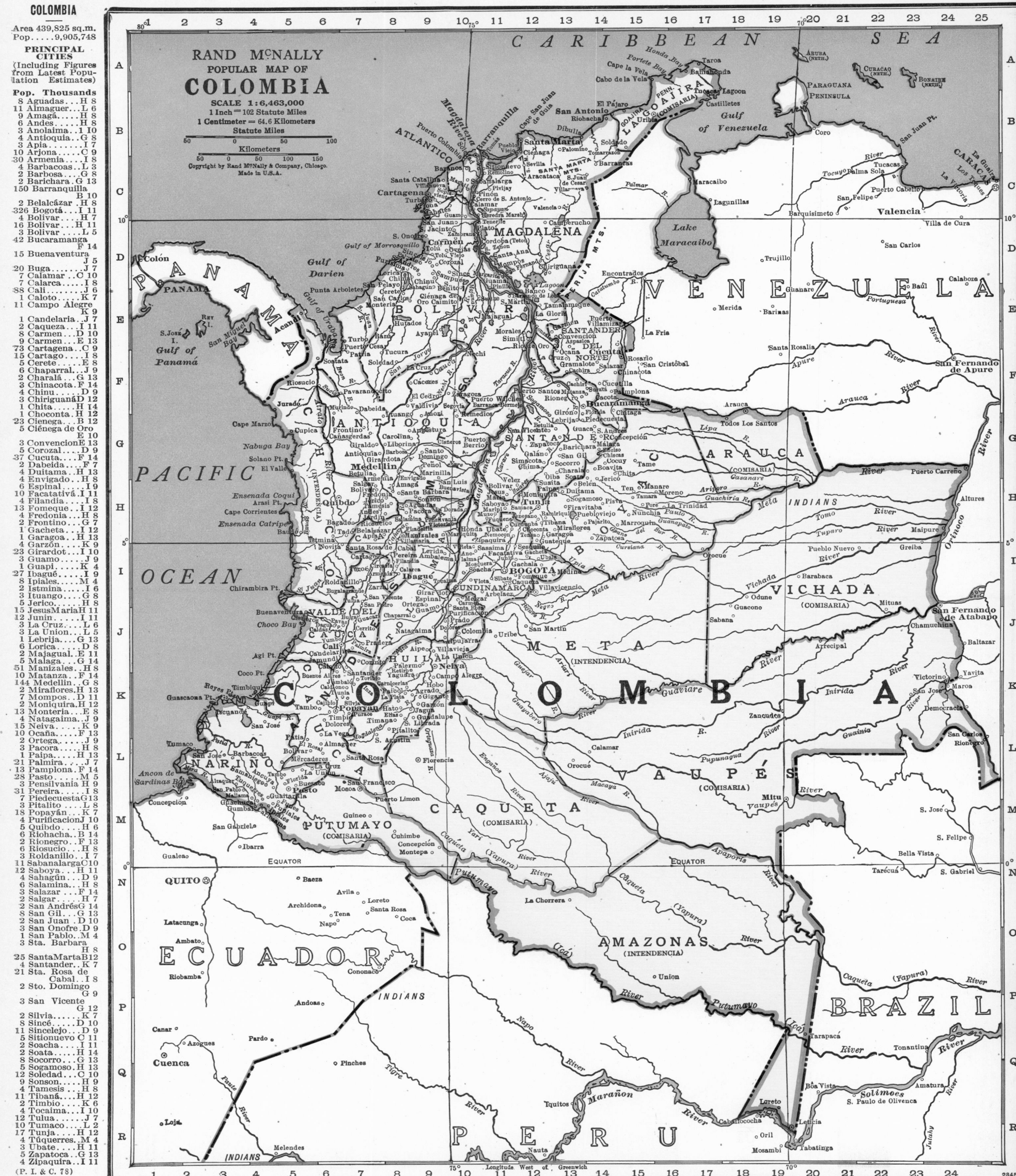

COLOMBIA

Area 439,525 sq. m.
Pop. 9,905,748

PRINCIPAL CITIES
(Including Figures from Latest Population Estimates)

RAND McNALLY
POPULAR MAP OF
COLOMBIA
SCALE 1:6,463,000
1 Inch = 102 Statute Miles
1 Centimeter = 64.6 Kilometers
Statute Miles
Kilometers
Copyright by Rand McNally & Company, Chicago.
Made in U.S.A.

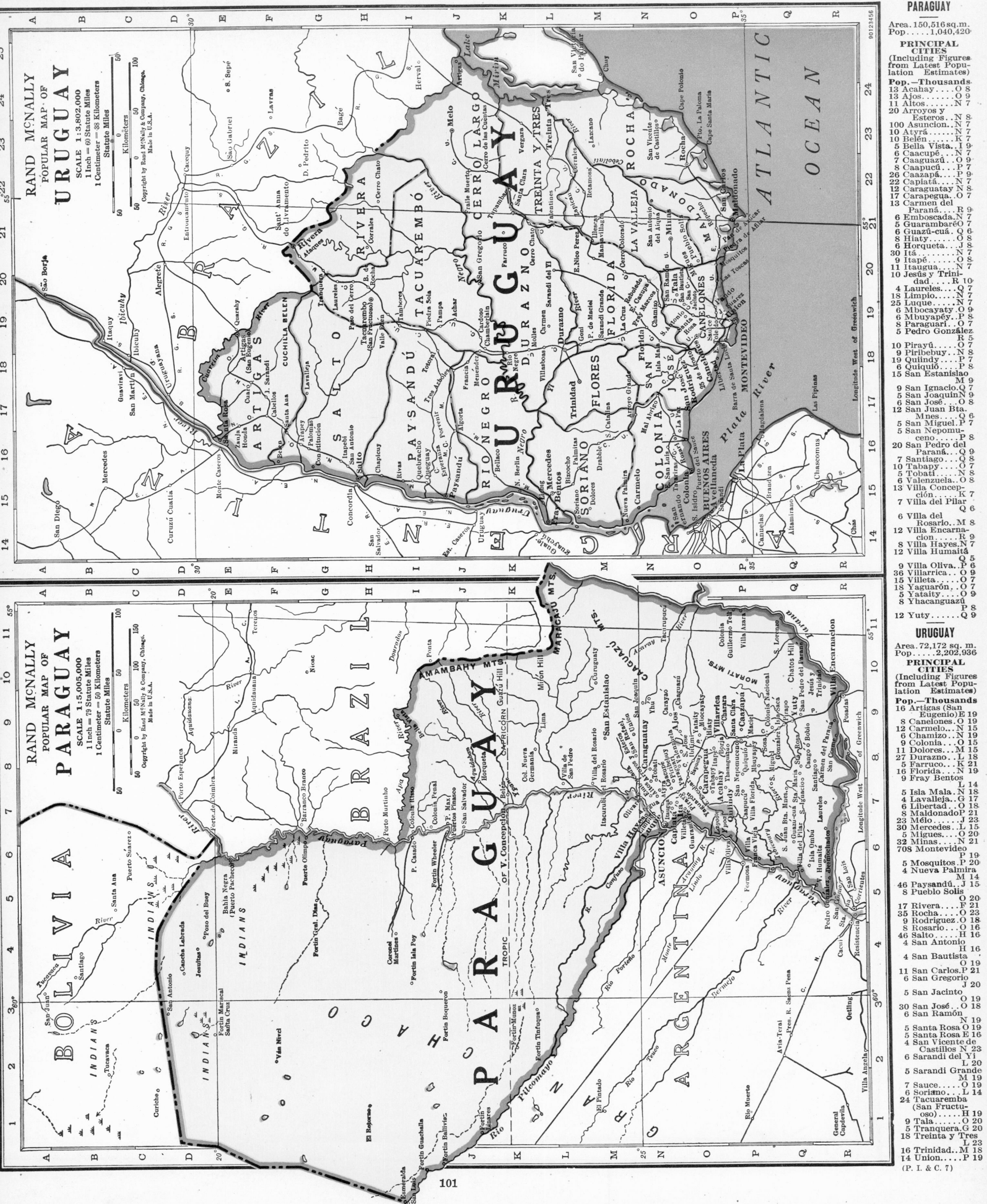

101

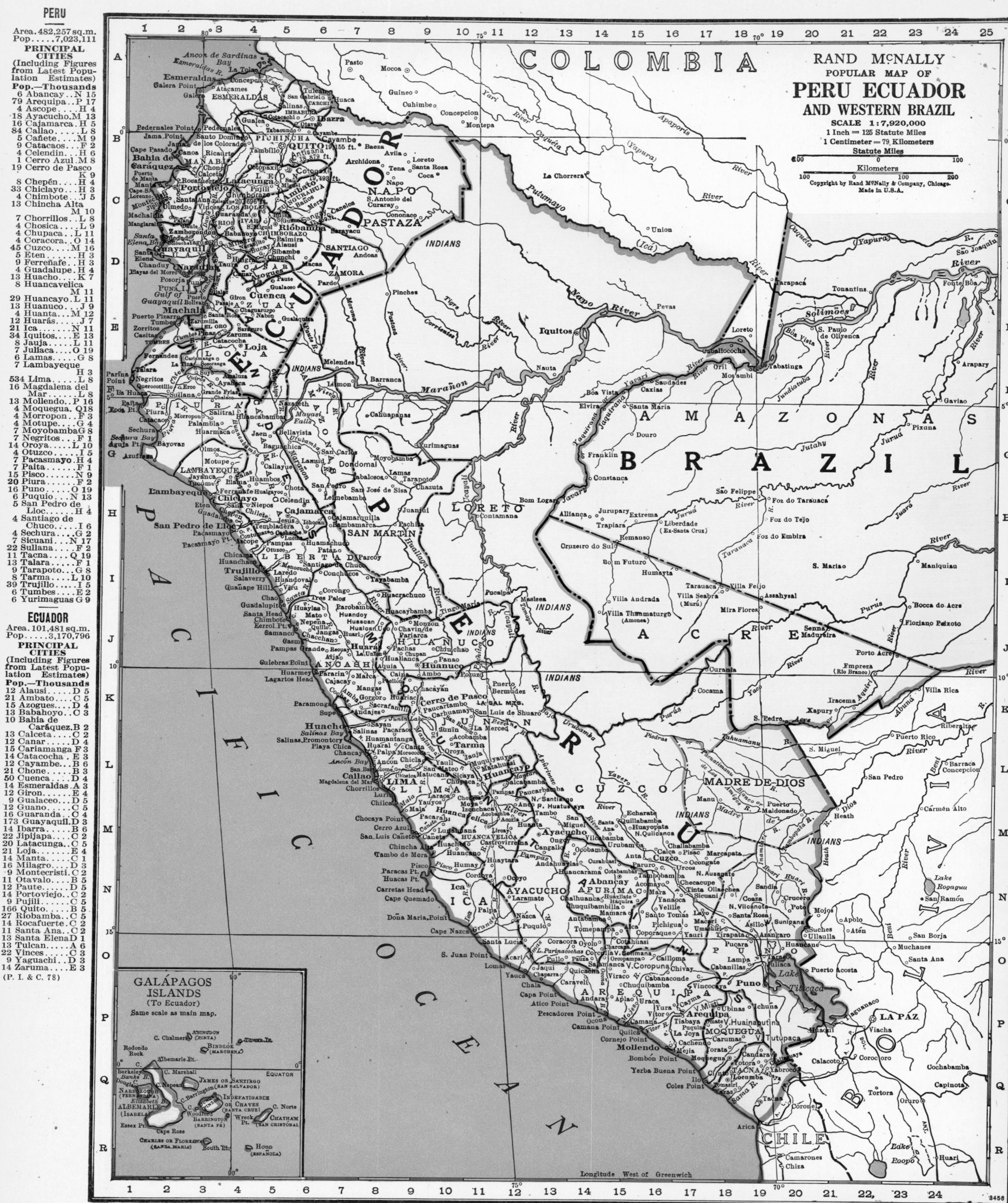

PERU

Area. 482,257 sq. m.
Pop.....7,023,111

PRINCIPAL CITIES
(Including Figures from Latest Population Estimates)

Pop.—Thousands
6 Abancay....N 15
79 Arequipa....P 17
4 Ascope....H 4
18 Ayacucho.M 13
16 Cajamarca. H 5
84 Callao....L 8
9 Cañete....M 9
5 Catacaos....F 2
1 Cerro Azul.M 8
19 Cerro de Pasco K 9
8 Chepén....H 4
33 Chiclayo...H 3
4 Chimbote....J 5
13 Chincha Alta M 10
7 Chorrillos..L 8
4 Chosica...L 11
4 Chupaca...L 11
4 Coracora...O 14
45 Cuzco....M 16
8 Eten....H 3
9 Ferreñafe..H 3
4 Guadalupe. H 4
13 Huacho....K 7
8 Huancavelica M 11
29 Huancayo..L 11
13 Huanuco....J 9
4 Huanta...M 12
12 Huaras....J 7
21 Ica....N 11
34 Iquitos....E 13
8 Jauja....L 11
7 Juliaca....O 19
6 Lamas....G 8
7 Lambayeque H 3
534 Lima....L 8
16 Magdalena del Mar....L 8
13 Mollendo..P 16
4 Moquegua. Q18
4 Moropon..F 2
4 Motupe....G 4
7 Moyobamba G 8
7 Negritos....F 1
14 Oroya....L 10
7 Otuzco....I 5
7 Pacasmayo. H 4
1 Paita....F 1
15 Pisco....N 9
20 Piura....F 2
16 Puno....O 19
5 Puquio....N 14
5 San Pedro de Lloc....H 4
4 Santiago de Chuco....I 6
4 Sechura....G 2
7 Sicuani....N 17
22 Sullana....F 2
11 Tacna....Q 19
13 Talara....F 1
7 Tarapoto..G 8
8 Tarma....L 10
39 Trujillo....I 5
6 Tumbes....E 2
6 Yurimaguas G 9

ECUADOR

Area. 101,481 sq.m.
Pop.....3,170,796

PRINCIPAL CITIES
(Including Figures from Latest Population Estimates)

Pop.—Thousands
12 Alausi....D 5
21 Ambato....C 5
15 Azogues....D 4
10 Babahoyo..C 3
10 Bahia de Caráquez.B 2
13 Calceta....C 2
12 Canar....D 4
15 Cariamanga F 3
14 Catacocha. E 3
12 Cayambe....B 6
21 Chone....B 3
50 Cuenca....D 4
14 Esmeraldas. A 3
12 Giron....E 4
9 Gualaceo. D 5
12 Guano....C 5
16 Guaranda.. C 4
173 Guayaquil.D 3
14 Ibarra....B 6
22 Jipijapa...C 2
14 Latacunga. C 5
20 Loja....E 4
14 Manta....C 1
16 Milagro....D 3
9 Montecristi. C 2
11 Otavalo....B 5
12 Paute....D 5
14 Portoviejo. C 2
9 Pujili....C 5
166 Quito....B 5
27 Riobamba.. C 5
14 Rocafuerte. C 2
14 Santa Ana.. C 2
13 Santa Elena D 1
13 Tulcan....A 6
22 Vinces....D 3
9 Yaguachi...D 3
14 Zaruma....E 3
(P. I. & C. 78)

RAND McNALLY
POPULAR MAP OF
PERU ECUADOR
AND WESTERN BRAZIL
SCALE 1:7,920,000
1 Inch = 125 Statute Miles
1 Centimeter = 79 Kilometers
Statute Miles

Kilometers

Copyright by Rand McNally & Company, Chicago.
Made in U.S.A.

GALÁPAGOS ISLANDS
(To Ecuador)
Same scale as main map.

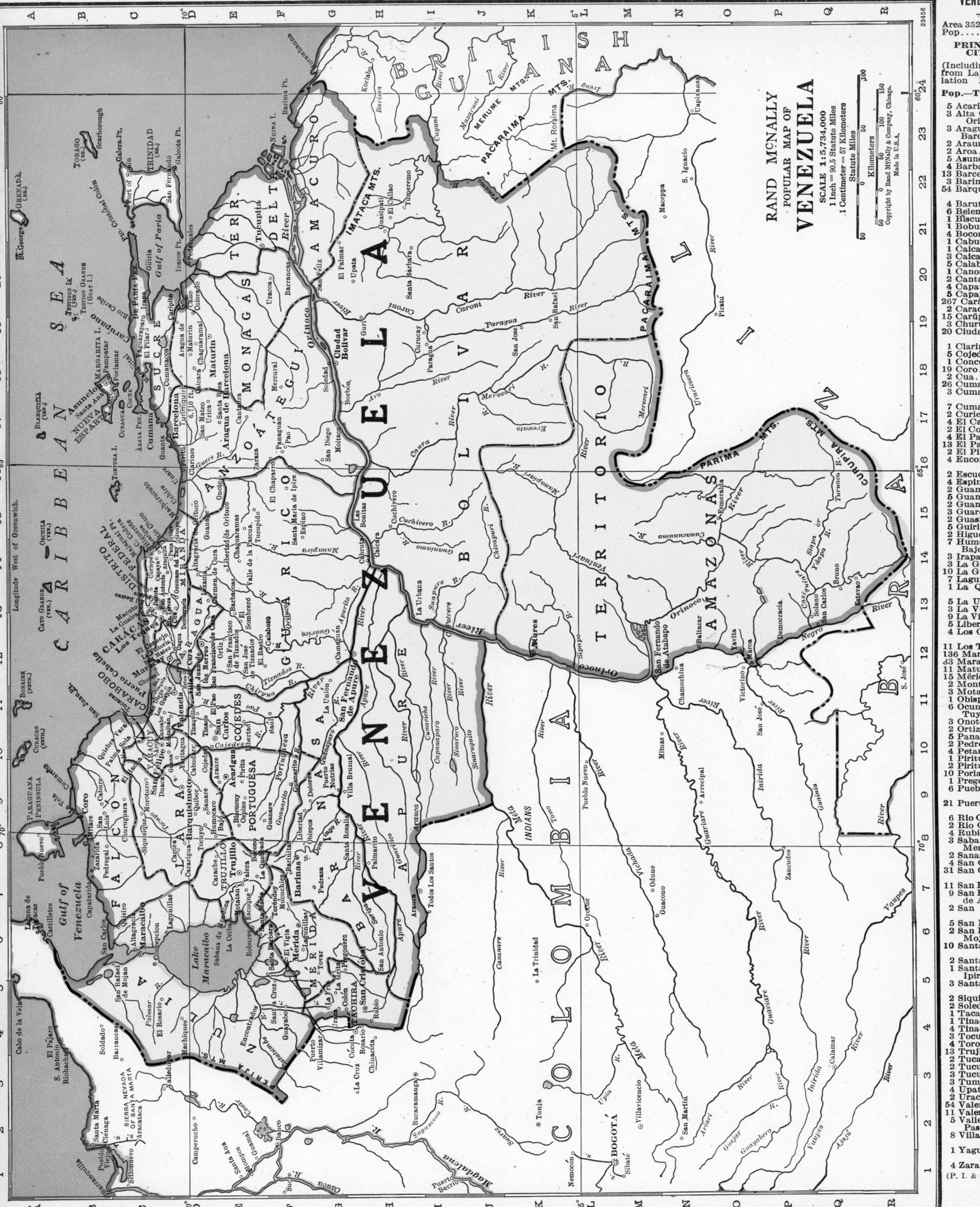

Area 352,141 sq. m.
Pop.....3,850,771

PRINCIPAL CITIES

(Including Figures
from Latest Popu-
lation Estimates)

Pop.—Thousands

5 Acarigua...E 9
3 Alta Gracia de
    Orituco..D 14
3 Aragua de
    Barcelona.E 16
2 Araure....E 9
2 Aroa......C 10
5 Asunción..B 18
4 Barbacoas..E 13
13 Barcelona.D 17
3 Barinitas..F 7
54 Barquisimeto
    D 9
4 Baruta.....C 13
6 Belen.....D 12
1 Biscucuy...E 8
4 Boburés....E 8
4 Bocono....E 8
1 Cabudare..D 10
1 Caicara...H 12
3 Caicara...D 18
3 Calabozo..F 12
1 Canoabo...C 11
2 Cantaura..C 17
4 Capatarida.B 7
5 Capaya....C 14
267 Caracas...C 13
2 Carache...D 8
15 Carúpano..C 19
3 Churuguara.C 9
20 Ciudad Bolivar
    D 18
1 Clarines...D 16
5 Cojedes...D 10
1 Concepción.C 5
19 Coro......C 9
2 Cua.......D 13
26 Cumana....C 17
3 Cumanacoa
    D 18
7 Cumarebo..B 9
2 Curiepe...C 14
2 El Callao..H 21
2 El Consejo.C 13
4 El Palmar.G 21
13 El Pao....E 11
2 El Pilar...C 19
2 Encontrados
    E 5
2 Escuque...E 7
4 Espino....F 15
2 Guama....D 10
5 Guanape...D 15
2 Guanare...F 9
2 Guarenas..C 13
4 Guaipati..H 21
5 Guiria....C 20
2 Higuerote.C 14
7 Humocaro
    Bajo....D 8
3 Irapa.....C 20
1 La Grita...G 5
10 La Guaira.C 13
7 Lagunillas..F 6
1 La Quebrada
    E 7
5 La Unión..G 12
3 La Vela....B 9
9 La Victoria.D 12
5 Libertad...F 11
4 Los Guayos
    D 11
11 Los Teques.C 13
136 Maracaibo..C 6
43 Maracay..D 12
11 Maturin...D 19
15 Mérida....F 6
2 Montalbán.D 11
3 Motatan...E 7
1 Obispos...F 8
6 Ocumare del
    Tuy....D 13
3 Onoto....E 16
2 Ortiz.....E 12
5 Panaquire.D 14
2 Pedregal...B 8
4 Petare....C 13
1 Piritu....E 9
2 Piritu....D 16
10 Porlamar..C 18
1 Pregonero..G 5
6 Pueblo Nuevo
    A 8
21 Puerto Cabello
    C 11
6 Rio Caribe.C 19
2 Rio Chico.D 14
4 Rubio.....F 5
2 Sabana de
    Mendoza..E 7
2 Sanare....E 8
4 San Carlos.D 10
31 San Cristóbal
    F 5
11 San Felipe.C 10
9 San Fernando
    de Apure.G 12
2 San Joaquin
    D 12
5 San Luis...E 8
2 San Rafael de
    Mojan...B 5
10 Santa Barbara
    F 5
4 Santa Cruz.F 5
1 Santa Maria de
    Ipire....F 16
3 Santa Teresa
    D 13
2 Siquisique.C 9
2 Soledad...G 18
1 Tacarigua.C 14
1 Tinaco....D 11
1 Tinaquillo.D 11
4 Tocuyo...D 8
4 Torondoy..F 6
13 Trujillo...E 7
2 Tucacas...C 11
2 Tucupido..E 15
3 Tucupita..F 21
2 Tumeremo.H 21
4 Upata....G 20
2 Uracoa...F 20
54 Valencia..D 11
11 Valera....E 7
5 Valle de la
    Pascua..E 15
2 Villa de Cura
    D 12
1 Yaguaraparo
    C 6
4 Zaraza....E 16

(P. I. & C. 7)

RAND McNALLY
POPULAR MAP OF
VENEZUELA
SCALE 1:5,734,000
1 Inch = 90.5 Statute Miles
1 Centimeter = 57 Kilometers
Statute Miles
Kilometers
Copyright by Rand McNally & Company, Chicago.
Made in U.S.A.

EUROPE

Ar. 3,771,000 sq. m.
Pop. . .532,600,000

COUNTRIES

ALBANIA . . . . . P 13
Area 10,629 sq. m.
Pop. 1,135,000
ANDORRA . . . . N 7
Area. . . 191 sq. m.
Pop. 6,000
AUSTRIA . . . . M 11
Area. 32,360 sq. m.
Pop 6,760,233
BELGIUM. . . . . K 9
Area. 11,752 sq. m.
Pop. 8,361,220
BULGARIA . . . . O 15
Area. 42,814 sq. m.
Pop 6,734,232
CZECHOSLOVAKIA . . . . L 12
Area. 49,373 sq. m.
Pop 14,004,179
DENMARK . . . H 11
Area. 16,571 sq. m.
Pop 3,776,328
FINLAND . . . . . E 14
Ar. 130,159 sq. m.
Pop 3,947,702
FRANCE . . . . L 8
Ar. 212,421 sq. m.
Pop 41,980,000
GERMANY . . . . . J 11
Area. 137,674 sq.m.
Pop 59,595,000
GIBRALTAR . . . . Q 3
Area . . . . . . 2 sq. m.
Pop. 21,372
GREAT BRITAIN and N. IRELAND H 6
Area. 94,278 sq. m.
Pop 46,688,814
GREECE . . . . . Q 14
Area. 51,145 sq. m.
Pop. 7,485,700
HUNGARY . . . M 13
Area. 35,849 sq. m.
Pop 9,034,815
ICELAND . . . . . . B 5
Area. 39,709 sq. m.
Pop 126,000
IRELAND . . . . . . I 5
Area. 26,592 sq. m.
Pop 2,944,000
ITALY . . . . O 11
Ar. . 116,793 sq. m.
Pop 44,530,000
LIECHTENSTEIN M 10
Area . . . . 65 sq. m.
Pop. 11,218
LUXEMBOURG . K 9
Area . . . . 998 sq.m.
Pop. 296,913
MALTA & GOZO R 11
Area . . . . 122 sq. m.
Pop. 268,668
MONACO . . . . . . N 9
Area . . . 0.5 sq. m.
Pop. 23,994
NETHERLANDS . J 9
Area. 13,202 sq. m.
Pop 9,075,870
NORWAY . . . . . E 11
Ar. . 124,984 sq. m.
Pop. 2,921,000
POLAND. . . . . . K 13
Area. 119,800 sq.m.
Pop 32,390,000
PORTUGAL . . . . O 3
Area. 34,904 sq. m.
Pop 7,185,143
ROMANIA. . . . M 15
Area. 91,600 sq. m.
Pop. . . 17,000,000
SAN MARINO. N 11
Area . . . . 38 sq. m.
Pop. 14,170
SOVIET UNION (Total) G 19
Ar. 8,439,000 sq. m
Pop . . . 195,000,000
SPAIN . . . . . O 4
Area. 190,768 sq.m.
Pop 25,608,000
SWEDEN . . . . . F 12
Ar. . 173,105 sq. m.
Pop. 6,406,474
SWITZERLAND. M 9
Area. 15,940 sq. m.
Pop 4,265,703
TURKEY (in Eur.) P 16
Area. . 9,254 sq. m.
Pop 1,516,000
VATICAN CITY. O 10
Area . . . . 0.5 sq. m.
Pop. 1,025
YUGOSLAVIA. . N 13
Area. 98,436 sq. m.
Pop 15,703,000

PRINCIPAL CITIES

(Including Figures from Latest Population Estimates)

Pop.—Thousands
167 Aberdeen . G 7
782 Amsterdam J 9
278 Anvers (Antwerp) . J 9
495 Athēnai (Athens) . Q 14
468 Baile Atha Cliath (Dublin) I 6
709 Baku . . . . N 23
1081 Barcelona O 7
201 Basel . . . . M 9
415 Belfast . . . . H 7
289 Beograd (Belgrade) N 13
4243 Berlin . . . J 11
151 Bern . . . . . M 9
195 Bilbao . . . . N 6
1013 Birmingham J 7
263 Bordeaux . M 7
324 Bremen . . J 10
625 Breslau . . K 12
411 Bristol . . . . J 7

(P. & I. 789)

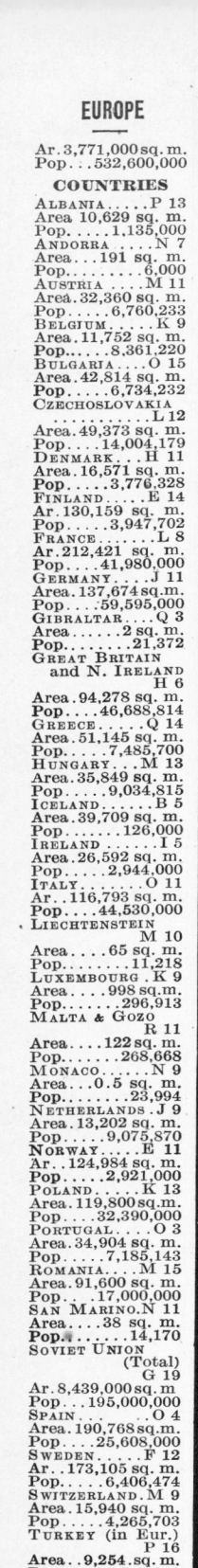

RAND McNALLY
14 x 21 INCH MAP OF
EUROPE
SCALE 1:13,750,000
1 Inch = 217 Statute Miles
1 Centimeter = 137.5 Kilometers
Statute Miles
Kilometers
Names of cities are spelled in their correct local form, which is the proper one to use for commerce and travel. The conventional form is given parenthetically when deemed necessary.
Copyright by Rand McNally & Company, Chicago.
Made in U.S.A.
Longitude West of Greenwich
Longitude East of Greenwich
ARCTIC
ATLANTIC OCEAN
NORTH SEA
English Channel
Bay of Biscay
ICELAND
GREAT BRITAIN
IRELAND
FRANCE
SPAIN
PORTUGAL
GERMANY
BELGIUM
SWITZERLAND
AUSTRIA
DENMARK
NORWAY
MOROCCO
ALGERIA
TUNISIA

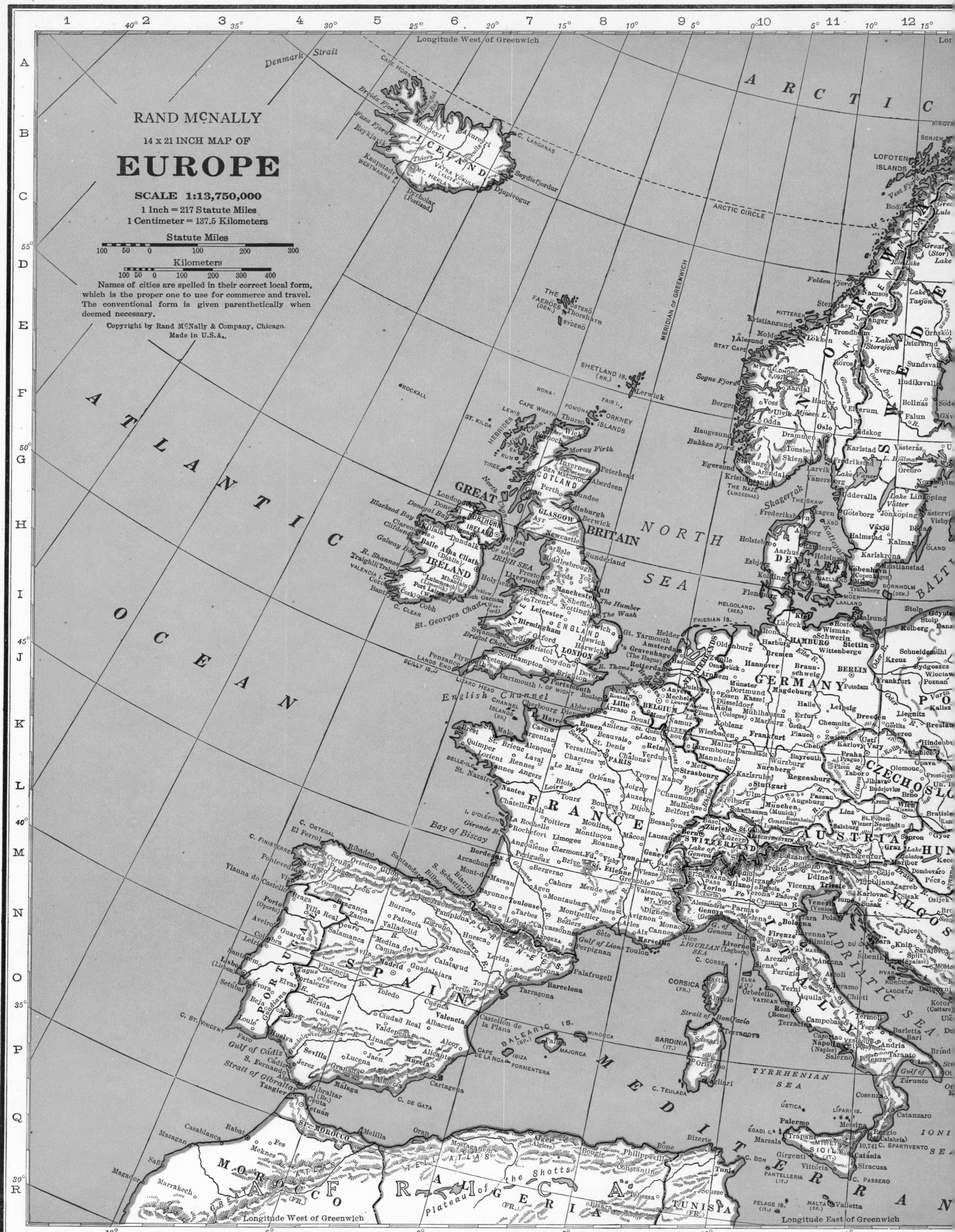

— — 1937 Boundaries in Central and Eastern Europe altered by World War II agreements

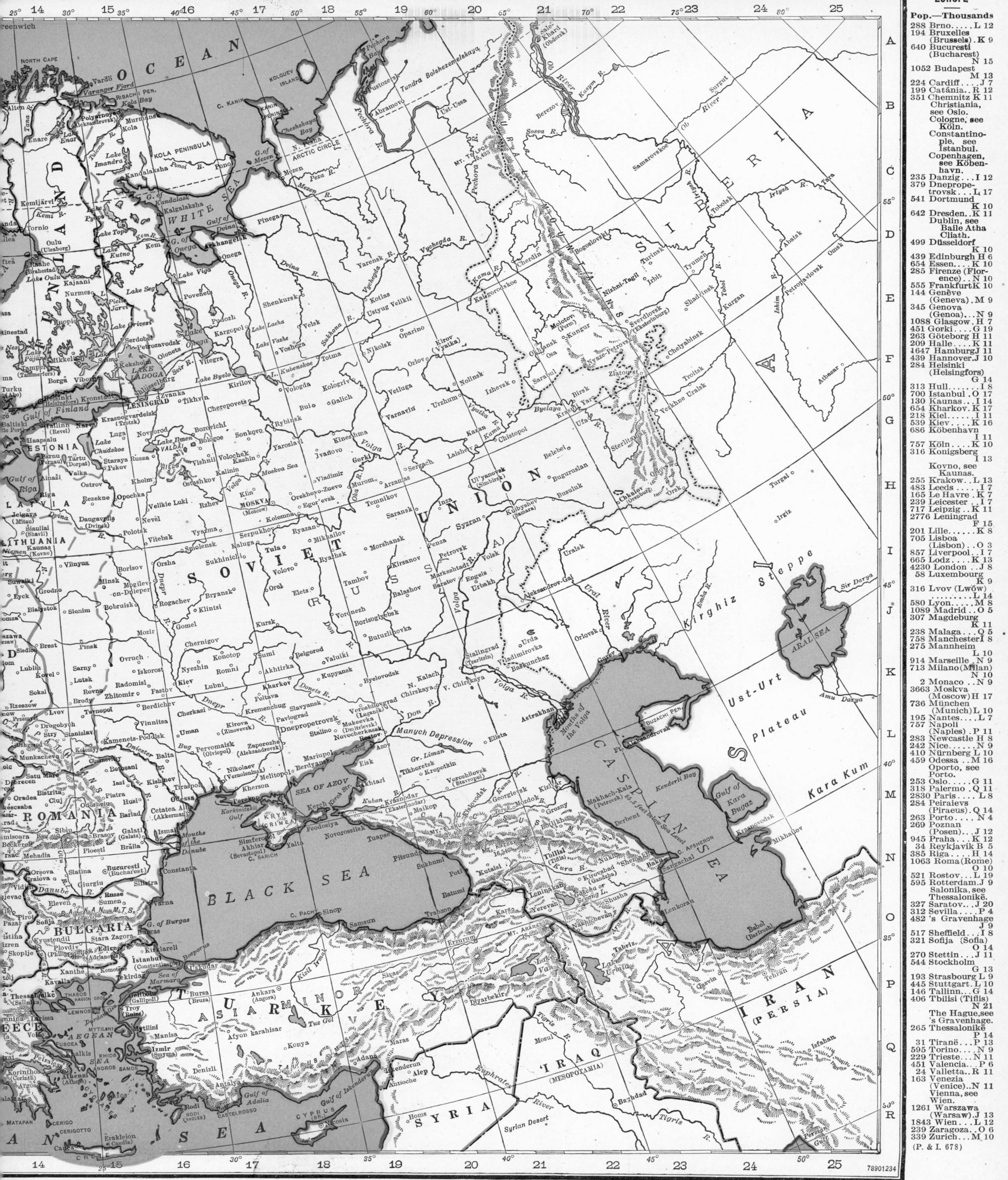

9

78901234

RAND McNALLY
POPULAR MAP OF
BRITISH ISLES
SCALE 1:4,055,000
1 Inch = 64 Statute Miles
1 Centimeter = 40.5 Kilometers
Statute Miles

Copyright by Rand McNally & Company, Chicago.
Made in U.S.A.

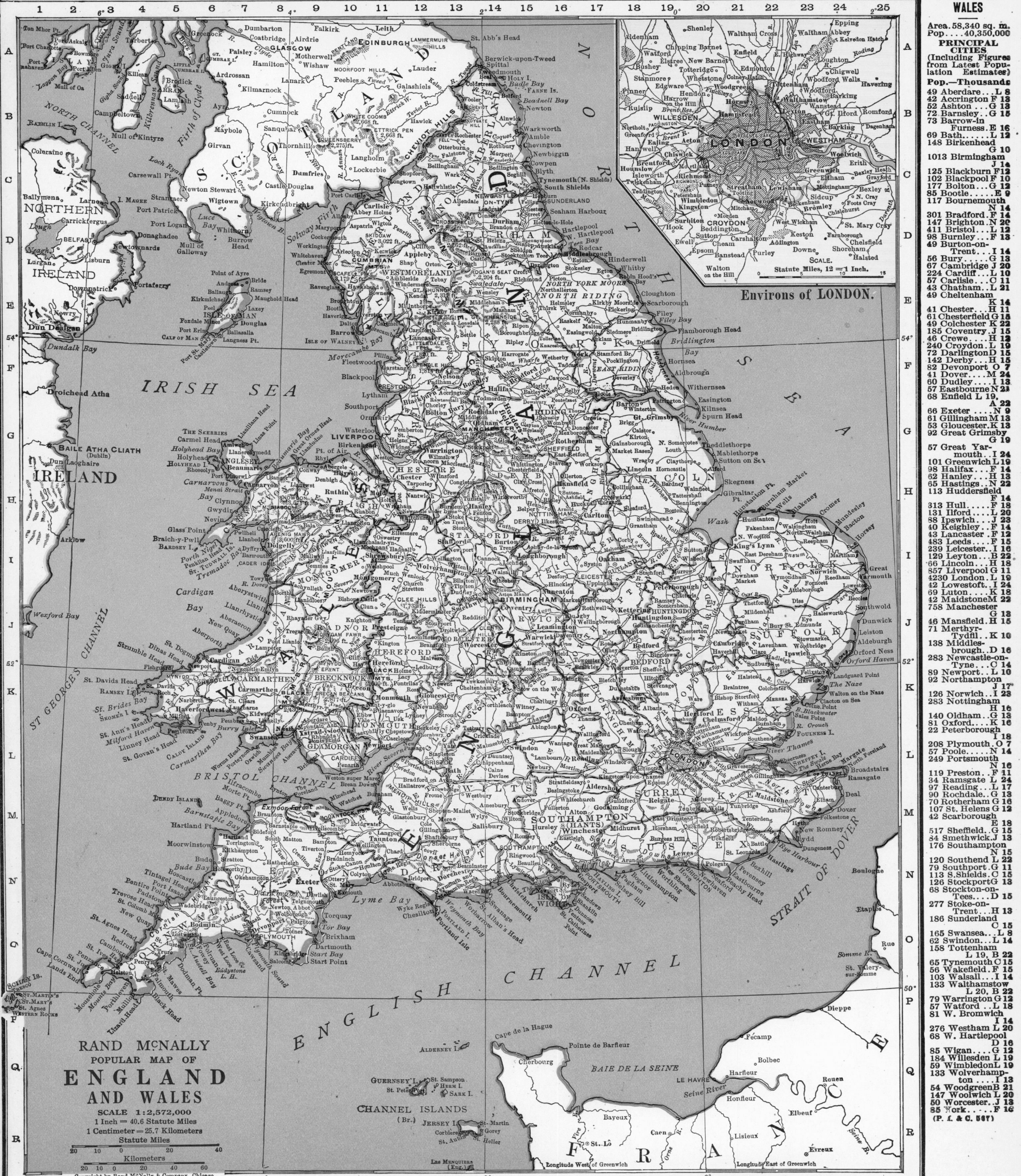

ENGLAND AND WALES

Area, 58,340 sq. m.
Pop....40,350,000

PRINCIPAL CITIES
(Including Figures from Latest Population Estimates)

Pop.—Thousands

49 Aberdare	L 8
42 Accrington	F 13
52 Ashton	G 13
72 Barnsley	G 15
73 Barrow-in Furness	E 16
69 Bath	L 12
148 Birkenhead	G 10
1013 Birmingham	
125 Blackburn	F 12
102 Blackpool	F 10
177 Bolton	F 13
85 Bootle	E 9
117 Bournemouth	N 14
301 Bradford	F 14
147 Brighton	N 20
411 Bristol	L 12
98 Burnley	F 13
49 Burton-on-Trent	I 14
56 Bury	I 12
67 Cambridge	J 20
224 Cardiff	L 9
57 Carlisle	C 11
43 Chatham	L 21
49 Cheltenham	K 14
41 Chester	H 11
61 Chesterfield	G 15
49 Colchester	K 22
185 Coventry	J 15
46 Crewe	H 11
240 Croydon	L 19
72 Darlington	D 15
142 Derby	I 15
82 Devonport	O 7
41 Dover	M 24
60 Dudley	I 13
57 Eastbourne	N 21
68 Enfield	L 19
	A 22
66 Exeter	N 9
61 Gillingham	M 13
53 Gloucester	K 13
92 Great Grimsby	G 19
57 Great Yarmouth	I 24
101 Greenwich	L 19
98 Halifax	F 14
62 Hanley	F 13
65 Hastings	N 22
113 Huddersfield	F 14
313 Hull	F 18
131 Ilford	L 20
88 Ipswich	J 23
40 Keighley	F 14
48 Lancaster	F 12
483 Leeds	F 15
239 Leicester	I 16
129 Leyton	B 22
66 Lincoln	H 18
857 Liverpool	G 11
4230 London	L 19
42 Lowestoft	I 24
69 Luton	K 18
42 Maidstone	M 22
758 Manchester	
	G 13
46 Mansfield	H 15
71 Merthyr-Tydfil	K 10
138 Middlesbrough	D 16
283 Newcastle-on-Tyne	C 14
89 Newport	L 10
92 Northampton	
	J 17
126 Norwich	I 23
283 Nottingham	
	H 16
140 Oldham	G 13
81 Oxford	K 17
22 Peterborough	
	I 18
208 Plymouth	O 7
57 Poole	N 14
249 Portsmouth	
	N 16
119 Preston	F 11
34 Ramsgate	L 24
97 Reading	L 17
90 Rochdale	G 13
70 Rotherham	G 16
107 St. Helens	G 12
42 Scarborough	
	D 18
517 Sheffield	G 16
84 Smethwick	J 13
176 Southampton	
	N 15
120 Southend	L 22
79 Southport	G 11
113 S. Shields	C 15
126 Stockport	G 13
68 Stockton-on-Tees	D 15
277 Stoke-on-Trent	H 13
186 Sunderland	
	C 15
165 Swansea	L 8
62 Swindon	L 14
158 Tottenham	
	L 19, B 22
65 Tynemouth	C 15
56 Wakefield	F 15
103 Walsall	I 14
133 Walthamstow	
	L 20, B 22
79 Warrington	G 12
57 Watford	L 18
81 W. Bromwich	
	I 14
276 Westham	L 20
68 W. Hartlepool	
	D 16
85 Wigan	G 12
184 Willesden	L 19
59 Wimbledon	L 19
133 Wolverhampton	I 13
54 Woodgreen	B 21
147 Woolwich	L 20
50 Worcester	J 13
85 York	F 16

(P. L. & C. 597)

Environs of LONDON.

SCALE.
Statute Miles, 12 = 1 Inch.

RAND McNALLY POPULAR MAP OF ENGLAND AND WALES

SCALE 1:2,572,000
1 Inch = 40.6 Statute Miles
1 Centimeter = 25.7 Kilometers
Statute Miles

Kilometers

Copyright by Rand McNally & Company, Chicago.
Made in U.S.A.

23456

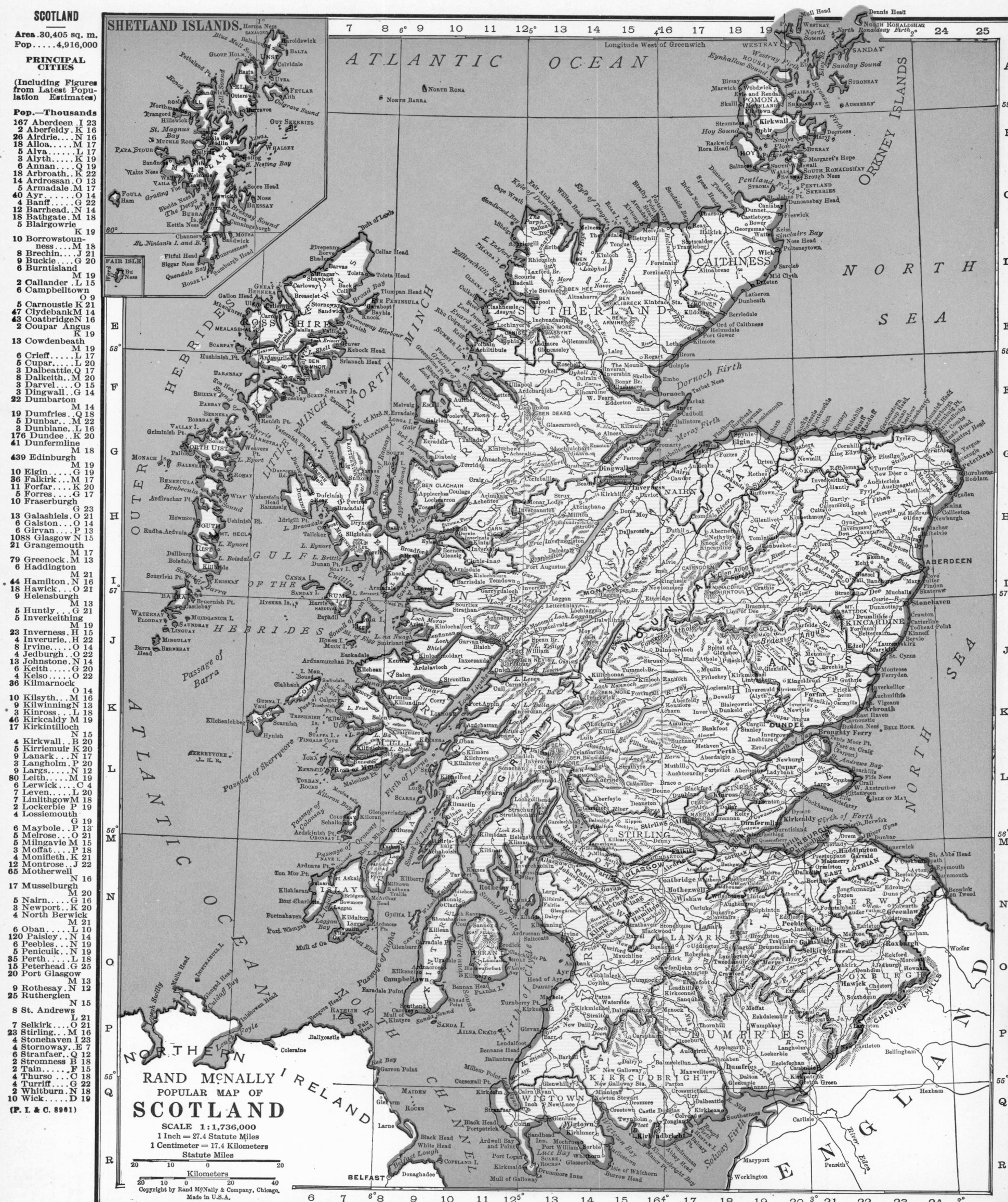

SCOTLAND

Area..30,405 sq. m.
Pop.....4,916,000

PRINCIPAL CITIES

(Including Figures
from Latest Popu-
lation Estimates)

Pop.—Thousands

167	Aberdeen..I 23	
2	Aberfeldy..K 16	
26	Airdrie....N 16	
18	Alloa.....M 17	
3	Alva.....L 17	
3	Alyth....K 19	
6	Annan....Q 19	
18	Arbroath..K 22	
14	Ardrossan..O 13	
5	Armadale..M 14	
40	Ayr......O 14	
4	Banff....G 22	
12	Barrhead..N 14	
18	Bathgate..M 18	
5	Blairgowrie..K 19	
10	Borrowstoun-	
	ness....M 18	
8	Brechin...J 21	
9	Buckie....G 20	
6	Burntisland..M 19	
2	Callander..L 15	
2	Campbelltown..O 9	
5	Carnoustie..K 21	
47	Clydebank..M 14	
43	Coatbridge..N 16	
2	Coupar Angus..K 19	
13	Cowdenbeath..M 19	
6	Crieff.....L 17	
5	Cupar....L 20	
5	Dalbeattie..Q 17	
8	Dalkeith..N 20	
3	Darvel....O 15	
3	Dingwall..G 14	
22	Dumbarton..M 13	
19	Dumfries..Q 18	
5	Dunbar...M 22	
3	Dunblane..L 16	
176	Dundee...K 20	
41	Dunfermline..M 18	
439	Edinburgh..N 19	
13	Elgin....G 19	
36	Falkirk...M 17	
11	Forfar....K 20	
5	Forres....G 17	
5	Fraserburgh..F 23	
13	Galashiels..O 21	
6	Galston...O 14	
6	Girvan....P 13	
1088	Glasgow..N 15	
21	Grangemouth..M 17	
79	Greenock..M 13	
6	Haddington..M 21	
44	Hamilton..N 16	
9	Hawick...O 21	
9	Helensburgh..M 13	
5	Huntly...G 21	
5	Inverkeithing..M 19	
23	Inverness..H 15	
4	Inverurie..H 22	
9	Irvine....O 14	
4	Jedburgh..O 22	
2	Johnstone..N 14	
6	Keith....G 20	
4	Kelso....O 22	
36	Kilmarnock..O 14	
10	Kilsyth...M 16	
9	Kilwinning..N 13	
3	Kinross...L 18	
46	Kirkcaldy..M 19	
17	Kirkintilloch..N 15	
4	Kirkwall..B 20	
4	Kirriemuir..K 20	
9	Lanark...N 17	
3	Langholm..P 20	
9	Largs....M 12	
80	Leith....M 19	
7	Leven....L 20	
7	Linlithgow..M 18	
2	Lockerbie..P 19	
2	Lossiemouth..G 18	
6	Maybole..P 13	
5	Melrose...O 21	
5	Milngavie..M 15	
7	Moffat....P 18	
4	Monifieth..K 21	
12	Montrose..J 22	
65	Motherwell..N 16	
17	Musselburgh..M 20	
5	Nairn....G 16	
4	Newport..K 20	
4	North Berwick..M 21	
8	Oban....L 10	
120	Paisley...N 14	
5	Peebles...N 19	
6	Penicuik..N 19	
35	Perth....L 18	
15	Peterhead..G 23	
20	Port Glasgow..M 13	
9	Rothesay..N 12	
25	Rutherglen..N 15	
8	St. Andrews..L 21	
7	Selkirk...O 21	
23	Stirling...M 16	
5	Stonehaven..I 23	
6	Stornoway..E 7	
6	Stranraer..Q 12	
2	Stromness..B 18	
2	Tain....F 15	
7	Thurso...C 18	
4	Turriff...G 22	
7	Whitburn..N 18	
10	Wick....D 19	

(P. I. & C. 8961)

SHETLAND ISLANDS.

ATLANTIC OCEAN

RAND McNALLY
POPULAR MAP OF
SCOTLAND

SCALE 1:1,736,000

1 Inch = 27.4 Statute Miles
1 Centimeter = 17.4 Kilometers

Statute Miles

Kilometers

Copyright by Rand McNally & Company, Chicago.
Made in U.S.A.

108

690123456

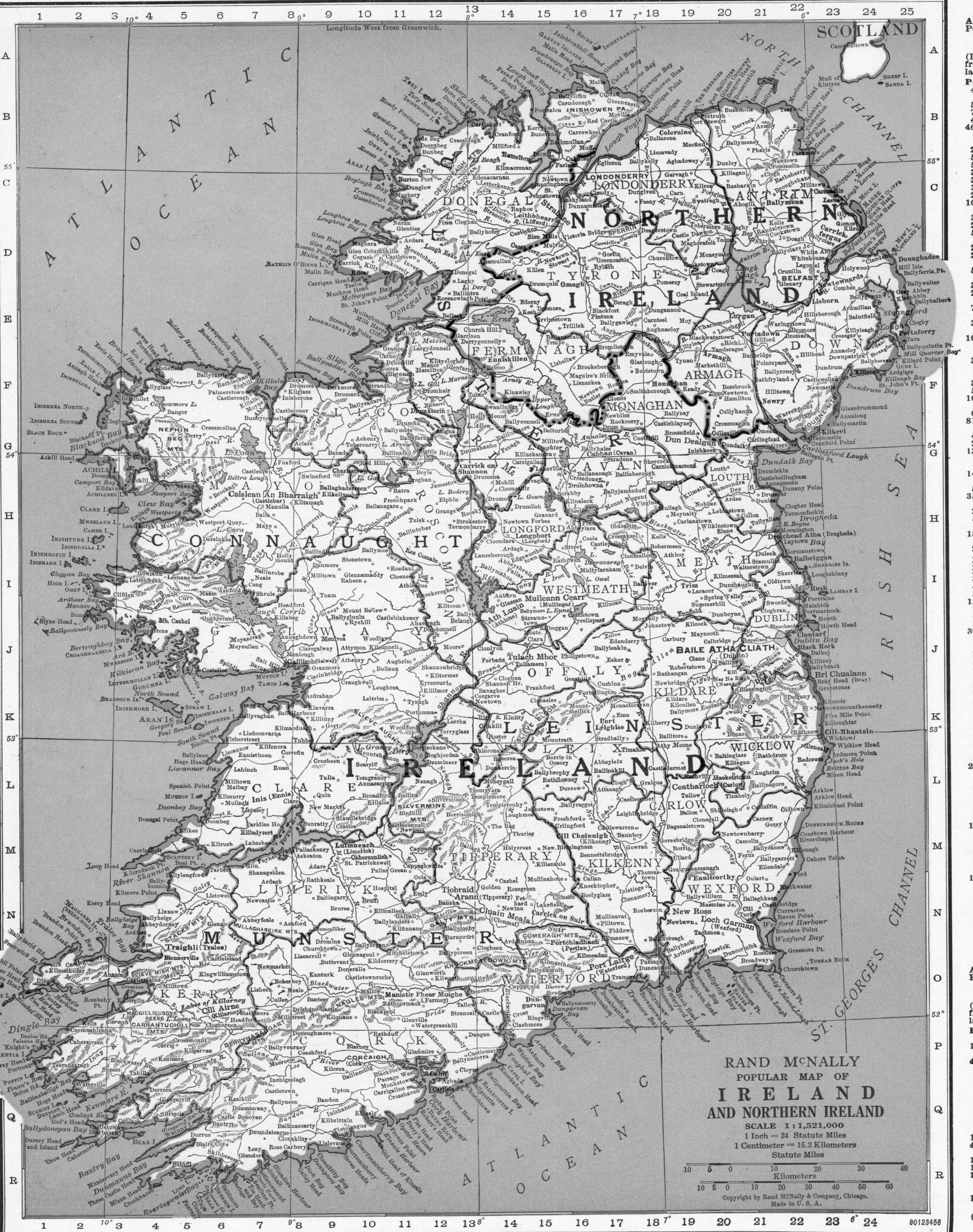

RAND McNALLY
POPULAR MAP OF
IRELAND
AND NORTHERN IRELAND
SCALE 1:1,521,000
1 Inch = 24 Statute Miles
1 Centimeter = 15.2 Kilometers
Statute Miles

Kilometers

Copyright by Rand McNally & Company, Chicago.
Made in U.S.A.

IRELAND

Area..26,592 sq. m.
Pop.....2,944,000
PRINCIPAL CITIES
(Including Figures from Latest Population Estimates)
Pop.—Thousands

4 An Uaimh (Nahan)..	H 20	
5 Arklow...	L 22	
7 Ath Luain..	J 13	
4 Athy...	K 18	
468 Baile Atha Cliath (Dublin)	J 22	
2 Balbriggan..	I 22	
5 Ballina...	G 7	
5 Ballinasloe..	J 12	
9 Bandon...	Q 9	
3 Bantry...	Q 6	
3 Birr.....	K 13	
2 Boyle...	G 12	
10 Bri Chualann..	J 22	
3 Cabhan..	G 16	
3 Cahersiveen	P 2	
5 Caislean An Bharraigh..	H 7	
2 Callan...	M 16	
2 Carrickmacross.....	G 19	
5 Carrick-on Suir.	N 16	
2 Cashel...	M 14	
2 Castleblayney	F 18	
7 Ceatharloch	L 18	
3 Cill Airne (Killarney).	O 5	
10 Cill Choinnigh (Kilkenny)..	M 17	
3 Cill Mhantain (Wicklow)..	K 23	
3 Clonakilty..	Q 8	
3 Clontarf..	J 22	
10 Cluain Meala..	N 15	
6 Cobh...	P 12	
81 Corcaigh (Cork)..	P 11	
4 Dalkey..	J 22	
2 Dingle...	O 2	
13 Droichead Atha (Drogheda)..	H 21	
14 Dun Dealgan (Dundalk).	G 21	
5 Dungarvan..	O 15	
35 Dun Laoghaire.....	J 22	
2 Edenderry..	J 18	
11 Enniscorthy..	N 20	
18 Gaillimh (Galway)..	J 8	
2 Gorey..	M 22	
2 Inis...	K 8	
2 Kildare...	K 18	
2 Kilkee...	M 4	
4 Kilrush...	M 5	
4 Kinsale..	Q 10	
2 Listowel..	N 6	
12 Loch Garman (Wexford)..	N 21	
4 Longphor..	H 14	
3 Loughrea..	K 12	
30 Luimneach (Limerick)..	M 10	
2 Macroom..	P 8	
5 Mallow...	O 10	
4 Manistir Fhear Muighe..	O 12	
3 Midleton..	P 12	
4 Monaghan.	F 18	
5 Muileann Cearr..	I 16	
3 Nas Na Riogh..	J 20	
4 Navan..	H 20	
5 Nenagh...	L 12	
2 Newbridge	K 19	
3 Newcastle..	N 8	
5 New Ross.	N 18	
27 Port Lairge (Waterford)..	O 17	
2 Rathkeale..	M 8	
2 Ros Comain..	I 12	
3 Roscrea..	L 14	
3 Skibbereen..	R 6	
12 Sligeach (Sligo)..	F 12	
2 Templemore	L 14	
5 Thurles..	M 14	
5 Tiobraid Arann (Tipperary)..	N 12	
10 Traighli (Tralee)..	O 4	
4 Tulach Mhor..	J 9	
5 Tullamore..	J 16	
4 Westport..	H 6	

NORTHERN IRELAND

Area..5,237 sq. m.
Pop.....1,279,753
PRINCIPAL CITIES
(Including Figures from Latest Population Estimates)
Pop.—Thousands

7 Armagh...	E 20	
11 Ballymena.	C 22	
3 Ballymoney	B 20	
415 Belfast..	D 23	
5 Carrickfergus	C 23	
8 Coleraine.	B 20	
4 Cookstown	D 19	
5 Downpatrick	D 24	
4 Dungannon	E 19	
5 Enniskillen	F 16	
8 Larne...	C 23	
12 Lisburn..	D 22	
45 Londonderry	C 16	
13 Lurgan...	D 20	
12 Newry...	F 21	
10 Newtownards	D 24	
5 Omagh...	D 16	
12 Portadown.	E 21	
5 Strabane..	C 16	

(P. I. & C. 901)

109

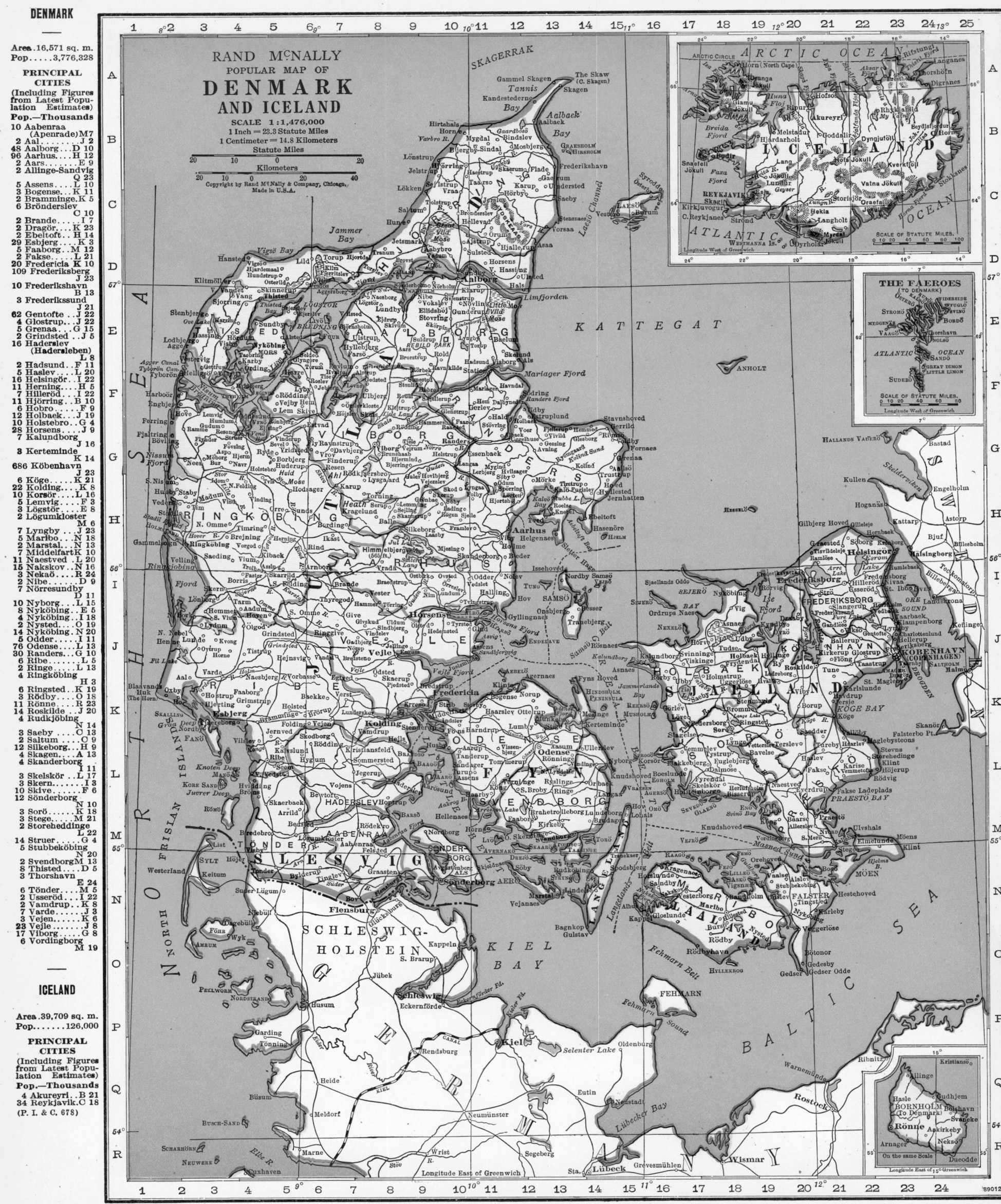

DENMARK

Area .16,571 sq. m.
Pop 3,776,328

PRINCIPAL CITIES
(Including Figures from Latest Population Estimates)
Pop.—Thousands

10 Aabenraa
(Apenrade)M7
28 Aal .... J 2
48 Aalborg ... D 10
98 Aarhus ... H 12
2 Aars ...... E 9
2 Allinge-Sandvig
Q 23
5 Assens .. L 10
3 Bogense .. K 11
6 Bramminge K 5
6 Bröndersev
C 10
2 Brande ... I 7
2 Dragör ... K 23
2 Ebeltoft .. H 14
29 Esbjerg .. K 3
5 Faaborg .. M 12
2 Fakse .... L 21
20 Fredericia K 10
109 Frederiksberg
J 23
10 Frederikshavn
B 13
3 Frederikssund
J 21
62 Gentofte .. J 22
3 Glostrup .. J 22
2 Grenaa ... G 15
2 Grindsted . J 5
16 Haderslev
(Haderleben)
L 8
2 Hadsund .. F 11
5 Haslev ... L 20
16 Helsingör . J 22
11 Herning .. H 5
7 Hilleröd .. I 22
6 Hobro .... F 9
12 Holbaek .. J 19
10 Holstebro . G 4
28 Horsens .. J 9
7 Kalundborg
J 16
3 Kerteminde
K 14
686 Köbenhavn
J 23
6 Köge .... K 21
22 Kolding ... K 8
10 Korsör ... L 16
5 Lemvig ... F 3
3 Lögstör ... E 8
2 Lögumkloster
M 6
7 Lyngby ... J 23
5 Maribo ... N 18
2 Marstal ... N 13
2 MiddelfartK 10
11 Naestved . L 20
15 Nakskov .. N 16
3 Nekaö ... R 24
2 Nibe ..... D 9
7 Nörresundby
C 10
10 Nyborg ... L 15
8 Nyköbing . E 5
4 Nyköbing . I 18
2 Nysted ... O 19
14 Nyköbing . N 20
6 Odder .... I 11
76 Odense ... L 13
30 Randers .. G 10
4 Ribe ..... L 5
3 Ringe .... L 13
4 Ringköbing
H 3
6 Ringsted .. K 19
8 Rödby .... O 18
11 Rönne .... R 23
14 Roskilde .. J 20
2 Rudkjöbing
N 14
3 Saeby ... C 13
2 Saltum ... O 9
12 Silkeborg . H 9
3 Skagen ... A 13
4 Skanderborg
J 11
3 Skelskör .. L 17
3 Skern .... I 3
10 Skive .... F 6
12 Sönderborg
N 10
3 Sorö .... K 18
3 Stege .... M 21
2 Storeheddinge
L 22
14 Struer ... G 4
5 Stubbeköbing
N 20
2 SvendborgM 13
8 Thisted ... D 5
3 Thorshavn
E 24
6 Tönder ... M 5
2 Usseröd .. I 22
2 Vamdrup .. K 8
7 Varde .... K 4
3 Vejen .... K 6
23 Vejle .... J 8
17 Viborg ... G 8
6 Vordingborg
M 19

ICELAND

Area .39,709 sq. m.
Pop 126,000

PRINCIPAL CITIES
(Including Figures from Latest Population Estimates)
Pop.—Thousands

4 Akureyri .. B 21
34 Reykjavik. C 18
(P. I. & C. 678)

110

RAND McNALLY
POPULAR MAP OF
FRANCE
SCALE 1:4,340,000
1 Inch = 68.5 Statute Miles
1 Centimeter = 43.4 Kilometers
Statute Miles

Copyright by Rand McNally & Company, Chicago.
Made in U.S.A.

DÉPARTEMENTS

1	Ain	45	Indre
2	Aisne	46	Indre-et-Loire
3	Allier	47	Isère
4	Alpes-Maritimes	48	Jura
5	Ardèche	49	Landes
6	Ardennes	50	Loir-et-Cher
7	Ariège	51	Loire
8	Aube	52	Loire-Inférieure
9	Aude	53	Loiret
10	Aveyron	54	Lot
11	Basses-Alpes	55	Lot-et-Garonne
12	Basses-Pyrénées	56	Lozère
13A	Belfort Ter.	57	Maine-et-Loire
14	Bouches-du-Rhône	58	Manche
15	Calvados	59	Marne
16	Cantal	60	Mayenne
17	Charente	61	Moselle
18	Charente-Inférieure	62	Meuse
19	Cher	63	Morbihan
20	Corrèze	64	Nièvre
21	Corse (Corsica)	65	Nord
22	Côte-d'Or	66	Oise
23	Côtes du Nord	67	Orne
24	Creuse	68	Pas-de-Calais
25	Deux-Sèvres	69	Puy-de-Dôme
26	Dordogne	70	Pyrénées-Orientales
27	Doubs	71	Rhône
28	Drôme	72	Saône-et-Loire
29	Eure	73	Sarthe
30	Eure-et-Loir	74	Savoie
31	Finistère	75	Seine
32	Gard	76	Seine-Inférieure
33	Gers	77	Seine-et-Marne
34	Gironde	78	Seine-et-Oise
35	Haute-Alpes	79	Somme
36	Haute-Garonne	80	Tarn
37	Haute-Loire	81	Tarn-et-Garonne
38	Haute-Marne	82	Var
39	Hautes-Pyrénées	83	Vaucluse
40	Haute-Saône	84	Vendée
41	Haute-Savoie	85	Vienne
42	Haute-Vienne	86	Vosges
43	Hérault	87	Yonne
44	Ille-et-Vilaine	88	Meurthe-et-Moselle
		89	Haut-Rhin

FRANCE

Area 212,421 sq.m.
Pop.... 41,980,000

PRINCIPAL CITIES
(Including Figures from Latest Population Estimates)

Pop.—Thousands

19	Abbeville	F 13
27	Agen	O 10
43	Aix	P 21
37	Ajaccio	Q 2
30	Albi	O 14
41	Alès	O 18
30	Alfortville	B 7
94	Amiens	F 13
88	Angers	J 8
39	Angouleme	M 10
59	Argenteuil	A 6
29	Arles	P 19
31	Arras	E 15
72	Asnières	A 4
56	Aubervilliers	A 6
24	Auxerre	I 16
59	Avignon	O 20
52	Bastia	P 4
31	Bayonne	P 6
40	Belfort	I 23
65	Besançon	J 22
73	Béziers	P 16
26	Blois	J 12
258	Bordeaux	N 7
52	Boulogne	E 12
97	Boulogne sur Seine	B 4
49	Bourges	I 14
79	Brest	H 1
29	Brive	M 13
61	Caen	G 9
68	Calais	D 13
30	Cambrai	F 15
49	Cannes	P 24
33	Carcassonne	P 14
29	Castres	P 14
33	Chalon-sur-Saône	K 19
36	Chalons-sur-Marne	G 18
28	Chambery	M 21
42	Chartres	H 12
29	Chateauroux	K 12
39	Cherbourg	F 7
23	Cholet	J 8
101	Clermont-Ferrand	L 15
56	Clichy	A 5
24	Colmar	I 23
62	Colombes	A 3
59	Courbevoie	A 3
26	Denain	E 15
26	Dieppe	F 12
96	Dijon	J 19
42	Douai	E 15
43	Drancy	A 7
31	Dunkerque (Dunkirk)	D 14
20	Epernay	G 17
22	Epinal	I 22
20	Fougères	H 7
19	Gennevilliers	A 5
96	Grenoble	M 21
44	Issy-les-Moulineaux	B 4
45	Ivry-sur-Seine	A 5
48	La Rochelle	L 8
32	Laval	I 8
29	Le Creusot	K 18
165	Le Havre	G 9
85	Le Mans	I 10
33	Lens	E 14
65	Levallois-Perret	A 5
201	Lille	E 15
95	Limoges	L 12
46	Lorient	I 4
24	Luneville	H 22
571	Lyon	L 20
914	Marseille	P 20
24	Maubeuge	E 16
83	Metz	G 21
43	Montluçon	K 14
91	Montpellier	P 17
72	Montreuil-sous-Bois	B 7
33	Montrouge	B 5
97	Mulhouse	I 23
12	Nancy	H 22
46	Nanterre	A 4
195	Nantes	J 7
30	Narbonne	P 16
34	Nevers	O 16
242	Nice	O 18
28	Niort	K 9
73	Orleans	I 13
38	Pantin	A 7
2830	Paris	H 14
40	Pau	P 8
26	Perigueux	M 11
72	Perpignan	Q 15
42	Poitiers	K 10
44	Puteaux	B 3
117	Reims	G 17
99	Rennes	I 6
41	Roanne	K 17
26	Rochefort	L 8
107	Roubaix	E 15
123	Rouen	G 12
32	St. Brieuc	H 4
78	St. Denis	A 6
190	St. Etienne	M 19
57	St. Maur-des-Fosses	B 8
43	St. Nazaire	J 4
51	St. Ouen sur Seine	A 6
49	St. Quentin	F 15
37	Sète	P 17
193	Strasbourg	H 24
35	Tarbes	P 10
150	Toulon	P 21
213	Toulouse	P 12
78	Tourcoing	E 15
84	Tours	I 11
58	Troyes	H 17
32	Valence	N 20
43	Valenciennes	E 16
74	Versailles	H 13
25	Vienne	M 19
25	Vichy	L 16
49	Vincennes	B 6
47	Vitry-sur-Seine	C 6

(P. I. & C. 789)

78901234

GERMANY

Area..137,674 sq.m.
Pop....59,595,000

PRINCIPAL CITIES

Pop. Thousands

162	Aachen (Aix la Chapelle)..K 2
177	Augsburg...P 8
4243	Berlin...G 12
121	Bielefeld...H 5
315	Bochum...I 3
99	Bonn.....J 3
63	Brandenburg...G 5
167	Braunschweig...G 8
324	Bremen...F 6
353	Charlottenburg..G 12
351	Chemnitz..K 11
	Cologne, see Köln.
90	Darmstadt.M 5
91	Dessau...H 10
541	Dortmund...I 4
642	Dresden...J 13
440	Duisburg–Hamborn..I 3
140	Erfurt....J 9
654	Essen...I 3
67	Flensburg..B 7
75	Frankfurt.G 14
555	Gera.....K 10
99	Freiburg..Q 3
77	Fürth.....N 8
336	Gelsenkirchen...I 3
194	Gladbach...J 2
92	Görlitz...J 14
48	Gotha....K 8
153	Graz....R 15
148	Hagen....I 4
209	Halle.....J 10
129	Hamborn..I 2
1047	Hamburg..D 8
439	Hannover..G 7
87	Heidelberg.N 5
60	Heilbronn..N 6
62	Hildesheim..H 7
57	Jena......K 9
99	Herne.....I 3
155	Karlsruhe..O 4
175	Kassel....I 6
218	Kiel......C 8
65	Koblenz..K 3
757	Köln.....J 3
165	Krefeld...I 2
717	Leipzig...J 10
138	Lübeck...D 8
106	Ludwigshafen...M 4
307	Magdeburg...H 9
143	Mainz....L 4
275	Mannheim...M 5
131	Mulheim..I 2
736	München (Munich)..Q 4
122	Münster..H 4
410	Nürnberg..N 9
102	Oberhausen.I 3
82	Offenbach.L 5
67	Oldenburg.E 5
94	Osnabrück.G 5
113	Plauen...L 10
70	Potsdam..G 12
106	Recklinghausen...O 10
81	Regensburg...O 10
101	Remscheid..J 3
93	Rostock...C 10
129	Saarbrücken...N 2
140	Solingen...I 3
270	Stettin....E 13
445	Stuttgart..O 5
77	Trier (Treves)..M 2
63	Ulm.....P 7
160	Wiesbaden.L 5
77	Wilhelmshaven...D 5
409	Wuppertal.J 3
101	Würzburg..M 7
87	Zwickau..K 11
(P. I. & C. 678)	

LEGEND

Zones of occupation
F..........French
U.S.........United States
U.S.S.R....Russian
B...........British
■ Joint Headquarters
(Berlin)

RAND McNALLY
POPULAR MAP OF
GERMANY
SCALE 1 : 3,295,000
1 Inch = 52 Statute Miles
1 Centimeter = 33 Kilometers
Statute Miles

Copyright by Rand McNally & Company, Chicago.
Made in U.S.A.

5678901234

RAND McNALLY POPULAR MAP OF ITALY

SCALE 1:4,815,000
1 Inch = 76 Statute Miles
1 Centimeter = 48 Kilometers
Statute Miles

Copyright by Rand McNally & Company, Chicago.
Made in U.S.A.

Environs of ROMA

SCALE.
Statute Miles, 3¼ = 1 Inch.

ITALY
Area 116,793 sq. m.
Pop.....44,530,000

PRINCIPAL CITIES
Pop.—Thousands

23	Acireale	O 17
40	Aderno	N 16
63	Alcamo	N 12
44	Alessandria	D 4
27	Altamura	J 19
67	Ancona	F 13
56	Andria	J 18
39	Aquila	H 13
19	Arezzo	G 10
25	Asti	D 3
164	Bari	J 20
50	Barletta	J 18
31	Benevento	J 15
22	Bergamo	C 8
27	Bitonto	J 19
199	Bologna	E 9
25	Bolzano	B 9
73	Brescia	C 8
35	Brindisi	J 22
81	Cagliari	L 4
31	Caltagirone	O 15
35	Caltanissetta	O 14
24	Carrara	F 6
28	Castellammare de Stabia	J 15
199	Catania	O 16
27	Catanzaro	M 19
36	Cerignola	J 18
21	Chieti	H 14
41	Como	C 5
48	Corato	J 19
15	Corleone	N 13
24	Cosenza	L 19
43	Cremona	D 6
72	Faenza	E 10
70	Ferrara	E 9
285	Firenze	F 9
53	Fiume	D 14
	Florence, see Firenze.	
50	Foggia	I 17
30	Forli	F 11
345	Genova (Genoa)	E 4
214	Girgenti	O 13
33	Gorizia	C 13
15	Imola	E 9
40	Lecce	K 22
112	Livorno (Leghorn)	F 7
22	Lodi	D 5
54	Lucca	F 7
13	Macerata	G 13
40	Mantova (Mantua)	D 8
31	Marsala	N 11
20	Mazarra del Valle	O 11
114	Messina	N 17
713	Milano (Milan)	D 5
51	Modena	E 8
56	Modica	P 16
45	Molfetta	J 19
37	Monza	C 5
757	Napoli (Naples)	J 14
17	Noto	P 16
45	Novara (Novarre)	D 4
83	Padova (Padua)	D 10
318	Palermo	N 13
69	Parma	E 7
21	Partinico	N 12
36	Pavia	D 5
24	Perugia	G 11
43	Piacenza	D 6
52	Pisa	F 7
53	Pistoia	F 8
27	Prato	F 8
33	Ragusa	O 16
94	Reggio	E 8
45	Reggio di Calabria	N 18
21	Rimini	F 11
1063	Roma (Rome)	B 21
1133	Roma (incl. suburbs)	B 21
34	Salerno	J 15
19	San Remo	F 2
33	San Severo	I 17
36	Sassari	J 3
52	Savona	E 3
20	Sciacca	O 12
32	Siena	G 9
40	Siracusa	O 17
76	Spezia, La	F 6
90	Taranto	K 21
27	Terni	H 11
595	Torino (Turin)	D 2
56	Trapani	N 11
31	Trento	C 8
30	Treviso	D 10
	Turin, see Torino.	
53	Udine	C 12
163	Venezia (Venice)	D 11
26	Vercelli	D 3
113	Verona	D 8
43	Vicenza	D 9
19	Vigevano	D 4
18	Viterbo	H 10
30	Vittoria	O 15
19	Vizzini	O 16
12	Zara	F 16

MALTA and GOZO
Area....122 sq. m.
Pop.....268,668
PRINCIPAL CITY
Pop.—Thousands
24 Valletta...Q 15

SAN MARINO
Area....38 sq. m.
Pop.....14,170
PRINCIPAL CITY
Pop.—Thousands
2 San Marino. F 11

TRIESTE FREE TER.
Area....285 sq. m.
Pop.....350,000
PRINCIPAL CITY
Pop.—Thousands
229 Trieste..D 13

(P. I. & C. 789)

NETHERLANDS

Area..13,202 sq. m.
Pop.....9,075,870

PRINCIPAL CITIES

Pop.—Thousands
28 Alkmaar...E 13
33 Almelo....F 23
39 Amersfoort G 17
782 Amsterdam
......F 14
67 Apeldoorn.G 19
84 Arnhem...H 19
18 Assen....D 22
51 Breda....J 13
51 Delft....H 11
36 Deventer..G 20
57 Dordrecht.I 13
31 Ede....H 18
100 Eindhoven
......J 16
41 Emmen...D 24
87 Enschede..G 23
Flushing, see
Vlissingen.
29 Gouda..H 13
115 Groningen
......C 22
129 Haarlem..F 12
47 Heerlen...L 19
29 Helder...D 13
25 Helmond..J 18
34 Hengelo..G 23
67 Hilversum.G 15
20 Kampen...F 19
16 Katwijk aan
Zee.....G 11
37 Kerkrade..L 19
48 Leeuwarden
......C 18
71 Leiden...G 12
31 Lonneker..G 24
61 Maastricht
......M 18
18 Middelburg.J 9
89 Nijmegen..I 18
25 Rheden...H 19
22 Roosendaal-en-
Nispen...J 12
595 Rotterdam
......H 12
61 Schiedam..H 12
482 's Gravenhage
......H 11
42 's Hertogen-
bosch...I 16
The Hague, see
's Gravenhage.
87 Tilburg...J 15
161 Utrecht..H 15
41 Velsen...F 13
24 Venlo...J 20
28 Vlaardingen
......H 11
22 Vlissingen..J 7
33 Zaandam..F 14
41 Zwolle....F 20

BELGIUM

Area..11,752 sq. m.
Pop.....8,361,220

PRINCIPAL CITIES

Pop.—Thousands
38 Alost....L 10
278 Anvers
(Antwerp)
......K 11
44 Berchem..K 12
19 Boom....L 11
54 Borgerhout K 12
51 Bruges...K 6
194 Bruxelles
(Brussels) M 12
28 Charleroi..N 12
18 Courcelles N 12
39 Courtrai
(Kortrijk) M 6
167 Gand....L 9
16 Gentbrugge L 9
19 Gheel....K 14
Ghent, see Gand
25 Gilly....N 12
26 Hasselt...L 16
25 Herstal...M 17
30 Hoboken..R 8
30 Jumet...N 12
39 Kortrijk
(Courtrai) M 6
32 Laeken...L 11
24 La Louviere
......N 11
40 Leuven
(Louvain) M 13
166 Liege....M 17
28 Lierre....K 12
24 Lokeren...L 9
40 Louvain
(Leuven) M 13
60 Malines
(Mechelen) L 12
22 Marcinelle O 12
60 Mechelen
(Malines) L 12
20 Menin....M 5
27 Merxem...M 11
27 Mons....N 10
30 Mouscron..M 6
30 Namur....N 13
49 Ostend...K 4
20 Ougree...N 17
24 Ronse (Renaix)
......M 7
28 Roulers...L 5
42 St. Nicolas K 11
123 Schaerbeek
......M 12
45 Seraing...N 17
36 Tourna....N 7
27 Turnhout..K 14
50 Uccle....M 11
41 Verviers..N 18
41 Vilvorde..L 12

LUXEMBOURG

Area....998 sq. m.
Pop......296,913

PRINCIPAL CITIES

Pop.—Thousands
4 Diekirch...Q 21
29 Esch....P 19
3 Grevenmacher
......Q 21
58 Luxembourg
......R 20

(P. I. & C. 67)

ANVERS (ANTWERP), GAND (GHENT), AND THE LOWER SCHELDT.

AMSTERDAM AND ITS ENVIRONS.

RAND McNALLY POPULAR MAP OF NETHERLANDS BELGIUM AND LUXEMBOURG
SCALE 1:1,609,000
1 Inch = 25.4 Statute Miles
1 Centimeter = 16.1 Kilometers
Copyright by Rand McNally & Company, Chicago.
Made in U.S.A.

114

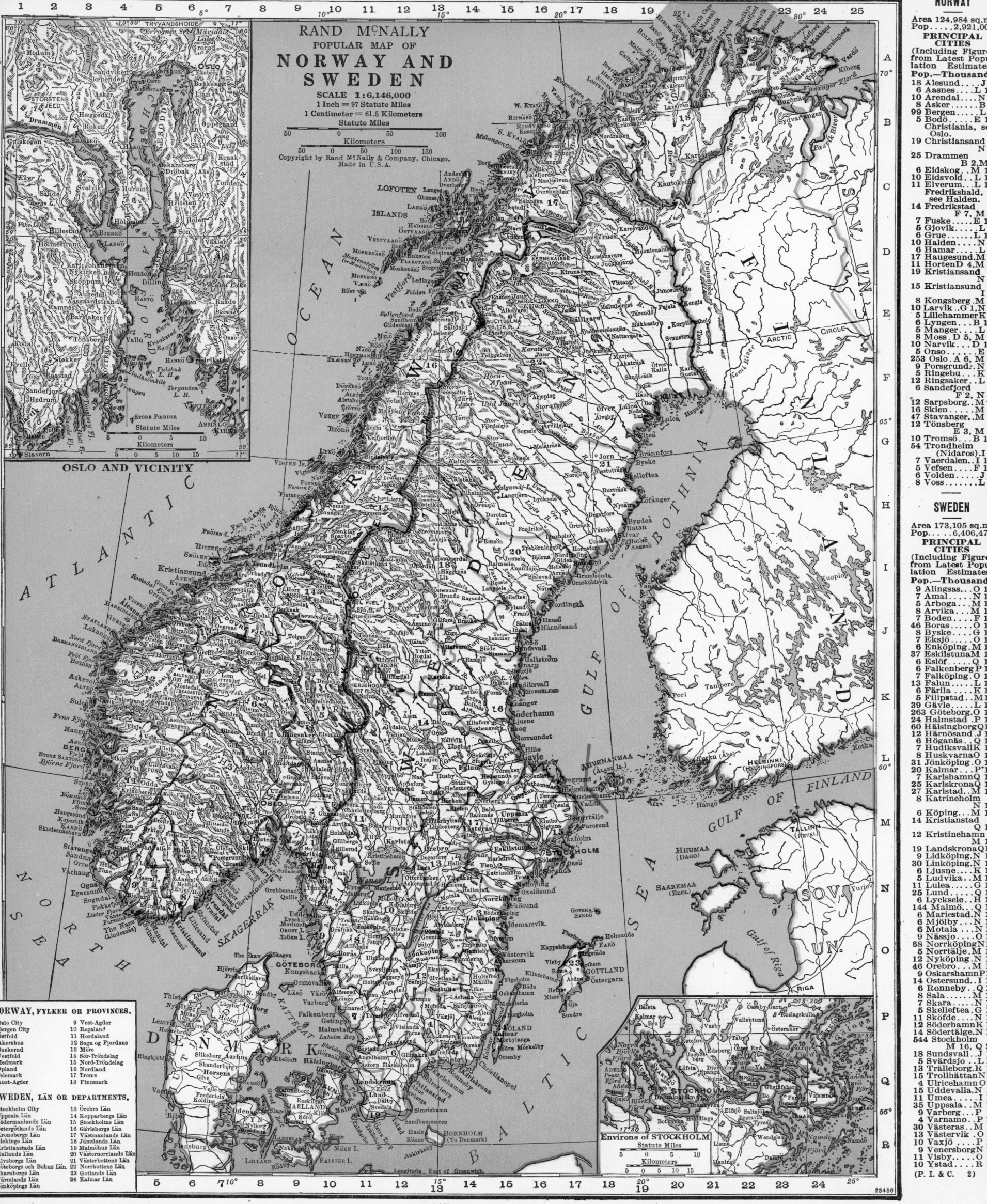

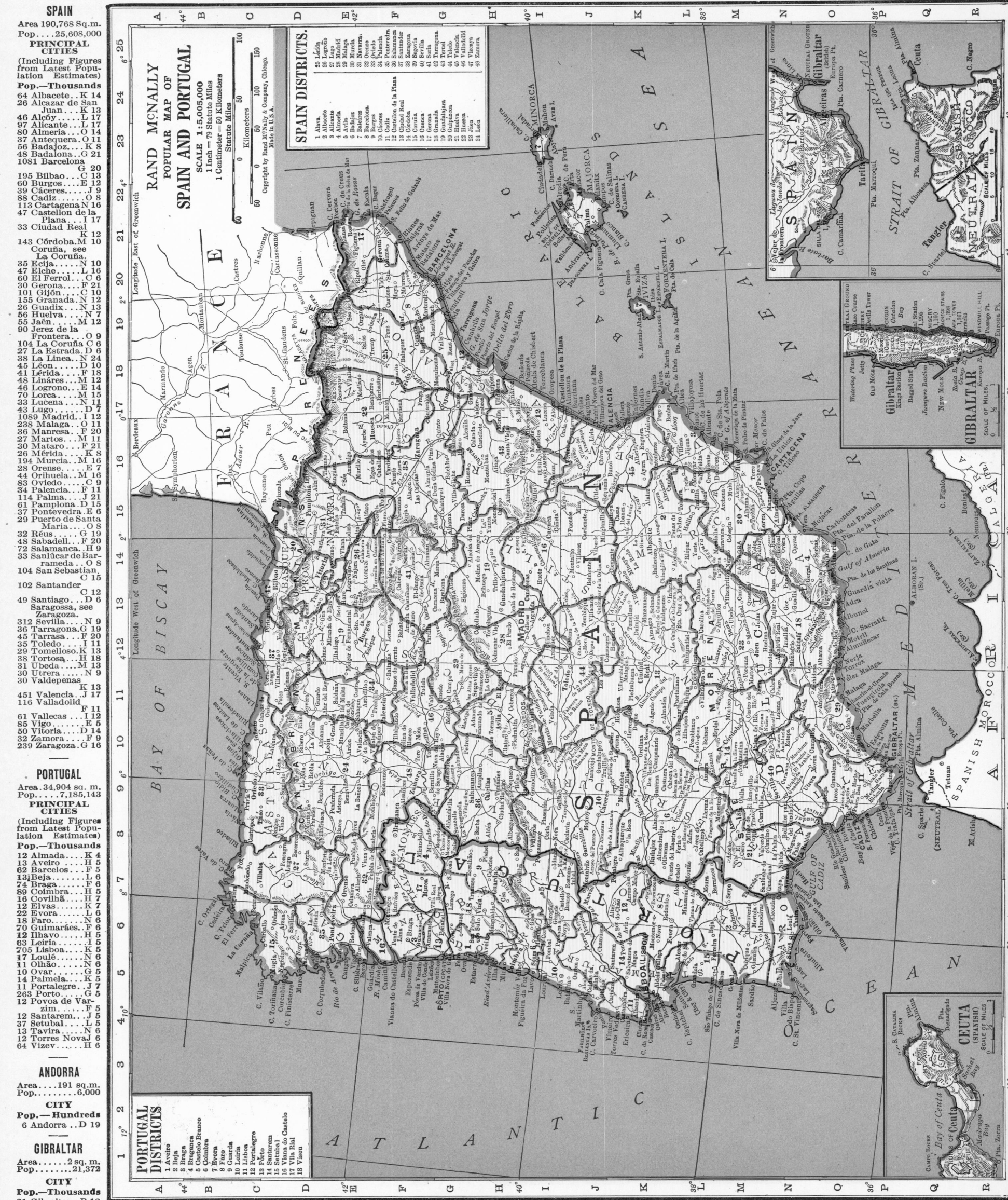

SPAIN

Area 190,768 Sq.m.
Pop....25,608,000

PRINCIPAL CITIES

(Including Figures from Latest Population Estimates)

Pop.—Thousands

64 Albacete....K 14	
26 Alcazar de San Juan...K 13	
46 Alcóy....L 17	
97 Alicante...L 17	
80 Almeria....O 14	
37 Antequera.O 11	
56 Badajoz....K 8	
48 Badalona..G 21	
1081 Barcelona G 20	
195 Bilbao....C 13	
60 Burgos....E 12	
39 Cáceres....J 9	
88 Cadiz....O 8	
113 Cartagena.M 16	
47 Castellon de la Plana..I 17	
33 Ciudad Real K 12	
143 Córdoba..M 10	
Coruña, see La Coruña.	
35 Ecija....N 10	
47 Elche....L 16	
60 El Ferrol...C 6	
30 Gerona....F 21	
101 Gijón....C 10	
155 Granada..N 12	
26 Guadix....N 13	
56 Huelva....N 7	
55 Jaén....M 12	
90 Jerez de la Frontera...O 9	
104 La Coruña C 6	
27 La Estrada.D 6	
38 La Linea..N 24	
45 Léon....D 10	
41 Lérida....F 18	
48 Lináres..M 12	
46 Logrono..E 14	
70 Lorca....M 15	
33 Lucena...N 11	
43 Lugo....D 7	
1089 Madrid..I 12	
238 Malaga..O 11	
36 Manresa..F 20	
27 Martos...M 11	
30 Mataro...F 21	
26 Mérida...K 8	
194 Murcia..M 16	
28 Orense....E 7	
44 Orihuela..M 16	
83 Oviedo....C 9	
34 Palencia..F 11	
114 Palma...J 21	
61 Pamplona.D 14	
37 Pontevedra.E 6	
29 Puerto de Santa Maria...O 8	
32 Réus....G 19	
48 Sabadell..F 20	
72 Salamanca..H 9	
33 Sanlúcar de Barrameda...O 8	
104 San Sebastian C 15	
102 Santander C 12	
49 Santiago...D 6	
Saragossa, see Zaragoza.	
312 Sevilla....N 9	
36 Tarragona.G 19	
45 Tarrasa..F 20	
35 Toledo...I 11	
29 Tomelloso.K 13	
38 Tortosa..H 18	
31 Ubeda...M 13	
30 Utrera....N 9	
30 Valdepeñas K 13	
451 Valencia..J 17	
116 Valladolid F 11	
61 Vallecas...I 12	
85 Vigo....E 5	
50 Vitoria...D 14	
32 Zamora....F 9	
239 Zaragoza.G 16	

PORTUGAL

Area 34,904 sq. m.
Pop....7,185,143

PRINCIPAL CITIES

(Including Figures from Latest Population Estimates)

Pop.—Thousands

12 Almada....K 4	
13 Aveiro....H 5	
62 Barcelos..F 5	
13 Beja....L 6	
74 Braga....F 6	
26 Coimbra...H 5	
16 Covilhã...K 7	
12 Elvas....K 7	
22 Evora....L 6	
18 Faro....N 6	
70 Guimarães..F 6	
12 Ilhavo...H 5	
63 Leiria....K 5	
705 Lisboa....K 5	
17 Loulé....N 6	
11 Olhão....N 6	
10 Ovar....G 5	
14 Palmela...K 5	
11 Portalegre..J 7	
263 Porto....G 5	
12 Povoa de Varzim...F 5	
12 Santarem..J 5	
37 Setubal...L 5	
13 Tavira...N 6	
12 Torres NovaJ 6	
64 Vizev....H 6	

ANDORRA

Area....191 sq.m.
Pop....6,000

CITY

Pop.—Hundreds

6 Andorra..D 19

GIBRALTAR

Area....2 sq. m.
Pop....21,372

CITY

Pop.—Thousands

21 Gibraltar..P 18

(P. I. & C. 67)

RAND McNALLY POPULAR MAP OF SPAIN AND PORTUGAL

SCALE 1:5,005,000
1 Inch = 79 Statute Miles
1 Centimeter = 50 Kilometers
Made in U.S.A.

Copyright by Rand McNally & Company, Chicago

SPAIN DISTRICTS.

1 Alava	25 Lérida
2 Albacete	26 Logroño
3 Alicante	27 Lugo
4 Almeria	28 Madrid
5 Avila	29 Malaga
6 Badajoz	30 Murcia
7 Baleares	31 Navarra
8 Barcelona	32 Orense
9 Burgos	33 Oviedo
10 Cáceres	34 Palencia
11 Cadiz	35 Pontevedra
12 Castellon de la Plana	36 Salamanca
13 Ciudad Real	37 Santander
14 Córdoba	38 Segovia
15 Coruña	39 Sevilla
16 Cuenca	40 Soria
17 Gerona	41 Tarragona
18 Granada	42 Teruel
19 Guadalajara	43 Toledo
20 Guipuzcoa	44 Valencia
21 Huelva	45 Valladolid
22 Huesca	46 Vizcaya
23 Jaén	47 Zamora
24 Léon	48 Zaragoza

PORTUGAL DISTRICTS

1 Aveiro	10 Leiria
2 Beja	11 Lisboa
3 Braga	12 Pórto
4 Braganca	13 Portalegre
5 Castelo Branco	14 Santarem
6 Coimbra	15 Setubal
7 Evora	16 Vianna do Castello
8 Faro	17 Villa Real
9 Guarda	18 Vizeu

GIBRALTAR

CEUTA (SPANISH)

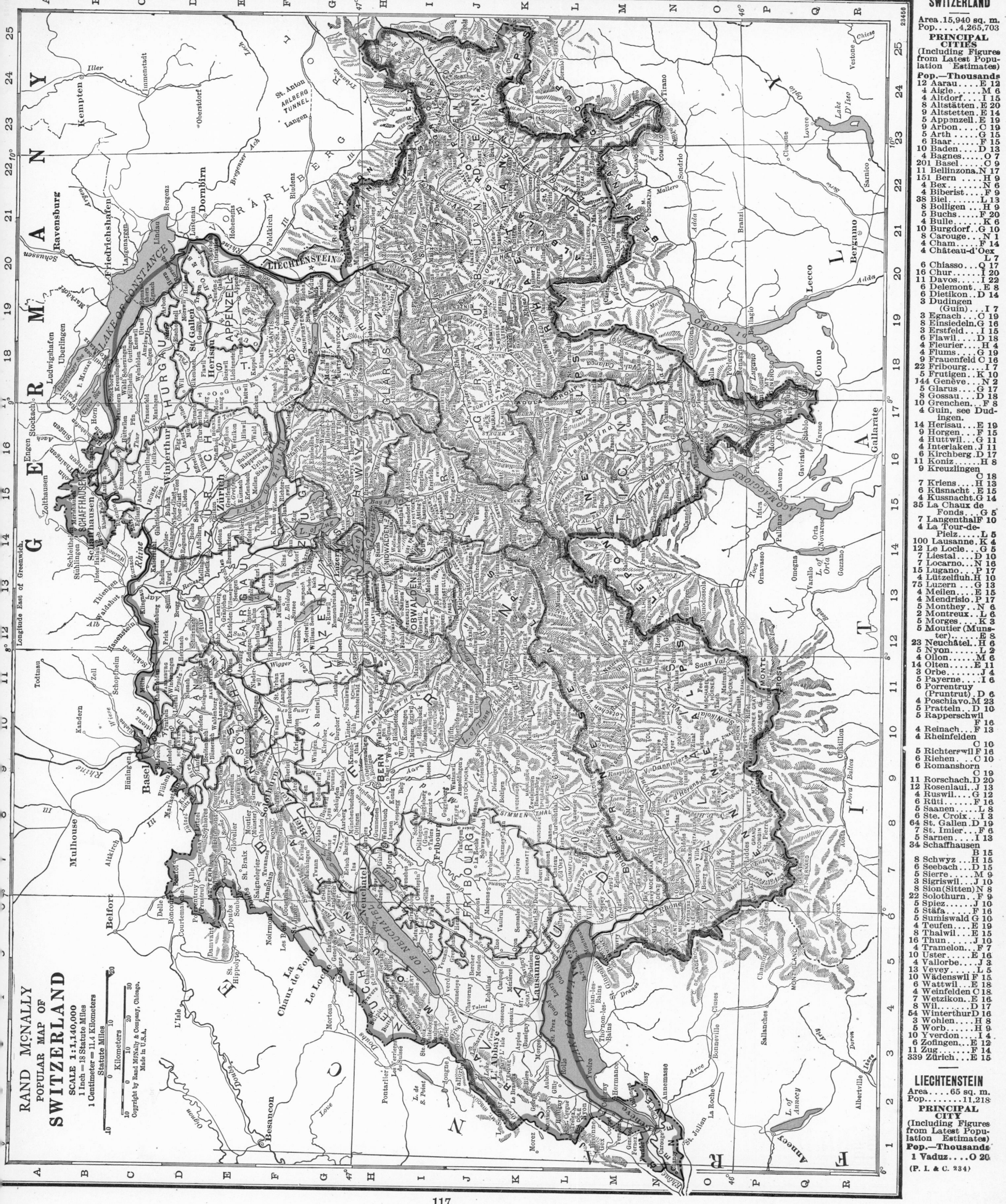

RAND McNALLY
POPULAR MAP OF
SWITZERLAND

SCALE 1:1,140,000
1 Inch = 18 Statute Miles
1 Centimeter = 11.4 Kilometers

Statute Miles

Kilometers

Copyright by Rand McNally & Company, Chicago.
Made in U.S.A.

SWITZERLAND

Area..15,940 sq. m.
Pop.....4,265,703

PRINCIPAL
CITIES
(Including Figures
from Latest Population Estimates)

Pop.—Thousands
12 Aarau........E 12
4 Aigle.........M 6
4 Altdorf.......I 15
8 Altstätten....E 20
9 Altstetten....E 14
5 Appenzell.....E 19
5 Arbon.........C 19
5 Arth..........G 15
6 Baar..........F 15
10 Baden.........D 13
4 Bagnes........O 7
201 Basel.........C 9
11 Bellinzona....N 17
151 Bern..........H 9
4 Bex...........N 6
4 Biberist......F 9
38 Biel..........L 13
8 Bolligen......H 9
4 Buchs.........F 20
4 Bulle.........K 6
10 Burgdorf......G 10
8 Carouge.......N 1
4 Cham..........F 14
4 Château-d'Oex
           L 7
6 Chiasso.......Q 17
16 Chur..........I 20
11 Davos.........I 22
6 Delemont......E 8
6 Dietikon......D 14
9 Dudingen
       (Guin)...I 7
3 Egnach........C 19
16 Einsiedeln....G 16
3 Erstfeld......I 15
4 Flawil........D 18
4 Fleurier......H 4
4 Flums.........G 19
6 Frauenfeld....D 16
22 Fribourg......I 7
5 Frutigen......K 10
144 Genève........N 2
5 Glarus........G 17
3 Gossau........D 18
10 Grenchen......F 8
4 Guin, see Dudingen.
14 Herisau.......E 19
9 Horgen........F 15
4 Huttwil.......G 11
8 Interlaken....J 11
6 Kirchberg.....I 17
11 Koniz.........H 8
9 Kreuzlingen
           C 18
7 Kriens........H 13
6 Küsnacht......E 15
4 Küssnacht.....G 14
35 La Chaux de
      Fonds.....G 5
7 Langenthal....F 10
4 La Tour-de-
      Pielz.....L 5
100 Lausanne......K 4
12 Le Locle......G 5
4 Liestal.......D 10
16 Locarno.......N 16
15 Lugano........P 17
4 Lützelfluh....H 10
75 Luzern........G 13
4 Meilen........E 15
4 Mendrisio.....P 17
4 Monthey.......N 6
5 Montreux......L 6
5 Morges........K 3
4 Moutier (Munster).......E 8
23 Neuchâtel.....H 6
5 Nyon..........L 2
4 Ollon.........M 6
14 Olten.........E 11
3 Orbe..........J 4
5 Payerne.......I 6
6 Porrentruy
      (Pruntrut).D 6
4 Poschiavo.....M 23
5 Pratteln......D 10
5 Rapperschwil
           F 16
4 Reinach.......F 13
4 Rheinfelden
           C 10
5 Richterswil...F 16
6 Riehen........C 10
5 Romanshorn
           C 19
11 Rorschach.....D 20
12 Rosenlaui.....J 13
4 Ruswil........G 12
6 Rüti..........F 16
4 Saanen........J 8
4 Ste. Croix....I 3
64 St. Gallen....D 19
7 St. Imier.....F 6
4 Sarnen........I 13
34 Schaffhausen
           B 15
8 Schwyz........H 15
6 Seebach.......D 15
5 Sierre........M 9
8 Sigriswil.....J 10
8 Sion (Sitten).N 8
22 Solothurn.....F 9
5 Spiez.........J 10
5 Stäfa.........F 16
6 Sumiswald.....G 10
4 Teufen........E 19
8 Thalwil.......E 15
16 Thun..........J 9
4 Tramelon......F 7
10 Uster.........E 16
4 Vallorbe......J 3
5 Vevey.........L 5
10 Wädenswil.....F 15
6 Wattwil.......E 18
4 Weinfelden....C 18
7 Wetzikon......E 16
5 Wil...........D 17
54 Winterthur....D 16
4 Wohlen........H 8
5 Worb..........H 9
10 Yverdon.......I 4
6 Zofingen......E 12
11 Zug...........F 14
339 Zürich........E 15

LIECHTENSTEIN

Area.....65 sq. m.
Pop........11,218

PRINCIPAL
CITY
(Including Figures
from Latest Population Estimates)
Pop.—Thousands
1 Vaduz....O 20

(P. I. & C. 234)

117

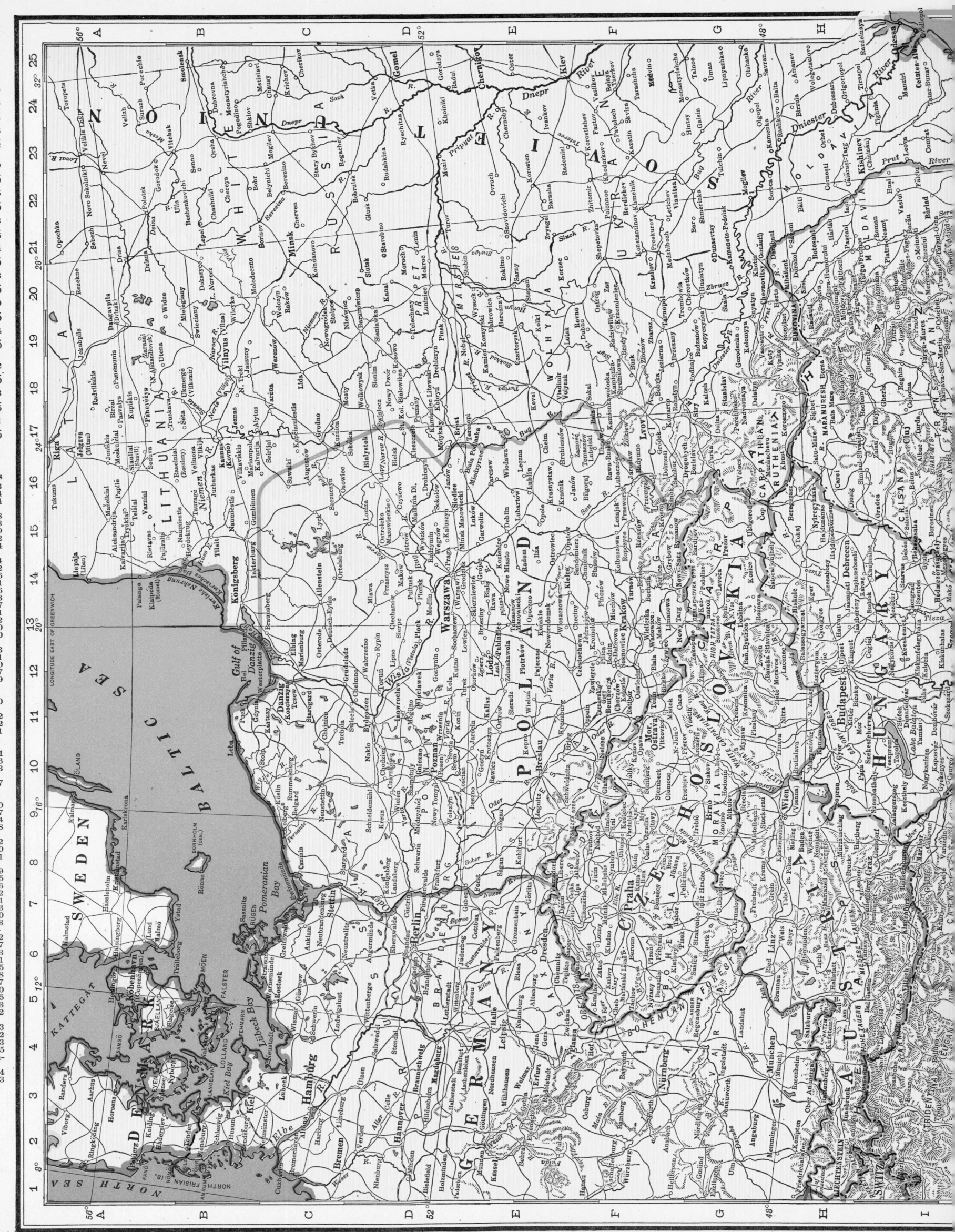

CENTRAL EUROPE

(Including Figures from Latest Population Estimates)

COUNTRIES

ALBANIA....M 13
Area..10,629 sq. m.
Pop.....1,135,000

AUSTRIA....H 6
Area..32,360 sq. m.
Pop.....6,760,233

BULGARIA....L 18
Area..42,814 sq. m.
Pop.....6,734,222

CZECHOSLOVAKIA
....G 9
Area..49,399 sq. m.
Pop.....15,215,000

GREECE....O 15
Area..51,145 sq. m.
Pop.....7,485,700

HUNGARY....I 13
Area..35,849 sq. m.
Pop.....9,034,815

ITALY....L-4
Area..116,793 sq.m.
Pop.....44,530,000

POLAND....D 13
Area..119,800 sq.m.
Pop.....32,390,000

ROMANIA....J 19
Area..91,600 sq. m.
Pop.....17,000,000

SAN MARINO..K 4
Area.....38 sq. m.
Pop.......14,170

TURKEY (In
Europe)....O 22
Area..9,254 sq. m.
Pop.....1,516,000

VATICAN CITY.M 3
Area....0.2 sq. m.
Pop.......1,025

YUGOSLAVIA.K 11
Area..98,436 sq. m.
Pop.....15,703,000

PRINCIPAL CITIES

Pop.—Thousands

96 Aarus....A 3
43 Allenstein..C 14
77 Arad....I 14
495 Athenai
(Athens)..P 18
177 Augsburg.G 3
22 Baden....H 9
48 Bedzin....F 12
49 Békéscsaba.I 14
289 Beograd (Bel-
grade)..J 14
66 Berdichev..R 22
4243 Berlin...D 6
101 Beuthen..F 11
105 Bialystok D 16
199 Bologna...J 3
42 Boryslaw..H 17
33 Botosani..H 21
68 Brăila....J 22
61 Brasov...J 20
133 Bratislava H 10
167 Braunschweig
D 3
324 Bremen...C 1
625 Breslau..E 10
48 Brest....D 17
288 Brno....G 9
640 Bucuresti
(Bucharest)
K 20
1052 Budapest.H 12
36 Burgas...L 22
36 Buzău...L 21
137 Bydgoszcz
(Bromberg)
D 11
199 Catania..P 6
37 Cegled...H 13
44 Ceské Bude-
jovice....G 7
111 Chernovitsy
(Cernauti)
G 20
99 Cluj....I 17
60 Constanta.K 24
63 Craiova..K 18
136 Czestochowa
F 12
42 Dabrowica.E 20
235 Danzig...C 11
43 Daugavpils
(Dvinsk)..A 19
120 Debrecen.H 15
642 Dresden...E 6
9 Durrës...M 12
45 Edrine...M 21
30 Eger....H 13
41 Erakleion.R 20
70 Ferrara....J 3
285 Firenze (Flor-
ence)....K 2
50 Fogcia...M 7
102 Galati...J 23
114 Gdynia..B 11
144 Gomel...D 25
153 Graz....H 8
50 Grodno..C 17
51 Györ....H 10
209 Halle....E 5
1647 Hamburg.C 3
439 Hannover. D 2
60 Hódmezővá-
sárhely....I 13
105 Iasi....H 22
61 Innsbruck..H 3
40 Insterburg C 15
789 Istanbul (Con-
stantinople)
M 24
30 Jászberény H 13
(P. & I. 789)

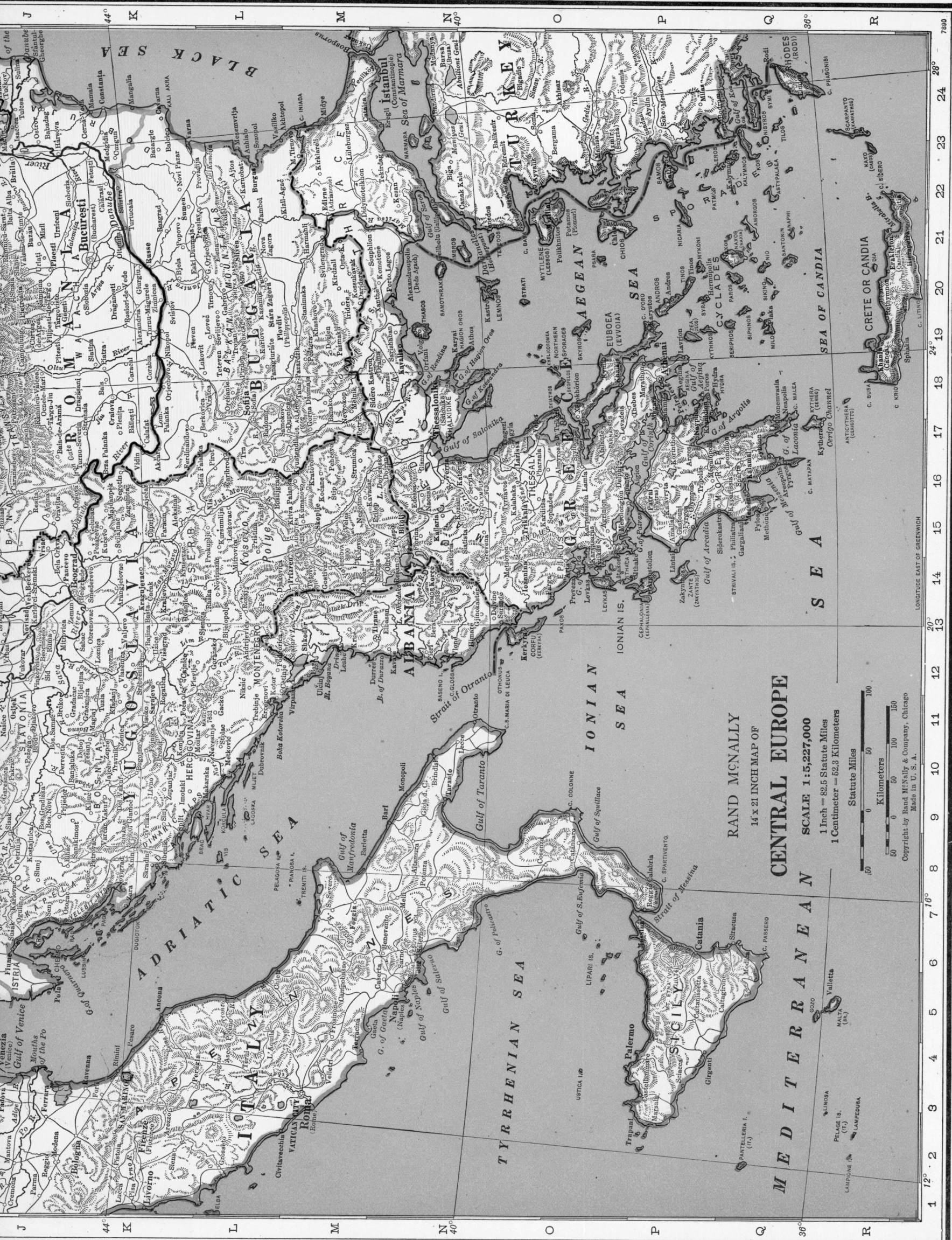

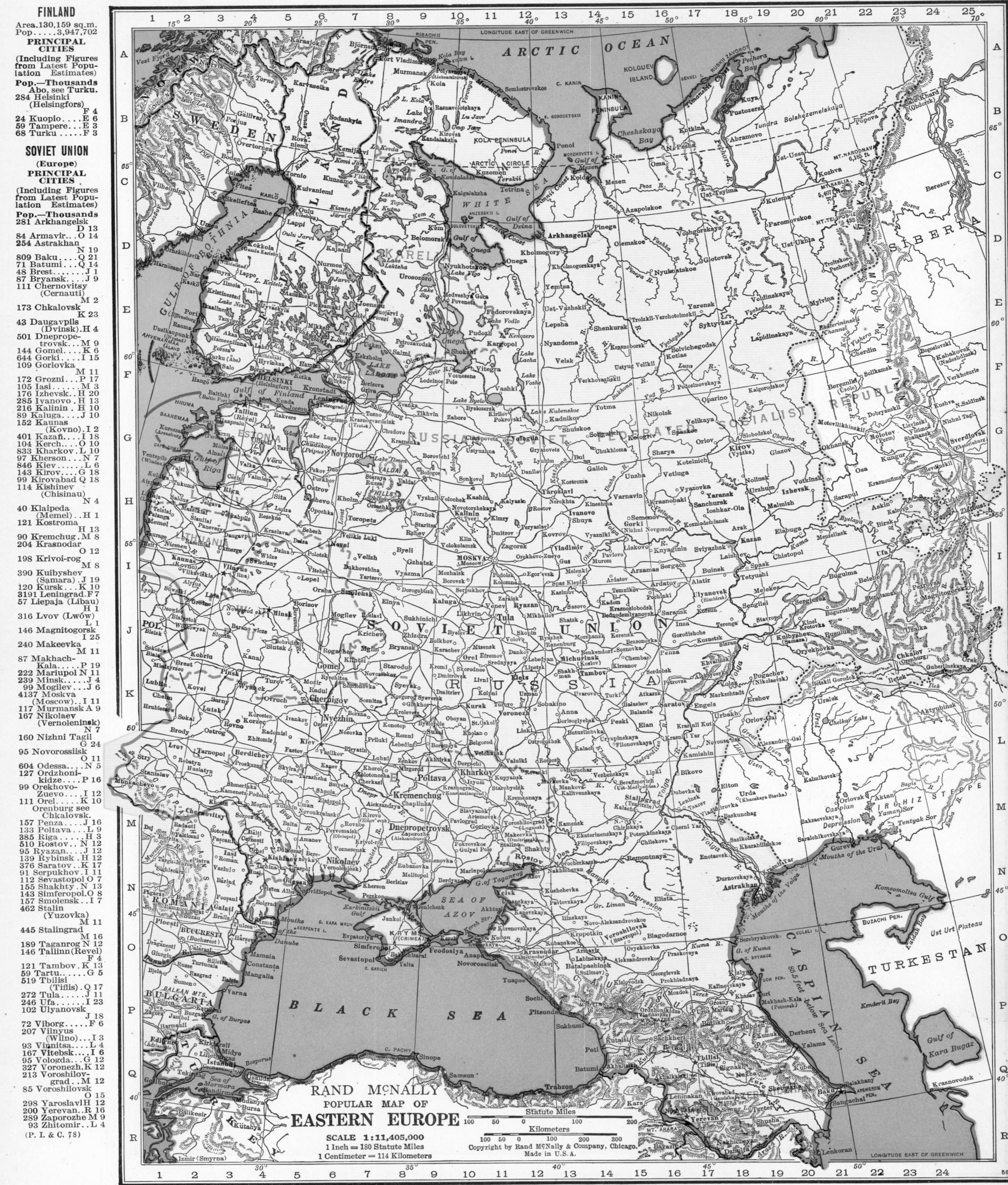

RAND MCNALLY
POPULAR MAP OF
EASTERN EUROPE

SCALE 1:11,405,000
1 Inch = 180 Statute Miles
1 Centimeter = 114 Kilometers

Copyright by Rand McNally & Company, Chicago.
Made in U.S.A.

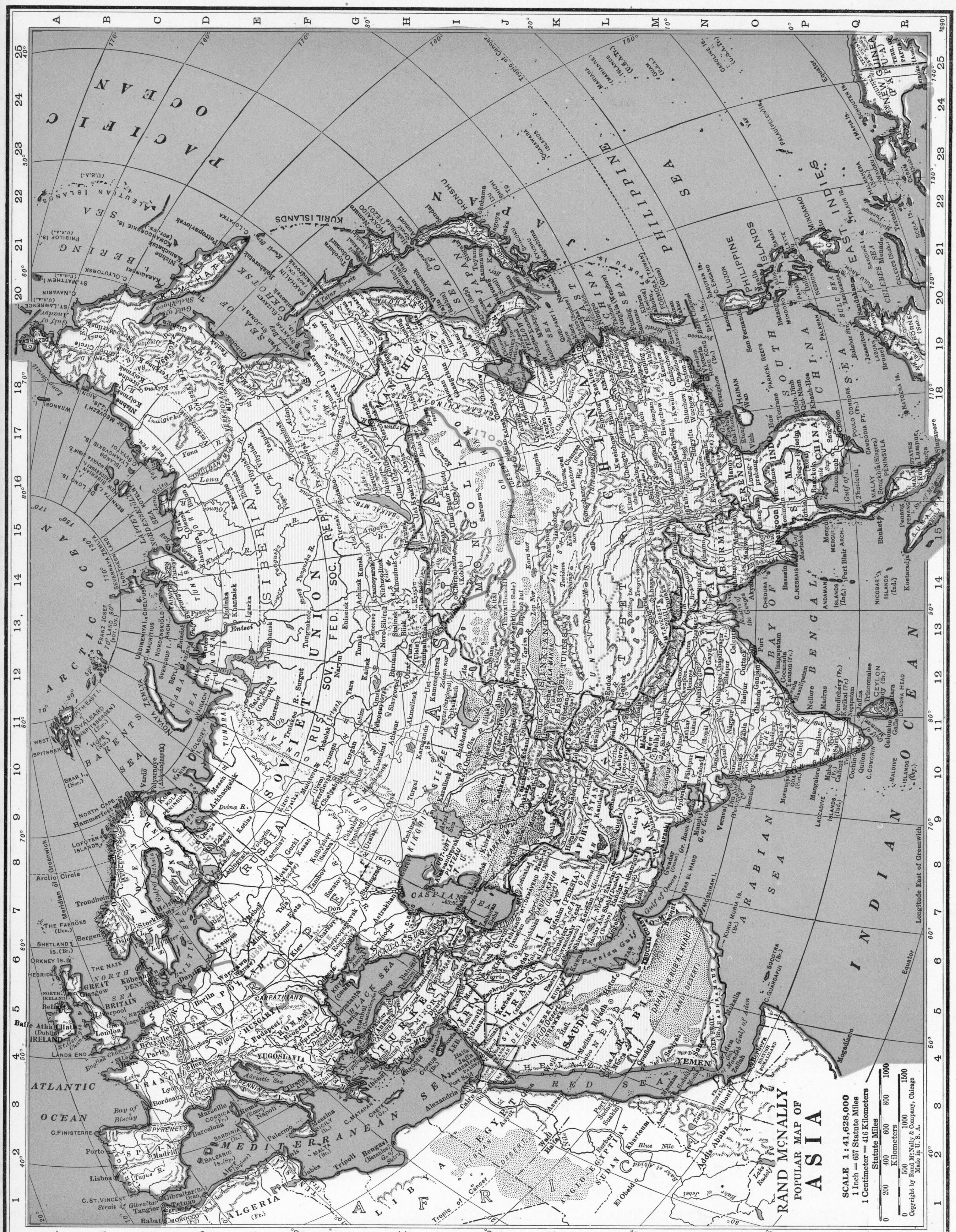

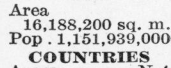

RAND MCNALLY
POPULAR MAP OF
ASIA
SCALE 1:41,628,000
1 Inch = 657 Statute Miles
1 Centimeter = 416 Kilometers
Statute Miles
Kilometers
Copyright by Rand McNally & Company, Chicago
Made in U. S. A.

ASIA

Area
16,188,200 sq. m.
Pop . 1,151,939,000

COUNTRIES

ADEN........N 4
Area..42,080 sq.m.
Pop.......100,000
AFGHANISTAN..L 9
Area 245,000 sq.m.
Pop....12,000,000
BAHREIN Is....L 6
Area...250 sq. m.
Pop.......120,000
BHUTAN.....M 13
Area.18,000 sq. m.
Pop.......300,000
BRITISH NORTH BORNEO...Q 19
Area.31,106 sq. m.
Pop.......299,311
BRUNEI.....R 19
Area..2,500 sq. m.
Pop........37,868
BURMA......N 15
Area.233,492 sq.m.
Pop....14,667,146
CEYLON.....R 11
Area.25,332 sq. m.
Pop......5,712,000
CHINA.......L 17
Ar.3,422,000 sq.m.
Pop...469,257,000
CYPRUS.......I 4
Area..3,584 sq. m.
Pop...... 377,000
FORMOSA (Taiwan)..M 19
Area.13,836 sq. m.
Pop.....5,872,000
FRENCH INDO-CHINA.....P 17
Area.284,522 sq.m.
Pop....23,250,000
GÔA..........P 10
Area..1,516 sq. m.
Pop.......579,969
HONG KONG.N 18
Area....391 sq. m.
Pop.....1,007,000
INDIA........N 12
Ar.1,228,267 sq.m.
Pop...330,000,000
IRAN (Persia).K 7
Area.628,000 sq.m.
Pop....15,055,115
IRAQ (Mesopotamia)....J 5
Area.143,240 sq.m.
Pop.....4,412,959
JAPAN........J 21
Area.147,889 sq.m.
Pop....72,222,000
KOREA (Chosen) J 20
Area.85,206 sq. m.
Pop....24,326,327
KUWAIT...... K 6
Area..1,930 sq. m.
Pop.........80,000
LEBANON......I 5
Area...3,474 sq.m.
Pop.......848,833
MACAU......N 18
Area.....4 sq. m.
Pop.......374,737
MALAYA, BR. R 16
Area..52,592 sq.m.
Pop.....5,300,137
MALDIVE Is..R 10
Area....115 sq. m.
Pop........79,000
NEPAL......M 12
Area.54,000 sq. m.
Pop.....5,600,000
NETHERLANDS INDIES....R 21
Area.733,790 sq.m.
Pop....70,000,000
NEW GUINEA TERRITORY.Q 25
Area.91,000 sq. m.
Pop.......755 882
NICOBAR Is..R 14
Area... 635 sq. m.
Pop........10,240
OMAN.........M 7
Area.82,000 sq. m.
Pop.......500,000
PAKISTAN....M 9
Area 350,000 sq. m.
Pop. ...70,000,000
PALESTINE....J 4
Area. 10,155 sq. m.
Pop.....1,677,000
PAPUA TERRITORY......R 25
Area.90,540 sq. m.
Pop.......276,366
PHILIPPINE Is.P 21
Area.115,600 sq.m.
Pop....16,000,303
SARAWAK....R 19
Area.42,000 sq. m.
Pop.......442,900
SAUDI ARABIA.L 5
Area......413,792
Pop.....5,500,000
SIAM.........P 16
Area.200,148 sq.m.
Pop....15,266,000
SOVIET UNION (Total).....F 14
Ar.8,439,000 sq.m.
Pop...195,000,000
SYRIA.........I 5
Area.72,723 sq. m.
Pop.....2,367,734
TRANSJORDAN..J 4
Area.......35,326
Pop.......400,000
TURKEY......H 5
Area.296,190 sq.m.
Pop....18,871,000
YEMAN.......N 4
Area.75,000 sq. m.
Pop.....3,500,000

(P. I. & C. 89)

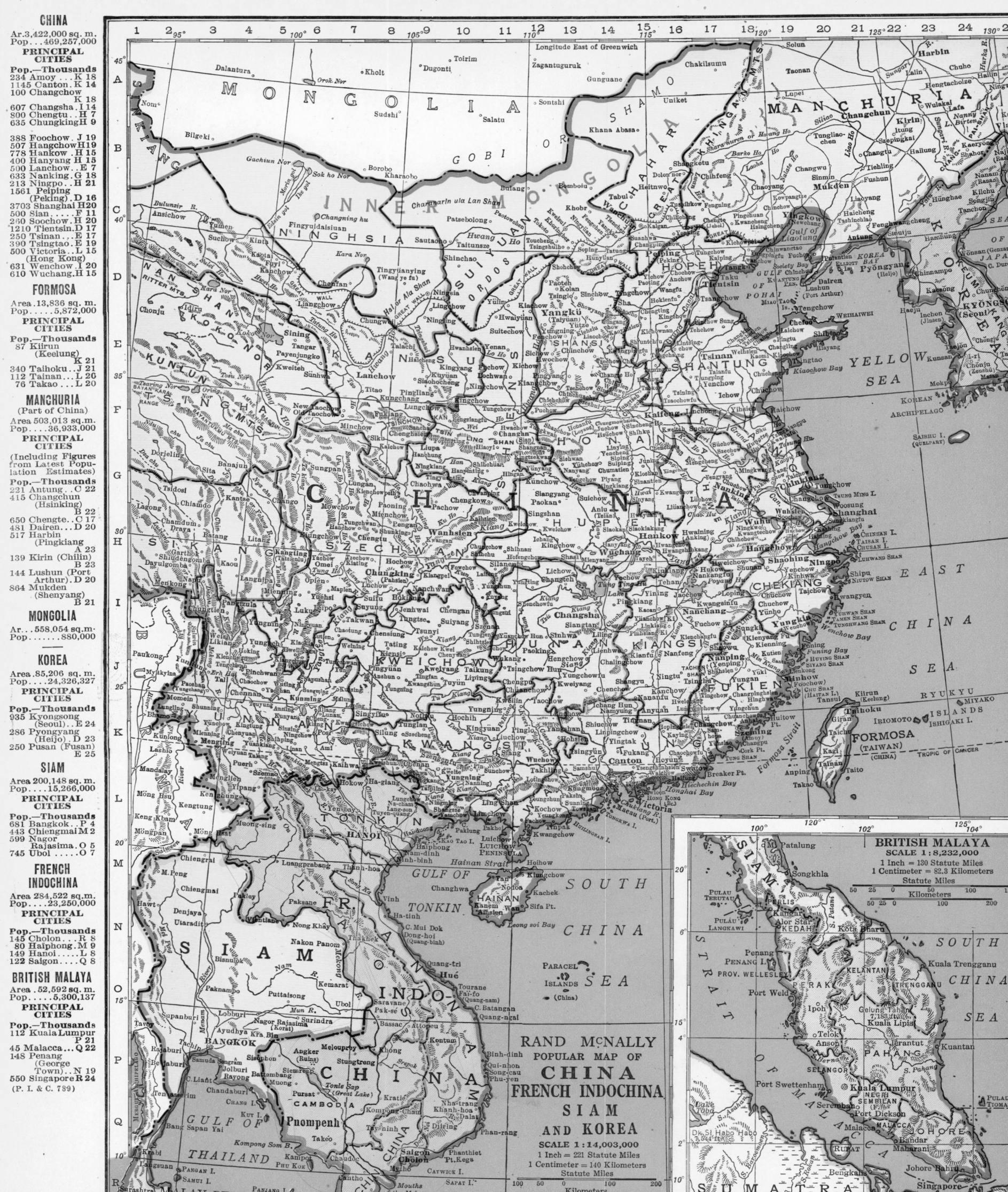

RAND McNALLY POPULAR MAP OF CHINA FRENCH INDOCHINA SIAM AND KOREA

SCALE 1:14,003,000
1 Inch = 221 Statute Miles
1 Centimeter = 140 Kilometers
Statute Miles

Copyright by Rand McNally & Company, Chicago.
Made in U.S.A.

BRITISH MALAYA
SCALE 1:8,232,000
1 Inch = 130 Statute Miles
1 Centimeter = 82.3 Kilometers
Statute Miles

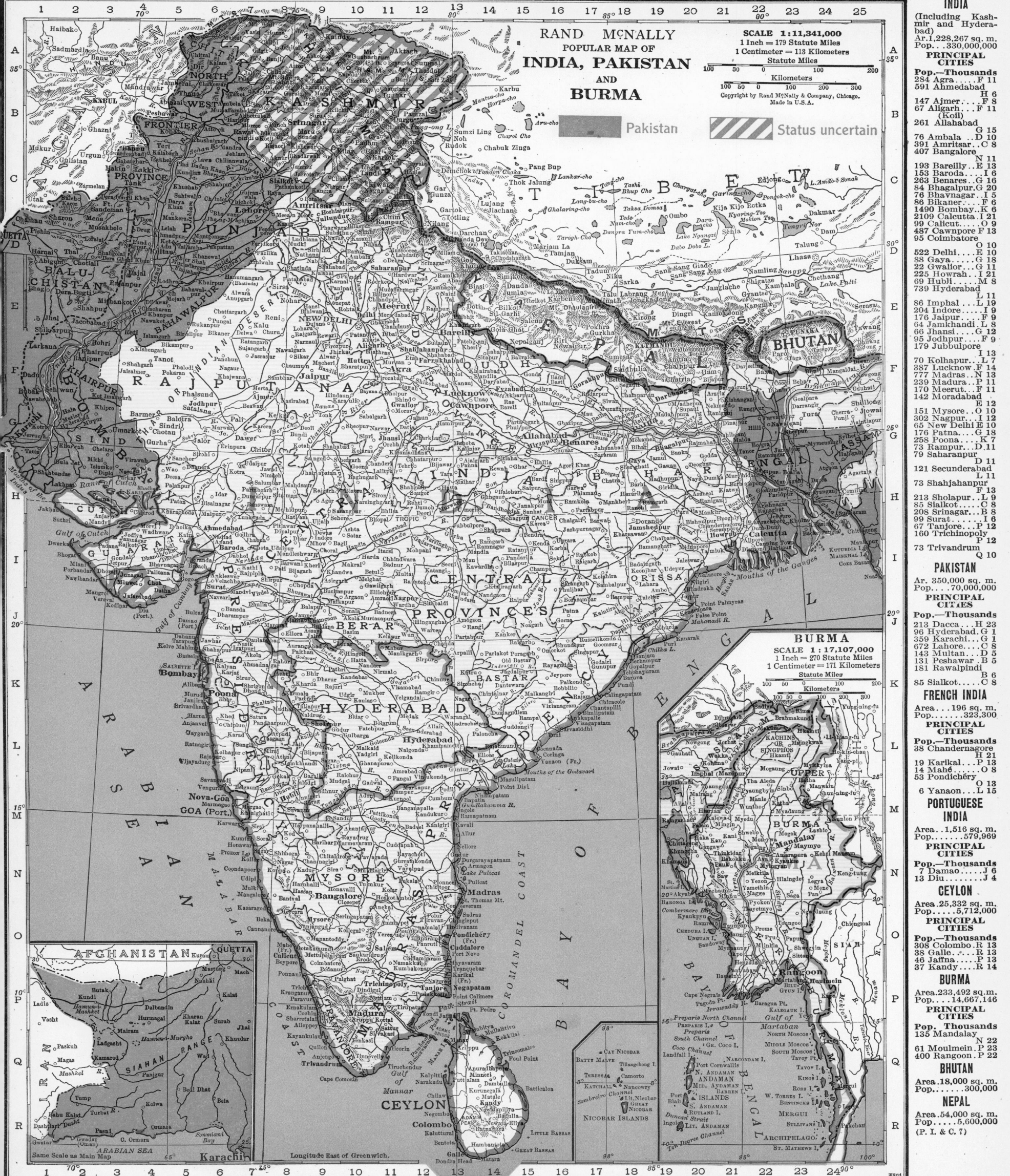

RAND McNALLY
POPULAR MAP OF
INDIA, PAKISTAN
AND
BURMA

SCALE 1:11,341,000
1 Inch = 179 Statute Miles
1 Centimeter = 113 Kilometers

Copyright by Rand McNally & Company, Chicago.
Made in U.S.A.

Pakistan
Status uncertain

BURMA
SCALE 1:17,107,000
1 Inch = 270 Statute Miles
1 Centimeter = 171 Kilometers

AFGHANISTAN

Same Scale as Main Map

Longitude East of Greenwich.

INDIA
(Including Kashmir and Hyderabad)
Ar.1,228,267 sq. m.
Pop..1,330,000,000

PRINCIPAL CITIES
Pop.—Thousands
284 Agra.....F 11
591 Ahmedabad...H 6
147 Ajmer...E 8
67 Allgarh...F 11
(Koil)
261 Allahabad...G 15
76 Ambala...D 10
391 Amritsar...C 8
407 Bangalore...N 11
193 Bareilly..E 13
153 Baroda...I 6
263 Benares..G 16
84 Bhagalpur.G 20
76 Bhavnagar..I 5
86 Bikaner...F 6
1490 Bombay...K 6
2109 Calcutta.I 21
99 Calicut...O 9
487 Cawnpore.F 13
95 Coimbatore...O 10
522 Delhi....E 10
88 Gaya....G 18
22 Gwalior..G 11
225 Howrah..I 21
69 Hubli....M 8
739 Hyderabad...L 11
86 Imphal...L 19
204 Indore...I 9
176 Jaipur...F 9
64 Jamkhandi.L 8
66 Jhansi...G 12
95 Jodhpur..F 9
179 Jubbulpore...I 13
70 Kolhapur...L 7
387 Lucknow..F 14
777 Madras..N 13
239 Madura...P 11
170 Meerut...E 11
142 Moradabad...E 12
151 Mysore...O 10
302 Nagpur...I 12
65 New Delhi..E 10
176 Patna....G 18
258 Poona....K 7
73 Rampur...D 11
79 Saharanpur...D 10
121 Secunderabad...L 11
73 Shahjahanpur..F 13
85 Sholapur..L 9
85 Sialkot...C 8
208 Srinagar...B 6
99 Surat....H 5
67 Tanjore...P 11
160 Trichinopoly...P 12
73 Trivandrum...Q 10

PAKISTAN
Ar. 350,000 sq. m.
Pop...70,000,000

PRINCIPAL CITIES
Pop.—Thousands
213 Dacca....H 23
96 Hyderabad.G 1
359 Karachi...G 1
672 Lahore....C 8
143 Multan....D 5
131 Peshawar..B 5
181 Rawalpindi...B 6
85 Sialkot...C 8

FRENCH INDIA
Area....196 sq. m.
Pop.....323,300

PRINCIPAL CITIES
Pop.—Thousands
38 Chandernagore..G 1
19 Karikal...P 13
14 Mahé....O 8
53 Pondichéry...O 13
6 Yanaon...L 15

PORTUGUESE INDIA
Area...1,516 sq. m.
Pop....579,969

PRINCIPAL CITIES
Pop.—Thousands
7 Damao.....J 6
13 Diu.....J 4

CEYLON
Area..25,332 sq. m.
Pop....5,712,000

PRINCIPAL CITIES
Pop.—Thousands
308 Colombo..R 13
38 Galle...R 13
46 Jaffna...P 13
37 Kandy...R 14

BURMA
Area.233,492 sq. m.
Pop..14,667,146

PRINCIPAL CITIES
Pop. Thousands
135 Mandalay...N 22
61 Moulmein..P 23
400 Rangoon..P 22

BHUTAN
Area.18,000 sq. m.
Pop....300,000

NEPAL
Area.54,000 sq. m.
Pop...5,600,000

(P. I. & C. 7)

123

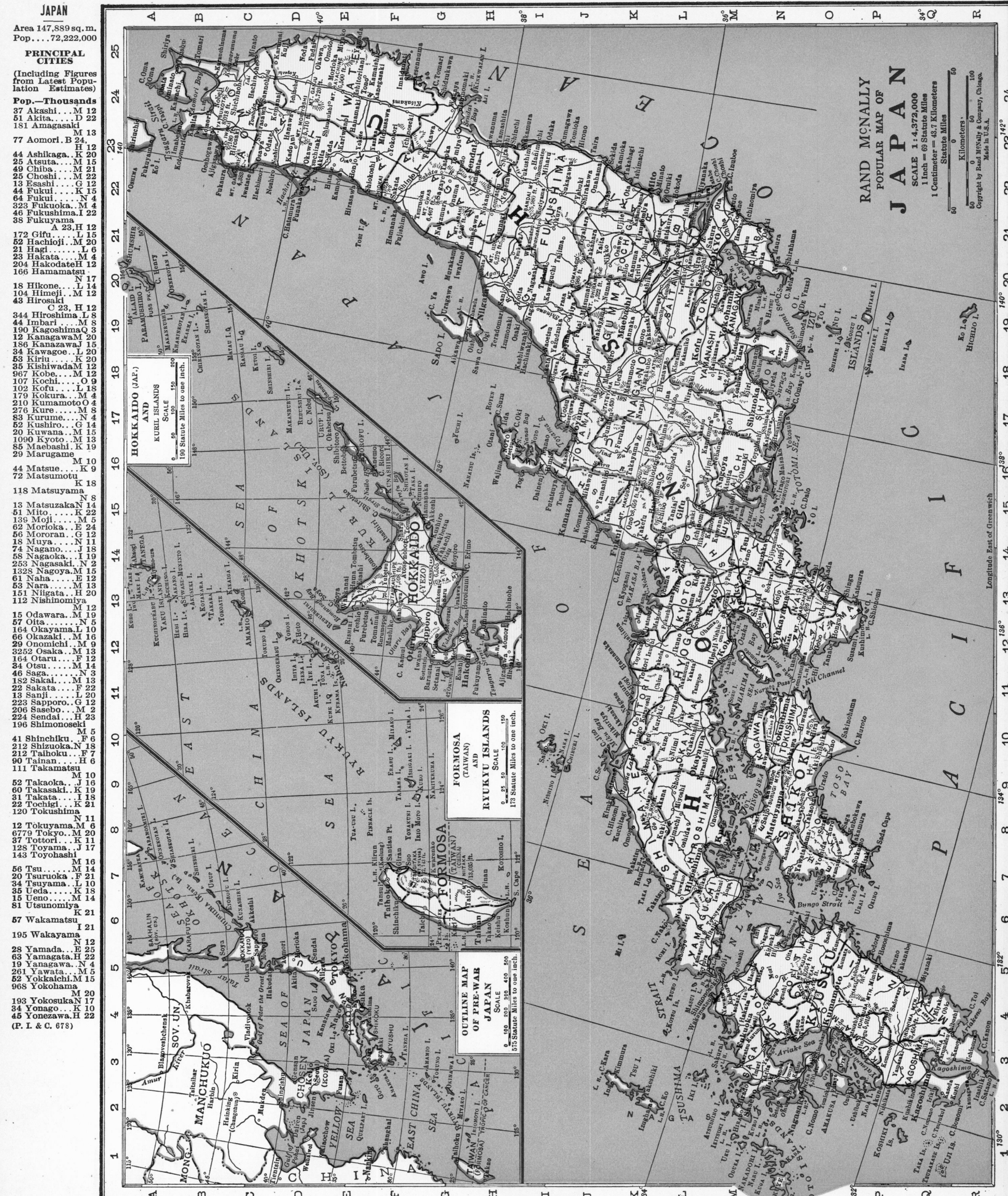

Area 147,889 sq. m.
Pop....72,222,000

**PRINCIPAL
CITIES**

(Including Figures
from Latest Popu-
lation Estimates)

Pop.—Thousands

37 Akashi....M 12
51 Akita....D 22
181 Amagasaki
M 13
77 Aomori.B 24
44 Ashikaga..K 20
25 Atsuta...M 15
49 Chiba....M 21
25 Choshi...M 22
6 Esashi...G 12
44 Fukui....K 15
64 Fukui....N 4
323 Fukuoka..M 4
46 Fukushima.I 22
38 Fukuyama
A 23, H 12
172 Gifu....L 15
52 Hachioji..M 20
21 Hagi....L 6
23 Hakata....M 4
204 HakodateH 12
166 Hamamatsu
N 17
18 Hikone...L 14
104 Himeji...M 12
43 Hirosaki
C 23, H 12
344 Hiroshima.L 8
44 Imbari...M 8
190 KagoshimaQ 3
12 KanagawaM 20
186 KanazawaJ 15
34 Kawagoe.L 20
53 Kiriu....K 20
35 KishiwadaM 12
967 Kobe....M 12
107 Kochi....O 9
102 Kofu....L 18
179 Kokura...M 4
210 KumamotoO 4
276 Kure....M 8
53 Kurume...N 4
52 Kushiro...G 14
20 Kuwana..M 15
1090 Kyoto...M 13
85 Maebashi.K 19
29 Marugame
M 10
44 Matsue...K 9
72 Matsumotu
K 18
118 Matsuyama
N 8
13 MatsuzakaN 14
51 Mito....K 22
139 Moji....M 5
62 Morioka...G 24
56 Mororan..G 12
18 Muya....N 11
74 Nagano...J 18
58 Nagaoka..J 19
253 Nagasaki..E 12
1328 Nagoya..M 15
61 Naha....E 12
53 Nara....M 13
151 Niigata...H 20
112 Nishinomiya
M 12
15 Odawara..M 19
57 Oita....N 5
164 Okayama.L 10
66 Okazaki..M 9
29 Onomichi..M 8
3252 Osaka...M 13
164 Otaru....F 12
34 Otsu....M 14
46 Saga....N 3
182 Sakai....M 13
22 Sakata...F 22
13 Sanji....L 20
223 Sapporo..G 12
206 Sasebo...M 2
224 Sendai...H 23
196 Shimonoseki
M 5
41 Shinchiku..P 6
212 Shizuoka.N 18
212 Taihoku...F 7
90 Tainan....H 6
111 Takamatsu
M 10
52 Takaoka..J 16
60 Takasaki..K 19
31 Takata...I 18
22 Tochigi...K 21
120 Tokushima
N 11
12 Tokuyama.M 6
6779 Tokyo...M 20
37 Tottori...K 11
128 Toyama...J 17
143 Toyohashi
M 16
56 Tsu....M 14
20 Tsuruoka .F 21
34 Tsuyama..L 10
15 Ueda....M 18
15 Ueno....M 14
81 Utsunomiya
K 21
57 Wakamatsu
I 21
195 Wakayama
M 12
28 Yamada...N 25
63 Yamagata.H 22
19 Yanagawa..N 4
261 Yawata...M 5
52 Yokkaichi.M 15
968 Yokohama
N 20
193 YokosukaN 17
34 Yonago...K 10
45 Yonezawa.H 22

(P. I. & C. 678)

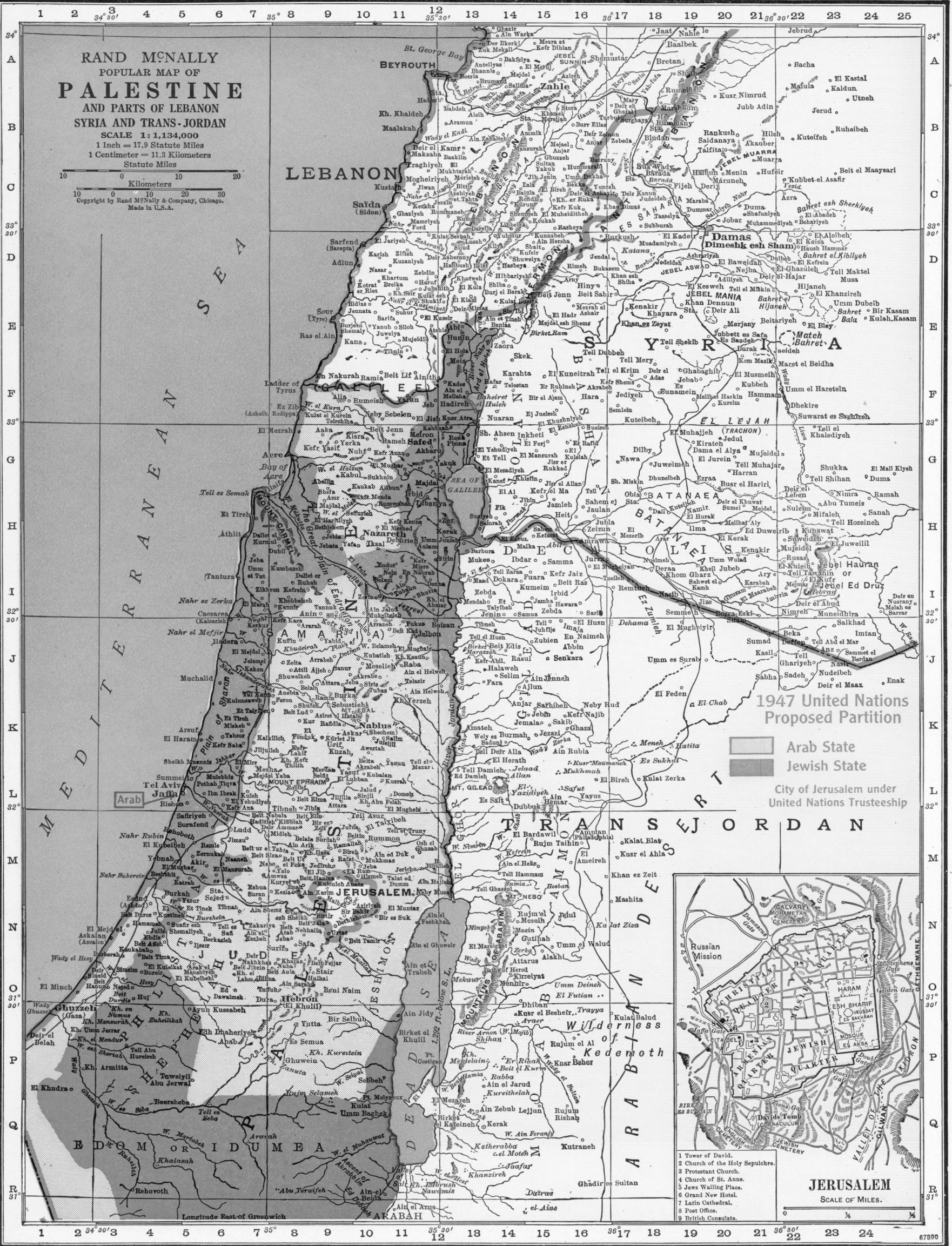

RAND McNALLY
POPULAR MAP OF
PALESTINE
AND PARTS OF LEBANON
SYRIA AND TRANS-JORDAN
SCALE 1: 1,134,000
1 Inch = 17.9 Statute Miles
1 Centimeter = 11.3 Kilometers
Statute Miles

Kilometers

Copyright by Rand McNally & Company, Chicago.
Made in U.S.A.

1947 United Nations
Proposed Partition

Arab State

Jewish State

City of Jerusalem under
United Nations Trusteeship

JERUSALEM
SCALE OF MILES.

1 Tower of David.
2 Church of the Holy Sepulchre.
3 Protestant Church.
4 Church of St. Anne.
5 Jews Wailing Place.
6 Grand New Hotel.
7 Latin Cathedral.
8 Post Office.
9 British Consulate.

PALESTINE
Area .10,155 sq. m.
Pop....1,677,000
PRINCIPAL CITIES
(Including Figures
from Latest Population
Estimates)
Pop.—Thousands
8 Acre ......G 8
7 Bethlehem .N 9
1 Bittir .....N 9
17 Gaza.......O 2
99 Haifa......H 7
18 Hebron...O 8
71 Jaffa......H 7
3 Jenin .....J 10
125 Jerusalem N 10
11 Ludd......M 6
17 Nablus
(Shechem) K 10
9 Nazareth..H 10
9 Safed ....G 12
4 Seffurieh ..H 10
Shechem,
see Nablus.
140 Tel Aviv..L 5
9 Tubariya..H 12

LEBANON
Area ..3,474 sq. m.
Pop......848 ,833
PRINCIPAL CITIES
Pop.—Thousands
161 Beyrouth A 12
14 Zahle....A 16

SYRIA
Area .72,723 sq. m.
Pop.....2,367,734
PRINCIPAL CITIES
(Including Figures
from Latest Population
Estimates)
Pop.—Thousands
5 Baalbek...A 18
319 Damas
(Damascus)
D 20
6 Sour (Tyre) E 9

TRANSJORDAN
Area .35,326 sq. m.
Pop......400,000
PRINCIPAL CITIES
(Including Figures
from Latest Population
Estimates)
Pop.—Thousands
15 Amman..M 16
10 Es Salt....L 14
3 Kerak.....Q 13
(P. I. & C. 78)

67896

IRAN
(PERSIA)

Area 628,000 sq.m.
Pop.... 15,055,115

PRINCIPAL CITIES

(Including Figures
from Latest Population Estimates)

Pop.—Thousands

40	Abadeh	K 7
20	Aderkan	P 8
6	Ahar	G 3
20	Amul	E 7
8	Anar	L 10
45	Ardebil	C 4
10	Ardistan	I 7
20	Asterabad	E 9
11	Babahan	L 5
30	Babol	E 8
12	Bahramabad	L 11
10	Bam	N 13
8	Bandar Abbas	P 11
19	Bandar Abu Shehr	N 6
	Barfrush, see Babul	
10	Binah	D 2
25	Birjand	J 13
8	Bujnurd	D 12
35	Burujird	H 4
	Bushire, see Bandar Abu Shehr	
6	Bustam	E 10
15	Damghan	F 9
5	Demavend	F 7
50	Dizful	J 3
	Enzelli, see Pahlevi	
15	Fesa	N 8
104	Hamadan	G 4
10	Hissar	E 2
205	Isfahan	H 7
40	Kashan	H 7
7	Kazerun	M 6
59	Kerman	L 11
89	Kermanshahan	G 2
6	Khaf	H 15
25	Khoi	B 1
16	Khonsar	I 5
22	Khorramshahr	I 3
6	Khur	H 9
35	Kom	N 10
17	Kuchan	E 13
	Kum, see Qum	
7	Lahijan	D 6
5	Lar	Q 9
9	Lingeh	Q 9
130	Mashhad	F 14
7	Mianeh	D 3
11	Minab	P 12
5	Nain	I 8
20	Nishapur	F 13
38	Pahlevi	D 5
60	Qazvin	F 5
39	Qum	O 9
122	Resht	D 5
50	Rezaieh	D 1
7	Sagzabad	F 5
20	Samnan	F 8
5	Sari	E 8
7	Sava	G 6
18	Sebzewar	F 12
5	Sehkoha	K 16
6	Shahpur (Dilman)	C 1
15	Shahrud	E 10
8	Shamsabad	K 8
7	Shehr-i-Babek	L 10
129	Shiraz	M 7
18	Shustar	J 4
55	Sultanabad	H 5
6	Tabbas	I 12
220	Tabriz	C 2
540	Tehran	F 7
	Urmia, see Rezaieh	
55	Yezd	K 9
10	Zenjan	E 4

AFGHANISTAN

Area 245,000 sq.m.
Pop.... 12,000,000

PRINCIPAL CITIES

(Including Figures
from Latest Population Estimates)

Pop.—Thousands

20	Andkhui	E 19
15	Balkh	E 20
6	Budwan	K 19
10	Ghazni	H 22
	(Ghuznee)	
10	Ghuznigik	K 22
100	Herat	H 16
200	Kabul	G 23
60	Kandahar	K 20
18	Sabzawar	
	Sebzar	I 17
15	Sir-i-pul	F 20
10	Tash-Kurgan	E 21

(P. I. & C. 678)

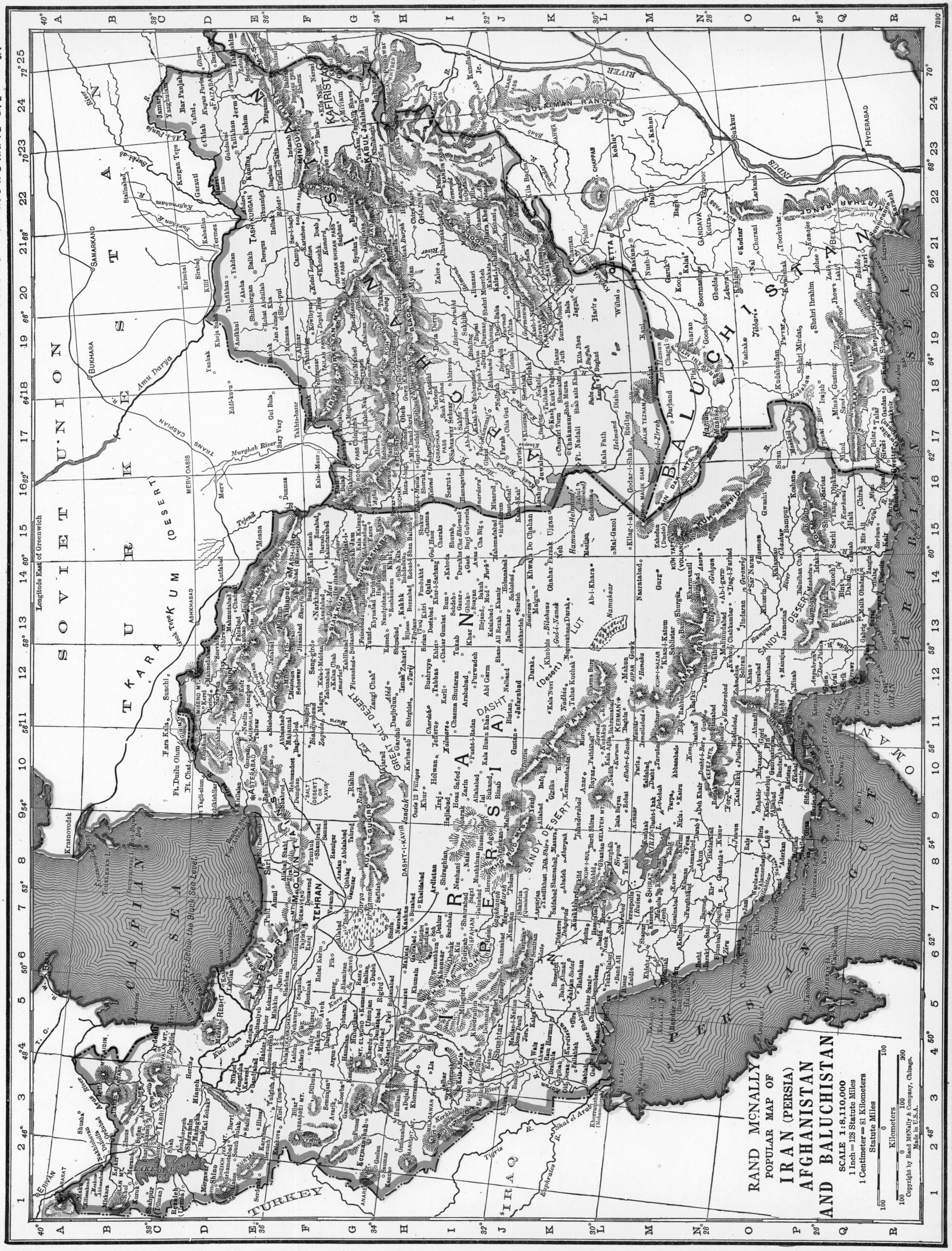

RAND MCNALLY POPULAR MAP OF IRAN (PERSIA) AFGHANISTAN AND BALUCHISTAN

SCALE 1:8,110,000
1 Inch = 128 Statute Miles
1 Centimeter = 81 Kilometers
Made in U.S.A.

Copyright by Rand McNally & Company, Chicago.

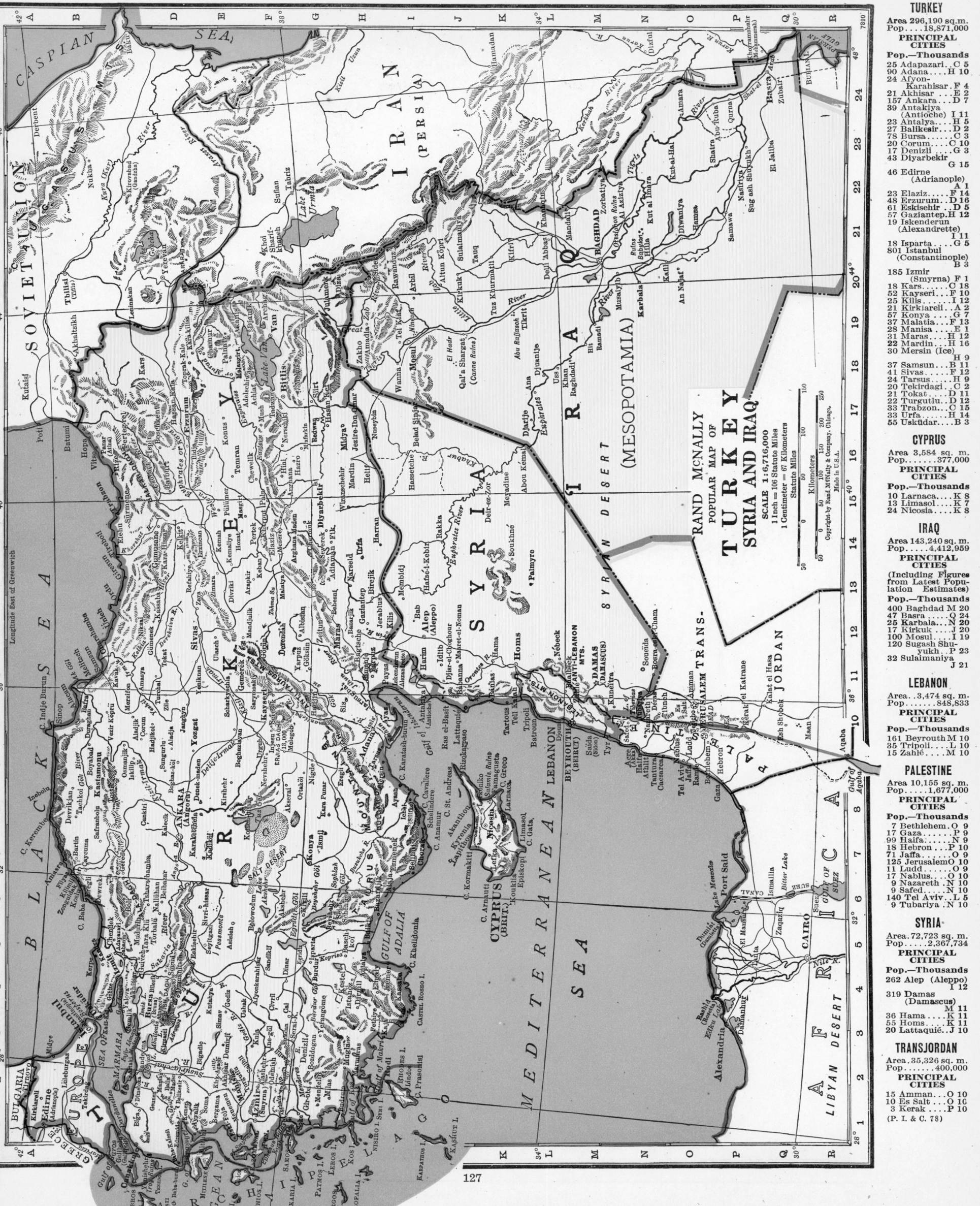

RAND McNALLY
POPULAR MAP OF
TURKEY
SYRIA AND IRAQ

SCALE 1:6,716,000
1 Inch = 106 Statute Miles
1 Centimeter = 67 Kilometers
Made in U. S. A.
Copyright by Rand McNally & Company, Chicago

TURKEY

Area 296,190 sq. m.
Pop....18,871,000
PRINCIPAL CITIES
Pop.—Thousands
25 Adapazari...C 5
90 Adana....H 10
24 Afyon-
Karahisar.F 4
21 Akhisar...E 2
157 Ankara...D 7
39 Antakiya
(Antioche) I 11
23 Antalya...H 5
27 Balikesir..D 2
78 Bursa....C 3
20 Corum...C 10
17 Denizli....G 3
43 Diyarbekir
G 15
46 Edirne
(Adrianople)
A 1
23 Elaziz....F 14
48 Erzurum..D 16
61 Eskisehir..D 5
57 Gaziantep.H 12
19 Iskenderun
(Alexandrette)
I 11
18 Isparta...G 5
801 Istanbul
(Constantinople)
B 3
185 Izmir
(Smyrna) F 1
18 Kars....C 18
52 Kayseri..F 10
25 Kilis....I 12
21 Kirklareli..A 2
17 Konya....G 7
37 Malatia..F 13
28 Manisa..E 1
31 Maras...H 12
22 Mardin..H 16
30 Mersin (Ice)
H 9
37 Samsun..B 11
41 Sivas....F 12
24 Tarsus...H 9
20 Tekirdagi..C 2
21 Tokat....D 11
22 Turgutlu..D 12
33 Trabzon..C 15
33 Urfa....H 14
55 Uskudar....B 3

CYPRUS

Area 3,584 sq. m.
Pop......377,000
PRINCIPAL CITIES
Pop.—Thousands
10 Larnaca...K 8
13 Limasol...K 7
24 Nicosia....K 8

IRAQ

Area 143,240 sq. m.
Pop....4,412,959
PRINCIPAL CITIES
(Including Figures
from Latest Popu-
lation Estimates)
Pop.—Thousands
400 Baghdad M 20
47 Basra...Q 24
25 Karbala..N 20
17 Kirkuk ..I 20
100 Mosul....I 19
120 Sugash Shu-
yukh...P 23
32 Sulaimaniya
J 21

LEBANON

Area...3,474 sq. m.
Pop......848,833
PRINCIPAL CITIES
Pop.—Thousands
161 Beyrouth M 10
35 Tripoli...L 10
15 Zahlé....M 10

PALESTINE

Area 10,155 sq. m.
Pop....1,677,000
PRINCIPAL CITIES
Pop.—Thousands
7 Bethlehem.O 9
17 Gaza...P 9
99 Haifa....N 9
18 Hebron...P 10
71 Jaffa....O 9
125 JerusalemO 10
11 Ludd...O 9
17 Nablus...O 10
9 Nazareth..N 10
9 Safed...N 10
140 Tel Aviv..L 5
9 Tubariya .N 10

SYRIA

Area 72,723 sq. m.
Pop....2,367,734
PRINCIPAL CITIES
Pop.—Thousands
262 Alep (Aleppo)
I 12
319 Damas
(Damascus)
M 11
36 Hama....K 11
55 Homs....K 11
20 Lattaquié..J 10

TRANSJORDAN

Area 35,326 sq. m.
Pop......400,000
PRINCIPAL CITIES
Pop.—Thousands
15 Amman...O 10
10 Es Salt ..O 10
3 Kerak ...P 10
(P. I. & C. 78)

RAND McNALLY
POPULAR MAP OF
AFRICA
SCALE 1:33,898,000
1 Inch = 535 Statute Miles
1 Centimeter = 339 Kilometers
Statute Miles

Kilometers

Copyright by Rand McNally & Company, Chicago.
Made in U.S.A.

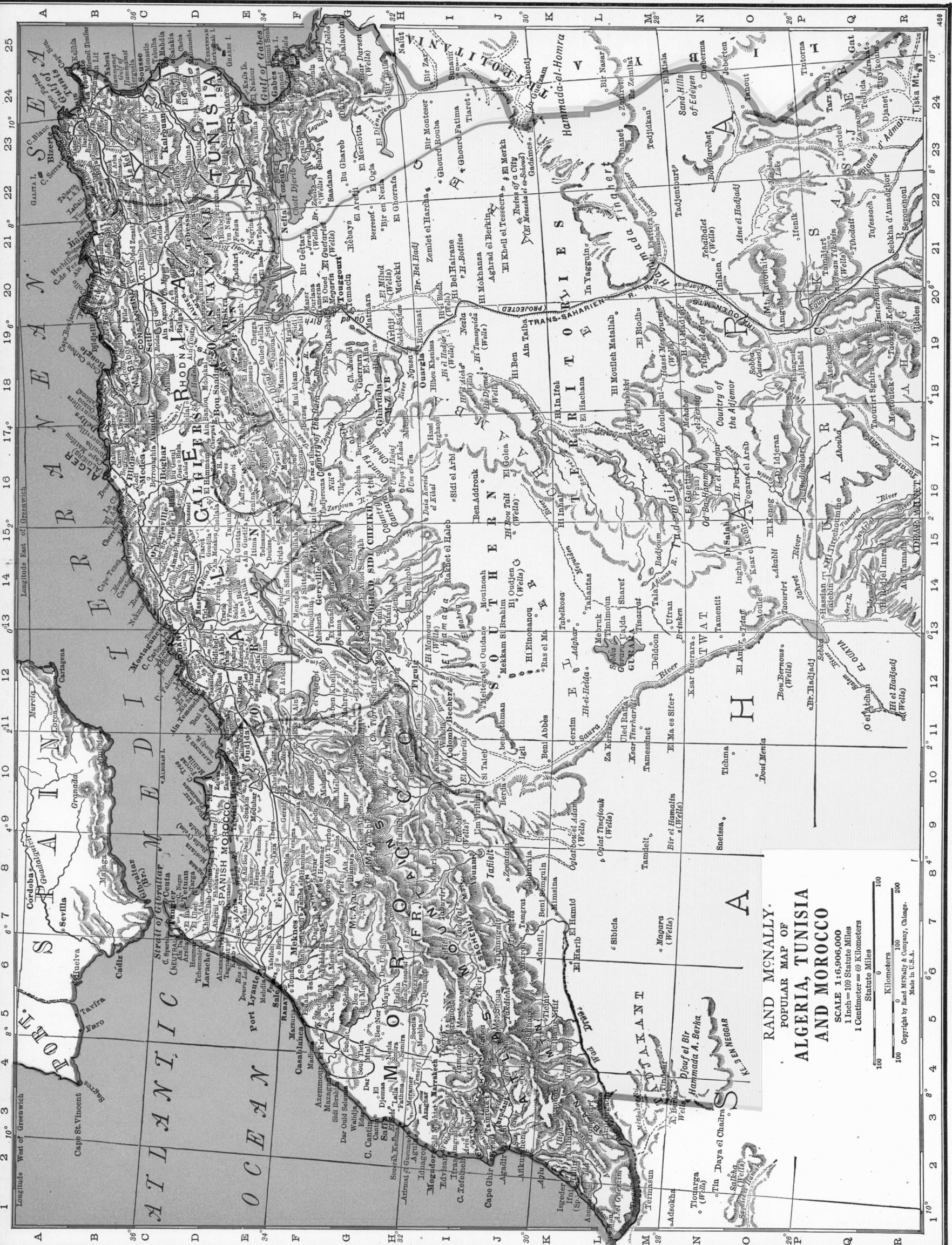

RAND McNALLY
POPULAR MAP OF
ALGERIA, TUNISIA
AND MOROCCO

SCALE 1:6,906,000
1 Inch = 109 Statute Miles
1 Centimeter = 69 Kilometers

Copyright by Rand McNally & Company, Chicago.
Made in U.S.A.

Statute Miles

Kilometers

ALGERIA

Area 847,818 sq.m.
Pop.....7,234,684

PRINCIPAL CITIES
(Including Figures
from Latest Population Estimates)
Pop.—Thousands

7 Affreville..O 16
14 Ain Beida..C 21
17 Ain Temouchent...D 11
264 Alger
(Algiers) B 16
5 Arzeu....C 12
4 Aumale...C 17
14 Batna....D 19
11 Biskra...E 19
30 Blida....C 16
86 Bône....B 21
6 Boufarik..C 16
25 Bougie...B 19
7 Bou Saada D 18
13 Cherchel..B-15
114 Constantine
C 20
5 Daya....E 12
11 Djidjelli,
(Jijelli)..B 19
6 Douera...E 16
5 Doussen..E 18
8 El Affroun C 16
12 El Oued..G 20
12 Géryville..F 14
12 Ghardaia..H 18
9 Guelma..B 21
5 Guerrara..G 18
8 Khenchela..D 21
10 Laghouat..E 16
24 Maison Carree
B 17
31 Mascara..C 13
16 Medea....C 16
7 Megarin..G 20
13 Millana...C 15
5 MograrFoukani
F 14
5 Mondovi..B 21
38 Mostaganem
C 13
6 Nedroma..C 11
201 Oran....D 12
9 Orleansville
C 15
6 Ouargla..G 19
18 Perregaux..D 13
51 Philippeville
B 20
9 Randon...B 21
15 Relizane..D 14
5 Rio SaladoD 12
5 Rouiba...B 17
14 Saida....D 14
11 St. Denis-du-
Sig....D 13
32 Setif....C 19
53 Sidi Bel Abbes
D 12
14 Souk-Ahras
B 22
5 Stitten...F 14
8 Tebessa...D 21
7 Temacin..G 20
7 Tenez....C 15
24 Tiaret...D 15
1 Timimoun..L 13
26 Tlemcen..D 12
12 Touggourt.G 20

MOROCCO

Area 200,000 sq.m.
Pop.....7,996,000

PRINCIPAL CITIES
(Including Figures
from Latest Population Estimates)
Pop.—Thousands

463 Casablanca
E 5
59 Ceuta....C 8
179 Fés (Fez)..F 8
15 Figuig...H 12
184 Marrakech
(Morocco)..I 4
113 Meknes
(Meknes) F 7
77 Melilla...D 10
21 Mogador..I 2
64 Oujda....E 11
122 Rabat....F 5
26 Safi.....H 3
44 Sale.....F 5
60 Tangier...D 7

TUNISIA

Area .48,300 sq. m.
Pop.....2,608,300

PRINCIPAL CITIES
(Including Figures
from Latest Population Estimates)
Pop.—Thousands

23 Bizerte..A 23
10 Gabes....F 24
22 Kairouan..C 24
8 Monastir..C 25
8 Nabeul..B 25
40 Sfax....D 25
25 Sousse...C 24
202 Tunis....B 24

(P. I. & C. 567)

129

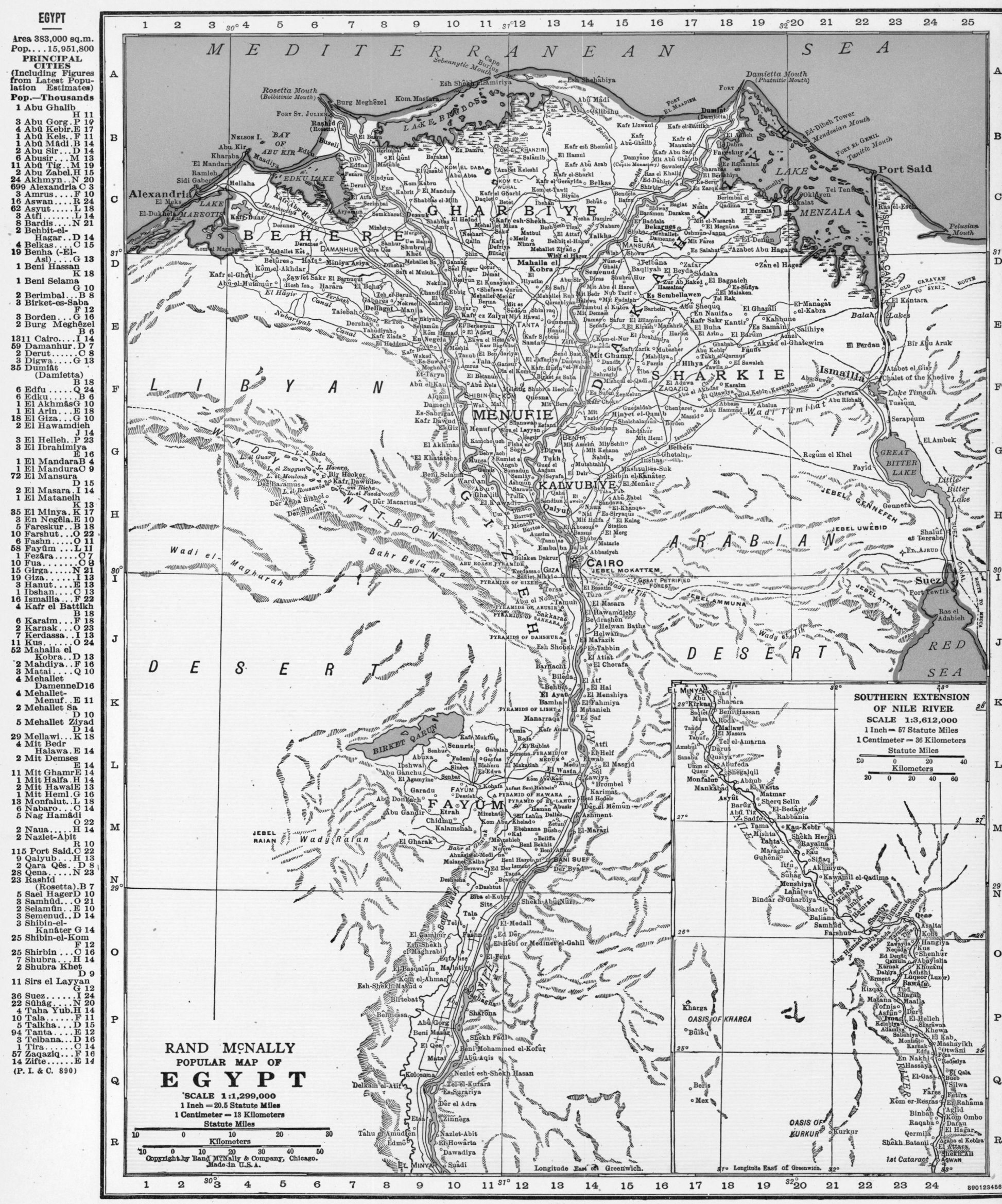

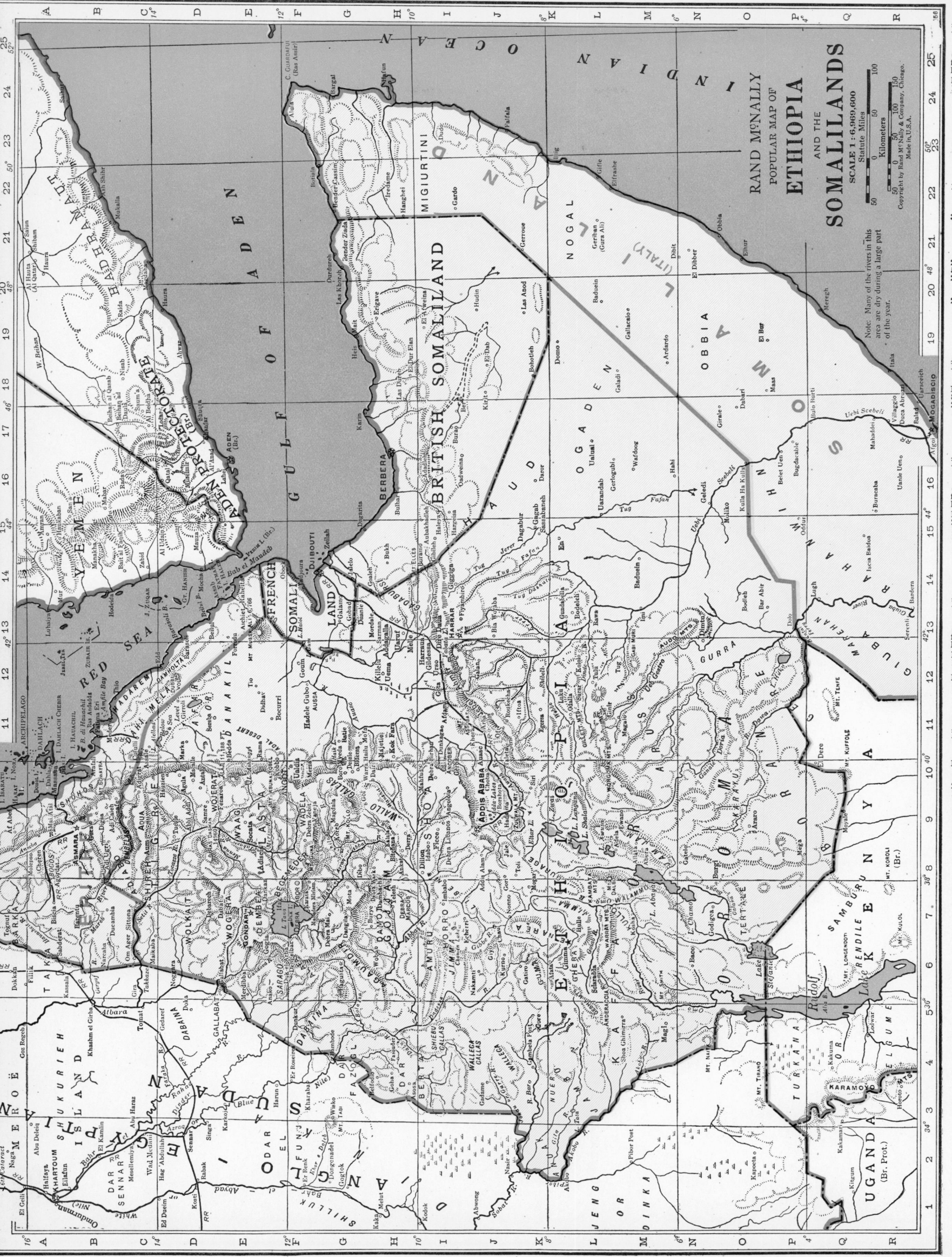

RAND McNALLY
POPULAR MAP OF
ETHIOPIA
AND THE
SOMALILANDS
SCALE 1:6,969,600

Copyright by Rand McNally & Company, Chicago.
Made in U.S.A.

Note: Many of the rivers in this area are dry during a large part of the year.

ETHIOPIA
Area..350,000 sq. m.
Pop.....7,500,000

PRINCIPAL CITIES
(Including Figures from Latest Population Estimates)

Pop. Thousands
129 Addis Abeba
.... J 9
2 Adigrat...C 10
5 Adua.....C 9
3 Afgoi.....R 17
5 Aksum....C 9
2 Alula.....F 24
2 Ancober...I 10
2 Anderaccia. L 5
1 Angolola...I 10
1 Antalo...E 10
3 Debra Birhan
.... I 10
10 Debra Marcos
.... H 7
3 Debra Tabor
.... F 8
30 Dire Daua. I 12
2 Ficce......I 9
3 Gambela Post
.... K 4
4 Giggiga ...I 14
3 Gondar ...E 7
20 Gore......K 5
50 Harrar ...I 13
20 Jiran ....K 6
3 Macalle ..D 10
3 Magdala ..G 9
21 MogadiscioR 17
3 Nakamiti..J 6
3 Samre.....D 9
1 Socota....E 9

ERITREA
Area..45,783 sq. m.
Pop.......596,944

PRINCIPAL CITIES
Pop.—Thousands
85 Asmara...A 9
20 Massaua..A 9

BRITISH SOMALILAND
Area..68,000 sq. m.
Pop.......344,768

PRINCIPAL CITIES
(Including Figures from Latest Population Estimates)

Pop. Thousands
20 Berbera..H 17
10 Burao ...I 17
17 Hargeisa..I 15
1 Zeilah....G 15

FRENCH SOMALILAND
Area..5,790 sq. m.
Pop.......46,391

PRINCIPAL CITIES
(Including Figures from Latest Population Estimates)

Pop. Thousands
10 Djibouti..F 14
3 Tadjoura..F 14
Pop. Hundreds
5 Obok.....F 14

SOMALILAND
(It.)
Area..190,000 sq. m.
Pop.......1,210,000

PRINCIPAL CITIES
Pop.—Thousands
3 Bardera ..P 13
3 Lugh.....P 14
21 Mogadiscio R 17
15 Villaggio Duca
Abruzzi..R 17

(P. & I. 678)

UNION OF SOUTH AFRICA

Area 472,550 sq. m.
Pop....10,160,000

PRINCIPAL CITIES
(Including Figures from Latest Population Estimates)
Pop.—Thousands

20 Beaconsfield J 15
8 Beaufort West O 12
6 Bethlehem. I 18
43 Bizana...M 20
51 Bloemfontein J 16
9 Bredasdorf. R 9
17 Bridgetown P 7
352 Capetown. Q 7
9 Cradock...O 15
270 Durban...L 21
47 East London P 18
68 Germiston.F 18
12 Graaf Reinet O 13
9 Graafwater O 7
20 Grahamstown P 16
9 Harrismith.I 19
10 Impendhle.L 19
554 Johannesburg F 18
39 Kimberley.J 14
10 King Williams Town P 17
6 Klerksdorp G 16
14 Kroonstad.I 17
55 Krugersdorp F 17
25 Kuruman.H 13
10 Ladysmith.J 20
26 Libode...N 19
26 Maclear..M 18
27 Marico...F 16
7 Mossel Bay Q 11
35 Mquanduli N 18
18 Oudtshoorn Q 11
19 Paarl...Q 7
47 Pietermaritzburg..K 21
118 Port Elizabeth Q 15
19 Potchefstroom G 16
138 Pretoria..F 18
7 Prieska...K 11
18 Queens Town N 16
34 Qumbu...M 18
23 Taungs...H 14
15 Ubombo..J 22
21 Uitenhage.Q 15
37 Umzimkulu L 19
8 Witbank...G 17
13 Wolmaransstadt...H 15
43 Worcester..Q 8
12 Zwart Kop L 10

BASUTOLAND

Area..11,716 sq. m.
Pop......562,311

PRINCIPAL CITY
(Including Figures from Latest Population Estimates)
Pop.—Thousands

2 Maseru..K 18

BECHUANALAND

Area 275,000 sq. m.
Pop......265,756

PRINCIPAL CITIES
(Including Figures from Latest Population Estimates)
Pop.—Thousands

8 Mochudi..D 15
20 Serowe...A 17

SOUTHWEST AFRICA

Area 322,393 sq. m.
Pop......288,000

PRINCIPAL CITIES
(Including Figures from Latest Population Estimates)
Pop.—Thousands

14 Grootfontein E 4
4 Keetmanshoop G 7
3 Lüderitz..G 3
9 Rehoboth..C 5
3 Swakopmund B 1
1 Walvis Bay C 1
20 Windhoek..B 5

SWAZILAND

Area..6,705 sq. m.
Pop......156,715

PRINCIPAL CITIES
(Including Figures from Latest Population Estimates)
Pop.— Hundreds

1 Bremersdorp G 22
2 Mbabane .G 22

(P. I. & C. 7890)

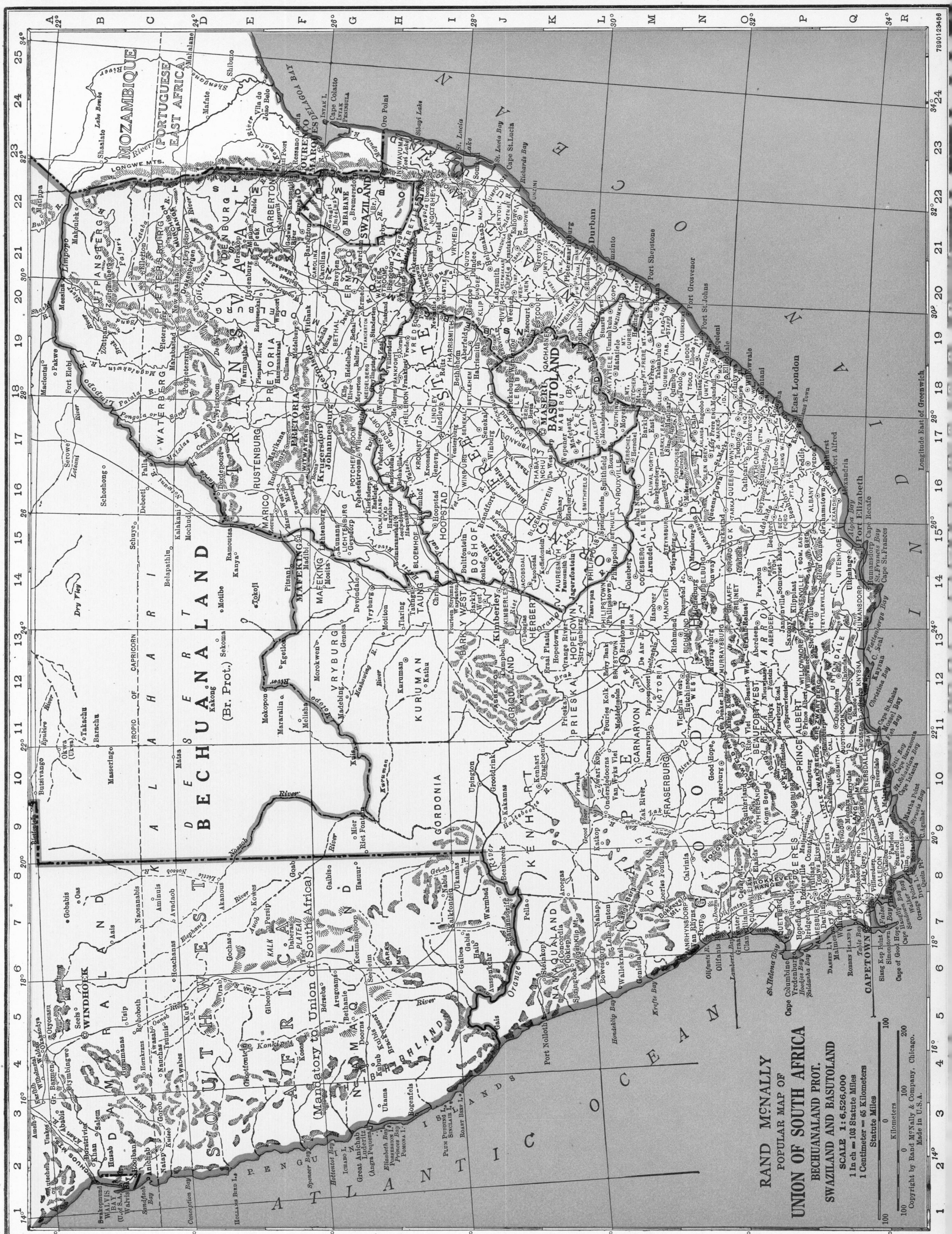

RAND McNALLY
POPULAR MAP OF
UNION OF SOUTH AFRICA
BECHUANALAND PROT.
SWAZILAND AND BASUTOLAND

SCALE 1:6,526,000
1 Inch = 103 Statute Miles
1 Centimeter = 65 Kilometers

Statute Miles

Kilometers

Copyright by Rand McNally & Company, Chicago.
Made in U.S.A.

ATLANTIC OCEAN

INDIAN OCEAN

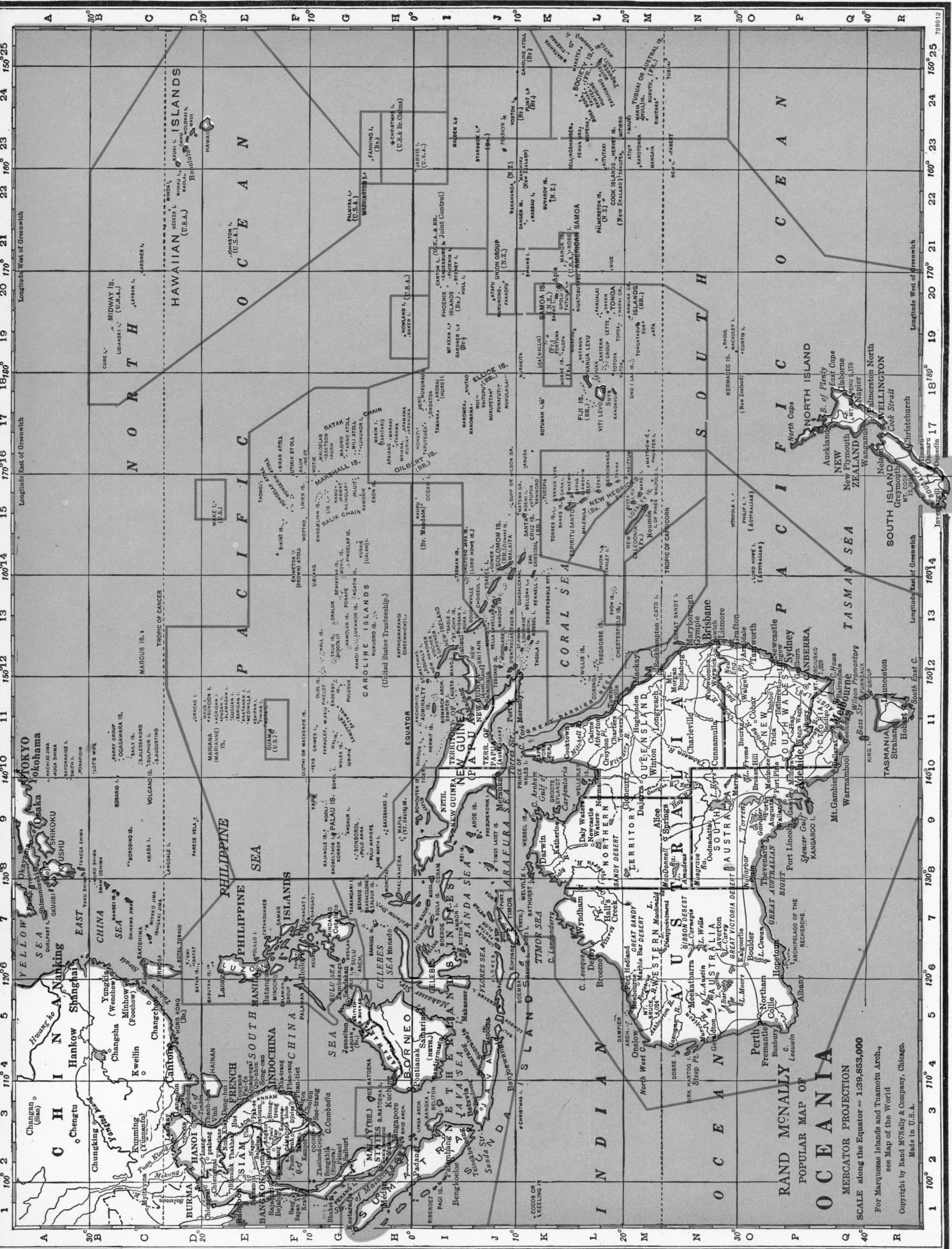

RAND MCNALLY
POPULAR MAP OF
OCEANIA

MERCATOR PROJECTION

SCALE along the Equator = 1:39,853,000

For Marquesas Islands and Tuamotu Arch.,
see Map of the World

Copyright by Rand McNally & Company, Chicago.
Made in U.S.A.

133

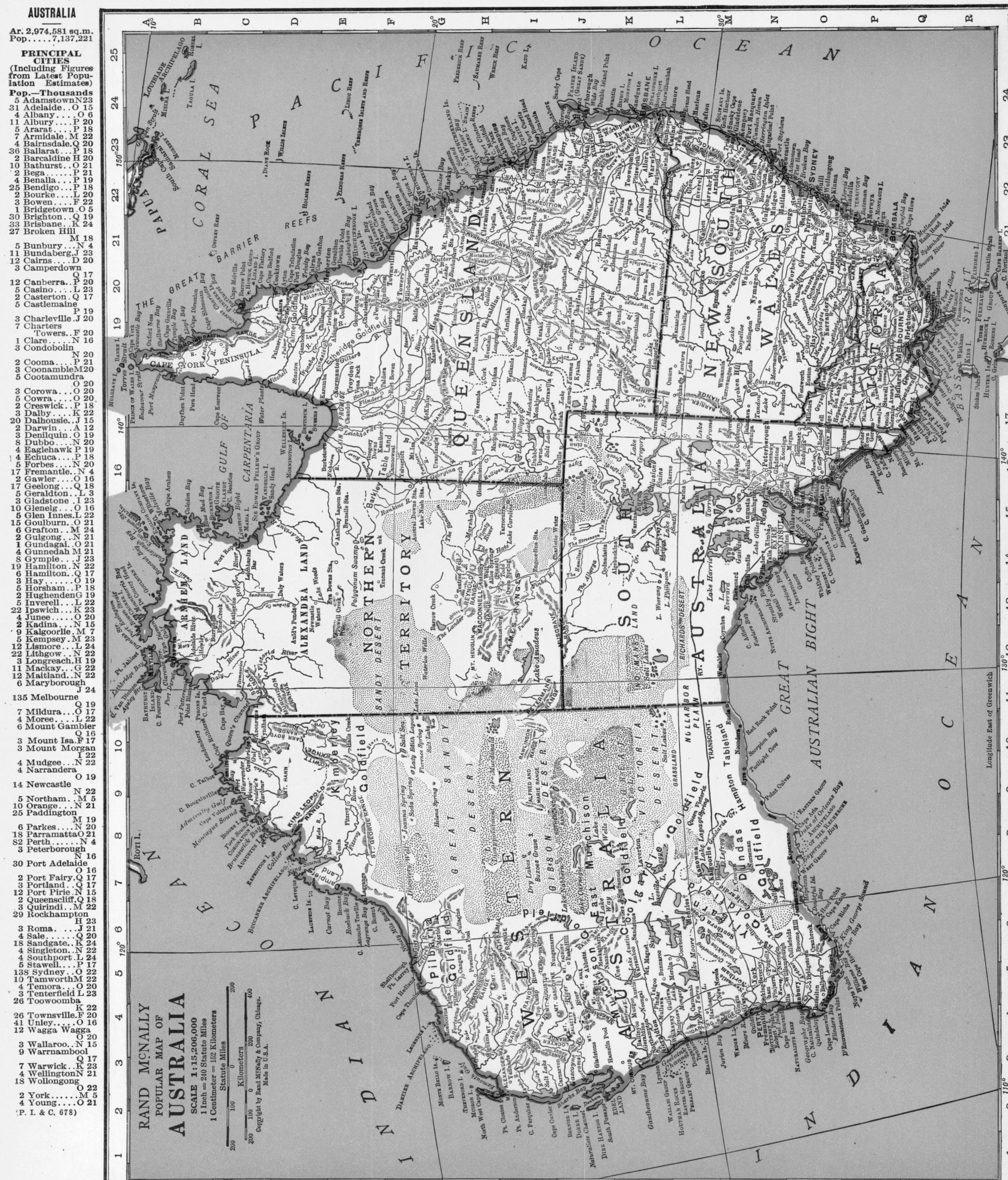

Ar. 2,974,581 sq. m.
Pop.....7,137,221

PRINCIPAL CITIES
(Including Figures from Latest Population Estimates)
Pop.—Thousands

RAND McNALLY
POPULAR MAP OF
AUSTRALIA
SCALE 1:15,206,000
1 Inch = 240 Statute Miles
1 Centimeter = 152 Kilometers

Statute Miles

Kilometers

Copyright by Rand McNally & Company, Chicago.
Made in U.S.A.

RAND MCNALLY
POPULAR MAP OF
NEW ZEALAND
TASMANIA AND FIJI ISLANDS
SCALE 1:4,879,000
1 Inch = 77 Statute Miles
1 Centimeter = 49 Kilometers
Statute Miles

Copyright by Rand McNally & Company, Chicago.
Made in U.S.A.

TASMANIA
SCALE 1:5,005,000
Statute Miles

FIJI ISLANDS
SCALE 1:5,069,000
Statute Miles

NEW ZEALAND

Area 103,862 sq. m.
Pop....1,618,093

PRINCIPAL CITIES
(Including Figures from Latest Population Estimates)

Pop.—Thousands

1 Ahaura....K 11
7 Ashburton N 11
107 Auckland D 17
2 Balclutha...Q 7
1 Belgrove...J 13
5 Blenheim..J 15
2 Cambridge E 18
2 Carterton..J 18
101 Christchurch
....M 12
2 Dargaville.C 15
2 Drury.....D 17
65 Dunedin...P 9
1 FeatherstonJ 18
1 Feilding...I 18
2 Foxton....I 18
14 Gisborne..G 23
9 Gore Junction
....Q 6
8 Greymouth L10
2 Greytown..J 18
18 Hamilton..E 18
14 Hastings..H 21
1 Havelock..J 15
5 Hawera...H 16
1 Helensville
....D 16
3 Hokitika...L 9
1 Huntly....E 18
1 Inglewood.G 16
23 Invercargill Q 5
2 Kaiapoi...M 12
1 Kaitangata.Q 7
1 Kelso.....Q 6
1 Levin.....I 18
1 Lyttelton..M 13
1 Marton...H 18
9 Masterton..J 18
2 Mataura...P 6
1 Mauriceville
....J 18
1 Methven..M 11
2 Milton....Q 8
2 Morrinsville
....E 18
2 Mosgiel Jc..P 8
2 Motueka...J 13
17 Napier....H 21
11 Nelson....J 14
18 New Plymouth
....G 15
8 Oamaru...O 9
1 Ohakune..G 18
11 Onehunga D 17
2 Opotiki...F 22
1 Orari.....N 10
2 Paeroa...E 19
24 Palmerston,
North....I 18
1 Patea....H 16
11 Petone...J 17
1 Picton...J 15
2 Rangiora..M 12
2 Reefton...K 11
1 Richmond..J 13
7 Rotorua..F 20
2 Selwyn....M 12
1 Shannon...I 18
2 Sheffield..M 11
2 Stratford..G 16
3 Taumarunui
....G 18
4 Tauranga..E 19
2 Te Aroha..E 19
3 Te Kuiti..F 17
4 Thames...D 18
18 Timaru...N 10
2 Waimate..O 10
1 Waipawa..H 20
1 Wallingford
....I 20
23 Wanganui.H 17
121 Wellington
....J 17
4 Westport..K 10
8 Whangarei B 16
1 Woodville..I 19

TASMANIA

Area..26,215 sq. m.
Pop.......241,171

PRINCIPAL CITIES
(Including Figures from Latest Population Estimates)

Pop.—Thousands

4 Burnie....B 5
2 Deloraine..C 6
5 Devonport.C 7
61 Hobart....E 6
1 Latrobe...C 7
28 Launceston.C 7
1 Longford..C 7
2 New Norfolk
....E 7
4 QueenstownD 4
1 St. Mary's.C 9
1 Scottsdale.C 8
1 Ulverstone..C 6
1 Westbury..C 7
2 Zeehan....C 4

FIJI ISLANDS

Area..7,083 sq. m.
Pop......227,280

PRINCIPAL CITY
(Including Figures from Latest Population Estimates)

Pop.—Thousands

8 Suva......Q 17
(P. I. & C. 67)

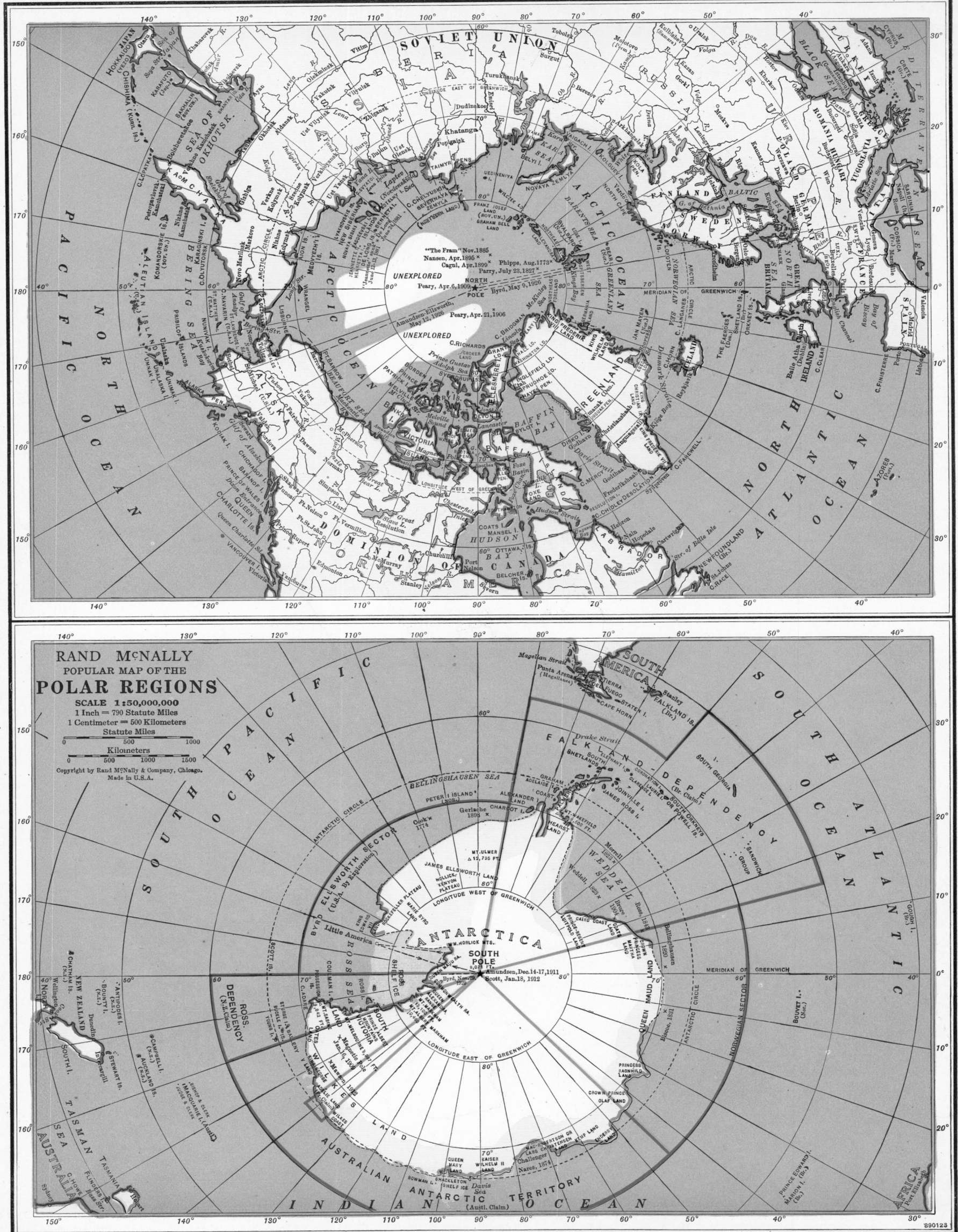

RAND McNALLY
POPULAR MAP OF THE
POLAR REGIONS
SCALE 1:50,000,000
1 Inch = 790 Statute Miles
1 Centimeter = 500 Kilometers
Statute Miles
Kilometers
Copyright by Rand McNally & Company, Chicago.
Made in U.S.A.

Counties of the United States

TOTAL NUMBER 3071

(Not including District of Columbia and Independent Cities in Virginia)

A list of the Counties of the United States, indexed alphabetically by states; with 1940 Census figure for each.

ALABAMA

COUNTIES.

TOTAL NUMBER 67

Pop.	County	Index
20,977	Autauga	I 13
32,324	Baldwin	P 7
32,722	Barbour	L 21
20,155	Bibb	H 11
29,490	Blount	E 14
19,810	Bullock	K 19
32,447	Butler	L 13
63,319	Calhoun	E 19
42,146	Chambers	H 21
19,928	Cherokee	D 19
27,955	Chilton	H 13
20,195	Choctaw	L 4
27,636	Clarke	L 7
16,907	Clay	G 18
13,629	Cleburne	F 20
31,987	Coffee	N 17
34,093	Colbert	B 7
25,489	Conecuh	N 11
13,460	Coosa	H 16
42,417	Covington	N 15
23,631	Crenshaw	M 15
47,343	Cullman	D 12
22,685	Dale	N 19
55,245	Dallas	K 11
43,075	DeKalb	C 19
34,546	Elmore	I 16
30,671	Escambia	O 10
72,580	Etowah	D 17
21,651	Fayette	E 8
27,552	Franklin	C 7
29,172	Geneva	O 18
19,185	Greene	H 6
25,533	Hale	I 8
21,912	Henry	M 22
45,665	Houston	O 21
41,802	Jackson	A 18
459,930	Jefferson	F 12
19,708	Lamar	E 6
46,230	Lauderdale	A 8
27,880	Lawrence	B 10
36,455	Lee	I 21
35,642	Limestone	A 11
22,661	Lowndes	K 13
27,654	Macon	J 19
66,317	Madison	A 14
35,736	Marengo	J 7
28,776	Marion	D 6
42,395	Marshall	C 15
141,974	Mobile	P 4
29,465	Monroe	M 9
114,420	Montgomery	K 16
48,148	Morgan	C 12
26,610	Perry	I 10
27,671	Pickens	G 6
32,493	Pike	L 18
25,516	Randolph	G 20
35,775	Russell	J 21
27,336	Saint Clair	E 16
28,962	Shelby	G 14
27,321	Sumter	J 5
51,832	Talladega	G 16
35,270	Tallapoosa	H 19
76,036	Tuscaloosa	G 9
64,201	Walker	E 10
16,188	Washington	M 4
26,279	Wilcox	L 9
18,746	Winston	D 10
2,832,961	Total	

ALASKA

DISTRICTS

TOTAL NUMBER 4

Pop.	District
25,241	First Judicial
11,877	Second Judicial
19,312	Third Judicial
16,094	Fourth Judicial
72,524	Total

ARIZONA

COUNTIES.

TOTAL NUMBER 14

Pop.	County	Index
24,095	Apache	G 23
34,627	Cochise	P 22
18,770	Coconino	E 13
23,867	Gila	K 18
12,113	Graham	L 22
8,698	Greenlee	L 24
186,193	Maricopa	K 11
8,591	Mohave	F 5
25,309	Navajo	F 20
72,838	Pima	O 13
28,841	Pinal	M 16
9,482	Santa Cruz	Q 18
26,511	Yavapai	H 11
19,326	Yuma	L 5
499,261	Tota	

ARKANSAS

COUNTIES.

TOTAL NUMBER 75

Pop.	County	Index
24,437	Arkansas	L 16
26,785	Ashley	Q 14
10,281	Baxter	A 12
36,148	Benton	B 4
15,860	Boone	B 9
18,097	Bradley	P 13
9,636	Calhoun	O 11
14,737	Carroll	A 7
27,452	Chicot	Q 17
24,402	Clark	M 9
28,386	Clay	A 20
13,134	Cleburne	E 14
12,570	Cleveland	N 13
29,822	Columbia	Q 8
21,536	Conway	G 11
47,200	Craighead	D 19
23,920	Crawford	E 4
42,473	Crittenden	H 21
26,046	Cross	G 19
14,471	Dallas	M 11
27,160	Desha	O 17
19,831	Drew	O 15
25,880	Faulkner	H 12
15,683	Franklin	E 6
10,253	Fulton	A 14
41,664	Garland	J 9
10,477	Grant	L 12
30,204	Greene	C 20
32,770	Hempstead	O 6
18,916	Hot Spring	L 9
16,621	Howard	M 6
25,643	Independence	E 16
12,834	Izard	C 14
26,427	Jackson	E 17
65,101	Jefferson	L 14
18,795	Johnson	E 8
16,851	Lafayette	Q 7
22,651	Lawrence	C 17
26,810	Lee	I 19
19,709	Lincoln	M 15
15,932	Little River	O 4
25,967	Logan	G 7
29,802	Lonoke	J 14
14,531	Madison	C 7
9,464	Marion	B 11
31,874	Miller	Q 6
80,217	Mississippi	D 22
21,133	Monroe	J 17
8,876	Montgomery	K 7
19,869	Nevada	O 8
10,881	Newton	D 9
31,151	Ouachita	O 10
8,392	Perry	I 10
45,970	Phillips	K 19
11,786	Pike	L 7
37,670	Poinsett	E 19
15,832	Polk	K 5
25,682	Pope	F 9
15,304	Prairie	J 16
156,085	Pulaski	I 12
18,319	Randolph	B 18
36,043	Saint Francis	H 19
19,163	Saline	J 11
13,300	Scott	I 5
11,942	Searcy	D 11
62,809	Sebastian	G 4
15,248	Sevier	M 4
11,497	Sharp	C 16
8,603	Stone	D 13
50,461	Union	Q 11
12,518	Van Buren	E 12
41,114	Washington	C 4
37,176	White	G 15
22,133	Woodruff	G 17
20,970	Yell	H 8
1,949,387	Total	

CALIFORNIA

COUNTIES.

TOTAL NUMBER 58

Pop.	County	Index
513,011	Alameda	I 6, F 22
323	Alpine	G 11
8,973	Amador	H 9
42,840	Butte	F 7
8,221	Calaveras	H 9
9,788	Colusa	F 5
100,450	Contra Costa	I 6, D 22
4,745	Del Norte	B 2
13,229	Eldorado	G 9
178,565	Fresno	K 10
12,195	Glenn	F 6
45,812	Humboldt	D 2
59,740	Imperial	Q 22
7,625	Inyo	K 16
135,124	Kern	M 13
35,168	Kings	L 11
8,069	Lake	G 4
14,479	Lassen	D 9
2,785,643	Los Angeles	N 15, Q 4
23,314	Madera	J 12
52,907	Marin	C 14, H 4
5,605	Mariposa	I 11
27,864	Mendocino	F 3
46,988	Merced	J 9
8,713	Modoc	B 9
2,299	Mono	H 13
73,032	Monterey	K 7
28,503	Napa	G 5, A 18
19,283	Nevada	F 9
130,760	Orange	P 17, R 6
28,108	Placer	G 9
11,548	Plumas	E 9
105,524	Riverside	P 19, R 9
170,333	Sacramento	H 8
11,392	San Benito	K 8
161,108	San Bernardino	N 18, P 9
289,348	San Diego	Q 19
634,536	San Francisco	I 5
134,207	San Joaquin	H 8
33,246	San Luis Obispo	M 10
111,782	San Mateo	I 5, G 17
70,555	Santa Barbara	N 11
174,949	Santa Clara	J 6, H 22
45,057	Santa Cruz	J 5
28,800	Shasta	D 6
3,025	Sierra	F 10
28,598	Siskiyou	B 5
49,118	Solano	H 6, B 22
69,052	Sonoma	G 3, A 15
74,866	Stanislaus	I 9
18,680	Sutter	G 7
14,316	Tehama	E 6
3,970	Trinity	D 4
107,152	Tulare	L 13
10,887	Tuolumne	H 10
69,685	Ventura	N 13
27,243	Yolo	G 6
17,034	Yuba	F 8
6,907,387	Total	

COLORADO

COUNTIES.

TOTAL NUMBER 63

Pop.	County	Index
22,481	Adams	F 17
10,484	Alamosa	P 12
32,150	Arapahoe	G 17
3,806	Archuleta	Q 8
6,207	Baca	Q 23
9,653	Bent	N 21
37,438	Boulder	E 14
8,109	Chaffee	J 11
2,964	Cheyenne	J 23
3,784	Clear Creek	G 13
11,648	Conejos	Q 11
7,533	Costilla	Q 13
5,398	Crowley	L 19
2,270	Custer	M 13
16,470	Delta	J 5
322,412	Denver	F 15
1,958	Dolores	O 3
3,496	Douglas	H 15
5,361	Eagle	G 9
5,460	Elbert	H 17
54,025	El Paso	K 16
19,742	Fremont	L 13
10,560	Garfield	G 4
1,625	Gilpin	F 13
3,587	Grand	E 11
6,192	Gunnison	K 8
349	Hinsdale	O 7
16,088	Huerfano	O 15
1,798	Jackson	C 10
30,725	Jefferson	G 14
2,793	Kiowa	L 23
7,512	Kit Carson	H 23
6,883	Lake	I 10
15,494	La Plata	P 6
35,539	Larimer	B 13
32,369	Las Animas	Q 18
5,882	Lincoln	J 20
18,370	Logan	B 21
33,791	Mesa	I 3
975	Mineral	O 8
5,086	Moffat	B 4
10,463	Montezuma	P 3
15,418	Montrose	L 4
17,214	Morgan	E 19
23,571	Otero	N 19
2,089	Ouray	M 5
3,272	Park	I 12
4,948	Phillips	C 24
1,836	Pitkin	I 8
12,304	Prowers	N 24
68,870	Pueblo	M 16
2,943	Rio Blanco	E 4
12,404	Rio Grande	P 10
10,525	Routt	C 8
6,173	Saguache	N 10
1,439	San Juan	O 6
3,664	San Miguel	N 3
5,294	Sedgwick	B 24
1,754	Summit	G 11
6,463	Teller	J 14
8,336	Washington	E 21
63,747	Weld	B 17
12,102	Yuma	E 24
1,123,296	Total	

CONNECTICUT

COUNTIES.

TOTAL NUMBER 8

Pop.	County	Index
418,384	Fairfield	N 5
450,189	Hartford	E 13
87,041	Litchfield	D 6
55.999	Middlesex	K 15
484,316	New Haven	K 11
125,224	New London	I 21
31,866	Tolland	D 18
56,223	Windham	D 23
1,709,242	Total	

DELAWARE

COUNTIES.

TOTAL NUMBER 3

Pop.	County	Index
34,441	Kent	H 21
179,562	New Castle	D 21
52,502	Sussex	K 22
266,505	Total	

DISTRICT OF COLUMBIA

DISTRICT

Pop.		Index
663,091	District of Columbia	J 11

FLORIDA

COUNTIES.

TOTAL NUMBER 67

Pop.	County	Index
38,607	Alachua	D 13
6,510	Baker	C 14
20,686	Bay	N 9
8,717	Bradford	C 14
16,142	Brevard	H 21
39,794	Broward	N 22
8,218	Calhoun	B 1
3,663	Charlotte	K 16
5,846	Citrus	G 13
6,468	Clay	C 15
5,102	Collier	N 19
16,859	Columbia	C 12
267,739	Dade	O 22
7,792	De Soto	K 16
7,018	Dixie	D 10
210,143	Duval	C 16
74,667	Escambia	M 2
3,008	Flagler	E 18
5,991	Franklin	D 3
31,450	Gadsden	B 3
4,250	Gilchrist	D 11
2,745	Glades	K 19
6,951	Gulf	P 11
9,778	Hamilton	B 10
10,158	Hardee	J 16
5,237	Hendry	L 19
5,641	Hernando	G 13
9,246	Highlands	K 19
180,148	Hillsborough	I 14
15,447	Holmes	M 9
8,957	Indian River	I 22
34,428	Jackson	A 1
12,032	Jefferson	B 7
4,405	Lafayette	C 10
27,255	Lake	G 16
17,488	Lee	M 16
31,646	Leon	B 5
12,550	Levy	E 12
3,752	Liberty	C 2
16,190	Madison	B 8
26,098	Manatee	J 14
31,243	Marion	E 15
6,295	Martin	K 22
14,078	Monroe	P 19
10,826	Nassau	B 16
12,900	Okaloosa	M 5
3,000	Okeechobee	J 20
70,074	Orange	G 18
10,119	Osceola	I 19
79,989	Palm Beach	L 23
13,981	Pasco	H 13
91,852	Pinellas	I 12
86,665	Polk	I 17
18,698	Putnam	D 16
20,012	Saint Johns	D 18
11,871	Saint Lucie	J 22
16,085	Santa Rosa	M 3
16,106	Sarasota	K 14
22,304	Seminole	G 18
11,041	Sumter	G 15
17,073	Suwannee	C 10
11,565	Taylor	C 8
7,094	Union	C 13
53,710	Volusia	F 18
5,463	Wakulla	C 5
14,246	Walton	M 7
12,302	Washington	M 9
1,897,414	Total	

GEORGIA

COUNTIES.

TOTAL NUMBER 159

Pop.	County	Index
14,497	Appling	M 18
7,093	Atkinson	N 15
8,096	Bacon	M 17
7,344	Baker	N 6
24,190	Baldwin	H 13
8,733	Banks	D 12
13,064	Barrow	E 10
25,283	Bartow	D 4
14,523	Ben Hill	M 13
15,370	Berrien	N 13
83,783	Bibb	I 10
9,655	Bleckley	J 12
6,871	Brantley	O 20
20,497	Brooks	P 11
6,288	Bryan	L 23
26,010	Bulloch	J 21
26,520	Burke	H 20
9,182	Butts	H 9
10,438	Calhoun	M 5
5,910	Camden	O 22
9,103	Candler	K 19
34,156	Carroll	G 3
12,199	Catoosa	B 3
5,256	Charlton	P 19
117,970	Chatham	L 24
15,138	Chattahoochee	K 4
18,532	Chattooga	C 2
20,126	Cherokee	D 6
28,398	Clarke	E 12
7,064	Clay	M 3
11,655	Clayton	G 7
6,437	Clinch	O 16
38,272	Cobb	E 6
21,541	Coffee	M 15
33,012	Colquitt	O 10
9,433	Columbia	G 19
11,919	Cook	O 12
26,972	Coweta	G 4
7,128	Crawford	I 9
17,540	Crisp	L 10
5,894	Dade	B 1
4,479	Dawson	D 8
22,234	Decatur	O 5
86,942	DeKalb	F 8
21,022	Dodge	K 13
16,886	Dooly	K 10
28,565	Dougherty	M 7
10,053	Douglas	F 5
18,679	Early	N 3
2,964	Echols	P 15
9,646	Effingham	K 24
19,618	Elbert	E 15
23,517	Emanuel	J 18
7,401	Evans	K 20
14,752	Fannin	B 7
8,170	Fayette	G 6
56,141	Floyd	D 2
11,322	Forsyth	D 8
15,612	Franklin	D 13
392,886	Fulton	F 7
9,001	Gilmer	C 6
4,547	Glascock	H 16
21,920	Glynn	N 22
18,445	Gordon	C 4
19,654	Grady	P 7
13,709	Greene	G 13
29,087	Gwinnett	E 9
14,771	Habersham	C 11
34,822	Hall	D 10
12,764	Hancock	H 14
14,377	Haralson	F 2
11,428	Harris	I 4
15,512	Hart	D 15
8,610	Heard	G 3
15,119	Henry	G 8
11,303	Houston	J 11
12,936	Irwin	M 13
20,089	Jackson	E 11
8,772	Jasper	G 10
8,841	Jeff Davis	M 16
20,040	Jefferson	H 17
11,843	Jenkins	I 20
12,953	Johnson	I 16
8,331	Jones	H 11
10,091	Lamar	H 8
5,632	Lanier	O 14
33,606	Laurens	J 15
7,837	Lee	M 8
8,595	Liberty	L 22
7,042	Lincoln	F 17
4,086	Long	M 21
31,860	Lowndes	P 13
6,223	Lumpkin	C 9
10,878	McDuffie	G 17
5,292	McIntosh	M 23
15,947	Macon	K 8
13,431	Madison	E 13
6,954	Marion	K 6
22,055	Meriwether	H 5
9,998	Miller	O 4
23,261	Mitchell	N 7
10,749	Monroe	H 9
9,668	Montgomery	K 17
12,713	Morgan	F 12
11,137	Murray	C 5
75,494	Muscogee	J 4
18,576	Newton	G 9
7,576	Oconee	F 12
12,430	Oglethorpe	F 14
12,832	Paulding	E 4
10,378	Peach	J 10
9,136	Pickens	D 6
11,800	Pierce	N 18
10,375	Pike	H 7
28,467	Polk	E 2
9,829	Pulaski	K 11
8,514	Putnam	G 12
3,435	Quitman	L 3
7,821	Rabun	B 12
16,609	Randolph	M 4
81,863	Richmond	G 19
7,724	Rockdale	F 9
5,033	Schley	K 7
20,353	Screven	I 22
8,492	Seminole	O 4
28,427	Spalding	H 7
12,972	Stephens	C 13
10,603	Stewart	L 4
24,502	Sumter	L 8
8,141	Talbot	I 6
6,278	Taliaferro	G 15
16,243	Tattnall	K 19
10,768	Taylor	J 8
15,145	Telfair	L 15
16,675	Terrell	M 6
31,289	Thomas	P 9
18,599	Tift	N 11
16,952	Toombs	K 18
4,925	Towns	B 10
7,632	Treutlen	J 17
43,879	Troup	H 3
10,846	Turner	M 11
9,117	Twiggs	J 12
7,680	Union	B 9
25,064	Upson	I 7
31,024	Walker	C 2
20,777	Walton	F 10
27,929	Ware	O 17
10,236	Warren	G 16
24,230	Washington	I 15
13,122	Wayne	M 20
4,726	Webster	L 6
8,535	Wheeler	L 16
6,417	White	C 10
26,105	Whitfield	C 3
12,755	Wilcox	L 12
15,084	Wilkes	F 16
11,025	Wilkinson	I 13
21,374	Worth	M 10
3,123,723	Total	

IDAHO

COUNTIES.

TOTAL NUMBER 44

Pop.	County	Index
50,401	Ada	O 5
3,407	Adams	K 4
34,759	Bannock	Q 19
7,911	Bear Lake	Q 22
7,332	Benewah	E 4
21,044	Bingham	O 19
5,295	Blaine	O 13
2,333	Boise	M 6
15,667	Bonner	B 5
25,697	Bonneville	N 18
5,987	Boundary	A 5
1,877	Butte	N 15
1,360	Camas	N 10
40,987	Canyon	N 4
2,284	Caribou	P 21
14,430	Cassia	R 14
1,005	Clark	M 18
8,243	Clearwater	F 7
3,549	Custer	L 12
5,518	Elmore	O 8
10,229	Franklin	R 20
10,304	Fremont	M 21
9,544	Gem	M 5
9,257	Gooding	P 10
12,691	Idaho	I 8
10,762	Jefferson	N 18
9,900	Jerome	P 12
22,283	Kootenai	E 5
18,804	Latah	F 4
6,521	Lemhi	J 11
4,666	Lewis	H 4
4,230	Lincoln	P 12
9,186	Madison	N 21
9,870	Minidoka	P 14
18,873	Nez Perce	H 3
5,417	Oneida	Q 17
5,652	Owyhee	Q 6
9,511	Payette	M 3
3,965	Power	Q 17
21,230	Shoshone	D 6
3,601	Teton	N 22
36,403	Twin Falls	Q 11
4,035	Valley	L 7
8,853	Washington	L 3
524,873	Total	

ILLINOIS

COUNTIES.

TOTAL NUMBER 102

Pop.	County	Index
65,229	Adams	I 5
25,496	Alexander	R 14
14,540	Bond	M 13
15,202	Boone	A 16
8,053	Brown	I 7
37,600	Bureau	D 12
8,207	Calhoun	L 7
17,987	Carroll	B 11
16,425	Cass	I 9
70,578	Champaign	H 19
38,564	Christian	J 14
18,842	Clark	K 21
18,947	Clay	M 18
22,912	Clinton	N 13
38,470	Coles	J 19
4,063,342	Cook	C 21
21,294	Crawford	L 21
11,698	Cumberland	K 19
34,388	De Kalb	C 16
18,244	De Witt	H 16
17,590	Douglas	J 19
103,480	Du Page	C 19
24,430	Edgar	J 21
8,974	Edwards	N 20
22,034	Effingham	L 17
29,159	Fayette	L 15
15,007	Ford	G 19
53,137	Franklin	O 16
44,627	Fulton	G 9
11,414	Gallatin	P 19
20,292	Greene	K 9
18,398	Grundy	E 18
13,454	Hamilton	O 17
26,297	Hancock	G 5
7,759	Hardin	Q 19
8,949	Henderson	F 6
43,798	Henry	D 10
32,496	Iroquois	G 21
37,920	Jackson	P 13
13,431	Jasper	L 19
34,375	Jefferson	N 16
13,636	Jersey	L 8
19,989	Jo Daviess	A 10
10,727	Johnson	Q 16
130,206	Kane	B 18
60,877	Kankakee	E 21
11,105	Kendall	D 18
52,250	Knox	F 9
121,094	Lake	A 20
97,801	La Salle	D 16
21,075	Lawrence	M 21
34,604	Lee	B 14
38,838	Livingston	F 17
29,438	Logan	H 13
26,944	McDonough	H 7
37,311	McHenry	A 18
73,930	McLean	G 16
84,693	Macon	I 15
46,304	Macoupin	K 11
149,349	Madison	M 11
47,989	Marion	M 16
13,179	Marshall	E 13
15,358	Mason	H 11
14,937	Massac	R 17
10,663	Menard	I 11
17,701	Mercer	E 7
12,754	Monroe	O 10
34,499	Montgomery	K 13
36,378	Morgan	J 10
13,477	Moultrie	J 17
29,869	Ogle	B 13
153,374	Peoria	F 11
23,438	Perry	O 13
14,659	Piatt	I 17
25,340	Pike	J 6
7,999	Pope	Q 17
15,875	Pulaski	R 15
5,289	Putnam	E 14
33,608	Randolph	O 11
17,137	Richland	M 20
113,323	Rock Island	D 8
166,899	Saint Clair	N 11
38,066	Saline	P 17
117,912	Sangamon	J 12
11,430	Schuyler	H 7
8,176	Scott	J 8
26,290	Shelby	K 16
8,881	Stark	E 11
40,646	Stephenson	A 12
58,362	Tazewell	G 12
21,528	Union	Q 14
86,791	Vermilion	H 21
13,724	Wabash	N 21
21,286	Warren	F 7
15,801	Washington	N 13
22,092	Wayne	N 18
20,027	White	O 19
43,338	Whiteside	C 11
114,210	Will	D 20
51,424	Williamson	Q 16
121,178	Winnebago	A 14
19,124	Woodford	F 14
7,897,241	Total	

INDIANA

COUNTIES.

TOTAL NUMBER 92

Pop.	County	Index
21,254	Adams	F 21
155,084	Allen	D 21
28,276	Bartholomew	L 16
11,117	Benton	F 7
13,783	Blackford	G 19
22,081	Boone	I 12
6,189	Brown	L 14
15,410	Carroll	F 11
36,908	Cass	E 13
31,020	Clark	O 17
25,365	Clay	K 8
28,411	Clinton	G 12
10,171	Crawford	P 12
26,163	Daviess	N 8
23,053	Dearborn	M 22
17,722	Decatur	L 18
24,756	De Kalb	C 21
74,963	Delaware	H 19
22,579	Dubois	P 9
72,634	Elkhart	B 16
19,411	Fayette	J 20
35,061	Floyd	P 16
18,299	Fountain	H 7
14,412	Franklin	K 21
15,577	Fulton	D 13
30,709	Gibson	P 5
55,813	Grant	G 17
31,330	Greene	M 9
24,614	Hamilton	I 15
17,302	Hancock	J 16
17,106	Harrison	P 15
20,151	Hendricks	J 12
40,208	Henry	I 18
47,752	Howard	G 14
29,931	Huntington	E 18
26,612	Jackson	N 15
14,397	Jasper	E 8
22,601	Jay	G 21
19,912	Jefferson	N 19
13,680	Jennings	M 18
22,493	Johnson	K 14
43,973	Knox	N 6
29,561	Kosciusko	C 16
14,352	Lagrange	B 18
293,195	Lake	C 7
63,660	La Porte	B 10
35,045	Lawrence	N 12
88,575	Madison	H 17
460,926	Marion	J 14
25,935	Marshall	C 13
10,300	Martin	O 10
27,926	Miami	E 15
36,534	Monroe	L 12
27,231	Montgomery	I 10
19,801	Morgan	K 12
10,775	Newton	E 7
22,776	Noble	C 18
3,782	Ohio	M 22
17,311	Orange	O 12
12,090	Owen	L 10
17,358	Parke	J 8
17,770	Perry	Q 11
17,045	Pike	P 7
27,836	Porter	C 8
19,183	Posey	Q 3
12,056	Pulaski	D 10
20,839	Putnam	J 10
26,766	Randolph	H 21
18,898	Ripley	M 20
18,927	Rush	J 18
161,823	Saint Joseph	B 13
8,978	Scott	N 17
25,953	Shelby	K 17
16,211	Spencer	Q 9

Pop.	County	Index
12,258	Starke	C 10
13,740	Steuben	B 21
27,014	Sullivan	M 6
8,167	Switzerland	N 22
51,020	Tippecanoe	G 9
15,135	Tipton	G 15
6,017	Union	J 22
130,783	Vanderburg	Q 5
21,787	Vermillion	I 6
99,709	Vigo	K 6
26,601	Wabash	E 16
9,055	Warren	G 7
19,435	Warrick	Q 7
17,008	Washington	O 14
59,229	Wayne	I 21
19,099	Wells	F 20
17,037	White	F 9
17,001	Whitley	D 18
3,427,796	Total	

IOWA

COUNTIES.

TOTAL NUMBER 99

Pop.	County	Index
13,196	Adair	M 8
10,156	Adams	N 7
17,184	Allamakee	C 20
24,245	Appanoose	O 15
11,790	Audubon	K 7
22,879	Benton	I 18
79,946	Black Hawk	G 17
29,782	Boone	J 10
17,932	Bremer	E 17
20,991	Buchanan	G 19
19,838	Buena Vista	F 6
17,986	Butler	F 15
17,584	Calhoun	H 8
22,770	Carroll	I 7
18,647	Cass	M 7
16,884	Cedar	J 21
43,845	Cerro Gordo	D 13
19,258	Cherokee	F 4
15,227	Chickasaw	C 17
10,233	Clarke	O 11
17,762	Clay	D 6
24,334	Clayton	E 20
44,722	Clinton	J 24
20,538	Crawford	I 5
24,649	Dallas	K 10
11,136	Davis	P 17
14,012	Decatur	P 11
18,487	Delaware	G 21
36,804	Des Moines	O 21
12,185	Dickinson	B 6
63,768	Dubuque	G 22
13,406	Emmet	B 8
29,151	Fayette	E 19
20,169	Floyd	D 15
16,379	Franklin	F 13
14,645	Fremont	P 4
16,599	Greene	I 9
13,518	Grundy	G 15
17,210	Guthrie	K 8
19,922	Hamilton	H 11
15,402	Hancock	D 11
22,530	Hardin	G 13
22,767	Harrison	K 3
17,994	Henry	N 20
13,531	Howard	B 17
13,459	Humboldt	E 9
11,047	Ida	G 4
17,016	Iowa	K 18
19,181	Jackson	H 23
31,496	Jasper	K 14
15,762	Jefferson	N 18
33,191	Johnson	K 20
19,950	Jones	I 21
18,406	Keokuk	M 18
26,630	Kossuth	C 10
41,074	Lee	P 21
89,142	Linn	I 20
11,384	Louisa	M 21
14,571	Lucas	N 13
15,374	Lyon	B 2
14,525	Madison	M 10
26,485	Mahaska	M 16
27,019	Marion	M 14
35,406	Marshall	I 14
15,064	Mills	N 4
14,121	Mitchell	B 15
18,238	Monona	I 2
14,553	Monroe	N 15
15,697	Montgomery	N 6
31,296	Muscatine	L 22
19,293	O'Brien	D 4
10,607	Osceola	B 4
24,887	Page	P 5
16,170	Palo Alto	D 8
23,502	Plymouth	E 2
16,266	Pocahontas	F 8
195,835	Polk	K 12
66,756	Pottawattamie	M 4
18,758	Poweshiek	K 16
11,137	Ringgold	P 9
17,639	Sac	G 6
84,748	Scott	K 24
16,720	Shelby	K 5
27,209	Sioux	C 2
33,434	Story	I 12
22,428	Tama	I 16
14,258	Taylor	P 7
16,280	Union	O 10
12,053	Van Buren	P 18
44,280	Wapello	O 17
17,695	Warren	M 12
20,055	Washington	M 19
13,308	Wayne	P 13
41,521	Webster	H 10
13,972	Winnebago	B 11
22,263	Winneshiek	B 19
103,627	Woodbury	G 2
11,449	Worth	B 13
20,038	Wright	F 11
2,538,268	Total	

KANSAS

COUNTIES.

TOTAL NUMBER 105

Pop.	County	Index
19,874	Allen	L 23
11,658	Anderson	J 23
22,222	Atchison	E 23
9,073	Barber	O 12
25,010	Barton	I 11
20,944	Bourbon	L 24
17,395	Brown	D 22
32,013	Butler	L 18
6,345	Chase	J 19
9,233	Chautauqua	O 20
29,817	Cherokee	N 24
6,221	Cheyenne	D 2
4,081	Clark	N 8
13,281	Clay	F 16
17,247	Cloud	E 15
12,278	Coffey	J 21
4,412	Comanche	O 10
38,139	Cowley	O 18
44,191	Crawford	M 24
7,434	Decatur	D 6
22,929	Dickinson	H 17
12,936	Doniphan	D 23
25,171	Douglas	H 23
6,377	Edwards	L 10
8,180	Elk	M 20
17,508	Ellis	G 10
9,855	Ellsworth	I 13
10,092	Finney	K 5
17,254	Ford	M 8
20,889	Franklin	I 23
15,222	Geary	G 18
4,793	Gove	H 6
6,071	Graham	F 8
1,946	Grant	M 3
4,773	Gray	M 6
1,638	Greeley	I 2
16,495	Greenwood	L 20
2,645	Hamilton	K 2
12,068	Harper	O 14
21,712	Harvey	K 16
2,088	Haskell	M 5
3,535	Hodgeman	K 8
13,382	Jackson	F 21
12,718	Jefferson	F 22
11,970	Jewell	D 13
33,327	Johnson	G 24
2,525	Kearny	K 3
12,001	Kingman	M 13
5,112	Kiowa	M 10
30,352	Labette	N 23
2,821	Lane	I 6
41,112	Leavenworth	F 24
8,338	Lincoln	G 13
11,969	Linn	J 24
3,688	Logan	G 4
26,424	Lyon	I 20
24,152	McPherson	J 15
18,951	Marion	J 17
20,986	Marshall	D 19
5,522	Meade	O 6
19,489	Miami	I 24
11,339	Mitchell	F 13
49,729	Montgomery	O 21
10,363	Morris	H 18
2,186	Morton	N 2
16,761	Nemaha	D 20
22,210	Neosho	M 23
6,864	Ness	I 8
9,831	Norton	D 8
15,118	Osage	H 21
9,835	Osborne	F 12
9,224	Ottawa	G 15
10,300	Pawnee	K 10
10,435	Phillips	D 10
14,015	Pottawatomie	F 19
12,348	Pratt	M 11
6,618	Rawlins	D 4
52,165	Reno	L 13
13,124	Republic	D 15
17,213	Rice	J 13
20,617	Riley	F 18
8,497	Rooks	F 10
8,285	Rush	I 10
13,464	Russell	H 11
29,535	Saline	H 15
3,773	Scott	I 5
143,311	Sedgwick	M 16
6,540	Seward	N 4
91,247	Shawnee	G 21
5,312	Sheridan	F 6
6,421	Sherman	E 2
10,582	Smith	D 11
10,487	Stafford	K 12
1,443	Stanton	M 2
3,193	Stevens	O 3
26,163	Sumner	O 16
6,425	Thomas	F 4
5,822	Trego	H 8
9,219	Wabaunsee	G 20
2,216	Wallace	G 2
15,921	Washington	D 17
2,185	Wichita	I 3
17,723	Wilson	M 21
8,014	Woodson	L 21
145,071	Wyandotte	F 25
1,801,028	Total	

KENTUCKY

COUNTIES.

TOTAL NUMBER 120

Pop.	County	Index
18,566	Adair	I 15
15,496	Allen	K 12
8,936	Anderson	F 16
9,480	Ballard	I 4
27,559	Barren	J 13
11,451	Bath	E 19
43,812	Bell	K 20
10,820	Boone	C 17
17,932	Bourbon	E 18
45,938	Boyd	E 23
17,075	Boyle	H 16
9,389	Bracken	D 19
23,946	Breathitt	H 21
17,744	Breckinridge	G 12
9,511	Bullitt	F 14
14,371	Butler	I 11
14,499	Caldwell	I 8
19,041	Calloway	K 6
71,918	Campbell	C 18
7,650	Carlisle	J 4
8,657	Carroll	D 15
25,545	Carter	E 21
19,962	Casey	I 16
36,129	Christian	J 9
17,988	Clark	F 18
23,901	Clay	I 20
10,279	Clinton	K 15
12,115	Crittenden	H 7
11,923	Cumberland	K 15
52,335	Daviess	G 10
11,344	Edmonson	I 12
8,713	Elliott	F 21
17,978	Estill	G 19
78,899	Fayette	F 17
13,327	Fleming	E 20
52,986	Floyd	H 22
23,308	Franklin	E 16
15,413	Fulton	K 4
4,307	Gallatin	C 16
11,910	Garrard	G 17
9,876	Grant	D 17
31,763	Graves	K 5
17,562	Grayson	H 12
12,321	Green	I 14
24,917	Greenup	D 22
6,807	Hancock	G 11
29,108	Hardin	G 13
75,275	Harlan	J 21
15,124	Harrison	D 18
17,239	Hart	I 13
27,020	Henderson	G 9
12,220	Henry	D 15
9,142	Hickman	K 4
37,789	Hopkins	I 8
16,339	Jackson	H 19
385,392	Jefferson	F 14
12,174	Jessamine	G 17
25,771	Johnson	G 22
93,139	Kenton	C 17
20,007	Knott	H 22
31,029	Knox	J 19
9,622	Larue	H 14
25,640	Laurel	I 19
17,275	Lawrence	F 22
10,860	Lee	G 20
14,981	Leslie	I 21
40,592	Letcher	J 22
15,686	Lewis	D 21
19,859	Lincoln	H 17
9,127	Livingston	I 6
23,345	Logan	J 11
9,067	Lyon	I 7
48,534	McCracken	J 5
16,451	McCreary	K 18
11,446	McLean	H 10
28,541	Madison	G 18
17,490	Magoffin	G 21
16,913	Marion	H 15
16,602	Marshall	J 6
10,970	Martin	G 23
19,066	Mason	D 19
8,827	Meade	F 12
5,691	Menifee	F 20
14,629	Mercer	G 16
10,853	Metcalfe	J 14
14,070	Monroe	K 14
12,280	Montgomery	F 19
16,827	Morgan	F 21
37,554	Muhlenberg	I 10
18,004	Nelson	G 15
8,617	Nicholas	E 19
24,421	Ohio	H 10
10,716	Oldham	E 14
10,942	Owen	D 17
8,957	Owsley	H 20
10,392	Pendleton	C 18
47,828	Perry	I 21
71,122	Pike	H 24
7,671	Powell	G 19
39,863	Pulaski	I 17
3,419	Robertson	D 19
17,165	Rockcastle	I 18
12,734	Rowan	F 21
13,615	Russell	J 16
14,314	Scott	E 17
17,759	Shelby	F 15
11,752	Simpson	K 11
6,757	Spencer	F 15
13,556	Taylor	H 15
14,234	Todd	J 10
12,784	Trigg	K 8
5,601	Trimble	D 15
17,411	Union	G 7
36,631	Warren	J 12
12,965	Washington	G 15
17,204	Wayne	J 16
19,198	Webster	H 8
33,186	Whitley	J 18
9,997	Wolfe	G 20
11,847	Woodford	F 17
2,845,627	Total	

LOUISIANA

PARISHES

TOTAL NUMBER 64

Pop.	Parish	Index
46,260	Acadia	M 10
17,540	Allen	K 8
21,215	Ascension	M 15
18,541	Assumption	N 15
39,256	Avoyelles	I 11
14,847	Beauregard	K 6
23,933	Bienville	D 7
33,162	Bossier	B 5
150,203	Caddo	C 4
56,506	Calcasieu	M 6
12,046	Caldwell	E 11
7,203	Cameron	N 5
14,618	Catahoula	G 12
29,855	Claiborne	A 7
14,562	Concordia	G 13
31,803	De Soto	E 4
88,415	East Baton Rouge	K 15
19,023	East Carroll	B 14
18,039	East Feliciana	J 15
30,497	Evangeline	K 9
32,382	Franklin	E 12
15,933	Grant	G 9
37,183	Iberia	N 12
27,721	Iberville	M 14
17,807	Jackson	D 9
50,427	Jefferson	O 18
24,191	Jefferson Davis	L 8
43,941	Lafayette	M 11
38,615	Lafourche	O 16
10,959	La Salle	F 10
24,790	Lincoln	C 8
17,790	Livingston	L 16
18,443	Madison	D 14
27,571	Morehouse	A 12
40,997	Natchitoches	F 7
494,537	Orleans	N 19
59,168	Ouachita	C 10
12,318	Plaquemines	O 19
24,004	Pointe Coupee	J 12
73,370	Rapides	I 9
15,881	Red River	E 6
28,829	Richland	D 12
23,586	Sabine	G 5
7,280	Saint Bernard	N 20
12,321	Saint Charles	N 17
9,542	Saint Helena	J 16
16,596	Saint James	M 16
14,766	Saint John the Baptist	M 17
71,481	Saint Landry	K 11
26,394	Saint Martin	M 12
31,458	Saint Mary	O 13
23,624	Saint Tammany	K 19
45,519	Tangipahoa	J 17
15,940	Tensas	E 13
35,880	Terrebonne	P 15
20,943	Union	A 9
37,750	Vermilion	N 9
19,142	Vernon	I 6
34,443	Washington	J 18
33,676	Webster	B 6
11,263	West Baton Rouge	L 13
19,252	West Carroll	B 13
11,720	West Feliciana	I 13
16,923	Winn	E 9
2,363,880	Total	

MAINE

COUNTIES.

TOTAL NUMBER 16

Pop.	County	Index
76,679	Androscoggin	N 6
94,436	Aroostook	D 16
146,000	Cumberland	O 5
19,896	Franklin	K 4
32,422	Hancock	L 17
77,231	Kennebec	M 9
27,191	Knox	N 13
16,294	Lincoln	O 10
42,662	Oxford	L 3
97,104	Penobscot	J 15
18,467	Piscataquis	G 12
19,123	Sagadahoc	O 8
38,245	Somerset	H 7
21,159	Waldo	M 13
37,767	Washington	J 21
82,550	York	Q 3
847,226	Total	

MARYLAND

COUNTIES.

TOTAL NUMBER 24

Pop.	County	Index
86,973	Allegany	L 6
68,375	Anne Arundel	H 14
155,825	Baltimore	D 13
859,100	Baltimore City	F 14
10,484	Calvert	M 14
17,549	Caroline	I 20
39,054	Carroll	C 10
26,407	Cecil	C 18
17,612	Charles	M 11
28,006	Dorchester	M 18
57,312	Frederick	D 8
21,981	Garrett	N 2
35,060	Harford	C 16
17,175	Howard	F 12
13,465	Kent	F 18
83,912	Montgomery	G 9
89,490	Prince Georges	J 12
14,476	Queen Annes	G 19
14,626	St. Marys	O 14
20,965	Somerset	P 20
18,784	Talbot	J 18
68,838	Washington	B 4
34,530	Wicomico	N 21
21,245	Worcester	O 23
1,821,244	Total	

MASSACHUSETTS

COUNTIES.

TOTAL NUMBER 14

Pop.	County	Index
37,295	Barnstable	M 24
122,273	Berkshire	F 3
364,637	Bristol	L 19
5,669	Dukes	P 23
496,313	Essex	C 20
49,453	Franklin	C 7
332,107	Hampden	I 7
72,461	Hampshire	F 7
971,390	Middlesex	D 17
3,401	Nantucket	R 14
325,180	Norfolk	H 18
168,824	Plymouth	J 22
863,248	Suffolk	F 19
504,470	Worcester	F 12
4,316,721	Total	

MICHIGAN

COUNTIES.

TOTAL NUMBER 83

Pop.	County	Index
5,463	Alcona	J 21
10,167	Alger	F 10
41,839	Allegan	P 12
20,766	Alpena	J 21
10,964	Antrim	J 15
9,233	Arenac	L 20
9,356	Baraga	E 4
22,613	Barry	P 14
74,981	Bay	M 19
7,800	Benzie	J 12
89,117	Berrien	Q 10
25,845	Branch	R 15
94,206	Calhoun	Q 16
21,910	Cass	Q 12
13,031	Charlevoix	I 16
13,644	Cheboygan	H 17
27,807	Chippewa	F 16
9,163	Clare	L 16
26,671	Clinton	O 17
3,765	Crawford	J 17
34,037	Delta	G 9
28,731	Dickinson	F 5
34,124	Eaton	P 16
15,791	Emmet	H 16
227,944	Genesee	O 21
9,385	Gladwin	L 18
31,797	Gogebic	C 22
23,390	Grand Traverse	J 14
32,205	Gratiot	N 17
29,092	Hillsdale	R 17
47,631	Houghton	D 2
32,584	Huron	L 23
130,616	Ingham	P 18
35,710	Ionia	O 16
8,560	Iosco	K 21
20,243	Iron	F 3
25,982	Isabella	M 16
93,108	Jackson	Q 18
100,085	Kalamazoo	Q 13
5,159	Kalkaska	J 15
246,338	Kent	O 14
4,004	Keweenaw	C 4
4,798	Lake	L 13
32,116	Lapeer	N 22
8,436	Leelanau	I 12
53,110	Lenawee	R 19
20,863	Livingston	P 20
7,423	Luce	E 13
9,438	Mackinac	F 15
107,638	Macomb	P 23
18,450	Manistee	K 12
47,144	Marquette	F 6
19,378	Mason	L 11
16,902	Mecosta	M 15
24,883	Menominee	H 7
27,094	Midland	M 18
8,034	Missaukee	K 15
58,620	Monroe	R 21
28,581	Montcalm	N 15
3,840	Montmorency	I 19
94,501	Muskegon	N 11
19,286	Newaygo	M 13
254,068	Oakland	P 22
14,812	Oceana	M 11
8,720	Ogemaw	K 19
11,359	Ontonagon	B 23
13,309	Osceola	L 15
2,543	Oscoda	J 19
5,827	Otsego	J 18
59,660	Ottawa	O 12
12,250	Presque Isle	H 19
3,668	Roscommon	K 17
130,468	Saginaw	N 20
76,222	Saint Clair	O 25
31,749	Saint Joseph	R 14
30,114	Sanilac	N 24
9,524	Schoolcraft	F 11
41,207	Shiawassee	O 19
35,694	Tuscola	N 22
35,111	Van Buren	Q 12
80,810	Washtenaw	Q 20
2,015,623	Wayne	Q 22
17,976	Wexford	K 13
5,256,106	Total	

MINNESOTA

COUNTIES.

TOTAL NUMBER 87

Pop.	County	Index
17,865	Aitkin	I 15
22,443	Anoka	M 16
26,562	Becker	H 6
26,107	Beltrami	E 10
16,106	Benton	L 13
10,447	Big Stone	L 3
36,203	Blue Earth	Q 13
25,544	Brown	P 10
24,212	Carlton	I 18
17,606	Carver	N 14
20,646	Cass	H 11
16,927	Chippewa	N 6
13,124	Chisago	L 18
25,337	Clay	H 3
11,153	Clearwater	F 8
3,030	Cook	B 21
16,143	Cottonwood	Q 8
30,226	Crow Wing	I 13
39,660	Dakota	O 17
12,931	Dodge	P 18
20,369	Douglas	K 7
23,941	Faribault	R 13
25,830	Fillmore	R 21
31,780	Freeborn	R 16
31,564	Goodhue	O 18
9,828	Grant	K 5
568,899	Hennepin	M 15
14,735	Houston	R 23
11,085	Hubbard	H 9
12,950	Isanti	L 16
32,996	Itasca	F 14
16,805	Jackson	R 8
9,651	Kanabec	K 16
26,524	Kandiyohi	N 9
10,717	Kittson	B 2
16,930	Koochiching	D 14
15,509	Lac qui Parle	N 4
6,956	Lake	F 23
5,975	Lake of the Woods	B 10
19,227	Le Sueur	P 14
10,797	Lincoln	O 4
21,569	Lyon	P 6
21,380	McLeod	N 12
8,054	Mahnomen	G 6
18,364	Marshall	C 4
24,656	Martin	R 11
19,277	Meeker	M 11
15,558	Mille Lacs	K 14
27,473	Morrison	K 12
36,113	Mower	R 18
15,060	Murray	Q 6
18,282	Nicollet	P 12
21,215	Nobles	R 6
14,746	Norman	G 3
42,658	Olmsted	P 20
53,192	Otter Tail	J 6
12,913	Pennington	D 5
21,478	Pine	J 18
13,794	Pipestone	Q 4
37,734	Polk	F 4
13,544	Pope	L 7
309,935	Ramsey	N 17
7,413	Red Lake	E 5
22,290	Redwood	O 8
24,625	Renville	O 9
32,160	Rice	P 16
10,933	Rock	R 4
15,103	Roseau	B 6
206,917	Saint Louis	F 19
15,585	Scott	O 15
10,456	Sherburne	L 14
16,625	Sibley	O 12
67,200	Stearns	L 11
19,749	Steele	Q 16
11,039	Stevens	L 5
15,469	Swift	M 6
27,438	Todd	K 9
8,283	Traverse	K 3
17,653	Wabasha	P 20
12,772	Wadena	I 9
15,186	Waseca	Q 15
26,430	Washington	N 17
13,902	Watonwan	Q 10
10,475	Wilkin	J 3
37,795	Winona	Q 22
27,550	Wright	M 13
16,917	Yellow Medicine	O 5
2,792,300	Total	

MISSISSIPPI

COUNTIES.

TOTAL NUMBER 82

Pop.	County	Index
27,238	Adams	N 4
26,969	Alcorn	A 21
21,892	Amite	O 7
30,227	Attala	H 15
10,429	Benton	A 17
67,574	Bolivar	E 7
20,893	Calhoun	D 16
20,651	Carroll	F 13
21,427	Chickasaw	D 19
13,548	Choctaw	F 17
12,810	Claiborne	L 6
20,596	Clarke	L 20
19,030	Clay	F 20
48,333	Coahoma	C 8
33,974	Copiah	L 10
17,030	Covington	M 15
26,663	De Soto	A 13
34,901	Forrest	O 17
12,504	Franklin	N 6
8,704	George	P 21
9,512	Greene	O 21
19,052	Grenada	E 13
11,328	Hancock	R 15
50,799	Harrison	R 18
107,273	Hinds	K 9
39,710	Holmes	G 12
26,257	Humphreys	G 9
6,433	Issaquena	I 6
19,922	Itawamba	C 22
20,601	Jackson	Q 21
19,484	Jasper	L 18
13,969	Jefferson	M 6
15,869	Jefferson Davis	N 13
49,227	Jones	M 17
21,867	Kemper	I 20
21,257	Lafayette	C 15
12,096	Lamar	O 16
58,247	Lauderdale	J 20
13,983	Lawrence	N 11
24,570	Leake	I 15
38,838	Lee	C 20
53,406	Leflore	F 10
27,506	Lincoln	N 9
35,245	Lowndes	G 22
37,504	Madison	I 12
24,085	Marion	O 13
25,522	Marshall	A 15
37,648	Monroe	E 21
15,703	Montgomery	F 14
27,882	Neshoba	I 18
24,249	Newton	J 18
25,669	Noxubee	G 21
22,151	Oktibbeha	G 19
34,421	Panola	C 12
19,125	Pearl River	Q 15
9,292	Perry	O 19
35,002	Pike	O 9
22,904	Pontotoc	C 18
20,921	Prentiss	B 21
27,191	Quitman	C 10
27,934	Rankin	K 12
23,144	Scott	J 15
15,433	Sharkey	I 7
22,024	Simpson	L 13
19,403	Smith	L 15
6,155	Stone	Q 18
61,007	Sunflower	F 8
34,166	Tallahatchie	D 11
19,309	Tate	B 12
19,680	Tippah	A 19
16,974	Tishomingo	A 23
22,610	Tunica	B 10
21,867	Union	B 18
17,534	Walthall	P 12
39,595	Warren	J 7
67,576	Washington	G 7
16,928	Wayne	M 20
14,160	Webster	F 17
15,955	Wilkinson	O 4
22,751	Winston	H 18
18,387	Yalobusha	D 14
40,091	Yazoo	I 10
2,183,796	Total	

MISSOURI

COUNTIES.

TOTAL NUMBER 115

Pop.	County	Index
20,246	Adair	O 12
13,015	Andrew	C 5
12,897	Atchison	A 3
22,673	Audrain	G 15
23,546	Barry	Q 8
14,148	Barton	N 6
19,531	Bates	J 6
11,142	Benton	J 10
12,898	Bollinger	O 21
34,991	Boone	H 13
94,067	Buchanan	E 5
34,276	Butler	H 22, Q 20
11,629	Caldwell	E 8
23,094	Callaway	H 14
8,971	Camden	L 11
37,775	Cape Girardeau	N 22
17,814	Carroll	F 9
6,226	Carter	P 18
19,534	Cass	I 6
11,697	Cedar	M 8
18,084	Chariton	E 11
13,538	Christian	P 10
10,166	Clark	B 15
30,417	Clay	F 6
13,261	Clinton	E 6
34,912	Cole	J 13
18,075	Cooper	H 12
12,693	Crawford	K 17
11,248	Dade	N 8
11,523	Dallas	M 11
13,398	Daviess	C 8
9,751	De Kalb	D 6
11,763	Dent	M 16
15,600	Douglas	P 12
44,957	Dunklin	J 24, R 21
33,868	Franklin	J 17
12,414	Gasconade	J 16
13,359	Gentry	B 6
90,541	Greene	N 9
15,716	Grundy	C 9
16,525	Harrison	B 8
22,313	Henry	J 8
6,506	Hickory	L 10
12,476	Holt	C 4
13,026	Howard	G 12
22,270	Howell	Q 14
10,440	Iron	M 18
477,828	Jackson	H 6
78,705	Jasper	O 6
32,023	Jefferson	J 19
21,617	Johnson	H 8
8,878	Knox	C 14
18,718	Laclede	M 12
27,856	Lafayette	G 8
24,637	Lawrence	O 8
11,490	Lewis	C 15
14,395	Lincoln	G 18
21,416	Linn	D 11
18,000	Livingston	D 9
15,749	McDonald	Q 6
21,396	Macon	D 12
9,656	Madison	N 20
8,638	Maries	K 14
31,576	Marion	D 16
8,766	Mercer	A 9
14,798	Miller	K 13
23,149	Mississippi	P 24
11,775	Moniteau	I 12
13,195	Monroe	E 14
12,442	Montgomery	H 16
11,140	Morgan	J 11
39,787	New Madrid	R 23
29,039	Newton	Q 6
25,556	Nodaway	A 5
13,390	Oregon	Q 16
12,375	Osage	J 15
10,766	Ozark	Q 13
46,857	Pemiscot	J 24
15,358	Perry	M 22
33,336	Pettis	I 10
17,437	Phelps	L 15
18,327	Pike	F 17
13,862	Platte	F 5
17,400	Polk	M 9
10,775	Pulaski	M 13
11,327	Putnam	A 11
10,040	Ralls	F 16
24,458	Randolph	F 12
18,584	Ray	F 8
9,370	Reynolds	N 18
12,606	Ripley	Q 18
25,562	Saint Charles	I 18
13,146	Saint Clair	K 8
10,905	Sainte Genevieve	L 21
35,950	Saint Francois	M 20
274,230	Saint Louis	I 20
816,048	Saint Louis City	I 20
29,416	Saline	G 10
6,627	Schuyler	A 12
8,557	Scotland	B 14
30,377	Scott	P 23
11,831	Shannon	O 16
11,224	Shelby	D 14
33,009	Stoddard	P 21
11,298	Stone	Q 9
13,701	Sullivan	B 11
10,323	Taney	Q 11
19,813	Texas	O 14
25,586	Vernon	L 6
7,734	Warren	I 17
17,492	Washington	L 18
12,794	Wayne	O 20
17,226	Webster	O 11
6,345	Worth	A 6
17,967	Wright	O 12
3,784,664	Total	

MONTANA

COUNTIES.

TOTAL NUMBER 56

Pop.	County	Index
6,943	Beaverhead	M 6
10,419	Big Horn	M 17
9,566	Blaine	D 15
3,451	Broadwater	J 9
11,865	Carbon	N 14
3,280	Carter	L 24

Counties of the United States

Pop.	County	Index
41,999	Cascade	H 9
7,316	Chouteau	F 11
10,422	Custer	J 22
4,563	Daniels	C 21
8,618	Dawson	G 23
13,627	Deerlodge	K 6
3,719	Fallon	J 24
14,040	Fergus	H 14
24,271	Flathead	D 4
13,269	Gallatin	M 10
2,641	Garfield	G 18
9,034	Glacier	C 6
1,607	Golden Valley	J 14
3,401	Granite	J 5
13,304	Hill	D 12
4,664	Jefferson	K 8
3,655	Judith Basin	H 12
13,490	Lake	F 4
22,131	Lewis and Clark	H 8
2,209	Liberty	D 11
7,882	Lincoln	C 2
3,798	McCone	F 21
7,294	Madison	N 8
2,237	Meagher	J 11
2,135	Mineral	H 2
29,038	Missoula	H 4
5,717	Musselshell	J 16
*11,609	Park	M 11
3,286	Petroleum	H 16
7,892	Phillips	E 17
6,716	Pondera	E 8
3,159	Powder River	M 22
6,152	Powell	H 6
2,410	Prairie	H 22
12,978	Ravalli	K 4
10,209	Richland	F 24
9,806	Roosevelt	D 22
6,477	Rosebud	I 19
6,926	Sanders	F 2
7,814	Sheridan	C 23
53,207	Silver Bow	L 7
5,694	Stillwater	M 14
3,719	Sweet Grass	L 13
6,922	Teton	F8
6,769	Toole	C9
1,499	Treasure	J 18
15,181	Valley	E 20
3,286	Wheatland	J 13
2,161	Wibaux	H 25
41,182	Yellowstone	K 16
(*Includes Yellowstone Nat'l. Park		43.)
559,456	Total	

NEBRASKA

COUNTIES.

TOTAL NUMBER 93

Pop.	County	Index
24,576	Adams	N 17
13,289	Antelope	G 18
1,045	Arthur	I 8
1,403	Banner	J 2
1,538	Blaine	H 12
12,127	Boone	I 18
10,736	Box Butte	G 4
6,060	Boyd	E 16
5,962	Brown	G 13
23,655	Buffalo	L 15
12,546	Burt	H 22
13,106	Butler	K 20
16,992	Cass	L 24
15,126	Cedar	F 20
5,310	Chase	M 7
9,637	Cherry	F 9
9,505	Cheyenne	J 4
10,445	Clay	N 18
10,627	Colfax	I 20
13,562	Cuming	H 21
22,591	Custer	J 13
23,928	Dakota	G 22
10,128	Dawes	E 3
17,890	Dawson	L 13
3,580	Deuel	K 5
10,413	Dixon	F 21
23,799	Dodge	J 22
247,562	Douglas	K 23
5,122	Dundy	N 7
11,417	Fillmore	N 19
7,740	Franklin	O 15
6,417	Frontier	M 11
10,098	Furnas	O 13
29,588	Gage	N 22
4,680	Garden	J 6
3,444	Garfield	H 15
3,687	Gosper	N 13
1,327	Grant	H 8
6,845	Greeley	J 16
27,523	Hall	L 16
9,982	Hamilton	L 18
7,130	Harlan	N 14
2,958	Hayes	N 9
6,404	Hitchcock	O 9
16,552	Holt	G 15
1,253	Hooker	H 9
8,422	Howard	K 16
15,532	Jefferson	O 20
8,662	Johnson	N 23
6,854	Kearney	N 15
8,333	Keith	K 8
3,235	Keya Paha	E 13
3,913	Kimball	K 2
16,478	Knox	F 18
100,585	Lancaster	M 22
25,425	Lincoln	L 10
1,742	Logan	J 11
1,777	Loup	H 14
1,175	McPherson	J 9
24,269	Madison	I 20
9,354	Merrick	K 18
9,806	Morrill	I 4
7,653	Nance	J 18
12,781	Nemaha	N 24
10,446	Nuckolls	O 18
18,994	Otoe	M 23
8,514	Pawnee	O 23
5,197	Perkins	L 8
8,452	Phelps	M 14
10,211	Pierce	G 19
20,191	Platte	J 19
8,748	Polk	K 19
11,051	Redwillow	O 11
19,178	Richardson	O 23
3,977	Rock	F 14
15,010	Saline	N 20
10,835	Sarpy	K 23
17,892	Saunders	K 22
33,917	Scotts Bluff	H 2
14,167	Seward	L 20
9,869	Sheridan	F 6
7,764	Sherman	K 15
4,001	Sioux	E 2
6,887	Stanton	H 20
12,262	Thayer	O 19
1,553	Thomas	H 11
10,243	Thurston	G 22
8,163	Valley	J 15
11,578	Washington	J 23
9,880	Wayne	G 20
8,071	Webster	O 17
2,170	Wheeler	H 16
14,874	York	L 19
1,315,834	Total	

NEVADA

COUNTIES.

TOTAL NUMBER 17

Pop.	County	Index
5,317	Churchill	G 8
16,414	Clark	O 21
2,056	Douglas	I 3
10,912	Elko	B 18
1,554	Esmeralda	K 10
1,361	Eureka	F 16
4,743	Humboldt	B 9
1,745	Lander	G 13
4,130	Lincoln	L 21
4,076	Lyon	H 5
2,342	Mineral	I 7
3,606	Nye	J 16
3,209	Ormsby	H 3
2,713	Pershing	E 8
1,216	Storey	G 4
32,476	Washoe	D 3
12,377	White Pine	G 21
110,247	Total	

NEW HAMPSHIRE

COUNTIES.

TOTAL NUMBER 10

Pop.	County	Index
24,328	Belknap	M 15
15,589	Carroll	J 16
34,953	Cheshire	Q 7
39,274	Coos	E 16
44,645	Grafton	J 12
144,888	Hillsborough	P 12
60,710	Merrimack	N 13
58,142	Rockingham	P 18
43,553	Strafford	N 18
25,442	Sullivan	N 8
491,524	Total	

NEW JERSEY

COUNTIES.

TOTAL NUMBER 21

Pop.	County	Index
124,066	Atlantic	N 13
409,646	Bergen	C 19
97,013	Burlington	L 13
255,727	Camden	L 10
28,919	Cape May	R 11
73,184	Cumberland	P 9
837,340	Essex	E 18
72,219	Gloucester	M 8
652,040	Hudson	E 20
36,766	Hunterdon	E 11
197,318	Mercer	I 18
217,077	Middlesex	G 16
161,238	Monmouth	I 18
125,732	Morris	D 14
37,706	Ocean	K 17
309,353	Passaic	C 18
42,274	Salem	N 7
74,390	Somerset	G 14
29,632	Sussex	B 14
328,344	Union	F 17
50,181	Warren	D 10
4,160,165	Total	

NEW MEXICO

COUNTIES.

TOTAL NUMBER 31

Pop.	County	Index
69,391	Bernalillo	G 10
4,881	Catron	J 3
23,980	Chaves	K 20
18,718	Colfax	C 18
18,159	Curry	I 24
3,725	De Baca	I 19
30,411	Dona Ana	O 10
24,311	Eddy	N 20
20,050	Grant	M 4
8,646	Guadalupe	H 18
4,374	Harding	E 21
4,821	Hidalgo	P 2
21,154	Lea	M 24
8,557	Lincoln	K 15
6,457	Luna	O 6
23,641	McKinley	F 4
10,981	Mora	E 18
10,522	Otero	N 13
12,111	Quay	G 23
25,352	Rio Arriba	C 9
14,549	Roosevelt	I 23
13,898	Sandoval	F 10
17,115	San Juan	C 3
27,910	San Miguel	F 18
30,826	Santa Fe	F 13
6,962	Sierra	L 7
11,422	Socorro	J 7
18,528	Taos	C 14
11,026	Torrance	H 14
9,095	Union	D 23
20,245	Valencia	H 4
531,818	Total	

NEW YORK

COUNTIES.

TOTAL NUMBER 62

Pop.	County	Index
221,315	Albany	O 23
39,681	Allegany	P 7
1,394,711	Bronx	H 6
165,749	Broome	Q 16
72,652	Cattaraugus	P 5
65,508	Cayuga	M 13
123,580	Chautauqua	P 3
73,718	Chemung	Q 12
39,776	Chenango	O 16
54,006	Clinton	D 23
41,464	Columbia	A, 6, Q 24
33,668	Cortland	O 15
40,989	Delaware	A 2, Q 10
120,542	Dutchess	C 6, R 23
798,377	Erie	O 5
34,178	Essex	G 23
44,286	Franklin	E 21
48,597	Fulton	L 21
44,481	Genesee	M 7
27,926	Greene	A 4, P 22
4,188	Hamilton	I 20
59,527	Herkimer	J 19
84,003	Jefferson	I 15
2,698,285	Kings	I 5
22,815	Lewis	I 17
38,510	Livingston	N 9
39,598	Madison	N 16
438,230	Monroe	L 9
59,142	Montgomery	N 21
406,748	Nassau	H 7
1,889,924	New York	H 5
160,110	Niagara	L 5
203,636	Oneida	L 17
295,108	Onondaga	M 14
55,307	Ontario	N 10
140,113	Orange	E 3
27,760	Orleans	L 7
71,275	Oswego	K 15
46,082	Otsego	O 19
16,555	Putnam	E 6
1,297,634	Queens	H 6
121,834	Rensselaer	N 24
174,441	Richmond	I 5
91,098	Saint Lawrence	F 17
65,606	Saratoga	L 23
122,494	Schenectady	N 22
20,812	Schoharie	O 21
12,979	Schuyler	P 12
25,732	Seneca	N 12
84,927	Steuben	Q 10
197,355	Suffolk	H 9
37,901	Sullivan	C 2, R 20
27,072	Tioga	Q 14
40,340	Tompkins	P 13
87,017	Ulster	C 4, R 21
36,035	Warren	J 22
46,726	Washington	K 24
52,747	Wayne	L 11
573,558	Westchester	F 6
31,394	Wyoming	N 7
16,381	Yates	O 11
13,479,142	Total	

NORTH CAROLINA

COUNTIES.

TOTAL NUMBER 100

Pop.	County	Index
57,427	Alamance	D 11
13,454	Alexander	E 4
8,341	Alleghany	C 4
28,443	Anson	I 8
22,664	Ashe	B 3
13,561	Avery	D 2
36,431	Beaufort	G 20
26,201	Bertie	D 20
27,156	Bladen	K 14
17,125	Brunswick	M 15
108,755	Buncombe	O 7
38,615	Burke	F 2
59,393	Cabarrus	G 6
35,795	Caldwell	E 3
5,440	Camden	C 23
18,284	Carteret	J 20
20,032	Caswell	C 11
51,653	Catawba	F 4
24,726	Chatham	F 11
18,813	Cherokee	Q 2
11,572	Chowan	D 21
6,405	Clay	R 3
58,055	Cleveland	G 3
45,663	Columbus	M 14
31,298	Craven	H 19
59,320	Cumberland	I 13
6,709	Currituck	C 23
6,041	Dare	F 24
53,377	Davidson	F 8
14,909	Davie	E 6
39,739	Duplin	I 16
80,244	Durham	D 13
49,162	Edgecombe	E 17
126,475	Forsyth	D 8
30,382	Franklin	D 15
87,531	Gaston	H 4
10,060	Gates	C 21
6,418	Graham	P 3
29,344	Granville	C 14
18,548	Greene	I 17
153,916	Guilford	E 9
56,512	Halifax	D 17
44,239	Harnett	H 13
34,804	Haywood	O 6
26,049	Henderson	P 8
19,352	Hertford	C 20
14,937	Hoke	I 11
7,860	Hyde	G 23
50,424	Iredell	E 5
19,366	Jackson	Q 6
63,798	Johnston	G 15
10,926	Jones	I 18
18,743	Lee	G 11
41,211	Lenoir	H 17
24,187	Lincoln	G 4
22,996	McDowell	F 1
15,880	Macon	Q 4
20,522	Madison	N 7
26,111	Martin	F 19
151,826	Mecklenburg	H 6
15,980	Mitchell	M 9
16,280	Montgomery	H 9
30,969	Moore	H 11
25,566	Nash	E 16
47,935	New Hanover	M 17
28,299	Northampton	C 18
17,939	Onslow	J 18
23,072	Orange	D 12
9,706	Pamlico	I 20
20,568	Pasquotank	C 22
17,710	Pender	K 16
9,773	Perquimans	D 22
25,029	Person	C 12
61,244	Pitt	G 18
11,874	Polk	P 9
44,554	Randolph	F 9
36,810	Richmond	I 10
76,860	Robeson	L 12
57,898	Rockingham	C 9
69,206	Rowan	F 7
45,577	Rutherford	G 1
47,440	Sampson	J 15
23,232	Scotland	J 11
32,834	Stanly	H 8
22,656	Stokes	C 6
41,783	Surry	C 4
12,177	Swain	O 4
12,241	Transylvania	Q 7
5,556	Tyrrell	F 22
39,097	Union	J 7
29,961	Vance	C 15
109,544	Wake	E 14
23,145	Warren	C 16
12,323	Washington	F 21
18,114	Watauga	D 3
58,328	Wayne	H 16
43,003	Wilkes	F 16
50,219	Wilson	F 18
20,657	Yadkin	D 6
17,202	Yancey	N 9
3,571,623	Total	

NORTH DAKOTA

COUNTIES.

TOTAL NUMBER 53

Pop.	County	Index
4,664	Adams	Q 6
17,814	Barnes	M 20
12,629	Benson	H 16
2,531	Billings	L 3
13,253	Bottineau	D 11
3,860	Bowman	Q 2
7,653	Burke	D 5
22,736	Burleigh	M 11
52,849	Cass	M 23
13,923	Cavalier	D 19
9,696	Dickey	Q 19
7,086	Divide	D 3
8,376	Dunn	K 6
5,741	Eddy	I 17
11,699	Emmons	P 13
5,824	Foster	K 18
3,498	Golden Valley	L 2
34,518	Grand Forks	H 22
8,264	Grant	P 9
5,818	Griggs	K 20
7,457	Hettinger	O 6
6,692	Kidder	M 15
10,298	La Moure	O 19
7,561	Logan	O 16
14,034	McHenry	G 12
8,984	McIntosh	Q 16
8,426	McKenzie	I 3
16,082	McLean	J 10
9,611	Mercer	K 8
20,184	Morton	O 11
10,482	Mountrail	G 6
9,129	Nelson	H 20
3,859	Oliver	L 10
15,671	Pembina	D 22
9,208	Pierce	G 14
15,626	Ramsey	G 18
1,061	Ransom	O 22
5,533	Renville	E 9
20,519	Richland	P 24
12,583	Rolette	D 15
8,693	Sargent	Q 22
6,616	Sheridan	J 13
4,419	Sioux	R 9
2,932	Slope	O 3
15,414	Stark	N 5
6,193	Steele	J 21
23,495	Stutsman	M 17
7,200	Towner	E 16
12,300	Traill	I 24
20,747	Walsh	F 21
31,981	Ward	G 10
11,198	Wells	J 15
16,315	Williams	F 3
641,935	Total	

OHIO

COUNTIES.

TOTAL NUMBER 88

Pop.	County	Index
21,705	Adams	P 9
73,303	Allen	G 7
29,785	Ashland	G 14
68,674	Ashtabula	C 20
46,166	Athens	N 15
28,037	Auglaize	H 7
95,614	Belmont	K 19
21,638	Brown	P 8
120,249	Butler	N 6
17,449	Carroll	H 19
25,258	Champaign	J 9
95,647	Clark	K 9
34,109	Clermont	O 7
22,574	Clinton	N 9
90,121	Columbiana	G 20
30,594	Coshocton	I 15
35,571	Crawford	G 12
1,217,250	Cuyahoga	D 17
38,831	Darke	J 6
24,367	Defiance	D 6
26,780	Delaware	I 12
43,201	Erie	D 13
48,490	Fairfield	L 13
21,385	Fayette	M 10
388,712	Franklin	K 11
23,626	Fulton	C 8
24,930	Gallia	P 14
19,430	Geauga	D 18
35,863	Greene	L 8
38,822	Guernsey	J 17
621,987	Hamilton	N 5
40,793	Hancock	F 8
27,061	Hardin	G 9
20,313	Harrison	I 19
22,756	Henry	E 8
27,099	Highland	O 9
21,504	Hocking	M 13
17,876	Holmes	H 15
34,800	Huron	E 13
27,004	Jackson	O 14
98,129	Jefferson	I 20
31,024	Knox	I 14
50,020	Lake	C 18
46,705	Lawrence	R 13
52,279	Licking	J 13
29,624	Logan	I 9
112,390	Lorain	E 15
344,333	Lucas	C 9
21,811	Madison	K 10
240,251	Mahoning	F 20
44,898	Marion	H 11
33,034	Medina	F 15
24,104	Meigs	O 15
26,266	Mercer	H 5
52,632	Miami	J 7
18,641	Monroe	L 19
295,480	Montgomery	L 7
14,227	Morgan	M 16
15,646	Morrow	H 12
69,795	Muskingum	K 15
14,587	Noble	L 17
24,360	Ottawa	C 11
15,527	Paulding	E 6
31,087	Perry	L 14
27,889	Pickaway	L 11
16,113	Pike	O 11
46,660	Portage	E 18
23,329	Preble	L 5
25,016	Putnam	F 7
73,853	Richland	G 13
52,147	Ross	N 11
41,014	Sandusky	D 11
86,565	Scioto	P 12
48,499	Seneca	E 11
26,071	Shelby	I 7
234,887	Stark	G 18
339,405	Summit	E 17
132,315	Trumbull	E 20
68,816	Tuscarawas	H 17
20,012	Union	I 10
26,759	Van Wert	G 6
11,310	Vinton	N 13
29,894	Warren	M 7
42,537	Washington	M 17
50,520	Wayne	G 15
25,510	Williams	C 6
51,796	Wood	D 9
19,218	Wyandot	G 10
6,907,612	Total	

OKLAHOMA

COUNTIES.

TOTAL NUMBER 77

Pop.	County	Index
15,755	Adair	G 24
14,129	Alfalfa	B 9
18,702	Atoka	O 18
8,648	Beaver	Q 8
22,169	Beckham	J 2
18,543	Blaine	G 8
38,138	Bryan	P 17
41,567	Caddo	K 8
27,329	Canadian	I 10
43,292	Carter	O 12
21,030	Cherokee	F 22
28,358	Choctaw	P 20
3,654	Cimarron	Q 2
27,728	Cleveland	J 12
12,811	Coal	M 17
38,988	Comanche	N 8
12,884	Cotton	O 8
21,083	Craig	B 21
55,503	Creek	G 17
23,068	Custer	H 6
18,592	Delaware	D 23
11,981	Dewey	F 5
8,466	Ellis	E 2
45,484	Garfield	D 10
31,150	Garvin	M 13
41,116	Grady	K 11
13,128	Grant	B 10
14,550	Greer	L 3
10,019	Harmon	M 2
6,454	Harper	B 3
17,324	Haskell	J 20
29,189	Hughes	K 17
22,708	Jackson	M 3
15,107	Jefferson	P 10
15,960	Johnston	O 15
47,084	Kay	B 13
15,617	Kingfisher	G 10
22,817	Kiowa	L 5
12,380	Latimer	L 21
45,866	Le Flore	L 24
29,529	Lincoln	H 14
25,245	Logan	F 12
11,433	Love	Q 13
19,205	McClain	K 12
41,318	McCurtain	P 23
24,097	McIntosh	I 20
11,946	Major	E 7
12,384	Marshall	P 15
21,668	Mayes	D 22
13,841	Murray	N 13
65,914	Muskogee	H 21
14,826	Noble	D 13
15,774	Nowata	B 20
26,279	Okfuskee	I 17
244,159	Oklahoma	H 12
50,101	Okmulgee	H 18
41,502	Osage	C 16
35,849	Ottawa	B 23
17,395	Pawnee	E 15
36,057	Payne	F 14
48,985	Pittsburg	L 19
39,792	Pontotoc	M 15
54,377	Pottawatomie	K 14
19,466	Pushmataha	N 21
10,736	Roger Mills	H 2
21,078	Rogers	D 20
61,201	Seminole	J 16
23,138	Sequoyah	I 24
31,090	Stephens	N 10
9,896	Texas	Q 5
20,754	Tillman	N 6
193,363	Tulsa	E 19
21,642	Wagoner	F 20
30,559	Washington	C 19
22,279	Washita	J 5
14,915	Woods	B 8
16,270	Woodward	D 4
2,336,434	Total	

OREGON

COUNTIES.

TOTAL NUMBER 36

Pop.	County	Index
18,297	Baker	G 22
18,629	Benton	H 5
57,130	Clackamas	E 8
21,327	Clatsop	B 5
20,971	Columbia	B 6
32,466	Coos	M 3
5,533	Crook	I 14
4,301	Curry	P 2
18,631	Deschutes	J 11
21,536	Douglas	M 6
2,844	Gilliam	D 14
6,380	Grant	H 18
5,374	Harney	M 18
11,580	Hood River	D 10
36,213	Jackson	Q 6
2,042	Jefferson	G 12
16,301	Josephine	Q 4
40,497	Klamath	O 10
6,293	Lake	O 13
69,096	Lane	J 5
14,549	Lincoln	H 4
30,485	Linn	H 7
19,767	Malheur	M 22
75,246	Marion	F 7
4,337	Morrow	D 16
355,099	Multnomah	D 8
19,989	Polk	F 5
2,321	Sherman	E 13
12,263	Tillamook	D 4
26,030	Umatilla	D 18
17,399	Union	E 20
7,623	Wallowa	C 23
13,069	Wasco	E 11
39,194	Washington	C 6
2,974	Wheeler	G 15
26,336	Yamhill	E 5
1,089,684	Total	

PENNSYLVANIA

COUNTIES.

TOTAL NUMBER 67

Pop.	County	Index
39,435	Adams	P 15
1,411,539	Allegheny	L 3
81,087	Armstrong	L 5
156,754	Beaver	L 2
40,809	Bedford	O 9
241,884	Berks	M 20
140,358	Blair	L 10
50,615	Bradford	E 17
107,715	Bucks	N 23
80,597	Butler	K 3
213,459	Cambria	M 8
6,852	Cameron	H 11
61,735	Carbon	L 21
52,608	Centre	K 12
135,626	Chester	P 21
38,410	Clarion	I 6
92,094	Clearfield	J 9
34,557	Clinton	H 13
51,413	Columbia	J 18
23,104	Crawford	C 4
74,806	Cumberland	O 14
177,410	Dauphin	M 16
310,756	Delaware	P 23
34,443	Elk	G 8
180,889	Erie	E 3
200,999	Fayette	Q 4
5,791	Forest	G 6
69,378	Franklin	P 13
10,673	Fulton	P 10
44,671	Greene	Q 2
41,836	Huntingdon	M 12
79,854	Indiana	L 6
14,090	Jefferson	I 7
15,373	Juniata	M 14
301,243	Lackawanna	G 21
212,504	Lancaster	O 19
96,877	Lawrence	J 2
72,641	Lebanon	M 18
177,533	Lehigh	L 22
441,518	Luzerne	I 20
93,633	Lycoming	H 15
56,673	McKean	E 9
101,039	Mercer	H 2
42,993	Mifflin	L 13
29,802	Monroe	I 23
289,247	Montgomery	N 22
15,466	Montour	J 17
168,959	Northampton	K 23
126,887	Northumberland	J 16
23,213	Perry	N 14
1,931,334	Philadelphia	P 24
7,452	Pike	H 23
18,201	Potter	F 12
228,331	Schuylkill	K 19
20,208	Snyder	L 15
84,957	Somerset	P 7
7,504	Sullivan	G 18
33,893	Susquehanna	E 20
35,004	Tioga	E 14
20,247	Union	J 15
63,958	Venango	H 4
42,789	Warren	F 6
210,852	Washington	O 2
29,934	Wayne	F 23
303,411	Westmoreland	M 5
16,702	Wyoming	G 19
178,022	York	P 17
9,900,180	Total	

RHODE ISLAND

COUNTIES.

TOTAL NUMBER 5

Pop.	County	Index
25,548	Bristol	G 20
58,311	Kent	H 9
46,696	Newport	J 20
550,298	Providence	D 8
32,493	Washington	L 10
713,346	Total	

SOUTH CAROLINA

COUNTIES.

TOTAL NUMBER 46

Pop.	County	Index
22,931	Abbeville	F 6
49,916	Aiken	I 10
13,040	Allendale	M 11
88,712	Anderson	D 5
18,643	Bamberg	L 13
20,138	Barnwell	K 11
22,037	Beaufort	Q 14
27,128	Berkeley	L 18
16,229	Calhoun	I 14
121,105	Charleston	N 19
33,290	Cherokee	A 10
32,579	Chester	C 12
35,963	Chesterfield	C 17
31,500	Clarendon	I 17
26,268	Colleton	M 14
45,198	Darlington	E 18
29,625	Dillon	E 21
19,928	Dorchester	L 16
17,894	Edgefield	H 9
24,187	Fairfield	E 13
70,582	Florence	G 19
26,352	Georgetown	J 21
136,580	Greenville	C 7
40,083	Greenwood	F 8
17,465	Hampton	N 12
51,951	Horry	G 23
11,011	Jasper	P 13
32,913	Kershaw	E 15
33,542	Lancaster	C 14
44,185	Laurens	E 8
24,908	Lee	F 17
35,994	Lexington	H 12
10,367	McCormick	H 7
30,107	Marion	G 21
33,281	Marlboro	D 19
33,577	Newberry	E 10
36,512	Oconee	C 3
63,707	Orangeburg	J 14
37,111	Pickens	B 5
104,843	Richland	G 14
17,192	Saluda	G 9
127,733	Spartanburg	B 8
52,463	Sumter	G 16
31,360	Union	C 10
41,011	Williamsburg	L 18
58,663	York	B 12
1,899,804	Total	

SOUTH DAKOTA

COUNTIES.

TOTAL NUMBER 68

Pop.	County	Index
42	Armstrong	G 11
5,387	Aurora	L 18
19,648	Beadle	I 19
3,983	Bennett	N 9
10,241	Bon Homme	O 21
16,560	Brookings	I 23
29,676	Brown	C 19
6,195	Brule	L 17
1,853	Buffalo	J 16
8,004	Butte	G 3
5,033	Campbell	C 13
13,449	Charles Mix	N 19
8,955	Clark	G 21
10,894	Clay	O 23
17,014	Codington	F 22
6,755	Corson	D 10
6,023	Custer	L 3
15,336	Davison	L 20
13,565	Day	E 20
8,450	Deuel	H 24
5,709	Dewey	E 11
6,348	Douglas	M 19
7,814	Edmunds	E 16
8,089	Fall River	N 2
5,168	Faulk	F 16
10,552	Grant	E 24
9,554	Gregory	N 16
3,515	Haakon	I 9
7,562	Hamlin	H 22
7,166	Hand	I 17
5,400	Hanson	L 21
3,010	Harding	D 3
6,624	Hughes	I 14
12,668	Hutchinson	N 21
3,113	Hyde	H 15
1,955	Jackson	K 9
4,752	Jerauld	K 18
2,509	Jones	K 12
10,831	Kingsbury	I 22
12,412	Lake	L 23
19,093	Lawrence	H 2
13,171	Lincoln	N 24
5,045	Lyman	K 14
9,793	McCook	L 22
8,353	McPherson	C 17
8,880	Marshall	C 21
9,735	Meade	H 5

Pop.	County	Index
4,107	Mellette	M 11
6,836	Miner	J 21
57,697	Minnehaha	L 24
9,341	Moody	J 24
23,799	Pennington	K 4
6,585	Perkins	D 6
4,614	Potter	F 14
15,887	Roberts	C 23
5,754	Sanborn	K 20
7,155	Shannon	N 6
12,527	Spink	G 19
1,959	Stanley	I 11
2,668	Sully	H 13
5,714	Todd	N 12
9,937	Tripp	N 14
13,270	Turner	N 23
11,675	Union	O 25
7,274	Walworth	E 14
1,980	Washabaugh	M 8
16,725	Yankton	O 22
2,875	Ziebach	G 9
642,961	Total	

TENNESSEE

COUNTIES.

TOTAL NUMBER 95

Pop.	County	Index
26,504	Anderson	M 18
23,151	Bedford	O 12
11,976	Benton	M 7
8,358	Bledsoe	O 15
41,116	Blount	O 19
28,498	Bradley	Q 16
31,131	Campbell	L 18
9,880	Cannon	N 13
25,978	Carroll	N 6
35,127	Carter	M 24
9,928	Cheatham	L 10
11,124	Chester	P 5
24,657	Claiborne	L 20
10,904	Clay	L 14
24,083	Cocke	N 22
18,959	Coffee	P 13
17,330	Crockett	N 4
15,592	Cumberland	N 16
257,267	Davidson	M 11
10,261	Decatur	O 7
14,588	De Kalb	N 13
19,718	Dickson	M 9
34,920	Dyer	M 3
30,322	Fayette	P 3
14,262	Fentress	M 16
23,892	Franklin	Q 12
44,835	Gibson	M 4
29,240	Giles	P 10
14,356	Grainger	M 20
39,405	Greene	M 22
11,552	Grundy	P 13
18,611	Hamblen	M 21
180,478	Hamilton	P 15
11,231	Hancock	L 21
23,590	Hardeman	P 4
17,806	Hardin	Q 6
28,523	Hawkins	L 22
27,699	Haywood	O 3
19,220	Henderson	O 6
25,877	Henry	L 6
14,873	Hickman	N 9
6,432	Houston	M 8
12,421	Humphreys	N 8
15,082	Jackson	M 14
18,621	Jefferson	M 20
12,998	Johnson	L 25
178,468	Knox	M 19
11,235	Lake	L 3
24,461	Lauderdale	N 2
28,726	Lawrence	P 9
5,849	Lewis	O 9
27,214	Lincoln	Q 11
19,838	Loudon	O 18
30,781	McMinn	P 17
20,424	McNairy	Q 5
14,904	Macon	L 13
54,115	Madison	O 5
19,140	Marion	Q 14
16,030	Marshall	P 11
40,357	Maury	O 10
6,393	Meigs	O 17
24,275	Monroe	P 18
33,346	Montgomery	L 9
4,093	Moore	P 12
15,242	Morgan	M 17
30,978	Obion	L 4
18,883	Overton	M 15
7,535	Perry	O 7
6,213	Pickett	K 16
15,473	Polk	Q 17
26,250	Putnam	M 14
16,353	Rhea	O 16
29,795	Roane	N 17
29,046	Robertson	L 11
33,604	Rutherford	N 12
15,966	Scott	L 17
5,038	Sequatchie	P 15
23,291	Sevier	N 20
358,250	Shelby	P 2
16,148	Smith	M 13
13,549	Stewart	L 8
69,085	Sullivan	K 24
32,719	Sumner	L 12
28,036	Tipton	O 2
6,113	Trousdale	L 13
14,128	Unicoi	M 23
9,030	Union	L 19
4,090	Van Buren	O 15
19,764	Warren	O 13
51,631	Washington	L 23
13,638	Wayne	P 8
29,498	Weakley	L 5
15,983	White	N 15
25,220	Williamson	N 10
25,267	Wilson	M 12
2,915,841	Total	

TEXAS

COUNTIES.

TOTAL NUMBER 254

Pop.	County	Index
37,092	Anderson	G 21
1,277	Andrews	F 8
32,201	Angelina	H 24
3,469	Aransas	O 19
7,599	Archer	C 15
2,495	Armstrong	D 4
19,275	Atascosa	N 16
17,384	Austin	K 20
6,318	Bailey	B 8
4,234	Bandera	L 15
21,610	Bastrop	K 18
7,755	Baylor	C 14
16,481	Bee	O 18
44,863	Bell	I 18
338,176	Bexar	L 16
4,264	Blanco	J 16
1,396	Borden	E 10
15,761	Bosque	G 17
50,208	Bowie	C 23
27,069	Brazoria	M 22
26,977	Brazos	I 20
6,478	Brewster	K 7
4,056	Briscoe	A 11
6,362	Brooks	E 4
25,924	Brown	G 15
18,334	Burleson	J 20
10,771	Burnet	I 17
24,893	Caldwell	K 18
5,911	Calhoun	N 20
11,568	Callahan	F 14
83,202	Cameron	P 5
10,285	Camp	D 22
6,624	Carson	C 4
33,496	Cass	D 24
4,631	Castro	A 9, E 2
7,511	Chambers	K 24
43,970	Cherokee	G 22
12,149	Childress	A 12, E 6
12,524	Clay	C 16
3,735	Cochran	C 8
4,590	Coke	G 12
20,571	Coleman	G 14
47,190	Collin	D 19
10,331	Collingsworth	D 6
17,812	Colorado	L 20
12,321	Comal	L 16
19,245	Comanche	G 16
6,192	Concho	H 13
24,909	Cooke	C 18
20,226	Coryell	H 17
7,079	Cottle	B 13
2,841	Crane	H 8
2,809	Crockett	I 10
10,046	Crosby	C 11
1,653	Culberson	G 4
6,494	Dallam	A 2
398,564	Dallas	E 19
15,367	Dawson	E 10
6,056	Deaf Smith	D 2
12,858	Delta	C 21
33,658	Denton	D 18
24,935	De Witt	M 18
7,847	Dickens	C 12
8,542	Dimmit	O 14
7,487	Donley	D 5
20,565	Duval	P 16
30,345	Eastland	F 15
15,051	Ector	F 8
2,933	Edwards	K 12
47,733	Ellis	F 19
131,067	El Paso	F 1
20,760	Erath	F 16
35,984	Falls	H 19
41,064	Fannin	C 20
29,246	Fayette	K 19
12,932	Fisher	E 12
10,659	Floyd	B 11
5,237	Foard	B 14
32,963	Fort Bend	L 22
8,378	Franklin	D 22
21,138	Freestone	G 20
9,207	Frio	N 15
8,136	Gaines	E 8
81,173	Galveston	L 23
5,678	Garza	D 11
10,670	Gillespie	J 15
1,193	Glasscock	G 10
8,798	Goliad	N 18
26,075	Gonzales	L 18
23,911	Gray	C 5
69,499	Grayson	C 19
58,027	Gregg	E 23
21,960	Grimes	I 21
25,596	Guadalupe	L 17
18,813	Hale	B 10
12,117	Hall	A 12, E 5
13,303	Hamilton	G 16
2,783	Hansford	A 4
11,073	Hardeman	A 13
15,875	Hardin	J 24
528,961	Harris	K 22
50,900	Harrison	E 24
1,873	Hartley	B 2
14,905	Haskell	D 13
15,349	Hays	K 17
4,170	Hemphill	B 6
31,822	Henderson	F 21
106,059	Hidalgo	P 4
38,355	Hill	G 18
12,693	Hockley	C 9
6,674	Hood	E 17
30,274	Hopkins	D 21
31,137	Houston	H 22
20,990	Howard	F 10
3,149	Hudspeth	G 2
48,793	Hunt	D 20
19,069	Hutchinson	B 4
1,963	Irion	H 11
10,206	Jack	D 16
11,720	Jackson	M 20
17,491	Jasper	I 25
2,375	Jeff Davis	I 5
145,329	Jefferson	K 25
5,449	Jim Hogg	R 16
20,239	Jim Wells	P 17
30,384	Johnson	F 18
23,378	Jones	E 13
19,248	Karnes	N 17
38,308	Kaufman	E 20
5,080	Kendall	K 16
700	Kenedy	R 18
3,413	Kent	D 12
11,650	Kerr	K 14
5,064	Kimble	J 14
1,066	King	C 12
4,533	Kinney	L 12
13,344	Kleberg	Q 18
10,090	Knox	C 13
50,425	Lamar	C 21
17,606	Lamb	B 9
9,167	Lampasas	H 16
8,003	La Salle	O 15
25,485	Lavaca	L 19
12,751	Lee	J 19
17,733	Leon	H 21
24,541	Liberty	J 23
33,781	Limestone	H 20
3,764	Lipscomb	A 6
9,799	Live Oak	O 17
5,996	Llano	I 16
285	Loving	G 6
51,782	Lubbock	C 10
11,931	Lynn	D 10
13,208	McCulloch	H 14
101,898	McLennan	G 18
1,374	McMullen	O 16
12,029	Madison	I 21
11,457	Marion	D 24
5,556	Martin	F 10
5,378	Mason	I 15
20,066	Matagorda	N 21
10,071	Maverick	N 12
16,106	Medina	L 15
4,521	Menard	I 14
11,721	Midland	G 9
33,120	Milam	I 19
7,951	Mills	H 16
12,477	Mitchell	F 11
20,442	Montague	C 17
23,055	Montgomery	J 22
4,461	Moore	B 3
9,810	Morris	D 23
4,994	Motley	A 12
35,392	Nacogdoches	G 23
51,308	Navarro	F 20
13,700	Newton	I 25
17,309	Nolan	F 12
92,661	Nueces	P 18
4,213	Ochiltree	A 5
1,385	Oldham	C 2
17,382	Orange	J 25
18,456	Palo Pinto	E 16
22,513	Panola	F 24
20,482	Parker	E 17
5,890	Parmer	A 8, E 1
8,185	Pecos	I 8
20,635	Polk	I 23
54,265	Potter	C 3
10,925	Presidio	J 5
7,334	Rains	D 21
7,185	Randall	D 3
1,997	Reagan	H 10
2,420	Real	K 13
29,769	Red River	C 22
8,006	Reeves	H 6
10,383	Refugio	O 19
1,289	Roberts	B 5
25,710	Robertson	I 20
7,051	Rockwall	D 20
18,903	Runnels	G 13
51,023	Rusk	F 23
10,896	Sabine	G 25
12,471	San Augustine	H 24
9,056	San Jacinto	J 22
28,871	San Patricio	P 18
11,012	San Saba	I 16
3,083	Schleicher	I 12
11,545	Scurry	E 11
6,211	Shackelford	E 14
29,235	Shelby	G 25
2,026	Sherman	A 3
69,090	Smith	E 22
3,071	Somervell	F 17
13,312	Starr	P 3, R 16
12,356	Stephens	E 15
1,404	Sterling	G 11
5,589	Stonewall	D 13
3,977	Sutton	J 12
6,528	Swisher	A 10, E 3
225,521	Tarrant	D 18
44,147	Taylor	F 13
2,952	Terrell	J 9
11,160	Terry	D 9
4,275	Throckmorton	D 14
19,228	Titus	D 22
39,302	Tom Green	H 12
111,053	Travis	J 18
13,705	Trinity	H 22
11,948	Tyler	I 24
26,178	Upshur	D 23
4,297	Upton	H 9
13,246	Uvalde	L 14
15,453	Val Verde	K 11
31,155	Van Zandt	E 21
23,741	Victoria	N 19
19,868	Walker	I 22
10,280	Waller	K 21
9,575	Ward	G 7
25,387	Washington	K 20
45,916	Webb	P 14
36,158	Wharton	M 20
12,411	Wheeler	C 6
73,604	Wichita	B 15
20,474	Wilbarger	B 14
13,230	Willacy	P 5
41,698	Williamson	I 18
17,066	Wilson	M 17
6,141	Winkler	G 7
19,074	Wise	D 17
24,360	Wood	D 22
5,354	Yoakum	D 8
19,004	Young	D 15
3,916	Zapata	R 15
11,603	Zavala	N 14
6,414,824	Total	

UTAH

COUNTIES.

TOTAL NUMBER 29

Pop.	County	Index
5,014	Beaver	M 5
18,832	Box Elder	C 7
29,797	Cache	B 12
18,459	Carbon	I 18
564	Daggett	E 23
15,784	Davis	D 11
8,958	Duchesne	G 18
7,072	Emery	K 17
5,253	Garfield	O 14
2,070	Grand	L 23
8,331	Iron	O 4
7,392	Juab	I 6
2,561	Kane	Q 11
9,613	Millard	K 6
2,611	Morgan	D 13
2,203	Piute	M 10
2,028	Rich	C 14
211,623	Salt Lake	F 11
4,712	San Juan	O 23
16,063	Sanpete	J 12
12,112	Sevier	L 12
8,714	Summit	E 17
9,133	Tooele	F 5
9,898	Uintah	G 23
57,382	Utah	G 12
5,754	Wasatch	G 15
9,269	Washington	Q 3
2,394	Wayne	M 16
56,714	Weber	D 12
550,310	Total	

VERMONT

COUNTIES.

TOTAL NUMBER 14

Pop.	County	Index
17,944	Addison	H 7
22,286	Bennington	P 7
24,320	Caledonia	E 17
52,098	Chittenden	E 8
6,490	Essex	C 21
29,601	Franklin	B 9
3,802	Grand Isle	B 5
11,028	Lamoille	D 11
17,048	Orange	I 14
21,718	Orleans	C 16
45,638	Rutland	L 8
41,546	Washington	F 12
27,850	Windham	P 7
37,862	Windsor	L 12
359,231	Total	

VIRGINIA

COUNTIES.

TOTAL NUMBER 100

Pop.	County	Index
33,030	Accomac	L 24
*44,052	Albemarle	K 12
*29,149	Alleghany	L 7
8,495	Amelia	N 14
20,273	Amherst	M 10
9,020	Appomattox	N 11
*90,563	Arlington	F 18
*56,109	Augusta	J 10
7,191	Bath	J 8
29,687	Bedford	N 8
6,731	Bland	O 2
16,447	Botetourt	M 7
19,575	Brunswick	Q 15
31,477	Buchanan	B 7
13,398	Buckingham	M 12
*70,589	Campbell	O 10
13,945	Caroline	K 17
25,904	Carroll	Q 3
4,275	Charles City	N 18
15,861	Charlotte	P 12
31,183	Chesterfield	N 16
7,158	Clarke	E 14
3,769	Craig	M 6
13,365	Culpeper	H 14
7,505	Cumberland	M 13
21,266	Dickenson	C 6
*48,797	Dinwiddie	O 16
*38,181	Elizabeth City	O 21
7,006	Essex	K 19
40,929	Fairfax	F 17
21,039	Fauquier	G 15
11,967	Floyd	P 5
7,088	Fluvanna	L 13
25,864	Franklin	P 7
*26,103	Frederick	E 13
14,635	Giles	N 4
9,548	Gloucester	M 20
8,454	Goochland	L 15
21,916	Grayson	Q 1
5,218	Greene	I 13
14,866	Greensville	Q 16
41,271	Halifax	Q 11
18,500	Hanover	L 17
*235,002	Henrico	M 17
*36,561	Henry	Q 7
4,875	Highland	I 8
13,381	Isle of Wight	Q 19
*8,849	James City	N 19
6,954	King and Queen	L 19
5,431	King George	I 18
7,855	King William	L 18
8,786	Lancaster	L 21
39,296	Lee	E 3
20,291	Loudoun	F 16
13,665	Louisa	K 14
13,844	Lunenburg	P 13
8,465	Madison	I 13
7,149	Mathews	M 21
31,933	Mecklenburg	Q 13
6,673	Middlesex	L 20
*28,196	Montgomery	O 5
*34,114	Nansemond	Q 20
16,241	Nelson	L 11
4,092	New Kent	M 19
*238,943	Norfolk	Q 21
17,597	Northampton	N 23
10,463	Northumberland	K 21
15,556	Nottoway	O 14
12,649	Orange	J 14
14,863	Page	H 12
16,613	Patrick	Q 5
*94,446	Pittsylvania	Q 9
5,671	Powhatan	M 15
14,922	Prince Edward	N 13
*20,905	Prince George	O 17
19,984	Princess Anne	Q 22
17,738	Prince William	G 16
22,767	Pulaski	O 3
7,208	Rappahannock	G 14
6,634	Richmond	K 19
*112,184	Roanoke	N 6
*26,719	Rockbridge	L 9
*40,057	Rockingham	H 11
26,627	Russell	D 7
26,989	Scott	E 5
20,898	Shenandoah	G 12
28,861	Smyth	D 9
26,442	Southampton	Q 18
*19,971	Spotsylvania	J 16
9,548	Stafford	I 16
6,193	Surry	O 19
12,485	Sussex	P 17
41,607	Tazewell	C 9
11,352	Warren	G 13
*46,315	Warwick	O 20
*47,965	Washington	E 8
9,512	Westmoreland	J 19
52,458	Wise	C 5
22,721	Wythe	P 2
8,857	York	N 20
*2,677,773	Total	

*Includes pop. for Indep. Cities.

WASHINGTON

COUNTIES.

TOTAL NUMBER 39

Pop.	County	Index
6,209	Adams	K 20
8,365	Asotin	N 24
12,053	Benton	N 16
34,412	Chelan	G 13
21,848	Clallam	F 3
49,852	Clarke	P 7
5,549	Columbia	N 22
40,155	Cowlitz	N 6
8,651	Douglas	H 16
4,701	Ferry	D 20
6,307	Franklin	M 18
3,383	Garfield	M 23
14,668	Grant	J 17
53,166	Grays Harbor	I 3
6,098	Island	E 7
8,918	Jefferson	G 3
504,980	King	H 9
44,387	Kitsap	H 6
20,230	Kittitas	J 13
11,357	Klickitat	P 13
41,393	Lewis	M 8
11,361	Lincoln	H 20
11,603	Mason	I 5
24,546	Okanogan	D 16
15,928	Pacific	M 3
7,156	Pend Oreille	D 23
182,081	Pierce	K 8
3,157	San Juan	D 6
37,650	Skagit	D 9
4,633	Skamania	O 9
88,754	Snohomish	F 10
164,652	Spokane	H 22
19,275	Stevens	D 22
37,285	Thurston	K 6
4,286	Wahkiakum	N 4
30,547	Walla Walla	N 20
60,355	Whatcom	C 10
27,221	Whitman	K 23
99,019	Yakima	M 13
1,736,191	Total	

WEST VIRGINIA

COUNTIES.

TOTAL NUMBER 55

Pop.	County	Index
19,869	Barbour	F 14
29,016	Berkeley	D 24
28,556	Boone	M 5
21,658	Braxton	I 10
25,513	Brooke	O 24
97,459	Cabell	K 2
12,455	Calhoun	H 8
15,206	Clay	J 9
10,923	Doddridge	E 10
80,628	Fayette	M 8
12,046	Gilmer	H 10
8,805	Grant	F 18
38,520	Greenbrier	M 12
12,974	Hampshire	E 21
31,572	Hancock	N 24
10,813	Hardy	G 20
82,911	Harrison	E 12
16,598	Jackson	H 5
16,762	Jefferson	E 25
195,619	Kanawha	L 6
22,271	Lewis	G 11
22,886	Lincoln	L 3
67,768	Logan	O 4
94,354	McDowell	Q 5
68,683	Marion	D 13
40,189	Marshall	B 11
22,270	Mason	H 4
68,289	Mercer	Q 9
22,215	Mineral	D 19
40,802	Mingo	O 3
51,252	Monongalia	C 13
13,577	Monroe	P 11
8,743	Morgan	D 22
24,070	Nicholas	L 10
73,115	Ohio	P 24
10,884	Pendleton	I 17
6,692	Pleasants	E 8
13,906	Pocahontas	L 14
30,416	Preston	D 16
19,511	Putnam	J 4
86,687	Raleigh	D 8
30,259	Randolph	H 15
15,389	Ritchie	F 9
20,787	Roane	I 7
20,409	Summers	P 10
19,919	Taylor	E 14
13,173	Tucker	F 16
12,559	Tyler	D 10
18,360	Upshur	H 13
35,566	Wayne	L 1
18,080	Webster	K 12
22,342	Wetzel	C 11
6,475	Wirt	G 7
62,399	Wood	F 6
29,774	Wyoming	P 6
1,901,974	Total	

WISCONSIN

COUNTIES.

TOTAL NUMBER 71

Pop.	County	Index
8,449	Adams	J 16
21,801	Ashland	G 6
34,289	Barron	D 10
15,827	Bayfield	E 5
83,109	Brown	O 14
16,090	Buffalo	D 14
11,382	Burnett	B 8
17,618	Calumet	O 15
40,703	Chippewa	E 11
33,972	Clark	G 13
32,517	Columbia	K 18
18,328	Crawford	F 19
130,660	Dane	K 20
54,280	Dodge	M 19
19,095	Door	Q 12
47,119	Douglas	C 5
27,375	Dunn	C 12
46,999	Eau Claire	E 13
4,177	Florence	N 8
62,353	Fond du Lac	N 17
11,805	Forest	M 9
40,639	Grant	G 21
23,146	Green	J 22
14,092	Green Lake	L 16
20,595	Iowa	I 20
10,049	Iron	H 6
16,599	Jackson	G 15
38,868	Jefferson	M 20
18,708	Juneau	I 16
63,505	Kenosha	O 22
16,680	Kewaunee	P 14
59,653	La Crosse	G 16
18,695	Lafayette	I 22
23,227	Langlade	L 10
22,536	Lincoln	J 10
61,617	Manitowoc	P 15
75,915	Marathon	J 12
36,225	Marinette	O 10
9,097	Marquette	K 17
766,885	Milwaukee	O 20
30,080	Monroe	G 16
27,075	Oconto	N 11
18,938	Oneida	J 9
70,032	Outagamie	N 14
18,985	Ozaukee	O 19
7,897	Pepin	C 13
21,471	Pierce	B 13
26,197	Polk	B 9
35,800	Portage	K 14
18,467	Price	H 9
94,047	Racine	O 21
20,381	Richland	H 19
80,173	Rock	L 21
17,737	Rusk	F 9
24,842	Saint Croix	B 11
33,700	Sauk	I 19
11,540	Sawyer	F 8
35,378	Shawano	M 12
76,221	Sheboygan	O 17
20,105	Taylor	H 11
24,381	Trempealeau	E 14
29,940	Vernon	G 18
8,894	Vilas	K 7
33,103	Walworth	N 22
12,496	Washburn	D 8
28,430	Washington	O 19
62,744	Waukesha	N 20
34,614	Waupaca	L 14
14,268	Waushara	K 15
80,507	Winnebago	M 15
44,465	Wood	I 14
3,137,587	Total	

WYOMING

COUNTIES.

TOTAL NUMBER 23

Pop.	County	Index
13,946	Albany	N 19
12,911	Big Horn	C 11
6,048	Campbell	D 19
12,644	Carbon	O 15
6,631	Converse	I 19
5,463	Crook	C 22
16,095	Fremont	J 9
12,207	Goshen	N 23
4,607	Hot Springs	G 10
4,980	Johnson	E 16
33,651	Laramie	P 22
10,286	Lincoln	K 2
23,858	Natrona	J 15
5,988	Niobrara	I 22
10,976	Park	D 7
8,013	Platte	M 21
19,255	Sheridan	B 14
2,778	Sublette	K 5
19,407	Sweetwater	O 8
2,543	Teton	F 3
7,223	Uinta	P 3
5,858	Washakie	F 12
4,958	Weston	F 22
416	Yellowstone National Park (part)	C 3
250,742	Total	

PRINCIPAL CITIES OF THE UNITED STATES

Including Population Figures from the 1940 Census

Page	Index	Name	Pop.
64	D 18	Aberdeen, S.D.	17,015
70	K 3	Aberdeen, Wash.	18,846
67	E 14	Abilene, Tex.	26,612
58	M 15	Ada, Okla.	15,143
57	F 17	Akron, Ohio	244,791
26	I 5	Alameda, Calif.	36,256
31	M 7	Albany, Ga.	19,055
53	N 23	Albany, N. Y.	130,577
51	G 10	Albuquerque, N. M.	35,449
38	H 9	Alexandria, La.	27,066
69	G 18	Alexandria, Va.	33,523
27	Q 5	Alhambra, Calif.	38,935
60	L 2	Aliquippa, Pa.	27,023
61	L 22	Allentown, Pa.	96,904
57	F 19	Alliance, Ohio	22,405
33	L 10	Alton, Ill.	31,255
60	M 10	Altoona, Pa.	80,214
66	D 3	Amarillo, Tex.	51,686
60	L 2	Ambridge, Pa.	18,968
53	M 22	Amsterdam, N. Y.	33,329
34	H 17	Anderson, Ind.	41,572
64	D 5	Anderson, S. C.	19,424
40	I 15	Annapolis, Md.	13,069
42	Q 20	Ann Arbor, Mich.	29,815
23	F 19	Anniston, Ala.	25,523
29	L 9	Ansonia, Conn.	19,210
72	N 14	Appleton, Wis.	28,436
58	P 14	Ardmore, Okla.	16,886
41	E 19	Arlington, Mass.	■40,013
69	G 18	Arlington, Va.	■57,040
50	I 21	Asbury Park, N. J.	14,617
54	O 8	Asheville, N. C.	51,310
37	D 23	Ashland, Ky.	29,537
57	B 19	Ashtabula, Ohio	21,405
31	E 13	Athens, Ga.	20,650
31	F 6	Atlanta, Ga.	302,288
50	P 16	Atlantic City, N. J.	64,094
41	J 17	Attleboro, Mass.	22,071
39	N 6	Auburn, Me.	19,817
53	M 13	Auburn, N. Y.	35,753
31	G 20	Augusta, Ga.	65,919
39	N 9	Augusta, Me.	19,360
33	C 18	Aurora, Ill.	47,170
43	R 17	Austin, Minn.	18,307
67	J 17	Austin, Tex.	87,930
27	M 13	Bakersfield, Calif.	29,252
40	F 14	Baltimore, Md.	859,100
39	L 14	Bangor, Me.	29,822
58	B 18	Bartlesville, Okla.	16,267
57	F 17	Barberton, Ohio	24,028
52	M 7	Batavia, N. Y.	17,267
38	L 14	Baton Rouge, La.	34,719
42	Q 15	Battle Creek, Mich.	43,453
42	M 20	Bay City, Mich.	47,956
50	E 19	Bayonne, N. J.	79,198
67	K 25	Beaumont, Tex.	59,061
60	K 2	Beaver Falls, Pa.	17,098
33	M 11	Belleville, Ill.	28,405
50	E 19	Belleville, N. J.	28,167
70	C 7	Bellingham, Wash.	29,314
41	E 18	Belmont, Mass.	■26,867
72	L 22	Beloit, Wis.	25,365
42	Q 10	Benton Hbr., Mich.	16,668
26	I 6	Berkeley, Calif.	85,547
49	F 17	Berlin, N. H.	19,084
33	C 21	Berwyn, Ill.	48,451
23	G 12	Bessemer, Ala.	22,826
61	L 23	Bethlehem, Pa.	58,490
41	C 21	Beverly, Mass.	25,537
27	Q 3	Beverly Hills, Calif.	26,823
37	Q 5	Biddeford, Me.	19,790
46	L 16	Billings, Mont.	23,261
44	R 19	Biloxi, Miss.	17,475
53	Q 16	Binghamton, N. Y.	78,309
23	F 13	Birmingham, Ala.	267,583
55	N 11	Bismarck, N. D.	15,496
50	E 18	Bloomfield, N. J.	41,623
33	G 15	Bloomington, Ill.	32,868
34	L 11	Bloomington, Ind.	20,870
71	R 8	Bluefield, Va. & W. Va.	24,562
33	C 21	Blue Island, Ill.	16,638
38	J 19	Bogalusa, La.	14,604
32	N 6	Boise, Idaho	26,130
41	F 20	Boston, Mass.	770,816
37	J 12	Bowling Green, Ky.	14,585
60	M 4	Braddock, Pa.	18,326
60	E 9	Bradford, Pa.	17,691
41	G 20	Braintree, Mass.	■16,378
70	H 6	Bremerton, Wash.	15,134
29	O 7	Bridgeport, Conn.	147,121
50	O 8	Bridgeton, N. J.	15,992
29	G 10	Bristol, Conn.	30,167
37	K 24	Bristol, Tenn. & Va.	23,772
41	I 20	Brockton, Mass.	62,343
41	F 19	Brookline, Mass.	■49,786
66	R 5	Brownsville, Tex.	22,083
31	O 22	Brunswick, Ga.	15,035
52	N 4	Buffalo, N. Y.	575,901
27	O 15	Burbank, Calif.	34,337
27	I 5	Burlingame, Calif.	15,940
35	P 22	Burlington, Ia.	25,832
69	E 6	Burlington, Vt.	27,686
60	K 4	Butler, Pa.	24,477
46	K 7	Butte, Mont.	37,081
41	E 18	Cambridge, Mass.	110,879
57	K 17	Cambridge, Ohio	15,044
50	K 9	Camden, N. J.	117,536
57	G 18	Canton, Ohio	108,401
45	O 23	Cape Girardeau, Mo.	19,426
61	F 22	Carbondale, Pa.	19,371
48	H 3	Carson City, Nev.	2,478
73	J 17	Casper, Wyo.	17,964
35	J 20	Cedar Rapids, Ia.	62,120
62	C 16	Central Falls, R. I.	25,248
33	M 15	Centralia, Ill.	16,343
60	P 12	Chambersburg, Pa.	14,852
33	H 19	Champaign, Ill.	23,302
63	N 19	Charleston, S. C.	71,275
71	K 6	Charleston, W. Va.	67,914
54	H 6	Charlotte, N. C.	100,899
69	K 12	Charlottesville, Va.	19,400
37	Q 15	Chattanooga, Tenn	128,163
41	E 19	Chelsea, Mass.	41,259
61	Q 23	Chester, Pa.	59,285
73	R 22	Cheyenne, Wyo.	22,474
33	C 21	Chicago, Ill.	3,396,808
33	D 21	Chicago Heights, Ill.	22,461
41	H 7	Chicopee, Mass.	41,664
56	N 12	Chillicothe, Ohio	20,129
33	C 21	Cicero, Ill.	64,712
56	O 6	Cincinnati, Ohio	455,610
60	N 4	Clairton, Pa.	16,381
71	E 12	Clarksburg, W. Va.	30,579
57	C 16	Cleveland, Ohio	878,336
57	O 24	Cleveland Heights, Ohio	54,992
50	D 21	Cliffside Park, N. J.	16,892
50	D 19	Clifton, N. J.	48,827
35	J 25	Clinton, Ia.	26,270
36	O 22	Coffeyville, Kan.	17,355
53	N 23	Cohoes, N. Y.	21,955
28	J 15	Colorado Sprs., Colo.	36,789
45	H 13	Columbia, Mo.	18,399
63	G 14	Columbia, S. C.	62,396
31	J 4	Columbus, Ga.	53,280
56	K 11	Columbus, Ohio	306,087
26	R 4	Compton, Calif.	16,198
54	G 6	Concord, N. C.	15,572
49	O 15	Concord, N. H.	27,171
52	Q 11	Corning, N. Y.	16,212
67	P 18	Corpus Christi, Tex.	57,301
67	F 20	Corsicana, Tex.	15,232
53	O 15	Cortland, N. Y.	15,881
35	M 3	Council Bluffs, Ia.	41,439
38	B 17	Covington, Ky.	62,018
62	E 14	Cranston, R. I.	47,085
40	L 6	Cumberland, Md.	39,483
57	F 18	Cuyahoga Falls, Ohio	20,546
67	E 19	Dallas, Tex.	294,734
29	L 3	Danbury, Conn.	22,339
33	H 22	Danville, Ill.	36,919
69	R 9	Danville, Va.	32,749
35	L 24	Davenport, Ia.	66.039
56	L 7	Dayton, Ohio	210,718
30	E 19	Daytona Beach, Fla.	22,584
42	Q 22	Dearborn, Mich.	63,584
23	B 12	Decatur, Ala.	16,604
31	F 8	Decatur, Ga.	16,561
33	I 15	Decatur, Ill.	59,305
67	B 19	Denison, Tex.	15,581
28	F 15	Denver, Colo.	322,412
35	L 12	Des Moines, Ia.	159,819
42	Q 23	Detroit, Mich.	1,623,452
23	O 21	Dothan, Ala.	17,194
49	O 20	Dover, N. H.	14,990
40	G 22	Dover, Del.	5,517
35	G 23	Dubuque, Ia.	43,892
43	H 21	Duluth, Minn.	101,065
52	O 2	Dunkirk, N. Y.	17,713
61	H 22	Dunmore, Pa.	23,086
60	N 4	Duquesne, Pa.	20,693
54	E 12	Durham, N. C.	60,195
34	B 6	E. Chicago, Ind.	54,637
57	C 17	E. Cleveland, Ohio	39,495
29	E 14	E. Hartford, Conn.	■18,615
57	G 21	E. Liverpool, Ohio	23,555
61	L 23	Easton, Pa.	33,589
50	E 18	E. Orange, N. J.	68,945
62	E 17	E. Providence, R.I.	■32,165
33	M 10	E. St. Louis, Ill.	75,609
72	E 12	Eau Claire, Wis.	30,745
25	Q 11	El Dorado, Ark.	15,858
33	B 18	Elgin, Ill.	38,333
50	F 18	Elizabeth, N. J.	109,912
34	B 15	Elkhart, Ind.	33,434
33	C 20	Elmhurst, Ill.	15,458
52	Q 12	Elmira, N. Y.	45,106
66	F 1	El Paso, Tex.	96,810
57	D 15	Elyria, Ohio	25,120
53	Q 15	Endicott, N. Y.	17,702
50	D 21	Englewood, N. J.	18,966
58	D 10	Enid, Okla.	28,081
60	C 3	Erie, Pa.	116,955
42	G 8	Escanaba, Mich.	14,830
56	C 17	Euclid, Ohio	17,866
59	I 6	Eugene, Ore.	20,838
26	D 1	Eureka, Calif.	17,055
33	B 21	Evanston, Ill.	65,389
34	R 5	Evansville, Ind.	97,062
41	E 19	Everett, Mass.	46,784
70	F 8	Everett, Wash.	30,224
71	D 13	Fairmont, W. Va.	23,105
44	M 19	Fall River, Mass.	115,428
55	M 25	Fargo, N. D.	32,580
54	I 13	Fayetteville, N. C.	17,428
42	P 23	Ferndale, Mich.	22,523
56	F 10	Findlay, Ohio	15,228
41	C 13	Fitchburg, Mass.	41,824
42	O 21	Flint, Mich.	151,543
23	A 8	Florence, Ala.	15,043
63	F 20	Florence, S. C.	16,054
72	N 17	Fond du Lac, Wis.	27,209
35	G 10	Fort Dodge, Ia.	22,904
30	M 24	Ft. Lauderdale, Fla.	17,996
25	F 4	Fort Smith, Ark.	36,584
34	D 20	Fort Wayne, Ind.	118,410
67	E 18	Fort Worth, Tex.	177,662
41	G 17	Framingham, Mass	■23,214
37	E 16	Frankfort, Ky.	11,492
40	E 8	Frederick, Md.	15,802
33	A 12	Freeport, Ill.	22,366
52	I 7	Freeport, N. Y.	20,410
56	E 11	Fremont, Ohio	14,710
27	K 11	Fresno, Calif.	60,685
23	D 18	Gadsden, Ala.	36,975
33	F 9	Galesburg, Ill.	28,876
67	M 23	Galveston, Tex.	60,862
41	D 13	Gardner, Mass.	20,206
50	D 20	Garfield, N. J.	28,004
56	P 23	Garfield Hts., Ohio	16,989
34	B 7	Gary, Ind.	111,719
54	H 4	Gastonia, N. C.	21,313
52	M 11	Geneva, N. Y.	15,555
27	O 15	Glendale, Calif.	82,582
53	K 24	Glens Falls, N. Y.	18,836
41	C 23	Gloucester, Mass.	24,046
53	M 21	Gloversville, N. Y.	23,329
54	H 16	Goldsboro, N. C.	17,274
55	H 24	Grand Forks, N. D.	20,228
47	L 17	Grand Island, Neb.	19,130
42	O 13	Grand R'pds Mich.	164,292
32	M 10	Granite City, Ill.	22,974
46	G 10	Great Falls, Mont.	29,928
28	D 16	Greeley, Colo.	15,995
72	P 14	Green Bay, Wis.	46,235
54	D 10	Greensboro, N. C.	59,319
60	N 5	Greensburg, Pa.	16,743
41	C 7	Greenfield, Mass.	■15,672
44	F 6	Greenville, Miss.	20,892
63	B 7	Greenville, S. C.	34,734
44	F 11	Greenwood, Miss.	14,767
44	R 18	Gulfport, Miss.	15,195
50	D 20	Hackensack, N. J.	26,279
40	B 6	Hagerstown, Md.	32,491
56	N 6	Hamilton, Ohio	50,592
34	B 5	Hammond, Ind.	70,184
42	P 23	Hamtramck, Mich.	49,839
45	E 16	Hannibal, Mo.	20,865
60	Q 16	Hanover, Pa.	■16,439
61	N 16	Harrisburg, Pa.	83,893
29	E 14	Hartford, Conn.	166,267
33	C 21	Harvey, Ill.	17,878
47	M 17	Hastings, Neb.	15,145
44	O 17	Hattiesburg, Miss.	21,026
41	A 19	Haverhill, Mass.	46,752
61	J 20	Hazleton, Pa.	38,009
46	J 8	Helena, Mont.	15,056
52	H 7	Hempstead, N. Y.	20,856
33	B 21	Highland Park, Ill	14,476
42	P 23	Highland Pk., Mich.	50,810
43	F 17	Hibbing, Minn.	16,385
54	E 9	High Point, N. C.	38,495
50	E 20	Hoboken, N. J.	50,115
42	O 11	Holland, Mich.	14,616
41	G 7	Holyoke, Mass.	53,750
60	M 3	Homestead, Pa.	19,041
25	K 9	Hot Springs, Ark.	21,370
52	P 9	Hornell, N. Y.	15,649
67	K 22	Houston, Tex.	384,514
71	K 2	Huntington, W. Va.	78,836
27	Q 4	Huntington Pk. Cal.	28,648
36	K 14	Hutchinson, Kan.	30,013
32	O 20	Idaho Falls, Idaho	15,024
45	G 6	Independence, Mo.	16,066
34	J 14	Indianapolis, Ind.	386,972
27	O 15	Inglewood, Calif.	30,114
35	K 20	Iowa City, Ia.	17,182
52	L 10	Irondequoit, N. Y.	■23,376
57	R 13	Ironton, Ohio	15,851
42	B 21	Ironwood, Mich.	13,369
50	E 18	Irvington, N. J.	55,328
52	P 13	Ithaca, N. Y.	19,730
42	Q 18	Jackson, Mich.	49,656
44	K 11	Jackson, Miss.	62,107
37	O 5	Jackson, Tenn.	24,332
30	B 16	Jacksonville, Fla.	173,065
33	J 9	Jacksonville, Ill.	19,844
52	Q 3	Jamestown, N. Y.	42,638
72	L 22	Janesville, Wis.	22,992
60	N 5	Jeannette, Pa.	16,220
45	I 14	Jefferson City, Mo.	24,268
50	E 20	Jersey City, N. J.	301,173
52	R 15	Johnson City, N. Y.	18,039
37	L 24	Johnson City, Tenn.	22,763
60	N 7	Johnstown, Pa.	66,668
33	D 19	Joliet, Ill.	42,365
45	O 6	Joplin, Mo.	37,144
42	Q 13	Kalamazoo, Mich.	54,097
33	E 20	Kankakee, Ill.	22,241
36	F 25	Kansas City, Kan.	121,458
45	G 6	Kansas City, Mo.	399,178
50	E 18	Kearny, N. J.	39,467
52	M 4	Kenmore, N. Y.	18,612
72	P 22	Kenosha, Wis.	48,765
35	R 21	Keokuk, Ia.	15,076
33	E 11	Kewanee, Ill.	16,901
53	R 22	Kingston, N. Y.	28,589
61	H 20	Kingston, Pa.	20,679
54	H 18	Kinston, N. C.	15,388
59	Q 9	Klamath Falls, Ore.	16,497
37	N 19	Knoxville, Tenn.	111,580
34	G 14	Kokomo, Ind.	33,795
52	N 4	Lackawanna, N. Y.	24,058
72	F 17	La Crosse, Wis.	42,707
34	G 9	La Fayette, Ind.	28,798
38	M 11	Lafayette, La.	19,210
31	H 3	Lagrange, Ga.	21,983
38	M 6	Lake Charles, La.	21,207
30	I 15	Lakeland, Fla.	22,068
57	C 16	Lakewood, Ohio	69,160
57	L 13	Lancaster, Ohio	21,940
61	P 18	Lancaster, Pa.	61,345
42	P 17	Lansing, Mich.	78,753
34	B 10	La Porte, Ind.	16,180
67	Q 14	Laredo, Tex.	39,274
44	M 18	Laurel, Miss.	20,598
41	B 18	Lawrence, Mass.	84,323
58	M 8	Lawton, Okla.	18,055
36	F 23	Leavenworth, Kan.	19,220
61	M 18	Lebanon, Pa.	27,206
41	D 14	Leominster, Mass.	22,226
39	N 6	Lewiston, Me.	38,598
37	F 17	Lexington, Ky.	49,304
56	G 7	Lima, Ohio	44,711
47	L 22	Lincoln, Neb.	81,984
42	Q 23	Lincoln Park, Mich.	15,236
50	F 18	Linden, N. J.	24,115
25	J 13	Little Rock, Ark.	88,039
52	L 5	Lockport, N. Y.	24,379
34	F 13	Logansport, Ind.	20,177
27	P 15	Long Beach, Calif.	164,271
50	H 21	Long Branch, N. J.	17,408
57	C 14	Lorain, Ohio	44,125
27	O 15	Los Angeles, Cal.	1,504,277
37	E 14	Louisville, Ky.	319,077
41	C 17	Lowell, Mass.	101,389
67	C 10	Lubbock, Tex.	31,853
52	H 7	Lynbrook, N. Y.	14,557
69	N 10	Lynchburg, Va.	44,541
50	E 19	Lyndhurst, N. J.	■17,454
41	E 20	Lynn, Mass.	98,123
60	N 4	McKeesport, Pa.	55,355
60	M 3	MeKees Rocks, Pa.	17,021
31	I 10	Macon, Ga.	57,865
72	J 20	Madison, Wis.	67,447
41	E 19	Malden, Mass.	58,010
49	P 15	Manchester, N. H.	77,685
72	Q 16	Manitowoc, Wis.	24,404
43	P 13	Mankato, Minn.	15,654
57	G 14	Mansfield, Ohio	37,154
34	G 17	Marion, Ind.	26,767
56	H 11	Marion, Ohio	30,817
41	F 15	Marlboro, Mass.	15,154
42	E 7	Marquette, Mich.	15,928
67	E 24	Marshall, Tex.	18,410
35	I 15	Marshalltown, Ia.	19,240
71	D 24	Martinsburg, W. Va.	15,063
56	J 20	Martins Ferry, Ohio	14,729
35	C 13	Mason City, Ia.	27,080
57	G 17	Massillon, Ohio	26,644
33	J 18	Mattoon, Ill.	15,827
33	C 20	Maywood, Ill.	26,648
60	F 3	Meadville, Pa.	18,919
41	E 19	Medford, Mass.	63,083
41	E 20	Melrose, Mass.	25,333
47	Q 1	Memphis, Tenn.	292,942
29	I 12	Meriden, Conn.	39,494
44	K 20	Meridian, Miss.	35,481
41	B 19	Methune, Mass.	■21,880
30	N 24	Miami, Fla.	172,172
30	O 24	Miami Beach, Fla.	28,012
34	B 9	Michigan City, Ind.	26,476
29	I 14	Middletown, Conn.	26,495
52	E 3	Middletown, N. Y.	21,908
56	M 7	Middletown, Ohio	31,220
50	O 10	Millville, N. J.	14,806
41	P 4	Milton, Mass.	■18,708
72	P 20	Milwaukee, Wis.	587,472
43	N 16	Minneapolis, Minn	492,370
55	G 10	Minot, N. D.	16,577
34	B 14	Mishawaka, Ind.	28,298
46	H 5	Missoula, Mont.	18,449
23	Q 5	Mobile, Ala.	78,720
26	I 8	Modesto, Calif.	16,379
33	D 8	Moline, Ill.	34,608
60	O 3	Monessen, Pa.	20,257
38	C 11	Monroe, La.	28,309
42	R 22	Monroe, Mich.	18,478
50	D 18	Montclair, N. J.	39,807
23	J 16	Montgomery, Ala.	78,084
68	G 12	Montpelier, Vt.	8,006
71	C 14	Morgantown, W. Va.	16,655
50	E 15	Morristown, N. J.	15,270
61	K 18	Mount Carmel, Pa.	17,780
33	N 16	Mt. Vernon. Ill.	14,724
52	G 6	Mount Vernon, N.Y.	67,362
34	H 19	Muncie, Ind.	49,720
35	L 22	Muscatine, Ia.	18,286
42	N 11	Muskegon, Mich.	47,697
42	N 11	Muskegon Heights, Mich.	16,047
58	H 21	Muskogee, Okla.	32,332
61	I 19	Nanticoke, Pa.	24,387
49	R 15	Nashua, N. H.	32,927
37	M 11	Nashville, Tenn.	167,402
44	N 3	Natchez, Miss.	15,296
29	J 9	Naugatuck, Conn.	15,388
34	P 16	New Albany, Ind.	25,414
50	E 19	Newark, N. J.	429,760
57	K 14	Newark, Ohio	31,487
41	M 20	New Bedford, Mass	110,341
29	G 13	New Britain, Conn.	68,685
50	G 16	New Brunswick, N.J.	33,180
52	D 5	Newburgh, N. Y.	31,883
34	I 19	New Castle, Ind.	16,620
60	J 2	New Castle, Pa.	47,638
29	M 10	New Haven, Conn.	160,605
60	M 4	New Kensington, Pa	24,055
29	L 21	New London, Conn.	30,456
38	N 19	New Orleans, La.	494,537
34	B 17	Newport, Ky.	30,631
62	L 18	Newport, R. I.	30,532
69	P 21	Newport News, Va.	37,067
52	G 6	New Rochelle, N. Y.	58,408
41	F 18	Newton, Mass.	69,873
52	I 5	New York, N. Y.	7,454,995
52	L 4	Niagara Falls, N. Y.	78,029
57	E 20	Niles, Ohio	16,273
69	P 21	Norfolk, Va.	144,332
61	O 23	Norristown, Pa.	38,181
41	B 3	North Adams, Mass.	22,213
41	F 8	Northampton, Mass	24,794
25	I 13	N. Little Rock, Ark.	21,137
52	L 5	N. Tonawanda, N.Y.	20,254
29	P 4	Norwalk, Conn.	39,849
29	I 21	Norwich, Conn.	23,652
56	O 7	Norwood, Ohio	34,010
50	E 19	Nutley, N. J.	21,954
26	I 6	Oakland, Calif.	302,163
33	C 21	Oak Park, Ill.	66,015
65	D 11	Ogden, Utah	43,688
53	D 17	Ogdensburg, N. Y.	16,356
60	G 4	Oil City, Pa.	20,379
58	I 11	Oklahoma Cy., Ok.	204,424
58	H 18	Okmulgee, Okla.	16,051
52	R 6	Olean, N. Y.	21,506
70	K 5	Olympia, Wash.	13,254
47	K 24	Omaha, Neb.	223,844
50	E 18	Orange, N. J.	35,717
30	G 18	Orlando, Fla.	36,736
72	N 16	Oshkosh, Wis.	39,089
52	F 6	Ossining, N. Y.	15,996
52	K 13	Oswego, N. Y.	22,062
33	D 16	Ottawa, Ill.	16,005
35	O 17	Ottumwa, Ia.	31,570
37	G 10	Owensboro, Ky.	30,245
37	J 5	Paducah, Ky.	33,765
26	F 20	Palo Alto, Calif.	16,774
67	C 21	Paris, Tex.	18,678
71	E 6	Parkersburg, W. Va.	30,103
56	D 17	Parma, Ohio	16,365
27	O 16	Pasadena, Calif.	81,864
50	D 19	Passaic, N. J.	61,394
50	D 19	Paterson, N. J.	139,656
62	D 16	Pawtucket, R. I.	75,797
41	D 20	Peabody, Mass.	21,711
52	E 5	Peekskill, N. Y.	17,311
33	G 12	Pekin, Ill.	19,407
30	N 3	Pensacola, Fla.	37,449
33	F 12	Peoria, Ill.	105,087
50	G 18	Perth Amboy, N. J.	41,242
69	O 17	Petersburg, Va.	30,631
23	J 24	Phenix City, Ala.	15,351
61	P 24	Philadelphia, Pa.	1,931,334
50	E 8	Phillipsburg, N. J.	18,314
24	K 12	Phoenix, Ariz.	65,414
64	I 13	Pierre, S. D.	4,322
25	L 14	Pine Bluff, Ark.	21,290
56	J 7	Piqua, Ohio	16,049
36	N 24	Pittsburg, Kan.	17,571
60	M 3	Pittsburgh, Pa.	671,659
41	E 2	Pittsfield, Mass.	49,684
61	H 21	Pittston, Pa.	17,828
50	F 16	Plainfield, N. J.	37,469
52	D 24	Plattsburg, N. Y.	16,351
61	I 20	Plymouth, Pa.	15,507
32	P 19	Pocatello, Idaho	18,133
27	O 17	Pomona, Calif.	23,539
58	C 13	Ponca City, Okla.	16,794
42	P 22	Pontiac, Mich.	66,626
67	K 25	Port Arthur, Tex.	46,140
52	G 7	Port Chester, N. Y.	23,073
42	O 25	Port Huron, Mich.	32,759
39	P 6	Portland, Me.	73,643
59	D 7	Portland, Ore.	305,394
49	O 21	Portsmouth, N. H.	14,821
56	Q 11	Portsmouth, Ohio	40,466
69	P 21	Portsmouth, Va.	50,745
61	N 22	Pottstown, Pa.	20,194
61	L 19	Pottsville, Pa.	24,530
52	C 6	Poughkeepsie, N. Y.	40,478
62	E 15	Providence, R. I.	253,504
65	G 12	Provo, Utah	18,071
28	L 16	Pueblo, Colo.	52,162
33	I 4	Quincy, Ill.	40,469
41	G 20	Quincy, Mass.	75,810
72	P 21	Racine, Wis.	67,195
50	F 17	Rahway, N. J.	17,498
54	F 14	Raleigh, N. C.	46,897
61	N 20	Reading, Pa.	110,568
48	G 3	Reno, Nev.	21,317
41	E 20	Revere, Mass.	34,405
26	H 5	Richmond, Calif.	23,642
34	J 22	Richmond, Ind.	35,147
69	M 17	Richmond, Va.	193,042
50	C 19	Ridgewood, N. J.	14,948
42	Q 23	River Rouge, Mich.	17,008
27	O 18	Riverside, Calif.	34,696
69	N 7	Roanoke, Va.	69,287
43	Q 19	Rochester, Minn.	26,312
52	L 9	Rochester, N. Y.	324,975
33	A 15	Rockford, Ill.	84,637
63	B 13	Rock Hill, S. C.	15,009
33	D 8	Rock Island, Ill.	42,775
52	I 7	Rockville Ctr., N. Y.	18,613
54	E 16	Rocky Mount, N. C.	25 568
31	D 3	Rome, Ga.	26,282
53	L 17	Rome, N. Y.	34,214
42	P 23	Royal Oak, Mich.	25,087
50	E 19	Rutherford, N. J.	15,466
68	L 8	Rutland, Vt.	17,082
26	G 7	Sacramento, Calif.	105,958
42	N 20	Saginaw, Mich.	82,794
43	L 12	St. Cloud, Minn.	24,173
45	D 5	St. Joseph, Mo.	75,711
45	I 20	St. Louis, Mo.	816,048
33	N 17	St. Paul, Minn.	287,736
30	I 12	St. Petersburg, Fla.	60,812
41	D 21	Salem, Mass.	41,213
58	F 6	Salem, Ore.	30,908
36	H 15	Salina, Kan.	21,073
54	F 6	Salisbury, N. C.	19,037
65	E 11	Salt Lake Cy., Utah	149,934
67	H 12	San Angelo, Tex.	25,802
67	L 16	San Antonio, Tex.	253,854
27	O 18	San Bernardino, Cal.	43,646
27	Q 19	San Diego, Calif.	203,341
56	D 13	Sandusky, Ohio	24,874
26	I 5	San Francisco, Cal.	634,536
27	J 7	San Jose, Calif.	68,457
27	D 20	San Leandro, Calif.	14,601
27	E 17	San Mateo, Calif.	19,403
27	P 17	Santa Ana, Calif.	31,921
27	O 11	Santa Barbara, Cal.	34,958
27	J 6	Santa Cruz, Calif.	16,896
51	E 14	Santa Fe, N. M.	20,325
27	O 14	Santa Monica, Calif.	53,500
41	E 20	Saugus, Mass.	■14,825
42	E 18	Sault S. Marie, Mich	15,847
31	K 25	Savannah, Ga.	95,996
53	N 22	Schenectady, N. Y.	87,549
61	H 21	Scranton. Pa.	140,404
70	H 8	Seattle, Wash.	368,302
45	I 10	Sedalia, Mo.	20,428
23	J 12	Selma, Ala.	19,834
56	D 16	Shaker Hts., Ohio	23,393
61	K 18	Shamokin, Pa.	18,810
60	I 1	Sharon, Pa.	25,622
58	J 15	Shawnee, Okla.	22,053
72	P 17	Sheboygan, Wis.	40,638
61	K 19	Shenandoah, Pa.	19,790
67	C 19	Sherman, Tex.	17,156
72	P 20	Shorewood, Wis.	15,184
38	C 5	Shreveport, La.	98,167
35	G 1	Sioux City, Ia.	82,364
64	M 24	Sioux Falls, S. D.	40,832
41	F 19	Somerville, Mass.	102,177
34	B 13	South Bend, Ind.	101,268
41	I 12	Southbridge, Mass.	■16,825
27	R 4	South Gate, Calif.	26,945
39	P 6	S. Portland, Me.	15,781
63	B 8	Spartanburg, S. C.	32,249
70	H 23	Spokane, Wash.	122,001
33	I 12	Springfield, Ill.	75,503
41	H 8	Springfield, Mass.	149,554
45	O 10	Springfield, Mo.	61,238
56	K 9	Springfield, Ohio	70,662
29	R 2	Stamford, Conn.	47,938
57	I 20	Steubenville, Ohio	37,651
72	K 14	Stevens Point, Wis.	15,777
26	H 8	Stockton, Calif.	54,714
29	O 8	Stratford, Conn.	■22,580
33	E 16	Streator, Ill.	14,930
50	E 17	Summit, N. J.	16,165
63	H 17	Sumter, S. C.	15,874
61	K 16	Sunbury, Pa.	15,462
72	C 4	Superior, Wis.	35,136
60	M 4	Swissvale, Pa.	15,919
53	M 15	Syracuse, N. Y.	205,967
70	J 7	Tacoma, Wash.	109,408
30	B 5	Tallahassee, Fla.	16,240
30	I 13	Tampa, Fla.	108,391
41	K 19	Taunton, Mass.	37,395
67	H 18	Temple, Tex.	15,344
34	K 6	Terre Haute, Ind.	62,693
67	C 24	Texarkana, Tex. & Ark.	28,840
56	F 11	Tiffin, Ohio	16,102
56	C 10	Toledo, Ohio	282,349
36	G 21	Topeka, Kan.	67,833
29	E 7	Torrington, Conn.	26,988
50	I 13	Trenton, N. J.	124,697
53	N 24	Troy, N. Y.	70,304
24	N 17	Tucson, Ariz.	36,818
58	E 19	Tulsa, Okla.	142,157
23	G 8	Tuscaloosa, Ala.	27,493
67	F 22	Tyler, Tex.	28,279
50	E 20	Union City, N. J.	56,173
60	P 4	Uniontown, Pa.	21,819
45	I 20	University City, Mo.	33,023
60	P 23	Upper Darby, Pa.	■56,883
53	L 18	Utica, N. Y.	100,518
31	P 12	Valdosta, Ga.	15,595
26	H 5	Vallejo, Calif.	20,072
53	H 6	Valley Stream, N.Y.	16,679
70	Q 7	Vancouver, Wash.	18,788
44	K 7	Vicksburg, Miss.	24,460
34	O 5	Vincennes, Ind.	18,228
67	G 19	Waco, Tex.	55,982
41	D 19	Wakefield, Mass.	■16,223
70	O 21	Walla Walla, Wash.	18,109
41	E 18	Waltham, Mass.	40,020
57	E 20	Warren, Ohio	42,837
60	E 7	Warren, Pa.	14,891
62	H 17	Warwick Neck, R. I.	28,757
40	J 11	Washington, D. C.	663,091
60	O 2	Washington, Pa.	26,166
29	I 9	Waterbury, Conn.	99,314
35	G 17	Waterloo, Ia.	51,743
41	M 2	Watertown, Mass.	■35,427
53	H 15	Watertown, N. Y.	33,385
39	M 10	Waterville, Me.	16,688
53	N 23	Watervliet, N. Y.	16,114
33	A 20	Waukegan, Ill.	34,241
72	N 20	Waukesha, Wis.	19,242
72	K 12	Wausau, Wis.	27,268
72	P 20	Wauwatosa, Wis.	27,769
31	O 17	Waycross, Ga.	16,763
45	I 20	Webster Groves, Mo.	18,394
72	O 20	West Allis, Wis.	36,364
41	H 6	Westfield, Mass.	18,793
50	F 17	Westfield, N. J.	18,458
29	E 13	W. Hartford, Conn	■33,776
29	N 10	W. Haven, Conn.	■30,021
50	E 21	W. New York, N. J.	39,439
50	E 18	W. Orange, N. J.	25,662
30	L 24	W. Palm Beach, Fla	33,693
41	H 7	W. Springfield, Mass.	■17,135
62	G 12	W. Warwick, R. I.	■18,188
71	Q 23	Wheeling, W. Va.	61,099
41	R 7	Weymouth, Mass.	■23,868
52	G 6	White Plains, N. Y.	40,327
27	O 16	Whittier, Calif.	16,115
36	M 16	Wichita, Kan.	114,966
67	B 16	Wichita Falls, Tex.	45,112
61	I 21	Wilkes-Barre, Pa.	86,236
60	M 4	Wilkinsburg, Pa.	29,853
61	H 16	Williamsport, Pa.	44,355
33	B 21	Wilmette, Ill.	17,226
40	B 22	Wilmington, Del.	112,504
54	M 17	Wilmington, N. C.	33,407
54	F 16	Wilson, N. C.	19,234
43	Q 23	Winona, Minn.	22,490
54	D 6	Winston-Salem, N.C.	79,815
41	M 6	Winthrop, Mass.	■16,768
41	D 18	Woburn, Mass.	19,751
50	F 18	Woodbridge, N. J.	■27,191
62	A 13	Woonsocket, R. I.	49,303
41	G 13	Worcester, Mass.	193,694
42	Q 23	Wyandotte, Mich.	30,618
70	M 14	Yakima, Wash.	27,221
52	G 5	Yonkers, N. Y.	142,598
61	P 17	York, Pa.	56,712
57	E 21	Youngstown, Ohio	167,720
57	K 16	Zanesville, Ohio	37,500

■Township district, or other minor civil division classified as urban.

GENERAL INDEX OF UNITED STATES CITIES

An index of 50,000 cities, towns and villages in the United States. (For index of cities in the U. S. Territories and Possessions, see pages following this Index).

The location of each place on the state maps is indicated by the letter and figure reference. Populations of incorporated places are in accordance with the 1940 Census.

▲ Figure includes population of entire township, district or other minor civil division.

■ Township, district, or other minor civil division classified as urban by U. S. Census Bureau.

* Not shown on map. Index refers to the county in which place is located.

MAP INDEX AND ABBREVIATIONS

Page No.	State	Abbrev.
23	Alabama	Ala.
24	Arizona	Ariz.
25	Arkansas	Ark.
26	California	Calif.
28	Colorado	Colo.
29	Connecticut	Conn.
40	Delaware	Del.
40	District of Columbia	D.C.
30	Florida	Fla.
31	Georgia	Ga.
32	Idaho	Idaho
33	Illinois	Ill.
34	Indiana	Ind.
35	Iowa	Ia.
36	Kansas	Kan.
37	Kentucky	Ky.
38	Louisiana	La.
39	Maine	Me.
40	Maryland	Md.
41	Massachusetts	Mass.
42	Michigan	Mich.
43	Minnesota	Minn.
44	Mississippi	Miss.
45	Missouri	Mo.
46	Montana	Mont.
47	Nebraska	Neb.
48	Nevada	Nev.
49	New Hampshire	N. H.
50	New Jersey	N. J.
51	New Mexico	N. M.
52	New York	N. Y.
54	North Carolina	N. C.
55	North Dakota	N. D.
56	Ohio	Ohio
58	Oklahoma	Okla.
59	Oregon	Ore.
60	Pennsylvania	Pa.
62	Rhode Island	R. I.
63	South Carolina	S. C.
64	South Dakota	S. D.
37	Tennessee	Tenn.
66	Texas	Tex.
65	Utah	Utah
68	Vermont	Vt.
69	Virginia	Va.
70	Washington	Wash.
71	West Virginia	W. Va.
72	Wisconsin	Wis.
73	Wyoming	Wyo.

A

Pop.	Place, Index	State
15	*Aaron, K 15	Ky.
320	Aaronsburg, K 14	Pa.
190	*Abanda, H 20	Ala.
23	*Abarr, E 24	Colo.
100	*Abba, M 13	Ga.
2080	Abbeville, M 22	Ala.
1010	Abbeville, L 13	Ga.
6672	Abbeville, N 11	La.
275	Abbeville, B 15	Miss.
4930	Abbeville, F 6	S. C.
920	Abbotsford, H 12	Wis.
300	Abbott, H 5	Ark.
....	Abbott, P 17	Ill.
....	Abbott, M 6	Ind.
75	*Abbott, F 20	Miss.
75	Abbott, L 17	Neb.
25	Abbott, D 20	N. M.
264	Abbott, G 19	Tex.
23	*Abbott, H 13	W. Va.
157	*Abbottsburg, K 14	N. C.
81	*Abbottsford, O 25	Mich.
441	Abbottstown, P 16	Pa.
200	Abbot Village, J 11	Me.
138	Abbyville, L 13	Kan.
25	Abdal, O 18	Neb.
50	*Abell, O 14	Md.
215	Abercrombie, O 25	N. D.
4	Aberdeen, J 16	Calif.
1016	Aberdeen, P 17	Idaho
84	*Aberdeen, I 11	Ky.
1525	Aberdeen, D 17	Md.
4746	Aberdeen, E 21	Miss.
1076	Aberdeen, I 11	N. C.
497	Aberdeen, Q 10	Ohio
17015	Aberdeen, D 18	S. D.
8	*Aberdeen, D 6	Tex.
18846	Aberdeen, K 3	Wash.
....	Aberdeen Jc., O 18	Idaho
....	Aberdeen Jc., H 13	Miss.
....	*Aberdeen Proving Ground C 16	Md.
315	*Abernant, G 8	Ala.
25	Abernathy, F 21	Ala.
847	Abernathy, B 10	Tex.
100	*Abeytas, J 10	N. M.
134	Abie, J 21	Neb.
5671	Abilene, H 17	Kan.
26612	Abilene, F 13	Tex.
48	*Abilene, P 12	Va.
3218	Abingdon, F 9	Ill.
60	Abingdon, N 18	Iowa
1300	Abingdon, D 16	Md.
3158	Abingdon, E 8	Va.
250	Abington, D 22	Conn.
289	Abington, E 5	La.
5708	■Abington, H 20	Mass.
20857	■*Abington, N 22	Pa.
530	▲Abiquiu, D 12	N. M.
528	Abita Springs, L 19	La.
395	Ableman, J 18	Wis.
10	*Ables, G 2	Tex.
10	*Abner, H 9	N. C.
....	Abney, P 5	Tex.
55	*Abney, O 8	W. Va.
25	*Abo, M 12	Mo.
150	Abo, I 12	N. M.
250	Abraham, J 7	Utah
30	*Abraham, O 8	W. Va.
319	Abram, P 3	Tex.
201	Abrams, O 13	Wis.
48	Absaraka, M 23	N. D.
400	Absarokee, M 14	Mont.
2084	Absecon, O 15	N. J.
40	*Absher, I 15	Ky.
75	Absher(Geneva), I 17	Mont.
....	*Abshers, C 5	N. C.
200	Academia, I 14	Ohio
150	Academia, M 14	Pa.
45	*Academy, K 10	Calif.
100	Academy, M 17	S. D.
600	Acadia, C 19	Me.
....	*Acadia Academy, L 10	La.
5	*Acahela, I 23	Pa.
30	*Acala, G 2	Tex.
250	*Acampo, H 8	Calif.
27	*Access, F 21	Ky.
236	Accident, M 2	Md.
36	*Accokeek, J 12	Md.
500	Accomac, L 24	Va.
165	*Accord, H 21	Mass.
359	Accord, C 4	N. Y.
90	*Accotink (Newington), F 17	Va.
1000	Accoville, O 5	W. Va.
400	*Ace, I 23	Tex.
110	Acequia, Q 14	Idaho
356	Achille, R 17	Okla.
20	*Achilles, D 4	Kan.
135	*Achilles, M 20	Va.
8	*Achsah, I 13	Va.
10	*Acidalia, R 20	N. Y.
250	*Ackerly, E 10	Tex.
1528	Ackerman, G 17	Miss.
397	Ackermanville, K 23	Pa.
110	*Ackert (Inman), G 6	Ga.
65	*Ackerville, L 10	Ala.
1586	Ackley, G 14	Iowa
50	Ackmen, O 3	Colo.
67	*Ackworth, M 12	Iowa
400	*Acmar, F 15	Ala.
150	*Acme H 12	La.
125	Acme, K 20	N. M.
196	*Acme, L 15	N. C.
275	Acme, M 10	Okla.
1300	*Acme, M 5	Pa.
250	Acme, A 13	Tex.
100	Acme, C 8	Wash.
515	Acme, M 7	W. Va.
200	Acme, A 15	Wyo.
50	Acoaxet, O 19	Mass.
....	*Acol, I 24	Tex.
10	*Acomita, H 4	N. M.
50	*Acorn, J 19	Va.
501	Acosta, O 7	Pa.
135	*Acra, P 22	N. Y.
200	Acree, M 9	Ga.
25	*Acres, N 8	Kan.
75	Acton, G 13	Ala.
95	Acton, N 15	Calif.
510	Acton, J 15	Ind.
94	Acton, Q 2	Me.
400	Acton, D 17	Mass.
50	Acton, L 15	Mont.
....	Acton, F 23	N. D.
10	*Acup, L 6	W. Va.
3000	Acushnet, M 20	Mass.
65	Acushnet (Ware), H 13	Mont.
1267	Acworth, E 5	Ga.
82	*Ackworth, M 12	Iowa
....	Acworth, O 7	N. H.
22	*Acworth, C 22	Tex.
15	*Acy, L 16	La.
200	*Ada, G 15	Kan.
450	Ada, O 14	Mich.
1938	Ada, G 3	Minn.
2368	Ada, G 9	Ohio
15143	Ada, M 16	Okla.
....	*Ada, I 6	Ore.
....	Ada, E 6	S. D.
200	*Ada, Q 9	W. Va.
300	Adah, P 3	Pa.
....	*Adahi, M 20	Calif.
375	Adair, G 7	Ill.
874	Adair, L 8	Iowa
9	*Adair, G 11	Ky.
256	Adair, G 12	Miss.
407	Adair, D 21	Okla.
827	Adairsville, D 4	Ga.
784	Adairville, K 11	Ky.
200	*Adako, E 3	N. C.
115	*Adam (Adamsburg), C 10	S. C.
68	▲Adamana, G 22	Ariz.
80	*Adamant, F 12	Vt.
90	*Adams, G 4	Calif.
50	*Adams (Adams City), F 15	Colo.
2	Adams, I 6	Idaho
225	Adams, I 5	Ill.
....	Adams, D 20	Ind.
275	Adams, L 18	Ind.
41	*Adams, M 13	Kan.
150	*Adams, F 22	Ky.
12608	■Adams, C 4	Mass.
....	Adams, R 17	Mich.
674	Adams, R 18	Minn.
100	*Adams (Adams Station), K 9	Miss.
516	Adams, N 22	Neb.
....	Adams, G 15	N. J.
1594	Adams, I 15	N. Y.
165	*Adams, D 3	N. C.
355	Adams, F 20	N. D.
50	*Adams, Q 5	Okla.
169	Adams, C 19	Ore.
512	Adams, K 10	Tenn.
1310	Adams, J 16	Wis.
150	Adams Basin, L 8	N. Y.
210	*Adamsburg, M 5	Pa.
115	*Adamsburg (Adam), C 10	S. C.
670	Adams Center, H 15	N. Y.
50	*Adams City (Adams), F 15	Colo.
110	*Adams Crossing (W. Lebanon), P 24	N. Y.
211	Adamsdale, J 17	Mass.
204	*Adamsdale, K 19	Pa.
....	Adamsdale Jc., J 17	Mass.
7	*Adams Diggings, J 3	N. M.
30	*Adams Grove, Q 17	Va.
155	*Adams Mills, K 15	Ohio
250	Adamson, L 20	Okla.
125	Adams Run, O 16	S. C.
45	*Adams Run (Osborn), N 17	S. C.
100	*Adams Station (Adams), K 9	Miss.
250	*Adamston, K 17	N. J.
300	Adamstown, F 8	Md.
955	Adamstown, N 20	Pa.
800	*Adamsville, F 12	Ala.
175	*Adamsville, K 15	Ohio
219	Adamsville, G 2	Pa.
530	Adamsville, J 24	R. I.
719	Adamsville, Q 6	Tenn.
60	*Adamsville H 16	Tex.
98	Adamsville, N 6	Utah
25	*Adaven, J 18	Nev.
100	*Adaza, I 9	Iowa
29	*Add, G 23	Ky.
500	*Addicks, K 22	Tex.
62	*Addie, A 5	Idaho
130	Addielee, F 24	Okla.
272	Addieville, N 13	Ill.
250	Addington, O 10	Okla.
492	Addis, L 14	La.
500	Addison, D 11	Ala.
425	Addison, F 15	Conn.
819	Addison, B 20	Ill.
90	*Addison, G 12	Ky.
400	Addison, L 20	Me.
60	▲Addison (Columbia), L 20	Me.
465	Addison, R 18	Mich.
1617	Addison, Q 10	N. Y.
4	Addison, N 24	N. D.
114	*Addison, P 14	Ohio
199	*Addison, P 7	Pa.
110	*Addison, D 19	Tex.
65	Addison, H 5	Vt.
1133	*Addison (Webster Springs), J 12	W. Va.
123	*Addor, H 11	N. C.
150	Addy, E 22	Wash.
1610	Addyston, O 5	Ohio
2134	Adel, O 12	Ga.
1740	Adel, L 10	Iowa
15	Adel, H 9	Mont.
10	Adel, N 20	Okla.
100	Adel, R 15	Ore.
5	Adelaide, F 19	S. D.
300	*Adelanto, N 18	Calif.
100	*Adelina, M 14	Md.
176	*Adeline, B 14	Ill.
31	*Adeline, F 22	Ky.
432	Adeline, O 13	La.
400	Adelino, H 10	N. M.
313	Adell, O 18	Wis.
414	Adelphi, M 13	Ohio
525	Adelphia, I 18	N. J.
25	Aden, O 9	N. M.
27	Adena, E 18	Colo.
1703	Adena, I 20	Ohio
300	*Adgateville, G 10	Ga.
600	Adger, G 11	Ala.
9	*Adial, L 11	Va.
300	Adin, C 8	Calif.
10	*Adirondack, J 22	N. Y.
50	*Adkins, M 17	Tex.
1027	*Admiralty (Eccles), O 7	W. Va.
270	Admire, I 20	Kan.
85	Adna, L 5	Wash.
100	*Adner, M 20	Va.
125	Adobe Hill, D 11	Wyo.
200	Adolph, H 20	Minn.
50	*Adolph, H 15	W. Va.
75	Adolphus, K 12	Ky.
....	*Adon, B 19	Wyo.
218	*Adona, H 10	Ark.
580	Adrian, J 17	Ga.
66	Adrian, G 5	Ill.
14230	Adrian, R 19	Mich.
1066	Adrian, R 5	Minn.
868	Adrian, J 6	Mo.
125	*Adrian, Q 10	N. Y.
100	Adrian, O 19	N. D.
75	*Adrian, E 11	Ohio
150	Adrian, K 24	Ore.
255	*Adrian (De Lancey), I 7	Pa.
122	*Adrian (Montgomeryville), L 5	Pa.
40	*Adrian, H 22	S. C.
119	*Adrian, C 2	Tex.
75	Adrian, I 17	Wash.
653	Adrian, H 13	W. Va.
....	Adrian Junction, H 13	W. Va.
100	*Adsit, Q 15	Va.
39	*Advance, C 12	Ark.
365	Advance, I 11	Ind.
125	*Advance (Cheap), D 22	Ky.
614	Advance, P 22	Mo.
186	Advance, E 7	N. C.
37	*Advance Mills, K 12	Va.
26	*Advent, H 5	W. Va.
18	*Adyeville, Q 11	Ind.
6	Aeneas, D 18	Wash.
105	*Aetna (Etna), J 19	Ill.
18	*Aetna, O 12	Kan.
60	Aetna, O 9	Tenn.
75	*Aetna Springs, G 5	Calif.
500	*Affinity, O 8	W. Va.
659	Affton (Gravois), I 26	Mo.
700	Aflex, G 24	Ky.
37	*Afton, D 8	Ga.
987	Afton, O 10	Iowa
185	*Afton, H 17	Mich.
132	Afton, N 17	Minn.
....	*Afton, N 9	N. M.
806	Afton, Q 17	N. Y.
1261	Afton, C 23	Okla.
150	*Afton, M 23	Tenn.
75	*Afton, C 12	Tex.
50	*Afton, L 11	Va.
136	*Afton, L 22	Wis.
1211	Afton, J 2	Wyo.
142	Agar, G 13	S. D.
135	Agate, G 18	Colo.
10	Agate, F 2	Neb.
16	Agate, E 15	N. D.
150	Agate Beach, G 3	Ore.
....	Agawam, G 18	Ky.
2700	Agawam, I 7	Mass.
34	Agawam, E 8	Mont.
....	Agawam Jc., I 7	Mass.
452	Agency (Agency City), O 17	Iowa
361	Agency, E 5	Mo.
....	Agency, H 12	Ore.
179	Agenda, E 16	Kan.
56	*Ager, B 5	Calif.
1050	*Ages, J 21	Ky.
250	*Aggie, G 9	Ark.
10	*Agnes, F 17	Ga.
10	Agness, P 3	Ore.
300	Agnew, G 22	Calif.
15	Agnew, C 11	Ill.
19	Agnew, L 21	Neb.
75	*Agnos, B 15	Ark.
187	Agosta (New Bloomington), H 10	Ohio
500	*Agoura, H 15	Calif.
406	Agra, D 10	Kan.
281	Agra, G 15	Okla.
450	Agricola, I 16	Fla.
50	*Agricola, H 16	Ga.
450	*Agricola, J 21	Kan.
250	*Agricola, P 21	Miss.
33	*Agricola, M 10	Va.
....	Agua, K 17	Okla.
20	Agua Caliente, L 8	Ariz.
60	*Agua Caliente, G 3	Calif.
112	*Agua Dulce, P 18	Tex.
12	*Aguanga, P 19	Calif.
50	*Agua Nueva, N 2	Tex.
40	Aguila, J 8	Ariz.
1397	Aguilar, P 16	Colo.
10	*Aguilares, P 14	Tex.
300	*Aguirre (Emery Park), N 17	Ariz.
15	*Ah-gwah-ching, H 11	Minn.
25	Ahloso, M 16	Okla.
475	Ahmeek, C 4	Mich.
25	Ahnberg, I 23	S. D.
20	*Aholt, E 11	Mo.
2313	Ahoskie, C 20	N. C.
150	Ahsahka, G 6	Idaho
164	Ahtanum, M 13	Wash.
50	*Ahwahnee, J 12	Calif.
260	*Aid, P 21	Mo.
49	*Aid, Q 14	Ohio
6168	Aiken, J 10	S. C.
50	*Aiken, B 11	Tex.
100	*Aikin, C 18	Md.
506	Ailey, K 17	Ga.
150	*Aily, C 6	Va.
25	*Aimwell, K 7	Ala.
14	*Aimwell, F 11	La.
415	Ainsworth, M 20	Iowa
359	Ainsworth, F 13	Neb.
65	Airedele, Q 16	Md.
51	*Airey, M 18	Md.
36	*Airlie, Q 4	Minn.
29	*Airlie, C 17	N. C.
40	Airlie, G 5	Ore.
....	Airline Jc., M 11	Conn.
35	*Airpoint, N 6	Va.
....	*Airport, I 6	Calif.
....	*Airport, D 16	Ohio
110	*Airville, P 17	Pa.
198	*Aitch (Marklesburg), M 12	Pa.
2063	Aitkin, I 14	Minn.
24	*Ajax, Q 9	Va.
450	Ajlune, M 7	Wash.
1100	Ajo, N 9	Ariz.
151	Akaska, E 13	S. D.
36	*Akela, O 6	N. M.
566	Akeley, H 10	Minn.
585	*Akeley, F 6	Pa.
250	*Akers (Manchac), L 17	La.
55	*Akers, O 16	Mo.
116	*Akersville, K 14	Ky.
150	Akin, O 15	Ill.
100	Akins, I 24	Okla.
37	Akra, D 21	N. D.
504	Akron, I 7	Ala.
1417	Akron, E 20	Colo.
990	Akron, E 15	Ind.
1314	Akron, E 1	Iowa
413	Akron, M 21	Mich.
2263	Akron, M 6	N. Y.
244791	Akron, F 17	Ohio
877	Akron, O 19	Pa.
....	Akron Jc., M 5	N. Y.
30	*Alabam, C 7	Ark.
150	*Alabama, M 7	N. Y.
90	*Alabama (Basom), M 7	N. Y.
....	Alabama and Vicksburg Jc., K 20	Miss.
8544	Alabama City, D 17	Ala.
300	Alabaster, L 21	Mich.
....	Alabaster Jc., L 21	Mich.
1081	Alachua, D 13	Fla.
23	Aladdin, C 22	Wash.
110	Aladdin, B 23	Wyo.
30	Alafla, I 15	Fla.
450	Alaflora, O 13	Ala.
450	*Alamance, D 11	N. C.
36256	Alameda, D 18, I 5	Calif.
2691	Alameda (North Pocatello), P 18	Idaho
506	Alameda, G 11	N. M.
24	Alameda, F 18	Wash.
69	*Alamo, B 21, I 6	Calif.
162	Alamo, O 15	Colo.
646	Alamo, K 16	Ga.
163	*Alamo, I 9	Ind.
125	*Alamo, Q 13	Mich.
150	Alamo, M 19	Nev.
214	Alamo, E 3	N. D.
1137	Alamo, N 4	Tenn.
1944	Alamo, P 4	Tex.
3950	Alamogordo, M 13	N. M.
5700	Alamo Heights, L 16	Tex.
5613	Alamosa, P 12	Colo.
40	*Alamota, I 6	Kan.
263	Alanreed, D 5	Tex.
330	Alanson, H 16	Mich.
56	*Alanthus, H 14	Va.
494	Alapaha, N 13	Ga.
200	*Alarka, O 4	N. C.
150	Alaska, O 14	Mich.
....	*Alaska see Fort Ashby	W. Va.
60	Alaska, Q 14	Wis.
450	Alba, J 16	Mich.
318	Alba, O 6	Mo.
154	*Alba, E 17	Pa.
675	Alba, E 21	Tex.
300	Albania, N 13	La.
11493	Albany, B 18	Calif.
19055	Albany, M 7	Ga.
492	Albany, C 9	Ill.
1623	Albany, H 20	Ind.
1259	Albany, K 15	Ky.
300	*Albany, L 17	La.
....	Albany, N 3	Me.
975	Albany, L 11	Minn.
2010	Albany, B 7	Mo.
17	Albany, D 6	Neb.
130577	Albany, N 24	N. Y.
551	Albany, N 15	Ohio
250	Albany, Q 18	Okla.
5654	Albany, G 6	Ore.
85	*Albany, M 20	Pa.
2230	Albany, E 14	Tex.
200	*Albany, C 16	Vt.
741	Albany, K 21	Wis.
35	Albany, Q 18	Wyo.
30	Albee, E 18	Ore.
114	Albee, F 25	S. D.
....	Albemarle, O 15	La.
4060	Albemarle, H 8	N. C.
318	Alberene, K 12	Va.
210	Alberhill, R 9	Calif.
225	Albers, M 13	Ill.
174	Albert, J 11	Kan.
36	*Albert, E 21	N. M.
300	Albert, J 8	Okla.
56	*Albert, J 15	Tex.
500	Albert (Douglas), F 16	W. Va.
200	*Alberta, L 10	Ala.
200	Alberta, D 7	La.
200	*Alberta, L 5	Minn.
416	Alberta, P 15	Va.
759	Albert City, E 7	Iowa
12200	Albert Lea, R 15	Minn.
500	Alberton, F 12	Md.
283	Alberton, H 3	Mont.
892	Albertson, H 6	N. Y.
....	Albertson, K 7	Vt.
2716	Albertville, C 16	Ala.
243	Albertville (St. Michaels Station), M 14	Minn.
5157	Albia	Iowa
27	*Albia, I 17	Ky.
57	Albin, E 14	Va.
160	Albin, P 24	Wyo.
75	Albion, F 2	Calif.
367	Albion, Q 14	Idaho
1855	Albion, N 20	Ill.
1234	Albion, C 19	Ind.
476	Albion, I 14	Iowa
840	Albion, M 11	Me.
8345	Albion, Q 16	Mich.
18	Albion, N 25	Mont.
2268	Albion, I 18	Neb.
4660	Albion, L 7	N. Y.
240	Albion, M 23	Okla.
1604	Albion, E 2	Pa.
1000	Albion, B 15	R. I.
206	Albion, L 24	Wash.
180	Albion, L 21	Wis.
50	Alborn, F 19	Minn.
....	Albright, K 24	Neb.
334	Albright, D 16	W. Va.
205	*Albrightsville, J 21	Pa.
35449	Albuquerque, G 11	N. M.
....	Alburg, D 20	N. Y.
638	Alburg (Alburgh), A 5	Vt.
25	Alburg Springs, A 6	Vt.
208	Alburnett, I 20	Iowa
885	Alburtis, M 22	Pa.
200	Alcalde, D 13	N. M.
....	Alcatraz, C 16	Calif.
581	Alcester, O 25	S. D.
213	Alco, D 12	Ark.
250	*Alco, H 7	La.
5131	Alcoa, N 19	Tenn.
365	Alcolu, H 17	S. C.
30	*Alcoma, M 12	Va.
25	*Alcorn, H 19	Ky.
150	Alcorn, M 5	Miss.
....	*Alcott, F 15	Colo.
50	Alcova, K 16	Wyo.
125	*Alcove, O 23	N. Y.
151	Alda, L 16	Neb.
2642	*Aldan, P 23	Pa.
800	*Alden, F 13	Ala.
187	Alden, A 18	Ill.
682	Alden, G 13	Iowa
321	Alden, K 13	Kan.
250	Alden, J 15	Mich.
544	Alden, R 15	Minn.
954	Alden, M 6	N. Y.
30	Alden, L 7	Okla.
1000	Alden, I 20	Pa.
250	*Alden Bridge, B 5	La.
99	*Aldenville, F 23	Pa.
8	Alder, F 14	Minn.
158	Alder, N 8	Mont.
265	Alder, L 8	Wash.
125	*Alder Creek, L 17	N. Y.
26	Alderdale, P 16	Wash.
150	*Alderpoint, D 2	Calif.
340	Alderson, L 20	Okla.
600	Alderson, H 20	Pa.
1493	Alderson, O 11	W. Va.
18	*Alder Springs (Oriental), F 6	Calif.
350	*Alderton, J 8	Wash.
500	*Alderwood Manor, G 8	Wash.
125	*Aldie, F 16	Va.
746	Aldora, H 8	Ga.
1013	Aldrich, H-13	Ala.
152	Aldrich, J 9	Minn.
239	Aldrich, N 9	Mo.
2593	Aledo, E 7	Ill.
22	Aledo, G 5	Okla.
517	*Aledo, E 17	Tex.
56	*Aleman, G 16	Tex.
100	*Aleppo, Q 2	Pa.
120	Alert, L 17	Ind.
500	*Alert, D 15	N. C.
544	Alex, L 11	Okla.
134	*Alexander, J 12	Ark.
300	*Alexander, H 20	Ga.
60	Alexander, P 21	Idaho
304	Alexander, J 9	Ill.
324	Alexander, E 13	Iowa
171	Alexander, J 9	Kan.
312	▲Alexander, J 22	Me.
265	Alexander M 7	N. Y.
1000	*Alexander O 8	N. C.
415	Alexander, I 2	N. D.
125	Alexander, F 16	Tex.
75	Alexander, H 13	W. Va.
6640	Alexander City, H 18	Ala.
819	*Alexander Mills, G 1	N. C.
....	Alexanders, Q 23	Ohio
250	*Alexandria, E 18	Ala.
4801	Alexandria, H 17	Ind.
430	Alexandria, C 18	Ky.
27066	Alexandria, H 9	La.
5051	Alexandria, K 7	Minn.
631	Alexandria, B 16	Mo.
369	Alexandria, O 20	Neb.
75	Alexandria, L 11	N. H.
425	Alexandria, J 13	Ohio
442	Alexandria, M 11	Pa.
746	Alexandria, L 21	S. D.
388	*Alexandria, M 13	Tenn.
33523	Alexandria, G 18	Va.
1748	Alexandria Bay, F 15	N. Y.
877	Alexis, E 8	Ill.
110	*Alexis, H 4	N. C.
28	Alexis, C 10	Ohio
14	*Alf, K 6	Ark.
112	Alfalfa, J 7	Okla.
2	Alfalfa, J 12	Ore.
50	Alfalfa, N 15	Wash.
40	*Alfonso, L 21	Va.
283	Alford, M 10	Fla.
65	*Alford, E 20	Pa.
106	Alfordsville, O 9	Ind.
600	Alfred, Q 3	Me.
694	Alfred, Q 8	N. Y.
500	Alfred, O 17	N. D.
32	*Alfred, N 15	Ohio
60	*Alfred, P 17	Tex.
750	*Alfred Station (Alfred), P 7	N. Y.
200	Alfredton, C 9	Va.
21	*Alger, I 20	Ky.
500	Alger, L 19	Mich.
811	Alger, G 9	Ohio
....	Alger, D 8	Wash.
22	*Algerita, I 16	Tex.
124	*Algiers, P 8	Ind.
134	Algoa, F 17	Ark.
63	Algoa, L 23	Tex.
290	Algodones, F 11	N. M.
183	Algoma, C 18	Miss.
250	Algoma, Q 10	Ore.
600	Algoma, Q 5	W. Va.
2652	Algoma, Q 13	Wis.
4954	Algona, D 9	Iowa
1000	*Algona, J 8	Wash.
1931	*Algonac, P 25	Mich.
926	Algonquin, B 18	Ill.
100	*Algonquin (Lamar), Q 7	W. Va.
609	Algood, M 15	Tenn.
38935	Alhambra, Q 5	Calif.
375	Alhambra, L 11	Ill.
100	Alhambra, J 9	Mont.
181	Alice, N 22	N. D.
28	*Alice, P 14	Ohio
7792	Alice, P 17	Tex.
300	Alicel, D 21	Ore.
64	*Aliceton, H 16	Ky.
1475	Aliceville, H 5	Ala.
125	*Aliceville, J 21	Kan.
333	Alicia, D 17	Ark.
150	Alicia, N 19	Mich.
500	Alicia, P 4	Pa.
30	Alida, B 9	Ind.
30	*Alida, F 8	Minn.
161	*Alief, K 22	Tex.
405	Aline, C 8	Okla.

Pop.	Place Index	State
27023	Aliquippa, L 2	Pa.
500	Alix, F 7	Ark.
40	Alkabo, D 2	N. D.
50	*Alkol, L 4	W. Va.
10	*All, M 7	Va.
200	Allaben, Q 21	N. Y.
2500	*Allais, I 21	Ky.
65	*Allamoore (Allamore), G 2	Tex.
75	Allamuchy, D 12	N. J.
75	*Allandale (Harbor Point), F 19	Fla.
....	Allantown, see Houck	Ariz.
5	Allard, L 16	Wash.
125	Allardt, L 16	Tenn.
5	*Allbright, N 20	Mo.
40	*Alledonia, K 19	Ohio
157	Alleene, N 4	Ark.
4526	Allegan, P 12	Mich.
494	▲Allegany (Zihlman), L5	Md.
1436	Allegany, Q 6	N. Y.
38	Allegany, L 3	Ore.
400	Alleghany, F 9	Calif.
120	*Alleghany, L 7	Va.
28	*Allegheny Spring, O 5	Va.
....	Allegheny, J 4	Pa.
47	*Allegre, J 10	Ky.
100	*Alleman, K 12	Iowa
650	Allemands (Des Allemands), O 17	La.
52	*Allen (Suggsville), M 7	Ala.
279	Allen, I 20	Kan.
284	*Allen, H 22	Ky.
125	Allen, O 21	Md.
244	Allen, R 16	Mich.
34	*Allen, (Allen Jct.) F 20	Minn.
26	*Allen, L 10	Miss.
76	*Allen (Nanachehaw, J 7	Miss.
404	Allen, F 21	Neb.
1389	Allen, L 17	Okla.
500	*Allen, O 14	Pa.
100	Allen, H 23	S. C.
10	Allen, N 8	S. D.
500	Allen, D 19	Tex.
12	*Allen, L 3	W. Va.
432	Allendale, M 21	Ill.
19	*Allendale, I 14	Ky.
212	*Allendale, A 6	Mo.
2058	Allendale, C 19	N. J.
2217	Allendale, M 12	S. C.
60	*Allendor, B 4	Iowa
116	*Allenfarm, I 20	Tex.
50	*Allenhurst, G 21	Fla.
360	Allenhurst, M 22	Ga.
520	Allenhurst, (Deal-Allenhurst), I 21	N. J.
34	Allen Jc., (Allen) F 20	Minn.
200	*Allen Junction, P 7	W. Va.
3487	*Allen Park, Q 22	Mich.
1078	*Allenport, O 2	Pa.
200	*Allens (West Bethel), M 2	Me.
141	Allens Creek (Ruppertown), P 8	Tenn.
15	*Allens Creek, L 11	Va.
319	Allens Grove, M 22	Wis.
60	Allenspark, D 13	Colo.
100	*Allen Springs, K 12	Ky.
1540	Allenstown (East Pembroke), O 15	N. H.
351	Allensville, K 10	Ky.
256	Allensville, N 13	Ohio
250	Allensville, M 12	Pa.
25	Allensworth, L 12	Calif.
110	Allenton, L 11	Ala.
139	*Allenton, O 25	Mich.
264	Allenton, J 19	Mo.
75	*Allenton, J 12	N. C.
962	Allenton, J 14	R. I.
310	Allenton, N 18	Wis.
83	*Allentown, G 13	Ill.
200	Allentown, J 11	Md.
766	Allentown, I 14	N. J.
191	Allentown, Q 7	N. Y.
96904	Allentown, L 22	Pa.
125	*Allenville, K 7	Ala.
240	Allenville, J 17	Ill.
200	Allenville, G 16	Mich.
190	Allenville, O 22	Mo.
60	*Allenville, M 15	Wis.
150	*Allenwood, I 18	N. J.
400	Allenwood, I 16	Pa.
303	Allerton, H 21	Ill.
782	Allerton, P 13	Iowa
200	Allerton, F 21	Mass.
100	*Alley, O 16	Mo.
200	Alleyton, L 20	Tex.
250	Allgood (Chepultepec), E 14	Ala.
50	Alliance, C 1	Calif.
100	*Alliance, M 12	Fla.
72	Alliance, O 21	Mo.
6253	Alliance, G 4	Neb.
409	Alliance, N 9	N. J.
500	*Alliance (West Alliance), I 20	N. C.
22405	Alliance, F 19	Ohio
400	Alliance Jc., F 19	Ohio
206	Alligator, D 8	Miss.
220	*Alligerville, C 4	N. Y.
20	Allingham, N 18	Tenn.
5000	Allingtown, M 10	Conn.
66	*Allison, H 6	Ala.
22	*Allison, D 13	Ark.
75	Allison, R 6	Colo.
708	Allison, E 15	Iowa
500	Allison, F 1	N. M.
50	Allison, Q 17	Okla.
1200	Allison, P 4	Pa.
50	*Allison, C 6	Tex.
150	*Allisona, N 12	Tenn.
500	*Allisonia, P 3	Va.
750	*Allison Park, L 3	Pa.
50	*Allister, C 11	W. Va.
10	*Allnutt, I 18	Va.
25	*Allock, I 21	Ky.
196	*Allons, M 15	Tenn.
800	Allouez, C 3	Mich.
....	Allouez, C 4	Wis.
600	Alloway, N 6	N. J.
....	Alloway Jc., N 6	N. J.
500	*Alloy (Boncar), M 8	W. Va.
412	Allport, J 11	Pa.
20	*Allred, L 15	Tenn.
250	*Allred, D 8	Tex.
16	*Allreds, H 9	N. C.
100	*Allsboro, B 7	Ala.
96	*Allsbrook, G 23	S. C.
....	*Allston, F 19	Mass.
300	Alluvial, N 20	La.
50	Alluwe, C 20	Okla.
125	Allyn, I 6	Wash.
40	*Alma, M 6	Ala.
774	Alma, F 5	Ark.
310	*Alma, J 6	Calif.
469	Alma, H 11	Colo.
1840	Alma, M 17	Ga.
465	Alma, M 15	Ill.
776	Alma, G 19	Kan.
7202	Alma, N 17	Mich.
366	Alma, G 9	Mo.
35	Alma, C 11	Mont.
1272	Alma, O 14	Neb.
95	Alma, L 1	N. M.
100	*Alma, P 7	N. Y.
150	Alma, K 11	N. C.
275	Alma, N 12	Okla.
250	Alma, F 20	Tex.
152	*Alma (Centreville), D 10	W. Va.
1139	Alma, C 14	Wis.
431	Alma Center, F 14	Wis.
166	*Alma City, Q 14	Minn.
....	*Almaden, J 6	Calif.
200	Almaden, L 10	Pa.
1200	Almagro, R 9	Va.
....	Alma Junction, N 18	Neb.
50	*Almartha, Q 13	Mo.
300	*Almeda, L 22	Tex.
125	*Almelund, L 18	Minn.
543	Almena, D 9	Kan.
350	Almena, C 10	Wis.
21	Almeria, I 13	Neb.
13	*Almira, C 5	Va.
466	Almira, H 19	Wash.
310	Almo, R 14	Idaho
154	Almo, K 6	Ky.
30	Almond, E 15	Ark.
533	Almond, P 8	N. Y.
300	*Almond, O 4	N. C.
449	Almond, K 15	Wis.
250	Almonesson, L 9	N. J.
32	Almont, J 9	Colo.
924	Almont, O 23	Mich.
232	Almont, N 9	N. D.
100	*Almont, N 23	Pa.
20	Almonte, B 14	Calif.
150	*Almora, J 7	Minn.
70	Almota, L 23	Wash.
140	Almy, Q 2	Wyo.
....	Almy Junction, Q 1	Wyo.
233	Almyra, K 16	Ark.
50	Alna (Alna Center), N 10	Me.
9	Aloe, C 9	Mont.
75	Aloha, G 8	La.
50	*Aloha, H 17	Mich.
500	*Aloha, C 6	Ore.
200	Aloha, J 2	Wash.
11	Aloys, I 21	Neb.
500	Alpaugh, L 12	Calif.
12808	Alpena, I 21	Mich.
440	Alpena, J 19	S. D.
115	Alpena, H 16	W. Va.
....	Alpena Jc., I 21	Mich.
313	Alpena (Alpena Pass) B 9	Ark.
75	Alpers, O 12	Okla.
10	*Alpha, K 7	Idaho
553	Alpha, E 9	Ill.
119	*Alpha, E 19	Iowa
23	*Alpha, K 16	Ky.
497	Alpha, G 3	Mich.
229	Alpha, R 9	Minn.
2301	Alpha, F 8	N. J.
4	Alpha, N 2	N. D.
300	*Alpha, L 8	Ohio
5	*Alpha, J 5	Ore.
125	*Alpha, M 13	Va.
6	Alpha, M 7	Wash.
647	Alpharetta, E 7	Ga.
350	*Alphoretta (Dinwood), H 23	Ky.
250	*Alpine, G 16	Ala.
165	Alpine, J 24	Ariz.
101	*Alpine, L 8	Ark.
200	*Alpine, Q 19	Calif.
30	*Alpine, K 20	Ind.
352	Alpine, J 17	Ky.
75	*Alpine, O 14	Mich.
626	Alpine, D 21	N. J.
150	*Alpine, P 12	N. Y.
100	Alpine, I 5	Ore.
150	*Alpine, M 15	Tenn.
3866	Alpine, J 6	Tex.
444	Alpine, F 12	Utah
21	*Alpine, K 2	Wyo.
....	Alpine Jc., I 6	Ore.
200	Alplaus, M 23	N. Y.
300	*Alpoca, P 7	W. Va.
60	Alpowa, M 24	Wash.
25	*Alps, K 18	Va.
45	*Alridge, O 18	Idaho
36	*Alsatia, B 14	La.
100	Alsea, H 4	Ore.
101	*Alsen, P 22	N. Y.
312	Alsen, E 18	N. D.
35	Alsen, O 24	S. D.
290	Alsey, J 8	Ill.
541	*Alsip, C 21	Ill.
....	*Alsop, J 16	Va.
300	Alstead, O 7	N. H.
213	Alston, K 17	Ga.
350	Alston, D 2	Mich.
....	Alston, F 12	S. C.
35	Alstown, H 15	Wash.
113	Alsuma, F 19	Okla.
113	*Alta, F 9	Calif.
78	Alta, F 12	Ill.
1269	Alta, F 5	Iowa
30	*Alta, J 4	Mont.
4	Alta, K 12	N. D.
4	Alta, (Peak), M 21	N. D.
313	Alta, F 12	Utah
....	*Altadena, O 16 (Pop. incl. in Pasadena)	Calif.
20	*Al Tahoe, G 9	Calif.
300	Altair, L 20	Tex.
1500	Alta Loma, Q 7	Calif.
350	Alta Loma, L 23	Tex.
26	*Altamaha, K 19	Ga.
300	Altamahaw, D 10	N. C.
64	*Altamont, I 6	Calif.
2111	Altamont, L 16	Ill.
642	Altamont, O 23	Kan.
35	*Altamont, N 3	Md.
274	Altamont, D 7	Mo.
890	Altamont, N 22	N. Y.
60	*Altamont, D 2	N. C.
144	Altamont, G 24	S. D.
238	Altamont, P 14	Tenn.
....	*Altamont (Akwenasa), P 3	Wyo.
551	*Altamonte Springs, G 18	Fla.
150	*Altapass, M 9	N. C.
320	*Altaville, H 9	Calif.
333	Alta Vista, C 17	Iowa
461	Alta Vista, H 19	Kan.
2919	Altavista, O 9	Va.
25	Altay, P 11	N. Y.
289	Altenburg, M 23	Mo.
350	Altha, B 1, N 11	Fla.
494	Altheimer, L 14	Ark.
27	*Altizer, H 8	W. Va.
304	Altmar, J 15	N. Y.
217	*Alto, C 11	Ga.
250	Alto, C 12	La.
300	Alto, O 14	Mich.
105	Alto, L 15	N. M.
75	*Alto, Q 12	Tenn.
1141	Alto, G 23	Tex.
11	*Alto, M 10	Va.
216	Alton, F 14	Ala.
255	Alton, D 1	Calif.
....	Alton, C 10	Fla.
31255	Alton, L 10	Ill.
78	*Alton, Q 13	Ind.
1025	Alton, D 3	Iowa
435	Alton, E 11	Kan.
112	*Alton, (Alton Station) F 16	Ky.
25	Alton, K 15	Me.
576	Alton, Q 16	Mo.
700	Alton, M 16	N. H.
200	*Alton, L 11	N. Y.
122	Alton, K 11	Ohio
58	Alton, (Mt. Alton) F 9	Pa.
113	*Alton, L 10	R. I.
150	Alton, P 8	Utah
100	*Alton, Q 11	Va.
150	*Alton, H 13	W. Va.
480	Altona, E 11	Ill.
340	Altona, C 20	Ind.
300	*Altona, M 15	Mich.
50	Altona, H 20	Neb.
600	*Altona, D 23	N. Y.
10	Altona, G 9	Okla.
300	Altonah, F 19	Utah
150	Alton Bay, M 16	N. H.
....	*Alton Park, Q 15	Tenn.
995	Altoona, D 16	Ala.
99	Altoona, F 17	Fla.
640	Altoona, K 12	Iowa
707	Altoona, M 22	Kan.
80214	Altoona, M 10	Pa.
150	Altoona, N 3	Wash.
1239	Altoona, E 13	Wis.
459	Alto Pass, P 14	Ill.
100	*Altro, H 21	Ky.
258	*Altura, Q 22	Minn.
2090	*Alturas, C 10	Calif.
200	Alturas, I 16	Fla.
541	Altus, F 7	Ark.
8593	Altus, M 4	Okla.
242	Alum Bank, O 9	Pa.
27	*Alumbaugh, G 19	Ky.
150	*Alum Bridge, G 11	W. Va.
161	*Alum Creek, L 6	W. Va.
30	*Alum Ridge, P 5	Va.
....	Alunite, M 9	Utah
540	Alva, L 17	Fla.
2600	*Alva, J 21	Ky.
5055	Alva, B 7	Okla.
42	Alva, B 23	Wyo.
86	*Alvada (Alveda), E 10	Ohio
40	Alvadore, J 5	Ore.
1000	Alvarado, I 5, E 21	Calif.
336	Alvarado, D 1	Minn.
1324	Alvarado, E 18	Tex.
54	*Alvarado, E 8	Va.
109	*Alvaton, H 5	Ga.
92	*Alvaton, J 12	Ky.
500	*Alverda (Sides), L 8	Pa.
500	Alverton, (Stoner) O 5	Pa.
339	Alvin, H 22	Ill.
35	* Alvin, K 19	S. C.
3087	Alvin, L 23	Tex.
100	Alvin, M 7	Wis.
677	Alviso, G 22	Calif.
215	Alvo, L 23	Neb.
50	*Alvon, M 12	W. Va.
306	Alvord, B 2	Iowa
821	Alvord C 17	Tex.
....	*Alvord, see Spencer	W. Va.
327	Alvordton, C 6	Ohio
60	*Alvwood, F 14	Minn.
100	Alvy, D 11	W. Va.
114	Aly, I 8	Ark.
50	Alzada, N 25	Mont.
650	Ama, N 18	La.
....	Amabel, F 15	Okla.
50	Amado, O 17	Ariz.
249	*Amador City, H 9	Calif.
150	*Amagon, E 17	Ark.
953	Amagansett, G 12	N. Y.
4	Amalia, B 16	N. M.
400	Amana, J 19	Iowa
561	Amanda, L 13	Ohio
120	*Amantha, C 2	N. C.
63	*Amaranth, P 11	Pa.
4	Amargo (Ave Marie), B 10	N. M.
51686	Amarillo, D 3	Tex
1000	Amasa, F 3	Mich.
100	*Amawalk, F 6	N. Y.
321	Amazonia, D 5	Mo.
60	*Amba, H 23	Ky.
82	*Amber, I 21	Iowa.
158	*Amber, M 14	N. Y.
300	Amber, K 10	Okla.
40	Amber, I 22	Wash.
600	Amberg, O 9	Wis.
466	Amberson, O 13	Pa.
603	Ambia, G 5	Ind.
70	Amble, N 14	Mich.
3953	Ambler, O 23	Pa.
95	*Amboy, N 20	Calif.
40	*Amboy, M 11	Ga.
1986	Amboy, C 14	Ill.
450	Amboy, F 15	Ind.
576	Amboy, Q 12	Minn.
....	Amboy, see Lester, O 17	Neb.
500	Amboy, A 20	Ohio
200	Amboy, P 7	Wash.
98	*Amboy, D 16	W. Va.
18968	Ambridge, L 2	Pa.
300	*Ambrose, M 15	Ga.
294	Ambrose, C 3	N. D.
77	*Ambrosia (Brosia), H 4	W. Va.
30	*Amburg, L 20	Va.
....	*A and M College, Q 9	Ark.
300	Ameagle, N 7	W. Va.
410	Amelia, O 15	La.
56	Amelia, G 15	Neb.
550	Amelia, O 7	Ohio
887	Amelia (Amelia C. H.), N 14	Va.
86	*Amelia City, B 16	Fla.
887	Amelia C.H. (Amelia), N 14	Va.
1200	Amenia, R 24	N. Y.
104	*Amenia, L 23	N. D.
116	*America (America Jc.), E 10	Ala.
50	*America, R 15	Ill.
50	America, R 25	Okla.
1439	American Falls, P 17	Idaho
3333	American Fork, G 12	Utah
800	*American Lake, K 7	Wash.
....	American Point, see Panasse	Minn.
9281	Americus, L 8	Ga.
406	Americus, I 20	Kan.
114	*Americus, H 16	Mo.
1461	Amery, B 10	Wis.
12555	Ames, I 12	Iowa
110	*Ames, E 15	Kan.
500	Ames, J 22	Neb.
180	*Ames, N 21	N. Y.
332	Ames, E 9	Okla.
64	*Ames, H 17	Tex.
10862	■Amesbury, A 20	Mass.
....	Ames Street Jc., L 9	N. Y.
286	Amesville, N 16	Ohio
102	Amherst, C 23	Colo.
150	*Amherst, K 16	Me.
6410	■Amherst, F 8	Mass.
238	Amherst, L 14	Neb.
361	Amherst, Q 13	N. H.
2876	Amherst, D 14	Ohio
150	Amherst, C 20	S. D.
749	Amherst, B 9	Tex.
930	Amherst, M 10	Va.
611	Amherst, K 14	Wis.
1900	Amherstdale, O 5	W. Va.
197	Amherst Junction, K 14	Wis.
102	Amidon, O 3	N. D.
250	Amigo, P 7	W. Va.
27	*Amiot, J 23	Kan.
85	*Amiret, P 6	Minn.
121	*Amissville, G 14	Va.
46	Amistad, E 25	N. M.
2499	Amite, K 17	La.
608	Amity, L 8	Ark.
65	*Amity, F 17	Ga.
172	Amity, D 6	Mo.
76	*Amity, E 3	N. Y.
545	Amity, E 6	Ore.
175	Amity, P 2	Pa.
5058	Amityville, H 7	N. Y.
....	Amityville, N 21	Pa.
100	*Amlin, K 11	Ohio
75	*Amma, I 7	W. Va.
217	Ammannsville, L 19	Tex.
50	*Ammie, I 20	Ky.
363	Ammon, O 20	Idaho
26	*Ammon, N 14	Va.
35	*Ammons, G 12	Ky.
288	Amo, J 11	Ind.
500	*Amonate, B 9	Va.
328	Amoret, K 6	Mo.
208	Amorita, A 9	Okla.
3727	Amory, D 21	Miss.
....	Amory Jc., D 21	Miss.
40	Amos, B 12	Ark.
....	*Ampere, E 18	N. J.
....	Amru, K 20	Ky.
162	Amsbry, M 9	Pa.
108	*Amsden, E 11	Ohio
400	*Amsterdam, O 5	Ga.
100	Amsterdam, Q 11	Idaho
172	*Amsterdam, J 6	Mo.
33329	Amsterdam, M 22	N. Y.
1177	Amsterdam, H 19	Ohio
200	*Amsterdam, N 7	Va.
100	Amston, H 18	Conn.
25	*Amy, O 10	Ark.
32	*Amy, I 6	Kan.
....	*Amy, see Auburn Hts.	Mich.
125	*Amy, B 3	N. C.
34	*Anabel, D 12	Mo.
305	Anacoco, I 6	La.
110	*Anaconda (Morrellton, J 17	Mo.
11004	Anaconda, K 6	Mont.
5875	Anacortes, D 7	Wash.
....	*Anacostia, I 11	D. C.
....	Anad, H 18	Mont.
5579	Anadarko, K 9	Okla.
11031	Anaheim, R 5	Calif.
513	Anahuac, L 24	Tex.
200	Analomink, I 23	Pa.
478	Anamoose, I 13	N. D.
4069	Anamosa, I 21	Iowa
3	Anan, N 17	Neb.
....	Anandale, I 9	La.
111	Anandale, see Anan	Neb.
37	*Anarene, C 15	Tex.
212	*Anastasia, D 18	Fla.
150	Anatone, O 25	Wash.
75	*Anatol, F 19	Minn.
450	*Anawalt (Jeanette), R 7	W. Va.
306	*Ancell, P 23	Mo.
16	Anceney, M 10	Mont.
150	Ancho, J 14	N. M.
185	Anchor, G 17	Ill.
321	Anchor, K 19	Ky.
....	*Anchor, I 20	Mo.
35	*Anchor, M 6	Ore.
10	*Anchor, F 9	Wyo.
690	Anchorage, E 14	Ky.
450	Anchorville, P 25	Mich.
300	Anco, I 21	Ky.
125	Ancona, E 16	Ill.
225	Ancram, R 24	N. Y.
....	*Ancram Lead Mines, see Ancramdale	N. Y.
200	Ancramdale, R 24	N. Y.
289	Andale, L 15	Kan.
6886	Andalusia, N 15	Ala.
365	Andalusia, D 7	Ill.
1200	Andalusia, O 24	Pa.
243	Anderson, A 10	Ala.
600	*Anderson, D 6	Calif.
41572	Anderson, I 17	Ind.
130	*Anderson, P 4	Iowa
25	Anderson, P 19	Mich.
938	Anderson, Q 6	Mo.
35	Anderson, L 18	Okla.
512	Anderson (Venita), N 3	Pa.
19424	Anderson, D 5	S. C.
310	Anderson, Q 13	Tenn.
500	Anderson, J 21	Tex.
....	Anderson Brick Yard, D 5	Calif.
96	*Andersonburg, N 14	Pa.
300	*Anderson Road (Wireton), L 3	Pa.
211	*Andersonville, L 8	Ga.
200	Andersonville, K 20	Ind.
275	*Andersonville, M 19	Tenn.
52	*Andersonville, M 12	Va.
20	Andes, E 24	Mont.
409	Andes, Q 20	N. Y.
....	Andes Jc., Q 20	N. Y.
82	*Andice, I 18	Tex.
300	*Anding, I 10	Miss.
280	Andover, F 18	Conn.
248	Andover, D 9	Ill.
72	*Andover, J 24	Iowa
100	*Andover, L 18	Kan.
757	▲Andover, L 3	Me.
11122	■Andover, C 19	Mass.
400	Andover, M 11	N. H.
512	Andover, C 12	N. J.
1290	Andover, Q 8	N. Y.
945	Andover, C 21	Ohio
....	*Andover, P 11	Pa.
350	Andover, E 20	S. D.
234	Andover, N 11	Vt.
535	Andover, D 5	Va.
....	Andover Jc., C 12	N. J.
65	Andrade (Cantu), Q 25	Calif.
50	*Andre (Lyral), P 12	Ohio
100	*Andreas, K 19	Pa.
263	Andrew, I 24	Iowa
110	*Andrew, N 11	La.
954	Andrews, E 18	Ind.
215	Andrews, N 18	Md.
50	Andrews, E 2	Neb.
1520	Andrews, Q 3	N. C.
60	Andrews, P 20	Ore.
2008	Andrews, J 20	S. C.
611	Andrews, F 8	Tex.
....	Andrico, M 6	Pa.
25	Andrix, P 20	Colo.
....	Andromeda, M 7	Ind.
35	*Andyville, F 12	Ky.
509	Aneta, I 21	N. D.
21	Angela, I 21	Mont.
928	Angelica, P 7	N. Y.
20	Angeline, O 16	Mo.
478	Angel Island, C 16	Calif.
285	*Angels, H 22	Pa.
1163	Angels Camp (Angels), H 9	Calif.
40	*Angelus, D 16	S. C.
187	Angie, J 19	La.
1028	Angier, G 14	N. C.
....	*Angle, N 10	Utah
1763	Angleton, M 22	Tex.
3141	Angola, B 21	Ind.
50	*Angola, N 23	Kan.
18	Angola, J 13	La.
1663	Angola, O 4	N. Y.
75	*Angora, F 19	Minn.
49	Angora, H 3	Neb.
493	Anguilla, H 7	Miss.
150	Angus, J 10	Iowa
80	*Angus, F 4	Minn.
65	*Angus, N 18	Neb.
100	*Angus, F 20	Tex.
62	*Angus, D 10	Wis.
300	*Angwin, G 5	Calif.
50	Animas, O 1	N. M.
712	Animas City, P 5	Colo.
1088	Anita, L 7	Iowa
375	Anita, J 7	Pa.
283	Aniwa, K 12	Wis.
100	Anjean, M 11	W. Va.
779	Ankeny, K 12	Iowa
64	*Ankona, J 22	Fla.
32	*Ankum, Q 15	Va.
15	Anlauf, K 6	Ore.
1200	Anmoore, E 13	W. Va.
4092	Anna, Q 14	Ill.
75	*Anna (Pawnee Sta.), L 24	Kan.
25	*Anna, J 12	Ky.
485	Anna, I 7	Ohio
509	Anna, C 19	Tex.
321	Annabella, L 10	Utah
110	*Annada, G 18	Mo.
....	*Annadale, I 4	N. Y.
158	*Anna Maria, J 12	Fla.
75	*Annamoriah, H 8	W. Va.
755	Annandale, M 12	Minn.
550	Annandale, F 11	N. J.
140	*Annandale on Hudson, R 23	N. Y.
219	*Annandale (Boyers), K 3	Pa.
75	*Annapolis, G 3	Calif.
206	Annapolis, K 21	Ill.
120	Annapolis, J 7	Ind.
13069	Annapolis, I 15	Md.
390	*Annapolis, N 18	Mo.
260	*Annapolis (Sulphur Springs) G 12	Ohio
500	Annapolis, H 7	Wash.
106	*Annapolis Junction (Ft. George G. Meade Jct.), G 13	Md.
29815	Ann Arbor, Q 20	Mich.
5	*Annarose, O 17	Tex.
578	Annawan, D 11	Ill.
50	*Annemanie (Arlington), L 10	Ala.
48	*Anness, M 16	Kan.
34	*Anneta, H 12	Ky.
63	Annis, N 20	Idaho
300	*Annisquam, C 22	Mass.
25523	Anniston, F 19	Ala.
379	Anniston, Q 24	Mo.
446	Annona, C 23	Tex.
....	Annpere, P 20	Mich.
3200	*Annville, N 18	Pa.
27	*Ano, I 17	Ky.
36	Anoka, F 13	Ind.
6426	Anoka, M 15	Minn.
117	Anoka, D 16	Neb.
100	Anona, I 11	Fla.
70	*Ansel, I 17	Ky.
41	Anselm, O 22	N. D.
47	*Anselma, P 21	Pa.
388	Anselmo, I 13	Neb.
71	*Ansley, M 18	Ala.
619	Ansley, C 9	La.
75	*Ansley, R 17	Miss.
253	Ansley, K 14	Neb.
75	*Anson, O 16	Kan.
600	Anson (Riverview), K 8	Me.
2338	Anson, E 13	Tex.
60	Anson, F 12	Wis.
19210	Ansonia, M 9	Conn.
712	Ansonia, I 5	Ohio
150	Ansonia, F 14	Pa.
519	Ansonville, I 8	N. C.
200	*Ansonville, J 9	Pa.
1422	Ansted, L 8	W. Va.
....	*Antassawamock Neck, M 22	Mass.
200	*Ante, Q 15	Va.
20	*Antelope, H 8	Calif.
42	*Antelope, J 17	Kan.
142	Antelope, C 24	Mont.
31	Antelope, M 7	N. D.
90	Antelope, F 13	Ore.
166	*Antelope, D 16	Tex.
600	Antes Fort, I 15	Pa.
881	Anthon, G 3	Iowa
4	Anthon, H 5	Okla.
369	Anthony, E 15	Fla.
2873	Anthony, O 14	Kan.
1200	Anthony, O 11	N. M.
2810	Anthony, G 11	R. I.
142	*Anthony, M 12	W. Va.
....	Anthracite, I 8	Colo.
250	*Anthras, L 18	Tenn.
9495	Antigo, L 11	Wis.
245	Antimony, N 11	Utah
5106	Antioch, B 24, H 7	Calif.
1098	Antioch, A 19	Ill.
25	*Antioch, A 8	La.
147	Antioch, H 5	Neb.
145	*Antioch, L 19	Ohio
55	Antioch, M 12	Okla.
300	*Antioch, M 11	Tenn.
50	*Antioch, D 19	W. Va.
310	Antiquity, P 16	Ohio
254	Antler, D 10	N. D.
100	Antlers, G 6	Colo.
3254	Antlers, P 20	Okla.
233	Antoine, M 8	Ark.
12	*Anton, E 21	Colo.
548	*Anton, C 9	Tex.
548	Anton Chico, G 17	N. M.
11	Antone, H 16	Ore.
260	*Antonino, G 10	Kan.
....	Antonio, N 9	Calif.
1220	Antonito, Q 11	Colo.
1540	*Antram (Palmer Mine), Q 4	Pa.
950	Antrim, P 10	N. H.
125	*Antrim, J 17	Ohio
412	Antrim, F 14	Pa.
817	Antwerp, G 17	N. Y.
1086	Antwerp, E 5	Ohio
150	*Anutt, M 16	Mo.
500	*Anvil Location, B 21	Mich.
15	*Anza, O 20	Calif.
45	Apache, O 25	Ariz.
1047	Apache, L 8	Okla.
160	*Apache Creek, J 4	N. M.
20	Apache Jc., K 15	Ariz.
255	Apalachee, F 12	Ga.
3268	Apalachicola, D 2	Fla.
300	Apalachin, R 14	N. Y.
160	*Apalona, Q 11	Ind.
28	*Apex, G 18	Mo.
....	Apex, M 7	Mont.
30	*Apex, Q 19	N. Y.
977	Apex, F 13	N. C.
20	*Apison, P 15	Tenn.
100	▲*Alpin, H 10	Ark.
588	Aplington, F 15	Iowa
3232	Apollo, M 5	Pa.
1312	Apopka, G 17	Fla.
3595	Appalachia, D 4	Va.
113	Appam, E 3	N. D.
....	*Appeal, L 14	Md.
109	Apperson, B 15	Okla.
....	Apple, O 7	Va.
10	Appleby, G 23	S. D.
495	Appleby, G 24	Tex.
510	Apple Creek, G 16	Ohio
14	*Apple Farm, H 8	W. Va.
250	Applegate (West Applegate), G 9	Calif.
231	Applegate, N 25	Mich.
30	Applegate, Q 6	Ore.
30	*Apple Grove, B 3	N. C.
100	*Apple Grove, K 14	Va.
240	*Apple Grove, H 4	W. Va.
461	Apple River, A 10	Ill.
500	Apple Springs, H 23	Tex.
200	Appleton, F 10	Ark.
59	*Appleton, E 9	Ill.
250	Appleton, N 12	Me.
1877	Appleton, M 5	Minn.
....	*Appleton, see Old Appleton,	Mo.
211	Appleton, K 5	N. Y.
198	Appleton, M 11	S. C.
67	*Appleton, P 9	Tenn.
103	Appleton, P 11	Wash.
28436	Appleton, N 15	Wis.
1188	Appleton City, K 7	Mo.
....	Appleton Jc., N 15	Wis.
....	Apple Valley, N 3	Idaho
450	Appling, G 18	Ga.
704	Appomattox, N 11	Va.
2200	Apponaug, G 14	R. I.
550	Aptos, J 7	Calif.
154	*Apulia, M 14	N. Y.
170	*Apulia Station, M 14	N. Y.
53	*Aqua (Decatur), L 9	Va.
300	Aquasco, L 13	Md.
329	*Aquashicola, J 21	Pa.
390	*Aquebogue, H 9	N. Y.
29	Aquilla, M 3	Ala.
300	Aquilla, G 18	Tex.
63	*Aquone, Q 4	N. C.
640	Arab, C 15	Ala.
19	*Arab, O 20	Mo.
197	▲Arabela, K 17	N. M.
388	Arabi, L 10	Ga.
262	Arabi, N 19	La.
65	*Arabia (South Fork), H 17	Ky.
8	Arabia, E 11	Neb.
8	*Arago, H 9	Minn.
150	Arago, N 2	Ore.
1800	Aragon, E 3	Ga.
150	Aragon, J 3	N. M.
....	Aragon Junction, G 5	Mich.
15	*Arah, E 11	Tex.
....	Aram, Q 14	Pa.
4095	Aransas Pass, P 19	Tex.
401	Arapaho, H 6	Okla.
120	Arapahoe, J 24	Colo.
1002	Arapahoe, N 12	Neb.
307	Arapahoe, I 20	N. C.
150	Arapahoe, J 10	Wyo.
200	Ararat, L 5	Ala.
100	*Ararat, C 7	N. C.
510	Ararat, E 22	Pa.
7	Aravaipa, L 20	Ariz.
....	Araz, Q 24	Calif.
12	*Arbaugh, D 8	Ark.
90	*Arbela, B 14	Mo.
48	Arboles, Q 7	Colo.
55	Arbon, Q 18	Idaho
4	Arbor, L 22	Neb.
75	Arborville, L 19	Neb.
55	*Arbor Vitae, J 8	Wis.
75	*Arbovale, L 14	W. Va.
331	Arbroth, K 14	La.
1000	Arbuckle, G 5	Calif.
12	*Arbuckle (Big Canyon), N 13	Okla.
200	*Arbuckle, H 4	W. Va.
489	Arbyrd, K 23	Mo.
....	*Arcade, I 11	D. C.
1683	Arcade, O 6	N. Y.
....	*Arcade, M 11	Tenn.
9122	Arcadia, Q 5	Calif.
4055	Arcadia, K 16	Fla.
968	Arcadia, H 15	Ind.
410	Arcadia, I 6	Iowa
843	Arcadia, M 25	Kan.
1601	Arcadia, C 8	La.
90	*Arcadia (Upperco), D 13	Md.
525	Arcadia, K 11	Mich.
346	Arcadia, N 19	Mo.
663	Arcadia, J 14	Neb.
481	Arcadia, F 10	Ohio
312	Arcadia, H 13	Okla.
500	Arcadia, K 8	Pa.
175	Arcadia, J 7	R. I.
1900	Arcadia, B 8	S. C.
50	Arcadia, K 23	Tenn.
158	Arcadia, L 23	Tex.
200	*Arcadia, G 19	Utah
100	*Arcadia, M 7	Va.
1830	Arcadia, E 15	Wis.
1188	Arcanum, K 6	Ohio
31	*Arcanum, M 12	Va.
1855	Arcata, C 1	Calif.
200	*Arch, I 23	N. M.
75	Arch, M 20	Okla.
8296	Archbald, G 22	Pa.
1236	Archbold, D 7	Ohio
10	*Arch Cape, B 5	Ore.
1097	*Archdale, F 9	N. C.
517	Archer, E 13	Fla.
400	Archer, N 21	Idaho
178	*Archer, D 4	Iowa
22	Archer, C 24	Mont.
113	Archer, K 18	Neb.
1675	Archer City, C 16	Tex.
40	*Archers Fork, M 17	Ohio
....	*Archey, E 12	Ark.
61	*Archibald, C 13	La.
50	*Archie, F 12	La.
293	Archie, J 6	Mo.
52	*Archville, Q 17	Tenn.
50	Arco, O 22	Ga.
548	Arco, N 16	Idaho
243	Arco, P 4	Minn.
57	*Arco, G 13	Va.
1837	Arcola, J 18	Ill.
260	Arcola, D 19	Ind.
113	*Arcola, J 17	La.
444	Arcola, G 7	Miss.
102	*Arcola, N 8	Mo.
62	*Arcola, C 16	N. C.
6	*Arcola, N 22	Pa.
....	Arcola, L 22	Tex.
43	*Arcola, F 16	Va.
210	*Arcola, K 12	W. Va.
50	*Arcola, Q 23	Wyo.
410	*Ardara, M 5	Pa.
80	*Ardel (Herbert), L 2	W. Va.
150	Arden, O 4	Ark.
40	*Arden, O 21	Nev.
100	*Arden, E 3	N. Y.
103	*Arden, O 7	N. C.
35	Arden, O 2	Pa.
1187	*Arden, G 13	S. C.
12	*Arden, H 11	Tex.
25	Arden, D 22	Wash.
200	*Arden, F 14	W. Va.
76	Ardena, I 19	N. J.
....	*Ardenvoir, G 14	Wash.
156	*Ardeola, P 22	Mo.
35	Ardilla, O 23	Ala.
250	Ardmore, I 12	Md.
20	Ardmore, E 12	Mo.
16886	Ardmore, P 14	Okla.
....	Ardmore, P 23 (Pop. 22000 incl. in Merion Sta.)	Pa.

Pop	Place Index	State
195	Ardmore, O 2	S. D.
700	Ardmore, Q 10	Tenn.
119	Ardoch, G 23	N. D.
25	*Ardon, L 22	Iowa
75	*Ardonia, C 4	N. Y.
....	Ardrossan, N 5	W. Va.
1423	*Ardsley, F 6	N. Y.
....	*Ardsley, O 23 (Pop. 1420 incl. in Abington)	Pa.
500	*Ardsley on Hudson, F-5	N.Y.
225	Aredale, E 14	Iowa
15	Arena, J 23	Colo.
216	Arena, Q 20	N. Y.
35	Arena, L 13	N. D.
278	Arena, I 20	Wis.
381	Arendtsville, P 14	Pa.
494	Arenzville, I 9	Ill.
....	*Arey, N 10	N. Y.
561	Argenta, I 16	Ill.
....	*Argentine, F 25	Kan.
250	Argentine, J 4	Pa.
100	*Argillite, D 22	Ky.
93	*Argo, F 12	Ala.
25	Argo, I 23	Del.
9000	*Argo, C 21	Ill.
45	*Argo (Middle Elk), H 24	Ky.
....	Argo, F 21	Minn.
60	Argo, C 23	Tex.
532	Argonia, N 14	Kan.
55	Argonne, J 21	S. D.
57	Argonne, N 3	W. Va.
256	Argonne, M 9	Wis.
10	*Argora, M 19	Idaho
1190	Argos, D 13	Ind.
100	*Argura, Q 6	N. C.
100	*Argus, N 23	Pa.
130	*Argusville, O 21	N. Y.
145	Argusville, L 24	N. D.
....	*Argyle, I 11	D. C.
135	Argyle, M 8	Fla.
278	Argyle, O 16	Ga.
96	Argyle, Q 20	Iowa
37	*Argyle, I 16	Ky.
100	*Argyle (Westbend P. O.), G 19	Ky.
90	Argyle, M 23	Mich.
857	Argyle, D 2	Minn.
209	Argyle, K 14	Mo.
226	Argyle, L 24	N. Y.
268	Argyle, D 18	Tex.
30	Argyle, D 6	Wash.
735	Argyle, I 22	Wis.
....	*Ariail, B 5	S. C.
30	Arickaree, F 21	Colo.
....	*Ariel, see Lake Ariel	Pa.
300	Ariel, O 7	Wash.
291	*Arimo, Q 19	Idaho
271	Arion, J 5	Iowa
48	*Aripeka, H 13	Fla.
60	*Aripine, H 19	Ariz.
149	*Arispe, O 10	Iowa
520	Arista, Q 8	W. Va.
500	*Aristes, J 18	Pa.
561	Ariton, M 20	Ala.
50	Arivaca, P 16	Ariz.
112	*Arizona, B 8	La.
15	Arizona, I 23	Neb.
34	*Arjay, K 20	Ky.
75	*Ark, M 20	Va.
200	*Arkabutla, B 12	Miss.
298	Arkadelphia, E 12	Ala.
5078	Arkadelphia, M 9	Ark.
30	*Arkana, B 12	Ark.
50	Arkansas Central Jc., F 4	Ark.
1446	Arkansas City, O 17	Ark.
12752	Arkansas City, O 17	Kan.
64	*Arkansas Post, L 16	Ark.
300	Arkansaw, C 13	Wis.
56	*Arkdale, J 16	Wis.
98	*Arkinda, N 4	Ark.
73	*Arkoe, A 5	Mo.
58	*Arkoma, L 24	Okla.
618	Arkport, P 9	N. Y.
500	Arkville, Q 20	N. Y.
36	Arkwright, G 15	Ala.
1500	*Arkwright (Fiskeville), G 12	R. I.
26	*Arlberg, D 12	Ark.
450	Arlee, H 4	Mont.
18	*Arlee, H 4	W. Va.
....	*Arleta, D 8	Ore.
63	Arletta, K 8	Wash.
53	*Arley, D 9	Ala.
18	Arling, L 6	Idaho
50	*Arlington (Annemanie) L 10	Ala.
150	*Arlington, L 10	Ala.
300	*Arlington, L 9	Ariz.
....	Arlington, R 8	Calif.
50	Arlington, L 20	Colo.
500	*Arlington, B 17	Fla.
1337	Arlington, N 4	Ga.
258	Arlington, D 14	Ill.
421	Arlington, J 18	Ind.
675	Arlington, F 19	Iowa
440	Arlington, L 14	Kan.
690	Arlington, K 4	Ky.
....	Arlington, E 13	Md.
40013	■Arlington, E 19	Mass.
1122	Arlington, O 12	Minn.
34	*Arlington, L 15	Mo.
569	Arlington, J 22	Neb.
....	*Arlington, E 20 (Pop. incl. in Kearny)	N. J.
2000	*Arlington, D 5	N. Y.
752	Arlington, G 9	Ohio
609	Arlington, C 15	Ore.
2500	Arlington, E 15	R. I.
1157	Arlington, I 23	S. D.
440	Arlington, P 2	Tenn.
4240	Arlington, E 19	Tex.
550	Arlington, P 7	Vt.
57040	■Arlington, G 18	Va.
1460	Arlington, F 9	Wash.
60	*Arlington, H 12	W. Va.
161	Arlington, K 19	Wis.
16	*Arlington, O 16	Wyo.
5668	Arlington Heights, B 20	Ill.
....	Arlington Heights, L 1	Mass.
1222	*Arlington Heights, N 5	Ohio
5	Arlington Jct., F 9	Wash.
65	*Arm, N 11	Miss.
1615	Arma, M 25	Kan.
16	Armada, E 5	Ark.
865	Armada, O 24	Mich.
163	*Armagh, L 6	Pa.
30	*Armathwaite, M 16	Tenn.
250	*Armbrust (Weavers Old Stand), M 5	Pa.
12	Armel, F 24	Colo.
....	Armells, G 14	Mont.
40	*Armet (Eula), I 6	Ore.
100	*Armijo, G 10	N. M.
299	Armington, H 14	Ill.
150	Armington, G 11	Mont.
....	*Armin, D 23	Ore.
100	Arminto, I 14	Wyo.
91	*Armistead, E 6	La.
250	Armona, K 12	Calif.
400	*Armonk, F 6	N. Y.
250	Armorel, D 23	Ark.
....	*Armory Place, E 14	Ky.
....	Armour, E 4	Mo.
28	Armour, O 23	Neb.
28	*Armour, M 14	N. C.
1013	Armour, N 19	S. D.
25	Armourdale, D 16	N. D.
50	Armstead, O 7	Mont.
50	*Armstrong (Lobman), K 17	Ala.
302	Armstrong, H 20	Ill.
33	*Armstrong, Q 4	Ind.
937	Armstrong, B 9	Iowa
30	*Armstrong, R 16	Minn
468	Armstrong, F 12	Mo.
55	Armstrong, P 17	Okla.
28	*Armstrong, R 18	Tex.
60	*Armstrong, J 8	Va.
150	Armstrong, Creek, M 9	Wis.
140	*Armstrong Mills, K 19	Ohio
25	*Armstrong Springs, G 14	Ark.
800	*Armuchee, D 2	Ga.
100	Army Point, A 20	Calif.
640	Arnaudville, L 12	La.
5	Arndt, D 16	N. D.
240	*Arneckeville, M 18	Tex.
222	Arnegard, I 3	N. D.
5	*Arnett, D 5	Ark.
....	*Arnett, H 20	Ky.
529	Arnett, E 2	Okla.
400	*Arnett, O 7	W. Va.
106	*Arnheim, E 4	Mich.
14	*Arno, C 5	Va.
9	*Arno (Wyarno), B 14	Wyo.
1000	*Arnold, H 9	Calif.
20	Arnold, E 10	Iowa
115	*Arnold, I 8	Kan.
14	*Arnold, H 10	Ky.
82	*Arnold, H 15	Md.
45	*Arnold (Watson), F 6	Mich.
200	Arnold, H 21	Minn.
50	Arnold, J 20	Mo.
884	Arnold, J 12	Neb.
10898	Arnold, L 4	Pa.
295	Arnold Mills, B 17	R. I.
125	*Arnoldsburg, H 8	W.Va.
855	Arnolds Park, B 6	Iowa
119	*Arnoldsville, F 14	Ga.
648	Arnot, F 15	Pa.
75	Arnott, K 14	Wis.
150	*Arock, L 22	Ore.
150	*Aroda, I 13	Va.
497	Aroma Park, E 21	Ill.
316	Arcmas, J 7	Calif.
503	*Arona, M 5	Pa.
1900	*Aronimink, P 23	Pa.
1150	*Aronimink Heights, P 23	Pa.
35	Aroya, J 21	Colo.
1139	*Arp, F 22	Tex.
13	Arpan, G 2	S. D.
60	Arpelar, L 18	Okla.
350	*Arpin, I 14	Wis.
100	*Arran, C 4	Fla.
298	Arrey, M 8	N. M.
286	Arriba, H 20	Colo.
100	Arrington, E 22	Kan.
50	*Arrington, N 10	Tenn.
120	*Arrington, L 11	Va.
25	Arriola, O 3	Colo.
65	*Arroll, O 14	Mo.
25	Arrow, O 8	Pa.
....	Arrowbear Lake, P 10.	Calif.
160	*Arrowhead Springs, P 10	Calif.
247	Arrow Rock, G 11	Mo.
123	*Arrowsic, O 9	Me.
294	Arrowsmith, G 17	Ill.
....	Arroyo, H 8	Pa.
150	Arroyo, M 24	W. Va.
1090	Arroyo Grande, M 10	Calif.
500	Arroyo Hondo, C 14	N. M.
....	Arroyo Park, Q 4	Calif.
620	Arroyoseco, C 15	N. M.
....	*Arsenal, I 19	Mo.
....	*Arsenal, M 3	Pa.
150	*Art, I 15	Tex.
209	Artas, C 14	S. D.
15	*Artemas, Q 10	Pa.
200	Artemus, J 19	Ky.
106	▲Artesia, M 22	Ariz.
3891	*Artesia, O 16, R 4	Calif.
50	*Artesia, H 21	Fla.
521	Artesia, F 21	Miss.
4071	Artesia, M 20	N. M.
502	Artesian, K 20	S. D.
150	Artesia Wells (Bart), O 14	Tex.
10	Artex, P 6	Ark.
....	Arthur, F 19	Ark.
1405	Arthur, J 18	Ill.
254	Arthur, H 5	Iowa
142	Arthur, J 8	Neb.
12	Arthur, C 18	Nev.
181	*Arthur (Bellarthur P.O.), G 18	N. C.
335	Arthur, L 23	N. D.
35	Arthur, N 11	Okla.
150	*Arthur, L 20	Tenn.
17	*Arthur, F 18	W. Va.
163	*Arthur City, C 21	Tex.
....	*Arthurdale, D 16	W. Va.
50	*Arthurmabel, G 21	Ky.
20	*Arthyde, I 15	Minn.
15	*Artia, B 7	Va.
21	*Artie, O 8	W. Va.
120	Artois, F 6	Calif.
63	*Artrip, D 7	Va.
40	*Artville, F 20	Ky.
1482	Arvada, F 14	Colo.
100	Arvada, B 18	Wyo.
50	*Arvel, H 19	Ky.
....	*Arverne, H 6	N. Y.
100	Arvilla, H 22	N. D.
35	*Arvilla, E 8	W. Va.
707	Arvin, M 14	Calif.
75	*Arvonia, M 12	Va.
34	*Ary, I 21	Ky.
15	*Asa, G 22	Ky.
150	*Asaph, E 14	Pa.
....	*Asberry, see Asbury	Ala.
10	*Asberrys, C 9	Va.
....	*Asbestos, see Cedarhurst	Md.
60	*Asbury (Asberry), J 17	Ala.
40	Asbury, H 18	Ky.
252	Asbury, O 6	Mo.
580	Asbury, E 10	N. J.
56	*Asbury, M 12	W. Va.
16	*Asbury Grove, C 21	Mass.
14617	Asbury Park, I 21	N. J.
300	*Asco, Q 5	W. Va.
125	Ascutney, M 14	Vt.
125	*Ash, M 16	N. C.
1000	Ashaway, M 5	R. I.
100	Ashboro, L 7	Ind.
676	*Ashbcurne, N 22	Pa.
2266	Ashburn, M 10	Ga.
159	*Ashburn, F 17	Mo.
190	Ashburn, F 16	Va.
800	Ashburnham, C 13	Mass.
90	*Ashby, H 11	Ala.
250	Ashby, B 13	Mass.
384	Ashby, J 6	Minn.
150	Ashby, H 7	Neb.
32	*Ashby, (Bayard) G 15	Va.
162	*Ashbyburg, I 8	Ky.
100	*Ashcamp, H 24	Ky.
....	Ashdale, B 11	Ill.
2332	Ashdown, O 4	Ark.
6981	Asheboro, F 9	N. C.
33	*Ashepoo, N 15	S. C.
50	*Asher, D 6	Ark.
25	*Asher, I 21	Ky.
507	Asher, K 14	Okla.
....	*Ashers Fork, I 20	Ky.
219	Asherton, K 16	Pa.
1538	Asherton, O 13	Tex.
42	Asherville, K 8	Ind.
200	*Asherville, F 13	Kan.
51310	Asheville, O 8	N. C.
100	*Asheville School, O 7	N. C.
278	Ashfield, D 6	Mass.
131	*Ashfield, J 21	Pa.
315	Ash Flat, B 15	Ark.
1224	Ashford, O 22	Ala.
20	Ashford, C 21	Conn.
100	Ashford, P 5	N. Y.
110	*Ashford, F 1	N. C.
165	Ashford, L 9	Wash.
108	*Ashford M 5	W. Va.
600	Ashfork, G 11	Ariz.
90	*Ash Grove, G 13	Kan.
1101	Ash Grove, O 9	Mo.
200	Ashippun, M 19	Wis.
337	Ashkum, F 20	Ill.
1608	Ashland, G 19	Ala.
21	*Ashland, D 13	Ga.
1139	Ashland, I 10	Ill.
1186	Ashland, O 8	Kan.
29537	Ashland, D 23	Ky.
210	Ashland, E 7	La.
2100	Ashland, D 16	Me.
110	Ashland, G 16	Mass.
354	Ashland, A 17	Miss.
434	Ashland H 13	Mo.
82	Ashland, L 21	Mont.
1709	Ashland, K 23	Neb.
1200	Ashland, K 13	N. H.
800	Ashland, L 9	N. J.
175	*Ashland, P 22	N. Y
234	*Ashland, B 3	N. C.
12453	Ashland, G 14	Ohio
142	Ashland, M 18	Okla.
4744	Ashland, Q 7	Ore.
7045	Ashland, K 19	Pa.
165	Ashland, E 23	Tex.
1297	Ashland, L 16	Va.
263	*Ashland, Q 5	W. Va.
11101	Ashland G 5	Wis.
957	Ashland City, M 10	Tenn.
720	Ashley, N 14	Ill.
675	Ashley, B 21	Ind.
466	Ashley, N 18	Mich.
187	Ashley, G 17	Mo.
1345	Ashley, Q 16	N. D.
762	Ashley, I 12	Ohio
30	Ashley, B 8	Okla.
6371	Ashley, I 20	Pa.
38	*Ashley, E 10	W. Va.
500	*Ashley Falls, I 2	Mass.
34	*Ashley Heights, I 11	N. C.
300	Ashley Jc., M 18	S. C.
454	Ashmore, J 20	Ill.
....	*Ashmore, E 8	Tex.
320	Ashokan, R 22	N. Y.
140	*Ash Point, O 13	Me.
210	Ashpcrt, M 2	Tenn.
21405	Ashtabula, B 20	Ohic
50	Ashtola, O 8	Pa.
27	*Ashtola, D 5	Tex.
1203	Ashton, M 21	Idaho
914	Ashton, C 14	Ill.
620	Ashton, C 4	Iowa
66	*Ashton, O 16	Kan.
....	*Ashton, N 13	La.
110	*Ashton, G 9	Md.
115	*Ashton, L 15	Mich.
60	Ashton, B 15	Mo.
488	Ashton, K 16	Neb.
52	*Ashton, K 16	N. C.
1000	Ashton, B 15	R. I.
59	*Ashton, M 13	S. C.
240	Ashton, F 18	S. D.
30	*Ashton, H 4	W. Va.
6	Ashue, M 14	Wash
500	Ashuelot, Q 6	N. H
175	Ashurst, L 21	Ariz
72	*Ash Valley, K 10	Kan.
385	Ashville, E 16	Ala.
114	*Ashville, M 18	Me
480	*Ashville, P 3	N. Y.
1101	Ashville, L 12	Ohio
511	Ashville, M 9	Pa.
28	Ashwood, G 13	Ore.
40	*Ashwood, O 10	Tenn.
163	*Ashwood, N 21	Tex.
11	*Aska, B 7	Ga.
1000	*Askam, I 20	Pa.
175	*Askel, D 2	Mich.
88	*Askew, C 12	Miss.
23	Askin, G 12	Ky.
312	Askov, J 18	Minn.
686	Asotin, N 25	Wash.
777	Aspen, H 9	Colo.
30	*Aspen, P 12	Va.
214	Aspen Hill, Q 10	Tenn.
25	*Aspentunnel (Aspen) P 3	Wyo.
1041	Aspermont, D 13	Tex.
414	*Aspers (Bendersville), P 15	Pa.
31	*Asphalt, I 12	Ky.
4	Asphaltum, O 11	Okla.
88	Aspinwall, J 6	Iowa
4716	Aspinwall, M 3	Pa.
232	Assaria, I 15	Kan.
50	*Assawoman, L 24	Va.
105	*Assinippi, H 22	Mass.
165	Associated (Avon), A 20	Calif.
3	*Association Camp, C 13	Colo.
1500	Assonet, L 19	Mass.
1561	Assumption, J 15	Ill.
20	*Assurance, P 11	W. Va.
70	*Assyria, P 14	Mich.
153	*Astatula, G 16	Fla.
105	*Asti, G 3	Calif.
48	*Astico, M 19	Wis.
150	Astor, F 17	Fla.
28	Astor, J 5	Iowa
....	*Astor, F 19	Mass.
1292	Astoria, H 9	Ill.
15	*Astoria, O 12	Mo.
....	*Astoria, H 6	N. Y.
10389	Astoria, A 4	Ore.
214	Astoria, H 25	S. D.
200	*Astor Park, F 17	Fla.
10	Asylum, K 11	Miss.
181	Atalissa, K 21	Iowa
85	*Atarque, H 3	N. M.
2000	Atascadero, M 9	Calif.
100	*Atascosa, L 16	Tex.
12	*Atchafalaya, M 12	La.
64	Atchee, G 3	Colo.
12648	Atchison, E 23	Kan.
1603	Atco, D 4	Ga.
1353	Atco, L 11	N. J.
588	Atglen, P 20	Pa.
263	Athalia, R 14	Ohio
12	*Athboy, D 10	S. D.
150	Athel, N 20	Md.
143	*Athelstan, P 7	Iowa
50	*Athelstane, O 10	Wis.
513	Athena, C 20	Ore.
4342	Athens, A 12	Ala.
74	*Athens, L 5	Ark.
20650	Athens, E 12	Ga.
1062	Athens, I 12	Ill.
186	*Athens, E 13	Ind.
206	Athens, G 17	Ky.
491	Athens, B 7	La.
300	Athens, K 9	Me.
658	Athens, Q 15	Mich.
1655	Athens, P 23	N. Y.
7696	Athens, N 15	Ohio
4215	Athens, E 17	Pa.
6930	Athens, P 17	Tenn.
4765	Athens, F 21	Tex.
682	Athens, Q 9	W. Va.
856	Athens, I 12	Wis.
200	Athensville, J 10	Ill.
1908	Atherton, F 18	Calif.
262	Atherton, K 6	Ind.
300	Athertonville, H 14	Ky.
53	*Athlone, J 9	Calif.
120	Athol, C 4	Idaho
248	Athol, D 11	Kan.
80	*Athol, G 19	Ky.
11180	■Athol, C 10	Mass.
117	*Athol, J 22	N. Y.
375	*Athol, M 20	Pa.
250	Athol, F 18	S. D.
....	Athol Jc., H 8	Mass.
324	Athol Springs, N 4	N. Y.
1332	Atkins, G 10	Ark.
330	Atkins, I 19	Iowa
300	Atkins, D 6	La.
40	*Atkins, G 17	S. C.
95	*Atkins, D 9	Va.
460	▲Atkinson, O 21	Ga.
719	Atkinson, D 10	Ill.
25	Atkinson, J 13	Me.
18	*Atkinson, I 18	Minn.
1350	Atkinson, F 15	Neb.
312	Atkinson, K 16	N. C.
225	*Atkinson (Atkinson Depot Q 18	N. H.
225	Atkinson Depot (Atkinson) Q 18	N. H.
120	*Atkinson Mills, L 13	Pa.
163	*Atlanta, R 9	Ark.
302288	Atlanta, F 6	Ga.
35	Atlanta, N 9	Idaho
1290	Atlanta, H 14	Ill.
479	Atlanta, H 15	Ind.
286	Atlanta, N 18	Kan.
120	Atlanta, F 9	La.
300	Atlanta, I 19	Mich.
507	Atlanta, D 12	Mo.
173	Atlanta, N 14	Neb.
600	Atlanta, O 9	N. Y.
200	*Atlanta, L 11	Ohio
2453	Atlanta, D 24	Tex.
....	Atlanta Jc., D 2	Ga.
5802	Atlantic, M 6	Iowa
445	Atlantic, N 16	Me.
....	Atlantic, (No. Quincy), P 5	Mass.
1100	*Atlantic (Atlantic Mine), D 2	Mich.
500	*Atlantic (Smithtown), Q 20	N. H.
711	Atlantic, J 22	N. C.
109	Atlantic, G 2	Pa.
150	Atlantic, K 24	Va.
468	*Atlantic Beach, B 18	Fla.
500	*Atlantic Beach, I 6	N. Y.
64094	Atlantic City, P 16	N. J.
50	Atlantic City, L 9	Wyo.
2335	Atlantic Highlands, H 20	N. J.
....	*Atlanticville, N 19	S. C.
....	Atlas, see Imo	Ark.
250	*Atlas, O 21	Mich.
3000	Atlas, K 18	Pa.
76	*Atlas, C 21	Tex.
78	*Atlas, B 9	Wis.
600	Atlasburg, N 2	Pa.
....	Atlee see Arkdelphia	Ark
10	Atlee, P 11	Okla.
60	*Atlee, L 17	Va.
3200	Atmore, O 8	Ala.
5	Atoka, M 20	N. M.
2548	Atoka, O 18	Okla.
255	Atoka, P 2	Tenn.
150	Atolia, M 17	Calif.
200	Atpontley (Cannon Creek) P 15	Tenn.
50	Attalia, O 19	Wash.
4885	Attalla, D 17	Ala.
315	Attapulgus, P 6	Ga.
100	*Atterberry, H 11	Ill.
25	*Atterson, I 16	Ky.
40	*Attica, B 18	Ark.
3760	Attica, H 7	Ind.
130	*Attica, M 14	Iowa
708	Attica, O 13	Kan.
220	Attica, O 23	Mich.
2379	Attica, N 6	N. Y.
780	Attica, F 12	Ohio
85	Attica Jc., (Siam), F 12	Ohio
25	*Attilla, H 14	Ky.
22071	Attleboro, J 17	Mass.
1200	Attleboro Falls, J 17	Mass.
....	Attleboro Jc., J 19	Mass.
162	*Attoyac, G 23	Tex.
1235	Atwater, J 9	Calif.
80	*Atwater, K 10	Ill.
815	Atwater, M 10	Minn.
480	Atwater, F 19	Ohio
51	*Atwater, M 19	Wis.
10	*Atwell, I 19	N. Y.
70	*Atwood, C 7	Ala.
235	Atwood, R 6	Calif.
250	Atwood, C 20	Cclo.
707	Atwood, I 18	Ill.
250	Atwood, D 15	Ind.
1408	Atwood, D 4	Kan.
217	Atwood, R 22	N. Y.
250	Atwood, L 17	Okla.
417	Atwood, N 5	Tenn.
....	Atwood Jc., O 21	Mich.
100	*Auberry, K 10	Calif.
300	Aubrey, J 18	Ark
472	Aubrey, D 19	Tex.
4652	Auburn, J 21	Ala.
4013	Auburn, G 9	Calf.
20	Auburn, O 10	Fla.
286	Auburn, E 10	Ga.
1952	Auburn, J 12	Ill
5415	Auburn, C 21	Ind.
383	Auburn, H 7	Iowa
110	*Auburn, G 21	Kan.
955	Auburn, J 11	Ky.
19817	Auburn, N 6	Me.
6629	■Auburn, H 14	Mass.
600	Auburn, M 19	Mich.
75	*Auburn, N 9	Miss.
3639	Auburn, N 24	Neb.
150	Auburn, P 16	N. H.
35753	Auburn, M 13	N. Y.
59	Auburn, E 22	N. D.
978	Auburn, L 20	Pa.
3500	Auburn, F 15	R. I.
4211	Auburn, J 8	Wash.
168	*Auburn, F 9	W. Va.
275	Auburn, J 2	Wyo.
2723	Auburndale, H 16	Fla.
....	Auburndale, F 18, N 1 (Pop. incl. in Newton).	Mass.
....	*Auburndale, C 10 (Wagon Works)	Ohio
342	Auburndale, I 13	Wis.
219	Auburn Jc., C 21	Ind.
....	Auburn Jc., P 13	N. Y.
1200	*Auburn Heights (Amy), P 23	Mich.
250	*Auburntown, N 13	Tenn.
300	Aucilla, B 7	Fla.
27	*Aud, I 15	Mo.
650	*Audenried, J 21	Pa.
26	*Audra, G 19	Ky.
2409	Audubon, K 7	Iowa
312	Audubon, H 5	Minn.
8906	Audubon, K 9	N. J.
110	*Audubon, N 22	Pa.
317	Au Gres, L 21	Mich.
2235	Augusta, G 16	Ark.
30	Augusta, O 16	Colo.
65919	Augusta, G 20	Ga.
972	Augusta, H 6	Ill.
240	Augusta (New Augusta) I 13	Ind.
200	Augusta, P 7	Ind.
87	*Augusta, O 21	Iowa
3821	Augusta, M 17	Kan.
1701	Augusta, C 19	Ky.
19360	Augusta, N 9	Me.
785	Augusta, Q 14	Mich.
252	Augusta, I 18	Mo.
410	Augusta, G 8	Mont.
75	Augusta, B 13	N. J.
260	Augusta, H 19	Ohio
24	*Augusta (Pattersonville) H 19	Ohio
100	*Augusta, H 22	Tex.
175	*Augusta, E 21	W. Va.
1519	Augusta, F 13	Wis.
250	*Augusta Springs, J 10	Va.
80	*Augustin, I 10	Ala.
4	*Aukum, G 10	Calif.
1057	Aulander, D 20	N. C.
178	*Aullville, G 8	Mo.
120	*Aulne, J 17	Kan.
761	Ault, C 16	Colo.
33	*Ault, F 21	Ky.
5	Aultman, H 13	Ariz.
400	Aultman, F 17	Ohio
600	Aultman, L 6	Pa.
174	Aumsville, G 7	Ore.
200	*Aura, M 8	N. J.
302	*Aura, E 3	Mich.
250	*Auraria, C 9	Ga.
752	Aurelia, F 5	Iowa
53	Aurelia, F 8	N. D.
60	*Auriesville, N 21	N. Y.
57	*Aurora, C 7	Ark.
3437	Aurora, F 15	Colo.
47170	Aurora, C 18	Ill.
4828	Aurora, M 22	Ind.
276	Aurora, F 19	Iowa
274	Aurora, F 16	Kan.
50	*Aurora, K 17	Me.
1528	Aurora, F 20	Minn.
4056	Aurora, P 8	Mo.
2419	Aurora, L 18	Neb.
100	Aurora, D 17	N. M.
372	Aurora, N 12	N. Y.
492	Aurora, H 21	N. C.
518	*Aurora, E 18	Ohio
1000	*Aurora (Aurora Station), E 18	Ohio
228	Aurora, E 7	Ore.
225	Aurora, I 24	S. D.
607	Aurora, L 11	Utah
162	*Aurora, D 16	W. Va.
100	Aurorahville, L 16	Wis.
150	*Aurora Station (Aurora), E 18	Ohio
61	Au Sable, K 22	Mich.
100	*Ausable Chasm, D 23	N. Y.
1800	Au Sable Forks, E 24	N. Y.
1229	Austell, F 5	Ga.
317	Austen, E 15	W. Va.
37	*Austerlitz, E 18	Ky.
150	*Austerlitz, Q 24	N. Y.
145	*Austin, H 14	Ark.
100	Austin, J 5	Colo.
1500	Austin, N 16	Ind
75	*Austin, J 13	Ky.
18307	Austin, R 17	Minn.
78	Austin, J 8	Mont.
....	Austin, K 15	Neb.
520	Austin, G 13	Nev.
98	Austin, H 20	Ore.
1050	Austin, F 11	Pa.
87930	Austin, J 17	Tex.
200	Austin, L 10	Utah
100	Austin, F 7	Wash.
350	Austinburg, B 20	Ohio
....	Austin Jc., K 18	Tex.
....	Austin Station; see Austin	Ark.
790	Austinville, B 12	Ala
164	*Austinville, F 15	Iowa
420	*Austinville, D 11	Va.
312	*Austonio, H 22	Tex.
301	Austwell, O 19	Tex.
456	Autaugaville, J 14	Ala.
25	Auto, M 12	W. Va.
75	Automba, I 17	Minn.
150	*Au Train, F 8	Mich.
100	Autreyville, O 10	Ga.
94	Autryville, J 15	N. C.
65	*Autumn, E 5	Va.
25	Autwine, B 13	Okla.
65	*Auvergne, F 17	Ark.
800	Auxier, G 22	Ky.
490	Auxvasse, H 15	Mo.
821	Ava, O 13	Ill
1393	Ava, P 12	Mo.
61	*Ava, L 17	N. Y.
225	Ava, L 17	Ohio
1637	*Avalon, N 15	Calif.
50	*Avalon (Mulat), M 3	Fla.
113	*Avalon, C 13	Ga.
65	*Avalon, J 18	Md.
25	*Avalon, F 13	Miss.
516	Avalon, E 9	Mo.
313	*Avalon, R 11	N. J.
6155	Avalon, M 3	Pa.
310	*Avalon, F 19	Tex.
28	*Avalon, K 21	Va.
85	Avalon, M 22	Wis.
10	Avance, G 7	S. D.
....	*Avans, B 1	Ga.
501	Avant, D 18	Okla.
126	Avard, C 6	Okla.
62	*Avawam. I 21	Ky.
2500	Avella, N 1	Pa.
19	Ave Marie, see Amargo	N. M.
50	*Avena, L 15	Ill.
4500	*Avenal, L 11	Calif.
627	*Avenel, G 16	N. J.
80	*Avenstoke, F 16	Ky.
14	*Avenue, O 14	Md.
298	Avera, H 17	Ga.
250	*Avera, O 21	Miss.
30	Averill, M 18	Mich.
34	*Averill, H 3	Minn.
9	*Averill, C 21	Vt.
700	Averill Park, O 24	N. Y.
134	*Avert, P 21	Mo.
64	*Avery, H 9	Calif.
200	*Avery, E 8	Idaho
300	Avery, N 16	Iowa
2505	Avery (Needham Heights), G 18	Mass.
21	*Avery, L 10	Mo.
130	*Avery, D 13	Ohio
100	Avery, G 15	Okla.
477	Avery, C 23	Tex.
347	*Avery Island (Salt Mine), N 11	La.
315	Avila, M 9	Calif.
534	Avilla, C 20	Ind.
178	Avilla, O 7	Mo.
25	*Avilton, N 2	Md.
624	Avinger, D 24	Tex.
41	▲Avis, M 16	N. M.
1161	Avis, I 14	Pa.
388	Aviston, M 12	Ill.
175	*Avoca, A 5	Ark.
500	Avoca, N 11	Ind.
1598	Avoca, L 5	Iowa
814	Avoca, O 15	La.
200	Avoca, O 25	Mich.
323	Avoca, Q 6	Minn.
197	Avoca, L 23	Neb.
940	Avoca, P 10	N. Y.
4771	Avoca, H 21	Pa.
262	Avoca, E 13	Tex.
417	Avoca, H 19	Wis.
165	Avon (Associated), A 20	Calif.
134	Avon, G 10	Colo.
1000	Avon, E 12	Conn.
25	*Avon (Vassar), F 4	Idaho
803	Avon, G 8	Ill.
22	Avon, L 13	Iowa
350	Avon, K 6	Me.
2200	Avon, H 20	Mass.
403	Avon, L 11	Minn.
100	*Avon (Pettit), G 7	Miss.
162	Avon, J 7	Mont.
1211	Avon (Avon by the Sea), I 21	N. J.
2339	Avon, M 8	N. Y.
500	Avon, H 25	N. C.
2118	Avon, D 15	Oho.
550	Avon, N 18	Pa.
728	Avon, O 20	S. D.
20	*Avon, L 11	Va.
25	*Avon, E 10	W. Va.
1211	Avon by the Sea (Avon), I 21	N.J.
23	Avondale (Litchfield), K 11	Ariz.
73	*Avondale (N. Avondale), L 17	Colo.
350	Avondale, M 17	Colo.
21	Avondale, O 18	La.
435	Avondale, G 6	Mo.
25	Avondale, C 20	Mont.
500	Avondale, H 2	N. C.
1042	Avondale, I 20	Pa.
754	Avondale, Q 21	Pa.
110	*Avondale (Ritter), Q 5	W. Va.
569	*Avondale Estates, F 8	Ga.
2274	Avon Lake (Beach Park), C 15	Ohio
1354	Avonmore, M 6	Pa.
3125	Avon Park, J 18	Fla.
150	*Awendaw, M 20	S. C.
40	Axial, D 6	Colo.
24	Axin, K 12	Mich.
247	*Axis, P 4	Ala.
11	*Axtel, G 12	Ky.
545	Axtell, D 20	Kan.
295	Axtell, N 15	Neb.
200	*Axtell, G 18	Tex.
250	Axtell, K 12	Utah
150	*Axton, Q 7	Va.
25	Aydelotte, I 14	Okla.
1884	Ayden, G 18	N. C.
310	Aydlett, C 24	N. C.
64	Ayer, N 18	Colo.
3572	■Ayer, D 15	Mass.
50	*Ayer (Haas), N 20	Wash.
....	*Ayers, J 18	Ky.
52	Ayers (Ayers Jc.), K 23.	Me.
82	*Ayersville, C 13	Ga.
....	*Ayersville, G 22	Ky.
100	Aylesworth, Q 16	Okla.
75	*Aylett, L 18	Va.
50	Aylmer, H 14	N. D.
107	*Aylor, I 13	Va.
537	Aynor, G 22	S. C.
152	Ayr, N 17	Neb.
107	Ayr, M 22	N. D.
391	Ayshire, D 7	Iowa
110	*Azalea, O 7	N. C.
200	Azalea, O 5	Ore.
125	*Azalia, R 21	Mich.
146	*Azle, D 18	Tex.
5	Aznoe, F 10	Mont.
31	Aztec, M 7	Ariz.
756	Aztec, C 5	N. M.
500	*Azucar, L 23	Fla.
5209	Azusa, Q 6	Calif.
65	*Azwell, G 13	Wash.

B

Pop	Place Index	State
25	Babb, C 6	Mont.
11	Babbitt, F 21	Minn.
22	Babcock (Boykin), O 5	Ga.
250	Babcock, I 15	Wis.
164	*Bablin, G 11	W. Va.
....	*Baboosic Lake, Q 12	N. H.
350	Babson Park, I 17	Fla.
4742	Babylon, H 8	N. Y.
50	Baca, F 5	N. M.
150	Bacaville, H 10	N. M.
166	Bacchus, F 10	Utah
150	*Bach, M 22	Mich.
120	Bache, L 20	Okla.
72	*Bachelor, G 4	Calif.
20	*Bachelor, H 14	Mo.
18	*Bachelor, H 19	N. C.
100	Bachmanville, N 17	Pa.
18	*Backbay, Q 23	Va.
40	Backoo, D 21	N. D.
334	Backus, H 11	Minn.
82	*Backus, E 9	Pa.
215	*Backus, N 9	W. Va.
50	Bacon (Bacons), M 22	Del.
....	Bacon, B 16	Tex.
225	Bacone, G 21	Okla.
160	*Bacons Castle, O 19	Va.
504	Baconton, N 7	Ga.
248	*Bacova, J 8	Va.
2624	Bad Axe, M 23	Mich.
....	Bade, B 20	Ore.
....	Baden, D 15	Calif.
165	*Baden, J 12	Md.
2135	Baden, L 2	Pa.
32	*Baden, C 6	Va.
221	Baden Baden, M 13	Ill.
120	*Bader, H 7	Ill.
39	*Badger, K 13	Calif.
251	Badger, F 10	Iowa
404	Badger, B 5	Minn.
170	Badger, H 23	S. D.
....	*Badger Basin, D 7	Wyo.
50	*Badgett (Maury Jc.), N 4	Tenn.
81	*Badham, L 15	S. C.
3063	Badin, G 8	N. C.
25	*Badnation (Runningville), L 13	S. D.
18	*Bado, O 14	Mo.
12	Badwater, H 14	Wyo.
36	*Bagby, I 11	Calif.
25	*Bagby, K 17	Va.
500	Bagdad, M 3	Fla.
500	Bagdad, E 16	Ky.
....	Bagdad, E 7	Mich.
350	Baggaley, N 6	Pa.
221	Baggs, R 12	Wyo.
427	Bagley, J 9	Iowa
12	*Bagley, C 16	Md.

Pop.	Place, Index	State
34	Bagley, H 6	Mich.
1241	Bagley, F 7	Minn.
293	Bagley, F 21	Wis.
....	Bagley Jc., I 9	Wash.
18*	Bagleys Mills, P 13	Va.
118	Bagnell, K 12	Mo.
....	Bagwell, P 15	S. C.
420*	Bagwell (Bagwells), C 22	Tex.
44*	Bahama, D 13	N. C.
360*	Baie de Wasai, F 16	Mich.
50	Bailey (Baileys), H 13	Colo.
50	Bailey, B 16	Iowa
160	Bailey, N 12	Mich.
....	Bailey, M 14	Minn.
66*	Bailey, J 20	Miss.
645	Bailey, F 16	N. C.
25	Bailey, M 11	Okla.
150*	Bailey, P 2	Tenn.
223	Bailey, C 20	Tex.
25*	Bailyboro, B 8	Tex.
250	Bailey Island, P 7	Me.
....	Bailey Jc., I 5	Ore.
36*	Baileys (Baileys Switch P.O.), J 19	Ky.
238	Baileys Harbor, R 11	Wis.
55*	Baileys Mills, K 19	Ohio
36*	Baileys Switch (Baileys), J 19	Ky.
50*	Baileysville, P 6	W. Va.
200	Baileyton, C 14	Ala.
229*	Baileyton, M 22	Tenn.
208	Baileyville, B 12	Ill.
636*	Baileyville, D 20	Kan.
50	Baileyville, I 19	Tex.
75*	Bain, I 15	Minn.
6352	Bainbridge, O 6	Ga.
414	Bainbridge, J 10	Ind.
1450	Bainbridge, P 17	N. Y.
913	Bainbridge, O 11	Ohio
500	Bainbridge, O 17	Pa.
403	Bainville, E 25	Mont.
250	Baird, F 9	Miss.
4	Baird, N 9	Okla.
....*	Baird, O 3	Pa.
1810	Baird, F 14	Tex.
1000	Bairdford, L 4	Pa.
125*	Bairdstown, F 14	Ga.
176*	Bairdstown, D 9	Ohio
250*	Bairoil, O 8	Wyo.
50*	Baisden, O 3	W. Va.
35*	Baizetown, H 11	Ky.
30*	Baker, D 11	Ark.
109*	Baker (Silver Lake), M 20	Calif.
260	Baker, M 5	Fla.
35	Baker, K 13	Idaho
75	Baker, D 22	Kan.
150*	Baker, K 15	La.
75*	Baker, H 3	Minn.
1304	Baker, J 25	Mont.
68	Baker, H 24	Nev.
70	Baker, G 15	N. D.
....	Baker, Q 6	Okla.
9342	Baker, F 22	Ore.
150*	Baker, G 20	W. Va.
100*	Bakerhill, L 21	Ala.
....	Bakers, C 11	Utah
....	Bakers Falls, K 24	N. Y.
29252	Bakersfield, M 13	Calif.
....	Bakersfield, K 8	Ill.
177	Bakersfield, R 14	Mo.
100*	Bakersfield, I 7	Tex.
325	Bakersfield, C 10	Vt.
....*	Bakers Island, D 22	Mass.
84*	Bakers Mills, J 22	N. Y.
100*	Bakers Run (Levi), I 10	W. Va.
150	Bakers Summit, N 10	Pa.
360*	Bakerstown, L 3	Pa.
150	Bakersville, P 22	Ariz.
300	Bakersville, D 9	Conn.
437	Bakersville, D 1, M 9	N. C.
100	Bakersville, I 17	Ohio
100*	Bakerton, K 15	Ky.
1500	Bakerton (Elmora), L 9	Pa.
518	Bakerton, E 25	W. Va.
75*	Bakerville, N 8	Tenn.
47*	Bakewell, P 15	Tenn.
68*	Bala, F 18	Kan.
....*	Bala-Cynwyd (Cynwyd), N 22 (Pop. 3000 incl. in Merion Station)	Pa.
....*	Balance Rock, D 3	Mass.
713	Balaton, P 5	Minn.
....	Balboa, P 16	Calif.
1000*	Balboa Island, O 17	Calif.
100*	Balch, F 18	Ark.
125	Balcom, Q 14	Ill.
....	Balcony Falls, M 9	Va.
33*	Bald Creek, N 9	N. C.
300	Bald Eagle, M 25	Minn.
100	Bald Eagle, L 11	Pa.
....	Bald Eagle Jc., J 13	Pa.
25	Baldhill, H 19	Okla.
26	Baldi, J 10	Wash.
1445	Bald Knob, G 15	Ark.
54*	Bald Knob, M 5	W. Va.
....*	Bald Mountain, K 4	Me.
500*	Bald Mountain, N 9	N. C.
50*	Baldock (Beldoc), M 11	S. C.
40	Bald Prairie, H 20	Tex.
37*	Baldrock, I 19	Ky.
39*	Baldwin, C 5	Ark.
126	Baldwin, J 8	Colo.
1002	Baldwin, C 15	Fla.
402*	Baldwin, C 11	Ga.
341	Baldwin, O 11	Ill.
210	Baldwin, I 23	Iowa
984	Baldwin, O 13	La.
316	Baldwin, D 15	Md.
612	Baldwin, M 12	Mich.
16300	Baldwin, I 7	N. Y.
....	Baldwin (Rogers Rock), I 24	N. Y.
250*	Baldwin, B 3	N. C.
150	Baldwin, M 12	N. D.
3000*	Baldwin, L 3	Pa.
81*	Baldwin, H 10	W. Va.
918	Baldwin, B 12	Wis.
1096	Baldwin City (Baldwin), H 23	Kan.
....*	Baldwin Mills, C 12	S. C.
8500*	Baldwin Park, Q 6	Calif.
425	Baldwin Place, E 6	N. Y.
2200	Baldwinsville, C 12	Mass.
3840	Baldwinsville, L 13	N. Y.
1279	Baldwyn, B 20	Miss.
25	Baldy, C 16	N. M.
29*	Balfe, F 9	Neb.
500*	Balfour (Smythe), P 8	N. C.
193	Balfour, H 12	N. D.
1000*	Balkan, K 20	Ky.
78	Balko, R 7	Okla.
50	Ball, H 10	La.
250	Ballantine, L 17	Mont.
50	Ballard, F 24	Okla.
24*	Ballard, P 11	W. Va.
....	Ballard Jc., B 11	Utah
1000	Ballard Vale, C 19	Mass.
184*	Ballclub, F 14	Minn.
75*	Ballengee, P 10	W. Va.
635▲*	Ballentine, F 12	S. C.
....*	Ballentine, P 21	Va.
711	Ball Ground, D 7	Ga.
5*	Ballico, J 9	Calif.
4472	Ballinger, G 13	Tex.
50	Ballot, G 22	Ky.
300	Ballouville, D 24	Conn.
35*	Balls Landing (Perry Park), D 17	Ky.
115	Ballston, F 6	Ore.
....*	Ballston, F 18	Va.
300*	Ballston Lake, L 23	N. Y.
4443	Ballston Spa, M 23	N. Y.
70*	Ballsville, M 15	Va.
250*	Ballwin, I 19	Mo.
613*	Bally, M 20	Pa.
108*	Balm, I 14	Fla.
175*	Balm, D 2	N. C.
250*	Balmat, E 18	N. Y.
283*	Balmorhea, H 6	Tex.
1350	Balnew (Turner), F 15	Md.
308*	Balsam, Q 6	N. C.
146*	Balsam Grove, Q 7	N. C.
452	Balsam Lake, B 10	Wis.
263	Balta, G 14	N. D.
1567	Baltic, H 21	Conn.
550*	Baltic, D 2	Mich.
492	Baltic, I 16	Ohio
270	Baltic, K 24	S. D.
859100	Baltimore, F 14	Md.
835	Baltimore, L 13	Ohio
....	Baltimore Park, B 14	Calif.
....*	Baltusrol, F 17	N. J.
10*	Balty, K 17	Va.
40*	Baltzer, F 8	Miss.
3000	Bamberg, K 13	S. C.
75*	Bamford, G 14	Ala.
159*	Bancker, M 11	La.
20*	Banco, I 13	Va.
29*	Banco, O 4	W. Va.
406	Bancroft, P 20	Idaho
959	Bancroft, C 10	Iowa
84*	Bancroft, D 20	Kan.
212	Bancroft, K 5	La.
102	Bancroft, H 18	Me.
150*	Bancroft (Middlefield), F 4	Mass.
581	Bancroft, O 19	Mich.
599	Bancroft, H 22	Neb.
....*	Bancroft, M 3	Ore.
126	Bancroft, I 21	S. D.
115*	Bancroft, J 4	W. Va.
150	Bancroft, K 15	Wis.
300	Bandana, I 4	Ky.
237*	Bandana, M 9	N. C.
470	Bandera, L 15	Tex.
40*	Bandon, Q 11	Ind.
1004	Bandon, N 2	Ore.
100*	Bandy, I 17	Ky.
800*	Bandy, C 9	Va.
80	Bandy, N 6	W. Va.
22*	Bane, N 4	Va.
....*	Bangall, C 6	N. Y.
25	Bangert, M 16	Mo.
75	Bangor, E 13	Ala.
450	Bangor, F 8	Calif.
70*	Bangor, F 21	Ky.
29822	Bangor, L 14	Me.
1409	Bangor, Q 11	Mich.
400	Bangor, C 21	N. Y.
319*	Bangor (North Bangor), E 21	N. Y.
5687	Bangor, K 23	Pa.
22	Bangor, D 6	Va.
157	Bangor, H 6	Wash.
847	Bangor, F 17	Wis.
68*	Bangs, I 14	Ohio
756	Bangs, G 15	Tex.
30*	Banida, R 20	Idaho
109	Bankers, R 16	Mich.
232	Bankersmith, K 15	Tex.
700	Bankhead, E 10	Ala.
252	Banks, M 19	Ala.
248	Banks, O 13	Ark.
25	Banks, M 6	Idaho
29*	Banks, J 22	Ky.
320	Banks, A 11	Miss.
10	Banks, H 4	N. D.
247	Banks, C 6	Ore.
205	Bankston, F 8	Ala.
....	Bank Street, Jc. I 9	Conn.
180	Bannack, N 6	Mont.
25*	Banner, E 14	Ark.
111*	Banner, H 22	Ky.
250	Banner, D 16	Miss.
25*	Banner (Brule), M 18	Mo.
95	Banner, I 11	Okla.
500*	Banner, C 5	Va.
47*	Banner, B 14	Wyo.
1	Bannerman, K 16	Wis.
344	Banners Elk, D 2	N. C.
40*	Banner Springs, M 16	Tenn.
3874	Banning, O 19, R 11	Calif.
300	Banning, G 3	Ga.
280*	Banning, Q 4	Pa.
350	Bannister, O 19	Mich.
232*	Bannock, K 19	Ohio
18	Bannockburn, N 14	Ga.
....*	Bannon, I 22	Ariz.
50*	Banock, I 11	Ky.
211	Banquete, P 18	Tex.
100*	Banta, H 8	Calif.
564	Bantam, F 6	Conn.
150*	Bantam, O 7	Ohio
250	Bantry, F 12	N. D.
50	Banty, P 18	Okla.
500*	Bapchula, L 14	Ariz.
60*	Baptist, G 20	Ky.
250*	Baptist, K 17	La.
150*	Baptistown, G 11	N. J.
6415	Baraboo, J 18	Wis.
132	Barada, N 25	Neb.
1110	Baraga, D 3	Mich.
610	Barataria, O 18	La.
8*	Barbeau, F 16	Mich.
34*	Barber, H 5	Ark.
300	Barber, N 6	Idaho
....	Barber, G 14	Mass.
90	Barber, J 14	Mont.
42	Barber, F 6	N. C.
47	Barber, G 23	Okla.
15*	Barber (Falling Spring), L 7	Va.
24028	Barberton, F 17	Ohio
325*	Barberville, E 18	Fla.
25*	Barbours Creek, M 6	Va.
250*	Barboursville, J 14	Va.
1550	Barboursville, K 2	W. Va.
2420	Barboursville, J 19	Ky.
83*	Barbreck, I 11	La.
....*	Barcamp, see Tipperary	Ark.
75*	Barclay, H 21	Kan.
119	Barclay, G 19	Md.
400*	Barco, C 23	N. C.
....*	Barcreek, I 20	Ky.
321*	Barcroft, F 18	Va.
30*	Bard, Q 22	Calif.
30	Bard, G 25	N. M.
71*	Bardane, E 25	W. Va.
67*	Bardley, Q 18	Mo.
32*	Bardo, J 21	Ky.
275	Bardolph, G 7	Ill.
200*	Bardonia, F 5	N. Y.
3152	Bardstown, G 14	Ky.
113	Bardstown, Jc. F 14	Ky.
1218	Bardwell, J 4	Ky.
266*	Bardwell, F 19	Tex.
....	Bardwell, M 22	Wis.
15	Barela, Q 17	Colo.
480*	Bareville, O 19	Pa.
50	Barfield, D 23	Ark.
750*	Bargaintown, N 13	N. J.
297	Bargersville, K 13	Ind.
75	Barham, H 6	La.
60	Barhamsville, M 19	Va.
4400	Bar Harbor, M 18	Me.
187	Baring, J 23	Me.
259	Baring, B 13	Mo.
95	Baring, H 10	Wash.
400*	Barium Springs, E 5	N. C.
452	Barker, K 6	N. Y.
90*	Barker, K 22	Tex.
200	Barkhamsted, C 10	Conn.
400*	Barking, L 3	Pa.
300	Bark River, H 7	Mich.
100	Barksdale, L 13	Tex.
63	Barksdale, F 4	Wis.
....*	Barksdale Field, C 5	La.
23*	Barkland, L 6	Miss.
343*	Barling, G 4	Ark.
584	Barlow, J 4	Ky.
46*	Barlow, L 10	Miss.
75	Barlow, J 17	N. D.
275*	Barlow, M 17	Ohio
52	Barlow, E 7	Ore.
219	Barlow Bend, N 8	Ala.
400*	Bar Mills, P 4	Me.
23*	Barn, Q 9	W. Va.
500	Barnabas (Barnabus), O 4	W. Va.
306	Barnard, G 14	Kan.
341	Barnard, B 5	Mo.
25*	Barnard, N 7	N. C.
60	Barnard, C 18	S. D.
109	Barnard, K 12	Vt.
500*	Barnardsville, N 8	N. C.
1200	Barnegat, M 18	N. J.
225*	Barnegat City, K 17	N. J.
130*	Barnerville, O 21	N. Y.
10	Barnes, E 6	Ark.
391	Barnes, E 18	Kan.
....	Barnes, E 6	Mich.
463	Barnes, F 7	Pa.
43*	Barnes, I 23	Tex.
3831	Barnesboro, L 8	Pa.
414	Barnes City, L 16	Ia.
133*	Barnes Corners, I 17	N. Y.
219	Barneston (Barnston) O 22	Neb.
50*	Barneston, P 21	Pa.
38*	Barnesville, C 17	Colo.
3535	Barnesville, H 8	Ga.
121*	Barnesville, G 8	Md.
40*	Barnesville Sta. (Sellman), G 8	Md.
1450*	Barnesville, H 3	Minn.
20*	Barnesville, J 12	N. C.
5002	Barnesville, K 19	Ohio
100*	Barnesville, K 19	Pa.
12*	Barnesville, P 12	Va.
200	Barnet, F 18	Vt.
100	Barnett, G 15	Ga.
80*	Barnett, L 20	Miss.
239	Barnett, J 12	Mo.
95*	Barnetts, N 18	Va.
250*	Barnetts Creek, G 22	Ky.
296*	Barneveld (Trenton), K 17	N. Y.
358	Barneveld, J 20	Wis.
154	Barney, O 11	Ga.
....	Barney, D 23	N. M.
197	Barney, P 24	N. D.
225*	Barnhart, J 19	Mo.
275*	Barnhart, H 11	Tex.
73*	Barnhill, N 18	Ill.
394	Barnhill, I 18	Ohio
65*	Barnitz, O 14	Pa.
189*	Barnrock, G 22	Ky.
1831	Barnsdall, C 18	Okla.
250	Barnsley, I 9	Ky.
84*	Barnsley, P 21	Pa.
8333■	Barnstable, M 25, N 13	Mass.
250	Barnstead, N 16	N. H.
219	Barnston (Barneston), O 22	Neb.
184	Barnum, G 9	Iowa
327	Barnum, I 18	Minn.
29*	Barnum, I 23	Tex.
152	Barnum, D 19	W. Va.
75	Barnum, G 19	Wis.
10	Barnum, G 15	Wyo.
12*	Barnumton, L 11	Mo.
89*	Barnwell, Q 7	Ala.
1922	Barnwell, L 11	S. C.
50*	Barnyard, J 19	Ky.
302	Baroda, R 10	Mich.
80	Baron, F 24	Okla.
45	Barr (Barr Lake), F 15	Colo.
8	Barr, I 12	Ill.
80*	Barr, B 12	Miss.
41*	Barr, (Barrs Mills), H 17	Ohio
210	Barr, N 2	Tenn.
....*	Barracks (see Jefferson Barracks)	Mo.
1000	Barrackville, D 13	W. Va.
5*	Barrallton, F 14	Ky.
16	Barranca, D 14	N. M.
36	Barratts, N 7	Mont.
2300	Barre, E 11	Mass.
10909	Barre, G 13	Vt.
300	Barre Center, L 7	N. Y.
130*	Barree, M 12	Pa.
....	Barre Jc., G 13	Vt.
50*	Barren Springs, D 11	Va.
900	Barre Plains, F 11	Mass.
....	Barre Transfer, G 13	Vt.
113*	Barrett, D 19	Kan.
384	Barrett, K 5	Minn.
360	Barrett (North Lisbon), H 11	N. H.
63*	Barrett, C 4	N. C.
....	Barrett, B 20	Ore.
319*	Barrett, M 5	W. Va.
25*	Barretts Ferry (Davidson), H 10	Ky.
25	Barretts Jc., G 9	Mass.
100*	Barretville, P 2	Tenn.
2*	Barrial, H 22	Mont.
250*	Barridge, I 21	Ky.
....	Barrie, O 24	N. D.
204	Barrineau Park, M 1	Fla.
3560	Barrington, B 19	Ill.
75	Barrington, O 18	N. H.
2329	Barrington, L 9	N. J.
6231■	Barrington, G 19	R. I.
45*	Barr Lake (Barr), F 15	Colo.
315	Barron, H 11	La.
2059	Barron, D 10	Wis.
225	Barronett, C 9	Wis.
75*	Barrow, K 9	Ill.
100*	Barrowsville, J 18	Mass.
41*	Barrs Mills (Barr), H 17	Ohio
1545	Barry, J 6	Ill.
116*	Barry, L 3	Minn.
319*	Barry, F 20	Tex.
35	Barry, F 18	Wash.
342	Barryton, M 15	Mich.
429	Barrytown, R 23	N. Y.
325	Barryville, D 1	N. Y.
2500	Barstow, M 19	Calif.
175	Barstow, D 9	Ill.
56*	Barstow, M 14	Md.
558	Barstow, G 7	Tex.
30*	Bart, J 16	Ky.
....	Bart, M 22	Mich.
130*	Bart, P 19	Pa.
....	Bart, see Artesia Wells	Tex.
300	Bartelso, N 13	Ill.
48*	Barterville, E 19	Ky.
160*	Barth, M 2	Fla.
25*	Barthell, K 17	Ky.
38*	Bartles, F 13	Ky.
48	Bartles, Q 13	Ohio
16267	Bartlesville, B 18	Okla.
70*	Bartlett, J 17	Calif.
608	Bartlett, B 19	Ill.
125*	Bartlett, P 4	Iowa
161	Bartlett, O 23	Kan.
40*	Bartlett, P 16	Mo.
176	Bartlett, I 16	Neb.
950	Bartlett, I 16	N. H.
78	Bartlett, H 19	N. D.
207	Bartlett, N 16	Ohio
....*	Bartlett, see Dighton	Okla.
65	Bartlett, B 22	Ore.
400*	Bartlett, P 2	Tenn.
1668	Bartlett, I 18	Tex.
100*	Bartlett Springs, F 4	Calif.
380	Bartley, O 11	Neb.
90*	Bartley, D 13	N. J.
500*	Bartley, Q 5	W. Va.
....*	Bartlick, B 6	Va.
150*	Barto, M 20	Pa.
109*	Barton, B 7	Ala.
75*	Barton, M 15	La.
781	Barton, N 4	Md.
200	Barton, R 13	N. Y.
157	Barton, F 13	N. D.
1200	Barton, J 20	Ohio
1263	Barton, C 16	Vt.
900	Barton, O 18	Wis.
16*	Barton City, J 21	Mich.
....	Barton Junction (Barton Crossing), K 19	Ark.
135*	Bartonsville, I 22	Pa.
120*	Bartonsville, P 11	Vt.
1879	Bartonville, G 12	Ill.
86*	Bartonville, E 13	Va.
6158	Bartow, I 16	Fla.
438*	Bartow, I 17	Ga.
29*	Bartow, L 14	W. Va.
75*	Bartville, O 20	Pa.
60	Bar View, C 4	Ore.
409	Barwick, O 10	Ga.
85*	Barwick, H 21	Ky.
212	Basalt, H 8	Colo.
252	Basalt (Monroe), O 19	Idaho
238	Basco, H 5	Ill.
50*	Basco, K 20	Wis.
300*	Bascom, A 1, M 12	Fla.
62*	Bascom, F 21	Ky.
25	Bascom, I 17	Mont.
400*	Bascom, F 11	Ohio
65*	Bascomville, C 13	S. C.
221	Basehor, F 24	Kan.
600*	Base Line, P 23	Mich.
11*	Basham, O 5	Va.
140*	Bashi, L 6	Ala.
36*	Basic City (Basic), L 20	Miss.
8*	Basil, M 13	Kan.
25*	Basil, I 15	Ky.
766	Basil, K 13	Ohio
1132	Basile, L 9	La.
250	Basin, J 8	Mont.
100*	Basin, P 6	W. Va.
1099	Basin, D 11	Wyo.
169*	Baskett, G 9	Ky.
330	Baskin, D 12	La.
1500	Basking Ridge, E 15	N. J.
90*	Basom (Alabama), M 7	N. Y.
17*	Bass, D 10	Ark.
60*	Bass (Bass Lake), D 11	Ind.
....*	Bass, K 14	La.
229	Bass, G 19	W. Va.
....	Bassenger, see Bassinger	Fla.
39*	Bassett, F 21	Ark.
40	Bassett, Q 5	Calif.
147*	Bassett, C 17	Iowa
931	Bassett, F 13	Neb.
63*	Bassett, C 23	Tex.
150*	Bassett (Bassetts), O 22	Wis.
3000	Bassetts, Q 6	Va.
....*	Bassetts Creek, M 4	Ala.
277	Bassfield, N 14	Miss.
....	Bassinger, J 19	Fla.
30*	Bass Lake, J 12	Calif.
60*	Bass Lake (Bass), D 11	Ind.
79*	Bass Lake, F 14	Minn.
260*	Bass River, N 13	Mass.
250*	Bass Station (Bass), A 17	Ala.
500*	Bastian, C 11, O 2	Va.
6626	Bastrop, B 12	La.
1976	Bastrop, K 18	Tex.
120*	Basye, F 12	Va.
....	Batan, D 6	Ore.
75*	Batavia, B 9	Ark.
5101	Batavia, C 18	Ill.
474	Batavia, O 18	Iowa
80*	Batavia, R 15	Mich.
17267	Batavia, M 7	N. Y.
1320	Batavia, O 7	Ohio
122	Batavia, O 18	Wis.
66*	Bat Cave, P 8	N. C.
229	Batchelor, J 12	La.
297	Batchtown, L 7	Ill.
30	Batemantown, H 13	Ohio
148	Bates, I 14	Ark.
513*	Bates (West Paris), M 4	Me.
18	Bates (Batesville), H 18	Ore.
2933	Batesburg, G 11	S. C.
103*	Bates City, G 8	Mo.
300*	Batesland, N 6	S. D.
143*	Batesville, L 21	Ala.
5267	Batesville, D 15	Ark.
3065	Batesville, L 20	Ind.
1815	Batesville, C 12	Miss.
194	Batesville, K 18	Ohio
....*	Batesville, see Bates	Ore.
625	Batesville, N 14	Tex.
150*	Batesville, K 12	Va.
358	Bath, H 10	Ill.
100	Bath, K 22	Ind.
14*	Bath, H 22	Ky.
10235	Bath, O 8	Me.
300	Bath, O 18	Mich.
430	Bath, H 10	N. H.
4696	Bath, P 10	N. Y.
380	Bath, G 21	N. C.
100	Bath, E 17	Ohio
1720	Bath, L 22	Pa.
1250	Bath, J 9	S. C.
128	Bath, D 19	S. D.
312	Bathgate, D 22	N. D.
35*	Bath Springs, O 7	Tenn.
60*	Batna, H 14	Va.
34719	Baton Rouge, L 14	La.
650	Batson, J 24	Tex.
300	Battenville, L 25	N. Y.
150	Battery Park, P 20	Va.
35	Battiest, N 23	Okla.
29*	Battle, J 15	La.
270	Battleboro, D 17	N. C.
4	Battle Creek, B 8	Colo.
827	Battle Creek, H 4	Iowa
43453	Battle Creek, Q 15	Mich.
702	Battle Creek, H 19	Neb.
53*	Battlecreek, C 2	S. C.
113*	Battlefield, N 9	Mo.
506	Battle Ground, G 10	Ind.
540	Battle Ground, P 7	Wash.
623	Battle Lake, J 6	Minn.
1120	Battle Mountain, D 13	Nev.
....	Battle River, E 10, see Quiring	Minn.
200	Battles Wharf, Q 6	Ala.
80*	Battletown, F 12	Ky.
52	Battleview, E 5	N. D.
6	Battrick, I 15	Mont.
1017	Baudette, B 1¹	Minn.
150*	Baugh, P 10	Tenn.
71*	Baughman, J 19	Ky.
500*	Bausman, O 19	Pa.
2000	Bauxite, J 12	Ark.
....	Bauxite Jc., J 12	Ark.
350*	Bavaria, H 15	Kan.
....*	Bavon, M 21	Va.
2916	Baxley, M 18	Ga.
218	Baxter, P 16	Ark.
50*	Baxter (Towle), N 18	Calif.
....*	Baxter, B 9	Ga.
623	Baxter, J 14	Iowa
750*	Baxter, J 21	Ky.
....	Baxter, see Lampe	Mo.
100*	Baxter, I 7	Pa.
15*	Baxter (Kneece), H 11	S. C.
576	Baxter, M 14	Tenn.
670	Baxter, D 13	W. Va.
760*	Baxter Estates, H 7	N. Y.
4921	Baxter Springs, O 25	Kan.
300	Baxterville, P 15	Miss.
357	Bay, E 20	Ark.
31*	Bay, G 3	Calif.
....*	Bay, E 11	La.
75*	Bay, J 16	Mo.
225*	Bayard, C 17	Fla.
703	Bayard, J 8	Iowa
39*	Bayard, L 23	Kan.
2121	Bayard, I 3	Neb.
764	Bayard, M 4	N. M.
121	Bayard, G 19	Ohio
32*	Bayard (Ashby), G 13	Va.
585	Bayard, E 17	W. Va.
428	Bayboro, H 21	N. C.
198*	Baybridge, D 13	Ohio
200	Bay Center, L 2	Wash.
47956	Bay City, M 20	Mich.
379	Bay City, D 4	Ore.
6594	Bay City, M 21	Tex.
30	Bay City, K 2	Wash.
299	Bay City, B 13	Wis.
372	Bayfield, P 6	Colo.
1212	Bayfield, F 4	Wis.
29*	Bayford, N 23	Va.
200*	Bay Harbor, N 10	Fla.
105	Bayhead, N 10	Fla.
499	Bayhead, J 20	N. J.
142*	Bay Horse, M 22	Mont.
44*	Bay Lake, E 15	Fla.
50*	Bayle (Bayle City, L15,	Ill.
25*	Bayles (Delta), D 6	Calif.
363	Baylis, J 6	Ill.
66	Baylor, C 20	Mont.
10	Bay Mills, J 10	Wis.
1763	Bay Minette, P 7	Ala.
82*	Baynesville, J 19	Va.
35	Bayocean, D 4	Ore.
79198	Bayonne, F 19	N. J.
40*	Bayou, I 6	Ky.
140*	Bayou, G 25	Tex.
110*	Bayou Chene, M 12	La.
119*	Bayou Current, I 12	La.
100*	Bayou George, N 10	Fla.
1031	Bayou Goula, M 14	La.
2000	Bayou La Batre, R 4	Ala.
....*	Bayou La Chute, see La Chute	La.
150*	Bayou Meto, L 16	Ark.
84	Bayou Sale, O 13	La.
....	Bayou Sara, K 13	La.
....*	Bay Pines, I 12	Fla.
....*	Bay Point; see Port Chicago	Calif.
20*	Bay Point, P 9	Me.
25*	Bayport, G 13	Fla.
537	Bay Port, L 22	Mich.
2633	Bayport, N 18	Minn.
1500	Bayport, H 9	N. Y.
57*	Bays, H 21	Ky.
12*	Bays, I 10	W. Va.
4138	Bay St. Louis, R 16	Miss.
100*	Bayshore (Samville), L 16	Fla.
125	Bayshore, I 15	Mich.
10000	Bay Shore, H 8	N. Y.
200	Bayside, D 1	Calif.
250	Bayside, M 16	Me.
83	Bayside, M 13	Me.
....	Bayside, O 5	N. J.
308	Bayside, O 19	Tex.
500*	Bayside, Q 22	Va.
217	Bay Springs, M 1	Fla.
1228	Bay Springs, L 17	Miss.
5194	Baytown, L 23	Tex.
300	Bay View, D 2	Calif.
136	Bayview, C 5	Idaho
3000*	Bay View, H 16	Mich.
....	Bay View, F 15	Md.
100	Bayview, B 19	Md.
75*	Bayview, G 4	Ore.
150*	Bayview, N 23	Va.
135	Bay View, D 7	Wash.
3356*	Bay Village (North Dover), O 20	Ohio
100*	Bayville, O 10	Me.
1200*	Bayville, K 17	N. J.
1516*	Bayville, H 7	N. Y.
275*	Baywood, K 14	La.
35*	Baywood, E 10	Va.
75*	Bazaar, J 19	Kan.
76	Bazile Mills, F 18	Neb.
465*	Bazine, I 8	Kan.
87*	Beach (Crawley), O 17	Ga.
....	Beach, see Forkville	Miss.
1178	Beach, M 1	N. D.
75*	Beach, N 16	Va.
3*	Beach, C 7	Wash.
277*	Beach Arlington (Ship Bottom-Beach Arlington), K 17	N. J.
600	Beach Bluff, J 8	Mass.
812	Beach City, H 17	Ohio
746	Beach Haven, N 18	N. J.
413*	Beach Haven (Loch Haven), I 20	Pa.
112*	Beach Haven Terrace, K 17	N. J.
269	Beachlake, F 23	Pa.
2274	Beach Park (Avon Lake), D 15	Ohio
140	Beachton, P 8	Ga.
102	Beachton, N 25	Okla.
250*	Beachville, O 14	Md.
650	Beachwood, K 19	N. J.
382	Beacon, M 16	Iowa
300	Beacon, E 5	Mich.
12572	Beacon, D 5	N. Y.
76*	Beacon, O 7	Tenn.
20*	Beacon Beach, N 9	Fla.
1300	Beacon Falls, K 9	Conn.
200*	Beacon Hill, D 2	Mich.
....	Beacon Park, N 3	Mass.
148*	Beaconsfield, P 9	Iowa
350*	Beadling, L 3	Pa.
90	Beagle, I 24	Kan.
2*	Beagle, P 7	Ore.
69	Bealeton, H 15	Va.
70*	Beallsville, G 9	Md.
450	Beallsville, K 19	Ohio
604*	Beallsville, O 3	Pa.
159*	Beals, G 9	Ky.
108	Beals, M 21	Me.
167	Beaman, H 15	Iowa
100*	Beaman, I 10	Mo.
62	Bean Blossom (Georgetown), L 13	Ind.
450	Bean Hill, I 21	Conn.
75*	Beans Creek, Q 12	Tenn.
500*	Bean Station (Tate), M 20	Tenn.
45*	Bear, D 21	Del.
47*	Bear, K 4	Idaho
....	Bear, K 17	Okla.
60*	Bear Branch, M 21	Ind.
12*	Bear Branch I 21	Ky.
....*	Bear Butte, H 5	S. D.
243	Bear Creek, C 8	Ala.
100*	Bear Creek, D 11	Ark.
58*	Bearcreek, M 8	Mo.
324	Bearcreek, N 14	Mont.
50	Bear Creek, F 11	N. C.
1	Bear Creek, I 5	Ore.
100*	Bear Creek, I 20	Pa.
409	Bear Creek, M 14	Wis.
4*	Bear Creek, I 19	Wyo.
....	Bear Creek Jc., M 4	Ark.
....	Bear Creek Jc., F 15	Md.
105*	Beard, L 14	W. Va.
961	Bearden, O 11	Ark.
150	Bearden, J 17	Okla.
2000	Bearden, N 19	Tenn.
700*	Beards Fork, M 8	W. Va.
....	Beardsley, J 11	Ariz.
64*	Beardsley, D 4	Kan.
537	Beardsley, L 2	Minn.
30	Beardsley, N 20	S. D.
6505	Beardstown, I 8	Ill.
50	Beardstown, O 8	Tenn.
12*	Beardwell, G 13	Neb.
124*	Bear Gap, J 16	Pa.
2*	Bear Island, L 15	N. H.
327	Bear Lake, K 11	Mich.
214*	Bear Lake, E 5	Pa.
50	Bearmouth, I 6	Mont.
100	Bearpaw, E 14	Mont.
200*	Bear Poplar, F 7	N. C.
265*	Bear River, C 8	Colo.
34*	Bear River, F 19	Minn.
429	Bear River City, C 10	Utah
350	Bear Spring, L 8	Tenn.
150*	Bearsville, R 21	N. Y.
100*	Bear Valley, I 11	Calif.
....	Bear Valley, K 17	Pa.
20*	Bear Wallow, B 7	Va.
305	Bear Wallow (Worth), Q 7	W. Va.
217*	Beasley, L 22	Tex.
252	Beason, H 14	Ill.
40*	Beaton, L 8	Ark.
....	Beaton, C 24	Mich.
410	Beatrice, M 10	Ala.
100*	Beatrice, D 2	Calif.
10883	Beatrice, N 22	Neb.
110*	Beatrice, F 9	W. Va.
389	Beattie, D 19	Kan.
200	Beatty, N 14	Nev.
81	Beatty, Q 11	Ore.
75*	Beatty, M 5	Pa.
1012	Beattyville, H 19	Ky.
42*	Beaty, A 3	Ark.
94*	Beaucoup, N 13	Ill.
12*	Beauchamp, I 4	Ark.
32*	Beaudry, J 10	Ark.
200*	Beaufort, J 17	Mo.
3272	Beaufort, J 21	N. C.
3185	Beaufort, P 15	S. C.
150*	Beaukiss, I 18	Tex.
378	Beaulieu, G 6	Minn.
39	Beaulieu, D 20	N. D.
2208	Beaumont, O 19, R 10	Calif.
150	Beaumont, M 19	Kan.
42*	Beaumont, J 14	Ky.
500	Beaumont, O 19	Miss.
59061	Beaumont, K 25	Tex.
....*	Beaumont, M 15	Va.
....	Beaupland, I 21	Pa.
223*	Beauregard, L 10	Miss.
446	Beauty (Himlerville), G 23	Ky.
20	Beaver, A 7	Ark.
126*	Beaver, J 10	Iowa
76	Beaver, I 12	Kan.
54*	Beaver, H 22	Ky.
10*	Beaver, J 9	La.
305	Beaver, P 12	Ohio
1166	Beaver, Q 8	Okla.
200	Beaver, E 4	Ore.
5641	Beaver, L 2	Pa.
1808	Beaver, N 7	Utah
50	Beaver, F 2	Wash.
1200*	Beaver (Glen Hedrick), O 8	W. Va.
150*	Beaver, O 10	Wis.
381▲*	Beaver Bay, G 23	Minn.
25*	Beaver Brook, I 20	Pa.
50*	Beaver Brook, D 8	Wis.
1015	Beaver City, O 13	Neb.
74*	Beavercreek, L 13	Ill.
254	Beaver Creek, R 3	Minn.
100	Beavercreek, E 8	Ore.
550	Beaver Crossing, M 20	Neb.
1643	Beaverdale, N 9	Pa.
1166	Beaver Dam, H 11	Ky.
377	Beaverdam, G 8	Ohio
300	Beaver Dam, K 16	Va.
10356	Beaver Dam, M 18	Wis.
....	Beaver Dam Jc., M 18	Wis.
250	Beaver Dams, P 11	N. Y.
600	Beaver Falls, H 17	N. Y.
17098	Beaver Falls, K 2	Pa.
....	Beaver Jc., H 22	Ky.
81*	Beaver Kill, R 20	N. Y.
27	Beaver Lake, B 15	N. J.
30*	Beaverlett, M 21	Va.
40*	Beaverlick, C 17	Ky.
32*	Beaver Meadow, O 16	N. Y.
2030	Beaver Meadows, J 20	Pa.
52*	Beaver River, J 19	N. Y.
600	Beaver Springs, L 15	Pa.
231*	Beaverton, E 5	Ala.
641	Beaverton, L 18	Mich.
38	Beaverton, D 18	Mont.
1052	Beaverton, D 7	Ore.
664	Beavertown, L 15	Pa.
425	Beaverville, F 21	Ill.
12*	Beazley, K 19	Va.
35*	Bebe, L 18	Tex.
8*	Bebee, C 11	W. Va.
500*	Beccaria, J 9	Pa.
587	Bechtelsville, N 21	Pa.
8*	Becida, H 9	Minn.
65	Beck (Tiernan), J 4	Ore.
900	Beckemeyer, M 13	Ill.
239	Becker, M 13	Minn.
150*	Becker, E 21	Miss.
25*	Becker (St. Albans), J 17	Mo.
267*	Beckersville, M 20	Pa.
200	Becket, F 4	Mass.
10	Becket, H 15	Mont.
....	Beckett, O 10	Okla.
....	Beckford Jc., C 21	N. C.
21*	Beckham, N 11	Va.
12852	Beckley, O 8	W. Va.
453	Beckville, F 24	Tex.

Pop. Place Index State
29*Beckwith, M 8 .... W. Va.
100*Beckwourth, E 10 .... Calif.
30*Beddington, K 18 .... Me.
5*Bedell, P 19 .... N. Y.
50*Bedford, J 6 .... Ill.
12514 Bedford, N 12 .... Ind.
2151 Bedford, P 8 .... Iowa
387 Bedford, D 15 .... Ky.
1800 Bedford, D 18 .... Mass.
250 Bedford, Q 15 .... Mich.
217 Bedford, D 10 .... Mo.
1500 Bedford, P 14 .... N. H.
1000*Bedford, F 6 .... N. Y.
23 Bedford, L 22 .... N. D.
7390 Bedford, D 17 .... Ohio
3268 Bedford, P 9 .... Pa.
3973 Bedford, N 8 .... Va.
265 Bedford, J 2 .... Wyo.
2000 Bedford Hills, F 6 .... N. Y.
165*Bedford Springs, O 10 .... Va.
100*Bedford Valley, O 9 .... Pa.
750 Bedias, I 21 .... Tex.
89*Bedington, D 24 .... W. Va.
68 Bedison, B 5 .... Mo.
500*Bedminister, G 14 .... N. J.
200*Bedminster, N 23 .... Pa.
100 Bedrock, L 2 .... Colo.
....*Bee, I 13 .... Ky.
205 Bee, L 20 .... Neb.
60 Bee, P 16 .... Okla.
61*Bee, C 6 .... Va.
1189 Beebe, H 14 .... Ark.
7 Beebe, K 22 .... Mont.
14 Beebe, D 16 .... S. D.
200 Beebe, G 16 .... Wash.
197*Beebe Plain, C 16 .... Vt.
250*Beebe River, K 13 .... N. H.
151*Bee Branch, F 12 .... Ark.
133 Beech, M 13 .... Iowa
100*Beech, H 21 .... Ky.
43 Beech, I 8 .... W. Va.
58*Beech Bluff, O 5 .... Tenn.
1200 Beechbottom (Beech Bottom), P 24 .... W. Va.
900 Beech Creek, I 10 .... Ky.
100*Beech Creek, D 2 .... N. C.
42 Beech Creek, H 18 .... Ore.
592*Beech Creek, H 13 .... Pa.
.... Beech Creek Jc., I 10 .... Ky.
742 Beecher, D 21 .... Ill.
506 Beecher City, K 16 .... Ill.
200 Beecher Falls A 23 .... Vt.
3*Beecher Island, E 23 .... Colo.
250*Beech Fork (Shea), L 18 .... Tenn.
125*Beech Grove, B 19 .... Ark.
3907 Beech Grove, J 14 .... Ind.
167 Beech Grove, H 9 .... Ky.
169*Beech Grove, P 13 .... Tenn.
10*Beech Grove, I 25 .... Tex.
25*Beech Hill, H 4 .... W. Va.
113*Beechtree, I 7 .... Pa.
....*Beechville, I 14 .... Ky.
32*Beechwood, P 12 .... Ind.
32*Beechwood, D 17 .... Ky.
510 Beechwood, G 21, R 9 .... Mass.
200*Beechwood, F 3 .... Mich.
500*Beechwood, L 9 .... N. Y.
650 Beechwood, C 14 .... W. Va.
.... Beechwood Sta., G 22, Q 10 .... Mass.
79*Beedeville, F 17 .... Ark.
11*Beefhide, J 22 .... Ky.
2*Beehive, M 13 .... Mont.
46*Bee House, H 17 .... Tex.
5 Beehunter, M 8 .... Ind.
50*Beelake, G 12 .... Miss.
89*Beeler, I 8 .... Kan.
125*Beelick Knob, N 9 .... W. Va.
330 Beelog, M 8 .... N. C.
585 Beemer, H 21 .... Neb.
100 Beemerville, A 13 .... N. J.
.... Beenham, D 22 .... N. M.
300*Bee Ridge, K 13 .... Fla.
75*Beerock, K 18 .... Ky.
30*Beersheba Springs, P 13 .... Tenn.
157*Beerston, Q 19 .... N. Y.
250 Beesleys Point, P 14 .... N. J.
.... Beeson, J 21 .... Ind.
25*Beeson, Q 9 .... W. Va.
100*Bee Springs, I 12 .... Ky.
23*Beetle, E 21 .... Ky.
150 Beetown, F 21 .... Wis.
6789 Beeville, O 18 .... Tex.
1823 Beggs, G 18 .... Okla.
12 Beidler, I 17 .... Ohio
200 Beirne (Bierne), N 9 .... Ark.
....*Beixedon, H 8 .... N. Y.
200 Bejou, F 5 .... Minn.
53*Bel, K 8 .... La.
1885 Bel Air, D 16 .... Md.
250*Bel Alton (Cox), M 11 .... Md.
45 Beland, H 20 .... Okla.
200*Belcamp, C 16 .... Md.
40 Belcher, M 22 .... Ala.
500*Belcher, H 24 .... Ky.
500 Belcher, B 4 .... La.
1000 Belchertown, G 9 .... Mass.
94*Belcherville, C 17 .... Tex.
200 Belcourt, D 15 .... N. D.
145*Belcross, C 23 .... N. C.
110*Belden, E 9 .... Calif.
17*Belden, J 18 .... Minn.
90 Belden, C 19 .... Miss.
235 Belden, F 20 .... Neb.
26 Belden, G 7 .... N. D.
66*Beldenville, B 13 .... Wis.
4089 Belding, O 15 .... Mich.
50*Beldoc (Baldock), M 11 .... S. C.
45*Beldor, H 11 .... Va.
159*Belden, C 10 .... Miss.
3038 Belen, H 10 .... N. M.
100*Belew Creek, D 8 .... N. C.
250*Belfair, I 5 .... Wash.
30*Belfast, K 12 .... Ark.
4 Belfast, B 10 .... Ind.
5540 Belfast, M 13 .... Me.
32 Belfast, I 16 .... Neb.
600 Belfast, P 7 .... N. Y.
140*Belfast, O 9 .... Ohio
356 Belfast, K 23 .... Pa.
150*Belfast, P 11 .... Tenn.
870 Belfield, M 4 .... N. D.
....*Belfield, Q 16 .... Va.
900 Belford, G 20 .... N. J.
8 Belford, D 15 .... Okla.
410*Belfry (Ep), H 23 .... Ky.
250 Belfry, N 15 .... Mont.
78*Belgique, M 22 .... Mo.
356*Belgium, O 19 .... Wis.
80 Belgrade, M 9 .... Me.
553 Belgrade, L 9 .... Minn.
1022▲Belgrade, M 18 .... Mo.
618 Belgrade, L 10 .... Mont.
406 Belgrade, J 18 .... Neb.
.... Belgrade Jc., L 10 .... Mont.
304 Belgrade Lakes, M 8 .... Me.
175 Belgreen, C 7 .... Ala.
86*Belgrove, H 5 .... W. Va.
2360 Belhaven, G 21 .... N. C.
62*Belinda, L 24 .... Va.
1517 Belington, G 14 .... W. Va.
125*Belk, E 7 .... Ala.
280 Belknap, Q 16 .... Ill.
102 Belknap, P 17 .... Iowa
44*Belknap, G 20 .... Ky.

Pop. Place Index State
113 Belknap, F 1 .... Mont.
11 Belknap Springs, I 9 .... Ore.
11264 Bell, Q 4 .... Calif.
183*Bell, D 11 .... Fla.
100 Bell, O 7 .... Pa.
89 Bellair, K 20 .... Ill.
100*Bellaire, D 11 .... Kan.
652 Bellaire, J 15 .... Mich.
13799 Bellaire, K 20 .... Ohio
1124 Bellaire, K 22 .... Tex.
317 Bellamy, J 5 .... Ala.
175*Bellamy, M 20 .... Va.
181*Bellarthur (Arthur), G 18 .... N. C.
13 Bella Vista, D 6 .... Calif.
410 Bellbrook, L 8 .... Ohio
355 Bell Buckle, O 12 .... Tenn.
75*Bellburn, M 12 .... W. Va.
264 Bell Center, G 19 .... Wis.
310 Bell City, N 7 .... La.
300 Bell City, P 22 .... Mo.
621 Belle, K 15 .... Mo.
5000*Belle, L 6 .... W. Va.
218*Belleair, I 12 .... Fla.
831 Belle Alliance, N 15 .... La.
835 Belle Center, H 9 .... Ohio
165 Belle Chester, P 19 .... Minn.
500*Belle Ellen, H 11 .... Ala.
425 Belle Flower (Bellflower) H 17 .... Ill.
100*Bellefont, M 8 .... Kan.
144*Bellefontaine, F 17 .... Miss.
9808 Bellefontaine, I 9 .... Ohio
250 Bellefonte, B 9 .... Ark.
2593 Bellefonte, A 22 .... Del.
5304 Bellefonte, J 13 .... Pa.
2496 Belle Fourche, H 2 .... S. D.
3806*Belle Glade, L 21 .... Fla.
900 BelleGlade-Chosen (Chosen), L 21 .... Fla.
200 Bellegrove, M 18 .... Pa.
....*Belle Harbor, C 4 .... Mich.
500 Belle Haven, M 23 .... Va.
51*Bellemead, G 14 .... N. J.
2061*Belle Meade, M 11 .... Tenn.
300*Belle Meade, G 15 .... Va.
140*Belle Mina, B 13 .... Ala.
35 Bellemont, G 14 .... Ariz.
30 Bellemont, I 15 .... Okla.
3202 Belle Plaine, J 17 .... Iowa
878 Belle Plaine, N 16 .... Kan.
1407 Belleplaine, O 14 .... Minn.
58*Belle Plaine, M 12 .... Wis.
25*Belle Point, G 20 .... Ky.
36*Bellepoint, P 10 .... W. Va.
67 Belle Prairie, N 17 .... Ill.
333 Belle Rive, N 16 .... Ill.
700 Bellerose, N 15 .... La.
1317*Bellerose, H 7 .... N. Y.
617 Belle Valley, L 17 .... Ohio
2463 Belle Vernon, O 4 .... Pa.
852*Bellevernon (Speers), O 4 .... Pa.
433 Belleview, F 15 .... Fla.
75*Belleview, K 7 .... Ill.
130*Belleview (Grant), C 17 .... Ky.
143*Belleview, M 18 .... Mo.
150*Belleview (Bellevue), M 11 .... Tenn.
175 Belleville, N 11 .... Ala.
411 Belleville, H 8 .... Ark.
28405 Belleville, M 11 .... Ill.
120 Belleville, J 12 .... Ind.
2580 Belleville, D 15 .... Kan.
1286 Belleville, Q 21 .... Mich.
28167 Belleville, E 19 .... N. J.
303 Belleville, I 15 .... N. Y.
1199*Belleville (Bellville), H 13 .... Ohio
21 Belleville, Q 12 .... Okla.
1156 Belleville, L 13 .... Pa.
.... Belleville, P 21 .... Va.
100 Belleville, F 5 .... W. Va.
594 Belleville, J 21 .... Wis.
.... Belleville Jc., P 21 .... Va.
319 Bellevue (Bellevue.), C 14 .... Colo.
100 Bellevue, A 22 .... Del.
502 Bellevue, N 12 .... Idaho
1771 Bellevue, H 24 .... Iowa
8741 Bellevue, B 17 .... Ky.
200*Bellevue, J 18 .... Md.
1011 Bellevue, P 16 .... Mich.
1184 Bellevue, K 24 .... Neb.
200 Bellevue, M 5 .... N. Y.
6127 Bellevue, E 13 .... Ohio
25 Bellevue, E 6 .... Ore.
10488 Bellevue, M 3 .... Pa.
150*Bellevue (Belleview), M 11 .... Tenn.
503 Bellevue, C 17 .... Tex.
100*Bellevue, N 8 .... Va.
800 Bellevue, H 8 .... Wash.
5220*Bellewood (Bellwood), C 21 .... Ill.
15 Bell Farm, K 17 .... Ky.
.... Bellfield, N 1 .... Pa.
10000 Bellflower, R 4 .... Calif.
425 Bellflower (Bell Flower), H 17 .... Ill.
218 Bellflower (Liege-Bellflower) H 16 .... Mo.
80 Bellfountain, H 5 .... Ore.
800 Bellingham (Midland), I 16 .... Mass.
456 Bellingham, M 4 .... Minn.
29314 Bellingham, C 7 .... Wash.
....*Belljellico, see Tinsley .... Ky.
1250 Bellmawr, L 9 .... N. J.
408 Bellmont, N 20 .... Ill.
320 Bellmore, J 8 .... Ind.
8200*Bellmore, H 7 .... N. Y.
174*Bellona, N 11 .... N. Y.
50*Bellona (Gage), N 11 .... N. Y.
89 Bellota, H 9 .... Calif.
4236 Bellows Falls, O 13 .... Vt.
650 Bellport, H 9 .... N. Y.
42 Bell Ranch, F 21 .... N. M.
210 Bellrun (Bells Landing), J 9 .... Pa.
1054 Bells, O 4 .... Tenn.
454 Bells, C 20 .... Tex.
15*Bells Cross Roads, K 14 .... Va.
210 Bells Landing (Bell Run), J 9 .... Pa.
263*Bellton, D 11 .... Ga.
319 Bellton (Denver), B 11, ... W. Va.
13 Belltower, L 25 .... Mont.
164*Belltown, P 18 .... Tenn.
250*Bellvale, E 3 .... N. Y.
400 Bellview, H 25 .... N. M.
300 Bellville (Belleville), K 20, ... Ga.
1199 Bellville (Belleville), H 13 .... Ohio
1347 Bellville, K 20 .... Tex.
319*Bellvue (Bellevue), C 14 .... Colo.
285*Bellwood, O 18 .... Ala.
5250*Bellwood (Bellewood), C 21 .... Ill.
61*Bellwood, G 7 .... La.
434 Bellwood, J 20 .... Neb.
2772 Bellwood, L 10 .... Pa.
75 Bellwood, N 17 .... Va.
300 Bellwood, N 10 .... W. Va.
65 Belmar, K 7 .... Neb.

Pop. Place Index State
3435 Belmar, I 20 .... N. J.
150 Belmar, H 4 .... Pa.
2109 Belmond, E 12 .... Iowa
1229 Belmont, F 18, I 5 .... Calif.
103 Belmont, D 10 .... Ga.
25*Belmont, E 5 .... Idaho
125*Belmont, M 13 .... Kan.
115*Belmont, F 14 .... Ky.
100*Belmont, F 5 .... La.
40 Belmont, M 12 .... Me.
26867■Belmont, E 18, M 2 .... Mass.
350*Belmont, O 13 .... Mich.
594 Belmont, B 23 .... Miss.
35 Belmont, K 15 .... Mont.
50 Belmont, F 3 .... Neb.
28 Belmont, I 13 .... Nev.
450 Belmont, M 14 .... N. H.
1146 Belmont, Q 7 .... N. Y.
4356 Belmont, H 5 .... N. C.
15 Belmont, J 24 .... N. D.
697 Belmont, J 19 .... Ohio
119*Belmont, L 18 .... Tex.
200 Belmont, M 10 .... Vt.
133*Belmont, J 16 .... Va.
145 Belmont, J 24 .... Wash.
500 Belmont, E 8 .... W. Va.
476 Belmont, H 21 .... Wis.
.... Belmont Avenue, J 12 .... Calif.
317 Belmont Center, C 22 .... N. Y.
238 Belmore, E 8 .... Ohio
.... Belmore, K 6 .... Wash.
95*Belo, O 3 .... W. Va.
75*Beloit, K 10 .... Ala.
100*Beloit, C 1 .... Iowa
3765 Beloit, F 14 .... Kan.
706 Beloit, F 19 .... Ohio
25365 Beloit, L 22 .... Wis.
.... Beloit Jc., L 22 .... Wis.
100*Belona, M 14 .... Va.
300 Belpre, L 10 .... Kan.
1717 Belpre, N 17 .... Ohio
219 Belsano, M 8 .... Pa.
50 Belsay, O 21 .... Mich.
100 Belsena, K 10 .... Pa.
500 Belspring, O 4 .... Va.
744 Belt, G 11 .... Mont.
.... Belt Jc., F 7 .... Ga.
.... Belt Jc., J 14 .... Ind.
.... Belt Jc., D 16 .... Ohio
75*Belton, M 6 .... Ark.
36*Belton (Yost), I 10 .... Ky.
971 Belton, H 6 .... Mo.
180 Belton, D 5 .... Mont.
2119 Belton, D 6 .... S. C.
3572 Belton, I 18 .... Tex.
55 Beltona, E 12 .... Ala.
213 Beltrami, F 3 .... Minn.
63*Beltsville, J 12 .... Md.
10 Belva, D 6 .... Okla.
125*Belva, L 10 .... W. Va.
37192■Belvedere, Q 4 .... Calif.
457*Belvedere, H 5, D 16 .... Calif.
3 Belvidere, L 6 .... Idaho
8094 Belvidere, A 16 .... Ill.
80 Belvidere, M 10 .... Kan.
325 Belvidere, N 19 .... Neb.
2060 Belvidere, D 9 .... N. J.
65 Belvidere, Q 7 .... N. Y.
101*Belvidere, D 21 .... N. C.
187 Belvidere, K 10 .... S. D.
60*Belvidere, Q 12 .... Tenn.
109 Belvidere Center, C 11 .... Vt.
65*Belvidere Corners, C 12 .... Vt.
409 Belview, O 7 .... Minn.
30*Belvoir, G 15 .... Va.
226 Belvue, F 20 .... Kan.
250*Belwood, G 3 .... N. C.
3789 Belzoni, G 9 .... Miss.
30*Belzoni, N 21 .... Okla.
1466 Bement, I 17 .... Ill.
9427 Bemidji, F 9 .... Minn.
15 Bemis, K 3 .... Me.
25 Bemis, G 24 .... S. D.
2700 Bemis, O 5 .... Tenn.
210*Bemis, H 15 .... W. Va.
290*Bemus Point, Q 2 .... N. Y.
24*Ben, E 14 .... Ark.
319*Bena, H 11 .... Minn.
200*Bena, N 21 .... Va.
308 Benarnold, I 19 .... Tex.
3081 Benavides, Q 16 .... Tex.
2516 Ben Avon, M 3 .... Pa.
200*Ben Bolt, P 17 .... Tex.
31*Benbow, C 2 .... Calif.
75*Benbrook, E 18 .... Tex.
350 Benbush, F 16 .... W. Va.
175 Bench, Q 21 .... Idaho
30 Benchland, H 13 .... Mont.
49*Benchley, I 20 .... Tex.
10021 Bend, J 11 .... Ore.
3*Bend, J 4 .... S. D.
105*Bend, I 16 .... Tex.
113 Ben Davis, J 13 .... Ind.
29*Bendavis, O 14 .... Mo.
84*Bendena, D 23 .... Kan.
425 Bendersville, P 15 .... Pa.
414*Bendersville (Aspers), P 15 .... Pa.
90*Bendon, J 12 .... Mich.
.... Bendon, M 17 .... S. D.
213 Benedict, M 21 .... Kan.
111*Benedict, M 14 .... Md.
20*Benedict, H 9 .... Minn.
221 Benedict, L 19 .... Neb.
167 Benedict, I 11 .... N. D.
300 Benedicta, G 17 .... Me.
190 Benevolence, L 5 .... Ga.
120*Benewah, E 4 .... Idaho
150*Benezett (Bennezett), H 10 .... Pa.
119*Benfer, K 15 .... Pa.
264 Benford, H 23 .... Tex.
321 Ben Franklin, C 21 .... Tex.
20*Beng, C 4 .... N. C.
10*Bengal, H 15 .... Ky.
78 Bengal, L 23 .... Okla.
90*Benge, I 19 .... Ky.
50 Benge, K 21 .... Wash.
161*Benhaden (Hilliardville), C 5 .... Fla.
3200 Benham, J 22 .... Ky.
50*Benham, C 5 .... N. C.
250*Benhams, E 7 .... Va.
101*Ben Hill, F 6 .... Ga.
20*Ben Hur, D 9 .... Ark.
75*Ben Hur, I 11 .... Calif.
217 Benhur, H 19 .... Tex.
62*Ben Hur, E 3 .... Va.
2419 Benicia, H 6, A 20 .... Calif.
.... Benicia Jc., A 20 .... Calif.
120*Benito, J 21 .... Ky.
599 Benjamin, C 13 .... Tex.
350 Benjamin, H 12 .... Utah
1448 Benkelman, O 8 .... Neb.
2444 Benld, L 11 .... Ill.
20*Benleo, I 11 .... Ky.
406 Ben Lomond, N 5 .... Ark.
600 Ben Lomond, J 5 .... Calif.
78*Benndale, P 20 .... Miss.
412 Bennet, M 22 .... Neb.
199 Bennett, F 16 .... Colo.
....*Bennett, N 9 .... Fla.
352 Bennett, K 22 .... Iowa
30*Bennett, D 22 .... Ky.
.... Bennett, F 18 .... Me.
14*Bennett, Q 18 .... Mo.
225*Bennett, M 24 .... N. M.
229 Bennett, G 10 .... N. C.
100*Bennett, L 18 .... Tenn.

Pop. Place Index State
118 Bennett, C 5 .... Wis.
260*Bennetts, E 16 .... Tex.
117*Bennettsburg, P 12 .... N. Y.
172*Bennetts Point, M 14 .... S. C.
27*Bennett Springs (Brice), M 11 .... Mo.
4895 Bennettsville, C 20 .... S. C.
150 Bennezette (Benezett), H 10 .... Pa.
250 Bennington, Q 22 .... Idaho
62*Bennington, N 20 .... Ind.
369 Bennington, G 16 .... Kan.
150 Bennington, O 18 .... Mich.
326 Bennington, J 23 .... Neb.
552 Bennington, P 10 .... N. H.
150 Bennington, N 6 .... N. Y.
513 Bennington, Q 18 .... Okla.
7268 Bennington, Q 6 .... Vt.
23*Benns Church, P 20 .... Va.
406 Benoit, F 6 .... Miss.
14*Benoit, G 13 .... Tex.
350*Benoit, F 6 .... Wis.
14*Benrud, D 22 .... Mont.
1869 Bensenville, B 20 .... Ill.
962 Benson, O 20 .... Ariz.
.... Benson, see Howard .... Fla.
358 Benson, F 14 .... Ill.
300 Benson, F 5 .... La.
30*Benson, C 15 .... Md.
2729 Benson, M 6 .... Minn.
1837 Benson, H 14 .... N. C.
408*Benson (Hollsopple), N 7 .... Pa.
600 Benson, K 5 .... Vt.
10*Benson, (Randall), A 9 .... Wis.
.... Benson Jc., O 20 .... Ariz.
.... Benson Jc., F 18 .... Fla.
250 Benson Mines, G 19 .... N. Y.
250 Benson Springs, F 18 .... Fla.
66*Bens Run, C 9 .... W. Va.
163*Ben Stockton (Stockton), M 16 .... Tenn.
200 Bent, L 14 .... N. M.
113*Bent Creek, M 11 .... Va.
17*Bentley, F 3 .... Calif.
89*Bentley, H 6 .... Ill.
98*Bentley, L 5 .... Iowa
205*Bentley, L 16 .... Kan.
75 Bentley, G 9 .... La.
150 Bentley, L 19 .... Mich.
....*Bentley, E 4 .... N. C.
110 Bentley, P 7 .... N. D.
32 Bentley, P 18 .... Okla.
140*Bentley Springs, C 13 .... Md.
3428 Bentleyville, O 3 .... Pa.
32*Bent Mountain, N 6 .... Va.
350 Benton, K 13 .... Ala.
3502 Benton, J 11 .... Ark.
100 Benton, I 14 .... Calif.
7372 Benton, O 16 .... Ill.
140*Benton, B 16 .... Ind.
189 Benton, P 9 .... Iowa
235 Benton, L 17 .... Kan.
1906 Benton, J 6 .... Ky.
519 Benton, B 5 .... La.
100*Benton, L 10 .... Me.
200 Benton, I 11 .... Miss.
408 Benton, P 23 .... Mo.
180 Benton, H 16 .... Ohio
786 Benton, I 18 .... Pa.
550 Benton, Q 17 .... Tenn.
835 Benton, H 22 .... Wis.
136*Benton City, G 15 .... Mo.
150 Benton City (Benton), N 17 .... Wash.
.... Benton Falls, L 10 .... Me.
16668 Benton Harbor, Q 10 .... Mich.
768*Benton Heights, J 7 .... N. C.
440 Bentonia, J 10 .... Miss.
304 Benton Ridge, F 9 .... Ohio
150*Bentonsport, P 19 .... Iowa
100*Benton Station, M 10 .... Me.
2359 Bentonville, A 5 .... Ark.
150 Bentonville, J 20 .... Ind.
25*Bentonville, K 9 .... Mo.
250 Bentonville, Q 10 .... Ohio
400 Bentonville, G 13 .... Va.
.... Bentonville Branch Jc. A 5 .... Ark.
109*Bentree, L 10 .... W. Va.
400*Ben Wheeler, E 21 .... Tex.
3608 Benwood, Q 24 .... W. Va.
47*Benz (Zero), I 22 .... Mont.
2*Benzien, G 18 .... Mont.
340 Benzonia, K 11 .... Mich.
200 Beowawe, D 15 .... Nev.
75*Bercail, J 14 .... Mont.
300 Berclair, O 18 .... Tex.
2176 Berea, H 18 .... Ky.
75 Berea, G 4 .... Neb.
4 Berea, M 20 .... N. D.
.... Berea, D 16, Q 21 .... Ohio
6025 Berea, Q 21 .... Ohio
22*Berea, I 16 .... Va.
55*Berea, G 9 .... W. Va.
.... Berea Br. Jc., Q 21 .... Ohio
25 Berenda, J 10 .... Calif.
100 Berenice, N 17 .... Idaho
100*Beresford, F 18 .... Fla.
1642 Beresford, N 24 .... S. D.
35*Berg, I 5 .... N. D.
658 Bergen, L 8 .... N. Y.
67 Bergen, H 12 .... N. D.
10275 Bergenfield, D 21 .... N. J.
175 Bergens, E 11 .... Ala.
15 Berger, Q 11 .... Idaho
213 Berger, I 17 .... Mo.
82*Bergey, N 22 .... Pa.
25*Bergheim, L 16 .... Tex.
1122 Bergholz, H 19 .... Ohio
600 Bergland B 23 .... Mich.
160*Bergman, B 10 .... Ark.
200*Bergoo, K 12 .... W. Va.
40*Bergton, G 11 .... Va.
25*Bering, I 23 .... Tex.
300 Berino, O 11 .... N. M.
85547 Berkeley, D 18, I 6 .... Calif.
284 Berkeley (Carlton), E 14 .... Ga.
216*Berkeley (Burkley), J 4 .... Ky.
2577*Berkeley (Kinlock Park), H 20 .... Mo.
1145 Berkeley Springs, C 23 .... W. Va.
248 Berkey, C 9 .... Ohio
350 Berkely, K 19 .... Mass.
6406 Berkley, P 22 .... Mich.
1000 Berkley Heights, F 16 .... N. J.
365 Berkshire, D 3 .... Mass.
264 Berkshire, P 14 .... N. Y.
200 Berkshire, A 11 .... Vt.
400*Berkshire Heights, M 20 .... Pa.
.... Berkshire Jc., K 4 .... Conn.
80*Berlamont, Q 12 .... Mich.
80*Berlin, K 10 .... Ala.
5230▲Berlin, H 12 .... Conn.
.... Berlin, H 13 .... Conn.
322 Berlin, O 11 .... Ga.
215 Berlin, J 11 .... Ill.
1435 Berlin, O 24 .... Md.
450 Berlin, F 15 .... Mass.
19084 Berlin, F 17 .... N. H.
1753 Berlin, L 11 .... N. J.
1200 Berlin, N 25 .... N. Y.
132 Berlin, P 19 .... N. D.
150 Berlin, H 16 .... Ohio
50 Berlin, I 3 .... Okla.
200 Berlin, H 7 .... Ore.
1602 Berlin, P 7 .... Pa.
350 Berlin, G 12 .... Vt.

Pop. Place Index State
4247 Berlin, L 16 .... Wis.
150*Berlin Center, F 20 .... Ohio
552*Berlin Heights, D 13 .... Ohio
113 Berlinsville, K 22 .... Pa.
200 Bermuda, M 11 .... Ala.
10*Bermuda, G 8 .... La.
157*Bermuda Hundred, N 16 .... Va.
45*Bermudian, P 16 .... Pa.
5*Bern, Q 22 .... Idaho
236 Bern, C 21 .... Kan.
2100 Bernalillo, G 11 .... N. M.
111*Bernard, G 22 .... Iowa
225*Bernard, N 16 .... Me.
400 Bernardston, C 8 .... Mass.
3405 Bernardsville, E 14 .... N. J.
2075 Berne, F 22 .... Ind.
260 Berne, O 22 .... N. Y.
152*Berne (Carlisle), L 17 .... Ohio
97*Berne, M 20 .... Pa.
.... Berne, G 12 .... Wash.
44*Berner, H 9 .... Ga.
200*Bernhards Bay (Bernhards), K 16 .... N. Y.
900*Bernharts, M 20 .... Pa.
27*Bernheimer, I 17 .... Mo.
24*Bernice, I 20 .... Ky.
1071 Bernice, B 9 .... La.
205 Bernice, C 23 .... Okla.
618 Bernice, G 18 .... Pa.
.... Bernice Jc., G 18 .... Pa.
1160 Bernie, H 24, Q 22 .... Mo.
33*Bernie, L 4 .... W. Va.
425 Bernstadt, I 18 .... Ky.
339 Bernville, M 20 .... Pa.
125*Beroun, J 18 .... Minn
11*Berrian, N 17 .... Wash.
241 Berrien Center, R 10 .... Mich.
1510 Berrien Springs, R 10 .... Mich.
300 Berros, M 10 .... Calif.
639 Berry, F 8 .... Ala.
363 Berry, D 18 .... Ky.
40 Berry, N 11 .... Mich.
.... Berry, M 8 .... N. M.
150 Berryburg, F 14 .... W. Va.
20 Berryburg Jc. (Close), F 14 .... W. Va.
100*Berry Creek, F 7 .... Calif.
60*Berrydale, H 9 .... Wash.
40*Berryman, L 17 .... Mo.
117 Berry Mills, L 5 .... Me.
426 Berrysburg, L 17 .... Pa.
15*Berrys Lick, I 11 .... Ky.
650 Berryton, D 1 .... Ga.
85*Berryton, H 22 .... Kan.
1482 Berryville, A 7 .... Ark.
1262 Berryville, E 14 .... Va.
5*Bert, I 19 .... Ky.
578 Bertha, J 9 .... Minn.
85*Bertha, Q 13 .... Mo.
10 Bertha, H 23 .... Neb.
26*Bertha, D 23 .... N. C.
62*Bertha, O 2 .... Pa.
27*Berthaville, I 18 .... Va.
428 Berthold, G 8 .... N. D.
811 Berthoud, D 14 .... Colo.
18*Bertis, F 20 .... Ky.
10 Berton, J 22 .... S. D.
108*Berton, N 4 .... Va.
700 Bertram, I 17 .... Tex.
377 Bertrand, P 23 .... Mo.
615 Bertrand, N 13 .... Neb.
56*Bertrand, L 21 .... Va.
313 Bertrandville, O 19 .... La.
150*Berville, O 25 .... Mich.
137 Berwick, F 8 .... Ill.
150*Berwick, K 12 .... Iowa
1906 Berwick, O 14 .... La.
1200 Berwick, R 2 .... Me.
92 Berwick, F 13 .... N. D.
70 Berwick, F 11 .... Ohio
13181 Berwick, J 19 .... Pa.
150 Berwind, P 16 .... Colo.
.... Berwind, N 14 .... Mont.
2900 Berwind, R 5 .... W. Va.
65*Berwindsdale, J 9 .... Pa.
48451 Berwyn, C 21 .... Ill.
1500 Berwyn, I 12 .... Md.
170 Berwyn, J 14 .... Neb.
227 Berwyn, O 14 .... Okla.
2500 Berwyn, P 22 .... Pa.
95 Beryl, O 2 .... Utah
18*Beryl, D 19 .... W. Va.
300*Besoco, O 8 .... W. Va.
.... Bess, L 6 .... Va.
22826 Bessemer, G 12 .... Ala.
4080 Bessemer, B 21 .... Mich.
....*Bessemer, D 9 .... N. C.
3567 Bessemer City, H 4 .... N. C.
1635 Bessemer (Walford), J 1 .... Pa.
.... Bessie, H 12 .... Ark.
210*Bessie, Q 6 .... N. C.
284 Bessie, I 6 .... Okla.
975 Bessmay, J 25 .... Tex.
49*Bessville, O 21 .... Mo.
....*Best, B 5 .... Ark.
350 Best, H 10 .... Tex.
62*Bestwater, A 5 .... Ark.
42*Beswick, B 5 .... Calif.
60*Bet, E 21 .... Ky.
1207 Bethalto, L 11 .... Ill.
100*Bethania, D 7 .... N. C.
5*Bethanna, G 21 .... Ky.
35*Bethany, I 7 .... Calif.
200 Bethany, K 10 .... Conn.
819 Bethany, J 16 .... Ill.
....*Bethany, G 20 .... Ky.
216 Bethany, C 4 .... La.
40 Bethany, Q 22 .... Minn.
85*Bethany, B 20 .... Miss.
2682 Bethany, B 8 .... Mo.
....*Bethany, L 22 (Pop. incl. in Lincoln) .... Neb.
110*Bethany, N 6 .... Ohio
2590 Bethany, I 11 .... Okla.
148*Bethany, F 22 .... Pa.
410*Bethany, O 24 .... W. Va.
152*Bethany Beach, K 22 .... Del.
300*Bethayres, O 24 .... Pa.
3200 Bethel, L 4 .... Conn.
245 Bethel, M 21 .... Del.
.... Bethel, M 17 .... Ill.
166*Bethel, G 24 .... Kan.
288*Bethel, E 19 .... Ky.
964 Bethel, M 3 .... Me.
188 Bethel, M 16 .... Minn.
217 Bethel, D 14 .... Mo.
125 Bethel, C 1 .... N. Y.
1333 Bethel, F 18 .... N. C.
1604 Bethel, P 8 .... Ohio
37 Bethel, O 23 .... Okla.
250*Bethel, M 19 .... Pa.
560 Bethel, Q 10 .... Tenn.
1500 Bethel, J 12 .... Vt.
305*Bethel, I 14 .... Wis.
....*Bethel College, see North Newton .... Kan.
300*Bethelridge, I 17 .... Ky.
573 Bethel Springs, P 5 .... Tenn.
15*Bethera (Herberta), L 19 .... S. C.
300 Bethesda, D 15 .... Ark.
25*Bethesda, J 16 .... Ky.
200 Bethesda, I 10 .... Md.
1127 Bethesda, K 19 .... Ohio
2000 Bethevan, G 17 .... Ind.
100 Bethlehem, H 7 .... Conn.
242 Bethlehem, E 10 .... Ga.
142*Bethlehem, P 17 .... Ind.
134*Bethlehem, D 15 .... Ky.

Pop. Place Index State
85*Bethlehem, K 19 .... Md.
500 Bethlehem, H 12 .... N. H.
58490 Bethlehem, L 22 .... Pa.
137*Bethlehem, (Pierce Bridge), H 13 .... N. H.
3500 Bethpage, H 7 .... N. Y.
250*Bethpage, L 12 .... Tenn.
.... Bethpage Jc., H 7 .... N. Y.
79 Bethune, H 23 .... Colo.
620 Bethune, E 16 .... S. C.
40*Betsey, J 16 .... Ky.
1000*Betsy Layne, H 22 .... Ky.
3143 Bettendorf, L 24 .... Iowa
250 Betteravia, M 9 .... Calif.
221 Betterton, E 18 .... Md.
200 Bettie, J 21 .... N. C.
300 Bettie, D 23 .... Tex.
13 Betts, L 20 .... S. D.
692 Bettsville, E 11 .... Ohio
.... Betty Baker, Q 3 .... Va.
150 Betula, F 10 .... Pa.
115 Between, F 10 .... Ga.
275 Beulah, M 15 .... Colo.
12 Beulah, D 21 .... Iowa
46*Beulah, N 25 .... Kan.
378 Beulah, K 11 .... Mich.
347 Beulah, E 6 .... Miss.
75*Beulah, M 14 .... Mo.
14 Beulah, E 15 .... N. M.
942 Beulah, L 8 .... N. D.
26 Beulah, J 21 .... Ore.
174▲Beulah, C 24 .... Wyo.
....*Beulah Beach, D 13 .... Ohio
462 Beulah Heights, P 18 .... Ill.
50*Beulah Heights, K 17 .... Ky.
46*Beulahville, L 18 .... Va.
567 Beulaville, J 17 .... N. C.
521 Beury, N 9 .... W. Va.
41*Bevan, M 18 .... Ohio
25*Bevans, B 14 .... N. J.
1276 Bevelle, H 18 .... Ala.
100 Beverly, J 6 .... Ill.
25 Beverly, J 19 .... Iowa
292 Beverly, G 14 .... Kan.
69*Beverly, J 20 .... Ky.
25537 Beverly, D 21 .... Mass.
500 Beverly Shores, B 9 .... Ind.
46 Beverly (Beverly Station), F 5 .... Mo.
37 Beverly, N 10 .... Neb.
2691 Beverly, J 11 .... N. J.
671 Beverly, M 17 .... Ohio
40 Beverly, K 16 .... Wash.
484 Beverly, H 15 .... W. Va.
.... Beverly Farms, D 21 .... Mass.
26823 Beverly Hills, Q 3 .... Calif.
1000*Beverly Park, F 10 .... Wash.
500*Beverly Shores, B 8 .... Ind.
46 Beverly Station (Beverly), F 5 .... Mo.
150*Beverlyville, K 21 .... Va.
600 Bevier, I 10 .... Ky.
1105 Bevier, D 12 .... Mo.
35*Bevington, M 11 .... Iowa
250*Bevinsville, H 22 .... Ky.
300 Bexar, D 5 .... Ala.
25*Bexar, B 14 .... Ark.
157*Bexley, P 21 .... Miss.
8705 Bexley, K 12 .... Ohio
515*Beyer (Wallopsburg), L 6 .... Pa.
148*Biardstown, C 22 .... Tex.
8*Biarly, D 22 .... Wash.
200*Bias, N 2 .... W. Va.
1631 Bibb City, J 3 .... Ga.
200 Bible Grove, M 18 .... Ill.
....*Bible School Park, Q 15 .... N. Y.
215 Bibo, G 8 .... N. M.
27 Bibon, F 6 .... Wis.
104 Bickleton, O 14 .... Wash.
100 Bickmore, K 8 .... W. Va.
5110 Bicknell, N 6 .... Ind.
100*Bicknell, M 11 .... Calif.
362 Bicknell, M 13 .... Utah
1*Bicycle, H 3 .... N. D.
19790 Biddeford, Q 4 .... Me.
100 Biddeford Pool, Q 5 .... Me.
2 Bidding Springs, G 24 .... Okla.
.... Biddle, J 13 .... Ark.
12 Biddle, N 22 .... Mont.
15*Bidville, D 5 .... Ark.
.... Bidwell, O 16 .... Iowa
350 Bidwell, P 14 .... Ohio
47*Bidwell, Q 4 .... Pa.
564 Bieber, C 8 .... Calif.
46*Biehle, M 22 .... Mo.
357 Bienville, C 8 .... La.
.... Bierd, K 11 .... Ill.
13 Bierman, O 2 .... N. D.
200 Bierne (Beirne), N 9 .... Ark.
50 Big Arm, F 4 .... Mont.
73*Big Bar, D 3 .... Calif.
....*Big Basin, J 6 .... Calif.
64 Big Bay (McNoel), Q 17 .... Ill.
700 Big Bay, D 6 .... Mich.
250*Big Bear City, M 21 .... Calif.
1500*Big Bear Lake (Pine Knot) N 18, P 9 .... Calif.
100*Big Bear Park, M 21 .... Calif.
73*Bigbee, N 4 .... Ala.
55*Bigbee Valley, G 22 .... Miss.
6*Big Bend, D 6 .... Calif.
60 Big Bend, L 22 .... Colo.
27*Big Bend, I 12 .... La.
62*Bigbend, G 8 .... W. Va.
298 Big Bend, N 21 .... Wis.
....*Bigbone, C 16 .... Ky.
270 Big Cabin, C 22 .... Okla.
200*Big Cane, K 11 .... La.
12*Big Canyon (Arbuckle), N 13 .... Okla.
30*Big Cedar, L 24 .... Okla.
162*Big Chimney, L 6 .... W. Va.
500 Big Clifty, H 12 .... Ky.
50*Big Cove Tannery, Q 11 .... Pa.
350 Big Creek, J 13 .... Calif.
250*Big Creek, I 20 .... Ky.
147*Big Creek, E 16 .... Miss.
450 Big Creek, M 4 .... W. Va.
377 Bigelow, H 11 .... Ark.
180*Bigelow, E 19 .... Kan.
250 Bigelow, R 6 .... Minn.
143 Bigelow, C 4 .... Mo.
52*Bigelow (Richville), D 17 .... N. Y.
509 Big Falls, D 14 .... Minn.
187 Big Falls, L 13 .... Wis.
210 Bigflat, C 12 .... Ark.
....*Big Flat, D 4 .... Calif.
500 Big Flats, Q 11 .... N. Y.
328▲Big Flats, J 15 .... Wis.
175 Bigfoot, M 15 .... Tex.
50*Big Fork, K 6 .... Ark.
....*Big Fork, I 21 .... Ky.
382*Bigfork, F 15 .... Minn.
250 Bigfork, E 4 .... Mont.
....*Big Four, F 10 .... Wash.
500 Big Four, Q 6 .... W. Va.
456 Biggers, B 19 .... Ark.
547 Biggs, F 7 .... Calif.
52 Biggs, C 13 .... Ore.
344 Biggsville, F 7 .... Ill.
13 Bigheart, B 18 .... Okla.
45*Bighill, G 18 .... Ky.
....*Big Hollow, see Maple-crest .... N. Y.
35 Big Horn, K 18 .... Mont.

Pop.	Place Index	State
144	Big Horn, B 15	Wyo.
154	*Big Indian, R 21	N. Y.
84	*Big Isaac, F 11	W. Va.
350	*Big Island, H 9	La.
500	Big Island, M 9	Va.
28	Biglake, D 21	Ark.
442	Big Lake, M 14	Minn.
763	Big Lake, H 10	Tex.
80	Biglake, E 8	Wash.
29	*Big Laurel, J 21	Ky.
25	*Big Laurel, N 8	N. C.
500	Bigler, J 10	Pa.
723	Biglerville, P 15	Pa.
200	*Biglick, N 17	Tenn.
125	*Big Moose, H 19	N. Y.
12	Bignell, L 11	Neb.
317	*Big Oak Flat, I 10	Calif.
67	*Big Otter, I 8	W. Va.
350	Bigpine, J 15	Calif.
36	*Big Pine, N 7	N. C.
100	*Big Piney, M 14	Mo.
241	Big Piney, K 4	Wyo.
32	*Bigpoint, Q 21	Miss.
125	Big Pool, C 4	Md.
200	Big Prairie, H 15	Ohio
4987	Big Rapids, M 14	Mich.
72	*Big Ridge, Q 5	N. C.
250	Big Rock, C 17	Ill.
97	*Big Rock, K 23	Iowa
....	*Big Rock, I 21	Ky.
196	*Big Rock, K 7	Tenn.
50	*Bigrock, B 7	Va.
963	Big Run, J 8	Pa.
25	*Big Run, C 11	W. Va.
596	Big Sandy, E 13	Mont.
601	Big Sandy, L 7	Tenn.
609	Big Sandy, E 23	Tex.
120	Big Sandy, Q 5	W. Va.
....	*Big Sandy, J 5	Wyo.
40	Bigspring, G 23	Kan.
100	Big Spring, G 12	Ky.
85	*Big Spring, C 5	Md.
569	Big Spring (Big Springs), K 6	Neb.
100	*Bigspring, P 16	Tenn.
2604	Big Spring, F 10	Tex.
10	*Big Springs, M 21	Idaho
30	Big Springs, I 12	Ind.
160	Bigsprings, H 10	Ohio
16	Big Springs, O 25	S. D.
92	*Big Springs, F 8	W. Va.
30	*Bigstone, F 21	Ky.
681	Big Stone City, E 24	S. D.
4331	Big Stone Gap, D 4	Va.
200	Big Suamico (Suamico), O 13	Wis.
75	*Big Sur, K 7	Calif.
1533	Bigtimber, L 13	Mont.
5	*Big Trails, F 12	Wyo.
89	*Bigtrees, H 10	Calif.
866	Bigwells, N 14	Tex.
28	*Big Woods, F 20	Ky.
10	*Bijou, G 10	Calif.
450	Bijou (Echo), I 10	La.
100	Bijou Hills, M 17	S. D.
4	*Bill, I 19	Wyo.
5000	Billerica, D 18	Mass.
....	Billet, M 21	Ill.
7	Billing, D 6	Neb.
452	Billings, P 9	Mo.
23261	Billings, L 16	Mont.
150	*Billings, C 6, R 23	N. Y.
661	Billings, C 12	Okla.
56	*Billings (Kyger), H 7	W. Va.
183	Billingsley, I 14	Ala.
16	*Billingsville, H 12	Mo.
100	*Billmeyer, O 17	Pa.
....	*Billows, H 18	Ky.
....	*Bills Place, P 11	Pa.
17475	Biloxi, R 19	Miss.
476	Biltmore, O 8	N. C.
50	*Bilvia, J 22	Ky.
100	*Bim, N 5	W. Va.
10	*Bimble, J 19	Ky.
26	*Bina, B 3	N. C.
109	*Binfield, O 19	Tenn.
311	Binford, J 19	N. D.
75	*Bingen, M 6	Ark.
221	Bingen, P 6	Ga.
600	Bingen, Q 11	Wash.
985	Bingen-White Salmon (White Salmon), Q 11	Wash.
840	Binger, J 8	Okla.
199	Bingham, L 14	Ill.
1200	Bingham, J 8	Me.
100	Bingham, H 6	Neb.
10	*Bingham, J 9	N. M.
101	*Bingham, D 20	S. C.
75	*Bingham, M 12	W. Va.
2834	Bingham Canyon (Bingham), F 10	Utah
251	Bingham Lake, Q 8	Minn.
78309	Binghamton, Q 16	N. Y.
....	Binghamton, P 1	Tenn.
200	*Binnewater, C 4, R 21	N. Y.
101	Binnsville, H 22	Miss.
200	Biola, J 11	Calif.
100	Biola Jc., J 11	Calif.
275	Bippus, E 18	Ind.
123	*Birch, Q 2	N. C.
....	*Birch, see Birchton	W. Va.
200	*Birchardville, D 20	Pa.
28	*Birchdale, C 14	Minn.
100	*Birch Harbor, L 18	Me.
70	*Birch Island, O 7	Me.
70	*Birchleaf, C 6	Va.
96	Birch River, J 10	W. Va.
600	Birch Run, N 20	Mich.
136	*Birchrunville, O 22	Pa.
250	*Birchton (Birch), N 8	W. Va.
495	Birch Tree, P 16	Mo.
107	*Birchwood, P 16	Tenn.
531	Birchwood, D 9	Wis.
10	*Bird, I 17	Ky.
694	Bird City, D 3	Kan.
60	*Birdell, B 17	Ark.
29	*Birdeye, F 19	Ark.
250	*Bird in Hand P 19	Pa.
1201	Bird Island, N 9	Minn.
2000	Bird Mills (East Walpole), H 18	Mass.
294	Birds, M 22	Ill.
100	*Birdsall, P 8	N. Y.
3313	Birdsboro, N 21	Pa.
370	Birdseye, P 10	Ind.
....	*Birdseye, G 12	Utah
42	*Birds Haven, F 12	Va.
26	*Birds Landing, B 23, H 6	Calif.
125	*Birdsnest, M 23	Va.
40	Birdsong, F 21	Ark.
50	*Birds Run, J 19	Ohio
200	Birdsview, D 9	Wash.
107	Birdsville, I 6	Ky.
....	*Birdville (Natrona Heights), L 4 (Pop. 1500 incl. in Harrison)	Pa.
197	*Birdville, D 18	Tex.
20	*Birkbeck, I 16	Ill.
70	Birkenfeld, B 6	Ore.
267583	Birmingham, F 13	Ala.
55	*Birmingham, H 7	Ill.
498	Birmingham, O 19	Iowa
60	*Birmingham, F 21	Kan.
312	Birmingham, J 7	Ky.
11196	Birmingham, P 22	Mich.
160	Birmingham, G 6	Mo.
200	Birmingham, K 13	N. J.
250	Birmingham, D 14	Ohio
198	*Birmingham, L 10	Pa.
556	Birnamwood, L 12	Wis.
14	Birney, M 20	Mont.
48	*Birome, G 19	Tex.
475	Biron, J 14	Wis.
58	*Birta, H 9	Ark.
116	*Birthright, D 22	Tex.
5853	Bisbee, P 22	Ariz.
393	Bisbee, E 16	N. D.
80	*Biscay, N 12	Minn.
402	Biscoe (Fredonia), I 16	Ark.
843	Biscoe, G 10	N. C.
70	*Biscoe, L 19	Va.
26	*Biscuit, H 24	Ky.
20	*Bishop, B 6	Ala.
1490	Bishop, I 15	Calif.
217	Bishop, F 12	Ga.
763	Bishop, N 25	Md.
1329	Bishop, Q 18	Tex.
75	Bishop (Shraders), C 9	Va.
150	*Bishop Creek, I 15	Calif.
75	Bishop Crossing, F 21	N. C.
199	Bishop Hill, E 10	Ill.
225	Bishops Head, O 18	Md.
50	*Bishopsville (Eldridge), F 17	Fla.
275	Bishopville, N 25	Md.
2995	Bishopville, F 17	S. C.
75	*Bismarck, L 9	Ark.
375	Bismarck, H 22	Ill.
1302	Bismarck, M 19	Mo.
15496	Bismarck, N 11	N. D.
113	*Bismarck, F 18	W. Va.
366	Bison, I 10	Kan.
6	Bison (Buelow), D 11	Mont.
228	Bison, E 10	Okla.
275	Bison, D 6	S. D.
....	Bisonte, P 22	Colo.
10	Bissell, J 20	Neb.
235	Biteley (Bitely), M 12	Mich.
79	*Bithlo, G 19	Fla.
50	Bitter Creek, P 10	Wyo.
150	*Bittinger, M 3	Md.
310	Bivalve, O 20	Md.
400	Bivalve, Q 9	N. J.
438	Bivins, D 24	Tex.
1304	Biwabik, F 19	Minn.
90	*Bixby, Q 17	Minn.
75	Bixby, M 17	Mo.
1291	Bixby, G 19	Okla.
17	Bixby, F 6	S. D.
100	Blabon, K 21	N. D.
12	Blachly, I 5	Ore.
348	Black, O 19	Ala.
25	*Black, F 19	Md.
26	*Black, N 18	Mo.
50	*Black, A 8, E 1	Tex.
....	Black Bayou Jc., E 11	Miss.
....	*Blackbear, B 5	Calif.
....	Black Bear, D 13	Okla.
39	*Blackberry, G 16	Minn.
550	Black Betsy, J 5	W. Va.
....	Blackbird Jc., O 18	Minn.
70	*Blackburn, D 5	Ark.
....	*Blackburn, G 19	Ky.
314	Blackburn, G 9	Mo.
198	Blackburn, D 16	Okla.
....	*Blackbutte, J 6	Ore.
5	Black Carbon, J 9	Wash.
133	*Black Creek, P 6	N. Y.
333	Black Creek, F 16	N. C.
542	Blackcreek, N 14	Wis.
700	Black Diamond, I 9	Wash.
753	Blackduck, F 11	Minn.
1000	Black Eagle, G 10	Mont.
531	Black Earth, J 20	Wis.
545	Blackey, I 22	Ky.
200	*Blackey, A 7	Va.
100	Black Field, P 7	Pa.
3681	Blackfoot, O 19	Idaho
175	Blackfoot, C 7	Mont.
271	*Blackford, H 7	Ky.
67	Blackford, D 8	Va.
35	Black Forest, E 21	Nev.
100	*Black Fork, I 4	Ark.
200	Blackfork, R 13	Ohio
48	Blackgum, H 23	Okla.
100	Black Hall (Lyme), M 19	Conn.
4	*Black Hammer, R 23	Minn.
289	Black Hawk (Blackhawk), F 13	Colo.
100	Blackhawk, L 7	Ind.
103	*Black Hawk, G 12	Miss.
60	Black Hawk, J 3	S. D.
....	Black Hollow, C 15	Colo.
....	Black Hollow Jc., C 15	Colo.
1000	Blackinton, B 3	Mass.
225	*Blackjoe, J 21	Ky.
114	*Black Lake, E 5	Idaho
100	*Blacklick, K 11	Ohio
1500	Black Lick, M 6	Pa.
211	Blacklog, M 13	Pa.
90	Blackman, L 5	Fla.
650	Blackmount (No. Haverhill) I 10	N. H.
1042	Black Mountain, O 9	N. C.
329	*Black Oak, D 20	Ark.
67	Black Pine, R 17	Idaho
5	*Blackpipe, N 9	S. D.
125	*Black Point (Grandview), H 4	Calif.
....	*Black Point Beach Club, I-20	Conn.
17	*Blackridge, Q 14	Va.
897	*Black River, G 16	N. Y.
2539	Black River Falls, F 15	Wis.
769	Black Rock, C 17	Ark.
46	*Black Rock, H 12	Ky.
150	Black Rock, F 5	Ore.
33	Black Rock, L 6	Utah
50	*Blackrun, J 16	Ohio
1917	Blacksburg, A 11	S. C.
2133	Blacksburg, O 5	Va.
78	*Blacks Ferry, K 15	Ky.
2010	Blackshear, N 19	Ga.
200	*Blacksher, P 7	Ala.
97	Black Springs, K 7	Ark.
175	Blackstock, D 12	S. C.
100	Blackstone, E 17	Ill.
4566	■Blackstone, I 16	Mass.
....	*Blackstone, D 3	N. C.
2699	Blackstone, O 14	Va.
261	Blacksville, C 13	W. Va.
20	Blacktail, I 1	S. D.
159	*Blackton, J 17	Ark.
150	*Blackville (Blackwell), G 10	Ark.
1456	Blackville, K 12	S. C.
350	Blackwater, L 15	Ariz.
36	*Blackwater, I 19	Ky.
389	Blackwater, H 11	Mo.
6	Blackwater, J 8	N. D.
80	*Blackwater, E 3	Va.
100	*Blackwell (Blackville), G 10	Ark.
91	*Blackwell, L 19	Mo.
8537	Blackwell, B 13	Okla.
100	Blackwell (Lloyd), G 14	Pa.
1500	Blackwell, F 12	Tex.
200	Blackwell, M 9	Wis.
....	Blackwell Jc., M 9	Wis.
35	Blackwells Mills, G 14	N. J.
50	*Black Wolf, H 13	Kan.
2000	Blackwood, L 9	N. J.
95	Blackwood, D 5	Va.
....	*Blackwood Terrace, M 8	N. J.
120	*Blade, F 10	La.
40	Bladen, N 22	Ga.
272	Bladen, N 16	Neb.
60	*Bladen, Q 15	Ohio
724	Bladenboro, K 13	N. C.
1220	Bladensburg, I 12	Md.
140	Bladensburg, I 14	Ohio
601	Blades, L 22	Del.
440	Bladon Springs, M 4	Ala.
....	Blaha, O 21	S. D.
280	Blain, N 14	Pa.
30	Blaine, O 23	Colo.
270	Blaine, E 19	Kan.
124	*Blaine, F 22	Ky.
750	Blaine, D 19	Me.
131	*Blaine, O 24	Mich.
150	*Blaine, F 9	Miss.
600	*Blaine, J 20	Ohio
30	Blaine, J 23	Okla.
9	Blaine, D 5	Ore.
15	*Blaine, M 20	Tenn.
1524	Blaine, B 7	Wash.
250	*Blaine, E 19	W. Va.
40	Blaineville (Blaine), M 20	Tenn.
50	*Blair, D 23	Kan.
....	Blair, E 24	Mont.
3289	Blair, J 23	Neb.
570	Blair, M 4	Okla.
75	*Blair (Blairs), E 11	S. C.
425	*Blair, O 4	W. Va.
856	Blair, E 15	Wis.
50	*Blairs (Blairs Corners), I 5	Pa.
65	*Blairs, O 17	Va.
276	Blairsburg, G 12	Iowa
50	*Blairs Corners (Blairs), I 5	Pa.
262	Blairsden, E 9	Calif.
72	*Blairs Mills, F 21	Ky.
84	Blairs Mills, N 13	Pa.
525	Blairstown, J 18	Iowa
214	Blairstown, I 8	Mo.
1000	Blairstown, C 10	N. J.
358	Blairsville, B 9	Ga.
200	*Blairsville, P 15	Ill.
5002	Blairsville, M 6	Pa.
100	Blairtown, P 7	Wyo.
100	Blaisdell, G 7	N. D.
36	*Blake, H 20	Ky.
16	Blake, B 19	Md.
42	Blake (Russell) M 3	Okla.
114	Blakeley, O 13	Minn.
150	Blakeley, K 7	W. Va.
2774	Blakeley, N 3	Ga.
8106	*Blakely, G 21	Pa.
100	*Blakeman, D 4	Kan.
14	*Blaker Mills, N 11	W. Va.
....	Blakes, D 16	Ill.
30	*Blakes, M 21	Va.
442	Blakesburg, G 12	Iowa
....	Blakes Jc., H 22	Ore.
13	*Blakeslee, H 16	Mont.
223	*Blakeslee (Perryville), N 16	N. Y.
164	*Blakeslee (Blakesly), B 6	Ohio
96	*Blakeslee, I 23	Pa.
....	Blakeslee Jc., L 6	Wash.
100	Blalack, M 3	Ariz.
16	Blalock, C 14	Ore.
407	Blanca, P 13	Colo.
75	*Blanch (Blanche), C 11	N. C.
30	*Blanchard, H 10	Calif.
150	*Blanchard, C 4	Idaho
259	Blanchard, Q 6	Iowa
200	Blanchard, B 4	La.
92	*Blanchard, J 10	Me.
280	Blanchard, N 15	Mich.
100	*Blanchard (Doretta) F 16	N. M
100	Blanchard, K 23	N. D.
1139	Blanchard, K 11	Okla.
531	*Blanchard, K 12	Pa.
63	*Blanchard, I 23	Tex.
150	Blanchard, D 8	Wash.
662	Blanchardville, J 21	Wis.
50	*Blanche, D 19	Ala.
315	Blanche, J 20	Ky.
50	*Blanche, Q 13	Mo.
262	Blanche, Q 11	Tenn.
1785	Blanchester, N 8	Ohio
....	Blanck, G 24	Okla.
81	*Blanco, K 6	Calif.
68	Blanco, C 6	N. M.
45	Blanco, M 19	Okla.
453	Blanco, K 16	Tex.
30	Blanconia, O 18	Tex.
565	Bland, J 16	Mo.
8	*Bland, H 18	Tex.
325	Bland, O 2	Va.
1821	Blandburg, K 10	Pa.
162	Blandford, H 5	Mass.
111	Blanding, O 23	Utah
914	Blandinsville, G 7	Ill.
15	*Blandlake, G 24	Tex.
800	Blandon, M 20	Pa.
201	Blandville, J 4	Ky.
79	*Blandville, E 10	W. Va.
49	*Blaney, F 11	Mich.
146	*Blaney, F 14	S. C.
800	Blanford, J 5	Ind.
200	*Blank (Blanks), J 12	La.
327	Blanket, G 15	Tex.
44	*Blansett, I 4	Ark.
84	*Blanton, J 21	Ala.
50	*Blanton, H 14	Fla.
175	*Blanton, I 7	Miss.
....	Blanton, D 10	Okla.
....	Blanton Jc., D 10	Okla.
20	*Blantons, K 16	Va.
2322	Blasdell, N 4	N. Y.
61	*Blaser, D 16	W. Va.
500	*Blauvelt, E 5	N. Y.
90	*Blawenburg, G 14	N. J.
2162	*Blawnox, L 4	Pa.
40	*Blaze, F 21	Ky.
175	Blazon, O 3	Wyo.
25	Blazon Jc., O 3	Wyo.
....	Bleachery, C 17	Mass.
68	Bleakwood, I 25	Tex.
240	*Bledsoe, J 21	Ky.
250	*Bledsoe, C 8	Tex.
108	Bleecker, J 23	Ala.
31	Bleiblerville, K 20	Tex.
367	Blencoe, J 2	Iowa
400	Blende, L 16	Colo.
237	Blenheim, D 20	S. C.
90	*Blenker (Sherry), I 14	Wis.
500	Blessing, N 21	Tex.
331	Blevins, N 7	Ark.
60	*Blevins, F 21	Ky.
54	Blewett, I 13	Wash.
500	*Blewett, L 13	Tex.
30	Blind Slough, A 5	Ore.
188	Bliss, P 10	Idaho
30	*Bliss, J 15	Ky.
100	*Bliss, K 18	Mo.
400	Bliss, O 6	N. Y.
2144	Blissfield, R 20	Mich.
100	*Blissfield, H 15	Ohio
26	Blitzen, P 18	Ore.
....	Blix, H 23	Tex.
100	*Blocher, O 16	Ind.
80	*Block, L 18	Tenn.
162	Blocker, K 20	Okla.
26	Blockhouse, P 12	Wash.
1000	Block Island, R 12	R. I.
50	*Blocksburg, C 2	Calif.
488	Blockton, Q 9	Iowa
1013	Blocton, H 11	Ala.
253	Blodgett, P 23	Mo.
12	Blodgett, G 5	Ore.
50	*Blodgett Landing, N 9	N. H.
175	*Blodgett Mills, O 15	N. Y.
110	*Blomkest, M 8	Minn.
100	*Bloodland, M 14	Mo.
51	Bloom, O 18	Colo.
150	*Bloom, N 8	Kan.
20	Bloom, M 19	N. D.
471	Bloomburg, D 24	Tex.
102	*Bloom City, H 19	Wis.
575	Bloomdale, E 10	Ohio
2204	Bloomer, E 11	Wis.
60	*Bloomery, E 22	W. Va.
75	*Bloomfield, G 3	Calif.
4309	▲Bloomfield, D 13	Conn.
2270	Bloomfield, M 10	Ind.
2732	Bloomfield, P 17	Iowa
535	Bloomfield, G 15	Ky.
1028	Bloomfield, P 22	Mo.
35	Bloomfield, G 23	Mont.
1467	Bloomfield, F 19	Neb.
41623	Bloomfield, E 18	N. J.
200	Bloomfield, C 5	N. M.
339	*Bloomfield (Bloomingdale), I 20	Ohio
....	*Bloomfield, M 3	Pa.
858	*Bloomfield (New Bloomfield), M 14	Pa.
47	*Bloomfield, C 19	Tex.
287	Bloomfield, C 22	Vt.
1281	Bloomfield Hills, P 22	Mich.
197	*Bloomingburg, R 20	N. Y.
567	Bloomingburg, M 11	Ohio
296	*Bloomingdale, L 24	Ga.
305	*Bloomingdale, C 19	Ill.
432	Bloomingdale, J 7	Ind.
553	Bloomingdale, P 12	Mich.
2606	*Bloomingdale, C 17	N. J.
446	Bloomingdale, F 22	N. Y.
339	*Bloomingdale (Bloomfield), I 20	Ohio
219	Bloomingdale, I 19	Pa.
313	*Blooming Glen, M 23	Pa.
184	*Blooming Grove, E 3	N. Y.
150	Blooming Grove, H 23	Pa.
821	Blooming Grove, F 19	Tex.
1205	Blooming Prairie, Q 17	Minn.
25	*Blooming Rose, L 15	Mo.
150	*Bloomingrose, L 5	W. Va.
2000	Bloomington, Q 9	Calif.
418	*Bloomington, R 21	Idaho
32868	Bloomington, G 16	Ill.
20870	Bloomington, M 11	Ind.
88	*Bloomington, F 11	Kan.
100	Bloomington, G 21	Ky.
338	Bloomington, N 4	Md.
2655	▲*Bloomington (Bloomington Lake), M 15	Minn.
361	Bloomington, O 15	Neb.
175	*Bloomington, R 22	N. Y.
400	Bloomington, N 19	Tex.
677	Bloomington, G 21	Wis.
174	*Bloomington Springs, M 14	Tenn.
50	Bloom Jc., Q 13	Ohio
9799	Bloomsburg, J 18	Pa.
704	Bloomsbury, F 9	N. J.
210	Bloomsdale, L 20	Mo.
200	Bloomsfield, C 5	N. M.
367	Bloomville, P 20	N. Y.
750	Bloomville, F 12	Ohio
29	*Bloss, I 18	Ky.
250	Blossburg, F 12	Ala.
75	*Blossburg (Schatz), J 7	Mont.
1955	Blossburg, F 15	Pa.
858	Blossom, B 22	Tex.
106	*Blossvale, K 16	N. Y.
200	*Blough, N 7	Pa.
36	*Blounts Creek, H 20	N. C.
150	Blount Springs, E 13	Ala.
1931	Blountstown, B 1, N 12	Fla.
576	Blountsville, D 14	Ala.
169	Blountsville, H 20	Ind.
250	Blountville, L 24	Tenn.
654	Blowing Rock, D 2	N. C.
150	*Blowing Rock, C 6	Va.
25	*Blowing Springs, I 13	Ky.
721	Blox, I 25	Tex.
20	*Bloxham, B 3	Fla.
400	Bloxom, K 24	Va.
30	*Bloyd, I 14	Ky.
80	*Blue, K 25	Ariz.
150	Blue, Q 18	Okla.
600	*Blue Ash, O 6	Ohio
82	*Blue Ball, I 6	Ark.
300	Blue Ball, O 19	Pa.
900	Blue Ball (West Decatur), K 10	Pa.
....	Blue Bell, I 12	Ariz.
500	*Blue Bell, N 23	Pa.
20	*Blue Bell, L 2	S. D.
85	Bluebell, G 19	Utah
162	Blueberry, D 6	Wis.
75	Blue Brick, F 21	S. C.
100	*Blue Canon, G 10	Calif.
155	*Blue Creek, P 9	Ohio
35	Blue Creek, B 9	Utah
76	Bluecreek, E 22	Wash.
310	Bluecreek, K 7	W. Va.
2000	Blue Diamond, H 21	Ky.
3702	Blue Earth, R 13	Minn.
125	*Blue Eye, R 9	Mo.
3921	Bluefield, N 1	Va.
24562	Bluefield, N 1	Va.-(W. Va.)
287	Blue Grass, L 23	Iowa
10	Bluegrass, N 9	N. D.
350	Bluegrove, C 16	Tex.
800	Blue Hill, M 15	Me.
565	Blue Hill, N 17	Neb.
400	*Blue Hill Falls, M 15	Me
200	*Bluehole, I 20	Ky.
16638	Blue Island, D 21	Ill.
349	Bluejacket, B 22	Okla.
200	*Blue Jay, P 9	Calif.
521	*Blue Jay, O 8	W. Va.
503	*Blue Lake, D 2	Calif.
45	Blue Lick, H 10	Mo.
200	Bluemont, E 15	Va.
....	*Blue Moon, H 22	Ky.
811	Blue Mound, J 15	Ill.
449	Blue Mound, K 24	Kan.
196	Blue Mounds, J 20	Wis.
687	Blue Mountain, E 18	Ala.
171	Blue Mountain, H 7	Ark.
544	Blue Mountain, B 18	Miss.
316	*Blue Mountain Lake, I 20	N. Y.
500	*Blue Pennant (Red Dragon), N 6	W. Va.
1100	*Blue Point, H 9	N. Y.
1433	Blue Rapids, E 18	Kan.
1362	Blue Ridge, B 8	Ga.
184	Blueridge, K 17	Ind.
40	*Blue Ridge, G 23	N. Y.
45	*Blue Ridge, O 8	N. C.
500	*Blue Ridge (Blue Ridge Summit), Q 14	Pa.
429	Blue Ridge, C 20	Tex.
500	*Blue Ridge, M 7	Va.
75	*Blue River, H 22	Ky.
73	Blue River, I 8	Ore.
381	Blue River, H 19	Wis.
65	*Blue Rock, K 16	Ohio
15	Blueslide, D 23	Wash.
10	*Bluespring, J 15	W. Va.
12	*Blue Spring Run (Cast Steel), L 7	Va.
167	*Blue Springs, L 21	Ala.
183	*Blue Springs, C 19	Miss.
788	Blue Springs, G 7	Mo.
681	Blue Springs, O 22	Neb.
50	Bluestem, H 21	Wash.
87	*Bluestone, F 21	Ky.
67	*Blue Sulphur Springs, M 12	W. Va.
250	Bluewater, G 5	N. M.
25	*Bluff, M 7	N. C.
25	Bluff, Q 20	Okla.
49	*Bluff (Warrens Bluff) O 6	Tenn.
70	Bluff, Q 23	Utah
59	*Bluff Boom, I 14	Ky.
150	Bluff City, O 9	Ark.
75	*Bluff City, H 7	Ill.
252	Bluff City, O 14	Kan.
700	Bluff City, L 24	Tenn.
300	*Bluff City (North Pearisburg), N 4	Va.
21	*Bluff Creek, J 15	La.
250	Bluff Dale, F 17	Tex.
400	*Bluff Point, N 11	N. Y.
....	Bluff Ridge, M 12	Ind.
839	Bluffs, J 8	Ill.
100	Bluffsprings, M 2	Fla.
93	*Bluff Springs, I 9	Ill.
100	*Bluffton, I 7	Ark.
246	Bluffton, M 4	Ga.
5417	Bluffton, E 19	Ind.
234	Bluffton, I 8	Minn.
30	*Bluffton, I 15	Mo.
2077	Bluffton, G 8	Ohio
459	Bluffton, Q 14	S. C.
48	*Bluffton, I 16	Tex.
463	Bluford, N 17	Ill.
50	*Bluit, I 23	N. M.
441	Blum, F 18	Tex.
50	*Blun, I 18	Ga.
150	*Blundale, I 18	Ga.
322	Blunt, I 14	S. D.
800	Bly, Q 12	Ore.
300	Blyn, F 6	Wash.
2355	Blythe, P 25	Calif.
181	Blythe, H 19	Ga.
55	*Blythebourne, I 5	N. Y.
266	Blythedale, A 8	Mo.
700	*Blythedale, N 4	Pa.
10652	Blytheville, D 22	Ark.
112	*Blythewood, F 13	S. C.
317	Boalsburg, K 12	Pa.
95	*Board Camp, J 5	Ark.
165	*Boardman, E 15	Fla.
159	Boardman, see South Boardman J 13	Mich.
158	Boardman, L 13	N. C.
110	Boardman, C 16	Ore.
110	*Boardman, A 11	Wis.
6	*Boat, H 20	Ky.
26	*Boatland, L 16	Tenn.
50	*Boatman, D 22	Okla.
1927	Boaz, D 17	Ala.
100	*Boaz, J 5	Ky.
10	Boaz, K 22	N. M.
100	*Boaz, F 6	W. Va.
230	Boaz, H 19	Wis.
110	*Bobo, D 8	Miss.
42	*Bobtown, I 17	Ky.
1900	*Bobtown, P 2	Pa.
25	*Boca, F 9	Calif.
....	Boca Chica, R 17	Fla.
700	Bocagrande, L 14	Fla.
723	Boca Raton, M 24	Fla.
125	*Bock, K 15	Minn.
319	Bodcaw, O 8	Ark.
533	Bode, E 9	Iowa
100	*Bodega, H 3	Calif.
40	*Bodfish, M 15	Calif.
135	Bodie, H 13	Calif.
120	Bodine (Bodines), H 16	Pa.
16	Boehler, P 19	Okla.
228	Boelus (Howard City) K 16	Neb.
2171	Boerne, L 16	Tex.
83	*Boeufcreek, J 17	Mo.
14604	Bogalusa, K 19	La.
334	Bogard, F 9	Mo.
379	Bogart, E 11	Ga.
800	Bogata, C 22	Tex.
12	*Boggs, J 11	W. Va.
125	Boggstown, K 16	Ind.
45	Boggy Depot, O 17	Okla.
68	*Bogota, L 19	Ill.
7346	Bogota, D 20	N. J.
500	*Bogota, M 3	Tenn.
55	*Bog Springs, K 4	Ark.
157	*Bogue, F 9	Kan.
76	*Bogue Banks, J 20	N. C.
384	Bogue Chitto, N 9	Miss.
66	*Bohannon, M 21	Va.
850	*Bohemia, H 8	N. Y.
100	*Bohri, D 14	Wis.
72	*Boiceville, C 3, R 21	N. Y.
100	*Boicourt, J 25	Kan.
613	*Boiling Springs, H 3	N. C.
800	Boiling Springs, O 15	Pa.
280	Bois (Dubois)	Ill.
290	Bois D'Arc, O 9	Mo.
26130	Boise, N 5	Idaho
1144	Boise City, R 2	Okla.
2500	Boissevain, B 10	Va.
581	Bokchito, Q 18	Okla.
55	*Bokeelia, L 15	Fla.
35	Bokhoma, R 25	Okla.
690	Bokoshe, J 24	Okla.
15	*Bolair, K 12	W. Va.
125	*Bolar, J 8	Va.
25	*Bolatusha, H 14	Miss.
341	Bolckow, C 5	Mo.
170	*Bolding, R 13	Ark.
121	*Boldman, H 23	Ky.
26	*Bold Spring, N 8	Tenn.
240	Bole, F 8	Mont.
95	*Boles, I 5	Ark.
15	*Boles, I 7	Idaho
70	Boles (West Vienna), Q 16	Ill.
25	*Boles, K 14	Ky.
942	Boley, I 16	Okla.
241	Boligee, I 6	Ala.
200	*Bolinas, H 4	Calif.
43	*Boling, L 21	Tex.
103	*Bolingbroke, I 10	Ga.
120	Bolinger, L 4	Ala.
25	Bolinger, A 5	La.
6	Bolivar, E 16	Ind.
53	*Bolivar, J 17	La.
2636	Bolivar, M 9	Mo.
1344	Bolivar, R 7	N. Y.
596	Bolivar, H 17	Ohio
811	Bolivar, M 7	Pa.
1314	Bolivar, P 4	Tenn.
628	Bolivar, E 25	W. Va.
203	*Bolivia, N 16	N. C.
8	Bolles, N 21	Wash.
369	*Bolling, M 13	Ala.
....	Bolling, M 13	Va.
86	Bolster Mills, N 4	Me.
35	*Bolt, O 7	W. Va.
504	Bolton, E 17	Conn.
....	Bolton, see Villa Tasso	Fla.
1000	*Bolton, F 7	Ga.
700	Bolton, E 15	Mass.
50	*Bolton, I 21	Mich.
627	Bolton, K 9	Miss.
150	Bolton, J 24	N. Y.
760	Bolton, L 15	N. C.
10	Bolton, F 9	Vt.
1200	Bolton Landing, J 24	N. Y.
105	*Boltonville, I 14	Vt.
175	Boltonville, O 18	Wis.
450	*Boltz, N 7	Pa.
65	*Bolyn, H 22	Ky.
147	*Boma, M 14	Tenn.
25	Bomar, Q 14	Okla.
185	Bomarton, C 14	Tex.
1000	Bombay, C 20	N. Y.
40	*Bomont, K 8	W. Va.
145	*Bomoseen, L 8	Vt.
100	Bon (Bon Jellico), K 18	Ky.
....	Bona, C 20	Tex.
371	Bon Air, G 16	Ala.
56	*Bonair, B 17	Iowa
340	Bon Air, N 15	Tenn.
125	*Bon Air, M 16	Va.
161	*Bonaire, J 11	Ga.
486	Bonanza, G 4	Ark.
140	Bonanza, L 11	Colo.
216	Bonanza, G 22	Ky.
233	Bonanza, R 11	Ore.
653	Bonaparte, P 19	Iowa
150	Bon Aqua, N 9	Tenn.
....	*Boncar, see Alloy	W. Va.
71	Boncarbo, (Bon Carbo) P 16	Colo.
500	Bond, I 19	Ky.
110	*Bond, J 8	La.
395	Bond, P 18	Miss.
1500	Bondsville, G 9	Mass.
288	Bondtown, D 6	Va.
661	Bonduel, N 13	Wis.
320	Bondurant, K 13	Iowa
75	Bondurant, I 3	Wyo.
228	Bondville, H 18	Ill.
100	*Bondville(Salvisa), G 16	Ky.
200	Bondville, O 9	Vt.
40	*Bone, N 20	Idaho
50	*Bone Cave, O 14	Tenn.
385	Bone Gap, N 20	Ill.
22	Boneita Springs, I 6	S. D.
532	Bonesteel, O 17	S. D.
31	*Boneville, G 17	Ga.
200	Boneta, G 19	Utah
45	Bonetraill, F 2	N. D.
116	Bonfield, E 20	Ill.
50	Bongards, O 13	Minn.
6349	Bonham, C 20	Tex.
200	Bon Homme, O 16	Miss.
....	Bon Homme, P 21	S. D.
1924	*Bonifay, M 9	Fla.
100	Bonilla, H 18	S. D.
....	Bonin, F 20	Mont.
100	Bonita, M 21	Ariz.
100	*Bonita, P 19	Calif.
422	Bonita, A 12	La.
200	*Bonita, J 21	Miss.
112	▲Bonita, I 5	Mont.
40	Bonita, I 22	Ore.
150	Bonita, B 17	Tex.
5	Bonita, N 11	Wis.
....	Bonita Jc., G 23	Tex.
356	Bonita Springs, M 16	Fla.
100	Bon Jellico (Bon), K 18	Ky.
228	Bonlee, F 11	N. C.
493	*Bonneau, K 19	S. C.
350	Bonner, I 4	Mont.
100	Bonnerdale, K 8	Ark.
1345	Bonners Ferry, A 5	Idaho
1837	Bonner Springs, G 24	Kan.
46	*Bonnerton, H 21	N. C.
3730	Bonne Terre, L 19	Mo.
500	*Bonneville, C 10	Ore.
20	Bonneville, H 11	Wyo.
177	Bonnie, O 16	Ill.
15	*Bonnie, I 10	W. Va.
278	Bonnieville, H 13	Ky.
250	*Bonnots Mill, J 15	Mo.
86	*Bonny, G 21	Ky.
2000	*Bonny Blue, E 3	Va.
520	Bonnyman, H 21	Ky.
248	Bono, D 19	Ark.
355	Bono, C 11	Ohio
54	*Bono, F 18	Tex.
50	Bonsal, F 13	N. C.
213	Bonsall, P 18	Calif.
550	Bon Secour, R 7	Ala.
100	Bonus, L 20	Tex.
600	*Bon Wier, I 25	Tex.
275	Boody, J 15	Ill.
27	Booge, L 25	S. D.
....	*Book, F 11	La.
386	Booker, A 6	Tex.
135	*Bookman, G 13	S. C.
29	Bookwalter, O 23	Neb.
150	Bookwalter (Buchwalter), L 10	Ohio
....	Boom, L 15	Tenn.
42	*Boomer (Forker), E 11	Mo.
60	*Boomer, E 4	N. C.
1213	Boomer, L 7	W. Va.
120	Boon, K 13	Mich.
250	Boone, L 17	Colo.
12373	Boone, I 11	Iowa
75	*Boone (Gap), H 18	Ky.
230	Boone, I 18	Neb.
1788	Boone, D 3	N. C.
....	Boone, P 21	Va.
219	*Boone, M 9	W. Va.
150	*Boone Grove, C 8	Ind.
377	*Boone Mill, O 7	Va.
63	*Boonesboro, G 11	Mo.
2324	Booneville, H 6	Ark.
62	*Booneville, L 11	Iowa
283	Booneville, H 20	Ky.
1893	Booneville, B 21	Miss.
149	*Booneville, I 14	Pa.
125	*Boonford, N 9	N. C.
938	Boonsboro, D 6	Md.
....	Boonesboro Jc., C 6	Md.
50	*Boons Camp, G 22	Ky.
25	*Boonshill, Q 11	Tenn.
125	*Boonsville, D 17	Tex.
6739	Boonton, D 16	N. J.
534	*Boonville, G 3	Calif.
4526	Boonville, Q 7	Ind.
6089	Boonville, H 12	Mo.
2076	Boonville, K 17	N. Y.
405	*Boonville, C 6	N. C.
....	*Booster, D 11	Ark.
107	Booth, J 14	Ala.
....	*Booth, G 20	Ky.
165	*Booth, M 5	Ore.
319	Booth, L 22	Tex.
100	*Booth, C 14	W. Va.
525	Boothbay, O 10	Me.
2250	Boothbay Harbor, P 10	Me.
213	Booth Corner, Q 22	Pa.
100	*Boothspoint, M 3	Tenn.
75	Boothsville, D 13	W. Va.
1300	Boothton, G 12	Ala.
350	*Boothville, P 21	La.
500	*Boothwyn, Q 22	Pa.
30	*Booton, L 1	W. Va.
150	Bordeaux, H 6	S. C.
500	Bordeaux, K 5	Wash.
263	▲Bordeaux, N 22	Wyo.
175	*Bordelonville, H 11	La.

Pop.	Place, Index	State
392	Borden (New Providence), P 15	Ind.
25	*Borden, G 16	S. C.
75	*Borden Springs, E 20	Ala.
4223	Bordentown, J 13	N. J.
93	Border, C 12	Minn.
37	Border, M 2	Wyo.
300	*Border City, M 12	N. Y.
262	*Borderland, O 2	W. Va.
100	*Bordley, H 8	Ky.
200	Bordulac, K 17	N. D.
12	*Borego, P 20	Calif.
42	*Boreing, J 19	Ky.
10018	Borger, C 4	Tex.
150	*Boring, D 13	Md.
200	Boring, D 8	Ore.
10	Borland, M 14	Mich.
199	*Borodino, M 14	N. Y.
500	*Boron, M 13	Calif.
123	Borton, J 21	Ill.
150	*Borup, G 3	Minn.
1359	▲Boscawen, N 13	N. H.
650	*Bosco (Hueysville), H 22	Ky.
101	*Bosco, D 11	La.
2008	Boscobel, G 20	Wis.
75	Bosler, P 19	Wyo.
....	*Bosley see Wardville,	N. C.
20	*Bosque, H 4	N. M.
58	*Boss, M 17	Mo.
18	Boss, R 24	Okla.
75	Bossburg, C 21	Wash.
5786	Bossier City, C 5	La.
226	Bostic, G 2	N. C.
591	Boston, D 7	Ala.
1099	Boston, P 10	Ga.
182	Boston, J 23	Ind.
175	*Boston, G 14	Ky.
770816	Boston, F 20, N 5	Mass.
54	*Boston, N 7	Mo.
300	Boston, O 5	N. Y.
300	Boston (Boston Mills), E 17	Ohio
600	*Boston, N 4	Pa.
25	Boston, C 24	Tex.
100	*Boston, H 14	Va.
98	Boston Corner, (Boston Corners) Q 24	N. Y.
400	*Bostonia, Q 19	Calif.
200	*Bostwick, D 16	Fla.
318	Bostwick, F 11	Ga.
80	Bostwick, O 18	Neb.
65	*Boswell (Omega), L 19	Ala.
100	*Boswell, C 14	Ark.
877	Boswell, F 6	Ind.
962	Boswell, Q 19	Okla.
1711	Boswell, O 7	Pa.
505	Bosworth, F 10	Mo.
794	Bothell, H 8	Wash.
150	*Botkinburg, E 11	Ark.
502	Botkins, I 7	Ohio
71	Botland, G 15	Ky.
50	Botna, J 6	Iowa
50	Botsford, L 6	Conn.
1739	Bottineau, D 12	N. D.
....	Botto, I 19	Ky.
25	Botzum, E 17	Ohio
300	Bouckville, M 17	N. Y.
100	Boughton, N 8	Ark.
12958	Boulder, E 14	Colo.
101	*Boulder, M 14	Ill.
510	Boulder, K 8	Mont.
150	*Boulder, O 12	Utah
80	*Boulder (Rangoon), F 13	W. Va.
36	Boulder, K 6	Wyo.
3000	Boulder City, P 21	Nev.
500	Boulder Creek, J 6	Calif.
....	Boulder Junction, P 20	Nev.
20	*Boulder Jc., J 7	Wis.
128	*Boulevard, Q 19	Calif.
....	*Boulevard, C 9	N. C.
150	*Boulevard (Windsor Shades), M 19	Va.
50	*Boulogne, A 15	Fla.
10	*Boundary, D 22	Wash.
....	Boundary Line, M 11	Ariz.
7616	Boundbrook, F 15	N. J.
3357	Bountiful, E 11	Utah
261	Bouquet, F 25	N. Y.
80	Bourbon, J 18	Ill.
1145	Bourbon, C 14	Ind.
50	*Bourbon, G 7	Miss.
360	Bourbon, K 17	Mo.
771	Bourbonnais, E 21	Ill.
420	Bourg, O 17	La.
86	*Bourne, G 17	Ky.
200	Bourne, L 23	Mass.
19	Bourne, G 20	Ore.
209	Bournedale, L 23	Mass.
147	*Bourneville, N 11	Ohio
100	Bouse, J 5	Ariz.
162	*Bouton, J 10	Iowa
310	Boutte, N 17	La.
....	*Bouty, J 18	Ky.
64	Bovee, N 18	S. D.
1355	Bovey, G 15	Minn.
447	Bovill, F 5	Idaho
100	Bovina, H 20	Colo.
100	*Bovina, K 8	Miss.
187	*Bovina, P 20	N. Y.
450	*Bovina, A 8	Tex.
150	*Bovina Center, P 20	N. Y.
15	*Bow, K 15	Ky.
780	Bow, O 14	N. H.
215	Bow, D 8	Wash.
787	Bowbells, D 7	N. D.
158	Bowden, F 18	Okla.
100	*Bowden, H 15	W. Va.
220	Bowdens, I 16	N. C.
375	Bowdil (North Lawrence), G 17	Ohio
757	Bowdle, D 15	S. D.
50	Bowdoin, O 8	Me.
70	Bowdoin, D 18	Mont.
302	Bowdoinham, O 8	Me.
1024	Bowdon, G 2	Ga.
348	Bowdon, K 15	N. D.
40	Bowdon Junction, F 2	Ga.
619	Bowen, H 5	Ill.
87	*Bowen (Filson), G 19	Ky.
227	Bowen, I 9	Mo.
20	Bowen, K 2	W. Va.
101	*Bowens, M 14	Md.
75	Bower, H 10	W. Va.
40	*Bowerbank, I 12	Me.
328	Bowers, H 23	Del.
....	*Bowers, M 22	Mont.
229	Bowers, M 21	Pa.
200	Bowers Hill (Bowers) Q 21	Va.
447	Bowerston, I 18	Ohio
284	Bowersville, D 14	Ga.
316	*Bowersville, L 8	Ohio
131	Bowesmont, D 23	N. D.
250	Bowie, N 23	Ariz.
350	Bowie, I 7	Colo.
767	Bowie, H 13	Md.
3470	Bowie, C 17	Tex.
500	Bowlegs, K 16	Okla.
12	Bowler, N 15	Mont.
315	Bowler, L 12	Wis.
40	*Bowlers Wharf, K 19	Va.
64	*Bowles, K 10	Calif.
38	*Bowles, L 3	W. Va.
55	*Bowlin (Bowling Green), A 12	S. C.
90	*Bowling (Greenmount), I 19	Ky.
950	Bowling Green, J 16	Fla.
219	Bowling Green, L 8	Ind.
14585	Bowling Green, J 12	Ky.
1975	Bowling Green, F 17	Mo.
7190	Bowling Green, D 9	Ohio
541	Bowling Green, J 17	Va.
200	*Bowlingtown, I 20	Ky.
304	Bowlus, K 11	Minn.
200	*Bowman, G 9	Calif.
634	Bowman, D 14	Ga.
967	Bowman, P 3	N. D.
799	Bowman, K 15	S. C.
200	Bowmansdale, O 16	Pa.
883	Bowmanstown, K 21	Pa.
500	*Bowmansville, O 5	N. Y.
400	*Bowmansville, O 20	Pa.
....	Bow Mills, O 14	N. H.
87	*Bowmont, N 4	Idaho
1000	*Bownemont (Elk), K 6	W. Va.
75	*Bowring, C 16	Okla.
60	*Bowser, I 16	Tex.
68	*Bowstring, F 15	Minn.
50	Bow Valley, E 20	Neb.
136	Bowyer, K 16	S. C.
20	Box, H 23	Okla.
35	Box, L 13	Okla.
342	Boxboro, D 16	Mass.
127	Box Elder, D 13	Mont.
30	*Box Elder, J 4	S. D.
136	▲*Boxelder, I 20	Wyo.
75	*Boxelder, C 23	Tex.
150	Boxford, C 20	Mass.
....	*Boxford see East Boxford C 20	Mass.
285	Boxholm, H 10	Iowa
44	*Boxley, D 9	Ark.
79	*Boxspring, I 6	Ga.
200	*Boxville, G 8	Ky.
40	*Boxwood, Q 7	Va.
15	*Boyce, K 12	Ky.
732	Boyce, H 9	La.
275	*Boyce, E 19	Tex.
342	Boyce, E 14	Va.
533	Boyceville, C 11	Wis.
13	*Boyd, C 8	Fla.
100	*Boyd, D 18	Ky.
523	Boyd, N 5	Minn.
33	*Boyd, M 15	Mont.
200	Boyd, R 7	Okla.
50	Boyd, D 12	Ore.
496	Boyd, D 18	Tex.
618	Boyd, F 12	Wis.
200	Boydell, P 16	Ark.
487	Boyden, C 3	Iowa
200	Boyds, G 9	Md.
60	Boyds, C 21	Wash.
300	*Boyds Creek, N 20	Tenn.
43	*Boyds Mills, F 23	Pa.
....	*Boydston, C 5	Tex.
210	Boydsville, A 20	Ark.
10	*Boyd Tavern, K 13	Va.
424	Boydton, Q 13	Va.
....	Boyer, F 7	Calif.
70	Boyer, H 5	Iowa
111	*Boyer, L 14	W. Va.
185	Boyero, I 20	Colo.
219	*Boyers (Anandale), K 3	Pa.
3983	Boyertown, N 21	Pa.
62	Boyes, M 23	Mont.
400	*Boyes Hot Springs, G 3 A 15	Calif.
369	▲*Boyett (Boyette), I 14	Fla.
9	*Boykin, F 15	S. C.
·699	Boykins, R 18	Va.
24	*Boyle, F 23	Kan.
742	Boyle, E 8	Miss.
....	Boyles, F 13	Ala.
100	*Boyleston, H 12	Ind.
1000	Boyleston Center, (Boyleston), F 14	Mass.
516	*Boylston, K 16	Ala.
....	Boylston Jc., C 5	Wis.
2904	Boyne City, I 15	Mich.
213	Boyne Falls, I 16	Mich.
50	Boynton, C 21	Ark.
1326	Boynton, M 24	Fla.
60	*Boynton, B 10	Mo.
842	Boynton, H 20	Okla.
800	Boynton, K 11	Pa.
79	Boy River, G 12	Minn.
254	*Boys Town, J 23	Neb.
40	*Boz, F 19	Tex.
8665	Bozeman, M 10	Mont.
....	Bozeman Hot Springs, M 10	Mont.
250	*Bozman, K 17	Md.
35	*Bozoo, Q 10	W. Va.
859	Bozrah, I 20	Conn.
....	*Bozrahville, see Gilman	Conn.
51	Braae, I 20	Wyo.
321	Braceville, E 19	Ill.
140	Braceville, E 19	Ohio
100	*Bracey, Q 14	Va.
6400	Brackenridge, L 4	Pa.
2653	Brackettville, M 12	Tex.
86	*Brackney, D 20	Pa.
28	*Brad, E 16	Tex.
150	*Bradbury (Hollis Center), Q 4	Me.
185	Braddock, O 14	N. D.
18326	Braddock, M 4	Pa.
150	*Braddock Heights, D 8	Md.
242	Braddyville, Q 6	Iowa
150	*Braden, J 25	Okla.
165	*Braden, P 2	Tenn.
7444	Bradenton, J 13	Fla.
700	Bradenville, N 6	Pa.
681	Bradford, F 16	Ark.
907	Bradford, E 12	Ill.
207	Bradford, P 15	Ind.
100	*Bradford, F 13	Iowa
47	*Bradford, H 20	Kan.
32	*Bradford, C 19	Ky.
46	Bradford, K 13	Me.
....	Bradford, B 19	Mass.
350	Bradford, N 10	N. H.
200	Bradford, P 11	N. Y.
1775	Bradford, J 7	Ohio
17691	Bradford, D 9	Pa.
1000	Bradford, N 6	R. I.
612	Bradford, M 5	Tenn.
693	Bradford, I 17	Vt.
500	Bradford Center, J 14	Me.
300	Bradfordsville, H 15	Ky.
374	*Bradfordwoods, L 3	Pa.
261	Bradgate, E 9	Iowa
54	Bradish, I 18	Neb.
409	Bradley, R 7	Ark.
70	*Bradley, L 8	Calif.
100	*Bradley, H 11	Ga.
3689	Bradley, E 21	Ill.
50	*Bradley, G 22	Ky.
500	Bradley, K 15	Me.
153	*Bradley, P 12	Mich.
125	*Bradley, G 18	Miss.
52	*Bradley, C 2	N. Y.
1200	*Bradley, J 20	Ohio
281	Bradley, L 11	Okla.
135	Bradley, G 7	S. C.
311	Bradley, F 21	S. D.
3468	Bradley Beach, I 21	N. J.
361	Bradley Jc., I 15	Fla.
107	*Bradley Junction, L 9	Pa.
165	*Bradleyton, L 16	Ala.
60	*Bradleyville, Q 11	Mo.
890	Bradner, E 10	Ohio
300	Bradrick, R 14	Ohio
325	*Bradshaw, H 19	Ky.
100	Bradshaw, E 16	Md.
339	Bradshaw, L 19	Neb.
311	Bradshaw, F 13	Tex.
30	*Bradshaw, N 5	Va.
....	Bradshaw, see Jolo	W. Va.
....	Bradshaw (Dan), R 5	W. Va.
27	*Bradshawmill, G 18	Ky.
400	Bradstreet, E 8	Mass.
75	*Bradwood, A 4	Ore.
428	Brady, E 9	Mont.
460	Brady (Brady Island), L 11	Neb.
3739	▲Brady, N 13	Okla.
2000	*Brady (Ranshaw) K 17	Pa.
5002	Brady, H 14	Tex.
....	Brady, K 4	Wash.
190	*Brady, C 14	W. Va.
460	Brady Island (Brady), L 11	Neb.
166	Brady Lake, E 18	Ohio
487	*Bradys Bend, L 5	Pa.
70	*Bradyville, O 12	Tenn.
1000	*Braeburn, L 4	Pa.
300	*Braeholm, O 5	W. Va.
26	Bragg, J 24	Tex.
300	*Braggadocio, J 24	Mo.
318	Bragg City, J 24	Mo.
200	*Braggs, K 13	Ala.
392	Braggs, H 22	Okla.
578	Braham, L 16	Minn.
1354	Braidwood, E 19	Ill.
37	*Brainard, G 22	Ky.
444	Brainard, K 21	Neb.
190	*Brainard (Brainard Sta.), O 24	N. Y.
37	*Brainards (Martins Creek) D 10	N. J.
190	*Brainard Station (Brainard), O 24	N. Y.
183	Brainardsville, C 22	N. Y.
12071	Brainerd, J 12	Minn.
....	*Brainerd, Q 15	Tenn.
16378	■Braintree, G 20	Mass.
85	Braintree, I 10	Vt.
....	Braintree Highlands, H 20	Mass.
250	Braithwaite, O 19	La.
40	Braithwaite, I 5	Okla.
427	Braman, A 13	Okla.
145	*Brampton, G 9	Mich.
68	Brampton, Q 21	N. D.
1494	Bramwell, R 7	W. Va.
390	Branch, G 6	Ark.
400	*Branch, L 10	La.
50	*Branch, L 11	Mich.
63	*Branch, L 11	Mo.
59	*Branch, C 4, R 21	N. Y.
....	*Branch, see Smoke Hole	W. Va.
150	Branch, P 15	Wis.
1150	Branch Dale, L 18	Pa.
100	*Branch Hill, N 7	Ohio
....	Branch Jc., N 15	Ill.
....	Branch Jc., L 20	Okla
518	Branchland, L 3	W. Va.
300	Branchport, O 11	N. Y.
77	Branchton, I 3	Pa.
100	*Branchville, E 15	Ala.
300	Branchville, N 5	Conn.
37	*Branchville, Q 11	Ind.
750	Branchville, H 12	Md.
715	Branchville, B 12	N. J.
1351	Branchville, K 14	S. C.
100	Branchville, I 19	Tex.
153	*Branchville, R 18	Va.
29	*Brandamore, O 21	Pa.
87	*Brandenberg, J 19	Mont.
561	Brandenburg, F 13	Ky.
94	Brandon, K 23	Colo.
600	*Brandon, I 14	Fla.
324	Brandon, H 18	Iowa
23	*Brandon, K 7	Ky.
25	*Brandon, J 13	La.
345	Brandon, K 7	Minn.
500	*Brandon (Value), K 12	Miss.
1184	Brandon, K 12	Miss.
40	*Brandon, L 7	Neb.
82	*Brandon, B 3	N. C.
75	Brandon, I 13	Ohio
192	Brandon, L 25	S. D.
236	Brandon, F 19	Tex.
1731	Brandon, J 7	Vt.
6	*Brandon (Deal), N 18	Va.
708	Brandon, M 17	Wis.
200	*Brandonville, J 19	Pa.
113	*Brandonville, C 16	W. Va.
56	*Brandreth, J 19	N. Y.
224	Brandsville, Q 15	Mo.
264	Brandt, K 8	Ohio
75	Brandt, D 22	Pa.
271	Brandt, H 24	S. D.
210	Brandy, H 15	Va.
67	*Brandy Camp, H 9	Pa.
150	Brandywine, K 12	Md.
49	*Brandywine, I 17	Va.
229	*Brandywine, I 18	W. Va.
200	*Brandywine Summit, Q 22	Pa.
2235	Branford, N 12	Conn.
684	Branford, D 11	Fla.
14	*Branscomb, F 2	Calif.
250	Branson, Q 18	Colo.
1011	Branson, Q 10	Mo.
....	Brant, J 13	Ind.
88	*Brant, N 20	Mich.
250	Brant, O 4	N. Y.
80	*Brant Beach, K 17	N. J.
125	Brantford, J 18	N. D.
55	*Brantingham, I 17	N. Y.
400	*Brant Lake (Horicon), I 24	N. Y.
1126	Brantley, M 16	Ala.
212	*Brant Rock, H 22	Mass.
150	Brantwood, I 9	Wis.
1900	*Branwood, A 6	S. C.
197	Braselton, E 10	Ga.
250	Brasfield, I 16	Ark.
345	Brashear, C 13	Mo.
500	*Brashear, D 21	Tex.
500	Brasher Falls, D 19	N. Y.
105	*Brassar, F 16	Mich.
150	*Brasstown, Q 3	N. C.
1350	*Bratenahl, D 17	Ohio
9622	Brattleboro, Q 12	Vt.
150	*Bratton, D 19	Ky.
467	Brave, Q 2	Pa.
110	*Bravo, P 11	Mich.
11718	Brawley, Q 22	Calif.
....	Brawley, C 15	Minn.
220	Braxton, L 12	Miss.
26	*Braxton, I 10	W. Va.
37	*Bray, C 6	Calif.
32	Bray, M 11	Okla.
933	Braymer, E 8	Mo.
52	*Brays, K 19	Va.
217	Brayton, L 7	Iowa
65	Brayton, J 16	Neb.
75	*Brazeau, M 22	Mo.
8126	Brazil, K 8	Ind.
530	Brazil, P 15	Iowa
27	*Brazil, H 18	Ky.
46	*Brazil, L 17	Mo.
....	Brazil Jc., J 6	Ind.
97	*Brazilton, M 24	Kan.
816	Brazoria, M 22	Tex.
200	*Brazos, E 17	Tex.
2567	*Brea, O 17	Calif.
12	*Bread Loaf, H 6	Vt.
135	Breakabeen, O 21	N. Y.
50	*Breaks, C 6	Va.
114	*Breathed (Breathedsville), B 4	Md.
1668	Breaux Bridge, M 12	La.
381	Breckenridge, G 11	Colo.
868	Breckenridge, N 17	Mich.
2745	Breckenridge, J 3	Minn.
728	Breckenridge, D 8	Mo.
5826	Breckenridge, E 15	Tex.
80	Breckinridge, D 11	Okla.
1900	Brecksville, D 17	Ohio
2	Breckwalker, E 15	Tex.
532	Breda, H 7	Iowa
100	*Bredette, D 22	Mont.
50	Breed, N 11	Wis.
....	*Breeden, (Breading), N 2	W. Va.
140	*Breeding, J 15	Ky.
184	*Breedsville, Q 11	Mich.
200	*Breen, P 5	Colo.
2206	Breese, M 13	Ill.
250	Breesport, Q 12	N. Y.
126	*Breezewood, O 9	Pa.
35	Breien, P 11	N. D.
93	*Breinigsville, L 22	Pa.
....	*Breitenbush, G 8	Ore.
60	*Bremen, D 12	Ala.
1708	Bremen, F 2	Ga.
2179	Bremen, C 14	Ind.
1030	Bremen, D 18	Kan.
239	*Bremen, H 10	Ky.
25	Bremen, O 11	Me.
105	Bremen, I 16	N. D.
1176	Bremen, L 14	Ohio
200	*Bremer, E 17	Iowa
15134	Bremerton, H 6	Wash.
82	*Bremo Bluff (Bremo), L 13	Va.
1106	Bremond, H 20	Tex.
6435	Brenham, K 20	Tex.
....	Brennan, N 6, see Wounded Knee	S. D.
829	Brent, H 11	Ala.
161	Brentford, F 19	S. D.
54	*Brentwood, D 5	Ark.
1500	*Brentwood, H 6	Calif.
2433	Brentwood, I 11	Md.
500	Brentwood, P 18	N. H.
495	Brentwood, H 8	N. Y.
7552	*Brentwood, L 3	Pa.
150	*Brentwood, N 11	Tenn.
125	Brereton, G 11	Ill.
45	Breslau, G 19	Neb.
....	*Bressler, M 16	Pa.
135	*Brethren, K 10	Mich.
....	*Breton Woods, K 17	N. J.
37	Bretton Woods, H 15	N. H.
26	*Bretz, C 15	W. Va.
3061	Brevard, Q 7	N. C.
22	*Brevik, G 12	Minn.
103	*Brevort, F 15	Mich.
14	*Brewer, E 13	Ark.
....	Brewer, H 22	Ill.
....	Brewer, M 19	Okla.
6510	Brewer Jc. (Brewer), L 14	Me.
42	*Brewers, J 6	Ky.
650	Brewerton, L 15	N. Y.
700	Brewster, I 15	Fla.
408	Brewster, F 3	Kan.
282	Brewster, M 14	Mass.
467	Brewster, R 7	Minn.
55	Brewster, H 13	Neb.
1863	Brewster, E 6	N. Y.
1534	Brewster, H 17	Ohio
447	Brewster, F 16	Wash.
104	*Brewstertown (Rose), M 16	Tenn.
3323	Brewton, O 11	Ala.
109	Brewton, J 15	Ga.
332	Briant (Bryant), G 22	Ind.
20	Briar, G 18	Mo.
1830	*Briarcliff Manor, F 6	N. Y.
316	Briar Creek, J 19	Pa.
60	*Briarton, N 13	Wis.
125	Briartown, J 22	Okla.
139	Brice (Bryceland), C 8	La.
....	Brice, see Bennett Springs	Mo.
58	*Brice (Kent), K 7	N. Y.
150	*Brice, K 12	Ohio
22	*Brice, E 5	Tex.
75	*Briceland, D 1	Calif.
601	Bricelyn, R 14	Minn.
205	Briceton, F 6	Ohio
1800	Briceville, M 18	Tenn.
18	*Brickchurch, L 5	Pa.
223	Brickerville, O 19	Pa.
90	*Brickeys, I 20	Ark.
75	*Brickeys, K 20	Mo.
....	*Bricks, E 17	N. C.
10	Brickton, L 15	Minn.
204	Bridal Veil, D 9	Ore.
100	*Bridge, Q 14	Idaho
150	Bridge, N 3	Ore.
250	Bridgeboro, N 9	Ga.
500	Bridgeboro, J 11	N. J.
1500	Bridgehampton, G 12	N. Y.
....	*Bridgeland, G 18	Utah
....	Bridge Jc., G 22	Ark.
....	Bridge Jc., K 6	Ind.
2031	Bridgeport, A 19	Ala.
200	Bridgeport, H 13	Calif.
147121	Bridgeport, O 7	Conn.
2143	Bridgeport, M 21	Ill.
500	*Bridgeport, J 13	Ind.
75	Bridgeport, I 15	Kan.
350	Bridgeport, N 20	Mich.
1520	Bridgeport, I 3	Neb.
600	Bridgeport, L 6	N. J.
350	*Bridgeport, L 16	N. Y.
4853	Bridgeport, J 20	Ohio
302	Bridgeport, I 8	Okla.
12	Bridgeport, H 22	Ore.
5904	Bridgeport, O 23	Pa.
28	*Bridgeport, N 21	Tenn.
1735	Bridgeport, D 17	Tex.
....	*Bridgeport, E 22	Utah
320	Bridgeport, F 16	Wash.
1581	Bridgeport, E 13	W. Va.
50	*Bridgeport, F 20	Wis.
783	Bridger, N 15	Mont.
4	Bridger, I 8	S. D.
59	*Bridges, N 20	Va.
250	Bridgeton, J 8	Ind.
169	*Bridgeton, I 20	Mo.
15992	Bridgeton, O 7	N. J.
616	*Bridgeton, I 20	N. C.
50	Bridgeton, Q 18	Pa.
532	Bridgeton, B 7	R. I.
108	*Bridgetown, B 15	Tex.
60	Bridgetown, M 23	Va.
300	*Bridgeville, D 2	Calif.
1180	Bridgeville, K 21	Del.
4459	Bridgeville, N 3	Pa.
175	Bridgewater, I 5	Conn.
302	Bridgewater, M 8	Iowa
400	Bridgewater (Bridgewater Center), E 19	Me.
8902	■Bridgewater, J 20	Mass.
884	▲Bridgewater, Q 20	Mich.
150	*Bridgewater, K 12	N. H.
238	Bridgewater, M 18	N. Y.
210	Bridgewater, F 2	N. C.
1621	*Bridgewater, (West Bridgewater), L 2	Pa.
790	Bridgewater, M 22	S. D.
240	Bridgewater, L 12	Vt.
993	Bridgewater, I 11	Va.
....	*Bridgewater Center, see Bridgewater	Me.
125	Bridgewater Corners, L 11	Vt.
774	Bridgman, R 10	Mich.
1625	Bridgton (Bridgton Center), O 3	Me.
114	Bridgton Jc., O 3	Me.
125	*Bridlecreek, E 11	Va.
100	Bridport, I 5	Vt.
54	*Brief, G 14	Wash.
961	Brielle, J 20	N. J.
20	*Brier, C 4	Mass.
98	Brierfield, H 12	Ala.
200	Brier Hill, E 16	N. Y.
125	*Brier Hill, P 4	Pa.
403	*Brigantine, N 13	N. J.
520	Briggs, I 17	Tex.
250	Briggsdale, C 17	Colo.
200	*Briggsdale, K 11	Ohio
300	*Briggsville, J 7	Ark.
175	Briggsville, B 4	Mass.
161	*Briggsville, K 17	Wis.
5641	Brigham, C 11	Utah
....	Bright, H 23	Wyo.
1377	Brighton, G 12	Ala.
50	Brighton, C 20	Ark.
1200	*Brighton, H 8	Calif.
4029	Brighton, E 15	Colo.
50	*Brighton, J 18	Fla.
697	Brighton, L 10	Ill.
791	Brighton, N. 19	Iowa
375	Brighton, F 17	Ky.
114	Brighton, J 9	Me.
1353	Brighton, P 20	Mich.
120	*Brighton, N. 10	Mo.
900	*Brighton, L 9	N. Y.
100	Brighton, C 4	Ore.
299	Brighton, O 2	Tenn.
....	Brighton, F 13	Utah
47	*Brightshade, J 20	Ky.
800	Brightsville D 19	S. C.
1562	*Brightwaters, H 8	N. Y.
65	*Brightwood, D 9	Ore.
33	Brightwood, I 14	Va.
143	*Brill, D 9	Wis.
600	Brilliant, D 7	Ala.
550	Brilliant, (Swastika), B 19	N. M.
1683	Brilliant, I 20	Ohio
1200	Brillion, O 15	Wis.
....	*Brim, Q 5	Va.
618	Brimfield, F 11	Ill.
174	Brimfield, C 19	Ind.
650	Brimfield, H 11	Mass.
....	Brimfield, F 18	Ohio
430	Brimley, F 17	Mich.
193	*Brimson, C 8	Mo.
300	Brimstone, M 6	La.
206	Bringhurst, G 12	Ind.
250	Brinkhaven, I 15	Ohio
3409	Brinkley, I 17	Ark.
18	Brinkley Branch Jc., J 17	Ark.
11	*Brinklow, G 11	Md.
12	Brinkman, D 11	Mont.
164	Brinkman, K 3	Okla.
33	*Brinktown, K 14	Mo.
130	Brinnon, H 6	Wash.
206	Brinsmade, G 16	N. D.
305	Brinson, O 4	Ga.
45	*Bris, I 13	Va.
15	Brisbane, D 20	Ill.
58	Brisbane, P 9	N. D.
501	*Brisbin, K 10	Pa.
61	*Briscoe, G 17	Mo.
125	*Briscoe, C 6	Tex.
17	*Bristersburg, G 15	Va.
200	Bristol, M 23	Colo.
30167	Bristol, G 10	Conn.
1000	Bristol, B 2	Fla.
114	Bristol, N 18	Ga.
464	Bristol, C 18	Ill.
694	Bristol, B 16	Ind.
160	Bristol, O 10	Me.
100	*Bristol, H 14	Md.
1200	Bristol, L 12	N. H.
11895	Bristol, O 25	Pa.
11159	■Bristol, H 20	R. I.
675	Bristol, E 21	S. D.
14004	Bristol, K 24	Tenn.
23772	Bristol, K 24	Tenn.-(Va.)
1236	Bristol, H 7	Vt.
9768	Bristol, E 7	Va.
250	Bristol, E 11	W. Va.
350	Bristol, O 22	Wis.
60	*Bristol, N 10	N. Y.
100	Bristol Ferry, I 19	R. I.
10	Bristol Silver, K 22	Nev.
500	*Bristolville, D 19	Ohio
402	*Bristolville, (Spokane) D 19	Ohio
102	*Bristow, Q 10	Ind.
318	Bristow, F 15	Iowa
100	*Bristow, J 12	Ky.
188	Bristow, E 16	Neb.
6050	Bristow, G 17	Okla.
40	Bristow, G 16	Va.
1813	Britt, D 11	Iowa
27	*Brittany, M 16	La.
23	Brittin, N 13	N. D.
300	*Brittmount, F 19	Minn.
409	*Britton, R 19	Mich.
2239	Britton, H 12	Okla.
1500	Britton, C 21	S. D.
250	*Britton, E 18	Tex.
19	*Brixey, Q 13	Mo.
50	*Broadacre, I 20	Ohio
1399	Broadalbin, L 22	N. Y.
46	Broadbent, N 3	Ore.
75	Broad Bottom, H 24	Ky.
1273	Broad Brook, C 15	Conn.
110	*Broad Cove, O 11	Me.
300	Broaddus, H 24	Tex.
250	Broad Ford, P 5	Pa.
600	*Broadford, D 9	Va.
100	*Broadkill (Harbeson), K 23	Del.
73	Broadland, I 19	S. D.
361	Broadlands, I 20	Ill.
50	Broadmead, F 6	Ore.
817	Broad Mountain, L 19	Pa.
....	Broad Ripple, J 14	Ind.
40	*Broad Run, F 15	Va.
610	*Broad Top (Broad Top City), M 12	Pa.
240	Broadus, M 22	Mont.
1457	Broadview, C 20	Ill.
140	Broadview, K 15	Mont.
30	*Broadview, H 24	N. M.
1141	*Broadview Heights, Cuyahoga, D 17	Ohio
344	Broadwater, I 4	Neb.
136	*Broadwater, N 24	Va.
150	Broadway, E 9	N. J.
338	Broadway, G 12	N. C.
300	Broadway, I 10	Ohio
506	Broadway, H 11	Va.
144	Broadwell, I 13	Ill.
120	*Brock, I 19	Ky.
373	Brock, N 24	Neb.
30	Brock, I 6	Ohio
90	Brock, P 13	Okla.
23	*Brockdell, O 15	Tenn.
291	Brocket, G 19	N. D.
30	*Brockett, B 18	Ark.
3590	Brockport, L 8	N. Y.
350	Brockport, I 9	Pa.
23	*Brockroad, I 16	Va.
33	Brocksburg, D 14	Neb.
62343	Brockton, I 20	Mass.
300	Brockton, E 23	Mont.
500	Brockton, L 20	Pa.
....	Brockville, P 15	Wis.
124	*Brockway, F 9	Calif.
229	*Brockway (St. Stephens), L 12	Minn.
130	Brockway, G 21	Mont.
62	Brockway, N 5	Ore.
2709	Brockway (Brockwayville), H 8	Pa.
125	*Brockwell, C 14	Ark.
449	Brocton, J 21	Ill.
1293	Brocton, P 2	N. Y.
50	*Brodbecks (Brodbeck), Q 16	Pa.
1500	*Broderick (Washington), G 7	Calif.
400	Brodhead Mine (Brodhead), O 16	Colo.
702	Brodhead, H 17	Ky.
68	*Brodhead, B 4	N. Y.
1750	Brodhead, K 22	Wis.
500	Brodheadsville, J 22	Pa.
536	Brodnax, Q 14	Va.
41	Brogan, I 23	Ore.
150	*Brogueville (Parks), Q 18	Pa.
145	*Brohard, F 9	W. Va.
40	Brohman, M 13	Mich.
477	Brokaw, J 12	Wis.
2074	Broken Arrow, F 19	Okla.
2968	Broken Bow, J 13	Neb.
2367	Broken Bow, P 24	Okla.
45	*Brokenburg, J 16	Va.
312	Bromide, O 16	Okla.
....	Bromide Jc., N 17	Okla.
876	Bromley, B 17	Ky.
25	*Bromo, H 17	Ky.
275	Brompton, F 15	Ala.
265	Bronaugh, M 6	Mo.
12	*Bronco, D 8	Tex.
758	Bronson, E 12	Fla.
25	Bronson, H 21	Ill.
....	*Bronson, see Losantville,	Ind.
250	*Bronson, G 2	Iowa
421	Bronson, L 24	Kan.
1871	Bronson, R 15	Mich.
350	*Bronson (Lake Bronson), B 3	Minn.
400	Bronson, H 25	Tex.
129	*Bronston, J 17	Ky.
754	Bronte, G 13	Tex.
437	Bronwood, L 7	Ga.
1394711	*Bronx Boro, H 6 (part of New York City)	N. Y.
6888	Bronxville, G 6	N. Y.
35	*Brood, I 17	W. Va.
888	Brook, E 6	Ind.
36	*Brookdale, J 6	Calif.
53	*Brooke, I 17	Va.
813	Brookeland, H 25	Tex.
98	Brooken, J 21	Okla.
300	Brooker, C 13	Fla
....	Brookes Mills, N 10	Pa.
100	*Brookesmith, H 15	Tex.
262	*Brookeville, G 9	Md.
425	Brookfield, J 4	Conn.
400	Brookfield, N 12	Ga.
10817	Brookfield, C 20	Ill.
700	Brookfield, G 11	Mass.
6174	Brookfield, D 11	Mo.
350	*Brookfield, N 17	N. Y.
300	Brookfield, E 21	Ohio
105	Brookfield, H 12	Vt.
70	Brookfield, N 4	Wash.
300	Brookfield, O 20	Wis.
97	Brookfield Center, K 4	Conn.
30	Brookfield Jc., K 4	Conn.
910	Brookford, F 4	N. C.
50	*Brook Forest (Jefferson), G 14	Colo.
75	*Brookgreen, K 21	S. C.
1500	*Brookhaven, F 7	Ga.
6232	Brookhaven, N 9	Miss.
510	Brookhaven, H 9	N. Y.
50	*Brook Hill, L 17	Va.
150	Brookings, B 19	Ark.
500	Brookings, R 2	Ore.
5346	Brookings, I 24	S. D.
271	Brookland, D 20	Ark.
1744	*Brookland (West Columbia), H 12	S. C.
311	Brooklandville, E 14	Md.
1919	Brooklawn, L 9	N. J.
503	Brooklet, K 22	Ga.
700	Brooklin, N 16	Me.
49786	■Brookline, F 19	Mass.
175	Brookline (Brookline Station), O 9	Mo.
150	Brookline, R 13	N. H.
175	Brookline Station (Brookline), O 9	Mo.
....	Brookline Jc., N 4	Mass.
275	Brooklyn, O 13	Ala.
....	*Brookline Village, F 19	Mass.
600	Brooklyn, E 23	Conn.
100	*Brooklyn, L 4	Ga.
162	Brooklyn, H 7	Ill.
2158	*Brooklyn (Lovejoy P.O.), N 11	Ill.
485	Brooklyn, K 13	Ind.
1408	Brooklyn, K 17	Iowa
75	*Brooklyn, I 11	Ky.
749	Brooklyn, Q 19	Mich.
300	Brooklyn, P 17	Miss.
2698285	Brooklyn Boro, I 5 (part of New York City)	N. Y.
1108	Brooklyn, P 22	Ohio
300	*Brooklyn, F 20	Pa.
230	*Brooklyn, M 3	Wash.
779	*Brooklyn (Finlow), M 8	W. Va.
449	Brooklyn, K 21	Wis.
1870	Brooklyn Center, M 16	Minn.
779	Brooklyn Jc. (Brooklyn), C 10	W. Va.
736	Brookneal, P 11	Va.
160	Brookpark (Brook Park), K 17	Minn.
1122	Brook Park, D 16	Ohio
1247	Brookport, R 18	Ill.
125	*Brooks (Eckhard), G 6	Calif.
134	Brooks, G 6	Ga.
200	*Brooks, O 7	Iowa
125	*Brooks, F 14	Ky.
20	*Brooks, J 13	La.
450	Brooks, M 13	Me.
150	Brooks, E 5	Minn.
21	Brooks, H 14	Mont.
150	Brooks, F 7	Ore.
115	*Brooks, J 17	Wis.
100	*Brooksburg, N 20	Ind.
600	Brookshire, K 21	Tex.
714	*Brookside, F 12	Ala.
196	Brookside, L 14	Colo.

Pop.	Place Index	State
....	*Brookside, J 21	Ky.
27	*Brookside, D 17	Mont.
140	*Brookside, E 14	N. J.
975	*Brookside, K 19	Ohio
826	Brookston, F 9	Ind.
135	Brookston, H 18	Minn.
120	Brookston, G 7	Pa.
375	Brookston, C 21	Tex.
48	*Brooksville, D 15	Ala.
1607	Brooksville, G 13	Fla.
656	Brooksville, D 19	Ky.
810	▲Brooksville, M 15	Me.
875	Brooksville(Brookville), G 21	Miss.
130	Brooksville, K 15	Okla.
100	*Brookton, D 10	Ga.
200	Brookton, I 20	Me.
150	*Brook Vale, L 21	Va.
155	Brookview, O 24	N. Y.
2194	Brookville, K 21	Ind.
221	Brookville, H 14	Kan.
600	Brookville, H 20	Mass.
764	*Brookville (Brooksville), G 21	Miss.
1653	Brookville, K 7	Ohio
4397	Brookville, I 7	Pa.
500	Brookwood, G 10	Ala.
800	*Broomall, P 23	Pa.
20	*Broome, G 12	Tex.
81	*Broomes Island, M 14	Md.
125	Broomfield, F 14	Colo.
676	Brooten, L 9	Minn.
162	Broseley, Q 21	Mo.
77	*Brosia (Ambrosia), H 4	W. Va.
51	Brosius (Hancock), C 23	W. Va.
....	*Broten, B 4	Idaho
55	Brothers, K 13	Ore.
216	*Brotherton, M 15	Tenn.
120	Brothertown, N 16	Wis.
387	Broughton, O 18	Ill.
123	Broughton, F 17	Kan.
2200	*Broughton, L 3	Pa.
250	*Brounland, K 6	W. Va.
791	Broussard, M 12	La.
112	*Browder, I 10	Ky.
786	Browerville, J 10	Minn.
27	*Brown, M 13	Calif.
23	*Brown, J 12	Md.
45	Brown, P 16	Okla.
250	*Brown, D 12	W. Va.
100	*Brownbranch, Q 11	Mo.
838	Brown City, N 23	Mich.
600	*Brown Deer, O 20	Wis.
519	Browndell, H 25	Tex.
162	Brownell, I 8	Kan.
75	Brownfield, Q 17	Ill.
689	▲Brownfield, O 2	Me.
901	Brownfield (East Brownfield), O 2	Me.
175	*Brownfield, A 19	Miss.
8	*Brownfield, M 13	Mo.
600	Brownfield, Q 4	Pa.
4009	Brownfield, D 9	Tex.
....	Browning, R 6	Calif.
402	Browning, H 8	Ill.
531	Browning, C 10	Mo.
1825	Browning, D 6	Mont.
261	Brownington, K 8	Mo.
75	Brownington, B 17	Vt.
40	*Brownlee, F 9	Neb.
30	*Brownlee, G 22	Ore.
50	Browns (Brown), J 9	Ala.
337	Browns, N 21	Ill.
56	*Browns Station (Browns) H 13	Mo.
67	*Brownsboro, A 14	Ala.
66	Brownsboro, P 7	Ore.
640	*Brownsboro, F 21	Tex.
1136	Brownsburg, I 12	Ind.
175	Brownsburg, K 9	Va.
21	*Browns Camp (Geneill), G 7	Miss.
....	*Browns Cove, J 12	Va.
51	*Browns Crossroads, K 15	Ky.
355	Brownsdale, R 18	Minn.
150	Brownsmead, A 5	Ore.
500	*Browns Mills, L 13	N. J.
....	Brownson, K 3	Neb.
21	*Browns Springs, P 9	Mo.
56	*Browns Station (Browns), H 13	Mo.
108	*Browns Store, K 21	Va.
100	*Browns Summit, E 9	N. C.
219	Brownstown, N 5	Ark.
825	Brownstown, L 16	Ill.
1860	Brownstown, N 14	Ind.
1598	Brownstown, N 8	Pa.
800	*Brownstown, O 19	Pa.
250	Brownstown, N 14	Wash.
51	*Browns Valley, F 8	Calif.
75	*Browns Valley, I 9	Ind.
1075	Browns Valley, L 1	Minn.
113	*Brownsville, F 8	Calif.
200	Brownsville, J 21	Ind.
451	Brownsville, I 12	Ky.
120	*Brownsville, B 4	Md.
298	Brownsville, R 25	Minn.
200	*Brownsville, J 13	Ohio
784	Brownsville, H 6	Ore.
8015	Brownsville, P 4	Pa.
85	Brownsville, E 20	S. C.
4012	Brownsville, O 3	Tenn.
22083	Brownsville, Q 5	Tex.
75	Brownsville, M 13	Vt.
15	Brownsville, H 6	Wash.
300	Brownsville, M 18	Wis.
723	Brownton, O 11	Minn.
370	*Brownton, F 14	W. Va.
339	Browntown, N 21	Ga.
400	*Browntown, F 13	Va.
271	Browntown, J 22	Wis.
65	*Brownview (Raccourci) J 12	La.
500	*Brownville, G 8	Ala.
125	Brownville, K 16	Fla.
1500	Brownville, I 13	Me.
581	Brownville, N 25	Neb.
907	*Brownville, G 15	N. Y.
900	Brownville Jc., I 13	Me.
234	Brownwood, P 21	Mo.
23	*Brownwood, C 3	N. C.
13398	Brownwood, G 15	Tex.
516	Brownwood (Lawton), N 9	W. Va.
908	Broxton, M 15	Ga.
466	▲*Bruce, N 8	Fla.
125	*Bruce, K 17	Ill.
34	Bruce, R 3	Minn.
1385	Bruce, D 16	Miss.
....	Bruce, H 18	Mont.
6	Bruce, H 5	Ore.
394	Bruce, I 24	S. D.
162	Bruce, P 21	Va.
35	*Bruce, L 10	W. Va.
596	Bruce, E 10	Wis.
127	*Bruce Crossing, B 23	Mich.
20	Bruce Jc., D 14	Miss.
70	*Bruce Lake, E 13	Ind.
350	*Bruceton, L 3	Pa.
1003	Bruceton, M 6	Tenn.
165	Bruceton Mills, C 16	W.Va.
345	Brucetown, E 14	Va.
700	Bruceville, N 6	Ind.
230	Bruceville, H 18	Tex.
218	*Bruckarts (Silver Springs), O 18	Pa.
110	*Bruin, F 22	Ky.
663	Bruin, J 4	Pa.
16	*Bruington, L 18	Va.
540	Bruins, I 21	Ark.
....	*Brule, see Banner	Mo.
374	Brule, K 7	Neb.
151	Brule, E 5	Wis.
75	*Brumfield, G 16	Ky.
121	Brumley, K 12	Mo.
75	*Brummitt, J 15	Ark.
119	*Brundage, N 14	Tex.
1909	Brundidge, M 19	Ala.
300	Bruneau, P 7	Idaho
75	*Bruner, P 11	Mo.
175	Brunerrun, P 6	Pa.
200	*Bruni, Q 15	Tex.
232	Bruning, N 19	Neb.
350	*Brunnerville, O 19	Pa.
110	*Bruno, B 11	Ark.
234	Bruno, J 18	Minn.
189	Bruno, K 21	Neb.
126	Bruno, O 18	Okla.
110	*Brunot, O 19	Mo.
542	*Brunson, M 13	S. C.
109	Brunsville, E 2	Iowa
15035	Brunswick, O 22	Ga.
7003	■Brunswick, O 8	Me.
3856	Brunswick, F 7	Md.
110	*Brunswick, N 11	Mich.
70	*Brunswick, J 6	Miss.
1749	Brunswick, F 10	Mo.
289	Brunswick, G 18	Neb.
227	Brunswick, L 13	N. C.
250	*Brunswick, D 16	Ohio
250	Brunswick, P 3	Tenn.
48	Brunswick, Q 15	Va.
3	Brusett, G 18	Mont.
2481	Brush, D 19	Colo.
50	*Brushart, D 22	Ky.
100	*Brush Creek (Orlando), H 18	Ky.
42	*Brush Creek, M 12	Mo.
175	*Brush Creek (North Alexandria), M 13	Tenn.
10	Brush Hill, I 20	Okla.
100	Brush Prairie, Q 7	Wash.
487	Brushton, D 20	N. Y.
15	*Brushvale, I 3	Minn.
175	*Brush Valley, M 7	Pa.
61	*Brushy, H 14	Ky.
100	Brushy, O 17	Mo.
32	*Brushyknob, P 12	Mo.
65	*Brushy Run, H 18	W. Va.
433	*Brusle Landing (Brusly Landing), L 14	La.
275	Brussels, L 8	Ill.
150	*Brussels, P 12	Wis.
25	*Brutus, H 20	Ky.
89	*Brutus, H 16	Mich.
27	*Bryan, J 16	Ky.
5404	Bryan, D 6	Ohio
11842	Bryan, J 20	Tex.
....	Bryan Mound, N 22	Tex.
94	*Bryans Mill, D 24	Tex.
311	Bryans Road, L 11	Md.
173	*Bryant, J 11	Ark.
387	Bryant, G 10	Ill.
332	Bryant (Briant), G 22	Ind.
60	*Bryant, I 25	Iowa
130	*Bryant, D 13	Miss.
75	*Bryant, P 12	Mo.
143	Bryant, I 18	Okla.
658	Bryant, H 22	S. D.
50	*Bryant, K 11	Va.
150	Bryant, E 8	Wash.
100	Bryant, L 11	Wis.
50	*Bryantown, M 11	Md.
350	Bryant Pond, M 4	Me.
52	*Bryants Store, K 19	Ky.
150	Bryantsville, G 17	Ky.
500	Bryantville, I 21	Mass.
831	Bryantville (Hanson), I 21	Mass.
22	*Bryarly, B 23	Tex.
95	*Bryce Canyon, O 12	Utah
139	Bryceland (Brice), C 8	La.
300	*Bryceville, B 15	Fla.
800	*Bryn Athyn, O 24	Pa.
500	*Bryn Mawr, Q 10	Calif.
....	Bryn Mawr, P 23 (Pop. 10206 incl. in Merion Sta.)	Pa.
800	Bryn Mawr, I 8	Wash.
30	Bryson, I 9	Mo.
806	Bryson, D 16	Tex.
1612	Bryson City (Bryson), P 4	N. C
500	*Bryte, G 8	Calif.
385	*Bucatunna, N 22	Miss.
220	Buchanan, J 16	Fla.
504	Buchanan, F 3	Ga.
48	*Buchanan, K 21	Iowa
125	*Buchanan, E 23	Ky.
4056	Buchanan, R 10	Mich.
60	*Buchanan, N 21	Mo.
20	Buchanan, I 18	N. M.
1600	*Buchanan, F 5	N. Y.
125	Buchanan, M 18	N. D.
20	Buchanan, H 5	Ore.
....	Buchanan, G 3	Pa.
15	*Buchanan, L 7	Tenn.
868	Buchanan, M 8	Va.
....	*Buchanan Dam, I 16	Tex.
10	Buchli, A 17	Calif.
775	Buchtel, M 15	Ohio
150	Buchwalter (Bookwalter) L 10	Ohio
55	*Buck, D 4	N. C.
....	Buck, I 23	Tex.
....	*Buck, O 10	W. Va.
300	Buck Creek, G 10	Ind.
1305	Buckeye, K 11	Ariz.
300	*Buckeye, D 6	Calif.
194	Buckeye, G 13	Iowa
109	*Buckeye, H 9	La.
....	*Buckeye, M 24	N. M.
25	Buckeye (Otho), K 16	Ohio
219	Buckeye, N 21	Tex.
300	Buckeye, G 23	Wash.
100	*Buckeye, L 13	W. Va.
....	Buckeye City, see Danville	Ohio
500	Buckeye Lake, K 14	Ohio
1425	Buckeyestown, E 8	Md.
343	Buckfield, N 5	Me.
80	Buckgrove, J 5	Iowa
4450	Buckhannon, G 13	W. Va.
15	*Buckhart, P 13	Mo.
214	Buckhead, G 12	Ga.
1500	*Buck Hill Falls, I 23	Pa.
515	*Buckholts, I 19	Tex.
125	*Buckhorn, I 21	Ky.
350	*Buckhorn, N 20	Mo.
50	*Buckhorn, L 2	N. M.
100	*Buckhorn (Purvis), Q 20	Va.
10	*Buckhorn, D 23	Wyo.
50	Buckingham, C 18	Colo.
100	*Buckingham, L 17	Fla.
149	Buckingham, F 19	Ill.
50	*Buckingham, H 16	Iowa
200	Buckingham, N 24	Pa.
190	Buckingham, M 12	Va.
200	*Buckingham Valley, N 24	Pa.
500	Buckland, E 15	Conn.
300	Buckland, C 6	Mass.
287	Buckland, H 7	Ohio
457	Buckley, G 19	Ill.
217	Buckley, K 13	Mich.
1170	Buckley, J 9	Wash.
832	Bucklin, M 9	Kan.
842	Bucklin, D 11	Mo.
186	Buckman, K 13	Minn.
250	*Buck Mountain, K 20	Pa.
450	Buckner, P 8	Ark.
927	Buckner, P 16	Ill.
125	*Buckner, E 15	Ky.
571	*Buckner, G 6	Mo.
30	*Buckner, N 8	N. C.
100	*Buckner, K 15	Va.
500	*Buckroe Beach, O 21	Va.
800	*Buck Run, K 19	Pa.
50	Buck Run, P 20	Pa.
50	*Bucks, O 6	Ala.
175	*Bucks Harbor, L 22	Me.
200	*Buckskin, P 6	Ind.
....	*Bucks Lake, E 9	Calif.
1500	Bucksport, L 14	Me.
28	*Bucksport, I 22	S. C.
75	Bucksport Center (Winterport Ferry), L 14	Me.
125	*Bucksville, L 23	Pa.
75	*Bucksville, I 22	S. C.
20	*Bucktail, I 7	Neb.
83	*Buck Valley, Q 10	Pa.
150	*Buckville, J 8	Ark.
541	Bucoda, L 6	Wash.
20	*Bucu, C 7	Va.
150	*Bucyrus, H 25	Kan.
27	*Bucyrus, N 14	Mo.
117	Bucyrus, Q 5	N. D.
9727	Bucyrus, G 12	Ohio
72	*Bud, J 16	Ky
500	*Bud, P 7	W. Va.
12	Buda, D 12	Fla.
734	Buda, E 13	Ill
50	Buda, M 15	Neb
400	Buda, K 17	Tex.
250	*Budd Lake, D 13	N. J.
71	*Budds Creek, N 12	Md.
261	Buddtown, K 13	N. J.
1207	Bude, N 7	Miss.
55	*Bueche, L 13	La.
800	*Buechel, E 14	Ky.
88	*Buell, H 16	Mo.
50	*Buell, E 5	Ore.
100	*Buell, Q 22	Va.
107	*Buellton, N 10	Calif.
6	*Buelow (Bison), D 11	Mont.
500	*Buena, N 11	N. J.
80	*Buena, I 14	Va.
400	Buena, M 14	Wash.
3500	*Buena Park, O 16	Calif.
198	Buena Vista, M 10	Ala.
90	Buena Vista, P 10	Ark.
779	Buena Vista, J 11	Colo.
1161	Buena Vista, K 6	Ga.
100	*Buena Vista, A 12	Ill.
50	*Buena Vista, G 17	Ky.
150	*Buena Vista (Cascade), B 4	Md.
350	Buena Vista, E 19	Miss.
210	*Buena Vista, E 17	N. M.
335	Buena Vista, R 11	Ohio
150	Buena Vista, G 6	Ore.
600	*Buena Vista, N 4	Pa.
50	Buenavista, H 8	Tex.
4336	Buena Vista, L 9	Va.
150	*Buena Vista Springs (Cascade), B 7	Md.
50	*Bueyeros, E 22	N. M.
125	*Buffalo, H 21	Ala.
60	Buffalo, B 12	Ark.
156	Buffalo (Buffalo Creek), H 14	Colo.
422	Buffalo, I 13	Ill.
150	*Buffalo, E 10	Ind.
588	Buffalo, L 23	Iowa
555	Buffalo, M 22	Kan.
230	Buffalo, H 14	Ky.
1695	Buffalo, M 13	Minn.
920	Buffalo, M 10	Mo.
125	Buffalo, I 13	Mont.
7	Buffalo, L 13	Neb.
575901	Buffalo, M 4	N. Y.
245	Buffalo, M 22	N. D.
900	*Buffalo, K 18	Ohio
1209	Buffalo, B 3	Okla.
83	*Buffalo, N 2	Pa.
2200	Buffalo, C 10	S. C.
250	Buffalo, D 2	S. D.
75	*Buffalo, N 8	Tenn.
737	Buffalo, H 21	Tex.
338	Buffalo, I 4	W. Va.
293	Buffalo, K 17	Wis.
2302	Buffalo, D 16	Wyo.
911	Buffalo Center, B 11	Iowa
100	*Buffalo City, F 23	N. C.
....	*Buffalo Cove, E 3	N. C.
156	*Buffalo Creek (Buffalo), H 14	Colo.
182	Buffalo Gap, M 3	S. D.
250	Buffalo Gap, F 13	Tex.
35	*Buffalo Hart, I 13	Ill.
....	Buffalo Jc., N 4	N. Y.
76	Buffalo Jc., R 12	Va.
637	Buffalo Lake, O 10	Minn.
....	*Buffalo Lithia Springs, see Buffalo Springs	Va.
117	Buffalo Mills, P 9	Pa.
200	*Buffalo Park (Park) G 6,	Kan.
45	Buffalo Prairie, E 6	Ill.
25	*Buffalo Ridge, Q 5	Va.
66	Buffalo Springs, P 3	N. D.
137	*Buffalo Springs, C 17	Tex.
....	Buffalo Springs see Buffalo Station	Va.
75	Buffalo Springs (Buffalo Lithia Sprgs.), Q 12	Va.
100	*Buffalo Station, M 11	Va.
250	*Buffalo Valley, M 14	Tenn.
140	*Buffaloville, Q 9	Ind.
125	Buffville, M 22	Kan.
30	*Buford, B 12	Ark.
40	Buford, E 6	Colo.
4191	Buford, E 9	Ga.
20	Buford (Fort Buford), H 1	N. D.
100	*Buford, O 9	Ohio
73	*Buford, P 10	Tenn.
100	Buford, Q 20	Wyo.
75	*Bug, K 15	Ky.
55	Bughill, M 14	N. C.
600	Buhl, G 7	Ala.
2414	Buhl, Q 10	Idaho
1600	Buhl, F 18	Minn.
634	Buhler, K 15	Kan.
17	Buick, H 18	Colo.
16	Buick, M 17	Mo.
118	*Buies, K 12	N. C.
435	Buies Creek, G 13	N. C.
50	*Bula, B 8	Tex.
40	*Bula, L 14	Va.
250	*Buladean, M 9	N. C.
350	*Bulan (Duane), H 21	Ky.
500	Bulger, M 2	Pa.
16	*Bulger, L 3	W. Va.
500	Bullard, F 22	Tex.
45	Bullards, M 2	Ore.
82	*Bullbeggar, L 24	Va.
75	*Bull Creek (Lancer), G 23	Ky.
70	Bullhead, C 10	S. D.
114	*Bullion (Hope Villa P. O.), M 15	La.
....	Bullochville, see Warm Springs	Ga.
100	*Bullock, C 14	N. C.
2	Bullock, C 2	S. D.
1200	Bullsgap, M 22	Tenn.
25	*Bulltown, I 11	W. Va.
225	*Bullville, D 4	N. Y.
....	Bulow, N 18	S. C.
50	Bulow Mines, N 18	S. C.
390	Bulpitt, J 13	Ill.
36	Bumble Bee, I 12	Ariz.
75	*Bumpass, K 14	Va.
6	Bumping Lake, L 11	Wash.
150	Bumpus Mills, K 8	Tenn.
414	Buna, J 25	Tex.
648	Bunceton, I 11	Mo.
61	*Bunch (Paris), P 17	Iowa
50	*Bunch, I 17	Ky.
500	Bunch, H 23	Okla.
241	Buncombe, Q 16	Ill.
75	*Bundick, K 20	Va.
8	Bundy, K 15	Mont.
25	*Bunell (Fitzsimons), F 17	Colo.
10	*Bunger, D 16	Tex.
726	Bunker, N 17	Mo.
1082	Bunker Hill, L 11	Ill.
561	Bunker Hill, F 14	Ind.
253	Bunkerhill, H 11	Kan.
246	Bunker Hill, E 24	W. Va.
80	*Bunkertown, M 14	Pa.
75	Bunkerville, N 24	Nev.
158	*Bunlevel, H 13	N. C.
3575	Bunkie, J 11	La.
245	▲*Bunn, M 12	Ark.
248	*Bunn, E 15	N. C.
1030	Bunnell, E 18	Fla.
20	Bunney, E 20	Ark.
500	* Bunola, N 4	Pa.
....	*Buntyn, Q 1	Tenn.
40	*Bunyan, B 9	Wis.
50	*Buras, G 12	Ky.
750	Buras, P 20	La.
47	*Burbank, N 4	Ala.
34337	Burbank, O 15	Calif.
263	*Burbank, E 15	Fla.
28	*Burbank, O 20	Mo.
348	Burbank, F 15	Ohio
329	Burbank, C 15	Okla.
200	Burbank, P 24	S. D.
49	Burbank, N 18	Wash.
47	*Burch, O 20	Mo.
125	Burch (Rusk), C 6	N. C.
20	Burch, C 20	S. D.
35	*Burchard, P 5	Minn.
263	Burchard, O 23	Neb.
56	*Burchinal, D 13	Iowa
....	*Burdal, F 6	Ga.
522	Burden, N 18	Kan.
320	Burdett, J 9	Kan.
408	Burdett, P 12	N. Y.
110	*Burdette, D 22	Ark.
43	*Burdette, F 13	Iowa
37	Burdette, H 18	S. D.
100	*Burdette, Q 19	Va.
150	*Burdick, I 18	Kan.
10	Burdock, M 1	S. D.
483	Bureau, E 13	Ill.
100	*Burem, L 22	Tenn.
28	*Burfield, K 16	Ky.
79	*Burfordville, N 21	Mo.
30	*Burg, L 5	Ark.
10	*Burg, F 21	Ky.
1476	Burgaw, K 17	N. C.
25	Burgdorf, J 7	Idaho
76	Burgess, E 8	Ill.
164	Burgess, N 6	Mo.
150	*Burgess, I 23	S. C.
10	Burgess Jc., D 16	Ill.
100	Burgess Store, K 21	Va.
2497	Burgettstown, M 2	Pa.
400	Burghill, D 21	Ohio
703	Burgin, G 17	Ky.
267	Burgoon, E 11	Ohio
200	*Burien, H 9	Wash.
2814	Burkburnett, B 16	Tex.
800	Burke, D 7	Idaho
5	*Burke, F 22	Ky.
344	Burke, C 22	N. Y.
602	Burke, N 16	S. D.
100	*Burke, N 16	Tenn.
210	Burke, H 23	Tex.
87	Burke, D 19	Vt.
100	*Burke, G 18	Va.
50	*Burke, K 20	Wis.
82	*Burkehaven, N 9	N. H.
620	Burkes Garden, O 1	Va.
1092	Burkesville, K 15	Ky.
216	Burket, D 15	Ind.
121	*Burketown, I 11	Va.
495	*Burkett, L 17	Neb.
325	*Burkett, F 15	Tex.
220	Burkettsville (Gilberts), I 6	Ohio
173	Burkettville, N 11	Me.
350	Burkeville, H 25	Tex.
658	Burkeville, O 14	Va.
50	*Burkhardt, A 12	Wis.
33	*Burkhart, G 21	Ky.
177	Burkittsville, E 6	Md.
216	*Burkley (Berkeley), J 4	Ky.
20	Burkmere, F 16	S. D.
30	*Burksville, O 10	Ill.
70	*Burkville, J 14	Ala.
28	*Burl, L 9	Ala.
50	Burleigh (Menoken) N 12	N. D.
573	*Burleson, E 18	Tex.
5329	Burley, Q 14	Idaho
150	*Burley, H 6,	Wash.
100	*Burleyville (East Wakefield) L 18	N. H.
15940	Burlingame, E 17	Calif.
1019	Burlingame, H 21	Kan.
350	*Burlingham, C 2	N. Y.
1280	Burlington, H 23	Colo.
705	Burlington, E 10	Conn.
235	Burlington, B 17	Ill.
615	Burlington, G 13	Ind.
25832	Burlington, P 22	Iowa
2379	Burlington, K 21	Kan.
600	Burlington, B 17	Ky.
2275	▲Burlington, D 18	Mass.
301	Burlington, J 16	Me.
198	Burlington, Q 15	Mich.
10905	Burlington, J 12	N. J.
12198	Burlington, D 11	N. C.
220	Burlington, G 9	N. D.
500	Burlington, R 14	Ohio
177	Burlington, A 8	Okla.
30	Burlington, C 7	Ore.
156	*Burlington, F 17	Pa
250	Burlington, I 19	Tex.
27686	Burlington, E 6	Vt.
1632	Burlington, D 8	Wash.
300	*Burlington, D 19	W. Va.
4414	Burlington, O 22	Wis.
250	Burlington, C 10	Wyo.
252	*Burlington Flats, N 18	N. Y.
....	Burlington Jc., I 23	Kan.
838	Burlington Jc., A 4	Mo.
52	*Burlison, O 2	Tenn.
70	*Burmah, P12	Idaho
107	Burmester, F 8	Utah
1000	*Burmont (Gladstone), P 23	Pa.
150	*Burna, I 6	Ky.
5	*Burnell, L 9	Miss.
1945	Burnet, I 16	Tex.
300	Burnett, K 7	Ind.
200	*Burnett, F 19	Minn.
75	Burnett, J 9	Wash.
250	Burnett, M 18	Wis.
23	*Burnetta, I 17	Ky.
15	Burnetts Lake, D 13	Fla.
436	Burnettsville, E 11	Ind.
800	*Burney, D 7	Calif.
225	Burney, L 17	Ind.
800	Burneyville, Q 13	Okla.
865	*Burnham, D 22	Ill.
120	Burnham Jc. (Burnham), L 11	Me.
74	*Burnham, P 14	Mo.
22	Burnham, M 21	Neb.
2997	*Burnham, L 13	Pa.
110	*Burnhams, P 3	N. Y.
....	*Burning Fork, G 21	Ky.
225	*Burning Springs, I 20	Ky.
250	Burning Springs, G 7	W.Va.
60	*Burningtown, Q 4	N. C.
125	Burnips, P 12	Mich.
28	*Burnleys, J 13	Va.
75	Burns, F 9	Colo.
409	Burns, K 18	Kan.
288	*Burns, K 15	Miss.
30	Burns, G 24	Mont.
150	*Burns, O 8	N. Y.
2566	Burns, L 18	Ore.
600	Burns, M 9	Tenn.
253	Burns, Q 24	Wyo.
160	Burns City, N 9	Ind.
110	Burns Flat, I 5	Okla.
1867	Burnside, E 15	Conn.
150	Burnside, G 6	Ill.
83	*Burnside, H 10	Iowa
880	Burnside, J 17	Ky.
200	*Burnside, M 15	La.
100	*Burnside, I 17	Miss.
100	Burnside, D 4	N. Y.
414	*Burnside, K 8	Pa.
200	Burnstad, P 15	N. D.
220	Burnsville, J 12	Ala.
449	Burnsville, A 22	Miss.
997	Burnsville, M 9	N. C.
22	*Burnsville, J 8	Va.
851	Burnsville, H 11	W. Va.
150	Burnt Cabins, O 12	Pa.
75	*Burnt Chimneys (Stockton) Q 7	Va.
50	Burntfork, R 5	Wyo.
390	*Burnt Hills, L 23	N. Y.
108	*Burnt House, G 9	W. Va.
202	*Burnt Prairie, (Liberty) O 19	Ill.
2	Burntside, E 21	Minn.
28	Burnt Woods (Tum Tum), H 4	Ore.
300	*Burnwell, F 11	Ala.
318	*Burnwell, M 7	W. Va.
78	*Burnwood, R 19	N. Y.
35	*Burr (Sparks Quarry), I 18	Ky.
49	*Burr, N 4	Minn.
126	Burr, M 23	Neb.
525	Burrage, I 21	Mass.
28	*Burrel, K 11	Calif.
13	Burress, M 19	Neb.
43	*Burr Hill, I 15	Va.
8185	■*Burrillville, D 8	R. I.
....	*Burris, K 10	Wyo.
1593	*Burr Oak (Calumet Park), C 21	Ill.
93	*Burr Oak, C 13	Ind.
150	Burroak, B 19	Iowa
560	Burr Oak, D 13	Kan.
706	Burr Oak, R 14	Mich.
77	*Burr Oak, F 16	Wis.
200	Burroughs, L 24	Ga.
250	*Burrows, F 12	Ind.
842	Burrton, K 15	Kan.
47	*Burrus, K 17	Va.
79	*Burrville, M 17	Tenn.
82	*Burrville, L 11	Utah
350	*Burrwood, O 19	La.
35	*Burson (Helisma), H 9	Calif.
175	Burstall, G 12	Ala.
613	Burt, C 10	Iowa
150	Burt, N 20	Mich.
150	Burt, K 5	N. Y.
125	Burt, P 7	N. D.
150	*Burt Lake, H 17	Mich.
280	*Burton, (Bypro) H 22	Ky.
100	*Burton, O 18	Mich.
105	Burton, D 13	Neb.
761	Burton, D 19	Ohio
75	*Burton (Burton Station), D 19	Ohio
110	*Burton, P 15	S. C.
350	Burton, K 20	Tex.
250	Burton, I 8	Wash.
300	Burton, C 12	W. Va.
100	Burton City, G 16	Ohio
75	*Burton Station (Burton), D 19	Ohio
58	*Burtonsville, G 9	Md.
40	*Burtonsville, N 21	N. Y.
82	*Burtonville, D 20	Ky.
297	Burtrum, K 10	Minn.
85	Burtsboro, D 8	Ga.
100	*Burtville, E 11	Pa.
200	*Burwell, G 3	Ga.
1412	Burwell, I 15	Neb.
38	Busby, M 19	Mont.
19	*Busch, A 6	Ark.
3	*Busch, E 17	Mo.
617	Bush, P 15	Ill.
200	Bush, J 19	Ky.
81	*Bush, K 19	La.
68	*Bush City, J 24	Kan.
10	Bush Hill, G 18	Va.
300	Buskilll, I 24	Pa.
82	*Bushland, D 2	Tex.
676	Bushnell, G 15	Fla.
2906	Bushnell, G 8	Ill.
252	Bushnell, K 1	Neb.
75	Bushnell, P 4	N. C.
134	Bushnell, I 24	S. D.
135	*Bushong, I 20	Kan.
10	Bushrod, M 8	Ind.
177	*Bushton, J 20	Ill.
473	Bushton, J 13	Kan.
50	*Bushville, C 2	N. Y.
....	Bushwick, G 22	Pa.
25	*Bushwood, O 13	Md.
52	*Bushy, M 21	Va.
100	Bushyhead, D 21	Okla.
300	*Busick, N 9	N. C.
50	*Buskirk (Thelma P. O.), G 22	Ky.
....	*Buskirk, F 21	Ky.
225	*Buskirk, M 25	N. Y.
50	*Bussey, O 8	Ark.
632	Bussey, N 15	Iowa
100	*Busseyville, F 23	Ky.
10	*Bustamante, R 15	Tex.
....	*Busy, I 21	Ky.
52	*Bustin's Island, P 7	Me.
55	*Butch, N 9	N. C.
670	Butler, K 4	Ala.
74	Butler, E 22	Ark.
1093	Butler, J 7	Ga.
246	Butler, L 13	Ill.
1794	Butler, C 22	Ind.
359	Butler, C 18	Ky.
100	*Butler, D 13	Md.
200	*Butler, I 7	Minn.
2958	Butler, J 6	Mo.
3351	Butler, C 17	N. J.
695	Butler, H 14	Ohio
428	Butler, H 5	Okla.
24477	Butler, K 4	Pa.
153	Butler, E 21	S. D.
608	Butler, L 25	Tenn.
778	*Butler, O 20	Wis.
....	Butler Jc., K 4	Pa.
80	*Butler Springs, M 13	Ala.
266	Butlerville, M 18	Ind.
37081	Butte, K 7	Mont.
623	Butte, E 15	Neb.
261	Butte, I 12	N. D.
250	Butte City, F 6	Calif.
112	*Butte Creek, G 18	Mont.
85	*Butte des Morts, M 15	Wis.
339	Butte Falls, P 7	Ore.
....	*Butte Meadows, F 7	Calif.
295	▲Butterfield, K 10	Ark.
511	Butterfield, Q 10	Minn.
150	Butterfield, Q 8	Mo.
12	*Butterfly, H 21	Ky.
90	Butternut, N 16	Mich.
669	Butternut, G 7	Wis.
85	*Butterworth, O 16	Va.
162	*Butte Valley, O 15	Colo.
500	*Buttonwillow, M 12	Calif.
....	Buttonwood (Christopher) G 15 (Pop. 900 incl. in Hanover)	Pa.
75	*Buttonwoods, H 9	R. I.
16	*Butts, L 17	Mo.
500	Buttzville, D 10	N. J.
32	Buttzville, O 22	N. D.
16	*Butylo, L 20	Va.
500	*Butztown, L 22	Pa.
4	Buxton, L 10	Colo.
....	Buxton, N 15	Iowa
1708	▲Buxton, P 4	Me.
500	*Buxton, F 25	N. C.
404	Buxton, J 23	N. D.
120	Buxton, C 6	Ore.
30	*Buyck, F 19	Minn.
375	*Buzzards Bay, M 23	Mass.
466	Byars, L 14	Okla.
75	*Bybee, G 18	Ky.
75	*Bybee, N 22	Tenn.
23	*Bybee, K 14	Va.
300	*Byer (Byers), O 13	Ohio
400	Byers, G 17	Colo.
153	Byers, L 11	Kan.
200	Byers, (Uwchland P. O.), O 21	Pa.
427	Byers, B 16	Tex.
2418	Byesville, K 17	Ohio
600	Byfield, B 20	Mass.
543	Byhalia, A 14	Miss.
100	Byhalia, I 10	Ohio
64	*Byington, N 19	Tenn.
500	*Bylas, L 21	Ariz.
50	*Byllesby, Q 3	Va.
46	Byng, L 15	Okla.
94	Bynum, E 8	Mont.
200	*Bynum, F 12	N. C.
250	*Bynum, G 19	Tex.
102	*Bynumville, E 12	Mo.
280	*Bypro (Burton) H 22	Ky.
350	Byram, K 11	Miss.
....	*Byram Cove, B 13	N. J.
5	*Byrds, G 15	Tex.
110	*Byrds Creek, G 19	Wis.
215	Byrdstown, L 15	Tenn.
6	*Byrdton, L 21	Va.
....	Byrne, H 12	Tex.
619	Byrnedale, H 10	Pa.
25	Byrnside, K 4	W. Va.
275	Byromville, K 9	Ga.
35	*Byron, B 14	Ark.
400	Byron, I 7	Calif.
305	Byron, J 10	Ga.
1113	Byron, B 14	Ill.
387	*Byron, O 19	Mich.
341	Byron, Q 19	Minn.
171	Byron, O 19	Neb.
200	Byron, L 7	N. Y.
177	Byron, A 9	Okla.
80	Byron, O 16	Wash.
55	*Byron, N 18	Wis.
700	Byron, (Mt. Clare), F 12	W. Va.
388	Byron, B 10	Wyo.
469	Byron Center, O 13	Mich.

C

Pop.	Place Index	State
164	▲*Caballo, L 8	N. M.
30	*Cabanal, B 8	Ark.
110	*Cabarrus, H 7	N. C.
65	*Cabarton, K 7	Idaho
150	*Cabazon, O 20	Calif.
27	*Cabell, J 16	Ky.
299	Cabery, F 19	Ill.
69	Cabezon, F 9	N. M.
840	Cabin Creek (Cabin Creek Junction), L 7	W. Va.
45	Cabinet, C 6	Idaho
1500	*Cabin John, G 9	Md.
210	Cable, J 9	Ohio
314	Cable, E 6	Wis.
1069	Cabool, O 14	Mo.
741	Cabot, H 14	Ark.
500	Cabot, K 4	Pa.
232	Cabot, F 15	Vt.
152	Cache, R 14	Ill.
620	Cache, M 7	Okla.
105	Cache Jc., B 11	Utah
225	*Cactus, K 12	Ariz.
59	Cactus, P 14	Tex.
75	*Cad, B 7	Ga.
60	Cadams, O 18	Neb.
100	Caddoa, M 21	Colo.
....	Caddo, B 11	Ala.
954	Caddo, P 18	Okla.
319	Caddo, E 16	Tex.
150	Caddo Gap, K 7	Ark.
390	Caddo Mills, D 21	Tex.
500	Cade, N 12	La.
75	Cade, P 18	Okla.
200	*Cades, I 19	S. C.
100	*Cades, L 3	Tenn.
25	*Cades Cove, O 19	Tenn.
150	*Cadet, L 18	Mo.
9855	Cadillac, L 14	Mich.
79	*Cadiz, D 19	Pa.
60	Cadiz, N 23	Calif.
1228	Cadiz, J 8	Ky.
2808	Cadiz, I 19	Ohio
32	*Cadiz, O 18	Tex.
25	Cadiz (Leiter), B 17	Wyo.
50	*Cadiz Jc. (Means), I 19	Ohio
50	*Cadmus, F 22	Ky.
100	*Cadmus, R 19	Mich.
500	*Cadogan, L 5	Pa.
300	Cadosia, R 18	N. Y.
676	Cadott, F 12	Wis.
291	Cadwell, K 14	Ga.
65	*Cadwell, J 17	Ill.
94	Cadys Falls, D 12	Vt.
265	*Cadyville, D 24	N. Y.
2	*Caesars Head, B 6	S. C.
....	Caffee Jc., G 11	Ala.
12	*Cagle, P 15	Tenn.
51	*Caglesville, F 10	Ark.
4	*Cahone, N 4	Colo.
25	*Cain City, J 15	Tex.
60	Caineville, M 16	Utah
100	*Cains, P 20	Pa.

Pop.	Place Index	State
75	*Cains Store, I 17	Ky
765	Cainsville, A 8	Mo.
45	Cainsville, N 12	Tenn.
1500	Cairnbrook, O 8	Pa.
20	Cairo, A 11	Ala.
100	*Cairo (Gainer), N 9	Fla.
4653	Cairo, O 7	Ga.
14407	Cairo, R 14	Ill.
254	Cairo, E 13	Mo.
411	Cairo, L 16	Neb.
800	Cairo, P 23	N. Y.
440	Cairo (West Cairo), G 8	Ohio
39	Cairo, N 18	Okla.
532	Cairo, F 8	W. Va.
20	Caisson, D 3	Colo.
50	Cajon, N 17, P 8	Calif.
....	*Calabar, see Sheffield	Mont
10	Calabasas, P 17	Ariz.
150	Calabasas, O 14, Q 2	Calif.
5161	Calais, J 23	Me.
75	Calais, F 13	Vt.
319	*Calallen, P 18	Tex.
64	*Calamine, C 16	Ark.
90	Calamine, I 21	Wis.
384	Calamus, J 23	Iowa
50	*Calcasieu, I 9	La.
100	*Calcis, F 15	Ala.
40	Calcite, L 12	Colo.
111	*Calcium, (Sanford Corners), H 16	N. Y.
47	*Calcium, M 20	Pa.
125	Calder, E 6	Idaho
188	Calderwood, P 19	Tenn.
....	Caldor, G 10	Calif.
50	*Caldwell, E 16	Ala.
64	*Caldwell, H 19	Ark.
7273	Caldwell, N 4	Idaho
1962	Caldwell, O 15	Kan.
10	Caldwell, B 16	Mont.
4932	Caldwell, D 17	N. J.
1705	Caldwell, L 17	Ohio
2165	Caldwell, J 20	Tex.
250	*Caldwell (North Caldwell), N 12	W. Va.
132	*Cale, O 8	Ark.
100	Caledonia, L 11	Ala.
212	Caledonia, A 16	Ill.
467	Caledonia, O 14	Mich.
1985	Caledonia, R 23	Minn.
240	*Caledonia, F 22	Miss.
139	*Caledonia, L 18	Mo.
1226	Caledonia, M 8	N. Y.
150	Caledonia, J 24	N. D.
629	Caledonia, H 12	Ohio
275	Caledonia, H 10	Pa.
31	*Caledonia, L 14	Va.
200	*Caledonia, O 21	Wis.
1092	Calera, H 13	Ala.
597	Calera, Q 17	Okla.
5415	Calexico, Q 23	Calif.
....	*Calf Creek, G 23	Ky.
....	*Calf Creek, H 14	Tex.
....	Calgary, G 24	Tex.
352	Calhan, I 17	Colo.
1000	*Calhoun, K 14	Ala.
2955	Calhoun, C 4	Ga.
197	Calhoun, M 20	Ill.
753	Calhoun, H 9	Ky.
278	Calhoun, C 10	La.
....	*Calhoun, N 15, M 22	Minn.
521	Calhoun, J 9	Mo.
....	*Calhoun, see Fort Calhoun,	Neb.
360	Calhoun, K 24	Okla.
761	Calhoun, C 4	S. C.
275	Calhoun, P 16	Tenn.
1171	Calhoun City, E 16	Miss.
1832	Calhoun Falls, G 5	S. C.
738	Calico Rock, C 13	Ark.
113	*Caliente, M 14	Calif.
1400	Caliente, L 22	Nev.
572	Califon, E 12	N. J.
100	California (California Jc.), L 2	Iowa
106	*California, C 18	Ky.
94	*California, O 14	Md.
....	California, O 6	Ohio
2525	California, I 12	Mo.
2614	California, O 4	Pa.
354	*California Hot Springs (Hot Springs), K 14	Calif.
100	California Jc., (California), L 2	Iowa
98	Calio, E 17	N. D.
712	Calion, Q 11	Ark.
200	*Calimesa, O 21	Calif.
1799	Calipatria, P 23	Calif.
45	*Calista, M 14	Kan.
1124	Calistoga, G 5	Calif.
22	Calkins, J 11	Mont.
....	*Calkinsville, see Rosebush.	Mich.
1500	Call, I 25	Tex.
....	*Calla, see Vancleve	Ky.
80	*Callahan, B 5	Calif.
685	Callahan, B 16	Fla.
75	*Callands, Q 9	Va.
398	Callao, D 12	Mo.
68	Callao, H 2	Utah
100	Callao, K 20	Va.
23	*Callaville, Q 15	Va.
25	*Callaway, K 20	Ky.
....	*Callaway, O 14	Md.
249	Callaway, H 5	Minn.
768	Callaway, K 12	Neb.
90	*Callaway, P 7	Va.
377	Callender, G 9	Iowa
289	Callensburg, I 5	Pa.
354	Callery, K 3	Pa.
850	Callicoon, C 1	N. Y.
331	*Callicoon Center, C 2	N. Y.
110	*Calliham, O 16	Tex.
50	*Callison, G 8	S. C.
....	Calloway, G 5	Ore.
903	Calmar, C 19	Iowa
26	*Calora, J 7	Neb.
300	Calpella, F 3	Calif.
53	*Calpet, J 5	Wyo.
600	Calpine, F 10	Calif.
....	Calpine Jc., E 10	Calif.
360	Calumet, E 10	Ala.
300	Calumet No. 1 (Delcarbon), O 15	Colo.
13241	Calumet City (West Hammond), C 22	Ill.
274	Calumet, D 4	Iowa
84	Calumet, O 14	La.
1460	Calumet (Red Jacket), C 3	Mich.
946	Calumet, G 16	Minn.
500	Calumet, H 9	Okla.
500	*Calumet, N 5	Pa.
125	Calumet Harbor (Pipe), N 16	Wis.
1593	*Calumet Park (Burr Oak), C 21	Ill.
100	Calumetville, N 16	Wis.
50	*Calva, L 22	Ariz.
500	Calvary, P 7	Ga.
96	*Calvary, H 15	Ky.
150	Calvary, N 17	Wis.
239	Calvert, O 5	Ala.
40	*Calvert, D 8	Kan.
319	Calvert (Calvert City) J 6	Ky.
75	Calvert, B 18	Md.
2366	Calvert, I 20	Tex.
319	Calvert City (Calvert), J 6	Ky.
822	Calverton, G 10	N. Y.
117	Calverton, H 16	Va.
45	*Calvin, O 19	Ill.
34	*Calvin, K 20	Ky.
250	*Calvin, E 9	La.
325	Calvin, D 17	N. D.
....	Calvin, O 15	Ohio
589	Calvin, L 17	Okla.
96	*Calvin, N 11	Pa.
200	*Calvin, E 3	Va.
14	*Calvin, L 10	W. Va.
210	*Calwa City (Calwa), J 12	Calif.
678	Calypso, I 16	N. C.
25	*Calyx, H 21	Miss.
360	Camak, G 16	Ga.
2	Camak Jc., G 16	Ga.
124	*Camanche, H 10	Calif.
814	Camanche, J 25	Iowa
257	Camargo, I 19	Ill.
289	Camargo, F 5	Okla.
300	Camarillo, O 13	Calif.
30	Camas, M 19	Idaho
100	Camas, F 3	Mont.
4433	Camas, Q 7	Wash.
302	Camas Valley, N 4	Ore.
60	*Cambra, H 18	Pa.
20	Cambray, O 8	N. M.
750	Cambria, L 8	Calif.
687	Cambria, (Reeves), P 15	Ill.
146	Cambria, P 13	Iowa
125	*Cambria, Q 13	Minn.
150	Cambria, L 19	Okla.
....	Cambria, M 18	Tenn.
50	Cambria, P 17	Tenn.
810	Cambria, O 5	Va.
688	Cambria, L 18	Wis.
405	Cambridge, L 4	Idaho
1312	Cambridge, D 10	Ill.
608	Cambridge, J 12	Iowa
246	Cambridge, N 18	Kan.
150	Cambridge, K 10	Me.
10102	Cambridge, L 18	Md.
110879	Cambridge, E 19, M 3,	Mass.
1592	Cambridge, L 16	Minn.
1084	Cambridge, N 12	Neb.
1572	Cambridge, M 25	N. Y.
15044	Cambridge, K 17	Ohio
65	*Cambridge, O 20	Pa.
237	Cambridge, D 9	Vt.
577	Cambridge, L 20	Wis.
2207	Cambridge City, J 20	Ind.
198	Cambridge Jc., D 10	Vt.
145	Cambridgeport, O 12	Vt.
1807	Cambridge Springs, E 3	Pa.
122	*Camby, J 14	Ind.
909	Camden, L 10	Ala.
8975	Camden, O 10	Ark.
682	Camden, G 22	Del.
157	Camden, H 7	Ill.
590	Camden, F 12	Ind.
3000	Camden, N 13	Me.
385	Camden, R 16	Mich.
....	*Camden (Camden Place) N 15, M 22	Minn.
300	Camden, I 13	Miss.
399	Camden, G 7	Mo.
117536	Camden, K 9	N. J.
2021	Camden, K 16	N. Y.
116	Camden, C 23	N. C.
991	Camden, L 5	Ohio
5747	Camden, F 15	S. C.
992	Camden, M 7	Tenn.
800	Camden, I 23	Tex.
25	Camden, F 24	Wash.
100	*Camden, G 11	W. Va.
373	Camden on Gauley, K 11	W. Va.
....	Camden Jc., L 10	Ala.
....	*Camden Place (Camden) N 15, M 22	Minn.
140	Camden Point, F 5	Mo.
893	Camdenton, L 12	Mo.
150	Cameo, I 4	Colo.
36	Cameo, L 15	W. Va.
10	Cameron, E 15	Ariz.
115	Cameron, G 4	Idaho
250	Cameron, F 8	Ill.
150	Cameron, O 6	La.
3615	Cameron, D 7	Mo.
125	Cameron, N 9	Mont.
5	Cameron, L 16	Neb.
....	*Cameron, H 24	N. M.
200	Cameron, Q 10	N. Y.
311	Cameron, H 12	N. C
127	Cameron, L 19	Ohio
203	Cameron, K 25	Okla.
60	Cameron, G 11	Pa.
624	Cameron, I 15	S. C.
5040	Cameron, I 19	Tex.
1998	Cameron, B 11	W. Va.
807	Cameron, D 10	Wis.
....	Cameron Jc., D 7	Mo.
135	*Cameron Mills, Q 10	N. Y.
....	*Cameronsville, A 17	Ala.
64	*Cameta, I 7	Miss.
2588	Camilla, N 7	Ga.
300	Camilla, J 23	Tex.
1133	Camillus, M 14	N. Y.
350	Camino, G 9	Calif.
50	Cammack, H 18	Ind.
230	Cammal, H 13	Pa.
....	*Camoochee, see Canoochee,	Ga.
121	*Camp, A 15	Ark.
27	*Camp, O 11	Ohio
15	*Camp, D 9	Va.
290	Camp (Procious), J 8	W. Va.
600	*Campaign, O 13	Tenn.
....	*Camp Alleghany, N 12	W. Va.
....	*Camp Allison, J 12	Tex.
100	Campania, G 18	Ga.
20	Camp Angelus, N 21, Q 11	Calif.
100	Camp Baldy, N 21, Q 7	Calif.
250	*Campbell, L 7	Ala.
183	*Campbell, D 12	Ark.
1800	Campbell, I 6, H 23	Calif.
328	Campbell, J 3	Minn.
1786	Campbell, R 21, I 23	Mo.
478	Campbell, N 16	Neb.
350	Campbell, Q 10	N. Y.
146	*Campbell (Kintyre), O 14	N. D.
13785	Campbell, F 21	Ohio
....	*Campbell, see Gore	Okla.
428	*Campbell, D 20	Tex.
150	*Campbell, K 12	Va.
275	Campbell Hall, D 4	N. Y.
401	Campbell Hill, O 13	Ill.
5	Campbell Jc., N 15	Tenn.
608	Campbellsburg, O 13	Ind.
350	Campbellsburg, D 15	Ky.
1094	Campbellsport, N 18	Wis.
81	Campellstown, L 5	Ohio
2488	Campellsville, I 15	Ky.
311	Campbellton, M 10	Fla.
38	Campbellton, N 17	Tex.
75	Campbelltown, P 6	Ind.
600	Campbelltown, N 17	Pa.
....	*Camp Connell, H 10	Calif.
25	*Camp Creek, Q 8	W. Va.
227	Camp Crook, D 1	S. D.
....	*Camp Curry, I 11	Calif.
....	*Camp Curtin, N 16	Pa.
....	*Camp Custer, Q 13	Mich.
327	*Camp Dennison, O 6	Ohio
....	*Camp Devens, see Fort Devens	Mass.
31	*Camp Dix, D 21	Ky.
....	Camp Dix, K 14	N. J.
445	Camp Douglas, H 16	Wis.
180	Camp Ellis, Q 5	Me.
200	*Campgaw, D 20	N. J.
100	Camp Grant, B 15	Ill.
215	Campgrove, E 12	Ill.
....	*Camp Ground, L 13	Ohio
....	*Camp Grounds, see Chester Heights	Pa.
1147	Camp Hill, I 19	Ala.
3630	Camp Hill, N 16	Pa.
....	Camp Jackson, G 14	S. C.
....	Camp Knox, see Fort Knox,	Ky.
128	*Camp Lake, O 22	Wis.
....	*Camp Lewis, see Fort Lewis	Wash.
25	*Camp McCoy (Sparta Military), G 6	Wis.
....	*Camp Meade, see Fort George G. Meade	Md.
....	*Camp Meade Jc., see Fort George G. Meade Jc.	Md.
125	*Camp Meeker, G 3, A 15	Calif.
109	*Camp Namanu, E 8	Ore.
16	*Camp Nelson, K 14	Calif.
100	Camp Nelson, G 17	Ky.
210	Campo, Q 20	Calif.
200	Campo, Q 22	Colo.
389	Campobello, A 7	S. C.
216	Campo Seco, H 9	Calif.
....	Camp Perry, C 11	Ohio
1084	Camp Point, I 5	Ill.
42	*Camp Richardson, G 10	Calif.
20	*Camp Rodgers, E 9	Calif.
....	*Camp Seale, I 23	Tex.
250	*Camp Sealth, I 9	Wash.
600	*Camp Ruby, I 23	Tex.
....	*Camp Sacramento, G 10	Calif.
100	*Camp San Saba, H 14	Tex.
30	*Camp Sherman, H 12	Ore.
4	*Camp Sierra, J 12	Calif.
10	*Campsite, G 10	Mont.
75	Camps Pass, M 22	Mont.
60	*Camp Springs, E 11	Tex.
....	Camp Stool, Q 23	Wyo.
....	*Camp Taylor, F 14	Ky.
1004	Campti, F 7	La.
190	Campton, F 10	Ga.
418	Campton, G 20	Ky.
300	Campton, J 13	N. H.
22	Campton Jc., G 20	Ky.
75	*Camptonville, F 8	Calif.
300	Camptown, F 19	Pa.
169	Campus, E 18	Ill.
25	*Campus, H 6	Kan.
350	Camp Verde, H 13	Ariz.
28	*Camp Verde, K 14	Tex.
118	Campville, F 8	Conn.
250	Campville, D 15	Fla.
....	*Camp Walton, see Fort Walton	Fla.
75	Camp Wood, H 9	Ariz.
778	Camp Wood, L 13	Tex.
50	*Cana, E 7	N. C.
35	*Cana, Q 3	Va.
100	*Canaan, D 11	Ark.
1500	Canaan, A 5	Conn.
100	Canaan, N 19	Ind.
184	Canaan, L 10	Me.
50	*Canaan, A 17	Miss.
500	Canaan, L 10	N. H.
500	Canaan, P 25	N. Y.
340	Canaan, A 23	Vt.
50	*Canaan, H 13	W. Va.
130	Canaan Center, L 9	N. H.
40	*Canada, J 17	Kan.
300	Canada, G 24	Ky.
....	*Canada Creek, I 19	Mich.
180	*Canada Lake (Green Lake), L 21	N. Y.
300	Canadensis, I 23	Pa.
385	Canadian, J 20	Okla.
2151	Canadian, B 6	Tex.
119	*Canadys (Cannadys), N 15	S. C.
2577	Canajoharie, M 20	N. Y.
....	Canal, C 20	Del.
1115	Canal Fulton, G 17	Ohio
419	Canalou, Q 23	Mo.
2000	Canal Point, L 22	Fla.
1046	Canal Winchester, L 12	Ohio
8321	Canandaigua, M 10	N. Y.
34	Canary, J 3	Ore.
698	Canaseraga, P 8	N. Y.
4150	Canastota, M 16	N. Y.
148	▲*Canaveral, H 21	Fla.
75	*Canby, B 9	Calif.
2099	Canby, O 3	Minn.
988	Canby, E 7	Ore.
7	Candelaria, K 9	Nev.
300	Candelaria K 4	Tex.
300	Candia, P 16	N. H.
200	*Candler, F 15	Fla.
50	*Candler, O 8	N. C.
50	*Candlewax, D 7	Va.
1282	Cando, F 16	N. D.
509	Candor, H 10	N. C.
661	Candor, Q 14	N. Y.
200	Caneadea, P 7	N. Y.
45	*Cane Beds, E 6	Ariz.
50	*Canebrake, H 13	La.
521	Canebrake, R 5	W. Va.
20	*Canecreek, I 19	Ky.
....	*Cane Creek, see Isom	Va.
200	Canehill, D 4	Ark.
250	*Cane River, N 9	N. C.
300	*Cane Valley, J 15	Ky.
2629	Caney, O 21	Kan.
200	Caney, G 21	Ky.
361	Caney, P 18	Okla.
....	*Caney Siding, see Esco	Ky.
10	*Caneyspring, P 11	Tenn.
399	Caneyville, H 12	Ky.
450	Canfield, Q 7	Ark.
6	*Canfield, I 8	Idaho
1141	Canfield, F 20	Ohio
45	*Canfield, I 10	W. Va.
2550	Canisteo, P 9	N. Y.
665	Canistota, L 22	S. D.
869	▲Canjilon, D 11	N. M.
250	*Canmer, I 13	Ky.
60	*Cannady, B 7	Va.
119	*Cannadys (Canadys), N 15	S. C.
145	Cannelburg, O 8	Ind.
226	Cannel City, G 21	Ky.
2240	Cannelton, R 10	Ind.
317	Cannelton, K 1	Pa.
521	*Cannelton, M 8	W. Va.
283	Cannelville, L 15	Ohio
100	Canning, I 14	S. D.
100	*Cannon, K 23	Del.
23	*Cannon, J 19	Ky.
100	Cannon Ball, P 12	N. D.
....	Cannon Ball Jc., P 12	N. D.
125	Cannon Beach, B 4	Ore.
35	*Cannon Creek, C 7	Ark.
....	*Cannon Creek, see Atpontley	Tenn.
250	Cannondale, O 4	Conn.
1544	Cannon Falls, O 17	Minn.
200	*Cannon Mines, L 18	Mo.
165	*Cannonsburg, O 13	Mich.
75	*Cannonsburg, M 5	Miss.
18	*Cannons Mill, K 15	Ky.
225	Cannonsville, Q 18	N. Y.
250	Cannonville, P 10	Utah
300	*Canobie Lake, P 18	N. H.
500	*Canoe, O 10	Ala.
100	*Canoe, H 21	Ky.
....	*Canoga Park (Owensmouth), N 16, Q 4, (Pop. incl. in Los Angeles)	Calif.
....	Canon, see Rock Springs	Ariz.
496	Canon, D 14	Ga.
6690	Canon City, K 14	Colo.
75	Canones, D 11	N. M.
12599	Canonsburg, N 2	Pa.
53	*Canoochee (Camoochee), J 18	Ga.
333	Canova, K 22	S. D.
500	Canterbury, G 23	Conn.
25	Canterbury, N 13	N. H.
16	*Cantil, M 14	Calif.
200	Canton, D 11	Conn.
100	Canton (Cantonment) M 2	Fla.
2651	Canton, D 6	Ga.
11577	Canton, G 10	Ill.
100	Canton, O 15	Ind.
796	Canton, J 16	Kan.
200	Canton, J 7	Ky.
800	Canton, M 6	Me.
6381	■Canton, H 19	Mass.
421	Canton, R 22	Minn.
6011	Canton, J 12	Miss.
2125	Canton, C 16	Mo.
23	Canton, J 9	Mont.
160	*Canton, N 6	N. J.
3018	Canton, E 18	N. Y.
5037	Canton, O 7	N. C.
148	Canton (Hensel), E 21	N. D.
108401	Canton, G 18	Ohio
775	Canton, F 7	Okla.
2040	Canton, F 16	Pa.
2518	Canton, N 25	S. D.
715	Canton, E 21	Tex.
100	Canton, D 10	Wis.
208	Canton Center, D 10	Conn.
....	*Canton Corner see Canton	Mass.
100	Cantonment (Canton), M 2	Fla.
105	*Canton Point, M 4	Me.
179	*Cantrall, I 12	Ill.
376	Cantril, Q 18	Iowa
65	*Cantu (Andrade), Q 25	Calif.
30	*Cantwell, M 20	Mo.
374	Canute, I 4	Okla.
700	*Canutillo, G 1	Tex.
14	*Canvas, L 10	W. Va.
50	*Canyon, H 6	Calif.
100	*Canyon, F 19	Minn.
2622	Canyon, D 3	Tex.
25	Canyon, C 15	W. Va.
5	*Canyon, B 3	Wyo.
312	Canyon City, I 18	Ore.
37	Canyon Creek, I 8	Mont.
....	*Canyondam, E 9	Calif.
20	Canyon Diablo, G 16	Ariz.
35	*Canyon Falls, G 19,	Ky.
50	Canyon Ferry, J 9	Mont.
....	Canyon Jc., J 2	S. D.
255	Canyonville, N 5	Ore.
85	Capa, J 11	S. D.
920	Capac, O 24	Mich.
175	Capahosic, N 20	Va.
115	Capay, G 6	Calif.
2299	Cape Charles, N 22	Va.
1025	Cape Cottage, P 6	Me.
5000	Cape Elizabeth, P 6	Me.
122	*Cape Fair, Q 9	Mo.
19426	Cape Girardeau, O 23	Mo.
2	*Capehart, H 4	W. Va.
300	Cape Henry, P 23	Va.
150	Cape Horn, Q 8	Wash.
....	Cape Jc., M 14	Me.
....	Cape Jc., N 23	Va.
1000	*Capels (Caples), Q 5	W. Va.
2583	Cape May, R 11	N. J.
1500	Cape May C. H., R 12	N. J.
126	Cape May Point, R 10	N.J.
218	Cape Neddick, R 4	Me.
6	*Capens, G 12	Me.
266	Cape Porpoise, Q 5	Me.
100	*Cape Rosier, L 17	Me.
....	Capers, N 16	Colo.
30	*Caperton, (Mincar), M 8	W. Va.
20	*Cape Sandy, P 12	Ind.
75	*Capeville, N 23	Va.
931	Cape Vincent, G 14	N. Y.
....	Capistrano Beach, see Doheny Park	Calif.
932	Capitan, K 15	N. M.
....	*Capital, O 10	Me.
175	Capitol, M 25	Mont.
500	Capitola, J 6	Calif.
80	Capitola, B 6	Fla.
812	Capitol Heights, J 16	Ala.
2036	Capitol Heights, J 12	Md.
160	*Capleville, Q 2	Tenn.
800	*Caples (Capels), Q 5	W. Va.
73	*Caplinger Mills, M 8	Mo.
201	*Capon Bridge, E 21	W. Va.
115	*Capon Road, G 12	Va.
162	*Capon Springs, E 21	W. Va.
150	*Capps, M 21	Ala.
23	*Capps, B 9	Ark.
800	Capps (Farr), O 16	Colo.
....	Capps, B 7	Fla.
....	Capps, B 4	Tex.
100	*Cappstown, Q 6	Ark.
100	Caprock, L 23	N. M.
487	Capron, A 16	Ill.
....	*Capron, see Van Cleve	Iowa
147	*Capron, A 7	Okla.
291	*Capron, Q 18	Va.
500	Capshaw, A 13	Ala.
180	*Captina (Captina Island), B 11	W. Va.
45	*Captiva, L 16	Fla.
106	Capulin, P 11	Colo.
150	Capulin, C 21	N. M.
35	Caputa, K 4	S. D.
36	*Caradan, H 16	Tex.
140	*Caratunk, I 7	Me.
477	Caraway, D 21	Ark.
4	Carbert, B 21	Mont.
50	Carbo, D 7	Va.
510	Carbon, K 8	Ind.
383	Carbon, N 7	Iowa
510	Carbon, L 20	Okla.
335	*Carbon, N 5	Pa.
459	Carbon, F 15	Tex.
324	*Carbon (South Carbon), K 6	W. Va.
75	Carbonado, K 9	Wash.
575	*Carbon Cliff, D 8	Ill.
50	*Carbondale, H 9	Calif.
437	Carbondale, H 8	Colo.
8550	Carbondale, P 14	Ill.
415	Carbondale, H 22	Kan.
120	Carbondale, I 8	Ky.
600	Carbondale, N 14	Ohio
....	*Carbondale (Pop incl. in Tulsa), E 19	Okla.
19371	Carbondale, F 22	Pa.
263	*Carbondale, C 24	Tex.
165	*Carbondale, M 8	W. Va.
80	Carbon Glow, I 22	Ky.
2555	Carbon Hill, E 9,	Ala.
141	Carbon Hill, D 18	Ill.
499	Carbon Hill, M 14	Ohio
....	*Carbon Station, see New Castle	Pa.
63	*Carbonton, F 11	N. C.
50	Carbur, D 9	Fla.
58	Carbury, D 12	N. D.
35	*Carcassonne, J 22	Ky.
750	*Cardale, P 4	Pa.
246	*Cardiff, F 12	Ala.
417	*Cardiff (Cardiff by the Sea) Q 20	Calif.
398	Cardiff, B 16	Md.
500	*Cardiff (Nettleton), M 8	Pa.
241	*Cardiff by the Sea (Cardiff), Q 20	Calif.
200	Cardiff Mines, H 9	Pa.
95	Cardigan (Grafton Center), L 10	N. H.
437	Cardin, A 23	Okla.
500	*Cardinal, K 20	Ky.
117	*Cardinal, M 21	Va.
1304	Cardington, H 12	Ohio
195	*Cardville, I 15	Me.
913	Cardwell, K 23	Mo.
100	Cardwell, L 8	Mont.
48	*Cardwell, L 15	Va.
18	*Cardy (La Crosse), D 12	Mo.
914	Carencro, M 11	La.
17	*Caress, I 10	W. Va.
47	*Caret, K 19	Va.
700	*Caretta (Juno), Q 5	W. Va.
600	Carey, O 13	Idaho
2984	Carey, F 10	Ohio
200	*Carey, A 13	Tex.
40	Careyhurst, J 19	Wyo.
25	*Careywood, C 5	Idaho
....	Cargile, Q 11	Ark.
52	*Caribou, E 9	Calif.
8000	Caribou, C 19	Me.
....	Carisbrook, B 20	N. M.
135	*Carl, E 10	Ga.
37	*Carl, L 10	W. Va.
68	*Carland, O 19	Mich.
81	*Carle Place, H 7	N. Y.
864	Carleton, Q 22	Mich.
350	Carleton, N 19	Neb.
112	*Carleton (Carlton), F 8	Okla.
34	Carley, P 16	Wash.
22	Carlile, C 21	Wyo.
832	Carlin, D 16	Nev.
61	*Carlin Bay, D 4	Idaho
4965	Carlinville, K 11	Ill.
1080	Carlisle, I 15	Ark.
874	Carlisle, M 6	Ind.
690	Carlisle, L 12	Iowa
1414	Carlisle, E 19	Ky.
150	*Carlisle, P 20	La.
747	▲Carlisle, D 17	Mass.
40	*Carlisle, I 6	Minn.
40	*Carlisle, L 6	Miss.
5	Carlisle, N 19	Neb.
150	Carlisle, N 21	N. Y.
152	*Carlisle (Berne), L 17	Ohio
390	Carlisle, M 7	Ohio
13984	Carlisle, O 15	Pa.
303	Carlisle, D 11	S. C.
519	Carlisle, I 23	Tex.
75	Carlisle, J 2	Wash.
250	Carlisle, N 8	W. Va.
....	Carlisle Jc., M 7	Ohio
1039	*Carl Jc., O 6	Mo.
375	Carlock, G 14	Ill.
3	Carlock, O 16	S. D.
13	*Carloover, K 7	Va.
100	Carlos (Carlos City), I 21	Ind.
515	Carlos, M 5	Md.
187	Carlos, K 8	Minn.
100	Carlos City (Carlos) I 21	Ind.
31	Carlos Jc. (National), M 5	Md.
45	Carlotta, D 1	Calif.
250	Carlowville, L 11	Ala.
2600	*Carlsbad, Q 20	Calif.
7116	Carlsbad, N 21	N. M.
150	*Carlsbad, H 12	Tex.
560	Carlsborg, F 5	Wash.
150	*Carlshend, E 6	Mich.
5644	Carlstadt, D 20	N. J.
30	*Carlton, L 7	Ala.
150	Carlton (Grote), M 23	Colo.
284	*Carlton (Berkeley), E 14	Ga.
101	Carlton, I 16	Kan.
700	Carlton, I 19	Minn.
112	*Carlton (Carleton), F 8	Okla.
864	Carlton, E 6	Ore.
75	*Carlton, F 3	Pa.
400	Carlton, G 17	Tex.
100	Carlton, E 15	Wash.
60	Carlton Center, P 15	Mich.
900	*Carlton Hill, D 19	N. J.
2591	Carlyle, M 13	Ill.
250	Carlyle, K 23	Kan.
85	Carlyle, I 25	Mont.
250	Carman, F 5	Ill.
5	Carman, J 8	Neb.
500	Carman, N 23	N. Y.
2837	Carmel (Carmel-by-the-Sea), K 6	Calif.
771	Carmel, I 14	Ind.
115	Carmel, L 13	Me.
250	Carmel, O 9	N. J.
1500	Carmel, E 6	N. Y.
2837	Carmel-by-the-Sea (Carmel), K 6	Calif.
....	Carmen, J 13	Idaho
29	*Carmen (Venters), H 24	Ky.
818	*Carmen, C 8	Okla.
....	*Carmenia, G 5	La.
4098	Carmi, O 19	Ill.
550	*Carmichael, H 8	Calif.
300	*Carmichael, L 21	Miss.
847	Carmichaels, P 3	Pa.
500	*Carmine, L 19	Tex.
175	Carmona, I 23	Tex.
....	Carnadero, J 7	Calif.
111	Carnarvon, H 6	Iowa
734	Carnation, H 9	Wash.
262	Carnegie, M 4	Ga.
1740	Carnegie, K 7	Okla.
12663	Carnegie, M 3	Pa.
70	*Carneiro, I 13	Kan.
....	*Carnelian Bay, G 9	Calif.
361	Carnesville, D 13	Ga.
250	Carney, H 6	Mich.
283	Carney, G 14	Okla.
3050	Carneys Point, M 5	N. J.
31	Carnforth, K 17	Iowa
6	*Carnot, O 2	Va.
25	*Carns, E 13	Neb.
200	Carnwath, K 10	Pa.
3070	Caro, N 22	Mich.
165	Caro, G 23	Tex.
70	*Caroga Lake, L 21	N. Y.
1740	Caroleen, H 2	N. C.
637	*Carolina Beach, L 17	N. C.
450	Carolina, L 8	R. I.
950	*Carolina, D 13	W. Va.
68	*Caroline (Caroline Depot), P 13	N. Y.
150	*Caroline, L 12	Wis.
100	Caroline Center, P 14	N. Y.
68	*Caroline Depot (Caroline), P 13	N. Y.
600	Carona, N 25	Kan.
66	*Carp, L 21	Nev.
78	*Carpenter, L 11	Ill.
156	*Carpenter, B 15	Iowa
32	*Carpenter, K 19	Ky.
165	*Carpenter, M 9	Miss.
15	Carpenter, D 14	N. D.
100	*Carpenter, O 15	Ohio
53	Carpenter, I 3	Okla.
90	Carpenter, H 20	S. D.
100	Carpenter, R 23	Wyo.
1289	Carpentersville, B 18	Ill.
206	Carpentersville (Carpenterville), F 8	N. J.
206	*Carpenterville (Carpentersville), F 8	N. J.
35	*Carpenterville, P 3	Ore.
1000	Carpinteria, N 12	Calif.
322	Carpio, F 8	N. D.
75	*Carp Lake, H 16	Mich.
65	Carr, B 15	Colo.
112	*Carrabassett, K 5	Me.
1019	Carrabelle, D 3	Fla.
40	Carraway, D 16	Fla.
1455	Carrboro, E 12	N. C.
50	*Carr Creek, H 22	Ky.
21	Carr Crossing, K 19	Colo.
....	Carrick, M 3	Pa.
36	*Carrie, H 22	Ky.
31	*Carrie, C 6	Va.
275	Carrier, D 9	Okla.
400	Carriere, Q 14	Miss.
2360	Carriers Mills, P 17	Ill.
....	*Carrigain, J 17	N. H.
1850	Carrington, K 17	N. D.
2494	Carrizo Springs, O 13	Tex.
1457	Carrizozo, K 13	N. M.
5389	Carroll, I 7	Iowa
100	Carroll, I 19	Me.
351	Carroll, G 20	Neb.
337	Carroll, L 13	Ohio
200	Carrolls, O 6	Wash.
626	Carrollton, G 5	Ala.
22	Carrollton, B 8	Ark.
6214	Carrollton, F 3	Ga.
2285	Carrollton, K 8	Ill.
2910	Carrollton, D 15	Ky.
102	*Carrollton, C 11	Md.
3100	Carrollton, N 20	Mich.
575	Carrollton, F 13	Miss.
469	Carrollton (Northcarrollton), F 13	Miss.
4070	Carrollton, F 9	Mo.
100	Carrollton, Q 5	N. Y.
2548	Carrollton, H 19	Ohio
921	*Carrollton, E 19	Tex.
20	*Carrollton, P 20	Va.
....	*Carrollton, see Carrolls,	Wash.
1289	Carrolltown, L 9	Pa.
650	Carrollville, P 21	Wis.
120	Carrothers, F 12	Ohio
18	*Carrs, D 21	Ky.
50	*Carrs Sta. (Carrs), H 14	Ga.
243	Carrsville, H 6	Ky.
100	Carrsville, Q 19	Va.
100	*Carrville, D 3	Calif.
5	*Carry Pond, I 7	Me.
85	*Carryville, B 20	Ark.
500	*Carson, N 4	Ala.
25	*Carson, E 22	Ark.
613	Carson, M 5	Iowa
5	Carson, K 6	La.
175	*Carson, N 13	Miss.
112	▲Carson, D 14	N. M.
473	Carson, P 9	N. D.
....	Carson, B 20	Ohio
35	Carson, J 18	Okla.
90	Carson, F 24	Ore.
200	*Carson, O 16	Va.
276	Carson, Q 9	Wash.
....	Carson, I 6	Wis.
1112	Carson City, N 16	Mich.
2478	Carson City, H 3	Nev.
50	*Carson Hill, H 10	Calif.
500	Carson Lake, F 17	Minn.
433	Carsonville, N 24	Mich.
....	Carswell, Q 6	W. Va.
30	*Cartago, K 17	Calif.
28	*Carta Valley, K 12	Tex.
160	*Cartecay, C 6	Ga.
....	Carter, see Hicks	Ark.
169	Carter, D 21	Ky.
350	*Carter, I 10	Miss.
105	Carter, F 11	Mont.
20	Carter, O 14	Neb.
15	Carter (Clearwater), I 19	N. Y.
535	Carter, J 3	Okla.
42	Carter, M 13	S. D.
500	*Carter, L 24	Tenn.
295	Carter, M 10	Wis.
40	Carter, P 3	Wyo.
....	*Carter Camp, see Carter Nine	Okla.
15	*Carter Camp, F 12	Pa.
11976	Carteret, F 18	N. J.
....	Carteret, F 18	N. J.
846	Carter Lake, M 3	Iowa
....	*Carter Nine (Carter Camp), C 16	Okla.
100	*Carters B 5,	Ga.
162	*Carters (W. Berlin), F 15	Mass.
25	*Carters Bridge, K 12	Va.
310	Cartersburg, J 12	Ind.
30	*Carters Creek, O 10	Tenn.
6141	Cartersville, E 4	Ga.
50	Cartersville, D 14	Iowa
27	Cartersville, J 20	Mont.
45	Cartersville, J 24	Okla.
178	Cartersville, G 18	S. C.
134	*Cartersville, M 13	Va.
95	*Carterton, D 7	Va.
2893	Carterville, P 15	Ill.
1582	Carterville, O 6	Mo.
687	Carthage, M 11	Ark.
2575	Carthage, G 5	Ill.
937	Carthage, J 18	Ind.
40	Carthage, L 5	Me.
....	Carthage, E 2	Minn.
1766	Carthage, I 15	Miss.
10585	Carthage, O 6	Mo.
24	Carthage, J 10	N. M.
4207	Carthage, H 17	N. Y.
1381	Carthage, H 11	N. C.
512	Carthage, J 21	S. D.
1512	Carthage, M 13	Tenn.
2178	Carthage, F 24	Tex.
12	*Carthage, P 5	Va.
3	Carthage Jc., E 2	Minn.
250	Carthagena, I 6	Ohio
25	*Cartney, B 12	Ark.

Pop. Place Index State
50*Cartter, M 16 .... Ill.
50*Cartwright, K 16 .... Ky.
50 Cartwright, H 2 .... N. D.
....*Cartwright, Q 17 .... Okla.
50 Cartwright, H 8 .... Pa.
121 Caruthers, K 11 .... Calif.
6612 Caruthersville, J 25 .... Mo.
75*Carvel (Cleveland), M 14 Kan.
37 Carver, G 22 .... Ky.
400 Carver, K 22 .... Mass.
519 Carver, O 14 .... Minn.
75 Carver, D 8 .... Ore.
15 Carver City, N 12 .... Okla.
....*Carversville, N 23 .... Pa.
10 Carwile, D 9 .... Okla.
707 Cary, B 18 .... Ill.
49*Cary, K 20 .... Ky.
287▲Cary, G 19 .... Me.
491*Cary, I 7 .... Miss.
1141 Cary, F 13 .... N. C.
50*Carysbrook, L 13 .... Va.
279 Caryville, M 9 .... Fla.
300*Caryville, H 18 .... Mass.
1500 Caryville, M 18 .... Tenn.
28 Caryville, D 13 .... Wis.
245 Casa, H 9 .... Ark.
400*Casa Blanca, O 21 .... Calif.
101 Casa Blanca, G 7 .... N. M.
1545 Casa Grande, L 14 .... Ariz.
108*Casanova, G 15 .... Va.
200*Casa Piedra, K 5 .... Tex.
310 Casar, F 2 .... N. C.
14 Cascabel, N 20 .... Ariz.
50*Cascade, J 16 .... Colo.
1029 Cascade, L 6 .... Idaho
1376 Cascade, H 22 .... Iowa
150*Cascade (Buena Vista), B 5 .... Md.
.... Cascade, E 7 .... Mich.
103*Cascade, O 20 .... Mo.
419 Cascade, H 9 .... Mont.
7*Cascade, F 9 .... Neb.
1000 Cascade, G 17 .... N. H.
109*Cascade, Q 9 .... Va.
355*Cascade, D 16 .... W. Va.
358 Cascade, O 17 .... Wis.
703 Cascade Locks, C 10 .... Ore.
....*Cascades, see North Bonneville .... Wash.
22*Cascade Summit, O 10 .... Ore.
100 Cascadia, H 8 .... Ore.
134*Cascilla, D 11 .... Miss.
350 Casco, O 4 .... Me.
292 Casco, P 13 .... Wis.
.... Casco Jc., P 14 .... Wis.
33*Case, I 17 .... Mo.
451 Caseville, L 22 .... Mich.
2543 Casey, K 20 .... Ill.
709 Casey, L 8 .... Iowa
35*Casey, I 11 .... Ky.
17 Casey, E 15 .... Okla.
30*Casey, N 20 .... Wash.
50*Casey Creek, J 15 .... Ky.
865 Caseyville, M 10 .... Ill.
67 Caseyville, H 7 .... Ky.
186*Cash, D 19 .... Ark.
29*Cash, I 13 .... Ky.
37 Cash, D 5 .... S. D.
266*Cash, D 20 .... Tex.
65*Cash, M 20 .... Va.
800 Cash Corner, H 21 .... N. C.
26 Cashel, F 22 .... Va.
353*Cashiers, Q 6 .... N. C.
200 Cashion, K 12 .... Ariz.
232 Cashion, G 11 .... Okla.
1465 Cashmere, I 14 .... Wash.
110*Cashmere, P 11 .... W. Va.
706 Cashton, G 17 .... Wis.
260 Cashtown, P 14 .... Pa.
185*Casma (Duncan), G 13 N. C.
181*Casmalia, N 11 .... Calif.
48*Casner, I 15 .... Ill.
289 Casnovia, N 13 .... Mich.
515 Cason, D 23 .... Tex.
250 Caspar, F 2 .... Calif.
17964 Casper, J 17 .... Wyo.
1797 Caspian G 2 .... Mich.
265 Caspiana, D 5 .... La.
32*Cass, E 6 .... Ark.
150*Cass, (Cass Sta.) D 4 .... Ga.
350 Cass, M 7 .... Ind.
597 Cass, K 15 .... W. Va.
14 Cassa, L 21 .... Wyo.
125*Cassadaga, F 19 .... Fla.
514*Cassadaga, Q 2 .... N. Y.
75*Cassandra, B 2 .... Ga.
514 Cassandra, M 9 .... Pa.
150*Cassard (Kermit), E 5 .... Va.
34*Cassatt, E 16 .... S. C.
1362 Cass City, M 22 .... Mich.
20*Casscoe, K 16 .... Ark.
50*Cassel, D 6 .... Calif.
213 Cassella, I 6 .... Ohio
135 Casselman, P 6 .... Pa.
1358 Casselton, M 23 .... N. D.
400*Cassia, G 16 .... Fla.
193*Cassie (Tripp), L 2 .... W. Va.
50*Cassity, H 15 .... W. Va.
1904 Cass Lake, G 11 .... Minn.
200 Cassoday (Sycamore Springs), K 19 .... Kan.
1488 Cassopolis, R 12 .... Mich.
150*Cass Station (Cass), D 4 Ga.
306 Casstown, J 8 .... Ohio
165 Cassville, D 4 .... Ga.
1214 Cassville, Q 8 .... Mo.
205 Cassville, J 17 .... N. J.
231 Cassville (Richfield Jc.), M 18 .... N. Y.
142*Cassville, N 11 .... Pa.
125*Cassville, C 14 .... W. Va.
645*Cassville (Ft. Gay), L 1 W. Va.
956 Cassville, F 21 .... Wis.
61*Castaic, N 15, P 3 .... Calif.
239 Castalia, D 19 .... Iowa
341 Castalia, D 16 .... N. C.
700 Castalia, D 12 .... Ohio
165*Castalian Springs, L 12 Tenn.
336 Castana, I 3 .... Iowa
600*Castanea, I 14 .... Pa.
70*Castell, I 16 .... Tex.
500*Castella, D 6 .... Calif.
902 Castile, O 7 .... N. Y.
59 Castilla, H 13 .... Utah
700 Castine, M 14 .... Me.
124*Castine, J 6 .... Ohio
....*Castle, see Green Castle, Mo.
....*Castle, F 6 .... N. Y.
242 Castle, I 17 .... Okla.
10 Castle, C 16 .... Ore.
427 Castleberry, N 12 .... Ala.
100*Castle Creek, Q 15 .... N. Y.
841 Castle Dale, J 16 .... Utah
265 Castleford, Q 10 .... Idaho
851 Castlegate, I 16 .... Utah
39*Castle Hayne, L 17 .... N. C.
50 Castle Hot Spring, J 11 Ariz.
100 Castle Hot Springs (Morristown), J 11 .... Ariz.
....*Castle Park, P 12 .... Mich.
23*Castle Point, C 6 .... N. Y.
580 Castle Rock, H 15 .... Colo.
84*Castle Rock, O 17 .... Minn.

Pop. Place Index State
3 Castle Rock, F 3 .... S. D.
1182 Castle Rock, N 6 .... Wash.
3970 Castle Shannon, N 3 .... Pa.
175 Castleton, E 12 .... Ill.
232 Castleton, I 15 .... Ind.
380 Castleton, L 14 .... Kan.
149*Castleton, C 16 .... Md.
1515 Castleton on Hudson, O 24 N. Y.
25 Castleton, L 24 .... Utah
800 Castleton, L 6 .... Vt.
4*Castleton, G 14 .... Va.
493 Castlewood, G 23 .... S. D.
250 Castlewood, D 7 .... Va.
....*Castolon, K 7 .... Tex.
144 Caston, K 23 .... Okla.
244 Castor, D 7 .... La.
309 Castorland, H 17 .... N. Y.
200 Castroville (Del Monte Junction), J 6 .... Calif.
1500 Castroville, M 15 .... Tex.
12*Cast Steel (Blue Spring Run), I 6 .... Va.
24*Caswell, R 8 .... Ala.
300 Caswell Plantation, C 19 Me.
100 Cataldo, D 5 .... Idaho
96 Catale, C 21 .... Okla.
200*Catalpa, E 7 .... Ark.
100*Cataract, L 9 .... Ind.
149*Cataract, G 16 .... Wis.
403 Catarina, O 14 .... Tex.
218 Cataro, K 11 .... La.
4764 Catasauqua, L 22 .... Pa.
250*Cataula, I 4 .... Ga.
200 Cataumet, M 23 .... Mass.
402 Catawba, F 5 .... N. C.
279 Catawba, K 9 .... Ohio
100 Catawba (Catawba Jc.), B 14 .... S. C.
200*Catawba, N 6 .... Va.
328 Catawba, D 14 .... W. Va.
290 Catawba, H 9 .... Wis.
462▲Catawba Island, C 12 .... Ohio
100*Catawba Jc. (Catawba), B 14 .... S. C.
100*Catawba Sanatorium, N 6 Va.
101*Catawissa, J 17 .... Mo.
2053 Catawissa, J 18 .... Pa.
300*Catchings, I 7 .... Miss.
100 Cat Creek, H 17 .... Mont.
750 Catechee, C 5 .... S. C.
184 Cates, I 7 .... Ind.
15 Catesby, D 2 .... Okla.
....*Catfish, See Sarah Furnace Pa.
712 Catharine, G 10 .... Kan.
44*Catharine Lake, J 18 N. C.
32*Catharpin, G 16 .... Va.
23*Cathay, I 11 .... Calif.
189 Cathay, J 16 .... N. D.
800*Cathedral City, O 21 .... Calif.
225 Catherine, K 9 .... Ala.
712*Catharine, H 10 .... Kan.
150*Catherine, J 16 .... Ky.
621 Cathlamet, N 4 .... Wash.
100*Cathro, I 21 .... Mich.
200 Catlett, H 16 .... Va.
4524 Catlettsburg, D 23 .... Ky.
845 Catlin, H 21 .... Ill.
150*Catlin, J 7 .... Ind.
....*Catlin, See Kelso .... Wash.
300*Cato, H 13 .... Ark.
50 Cato, P 6 .... Ind.
19*Cato, Q 8 .... Mo.
.... Cato, I 23 .... Mont.
412 Cato, L 13 .... N. Y.
....*Cato, see Kato .... Pa.
125 Cato, P 15 .... Wis.
50*Catoctin (Lander), D 8 .... Md.
7647 Catonsville, F 13 .... Md.
405 Catoosa, E 20 .... Okla.
275 Catoosa, N 16 .... Tenn.
.... Cator, B 4 .... Tex.
259*Catron, Q 23 .... Mo.
5429 Catskill, Q 23 .... N. Y.
500 Cat Spring, K 20 .... Tex.
1145 Cattaraugus, P 4 .... N. Y.
50 Caughdenoy, K 14 .... N. Y.
50*Caulfield, Q 15 .... Mo.
100*Causey, I 21 .... Ky.
20*Causey, J 4 .... N. M.
150*Cauthornville, L 19 .... Va.
150 Cauthron, H 4 .... Ark.
20*Caution, D 3 .... Calif.
1105 Cavalier, D 21 .... N. D.
50*Cave, D 4 .... Ga.
262 Cave (Weyers Cave), I 11 Va.
27*Cave, I 17 .... W. Va.
427 Cave City, D 16 .... Ark.
960 Cave City, J 13 .... Ky.
175 Cavecreek, L 13 .... Ariz.
14*Cavecreek, D 9 .... Ark.
486 Cave in Rock, Q 19 .... Ill.
20 Cavell, G 17 .... Ky.
30 Cavendish, G 5 .... Idaho
539 Cavendish, M 12 .... Vt.
18*Cave Ridge, J 14 .... Ky.
982 Cave Spring, E 2 .... Ga.
54*Cave Spring, J 10 .... Ky.
50 Cave Spring, O 6 .... Va.
285*Cave Springs, B 5 .... Ark.
250*Cavetown, C 5 .... Md.
75*Caviness, C 21 .... Tex.
138 Cavour, I 20 .... S. D.
160 Cavour, M 9 .... Wis.
657 Cawker City, E 13 .... Kan.
800*Cawood, J 21 .... Ky.
45*Cawood, C 5 .... Mo.
67*Cawthon, J 20 .... Tex.
....*Caxambas, see Collier City Fla.
131 Cayce, K 4 .... Ky.
1476 Cayce, G 13 .... S. C.
26*Cayton, D 6 .... Calif.
260 Cayucos, M 8 .... Calif.
1126 Cayuga, I 6 .... Ind.
472 Cayuga, M 12 .... N. Y.
196 Cayuga, Q 23 .... N. D.
75*Cayuga, G 21 .... Tex.
100*Cayuga, G 6 .... Wis.
.... Cayuga Jc., N 12 .... N. Y.
651*Cayuga Heights, P 13. N. Y.
32 Cayuse, C 19 .... Ore.
40*Cayuta, P 12 .... N. Y.
20*Cayuta, F 7 .... Tex.
150 Cazadero, G 3 .... Calif.
96*Cazenovia, F 14 .... Ill.
1689 Cazenovia, M 16 .... N. Y.
370 Cazenovia, I 18 .... Wis.
12 Cebolla, K 8 .... Colo.
480 Cebolla, C 10 .... N. M.
117*Cecil, K 14 .... Ala.
88*Cecil, F 6 .... Ark.
216 Cecil, O 12 .... Ga.
266 Cecil, E 6 .... Ohio
25 Cecil, C 15 .... Ore.
1000*Cecil, N 2 .... Pa.
52*Cecil, E 14 .... W. Va.
370 Cecil, N 12 .... Wis.
500 Cecilia, H 13 .... Ky.
498 Cecilton, E 19 .... Md.
20*Cecilville, B 5 .... Calif.
1*Cedar, M 4 .... Colo.
113*Cedar, D 11 .... Iowa
144*Cedar, D 1 .... Kan.
.... Cedar, H 18 .... Mass.

Pop. Place Index State
300 Cedar (Cedar City), J 13 Mich.
64 Cedar, M 16 .... Minn.
164 Cedar (Urland), P 3. W. Va.
83*Cedar, H 6 .... Wis.
300 Cedar Bayou, K 23 .... Tex.
....*Cedar Beach, E 7 .... Vt.
500 Cedar Bluff, D 20 .... Ala.
59*Cedar Bluff, K 22 .... Iowa
126*Cedarbluff (Cedar Bluff), E 20 .... Miss.
823 Cedar Bluff, C 9 .... Va.
500*Cedar Bluffs, D 6 .... Kan.
504 Cedar Bluffs, J 22 .... Neb.
350 Cedar Brook, M 11 .... N. J.
2245 Cedarburg, O 19 .... Wis.
5 Cedarbutte, L 15 .... S. D.
10 Cedar Canyon, F 5 .... S. D.
300*Cedar City (Cedar), J 13 Mich.
275 Cedar City, I 14 .... Mo.
4695 Cedar City, O 5 .... Utah
159*Cedar Cove (Dudley), G 8 Ala.
20 Cedar Creek, K 6 .... Colo.
300*Cedarcreek, Q 11 .... Mo.
100 Cedar Creek, K 23 .... Neb.
80*Cedar Creek, I 13 .... N. C.
42*Cedarcreek, M 22 .... Tenn.
150 Cedar Creek, K 18 .... Tex.
....*Cedar Crest, J 12 .... Calif.
....*Cedarcrest, K 16 .... Ky.
200 Cedar Crest, G 10 .... N. M.
....*Cedar Crossing, see Lyons Ga.
25 Cedardale, E 5 .... Okla.
556 Cedaredge, J 5 .... Colo.
9349 Cedar Falls, G 16 .... Iowa
500 Cedar Falls, F 10 .... N. C.
200 Cedar Falls, I 10 .... Wash.
.... Cedar Falls Jc., G 17 .... Iowa
135*Cedar Gap, O 12 .... Mo.
100*Cedar Glades, J 8 .... Ark.
100*Cedar Glen, N 18, P 9 Calif.
50*Cedar Grove, B 2 .... Ga.
204 Cedar Grove, L 22 .... Ind.
.... Cedar Grove, C 5 .... La.
45*Cedar Grove, N 10 .... Me.
37*Cedargrove, O 16 .... Mo.
100*Cedar Grove, D 12 .... N. C.
2000 Cedar Grove, D 18 .... N. J.
25*Cedar Grove, N 6 .... Tenn.
907 Cedar Grove, P 18 .... Wis.
1411 Cedar Grove, L 7 .... W. Va.
493 Cedar Heights, G 17 .... Iowa
82 Cedarhill, Q 18 .... Idaho
89*Cedar Hill, K 19 .... Mo.
200 Cedar Hill, B 6 .... N. M.
900 Cedar Hill, K 10 .... Tenn.
476*Cedar Hill, E 19 .... Tex.
75*Cedarhurst (Asbestos), C 11 .... Md.
5463 Cedarhurst, I 6 .... N. Y.
988 Cedar Keys (Cedar Key), F 10 .... Fla.
650*Cedar Knolls (Monroe-Cedar Knoll) D 15 .... N. J.
200 Cedar Lake, C 6 .... Ind.
500*Cedar Lake, N 15 .... Mich.
.... Cedar Lake, I 14 .... Minn.
250 Cedar Lake, N 22 .... Tex.
21*Cedar Lane, N 21 .... Tex.
76*Cedar Mills, M 11 .... Minn.
30*Cedar Mtn., Q 7 .... N. C.
250*Cedar Park, J 18 .... Tex.
60*Cedarpines Park, O 21 Calif.
279*Cedar Point, D 16 .... Ill.
140*Cedar Point, J 19 .... Kan.
....*Cedar Point, D 13 .... Ohio
62120 Cedar Rapids, J 20 .... Iowa
695 Cedar Rapids, J 17 .... Neb.
....*Cedar Rapids, see Ucross Wyo.
88 Cedar River, H 7 .... Mich.
200 Cedar Run, M 18 .... N. J.
100*Cedar Run, G 14 .... Pa.
25*Cedars, J 25 .... Okla.
75*Cedars, O 22 .... Pa.
75*Cedar Springs, N 4 .... Ga.
1101 Cedar Springs, N 13 .... Mich.
35*Cedar Springs, M 8 .... Mo.
162*Cedar Spring (Delmar) B 9 .... S. C.
70*Cedar Springs, D 10 .... Va.
9025 Cedartown, E 2 .... Ga.
952 Cedar Vale, O 19 .... Kan.
50 Cedarvale, I 14 .... N. M.
....*Cedar Valley, J 17 .... Tex.
.... Cedar Valley, G 10 .... Utah
100 Cedarview, G 20 .... Utah
25 Cedarville, I 8 .... Ala.
111*Cedarville, E 4 .... Ark.
650 Cedarville, B 11 .... Calif.
420 Cedarville, A 12 .... Ill.
36*Cedarville, I 18 .... Md.
250*Cedarville, F 15 .... Mich.
1900 Cedarville, P 8 .... N. J.
100*Cedarville (Chepachet), J 19 .... N. Y.
1034 Cedarville, L 9 .... Ohio
150 Cedarville, N 21 .... Pa.
92*Cedarville, F 14 .... Va.
25 Cedarville, K 5 .... Wash.
82*Cedarville, G 10 .... W. Va.
30 Cedarwood, N 16 .... Colo.
25*Cedon K 17 .... Va.
26 Cedonia, F 21 .... Wash.
.... Cee Vee, A 12 .... Tex.
730 Celeste, D 20 .... Tex.
80*Celestine, P 9 .... Ind.
47 Celilo, C 13 .... Ore.
4*Celina, Q 11 .... Ind.
4841 Celina, H 6 .... Ohio
864 Celina, L 14 .... Tenn.
994 Celina, C 19 .... Tex.
36*Celo, N 9 .... N. C.
1349 Celoron, Q 2 .... N. Y.
5*Celt, M 11 .... Ark.
....*Celynda, see Gatewood. Mo.
.... Cement, H 6 .... Calif.
1039 Cement, L 9 .... Okla.
525 Cement City, Q 18 .... Mich.
520*Cementon, P 22 .... N. Y.
2300 Cementon, L 22 .... Pa.
.... Cement Works, J 2 .... Pa.
44*Centaur (Centaur Sta.), I 20 .... Mo.
33*Centenary, G 21 .... S. C.
4 Centennial, C 9 .... Ohio
400 Centennial, Q 18 .... Wyo.
1012 Center (Centre), D 20 .... Ala.
75*Center, C 16 .... Ark.
1515 Center, N 11 .... Colo.
117*Center, K 10 .... Ga.
225 Center, G 15 .... Ind.
144*Center, J 14 .... Ky.
150*Center, H 15 .... Miss.
486 Center, E 16 .... Mo.
146 Center, F 18 .... Neb.
509 Center, L 10 .... N. D.
200 Center, L 15 .... Okla.
500*Center, N 14 .... Pa.
19 Center, K 22 .... S. D.
3010 Center, G 24 .... Tex.
288 Center (Newport Center), B 15 .... Vt.
320 Center Barnstead, N 16 N. H.

Pop. Place Index State
500*Center Belpre (Porterfield), N 17 .... Ohio
110*Center Berlin, N 25 .... N. Y.
500*Centerbrook, J 16 .... Conn.
779 Centerburg, I 13 .... Ohio
251 Center City, M 18 .... Minn.
200 Center Conway (Conway Center), J 18 .... N. H.
150*Center Cross, K 19 .... Va.
15*Centerdale, K 22 .... Iowa
2140 Centerdale (Centredale), D 13 .... R. I.
600*Centereach, H 9 .... N. Y.
83*Center Effingham, J 17 N. H.
598 Centerfield, K 12 .... Utah
200 Center Harbor, K 15 .... N. H.
545 Center Hill, G 15 .... Fla.
12155*Center Hill, F 7 .... Ga.
200 Center Jc., I 22 .... Iowa
155*Center Lebanon (New Lebanon Center), Q 24 N. Y.
....*Center Lincolnville, see Lincolnville Center .... Me.
3198*Center Line, P 23 .... Mich.
270 Center Lovell, N 2 .... Me.
382 Center Montville, M 18 Me.
130*Center Moreland, G 20 .... Pa.
1451 Center Moriches, H 10 N. Y.
500 Center Ossipee (Mountainview), K 17 .... N. H.
800 Center Point, F 12 .... Ala.
244 Center Point, M 6 .... Ark.
332 Centerpoint (Center Point) K 8 .... Ind.
861 Center Point, I 19 .... Iowa
75*Center Point, K 14 .... Ky.
21*Center Point, I 11 .... La.
136*Center Point (Worcester), N 22 .... Pa.
25 Centerpoint, N 23 .... S. D.
500 Center Point, K 15 .... Tex.
211 Center Point, E 11 .... W. Va.
490*Centerport, H 9 .... N. Y.
191*Centerport, M 20 .... Pa.
164*Center Ridge, F 11 .... Ark.
94*Center Road, F 2 .... Pa.
700 Center Rutland, L 8 .... Vt.
300 Center Sandwich, K 15 N. H.
500*Center Square, N 22 .... Pa.
100 Center Strafford, N 18 N. H.
219 Centerton, A 4 .... Ark.
175 Centerton, K 12 .... Ind.
132*Centerton, N 6 .... N. J.
424 Centertown, H 10 .... Ky.
271 Centertown, I 13 .... Mo.
150 Center Tuftonboro, L 17 N. H.
400 Centervale (St. Johnsbury Center), E 18 .... Vt.
525*Center Valley, L 22 .... Pa.
48*Centerview, L 10 .... Kan.
198 Centerview, I 8 .... Mo.
....*Center Village, see Folkston, Ga.
100*Center Village, (Centre Village), Q 16 .... N. Y.
893 Centerville, H 11 .... Ala.
175 Centerville, H 9 .... Ark.
2000 Centerville, E 22 .... Calif.
210 Centerville, A 21 .... Del.
95 Centerville, M 6 .... Idaho
1162 Centerville, J 21 .... Ind.
8413 Centerville, P 15 .... Iowa
200*Centerville, J 24 .... Kan.
75 Centerville, E 18 .... Ky.
300 Centerville, E 13 .... La.
97*Centerville, J 21 .... Me.
1141 Centerville (Centreville) H 18 .... Md.
400 Centerville, M 25, N 12 Mass.
812 Centerville, R 13 .... Mich.
195 Centerville, M 17 .... Minn.
300 Centerville, N 18 .... Mo.
.... Centerville (Pop. incl. in Butte), K 7 .... Mont.
....*Centerville, see Mountainview .... N. H.
20*Centerville, C 23 .... N. M.
100*Centerville, P 7 .... N. Y.
561 Centerville, M 7 .... Ohio
113*Centerville (Thurman), P 14 .... Ohio
273 Centerville, F 4 .... Pa.
....*Centerville, see Dickinson Pa.
....*Centerville, see Kersey .... Pa.
6317 Centerville, P 3 .... Pa.
1046 Centerville, N 24 .... S. D.
1030 Centerville, O 9 .... Tenn.
900 Centerville, H 21 .... Tex.
691 Centerville, E 11 .... Utah
125 Centerville, Q 12 .... Wash.
200*Centerville Sta. (Church), N 11 .... Ill.
200 Centrahoma, M 17 .... Okla.
100 Central, I 17 .... Ala.
290 Central, L 22 .... Ariz.
225 Central, P 21 .... Idaho
50*Central, Q 14 .... Ind.
132*Central, N 16 .... La.
750 Central, M 4 .... N. M.
1496 Central, C 5 .... S. C.
70*Central, C 5 .... Utah
25 Central, E 22 .... Vt.
....*Central (Central Sta.), E 10 .... W. Va.
275 Central Bridge, N 21 N. Y.
706 Central City, F 13 .... Colo.
1562 Central City, M 15 .... Ill.
150 Central City, H 20 .... Iowa
4199 Central City, I 10 .... Ky.
2460 Central City, K 18 .... Neb.
2083 Central City, O 8 .... Pa.
302 Central City, I 2 .... S. D.
510 Central Falls, F 9 .... N. C.
25248 Central Falls, C 16 .... R. I.
....*Central Ferry, M 23 .... Wash.
201 Centralhatchee, G 3 .... Ga.
16343 Centralia, M 15 .... Ill.
57 Centralia, G 23 .... Iowa
200 Centralia, D 20 .... Kan.
1996 Centralia, G 14 .... Mo.
378 Centralia, B 23 .... Pa.
2449 Centralia, K 18 .... Pa.
164*Centralia, H 23 .... Tex.
60*Centralia, N 16 .... Va.
7414 Centralia, L 6 .... Wash.
300 Centralia, J 11 .... W. Va.
.... Centralia Jc., L 6 .... Wash.
2000 Central Islip, H 8 .... N. Y.
50 Central Jc., L 24 .... Ga.
659 Central Lake, I 15 .... Mich.
.... Central Massachusetts Jc., F 16 .... Mass.
70 Central Mills, K 9 .... Ala.
25 Central Park, L 10 .... Mont.
3500*Central Park, H 7 .... N. Y.
906 Central Point, Q 6 .... Ore.
12*Central Point, K 17 .... Va.
568 Central Square, K 15 N. Y.
200*Central Station (Central), E 10 .... W. Va.
5500*Central Valley, D 6 .... Calif.

Pop. Place Index State
1049 Central Valley, E 4 .... N. Y.
720 Central Village, F 23 .... Conn.
300 Central Village, N 19 .... Mass.
1012 Centre (Center), D 20 .... Ala.
2140*Centredale (Centerdale) D 13 .... R. I.
738 Centre Hall, K 13 .... Pa.
300 Centre Hill (Tyner) D 21 N. C.
100*Centre Village (Center Village) Q 16 .... N. Y.
1141*Centreville (Centerville) H 18 .... Md.
1163 Centreville, P 5 .... Miss.
152*Centreville (Alma), D 10 W. Va.
411 Centuria, B 10 .... Wis.
2000 Century, L 2 .... Fla.
450*Century (Douthat), A 23 Okla.
525 Century, F 13 .... W. Va.
30 Century Jc., G 14 .... W. Va.
41*Ceralvo, H 10 .... Ky.
75*Cereal, M 5 .... Pa.
1212 Ceredo, K 1 .... W. Va.
1332 Ceres, I 8 .... Calif.
370 Ceres, R 6 .... N. Y.
10 Ceres, D 13 .... Okla.
46*Ceres, O 2 .... Va.
15 Ceres, M 5 .... Wash.
250 Ceresco, Q 15 .... Mich.
342 Ceresco, K 22 .... Neb.
4603 Cerrillos (Los Cerrillos), F 13 .... N. M.
6137 Cerrito (El Cerrito), B 18 Calif.
630▲Cerro, C 15 .... N. M.
1016 Cerro Gordo, I 16 .... Ill.
379 Cerro Gordo, L 13 .... N. C.
150*Cerrogordo, P 23 .... Okla.
20*Cerro Gordo, Q 6 .... Tenn.
213 Cerulean (Cerulean Springs) J 8 .... Ky.
175*Cessna, O 9 .... Pa.
27 Cestos, E 5 .... Okla.
549 Ceylon, R 10 .... Minn.
50 Ceylon, D 13 .... Ohio
334 Chacahoula, O 16 .... La.
400 Chacon, D 16 .... N. M.
127 Chadborn (Chadbourn) L 11 .... Mont.
1576 Chadbourn, L 13 .... N. C.
200*Chadds Ford, Q 22 .... Pa.
60*Chadds Ford Jc., Q 22 .... Pa.
4262 Chadron, E 4 .... Neb.
581 Chadwick, B 11 .... Ill.
250 Chadwick, P 11 .... Mo.
....*Chadwick, see Normandy Beach .... N. J.
....*Chadwick, H 6 .... N. C.
800*Chadwicks, (Chadwick), L 17 .... N. Y.
300 Chafee (Chaffee), O 6 N. Y.
3049 Chaffee, O 23 .... Mo.
125 Chaffee, N 23 .... N. D.
....*Chafin, see Mount Gay W. Va.
2505 Chagrin Falls, D 18 .... Ohio
200*Chaires, B 5 .... Fla.
69 Chalco, K 23 .... Neb.
1372*Chalfant, L 3 .... Pa.
470 Chalfont, N 23 .... Pa.
65*Chalk, B 13 .... Tex.
6 Chalkbutte, H 5 .... S. D.
60*Chalk Buttes, L 24 .... Mont.
100*Chalkhill, Q 15 .... Pa.
30*Chalk Level, P 9 .... Va.
....*Chalkton, see Otis Chalk .... Tex.
61*Challenge, F 8 .... Calif.
620 Challis, L 12 .... Idaho
450 Chalmers, F 9 .... Ind.
550 Chalmette, N 19 .... La.
199*Chalybeate, A 19 .... Miss.
30*Chalybeate, O 15 .... Tenn.
150*Chalybeate (Chalybeate Springs), G 13 .... N. C.
350 Chama, J 13 .... Colo.
4 Chama, M 1 .... N. D.
700 Chama, B 11 .... N. M.
275 Chamberino, O 10 .... N. M.
19*Chamberlain, O 10 .... Me.
1626 Chamberlain, L 16 .... S. D.
100*Chamberlin, L 14 .... Ill.
25 Chambers, G 23 .... Ariz.
20*Chambers, G 11 .... Ky.
142*Chambers (Wyandotte), E 7 .... Miss.
388 Chambers, G 16 .... Neb.
40*Chambers, Q 12 .... Tex.
178 Chambersburg, I 7 .... Ill.
14852 Chambersburg, P 13 .... Pa.
75*Chambersburg, (Eureka) Q 15 .... Ohio
....*Chambers Lodge, F 10. Calif.
....*Chambers Prairie, see East Olympia .... Wash.
200 Chambersville, L 7 .... Pa.
1081 Chamblee, E 7 .... Ga.
95 Chamisal, D 14 .... N. M.
275 Chamita, E 13 .... N. M.
771 Chamois, I 15 .... Mo.
125*Champ, Q 20 .... Md.
14*Champ, O 16 .... Va.
23302 Champaign, H 19 .... Ill.
100 Champion, E 5 .... Mich.
300 Champion, N 7 .... Neb.
128*Champion, D 4 .... N. C.
68*Champion, Q 5 .... Pa.
950 Champion Heights, D 19 .... Ohio
1354 Champlain, C 24 .... N. Y.
83*Champlain, K 19 .... Va.
75 Champlin, F 17 .... Ill.
350 Champlin, M 15 .... Minn.
400 Chana, B 14 .... Ill.
170*Chance, M 6 .... Ala.
50*Chance, J 15 .... Ky.
711 Chance, P 19 .... Md.
400 Chance, N 14 .... Mont.
12 Chance, F 24 .... Okla.
31 Chance, E 7 .... S. D.
119*Chance, K 18 .... Tex.
298*Chancellor, O 18 .... Ala.
232 Chancellor, M 23 .... S. D.
25*Chancellor, J 16 .... Va.
.... Chancy, D 10 .... Miss.
1239 Chandler, K 14 .... Ariz.
150 Chandler, J 10 .... Ind.
650 Chandler, G 6 .... Ind.
363 Chandler, Q 5 .... Minn.
60*Chandler, F 6 .... Mo.
2738 Chandler, F 20 .... Okla.
500 Chandler, F 22 .... Tex.
125*Chandler Heights, K 11 Ariz.
125 Chandlers Valley, E 6 .... Pa.
153 Chandlersville, K 16 .... Ohio
874 Chandlerville, I 10 .... Ill.
34*Chandlerville, G 22 .... Ky.
102*Chaney, M 14 .... Md.
9 Chaney, C 2 .... Okla.
200 Chaneysville, Q 10 .... Pa.
200 Changewater, E 10 .... N. J.
1332 Chanhassen, N 21 .... Minn.
250 Channahon, D 19 .... Ill.
....*Channel Five, see Craig. Fla.
1000*Channelview, K 22 .... Tex.
800 Channing, F 4 .... Mich.

Pop. Place Index State
450 Channing, C 2 .... Tex.
....*Chant, see McCurtain. Okla.
10142 Chanute, M 23 .... Kan.
52*Chanute, L 15 .... Tenn.
82*Chanola, O 20 .... Mo.
98*Chapanoke, D 22 .... N. C.
26*Chapel, N 3 .... Va.
7*Chapel, I 10 .... W. Va.
3654 Chapel Hill, E 12 .... N. C.
391 Chapel Hill, O 11 .... Tenn.
600 Chapel Hill, K 20 .... Tex.
40*Chapelle, F 18 .... N. M.
86*Chapelle (Riffle), I 10 W. Va.
100 Chaperito, G 18 .... N. M.
554 Chapin, I 8 .... Ill.
150 Chapin, E 14 .... Iowa
110*Chapin, M 10 .... N. Y.
311 Chapin, F 11 .... S. C.
104 Chaplin, E 21 .... Conn.
187*Chaplin, G 14 .... Ky.
1167 Chapman, M 13 .... Ala.
782 Chapman, G 17 .... Kan.
100 Chapman, D 18 .... Me.
.... Chapman, F 10 .... Mich.
21 Chapman, C 16 .... Mont.
204 Chapman, L 17 .... Neb.
135 Chapman, L 16 .... Pa.
244*Chapman Quarries, K 22 Pa.
....*Chapman Ranch, P 18. Tex.
100*Chapmansboro, M 10. Tenn.
300 Chapmanville, M 4. W. Va.
3000*Chappaqua, F 6 .... N. Y.
75*Chappell, I 21 .... Ky.
74 Chappell (Loma) F 12 Mont.
1093 Chappell, K 5 .... Neb.
195 Chappell (Chappells), F 9 S. C.
50*Chaptico, O 14 .... Md.
50 Charbonneau, H 2 .... N. D.
163*Charco, N 18 .... Tex.
9*Chardon, D 4 .... Kan.
2001 Chardon, C 18 .... Ohio
418*Charenton, O 13 .... La.
100 Charing, J 7 .... Ga.
5754 Chariton, O 13 .... Iowa
110*Charity, M 11 .... Mo.
250 Charlemont, C 5 .... Mass.
10784 Charleroi, O 4 .... Pa.
43*Charles, E 5 .... N. C.
100 Charlesburg, O 16 .... Wis.
8681 Charles City, D 16 .... Iowa
25 Charles City, N 18 .... Va.
....*Charles River, H 18 .... Mass.
958 Charleston, E 16 .... Ark.
8197 Charleston, J 19 .... Ill.
40*Charleston, P 21 .... Iowa
30*Charleston, L 6 .... Kan.
150 Charleston, J 13 .... Me.
2100 Charleston, D 12 .... Miss.
5182 Charleston, P 24 .... Mo.
50 Charleston, L 19 .... Neb.
....*Charleston, see South Charleston .... Ohio
60*Charleston, C 19 .... Nev.
150*Charleston, M 3 .... Ore.
71275 Charleston, N 18 .... S. C.
480 Charleston, P 16 .... Tenn.
218 Charleston, C 22 .... Tex.
323 Charleston, F 13 .... Utah
67914 Charleston, K 6 .... W. Va.
....*Charleston Navy Yard, See Navy Yard .... S. C.
2500 Charleston North, M 18 S. C.
939 Charlestown, P 17 .... Ind.
307*Charlestown, C 19 .... Md.
4000 Charlestown, M 4 .... Mass.
1000 Charlestown, N 6 .... N. H.
100 Charlestown, N 9 .... R. I.
2926 Charles Town, E 25. W. Va.
2299 Charlevoix, I 15 .... Mich.
50*Charley, F 22 .... Ky.
37*Charleys Branch, M 18 Tenn.
150 Charlie, B 16 .... Tex.
53*Charlie Hope, Q 15 .... Va.
81 Charlo, G 4 .... Mont.
86*Charlotte, D 16 .... Ark.
393 Charlotte, J 24 .... Iowa
219 Charlotte, K 23 .... Me.
5544 Charlotte, P 16 .... Mich.
100899 Charlotte, H 6 .... N. C.
.... Charlotte, L 9 .... N. Y.
470 Charlotte, M 9 .... Tenn.
1750 Charlotte, N 16 .... Tex.
83 Charlotte, F 5 .... Vt.
399 Charlotte Court House, O 12 .... Va.
20*Charlotte Furnace, E 22. Ky.
82*Charlotte Hall, O 14 .... Md.
225 Charlotte Harbor, L 15. Fla.
500 Charlottesville (Charlottsville), J 18 .... Ind.
19400 Charlottesville, K 12 .... Va.
99 Charlotteville, O 20 .... N. Y.
900 Charlottsville (Charlottesville) J 18 .... Ind.
41 Charlson, H 5 .... N. D.
60 Charlton, E 15 .... Md.
250*Charlton (Charlton Depot), H 12 .... Mass.
2557▲Charlton, H 12 .... Mass.
.... Charlton, B 7 .... Ore.
670 Charlton City, H 12 .... Mass.
250 Charlton Depot (Charlton) H 12 .... Mass.
122*Charmian, Q 14 .... Pa.
69*Charter Grove, B 16 .... Ill.
75*Charmco, N 12 .... W. Va.
300*Charter Oak, N 16 .... Calif.
776 Charter Oak, I 4 .... Iowa
25*Charteroak, (Charter Oak) P 22 .... Pa.
50*Charters, D 21 .... Ky.
525 Chartley, J 18 .... Mass.
300 Chase, A 14 .... Ala.
825 Chase, J 13 .... Kan.
63*Chase, E 12 .... La.
316 Chase, E 16 .... Md.
298 Chase, N 13 .... Mich.
4 Chase, M 7 .... Neb.
258 Chaseburg, F 17 .... Wis.
1896 Chase City, Q 13 .... Va.
85 Chaseley, K 15 .... N. D.
75*Chase Mills, E 18 .... N. Y.
1927 Chaska, H 15, N 21 .... Minn.
95*Chaska, L 18 .... Tenn.
805 Chassell, D 3 .... Mich.
....*Chastang, P 5 .... Ala.
75*Chastine (Chastain, P. O.) B 12 .... Ark.
259 Chataignier, K 10 .... La.
22*Chatawa, O 9 .... Miss.
45 Chatcolet, E 4 .... Idaho
1183 Chateaugay, C 22 .... N. Y.
250*Chatfield, G 21 .... Ark.
1640 Chatfield, Q 20 .... Minn.
216 Chatfield, F 12 .... Ohio
95*Chatfield, F 20 .... Tex.
.... Chatfield Jc., Q 20 .... Minn.
867 Chatham, J 12 .... Ill.
605*Chatham, D 9 .... La.
1250 Chatham, N 15 .... Mass.
150 Chatham, F 9 .... Mich.
500*Chatham, G 6 .... Miss.
4888 Chatham, E 16 .... N. J.

Pop.	Place, Index	State
2254	Chatham, P 24	N. Y.
210	Chatham, E 15	Ohio
300	Chatham, Q 21	Pa.
1230	Chatham, Q 9	Va.
200	Chatham (Winchester) F 11	Wyo.
227	*Chatham Center, P 24	N. Y.
100	*Chatham Hill, D 9	Va.
500	Chatom, N 4	Ala.
....	Chatsworth, N 14 Q 2 (Pop. incl. in Los Angeles)	Calif.
1001	Chatsworth, C 5	Ga.
1036	Chatsworth, F 18	Ill.
144	*Chatsworth, D 2	Iowa
350	Chatsworth, L 15	N. J.
3000	Chattahoochee, B 2	Fla.
2500	Chattahoochee, F 6	Ga.
150	Chattanooga, H 5	Ohio
365	Chattanooga, N 6	Okla.
128163	Chattanooga, Q 15	Tenn.
65	Chattaroy, G 24	Wash.
526	Chattaroy, O 2	W. Va.
75	*Chatterton, I 18	Va.
534	Chaumont, G 15	N. Y.
387	Chauncey, L 14	Ga.
115	*Chauncey, M 21	Ill.
....	*Chauncey, see Hugo	Mo.
200	*Chauncey, F 6	N. Y.
1234	Chauncey, N 15	Ohio
20	*Chautauqua, L 9	Ill.
254	Chautauqua, O 20	Kan.
540	Chautauqua, Q 2	N. Y.
70	*Chautauqua, L 7	Ohio
257	Chauvin, P 17	La.
....	*Chaves, K 20	N. M.
53	*Chavies, C 19	Ala.
500	Chavies, H 21	Ky.
500	Chazy, C 24	N. Y.
125	*Cheap, (Advance) D 22	Ky.
100	*Cheapside, M 18	Tex.
....	*Cheat Haven, see Lake Lynn	Pa.
45	*Cheat Bridge, H 15	W. Va.
603	Chebanse, E 20	Ill.
300	Chebeague Island, P 7	Me.
5673	Cheboygan, H 17	Mich.
100	*Check, P 5	Va.
2126	Checotah, I 21	Okla.
50	Cheek, P 13	Okla.
6000	*Cheektowaga, N 5	N. Y.
205	Cheesequake, G 18	N. J.
4857	Chehalis, L 6	Wash.
....	Chehaw, J 19	Ala.
1738	Chelan, G 15	Wash.
100	Chelan Falls, G 15	Wash.
2500	Chelmsford, C 17	Mass.
200	Chelsea, G 14	Ala.
540	Chelsea, J 17	Iowa
600	Chelsea, N 9	Me.
41259	Chelsea, E 20, M 5	Mass.
2246	Chelsea, Q 19	Mich.
150	*Chelsea, C 6, R 24	N. Y.
1642	Chelsea, C 20	Okla.
51	Chelsea, F 18	S. D.
400	Chelsea, I 14	Vt.
110	Chelsea, H 10	Wis.
37	*Cheltenham, J 12	Md.
19082	■*Cheltenham, O 23	Pa.
1397	Chelyan, L 6	W. Va.
700	Chemawa, F 7	Ore.
55	Chemult, M 10	Ore.
145	Chemung, A 16	Ill.
350	Chemung, R 13	N. Y.
84	*Chenal, K 13	La.
100	*Chenango, M 22	Tex.
500	Chenango Bridge, Q 16	N. Y.
536	Chenango Forks, Q 16	N. Y.
35	*Chenault, G 12	Ky.
714	Cheney, M 15	Kan.
....	*Cheney, see Eden	Minn.
80	*Cheney (Cheneys) M 22	Neb.
1551	Cheney, I 23	Wash.
6	Cheneycenter, N 24	Colo.
80	*Cheneys (Cheney), M 22	Neb.
130	Cheneyville, G 22	Ill.
913	Cheneyville, J 10	La.
57	Cheniere, C 10	La.
1401	Chenoa, F 16	Ill.
150	*Chenoa, K 20	Ky.
350	Cheoah, P 3	N. C.
100	*Chepachet (Cedarville), J 19	N. Y.
1000	Chepachet, C 8	R. I.
250	Chepultepec (Allgood), E 14	Ala.
184	Cheraw, M 19	Colo.
4497	Cheraw, C 18	S. C.
500	Cheriton, N 23	Va.
786	Cherokee, B 6	Ala.
225	Cherokee, F 7	Calif.
7469	Cherokee, E 4	Iowa
1101	Cherokee, N 25	Kan.
80	*Cherokee, E 14	Ky.
72	*Cherokee, F 22	Ky.
225	*Cherokee, P 4	N. C.
2553	Cherokee, B 8	Okla.
2000	Cherokee, N 18	S. C.
450	Cherokee, I 16	Tex.
100	Cherokee City, B 3	Ark.
725	Cherokee Falls, A 11	S. C.
75	*Cherry, H 11	Ariz.
583	Cherry, D 14	Ill.
....	*Cherry, see Iron	Minn.
6	Cherry, G 9	Neb.
50	*Cherry. N 2	Tenn.
44	*Cherry Box, D 14	Mo.
26	Cherry Creek (Dewey) H 12	Ariz.
56	*Cherry Creek, G 21	Nev.
529	Cherry Creek, P 3	N. Y.
100	Cherry Creek, H 9	S. D.
1100	Cherryfield, L 19	Me.
....	Cherryfield, Q 7	N. C.
....	*Cherry Ford Station, see Laurys Station	Pa.
219	Cherry Fork, P 10	Ohio
....	*Cherry Grove, G 9	N. Y.
250	Cherry Grove, D 6	Ore.
130	*Cherry Grove, I 17	W. Va.
60	Cherry Hill, (Egger) K 5	Ark.
250	Cherry Hill, B 19	Md.
200	*Cherry Hill, G 16	Va.
55	*Cherry Lane, B 5	N. C.
63	*Cherrylog, C 6	Ga.
209	Cherryplain, O 25	N. Y.
150	*Cherry Run, D 22	W. Va.
529	Cherry Tree, L 8	Pa.
3185	Cherryvale, N 22	Kan.
75	▲*Cherry Vale, F 18	N. M.
425	Cherry Valley, F 19	Ark.
583	Cherry Valley, A 15	Ill.
....	Cherry Valley, G 13	Mass.
8	Cherry Valley, L 17	Mo.
104	Cherry Valley, N 20	N. Y.
100	Cherry Valley, C 20	Ohio
300	Cherry Valley, N 2	Pa.
....	Cherry Valley Jc., L 16	Mo.
25	*Cherryville, L 17	Mo.
3225	Cherryville, H 4	N. C.
110	Cherryville, D 9	Ore.
200	*Cherryville, K 22	Pa.
1807	Chesaning, N 19	Mich.
1068	Chesapeake, R 14	Ohio
150	*Chesapeake (Cobbs), N 23	Va.
100	*Chesapeake, K 6	W. Va.
326	Chesapeake Beach, K 15	Md.
1094	Chesapeake City, C 20	Md.
202	▲Chesaw, B 18	Wash.
129	*Chesham, P 8	N. H.
1000	Cheshire, J 11	Conn.
40	Cheshire (West Cheshire), J 11	Conn.
1100	Cheshire, D 3	Mass.
25	Cheshire, P 12	Mich.
210	Cheshire, N 10	N. Y.
320	Cheshire, P 15	Ohio
33	Cheshire, I 5	Ore.
308	Chesilhurst, M 11	N. J.
827	Chesnee, A 9	S. C.
33	*Chesnutburg, I 26	Ky.
110	*Chesson, J 19	Ala.
207	Chester, E 5	Ark.
25	*Chester, E 9	Calif.
1200	Chester, K 17	Conn.
281	Chester, K 13	Ga.
342	Chester, M 21	Idaho
5110	Chester, O 11	Ill.
234	Chester, B 17	Iowa
....	Chester, I 16	Me.
366	Chester, I 16	Md.
1000	Chester, G 5	Mass.
100	*Chester (Haverhill), Q 20	Minn.
25	Chester, G 17	Miss.
548	Chester, D 11	Mont.
634	Chester, O 19	Neb.
702	▲Chester, P 16	N. H.
650	Chester, E 13	N. J.
1140	Chester, E 4	N. Y.
200	*Chester, O 15	Ohio
45	Chester, E 6	Okla.
59285	Chester, Q 23	Pa.
6392	Chester, C 12	S. C.
180	Chester, K 23	S. D.
500	Chester, I 24	Tex.
182	Chester, J 13	Utah
749	Chester, N 12	Vt.
1500	Chester, N 17	Va.
76	Chester, H 24	Wash.
3805	Chester, M 24	W. Va.
15	Chester Center, J 16	Iowa
380	Chester Depot, N 12	Vt.
62	Chesterfield, K 20	Conn.
196	Chesterfield, P 20	Idaho
....	*Chesterfield (91st Street), C 21	Ill.
299	Chesterfield, K 10	Ill.
581	*Chesterfield, H 17	Ind.
200	Chesterfield, F 6	Mass.
139	*Chesterfield, I 20	Mo.
200	Chesterfield, Q 6	N. H.
1263	Chesterfield, C 18	S. C.
100	*Chesterfield, O 6	Tenn.
150	Chesterfield, N 16	Va.
300	*Chester Heights, P 22	Pa.
442	Chesterhill, M 16	Ohio
885	*Chester Hill (Wigton), J 9	Pa.
150	*Chesterland, D 18	Ohio
179	*Chester Springs, O 22	Pa.
2470	Chesterton, B 9	Ind.
2760	Chestertown, G 18	Md.
500	Chestertown, I 23	N. Y.
100	*Chesterville, I 19	Ill.
450	Chesterville, L 7	Me.
....	*Chesterville, see Westerlo	N. Y.
188	*Chesterville, H 13	Ohio
50	*Chesterville, L 20	Tex.
50	*Chestnut, M 10	Ala.
300	Chestnut, I 14	Ill.
50	Chestnut, E 7	La.
....	Chestnut. M 11	Mont.
185	*Chestnut Hill, I 21	Conn.
....	*Chestnut Hill, E 17	Mass.
100	Chestnut Mound, M 13	Tenn.
26	*Chestnutridge, P 10	Mo.
775	*Chestnut Ridge, P 4	Pa.
114	*Chestnut Yard (Monarat), Q 3	Va.
183	*Chest Springs, L 9	Pa.
66	Chesuncook, F 11	Me.
1241	*Cheswick, M 4	Pa.
232	Cheswold, F 21	Del.
1227	Chetek, D 10	Wis.
56	Cheto (Sanders), F 24	Ariz.
1606	Chetopa, O 24	Kan.
100	*Cheviot, Q 24	N. Y.
9043	Cheviot, O 6	Ohio
1500	*Chevrolet, J 21	Ky.
8000	Chevy Chase, I 11	Md.
123	*Chewalla, Q 5	Tenn.
1565	Chewelah, E 22	Wash.
20	Chewey, E 24	Okla.
405	*Chews, (Chews Landing), L 10	N. J.
405	*Chews Landing (Chews), L 10	N. J.
208	*Chewsville, C 5	Md.
315	Chewton, K 2	Pa.
1070	Cheyenne, H 2	Okla.
15	Cheyenne, G 7	Tex.
22474	Cheyenne, Q 22	Wyo.
121	Cheyenne Agency, F 13	S.D.
....	Cheyenne Jc., Q 22	Wyo.
695	Cheyenne Wells, J 23	Colo.
280	Cheyney, P 22	Pa.
200	*Chic, M 3	Tenn.
3396808	Chicago, C 21	Ill.
....	Chicago, see Saint Francis	Ky.
22461	Chicago Heights, D 21	Ill.
16	*Chicago Park, F 9	Calif.
376	*Chicago Ridge, C 21	Ill.
170	*Chicamuxen, M 11	Md.
200	Chichester, N 15	N. H.
70	Chichester, N 16	N. H.
300	Chichester, Q 21	N. Y.
76	Chickalah, G 8	Ark.
1665	Chickamauga, B 2	Ga.
109	*Chickamauga (Shepherd), Q 15	Tenn.
1500	Chickasaw, P 5	Ala.
141	Chickasaw, H 6	Ohio
378	Chickasaw, J 5	Pa.
....	Chickasawba, D 22	Ark.
14111	Chickasha, K 9	Okla.
150	Chick Springs, B 7	S. C.
9287	Chico, E 7	Calif.
10	Chico, N 11	Mont.
20	Chico, C 21	N. M.
700	Chico, D 17	Tex.
298	*Chicod(Simpson),G 18	N. C.
....	*Chicopee, D 10	Ga.
41664	Chicopee, H 7	Mass.
251	Chicopee, P 18	Mo.
....	Chicopee Falls, H 8	Mass.
150	*Chicora, M 21	Miss.
987	Chicora (Millerstown), J 4	Pa.
3000	Chicora Place, N 18	S. C.
160	*Chicot, Q 17	Ark.
500	*Chicota, C 21	Tex.
508	Chidester, O 9	Ark.
43	*Chief (Chief Lake), K 12	Mich.
43	*Chief Lake (Chief) K 12	Mich.
572	Chiefland, E 11	Fla.
....	Chigley, N 14	Okla.
88	*Chilcoot, E 9	Calif.
40	*Chilco, D 4	Idaho
30	Childers, B 21	Okla.
515	Childersburg, G 15	Ala.
6464	Childress, A 13	Tex.
112	*Childress, O 5	Va.
61	Childs, B 19	Md.
326	Childs, G 22	Pa.
....	Childs, H 13	S. C.
83	Childwold, G 20	N. Y.
40	*Chiles, I 24	Kan.
112	*Chilesburg, F 17	Ky.
50	*Chilesburg, K 17	Va.
415	Chilhowee, I 8	Mo.
250	Chilhowee, O 19	Tenn.
889	Chilhowie, E 9	Va.
250	Chili, E 15	Ind.
50	*Chili, L 8	N. Y.
100	*Chili (Pearl), I 16	Ohio
200	Chili, H 13	Wis.
....	Chili Jc., L 8	N. Y.
250	Chilili, H 12	N. M.
2303	Chillicothe, F 13	Ill.
173	*Chillicothe, N 17	Iowa
8012	Chillicothe, D 9	Mo.
20129	Chillicothe, N 12	Ohio
1423	Chillicothe, A 14	Tex.
....	Chillum, I 11	D. C.
92	Chilly, M 13	Idaho
130	Chilmark, P 22	Mass.
250	Chilo, O 7	Ohio
200	*Chilocco, B 13	Okla.
741	Chiloquin, P 10	Ore.
168	*Chilson, G 23	N. Y.
6	*Chilton, I 16	Ky.
70	*Chilton, P 18	Mo.
500	Chilton, H 19	Tex.
2203	Chilton, O 16	Wis.
12	*Chiltons, J 19	Va.
300	Chiltonville, J 23	Mass.
364	Chimacum, F 6	Wash.
500	Chimayo, E 13	N. M.
13	*Chimes, E 11	Ark.
50	Chimney Rock, I 3	Neb.
209	*Chimney Rock, G 1	N. C.
30	China, N 19	Ind.
250	China, M 10	Me.
432	China, K 24	Tex.
1567	China Grove, G 7	N. C.
285	China Spring, G 18	Tex.
80	*Chinati, K 5	Tex.
500	*Chinchilla, F 21	Pa.
2142	Chincoteague Island, K 25	Va.
237	*Chinese (Chinese Camp), H 11	Calif.
65	Chin Lee, D 22	Ariz.
....	*Chinnville, see Raceland	Ky.
4204	Chino, O 17, Q 7	Calif.
2051	Chinook, D 14	Mont.
500	Chinook, N 3	Wash.
350	Chino Valley, H 11	Ariz.
250	Chinquapin, J 17	N. C.
....	*Chipita Park, J 16	Colo.
2167	Chipley, M 10	Fla.
709	Chipley, I 4	Ga.
....	*Chipola, J 16	La.
85	*Chippewa Bay, E 19	N. Y.
10368	Chippewa Falls, E 12	Wis.
100	Chippewa Lake, M 14	Mich.
42	*Chippewa Lake (Chippewa on the Lake), E 16	Ohio
....	Chipps, A 23	Calif.
1000	Chireno, G 24	Tex.
510	Chisago City, M 17	Minn.
150	*Chisford, J 19	Va.
1200	Chisholm, M 6	Me.
7487	Chisholm, F 17	Minn.
75	Chisholm, O 15	S. C.
125	*Chisholm, D 20	Tex.
33	Chism, L 14	Okla.
71	*Chisolm, P 14	S. C.
....	*Chisville, Wash., see Griggs.	
885	Chittenango, M 16	N. Y.
200	*Chittenango Station (North Chittenango), M 16	N. Y.
125	Chittenden, K 9	Vt.
20	Chitwood, G 4	Ore.
65	Chivington, K 22	Colo.
11	*Chloe, K 8	Mo.
36	*Chloe, H 8	W. Va.
185	Chloride, F 4	Ariz.
86	*Chloride, N 19	Mo.
12	Chloride, L 6	N. M.
10	Choate, B 24	Mich.
268	Choccolocco, F 19	Ala.
59	Chockie, N 19	Okla.
125	*Chocolate Bayou, M 22	Tex.
189	▲Choconut, D 20	Pa.
325	Chocorua, J 17	N. H.
150	Chocowinity (Marsden), G 19	N. C.
....	Choctaw, Q 5	Ala.
65	*Choctaw, F 12	Ark.
289	Choctaw, I 13	Okla.
500	*Choctaw Bluff, N 7	Ala.
263	*Choctaw City, K 5	Ala.
400	*Choestoe, B 9	Ga.
211	*Choice, G 24	Tex.
30	*Chokecherry, N 21	Idaho
492	Chokio, L 4	Minn.
128	*Chokoloskee, N 18	Fla.
100	*Cholame, L 10	Calif.
....	Chopaka, B 16	Wash.
34	*Chopin, F 7	La.
236	Choptank, K 19	Md.
900	*Chosen, (Belle Glade-Chosen), L 21	Fla.
1181	Choteau, F 8	Mont.
400	Choteau, E 21	Okla.
438	Choudrant, C 9	La.
1957	Chowchilla, J 10	Calif.
750	*Chriesman, J 20	Tex.
1112	Chrisman, I 21	Ill.
437	Chrisney, Q 8	Ind.
100	Christchurch, M 20	Va.
250	*Christian, O 4	W. Va.
500	Christiana, B 21	Del.
1062	Christiana, P 20	Pa.
250	Christiana, O 12	Tenn.
130	Christianburg, E 15	Ky.
536	Christiansburg, J 8	Ohio
2299	Christiansburg, O 5	Va.
....	*Christian Springs, see Nazareth	Pa.
100	Christie, F 24	Okla.
40	*Christie, Q 11	Va.
20	Christina, G 14	Mont.
30	*Christine, J 15	Ky.
175	Christine, O 25	N. D.
286	Christine, N 16	Tex.
412	*Christmans, J 21	Pa.
129	Christmas, L 18	Ariz.
250	*Christmas (Fort Christmas), G 18	Fla.
40	*Christmas Cove, N 10	Me.
3833	Christopher, O 15	Ill.
320	*Christopher, I 21	Ky.
....	*Christopher (Buttonwood), G 15, (Pop. 900 incl. in Hanover)	Pa.
600	Christoval, H 12	Tex.
85	*Christy, E 21	Ky.
....	Chrome, F 18	N. J.
203	Chrome, Q 9	Colo.
....	*Chrysler, M 9	Ala.
250	*Chualar, L 9	Calif.
18	*Chubbuck, N 18, P 9	Calif.
250	*Chuckatuck, Q 20	Va.
300	Chuckey, M 23	Tenn.
245	Chugwater, O 22	Wyo.
75	*Chula, H 8	Ark.
200	Chula, M 11	Ga.
439	Chula, D 9	Mo.
100	*Chula, N 15	Va.
5138	Chula Vista, Q 19	Calif.
124	Chuluota, G 19	Fla.
....	Chumuckla, M 2	Fla.
200	Chunchula, P 4	Ala.
228	Chunky, K 19	Miss.
200	*Church (Centerville Sta), N 11	Ill.
40	*Church, C 21	Iowa
300	Church Creek, M 18	Md.
316	Church Hill, G 19	Md.
90	*Church Hill, M 5	Miss.
400	Church Hill, K 23	Tenn.
200	*Churchill, Q 14	Idaho
145	Churchland, P 21	Va.
1892	Church Point, L 10	La.
165	*Church Road, O 16	Va.
244	Churchs Ferry, G 17	N. D.
600	Churchton, J 14	Md.
200	*Churchtown, O 20	Pa.
100	*Church View, L 20	Va.
80	*Churchville, M 12	Iowa
219	Churchville, C 17	Md.
601	Churchville, L 8	N. Y.
300	*Churchville, O 24	Pa.
325	Churchville, J 10	Va.
677	Churdan, I 9	Iowa
1122	Churubusco, D 19	Ind.
350	*Churubusco, D 23	N. Y.
50	Cibecue, I 19	Ariz.
262	*Cibolo, L 17	Tex.
64712	Cicero, C 21	Ill.
943	Cicero, H 15	Ind.
400	*Cicero, M 14	N. Y.
33	*Cicerone, I 7	W. Va.
....	Cico, F 11	Mich.
15	*Cid, F 8	N. C.
26	*Cienega, N 14	N. M.
80	*Cima, N 20	Calif.
42	Cimarron, K 7	Colo.
1004	Cimarron, L 6	Kan.
744	Cimarron, C 17	N. M.
859	Cincinnati, Q 15	Iowa
455610	Cincinnati, O 6	Ohio
645	Cincinnatus, O 15	N. Y.
425	Cinclare, L 14	La.
300	Cinco, K 7	W. Va.
18	*Cinda, I 21	Ky.
200	Cinderella, O 3	W. Va.
75	*Cinebar, M 8	Wash.
29	*Cipres, P 4	Tex.
685	Circle, G 22	Mont.
54	*Circle Back, B 8	Tex.
216	Circleville, E 21	Kan.
100	*Circleville, E 4	N. Y.
7982	Circleville, M 12	Ohio
683	Circleville, N 9	Utah
600	*Circleville, I 17	W. Va.
11	*Cisco, A 8	Ark.
26	*Cisco, F 10	Calif.
31	*Cisco, B 5	Ga.
357	Cisco, I 16	Ill.
185	*Cisco, G 21	Ky.
9	Cisco, E 5	Minn.
4868	Cisco, F 15	Tex.
75	*Cisco, K 23	Utah
....	Cisco Lake, C 23	Mich.
17	*Cismont, K 12	Va.
628	Cisne, M 18	Ill.
....	Cissna Jc., G 21	Ill.
582	Cissna Park, G 20	Ill.
100	*Cistern, K 19	Tex.
200	*Citadel (Coram), D 4	Mont.
46	*Cito, P 12	Pa.
485	Citra, E 15	Fla.
69	Citra, M 17	Okla.
39	*Citron, B 4	N. C.
1057	Citronelle, O 4	Ala.
100	Citronelle, F 13	Fla.
....	Citrus, G 8	Calif.
150	City Mills, H 17	Mass.
300	*City Point, H 21	Fla.
84	Citypoint, M 13	Me.
....	City Point, N 17	Va.
100	*City Point, G 15	Wis.
....	City Point Branch Jc., N 17	Va.
....	*City Terrace, N 16	Calif.
60	Civit, M 14	Okla.
600	Clackamas, D 8	Ore.
747	Claflin, I 12	Kan.
30	Clagstone, C 4	Idaho
146	*Claiborne, M 9	Ala.
156	Claiborne, J 16	Md.
125	*Claiborne, I 10	Ohio
149	Claire City, C 22	S. D.
150	Clairemont, D 12	Tex.
219	Clairette, F 17	Tex.
2000	Clairfield, K 19	Tenn.
45	*Clairmont Springs, G 18	Ala.
16381	Clairton, N 4	Pa.
200	Clallam Bay, E 2	Wash.
32	Clam, K 24	Va.
120	*Clam Falls, B 9	Wis.
47	Clam Lake, G 7	Wis.
....	*Clam River, I 15	Mich.
200	Clancey, J 8	Mont.
3982	Clanton, I 14	Ala.
12	*Clapham, C 23	N. M.
103	*Clara, N 21	Md.
75	*Clara, M 20	Miss.
18	*Clara, O 14	Mo.
57	*Clara, J 14	Mont.
845	Clara City, N 7	Minn.
....	*Claraville, M 13	Calif.
75	Clarcona, G 17	Fla.
75	*Clare, B 16	Ill.
232	Clare, F 9	Iowa
50	Clare, H 24	Kan.
1844	Clare, M 16	Mich.
3057	*Claremont, N 16, Q 4	Calif.
205	Claremont, M 20	Ill.
398	Claremont, Q 17	Minn.
12144	■Claremont, N 7	N. H.
467	Claremont, F 5	N. C.
271	Claremont, C 20	S. D.
380	Claremont, N 19	Va.
225	Claremont, N 9	W. Va.
175	Claremont Jc., N 6	N. H.
4134	Claremore, E 20	Okla.
218	*Claren (Hensley), Q 5	W.Va.
100	Clarence, G 20	Ill.
685	Clarence, J 22	Iowa
84	*Clarence, I 17	Ky.
94	*Clarence, F 7	La.
1157	Clarence, D 13	Mo.
900	Clarence, M 5	N. Y.
800	*Clarence (Snow Shoe), J 12	Pa.
450	*Clarence Center, N 5	N. Y.
2551	Clarendon, J 17	Ark.
200	*Clarendon, L 7	N. Y.
150	*Clarendon, M 14	N. C.
824	Clarendon, E 7	Pa.
2431	Clarendon, D 5	Tex.
100	Clarendon, L 9	Vt.
....	*Clarendon, F 18	Va.
1281	*Clarendon Hills, C 19	Ill.
7	Clareton, F 22	Wyo.
419	Clareville, O 17	Tex.
1200	Claridge, N 5	Pa.
200	Claridon, C 18	Ohio
4905	Clarinda, P 6	Iowa
490	Clarington, L 20	Ohio
175	Clarington, H 7	Pa.
2971	Clarion, F 11	Iowa
110	*Clarion (Walloon Lake Station), I 15	Mich.
3798	Clarion, I 6	Pa.
250	*Clarion (Lynch Station), O 10	Va.
....	Clarion Jc., G 9	Pa.
519	Clarissa, J 9	Minn.
191	Clarita, N 16	Okla.
12	Clark, C 9	Colo.
273	Clark, F 13	Mo.
210	Clark (Clarks), I 19	N. C.
200	Clark, I 16	Ohio
279	*Clark (Clarksville), H 2	Pa.
1291	Clark, G 21	S. D.
200	*Clark, K 24	Tex.
150	Clark, A 8	Wyo.
2800	Clarkdale, H 13	Ariz.
50	Clarkdale (Clarkedale) G 21	Ark.
650	*Clarkdale, E 6	Ga.
....	Clarke, E 8	Ala.
50	Clarkedale (Clarkdale) G 21	Ark.
850	Clarkesville, C 11	Ga.
965	Clarkfield, N 5	Minn.
430	Clark Fork, C 6	Idaho
75	Clarkia, F 6	Idaho
240	*Clark Island, N 12	Me.
140	*Clarklake (Clarks Lake), Q 18	Mich.
1266	Clark Mills, L 17	N. Y.
100	*Clarkrange, L 16	Tenn.
14	*Clarkridge, A 12	Ark.
2000	Clarks, E 11	La.
454	Clarks, K 18	Neb.
210	*Clarks (Clark), I 19	N. C.
500	Clarksboro, L 7	N. J.
321	Clarksboro (Clarksville) H 2	Pa.
100	*Clarksburg, G 6	Calif.
79	*Clarksburg, K 16	Ill.
400	Clarksburg, K 19	Ind.
150	*Clarksburg, G 10	Md.
600	Clarksburg, B 4	Mass.
393	Clarksburg, I 12	Mo.
850	Clarksburg, I 16	N. J.
390	Clarksburg, M 11	Ohio
200	*Clarksburg, M 6	Pa.
255	Clarksburg, N 6	Tenn.
30579	Clarksburg, E 12	W. Va.
51	Clarksdale, J 13	Ill.
12168	Clarksdale, C 9	Miss.
307	Clarksdale, D 6	Mo.
350	*Clarks Falls, I 21	Conn.
100	Clarksfield, E 14	Ohio
726	*Clarks Green, G 21	Pa.
203	Clarks Grove, Q 16	Minn.
381	Clarks Hill, (Clarkshill), H 10	Ind.
120	*Clarks Hill, H 7	S. C.
140	*Clarks Lake (Clarklake), Q 18	Mich.
106	Clarks Mills, H 3	Pa.
280	Clarks Mills, P 16	Wis.
390	Clarkson, H 12	Ky.
829	Clarkson, I 20	Neb.
307	*Clarkson, L 9	N. Y.
153	*Clarkson, G 20	Ohio
2691	Clarks Summit, G 21	Pa.
921	Clarkston, F 8	Ga.
653	*Clarkston, P 22	Mich.
3	*Clarkston, K 10	Mont.
579	Clarkston, B 11	Utah
3116	Clarkston, M 25	Wash.
3118	Clarksville, F 8	Ark.
100	*Clarksville, K 23	Del.
150	Clarksville, B 1, N 11	Fla.
2386	Clarksville, P 16	Ind.
1240	Clarksville, E 16	Iowa
2304	▲*Clarksville, F 12	Md.
309	Clarksville, O 15	Mich.
879	Clarksville, F 18	Mo.
400	Clarksville, O 23	N. Y.
430	Clarksville, N 8	Ohio
120	Clarksville, G 20	Okla.
428	Clarksville, P 3	Pa.
321	*Clarksville (Clark), H 2	Pa.
....	*Clarksville (Clarksboro), H 2	Pa.
11831	Clarksville, L 9	Tenn.
4095	Clarksville, C 22	Tex.
826	Clarksville, R 12	Va.
....	Clarksville Jc., R 12	Va.
733	Clarkton, R 22, I 24	Mo.
484	Clarkton, L 14	N. C.
40	*Clarkton, Q 11	Va.
25	*Clarkville, E 24	Colo.
500	*Clarkwood, P 18	Tex.
4	*Clarno, G 15	Ore.
6	Clarno, K 22	S. D.
115	*Clarno, J 22	Wis.
75	Claro, D 13	N. M.
120	*Clarrissa, M 9	N. C.
101	Claryville (West Chester), L 22	Mo.
132	*Claryville, C 2, R 20	N. Y
12	Clasoil, J 9	Mont.
194	Clatonia, N 21	Neb.
708	Clatskanie, A 6	Ore.
7	*Claud, N 10	Okla.
19	*Claud, M 7	Tenn.
761	Claude, D 4	Tex.
52	*Claudell, D 12	Kan.
109	*Claudville, Q 5	Va.
50	*Claunch, J 10	N. M.
50	*Claussen, G 19	S. C.
329	*Claussville, L 21	Pa.
500	*Claverack, P 24	N. Y.
60	Claverhouse, L 9	N. Y.
....	Clavicle, K 15	Calif.
4006	Clawson, P 23	Mich.
262	Clawson, H 23	Tex.
78	*Clawson, K 17	Utah
1808	Claxton, K 20	Ga.
56	*Claxton, I 8	Ky.
200	Clay, F 14	Ala.
53	*Clay, H 8	Calif.
1429	Clay, H 8	Ky.
200	*Clay, D 9	La.
98	*Clay, M 14	N. Y.
70	*Clay, O 19	Pa.
500	*Clay, J 20	Tex.
511	Clay (Henry), K 9	W. Va.
12	Clay, G 14	Wis.
100	*Clay Bank, M 20	Va.
180	*Clayburg, D 24	N. Y.
4518	Clay Center, F 17	Kan.
715	Clay Center, N 18	Neb.
400	Clay Center, C 10	Ohio
1136	Clay City, M 18	Ill.
1117	Clay City, L 8	Ind.
627	Clay City, G 19	Ky.
....	*Clay Court House, See Clay	W. Va.
77	*Clayhill, F 17	Ga.
....	*Clay Hill, See Hoxeyville	Mich.
170	*Clayhole, H 21	Ky.
5500	Claymont, A 22	Del.
....	Claymont, M 25	Minn.
1500	Claypool, K 18	Ariz.
423	Claypool, D 16	Ind.
38	*Claypool, J 12	Ky.
15	Claypool, P 10	Okla.
100	Claypool, N 9	W. Va.
....	*Clay Root, See Bragg City	Mo.
597	Claysburg, P 17	Ind.
1400	Claysburg, N 10	Pa.
154	Clay Springs, I 20	Ariz.
72	*Claysville, J 17	Ohio
970	Claysville, O 1	Pa.
1813	Clayton, L 21	Ala.
164	*Clayton, H 6, B 22	Calif.
890	Clayton, F 21	Del.
1088	Clayton, B 12	Ga.
42	Clayton, M 12	Idaho
1028	Clayton, I 6	Ill.
558	Clayton, J 12	Ind.
161	Clayton, E 21	Iowa
153	Clayton, D 7	Kan.
500	*Clayton, H 12	La.
375	Clayton, R 19	Mich.
201	*Clayton, B 10	Miss.
13069	Clayton, I 20	Mo.
2320	Clayton, M 9	N. J.
3188	Clayton, D 25	N. M.
1999	Clayton, G 15	N. Y.
1711	Clayton, F 15	N. C.
460	*Clayton, L 7	Ohio
110	Clayton, N 21	Okla.
52	Clayton, M 21	S. D.
100	*Clayton, F 24	Tex.
200	Clayton, F 23	Wash.
46	*Clayton, O 10	W. Va.
367	Clayton, C 10	Wis.
220	Claytonia, J 3	Pa.
....	Clayton Jc., G 13	La.
16	*Clayton Lake, D 15	Me.
109	Claytonville, G 21	Ill.
711	Clayville, M 18	N. Y.
....	*Clayville, see Punxsutawney	Pa.
212	Clayville, F 8	R. I.
256	Clayville, M 15	Va.
....	Clearbranch, see Mountain Dale	Tenn.
425	Clearbrook, F 7	Minn.
25	*Clearbrook (Clear Brook), E 13	Va.
....	Clearbrook, B 8	Wash.
152	*Clearco, N 12	W. Va.
100	*Clear Creek, A 5	Calif.
200	Clear Creek, M 12	Ind.
....	*Clear Creek, see League City	Tex.
150	Clearcreek, I 15	Utah
200	*Clear Creek, O 8	W. Va.
100	*Clear Creek Jc. (Fed), H 23	Ky.
615	Clearfield, P 9	Iowa
550	Clearfield, F 20	Ky.
9372	Clearfield, J 10	Pa.
30	Clearfield, N 14	S. D.
1053	Clearfield, D 11	Utah
....	Clearfield Jc., J 10	Pa.
500	*Clear Fork, P 6	W. Va.
76	*Clearlake, F 4	Calif.
3764	Clear Lake, D 13	Iowa
25	*Clear Lake, F 7	La.
285	Clear Lake, L 13	Minn.
39	Clear Lake, R 9	Okla.
997	Clear Lake, G 24	S. D.
50	*Clearlake, D 19	Tex.
12	Clear Lake (Clearlake), K 7	Utah
800	Clear Lake (Clearlake), D 8	Wash.
733	Clear Lake, B 10	Wis.
255	*Clearlake Highlands, F 4	Calif.
200	*Clearlake Oaks (Stubbs), F 4	Calif.
243	Clearmont, A 4	Mo.
215	Clearmont, B 17	Wyo.
75	*Clear Ridge, O 12	Pa.
500	Clear Spring, B 4	Md.
....	*Clearspring, see Big Spring	Md.
80	Clear Springs (Mooney), M 15	Ind.
28	*Clear Springs, O 14	Mo.
420	Clearview, I 17	Okla.
140	*Clearville, P 10	Pa.
3800	*Clearwater, N 16	Calif.
10136	Clearwater, I 12	Fla.
58	Clearwater, H 7	Idaho
591	Clearwater, N 16	Kan.
241	Clearwater, M 13	Minn.
100	*Clearwater, L 21	Mo.
568	Clearwater, G 17	Neb.
15	*Clearwater (Carter), I 19	N. Y.
900	*Clearwater, J 10	S. C.
70	Clearwater, H 2	Wash.
676	Clearwater Lake, K 8	Wis.
725	Cleaton, I 10	Ky.
20	Cleator, I 12	Ariz.
300	*Clebit, P 23	Okla.
210	Cleburne, E 18	Kan.
10558	Cleburne, F 18	Tex.
2230	Cle Elum, J 12	Wash.
12	*Clegg, O 17	Tex.
236	Cleghorn, E 4	Iowa
200	Cleghorn, E 13	Wis.
175	*Clell, B 7	Va.
85	*Clem, F 3	Ga.
6	Clem, D 15	Ore.
12	*Clem, I 10	W. Va.
800	Clemenceau, H 13	Ariz.
375	Clement (West Barnstable), N 12	Mass.
14	Clement, Q 20	N. D.
2866	Clementon, L 10	N. J.
419	Clements, H 8	Calif.
115	*Clements, J 19	Kan.
75	*Clements, O 14	Md.
240	*Clements, P 8	Minn.
10	*Clementson, B 10	Minn.
7	Clementsville, M 22	Idaho
70	*Clementsville, I 16	Ky.
16	Clementsville, L 19	N. D.
65	*Clemmons, D 8	N. C.
207	Clemons (Clemons Grove), I 14	Iowa
500	*Clemons, I 21	Ky.
510	*Clemons, K 25	N. Y.
207	Clemons Grove (Clemons), I 14	Iowa
200	*Clemscot, O 12	Okla.
1300	Clemson, C 4	S. C.
250	Clemville, N 21	Tex.
1200	Clendenin (Clendennin), J 7	W. Va.
386	*Cleo, (Cleo Springs), D 8	Okla.
36	*Cleo, J 13	Tex.
33	Cleodell, P 14	Wash.
1108	Cleona, N 18	Pa.
75	Cleora, C 22	Okla.
386	Cleo Springs (Cleo), D 8	Okla.
1631	Clermont, G 16	Fla.
297	Clermont, D 10	Ga.
465	Clermont, J 13	Ind.
626	Clermont, D 20	Iowa
200	Clermont, F 14	Ky.
309	Clermont, Q 12	N. J.
600	*Clermont, Q 24	N. Y.
400	Clermont, F 9	Pa.
....	Clermont Branch Jc., E 10	Pa.

Pop. *Place* *Index* *State*
100*Clermont Harbor, R 15 Miss.
300*Cleveland, D 14 Ala.
99*Cleveland, F 11 Ark.
95*Cleveland, L 16 Fla.
471 Cleveland, C 10 Ga.
243 Cleveland, Q 21 Idaho
80 Cleveland, D 9 Ill.
75*Cleveland (Carvel), M 14 Kan.
.... Cleveland, A 17 Me.
313 Cleveland, P 14 Minn.
4189 Cleveland, E 8 Miss.
146 Cleveland, I 6 Mo.
30 Cleveland, E 15 Mont.
776▲Cleveland, E 16 N. M.
440 Cleveland, L 16 N. Y.
506 Cleveland, F 6 N. C.
246 Cleveland, M 17 N. D.
878336 Cleveland, D 16, O 23 Ohio
2510 Cleveland, D 16 Okla.
150*Cleveland, B 6 S. C.
11351 Cleveland, Q 16 Tenn.
1783 Cleveland, J 23 Tex.
447 Cleveland, J 17 Utah
500 Cleveland, D 7 Va.
60*Cleveland, J 12 W. Va.
235 Cleveland, P 16 Wis.
54992 Cleveland Heights, (Heights), O 24 Ohio
291 Clever, P 9 Mo.
27*Cleverdale, J 23 N. Y.
103 Cleversburg, P 14 Pa.
.... Cleversburg Jc., P 14 Pa.
50*Cleves, G 13 Iowa
1871 Cleves, O 5 Ohio
1338*Clewiston, L 20 Fla.
100*Cliff, H 22 Ky.
161 Cliff, M 2 N. M.
....*Cliff Haven, D 24 N. Y.
100*Cliffield, C 9 Va.
200 Cliff Island, P 7 Me.
37*Cliff Lake, N 8 Mont.
188*Clifford, L 16 Ind.
80*Clifford, F 22 Ky.
500*Clifford, L 19 Mass.
321 Clifford, N 22 Mich.
169 Clifford, K 23 N. D.
100 Clifford, F 21 Pa.
105 Clifford, M 10 Va.
20 Clifford, I 9 Wis.
10*Cliffs, Q 6 Idaho
40*Cliffs, P 13 Wash.
....*Cliffside, see Cliffside Park N. J.
1836 Cliffside, H 2 N. C.
.... Cliffside Jc., H 2 N. C.
16892 Cliffside Park (Cliffside) D 21 N. J.
325 Clifftop, M 9 W. Va.
550*Cliffwood, I 18 N. J.
2668 Clifton, L 24 Ariz.
300 Clifton, I 4 Colo.
268 Clifton, R 20 Idaho
580 Clifton, F 20 Ill.
670 Clifton, E 16 Kan.
81*Clifton, J 19 La.
....*Clifton, F 14 Md.
610 Clifton, J 8 Mass.
278 Clifton (Clifton Hill), F 12 Mo.
48827 Clifton, D 19 N. J.
120*Clifton, L 8 N. Y.
200*Clifton, C 3 N. C.
4*Clifton, G 14 N. D.
187 Clifton, L 9 Ohio
150 Clifton, A 5 Ore.
1200 Clifton, B 9 S. C.
850 Clifton, P 7 Tenn.
1732 Clifton, G 18 Tex.
194 Clifton G 17 Va.
....*Clifton, see Belfair Wash.
300 Clifton, G 4 W. Va.
20*Clifton, F 22 Wyo.
150*Clifton City, H 11 Mo.
3500 Cliftondale, K 5 Mass.
6461 Clifton Forge, L 7 Va.
4921 Clifton Heights, P 22 Pa.
278 Clifton Hill (Clifton), F 12 Mo.
51*Clifton Mills, D 16 W. Va.
1413 Clifton Springs, M 11 N. Y.
175*Cliftonville, H 21 Miss.
40 Cliftonville, O 24 W. Va.
73*Clifty, C 7 Ark.
152 Clifty (Milford), L 17 Ind.
110*Clifty, J 10 Ky.
192 Clifty, N 15 Tenn.
168*Clifty, M 9 W. Va.
250 Climax, H 11 Colo.
372 Climax, O 6 Ga.
157*Climax, L 20 Kan.
56*Climax, H 18 Ky.
460 Climax, Q 14 Mich.
253 Climax, F 2 Minn.
75 Climax, E 10 N. C.
58*Climax, P 22 N. Y.
10 Climax, Q 7 Ore.
250*Climax, J 6 Pa.
264 Climax Springs, K 11 Mo.
150*Climbing Hill, G 2 Iowa
20*Clinch, E 5 Va.
300*Clinchburg, E 8 Va.
1450*Clinchco, C 6 Va.
160*Clinchfield, J 10 Ga.
100 Clinchfield, D 7 Va.
500*Clinchmore, L 18 Tenn.
346 Clinchport, E 5 Va.
86*Cline, M 13 Tex.
600 Clint, G 1 Tex.
125*Clinton, H 6 Ala.
915 Clinton, E 12 Ark.
1200 Clinton, N 16 Conn.
200 Clinton, H 11 Ga.
6331 Clinton, H 15 Ill.
7092 Clinton, J 6 Ind.
26270 Clinton, J 25 Iowa
1540 Clinton, K 4 Ky.
998 Clinton, J 15 La.
12440■Clinton, E 15 Mass.
200*Clinton, J 12 Md.
1200 Clinton, L 10 Me.
1126 Clinton, Q 20 Mich.
630 Clinton, L 3 Minn.
916 Clinton, K 10 Miss.
6041 Clinton, J 8 Mo.
50 Clinton, I 5 Mont.
119 Clinton, E 6 Neb.
1066 Clinton, F 11 N. J.
1478 Clinton, M 17 N. Y.
3557 Clinton, I 15 N. C.
367 Clinton, F 17 Ohio
6736 Clinton, I 6 Okla.
200*Clinton, M 2 Pa.
5704 Clinton, D 9 S. C.
2761 Clinton, M 18 Tenn.
88*Clinton, D 20 Tex.
55 Clinton, L 22 Tex.
36*Clinton, F 7 Wash.
903 Clinton (Clinton Jc.), M 22 Wis.
200 Clinton Corners, C 6 N. Y.
603 Clintondale, C 4 N. Y.
184*Clintondale, J 14 Pa.
.... Clinton Jc., E 14 Mass.
.... Clinton Jc., H 5 Okla.
903*Clinton Jc. (Clinton), M 22 Wis.

Pop. *Place* *Index* *State*
500 Clintonville (Northford), L 12 Conn.
150*Clintonville, E 18 Ky.
244*Clintonville (Rogers), E 24 N. Y.
329 Clintonville, I 4 Pa.
100*Clintonville, N 11 W. Va.
4134 Clintonville, M 13 Wis.
1106 Clintwood, C 6 Va.
841 Clio, M 20 Ala.
62*Clio, E 9 Calif.
200 Clio, Q 12 Iowa
36*Clio, K 18 Ky.
78*Clio, L 16 La.
1711 Clio, O 21 Mich.
821 Clio, D 20 S. C.
19*Clio, I 7 W. Va.
200 Clipper, C 8 Wash.
59*Clippergap, G 9 Calif.
143*Clipper Mills, F 7 Calif.
54*Cliquot, M 9 Mo.
172*Clitherall (Clitheral), I 6 Minn.
55*Clito, J 21 Ga.
100 Clive, K 11 Iowa
190*Clockville, M 16 N. Y.
25*Clodine, L 21 Tex.
380 Cloe, J 8 Pa.
25*Clonmel, M 16 Kan.
....*Clonsilla, see Drumb Okla.
230 Clontarf, M 6 Minn.
150*Clopton, M 21 Ala.
75 Clopton, M 17 Va.
80*Clopton, M 20 Va.
7304 Cloquet, I 19 Minn.
....*Close, see Berryburg Jc., W. Va.
.... Closplint, J 21 Ky.
3*Closson, H 5 N. M.
2603 Closter, C 21 N. J.
200 Clothier, N 5 W. Va.
26*Cloud, G 14 Va.
112 Cloud Chief, J 6 Okla.
300 Cloudcroft, M 14 N. M.
....*Cloudland, C 2 Ga.
50*Clouds, L 20 Tenn.
31 Cloudy, O 21 Okla.
.... Clough, J 19 Ala.
7 Clough, H 5 S. D.
140 Cloutierville, G 8 La.
3067 Clover, A 12 S. C.
7 Clover, G 8 Utah
252 Clover, Q 12 Va.
30*Clover, I 7 W. Va.
174*Clover Bottom, H 19 Ky.
13*Clover Creek, I 8 Va.
.... Clover Creek Jc., M 11 Pa.
100 Cloverdale, A 7 Ala.
180 Cloverdale, K 16 Ala.
809 Cloverdale, G 3 Calif.
75*Cloverdale, C 19 Ill.
657 Cloverdale, K 10 Ind.
117*Cloverdale, P 14 Mich.
94▲Cloverdale, Q 1 N. M.
185*Cloverdale, F 7 Ohio
72 Cloverdale, E 4 Ore.
200 Cloverdale, N 7 Va.
30*Cloverdale, I 16 Wis.
35 Clover Fork, J 22 Ky.
326 Clover Hills, L 11 Iowa
350 Clover Hill, C 9 Miss.
25 Cloverland, N 24 Wash.
175 Clover Lick, K 14 W. Va.
1402 Cloverport, G 11 Ky.
50*Cloverton, J 18 Minn.
1626 Clovis, J 12 Calif.
10065 Clovis, I 25 N. M.
.... Clowry, E 5 Mich.
63*Cloyds Landing, K 15 Ky.
30*Clubb, O 20 Mo.
750*Clune (Ray), L 7 Pa.
100*Cluster Springs, Q 11 Va.
354 Clutier, I 17 Iowa
215*Cly, O 17 Pa.
100*Clyattville, (Clyatteville) P 13 Ga.
.... Clybourn, B 21 Ill.
40*Clyde, D 4 Ark.
125 Clyde, L 23 Ga.
1060 Clyde, E 16 Kan.
215*Clyde, P 22 Mich.
148 Clyde, B 6 Mo.
20 Clyde, K 9 N. M.
2356 Clyde, M 12 N. Y.
516 Clyde, O 6 N. C.
150 Clyde, E 17 N. D.
3174 Clyde, E 12 Ohio
10 Clyde, B 11 Okla.
40*Clyde, L 6 Pa.
800 Clyde, F 14 Tex.
16 Clyde, M 20 Wash.
....*Clyde Center, see Bravo Mich.
216 Clyde Park (Clydepark), L 11 Mont.
230 Clyman, M 19 Wis.
535 Clymer, R 1 N. Y.
3082 Clymer, L 7 Pa.
42 Clymers, F 12 Ind.
300 Clyo, J 24 Ga.
1150 Coachella, O 21 Calif.
295 Coahoma, C 9 Miss.
574 Coahoma, F 11 Tex.
26*Coakley, I 14 Ky.
57*Coal, J 8 Mo.
200*Coal Bluff, L 10 Ala.
325 Coal Bluff, K 7 Ind.
100*Coalburg, F 12 Ala.
300 Coalburg, E 21 Ohio
293 Coalburg, L 7 W. Va.
705*Coal Center, O 3 Pa.
.... Coal City, see Wattsville Ala.
1852 Coal City, E 18 Ill.
450 Coal City, L 8 Ind.
65*Coal City, P 15 Iowa
200*Coal City, O 8 W. Va.
261 Coalcreek, L 14 Colo.
150 Coal Creek, I 6 Ind.
15 Coal Creek, J 24 Okla.
.... Coal Creek, see Lake City Tenn.
125 Coaldale, E 13 Ala.
2 Coaldale, I 4 Ark.
125 Coaldale, L 12 Colo.
.... Coal Dale, I 23 Ky.
273*Coaldale (Six Mile Run), P 9 Pa.
6163 Coaldale, K 20 Pa.
50*Coaldale, Q 8 W. Va.
100 Coal Dale Jc., I 23 Ky.
25*Coaledo, M 3 Ore.
800 Coalfield, N 17 Tenn.
600 Coal Fork, K 6 W. Va.
2118 Coalgate, N 18 Okla.
338 Coal Glen, I 8 Pa.
2351 Coal Grove, R 13 Ohio
1169 Coal Hill, F 7 Ark.
465*Coaling, G 10 Ala.
5026 Coalinga, K 10 Calif.
.... Coal Jc., O 7 Pa.
113 Coalmont, G 12 Ala.
300 Coalmont, C 10 Colo.
550 Coalmont, L 7 Ind.
162 Coalmont, N 11 Pa.
600 Coalmont, P 14 Tenn.
1121 Coalport, L 9 Pa.

Pop. *Place* *Index* *State*
20 Coalridge, C 25 Mont.
162*Coal Run, H 24 Ky.
201 Coal Run, M 17 Ohio
150 Coal Springs, D 7 S. D.
459 Coalton, K 14 Ill.
100 Coalton, E 22 Ky.
623 Coalton, O 13 Ohio
259 Coalton, I 18 Okla.
417 Coalton (Womelsdorf), H 15 W. Va.
495*Coal Valley, E 10 Ala.
243*Coal Valley, D 8 Ill.
250*Coal Valley, L 3 Pa.
150 Coalville, G 10 Iowa
949 Coalville, E 14 Utah
13 Coalwood, L 22 Mont.
650 Coalwood, Q 5 W. Va.
210 Coan, K 21 Va.
37*Coarsegold, I 12 Calif.
.... Coastine, O 15 Ga.
377 Coatesville, J 11 Ind.
107*Coatesville (Coatesville) A 12 Mo.
14006 Coatesville, P 21 Pa.
50*Coatopa, I 4 Ala.
310 Coats, N 11 Kan.
827 Coats, G 14 N. C.
189 Coatsburg, I 5 Ill.
107 Coatsville (Coatesville), A 12 Mo.
150 Cobalt, I 15 Conn.
25*Cobb, G 4 Calif.
150*Cobb, L 7 Ga.
25*Cobb, I 8 Ky.
276 Cobb, H 20 Wis.
66 Cobban, F 11 Wis.
150*Cobbs (Chesapeake), N 23 Va.
100 Cobbs Creek, M 21 Va.
275 Cobbtown, K 19 Ga.
834▲*Cobbville, L 15 Ga.
1098 Cobden, Q 14 Ill.
136*Cobden, P 10 Minn.
....*Cobden (Lozeau), G 2 Mont.
41*Cobham, K 12 Va.
30*Cobhill, G 19 Ky.
100*Coble, N 9 Tenn.
2617 Cobleskill, N 21 N. Y.
45 Cobre, C 22 Nev.
162*Coburg, O 6 Iowa
30*Coburg, J 15 Ky.
33 Coburg, D 16 Mont.
456 Coburg, I 6 Ore.
.... Coburn, F 22 Neb.
.... Coburn, O 23 N. D.
800 Coburn, K 14 Pa.
200*Coburn, C 11 W. Va.
207*Coburn Gore, K 4 Me.
200*Cochecton, C 2, R 20 N. Y.
200*Cochecton Center, C 2, R 20 N. Y.
225 Cochesett, I 20 Mass.
36 Cochetopa, L 9 Colo.
65 Cochise, N 21 Ariz.
1350 Cochituate, F 17 Mass.
2464 Cochran, J 12 Ga.
875 Cochran, M 22 Ind.
40 Cochran, C 5 Ore.
46*Cochran, Q 15 Va.
80 Cochrane, H 4 Ala.
458 Cochrane, D 15 Wis.
....*Cochranton, see Meeker Ohio
793 Cochranton, G 3 Pa.
200 Cochranville, P 20 Pa.
....*Cockburn, see Mount Marion N. Y.
1515 Cockeysville, D 14 Md.
1246*Cockrell Hill, E 19 Tex.
75*Cockrum, A 12 Miss.
140*Coco, K 6 W. Va.
3098 Cocoa, H 21 Fla.
49*Cocoa Beach, H 21 Fla.
25 Cocolalla, C 4 Idaho
100*Cocolamus, L 15 Pa.
.... Coconut Grove, O 23 Fla.
15*Coddington, K 14 Wis.
100*Codell, F 10 Kan.
300 Coden, R 4 Ala.
400 Codorus (Jefferson), Q 16 Pa.
530 Cody, B 6 Fla.
24*Cody, I 22 Ky.
395 Cody, D 9 Neb.
2536 Cody, C 8 Wyo.
50 Coe, P 7 Ind.
5*Coe, K 14 Ky.
28*Coe, K 10 W. Va.
764 Coeburn, D 6 Va.
601*Coello, O 16 Ill.
150 Coesse, D 19 Ind.
10049 Coeur d'Alene, D 4 Idaho
1500 Coeymans, O 23 N. Y.
160*Coeymans Hollow, O 23 N. Y.
33*Cofer, J 14 Ky.
75*Coffee, D 3 Calif.
250*Coffee, M 17 Ga.
158 Coffee Creek, G 13 Mont.
704 Coffeen, L 13 Ill.
196 Coffee Springs, O 18 Ala.
112 Coffeeville, M 5 Ala.
481 Coffeeville, D 14 Miss.
245 Coffey (Salem), C 8 Mo.
17355 Coffeyville, O 22 Kan.
150*Coffinton, L 4 Ga.
46*Coffman, L 21 Mo.
200*Cofield, C 20 N. C.
....*Cofoco, see Ohley W. Va.
83 Cogan House, H 15 Pa.
26 Cogan Valley (Cogan Sta.), H 15 Pa.
63 Cogar, J 9 Okla.
600*Cogdell, O 16 Ga.
46*Coger (Gem), I 10 W. Va.
512 Coggon, H 20 Iowa
60*Cognac, I 10 N. C.
50*Cogswell, E 20 Ky.
430 Cogswell, Q 21 N. D.
200 Cohagen, H 20 Mont.
2500 Cohasset, G 21, Q 10 Mass.
389 Cohasset, G 14 Minn.
55*Cohasset (Fork Union), L 13 Va.
1092 Cohay, L 14 Miss.
150 Cohoctah, P 20 Mich.
931 Cohocton, O 9 N. Y.
21955 Cohoes, N 24 N. Y.
70*Cohoke, L 18 Va.
300 Cohutta, B 4 Ga.
150*Coila, F 12 Miss.
516 Coiltown, I 8 Ky.
26*Coin, B 7 Ark.
457 Coin, P 6 Iowa
216 Coinjock, C 24 N. C.
1175 Cokato, N 12 Minn.
165*Coke, M 20 Va.
1415 Cokeburg, O 3 Pa.
500 Cokedale, Q 16 Colo.
49*Cokeleys, F 9 W. Va.
127*Coker, G 7 Ala.
10*Cokercreek, P 18 Tenn.
117 Cokesbury, F 7 S. C.
300 Coketon, F 16 W. Va.
625 Cokeville, M 6 Pa.
452 Cokeville, M 2 Wyo.
345 Colbert, E 13 Ga.

Pop. *Place* *Index* *State*
602 Colbert, Q 17 Okla.
49 Colbert (Dean), G 24 Wash.
30 Colburn, B 5 Idaho
191 Colburn, G 10 Ind.
2458 Colby, E 4 Kan.
55 Colby, H 7 Wash.
903 Colby, H 12 Wis.
1234 Colchester, I 18 Conn.
1426 Colchester, G 7 Ill
150 Colchester, D 5 Vt.
10 Colclesser, F 5 Neb.
94*Colcord (Row), D 23 Okla.
113*Colcord, O 8 W. Va.
271*Cold Brook, J 19 N. Y.
210 Coldbrook (White Valley), F 12 Mass.
575 Colden, O 5 N. Y.
10*Coldiron, J 21 Ky.
50*Cold Spring (Cold Springs) L 22 Ind.
1564*Cold Spring, C 18 Ky.
....*Coldspring, see Westford, Mass.
1427 Cold Spring (Cold Springs), L 11 Minn.
15*Coldspring, P 13 Mo.
1897 Cold Spring, E 5 N. Y.
....*Cold Spring, F 2 N. C.
2*Cold Spring (Lotell), N 18 Pa.
850 Coldspring, J 23 Tex.
29*Cold Spring (Ellard), J 10 Va.
20*Coldspring, O 19 Wyo.
.... Cold Spring Harbor, R 12 N. J.
982*Cold Spring Harbor, H 9 N. Y.
50*Cold Springs (Cold Spring) L 22 Ind.
100 Cold Springs, K 8 Ohio
100 Cold Springs, L 6 Okla.
42*Cold Stream, E 21 W. Va.
400 Coldwater, K 11 Ariz.
1214 Coldwater, O 10 Kan.
7343 Coldwater, R 15 Mich.
690 Coldwater, A 12 Miss.
78*Coldwater, O 20 Mo.
270*Cold Water, L 8 N. Y.
2019 Coldwater, H 6 Ohio
72*Coldwater, Q 11 Tenn.
145*Coldwater, E 10 W. Va.
.... Cole, B 5 Calif.
40 Cole, K 12 Okla.
10 Cole, C 6 S. D.
750 Coleanor, H 11 Ala.
250 Colebrook, B 8 Conn.
1990 Colebrook, D 14 N. H.
739▲Colebrook, C 20 Ohio
146*Colebrook, M 18 Pa.
225 Colebrook River, A 9 Conn.
753 Cole Camp, J 10 Mo.
125*Colegrove, F 10 Pa.
150 Coleharbor, J 10 N. D.
8 Cole Jc., I 13 Mo.
764 Coleman, G 15 Fla.
375 Coleman, G 15 Ga.
270 Coleman, M 4 Ga.
.... Coleman, C 4 Idaho
100*Coleman, H 24 Ky.
722 Coleman, M 17 Mich.
250 Coleman, O 17 Okla.
6054 Coleman, G 14 Tex.
150*Coleman (Colemans Falls) N8 Va.
50*Coleman (Sidney), L 1 W. Va.
562 Coleman, O 11 Wis.
159*Colemans (Colemans Station), C 6, R 24 N. Y.
150*Colemans Falls (Coleman), N 8 Va.
159*Colemans Sta. (Colemans), C 6, R 24 N. Y.
307 Colerain, D 20 N. C.
150*Colerain, K 19 Ohio
1325 Coleraine, G 15 Minn.
.... Coleraine Jc., H 19 Minn.
627 Coleridge, F 20 Neb.
500*Coleridge, F 9 N. C.
75*Coles, J 17 Ill.
150*Coles, O 7 Miss.
300 Coles (Petroleum), E 21 Ohio
20*Coles (Coles Summit), N 12 Pa.
306 Colesburg, F 21 Iowa
175 Colesburg, G 14 Ky.
30 Colesburg, M 9 Tenn.
109*Coles Point, J 19 Va.
20*Coles Summit (Coles), N 12 Pa.
50 Colestin, R 7 Ore.
213 Colesville, A 14 N. J.
184*Coleta, C 11 Ill.
150*Coleville, H 13 Calif.
794 Colfax, F 9 Calif.
821 Colfax, G 17 Ill.
717 Colfax, H 11 Ind.
2252 Colfax, K 13 Iowa
50*Colfax, E 20 Ky.
1354 Colfax, G 9 La.
40 Colfax, C 18 N. M.
150*Colfax, D 9 N. C.
125 Colfax, O 24 N. D.
2853 Colfax, K 24 Wash.
130*Colfax, D 13 W. Va.
992 Colfax, D 12 Wis.
97 Colgan, C 3 N. D.
51 Colgate, K 22 N. D.
65*Colgate, O 19 Wis.
....*Colie, H 22 Ky.
200*Colington, F 24 N. C.
108*Collbran, C 19 Ala.
301 Collbran, H 5 Colo.
20*College, M 15 Ga.
2643*College (College Hill), K 2 Pa.
200 College, B 11 Utah
550*Collegeboro, J 21 Ga.
....*College Camp, N 22 Wis.
150 College City, G 6 Calif.
900 College Corner, K 22 Ind.
379 College Corner, M 5 Ohio
425*Collegedale, Q 15 Tenn.
300 College Grove, N 11 Tenn.
50 College Hill, G 18 Ky.
150 College Hill, B 15 Miss.
2643 College Hill (College), K 2 Pa.
84*College Mound, D 12 Mo.
.... College Park, I 6, G 23 Calif.
8213 College Park (Collegepark), F 6 Ga.
316 College Park, I 12 Md.
2000 College Place (Columbia College), G 13 S. C.
1505 College Place, O 21 Wash.
118 Collegport, N 21 Tex.
430 College Springs, Q 6 Iowa
2184*College Sta., I 20 Tex.
....*College View (Pop. incl. in Lincoln), L 22 Neb.
375*Collegeville, E 8 Ind.
200*Collegeville, L 10 Minn.
976 Collegeville, O 22 Pa.
136*Collettsville, E 3 N. C.

Pop. *Place* *Index* *State*
100*Colley, G 18 Pa.
48*Colley, C 6 Va.
619*Collier, Q 4 Pa.
342 Collier City, N 17 Fla.
100*Colliers (Colliersville), O 19 N. Y.
100 Colliers, I 8 S. C.
700 Colliers (Collier), O 24 W. Va.
150 Collierstown, L 8 Va.
100*Colliersville (Colliers), O 19 N. Y.
1042 Collierville, Q 2 Tenn.
8162*Collingdale, P 23 Pa.
12685 Collingswood, K 9 N. J.
200*Collins, P 15 Ark.
712 Collins, K 19 Ga.
.... Collins, O 11 Ill.
516 Collins, J 13 Iowa
1100 Collins, M 15 Miss.
193 Collins, L 9 Mo.
45 Collins, F 9 Mont.
500 Collins, O 4 N. Y.
120 Collins, E 14 Ohio
200 Collins, O 16 Wis.
400 Collins Center, O 4 N. Y.
482 Collinston, B 12 La.
122 Collinston, B 10 Utah
957 Collinsville, C 18 Ala.
100 Collinsville, A 24 Calif.
1200 Collinsville, E 10 Conn.
9767 Collinsville, M 10 Ill.
2000 Collinsville, B 17 Mass.
75*Collinsville (Schamberville), J 20 Miss.
106 Collinsville, M 6 Ohio
1927 Collinsville, D 19 Okla.
653 Collinsville, C 19 Tex.
.... Collinwood, C 17, N 24 Ohio
600 Collinwood, Q 8 Tenn.
50*Collirene, K 14 Ala.
47*Collis, K 3 Minn.
110 Collison, H 21 Ill.
10*Collista, G 22 Ky.
65*Collosse (Colosse), Q 19 Va.
210 Colly, I 22 Ky.
268*Collyer, H 8 Kan.
1800 Colma, I 5, D 16 Calif.
462 Colman, K 24 S. D.
50 Colmar, H 6 Ill.
400*Colmar, K 20 Ky.
500*Colmar, N 22 Pa.
700 Colmesneil, I 24 Tex.
150 Colmor, D 18 N. M.
539 Colo, I 13 Iowa
427 Cologne, N 14 Minn.
52 Cologne, N 13 N. J.
30*Cologne, L 19 Va.
85*Coloma, G 10 Calif.
960 Coloma, Q 10 Mich.
400 Coloma, J 16 Wis.
509 Colome, N 15 S. D.
896 Colon, R 14 Mich.
88 Colon, K 22 Neb.
103 Colon, G 12 N. C.
100 Colona, L 6 Colo.
264 Colona, D 9 Ill.
.... Colona, L 2 Pa.
.... Colonel, P 4 W. Va.
125 Colonia, F 17 N. J.
1105 Colonial Beach, I 19 Va.
3194*Colonial Heights, N 16 Va.
800*Colonial Manor, M 8 N. J.
300*Colonial Park, M 16 Pa.
164▲Colonias, G 18 N. M.
1407*Colonie, O 23 N. Y.
420 Colony, K 23 Kan.
300 Colony, J 7 Okla.
100*Colony, M 10 Va.
141▲Colony, A 23 Wyo.
70 Colony Bay, E 11 Mont.
154*Colony Town, F 10 Miss.
160 Colora, B 18 Md.
.... Colorado, Q 25 Calif.
5213 Colorado City, E 11 Tex.
36789 Colorado Springs, J 15 Colo.
152*Colosse, K 15 N. Y.
323 Colp, P 15 Ill.
1416 Colquitt, O 5 Ga.
215 Colrain, C 7 Mass.
....*Colsby, I 15 Ky.
32 Colson, I 22 Ky.
160 Colstrip, L 20 Mont.
267 Colt, H 19 Ark.
.... Coltexo, C 5 Tex.
9686 Colton, O 18, Q 9 Calif.
500 Colton, E 19 N. Y.
148*Colton, D 8 Ohio
125 Colton, E 8 Ore.
615 Colton, L 23 S. D.
45 Colton, H 16 Utah
262 Colton, M 25 Wash.
300*Colts Neck, I 19 N. J.
829 Columbia, N 23 Ala.
200*Columbia, H 11 Calif.
200 Columbia, F 19 Conn.
.... Columbia, F 20 Conn.
1871 Columbia, N 9 Ill.
160 Columbia, N 14 Iowa
1372 Columbia, I 15 Ky.
947 Columbia, E 11 La.
60 Columbia (Addison), L 20 Me.
6064 Columbia, O 13 Miss.
18399 Columbia, H 13 Mo.
....*Columbia, see Columbia Bridge N. H.
287 Columbia, D 9 N. J.
1090 Columbia, E 23 N. C.
75 Columbia (Columbia Sta.), Q 20 Ohio
11547 Columbia, P 18 Pa.
62396 Columbia, G 13 S. C.
275 Columbia, D 19 S. D.
10579 Columbia, O 10 Tenn.
500 Columbia, I 19 Utah
144*Columbia, L 13 Va.
50 Columbia Bridge (Columbia), D 14 N. H.
4219 Columbia City, D 18 Ind.
327 Columbia City, B 7 Ore.
2000*Columbia College (College Place), G 13 S. C.
150 Columbia Cross Roads, E 16 Pa.
175 Columbia Falls, L 20 Me.
637 Columbia Falls, D 4 Mont.
70*Columbia Furnace, G 12 Va.
6035 Columbia Heights, M 23 Minn.
.... Columbia Jc., I 19 Utah
1197 Columbiana, G 14 Ala.
2687 Columbiana, G 20 Ohio
300*Columbia Park, O 6 Ohio
.... Columbia River, I 15 Wash.
75*Columbia Sta. (Columbia), Q 20 Ohio
664 Columbiaville, O 22 Mich.
530*Columbiaville (Stockport), P 24 N. Y.
11 Columbine, B 9 Colo.
200*Columbine, J 15 Wyo.
259 Columbus, N 6 Ark.
53280 Columbus, J 3 Ga.
100*Columbus, I 5 Ill.
11738 Columbus, L 16 Ind.
3402 Columbus, N 25 Kan.
552 Columbus, K 4 Ky.

Pop. *Place* *Index* *State*
....*Columbus, G 5 La.
12*Columbus, O 24 Mich.
13645 Columbus, F 22 Miss.
962 Columbus, M 14 Mont.
7632 Columbus, J 20 Neb.
600 Columbus, J 13 N. J.
265 Columbus, P 6 N. M.
100 Columbus, O 17 N. Y.
390 Columbus, Q 9 N. C.
506 Columbus, D 5 N. D.
306087 Columbus, K 12 Ohio
425 Columbus, E 5 Pa.
2422 Columbus, L 20 Tex.
....*Columbus, see Maryhill Wash.
2760 Columbus, L 19 Wis.
....*Columbus Circle, H 5 N. Y.
326 Columbus City, M 21 Iowa
1737 Columbus Grove, F 8 Ohio
975 Columbus Jc., M 21 Iowa
2285 Colusa, F 6 Calif.
104 Colusa, G 5 Ill.
1800 Colver, M 8 Pa.
.... Colver Hts., M 8 Pa.
2418 Colville, D 22 Wash.
93*Colwell, D 15 Iowa
284 Colwich, L 16 Kan.
10 Colwood, M 22 Mich.
2202*Colwyn, P 23 Pa.
29 Comanche, K 15 Mont.
1533 Comanche, O 10 Okla.
3209 Comanche, G 16 Tex.
400*Combes, P 5 Tex.
625*Combined Locks, N 14 Wis.
214 Combs, D 6 Ark.
861*Combs (Dolan), H 21 Ky.
....*Combs Ridge, B 7 Va.
875 Comer, L 21 Ala.
811 Comer, E 14 Ga.
150*Comers Rock, E 10, Q 2 Va.
104 Comertown, B 24 Mont.
75*Comet, C 3 N. C.
400*Comfort, I 18 N. C.
14*Comfort, Q 14 Tenn.
900 Comfort, K 15 Tex.
600*Comfort, M 5 W. Va.
555 Comfrey, P 9 Minn.
100 Comins, J 19 Mich.
531▲*Cominto, O 15 Ark.
500*Commack, G 9 N. Y.
200 Commerce, M 12 Ala.
3294 Commerce, D 12 Ga.
160*Commerce, K 12 Iowa
....*Commerce, N 15 Minn.
413 Commerce, O 23 Mo.
2422 Commerce, A 23 Okla.
4699 Commerce, D 21 Tex.
207 Commercial Point, L 11 Ohio
300 Commiskey, N 17 Ind.
450 Commodore, L 8 Pa.
64 Commonwealth, N 8 Wis.
10*Community, M 18 N. D.
95 Como, H 12 Colo.
.... Como, H 8 Ky.
819 Como, B 12 Miss.
117*Como, Q 23 Mo.
500 Como, C 20 N. C.
....*Como, see Ahnberg S. D.
125*Como, L 6 Tenn.
412 Como, D 22 Tex.
36*Comorn, I 18 Va.
200 Compass Lake, M 10 Fla.
50*Competition, M 12 Mo.
....*Complete, J 20 Miss.
9 Compro, J 11 Ill.
175 Comptche, F 2 Calif.
20*Compton, C 9 Ark.
16198 Compton, R 4 Calif.
300 Compton, C 15 Ill.
30*Compton, O 14 Md.
85*Compton, H 12 Va.
750 Comstock, Q 13 Mich.
134 Comstock, I 2 Minn.
408 Comstock, J 14 Neb.
2000 Comstock, J 25 N. Y.
5 Comstock, K 5 Ore.
319 Comstock, L 11 Tex.
100*Comstock, D 10 Wis.
800 Comstock Park, O 13 Mich.
22*Comus, G 10 Md.
45*Comyn, G 16 Tex.
32*Conant (Conants), O 13 Ill.
500*Conasauga, Q 17 Tenn.
35 Conata, L 7 S. D.
47 Concan, L 14 Tex.
50*Concepcion, N 11 Calif.
500 Concepcion M 3 Tex.
200*Conception, B 5 Mo.
441 Conception (Conception Jc.), B 5 Mo.
1000 Conchas Dam, F 21 N. M.
.... Concho, H 23 Ariz.
290 Concho, H 10 Okla.
18*Concho, H 13 Tex.
319*Concho, M 9 W. Va.
187 Conconully, D 16 Wash.
1373 Concord, B 21 Calif.
150 Concord, L 22 Del.
300 Concord, B 5 Fla.
403 Concord, H 6 Ga.
257 Concord, I 9 Ill.
160*Concord, D 21 Ky.
7972■Concord, E 17 Mass.
618 Concord, Q 17 Mich.
242 Concord, G 21 Neb.
27171 Concord, O 14 N. H.
15572 Concord, G 6 N. C.
.... Concord, C 18 Ohio
120*Concord, O 13 Pa.
700 Concord, N 18 Tenn.
163*Concord, H 21 Tex.
313 Concord, E 20 Vt.
500 Concord (Concord Depot), N 11 Va.
937▲Concord, M 20 Wis.
500 Concord Depot (Concord), N 11 Va.
6255 Concordia, E 15 Kan.
100*Concordia, F 12 Ky.
.... Concordia, G 13 La.
1077 Concordia, H 9 Mo.
....*Concord Jc., see West Concord Mass.
300*Concordville, P 22 Pa.
200 Concordville (Ward), P 22 Pa.
100*Concord Wharf, M 23 Va.
35 Concrete, L 15 Colo.
38 Concrete, E 21 N. D.
859 Concrete, D 10 Wash.
300 Conda, P 22 Idaho
395 Conde, F 20 S. D.
47*Conde, G 15 Va.
121 Condit, I 12 Ohio
856 Condon, E 15 Ore.
302 Cone (Conesville), M 21 Iowa
6 Cone, E 23 N. M.
110*Cone, C 11 Tex.
152*Conehatta, J 18 Miss.
90 Conejos, Q 11 Colo.
.... Conemaugh, N 8 Pa.
500 Conestee, C 6 S. C.
600*Conestoga, P 19 Pa.
250 Conesus, N 9 N. Y.

Pop.	Place, Index	State
302	Conesville (Cone), M 21	Iowa
500	Conesville, J 16	Ohio
194*	Conetoe, E 18	N. C.
200	Conewango, Q 3	N. Y.
201*	Conewango (Conewango Valley), Q 3	N. Y.
201	Conewango Valley (Conewango), Q 3	N. Y.
60	Confidence, J 5	W. Va.
200*	Confluence, I 21	Ky.
1035	Confluence, Q 6	Pa.
....	Congamond, I 6	Mass.
50*	Congaree, G 14	S. C.
131*	Conger, R 16	Minn.
1800	Congers, F 5	N. Y.
150	Congerville, G 14	Ill.
....*	Congleton, G 19	Ky.
69*	Congo, I 19	Ky.
50*	Congo, D 4	N. C.
350*	Congo, L 15	Ohio
250	Congo, M 24	W. Va.
50	Congress (Congress Jc. P. O.), I 9	Ariz.
....	Congress Jc., H 22	Calif.
1800*	Congress Park, C 21	Ill.
114*	Conicut (South Newbury), H 14	Vt.
126*	Conicville, G 12	Va.
100	Conifer, G 14	Colo.
125*	Conifer, E 19	N. Y.
50	Conifer, I 7	Pa.
1500	Conimicut, G 16	R. I.
225	Conklin, O 12	Mich.
200*	Conklin, Q 16	N. Y.
25*	Conkling, H 20	Ky.
24*	Conkling Park, D 4	Idaho
50*	Conklingville, L 23	N. Y.
50*	Conlen, A 2	Tex.
75*	Conley, G 7	Ga.
27*	Conley, G 22	Ky.
9355	Conneaut, A 21	Ohio
....	Conneaut Harbor, A 21	Ohio
598	Conneaut Lake, G 2	Pa.
500	Conneaut Lake Park, F 2	Pa
965	Conneautville, E 2	Pa.
365	Connell, L 19	Wash.
13608	Connellsville, P 5	Pa.
850*	Connelly, C 4, R 22	N. Y.
384	Connellys Springs, (Connelly Springs), F 3	N. C.
108	Connelsville, B 12	Mo.
75*	Conner, E 15	Fla.
....	Conner, K 4	Mont.
12895	Connersville, K 21	Ind.
650*	Connerton, J 19	Pa.
150	Connerville, N 15	Okla.
10*	Connor, A 7	Ark.
....*	Connor, see Wolcott	Kan.
250*	Connor (Connorville), I 20	Ohio
250*	Connorville (Connor), I 20	Ohio
441*	Conoquenessing, K 3	Pa.
60*	Conotton, I 19	Ohio
49	Conover, C 19	Iowa
1195	Conover, F 4	N. C.
110	Conover, J 8	Ohio
60	Conover, K 7	Wis.
150	Conowingo, B 17	Md.
591	Conrad, H 15	Iowa
1471	Conrad, E 9	Mont.
385*	Conrad (Hull), F 12	Pa.
129	Conran, R 23	Mo.
35*	Conrard, I 17	Ky.
128*	Conrath, F 10	Wis.
4624	Conroe, J 22	Tex.
160*	Conroy, K 18	Iowa
4	Conroy, O 3	Wyo.
10776	Conshohocken, O 23	Pa.
503	Consol, N 14	Iowa
....	Consolidation Mine, E 13	W. Va.
175*	Constable, E 21	N. Y.
340	Constableville, J 17	N. Y.
87*	Constance, C 17	Ky.
18*	Constance, M 16	Minn.
500*	Constantia, K 15	N. Y.
52*	Constantine, G 12	Ky.
1384	Constantine, R 13	Mich.
23*	Constellation, H 11	Ariz.
100*	Constitution, M 17	Ohio
96*	Consul, K 8	Ala.
200*	Consumers, I 18	Utah
37	Contact, M 12	Mont.
146	Contact, A 21	Nev.
10	Content, E 18	Mont.
10	Contentnea, F 16	N. C.
22	Continental, O 17	Ariz.
1059	Continental, E 7	Ohio
800	Contoocook, O 12	N. H.
70	Contreras, I 10	N. M.
76*	Convene, P 5	Me.
500	Convent, N 16	La.
25*	Convent (Convent Sta.) D 14	N. J.
25*	Convent Sta. (Convent), D 14	N. J.
943	Converse, F 16	Ind.
314	Converse, F 5	La.
43*	Converse, E 6	Mo.
84*	Converse (South Danbury), N 13	N. H.
1500	Converse, B 9	S. C.
175*	Converse, M 16	Tex.
817	Convoy, F 5	Ohio
5782	Conway, H 12	Ark.
600	Conway, G 18	Fla.
246	Conway, P 8	Iowa
849*	Conway, J 15	Kan.
219	Conway, H 18	Ky.
600	Conway, D 7	Mass.
72*	Conway, H 16	Mich.
62*	Conway, I 15	Miss.
516	Conway, N 11	Mo.
1300	Conway, J 17	N. H.
449	Conway, C 19	N. C.
120	Conway, G 21	N. D.
1865	Conway, L 2	Pa.
5066	Conway, H 23	S. C.
32*	Conway, D 4	Tex.
742▲	Conway, E 8	Wash.
200	Conway Center (Center Conway), J 18	N. H.
878	Conway Springs, N 15	Kan.
1619	Conyers, F 9	Ga.
744	Conyngham, J 19	Pa.
10	Coodys Bluff, C 21	Okla.
470	Cook, E 18	Minn.
305	Cook, N 23	Neb.
150	Cook, (Cooks), Q 10	Wash.
45	Cooke, N 13	Mont.
4364	Cookeville, M 14	Tenn.
470	Cook Place, L 15	Tenn.
100	Cooks, G 10	Mich.
115*	Cooks (Cook Station), L 17	Mo.
....	Cooks, L 24	N. Y.
150*	Cooks (Cook), Q 10	Wash.
80*	Cooksburg, O 23	N. Y.
164*	Cooksburg, G 6	Pa.
300	Cooks Falls, R 19	N. Y.
35	Cookson, H 22	Okla.
437	Cooks Point, J 20	Tex.
15	Cooks Run, I 12	Pa.
200*	Cooks Springs, E 16	Ala.
115*	Cook Station (Cooks), L 17	Mo.
110*	Cookstown, L 13	N. J.
269	Cooksville, G 16	Ill.
42*	Cooksville, F 12	Md.
14*	Cooksville, H 21	Miss.
48*	Cookville, M 14	Mo.
518	Cookville, D 23	Tex.
10*	Cool, G 10	Calif.
50*	Coolbaugh, I 24	Pa.
....	Cooledge, see Coolidge	Tex.
1842	Cooleemee, E 7	N. C.
....	Cooleemee Jc., E 6	N. C.
159*	Cooley, F 14	Minn.
1200	Coolidge, L 15	Ariz.
608	Coolidge, O 9	Ga.
132*	Coolidge, K 2	Kan.
50*	Coolidge, F 4	N. M.
1102*	Coolidge, G 20	Tex.
50*	Coolidge Dam, K 18	Ariz.
1100*	Coolidge, G 20	Tex.
100	Coolin, B 4	Idaho
200*	Cool Ridge, O 8	W. Va.
163*	Coolspring, I 7	Pa.
463	Coolville, N 16	Ohio
....	Coon, K 13	La.
1080	Coon Creek, M 23	Minn.
1533	Coon Rapids, J 8	Iowa
469	Coon Valley, F 17	Wis.
300*	Cooper, I 14	Ala.
157*	Cooper I 9	Iowa
50*	Cooper, K 16	Ky.
50*	Cooper, K 21	Me.
100	Cooper, Q 13	Mich.
150	Cooper, B 15	Okla.
33*	Cooper, I 20	S. C.
11	Cooper, G 7	S. D.
2537	Cooper, C 21	Tex.
115*	Cooper, L 20	Va.
300*	Cooper (Coopers) Q 8,	W. Va.
250*	Co-operative, K 17	Ky.
70*	Cooperdale, I 16	Ohio
34*	Cooper Heights, C 2	Ga.
47*	Cooper Hill, J 15	Mo.
296*	Coopers (Coopers Plains), Q 11	N. Y.
300*	Coopers (Cooper), Q 8	W. Va.
1193	Coopersburg, M 22	Pa.
135	Coopers Mills, N 10	Me.
296	Coopers Plains (Coopers), Q 11	N. Y.
189	Cooperstown, I 7	Ill.
2599	Cooperstown, N 19	N. Y.
1077	Cooperstown, K 20	N. D.
205*	Cooperstown, H 4	Pa.
125	Cooperstown, P 15	Wis.
25	Cooperstown, Jc., O 19	N. Y.
76*	Coopersville, K 16	Ky.
1083	Coopersville, O 12	Mich.
57*	Coopersville, O 11	Ohio
187	Cooperton, L 6	Okla.
100*	Coosa, D 2	Ga.
175*	Coosada Sta., J 17	Ala.
....	Coosaw, O 14	S. C.
160*	Coosawhatchie, O 13	S. C.
....*	Coos Bay, see Marshfield	Ore.
25	Coos Jc., F 14	N. H.
100	Cooston, L 3	Ore.
466	Cooter, K 24	Mo.
25*	Cootes Store, H 11	Va.
550	Copake, Q 24	N. Y.
350	Copake Falls, Q 24	N. Y.
....	Copalis, J 2	Wash.
400	Copalis Beach, J 2	Wash.
160*	Copalis Crossing, J 3	Wash.
549	Copan, A 19	Okla.
100*	Copas (Scandia), M 18	Minn.
88*	Copco, B 5	Calif.
94	Cope, G 21	Colo.
280	Cope, K 13	S. C.
75*	Copebranch, H 21	Ky.
64*	Copeland, N 4	Ala.
61*	Copeland, E 11	Ark.
120	Copeland, A 5	Idaho
262	Copeland, M 5	Kan.
241	Copemish, K 12	Mich.
250*	Copen, I 10	W. Va.
9	Copenhagen, G 18	Neb.
608	Copenhagen, H 16	N. Y.
124*	Copeville, D 20	Tex.
2000*	Copiague, H 9	N. Y.
75*	Copland (Saldee), H 21	Ky.
3109*	Coplay, L 22	Pa.
....*	Copley, G 23	Ky.
322	Copley, F 17	Ohio
150	Copopa, R 20	Ohio
419*	Coppell, E 19	Tex.
....	Copper, H 11	Ariz.
356	Copperas Cove, H 17	Tex.
479	Copper City, C 4	Mich.
16	Copper Creek, M 19	Ariz.
8	Copperfield, F 24	Ore.
50*	Copper Harbor, C 4	Mich.
5	Copper Hill, K 18	Ariz.
1005	Copperhill, Q 18	Tenn.
130*	Copper Hill, P 5	Va.
250*	Copperopolis, H 10	Calif.
26*	Copper Spur (Coppertown) G 10	Colo.
26*	Coppertown (Copper Spur), G 10	Colo.
12*	Copper Valley, P 5	Va.
93	Coppock, N 20	Iowa
3327	Coquille, M 3	Ore.
50*	Cora (Cora City), P 13	Ill.
27*	Cora, I 7	La.
47*	Cora, C 10	Mo.
260	Cora, N 4	W. Va.
96	Cora, J 5	Wyo.
....	*Cora City, see Cora	Ill.
350	Coral, N 14	Mich.
625	Coral, M 7	Pa.
8294	Coral Gables, O 23	Fla.
800*	Coral Ridge, F 14	Ky.
200	Coram (Citadel), D 4	Mont.
250*	Coram, G 9	N. Y.
20	Coran, L 22	Tenn.
11086	Coraopolis, M 3	Pa.
55*	Corapeake, C 21	N. C.
75*	Corbett, D 14	Md.
153*	Corbett, Q 19	N. Y.
32	Corbett, L 13	Okla.
90	Corbett, C 9	Ore.
150	Corbettsville, R 16	N. Y.
35	Corbin, D 4	Idaho
123*	Corbin, O 16	Kan.
7893	Corbin, J 19	Ky.
110*	Corbin, L 16	La.
....*	Corbin, see Eveleth	Minn.
60	Corbin, J 8	Mont.
220*	Corbin (Corbin City), N 13	N. J.
60*	Corbin, K 17	Va.
256*	Corbin City (Corbin) N 13	N. J.
2092	Corcoran, K 12	Calif.
100*	Cord, D 16	Ark.
500	Cordaville, G 16	Mass.
7929	Cordele, L 10	Ga.
2*	Cordele, N 20	Tex.
150	Cordelia, A 20	Calif.
50*	Cordell, F 22	Ky.
2776	Cordell, J 6	Okla.
100*	Cordell, L 17	Tenn.
630	Corder, G 9	Mo.
15	Cordes, I 12	Ariz.
113*	Cordesville, L 19	S. C.
23*	Cordia, H 22	Ky.
1565	Cordova, E 11	Ala.
....	Cordova, H 14	Fla.
364	Cordova, C 9	Ill.
28*	Cordova, M 14	Iowa
211*	Cordova, K 18	Md.
188	Cordova, M 20	Neb.
320	Cordova, E 14	N. M.
900*	Cordova, I 10	N. C.
139*	Cordova, J 14	S. C.
200*	Cordova, Q 2	Tenn.
15*	Cordova, N 12	W. Va.
100*	Core, C 14	W. Va.
203	Corea, M 19	Me.
36*	Corey (McGlone), E 22	Ky.
60*	Coreys, E 21	N. Y.
462	Corfu, M 6	N. Y.
25	Corfu, L 17	Wash.
200	Corinna, K 12	Me.
80*	Corinne (Viola), F 15	Mich.
60	Corinne, P 21	Okla.
411	Corinne, C 10	Utah
494	Corinne, P 7	W. Va.
....	Corinne Jc., C 10	Utah
119	Corinth, M 6	Ark.
144	Corinth, H 3	Ga.
210	Corinth, D 17	Ky.
7818	Corinth, A 21	Miss.
35	Corinth, L 17	Mont.
35	Corinth, L 17	Mont.
3054	Corinth, K 23	N. Y.
70*	Corinth, F 12	N. C.
50	Corinth, E 4	N. D.
187	Corinth, H 15	Vt.
200*	Corinth, D 16	W. Va.
56*	Cork, H 9	Ga.
8*	Cork, J 14	Ky.
29*	Corkery, M 11	Mo.
6	Corlett Jc., R 22	Wyo.
72*	Corley, G 7	Ark.
75*	Corley, K 5	Iowa
100*	Corley, C 24	Tex.
53*	Corley, I 11	W. Va.
19*	Corliss, M 9	W. Va.
....*	Corliss, see Sturtevant	Wis.
....	Cormier, O 13	Wis.
450	Corn, I 7	Okla.
1808	Cornelia, C 11	Ga.
....	Cornelia, O 14	Ohio
1195	Cornelius, G 5	N. C.
637	Cornelius, D 6	Ore.
16	Cornell, Q 1	Calif.
478	Cornell, E 16	Ill.
21*	Cornell, D 6	Iowa
50*	Cornell, G 9	Mich.
1759	Cornell, F 11	Wis.
40*	Corner, G 18	W. Va.
100	Cornerstone, L 15	Ark.
343	Cornersville, P 11	Tenn.
132*	Cornerville, N 14	Ark.
....*	Cornette, I 19	Ky.
75*	Cornettsville, I 21	Ky.
1550	Corning, A 20	Ark.
1472	Corning, E 6	Calif.
2162	Corning, O 8	Iowa
352	Corning, E 20	Kan.
269	Corning, B 3	Mo.
16212	Corning, Q 11	N. Y.
1433	Corning, M 15	Ohio
72*	Corning, M 22	Pa.
700*	Corning, J 10	Wis.
140	Cornish, C 16	Colo.
....	Cornish, M 17	Ill.
88	Cornish, P 3	Me.
....*	Cornish, see Cornish Flat,	N. H.
234	Cornish, P 11	Okla.
221	Cornish, A 11	Utah
115	Cornish Flat (Cornish), M 7	N. H.
190	Cornishville, G 16	Ky.
160	Cornland, I 13	Ill.
67	Cornlea, I 19	Neb.
51*	Cornor, J 13	La.
20*	Cornstalk, N 11	W. Va.
355	Cornucopia, F 23	Ore.
159*	Cornucopia, F 5	Wis.
51*	Corn Valley, D 7	Va.
5*	Cornville, H 11	Ariz.
....	Cornville, K 9	Me.
150	Cornwall, D 5	Conn.
50*	Cornwall, N 20	Mo.
1978*	Cornwall, E 4	N. Y.
1680	Cornwall, N 18	Pa.
89	Cornwall, I 6	Vt.
97*	Cornwall, L 9	Va.
100*	Cornwall Bridge, E 6	Conn.
142	Cornwallis, F 8	W. Va.
100*	Cornwall Landing, E 4	N. Y.
2000	Cornwall-on-the-Hudson, D 5	N. Y.
65*	Cornwallville, P 22	N. Y.
....*	Cornwell, J 18	Fla.
260*	Cornwells Heights, N 24	Pa.
110*	Corolla, C 24	N. C.
300	Corona, E 9	Ala.
8764	Corona, O 17, R 8	Calif.
550	Corona, J 15	N. M.
177	Corona, E 24	S. D.
192*	Coronaca (Coronaco), F 8	S. C.
450*	Corona Del Mar, O 17	Calif.
6932	Coronado, Q 18	Calif.
328*	Coronado Beach, F 19	Fla.
400	Coronet, I 14	Fla.
57301	Corpus Christi, P 18	Tex.
180	Corral, O 10	Idaho
1151	Correctionville, G 3	Iowa
151*	Correll, L 3	Minn.
35	Correo (Suwanee), H 8	N. M.
54	Corridon, N 17	Mo.
1402	Corrigan, I 23	Tex.
600	Corriganville (Kreigbaum), L 6	Md.
6935	Corry, D 5	Pa.
250*	Corryton, N 19	Tenn.
481*	Corsica, I 7	Pa.
452	Corsica, M 19	S. D.
15232	Corsicana, F 20	Tex.
29*	Corso, G 18	Mo.
37	Corson, L 25	S. D.
250	Cortaro, N 17	Ariz.
160*	Cortelyou, N 4	Ala.
1098	Corte Madera, B 15	Calif.
1778	Cortez, P 3	Colo.
263*	Cortez, J 14	Fla.
45*	Cortez, F 13	Nev.
....*	Cortez, see Red Oak	Pa.
230	Cortland, B 17	Ill.
125*	Cortland, N 15	Ind.
....*	Cortland, see Lucky Fork	Ky.
307	Cortland, N 21	Neb.
15881	Cortland, O 14	N. Y.
1014	Cortland, D 20	Ohio
70*	Cortner, P 12	Tenn.
50*	Corton, K 6	W. Va.
....	Corum, O 9	Okla.
278	Corunna, C 20	Ind.
2017	Corunna, O 19	Mich.
275	Corvallis, J 4	Mont.
8392	Corvallis, H 6	Ore.
6	Corvallis Jc., G 6	Ore.
32*	Corvuso, M 11	Minn.
110*	Corwin, O 14	Kan.
163*	Corwin, (Waynesville), M 8	Ohio
8*	Corwine Center, E 17	Mont.
14	Corwin Springs, N 11	Mont.
481	Corwith, D 11	Iowa
17*	Cory, J 5	Colo.
155	Cory, L 7	Ind.
1865	Corydon, Q 14	Ind.
1872	Corydon, P 13	Iowa
787	Corydon, G 8	Ky.
250	Corydon, D 8	Pa.
225	Coryell, H 18	Tex.
....*	Coryell Islands, G 16	Mich.
400	Coryville, E 10	Pa.
162	Cosby, D 5	Mo.
40*	Cosby, N 22	Tenn.
591	Cos Cob, R 2	Conn.
11509	Coshocton, I 16	Ohio
1207	Cosmopolis, K 3	Wash.
357*	Cosmos, M 11	Minn.
150*	Cossayuna, K 25	N. Y.
55*	Cost, M 18	Tex.
162*	Costa (Brushton), M 5	W. Va.
1800	Costa Mesa, R 6	Calif.
75	Costello, G 11	Pa.
27*	Coster, M 14	Md.
75	Costigan, K 15	Me.
400	Costilla, B 15	N. M.
57*	Costonia, I 20	Ohio
1000*	Cotati, G 4	Calif.
125	Coteau, D 7	N. D.
134	Cotesfield, K 16	Neb.
238	Cotopaxi, L 12	Colo.
....*	Cottage City, see Oak Bluffs	Mass.
....	Cottage Farm, N 3	Mass.
....*	Cottage Grove, I 17	Ala.
100	Cottage Grove, K 22	Ind.
57*	Cottage Grove, N 17	Minn.
2626	Cottage Grove, K 6	Ore.
172	Cottagegrove, L 6	Tenn.
310	Cottage Grove, L 20	Wis.
300*	Cottage Hill (Cottagehill), M 2	Fla.
544	Cottageville, M 16	S. C.
275	Cottageville, H 5	W. Va.
400*	Cottekill, R 21, C 4	N. Y.
1064	Cotter, B 12	Ark.
72*	Cotter, M 21	Iowa
407▲*	Cottier, M 23	Wyo.
25*	Cottle, F 21	Ky.
136	Cottleville, I 19	Mo.
125*	Cotton, N 7	Ga.
250	Cotton, G 19	Minn.
36*	Cottonburg, G 18	Ky.
350	Cottondale, G 9	Ala.
719	Cottondale, M 10	Fla.
22*	Cottongin, I 20	Ky.
1689	Cotton Plant, H 17	Ark.
150*	Cotton Plant, A 19	Miss.
1196	Cottonport, J 11	La.
98*	Cottonton, K 23	Ala.
59*	Cottontown, L 12	Tenn.
1133	Cotton Valley, A 6	La.
300*	Cotton Valley (East Wolfeboro), L 18	N. H.
600	Cottonwood, O 22	Ala.
1700	Cottonwood, H 13	Ariz.
450	Cottonwood, D 6	Calif.
673	Cottonwood, H 5	Idaho
15*	Cottonwood, P 21	Iowa
150	Cottonwood, O 19	Ill.
690	Cottonwood, O 6	Minn.
....	Cottonwood, H 6	Mont.
118	Cottonwood, K 8	S. D.
264	Cottonwood, F 14	Tex.
1078	Cottonwood Falls, J 19	Kan.
450	Cotuit, M 24, N 12	Mass.
500*	Cotula, L 18	Tenn.
3633	Cotulla, O 14	Tex.
80*	Couch, Q 16	Mo.
200*	Couchwood, B 6	La.
189	Couderay, E 8	Wis.
3197	Coudersport, F 11	Pa.
100*	Coudley (Frenchville), I 10	Pa.
25	Cougar, O 8	Wash.
30*	Coughran, N 16	Tex.
82	Coulee, F 7	N. D.
744	Coulee, H 17	Wash.
....*	Coulee Dam, J 17	Wash.
....*	Coulstone, M 16	Mo.
236	Coulter, F 13	Iowa
350*	Coulters, M 3	Pa.
380	Coulterville, I 11	Calif.
1284	Coulterville, O 12	Ill.
175	Coulwood (Finney), D 8	Va.
1500*	Counce, Q 6	Tenn.
75*	Council, O 16	Ga.
692	Council, K 5	Idaho
90	Council (Councils), L 15	N. C.
15	Council, I 12	Okla.
150*	Council, B 7	Va.
41439	Council Bluffs, M 3	Iowa
....*	Council Corners, see Clawson	Mich.
2875	Council Grove, I 19	Kan.
171	Council Hill, H 19	Okla.
73*	Councils (Council), L 15	N. C.
....*	Country Club Estates, see Miami Springs	Fla.
3*	Countsville, I 7	W. Va.
500*	Countyline, P 13	Okla.
325	Coupeville, E 7	Wash.
200	Coupland, J 18	Tex.
600*	Coupon, M 8	Pa.
1039*	Courtdale, I 20	Pa.
297	Courtenay, L 19	N. D.
454	Courtland, B 10	Ala.
50	Courtland, O 22	Ariz.
750*	Courtland, G 8	Calif.
383	Courtland, D 14	Kan.
291*	Courtland, P 12	Minn.
237	Courtland, C 12	Miss.
459	Courtland, Q 18	Va.
80*	Courtney, G 6	Mo.
69	Courtney, Q 12	Okla.
617*	Courtney, N 3	Pa.
317	Courtney, J 21	Tex.
50*	Courtois, L 18	Mo.
67*	Courtrock, H 18	Ore.
1289	Coushatta, E 6	La.
83*	Cousins Island, P 5	Me.
260	Coutolenc, F 7	Calif.
55	Covada, E 21	Wash.
482	Cove, K 4	Ark.
371	Cove (Cove City), I 19	N. C.
25*	Cove, O 13	Ohio
321	Cove, E 22	Ore.
300*	Cove, L 24	Tex.
241*	Cove, I 9	Wash.
371*	Cove City (Cove), I 19	N. C.
33*	Cove Creek, O 6	N. C.
52*	Cove Creek, C 9	Va.
200*	Cove Gap, P 12	Pa.
25*	Cove Gap, L 2	W. Va.
200*	Covel, P 6	W. Va.
600	Covelo, E 3	Calif.
105*	Covena, J 18	Ga.
400	Coventry, G 9	R. I.
180	Coventry, B 16	Vt.
50	Cove Orchard, D 6	Ore.
33	Cove Point, N 16	Md.
130*	Coverdale, M 3	Pa.
75*	Covert, F 11	Kan.
600	Covert, Q 10	Mich.
....	Coverts, J 2	Pa.
185	Covesville, K 12	Va.
100*	Covin, F 7	Ala.
3049*	Covina, N 15	Calif.
3900	Covington, F 10	Ga.
2096	Covington, H 6	Ind.
62018	Covington, B 17	Ky.
4123	Covington, L 18	La.
100	Covington, E 3	Mich.
1945	Covington, J 7	Ohio
780	Covington, E 11	Okla.
500	Covington, F 15	Pa.
3513	Covington, O 2	Tenn.
413	Covington, F 18	Tex.
6300	Covington, L 6	Va.
150	Covode, K 7	Pa.
212	Cowan, H 19	Ind.
174*	Cowan, E 20	Ky.
100*	Cowan, J 16	Pa.
1461	Cowan, Q 13	Tenn.
133	Cowanesque, E 14	Pa.
....	Cowans, Q 24	Ohio
175*	Cowansburg (Lash), N 5	Pa.
300*	Cowansville, K 5	Pa.
500*	Coward, G 19	S. C.
97*	Cowart, K 21	Va.
800	Cowarts, O 22	Ala.
....*	Cowarts, Q 6	N. C.
250*	Cowcreek, H 20	Ky.
100	Cow Creek, F 21	Mont.
709	Cowden, K 16	Ill.
25	Cowdrey, B 11	Colo.
14*	Cowell, D 9	Ark.
110	Cowell, H 6, B 22	Calif.
539	Cowen, K 11	W. Va.
200	Cowenton, E 15	Md.
41	Cowentown, B 20	Md.
42*	Cowesett, H 10	R. I.
1455	Coweta, F 20	Okla.
338	Cowgill, E 8	Mo.
500	Cowiche, L 13	Wash.
158	Cowles, O 17	Neb.
50*	Cowles, F 18	N. M.
400*	Cowlesville, N 7	N. Y.
48*	Cowley (Granville Summit), E 17	Pa.
491	Cowley, A 10	Wyo.
114*	Cowling, N 21	Ill.
224	Cowlington, J 24	Okla.
....	Cowlitz, M 7	Wash.
1343	Cowpens, A 9	S. C.
250*	Cox (Bel Alton), M 11	Md.
....	Cox, D 10	Utah
251*	Cox City, K 10	Okla.
300*	Coxey, A 12	Ala.
31	Coxheath, K 6	Ala.
2352	Coxsackie, P 23	N. Y.
....*	Coxsackie Station, see Newton Hook	N. Y.
40*	Coxs Creek, G 14	Ky.
102*	Coxs Mills, G 10	W. Va.
1000*	Coxton, J 21	Ky.
750*	Coy, L 10	Ala.
75*	Coy, J 14	Ark.
33*	Coy City, N 17	Tex.
440	Coyle, G 13	Okla.
....	Coyne, J 14	Wis.
100	Coyote, J 7	Calif.
100	Coyote, D 11	N. M.
5	Coyote Canyon, F 2	N. M.
2000*	Coytesville, D 20	N. J.
175	Coyville, M 21	Kan.
2156	Cozad, L 12	Neb.
206	Cozaddale, N 7	Ohio
55*	Cozahome, D 11	Ark.
115*	Crabbottom, I 8	Va.
300	Crab Orchard, P 16	Ill.
705	Crab Orchard, H 17	Ky.
218	Crab Orchard (Craborchard), N 22	Neb.
700	Crab Orchard, N 16	Tenn.
700*	Crab Orchard, O 8	W. Va.
6*	Crabtree, E 11	Ark.
136	Crabtree, G 7	Ore.
1500	Crabtree, N 5	Pa.
30*	Cracker, H 22	Ky.
8*	Craddock, L 15	Mo.
200*	Craddockville, L 24	Va.
7163	Crafton, M 3	Pa.
....	Crafton, G 8	S. C.
220*	Crafts, E 6	N. Y.
142	Craftsbury, D 14	Vt.
110*	Craftsbury Common (North Craftsbury), C 15	Vt.
21*	Crag, N 12,	W. Va.
120	Cragford, G 20	Ala.
70*	Craggie Hope, L 10	Tenn.
150*	Cragmor, J 16	Colo.
60*	Cragsmoor, C 4, R 22	N. Y.
2123	Craig, C 7	Colo.
56*	Craig (Channel Five), P 19	Fla.
150*	Craig (Winkle), O 13	Ill.
165	Craig, E 1	Iowa
....	Craig, see Craigville	Minn.
10*	Craig, I 10	Miss.
718	Craig, B 3	Mo.
103	Craig, H 8	Mont.
437	Craig, I 23	Neb.
....*	Craige, N 24	Wash.
28*	Craig Healing Springs (Springs), M 6	Va.
....	Craig Jc., H 5	Idaho
528	Craigmont, H 5	Idaho
158*	Craigsville, E 4	N. Y.
135	Craigsville, K 5	Pa.
1000	Craigsville, J 9	Va.
175	Craigsville, K 11	W. Va.
180	Craigville, F 21	Ind.
85	Craigville (Craig), E 14	Minn.
35*	Craigville, N 12	Mass.
53*	Crailhope, I 14	Ky.
11*	Crain (Matthews), O 13	Ill.
381	Crainville, P 15	Ill.
225*	Craley, P 17	Pa.
150*	Cramer, L 7	Pa.
500*	Cramer (Stump Creek), I 7	Pa.
2000	Cramerton, H 4	N. C.
350	Cranberry, D 2	N. C.
232*	Cranberry, H 4	Pa.
....*	Cranberry, see Woodbine,	W. Va.
262*	Cranberry, O 8	W. Va.
150	Cranberry Creek, L 22	N. Y.
200	Cranberry Isles, N 17	Me.
45*	Cranberry Lake, B 13	N. J.
250	Cranberry Lake, G 19	N. Y.
850	Cranbury, H 15	N. J.
56*	Cranbury Sta. (Cranbury), H 16	N. J.
213*	Crandall, B 5	Ga.
50	Crandall, G 13	Ill.
146	Crandall, P 14	Ind.
650	Crandall, L 21	Miss.
50	Crandall, F 20	S. D.
750	Crandall, E 20	Tex.
150	Crandon, G 19	S. D.
50*	Crandon, O 2	Va.
2000	Crandon, L 9	Wis.
200*	Cranduil, L 25	Tenn.
1013	Crane, P 9	Mo.
150	Crane, F 24	Mont.
145	Crane, M 19	Ore.
1420*	Crane, H 8	Tex.
97*	Crane Hill, D 13	Ala.
40*	Crane Lake, F 19	Minn.
110*	Crane Nest, J 19	Ky.
60*	Cranes Mill, L 17	Tex.
....*	Cranes Nest, C 5	Va.
548	Cranesville, E 2	Pa.
50*	Craney, E 20	Ky.
400*	Cranfills Gap, G 18	Tex.
12860■	Cranford, F 17	N. J.
30*	Cranks, J 21	Ky.
300	Crannell, C 1	Calif.
53*	Cranston, L 22	Iowa
27*	Cranston, E 20	Ky.
47085	Cranston, F 14	R. I.
160*	Crapo, M 18	Md.
267	Crary, H 18	N. D.
500*	Craryville, Q 24	N. Y.
21*	Crater (Pershing), C 8	Colo.
....*	Craterclub, G 23	N. Y.
10	Crater Lake, O 8	Ore.
5	Craven, D 17	S. D.
70	Crawford, J 22	Ala.
221	Crawford, J 6	Colo.
116	Crawford, B 15	Fla.
812	Crawford, F 13	Ga.
36*	Crawford, J 13	Kan.
25*	Crawford, I 19	Ky.
125*	Crawford, J 21	Me.
380	Crawford, G 21	Miss.
1845	Crawford, E 3	Neb.
42	Crawford, G 2	Okla.
331	Crawford, M 15	Tenn.
471	Crawford, H 18	Tex.
60	Crawford, P 7	Wash.
65*	Crawford, G 11	W. Va.
....	Crawford, F 20	Wis.
25*	Crawford House (Crawfords), E 16	N. H.
....	Crawford Jc., D 3	N. Y.
25*	Crawfords (Crawford House), E 16	N. H.
612	Crawfordsville (Crawfordville), G 21	Ark.
11089	Crawfordsville, I 9	Ind.
316	Crawfordsville, N 20	Iowa
117	Crawfordsville, I 7	Ore.
500	Crawfordville, C 5	Fla.
1056	Crawfordville, G 15	Ga.
163*	Crawley (Beach), O 17	Ga.
40	Crawley, N 11	W. Va.
35*	Craycraft, J 15	Ky.
129*	Crayne, I 7	Ky.
43*	Craynor, H 22	Ky.
950	Creal Springs, P 16	Ill.
155*	Creamery, N 22	Pa.
6*	Creamery, P 11	W. Va.
200*	Creamridge (Cream Ridge), I 18	N. J.
613	Creasy (Mifflinville), J 18	Pa.
47*	Crecy, H 23	Tex.
670	Creede, N 8	Colo.
640	Creedmoor, D 14	N. C.
160*	Creedmoor, J 18	Tex.
70*	Creeds, Q 23	Va.
....	Creek, see Austonio	Tex.
325*	Creek Locks, R 21, C 4	N. Y.
42*	Creekmore, K 17	Ky.
606	Creekside, L 7	Pa.
84*	Creekvale, E 21	W. Va.
25*	Creekville, I 20	Ky.
100*	Creelsboro, J 16	Ky.
15	Creighton, F 11	Mich.
272	Creighton, J 7	Mo.
1272	Creighton, F 18	Neb.
1600*	Creighton, M 3	Pa.
9	Creighton, J 7	S. D.
....	Creighton, O 23	Wyo.
10	Crekola (Creekola), H 21	Okla.
600	Crellin, O 1	Md.
24*	Cremo, H 8	W. Va.
623	Crenshaw, B 11	Miss.
500*	Crenshaw, I 7	Pa.
100*	Creola, P 4	Ala.
90*	Creola, N 14	Ohio
25*	Creole, N 6	La.
505	Creosote (Crumps Park), I 10	Ga.
250*	Creosote, H 7	Wash.
55*	Cresaptown, L 6	Md.
288	Cresbard, F 17	S. D.
150	Crescent, M 23	Ga.
275	Crescent, M 3	Iowa
75*	Crescent, I 20	Mo.
1301	Crescent, F 11	Okla.
60	Crescent, L 10	Ore.
320	Crescent, F 11	Utah
259*	Crescent Beach, I 21	Conn.
....*	Crescent Beach, D 18	Fla.
1363	Crescent City, B 1	Calif.
1124	Crescent City, E 17	Fla.
332	Crescent City, F 20	Ill.
210	Crescent Lake, O 5	Me.
97*	Crescent Lake, O 10	Ore.
300*	Crescent Mills, E 9	Calif.
3530	Cresco, B 18	Iowa
400	Cresco, I 23	Pa.
34*	Cressey, J 9	Calif.
17*	Cressey, P 14	Mich.
2246	Cresskill, D 21	N. J.
....*	Cressman, see Trumbauersville	Pa.
48*	Cressmont, G 19	Ky.
72*	Cressmont, J 9	W. Va.
2500	Cresson, M 9	Pa.
250	Cresson, E 18	Tex.
1695	Cressona, L 19	Pa.
50*	Cressy (Parvin), G 19	Ky.
100	Crest, I 6	Ga.
250*	Cresta Blanca, I 6	Calif.
1145	Crested Butte, J 8	Colo.
20*	Cresthill, G 13	Va.
1000*	Crestline, N 20	Calif.
190*	Crestline, N 25	Kan.
4337	Crestline, G 13	Ohio
....*	Crestmont, G 17	Pa.
66	Creston, L 10	Calif.
284	Creston, B 15	Ill.
8033	Creston, N 9	Iowa
37*	Creston, I 16	Ky.
37*	Creston, F 7	La.
20	Creston, E 4	Mont.
302	Creston, I 20	Neb.
400*	Creston, C 3	N. C.
1110	Creston, F 16	Ohio
25*	Creston, M 22	Ore.
25	Creston, K 5	S. D.
125*	Creston, N 16	Tenn.
281	Creston, G 20	Wash.
159*	Creston, G 7	W. Va.
172	Crestone, M 12	Colo.
65*	Crestonio, Q 16	Tex.
2252	Crestview, M 5	Fla.
....	Crestview, C 4	Mich.
372*	Crestview, P 9	Tenn.
500*	Crestwood, E 14	Ky.
42*	Creswell, C 14	Ark.
459	Creswell, E 22	N. C.
497	Creswell, J 6	Ore.
150*	Creswell, O 18	Pa.
5	Creta, N 3	Okla.
1772	Crete, D 21	Ill.
3038	Crete, M 21	Neb.
107	Crete, Q 21	N. D.
....*	Crete, B5	S. C.
3535*	Creve Coeur, G 12	Ill.
2048	Crewe, O 14	Va.

Pop. Place Index State
100*Crews, E 9 ... La.
78*Crews Depot, E 6 ... Ala.
4000 Crichton, Q 5 ... Ala.
75*Crichton, N 12 ... W. Va.
146 Cricket (Omaha), A 9 ... Ark.
750*Cricket, C 4 ... N. C.
19*Cricket Hill, M 21 ... Va.
52*Crickmer, M 8 ... W. Va.
110*Crider, I 8 ... Ky.
18*Criders, H 11 ... Va.
581 Cridersville, H 7 ... Ohio
50*Criehaven, N 13 ... Me.
80 Crigler, M 15 ... Ark.
100*Criglersville, I 13 ... Va.
60*Crimora, J 10 ... Va.
....*Crimson, see Odd ... W. Va.
75*Criner, K 12 ... Okla.
2358 Cripple Creek, J 14 ... Colo.
500 Cripple Creek, Q 2 ... Va.
29 Crisfield, O 14 ... Kan.
3908 Crisfield, R 20 ... Md.
21*Crisp, N 8 ... Mo.
121*Crisp, F 19 ... Tex.
8 Critchell, G 14 ... Colo.
232*Crittenden, D 17 ... Ky.
148*Crittenden, N 5 ... N. Y.
200*Crittenden, Q 20 ... Va.
75*Critz, Q 5 ... Va.
447 Crivitz (Ellis Jc.), O 11 ... Wis.
12*Crocheron, M 18 ... Md.
80*Crocker (Croker), D 14 ... Ark.
100 Crocker, B 8 ... Ind.
453 Crocker, L 13 ... Mo.
100 Crocker, F 21 ... S. D.
5000 Crockett, A 19, H 5 ... Calif.
125*Crockett, F 21 ... Ky.
4536 Crockett, H 22 ... Tex.
150 Crockett, P 2 ... Va.
200*Crockett Mills, N 4 ... Tenn.
80*Crocketts Bluff, K 17 ... Ark.
500 Crockettsville, H 20 ... Ky.
150 Crocketville, M 13 ... S. C.
15*Crocus, J 15 ... Ky.
35 Crocus, E 17 ... N. D.
9 Croff, I 5 ... N. D.
16*Croft (Crofts), M 12 ... Kan.
688 Crofton, J 9 ... Ky.
600 Crofton, E 19 ... Neb.
16*Crofts (Croft), M 12 ... Kan.
801 Croghan, H 17 ... N. Y.
.... Croghan, N 18 ... S. C.
80*Croker (Crocker), D 14 ... Ark.
72 Cromanton, O 9 ... Fla.
65*Cromers, E 11 ... Ohio
75*Cromona, I 22 ... Ky.
....*Crompond, F 6 ... N. Y.
.... Crompton, H 12 ... R. I.
20 Cromwell, K 4 ... Ala.
2700 Cromwell, H 14 ... Conn.
399 Cromwell, C 17 ... Ind.
165*Cromwell, N 9 ... Iowa
250*Cromwell, H 11 ... Ky.
214*Cromwell, I 18 ... Minn.
451 Cromwell, I 16 ... Okla.
....*Cronly, see Acme ... N. C.
236 Crook, B 21 ... Colo.
450*Crooked Creek, F 15 ... Pa.
25*Crooked Lake, B 21 ... Ind.
180 Crooks, L 24 ... S. D.
7161 Crookston, E 3 ... Minn.
262 Crookston, D 10 ... Neb.
2890 Crooksville, L 15 ... Ohio
150 Croom, G 14 ... Fla.
27*Croom, J 12 ... Md.
91*Croom Sta., (Croom), J 12 ... Md.
14*Cropp, I 16 ... Va.
250 Cropper, E 16 ... Ky.
350 Cropsey, G 17 ... Ill.
500*Cropseyville, N 24 ... N. Y.
189*Cropwell, F 16 ... Ala.
2954 Crosby, I 13 ... Minn.
.... Crosby, see Etal ... Miss.
1489*Crosby, O 7, O 4 ... Miss.
1404 Crosby, D 4 ... N. D.
300*Crosby, E 10 ... Pa.
1615 Crosby, K 23 ... Tex.
303 Crosby, F 11 ... Wyo.
1250 Crosbyton, C 11 ... Tex.
220*Crosland, N 10 ... Ga.
.... Cross, B 14 ... Okla.
75*Cross, L 18 ... S. C.
250 Cross Anchor, C 9 ... S. C.
1869 Cross City, D 10 ... Fla.
250*Cross Creek, O 2 ... Pa.
100*Cross Cut, G 15 ... Tex.
150*Crosses, C 7 ... Ark.
4891 Crossett, R 14 ... Ark.
40 Cross Fork, G 12 ... Pa.
525 Cross Hill, E 8 ... S. C.
28*Cross Jc., E 13 ... Va.
500 Cross Keys, M 9 ... N. J.
34*Crosslake, I 13 ... Minn.
48 Cross Mtn., D 5 ... Colo.
266*Crossnore, D 2 ... N. C.
146 Cross Plains, M 20 ... Ind.
200*Cross Plains, L 11 ... Tenn.
1229 Cross Plains, F 15 ... Tex.
374 Cross Plains, J 20 ... Wis.
250*Cross River, F 6 ... N. Y.
....*Cross Roads, M 20 ... Calif.
248*Cross Roads (Nanjemoy), M 12 ... Md.
19*Cross Roads, P 12 ... Mo.
132*Crossroads, M 24 ... N. M.
175 Crossroads, K 22 ... Pa.
250 Cross Timbers, L 10 ... Mo.
139 Crosstown, M 22 ... Mo.
230 Cross Village, H 15 ... Mich.
436 Crossville, C 18 ... Ala.
666 Crossville, O 20 ... Ill.
1511 Crossville, N 16 ... Tenn.
1381 Croswell, N 25 ... Mich.
275 Crosswicks, J 14 ... N. J.
80*Crothers (Taylorstown Station), O 2 ... Pa.
1169 Crothersville, N 16 ... Ind.
353 Croton (Hartford), J 13 ... Ohio
35*Croton, D 19 ... Wyo.
600*Croton Falls, F 6 ... N. Y.
40*Croton Lake, F 6 ... N. Y.
....*Croton Landing, see Croton-on-Hudson ... N. Y.
3843 Croton-on-Hudson, F 5 ... N. Y.
1235*Crotty (Seneca), D 17 ... Ill.
75*Crouch, L 19 ... Va.
221 Crouse, G 4 ... N. C.
350 Crouseville, D 18 ... Me.
33 Crow, J 5 ... Ore.
109*Crow, E 22 ... Tex.
30*Crow, N 7 ... W. Va.
350 Crow Agency, M 18 ... Mont.
25*Crow Creek, B 5 ... S. C.
454 Crowder, D 11 ... Miss.
144*Crowder, P 23 ... Mo.
378 Crowder, K 19 ... Okla.
265*Croweburg, M 24 ... Kan
39 Crowell, I 21 ... Neb.
1817 Crowell, B 13 ... Tex.
32*Crowheart, J 10 ... Wyo.
5 Crowlake, K 18 ... S. D.
65*Crowl, K 17 ... Pa.
318 Crowley, M 18 ... Colo.
9523 Crowley, M 10 ... La.
18 Crowley, M 22 ... Ore.
500*Crowley, E 18 ... Tex.
.... Crowleys Jc., O 7 ... Me.
20*Crown, I 22 ... Ky.
40*Crown, I 6 ... Pa.
250*Crown (Lax), N 4 ... W. Va.
364 Crown City, Q 15 ... Ohio
550*Crown Hill, K 6 ... W. Va.
70 Crown King, I 11 ... Ariz.
4643 Crown Point, C 6 ... Ind.
90 Crownpoint, F 4 ... N. M.
900 Crown Point, H 25 ... N. Y.
210 Crown Point Center, H 24 ... N. Y.
5 Crow Rock, H 21 ... Mont.
95 Crows Landing, I 8 ... Calif.
16*Crow Summit, H 5 ... W. Va.
119*Crowville, E 12 ... La.
10 Crow Wing, J 12 ... Minn.
....*Croxton, K 17 ... Va.
75 Croydon, M 8 ... N. H.
1300*Croydon, N 24 ... Pa.
107 Croydon, D 13 ... Utah
712 Crozet, J 12 ... Va.
50*Crozier, L 15 ... Va.
35 Crucero, M 21 ... Calif.
1800*Crucible, P 2 ... Pa.
450 Cruger, G 11 ... Miss.
250*Crugers, F 6 ... N. Y.
.... Cruik, K 16 ... Idaho
30*Cruise, I 19 ... Ky.
119*Cruise, L 18 ... Mo.
250*Crum, L 2 ... W. Va.
135 Crum Creek, N 20 ... Okla.
950*Crum Lynne (Leiperville), P 23 ... Pa.
300 Crummies, J 21 ... Ky.
3 Crump, L 10 ... Calif.
57 Crump, M 19 ... Mich.
35*Crump, N 23 ... Mo.
100*Crump, Q 6 ... Tenn.
600*Crumpier, C 3 ... N. C.
125*Crumpler, Q 6 ... W. Va.
66*Crumps Bottom, P 9 ... W. Va.
505*Crumps Park (Creosote), I 10 ... Ga.
243 Crumpton, F 19 ... Md.
40*Crumrod (Ferguson), L 18 ... Ark.
.... Cruse, M 17 ... Ill.
.... Crusher, N 16 ... Okla.
15*Cruso, O 6 ... N. C.
118*Crutchfield, K 4 ... Ky.
65*Crutchfield, C 6 ... N. C.
115*Crystal, P 17 ... Idaho
50*Crystal, G 19 ... Ky.
75 Crystal, G 17 ... Me.
450 Crystal, N 16 ... Mich.
2373 Crystal, M 22, N 16 ... Minn.
125*Crystal, E 16 ... N. H.
7 Crystal, E 1 ... N. M.
428 Crystal, E 21 ... N. D.
36 Crystal, P 19 ... Okla.
32*Crystal, P 9 ... Ore.
.... Crystal, L 12 ... Utah
200 Crystal, Q 7 ... W. Va.
250*Crystal Bay, N 15 ... Minn.
....*Crystal Bay, D 3 ... Nev.
144*Crystal Beach, I 12 ... Fla.
3417 Crystal City, K 20 ... Mo.
6529 Crystal City, N 13 ... Tex.
2641 Crystal Falls, F 3 ... Mich.
119 Crystal Falls, E 15 ... Tex.
150*Crystal Hill Q 11 ... Va.
....*Crystal Lake, M 9 ... Fla.
3917 Crystal Lake, A 18 ... Ill.
301 Crystal Lake, C 11 ... Iowa
927 Crystal River, F 12 ... Fla.
152*Crystal Run, E 4 ... N. Y.
82*Crystal Spring, P 11 ... Pa.
101*Crystal Springs, J 9 ... Ark.
200*Crystal Springs, H 14 ... Fla.
64*Crystalsprings (Eula), O 14 ... Kan.
2855 Crystal Springs, L 10 ... Miss.
55 Crystal Springs, M 16 ... N. D.
125*Crystal Springs, G 17 ... Ohio
100 Crystal Valley, M 11 ... Mich.
557 Cuba, J 4 ... Ala.
1620 Cuba, G 9 ... Ill.
363 Cuba, D 16 ... Kan.
1033 Cuba, K 16 ... Mo.
700 Cuba, E 9 ... N. M.
1699 Cuba, Q 6 ... N. Y.
22 Cuba, N 21 ... N. D.
160*Cuba, N 9 ... Ohio
1259 Cuba City, H 22 ... Wis.
37*Cubage, K 20 ... Ky.
340*Cuba Landing, M 8 ... Tenn.
300 Cubero, G 7 ... N. M.
89*Cub Run, I 13 ... Ky.
3000*Cucamonga, M 20 ... Calif.
.... Cuchara, O 16 ... Colo.
25*Cuchara Camps, O 15 ... Colo.
200 Cuchillo, L 8 ... N. M.
53*Cuckoo, K 15 ... Va.
16*Cucumber, R 6 ... W. Va.
....*Cudahy, N 16, Q 4 ... Calif.
10561 Cudahy, P 20 ... Wis.
200*Cuddebackville, E 4 ... N. Y.
2000*Cuddy (Treveskyn), M 2 ... Pa.
5474 Cuero, M 19 ... Tex.
150 Cuervo, G 19 ... N. M.
40*Cuevas, R 18 ... Miss.
98*Culberson, Q 2 ... N. C.
585 Culbertson, E 24 ... Mont.
815 Culbertson, O 10 ... Neb.
75 Culbertson, Q 13 ... Ohio
219 Culdesac, G 4 ... Idaho
32*Cullasaja, Q 5 ... N. C.
1400*Cullen, B 6 ... La.
30*Cullen, P 12 ... Va.
....*Cullendale, P 10 ... Ark.
500 Culleoka (Pleasant Grove), O 10 ... Tenn.
239 Cullison, M 11 ... Kan.
5074 Cullman, D 13 ... Ala.
251 Culloden, I 8 ... Ga.
110*Culloden, K 3 ... W. Va.
509 Cullom, F 18 ... Ill.
67*Cullomburg, L 4 ... Ala.
700*Cullowhee, P 5 ... N. C.
162*Culp, B 12 ... Ark.
60*Culp Creek, J 7 ... Ore.
2316 Culpeper, H 14 ... Va.
....*Culton, I 20 ... Ky.
1605 Culver, D 12 ... Ind.
195 Culver, H 15 ... Kan.
141*Culver, F 21 ... Ky.
150 Culver, H 19 ... Minn.
.... Culver, D 12 ... Ohio
50 Culver, H 12 ... Ore.
8976 Culver City, O 15, Q 3 ... Calif.
150 Culverton, G 15 ... Ga.
.... Cumback, O 7 ... Ind.
500 Cumberland, J 15 ... Ind.
578 Cumberland, M 7 ... Iowa
4149*Cumberland (Poor Fork), J 22 ... Ky.
39483 Cumberland, L 6 ... Md.
500 Cumberland, P 6 ... Me.
145*Cumberland, F 17 ... Miss.
100 Cumberland, O 10 ... N. J.
80*Cumberland, I 13 ... N. C.
521 Cumberland, K 17 ... Ohio
103 Cumberland, Q 16 ... Okla.
10625■*Cumberland (Cumberland Hill), B 14 ... R. I.
130 Cumberland, M 13 ... Va.
225 Cumberland, J 9 ... Wash.
1539 Cumberland, C 9 ... Wis.
20 Cumberland, O 3 ... Wyo.
705 Cumberland Center, P 6 ... Me.
31*Cumberland City, K 16 ... Ky.
313 Cumberland City, L 8 ... Tenn.
200*Cumberland Falls (Parkers Lake), K 17 ... Ky.
30*Cumberland Falls, K 17 ... Ky.
200 Cumberland Furnace, M 9 ... Tenn.
409*Cumberland Gap, L 20 ... Tenn.
10625■Cumberland Hill (Cumberland), B 14 ... R. I.
.... Cumberland Mills, P 5 (Pop. incl. in Westbrook) ... Me.
....*Cumberland Valley see Bedford Valley ... Pa.
....*Cumberstone, H 14 ... Md.
1700 Cumbola, L 19 ... Pa.
642 Cumby, D 21 ... Tex.
75*Cumi, B 12 ... Ark.
85*Cummaquid, N 13 ... Mass.
958 Cumming, D 8 ... Ga.
139 Cumming, L 11 ... Iowa
56*Cummings, F 3 ... Calif.
76*Cummings, E 23 ... Kan.
.... Cummings, R 2 ... Me.
100 Cummings, J 23 ... N. D.
1250*Cummingsville, O 14 ... Tenn.
428 Cummington, E 5 ... Mass.
210 Cumnock, G 12 ... N. C.
25*Cumnor, L 19 ... Va.
12 Cumro, K 13 ... Neb.
600*Cunard, M 9 ... W. Va.
50*Cundiff, J 15 ... Ky.
120*Cundiyo, F 13 ... N. M.
215 Cundys Harbor, P 8 ... Me.
260*Cuney, G 22 ... Tex.
5*Cunico, C 19 ... N. M.
....*Cunningham, L 5 ... Ala.
350*Cunningham, G 4 ... Calif.
451 Cunningham, M 13 ... Kan.
100*Cunningham, J 4 ... Ky.
....*Cunningham see Powers, ... Ore.
188*Cunningham (Lone Oak), L 9 ... Tenn.
413*Cunningham, B 21 ... Tex.
37 Cunningham, L 19 ... Wash.
3800 Cupertino, G 22 ... Calif.
14*Cuprum, K 5 ... Idaho
211 Curdsville, G 9 ... Ky.
50*Curdsville, M 12 ... Va.
6*Cureall, Q 15 ... Mo.
35 Curl, J 4 ... Ala.
183 Curlew, D 8 ... Iowa
100 Curlew, B 20 ... Wash.
169*Curllsville, I 5 ... Pa.
215 Curran, J 11 ... Ill.
300 Curran, J 20 ... Mich.
50 Currant, I 19 ... Nev.
524 Currie, Q 6 ... Minn.
42 Currie, E 21 ... Nev.
100*Currie, K 16 ... N. C.
94 Currituck, C 23 ... N. C.
40*Curry, C 2, R 20 ... N. Y.
31*Curry, N 4 ... W. Va.
104*Curry (Curryville), M 10 ... Pa.
150 Curry Run, K 9 ... Pa.
55*Curryville, C 4 ... Ga.
266 Curryville, F 16 ... Mo.
104*Curryville (Curry), M 10 ... Pa.
....*Curt, G 21 ... Ky.
425 Curtice, C 10 ... Ohio
26 Curtin, K 5 ... Ore.
12 Curtin, L 11 ... W. Va.
520 Curtis, M 9 ... Ark.
300 Curtis, F 13 ... Mich.
.... Curtis, R 16 ... Minn.
952 Curtis, M 11 ... Neb.
123 Curtis, D 5 ... Okla.
28 Curtis, M 5 ... Wash.
.... Curtis Bay, F 14 ... Md.
200 Curtis Corner, N 7 ... Me.
171*Curtiss, G 13 ... Wis.
210*Curtis Station, C 11 ... Miss.
150 Curtisville, H 16 ... Ind.
12*Curtisville, J 21 ... Mich.
1200 Curtisville, L 4 ... Pa.
30*Curve, N 2 ... Tenn.
3422 Curwensville, J 9 ... Pa.
....*Cuscowilla, Q 13 ... Va.
30 Cush Creek Jc., K 8 ... Pa.
258 Cushing, G 4 ... Iowa
200 Cushing, A 21 ... Mass.
91*Cushing, K 12 ... Minn.
102 Cushing, K 17 ... Neb.
7703 Cushing, F 15 ... Okla.
473 Cushing, G 23 ... Tex.
200 Cushing, B 9 ... Wis.
412 Cushman, D 15 ... Ark.
225 Cushman, E 8 ... Mass.
25 Cushman, K 15 ... Mont.
200 Cushman, J 3 ... Ore.
404 Cusick, E 24 ... Wash.
10 Cusino, E 11 ... Mich.
320 Cusseta, I 22 ... Ala.
357 Cusseta, K 4 ... Ga.
250 Custar, E 9 ... Ohio
16*Custer, B 12 ... Ark.
40*Custer, L 12 ... Idaho
.... Custer, E 14 ... Ill.
69*Custer, G 12 ... Ky.
237 Custer, L 11 ... Mich.
35*Custer, N 16 ... Mo.
150 Custer, K 18 ... Mont.
641 Custer (Custer City), H 6 ... Okla.
1845 Custer, L 2 ... S. D.
250 Custer, B 7 ... Wash.
132*Custer, K 14 ... Wis.
641 Custer City (Custer), H 6 ... Okla.
325 Custer City, E 9 ... Pa.
100*Custer Park, D 20 ... Ill.
2509 Cut Bank, C 8 ... Mont.
1000 Cutchogue, F 11 ... N. Y.
131*Cuthand, C 22 ... Tex.
3447 Cuthbert, L 4 ... Ga.
50 Cuthbert, K 19 ... S. D.
21*Cuthbert, F 11 ... Tex.
3235 Cuthbert Jc., M 4 ... Ga.
1200 Cutler, K 13 ... Calif.
590 Cutler, O 12 ... Ill.
300 Cutler, G 12 ... Ind.
463 Cutler, L 23 ... Me.
125*Cutler, M 17 ... Ohio
40*Cutler, I 16 ... Wis.
50*Cutler City, G 4 ... Ore.
50*Cutlips, I 10 ... W. Va.
476 Cut Off, P 18 ... La.
115*Cutshin, I 21 ... Ky.
600*Cutten, D 2 ... Calif.
20*Cutter, L 7 ... N. M.
328 Cuttingsville, L 9 ... Vt.
77*Cuttyhunk, P 23 ... Mass.
6*Cutuno (Gent), G 22 ... Ky.
20546 Cuyahoga Falls, E 17 ... Ohio
674*Cuyahoga Heights, D 17 ... Ohio
.... Cuyler, K 23 ... Ga.
120*Cuyler, O 15 ... N. Y.
300 Cuylerville, N 8 ... N. Y.
176 Cuyuna, I 13 ... Minn.
30*Cuzco, P 9 ... Ind.
26*Cuzick, G 18 ... Ky.
80*Cuzzart, C 16 ... W. Va.
28*Cuzzie, L 3 ... W. Va.
49*Cybur, Q 15 ... Miss.
100*Cycle, D 6 ... N. C.
8*Cyclone, Q 6 ... Mo.
700*Cyclone (Simpson), E 9 ... Pa.
66*Cyclone, P 6 ... W. Va.
569 Cygnet, E 9 ... Ohio
175*Cylinder, D 8 ... Iowa
125 Cylon, B 11 ... Wis.
.... Cynthina, N 12 ... Ark.
535 Cynthiana, Q 4 ... Ind.
4840 Cynthiana, E 18 ... Ky.
179*Cynthiana, O 11 ... Ohio
....*Cynwyd (Bala-Cynwyd), N 22 (Pop. 3000, incl. in Merion Sta.) ... Pa.
165*Cypress, I 8 ... Ala.
610*Cypress, O 17 ... Calif.
212 Cypress, A 2, M 12 ... Fla.
407 Cypress, Q 15 ... Ill.
100 Cypress, G 7 ... La.
50*Cypress, Q 5 ... Tenn.
48*Cypress, K 22 ... Tex.
12*Cypress (Cypress Chapel), Q 20 ... Va.
892*Cypress Inn, Q 8 ... Tenn.
46*Cypress Mill, K 16 ... Tex.
....*Cypress Top, see Cypress ... Tex.
175*Cyrene, O 5 ... Ga.
69*Cyrene, F 17 ... Mo.
27*Cyril, L 4 ... Ala.
972 Cyril, L 9 ... Okla.
75*Cyrus, G 22 ... Ky.
....*Cyrus, see Rowe ... Mass.
357 Cyrus, L 6 ... Minn.
100*Cyrus (Whites Creek), L 1 ... W. Va.
50*Czar, H 15 ... W. Va.
....*Czizek, I 8 ... Idaho

D

24*Dabney, E 11 ... Ark.
36*Dabney, I 17 ... Ky.
.... Dabney, M 13 ... Tex.
217 Dabney (Kleenkoal), O 4 ... W. Va.
150*Dabneys, K 15 ... Va.
55*Dabob, G 3 ... Wash.
274 Dacoma, C 7 ... Okla.
296 Dacono, E 15 ... Colo.
75 Da Costa, N 12 ... N. J.
49*Dacosta (Da Costa), N 19 ... Tex.
500*Dacota (Decota), K 6 ... W. Va.
315 Dacula, E 9 ... Ga.
100*Dacus, J 22 ... Tex.
30*Dacusville, B 5 ... S. C.
11 Dad, Q 12 ... Wyo.
2561 Dade City, H 14 ... Fla.
2025 Dadeville, I 19 ... Ala.
248 Dadeville, N 9 ... Mo.
53*Dady, M 9 ... Fla.
90 Dafter, F 18 ... Mich.
112 Daggett, M 19 ... Calif.
283 Daggett, H 6 ... Mich.
50 Dagmar, C 25 ... Mont.
222 Dagsboro, L 24 ... Del.
250 Daguscahonda, H 9 ... Pa.
800 Dagus Mines, H 9 ... Pa.
175 Dahinda, F 10 ... Ill.
28*Dahl, I 17 ... Ky.
75 Dahlen, G 21 ... N. D.
595 Dahlgren, O 16 ... Ill.
800 Dahlgren, I 18 ... Va.
120*Dahlia, G 16 ... N. M.
1294 Dahlonega, C 8 ... Ga.
75 Dahoga, G 9 ... Pa.
150 Dailey, C 22 ... Colo.
100*Dailey, H15 ... W. Va.
.... Dain (La Frank), L 11 ... W. Va.
1032 Daingerfield, D 23 ... Tex.
21 Dairy, Q 10 ... Ore.
.... Dairyland, J 11 ... Calif.
72*Dairyland, C 3 ... N. Y.
2000*Daisetta, K 23 ... Tex.
100*Daisy, L 6 ... Ark.
294 Daisy, K 21 ... Ga.
50*Daisy, J 21 ... Ky.
44*Daisy, N 22 ... Mo.
84 Daisy, N 20 ... Okla.
1600 Daisy (Melville), Q 15 ... Tenn.
80 Daisy, E 21 ... Wash.
2000*Daisytown, P 4 ... Pa.
268 Dakota, A 13 ... Ill.
300 Dakota, Q 24 ... Minn.
537 Dakota City, F 10 ... Iowa
477 Dakota City, F 22 ... Neb.
.... Dakota Jc., D 4 ... Minn.
.... Dakota Jc., E 4 ... Neb.
157 Dalark, M 10 ... Ark.
58*Dalbo, L 16 ... Minn.
450 Dalby Springs, C 23 ... Tex.
41*Dalcour, O 19 ... La.
48*Dale, E 7 ... Ark.
132*Dale (Dales), O 18 ... Ill.
763 Dale, Q 9 ... Ind.
79 Dale, L 9 ... Iowa
63*Dale, G 21 ... Ky.
30*Dale, H 5 ... Minn.
.... Dale, J 23 ... Neb.
180*Dale, N 7 ... N. Y.
372 Dale, I 14 ... Okla.
5 Dale, F 18 ... Ore.
3291 Dale, N 8 ... Pa.
300*Dale, O 15 ... S. C.
500 Dale, K 18 ... Tex.
50*Dale, D 11 ... W. Va.
300 Dale, M 15 ... Wis.
56*Dale Enterprise, H 17 ... Va.
....*Dalerose, R 20 ... Colo.
50*Dalesburg (Valjean), H 21 ... Ky.
45 Dalesberg, O 24 ... S. D.
35 Daleview, B 23 ... Mont.
500 Daleville, N 19 ... Ala.
914 Daleville, H 18 ... Ind.
118*Daleville, J 20 ... Miss.
80*Daleville, N 7 ... Va.
36 Daley, I 21 ... Ky
4682 Dalhart, B 2 ... Tex.
10 Dalies, H 9 ... N. M.
350 Dalkena, E 23 ... Wash.
1922 Dallas, E 4 ... Ga.
566 Dallas, M 13 ... Iowa
1704 Dallas, H 4 ... N. C.
3579 Dallas, F 5 ... Ore.
1484*Dallas, H 20 ... Pa.
278 Dallas, N 15 ... S. D.
294734 Dallas, E 19 ... Tex.
125 Dallas, A 11, Q 24 ... W. Va.
436 Dallas, D 10 ... Wis.
865 Dallas Center, K 11 ... Iowa
1149 Dallas City, G 5 ... Ill.
20*Dallas City, D 9 ... Pa.
2000 Dallas Mills, B 14 ... Ala.
2917 Dallastown, P 17 ... Pa.
80*Dallesport, P 13 ... Wash.
425 Dalmatia, L 16 ... Pa.
76*Dalton, A 17 ... Ark.
10448 Dalton, C 3 ... Ga.
.... Dalton, see West Le Mars, ... Iowa
65*Dalton, O 16 ... Kan.
114*Dalton, I 8 ... Ky.
4206■Dalton, E 3 ... Mass.
226 Dalton, J 5 ... Minn.
342 Dalton, F 11 ... Mo.
358 Dalton, J 4 ... Neb.
250 Dalton, G 13 ... N. H.
540 Dalton, O 8 ... N. Y.
59*Dalton, D 7 ... N. C.
774 Dalton, G 16 ... Ohio
1090 Dalton, G 21 ... Pa.
.... Dalton, F 10 ... Utah
240 Dalton, L 17 ... Wis.
354 Dalton City, J 16 ... Ill.
534 Dalworth (Dalworth Park), E 19 ... Tex.
9625 Daly City, D 16 ... Calif.
496 Dalzell, D 14 ... Ill.
80 Dalzell, G 16 ... S. C.
40 Dalzell, I 6 ... S. D.
850 Damariscotta, O 10 ... Me.
290 Damariscotta Mills, O 10 ... Me.
336 Damascus, F 12 ... Ark.
477 Damascus, N 4 ... Ga.
250*Damascus, F 10 ... Md.
250*Damascus, Q 17 ... N. Y.
425*Damascus, F 19 ... Ohio
150 Damascus, D 8 ... Ore.
250*Damascus, F 23 ... Pa.
1441 Damascus, E 8 ... Va.
50*Dameron, O 15 ... Md.
50*Dameron, P 16 ... Md.
64*Dames Ferry, H 10 ... Ga.
347▲Dames Quarter, P 20 ... Md.
363 Damon, M 21 ... Tex.
39*Dan, F 20 ... Ky.
.... Dan, see Bradshaw ... W. Va.
24*Dana, C 7 ... Calif.
253 Dana, F 15 ... Ill.
845 Dana, J 5 ... Ind.
153 Dana, I 10 ... Iowa
50*Dana, H 23 ... Ky.
200*Dana, P 8 ... N. C.
4 Dana, O 13 ... N. D.
.... Dana, see Reed ... W. Va.
125*Dana Point, R 7 ... Calif.
125*Danboro, N 24 ... Pa.
203 Danburg, E 16 ... Ga.
22339 Danbury, L 3 ... Conn.
728 Danbury, H 4 ... Iowa
236 Danbury, O 11 ... Neb.
490 Danbury, M 11 ... N. H.
300 Danbury, C 8 ... N. C.
90 Danbury, D 13 ... Ohio
500 Danbury, M 22 ... Tex.
285 Danbury, C 7 ... Wis.
40*Danby, K 20 ... Mo.
50 Danby (Mount Tabor), N 8 ... Vt.
75*Danciger, M 22 ... Tex.
85*Dancy, H 4 ... Ala.
50*Dancy, E 18 ... Miss.
155*Dancy, J 13 ... Wis.
488 Dandridge, N 20 ... Tenn.
215 Dandy, N 21 ... Va.
10 Dane, E 7 ... Okla.
301 Dane, K 19 ... Wis.
53*Danese, N 9 ... W. Va.
550 Danevang, M 21 ... Tex.
362 Danforth, F 20 ... Ill.
1400 Danforth, H 19 ... Me.
2902 Dania, N 24 ... Fla.
36 Daniel, H 22 ... Tex.
6*Daniel, J 14 ... Va.
44 Daniel, J 5 ... Wyo.
155*Daniel Boone, I 9 ... Ky.
.... Daniels, Q 17 ... Idaho
150*Daniels, O 8 ... W. Va.
27*Daniels Landing, N 7 ... Tenn.
4507 Danielson, E 24 ... Conn.
333 Danielsville, E 13 ... Ga.
945 Danielsville, K 22 ... Pa.
25*Danieltown, P 15 ... Va.
379 Dannebrog, K 16 ... Neb.
4830 Dannemora, D 23 ... N. Y.
50 Danner, N 23 ... Ore.
33 Dannevirke, K 16 ... Neb.
25*Danripple, Q 10 ... Va.
351 Dansville, P 17 ... Mich.
4976 Dansville, O 9 ... N. Y.
49*Dant (Dants), H 15 ... Ky.
118 Dante, O 20 ... S. D.
2700*Dante, D 6 ... Va.
49*Dants (Dant), H 15 ... Ky.
350 Danube, N 8 ... Minn.
705 Danvers, G 14 ... Ill.
14179■Danvers, D 20 ... Mass.
184 Danvers, M 6 ... Minn.
51 Danvers, G 13 ... Mont.
450 Danville, C 11 ... Ala.
761 Danville, H 8 ... Ark.
600 Danville, C 22 ... Calif.
423 Danville, J 13 ... Ga.
36919 Danville, H 21 ... Ill.
2093 Danville, J 11 ... Ind.
309 Danville, O 21 ... Iowa
134*Danville, N 14 ... Kan.
6734 Danville, H 16 ... Ky.
18*Danville, D 8 ... La.
150*Danville (Danville Jc.), N 6 ... Me.
63 Danville, H 16 ... Mo.
275 Danville, P 18 ... N. H.
790 Danville, I 15 ... Ohio
205 Danville, O 9 ... Ohio
7122 Danville, J 17 ... Pa.
162*Danville, L 7 ... Tenn.
500 Danville, F 17 ... Vt.
32749 Danville, R 9 ... Va.
75 Danville, B 20 ... Wash.
417 Danville, M 5 ... W. Va.
150 Danville Jc. (Danville), O 6 ... Me.
75 Danzig, Q 16 ... N. D.
630 Daphne, P 6 ... Ala.
481 Darby, K 4 ... Mont.
29 Darby, D 4 ... N. C.
10334 Darby, P 23 ... Pa.
44 Darbyville, P 15 ... Iowa
256 Darbyville, L 11 ... Ohio
.... Darbyville, D 3 ... Va.
1832 Dardanelle, G 9 ... Ark.
.... Dardanelles, see Nason Creek ... Wash.
210 Darden, O 6 ... Tenn.
175*Dardens (Darden, F 20 ... N. C.
250 Dare, O 21 ... Va.
400 Darent (Lemont Furnace), P 5 ... Pa.
20*Dares Wharf (Dares), L 15 ... Md.
175*Daretown, N 7 ... N. J.
400*Darfork, I 21 ... Ky.
132*Darfur, Q 10 ... Minn.
3000 Darien, Q 3 ... Conn.
1015 Darien, N 23 ... Ga.
45*Darien, M 16 ... Mo.
175*Darien, M 6 ... N. Y.
410 Darien, M 22 ... Wis.
300 Darien Center, M 6 ... N. Y.
104 Darke, E 5 ... W. Va.
200 Darkesville, D 23 ... W. Va.
110 Darkharbor, N 14 ... Me.
.... Dark Swamp, C 14 ... La.
200*Darling, C 11 ... Miss.
60*Darling (Darlington), P 22 ... Pa.
....*Darlington, L 10 ... Ala.
145*Darlington, L 8 ... Fla.
100 Darlington, N 15 ... Idaho
683 Darlington, H 10 ... Ind.
35*Darlington, J 16 ... La.
500 Darlington, B 17 ... Md.
274 Darlington, B 6 ... Mo.
75 Darlington, K 15 ... Ohio
444 Darlington, K 1 ... Pa.
60 Darlington (Darling), P 22 ... Pa.
6236 Darlington, F 18 ... S. C.
2002 Darlington, H 22 ... Wis.
73*Darlington Heights, N 13 ... Va.
27*Darlove, G 7 ... Miss.
102 Darmstadt, N 12 ... Ill.
300*Darnell, B 14 ... La.
18 Darr, L 13 ... Neb.
409*Darragh (Madison), M 5 ... Pa.
400 Darrington, E 11 ... Wash.
500*Darrouzett, A 6 ... Tex.
300 Darrow, M 15 ... La.
.... Darrow, F 8 ... Okla.
100*Darrowville, D 17 ... Ohio
150 Darrtown, M 5 ... Ohio
20*Dart, M 18 ... Ohio
25*Dartmont (Javins), L 5 ... W. Va.
178*Dartmoor, G 14 ... W. Va.
9011■Dartmouth, N 20 ... Mass.
80*Darwin, K 17 ... Calif.
100 Darwin, K 22 ... Ill.
224*Darwin, M 12 ... Minn.
10 Darwin, O 20 ... Okla.
.... Darwin, P 14 ... Tex.
56*Darwin, C 6 ... Va.
297*Dash Point, K 8 ... Wash.
872 Dassel, N 12 ... Minn.
....*Date, D 5 ... S. D.
....*Datha, H 19 ... Ky.
61 Datil, J 5 ... N. M.
275 Datto, A 19 ... Ark.
100*Dauberville, M 20 ... Pa.
600*Daufuskie Island, R 14 ... S. C.
52*Daugherty, L 24 ... Va.
620 Dauphin, N 16 ... Pa.
250*Dauphin Island, P 4 ... Ala.
30*Daus, P 15 ... Tenn.
415*Davant, N 20 ... La.
17*Davella, G 23 ... Ky.
550 Davenport, J 5 ... Calif.
640*Davenport, H 17 ... Fla.
66039 Davenport, L 24 ... Iowa
30*Davenport, I 11 ... Ky.
450 Davenport, N 19 ... Neb.
173 Davenport, P 20 ... N. Y.
147 Davenport, N 24 ... N. D.
975 Davenport, H 15 ... Okla.
300*Davenport, C 22 ... Tex.
125*Davenport, B 7 ... Va.
1337 Davenport, H 21 ... Wash.
185*Davenport Center, Q 10 ... N. Y.
125 Davey, L 21 ... Neb.
75 David, I 17 ... Ala.
31*David, G 15 ... Va.
2272 David City, K 20 ... Neb.
250 Davisburg, P 21 ... Mich.
40*Davidson, E 3 ... Ark.
25*Davidson (Barretts Ferry), H 11 ... Ky.
57 Davidson, G 16 ... Me.
1550 Davidson, G 5 ... N. C.
507 Davidson, O 5 ... Okla.
550 Davidson, L 15 ... Tenn.
54*Davidsonville, I 14 ... Md.
282*Davidsville, O 7 ... Pa.
421*Davilla, I 19 ... Tex.
100 Davin, O 5 ... W. Va.
1672 Davis, G 7 ... Calif.
317 Davis, A 13 ... Ill.
100 Davis, O 23 ... Mich.
60 Davis, G 18 ... Mo.
.... Davis, H 19 ... N. C.
525 Davis, J 22 ... N. C.
1698 Davis, N 14 ... Okla.
290*Davis (Gifford), D 9 ... Pa.
230 Davis, N 23 ... S. D.
1454 Davis, G 17 ... W. Va.
533 Davisboro, I 16 ... Ga.
250 Davisburg, O 21 ... Mich.
556 Davis City, Q 11 ... Iowa
84*Davis Creek, B 10 ... Calif.
311 Davis Jct., B 15 ... Ill.
1397 Davison, O 21 ... Mich.
20*Davisport, G 23 ... Ky.
301*Davis Sta., I 17 ... S. C.
124*Daviston, I 19 ... Ala.
95*Davistown, Q 3 ... Pa.
85*Davisville, F 22 ... Ky.
40*Davisville, K 17 ... Mo.
50*Davisville, N 12 ... N. H.
109*Davisville, N 23 ... Pa.
300 Davisville, I 14 ... R. I.
75*Davisville, F 7 ... W. Va.
112*Davis Wharf, L 24 ... Va.
113*Davy, M 18 ... Tex.
900 Davy, Q 6 ... W. Va.
35 Daw, C 8 ... Va.
150 Dawes, Q 4 ... Ala.
200*Dawes, L 6 ... W. Va.
....*Dawkins, E 11 ... S. C.
168 Dawn, E 9 ... Mo.
50*Dawn, D 2 ... Tex.
75*Dawson, C 18 ... Ala.
3681 Dawson, M 6 ... Ga.
396 Dawson, I 13 ... Ill.
289 Dawson, J 10 ... Iowa
1646 Dawson, N 5 ... Minn.
25*Dawson, O 13 ... Mo.
394 Dawson, O 24 ... Neb.
2000 Dawson, C 18 ... N. M.
263 Dawson, N 15 ... N. D.
1086 Dawson, E 19 ... Okla.
50 Dawson, H 5 ... Ore.
732*Dawson, P 5 ... Pa.
1155 Dawson, G 20 ... Tex.
125*Dawson, N 10 ... W. Va.
2560 Dawson Springs, I 8 ... Ky.
319 Dawsonville, D 8 ... Ga.
56*Dawsonville, J 13 ... Va.
82*Day, B 15 ... Ark.
40*Day, B 9 ... Calif.
100 Day, C 9 ... Fla.
....*Day, J 22 ... Ky.
16*Day, Q 11 ... Mo.
318 Day Book, M 9 ... N. C.
300*Dayhoit (Wilhoit), J 21 ... Ky.
165 Daykin, N 20 ... Neb.
100*Daylight, N 13 ... Tenn.
130*Daylo, C 4 ... N. C.
40*Daysboro, G 21 ... Ky.
138 Days Creek, N 6 ... Ore.
250*Daysville, N 16 ... Tenn.
153 Dayton, J 8 ... Ala.
29*Dayton, Q 16 ... Ga.
364 Dayton, R 20 ... Idaho
125 Dayton, D 16 ... Ill.
690 Dayton, G 11 ... Ind.
732 Dayton, H 10 ... Iowa
8379 Dayton, B 17 ... Ky.
225*Dayton, F 11 ... Md.
250*Dayton, R 8 ... Mich.
253 Dayton, M 15 ... Minn.
43 Dayton, F 4 ... Mont.
200 Dayton, H 3 ... Nev.
360 Dayton, H 15 ... N. J.
105 Dayton, M 20 ... N. M.
225 Dayton, P 4 ... N. Y.
210718 Dayton, L 7 ... Ohio

Pop.	Place Index	State
506	Dayton, E 6	Ore.
882	Dayton, K 6	Pa.
1870	Dayton, P 16	Tenn.
1279	Dayton, K 23	Tex.
632	Dayton, I 11	Va.
3026	Dayton, N 22	Wash.
60	Dayton, K 21	Wis.
240	Dayton, B 14	Wyo.
22584	Daytona Beach, E 19	Fla.
700	Dayville (Killingly), D 24	Conn.
136	Dayville, H 16	Ore.
215	Dazey, L 20	N. D.
75*	Dead River, J 7	Me.
309*	Deadwater, J 9	Me.
4100	Deadwood, I 2	S. D.
312	Deadwood, F 24	Tex.
917	Deal, I 21	N. J.
....	Deal, see Brandon	Va.
50*	Deale, H 14	Md.
1048▲	Deal Island, P 19	Md.
92*	Dean, Q 16	Iowa
25*	Dean, M 14	Mont.
107	Dean, L 10	Pa.
....*	Dean, E 17	Tenn.
49	Dean (Colbert), H 22	Wash.
20*	Dean, C 11	W. Va.
36*	Deane, I 22	Ky.
129	Dean Lake (Snyder), E 10	Mo.
50	De Ann, N 7	Ark.
200*	Deans, H 15	N. J.
150	Deansboro, M 17	N. Y.
15	Deans Island, F 22	Ark.
250	Deanville, J 19	Tex.
....	Dearborn, M 22	Ind.
63584	Dearborn, Q 22	Mich.
456	Dearborn, E 5	Mo.
273	Dearing, G 18	Ga.
273	Dearing, O 21	Kan.
57*	Dearing (Black Wolf), R 6	W. Va.
25	Dearman, D 22	Ark.
200*	De Armanville, F 19	Ala.
320	Deary, F 5	Idaho
100	Death Valley, K 22	Calif.
350	Deatsville, I 15	Ala.
13*	Deatsville, F 14	Ky.
111	Deaver, A 10	Wyo.
192	Deavertown, L 15	Ohio
100*	De Bardeleben (Empire), E 10	Ala.
280	De Beque, H 5	Colo.
350*	De Berry, E 24	Tex.
51*	Deblois, L 19	Me.
50*	Deborah, C 9	Miss.
15*	Debord, G 23	Ky.
125	Deborgia, G 2	Mont.
75*	Debruce, R 20	N. Y.
20	De Camp, L 16	Mo.
16604	Decatur, B 12	Ala.
413	Decatur, A 4	Ark.
16561	Decatur, F 8	Ga.
59305	Decatur, I 15	Ill.
5861	Decatur, E 22	Ind.
275	Decatur, P 11	Iowa
5*	Decatur, I 16	Ky.
1599	Decatur, Q 12	Mich.
773	Decatur, J 18	Miss.
905	Decatur, H 23	Neb.
150	Decatur, P 9	Ohio
205	Decatur, P 16	Tenn.
2578	Decatur, D 18	Tex.
38*	Decatur (Agua), L 9	Va.
57	Decatur, D 7	Wash.
282	Decatur City, P 11	Iowa
....	Decatur Jc., B 12	Ala.
29*	Decaturville, L 12	Mo.
433	Decaturville, O 7	Tenn.
868	Decherd, Q 13	Tenn.
....	Decide, K 16	Ky.
466	Decker, O 5	Ind.
10*	Decker, H 11	Ky.
125	Decker, N 23	Mich.
20	Decker, N 20	Mont.
42	Deckerville, F 21	Ark.
647	Deckerville, M 24	Mich.
238	Declo, Q 14	Idaho
5303	Decorah, C 19	Iowa
500*	Decota (Dacota), L 6	W.Va.
1500	Decoto, E 21	Calif.
26*	Decoy, H 22	Ky.
62*	Dederick, L 7	Mo.
392	Dedham, J 7	Iowa
293▲	Dedham, L 15	Me.
15508■	Dedham, G 18, Q 2	Mass.
....	Dee, see Ridge	Ark.
100	Dee, C 10	Ore.
150	Deedsville (Deeds), E 14	Ind.
....*	Deel, B 7	Va.
200*	Deemer, I 18	Miss.
710*	Deemston, O 2	Pa.
27	Deep, E 11	N. D.
112*	Deepcreek, C 8	Colo.
500	Deep Creek, Q 22	Va.
35	Deepcreek, H 22	Wash.
200*	Deep Gap, D 3	N. C.
1026	Deephaven, N 15	Minn.
....	Deep Lake, N 17	Fla.
2400	Deep River, L 17	Conn.
443	Deep River, L 17	Iowa
50	Deep River, M 4	Wash.
150*	Deep Run, I 17	N. C.
174*	Deepstep, H 14	Ga.
225*	Deep Valley, Q 1	Pa.
956	Deepwater, J 8	Mo.
395	Deepwater, M 5	N. J.
125*	Deepwater (Deep Water), M 8	W. Va.
160*	Deer, D 9	Ark.
50*	Deerbrook, G 21	Miss.
100*	Deerbrook, K 11	Wis.
469	Deer Creek, G 13	Ill.
405	Deer Creek, J 8	Minn.
250	Deer Creek, B 12	Okla.
61	Deerfield, L 18	Ark.
2283	Deerfield, A 20	Ill.
356	Deerfield, K 4	Kan.
31*	Deerfield (Lantz), D 8	Md.
600	Deerfield, D 7	Mass.
569	Deerfield, R 21	Mich.
165	Deerfield, L 6	Mo.
150	Deerfield, O 17	N. H.
435	Deerfield, F 19	Ohio
5*	Deerfield, K 4	S. D.
100*	Deerfield, J 9	Va.
611	Deerfield, L 20	Wis.
1850	Deerfield Beach, M24	Fla.
65	Deerfield Center, O 17	N. H.
15	Deerfield Jc., D 7	Mass.
75*	Deerfield Street, P 9	N. J.
52*	Deerford, K 14	La.
98	Deer Grove, D 12	Ill.
75	Deer Harbor, C 5	Wash.
20	Deerhead, F 24	N. Y.
187	Deering, J 24	Mo.
140	Deering, F 11	N. D.
1000	Deering Jc., P 6	Me.
75	Deer Island, B 7	Ore.
500	Deer Isle, N 15	Me.
65*	Deerland, H 20	N. Y.
....*	Deer Lick, L 20	Ky.
3278	Deer Lodge, J 7	Mont.
155*	Deer Lodge, M 16	Tenn.
300	Deer Park, N 4	Ala.
20	Deer Park (Ross), O 17	Ark.
172▲	Deer Park, H 20	Fla.
31*	Deerpark, G 13	La.
329	Deer Park, N 2	Md.
150*	Deer Park, H 9	N. Y.
3510	Deer Park, N 6	Ohio
350*	Deer Park, E 24	Tex.
1070	Deer Park, F 23	Wash.
203	Deer Park, C 11	Wis.
62*	Deer Plain, L 8	Ill.
67*	Deer Range (Range), N 10	Ala.
987	Deer River, G 14	Minn.
100	Deer River, H 17	N. Y.
118*	Deersville, I 18	Ohio
124*	Deerton, F 12	Mich.
387	Deertrail, G 18	Colo.
87*	Deerun, I 17	W. Va.
570	Deerwood, I 14	Minn.
30*	Deeson, D 7	Miss.
75	Deeth, C 19	Nev.
10*	Deevert, E 21	Ky.
32*	Defeated Creek, J 22	Ky.
620	Deferiet, G 16	N. Y.
428	Defiance, J 6	Iowa
90*	Defiance, I 18	Mo.
9744	Defiance, D 6	Ohio
350*	Defiance, O 9	Pa.
136*	Defoe, E 15	Ky.
138	Deford, M 22	Mich.
598	De Forest, L 19	Wis.
2570	De Funiak Springs, M 7	Fla.
27*	Degolia, D 9	Pa.
37*	De Graff, K 18	Kan.
291	De Graff, M 7	Minn.
796	Degraff, I 9	Ohio
112*	Degrasse, F 18	N. Y.
100*	Degray, L 8	Ark.
13	De Grey, J 14	S. D.
15*	Dehart, F 20	Ky.
130*	Dehart, D 5	N. C.
56*	Dehaven, D 14	Va.
....*	Dehue (Dehu), O 4	W. Va.
38	Deisem, O 18	N. D.
95*	De Jarnette, J 17	Va.
9146	De Kalb, B 16	Ill.
866	De Kalb, I 20	Miss.
314*	De Kalb, E 5	Mo.
1287	De Kalb, C 23	Tex.
30*	Dekalb, G 9	W. Va.
450	De Kalb Jc., E 17	N. Y.
296	Dekoven, H 7	Ky.
32*	Dela, N 21	Okla.
50	Delacroix, N 12	La.
100*	Delafield, O 17	Ill.
450	Delafield, N 20	Wis.
422	Delagua, P 16	Colo.
250	Delair, K 9	N. J.
....*	Delake, H 4	Ore.
12	De Lamar, P 3	Idaho
150	De Lamere, P 23	N. D.
255*	DeLancey (Adrian), I 17	Pa.
1272	Delanco, J 11	N. J.
200	De Lancy, A 1, Q 19	N. Y.
7041	De Land, F 18	Fla.
487	De Land, H 17	Ill.
....	De Land Sta., F 18	Fla.
300*	Delaney, D 6	Ark.
4573	Delano, L 13	Calif.
1094	Delano, N 14	Minn.
800	Delano, K 19	Pa.
175*	Delano, Q 17	Tenn.
40*	Delano, L 1	W. Va.
326	Delanson, N 22	N. Y.
161*	Delaplaine, B 19	Ark.
100*	Delaplane, F 15	Va.
....	De Lassus, M 20	Mo.
1181	Delavan, H 12	Ill.
150*	Delavan, I 18	Kan.
321	Delavan, Q 13	Minn.
3444	Delavan, M 22	Wis.
511	Delawanna, C 18	N. J.
125*	Delaware, G 8	Ark.
190	Delaware, M 20	Ind.
198	Delaware, G 21	Iowa
91*	Delaware, G 9	Ky.
100*	Delaware, O 16	Mo.
205*	Delaware, D 9	N. J.
8944	Delaware, I 11	Ohio
542	Delaware, B 20	Okla.
....	Delaware Bend, see Orlena	Tex.
1163	Delaware City, C 21	Del.
....	Delaware, Lackawanna and Western Jc., M 8	N. Y.
410	Delaware Water Gap, J 23	Pa.
325	Delbarton, O 3	W. Va.
....*	Del Bonita, C 6	Mont.
1255	Delcambre, N 11	La.
300*	Delcarbon (Calumet No. 1), O 15	Colo.
196*	Delco, R 14	Idaho
263	Delco, M 15	N. C.
1971	De Leon, F 16	Tex.
450	Deleon Springs, F 18	Fla.
100*	Delevan, F 6	Calif.
554	Delevan, O 6	N. Y.
2802	Delford (Oradell), C 20	N. J.
115*	Delft, Q 9	Minn.
500*	Delhi, I 9	Calif.
25	Delhi, Q 18	Colo.
36*	Delhi, L 9	Ill.
421	Delhi, G 21	Iowa
1192	Delhi, C 13	La.
174*	Delhi, O 9	Minn.
1841	Delhi, P 20	N. Y.
79	Delhi, J 2	Okla.
222	Delia, F 21	Kan.
100*	Delia, G 19	Tex.
408	Delight, M 7	Ark.
150*	De Lisle, R 17	Miss.
267	Dell, D 22	Ark.
20	Dell, O 7	Mont.
....*	Delle, E 6	Utah
200*	Delleker, E 9	Calif.
....*	Del Loma, D 3	Calif.
1706	Dell Rapids, K 24	S. D.
200*	Dellrose, Q 11	Tenn.
335	Dellroy (Dell Roy), H 19	Ohio
100*	Dellslow, C 15	W. Va.
36*	Dellvale, D 8	Kan.
155*	Dellwood, O 6	N. C.
....*	Dellwood, M 3	Ore.
114*	Dellwood (Holmsville), J 16	Wis.
250*	Delmar, D 8	Ala.
17*	Delmar, B 8	Ark.
680	Del Mar, P 18	Calif.
881	Delmar, M 22	Del.
....	Delmar, E 21	Ill.
434	Delmar, I 24	Iowa
1184*	Delmar, M 22	Md.
2065	Delmar	Del.-Md.
4500	Delmar, O 23	N. Y.
30	Delmar, M 2	Ore.
162*	Delmar (Cedar Springs), B 9	S. C.
....*	Del Mar, P 6	Tex.
116*	Delmar (Vestal), E 8	Va.
23*	Delmer, J 17	Ky.
650*	Delmita (Zaragoza), O 3	Tex.
278	Delmont, Q 11	N. J.
705	Delmont, M 5	Pa.
461	Delmont, N 20	S. D.
750*	Del Monte, K 6	Calif.
....	Del Monte Jc., see Castroville	Calif.
1923	Del Norte, N 10	Colo.
281	Deloit, I 5	Iowa
50*	Delombre, J 14	La.
80	De Long, F 9	Ill.
115	Delong, D 12	Ind.
50	Delorme (Edgarton), P 3	W. Va.
800*	Del Paso Heights (Del Paso), G 8	Calif.
2213	Delphi, F 11	Ind.
50*	Delphi (Zieglersville), N 22	Pa.
50*	Delphia, J 22	Ky.
40	Delphia, J 16	Mont.
265*	Delphi Falls, M 15	N. Y.
90*	Delphos, P 9	Iowa
714	Delphos, F 15	Kan.
68	Delphos, J 24	N. M.
5746	Delphos, G 7	Ohio
31*	Delpiedra (Piedra), J 13	Calif.
13*	Delray, F 21	W. Va.
3737	Delray Beach, M 24	Fla.
1000*	Del Rey, J 12	Calif.
89*	Delrey, G 20	Ill.
300	Del Rio, N 22	Tenn.
13343	Del Rio, M 11	Tex.
8	Delrio, F 18	Wash.
550*	Del Rosa, O 18	Calif.
219*	Delta, F 19	Ala.
73*	Delta (Bayles), C 5	Calif.
3717	Delta, J 5	Colo.
602	Delta, M 17	Iowa
30*	Delta, J 17	Ky.
183*	Delta (Delta Point), D 15	La.
21*	Delta Farms, P 17	La.
183*	Delta Point (Delta), D 15	La.
320	Delta, O 22	Mo.
1773	Delta, C 8	Ohio
724	Delta, Q 18	Pa.
1304	Delta, J 8	Utah
23*	Delta, E 5	Wis.
21*	Delta Farms, N 18	La.
750	Deltaville, M 21	Va.
300	Delton, P 14	Mich.
60*	Delton, P 4	Va.
....*	Delton, see Lake Delton	Wis.
180*	De Luz, P 20	Calif.
75*	Delvalle, K 18	Tex.
15*	Delvinta, G 20	Ky.
83*	Delwin, C 12	Tex.
60*	Delwood, Q 18	Ill.
160*	Dema, H 22	Ky.
1165	Demarest, C 21	N. J.
....	Demers, B 9	Mont.
3608	Deming, O 6	N. M.
250	Deming, C 8	Wash.
75*	Democrat, J 22	Ky.
165*	Democrat, N 8	N. C.
4137	Demopolis, J 7	Ala.
820	Demorest, C 11	Ga.
55*	Demory Hill, D 10	Fla.
8	De Moss, D 13	Ore.
175*	De Mossville, C 17	Ky.
600	Demotte, D 8	Ind.
10	Dempsey, J 7	Mont.
....	Dempster, G 11	Ky.
103	Dempster, H 23	S. D.
75	Demster J 14	N. Y.
30*	Demund, G 21	Ky.
437	Denair, I 9	Calif.
105*	Denaud, L 17	Fla.
55	Denbigh, G 12	N. D.
100	Denbigh, O 20	Va.
1800*	Denbo, O 2	Pa.
10*	Denby, N 6	S. D.
465	Dendron, O 19	Va.
120*	Denham, D 10	Ind.
90*	Denham, J 18	Minn.
1233	Denham Springs, L 15	La.
75*	Denhawken, M 17	Tex.
113	Denhoff, K 13	N. D.
50	Denio, R 20	Ore.
4361	Denison, I 5	Iowa
176	Denison, F 21	Kan.
20*	Denison, I 13	Ky.
15581	Denison, B 19	Tex.
40	Denison, G 23	Wash.
5	Denman, M 16	Neb.
....*	Denmar, M 13	W. Va.
100*	Denmark, F 15	Ark.
200	Denmark, P 21	Iowa
200	Denmark, O 3	Me.
75*	Denmark, C 16	Miss.
113*	Denmark, H 16	N. Y.
96	Denmark, N 2	Ore.
2056	Denmark, K 12	S. C.
81	Denmark, O 4	Tenn.
864	Denmark, P 14	Wis.
....	Denmark, Jc. N 21	Mich.
33*	Dennard, E 12	Ark.
37*	Denney, K 17	Ky.
384	Denning, F 6	Ark.
50	Dennis, H 13	Ga.
212	Dennis, N 23	Kan.
10*	Dennis, E 22	Ky.
300	Dennis, M 13	Mass.
194	Dennis, B 23	Miss.
75*	Dennis (Salem Chapel), D 8	N. C.
7*	Dennis, D 23	Okla.
41*	Dennis, E 17	Tex.
112*	Dennis, N 10	W. Va.
63*	Dennis Mills, K 16	La.
90*	Dennison, K 22	Ill.
40*	Dennison, O 12	Mich.
216	Dennison, O 17	Minn.
4413	Dennison, I 18	Ohio
750	Dennis Port, N 14	Mass.
37*	Denniston, F 20	Ky.
200	Denniston, R 11	Va.
400	Dennisville, Q 12	N. J.
45*	Denny, C 3	Calif.
123*	Denny, D 3	N. C.
450	Dennysville, K 23	Me.
26	De Nova, F 21	Colo.
100	Denoya, B 16	Okla.
18	Denrock, C 11	Ill.
140*	Densmore, E 8	Kan.
9	Denson, C 8	Ohio
37*	Densons Landing, O 7	Tenn.
25	Dent, G 6	Idaho
204	Dent, I 6	Minn.
50*	Denton, C 17	Ark.
254	Denton, M 16	Ga.
156*	Denton, D 23	Kan.
250	Denton, E 22	Ky.
1572	Denton, J 20	Md.
144*	Denton, I 8	Mo.
406	Denton, G 13	Mont.
126	Denton, M 21	Neb.
677	Denton, F 9	N. C.
3	Denton, M 9	Okla.
11192	Denton, D 18	Tex.
....	Denton Branch Jc., I 19	Md.
25	Dents, G 13	S. C.
100	Dents Run, H 10	Pa.
36*	Dentsville, N 13	Md.
60*	Denver, A 8	Ark.
322412	Denver, F 15	Colo.
....*	Denver, D 16	Fla.
150	Denver, H 6	Ill.
483	Denver, E 14	Ind.
556	Denver, F 17	Iowa
100*	Denver, G 22	Ky.
213	Denver, B 7	Mo.
100*	Denver, Q 20	N. Y.
254	Denver, G 4	N. C.
77*	Denver, N 12	Ohio
1428	Denver, N 19	Pa.
56	Denver, M 7	Tenn.
319	Denver (Bellton), B 11	W. Va.
160*	Denver, D 16	W. Va.
700	Denver City, D 8	Tex.
1500	Denville, D 15	N. J.
....*	Denworth, D 5	Tex.
13	Denzer, H 4	Ore.
4	Deora, O 22	Colo.
300*	Depauville, G 15	N. Y.
150	Depauw, P 13	Ind.
6373	De Pere, O 14	Wis.
6084	Depew, M 5	N. Y.
876	Depew, G 16	Okla.
250*	De Peyster, E 17	N. Y.
822	Deport, C 22	Tex.
2028	Deposit, R 17	N. Y.
100*	Depoy, I 9	Ky.
2296	Depue, D 14	Ill.
179	Deputy, N 17	Ind.
3055	De Queen, M 4	Ark.
3252	De Quincy, L 6	La.
83*	Derby, F 15	Colo.
10287	Derby, M 8	Conn.
20*	Derby, P 17	Ill.
150*	Derby, Q 11	Ind.
269	Derby, O 13	Iowa
256	Derby, M 16	Kan.
500	Derby, J 13	Me.
800	Derby, N 4	N. Y.
307	Derby, L 10	Ohio
62*	Derby, M 15	Tex.
346	Derby (Derby Center), B 17	Vt.
1000	Derby, D 4	Va.
661	Derby Line, A 17	Vt.
68*	Derden, G 18	Tex.
3750	De Ridder, J 6	La.
....*	Derinda Center, A 9	Ill.
500*	Derita, H 6	N. C.
477	Derma, E 16	Miss.
3083	Dermott, P 16	Ark.
64*	Dermott, E 11	Tex.
70*	Deronda, B 10	Wis.
200*	De Rossett, N 15	Tenn.
68	Derrick, F 19	N. D.
150	Derrick City, E 9	Pa.
....	Derry, see Hawk	Kan.
367	Derry, G 8	La.
5400■	Derry, Q 16	N. H.
200	Derry, M 8	N. M.
3003	Derry, N 6	Pa.
1000*	Derry Church, M 16	Pa.
526	De Ruyter, N 16	N. Y.
500*	Derwent, K 17	Ohio
200*	Derwood, G 10	Md.
150*	De Sabla, E 7	Calif.
650	DesAllemands (Allemands), O 17	La.
1348	Des Arc, H 16	Ark.
399	Des Arc, O 19	Mo.
27	De Sart, O 4	N. D.
230*	Descanso, Q 20	Calif.
....	Deschutes, I 12	Ore.
198	Desdemona, F 16	Tex.
375	Deseret, J 7	Utah
125*	Desert Center, O 21	Calif.
....	Desert Mound, O 4	Utah
14*	Des Glaise, M 12	La.
475*	Desha, D 15	Ark.
1037	Deshler, O 19	Neb.
1570	Deshler, E 9	Ohio
150	Desire, J 8	Pa.
31*	Deskins, C 7	Va.
197	Deslacs, G 9	N. D.
60*	Deslet, O 17	Mo.
1394	Desloge, L 19	Mo.
250	Desmet, E 3	Idaho
25	De Smet, H 4	Mont.
1016	De Smet, I 21	S. D.
159819	Des Moines, L 12	Iowa
289	Des Moines, C 22	N. M.
600	Des Moines, I 8	Wash.
295	De Soto, L 8	Ga.
656	De Soto, P 14	Ill.
95	Desoto, H 19	Ind.
274	De Soto, L 10	Iowa
383	De Soto, G 24	Kan.
176	De Soto, L 20	Miss.
5121	De Soto, K 20	Mo.
17	Desoto, J 24	Neb.
400	De Soto, F 18	Wis.
131*	De Soto City, J 17	Fla.
17*	De Spains, I 14	Ky.
9518	Des Plaines, B 20	Ill.
20*	Dess, G 5	La.
100	Destin, N 6	Fla.
900*	Destrehan, N 17	La.
	Deter, R 7, see Colestin	Ore.
125*	Detonti, K 12	Ark.
110*	Detour, C 9	Md.
595	Detour, G 20	Mich.
27*	Detrick, F 13	Va.
200	Detroit, D 5	Ala.
140*	Detroit, J 7	Ill.
204	Detroit, H 17	Kan.
148	Detroit, L 11	Me.
1623452	Detroit, Q 23	Mich.
5015	Detroit Lakes, H 6	Minn.
111	Detroit, G 9	Ore.
1064	Detroit, B 22	Tex.
....	Detroit Harbor, see Washington Island	Wis.
150*	Deucher, M 18	Ohio
45	Deunquat, G 11	Ohio
672	De Valls Bluff, I 16	Ark.
300*	Devault, O 22	Mo.
50*	Deventer, P 24	Mo.
....	Dever, G 6	Ore.
200	Devereux, H 14	Ga.
213	Devers, K 24	Tex.
....	Devils Elbow, M 14	Mo.
117*	Devils Lake, R 19	Mich.
6204	Devils Lake, H 18	N. D.
....	Devils Lake, J 18	Wis.
320	Devils Slide, D 13	Utah
75*	Devils Tower, B 21	Wyo.
80	Devine, M 17	Colo.
1398	Devine, M 15	Tex.
20	Devitt, G 5	Ore.
...*	Devitts Camp, I 16	Pa.
208	Devol, P 7	Okla.
....	Devon, O 8	Conn.
200*	Devon, L 25	Kan.
27	Devon, H 24	Ky.
40	Devon, D 10	Mont.
136*	Devon, O 22	Pa.
163*	Devon (Okeeffe), P 3	W.Va.
154*	Devonia, M 18	Tenn.
....*	Devotion, C 6	N. C.
128*	Dewalt, L 22	Tex.
84*	Dewar, G 18	Iowa
778	Dewar, I 19	Okla.
10	Deward, J 16	Mich.
289	Dewart, I 16	Pa.
58	Dewatto, I 6	Wash.
31*	Dewdrop, F 21	Ky.
134	Deweese, N 18	Neb.
26*	Dewey (Cherry Creek), I 12	Ariz.
140	Dewey, H 18	Ill.
60*	Dewey, G 22	Ky.
....	Dewey, L 6	Mont.
....*	Dewey, L 9	N. Y.
2114	Dewey, B 19	Okla.
75	Dewey, M 1	S. D.
256	Dewey (Deweyville), B 11	Utah
2000	Deweyville, J 25	Tex.
256*	Deweyville (Dewey), B 11	Utah
2498	De Witt, L 16	Ark.
247	Dewitt, H 17	Ill.
2205	Dewitt, J 24	Iowa
100*	Dewitt, J 19	Ky.
651	De Witt, O 17	Mich.
314	De Witt, F 10	Mo.
490	De Witt, N 21	Neb.
500*	De Witt, M 15	N. Y.
150*	Dewitt, P 16	Va.
153*	Dewittville, Q 2	N. Y.
250	Dewmaine, P 15	Ill.
....*	Dewright, J 16	Okla.
45*	Dewville, L 17	Tex.
260*	Dewyrose, E 15	Ga.
324	Dexter, J 14	Ga.
50*	Dexter, Q 12	Ind.
760	Dexter, L 10	Iowa
424	Dexter, O 18	Kan.
243	Dexter, K 6	Ky.
2500	Dexter, K 12	Me.
1087	Dexter, Q 20	Mich.
303	Dexter, R 18	Minn.
3108	Dexter, Q 22	Mo.
734	Dexter, L 20	N. M.
1109	Dexter, H 15	N. Y.
300	Dexter, O 15	Ohio
100	Dexter, J 7	Ore.
317	Dexter, B 19	Tex.
191	Dexter City, L 18	Ohio
....	Dexter Jc., H 15	N. Y.
36*	Dexterville, I 11	Ky.
90	Dexterville, I 14	Wis.
163*	De Young (Russell City), G 8	Pa.
700	D'Hanis, M 15	Tex.
300	Diablock, I 21	Ky.
603	Diagonal, P 9	Iowa
100*	Dial (Swan), C 8	Ga.
100*	Dial, B 4	Tex.
219	Dialville, F 22	Tex.
1000	Diamond Spring, G 9	Calif.
250*	Diamond, C 7	Ga.
150	Diamond, J 7	Ind.
200	Diamond, P 20	La.
486	Diamond, P 6	Mo.
300	Diamond (Palmyra), F 19	Ohio
12	Diamond, N 19	Ore.
140*	Diamond, H 4	Pa.
50	Diamond, K 23	Wash.
650	Diamond, L 6	W. Va.
56	Diamond, O 21	Wyo.
150	Diamond Bluff, B 13	Wis.
265	Diamond Hill, A 16	R. I.
6*	Diamond Lake, M 6	Ore.
200*	Diamond Point, J 22	N. Y.
586	Diamondville, O 3	Wyo.
200*	Diana, P 10	Tenn.
212	Diana, J 12	W. Va.
....*	Diana Mills, M 12	Va.
50	Diantha, K 15	Ark.
80*	Dias, M 7	Pa.
50*	Diascond (Diascund), M 19	Va.
256	Dias Creek, Q 11	N. J.
240	Diaz, E 17	Ark.
97	Dibble, K 11	Okla.
1363	Diboll, H 23	Tex.
26*	Dice, I 21	Ky.
378	Dickens, C 7	Iowa
40*	Dickens, Q 11	Mo.
115	Dickens, L 9	Neb.
465	Dickens, C 12	Tex.
65*	Dickensonville, E 6	Va.
200	Dickerson, F 8	Md.
25	Dickerson, D 14	N. C.
1000*	Dickerson Run, P 5	Pa.
203	Dickey, O 19	N. D.
200	Dickeysville, G 22	Wis.
16	Dickie, E 9	Wyo.
165*	Dickinson, L 7	Ala.
5839	Dickinson, M 5	N. D.
163*	Dickinson, O 14	Pa.
81	Dickinson, L 23	Tex.
350	Dickinson (Quincy), L 6	W. Va.
500	Dickinson Center, D 20	N. Y.
110*	Dicks (Dix), P 18	Colo.
25	Dickson, I 13	Okla.
11548	Dickson (Dickson City), G 21	Pa.
3504	Dickson, M 9	Tenn.
....	Dickworsham, B 16	Tex.
159*	Diehlstadt, P 23	Mo.
143*	Dieringer, J 8	Wash.
1544	Dierks, M 5	Ark.
100*	Dies, I 24	Tex.
477	Dieterich, L 18	Ill.
300	Dietrich, P 12	Idaho
100	Dietz, B 15	Wyo.
31*	Diffee, P 5	Ga.
150	Difficult, L 13	Tenn.
50*	Difficulty, N 16	Wyo.
128*	Diggins, O 11	Mo.
250*	Diggs, M 22	Va.
974	Dighton, J 6	Kan.
500	Dighton, K 19	Mass.
123	Dighton, L 14	Mich.
37	Dighton, I 18	Okla.
408	Dike, G 16	Iowa
150*	Dike, C 22	Tex.
561▲	Dilia, G 17	N. M.
2	Dilkon, F 20	Ariz.
511	Dill (Dill City), J 5	Okla.
4	Dill, J 22	Wis.
204*	Dillard, B 12	Ga.
43*	Dillard, K 17	Mo.
250	Dillard, P 12	Okla.
11	Dillard, N 5	Ore.
500*	Dille (Dilles Bottom), K 20	Ohio
164*	Dille, J 10	W. Va.
75*	Dillen, E 9	Ark.
378	Diller, O 21	Neb.
500*	Dilles Bottom (Dille), K 20	Ohio
150	Dilley, D 6	Ore.
1244	Dilley, N 15	Tex.
161	Dillon, G 11	Colo.
....	Dillon, B 12	Ind.
42*	Dillon, J 15	Iowa
55*	Dillon (Swayne), I 17	Kan.
100	Dillon, L 15	Mo.
3014	Dillon, N 7	Mont.
....	Dillon, C 19	N. M.
3867	Dillon, E 21	S. C.
20*	Dillon Beach, A 14	Calif.
27*	Dillons Run, F 21	W. Va.
1652	Dillonvale, J 20	Ohio
558	Dillsboro, M 21	Ind.
290	Dillsboro, P 5	N. C.
1054	Dillsburg, O 16	Pa.
68*	Dilltown, M 7	Pa.
436	Dillwyn, M 13	Va.
1068	Dilworth, H 2	Minn.
50*	Dilworth, L 18	Tex.
219	Dime Box, J 19	Tex.
943	Dimmitt, A 9	Tex.
65	Dimock, E 20	Pa.
200	Dimock, M 20	S. D.
604	Dimondale, P 17	Mich.
33*	Dimple, I 11	Ky.
150*	Dinero, O 17	Tex.
225	Dines, O 8	Wyo.
400	Dingess, N 3	W. Va.
300	Dingle, Q 23	Idaho
200	Dingmans Ferry, I 24	Pa.
10*	Dingus, F 21	Ky.
35*	Dingy, I 9	W. Va.
15*	Dink, J 9	W. Va.
800*	Dinkey Creek, J 12	Calif.
75*	Dinsdale, H 16	Iowa
36*	Dinsmore, C 8	Ark.
708▲*	Dinsmore, B 16	Fla.
3790	Dinuba, K 12	Calif.
200	Dinwiddie, O 16	Va.
350*	Dinwood (Alphoretta), H 22	Ky.
25*	Dione, J 21	Ky.
210	Diorite, E 5	Mich.
184*	Direct, C 21	Tex.
215	Dirgin, F 23	Tex.
28*	Dirigo, J 15	Ky.
....	Dirk, see Carr Creek	Ky.
114*	Disautel, D 16	Wash.
30*	Disco, F 15	Wis.
300	Dishman, H 24	Wash.
100	Disko, E 15	Ind.
2000	Disney, C 22	Okla.
75*	Disputanta, H 18	Ky.
120*	Disputanta, O 18	Va.
....	Disque, F 4	Wash.
12	Disston, K 7	Ore.
658*	Distant, L 5	Pa.
211*	Ditchley, L 21	Va.
9*	Dittmer, J 19	Mo.
1033	Divernon, J 12	Ill.
30	Divide, J 14	Colo.
....	Divide, F 21	Minn.
113	Divide, L 7	Mont.
....	Divide, see Winchester	Wis.
116*	Divide, P 22	Wyo.
150	Dividend, H 10	Utah
900	Dividing Creek, P 9	N. J.
64*	Divine Corners, C 2	N. Y.
....*	Division, O 13	Mich.
24*	Divot, M 15	Tex.
110*	Dix (Dicks) P 18	Colo.
189	Dix, N 16	Ill.
199	Dix, K 2	Neb.
1200	Dixfield, M 5	Me.
2000	Dixiana, E 14	Ala.
34*	Dixie, H 16	Ark.
221	Dixie, P 11	Ga.
30*	Dixie, I 8	Idaho
350*	Dixie, B 4	La.
129	Dixie, O 11	Okla.
15	Dixie, H 23	Ore.
22*	Dixie, M 21	Va.
200	Dixie, O 21	Wash.
250	Dixie, L 10	W. Va.
35	Dixie Springs (Dixie), E 10	Ala.
75	Dixmont, L 12	Ala.
188*	Dixmont, M 3	Pa.
1022*	Dixmoor (Specialville), C 21	Ill.
1108	Dixon, H 6	Calif.
10671	Dixon, C 13	Ill.
226*	Dixon, K 23	Iowa
642	Dixon, H 8	Ky.
200*	Dixon, I 17	Miss.
741	Dixon, L 14	Mo.
132	Dixon, G 4	Mont.
226	Dixon, F 21	Neb.
800	Dixon, D 14	N. M.
250*	Dixon, K 18	N. C.
157*	Dixon, G 6	Ohio
70	Dixon, M 15	S. D.
94	Dixon, R 13	Wyo.
13*	Dixondale, M 21	Va.
150*	Dixons Mills, K 7	Ala.
28*	Dixon Springs, Q 17	Ill.
25*	Dixon Springs (Renshaw) Q 17	Ill.
250	Dixon Springs, M 13	Tenn.
40	Dixonville, M 6	Ore.
1000	Dixonville, L 8	Pa.
28*	Dixville Notch, D 16	N. H.
85*	Dizney, J 21	Ky.
400	D'Lo, L 13	Miss.
25*	Doans, M 9	Ind.
300*	Doanville (Myers Crossing), M 15	Ohio
200	Dobbin, J 21	Tex.
42*	Dobbins, F 8	Calif.
23*	Dobbins, F 21	Ky.
5883	Dobbs Ferry, G 5	N. Y.
520	Dobson, C 6	N. C.
65*	Dock, G 22	Ky.
55	Dockery, E 8	Miss.
60*	Dockery, C 5	N. C.
25	Dock Jc., C 3	Pa.
200	Dockton, I 7	Wash.
52	Doctor Phillips, G 18	Fla.
300*	Doctors Inlet, C 16	Fla.
59*	Doctortown, M 21	Ga.
317	Doddridge, R 6	Ark.
308	Dodds (Dodd City), C 20	Tex.
262	Doddsville, F 9	Miss.
240	Dodge, H 13	Mass.
656	Dodge, I 21	Neb.
234	Dodge, K 7	N. D.
53	Dodge, C 24	Okla.
467	Dodge, I 22	Tex.
208	Dodge, E 15	Wis.
1029	Dodge Center, Q 18	Minn.
8487	Dodge City, L 8	Kan.
550	Dodgeville, J 18	Mass.
510*	Dodgeville, D 2	Mich.
2269	Dodgeville, I 20	Wis.
8*	Dodlyt, K 21	Va.
442	Dodson, E 9	La.
11	Dodson, O 3	Md.
250	Dodson, G 6	Mo.
397	Dodson, D 16	Mont.
46	Dodson, K 6	Ohio
357	Dodson, E 6	Tex.
40*	Dodson, Q 6	Va.
100*	Doe (Doeville), L 25	Tenn.
104	Doebay, C 7	Wash.
60*	Doe Hill, H 9	Va.
35*	Doering, K 11	Wis.
832	Doerun, N 9	Ga.
962	Doe Run, M 20	Mo.
50	Doe Run, P 21	Pa.
....	Doe Run, M 19	Mo.
....	Dogden, see Butte	N. D.
35*	Dogie, I 23	Wyo.
40*	Dogue, I 17	Va.
325*	Dogwood (Underwood), H 13	Ala.
....*	Dogwood, K 18	Ky.
549*	Doheny Park, R 7	Calif.
223	Dola, G 9	Ohio
162*	Dola, E 12	W. Va.
861*	Dolan, I 21	Ky.
542	Doland, G 20	S. D.
25	Dolberg, M 14	Okla.
....	Dole (Ruckles), N 5	Ore.
....	Dole Jc., R 5	N. H.
85*	Doles, M 10	Ga.
3195	Dolgeville, L 20	N. Y.
850	Dollar Bay, D 3	Mich.
190	Dollarville, F 13	Mich.
179*	Dolliver, B 8	Iowa
3000*	Dolomite, F 12	Ala.
....	Dolomite, F 8	Utah
804	Dolores, O 3	Colo.
500	Dolores, P 14	Tex.
100*	Doloroso, O 4	Miss.
12*	Dolph, B 13	Ark.
84	Dolph, E 4	Ore.

Pop. Place Index State
35*Dolphin, P 16....Va.
.... Dolphin, C 6....Wash.
3068*Dolton, D 22....Ill.
121 Dolton, M 22....S. D.
6 Dombey, Q 6....Okla.
113 Dome, M 3....Ariz.
37*Dome, O 7....N. C.
100 Domingo, F 12....N. M.
.... Dominguez Junction, R 4....Calif.
5*Dominion, D 22....Wash.
.... Dona, O 8....N. M.
133*Dona, F 4....Va.
500 Dona Ana, N 10....N. M.
.... Donahue, A 15....Calif.
89*Donahue, K 24....Iowa
164 Donald, E 7....Ore.
103 Donald, M 14....Wash.
10 Donald, F 11....Wis.
271 Donalds, E 6....S. C.
108*Donaldson, L 10....Ark.
128*Donaldson, C 12....Ind.
120*Donaldson, C 2....Minn.
1000 Donaldson, L 18....Pa.
3889 Donaldsonville, N 15....La.
1718 Donalsonville, O 4....Ga.
65*Donansburg, I 14....Ky.
30*Doncaster, N 10....Md.
258*Donegal, M 5....Pa.
1500*Donelson, M 11....Tenn.
64*Donerail, F 17....Ky.
23*Dongola, D 11....Ark.
638 Dongola, Q 14....Ill.
15*Dongola, I 22....Ky.
30*Dongola, L 15....Va.
218 Donie, H 21....Tex.
150*Doniphan, E 23....Kan.
1604 Doniphan, Q 18....Mo.
395 Doniphan, M 17....Neb.
75 Don Luis, P 22....Ariz.
175 Donna (Mohawk), I 7....Ore.
4712 Donna, Q 4....Tex.
40*Donnaha (Donnoha)....N. C.
51 Donnan, E 19....Iowa
110*Donnels, N 12....Tenn.
356 Donnellson, L 13....Ill.
515 Donnellson, Q 20....Iowa
325 Donnelly, K 6....Idaho
370 Donnelly, L 5....Minn.
400 Donner, O 15....La.
40 Donnoha (Donnaha), D 7....N. C.
215 Donnybrook, F 8....N. D.
18*Donohue (Silver Run), F 8....W. Va.
13180 Donora, O 4....Pa.
80*Donovan, I 16....Ga.
381 Donovan, F 21....Ill.
.... Donovan, K 17....Okla.
25*Dont, M 15....Ky.
527*Donwood, L 7....W. Va.
16*Dony, H 22....Ky.
12*Doogan, B 5....Ga.
500*Doole, H 14....Tex.
200 Dooley, B 24....Mont.
184*Dooling, K 9....Ga.
14*Doolittle Mills, P 11....Ind.
576 Doon, C 2....Iowa
.... *Doorway, H 20....Ky.
1032 Dora, E 11....Ala.
100*Dora, Q 13....Mo.
30*Dora, J 24....N. M.
120*Dora, M 3....Ore.
350*Dora, J 7....Pa.
26*Dora, F 13....Tex.
75 Dora, O 3....Va.
128*Doran, J 3....Minn.
112 Doran, C 8....Va.
300*Doraville, E 7....Ga.
30*Dorcas, G 18....W. Va.
222 Dorchester, M 23....Ga.
185 Dorchester, L 11....Ill.
102*Dorchester, B 20....Iowa
558 Dorchester, M 20....Neb.
165 Dorchester, P 10....N. J.
160 Dorchester, L 16....N. C.
100*Dorchester, C 19....Tex.
600*Dorchester, D 5....Va.
456 Dorchester, H 12....Wis.
300 Dorcyville, M 14....La.
35 Dore, H 1....N. D.
300*Dorena, Q 24....Mo.
40*Dorena, K 7....Ore.
100 Dorfee, K 8....W. Va.
100*Dorloo, N 20....N. Y.
25 Dorman, L 20....Me.
50*Dormansville, O 23....N. Y.
.... *Dormers, K 20....Ky.
12974*Dormont, L 3....Pa.
134*Dornsife, K 17....Pa.
23*Dorothy, E 4....Minn.
464 Dorothy, O 12....N. J.
60*Dorothy, M 6....W. Va.
224 Dorr, P 13....Mich.
19*Dorr, P 11....W. Va.
414 Dorrance, H 12....Kan.
100*Dorrance, I 20....Pa.
863 Dorris, B 6....Calif.
54*Dorset, H 10....Minn.
350 Dorset, C 20....Ohio
100 Dorset, N 7....Vt.
.... Dorsey, A 23....Colo.
3 Dorsey, E 8....Idaho
60*Dorsey, L 11....Ill.
181*Dorsey, G 13....Md.
21*Dorsey (Sundell), F 12 Mich.
40 Dorsey, C 21....Miss.
46*Dorsey, E 17....Neb.
75*Dorsey, P 4....N. C.
45*Dortha (Dorthae), J 19 Ky.
150*Dorton, I 23....Ky.
16 Dory, P 18....Va.
262*Dos Cabezos, Q 23....Ariz.
170*Dos Palos (South Dos Palos) J 9....Calif.
978 Dos Palos, J 9....Calif.
20 Dos Rios, E 2....Calif.
12*Doss, N 16....Mo.
50*Doss, J 14....Tex.
15 Dossett, M 18....Tenn.
50*Dossville, I 15....Miss.
40*Doster, P 12....Mich.
250 Doswell, K 17....Va.
65*Dot, K 10....Ky.
17194 Dothan, N 21....Ala.
30 Dothan (West Fork), O 5....Ore.
79*Dothan, E 15....Tex.
400*Dothan, M 8....W. Va.
25*Dott, P 11....Pa.
350 Dott (Wenonah), Q 8 W. Va.
.... Dottelle, N 9....Ala.
.... Doty, Q 20....Minn.
287 Doty, L 5....Wash.
263 Double Bayou, L 24....Tex.
75 Double Run, L 11....Ga.
400 Double Springs, D 9....Ala.
155*Double Springs, M 14 Tenn.
235*Doubs, D 8....Md.
519 Doucette, I 24....Tex.
.... Doud, C 9....Tex.
216 Douds, P 18....Iowa
45 Dougherty, D 8....Ga.
215 Dougherty, E 14....Iowa
464 Dougherty, O 14....Okla.
140*Dougherty, B 11....Tex.
8623 Douglas, P 23....Ariz.
5175 Douglas, M 14....Ga.
100 Douglas, E 9....Ill.
397 Douglas, I 14....Mass.
421 Douglas, P 11....Mich.
87 Douglas, P 19....Minn.
234 Douglas, M 23....Neb.
313 Douglas, I 9....N. D.
140 Douglas, E 11....Okla.
60 Douglas, H 15....Wash.
50*Douglas, H 8....W. Va.
500*Douglas (Albert), G 16 W. Va.
2205 Douglas, K 19....Wyo.
62*Douglas City, D 4....Calif.
85*Douglasflat, H 10....Calif.
25*Douglas Hill, O 3....Me.
.... Douglas Jc., I 14....Mass.
.... *Douglaslodge, H 9....Minn.
40*Douglass, D 19....Iowa
760 Douglass, M 17....Kan.
20*Douglass (Bell), J 9....Ky.
225*Douglass, G 23....Tex.
575*Douglassville, M 20....Pa.
328*Douglassville, C 24....Tex.
2555 Douglasville, F 5....Ga.
272 Dousman, N 20....Wis.
450 Douthat, A 23....Okla.
40*Dove (Robbins), O 12 Ohio
418 Dove Creek, N 2....Colo.
510 Dover, F 9....Ark.
8 Dover, B 15....Colo.
5517 Dover, G 22....Del.
450*Dover, I 14....Fla.
200 Dover, J 21....Ga.
125 Dover, C 4....Idaho
155*Dover, D 13....Ill.
150*Dover (Kelso), L 22....Ind.
200 Dover, G 21....Kan.
353 Dover, C 19....Ky.
500 Dover, G 18....Mass.
269 Dover, Q 21....Minn.
233 Dover, G 9....Mo.
45 Dover, H 12....Mont.
14990 Dover, O 20....N. H.
10491 Dover, D 15....N. J.
623 Dover, H 18....N. C.
2 Dover, K 16....N. D.
9691 Dover, H 17....Ohio
390 Dover, F 10....Okla.
733 Dover, P 16....Pa.
600 Dover, L 8....Tenn.
175 Dover, Q 10....Vt.
.... Dover Bay, O 20....Ohio
3200 Dover Center (Westlake), C 15....Ohio
3000 Dover-Foxcroft, J 12....Me.
110 Dover Furnace, C 6....N. Y.
1100 Dover Plains, C 7....N. Y.
25 Dover South Mills, J 12 Me.
190*Dovesville, E 19....S. C.
8*Dovetail, H 16....Mont.
125*Dovray, F 7....Minn.
200 Dow, L 9....Ill.
200 Dow, L 20....Okla.
.... *Dowagiac, see Pike View Ky.
5007 Dowagiac, R 11....Mich.
642 Dow City, J 5....Iowa
.... Dowd, D 22....Mont.
35*Dowdy, E 16....Ark.
704*Dowell, P 14....Ill.
.... *Dowell, M 15....Md.
267 Dowelltown, N 13....Tenn.
35*Dowlingsville, D 17....Ky.
120*Dowling, P 13....Mich.
100*Dowling, C 10....Ohio
5 Dowling, I 7....S. D.
500 Dowling Park, C 10....Fla.
74*Downer, H 3....Minn.
76*Downer, M 9....N. J.
9526 Downers Grove, C 20....Ill.
15000*Downey, Q 4....Calif.
673 Downey, Q 20....Idaho
111*Downey, K 21....Iowa
450 Downieville, F 9....Calif.
150 Downieville, L 3....Pa.
64*Downing (Kelso), H 19 Kan.
507 Downing, A 13....Mo.
300*Downing, C 11....Wis.
6 Downing Jc., C 11....Wis.
75*Downings, K 21....Va.
100*Downington, O 15....Ohio
4645 Downingtown, P 21....Pa.
225*Downs, K 19....Ala.
301 Downs, H 16....Ill.
1219 Downs, E 12....Kan.
5 Downs, I 21....Wash.
112*Downsville, C 10....La.
352 Downsville, L 19....N. Y.
200 Downsville, D 12....Wis.
945 Dows, F 12....Iowa
154 Doxey, J 3....Okla.
65*Doyle, D 9....Calif.
100 Doyle (Doyleville), L 10 Colo.
30*Doyle, K 6....Ga.
600*Doyle, J 17....La.
15*Doyle, P 15....Minn.
40 Doyle, M 11....Okla.
500 Doyle, N 14....Tenn.
61*Doylesburg, N 13....Pa.
48*Doyles Mills, M 13....Pa.
1259 Doylestown, F 16....Ohio
4976 Doylestown, P 24....Pa.
253 Doylestown, K 18....Wis.
35*Doylesville, J 12....Va.
100*Doyleville (Doyle), L 10 Colo.
600 Doyline, B 6....La.
120 Doyon, H 19....N. D.
399 Dozier, M 15....Ala.
75*Dozier, D 6....Tex.
7339■*Dracut, D 17....Mass.
18 Drady, G 9....N. D.
64*Draffin, I 24....Ky.
4*Dragonville, L 20....Va.
60 Dragoon, N 21....Ariz.
597 Drain, K 5....Ore.
150 Drake, G 11....Ariz.
60 Drake, D 14....Colo.
75 Drake, J 8....Ill.
50*Drake, J 12....Ky.
97*Drake, J 11....Mo.
654 Drake, I 5....N. D.
5 Drake, O 15....Okla.
176*Drake, E 20....S. C.
1255 Drakesboro, I 10....Ky.
438 Drakes Branch, P 12....Va.
25 Drakes Creek, C 6....Ark.
100*Drakestown, M 21....N. J.
252 Drakesville, P 17....Iowa
300*Draketown, F 3....Ga.
2000 Draper, B 9....N. C.
300 Draper, K 12....S. D.
1250 Draper, F 11....Utah
241*Draper, P 3....Va.
125*Draper, H 5....Wis.
345*Drasco, E 14....Ark.
319 Draughon, N 13....Ark.
2277 Dravosburg, N 3....Pa.
75*Drayden, P 15....Md.
688 Drayton, E 23....N. D.
1200 Drayton, A 9....S. C.
.... *Drayton Island, D 16....Fla.
100*Drehersville, L 20....Pa.
1250 Drayton Plains, P 22 Mich.
90*Drefus, G 18....Ky.
65*Drennen, L 9....W. Va.
16*Drennon Springs, D 15 Ky.
200*Dresbach, Q 25....Minn.
180 Dresden, E 6....Kan.
180 Dresden, N 9....Me.
120*Dresden, I 10....Mo.
257 Dresden, N 11....N. Y.
180 Dresden, D 19....N. D.
1350 Dresden, J 16....Ohio
1115 Dresden, M 5....Tenn.
182 Dresden Mills, N 9....Me.
100 Dresden Sta., I 24....N. Y.
200*Dresher, N 22....Pa.
.... Dresser, J 21....Ky.
294 Dresser, B 10....Wis.
30*Dressor, L 15....Ill.
.... Drew, H 18....Me.
1579 Drew, E 9....Miss.
86 Drew, N 6....Ore.
90*Drewersburg, L 22....Ind.
65*Drewry, N 10....Ala.
40*Drewrys Bluff, M 17....Va.
250*Drewryville, Q 17....Va.
58 Drewsey, K 20....Ore.
100*Drewsville, O 6....N. H.
450*Drexel, J 6....Mo.
16*Drexel, H 3....Mont.
881 Drexel, E 2....N. C.
2550*Drexel, L 7....Ohio
1197 Drexel Hill, P 23....Pa.
90*Dreyfus, G 18....Ky.
200*Drift, H 22....Ky.
56*Drifting, I 11....Pa.
45 Drifton, B 7....Fla.
1200 Drifton, J 20....Pa.
.... Drifton Jc., J 21....Pa.
75*Driftwood, C 17....Ark.
61 Driftwood, B 8....Okla.
293 Driftwood, H 11....Pa.
57*Driftwood, K 17....Tex.
.... Driftwood Jc., H 11....Pa.
75*Driggs, G 6....Ark.
1040 Driggs, N 23....Idaho
100*Drill, C 8....Va.
110*Dripping Springs, J 16 Tex.
62*Drip Rock, H 19....Ky.
235 Driscoll, N 14....N. D.
500*Driscoll, P 18....Tex.
25*Driver, E 22....Ark.
125 Driver, P 21....Va.
27*Drum, I 17....Ky.
30 Drumb (Clonsilla), L 21 Okla.
100*Drumhill, C 20....N. C.
66 Drummond, M 22....Idaho
150*Drummond, F 16....Mich.
150 Drummond, I 6....Mont.
245 Drummond, E 10....Okla.
250 Drummond, H 8....Pa.
300 Drummond, E 6....Wis.
50*Drummonds, P 2....Tenn.
50*Drumore, Q 19....Pa.
4303 Drumright, F 16....Okla.
265 Drums, J 20....Pa.
21*Drury, J 14....Md.
87*Drury, C 5....Mass.
64*Drury, P 13....Mo.
300 Dryad, L 5....Wash.
300*Drybranch, I 12....Ga.
506*Drybranch, L 6....W. Va.
250*Dryburg, D 19....Mich.
57*Dry Creek, K 7....La.
75*Dry Creek, N 7....W. Va.
1100*Dryden (Wilton), L 7....Me.
411 Dryden, O 22....Mich.
471 Dryden, O 14....N. Y.
110 Dryden, Q 4....Ore.
150*Dryden, D 10....Tex.
300*Dryden, E 4....Va.
250 Dryden, H 14....Wash.
161*Dryfork, B 7....Ark.
22*Dryfork, J 13....Ky.
150*Dry Fork, Q 9....Va.
800*Dryfork, G 16....W. Va.
40 Dry Grove, L 9....Miss.
15*Dryhead, N 14....Mont.
34*Dryhill, H 20....Ky.
.... *Dry Lake, O 21....Nev.
125 Dry Mills, O 5....Me.
56*Drynob, M 13....Mo.
520*Dry Prong, G 9....La.
257*Dry Ridge, D 17....Ky.
75 Dry Run, B 4....Md.
200 Dry Run, O 13....Pa.
150*Drytown, H 9....Calif.
350*Duane (Bulan), K 5....Ky.
10 Duane, D 20....Mo.
12 Duane, Q 19....N. D.
50*Duane, K 17....Va.
100 Duanesburg, N 22....N. Y.
2000*Duarte, P 6....Calif.
749 Dubach, B 9....La.
150*Dubard, F 13....Miss.
250 Dubberly, C 7....La.
7814 Dublin, J 15....Ga.
751 Dublin, J 20....Ind.
111*Dublin, K 5....Ky.
300*Dublin, D 9....Miss.
60*Dublin, Q 9....N. H.
325*Dublin, K 13....N. C.
351*Dublin, J 11....Ohio
237 Dublin, N 23....Pa.
2546 Dublin, F 16....Tex.
576 Dublin, D 4....Va.
332 Dubois, M 19....Idaho
280 Dubois (Bois), N 14....Ill.
45*Dubois, O 10....Ind.
315 Du Bois, O 24....Neb.
12080 Du Bois, I 9....Pa.
412 Dubois, G 6....Wyo.
1047 Duboistown, I 15....Pa.
23 Dubose, Q 6....Ala.
.... *Dubre, K 15....Ky.
.... Dubuisson, K 11....La.
43892 Dubuque, G 24....Iowa
907 Duchesne, G 19....Utah
130*Duck, D 24....N. C.
62*Duck (Villa Nova), J 9 W. Va.
90 Duckabush, H 5....Wash.
35*Duck Creek, K 19....N. C.
1650 Duck Creek, O 13....Wis.
150 Duckers, F 17....Ky.
537 Duck Hill, F 14....Miss.
118*Duck River, O 9....Tenn.
150*Ducktown, K 18....Ky.
1600 Ducktown, Q 18....Tenn.
250*Ducktown (Postelle), Q 18 Tenn.
50 Duckwater, I 18....Nev.
36*Duco, G 21....Va.
100 Ducor, L 13....Calif.
58*Dudie, G 14....Va.
159*Dudley (Cedar Cove), G 11....Ala.
259 Dudley, J 13....Ga.
50 Dudley, D 5....Idaho
125*Dudley, J 21....Ill.
64*Dudley, N 16....Iowa
4616■Dudley, I 13....Mass.
339 Dudley, Q 21....Mo.
152 Dudley, H 16....N. C.
60*Dudley, L 17....Ohio
410 Dudley, O 11....Pa.
29*Due, B 7....Ga.
500 Duenweg, O 6....Mo.
40*Duet, H 14....Va.
593 Due West, E 7....S. C.
82*Duff, P 8....Ind.
8*Duff, G 13....Neb.
125*Duff, L 18....Tenn.
220*Duffau, F 17....Tex.
75 Duffee, J 19....Miss.
83*Duffield, E 4....Va.
75*Duffy, L 20....Ohio
386 Duffy, H 12....W. Va.
392 Dufur, D 12....Ore.
1406 Dugger, M 6....Ind.
42*Dugginsville, R 12....Mo.
14*Dugspur, Q 4....Va.
150*Duhring, R 7....W. Va.
29*Duke, E 18....Ala.
37*Duke, M 14....Mo.
37*Duke, P 11....Ohio
412 Duke (East Duke), M 3....Okla.
1200 Duke Center, E 10....Pa.
125 Dukedom, L 5....Tenn.
50*Dukes, C 13....Fla.
16*Dukehurst, H 10....Ky.
75*Dukes (Ruse), F 6....Mich.
83*Dulac, Q 16....La.
100*Dulah, M 14....N. C.
34*Dulaney, I 7....Ky.
29*Dulany, M 22....Tenn.
44 Dulce, B 9....N. M.
.... *Duley, K 13....Md.
40*Dull Center, H 21....Wyo.
626 Duluth, E 8....Ga.
67*Duluth, E 20....Kan.
27*Duluth, G 18....Ky.
101065 Duluth, H 21....Minn.
45*Dulworth, I 15....Ky.
2323 Dumas, N 16....Ark.
150*Dumas, B 19....Miss.
2117 Dumas, B 3....Tex.
15*Dumbarton, M 17....Va.
480*Dumfries, L 18....Va.
40 Dummerston (Dummeston Sta.) Q 13....Vt.
43 Dumont, F 13....Colo.
762 Dumont, F 14....Iowa
238 Dumont, K 3....Minn.
7556 Dumont, O 21....N. J.
35 Dumont, J 2....S. D.
982*Dumont (South Houston), L 23....Tex.
500 Dumont, B 12....Tex.
115*Dunavant (Dunnavant), F 14....Ala.
14*Dunavant, I 16....Va.
50*Dunbar, I 11....Ky.
114*Dunbar, F 14....Minn.
336 Dunbar, M 24....Neb.
10*Dunbar, N 20....Okla.
1390 Dunbar, P 5....Pa.
275*Dunbar, D 20....S. C.
40*Dunbar, D 5....Va.
5266 Dunbar, K 5....W. Va.
150*Dunbar, N 9....Wis.
75 Dunbarton, O 13....N. H.
231*Dunbarton, L 11....S. C.
26*Dunbarton, I 22....Wis.
240 Dunbridge, D 10....Ohio
50*Dunbrooke, K 19....Va.
887 Duncan, M 25....Ariz.
150*Duncan, G 16....Ky.
419 Duncan, D 8....Miss.
25 Duncan, O 12....Mo.
241 Duncan, J 19....Neb.
185 Duncan (Casma), G 13....N. C.
9207 Duncan, N 9....Okla.
30*Duncan, D 20....Ore.
631 Duncan, B 7....S. C.
20*Duncan, H 6....W. Va.
49*Duncan, M 10....Wyo.
500 Duncan Falls, K 16....Ohio
73 Duncan Mills (Duncans Mills), G 3....Calif.
1707 Duncannon, M 15....Pa.
70*Duncans Bridge, E 13....Mo.
1415 Duncansville, N 10....Pa.
150 Duncanville, H 9....Ala.
57*Duncanville, L 22....Ill.
350*Duncanville, E 19....Tex.
300 Duncanwood, J 19....Ohio
341 Duncombe, G 11....Iowa
1000*Duncott, K 19....Pa.
50*Dundalk, J 4....Ga.
2210 Dundalk, F 15....Md.
157 Dundas, M 20....Ill.
456 Dundas, O 16....Minn.
16 Dundas, J 17....N. D.
300 Dundas, O 14....Ohio
150*Dundas, I 19....Va.
96*Dundas, O 15....Wis.
100*Dundee, O 18....Ala.
694 Dundee, I 17....Fla.
3137 Dundee, B 18....Ill.
.... *Dundee, see Roll....Ind.
193*Dundee, F 20....Iowa
32*Dundee, J 11....Kan.
150 Dundee, H 11....Ky.
1699 Dundee, R 21....Mich.
22*Dundee, R 6....Minn.
300*Dundee, B 10....Miss.
250 Dundee, D 19....N. Y.
1168 Dundee, O 11....N. Y.
356 Dundee, H 17....Ohio
209 Dundee, E 6....Ore.
300 Dundee, B 15....Tex.
59*Dundon, J 9....W. Va.
1758 Dunedin, I 12....Fla.
5360 Dunellen, F 16....N. J.
15 Dunfermline, G 10....Ill.
333 Dungannon, D 6....Va.
150 Dungeness, F 6....Wash.
140*Dunglen, I 20....Ohio
105 Dunham, I 23....Ky.
102*Dunhams Hollow, O 24 N. Y.
75 Dunkard, Q 3....Pa.
360 Dunkerton, G 18....Iowa
2942 Dunkirk, G 20....Ind.
.... *Dunkirk, M 14....Md.
25 Dunkirk, D 9....Mont.
17713 Dunkirk, O 2....N. Y.
922 Dunkirk, G 10....Ohio
40 Dunkley, D 8....Colo.
52*Dunksburg, H 8....Mo.
61*Dunlap, K 10....Calif.
10 Dunlap, E 13....Ill.
400*Dunlap, F 12....Ill.
1550 Dunlap, J 4....Iowa
219 Dunlap, I 19....Kan.
150*Dunlap, C 9....Mo.
19 Dunlap, F 4....Neb.
15*Dunlap, J 19....N. M.
680*Dunlap, E 6....Ohio
53 Dunlap, C 3....Okla.
721 Dunlap, P 15....Tenn.
175*Dunlay, L 16....Tex.
100*Dunleary, H 24....Ky.
100*Dunleith, F 7....Miss.
80*Dunleith (Buffalo Creek), K 1....W. Va.
367*Dunlevy, O 2....Pa.
2000 Dunlo, N 9....Pa.
524 Dunloop, N 8....W. Va.
50 Dunlow, M 2....W. Va.
158*Dunmor, J 10....Ky.
23086 Dunmore, H 22....Pa.
50*Dunmore, K 15....W. Va.
6*Dunmovin, K 16....Calif.
59*Dunn (Dunns), C 13....La.
35*Dunn (Impo), O 14....Mo.
5256 Dunn, H 14....N. C.
58*Dunn (Dunns Sta.), P 2 Pa.
163*Dunn, E 11....Tex.
115*Dunnavant, F 14....Ala.
238 Dunn Center, K 6....N. D.
150 Dunnegan, M 9....Mo.
239 Dunnell, R 10....Minn.
1217 Dunnellon, F 13....Fla.
141*Dunnigan, G 6....Calif.
12*Dunning (Dunningville), P 12....Mich.
272 Dunning, I 12....Neb.
7 Dunning, E 11....N. D.
24 Dunnings Creek Jc., P 9 Pa.
12*Dunningville (Dunning), P 12....Mich.
32*Dunn Loring, F 17....Va.
569▲*Dunns (N. Yarmouth), O 6....Me.
59*Dunns (Dunn), C 13....La.
34*Dunns, P 9....W. Va.
58*Dunns Sta. (Dunn), P 2 Pa.
205 Dunnsville, K 19....Va.
200*Dunnville, I 16....Ky.
250*Du Noir, J 9....Wyo.
50*Dunphy, D 15....Nev.
114*Dunraven, I 21....Ky.
13*Dunraven, Q 20....N. Y.
30 Dunreath, L 14....Iowa
187 Dunreith, J 19....Ind.
719 Dunseith, D 14....N. D.
2359 Dunsmuir, C 6....Calif.
300*Dunstable, C 17....Mass.
483*Dunstan (W. Scarboro), O 6....Me.
25 Dunton, N 5....Colo.
.... *Dunvilla (Lake Lizzie) J 6....Minn.
190*Dunwoody, E 7....Ga.
85*Duo, M 12....W. Va.
25*Duoro, I 17....N. M.
25*Duplessis, M 15....La.
2073 Dupo, M 9....Ill.
200*Dupont, F 15....Colo.
332 Dupont, O 15....Ga.
300 Dupont, N 19....Ind.
28*Dupont, N 15....La.
217 Dupont, F 7....Ohio
5278 Dupont, H 21....Pa.
100 Dupont, N 18....S. C.
400*Du Pont, J 7....Wash.
460 Dupree, F 9....S. D.
45*Dupuyer, B 7....Mont.
164 Duquesne, P 18....Ariz.
20693 Duquesne, N 4....Pa.
10*Duquette, J 19....Minn.
7515 Duquoin, O 14....Ill.
43*Duquoin, N 14....Kan.
181 Durand, I 4....Ga.
592 Durand, A 13....Ill.
3127 Durand, O 19....Mich.
1858 Durand, D 13....Wis.
5887 Durango, P 5....Colo.
42*Durango, G 23....Iowa
810 Durant, K 22....Iowa
2510 Durant, H 13....Miss.
.... Durant, K 6....Mont.
10027 Durant, Q 17....Okla.
10 Durban, R 21....Mich.
10 Durbin, E 23....Ky.
23 Durbin, N 23....N. D.
533 Durbin, J 15....W. Va.
150*Durham, C 5....Ark.
1500 Durham, F 6....Calif.
800*Durham, J 14....Conn.
310 Durham (Pittsburg), B 2 Ga.
245 Durham, I 16....Kan.
40 Durham, O 7....Me.
210 Durham, C 15....Mo.
1200 Durham, O 19....N. H.
250*Durham, P 22....N. Y.
60195 Durham, E 12....N. C.
140 Durham, G 2....Okla.
60*Durham, N 23....Pa.
.... Durham, I 9....Wash.
407 Durham Center, J 14 Conn.
625 Durhamville, L 16....N. Y.
100 Durkee, G 23....Ore.
50 Durwood, F 14....Okla.
8275 Duryea, H 21....Pa.
739 Dushore, G 18....Pa.
36*Dusk, H 10....W. Va.
463 Duson, M 11....La.
314 Duster, F 16....Tex.
25*Dustin, E 15....Neb.
652 Dustin, I 9....Okla.
6 Dusty, K 6....N. M.
24 Dusty, L 22....Wash.
24*Dutch, I 11....W. Va.
79 Dutchess Jc., D 5....N. Y.
90*Dutch Flat, F 9....Calif.
336▲*Dutch Mills, D 4....Ark.
106*Dutch Neck, I 14....N. J.
77*Dutch Town, L 16....La.
66*Dutchtown, O 22....Mo.
200*Duthie, E 7....Idaho
130*Dutton, B 17....Ala.
60*Dutton, D 6....Ark.
115*Dutton, O 14....Mich.
447 Dutton, F 9....Mont.
54*Dutton, M 21....Va.
60*Duty, C 7....Va.
73*Dutzow, I 17....Mo.
15 Duvall, N 16....Ala.
90*Duvall (Duvalls), L 11 Ohio
234 Duvall, H 9....Wash.
1200 Duxbury, I 23....Mass.
200*Duxbury (Millbrook), I 23 Mass.
10 Duxbury, E 18....S. D.
553 Duxbury, F 9....Vt.
260 Dwale, H 22....Ky.
52*Dwale, C 6....Va.
118*Dwarf, H 21....Ky.
2499 Dwight, E 18....Ill.
295 Dwight, H 19....Kan.
294 Dwight, K 21....Neb.
168 Dwight, P 25....N. D.
40*Dwight, B 7....Va.
120 Dwyer, N 6....N. M.
171▲Dwyer, M 21....Wyo.
50*Dyas, O 7....Ala.
50*Dyberry, E 23....Pa.
30 Dyckesville, P 13....Wis.
178*Dycusburg, I 7....Ky.
50*Dye, D 7....Va.
425 Dyer, F 5....Ark.
976*Dyer, B 6....Ind.
31*Dyer, G 12....Ky.
18*Dyer, L 9....Nev.
1185 Dyer, M 4....Tenn.
50 Dyer Brook, F 18....Me.
10034 Dyersburg, M 3....Tenn.
2138 Dyersville, G 22....Iowa
2500 Dyess, E 21....Ark.
10*Dyke, P 8....Colo.
55*Dyke, J 12....Va.
42 Dykes, J 18....Ky.
13*Dykesville, A 7....La.
100*Dynard, O 13....Md.
986 Dysart, I 17....Iowa
50*Dysart, L 9....Pa.
75*Dysortville, F 1....N. C.

E

700 Eads, K 22....Colo.
105*Eads, P 2....Tenn.
100*Eadston (Gates), E 21 Ky.
40*Eadsville, J 16....Ky.
1000*Eagan (Egan), L 20....Tenn.
400 Eagar, I 24....Ariz.
251*Eagarville, K 11....Ill.
518 Eagle, G 9....Colo.
650 Eagle, N 5....Idaho
112*Eagle (Eagle Station), D 15....Ky.
27*Eagle, N 14....Me.
147*Eagle, O 17....Mich.
289 Eagle, L 22....Neb.
310 Eagle, M 17....S. D.
55*Eagle, L 24....Tex.
1536 Eagle, L 7....W. Va.
391 Eagle, N 21....Wis.
30*Eagle Bay, H 19....N. Y.
682 Eagle Bend, J 9....Minn.
50*Eaglebend, J 7....Miss.
300 Eagle Bridge, M 24....N. Y.
374 Eagle Butte, F 10....S. D.
225 Eagle City, G 7....Okla.
16 Eaglecliff, N 5....Wash.
70*Eagle Creek, M 7....Tenn.
263 Eagle Ford, E 19....Tex.
.... Eagle Gorge, see Baldi, Wash.
4024 Eagle Grove, F 11....Iowa
75 Eagle Harbor, C 4....Mich.
217*Eagle Harbor, L 7....N. Y.
862*Eagle Lake, I 16....Fla.
1200 Eagle Lake, B 15....Me.
269 Eagle Lake, P 13....Minn.
2124 Eagle Lake, L 20....Tex.
350 Eagle Mills, O 11....Ark.
800*Eagle Mtn., L 7....Va.
21*Eagle Nest (Therma), C18 N. M.
4*Eagle Nest, H 21....N. Y.
6459 Eagle Pass, N 12....Tex.
243 Eaglepoint, P 7....Ore.
85*Eagleport, L 17....Ohio
81 Eagle River, C 4....Mich.
1491 Eagle River, K 8....Wis.
30*Eagle Rock, R 8....Mo.
100*Eagle Rock, F 14....N. C.
526 Eagle Rock, M 7....Va.
175*Eagles Mere, G 17....Pa.
10*Eagles Mere Park, F 17..Pa.
300 Eagle Springs, H 11....N. C.
112*Eagle Sta. (Eagle), D 16 Ky.
440*Eagleton, J 4....Ark.
24*Eagleton, F 12....Mont.
75 Eagletown, I 14....Ind.
300 Eagletown, P 25....Okla.
210 Eagleville, C 10....Calif.
75 Eagleville, E 19....Conn.
353 Eagleville, A 8....Mo.
500*Eagleville, N 22....Pa.
.... Eagleville, I 13....Pa.
500 Eagleville, O 11....Tenn.
231 Eakly, J 7....Okla.
2062 Earl (Earle), G 20....Ark.
15 Earl, P 17....Colo.
.... Earl, K 10....Kan.
300*Earl, H 3....N. C.
2062 Earle (Earl), G 20....Ark.
200*Earlehurst, M 6....Va.
.... Earles, I 9....Ky.
25*Earleton, D 15....Fla.
166 Earleton, M 22....Kan.
60*Earleville, D 15....Md.
525 Earleys, C 20....N. C.
75*Earlham, J 21....Ind.
865 Earlham, L 10....Iowa
1000*Earlimart, L 13....Calif.
320 Earling, J 5....Iowa
350*Earling (Manbar), O 4 W. Va.
2858 Earlington, I 9....Ky.
125*Earlington, N 22....Pa.
250 Earlington, I 8....Wash.
507 Earl Park, F 6....Ind.
15*Earls, N 14....Va.
486 Earlsboro, J 15....Okla.
500 Earlston, P 10....Pa.
1000*Earlston Furnace, O 9...Pa.
174*Earlton, M 23....Kan.
197*Earlton, P 22....N. Y.
1103 Earlville, D 15....Ill.
687 Earlville, G 21....Iowa
864 Earlville, N 16....N. Y.
.... Earlville, E 18....Ohio
100*Earlville, N 21....Pa.
644 Early, G 6....Iowa
200*Early Branch, N 14...S. C.
.... Earnest, O 21....Va.
46*Earnestville, H 19....Ky.
10 Earp, O 25....Calif.
400*Earth, B 9....Tex.
33 Easby, E 19....N. D.
10*Easley, H 13....Mo.
5183 Easley, B 6....S. C.
32 Easley, K 24....Tenn.
100*Easonville, E 16....Ala.
.... East, Q 3....Tex.
500*Eastaboga, F 17....Ala.
445 Eastabutchie (Estabutchie), N 17....Miss.
350 East Alburgh Jc., A 7...Vt.
150 East Alstead, O 7....N. H.
4680 East Alton, L 10....Ill.
126*East Andover, L 3....Me.
200*East Andover (Halcyon), M 11....N. H.
156*Eastanollee, D 13....Ga.
....*East Arlington, N 5..Mass.
500 East Arlington, P 7....Vt.
56*Eastatoe, B 5....S. C.
5253 East Aurora, N 6....N. Y.
200 East Avon, M 9....N. Y.
250 East Baldwin (Mattocks), P 4....Me.
966 East Bangor, K 23....Pa.
601 Eastbank, L 7....W. Va.
200 East Barnard, J 12....Vt.
250 East Barnet (Inwood), F 18....Vt.
650 East Barre, G 14....Vt.
83 East Barrington, O 19.N. H.
410*East Beckley (Sylvia), O 8 W. Va.
1262 East Bend, D 7....N. C.
300 East Berkshire, B 11....Vt.
835 East Berlin, H 13....Conn.
792 East Berlin, P 16....Pa.
600*East Bernard, L 21....Tex.
60*East Berne, O 22....N. Y.
700 East Bernstadt, I 18...Ky.
125 East Bethany, M 7...N. Y.
115*East Bethel, L 12....Vt.
2000 East Blackstone, I 16.Mass.
365*East Bloomfield, M 10.N.Y.
250 East Blue Hill, M 16...Me.
300 East Boothbay, O 10...Me.
.... East Boston, F 20....Mass.
120*East Boxford, C 20...Mass.
1427 East Brady, J 5....Pa.
5300 East Braintree, R 6..Mass.
75 East Braintree, I 11....Vt.
310 East Branch, R 19...N. Y.
95*Eastbranch, F 6....Pa.
155 East Brewster, M 15..Mass.
1340 East Brewton, O 11...Ala.
150 East Bridgeton, O 8...N. J.
2250 East Bridgewater, I 20 Mass.
60 East Brimfield, H 10..Mass.
380 Eastbrook, L 17....Me.
210 East Brook, J 2....Pa.
500 East Brookfield, G 12.Mass.
200 East Brookfield, H 12...Vt.

Pop.	Place Index	State
901	East Brownfield (Brownfield), O 2	Me.
....	East Buffalo, M 5	N. Y.
250	East Burke, D 19	Vt.
559	East Butler, K 4	Pa.
25	East Cairo, J 4	Ky.
104	East Calais, F 14	Vt.
....*	East Camp, M 4	N. M.
400	East Canaan, A 6	Conn.
200*	East Candia, P 16	N. H.
75	East Canterbury, N 14	N. H.
919	East Canton, G 18	Ohio
416	East Carondelet, N 9	Ill.
75	East Charleston, B 18	Vt.
28	East Charlotte, F 6	Vt.
250*	East Chatham, P 24	N. Y.
....	East Chattanooga, Q 15	Tenn.
54637	East Chicago, B 6	Ind.
50	East Clarendon, L 9	Vt.
123*	East Claridon, C 19	Ohio
39495	East Cleveland, C 17	Ohio
149	East Clinton, C 10	Ill.
525	East Columbia, M 22	Tex.
1958	East Columbus, K 12	Ohio
....	East Concord, O 14	N. H.
200*	East Concord, O 5	N. Y.
285*	East Concord (Mayo), C 21	Vt.
4810*	East Conemaugh, N 8	Pa.
100	East Conway, I 19	N. H.
400	East Corinth, K 13	Me.
440	East Corinth, H 16	Vt.
83	East Craftsbury, D 15	Vt.
33*	East Creek, M 20	N. Y.
140*	East Danville (Winkle), O 9	Ohio
....	East Dedham, G 19	Mass.
800	East Dennis, M 14	Mass.
390	East Derry, Q 16	N. H.
8584	East Detroit, P 24	Mich.
214	East Dixfield, L 6	Me.
350	East Dorset, N 8	Vt.
1650	East Douglas, I 14	Mass.
75	East Dover, J 12	Me.
60	East Dover, Q 10	Vt.
....	East Downington, P 21	Pa.
1475	East Dubuque, A 8	Ill.
412	East Duke (Duke) M 3	Okla.
280	East Dummerston, Q 12	Vt.
....*	East Dundee, see Dundee	Ill.
375	East Durham, P 22	N. Y.
....	East Durham, E 13	N. C.
10	East Eagle, G 17	Iowa
56*	East Earl, O 20	Pa.
230	East Eddington, L 16	Me.
28	Eastedge, N 21	N. D.
150*	East Edgecomb, O 10	Me.
460	East Ellijay, C 6	Ga.
500	East Ellsworth, B 13	Wis.
600	East Ely, H 21	Nev.
....	East End, R 11	Mich.
175	East Enterprise, N 21	Ind.
15*	Easteday, D 15	Ky.
300*	Easterly, I 21	Tex.
187*	Eastern, H 22	Ky.
300	East Fairfield, C 10	Vt.
1000	East Falls Church, F 18	Va.
500	East Falmouth, N 23	Mass.
....	East Farms, I 10	Conn.
86*	East Farms, H 22	Wash.
60*	East Fishkill, E 5	N. Y.
1103	East Flat Rock (Flat Rock), Q 8	N. C.
....*	East Florence, A 8	Ala.
212	East Florence, K 16	N. Y.
250	Eastford, C 21	Conn.
65*	Eastfork, J 14	Ky.
152*	East Fort Madison (Niota), G 5	Ill.
500	East Foxboro, I 18	Mass.
86	East Franklin, L 18	Me.
50*	East Franklin, A 10	Vt.
348*	East Freedom, M 10	Pa.
800	East Freetown, L 20	Mass.
27*	East Freetown, O 15	N. Y.
621	East Fultonham, K 15	Ohio
1300	East Gaffney, A 10	S. C.
605*	East Galesburg (Randall), F 9	Ill.
3401	East Gary, B 7	Ind.
103*	East Georgia (Georgia), B 9	Vt.
305*	East Germantown (Pershing), D 13	Ind.
375	East Glastonbury, G 15	Conn.
75	East Grafton, L 10	N. H.
500	East Granby, B 13	Conn.
3511	East Grand Forks, E 1	Minn.
4899	East Grand Rapids, N 11	Mich.
150*	East Granville, H 7	Vt.
616*	East Greenbush, N 24	N. Y.
360	East Greenville, G 16	Ohio
1776	East Greenville, M 22	Pa.
93*	East Greenwich, K 25	N. Y.
3842■	East Greenwich, H 13	R. I.
54*	Eastgulf, P 7	W. Va.
1000	East Haddam, J 17	Conn.
500	Eastham, L 15	Mass.
....*	Eastham, K 12	Va.
325	East Hampden, L 14	Me.
175*	East Hampstead, Q 18	N.H.
2955▲	East Hampton, I 16	Conn.
10316■	Easthampton, H 7	Mass.
1756	Easthampton, G 12	N. Y.
44	East Hannibal, I 4	Ill.
70	East Hardin, K 7	Ill.
510	East Hardwick (Lamoille), E 15	Vt.
18615■	East Hartford, E 14	Conn.
296	East Hartland, B 11	Conn.
325	East Harwich, M 14	Mass.
6000	East Haven, N 11	Conn.
30*	East Haven, C 21	Vt.
125	East Haverhill (Oliverian), I 10	N. H.
130*	East Hebron, (Hebron Sta.), N 5	Me.
85*	East Hebron, L 13	N. H.
1143	East Helena, I 9	Mont.
....	East Hiawatha, J 15	Utah
361	East Hickory, G 6	Pa.
300*	East Highgate (Ritford), B 9	Vt.
300*	East Highlands, O 18	Calif.
330	East Hiram, O 3	Me.
215	East Holden (Holden), L 15	Me.
121*	East Holliston, G 17	Mass.
80*	East Homer, N 14	N. Y.
115	East Hope, C 5	Idaho
2000	East Islip, H 8	N. Y.
240	East Jackson, L 12	Me.
2110	East Jaffrey, Q 10	N. H.
75*	East Jamaica (Wardsboro), P 7	Vt.
200	East Jewett, A 4	N. Y.
50	East Johnson, D 12	Vt.
....	East Joliet, D 20	Ill.
1725	East Jordan, I 15	Mich.
....	East Jc., J 18	Mass.
600	East Kane, F 9	Pa.
188*	East Kansas City (Randolph), G 6	Mo.
1000	East Killingly, D 25	Conn.
270	East Kingston, P 19	N. H.
150	Eastlake (East Lake), F 15	Colo.
412	East Lake, L 11	Mich.
18*	East Lake, I 16	Minn.
200	East Lake, E 24	N. C.
160*	Eastlake Weir, F 16	Fla.
236	Eastland, N 15	Tenn.
3849	Eastland, F 15	Tex.
3323*	East Lansdowne, P 23	Pa.
5839	East Lansing, P 17	Mich.
200	East Laport, P 6	N. C.
6421	East Las Vegas, F 17	N. M.
890	East Laurinburg, J 11	N. C.
9*	East Leake, L 15	Va.
68	East Leavenworth, F 5	Mo.
269	East Lebanon (Eastwood), Q 2	Me.
240	East Lee, F 3	Mass.
35*	Eastlemon, F 20	Pa.
140*	East Lempster, N 8	N. H.
105*	East Leroy, Q 16	Mich.
110*	East Leroy, Q 16	Wash.
4000	East Lexington, E 18	Mass.
60*	East Lexington, L 8	Va.
406	East Liberty, I 9	Ohio
209	East Limington, P 3	Me.
400	East Livermore (Norlands), M 7	Me.
23555	East Liverpool, G 21	Ohio
1800	East Longmeadow, I 8	Mass.
8000	East Los Angeles, Q 4	Calif.
1039	East Lumberton, K 12	N. C.
600	East Lyme, L 20	Conn.
1312	East Lyme (Niantic), M 20	Conn.
300	East Lynn, G 21	Ill.
....	East Lynn, K 7	Mass.
225	East Lynn, L 2	W. Va.
236	East Lynne, I 7	Mo.
1183▲	East Machias, L 22	Me.
3026*	East McKeesport, M 4	Pa.
575	East Madison, K 9	Me.
51*	East Madison, J 18	N. H.
3311	Eastman, K 13	Ga.
348	Eastman, F 19	Wis.
270*	East Marion, H 9	N. Y.
95*	East Masonville, P 18	N. Y.
400	East Mattapoisett, M 22	Mass.
3392*	East Mauch Chunk, J 21	Pa.
200	East Meredith, P 19	N. Y.
325	East Middlebury, I 7	Vt.
520	East Milford, Q 13	N. H.
1500	East Millinocket, H 15	Me.
300*	East Millsboro, O 3	Pa.
387	East Millstone, G 14	N. J.
5245	East Milton, P 5	Mass.
....	East Minneapolis, M 23	Minn.
62*	East Mobridge, E 14	S. D.
12359	East Moline, D 9	Ill.
450	East Monbo, F 5	N. C.
200*	East Monongahela (Manown), N 4	Pa.
125*	East Monroe, N 8	Ohio
158	East Montpelier, F 13	Vt.
800	East Moriches, H 10	N. Y.
221*	East Nassau, O 24	N. Y.
....	East Nekoosa Jc., I 14	Wis.
2273*	East Newark, E 19	N. J.
267	East New Market, L 19	Md.
50*	East Newport, K 12	Me.
99*	East New Portland, K 7	Me.
64*	East Nicolaus, H 7	Calif.
....	East Northfield, B 9	Mass.
....*	East Northfield (S. Vernon), B 9	Mass.
2120*	East Northport (Northport), G 8	N. Y.
525	East Norton (Norton), J 19	Mass.
5327	East Norwalk, Q 4	Conn.
731*	East Norwich, H 7	N. Y.
....	Easton, N 5	Conn.
442	Easton, H 11	Ill.
255	Easton, F 23	Kan.
450	Easton, D 19	Me.
4528	Easton, J 18	Md.
500	Easton, I 19	Mass.
332	Easton, Q 13	Minn.
214	Easton, D 6	Mo.
200	Easton, L 24	N. Y.
33589	Easton, L 23	Pa.
251	Easton, J 11	Wash.
107	Easton, P 20	Wis.
500	Eastondale, I 19	Mass.
104	Eastonville, I 16	Colo.
68945	East Orange, E 18	N. J.
76	East Orange, H 15	Vt.
135	East Orland, M 15	Me.
150	East Orleans, M 15	Mass.
300	East Orwell, D 20	Ohio
96*	East Otis, H 4	Mass.
238	East Otisfield, N 4	Me.
250	East Otto, P 5	N. Y.
473	Eastover, G 15	S. C.
1000	East Palatka, D 17	Fla.
5123*	East Palestine, F 21	Ohio
300*	East Palmyra, L 11	N. Y.
2000	East Palo Alto, H 20	Calif.
135	East Parsonfield, P 2	Me.
8044	East Pasadena (Lamanda Park), Q 4	Calif.
600*	East Patchogue, G 9	N. Y.
4937*	East Paterson, C 19	N. J.
70	East Peacham, F 17	Vt.
116*	East Pembroke, I 22	Mass.
1540	East Pembroke (Allenstown), O 15	N. H.
500*	East Pembroke, L 6	N. Y.
6807	East Peoria, F 12	Ill.
2000	East Pepperell (Pepperell), C 16	Mass.
90*	East Peru (Worthley), M 5	Me.
918	East Petersburg, O 18	Pa.
50*	East Pharsalia, O 16	N. Y.
6079	East Pittsburgh, N 3	Pa.
72*	East Pittston, N 9	Me.
500	East Pleasant Plain, N 19	Iowa
67*	Eastpoint, D 2	Fla.
12403	East Point, F 7	Ga.
265	East Point, G 22	Ky.
113*	East Point, E 6	La.
368	East Poland (Empire Road), N 5	Me.
50	Eastport, B 17	Fla.
40	Eastport, A 6	Idaho
3466	Eastport, K 24	Me.
....	Eastport, I 15	Md.
60*	Eastport, J 15	Mich.
800	Eastport, G 10	N. Y.
50	East Portal (Newcomb), F 13	Colo.
5450	East Port Chester, R 1	Conn.
306	East Poultney, L 6	Vt.
1385	East Prairie, Q 24	Mo.
178	East Princeton, E 13	Mass.
419	East Prospect, P 17	Pa.
32165■	East Providence, E 17	R. I.
500	East Quogue, H 11	N. Y.
....*	East Radford, see Radford	Va.
1515	East Rainelle, M 10	W. Va.
496*	East Randolph, Q 4	N. Y.
122	East Randolph, I 13	Vt.
100	East Raymond, O 5	Me.
100	East Richford (Missiquoi), A 13	Vt.
180	East Rindge, R 10	N. H.
200	East River, N 14	Conn.
1000	East Rochester (Ringdemere), N 19	N. H.
6691	East Rochester, L 10	N. Y.
208	East Rochester, G 19	Ohio
706*	East Rochester, L 2	Pa.
7000*	East Rockingham (Roberdel), J 10	N. C.
5610*	East Rockaway, G 6	N. Y.
....	East Rockford, A 15	Ill.
25	East Roxbury, H 11	Vt.
7268*	East Rutherford, C 19	N. J.
225	East Ryegate, G 18	Vt.
75609	East St. Louis, M 10	Ill.
....	East Salamanca, Q 5	N. Y.
123*	East Sandwich (Royal), L 25	Mass.
....	East Sandy, H 4	Pa.
....	East San Pedro, R 4	Calif.
....	East Saratoga Jc., M 23	N. Y.
100*	East Saugatuck, P 12	Mich.
2500	East Saugus, K 6	Mass.
238*	East Schodack, O 24	N. Y.
1259*	East Scobey (Scobey), C 24	Mont.
210	East Sebago, O 4	Me.
1500	East Setauket, G 8	N. Y.
25	East Shoreham (Shoreham), H 7	Vt.
250	Eastside, R 22	Miss.
638	Eastside, M 3	Ore.
....	East Sioux Falls, M 25	S. D.
200*	East Smethport (Smethport), E 10	Pa.
330	East Smithfield, E 16	Pa.
....	East Somerville, F 19	Mass.
150	East Sound, C 6	Wash.
690	East Sparta, G 18	Ohio
2181	East Spencer, F 8	N. C.
350*	East Springfield, N 18	N. Y.
315	East Springfield, H 20	Ohio
415	East Springfield, D 2	Pa.
359	East Stanwood, E 8	Wash.
25	East Steamburg, P 12	N. Y.
476	East Stone Gap (Elverton), D 5	Va.
129*	East Stoneham, N 3	Me.
6404	East Stroudsburg, J 23	Pa.
126*	East Sullivan, P 8	N. H.
188	East Sumner, M 5	Me.
200	East Surry, M 16	Me.
....	East Swanton, B 7	Vt.
400	East Swanzey, Q 7	N. H.
	East Sylamore, see Sylamore	Ark.
4520	East Syracuse, L 15	N. Y.
3000	East Tallassee, J 18	Ala.
250	East Tampa (Gibsonton), I 13	Fla.
3030	East Taunton, K 20	Mass.
1670	East Tawas, K 21	Mich.
1000	East Templeton, D 11	Mass.
320*	East Texas, L 22	Pa.
30*	East Thetford, I 14	Vt.
3590	East Thomaston, I 8	Ga.
....	East Thompson, A 25	Conn.
925	East Troy, N 21	Wis.
1108*	East Tupelo, C 20	Miss.
....	East Tyrone, L 11	Pa.
300*	East Union, N 12	Me.
573*	Eastvale, K 2	Pa.
2005	East Vandergrift, L 5	Pa.
142	East Vassalboro, M 10	Me.
423	East Vaughn, H 17	N. M.
49*	Eastview, H 13	Ky.
1000*	Eastview, G 6	N. Y.
....	East Village, I 14	Mass.
316	Eastville, N 23	Va.
200	Eastville Sta., N 23	Va.
100*	East Wakefield (Burleyville), L 19	N. H.
190	East Wallingford, M 9	Vt.
2000*	East Walpole (Bird Mills), H 19	Mass.
675	East Wareham, L 22	Mass.
2106	East Washington, O 2	Pa.
143	East Waterboro (Westcot), Q 3	Me.
175	East Waterford, N 3	Me.
175	East Waterford, N 13	Pa.
....*	East Watertown, M 3	Mass.
380	East Weare, O 13	N. H.
268*	East Wenatchee, I 14	Wash.
175*	East Westmoreland (Gilboa), P 6	N. H.
7500	East Weymouth, G 21	Mass.
450	East Whately, E 8	Mass.
34	East White Bluffs, L 17	Wash.
110*	East White Plains, F 6	N. Y.
300*	East Williamson, K 11	N. Y.
1152*	East Williston, G 6	N. Y.
250	East Wilton (Tyngston), L 6	Me.
110*	East Windham, P 22	N. Y.
200	East Windsor (Scantic), C 15	Conn.
40*	East Windsor, Q 16	N. Y.
500	East Windsor Hill, D 15	Conn.
80*	East Winfield (Winfield), M 18	N. Y.
83	East Winn, I 17	Me.
....	East Winona, E 16	Wis.
94*	East Winthrop, N 8	Me.
300	East Wolfeboro (Cotton Valley), L 18	N. H.
250*	Eastwood, F 14	Ky.
269*	East Wood (East Lebanon), Q 2	Me.
....	Eastwood, L 15	N. Y.
180	East Woodstock, B 23	Conn.
500	East Worcester, O 20	N. Y.
55*	Eaton, C 18	Ark.
1322	Eaton, C 16	Colo.
350	Eaton, L 21	Ill.
1453	Eaton, G 19	Ind.
115	Eaton, H 20	Me.
500*	Eaton, M 16	N. Y.
3552	Eaton, L 6	Ohio
125	Eaton, N 4	Tenn.
66*	Eaton Center, J 18	N. H.
150*	Eaton Park, I 16	Fla.
3060	Eaton Rapids, P 17	Mich.
38*	Eatons (Eaton), F 7	W. Va.
2399	Eatonton, G 12	Ga.
1758	Eatontown, H 20	N. J.
996	Eatonville, K 8	Wash.
328	Eau Claire, R 10	Mich.
349	Eau Claire, I 4	Pa.
3508	Eau Claire, G 13	S. C.
30745	Eau Claire, E 12	Wis.
216*	Eau Galle, C 13	Wis.
873	Eau Gallie, H 21	Fla.
152*	Ebb, B 8	Fla.
400*	Eben (Eben Jc.), F 8	Mich.
118*	Ebenezer, H 12	Miss.
2600*	Ebenezer, O 5	N. Y.
298	Ebenezer, F 18	S. C.
116*	Ebenezer, M 19	Tenn.
400	Eben Jc. (Eben), F 8	Mich.
3719	Ebensburg, M 8	Pa.
....*	Eberle, H 19	Ky.
580*	Ebervale, I 20	Pa.
....	Ebner, B 10	Ill.
153*	Ebon, F 21	Ky.
113*	Ebony, H 15	Tex.
16*	Ebony, R 15	Va.
633▲*	Ebro, M 8	Fla.
75*	Ebro, F 7	Minn.
50*	Eby, E 21	Ky.
1027	Eccles, O 7	W. Va.
50*	Eccleston, E 14	Md.
19	Echeta, C 18	Wyo.
450	Echo (Bijou), I 10	La.
477	Echo, O 7	Minn.
280	Echo, C 18	Ore.
125	Echo, K 6	Pa.
160	Echo (Echo City), E 14	Utah
5	Echo, C 22	Wash.
....	Echo, L 1	W. Va.
55	Echola, G 7	Ala.
....*	Echo Lake, G 9	Calif.
....*	Echo Lake, I 24	Pa.
257*	Echols, G 11	Ky.
80	Eckelson, M 20	N. D.
200*	Eckerman, F 16	Mich.
125	Eckert, J 5	Colo.
61	Eckert, J 15	Tex.
240	Eckerty, P 11	Ind.
125*	Eckhard (Brooks), G 6	Calif.
1500*	Eckhart (Eckhart Mines), M 5	Md.
....	Eckhart Jc., L 6	Md.
1500*	Eckhart Mines (Eckhart)	Md.
13*	Eckington, I 15	Va.
25*	Ecleto, N 17	Tex.
358	Eckley, E 22	Colo.
1100*	Eckley, I 20	Pa.
66	Eckman, E 11	N. D.
800	Eckman, Q 6	W. Va.
606	Eclectic, I 17	Ala.
10*	Ecleto, N 17	Tex.
315*	Eclipse, Q 19	Va.
251	Economy, I 21	Ind.
13209*	Ecorse, Q 22	Mich.
601	Ecru, C 18	Miss.
457	Ector, C 20	Tex.
35*	Ed, I 16	Ky.
1758	Edcouch, P 4	Tex.
375	Eddiceton, N 7	Miss.
200	Eddington, K 15	Me.
800	Eddington, O 25	Pa.
40	Eddy, F 2	Mont.
50*	Eddy, F 17	N. Y.
38	Eddy, B 12	Okla.
407	Eddy, H 18	Tex.
2493*	Eddystone, Q 23	Pa.
144*	Eddyville, Q 17	Ill.
984	Eddyville, N 16	Iowa
2407	Eddyville, J 7	Ky.
237	Eddyville, L 13	Neb.
640	Eddyville, R 23	N. Y.
41	Eddyville, G 4	Ore.
25	Eddyville, J 6	Pa.
70*	Edella, F 21	Pa.
125*	Edelstein, F 12	Ill.
329*	Eden, F 16	Ala.
350	Eden, L 22	Ariz.
106*	Eden, K 24	Ga.
413	Eden, Q 12	Idaho
69*	Eden, F 12	Ill.
	Eden, see Inez	Ky.
70*	Eden, I 11	Ky.
156*	Eden, P 20	Md.
50*	Eden, P 18	Mich.
25	Eden (Cheney), P 18	Minn.
292	Eden, H 10	Miss.
38	Eden, H 10	Mont.
870	Eden, N 4	N. Y.
171	Eden, D 22	S. D.
1603	Eden, H 13	Tex.
120	Eden, D 12	Utah
52	Eden, C 13	Vt.
85	Eden, N 3	Wash.
223*	Eden, N 17	Wis.
200	Eden, N 7	Wyo.
1500	Edenborn, Q 3	Pa.
1098	Edenburg (Knox), I 5	Pa.
650	Edenburg (Edinburg), J 1	Pa.
870	Eden Center (Eden), N 4	N. Y.
30	Eden Mills, C 13	Vt.
75*	Eden Prarie, N 16	Minn.
20*	Edenton, G 18	Ky.
3835	Edenton, D 21	N. C.
75	Edenton, N 8	Ohio
716	Eden Valley, M 11	Minn.
379	Edenville (Rhodes)	Iowa
95*	Edenville, M 18	Mich.
1000	Edenwold, M 11	Tenn.
....	Edgar, R 10	Ark.
22*	Edgar, D 15	Fla.
76	Edgar, J 21	Ill.
20*	Edgar, H 23	Ky.
111	Edgar, M 15	Mont.
708	Edgar, N 18	Neb.
75*	Edgar, L 19	Tex.
111	Edgar, K 17	Va.
694	Edgar, I 12	Wis.
268	Edgard, N 17	La.
150	Edgar Springs, M 15	Mo.
50*	Edgarton (Delorme), P 3	W. Va.
1250	Edgartown, P 24	Mass.
57	Edge, I 20	Tex.
411▲	Edgecomb, O 10	Me.
150	Edgecomb, F 9	Wash.
2119	Edgefield, H 8	S. C.
....*	Edge Hill, N 22 (Pop. 900 incl. in Abington)	Pa.
63*	Edgehill, J 18	Va.
803	Edgeley, P 18	N. D.
15*	Edgemere, B 5	Idaho
66*	Edgemere, G 24	Pa.
96*	Edgemont, E 13	Ark.
500	Edgemont, B 7	Md.
50	Edgemont, D 3	N. C.
30*	Edgemont, P 23	Pa.
1002	Edgemont, N 1	S. D.
1008	Edge Moor, A 22	Del.
217	Edgemoor (Edgmoor), B 13	S. C.
75*	Edgemoor, M 18	Tenn.
300*	Edgerley, M 5	La.
100	Edgerton, D 23	Ind.
264	Edgerton, H 24	Kan.
200*	Edgerton, O 14	Mich.
815	Edgerton, Q 4	Minn.
427	Edgerton, E 6	Mo.
1082	Edgerton, D 6	Ohio
65*	Edgerton, Q 15	Va.
3266	Edgerton, L 21	Wis.
232	Edgerton, H 17	Wyo.
15	Edgerton Junction, E 6	Mo.
1648*	Edgewater, F 14	Colo.
477*	Edgewater, F 20	Fla.
29*	Edgewater, I 15	Md.
4028	Edgewater, D 21	N. J.
50*	Edgewater, E 8	Wis.
....*	Edgewater Park, R 18	Miss.
400	Edgewater Park, J 11	N. J.
30	Edgewick, I 10	Wash.
200*	Edgewold, G 13	S. C.
250*	Edgewood, C 5	Calif.
467	Edgewood, L 17	Ill.
716	Edgewood, F 21	Iowa
300*	Edgewood, C 16	Md.
118*	Edgewood, F 17	Mo.
4697	Edgewood (Edgewood Park), M 4	Pa.
....	Edgewood, E 16	R. I.
....*	Edgewood Arsenal, C 16	Md.
4697*	Edgewood Park (Edgewood), M 4	Pa.
738*	Edgewood, E 21	Tex.
6390	Edgeworth, L 4	Mass.
1696	Edgeworth, L 3	Pa.
60*	Edgington, D 7	Ill.
217*	Edgmoor (Edgemoor), C 13	S. C.
57*	Edgoten, J 9	Ky.
17	Edholm, J 20	Neb.
5855*	Edina, M 15	Minn.
1637	Edina, C 14	Mo.
804	Edinboro, E 3	Pa.
919	Edinburg, J 13	Ill.
2466	Edinburg, L 15	Ind.
1000	Edinburg, I 16	Miss.
110	Edinburg, C 9	Mo.
534	Edinburg, L 22	N. Y.
378	Edinburg, F 21	N. D.
650	Edinburg (Edenburg), I 1	Pa.
8718	Edinburg, Q 4	Tex.
565	Edinburg, G 12	Va.
1241	Edison, M 4	Ga.
321	Edison, N 13	Neb.
8	Edison, C 14	N. J.
419	Edison, H 12	Ohio
300*	Edison, N 24	Pa.
250	Edison, D 7	Wash.
1000	Edisto Island, O 16	S. C.
31	Edith, B 5	Okla.
15*	Edith, G 12	Tex.
....	Edler, P 22	Colo.
650	Edmeston, O 18	N. Y.
185*	Edmon, L 5	Pa.
180	Edmond, E 8	Kan.
4002	Edmond, H 12	Okla.
20*	Edmond, M 9	W. Va.
45*	Edmonds (Snipe), M 22	Tex.
1288	Edmonds, G 8	Wash.
302	Edmondson, H 21	Ark.
934*	Edmonston, J 12	Md.
403	Edmonton, J 14	Ky.
825	Edmore, N 15	Mich.
453	Edmore, F 19	N. D.
150*	Edmund, H 20	Wis.
500	Edmunds, K 23	Me.
75	Edmunds, L 17	N. D.
75*	Edna, K 6	Ala.
100	Edna, M 9	Calif.
35*	Edna, B 2	Iowa
507	Edna, O 23	Kan.
21*	Edna, G 21	Ky.
....	Edna, L 8	La.
50	Edna, H 18	Okla.
2724	Edna, M 20	Tex.
100*	Edneyville, Q 9	N. C.
49*	Ednor, G 10	Md.
20*	Edo, H 24	Ky.
	Edom, see Thousand Palms	Calif.
300*	Edom, F 21	Tex.
42*	Edom, H 11	Va.
635	Edon, C 6	Ohio
125*	Edray, L 13	W. Va.
515	Edri, M 6	Pa.
80*	Edson, F 3	Kan.
30*	Edson, Q 16	N. Y.
20	Edson, F 7	S. D.
....	Edson, G 17	Tex.
150	Edwall, I 21	Wash.
....	Edward, L 25	Kan.
142*	Edward, H 21	N. C.
83	Edwards, G 10	Colo.
400	Edwards, F 11	Ill.
456	Edwards, K 8	Miss.
60*	Edwards, K 10	Mo.
7	Edwards, H 18	Mont.
624	Edwards, F 18	N. Y.
8	Edwards, E 15	Ore.
482	Edwardsburg, R 11	Mich.
16*	Edwards Crossroads, B 4	N. C.
1350	Edwardsport, N 7	Ind.
194	Edwardsville, F 20	Ala.
8008	Edwardsville, M 11	Ill.
243	Edwardsville, G 24	Kan.
7998	Edwardsville, H 20	Pa.
121*	Edwardsville, K 21	Va.
500	Edwight, N 6	W. Va.
60*	Eel Rock, E 2	Calif.
15*	Effie, I 10	La.
100*	Effie, I 14	Minn.
6180	Effingham, L 17	Ill.
676	Effingham, E 22	Kan.
40	Effingham, K 19	N. H.
200*	Effingham, G 19	S. C.
86	Effingham Falls, K 18	N. H.
225*	Effort, J 22	Pa.
220*	Efland, E 12	N. C.
1200*	Egan (Fernside), F 7	Ga.
36*	Egan, B 13	Ill.
52*	Egan, M 9	La.
418	Egan, K 24	S. D.
35*	Egan (Eagan), L 20	Tenn.
250	Egan, E 18	Tex.
55	Egbert, Q 24	Wyo.
275	Egeland, E 17	N. D.
112*	Egeria, N 7	W. Va.
....*	Eggers, C 13	Colo.
520*	Eggertsville, O 5	N. Y.
3589	Egg Harbor (Egg Harbor City), N 14	N. J.
150*	Egg Harbor, Q 11	Wis.
200*	Eggleston, N 4	Va.
5*	Eglon, H 19	Ky.
25*	Eglon, G 7	Wash.
225	Eglon, E 16	W. Va.
100	Egnar, M 2	Colo.
463▲	Egremont, H 1	Mass.
41*	Egremont, I 7	Miss.
33	Egypt, D 18	Ark.
300	Egypt, J 22	Ga.
37*	Egypt, H 19	Ky.
600*	Egypt, G 22	Mass.
1489	Egypt, L 22	Pa.
75*	Egypt, L 21	Tex.
46*	Eheart, J 13	Va.
78*	Ehren, H 13	Fla.
1100*	Ehrenfeld, M 8	Pa.
407	Ehrhardt, L 13	S. C.
140	Eidenau (Harmony Jc.), J 3	Pa.
100*	Eidson, L 22	Tenn.
64*	Eidsvold, G 12	Wis.
200*	Eifort, P 13	Ohio
30*	Eight, Q 5	W. Va.
2*	Eightmile, D 16	Ore.
75*	Eighty-Eight, J 14	Ky.
45*	Eightyfour, N 3	Pa.
301*	Eileen (Pequot), E 18	Ill.
....*	Eiler, L 4	Ala.
136	Eitzen, R 24	Minn.
....	Ekal, G 15	Fla.
719	Ekalaka, K 24	Mont.
154*	Ekron, G 12	Ky.
65*	Ela, P 5	N. C.
511	Elaine, L 18	Ark.
25*	Elams, C 16	N. C.
52*	Elamsville, Q 6	Va.
200*	Elamton, G 22	Ky.
89	Elamville, M 19	Ala.
25*	Elana, I 8	W. Va.
296	Eland, L 12	Wis.
2363	Elba, N 17	Ala.
377*	Elba, D 12	Ark.
10	Elba, F 20	Colo.
250	Elba, R 14	Idaho
43*	Elba, J 13	La.
150*	Elba, N 21	Mich.
159*	Elba, Q 22	Minn.
270	Elba, K 16	Neb.
614	Elba, L 7	N. Y.
100	Elba, M 18	Ohio
	Elba, see Gretna	Va.
175	Elbe, L 8	Wash.
520	Elberfeld, Q 5	Ind.
256	Elberon, I 17	Iowa
500*	Elberon, I 18	N. J.
35*	Elberon, D 15	N. C.
30*	Elberon, O 19	Va.
325	Elbert, H 16	Colo.
1200*	Elbert, Q 4	W. Va.
115	Elberta, Q 8	Ala.
617	Elberta, K 11	Mich.
10*	Elberta, K 4	N. Y.
98	Elberta, H 11	Utah
6188	Elberton, E 15	Ga.
151	Elberton, K 24	Wash.
101	Elbing, K 17	Kan.
75	Elbon, H 9	Pa.
5	Elbon, J 8	S. D.
1150	Elbow Lake, K 5	Minn.
139*	Elbowoods, J 7	N. D.
497*	Elbridge, L 13	N. Y.
95*	Elbridge, M 3	Tenn.
624	Elburn, C 18	Ill.
1471	El Cajon, Q 19	Calif.
3906	El Campo, M 21	Tex.
10017	El Centro, Q 23	Calif.
6137	El Cerrito (Cerrito), B 18	Calif.
400	Elcho, L 10	Wis.
500	Elco, Q 14	Ill.
619*	Elco (Wood Run), O 3	Pa.
200*	Elcor, I 19	Minn.
158	El Dara, J 6	Ill.
76*	Eldena, C 14	Ill.
249	Elderon, K 13	Wis.
150*	Eldersville, O 2	Pa.
354	Elderton, L 6	Pa.
1676	Eldon, O 18	Iowa
2590	Eldon, J 12	Mo.
150	Eldon, F 23	Okla.
31*	Eldora, F 13	Colo.
3553	Eldora, H 14	Iowa
15858	El Dorado, Q 11	Ark.
150*	El Dorado, H 9	Calif.
380*	Eldorado (Fender), N 12	Ga.
4891	Eldorado, P 18	Ill.
103*	Eldorado, E 19	Iowa
10045	Eldorado, L 18	Kan.
....	Eldorado, L 20	Md.
10*	Eldorado, J 16	Mich.
30	Eldorado, M 18	Neb.
290*	Eldorado, G 9	N. C.
311	Eldorado, K 5	Ohio
929	Eldorado, N 3	Okla.
310*	Eldorado, M 10	Pa.
1530	Eldorado, I 12	Tex.
....	Eldora Jc., H 14	Iowa
147*	El Dorado, M 17	Wis.
25*	Eldorado Springs (Hawthorne), E 14	Colo.
2342	El Dorado Springs, L 7	Mo.
150*	Eldorendo, O 6	Ga.
100*	Eldred, J 22	Fla.
340	Eldred, K 8	Ill.
35	Eldred, F 2	Minn.
157*	Eldred, C 1	N. Y.
1051	Eldred, E 10	Pa.
111*	Eldredsville, F 17	Pa.
575*	Eldridge, E 8	Ala.
50	Eldridge (Bishopsville), E 17	Fla.
283	Eldridge (Eldridge Jc.), K 24	Iowa
10*	Eldridge, F 21	Ky.
88*	Eldridge, M 12	Mo.
80	Eldridge, M 18	N. D.
400	Eldridge, L 20	Tex.
283*	Eldridge Jc. (Eldridge), K 24	Iowa
5*	Eldridge, M 10	Mont.
100*	Eleanor, K 10	Ala.
120	Eleanor, I 7	Pa.
....	Eleanor, H 21	Wash.
33*	Eleazer, G 9	N. C.
5588	Electra, B 15	Tex.
1500	Electric City, G 18	Wash.
1205	Electric Mills, I 22	Miss.
....*	Electric Mills Jc., I 21	Miss.
....	Electron, K 9	Wash.
162*	Elena, L 23	Tex.
15	Elephant Butte, L 9	N. M.
90*	Eleroy, A 12	Ill.
406	Eleva, E 13	Wis.
10*	Elevenpoint, B 18	Ark.
150*	Elevon, K 19	Va.
256*	Elfers, H 12	Fla.
14*	Elfrida, P 22	Ariz.
44	Elgin, O 19	Ariz.
38333	Elgin, B 18	Ill.
638	Elgin, D 20	Iowa
336	Elgin, O 20	Kan.
36*	Elgin, I 17	Ky.
468	Elgin, P 20	Minn.
27*	Elgin, D 14	Mo.
853	Elgin, H 18	Neb.
60*	Elgin, M 23	Nev.
583	Elgin, P 8	N. D.
116*	Elgin, G 6	Ohio
381	Elgin, M 9	Okla.
997	Elgin, C 21	Ore.
224*	Elgin, E 4	Pa.
150*	Elgin (Rugby Road), L 17	Tenn.
2008	Elgin, J 18	Tex.
33*	Elgin (Kimball), G 13	Va.
108	Elgin, K 8	Wash.
31*	Elgood, Q 9	W. Va.
122*	El Granada, G 16, I 5	Calif.
75*	Eli, J 16	Ky.
84	Eli, D 8	Neb.
75*	Elias, J 19	Ky.
750*	Eliasville, D 15	Tex.
330	Elida, J 22	N. M.
551	Elida, G 7	Ohio
70*	Elihu, I 17	Ky.
34*	Elijah, R 14	Mo.
500*	Elijah (Stainville), M 18	Tenn.
83*	Elimsport, I 16	Pa.
100*	El Indio, N 12	Tex.
1200	Eliot, R 3	Me.
300	Eliot, O 1	Mass.
214	Elizabeth, B 13	Ark.
275	Elizabeth, H 16	Colo.
800	Elizabeth, E 6	Ga.
694	Elizabeth, A 9	Ill.
209*	Elizabeth, Q 15	Ind.
3000	Elizabeth, J 8	La.
176*	Elizabeth, I 5	Minn.
221	Elizabeth, F 7	Miss.
109912	Elizabeth, F 18	N. J.
2976	Elizabeth, N 4	Pa.
685	Elizabeth, G 7	W. Va.
11564	Elizabeth City, C 22	N. C.
8516	Elizabethton, L 24	Tenn.
622	Elizabethtown, Q 19	Ill.
319	Elizabethtown, M 16	Ind.
3667	Elizabethtown, G 13	Ky.
....	Elizabethtown, C 17	N. M.

Pop.	Place	Index	State
640	Elizabethtown	G 23	N. Y.
1123	Elizabethtown	K 14	N. C.
4315	Elizabethtown	O 18	Pa.
1410	Elizabethville	M 16	Pa.
75	*Elizaville	H 13	Ind.
150	Elizaville	E 19	Ky.
124	Elizaville	Q 24	N. Y.
98	*El Jobean (Southland)	L 15	Fla.
200	Elk	F 2	Calif.
17	Elk	M 16	N. M.
250	Elk	F 24	Wash.
1000	*Elk (Bownemont)	K 6	W. Va.
200	*Elk (Elk Lick)	G 16	W. Va.
102	*Elk	E 4	Wyo.
1556	Elkader	E 20	Iowa
7	*Elkader	G 4	Kan.
200	*Elka Park	Q 22	N. Y.
140	*Elkatawa (Gentry)	G 20	Ky.
125	Elk Basin	A 9	Wyo.
150	Elk City	I 8	Idaho
680	Elk City	N 21	Kan.
50	Elk City	J 23	Neb.
5021	Elk City	I 3	Okla.
43	Elk City	G 4	Ore.
117	*Elk Creek	E 5	Calif.
54	*Elk Creek	F 15	Ky.
19	*Elk Creek	O 14	Mo.
199	Elk Creek	N 23	Neb.
60	*Elk Creek	O 19	N. Y.
100	*Elk Creek	E 11	Va.
294	Elk Falls	N 20	Kan.
10	*Elkfork	F 21	Ky.
500	*Elk Garden	D 8	Va.
342	Elk Garden	E 18	W. Va.
1000	Elk Grove	H 8	Calif.
30	*Elkgrove	I 22	Wis.
436	Elkhart	I 13	Ill.
33434	Elkhart	B 15	Ind.
215	*Elkhart	K 12	Iowa
902	Elkhart	O 2	Kan.
751	Elkhart	G 22	Tex.
571	Elkhart Lake	O 16	Wis.
33	*Elkhead	P 11	Mo.
89	*Elk Hill	L 14	Va.
....	Elk Home	H 10	Pa.
486	Elkhorn	L 6	Iowa
72	*Elk Horn	H 15	Ky.
429	Elkhorn	K 23	Neb.
1400	Elkhorn	Q 7	W. Va.
2382	Elkhorn	M 22	Wis.
21	Elkhorn	L 8	Wyo.
1030	Elkhorn City (Praise)	I 24	Ky.
....	Elkhorn Jc.	K 24	Neb.
....	Elkhorn Mines	M 6	Mont.
....	Elkhurst	A 14	Vt.
119	*Elkhurst	J 8	W. Va.
2737	Elkin	D 5	N. C.
243	Elkins	C 5	Ark.
150	*Elkins	M 10	N. H.
35	Elkins	K 22	N. M.
8133	Elkins	G 15	W. Va.
20	Elkins Jc.	H 15	W. Va.
59	*Elkins Park	N 22	Pa.
32	*Elkinsville	M 14	Ind.
....	*Elk Lake	J 10	Ore.
75	Elk Lake	F 20	Pa.
79	Elkland	N 11	Mo.
136	Elkland (Todd)	C 3	N. C.
2400	Elkland	D 14	Pa.
....	Elk Lick, see Salisbury		Pa.
200	*Elk Lick (Elk)	G 16	W. Va.
500	Elk Mills	B 20	Md.
185	Elkmont	A 12	Ala.
110	Elkmont	O 20	Tenn.
338	Elk Mound	D 12	Wis.
....	Elk Mtn.	L 1	S. D.
107	Elk Mtn.	O 16	Wyo.
189	Elko	K 10	Ga.
62	*Elko	O 16	Minn.
4094	Elko	D 17	Nev.
206	*Elko	K 12	S. C.
55	*Elko	N 17	Va.
46	Elkol	O 3	Wyo.
6	Elk Park	K 7	Mont.
467	Elk Park	D 2, M 10	N. C.
1483	Elk Point	P 25	S. D.
130	Elkport	F 21	Iowa
65	*Elk Ranch	A 7	Ark.
690	Elk Rapids	J 14	Mich.
....	Elkridge (Elk Ridge)	G 13	Md.
500	*Elkridge	M 8	W. Va.
337	Elk River	F 6	Idaho
1245	Elk River	M 15	Minn.
11	Elk River Jc.	I 25	Iowa
28	*Elk Springs	D 4	Colo.
50	Elkton	J 14	Colo.
200	*Elkton	D 18	Fla.
50	Elkton	O 13	Ill.
1214	Elkton	K 10	Ky.
3518	Elkton	C 19	Md.
539	Elkton	M 22	Mich.
117	*Elkton	R 19	Minn.
150	*Elkton	L 9	Mo.
50	*Elkton	L 14	N. C.
133	*Elkton	G 20	Ohio
90	Elkton	K 5	Ore.
779	Elkton	J 25	S. D.
500	Elkton	Q 11	Tenn.
1050	Elkton	I 12	Va.
650	Elk Valley	L 18	Tenn.
35	*Elk View	Q 21	Pa.
27	*Elk View	K 6	W. Va.
951	Elkville	O 14	Ill.
100	Elkwater (Old Fort)	J 14	W. Va.
140	*Elkwood	A 14	Ala.
51	*Elkwood	H 15	Va.
45	*Ella	I 15	Ky.
100	Ellabell	K 23	Ga.
50	*Ella Gap	C 6	Ga.
519	Ellamore	H 14	W. Va.
29	*Ellard (Cold Spring)	K 10	Va.
100	*Ellaville	B 10	Fla.
928	Ellaville	K 7	Ga.
36	*Ellen	F 22	Ky.
471	Ellenboro	G 2	N. C.
277	Ellenboro	E 9	W. Va.
180	*Ellenburgh (Ellenburg Depot)	C 23	N. Y.
2428	▲*Ellenburg	C 23	N. Y.
300	*Ellenburg Center	C 23	N. Y.
180	*Ellenburg Depot (Ellenburgh)	C 23	N. Y.
287	Ellendale	J 23	Del.
322	Ellendale	P 16	La.
430	Ellendale	Q 16	Minn.
1517	Ellendale	Q 19	N. D.
250	*Ellendale	P 2	Tenn.
5944	Ellensburg	K 14	Wash.
844	Ellenton	J 13	Fla.
427	*Ellenton	N 10	Ga.
125	*Ellenton	G 16	Pa.
532	Ellenton	L 9	S. C.
4000	Ellenville	C 4	N. Y.
200	*Ellenwood	F 8	Ga.
693	Ellerbe	I 10	N. C.
....	Ellerbeck	E 8	Utah
550	*Ellerslie	I 5	Ga.
650	Ellerslie	L 6	Md.
110	*Ellerson	M 17	Va.
5	*Ellerville	G 23	Okla.
98	*Ellery	N 19	Ill.
3700	Ellet, (North Springfield)	F 18	Ohio
863	Ellettsville	L 11	Ind.
20	Ellicott	O 5	N. Y.
1216	Ellicott City	F 13	Md.
1024	Ellicottville	P 5	N. Y.
1497	Ellijay	C 7	Ga.
300	*Ellijay	Q 5	N. C.
223	Ellinger	K 20	Tex.
7	Ellingson	C 5	S. D.
136	Ellington	C 16	Conn.
27	*Ellington	K 15	Ky.
849	Ellington	O 18	Mo.
500	*Ellington	Q 3	N. Y.
35	Ellinor	I 19	Kan.
2059	Ellinwood	J 12	Kan.
128	*Elliot	E 13	Miss.
41	*Elliot	J 15	N. C.
33	*Elliot	L 9	W. Va.
60	Elliott	D 22	Conn.
332	Elliott	G 19	Ill.
548	Elliott	N 6	Iowa
263	Elliott	O 19	Md.
128	*Elliott	E 14	Miss.
118	Elliott	P 21	N. D.
20	Elliott	A 20	Okla.
276	Elliott	F 17	S. C.
103	*Elliottsburg	M 15	Pa.
64	*Elliottsville	Q 5	Pa.
121	*Elliottville	F 21	Ky.
100	*Ellis	L 12	Idaho
2042	Ellis	H 9	Kan.
25	*Ellis	L 10	La.
100	Ellis	O 21	Neb.
42	Ellis	L 24	S. D.
50	Ellisburg	H 16	Ky.
253	Ellisburg	I 14	N. Y.
50	*Ellisburg	E 12	Pa.
75	Ellisdale	J 15	N. J.
125	*Ellisford	C 17	Wash.
290	*Ellisgrove	O 11	Ill.
15	*Ellison	P 9	W. Va.
150	*Ellison Bay	Q 11	Wis.
412	Ellisport	I 7	Wash.
25	*Ellis Prairie	N 14	Mo.
30	Elliston	M 9	Ind.
53	*Elliston	D 17	Ky.
225	Elliston	J 7	Mont.
150	*Elliston	C 11	Ohio
309	Elliston	O 5	Va.
80	*Ellisville	O 12	Ark.
216	Ellisville	G 9	Ill.
2607	Ellisville	N 17	Miss.
288	*Ellisville	I 19	Mo.
117	*Ellisville	P 14	Wis.
1123	Elloree	J 15	S. C.
967	*Ellport	J 2	Pa.
....	*Ellsburg, see Melrude	G 19	Minn.
195	Ellston	O 10	Iowa
255	Ellsworth	H 16	Ill.
405	Ellsworth	H 12	Iowa
2227	Ellsworth	H 13	Kan.
3911	Ellsworth	M 16	Me.
347	Ellsworth	I 15	Mich.
660	Ellsworth	R 5	Minn.
30	Ellsworth	H 6	Neb.
162	Ellsworth	F 19	Ohio
1975	Ellsworth	O 3	Pa.
60	Ellsworth	Q 7	Wash.
1340	Ellsworth	A 13	Wis.
1040	Ellsworth Falls (The Falls)	L 16	Me.
....	Ellsworth Jc.	G 16	Fla.
63	*Ellwood (Jonacy)	J 23	Ky.
12329	Ellwood City	K 2	Pa.
55	*Elly	I 14	Va.
155	*Ellzey	E 12	Fla.
....	Elm	D 16	Colo.
228	Elm	M 12	N. J.
115	*Elm	O 19	Pa.
790	Elma	C 16	Iowa
800	Elma	N 5	N. Y.
150	*Elma (Elmington)	L 11	Va.
1370	Elma	K 4	Wash.
946	Elm City	F 17	N. C.
730	Elm Creek	M 14	Neb.
239	Elmdale	J 18	Kan.
40	Elmdale	O 14	Mich.
14	*Elmdale	E 23	Mont.
700	Elmendorf	M 16	Tex.
46	*Elmer	I 8	La.
4	*Elmer	G 18	Minn.
238	Elmer	D 12	Mo.
1344	Elmer	N 8	N. J.
249	Elmer	N 3	Okla.
20	Elmer (Yvonne)	E 13	Pa.
1500	*Elmer City	D 16	Wash.
100	*Elmgrove (Wellsburg)	C 19	Ky.
49	*Elmgrove	C 5	La.
43	*Elm Grove	O 11	Ohio
75	Elm Grove	P 4	Pa.
500	Elm Grove	O 20	Wis.
119	Elm Hall	N 17	Mich.
....	Elmhurst	D 20	Calif.
15458	Elmhurst	C 20	Ill.
684	Elmhurst	H 22	Pa.
....	Elmhurst, see Oakton		Wis.
517	Elmina	J 22	Tex.
200	Elmira	H 6	Calif.
74	Elmira	B 5	Idaho
150	*Elmington (Elma)	L 11	Va.
12	Elmira	K 21	Iowa
150	Elmira	I 16	Mich.
159	*Elmira	E 7	Mo.
45106	Elmira	Q 12	N. Y.
115	*Elmira	C 7	Ohio
200	Elmira	J 5	Ore.
150	*Elmira	I 9	W. Va.
4829	Elmira Heights	Q 12	N. Y.
137	*Elm Mott	G 19	Tex.
	Elmo, see Macks		Ark.
200	*Elmo	I 16	Kan.
318	Elmo	A 4	Mo.
16	Elmo	F 4	Mont.
5	Elmo	G 19	N. D.
362	Elmo	E 20	Tex.
198	Elmo	J 17	Utah
134	Elmo	N 16	Wyo.
60	*Elmodel	N 6	Ga.
600	*El Modeno	O 17	Calif.
25	*Elmonica	D 7	Ore.
52	*Elmont	G 21	Kan.
492	*Elmont	H 7	N. Y.
300	*Elmont	C 19	Tex.
100	*Elmont	L 17	Va.
4746	*El Monte	Q 5	Calif.
206	El Moro	P 16	Colo.
1500	*Emora (Bakerton)	L 9	Pa.
100	Elmore	I 15	Ala.
200	Elmore	F 11	Ill.
935	Elmore	R 13	Minn.
1103	Elmore	D 11	Ohio
75	Elmore	E 13	Vt.
494	Elmore City	N 12	Okla.
4	*El Morro	H 4	N. M.
50	*Elm Park	J 14	La.
47	*Elmrock	H 22	Ky.
3078	*Elmsford	G 6	N. Y.
182	*Elm Springs	B 5	Ark.
78	*Elm Tree	L 6	Tenn.
5000	Elmwood	F 13	Conn.
1348	Elmwood	F 10	Ill.
100	Elmwood	O 16	Me.
300	Elmwood	I 20	Mass.
456	Elmwood	L 23	Neb.
4	Elmwood	P 10	N. H.
164	*Elmwood	F 6	N. C.
8	Elmwood	R 8	Okla.
60	*Elmwood	L 12	Tenn.
53	*Elmwood	I 5	W. Va.
828	Elmwood	C 13	Wis.
13689	*Elmwood Park	C 21	Ill.
4248	*Elmwood Place	N 5	Ohio
30	*Elna	F 22	Ky.
250	*El Nido	J 10	Calif.
799	Elnora	N 9	Ind.
50	*Elnora	M 23	N. Y.
19	*Elo	D 2	Mich.
1700	*Eloise	P 22	Mich.
45	*Eloise	H 19	Tex.
494	Elon College	D 11	N. C.
600	Elora	Q 12	Tenn.
400	Eloy	M 15	Ariz.
217	El Paso	H 13	Ark.
1621	El Paso	F 15	Ill.
96810	El Paso	F 1	Tex.
25	*El Paso Gap	O 20	N. M.
11	Elphis	G 22	Colo.
100	El Portal	I 11	Calif.
200	*El Porvenir	F 18	N. M.
6	El Prado	J 12	Calif.
20	El Rain	P 5	Tex.
1200	*Elrama	N 3	Pa.
10078	El Reno	I 9	Okla.
....	Elrick	N 22	Iowa
500	*El Rito	D 12	N. M.
825	*Elrod	G 7	Ala.
27	*Elrod	I 18	Ky.
132	Elrod	K 11	N. C.
92	Elrod	G 21	S. D.
187	*Elrosa	L 10	Minn.
115	*Elroy	N 23	Pa.
1850	Elroy	I 17	Wis.
1006	*Elsa	P 4	Tex.
175	*Elsah	L 8	Ill.
....	*El Sauz	O 2	Tex.
1548	Elsberry	G 18	Mo.
3738	El Segundo	R 2	Calif.
116	*Elsey	P 9	Mo.
16	*Elsie	G 21	Ky.
773	Elsie	O 18	Mich.
223	Elsie	L 8	Neb.
68	Elsie	B 5	Ore.
....	Elsiecoal, see Hot Spot		Ky.
1552	Elsinores	R 9	Calif.
172	*Elsinore (Forks of Elkhorn)	E 17	Ky.
267	Elsinore (Ellsinore)	P 19	Mo.
674	Elsinore	L 10	Utah
15	Elsinore Jc.	O 18, R 9	Calif.
2885	Elsmere	C 17	Ky.
12	Elsmere	G 12	Neb.
1200	*Elsmere	N 23	N. Y.
180	Elsmore	L 23	Kan.
50	*Elsom	M 19	Va.
84	*Elston	I 13	Mo.
901	Elton	L 8	La.
46	*Elton	O 6	N. Y.
195	Elton	N 8	Pa.
10	*Elton	C 12	Tex.
70	*Elton	P 10	W. Va.
500	Elton	L 11	Wis.
85	Eltopia	M 19	Wash.
108	*El Toro	P 17	Calif.
63	*Elva	J 6	Ky.
125	*Elva	L 17	Tenn.
....	El Vado	C 10	N. M.
2	El Valle	M 14	N. M.
226	Elvaston	G 5	Ill.
518	*El Verano	G 3	Calif.
316	Elverson	O 21	Pa.
196	*Elverta	G 8	Calif.
476	Elverton (East Stone Gap)	D 5	Va.
262	Elverton	M 9	W. Va.
2367	Elvins	L 19	Mo.
13	*Elway	D 8	Va.
175	Elwell	N 17	Mich.
60	Elwha	F 4	Wash.
110	*Elwin	J 16	Ill.
248	Elwood	D 19	Ill.
10913	Elwood	H 16	Ind.
100	Elwood	J 23	Iowa
1014	Elwood	D 24	Kan.
67	*Elwood	O 9	Mo.
633	Elwood	M 13	Neb.
500	Elwood	N 13	N. J.
535	*Elwood	C 7	Utah
....	Elwood Jc.	K 2	Pa.
172	*Ely	J 20	Iowa
....	*Ely, see Ash Valley		Kan.
5970	Ely	E 21	Minn.
4140	Ely	H 21	Nev.
50	*Ely (S. Fairlee)	I 14	Vt.
75	*Elyria	J 15	Kan.
77	Elyria	I 15	Neb.
25120	Elyria	D 15	Ohio
158	*Elys	K 20	Ky.
625	Elysburg	K 18	Pa.
382	Elysian	P 14	Minn.
321	Elysian Fields	E 24	Tex.
200	*Elza	L 19	Ga.
31	Emad	L 8	La.
100	*Emanuel	J 19	Ky.
5	Emanuel	G 8	Okla.
20	Emathla	E 14	Fla.
25	Embar	G 9	Wyo.
150	*Embarrass	F 20	Minn.
335	Embarrass	M 13	Wis.
....	Embden	K 8	Me.
70	Embden	N 22	N. D.
50	*Emberton	K 14	Ky.
250	Emblem	C 11	Wyo.
16	*Embree	O 12	Mo.
500	*Embreeville	P 21	Pa.
500	Embreeville	M 23	Tenn.
70	*Embry	E 16	Miss.
....	*Embryfield	I 22	Tex.
6	Embudo	D 13	N. M.
396	Emden	H 13	Ill.
119	*Emden	D 15	Mo.
400	*Emeigh	M 8	Pa.
318	Emelle	I 4	Ala.
150	Emerado	H 22	N. D.
125	Emerald	L 21	Neb.
500	*Emerald	K 21	Pa.
153	Emerald	C 11	Wis.
50	*Emerald Bay	G 9	Calif.
373	Emerson	R 9	Ark.
453	*Emerson	E 5	Ga.
70	*Emerson	C 12	Ill.
498	Emerson	O 5	Iowa
100	*Emerson	E 21	Ky.
879	Emerson	G 21	Neb.
1487	Emerson	C 20	N. J.
134	*Emerson (Portersville)	L 14	N. C.
45	*Emery	C 16	Ark.
482	Emery	L 21	S. D.
618	Emery	K 14	Utah
214	*Emery Mills	Q 3	Me.
300	*Emery Park (Aguirre)	N 17	Ariz.
2521	Emeryville	C 18	Calif.
100	Emeryville	F 17	N. Y.
100	Emet	P 16	Okla.
281	*Emhouse	F 20	Tex.
200	Emida	E 4	Idaho
42	Emigrant	M 11	Mont.
100	*Emigrant Gap	F 10	Calif.
700	Emigsville	P 17	Pa.
60	*Emilee	I 24	Tex.
99	*Emily	H 14	Minn.
150	Eminence	K 11	Ind.
3	*Eminence	K 5	Kan.
1411	Eminence	E 15	Ky.
417	Eminence	O 17	Mo.
160	Emington	F 18	Ill.
145	*Emison	N 6	Ind.
986	Emlenton	I 4	Pa.
35	*Emlyn	K 18	Ky.
23	*Emma	H 8	Colo.
....	*Emma	D 8	Ga.
125	*Emma	O 20	Ill.
110	*Emma	H 23	Ky.
180	*Emma	H 9	Mo.
200	Emma	O 7	N. C.
36	*Emmalena	H 21	Ky.
6731	Emmaus	L 22	Pa.
42	*Emmerich	J 12	Wis.
33	*Emmerton	K 20	Va.
387	Emmet	O 8	Ark.
89	Emmet	F 15	Neb.
3	*Emmet	J 9	N. D.
3374	Emmetsburg	D 8	Iowa
3203	Emmett	M 4	Idaho
191	Emmett	F 20	Kan.
229	Emmett	N 24	Mich.
50	*Emmett	L 25	Tenn.
230	*Emmett	O 4	W. Va.
1412	Emmitsburg	B 9	Md.
60	Emmitsburg Jc. (Rocky Ridge)	C 8	Md.
334	Emmons	R 15	Minn.
125	*Emmons	L 6	W. Va.
....	*Emory (Emory University)	F 7	Calif.
30	Emory	J 15	Mont.
750	Emory	D 21	Tex.
192	*Emory	E 8	Va.
500	*Emory Gap	N 17	Tenn.
....	Emory Grove	D 12	Md.
20	Emoryville	E 18	W. Va.
100	*Empire (De Bardeleben R. R.)	E 10	Ala.
600	Empire	I 9	Calif.
174	*Empire	F 12	Colo.
162	Empire	K 12	Ga.
550	Empire	P 20	La.
266	Empire	J 12	Mich.
618	Empire	H 20	Ohio
665	Empire	L 2	Ore.
43	Empire	O 17	Minn.
80	Empire City	N 10	Okla.
....	Empire Mine	J 9	Ky.
368	Empire Road (East Poland)	O 5	Me.
212	*Emporia	E 17	Fla.
13188	Emporia	J 20	Kan.
2735	Emporia	Q 16	Va.
3775	Emporium	G 10	Pa.
....	Emporium Jc.	G 11	Pa.
18	Emrick	J 16	N. D.
2765	Emsworth	M 3	Pa.
75	Enaville	D 5	Idaho
331	Encampment	Q 15	Wyo.
417	*Encanto	Q 18	Calif.
963	Encinal	P 15	Tex.
2600	Encinitas	P 18	Calif.
....	*Encino, N 15, Q 4, (Pop. incl. in Los Angeles)		Calif.
652	Encino	H 16	N. M.
510	Encino	R 17	Tex.
50	*Encinoso	K 15	N. M.
....	Enda	C 10	Utah
200	Endeavor	G 6	Pa.
420	Endeavor	K 17	Wis.
23	*Endee	H 20	Ky.
237	▲Endee	G 25	N. M.
1593	Enderlin	O 22	N. D.
100	Enders	N 8	Neb.
110	*Enders	M 16	Pa.
6	Enderslake	G 12	Neb.
15	*Endicott	G 23	Ky.
246	Endicott	O 21	Neb.
17702	Endicott	Q 15	N. Y.
33	*Endicott	P 6	Va.
495	Endicott	K 22	Wash.
41	*Endicott	C 11	W. Va.
....	*Endless Caverns	H 11	Va.
2500	Endwell (Hooper)	Q 15	N. Y.
458	*Energy	P 15	Ill.
67	*Energy	G 16	Tex.
1000	Enfield	B 15	Conn.
875	Enfield	O 18	Ill.
979	▲Enfield	J 15	Me.
45	*Enfield	M 14	Minn.
850	Enfield	L 8	N. H.
2208	Enfield	D 18	N. C.
9	Enfield	M 18	Va.
200	Enfield Center	L 9	N. H.
150	Engadine	F 14	Mich.
40	*Engelberg	B 18	Ark.
340	Engelhard	G 24	N. C.
2130	England	K 14	Ark.
117	*Engle	H 21	Ky.
50	Engle	L 9	N. M.
50	*Engle	L 19	Tex.
83	*Engle	E 25	W. Va.
600	Englehard	G 24	N. C.
174	*Englevale	M 25	Kan.
200	Englevale	P 21	N. D.
9680	Englewood	G 15	Colo.
450	*Englewood	K 13	Fla.
....	Englewood	C 21	Ill.
377	Englewood	O 7	Kan.
18966	Englewood	D 21	N. J.
531	Englewood	K 7	Ohio
77	Englewood	I 2	S. D.
1342	Englewood	P 18	Tenn.
888	*Englewood Cliffs	C 19	N. J.
757	English	P 12	Ind.
150	*English	D 16	Ky.
213	English	B 23	Tex.
300	English (Lakewood)	E 8	Wash.
161	*English	R 5	W. Va.
75	*English Center	G 14	Pa.
283	English Creek	P 14	N. J.
210	English Lake	C 10	Ind.
25	English Lookout	M 20	La.
815	Englishtown	H 17	N. J.
3000	*Enhaut	N 16	Pa.
121	*Enid	D 12	Miss.
73	Enid	F 23	Mont.
28081	Enid	D 10	Okla.
529	Enigma	N 12	Ga.
275	Enloe	C 21	Tex.
50	*Ennice	B 5	N. C.
26	Enning	H 5	S. D.
20	*Ennis	I 10	Ky.
400	Ennis	N 9	Mont.
7087	Ennis	F 19	Tex.
56	*Enoch	J 9	W. Va.
57	*Enochs	B 8	Tex.
250	*Enola	G 13	Ark.
54	Enola	H 19	Neb.
2600	Enola	N 16	Pa.
46	*Enon	A 8	Ark.
97	*Enon	P 12	Miss.
68	*Enon	I 13	Mo.
281	Enon	K 8	Ohio
368	Enon (Enon Valley	K 1	Pa.
28	*Enon	L 9	W. Va.
132	*Enondale	I 20	Miss.
368	*Enon Valley (Enon)	K 1	Pa.
10	*Enonville	M 13	Va.
1800	Enoree	C 9	S. C.
1168	Enosburg Falls	B 10	Vt.
....	Enosville	P 6	Ind.
26	*Enough	M 18	Mo.
32	*Enright	G 16	Ark.
14	*Enright	E 2	Ore.
375	Ensenada	C 12	N. M.
202	Ensign	M 7	Kan.
402	*Ensign	G 9	Mich.
....	Ensley	F 12	Ala.
4353	Enterprise	N 18	Ala.
....	Enterprise, see Benson Spgs.		Fla.
35	Enterprise	K 12	Iowa
671	Enterprise	H 17	Kan.
36	*Enterprise	E 21	Ky.
18	*Enterprise	F 12	La.
757	Enterprise	K 20	Miss.
125	*Enterprise	M 14	Ohio
100	Enterprise	J 21	Okla.
1709	Enterprise	D 23	Ore.
110	Enterprise	F 5	Pa.
....	Enterprise	O 17	S. C.
619	Enterprise	P 2	Utah
1000	*Enterprise	D 13	W. Va.
290	Entiat	H 14	Wash.
186	*Entriken	M 12	Pa.
15	Entro	H 11	Ariz.
2627	Enumclaw	J 8	Wash.
250	Enville	Q 14	Okla.
500	*Enville	P 6	Tenn.
119	Eola	C 18	Ill.
150	Eola	J 11	La.
25	Eola	N 12	Okla.
116	*Eola	G 13	Tex.
10	*Eolia	J 23	Ky.
410	Eolia	G 18	Mo.
56	*Eolian	D 15	Tex.
125	*Eoline	H 10	Ala.
410	*Ep (Belfry)	H 24	Ky.
328	Epes	I 5	Ala.
2094	Ephraim	J 13	Utah
254	*Ephraim	R 11	Wis.
6199	Ephrata	O 19	Pa.
951	Ephrata	J 17	Wash.
70	Epiphany	K 21	S. D.
131	*Epoufette	F 15	Mich.
60	*Epperly	P 8	W. Va.
....	*Epperson	P 18	Tenn.
800	Epping	P 18	N. H.
154	Epping	G 3	N. D.
391	Epps	B 13	La.
150	Epsie	M 22	Mont.
....	Epsom	P 17	Minn.
52	Epsom	O 16	N. H
67	Epsom	O 16	N. H.
75	*Epson	G 21	Ky.
241	*Epworth	B 7	Ga.
31	*Epworth	O 20	Ill.
454	Epworth	G 22	Iowa
221	Epworth	D 20	Ky.
3	Epworth	L 10	Mich.
12	Epworth	G 7	N. D.
21	*Epworth	L 18	Va.
196	Equality	I 17	Ala.
971	Equality	P 18	Ill.
60	*Equality (Kronos)	H 11	Ky.
425	Equinunk	E 23	Pa.
....	Equity	M 17	Ohio
263	Era	C 18	Tex.
29	*Era	O 16	Va.
175	Eram	H 19	Okla.
54	*Erastus	Q 6	N. C.
1408	Erath	N 11	La.
25	*Erath	G 18	Tex.
....	Eraw	P 4	W. Va.
200	Erbacon	J 11	W. Va.
....	*Erbie	D 9	Ark.
90	*Ercildoun	P 20	Pa.
112	*Erdahl	K 6	Minn.
1000	*Erdenheim	N 22	Pa.
121	*Erhard (Erharts)	I 5	Minn.
100	Erhart	E 16	Ohio
121	*Erharts (Erhard)	I 5	Minn.
35	*Erica	J 19	Va.
1591	Erick	J 2	Okla.
520	Erico (Soppitt)	I 4	Pa.
110	*Ericsburg	D 14	Minn.
279	Ericson	I 16	Neb.
1019	Erie	E 14	Colo.
1052	Erie	C 10	Ill.
1286	Erie	M 23	Kan.
590	Erie	R 21	Mich.
50	*Erie	D 5	Minn.
215	Erie	L 23	N. D.
116955	Erie	C 3	Pa.
25	*Erie	O 18	Tenn.
....	Erie Jc.	L 23	N. D.
25	Erie Jc.	H 8	Pa.
150	Erieville (Eritown)	N 16	N. Y.
33	*Eriline	I 20	Ky.
216	*Erin	Q 13	N. Y.
905	Erin	L 8	Tenn.
150	Erin Springs	L 11	Okla.
150	*Eritown (Erieville)	N 16	N. Y.
2416	*Erlanger	B 17	Ky.
1400	Erlanger	E 7	N. C.
....	*Erlton	K 9	N. J.
204	Erma	R 11	N. J.
50	*Ermine	I 22	Ky.
1500	*Ernest	L 6	Pa.
100	Ernul	H 19	N. C.
289	Eros	C 9	La.
5	*Erose	J 20	Ky.
90	Errol	D 17	N. H.
581	Erskine	F 5	Minn.
3	*Ervay	J 16	Wyo.
15	Ervin	Q 21	Okla.
500	Erving	C 9	Mass.
150	*Erwin	H 6	Miss.
3500	Erwin	H 14	N. C.
182	Erwin	H 22	S. D.
3350	Erwin	M 24	Tenn.
200	*Erwin	E 16	W. Va.
100	Erwinna	M 24	Pa.
75	Erwinville	L 14	La.
292	Esbon	D 13	Kan.
1106	Escalante	O 13	Utah
50	*Escalante Forks	I 4	Colo.
785	*Escalon	I 9	Calif.
14830	Escanaba	G 8	Mich.
400	*Escatawpa	N 3	Ala.
600	*Escatawpa	R 22	Miss.
160	*Esco (Penny)	I 23	Ky.
110	*Escoheag	L 10	R. I.
4560	Escondido	P 19	Calif.
....	Escondido Jc.	P 18	Calif.
200	*Escuela	N 14	Ariz.
30	Eshbach	M 21	Pa.
800	Eskdale	M 7	W. Va.
20	*Eskay	F 12	Mont.
....	*Esko	I 18	Minn.
5	Eskota	N 8	N. C.
50	*Eskota	E 13	Tex.
648	Eskridge	H 20	Kan.
....	*Esmerelda	H 10	Calif.
350	Esmond	B 15	Ill.
449	Esmond	H 15	N. D.
1000	Esmond	D 12	R. I.
96	Esmond	J 21	S. D.
515	Esmont	L 12	Va.
364	*Esom Hill (Esom)	E 2	Ga.
400	*Esopus	C 5	N. Y.
472	▲*Espanola	E 18	Fla.
643	Espanola	E 12	N. M.
31	Espanola	H 22	Wash.
300	Esparto	G 6	Calif.
219	*Esperance	N 22	N. Y.
200	Esperanza	C 18	Miss.
410	Espinoza	Q 11	Colo.
600	Espy	J 18	Pa.
200	Espyville (Espyville Sta.)	F 2	Pa.
500	*Esserville	D 5	Va.
30	*Essex	M 21	Calif.
1500	Essex	L 17	Conn.
211	Essex	E 19	Ill.
762	Essex	O 5	Iowa
3500	Essex	E 15	Md.
1384	▲Essex	C 22	Mass.
118	*Essex	C 11	Miss.
639	Essex	Q 22	Mo.
150	Essex (Walton)	D 5	Mont.
250	*Essex	G 23	N. Y.
45	Essex	D 16	N. C.
125	Essex (Essex Center)	E 8	Vt.
67	*Essex (North Concord)	E 20	Vt.
1466	*Essex Fells	D 18	N. J.
1901	Essex Jc.	E 7	Vt.
2390	Essexville	L 19	Mich.
....	*Essie	I 21	Ky.
65	*Essig	P 11	Minn.
1500	Essington	P 23	Pa.
44	*Estabrook	I 12	Colo.
445	Estabutchie (Eastabuchie)	N 17	Miss.
526	Estacada	E 9	Ore.
668	Estancia	H 13	N. M.
250	*Estatoe	N 10	N. C.
6	Estella	C 21	Okla.
210	*Estelle (Tunnel)	C 2	Ga.
627	Estelline	H 23	S. D.
603	Estelline	A 12	Tex.
423	*Estell Manor	N 13	N. J.
56	Esterbrook	L 20	Wyo.
825	*Esterly	N 21	Pa.
300	*Estero	M 16	Fla.
45	*Estes	J 14	Ky.
100	*Estes	H 18	Miss.
25	Estes	P 19	Tex.
29	*Estes	H 14	Va.
994	Estes Park	D 13	Colo.
81	*Esther	N 10	La.
817	Esther	L 20	Mo.
5651	Estherville	B 7	Iowa
539	Estherwood	M 9	La.
60	*Estill	H 22	Ky.
50	*Estill	G 7	Miss.
34	*Estill	G 12	Mo.
1280	*Estill	N 11	S. C.
106	*Estillfork	A 17	Ala.
500	Estill Springs	P 12	Tenn.
213	Esto	M 9	Fla.
70	*Esto	J 15	Ky.
20	Estrella	L 11	Ariz.
14	*Estrella	F 4	N. M.
13	*Esty	M 12	W. Va.
57	*Etam	E 15	W. Va.
324	Ethan	M 20	S. D.
353	*Ethanac	O 18	Calif.
33	*Ethel	L 17	Ark.
90	Ethel	P 12	Ind.
150	Ethel	J 14	La.
828	Ethel	H 16	Miss.
317	Ethel	D 12	Mo.
56	Ethel	P 20	Okla.
125	*Ethel	K 19	Va.
300	Ethel	M 6	Wash.
411	Ethel	N 4	W. Va.
500	*Ethelsville	G 5	Ala.
95	*Ether	G 10	N. C.
200	*Ethete	J 10	Wyo.
45	*Ethlyn	H 18	Mo.
40	Ethridge	D 8	Mont.
350	Ethridge	P 9	Tenn.
1000	*Etiwanda	N 18	Calif.
7	Etlah	I 16	Mo.
28	*Etlan	I 13	Va.
456	Etna	C 4	Calif.
105	*Etna (Aetna)	K 18	Ill.
123	Etna	K 13	Me.
450	Etna	K 7	N. H.
200	Etna	P 14	N. Y.
11	*Etna	P 5	N. C.
300	Etna	K 13	Ohio
7223	Etna	M 3	Pa.
....	*Etna	B 2	Utah
28	Etna	P 7	Wash.
60	Etna	I 2	Wyo.
433	Etna Green	D 15	Ind.
16	*Etna Mills	L 17	Va.
60	*Etoile	J 14	Ky.
100	*Etoile	H 24	Tex.
239	Eton	B 5	Ga.
175	*Etowah	D 21	Ark.
35	*Etowah	P 8	N. C.
30	Etowah	K 13	Okla.
3362	Etowah	P 18	Tenn.
50	*Etta	B 17	Miss.
12	*Etta	J 18	Va.
40	Etter	B 3	Tex.
478	Etters (Goldsboro)	O 16	Pa.
68	*Ettersburg	D 2	Calif.
98	*Etterville	K 12	Mo.
300	Ettrick	E 15	Wis.
1000	Ettricks	N 17	Va.
114	*Etty	I 23	Ky.
303	Eubank	I 17	Ky.
33	Eubanks	O 21	Okla.
113	Eucha	D 23	Okla.
17	*Euclid	E 22	Ky.
150	Euclid	E 3	Minn.
201	*Euclid	L 14	N. Y.
17866	Euclid	C 17	Ohio
60	Euclid	J 4	Pa.
25	Euclid	P 22	Va.
3	*Euclid	H 8	W. Va.
50	*Eucutta	M 20	Miss.
2020	Eudora	R 17	Ark.
603	Eudora	G 24	Kan.
75	*Eudora	N 9	Mo.
6269	Eufaula	L 23	Ala.
2355	Eufaula	J 20	Okla.
63	*Eufola	F 5	N. C.
400	Eugene	I 5	Ind.
232	Eugene	J 13	Mo.
20838	Eugene	I 6	Ore.
30	*Eula	D 10	Ark.
64	*Eula (Crystalsprings)	N 14	Kan.
35	Eulogy	F 18	Tex.
200	*Eulonia	N 23	Ga
24	*Eunice	I 15	Ky
5242	Eunice	L 10	La.
35	*Eunice	O 15	Mo.
1227	Eunice	N 25	N. M.
....	*Eunice	O 8	W. Va.
1377	Eupora	F 17	Miss.
200	*Eure	C 20	N. C.
....	Eureka	H 15	Ala.
17055	Eureka	D 1	Calif.
7	Eureka	N 6	Colo.
150	Eureka	E 16	Fla.
1714	Eureka	F 14	Ill.
3803	Eureka	L 20	Kan.
200	Eureka	N 16	Mich.
75	*Eureka	M 15	Minn.
700	Eureka	J 19	Mo.
912	Eureka	B 3	Mont.
600	Eureka	G 17	Nev.
100	*Eureka	C 3	N. Y.
194	*Eureka	G 16	N. C.
202	*Eureka (Chambersburg)	Q 15	Ohio
340	*Eureka	N 23	Pa.
1457	Eureka	C 15	S. D.
162	*Eureka	F 20	Tex.
2292	Eureka	H 10	Utah
30	Eureka	N 20	Wash.
100	Eureka	E 8	W. Va.
318	Eureka	M 16	Wis.
1770	Eureka Springs	A 7	Ark
513	Eustace	F 21	Tex.

Pop.	Place	Index	State
2930	Eustis	F 16	Fla.
80	Eustis	J 5	Me.
459	Eustis	M 12	Neb.
1895	Eutaw	I 7	Ala.
....	*Eutaw	E 7	Miss.
496	Eutawville	J 16	S. C.
150	*Eva	C 13	Ala.
34	*Eva	H 12	La.
400	Eva	M 7	Tenn.
....	Eva, see Palito Blanco		Tex.
25	*Eva	G 9	W. Va.
515	Evadale	J 25	Tex.
....	Evadale Jc.	E 22	Ark.
145	Evan	P 10	Minn.
350	Evangeline	M 9	La.
792	Evans	D 16	Colo.
82	*Evans	G 19	Ga.
98	Evans	M 16	Iowa
370	Evans	I 5	La.
50	*Evans	H 10	Mont.
55	Evans (Lostine	D 23	Ore.
50	Evans	C 21	Wash.
250	*Evans	H 5	W. Va.
1604	Evans City (Evansburg)	K 3	Pa.
425	*Evans Landing	Q 15	Ind.
523	Evans Mills	G 16	N. Y.
200	Evansport	D 6	Ohio
65389	Evanston	B 21	Ill.
45	*Evanston	Q 10	Ind.
....	Evanston	P 21	Miss.
10	Evanston	N 12	Pa.
3605	Evanston	Q 2	Wyo.
163	*Evansville	D 4	Ark.
693	Evansville	O 11	Ill.
97062	Evansville	R 5	Ind.
439	Evansville	K 6	Minn.
175	*Evansville	B 10	Miss.
26	*Evansville	F 13	Mo.
47	*Evansville	M 20	Pa.
135	Evansville	C 17	Vt.
2321	Evansville	K 21	Wis.
206	Evansville	J 17	Wyo.
350	Evant	H 17	Tex.
25	Evaro	H 4	Mont.
1335	Evart	L 15	Mich.
1642	Evarts	J 21	Ky.
216	Evarts (North Hartland)	L 14	Vt.
43	*Eve	I 14	Ky.
50	Eve	L 6	Mo.
6887	Eveleth	F 19	Minn.
126	*Evelyn	G 19	Ky.
....	Evelyn	F 10	Mich.
325	Evening Shade	C 15	Ark.
45	*Eveningshade	N 13	Mo.
150	*Evensville	O 16	Tenn.
25	Evenwood	H 16	W. Va.
55	*Ever	G 22	Ky.
375	Everest	D 22	Kan.
100	Everest	M 23	N. D.
168	Everett (Everett City)	N 22	Ga.
110	*Everett	J 10	Ky.
46784	Everett	E 19, M 5	Mass.
9	Everett	I 22	Neb.
180	Everett	H 19	N. J.
80	Everett	E 17	Ohio
2425	Everett	P 10	Pa.
30224	Everett	F 8	Wash.
168	*Everett City (Everett)	N 22	Ga.
265	Everetts	F 19	N. C.
200	*Everettville	C 14	W. Va.
518	Everglades	N 18	Fla.
2216	Evergreen	N 12	Ala.
314	Evergreen	G 25	Calif.
275	Evergreen	G 14	Colo.
384	Evergreen	J 11	La.
279	*Evergreen	L 13	N. C.
150	*Evergreen	N 11	Va.
3313	Evergreen Park	C 22	Ill.
320	Everitt	J 22	Tex.
523	Everly	C 5	Iowa
22	*Everman	E 22	Ky.
200	*Everman	E 18	Tex.
50	Eversole	H 20	Ky.
1809	Everson	O 5	Pa.
295	Everson	B 8	Wash.
180	Everton	B 10	Ark.
116	*Everton	K 21	Ind.
368	Everton	N 8	Mo.
110	*Evesboro	L 13	N. J.
113	*Evington	N 9	Va.
200	*Evinston	E 14	Fla.
13	*Evona	I 16	Ky.
200	Ewan	M 8	N. J.
150	Ewan	J 23	Wash.
100	Ewart	K 16	Iowa
35	*Ewart	M 9	N. C.
450	Ewell	R 19	Md.
10	Ewell	I 16	Utah
800	Ewen	B 24	Mich.
339	Ewing	O 16	Ill.
500	Ewing	N 15	Ind.
525	Ewing	D 19	Ky.
309	Ewing	C 15	Mo.
681	Ewing	G 17	Neb.
10146	▲Ewing	I 12	N. J.
....	Ewing	H 6	Okla
131	*Ewing	H 24	Tex.
500	Ewing	E 2	Va.
....	*Ewing	B 22	Wyo.
120	*Ewington	P 14	Ohio
250	Ewingville	I 12	N. J.
85	Excel	N 10	Ala.
....	Excell	C 3	Tex.
125	*Excello	E 13	Mo.
307	Excello (North Excello)	M 7	Ohio
150	Excelsior	G 4	Ark.
1422	Excelsior	N 21	Minn.
857	Excelsior	K 18	Pa.
700	*Excelsior	R 5	W. Va.
150	*Excelsior	G 19	Wis.
4864	Excelsior Springs	F 7	Mo.
....	Excelsior Spgs. Jc.	F 7	Mo.
268	Exchange	I 17	Pa.
100	*Exchange	I 10	W. Va.
194	Exeland	E 9	Wis.
8	Exendine	I 7	Okla.
3883	Exeter	K 13	Calif.
126	*Exeter	J 8	Ill.
85	Exeter	K 12	Me.
249	Exeter	Q 8	Mo.
841	Exeter	M 19	Neb.
5398	■Exeter	P 19	N. H.
5802	Exeter	H 20	Pa.
125	Exeter	I 15	R. I.
14	Exeter	D 4	Va.
58	*Exie	I 15	Ky.
1046	Exira	L 7	Iowa
481	Exline	Q 15	Iowa
800	Exmore	M 23	Va.
....	Expedit, see Twin Rocks		Pa.
33	*Experiment	Q 8	Ark.
1900	Experiment	H 8	Ga.
1990	Export	M 5	Pa.
86	*Extension	E 12	La.
99	*Exton	P 22	Pa.
....	Exum, see Magic City		Tex.
84	*Eyers Grove	I 18	Pa.
2540	Eynon	G 21	Pa.
438	Eyota	Q 20	Minn.
100	*Ezel (Linwood)	M 18	Ala.
147	*Ezel	G 20	Ky.

F

Pop.	Place	Index	State
1623	Fabens	G 1	Tex.
24	*Faber	L 10	Ark.
250	*Faber	K 11	Va.
40	*Fabius	A 17	Ala.
20	Fabius	B 14	Mo.
308	Fabius	N 15	N. Y.
19	*Fabius	F 20	W. Va.
450	*Fabyan	A 23	Conn.
25	Fabyan House	H 15	N. H.
500	Faceville	P 5	Ga.
175	*Fackler	B 18	Ala.
893	Factoryville	G 20	Pa.
24	*Fagan	G 20	Ky
150	*Fagus	I 22, R 20	Mo.
500	*Fairaces	O 10	N. M.
110	Fairbank	O 20	Ariz.
631	Fairbank	F 18	Iowa
150	*Fairbank	K 17	Md.
500	Fairbank	P 4	Pa.
21	Fairbank	G 12	S. D.
200	*Fairbanks	D 14	Fla.
100	Fairbanks	L 5	Ind.
52	*Fairbanks	B 11	La.
320	Fairbanks	L 7	Me.
30	*Fairbanks	F 19	Minn.
148	*Fairbanks	K 22	Tex.
970	Fair Bluff	L 12	N. C.
1502	Fairburn	G 6	Ga.
120	Fairburn	L 3	S. D.
2300	Fairbury	F 17	Ill.
6304	Fairbury	O 20	Neb.
1855	Fairchance	Q 4	Pa.
6	Fairchild	D 12	Mont.
639	Fairchild	F 13	Wis.
149	Fairdale	B 16	Ill.
187	Fairdale	F 20	N. D.
50	Fairdale	E 20	Pa.
100	*Fairdale	H 25	Tex.
....	*Fairdale	D 8	W. Va.
30	Fairdealing	Q 19	Mo.
2000	Fairfax	I 22	Ala.
2198	*Fairfax	H 4	Calif.
100	*Fairfax	N 16	Ga.
262	Fairfax	J 19	Iowa
437	Fairfax	R 14	Mich.
1116	Fairfax	O 10	Minn.
813	Fairfax	B 3	Mo.
2327	Fairfax	C 16	Okla.
1379	Fairfax	M 12	S. C.
338	Fairfax	O 17	S. D.
500	Fairfax	C 8	Vt.
979	Fairfax	G 17	Va.
40	*Fairfax (Fairfax Sta.)	G 17	Va.
200	Fairfax	K 9	Wash.
11703	Fairfield	F 12	Ala.
1312	Fairfield	H 6	Calif.
5000	Fairfield	P 6	Conn.
665	▲*Fairfield	E 14	Fla.
511	Fairfield	O 10	Idaho
4008	Fairfield	N 18	Ill.
185	Fairfield	K 22	Ind.
150	*Fairfield (Oakford)	G 15	Ind.
6773	Fairfield	O 19	Iowa
10	Fairfield	G 15	Ky.
3420	■Fairfield	L 10	Me.
150	*Fairfield	K 10	Mo.
185	Fairfield	F 9	Mont.
640	Fairfield	N 18	Neb.
200	Fairfield	L 19	N. Y.
200	Fairfield	G 23	N. C.
15	Fairfield	L 4	N. D.
2549	Fairfield	L 8	Ohio
431	Fairfield	Q 14	Pa.
1047	Fairfield	G 20	Tex.
110	Fairfield	G 10	Utah
136	Fairfield	C 9	Vt.
150	*Fairfield	K 9	Va.
364	Fairfield	I 24	Wash.
159	*Fairfield Center	L 10	Me.
10	Fairfield Center	H 16	Pa.
112	*Fairford	O 5	Ala.
600	Fair Forest	A 8	S. C.
95	*Fairgrange	J 19	Ill.
55	Fairground (Sheldon Jc)	B 9	Vt.
481	Fairgrove	M 20	Mich.
361	*Fair Grove	N 10	Mo.
31	Fair Haven	K 14	Md.
10938	■Fairhaven	M 21	Mass.
800	*Fair Haven	O 24	Mich.
200	Fair Haven	M 13	Minn.
2491	Fair Haven	H 20	N. J.
471	Fairhaven	K 13	N. Y.
1968	Fair Haven	L 5	Vt.
1845	Fairhope	Q 6	Ala.
75	Fairhope	Q 8	Pa.
168	*Fairland	I 20	Ill.
600	Fairland	K 16	Ind.
786	Fairland	B 23	Okla.
60	Fairland	I 16	Tex.
9017	Fair Lawn	C 19	N. J.
....	Fairlawn	F 17	Ohio
375	Fairlee	I 17	Vt.
120	*Fairlie	D 20	Tex.
75	*Fairmead	J 12	Calif.
100	*Fairmont	N 15	Calif.
6988	Fairmont	R 11	Minn.
75	Fairmont	B 15	Mo.
810	Fairmont	M 19	Neb.
1993	Fairmont	K 12	N. C.
153	Fairmont	D 11	Okla.
50	Fairmont (Fairmount)	J 4	Pa.
450	*Fairmont	B 8	S. C.
23105	Fairmont	D 13	W. Va.
1905	*Fairmont City	N 11	Ill.
1000	Fairmont Mills	B 8	S. C.
50	*Fairmount	K 24	Del.
474	Fairmount	D 5	Ga.
775	Fairmount	H 21	Ill.
2382	Fairmount	G 17	Ind.
500	*Fairmount	Q 20	Md.
2505	*Fairmount	H 6	Mo.
705	Fairmount	Q 25	N. D.
50	*Fairmount (Fairmont)	J 4	Pa.
100	*Fairmount	H 25	Tex.
50	Fairmount	F 6	Wash.
900	Fairmount City (Helper)	J 6	Pa.
40	*Fairmount Springs	I 20	Pa.
160	Fair Oaks	G 18	Ark.
1000	Fairoaks	G 8	Calif.
500	Fairoaks	D 7	Ind.
1100	*Fairoaks (Fair Oaks)	L 2	Pa.
54	*Fairplain	H 6	W. Va.
100	*Fair Play	G 10	Calif.
739	Fair Play	H 12	Colo.
50	*Fairplay	J 15	Ky.
102	*Fair Play	B 4	Md.
431	Fair Play	M 9	Mo.
150	*Fair Play	D 4	S. C.
164	*Fairplay	G 22	Wis.
1000	*Fairpoint	J 20	Ohio
150	Fairpoint	G 5	S. D.
150	Fairport	L 23	Iowa
50	*Fairport	G 11	Kan.
263	Fairport	C 7	Mo.
4644	Fairport	L 10	N. Y.
700	Fair Port	K 21	Va.
4528	Fairport Harbor	B 18	Ohio
400	Fairton	O 8	N. J.
32	Fairvalley	B 6	Okla.
414	Fairview	R 20	Idaho
528	Fairview	G 10	Ill.
50	*Fairview	N 21	Ind.
333	Fairview	D 21	Kan.
175	Fairview	J 9	Ky.
150	*Fairview	H 12	La.
....	*Fairview	G 8	Mass.
150	*Fairview	I 18	Mich.
304	Fairview	Q 7	Mo.
901	Fairview	E 25	Mont.
8770	Fairview	D 20	N. J.
....	*Fair View, see Winston		N. M.
206	Fairview	J 18	Ohio
4700	*Fairview	D 16	Ohio
1913	Fairview	E 7	Okla.
305	Fairview	C 8	Ore.
555	Fairview	D 2	Pa.
214	*Fairview	J 5	Pa.
150	Fairview	N 25	S. D.
1100	*Fairview, (Jingo)	N 10	Tenn.
1314	Fairview	I 14	Utah
....	*Fairview	O 10	Va.
65	*Fairview	E 4	Va.
831	Fairview	C 13	W. Va.
425	Fairview	K 2	Wyo.
....	Fairview Jc.	P 25	N. D.
1074	Fairview Park	J 6	Ind.
90	*Fairview Village	O 23	Pa.
109	*Fairville	Q 22	Pa.
293	Fairwater	M 17	Wis.
....	Fair Weather	I 5	Ill.
127	*Fairy	G 17	Tex.
751	Faison	I 16	N. C.
....	Faith	K 13	Mo.
449	Faith	G 7	N. C.
522	Faith	F 7	S. D.
300	Faithorn, (Faithorn Jc.)	G 5	Mich.
80	Falco	O 14	Ala.
75	Falcon	J 16	Colo.
75	Falcon	G 22	Ky.
150	*Falcon	C 11	Miss.
26	*Falcon	L 13	Mo.
206	Falcon	H 14	N. C.
3222	Falconer	Q 3	N. Y.
....	Falconer Jc.	Q 3	N. Y.
45	*Falfa	P 6	Colo.
2641	Falfurrias	Q 17	Tex.
216	Falk	D 1	Calif.
45	Falkirk	K 10	N. D.
188	*Falkland	F 17	N. C.
275	*Falkner	A 18	Miss.
....	Falks	M 4	Idaho
567	Falkville	C 12	Ala.
500	*Fall Branch	L 23	Tenn.
887	Fall Brook	P 18	Calif.
....	Fall Brook Jc.	P 18	Calif.
400	Fall City	I 9	Wash.
3	*Fall Creek	M 4	Colo.
50	Fall Creek	I 4	Ill.
35	Fall Creek	J 7	Ore.
572	Fall Creek	E 13	Wis.
1	*Fallen Leaf	G 9	Calif.
580	*Fallentimber	M 8	Pa.
250	Falling Creek	M 17	Va.
180	*Falling Rock (Weir)	L 6	W. Va.
388	Falling Spring (Renick)	M 12	W. Va.
15	Falling Springs	N 15	Pa.
300	*Falling Waters	C 24	W.Va.
17	*Fallis	D 15	Ky.
137	Fallis	G 13	Okla.
20	*Fallon	H 4	Calif.
200	Fallon	I 23	Mont.
1911	Fallon	G 6	Nev.
15	Fallon	O 10	N. D.
25	Fallon	Q 21	Okla.
....	Fallon	K 24	Wash.
336	Fall River	M 20	Kan.
115428	Fall River	M 19	Mass.
425	Fall River	L 19	Wis.
400	Fall River Mills	C 8	Calif.
20	*Fall Rock	I 20	Ky.
300	*Falls	G 19	Pa.
100	*Fallsburg	F 23	Ky.
200	*Fallsburg	C 3	N. Y.
1500	Fallsburg (South Fallsburg)	C 3	N. Y.
2576	Falls Church	F 18	Va.
50	*Falls City	D 10	Ala.
6146	Falls City	O 25	Neb.
715	Falls City	F 5	Ore.
350	Falls City	M 17	Tex.
1258	Falls Creek	I 9	Pa.
50	*Fallsvale	M 21	Calif.
600	*Fallsington	N 23	Pa.
....	Falls Jc.	C 16	Minn.
218	Falls Jc., (Glenwillow)	D 17	Ohio
85	*Fallsmill	I 11	W. Va.
300	*Falls Mills	B 10	Va.
150	Falls of Rough	H 11	Ky.
100	Fallston	D 15	Md.
300	Fallston	G 3	N. C.
628	Fallston	L 2	Pa.
500	Falls Village	B 5	Conn.
25	*Fallsville	D 8	Ark.
150	*Falmouth	B 10	Fla.
80	Falmouth	J 19	Ind.
2099	Falmouth	D 18	Ky.
272	Falmouth	P 6	Me.
3000	Falmouth	N 23	Mass.
250	Falmouth	K 14	Mich.
....	Falmouth	O 17	Pa.
500	Falmouth	I 17	Va.
252	Falmouth Foreside	P 6	Me.
160	*Falmouth Heights	N 24	Mass.
125	Falun	I 15	Kan.
90	Falun	B 8	Wis.
163	Fame	J 20	Okla.
....	*Fame	I 17	W. Va.
63	Family	D 7	Mont.
110	Famoso	L 13	Calif.
100	*Fancher	L 7	N. Y.
417	Fancy Farm	J 5	Ky.
50	*Fancy Gap	Q 4	Va.
110	*Fancy Prairie	I 13	Ill.
60	*Fandon	H 7	Ill.
50	Fanlew	C 6	Fla.
250	Fannett	K 25	Tex.
198	Fannettsburg	O 12	Pa.
24	*Fannin	F 21	Ky.
150	Fannin	J 13	Miss.
150	*Fannin	N 19	Tex.
54	*Fanning	L 16	Mo.
....	*Fanrock	P 6	W. Va.
150	Fanshawe	K 23	Okla.
....	Fanton	B 9	Vt.
2310	Fanwood	F 16	N. J.
....	Faraday, see Amonate		Va.
386	Farber	F 16	Mo.
37	Fargo	I 17	Ark.
250	Fargo	P 17	Ga.
112	Fargo	N 24	Mich.
32580	Fargo	M 25	N. D.
291	Fargo	D 3	Okla.
574	Far Hills	E 14	N. J.
14527	Faribault	P 16	Minn.
....	Faribault Jc.	P 16	Minn.
804	Farina	M 16	Ill.
300	*Farisita	O 15	Colo.
150	*Fariston	J 19	Ky.
25	*Farler	I 21	Ky.
11	*Farley	F 3	Calif.
739	Farley	G 22	Iowa
138	*Farley	D 9	Mass.
111	Farley	F 5	Mo.
175	Farley	D 21	N. M.
75	*Farlin	I 9	Iowa
132	*Farlington	M 24	Kan.
40	*Farmdale	N 9	Fla.
....	Farmdale	G 13	Ill.
100	*Farmdale (Kinsman)	D 20	Ohio
110	*Farmer	G 9	N. C.
930	▲Farmer	D 6	Ohio
130	Farmer	L 21	S. D.
81	Farmer	H 16	Wash.
1833	Farmer City	H 17	Ill.
236	Farmers	F 20	Ky.
1005	Farmersburg	L 6	Ind.
296	Farmersburg	D 21	Iowa
300	*Farmers Exchange	O 8	Tenn.
30	*Farmers Fork	J 19	Va.
....	*Farmers Store	K 17	Va.
60	*Farmersville	K 12	Ala.
800	Farmersville	K 13	Calif.
558	Farmersville	J 12	Ill.
50	Farmersville (Farmersville Sta.)	P 6	N. Y.
464	Farmersville	L 6	Ohio
200	*Farmersville	O 19	Pa.
2206	Farmersville	D 20	Tex.
19	*Farmersville	M 19	Wis.
50	*Farmersville Sta. (Farmersville)	P 6	N. Y.
1428	Farmerville	B 10	La.
125	*Farmhaven	I 12	Miss.
....	Farmingdale	N 9	Me.
609	Farmingdale	I 19	N. J.
3524	Farmingdale	H 7	N. Y.
50	Farmingdale	K 4	S. D.
40	*Farmington	C 5	Ark.
263	*Farmington	H 9	Calif.
1323	Farmington	F 12	Conn.
....	Farmington	F 11	Conn.
120	*Farmington	H 21	Del.
165	*Farmington	F 13	Ga.
2225	Farmington	F 10	Ill.
968	Farmington	Q 19	Iowa
54	*Farmington	E 23	Kan.
134	*Farmington	K 6	Ky.
1737	Farmington	L 7	Me.
110	*Farmington	B 18	Md.
1510	Farmington	P 22	Mich.
1580	Farmington	O 17	Minn.
3738	Farmington	M 20	Mo.
20	Farmington	F 8	Mont.
2500	Farmington	N 18	N. H.
2161	Farmington	C 4	N. M.
150	Farmington	E 6	N. C.
650	Farmington	D 19	Ohio
385	*Farmington	Q 5	Pa.
155	*Farmington	P 11	Tenn.
1211	Farmington	E 11	Utah
341	Farmington	J 25	Wash.
880	Farmington	D 13	W. Va.
445	Farmington Falls	L 7	Me.
914	Farmland	H 21	Ind.
2980	Farmville	F 18	N. C.
3475	Farmville	N 13	Va.
346	Farnam	M 12	Neb.
250	Farnams	D 3	Mass.
200	*Farner	Q 18	Tenn.
388	Farnham	O 3	N. Y.
200	*Farnham	K 20	Va.
425	Farnhamville	H 9	Iowa
250	Farnhurst	B 21	Del.
10	Farnsworth	J 20	S. D.
25	*Farnsworth	A 5	Tex.
1500	Farnumsville	H 15	Mass.
8	*Faro	N 20	Mo.
800	Farr (Capps)	O 16	Colo.
500	*Farraday	J 22	Ky.
496	Farragut	P 5	Iowa
225	Farrandsville	I 13	Pa.
16	*Farrar	G 11	Ga.
36	*Farrar	K 13	Iowa
75	*Farrar	M 22	Mo.
120	Farrar	H 20	Tex.
175	Farrell	C 8	Miss.
13899	Farrell	I 1	Pa.
200	Farrington (West Danville)	E 16	Vt.
300	Farris	P 19	Okla.
57	*Farrsville	H 25	Tex.
25	Farry	B 6	Okla.
300	Farris	O 19	Okla.
....	*Far Rockaway	H 6	N. Y.
86	*Farson	N 18	Iowa
45	Farson	M 7	Wyo.
538	Farwell	M 16	Mich.
132	Farwell	K 7	Minn.
200	Farwell	K 16	Neb.
20	Farwell	K 20	S. D.
647	Farwell	A 7	Tex.
350	*Fashing	N 16	Tex.
300	*Fastrill	G 22	Tex.
127	*Fate	D 20	Tex.
50	*Faubin	D 10	Ore.
45	*Faubush	J 17	Ky.
150	*Faucett	E 5	Mo.
50	*Faulkner	F 14	Iowa
80	*Faulkner	O 24	Kan.
50	Faulkner (Lothair)	N 11	Md.
5	Faulkner	A 5	Okla.
747	Faulkton	F 16	S. D.
185	Faunsdale	J 8	Ala.
200	Faust (Tupper Lake Jc.)	G 20	N. Y.
20	*Faust	N 8	N. C.
150	Favoretta (Favorite)	E 19	Fla.
13	Fawn	I 21	Okla.
320	Fawn Grove	R 18	Pa.
50	*Fawnskin	M 21	Calif.
178	Faxon	N 7	Okla.
43	*Faxon	L 7	Tenn.
150	Fay	B 10	Ill.
6	Fay	M 19	Ohio
115	Fay	G 7	Okla.
400	Fayal	F 19	Minn.
100	*Faye	F 21	Ky.
2668	Fayette	E 7	Ala.
....	Fayette	I 13	Ind.
1162	Fayette	E 19	Iowa
....	Fayette	K 7	La.
68	Fayette	M 7	Me.
50	*Fayette	G 9	Mich.
907	Fayette	M 5	Miss.
2608	Fayette	G 12	Mo.
250	Fayette	N 12	N. Y.
10	Fayette	K 5	N. D.
912	Fayette	C 7	Ohio
207	Fayette	J 11	Utah
40	Fayette	M 9	W. Va.
1598	Fayette City	O 4	Pa.
80	*Fayette Jc. (Vale)	C 5	Ark.
643	*Fayetteville	H 15	Ala.
8212	Fayetteville	C 5	Ark.
832	Fayetteville	G 5	Ga.
2172	Fayetteville	M 15	N. Y.
17428	Fayetteville	I 13	N. C.
394	*Fayetteville	N 8	Ohio
25	Fayetteville	H 6	Ore.
800	Fayetteville (West Fayetteville)	P 13	Pa.
4684	Fayetteville	Q 11	Tenn.
445	Fayetteville	K 20	Tex.
1347	Fayetteville	M 8	W. Va.
10	Faysville	Q 4	Tex.
525	Fayville	G 16	Mass.
50	Faywood	N 5	N. M.
50	Faywood	N 4	N. M.
62	*Fazenda	D 23	Tex.
61	Fearer	L 1	Md.
150	*Fearns Springs	H 19	Miss.
163	*Feasterville	O 24	Pa.
750	*Feather Falls	E 8	Calif.
103	Featherston	K 21	Okla.
....	Featherville	N 8	Idaho
100	Fed (Clear Creek Jc.)	H 23	Ky.
....	Federal, see Flat River		Mo.
375	*Federal	N 2	Pa.
35	Federal	E 8	W. Va.
10	Federal	Q 21	Wyo.
269	Federal Dam	G 12	Minn.
275	Federal Point	D 17	Fla.
1748	Federalsburg	K 20	Md.
5	Federman	R 21	Mich.
225	Fedora	K 21	S. D.
60	*Fedscreek	H 24	Ky.
1800	Feeding Hills	I 7	Mass.
154	*Feesburg	P 8	Ohio
400	*Felch	D 9	Mich.
500	*Felda	L 19	Fla.
40	Feldman	L 18	Ariz.
641	Felicity	P 8	Ohio
12	*Felicity Jc.	P 8	Ohio
260	Felida	Q 6	Wash.
....	*Felix	M 19	N. M.
150	*Felix (Ogletown)	P 7	Pa.
21	*Felixville	J 15	La.
1500	Fellows	M 12	Calif.
68	*Fellsburg	L 10	Kan.
643	Fellsmere	I 21	Fla.
208	Felsenthal	R 13	Ark.
50	Felt	M 23	Idaho
200	Felt	R 1	Okla.
350	Felton	K 6	Calif.
442	Felton	H 22	Del.
100	*Felton	E 2	Ga.
200	*Felton	G 3	Minn.
421	Felton	Q 18	Pa.
....	Felts	P 1	Tenn.
500	*Felts Mills	H 16	N. Y.
....	*Felty	I 20	Ky.
125	*Fence	N 8	Wis.
380	*Fender (Eldorado)	N 12	Ga.
28	Fendley	L 8	Ark.
90	*Fenelton	K 4	Pa.
57	Fenn	H 5	Idaho
25	*Fenner	N 18	Calif.
1592	Fennimore	G 20	Wis.
643	Fennville	P 11	Mich.
68	*Fenter	K 11	Ark.
100	Fenton	C 10	Ill.
385	Fenton	C 9	Iowa
350	*Fenton	L 8	La.
3377	Fenton	O 20	Mich.
171	*Fenton	J 19	Mo.
55	*Fentress	G 17	Miss.
269	Fentress	L 18	Tex.
265	Fentress	Q 22	Va.
15	*Fenwick	M 11	Md.
100	Fenwick	N 14	Mich.
....	Fenwick	O 15	S. C.
550	Fenwick	K 10	W. Va.
156	*Fenwood	I 13	Wis.
86	*Ferda	K 14	Ark.
150	*Ferdig	H 14	Mont.
223	Ferdinand	H 5	Idaho
990	Ferdinand	Q 10	Ind.
6	Fergus	H 15	Mont.
10848	Fergus Falls	J 5	Minn.
40	*Ferguson (Crumrod)	L 18	Ark.
183	Ferguson	J 15	Iowa
50	*Ferguson	J 10	Ky.
517	Ferguson (Luretha)	J 17	Ky.
5724	Ferguson	I 20	Mo.
60	*Ferguson	D 4	N. C.
64	Ferguson	F 8	Okla.
....	Ferguson	J 17	S. C.
82	*Ferguson	M 2	W. Va.
25	*Fern	D 6	Calif.
160	*Fern	H 5	Pa.
50	*Fern	N 8	Wis.
110	*Fernald	I 13	Iowa
3492	Fernandina	B 17	Fla.
20	*Fernando	Q 5	Tex.
80	*Fernbank	F 5	Ala.
17	*Ferncliff	K 14	Va.
20	*Ferndale	I 11	Ark.
901	Ferndale	D 1	Calif.
200	*Ferndale	G 17	Fla.
1200	Ferndale	G 14	Md.
22523	Ferndale	P 22	Mich.
500	*Ferndale	C 2	N. Y.
....	Ferndale	B 20	Ore.
150	Ferndale	M 23	Pa.
2740	Ferndale	N 7	Pa.
717	Ferndale	C 7	Wash.
200	*Ferndale (Garrison)	N 6	W. Va.
100	Ferney	E 20	S. D.
800	*Fern Glen	J 19	Pa.
418	Fernley	G 4	Nev.
120	*Fern Park	G 19	Fla.
54	*Fernridge	J 22	Pa.
1200	*Fernside (Egan)	E 8	Ga.
150	Fernwood	E 5	Idaho
800	Fernwood	O 9	Miss.
212	Fernwood	J 15	N. Y.
700	*Fernwood	P 23	Pa.
14	Fero	F 14	N. D.
31	*Ferrell	I 18	Va.
20	*Ferrellsburg	M 3	W. Va.
134	*Ferrelview	F 5	Mo.
2857	Ferriday	G 13	La.
272	Ferris	G 5	Ill.
....	Ferris	I 4	Pa.
1436	Ferris	E 19	Tex.
350	Ferrisburg	G 5	Vt.
515	Ferron	K 15	Utah
5	*Ferron Park	C 8	Wis.
521	Ferrum	P 6	Va.
128	*Ferry	M 11	Mich.
10	Ferry	B 19	Wash.
	Ferry Point, see Richmont Point		Calif.
500	Ferrysburg	O 11	Mich.
306	Ferryville	F 19	Wis.
75	*Fertigs	H 5	Pa.
276	Fertile	C 13	Iowa
907	Fertile	F 4	Minn.
50	Fessenden	E 14	Fla.
902	Fessenden	J 15	N. D.
160	*Festina	B 19	Iowa
4620	Festus	K 20	Mo.
28	*Feterita	O 3	Kan.
300	*Fetters Hot Springs	G 3	Calif.
12	*Fetzer	K 21	Tex.
350	*Feura Bush	O 23	N. Y.
16	Fewell	N 23	Okla.
175	Fiatt	G 10	Ill.
60	Fiborn (Fibron Quarry)	F 15	Mich.
....	Fiborn Jc.	F 15	Mich.
60	*Fibre	F 16	Mich.
182	*Ficklin	G 16	Ga.
60	*Ficklin	J 19	Ill.
250	*Fiddletown	G 10	Calif.
146	Fidelity	K 10	Ill.
50	Fidelity (Shoopman)	K 17	Ky.
200	Fidelity	K 7	Ohio
....	*Field	I 20	Mo.
519	▲Field	H 23	N. M.
59	Field (Puertecito)	I 8	N. M.
17	Field (Fields Sta.)	G 15	Pa.
1800	Fieldale	Q 7	Va.
100	Fieldbrook	C 1	Calif.
63	*Field Creek	I 15	Tex.
114	*Fielden	F 22	Ky.
329	Fielding	B 10	Utah
100	*Fieldmore Springs (East Titusville)	F 3	Pa.
217	*Fieldon	L 8	Ill.
25	*Fields	J 5	La.
25	Fields	Q 20	Ore.
537	Fieldsboro	J 13	N. J.
178	*Fieldsboro (Walstonburg)	G 17	N. C.
200	*Fields Landing	D 1	Calif.
105	*Fieldton	B 9	Tex.
500	Fierro	M 5	N. M.
100	Fife	G 6	Ga.
32	Fife	G 11	Mont.
10	Fife	K 16	Ore.
31	Fife	H 14	Tex.
125	Fife	L 14	Va.
303	Fife Lake	I 13	Mich.
200	Fifield	H 8	Wis.
25	*Fifty Lakes	H 12	Minn.
40	*Fifty-six	C 13	Ark.
100	*Fig	C 3	N. C.
100	*Figarden	K 10	Calif.
19	*Figsboro	Q 7	Va.
18	*Figure Five	F 4	Ark.
130	*Filbert	A 12	S. C.
1231	Filbert	R 6	W. Va.
18	*File	K 17	Va.
1239	Filer	Q 11	Idaho
320	Filer City	K 11	Mich.
5	*Filion	K 23	Mich.
174	Filley	N 22	Neb.
3252	Fillmore	N 14	Calif.
458	Fillmore	L 14	Ill.
350	Fillmore	J 10	Ind.
36	*Fillmore	H 19	Ky.
269	Fillmore	C 4	Mo.
518	Fillmore	P 7	N. Y.
95	Fillmore	G 15	N. D.
113	Fillmore	O 17	Okla.
1785	Fillmore	K 9	Utah
150	Fillmore	O 18	Wis.
36	*Fillmore	G 20	Ky.
51	*Filson	J 19	Ill.
87	*Filson (Bowen)	G 19	Ky.
50	*Filston (Phillipston)	K 13	La.
72	*Fincastle	G 20	Ky.
67	*Fincastle	O 9	Ohio
442	Fincastle	M 7	Va.
9	Finch	K 19	Mont.
52	*Finchburg	M 9	Ala.
....	Fincher	B 7	Fla.
44	*Finchley	Q 13	Va.
115	*Finchville	F 15	Ky.
55	*Finchville	M 18	Md.
5	Finchville	J 12	Neb.
150	Finderne	F 14	N. J.
688	Findlay	J 16	Ill.
20228	Findlay	F 10	Ohio
257	Findley Lake	Q 1	N. Y.
42	*Findon	J 11	Mont.
200	*Fine	F 18	N. Y.
75	*Fine Creek Mills	M 15	Va.
14	*Fines	I 16	Va.
296	*Finesville	D 10	N. J.
20	*Fineview	H 15	N. Y.
300	Fingal	N 21	N. D.
350	Finger	P 5	Tenn.
350	Fingerville	A 8	S. C.
100	Finkbine	K 13	Miss.
310	*Finksburg	C 10	Md.
16	*Finland	F 23	Minn.
62	*Finlay	H 2	Tex.
225	Finlayson	J 17	Minn.
33	*Finley	G 5	Calif.
35	*Finley	H 15	Ky.
19	*Finley	D 3	N. C.
677	Finley	J 21	N. D.
145	Finley	O 21	Okla.
350	Finley	M 3	Tenn.
583	*Finley	O 18	Wash.
25	*Finley	H 15	Wis.
129	Finleyson	K 11	Ga.
699	Finleyville	N 3	Pa.
....	Finlow, see Brooklyn		W. Va.
89	*Finly (Reedville)	J 16	Ind.
17	*Finn	H 6	Mont.
49	*Finney	J 13	Ky.
175	Finney (Coulwood)	D 7	Va.
43	*Finneywood	P 12	Va.
200	Fir	E 8	Wash.
704	Firebaugh	J 9	Calif.
250	Firebrick	C 21	Ky.
100	*Firebrick	R 13	Ohio
250	Fireco	P 8	W. Va.
212	*Fire Creek	M 8	W. Va.
148	Firesteel	E 10	S. D.
262	Firestone	E 15	Colo.
....	*Firestone Park, (Florence)	N 16	Calif.
60	*Firstfork	H 11	Pa.
31	Firstview	J 22	Colo.
242	*Firth	O 19	Idaho
323	Firth	M 22	Neb.
500	Firthcliffe	E 3	N. Y.
35	*Fischer Store	K 17	Tex.
20	*Fish Camp	I 11	Calif.
75	*Fish Creek	L 16	N. Y.
250	Fish Creek	R 11	Wis.
84	*Fishdam	K 24	Tenn.
259	Fisher	F 18	Ark.
754	Fisher	H 18	Ill.
50	*Fisher	H 12	Ky.
500	Fisher	G 6	La.
333	Fisher	E 2	Minn.
68	Fisher	F 17	Okla.
13	Fisher	H 4	Ore.
311	Fisher	H 6	Pa.
134	Fisher	Q 7	Wash.
125	*Fisher	G 19	W. Va.
164	Fishers (Fishers Station)	I 15	Ind.
220	Fishers	M 10	N. Y.
100	Fishers Ferry	K 17	Pa.
75	*Fishers Hill	F 13	Va.
750	*Fishers Island	H 8	N. Y.
62	*Fishers Landing	H 15	N. Y.
118	*Fishersville	J 11	Va.
190	*Fishertown	O 9	Pa.
60	*Fisherville	E 15	Ky.
1375	Fisherville	H 15	Mass.
105	*Fisherville	M 16	Pa.
125	Fish Haven	R 22	Idaho
150	Fish House	K 9	N. J.
....	*Fishing Bridge	B 3	Wyo.
893	Fishing Creek	O 17	Md.
258	Fishing Creek	R 11	N. J.
720	Fishkill	D 5	N. Y.
65	*Fishkill Plains	D 5	N. Y.
231	Fishs Eddy	R 18	N. Y.
42	Fishtail	M 14	Mont.
250	*Fishtrap	H 24	Ky.
2	Fishtrap	L 5	Mont.
50	Fishtrap	I 22	Wash.
50	Fisk	A 14	Ala.
386	Fisk	Q 21	Mo.
31	*Fisk	H 14	Tex.
60	*Fisk	M 16	Wis.
271	Fiskburg	C 17	Ky.
650	Fiskdale	H 11	Mass.

Pop.	Place	Index	State

1500 Fiskeville (Arkwright), G 12....R. I.
29*Fitch, B 21.....Ky.
46*Fitchburg, G 19....Ky.
41824 Fitchburg, C 14....Mass.
80*Fitchburg, J 20....Wis.
85*Fitchetts, M 21....Va.
350*Fitchville, I 20....Conn.
200 Fitchville, E 14....Ohio
423 Fithian, H 21....Ill.
45*Fitler, I 6....Miss.
7388 Fitzgerald, M 13....Ga.
70*Fitzhugh, F 17....Ark.
19*Fitzhugh, E 9....Miss.
250 Fitzhugh, M 15....Okla.
29*Fitzhugh, G 16....Va.
100 Fitzpatrick, K 18....Ala.
620*Fitzpatrick, O 8....W. Va.
....*Fitzsimmons (Bunell), F 17....Colo.
250 Fitzwilliam, R 8....N. H.
168 Fitzwilliam (Fitzwilliam Depot), R 8....N. H.
170*Five Corners, N 13....N. Y.
....*Five Forks, H 8....W. Va.
150 Five Islands, P 9....Me.
....; Fivemile, I 9....Ala.
778 Fivepoints, H 21....Ala.
....; Five Points, D 11....Utah
....; Five Points Jc., D 11....Utah
25*Fixer, G 20....Ky.
217▲Flag, D 12....Ark.
50 Flag Center, B 15....Ill.
44*Flagg, N 4....Tex.
506 Flagler, H 21....Colo.
175 Flagler, L 14....Iowa
133*Flagler Beach (Ocean City), E 19....Fla.
1500*Flag Pond, F 13....Tenn.
5050 Flagstaff, G 14....Ariz.
125 Flagstaff, J 1....Me.
65*Flagtown, G 11....N. J.
663 Flanagan, F 16....Ill.
350 Flanders, B 13....N. J.
2212 Flandreau, J 25....S. D.
25 Flanigan, E 2....Nev.
357 Flasher, O 10....N. D.
74*Flat, G 20....Ky.
75*Flat, L 15....Mo.
113*Flat, H 18....Tex.
102*Flatbrookville, B 14....N. J.
600 Flat Creek, F 11....Ala.
30*Flat Creek, F 10....La.
121*Flatcreek, O 12....Tenn.
124*Flatgap, G 22....Ky.
67*Flat Gap, 3C 5....Va.
500 Flat Lick, J 19....Ky.
1024 Flatonia, L 19....Tex.
31*Flatbridge, E 10....Va.
5401 Flat River (Federal), L 19....Mo.
75*Flat Rock, A 17....Ala.
585 Flat Rock, L 22....Ill.
190 Flat Rock, L 16....Ind.
40*Flat Rock, K 17....Ky.
1467 Flat Rock, Q 22....Mich.
319 Flat Rock, Q 8....N. C.
1103*Flat Rock (East Flat Rock), Q 8....N. C.
360 Flat Rock, E 12....Ohio
27 Flatrun, I 15....Va.
7 Flats, I 9....Neb.
100*Flats, Q 4....N. C.
28*Flats, E 19....W. Va.
220*Flattop, F 12....Ala.
80*Flattop, P 15....Tenn.
50*Flat Top, P 8....W. Va.
10 Flat Top, K 22....Wyo.
100 Flat Top Yard (Yards), ...Va.
126 Flatwillow, I 16....Mont.
10*Flatwood, K 9....Ala.
125*Flatwoods, D 22....Ky.
45*Flatwoods, K 8....La.
172 Flatwoods, Q 19....Mo.
57*Flat Woods, O 7....Tenn.
308 Flat Woods, I 11....W. Va.
362 Flaxton, D 7....N. D.
250 Flaxville, C 22....Mont.
312 Fleeton, K 21....Va.
279 Fleetville, F 21....Pa.
300*Fleetwood, C 3 N C.
60 Fleetwood, Q 11....Okla.
2254 Fleetwood, M 21....Pa.
546 Fleischmanns, Q 21....N. Y.
400 Fleming, C 21....Colo.
50*Fleming, L 23....Ga.
1193 Fleming, L 23....Ky.
50 Fleming, G 7....Mo.
68*Fleming, M 13....N. Y.
4*Fleming, N 17....Ohio
350 Fleming, K 12....Pa.
1542 Flemingsburg, E 19....Ky.
30 Flemingsburg Jc., D 19....Ky.
14 Flemington, L 22....Ga.
255 Flemington, M 9....Mo.
2617 Flemington, G 11....N. J.
1301 Flemington, I 13....Pa.
690 Flemington, E 13....W. Va.
22*Flener, I 11....Ky.
272 Flensburg, K 11....Minn.
75*Fletcher, D 10....Fla.
30*Fletcher, J 19....Ind.
125*Fletcher, K 18....Mo.
500*Fletcher, P 8....W. Va.
436 Fletcher, J 8....Ohio
789 Fletcher, L 9....Okla.
90 Fletcher, J 25....Tex.
200 Fletcher, O 9....Vt.
75*Fletcher, I 13....W. Va.
86*Fletcher, I 6....W. Va.
152*Fletcher Bay, N 7....Wash.
200*Fletcher Park, O 19....Wyo.
200*Flicksville, K 23....Pa.
100*Flint, N 8....Ga.
100*Flint, J 22....Ind.
....*Flint (Flint Village), M 19....Mass.
151543 Flint, M 20....Mich.
25 Flint, E 24....Okla.
200*Flint, P 7....Va.
123*Flint, H 15....W. Va.
61*Flinthill, H 18....Mo.
250 Flint Hill, G 14....Va.
10 Flinton, O 10....Ill.
150 Flinton, L 9....Pa.
18*Flintsprings, H 10....Ky.
142*Flintstone, J 8....Ga.
150 Flint Stone, L 8....Md.
....*Flint Village (Flint), M 19....Mass.
350*Flintville, Q 12....Tenn.
245*Flippen, B 11....Ga.
325*Flippin, B 11....Ark.
75*Flippin, K 14....Ky.
13*Flog, P 1....W. Va.
95*Flom, G 5....Minn.
837 Flomaton, O 10....Ala.
212*Flomot, A 11....Tex.
571 Floodwood, H 17....Minn.
....Flora, A 16....La.
5474 Flora, M 18....Ill.
1468 Flora, F 12....Ind.
110*Flora, G 7....La.
509 Flora, J 10....Miss.
50 Flora, H 16....N. D.
153*Flora, O 16....Ohio
64 Flora, B 23....Ore.
50*Flora Dale, P 14....Pa.

50*Florahome, D 16....Fla.
92*Floral, F 15....Ark.
15*Floral, G 11....Ill.
2999 Florala, O 16....Ala.
300 Floral City, G 14....Fla.
12950 Floral Park, H 6....N. Y.
300 Flora Vista, C 5....N. M.
50*Floreffe, N 3....Pa.
15043 Florence, B 8....Ala.
1383 Florence, L 15....Ariz.
46*Florence, N 15....Ark.
....*Florence (Firestone Park), N 16....Calif.
2632 Florence, K 14....Colo.
89*Florence, L 3....Ga.
105*Florence, J 6....Ill.
139*Florence (Florence Sta.), B 12....Ill.
150 Florence, N 22....Ind.
1329 Florence, J 18....Kan.
776*Florence, B 17....Ky.
3500 Florence, F 7....Mass.
149*Florence, P 5....Minn.
368 Florence, K 11....Miss.
78*Florence, I 4....Mont.
150 Florence, I 4....Mont.
3800 Florence, J 12....N. J.
130*Florence, K 16....N. Y.
180*Florence, J 21....N. C.
43 Florence, J 3....Ore.
150*Florence, M 1....Pa.
16054 Florence, F 20....S. C.
254 Florence, F 22....S. D.
421 Florence, I 18....Tex.
300 Florence, K 7....Va.
300 Florence, R 8....Wash.
1353 Florence, N 8....Wis.
15 Florence Jc., L 15....Ariz.
....Florence Jc., K 7....Vt.
139*Florence Sta. (Florence), B 12....Ill.
928*Florence Villa, H 16....Fla.
....Florentine, K 7....Vt.
125*Florenton, H 19....Minn.
....Florenville, L 19....La.
1708 Floresville, M 17....Tex.
17*Florey, E 4....Tex.
1609 Florham Park, E 16....N. J.
100 Florida, B 4....Mass.
200 Florida, F 15....Mo.
25*Florida, N 6....N. M.
1000 Florida, E 3....N. Y.
752 Florida City, O 22....Fla.
53*Floridatown, M 3....Fla.
264 Florien, H 6....La.
200 Florin, G 8....Calif.
1100 Florin, O 18....Pa.
247 Floris, I 17....Iowa
20 Floris, Q 7....Okla.
62 Florissant, J 14....Colo.
1369 Florissant (St. Ferdinand), H 20....Mo.
38*Floriston, F 9....Calif.
35*Florosa, M 5....Fla.
56*Florress, F 21....Ky.
1270*Flossmoor, C 21....Ill.
16*Flournoy, E 6....Calif.
240 Flournoy, G 7....Ky.
1150*Flourtown, O 23....Pa.
240 Flovilla, H 9....Ga.
1*Flower, I 10....W. Va.
59*Floweree, J 7....Miss.
23 Floweree, F 10....Mont.
150*Flowerfield, N 14....Mich.
50*Flowerfield, H 8....N. Y.
666*Flower Hill, H 7....N. Y.
506 Flowery Branch, E 9....Ga.
15 Flowing Wells, C 19....Tex.
352 Floyd, O 16....Iowa
100 Floyd, B 13....La.
20*Floyd, J 23....N. M.
25 Floyd, H 4....Pa.
....Floyd, H 11....Pa.
250*Floyd, C 20....Tex.
479*Floyd, P 5....Va.
2726 Floydada, B 11....Tex.
95*Floydale (Floyd Dale), ...S. C.
35 Floyd Hill, G 13....Colo.
182 Floyds Knobs, P 16....Ind.
....Fluff, see Ellwood.
....Md.
31*Fluker, J 17....La.
1806 Flushing, N 19....Mich.
....Flushing, G 6....N. Y.
1217 Flushing, J 18....Ohio
127*Fluvanna, Q 3....N. Y.
265 Fluvanna, D 11....Tex.
11 Flux, F 8....Utah
200*Fly, M 19....Ohio
325 Flycreek, N 19....N. Y.
19*Flying H, K 20....N. M.
419 Flynn, H 21....Tex.
350*Foard City, B 13....Tex.
50*Fob, Q 15....Okla.
35*Fodice, M 22....Tex.
34 Fogel, M 25....Okla.
513*Fogelsville, M 22....Pa.
38*Fogertown, I 19....Ky.
2729 Foggsburg, G 21....Ark.
16*Foil, Q 13....Ark.
....Fola, K 8....W. Va.
1592*Folcroft, P 23....Pa.
864 Foley, Q 7....Ala.
1200*Foley, C 8....Fla.
961 Foley, L 13....Minn.
197 Foley, S 18....Ala.
12 Foley, K 20....Neb.
....Foley, H 6....Okla.
7 Foley, Q 3....S. D.
6*Foleysprings, J 5....Ore.
1024 Folkston, P 20....Ga.
53*Folkstone, M 18....N. C.
178 Follansbee, O 24....W. Va.
80 Folly, D 15....Md.
30*Folly, K 21....Va.
55*Folly Beach, O 19....S. C.
9 Follyfarm, N 9....Ore.
1500 Folsom (Folsom City), G 8....Calif.
450 Folsom, K 18....La.
229 Folsom, N 12....N. J.
360 Folsom, B 22....N. M.
22 Folsom, P 17....Okla.
114*Folsom, Q 23....Pa.
30 Folsom, K 4....S. D.
500 Folsom, D 11....W. Va.
200 Folsomdale, K 5....Ohio
100 Folsomville, Q 7....Ind.
50*Fombell, K 8....Pa.
1188 Fonda, F 7....Iowa
1123 Fonda, M 21....N. Y.
13 Fonda, B 14....N. D.
16 Fonda, B 7....Pa.
....Fonda, B 7....Pa.
10 Fonds, H 16....Colo.
27200 Fond du Lac, N 17....Wis.
800 Fonde, K 19....Ky.
....Fonesswood, J 19....Va.
7200 Fontana, K 7....Calif.
174 Fontana, I 24....Kan.
150 Fontana, P 3....N. C.
60*Fontana, N 18....Pa.
461 Fontana, M 18....Wis.
797 Fontanelle, M 8....Iowa
128 Fontelle, J 22....Neb.
90*Fontenelle, K 2....Wyo.
450 Fontanet, K 7....Ind.

40*Fonthill, I 16....W. Va.
21 Fonzo, G 9....W. Va.
250 Foosland, H 18....Ill.
50*Foote, H 6....Miss.
130 Footville, C 19....Ohio
459 Footville, K 22....Wis.
96 Forada, K 8....Minn.
67 Ford City, C 6....Mo.
5795 Ford City, K 5....Pa.
585*Ford Cliff, K 5....Pa.
85 Forder, K 19....Colo.
331 Fordland, O 11....Mo.
....Fordney, N 19....Mich.
261 Fort Atkinson, C 18....Iowa
6153 Fort Atkinson, M 20....Wis.
325 Fort Barnwell, H 18....N. C.
4746 Fords, G 17....N. J.
457 Fords Branch, H 23....Ky.
250*Fords Ferry, H 7....Ky.
587 Fordsville, H 11....Ky.
30*Fordtown, L 24....Tenn.
65*Fordtran, M 19....Tex.
439 Fordville, C 21....N. D.
500 Fordwick, J 9....Va.
3429 Fordyce, N 12....Ark.
202 Fordyce, E 20....Neb.
16*Forecamp, H 9....Wash.
1007 Foreman (New Rocky Comfort), N 4....Ark.
....Fore River, G 20....Mass.
100 Forest, K 9....Calif.
....Forest, see Blackbird....Del.
33 Forest, H 4....Idaho
450 Forest, G 13....Ind.
100*Forest, B 13....La.
60*Forest (Forest Station), H 20....Me.
2735 Forest, K 15....Miss.
116*Forest, C 23....N. Y.
1083 Forest, G 10....Ohio
500*Forest, G 22....Tex.
100 Forest, N 9....Va.
25 Forest, M 6....Wash.
300 Forestburg, K 20....S. D.
200 Forestburg, C 17....Tex.
240 Forest City, H 11....Ill.
2545 Forest City, C 12....Iowa
64 Forest City, H 20....Me.
548 Forest City, K 9....N. C.
5035 Forest City, H 1....N. C.
4266 Forest City, F 22....Pa.
65 Forest City, F 13....S. D.
6*Forest Cottage, K 15....Ky.
61*Forestdale, M 24....Mass.
765 Forestdale, A 11....R. I.
33 Forest Dale, J 7....Vt.
1306 Forester, I 6....Ark.
64*Forest Glen, E 3....Calif.
462▲*Forest Glen, L 13....Ga.
1000*Forest Glen, G 9....Md.
95*Forest Green, F 11....Mo.
50*Forestgrove, I 15....Mont.
2440 Forest Grove, D 6....Ore.
60*Forest Grove, N 24....Pa.
200 Foresthill, G 9....Calif.
302 Forest Hill, I 9....La.
400 Forest Hill, C 16....Md.
127 Forest Hill, N 17....Mich.
670 Forest Hill, Q 2....Tenn.
200*Forest Hill, P 10....W. Va.
....Forest Hills, F 19, O 4 Mass.
5248*Forest Hills, L 3....Pa.
125 Forest Home, L 12....Ala.
....*Forest Home, M 21....Ala.
250 Forest Jc., O 15....Wis.
500*Forest Knolls, C 14, H 4 ....Calif.
220 Forest Lake, D 12....Mich.
1120 Forest Lake, M 17....Minn.
265 Foreston, L 14....Minn.
210*Foreston, I 15....S. C.
577*Forest Park, F 6....Ga.
14840*Forest Park, C 21....Ill.
598 Forest Park, P 8....Mo.
....*Forest Park, H 24....N. Y.
416 Forestport, J 18....N. Y.
100*Forest Ranch, F 7....Calif.
207 Forest River, D 21....Mass.
50*Forest River, G 22....N. D.
20 Forest Run, O 16....Ohio
60*Forest Sta. (Forest), H 20 ....Mo.
350 Forestville, H 4....Calif.
400 Forestville, G 11....Conn.
12*Forestville, I 13....Ky.
500 Forestville, J 12....Md.
156 Forestville, L 24....Mich.
692 Forestville, P 3....N. Y.
626 Forestville (Harrisville), I 3....Pa.
10 Forestville, F 23....S. D.
66*Forestville, G 12....Va.
246 Forestville, P 13....Wis.
428 Forgan, Q 8....Okla.
311 Fork, Laramie, W 23....Pa.
178 Forestell, H 18....Mo.
80 Fork, D 15....Md.
40 Fork, E 7....N. C.
168*Fork, F 22....S. C.
512 Forked River, L 19....N. J.
42*Forker (Boomer), E 11.Mo.
75*Fork Mtn., M 18....Tenn.
800 Fork Logan, G 14....Colo.
75*Fork Ridge, K 19....Minn.
75*Fork Ridge, C 9....Tenn.
6*Forks, E 17....Mont.
....Forks, E 10....N. M.
....Forks, see Cheektowaga, N 5....N. Y.
600 Forks, F 2....Wash.
371 Forkshoals, D 6....S. C.
47 Forks of Buffalo, I 11....Va.
172*Forks of Elkhorn (Elsinore), E 16....Ky.
100*Forks of Salmon, B 5.Calif.
100 Forkton, G 19....Pa.
108*Forksville, G 17....Pa.
50*Forksville (Skelton), Q 14 ....Va.
100*Forkton, K 14....Ky.
200*Fork Union, L 13....Va.
55*Fork Union (Cohasset), ...Va.
65*Forkville (Beach), J 15 Miss.
15 Forman, Q 16....Ill.
500 Forman, Q 22....N. D.
23*Forman, F 19....Ark.
170*Formosa, F 12....Ark.
200*Formosa, G 18....Fla.
25*Formosa, P 12....Pa.

....Formosa Jc., M 11....Ill.
293 Formoso, D 14....Kan.
125*Forney, J 21....Ala.
50 Forney, K 12....Idaho
1295 Forney, N 20....Okla.
1504 Fornfelt, O 23....Mo.
110 Forrest, J 20....Ill.
947 Forrest, F 18....Ill.
200 Forrest, H 9....Ohio
222 Forrest, B 16....Okla.
250 Forbes, F 18....Minn.
130 Forbes, D 4....Mo.
52*Forbes, M 9....N. C.
268 Forbes, R 18....N. D.
619*Forbes Road, N 5....Pa.
231 Forbestown, P 8....Calif.
63*Forbing, D 5....La.
200*Forbus, L 5....Tenn.
1200*Force, I 10....Pa.
296 Ford, M 8....Kan.
250 Ford, G 13....Ky.
....Ford, Q 20....Mich.
310 Ford, R 22....Miss.
210 Ford, O 16....Va.
50 Ford, G 22....Wash.
59 Forrest (Plain), H 24..N. M.
5699 Forrest City, H 19....Ark.
20 Forrest Hall, N 13....Md.
992 Forreston, B 12....Ill.
300*Forreston, F 19....Tex.
....Forrestville, D 3....Ga.
175*Forsan, F 11....Tex.
91*Forshee, M 19....Va.
2372 Forsyth, H 10....Ga.
350 Forsyth, I 15....Ill.
200 Forsyth (Little Lake), ...Mich.
290*Forsyth, N 10....Mo.
1096 Forsyth, K 20....Mont.
550 Forsythe (Oakville), Q 1....Tenn.
200*Fort Adams, P 3....Miss.
450 Fort Adams, L 17....R. I.
439 Fort Ann, K 24....N. Y.
600 Fort Apache, J 21....Ariz.
325*Fort Ashby (Alaska), E 19....W. Va.
261 Fort Atkinson, C 18....Iowa
....Fort Barrancas, M 2....Fla.
40 Fort Barry, C 15....Calif.
1000*Fort Bayard, M 4....N. M.
19 Fort Belknap, D 15....Mont.
131*Fort Bellefontaine (Ruegg), H 19....Mo.
....*Fort Belvoir, G 17....Va.
490 Fort Benning, K 4....Ga.
1227 Fort Benning Jc., J 3....Ga.
1227 Fort Benton, F 12....Mont.
462 Fort Bidwell, B 11....Calif.
500*Fort Blackmore, E 6....Va.
....Fort Bliss, G 1....Tex.
3235 Fort Bragg, F 2....Calif.
1552 Fort Bragg, I 12....N. C.
205*Fort Branch, O 4....W. Va.
100*Fort Bridger, Q 3....Wyo.
500 Fort Brown, Q 5....Tex.
2 Fort Browning, D 7 .Mont.
20 Fort Buford (Buford), H 1....N. D.
329 Fort Calhoun, J 24....Neb.
35 Fort Casey, F 17....Wash.
128*Fort Chadbourne, F 12..Tex.
....Fort Christmas, see Christmas....Fla.
41 Fort Clark, I 10....N. D.
699 Fort Cobb, K 8....Okla.
12251 Fort Collins, C 14....Colo.
813 Fort Covington, C 20.N. Y.
75 Fort Crook, K 24....Neb.
425 Fort Davis, K 19....Ala.
800 Fort Davis, I 6....Tex.
600 Fort Defiance, E 24....Ariz.
....*Fort Defiance, J 11....Va.
1351 Fort Dennis, L 14....Ala.
1800 Fort Des Moines, L 12.Iowa
....*Fort Devens, H 15....Mass.
75*Fort Dick, B 1....Calif.
2904 Fort Dodge, G 10....Iowa
550 Fort Dodge, L 8....Kan.
50*Fort Douglas, E 8....Ark.
1071 Fort Douglas, E 8....Utah
100*Fort Drum, J 21....Pa.
104 Fort Duchesne, O 21....Utah
3620 Fort Edward, K 24....N. Y.
175*Fortescue, C 3....N. J.
250*Fortescue, P 19....N. J.
16 Fort Estill Jc., G 18....Ky.
50*Fort Ethan Allen, E 8...Vt.
250 Fort Eustis, N 20....Va.
2693■Fort Fairfield, C 20....Me.
139▲Fort Fred Steele (Fort Steele), N 14....Wyo.
44*Fort Gage, P 1....Ill.
1357 Fort Gaines, M 2....Ga.
1413 Fort Garland, H 23....Colo.
645 Fort Gay, L 1....W. Va.
50*Fort George C 16....Fla.
....Fort George G. Meade, H 13....Md.
15 Fort George G. Meade Jc., G 12....Md.
1233 Fort Gibson, G 22....Okla.
76*Fort Grant, L 21....Ariz.
150 Fort Green, I 21....Fla.
133*Fort Griffin, D 14....Tex.
100 Fort Hall, O 19....Idaho
200*Fort Hancock, H 2....Tex.
550*Fort Harrison, H 8....Mont.
50*Fort Henry, L 7....Tenn.
53*Fort Hill, Q 6....Pa.
1200*Fort Howard, D 13....Md.
1500 Fort Huachuca, P 20....Ariz.
300 Fort Hunter, M 16....Pa.
100 Fortine, C 3....Mont.
225*Fort Jackson, F 17....N. Y.
326 Fort Jennings, F 7....Ohio
868 Fort Johnson, M 22....N. Y.
360 Fort Jones, B 4....Calif.
2245 Fort Kent, A 15....Me.
133 Fort Keogh, J 21....Mont.
200 Fort Klamath, E 7....Ore.
310 Fort Landing, E 23....N. C.
311 Fort Laramie, W 23....Pa.
17996 Fort Lauderdale, M 24 Fla.
168 Fort Lawn, O 14....S. C.
4982 Fort Leavenworth, F 24 ....Kan.
9468 Fort Lee, D 21....N. J.
....Fort Lewis, J 7....Wash.
75*Fort Littleton, P 12....Pa.
800 Fort Logan, G 14....Colo.
....*Fort Lookout, K 15....S. D.
507 Fort Loramie (Loramie), I 6....Ohio
400 Fort Loudon, P 12....Pa.
1692*Fort Lupton (Lupton), M 15....Colo.
1180 Fort Lyon, M 20....Colo.
78*Fort Lyon, I 9....Mo.
400*Fort McCoy, K 15....Fla.
110*Fort McKavett, L 13....Tex.
14063 Fort Madison, O 21....Iowa
41*Fort Maginnis, H 14 Mont.
1000*Fort Meade, J 9....Fla.
....Fort Meade, I 16....Fla.
850*Fort Meade, K 3....S. D.
2919 Fort Mill, A 13....S. C.
314*Fort Mitchell, K 24....N. Y.
100*Fort Mitchell, J 23....Ala.
....Fort Monroe (Fortress Monroe), O 21....Va.
850 Fort Montgomery, E 5 ....N. Y.
4884 Fort Morgan, D 18....Colo.
386 Fort Motte, I 14....S. C.
2500 Fort Myer, F 18....Va.
....Fort Myer Heights, F18.Va.
10604 Fort Myers, L 16....Fla.

....*Fort Neal, F 7....W. Va.
46*Fort Necessity, E 12....La.
250 Fort Ogden, J 15....Fla.
800 Fort Oglethorpe, B 2....Ga.
41*Fort Palmer, M 5....Pa.
4424 Fort Payne, C 19....Ala.
4000 Fort Peck, E 20....Mont.
8040 Fort Pierce, J 23....Fla.
764 Fort Pierre, I 12....S. D.
59*Fort Pillow, N 2....Tenn.
2770 Fort Plain (South Fort Plain), M 20....N. Y.
85 Fort Ransom, O 21....N. D.
1123 Fort Recovery, I 5....Ohio
2000*Fortress Monroe (Fort Monroe), O 21....Va.
50 Fort Rice, O 12....N. D.
3500 Fort Riley, R 18....Kan.
126*Fort Ripley, J 12....Minn.
150*Fort Ritner, N 13....Ind.
175 Fort Robinson, E 3....Neb.
6 Fort Rock, M 12....Ore.
60*Fort Run, Q 20....W. Va.
550 Fort Russel, see Russell Q 1....Wyo.
....*Fort Sam Houston, M 16
100 Fort Saint Philip, Q 21..La.
10557 Fort Scott, K 25....Kan.
325*Fort Screven, L 5....Ga.
100 Fort Selden, N 10....N. M.
115*Fort Seneca, E 11....Ohio
28*Fort Seward, E 2....Calif.
15*Fort Seybert, I 18....W. Va.
85 Fort Shaw, G 9....Mont.
2600*Fort Sheridan, A 19....Ill.
....*Fort Sill, M 8....Okla.
....*Fort Slocum, F 6....N. Y.
36584 Fort Smith, F 4....Ark.
150*Fortson, J 3....Ga.
200 Fortson, E 7....W. Va.
50*Fort Spring, M 12....W. Va.
490 Fort Stanton, K 16....N. M.
139 Fort Steele, N 14....Wyo.
120 Fort Stevens, A 4....Ore.
3294 Fort Stockton, I 8....Tex.
1669 Fort Sumner, I 21....N. M.
100 Fort Terry, F 12....N. Y.
250 Fort Thomas, L 21....Ariz.
11034 Fort Thomas, B 18....Ky.
180 Fort Thompson, J 16...S. D.
50 Fort Ticonderoga, H 24....N. Y.
125 Fort Totten, H 17....N. D.
501 Fort Towson, P 22....Okla.
1413 Fortuna, D 1....Calif.
213 Fortuna, I 11....Mo.
214 Fortuna, C 2....N. D.
120 Fort Union, E 24....Mont.
4953 Fort Valley, J 9....Ga.
1463*Fortville, I 16....Ind.
150*Ft. Walton, M 5....Fla.
775*Fort Warren (Russell), ...Wyo.
150 Fort Washakie, J 9....Wyo.
415 Fort Washington, K 11.Md.
800*Fort Washington, O 23...Pa.
118410 Fort Wayne, D 19....Ind.
....Fort Wayne Jc., R 17.Mich.
317 Fort White, D 12....Fla.
14 Fort Wingate, F 3....N. M.
177662 Fort Worth, E 18....Tex.
50*Fort Wright, H 23....Wash.
1000 Fort Yates, Q 12....N. D.
6293 Forty Fort, H 20....Pa.
80*Forty Four, C 14....Ark.
25*Forum, C 7....Ark.
306 Foss, I 5....Okla.
78*Foss, C 4....Mo.
532 Fossil, F 15....Ore.
100 Fossil, N 3....Wyo.
50 Fossilville, O 9....Pa.
10 Fosston, C 7....Colo.
1271 Fosston, F 6....Minn.
94*Foster, C 18....Ky.
30*Foster, M 14....Ky.
293 Foster, K 6....Ore.
128 Foster, G 19....Neb.
100 Foster (Fosters), N 7..Ohio
141 Foster, M 12....Okla.
100 Foster, H 7....Ore.
375 Foster (Hop Bottom), F 21
250 Foster, D 7....R. I.
15*Foster, L 22....Tex.
22*Foster, M 21....Va.
33*Foster, M 5....W. Va.
650 Foster Center, E 5....R. I.
91 Foster City, G 6....Mich.
112*Fosterdale, O 1....N. Y.
49*Fosters, G 7....Ala.
150*Fosters, M 19....Mich.
315 Fosters Falls, P 3....Va.
311 Fostersville, O 12....Tenn.
35*Fostoria, K 14....Ala.
136 Fostoria, C 6....Iowa
104*Fostoria, F 19....Kan.
400 Fostoria, M 21....Mich.
13453 Fostoria, D 10....Ohio
1518 Fostoria, J 23....Tex.
363 Fouke, Q 6....Ark.
30*Fouke, L 18....Miss.
45*Foules, F 12....La.
....Foundry, N 20....N. H.
175*Foundryville, I 19....Pa.
163*Fount, J 19....Ky.
360*Fountain, M 10....Ala.
577 Fountain, J 16....Colo.
250 Fountain, N 10....Fla.
235 Fountain, L 11....Mich.
306 Fountain, R 21....Minn.
483 Fountain (Fountains), F 17....N. C.
15 Fountain, J 22....Ind.
491 Fountain City, L 22....Ind.
3917 Fountain City, M 19....Tenn.
985 Fountain City, D 15....Wis.
140*Fountain Green, G 7....Ill.
988 Fountain Green, I 13....Utah
71*Fountain Grove, E 10....Mo.
200*Fountain Head, L 12....Tenn.
215*Fountain Hill, Q 14....Ark.
4804 Fountain Hill, L 23....Pa.
1346 Fountain Inn, C 7....S. C.
334 Fountain Run, K 13....Ky.
250*Fountain Springs, K 18.Pa.
210 Fountaintown, I 19....Ind.
500*Fountainville, M 24....Pa.
35*Four Buttes, C 22....Mont.
20 Four Corners, E 24....Wyo.
500*Four Holes, K 15....S. C.
125*Four Lakes, K 23....Wash.
500*Fourmile, J 20....Ky.
828 Four Oaks, G 15....N. C.
500 Four States, D 12....W. Va.
20 Fowler, M 11....Ariz.
1531 Fowler, K 12....Calif.
968 Fowler, M 18....Colo.
100 Fowler, I 21....Ind.
1903 Fowler, M 18....Mich.
563 Fowler, N 7....Kan.
579 Fowler, O 17....Mich.
14 Fowler, D 17....Mont.
125 Fowler, F 17....N. Y.
500*Fowler (Nutwood), D 20....Ohio
15 Fowler Jc., E 12....Calif.
36 Fowler Knob, L 10...W. Va.

30*Fowlersville, I 18....Pa.
255 Fowlerton, G 18....Ind.
275 Fowlerton, O 15....Tex.
1118 Fowlerville, O 15....Mich.
250 Fowlerville, M 8....N. Y.
400 Fowlkes, N 3....Tenn.
100 Fowlstown, P 5....Ga.
25*Fox, D 13....Ark.
42*Fox, O 19....Ky.
93*Fox, H 6....Mich.
38 Fox, O 13....Okla.
20 Fox, G 18....Ore.
87*Fox, E 10....Tex.
4000 Foxboro, I 18....Mass.
125*Foxboro, C 5....Wis.
441 Foxburg, I 4....Pa.
1080*Fox Chapel Boro, L 3....Pa.
1000 Fox Hill (Riprapps), O 21.Va.
....Foxcroft, see Dover Foxcroft....Me.
250 Foxholm, F 9....N. D.
240 Foxhome, J 4....Minn.
1110 Fox Lake, A 19....Ill.
100 Foxlake, R 10....Minn.
1016 Fox Lake, R 18....Wis.
100 Fox Lake Jc., M 18....Wis.
100 Foxpark, R 18....Wyo.
1180*Fox Point, O 20....Wis.
7*Fox Ridge, G 6....S. D.
693*Fox River Grove, B 19...Ill.
5*Foxton, H 14....Colo.
....*Foxtown, H 19....Ky.
55*Foxwells, L 21....Va.
500 Foxworth, O 13....Miss.
78 Foyil, S 20....Okla.
8035*Frackville, K 19....Pa.
115*Fragaria, I 7....Wash.
100 Frame, J 7....W. Va.
175*Frametown, I 10....W. Va.
33214 Framingham, G 17....Mass.
....Framingham Center, F 16
150 Frances, O 17, R 6....Calif.
50 Frances, M 4....Wash.
804 Francesville, E 10....Ind.
5 Francis, G 15....Mo.
18*Francis, M 10....Mont.
370 Francis, L 19....Okla.
....Francis, J 8....Ore.
400 Francis, D 12....W. Va.
55*Francisco, A 16....Ala.
611 Francisco, D 21....Ind.
65*Francisco, C 7....Tex.
200 Francis Creek, P 15....Wis.
120 Francitas, M 20....Tex.
500 Franconia, H 12....N. H.
160*Franconia, N 23....Pa.
81*Frank, D 2....N. C.
650*Frank (Scott Haven Station), J 3....Pa.
300*Frank, K 19....Pa.
32*Frank, O 19....Va.
350 Frankclay, L 19....Mo.
417*Frankell, E 15....Tex.
1100 Frankenlust, L 19....Mich.
1000*Frankenmuth, M 20....Mich.
104*Frankewing, P 16....Tenn.
563 Frankford, M 24....Del.
471 Frankford, F 17....Mo.
140*Frankford, N 12....W. Va.
568 Frankford, P 21....Pa.
13706 Frankfort, H 12....Ind.
1243 Frankfort, D 19....Kan.
11492 Frankfort, E 16....Ky.
407 Frankfort, L 14....Me.
1642 Frankfort, J 11....Mich.
3859 Frankfort, M 18....N. Y.
839 Frankfort, N 11....Ohio
335 Frankfort, G 19....S. D.
39*Frankfort, M 16....Tenn.
....Frankfort Heights, P 16..Ill.
147*Frankfort Springs, L 2...Pa.
500*Franklin, N 9....Ala.
....Franklin, M 25....Ariz.
120 Franklin, B 14....Ark.
100 Franklin, B 7....Calif.
94 Franklin, H 21....Conn.
390 Franklin, H 3....Ga.
523 Franklin, R 20....Idaho
515 Franklin, J 10....Ill.
6264 Franklin, H 15....Ind.
650*Franklin, M 9....Kan.
3940 Franklin, K 11....Ky.
4274 Franklin, O 13....La.
950 Franklin, I 17....Me.
7303*Franklin, I 17....Mass.
233*Franklin, O 21....Mich.
502 Franklin, O 9....Minn.
325 Franklin, G 12....Mo.
12 Franklin, J 14....Mont.
1272 Franklin, O 15....Neb.
6749 Franklin, M 13....N. H.
311 Franklin, B 14....N. J.
481*Franklin, P 19....N. Y.
100 Franklin (Franklin Depot), P 19
1249 Franklin, O 5....Ohio
4511 Franklin, M 7....Ohio
25 Franklin, K 14....Okla.
9948 Franklin, H 1....Pa.
2297 Franklin, M 8....Pa.
4120 Franklin, N 11....Tenn.
1087 Franklin, I 20....Tex.
200 Franklin, A 9....Vt.
3466 Franklin, Q 19....Va.
613 Franklin, I 17....W. Va.
....Franklin & Abbeville Jc., O 13....La.
250 Franklin City, K 25....Va.
219 Franklin Corners, E 3..Pa.
100*Franklin Depot (Franklin), P 19....N. Y.
....*Franklin Furnace, see Franklin
131*Franklin Furnace, Q 13.Ohio
645 Franklin Grove, C 14....Ill.
1203*Franklin Lakes, C 19...N. J.
1592*Franklin Jc., I 17....Mass.
900 Franklin Mine, O 3....Mich.
3007 Franklin Park, B 20....Ill.
450 Franklin Park, G 14...N. J.
116*Franklin Springs, D 13...Ga.
360*Franklin Springs, M 17 ....N. Y.
4000*Franklin Square, H 7, V 3.Ohio
100 Franklinton, I 11....Ga.
150*Franklinton, E 15....Ky.
1579 Franklinton, L 18....La.
1273 Franklinton, C 15....N. C.
296*Franklinton, O 16....Pa.
500 Franklinville, N 9....N. J.
1884 Franklinville, P 6....N. Y.
851 Franklinville, F 10....N. C.
27*Franks, L 14....Miss.
100 Franks, O 16....Okla.
1216 Franks, F 22....Tex.
824 Frankton, H 16....Ind.
125 Franktown, M 23....Colo.
350 Franktville, M 5....Ala.
92 Frannie, A 9....Wyo.
260 Fraser, F 12....Colo.
97 Fraser, G 6....Idaho
263 Fraser, I 11....Iowa

Pop.	Place	Index	State
747	Fraser	P 24	Mich.
25*	Fraser	P 19	Minn.
1167	Frazee	H 6	Minn.
327*	Frazer	J 16	Ky.
56*	Frazer (Frazier)	E 5	Mo.
300	Frazer	E 21	Mont.
100*	Frazer	O 22	Pa.
640*	Frazeysburg	K 15	Ohio
56*	Frazier (Frazer)	E 5	Mo.
...	Frazier	J 19	N. D.
81*	Fraziers Bottom	J 4	W. Va.
5*	Freck	C 11	Ark.
175*	Fred	I 24	Tex.
160	Freda	B 6	Mich.
22	Freda	P 10	N. J.
54	Frederic (Fredric)	N 16	Iowa
75	Frederic	J 17	Mich.
680	Frederic	B 9	Wis.
645	Frederica	H 8	Del.
652	Frederick	E 15	Colo.
327	Frederick	H 3	Kan.
84	Frederick	J 13	Kan.
15802	Frederick	E 8	Md.
5109	Frederick	N 6	Okla.
253	Frederick	N 22	Pa.
422	Frederick	C 18	S. D.
725*	Frederick	B 9	Wis.
4	Frederick	L 23	Wyo.
10	Frederick Jc.	E 8	Md.
205	Fredericksburg	P 13	Ind.
649	Fredericksburg	D 17	Iowa
485	Fredericksburg	G 15	Ohio
750	Fredericksburg	M 18	Tex.
3544	Fredericksburg	J 15	Tex.
10066	Fredericksburg	I 17	Va.
...	Fredericksburg Jc.	K 16	Tex.
75*	Fredericks Hall	J 15	Va.
150	Frederickson	J 8	Wash.
81	Fredericktown	E 19	Md.
3414	Fredericktown	M 20	Mo.
1297	Fredericktown	I 14	Ohio
1050*	Fredericktown	P 3	Pa.
236	Frederika	E 17	Iowa
264	Fredonia	H 22	Ala.
402*	Fredonia (Biscoe)	I 16	Ark.
220	Fredonia	B 11	Ariz.
50*	Fredonia	Q 12	Ind.
147	Fredonia	M 21	Iowa
3524	Fredonia	M 21	Kan.
446	Fredonia	I 7	Ky.
5738	Fredonia	P 3	N. Y.
309	Fredonia	P 17	N. D.
536	Fredonia	H 2	Pa.
184*	Fredonia	I 15	Tenn.
356	Fredonia	P 18	Wis.
54*	Fredric (Frederic)	N 16	Iowa
18*	Fredvile	G 22	Ky.
252	Freeborn	Q 15	Minn.
1507	Freeburg	N 11	Ill.
50*	Freeburg	R 24	Minn.
395	Freeburg	J 14	Mo.
467	Freeburg	K 16	Pa.
113*	Freed	G 8	W. Va.
350*	Freedom	J 5	Calif.
400	Freedom	I 9	Ind.
50*	Freedom	J 13	Ky.
492▲	Freedom	M 11	Me.
40*	Freedom	J 15	Mo.
16	Freedom	N 11	Neb.
16	Freedom	K 18	N. H.
175*	Freedom	O 6	N. Y.
75*	Freedom (Freedom Sta.)	E 18	Ohio
364*	Freedom	B 5	Okla.
3227	Freedom	L 2	Pa.
68	Freedom	I 13	Utah
450*	Freedom	I 2	Wyo.
75*	Freedom Sta. (Freedom)	E 18	Ohio
6952	Freehold	I 18	N. J.
250*	Freehold	P 22	N. Y.
...	Freehold	E 6	Pa.
100	Free Home	D 7	Ga.
80*	Freeland	D 13	Md.
850	Freeland	M 18	Mich.
250	Freeland	M 14	N. C.
6593	Freeland	J 20	Pa.
300	Freeland	F 7	Wash.
60*	Freeland	J 16	Wis.
120	Freeland Park	N 6	Ind.
625	Freelandville	N 6	Ind.
21*	Freeling	C 6	Va.
...	Freeman	A 7	Ark.
258*	Freeman (Freeman Spur)	P 16	Ill.
219*	Freeman	K 6	Me.
302	Freeman	I 6	Mo.
60	Freeman	R 10	N. Y.
976	Freeman	M 22	S. D.
20*	Freeman	Q 16	Va.
100	Freeman	H 24	Wash.
800*	Freeman (Simmons)	Q 9	W. Va.
36*	Freeman	F 19	Wis.
1728	Freemansburg	F 21	Pa.
50*	Freemansburg	F 11	W. Va.
258*	Freeman Spur (Freeman)	P 16	Ill.
250*	Freemanville	O 11	Ala.
50	Freeport	N 7	Fla.
22366	Freeport	A 12	Ill.
67*	Freeport	O 15	Kan.
973	Freeport	O 7	Me.
405	Freeport	O 14	Mich.
548	Freeport	L 10	Minn.
20410	Freeport	I 7	N. Y.
636*	Freeport (Wayne)	E 10	Ohio
562	Freeport	O 7	Ohio
2710	Freeport	L 5	Pa.
2579	Freeport	M 22	Tex.
40*	Freeport	M 21	Tex.
2346*	Freeport	F 16	Tex.
236	Free Soil	L 11	Mich.
113*	Freestone	H 4	Calif.
103*	Freestone	O 12	Tex.
50	Freestone	Q 20	Tex.
350	Freetown	M 14	Ind.
57	Free Union	J 12	Va.
379	Freeville	O 14	N. Y.
825	Freewater	B 20	Ore.
132*	Freistadt	O 19	Wis.
132	Freistatt	P 8	Mo.
106*	Fremont	J 2	Ala.
855	Fremont	B 22	Ind.
490	Fremont	N 17	Iowa
2520	Fremont	M 12	Tenn.
208	Fremont	P 17	Mo.
11862	Fremont	P 22	Neb.
234	Fremont	P 18	N. H.
1264	Fremont	C 16	N. C.
14710	Fremont	E 11	Ohio
...	Fremont	L 12	Ore.
10	Fremont	O 14	Tenn.
50	Fremont	M 13	Utah
250	Fremont	C 6	Va.
437	Fremont	M 15	Wis.
154*	Fremont Center	C 2	N. Y.
28*	French	A 15	Ark.
23	French	M 4	Idaho
218	French	N 11	N. M.
31*	French (South Branch)	E 21	W. Va.
50*	French	O 15	Wyo.
75*	French Broad	N 22	Tenn.
289	Frenchburg	F 20	Ky.
600	French Camp	I 7	Calif.
172	French Camp	G 16	Miss.
153*	French Corral	F 8	Calif.
200	French Creek	H 13	W. Va.
34*	Frenchglen	C 18	Ore.
618	French Gulch	D 4	Calif.
2042	French Lick	O 11	Ind.
33*	Frenchmans Bayou	F 21	Ark.
34*	French Mills	N 19	Mo.
109*	French Mtn.	J 22	N. Y.
1707	French River	F 19	Minn.
750*	French Settlement	L 16	La.
300	Frenchton	H 12	W. Va.
300	Frenchtown	H 4	Mont.
1238	Frenchtown	G 9	N. J.
40	French Village	L 20	Mo.
1500	Frenchville	A 17	Me.
450	Frenchville	I 11	Pa.
100	Frenchville (Coudley)	I 11	Pa.
44*	Frenier	M 17	Tex.
23*	Freshwater	D 2	Calif.
60685	Fresno	K 12	Calif.
12	Fresno	D 13	Mont.
200	Fresno	I 17	Ohio
50*	Fresno	L 22	Tex.
23*	Frew	I 21	
1193	Frewsburg	R 3	N. Y.
...	Frey	F 16	Okla.
298*	Freybush	N 21	N. Y.
500	Friant	J 12	Calif.
80*	Friars Hill	M 12	W. Va.
940	Friars Point (Friar Point)	C 25	Miss.
179*	Fricks	N 24	Pa.
250*	Friday	H 22	Tex.
658	Friday Harbor	D 5	Wash.
1392▲	Fridley	M 16	Minn.
42	Fried	M 18	N. D.
900	Friedens	P 8	Pa.
199*	Friedensburg (Oley)	N 21	Pa.
164*	Friedensburg	L 19	Pa.
80*	Friedheim	N 22	Mo.
58*	Friend	F 5	Kan.
1169	Friend	N 20	Neb.
21	Friend	D 11	Ore.
148*	Friendly	D 9	W. Va.
450	Friendship	M 20	Ind.
140	Friendship	M 20	Ind.
500*	Friendship	O 7	N. Y.
1148	Friendship	Q 11	Ohio
451	Friendship	N 3	Tenn.
453	Friendship	J 16	Wis.
569	Friendsville	L 1	Md.
76*	Friendsville	E 20	Tenn.
300*	Friendswood	L 23	Tex.
375	Frierson	D 5	La.
1677	Fries	Q 2	Va.
...	Fries Jc.	Q 2	Va.
300	Friesland	L 18	Wis.
81*	Frijole	H 4	Tex.
100*	Frink	B 1, N 11	Fla.
23	Frio	H 23	N. M.
803	Friona	E 1	Tex.
67*	Frio Town	M 15	Tex.
16*	Frisby	J 16	Ky.
60	Frisco	G 11	Colo.
75	Frisco	K 13	La.
100	Frisco	Q 22	Mo.
115	Frisco	H 25	N. C.
105	Frisco	K 2	N. M.
219	Frisco	M 16	Ohio
100	Frisco	K 2	Pa.
670	Frisco	D 19	Tex.
4	Frisco	M 4	Utah
994	Frisco City	N 8	Ala.
...	Frisco Jc.	P 14	Okla.
114*	Fristoe	J 10	Mo.
500*	Fritch	B 4	Tex.
200	Fritchton	O 6	Ind.
110	Frizellburg	C 11	Md.
40*	Froelich	D 21	Iowa
43*	Frogmore	G 12	La.
150*	Frogmore	P 16	S. C.
30*	Frogue	K 15	Ky.
80	Frogville	Q 21	Okla.
210	Frohna	M 23	Mo.
441	Froid	D 24	Mont.
17*	Frolona	G 2	Ga.
533	Fromberg	M 15	Mont.
1766	Frontenac	M 22	Kan.
280	Frontenac	O 20	Minn.
25	Frontenac	O 15	N. Y.
200	Frontier	R 16	Mich.
268	Frontier	D 14	Minn.
522	Frontier (North Kemmerer)	N 3	Wyo.
3831	Front Royal	F 14	Va.
...	Front Royal Jc.	F 14	Va.
45*	Frosa	G 19	Tex.
100*	Frost	I 16	La.
278	Frost	R 13	Minn.
35	Frost (Frosts)	N 16	Ohio
671	Frost	F 19	Tex.
50*	Frost	L 15	W. Va.
7659	Frostburg	M 5	Md.
110	Frostburg	I 7	Pa.
1704	Frostproof	I 17	Fla.
15*	Frosts (Pigeon)	G 7	Pa.
360*	Frozen Creek	G 20	Ky.
203	Frozen	I 9	W. Va.
96	Frugality	L 10	Pa.
1466	Fruita	J 4	Colo.
300	Fruitdale	N 3	Ala.
21*	Fruitdale	L 7	Va.
89	Fruitdale	H 2	S. D.
281	Fruithurst	E 21	Ala.
65	Fruitland	P 15	Ga.
500	Fruitland	M 3	Idaho
150	Fruitland	I 11	Kan.
956	Fruitland	I 7	Md.
150	Fruitland	M 22	Iowa
300	Fruitland	O 21	Md.
117	Fruitland	N 22	Mo.
200	Fruitland	C 3	N. M.
50*	Fruitland	N 5	Tenn.
100*	Fruitland	C 17	Utah
68	Fruitland	O 17	Wash.
35*	Fruitland	D 17	Wash.
362*	Fruitland Park	F 15	Fla.
64*	Fruitland Park	P 18	Md.
458	Fruitport	N 11	Mich.
...	Fruitport Jc.		Mich.
150	Fruitvale	D 19	Calif.
150*	Fruitvale	N 5	Idaho
105*	Fruitvale	N 4	Tenn.
150*	Fruitvale	E 21	N. Y.
300*	Fruitvale	J 13	Fla.
500*	Frum	C 13	W. Va.
500	Fruto	F 5	Calif.
38*	Fry	B 7	Ga.
75*	Fry	I 14	Ky.
50*	Fryatt	A 15	Ark.
50	Fryburg	M 3	N. D.
327	Fryburg	H 6	Pa.
180*	Frye	L 4	Me.
513*	Frye (Ivanhoe)	O 2	Pa.
128	Fryeburg	O 7	Me.
789	Fryeburg	O 2	Me.
47*	Frymire	F 22	Ky.
75*	Fuget	F 22	Ky.
225	Fulbright	C 22	Tex.
76	Fulda	Q 10	Ind.
984	Fulda	O 6	Minn.
75*	Fulks Run	H 11	Va.
13	Fuller	O 13	Mich.
...	*Fuller Road	N 23	N. Y.
61*	Fullers	P 9	N. C.
75	Fullers	O 23	N. Y.
200	Fullerton	P 13	Ark.
10442	Fullerton	R 6	Calif.
5*	Fullerton	H 15	Ill.
1237	Fullerton	D 22	Ky.
148	Fullerton	I 7	La.
4829	Fullerton	E 15	Md.
1813	Fullerton	F 15	Md.
1707	Fullerton	J 15	Neb.
184	Fullerton	Q 19	N. D.
3075	Fullerton	L 22	Pa.
6	Fulshear	L 21	Tex.
200	Fulton	L 7	Ala.
707	Fulton	I 7	Ark.
593	Fulton	O 6	Ark.
250	Fulton	G 4	Calif.
2585	Fulton	C 10	Ill.
373	Fulton	E 13	Ind.
77*	Fulton	I 23	Iowa
309	Fulton	K 25	Kan.
3308	Fulton	L 5	Ky.
52	Fulton	L 6	Ky.
100*	Fulton	Q 12	Md.
1154	Fulton	C 22	Miss.
8297	Fulton	H 14	Mo.
...	Fulton, see Ilfeld		N. M.
13362	Fulton	K 13	N. Y.
275	Fulton	I 12	Ohio
168	Fulton	L 21	S. D.
108*	Fulton	O 2	Tenn.
200*	Fulton	M 17	Va.
200*	Fultonham	O 21	N. Y.
240	Fultonham (Union-town)	K 15	Ohio
806	Fultonville	M 21	N. Y.
88*	Fultz	O 10	Ill.
12	Fultz	E 22	Ky.
120	Funk	N 14	Neb.
26	Funkley	E 11	Minn.
798	Funkstown	C 6	Md.
199*	Funston	O 9	Ga.
17	Funston	H 13	N. D.
...	Fuqua	J 23	Tex.
1323	Fuquay Springs	G 14	N. C.
50	Furches	C 4	N. C.
113*	Furley	L 17	Kan.
200*	Furlong	N 24	Pa.
229*	Furman	L 12	Ala.
380	Furman	V 12	S. C.
37*	Furnace	G 19	Ky.
...	*Furnace (Old Furnace)		
11	Furnace	I 11	Mass.
150*	Furnessville	B 9	Ind.
50	Furniss	Q 19	Pa.
50*	Furport	D 23	Wash.
60*	Furrh	F 24	Tex.
80*	Furth	N 15	Ark.
...	Fuson, see Fusonia		Ky.
50	Fusonia	J 22	Ky.
10	Futrell	I 5	Ky.
500*	Fyffe	C 19	Ala.

G

Pop.	Place	Index	State
60	Gaars Mills	E 9	La.
773	Gaastra	F 2	Mich.
50*	Gabbard (Sebastian)	H 20	Ky.
55*	Gabbettville	I 2	Ga.
29*	Gabe	I 14	Ky.
46*	Gable	H 17	S. C.
6	Gabriel	F 23	Okla.
200	Gabriels	E 21	N. Y.
537	Gackle	O 17	N. D.
13*	Gad	L 9	W. Va.
100*	Gadberry	J 15	W. Va.
100*	Gaddistown	B 9	Ga.
36975	Gadsden	D 18	Ala.
907▲	Gadsden	M 1	Ariz.
400*	Gadsden	H 14	S. C.
50	Gadsden	N 4	Tenn.
60*	Gads Hill	O 19	Mo.
7636	Gaffney	A 10	S. C.
31	Gage	J 16	Mont.
12	Gage	O 4	Okla.
829	Gage (Bellona)	N 11	N. Y.
684	Gage	D 3	Okla.
31*	Gagedy	C 6	Tex.
125	Gagen	L 9	Wis.
425	Gahanna	K 12	Ohio
100	Gail	E 10	Tex.
...	*Gaillard	J 9	Ga.
100*	Gainer (Cairo)	N 10	Fla.
268	Gaines	O 19	Mich.
130	Gaines	N 7	Pa.
175*	Gaines	E 14	Pa.
15	Gaines	S 8	S. C.
118	Gaines	H 13	W. Va.
671	Gainesboro	I 14	Tenn.
77*	Gainesboro	E 13	Va.
115	Gaines Jc. (Watrous)	F 13	Pa.
261*	Gainesmore	M 22	Tex.
150*	Gainestown	N 7	Ala.
283	Gainesville	I 5	Ala.
113*	Gainesville	B 20	Ark.
3757	Gainesville	D 13	Fla.
10243	Gainesville	D 9	Ga.
255	Gainesville	R 13	Mo.
283	Gainesville	O 7	Mo.
9651	Gainesville	C 18	Tex.
100*	Gainesville	O 16	Va.
100*	Gainesville	C 11	Mo.
1021	Gaithersburg	G 10	Md.
21*	Gala	L 7	Va.
89	Galata	D 10	Mont.
30	Galatea	K 21	Colo.
45	Galatea	E 10	Ohio
3195	Galax	D 13	Va.
...	*Galbraith Springs	L 23	Tenn.
65	Galchutt	O 25	N. D.
150	Galdia	G 22	Ky.
150	Gale	K 13	Ill.
185*	Gale (West Andover)	M 11	N. H.
4126	Galena	A 9	Ill.
152	Galena	P 15	Ind.
4375	Galena	K 2	Kan.
250	Galena	R 9	Md.
507	Galena	Q 9	Mo.
180	Galena (North Norwich)	O 17	N. Y.
355	Galena	J 12	Ohio
90	Galena	D 7	Okla.
38	Galena	O 18	Ore.
1562▲	Galena Park	K 23	Tex.
28876	Galesburg	F 9	Ill.
165	Galesburg	K 23	Kan.
1040	Galesburg	O 14	Mich.
280	Galesburg	K 23	N. D.
122	Gales Creek	O 9	Ore.
200*	Gales Ferry	K 21	Conn.
265	Galesville	J 20	Wis.
260	Galesville	J 14	Wis.
1147	Galesville	E 15	Wis.
110	Galeton	A 5	N. M.
200	Galeton	C 16	Colo.
1820	Galeton	F 13	Pa.
291	Galice	K 19	Ore.
355	Galien	K 10	Mich.
567	Galien	R 10	Mich.
38	Galilee	F 23	Pa.
8685	Galion	H 12	Ohio
231*	Galisteo	F 14	N. M.
250*	Galivantes Ferry	G 22	S. C.
415*	Gallagher	L 7	W. Va.
50*	Gallant	D 16	Ala.
1642	Gallatin	D 8	Mo.
600	Gallatin	N 4	Pa.
4829	Gallatin	I 12	Tenn.
300	Gallatin	J 15	Tex.
160	Gallatin Gateway	M 10	Mont.
100*	Gallaway	P 2	Tenn.
113*	Gallegos	F 23	N. M.
80	Gallia	P 14	Ohio
10	Gallina	D 10	N. M.
175	Gallion	J 8	Ala.
69*	Gallion	B 12	La.
7832	Gallipolis	P 14	Ohio
112*	Gallipolis Ferry (Gallipolis)	H 3	W. Va.
3618	Gallitzin	M 9	Pa.
60	Galliver	M 5	Fla.
180*	Gallman	L 10	Miss.
50	Galloway	E 9	Ala.
28*	Galloway	O 10	Mo.
280	Galloway	K 11	Ohio
300	Galloway	F 13	W. Va.
77*	Galloway	J 13	Wis.
50*	Gallup	F 23	Ky.
7041	Gallup	F 2	N. M.
50*	Gallup City	E 8	Mont.
200*	Gallupville	N 22	N. Y.
700	Galt	H 8	Calif.
25	Galt	I 6	Iowa
156*	Galt	F 12	Iowa
355	Galt	J 14	Kan.
525	Galt (Gault)	C 10	Mo.
75*	Galton	J 19	Ill.
2812	Galva	E 10	Ill.
496	Galva	G 5	Iowa
463	Galva	I 3	Kan.
10	Galvatas	G 20	Ga.
735	Galveston	B 13	Ind.
35*	Galveston	H 23	Ky.
60862	Galveston	M 23	Tex.
50	Galvez	L 16	La.
4285	Galvin	L 1	Wash.
938	Galvin	H 22	Ky.
50	Galva Jc.	C 15	Minn.
161*	Galway	L 23	N. Y.
150*	Gamaliel	A 13	Ark.
150	Gamaliel	I 14	Ky.
470	Gambier	I 14	Ohio
50*	Gambrills	H 13	Md.
27*	Gamoca	L 8	W. Va.
150	Ganado	E 23	Ariz.
717	Ganado	M 20	Tex.
135*	Gandeeville	I 7	W. Va.
125*	Gandy	H 6	La.
169	Gandy	J 11	Neb.
50	Gandy	J 1	Utah
41*	Grandy Bridge	I 14	Fla.
100*	Ganges	P 2	Mich.
300	Ganister	M 11	Pa.
100	Gann	O 12	Ohio
125	Gannvalley	K 17	S. D.
150	Gano	F 15	Okla.
150*	Ganotown	D 23	W. Va.
204	Gans	L 24	N. Y.
288	Gans	Q 4	Pa.
400	Gans	N 14	Ala.
25*	Gansevoort	L 24	N. Y.
30	Gantts Jc.	H 17	Ala.
456	Gantts Quarry	H 16	Ala.
75*	Gap (Boone)	H 18	N. Y.
15	Gap	M 19	Okla.
1050	Gap	P 20	Pa.
38*	Gap	F 1	Tex.
98*	Gapcreek	K 16	Ky.
200*	Gapland	B 4	Md.
50*	Gapmills	P 12	W. Va.
183*	Gapville	G 22	Pa.
75*	Gards Fort	Q 3	Pa.
30*	Garber	B 9	Ark.
16*	Garber	G 18	Ill.
158*	Garber	F 21	Iowa
25*	Garber	Q 10	Mo.
1086	Garber	D 11	Okla.
80*	Garber	M 24	Tenn.
500*	Garberville	E 2	Calif.
300	Garbutt	M 9	N. Y.
650	Garcias (Garciasville)	L 24	Tex.
650	Garcia	Q 13	Colo.
7*	Gard	F 10	Neb.
90	Gardar	E 21	N. D.
462	Garden	G 10	Mich.
5909	Gardena	M 3	Calif.
125	Gardena	E 12	N. D.
75*	Garden Canyon	P 20	Ariz.
400	Garden City	D 13	Ala.
85*	Garden City	H 13	Iowa
6285	Garden City	L 5	Kan.
250	Garden City	J 5	Mo.
4096*	Garden City	Q 22	Minn.
320	Garden City	O 4	N. D.
599	Garden City	I 7	Mo.
11223	Garden City	H 7	N. Y.
520*	Garden City	E 19	Okla.
272	Garden City	F 21	S. D.
250	Garden City	L 5	Tex.
261	Garden City	B 14	Utah
210	Gardendale	O 15	Tex.
2500*	Garden Grove	R 6	Calif.
558	Garden Grove	P 12	Iowa
60*	Garden Home	C 9	Ore.
323	Garden Plain	M 15	Kan.
204*	Garden Prairie	A 16	Ill.
15*	Garden Valley	H 9	Calif.
32*	Garden Valley	M 7	Idaho
214*	Garden Valley	F 27	Tex.
...	Gardenville, see Remlap		Fla.
1000	Gardenville	N 5	N. Y.
120*	Gardenville	M 24	Pa.
1500*	Gardenville	K 8	Wash.
200*	Gardi	N 20	Ga.
6044	Gardiner	N 9	Me.
500	Gardiner	N 11	Mont.
150	Gardiner	B 19	N. M.
150	Gardiner	C 4	N. Y.
350	Gardiner	K 3	Ore.
86	Gardiner	G 3	Wash.
125	Gardner	N 14	Colo.
200*	Gardner	K 16	Fla.
20	Gardner	O 19	Idaho
20206	Gardner	D 13	Mass.
103	Gardner	L 24	Tenn.
100	Gardner	L 4	Tenn.
49	Gardner	B 12	Mont.
105*	Gardners	O 8	Va.
400	Gardners	I 3	Nev.
186*	Gardner	E 21	Md.
110	Garfield	A 5	Wash.
43	Garfield	K 19	Colo.
355	Garfield	K 10	Kan.
100*	Garfield	G 12	Ill.
1800	Garfield	L 8	W. Va.
203*	Garfield	K 8	Minn.
28044	Garfield	D 20	N. J.
200	Garfield	M 8	N. M.
257	Garfield	F 19	Ohio
2010	Garfield	E 10	Utah
674	Garfield	K 24	Wash.
16989	Garfield Heights	P 24	Ohio
400	Garfield Smelter	F 10	Utah
61*	Gargatha	L 24	Va.
500	Garibaldi	C 4	Ore.
75*	Garita	F 19	N. M.
250	Garland	M 12	Ala.
370	Garland (Garland City)	P 6	Ark.
191	Garland	L 25	Kan.
125	Garland	K 12	Me.
205	Garland	L 21	Neb.
484	Garland	J 15	N. C.
300	Garland	J 5	Pa.
1233	Garland	B 17	Tenn.
926	Garland	B 10	Utah
88	Garland	B 9	Wyo.
210	Garlandville	K 18	Miss.
50*	Garlin	J 15	Ky.
461	Garnavillo	E 21	Iowa
160	Garneill	I 13	Mont.
1549	Garner	D 12	Iowa
768	Garner	F 14	N. C.
100*	Garner	E 18	Tex.
1200*	Garnerville	F 5	N. Y.
80*	Garnet	F 15	Mich.
25	Garnet	I 6	Mont.
17*	Garnet	L 2	Ill.
156*	Garnet	F 12	Iowa
10*	Garnet Lake	J 22	N. Y.
2607	Garnett	J 24	Kan.
50*	Garnett	E 19	Okla.
50*	Garnett	O 12	S. C.
55	Garnettsville	F 13	Ky.
48*	Garnsey	H 12	Ala.
36*	Garo (Garos)	I 12	Colo.
25*	Garoga	J 21	N. Y.
36	Garos (Garo)	I 12	Colo.
43*	Garrard	I 20	Ky.
125	Garrattsville	O 19	N. Y.
656	Garretson	L 25	S. D.
252	Garrett	I 15	Ind.
4285	Garrett	C 20	Ind.
938	Garrett	H 22	Ky.
872	Garrett	Q 7	Pa.
200	Garrett	F 19	Tex.
24*	Garrett	M 19	Wyo.
950*	Garrettford	P 23	Pa.
100*	Garrett Hill	P 23	Pa.
400*	Garrett Park	G 9	Md.
60*	Garretts Bend	L 4	W. Va.
90*	Garretts Bluff	C 21	Tex.
1264	Garrettsville (Garrettsville Hiram)	E 18	Ohio
5*	Garrison	D 7	Pa.
459	Garrison	I 18	Iowa
116	Garrison	E 18	Kan.
231	Garrison	D 21	Ky.
475*	Garrison (Garrison Forest)	E 13	Md.
211*	Garrison	J 14	Minn.
45*	Garrison	Q 11	Mo.
100	Garrison	J 7	Mont.
124	Garrison	K 20	Neb.
4	Garrison	J 24	N. M.
1117	Garrison	J 9	N. D.
115*	Garrison	Q 1	Pa.
770	Garrison	G 24	Tex.
75	Garrison	K 1	Utah
200*	Garrison	N 6	W. Va.
200*	Garrisonville	H 17	Va.
50*	Garryowen	M 17	Mont.
45	Garske	F 18	N. D.
30*	Garten	M 8	W. Va.
350	Garvin	P 6	Minn.
170	Garvin	Q 3	Okla.
...	*Garway, see Hastings Branch Jc.		Pa.
517	Garwin	I 16	Iowa
50	Garwood	X 4	Idaho
25*	Garwood	N 18	Mo.
3622	Garwood	F 17	N. J.
600	Garwood	K 22	Tex.
115*	Garwoods (Whitney Crossings)	O 8	N. Y.
4*	Gary	E 19	Colo.
1	Gary	I 13	Fla.
111719	Gary	B 7	Ind.
300	Gary	F 4	Minn.
566	Gary	G 25	S. D.
300*	Gary	P 24	Tex.
30*	Gary	P 14	W. Va.
3000	Gary	Q 6	W. Va.
320	Garysburg	C 18	N. C.
64*	Garysville	O 17	La.
1800	Garyville	N 17	La.
16*	Gasburg	R 15	Va.
357	Gas, L 23		Kan.
3488	Gas City	G 17	Ind.
50	Gas City	N 9	Okla.
1455	Gasconade	D 11	Mo.
494	*Gasconade	I 16	Mo.
48	Gascoyne	Q 4	N. D.
700*	Gashland	F 6	Mo.
250	Gaskin	I 7	Fla.
114*	Gasoline	A 11	Tex.
110*	Gasparilla	L 14	Fla.
900	Gasport	L 6	N. Y.
36*	Gasque	R 6	S. C.
101*	Gassaway	N 13	Tenn.
1429	Gassaway	I 10	W. Va.
57*	Gassetts	L 12	Vt.
227*	Gassville	B 12	Ark.
677	Gaston	H 18	Ind.
323	Gaston	C 18	N. C.
233	Gaston	D 7	Ore.
125*	Gaston	D 13	S. C.
136*	Gastonburg	K 10	Ala.
21313	Gastonia	H 4	N. C.
40	Gaston Jc.	D 13	W. Va.
500*	Gastonville	H 3	Pa.
42*	Gatchel	Q 11	Ind.
243	Gate, B I	Q 9	Okla.
133	Gate	L 5	Pa.
1565	Gate City	E 5	Va.
...	*Gateley	R 15	Ill.
100*	Gates (Eadston)	E 21	Ky.
18	Gates	I 13	Neb.
50	Gates	B 20	N. C.
48	Gates	Q 3	Ore.
383	Gates	N 3	Tenn.
18*	Gates	P 11	W. Va.
906	Gates Mills	D 18	Ohio
106*	Gatesville	L 10	Miss.
50*	Gatesville	C 21	N. C.
3177*	Gatesville	H 17	Tex.
10	Gatewood	H 22	Mo.
50*	Gatewood	M 4	Ark.
65	Gateway	J 2	Colo.
134	Gateway	B 22	Mont.
49	Gateway	G 12	Ore.
668*	Gatewood	R 17	Mo.
1000	Gatliff	K 19	Ky.
186*	Gatlinburg	O 20	Tenn.
186*	Gattman (Gatman)	E 21	Miss.
29*	Gatton	H 14	Ky.
291	Gaty	E 22	Ark.
46	Gatzke	C 4	Minn.
1800	Gauley Bridge	L 8	W. Va.
275	Gauley Mills	K 11	W. Va.
525	Gault (Galt)	C 10	Mo.
100*	Gausdale	K 19	Ky.
500	Gause	J 19	Tex.
116*	Gautier	R 21	Miss.
12*	Gavilan	D 9	N. M.
157	Gaviota	O 10	Calif.
262	Gay	H 5	Ga.
228	Gay	C 4	Mich.
450*	Gay	P 5	N. C.
30	Gay	Q 6	Okla.
516*	Gay (Mount Gay)	N 4	W. Va.
65*	Gay	I 6	W. Va.
100	Gay Head	P 21	Mass.
52*	Gayhead	P 23	N. Y.
216*	Gay Hill	J 20	Tex.
140*	Gayler	D 5	Ark.
183	Gaylesville	C 20	Ala.
245	Gaylord	E 11	Kan.
2055	Gaylord	H 15	Mich.
1049	Gaylord	O 13	Minn.
100*	Gaylord	N 3	Ore.
30*	Gaylord	E 14	Va.
331	Gaylordsville	H 3	Conn.
261	Gays	K 17	Ill.
30*	Gays Creek	I 21	Ky.
737	Gays Mills	G 19	Wis.
100*	Gayport (Merriam)	L 16	Ohio
1145*	Gaysport	M 10	Pa.
200	Gaysville	J 11	Vt.
278	Gayville	O 23	S. D.
118*	Gaza	D 9	Ark.
116*	Gazelle	D 5	Calif.
319	Gearhart	A 4	Ore.
4*	Geary	I 5	Calif.
1634	Geary	M 15	La.
260	Geauga Lake	D 18	Ohio
36*	Gebo	B 17	Wyo.
500	Ged	N 5	La.
581	Geddes	N 18	S. D.
15*	Gee	F 15	Ky.
8	Geer	F 7	Ore.
288	Geff	N 18	Ill.
192*	Geiger	H 4	Ala.
...	*Geiger Mills, see Geigertown		Pa.
315	Geigertown	O 21	Pa.
200	Geismar	M 15	La.
1037*	Geistown	N 8	Pa.
315	Gelatt	E 21	Pa.
250	Gem	J 2	Idaho
125	Gem	E 5	Kan.
83*	Gem	C 6	Tex.
46*	Gem (Coger)	I 11	W. Va.
100*	Gemmell	E 13	Minn.
100*	Geneill (Browns Camp)		Miss.
...	General Grant National Park, see Kings Canyon National Park		Calif.
20*	Genesee	E 9	Calif.
678	Genesee	G 3	Idaho
300*	Genesee	N 7	Mich.
400	Genesee	D 12	Pa.
150*	Genesee (Genesee Depot)	N 20	Wis.
1400*	Genesee	E 6	N. Y.
3824	Geneseo	H 9	Ill.
632	Geneseo	J 14	Kan.
2144	Geneseo	N 8	N. Y.
180	Geneseo	O 23	N. D.
2803	Geneva	O 18	Ala.
489▲*	Geneva	G 19	Fla.
203	Geneva	J 6	Ga.
50	Geneva	Q 23	Idaho
4101	Geneva	C 18	Ill.
966	Geneva	E 22	Ind.
268	Geneva	F 14	Iowa
75*	Geneva	K 22	Kan.
300*	Geneva	G 9	Ky.
313	Geneva	Q 17	Minn.
75	Geneva (Absher)	I 17	Mont.
1888	Geneva	M 19	Neb.
15555	Geneva	M 11	N. Y.
4171	Geneva	B 19	Ohio
246*	Geneva	E 2	Pa.
187*	Geneva	H 25	Tex.
...	*Geneva Lake Sta.	N 22	Wis.
172*	Geneva-on-the-Lake	C 20	Ohio
60	Genevieve	C 18	Mont.
45	Gennett	L 18	Ark.
120*	Genoa	P 5	Ark.
214	Genoa	H 19	Colo.
1290	Genoa	B 17	Ill.
1231	Genoa	J 19	Neb.
75	Genoa	H 2	Nev.
500	Genoa	N 13	N. Y.
50	Genoa	G 11	N. D.
1455	Genoa	D 11	Ohio
1000*	Genoa	K 22	Tex.
35*	Genoa	L 2	W. Va.
339	Genoa	F 18	Wis.
715	Genoa City	N 22	Wis.
75	Genola	N 13	Minn.
200	Genola	H 11	Utah
46	Genou	E 10	Mont.
...	Gent, see Cutuno		Ky.
120*	Gentilly	E 4	Minn.
779	Gentry	B 4	Ark.
140*	Gentry (Elkatawa)	H 21	Ky.
196	Gentry	B 6	Mo.
31*	Gentrys Mill	J 15	Ky.
258	Gentryville	O 8	Ind.
90	Gentryville	C 7	Mo.
1107	George	B 3	Iowa
65	George (Woodland)	C 19	N. C.
300	George	P 2	Pa.
100	George	I 21	Tex.
104*	Georges Creek	F 23	Ky.
86*	Georges Creek	F 17	Md.
...	Georges Creek Jc.	L 5	Md.
200*	Georges Fork	C 6	Va.
125*	Georges Mills	M 9	N. H.
150*	Georges River (South Warren)	N 4	Me.
139	Georgesville	L 11	Ohio
198*	Georgetown	M 8	Calif.
500	Georgetown	H 9	Calif.
391	Georgetown	F 12	Colo.
910	Georgetown	N 4	Conn.
1820	Georgetown	K 23	Del.
250	Georgetown	E 17	Fla.
463	Georgetown	L 2	Ga.
3235	Georgetown	Q 22	Idaho
...	Georgetown, see Bean Blossom		Ind.
377	Georgetown	P 14	Ind.
4420	Georgetown	E 17	Ky.
677	Georgetown	F 10	La.
420*	Georgetown	F 9	Me.
1800	Georgetown	B 20	Mass.
193*	Georgetown	S 2	Minn.
415	Georgetown	L 11	Miss.
100	Georgetown	N 16	N. Y.
1848	Georgetown	P 8	Ohio
253*	Georgetown	K 1	Pa.

Pop. Place Index State
2000*Georgetown, I 20.......Pa.
5559 Georgetown, K 21....S. C.
175*Georgetown, Q 16....Tenn.
3682 Georgetown, J 18......Tex.
.... Georgetown Jc., H 11..Md.
28*Georgetown Sta., N 16 N. Y.
63*Georgeville, L 10.....Minn.
500 George West, O 17....Tex.
75*Georgia (East Georgia), B 9.......Vt.
500 Georgia Center, C 7....Vt.
1627 Georgiana, M 13.......Ala.
600 Georgiaville, C 13.....R. I.
65*Gera, M 19..........Mich.
100*Gera, J 18..........Va.
7*Gerald, Q 11..........Ind.
371 Gerald, J 17..........Mo.
132*Geraldine, C 19.......Ala.
262 Geraldine, F 13......Mont.
10*Gerard, I 7..........Me.
1000 Gerber, E 6..........Calif.
4 Gerber, G 10.........Mont.
50*Geren (Ruby), F 10...Miss.
3104 Gering, H 2..........Neb.
150 Gerlach, D 4..........Nev.
28 Gerlane, O 12.........Kan.
60*Gerlaw, F 8..........Ill.
32 Gerled, B 10.........Iowa
18*German, H 23..........Ky.
75*Germania, J 10.......Miss.
250 Germania, F 13.........Pa.
10*Germania, G 10........Tex.
200 Germania, F 21......Wash.
180*Germano, L 7........Ohio
183*Germansville, L 21....Pa.
140*Germanton, D 8......N. C.
796 Germantown, M 13.....Ill.
304 Germantown, D 19.....Ky.
313 Germantown, G 9.....Md.
250 Germantown, Q 23.... N. Y.
2095 Germantown, M 6....Ohio
....*Germantown, P 23.....Pa.
402 Germantown (Neshoba), Q 2..........Tenn.
292 Germantown, O 19....Wis.
180 German Valley (Baalton), B 13..........Ill.
250 Germfask, F 12......Mich.
210 Gernt, L 16.........Tenn.
35 Gerome, F 21.......Wash.
114 Geronimo, L 21.......Ariz.
117 Geronimo, N 8........Okla.
178*Geronimo, L 17........Tex.
200 Gerrardstown, E 23.W. Va.
300*Gerrish, N 13.........N. H.
....*Gerry, K 14...........Me.
150 Gerry, Q 3...........N. Y.
108*Gerster, L 9..........Mo.
146*Gerton, P 9..........N. C.
265*Gertrude, J 7........Wash.
206 Gerty, L 17.........Okla.
332 Gervais, E 7..........Ore.
....*Gesling, E 22..........Ky.
124*Gessie, J 5...........Ind.
149*Gest, E 16............Ky.
100 Getchell, F 9........Wash.
22*Gether, K 17...........Va.
25 Gethsemane, K 14.....Ark.
50*Gethsemane, G 14.....Ky.
440 Gettysburg, J 6.......Ohio
5916 Gettysburg, Q 15.......Pa.
1324 Gettysburg, F 14.....S. D.
20 Gettysburg, E 3.....Wash.
.... Gettysburg Jc., N 15...Pa.
65 Getzville, M 5........N. Y.
275 Geuda Springs, O 17...Kan.
....*Gewhitt, B 4..........Tex.
175 Geyser, H 12........Mont.
619 Geyserville, G 4......Calif.
92 Gheen, F 19.........Minn.
530 Gheens, O 17............La.
414 Ghent, D 16............Ky.
341 Ghent, O 5..........Minn.
750 Ghent, P 24..........N. Y.
163 Ghent, E 17..........Ohio
100*Ghent, P 8..........W. Va.
250*Ghio, J 10............N. C.
55 Gholson, H 20........Miss.
52*Gholsonville, Q 15......Va.
120*Giant, I 7...........Calif.
.... Giant Forest, see Sequoia National Park......Calif.
250 Giatto, Q 8.........W. Va.
761 Gibbon, O 11........Minn.
836 Gibbon, M 16.........Neb.
25 Gibbon, A 10.........Okla.
100 Gibbon, C 20..........Ore.
56*Gibbon Glade, Q 5.....Pa.
30*Gibbons, M 6........Mont.
47 Gibbonsville, I 13....Idaho
130 Gibbs, D 4..........Idaho
30*Gibbs, J 19.............Ky.
150*Gibbs, I 19...........Mich.
152 Gibbs, C 13............Mo.
75 Gibbs, L 4............Tenn.
713 Gibbsboro, L 11.......N. J.
150 Gibbs City, F 2.......Mich.
1023 Gibbsland (Gibsland), C 7 La.
208 Gibbstown, L 7........N. J.
75 Gibbsville, P 17.......Wis.
50*Gibisonville, M 14....Ohio
800 Gibralter, N 20.........Pa.
1023*Gibsland (Gibbsland), C 7 La.
474 Gibson, H 17...........Ga.
400*Gibson, B 6...........Ind.
125*Gibson, L 17..........Iowa
500 Gibson, O 15............La.
40 Gibson, E 20..........Miss.
144 Gibson, I 24, R 21.....Mo.
2 Gibson, K 13.........Mont.
175 Gibson, F 2..........N. M.
280 Gibson, Q 11..........N. Y.
435 Gibson, J 10..........N. C.
55*Gibson, K 18.........Ohio
110 Gibson, G 21.........Okla.
1 Gibson, E 21............Pa.
284 Gibson, N 5..........Tenn.
2169 Gibsonburg, D 10.....Ohio
10 Gibsonburg Jc., C 10..Ohio
2401 Gibson City, G 18........Ill.
500*Gibsonia, L 3...........Pa.
....*Gibson Island, H 14....Md.
200 Gibsons Station (Gibson Sta.), E 3...........Va.
250*Gibsonton (East Tampa) I 13...............Fla.
1753 Gibsonville, D 11.....N. C.
....*Gibtown, see Klein...Mont.
7*Gid, D 14............Ark.
2166 Giddings, K 19.........Tex.
1606 Gideon, I 24, R 22......Mo.
25 Gideon, F 22.........Okla.
23*Giese, I 15..........Minn.
.... Giffen, G 10..........Mont.
500*Gifford, J 23............Fla.
70 Gifford, G 5..........Idaho
359 Gifford, H 20............Ill.
200 Gifford, H 14..........Iowa
30*Gifford, G 21...........Ky.
290*Gifford Davis, D 9.....Pa.
85*Gifford, N 13.........S. C.
39 Gifford, E 21........Wash.
51*Gift, A 20...........Miss.
1200 Gig Harbor, I 7.....Wash.
400 Gila (Gila Bend, L 10),Ariz.

Pop. Place Index State
50 Gila, M 2............N. M.
837 Gilbert, K 14...........Ariz.
116*Gilbert, C 11...........Ark.
226 Gilbert, I 12...........Iowa
428 Gilbert, E 12.............La.
2504 Gilbert, F 19.........Minn.
50 Gilbert, K 9............Nev.
25 Gilbert, B 10...........Okla.
327 Gilbert, J 22.............Pa.
153 Gilbert (Lewiedale), G 11 ....S. C.
22 Gilbert (Priddys), K 12.Va.
490*Gilbert, O 3.........W. Va.
3710*Gilberton, K 19.........Pa.
425 Gilbertown, L 4........Ala.
170*Gilberts, B 18...........Ill.
220 Gilberts (Burkettsville), I 6...............Ohio
329 Gilbertsville, J 6.......Ky.
377 Gilbertsville, P 17....N. Y.
521*Gilbertsville, N 22......Pa.
259 Gilbertville, G 17.....Iowa
1517 Gilbertville, F 11....Mass.
175*Gilboa (East Westmoreland), P 6..........N. H.
60 Gilboa, O 21..........N. Y.
209*Gilboa, E 6............Ohio
10*Gilboa, L 9..........W. Va.
255 Gilby, G 22..........N. D.
50 Gilchrist. E 7............Ill.
300*Gilchrist, O 10.........Ore.
352 Gilcrest, D 15.........Colo.
1100 Gildersleeve, H 14....Conn.
250 Gildford, D 12........Mont.
500 Gile, H 5...............Wis.
130 Gilead, G 17..........Conn.
....*Gilead, J 15..............La.
197*Gilead, M 2.............Me.
148 Gilead, O 20...........Neb.
70*Giles, A 14..............Ala.
100*Giles, D 5...............Tex.
200 Gilford, M 20..........Mich.
200 Gilford, L 15..........N. H.
70*Gilfoyle (Gilfoyl), G 6...Pa.
100 Gilkey, D 1, P 10....N. C.
350 Gill, D 16..............Colo.
50 Gill, C 8..............Mass.
3 Gill, E 4...............S. D.
28*Gill, M 3............W. Va.
150*Gillentine, O 15.......Tenn.
4440 Gillespie, K 11...........Ill.
40*Gillespie (Hyer), I 10 W. Va.
.... Gillespieville, see Londonderry..............Ohio
870 Gillett, M 16............Ark.
35*Gillett, K 19..........N. C.
247 Gillett, E 16..............Pa.
267 Gillett, M 18............Tex.
1145 Gillett, N 12............Wis.
500*Gillette, D 14..........N. J.
2177 Gillette, D 20..........Wyo.
150*Gillett Grove, D 6....Iowa
.... Gillett Jc., N 12.......Wis.
19*Gilley, I 22..............Ky.
63*Gillford, F 21...........Ohio
242 Gillham, L 4.............Ark.
750 Gilliam, A 4..............La.
308 Gilliam, G 11............Mo.
27*Gilliam, Q 7.........W. Va.
50*Gilliland, C 14..........Tex.
100*Gillingham, H 18.......Wis.
.... Gillintown, J 12...........Pa.
23*Gillises Mills, Q 7....Tenn.
80*Gillmore, G 20...........Ky.
62*Gilmore, H 17..........Ohio
150 Gillsburg, P 8..........Miss.
157 Gillsville, D 11...........Ga.
15 Gilluly, H 15...........Utah
225 Gilman, (Rex), G 10..Colo.
100 Gilman (Bozrahville), I 19 Conn.
1554 Gilman, F 20..............Ill.
483 Gilman, J 15...........Iowa
140*Gilman, K 14.........Minn.
535 Gilman City, C 8.......Mo.
35 Gilman, G 8..........Mont.
750*Gilman, C 21..............Vt.
440 Gilman, G 11............Wis.
555 Gilman City (Gilman), C 8, Mo.
....*Gilman Hot Springs, P 19, R 9..........Calif.
708▲Gilmanton, M 15.....N. H.
275 Gilmanton, D 14.....Wis.
111 Gilmanton Iron Works, M 16..............N. H.
3138 Gilmer, E 23............Tex.
100*Gilmer, H 10........W. Va.
250 Gilmerton, Q 21..........Va.
263 Gilmore, F 21............Ark.
50 Gilmore, L 16..........Idaho
155 Gilmore, H 18............Mo.
15 Gilmore, K 24..........Neb.
.... Gilmore, J 18............Ohio
908 Gilmore City, F 9......Iowa
176 Gilmour, M 7.............Ind.
.... Gilpin, M 21............Colo.
100 Gilpin, I 16..............Ky.
13*Gilpin, D 12.............Tex.
44*Gilreath, D 5..........N. C.
3615 Gilroy, J 7.............Calif.
205 Gilson, F 9...............Ill.
45*Gilstrap, I 11............Ky.
200 Gilsum, P 7............N. H.
25 Giltedge, H 14........Mont.
325 Giltner (Huntington), M 17 Neb.
150*Gimlet, E 21..............Ky.
105*Ginter, K 10..............Pa.
143*Gip, I 9..............W. Va.
220 Gipsy, A 11..............Ala.
7*Gipsy, O 20..............Mo.
235 Gipsy, K 8.................Pa.
600*Girard, P 5.............Calif.
300 Girard, H 21...............Ga.
1741 Girard, J 11...............Ill.
2554 Girard, M 25.............Kan.
107*Girard, C 12................La.
240 Girard, Q 16.............Mich.
30 Girard, F 24............Mont.
9805 Girard, E 20............Ohio
1732 Girard, D 2.................Pa.
500*Girard, D 12.............Tex.
.... Girard Jc., D 2.............Pa.
4602 Girardville, K 19.........Pa.
75 Girdler, J 19..............Ky.
375 Girdletree, Q 23.........Md.
50*Girdner, P 12.............Mo.
263 Girta, F 8...........W. Va.
36*Girvin, I 8...............Tex.
35 Gist, J 25................Tex.
75*Gittings (Long Green), E 14..............Md.
28 Given, I 5............W. Va.
40 Givens Springs, O 4..Idaho
50 Givin, M 16.............Iowa
22 Glace, P 12.........W. Va.
87 Glacier, B 9..........Wash.
476 Glacier Park, D 6.....Mont.
945 Gladbrook, I 15.........Iowa
11*Gladden, N 16.............Mo.
90 Gladdens, Q 8..............Pa.
70*Glade, A 6...............Ark.
218 Glade, E 10..............Kan.
160*Glade, H 12................La.
123*Glade, P 6..................Pa.
5*Glade Farms, D 16..W. Va.
69*Gladehill, P 7..............Va.

Pop. Place Index State
60 Glade Mills, L 5..........Pa.
150 Glade Park, I 3........Colo.
.... Glade Run, K 11.......Ohio
686 Glade Spring, E 9........Va.
75*Glade Valley, C 4....N. C.
150*Gladeville, M 12......Tenn.
....*Gladeville, see Wise,....Va.
4454 Gladewater, E 23.......Tex.
102*Gladhill (Greenstone), Q 14................Pa.
50*Gladehill, P 7...............Va.
4*Gladiola, L 25..........N. M.
413 Gladstell, J 23............Tex.
367 Gladstone, F 6..............Ill.
4972 Gladstone, G 8........Mich.
Gladstone, see Gloster,Minn.
100 Gladstone, O 20.......Neb.
.... Gladstone, E 13.........N. J.
30 Gladstone, D 22......N. M.
278 Gladstone, M 6.......N. D.
1629 Gladstone, D 8..........Ore.
1000*Gladstone (Burmont), P 23.................Pa.
66*Gladstone, I 22.........Tex.
165*Gladstone, M 10..........Va.
4*Glad Valley, G 9.....S. D.
1600 Gladwin, L 18..........Mich.
....*Gladwyne, O 23 (Pop. 1236 incl. in Merion)..Pa.
200 Glady, H 15..........W. Va.
65*Gladys, F 22..............Ky.
300*Gladys, O 10..............Va.
....*Glamis, Q 22............Calif.
650 Glamorgan, D 5.............Va.
45*Glancy, L 9..............Miss.
483 Glandorf, F 7..............Ohio
741 Glasco, F 15..............Kan.
1409 Glasco, B 5, R 23....N. Y.
782 Glasford, G 11...............Ill.
358 Glasgo, I 24............Conn.
222 Glasgow, J 8.................Ill.
5815 Glasgow, J 13...............Ky.
1490 Glasgow, G 11..............Mo.
3799 Glasgow, E 19...........Mont.
204 Glasgow (Smiths Ferry), L 1.......................Pa.
250 Glasgow, L 10...............Pa.
938 Glasgow, M 9.................Va.
725 Glasgow, L 7..........W. Va.
354 Glasgow Jc. (Park City), J 14........................Ky.
210 Glass, I 22..................Ala.
75 Glass, L 3................Tenn.
46*Glass, N 20..................Va.
4925 Glassboro, M 9..........N. J.
....*Glasser, C 13............N. J.
1500 Glassmere, L 4.............Pa.
8748*Glassport, M 4..............Pa.
160 Glasston, E 22.........N. D.
4000 Glastonbury, F 15...Conn.
83*Glatfelters (Glatfelter), Q 17........................Pa.
125 Glazier, B 6...............Tex.
21*Gleanings, H 14...........Ky.
883 Gleason, M 5............Tenn.
250 Gleason, J 10..............Wis.
255 Gleasondale, E 16.....Mass.
500 Gleasonton, H 13..........Pa.
50 Gleed, L 13............Wash.
65 Gleeson, O 22............Ariz.
10*Glen, I 16................Minn.
50*Glen, A 22................Miss.
35 Glen (Reichle), M 7..Mont.
11 Glen, E 2...................Neb.
305 Glen, I 17..................N. H.
200*Glen, M 21...............N. Y.
250 Glen, K 8...............W. Va.
110*Glenada, J 5................Ore.
200*Glenalice, N 17..........Tenn.
275 Glen Allan (Glen Allen), H 6........................Miss.
130*Glen Allen, E 7..........Ala.
118*Glenallen, O 21.............Mo.
200*Glenallen, M 16.............Va.
10*Glen Alpine, G 9.......Calif.
665 Glen Alpine, E 2.......N. C.
300 Glenalum, P 4.........W. Va.
109*Glen Arbor, I 12.......Mich.
205 Glenarm, J 13................Ill.
150 Glenarm, E 15..............Md.
75*Glen Aubrey, P 15.....N. Y.
250 Glenbar, L 22..............Ariz.
357 Glenbeulah, O 17..........Wis.
10 Glenblair, F 2............Calif.
.... Glenblair Jc., F 2.......Calif.
2140 Glenbrook, Q 3...........Conn.
9*Glenbrook, H 2..............Nev.
20 Glenbrook, H 5..............Ore.
....*Glen Burke, see Clora....Va.
34*Glenburn, D 6.............Calif.
100 Glenburn, K 14..............Me.
190 Glenburn, F 10...........N. D.
1044 Glenburnie, G 14............Md.
250*Glenburnie (Glenburnie-on-Lake George), K 24 N. Y.
50*Glencairn, G 20...............Ky.
612*Glenn Campbell, L 6.....Pa.
1091*Glen Carbon, M 11.........Ill.
109*Glen Carbon, K 19..........Pa.
85 Glencarlyn, F 18............Va.
200*Glencliff, I 6..............N. H.
669 Glencoe, E 18................Ala.
19*Glencoe, B 15................Ark.
6825 Glencoe, B 21...................Ill.
300 Glencoe, D 16..................Ky.
....*Glencoe, M 13...................La.
215 Glencoe, C 14..................Md.
2387 Glencoe, N 12..............Minn.
67 Glencoe, I 19..................Mo.
575 Glencoe, L 15...............N. M.
500*Glencoe, J 19...............Ohio
337 Glencoe, E 14...............Okla.
83*Glencoe, P 8....................Pa.
....*Glen Cove, G 14............Tex.
200 Glencoe, O 3................Wyo.
.... Glencoe Jc., O 3...........Wyo.
....*Glen Cove (Oakland), N 12........................Me.
12415 Glen Cove, G 6.......N. Y.
51*Glen Cove, G 14............Tex.
61*Glencross, E 11...........S. D.
400*Glencullen, D 8..............Ore.
4855 Glendale, K 12..............Ariz.
82582 Glendale, O 15, P 3..Calif.
75*Glendale, H 14..............Kan.
175*Glendale, H 13................Ky.
250*Glendale, G 2...............Mass.
.... Glendale. E 18..............Minn.
2526*Glendale, I 20..................Mo.
2359 Glendale, N 6................Ohio
.... Glendale, P 24................Ohio
3 Glendale, L 24..............Okla.
557 Glendale, O 5..................Ore.
2500*Glendale, L 3....................Pa.
400 Glendale, A 9................R. I.
1150 Glendale, B 9...............S. C.
200*Glendale, O 11..............Tenn.
200*Glendale, I 22.................Tex.
50 Glendale, Q 8................Utah
50 Glendale, E 7................Wash.
1348 Glen Dale, A 10.......W. Va.
30*Glendale Springs, C 3.N. C.
216*Glen Daniel, O 8......W. Va.
155 Glen Dean, G 11................Ky.
20 Glendevey, B 12.............Colo.
60*Glendie, I 16......................Va.
4524 Glendive, H 24...............Mont.
2 Glendo, C 4...................S. D.
162 Glendo, L 21...................Wyo.

Pop. Place Index State
45*Glendon, G 11........N. C.
552 Glendon, L 23...............Pa.
10*Glendon, J 9..........W. Va.
2822 Glendora, O 17, Q 6...Calif.
.... Glendora, M 6...............Ind.
100*Glendora, Q 10...........Mich.
247 Glendora, E 10.............Miss.
125*Glen Easton, B 11..W. Va.
395 Glen Echo, I 10..............Md.
....*Glen Echo, F 13...............Va.
35*Gleneden Beach, G 3...Ore.
555 Glen Elder, E 13.........Kan.
107*Glenelg, F 11..................Md.
220 Glen Ellen, H 5...........Calif.
45 Glen Ellen, K 9...........Tenn.
8055 Glen Ellyn, C 20..............Ill.
155*Glen Este, O 7................Ohio
46*Glen Eyre, G 24.................Pa.
500*Glenfawn, G 24...............Tex.
700 Glen Ferris, L 8.......W. Va.
260 Glenfield, I 17................N. Y.
110*Glenfield, K 19..............N. D.
911 Glenfield, M 3....................Pa.
500 Glenflora, L 21...............Tex.
140*Glen Flora, G 10...........Wis.
75*Glenford, R 22................N. Y.
231*Glenford, K 15................Ohio
....*Glen Fork, P 6..........W. Va.
536 Glen Gardner, E 11...N. J.
35 Glengarry, H 14...........Mont.
57*Glengarry, E 23............Idaho
50*Glengarry, E 23........W. Va.
600*Glenham, D 6...............N. Y.
131 Glenham, D 13..............S. D.
15*Glen Haven, C 13.......Colo.
75*Glen Haven, I 12.......Mich.
200 Glenhaven, F 21..............Wis.
75*Glenhayes, M 1........W. Va.
2500*Glen Head, H 6............N. Y.
1200*Glen Hedrick (Beaver), O 8.........................W. Va.
185 Glenhope, K 9....................Pa.
146*Gleniron, I 15...................Pa.
....*Glen Island, I 24..........N. Y.
....*Glenita, see Natural Tunnel..........................Va.
.... Glen Jean, O 12..............Ohio
1000 Glen Jean, N 8.........W. Va
14*Glenlake, J 22................N. Y.
220*Glen Lake, M 15.........Minn.
30*Glenloch, J 23................Kan.
200*Glenloch, O 22.....................Pa.
259*Glenlyn, N 3.......................Va.
6200 Glen Lyon, I 20..................Pa.
400 Glenmary, M 17............Tenn.
....*Glenmere, N 13.................Me.
289 Glen Mills, P 22..................Pa.
100*Glenmont, N 23...............N. Y.
281 Glenmont, H 15.................Ohio
163 Glenmoore, O 21...................Pa.
1452 Glenmora, J 9......................La.
25 Glenmore, O 17.....................Ga.
20*Glenmore, J 12......................Ky.
125*Glenmore, F 6....................Ohio
953▲*Glenmore, O 14..............Wis.
100 Glen Morgan, O 8...W. Va.
150*Glen Morrison (Morri), O 6...........................W. Va.
100*Glenn, F 6....................Calif.
48*Glenn, H 2............................Ga.
....*Glenn, see East Glenn..Ind.
100 Glenn, P 11....................Mich.
2239*Glenn (Heidelberg), L 3.Pa.
....*Glenn, C 12.......................Tex.
205*Glenn Dale, I 13................Md.
500 Glennie, J 20...................Mich.
27*Glennonville, J 24..............Mo.
50*Glenn Ranch, M 21...Calif.
53*Glenns, M 20.........................Va.
1290 Glenns Ferry, P 8....Idaho
134*Glenn Springs, B 9.....S. C.
950*Glen Ullin, O 11...........N. D.
50*Glennville, M 14..........Calif.
1674 Glennville, L 20....................Ga.
21*Glen Oak, K 17.....................Wis.
4825 Glenolden (Glen Olden), P 23.................................Pa.
450 Glenoma, M 8...............Wash.
16*Glenora, J 15........................Va.
523 Glen Park, H 15..............N. Y.
284 Glenpool, F 19.................Okla.
225 Glen Raven, D 10.........N. C.
85*Glenray, P 10..............W. Va.
250 Glen Richey, J 10..............Pa.
1000 Glen Riddle, P 22...............Pa.
332 Glenridge (Junction City), M 15.....................................Ill.
7331 Glen Ridge, E 18...........N. J.
80 Glenrio, G 25.................N. M.
15*Glen Robbins, I 20.......Ohio
30 Glenrock (Glen Rock), N 24.................................Neb.
5177 Glenrock, C 19...............N. J.
1412 Glen Rock, Q 17...................Pa.
1014 Glenrock, J 18.................Wyo.
200 Glen Rogers, O 7...W. Va.
1050 Glen Rose, F 17...............Tex.
150 Glenroy, O 13...................Ohio
215*Glen St. Mary, C 14.....Fla.
150 Glensboro, F 16...................Ky.
18836 Glens Falls, K 24.....N. Y.
1500 Glenshaw, L 3.....................Pa.
.... Glenside, O 24 (Pop. 13000 incl. in Abington)......Pa.
150*Glen Spey, C 2.............N. Y.
27*Glen Springs, D 21.........Ky.
61*Glensted, J 11....................Mo.
75 Glentana, C 20..............Mont.
976 Glen Ullin (Glenullen), N 8.............................N. D.
....*Glen Union, H 13..............Va.
2500 Glenview, B 21.....................Ill.
100*Glenview, F 14....................Ky.
285 Glenvil, N 17......................Neb.
185*Glenville, P 8....................Ark.
500 Glenville, R 1..................Conn.
615 Glenville, R 16................Minn.
400*Glenville, P 5.................N. C.
130*Glenville, Q 17....................Pa.
588 Glenville, G 10.........W. Va.
230 Glenwhite, M 9.....................Pa.
519 Glen White, O 7.......W. Va.
170*Glen Wild, B 3..............N. Y.
1600*Glenwillard (Shousetown), M 3..............................Pa.
218 Glenwillow (Falls Jc.), D 17................................Ohio
325 Glen Wilton, L 7..................Va.
393 Glenwood, M 16..................Ala.
1310 Glenwood, L 7....................Ark.
25*Glenwood, J 6.................Calif.
1825 Glenwood (Glenwood Springs), G 7...............Colo.
321*Glenwood, F 18....................Fla.
625 Glenwood, K 16....................Ga.
35 Glenwood, H 7..................Idaho
643 Glenwood, D 21......................Ill.
338 Glenwood, K 19....................Ind.
4501 Glenwood, N 3..................Iowa
85*Glenwood, E 22......................Ky.
175*Glenwood, F 12....................Md.
200*Glenwood, R 12..................Mich.
2564 Glenwood, L 7...................Minn.
315 Glenwood, A 12......................Mo.
309 Glenwood, A 15..................N. J.
58 Glenwood, L 2...................N. M.
100*Glenwood, N 5.................N. Y.
176*Glenwood (Nealsville), F 1...................................N. C.

Pop. Place Index State
40*Glenwood, K 17.........Ohio
200 Glenwood, C 6.............Ore.
385 Glenwood, L 11..........Utah
96 Glenwood, O 11........Wash.
166*Glenwood, J 3.......W. Va.
811 Glenwood City, C 11..Wis.
3 Glenwood Jc., A 12....Mo.
.... Glenwood Jc., E 3....N. Y.
350*Glenwood Landing, H 6 N. Y.
5 Glenwood Park, M 15.Neb.
2253 Glenwood Springs (Glenwood), G 7..............Colo.
40*Glenys, P 22..............Wyo.
250*Glezen, P 7....................Ind.
941 Glidden, I 8...................Iowa
360 Glidden, L 20....................Tex.
1150 Glidden, G 7.....................Wis.
50 Glide, M 6.........................Ore.
450*Glo, H 22..............................Ky.
6141 Globe, K 18......................Ariz.
30*Globe, E 22............................Ky.
12 Globe, N 21....................N. M.
125*Globe, E 3......................N. C.
.... Globe, M 4....................Wash.
58 Globe Mills, K 15..............Pa.
1000 Glomawr, I 21......................Ky.
280 Glorieta, F 14................N. M.
700*Gloryetta, P 16..............Calif.
125*Gloster, F 8........................Ga.
500 Gloster, D 4..........................La.
250 Gloster, M 25..................Minn.
1232 Gloster, O 6.....................Miss.
24046 Gloucester, C 22.....Mass.
13692*Gloucester (Gloucester City), K 9..................N. J.
148*Gloucester, K 21..........N. C.
300 Gloucester, M 20..................Va.
13692 Gloucester City (Gloucester), K 9...N. J.
109*Gloucester Heights, K 9 N. J.
160*Gloucester Point, N 21..Va.
2847 Glouster, M 15................Ohio
82*Glover, M 7......................Ala.
12 Glover, H 20..........................Ill.
78*Glover, N 19........................Mo.
80 Glover, P 20....................N. D.
23 Glover, P 23......................Okla.
216 Glover, C 16..........................Vt.
200*Glovergap, D 12.......W. Va.
23329 Gloversville, M 21...N. Y.
.... Gluck, C 3.............................Tex.
31 Gluek, N 7........................Minn.
490 Glyndon, D 12......................Md.
405 Glyndon, H 3...................Minn.
84*Glynn, J 14.............................La.
876 Gnadenhutten, I 18...Ohio
100*Gneiss, Q 5....................N. C.
319*Gober, D 21........................Tex.
90 Goble. B 7............................Ore.
25*Gobler, J 24..........................Mo.
616 Gobles, Q 12....................Mich.
112*Goddard, E 20.........................Ky.
248 Goddard, M 15....................Kan.
112*Goddard, E 20.........................Ky.
30*Godeffroy, D 3.................N. Y.
197 Godfrey, G 11..........................Ga.
300 Godfrey, L 10.........................Ill.
12 Godfrey, L 25........................Kan.
317 Godley, E 18..........................Tex.
123 *Godwin, I 14.................N. C.
125 Goehner, L 20......................Neb.
300*Goessel, K 16......................Kan.
57 Goethite, G 11......................Ala.
75*Goetzville, F 16..................Mich.
339 Goff, E 21..............................Kan.
.... Goff-Kirby Jc. J 4..................Pa.
60*Goffs, G 9.........................W. Va.
265*Goffs Falls, P 15..............N. H.
850 Goffstown, P 13................N. H.
....*Gogganville, see Goggins, Ga.
125*Goggins, H 8..........................Ga.
22*Goin, L 20.........................Tenn.
.... Golah, M 9.......................N. Y.
19*Golansville, K 16....................Va.
1301 Golconda, Q 18......................Ill.
269 Golconda, C 11....................Nev.
96*Gold, F 12..................................Pa.
307 Gold Bar (Goldbar), G 10 Wash.
500 Gold Beach, P 2..................Ore.
32*Goldbug, J 18..........................Ky.
75*Goldburg, L 12..................Idaho
35 Goldbutte, C 10................Mont.
35 Gold Creek, I 7..............Mont.
62 Gold Creek, B 18...............Nev.
99*Gold Dust, I 11.......................La.
217 Golddust, N 2.....................Tenn.
3175 Golden, F 14......................Colo.
150 Golden, I 7........................Idaho
624 Golden, H 6................................Ill.
340 Golden, A 23......................Miss.
114*Golden, R 9............................Mo.
50 Golden, G 13......................N. M.
40 Golden, P 24........................Okla.
163*Golden, E 23.........................Tex.
500 Goldenbridge, E 6.....N. Y.
867 Golden City, N 7...................Mo.
1584 Goldendale, P 13.........Wash.
....*Golden Eagle, L 8...................Ill.
248 Goldengate, N 19......................Ill.
275 Golden Hill, N 17.....................Md.
75 Golden Lake, E 22..............Ark.
300*Golden Meadow, P 18...La.
74*Golden Pond, J 7..................Ky.
2048*Golden Valley, M 15.Minn.
400 Goldenvalley, K 7.......N. D.
195 Goldfield, K 14.................Colo.
715 Goldfield, F 11....................Iowa
325 Goldfield, L 12......................Nev.
32*Goldfinch, M 16....................Tex.
72*Gold Hill (Gold Ridge), I 21...................................Ala.
50 Goldhill, E 13.......................Colo.
30*Gold Hill, H 3........................Nev.
249 Gold Hill, G 7.....................N. C.
536 Gold Hill, P 6............................Ore.
75 Gold Hill, G 2........................Utah
256*Goldonna, E 8..............................La.
20 Gold Point, M 12.....................Nev.
72*Gold Ridge (Gold Hill), J 21....................................Ala.
....*Goldroad, F 5..........................Ariz.
114*Gold Run, H 9......................Calif.
50*Goldsberry, D 12....................Mo.
197 Goldsboro, H 20........................Md.
17274 Goldsboro, H 16.....N. C.
478 Goldsboro (Etters), O 16.Pa.
150*Goldsboro, F 14....................Tex.
200 Goldsmith, H 14.....................Ind.
1000*Goldsmith, F 8......................Tex.
416 Goldston, F 11..................N. C.
8 Gold Stone, C 12.............Mont.
1414 Goldthwaite, H 16..............Tex.
14*Goldvein, G 15..........................Va.
1200 Goldville, E 9......................S. C.
45 Goldwin, L 17......................N. D.
1200 Goleta, N 11.......................Calif.
158*Golf, B 20..................................Ill.
1446 Goliad, N 18............................Tex.
330*Goltry, C 9...........................Okla.
80*Golts (Golt), F 18.....................Md.
128 Golva, N 1.............................N. D.
270 Gomer, G 8...........................Ohio
3*Gonce, B 17...............................Ala.
400*Gonic (West Gonic), N 19 N. H.

Pop. Place Index State
317 Gonvick, E 7...........Minn.
30*Gonyon, K 21..................Va.
1200 Gonzales, K 7..............Calif.
857 Gonzales, M 16..................La.
4722 Gonzales, L 18...............Tex.
500*Gonzalez, M 2.................Fla.
62 Goochland, L 15...............Va.
50*Goodbee, K 18....................La.
75*Goode (Goodes), N 8...Va.
236 Goodell, E 12....................Iowa
250*Goodells, N 24..................Mich.
100 Goodenow, D 21......................Ill.
150 Goodfield, G 14......................Ill.
110*Good Hart, H 16.............Mich.
125*Good Hope, J 17.................Ala.
219 Good Hope, F 11....................Ga.
366 Good Hope, G 7.......................Ill.
500*Goodhope, M 18......................La.
50 Goodhope, J 14..................Miss.
250 Good Hope, M 11..............Ohio
480 Goodhue, O 19....................Minn.
2568 Gooding, P 10......................Idaho
1097 Goodland, E 7..........................Ind.
3306 Goodland, F 2.......................Kan.
39*Goodland, I 14.....................Minn.
27*Goodland, M 18........................Mo.
....*Goodland, B 8........................Tex.
113*Goodlett, A 13........................Tex.
1500 Goodlettsville (Goodletts), L 11.................................Tenn.
55*Goodloe, H 22............................Ky.
34*Goodluck, J 15............................Ky.
609 Goodman, H 13.....................Miss.
321 Goodman, Q 6............................Mo.
1000 Goodman, N 9..........................Wis.
86*Good Mills, H 11..........................Va.
22 Goodnight, G 14.....................Okla.
180 Goodnight, D 4..........................Tex.
144*Goodnoe Hills, P 14..Wash.
600 Good Pine, F 11..........................La.
50*Goodrich, D 18.......................Colo.
33 Goodrich, K 4.......................Idaho
113*Goodrich, J 24..........................Kan.
.... Goodrich, C 19............................Me.
380 Goodrich, O 21.......................Mich.
476 Goodrich, K 14......................N. D.
500*Goodrich, J 23..........................Tex.
50 Goodrich, I 11.............................Wis.
174 Goodridge, D 6.....................Minn.
36 Goodridge, Q 21......................Utah
25 Goods Mills, I 12......................Va.
77*Goodson, M 10..........................Mo.
110*Goodspeeds (Tylerville), K 15.......................................Conn.
104*Goodspring, L 18..........................Pa.
50*Goodspring, Q 10.....................Tenn.
125 Goodsprings, F 10.....................Ala.
80 Goodsprings, P 19.....................Nev.
457 Good Thunder, Q 13.Minn.
75*Goodview, N 8................................Va.
229*Goodville, O 20................................Pa.
1028 Good Water, H 17....................Ala.
30*Good Water, M 17....................Mo.
119*Goodwater, Q 25...................Okla.
75*Goodway, N 10............................Ala.
360 Goodwell, R 5..........................Okla.
300 Goodwill, Q 7..................W. Va.
75*Goodwin, H 18..........................Ark.
30 Goodwin, F 22..........................Neb.
152 Goodwin, G 24........................S. D.
85 Goodwine, G 21............................Ill.
46*Goodwins Ferry, O 4...Va.
19*Goody, H 24.................................Ky.
140 Goodyear, L 14........................Ariz.
784 Goodyear, D 23.....................Conn.
35*Goodyear, O 15..............................Pa.
60*Goodyears Bar, F 9...Calif.
77*Goose Bill, F 11.................Mont.
6929 Goose Creek, L 23.............Tex.
....*Goose Egg, J 15..................Wyo.
145*Gooselake, J 25...................Iowa
25*Gooseprairie, L 12...Wash.
100*Gooserock, I 20............................Ky.
13 Gopher, D 8.............................S. D.
12*Gorby, C 13..................................Ark.
934 Gordo, G 6...................................Ala.
327 Gordon, O 23..............................Ala.
81 Gordon, O 15..............................Colo.
1524 Gordon, I 12...................................Ga.
50*Gordon, M 17..............................Kan.
22*Gordon, J 22.................................Ky.
100*Gordon (Gordonville), R 17.......................................Minn.
1967 Gordon, E 6................................Neb.
178*Gordon, K 6...............................Ohio
1062*Gordon, K 19...............................Pa.
532 Gordon, E 16..............................Tex.
65*Gordon, N 5..........................W. Va.
225 Gordon, D 6.................................Wis.
315 Gordonsburg, O 9.........Tenn.
85*Gordonsville, K 13..............Ala.
100*Gordonsville (Gordon), R 17.......................................Minn.
250 Gordonsville, M 13...Tenn.
508 Gordonsville, J 14....................Va.
319 Gordontown, I 6......................Pa.
154*Gordonville, N 22..................Mo.
250*Gordonville, P 20.....................Pa.
250*Gordonville, C 19..................Tex.
35*Gore, C 2...Ga.
30*Gore, I 16......................................Mo.
350*Gore, M 13...................................Ohio
334 Gore, I 22.....................................Okla.
200*Gore (Cornwell), E 13..Va.
425 Goree, C 14...................................Tex.
508 Goreville, Q 15..............................Ill.
500*Gorgas, E 10.................................Ala.
91*Gorham (Marshall), E 13 Colo.
595 Gorham, P 13......................................Ill.
275 Gorham, H 11...................................Kan.
1088 Gorham, P 5.....................................Me.
2000 Gorham, G 17..............................N. H.
500 Gorham, N 11..............................N. Y.
10 Gorham, L 3..................................N. D.
500 Gorin, B 14..Mo.
35*Gorman, N 14...........................Calif.
35 Gorman, G 13..............................S. D.
82*Gorman, M 8.............................Tenn.
1157 Gorman, F 15................................Tex.
373 Gormania, E 17................W. Va.
36*Gorum, H 8..La.
.... Gosford, M 13...............................Calif.
96*Goshen (Goshen Jc.), K 12...Calif.
356 Goshen, M 17.................................Ala.
75*Goshen, C 5.......................................Ark.
300 Goshen, D 6...................................Conn.
11375 Goshen, B 16..............................Ind.
30*Goshen, E 14..Ky.
150 Goshen, E 6.....................................Mass.
400 Goshen, Q 12..................................N. J.
3073 Goshen, E 4.................................N. Y.
88*Goshen, D 4....................................N. C.
200*Goshen, N 7....................................Ohio
93 Goshen, J 6..Ore.
.... Goshen, O 17....................................S. C.
616 Goshen, H 11......................................Utah
187*Goshen, K 9..Va.
10 Goshen, B 8..Wash.
96 Goshen Jc. (Goshen), K 12...Calif.
.... Goshen Jc., O 19.......................Idaho
45*Goshen Springs, J 13..Miss.
115*Gosneyville, G 20......................Ky.
25*Gosport, M 6.....................................Ala.
729 Gosport, L 11..Ind.
.... Gosport Jc., L 11..................................Ind.
36*Goss, O 13...Miss.

Pop. Place Index State
26*Goss, F 14 ... Mo.
155 Gossville, O 16 ... N. H.
607 Gotebo, K 6 ... Okla.
200*Gotha, G 17 ... Fla.
300 Gotham, H 19 ... Wis.
2330 Gothenburg, L 12 ... Neb.
200*Goudeau, J 11 ... La.
200*Gough, H 19 ... Ga.
245*Gough, L 19 ... S. C.
121*Gouglersville, N 20 ... Pa.
827 Gould, M 16 ... Ark.
... Gould, I 7 ... Mont.
391 Gould, M 2 ... Okla.
200*Gouldbusk, H 15 ... Tex.
200*Gould City, F 15 ... Mich.
490 Goulds, O 23 ... Fla.
280 Gouldsboro, M 19 ... Me.
621 Gouldsboro (Sand Cut), H 22 ... Pa.
....*Gourd, See Ulvah ...
50 Gourdin, J 18 ... S. C.
4478 Gouverneur, F 17 ... N. Y.
.... Gouverneur and Oswegatchie Jc., F 17 ... N. Y.
113*Govan, L 13 ... S. C.
28 Govan, G 19 ... Wash.
284 Gove, G 6 ... Kan.
10*Governador, C 8 ... N. M.
50*Government Camp, E 10 Ore.
....*Governors Island, I 5 . N. Y.
3 Govert, E 4 ... S. D.
207*Gowan (Mirbat), F 19 Minn.
3156 Gowanda, O 4 ... N. Y.
600*Gowdey, K 9 ... Miss.
128 Gowen, M 13 ... Mich.
400*Gowen City, J 16 ... Pa.
386 Gower, E 6 ... Mo.
1028 Gowrie, H 9 ... Iowa
100 Graafschap, O 11 ... Mich.
82*Grab, J 14 ... Ky.
288 Grabill, C 21 ... Ind.
60*Grabners, K 10 ... Calif.
701 Grace, Q 21 ... Idaho
.... Grace, I 20 ... Ky.
30 Grace, H 19 ... Mich.
100*Grace, H 6 ... Miss.
18 Grace, L 8 ... Mont.
100 Grace City, J 18 ... N. D.
150 Graceham, C 8 ... Md.
.... Graceland, C 8 ... Va.
328 Gracemont, J 8 ... Okla.
41*Graceton, C 10 ... Minn.
500 Graceton, M 7 ... Pa.
1181 Graceville, M 10 ... Fla.
1020 Graceville, L 3 ... Minn.
500*Gracewood, H 19 ... Ga.
234 Gracey, J 8 ... Ky.
45*Grade, J 18 ... Ky.
175*Grady, K 17 ... Ala.
496 Grady, M 15 ... Ark.
112 Grady, E 2 ... Ga.
237 Grady, H 24 ... N. M.
64 Grady, Q 11 ... Okla.
150*Gradyville, J 15 ... Ky.
110*Gradyville, P 22 ... Pa.
150 Graeagle, E 9 ... Calif.
928 Graettinger, C 8 ... Iowa
47 Graf, G 23 ... Iowa
64 Graf, N 24 ... Neb.
10*Graff, O 13 ... Mo.
804 Graford, D 16 ... Tex.
.... Grafton, see Knights Landing ... Calif.
1110 Grafton, L 8 ... Ill.
256 Grafton, C 14 ... Iowa
1000 Grafton, G 15 ... Mass.
240 Grafton, M 19 ... Neb.
75 Grafton, L 10 ... N. H.
750*Grafton, N 24 ... N. Y.
4070 Grafton, F 22 ... N. D.
971 Grafton, E 15 ... Ohio
150 Grafton, O 12 ... Vt.
200*Grafton, O 21 ... Va.
7431 Grafton, E 14 ... W. Va.
1150 Grafton, P 19 ... Wis.
95 Grafton Center (Cardigan), M 16 ... N. H.
26*Gragg, E 2 ... N. C.
233 Graham, F 21 ... Ala.
150*Graham, C 14 ... Fla.
165 Graham, M 17 ... Ga.
56*Graham, F 22 ... Iowa
1200 Graham, I 9 ... Ky.
336 Graham, B 4 ... Mo.
35 Graham, M 22 ... Mont.
46 Graham, E 2 ... N. Y.
4339 Graham, E 10 ... N. C.
115 Graham, O 12 ... Okla.
121*Graham, N 9 ... Tenn.
5175 Graham, D 16 ... Tex.
250 Graham, K 8 ... Wash.
50*Graham (Graham Sta.), G 5 ... W. Va.
210 Grahams Forge, P 3 ... Va.
235*Grahamsville, C 3 ... N. Y.
300 Grahamton, G 13 ... Ky.
325 Grahn, E 21 ... Ky.
341 Grainfield, G 6 ... Kan.
157 Grainola, A 16 ... Okla.
100 Grainton, L 9 ... Neb.
362 Grain Valley, G 7 ... Mo.
250*Grambling, C 8 ... La.
2000*Gramercy, M 17 ... La.
150*Gramling (Gramlin), A 8 ... S. C.
.... Gramm, R 18 ... Wyo.
153*Grammer, L 17 ... Ind.
632 Grampian, J 9 ... Pa.
342 Granada, M 23 ... Colo.
431 Granada, R 12 ... Minn.
1166 Granbury, E 17 ... Tex.
251 Granby, E 12 ... Colo.
625 Granby, B 12 ... Conn.
56 Granby, G 8 ... Mass.
1455 Granby, P 6 ... Mo.
15*Granby, D 20 ... Vt.
16*Grancer, I 11 ... Ky.
113 Grand, F 2 ... Okla.
300*Grandale, Q 22 ... Mich.
500*Grand Bay, Q 4 ... Ala.
83*Grand Bayou, E 6 ... La.
319 Grand Beach, R 9 ... Mich.
1012 Grand Blanc, N 20 ... Mich.
377 Grand Cane, E 4 ... La.
550*Grand Canyon, D 12 . Ariz.
406 Grand Chain (New Grand Chain), Q 15 ... Ill.
250*Grand Chenier, O 8 ... La.
662 Grand Coteau, L 11 ... La.
3659*Grand Coulee, J 17 . Wash.
200*Grand Crossing (Moncrief), B 15 ... Fla.
.... Grand Crossing, C 21 ... Ill.
30 Grand Falls, P 6 ... Mo.
653*Grand Falls, G 8 ... Tex.
1116 Grandfield, O 6 ... Okla.
20228 Grand Forks, H 24 . N. D.
80*Grandglaise, F 16 ... Ark.
600 Grand Gorge, P 21 ... N. Y.
12 Grand Gulf, L 6 ... Miss.
12 Grand Harbor, G 17 . N. D.
8799 Grand Haven, O 11 ... Mich.
60*Grand Hotel (Highmount), R 21 ... N. Y.
150*Grandin, D 15 ... Fla.
294 Grandin, Q 18 ... Mo.
158 Grandin, K 24 ... N. D.

Pop. Place Index State
198*Grand Island, F 16 ... Fla.
19130 Grand Island, L 17 ... Neb.
500*Grand Island, O 5 ... N. Y.
575 Grand Isle, Q 19 ... La.
1000 Grand Isle, A 18 ... Me.
815 Grand Isle, C 5 ... Vt.
12479 Grand Jc., I 3 ... Colo.
4 Grand Jc., D 3 ... Idaho
1125 Grand Jc., I 10 ... Iowa
168 Grand Jc., P 11 ... Mich.
560 Grand Jc., Q 4 ... Tenn.
50*Grand Lake, R 17 ... Ark.
200 Grand Lake, D 12 ... Colo.
100 Grand Lake Stream, J 20 Me.
3899 Grand Ledge, O 17 ... Mich.
500 Grand Marais, E 12 . Mich.
855 Grand Marais, B 22 . Minn.
202 Grand Marsh, J 17 ... Wis.
700 Grand Meadow, R 19 . Minn.
....*Grand Mesa, I 6 ... Colo.
526 Grandmound, J 23 ... Iowa
200 Grand Mound, L 5 ... Wash.
115*Grand Pass, G 9 ... Mo.
136*Grand Portage, B 21 . Minn.
1595 Grand Prairie, E 19 ... Tex.
164292 Grand Rapids, O 13 . Mich.
4875 Grand Rapids, G 15 . Minn.
60 Grand Rapids, O 20 . N. D.
641 Grand Rapids, D 9 ... Ohio
300 Grand Ridge, B 2 ... Fla.
385 Grand Ridge, E 16 ... Ill.
374 Grand River, P 11 ... Iowa
305 Grand River, A 18 ... Ohio
499 Grand Rivers, J 7 ... Ky.
350 Grand Ronde, F 5 ... Ore.
1641 Grand Saline, E 21 ... Tex.
1043 Grand Tower, P 13 ... Ill.
230 Grand Valley, G 5 ... Colo.
445▲Grand Valley, R 6 ... Okla.
268 Grand Valley, F 5 ... Pa.
50*Grand View, A 7 ... Ark.
125*Grandview, H 5 ... Calif.
.... Grand View, P 5 ... Idaho
607 Grand View, R 9 ... Ind.
315 Grandview, M 22 ... Iowa
596 Grandview, H 6 ... Mo.
100*Grandview, Q 2 ... N. C.
250 Grandview, M 18 ... Ohio
1*Grandview, H 11 ... Ore.
80*Grandview, N 16 ... Tenn.
823 Grand View, F 18 ... Tex.
1449 Grandview, N 16 ... Wash.
200*Grandview, N 9 ... W. Va.
412 Grandview, F 6 ... Wis.
6960 Grandview Heights, K 12 Ohio
1566 Grandville, O 13 ... Mich.
150*Grandy, L 17 ... Minn.
105*Grandy, D 24 ... N. C.
35*Grange, C 16 ... Ark.
.... Grange, M 12 ... Miss.
56*Grange, J 7 ... Pa.
231 Grangeburg, O 22 ... Ala.
165*Grange City, E 20 ... Ky.
271 Granger, A 14 ... Ind.
324 Granger, K 11 ... Iowa
160*Granger, R 21 ... Minn.
180*Granger, A 14 ... Mo.
1723 Granger, I 18 ... Tex.
.... Granger, F 11 ... Utah
752 Granger, N 15 ... Wash.
163 Granger, O 5 ... Wyo.
162*Grangeville, K 11 ... Calif.
1929 Grangeville, H 6 ... Idaho
60 Grangeville, K 16 ... La.
50*Granite (Yale), I 11 ... Colo.
102 Granite, C 4 ... Idaho
51*Granite, B 1 ... Iowa
500 Granite, D 13 ... Md.
50*Granite, K 18 ... N. H.
1058 Granite, L 4 ... Okla.
86 Granite, G 20 ... Ore.
100 Granite Canon, Q 20 . Wyo.
22974 Granite City, M 10 ... Ill.
2388 Granite Falls, N 7 ... Minn.
1873 Granite Falls, E 4 ... N. C.
683 Granite Falls, F 9 ... Wash.
35*Granite Heights (Heights), J 11 ... Wis.
20*Granite Hill, H 14 ... Ga.
555 Granite Quarry, F 7 . N. C.
207*Granite Springs, E 6 . N. Y.
12*Granite Springs, J 15 ... Va.
150 Graniteville, F 9 ... Calif.
1200 Graniteville, C 16 ... Mass.
600 Graniteville, M 19 ... Mo.
2560 Graniteville, I 9 ... S. C.
1000 Graniteville, G 13 ... Vt.
25*Grannie, G 20 ... Ky.
325 Grannis, L 4 ... Ark.
57 Grano, E 9 ... N. D.
96*Granogue, D 21 ... Del.
35*Gran Quivera, I 13 ... N. M.
205*Grant, B 16 ... Ala.
25 Grant, H 13 ... Colo.
150*Grant, I 21 ... Fla.
.... Grant, N 19 ... Idaho
23 Grant, N 6 ... Iowa
....*Grant, see Belleview ... Ky.
150*Grant, J 7 ... La.
552 Grant, M 11 ... Mich.
125 Grant, N 6 ... Mont.
897 Grant, L 7 ... Neb.
25*Grant, K 18 ... N. Y.
309 Grant, Q 20 ... Okla.
.... Grant, J 25 ... S. D.
75*Grant, E 10 ... Va.
37*Grant Center, I 2 ... Iowa
1209 Grant City, A 6 ... Mo.
110 Grantham, M 9 ... N. H.
150*Grantham, O 14 ... Pa.
50*Granton, Q 19 ... N. Y.
300 Granton, H 13 ... Wis.
120*Grant Orchards (Soap Lake), J 17 ... Wash.
519 Grant Park, E 21 ... Ill.
25 Grants (Kennebago), J 4 Me.
800 Grants (Grant), G 5 . N. M.
500*Grants (Grantsboro), I 20 N. C.
500*Grantsboro (Grants), I 20 N. C.
110 Grantsburg, Q 17 ... Ill.
125 Grantsburg, P 12 ... Ind.
874 Grantsburg, B 8 ... Wis.
90 Grantsdale, K 4 ... Mont.
1411▲*Grants Lick, C 18 ... Ky.
6028 Grants Pass, P 5 ... Ore.
465*Grantsville, N 2 ... Md.
1242 Grantsville, F 9 ... Utah
1052 Grantsville, G 9 ... W. Va.
3000 Grant Town, C 13 ... W. Va.
1267 Grantville, H 4 ... Ga.
100 Grantville, G 22 ... Kan.
150*Grantville, N 17 ... Pa.
....*Grantwood, C 19 ... N. J.
1038 Granville, E 14 ... Ill.
361 Granville, D 3 ... Iowa
360 Granville, I 5 ... Mass.
98 Granville, E 14 ... Mo.
3173 Granville, K 25 ... N. Y.
443 Granville, G 11 ... N. D.
1502 Granville, K 14 ... Ohio
500 Granville, M 13 ... Pa.
300 Granville, M 14 ... Tenn.
247▲Granville, I 10 ... Vt.
318*Granville (Mona), ... W. Va.

Pop. Place Index State
175*Granville, O 19 ... Wis.
90*Granville Center, I 6 . Mass.
48*Granville Summit (Cowley), F 17 ... Pa.
....*Grape, J 17 ... Ky.
400 Grape Creek, H 22 ... Ill.
83*Grapefield, C 11 ... Va.
6*Grapeland, F 7 ... Miss.
1327 Grapeland, G 22 ... Tex.
100 Grapeview, I 6 ... Wash.
1400*Grapeville, N 5 ... Pa.
50 Grapevine, L 12 ... Ark.
15*Grapevine, M 14 ... Calif.
1043 Grapevine, D 18 ... Tex.
200 Grasmere, P 14 ... N. H.
850 Grasonville, I 17 ... Md.
25 Grasscreek, E 13 ... Ind.
60 Grass Creek, E 14 ... Utah
482 Grass Creek, F 9 ... Wyo.
.... Grass Creek Jc., E 14 Utah
1100 Grasselli, F 12 ... Ala.
.... Grasselli, B 6 ... Ind.
510 Grasselli, F 18 ... N. J.
83*Grassfield, O 2 ... Va.
1200 Grassflat, J 11 ... Pa.
810 Grass Lake, P 18 ... Mich.
38*Grassland, I 12 ... Ky.
27*Grassland, I 15 ... Va.
206 Grass Range, H 14 ... Mont.
144 Grasston, K 16 ... Minn.
5701 Grass Valley, F 8 ... Calif.
204 Grass Valley, D 13 ... Ore.
75*Grassy, P 20 ... Mo.
50*Grassy, M 1 ... W. Va.
40*Grassy Butte, I 3 ... N. D.
58*Grassy Cove, O 16 ... Tenn.
47*Grassy Creek, F 21 ... Ky.
350*Grassy Creek, B 4 ... N. C.
42*Grassy Meadows, M 12 W. Va.
200*Grassy Point, F 5 ... N. Y.
.... Grassy Run Jc., G 7 ... Pa.
400*Graterford (Graters Ford), N 22 ... Pa.
257 Gratiot, K 14 ... Ohio
297 Gratiot, I 22 ... Wis.
435 Gratis, L 6 ... Ohio
500*Graton, G 3 ... Calif.
95▲*Grattan, F 12 ... Minn.
19*Gratton, C 10 ... Va.
139 Gratz, D 16 ... Ky.
692 Gratz, L 17 ... Pa.
....*Grave Creek, O 5 ... Ore.
138*Gravelly, I 7 ... Ark.
70*Gravelly Springs, A 7 . Ala.
41*Gravelridge, P 12 ... Ark.
125*Gravel Switch, H 15 ... Ky.
100*Gravelton, O 20 ... Mo.
63*Graves, L 6 ... Ga.
13*Graves Mill, I 13 ... Va.
....*Graves Sta., see Graves . Ga.
60*Gravesville, K 19 ... N. Y.
812 Gravette, A 4 ... Ark.
514 Gravity, P 8 ... Iowa
165*Gravity, G 22 ... Pa.
500 Gravois (Affton), I 20 . Mo.
59*Gravois Mills, J 11 ... Mo.
150 Grawn, J 13 ... Mich.
698 Gray, H 12 ... Ga.
....*Gray, O 21 ... Idaho
182*Gray, J 7 ... Iowa
500 Gray (Grays), J 19 ... Ky.
200*Gray, O 16 ... La.
500 Gray, O 6 ... Me.
135*Gray (East Gray), O 6 . Me.
14*Gray, R 7 ... Okla.
.... Gray, R 7 ... Okla.
800 Gray, O 7 ... Pa.
20 Gray, Q 17 ... Va.
14 Gray (Grays), F 22 . Wash.
....*Grayback, B 15 ... Tex.
474 Grayburg, K 24 ... Tex.
401 Gray Court, D 7 ... S. C.
32*Graydon, L 8 ... W. Va.
50*Graydon Springs, N 9 . Mo.
35*Grayfox, F 21 ... Ky.
125*Gray Hawk, H 19 ... Ky.
500 Gray (Grays), J 19 ... Ky.
63 Gray Horse, C 16 ... Okla.
200 Grayland, L 2 ... Wash.
2124 Grayling, J 17 ... Mich.
10*Grayling, M 10 ... Mont.
1019*Graymont, J 18 ... Ga.
102 Graymont, F 16 ... Ill.
250*Grayridge, P 21 ... Mo.
62 Grayrocks, M 22 ... Wyo.
80*Grays, G 17 ... Ark.
500*Grays (Gray), J 19 ... Ky.
14 Grays (Gray), F 22 . Wash.
250*Grays Branch (Mackoy), D 22 ... Ky.
225*Grays Chapel, B 18 ... Ala.
150*Grays Knob, K 21 ... Ky.
1182 Grayslake, A 19 ... Ill.
500 Grays Landing, Q 4 ... Pa.
228 Grayson, E 9 ... Ga.
1176 Grayson, E 22 ... Ky.
407 Grayson, E 11 ... La.
51*Grayson, E 6 ... Mo.
74*Grayson, B 3 ... N. C.
....*Grayson, see Wildcat . Okla.
694 Graysonia, M 8 ... Ark.
100*Graysport, E 14 ... Miss.
40 Grays River, N 4 ... Wash.
215 Gray Summit, J 18 ... Mo.
126*Graysville, B 3 ... Ga.
100 Graysville, M 5 ... Ind.
170*Graysville, L 18 ... Ohio
240 Graysville, P 1 ... Pa.
846 Graysville, P 16 ... Tenn.
25*Grayton, N 10 ... Md.
129*Graytown, C 11 ... Ohio
2240 Grayville, N 20 ... Ill.
200*Greaney, F 19 ... Minn.
200*Greason, O 14 ... Pa.
47*Greasy Creek, I 23 ... Ky.
50*Greasy Ridge, Q 14 ... Ohio
5824■Great Barrington, G 2 . Mass.
9044 Great Bend, J 11 ... Kan.
400 Great Bend, H 16 ... N. Y.
198 Great Bend, P 25 ... N. D.
742 Great Bend, D 21 ... Pa.
525 Great Cacapon, C 23 . W. Va.
23 Great Divide, B 6 ... Colo.
75 Greaterville, O 18 ... Ariz.
29928 Great Falls, G 10 ... Mont.
4300 Great Falls, D 14 ... S. C.
....*Great Lakes, A 20 ... Ill.
250*Great Meadows, D 11 . N. J.
75 Great Mills, O 15 ... Md.
6167*Great Neck, G 7 ... N. Y.
1969*Great Neck Estates, H 7 N. Y.
2031*Great Neck Plaza, H 7 . N. Y.
500*Great Notch, D 19 ... N. J.
50 Great Pond, K 17 ... Me.
125*Great River, H 8 ... N. Y.
190 Great Valley, Q 5 ... N. Y.
200 Great Western, F 4 ... Mich.
413 Great Works, K 15 ... Me.
35*Greear, F 21 ... Ky.
525 Greeley, G 10 ... Ala.
15995 Greeley, D 16 ... Colo.
403 Greeley, F 21 ... Iowa
387 Greeley, J 23 ... Kan.
17*Greeley, G 20 ... Ky.
30 Greeley, N 17 ... Mo.
891 Greeley, J 16 ... Neb.
300 Greeley, G 24 ... Pa.

Pop. Place Index State
633 Greelyville, J 18 ... S. C.
246 Green, F 17 ... Kan.
20*Green, F 21 ... Ky.
185 Green, M 5 ... Ore.
110*Green, N 17 ... Tex.
304 Greenacres City, L 23 . Fla.
700 Greenacres, H 24 ... Wash.
600*Greenback, O 18 ... Tenn.
408 Greenbackville, K 25 ... Va.
230 Green Bank, N 15 ... N. J.
16 Greenbank, O 19 ... Pa.
100 Greenbank, F 7 ... Wash.
175*Green Bank, K 15 ... W. Va.
125 Green Bay, O 13 ... Va.
46235 Green Bay, P 14 ... Wis.
.... Green Bay Jc., O 13 ... Wis.
2831*Greenbelt, J 12 ... Md.
4 Green Bluff, H 22 ... Wash.
300 Greenbrier, G 12 ... Ark.
110*Greenbrier, O 21 ... Mo.
10 Greenbrier, L 19 ... Ohio
795 Greenbrier, L 11 ... Tenn.
150*Greenburr, I 13 ... Pa.
103*Greenbush, G 8 ... Ill.
100 Greenbush, J 15 ... Me.
318 Greenbush, H 22 ... Mass.
150*Greenbush, I 21 ... Mich.
556 Greenbush, C 5 ... Minn.
50 Greenbush, M 6 ... Ohio
146*Greenbush, L 24 ... Va.
149*Greenbush, O 17 ... Wis.
327 Green Camp, H 11 ... Ohio
4872 Greencastle, K 10 ... Ind.
342 Green Castle, B 11 ... Mo.
2511 Greencastle, Q 13 ... Pa.
697 Green City, B 11 ... Mo.
50*Green Cove, E 9 ... Va.
1752 Green Cove Springs, C 16 Fla.
52 Greencreek, H 5 ... Idaho
372 Green Creek, R 11 ... N. J.
5 Greendale, M 17 ... Ill.
1548 Greendale, M 22 ... Ind.
80*Greendale, F 17 ... Ky.
305*Greendale, R 24 ... N. Y.
300*Greendale, M 14 ... Ohio
80*Greendale, E 7 ... Va.
.... Greendale, L 8 ... W. Va.
2527*Greendale, O 20 ... Wis.
111*Greendell, B 14 ... N. J.
1303 Greene, E 15 ... Iowa
575 Greene, N 7 ... Me.
35 Greene, E 9 ... N. D.
1431 Greene, P 16 ... N. Y.
213 Greene, Q 19 ... Pa.
100 Greene, H 6 ... R. I.
.... Greene Jc., P 5 ... Pa.
6784 Greeneville, M 22 ... Tenn.
50 Greenfield, E 19 ... Ark.
1000*Greenfield, K 7 ... Calif.
1006 Greenfield, K 9 ... Ill.
4821 Greenfield, J 16 ... Ind.
1869 Greenfield, M 9 ... Iowa
15672■Greenfield, C 7 ... Mass.
15*Greenfield, K 12 ... Miss.
1353 Greenfield, N 8 ... Mo.
369 Greenfield, P 11 ... N. H.
30 Greenfield, L 20 ... N. M.
175 Greenfield, L 23 ... N. Y.
4228 Greenfield, N 11 ... Ohio
303 Greenfield, H 8 ... Okla.
310*Greenfield, I 2 ... Pa.
35 Greenfield, P 24 ... S. D.
1509 Greenfield, M 5 ... Tenn.
37*Greenfield, K 11 ... Va.
100 Greenfield Center, L 23 N. Y.
460 Greenfield Hill, P 6 ... Conn.
200 Greenfield Park, R 21 . N. Y.
200 Greenford, F 20 ... Ohio
745 Green Forest, B 8 ... Ark.
254 Green Garden, E 7 ... Mich.
48*Green Grove, K 16 ... Ky.
10 Greengrove, D 7 ... Miss.
62*Green Hall, H 19 ... Ky.
84*Green Harbor, I 23 ... Mass.
60*Green Hill, C 11 ... W. Va.
2677*Greenhills, N 5 ... Ohio
350*Greenhurst, P 3 ... N. Y.
148 Green Island, I 25 ... Iowa
3988*Green Island, N 24 ... N. Y.
376 Green Isle, O 13 ... Minn.
85*Greenlake, L 16 ... Me.
.... Green Lake, see Canada Lake ... N. Y.
....*Green Lake, N 20 ... Tex.
661 Green Lake, L 17 ... Wis.
127*Greenland, C 5 ... Ark.
30 Greenland, I 15 ... Colo.
600 Greenland, D 1 ... Mich.
250 Greenland, P 20 ... N. H.
29*Greenland, E 18 ... W. Va.
8 Greenland Jc., D 1 ... Mich.
478 Green Lane, N 22 ... Pa.
1237*Greenlawn, G 9 ... N. Y.
110*Greenleaf, N 4 ... Idaho
739 Greenleaf, D 17 ... Kan.
10 Greenleaf, H 22 ... Okla.
20*Greenleaf, J 4 ... Ore.
250 Greenleaf, O 15 ... Wis.
.... Greenlee, O 3 ... Pa.
28*Greenlee, M 9 ... Va.
474*Greeleyville, I 19 ... S. C.
90*Greenmount (Bowling), I 19 ... Ky.
150*Greenmount, C 12 ... Md.
163*Green Mtn., I 15 ... Iowa
200*Greenmountain, M 10 . N. C.
87 Green Mtn. Falls, I 15 . Colo.
40*Greenock, H 14 ... Md.
1050*Greenock, L 3 ... Pa.
280*Greenough, H 5 ... Mont.
100*Greenpark, M 14 ... Pa.
150*Green Pond, G 11 ... Ala.
109*Green Pond, C 15 ... N. J.
285 Green Pond, O 15 ... S. C.
.... Green Pond Jc., C 16 . N. J.
3259 Greenport, F 11 ... N. Y.
.... Green Ridge, K 11 ... Ill.
350 Green Ridge, I 9 ... Mo.
50*Green Ridge (Brodbecks), Pa.
25*Green River, I 10 ... Ky.
470 Greenriver, K 20 ... Utah
60 Green River, R 12 ... Vt.
2640 Green River, P 6 ... Wyo.
2034 Greensboro, I 8 ... Ala.
443 Greensboro, B 3 ... Fla.
2459 Greensboro, G 13 ... Ga.
222 Greensboro, J 20 ... Ind.
737 Greensboro, I 20 ... Md.
59319 Greensboro, D 10 ... N. C.
625 Greensboro, Q 3 ... Pa.
330 Greensboro (Greensboro Bend), E 16 ... Vt.
400 Greensboro, D 15 ... Vt.
6065 Greensburg, L 18 ... Ind.
1417 Greensburg, M 10 ... Kan.
1176 Greensburg, I 14 ... Ky.
389 Greensburg, J 16 ... La.
40*Greensburg, B 13 ... Mo.
300*Greensburg, F 18 ... Ohio
100 Greensburg, D 20 ... Ohio
16743 Greensburg, N 5 ... Pa.
200*Greens Creek, P 5 ... N. C.
150*Green Sea, F 23 ... S. C.
.... Greens Farm, J 4 ... Me.
275 Greens Farms, P 5 ... Conn.
413 Greens Fork, I 21 ... Ind.

Pop. Place Index State
4*Greens Gap, J 3 ... N. M.
45 Greenspot, O 18 ... Calif.
30 Green Spring, D 21 . W. Va.
200*Green Spring Depot (Green Springs), J 14 ... Va.
.... Green Spring Jc., E 13 . Md.
930 Green Springs, E 12 ... Ohio
102*Greenstone (Gladhill), Q 14 ... Pa.
100*Green Sulphur Springs, O 10 ... W. Va.
268 Greentop, B 12 ... Mo.
1060 Greentown, G 15 ... Ind.
354*Greentown, F 18 ... Ohio
50*Greentown, H 22 ... Pa.
1880*Greentree, L 3 ... Pa.
1410 Greenup, K 20 ... Ill.
1063 Greenup, D 22 ... Ky.
1500*Greenvale, H 6 ... N. Y.
516 Green Valley, G 12 ... Ill.
185*Green Valley, O 6 ... Minn.
100 Green Valley, N 13 ... Wis.
20*Green Valley Lake, N 18, P 9 ... Calif.
94*Greenview, B 4 ... Calif.
749 Greenview, I 11 ... Ill.
300*Greenview, M 5 ... W. Va.
450*Green Village, D 14 ... N. J.
160 Green Village, P 13 ... Pa.
5075 Greenville, L 14 ... Ala.
520 Greenville, E 9 ... Calif.
.... Greenville, I 22 ... Conn.
50*Greenville, D 21 ... Del.
1114 Greenville, B 8 ... Fla.
683 Greenville, H 5 ... Ga.
3391 Greenville, L 13 ... Ill.
285 Greenville, P 15 ... Ind.
169*Greenville, D 6 ... Iowa
2347 Greenville, I 10 ... Ky.
1000 Greenville, I 10 ... Me.
5321 Greenville, N 15 ... Mich.
20892 Greenville, F 6 ... Miss.
572 Greenville, O 20 ... Mo.
1350 Greenville, R 12 ... N. H.
467*Greenville, P 22 ... N. Y.
12674 Greenville, G 18 ... N. C.
7745 Greenville, J 5 ... Ohio
8149 Greenville, H 1 ... Pa.
1230 Greenville, D 11 ... R. I.
34734 Greenville, B 7 ... S. C.
13995 Greenville, D 21 ... Tex.
173 Greenville, N 7 ... Utah
400 Greenville, K 10 ... Va.
100*Greenville, P 11 ... W. Va.
160*Greenville, N 15 ... Wis.
26*Greenville Center, P 22 N. Y.
600*Greenville Jc., I 10 ... Me.
233*Greenwald, L 9 ... Minn.
....*Greenway, N 14 ... Ariz.
367 Greenway, B 21 ... Ark.
101 Greenway, B 15 ... S. D.
....*Greenway, F 17 ... Va.
130 Greenwell Springs, K 14 . La.
5981 Greenwich, R 1 ... Conn.
60*Greenwich, L 17 ... Kan.
25 Greenwich, O 6 ... N. J.
2270 Greenwich, L 24 ... N. Y.
996 Greenwich, F 14 ... Ohio
86*Greenwich, M 11 ... Utah
.... Greenwich Jc., L 24 . N. Y.
.... Greenwich Pier, O 6 ... N. J.
96*Greenwich Village, E 10 Mass.
1219 Greenwood, G 4 ... Ark.
584▲Greenwood, G 9 ... Calif.
30 Greenwood, M 14 ... Colo.
573 Greenwood, J 22 ... Del.
293 Greenwood, M 11 ... Fla.
2499 Greenwood, K 14 ... Ind.
300 Greenwood, J 17 ... Ky.
350 Greenwood, C 4 ... La.
3500 Greenwood, J 4 ... Mass.
50 Greenwood, M 4 ... Me.
14767 Greenwood, F 11 ... Miss.
250 Greenwood, H 6 ... Mo.
350 Greenwood, L 23 ... Neb.
400 Greenwood, Q 9 ... N. Y.
13020 Greenwood, F 7 ... S. C.
200 Greenwood, O 19 ... S. D.
120*Greenwood, N 13 ... Tenn.
87 Greenwood, C 18 ... Tex
52*Greenwood, J 11 ... Va.
400 Greenwood, E 10 ... W. Va.
776 Greenwood, G 13 ... Wis.
.... Greenwood Jc., I 25 ... Okla.
483*Greenwood Lake, F 4 . N. Y.
117 Greenwood Springs, E 23 Miss.
111 Greer, G 6 ... Idaho
87*Greer, Q 16 ... Mo.
100*Greer, H 15 ... Ohio
2940 Greer, B 7 ... S. C.
40*Greer, C 13 ... W. Va.
100*Greggs, M 4 ... Pa.
70 Greggs (Chisville), C 8 Wash.
.... Gregor, L 21 ... Wash.
100 Gregory, H 16 ... Ark.
25*Gregory, K 17 ... Ky.
150 Gregory, P 18 ... Mich.
86*Gregory (Gregory Landing) B 14 ... Mo.
160*Gregory, C 23 ... N. C.
50*Gregory (Colestin), R 7 Ore.
1246 Gregory, N 16 ... S. D.
517 Gregory, P 19 ... Tex.
14*Gregory, I 10 ... W. Va.
10*Gregoryville, E 21 ... Ky.
14 Gregson, K 6 ... Mont.
70*Gregville (Wilcox), M 12 Ala.
160*Greig, I 17 ... N. Y.
45 Greigsville, N 8 ... N. Y.
213*Greismore (Mentcle), L 8 Pa.
250 Grelton, D 8 ... Ohio
300 Grenada, B 5 ... Calif.
5831 Grenada, E 13 ... Miss.
4 Grenada Jc., F 11 ... Miss.
14*Grenell, G 15 ... N. Y.
255 Grenloch, L 9 ... N. J.
517 Grenola, N 19 ... Kan.
425 Grenora, E 2 ... N. D.
143 Grenville, C 23 ... N. M.
260 Grenville, D 22 ... S. D.
352 Gresham, L 20 ... Neb.
.... Gresham, R 1 ... Okla.
1951 Gresham, D 8 ... Ore.
200*Gresham, H 21 ... S. C.
295 Gresham, M 12 ... Wis.
55*Greshamville, F 13 ... Ga.
200 Gressitt, M 20 ... Va.
65*Gresston, K 13 ... Ga.
.... Greta, O 19 ... Tex.
30*Greta, K 24 ... Va.
27*Grethel, H 22 ... Ky.
200*Gretna, B 3 ... Fla.
45*Gretna, D 10 ... Kan.
10879 Gretna, N 19 ... La.
482 Gretna, K 23 ... Neb.
3 Gretna, D 15 ... S. D.
619 Gretna, P 9 ... Va.
75 Greve, B 18 ... Mont.
1828 Greybull, C 12 ... Wyo.
85 Greycliff, L 13 ... Mont.
100 Greycourt, E 4 ... N. Y.
428 Grey Eagle, K 10 ... Minn.
125*Greyeagle, N 2 ... W. Va.
75*Greystone, C 5 ... Colo.

Pop. Place Index State
1400 Greystone, D 13 ... R. I.
....*Greystone Park, D 15 . N. J.
250 Greythorne (Walnut Bottom), P 14 ... Pa.
33*Grider, J 15 ... Ky.
2338 Gridley, F 7 ... Calif.
745 Gridley, F 16 ... Ill.
10 Gridley, B 8 ... Iowa
418 Gridley, K 21 ... Kan.
50 Griegos, G 10 ... N. M.
100 Griffin, P 11 ... Ark.
13222 Griffin, H 7 ... Ga.
386 Griffin, Q 2 ... Ind.
67 Griffin, P 2 ... N. D.
15*Griffinsburg, H 14 ... Va.
2116 Griffith, B 6 ... Ind.
500 Griffithsville, L 4 ... W. Va.
238 Griffithville, H 15 ... Ark.
456 Grifton, H 18 ... N. C.
4*Griggs, Q 2 ... Okla.
35 Griggstown, G 15 ... N. J.
1266 Griggsville, J 7 ... Ill.
109 Grigsby, G 24 ... Tex.
57*Grigston, I 5 ... Kan.
70 Grim (Grims Landing), I 4 W. Va.
110 Grimes, N 21 ... Ala.
350*Grimes, F 5 ... Calif.
489 Grimes, K 11 ... Iowa
40 Grimes, I 2 ... Okla.
40*Grimes, D 14 ... Va.
405 Grimesland, F 19 ... N. C.
.... Grimes Mill, C 19 ... Me.
....*Grimes Pass, M 6 ... Idaho
149*Grimms, P 15 ... Wis.
50*Grimsley, M 16 ... Tenn.
650 Grimstead, M 21 ... Va.
58*Grindstone, H 15 ... Me.
41*Grinsdtone, H 14 ... N. Y.
528*Grindstone, P 4 ... Pa.
21 Grindstone, J 8 ... S. D.
100 Grindstone City, K 23 Mich.
5210 Grinnell, K 16 ... Iowa
289 Grinnell, G 6 ... Kan.
.... Grinnell & Montezuma Jc., L 16 ... Iowa
66 Grippe, L 5 ... W. Va.
30*Grisdella, G 19 ... Mont.
17*Grisham, O 21 ... Mo.
1132 Griswold, M 6 ... Iowa
132*Griswoldville, C 7 ... Mass.
20*Grit, I 15 ... Tex.
16 Grizzly (Egan), D 5 . Mont.
25 Grizzly, H 13 ... Ore.
110*Grizzly Flats, G 10 ... Calif.
2272 Groesbeck, G 20 ... Tex.
25*Grogan, O 15 ... Mo.
50 Groningen, J 17 ... Minn.
2 Gronna, D 15 ... N. D.
475 Groom, D 4 ... Tex.
100*Groom Creek, H 11 ... Ariz.
65*Groseclose, D 10 ... Va.
23 Gross, D 16 ... Neb.
2000 Grosse Isle, Q 22 ... Mich.
6179*Grosse Point, P 23 ... Mich.
7217*Grosse Pointe Farms, P 23 ... Mich.
12646 Grosse Pointe Park, P 23 Mich.
801*Grosse Pointe Shores, P 23 ... Mich.
382 Grosse Tete, L 13 ... La.
175*Grossmont, Q 19 ... Calif.
60 Grosvenor, G 15 ... Tex.
490 Grosvenor Dale, B 23 . Conn.
150*Grote (Carlton), M 23 . Colo.
4719 Groton, L 22 ... Conn.
1950 Groton, C 15 ... Mass.
182▲*Groton, K 11 ... N. H.
2087 Groton, O 14 ... N. Y.
946 Groton, D 19 ... S. D.
419 Groton, G 16 ... Vt.
....*Groton Long Point, I 21 Conn.
60*Grotons, K 24 ... Va.
65*Grotto, H 9 ... Wash.
759 Grottoes, I 11 ... Va.
40*Grouse, L 13 ... Idaho
300 Grouse Creek, B 2 ... Utah
.... Grove, G 12 ... Ill.
.... Grove, K 18 ... Ky.
132*Grove, B 6 ... La.
104 Grove, K 22 ... Me.
1093 Grove, C 24 ... Okla.
....*Grove Beach, N 16 ... Conn.
200*Grove Center, G 7 ... Ky.
71 Grove City, J 14 ... Ill.
447 Grove City, M 10 ... Minn.
1787 Grove City, K 12 ... Ohio
6296 Grove City, I 3 ... Pa.
730 Grove Hill, M 7 ... Ala.
40*Grove Hill, D 16 ... N. C.
300 Groveland, I 10 ... Calif.
411 Groveland, G 16 ... Fla.
97 Groveland, K 21 ... Ga.
300 Groveland, G 13 ... Ill.
5*Groveland, J 15 ... Kan.
1600 Groveland, B 19 ... Mass.
550 Groveland, O 9 ... N. Y.
61*Groveoak, C 19 ... Ala.
165*Grove Park, D 14 ... Fla.
1052 Groveport, L 12 ... Ohio
137 Grover, B 17 ... Colo.
150*Grover, I 20 ... Mo.
469 Grover, H 3 ... N. C.
.... Grover, see Tiltonsville, Ohio
200 Grover, F 16 ... Pa.
57*Grover, L 15 ... S. C.
38 Grover, G 22 ... S. D.
70*Grover, N 14 ... Utah
350*Grover, J 2 ... Wyo.
478 Grover Hill, F 6 ... Ohio
75*Grovertown, C 12 ... Ind.
.... Groves, see Falmouth . Ind.
3500*Groves, K 24 ... Tex.
133 Grovespring, N 12 ... Mo.
1923 Groveton, F 14 ... N. H.
800*Groveton, L 2 ... Pa.
940 Groveton, H 23 ... Tex.
267 Grovetown, G 19 ... Ga.
500 Groveville, I 13 ... N. J.
51 Grovont, G 3 ... Wyo.
750*Grow, B 12 ... Tex.
161 Growmore, M 13 ... Wash.
366 Grubbs, E 18 ... Ark.
150*Grubbs, D 21 ... Del.
40*Grubville, K 19 ... Mo.
319 Gruetli, P 14 ... Tenn.
1800 Grulla, Q 3 ... Tex.
1476 Grundy, B 7 ... Va.
2012 Grundy Center, H 15 . Iowa
10 Grundy Jc., J 10 ... Wis.
138 Gruver, B 8 ... Iowa
330 Gruver, A 4 ... Tex.
183 Grygla, D 7 ... Minn.
2000 Guadalupe, M 9 ... Calif.
43 Guadalupe, N 19 ... Tex.
312 Guadalupita, D 17 ... N. M.
50*Guage, G 21 ... Ky.
80*Guajillo, P 16 ... Tex.
15*Gualala, G 2 ... Calif.
18*Guardian (Removable), J 11 ... W. Va.
600*Guasti, O 17 ... Calif.
50*Guatay, Q 20 ... Calif.
132*Guckeen, R 13 ... Minn.
100 Guelph, Q 20 ... N. D.

Pop.	Place Index	State
....	Guerette, B 18	Me.
800	*Guerneville, H 4	Calif.
50	*Guernewood Park, G 3	Calif.
177	*Guernsey, K 17	Iowa
61	*Guernsey, J 17	Ohio
38	*Guernsey, P 15	Pa.
603	Guernsey, M 21	Wyo.
96	Guerra, R 16	Tex.
40	*Guerrant, H 21	Ky.
124	*Guerryton, K 20	Ala.
1506	Gueydan, N 9	La.
26	Guffey, J 13	Colo.
75	Guffey, K 24	Tex.
596	Guide Rock, O 17	Neb.
50	Guild, L 22	Idaho
149	*Guild, N 8	N. H.
115	Guild, Q 14	Tenn.
123	*Guilderland, N 23	N. Y.
70	*Guilderland Center, N 23	N. Y.
100	Guildhall, D 22	Vt.
1986	Guildford, N 14	Conn.
140	Guilford, M 22	Ind.
1880	Guilford, J 11	Me.
201	Guildford, C 5	Mo.
400	Guildford, P 17	N. Y.
400	*Guilford, E 9	N. C.
50	Guilford, Q 12	Vt.
600	Guilford College, D 9	N. C.
1175	Guin, E 7	Ala.
235	Guinda, G 5	Calif.
200	*Guinea, J 17	Va.
24	*Guinea Mills, M 13	Va.
288	Guion, D 14	Ark.
24	Guion, J 8	Ind.
25	*Guion, F 13	Tex.
74	*Guldens, Q 15	Pa.
50	Guler, O 10	Wash.
200	Gulf, G 11	N. C.
400	Gulf, N 21	Tex.
150	*Gulf Breeze, M 3	Fla.
....	Gulf Crossing, D 9	La.
800	*Gulf Hammock, E 12	Fla.
....	Gulf Jc., M 13	Okla.
1581	Gulfport, I 12	Fla.
15195	Gulfport, R 18	Miss.
101	*Gulf Summit, R 17	N. Y.
30	*Gullett, G 21	Ky.
210	Gullett, K 17	La.
....	Gulling, E 10	Calif.
30	*Gulliver, F 11	Mich.
318	*Gull Point, N 3	Fla.
164	Gully, E 7	Minn.
35	*Gulnare, Q 18	Colo.
55	*Gulnare, G 23	Ky.
12	*Gulrock, G 23	N. C.
140	Gumberry, C 18	N. C.
50	*Gum Fork, N 20	Va.
100	Gumlog, G 9	Ark.
1198	▲Gum Neck, F 23	N. C.
500	*Gum Run (Sugarloaf), J 19	Pa.
50	*Gum Spring, L 15	Va.
....	*Gunlock, G 21	Ky.
127	*Gunlock, Q 2	Utah
	Gunn, see Wolverine	Ky.
....	Gunn, G 15	Minn.
2	Gunn, O 8	Wyo.
59	*Gunn City, I 7	Mo.
2177	Gunnison, K 8	Colo.
396	Gunnison, D 6	Miss.
1115	Gunnison, K 12	Utah
....	Gunn Jc., P 8	Wyo.
....	*Gunntown, see Gulf Hammock	Fla.
....	Gunsight, C 6	Mont.
91	*Gunsight, E 15	Tex.
15	Gunter, K 4	Ore.
60	*Gunter, L 15	Tenn.
481	*Gunter, C 19	Tex.
4398	Guntersville, C 16	Ala.
349	Guntown, B 20	Miss.
75	*Gupton, D 15	N. C.
35	Gurdane, E 18	Ore.
2172	Gurdon, N 9	Ark.
581	Gurley, B 15	Ala.
19	*Gurley, J 15	La.
203	Gurley, J 4	Neb.
115	*Gurley, G 23	S. C.
118	Gurleyville, E 20	Conn.
661	Gurnee, A 20	Ill.
....	Gurnee Jc., G 12	Ala.
57	*Gurney, H 5	Wis.
99	*Gurneyville, N 9	Ohio
35	*Gurnspring, L 23	N. Y.
25	*Gus, I 10	Ky.
50	*Gusdorf, C 14	N. M.
250	Gusher, G 21	Utah
5	*Gustave, E 2	S. D.
95	Gustavus, D 21	Ohio
1355	Gustine, I 8	Calif.
409	Gustine, G 16	Tex.
80	*Guston, F 12	Ky.
69	Guthrie, G 18	Ill.
200	Guthrie, M 12	Ind.
1253	Guthrie, K 10	Ky.
58	Guthrie, B 11	La.
143	*Guthrie, G 10	Minn.
75	*Guthrie, I 14	Mo.
100	Guthrie, H 13	N. D.
10018	Guthrie, G 12	Okla.
318	Guthrie, C 13	Tex.
....	Guthrie, L 12	Va.
2066	Guthrie Center, K 8	Iowa
1860	Guttenberg, E 22	Iowa
6200	Guttenberg, E 21	N. J.
200	Guy, G 12	Ark.
25	*Guy, I 11	Ky.
10	Guy, C 24	N. M.
29	*Guy, L 22	Tex.
206	Guyan, P 5	W. Va.
....	Guyandotte, K 2	W. Va.
65	*Guyaux, Q 3	Pa.
52	*Guyaz, O 21	Idaho
46	Guymard (Graham), E 2	N. Y.
2290	Guymon, R 5	Okla.
90	*Guys, Q 5	Tenn.
321	Guys Mills, F 3	Pa.
14	Guyson, P 17	N. D.
150	Guysville, N 16	Ohio
549	Guyton, K 23	Ga.
35	Gwendolen, D 15	Ore.
50	*Gwenford, Q 18	Idaho
....	Gwin, G 11	Miss.
1300	Gwinn, F 7	Mich.
200	Gwinner, P 22	N. D.
164	*Gwynedd, O 23	Pa.
400	*Gwynedd Valley, O 23	Pa.
540	Gwynn, M 21	Va.
250	Gwynneville, J 17	Ind.
245	Gypsum, G 9	Colo.
25	Gypsum, G 10	Iowa
615	Gypsum, H 15	Kan.
740	Gypsum, C 12	Ohio
8	Gypsum, H 23	Ore.
....	Gypsum City, see Gypsum	Kan.
....	*Gypsy, G 21	Ky.
100	*Gypsy, G 17	Okla.
163	*Gypsy, E 12	W. Va.

H

Pop.	Place Index	State
30	Haas (Ayer), M 21	Wash.
15	*Habberton, C 5	Ark.
1000	*Habersham, C 12	Ga.
250	*Habersham, M 19	Tenn.

Pop.	Place Index	State
....	Hachita, P 3	N. M.
50	*Hacienda, L 14	Tex.
85	Hackberry, F 6	Ariz.
800	*Hackberry, N 5	La.
40	*Hackberry, L 19	Tex.
264	Hackensack, H 11	Minn.
26279	Hackensack, D 20	N. J.
150	*Hacker Valley, I 12	W. Va.
316	Hackett, G 4	Ark.
3289	Hackettstown, D 11	N. J.
492	Hackleburg, C 7	Ala.
25	*Hackley, J 19	La.
162	*Hacksneck, L 23	Va.
300	*Hacoda, O 16	Ala.
133	Hadar, H 19	Neb.
700	Haddam, J 16	Conn.
384	Haddam, D 16	Kan.
52	*Haddix, H 21	Ky.
400	Haddock, I 12	Ga.
8857	Haddonfield, K 10	N. J.
12	*Haddonfield, C 5	Va.
5555	Haddon Heights, L 9	N. J.
10	*Hadensville, L 15	Va.
75	*Hadley, D 20	Ind.
37	*Hadley, I 12	Ky.
1400	Hadley, F 8	Mass.
150	Hadley, O 21	Mich.
162	*Hadley, Q 6	Minn.
1	*Hadley, N 18	Mo.
933	Hadley, K 23	N. Y.
147	Hadley, H 2	Pa.
75	*Hadlock, M 23	Va.
176	Hadlock, F 6	Wash.
310	Hadlyme, K 17	Conn.
302	Hadlyme, K 16	Conn.
160	*Haffey (Milltown), M 4	Pa.
35	Hagaman, K 10	Ill.
867	*Hagaman, M 22	N. Y.
685	Hagan, K 20	Ga.
15	Hagan, G 12	N. M.
120	*Hagan, E 3	Va.
647	Hagan Jc., F 12	N. M.
120	Hagans, E 2	Va.
100	*Hagarstown, L 15	Ill.
420	*Hagarville, F 8	Ark.
5	Hageman, N 7	Ohio
40	*Hager, G 21	Ky.
25	*Hager, L 3	W. Va.
104	*Hager City, B 13	Wis.
50	*Hager Hill, G 22	Ky.
435	Hagerman, P 10	Idaho
854	Hagerman, L 21	N. M.
125	*Hagerman, B 19	Tex.
1638	Hagerstown, I 20	Ind.
32491	Hagerstown, B 6	Md.
....	Hagerstown Jc., B 5	Md.
71	Hagevo, O 8	Pa.
12	*Haggard, M 6	Kan.
55	*Hagler, L 16	Ark.
....	Hagley, A 21	Del.
215	*Hagood, G 15	S. C.
45	*Hagood (Marengo), O 13	Va.
250	Hague, D 13	Fla.
650	*Hague, H 24	N. Y.
442	Hague, Q 14	N. D.
57	*Hague, J 20	Va.
980	Hahira, O 12	Ga.
49	*Hahn, O 21	Mo.
40	Hahns Peak, B 9	Colo.
300	Hahnville, N 17	La.
270	Haig, H 1	Neb.
507	Haigler, O 7	Neb.
35	*Hail, J 17	Ky.
95	*Haile, B 11	La.
258	*Hailesboro, F 17	N. Y.
1443	Hailey, N 12	Idaho
1183	Haileyville, M 20	Okla.
377	Haines, F 21	Ore.
150	Hainesburg, C 9	N. J.
3890	Haines City, H 17	Fla.
590	Haines Falls, Q 22	N. Y.
250	Hainesport, K 12	N. J.
311	Hainesville, A 12	N. J.
209	Halbur, I 7	Iowa
273	▲Halcott Center, Q 21	N. Y.
119	*Halcottville (Halcottsville), Q 20	N. Y.
100	*Halcyon, M 9	Calif.
200	Halcyon (East Andover), M 12	N. H.
75	Halcyon, M 3	W. Va.
50	*Halcyondale (Halcyon Dale), I 22	Ga.
75	*Haldane, B 14	Ill.
387	Haldeman, E 21	Ky.
40	Halder, J 13	Wis.
32	Hale, G 24	Colo.
77	Hale, I 22	Iowa
250	*Hale, J 19	Mich.
562	Hale, E 10	Mo.
10	*Hale (Parsley), O 3	W. Va.
232	*Haleburg, N 22	Ala.
836	Hale Center, B 10	Tex.
5303	Haledon, C 18	N. J.
125	*Hale Eddy, Q 19	N. Y.
700	Hales Corners, O 20	Wis.
500	*Halesite, H 7	N. Y.
252	Hales Point, N 2	Tenn.
1831	Halethorpe, F 13	Md.
40	Haley, R 4	N. D.
75	*Haley, P 12	Tenn.
75	*Haleys Mill, I 9	Ky.
2427	Haleyville, D 8	Ala.
225	Haleyville, P 10	N. J.
100	Half Moon, D 4	Mont.
800	Half Moon Bay, H 17	Calif.
18	*Halford, F 5	Kan.
38	*Halfway, J 12	Ky.
135	*Half Way, M 10	Mo.
416	Halfway, F 24	Ore.
20	Halfway, J 4	Wyo.
867	▲Halifax, J 21	Mass.
374	Halifax, C 17	N. C.
813	Halifax, M 16	Pa.
130	Halifax, R 11	Vt.
536	Halifax, Q 11	Va.
....	Halite, N 8	N. Y.
150	Hall, K 12	Ind.
100	*Hall, I 22	Ky.
50	*Hall, J 12	Md.
90	Hall, J 6	Mont.
178	Hall, N 11	N. Y.
50	*Hall, H 15	Tex.
25	Hall, P 7	Wash.
32	*Hall, F 13	W. Va.
168	Hallam, M 21	Neb.
799	Hallam (Hellam), P 18	Pa.
1827	Hallandale, N 24	Fla.
66	*Hallburg, I 9	W. Va.
185	Halldale, M 12	Me.
350	Halleck (Oro Grande), N 18	Calif.
30	Halleck, C 18	Nev.
159	Hallett, E 16	Okla.
1581	Hallettsville, L 19	Tex.
120	Halley, P 17	Ark.
395	Halliday, K 6	N. D.
425	Hallidayboro, P 14	Ill.
10	*Hallie, I 22	Ky.
275	Hallieford, M 21	Va.
25	Hallison, G 10	N. C.
1353	Hallock, B 2	Minn.
205	*Hallowell, N 24	Kan.
2906	Hallowell, N 9	Me.
150	*Hallowell, N 22	Pa.
138	*Hall Quarry, M 17	Me.
150	Halls (Linwood), D 4	Ga.
50	Halls, E 4	Mo.

Pop.	Place Index	State
25	Halls, I 16	Pa.
....	Halls, K 18	S. C.
1511	Halls, N 3	Tenn.
250	*Hallsboro, L 14	N. C.
30	*Hallsboro, M 16	Va.
....	*Halls Gap, H 17	Ky.
40	*Halls Mills, D 4	N. C.
8	Hallson, D 21	N. D.
105	Halls Summit, J 21	Kan.
1293	Hallstead, D 21	Pa.
750	Hall Summit, (Halls Summit), D 6	La.
227	Hallsville, H 15	Ill.
224	Hallsville, G 13	Mo.
210	Hallsville, N 13	Ohio
600	Hallsville, E 23	Tex.
344	Hallton, H 8	Pa.
168	*Halltown, O 9	Mo.
150	Halltown, E 25	W. Va.
210	Hallville, J 22	Conn.
367	*Hallwood, K 24	Va.
263	Hallwood (Spilman), G 4	W. Va.
158	*Halma, C 3	Minn.
100	*Halo, H 22	Ky.
68	*Halo (Marcus), K 11	W. Va.
117	*Halsell, K 4	Ala.
130	Halsey, H 11	Neb.
100	Halsey, C 13	N. J.
305	Halsey, H 6	Ore.
200	*Halsey Valley, Q 13	N. Y.
570	Halstad, G 2	Minn.
1397	Halstead, K 16	Kan.
....	Halvern, F 21	Calif.
135	Hamar, I 19	N. D.
100	Hambden, C 19	Ohio
164	Hamberg, I 16	N. D.
394	Hambleton, F 16	W. Va.
6	Hambone, C 7	Calif.
100	*Hamburg, J 10	Ala.
1939	Hamburg, Q 14	Ark.
70	*Hamburg, B 4	Calif.
263	Hamburg, L 18	Conn.
300	Hamburg, K 7	Ill.
2187	Hamburg, Q 4	Iowa
63	Hamburg, I 12	La.
224	*Hamburg, P 19	Mich.
198	*Hamburg, N 14	Minn.
102	*Hamburg, N 5	Miss.
210	Hamburg, I 19	Mo.
1116	Hamburg, B 14	N. J.
5467	Hamburg, N 4	N. Y.
3717	Hamburg, M 20	Pa.
300	Hamburg (West Hamburg), M 20	Pa.
....	Hamburg, J 9	S. C.
188	*Hamburg, Q 6	Tenn.
5	Hamburg, J 11	Wis.
70	Hamby, E 14	Tex.
5000	Hamden, L 11	Conn.
13	*Hamden, E 11	Mo.
200	Hamden, Q 19	N. Y.
924	Hamden, O 14	Ohio
25	Hamden, P 20	Okla.
250	*Hamel, M 15	Minn.
50	Hamer, N 19	Idaho
170	*Hamer, D 21	S. C.
349	Hamersville, P 9	Ohio
240	*Hamil, A 17	Ark.
90	Hamill, M 15	S. D.
1002	Hamilton, D 6	Ala.
500	*Hamilton (Hamilton City), F 6	Calif.
40	Hamilton, D 7	Colo.
473	Hamilton, I 4	Ga.
1642	Hamilton, H 4	Ill.
392	Hamilton, B 22	Ind.
291	Hamilton, N 15	Iowa
519	Hamilton, K 20	Kan.
80	*Hamilton, F 18	Ky.
500	Hamilton, C 21	Mass.
500	Hamilton, O 10	Mich.
115	*Hamilton, E 22	Miss.
1655	Hamilton, D 8	Mo.
2332	Hamilton, J 4	Mont.
25	Hamilton, H 19	Nev.
1790	Hamilton, N 17	N. Y.
524	Hamilton, E 19	N. C.
255	Hamilton, D 22	N. D.
50592	Hamilton, N 6	Ohio
25	Hamilton, G 17	Ore.
125	*Hamilton, K 7	Pa.
415	Hamilton, J 14	R. I.
2716	Hamilton, G 17	Tex.
409	Hamilton, E 16	Va.
229	Hamilton, D 9	Wash.
25	*Hamilton, N 17	Wis.
1700	*Hamilton (Montreal), I 6	Wis.
1500	Hamilton and Wenham (S. Hamilton), C 21	Mass.
....	Hamilton Belt Jc., N 5	Ohio
300	*Hamilton City (Hamilton), F 6	Calif.
100	*Hamilton Dome, F 10	Wyo.
2000	Hamilton Square, I 14	N. J.
475	Hamler, E 8	Ohio
519	Hamlet, C 12	Ind.
220	Hamlet, N 9	Neb.
115	*Hamlet, P 3	N. Y.
5111	Hamlet, J 10	N. C.
75	Hamlet, E 5	N. D.
200	*Hamlet, O 7	Ohio
35	*Hamlet, B 5	Ore.
115	*Hamlet, O 8	W. Va.
192	Hamletsburg, R 18	Ill.
150	*Hamlin, K 7	Iowa
174	Hamlin, C 22	Kan.
50	*Hamlin, K 7	Ky.
....	Hamlin, B 20	Me.
600	Hamlin, K 8	N. Y.
35	Hamlin, F 10	Pa.
300	Hamlin, G 22	Pa.
2406	Hamlin, D 13	Tex.
850	Hamlin, L 3	W. Va.
75	Hammer, B 23	S. D.
100	*Hammer, M 20	Tenn.
48	*Hammersley Fork, H 12	Pa.
50	Hammett, J 8	Ga.
234	Hammett, O 8	Idaho
25	Hammett, D 4	Pa.
705	Hammon, H 4	Okla.
100	*Hammon (Summit Sta.), L 19	Pa.
470	Hammond, I 18	Ill.
70184	Hammond, B 6	Ind.
34	*Hammond, L 24	Kan.
6033	Hammond, L 17	La.
252	Hammond, P 20	Minn.
48	*Hammond, Q 12	Mo.
323	Hammond, E 16	N. Y.
422	Hammond, A 4	Ore.
100	*Hammond, H 24	S. C.
183	*Hammond, I 20	Tex.
105	Hammond, D 13	W. Va.
467	Hammond, B 12	Wis.
1112	Hammondsport, P 10	N. Y.
500	Hammondsville, H 20	Ohio
25	Hammon Jc., H 4	Okla.
300	Hammonton, F 7	Calif.
7668	Hammonton, M 12	N. J.
50	*Hamner, I 4	Ala.
50	Hampden, L 14	Me.
250	Hampden, I 9	Mass.
193	Hampden, F 18	N. D.
....	Hampden, see Hampden Sydney	Va.
....	*Hampden, O 3	W. Va.
2	Hampden, K 19	Wis.

Pop.	Place Index	State
500	Hampden Highlands, L 14	Me.
300	*Hampden Sydney, O 13	Va.
....	Hample, Q 21	N. D.
757	Hampshire, B 17	Ill.
200	Hampshire, O 9	Tenn.
5	Hampshire, G 21	Wyo.
664	Hampstead, C 12	Md.
700	Hampstead, Q 17	N. H.
146	*Hampstead (West Hampstead), Q 17	N. H.
350	*Hampstead, K 16	N. C.
669	Hampton, P 12	Ark.
150	Hampton, D 22	Conn.
478	Hampton, D 14	Fla.
619	Hampton, G 8	Ga.
532	Hampton, D 8	Ill.
4006	Hampton, F 13	Iowa
47	*Hampton (Simpson), G 21	Ky.
163	*Hampton, I 6	Ky.
224	Hampton, O 17	Minn.
50	Hampton, H 6	Miss.
310	Hampton, L 18	Neb.
1000	Hampton, P 20	N. H.
864	Hampton, E 10	N. J.
200	*Hampton, K 24	N. Y.
297	*Hampton (Ruth), G 1	N. C.
31	Hampton, K 14	Ore.
200	*Hampton, P 15	Pa.
997	Hampton, M 13	S. C.
600	Hampton, L 24	Tenn.
375	Hampton, I 24	Tex.
5398	Hampton, O 21	Va.
8	Hampton, B 8	Wash.
150	*Hampton (Ivanhoe), G 13	W. Va.
600	Hampton Bays, G 11	N. Y.
200	*Hampton Beach, P 21	N. H.
....	*Hamptonburgh, E 3	N. Y.
350	Hampton Falls, P 20	N. H.
....	Hampton Jc., G 13	W. Va.
....	*Hampton Roads, P 21	Va.
150	Hampton Springs, C 8	Fla.
134	*Hampton Station (Beldon), L 9	Tenn.
75	*Hamptonville, D 6	N. C.
200	*Hamshire, K 24	Tex.
49839	Hamtramck, P 23	Mich.
650	Hanceville, D 13	Ala.
80	Hancock, D 21	Ark.
256	Hancock, M 5	Iowa
76	Hancock, M 17	Me.
940	Hancock, B 2	Md.
250	Hancock, D 2	Mass.
5554	Hancock, C 3	Mich.
827	Hancock, L 6	Minn.
134	*Hancock, M 13	Mo.
515	Hancock, P 10	N. H.
1581	Hancock, R 18	N. Y.
51	*Hancock, M 21	Pa.
85	*Hancock (Osceola), B 14	S. C.
198	Hancock, I 10	Vt.
51	Hancock (Brosius), C 23	W. Va.
481	Hancock, K 15	Wis.
130	*Hancock Point, M 17	Me.
146	*Hancocks Bridge, N 7	N. J.
65	*Hand, B 13	Ark.
....	*Hand, H 23	S. C.
50	*Hand (Handsom), Q 18	Va.
2000	*Handley, E 18	Tex.
550	Handley, L 7	W. Va.
25	*Handleyton, L 11	Tenn.
1200	Handsboro, R 19	Miss.
12	*Handshoe, H 22	Ky.
15	Handy, G 6	Ind.
60	*Handy, Q 17	Mo.
600	*Hanes, D 8	N. C.
25	*Haneyville, H 13	Pa.
8234	Hanford, K 12	Calif.
223	*Hanford, K 11	Ohio
250	Hanford, M 17	Wash.
21	*Hanger, B 7	Va.
52	*Hanging Limb, M 15	Tenn.
481	Hanging Rock, R 12	Ohio
65	*Hanging Rock, E 21	W. Va.
95	Hankamer, K 24	Tex.
125	*Hankins, C 1	N. Y.
1000	*Hankins (Harman), B 7	Va.
23	*Hankinson, L 6	Miss.
1420	Hankinson, Q 24	N. D.
192	Hanks, E 2	N. D.
80	*Hanksville, M 17	Utah
336	Hanley Falls, O 6	Minn.
35	*Hanlin (Hanlin Sta.), O 2	Pa.
260	Hanlontown, C 13	Iowa
633	Hanna (Hanna City), G 11	Ill.
410	Hanna, C 10	Ind.
58	*Hanna, E 6	La.
26	*Hanna, M 13	Mo.
344	Hanna, J 19	Okla.
150	Hanna, G 16	Utah
1127	Hanna, N 16	Wyo.
59	*Hannacroix (New Baltimore), O 23	N. Y.
405	Hannaford, K 20	N. D.
56	*Hannah, F 22	Ky.
261	Hannah, D 18	N. D.
....	Hannah Jc., H 21	N. D.
750	*Hannastown, N 5	Pa.
301	Hannawa Falls, E 19	N. Y.
20865	Hannibal, E 16	Mo.
437	Hannibal, K 13	N. Y.
516	Hannibal, L 19	Ohio
300	Hannibal, G 10	Wis.
270	Hannibal Center, K 13	N. Y.
350	*Hannon, K 20	Ala.
50	*Hannon, M 6	Mo.
15	Hannover, L 9	N. D.
280	*Hanover, D 13	Ark.
389	Hanover, G 22	Conn.
899	Hanover, A 10	Ill.
406	Hanover, N 18	Ind.
896	Hanover, D 17	Kan.
178	▲*Hanover, M 4	Me.
150	*Hanover, G 13	Md.
400	Hanover, H 22	Mass.
402	Hanover, Q 16	Mich.
241	*Hanover, M 15	Minn.
150	Hanover, H 14	Mont.
2500	Hanover, K 7	N. H.
400	Hanover, E 17	N. J.
300	Hanover, M 5	N. M.
325	Hanover, J 14	Ohio
13076	Hanover, Q 16	Pa.
16439	■*Hanover, I 20	Pa.
63	Hanover, L 17	Va.
260	Hanover, P 5	W. Va.
230	Hanover, J 22	Wis.
125	*Hanover Center, H 22	Mass.
128	*Hanover Jc., Q 17	Pa.
292	Hanoverton, G 19	Ohio
196	Hansboro, D 16	N. D.
....	Hansell, H 11	Ala.
183	*Hansell, F 14	Iowa
527	Hansen, Q 12	Idaho
59	Hansen, M 17	Neb.
44	*Hansford, I 18	Ky.
....	Hansford, A 4	Tex.
200	Hansford, L 7	W. Va.
461	Hanska, P 11	Minn.
364	Hanson, H 9	Ky.
831	Hansom (Bryantville), I 21	Mass.

Pop.	Place Index	State
250	Hanson, I 24	Okla.
3	Hanson, N 22	S. D.
28	*Hansonville, E 7	Va.
251	Hanston (Olney), K 8	Kan.
105	Hansville, G 7	Wash.
5	Hanton (Cactus), G 23	S. D.
5059	Hapeville, F 6	Ga.
100	*Happy, I 21	Ky.
576	Happy, E 3	Tex.
250	*Happy Camp, B 5	Calif.
95	*Happy Creek, F 14	Va.
83	*Happy Jack, P 20	La.
1082	*Harahan, O 18	La.
....	Harahan Jc., N 18	La.
108	*Haralson, H 6	Ga.
....	Harber, J 20	Ky.
50	*Harbert, R 7	Mich.
100	*Harbeson (Broadkill), K 22	Del.
63	Harbine, O 21	Neb.
525	*Harbinger, D 24	N. C.
....	Harbor, B 20	Ohio
15	Harbor, R 2	Ore.
2186	Harbor Beach, L 24	Mich.
2500	*Harbor City, O 15	Calif.
311	*Harborcreek, C 4	Pa.
....	*Harbor Point (Allandale), F 19	Fla.
85	Harborside, M 14	Me.
1423	Harbor Springs, H 15	Mich.
357	Harborton, L 23	Va.
361	*Harbor View, C 9	Ohio
52	*Harbourton, H 13	N. J.
650	Harco, P 17	Ill.
282	Harcourt, H 10	Iowa
100	*Harcum, M 21	Va.
500	Hardaway, K 19	Ala.
1100	Hardburly, H 21	Ky.
27	*Hardeetown, E 11	Fla.
1361	Hardeeville, Q 13	S. C.
500	Harden City, M 16	Okla.
25	*Hardenville, Q 13	Mo.
25	Hardin, D 17	Colo.
838	Hardin, L 7	Ill.
414	Hardin, K 6	Ky.
805	Hardin, F 8	Mo.
1886	Hardin, L 18	Mont.
216	*Hardin, J 23	Tex.
1500	*Harding, G 18	Mass.
117	*Harding, K 12	Minn.
17	Harding, D 2	S. D.
136	*Harding, H 15	W. Va.
100	*Hardings, L 21	Va.
112	*Hardingville, M 8	N. J.
275	Hardinsburg, P 13	Ind.
930	Hardinsburg, G 12	Ky.
20	*Hardin Springs, G 13	Ky.
83	Hardman, E 16	Ore.
28	*Hardman, H 10	W. Va.
71	*Hardshell, H 21	Ky.
313	Hardtner, O 12	Kan.
43	*Hardware, L 13	Va.
139	*Hardwick, L 11	Calif.
112	*Hardwick, H 14	Ga.
300	Hardwick, F 10	Mass.
273	Hardwick, Q 4	Minn.
1607	Hardwick, E 14	Vt.
....	*Hardwood, I 13	La.
100	*Hardwood, F 5	Mich.
113	Hardwood, N 17	Okla.
508	Hardy, B 16	Ark.
168	*Hardy, E 10	Iowa
809	Hardy, H 24	Ky.
341	Hardy, O 18	Neb.
41	Hardy, A 15	Okla.
78	*Hardy, N 8	Va.
225	*Hardyville, I 13	Ky.
90	*Hardyville, L 20	Va.
150	*Harford (North Harford), O 15	N. Y.
296	Harford, E 21	Pa.
100	*Harford Mills (Mills), O 15	N. Y.
75	*Harg (Hargett), G 19	Ky.
350	Hargill, P 4	Tex.
50	*Hargis, J 17	Ky.
18	*Hargrave, I 10	Kan.
16	Harjo, J 15	Okla.
1000	Harkers Island, K 21	N. C.
500	Harlan, D 22	Ind.
3727	Harlan, K 5	Iowa
200	Harlan, E 12	Kan.
5122	Harlan, J 21	Ky.
200	Harlan, H 4	Ore.
....	Harlan Jc., L 5	Iowa
100	Harlansburg, J 3	Pa.
585	*Harleigh, J 20	Pa.
736	Harlem, G 18	Ga.
1166	Harlem, D 15	Mont.
220	Harlem Springs, H 19	Ohio
513	Harleton, E 23	Tex.
433	*Harleysville, N 23	Pa.
381	Harleyville, K 16	S. C.
175	Harlingen, G 15	N. J.
13306	Harlingen, Q 5	Tex.
125	Harlow, G 16	N. D.
1547	Harlowton, J 13	Mont.
1000	*Harman (Hankins), B 7	Va.
184	*Harman, H 15	W. Va.
307	Harmans (Harman), G 13	Md.
900	*Harmarville, L 3	Pa.
201	Harmon, C 13	Ill.
58	*Harmon, E 6	La.
1500	*Harmon (Harmon-on-Hudson), F 6	N. Y.
16	Harmon, M 11	N. D.
118	Harmon, G 17	Ohio
54	Harmon, E 3	Okla.
250	Harmonsburg, F 2	Pa.
75	*Harmony, E 7	Ark.
75	*Harmony, M 10	Calif.
....	Harmony, C 14	Colo.
1080	Harmony, K 9	Ind.
335	Harmony, K 10	Me.
50	Harmony, D 7	Md.
890	Harmony, R 21	Minn.
100	Harmony, E 8	N. J.
348	Harmony, E 6	N. C.
846	Harmony, K 3	Pa.
200	*Harmony, D 10	R. I.
62	*Harmony, R 11	Va.
15	*Harmony, I 7	W. Va.
166	*Harmony Village, M 21	Va.
68	*Harms, Q 11	Tenn.
175	*Harned, G 12	Ky.
80	*Harnedsville, Q 6	Pa.
10	*Harness, E 12	Ark.
100	*Harney, I 20	Minn.
3	Harney, K 19	Ore.
100	*Harold, M 4	Fla.
150	*Harold, H 23	Ky.
12	Harold, F 3	Minn.
208	Harper, M 18	Iowa
1695	Harper, N 14	Kan.
29	*Harper, G 21	Ky.
165	Harper, J 22	Ore.
500	*Harper, J 15	Tex.
250	Harper, I 7	Wash.
201	*Harper, O 7	W. Va.
361	Harpers Ferry, C 21	Iowa
665	Harpers Ferry, E 25	W. Va.
180	*Harpersfield, P 20	N. Y.
75	*Harpers Home, P 15	Va.
200	Harpersville, G 14	Ala.
84	Harpersville, O 21	Va.
179	*Harperville, J 16	Miss.
40	Harpster, H 6	Idaho
203	Harpster, G 10	Ohio

Pop.	Place Index	State
300	*Harpursville, Q 16	N. Y.
150	Harpwell Center, P 7	Me.
620	Harrah, I 13	Okla.
650	Harrah, N 13	Wash.
316	Harrell, P 12	Ark.
154	Harrellsville, C 20	N. C.
20	*Harriet, D 12	Ark.
....	Harriet, O 9	Ohio
208	Harrietta, J 11	Mich.
200	Harriettsville, L 18	Ohio
703	*Harriman, E 4	N. Y.
2056	*Harriman, O 25	Pa.
5620	Harriman, N 17	Tenn.
2113	Harrington, I 22	Del.
800	Harrington, L 20	Me.
1389	Harrington Park, C 21	N. J.
11	*Harrington, N 9	S. D.
545	Harrington, I 20	Wash.
68	*Harris, C 5	Ark.
123	*Harris, E 3	Calif.
106	Harris, I 4	Ga.
309	Harris, B 5	Iowa
127	*Harris, J 22	Kan.
609	Harris, L 17	Minn.
263	Harris, B 10	Mo.
109	*Harris, C 2	N. Y.
70	*Harris, H 2	N. C.
110	Harris, R 24	Okla.
75	*Harris, L 4	Tenn.
1111	Harrisburg, E 19	Ark.
11453	Harrisburg, P 17	Ill.
108	*Harrisburg, G 13	Mo.
62	Harrisburg, I 2	Neb.
200	*Harrisburg, H 6	N. C.
294	Harrisburg, L 11	Ohio
15	Harrisburg, N 11	Okla.
622	Harrisburg, I 6	Ore.
83893	Harrisburg, N 16	Pa.
241	Harrisburg, M 25	S. D.
....	Harrisburg, L 22	Tex.
10	*Harris Ferry, F 5	W. Va.
322	Harris Grove, N 21	Va.
....	Harris Jc., G 21	Minn.
4238	Harrison, B 9	Ark.
....	*Harrison, see Loma Mar	Calif.
298	Harrison, I 15	Ga.
362	Harrison, E 4	Idaho
....	Harrison, P 14	Ill.
500	Harrison, N 4	Me.
727	Harrison, K 15	Mich.
151	Harrison, M 9	Mont.
500	Harrison, E 1	Neb.
14171	Harrison, E 19	N. J.
8500	Harrison, G 6	N. Y.
1656	Harrison, N 5	Ohio
13161	■*Harrison, L 3	Pa.
....	Harrison, O 7	Pa.
159	Harrison, M 18	S. D.
220	Harrison, Q 15	Tenn.
....	Harrison, E 18	W. Va.
30	*Harrison, J 9	W. Va.
50	Harrison, K 10	Wis.
422	Harrisonburg, F 12	La.
8768	Harrisonburg, I 11	Va.
500	*Harrison City, N 5	Pa.
250	Harrison Valley, E 13	Pa.
411	Harrisonville, E 12	Md.
2322	Harrisonville, I 6	Mo.
115	Harrisonville, M 7	N. J.
442	Harrisonville, O 15	Ohio
125	*Harrisonville, P 11	Pa.
277	Harriston, M 6	Miss.
100	*Harriston, J 11	Va.
190	Harristown, I 15	Ill.
437	Harrisville, J 22	Mich.
75	*Harrisville, L 11	Miss.
300	Harrisville, P 9	N. H.
832	Harrisville, G 18	N. Y.
583	Harrisville, I 3	Pa.
626	Harrisville (Forestville), I 3	Pa.
1700	Harrisville, B 7	R. I.
110	Harrisville, D 11	Utah
1338	Harrisville, F 9	W. Va.
422	Harrod (Harrods), G 8	Ohio
400	Harrodsburg, M 12	Ind.
4673	Harrodsburg, G 16	Ky.
75	*Harrods Creek, E 14	Ky.
800	*Harrogate, K 20	Tenn.
229	Harrold, I 14	S. D.
200	Harrold, B 15	Tex.
70	*Harryhogan, K 21	Va.
150	Harshaw, P 18	Ariz.
10	*Harshaw, J 9	Wis.
227	Harshman, (Riverside) L 8	Ohio
1922	Hart, L 8	Mich.
300	*Hart, A 9	Tex.
30	Hartburg, J 25	Tex.
300	*Hartfield (Lot), M 21	Va.
1494	Hartford, O 19	Ala.
1210	Hartford, H 4	Ark.
166267	Hartford, E 14	Conn.
1842	Hartford, M 10	Ill.
207	Hartford, L 13	Iowa
491	Hartford, J 20	Kan.
1385	Hartford, H 11	Ky.
700	Hartford, M 5	Me.
1694	Hartford, O 11	Mich.
250	*Hartford, K 11	N. J.
200	Hartford, K 25	N. Y.
162	Hartford, E 21	Ohio
353	Hartford (Croton), J 13	Ohio
647	Hartford, L 23	S. D.
175	*Hartford, N 22	Tenn.
550	Hartford, K 15	Vt.
200	*Hartford, F 9	Wash.
467	Hartford, G 4	W. Va.
3910	Hartford, N 19	Wis.
6946	Hartford City, G 19	Ind.
1688	Hartington, F 20	Neb.
65	*Hartland, A 18	Ill.
1205	Hartland, K 11	Me.
224	Hartland, Q 15	Minn.
200	*Hartland, L 6	N. Y.
129	Hartland, F 8	N. D.
200	Hartland, L 14	Vt.
80	Hartland, K 8	W. Va.
998	Hartland, N 20	Wis.
116	*Hartland Four Corners, L 14	Vt.
208	*Harleton, J 15	Pa.
1503	Hartley, C 5	Iowa
112	*Hartley, I 23	Ky.
12	*Hartley, I 8	S. D.
250	*Hartley, B 2	Tex.
168	Hartline, H 18	Wash.
200	Hart Lot (Skaneateles Jc.), M 14	N. Y.
125	Hartly, G 21	Del.
542	Hartman, F 7	Ark.
148	Hartman, M 24	Colo.
8	Hartmansville, E 18	W. Va.
125	*Harts, M 3	W. Va.
269	Hartsburg, H 13	Ill.
154	Hartsburg, I 13	Mo.
....	Hartsdale, B 6	Ind.
3500	*Hartsdale, G 6	N. Y.
50	Hartsel, I 11	Colo.
2584	Hartselle, C 12	Ala.
300	*Hartsfield, N 9	Ga.
85	Hartsgrove, C 19	Ohio
135	Hartshorn, O 15	Mo.
2596	Hartshorne, M 20	Okla.
193	*Hartstown, G 2	Pa.
318	Hartsville, L 16	Ind.
179	*Hartsville, H 3	Mass.

Pop. Place Index State

626*Hartsville, N 24........Pa.
5399 Hartsville, E 17......S. C.
1095 Hartsville, L 12......Tenn.
.... Hartsville Jc., L 12...Tenn.
393 Hartville, O 12........Mo.
1200 Hartville, F 18........Ohio
179 Hartville, L 22........Wyo.
39*Hartwell, C 6..........Ark.
2372 Hartwell, D 15..........Ga.
116*Hartwell, J 8..........Mo.
.... Hartwell, O 23.........Ohio
750*Hartwell (Vallscreek), Q 5 W. Va.
122*Hartwick, K 17.......Iowa
450 Hartwick, O 19.......N. Y.
75*Hartwick Seminary, O 19 N. Y.
50*Hartwood, I 16.........Va.
140*Hartzell, R 22.........Mo.
45 Harvard, F 4.........Idaho
3121 Harvard, A 17...........Ill.
130*Harvard, P 13.........Iowa
800 Harvard, D 15.......Mass.
30 Harvard, N 12.......Mich.
704 Harvard, M 18........Neb.
150*Harvard, R 19........N. Y.
319 Harvel, K 13.............Ill.
118*Harvest, A 14..........Ala.
28 Harvest, B 11............Ga.
35*Harvey, I 6..............Ark.
17878 Harvey, D 21...........Ill.
418 Harvey, M 15.........Iowa
1200 Harvey, N 18.............La.
1851 Harvey, I 14..........N. D.
30*Harvey, N 8........W. Va.
74*Harvey Cedars, (High-point) M 19.........N. J.
354 Harveysburg, M 8....Ohio
1000 Harveyton, H 21.........Ky.
302 Harveyville, H 20.....Kan.
289 Harveyville, I 19..........Pa.
208 Harviell, Q 20............Mo.
33*Harvin, H 17..........S. C.
700 Harwich, M 14........Mass.
500 Harwich Port, N 15..Mass.
1600*Harwick, L 4..............Pa.
100 Harwinton, E 9.......Conn.
75*Harwood, J 14..........Md.
167 Harwood, L 7............Mo.
100 Harwood, M 24........N. D.
222 Harwood, L 18...........Tex.
840*Harwood Mines, J 20...Pa.
6716 Hasbrouck Hts., D 20..N. J.
180*Haskell (Haskells), K 11 Ark.
....*Haskell, see Highland City, Fla.
27 Haskell (Haskells), B 9.Ind.
3 Haskell, I 6..........Mont.
845 Haskell, C 17...........N. J.
1572 Haskell, G 19..........Okla.
3051 Haskell, D 13...........Tex.
83*Haskins, M 20..........Iowa
447 Haskins, D 9...........Ohio
527 Haslam, F 24.............Tex.
300*Haslet, D 18..............Tex.
250 Haslett, O 17.........Mich.
15 Hassan, L 21..........Minn.
145 Hasse, G 16..............Tex.
31 Hassell, H 21..........N. M.
150*Hassell, E 19..........N. C.
157 Hasslers (Rock Crusher), G 14.................Tex.
50*Hastain, K 10...........Mo.
30 Hastie, L 12.............Iowa
307 Hastings, P 16.........Colo.
1035 Hastings, D 17...........Fla.
403 Hastings, N 4.............Iowa
143*Hastings (North Eastham), L 15...............Mass.
5175 Hastings, P 15.......Mich.
5662 Hastings, O 18.......Minn.
15145 Hastings, M 17.......Neb.
100 Hastings (Morse), K 15 N. Y.
140 Hastings, N 20.......N. D.
352 Hastings, P 9.........Okla.
2105 Hastings, L 9............Pa.
288*Hastings, D 11......W. Va.
.... Hastings Branch Jc., L 8 Pa.
7057 Hastings-on-Hudson, G 5.................N. Y.
175*Hasty, C 9...............Ark.
90 Hasty, M 21...........Colo.
30 Hasty, M 13..........Minn.
250*Hasty, K 11...........N. C.
163 Haswell, K 20.........Colo.
2605 Hatboro, O 23..............Pa.
50 Hatch, I 8...............Calif.
822 Hatch, N 8..............N. M.
37*Hatch, O 11.............Ohio
294 Hatch, O 8...............Utah
140 Hatchechubbee, K 22...Ala.
180*Hatchel, G 13...........Tex.
62*Hatcher, L 3...............Ga.
35*Hatcher, I 15.............Ky.
40*Hatchie, P 4..........Tenn.
.... Hatchs Crossing, J 13 Mich.
50 Hat Creek, J 23.......Wyo.
382 Hatfield, K 4............Ark.
440 Hatfield, R 7.............Ind.
2000 Hatfield, F 8..........Mass.
200*Hatfield (West Hatfield), F 8.................Mass.
73*Hatfield, Q 4.........Minn.
120*Hatfield, A 7...............Mo.
1301 Hatfield, N 23..............Pa.
55 Hatfield, G 14...........Wis.
50 Hathaway, J 21.....Mont.
146*Hathorne, D 20.......Mass.
40 Hatley, L 10...............Ga.
270 Hatley, K 12...............Wis.
600 Hatteras, H 25.........N. C.
21026 Hattiesburg, O 17...Miss.
75*Hattieville, G 10.......Ark.
160*Hatton, K 4..............Ark.
30*Hatton, E 16..............Ky.
22*Hatton, H 14..............Mo.
933 Hatton, J 22.............N. D.
106*Hatton, D 9..............Ohio
59*Hatton, K 6..............Utah
125*Hatton, L 12...............Va.
43 Hatton, L 19..........Wash.
762 Haubstadt, Q 5.........Ind.
75*Hauer, F 8..................Wis.
125 Haugan, G 1..........Mont.
268 Haugen, D 9...............Wis.
409 Haughton, B 5.............La.
200 Hauser, D 3............Idaho
126*Hauser, M 3.............Ore.
400 Hauto, K 20................Pa.
500*Havaco, Q 5.........W. Va.
150 Havana, H 8...............Ala.
370 Havana, H 7...............Ark.
1221 Havana, B 4...............Fla.
3999 Havana, H 10...............Ill.
253 Havana, O 21.............Kan.
305 Havana, R 22...........N. D.
125 Havana, E 13.............Ohio
326 Havelock, E 8............Iowa
.... Havelock, L 22..........Neb.
100*Havelock, H 19.........N. C.
100 Havelock, O 5...........N. D.
14*Havelock, K 19..............Va.
653 Haven, L 15...............Kan.
101*Haven, N 15...............Me.
60*Haven, O 17...............Wis.
22 Havens, K 19............Neb.
232 Havensville, E 20.....Kan.

Pop. Place Index State

....*Haverford, N 22 (Pop. 3000 incl. in Merion Sta.)..Pa.
27594■*Haverford, P 23......Pa.
115*Haverhill, I 14.........Iowa
46752 Haverhill, A 19.....Mass.
100*Haverhill (Chester), P 20 Minn.
500 Haverhill, I 10.........N. H.
91*Haverhill, P 12..........Ohio
5909 Haverstraw, F 5.......N. Y.
499 Haviland, M 9............Kan.
210 Haviland, F 5..............Ohio
16 Havillah, B 18.........Wash.
6427 Havre, D 13..............Mont.
4967 Havre de Grace, C 18..Md.
2681 Hawarden, D 1...........Iowa
896 Hawesville, G 11..........Ky.
40*Hawick, N 9............Minn.
500*Hawk, M 10.............N. C.
80*Hawks (Hawk), N 13..Ohio
544 Hawkeye, E 18...........Iowa
64*Hawkeye, L 13.............Mo.
73 Hawkeye, E 23.........N. Y.
250*Hawkins, E 22.............Tex.
496 Hawkins, G 9...............Wis.
3000 Hawkinsville, K 12.......Ga.
81 Hawkinsville, J 18....N. Y.
279 Hawk Point, H 17.......Mo.
663 Hawk Run, K 11............Pa.
75 Hawks (LaRocque), H 20 Mich.
25 Hawks Nest, M 8...W. Va.
74▲*Hawk Springs, M 23.Wyo.
13 Hawley, E 10.........Calif.
35 Hawley, M 19..........Colo.
15 Hawley, C 12............Iowa
54*Hawley, C 7............Mass.
1122 Hawley, H 4............Minn.
30 Hawley, B 10............Okla.
1778*Hawley, G 23...............Pa.
200 Hawley, E 13..............Tex.
106 Hawleyville, K 5......Conn.
28*Hawlin, H 14...............Va.
1419 Haworth, C 20.........N. J.
232 Haworth, Q 24..........Okla.
2300 Haw River, E 11......N. C.
210*Haws (Hawstone), L 14 Pa.
125*Hawthorn, N 5............Ala.
741*Hawthorn (Hawthorne), D 15....................Fla.
200 Hawthorn, I 6...............La.
628 Hawthorn, J 6...............Pa.
8263 Hawthorne, Q 2........Calif.
25*Hawthorne (Eldorado Springs), E 14.........Colo.
750 Hawthorne, J 7...........Nev.
12610 Hawthorne, D 19.....N. J.
2000*Hawthorne, F 6........N. Y.
75 Hawthorne, D 5...........Wis.
.... Hawton, M 6...............Ind.
4*Haxby, G 18............Mont.
985 Haxtun, C 22...........Colo.
130 Hay, L 22...............Wash.
....*Haycock Run, M 23.....Pa.
27 Hay Creek, G 13.........Ore.
350*Hayden, D 14.............Ala.
1800 Hayden, L 18............Ariz.
640 Hayden, C 8..............Colo.
200 Hayden, M 17...............Ind.
10*Hayden, K 14...............Mo.
34 Hayden, E 24............N. M.
5 Hayden, C 21............Okla.
225 Hayden, F 21..............Utah
50*Haydenburg, L 14....Tenn.
25*Hayden Jc., M 17.......Ariz.
50 Hayden Lake, D 4....Idaho
.... Haydens, C 14.........Conn.
1000 Haydenville, F 6.....Mass.
1100 Haydenville, M 14.....Ohio
145 Haydraw, I 5...........S. D.
200*Hayes, N 7..................La.
175*Hayes (North Rochester), N 19....................N. H.
40 Hayes, I 11...............S. D.
25 Hayes, M 12...............Wis.
314 Hayes Center, N 9....Neb.
49*Hayes Store, N 21.........Va.
120*Hayesville, M 18.......Iowa
336 Hayesville, Q 3.........N. C.
363 Hayesville, G 14........Ohio
25*Haysville, K 13.........Tenn.
160*Hayfield, C 12............Iowa
742 Hayfield, Q 18...........Minn.
100*Hayfield, E 13...............Va.
.... Hayfield Jc., D 12.......Iowa
500 Hayfork, D 3...........Calif.
6 Hay Jc., J 7...............Wyo.
25 Hayland, M 16..........Neb.
45 Haylow, P 15...............Ga.
28*Haymakertown, M 7.....Va.
156*Haymarket, G 16..........Va.
23*Hayne, I 14............N. C.
15 Hayne, A 8...............S. C.
25*Haynes, I 13................Ala.
275 Haynes, I 19................Ark.
100 Haynes, D 7...............N. M.
210 Haynes, R 6...............N. D.
100 Haynes, G 21..............Okla.
2418 Haynesville, A 7............La.
100 Haynesville, G 19.........Me.
100*Haynesville, K 20............Va.
525 Hayneville, K 14.........Ala.
4 Haynor, N 13............Mich.
35 Haynesworth (Haines-worth), D 13..............Fla.
6385 Hays, H 10.................Kan.
412 Hays, E 15...............Mont.
100*Hays, C 4..................N. C.
.... Hays, N 3.....................Pa.
623 Haysi, C 6...................Va.
819 Hay Springs, E 5.......Neb.
150*Hayston, G 10...............Ga.
175 Haysville, O 9..............Ind.
50*Haysville, M 16...........Kan.
169*Haysville, L 2...............Pa.
73 Hayt Corners, O 12...N. Y.
2628 Hayti, J 24...................Mo.
370 Hayti, H 22...............S. D.
200 Hayton, O 16...............Wis.
6736 Hayward, I 6...........Calif.
184*Hayward, R 17..........Minn.
156 Hayward, E 12............Okla.
81*Haywood, E 12........W. Va.
1571 Hayward, E 7...............Wis.
187*Haywood, G 12..........N. C.
35 Haywood, L 18...........Okla.
30*Haywood, I 13.................Va.
81 Haywood, E 12........W. Va.
7397 Hazard, I 21...................Ky.
142 Hazard, K 15...............Neb.
.... Hazard, G 23.............Wash.
396 Hazel, L 6......................Ky.
.... Hazel, D 6...................Mich.
65*Hazel, E 5.................Minn.
5 Hazel, H 22...............Mont.
125 Hazel, K 15................Okla.
182 Hazel, G 22...............S. D.
132*Hazel, D 7......................Va.
34 Hazel, E 9..................Wash.
69*Hazel Creek (Sims), C 6 Calif.
1299*Hazel Crest, D 21............Ill.
200 Hazel Dell, L 20.............Ill.
250 Hazel Green, A 14.........Ala.
311 Hazel Green, G 20.........Ky.
18*Hazelgreen, G 9.....W. Va.
582 Hazel Green, H 22.....Wis.
26*Hazelhurst, B 12............Ill.

Pop. Place Index State

650 Hazelhurst (Hazel Hurst), F 9.......................Pa.
191 Hazelhurst, J 8..........Wis.
.... Hazel Park, P 23.......Mich.
185*Hazel Patch, (Hazle Patch), I 19.........................Ky.
126*Hazel Run, N 6.......Minn.
417 Hazelton, Q 13.........Idaho
260 Hazelton, O 11...........Kan.
500 Hazelton, O 13.........N. D.
75*Hazelton, C 16......W. Va.
15*Hazel Valley, D 6.......Ark.
86 Hazelwood, J 12............Ind.
1508 Hazelwood, P 6.........N. C.
100 Hazelwood, H 8.......Wash.
45*Hazen, K 11..................Ala.
787 Hazen, I 15...................Ark.
100 Hazen, G 5...................Nev.
.... Hazen, E 9...................N. J.
662 Hazen, K 9..................N. D.
32*Hazen, H 7......................Pa.
25 Hazen, G 14..................N. H.
34*Hazelbrook, I 20..............Pa.
64*Hazlegreen, M 13............Mo.
1732 Hazlehurst, L 17.............Ga.
3124 Hazlehurst, M 10.........Miss.
516 Hazleton, O 5..................Ind.
536 Hazleton, F 19...............Iowa
6*Hazleton, N 14..................Mo.
38009 Hazleton, J 20..................Pa.
60*Hazlettville, G 20............Del.
21 Hazy (Hazy Creek), N 6 W. Va.
313*Hazzard, N 3......................Pa.
2052 Headland, N 21................Ala.
12*Headlee Ranch, M 8..S. D.
42*Head of Grassy, E 21...Ky.
50*Head of Island, M 16....La.
75 Headquarters, G 6...Idaho
174 Headrick, M 4.............Okla.
27*Head River, B 1...............Ga.
25*Heads, F 7.....................Miss.
46*Headsville, D 20.....W. Va.
54*Head Tide, N 9..................Me.
16*Head Waters, I 9...............Va.
38 Heafford Jc. (Bradley), J 9.............................Wis.
2507 Healdsburg, G 4..........Calif.
2067 Healdton, O 12............Okla.
105*Healdville, L 8....................Vt.
65*Healing Springs, M 4...Ala.
114*Healing Springs, B 4...Ark.
195*Healing Springs, K 7.....Va.
18*Health, D 6....................Ark.
230 Healy, I 6......................Kan.
45 Healys, M 20....................Va.
350*Heardmont, E 16...............Ga.
55*Heards, K 12....................Va.
3511 Hearne, I 20....................Tex.
20*Hearst, F 3.....................Calif.
30*Heart, B 15......................Ark.
21 Heart Butte, E 7.........Mont.
50*Heart Prairie, N 22.......Wis.
20 Heartstrong, E 22........Colo.
141 Heartwell, M 16.............Neb.
100*Heaters, I 11..........W. Va.
67 Heath, C 5.....................Mass.
200 Heath, K 14....................Ohio
50*Heathman, F 8...............Miss.
570 Heath Springs, C 15...S. C.
30*Heathsville, D 17.........N. C.
350 Heathsville, K 21..............Va.
101*Heathville, I 7....................Pa.
500*Heaton, D 2....................N. C.
400 Heaton, K 16..................N. D.
.... Heaton, C 5.......................Tex.
100*Heatoncreek, M 24.....Tenn.
2215 Heavener, L 24.............Okla.
300 Hebardsville, N 17..........Ga.
200 Hebbardsville, G 9.........Ky.
20*Hebbertsburg, N 16..Tenn.
2742 Hebbronville, Q 16.........Tex.
80 Heber, H 19....................Ariz.
240 Heber, Q 22..................Calif.
2748 Heber, F 14....................Utah
1656 Heber Springs, F 14......Ark.
150*Hebert, D 11.......................La.
275 Hebo, E 4..........................Ore.
250 Hebron, G 18..................Conn.
627 Hebron, A 18........................Ill.
949 Hebron, C 8..........................Ind.
125*Hebron, B 17..........................Ky.
150 Hebron, N 5...........................Me.
804 Hebron, N 21.........................Md.
1909 Hebron, O 19......................Neb.
151▲*Hebron, L 11.................N. H.
.... Hebron, C 20....................N. M.
1267 Hebron, M 7....................N. D.
723 Hebron, K 14......................Ohio
600*Hebron, M 18........................Pa.
131*Hebron, D 19.......................Tex.
160*Hebron, O 15..........................Va.
113*Hebron, E 9....................W. Va.
130 Hebron Sta. (East Hebron), N 5.........................Me.
650 Hebronville, K 18.........Mass.
205 Hecker, O 11..........................Ill.
96*Heckscherville, K 19......Pa.
85 Hecla, C 17..........................Ind.
40 Hecla, H 9...........................Neb.
2000 Hecla (Southwest), N 5.Pa.
555 Hecla, B 19.......................S. D.
250*Hector, F 10.......................Ark.
45*Hector, I 20...........................Ky.
1044 Hector, N 10....................Minn.
60*Hector, O 12......................N. Y.
28*Hedding, P 18.....................N. H.
85 Hedgesville, J 14..........Mont.
403 Hedgesville, C 24...W. Va.
34*Hedgeville, H 17................Ky.
637 Hedley, E 5..........................Tex.
94*Hedrick, H 6........................Ind.
731 Hedrick N 17......................Iowa
....*Heeney, G 11.....................Colo.
1684 Heflin, F 20..........................Ala.
61 Heflin, C 7................................La.
1000*Hegins, K 18...........................Pa.
41*Hegira, K 15..............................Ky.
4 Heglar, Q 16........................Idaho
200*Heiberger, I 10......................Ala.
2879▲Heidelberg, H 19..............Ky.
615 Heidelberg, L 19................Miss.
2239*Heidelberg (Glenn), L 3 .Pa.
166 Heidenheimer, I 18..........Tex.
400*Heidrick, J 19.........................Ky.
.... Heidrick Jc., I 7......................Pa.
54992*Heights (Cleveland Heights), O 24..............Ohio
.... Heights, H 3..................W. Va.
35*Heights (Granite Heights), J 11..............................Wis.
100 Heil, P 9............................N. D.
1000 Heilwood, L 8..........................Pa.
130 Heimdal, I 15....................N. D.
200 Heiner, I 16...........................Utah
60*Heise, N 18.........................Idaho
215*Heiskell, M 19....................Tenn.
365 Heislerville, Q 10..............N. J.
75 Heisson (Heison), P 7.Wash.
110*Heizer, J 11...........................Kan.
59*Helechawa, G 21.....................Ky.
198*Helen, C 10..............................Ga.
12*Helen, O 14..............................Md.
.... Helen, P 4.................................Pa.
52*Helen, O 8........................W. Va.
667 Helena, G 12..........................Ala.
8546 Helena, K 20..........................Ark.
62*Helena, D 4.........................Calif.
1073 Helena, L 14..............................Ga.

Pop. Place Index State

70*Helena (Helena Sta.), D 19...........................Ky.
....*Helena, see Clam River, J 15..........................Mich.
210 Helena, D 6...........................Mo.
15056 Helena, J 8......................Mont.
160 Helena, C 20.....................N. Y.
300*Helena (Timberlake), C 13.............................N. C.
268 Helena, D 11.......................Ohio
776 Helena, C 9..........................Okla.
497 Helena, E 10.........................S. C.
18*Helena, L 16........................Tenn.
120*Helena, N 17...........................Tex.
.... Helena Crossing, K 20.Ark.
30*Helendale (Judson), N 18 Calif.
25*Helen Furnace, H 6.......Pa.
200*Helenville, M 20...........Wis.
700 Helenwood, L 17.........Tenn.
475*Helfenstein, K 18..............Pa.
35*Helisma(Burson, H 9.Calif.
8 Helium, D 14..................N. D.
121 Helix, B 19..........................Ore.
799 Hellam (Hallam), P 18..Pa.
4031 Hellertown, L 23...............Pa.
33*Hellgate, F 20...............Wash.
606 Hellier, I 23............................Ky.
....*Hells Half Acre, J 15.Wyo.
175*Helm, K 11.......................Calif.
30*Helm, J 15................................Ky.
70 Helm, F 7..............................Miss.
50 Helmer, F 5.........................Idaho
100 Helmer, B 20............................Ind.
60*Helmet, L 19...............................Va.
667 Helmetta, H 16....................N. J.
122*Helmsburg, L 13...................Ind.
200 Helmville, I 6....................Mont.
380 Helotes, L 16.........................Tex.
900*Helper (Fairmount City), J 6...Pa.
2843 Helper, I 16.............................Utah
22 Helsel, K 13............................Okla.
47*Helton, J 21................................Ky.
964▲Helton, B 3........................N. C.
602 Heltonville, N 13..................Ind.
500 Helvetia (Helvetia Mines), I 8...Pa.
290 Helvetia, I 13....................W. Va.
60 Helvey, N 20............................Neb.
30 Heman, C 6.............................Okla.
213 Hematite, K 19..........................Mo.
75*Hematite, L 6.............................Va.
50 Hembree, M 18......................Tenn.
2595 Hemet, P 19..........................Calif.
792 Hemingford, G 4.....................Neb.
536 Hemingway, I 20...................S. C.
310 Hemlock, G 15..........................Ind.
650 Hemlock, N 19........................Mich.
317 Hemlock, N 9...........................N. Y.
600*Hemlock, B 3...........................N. C.
353 Hemlock, M 15........................Ohio
25 Hemlock, D 4..............................Ore.
28*Hemlock, I 13....................W. Va.
65*Hemlock Grove, O 15.Ohio
60*Hemp, B 8....................................Ga.
972*Hemp, G 10.............................N. C.
739 Hemphill, H 25.........................Tex.
500 Hemphill, Q 6....................W. Va.
100*Hemple, E 6...............................Mo.
20856 Hempstead, H 7.........N. Y.
.... Hempstead, L 7......................Ohio
1674 Hempstead, K 21.................Tex.
200*Henagar, B 19...........................Ala.
48*Henderson, A 13.....................Ark.
150 Henderson, F 15...................Colo.
75 Henderson, K 9...........................Ga.
152*Henderson, F 9.............................Ill.
100 Henderson, J 18..........................Ind.
217 Henderson, N 5...........................Iowa
13160 Henderson, G 9.......................Ky.
147*Henderson, H 20.....................Md.
2500 Henderson, O 19.................Mich.
820 Henderson, O 13.................Minn.
.... Henderson, G 2.....................Mont.
495 Henderson, L 18......................Neb.
262 Henderson, I 14......................N. Y.
7647 Henderson, C 15...................N. C.
15 Henderson. K 13.....................Okla.
1771 Henderson, P 5.....................Tenn.
6437 Henderson, F 23......................Tex.
.... Henderson, O 10....................Utah
398 Henderson, H 3...............W. Va.
68*Henderson Harbor, G 14 N. Y.
5381 Hendersonville, P 8...N. C.
319*Hendersonville, N 2.........Pa.
316 Hendersonville, N 14..S. C.
750 Hendersonville, L 11..Tenn.
147 Hendley, O 12.........................Neb.
6*Hendon, O 15.........................Tenn.
114*Hendricks, G 21........................Ky.
740 Hendricks, O 3........................Minn.
64*Hendricks, N 22..........................Pa.
539 Hendricks, G 16................W. Va.
115 Hendrickson, P 20.................Mo.
25*Hendrix, D 3.........................N. C.
145 Hendrix (Kemp City), R 17..Okla.
341 Hendrum, G 2........................Minn.
300 Hendrysburg, J 18.............Ohio
335 Henefer, E 13.........................Utah
219*Henlawson, N 4..............W. Va.
87*Henley, J 13...................................Mo.
107*Henley, P 11...........................Ohio
25 Henly, K 17.................................Tex.
396 Hennepin, E 13...........................Ill.
250 Hennepin, N 13.........................Okla.
1342 Hennessey, F 11....................Okla.
1000 Henniker, O 11......................N. H.
.... Henniker Jc., O 12.............N. H.
259 Henning, H 21...............................Ill.
948 Henning, J 7............................Minn.
415 Henning, O 2............................Tenn.
33*Henrico, C 17..........................N. C.
65 Henrietta, P 17........................Mich.
5*Henrietta, H 8..............................Mo.
544 Henrietta, F 8................................Mo.
1800*Henrietta, L 9.......................N. Y.
1400 Henrietta, H 2.......................N. C.
185 Henrietta, N 10...........................Pa.
2391 Henrietta, B 16........................Tex.
5*Henrietta, H 9.....................W. Va.
148 Henriette, K 17.......................Minn.
241 Henrieville, P 10.....................Utah
22 Henry, P 22...............................Idaho
1877 Henry, E 13.....................................Ill.
145*Henry, N 9...La.
11 Henry, K 12.................................Mich.
176 Henry, H 1....................................Neb.
31*Henry, I 20...............................S. C.
322 Henry, G 22...............................S. D.
232 Henry, M 6................................Tenn.
156*Henry, Q 6..Va.
Henry, see Clay.........W. Va.
6905 Henryetta, I 18.........................Okla.
360 Henry River, F 3.......................N. C.
25 Henrys, I 9.................................Wash.
15*Henryton, C 10.............................Md.
400 Henryville, O 17..........................Ind.
450 Henryville, E 19............................Ky.
75*Henryville, H 23............................Pa.
161*Henryville, P 9.......................Tenn.
148 Hensel (Canton), E 21.N. D.
112*Hensel, Q 19.......................................Pa.
151 Henshaw, G 7...................................Ky.
34 Hensler, L 11.............................N. D.
25*Hensley, I 20.....................................Ky.
218*Hensley (Claren), Q 5.W.Va.

Pop. Place Index State

28*Henson, P 23.........................Mo.
300*Hensonville, P 22....N. Y.
95*Henton, K 16...........................Ill.
81*Hepburn, P 6.........................Iowa
256 Hepburn, H 10.......................Ohio
.... Hepburn, H 16..............................Pa.
80*Hepburnville, H 15.............Pa.
516 Hephzibah, G 19......................Ga.
259*Hepler, L 24.............................Kan.
22*Hepners, G 11.............................Va.
1140 Heppner, D 17.........................Ore.
125*Heppner, N 2...........................S. D.
2 Hepner Jc., C 15...................Ore.
35*Hepzibah, E 12.................W. Va.
30*Herald, H 8..............................Calif.
50*Herald, P 19.................................Ill.
250*Herald, C 6...................................Va.
36*Heraline, I 15................................Ky.
49 Herbert, N 13..............................Ala.
80*Herbert (Ardel), L 2.W. Va.
15*Herberta (Bethera), L 19 S. C.
85*Herbertsville, J 19....N. J.
25*Herbine, N 14..........................Ark.
280 Herbst, F 16.................................Ind.
25*Herbster, E 4...............................Wis.
1800 Herculaneum, K 20....Mo.
343 Hercules, A 18.....................Calif.
57*Hercules, Q 11.............................Mo.
50 Herd, H 19.......................................Ky.
100 Herd, B 17..................................Okla.
60 Hereford, P 21............................Ariz.
100 Hereford, B 17..........................Colo.
250 Hereford, C 13.............................Md.
.... Hereford, F 14..........................Ohio
32 Hereford, H 21............................Ore.
175*Hereford, M 22................................Pa.
2*Hereford, I 5.............................S. D.
2584 Hereford, E 2.............................Tex.
3804 Herington, I 17.........................Kan.
152 Herkimer, D 18...........................Kan.
9617 Herkimer, L 19.......................N. Y.
32 Herman, E 20...................................Ark.
300 Herman, C 7...............................Mich.
703 Herman, K 4................................Minn.
427 Herman, I 23..................................Neb.
200*Herman, J 4.......................................Pa.
40 Hermanas, P 5...........................N. M.
2308 Hermann, I 16.................................Mo.
1615 Hermansville, G 7............Mich.
52*Hermanville, O 16....................Md.
206 Hermanville, L 7....................Miss.
2500 Herminie, N 4.................................Pa.
803 Hermiston, B 17..........................Ore.
419 Hermitage, P 13............................Ark.
124*Hermitage, D 3................................Ga.
300 Hermitage, K 13..............................La.
321 Hermitage, L 10...........................Mo.
206 Hermitage, O 6..........................N. Y.
250*Hermitage, M 11......................Tenn.
150*Hermitage Springs, L 14 Tenn.
404 Hermleigh, E 12.............................Tex.
84*Hermon, F 9..Ill.
.... Hermon, K 14......................................Me.
487 Hermon, E 18................................N. Y.
22*Hermondale, J 24.........................Mo.
121 Hermosa, K 4...............................S. D.
204▲Hermosa (Tie Siding), R 19...........................Wyo.
7197 Hermosa Beach, O 15.Calif.
12*Hernandez, C 9..........................N. M.
402 Hernando, F 13..............................Fla.
1072 Hernando, A 12.......................Miss.
60*Herndon, K 11..........................Calif.
210*Herndon, J 19.................................Ga.
112 Herndon, J 9...................................Iowa
448 Herndon, C 5...................................Kan.
85*Herndon, K 8..Ky.
687 Herndon, L 17......................................Pa.
1046 Herndon, F 17......................................Va.
600 Herndon, Q 7..............................W. Va.
85 Hernshaw, L 6..........................W. Va.
26*Herod, Q 18..Ill.
15*Herold, J 10...................................W. Va.
215 Heron, E 1.......................................Mont.
180*Heron Island, P 10.....................Me.
852 Heron Lake, Q 8.......................Minn.
30*Herpel, D 14..Ark.
592 Herreid, C 13..................................S. D.
616 Herrick, K 15..Ill.
246 Herrick, O 16..................................S. D.
140 Herrick Center, F 22.............Pa.
57 Herrickville, E 19..........................Pa.
289 Herriman, F 10............................Utah
9352 Herrin, P 15..Ill.
35*Herring, H 6.......................................Iowa
232*Herring, H 15.............................N. Y.
27 Herring, H 3.......................................Okla.
81*Herrold, K 12...................................Iowa
.... Herron, I 19..Ky.
50*Herron, J 21......................................Mich.
416 Herscher, E 19...Ill.
202 Hersey, L 14.......................................Mich.
150 Hersey, C 12..Wis.
487 Hershey, K 9...Neb.
2000 Hershey, N 17..Pa.
126 Hersman, I 7...Ill.
17*Hertel, C 8...Wis.
1959 Hertford, D 22..N. C.
.... Hervey City, J 15..Ill.
100*Heshbon, L 7...Pa.
8 Heslop, M 18..Ohio
749▲Hesper, B 19...Iowa
32 Hesper, L 15...Mont.
80 Hesper, H 15...N. D.
148*Hesperia, N 18...Calif.
535 Hesperia, M 12..Mich.
125 Hesperus, P 5...Colo.
215 Hess, N 3..Okla.
25*Hessdale, P 19..Pa.
200 Hessel, G 18..Mich.
500 Hessmer, I 11..La.
40 Hesston, A 11...Ind.
403 Hesston, K 16..Kan.
98*Hesston, M 11...Pa.
6000*Hessville, B 6...Ind.
100 Hessville, D 11...Ohio
57*Hestand, K 14..Ky.
110*Hester, L 17...La.
90*Hester, D 14..N. C.
44 Hester, L 4...Okla.
7 Hetch Hetchy, I 12...Calif.
10 Hetch Hetchy Jc., I 10 Calif.
60 Heth, H 20...Ark.
199 Hetland, I 22...S. D.
290 Hettick, K 11...Ill.
16*Hettie, I 10...W. Va.
1138 Hettinger, Q 5...N. D.
312 Hetzel N 4...W. Va.
620 Heuvelton, E 17..N. Y.
20 Hewes-Kirkwood, D 13 Colo.
125*Hewett, N 5..W. Va.
200 Hewins, O 19..Kan.
294 Hewitt, J 9...Minn.
216 Hewitt B 17...N. J.
162*Hewitt, G 18...Tex.
150 Hewitt, I 13..Wis.
32*Hewlet (Merideth), L 1 W. Va.
550*Hewlett, H 7...N. Y.
438*Hewlett Bay Park, H 7 N. Y.
75*Hewlett, L 17...Va.
49*Hext, I 14..Tex.
413 Heyburn, Q 14..Idaho
30 Heyburn, G 17...Okla.

Pop. Place Index State

.... Heyser, N 19...............Tex.
996 Heyworth, H 16...............Ill.
3958 Hialeah, N 23.................Fla.
125 Hiattville, L 24...............Kan.
200 *Hiawassa (Hiwasse), O 3 Va.
163 Hiawassee, B 11...............Ga.
3238 Hiawatha, D 21..............Kan.
160 Hiawatha, F 11..............Mich.
20 Hiawatha, N 8................Neb.
858 Hiawatha (Kingmine), J 16...................................Utah
118*Hiawatha, Q 8.............W. Va.
150 Hibbard, C 12......................Ind.
12 Hibbard, I 18...................Mont.
19*Hibbetts, H 19...................Ohio
16385 Hibbing, F 17...................Minn.
50*Hibbs, P 4..............................Pa.
55*Hibernia, H 14........................Ky.
32*Hibernia (Holts Summit), I 14...Mo.
1395 Hibernia, D 15...................N. J.
2 Hickey, L 21.............................Tex.
250*Hickman, C 23..........................Ark.
58*Hickman, I 9............................Calif.
150 Hickman, J 21..............................Del.
2268 Hickman, K 4...............................Ky.
320 Hickman, M 22...........................Neb.
525*Hickman, M 2.................................Pa.
214 Hickman, M 13...........................Tenn.
200 Hickman Mills, H 6....Mo.
28*Hickoria (Hicoria), A 18 Ark.
234 Hickory (Hickory Grove), K 5..Ky.
724 Hickory, K 18.........................Miss.
33 Hickory (Hickory Creek), C 9...Mo.
13487 Hickory, E 3........................N. C.
224 Hickory, N 14..........................Okla.
600 Hickory, N 2.................................Pa.
180 Hickory Corners, P 13.Mich.
300*Hickory Corners, L 16..Pa.
33 Hickory Creek (Hickory), C 9...Mo.
15*Hickory Flat, K 12..........Ky.
352 Hickory Flat, B 17.........Miss.
153*Hickory Ground (Hickory), Q 22.....................................Va.
234 Hickory Grove (Hickory), K 5..Ky.
272 Hickory Grove, B 10..S. C.
200 Hickory Plains, H 14..Ark.
40*Hickory Pt., L 9.........Tenn.
350 Hickory Ridge, F 18...Ark.
55*Hickory Ridge, M 20.Tenn.
400 Hickory Valley, Q 4..Tenn.
76*Hickory Withe, P 3...Tenn.
83*Hickox, N 20........................Ga.
16 Hicks (Carter), D 5...Ark.
12 Hicks. H 16...............................Iowa
28*Hicksbaugh, J 24...................Tex.
75 Hickson, N 25.......................N. D.
6772 Hicksville, H 7....................N. Y.
2549 Hicksville, D 6......................Ohio
200 Hicks Wharf, M 21...............Va.
89*Hico, B 9......................................La.
1242 Hico, F 17...................................Tex.
40*Hico, M 9...........................W. Va.
28*Hicoria (Hickoria), A 18 Ark.
191 Hidalgo, L 19..................................Ill.
15*Hidalgo, K 16...............................Ky.
630 Hidalgo, R 3................................Tex.
450 Hiddenite, E 4..........................N. C.
12*Hidden Timber, N 11 S. D.
.... Higbee, N 19...........................Colo.
877 Higbee, F 12................................Mo.
15 Higby, O 12...............................Ohio
158*Higby, I 6...........................W. Va.
142 Higden, E 13...............................Ark.
12*Higdon, M 20...............................Mo.
56*Higdons Store, B 6.........Ga.
800 Higganum, J 16......................Conn.
65*Higgins, M 9..........................N. C.
741 Higgins, B 6...................................Tex.
35*Higgins Bay (Spy Lake), I 20..N. Y.
195 Higginson, G 15.......................Ark.
373 Higginsport, P 8........................Ohio
3533 Higginsville, G 8.........................Mo.
32*Higginsville, E 21...W. Va.
141*Higgston, K 17.............................Ga.
12*High, A 7.......................................Ark.
105*High, J 19......................................Iowa
92*High, C 21...Tex.
212*Highbank, I 19..............................Tex.
224*High Bridge, G 17.......Ky.
1781 High Bridge, F 11......N. J.
30 High Bridge, G 6.............Wis.
20 High Cliff, K 19.............Tenn.
50 Highcliff, N 15......................Wis.
60 High Cliff Jc., N 15......Wis.
117*Highcoal, N 6...............W. Va.
450 High Falls, B 4..............N. Y.
220*Highfalls, G 10...............N. C.
450*Highfield, B 4..........................Md.
800*Highfield, K 3...............................Pa.
46*Highfill, B 4...............................Ark.
31*High Gate, K 15..........................Mo.
437 Highgate Center (High-gate), B 8.....................................Vt.
100 Highgate Springs, A 7...Vt.
900*Highgrove, Q 10...............Calif.
188 High Hill, H 16..........................Mo.
800 High Island, L 24...............Tex.
68*Highknob, I 19...............................Ky.
110 Highland, M 6...............................Ark.
1500 Highland, O 18.......................Calif.
.... Highland, I 13...........................Conn.
100 Highland, C 15..............................Fla.
3820 Highland, M 12...............................Ill.
1553 Highland, B 6...................................Ind.
*Highland, see Highland Center....................................Iowa
764 Highland, C 23.............................Kan.
27*Highland, E 14...................................La.
100*Highland (East Warren), N 12..Me.
62*Highland, G 12..............................Md.
220 Highland. P 21......................Mich.
45*Highland (Marcy), F 23 Minn.
1714 Highland, C 5.........................N. Y.
262 Highland, N 10.........................Ohio
780*Highland, I 20...................................Pa.
26*Highland, F 9.......................W. Va.
902 Highland, H 20...........................Wis.
100*Highland Center (High-land), O 17...........................Iowa
500*Highland City (Haskell), I 16..Fla.
210 Highlandale, E 10..........Miss.
3711 Highland Falls, E 5...N. Y.
200*Highland Home, L 16..Ala.
.... Highland Jc., P 10....Calif.
150*High Landing, D 6...Minn.
350 Highland Lake, P 5....Me.
65*Highland Lake, D 2..N. Y.
650*Highland Mills, E 3..N. Y.
300 Highland Park, F 16..Conn.
14476 Highland Park, B 21...Ill.
....*Highland Park, F 14...Ky.
50810 Highland Park, P 22 Mich.
9002 Highland Park, G 16..N. J.
10288*Highland Park, E 19..Tex.
25*Highlands (Bennetts Landing), G 15....N. H.

Pop.	Place	Index	State
2076	Highlands	H 21	N. J.
569	Highlands	R 5	N. C.
1000	*Highlands	K 22	Tex.
1000	*Highland Springs	M 17	Va.
56	Highlandville	B 19	Iowa
76	*Highlandville	P 10	Mo.
....	High Level	F 10	Ala.
1136	Highmore	I 15	S. D.
60	*Highmount (Grand Hotel)	C 4	N. Y.
165	*Highpine	Q 4	Me.
25	*High Point	F 10	La.
80	*Highpoint	H 18	Miss.
110	*High Point	J 12	Mo.
	*Highpoint, see Harvey Cedars		N. J.
38495	High Point	E 9	N. C.
150	High Point	H 9	Wash.
40	High Ridge	G 12	Md.
250	*High Ridge	J 20	Mo.
	*High Rock, see Dawson	L 6	Md.
80	High Rock	G 8	N. C.
650	*Highrock	P 18	Pa.
217	High Shoals	F 11	Ga.
1000	Highshoals	G 4	N. C.
2371	High Spire	O 17	Pa.
2000	*Highsplint	J 21	Ky.
2010	High Springs	D 12	Fla.
97	*Hightower	F 21	Ala.
34	*Hightower	J 23	Tex.
....	Hightower	M 21	Wyo.
20	*Hightown	I 8	Va.
3486	Hightstown	I 15	N. J.
125	*Highview	C 2	N. Y.
57	*High View	E 21	W. Va.
52	*Highway	K 15	Ky.
500	*Highway Highlands	N 15	Calif.
3707	Highwood	B 21	Ill.
60	*Highwood	L 18	Mich.
225	Highwood	F 11	Mont.
200	Higley	L 14	Ariz.
105	*Hika	P 16	Wis.
13	*Hike	E 21	Ky.
32	*Hiland	J 15	Wyo.
607	Hilbert (Hilbert Junction)	O 15	Wis.
100	*Hilda	F 20	Ky.
8	*Hilda	Q 11	Mo.
246	*Hilda	L 12	S. C.
357	*Hildebran	F 2	N. C.
12	Hildebrand	Q 11	Ore.
15	*Hilderbrand	M 22	Mo.
30	*Hildreth	D 11	Fla.
361	Hildreth	N 15	Neb.
350	Hiles	L 8	Wis.
....	Hiles Jc.	K 8	Wis.
100	Hilgard	D 20	Ore.
225	Hilger	H 14	Mont.
254	Hilham	L 14	Tenn.
	Hill, see Sorrento		Calif.
300	Hill	M 12	N. H.
37	Hill	N 10	N. M.
75	Hill	K 25	Okla.
50	*Hill (Groveland)	O 10	Tenn.
100	*Hill	E 5	Va.
6	Hilland	J 8	S. D.
1161	*Hillburn	F 4	N. Y.
116	*Hill City	C 3	Ga.
58	Hill City	O 9	Idaho
1115	Hill City	F 8	Kan.
641	Hill City	H 14	Minn.
225	Hill City	K 2	S. D.
	*Hillcoke, see Isabella	P 4	Pa.
....	Hillcrest	H 4	Ark.
....	Hillcrest	C 5	Wis.
55	*Hilleman (Hillemann)	H 18	Ark.
1500	*Hiller	P 5	Pa.
150	*Hillgirt	P 8	N. C.
60	Hill Grove	J 5	Ohio
175	*Hillham	O 10	Ind.
103	Hillhead	C 22	S. D.
75	*Hillhouse	D 7	Miss.
550	Hilliard	B 15	Fla.
58	*Hilliards	P 12	Mich.
583	Hilliards	K 11	Ohio
400	Hilliards	J 4	Pa.
161	*Hilliardville, (Benhaden)	C 5	Fla.
218	Hillisburg	H 13	Ind.
180	*Hillister	I 24	Tex.
27	*Hillman	G 15	Ga.
363	Hillman	H 18	Mich.
110	*Hillman	K 14	Minn.
15	Hillman	K 8	Pa.
122	*Hillpoint	I 19	Wis.
177	Hillrose	D 19	Colo.
232	Hills	L 20	Iowa
450	Hills	R 3	Minn.
2100	*Hills (Lawrence)	J 2	Pa.
292	Hillsboro	B 10	Ala.
334	Hillsboro	H 11	Ga.
4514	Hillsboro	L 13	Ill.
280	Hillsboro	P 20	Iowa
1580	Hillsboro	J 17	Kan.
146	*Hillsboro	E 20	Ky.
181	Hillsboro	I 19	Md.
200	*Hillsboro	J 15	Miss.
256	Hillsboro	K 19	Mo.
25	*Hillsboro	N 15	Mont.
1840	Hillsboro	O 11	N. H.
350	Hillsboro	M 7	N. M.
1311	Hillsboro	D 12	N. C.
1338	Hillsboro	K 24	N. D.
4713	Hillsboro	O 10	Ohio
3747	Hillsboro	D 6	Ore.
200	*Hillsboro	P 13	Tenn.
7799	Hillsboro	F 19	Tex.
115	*Hillsboro	E 15	Va.
224	Hillsboro	M 13	W. Va.
1146	Hillsboro	H 17	Wis.
175	Hillsboro Lower Village	O 10	N. H.
2747	Hillsborough	E 17	Calif.
70	Hillsboro Upper Village	O 10	N. H.
516	Hillsborough (Hillsboro)	H 8	Ind.
250	Hillsdale	D 10	Ill.
500	Hillsdale	J 6	Ind.
142	Hillsdale	H 24	Kan.
6381	Hillsdale	R 16	Mich.
515	Hillsdale	P 15	Miss.
3438	Hillsdale	C 20	N. J.
500	Hillsdale	Q 24	N. Y.
131	Hillsdale	C 10	Okla.
410	*Hillsdale	K 7	Pa.
100	*Hillsdale	L 13	Tenn.
182	*Hillsdale	D 10	Wis.
125	Hillsdale	Q 23	Wyo.
100	Hillsgrove	G 17	Pa.
1000	Hills Grove (Hillsgrove)	G 15	R. I.
27	Hillside	I 9	Ariz.
8	Hillside	L 13	Colo.
1080	*Hillside	C 21	Ill.
520	Hillside	I 10	Ky.
30	*Hillside	O 3	Me.
35	Hillside	H 20	Mont.
18556	■Hillside	F 18	N. J.
284	*Hillside	M 6	Pa.
8	Hillside	M 20	S. D.
160	Hillsview	D 15	S. D.
2000	*Hillsville	I 1	Pa.
656	Hillsville	Q 3	Va.
246	Hilltonia	I 22	Ga.
5	*Hill Top	B 8	Ark.
110	Hill Top	G 16	Colo.
71	*Hilltop	K 20	Kan.
800	▲*Hill Top	N 10	Md.
115	Hilltop	E 14	Nev.
908	Hilltop	N 8	W. Va.
110	*Hilltown	M 23	Pa.
544	Hillview	K 7	Ill.
25	*Hillview (Paddock)	J 6	Minn.
100	*Hilly	B 9	La.
....	Hillyard	G 23	Wash.
100	Hilmar	I 9	Calif.
....	Hilo	J 21	Ky.
....	Hilo Jc.	N 16	Minn.
500	Hilt (Hilts)	B 5	Calif.
110	*Hilton	G 4	Calif.
93	*Hilton	N 3	Ga.
....	*Hilton (Newark Heights)	E 18	N. J.
895	Hilton	K 8	N. Y.
1035	*Hiltonhead	Q 14	S. C.
250	*Hiltons (Hilton)	E 6	Va.
1600	*Hilton Village	P 21	Va.
210	*Hima	I 20	Ky.
11	Himes	B 11	Wyo.
446	*Himlerville (Beauty)	G 23	Ky.
350	Himrod	O 11	N. Y.
100	*Himyar	J 19	Ky.
50	*Hinch	K 17	Mo.
13	*Hinch	P 4	W. Va.
11	*Hinchcliff	C 11	Miss.
5	Hinchley	F 6	Neb.
710	Hinckley	C 17	Ill.
150	*Hinckley	L 9	Me.
873	Hinckley	K 17	Minn.
250	Hinckley	K 18	N. Y.
637	Hinckley	J 7	Utah
75	*Hindes	N 16	Tex.
625	Hindman	H 22	Ky.
407	Hindsboro	J 20	Ill.
175	Hindsville	B 6	Ark.
203	*Hi Nella	L 10	N. J.
210	Hines	F 11	Minn.
677	Hines	L 18	Ore.
....	*Hines	M 12	W. Va.
10	*Hines	D 5	Wis.
600	Hinesburg	F 7	Vt.
5	Hines Jc.	H 17	N. C.
2113	▲*Hineston	I 8	La.
630	Hinesville	L 21	Ga.
8003	■Hingham	G 21	Mass.
205	Hingham	D 12	Mont.
150	Hingham	P 17	Wis.
1650	Hingham Center	G 21	Mass.
19	*Hinkle	J 19	Ky.
16	*Hinkle	K 16	Mo.
7	Hinkle	C 17	Ore.
200	*Hinkley	N 18	Calif.
58	*Hinnom	J 19	Va.
7336	Hinsdale	C 20	Ill.
900	Hinsdale	E 4	Mass.
359	Hinsdale	D 19	Mont.
1000	Hinsdale	Q 5	N. H.
300	Hinsdale	Q 6	N. Y.
100	*Hinson	B 4	Fla.
60	*Hinsonton	N 7	Ga.
340	Hinton	F 2	Iowa
145	*Hinton	E 17	Ky.
842	Hinton	I 8	Okla.
57	*Hinton	I 11	Va.
5815	Hinton	O 10	W. Va.
75	*Hinze	H 17	Miss.
60	*Hipass	Q 20	Calif.
100	*Hiram	F 14	Ark.
282	Hiram	F 4	Ga.
650	Hiram	O 3	Me.
45	*Hiram	O 20	Mo.
389	Hiram	E 19	Ohio
15	*Hisega	K 3	S. D.
196	*Hiseville	I 13	Ky.
9	*Hisle	M 8	S. D.
100	*Hissop	H 17	Ala.
222	Hitchcock	F 8	Okla.
246	Hitchcock	H 19	S. D.
700	Hitchcock	L 23	Tex.
303	*Hitchins	E 22	Ky.
206	Hitchita	I 20	Okla.
....	*Hitchland	A 4	Tex.
29	*Hite	H 22	Ky.
600	Hiteman	N 15	Iowa
40	*Hitt	A 13	Mo.
268	Hitterdal	H 4	Minn.
25	*Hiwannee	M 21	Miss.
25	Hiwasse	A 4	Ark.
200	*Hiwassee (Hiawassee)	O 3	Va.
24	*Hiwassee	Q 1	N. C.
50	*Hiwassee (Hiawassa)	P 4	Va.
....	Hiwasee Dam	Q 1	N. C.
10	*Hiwood	C 8	Minn.
15	Hix	M 25	Okla.
....	*Hixon, see Fountain		Ala.
500	*Hixson (Hixon)	Q 15	Tenn.
301	Hixton	F 14	Wis.
79	*Hoadly	H 17	Va.
57	Hoag	N 21	Neb.
300	Hoagland	E 21	Ind.
25	Hoagland	J 11	Neb.
15	*Hoback	F 2	Wyo.
350	*Hoban Heights (Whites Ferry)	G 20	Pa.
7166	Hobart	B 7	Ind.
40	*Hobart	M 15	La.
50	*Hobart	K 13	Mich.
638	Hobart	P 20	N. Y.
5177	Hobart	K 5	Okla.
125	Hobart	I 9	Wash.
400	Hobart Mills	F 11	Calif.
75	Hobbieville	M 10	Ind.
175	Hobbs	H 15	Ind.
60	*Hobbs	J 20	Md.
10619	Hobbs	M 25	N. M.
60	Hobbsville	C 21	N. C.
80	*Hobby	L 22	Tex.
83	*Hoberg	P 8	Mo.
629	Hobgood	E 18	N. C.
386	Hoboken	O 19	Ga.
50115	Hoboken	E 20	N. J.
239	*Hobson	H 13	Mont.
75	Hobson	P 15	Ohio
210	Hobson	M 17	Tex.
36	*Hobson	P 21	Va.
508	Hobson City	F 18	Ala.
403	Hobucken	H 22	N. C.
513	Hochatown	P 25	Okla.
273	Hochheim	M 18	Tex.
1000	Hockanum	F 14	Conn.
900	Hockerville	A 24	Okla.
354	Hockessin	A 20	Del.
....	Hocking	O 15	Iowa
100	Hocking	N 15	Ohio
230	Hockingport	N 16	Ohio
410	Hockley	K 21	Tex.
11	*Hockley	M 20	Va.
250	*Hockman (West Graham)	C 9	Va.
35	*Hode	G 23	Ky.
500	Hodgdon	F 20	Me.
60	*Hodge (Palliser)	N 18	Calif.
1445	Hodge	D 8	La.
75	*Hodge	G 9	Mo.
....	Hodge	E 18	Tex.
150	Hodgens (Hodgen)	L 24	Okla.
1348	Hodgenville	H 14	Ky.
260	Hodges	C 6	Ala.
50	Hodges	H 24	Mont.
303	Hodges	F 7	S. C.
320	Hoehne	P 17	Colo.
2	Hoffland	H 5	Neb.
47	*Hofflin (Hofflins)	K 16	Mo.
175	Hoffman	N 14	Ill.
....	Hoffman	M 5	Md.
504	Hoffman	K 6	Minn.
395	Hoffman	I 11	N. C.
432	Hoffman	H 19	Okla.
200	*Hoffmans	M 22	N. Y.
20	*Hoffmeister	K 20	N. Y.
89	*Hogan	N 18	Mo.
245	*Hogansburg	C 20	N. Y.
3886	Hogansville	H 3	Ga.
125	Hogeland	C 15	Mont.
40	*Hoges Store	N 4	Va.
75	*Hogsett	H 4	W. Va.
....	Hogstrom, see Lawson		Mich.
35	*Hogue	I 17	Ky.
67	Hoh	G 1	Wash.
50	*Hohenlinden	E 17	Miss.
137	*Hohen Solms	M 15	La.
1086	Hohenwald	O 9	Tenn.
1626	Hohokus	C 19	N. J.
3719	Hoisington	I 11	Kan.
546	Hokah	Q 24	Minn.
1298	*Hokendauqua	K 22	Pa.
63	Holabird	I 15	S. D.
1184	Holbrook	G 20	Ariz.
240	Holbrook	R 17	Idaho
25	*Holbrook	K 18	Iowa
2700	Holbrook	H 20	Mass.
441	Holbrook	N 12	Neb.
321	Holbrook	H 8	N. Y.
25	Holbrook	C 7	Ore.
140	*Holbrook	Q 2	Pa.
172	Holcomb	B 15	Ill.
215	*Holcomb	K 4	Kan.
232	Holcomb	E 12	Miss.
388	Holcomb	R 22	Mo.
304	*Holcomb	M 10	N. Y.
175	Holcomb	M 3	Wash.
75	*Holcomb	L 11	W. Va.
300	Holcombe	E 11	Wis.
70	*Holcombs Rock (Holcomb Rock)	N 8	Va.
15	*Holcut	A 22	Miss.
40	*Holdcroft	N 19	Va.
150	Holden	L 16	La.
215	Holden (East Holden)	L 15	Me.
2500	Holden	F 13	Mass.
1818	*Holden	I 8	Mo.
500	Holden	K 9	Utah
475	*Holden	G 13	Wash.
3000	Holden	N 3	W. Va.
6632	Holdenville	K 17	Okla.
179	Holder (Ladonia)	F 13	Fla.
100	Holder	G 16	Ill.
209	*Holderness	K 13	N. H.
527	Holdingford, (Holding)	L 11	Minn.
30	Holdman	B 18	Ore.
3360	Holdredge	N 14	Neb.
60	*Holeb	H 5	Me.
1050	Holgate	E 7	Ohio
45	*Holicong	N 23	Pa.
200	*Holladay	N 7	Tenn.
200	Holladay	F 12	Utah
109	*Holladay	J 15	Va.
219	Holland	G 13	Ark.
40	Holland	I 3	Colo.
110	*Holland	D 2	Ga.
380	Holland	P 8	Ind.
202	Holland	G 15	Iowa
167	*Holland	K 13	Ky.
14616	Holland	O 11	Mich.
303	Holland	P 4	Minn.
390	Holland	K 24	Mo.
90	Holland	M 22	Neb.
1150	▲Holland	F 8	N. J.
825	Holland	O 6	N. Y.
607	Holland	C 9	Ohio
50	Holland	R 4	Ore.
200	*Holland	N 24	Pa.
741	Holland	I 18	Tex.
30	Holland	A 18	Vt.
378	Holland	Q 20	Va.
219	*Hollandale	R 16	Minn.
1606	Hollandale	G 7	Miss.
290	Hollandale	I 21	Wis.
388	Holland Patent	K 18	N. Y.
280	Hollandsburg	K 5	Ohio
128	Hollenberg	C 17	Kan.
44	Hollene	H 25	N. M.
400	*Holler	D14	Minn.
1230	Holley	L 7	N. Y.
50	Holley	H 7	Ore.
80	*Holliday	K 16	Ill.
150	Holliday	G 24	Kan.
25	*Holliday	F 21	Ky.
207	Holliday	F 14	Mo.
132	Holliday	N 7	Okla.
798	Holliday	B 15	Tex.
5910	Hollidaysburg	N 10	Pa.
6173	Hollidays Cove	N 24	W. Va.
48	*Hollifield	F 1	N. C.
40	Hollinger	O 13	Neb.
56	*Hollinger	O 19	Pa.
150	Hollins	H 17	Ala.
75	Hollins	N 7	Va.
....	*Hollins College	N 7	Va.
114	*Hollis	I 9	Ark.
44	Hollis	G 12	Ill.
94	Hollis	E 16	Kan.
230	Hollis	R 13	N. H.
....	*Hollis (Hollis Depot)	R 13	N. H.
50	*Hollis	G 2	N. C.
2732	Hollis	M 1	Okla.
150	Hollis Center (Bradbury)	Q 3	Me.
3881	Hollister	J 8	Calif.
150	Hollister	D 17	Fla.
100	Hollister	Q 11	Idaho
370	Hollister	Q 10	Mo.
200	Hollister	D 16	N. C.
531	Hollister	M 15	Ohio
200	Hollister	O 6	Okla.
....	Hollister	K 7	Vt.
130	*Hollister	L 10	Wis.
250	Hollisterville	H 22	Pa.
2500	Holliston	G 16	Mass.
25	*Hollonville	G 21	Ky.
56	*Hollow	I 20	Mo.
22	Hollow	B 21	Okla.
100	*Holloway	R 19	Mich.
286	*Holloway	M 6	Minn.
733	Holloway	J 18	Ohio
422	*Hollow Rock	M 6	Tenn.
140	*Hollowville	Q 24	N. Y.
408	*Hollsopple (Benson)	N 7	Pa.
864	Holly	M 24	Colo.
2343	Holly	O 20	Mich.
100	Holly	I 11	W. Va.
150	*Holly Bluff	I 10	Miss.
60	*Hollybush	H 22	Ky.
741	Holly Grove	J 17	Ark.
50	*Holly Grove (Hudnall)	L 7	W. Va.
45	*Holly Grove	I 12	W. Va.
1665	Holly Hill	E 19	Fla.
47	*Hollyhill	K 18	Ky.
1062	Holly Hill	K 16	S. C.
....	Holly Jc.	I 11	W. Va.
26	*Hollyknowe	G 8	Miss.
500	Holly Oak (Hollyoak)	A 22	Del.
226	*Holly Pond	D 12	Ala.
450	Holly Ridge	C 13	La.
50	*Holly Ridge	F 9	Miss.
69	*Hollyridge	L 18	N. C.
150	*Holly Springs	N 11	Ark.
256	*Hollysprings	D 6	Ga.
2750	Holly Springs	A 16	Miss.
394	Holly Springs	F 13	N. C.
50	*Hollytree	A 16	Ala.
40	*Hollyville	K 22	Del.
311	Hollywood	B 17	Ala.
108	*Hollywood	M 8	Ark.
....	Hollywood	O 15, Q 3	Calif.
6239	Hollywood	N 24	Fla.
160	*Hollywood	C 11	Ga.
304	*Hollywood	C 20	Ill.
260	Hollywood	O 14	Md.
50	Hollywood	A 10	Miss.
140	*Hollywood	K 23	Mo.
33	*Hollywood	P 12	W. Va.
65	*Holman	G 7	Ala.
50	Holman	E 16	N. M.
250	Holmdel	H 19	N. J.
477	Holmen	F 16	Wis.
210	*Holmes	D 3	Calif.
46	*Holmes	F 11	Iowa
46	*Holmes	J 15	Ky.
75	*Holmes (Holmes Park)	H 6	Mo.
150	*Holmes	B 6	N. Y.
150	*Holmes	P 23	Pa.
50	*Holmes	O 19	Wyo.
....	*Holmesburg	P 24	Pa.
100	*Holmes City	K 7	Minn.
50	*Holmeson	I 81	N. J.
72	*Holmesville	O 10	Miss.
149	Holmesville	O 22	Neb.
250	Holmesville	O 18	N. Y.
375	Holmesville	H 16	Ohio
....	*Holm Lodge	C 6	Wyo.
85	Holmquist	E 21	S. D.
....	*Holmsville, see Dellwood		Wis.
1000	*Holopaw	H 19	Fla.
63	*Holstead	J 11	W. Va.
1296	Holstein	G 4	Iowa
125	Holstein	I 17	Mo.
241	Holstein	N 16	Neb.
100	*Holston	D 7	Va.
1500	Holt	G 9	Ala.
125	Holt	H 7	Calif.
....	*Holt, see Holts		Fla.
1	*Holt	F 11	Ky.
1000	Holt	P 18	Mich.
209	Holt	D 5	Minn.
320	Holt	F 6	Mo.
40	*Holt	I 9	Wyo.
....	Holt Jc.	G 9	Ala.
59	*Holtland (Holts Corner)	O 11	Tenn.
400	Holton	M 19	Ind.
2885	Holton	E 21	Kan.
350	Holton	N 11	Mich.
303	Holts	M 5	Fla.
59	*Holts Corner (Holtland)	O 11	Tenn.
32	*Holts Summit (Hibernia)	I 14	Mo.
260	*Holtsville	G 9	N. Y.
1772	Holtville	Q 23	Calif.
600	Holtwood	Q 19	Pa.
21	Holum	E 11	La.
1150	Holyoke	C 23	Colo.
53750	Holyoke	G 7	Mass.
40	*Holyoke	I 18	Minn.
559	Holyrood	I 12	Kan.
100	Homan	O 6	Ark.
14	Home	C 12	Colo.
175	Home	D 19	Kan.
25	Home	H 23	Ore.
130	*Home	L 7	Pa.
....	*Home Creek	A 7	Va.
857	Homedale	N 3	Idaho
300	Homeland	I 16	Fla.
213	*Homeland	P 20	Ga.
50	Home Place	I 15	Ind.
182	*Homeplace	O 21	La.
283	Homer	D 12	Ga.
983	Homer	I 20	Ill.
121	Homer	K 18	Ind.
34	*Homer	J 10	Ky.
3497	Homer	B 7	La.
1145	Homer	Q 15	Mich.
125	*Homer	Q 23	Minn.
477	Homer	G 22	Neb.
2928	Homer	O 14	N. Y.
15	Homer	N 18	N. D.
110	*Homer (Homerville)	E 16	Ohio
300	Homer	J 13	Ohio
	*Homer, see Hennepin		Okla.
2078	Homer City	M 7	Pa.
1522	Homerville	O 16	Ga.
16	Homestake	L 7	Mont.
3154	Homestead	O 22	Fla.
285	Homestead	K 19	Iowa
267	Homestead	D 24	Mont.
287	Homestead	E 8	Okla.
150	Homestead	E 24	Ore.
19041	Homestead	M 3	Pa.
....	*Homestead	I 18	R. I.
....	*Homestead Park	M 4	Pa.
8	*Homevalley	Q 10	Wash.
18	*Homeville	P 17	Va.
7397	*Homewood	F 12	Ala.
20	*Homewood	G 11	Calif.
4078	Homewood	D 22	Ill.
80	*Homewood	I 23	Kan.
250	*Homewood	K 15	Miss.
357	*Homewood Jc (Racine)	K 2	Pa.
403	Homeworth	G 19	Ohio
3267	Hominy	D 17	Okla.
30	*Hominy Falls	M 10	W. Va.
350	Homosassa	G 12	Fla.
150	*Hon	H 5	Ark.
55	*Honaker	H 22	Ky.
851	Honaker	C 8	Va.
150	Honcut	F 7	Calif.
5	Hondale	O 5	N. M.
200	Hondo	L 16	N. M.
2500	Hondo	M 15	Tex.
2765	Honea Path	E 6	S. C.
275	*Honeoye	M 9	N. Y.
1274	Honeoye Falls	M 9	N. Y.
5687	Honesdale	F 23	Pa.
42	*Honeybee	K 18	Ky.
43	*Honey Bend	K 13	Ill.
766	Honey Brook	O 20	Pa.
150	*Honeycamp	C 6	Va.
145	*Honey Creek	I 19	Ind.
100	*Honey Creek	L 3	Iowa
200	Honey Creek	N 21	Wis.
175	*Honeycutt	M 9	N. C.
68	Honeyford	H 22	N. D.
279	Honey Grove	M 14	Pa.
2456	Honey Grove	C 21	Tex.
78	*Honeyhill	L 20	S. C.
63	*Honey Island	J 24	Tex.
596	Honeyville	C 10	Utah
6	Hong	F 15	N. D.
136	*Honga	N 17	Md.
284	Honor	J 11	Mich.
85	*Honoraville	L 15	Ala.
100	*Hood	H 8	Calif.
....	*Hood	B 4	Md.
12	*Hood	I 13	Va.
3280	Hood River	C 11	Ore.
500	Hoodsport	I 5	Wash.
33	*Hooes	I 18	Va.
52	*Hookdale	M 14	Ill.
37	*Hooker	J 20	Ky.
120	*Hooker	L 14	Mo.
1146	Hooker	Q 5	Okla.
43	Hooker	N 23	S. D.
37	*Hookersville	K 10	W. Va.
319	Hookerton	H 17	N. C.
160	Hooks	C 24	Tex.
1000	Hooksett	O 14	N. H.
....	*Hooks Mills	E 21	W. Va.
239	*Hookstown	L 2	Pa.
20	*Hoopa	C 2	Calif.
170	Hooper	N 12	Colo.
40	Hooper	P 13	Mich.
802	Hooper	I 22	Neb.
2500	*Hooper (Endwell)	Q 15	N. Y.
1100	Hooper	D 10	Utah
75	Hooper	L 21	Wash.
275	Hoopersville	O 17	Md.
5381	Hoopeston	G 22	Ill.
346	Hoople	E 21	N. D.
200	Hooppole	D 11	Ill.
42	*Hoopup	P 21	Colo.
150	Hoosac Tunnel	B 5	Mass.
29	*Hooser	O 19	Kan.
400	Hooscik	M 25	N. Y.
4279	Hoosick Falls	M 25	N. Y.
5	Hoosick Jc.	M 25	N. Y.
....	Hoosier	N 12	Ind.
500	*Hooven	N 5	Ohio
10	Hoover	N 13	Okla.
6	Hoover	F 4	S. D.
50	*Hoover	C 5	Tex.
218	Hoover Hill	F 9	N. C.
65	Hoovers	E 14	Ind.
1364	Hooversville	O 8	Pa.
660	*Hopatcong	D 14	N. J.
....	Hopatcong Jc.	D 14	N. J.
375	Hop Bottom (Foster)	E 21	Pa.
7475	Hope	O 7	Ark.
116	Hope	B 6	Idaho
1046	Hope	L 16	Ind.
500	Hope	H 17	Kan.
45	*Hope	F 19	Ky.
	*Hope, see Fryeburg		La.
200	Hope	N 12	Me.
48	*Hope	M 18	Mich.
125	*Hope	Q 17	Minn.
44	*Hope	J 15	Mo.
200	Hope	D 10	N. J.
289	Hope	M 19	N. M.
474	Hope	K 21	N. D.
....	Hope	J 23	Ore.
500	Hope	G 11	R. I.
545	Hopedale	G 13	Ill.
3113	■Hopedale	H 15	Mass.
901	Hopedale	I 19	Ohio
50	*Hope Hull (McGehees)	K 15	Ala.
386	*Hopeland	N 19	Pa.
900	Hope Mills	I 13	N. C.
475	*Hopemont	D 16	W. Va.
50	Hopeton	C 7	Okla.
231	*Hopeton	L 24	Va.
725	Hope Valley	K 6	R. I.
114	*Hope Villa (Bullion)	L 15	La.
104	Hopewell	F 21	Ala.
125	*Hopewell	B 13	Ark.
40	*Hopewell	L 11	Kan.
35	*Hopewell	D 22	Ky.
250	*Hopewell	L 11	Miss.
1678	Hopewell	H 12	N. J.
250	Hopewell (Mount Sterling)	K 15	Ohio
50	Hopewell	E 6	Ore.
405	Hopewell	O 10	Pa.
8679	Hopewell	N 17	Va.
230	Hopewell Jc.	D 6	N. Y.
150	Hopkins	H 21	Fla.
45	Hopkins	O 17	Ga.
455	Hopkins	P 13	Mich.
4100	Hopkins	N 15, N 22	Minn.
834	Hopkins	A 5	Mo.
925	*Hopkins	H 14	S. C.
101	*Hopkins	L 24	Va.
....	Hopkins, Jc.	N 15	Minn.
59	*Hopkins Park	E 21	Ill.
11724	Hopkinsville	J 9	Ky.
841	Hopkinton	H 21	Iowa
2000	Hopkinton	G 16	Mass.
500	*Hopkinton	O 12	N. H.
1300	*Hopkinton	F 17	N. Y.
150	Hopkinton	L 5	R. I.
860	Hopland	G 3	Calif.
40	*Hopmere	F 8	Ore.
37	*Hopper	K 7	Ark.
290	*Hopper	E 19	Minn.
35	*Hopson (White Rock)	M 24	Tenn.
1500	Hopwood	Q 4	Pa.
10835	Hoquiam	K 2	Wash.
234	Horace	I 2	Kan.
60	Horace	J 16	Neb.
250	Horace	N 24	N. D.
1028	Horatio	M 4	Ark.
85	Horatio	J 7	Pa.
33	*Horatio	H 16	S. C.
160	Hordville	K 18	Neb.
400	Horicon (Brant Lake)	I 23	N. Y.
2253	Horicon	M 18	Wis.
125	Horine	K 20	Mo.
382	Hornbeak	L 3	Tenn.
481	Hornbeck	H 6	La.
300	Hornbrook	B 5	Calif.
....	Hornby	G 21	Minn.
15649	Hornell	P 9	N. Y.
120	*Horner	H 12	W. Va.
46	*Horners	J 29	Va.
964	Hornersville	K 23	Mo.
31	Horn Hill	G 20	Tex.
291	Hornick	H 2	Iowa
500	*Horning	M 3	Pa.
159	*Hornitos	I 11	Calif.
219	Horn Lake	A 12	Miss.
40	*Hornsby	L 11	Ill.
207	Hornsby	Q 5	Tenn.
250	Hornsbyville (Tampico)	O 20	Va.
150	Horntown	K 25	Va.
....	Hornville	O 22	Colo.
75	Horse Branch	H 11	Ky.
1278	Horse Cave	I 13	Ky.
14	Horse Creek	P 21	Wyo.
....	Horse Creek, Jc.	I 20	Ky.
40	*Horse Haven	G 12	Ore.
28	*Horse Head	K 21	Va.
2570	Horseheads	Q 12	N. Y.
127	*Horse Lick	I 18	Ky.
150	*Horsepen	B 10	Va.
18	*Horseshoe	F 17	N. Y.
30	*Horse Shoe	P 8	N. C.
200	Horse Shoe Bend	M 5	Idaho
60	*Horse Shoe Bottom	J 16	Ky.
75	*Horseshoe Run	D 16	W. Va.
310	▲*Horse Springs	J 3	N. M.
26	*Horsey	K 24	Va.
800	*Horsham	N 22	Pa.
325	Hortense	N 20	Ga.
50	Hortense	I 23	Tex.
140	*Horton	D 16	Ala.
134	Horton (Hortonville)	H 13	Ind.
2872	Horton	D 22	Kan.
150	*Horton	H 11	Ky.
188	Horton	Q 16	Mich.
98	*Horton	L 6	Mo.
91	*Horton	R 19, A 3	N. Y.
80	Horton	I 5	Ore.
....	Horton	Q 11	Ore.
528	Horton	H 16	W. Va.
52	Horton	E 23	Wyo.
150	*Hortons Summit (Sunbright)	E 5	Va.
225	*Hortonville	C 2	N. Y.
968	Hortonville	M 14	Wis.
364	Hoschton	E 11	Ga.
50	*Hosensack	M 22	Pa.
500	Hosford	B 3	Fla.
212	Hoskins	H 20	Neb.
119	Hoskins	G 5	Ore.
....	Hoskins	M 23	Tex.
38	*Hoskinston	J 21	Ky.
579	Hosmer	D 15	S. D.
592	Hospers	D 3	Iowa
500	Hosston	A 4	La.
131	*Host	M 20	Pa.
65	*Hosterman	K 15	W. Va.
725	Hostetter	N 6	Pa.
653	Hotchkiss	J 6	Colo.
30	*Hotchkiss	K 8	Va.
50	*Hotchkiss	P 7	W. Va.
365	Hotchkissville	H 7	Conn.
....	*Hotel Greenbrier (White Sulphur Spgs.)	N 12	W. Va.
12	Hotevilla	E 18	Ariz.
250	Hot Lake	E 21	Ore.
50	Hot Springs (Castle Hot Springs)	J 11	Ariz.
21370	Hot Springs	K 9	Ark.
354	*Hot Springs (California Hot Springs)	K 14	Calif.
663	Hot Springs	F 3	Mont.
1	Hot Springs	K 8	Mont.
....	*Hot Springs, see Montezuma College		N. M.
2940	Hot Springs	L 7	N. M.
773	Hot Springs	M 7	N. C.
4083	Hot Springs	M 3	S. D.
6	*Hot Springs	L 7	Tex.
....	Hot Springs	M 6	Utah
1000	Hot Springs	K 7	Va.
100	Hot Springs Jc. (Morristown)	J 10	Ariz.
....	Hot Springs Jc.	J 12	Ark.
235	Hot Sulphur Springs (Sulphur Springs)	E 11	Colo.
10	*Hottelville	G 7	Pa.
60	Houck (Allantown)	F 24	Ariz.
37	*Houckville	F 23	Ky.
40	Hough	Q 5	Okla.
60	*Houghton	P 20	Iowa
3693	Houghton	C 3	Mich.
300	*Houghton	O 7	N. Y.
200	Houghton	C 19	S. D.
260	Houghton	H 9	Wash.
150	*Houghton Lake	K 17	Mich.
675	Houlka	D 18	Miss.
132	*Hoult	D 13	W. Va.
6000	Houlton	F 19	Me.
1000	Houlton	B 7	Ore.
228	Houlton	A 11	Wis.
89	Houltonville	L 18	La.
9052	Houma	P 16	La.
2000	Housatonic	G 2	Mass.
115	House	H 22	N. M.
95	*House Springs	J 19	Mo.
39	*Houton	D 10	Ala.
345	Houston	H 11	Ark.
296	Houston (Houston Station)	I 22	Del.
80	*Houston	C 11	Fla.
140	*Houston	O 12	Ill.
31	*Houston	H 21	Ky.
977	Houston	Q 23	Minn.
1729	Houston	E 18	Miss.
820	Houston	O 14	Mo.
10	Houston	L 19	Neb.
150	Houston	J 7	Ohio
1610	Houston	N 2	Pa.
42	*Houston	P 7	Tenn.
384514	Houston	K 22	Tex.
....	Houston Heights	K 22	Tex.
326	Houstonia	H 10	Mo.
40	*Houstonville	E 5	N. C.
1430	Houtzdale	K 10	Pa.
369	Hoven	E 14	S. D.
90	Hover	O 18	Wash.
20	Hoving	P 22	N. D.
225	Hovland	B 23	Minn.
200	Howard	K 12	Colo.
200	*Howard	J 8	Ga.
1170	Howard	N 19	Kan.
....	Howard	E 20	N. C.
400	*Howard	P 9	N. Y.
250	Howard	I 14	Ohio
100	Howard	E 9	Pa.
726	Howard	J 13	Pa.
5000	Howard	F 14	R. I.
1193	Howard	K 22	S. D.
27	*Howard	C 11	W. Va.
839	Howard City	N 14	Mich.
....	Howard City, see Boelus		Neb.
847	Howard Lake	N 13	Minn.
600	Howards Grove	P 17	Wis.
69	*Howards Ridge	Q 13	Mo.
64	*Howardstown	H 15	Ky.
80	Howardsville	L 12	Va.
10	Howbert	J 13	Colo.
150	Howe	N 17	Idaho
810	Howe	A 19	Ind.
178	Howe	N 24	Neb.
640	Howe	L 25	Okla.
546	Howe	C 19	Tex.
21	*Howel	J 9	Ky.
169	*Howell	H 17	Ark.
174	*Howell	P 15	Ga.
3748	Howell	O 19	Mich.
861	Howells	I 21	Neb.
195	*Howell	P 11	Tenn.
70	Howell	B 9	Utah
....	Howells	F 7	Ga.
260	Howells	D 3	N. Y.
60	*Howertons	L 19	Va.
3	*Howes	H 5	S. D.
200	*Howes Cave	N 21	N. Y.
50	*Howes Mill	M 17	Mo.
225	Howesville	D 15	W. Va.
203	*Howey in the Hills	G 16	Fla.
15	Howison	Q 18	Miss.
36	*Howison	J 15	Va.
1000	Howland	J 15	Me.
145	Howland	C 21	Tex.
20	Hoxbar	P 14	Okla.
85	*Hoxeyville	K 13	Mich.
1448	Hoxie	C 18	Ark.
957	Hoxie	F 6	Kan
135	*Hoxsie	H 9	R. I.
....	Hoy	J 8	La.
35	*Hoy	E 21	W. Va.
41	*Hoyes	M 2	Md.
401	Hoyleton	N 14	Ill.
53	Hoyt	E 18	Colo.
238	Hoyt	F 21	Kan.
....	Hoyt	M 19	Mich.

Pop. Place Index State
320 Hoyt, J 21....Okla.
36 Hoyt, E 22....Tex.
300 Hoytsville, E 14....Utah
361 Hoytville, E 9....Ohio
572 Hoytville, G 15....Pa.
35*Hub, O 14....Miss.
110*Hubball, L 3....W. Va.
779 Hubbard, H 13....Iowa
108*Hubbard, H 10....Minn.
188 Hubbard, F 22....Neb.
.... Hubbard, B 21....Nev.
4189 Hubbard, E 21....Ohio
387 Hubbard, E 7....Ore.
1871 Hubbard, G 19....Tex.
75 Hubbard Lake, I 20..Mich.
80*Hubbard Springs, E 3...Va.
450 Hubbardston, D 12...Mass.
391 Hubbardston, N 14...Mich.
100 Hubbardstown, L 1.W. Va.
250 Hubbardsville, N 17..N. Y.
250 Hubbardton, K 6....Vt.
....*Hubbard Woods, B 21...Ill.
1100 Hubbell, C 3....Mich.
250 Hubbell, O 20....Neb.
58*Hubbleton, M 19....Wis.
75*Huber, J 12....Ga.
22*Huber, C 6....Ore.
....*Hubert, see Lake Hubert Minn.
70*Hubert, K 19....N. C.
100*Hubertus (St. Huberts), O 19....Wis.
100*Hublersburg, J 13....Pa.
50 Huching (Hutchings), F 14 Ga.
125 Huckabay, F 16....Tex.
93 Huddleston, O 9....Va.
22*Hudgins, I 14....Ky.
12 Hudgins, M 21....Va.
50*Hudnall (Holly Grove), L 7....W. Va.
295 Hudson, E 16....Colo.
160 Hudson, H 12....Fla.
324 Hudson, G 15....Ill.
437 Hudson, B 21....Ind.
492 Hudson, G 17....Iowa
221 Hudson, K 12....Kan.
36*Hudson, H 12....Ky.
.... Hudson, K 14....Me.
8042■Hudson, F 16....Mass.
2426 Hudson, R 17....Mich.
1 Hudson, I 4....Nev.
2000 Hudson, R 15....N. H.
50 Hudson, G 23....N. M.
11517 Hudson, P 24....N. Y.
748 Hudson, E 3....N. C.
1417 Hudson, E 18....Ohio
.... Hudson, H 21 (Pop. 2050 incl. in Plains)....Pa.
478 Hudson, N 25....S. D.
2987 Hudson, A 12....Wis.
330 Hudson, J 9....Wyo.
6654 Hudson Falls, K 24...N. Y.
2500 Hudson Heights, E 21.N. J.
837 Hudsonville, O 12....Mich.
40*Hudsonville, A 16....Miss.
.... Hueneme, see Port Hueneme....Calif.
163*Huey, M 14....Ill.
150*Huey, I 5....Pa.
650*Hueysville (Bosco), H 23 Ky.
175*Huff, E 15....Ark.
30*Huff, H 12....Ky.
39 Huff, O 12....N. D.
175*Huff, L 6....Pa.
400 Huffman, F 12....Ala.
175*Huffman, C 23....Ark.
10*Huffman, K 22....Tex.
24 Huffton, D 19....S. D.
50 Huffville, O 5....Va.
158*Hufsmith, J 22....Tex.
25*Huger, L 19....S. C.
19*Huggins, O 13....Mo.
15*Hughart, M 12....W. Va.
815 Hughes, I 20....Ark.
20 Hughes, F 22....Colo.
50*Hughes, D 2....N. C.
55 Hughes, L 23....Okla.
918 Hughesdale, E 12....R. I.
767 Hughes Springs, D 24..Tex.
2340*Hughestown, I 20....Pa.
219*Hugheston, L 6....W. Va.
500 Hughesville, M 13....Md.
162 Hughesville, H 10....Mo.
66*Hughesville, G 12....Mont.
20 Hughesville, F 8....N. J.
1947 Hughesville, I 17....Pa.
46*Hughett, L 17....Tenn.
500 Hughson, I 9....Calif.
250*Hughsonville, D 6....N. Y.
40*Hugo, K 8....Ala.
852 Hugo, I 19....Colo.
.... Hugo, D 20....Ind.
348 Hugo, L 25....Minn.
20*Hugo, L 12....Mo.
5909 Hugo, Q 21....Okla.
150 Hugo, P 5....Ore.
1349 Hugoton, O 3....Kan.
500*Huguenot, E 3....N. Y.
40 Hulah, A 18....Okla.
325 Hulbert, H 21....Ark.
300*Hulbert, F 16....Mich.
300 Hulbert, F 22....Okla.
420*Hulberton, L 7....N. Y.
100*Hulen (Felder), K 20...Ky.
12 Hulen, N 9....Okla.
150 Hulett, B 22....Wyo.
160 Hulette, F 23....Ky.
42*Huletts Landing, K 24 N. Y.
360 Hull, H 8....Ala.
200 Hull, K 15....Fla.
133*Hull, E 13....Ga.
572 Hull (Hulls), J 5....Ill.
1072 Hull, C 2....Iowa
1500 Hull, F 20....Mass.
34 Hull, Q 14....N. D.
385 Hull (Conrad), G 12...Pa.
900 Hull, K 24....Tex.
265*Hull (Litwar), Q 5..W. Va.
.... Hulldale, H 12....Tex.
.... Hull Jc., G 17....Minn.
175 Hulls Cove, M 17....Me.
150 Hullt, F 8....Ore.
694*Hulmeville, N 23....Pa.
786 Humansville, M 9....Mo.
35*Humarock, H 22....Mass.
319 Humbert, Q 6....Pa.
315 Humbird, G 13....Wis.
1371 Humble, K 23....Tex.
175 Humboldt, H 12....Ariz.
334 Humboldt, J 19....Ill.
2819 Humboldt, F 10....Iowa
2290 Humboldt, L 23....Kan.
100 Humboldt, E 5....Mich.
139*Humboldt, B 1....Minn.
1386 Humboldt, O 24....Neb.
417 Humboldt, L 23....S. D.
5160 Humboldt, N 4....Tenn.
25*Hume, K 10....Calif.
489 Hume, I 21....Ill.
487 Hume, K 6....Mo.
300 Hume, O 7....N. Y.
75*Hume, G 7....Ohio
300*Hume, G 14....Va.
903 Humeston, O 12....Iowa
40*Hummel (Langford), I 18 Ky.

Pop. Place Index State
3264 Hummelstown, N 17....Pa.
800*Hummels Wharf, L 15..Pa.
250*Humnoke, K 15....Ark.
595 Humphrey, K 15....Ark.
53*Humphrey, L 19....Idaho
803 Humphrey (Tovey), K 13 Ill.
20*Humphrey, I 16....Ky.
841 Humphrey, I 19....Neb.
45*Humphrey, P 6....N. Y.
450 Humphrey, N 5....Pa.
112*Humphrey Center, P 6 N. Y.
150*Humphreys, P 15....La.
247 Humphreys, C 10....Mo.
110 Humphreys, N 5....Okla.
100 Humptulips, I 2....Wash.
75 Humrick, I 22....Ill.
706 Hundred, C 12....W. Va.
70*Hungerford (Turnpike), P 17....Pa.
128*Hungerford, L 21....Tex.
348*Hunkers, N 5....Pa.
525*Hunlock Creek, I 20....Pa.
166 Hunnewell, O 16....Kan.
12*Hunnewell, E 22....Ky.
312 Hunnewell, E 15....Mo.
.... Hunt, H 23....Ariz.
130*Hunt (Hunt City), L 20.Ill.
85*Hunt, O 8....N. Y.
116*Hunt, J 14....Tex.
38*Huntdale, M 9....N. C.
293 Hunter, H 17....Ark.
199 Hunter, F 13....Kan.
35*Hunter, H 22....Ky.
.... Hunter, F 4....La.
208 Hunter, P 18....Mo.
626 Hunter, Q 22....N. Y.
414 Hunter, L 23....N. D.
291 Hunter, C 11....Okla.
178 Hunter, K 17....Tex.
....*Hunter Lake, C 2, R 20....N. Y.
40*Hunters, I 22....Ga.
200 Hunters, F 20....Wash.
29 Hunters Hotsprings, L 12 Mont.
100*Huntersville, K 16....Ky.
763 Huntersville, G 6....N. C.
100 Huntersville, L 14...W. Va.
400 Huntertown, C 20....Ind.
10 Huntimer (Charles City), K 23....S. D.
50 Hunting, L 13....Wis.
3816 Huntingburg, P 10....Ind.
7170 Huntingdon, M 12....Pa.
1432 Huntingdon, N 6....Tenn.
500 Huntingdon Valley, O 24 Pa.
100 Hunting Ground, I 17 W. Va.
813 Huntington, H 4....Ark.
75 Huntington, M 8....Conn.
200*Huntington, E 17....Fla.
13903 Huntington, E 17....Ind.
35*Huntington, B 8....Iowa
1000 Huntington, G 5....Mass.
35*Huntington, E 15....Mo.
.... Huntington, see Giltner Neb.
11250 Huntington P. O., G 7 N. Y.
190 Huntington, F 15....Ohio
741 Huntington, H 23....Ore.
969 Huntington, H 24....Tex.
997 Huntington, J 16....Utah
221 Huntington, F 8....Vt.
78836 Huntington, K 2...W. Va.
408*Huntington Bay, G 8.N. Y.
3738 Huntington Beach, P 16 Calif.
310 Huntington Center, F 8.Vt.
45*Huntington Lake, J 10.Calif.
169*Huntington Mills, H 19.Pa.
28648 Huntington Park, O 15, Q 5....Calif.
5000 Huntington (Huntington Station), G 8....N. Y.
50*Huntingtown, L 14....Md.
303 Huntland, Q 12....Tenn.
674 Huntley, B 18....Ill.
100*Huntley, Q 13....Minn.
150 Huntley, L 16....Mont.
148 Huntley, O 14....Neb.
75*Huntley, N 24....Wyo.
3*Huntly, G 14....Va.
.... Huntoon, A 5....Tex.
120 Huntsburg, D 19....Ohio
75*Huntsdale, H 13....Mo.
160 Huntsdale, O 15....Pa.
14 Huntsman, K 4....Neb.
86*Hunts Spur (Huntspur), D 15....Mich.
13050 Huntsville, B 14....Ala.
602 Huntsville, C 7....Ark.
87 Huntsville, H 6....Ill.
127*Huntsville, I 11....Ky.
1739 Huntsville, F 12....Mo.
50 Huntsville, C 12....N. J.
353 Huntsville, I 9....Ohio
400 Huntsville, L 17....Tenn.
5108 Huntsville, I 22....Tex.
496 Huntsville, D 12....Utah
150 Huntsville, N 22....Wash.
29*Hur, H 8....W. Va.
14 Hurd, E 10....N. D.
311 Hurdland, C 13....Mo.
75*Hurdle Mills, D 12...N. C.
258 Hurdsfield, K 14....N. D.
221*Hurley, Q 22....Miss.
235 Hurley, P 9....Mo.
2000 Hurley, M 4....N. M.
400*Hurley, B 5, R 21....N. Y.
586 Hurley, N 23....S. D.
500*Hurley, A 7....Va.
3375 Hurley, I 5....Wis.
800 Hurleyville (Luzon), C 2 N. Y.
800 Hurlock, L 19....Md.
12*Hurlwood, C 10....Tex.
30*Huron, K 10....Calif.
245*Huron, N 11....Ind.
163*Huron, D 23....Kan.
1827 Huron, D 13....Ohio
.... Huron, Q 3....Pa.
10843 Huron, I 19....S. D.
41*Huron, O 6....Tenn.
119*Hurricane, P 6....Ala.
8*Hurricane, N 21....Mo.
1524 Hurricane, Q 4....Utah
1103 Hurricane, K 4....W. Va.
117*Hurricane Mills, N 8.Tenn.
100 Hurry, O 13....Md.
400 Hursley (Stockton), Q 23 Md.
200*Hurst, B 8....Ga.
1012 Hurst, P 15....Ill.
60*Hurst, G 10....W. Va.
89*Hurstville, I 23....Iowa
150*Hurt, O 9....Va.
894 Hurtsboro, K 21....Ala.
100 Husband, P 7....Pa.
250*Hushpuckena, D 8....Miss.
66*Husk, C 3....N. C.
30 Huson, H 4....Mont.
250 Husser, K 18....La.
564 Hustisford, N 19....Wis.
.... Hustle, G 21....Ill.
125*Hustle, K 18....Va.

Pop. Place Index State
167*Hustler, H 16....Wis.
51*Huston, N 4....Idaho
127 Hustontown, P 11....Pa.
443 Hustonville, H 16....Ky.
200 Husum, P 11....Wash.
50 Hutchings (Huching), F 14....Ga.
60 Hutchins, F 9....Pa.
400 Hutchins, E 19....Tex.
30013 Hutchinson, K 14....Kan.
3887 Hutchinson, N 11....Minn.
.... Hutchinson, D 13...W. Va.
.... Hutchinson Jc., N 15.Minn.
714 Hutsonville, L 21....Ill.
1386 Huttig, R 13....Ark.
597 Hutto, J 18....Tex.
250*Hutton, I 7....La.
156 Hutton, N 1....Md.
308 Huttonsville, I 14...W. Va.
100*Hutton Valley, P 15....Mo.
392 Huxley, J 12....Iowa
52 Huyett, C 5....Md.
20*Huzzah, L 17....Mo.
39*Hyacinth, K 20....Va.
60 Hyak, I 11....Wash.
31 Hyampom, E 4....Calif.
1800 Hyannis, N 13....Mass.
449 Hyannis, H 7....Neb.
300*Hyannis Port, N 13..Mass.
.... Hyannis Wharf, O 13.Mass.
200 Hyatt, J 24....Tex.
103 Hyattstown, F 9....Md.
6575 Hyattsville, I 12....Md.
120 Hyattville, D 13....Wyo.
16*Hyde, E 22....Colo.
150*Hyde (Hydes), D 15...Md.
268 Hyde, J 10....Pa.
500 Hyden, I 20....Ky.
517*Hyde Park, Q 2....Calif.
2000 Hyde Park, G 19....Mass.
1200*Hyde Park, C 6....N. Y.
50 Hyde Park, N 18....N. Y.
717 Hyde Park, L 5....Pa.
696 Hyde Park, B 12....Utah
330 Hyde Park, D 12....Vt.
200*Hydesville (Newell), D 2 Calif.
446 Hydetown, F 5....Pa.
800*Hyde Villa, M20....Pa.
500 Hydeville, L 6....Vt.
9*Hydrate (Volcano), F 9 Colo.
5 Hydro, B 14....Mont.
759 Hydro, I 7....Okla.
260*Hye, K 16....Tex.
10 Hyer, G 13....N. M.
250 Hygiene, D 14....Colo.
25*Hylas, L 16....Va.
75*Hylton, H 24....Ky.
212 Hylton, F 13....Tex.
31*Hyman, F 11....Tex.
75*Hyman, G 20....S. C.
450*Hymel (St. Amelia), M 16 La.
64*Hymer, J 18....Kan.
1298 Hymera, L 7....Ind.
29*Hymon (Hyman), K 6..Ky.
1325 Hyndman, Q 9....Pa.
134*Hyndsville, N 21....N. Y.
300 Hyner, H 13....Pa.
5000*Hynes, Q 4....Calif.
75 Hyper-Humus (Warbasse)....N. J.
1874 Hyrum, B 11....Utah
392 Hysham, K 19....Mont.

I

986 Iaeger, Q 5....W. Va.
115*Iago, L 21....Tex.
250 Iantha, N 6....Mo.
150*Iatan, F 4....Mo.
213 Ibapah, H 1....Utah
486 Iberia, K 12....Mo.
211 Iberia, H 12....Ohio
30 Iberia, and Vermillion Jc., N 12....La.
53*Iberis, L 21....Va.
16*Iberville, L 15....La.
.... Ibex, H 11....Colo.
20*Ibex, F 21....Ky.
150*Ibex, E 14....Tex.
275*Icard, F 4....N. C.
527 Icemorlee, I 6....N. C.
238 Ickesburg, M 14....Pa.
48*Iconium, K 9....Mo.
12*Ida (Idella), G 16....Ala.
5*Ida, K 16....Ky.
750 Ida, A 4....La.
600 Ida, R 20....Mich.
.... Ida, see Battiest....Okla.
3689 Idabel, Q 24....Okla.
2238 Ida Grove, G 5....Iowa
60*Idaho, O 11....Ohio
273 Idaho City, N 7....Idaho
15024 Idaho Falls, O 20...Idaho
48 Idahome, Q 15....Idaho
2112 Idaho Springs, F 13..Colo.
198 Idalia, F 23....Colo.
75*Idalia, P 21....Mo.
503 Idalou, C 10....Tex.
188 Idamar, K 7....Pa.
215 Idamay, H 19....Ky.
600*Idamay (Ida May), D 13 W. Va.
170 Idana, F 16....Kan.
60 Idanha, G 9....Ore.
500 Idaville, E 11....Ind.
165*Idaville, O 15....Pa.
.... Ideal, O 15....Colo.
238 Ideal, K 8....Ga.
104*Ideal, M 14....S. D.
22*Ideal, K 17....Va.
12*Idella (Ida), G 16....Ala.
150 Idetown, H 20....Pa.
50*Idlewild, D 3....N. C.
150*Idlewild, M 5....Tenn.
650*Idlewood, L 3....Pa.
50*Idleyld Park, M 6....Ore.
....*Idol, see Thorn Hill..Tenn.
45*Idria, K 8....Calif.
376*Idyllwild, P 19....Calif.
135 Ignacio, H 4....Calif.
555 Ignacio, Q 6....Colo.
40*Igo, D 6....Calif.
12*Igo, I 17....Va.
174 Ihlen, Q 3....Minn.
72*Ijamsville, E 9....Md.
224 Ila, E 13....Ga.
20*Ilasco, E 16....Mo.
92*Ilchester, F 13....Md.
28 Ilers, E 11....Ohio
20 Iles, J 12....Ill.
31*Ilfeld, F 15....N. M.
.... Ilford, L 18....Tenn.
22 Iliad, F 13....Mont.
322 Iliff, B 21....Colo.
8927 Ilion, M 19....N. Y.
25 Illahe, O 3....Ore.
16 Illco, I 16....Wyo.
75*Illinois Bend, C 18....Tex.
.... Illinois Central Jc., G 15.Ill.
.... Illinois Jc., F 5....Ill.
714 Illiopolis, I 14....Ill.
1224 Illmo, O 23....Mo.
100*Ilsley, I 8....Ky.
656 Ilwaco, N 2....Wash.
60 Ima, H 21....N. M.

Pop. Place Index State
90 Image, Q 7....Wash.
182 Imbler, D 21....Ore.
564 Imboden, B 17....Ark.
84 Imboden, D 4....Va.
200 Imlay, D 9....Nev.
23 Imlay, L 6....S. D.
1446 Imlay City, N 22....Mich.
125*Imlaystown, I 18....N. J.
30*Imlaystown (Nelsonville), J 15....N. J.
113*Imler, N 9....Pa.
190*Immaculata, O 22....Pa.
800 Immokalee, M 18....Fla.
45 Imnaha, C 24....Ore.
19*Imo (Atlas), D 11....Ark.
.... Imo, D 10....Okla.
280 Imogene, O 5....Iowa
12 Imogene, R 12....Minn.
25 Imogene, F 5....S. D.
25 Impach, E 20....Wash.
1493 Imperial, Q 22....Calif.
1195 Imperial, N 7....Neb.
2000 Imperial, M 2....Pa.
75*Imperial, H 8....Tex.
90*Imperial, H 13....W. Va.
113*Imperial Beach, Q 18.Calif.
35*Impo (Dunn), N 14....Mo.
501 Ina, O 16....Ill.
105*Inadale, E 11....Tex.
200 Inavale, O 16....Neb.
150 Inchelium, E 21....Wash.
.... Incline, B 15....Ala.
84*Incline, J 21....Ky.
600 Independence, J 16...Calif.
80*Independence, K 14...Colo.
178 Independence, G 8....Ind.
4342 Independence, G 19....Iowa
11565 Independence, N 21..Kan.
253 Independence, C 17....Ky.
1498 Independence, K 17....La.
159*Independence, B 13...Miss.
16066 Independence, G 6....Mo.
15 Independence, P 20...N. D.
1815 Independence, D 17...Ohio
11 Independence, G 5....Okla.
1372 Independence, F 6....Ore.
200*Independence, N 1....Pa.
319 Independence, J 20....Tex.
429 Independence, E 11, R 2.Va.
.... Independence, L 5...Wash.
325 Independence, E 15.W. Va.
1036 Independence, D 14....Wis.
67*Index, F 21....Ky.
37*Index, J 18....Va.
217 Index, G 10....Wash.
5*Index, H 9....W. Va.
337 Indiahoma, M 7....Okla.
200 Indian, C 9....Va.
10050 Indiana, L 7....Pa.
.... Indiana Harbor, B 7...Ind.
386972 Indianapolis, J 15....Ind.
50 Indianapolis, H 6....Okla.
150*Indian Bayou, M 10....La.
40*Indiancreek, J 19....Ky.
35 Indian Creek, P 5....Pa.
113*Indian Creek, G 15....Tex.
45*Indian Fields, F 19....Ky.
154*Indian Gap, G 17....Tex.
1104 Indian Head, M 9....Md.
400*Indian Head, Q 4....Pa.
40*Indianhill, P 22....Wyo.
100*Indian Hills, G 14....Colo.
350 Indian Lake, I 21....N. Y.
117*Indian Mills, Q 10..W. Va.
37*Indianmound, K 15....La.
157*Indian Mound, K 8,..Tenn.
22*Indian Neck, K 18....Va.
400 Indian Oasis, P 13....Ariz.
411 Indianola, I 21....Ill.
4123 Indianola, M 12....Iowa
3604 Indianola, F 8....Miss.
800 Indianola, O 11....Neb.
311 Indianola, K 19....Okla.
532*Indianola, M 4....Pa.
108 Indianola, I 13....Utah
.... Indianola Jc., N 13....Iowa
.... Indian Orchard, H 8..Mass.
125 Indian River, L 21....Me.
300 Indian River, G 16...Mich.
120*Indian River City, G 20.Fla.
50*Indian Rock, M 8....Va.
80*Indian Rocks, I 11....Fla.
378 Indianrun, D 22....Ky.
65*Indian Springs, G 9....Ga.
150 Indian Springs, N 10....Ind.
60 Indian Springs, L 24..Tenn.
343*Indian Town, K 22....Fla.
45*Indian Town, C 23...N. C.
225 Indian Trail, I 7....N. C.
250 Indian Valley, L 5....Idaho
50*Indian Valley, P 4....Va.
.... Indian Village, M 14....La.
16 Indian Wells, F 21....Ariz.
2296 Indio, P 20....Calif.
32*Indore, K 8....W. Va.
20*Indus, C 13....Minn.
200 Industrial City, D 5....Mo.
....*Industrial School (Industrial), E 11....W. Va.
576 Industry, H 7....Ill.
250 Industry, L 1....Pa.
518 Industry, K 20....Tex.
119*Industry, G 8....W. Va.
500 Inez (Eden), G 23....Ky.
40 Inez, J 25....N. M.
50 Inez, G 15....Neb.
52*Inez, D 16....N. C.
210 Inez, N 19....Tex.
25 Inez, J 19....Wyo.
25 Inga, E 12....Mont.
202*Ingalls, P 13....Ark.
442 Ingalls, I 16....Ind.
187 Ingalls, L 6....Kan.
75 Ingalls, H 6....Mich.
250*Ingalls, D 2....N. C.
50 Ingalton, B 19....Ill.
100*Inger, F 14....Minn.
134 Ingersoll, B 8....Okla.
15 Ingham, M 11....Neb.
.... Inghams, L 20....N. Y.
.... Ingle, K 10....Calif.
60*Ingle (Inglefield), Q 5..Ind.
23*Ingle, I 17....Ky.
30 Ingleford, G 23....Wash.
10 Ingleside, F 16....Ark.
98*Ingleside, A 19....Ill.
216 Ingleside, H 19....Md.
10 Ingleside, H 17....Mich.
1699*Ingleside, M 17....Neb.
1000*Ingleside, P 17....Tex.
100 Ingleside, R 9....W. Va.
30114 Inglewood, O 15, R 3. Calif.
136 Inglis, F 12....Fla.
31*Ingo, G 11....W. Va.
300*Ingold, J 15....N. C.
262 Ingomar, C 18....Miss.
300 Ingomar, I 18....Mont.
60*Ingomar, L 6....Ohio
2000*Ingomar, M 3....Pa.
100 Ingot, D 6....Calif.
150 Ingraham, M 18....Ill.
150*Ingram, A 18....Ark.
42*Ingram, K 19....Ky.
.... Ingram, P 25....N. D.
3904 Ingram, M 3....Pa.
200*Ingram, K 15....Tex.
88*Ingram, Q 10....Va.
174*Ingram, G 9....Wis.

Pop. Place Index State
419*Ingram Branch, M 8.W. Va.
20*Ink, J 5....Ark.
31*Ink, O 16....Mo.
527*Inkerman, I 20....Pa.
17*Inkerman, F 20....W. Va.
500 Inkom, P 19....Idaho
7044 Inkster, Q 22....Mich.
310 Inkster, G 21....N. D.
15 Inland, E 14....Ala.
100 Inland, M 17....Neb.
5 Inland, F 5....S. D.
100*Inlet, I 20....N. Y.
110*Inman (Ackert), G 6...Ga.
507 Inman, J 15....Kan.
206 Inman, G 16....Neb.
52*Inman (Loon Lake), E 22 N. Y.
1115 Inman, A 6....S. C.
50 Inman, Q 14....Tenn.
50*Inman, D 5....Va.
100*Innis, I 13....La.
75*Ino, L 20....Va.
395 Inola, E 20....Okla.
48*Inroad, J 15....Ky.
900*Inskip, M 19....Tenn.
31*Insko (Adele), G 21....Ky.
450 Inspiration, K 17....Ariz.
5 Instanter, G 9....Pa.
500 Institute, K 5....W. Va.
45 Intake, G 24....Mont.
400 Intercourse, O 20....Pa.
182 Interior, L 7....S. D.
100*Interior, N 4....Va.
251*Interlachen, D 15....Fla.
65*Interlaken, F 2....Mass.
787*Interlaken, I 18....N. J.
661 Interlaken, O 13....N. Y.
80 Interlochen, J 13....Mich.
15*Intermont, E 21....W. Va.
.... International, F 10....Utah
5626 International Falls, C 15 ....Minn.
....*Interstate, see Irona.W. Va.
166*Intervale (New Gloucester), O 6....Me.
200 Intervale, I 17....N. H.
....*Intervilla, see West Lawn, Pa.
502 Inver Grove (Invergrove), N 25....Minn.
38*Invermere (Irona), D 15 ....W. Va.
150 Inverness, L 19....Ala.
200*Inverness, H 4....Calif.
1075 Inverness, F 14....Fla.
677 Inverness, G 9....Miss.
137 Inverness, D 11....Mont.
150 Inwood, C 14....Ind.
634 Inwood, C 1....Iowa
8116 Inwood, I 6....N. Y.
250*Inwood (E. Barnet), E 17 Vt.
300*Inwood, E 24....W. Va.
25*Inyokern, M 13....Calif.
225*Ioka, G 18....Utah
100 Iola, K 8....Colo.
256 Iola, M 17....Ill.
7244 Iola, L 23....Kan.
318 Iola, I 21....Tex.
746 Iola, L 14....Wis.
518 Iona, N 20....Idaho
200*Iona, M 8....N. J.
.... Iona, M 14....Okla.
95 Iona, M 16....S. D.
365 Iona Lake (Iona), Q 6 Minn.
63*Ione, H 5....Ark.
1200 Ione, H 9....Calif.
100*Ione, B 17....Colo.
40 Ione, I 11....Nev.
262 Ione, D 16....Ore.
681 Ione, C 23....Wash.
283 Ionia, D 16....Iowa
150 Ionia, E 13....Kan.
100*Ionia, I 19....Ky.
6392 Ionia, O 15....Mich.
116*Ionia, J 10....Mo.
214 Ionia, M 10....N. Y.
1000 Iota, L 9....La.
113*Iowa, L 8....La.
17182 Iowa City, K 20....Iowa
25*Iowa Colony, M 22....Tex.
4425 Iowa Falls, G 13....Iowa
100*Iowa Hill, F 9....Calif.
6 Iowa Jc., F 6....Ill.
.... Iowa Jc., G 12....Ill.
1980 Iowa Park, B 15....Tex.
75 Iowa Point, C 23....Kan.
629 Ipava, H 9....Ill.
6348■Ipswich, B 21....Mass.
1002 Ipswich, D 17....S. D.
3 Ipswich, H 21....Wis.
80*Ira, K 14....Iowa
13*Ira, L 11....Mo.
70*Ira, M 13....N. Y.
.... Ira, E 17....Ohio
150 Ira, E 11....Tex.
50*Ira, B 7....Va.
287 Ira, L 7....Vt.
75*Ira, J 9....W. Va.
1500*Iraan, I 8....Tex.
81*Irad, F 23....Ky.
400 Irasburg, C 15....Vt.
40 Irby, I 19....Wash.
483 Iredell, F 17....Tex.
263 Ireland, P 9....Ind.
357 Ireland, G 17....Tex.
100*Ireland, H 12....W. Va.
39*Irene, B 16....Ill.
391 Irene, O 23....S. D.
267 Irene, G 19....Tex.
150 Irene, L 5....W. Va.
653 Ireton, D 1....Iowa
100*Irma, J 10....Wis.
230 Irmo, G 12....S. C.
210*Irona, C 23....N. Y.
75 Ironaton, F 18....Ala.
800 Iron Belt, H 6....Wis.
....*Ironbridge, see Rahns, N 22....Pa.
289 Iron City, O 4....Ga.
750 Iron City, Q 8....Tenn.
1486 Irondale, F 13....Ala.
446 Irondale, L 19....Mo.
1000 Irondale, H 20....Ohio
23376■Irondequoit, L 10...N. Y.
719 Iron Gate, L 7....Va.
47*Iron Hill (Ironhill), C 18 Md.
11 Ironhub, I 13....Minn.
67*Ironia, D 14....N. J.
107*Iron Jc. (Iron), F 19..Minn.
.... Iron King, H 10....Utah
11080 Iron Mountain, G 4.Mich.
200*Iron Mountain, M 19..Mo.
.... Iron Mountain, P 4...Utah
35*Iron Mountain, P 22..Wyo.
23*Iron Nation, K 14....S. D.
273 Iron Ridge, N 18....Wis.
4416 Iron River, F 2....Mich.
800 Iron River, E 5....Wis.
26*Irons, L 13....Mich.
50*Ironsburg, P 19....Tenn.
81 Ironshire, O 24....Md.
7 Ironside, I 21....Ore.
10*Ironsides, M 10....Md.
150 Ironspot, L 15....Ohio
50*Iron Springs, Q 14....Pa.
43 Iron Springs, O 5....Utah

Pop. Place Index State
96 Iron Station (Iron), G 4 N. C.
100*Ironto, O 5....Va.
20*Ironton, K 7....Ky.
106*Ironton, H 16....Mich.
827 Ironton, I 13....Minn.
1083 Ironton, M 19....Mo.
15851 Ironton, R 13....Ohio
130*Ironton, F 22....Tex.
120 Ironton, G 13....Utah
213*Ironton, I 18....Wis.
.... Ironton Jc., O 13....Ohio
.... Ironville, C 10....Ohio
13369 Ironwood, B 21....Mich.
242 Iroquois, F 22....Ill.
413 Iroquois, I 21....S. D.
65 Irrigon, B 17....Ore.
300 Irvin, G 24....Wash.
250*Irvine, P 17, R 7....Calif.
150*Irvine, E 14....Fla.
3631 Irvine, G 19....Ky.
375 Irvineton (Irvine), E 6..Pa.
588 Irving, L 13....Ill.
74*Irving, J 17....Iowa
310 Irving, E 19....Kan.
350 Irving, O 4....N. Y.
100 Irving, I 6....Ore.
1089*Irving, D 19....Tex.
53*Irving College, O 14..Tenn.
....*Irvings, see West Portal, Colo.
469 Irvington, Q 4....Ala.
1000 Irvington, F 22....Calif.
418 Irvington, N 14....Ill.
80*Irvington, D 10....Iowa
790 Irvington, G 12....Ky.
150 Irvington, J 23....Neb.
55328 Irvington, E 18....N. J.
3272 Irvington, G 6....N. Y.
700 Irvington, L 21....Va.
30*Irvins Store, I 16....Ky.
1049 Irvona, K 9....Pa.
250*Irwin, I 9....Calif.
258 Irwin, N 22....Idaho
66*Irwin, F 20....Ill.
345 Irwin, J 6....Iowa
57*Irwin, M 6....Mo.
105 Irwin, E 7....Neb.
150*Irwin, K 10....Ohio
3441 Irwin, N 5....Pa.
10*Irwin, L 15....Va.
125*Irwindale, O 16....Calif.
589 Irwinton, I 12....Ga.
150 Irwinville, M 11....Ga.
650*Isaban, P 5....W. Va.
200 Isabel, J 21....Ill.
252 Isabel, N 12....Kan.
50*Isabel, L 11....Minn.
490 Isabel, E 9....S. D.
200*Isabella, L 15....Calif.
25 Isabella, M 9....Ga.
227 Isabella, E 13....Mich.
94*Isabella, E 24....Minn.
18*Isabella, R 12....Mo.
97 Isabella, E 9....Okla.
350*Isabella, Q 4....Pa.
450 Isabella, Q 18....Tenn.
53*Isadora, A 6....Mo.
354 Isanti, L 16....Minn.
125 Isbell, C 7....Ala.
12*Isbell (Isbell Station), I 15....Mo.
209 Ischua, Q 6....N. Y.
710*Iselin, F 17....N. J.
2050 Iselin, M 6....Pa.
.... Iser, G 2....Tex.
158*Ishawooa, C 6....Wyo.
9491 Ishpeming, E 6....Mich.
5 Isinours, R 21....Minn.
.... Isinours Jc., R 21....Minn.
180*Islamorado, Q 22....Fla.
626 Island, H 9....Ky.
45*Island, L 15....Va.
45*Islandbranch, J 6...W. Va.
75*Island City, H 20....Ky.
177 Island City, D 21....Ore.
32*Island Creek, N 14....Md.
200*Island Creek, I 22....Mass.
1000 Island Falls, G 17....Me.
27 Island Ford (Islandford), I 12....Va.
275*Island Grove, D 15....Fla.
392*Island Heights, K 19..N. J.
25*Island Mountain, E 3.Calif.
50*Island Park, L 22....Idaho
526*Island Park, M 15...Minn.
1531*Island Park, H 7....N. Y.
.... Island Park, I 21....R. I.
2001 Island Pond, C 20....Vt.
66*Islandton, M 13....S. C.
.... Islay, Q 21....Wyo.
567 Isle, J 15....Minn.
97▲*Isle au Haut, N 15....Me.
335▲Isle La Motte, B 5....Vt.
25*Isle of Palms, N 18....S. C.
110 Isle of Wight, P 20....Va.
300 Islesboro, N 14....Me.
159*Islesford, N 18....Me.
80*Isle St. George (N. Bass Island), C 11....Ohio
1000 Isleta, H 11....N. M.
190*Isleta, J 17....Ohio
1837 Isleton, H 7....Calif.
700 Islington, G 18, Q 2..Mass.
....*Islington (Les Cheneaux) F 15....Mich.
4000 Islip, H 8....N. Y.
946*Islip Terrace, H 9....N. Y.
250 Islitas, P 14....Tex.
176 Ismay, I 24....Mont.
161*Isney, M 3....Ala.
449 Isola, G 9....Miss.
200 Isoline, M 16....Tenn.
25*Isom, I 22....Ky.
27*Isom, C 6....Va.
40 Isom Springs, Q 15....Okla.
50*Isonville, F 22....Ky.
812 Issaquah, I 9....Wash.
60 Issaquena, I 6....Miss.
203*Issue, N 11....Md.
150 Istachatta, G 14....Fla.
14*Istrouma, K 15....La.
.... Italian Swiss Colony, J 10....Calif.
1224 Italy, F 19....Tex.
787 Itasca, B 20....Ill.
1759 Itasca, F 19....Tex.
.... Itasca, D 4....Wis.
125*Itaska, P 16....N. Y.
2000 Ithaca, M 16....Mich.
139 Ithaca, K 22....Neb.
19730 Ithaca, P 13....N. Y.
142*Ithaca, K 6....Ohio
350*Ithan, O 23....Pa.
.... Itmann, P 7....W. Va.
1795 Itta Bena, F 10....Miss.
51 Iuka, B 13....Ark.
470 Iuka, M 16....Ill.
183 Iuka, L 11....Kan.
55*Iuka, I 7....Ky.
1664 Iuka, A 23....Miss.
43*Iuka, D 10....W. Va.
1285 Iva, E 5....S. C.
64*Ivan, N 12....Ark.
100*Ivan, I 22....Ky.
48*Ivan, D 15....Tex.
42*Ivan, G 7....W. Va.
1000*Ivanhoe, L 13....Calif.
606 Ivanhoe, O 4....Minn.

Pop.	Place, Index	State
146	*Ivanhoe, K 15	N. C.
513	*Ivanhoe (Frye), O 2	Pa.
60	*Ivanhoe, C 20	Tex.
1200	Ivanhoe, Q 3	Va.
150	*Ivanhoe (Hampton), G 13	W. Va.
55	*Ivel, H 22	Ky.
259	Ives, P 21	Wis.
386	Ivesdale, I 18	Ill.
27	*Ivey, I 13	Ga.
83	*Ivins, Q 3	Utah
200	*Ivis, H 22	Ky.
25	*Ivondale, K 19	Va.
339	Ivor, P 19	Va.
750	Ivoryton, L 17	Conn.
140	*Ivy, N 11	Ark.
43	*Ivy, N 8	N. C.
38	*Ivy, P 18	Tenn.
500	*Ivy Depot, K 12	Va.
1963	▲Ivydale (Otter), J 9	W. Va.
318	*Ivyland, N 24	Pa.
100	*Ivyton, G 21	Ky.
1472	Ivywild, J 15	Colo.
34	*Ivywood, K 4	Pa.
120	*Ixonia, N 19	Wis.
50	Izee, J 17	Ore.
32	*Izoro, H 17	Tex.

J

Pop.	Place, Index	State
100	*Jabez, J 16	Ky.
14	*Jachin, K 5	Ala.
10	Jacinto, K 3	Neb.
8	*Jack, N 15	Mo.
....	Jack, O 16	Va.
50	*Jackhorn, I 22	Ky.
800	Jackman, H 6	Me.
500	Jackman Sta. (Jackman), H 6	Me.
1200	Jacksboro, L 18	Tenn.
2368	Jacksboro, D 16	Tex.
150	*Jacks Creek, O 6	Tenn.
21	*Jacks Fork, O 17	Mo.
2039	Jackson, M 6	Ala.
2024	Jackson, H 9	Calif.
1917	Jackson, G 10	Ga.
....	Jackson, J 6	Ind.
2099	Jackson, G 21	Ky.
5384	Jackson, J 14	La.
37	Jackson, L 12	Me.
50	Jackson, C 18	Md.
49656	Jackson, Q 17	Mich.
2840	Jackson, R 9	Minn.
62107	Jackson, J 11	Miss.
3113	Jackson, N 22	Mo.
52	Jackson, M 5	Mont.
226	Jackson, F 22	Neb.
409	▲Jackson, I 17	N. H.
758	Jackson, C 19	N. C.
6295	Jackson, O 13	Ohio
85	Jackson, Q 19	Okla.
198	Jackson, E 21	Pa.
700	*Jackson, K 19	Pa.
150	*Jackson, L 10	S. C.
24332	Jackson, O 5	Tenn.
302	Jackson, O 19	Wis.
1046	Jackson, G 3	Wyo.
75	*Jacksonboro, N 16	S. C.
175	*Jacksonburg, C 11	W. Va.
566	Jackson Center, I 8	Ohio
268	Jackson Center, H 3	Pa.
39	*Jackson Hill, G 8	N. C.
122	Jackson Jc., D 18	Iowa
196	Jacksonport, E 17	Ark.
124	Jacksonport, Q 12	Wis.
72	*Jacksons Creek, F 9	N. C.
199	Jackson Springs, H 10	N. C.
50	*Jackson Summit, D 16	Pa.
313	Jacksontown, K 14	Ohio
2995	Jacksonville, E 19	Ala.
500	Jacksonville, I 13	Ark.
173065	Jacksonville, B 16	Fla.
100	Jacksonville, M 14	Ga.
19844	Jacksonville, J 10	Ill.
275	*Jacksonville, L 23	Me.
181	Jacksonville, E 13	Mo.
47	*Jacksonville, P 13	N. Y.
873	Jacksonville, J 19	N. C.
812	*Jacksonville, N 15	Ohio
761	Jacksonville, Q 6	Ore.
232	*Jacksonville, L 21	Pa.
7213	Jacksonville, F 22	Tex
240	Jacksonville, R 10	Vt.
3566	Jacksonville Beach, C 17	Fla.
65	*Jacksonwald, N 21	Pa.
75	*Jacob, P 13	Ill.
29	*Jacobs, E 21	Ky.
100	*Jacobsburg, K 19	Ohio
550	*Jacobs Creek, O 4	Pa.
300	Jacobson, H 16	Minn.
125	*Jacobstown, J 13	N. J.
163	Jacobsville, B 7	Mich.
552	Jacobus, Q 17	Pa.
290	Jacoby, J 12	La.
5	*Jacox, L 14	W. Va.
400	*Jacumba (Jacumba Hot Springs), Q 21	Calif.
113	Jadie, Q 25	Okla.
58	*Jadwin, N 16	Mo
300	Jaffrey, Q 9	N. H.
50	*Jahile, C 6	Va.
62	Jaite, R 23	Ohio
25	Jakajones, N 7	Ark.
264	Jakin, O 3	Ga.
1157	Jal, O 25	N. M.
....	*Jalong, see Longhurst	N. C.
81	Jamaica, I 21	Ill.
283	Jamaica, J 9	Iowa
....	Jamaica, H 6	N. Y.
350	Jamaica, O 10	Vt.
25	*Jamaica, L 20	Va.
510	*Jamaica Square (South Floral), H 7	N. Y.
160	*Jamboree, H 24	Ky.
110	*James, I 12	Ga.
39	James, F 1	Iowa
259	James, M 16	Md.
61	*James, G 6	Miss.
30	James, D 19	S. D.
108	James, E 23	Tex.
2128	Jamesburg, H 16	N. J.
600	James City, I 19	N. C.
800	*James City, G 8	Pa.
200	*James Creek, M 11	Pa.
223	Jameson, C 8	Mo.
761	Jamesport, C 8	Mo.
353	Jamesport, G 10	N. Y.
....	James River Jc., Q 17	Va.
150	*James Store, M 21	Va.
75	*Jamestown, C 20	Ala.
66	*Jamestown, E 15	Ark.
1000	Jamestown, H 10	Calif.
190	Jamestown, E 13	Colo.
583	Jamestown, I 12	Ind.
490	Jamestown, E 14	Kan.
476	Jamestown, J 16	Ky.
63	*Jamestown, D 7	La.
200	Jamestown, O 13	Mich.
269	Jamestown, I 12	Mo.
42638	Jamestown, Q 3	N. Y.
900	*Jamestown, E 9	N. C.
8790	Jamestown, M 18	N. D.
1079	Jamestown, L 9	Ohio
819	Jamestown, G 1	Pa.
1744	▲Jamestown, K 17	R. I.
43	*Jamestown, K 20	S. C.
1230	Jamestown, L 16	Tenn.
28	*Jamestown, I 25	Tex.
6	*Jamestown, N 19	Va.
....	Jamestown Jc., M 18	N. D.
....	James Valley Jc., I 19	S. D.
800	*Jamesville, M 15	N. Y.
499	Jamesville, F 20	N. C.
255	Jamesville, M 23	Va.
169	*Jamieson, B 4	Fla.
27	Jamieson, I 23	Ore.
65	*Jamison, N 12	Iowa
150	Jamison, D 14	Neb.
93	*Jamison, N 24	Pa.
70	*Jamison, I 14	S. C.
30	Jamison City, H 18	Pa.
300	*Jamul, Q 19	Calif.
86	*Jane, R 6	Mo.
143	*Jane, B 6	Va.
505	*Jane Lew, F 12	W. Va.
200	*Janesville, D 10	Calif.
250	Janesville, K 19	Ill.
366	Janesville, F 16	Iowa
1296	Janesville, P 14	Minn.
22992	Janesville, L 22	Wis.
24	Janousek, O 22	S. D.
30	Jansen, P 16	Colo.
255	Jansen, O 21	Neb.
211	Janvier, N 10	N. J.
380	*Japan, P 3	N. C.
55	*Japton, C 6	Ark.
700	Jarales, H 10	N. M.
68	*Jarbalo, F 23	Kan.
150	*Jarbidge, A 18	Nev.
134	*Jardin, C 21	Tex.
25	*Jared, D 24	Wash.
150	Jaroso, Q 13	Colo.
458	Jarratt, Q 17	Va.
107	*Jarreau, K 14	La.
215	Jarrell, I 18	Tex.
300	*Jarrettown, N 22	Pa.
265	*Jarrettsville, C 16	Md.
50	Jarrolds Valley, N 6	W. Va.
550	Jarvisburg, D 24	N. C.
40	*Jarvis Store, J 19	Ky.
3418	Jasonville, M 7	Ind.
6847	Jasper, E 10	Ala.
385	Jasper, C 9	Ark.
1722	Jasper, B 11	Fla.
576	Jasper, D 6	Ga.
5041	Jasper, P 10	Ind.
275	Jasper, R 18	Mich.
880	Jasper, Q 3	Minn.
804	Jasper, N 6	Mo.
250	Jasper, Q 10	N. Y.
240	Jasper, O 11	Ohio
70	Jasper, J 7	Ore.
1251	Jasper, Q 14	Tenn.
3497	Jasper, I 25	Tex.
493	Java, D 14	S. D.
257	Java, P 10	Va.
100	*Java Center, O 6	N. Y.
....	Java Jc., D. 14	S. D.
225	*Java Village, O 6	N. Y.
400	*Jay, L 3	Fla.
....	Jay, O 17	La.
350	Jay (T e Bridge), M 6	Me.
400	*Jay, F 23	N. Y.
741	Jay, D 23	Okla.
....	Jay, O 8	W. Va.
....	Jay Junction, O 8	W. Va.
48	Jay Em, L 23	Wyo.
89	*Jayess, N 11	Miss.
....	Jaype, G 7	Idaho
770	Jayton, D 12	Tex.
100	*Jean, F 22	Ky.
310	Jean, D 15	Tex.
3362	Jeanerette, N 12	La.
400	Jeanesville, J 20	Pa.
16220	Jeanette, N 5	Pa.
200	*Jedburg (Sherman), I 19	Mo.
200	*Jedburg, M 17	S. C.
115	Jeddo, N 24	Mich.
327	*Jeddo, J 20	Pa.
120	*Jeff, A 13	Ala.
125	*Jeff, I 22	Ky.
648	Jeffers, Q 8	Minn.
40	Jeffers, N 9	Mont.
825	Jefferson, J 7	Ala.
50	Jefferson, H 12	Colo.
1839	Jefferson, E 12	Ga.
126	Jefferson, H 12	Ind.
4088	Jefferson, I 9	Iowa
50	*Jefferson. O 22	Kan.
300	Jefferson, N 11	Me.
300	Jefferson, E 7	Md.
861	Jefferson, F 13	Mass.
68	Jefferson (Jefferson City), J 8	Mont.
200	Jefferson (Meadows), G 14	N. H.
250	Jefferson, P 20	N. Y.
304	Jefferson, C 3	N. C.
1676	Jefferson, C 20	Ohio
229	Jefferson, B 11	Okla.
479	Jefferson, G 6	Ore.
400	Jefferson (Codorus), Q 17	Pa.
557	Jefferson, P 3	Pa.
547	Jefferson, C 16	S. C.
469	Jefferson, Q 25	S. D.
2797	Jefferson, D 24	Tex.
11	*Jefferson, L 15	Va.
3059	Jefferson, M 20	Wis.
....	Jefferson Barracks, J 20	Mo.
24268	Jefferson Cty, I 14	Mo.
2576	Jefferson City, M 19	Tenn.
162	*Jefferson Highland, G 15	N. H.
150	*Jefferson Island, M 12	La.
45	Jefferson Island, L 9	Mont.
15	Jefferson Jc., L 20	Wis.
62	*Jefferson Springs (Jefferson), K 13	Ark.
82	*Jeffersonton, H 14	Va.
899	Jeffersontown, E 14	Ky.
130	*Jefferson Valley, E 5	N. Y.
804	Jeffersonville, I 13	Ga.
....	Jeffersonville, see Geff	Ill.
11493	Jeffersonville, P 17	Ind.
84	*Jeffersonville, F 19	Ky.
403	Jeffersonville, C 2	N. Y.
785	Jeffersonville, L 10	Ohio
287	Jeffersonville, D 10	Vt.
200	*Jeffery, M 5	W. Va.
60	Jeffress, Q 12	Va.
48	*Jeffrey, K 13	Ky.
35	*Jeffries, B 9	Miss.
50	*Jeffriesburg, J 17	Mo.
40	Jeffris, H 9	Wis.
4	Jeffris Jc., J 9	Wis.
90	*Jeffs, O 21	Va.
216	Jeiseyville, J 13	Ill.
....	Jelks, see Patterson	Ark.
1581	Jellico, K 18	Tenn.
100	*Jellicocreek, K 18	Ky.
10	*Jelm, O 19	Wyo.
650	Jemes (Jemez), F 11	N. M.
200	Jemez Springs, E 10	N. M.
456	Jemison, H 13	Ala.
101	Jemtland, B 18	Me.
250	*Jena, D 9	Fla.
946	Jena, G 11	La.
262	Jenera, G 9	Ohio
138	Jenifer, F 18	Ala.
175	*Jenison, O 12	Mich.
800	Jenkinjones, R 7	W. Va.
9428	Jenkins, I 23	Ky.
206	Jenkins, I 12	Minn.
52	**Jenkins, Q 8	Mo.
80	*Jenkins Bridge, K 23	Va.
166	Jenkinsburg, G 9	Ga.
35	*Jenkinsville, F 12	S. C.
5024	Jenkintown, O 24	Pa.
1026	Jenks, F 19	Okla.
127	*Jenky, L 9	W. Va.
160	*Jenner, H 3	Calif.
1500	Jenners, O 7	Pa.
369	*Jennerstown, O 7	Pa.
120	*Jennie, Q 17	Ark.
55	*Jenning (Jennings Ordinary), O 14	Va.
499	Jennings, B 10	Fla.
311	Jennings, D 6	Kan.
7343	Jennings, M 8	La.
200	*Jennings, M 3	Md.
109	Jennings, K 15	Mich.
....	*Jennings, C 20	Mo.
80	Jennings, D 2	Mont.
....	*Jennings, see Union Grove	N. C.
453	Jennings, E 15	Okla.
....	Jennings, C 11	Wash.
60	Jennings, J 9	W. Va.
800	*Jennings Lodge, E 8	Ore.
75	*Jenningston, G 16	W. Va.
50	*Jenny Lake, F 2	Wyo.
517	Jenny Lind, G 4	Ark.
100	*Jenny Lind, H 9	Calif.
85	Jens, I 6	Mont.
96	Jensen, J 23	Fla.
350	Jensen, G 24	Utah
....	Jenson, G 4	Ark.
50	*Jenson, K 20	Ky.
36	*Jeptha, G 21	Ky.
250	*Jere, C 13	W. Va.
80	*Jeremiah, I 22	Ky.
....	Jericho, I 10	Ala.
225	Jericho, G 21	Ark.
60	*Jericho, E 15	Ky.
500	*Jericho, H 7	N. Y.
46	*Jericho, D 5	Tex.
254	*Jericho, E 8	Vt.
380	Jericho Center, E 8	Vt.
254	Jerico Springs, M 7	Mo.
30	*Jeriel, F 22	Ky.
3238	Jermyn, G 22	Pa.
320	Jermyn, D 16	Tex.
2295	Jerome, H 12	Ariz.
97	Jerome, P 16	Ark.
3537	Jerome, P 11	Idaho
60	Jerome, G 16	Ind.
275	Jerome, P 14	Iowa
38	*Jerome, H 6	Kan.
100	Jerome, Q 18	Mich.
190	*Jerome, L 14	Mo.
1500	Jerome, O 7	Pa.
160	*Jerome, F 11	Va.
....	Jerome Jc., O 8	Pa.
474	Jeromesville, G 15	Ohio
418	Jerry, E 23	N. C.
25	Jerry, N 24	Wash.
335	Jerry City, E 10	Ohio
38	*Jersey, P 12	Ark.
188	Jersey, F 10	Ga.
200	Jersey, J 13	Ohio
....	*Jersey, I 18	Va.
301173	Jersey City, E 20	N. J.
10	Jersey City, J 9	Wis.
698	*Jersey Homesteads, H 13	N. J.
80	Jersey Mills, H 14	Pa.
5432	Jersey Shore, H 14	Pa.
900	Jersey Shore Jc., I 14	Pa.
216	*Jerseytown, I 17	Pa.
4809	Jerseyville, L 8	Ill.
162	*Jerusalem, F 10	Ark.
186	Jerusalem. K 18	Ohio
100	Jesse, M 17	Okla.
171	*Jesse, P 6	W. Va.
75	Jessie, J 20	N. D.
60	Jesse Lake, F 13	Minn.
250	*Jessieville, J 9	Ark.
78	*Jessup (Jessups), J 7	Ind.
....	Jessup; G 22	Pa.
161	*Jessups (Jessup), G 13, H 14	Md.
25	Jester, K 2	Okla.
316	Jesterville, O 20	Md.
75	Jesuit Bend, O 19	La.
50	*Jesup, C 17	Ark.
2903	Jesup, M 20	Ga.
902	Jesup, G 18	Iowa
442	*Jet, C 9	Okla.
175	Jetersville, N 14	Va.
25	*Jethro, E 6	Ark.
881	Jetmore, K 7	Kan.
26	*Jetson, I 11	Ky.
165	*Jetsville, L 11	W. Va.
80	*Jett, E 16	Ky.
....	*Jettie, H 24	Ky.
75	*Jetts Creek, H 20	Ky.
75	Jewell, H 16	Ga.
1051	Jewell, H 12	Iowa
669	Jewell, E 14	Kan.
33	*Jewell, K 4	Md.
140	*Jewell, L 16	N. Y.
150	Jewell, D 7	Ohio
167	*Jewell, B 5	Ore.
1000	Jewell (Jewell Ridge), C 8	Va.
482	Jewella, C 4	La.
204	Jewett, K 19	Ill.
75	Jewett, R 3	Me.
26	*Jewett, N 19	Mo.
200	*Jewett, P 22	N. Y.
1031	Jewett, I 19	Ohio
515	Jewett, H 21	Tex.
50	*Jewett, B 11	Wis.
3682	Jewett City, H 23	Conn.
300	*Jewell Valley, B 7	Va.
100	Jicarilla, J 15	N. M.
301	Jigger, E 12	La.
76	Jiggs, E 18	Nev.
100	*Jim Falls, F 11	Wis.
....	Jingo, see Fairview	Tenn.
25	*Jinks, H 19	Ky.
16	Jireh, J 22	Wyo.
....	Jacksonville Mine Jc., L 6	Pa.
60	*Joanna, M 20	Pa.
487	Joaquin, F 25	Tex.
27	*Job, F 23	Ky.
50	*Job, Q 16	Mo.
184	*Job, H 16	W. Va.
210	Jobstown, J 13	N. J.
50	*Jocassee, C 3	S. C.
25	Jochin, M 8	W. Va.
40	*Jodie, L 8	W. Va.
75	*Joe, N 6	N. C.
....	*Joe Creek, I 14	S. D.
29	*Joel, C 10	Wis.
35	*Joelton, M 11	Tenn.
45	Joes, G 22	Colo.
750	*Joffre (Raccoon), N 2	Pa.
100	Johannesburg, M 17	Calif.
721	Johannesburg, H 17	Mich.
1	Johannott, G 22	Ill.
708	John Day, H 18	Ore.
36	*Johnetta, H 18	Ky.
6	Johnetta, L 5	Pa.
39	*Johnnie Mine, J 16	Nev.
344	Johns, G 11	Ala.
85	*Johns, K 13	Miss.
100	Johns, K 10	N. C.
176	Johnsburg, A 19	Ill.
276	*Johnsburg, J 23	N. Y.
100	Johnsburg, O 16	Wis.
14	Johnsdale, K 14	Minn.
2000	Johns Island, N 17	S. C.
165	*Johnson (Johnsons), C 4	Ark.
65	*Johnson (Woodlawn), D 15	Fla.
524	Johnson, M 1	Kan.
101	*Johnson, L 4	Minn.
301	Johnson, N 24	Neb.
500	*Johnson, E 3	N. Y.
20	*Johnson, Q 11	Utah
753	Johnson, D 11	Vt.
39	*Johnson (Wealthia), L 13	Va.
150	Johnson, L 24	Wash.
162	*Johnsonburg, D 11	N. J.
276	Johnsonburg, N 6	N. Y.
4955	Johnsonburg, G 9	Pa.
....	Johnsonburg and Bedford Jc., F 9	Pa.
18039	Johnson City, R 15	N. Y.
25332	Johnson City, L 24	Tenn.
500	Johnson City, J 16	Tex.
511	Johnson Creek, M 20	Wis.
400	*Johnsondale, L 13	Calif.
165	*Johnsons (Johnson), C 5	Ark.
	Johnsons Corners, F 16	Ohio
60	*Johnsons Mill, E 4	Va.
26	*Johnsons Springs, L 15	Va.
50	*Johnsontown, N 23	Va.
98	*Johnsonville, N 18	Ill.
575	Johnsonville, M 24	N. Y.
464	Johnsonville, H 21	S. C.
354	Johnsonville, M 7	Tenn.
120	*Johns Run, E 22	Ky.
200	*Johnston, K 12	Iowa
10672	■*Johnston, D 8	R. I.
1100	Johnston, H 9	S. C.
121	Johnston (Johnstons Sta.) O 9	Miss.
5418	Johnston City, P 16	Ill.
13	*Johnstonville, D 10	Calif.
961	Johnstown, D 15	Colo.
75	*Johnstown, C 14	Fla.
173	Johnstown, F 12	Neb.
10666	Johnstown, M 21	N. Y.
26	Johnstown, G 22	N. D.
1064	Johnstown, J 13	Ohio
66668	Johnstown, N 7	Pa.
80	Johnstown, F 12	W. Va.
105	*Johnsville, P 14	Ark.
66	*Johnsville, E 9	Calif.
190	Johnsville (Shauck), H 13	Ohio
300	*Johnsville, O 24	Pa.
20	Johnsville, F 17	Tex.
100	Johns Wood, G 21	Mich.
500	*Johntown, C 22	Tex.
263	Joice, B 13	Iowa
306	Joiner, F 21	Ark.
....	*Joinerville, F 23	Tex.
40	Jo-Jo Jc., F 8	Pa.
400	Jokake, K 15	Ariz.
68	*Joker, H 8	W. Va.
42365	Joliet, D 19	Ill.
476	Joliet, M 15	Mont.
150	*Joliet† (Keffers), L 18	Pa.
150	Joliette, D 23	N. D.
100	Jolietville, I 13	Ind.
54	Joller, O 11	Pa.
161	Jolley, G 8	Iowa
96	*Jolly, B 16	Tex.
150	*Jollytown, Q 2	Pa.
300	*Jolo (Bradshaw), R 5	W. Va.
20	Jolon, L 8	Calif.
160	*Jonah, I 18	Tex.
63	*Jonancy (Elwood), H 22	Ky.
40	*Jonas, J 22	Pa.
50	*Jonas Ridge, E 2	N. C.
112	*Jonben, P 8	W. Va.
195	*Jones, J 12	Ala.
40	*Jones, M 23	Ga.
100	*Jones, A 12	La.
250	*Jones, R 11	Mich.
260	Jones, H 13	Okla.
100	*Jones, O 3	Tenn.
105	*Jones (Jones Spur), M 10	Wis.
11729	Jonesboro, D 19	Ark.
1204	Jonesboro, G 8	Ga.
1521	Jonesboro, Q 14	Ill.
1791	Jonesboro, G 17	Ind.
2639	Jonesboro, D 8	La.
268	Jonesboro, L 21	Me.
928	Jonesboro, G 11	N. C.
976	Jonesboro, M 23	Tenn.
462	Jonesboro, G 17	Tex.
422	Jonesburg, H 16	Mo.
65	*Jonesdale, I 21	Wis.
....	Jones Mills, see Frisco City	Ala.
300	*Jones Mills, O 6	Pa.
100	*Jonespoint, E 5	N. Y.
1200	Jonesport, M 21	Me.
200	*Jones Prairie, I 19	Tex.
101	*Jones Springs, D 23	W. Va.
105	*Jones Spur (Jones), M 10	Wis.
27	*Jones Store, J 15	Va.
706	Jonestown, C 9	Miss.
48	*Jonestown (Tokio), G 6	Ohio
721	Jonestown, M 18	Pa.
181	Jonesville, M 15	Ind.
133	*Jonesville, D 17	Ky.
2080	Jonesville, G 12	La.
1302	Jonesville, Q 16	Mich.
150	*Jonesville, M 24	N. Y.
1733	Jonesville, D 6	N. C.
1182	Jonesville, B 10	S. C.
88	Jonesville, E 24	Tex.
400	Jonesville, F 9	Vt.
588	Jonesville, E 3	Va.
37144	Joplin, O 6	Mo.
250	Joplin, D 11	Mont.
125	*Joplin, H 17	Va.
148	Joppa, C 14	Ala.
587	Joppa, R 16	Ill.
14	*Joppa, I 15	Ky.
50	*Joppa, D 16	Md.
....	Joppa, J 20	Mont.
100	*Joppa, M 20	Tenn.
150	Joppa Jc., Q 15	Ill.
....	Jordan, O 17	Ill.
113	*Jordan, K 4	Ky.
1422	Jordan, O 14	Minn.
26	*Jordan, L 10	Mo.
500	Jordan, G 19	Mont.
181	▲Jordan, H 22	N. M.
1115	Jordan, L 14	N. Y.
133	*Jordan (Pleasant Corners), L 21	Pa.
318	Jordan, I 17	S. C.
100	*Jordan, D 13	W. Va.
1500	Jordania (Lonsdale), D 4	S. C.
100	*Jordan Mines, L 6	Va.
25	*Jordan Run, F 17	W. Va.
274	Jordan Valley, N 24	Ore.
275	Jordanville, M 19	N. Y.
69	*Jordan, I 11	Iowa
35	Joseco, L 24	Nev.
85	*Joseph, I 4	Idaho
....	Joseph, C 17	Mont.
593	Joseph, D 23	Ore.
297	Joseph, L 10	Utah
400	Joseph City, G 20	Ariz.
95	*Josephine, Q 8	Ala.
9	Josephine, H 16	N. D.
500	Josephine, M 7	Pa.
360	Josephine, D 20	Tex.
103	*Josephs Mills, D 10	W. Va.
850	*Joshua, E 18	Tex.
60	Joslin, Q 8	N. H.
5	Josselyn, M 13	Neb.
125	Josserand, H 23	Tex.
25	Joubert, M 18	S. D.
950	Jourdanton, N 16	Tex.
470	Joy, E 7	Ill.
35	*Joy, H 6	Ky.
5	*Joy, N 15	Mo.
20	*Joy, E 2	N. C.
37	*Joy, C 16	Tex.
100	*Joyce, E 10	La.
240	Joyce, P 14	Tex.
75	Joyce, F 4	Wash.
100	*Joyner, Q 18	Va.
26	*Joynes, C 5	N. C.
125	*Jozye, I 21	Tex.
39	*Juan, H 20	Ky.
88	Juanita, J 18	N. D.
400	Juanita, H 8	Wash.
202	Jud, O 18	N. D.
300	Juda, K 22	Wis.
212	Judith Gap, I 13	Mont.
12	*Judkin (Judkins), G 8	Tex.
30	*Judson (Helendale), N 18	Calif.
124	*Judson, J 8	Ind.
150	*Judson, P 13	Minn.
75	Judson, P 4	N. C.
250	Judson, N 10	N. D.
19	*Judson, O 10	W. Va.
1123	Judsonia, G 15	Ark.
200	Judyville, G 7	Ind.
1619	Julesburg, A 23	Colo.
200	*Julia (Union), K 4	Ga.
337	Juliaetta, G 4	Idaho
250	Julian, Q 20	Calif.
136	Julian, N 24	Neb.
215	Julian, E 10	N. C.
172	Julian, K 12	Pa.
42	*Julian, L 5	W. Va.
200	*Juliette, H 10	Ga.
43	*Juliff, L 21	Tex.
18	*Julip, J 18	Ky.
300	Juliustown, J 13	N. J.
85	*Jumbo, C 14	Ark.
27	Jumbo, N 20	Okla.
155	*Jumping Branch, P 9	W. Va.
75	Jump River, G 10	Wis.
....	Junction, A 7	Ark.
320	Junction, P 19	Ill.
75	Junction, E 7	Ohio
2086	Junction, J 14	Tex.
393	Junction, N 10	Utah
45	*Junction, E 20	W. Va.
814	Junction City, R 11	Ark.
94	*Junction City, D 4	Calif.
326	Junction City, J 7	Ga.
8507	Junction City, G 18	Kan.
694	Junction City, H 16	Ky.
355	Junction City, A 9	La.
813	Junction City. L 14	Ohio
1187	Junction City, I 5	Ore.
166	Junction City, K 3	Wash.
308	Junction City, J 13	Wis.
....	Junction Switch, H 21	Iowa
....	*June, see Ilfeld	N. M.
200	Juneau, K 7	Pa.
1301	Juneau, M 18	Wis.
595	*Junedale (Leviston), J 20	Pa.
50	Jungo, D 8	Nev.
338	Juniata, M 17	Neb.
....	Juniata, M 10	Pa.
500	*Juniata (Juniataville), P 5	Pa.
533	Junior, G 14	W. Va.
125	*Juniper, J 5	Ga.
3	Juniper Springs, C 6	Colo.
75	Junius, K 22	S. D.
20	Juno, D 4	Ore.
93	*Juno. K 11	Tex.
700	Juno (Caretta), R 5	W. Va.
10	*Junta, P 10	W. Va.
167	Juntura, K 21	Ore.
215	Jupiter, K 24	Fla.
150	*Just, N 8	N. C.
....	*Justell, H 22	Ky.
65	*Justice, O 3	W. Va.
200	*Justiceburg, D 11	Tex.
600	Justin, D 18	Tex.
120	*Justisville, K 24	Va.
322	Justus, G 17	Ohio
45	Justus, G 21	Pa.
77	*Jutland, F 10	N. J.

K

Pop.	Place, Index	State
....	Kaaterskill, Q 23	N. Y.
....	Kaaterskill Jc., Q 22	N. Y.
....	*Kables, J 10	Va.
63	*Kackley, E 14	Kan.
464	Kadoka, L 9	S. D.
163	Kahlotus, M 20	Wash.
100	*Kahns, K 14	La.
....	Kahoka, D 14	Ark.
1781	Kahoka, B 15	Mo.
175	*Kaiser, G 8	Wis.
76	*Kalaloch, H 3	Va.
1028	Kalama, O 6	Wash.
54097	Kalamazoo, Q 13	Mich.
300	Kaleva, K 12	Mich.
51	*Kalgary, C 11	Tex.
521	Kalida, F 7	Ohio
4	Kalinke, K 11	Wis.
17	*Kalish (Strickland), E 10	Wis.
8245	Kalispell, E 4	Mont.
1132	Kalkaska, J 15	Mich.
....	*Kalmia, M 9	N. C.
100	Kalo, G 10	Iowa
765	Kalona, L 20	Iowa
49	*Kalvesta, K 5	Kan.
....	Kam, see Red Dragon	W. Va.
683	Kamas, F 14	Utah
800	*Kamay, B 15	Tex.
27	Kamela, D 20	Ore.
568	Kamiah, H 6	Idaho
5	Kamilche, J 5	Wash.
67	Kampeska, G 22	S. D.
432	Kampsville, K 7	Ill.
288	Kamrar, G 12	Iowa
1365	Kanab, Q 8	Utah
64	*Kanaranzi, R 5	Minn.
309	Kanarraville, P 5	Utah
50	*Kanaskat, I 9	Wash.
250	Kanauga, P 15	Ohio
767	Kanawha, E 11	Iowa
275	Kanawha, B 22	Tex.
63	*Kanawha (Kanawha Sta.), F 7	W. Va.
200	*Kanawha Falls, L 8	W. Va.
40	*Kanawha Head, H 12	W. Va.
271	*Kandiyohi, M 9	Minn.
490	Kane, L 7	Ill.
6133	Kane, F 8	Pa.
30	Kane, B 11	Wyo.
....	Kane Jc., F 9	Pa.
190	Kaneville, C 17	Ill.
211	Kaneville, G 5	Pa.
239	Kangley, E 16	Ill.
....	Kangley Jc., I 9	Wash.
80	Kanima, J 22	Okla.
22241	Kankakee, E 21	Ill.
12661	Kannapolis, G 7	N. C.
100	*Kanona, D 6	Kan.
200	Kanona, P 10	N. Y.
868	Kanopolis, H 13	Kan.
322	Kanorado, F 2	Kan.
526	Kanosh, L 9	Utah
650	*Kansas, E 9	Ala.
875	Kansas, J 21	Ill.
350	Kansas, E 10	Ohio
163	Kansas, E 24	Okla.
121458	Kansas City, F 25	Kan.
399178	Kansas City, G 6	Mo.
....	Kansas City & Omaha Jc., O 20	Neb.
80	Kansasville, O 22	Wis.
300	*Kantner, P 8	Pa.
2838	Kaplan, N 10	La.
445	▲Kapowsin, K 8	Wash.
141	*Kappa, G 15	Ill.
40	Karbers Ridge, Q 19	Ill.
25	Karinen, B 2	S. D.
35	*Karlin, I 11	Mich.
15	*Karlin, N 9	Mo.
289	Karlsruhe, H 12	N. D.
501	Karlstad, C 3	Minn.
250	*Karnack, E 24	Tex.
....	Karnak, G 7	Calif.
893	Karnak, R 16	Ill.
40	Karnak, K 20	N. D.
1571	Karnes City, N 17	Tex.
5	Karns, H 9	Okla.
453	*Karns City, J 4	Pa.
4	*Kartar, D 16	Wash.
550	Karthaus, I 11	Pa.
70	Karval, J 19	Colo.
12	*Kary, M 11	S. D.
100	*Kasbeer, D 13	Ill.
500	*Kaska, K 20	Pa.
604	Kasota, P 13	Minn.
1230	Kasson, Q 18	Minn.
14	Kasson, F 10	Pa.
30	*Kasson, F 15	W. Va.
14	*Katahdin Iron Works, I 13	Me.
55	Kateland, H 9	La.
62	*Katemcy, I 15	Tex.
1200	Kathleen, H 15	Fla.
55	*Kathleen, J 11	Ga.
229	Kathryn, N 21	N. D.
25	*Kathryn, N 8	W. Va.
60	*Kathwood, K 9	S. C.
125	Kato, J 12	Pa.
1800	Katonah, E 6	N. Y.
26	*Kattskill Bay, J 22	N. Y.
450	Katy, K 21	Tex.
2654	Kaufman, E 20	Tex.
7382	Kaukauna, N 14	Wis.
809	Kaw (Kaw City), B 15	Okla.
100	*Kaweah, K 13	Calif.
250	Kawkawlin, L 19	Mich.
210	Kaycee, F 15	Wyo.
40	Kayenta, C 20	Ariz.
750	Kayford, M 7	W. Va.
30	*Kaylong (Maggie), H 4	W. Va.
200	Kaylor, J 5	Pa.
200	Kaylor, N 21	S. D.
700	Kay Moor, M 9	W. Va.
....	Kays, K 10	Ohio
1211	Kaysville, E 11	Utah
375	Keachie (Keatchie), D 4	La.
150	Keams Canyon, E 20	Ariz.
2904	Keansburg, G 19	N. J.
543	Kearney, F 6	Mo.
9643	Kearey, M 15	Neb.
319	Kearney, O 11	Pa.
25	Kearney, C 15	Wyo.
125	*Kearney Park, J 11	Calif.
500	Kearneysville, E 25	W. Va.
30	Kearns, Q 8	Colo.
39467	Kearny, E 18	N. J.
250	Kearsarge, I 18	N. H.
98	*Keasbey (Keasbeys), G 17	N. J.
50	*Keasey, B 6	Ore.
375	Keatchie (Keachie), D 4	La.
68	Keating, F 23	Ore.
75	Keating, I 12	Pa.
150	Keating Summit, F 11	Pa.
55	*Keaton, F 22	Ky.
97	*Keats, F 18	Kan.
10	*Keavy, J 19	Ky.
....	*Kebler, see Tioga	Colo.
120	*Kechi, L 16	Kan.
38	*Keck, H 20	Ky.
1900	Kecoughtan, P 21	Va.
150	Keddie, E 9	Calif.
75	*Kedron, M 13	Ark.
52	Kedron, O 10	Tenn.
28	Kedron, H 14	W. Va.
50	Keechelus, I 11	Wash.
40	*Keechi, G 21	Tex.
404	Keedysville, D 6	Md.
102	Keefeton, H 21	Okla.
800	Keegan, B 19	Me.
2000	*Keego Harbor, O 21	Mich.
300	Keeler, K 16	Calif.
150	*Keeler, Q 11	Mich.
49	Keeline, J 22	Wyo.
125	*Keeling, P 3	Tenn.
37	*Keeling, Q 9	Va.
....	Keenan, G 18	Minn.
150	Keenan, J 22	Tex.
50	*Keenan, P 12	W. Va.
164	*Keene, M 14	Calif.
500	Keene, F 17	Ky.
100	Keene, N 15	Neb.
13832	Keene, P 7	N. H.
600	Keene, F 23	N. Y.
20	Keene, H 5	N. D.
125	*Keene, J 16	Ohio
800	*Keene, F 18	Tex.
21	*Keene, L 12	Va.
100	*Keener, D 18	Ala.
19	*Keener, B 10	Ark.
245	Keenes, N 17	Ill.
284	Keenesburg, E 16	Colo.
511	*Keene Valley, F 22	N. Y.
50	Keeneyville, E 14	Pa.
250	*Keen Mountain, B 7	Va.
421	Keensburg, N 21	Ill.
321	Keep Tryst, B 4	Md.
1921	Keeseville, E 24	N. Y.
50	▲Keetley, F 14	Utah
....	Keetley Jc., F 14	Utah
150	*Keevil, I 17	Ark.
1942	Keewatin, G 17	Minn.
102	*Keewaydin, J 9	Pa.
150	Keezletown, I 11	Va.
150	*Keffers (Joliett), L 18	Pa.
160	*Kegg, O 9	Pa.
300	*Kegley, Q 8	W. Va.
62	*Kehoe, E 22	Ky.
800	*Keifertown (Kifertown), Q 4	Pa.
59	*Keighley, M 19	Kan.
75	*Keirn, G 11	Miss.
600	Keiser, E 22	Ark.
2000	*Keiser, J 16	Pa.
....	Keister Jc., P 4	Pa.
500	*Keisterville, P 4	Pa.
....	*Keith, J 21	Ky.
11	*Keith, L 18	Va.
50	*Keith, M 5	W. Va.
1130	Keithsburg, E 6	Ill.
115	Keithville, C 4	La.
1527	Kelayres. K 20	Pa.

Pop.	Place	Index	State
30	Keldron	B 8	S. D.
456	Kelford	D 19	N. C.
....	Kelim	D 15	Colo.
216	Kell	N 16	Ill.
12	*Kellacey	F 21	Ky.
3	Keller	P 13	Okla.
400	*Keller	D 18	Tex.
530	Keller	L 23	Va.
100	Keller	F 19	Wash.
200	Kellerman	G 10	Ala.
83	*Kellers Church	M 23	Pa.
563	Kellerton	P 10	Iowa
60	*Kellerville	I 6	Ill.
....	*Kellerville	C 6	Tex.
839	Kellettville	G 7	Pa.
159	Kelley	J 12	Iowa
564	Kelleys Island	C 13	Ohio
357	Kelliher	E 11	Minn.
250	Kellnersville	P 15	Wis.
4235	*Kellogg (Kellogg-Wardner)		Idaho
12	Kellogg	O 10	Ill.
648	Kellogg	K 15	Iowa
403	Kellogg	P 21	Minn.
....	Kellogg	N 5	N. Y.
4235	Kellogg-Wardner (Kellogg)	D 6	Idaho
125	*Kelly	G 11	Ga.
80	Kelly	D 21	Kan.
227	Kelly	J 9	Ky.
250	*Kelly	E 10	La.
100	Kelly	J 8	N. M.
60	*Kelly	L 15	N. C.
28	Kellys	H 23	N. D.
150	*Kelly (Kelly Station)	L 5	Pa.
8	Kelly	G 4	Wyo.
80	*Kelly Corners	A 2, Q 20	N. Y.
....	*Kelly Field	L 16	Tex.
350	Kelly Lake	G 17	Minn.
27	*Kellys (Princetown)	N 22	N. Y.
53	Kelly	K 12	Wis.
300	*Kellysville	Q 9	W. Va.
168	Kellyton	H 17	Ala.
647	Kellyville	G 17	Okla.
33	*Kelsa	B 7	Va.
150	*Kelsey	G 10	Calif.
50	*Kelsey	G 19	Minn.
75	*Kelsey	R 17	N. Y.
....	Kelsey City, see Lake Park		Fla.
200	Kelseyville	G 4	Calif.
134	Kelso	N 17	Ark.
79	*Kelso	N 18	Calif.
150	Kelso (Dover)	L 22	Ind.
64	*Kelso (Downing)	H 19	Kan.
....	Kelso	I 7	Miss.
223	*Kelso	P 23	Mo.
28	Kelso	K 24	N. D.
....	Kelso	B 22	Okla.
50	Kelso	D 9	Ore.
95	*Kelso	Q 12	Tenn.
6749	Kelso	O 6	Wash.
30	Kelso Jc.	F 4	Mich.
1369	▲*Keltner	J 14	Ky.
7	*Keltner	P 11	Mo.
30	Kelton	Q 22	Ariz.
75	*Kelton	Q 20	Pa.
62	*Kelton	C 10	S. C.
43	Kelton	B 6	Utah
399	Keltys	H 23	Tex.
125	Kelvin	L 17	Ariz.
5	Kelvin	D 14	N. D.
250	Kemah	L 23	Tex.
200	*Kemblesville	Q 21	Pa.
2026	Kemmerer	N 4	Wyo.
100	*Kemp	J 19	Ill.
35	*Kemp	J 15	Ky.
204	Kemp	R 17	Okla.
145	*Kemp City (Hendrix)		Okla.
1000	Kemp	E 20	Tex.
105	*Kemper	K 10	Ill.
40	*Kemper (Bennetts)	H 11	W. Va.
200	*Kempner	I 17	Tex.
52	*Kempster	L 10	Wis.
100	Kempsville	P 22	Va.
259	Kempton	F 19	Ill.
403	Kempton	H 14	Ind.
65	Kempton	I 22	N. D.
110	*Kempton	L 20	Pa.
350	Kempton	F 16	W. Va.
350	*Kenansville	I 20	Fla.
571	Kenansville	J 16	N. C.
50	Kenaston	E 7	N. D.
155	*Kenberma	G 21	Mass.
847	Kenbridge	P 14	Va.
100	*Kendaia	N 12	N. Y.
228	*Kendal (Kendall)	O 22	Fla.
560	Kendal Green	F 18	Mass.
47	*Kendalia	K 16	Tex.
150	*Kendall	L 2	Kan.
....	Kendall	M 2	Md.
248	Kendall	Q 12	Mich.
263	Kendall	K 8	N. Y.
100	*Kendall	D 8	Ore.
289	Kendall	B 9	Wash.
478	Kendall (Kendalls)	H 17	Wis.
63	*Kendall Grove	M 23	Va.
5431	Kendallville	C 19	Ind.
68	*Kendleton	L 21	Tex.
19	Kendrick	J 18	Colo.
500	*Kendrick	E 15	Fla.
407	Kendrick	G 4	Idaho
125	*Kendrick	A 22	Miss.
256	Kendrick	G 15	Okla.
200	Kenduskeag	K 14	Me.
2891	Kenedy	N 17	Tex.
227	Kenefick (Kenefic)	P 17	Okla.
50	Kenel	B 12	S. D.
551	Kenesaw	M 16	Neb.
2935	Kenilworth	B 21	Ill.
2451	Kenilworth	F 17	N. J.
....	Kenilworth	E 12	Mont.
325	Kenilworth	I 17	Utah
....	Kenilworth Jc.	I 16	Utah
1095	Kenly	F 15	N. C.
1528	Kenmare	E 7	N. D.
18612	Kenmore	M 5	N. Y.
....	Kenmore	F 17	Ohio
250	Kenmore	H 8	Wash.
105	▲Kenna	J 22	N. M.
160	*Kenna	I 6	W. Va.
256	Kennan	G 9	Wis.
522	Kennard	I 18	Ind.
315	Kennard	J 23	Neb.
80	*Kennard	G 2	Pa.
610	Kennard	H 22	Tex.
....	*Kennard	K 20	Va.
25	Kennebago (Grants)	J 3	Me.
15	*Kennebago Lake	J 4	Me.
....	Kennebec	M 9	Me.
390	Kennebec	K 14	S. D.
2200	Kennebunk	Q 4	Me.
....	*Kennebunk Beach	Q 5	Me.
750	Kennebunk Port	Q 5	Me.
700	*Kennedale	E 18	Tex.
367	Kennedy	F 6	Ala.
338	Kennedy	C 2	Minn.
12	Kennedy	F 10	Neb.
....	Kennedy	F 14	N. M.
485	Kennedy	Q 3	N. Y.
91	*Kennedy	G 8	Wis.
160	Kennedyville	E 19	Md.
2375	Kenner	N 18	La.
100	*Kennerdell	H 4	Pa.
....	Kenner Jc.	N 18	La.
436	Kennesaw	E 5	Ga.
75	Kenneth (Mastin)	H 25	Kan.
148	*Kenneth	Q 5	Minn.
124	Kennett (Kennet)	D 6	Calif.
6335	Kennett	J 23	Mo.
3375	Kennett Square	Q 21	Pa.
1918	Kennewick	O 18	Wash.
483	Kenney	I 14	Ill.
160	*Kenney	K 20	Tex.
400	Kennydale	I 8	Wash.
175	*Keno	J 17	Ky.
150	Keno	R 9	Ore.
129	*Kenoma	N 7	Mo.
48765	Kenosha	P 22	Wis.
3902	Kenova	K 1	W. Va.
119	*Kenoza Lake	D 1	N. Y.
356	Kensal	K 18	N. D.
889	Kensett	G 15	Ark.
392	Kensett	B 13	Iowa
....	*Kensico, see Valhalla		N. Y.
2443	Kensington	H 12	Conn.
25	*Kensington	B 2	Ga.
....	Kensington	C 21	Ill.
597	Kensington	D 11	Kan.
931	Kensignton	H 10	Md.
337	Kensington	K 6	Minn.
200	Kensington	P 19	N. H.
933	*Kensington	H 7	N. Y.
450	Kensington	G 19	Ohio
1245	▲Kent	F 3	Conn.
400	Kent	B 11	Ill.
100	*Kent	N 18	Ind.
138	*Kent	O 9	Iowa
146	*Kent	I 3	Minn.
58	*Kent (Brice)	K 7	N. Y.
8581	Kent	E 18	Ohio
94	Kent	E 13	Ore.
172	Kent	P 6	Pa.
50	*Kent	H 5	Tex.
2586	Kent	I 8	Wash.
....	Kent	M 11	Wis.
440	Kent City	N 11	Mich.
55	*Kent Cliffs	E 6	N. Y.
1000	*Kentfield	B 15, H 5	Calif.
1608	Kentland	F 6	Ind.
....	Kentmere Jc.	A 22	Del.
233	Kenton	F 21	Del.
100	*Kenton	C 17	Ky.
400	Kenton	C 6	Mich.
35	*Kenton (Linden)	P 10	Mo.
7593	Kenton	H 10	Ohio
250	Kenton	Q 1	Okla.
809	Kenton	M 4	Tenn.
90	*Kents Hill	M 7	Me.
19	*Kents Store	J 15	La.
60	*Kents Store	K 14	Va.
30	*Kentuck	J 6	W. Va.
....	Kentucky House	H 8	Calif.
1854	Kentwood	J 17	La.
1000	Kenvil	D 14	N. J.
2500	Kenvir	J 21	Ky.
150	*Kenwood	H 5	Calif.
....	Kenwood	M 14	Colo.
5	Kenwood	E 15	Fla.
133	*Kenwood	G 7	Ga.
30	*Kenwood	F 22	Ky.
150	Kenwood	I 19	Ohio
100	*Kenwood	D 23	Okla.
....	Kenwood Park	I 20	Iowa
1530	Kenyon	P 17	Minn.
250	Kenyon (Kenyons)	L 9	R. I.
267	Keo	J 14	Ark.
250	Keokee	D 4	Va.
15076	Keokuk	R 21	Iowa
30	Keokuk Falls	I 15	Okla.
1040	Keosauqua	P 19	Iowa
34	Keota	C 18	Colo.
1032	Keota	M 19	Iowa
25	Keota	E 12	Mo.
525	Keota	J 23	Okla.
200	Kerby	Q 4	Ore.
51	*Kerbyknob	H 18	Ky.
1287	Kerens	F 20	Tex.
80	*Kerens	G 15	W. Va.
560	*Kerhonkson	C 4	N. Y.
607	Kerkhoven	M 8	Minn.
250	Kerman	J 10	Calif.
23	Kermit	D 4	N. D.
2584	Kermit	G 7	Tex.
150	*Kermit (Cassard)	E 5	Va.
811	Kermit	N 2	W. Va.
62	*Kernan	E 17	Ill.
50	*Kernan	L 6	La.
2103	Kernersville	D 8	N. C.
25	*Kernie	G 21	Ky.
75	*Kerns	N 4	Va.
135	*Kernstown	E 14	Va.
175	*Kernville	L 14	Calif.
300	*Kernville	F 4	Ore.
100	Kerr (Kerrs)	I 13	Ark.
150	Kerr	F 17	Minn.
25	*Kerr	J 15	N. C.
100	*Kerrick	J 19	Minn.
50	Kerrick	A 2	Tex.
61	Kerriston	I 9	Wash.
140	Kerrmoor	K 9	Pa.
160	*Kerrs (Kerr)	P 15	Ohio
650	*Kerrtown	F 3	Pa.
225	Kerrville	P 2	Tenn.
5572	Kerrville	K 15	Tex.
82	Kerry	A 6	Ore.
268	Kersey	D 16	Colo.
80	Kersey	D 8	Ind.
700	Kersey	H 9	Pa.
1264	Kershaw	D 15	S. C.
500	*Keshena	N 12	Wis.
39	*Keslers Cross Lanes	L 9	W. Va.
123	*Kesley	F 15	Iowa
40	*Kessel	G 19	W. Va.
30	*Kessinger	I 13	Ky.
....	*Kessler	M 12	W. Va.
20	*Kester	I 18	W. Va.
....	*Kestler, see Damsacus		Ga.
307	Keswick	L 17	Iowa
63	*Keswick	K 12	Va.
220	Ketchum	N 12	Idaho
611	Ketchum	C 22	Okla.
600	Ketona	F 13	Ala.
560	*Ketron	K 8	Wash.
49	*Ketterman	F 18	W. Va.
40	*Kettle	K 15	Ky.
66	*Kettle	J 7	W. Va.
414	Kettle Falls	D 21	Wash.
800	Kettle Island	J 20	Ky.
....	Kettle Point	R 25	R. I.
221	Kettle River	I 17	Minn.
131	*Kettlersville	I 7	Ohio
17	*Keuka	Q 11	N. Y.
45	*Keuka Park (Keuka)	O 11	N. Y.
68	Keuterville	H 5	Idaho
209	Kevil	I 4	Ky.
360	Kevin	C 9	Mont.
....	*Kewa	E 21	Wash.
150	Kewadin	L 23	Mich.
16901	Kewanee	E 10	Ill.
150	*Kewanee	J 20	Miss.
28	*Kewanee	Q 22	Mo.
701	Kewanna	D 13	Ind.
880	Kewaskum	N 18	Wis.
2533	Kewaunee	Q 14	Wis.
100	Keweenaw Bay	D 3	Mich.
37	*Key	G 20	Ky.
8	*Keyapaha	O 13	S. D.
150	Keyes	I 8	Calif.
227	Keyes	Q 3	Okla.
547	*Keyesport	M 14	Ill.
50	*Key Largo	P 23	Fla.
210	Keymar	C 10	Md.
5147	Keyport	G 19	N. J.
190	Keyport	H 7	Wash.
37	*Keyrock	P 7	W. Va.
6177	Keyser	D 19	W. Va.
20	Keysor	I 18	Colo.
200	*Keystone	G 13	Ala.
9	Keystone	G 12	Colo.
250	Keystone	F 20	Ind.
466	Keystone	I 18	Iowa
125	Keystone	K 8	Neb.
406	Keystone	E 17	Okla.
250	Keystone	K 3	S. D.
....	Keystone	J 21	Wash.
2942	Keystone	Q 8	W. Va.
145	*Keystone Heights	D 15	Fla.
385	*Keysville	I 15	Fla.
363	*Keysville	H 19	Ga.
49	*Keysville	L 16	Mo.
607	Keysville	P 13	Va.
854	Keytesville	F 11	Mo.
12927	Key West	R 16	Fla.
22	Keywest	E 2	Minn.
883	Kezar Falls	O 2	Me.
100	*Kiahsville	L 1	W. Va.
150	*Kiamesha Lake	D 2	N. Y.
100	Kiamichi	M 22	Okla.
50	*Kibbee (Kibbee-Tiger)	K 17	Ga.
138	*Kibbie	Q 12	Mich.
50	*Kiblah	R 6	Ark.
124	*Kibler	R 5	Va.
510	Kickapoo	I 23	Tex.
8	Kidd	N 15	Mich.
37	*Kidder	J 17	Ky.
270	Kidder	D 7	Mo.
190	Kidder	B 21	S. D.
15	Kidders	M 14	Me.
33	*Kidds Crossing	J 17	Ky.
26	*Kidds Fork	K 17	Va.
25	*Kidds Store	I 16	Ky.
150	*Kidron	G 15	Ohio
....	Kidville	O 21	N. D.
159	Kief	I 12	N. D.
330	Kiefer	F 18	Okla.
51	*Kieffer	N 11	W. Va.
1898	Kiel	O 16	Wis.
8	*Kiene	H 19	Iowa
34	*Kienstra	N 4	Miss.
30	Kiersey	Q 16	Okla.
407	*Kiester	R 13	Minn.
800	*Kifertown (Keifertown)	Q 4	Pa.
70	Kila	E 3	Mont.
....	Kilarm Jc.	D 13	W. Va.
40	*Kilbourn (Kilbourne)	P 19	Iowa
....	Kilbourn, see Wisconsin Dells		Wis.
360	Kilbourne	H 10	Ill.
164	*Kilbourne	A 13	La.
219	Kilbourne	I 12	Ohio
....	*Kilbuck	L 3	Pa.
....	Kilby	Q 20	Va.
50	Kildare	J 23	Ga.
65	*Kildare	F 20	N. Y.
137	Kildare	B 14	Okla.
261	Kildare	D 24	Tex.
419	Kildav	J 21	Ky.
15	*Kile (Kileville)	J 11	Ohio
116	Kilgore	L 20	Idaho
173	Kilgore	D 10	Neb.
112	Kilgore	I 19	Ohio
6708	Kilgore	E 23	Tex.
214	Kilkenny	P 15	Minn.
700	Killarney	P 7	W. Va.
200	Killawog	P 15	N. Y.
250	Kill Buck	Q 5	N. Y.
716	Killbuck	H 16	Ohio
650	Killdeer	K 5	N. D.
....	*Kill Devil Hills	F 24	N. C.
90	*Killduff	L 15	Iowa
1263	Killeen	H 17	Tex.
210	Killen	A 9	Ala.
22	*Killian	L 17	La.
700	Killingly, (Dayville)	D 24	Conn.
87	*Killona	N 17	La.
614	Kilmarnock	L 21	Va.
556	Kilmichael	F 15	Miss.
350	Kiln	R 16	Miss.
200	*Kilsyth	N 8	W. Va.
18	*Kilts	G 13	Ore.
200	*Kim	P 20	Colo.
50	Kimama	P 13	Idaho
100	Kimball (Kimbal)	M 23	Kan.
45	Kimball	R 15	Ark.
505	Kimball	M 12	Minn.
1725	Kimball	K 2	Neb.
100	Kimball	D 13	Ohio
997	Kimball	L 17	S. D.
105	*Kimball (Willoughby)	D 17	Vt.
23	*Kimball (Elgin)	G 13	Va.
1580	Kimball	Q 6	W. Va.
48	Kimball	H 5	Wis.
349	Kimballton	K 6	Iowa
44	*Kimballton	N 4	Va.
....	*Kimberling	O 2	Va.
250	*Kimberlin Heights	N 20	Tenn.
800	Kimberly	E 13	Ala.
963	Kimberly	Q 11	Idaho
25	Kimberly	I 15	Minn.
200	Kimberly	H 20	Nev.
45	*Kimberly	H 18	Ore.
600	*Kimberly	L 7	W. Va.
2618	Kimberly	N 15	Wis.
300	Kimberton	O 21	Pa.
25	*Kimble	N 15	Mo.
95	*Kimble (Kimbles)	G 23	Pa.
214	Kimbolton	J 17	Ohio
41	*Kimbrell	G 19	Ky.
90	Kimbrough	K 8	Ala.
350	Kimbrough	L 4	Ga.
87	*Kimesville	E 10	N. C.
300	Kimmell	C 17	Ind.
216	Kimmelton	P 8	Pa.
200	Kimmins	O 9	Tenn.
172	*Kimmswick	J 20	Mo.
32	*Kimper	H 24	Ky.
25	Kinard	Q 12	Ark.
500	*Kinard	C 1, N 12	Fla.
234	Kinards	E 10	S. C.
107	*Kinbrae	Q 7	Minn.
1749	Kincaid	J 13	Ill.
401	Kincaid	K 23	Kan.
321	Kincaid	M 7	W. Va.
54	*Kincheloe (Mineral)	F 12	W. Va.
503	Kinde	K 23	Mich.
1415	Kinder	L 8	La.
336	Kinderhook	J 5	Ill.
745	Kinderhook	P 24	N. Y.
85	Kinderhook	R 16	Mich.
20	*Kinderpost	N 14	Mo.
450	Kindred	N 24	N. D.
50	*Kindrick	E 10, R 1	Va.
350	Kineo (Rockwood)	H 9	Me.
12	Kineo	H 9	Me.
90	*Kings (King)	L 4	Ark.
30	*King	J 19	Ky.
550	King	C 8	N. C.
7	*King	H 17	Tex.
30	King and Queen C. H.	L 19	Va.
1768	King City	K 8	Calif.
1103	King City	C 6	Mo.
600	King Ferry	N 13	N. Y.
1000	Kingfield	K 7	Me.
3352	Kingfisher	G 11	Okla.
150	King George	I 18	Va.
150	King Hill	P 9	Idaho
2200	Kingman	G 5	Ariz.
549	Kingman	I 8	Ind.
3213	Kingman	M 14	Kan.
350	Kingman	H 17	Me.
....	Kingman	M 9	Ohio
11	*King Mills	B 16	Ark.
858	*Kingmine (Hiawatha)	J 16	Utah
150	*Kingmount	D 13	W. Va.
129	*King of Prussia	N 22	Pa.
130	Kings	B 15	Ill.
1504	Kingsburg	K 12	Calif.
50	Kingsburg	O 21	S. D.
250	Kingsbury	B 11	Ind.
45	*Kingsbury, (Mayfield)	J 10	Me.
300	Kingsbury	L 17	Tex.
....	*Kings Canyon National Park (General Grant National Park)	L 13	Calif.
21	*Kings Creek	J 22	Ky.
12	Kings Creek	P 21	Md.
36	Kings Creek	E 4	N. C.
247	Kings Creek	J 8	Ohio
100	*Kings Creek	A 11	S. C.
50	*Kingsdale	J 18	Minn.
114	*Kingsdale	Q 16	Pa.
150	*Kingsdown	M 8	Kan.
50	Kings Ferry	A 16	Fla.
5771	Kingsford	G 5	Mich.
328	Kingsland	N 12	Ark.
619	Kingsland	P 21	Ga.
80	Kingsland	E 20	Ind.
150	Kingsland	I 16	Tex.
1145	Kingsley	F 3	Iowa
385	Kingsley	J 14	Mich.
210	*Kingsley	F 21	Pa.
300	*Kings Mill	C 5	Tex.
800	Kings Mills	N 7	Ohio
400	Kings Mountain	I 17	Ky.
6547	Kings Mountain	H 3	N. C.
2500	Kings Park	G 8	N. Y.
1247	*Kings Point	H 7	N. Y.
14404	Kingsport	L 23	Tenn.
166	Kingston	C 8	Ark.
....	Kingston	E 19	Fla.
653	Kingston	D 4	Ga.
200	Kingston	D 5	Idaho
259	Kingston	B 16	Ill.
90	*Kingston	O 22	Iowa
300	Kingston	D 5	La.
120	*Kingston	P 22	Md.
....	Kingston	I 22	Mass.
314	Kingston	M 22	Mich.
394	Kingston	E 7	Mo.
750	Kingston	P 18	N. H.
313	Kingston	H 14	N. J.
28	Kingston	M 6	N. M.
28589	Kingston	R 22	N. Y.
864	Kingston	M 12	Ohio
481	Kingston	Q 15	Okla.
1	Kingston	G 7	Ore.
20679	Kingston	H 20	Pa.
1000	Kingston	L 12	R. I.
1000	Kingston (West Kingston)	L 11	R. I.
880	Kingston	N 17	Tenn.
150	Kingston	D 20	Tex.
63	Kingston	N 10	Utah
175	Kingston	G 7	Wash.
1500	Kingston	N 7	W. Va.
295	Kingston	L 17	Wis.
390	Kingston Mines	G 11	Ill.
150	*Kingston Springs	M 10	Tenn.
3182	Kingstree	I 18	S. C.
10	Kings Valley	Q 6	Mo.
129	Kings Valley	G 5	Ore.
50	Kingsville	D 15	Md.
212	Kingsville	H 7	Mo.
834	Kingsville (N. Kingsville)	B 20	Ohio
750	*Kingsville	B 20	Ohio
7782	Kingsville	Q 18	Tex.
161	Kingswood	G 12	Ky.
100	Kingville	H 14	S. C.
100	King William	L 18	Va.
18	Kingwood	O 10	Ga.
35	Kingwood	G 9	N. J.
1676	Kingwood	D 16	W. Va.
2577	Kinloch Park (Berkeley)	H 20	Mo.
....	Kinlock	Q 15	Okla.
1015	Kinmundy	M 16	Ill.
745	*Kinnelon	D 14	N. J.
462	Kinney	F 18	Minn.
2	Kinney	O 22	Neb.
....	Kinney	N 10	Va.
42	*Kinniconick (Summer P. O.)	D 21	Ky.
....	Kinnickinnick	N 12	Ohio
150	*Kino	K 19	Va.
50	Kinport	L 8	Pa.
109	*Kinross	L 19	Iowa
55	Kinross	C 19	Mich.
200	Kinsale	K 20	Va.
75	*Kinsey	L 20	Mo.
18	Kinsey	I 22	Mont.
2178	Kinsley	L 9	Kan.
164	Kinsman	E 17	Ill.
100	*Kinsman (Farmdale)	D 21	Ohio
600	Kinsman	D 21	Ohio
343	Kinston	O 16	Ala.
15388	Kinston	H 18	N. C.
221	Kinta	K 22	Okla.
150	*Kintnersville	M 23	Pa.
210	*Kinton	G 19	Ark.
146	Kintyre (Campbell)	O 14	N. D.
228	*Kinzer (Kinzers)	P 20	Pa.
600	Kinzua	F 15	Ore.
460	Kinzua	E 7	Pa.
40	Kiomatia	B 22	Tex.
50	Kiona	N 17	Wash.
195	Kiowa	H 16	Colo.
1379	Kiowa	O 12	Kan.
802	Kiowa	M 19	Okla.
400	*Kipling	G 8	Mich.
30	Kipling	I 20	Miss.
75	*Kipling	G 13	N. C.
304	Kipling	K 17	Ohio
100	*Kipp	H 16	Kan.
40	Kippen	C 10	Mont.
275	Kipton	E 14	Ohio
100	Kiptopeke	O 23	Va.
300	*Kirby	L 7	Ark.
5	Kirby	N 19	Mont.
137	*Kirby	G 10	Ohio
48	*Kirby (Newtown)	Q 3	Pa.
15	*Kirby	F 20	W. Va.
107	Kirby	F 11	Wyo.
99	*Kirbyville	R 10	Mo.
1088	Kirbyville	I 25	Tex.
150	Kire	M 4	Va.
100	Kirk	G 22	Colo.
56	*Kirk	G 12	Ky.
....	Kirk	I 2	Neb.
42	Kirk	O 10	Ore.
9	*Kirk	N 3	W. Va.
264	Kirkersville	K 13	Ohio
100	Kirkland	I 10	Ariz.
250	*Kirkland	N 14	Ga.
570	Kirkland	B 16	Ill.
250	*Kirkland	M 17	N. Y.
500	Kirkland	A 13	Tex.
2084	Kirkland	H 8	Wash.
712	Kirklin	H 13	Ind.
1500	*Kirklyn	P 23	Pa.
185	Kirkman	K 5	Iowa
197	*Kirkmansville	J 10	Ky.
44	Kirkpatrick	H 10	Ind.
150	Kirksey	K 6	Ky.
40	Kirksey	G 8	S. C.
61	Kirksville	J 16	Ill.
100	Kirksville	G 18	Ky.
10080	Kirksville	C 12	Mo.
241	Kirkville	N 16	Iowa
75	Kirkville	B 21	Miss.
300	Kirkville	L 15	N. Y.
12	*Kirkwood	E 6	Calif.
200	*Kirkwood	C 21	Del.
....	Kirkwood	F 7	Ga.
746	Kirkwood	F 7	Ill.
12132	Kirkwood	I 20	Mo.
550	Kirkwood	L 10	N. J.
200	Kirkwood	R 16	N. Y.
79	Kirkwood	Q 19	Pa.
62	*Kirkwood	K 10	W. Va.
37	Kirley	H 10	S. D.
260	Kiron	H 5	Iowa
72	Kirtland	C 4	N. M.
206	*Kirtland	C 18	Ohio
50	*Kirtley	K 19	Tex.
50	*Kirtley	I 23	Wyo.
231	Kirven (Kirvin)	G 20	Tex.
392	Kirwin	E 10	Kan.
23	*Kisatchie	H 7	La.
301	*Kis-Lyn	I 20	Pa.
....	Kismet	J 11	Calif.
227	*Kismet	N 4	Kan.
70	Kissee Mills	Q 11	Mo.
3225	Kissimmee	H 18	Fla.
135	*Kissimmee Park	H 18	Fla.
494	*Kistler	L 13	Pa.
750	Kistler	O 4	W. Va.
325	Kit Carson	J 22	Colo.
100	*Kitchiwan	F 6	N. Y.
60	*Kitchel (Kitchell)	J 22	Ind.
472	Kite	J 17	Ga.
50	*Kite	I 22	Ky.
100	*Kitsap	H 6	Wash.
7550	Kittanning	K 5	Pa.
35	Kittanning Point	M 10	Pa.
4800	Kittery (Kittery Navy Yard)	R 3	Me.
....	Kittery Jct.	R 3	Me.
1000	Kittery Point	R 3	Me.
501	Kittitas	K 14	Wash.
350	*Kittredge	G 14	Colo.
....	Kittredge	B 12	Ill.
184	Kittrell	D 15	N. C.
500	Kitts	J 21	Ky.
62	*Kitts Hill	R 14	Ohio
9	Kittson	F 3	Minn.
250	Kitty Hawk	D 25	N. C.
870	Kitzmiller	O 3	Md.
....	Kitzville	F 18	Minn.
92	*Kiz	I 18	Utah
25	*Kizer (Kiser)	O 19	Tenn.
21	*Klaber	M 8	Wash.
150	Klamath Agency	P 9	Ore.
16497	Klamath Falls	Q 9	Ore.
115	*Kleberg	E 20	Tex.
1450	Kleenburn (Carneyville)	B 14	Wyo.
217	Kleenkoal (Dabney)	O 4	W. Va.
850	Klein (Gibtown)	J 16	Mont.
250	*Kleinfeltersville	M 18	Pa.
528	Klemme	D 12	Iowa
30	*Klevenville	J 20	Wis.
830	Klickitat	P 12	Wash.
56	Kline	P 5	Colo.
282	Kline	L 11	S. C.
8	*Kline	I 8	W. Va.
25	*Klinger Lake (Klingers)	R 14	Mich.
100	*Klingerstown	L 19	Pa.
11	Klockman	A 4	Idaho
....	Klondike	N 21	Calif.
100	*Klondike	I 18	Mo.
6	*Klondike	Q 6	Mo.
36	Klondike	C 14	Ore.
100	*Klondike	L 21	Tenn.
500	Klondike	C 21	Tex.
19	Klondike	M 20	Ariz.
....	Klondike	H 21	Ohio
62	*Klossner	P 12	Minn.
160	Kloten	I 20	N. D.
300	*Klotzville	N 15	La.
6	Kloze	N 18	N. D.
102	Knapps (North Stockholm)	D 19	N. Y.
21	*Knapp	E 11	Tex.
....	Knapp	P 6	Wash.
28	Knapp	H 10	W. Va.
436	Knapp	C 12	Wis.
74	Knappa	A 5	Ore.
207	*Knapp Creek	P 5	N. Y.
39	Knappton	N 3	Wash.
15	Kneece (Baxter)	H 11	S. C.
215	Knickerbocker	H 12	Tex.
159	*Knierim	H 8	Iowa
350	Knife River	H 22	Minn.
300	Knifley	I 15	Ky.
60	*Knight	K 7	Ky.
23	*Knight	I 6	La.
68	*Knight	I 23	Tex.
352	*Knightdale	F 14	N. C.
50	*Knights	H 15	Fla.
....	Knights	I 13	Me.
80	*Knights Ferry	I 10	Calif.
600	Knights Landing (Grafton)	G 7	Calif.
2323	Knightstown	J 18	Ind.
677	Knightsville	K 9	Ind.
35	*Kniman	D 8	Ind.
200	*Knippa	M 14	Tex.
42	Knob	D 4	Calif.
110	*Knob Creek	C 14	Ark.
486	Knobel	B 19	Ark.
75	*Knob Fork	C 11	W. Va.
87	*Knob Lick	I 14	Ky.
250	Knob Lick	M 20	Mo.
640	Knobnoster (Knob Noster)	H 9	Mo.
7	Knobs	K 25	Mont.
125	*Knobs	O 11	W. Va.
106	*Knobsville	P 11	Pa.
....	*Knobview, see Rosati		Mo.
50	*Knoke	G 8	Iowa
90	*Knott	E 10	Tex.
279	Knotts Island	B 24	N. C.
178	Knottsville	G 11	Ky.
75	*Knottville	D 5	N. C.
75	Knowles	J 11	Calif.
30	Knowles	M 25	N. M.
105	Knowles	Q 8	Okla.
87	*Knowles	N 18	Wis.
....	Knowles Jc.	J 11	Calif.
250	*Knowlesville	L 7	N. Y.
258	Knowlton	M 18	Ark.
100	Knowlton	O 9	Iowa
40	*Knowlton	G 19	Ky.
102	Knowlton	J 23	Mont.
150	*Knowlton	J 13	Wis.
2165	Knox	C 12	Ind.
22	Knox	L 12	Me.
419	Knox (Knox City)	C 14	Mo.
144	Knox	N 22	N. Y.
189	Knox	G 15	N. D.
....	Knox	I 13	Ohio
1098	Knox (Edenburg)	I 5	Pa.
270	*Knoxboro	M 17	N. Y.
1127	Knox City	C 13	Tex.
315	Knox Dale	J 7	Pa.
38	*Knoxfork	J 19	Ky.
80	Knoxo	O 12	Miss.
350	*Knoxville	H 7	Ala.
400	Knoxville	F 8	Ark.
100	Knoxville	I 9	Ga.
2241	Knoxville	F 10	Ill.
6936	Knoxville	M 14	Iowa
335	Knoxville	E 6	Md.
110	*Knoxville	O 6	Miss.
31	Knoxville	E 17	Neb.
664	Knoxville	D 14	Pa.
111580	Knoxville	N 19	Tenn.
....	Knoxville Jc.	F 8	Ark.
....	Koch	J 13	Miss.
900	Koch	J 20	Mo.
78	*Koch Ridge	E 11	Ark.
13	*Kodak	I 22	Ky.
20	*Kodak	N 20	Tenn.
125	*Kodol	C 11	W. Va.
25	Koehler	C 18	N. M.
....	Koehler Jc.	C 19	N. M.
265	Koeltztown	J 14	Mo.
98	*Koenton	M 4	Ala.
54	Koepenick	K 10	Wis.
1789	*Kohler	P 17	Wis.
50	Kohler	O 18	Wis.
30	*Kohls Ranch	K 18	Ariz.
4	Kohr	J 7	Mont.
18	*Kokadjo	H 11	Me.
101	Kokomo	H 11	Colo.
33795	Kokomo	G 13	Ind.
100	*Kokomo	O 12	Miss.
100	*Koleen	M 8	Ind.
250	Kolin	H 10	La.
50	Kolin	H 13	Mont.
50	Kollock (Kollocks)	C 19	S. C.
25	Komalty	K 6	Okla.
34	*Kona (Mater)	J 22	Ky.
50	*Kona	M 9	N. C.
2205	Konawa	L 15	Okla.
15	Kongsberg	I 11	N. D.
500	Konnarock	E 9	Va.
....	Koontz	M 4	Md.
375	Koosharem	M 11	Utah
490	Kooskia	H 7	Idaho
214	Kootenai	B 4	Idaho
1064	Koppel	K 2	Pa.
350	*Kopperl	F 18	Tex.
....	*Kopperstown	P 6	W. Va.
350	Korbel	C 2	Calif.
17	*Korea	H 14	Va.
40	Kornman	L 22	Colo.
100	*Korona	E 19	Fla.
4291	Kosciusko	H 15	Miss.
282	Koshkonong	R 15	Mo.
5	*Koshopah	G 12	Neb.
18	*Kosmos	M 8	Wash.
67	*Kosmosdale	F 13	Ky.
61	Kosoma	O 20	Okla.
881	Kosse	H 20	Tex.
238	Kossuth	A 20	Miss.
275	*Kossuth	H 5	Pa.
110	*Kost	L 17	Minn.
1000	Kountze	J 24	Tex.
732	Kouts	C 8	Ind.
....	Kowanda	K 5	Neb.
110	*Kraemer	N 16	La.
50	*Kragnes	H 2	Minn.
40	*Krakow	J 17	Mo.
146	*Krakow	O 13	Wis.
....	Kramer	M 17	Calif.
500	Kramer	G 7	Ind.
60	Kramer	M 21	Neb.
220	Kramer	E 12	N. D.
140	Kranzburg	G 23	S. D.
....	Krause	N 9	Ill.
211	*Krayn	N 8	Pa.
200	*Kreamer	K 16	Pa.
1436	Krebs	L 19	Okla.
....	Krebs, see Coalfield		W. Va.
110	Kregar	O 6	Pa.
40	Krem	K 9	N. D.
52	Kremis	H 2	Pa.
85	Kremlin	C 13	Mont.
146	Kremlin	C 10	Okla.
567	Kremmling	E 10	Colo.
345	*Kreole	Q 21	Miss.
227	Kresgeville	J 22	Pa.
400	Kress	A 10	Tex.
75	Kress City	Q 7	Ark.
140	Kresson	L 11	N. J.
182	*Kristenstad	F 17	Tex.
212	*Krollitz	Q 5	W. Va.
50	Kronborg	L 18	Neb.
60	*Kronos (Equality)	H 10	Ky.
630	Krotz Springs	L 12	La.
475	Krum	D 18	Tex.
52	*Krumville	R 22	N. Y.
25	*Krupp	J 18	Ky.
94	*Krupp (Marlin)	I 19	Wash.
25	Kruse	F 9	Wash.
148	*Krypton	H 21	Ky.
....	Kubler	J 8	Colo.
10	Kublia	Q 6	Ore.
734	Kulm	P 18	N. D.
6159	Kulpmont	K 18	Pa.
475	*Kulpsville	N 23	Pa.
....	Kulshan	C 9	Wash.
75	Kummer	J 9	Wash.
443	Kuna	N 5	Idaho
20	Kuner	D 16	Colo.
296	Kunkle	C 6	Ohio
200	Kunkletown	K 22	Pa.
15	Kuroki	D 10	N. D.
35	*Kurten	I 21	Tex.
850	Kurthwood	H 7	La.
173	Kurtz	M 14	Ind.
99	Kusa	I 19	Okla.
140	Kushequa	F 9	Pa.
38	Kutch	J 18	Colo.
1125	Kuttawa	J 7	Ky.
2966	Kutztown	M 21	Pa.
35	*Kyana	P 10	Ind.
10	*Kyburz	G 10	Calif.
110	*Kyger	O 15	Ohio
56	*Kyger (Billings)	H 7	W. Va.
200	*Kyle	Q 4	N. C.
50	Kyle	M 7	S. D.
874	Kyle	K 17	Tex.
700	*Kyle	Q 5	W. Va.
15	*Kyle	O 15	Wyo.
500	*Kylertown	J 11	Pa.
50	*Kyles Ford	K 21	Tenn.
963	▲Kynesville	M 11	Fla.
631	Kyrock	I 12	Ky.
107	*Kyserike	R 22, B 5	N. Y.

L

Pop.	Place	Index	State
20	*Laager	O 14	Tenn.
150	*Laana	H 23	Pa.
400	Labadie	J 18	Mo.

Pop.	Place	Index	State
600	Labadieville	O 15	La.
150	*Laban	M 21	Va.
15	Labarge	O 14	Mich.
150	*La Barge (Tulsa)	M 3	Wyo.
125	*Labarre	K 13	La.
837	La Belle	L 18	Fla.
833	La Belle	C 14	Mo.
500	*La Belle	P 3	Pa.
140	Labette	N 23	Kan.
115	*La Blanca	P 4	Tex.
14	La Boca	Q 6	Colo.
127	Labolt	F 24	S. D.
18	*Labranche	D 10	Mich.
3800	*La Canada	O 16, P 4	Calif.
175	Lacarne	D 11	Ohio
100	*Lacassine	M 8	La.
55	*Lacassine	M 6	La.
888	Lac du Flambeau	J 7	Wis.
591	La Center	J 4	Ky.
193	La Center	P 7	Wash.
75	Lacey	M 16	Iowa
27	*Lacey	G 21	Ky.
5	Lacey	L 18	N. J.
20	Lacey	F 10	Okla.
500	Lacey	K 6	Wash.
150	*Lacey Spring	H 11	Va.
500	Laceys Spring	B 14	Ala.
491	Laceyville	F 19	Pa.
100	Lachine	I 20	Mich.
200	*Lackawack	R 22	N. Y.
24058	Lackawanna	N 4	N. Y.
500	Lackawaxen	G 24	Pa.
472	Lackey	H 22	Ky.
31	*Lackey	N 20	Va.
50	Laclede	C 4	Idaho
200	Laclede (La Clede)	L 17	Ill.
642	Laclede	D 10	Mo.
10	Lacoleman	K 17	Ky.
41	Lacomb	G 7	Ore.
900	Lacombe	M 19	La.
80	*Lacon	C 12	Ala.
1627	Lacon	E 14	Ill.
424	Lacona	N 13	Iowa
413	Lacona	J 15	N. Y.
83	*Laconia	Q 14	Ind.
13484	Laconia	M 15	N. H.
14	*Laconia	P 3	Tenn.
624	La Conner	E 7	Wash.
1000	Lacoochee	G 14	Fla.
521	Lacoste	M 15	Tex.
51	*Lacota	E 15	Fla.
250	*Lacota	Q 12	Mich.
63	*Lacour	J 13	La.
70	Lac qui Parle	N 5	Minn.
815	La Crescent	Q 24	Minn.
3000	*La Crescenta	Q 4	Calif.
....	La Crew	P 20	Iowa
50	*La Cross (La Crosse)	K 7	Ga.
125	*La Crosse	C 14	Ark.
192	La Crosse	D 13	Fla.
574	La Crosse	C 10	Ind.
1407	La Crosse	I 9	Kan.
18	*La Crosse (Cardy)	C 12	Mo.
524	La Crosse (Lacrosse)	Q 14	Va.
475	La Crosse (Lacrosse)	K 22	Wash.
42707	La Crosse	F 17	Wis.
425	▲La Cueva	E 17	N. M.
3	*Lacy	I 11	S. D.
932	La Cygne	J 25	Kan.
1156	Ladd	D 14	Ill.
57	*Ladd	O 11	Ohio
588	Laddonia	G 15	Mo.
76	*Ladelle	P 15	Ark.
30	*Laden	J 21	Ky.
25	Ladessa	L 3	Okla.
55	*Ladiesburg	D 8	Md.
39	*Ladleton	R 21	N. Y.
7	*Ladner	C 2	S. D.
936	Ladoga	I 10	Ind.
....	Ladoga	F 8	Mich.
179	Ladonia (Holder)	F 13	Fla.
1279	Ladonia	C 21	Tex.
300	Ladora	K 18	Iowa
42	Ladson	M 18	S. C.
42	La Due	J 8	Mo.
3981	*Ladue (Price)	I 20	Mo.
309	*Lady Lake	F 15	Fla.
....	*Ladysmith	J 17	Va.
3671	Ladysmith	F 10	Wis.
921	La Farge	H 18	Wis.
408	La Fargeville	G 15	N. Y.
2138	Lafayette	H 21	Ala.
750	*Lafayette	I 6	Calif.
2052	Lafayette	E 14	Colo.
3509	La Fayette	C 3	Ga.
295	La Fayette	E 10	Ill.
28798	La Fayette	G 9	Ind.
229	La Fayette (Lafayette)	K 8	Ky.
19210	Lafayette	M 11	La.
400	Lafayette	O 12	Minn.
300	Lafayette	B 13	N. J.
185	*La Fayette (Onativa)	M 15	N. Y.
411	Lafayette (La Fayette)	G 8	Ohio
219	Lafayette	K 10	Ohio
409	Lafayette	E 6	Ore.
600	Lafayette	J 13	R. I.
850	Lafayette	L 13	Tenn.
250	*La Fayette	D 23	Tex.
150	*Lafayette	O 5	Va.
	*La Fayette, see Rhoadesville		Va.
800	*Lafayette Hill	N 22	Pa.
151	*Lafayette Springs	C 15	Miss.
105	*Lafe	B 20	Ark.
1644	La Feria	Q 4	Tex.
1200	*Lafferty	J 19	Ohio
500	*Lafitte	N 19	La.
23	*Lafleur	F 17	Wash.
20	*Laflin	O 21	Mo.
4010	Lafollette	L 18	Tenn.
554	La Fontaine	F 17	Ind.
190	*La Fontaine (Lafontaine)	N 21	Kan.
500	*Lafourche	O 16	La.
60	*Lafox	C 18	Ill.
1000	*La France	D 5	S. C.
....	*La Frank (Dain)	L 10	W. Va.
65	*Lagan	N 16	La.
49	La Garita	N 11	Colo.
184	*Lagarto	O 17	Tex.
160	Lago	Q 20	Idaho
176	*Lagoon	K 15	N. C.
7747	La Grande	E 20	Ore.
105	La Grande	K 7	Wash.
250	La Grange	J 19	Ark.
102	La Grange	I 10	Calif.
21983	La Grange	H 2	Ga.
10479	La Grange	C 20	Ill.
1814	Lagrange	B 19	Ind.
1334	La Grange	E 15	Ky.
508	▲La Grange	J 14	Me.
1222	La Grange	C 16	Mo.
140	*La Grange (Lagrangeville)	R 23	N. Y.
1647	La Grange	H 17	N. C.
546	Lagrange	E 15	Ohio
157	*La Grange (Osterhout)	G 20	Pa.
243	La Grange (Lagrange)	Q 3	Tenn.
2531	Lagrange	K 19	Tex.
20	*Lagrange	I 15	Va.
211	Lagrange	O 24	Wyo.
3406	*La Grange Park	C 21	Ill.
542	Lagro	E 17	Ind.
15	Laguna	M 3	Ariz.
50	Laguna (New Laguna)	G 7	N. M.
500	*Laguna	G 17	N. M.
43	*Laguna	L 13	Tex.
4460	Laguna Beach	P 16	Calif.
100	Lagunitas	H 4	Calif.
2499	*La Habra	Q 6	Calif.
1322	La Harpe	G 6	Ill.
624	La Harpe	K 23	Kan.
218	Lahaska	K 24	Pa.
150	*Lahey	D 9	Tex.
52	*Lahmansville	F 19	W. Va.
53	La Hogue	F 20	Ill.
195	Lahoma	D 9	Okla.
250	*La Honda	I 5	Calif.
21	*Lahore	I 14	Va.
	*Lahoward, see Howard		La.
20	*Laidig	O 11	Pa.
124	*Laing	M 6	W. Va.
50	*Laings	L 19	Ohio
896	Laingsburg	O 17	Mich.
165	Laird	E 24	Colo.
112	Lairdsville	I 17	Pa.
897	La Jara	P 12	Colo.
417	*Lajitas	L 5	Tex.
....	La Jolla	Q 18	Calif.
200	La Jose	K 9	Pa.
382	▲Lajoya	I 9	N. M.
....	*La Joya (Sam Fordyce)	P 4	Tex.
7040	La Junta	M 19	Colo.
100	Lake	K 22	Idaho
45	*Lake	J 19	Ky.
325	Lake	K 16	La.
150	Lake	L 16	Mich.
437	Lake	K 16	Miss.
100	Lake	F 4	N. Y.
....	Lake	F 18	Okla.
18	Lake	M 13	Ore.
103	*Lake	K 20	Va.
....	*Lake, see Mesa		Wash.
135	*Lake	N 4	W. Va.
40	Lake	P 20	Wis.
....	Lake Almanor	E 9	Calif.
920	Lake Alfred	H 16	Fla.
....	Lake Allyn	O 7	Ohio
785	Lake Andes	N 19	S. D.
37	*Lake Ann	I 11	Mich.
2500	Lake Ariel (Ariel)	G 23	Pa.
300	Lake Arrowhead	P 9	Calif.
2131	Lake Arthur	N 8	La.
279	Lake Arthur	M 19	N. M.
250	*Lakebay	J 7	Wash.
961	Lake Benton	P 3	Minn.
101	*Lake Beulah	O 21	Wis.
1729	Lake Bluff	A 21	Ill.
350	Lake Bronson (Bronson)	B 3	Minn.
923	Lake Butler	C 13	Fla.
300	*Lake Carey	F 20	Pa.
21207	Lake Charles	M 6	La.
....	Lake Charm	G 19	Fla.
101	*Lake Church	O 19	Wis.
50	*Lake Cicott (Lake Ciecott)	E 13	Ind.
760	Lake City	D 20	Ark.
80	*Lake City	B 9	Calif.
185	Lake City	M 7	Colo.
5836	Lake City	C 12	Fla.
150	Lake City	J 16	Ill.
2216	Lake City	H 8	Iowa
200	*Lake City	N 11	Kan.
693	Lake City	K 15	Mich.
3204	Lake City	O 20	Minn.
2522	Lake City	H 19	S. C.
168	Lake City	C 22	S. D.
1520	Lake City (Coal Creek)	M 18	Tenn.
....	Lake City Jc.	C 12	Fla.
300	Lake Clear Jc.	F 21	N. Y.
34	Lake Comfort	G 23	N C.
88	Lake Como	E 17	Fla.
190	*Lake Como	L 17	Miss.
230	Lake Como	I 20	N. J.
240	Lake Como	E 23	Pa.
207	Lake Cormorant	A 11	Miss.
200	Lakecreek	Q 7	Ore.
150	*Lake Creek	C 22	Tex.
1319	Lake Crystal	P 12	Minn.
75	*Lakedale	I 13	N. C.
300	*Lake Dallas	D 18	Tex.
250	Lake Delton (Delton)	J 18	Wis.
10	Lake Dick	L 14	Ark.
5	*Lake Dunmore	I 7	Vt.
265	*Lake Elmo	M 25	Minn.
157	*Lake End	E 6	La.
50	Lakefarm (Swan Lake)	L 15	Ark.
1699	Lakefield	R 8	Minn.
6885	Lake Forest	A 21	Ill.
200	Lake Fork	I 13	Ill.
188	*Lake Fremont (Zimmerman)	L 15	Minn.
53	*Lake Geneva	D 15	Fla.
3258	Lake Geneva	N 22	Wis.
100	Lake George	I 14	Colo.
110	*Lake George	L 16	Mich.
803	Lake George	K 23	N. Y.
401	*Lake Grove	H 9	N. Y.
800	*Lake Grove	D 8	Ore.
344	Lake Hamilton	H 17	Fla.
260	Lake Harbor	L 21	Fla.
18	*Lake Harmony	I 21	Pa.
587	Lake Helen	F 18	Fla.
....	*Lake Hiawatha	D 14	N. J.
58	*Lake Hill	R 22	N. Y.
700	*Lake Hopatcong (Landing)	D 14	N. J.
225	Lake Hopatcong	C 14	N. J.
31	*Lake Hubert	I 12	Mich
98	*Lake Hughes	Q 4	Calif.
400	*Lake Huntington	R 20	N. Y.
827	Lakehurst	K 17	N. J.
10	*Lake Itasca	G 8	Minn.
....	*Lake James	B 21	Ind.
69	*Lake Jem	G 17	Fla.
....	*Lake Jovita, see San Antonio		Fla.
17	*Lake Junaluska	O 6	N. C.
200	*Lake Katrine	R 21	N. Y.
15	*Lake Kerr	E 16	Fla.
....	*Lake Kirkwood	G 9	Calif.
10	*Lake Kushaqua	E 22	N. Y.
22068	Lakeland	I 15	Fla.
1502	Lakeland	O 14	Ga.
55	*Lakeland	F 14	Ky.
110	*Lakeland	L 14	La.
200	Lakeland	P 19	Mich.
350	Lakeland	N 18	Minn.
10	Lake Landing	G 23	N. C.
150	Lake Leelanau (Provemont)	I 13	Mich.
271	Lake Lillian	N 10	Minn.
1631	Lake Linden	C 4	Mich.
212	*Lake Lure	G 1	N. C.
800	*Lake Luzerne (Luzerne)	J 22	N. Y.
500	Lake Lynn	Q 4	Pa.
463	Lake Maitland (Maitland)	G 18	Fla.
....	Lake Majella	K 6	Calif.
331	*Lake Mary	I 21	Fla.
20	Lake McDonald	C 5	Mont.
1677	Lake Mills	B 12	Iowa
2219	Lakemills	L 20	Wis.
75	*Lake Mine	B 23	Mich.
450	*Lake Monroe	F 18	Fla
75	*Lakemont	C 12	Ga.
200	*Lakemont	P 12	N. Y.
1256	Lakemont	M 10	Pa.
1832	Lakemore	E 17	Ohio
120	*Lakenan	E 14	Mo.
357	Lake Nebagamon	D 5	Wis.
....	*Lake Nekopen	D 9	Calif.
463	Lake Norden	H 22	S. D.
1933	*Lake Orion (Orion)	P 22	Mich.
1417	Lake Odessa	O 13	Mich.
....	*Lake Outlet	C 3	Wyo.
379	Lake Park (Kelsey City)	L 24	Fla.
387	Lake Park	P 13	Ga.
828	Lake Park	B 5	Iowa
654	Lake Park	H 5	Minn.
340	Lake Placid	K 19	Fla.
3136	*Lake Placid	F 22	N. Y.
800	Lake Placid (Newman)	G 23	N. Y.
....	Lake Placid Club	F 22	N. Y.
54	*Lake Pleasant	C 8	Mass.
180	Lake Pleasant	J 21	N. Y.
250	Lake Point	F 10	Utah
1490	Lakeport	G 3	Calif.
80	*Lakeport	K 19	Fla.
....	Lakeport	L 15	N. H.
6	Lakeport	O 21	S. D.
886	Lake Preston	I 22	S. D.
3711	Lake Providence	B 14	La.
1000	*Lake Ronkonkoma	H 8	N. Y.
11	*Lake Sheridan	G 21	Pa.
....	Lakeshore	M 9	Me.
20	Lake Shore	P 24	Mich.
200	Lakeshore	R 16	Miss.
350	Lake Shore	G 12	Utah
425	Lakeside	I 21	Ariz.
....	Lakeside	Q 19	Calif.
137	*Lakeside	G 6	Conn.
....	*Lakeside	P 23	Mich.
300	*Lakeside	Q 10	Mich.
200	Lakeside	H 6	Neb.
425	Lakeside	C 13	Ohio
134	Lakeside	K 3	Ore.
49	Lakeside	D 7	Utah
50	Lakeside	M 17	Va.
241	Lakeside	G 15	Wash.
38	*Lake Spring	M 15	Mo.
2000	Lake Stevens	F 9	Wash.
165	*Lakesville	N 18	Md.
105	*Lake Tomahawk	J 8	Wis.
350	Laketon	E 17	Ind.
103	*Laketon	H 20	Pa.
50	*Laketon	C 5	Tex.
275	*Laketown	B 14	Utah
125	Lake Toxaway	Q 6	N. C.
55	Lake Valley	M 7	N. M.
100	*Lake Victor	I 17	Tex.
200	Lakeview	O 19	Calif.
....	Lakeview	F 9	Ga.
50	Lakeview	C 5	Idaho
1082	Lake View	H 6	Iowa
33	Lake View	I 14	Me.
824	Lakeview	N 15	Mich.
200	Lake View	A 11	Miss.
27	Lakeview	P 9	Mont.
550	Lake View	N 4	N. Y.
1200	*Lake View	H 7	N. Y
120	*Lakeview	H 11	N. C.
726	Lakeview	I 8	Ohio
2466	Lakeview	R 14	Ore.
532	Lake View	E 22	S. C.
40	Lakeview	O 12	S. D.
330	Lakeview	E 5	Tex.
107	Lake View	G 12	Utah
300	Lakeview	J 7	Wash.
438	Lake Villa	A 20	Ill.
2045	Lake Village	Q 17	Ark.
250	*Lake Village	D 6	Ind.
1800	Lakeville	B 4	Conn.
567	Lakeville	B 13	Ind.
75	*Lakeville	G 21	Ky.
50	Lakeville	K 20	Mass.
60	*Lakeville	O 22	Mich.
543	Lakeville	O 16	Minn.
....	Lakeville	F 4	N. Y.
400	Lakeville	N 9	N. Y.
144	Lakeville	H 14	Ohio
....	Lakeville	E 4	Pa.
65	*Lakeville	G 23	Pa.
4	Lake Vista	O 3	Colo.
429	Lake Waccamaw	L 14	N. C.
5024	Lake Wales	I 17	Fla.
83	Lake Williams	L 15	N. D.
421	Lake Wilson	Q 5	Minn.
800	*Lake Winola	G 20	Pa.
....	*Lakewood	G 14	Colo.
123	Lakewood	L 7	Fla.
125	Lakewood	K 15	Ill.
50	*Lakewood (Ossipee Valley)	K 17	N. H.
8000	Lakewood	J 18	N. J.
75	Lakewood	N 20	N. M.
2314	Lakewood	Q 2	N. Y
69160	Lakewood	C 16	Ohio
119	*Lakewood	E 22	Pa.
1500	Lakewood	F 16	R. I.
300	Lakewood (English)	F 8	Wash.
150	*Lakewood	N 10	Wis.
10	*Lakewood Club	N 11	Mich.
7408	Lake Worth	L 24	Fla.
421	Lake Zurich	B 19	Ill.
709	Lakin	L 4	Kan.
50	*Lakin	H 4	W. Va.
457	Lakota	B 10	Iowa
907	Lakota	H 19	N. D.
28	*Lakota	H 15	Va.
70	La Lande	I 21	N. M.
....	La Leona	Q 5	Tex.
100	La Liendre	F 17	N. M.
10	Lallie	H 17	N. D.
105	La Luz	M 14	N. M.
342	▲La Madera	D 13	N. M.
3044	*Lamanda Park (East Pasadena)	Q 4	Calif.
....	Lamar, see Woodland		Ala.
449	Lamar	F 8	Ark.
4445	Lamar	M 22	Colo.
75	*Lamar	Q 8	Ind.
33	*Lamar	F 15	Kan.
100	*Lamar (Algonquin)	Q 7	W. Va.
68	*Lamar	A 16	Miss.
2992	Lamar	N 7	Mo.
120	Lamar	M 7	Neb.
296	Lamar	K 18	Okla.
183	Lamar	J 14	Pa.
921	Lamar	F 17	S. C.
....	Lamar	N 20	Wash.
740	*La Marque (Lamarque)	L 23	Tex.
7	La Mars	Q 25	N. D.
60	*Lamartine (Perryville)	H 19	Ohio
175	*Lamartine	H 5	Pa.
75	*Lamasco	J 7	Ky.
36	*Lamb	K 14	Ky.
280	*Lambert	K 9	Ark.
218	Lambert (Walthourville)	M 22	Ga.
75	Lambert	C 20	Ill.
1016	Lambert	C 9	Miss.
238	Lambert	F 24	Mont.
99	Lambert	C 8	Okla.
1000	Lambert (Lamberton)	P 4	Pa.
75	*Lambert Lake	I 21	Me.
922	Lamberton	P 8	Minn.
....	Lamberton	P 21	Wis.
350	*Lambertville	R 20	Mich.
4447	Lambertville	H 11	N. J.
....	Lambeth	L 8	Ohio
10	*Lambric	G 21	Ky.
400	*Lambsburg	R 3	Va.
125	Lambs Creek	E 15	Pa.
55	Lambs Jc.	N 18	S. C.
89	Lame Deer	L 20	Mont.
3925	La Mesa	Q 19	Calif.
600	La Mesa	O 10	N. M.
6038	Lamesa	E 9	Tex.
60	*Lamine (La Mine)	H 11	Mo.
200	*Lamira	K 20	Ohio
300	*La Mirada	Q 4	Calif.
125	Lamison	K 8	Ala.
50	*Lamkin	H 10	Miss.
100	*Lamkin	G 16	Tex.
509	La Moille	D 14	Ill.
113	*Lamoille	I 14	Iowa
35	*Lamoille	Q 24	Minn.
68	Lamoille	D 18	Nev.
150	Lamoille (East Hardwick)	E 17	Vt.
100	*La Moine	C 5	Calif.
600	Lamoine	M 17	Me.
75	Lamona	I 20	Wash.
1567	Lamoni	Q 11	Iowa
250	Lamont	B 7	Fla.
11	*Lamont	M 22	Idaho
589	Lamont	F 20	Iowa
100	Lamont (Wilbur)	K 20	Kan.
....	*Lamont	I 21	Ky.
25	*Lamont	J 5	Ky.
150	Lamont	O 12	Mich.
5	Lamont	F 6	Miss.
577	Lamont	C 11	Okla.
118	La Mont	G 8	Pa.
135	Lamont	J 22	Wash.
50	*Lamont	O 15	Wyo.
....	Lamonta	H 12	Ore.
491	Lamonte (La Monte)	H 9	Mo.
272	Lamotte	H 24	Iowa
990	La Moure	P 19	N. D.
....	Lamourie	I 10	La.
3426	Lampasas	I 17	Tex.
65	*Lampe (Baxter)	Q 9	Mo.
500	*Lampeter	P 19	Pa.
41	*Lampson	D 7	Wis.
50	*Lamson	L 14	N. Y.
306	Lamy	F 14	N. M.
100	*Lanahan (Waidsboro)	P 7	Va.
340	*Lanagan	Q 6	Mo.
10	Lanare	K 11	Calif.
1292	Lanark	B 11	Ill.
16	Lanark	E 24	Mont.
525	Lanark	O 8	W. Va.
2400	*Lancaster	N 16	Calif.
125	Lancaster	N 20	Ill.
20	Lancaster	M 18	Iowa
163	*Lancaster	E 23	Kan.
1999	Lancaster	H 17	Ky.
2963	▲Lancaster	E 14	Mass.
473	Lancaster	B 2	Minn.
886	Lancaster	A 12	Mo.
2200	Lancaster	F 14	N. H.
7236	Lancaster	M 5	N. Y.
21940	Lancaster	L 13	Ohio
....	Lancaster	I 23	Ore.
61345	Lancaster	P 18	Pa.
4430	Lancaster	C 15	S. C.
115	*Lancaster	M 13	Tenn.
1151	Lancaster	E 19	Tex.
221	Lancaster	L 21	Va.
75	Lancaster (Willada)	K 22	Wash.
2963	Lancaster	G 21	Wis.
....	Lancaster, Jc.	H 20	Wis.
100	Lance Creek	I 22	Wyo.
75	Lancer (Bull Creek)	G 23	Ky.
250	*Lancing	M 17	Tenn.
56	*Land	L 5	Ala.
149	Landa	D 11	N. D.
50	Landaff	I 12	N. H.
....	Landax	J 7	Ore.
....	Landco	M 13	Calif.
13	Landeau	D 12	S. D.
350	Landenberg	Q 21	Pa.
35	Landenberg Jc.	B 21	Del.
50	*Lander (Catoctin)	F 7	Md.
200	Lander	E 6	Pa.
2594	Lander	J 9	Wyo.
1834	▲Landers (New Hartford)	C 10	Conn.
375	Landersville	C 10	Ala.
....	Landes	J 20	Tex.
125	*Landes	G 18	W. Va.
1000	*Landgraff	Q 6	W. Va.
700	Landing (Lake Hopatcong)	D 14	N. J.
255	Landingville	L 20	Pa.
79	*Landis	D 12	Ark.
1650	Landis	G 6	N. C.
266	*Landisburg	N 14	Pa.
420	Landisburg	M 9	W. Va.
65	*Landis Store	M 21	Pa.
790	*Landisville	N 11	N. J.
670	Landisville	O 18	Pa.
800	Lando	C 13	S. C.
315	*Land O'Lakes	K 7	Wis.
50	Landon	R 18	Miss.
215	*Landover	I 12	Md.
1289	Landrum	A 8	S. C.
40	*Landsaw	G 20	Ky.
20	Landsdown	F 11	N. J.
120	Landusky	F 15	Mont.
161	*Landville	O 4	W. Va.
40	Lane	D 5	Idaho
175	Lane (Lanes)	I 15	Ill.
234	Lane	I 23	Kan.
10	*Lane	F 23	Mont.
....	Lane	K 23	Neb.
32	Lane	O 18	Okla.
214	Lane	J 19	S. D.
68	*Lane	M 3	Tenn.
75	*Laneburg	O 8	Ark.
150	*Lane City	M 21	Tex.
75	Lane Park	G 16	Fla.
297	Lanes (Lane)	J 19	S. C.
289	Lanesboro	H 8	Iowa
900	Lanesboro	D 2	Mass.
1100	Lanesboro	R 21	Minn.
637	Lanesboro	D 21	Pa.
131	Lanes Mills	I 9	Pa.
57	*Lanes Prarie	K 15	Mo.
64	*Lanesville	J 12	Ill.
267	Lanesville	P 15	Ind.
....	Lanesville	B 23	Mass.
110	*Lanesville	Q 22	N. Y.
20	*Lanesville	M 19	Va.
6141	Lanett	H 22	Ala.
75	*Laneview	L 20	Va.
300	Laneville	F 23	Tex.
70	*Lanexa	N 18	Va.
5	Laney	N 13	Wis.
100	*Lanford (Lanford Sta.)	D 9	S. C.
1800	Langdale	I 22	Ala.
60	*Langdon	C 7	Iowa
208	Langdon	L 13	Kan.
45	Langdon	B 3	Mo.
30	Langdon	O 6	N. H.
1546	Langdon	D 19	N. D.
50	*Langdondale	O 9	Pa.
2000	Langeloth	M 1	Pa.
12	Langford	F 18	Md.
216	Langford	O 5	N. Y.
452	Langford	D 20	S. D.
1221	Langhorne	O 25	Pa.
477	*Langhorne Manor	N 23	Pa.
83	*Langley	K 6	Ark.
72	*Langley	I 14	Kan.
100	*Langley	H 22	Ky.
838	*Langley	D 22	Okla.
3500	Langley	J 9	S. C.
338	Langley	F 7	Wash.
....	*Langley Field	O 21	Va.
350	*Langleyville	J 14	Ill.
250	Langlois	N 2	Ore.
30	*Langnau	I 19	Ky.
25	Langrell	F 23	Ore.
41	*Langsdale	L 21	Miss.
600	Langston	B 17	Ala.
514	Langston	G 13	Okla.
50	*Langsville	O 15	Ohio
325	*Langtry	K 10	Tex.
100	*Langworthy	H 21	Iowa
900	*Lanham	I 12	Md.
100	*Lanham	O 21	Neb.
110	*Lanham	J 5	W. Va.
55	*Lanier	K 22	Ga.
....	Lankershim, see N. Hollywood		Calif.
283	Lankin	F 21	N. D.
378	Lannon	O 19	Wis.
213	Lanoka Harbor	L 19	N. J.
9316	Lansdale	N 23	Pa.
2000	Lansdowne	F 14	Md.
10837	Lansdowne	P 23	Pa.
2564	L'Anse	D 3	Mich.
300	*Lanse	J 9	Pa.
300	Lansford	E 10	N. D.
8710	Lansford	K 21	Pa.
4462	*Lansing	C 21	Ill.
1388	Lansing	B 21	Iowa
988	Lansing	F 24	Kan.
78753	Lansing	P 17	Mich.
196	*Lansing	Q 18	Minn.
50	Lansing	K 13	N. Y.
274	*Lansing	B 3	N. C.
1509	*Lansing	K 19	Ohio
424	*Lansing	M 8	W. Va.
....	Lansingburg	N 24	N. Y.
234	*Lantana	L 24	Fla.
83	*Lanton	Q 14	Mo.
40	Lantry	F 9	S. D.
80	*Lantry	G 11	Ark.
31	*Lantz, (Deerfield)	D 8	Md.
162	*Lantz Mills	G 12	Va.
105	*Lanyon	H 10	Iowa
157	Laona	P 3	N. Y.
1800	Laona	M 9	Wis.
....	Laona Jc.	M 9	Wis.
300	Laotto	C 20	Ind.
500	*La Paloma	P 5	Tex.
....	La Paloma Jc.	R 5	Tex.
375	*Lapaz	C 13	Tex.
429	Lapaz	B 13	Ind.
....	Lapeer	R 13	Ark.
5365	Lapeer	O 22	Mich.
1146	Lapel	H 16	Ind.
95	*Lapile	R 12	Ark.
360	Lapine	L 16	Ala.
50	Lapine	K 11	Ore.
400	La Place	J 19	Ala.
290	La Place	I 17	Ill.
175	*Laplace (La Place)	L 18	La.
61	La Plant (Laplant)	F 12	S. D.
488	La Plata	M 11	Md.
1421	La Plata	C 12	Mo.
300	Laplata	B 5	N. M.
79	La Platte	K 24	Neb.
332	La Plume (Laplume)	G 21	Pa.
150	Lapoint	G 22	Utah
92	La Pointe	G 4	Wis.
250	*La Porte	E 9	Calif.
100	Laporte	C 14	Colo.
16180	Laporte	B 11	Ind.
213	Laporte	G 10	Minn.
206	Laporte	H 18	Pa.
3072	La Porte	L 23	Tex.
1594	Laporte City	H 18	Iowa
....	La Posta, see Posta		Colo.
141	La Prairie	H 6	Ill.
702	La Pryor	N 13	Tex.
10	*La Puente	C 9	N. M.
270	Lapush	G 1	Wash.
426	Lapwai	G 3	Idaho
34	*Laquey	M 13	Mo.
85	Laquin	F 17	Pa.
10627	Laramie	Q 20	Wyo.
32	*Laran	A 10	La.
50	Larch	G 8	Mich.
5970	Larchmont	G 6	N. Y.
405	Larchwood	B 1	Iowa
544	Laredo	C 9	Mo.
225	Laredo	D 13	Mont.
39274	Laredo	Q 14	Tex.
75	*Larew (Trowbridge)	D 16	W. Va.
319	*Large	L 3	Pa.
50	L'Argent	F 13	La.
65	*Largent	D 22	W. Va.
1031	Largo	I 12	Fla.
46	*Lariat	E 1	Tex.
1527	*Larimer	M 5	Pa.
1222	Larimore	H 22	N. D.
125	Lark	O 9	N. D.
20	Lark	Q 15	Okla.
....	*Lark	C 4	Tex.
350	Lark	F 10	Utah
60	*Larkin	C 14	Ark.
....	Larkins, see South Miami		Fla.
113	*Larkinburg	E 22	Kan.
225	Larkinsville	B 17	Ala.
1558	Larkspur	B 14	Calif.
150	Larkspur	H 15	Colo.
8467	Larksville	H 20	Pa.
3533	Larned	J 10	Kan.
....	*LaRoche	I 11	S. D.
75	La Rocque (Hawks)	H 19	Mich.
179	La Rose	F 14	Ill.
600	Larose	P 18	La.
....	La Rosen	C 4	La.
139	Larrabee	E 4	Iowa
110	*Larrabee	L 22	Me.
47	Larrys Creek	H 14	Pa.
111	*Larryville	I 15	Pa.
98	*Larsen	M 15	Wis.
170	Larslan	C 20	Mont.
79	Larson	D 5	N. D.
100	Larson	C 8	Wash.
6	*Larue	B 6	Ark.
57	*Larue	I 19	Ky.
714	La Rue	H 10	Ohio
56	*Larue	Q 17	Pa.
300	*La Rue (Larue)	F 22	Tex.
319	Larwill	D 18	Ind.
200	*La Sal	M 24	Utah
755	La Salle	D 16	Colo.
12812	La Salle	D 15	Ill.
40	*La Salle	R 21	Mich.
139	*La Salle	P 11	Minn.
....	La Salle	L 4	N. Y.
85	*La Salle (Bennview)	M 20	Tex.
3232	Las Animas	M 20	Colo.
400	*La Sara (Lasara)	O 5	Tex.
150	Lasauses	P 12	Colo.
50	Lascar	N 15	Colo.
86	*Lascassas	N 12	Tenn.
8385	Las Cruces	N 10	N. M.
175	*Lash (Cowansburg)	N 4	Pa.
57	*Lashley	Q 10	Pa.
100	*Lashmeet	O 9	W. Va.
169	Lasker	C 19	N. C.
87	Las Palomas	M 8	N. M.
....	Lass	C 10	Ill.
175	Lassater	D 24	Tex.
150	Las Tablas	C 13	N. M.
128	*Lastrup	J 13	Minn.
8422	Las Vegas	P 20	Nev.
5941	Las Vegas	F 16	N. M.
6421	*Las Vegas (town) (East Las Vegas)	F 18	N. M.
270	Latah	I 24	Wash.
66	*Latcha (Latchie)	C 10	Ohio
500	*Latexo	H 22	Tex.
369	Latham	I 14	Ill.
307	Latham	M 18	Kan.
148	Latham	I 12	Mo.
200	*Latham	O 23	N. Y.
87	*Latham	O 11	Ohio
250	Lathrop	I 7	Calif.
150	*Lathrop	G 9	Mich.
1049	Lathrop	E 7	Mo.
85	Lathrop	M 15	Ohio
416	Latimer	E 13	Iowa
84	*Latimer	I 18	Kan.
....	Latimer	D 21	Ohio
....	Latimer	F 5	S. C.
750	Laton	K 12	Calif.
....	Latonia	B 17	Ky.
101	*Latour	I 7	Mo.
45	Latourell	D 9	Ore.
220	Latrobe	G 9	Calif.
11111	Latrobe	N 6	Pa.
1334	Latta	E 20	S. C.
1850	Lattimer Mines	J 20	Pa.
342	Lattimore	H 3	N. C.
293	Latty	E 6	Ohio
30	Latuda	I 16	Utah
....	*La Tuna	G 1	Tex.
133	Laud	D 19	Ind.
270	*Lauderdale	J 22	Miss.
285	*Laughlintown	O 6	Pa.
300	La Union	O 10	N. M.
127	Laura	F 11	Ill.
15	*Laura	G 23	Ky.
30	Laura	N 15	La.
317	Laura	K 6	Ohio
20	Laura	M 22	Okla.
65	*Lauratown	D 17	Ark.
11	*Lauraville	K 17	Va.
60	*Laurel	J 7	Calif.
2884	Laurel	L 22	Del.
165	*Laurel	K 13	Fla.
533	Laurel	K 21	Ind.
232	Laurel	J 15	Iowa
2823	Laurel	H 12	Md.
20598	Laurel	M 18	Miss.
2754	Laurel	M 15	Mont.
861	Laurel	F 20	Neb.
150	*Laurel	G 11	N. Y.
35	*Laurel	Q 17	Pa.
200	Laurel	L 15	Va.
100	Laurel	P 11	Wash.
200	*Laurel (Laurel Creek)	N 9	W. Va.
240	*Laurel Bloomery	K 25	Tenn.
20	*Laurelburg	N 14	Tenn.
125	*Laurel Creek	I 20	Ky.
200	*Laurel Creek (Laurel)	N 9	W. Va.
3397	*Laureldale	M 20	Pa.
17	*Laurel Dale	D 18	W. Va.
49	*Laurel Fork	Q 4	Va.
....	Laurel Furnace	C 15	W. Va.
595	*Laurel Gardens	M 3	Pa.
350	Laurel Hill	L 6	Fla.
33	*Laurel Hill	J 13	La.
400	Laurel Hill	J 10	N. C.
1057	Laurel Run	I 21	Pa.
1344	Laurel Springs	L 10	N. J.
100	*Laurel Springs	C 4	N. C.
212	Laurelton	J 20	N. J.
327	Laurelton	K 15	Pa.
491	Laurelville	M 13	Ohio
1304	Laurens	E 7	Iowa
203	Laurens	O 18	N. Y.
6894	Laurens	D 9	S. C.
....	Laurette	H 17	Ill.
35	Laurier	B 21	Wash.
45	Laurin	M 8	Mont.
5685	Laurinburg	J 11	N. C.
3929	Laurium	C 3	Mich.
220	Laurys Station	L 22	Pa.
40	*Lauzon	L 1	S. D.
163	*Lavaca	K 5	Ala.
319	Lavaca	F 5	Ark.
647	Lava Hot Springs	P 20	Idaho
100	*Lavalette	K 2	W. Va.
50	*La Valle	Q 22	Mo.
408	La Valle	I 18	Wis.
315	*Lavallette	K 17	N. J.
340	Lavalley	Q 13	Colo.
100	Laveen	K 12	Ariz.
1200	*Lavelle	K 18	Pa.
122	La Ventana	E 9	N. M.
183	Lavergne (La Vergne)	N 12	Tenn.
349	La Verkin	Q 4	Utah
3092	La Verne	P 7	Calif.
816	Laverne	B 2	Okla.
480	Lavernia	M 17	Tex.
50	Laverty	L 9	Okla.
897	La Veta	O 14	Colo.
100	Lavier (Moskee)	C 22	Wyo.
200	*LaVilla	P 4	Tex.
199	Lavina	J 15	Mont.
61	*Lavinia	G 8	Iowa
50	*Lavinia	F 10	Minn.
30	*Lavinia	N 5	Tenn.
50	*Lavon	D 20	Tex.
1667	Lavonia	D 14	Ga.
10	Lavoye	H 17	Wyo.
28	*La Ward	M 20	Tex.
50	Lawen	L 18	Ore.
18	*Lawford	F 9	W. Va.
70	*Lawhon	C 7	La.
542	Lawler	D 18	Iowa
95	Lawler	I 16	Minn.
175	*Lawley	H 12	Ala.
204	Lawn	O 18	Pa.
306	Lawn	F 14	Tex.
45	*Lawn	M 12	W. Va.
2365	*Lawndale	Q 4	Calif.
152	*Lawndale	H 14	Ill.
30	*Lawndale	I 4	Minn.
1006	Lawndale	G 3	N. C.
....	Lawndale	F 17	Ohio
50	*Lawn Hill	H 14	Iowa
1270	*Lawnside	L 9	N. J.

Pop.	Place, Index	State
....	Linton, E 13	Ala.
200	Linton, H 14	Ga.
6263	Linton, M 8	Ind.
21	Linton, K 25	Kan.
135*	Linton, K 7	Ky.
1602	Linton, P 13	N. D.
100*	Linville, A 11	La.
500	Linville, D 2	N. C.
200	Linville, H 11	Va.
52*	Linville Falls, E 2	N. C.
302*	Linwood (Ezel), L 18	Ala.
150	Linwood (Halls), D 4	Ga.
200	Linwood (White Sulphur), L 23	Iowa
299	Linwood, G 24	Kan.
75*	Linwood, H 23	Ky.
75*	Linwood, C 10	Md.
1550	Linwood (Whitins), I 15	Mass.
217	Linwood, M 20	Mich.
247	Linwood, J 21	Neb.
1479	Linwood, P 15	N. J.
60*	Linwood, M 8	N. Y.
250	Linwood, F 8	N. C.
4000*	Linwood, P 23	Pa.
23	Linwood, E 22	Utah
250*	Linworth, K 11	Ohio
25*	Lionilli, H 24	Ky.
....	Lionkol, O 8	Wyo.
....	Lionkol Jc., O 7	Wyo.
500*	Lions, M 17	La.
150	Lionville, O 21	Pa.
375	Lipan, E 17	Tex.
50	Lipe (Zach), M 7	Tenn.
31*	Lipps, J 20	Ky.
1740	Lipscomb, G 12	Ala.
200	Lipscomb, A 6	Tex.
20*	Lipscomb, J 10	Va.
50*	Lisabeula, H 9	Wash.
300*	Lisbon, F 16	Fla.
56*	Lisbon, F 17	Ga.
206	Lisbon, D 18	Ill.
873	Lisbon, J 21	Iowa
146*	Lisbon, B 8	La.
800	Lisbon, O 7	Me.
176*	Lisbon, F 12	Md.
1700	Lisbon, H 11	N. H.
250*	Lisbon, F 17	N. Y.
1997	Lisbon, O 22	N. D.
3379	Lisbon, G 20	Ohio
132*	Lisbon Center, O 7	Me.
2500	Lisbon Falls, O 7	Me.
238	Lisco, J 4	Neb.
340	Liscomb, I 14	Iowa
1500	Lisle, C 19	Ill.
25*	Lisle, I 6	Mo.
342	Lisle, P 15	N. Y.
545	Lisman, K 4	Ala.
100	Lisman, H 8	Ky.
55	Lisman, Q 14	Ohio
75*	Lismore, F 13	La.
311	Lismore, Q 5	Minn.
100*	Lissie, L 21	Tex.
650*	Listie, P 7	Pa.
250	Listonburg, Q 6	Pa.
23	Litchfield (Avondale), K 11	Ariz.
50*	Litchfield, D 10	Calif.
1234	Litchfield, F 7	Conn.
7048	Litchfield, L 12	Ill.
48	Litchfield, N 8	Me.
717	Litchfield, Q 15	Mich.
3920	Litchfield, M 11	Minn.
412	Litchfield, K 15	Neb.
779▲*	Litchfield, L 18	N. Y.
175*	Litchfield, E 16	Ohio
68	Litchfield Corners, N 8	Me.
430	Litchville, N 20	N. D.
112*	Literberry, I 10	Ill.
600*	Lithia, I 14	Fla.
83*	Lithia, E 6	Mass.
176*	Lithia, N 7	Va.
222	Lithia Springs, F 4	Ga.
91*	Lithium, L 21	Mo.
1554	Lithonia, F 8	Ga.
288	Lithopolis, L 13	Ohio
4840	Lititz, O 19	Pa.
46*	Litroe (Litro), A 11	La.
35*	Littcarr, H 22	Ky.
100	Littell, L 5	Wash.
264	Littig, J 18	Tex.
50	Little (Littles), O 7	Ind.
25	Little, J 15	Okla.
....*	Little Barren, I 14	Ky.
105*	Little Birch, J 10	W. Va.
50*	Little Blue, H 6	Mo.
....*	Littleboro, see North Leeds, N 7	Me.
208*	Little Britain, E 4	N. Y.
98	Little Cedar, B 15	Iowa
3360	Little Chute, N 14	Wis.
110	Little Compton, K 22	R. I.
28*	Littlecrab, L 16	Tenn.
242*	Little Creek, G 22	Del.
12*	Littlecreek, G 11	La.
450	Little Deer Isle, N 14	Me.
40	Little Eagle, C 11	S. D.
107*	Little Elm, D 19	Tex.
6047	Little Falls, K 12	Minn.
3000	Little Falls, D 18	N. J.
10163	Little Falls, L 20	N. Y.
....*	Little Falls, see Vader	Wash.
33*	Little Falls, D 14	W. Va.
4545*	Little Ferry, D 20	N. J.
3817	Littlefield, B 9	Tex.
608	Littlefork, C 15	Minn.
400	Little Gap, K 22	Pa.
253	Little Genesee, R 7	N. Y.
200	Little Hocking, O 17	Ohio
10*	Littlejohn Island, P 7	Me.
23*	Little Lake, K 16	Calif.
200	Little Lake (Forsyth), D 10	Mich.
190*	Littlelot, N 9	Tenn.
150*	Little Marais, F 24	Minn.
100	Little Marsh, E 14	Pa.
156*	Little Meadows, E 19	Pa.
20*	Little Medicine, O 19	Wyo.
251	Little Mountain, F 11	S. C.
110*	Little Orleans, N 6	Md.
100*	Little Otter (Quickle), I 10	W. Va.
81*	Little Plymouth, M 19	Va.
170*	Littleport, F 20	Iowa
150*	Little Rapids, O 14	Wis.
275*	Little River, N 7	Ala.
152*	Littleriver, F 1	Calif.
....	Little River, N 24	Fla.
603	Little River, J 13	Kan.
255	Little River, H 25	S. C.
200	Little River, I 18	Tex.
....	Little River Jc., C 2	Calif.
60	Littlerobe, F 2	Okla.
88039	Little Rock, J 13	Ark.
300*	Littlerock, N 16	Calif.
633	Little Rock, B 3	Iowa
150	Little Rock, E 19	Ky.
12*	Little Rock, J 19	Miss.
274*	Little Rock, E 21	S. C.
250	Littlerock (Little Rock), K 5	Wash.
150*	Littlerock Creek, M 9	N. C.
50	Littles, see Little, O 7	Ind.
27*	Littlesandy, F 21	Ky.
75*	Little Sauk, K 10	Minn.
1461	Little Silver, H 20	N. J.
434	Little Sioux, J 3	Iowa
2463	Littlestown, Q 15	Pa.
150	Little Suamico, P 13	Wis.
100	Little Swan, G 17	Minn.
163*	Little Switzerland, N 10	N. C.
427	Littleton, F 12	Ala.
2244	Littleton, G 15	Colo.
277	Littleton, H 8	Ill.
800	Littleton, F 19	Me.
1651▲	Littleton, D 16	Mass.
4571■	Littleton, G 12	N. H.
1200	Littleton, C 16	N. C.
180*	Littleton, P 18	Va.
539	Littleton, C 11	W. Va.
1000	Littleton Common, D 16	Mass.
1234	Little Valley, Q 5	N. Y.
318	Little York, E 7	Ill.
132*	Little York, N 14	Ind.
110*	Little York, F 11	N. J.
151*	Little York, N 15	N. Y.
100*	Litton, O 16	Tenn.
112*	Litwalton, L 20	Va.
265*	Litwar (Hull), Q 5	W. Va.
210*	Lively, L 21	Va.
800*	Live Oak, F 7	Calif.
3427	Live Oak, C 11	Fla.
2885	Livermore, I 6	Calif.
285	Livermore, B 14	Colo.
736	Livermore, E 10	Iowa
1601	Livermore, H 10	Ky.
300	Livermore, M 6	Me.
113*	Livermore, M 6	Pa.
....	Livermore Center, M 6	Me.
3600	Livermore Falls, M 7	Me.
216*	Liverpool, H 10	Ill.
18	Liverpool, B 7	Ind.
50*	Liverpool, J 16	La.
2500	Liverpool, L 15	N. Y.
607	Liverpool, L 15	Pa.
210*	Liverpool, L 22	Tex.
75*	Liverpool, H 6	W. Va.
8	Livesey, L 15	Colo.
....	Livesley, see Roberts	Ore.
29*	Livia, G 10	Ky.
9*	Living Springs, J 13	Mont.
1172	Livingston, I 5	Ala.
895	Livingston, I 9	Calif.
1115	Livingston, L 11	Ill.
669	Livingston, I 18	Ky.
425	Livingston, L 16	La.
6642	Livingston, M 12	Mont.
1000	Livingston, E 17	N. J.
406*	Livingston, Q 24	N. Y.
178*	Livingston, J 13	S. C.
1527	Livingston, L 15	Tenn.
1851	Livingston, I 23	Tex.
520	Livingston, H 21	Wis.
1612	Livingston Manor, R 20	N. Y.
60	Livingstonville, O 22	N. Y.
40*	Livona, O 13	N. D.
500	Livonia, K 13	La.
220	Livonia, A 12	Mo.
751	Livonia, N 9	N. Y.
200*	Livonia (Livonia Center), N 9	N. Y.
26*	Livonia, K 14	Pa.
16*	Lixville, O 21	Mo.
202*	Lizella, I 10	Ga.
521	Lizemores, K 8	W. Va.
200	Lizton, I 12	Ind.
....*	Llanerch, P 23 (Pop. 210 incl. in Haverford)	Pa.
....	Llanfair, N 9	Pa.
100*	Llano, Q 4	Calif.
2658	Llano, I 16	Tex.
526	Llewellyn, L 19	Pa.
250*	Lloyd, B 6	Fla.
75	Lloyd, D 14	Mont.
100	Lloyd (Blackwell), G 14	Pa.
1000*	Lloydell, N 8	Pa.
35*	Lloyds, K 18	Va.
1588*	Llyswen, M 10	Pa.
396	Loa, M 12	Utah
360	Loachapoka, I 20	Ala.
32*	Load, D 22	Ky.
5	Loaf, D 21	Okla.
37*	Loam, H 18	Ky.
488	Loami, J 11	Ill.
35*	Lobata, P 3	W. Va.
25	Lobatos, Q 12	Colo.
10*	Lobb, H 14	Ky.
150*	Lobdell, K 14	La.
75*	Lobdell, E 6	Miss.
75*	Lobeco, O 14	S. C.
64*	Lobelia, L 4	W. Va.
380	Lobelville, N 8	Tenn.
50*	Lobman (Armstrong), J 19	Ala.
15*	Lobo, G 4	Tex.
250	Lochgelly, M 8	W. Va.
....*	Loch Haven, see Beach Haven	Pa.
61*	Loch Lomond, B 11	La.
100*	Lochloosa, E 15	Fla.
420	Lochloy, F 9	Wash.
339	Loch Lynn Heights, O 2	Md.
450	Lochmere, M 14	N. H.
120*	Loch Raven, E 14	Md.
240*	Loch Sheldrake, R 20	N. Y.
65*	Lochvale, K 6	Pa.
114*	Lock Berlin, L 11	N. Y.
372	Lockbourne, L 11	Ohio
17*	Lockbridge, O 10	W. Va.
35*	Locke, E 5	Ark.
45*	Locke, H 7	Calif.
650	Locke, O 14	N. Y.
50*	Locke, D 23	Wash.
619	Lockeford, H 8	Calif.
200	Locke Mills, M 4	Me.
60*	Locker, H 15	Tex.
12	Lockerby, O 25	Utah
747	Lockesburg, M 5	Ark.
910	Lockhart, O 15	Ala.
204	Lockhart, G 18	Fla.
95*	Lockhart, F 3	Minn.
75*	Lockhart, J 22	Miss.
2300	Lockhart, C 10	S. C.
5018	Lockhart, K 18	Tex.
25	Lockhart Jc., B 9	S. C.
....	Lock Haven, L 9	Ill.
10810	Lock Haven, I 14	Pa.
....*	Lockheart, see Dowdy	Ark.
5601	Lockland, N 5	Ohio
19*	Locklies, L 21	Va.
....	Lockmoor, M 6	La.
1231	Lockney, B 11	Tex.
77*	Lockney, H 10	W. Va.
618*	Lock Number Four, N 3	Pa.
95*	Lock Number Three, L 3	Pa.
3475	Lockport, D 19	Ill.
151*	Lockport, E 16	Ky.
877	Lockport, O 17	La.
24379	Lockport, L 5	N. Y.
225*	Lockport (Lockport Sta.), M 5	Pa.
....	Lockport Jc., L 5	N. Y.
279	Lockridge, O 19	Iowa
45	Lockridge, H 12	Okla.
214*	Lock Seven, K 5	W. Va.
122*	Lock Seventeen (Seventeen) I 17	Ohio
191	Lock Springs, D 8	Mo.
2*	Lockwood, L 8	Calif.
841	Lockwood, N 8	Mo.
115*	Lockwood, Q 13	N. Y.
100	Lockwood, D 20	Ohio
27*	Lockwood, L 9	W. Va.
17*	Loco, F 17	Ga.
268	Loco, O 11	Okla.
100*	Loco, E 6	Tex.
5	Locust, D 15	Ky.
22*	Locust, R 12	Mo.
100*	Locust, I 18	N. J.
263*	Locust, M 13	W. Va.
65*	Locust Branch, G 19	Ky.
620	Locustdale, K 18	Pa.
12*	Locust Dale, I 14	Va.
1442	Locust Gap, K 18	Pa.
28*	Locust Grove, E 15	Ark.
349	Locust Grove, G 9	Ga.
100	Locust Grove, O 10	Ohio
545	Locust Grove, E 22	Okla.
18*	Locustgrove, I 15	Va.
22*	Locust Hill, G 12	Ky.
112*	Locust Hill, M 20	Va.
20*	Locust Point, Q 14	Ind.
1800*	Locust Valley, G 6	N. Y.
100*	Locustville, L 24	Va.
507	Loda, G 20	Ill.
200	Lodge, I 17	Ill.
60*	Lodge, N 20	Mo.
242	Lodge, L 13	S. C.
125*	Lodge, Q 13	Tenn.
50	Lodge, E 5	Tex.
89*	Lodge, K 20	Va.
839	Lodge Grass, M 18	Mont.
479	Lodgepole (Lodge Pole), K 5	Neb.
34	Lodgepole, C 6	S. D.
11079	Lodi, H 8	Calif.
60	Lodi, F 15	Miss.
65	Lodi, O 20	Mo.
11552	Lodi, D 20	N. J.
366*	Lodi, O 12	N. Y.
1304	Lodi, F 16	Ohio
33	Lodi, K 22	Okla.
250*	Lodi, D 24	Tex.
1116	Lodi, K 19	Wis.
30*	Lodiburg, F 11	Ky.
16*	Loesch, L 22	Mont.
25	Lofall, G 7	Wash.
45*	Lofgreen, H 9	Utah
55*	Lofton, K 10	Va.
101*	Lofty, J 20	Pa.
63*	Logan, D 12	Ala.
474	Logan, P 16	Ill.
1700	Logan, K 3	Iowa
703	Logan, D 9	Kan.
112*	Logan, P 9	Mo.
125	Logan, L 10	Mont.
34	Logan, J 12	Neb.
400	Logan, F 23	N. M.
42	Logan, G 10	N. D.
6177	Logan, M 14	Ohio
2	Logan, R 8	Okla.
11868	Logan, B 12	Utah
....*	Logan, J 15	Va.
5166	Logan, N 4	W. Va.
100	Logandale, N 23	Nev.
65*	Logan Mills, H 13	Pa.
1600*	Logans Ferry, L 3	Pa.
20177	Logansport, F 12	Ind.
57*	Logansport, I 11	Ky.
1222	Logansport, E 4	La.
297	Loganton, J 14	Pa.
627	Loganville, F 9	Ga.
100	Loganville, I 8	Ohio
408*	Loganville, Q 17	Pa.
236	Loganville, I 18	Wis.
19*	Logcabin, B 13	Colo.
25*	Logdell, I 17	Ore.
43*	Loglick, F 19	Ky.
200*	Logmont, K 19	Ky.
38	Logsden, G 4	Ore.
500	Logtown, R 15	Miss.
70*	Logville, G 21	Ky.
100*	Lohman, I 13	Mo.
63	Lohman, D 14	Mont.
110*	Lohn, H 15	Tex.
776	Lohrville, H 8	Iowa
191	Lohrville, L 16	Wis.
10*	Lokoya, G 5	Calif.
135*	Lola, I 7	Ky.
....	Lola, J 22	N. C.
400	Loleta, D 1	Calif.
215	Lolita, N 20	Tex.
135*	Lollie (Minter), J 15	Ga.
200	Lolo, I 4	Mont.
*	Lolo, see Valley Falls	S. C.
17*	Lolo Hot Springs, I 3	Mont.
460	Loma, H 3	Colo.
74	Loma (Chappell), F 11	Mont.
60	Loma, K 21	Neb.
256	Loma, E 19	N. D.
2500*	Loma Linda, P 9	Calif.
60	Loma Mar (Harrison), J 5	Calif.
75	Loman, C 14	Minn.
150	Lomax, H 14	Ala.
520	Lomax, G 5	Ill.
25	Lomax, H 22	Kan.
38*	Lomax, D 5	N. C.
7075	Lombard, C 20	Ill.
65*	Lombard, F 19	Ky.
35	Lombard, K 10	Mont.
65	Lombardy, E 8	Miss.
915	Lometa, H 16	Tex.
659	Lomira, N 18	Wis.
7052	Lomita, Q 3	Calif.
1000	Lomita Park, F 17	Calif.
3379	Lompoc, N 9	Calif.
2429	Lonaconing, M 5	Md.
355	London, G 9	Ark.
105	London, K 16	Ind.
2263	London, I 19	Ky.
77*	London, R 16	Minn.
4697	London, K 10	Ohio
50	London, K 6	Ore.
200*	London, I 14	Tex.
218*	London, L 7	W. Va.
200*	London, L 20	Wis.
112*	Londonbridge, P 23	Va.
750	Londonderry, Q 15	N. H.
200*	Londonderry, N 12	Ohio
200	Londonderry, N 10	Vt.
579	London Mills, G 9	Ill.
52*	Loneash, D 11	Va.
50*	Lone Cedar, G 5	W. Va.
14*	Lonedell, K 18	Mo.
97*	Lone Elm, K 23	Kan.
34*	Lone Fountain, J 10	Va.
350	Lone Grove, P 13	Okla.
40*	Lone Grove, I 16	Tex.
350*	Lonejack, H 7	Mo.
35*	Lonely, N 8	Tenn.
275	Lone Mountain, L 20	Tenn.
188*	Lone Oak (Cunningham), L 9	Tenn.
735	Lone Oak, D 21	Tex.
625	Loneoak, J 5	Ky.
900	Lone Pine, K 16	Calif.
100*	Lonepine, J 10	La.
500	Lonepine, F 3	Mont.
25	Lone Rock, B 12	Ark.
170*	Lone Rock, (Lonerock), C 9	Iowa
46	Lonerock, E 15	Ore.
502	Lone Rock, I 19	Wis.
46*	Lone Star, H 23	Kan.
123*	Lone Star (Lonestar), I 15	S. C.
651	Lone Tree, L 21	Iowa
43	Lone Tree (Lonetree), G 9	N. D.
6	Lonetree, R 4	Wyo.
5*	Lonewillow, I 8	W. Va.
783	Lone Wolf, K 4	Okla.
....*	Long, L 6	Md.
120*	Long, F 7	Miss.
175	Long, I 25	Okla.
700*	Longacre, M 7	W. Va.
164271	Long Beach, P 15, R 4	Calif.
14*	Longbeach, J 12	Fla.
455	Long Beach, A 10	Ind.
1495	Long Beach, R 18	Miss.
9036	Long Beach, I 7	N.Y.
620	Long Beach, M 2	Wash.
25*	Long Bottom, J 16	Ky.
163*	Long Bottom, O 16	Ohio
17408	Long Branch, H 21	N. J.
250	Long Branch, F 23	Tex.
300*	Longbranch, J 7	Wash.
31*	Long Branch, N 8	W. Va.
300	Long Bridge (Longbridge) I 11	La.
260	Long Bridge (McCance), N 6	Pa.
....	Long Bridge Jc., I 11	La.
176*	Longcove, O 12	Me.
238	Long Creek, G 18	Ore.
195*	Longcreek, C 3	S. C.
291	Longdale, F 7	Okla.
80*	Long Dale, L 7	Va.
250*	Long Eddy, R 20	N. Y.
160*	Longford, G 16	Kan.
38*	Longfork, C 6	Va.
210	Long Green, D 15	Md.
75*	Long Green (Gittings), D 15	Md.
139*	Long Grove, K 24	Iowa
47*	Long Grove (Hansbrough), H 13	Ky.
1014	Long Hill, N 6	Conn.
500	Longhurst (Jalong), C 12	N. C.
100*	Long Island, A 17	Ala.
257	Long Island, C 9	Kan.
150	Longisland, F 4	N. C.
100*	Long Island, O 10	Va.
155*	Long Key, Q 21	Fla.
35*	Long Lake, L 16	Mich.
57*	Long Lake, K 21	Mich.
260	Long Lake, N 15	Minn.
1000	Long Lake, H 21	N. Y.
66	Longlake, C 16	S. D.
25	Long Lake, H 20	Wash.
300*	Long Lake, M 8	Wis.
100*	Long Lane, M 11	Mo.
300	Longleaf, I 9	La.
5790■*	Longmeadow, I 7	Mass.
50	Longmeadow, G 16	R. I.
....*	Longmire, L 10	Wash.
7406	Longmont, E 14	Colo.
100*	Long Mott, N 20	Tex.
824	Long Pine, F 13	Neb.
1500	Long Plain, L 21	Mass.
278	Long Point, F 16	Ill.
131*	Long Pond, H 7	Me.
147	Long Pond, I 22	Pa.
303	Longport, P 15	N. J.
2311	Long Prairie, K 10	Minn.
100	Long Rapids, H 19	Mich.
25*	Long Reach, D 9	W. Va.
....	Long Ridge, P 2	Conn.
115*	Long Ridge, D 16	Ky.
30*	Long Run (Longrun), E 14	Ky.
250*	Long Run, F 11	W. Va.
250*	Longs, G 24	S. C.
60	Longs, J 24	Tex.
40	Longsdale, Q 16	Colo.
130*	Longshoal, P 4	Va.
57*	Long Siding, (Long), L 15	Minn.
13*	Longs Peak, B 13	Colo.
8*	Longspur, C 11	Va.
263*	Longstreet, E 4	La.
50*	Longstreet, D 10	Miss.
200	Longstreth, N 16	Ohio
629	Longton, N 20	Kan.
265	Longtown, B 11	Miss.
138*	Longtown, M 22	Mo.
40*	Longtown, E 14	S. C.
18*	Longvale, F 3	Calif.
550	Long Valley, E 12	N. J.
16*	Longvalley, M 8	S. D.
100	Longview, G 13	Ala.
259	Longview, I 20	Ill.
362	Longview (West Falmouth), M 23	Mass.
227	Longview, G 19	Miss.
1262	Long View, E 3	N. C.
13758	Longview, E 23	Tex.
12385	Longview, O 5	Wash.
350	Longville, K 6	La.
56*	Longville, H 11	Minn.
406*	Longwood, G 18	Fla.
37*	Longwood, H 6	Miss.
110*	Longwood, H 10	Mo.
45*	Longwoods, J 18	Md.
130*	Longworth, E 13	Tex.
....	Lono, see Rolla	Ark.
28*	Lonoak, L 8	Calif.
1715	Lonoke, I 14	Ark.
153*	Lonsdale, K 10	Ark.
545	Lonsdale, O 15	Minn.
4500	Lonsdale, C 16	R. I.
1500*	Lonsdale (Jordania), D 4	S. C.
80	Loogootee, L 16	Ill.
2325	Loogootee, N 9	Ind.
279	Lookeba, I 8	Okla.
50	Lookingglass, M 4	Ore.
80	Lookout, B 9	Calif.
1500*	Lookout, H 24	Ky.
20	Lookout, A 5	Okla.
300	Lookout, E 23	Pa.
500	Lookout, M 9	W. Va.
25*	Lookout, O 19	Wyo.
1545	Lookout Mountain, Q 15	Tenn.
32*	Loom, E 21	W. Va.
500*	Loomis, G 8	Calif.
60	Loomis, L 17	Mich.
249	Loomis, N 14	Neb
500*	Loomis, C 2	N. Y.
100	Loomis, L 20	S. D.
180	Loomis, C 17	Wash.
25*	Loomis, O 11	Wis.
50*	Looneyville, I 7	W. Va.
110*	Loon Lake, E 22	N. Y.
52*	Loon Lake (Inman), E 22	N. Y.
200	Loon Lake, F 23	Wash.
70*	Loop, L 6	Pa.
23*	Loop, E 8	Tex.
200*	Loose Creek, J 14	Mo.
50*	Looxahoma, B 13	Miss.
500	Lopeno (San Pedro), R 15	Tex.
900	Lopez, G 19	Pa.
51	Lopez, D 6	Wash.
100	Lord, M 4	Md.
400	Lorado, O 5	W. Va.
1373*	Lorain, M 8	Pa.
74	Lorain, D 9	N. D.
44125	Lorain, C 14	Ohio
346	Loraine, H 5	Ill.
700	Loraine, E 12	Tex.
75*	Loraine, C 9	Wis.
507*	Loramie (Fort Loramie), I 6	Ohio
150*	Lorane, I 10	Ga.
52	Lorane, K 6	Ore.
115*	Lorane, M 20	Pa.
150*	Loranger, J 18	La.
58*	Loray, F 5	N. C.
550	Lorberry Jc. (Ravine), L 18	Pa.
3101	Lordsburg, N 2	N. M.
75*	Lords Valley, H 23	Pa.
75*	Lordville, Q 19	N. Y.
490	Loreauville, N 13	La.
606	Lore City, K 18	Ohio
....	Lorella, R 12	Ore.
300	Lorena, K 15	Miss.
*	Lorena see Turpin	Okla.
400	Lorena, H 18	Tex.
262	Lorentz, G 13	W. Va.
20*	Lorenzen, I 7	Miss.
1000	Lorenzo (San Lorenzo), D 20	Calif.
250	Lorenzo, N 20	Idaho
30	Lorenzo, K 4	Neb.
616	Lorenzo, C 10	Tex.
300	Loretta, G 8	Wis.
420*	Loretto, H 15	Ky.
500	Loretto, G 5	Mich.
149	Loretto, N 14	Minn.
175	Loretto, I 18	Neb.
504*	Loretto, M 9	Pa.
900	Loretto, Q 9	Tenn.
34*	Loretto, K 19	Va.
150*	Lorida (Lake Istokpoga), K 19	Fla.
614	Lorimor, N 10	Iowa
31*	Loring, F 25	Kan.
500*	Loring (Sterling), E 14	Mass.
17*	Loring, O 12	Mo.
1238	Loris, F 24	S. C.
200*	Lorman, M 6	Miss.
100*	Lorne, K 17	Va.
236	Lorraine, I 13	Kan.
109	Lorraine, I 15	N. Y.
65	Lorton, M 24	Neb.
60*	Lorton, G 17	Va.
160	Lory, M 5	W. Va.
800	Los Alamitos, R 4	Calif.
500	Los Alamos, N 10	Calif.
50	Los Alamos, E 16	N. M.
4300	Los Altos, G 21	Calif.
1504277	Los Angeles, Q 3	Calif.
85*	Los Angeles, O 15	Tex.
253*	Losantville (Bronson), H 21	Ind.
2214	Los Banos, J 9	Calif.
403	Los Cerrillos (Cerrillos), F 13	N. M.
50	Los Cerritos, Q 12	Colo.
78*	Lose (Oakgrove), M 5	Pa.
500	Los Ebanos, Q 3	Tex.
500*	Los Fresnos, Q 5	Tex.
3597	Los Gatos, J 6	Calif.
28*	Losie, H 8	W. Va.
162	Los Indios, R 4	Tex.
686	Los Lunas, H 11	N. M.
500	Los Molinos, E 6	Calif.
1000*	Los Nietos, Q 5	Calif.
193	Los Olivos, N 10	Calif.
600*	Los Saenz, R 16	Tex.
399	Lostant, E 15	Ill.
34	Lost Cabin, H 13	Wyo.
250*	Lost City, G 20	W. Va.
40*	Lost Creek	Ky.
1621*	Lost Creek, K 19	Pa.
58	Lost Creek, C 23	Wash.
450	Lost Creek, F 12	W. Va.
25	Lost Corner, F 10	Ark.
200*	Lost Hills, L 12	Calif.
204	Lostine, D 22	Ore.
55	Lostine (Evans), D 23	Ore.
5	Lost Lake, C 16	Mont.
493	Lost Nation, J 23	Iowa
214	Lost River, G 20	W. Va.
38	Lost Spring (Lost Springs), J 22	Wyo.
255	Lost Springs, I 17	Kan.
70	Lostwood, F 6	N. D.
300*	Lot (Hartfield), M 21	Va.
2*	Lotell (Cold Spring), M 17	Pa.
65*	Lothian, H 14	Md.
2500	Lothair, I 21	Ky.
50	Lothair (Faulkner), N 11	Md.
149	Lothair, D 10	Mont.
1021	Lott, H 19	Tex.
160*	Lottie, L 12	La.
260*	Lottsburg, K 21	Va.
50	Lottsville, E 6	Pa.
100*	Lotus, G 9	Calif.
78	Lotus, H 18	Ill.
....*	Lou, see Welch	Tex.
492	Louann, P 10	Ark.
675	Loudon, N 15	N. H.
3017	Loudon, O 18	Tenn.
527*	Loudonville, N 23	N. Y.
2334	Loudonville, H 14	Ohio
84	Loudville, O 11	Me.
1800*	Louellen, J 21	Ky.
	Lough, G 9	W. Va.
750*	Loughman, H 17	Fla.
485	Louin, L 17	Miss.
2023	Louisa, F 23	Ky.
75*	Louisa (Cypremont), O 13	La.
365	Louisa, K 14	Va.
590	Louisburg, H 25	Kan.
94*	Louisburg, N 4	Minn.
175*	Louisburg, M 10	Mo.
2309	Louisburg, D 15	N. C.
100	Louisburg, G 22	Wis.
456	Louise, H 9	Miss.
30	Louise, L 9	Tenn.
327	Louise, M 20	Tex.
4669	Louisiana, F 17	Mo.
10	Louisiana Western Jc., M 7	La.
662	Louisville, L 20	Ala.
2023	Louisville, E 14	Colo.
1803	Louisville, H 18	Ga.
925	Louisville (Louis), M 18	Ill.
188	Louisville, F 20	Kan.
319077	Louisville, E 14	Ky.
3451	Louisville, H 18	Miss.
977	Louisville, L 23	Neb.
100	Louisville, C 18	N. Y.
3379	Louisville, G 18	Ohio
500	Louisville, N 19	Tenn.
250*	Lounsberry, R 14	N. Y.
1675	Loup City, K 15	Neb.
10*	Loupurex, M 3	Pa.
220	Louvale, K 4	Ga.
350	Louviers, G 15	Colo.
50*	Love, I 11	Ky
71*	Love, A 12	Miss.
18*	Love, L 10	Va.
114	Lovejoy (Lovejoys Sta.), G 7	Ga.
2158*	Lovejoy (Brooklyn), N 11	Ill.
5	Lovejoy, C 17	Mont.
300*	Lovelaceville, J 5	Ky.
542	Lovelady, H 22	Tex.
6145	Loveland, D 14	Colo.
120*	Loveland, L 3	Iowa
1904	Loveland, N 7, O 25	Ohio
101	Loveland, O 6	Okla.
100	Lovell, N 2	Me.
120	Lovell, F 12	Okla.
2175	Lovell, A 11	Wyo.
40*	Lovells, I 16	Mich.
1294	Lovelock, E 8	Nev.
100	Love Point, H 16	Md.
75*	Lovern, Q 10	W. Va.
16*	Lovesmill, P 13	Va.
50*	Lovett, B 8	Fla.
125	Lovett, J 15	Ga.
300	Lovett (Sidman), N 9	Pa.
248*	Lovettsville, F 15	Va.
83*	Loveville, N 13	Md.
106*	Lovewell, D 14	Kan.
119*	Lovick, F 12	Ala.
852	Lovilia, N 15	Iowa
115*	Lovill, C 2	N. C.
50*	Loving, B 8	Ga.
600	Loving, O 21	N. M.
25	Loving, L 25	Okla.
200*	Loving, D 16	Tex.
250	Lovingston, L 11	Va.
1215	Lovington, J 17	Ill.
1916	Lovington, M 23	N. M.
1000	Low (Twila), K 21	Ky.
....	Low, M 15	Miss.
13*	Lowake, H 13	Tex.
718*	Lowber, N 4	Pa.
645	Lowden, J 22	Iowa
250	Lowden, O 20	Wash.
125*	Lowder, J 11	Ill.
24*	Lowe, O 20	Kan.
72*	Lowe (Weyanoke), Q 7	W. Va.
....	Lowell, P 22	Ariz.
271	Lowell, B 5	Ark.
102*	Lowell, E 14	Fla.
76	Lowell, E 15	Ill.
1448	Lowell, C 7	Ind.
56*	Lowell, O 21	Iowa
161▲	Lowell, J 16	Me.
101389	Lowell, C 17	Mass.
1944	Lowell, O 14	Mich.
76	Lowell, M 16	Neb.
1826	Lowell, H 4	N. C.
528	Lowell, M 17	Ohio
175	Lowell, J 7	Ore.
150	Lowell, C 14	Vt.
740	Lowell, G 8	Wash.
200*	Lowell, P 10	W. Va.
282	Lowell (North Lowell), M 19	Wis.
2359	Lowellville, F 21	Ohio
60*	Lowemont, F 23	Kan.
20	Lower Bridge, H 11	Ore.
50	Lower Brule, J 15	S. D.
42*	Lower Buffalo, G 20	Ky.
116	Lower Cabot, F 15	Vt.
300	Lower Lake, G 4	Calif.
200	Lower Marlboro, L 14	Md.
39566■*	Lower Merion (Merion Station), P 23	Pa.
200	Lower Peach Tree, L 8	Ala.
263	Lower Rochester, E 9	Nev.
135*	Lower Salem, M 18	Ohio
32*	Lower Waterford, F 17	Vt.
219	Lowes, J 5	Ky.
200*	Lowesville, L 10	Va.
150*	Lowgap, C 8	Ark.
300*	Lowgap, C 6	N. C.
40	Lowgap (Low Gap), M 5	W. Va.
32*	Lowland, H 21	N. C.
12	Lowman, M 8	Idaho
100*	Lowman, R 12	N. Y.
100*	Lowmansville, F 22	Ky.
252	Low Moor, J 22	Iowa
500	Lowmoor, L 7	Va.
200*	Lowndes, O 20	Mo.
445	Lowndesboro, K 14	Ala.
155*	Lowndesboro (St. Clair), J 14	Ala.
201	Lowndesville, F 4	S. C.
215	Lowpoint, F 14	Ill.
100	Lowrane, C 17	Mont.
8*	Lowry, A 10	Ark.
273	Lowry, L 7	Minn.
8	Lowry, G 8	Mont.
90	Lowry, E 14	S. D.
101*	Lowry, N 9	Va.
488	Lowry City, K 8	Mo.
315*	Lowrys, C 12	S. C.
3578	Lowville, I 17	N. Y.
110*	Low Wassie, P 17	Mo.
476	Loxley, P 7	Ala.
59*	Loy, C 7	Ark.
1600	Loyal (Shonn), J 21	Ky.
177	Loyal, F 10	Okla.
921	Loyal, H 13	Wis.
800*	Loyalhanna, N 6	Pa.
72	Loyalsock, H 16	Pa.
925	Loyalton, F 11	Calif.
350	Loyalton, M 17	Pa.
89	Loyalton, E 16	S. D.
50*	Loys, C 9	Md.
318	Loysburg, O 10	Pa.
150*	Loyston, L 19	Tenn.
700	Loysville, N 15	Pa.
204*	Luana, D 20	Iowa
31853	Lubbock, C 10	Tex.
1500	Lubec, K 24	Me.
16*	Luber, E 14	Ark.
148	Lublin, G 11	Wis.
362	Lucama, F 16	N. C.
226*	Lucan, O 8	Minn.
534	Lucas, O 13	Iowa
648	Lucas, G 12	Kan.
75*	Lucas, J 13	Ky.
....	Lucas, C 5	La.
119*	Lucas, K 15	Mich.
484	Lucas, H 14	Ohio
54	Lucas, N 16	S. D.
....	Lucas, P 3	Va.
65	Lucaston, L 10	N. J.
1000	Lucasville, P 12	Ohio
70	Lucca, N 22	N. D.
62*	Luce, I 7	Minn.
5	Luce, L 16	Neb.
1204	Lucedale, P 21	Miss.
200	Luce Farms, P 22	Miss.
....	Luce Line Jc., M 22	Minn.
75	Lucerne, C 16	Colo.
215	Lucerne, E 13	Ind.
20*	Lucerne, E 7	Kan.
258	Lucerne, A 10	Mo.
....	Lucerne,	Utah
10*	Lucerne, F 14	Wash.
150	Lucerne, F 11	Wyo.
....	Lucerne Jc., L 7	Pa.
1200*	Lucerne Mines (Lucernemines), L 7	Pa.
100	Lucerne Park, H 16	Fla.
500	Lucerne Valley, N 19	Calif.
150	Lucero, E 17	N. M.
100*	Lucien, N 6	Miss.
150	Lucien, E 12	Okla.
46	Lucile, I 6	Idaho
30*	Lucile, F 21	Ky.
82	Lucin, C 2	Utah
319	Lucinda, H 6	Pa.
100	Luciusboro, M 7	Pa.
617	Luck, B 9	Wis.
25*	Luckenbach, K 16	Tex.
51*	Lucketts, E 16	Va.
720	Luckey, C 10	Ohio
58*	Lucknow, N 16	Pa.
40*	Lucknow, E 17	S. C.
32*	Lucky Fork (Cortland), H 20	Ky.
400*	Lucy, M 17	La.
25*	Lucy, H 14	N. M.

Pop.	Place Index	State
125	*Lucy, P 1	Tenn.
150	Ludden, Q 20	N. D.
400	Ludell, D 5	Kan.
25	Ludington, J 6	La.
8701	Ludington, L 10	Mich.
150	Ludlow, N 21	Calif.
210	Ludlow, P 16	Colo.
318	Ludlow H 20	Ill.
6185	Ludlow, B 17	Ky.
50	Ludlow, F 19	Me.
8181	■Ludlow, H 7	Mass.
200	*Ludlow, J 14	Miss.
265	Ludlow, E 9	Mo.
....	Ludlow, F 10	N. J.
12	*Ludlow, L 24	Okla.
1400	Ludlow, F 8	Pa.
4	Ludlow, C 3	S. D.
1780	Ludlow, M 11	Vt.
....	Ludlow Center, H 9	Mass.
212	Ludlow Falls, K 7	Ohio
271	*Ludlowville, O 13	N. Y.
866	Ludowici, M 22	Ga.
30	Ludwig, I 4	Nev.
28	*Luebbering, K 18	Mo.
328	Lueders, E 14	Tex.
110	*Luella, G 8	Ga.
9567	Lufkin, H 23	Tex.
....	Luger Jc., H 8	Wis.
200	Lugert, L 4	Okla.
510	Lugerville, G 8	Wis.
200	*Lugoff, F 15	S. C.
10	Lukachukai, C 24	Ariz.
988	Luke, N 4	Md.
150	*Lukens, J 21	N. C.
316	Lula, D 10	Ga.
47	*Lula, J 16	Ky.
503	Lula, B 9	Miss.
215	Lula, M 16	Okla.
14	*Lula, P 6	Tenn.
950	Luling, N 17	La.
4437	Luling, L 18	Tex.
300	Lulu, C 13	Fla.
75	*Lulu, R 20	Mich.
263	Lum, N 22	Mich.
300	Lumber, J 9	Pa.
150	Lumber, E 19	S. C.
196	Lumber Bridge, J 11	N. C.
1044	Lumber City, L 16	Ga.
1285	Lumberport, E 12	W. Va.
1485	Lumberton, P 16	Miss.
700	Lumberton, K 12	N. J.
350	Lumberton, B 9	N. M.
5803	Lumberton, K 13	N. C.
275	Lumberville, M 24	Pa.
1210	Lumpkin, L 4	Ga.
273	▲*Luna, J 1	N. M.
....	Luna Landing, P 17	Ark.
120	Lund, P 19	Idaho
195	Lund, I 20	Nev.
75	Lund, N 3	Utah
525	Lundale, O 5	W. Va.
30	*Lunday, M 9	N. C.
63	*Lundell, L 18	Ark.
43	Lunds Valley (Lundsvalley) F 6	N. D.
13	Lundville, D 22	Mont.
260	Lundys Lane, E 2	Pa.
336	▲*Lunenburg, C 14	Ark.
1500	Lunenburg, C 14	Mass.
650	Lunenburg, E 21	Vt.
150	*Lunenburg (South Lunenburg), E 21	Vt.
30	Lunenburg, P 13	Va.
35	Luning, J 8	Nev.
100	Lunsford, D 20	Ark.
25	*Lupton, F 24	Ariz.
1692	Lupton (Fort Lupton), E 15	Colo.
60	*Lupton, K 19	Mich.
200	*Lupton City, P 15	Tenn.
127	*Lupus, I 12	Mo.
392	Luray, G 12	Kan.
202	*Luray, B 15	Mo.
162	*Luray, N 12	S. C.
200	Luray, O 6	Tenn.
1511	Luray, G 13	Va.
517	*Luretha (Ferguson), J 17	Ky.
52	*Lurgan, P 13	Pa.
90	*Lurich, N 3	Va.
94	*Lurton, D 9	Ark.
29	*Lusby, M 14	Md.
126	Lushton, M 19	Neb.
300	*Lusk, D 15	Tex.
1814	Lusk, J 23	Wyo.
40	Lustre, D 21	Mont.
2167	Lutcher, N 16	La.
581	Lutesville, O 21	Mo.
145	*Luther, J 11	Iowa
343	Luther, L 13	Mich.
40	Luther, N 14	Mont.
425	Luther, H 13	Okla.
27	*Luther, L 21	Tenn.
3	*Luther, F 10	Tex.
284	Luthersburg, J 9	Pa.
354	Luthersville, H 5	Ga.
50	*Lutherville, F 9	Ark.
500	Lutherville, E 14	Md.
45	Lutie, L 21	Okla.
130	Luton, G 2	Iowa
25	*Lutsen, B 20	Minn.
300	Luttrell, M 19	Tenn.
100	*Luttrellville, K 21	Va.
150	*Lutts, P 8	Tenn.
500	*Lutz, H 13	Fla.
82	*Lutzville, O 9	Pa.
2243	Luverne, M 16	Ala.
576	Luverne, E 10	Iowa
3114	Luverne, R 4	Minn.
187	Luverne, K 21	N. D.
124	*Luxemburg, G 22	Iowa
468	Luxemburg, P 13	Wis.
86	*Luxomni, E 8	Ga.
725	*Luxor, N 5	Pa.
1258	Luxora, D 22	Ark.
135	*Luzerne, J 18	Iowa
114	*Luzerne, I 10	Ky.
25	*Luzerne, J 19	Mich.
....	Luzerne, see Lake Luzerne	N. Y.
7082	*Luzerne, H 20	Pa.
800	Luzon (Hurleyville), C 2	N. Y.
44	*Lyburn, O 4	W. Va.
15	Lycan, O 24	Colo.
190	*Lycippus, N 5	Pa.
320	Lycoming, J 14	N. Y.
38	*Lydalisk, D 13	Ark.
188	*Lyden, C 9	N. M.
114	*Lydia, N 12	La.
85	*Lydia (Saint James), B 4	Md.
250	Lydia, E 17	S. C.
6	*Lydia, I 12	Va.
350	Lydick, B 12	Ind.
80	*Lyells, K 20	Va.
368	Lyerly, D 2	Ga.
200	Lyford, J 7	Ind.
891	Lyford, Q 4	Tex.
100	Lykens, F 12	Ohio
3048	Lykens, M 17	Pa.
150	*Lykesland (Lykes), H 14	S. C.
61	*Lykins, G 21	Ky.
513	Lyle, R 17	Minn.
250	Lyle, Q 11	Wash.
250	*Lyles (Lyle), N 9	Tenn.
100	Lyman, R 18	Miss.
672	*Lyman, H 2	Neb.
50	Lyman, H 10	N. H.
100	Lyman, B 15	Okla.
1675	Lyman, B 8	S. C.
40	*Lyman, K 14	S. D.
200	Lyman, M 13	Utah
376	Lyman, D 9	Wash.
378	Lyman, Q 4	Wyo.
1500	Lymansville, D 13	R. I.
100	Lyme (Black Hall), M 19	Conn.
300	Lyme, K 8	N. H.
285	Lyme Center, K 8	N. H.
14557	Lynbrook, H 7	N. Y.
....	Lynces Jc., G 2	Pa.
10000	Lynch, J 22	Ky.
255	*Lynch, F 18	Md.
487	Lynch, E 16	Neb.
44	*Lynchburg, M 12	Mo.
21	Lynchburg, N 23	N. D.
833	Lynchburg, N 9	Ohio
382	Lynchburg, G 17	S. C.
390	Lynchburg, P 12	Tenn.
44541	Lynchburg, N 10	Va.
250	*Lynch Sta. (Clarion), O 9	Va.
218	Lynd, P 5	Minn.
60	*Lyndell, O 21	Pa.
1696	Lynden, B 7	Wash.
17454	■Lyndhurst, E 19	N. J.
2391	Lyndhurst, O 25	Ohio
22	*Lyndhurst, L 11	S. C.
160	*Lyndhurst, J 11	Va.
151	*Lyndhurst, M 12	Wis.
476	Lyndon, C 11	Ill.
751	Lyndon, I 21	Kan.
250	*Lyndon, E 14	Ky.
100	*Lyndon, N 11	Ohio
275	Lyndon, E 18	Vt.
354	Lyndon (Lyndon Sta.), J 17	Wis.
283	Lyndon Center, E 18	Vt.
745	Lyndonville, K 6	N. Y.
1444	Lyndonville, E 18	Vt.
5000	Lyndora, K 4	Pa.
25	Lynhams, L 21	Va.
98	*Lynn, D 9	Ala.
200	*Lynn, C 17	Ark.
68	*Lynn (Lynn Center), E 9	Ill.
1014	Lynn, I 22	Ind.
77	*Lynn (Boston), C 18	Ky.
98123	Lynn, E 20, K 7	Mass.
250	Lynn, Q 9	N. C.
125	*Lynn, F 20	Pa.
60	*Lynn, B 2	Utah
310	Lynn, P 3	W. Va.
50	Lynn, H 13	Wis.
10	*Lynn Camp, J 19	Ky.
125	Lynndyl, I 9	Utah
150	*Lynne, E 16	Fla.
600	Lynnfield, D 19	Mass.
650	Lynnfield Center, D 19	Mass.
33	*Lynn Grove, K 6	Ky.
1246	Lynn Haven, N 9	Fla.
300	Lynnhaven, P 22	Va.
300	*Lynnport, L 21	Pa.
....	*Lynn Spring, D 7	Va.
371	Lynnville, Q 7	Ind.
427	Lynnville, L 15	Iowa
100	*Lynnville, K 5	Ky.
374	Lynnville, P 10	Tenn.
....	Lynnville Jc., L 15	Iowa
125	*Lynnwood, I 11	Va.
10982	Lynwood, Q 4	Calif.
50	*Lynx, P 9	Ohio
233	Lynxville, F 19	Wis.
339	Lyon, C 9	Miss.
1136	Lyon Mtn., D 22	N. Y.
654	Lyons, D 14	Colo.
1900	Lyons (Cedar Crossing), K 18	Ga.
4960	*Lyons, C 21	Ill.
794	Lyons, M 8	Ind.
4497	Lyons, J 13	Kan.
57	*Lyons, H 14	Ky.
596	Lyons, N 14	Mich.
1033	Lyons, H 22	Neb.
3863	Lyons, M 11	N. Y.
464	Lyons, C 8	Ohio
12	Lyons, G 24	Okla.
175	Lyons, G 8	Ore.
518	*Lyons (Lyon Sta.), M 21	Pa.
54	Lyons, L 24	S. D.
500	Lyons, J 20	Tex.
315	Lyons, N 22	Wis.
818	Lyons Falls, J 17	N. Y.
....	Lyonsville, C 7	Mass.
5	*Lyonville, L 17	S. D.
25	Lyoth, I 7	Calif.
50	*Lyra (Andre), Q 13	Ohio
250	Lyra, E 16	Tex.
280	Lysander, L 13	N. Y.
75	*Lysite, I 12	Wyo.
125	*Lytle, M 7	Ohio
423	Lytle, M 16	Tex.
50	*Lytten, F 21	Ky.
220	*Lytton, G 4	Calif.
335	Lytton, G 7	Iowa
300	Lytton Springs K 18	Tex.

M

Pop.	Place Index	State
35	Mabana, F 7	Wash.
988	Mabank, F 20	Tex.
220	*Mabe, E 5	Va
741	Mabel, R 22	Minn.
100	*Mabel, C 2	N. C.
38	Mabel, I 7	Ore.
58	*Mabelle, C 15	Tex.
95	*Mabelvale, J 13	Ark.
300	*Maben, F 11	Ala.
675	Maben, F 18	Miss.
300	*Maben, P 7	W. Va.
311	Mabie, H 14	W. Va.
310	*Mableton, F 5	Ga.
1473	Mabscott, O 8	W. Va.
485	Mabton, N 15	Wash.
771	*Macclenny (McClenny), C 14	Fla.
32	*McAdams, H 14	Miss.
887	McAdenville, H 5	N. C.
5127	McAdoo, K 20	Pa.
27	McAdoo, C 12	Tex.
100	*McAfee, G 16	Ky.
209	McAfee, B 15	N. J.
12401	McAlester, K 19	Okla.
75	*McAlevy's Fort, L 12	Pa.
20	McAlister, H 22	N. M.
570	McAlisterville, L 15	Pa.
25	*McAllaster, G 3	Kan.
11877	McAllen, Q 3	Tex.
75	McAllister, M 9	Mont.
2	McAllister, H 13	Ore.
17	*McAllister, P 10	Wis.
300	*McAlisterville, L 14	Pa.
79	*McAlpin, C 11	Fla.
500	*McAlpin (Macalpin), O 7	W. Va.
750	*McAndrews, H 24	Ky.
112	*McArthur, C 7	Calif.
40	McArthur, B 5	Idaho
1288	McArthur, N 14	Ohio
489	McBain, L 15	Mich.
131	McBaine, H 13	Mo.
75	*McBean, H 20	Ga.
587	McBee, D 16	S. C.
150	*McBeth (Macbeth), L 18	S. C.
45	*McBeth (Mac Beth), O 4	W. Va.
25	*McBride, M 6	Miss.
100	*McBride, M 22	Mo.
24	McBride, G 22	Okla.
186	McBrides, M 14	Mich.
875	McCall, K 6	Idaho
11	*McCall, H 5	Ill.
....	*McCall, see Taylor	Ky.
710	McCall, M 15	La.
169	McCall (McCall Creek), N 8	Miss.
48	*McCalla, G 12	Ala.
278	McCallsburg, I 13	Iowa
2595	McCamey, H 9	Tex.
489	McCammon, P 19	Idaho
260	McCance (Long Bridge), N 6	Pa.
....	McCandless, N 25	Neb.
45	*McCann, D 2	Calif.
100	McCanna, H 21	N. D.
50	*McCarley, F 14	Miss.
100	*McCarr, H 24	Ky.
9	McCarty, M 12	Okla.
236	McCaskill, N 7	Ark.
7	*McCauley, G 20	W. Va.
350	McCaulley, E 13	Tex.
115	*McCausland, K 24	Iowa
1832	McCaysville, B 7	Ga.
200	*McClelland, H 16	Ark.
....	McClainville, K 20	Ohio
58	*McClanahan, H 19	Tex.
250	McClave, M 21	Colo.
1200	McCleary, J 4	Wash.
92	*McClelland, H 16	Ark.
165	McClelland, M 4	Iowa
1060	*McClellandtown, P 3	Pa.
....	*McCellan Field, H 8	Calif.
431	McClellanville, L 21	S. C.
771	McClenny (Macclenny), C 14	Fla.
2000	*McCloud, C 6	Calif.
50	*McCloud, L 22	Tenn.
26	*McClung, K 8	Va.
450	McClure, Q 13	Ill.
19	*McClure, G 23	Ky.
467	McClure, D 8	Ohio
850	McClure, L 14	Pa.
700	*McClure, C 6	Va.
12	*McClurg, Q 12	Mo.
22	*McClusky, L 9	Ill.
924	McClusky, K 13	N. D.
2391	McColl, C 20	S. C.
1000	McComas, Q 7	W. Va.
9898	McComb, O 9	Miss.
976	McComb, E 9	Ohio
201	*McComb (Macomb), K 14	Okla.
....	McCombs, F 14	Ala.
25	*McCombs, G 23	Ky.
78	McConchie, M 10	Md.
75	*McCondy, E 19	Miss.
400	McCone City, E 20	Mont.
200	McConnell, A 12	Ill.
36	McConnell, G 10	N. C.
56	*McConnell, L 5	Tenn.
80	*McConnell, O 4	W. Va.
25	*McConnells, F 8	Ala.
263	McConnells (McConnellsville), B 12	S. C.
1055	McConnellsburg, P 11	Pa.
362	*McConnellstown, M 11	Pa.
200	McConnellsville, K 16	N. Y.
279	*McConnellsville (McConnells), B 12	S. C.
1895	McConnelsville, L 16	Ohio
....	McConnico, G 5	Ariz.
6212	McCook, O 11	Neb.
100	McCool, B 8	Ind.
373	McCool, G 16	Miss.
272	McCool Jc., M 19	Neb.
30	McCord, J 9	Wis.
100	*McCords, O 14	Mich.
313	McCordsville, I 16	Ind.
200	*McCorkle (MacCorkle), K 3	W. Va.
1456	McCormick, G 7	S. C.
50	McCormick, M 5	Wash.
75	*McCoy, F 9	Colo.
20	*McCoy, H 12	Ky.
38	McCoy, F 6	Ore.
33	*McCoy, N 17	Tex.
50	*McCoy, N 5	Va.
100	McCoysburg, E 8	Ind.
52	*McCoysville, M 13	Pa.
534	McCracken, I 8	Kan.
500	*McCrady, D 9	Va.
53	*McCrea, N 14	Pa.
6	McCreanor, I 14	Ark.
100	*McCredie, H 14	Mo.
60	*McCredie Springs, K 8	Ore.
52	*McCreery, O 8	W. Va.
1010	McCrory, G 17	Ark.
....	McCrory, K 10	Va.
130	McCullem, E 10	Ala.
86	*McCullers, E 14	N. C
360	McCullough, O 8	Ala.
130	McCullum, E 10	Ala.
556	*McCune, N 24	Kan.
175	*McCuneville, L 14	Ohio
870	McCurtain, J 23	Okla.
345	McCutchenville, F 11	Ohio
58	*McDade, D 6	La.
400	McDade, J 19	Tex.
61	*McDaniel, J 17	Md.
197	*McDaniels, H 12	Ky.
300	McDavid, M 2	Fla.
2000	McDermitt, A 10	Nev.
850	*McDermott, P 12	Ohio
16	McDonald, G 19	Ark.
425	McDonald, D 3	Kan.
76	*McDonald, Q 12	Mich.
150	*McDonald, I 18	Miss.
8	McDonald, L 24	N. M.
250	*McDonald, E 21	N. Y.
1529	McDonald, E 20	Ohio
....	McDonald, G 6	Pa.
3530	McDonald, N 2	Pa.
62	*McDonald, Q 16	Tenn.
127	*McDonald (McDonalds), K 12	N. C.
246	*McDonogh, D 13	Md.
....	McDonoghville, N 19	La.
1232	McDonough, G 8	Ga.
250	McDonough, O 16	N. Y.
258	*McDougal, A 20	Ark.
120	*McDowell, I 4	Ala.
500	*McDowell, H 23	Ky.
34	McDowell, Q 8	Mo.
110	*McDowell, I 9	Va.
500	McDowell, Q 7	W. Va.
465	McElhattan (Youngdale) I 14	Pa
10	McElroy, B 24	Mont
150	McEwen, G 21	Ore.
617	McEwen, M 8	Tenn.
261	McEwensville, J 17	Pa.
163	*McFadden, F 17	Ark.
14	*McFadden, O 15	Wyo.
89	*McFaddin, N 19	Tex.
393	McFall, C 7	Mo.
184	McFarlan, J 8	N. C.
750	McFarland, L 13	Calif.
336	McFarland, G 20	Kan.
400	*McFarland (Turin), F 6	Mich.
463	McFarland, L 20	Wis.
20	McFerrin, D 22	Ark.
60	*McGaffey, F 3	N. M.
400	McGaheysville, I 11	Va.
8	McGary, P 4	Ind.
15	*McGee, P 20	Mo.
115	McGees (McGees Mills), K 8	Pa.
3663	McGehee, O 16	Ark.
50	*McGehees (Hope Hull), K 16	Ala.
26	*McGhee, O 18	Tenn.
3000	McGill, G 21	Nev.
20	*McGinn, J 21	Mich.
150	*McGirk, I 13	Mo.
36	*McGlone (Corey), E 21	Ky.
180	McGlynn (Penn), E 7	Ore.
50	*McGonigle, M 6	Ohio
20	McGowan, N 3	Wash.
30	*McGrady, C 4	N. C.
500	*McGrann, K 5	Pa.
138	*McGrath, J 16	Minn.
1201	McGraw (McGrawville), O 15	N. Y.
....	McGraws, see Ravencliff	W. Va.
50	*McGrawsville, F 15	Ind.
1201	*McGrawville (McGraw), O 15	N. Y.
100	McGregor, C 8	Colo.
55	*McGregor, K 17	Ga.
1309	McGregor, D 21	Iowa
80	McGregor, M 24	Mich.
311	McGregor, I 16	Minn.
118	McGregor, E 5	N. D.
2062	McGregor, H 18	Tex.
139	McGrew, I 2	Neb.
100	McGrew Jc., O 21	Mich.
618	McGuffey, G 9	Ohio
1596	McHenry, A 18	Ill.
....	*McHenry (West McHenry), A 18	Ill.
722	McHenry, H 10	Ky.
31	*McHenry, M 2	Md.
630	McHenry, Q 18	Miss.
250	McHenry, J 19	N. D.
14	*McHenry, J 15	Va.
200	*McHue, E 16	Ark.
325	McIndoes Falls (McIndoe), G 18	Vt.
300	McIntire, B 16	Iowa
175	McIntosh, N 6	Ala.
397	McIntosh, E 14	Fla.
200	McIntosh, M 23	Ga.
903	McIntosh, F 6	Minn.
184	▲McIntosh, H 13	N. M.
626	McIntosh, B 9	S. D.
....	McIntosh, L 6	Wash.
209	*McIntyre, I 13	Ga.
800	*McIntyre, M 6	Pa.
30	*McIvor, K 20	Mich.
76	*McJester, F 14	Ark.
3	McKain, I 25	S. D.
75	McKamie, Q 7	Ark.
320	*McKean (Middleboro), D 3	Pa.
237	*McKeansburg, L 19	Pa.
190	McKee, H 19	Ky.
15	McKee, E 7	Ore.
....	McKee, B 3	Tex.
180	*McKee, N 10	Pa.
180	*McKee City, O 14	N. J.
180	*McKeefry, B 11	W. Va.
125	McKees Half Falls, L 16	Pa.
55355	McKeesport, N 4	Pa.
17021	McKees Rocks, M 3	Pa.
....	McKeever, E 1	Mich.
25	*McKeever, J 18	N. Y.
80	*McKendree, N 9	W. Va.
20	McKenna, K 7	Wash.
453	McKenney, P 16	Va.
504	McKenzie, N 13	Ala.
....	McKenzie, M 6	Md.
125	McKenzie, N 13	N. D.
2019	McKenzie, M 6	Tenn.
23	McKenzie Bridge, I 9	Ore.
....	*McKeon, G 8	Calif.
50	McKey, I 23	Okla.
100	*McKinley, K 8	Ala.
300	McKinley, N 17	Me.
235	McKinley, F 19	Minn.
95	McKinley, M 3	Ore.
50	McKinley, K 21	Wyo.
20	*McKinney (Chambers Lodge), F 10	Calif.
500	McKinney, H 17	Ky.
8555	McKinney, D 19	Tex.
71	*McKinnon, M 20	Ga.
200	*McKinnon, L 7	Tenn.
161	*McKinnon, O 8	Wyo.
450	McKittrick, M 12	Calif.
124	*McKittrick, I 16	Mo.
250	*McKnightstown, Q 14	Pa.
350	McLain, O 20	Miss.
80	McLain, H 21	Okla.
660	McLaughlin, C 11	S. D.
170	McLaurin, O 17	Miss.
652	McLean, H 14	Ill.
82	McLean, G 19	Neb.
225	McLean, O 14	N. Y.
1489	McLean, D 5	Tex.
200	*McLean, F 18	Va.
2528	McLeansboro, O 18	Ill.
150	*McLeansville, D 10	N. C.
315	McLemoresville, N 5	Tenn.
40	*McLeod, G 22	Miss.
15	McLeod, M 12	Mont.
185	McLeod, P 23	N. D.
616	McLoud, I 13	Okla.
515	McLouth, F 23	Kan.
95	*McLuney, L 15	Ohio
70	*McMahan, K 18	Tex.
127	McMan, P 11	Okla.
17	*McManus, I 15	La.
3726	McMechen, A 10	W. Va.
300	McMillan, C 16	Mich.
30	McMillan, P 15	Okla.
300	McMillin (McMillan), J 8	Wash.
3706	McMinnville, E 6	Ore.
4649	McMinnville, O 13	Tenn.
11	*McMullen, I 12	Va.
224	McMurray, E 8	Wash.
144	*McNab, N 6	Ark.
150	McNabb, E 14	Ill.
10	McNair, C 5	Ark.
101	McNair, M 6	Miss.
147	*McNairy, P 5	Tenn.
55	McNary, I 22	Ariz.
50	*McNary, I 9	Ky.
151	McNary, J 9	La.
42	*McNary, G 2	Tex.
120	*McNaughton, K 8	Wis.
9	McNeal, P 23	Ariz.
278	McNeil, Q 9	Ark.
100	McNeil, J 18	Tex.
500	McNeill, Q 15	Miss.
50	*McNeill, F 19	W. Va.
64	*McNoel (Big Bay), Q 17	Ill.
47	*McPaul, P 3	Iowa
48	*McPhearson, C 13	Ark.
350	*McPhee, P 3	Colo.
7194	McPherson, J 15	Kan.
111	*McPhersonville, O 13	S. C.
68	*McQuady, G 11	Ky.
14	McQueen, M 2	Okla.
500	McQueeney, L 17	Tex.
420	McRae, H 15	Ark.
1595	McRae, L 15	Ga.
24	McRae, L 18	Mont.
....	McRae Jc., L 15	Ga.
2146	McRoberts, I 23	Ky.
68	*McShan, G 5	Ala.
2128	McSherrystown, Q 15	Pa.
....	McSweeney, K 11	Nev.
1298	McVeigh, H 24	Ky.
581	McVeytown, M 13	Pa.
548	McVille, I 20	N. D.
80	*McWhorter, I 19	Ky.
250	McWhorter, F 12	W. Va.
248	*McWilliams, L 11	Ala.
20	McWillie, C 9	Okla.
20	*Mac, H 14	Ky.
28	Macall, J 21	Wash.
....	*Macalpin, see McAlpin,	W. Va.
50	*Macanie, G 12	Va.
300	*Macatawa, O 12	Mich.
....	MacBain, B 11	Tex.
150	*Macbeth (McBeth), L 18	S. C.
616	*Macclenny (McClenny), C 14	Fla.
367	Macclesfield, F 18	N. C.
150	*Macdoel, B 6	Calif.
123	*Macdona, M 15	Tex.
1175	Macdonald, N 8	W. Va.
1035	Macdonaldton, P 8	Pa.
42	*MacDougall, N 12	N. Y.
....	*MacDunn, M 8	W. Va.
41	*Mace, K 14	W. Va.
557	Macedon, L 10	N. Y.
150	*Macedon Center, L 10	N. Y.
147	Macedonia, O 17	Ill.
329	Macedonia, N 5	Iowa
734	Macedonia, E 17	Ohio
25	Macel, E 11	Miss.
350	*Maceo, F 9	Ky.
60	*Maces Spring, E 6	Va.
150	*Macfarlan, F 8	W. Va.
131	Machen, G 11	Ga.
75	Machens, H 20	Mo.
2200	Machias, L 22	Me.
585	Machias, P 6	N. Y.
100	*Machias (Machias Jct.), P 6	N. Y.
200	Machias, G 9	Wash.
100	Machias Junction (Machias), P 6	N. Y.
300	Machiasport, L 22	Me.
115	*Machipongo, M 23	Va.
110	*Machodoc, K 19	Va.
250	Mack, H 3	Colo.
....	Mack, see Talmoon	Minn.
28	*Mackall, N 15	Md.
776	Mackay, M 14	Idaho
300	*Mackay, M 20	Tex.
2	Mackenzie, J 24	Mont.
175	Mackey, P 6	Ind.
175	Mackeys, E 21	N. C.
160	*Mackeyville, I 13	Pa.
508	Mackinac Island, G 17	Mich.
845	Mackinaw, G 13	Ill.
922	Mackinaw City (Mackinaw), G 17	Mich.
....	Mackoy, see Grays Branch	Ky.
60	*Macks (Elmo), E 17	Ark.
255	Macksburg, N 10	Iowa
283	Macksburg, M 18	Ohio
147	*Macks Creek, L 11	Mo.
5	*Macks Inn, M 21	Idaho
3729	Macksville (West Terre Haute), K 5	Ind.
723	Macksville, L 11	Kan.
51	*Macksville, H 17	W. Va.
244	Mackville, G 15	Ky.
43	Macleay, F 7	Ore.
....	*MacMahan, O 8	Me.
8764	Macomb, G 7	Ill.
100	Macomb, O 23	Mich.
75	*Macomb, P 13	Mo.
201	Macomb (McComb), K 14	Okla.
57865	Macon, I 11	Ga.
875	Macon, J 15	Ill.
23	*Macon, H 13	Ky.
300	Macon, Q 19	Mich.
2261	Macon, H 21	Miss.
4206	Macon, D 13	Mo.
64	Macon, O 15	Neb.
197	*Macon, C 16	N. C.
75	Macon, O 9	Ohio
220	Macon, Q 3	Tenn.
115	*Macon, M 14	Va.
....	Macon, Dublin & Savannah Jc., J 15	Ga.
30	*Macoupin, K 11	Ill.
50	*Macune, H 25	Tex.
856	Macungie, M 22	Pa.
275	Macy, D 14	Ind.
22	Macy, G 14	Iowa
203	Macy, H 23	Neb.
200	Madalin, Q 23	N. Y.
45	*Madam Creek, P 10	W. Va.
....	Madart, N 17	Minn.
3800	Madawaska, A 17	Me.
401	▲Madbury, O 19	N. H.
75	*Madden, I 16	Miss.
27	*Maddensville, O 12	Pa.
691	Maddock, H 16	N. D.
45	*Maddox, N 13	Md.
30	*Maddus, D 15	Mont.
1384	Madeira, P 25	Ohio
1652	Madelia, Q 11	Minn.
250	*Madeline (Malco), O 8	W. Va.
60	Madeline, C 10	Calif.
6457	Madera, J 11	Calif.
2000	Madera, K 10	Pa.
40	*Madera Canyon, P 18	Ariz.
116	*Madera Springs, I 5	Tex.
2594	Madill, P 15	Okla.
455	Madison, B 13	Ala.
838	Madison, H 19	Ark.
150	*Madison, G 7	Calif.
1155	Madison, N 15	Conn.
2730	Madison, B 9	Fla.
2045	Madison, F 12	Ga.
7782	Madison, M 10	Ill.
6923	Madison, N 19	Ind.
1198	Madison, K 20	Kan.
2581	■Madison, K 8	Me.
200	Madison, M 17	Md.
2312	Madison, N 4	Minn.
325	Madison (Madison Sta.), J 11	Miss.
625	Madison, F 13	Mo.
1812	Madison, I 19	Neb.
225	Madison (Silver Lake), J 18	N. H.
300	Madison, J 17	N. H.
7944	Madison, E 16	N. J.
300	*Madison, M 17	N. Y.
1683	Madison, C 9	N. C.
979	Madison, B 19	Ohio
409	*Madison (Darragh), Q 5	Pa.
80	Madison, D 3	S. C.
5018	Madison, K 23	S. D.
900	*Madison, L 11	Tenn.
281	Madison, I 13	Va.
1205	Madison, M 5	W. Va.
67447	Madison, N 15	Wis.
189	*Madisonburg, K 14	Pa.
2700	Madison Heights, N 10	Va.
377	Madison Lake, P 14	Minn.
175	*Madison Mills, L 10	Ohio
27	*Madison Mills, I 13	Va.
150	*Madison Run, J 14	Va.
325	*Madison Station (Madison), J 11	Miss.
....	*Madison Square, O 13	Mich.
8209	Madisonville, I 9	Ky.
915	Madisonville, L 18	La.
....	Madisonville, O 6	Ohio
965	Madisonville, P 18	Tenn.
2095	Madisonville, I 21	Tex.
150	*Madisonville, O 12	Va.
81	*Madley, P 9	Pa.
45	*Madoc, C 21	Mont.
7	Madra, B 14	S. D.
99	*Madras, G 5	Ga.
412	Madras, G 12	Ore.
276	Madras, B 22	Tex.
229	*Madrid, O 21	Ala.
2074	Madrid, J 11	Iowa
25	*Madrid, G 12	Ky.
50	Madrid, K 5	Me.
410	Madrid, L 8	Neb.
1056	▲Madrid, F 12	N. M.
900	Madrid, D 18	N. Y.
10	*Mad River, D 3	Calif.
37	*Madrone, J 7	Calif.
100	*Mae, J 17	Wash.
100	Maes, E 19	N. M.
160	Maeystown, N 9	Ill.
100	Magalia, E 7	Calif.
900	*Magazine, P 5	Ala.
385	Magazine, G 6	Ark.
1323	Magdalena, J 8	N. M.
10	Magee, B 11	Ind.
1221	Magee, L 14	Miss.
28	*Magenta, D 2	Tex.
....	Magenta, E 12	Wis.
....	*Maggard, G 22	Ky.
166	*Maggie, O 6	N. C.
33	*Maggie, M 6	Va.
....	*Maggie, see Kaylong	W. Va.
....	*Magic City, C 6	Tex.
15	Magley, E 21	Ind.
25	Magma, L 15	Ariz.
4000	Magna, F 10	Utah
....	Magnesite, L 14	Calif.
226	*Magness, E 16	Ark.
252	*Magnet, K 10	Ark.
35	*Magnet, Q 12	Ind.
152	Magnet, F 19	Neb.
50	*Magnet, M 21	Tex.
246	*Magnetic Springs, I 11	Ohio
100	Magnolia, K 8	Ala.
4326	Magnolia, Q 9	Ark.
218	Magnolia, H 22	Del.
329	Magnolia, E 14	Ill.
242	Magnolia, K 3	Iowa
200	*Magnolia, H 14	Ky.
450	*Magnolia, D 16	Md.
1620	Magnolia, C 22	Mass.
273	Magnolia, R 4	Minn.
2125	Magnolia, O 9	Miss.
40	*Magnolia, I 8	Mo.
1552	Magnolia, L 10	N. J.
730	Magnolia, J 16	N. C.
819	Magnolia, H 18	Ohio
75	*Magnolia, K 21	Tex.
114	Magnolia, Q 20	Va.
150	Magnolia, C 22	W. Va.
91	*Magnolia Beach, O 20	Tex.
90	*Magnolia Beach, H 9	Wash.
263	Magnolia Springs, R 7	Ala.
500	*Magnolia Springs, I 25	Tex.
....	*Magnolia Terminal, K 7	Ala.
15	*Magotha, Q 23	Va.
37	Maguire, K 13	Okla.
....	Magunden, M 14	Calif.
609	Mahaffey, J 8	Pa.
50	Mahalasville, L 12	Ind.
217	*Mahan, M 7	W. Va.
13442	Mahanoy City, K 19	Pa.
1800	*Mahanoy Plane, K 19	Pa.
1000	*Mahanoy Tunnel, K19	Pa.
197	Mahaska, C 16	Kan.
100	*Maher, K 5	Colo.
1429	Mahnomen, G 5	Minn.
823	Mahomet, H 18	Ill.
250	Mahon, E 24	Tex.
32	*Mahone, F 8	W. Va.
87	Mahoning, J 5	Pa.
....	Mahoningtown, J 2 (Pop. 4800 incl. with New Castle)	Pa.
1500	Mahopac, E 6	N. Y.
800	*Mahopac Falls, E 6	N. Y.
55	Mahto, C 12	S. D.
876	Mahtomedi, M 17	Minn.
150	Mahtowa, I 18	Minn.
874	Mahwah, B 19	N. J.
42	Maida, D 19	N. D.
1803	Maiden, G 4	N. C.
154	*Maiden Creek, M 20	Pa.
291	Maiden Rock, B 13	Wis.
22	*Maidens, L 15	Va.
80	*Maidsville, C 14	W. Va.
30	*Maine (Parks), G 13	Ariz.
400	Maine, Q 15	N. Y.
150	Mainesburg, F 16	Pa.
55	*Mainland, N 23	Pa.
205	Mainstream, K 10	Me.
150	Mainville, J 18	Pa.
463	Maitland (Lake Maitland), G 18	Fla.
539	Maitland, B 4	Mo.
750	Maitland, Q 6	W. Va.
198	*Maize, L 16	Kan.
75	Majenica, (Kelso), E 18	Ind.
700	*Majestic, H 24	Ky.
35	*Major, H 20	Ky.
130	*Majorsville, B 11	W. Va.
258	Makanda, P 14	Ill.
75	*Makemie Park, K 24	Va.
20	*Makinen, F 19	Minn.
212	Makoti, H 8	N. D.
169	*Malabar, I 21	Fla.
18	Malachite, N 14	Colo.
2731	Malad City (Malad), R 19	Idaho
125	*Malaga, K 10	Calif.
47	*Malaga, G 21	Ky.
410	Malaga, N 10	N. J.
701	Malaga, O 21	N. M.
100	*Malaga, L 18	Ohio
80	Malaga, I 14	Wash.
2000	Malakoff, F 21	Tex.
250	*Malcol (Madeleine), O 8	W. Va.
75	*Malcolm, N 4	Ala.
79	*Malcolm (Woodville), M 11	Md.
9	*Malcolm, D 8	Minn.
121	Malcolm, L 21	Neb.
447	Malcolm, K 16	Iowa
237	Malden, D 13	Ill.
75	*Malden, C 8	Ind.
58010	Malden, L 4	Mass.
2673	Malden, I 24	Mo.
325	Malden, J 23	Wash.
500	Malden, K 6	W. Va.
220	*Malden Bridge, Q 24	N. Y.
400	Malden on Hudson, A 5	N. Y.
125	*Malesus, O 5	Tenn.
21	Malheur, H 22	Ore.
12	Malheur Jc., J 24	Ore.
535	Malin, R 11	Ore.
340	Malinta, D 8	Ohio
438	Mallard, D 8	Iowa
20	Mallard Jc., M 7	La.
200	Mallet Creek, E 16	Ohio

Pop.	Place Index	State
....	Malletts Bay, D 6	Vt.
45	*Mallie, H 22	Ky.
150	Mallory, K 15	N. Y.
....	*Mallory, Q 1	Tenn.
212	*Mallory, O 5	W. Va.
27	Mallow, L 7	Va.
50	*Malmo, I 15	Minn.
167	Malmo, K 21	Neb.
90	Malo, C 20	Wash.
75	*Malone, G 21	Ala.
442	Malone, A 1, L 11	Fla.
120	*Malone, G 21	Ky.
8743	Malone, C 21	N. Y.
429	Malone, G 19	Tex.
300	Malone, K 5	Wash.
48	*Malone, N 16	Wis.
....	Malone Jc., C 21	N. Y.
24	*Maloneton, D 22	Ky.
....	*Maloney (Hosmer), P 12	Va.
381	Malott, E 16	Wash.
112	Maloy, P 9	Iowa
8	*Malpie, C 18	N. M.
43	*Malt, H 14	Ky.
38	Malta, H 10	Colo.
235	Malta, Q 15	Idaho
455	Malta, B 16	Ill.
2215	Malta, D 17	Mont.
938	Malta, L 16	Ohio
150	Malta, C 23	Tex.
355	Malta Bend, G 10	Mo.
....	Maltby, H 20 (Pop. incl. in Swoyersville)	Pa.
125	Maltby, G 9	Wash.
210	*Malung, B 7	Minn.
190	*Malvern, O 20	Ala.
5290	Malvern, K 10	Ark.
75	*Malvern, C 11	Ill.
1325	Malvern, O 4	Iowa
1177	Malvern, H 19	Ohio
1680	Malvern, P 22	Pa.
5153	*Malverne, H 7	N. Y.
50	*Malvina, E 7	Miss.
13034	Mamaroneck, G 6	N. Y.
250	*Mamers, G 13	N. C.
518	Mamie, D 24	N. C.
200	Mammoth, M 18	Ariz.
....	Mammoth, B 8	Calif.
29	*Mammoth, R 12	Mo.
550	Mammoth, O 5	Pa.
650	Mammoth, I 6	Utah
1500	Mammoth, L 7	W. Va.
....	Mammoth, I 17	Wyo.
96	Mammoth Cave, I 13	Ky.
25	Mammoth Jc., O 5	Pa.
....	Mammoth Jc., H 10	Utah
18	*Mammoth Lakes, H 13	Calif.
666	Mammoth Spring, A 16	Ark.
21	*Mamont, M 5	Pa.
1379	Mamou, K 9	La.
1342	Man, O 4	W. Va.
187	*Manadahill, N 17	Pa.
900	Manahawkin, M 18	N. J.
300	*Manakin, M 16	Va.
40	Manalapan, I 16	N. J.
2340	Manasquan, J 20	N. J.
1008	Manassa, Q 12	Colo.
165	Manassas, K 20	Ga.
1302	Manassas, G 16	Va.
110	*Manatawny, N 21	Pa.
3595	Manatee, J 13	Fla.
75	*Manavista, J 14	Fla.
791	Manawa, M 14	Wis.
....	*Manayunk, P 23	Pa.
1173	Mancelona, I 14	Mich.
155	*Manchac (Akers), L 17	La.
125	*Manchaca, K 17	Tex.
1490	*Manchaug, I 14	Mass.
518	Manchester, E 10	Ala.
75	*Manchester, G 2	Calif.
23000	Manchester, E 15	Conn.
3462	Manchester, I 5	Ga.
348	Manchester, J 9	Ill.
115	Manchester, L 21	Ind.
3762	Manchester, G 20	Iowa
215	Manchester, G 17	Kan.
1509	Manchester, I 20	Ky.
492	Manchester, M 8	Me.
763	Manchester, B 12	Md.
2200	Manchester, C 22	Mass.
1100	Manchester, Q 18	Mich.
100	*Manchester, Q 16	Minn.
600	Manchester, I 19	Mo.
20	Manchester, G 10	Mont.
77685	Manchester, P 15	N. H.
1330	Manchester, M 10	N. Y.
49	*Manchester, I 12	N. C.
2163	Manchester, Q 9	Ohio
269	Manchester, A 10	Okla.
1004	Manchester, P 17	Pa.
150	Manchester, I 21	S. D.
1715	Manchester, P 13	Tenn.
500	*Manchester, B 22	Tex.
325	Manchester, O 7	Vt.
....	Manchester (Manchester Depot), O 8	Vt.
100	*Manchester, H 7	Wash.
200	Manchester, L 17	Wis.
765	Manchester Center, O 7	Vt.
....	Manchester Depot (Manchester), O 8	Vt.
....	Manchester Green, E 16	Conn.
....	Manchester Jc., Q 19	Mich.
750	*Manco, I 23	Ky.
748	Mancos, P 4	Colo.
200	Mandalay, D 21	Ark.
6685	Mandan, N 11	N. D.
500	*Mandarin, C 17	Fla.
100	*Mandata, L 16	Pa.
200	Manderson, N 6	S. D.
130	Manderson, D 12	Wyo.
300	*Mandeville, P 5	Ark.
1326	Mandeville, L 19	La.
25	*Mandeville, O 10	W. Va.
20	Mandt, E 22	N. D.
103	*Manes, N 13	Mo.
400	*Manette, H 7	Wash.
125	Manfred, J 15	N. D.
45	Mangas, J 4	N. M.
572	Mangham, D 12	La.
200	*Mango, I 14	Fla.
300	*Mangohick, L 17	Va.
37	*Mangum, I 16	Ky.
4193	Mangum, L 3	Okla.
20	Mangum, F 15	Tex.
2557	Manhasset, H 6	N. Y.
6398	*Manhattan (Manhattan Beach), R 3	Calif.
601	Manhattan, D 20	Ill.
200	*Manhattan, K 9	Ind.
11659	Manhattan, F 18	Kan.
646	Manhattan, L 10	Mont.
157	Manhattan, J 12	Nev.
6398	Manhattan Beach (Manhattan), R 3	Calif.
86	*Manhattan Beach, I 13	Minn.
40	Manhattan Beach, C 4	Ore.
1889924	*Manhattan Boro (part of New York City), I 5	N. Y.
3831	*Manheim, O 18	Pa.
400	*Manheim, E 16	W. Va.
85	*Manifest, G 11	La.
80	*Manifold, O 3	Pa.
1248	Manila, D 21	Ark.
75	*Manila, G 22	Ky.
4	Manila, I 9	S. D.
116	Manila, E 22	Utah
35	*Manila, N 4	W. Va.
300	Manilla, K 17	Ind.
1040	Manilla, J 6	Iowa
8649	Manistee, K 11	Mich.
....	Manistee Jc., N 10	Ala.
5399	Manistique, G 11	Mich.
776	Manito, G 11	Ill.
125	*Manitou, H 8	Ky.
2	*Manitou, C 13	Minn.
43	Manitou, F 6	N. D.
258	Manitou, N 6	Okla.
150	Manitou Beach, Q 17	Mich.
1462	Manitou Springs, J 15	Colo.
30	*Manitowish, I 7	Wis.
24404	Manitowoc, Q 16	Wis.
1426	Mankato, D 13	Kan.
15654	Mankato, P 13	Minn.
95	*Mankins, B 15	Tex.
15	Manley, R 3	Minn.
130	Manley, L 23	Neb.
319	Manlius, D 12	Ill.
1520	Manlius, M 15	N. Y.
1445	Manly, C 13	Iowa
249	*Manly, I 11	N. C.
....	Mann, Q 4	Ala.
58	*Mannboro, O 15	Va.
403	Mannford, F 17	Okla.
12	Mannhaven, K 9	N. D.
334	Manning, M 10	Ark.
1748	Manning, J 6	Iowa
40	*Manning, I 5	Kan.
113	Manning, L 5	N. D.
100	Manning, C 6	Ore.
2381	Manning, I 17	S. C.
715	Manning, H 24	Tex.
....	Manning Jc., G 23	Pa.
200	*Mannington, I 8	Ky.
3145	Mannington, D 12	W. Va.
306	Manns Choice, P 9	Pa.
280	Manns Harbor, E 24	N. C.
103	*Mannsville, H 15	Ky.
348	Mannsville, H 15	N. Y.
359	Mannsville, P 15	Okla.
249	*Mannville, D 15	Fla.
200	*Manokin, P 21	Md.
350	Manomet, J 24	Mass.
....	Manor, H 4	Calif.
250	Manor, O 16	Ga.
1289	Manor, N 5	Pa.
688	Manor, J 18	Tex.
25	*Manor Hill, M 12	Pa.
50	Manor Kill, P 21	N. Y.
....	Manor No. 1, N 2	Md.
650	Manorville, G 9	N. Y.
604	Manorville, K 5	Pa.
200	*Manown (East Monongahela), O 4	Pa.
29	*Manquin, L 18	Va.
17	Manring, L 19	Tenn.
300	Manset, N 17	Me.
1002	Mansfield, H 4	Ark.
100	Mansfield, D 19	Conn.
300	*Mansfield (Mansfield Depot), E 19	Conn.
432	Mansfield, G 10	Ga.
693	Mansfield, H 17	Ill.
100	Mansfield, J 8	Ind.
4065	Mansfield, E 5	La.
6530	■Mansfield, I 19	Mass.
922	Mansfield, O 12	Mo.
37154	Mansfield, G 14	Ohio
1880	Mansfield, F 16	Pa.
106	Mansfield, E 18	S. D.
150	*Mansfield, M 6	Tenn.
774	*Mansfield, D 19	Tex.
349	Mansfield, G 17	Wash.
168	Mansfield Center, F 20	Conn.
300	Mansfield Depot (Mansfield), E 19	Conn.
70	*Manson, B 18	Ark.
40	Manson, H 12	Ind.
1429	Manson, G 8	Iowa
65	Manson, E 8	Mont.
70	Manson, C 15	N. C.
27	*Manson, M 15	Tenn.
300	Manson, G 15	Wash.
1138	Mansura, I 11	La.
238	*Mantachie, C 22	Miss.
128	Mantador, P 24	N. D.
10	Mante, C 6	Ark.
1981	Manteca, I 8	Calif.
241	Mantee, E 18	Miss.
1537	Manteno, E 20	Ill.
571	Manteo, E 25	N. C.
127	*Manteo, M 12	Va.
133	Manter, M 1	Kan.
2268	Manti, J 13	Utah
58	*Mantoloking, K 17	N. J.
47	*Manton, D 7	Calif.
1006	Manton, K 14	Mich.
600	Manton, O 17	R. I.
486	*Mantorville, P 18	Minn.
20	*Mantua, H 6	Ala.
1500	Mantua, L 8	N. J.
870	Mantua, E 18	Ohio
319	Mantua, C 11	Utah
53	*Manuel, I 21	Ky.
47	Manuelito, F 2	N. M.
....	Manumuskin, P 10	N. J.
....	Manunka Chunk, D 9	N. J.
209	Manvel, G 23	N. D.
208	Manvel, L 22	Tex.
....	Manver, L 8	Pa.
44	*Manville, F 17	Ill.
6065	Manville, G 14	N. J.
4590	Manville, B 15	R. I.
240	Manville, J 23	Wyo.
1474	Many, G 5	La.
25	*Many Islands, B 16	Ark.
45	Manzanita, C 4	Ore.
25	Manzanita, H 7	Wash.
....	*Manzanita Lake, D 6	Calif.
500	Manzano, H 12	N. M.
531	Manzanola, M 18	Colo.
58	Mapes, H 20	N. D.
32	*Maple, H 14	Ky.
6	*Maple, C 23	N. C.
20	Maple, I 25	Okla.
....	*Maple, A 8	Tex.
40	Maple, D 5	Wis.
76	*Maplebay, F 5	Minn.
80	*Maple City, O 18	Kan.
145	*Maple City, H 11	Mich.
150	*Maplecrest, Q 22	N. Y.
40	*Mapledale, R 21	N. Y.
150	Maple Falls, B 9	Wash.
46	*Mapleglen, O 23	Pa.
....	Maplegrove, D 19	Me.
50	Maple Grove, E 10	Ohio
315	Maple Grove, I 24	Pa.
34	*Maplegrove, I 18	Va.
6728	*Maple Heights, D 17	Ohio
84	Maple Hill, B 8	Iowa
247	Maplehill, G 20	Kan.
250	*Maple Hill, K 17	N. C.
30	Maplehill, I 16	Pa.
637	Maple Lake, M 14	Minn.
30	Mapleleaf, B 11	S. D.
....	*Maple Mount, G 10	Ky.
398	Maple Park, C 17	Ill.
360	Maple Plain, N 14	Minn.
580	Maple Rapids, N 17	Mich.
201	*Maple Ridge, P 7	Pa.
100	Maple River, I 7	Iowa
50	*Maples, E 21	Ind.
18	*Maples, N 15	Mo.
5900	Maple Shade, K 10	N. J.
200	*Maple Springs, Q 2	N. Y.
456	Maplesville, I 12	Ala.
121	*Maplesville, I 19	Ky.
250	Mapleton, G 12	Ill.
1824	Mapleton, H 3	Iowa
226	Mapleton, K 24	Kan.
150	Mapleton, D 18	Me.
500	Mapleton, F 3	Mich.
1070	Mapleton, Q 13	Minn.
300	Mapleton (Stratford), E 14	N. H.
21	*Mapleton, L 13	N. Y.
180	Mapleton, M 24	N. D.
162	Mapleton, G 19	Ohio
300	Mapleton, J 4	Ore.
803	Mapleton Depot (Mapleton), N 12	Pa.
907	Mapleton, H 13	Utah
225	*Mapletown, Q 3	Pa.
250	Maplevalley, I 10	Wash.
150	*Maple View, K 14	N. Y.
93	*Mapleville, C 4	Md.
800	Mapleville, B 9	R. I.
125	*Maplewood, I 12	Ind.
98	*Maplewood, P 2	Me.
12875	Maplewood, I 20	Mo.
56	*Maplewood, H 13	N. H.
23139	■Maplewood, E 17	N. J.
162	*Maplewood, H 8	Ohio
200	*Maplewood, D 8	Ore.
210	Maplewood, G 23	Pa.
200	*Maplewood, M 8	W. Va.
124	Maplewood, Q 13	Wis.
55	*Mappsburg, M 24	Va.
176	*Mappsville, K 24	Va.
53	Maquam, B 6	Vt.
4076	Maquoketa, I 23	Iowa
429	Maquon, F 10	Ill.
271	Maramec, E 15	Okla.
275	Marana, N 16	Ariz.
5	*Maranacook, M 8	Me.
100	Marathon, Q 19	Fla.
597	Marathon, E 7	Iowa
....	Marathon, H 6	Miss.
955	Marathon, P 15	N. Y.
165	*Marathon, O 8	Ohio
750	Marathon, J 7	Tex.
823	Marathon City (Marathon) J 12	Wis.
150	*Marble, C 7	Ark.
240	Marble, I 8	Colo.
792	Marble, G 16	Minn.
356	Marble, Q 2	N. C.
115	*Marble, H 6	Pa.
28	*Marble, C 22	Wash.
31	Marble Canyon, C 14	Ariz.
214	Marble City, H 23	Okla.
331	Marble Cliff, K 12	Ohio
25	Marble Creek, E 6	Idaho
110	Marble Dale, G 5	Conn.
....	Marble Falls, C 9	Ark.
1021	Marble Falls, J 16	Tex.
121	*Marblehead, I 4	Ill.
10856	■Marblehead, D 21	Mass.
915	Marblehead, C 13	Ohio
105	Marblehead, N 17	Wis.
....	Marblehead Neck, D 21	Mass.
500	Marblehill, D 7	Ga.
30	*Marblehill, N 19	Ind.
421	Marblehill, O 21	Mo.
55	Marblemount, D 11	Wash.
660	Marble Rock, D 15	Iowa
....	Marbleton, H 15	Ala.
43	Marbleton, K 5	Wyo.
161	*Marburg, P 17	Pa.
200	Marbury, I 15	Ala.
500	*Marbury, M 10	Md.
75	*Marcel, N 12	La.
3206	Marceline, D 11	Mo.
20	Marcell, F 14	Minn.
89	*Marcella, D 14	Ark.
992	Marcellus, Q 12	Mich.
1112	Marcellus, M 14	N. Y.
43	Marcellus, J 21	Wash.
158	*Marcellus Falls, M 14	N. Y.
6	*March, I 13	Va.
130	*Marchand, L 6	Pa.
....	Marchant, G 7	Calif.
....	*March Field, Q 9	Calif.
50	*Marcia, M 15	N. M.
175	Marco, M 7	Ind.
500	Marco, G 8	La.
500	Marcola, I 7	Ore.
20	*Marcum, I 20	Ky.
1206	Marcus, E 3	Iowa
37	Marcus, H 7	S. D.
393	Marcus, C 21	Wash.
68	*Marcus (Halo), K 11	W. Va.
....	Marcuse, G 7	Calif
4123	Marcus Hook, Q 23	Pa
45	*Marcy (Highland), F 23	Minn.
4528	▲*Marcy, L 18	N. Y.
....	Marcy, D 17	Ohio
418	Mardela Springs, M 20	Md.
....	Mardock, J 13	Okla.
500	Mare Island, A 19	Calif.
118	*Marengo, K 7	Ala.
2034	Marengo, A 17	Ill.
812	Marengo, P 12	Ind.
2260	Marengo, K 18	Iowa
275	Marengo, I 13	Ohio
45	*Marengo (Hagood), Q 14	Va.
35	Marengo, K 21	Wash.
100	Marengo, G 5	Wis.
400	Marenisco, C 22	Mich.
41	*Maretburg, H 18	Ky.
3805	Marfa, J 5	Tex.
600	Marfork, D 8	W. Va.
875	Marfrance, M 11	W. Va.
1200	Margaret, F 15	Ala.
95	*Margaret (Margarettsville). C 18	N. C.
200	Margaret, B 14	Tex.
812	Margaretville, Q 20	N. Y.
3266	Margate, P 15	N. J.
100	*Margerum, B 6	Ala.
150	Margie, D 13	Minn.
23	*Margo, J 16	Va.
100	*Margret, B 6	Ga.
600	*Marguerite, M 5	Pa.
100	Mariah Hill, Q 8	Ind.
62	Marial, O 4	Ore.
4449	Marianna, I 19	Ark.
5079	Marianna, A 1, M 11	Fla.
1493	Marianna, P 2	Pa.
6	*Marias, C 11	Mont.
450	Maria Stein, I 6	Ohio
40	Mariaville, E 14	Neb.
200	*Mariaville, M 22	N. Y.
72	*Mariba, F 20	Ky.
128	*Maribel, I 21	N. C.
175	Maribel, O 15	Wis.
25	Maricopa, L 13	Ariz.
670	Maricopa, M 12	Calif.
32	*Marie, E 22	Ark.
13	*Marie, G 13	Tex.
50	*Marie, P 10	W. Va.
....	*Mariemont, O 6	Ohio
50	*Marienthal, I 4	Kan.
700	Marienville, G 7	Pa.
8667	Marietta, E 6	Ga.
193	Marietta, G 9	Ill.
150	Marietta, K 16	Ind.
50	*Marietta, D 18	Kan.
400	Marietta, N 3	Minn.
200	*Marietta, B 22	Miss.
125	*Marietta, M 14	N. Y.
71	*Marietta, J 12	N. C.
14543	Marietta, M 18	Ohio
1837	Marietta, Q 13	Okla.
2128	*Marietta, O 18	Pa.
300	*Marietta, B 6	S. C.
250	*Marietta, D 24	Tex.
200	Marietta, C 7	Wash.
242	*Marilla, N 5	N. Y.
400	*Marina, K 7	Calif.
....	*Marina, I 5	Calif.
4	Marindahl, O 22	S. D.
557	Marine, M 12	Ill.
338	Marine (Marine on St. Croix), M 18	Minn.
....	*Marine Barracks, A 19	Calif.
....	*Marine Barracks, N 18	S. C.
3633	Marine City, O 25	Mich.
....	*Marineland, E 18	Fla.
338	Marine on St. Croix (Marine), M 18	Minn.
300	*Marines, K 19	N. C.
....	Marinette, K 12	Ariz.
14183	Marinette, P 11	Wis.
708	Maringouin, L 13	La.
2382	Marion, J 10	Ala.
758	Marion, G 21	Ark.
258	Marion, I 11	Conn.
45	*Marion, C 6	Ga.
9251	Marion, P 15	Ill.
26767	Marion, F 17	Ind.
4721	Marion, I 20	Iowa
2086	Marion, J 17	Kan.
2163	Marion, I 7	Ky.
481	Marion, A 10	La.
77	Marion, K 23	Me.
650	*Marion (Marion Station), R 20	Md.
2030	▲Marion, L 21	Mass.
710	Marion, L 15	Mich.
54	*Marion, J 21	Miss.
100	*Marion, I 13	Mo.
10	Marion, E 3	Mont.
150	Marion, O 11	Neb.
700	Marion, L 11	N. Y.
2889	Marion, F 1, N 10	N. C.
242	Marion, O 20	N. D.
30817	Marion, H 11	Ohio
18	Marion, I 12	Okla.
81	Marion, G 6	Ore.
500	Marion, Q 13	Pa.
5746	Marion, F 21	S. C.
765	Marion (Marion Junction), M 22	S. D.
373	Marion, L 17	Tex.
5177	Marion, D 10	Va.
1034	Marion, L 13	Wis.
439	*Marion Center, L 6	Pa.
2068	*Marion Heights, J 16	Pa.
300	Marion Jc., J 10	Ala.
765	Marion Junction (Marion), M 22	S. D.
600	Marion Station (Marion), R 20	Md.
1127	Marionville, P 9	Mo.
383	Mariposa, I 11	Calif.
35	*Mariposa, O 16	N. Y.
....	Mariska, F 19	Minn.
1657	Marissa, N 12	Ill.
529	Mark, E 14	Ill.
40	*Mark, P 16	Iowa
220	Mark, L 14	La.
10	Mark, D 16	Mo.
202	Mark Center, D 5	Ohio
2685	Marked Tree, E 20	Ark.
48	Markelsville, M 14	Pa.
912	Markesan, L 17	Wis.
1388	*Markham, J 9	Ill.
45	*Markham, P 22	Pa.
400	Markham, M 21	Tex.
110	*Markham, F 14	Va.
260	Markham, K 3	Wash.
100	Markland, N 21	Ind.
671	Markle, E 19	Ind.
54	Markleeville, G 11	Calif.
198	Marklesburg (Aitch), N 11	Pa.
125	*Markleton, P 6	Pa.
266	Markleville, I 17	Ind.
46	*Markley, D 15	Tex.
297	*Markleysburg, Q 5	Pa.
1818	Marks, C 9	Miss.
1811	Marksville, I 11	La.
10	*Markton, L 10	Wis.
150	Markville, J 18	Minn.
257	Marland, C 14	Okla.
....	Marlboro, O 17	Calif.
300	Marlboro, G 16	Conn.
....	*Marlboro, M 17 (Pop. incl. in Hancock)	Me.
15154	Marlboro, F 15	Mass.
1000	Marlboro, Q 8	N. H.
500	Marlboro, H 18	N. J.
3000	Marlboro (Marlborough), D 5	N. Y.
300	Marlboro, F 18	Ohio
15	Marlboro, Q 11	Vt.
127	*Marlboro, E 13	Va.
....	Marlboro Depot, see Webb Q 8	N. H.
....	Marlboro Jc., F 15	Mass.
12	*Marlbrook, L 8	Va.
1161	Marlette, N 23	Mich.
495	*Mar Lin, K 19	Pa.
6542	Marlin, H 19	Tex.
94	Marlin (Krupp), I 19	Wash.
35	*Marling, G 16	Mo.
1644	Marlinton, L 14	W. Va.
150	*Marlow, K 23	Ga.
35	*Marlow, K 16	Ky.
300	Marlow, O 8	N. H.
2889	Marlow, M 10	Okla.
15	Marlow, B 22	S. D.
600	Marlton, K 11	N. J.
677	Marmaduke, B 20	Ark.
626	Marmarth, P 1	N. D.
1814	Marmet, L 6	W. Va.
10	*Marmon, E 3	N. D.
220	Marmora, P 14	N. J.
10	Marmot, D 9	Ore.
....	Marne, I 7	Ga.
245	Marne, L 6	Iowa
400	Marne (Berlin), O 12	Mich.
....	Marnel, N 16	Colo.
1033	Maroa, I 15	Ill.
150	Marquam, F 7	Ore.
403	Marquand, N 21	Mo.
747	Marquette, D 21	Iowa
609	Marquette, I 15	Kan.
15928	Marquette, E 7	Mich.
245	Marquette, L 18	Neb.
185	Marquette, L 17	Wis.
100	Marquez, G 8	N. M.
381	Marquez, H 21	Tex.
150	*Marquisville, K 12	Iowa
8	*Marr, L 18	Ohio
2500	Marrero, N 18	La.
112	*Marriottsville, E 12	Md.
160	Marrowbone, J 15	Ky.
217	Marrowbone (Regina), H 23	Ky.
1318	Mars, L 3	Pa.
460	Mars Bluff, F 20	S. C.
150	Marsden (Chocowinity), G 19	N. C.
59	Marsden, Q 13	Okla.
4455	Marseilles, D 16	Ill.
65	*Marsena, C 9	Ark.
15	Marsh, O 19	Ariz.
50	Marsh, H 23	Mont.
822	Marshall, D 11	Ark.
19	*Marshall, H 4	Calif.
2758	Marshall, K 21	Ill.
321	Marshall, I 7	Ind.
75	Marshall (North Fork), D 19	Ky.
5253	Marshall, Q 16	Mich.
4590	Marshall, O 6	Minn.
8533	Marshall, G 10	Mo.
1160	Marshall, N 8	N. C.
12	Marshall, L 7	N. D.
382	Marshall (New Marshall), F 12	Okla.
18410	Marshall, E 24	Tex.
550	Marshall, F 15	Va.
55	Marshall, H 23	Wash.
447	Marshall, L 19	Wis.
20	Marshall, M 18	Wyo.
500	*Marshallberg, J 20	N. C.
....	*Marshall Ford Dam, J 18	Tex.
155	*Marshall Hall, M 11	Md.
75	Marshall Jc., G 10	Mo.
....	Marshall Jc., O 6	Wis.
7	*Marshall Pass, M 11	Colo.
125	*Marshalls Creek, I 23	Pa.
1500	Marshallton, B 21	Del.
19240	Marshalltown, I 15	Iowa
905	Marshallville, J 9	Ga.
373	Marshallville, G 16	Ohio
20	*Marshburg, G 21	Pa.
52	*Marshes Siding, K 18	Ky.
110	*Marshfield, H 6	Ind.
800	Marshfield, H 22	Mass.
1764	Marshfield, N 11	Mo.
5259	Marshfield, L 2	Ore.
292	Marshfield, F 15	Vt.
10359	Marshfield, H 13	Wis.
265	Marshfield Hills, H 22	Mass.
....	Marshfield Jc., I 13	Wis.
90	*Marsh Hill (Marsh Hill Jc.), G 15	Pa.
900	Mars Hill, D 19	Me.
517	Mars Hill, N 8	N. C.
90	Marsh Hill Jc., (Marsh Hill), G 15	Pa.
67	Marshland, A 6	Ore.
35	Marshland, D 15	Wis.
....	Marshs, H 10	Ohio
1007	Marshville, I 6	N. C.
58	*Marshville (Theresa), N 18	Wis.
100	Marsing, N 3	Idaho
123	Marsland, F 3	Neb.
1200	Marsteller, L 8	Pa.
20	Marston, J 19	La.
468	Marston, I 25, R 23	Mo.
125	*Marston, I 10	N. C.
600	Marstons Mills, M 12, M 25	Mass.
2856	Mart, G 19	Tex.
150	Martaban, G 11	Ala.
102	Martel, M 21	Neb.
150	Martel, H 12	Ohio
250	*Martel, N 18	Tenn.
150	Martell, H 9	Calif.
125	Martell, B 12	Wis.
215	*Martelle, I 21	Iowa
172	Martensdale, M 11	Iowa
125	*Martha, F 22	Ky.
....	Martha, G 16	Neb.
242	Martha, M 4	Okla.
63	*Martha (Martha Furnace), K 12	Pa.
24	*Martha, L 12	Tenn.
63	*Martha Furnace (Martha), K 12	Pa.
25	*Martha Gap, C 6	Va.
321	Marthasville, I 18	Mo.
243	Marthaville, F 6	La.
53	*Martin, E 14	Fla.
242	Martin, C 13	Ga.
5	*Martin, N 15	Idaho
957	Martin (Smalley), H 22	Ky.
12	*Martin (Queens), D 21	Ky.
55	*Martin, O 11	Me.
400	Martin, P 13	Mich.
228	Martin, I 14	N. D.
250	Martin, C 11	Ohio
600	Martin, Q 3	Pa.
300	*Martin, M 11	S. C.
1013	Martin, N 8	S. D.
3587	Martin, L 4	Tenn.
15	Martin, J 11	Wash.
27	*Martin, E 18	W. Va.
183	*Martin City, H 6	Mo.
200	*Martindale, O 20	Pa.
550	Martindale, K 17	Tex.
150	*Martindale Depot (Martindale), Q 24	N. Y.
7381	Martinez, A 20, H 6	Calif.
175	*Martinez, G 19	Ga.
200	Marting, L 7	W. Va.
150	Martinsburg, P 15	Ind.
218	Martinsburg, N 18	Iowa
184	*Martinsburg (Sandy Hook), F 21	Ky.
422	Martinsburg, G 15	Mo.
105	Martinsburg, F 21	Neb.
239	Martinsburg, I 17	N. Y.
215	Martinsburg, J 14	Ohio
1396	Martinsburg, N 10	Pa.
15063	Martinsburg, D 24	W. Va.
37	*Martins Creek (Brainards), D 10	N. J.
500	Martins Creek, K 23	Pa.
100	Martinsdale, J 12	Mont.
14729	*Martins Ferry, J 20	Ohio
75	Martins Mills, Q 7	Tenn.
89	*Martins Mills, E 21	Tex.
80	*Martins Point, O 17	S. C.
34	*Martin Springs (Dove), Q 14	Tenn.
30	*Martin Springs, D 21	Tex.
1296	Martinsville, K 20	Ill.
5009	Martinsville, K 12	Ind.
15	*Martinsville, M 10	Miss.
119	*Martinsville, B 7	Mo.
352	*Martinsville, F 15	N. J.
409	Martinsville, N 9	Ohio
350	*Martinsville, G 24	Tex.
10080	Martinsville, Q 7	Va.
280	Martinton, F 21	Ill.
117	*Martintown, J 22	Wis.
250	*Martinville, G 12	Ark.
50	Martland, N 19	Neb.
120	*Martling, C 16	Ala.
125	*Martville, M 13	N. Y.
259	*Martwick, I 10	Ky.
400	*Marty, N 18	S. D.
....	*Martz, see Clay City	Ind.
20	*Marumsco, P 20	Md.
800	Marvel, H 12	Ala.
830	Marvell, J 18	Ark.
16	*Marvin, J 12	Mo.
164	Marvin, E 23	S. D.
30	*Marvin, C 8	Va.
....	*Mar Vista, N 15	Calif.
300	Marvyn, J 22	Ala.
150	*Marwood, K 4	Pa.
20	*Mary, G 20	Ky.
100	Mary, O 17	La.
....	*Mary, F 13	Neb.
500	*Maryd, K 20	Pa.
127	Marydel, G 20	Md.
116	*Marydell, I 19	Ky.
18	*Marye, J 16	Va.
24	*Mary Esther, N 5	Fla.
90	Maryhill, P 12	Wash.
375	*Maryknoll, F 6	N. Y.
250	Maryland, O 20	N. Y.
....	Maryland Jc., C 20	W. Va..
2000	*Maryland Heights, I 20	Mo.
140	*Maryland Line, B 14	Md.
250	*Marylhurst, E 8	Ore.
125	*Maryneal, E 12	Tex.
626	Marysvale, M 9	Utah
6646	Marysville, F 7	Calif.
218	Marysville, M 22	Idaho
....	*Marysville, see Potomac	Ill.
80	*Marysville, O 17	Ind.
4055	Marysville, D 18	Kan.
1777	Marysville, N 25	Mich.
150	Marysville, I 8	Mont.
4037	Marysville, J 10	Ohio
1882	Marysville, N 16	Pa.
162	*Marysville, B 18	Tex.
1748	Marysville, F 8	Wash.
360	*Marytown, Q 5	W. Va.
140	Marytown, O 16	Wis.
250	*Maryus, M 20	Va.
536	Maryville, M 10	Ill.
5700	Maryville, B 5	Mo.
5609	Maryville, O 19	Tenn.
....	Maryville Jc., N 15	Iowa
300	Masardis, E 17	Me.
100	Mascoma (East Lebanon), L 8	N. H.
262	*Mascot, N 23	Ariz.
45	Mascot, N 13	Neb.
1800	Mascot, M 19	Tenn.
12	*Mascot, L 19	Va.
239	*Mascotte, M 16	Fla.
2294	Mascoutah, N 12	Ill.
406	Masena, H 12	Ala.
18	Masham, D 15	Okla.
100	*Mashfork, G 21	Ky.
105	*Mashoes, E 24	N. C.
200	Mashpee, N 12, M 24	Mass.
200	*Mashulaville, H 20	Miss.
138	Maskell, E 21	Neb.
330	Mason, L 17	Ill.
50	*Mason, D 17	Ky.
2867	Mason, P 17	Mich.
396	Mason (Mason City), K 14	Neb.
259	Mason, I 5	Nev.
50	Mason, R 12	N. H.
902	Mason, N 7	Ohio
32	Mason, H 17	Okla.
35	Mason, E 3	S. D.
448	Mason, P 3	Tenn.
1535	Mason, I 15	Tex.
47	*Mason, Q 17	Va.
795	Mason (Mason City), G 4	W. Va.
152	Mason, F 5	Wis.
30	*Mason, J 5	Wyo.
50	*Mason and Dixon, Q 13	Pa.
1984	Mason City, H 12	Ill.
27080	Mason City, C 13	Iowa
396	Mason City (Mason), K 14	Neb.
3000	Mason City, G 18	Wash.
80	*Masonia, E 6	Idaho
....	*Masonic Home, E 14	Ky.
3721	Masontown, Q 4	Pa.
869	Mason Town, D 15	W. Va.
130	*Masonville, O 16	Ark.
105	Masonville, D 14	Colo.
176	Masonville, G 20	Iowa
100	*Masonville, G 9	Mich.
300	*Masonville, L 13	N. J.
75	*Masonville, Q 19	N. Y.
31	*Masonville, F 18	W. Va.
350	Mass, D 1	Mich.
19	*Massack, E 9	Calif.
1260	*Massapequa, I 7	N. Y.
488	*Massapequa Park, I 7	N. Y.
24	*Massbach, A 9	Ill.
479	Massena, M 7	Iowa
11328	Massena P.O., C 19	N. Y.
....	*Massena (Massena Springs), C 19	N. Y.
....	Massena Springs, see Massena	N. Y.
125	Massey, F 20	Md.
....	Massey, K 20	Okla.
12	*Massey Lake, G 21	Tex.
212	Massies Mill, L 10	Va.
250	Massieville, N 11	Ohio
40	*Massillon, J 10	Ala.
47	*Massillon, J 22	Iowa
26644	Massillon, G 17	Ohio
31	Masten, G 17	Pa.
17	Masters, D 17	Colo.
800	Masters (Winona), M 9	W. Va.
50	Masthope, G 24	Pa.
750	*Mastic, H 9	N. Y.
10	*Mastic Beach, H 9	N. Y.
....	Mastodon, F 3	Mich.
100	*Masury, D 21	Ohio
1376	Matador, B 12	Tex.
510	Matagorda, C 9	Miss.
805	Matagorda, N 21	Tex.
1735	Matamoras, H 25	Pa.
74	*Matawan, Q 15	Minn.
2758	Matawan, G 18	N. J.
400	*Matchwood, B 23	Mich.
27	*Mateer, L 5	Pa.
34	*Mater (Kona), J 22	Ky.
905	Matewan, P 3	W. Va.
400	Matfield, I 20	Mass.
146	Matfield Green, K 19	Kan.
9	*Mather, H 11	Calif.
1500	Mather, P 3	Pa.
125	*Mather, I 16	Wis.
115	*Mathers (Quaker), L 1	W. Va.
252	Matherton, O 16	Mich.
565	Matherville, E 7	Ill.
100	*Matherville, M 20	Miss.
359	*Matheson, D 6	Calif.
200	Matheson, I 18	Colo.
600	Mathews, K 18	Ala.
500	Mathews, O 17	La.
37	*Mathews (North Wakefield), L 18	N. H.
....	Mathews, P 25	N. D.
500	Mathews, M 21	Va.
110	*Mathias, H 20	W. Va.
160	*Mathias Point, I 18	Va.
1950	Mathis, O 18	Tex.
549	Mathiston, F 18	Miss.
150	*Matinicus (Matinicus Isle), O 14	Me.
112	*Matlock, C 3	Iowa
25	*Matlock, J 5	Wash.
21	*Matney, D 2	N. C.
	*Matney, see Stacy	Va.
800	Matoaca, N 17	Va.
926	Matoaka, Q 8	W. Va.
25	Matoy, P 18	Okla.
65	*Matson, I 18	Mo.
5000	Mattapan, G 19, P 4	Mass.
1000	Mattapoisett, M 21	Mass.
125	*Mattaponi, L 19	Va.
700	Mattawamkeag, I 17	Me.
312	Mattawan, Q 13	Mich.
250	*Mattawana, M 13	Pa.
....	*Matteawan (Beacon), D 5	N. Y.
819	Matteson, D 21	Ill.
15	*Matthew, F 21	Ky.
27	Matthews, C 17	Colo
145	Matthews, H 18	Ga.
11	*Matthews (Crain), O 14	Ill.
468	Matthews, G 18	Ind.

Pop.	Place	Index	State
448	Matthews	Q 23	Mo.
486	Matthews	I 6	N. C.
....	Matthie	J 10	Ariz.
100*	Mattie	F 22	Ky.
1938	Mattituck	F 10	N. Y.
37*	Mattoax	N 14	Va.
250	Mattocks (E. Baldwin)	P 4	Me.
15287	Mattoon	J 18	Ill.
524	Mattoon	L 12	Wis.
....	Mattoon Jc.	L 12	Wis.
....	Mattox	C 15	Fla.
200	Mattson	D 9	Miss.
....	Mattsville	O 25	Neb.
3009	Mauch Chunk	K 21	Pa.
154	Mauckport	Q 14	Ind.
45*	Maud	B 6	Ala.
80*	Maud	G 15	Ky.
75*	Maud	B 10	Miss.
300*	Maud (Mauds)	N 6	Ohio
2036	Maud	K 15	Okla.
600	Maud	C 24	Tex.
88*	Maud	C 10	W. Va.
43	Maudlow	K 10	Mont.
500	Maugansville	B 5	Md.
123*	Mauk	J 7	Ga.
34*	Maulden	H 19	Ky.
....	Mauldin	J 7	Ark.
25*	Maumee	C 10	Ark.
4683	Maumee	C 9	Ohio
521	Maunie	O 20	Ill.
80*	Maupin	K 18	Mo.
267	Maupin	E 12	Ore.
163*	Maurepas	L 17	La.
....	Maurer	G 18	N. J.
300*	Maurertown	F 12	Va.
272	Maurice	D 2	Iowa
420	Maurice	N 10	La.
300	Maurice River	Q 10	N. J.
450	Mauricetown	P 10	N. J.
400	Mauriceville	J 25	Tex.
12*	Maurine	H 5	S. D.
274	Maury	G 17	N. C.
412	Maury City	N 4	Tenn.
50*	Maury Jc. (Badgett)	N 4	Tenn.
2621	Mauston	I 17	Wis.
50*	Maverick	F 13	Tex.
40*	Mavie	D 6	Minn.
18*	Mavis	I 10	W. Va.
....*	Mavisdale	B 7	Va.
33*	Mawrglen (Glen Mawr)	H 17	Pa.
40*	Max	I 12	Ind.
....*	Max	F 13	Minn.
21*	Max	M 17	Mo.
155	Max	O 8	Neb.
423	Max	I 10	N. D.
113*	Maxatawny	P 21	Pa.
215	Maxbass	E 10	N. D.
226	Maxeys	F 14	Ga.
150	Maxie	P 17	Miss.
100*	Maxie	B 7	Va.
300	Maximo	G 19	Ohio
54*	Maxinkuckee	D 13	Ind.
700	Max Meadows	P 3	Va.
....	Maxon	N 15	Iowa
150*	Maxon (West Paducah)	I 5	Ky.
1656	Maxton	J 11	N. C.
250*	Maxville	D 19	Fla.
50*	Maxville	J 6	Mont.
506	Maxwell	F 5	Calif.
350	Maxwell	I 17	Ind.
812	Maxwell	J 13	Iowa
480	Maxwell	K 11	Neb.
483	Maxwell	C 19	N. M.
50	Maxwell	L 15	Okla.
100*	Maxwell	Q 12	Tenn.
395	Maxwell	K 17	Tex.
50*	Maxwell	C 9	Va.
31*	Maxwell	E 8	W. Va.
....*	Maxwell Field	K 16	Ala.
16	Maxwelton	G 7	Wash.
45*	Maxwelton	N 12	W. Va.
300	May	L 13	Idaho
....*	May	H 22	Ky.
239	May	C 2	Okla.
450	May	F 15	Tex.
47*	Mayaro	E 7	Calif.
390	Maybee	Q 20	Mich.
107	Maybell	C 5	Colo.
110	Mayberry	N 23	Neb.
2000	Maybeury	Q 7	W. Va.
1189	Maybrook	D 4	N. Y.
21*	Maybrook	N 4	Va.
75	Mayburg	G 7	Pa.
45*	May Day	E 18	Kan.
500*	Maydelle	G 22	Tex.
400	Mayer	I 12	Ariz.
146*	Mayer	N 14	Minn.
136	Mayersville	H 6	Miss.
57*	Mayesville	K 23	Iowa
649	Mayesville	G 17	S. C.
275	Mayetta	F 21	Kan.
125*	Mayetta	M 18	N. J.
....	Mayfair	B 21	Ill.
170*	Mayfield	B 6	Ark.
1800	Mayfield	G 20, I 5	Calif.
175*	Mayfield	G 16	Ga.
150*	Mayfield	O 7	Idaho
150	Mayfield	N 15	Kan.
8619	Mayfield	K 5	Ky.
45*	Mayfield (Kingsbury)	J 10	Me.
100*	Mayfield	I 12	Mich.
50*	Mayfield	N 21	Mo.
759	Mayfield	L 22	N. Y.
448	Mayfield	C 18	Ohio
34	Mayfield	J 2	Okla.
3172	Mayfield	G 22	Pa.
473*	Mayfield	K 12	Utah
92*	Mayfield	M 7	Wash.
2696	Mayfield Heights	D 25	Ohio
165*	Mayflower	H 12	Ark.
10*	Mayflower	H 24	Ky.
29*	Mayflower	I 25	Tex.
200	Mayger	A 6	Ore.
172*	Mayhew	G 22	Miss.
300	Mayhill	M 15	N. M.
100	Mayking	I 23	Ky.
100	Maylene	H 13	Ala.
123*	Maymead (Vaughtsville)	L 25	Tenn.
14*	Mayna	G 12	La.
266	Maynard	A 18	Ark.
5	Maynard	B 6	Ind.
432	Maynard	E 19	Iowa
6812■	Maynard	E 17	Mass.
580	Maynard	N 7	Minn.
600	Maynard	J 19	Ohio
500	Maynardville	M 19	Tenn.
216*	Maynor	N 7	W. Va.
915	Mayo	C 10	Fla.
25*	Mayo	G 16	Ky.
250*	Mayo	I 7	La.
700*	Mayo	H 14	Md.
155*	Mayo	A 9	S. C.
285*	Mayo (East Concord)	E 20	Vt.
40*	Mayo	R 11	Va.
2353	Mayodan	C 8	N. C.
20	Mayo Jc.	C 9	Fla.
67	Mayoworth	F 16	Wyo.
377*	Maypearl	F 19	Tex.
511	Mayport	B 17	Fla.
100	Mayport	J 6	Pa.
175	Mays	J 19	Ind.
12	Maysdorf	E 19	Wyo.
....*	Maysel	K 8	W. Va.
159*	Maysfield	I 20	Tex.
2800	Mays Landing	O 13	N. J.
327	Mays Lick	D 19	Ky.
150	Maysville	B 15	Ala.
175	Maysville	A 3	Ark.
514	Maysville	D 11	Ga.
28	Maysville	J 7	Ill.
6572	Maysville	D 20	Ky.
....	Maysville	C 19	Me.
1026	Maysville	D 6	Mo.
732	Maysville	J 19	N. C.
880	Maysville	M 12	Okla.
160*	Maysville	F 18	W. Va.
....	Mayton	N 11	Tenn.
154	Maytown	G 20	Fla.
520*	Maytown	O 18	Pa.
75	Maytown	K 6	Wash.
....	May Valley	L 22	Colo.
....*	Mayview	H 20	Ill.
325	Mayview	G 8	Mo.
420*	Mayview	L 3	Pa.
28	May View	L 23	Wash.
736	Mayville	M 21	Mich.
1354	Mayville	Q 2	N. Y.
1351	Mayville	J 23	N. D.
75	Mayville	E 14	Ore.
2754	Mayville	N 18	Wis.
10731*	Maywood	N 5, Q 4	Calif.
26648	Maywood	C 20	Ill.
500*	Maywood	J 14	Ind.
75*	Maywood	H 17	Ky.
165	Maywood	D 15	Mo.
426	Maywood	M 11	Neb.
4052	Maywood	D 20	N. J.
300	Maywood (Sidney Center)	P 18	N. Y.
66*	Maza	F 17	N. D.
21*	Mazama	D 16	Wash.
545	Mazeppa	P 19	Minn.
30*	Mazie	F 22	Ky.
200	Mazie	E 21	Okla.
851	Mazomanie	J 19	Wis.
512	Mazon	E 18	Ill.
....	Mazonia	E 18	Ill.
70	Meacham	D 20	Ore.
191*	Mead	B 17	Colo.
260	Mead	K 22	Neb.
150	Mead	Q 16	Okla.
103	Mead	G 24	Wash.
150*	Meade	O 8	W. Va.
1400	Meade	N 7	Kan.
100*	Mead Lake (Nepac)	O 21	Nev.
60*	Meador	J 13	Ky.
190*	Meador	P 3	W. Va.
35*	Meadow	K 23	Neb.
60	Meadow	D 7	S. D.
300*	Meadow	N 18	Tenn.
408	Meadow	C 9	Tex.
422	Meadow	K 9	Utah
16	Meadow	M 17	Va.
31*	Meadow Bluff	M 11	W. Va.
477	Meadow Bridge	N 10	W. Va.
66*	Meadow Brook	D 18	Minn.
150*	Meadowbrook	E 4	N. Y.
....*	Meadowbrook	N 22 (Pop. 400 incl. in Abington)	Pa.
262	Meadowbrook	E 13	W. Va.
38*	Meadow Creek	A 6	Idaho
600	Meadow Creek	O 9	W. Va.
150	Meadowdale	G 8	Wash.
150	Meadowdale	K 22	Wyo.
479	Meadow Grove	H 19	Neb.
142*	Meadow Lands	H 18	Minn.
1500	Meadow Lands	N 2	Pa.
55*	Meadow Lawn	F 13	Ky.
....	Meadows	F 4	Ark.
150*	Meadows	K 5	Idaho
150	Meadows	F 16	Ill.
200	Meadows	J 12	Md.
200*	Meadows (Jefferson)	G 14	N. H.
25*	Meadows of Dan	Q 5	Va.
112*	Meadow Valley	E 9	Calif.
43*	Meadow Valley	I 15	Wis.
20	Meadow View	I 5	Ore.
596	Meadowview	E 8	Va.
510	Meadville	N 7	Miss.
509	Meadville	D 10	Mo.
10	Meadville	E 13	Neb.
18919	Meadville	F 3	Pa.
75*	Meadville	P 10	Va.
46*	Meadville	D 9	W. Va.
....	Meadville Jc.	F 2	Pa.
75*	Meally	G 22	Ky.
160*	Means (Chambers)	F 20	Ky.
50	Means (Cadiz Jc.)	I 19	Ohio
193	Meansville	H 7	Ga.
912	Mears	M 10	Mich.
19*	Mears	L 24	Va.
6	Mears Jc.	K 11	Colo.
26*	Meat Camp	C 3	N. C.
55	Meauwataka	K 14	Mich.
....*	Meaux	N 10	La.
2060	Mebane	D 12	N. C.
17	Mecaha	G 17	Mont.
500*	Mecca	P 19	Calif.
1000	Mecca	J 7	Ind.
123	Mecca	D 20	Ohio
1500	Mechanic Falls	N 5	Me.
423	Mechanicsburg	I 13	Ill.
130	Mechanicsburg	I 18	Ind.
50*	Mechanicsburg	H 13	Ind.
50*	Mechanicsburg	J 9	Miss.
1653	Mechanicsburg	J 10	Ohio
5709	Mechanicsburg	N 15	Pa.
125*	Mechanicsburg	O 2	Va.
107	Mechanicstown	H 19	Ohio
....*	Mechanics Valley, see Spring Valley		Pa.
....	Mechanicsville	B 24	Conn.
821	Mechanicsville	J 21	Iowa
1801▲	Mechanicsville	N 13	Md.
748*	Mechanicsville	L 19	Pa.
95*	Mechanicsville	L 17	Va.
7449	Mechanicville	M 24	N. Y.
35	Mechum River	K 12	Va.
110	Meckinock (Mekinock)	H 22	N. D.
180*	Mecklenburg	O 12	N. Y.
144	Meckling	P 23	S. D.
38	Meckville	M 20	Pa.
254	Mecosta	M 15	Mich.
75*	Meda	H 13	Ga.
703	Medaryville	D 10	Ind.
24	Medberry	P 19	N. D.
10*	Meddybemps	K 23	Me.
50*	Mederville	E 21	Iowa
1899	Medfield	G 18	Mass.
....	Medfield Jc.	G 17	Mass.
57	Medford	J 14	Me.
50*	Medford	D 11	Md.
63083	Medford	L 4	Mass.
342	Medford	P 16	Minn.
50*	Medford	I 8	Mo.
1000	Medford	K 12	N. J.
1121	Medford	B 10	Okla.
11281	Medford	Q 6	Ore.
2361	Medford	H 11	Wis.
94	Medford Center	J 14	Me.
....*	Medford Hillside	L 3	Mass.
....	Medford Jc.	L 4	Mass.
1500	Medford Station	H 9	N. Y.
187*	Media	F 7	Ill.
5351	Media	P 22	Pa.
806	Mediapolis	N 22	Iowa
2114	Medical Lake	H 22	Wash.
40	Medical Springs	F 22	Ore.
338	Medicine Bow	N 18	Wyo.
396	Medicine Lake	C 24	Mont.
1870	Medicine Lodge	N 12	Kan.
210	Medicine Mound	B 14	Tex.
50*	Medicine Park	M 8	Okla.
162	Medill	B 15	Mo.
30*	Medill	B 22	Tex.
140*	Medimont	E 5	Idaho
75*	Medina	R 19	Mich.
5871	Medina	L 6	N. Y.
500	Medina	M 16	N. D.
4359	Medina	E 16	Ohio
414	Medina	N 5	Tenn.
300	Medina	L 15	Tex.
600*	Medina	H 9	Wash.
225	Medina	M 15	Wis.
100*	Medinah	B 20	Ill.
150*	Medina Lake (Mico)	L 15	Tex.
100	Medix Run	I 10	Pa.
48*	Medley	F 19	W. Va.
160	Medomak	O 11	Me.
97*	Medon	P 5	Tenn.
438	Medora	K 10	Ill.
722	Medora	N 14	Ind.
135	Medora	K 15	Kan.
210	Medora	M 3	N. D.
110	Medusa	P 22	N. Y.
500	Medway	H 16	Me.
2000	Medway	H 17	Mass.
255	Medway	K 8	Ohio
63*	Meece	J 17	Ky.
84*	Meehan Junction	K 20	Miss.
4	Meek	E 16	Neb.
1399	Meeker	E 6	Colo.
52*	Meeker	I 10	La.
130	Meeker	H 11	Ohio
502	Meeker	I 14	Okla.
23*	Meeker	D 10	W. Va.
88*	Meeks	J 17	Ga.
25*	Meeks Bay	G 9	Calif.
6	Meers	M 7	Okla.
373	Meeteetse	E 9	Wyo.
60*	Megargel	N 9	Ala.
531	Megargel	C 15	Tex.
150	Megeath (Winton)	O 8	Wyo.
1500	Meggett (Meggetts)	N 17	S. C.
....	Megler	N 3	Wash.
150	Mehama	F 8	Ore.
86	Mehan	F 14	Okla.
12*	Meharry	C 19	Mont.
250	Meherrin	O 13	Va.
418	Mehoopany	G 19	Pa.
927	Meigs	O 8	Ga.
110	Mekinock (Meckinock)	H 22	N. D.
213	Melba	O 4	Idaho
400*	Melber	J 5	Ky.
150*	Melbern	C 6	Ohio
145	Melbeta	I 2	Neb.
567	Melbourne	C 14	Ark.
2622	Melbourne	H 21	Fla.
480	Melbourne	J 14	Iowa
337*	Melbourne	B 18	Ky.
144*	Melbourne	C 8	Mo.
100	Melbourne	K 4	Wash.
90*	Melbourne Beach	H 21	Fla.
80*	Melby	J 7	Minn.
1290	Melcher	M 13	Iowa
500*	Melcroft	O 6	Pa.
50*	Melder	I 9	La.
300	Meldrim	K 23	Ga.
321	Melfa	L 24	Va.
50	Melham	H 21	S. D.
500*	Melissa	D 20	Tex.
15*	Mell	I 14	Ky.
1598	Mellen	G 6	Wis.
475	Mellenville	Q 24	N. Y.
25	Mellette	J 19	Okla.
332	Mellette	F 18	S. D.
25*	Mellin	F 9	W. Va.
302	Mellott	H 8	Ind.
75*	Mellwood	L 18	Ark.
255	Melmore	F 11	Ohio
110*	Melon	N 15	Tex.
75*	Melones	H 10	Calif.
22*	Melrose	E 14	Ark.
....	Melrose	D 19	Calif.
200	Melrose	B 16	Conn.
500	Melrose	D 15	Fla.
71	Melrose	G 5	Idaho
451	Melrose	O 14	Iowa
350	Melrose	G 8	La.
25333	Melrose	E 20, K 5	Mass.
2015	Melrose	L 10	Minn.
100	Melrose	M 7	Mont.
851	Melrose	I 23	N. M.
310	Melrose	M 24	N. Y.
249	Melrose	F 6	Ohio
400	Melrose	M 5	Ore.
462	Melrose	G 15	Wis.
....	Melrose Highlands	K 5 (Pop. incl. in Melrose)	Mass.
10933*	Melrose Park	B 20	Ill.
20*	Melrude	F 20	Mich.
203	Melstone	I 17	Mont.
....*	Meltonia	E 7	Miss.
120*	Meltons	J 14	Va.
52*	Meltonville	B 14	Iowa
368	Melvern	I 21	Kan.
1828	Melville	K 12	La.
80	Melville	K 13	Mont.
100	Melville	K 17	N. D.
....	Melville, see Daisy		Tenn.
150*	Melvin	L 3	Ala.
470	Melvin	G 19	Ill.
328	Melvin	C 4	Iowa
28*	Melvin	H 22	Ky.
152	Melvin	N 23	Mich.
10*	Melvin	F 4	Minn.
79*	Melvin (Melvin Mills)	N 11	N. H.
80*	Melvin	M 9	Ohio
500	Melvin	H 14	Tex.
135	Melvina	F 17	Wis.
4764*	Melvindale	Q 22	Mich.
90*	Melvin Hill	Q 10	N. C.
79*	Melvin Mills (Melvin)	N 11	N. H.
190	Melvin Village	L 16	N. H.
200*	Memorial	K 14	Tenn.
200*	Memory	D 2	N. C.
200	Memphis	O 16	Ind.
630	Memphis	O 24	Mich.
1935	Memphis	A 14	Mo.
103	Memphis	K 22	Neb.
250*	Memphis	L 14	N. Y.
292942	Memphis	Q 1	Tenn.
3869	Memphis	E 6	Tex.
25	Memphis Jc.	J 12	Ky.
....	Memphis Jc.	E 13	Miss.
3510	Mena	J 4	Ark.
768	Menahga	H 9	Minn.
432	Menan	N 20	Idaho
1764*	Menands	O 23	N. Y.
22*	Menard	P 12	Ill.
12	Menard	L 10	Mont.
2375	Menard	I 14	Tex.
10481	Menasha	N 15	Wis
10	Menchville	O 20	Va.
1282	Mendenhall	L 13	Miss.
127*	Mendenhall	Q 21	Pa.
154	Mendes	L 20	Ga.
1343	Mendham	E 14	N. J.
500	Mendocino	F 2	Calif.
637	Mendon	H 4	Ill.
960	Mendon	H 16	Mass.
667	Mendon	Q 12	Mich.
350	Mendon	E 10	Mo.
350*	Mendon	L 9	N. Y.
547	Mendon	G 6	Ohio
454	Mendon	B 11	Utah
500	Mendota	J 10	Calif.
4215	Mendota	D 15	Ill.
228	Mendota	N 16, N 24	Minn.
45*	Mendota	A 11	Mo.
77*	Mendota	B 6	Tex.
173	Mendota	E 6	Va.
....	Mendota	L 6	Wash.
60*	Mendota	K 20	Wis.
....	Menefee	F 9	La.
50*	Menemsha	P 22	Mass.
93*	Menfro	M 22	Mo.
425	Mengelwood	M 2	Tenn.
165*	Menges Mills	P 16	Pa.
35*	Menifee	H 11	Ark.
414	Menlo	C 1	Ga.
441	Menlo	L 9	Iowa
144*	Menlo	F 5	Kan.
400	Menlo	L 3	Wash.
3258	Menlo Park	F 19	Calif.
355	Menlo Park	F 17	N. J.
966	Menno	N 22	S. D.
180	Meno	D 9	Okla.
15	Menoken	G 21	Kan.
50	Menoken (Burleigh)	N 12	N. D.
10230	Menominee	I 6	Mich.
1469	Menominee Falls	O 19	Wis.
6582	Menomonie	C 12	Wis.
125	Menomonie Jc.	D 12	Wis.
213*	Mentcle (Greismore)	L 6	Pa.
25*	Mentha	Q 12	Mich.
350	Mentmore	F 1	N. M.
154*	Mentone	B 20	Ala.
731	Mentone	D 15	Ind.
600*	Mentone	G 6	Tex.
30*	Mentor	H 15	Kan.
250	Mentor	C 18	Ky.
287	Mentor	F 5	Minn.
1827	Mentor	C 18	Ohio
150	Mentor	N 19	Tenn.
538*	Mentor on the Lake	C 18	Ohio
146	Meppen	L 7	Ill.
....*	Meramec	I 20	Mo.
....*	Meramec Highlands, see Osage Hills		Mo.
175*	Meraux	N 19	La.
10135	Merced	I 10	Calif.
7624	Mercedes	R 4	Tex.
500*	Merced Falls	I 10	Calif.
500	Mercer	I 10	Ky.
100	Mercer	L 7	Me.
430	Mercer	A 9	Mo.
250	Mercer	K 12	N. D.
322	Mercer	H 6	Ohio
2272	Mercer	I 2	Pa.
250	Mercer	O 4	Tenn.
800	Mercer	I 7	Wis.
1069*	Mercer Island	H 9	Wash.
1763	Mercersburg	Q 12	Pa.
10	Mercersburg Jc.	Q 12	Pa.
164*	Mercerville	I 13	N. J.
35*	Mercerville	Q 15	Ohio
10	Mercerville	K 15	Va.
200*	Merchant	Q 15	Va.
3679	Merchantville	K 9	N. J.
50*	Mercier	D 22	Kan.
358*	Mercur	F 5	Utah
101	Mercury	H 15	Tex.
35	Meredith	H 9	Colo.
15	Meredith	E 12	Fla.
1200	Meredith	L 14	N. H.
1295▲*	Meredith	P 19	N. Y.
200	Meredith (Radnor)	I 11	Ohio
141*	Meredith Center	L 14	N. H.
....*	Meredith College	F 14	N. C.
75*	Meredithville	Q 15	Va.
998	Meredosia	I 8	Ill.
25*	Merepoint	O 7	Me.
80*	Mereta	H 13	Tex.
146*	Meridale	P 19	N. Y.
40*	Meridean	D 13	Wis.
39494	Meriden	I 12	Conn.
65*	Meriden	D 15	Ill.
200	Meriden	E 4	Iowa
421	Meriden	F 22	Kan.
108*	Meriden	P 16	Minn.
425	Meriden	L 7	N. H.
150*	Meriden	F 14	W. Va.
12*	Meriden	K 22	Wyo.
32*	Merideth (Hewlet)	L 1	W. Va.
350*	Meridian	F 7	Calif.
53*	Meridian	N 23	Ga.
1465	Meridian	N 5	Idaho
....	Meridian	J 10	La.
35481	Meridian	K 20	Miss.
307	Meridian	L 13	N. Y.
210	Meridian	G 13	Okla.
1016	Meridian	G 18	Tex.
453	Meridianville	A 14	Ala.
704	Merigold	E 8	Miss.
259	Merino	C 20	Colo.
65	Merino	H 12	Mont.
39566■*	Merion Station (Lower Merion)	P 23	Pa.
340*	Merit	D 20	Tex.
80*	Meriwether	I 8	S. C.
2005	Merkel	E 13	Tex.
....	Merle	P 8	Iowa
138	Merlin	P 5	Ore.
571	Mermentau	M 9	La.
100*	Mermet	R 16	Ill.
119*	Mermill	E 10	Ohio
65*	Merna	G 16	Ill.
250	Merna	J 21	Ky.
414	Merna	J 13	Neb.
12*	Merna	K 5	Wyo.
499	Merom	M 6	Ind.
75	Merom (Sta.)	M 5	Ind.
49*	Merriam	N 19	Ill.
1500	Merriam	G 25	Kan.
....	Merriam	O 15	Minn.
10	Merriam	K 16	Ohio
....	Merrick	H 7	Mass.
7000*	Merrick	H 7	N. Y.
220	Merrick	G 14	Okla.
122*	Merrickville	P 18	N. Y.
153	Merricourt	P 18	N. D.
....*	Merriewold	C 1	N. Y.
65*	Merrifield	I 13	Minn.
18	Merrifield	I 23	N. D.
36*	Merrifield	G 17	Va.
547	Merrill	E 2	Iowa
711	Merrill	M 17	Mich.
105	Merrill	P 20	Miss.
53*	Merrill	D 22	N. Y.
648	Merrill	R 10	Ore.
8711	Merrill	J 11	Wis.
591	Merrillan	F 14	Wis.
375	Merrillville	B 7	Ind.
157*	Merrimac	H 15	Ky.
2000	Merrimac	A 19	Mass.
....	Merrimac	O 5	Va.
200*	Merrimac	P 2	W. Va.
234	Merrimac	J 19	Wis.
150	Merrimack	Q 14	N. H.
102*	Merrimac Mines	O 4	Va.
200	Merrimacport	A 20	Mass.
321	Merriman	D 8	Neb.
250*	Merrimon	I 21	N. C.
91*	Merritt	J 9	Ill.
30*	Merritt	J 14	Mich.
219	Merritt	I 21	N. C.
25	Merritt	G 12	Wash.
200*	Merritt Island	H 21	Fla.
78*	Merrittstown	P 3	Pa.
....*	Merriweather	B 23	Mich.
713	Mer Rouge	B 12	La.
125*	Merrow	D 18	Conn.
100	Merry Hill	E 20	N. C.
....*	Merry Mount, see Paschall		N. C.
157*	Merry Oaks	G 12	N. C.
75*	Merry Point	N 21	Va.
1216	Merryville	K 5	La.
225*	Mershon	N 18	Ga.
150	Mershon	N 20	Mich.
3*	Mershons	I 18	Ky.
251	Mertens	F 19	Tex.
....*	Mertie	C 4	N. C.
254	Merton	N 20	Wis.
31*	Mertz	H 11	Ala.
869	Mertzon	H 11	Tex.
102*	Mertztown	L 21	Pa.
75*	Merwin	J 6	Mo.
7224	Mesa	K 14	Ariz.
25	Mesa	I 16	Ark.
92	Mesa	I 5	Colo.
150	Mesa	K 5	Idaho
45	Mesa	M 18	Wash.
10	Mesaba	F 20	Minn.
20*	Mesa Grande	Q 19	Calif.
2000	Mesa Rica	F 20	N. Mex.
14	Mescal	O 19	Ariz.
300	Mescalaro	L 15	N. M.
282	Meservey	E 12	Iowa
74*	Meshack	K 14	Ky.
....	Meshanticut	F 13	R. I.
580	Meshoppen	F 20	Pa.
1025	Mesic	H 21	N. C.
327	Mesick	K 13	Mich.
2000	Mesilla	N 9	N. M.
1826▲	Mesilla Park	O 11	N. M.
250	Mesita	Q 13	Colo.
150	Mesopotamia	D 19	Ohio
50	Mesquite	N 24	Nev.
100	Mesquite	O 11	N. M.
1045*	Mesquite	E 19	Tex.
46	Messer	P 21	Okla.
45	Messex	D 20	Colo.
2040	Messick	O 21	Va.
62*	Messler	P 22	Mo.
210*	Messmore	P 4	Pa.
18	Messner	C 16	Ore.
75*	Messongo	K 24	Va.
50*	Meta	H 24	Ky.
381	Meta	J 14	Mo.
....*	Metaire	O 18	La.
125	Metaline	B 23	Wash.
453	Metaline Falls	B 23	Wash.
35*	Metalton	A 7	Ark.
65*	Metalton	O 8	W. Va.
896	Metamora	F 13	Ill.
250	Metamora	K 20	Ind.
281	Metamora	O 22	Mich.
490	Metamora	C 8	Ohio
169	Metasville	F 17	Ga.
235	Metcalf	L 24	Ariz.
161	Metcalf	P 9	Ga.
328	Metcalf	J 21	Ill.
14*	Metcalf (Blackstone)	Q 16	Kan.
100	Metcalfe	F 6	Miss.
51*	Meter	J 20	Va.
300*	Method	E 14	N. C.
54	Methow	F 15	Wash.
21880■	Methuen	B 19	Mass.
40	Metolius	H 12	Ore.
6287	Metropolis	R 17	Ill.
127	Metropolis	C 20	Nev.
350	Metropolitan	G 5	Mich.
1823	Metter	K 19	Ga.
6557	Metuchen	G 17	N. J.
150	Metz	B 22	Ind.
150*	Metz	H 19	Mich.
223	Metz	L 6	Mo.
165*	Metz	D 12	W. Va.
106*	Mexboro	M 9	Ala.
20	Mexhoma	B 1	Okla.
200*	Mexia	M 9	Ala.
6410	Mexia	G 20	Tex.
150*	Mexican Springs	F 4	N. M.
510	Mexico	E 14	Ind.
45*	Mexico	I 8	Ky.
2500	Mexico	L 4	Me.
9053	Mexico	G 15	Mo.
1348	Mexico	K 14	N. Y.
325	Mexico	M 14	Pa.
75	Meyer	B 16	Iowa
45*	Meyers	J 9	Ark.
50*	Meyers	G 10	Calif.
....*	Meyers Cove	J 12	Idaho
3250	Meyersdale	Q 7	Pa.
200	Meyers Falls	C 22	Wash.
50*	Meyers Mill	L 10	S. C.
256	Meyersville	N 18	Tex.
4722	Miami	K 17	Ariz
172172	Miami	N 23	Fla.
200	Miami	F 15	Ind.
275	Miami	F 10	Mo.
100*	Miami (Miami Station)	F 10	Mo.
530	Miami	D 18	N. M.
8345	Miami	B 23	Okla.
713	Miami	C 5	Tex.
100*	Miami	L 7	W. Va.
28012	Miami Beach	O 24	Fla.
....	Miami City	L 7	Ohio
5544	Miamisburg	M 7	Ohio
1956	Miami Shores	N 24	Fla.
100*	Miami Station (Miami)	F 10	Mo.
898*	Miami Springs (Country Club Estates)	O 22	Fla.
275	Miamitown	N 5	Ohio
200*	Miamiville	N 7	Ohio
1000	Mianus	R 2	Conn.
115*	Mica	N 10 E 1	N. C.
14*	Mica	J 17	Va.
150	Mica	H 24	Wash.
720	Micanopy	E 14	Fla.
10	Micanopy Jc.	E 14	Fla.
118*	Micaville	N 10	N. C.
40	Micawber	H 16	Okla.
100*	Micco	I 22	Fla.
110*	Micco	O 4	W. Va.
500*	Miccosukee	B 6	Fla.
42*	Michael	K 8	Ill.
37*	Michaux	M 15	Va.
10	Michelson	J 15	Mich.
110*	Michie	Q 6	Tenn.
300	Michigamme	C 8	Mich.
113*	Michigan (Michigan Valley)	I 22	Kan.
491	Michigan	H 20	N. D.
123*	Michigan Bar	G 8	Calif.
75*	Michigan Bluff	G 8	Calif.
2500*	Michigan Center	Q 18	Mich.
26476	Michigan City	A 9	Ind.
55*	Michigan City	A 16	Miss.
417	Michigantown	G 13	Ind.
113*	Michigan Valley (Michigan)	I 22	Kan.
27*	Michillinda	M 9	Mich.
16*	Mickey	A 11	Tex.
150*	Mickleton	L 7	N. J.
60*	Mico (Medina Lake)	M 15	Tex.
289	Micro	F 16	N. C.
25*	Midas	C 4	Idaho
150	Midas	C 14	Nev.
285*	Middle	J 19	Iowa
400	Middle Amana	K 19	Iowa
210*	Middle Bass	B 12	Ohio
50	Middleberg	K 10	Okla.
9032■	Middleboro	J 21	Mass.
320*	Middleboro (McKean)	E 3	Pa.
733	Middlebourne	D 19	W. Va.
12	Middlebranch	F 17	Neb.
550	Middlebranch (Middle Branch)	G 18	Ohio
35*	Middlebrook	A 18	Ark.
133*	Middle Brook	M 19	Mo.
250	Middlebrook	K 10	Va.
150	Middleburg	C 15	Fla.
67*	Middleburg	C 3	Iowa
200*	Middleburg	H 16	Ky.
150*	Middleburg	C 10	Md.
1074	Middleburg	O 22	N. Y.
181*	Middleburg	C 15	N. C.
240	Middleburg	I 9	Ohio
1124	Middleburg	K 15	Pa.
629	Middleburg	F 15	Va.
1225*	Middleburgh Heights	D 17	Ohio
1100	Middlebury	I 8	Conn.
722	Middlebury	A 16	Ind.
45*	Middlebury (Middlebury Center)	E 15	Pa.
2123	Middlebury	H 6	Vt.
45*	Middlebury Center (Middlebury)	E 15	Pa.
100*	Middlebush	G 15	N. J.
38*	Middle Creek	K 15	Pa.
....	Middle Creek	H 1	S. D.
11*	Middledam	L 2	Me.
....*	Middle Elk, see Argo		Ky.
419*	Middle Falls	L 24	N. Y.
1230▲	Middlefield	J 13	Conn.
150	Middlefield	F 5	Mass.
150*	Middlefield (Brancoft)	F 4	Mass.
100*	Middlefield	N 19	N. Y.
932	Middlefield	D 19	Ohio
50*	Middlefork	H 12	Ind.
36*	Middlefork	H 20	Ky.
650*	Middle Granville	K 25	N. Y.
185*	Middlegrove	G 10	Ill.
100	Middle Grove	L 22	N. Y.
300	Middle Haddam	I 16	Conn.
320*	Middle Hope	E 3	N. Y.
75*	Middle Inlet	O 10	Wis.
350*	Middle Island	G 9	N. Y.
586	Middle Point	G 6	Ohio
1575	Middleport	L 6	N. Y.
3356	Middleport	P 15	Ohio
1077	Middleport	L 20	Pa.
20	Middleport	D 22	Wash.
77*	Middle River	H 8	Calif.
112	Middle River	M 9	Iowa
161*	Middle River	D 13	Md.
328	Middle River	C 5	Minn.
11777	Middlesboro (Middlesborough)	K 20	Ky.
3763*	Middlesex (Lincoln)	G 16	N. J.
300	Middlesex	N 10	N. Y.
545	Middlesex	F 16	N. C.
817▲	Middlesex	F 11	Vt.
224*	Middleton	E 16	Ga.
477	Middleton	N 4	Idaho
1000	Middleton	C 19	Mass.
450	Middleton	N 17	Mich.
40	Middleton	G 20	Ohio
430	Middleton	Q 4	Tenn.
66*	Middleton	H 20	Tex.
1358	Middleton	J 20	Wis.
200	Middletons (West Middleton)	G 14	Ind.
450	Middletown	G 5	Calif.
26495	Middletown	I 14	Conn.
1529	Middletown	D 20	Del.
496	Middletown	H 12	Ill.
1520	Middletown	I 18	Ind.
134*	Middletown	P 21	Iowa
1000*	Middletown	F 18	Ky.
320	Middletown (Lincoln Center)	I 16	Me.
839	Middletown	D 7	Md.
243	Middletown	G 16	Mo.
11018▲	Middletown	H 19	N. J.
21908	Middletown	E 3	N. Y.
225	Middletown	G 24	N. C.
31220	Middletown	M 7	Ohio
7046	Middletown	N 17	Pa.
....	Middletown	J 19	R. I.
361	Middletown	F 13	Va.
....	Middletown Jc.	N 7	Ohio
150	Middletown Springs	L 7	Vt.
211	Middle Valley	E 12	N. J.
833	Middleville	P 14	Mich.
45*	Middleville	B 14	N. J.
612	Middleville	L 19	N. Y.
40*	Middle Water	B 2	Tex.
226	Middleway	E 24	W. Va.
150*	Midfields	M 21	Tex.
60*	Midian	L 17	Kan.
100*	Midkiff	L 3	W. Va.
5*	Midlake	F 4	Calif.
560	Midland	H 4	Ark.
100*	Midland	O 24	Calif.
107*	Midland	J 5	Ga.
475	Midland	M 8	Ind.
375	Midland	M 9	La.
935	Midland	M 5	Md.
800	Midland (Bellingham)	I 16	Mass.
10329	Midland	M 18	Mich.
250*	Midland	G 7	N. C.
285	Midland (Midland City)	N 9	Ohio
80	Midland	R 10	Ore.
6373	Midland	L 1	Pa.
282	Midland	J 10	S. D.
9352	Midland	F 9	Tex.
78*	Midland	H 15	Va.
647	Midland City	N 21	Ala.
100	Midland City	H 14	Ill.
285	Midland City (Midland)	N 9	Ohio
....	Midland Jc.	M 5	Md.
....	Midland Jc.	P 21	Minn.
4525	Midland Park	C 19	N. J.
2430*	Midlothian	D 21	Ill.
116*	Midlothian	L 6	Md.
65	Midlothian	H 14	Okla.
1027	Midlothian	E 19	Tex.
200	Midlothian	M 16	Va.
250	Midnight	H 9	Miss.
....*	Midridge	O 17	Mo.
262	Midvale	L 4	Idaho
319*	Midvale	I 12	Iowa
432	Midvale	C 17	N. J.
670	Midvale	I 17	Ohio
53*	Midvale	P 13	Pa.
2875	Midvale	F 11	Utah

Pop.	Place Index	State
....	Midvale, N 15	Wash.
900*	Midvalley, J 18	Pa
780	Midville, J 19	Ga.
617	Midway, L 21	Ala.
....	Midway, M 11	Ark.
....	Midway, M 22	Conn.
200*	Midway, B 4	Fla.
96*	Midway, C 2	Ga.
500*	Midway, P 15	Ind.
100*	Midway, Q 9	Ind.
886	Midway, F 17	Ky.
278	Midway (Sedalia), L 10	Ohio
988	Midway, M 2	Pa.
300*	Midway, M 22	Tenn.
530	Midway, I 21	Tex.
801	Midway, F 13	Utah
29*	Midway (Midway Mills), L 11	Va.
500*	Midway, H 9	Wash.
112*	Midway, F 16	Wis.
1000*	Midway City, O 17	Calif.
29*	Midway Mills (Midway), L 11	Va.
92	Midwell, Q 4	Okla.
1021	Midwest, H 10	Wyo.
100*	Mier, F 16	Ind.
25	Miesse, N 7	N. M.
50*	Mifflin, P 12	Ind.
860	Mifflin, M 14	Pa.
100	Mifflin, H 21	Wis.
2090	Mifflinburg, J 15	Pa.
1097	Mifflintown, L 14	Pa.
613*	Mifflinville (Creasy), I 18	Pa.
325*	Miflin, P 7	Ala.
2407	Mignon, H 16	Ala.
125	Mikado, J 22	Mich.
125*	Mikana, D 9	Wis.
518	Mikeska, O 17	Tex.
17	Mikkalo, D 15	Ore.
104*	Mila, L 21	Va.
1627	Milaca, K 14	Minn.
....	Milaca Jc., K 14	Minn.
750*	Milam, G 25	Tex.
100*	Milam, G 19	W. Va
748	Milan, L 14	Ga.
1210	Milan, D 8	Ill.
1000	Milan, M 21	Ind.
224	Milan, O 15	Kan.
2340	Milan, Q 20	Mich.
624	Milan, M 5	Minn.
2016	Milan, B 10	Mo.
719▲	Milan, F 17	N. H.
719	Milan, E 13	Ohio
187*	Milan, E 17	Pa.
3035	Milan, N 5	Tenn.
115	Milan, F 24	Wash.
150*	Milan, I 12	Wis.
500	Milano, I 19	Tex.
246	Milanville, F 23	Pa.
2745	Milbank, E 24	S. D.
250	Milburg, Q 10	Mich.
225	Milburn, K 4	Ky.
39	Milburn, I 13	Neb.
442	Milburn, P 16	Okla.
100	Milburn, H 15	Tex.
550	Milburn, M 7	W. Va.
110*	Mildred, F 22	Colo.
155	Mildred, K 23	Kan.
35*	Mildred, I 19	Ky.
24*	Mildred, H 12	Minn.
150	Mildred, I 23	Mont.
1200	Mildred, G 18	Pa.
314	Miles, I 25	Iowa
18*	Miles, C 5	N. C.
20	Miles, B 21	Okla.
814	Miles, G 13	Tex.
20	Miles, G 20	Wash.
681	Milesburg, J 13	Pa.
7313	Miles City, J 22	Mont.
100*	Mileses, C 1	N. Y.
20*	Mileston, H 11	Miss.
27*	Miles Store, M 21	Va.
45*	Milestown, O 14	Md.
210*	Milesville (Sunny Side), M 4	Pa.
100	Milesville, I 8	S. D.
50*	Miletus, F 11	W. Va.
475*	Miley, M 13	S. C.
193	Milfay, H 15	Okla.
69*	Milford, D 10	Calif.
11300	Milford, O 9	Conn.
4214	Milford, I 23	Del.
60*	Milford, N 6	Ga.
1628	Milford, G 21	Ill.
901	Milford, C 15	Ind.
*	Milford, see Clifty	Ind.
1202	Milford, C 6	Iowa
271	Milford, G 17	Kan.
150*	Milford, D 18	Ky.
900	Milford, K 15	Me.
15388■	Milford, H 16	Mass.
1637	Milford, P 21	Mich.
116*	Milford, M 7	Mo.
759	Milford, M 21	Neb.
3927■	Milford, Q 13	N. H.
933	Milford, F 8	N. J.
460	Milford, O 19	N. Y.
2139	Milford, P 25, O 7	Ohio
901	Milford, H 25	Pa.
767	Milford, F 19	Tex.
1393	Milford, M 5	Utah
300*	Milford, K 17	Va.
686	Milford Center, J 10	Ohio
....	Milford Jc., G 21	Ill.
96	Milford Jc., C 15	Ind.
100*	Milford Square, M 23	Pa.
....	Military, O 25	Kan.
....	Military Jc., I 13	Ark.
....	Mill, G 21	Nev.
226	Milladore, I 13	Wis.
....	Millard, G 7	Ark.
125*	Millard, I 11	Kan.
100*	Millard, H 23	Ky.
350	Millard, Q 15	Miss.
123*	Millard, C 12	Mo.
315	Millard, K 23	Neb.
50	Millard, I 16	S. C.
15	Millard, F 16	S. D.
75*	Millard, C 6	Va.
45*	Millard, N 21	Wis.
67	Millarton, N 18	N. D.
50	Millboro, O 14	S. D.
400	Millboro, K 8	Va.
40*	Millboro Spring, K 9	Va.
2500	Millbrae, E 17	Calif.
1150	Millbridge, M 19	Me.
25*	Millbrook, I 17	Ala.
100	Millbrook, D 17	Ill.
200*	Millbrook (Duxbury), I 22	Mass.
75	Millbrook (West Millbrook), M 15	Mich.
1340	Millbrook, C 6	N. Y.
....*	Millbrook, E 14	N. C.
....*	Millbrook, E 21	W. Va.
....	Millbrook, P 18	Wyo.
11652■	Millburn, E 17	N. J.
50*	Millburne, P 3	Wyo.
6983■	Millbury, G 14	Mass.
428	Millbury, C 10	Ohio
525	Millbury Jc., G 14	Mass.
21	Mill City, D 9	Nev.
1200	Mill City, G 8	Ore.
265*	Mill City, G 19	Pa.
210*	Mill Creek, R 14	Ill.
100*	Mill Creek, B 10	Ind.
300	Mill Creek (South Orrington), L 14	Me.
100*	Millcreek, N 20	Mo.
459	Mill Creek, O 15	Okla.
362	Mill Creek, M 12	Pa.
732	Mill Creek. I 14	W. Va.
....	Mill Creek Jc., O 21	Wash.
1000	Milldale, I 11	Conn.
....	Milldale, B 16	Fla.
20	Milldale, J 12	Neb.
27*	Milldale, F 14	Va.
6778	Milledgeville, H 13	Ga.
808	Milledgeville, B 11	Ill.
178	Milledgeville, M 10	Ohio
250*	Milledgeville, P 6	Tenn.
2820	Millen, I 20	Ga.
102*	Millenbeck, L 20	Va.
64*	Miller, F 13	Ark.
....	Miller, B 7 (Pop incl. in Gary)	Ind.
70*	Miller, C 12	Iowa
125*	Miller, I 20	Kan.
165*	Miller, A 13	Miss.
519	Miller, O 8	Mo.
205	Miller, L 14	Neb.
355	Miller (Millersport), R 14	Ohio
29*	Miller, O 20	Okla.
11*	Miller, E 13	Ore.
1460	Miller, I 17	S. D.
54*	Miller, M 9	W. Va.
157*	Miller City, R 14	Ill.
174*	Miller City, F 7	Ohio
600*	Miller Grove, D 22	Tex.
155*	Miller Place, G 9	N. Y.
114	Miller River, H 10	Wash.
600*	Millers, C 10	Md.
....	Millers, K 11	Nev.
2	Millers, K 18	N. D.
349	Millersburg, E 7	Ill.
384	Millersburg, B 17	Ind.
50*	Millersburg, Q 7	Ind.
177	Millersburg, L 18	Iowa
850	Millersburg, E 18	Ky.
306	Millersburg, G 18	Mich.
40*	Millersburg, H 14	Mo.
2239	Millersburg, H 15	Ohio
2959	Millersburg, L 16	Pa.
174*	Millers City (Miller City) E 7	Ohio
60*	Millers Creek, G 19	Ky.
50*	Millers Creek, C 4	N. C.
1800	Millers Falls, D 9	Mass.
27*	Millers Ferry, L 10	Ala.
50*	Millers Ferry, M 9	Fla.
127*	Millers Mills, J 19	N. Y.
....*	Miller School, K 12	Va.
460	Millersport, K 14	Ohio
355	Millersport (Miller), R 14	Ohio
45*	Millers Tavern, L 19	Va.
110*	Millerstown, H 13	Ky.
684	Millerstown, M 15	Pa.
987	Millerstown (Chicora), J 4	Pa.
263	Millersview, H 14	Tex.
400	Millersville, I 15	Ind.
105*	Millersville, H 14	Md.
108*	Millersville, N 22	Mo.
119*	Millersville, D 11	Ohio
1867	Millersville, P 18	Pa.
163*	Millerton, O 13	Iowa
30	Millerton, K 20	Neb.
953	Millerton, B 6, R 24	N. Y.
255	Millerton, Q 23	Okla.
210	Millerton, E 16	Pa.
250*	Millerville, G 18	Ala.
18	Miller Yard, D 6	Va.
200	Millett, O 17	Mich.
25	Millett, H 12	Nev.
150*	Millett (Millettville), M 11	S. C.
143	Millett, N 15	Tex.
150*	Millettville (Millett), M 11	S. C.
400*	Millfield, N 15	Ohio
50*	Mill Gap, I 8	Va.
150	Millgrove, G 20	Ind.
139*	Mill Grove, B 8	Mo.
1513	Mill Hall, I 14	Pa.
60	Millhaven, I 22	Ga.
682	Millheim, K 14	Pa.
108*	Milhousen, L 18	Ind.
10	Millican, K 13	Ore.
500	Millican, J 21	Tex.
250	Milligan, M 5	Fla.
22*	Milligan, J 7	Ind.
392	Milligan, N 20	Neb.
261*	Milligan College, M 24	Tenn.
531	Milliken, D 15	Colo.
105	Milliken, A 14	La.
248	Millington, D 18	Ill.
307	Millington, F 19	Md.
813	Millington, M 20	Mich.
600	Millington, F 15	N. J.
300	Millington, L 4	Ore.
730	Millington, P 1	Tenn.
6000	Millinocket, H 15	Me.
47*	Million, G 18	Ky.
4*	Mill Iron, L 24	Mont.
1500	Millis, H 17	Mass.
39	Mill Mine, D 3	Mich.
170*	Millmont, J 15	Pa.
101*	Mill Neck, H 7	N. Y.
300	Mill Plain, L 3	Conn.
200*	Mill Point, M 13	W. Va.
50*	Mill Pond, I 20	Ky.
700	Millport, F 5	Ala.
27*	Millport, H 10	Ky.
340	Mill Port, Q 12	N. Y.
150*	Millport, F 12	Pa.
102*	Millrift, G 24	Pa.
270	Mill River, H 3	Mass.
249	Mill Run, P 6	Pa.
500	Millry, M 4	Ala.
50*	Mills, G 8	Calif.
100*	Mills, J 20	Ky.
23	Mills, D 14	Neb.
136	Mills, D 20	N. M.
100	Mills (Hartford Mills), P 14	N. Y.
411	Mills, E 13	Pa.
....*	Mills, D 5	S. C.
....*	Mills, B 19	Tex.
100*	Mills, J 10	Utah
379	Mills, J 16	Wyo.
815	Millsap, E 17	Tex.
432	Millsboro, L 24	Del.
2000*	Millsboro, O 2	Pa.
978*	Mills College, D 20	Calif.
537	Mill Shoals, N 18	Ill.
275	Mill Spring, P 19	Mo.
160*	Mill Spring, P 9	N. C.
75*	Mill Springs, J 17	Ky.
1290	Millstadt, N 10	Ill.
....	Millstadt Jc., N 8	Ill.
125*	Millston, G 15	Wis.
50	Millstone, M 20	Conn.
1000*	Millstone, I 22	Ky.
252*	Millstone, G 14	N. J.
200	Millstone, O 4	W. Va.
150*	Milltown, H 20	Ala.
760	Milltown, P 13	Ind.
125*	Milltown, I 15	Ky.
....	Milltown, J 23 (Pop incl. in Calais)	Me.
552	Milltown, H 5	Mont.
3515	Milltown, G 16	N. J.
160*	Milltown (Haffey) M 4	Pa.
52	Milltown, M 20	S. D.
7	Milltown, E 8	Wash.
469	Milltown, B 9	Wis.
7811	Millvale, M 3	Pa.
4847	Mill Valley, H 4	Calif.
450	Millview, N 2	Fla.
100	Mill Village, N 8	N. H.
259	Mill Village, E 4	Pa.
100	Millville, O 11	Ark.
65	Millville, D 6	Calif.
184*	Millville, K 22	Del.
2500*	Millville, N 9	Fla.
....	Millville, I 20	Ind.
150	Millville, E 16	Ky.
....	Millville (Millville Heights) I 15	Mass.
175*	Millville, P 21	Minn.
14806	Millville, O 10	N. J.
335	Millville, N 5	Ohio
761	Millville, I 18	Pa.
439	Millville, B 12	Utah
156*	Millville, E 25	W. Va.
75*	Millville, F 20	Wis.
....	Millville Heights (Millville), I 15	Mass.
300*	Millway, P 19	Pa
250*	Millwood, N 16	Ga.
160*	Millwood, H 12	Ky.
400*	Millwood, F 6	N. Y.
8	Millwood, L 4	Ore.
500	Millwood, E 14	Va.
242	Millwood, H 23	Wash.
362	Millwood, H 5	W. Va.
78*	Milmay, N 13	N. J.
140	Milmine, I 17	Ill.
1750*	Milmont Park, P 23	Pa.
75	Milner, D 8	Colo.
352	Milner, H 8	Ga.
85*	Milner, Q 11	Idaho
150	Milnesand, K 23	N. M.
520	Milnesville, J 20	Pa.
677	Milnor, P 22	N. D.
30*	Milo, Q 14	Ark.
528	Milo, M 13	Iowa
46*	Milo, G 23	Ky.
2000	Milo, J 13	Me.
129*	Milo, M 6	Mo.
550	Milo, O 13	Okla.
12*	Milo, M 6	Ore.
52*	Milo, O 15	Tenn.
20*	Milo, I 8	W. Va.
46	Miloma, Q 7	Minn.
450	Milpitas, G 23	Calif.
750	Milroy, K 19	Ind.
261*	Milroy, O 7	Minn.
1800	Milroy, L 13	Pa.
57*	Milroy, I 11	W. Va.
200	Milstead, J 18	Ala.
1200	Milstead, F 9	Ga.
200	Milton, H 9	Calif.
1198	Milton, J 24	Del.
1851	Milton, M 3	Fla.
327	Milton, J 7	Ill.
646	Milton, J 21	Ind.
809	Milton, Q 18	Iowa
163	Milton, N 14	Kan.
347	Milton, D 15	Ky.
200	Milton, M 11	La.
18708■	Milton, P 4	Mass.
700	Milton, M 19	N. H.
303	Milton, C 15	N. J.
1505	Milton, D 5	N. Y.
329	Milton, C 11	N. C.
310	Milton, E 20	N. D.
226*	Milton (Milton Center), D 9	Ohio
100	Milton, K 23	Okla.
1744	Milton, B 20	Ore.
8313	Milton, J 16	Pa.
72	Milton, N 12	Tenn.
250	Milton, E 12	Utah
729	Milton, D 7	Vt.
671	Milton, J 8	Wash.
1641	Milton, K 3	W. Va.
1266	Milton, M 21	Wis.
116*	Miltona, J 8	Minn
226*	Milton Center (Milton), D 9	Ohio
1000	Milton Jc., L 21	Wis.
400	Milton Mills, M 19	N. H.
86*	Miltonsburg, K 20	Ohio
800	Miltonvale, F 15	Kan.
30	Milvid, J 23	Tex.
291*	Milwaukee, C 19	N. C.
587472	Milwaukee, P 20	Wis.
1871	Milwaukie, D 8	Ore.
126*	Mima, G 22	Ky.
100	Mimbres, M 5	N. M.
700*	Mims, G 20	Fla.
44	Mimsville, N 6	Ga.
400	Mina, J 9	Nev.
57	Mina, D 18	S. D.
60	Minam, C 22	Ore.
1125	Minatare, I 2	Neb.
335	Minburn, K 10	Iowa
....	Mincar, see Caperton	W. Va.
921	Minco, J 10	Okla.
20*	Mincy, R 10	Mo.
310	Minden, L 4	Iowa
6677	Minden, B 6	La.
787	Minden (Mindenmines), N 6	Mo.
1848	Minden, N 15	Neb.
200	Minden, I 3	Nev.
500	Minden, F 23	Tex.
1500*	Minden, N 8	W. Va.
321	Minden City, M 24	Mich.
550	Mindenmines (Minden), N 6	Mo.
126	Mindoro, F 16	Wis.
10*	Minefork, G 21	Ky.
1100	Mine Hill, D 14	N. J.
200	Mine Lamotte, M 20	Mo.
....	Mine No. 40, L 21	Okla.
109*	Mineola, L 5	Ark.
135*	Mineola, N 4	Iowa
490*	Mineola (Minneola), N 7	Kan.
86*	Mineola, H 16	Mo.
10064	Mineola, H 6	N. Y.
3223	Mineola, E 22	Tex.
55*	Miner, L 12	Mont.
....	Miner, I 15	Wis.
50*	Mineral, L 4	Ark.
50*	Mineral, E 7	Calif.
307	Mineral, D 11	Ill.
80*	Mineral, M 8	Ind.
100	Mineral, N 24	Kan.
215	Mineral, N 14	Ohio
400	Mineral, O 18	Tex.
427	Mineral, K 15	Va.
500	Mineral, L 8	Wash.
23*	Mineral (Kincheloe), E 12	W. Va.
181	Mineralbluff, B 7	Ga.
19*	Mineral Center, B 21	Minn.
820	Mineral City, H 18	Ohio
90*	Mineral Hill, F 15	N. M.
344	Mineral Hills, F 2	Mich.
25	Mineral Hot Springs, M 12	Colo.
....*	Mineralking, K 14	Calif.
58*	Mineral Park, Q 16	Tenn.
350	Mineral Point, L 19	Mo.
300	Mineral Point, N 8	Pa.
2275	Mineral Point, I 21	Wis.
1600	Mineral Ridge, E 19	Ohio
52	Mineral Springs (Watson), F12	Ala.
731	Mineral Springs, N 6	Ark.
89*	Mineral Springs, J 6	N. C.
800*	Mineral Springs, J 10	Pa.
200*	Mineral Wells, A 13	Miss.
6303	Mineral Wells, E 17	Tex.
30*	Mineralwells, F 6	W. Va.
....	Miners Mills, H 21	Pa.
....*	Minersville, D 4	Calif.
....	Minersville, M 24	Neb.
500	Minersville, O 16	Ohio
8686	Minersville, L 19	Pa.
570	Minersville, N 6	Utah
50*	Mine Run (Tinder), J 15	Va.
20	Minerva, I 14	Iowa
127*	Minerva, D 19	Ky.
94*	Minerva, N 16	La.
200*	Minerva, H 23	N. Y.
2937	Minerva, G 19	Ohio
118*	Minerva, I 18	Tex.
225*	Mines (Oreminea), M 10	Pa.
500*	Minetto, K 15	N. Y.
687	Mineville, G 24	N. Y.
200*	Minford, P 12	Ohio
290	Mingo, K 13	Iowa
65	Mingo, F 4	Kan.
....	Mingo, see Tutor Key	Ky.
150*	Mingo, J 8	Ohio
80*	Mingo, I 14	W. Va.
5192	Mingo Jc., I 20	Ohio
86*	Mingoville, J 13	Pa.
570	Mingus, E 16	Tex.
174	Minidoka, P 14	Idaho
737	Minier, G 14	Ill.
22*	Minimum, N 19	Mo.
32*	Mining City, I 11	Ky.
175*	Minisink Hills (Water Gap), J 23	Pa.
1	Mink, G 23	Mont.
170	Minkcreek, Q 21	Idaho
45	Minkler, J 12	Calif.
2087	Minneapolis, G 16	Kan.
492370	Minneapolis, M 23, N 16	Minn.
450*	Minneapolis, M 10, D 2	N. C.
....	Minneapolis Jc., M 23	Minn.
....	Minneapolis & Duluth Jc., M 25, N 17	Minn.
....*	Minnehaha, M 23	Minn.
68*	Minnehaha Springs, L 13	W. Va.
187	Minneiska, P 22	Minn.
10	Minnekahta, M 2	S. D.
....*	Minnelusa, N 19	Calif.
269*	Minneola, G 16	Fla.
490	Minneola (Mineola), N 7	Kan.
1065	Minneota, O 5	Minn.
211	Minnesota City, P 22	Minn.
148	Minnesota Jc., M 19	Wis.
526	Minnesota Lake Q 14	Minn.
229*	Minnetonka Beach, M 15	Minn.
50*	Minnewaska, C 4	N. Y.
521	Minnewaukan, H 16	N. D.
80*	Minnie, H 23	Ky.
35	Minnith, M 21	Mo.
37*	Minnora, I 8	W. Va.
902	Minoa, L 15	N. Y.
990	Minocqua, J 8	Wis.
308	Minong, D 7	Wis.
1897	Minonk, F 15	Ill.
....	Minonk Jc., F 15	Ill.
317	Minooka, D 18	Ill.
4000	Minooka H 21	Pa.
11*	Minor, F 21	Ky.
108*	Minor, L 19	Va.
65*	Minorca, A 18	Ark.
500*	Minor Hill, P 10	Tenn.
206	Minortown, H 7	Conn.
101	Minot, N 6	Me.
125	Minor, G 22	Mass.
16577	Minot, G 10	N. D.
530	Minotola, N 10	N. J.
100*	Minpro, E 1	N. C.
1504	Minster, I 6	Ohio
250	Minter, K 12	Ala.
135*	Minter (Lollie), K 15	Ga.
350	Minter City, E 10	Miss.
....*	Mint Hill, J 15	Mo.
200*	Minthill, H 6	N. C.
630	Minto, F 22	N. D.
86*	Mintonville, I 16	Ky.
30*	Mints, (Mintz) J 15	N. C.
57*	Mint Springs, J 10	Va.
133	Minturn, C 18	Ark.
596	Minturn, G 10	Colo.
156	Minturn, N 16	Me.
64*	Minturn, D 21	S. C.
30*	Mintz (Mints), J 15	N. C.
350	Mio, J 19	Mich.
200*	Miola, I 6	Pa.
300*	Miquon, N 22	Pa.
300	Mira, A 4	La.
115*	Mirabile, E 7	Mo.
25*	Miracle, K 20	Ky.
12	Mirage, M 12	Colo.
800*	Mira Loma (Wineville), P 9	Calif.
50*	Miramar, P 19	Calif.
47*	Miramonte, K 10	Calif.
44*	Miranda, D 2	Calif.
70	Miranda, G 17	S. D.
1200	Mirando City, P 15	Tex.
207*	Mirbat (Gowan), F 19	Minn.
100	Mirror Lake, L 16	N. H.
....*	Mirror Lake, see Lake Delton	Wis.
250*	Misenheimer (Misenheimer Springs), G 8	N. C.
28298	Mishawaka, B 14	Ind.
600	Mishicot, Q 15	Wis.
25*	Miskimon, L 21	Va.
38*	Misquamicut (Pleasant View), N 3	R. I.
....	Missaukee Jc., K 14	Mich.
3000*	Mission, G 24	Kan.
....	Mission, L 12	Mont.
40	Mission, C 19	Ore.
452	Mission, N 12	S. D.
5982	Mission, Q 3	Tex.
195	Missionhill, O 23	S. D.
26*	Mission Home, I 13	Va.
4*	Mission Ridge, I 11	S. D.
531*	Mission San Jose, G 23	Calif.
100	Missisquoi (East Richford), A 13	Vt.
1000	Mississippi City, R 19	Miss.
18449	Missoula, H 5	Mont.
....*	Missouri Branch, L 1	W. Va.
323	Missouri City, F 7	Mo.
200*	Missouri City, L 22	Tex.
3994	Missouri Valley, L 3	Iowa
39*	Mist, Q 15	Ark.
80	Mist, B 6	Ore.
27*	Mistletoe, H 20	Ky.
300*	Miston, M 4	Tenn.
75	Mitch, I 23	Okla.
310	Mitchell (Mitchell Station), K 18	Ala.
208*	Mitchell, B 14	Ark.
228	Mitchell, H 16	Ga.
300	Mitchell, M 10	Ill.
3393	Mitchell, N 11	Ind.
161	Mitchell, C 15	Iowa
85*	Mitchell, J 14	Kan.
100*	Mitchell, F 5	La.
2181	Mitchell, H 2	Neb.
219	Mitchell, H 15	Ore.
10633	Mitchell, L 20	S. D.
90*	Mitchells, I 14	Va.
250	Mitchellsburg, H 16	Ky.
15*	Mitchell Mill, H 9	Calif.
40	Mitchellsville, P 18	Ill.
769	Mitchellville, K 13	Iowa
18*	Mitchellville (Mullikin), I 14	Md.
216*	Mitchellville, K 11	Tenn.
....*	Mitiwanga, C 14	Ohio
60*	Mitterhofer, G 11	Wis.
....*	Mittie, K 8	La.
....	Mittineague, see West Springfield	Mass.
85	Mix, K 13	La.
40*	Mixersville, K 23	Ind.
35*	Mize, C 13	Ga.
15*	Mize, G 21	Ky.
561*	Mize, M 16	Miss.
173	Mizpah, E 13	Minn.
12*	Mizpah, K 22	Mont.
500*	Mizpah, O 12	N. J.
1084	Moab, L 23	Utah
200	Moapa, N 22	Nev.
119*	Moark, A 20	Ark.
120*	Moatsville, F 14	W. Va.
667	Mobeetie, C 6	Tex.
35*	Moberly, G 18	Ky.
12920	Moberly, F 13	Mo.
78720	Mobile, P 5	Ala.
40*	Mobile, L 11	Ariz.
211	Mobjack, N 21	Va.
28*	Mobley, D 16	Ark.
22*	Mobley, L 8	Tenn.
3008	Mobridge, D 12	S. D.
2300*	Mocanaqua, I 20	Pa.
3	Mocane, Q 8	Okla.
61*	Moccasin, B 10	Ariz.
40*	Moccasin, H 10	Calif.
107	Moccasin, K 16	Ill.
85	Moccasin, H 13	Mont.
65	Moccasin Gap, E 5	Va.
15*	Mock, D 4	Mont.
1607	Mocksville, E 6	N. C.
300	Moclips, J 2	Wash.
30*	Moct, H 21	Ky.
385	Modale, K 3	Iowa
64*	Moddersville, K 14	Mich.
118	Mode, K 16	Ill.
150	Model, P 17	Colo.
154*	Model, K 7	Tenn.
127	Modeltown (Model City), L 4	N. Y.
95*	Modena, B 9	Mo.
257*	Modena, D 4	N. Y.
599*	Modena, P 21	Pa.
100	Modena, O 1	Utah
150	Modena, D 14	Wis.
45*	Modeste, L 15	La.
16379	Modesto, I 8	Calif.
276	Modesto, K 11	Ill.
79*	Modest Town, L 24	Va.
220	Modoc, J 18	Ga.
114	Modoc, O 10	Ill.
237	Modoc, I 21	Ind.
52*	Modoc, I 4	Kan.
90*	Modoc, I 8	S. C.
200	Modoc Point, P 10	Ore.
10	Moe, N 25	S. D.
5	Moenville, I 9	S. D.
25	Moeville, B 13	Wis.
149	Moffat, M 12	Colo.
40	Moffat, H 18	Tex.
10	Moffatt, L 4	Tenn.
130*	Moffatts Creek (Newport), K 9	Va.
....*	Moffets, see North Bonneville	Wash.
538	Moffett, I 25	Okla.
300*	Moffet Field, G 21	Calif.
128	Moffit, N 13	N. D.
150*	Moffitsville, C 23	N. Y.
....	Moffitt, J 16	Fla.
1616	Mogadore, F 18	Ohio
295	Mogollon, L 2	N. M.
50	Mogote, Q 11	Colo.
25	Mogul, I 11	Ga.
687	Mohall, C 9	N. D.
12	Mohave City, G 3	Ariz.
125	Mohawk, M 6	Ariz.
30*	Mohawk, G 16	Fla.
100	Mohawk, I 16	Ind.
1200	Mohawk, C 3	Mich.
2882	Mohawk, M 19	N. Y.
117*	Mohawk (Nellie), I 16	Ohio
175	Mohawk (Donna), I 7	Ore.
330	Mohawk, M 22	Tenn.
100	Mohawk, P 4	W. Va.
....	Mohawk Jc., J 6	Ore.
150*	Mohegan, Q 5	W. Va.
600*	Mohegan Lake, F 6	N. Y.
46	Mohler, G 5	Idaho
50	Mohler, C 4	Ore.
100	Mohler, I 20	Wash.
1853*	Mohnton, N 20	Pa.
40*	Mohonk Lake, C 4, R 22	N. Y.
....	Mohr, C 11	Ore.
512	Mohrland, J 15	Utah
400	Mohrsville, M 20	Pa.
5	Moiese, G 4	Mont.
700	Moira, D 20	N. Y.
750	Mojave, M 15	Calif.
544	Mokane, I 15	Mo.
624▲	Mokelumne Hill, H 9	Calif.
657	Mokena, D 20	Ill.
26*	Moko, A 14	Ark.
907	Molalla, E 8	Ore.
4	Molan, N 22	S. D.
5*	Mold, G 17	Wash.
152*	Mole Hill, F 9	W. Va.
310	Molena, H 6	Ga.
100	Molina, H 5	Colo.
34608	Moline, D 8	Ill.
870	Moline, N 20	Kan.
300	Moline, O 13	Mich.
40*	Moline, H 16	Tex.
438	Molino, M 2	Fla.
45*	Molino, F 15	Mo.
400*	Mollenaur, L 3	Pa.
32*	Mollie (Birch Run), K 8	W. Va.
25	Mollus, B 19	Ark.
100*	Mollusk, L 20	Va.
81	Molson, B 18	Wash.
20	Molt (Stickley), L 15	Mont.
500*	Molus, J 21	Ky.
33*	Mombaccus, C 4, R 22	N. Y.
2425	Momence, E 21	Ill.
75	Momeneetown, C 11	Ohio
55	Mona, E 23	Mont.
6	Mona, D 20	N. D.
357	Mona, H 11	Utah
318	Mona (Granville), C 14	W. Va.
35*	Mona, B 22	Wyo.
7061	Monaca, L 2	Pa.
3944	Monahans, G 8	Tex.
175	Monango, Q 19	N. D.
114*	Monarat (Chestnut Yard), Q 3	Va.
9*	Monarch, B 11	Ark.
....	Monarch, K 11	Colo.
66	Monarch, H 11	Mont.
120	Monarch. A 23	Okla.
300	Monarch, D 10	S. C.
500	Monarch, A 15	Wyo.
210	Monarda, G 17	Me.
105*	Monaskon, L 20	Va.
211*	Monaville, O 4	W. Va.
111*	Monches, N 20	Wis.
1165	Moncks Corner, L 17	S. C.
10*	Moncla, I 11	La.
620*	Monclo, O 4	W. Va.
107*	Monclova, B 9	Ohio
108	Moncrief (Grand Crossing), B 16	Fla.
144	Moncure, F 12	N. C.
610	Mondamin, K 2	Iowa
20	Mondovi, G 21	Wash.
2077	Mondovi, D 13	Wis.
427	Monee, D 21	Ill.
120*	Monegaw Springs, L 8	Mo.
150	Monero, B 10	N. M.
20257	Monessen, O 3	Pa.
....*	Moneta, N 15	Calif.
115*	Moneta, D 5	Iowa
200*	Moneta, O 8	Va.
20	Moneta, I 12	Wyo.
4395	Monett, P 8	Mo.
242*	Monetta, H 10	S. C.
1074	Monette, D 21	Ark.
60*	Money, E 11	Miss.
25*	Monford, I 12	Ky.
62*	Mongaup, C 2	N. Y.
200*	Mongaup Valley, C 2	N. Y.
225	Mongo, A 1	Ind.
100*	Monhegan, P 11	Me.
100	Moniac, Q 19	Ga.
169	Monica, F 11	Ill.
175	Monico, L 9	Wis.
50	Monida, P 7	Mont.
212	Monie, P 20	Md.
88	Monitor, E 7	Ore.
165	Monitor, I 14	Wash.
550*	Monitor (Wilkinson), N 4	W. Va.
150*	Monk, C 8	Va.
150	Monkstown, B 21	Tex.
100	Monkton, C 14	Md.
575▲	Monkton, G 7	Vt.
215	Monktonridge, G 7	Vt.
40	Monmouth, E 13	Ala.
9096	Monmouth, F 7	Ill.
100*	Monmouth, F 22	Ind.
190	Monmouth, I 23	Iowa
75*	Monmouth, N 24	Kan.
1350	Monmouth, N 7	Me.
965	Monmouth, F 5	Ore.
584	Monmouth Beach, H 21	N. J.
500	Monmouth Jc., H 15	N. J.
300	Monocacy, N 21	Pa.
300*	Monocacy Station (Monocacy), N 21	Pa.
75	Monohon, H 9	Wash.
25*	Mono Lake, H 13	Calif.
261*	Monolith, M 13	Calif.
1262	Monon, E 10	Ind.
1191	Monona, D 21	Iowa
1790	Monongah, D 13	W. Va.
8825	Monongahela, O 3	Pa.
300*	Monoville, L 13	Tenn.
99	Monowi, E 17	Neb.
61*	Monponsett, I 21	Mass.
118*	Monroe, J 18	Ark.
1728▲	Monroe, L 7	Conn.
4168	Monroe. F 10	Ga.
259*	Monroe (Basalt), O 19	Idaho
405	Monroe, F 22	Ind.
1015	Monroe, L 17	Iowa
28309	Monroe, C 11	La.
500	Monroe, L 13	Me.
18478	Monroe, Q 22	Mich.
136*	Monroe, N 7	Miss.
315	Monroe, J 19	Neb.
200	Monroe, H 10	N. H.
125*	Monroe, B 14	N. J.
1616	Monroe, E 4	N. Y.
6475	Monroe, I 6	N. C.
307	Monroe, M 7	Ohio
225	Monroe, L 25	Okla.
311	Monroe, I 5	Ore.
100*	Monroe, I 5	Pa.
219	Monroe, M 23	S. D.
69*	Monroe, L 15	Tenn.
1292	Monroe, L 10	Utah
600	Monroe, M 10	Va.
1590	Monroe, G 9	Wash.
6182	Monroe, K 22	Wis.
250	Monroe Bridge, B 5	Mass.
650	Monroe-Cedar Knoll (Cedar Knolls), D 14	N.J.
200	Monroe Center, B 15	Ill.
50	Monroe Center, B 21	Ohio
518	Monroe City, O 6	Ind.
1978	Monroe City, E 15	Mo.
30	Monroe Hall, I 19	Va.
40	Monroeton, N 10	Ala.
500	Monroeton, F 18	Pa.
1724	Monroeville, M 10	Ala.
994	Monroeville, D 23	Ind.
250*	Monroeville, N 7	N. J.
1173	Monroeville, E 13	Ohio
12807	Monrovia, O 16	Calif.
450	Monrovia, K 12	Ind.
76*	Monrovia, E 9	Md.
359*	Monsanto, N 11	Ill.
30	Monse, F 16	Wash.
500*	Monsey, G 4	N. Y.
1000	Monson, I 11	Me.
3500	Monson, H 9	Mass.
100	Monson Jc., J 11	Me.
....	Mont, M 11	Ill.
463	Montague, B 5	Calif.
7582■	Montague, D 8	Mass.
1099	Montague, N 10	Mich.
53	Montague, F 12	Mont.
12*	Montague, L 16	N. C.
250	Montague, C 17	Tex.
56*	Montague, L 19	Va.
635	Montague City, C 8	Mass.
125*	Montalba, G 21	Tex.
661	Mont Alto, Q 14	Pa.
....	Mont Alto Park, Q 14	Pa.
300	Montalvo, O 13	Calif.
275	Montana, F 7	Ark.
300	Montana Mines (Montana), D 14	W. Va.
250*	Montandon, J 16	Pa.
177*	Montara, F 18	Calif.
25*	Montauk, N 15	Mo.
608	Montauk, H 13	N. Y.
....	Monta Vista, H 21	Calif.
1800*	Mont Belvieu, K 23	Tex.
80	Montborne, E 8	Wash.
150	Montbrook, E 13	Fla.
100*	Montcalm, Q 8	W. Va.
125*	Montchanin, A 21	Del.
40*	Montclair, J 11	Ind.
39807	Montclair, D 18	N. J.
900*	Mont Claire, O 22	Pa.
250*	Mont Clare (Montclare), E 18	S. C.
150*	Montcoal, O 8	W. Va.
600	Monteagle, P 13	Tenn.
8016	Montebello, Q 5	Calif.
47*	Montebello, K 10	Va.
2000	Montecito, N 12	Calif.

Pop. *Place* *Index* *State*

250*Monte Clare (Montclare), E 19....S. C.
30 Monte Cristo, G 11..Wash.
210 Montegut, P 17....La.
78*Monteith, K 9....Iowa
.... Monteith Jc., K 6....Mo.
30*Montela, C 3....N. Y.
250*Montell, L 13....Tex.
350 Montello, C 23....Nev.
1138 Montello, K 17....Wis.
86*Monte Ne (Silver Springs), B 5....Ark.
400 Monterey, L 12....Ala.
10084 Monterey, K 6....Calif.
288 Monterey, D 11....Ind.
35*Monterey, Q 16....Iowa
203 Monterey, E 16....Ky.
495*Monterey, H 12....La.
75*Monterey, H 3....Mass.
311 Monterey, Q 10....Minn.
260*Monterey, N 18....Mo.
277 Monterey, P 11....N. Y.
75*Monterey, O 8....Ohio
1742 Monterey, M 15....Tenn.
309 Monterey, I 8....Va.
8531 Monterey Park, Q 5..Calif.
300*Monte Rio, G 3....Calif.
3*Monterville, H 15...W. Va.
2242 Montesano, K 3....Wash.
100*Montessori School, M 23 Pa.
1490 Montevallo, H 12....Ala.
69*Montevallo, M 7....Mo.
5220 Montevideo, N 6....Minn.
43*Monteview, N 19....Idaho
3208 Monte Vista, O 11....Colo.
165 Montevue, D 8....Md.
59 Montezuma, G 12....Colo.
2346 Montezuma, K 9....Ga.
1366 Montezuma, J 6....Ind.
1477 Montezuma, L 16....Iowa
340 Montezuma, M 6....Kan.
30*Montezuma (Montezuma College), F 16....N. M.
200*Montezuma, L 13....N. Y.
150*Montezuma, E 2....N. C.
232*Montezuma, H 6....Ohio
120*Montezuma, P 5....Tenn.
30 Montezuma College (Montezuma), F 16....N. M.
615 Montfort, H 20....Wis.
.... Montfort Jc., H 20....Wis.
78084 Montgomery, K 16...Ala.
200*Montgomery Creek, C 6 Calif.
607 Montgomery, C 18....Ill.
510 Montgomery, O 9....Ind.
300*Montgomery, B 6....Iowa
383 Montgomery, F 8....La.
120 Montgomery, G 5....Mass.
313 Montgomery, R 15....Mich.
1741 Montgomery, O 15...Minn.
1671 Montgomery (Montgomery City), H 16....Mo.
844 Montgomery, D 4....N. Y.
461 Montgomery, N 5....Ohio
1893 Montgomery, I 16....Pa.
800 Montgomery, J 22....Tex.
165 Montgomery, B 12....Vt.
3231 Montgomery, L 7...W. Va.
600 Montgomery Center, B 12 Vt.
1671 Montgomery City (Montgomery), H 16....Mo.
.... Montgomery Jc., L 18 Tenn.
199*Montgomerys Ferry, N 14 Pa.
122*Montgomeryville (Adrian), K 5....Pa.
183*Montgomeryville, N 23 .Pa.
60*Monthalia, L 18....Tex.
3650 Monticello, O 15....Ark.
100*Monticello, G 5....Calif.
2042 Monticello, B 7....Fla.
1746 Monticello, G 11....Ga.
2523 Monticello, I 17....Ill.
3153 Monticello, E 9....Ind.
2546 Monticello, H 21....Iowa
1733 Monticello,K 16....Ky.
1467 Monticello, E 19....Me.
1076 Monticello, M 14....Minn.
802 Monticello, N 12....Miss.
198 Monticello, C 15....Mo.
175 Monticello, L 8....N. M.
3737 Monticello, D 2....N. Y.
50*Monticello, E 12....S. C.
667 Monticello, O 24....Utah
....*Monticello, K 12....Va.
716 Monticello, J 21....Wis.
146 Mont Ida, J 23....Kan.
147*Montier, P 16....Mo.
.... Montlake, Q 15....Tenn.
350 Montmorenci, G 8....Ind.
150*Montmorenci, J 10....S. C.
100 Montour, M 5....Idaho
393 Montour, J 15....Iowa
1345 Montour Falls, P 11..N. Y.
3019*Montoursville, I 16....Pa.
300 Montowese, M 12....Conn.
75 Montoya, G 21....N. M.
49*Montpelier, I 9....Calif.
2824 Montpelier, Q 22....Idaho
1800 Montpelier, F 20....Ind.
125 Montpelier, L 23....Iowa
45*Montpelier, I 15....Ky.
100 Montpelier, K 16....La.
250*Montpelier, F 20....Miss.
133 Montpelier, N 19....N. D.
3703 Montpelier, C 6....Ohio
8006 Montpelier, G 12....Vt.
175*Montpelier (Montpelier Station), J 14....Va.
.... Montpelier, Jc. G 12....Vt.
175*Montpelier Station (Montpelier), J 14....Va.
95*Montreal, L 12....Mo.
1700 Montreal (Hamilton), I 6 Wis.
100*Montreat, N 7....N. C.
75*Montrose, Q 6....Ala.
343 Montrose, Q 16....Ark.
3500*Montrose, O 15....Calif.
4764 Montrose, K 6....Colo.
90 Montrose, J 13....Ga.
334 Montrose, K 18....Ill.
592 Montrose, Q 21....Iowa
75*Montrose, D 13....Kan.
500 Montrose, G 7....La.
675 Montrose, N 19....Mich.
275 Montrose, N 13....Minn.
278 Montrose, K 17....Miss.
487 Montrose, K 8....Mo.
12 Montrose, D 2....Neb.
214 Montrose, F 5....N. Y.
1977 Montrose, E 20....Pa.
506 Montrose, L 23....S. D.
122*Montrose, G 15....W. Va
200 Montross, J 19....Va.
148*Montserrat, I 9....Mo.
.... Montvale, E 18....Mass.
1342 Montvale, C 20....N. J.
300 Montvale, N 8....Va.
312*Montverde, G 16....Fla.
110 Mont Vernon, Q 13...N. H.
.... Montview, N 10....Va.
4135▲Montville, K 21....Conn.
850 Montville, K 21....Conn.
605▲Montville, M 12....Me.

Pop. *Place* *Index* *State*

98*Montville, H 3....Mass.
1200 Montville, D 16....N. J.
50 Montville, C 19....Ohio
175 Monument, I 15....Colo.
156*Monument, G 4....Kan.
55 Monument, N 24....N. M.
118 Monument, G 17....Ore.
300*Monument, I 13....Pa.
500 Monument Beach, L 23 Mass.
25*Monument City, E 18..Ind.
400 Mooar, R 21....Iowa
1137 Moodus, J 17....Conn.
.... Moody, K 22....Kan.
135*Moody, R 4....Me.
175*Moody, R 14....Mo.
50*Moody, G 20....N. Y.
5 Moody, C 13....Ore.
931 Moody, H 18....Tex.
.... Moody, J 7....Utah
50 Moodys, F 22....Okla.
42*Moodyville, L 16....Tenn.
477*Mooers, C 24....N. Y.
200 Mooers Forks, C 23..N. Y.
30*Mook, G 12....Ky.
50*Mooleyville, F 12....Ky.
72*Moon, F 21....Ky.
4*Moon, K 2....S. D.
110*Moon, M 21....Va.
1554*Moonachie, D 20....N. J.
81*Mooncreek, J 22....Mont.
.... Mooney, see Clear Springs Ind.
.... Moonlake, see Switzerland Calif.
1267 Moon Run, M 3....Pa.
75 Moons, N 10....Ohio
387 Moorcroft, D 21....Wyo.
28*Moore, E 10....Ark.
50 Moore, N 15....Idaho
241 Moore, I 13....Mont.
499 Moore, J 12....Okla.
66*Moore, C 9....S. C.
575 Moore, M 15....Tex.
35*Moore (Rochester), K 17 Utah
10 Moore, E 14....Wash.
163*Moore, F 15....W. Va.
71*Moorefield, D 16....Ark.
79*Moorefield, N 20....Ind.
200 Moorefield, E 19....Ky.
97 Moorefield, M 11....Neb.
154*Moorefield, I 18....Ohio
.... Moorefield (New Moorefield,) K 10....Ohio
1291 Moorefield, F 19....W. Va.
831 Moore Haven, L 19....Fla.
496 Mooreland, I 19....Ind.
811 Mooreland, C 4....Okla.
124*Moorepark, Q 11....Mich.
5100*Moores (Prospect Park), P 23....Pa.
296 Mooresboro, H 2....N. C.
26 Moores Bridge, F 7....Ala.
85*Mooresburg, J 17....Pa.
200*Mooresburg, L 22....Tenn.
40*Moores Corner, D 9..Mass.
50*Moores Creek, H 19....Ky.
.... Moores Dock, M 14. W. Va.
75 Moores Ferry, F 20....Ky.
359 Moores Hill, M 20....Ind.
20 Moores Jc., N 17....Ohio
99*Moores Mill, C 6....N. Y.
14*Moores Springs, C 8..N. C.
75*Moores Store, G 11....Va.
64*Moorestown, J 14....Mich.
6500 Moorestown, K 10....N. J.
129*Mooresville, B 12....Ala.
1979 Mooresville, K 13....Ind.
170*Mooresville, D 9....Mo.
6682 Mooresville, F 5....N. C.
146 Mooreton, P 24....N. D.
150*Mooreville, C 20....Miss.
80 Moorewood, G 4....Okla.
421 Moorehead, J 3....Iowa
9491 Moorhead, H 2....Minn.
1504 Moorhead, F 9....Miss.
25 Moorhead, N 21....Mont.
5 Moorhead, C 4....Pa.
748 Mooringsport, B 4....La.
215 Moorland, G 9....Iowa
296 Moorland (North Truro), J 15....Mass.
55*Moorland, G 16....Ohio
200 Moorman, H 10....Ky.
34*Moormans River, J 12..Va.
1000 Moorpark, N 14....Calif.
37*Moose, E 2....Wyo.
35*Moosehead, H 9....Me.
995*Mooseheart, C 18....Ill.
....*Moosehorn, J 3....Me.
1432 Moose Lake I 18....Minn.
250 Moose River, H 6....Me.
4568 Moosic, H 21....Pa.
3481 Moosup, F 24....Conn.
36*Moquah, F 5....Wis.
35*Mora, H 8....La.
1494 Mora, K 16....Minn.
40*Mora, J 10....Mo.
1000 Mora, E 16....N. M.
10 Mora, F 1....Wash.
61*Moraga, C 21....Calif.
6 Moragne, D 17....Ala.
.... Moraine, P 9....N. Y.
68*Morales, M 20....Tex.
40*Moran, I 9....Ga.
150 Moran, G 12....Ind.
224*Moran, K 11....Iowa
592 Moran, K 24....Kan.
260 Moran, G 16....Mich.
710 Moran, F 15....Tex.
28 Moran, F 3....Wyo.
500 Morann, K 10....Pa.
400 Morattico, L 20....Va.
110 Moravia, B 5....Idaho
731 Moravia, O 15....Iowa
1231 Moravia, N 14....N. Y.
26 Moravia, K 3....Okla.
250*Moravian Falls, D 4..N. C.
35*Moray, D 23....Kan.
....*Mordue, see Jane...W. Va.
1000 Morea Colliery, K 19...Pa.
....*Moreau, E 11....S. D.
.... Moreau Jc., D 12....S. D.
815 Moreauville, I 11....La.
....*Moree, G 23....Ky.
17 Morefield, L 24....S. D.
125*Morehead, M 23....Kan.
1901 Morehead, E 20....Ky.
3695 Morehead City, K 20.N. C.
1598 Morehouse, Q 22....Mo.
75*Moreland, F 10....Ark.
321 Moreland, G 4....Ga.
400 Moreland, O 18....Idaho
500 Moreland, H 16....Ky.
350 Moreland, H 17....Pa.
561*Moreland Hills, D 17..Ohio
1500 Morenci, L 23....Ariz.
1845 Morenci, R 18....Mich.
400*Moreno, O 19....Calif.
300 Moretown, G 11....Vt.
282 Morgan, M 6....Ga.
70*Morgan, D 18....Ky.
86*Morgan, C 10....Md.
846 Morgan, O 9....Minn.
76*Morgan, N 12....Mo.
500*Morgan (Lawrence Harbor), G 16....N. J.
25*Morgan, D 16....Ore.

Pop. *Place* *Index* *State*

375*Morgan, L 3....Pa.
503 Morgan, F 18....Tex.
1078 Morgan, D 12....Utah
108 Morgan, B 18....Vt.
200*Morgana, I 8....S. C.
100*Morgan Center, B 16...Vt.
6969 Morgan City, O 14....La.
193*Morgan City, G 10...Miss.
163*Morganette, see Beelicks Knob,....W. Va.
3077 Morganfield, G 8....Ky.
1014 Morgan Hill, J 7....Calif.
261*Morgan Hill, E 16....Tex.
75*Morgan Place, L 7....Ohio
.... Morgan Run, I 16....Ohio
90*Morgan Springs, O 16..Tenn.
.... Morgans Run, C 15.W. Va.
54 Morgansville, E 11..W. Va.
250*Morganton, F 12....Ark.
285*Morganton, B 7....Ga.
7670 Morganton, E 2....N. C.
724 Morgantown, K 13....Ind.
859 Morgantown, I 11....Ky.
4 Morgantown, N 11....Md.
100*Morgantown, O 13...Miss.
75*Morgantown, O 11....Ohio
250*Morgantown, M 20....Pa.
16655 Morgantown, B 14. W. Va.
60*Morganville (Tyson), K 15....Ala.
264 Morganville, E 17....Kan.
250*Morganville, H 18....N. J.
744 Morganza, K 13....La.
36*Morganza, O 14....Md.
900*Morganza, N 2....Pa.
500*Moriah, G 24....N. Y.
500*Moriah Center, G 24..N. Y.
275 Moriarty, G 13....N. M.
450 Moriches, H 10....N. Y.
6 Moritz, G 24....S. D.
356*Morland, F 7....Kan.
600 Morley, Q 16....Colo.
119*Morley, I 21....Iowa
366 Morley, M 14....Mich.
522 Morley, P 23....Mo.
204*Morley, F 17....N. Y.
200*Morley, L 19....Tenn.
3*Mormon Lake, G 15...Ariz.
....*Morningdale, F 14...Mass.
1282*Morningside, M 15...Minn.
861 Morning Sun, N 22....Iowa
101*Morning Sun, L 5....Ohio
59*Morning View, C 17....Ky.
278 Moro, I 18....Ark.
150 Moro, L 11....Ill.
309 Moro, D 13....Ore.
85*Morobay, Q 12....Ark.
1151 Morocco, E 6....Ind.
1158 Moroni, I 13....Utah
398 Morral, H 11....Ohio
....*Morrell (Morrell Park), F 14....Md.
110*Morrellton (Anaconda), J 17....Mo.
150 Morri (Glen Morrison), O 6....W. Va.
452 Morrice, O 19....Mich.
387 Morrill, C 21....Kan.
....*Morrill, H 19....Ky.
100 Morrill, M 12....Me.
877 Morrill, H 1....Neb.
40*Morrill, G 22....Tex.
4608 Morrillton, H 11....Ark.
315*Morris, E 13....Ala.
344 Morris, G 7....Conn.
6145 Morris, D 18....Ill.
298 Morris, L 21....Ind.
105*Morris, F 25....Kan.
3214 Morris, L 5....Minn.
599 Morris, O 18....N. Y.
1197 Morris, H 19....Okla.
140 Morris, G 14....Pa.
25*Morris, J 10....W. Va.
65*Morris Chapel, P 6...Tenn.
.... Morris Creek Jc., L 7 W. Va.
600 Morrisdale, J 11....Pa.
140*Morrisey, F 22....Wyo.
....*Morris Fork, H 20....Ky.
216*Morrison(Mount Morrison), G 14....Colo.
3187 Morrison, C 11....Ill.
161 Morrison, H 16....Iowa
271 Morrison, I 15....Mo.
333 Morrison, E 14....Okla.
5 Morrison, G 4....Ore.
100 Morrison, E 8....Pa.
278 Morrison, O 13....Tenn.
521 Morrison, O 21....Va.
1206 Morrisonville, K 13....Ill.
750 Morrisonville, D 23...N. Y.
190 Morrisonville, K 19....Wis.
2018 Morris Plains, D 16...N. J.
140 Morris Ranch, K 15....Tex.
2352 Morris Run, F 16....Pa.
....*Morrissey, see Sulphurdale, Utah
195*Morriston, B 15....Ark.
200 Morriston, E 13....Fla.
....*Morristown, see Castle Hot Springs....Ariz.
665 Morristown, J 17....Ind.
677 Morristown, P 15....Minn.
15270 Morristown, E 15....N. J.
540 Morristown, E 16....N. Y.
410*Morristown, K 19....Ohio
217 Morristown, B 8....S. D.
8050 Morristown, M 21....Tenn.
65 Morristown, E 12....Vt.
100*Morrisvale, M 5....W. Va.
329 Morrisville, N 9....Mo.
666 Morrisville, N 16....N. Y.
161*Morrisville, F 13....N. C.
5493 Morrisville, N 25....Pa.
1967 Morrisville, D 12....Vt.
150*Morrisville, H 15....Va.
35*Morrisville Station, M 17 N. Y.
1100*Morro Bay, M 9....Calif.
65*Morrow, D 4....Ark.
450*Morrow, F 6....Ga.
250 Morrow (Morrows), J 11 La.
840 Morrow, N 8....Ohio
308 Morrowville, D 16....Kan.
70*Morse, K 21....Iowa
39 Morse, G 25....Kan.
742 Morse, M 9....La.
100*Morse (Hastings), K 15 N. Y.
50 Morse, I 17....Okla.
100 Morse, B 4....Tex.
153 Morse, G 7....Wis.
170 Morse Bluff, J 21....Neb.
50*Moseley, M 15....Va.
62*Morse Mill, K 19....Mo.
....*Morses Creek, F 18...N. J.
50 Mortimer, L 9....N. Y.
42*Mortimer, E 3....N. C.
11 Mortimer, J 19....N. D.
50 Mortimer, F 9....Ohio
28*Morton, G 17....Ark.
35*Morton, C 4....Idaho
2241 Morton, G 13....Ill.
1068*Morton (Mortons Gap), I 9....Ky.
904 Morton, O 9....Minn.
934 Morton, K 14....Miss.
127*Morton, K 7....N. Y.

Pop. *Place* *Index* *State*

1316*Morton, P 23....Pa.
1137 Morton, B 8....Tex.
778 Morton, M 8....Wash.
25 Morton, I 9....Wyo.
2010 Morton Grove, B 21....Ill.
69*Morton Mills, N 7....Iowa
1072 Mortons Gap (Morton), I 9....Ky.
.... Mortonsville, F 16....Ky.
200*Mortonville, P 21....Pa.
512 Morven, O 11....Ga.
602 Morven, J 8....N. C.
80*Morville, G 13....La.
52*Morvin, L 6....Ala.
25 Morvin, J 14....Okla.
100*Morwood, N 23....Pa.
218*Mosby (Moseby), F 7..Mo.
6 Mosby, H 17....Mont.
75 Mosca, O 12....Colo.
225*Moscow, M 15....Ark.
6014 Moscow, F 3....Idaho
50*Moscow, K 18....Ind.
153 Moscow, L 22....Iowa
177*Moscow, N 4....Kan.
200 Moscow, K 4....Ky.
50*Moscow, H 7....Me.
175 Moscow, N 5....Md.
902▲Moscow, Q 16....Mich.
347 Moscow (Moscow Mills), N 18....Mo.
309 Moscow, P 7....Ohio
1097 Moscow, H 22....Pa.
309 Moscow, Q 3....Tenn.
263 Moscow, I 23....Tex.
200 Moscow, E 11....Vt.
347 Moscow Mills (Moscow), H 18....Mo.
30 Mose, J 19....N. D.
218 Moseby (Mosby), F 7..Mo.
60 Moselem, M 20....Pa.
50 Moseley, D 23....Okla.
50 Moseley, M 15....Va.
30 Moseley Hall, C 8....Fla.
204 Moselle, N 17....Miss.
80*Moselle, J 18....Mo.
162▲Moses, C 25....N. M.
326 Moses Lake (Neppel), J 17 Wash.
120 Mosgrove, K 6....Pa.
148*Moshannon, J 11....Pa.
400 Mosheim, M 22....Tenn.
265 Mosheim, G 18....Tex.
25*Mosher, M 11....S. D.
125*Mosherville, Q 15....Mich.
216 Mosier, C 11....Ore.
100 Mosiertown, E 2....Pa.
1361 Mosinee, J 12....Wis.
100 Moskee (Lavier), C 22. Wyo.
742 Mosquero, E 20....N. M.
75*Moss (Mossville), M 18 Miss.
150*Moss, K 14....Tenn.
10*Moss, H 10....W. Va.
416 Moss Beach, F 15....Calif.
150*Moss Landing, K 6...Calif.
150 Mossmain, M 16....Mont.
2*Moss Neck, J 17....Va.
3042 Moss Point, R 22....Miss
120 Mossville, D 8....Ark.
150*Mossville, F 13....Ill.
.... Mossville, M 6....La.
75*Mossville (Moss), M 18 Miss.
136*Mossy Bottom, H 23...Ky.
150*Mossyhead, M 6....Fla.
225 Mossyrock, M 7....Wash.
3 Motala, N 15....Neb.
150*Motbridge, H 17....S. C.
368 Motley, J 11....Minn.
33*Motoque, Q 1....Utah
247 Motordale (New Germany) N 13....Minn.
230 Motorun, N 21....Va.
1220 Mott, P 6....N. D.
30 Motters, B 9....Md.
25 Mottinger, O 18....Wash.
500 Mottville, M 13....N. Y.
752 Moulton, C 10....Ala.
1181 Moulton, P 16....Iowa
74*Moulton, H 14....Mont.
5 Moulton, I 13....Neb.
643 Moulton, L 19....Tex.
100 Moultonboro, K 15...N. H.
225 Moultonville, K 17...N. H.
500*Moultrie, D 18....Fla.
10147 Moultrie, N 9....Ga.
15*Moultrie, G 19....Ohio
515 Moultrieville, N 19....S. C.
145 Mound, D 15....La.
1189 Mound, N 14....Minn.
100*Mound, O 2....N. D.
100*Mound, H 17....Tex.
806 Mound Bayou, E 8...Miss.
2465 Mound City, R 15....Ill.
703 Mound City, J 24....Kan.
1606 Mound City, C 4....Mo.
195 Mound City, C 13....S. D.
5 Mound House, H 3....Nev.
50*Mound Prairie, R 23 Minn.
864 Moundridge, J 16....Kan.
2144 Mounds, R 14....Ill.
627 Mounds, G 18....Okla.
20 Mounds, J 18....Utah
14168 Moundsville, A 10, R 23 W. Va.
648 Mound Valley, N 22..Kan.
812 Moundville, H 8....Ala.
247 Moundville, M 6....Mo.
62*Mount, H 17....Va.
.... Mount Abram Jc., K 6.Me.
250 Mount Aetna, M 19....Pa.
205 Mountain, E 21....N. D.
150*Mountain, N 11....Wis.
1477 Mountainair, I 13..N. M.
700*Mountain Ash, K 19...Ky.
185 Mountainburg, E 5....Ark.
524 Mountain City, B 12...Ga.
100 Mountain City, A 17..Nev.
1021 Mountain City, L 25. Tenn.
300 Mountain Creek, I 14..Ala.
70*Mountaincrest, E 6....Ark.
450 Mountain Dale, D 3..N. Y.
25*Mountaindale, C 6....Ore.
300 Mountaindale, L 10....Pa.
100 Mountain Dale, (Clear branch), M 23....Tenn.
40*Mountain Falls, E 13...Va.
2431 Mountain Grove, O 13.Mo.
137*Mountain Grove, J 7...Va.
927 Mountain Home, B 12.Ark.
1193 Mountain Home, O 7,.Idaho
5*Mountain Home, P 8..N. C.
700 Mountainhome, I 23....Pa.
....*Mountain Home, L 23 Tenn.
25*Mountain Home, J 14 .Tex.
120 Mountain Home, G 19.Utah
1492 Mountain Iron, F 18.Minn.
30 Mountain Island, H 5.N. C.
1745 Mountain Lake, Q 9..Minn.
30*Mountain Lake (Summer), N 4....Va.
551 Mountain Lake Park, O 2 Md.
2205 Mountain Lakes, D 16.N. J.
200 Mountain Park, M 14.N. M.
90*Mountain Park, C 6..N. C.
441 Mountain Park, M 6.Okla.

Pop. *Place* *Index* *State*

1000 Mountain Pine, J 9....Ark.
13*Mountain Ranch, H 9.Calif.
29*Mountain Rest, B 3..S. C.
1148 Mountainside, E 16..N. J.
41*Mountain Springs, H 19.Pa.
60*Mountain Top, E 6...Ark.
1150*Mountaintop, H 21....Pa.
150 Mountain Valley, J 9..Ark.
....*Mountain Valley, H 21.Ky.
745 Mountain View, D 13..Ark.
3946 Mountain View, G 21.Calif.
400*Mountain View, F 7...Ga.
725 Mountain View, P 15..Mo.
500 Mountainview (Center Osspee), K 17....N. H.
1600*Mountain View, C 18..N. J.
91*Mountain View, D 22.N. Y.
1075 Mountain View, K 6..Okla.
115*Mountainview, I 16....Va.
60*Mountain View, N 24.Wash.
100 Mountainview, Q 4..Wyo.
460*Mountainville, D 4..N. Y.
.... Mountainville, L 22...Pa.
437 Mount Airy, C 12....Ga.
250*Mount Airy, L 17....La.
791 Mount Airy, E 10....Md.
6286 Mount Airy, B 6....N. C.
25*Mountairy, P 15....Tenn.
30 Mount Airy Jc., E 10..Md.
....*Mount Alto, H 5....W. Va.
58 Mount Alton (Alton), F 9 Pa.
325 Mount Andrew, L 20...Ala.
1032 Mount Angel, F 7....Ore.
15*Mount Arab, F 17....N. Y.
456 Mount Arlington, D 14 N. J.
471 Mount Auburn, I 14....Ill.
161*Mount Auburn, K 16..Ind.
223 Mount Auburn, H 18..Iowa
207 Mount Ayr, D 7....Ind.
1930 Mount Ayr, P 10....Iowa
900*Mount Berry, D 2....Ga.
450 Mount Bethel, J 24....Pa.
442 Mount Blanchard, F 10 Ohio
800 Mount Braddock, P 5...Pa.
100*Mount Bullion, I 11...Calif.
525 Mount Calm, G 19....Tex.
500 Mount Calvary, N 17..Wis.
311*Mount Carbon, L 19....Pa.
475 Mount Carbon, L 7.W. Va.
1200 Mount Carmel, K 11.Conn.
6987 Mount Carmel, N 21....Ill.
120*Mount Carmel, K 22...Ind.
56*Mount Carmel, I 7....Iowa
55*Mount Carmel, D 20...Ky.
190 Mount Carmel, D 19.N. D.
17780 Mount Carmel, K 18...Pa.
114 Mount Carmel, G 6...S. C.
125 Mount Carmel, Q 7...Utah
.... Mount Carrigain, see Willey House....N. H.
1845 Mount Carroll, B 11....Ill.
40*Mountcastle, N 18....Va.
331 Mount Clare, L 11....Ill.
200 Mount Clare, O 17....Neb.
700 Mount Clare (Byron), F 12....W. Va.
14389 Mount Clemens, P 24 Mich.
241 Mount Clinton, H 10...Va.
100*Mount Comfort, I 15...Ind.
273 Mount Cory, F 9....Ohio
290 Mount Crawford, I 11..Va.
110*Mount Crawford (North River), I 11....Va.
209 Mount Croghan, C 17.S. C.
523 Mount de Chaute (Clator), Q 24....W. Va.
100 Mount Desert, M 17...Me.
179 Mount Desert Ferry, M 18 Me.
1880 Mount Dora, F 17....Fla.
250*Mount Dora, C 24...N. M.
200*Mount Eaton, G 16...Ohio
500*Mount Eden, F 20, I 6Calif.
350 Mount Eden, F 15....Ky.
280 Mount Emmons, G 19.Utah
622 Mount Enterprise, F 23Tex.
2319 Mount Ephraim, L 9..N. J.
125 Mount Ephraim, L 18.Ohio
200 Mount Erie, N 19....Ill.
139*Mount Etna, E 18....Ind.
106*Mount Etna, N 8....Iowa
28*Mountfair, J 12....Va.
500*Mount Forest, C 21....Ill.
50 Mountforest, L 18....Mich.
219 Mount Freedom, D 14.N. J.
516*Mount Gay (Gay), N 4 W. Va.
915 Mount Gilead, H 9...N. C.
2008 Mount Gilead, H 13...Ohio
1441*Mount Greenwood, C 21.Ill.
42*Mount Gretna, N 18....Pa.
82*Mount Hamill (Hamill), P 20....Iowa
57*Mount Hamilton (Lick Observatory), I 7...Calif.
30*Mount Harmony (Paris), K 15....Md.
1500 Mount Harris, C 8....Colo.
....*Mount Hays, D 13....Md.
3997 Mount Healthy, O 22, N 6 Ohio
50*Mount Hebron, H 6....Ala.
200*Mount Hebron, B 6...Calif.
50*Mount Hermon, J 6...Calif.
36*Mount Hermon, K 14..Ky.
200 Mount Hermon, J 18...La.
600*Mount Hermon, B 8..Mass.
200*Mount Heron, B 7....Va.
400 Mount Holly, Q 9....Ark.
6892 Mount Holly, K 12...N. J.
2055 Mount Holly, H 5....N. C.
250*Mount Holly, M 18...S. C.
250 Mount Holly, M 10....Vt.
24*Mount Holly, J 19....Va.
1260 Mount Holly Springs, O 15 Pa.
65*Mount Hood, D 11....Ore.
250 Mount Hope, C 9....Ala.
442 Mount Hope, L 15....Kan.
1000 Mount Hope, D 15....N. J.
120*Mount Hope, G 16....Ohio
50 Mount Hope, H 22...Wash.
2431 Mount Hope, N 8...W. Va.
256 Mount Hope, F 20....Wis.
1610 Mount Horeb, J 20....Wis.
490 Mount Ida, J 7....Ark.
70 Mount Idaho, H 6...Idaho
562 Mount Jackson, G 12...Va.
1445 Mount Jewett, F 9....Pa.
40*Mount Joy, K 24....Iowa
2855 Mount Joy, O 18....Pa.
78*Mount Judea, D 9....Ark.
550 Mount Juliet, M 11..Tenn.
5941 Mount Kisco, F 6....N. Y.
29*Mount Laguna (Resort), P 20....Calif.
55*Mount Landing, K 19...Va.
200 Mount Laurel, K 11...N. J.
100*Mount Lebanon, C 7....La.
19571■*Mount Lebanon, M 3. Pa.
150 Mount Leonard, G 9...Mo.
49*Mount Levi, E 8....Ark.
150 Mount Liberty, I 13...Ohio
163*Mount Lookout, L 9.W.Va.
25*Mount Lowe, O 16...Calif.

Pop. *Place* *Index* *State*

500*Mount McGregor, L 23 N. Y.
....*Mount Mansfield, D 11.Vt.
....*Mount Marion, R 21.N. Y.
110*Mount Meigs, J 16....Ala.
180*Mount Mitchell (Switzerland), M 10....N. C.
9*Mount Montgomery, I 7 Nev.
276 Mount Moriah, B 8....Mo.
2304 Mount Morris, B 13....Ill.
2237 Mount Morris, N 21..Mich.
3530 Mount Morris, N 8...N. Y.
432 Mount Morris, Q 2....Pa.
110 Mount Morris, L 16...Wis.
216*Mount Morrison (Morrison) G 14....Colo.
150*Mount Mourne, E 5..N. C.
206 Mount Nebo, L 10..W. Va.
1800*Mount Olive, F 12....Ala.
138▲*Mount Olive, C 14...Ark.
2559 Mount Olive, L 11....Ill.
75*Mount Olive .O 10....Ind.
775 Mount Olive, M 14...Miss.
2929 Mount Olive, H 16...N. C.
6981*Mount Oliver, M 3....Pa.
573 Mount Olivet, D 19....Ky.
589 Mount Orab (Mount Oreb), O 9....Ohio
150*Mount Palatine, E 14...Ill.
3654*Mount Penn, N 20....Pa.
150*Mount Perry, K 15....Ohio
500*Mount Pinson (Pinson), F 12....Ala.
84*Mount Pisgah, K 17....Ky.
10*Mount Pleasant, N 8...Ala.
300 Mount Pleasant, C 15..Ark.
201 Mount Pleasant, D 20..Del.
200*Mount Pleasant, B 3...Fla.
50*Mount Pleasant, M 20..Ga.
40*Mount Pleasant, H 19..Ind.
60*Mount Pleasant, Q 11..Ind.
4610 Mount Pleasant, O 20.Iowa
8413 Mount Pleasant, L 15Mich.
107*Mount Pleasant, A 15 Miss.
1017 Mount Pleasant, G 7..N. C.
50*Mount Pleasant, C 3.N. Y.
717*Mount Pleasant, I 20..Ohio
5824 Mount Pleasant, O 5....Pa.
1698 Mount Pleasant, N 19.S. C.
3089 Mountpleasant, O 10.Tenn.
4528 Mount Pleasant, D 22.Tex.
2382 Mount Pleasant, I 13..Utah
300 Mount Pleasant Mills, L 15....Pa.
50*Mount Plymouth, G 16.Fla.
648 Mount Pocono, I 22....Pa.
25 Mount Princeton Hot Springs, J 11....Colo.
1720 Mount Prospect, B 20...Ill.
1378 Mount Pulaski, I 14....Ill.
4830 Mount Ranier, I 11....Md.
50 Mount Riga, R 24....N. Y.
685*Mount Royal, L 7....N. J.
25*Mount St. Francis, P 16 Ind.
3*Mount St. Joseph, O 6.Ohio
36*Mount Salem, H 17....Ky.
3500 Mount Savage, L 5....Md.
.... Mount Savage Jc., L 6.Md.
200*Mount Selman, F 22...Tex.
200*Mount Sharp, E 22....Tex.
1618 Mount Shasta, (Sisson) C 5....Calif.
200 Mount Sherman, C 9..Ark.
51*Mount Sherman, H 14..Ky.
250 Mount Sidney, I 11....Va.
500*Mount Sinai, G 9....N. Y.
.... Mount Solo, N 5....Wash.
96 Mount Solon, I 10....Va.
150 Mount Sterling, K 5...Ala.
2140 Mount Sterling, I 6....Ill.
30*Mount Sterling, N 21..Ind.
165*Mount Sterling, Q 19..Iowa
4782 Mount Sterling, F 19...Ky.
50*Mount Sterling, J 15...Mo.
250*Mount Sterling, N 6..N. C.
1115 Mount Sterling, L 9...Ohio
.... Mount Sterling, see Hopewell....Ohio
1047 Mount Sterling, Q 3....Pa.
264 Mount Sterling, F 19...Wis.
25*Mount Storm, F 18. W. Va.
265 Mount Summit, I 18...Ind.
65*Mount Sunapee, N 8.N. H.
181*Mount Sylvan, E 21...Tex.
500*Mount Tabor (Tabor), D 15....N. J.
.... Mount Tabor see Tabor City....N. C.
55*Mount Tabor (Robat), C 11....S. C.
50 Mount Tabor (Danby), N 8....Vt.
25*Mount Tabor, H 17...Wis.
240 Mount Tom, F 7....Mass.
172*Mount Tremper (The Corners), R 22....N. Y.
100*Mount Trumbull, C 7.Ariz.
20*Mount Ulla, G 6....N. C.
186 Mount Union, N 21...Iowa
4763 Mount Union, N 12....Pa.
400 Mount Upton, P 18..N. Y.
810 Mount Vernon, O 5....Ala.
200 Mount Vernon, G 13...Ark.
900 Mount Vernon, K 15...Ga.
14724 Mount Vernon, N 16...Ill.
5638 Mount Vernon, R 3....Ind.
1489 Mount Vernon, J 21...Iowa
1100 Mount Vernon, H 18....Ky.
500 Mount Vernon, O 20...Md.
300 Mount Vernon, M 8....Me.
1982 Mount Vernon, O 8....Mo.
67362 Mount Vernon, G 6..N. Y.
10122 Mount Vernon, I 13..Ohio
75 Mount Vernon, H 18...Ore.
405 Mount Vernon, L 19..S. D.
52*Mount Vernon, P 18..Tenn.
1443 Mount Vernon, D 22...Tex.
101 Mount Vernon, G 17...Va.
4278 Mount Vernon, E 7..Wash.
128*Mount Vernon, J 20...Wis.
.... Mount Vernon. Jc., P 5.Ind.
75 Mount Vernon Springs (Ore Hill), F 11....N. C.
15*Mount Victoria, N 12..Md.
37*Mount Victory, J 18....Ky.
645 Mount Victory, H 10...Ohio
35*Mountview, P 9....W. Va.
298 Mountville, H 4....Ga.
967 Mountville, P 18....Pa.
139 Mountville, E 9....S. C.
50*Mountville, E 15....Va.
150 Mount Vision, O 18..N. Y.
350 Mount Washington, F 14 Ky.
2500 Mount Washington, G 6. Mo.
90 Mount Washington, H 16 N. H.
.... Mount Washington, O 7 Ohio
100*Mount Whittier (West Ossipee), L 17....N. H.
30*Mount Williams, E 13..Va.
300 Mount Willing, K 13...Ala.
29*Mount Wilson, N 15..Calif.
225*Mount Wilson, E 13...Md.
970 Mount Wolf, O 17....Pa.

Pop. Place Index State
84*Mount Zion, F 2.......Ga.
384 Mount Zion, J 16.......Ill.
60 Mount Zion, F 20.....Ind.
40 Mount Zion, P 19.....Iowa
100*Mount Zion, D 3.....N. C.
31*Mount Zion, H 8....W. Va.
50*Mount Zion, G 19.....Wis.
81 Mous, N 10..........Ala.
20 Mouser, Q 5.........Okla.
63*Mousie, H 22.........Ky.
263 Mouthcard, I 24.......Ky.
31*Mouth of Laurel (Camp Dix), D 21.........Ky.
65*Mouth of Seneca, H 17 W. Va.
20 Mouzons, I 19........S. C.
24*Movico, P 4..........Ala.
973 Moville, G 2..........Iowa
15 Mowbray, D 19.......N. D.
1366 Moweaqua, J 16........Ill.
35*Mowersville, O 13......Pa.
325*Mowry, K 18..........Pa.
427 Mowrystown, O 9....Ohio
410 Moxahala, M 15.......Ohio
335 Moxee City, M 14...Wash.
89*Moxley, D 16..........Ky.
.... Moxley, C 4.........N. C.
10 Moyer Jc., O 2.......Wyo.
213 Moyers, O 20.........Okla.
19*Moyers, J 17.......W. Va.
100*Moyie Springs, A 5....Idaho
359*Moylan (Moylan-Rose Valley), P 23.........Pa.
500 Moyock, B 22........N. C.
20*Mozart, D 13.........Ark.
80*Mozelle, I 21..........Ky.
25*Mozer, I 17........W. Va.
301 Mozier, K 7...........Ill.
25*Mud, M 4..........W. Va.
3*Mud Butte, G 6......S. D.
23*Mudbaden, O 15.....Minn.
20*Mud Camp, K 14......Ky.
575*Muddy, P 18...........Ill.
56*Muddy Creek Forks, Q 18 Pa.
17*Mudfork, H 8......W. Va.
55 Mudlick, K 14.........Ky.
599 Muenster, C 18.......Tex.
6000*Muhlenburg, M 20.....Pa.
52*Muir, F 18............Ky.
447 Muir, O 16..........Mich.
750*Muir, L 18............Pa.
109*Muirkirk, H 12.......Md.
450 Mukilteo, G 8.......Wash.
855 Mukwonago, O 21.....Wis.
50*Mulat (Avalon), M 3...Fla.
973 Mulberry, F 5.........Ark.
1502 Mulberry, I 15.........Fla.
860 Mulberry, G 11........Ind.
1175 Mulberry, M 25......Kan.
200 Mulberry, N 6.........Mo.
300*Mulberry (New Salsbury), O 7..............Ohio
210 Mulberry, P 12......Tenn.
702 Mulberry Grove, L 13...Ill.
37*Mulch, K 20...........Va.
75 Muldon, E 20........Miss.
35*Muldoon, O 13.......Idaho
600*Muldoon (Mulldoon), K 19 Tex.
200*Muldraugh, G 13......Ky.
638 Muldrow, I 24........Okla.
100*Mule Creek, M 4....N. M.
50*Mule Creek, E 22....Wyo.
1327 Muleshoe, A 8........Tex.
.... Mulford, D 19.......Calif.
2000*Mulga, F 12...........Ala.
406 Mulhall, F 12.........Okla.
200 Mulino (Howard), E 8.Ore.
30 Mulkey, O 14.........Okla.
450 Mulkeytown, P 14......Ill.
16*Mull, C 11............Ark.
2291 Mullan, E 7..........Idaho
600*Mulldoon (Muldoon), K 19 Tex.
725 Mullen, H 9..........Neb.
404 Mullen (Mullin), G 16.Tex.
3026 Mullens, P 7.......W. Va.
50*Mullet Lake, F 16...Mich.
350 Mullica Hill, M 7.....N. J.
338 Mulliken, O 14......Mich.
36*Mullikin, I 6...........Ky.
18*Mullikin (Mitchellville), I 12...............Md.
75*Mullins (Withers), H 18 Ky.
4392 Mullins, F 22.........S. C.
428 Mullinville, M 9.......Kan.
3000 Multnomah, D 7.......Ore.
940 Mulvane, N 17.........Kan.
530*Mumford, M 8........N. Y.
215 Mumford, I 20.........Tex.
30*Mummie, H 19.........Ky.
....*Mumper, I 5..........Neb.
200 Muncie, H 21...........Ill.
49720 Muncie, H 18.........Ind.
30 Muncie, F 25.........Kan.
50*Muncy, H 19..........Ky.
2606 Muncy, I 17............Pa.
220 Muncy Valley, H 17....Pa.
1545 Munday, C 14..........Tex.
30*Munday, G 8.......W. Va.
1328*Mundelein, A 20........Ill.
135*Mundell, B 6...........Ark.
193 Munden, D 15.........Kan.
200 Munden, R 23..........Va.
100 Mundy, O 20.........Mich.
50*Mundy Point, K 20....Va.
450 Munford, F 18.........Ala.
407 Munford, O 2.......Tenn.
832 Munfordville, I 13.....Ky.
.... Munger, B 19..........Ill.
96 Munger, M 19......Mich.
25*Munger, G 19.........Tex.
13900 Munhall, N 3............Pa.
216 Munich, E 18........N. D.
4409 Munising, E 10......Mich.
.... Munising Jc., F 9....Mich.
218 Munith, P 19.........Mich.
58*Munition, N 7.......W. Va.
75*Munjor, H 10.........Kan.
50*Munk, D 16............Ky.
50*Munnerlyn, H 20.......Ga.
357*Munnsville (Munns), M 16 N. Y.
511 Munroe Falls, E 18....Ohio
1456*Munsey Park, H 7...N. Y.
150*Munson, M 4..........Fla.
58*Munson, R 19........Mich.
600 Munson, J 11...........Pa.
75*Munsonville, P 8.....N. H.
16 Munster, E 16..........Ill.
1751 Munster, B 6...........Ind.
.... Munster, I 16.........N. D.
....*Munuscono (Thorice), F 19..............Mich.
32*Murat, L 8.............Va.
14 Murchison, D 4......S. D
407 Murchison, F 21.......Tex.
680 Murdo (Murdo Mackenzie), K 11...............S. D.
75 Murdock, K 15........Fla.
220 Murdock, J 20..........Ill.
140*Murdock, M 14........Kan.
334 Murdock, M 7.......Minn.
199 Murdock, L 23.........Neb.
25 Murdock, P 7...........Pa.
680 Murdo Mackenzie (Murdo), K 11.....S. D.

Pop. Place Index State
100*Muren, P 7...........Ind.
835 Murfreesboro, M 7....Ark.
1550 Murfreesboro, C 20...N. C.
9495 Murfreesboro, N 12..Tenn.
.... Muriel, N 17.........Neb.
75*Murl, J 17.............Ky.
100*Muroc, M 13.........Calif.
600 Murphy, H 10.......Calif.
75 Murphy, O 4........Idaho
30*Murphy, G 7.........Miss.
47 Murphy, L 18.........Neb.
1873 Murphy, Q 2..........N. C.
150 Murphy, E 22.........Okla.
50 Murphy, Q 5..........Ore.
400 Murphy, D 19.........Tex.
13*Murphy, C 7............Va.
....*Murphyfork, G 21.....Ky.
.... Murphy Jc., B 7........Ga.
25 Murphy Jc., O 7.......N. C.
8976 Murphysboro, P 14......Ill.
50 Murphysville, D 20....Ky.
333▲*Murray, C 8..........Ark.
150*Murray, L 11.........Calif.
175 Murray, D 7.........Idaho
60*Murray, E 20..........Ind.
857 Murray, N 11.........Iowa
3773 Murray, K 6............Ky.
209 Murray, L 24..........Neb.
.... Murray, J 23.........N. D.
25*Murray, D 15.........Tex.
5740 Murray, F 11..........Utah
.... Murray, see Jordan .W. Va.
1009 Murray City, M 15 ...Ohio
500*Murray Hill, F 17....N. J.
10*Murrayisle, H 15.....N. Y.
700 Murraysville (Murrysville), M 5..................Pa.
115*Murraysville, H 5...W. Va.
750*Murrayville, D 9.......Ga.
478 Murrayville, J 10.......Ill.
210 Murrells Inlet, I 23...S. C.
1000*Murrieta, O 19.......Calif.
700*Murrysville (Murraysville), M 5..................Pa.
125*Murrycross, D 18......Ala.
272 Murtaugh, Q 12.....Idaho
98*Muscadine, F 20.......Ala.
18286 Muscatine, L 22.....Iowa
1113 Muscle Shoals, B 8....Ala.
902 Muscoda, H 20........Wis.
200 Muscogee, M 2.........Fla.
.... Muscogee, J 3..........Ga.
331 Muscotah, E 22........Kan.
450 Muse, M 24...........Okla.
2100*Muse, N 2...............Pa.
100*Musella, I 9............Ga.
46*Muses Mills, E 20.....Ky.
100*Museville, Q 9...........Va.
40*Music, E 22.............Ky.
300 Muskego (Muskego Center), O 20....................Wis.
47697 Muskegon, N 11....Mich.
16047 Muskegon Heights, N 11 Mich.
32332 Muskogee, H 21.....Okla.
29*Musselfork, E 11.......Mo.
350 Musselshell, J 17....Mont.
35 Mustang, N 16........Colo.
214 Mustang, J 11.........Okla.
29*Mustoe, I 8.............Va.
335*Muttontown, H 7....N. Y.
29*Mutual, M 14.........Md.
120*Mutual, J 9..........Ohio
179 Mutual, E 5..........Okla.
250 Mutual, N 5.............Pa.
213 Mutual, I 16..........Utah
95*Muzette, G 6............Pa.
125*Myakka City, K 15....Fla.
150 Myers, E 19.............Ky.
42 Myers, K 18........Mont.
228*Myers, O 13.........N. Y.
60 Myers, C 4..........N. C.
800 Myers, N 18.........S. C.
300*Myers Crossing (Doanville). N 15..............Ohio
2692 Myerstown, M 19.......Pa.
310 Myersville, D 7........Md.
100*Myles, L 10..........Miss.
89 Mylo, E 15..........N. D.
40*Mynard, L 23.........Neb.
10 Myndus, O 7........N. M.
120*Myra, H 24.............Ky.
12 Myra, N 9...............Pa.
250 Myra, C 18............Tex.
64*Myra, L 3..........W. Va.
70*Myra, O 18............Wis.
.... Myren, F 10..........Mich.
15*Myricks (Lay), J 19....Ky.
.... Myricks, K 20........Mass.
25*Myron, B 15...........Ark.
75 Myrtis, A 4.............La.
25*Myrtle, A 9............Ark.
24 Myrtle, G 4..........Idaho
50*Myrtle, H 22............Ky.
133*Myrtle, R 17.........Minn.
349 Myrtle, B 18..........Miss.
52*Myrtle, Q 16...........Mo.
27*Myrtle, Q 20............Va.
1597 Myrtle Beach, I 24....S. C.
441 Myrtle Creek, N 5.....Ore.
600*Myrtle Grove, M 2.....Fla.
34*Myrtle Grove, O 19....La.
1296 Myrtle Point, N 3.....Ore.
800 Myrtlewood, K 6.......Ala.
....*Mystic, C 8...........Colo.
2547 Mystic, L 23.........Conn.
256 Mystic, M 12...........Ga.
1884 Mystic, P 15...........Iowa
50*Mystic, G 12.............Ky.
40 Mystic, J 2............S. D.
437 Myton, G 20..........Utah

N

1 Na-Ah-Tee Canyon, F 20 Ariz.
100*Nabb (Nabbs), O 17...Ind.
....*Nabnasset (Brookside), C 17..............Mass.
185*Naborton, E 5...........La.
27*Nace, N 7...............Va.
536 Naches, L 13........Wash.
129*Nachusa, C 14..........Ill.
250 Naco, P 21............Ariz.
7538 Nacogdoches, G 23....Tex.
200 Nacoochee, C 10........Ga.
37 Nacora, G 21..........Neb.
58*Nada, L 21.............Tex.
28 Nada, N 4............Utah
....*Nadaburg, see Wittmann, Ariz.
93 Nadawah, L 10.........Ala.
200 Nadeau, H 6..........Mich.
82*Nady, M 17............Ark.
90 Naf, R 15.............Idaho
110 Nafton, A 5............Utah
600 Nagog, D 17..........Mass.
25 Nagrom, J 10.........Wash.
45*Nags Head, F 24.....N. C.
1200 Nahant, E 21.........Mass.
83 Nahcotta, M 2.......Wash.
900 Nahma, G 10.........Mich.
10 Nahon, E 19..........S. D.
561 Nahunta, O 20..........Ga.
17*Nail, D 8..............Ark.
250 Nairn, P 20..............La.
....*Naker, I 11...............Ky.
200*Nakina, M 13.........N. C.

Pop. Place Index State
5 Nakoda, C 15........Minn.
.... Nakomis, J 9..............Ga.
500 Nallen, M 10........W. Va.
24 Nallpee, M 3..........Wash.
534 Nambe, E 14.........N. M.
2701*Nameoki, M 10..........Ill.
12149 Nampa, N 4..........Idaho
76*Nanachehaw (Allen), J 7 Miss.
200 Nanafalia, K 6..........Ala.
358*Nancy, I 17..............Ky.
250*Nancy, H 23............Tex.
50*Nancy, C 7...............Va.
48*Nandua, L 23............Va.
248*Nanjemoy, M 11........Md.
250*Nankin, F 14..........Ohio
12 Nansen, J 22..........S. D.
81 Nanson, E 15..........N. D.
49*Nantahala, P 4........N. C.
1365 Nantasket, P 8........Mass.
.... Nantasket Jc., G 21..Mass.
400 Nanticoke, O 20.........Md.
50*Nanticoke, Q 16.....N. Y.
24387 Nanticoke, I 19..........Pa.
3401■Nantucket, R 15.......Mass.
6217 Nanty Glo, M 8..........Pa.
1500 Nanuet, G 5...........N. Y.
8*Naola, M 9...............Va.
....*Naoma, O 8.........W. Va.
71*Naomi, I 17..............Ky.
75 Naomi, O 19..............La.
.... Naomi, M 24..........S. D.
.... Naomi Pines, see Pocono Pines..............Pa.
7740 Napa, H 5..........Calif.
.... Napa, O 22............S. D.
40 Napa Jc., H 5, A 18..Calif.
750 Napanoch, C 3........N. Y.
220 Napavine, M 6........Wash.
195 Naper, D 15............Neb.
5272 Naperville, C 19..........Ill.
100*Napfor, I 21...............Ky.
25*Napier, I 20...............Ky.
70 Napier, C 4..............Mo.
23*Napier, I 10.........W. Va.
1500 Naples, N 11..........Calif.
1253 Naples, M 16.............Fla.
327 Naples, B 5............Idaho
260 Naples, J 8..............Ill.
25*Naples, E 23.............Ky.
310 Naples, I 12...............La.
185 Naples, O 4..............Me.
1152 Naples, O 10..........N. Y.
33*Naples, P 8............N. C.
84 Naples, G 22...........S. D.
821 Naples, C 23...........Tex.
100*Naples, I 8................Va.
325 Napoleon, L 20..........Ind.
350 Napoleon, Q 17........Mich.
132*Napoleon, G 7............Mo.
982 Napoleon, O 15........N. D.
4825 Napoleon, D 7..........Ohio
1301 Napoleonville, N 15.....La.
272 Naponee, O 15...........Neb.
3028 Nappanee, C 15..........Ind.
105 Napton, G 11..............Mo.
500*Naranja, O 23............Fla.
300 Nara Visa, F 24.....N. M.
5217*Narberth, O 23............Pa.
75 Narcissa, B 23..........Okla.
5 Narcisso, B 12...........Tex.
48 Narcoossee, H 19.......Fla.
217 Nardin, B 12............Okla.
....*Narehood, H 12...........Pa.
60 Narenta, G 7...........Mich.
193 Narka, C 16..............Kan.
1000 Narragansett (Narragansett Pier), M 15..............R. I.
20 Narrows, M 18..........Ore.
1489 Narrows, N 3..............Va.
500 Narrowsburg, D 1....N. Y.
125*Naruna, O 10..............Va.
42*Narvel, K 16..............Ky.
150*Narvon, O 20..............Pa.
100*Naselle, N 3...........Wash.
26 Nash, F 22..............N. D.
348 Nash (Nashville), C 10 Okla.
500 Nash, C 24...............Tex.
29*Nash, L 10................Va.
70*Nashmead, E 3..........Calif.
110 Nashoba, N 22..........Okla.
105 Nashotah, N 20..........Wis.
150*Nashport, J 15..........Ohio
1439 Nashua, D 16............Iowa
177*Nashua, J 4............Minn.
126*Nashua, F 6..............Mo.
943 Nashua, E 20..........Mont.
32927 Nashua, R 15..........N. H.
2782 Nashville, M 6...........Ark.
2449 Nashville, N 13............Ga.
2418 Nashville, N 13.............Ill.
493 Nashville, L 13...........Ind.
212 Nashville, M 12..........Kan.
1279 Nashville, P 15.........Mich.
85*Nashville, N 6.............Mo.
1171 Nashville, E 16..........N. C.
200 Nashville, H 15..........Ohio
348 Nashville,(Nash),C 10. Okla.
130 Nashville, G 4............Ore.
167402 Nashville, M 11....Tenn.
100 Nashville, L 9............Wis.
2228 Nashwauk, G 16.........Minn.
271 Nason, O 15...............Ill.
28 Nason Creek (Dardanelles), G 13.................Wash.
73*Nasons, I 14...............Va.
300 Nasonville, A 9..........R. I.
165*Nass, E 16..............Minn.
51*Nassau, K 22..............Del.
208*Nassau, M 3............Minn.
698*Nassau, O 24.........N. Y.
250 Nassawadox, M 23.....Va.
125*Nat, I 4...............W. Va.
....*Natal, B 9..................Ga.
225 Natalbany, K 17..........La.
278*Natalia, M 15............Tex.
268*Natalie, K 18...............Pa.
30*Natchez, M 11..........Ala.
100*Natchez, G 7...............La.
15296 Natchez, N 3...........Miss.
6812 Natchitoches, F 7......La.
110 Nathalie, P 11..............Va.
50 Nathan, E 9...........Mich.
65*Nathans Creek, C 3...N. C.
40 Nathrop, J 11...........Colo.
13851■Natick, F 17..........Mass.
5488 Natick, G 14..........R. I.
31*National (Carlos Jc.), M 5..................Md.
300 National, I 15............Utah
300 National, L 9..........Wash.
10344 National City, Q 19..Calif.
244*National City (National Stock Yards), N 11...Ill.
82 National City, F 20..Mich.
70*National Gardens (Volusia), E 19..................Fla.
....*National Military, P 10 N. Y.
....*National Military Home, Q 4..................Calif.
.... National Military Home, see Veterans Administration Hospital....Ind.
.... National Military Home, see Veterans Administration Home......Kan.
.... National Military Home, L 7..................Ohio

Pop. Place Index State
700 National Mine (Winthrop Mine), E 9........Mich.
1977 National Park, L 8....N. J.
....*National Soldiers Home, see Veterans Administration Home..............Me.
1900*National Soldiers Home, (Veterans Administration Home), O 21........Va.
244*National Stock Yards, N 11..................Ill.
106*Natoma, G 8........Calif.
651 Natoma, G 11.........Kan.
75*Natrona, H 12.........Ill.
.... Natrona, L 4 (Pop. 7591 incl. in Harrison).....Pa.
150*Natrona, G 14........Wyo.
.... Natrona Heights(Birdville), L 4, (Pop. 1500 incl. in Harrison)...........Pa.
832▲Natura, G 18..........Okla.
100 Natural Bridge, D 8....Ala.
22*Natural Bridge, G 20...Ky.
....*Natural Bridge (Yeatman), I 20..................Mo.
600 Natural Bridge, H 17.N. Y.
70 Natural Bridge, L 9....Va.
100*Natural Bridge Station, M 8...................Va.
25*Natural Dam, E 4.....Ark.
130*Natural Dam, F 17...N. Y.
85*Natural Steps, I 11....Ark.
57*Natural Tunnel, (Glenita), E 5.....................Va.
145 Naturita, L 3..........Colo.
.... Natwick, N 21.........Wyo.
183*Naubinway, F 15....Mich.
4*Naugart, J 11..........Wis.
15388 Naugatuck, J 9.....Conn.
200 Naugatuck, O 2....W. Va.
78 Naughright, E 12.....N. J.
2000*Naukeag (North Ashburnham), C 13 ...Mass.
16*Naulakla, K 17.........Va.
533 Nauvoo, D 9............Ala.
1088 Nauvoo, G 4...........Ill.
40*Nauvoo, R 9............Mo.
2500*Nauvoo, P 11..........Ohio
125 Nauvoo, G 15...........Pa.
....*Nava, see Newcomb, N. M.
....*Naval Academy, I 15..Md.
....*Naval Air Station, Naval Operating Base, P 21.Va.
....*Naval Training Station-War College, L 19..R. I.
15 Navajo, G 23..........Ariz.
15 Navajo, C 23.........Mont.
125*Navarino, N 13..........Wis.
125 Navarre, H 17..........Kan.
1703 Navarre, G 17.........Ohio
140 Navarro, F 2..........Calif.
100 Navarro, F 20...........Tex.
6138 Navasota, J 21...........Tex.
225 Navassa, M 16.........N. C.
200*Navco, P 4...............Ala.
608 Navesink, H 20..........N. J.
28*Navidad, M 20...........Tex.
43 Navina, G 11...........Okla.
....*Navy Yard, P 21..........Va.
1025 Navy Yard, M 19......S. C.
52*Naxera, N 21.............Va.
34*Nay Aug, G 21...........Pa.
261 Naylor, O 14...............Ga.
32*Naylor, K 13..............Md.
507 Naylor, R 19..............Mo.
58 Naylors, K 19..............Va.
19*Naytahwaush, G 6...Minn.
....*Nazareth, G 14...........Ky.
350*Nazareth, P 12.........Mich.
200*Nazareth, F 14.........N. C.
5721 Nazareth, K 23...............Pa.
100*Nazareth, E 3..............Tex.
75*Nead, F 15..................Ind.
40*Neafus, H 12...............Ky.
750 Neah Bay, D 1.........Wash.
150*Neal, L 20..................Kan.
50 Neal, I 21..................Tex.
150*Neals Run, E 21.....W. Va.
.... Neal Springs, M 4.......Ark.
176*Nealsville (Glenwood), F 8 N. C.
.... Neame, J 6..................La.
154*Neapolis, C 9.............Ohio
....*Neath, D 18..................Pa.
312 Neavitt, K 16................Md.
30*Nebish, E 10...........Minn.
521 Nebo, K 7.....................Ill.
272 Nebo, I 8......................Ky.
250*Nebo, G 10....................La.
25*Nebo, N 13...................Mo.
235 Nebo, F 1..................N. C.
6 Nebo, O 14.................Okla.
28*Nebo, D 10....................Va.
20*Nebo, J 9................W. Va.
.... Nebo Jc., I 12............Utah
84*Nebraska, M 18............Ind.
100 Nebraska, G 6...............Pa.
7339 Nebraska City, M 24..Neb.
838 Necedah, I 16..............Wis.
15 Necessity, E 15............Tex.
25*Nechanitz, K 19...........Tex.
565 Neche, C 22..............N. D.
500 Neches, G 22...............Tex.
.... Neches Jc., K 25.........Tex.
358 Neck, O 6...................Mo.
100 Ned, H 21......................Ky.
100*Ned, Q 1........................Pa.
384 Nederland, E 13..........Colo.
3000*Nederland, K 25...........Tex.
247*Nedrow, M 14.........N. Y.
65*Neebish, F 16............Mich.
364*Neeces (Neeses), J 13.S. C.
75*Needham, L 4..............Ala.
100 Needham, K 15..............Ind.
12445■Needham, G 18.........Mass.
2505 Needham Heights (Avery), F 18.................Mass.
3624 Needles, M 24...........Calif.
300 Needmore, M 12............Ind.
130*Needmore, L 13.............Ind.
50*Needmore, P 4..........N. C.
25 Needmore, K 13...........Okla.
81*Needmore, P 11..............Pa.
52*Needmore, G 20.....W. Va.
475*Needville, L 21..............Tex.
65*Neely, O 20...............Miss.
45 Neely (Neelys), O 4..Tenn.
69*Neelys Landing (Neelys), N 23..................Mo.
150 Neelyton, O 12...............Pa.
280 Neelyville, I 22, R 19..Mo.
25*Neenah, L 10...............Ala.
50*Neenah, J 20.................Va.
10645 Neenah, N 15...........Wis.
320 Neeses (Neeces), J 13.S. C.
3000 Neffs, K 20...............Ohio
300 Neffs, L 22.....................Pa.
28*Neffs Mills, L 12...........Pa.
975*Neffsville, O 19...............Pa.
6813 Negaunee, E 6..........Mich.
400 Negley, G 21...............Ohio
15 Negra, H 15...............N. M.
125*Negreet, H 5...................La.
247 Nehalem, C 4...............Ore.
11*Nehasane, I 20..........N. Y.
353 Nehawka, L 24............Neb.
150*Neibert, N 4..........W. Va.
466 Neihart, I 11.............Mont.
2562 Neillsville, H 14...........Wis.

Pop. Place Index State
100 Neilton, I 3.........Wash.
21*Neita, J 12...............La.
60*Nekoma, E 9...............Ill.
96*Nekoma, J 9.............Kan.
184 Nekoma, E 19.........N. D.
2212 Nekoosa, I 15..............Wis.
174 Nelagoney, C 17.......Okla.
1796 Neligh, G 18..............Neb.
....*Nell, I 15....................Ky.
63*Nella, I 5....................Ark.
30*Nellie, O 6................N. C.
121*Nellie (Mohawk), I 15 Ohio
300*Nellis, M 5...........W. Va.
638*Nelliston, M 20.......N. Y.
50 Nellita, H 6...........Wash.
65*Nellysford, K 11.........Va.
40*Nelma, M 8.................Wis.
150*Nelscott, F 4...............Ore.
....*Nelse, H 21....................Ky.
200 Nelson, F 8.................Ariz.
200*Nelson, F 7..............Calif.
679 Nelson, D 7....................Ga.
265 Nelson, C 13...................Ill.
513 Nelson, I 10...................Ky.
98*Nelson (Taylor), C 7....La.
159*Nelson, M 16...............Minn.
334 Nelson, H 11....................Mo.
34 Nelson, I 9.................Mont.
963 Nelson, O 18..................Neb.
20*Nelson, O 21..................Nev.
31*Nelson, P 20.................Okla.
415 Nelson, E 15.....................Pa.
.... Nelson, B 9....................Utah
60*Nelson, R 12......................Va.
350 Nelson, C 14....................Wis.
160*Nelsonville, G 14...........Ky.
20*Nelsonville, D 15..........Mo.
....*Nelsonville, see Imlaystown....................N. J.
457*Nelsonville, E 5..........N. Y.
5368*Nelsonville, N 15...........Ohio
180*Nelsonville, L 14...........Wis.
2418*Nemacolin, P 3..................Pa.
7 Nemadji, I 19..............Minn.
169*Nemaha, G 6.................Iowa
379 Nemaha, N 25.................Neb.
.... Nemo, F 8........................Ill.
280 Nemo, J 3....................S. D.
48*Nemo, F 17......................Tex.
65*Nemours, Q 9..........W. Va.
125 Nenzel (Nenzil), D 9..Neb.
3376 Neodesha, N 21..............Kan.
75 Neodesha, F 21.............Okla.
1062 Neoga, K 18.....................Ill.
.... Neoga, M 3....................Iowa
841 Neola, L 4........................Iowa
50 Neola, F 20.....................Utah
87*Neola, N 13...............W. Va.
1187*Neon, I 22..........................Ky.
800*Neopit, L 12....................Wis.
5318 Neosho, P 6.......................Mo.
255 Neosho, N 19....................Wis.
452 Neosho Falls, K 22....Kan.
253 Neosho Rapids, J 21...Kan.
126*Neotsu, F 4.......................Ore.
128*Nepac (Mead Lake) O 21 Nev.
10 Nepesta, M 17..............Colo.
2835 Nephi, I 12.....................Utah
520 Neponset, E 12.................Ill.
.... Neponset, F 20..........Mass.
81*Neponset, Q 10.....W. Va.
.... Neppel, see Moses Lake Wash.
300 Nepton, D 19......................Ky.
2392 Neptune (Neptune City) I 20..........................N. J.
100*Neptune, L 10..............Tenn.
1363*Neptune Beach, C 16...Fla.
10*Nerinx, H 15......................Ky.
210 Nero, O 19..........................La.
159 Nerotown, J 20................Okla.
251 Nerstrand, P 17..............Minn.
156*Nesbitt, A 12..................Miss.
2100*Nesconset, H 8.............N. Y.
1805 Nescopeck, J 19...................Pa.
275*Neshaminy, N 24...............Pa.
1000*Neshaming Falls (Oakford), N 23.........................Pa.
15*Neshannock, H 2................Pa.
70 Neshannock Falls, I 2...Pa.
350 Neshanic (Neshanic Sta.), G 13..........................N. J.
301 Neshkoro, K 16..................Wis.
150 Neshoba, J 18..................Miss.
402 Neshoba (Germantown), Q 2..........................Tenn.
65 Neskowin, E 4..................Ore.
200 Neslen (Sego), K 22... Utah
176 Nesmith (Rickreall), F 6 Ore.
150*Nesmith, I 20..............S. C.
36*Nesom, I 6..........................La.
300 Nespelem, F 18............Wash.
4176 Nesquehoning, J 21.......Pa.
1355 Ness City, J 8...............Kan.
123*Nesting, L 20.....................Va.
150*Nestor, Q 19.................Calif.
25 Nestoria, E 4.................Mich.
215 Nestorville, F 15....W. Va.
80 Netarts, D 4......................Ore.
226 Netawaka, E 21.................Kan.
2158 Netcong, D 13..................N. J.
26*Nethers, H 13......................Va.
214 Nettie, L 11...............W. Va.
....*Nett Lake, F 19...........Minn.
200*Nettleboro, M 6..................Ala.
57*Nettle Hill, Q 2.....................Pa.
.... Nettleridge, Q 5......................Va.
909 Nettleton, D 19..................Ark.
861 Nettleton, D 21...............Miss.
210 Nettleton, D 8.......................Mo.
200*Nettleton (Cardiff), M 8 Pa.
62*Netty, G 21..........................Ky.
34*Neubert, N 19..................Tenn.
50*Neuse, E 13......................N. C.
175*Neuville, G 24.....................Tex.
.... Neva, I 19......................Kan.
125*Neva, L 25........................Tenn.
130*Nevada, G 15......................Ind.
3353 Nevada, I 13......................Iowa
50 Nevada, G 16.........................Ky.
8181 Nevada, L 6...........................Mo.
741 Nevada, G 11......................Ohio
386 Nevada, D 20......................Tex.
2445 Nevada City, F 8............Calif.
300 Neversink, C 2..................N. Y.
15 Neverstil, B 5......................Ore.
127*Neville, P 8......................Ohio
1200*Neville, L 3..........................Pa.
....*Neville Island, M 3..........Pa.
102 Nevinville, N 8..................Iowa
358 Nevis, H 10.......................Minn.
31*Nevisdale, K 19....................Ky.
55*New, O 9..................W. Va.
69*Newagen, O 9......................Me.
200*Newala, G 14.........................Ala.
25414 New Albany, P 15..........Ind.
165 New Albany, M 21.......Kan.
3602 New Albany, B 18.......Miss.
221 New Albany, J 13........Ohio
334 New Albany, F 18..........Pa.
602 New Albin, B 21.............Iowa
125 New Albion, P 4.........N. Y.
300*Newald, M 8.......................Wis.
328*New Alexandria, I 20..Ohio
639 New Alexandria, N 5....Pa.
116 Newalla, I 13..................Okla.
125*New Almelo, D 7...........Kan.

Pop. Place Index State
100 New Alsace, L 22......Ind.
86*New Amsterdam, Q 13.Ind.
802 Newark, E 16.........Ark.
2500 Newark, F 21........Calif.
4502 Newark, B 20.........Del.
425 Newark, D 18...........Ill.
75*Newark, M 8............Ind.
250*Newark (Queponco), O 24 Md.
187 Newark, C 14..........Mo.
28 Newark, M 15........Neb.
429760 Newark, E 19.......N. J.
9646 Newark, L 11.......N. Y.
31487 Newark, K 14.......Ohio
147 Newark, B 20........S. D.
300 Newark, D 18..........Tex.
50 Newark, C 19............Vt.
85*Newark, F 7.......W. Va.
.... Newark Heights (Hilton), E 18.................N. J.
949 Newark Valley, Q 15..N. Y.
1355 New Athens, N 12......Ill.
508 New Athens, J 19.....Ohio
263 New Auburn, O 12...Minn.
398 New Auburn, E 11....Wis.
.... New Augusta, G 16....Ark.
240 New Augusta (Augusta), I 13...................Ind.
350 New Augusta, O 18...Miss.
1282 Newaygo, N 13......Mich.
1176 New Baden, N 12.......Ill.
185*New Baden, I 20.......Tex.
1434 New Baltimore, O 24.Mich.
650 New Baltimore, P 23.N. Y.
50*New Baltimore (Hannacroix), O 23.........N. Y.
125 New Baltimore, F 18..Ohio
260*New Baltimore, O 8....Pa.
107 New Bavaria, E 8.....Ohio
250 New Bedford, D 12.....Ill.
110341 New Bedford, M 20.Mass.
102*New Bedford, I 16.....Ohio
300*New Bedford, I 1.......Pa.
2960 Newberg, E 7.........Ore.
631 New Berlin, J 11.......Ill.
999 New Berlin, O 17....N. Y.
583 New Berlin, K 16........Pa.
.... New Berlin Jc., P 17..N. Y.
600*New Berlinville, N 21...Pa.
388 Newbern, J 8............Ala.
200*Newbern, L 9............Ill.
70 Newbern, L 16..........Ind.
70*Newbern, N 13........Iowa
11815 New Bern, I 19......N. C.
25*Newbern, I 6............Ky.
1740 Newbern, M 3........Tenn.
205*Newbern, O 4............Va.
60*Newberne, G 10....W. Va.
175*Newberry, N 19......Calif.
735 Newberry, D 12........Fla.
360 Newberry, M 9.........Ind.
2732 Newberry, E 14.......Mich.
....*Newberry, I 15..........Pa.
7510 Newberry, E 10.......S. C.
20 Newberry Jc., I 15......Pa.
1622 New Bethlehem, J 6....Pa.
200*New Blaine, G 8.......Ark.
500 New Bloomfield, I 14...Mo.
858 New Bloomfield, M 14..Pa.
187 New Bloomington (Agosta), H 11................Ohio
307 Newborn, G 11.........Ga.
801 New Boston, E 6........Ill.
100*New Boston (Huff), Q 8 Ind.
100 New Boston, Q 21....Iowa
250 New Boston, I 3.....Mass.
704*New Boston, Q 22....Mich.
81*New Boston, D 11.....Mo.
500 New Boston, P 12....N. H.
6024 New Boston, Q 12.....Ohio
648*New Boston, K 19......Pa.
1111 New Boston, C 23.....Tex.
150 New Braintree, F 12..Mass.
6976 New Braunfels, L 17...Tex.
133 New Bremen, I 17....N. Y.
1484 New Bremen, I 7.....Ohio
70 New Bridge, F 23.....Ore.
658 New Brighton, M 24 Minn.
9630 New Brighton, K 2.....Pa.
68685 New Britain, G 12..Conn.
476*New Britain, N 23.....Pa.
878 New Brockton, N 18...Ala.
.... New Brookland, see West Columbia...........S. C.
30 New Brunswick, I 11..Ind.
33180 New Brunswick, G 16 N. J.
172 New Buena Vista, P 8..Pa.
1190 New Buffalo, R 9....Mich.
101*New Buffalo, M 16.....Pa.
150*Newburg, C 7.........Ala.
96*Newburg, C 14........Ark.
1374 Newburg, Q 6..........Ind.
135 Newburg, J 15.........Iowa
75*Newburg, K 6...........Ky.
27*Newburg, N 12.........Md.
400 Newburg, L 13.........Me.
1056 Newburg, L 15.........Mo.
119 Newburg, E 11......N. D.
....*Newburg (Newburgh), D 17..................Ohio
278*Newburg, O 14..........Pa.
183*Newburg, J 9............Pa.
696 Newburg, E 15.....W. Va.
235 Newburg, O 18.........Wis.
1374 Newburgh, (Newburg), R 6 Ind.
31883 Newburgh, D 5.....N. Y.
3830 Newburg Hts., D 17...Ohio
.... Newburgh Jc., E 4...N. Y.
350 New Burlington, M 8..Ohio
299 New Burnside, Q 17.....Ill.
150 Newbury, N 9.........N. H.
391 Newbury, H 17...........Vt.
135*Newbury Park, N 13..Calif.
13916 Newburyport, A 21..Mass.
800 New Butler, (Butler), O 20 Wis.
36*Newby, G 18............Ky.
44 Newby, H 17..........Okla.
121*Newby, H 20...........Tex.
144*New Cambria, H 16...Kan.
318 New Cambria, D 12....Mo.
2372 New Canaan, P 3....Conn.
157*New Caney, J 22.......Tex.
517 New Canton, J 5.........Ill.
75 New Canton, L 13.......Va.
747 New Carlisle, A 13.....Ind.
1237 New Carlisle, K 8.....Ohio
1200 New Castle, F 13.......Ala.
500 Newcastle, G 8.......Calif.
484 New Castle, G 7......Colo.
4414 New Castle, B 21.......Del.
16620 New Castle, I 19.....Ind.
487 New Castle, E 15.......Ky.
350 New Castle, O 10.......Me.
447 Newcastle, E 21.......Neb.
100 New Castle, O 21....N. H.
120 Newcastle, I 15.......Ohio
150 Newcastle, J 11.......Okla.
47638 New Castle, J 2.........Pa.
1044 Newcastle, D 15.......Tex.
100 Newcastle, O 3........Utah
253 New Castle, M 6.........Va.
20 Newcastle, I 8........Wash.
1962 Newcastle, F 23.......Wyo.
10 New Castle Jc., J 2.....Pa.

Pop. Place Index State

144*New Centerville, P 7....Pa.
466 New Chicago, B 8.....Ind.
300 New Church, K 24.....Va.
35*New City, J 12.........Ill.
1000 New City, F 5.......N. Y.
66*New Coeln, P 20......Wis.
75*New Columbia, R 17....Ill.
415 New Columbia, J 16....Pa.
.... Newcomb, see East Portal Colo.
77*Newcomb, K 17.......Md.
37*Newcomb (Nava), D 3 N. M.
300*Newcomb, G 22......N. Y.
650 Newcomb, L 18......Tenn.
113*Newcombe, F 21.......Ky.
4564 Newcomerstown, J 17..Ohio
75*New Concord, K 6.....Ky.
1067 New Concord, K 17...Ohio
105 New Corydon, F 22....Ind.
110*Newcreek, E 19.....W. Va.
90*New Cumberland, H 17 Ohio
4525 New Cumberland, O 16.Pa.
2098 New Cumberland, N 24 W. Va.
5*New Cummer, F 21....Ky.
356*Newdale, M 21......Idaho
26*Newdale, N 9........N. C.
130*New Danville, P 18.....Pa.
1000 New Deal, D 19.....Mont.
75*New Dennison, Q 16....Ill.
400*New Derry, M 6.......Pa.
300 New Diggings, H 22...Wis.
....*New Dorp, I 4.......N. Y.
345 New Douglas, L 12.....Ill.
125 New Dover, I 10......Ohio
175 New Durham, M 17..N. H.
.... New Durham, E 20..N. J.
1936 New Eagle, N 3........Pa.
400 New Edinburg, N 13...Ark.
344 New Effington, B 23..S. D.
500 New Egypt, J 15.....N. J.
100*Newell, F 20..........Ala.
....*Newell, see Hydesville. Calif.
852 Newell, F 7..........Iowa
854*Newell, H 6.........N. C.
800 Newell, P 4............Pa.
683 Newell, H 3..........S. D.
2200 Newell, M 24.......W. Va.
100*Newell Run, M 18....Ohio
789 Newellton, E 14........La.
895 New England, O 5....N. D.
36*New England, F 5...W. Va.
125*New England Mills, (Weimar), G 8.....Calif.
212 New Enterprise, O 10...Pa.
28*New Era, H 12..........La.
252 New Era, M 10.......Mich.
48 New Era, E 8..........Ore.
.... New Fairfield, J 3....Conn.
1200 Newfane, K 5.......N. Y.
160 Newfane, P 12..........Vt.
201 Newfield, P 2..........Me.
889 Newfield, N 10.......N. J.
165 Newfield, P 13.......N. Y.
50 Newfield, E 12..........Pa.
.... Newfield Jc., E 12......Pa.
150 Newfields, P 19......N. H.
565 New Florence, H 16....Mo.
864*New Florence, M 5.....Pa.
300 Newfolden, D 4......Minn.
24*Newfound, I 20.........Ky.
20*Newfoundland, F 21....Ky.
565 Newfoundland, C 16..N. J.
500 Newfoundland, H 22....Pa.
125*New Franken, P 13....Wis.
97 New Frankfort, F 11...Mo.
1144*New Franklin, G 12....Mo.
1137 New Freedom, Q 17....Pa.
100 New Freeport, Q 1......Pa.
534*New Galilee, K 1.......Pa.
100*New Garden, P 21......Pa.
410 New Geneva, Q 4.......Pa.
128 New Germantown, N 13 Pa.
247 New Germany (Motordale), N 13..............Minn.
1068 New Glarus, J 21......Wis.
148*New Glasgow, M 11....Va.
250 New Gloucester, O 6...Me.
166*New Gloucester (Intervale), O 6................Me.
500*New Goshen, K 6......Ind.
406*New Grand Chain (Grand Chain), R 15.........Ill.
93*New Grenada, O 11.....Pa.
958 New Gretna, N 16....N. J.
....*New Gulf, M 20.......Tex.
65*New Hackensack, R 23 N. Y.
.... Newhalem, C 11.....Wash.
1800 Newhall, N 15.......Calif.
330 Newhall, I 18.........Iowa
312 Newhall, R 6.......W. Va.
137*New Hamburg, O 22...Mo.
320*New Hamburg, R 23..N. Y.
215 New Hampshire, H 9..Ohio
2933 New Hampton, D 17..Iowa
412 New Hampton, B 7.......Mo.
177 New Hampton, L 13..N. H.
105*New Hampton, G 11..N. J.
400*New Hampton, E 4...N. Y.
50*New Hanover, N 10.....Ill.
200 New Hanover, N 22....Pa.
305 New Harbor, O 10.....Me.
1390 New Harmony, Q 3....Ind.
170 New Harmony, P 4...Utah
1834▲New Hartford (Lander), D 9..............Conn.
125*New Hartford, J 7.......Ill.
548 New Hartford, F 16...Iowa
50*New Hartford, G 16...Mo.
1914 New Hartford, M 18..N. Y.
160605 New Haven, M 10.Conn.
695 New Haven, P 20.......Ill.
1872 New Haven, D 22.....Ind.
549 New Haven, G 14......Ky.
904 New Haven, O 24....Mich.
1002 New Haven, I 17.......Mo.
300 New Haven, J 14....N. Y.
225*New Haven, E 13.....Ohio
150 New Haven, N 5......Ohio
106 New Haven, H 5.......Vt.
200 New Haven, P.O., H 6..Vt.
606 New Haven, G 4....W. Va.
17 New Haven, B 21.......Wyo.
106 New Haven, H 6.........Vt.
.... New Haven Mills, H 7..Vt.
75*New Hebron, L 21.......Ill.
298 Newhebron, M 12....Miss.
120*Newhill, F 13.........N. C.
208 New Holland, D 10.....Ga.
336 New Holland, H 12.....Ill.
111 New Holland, G 22...N. C.
777 New Holland, M 11...Ohio
2153 New Holland, O 20.....Pa.
100 New Holland, M 18...S. D.
1502 New Holstein, O 16....Wis.
446 New Hope, B 16.......Ala.
136*Newhope, L 6..........Ark.
201 New Hope, G 14.........Ky.
.... Newhope, N 24.........Md.
4 Newhope, K 24......N. M.
16*Newhope, E 5........N. C.
150 New Hope, L 5.......Ohio
1053 New Hope, M 24.........Pa.
250*New Hope, J 10.........Va.

Pop. Place Index State

41*New Hope (Golddale), J 14 Va.
115 Newhouse, M 4.......Utah
40*New Hradec, K 6....N. D.
300*New Hudson, P 22...Mich.
4691*New Hyde Park, G 6.N. Y.
13747 New Iberia, N 12......La.
5449▲Newington, G 13.....Conn.
366 Newington, J 23..........Ga.
100 Newington, O 20.....N. H.
90*Newington, (Accotink), G 18..................Va.
....*Newington Jc., see North Newington........Conn.
400 New Ipswich, R 11...N. H.
5 New Kamilche, J 5...Wash.
24055 New Kensington, M 4..Pa.
40 New Kent, M 19.........Va.
63*New Kingston, Q 20..N. Y.
300 New Kingstown, N 15..Pa.
150 Newkirk, G 20......N. M.
2283 Newkirk, B 14.......Okla.
557 New Knoxville, H 7...Ohio
30*New Lancaster, I 25...Kan.
75*Newland, D 9...........Ind.
471 Newland, D 2.........N. C.
325 Newland, J 19..........Va.
170*New Lebanon, M 5....Ind.
350 New Lebanon, O 24...N. Y.
229*New Lebanon (Potsdam), J 7......................Ohio
534 New Lebanon, L 6....Ohio
127*New Lebanon Center (Center Lebanon), Q 24.N. Y.
366 New Leipzig, P 8.....N. D.
700 New Lenox, D 20.........Ill.
50 New Lenox, E 2.......Mass.
4049 New Lexington, L 14..Ohio
40*New Liberty, R 18.......Ill.
125*New Liberty, K 23...Iowa
190*New Liberty, D 16.....Ky.
127*New Liberty, P 17.....Mo.
150*New Lima, J 16........Okla.
200 New Limerick, F 19....Me.
211 Newlin, E 5.............Tex.
250 New Lisbon, I 20........Ind.
213*New Lisbon, K 14.....N. J.
150 New Lisbon, O 18....N. Y.
1215 New Lisbon, I 17.......Wis.
350*Newllano, I 6...........La.
80*New London, Q 12.....Ark.
30456 New London, L 21..Conn.
200*New London, G 13.....Ind.
1340 New London, O 21....Iowa
578 New London, M 9...Minn.
1005 New London, E 16.....Mo.
800 New London, M 10...N. H.
243 New London, G 8.....N. C.
1656 New London, F 13.....Ohio
250*New London, Q 21......Pa.
750*New London, F 23.....Tex.
4825 New London, M 14....Wis.
350*New Lothrop, N 18...Mich.
....*New Lots, H 5.......N. Y.
729▲New Lyme, C 20......Ohio
627*New Lyme Sta. (New Lyme), B 19..........Ohio
616 New Madison, K 5.....Ohio
2450 New Madrid, R 23.....Mo.
186*New Mahoning, K 21...Pa.
1214 Newman, J 8..........Calif.
1103 Newman, J 20.............Ill.
64*Newman, G 22...........Kan.
75*Newman, G 10............Ky.
50*Newman, N 13.......N. M.
800*Newman (Lake Placid), F 22.....................N. Y.
75*Newman, G 1............Tex.
1036 Newman Grove, I 18..Neb.
100*Newman Lake, G 24.Wash.
1100*Newmanstown, N 19....Pa.
30*Newmansville, I 10.....Ill.
40*Newmansville, I 6.......Pa.
125 New Marion, M 19....Ind.
300 New Market, A 15.....Ala.
323 New Market, I 9.......Ind.
681 New Market, P 7.....Iowa
107 Newmarket, H 15.......Ky.
360 New Market, E 9........Md.
199 New Market, O 16...Minn.
75*New Market, E 5.......Mo.
2500 Newmarket, P 19....N. H.
2000 New Market, F 16....N. J.
75 Newmarket, O 10.....Ohio
500 New Market, M 20...Tenn.
629 New Market, G 12......Va.
150 New Marlboro, H 3..Mass.
382*New Marshall (Marshall), E 11.......................Okla.
435 New Marshfield, N 14.Ohio
100 New Martinsburg, N 10 Ohio
3491 New Martinsville, C 10 W. Va.
793 New Matamoras, M 18Ohio
75*New Maysville, J 10...Ind.
264 New Meadows, K 5..Idaho
218 New Melle, I 18.........Mo.
150 New Memphis, N 12....Ill.
1443*New Miami, N 5......Ohio
309 New Middleton, M 13Tenn.
115*New Middletown, Q 14.Ind.
227*New Middletown, F 20Ohio
90*New Midway, C 9......Md.
3000 New Milford, I 4.....Conn.
300 New Milford, B 15........Ill.
3215 New Milford, C 20....N. J.
300*New Milford, F 4....N. Y.
310*New Milford (Rootstown), E 18...........................Ohio
807 New Milford, E 21......Pa.
200*New Millport, J 9.......Pa.
450*New Milton, E 10...W. Va.
152 New Minden, N 13........Ill.
400*New Monmouth, H 19 N. J.
.... New Moorefield, see Moorefield, K 10....Ohio
40*New Mount Pleasant, G 21 Ind.
305 New Munich, L 10...Minn.
213*New Munster, O 22...Wis.
7182 Newnan, G 4..........Ga.
85*Newnata, D 13........Ark.
198*New Offenburg, L 20...Mo.
494537 New Orleans, N 19...La.
1194 New Oxford, O 15.......Pa.
35*New Palestine, P 11.....Ill.
448 New Palestine, J 16....Ind.
1492 New Paltz, C 5.......N. Y.
634 New Paris, B 15.......Ind.
989 New Paris, K 5........Ohio
201*New Paris, O 9...........Pa.
250*New Park, P 17..........Pa.
434*Pekin, O 14..............Ind.
100 New Petersburg, N 9..Ohio
150 New Philadelphia, G 9..Ill.
120*New Philadelphia, O 15Ind.
12328 New Philadelphia, H 18 Ohio
2453*New Philadelphia (Silver Creek), K 19..........Pa.
200 New Pine Creek, R 14..Ore.
50*New Pittsburg, H 22...Ind.
804 New Plymouth, M 3..Idaho
135*New Plymouth, N 14..Ohio
328 New Point, L 20.......Ind.
100*New Point, C 4.........Mo.
25 New Point, N 21........Va.
4321 Newport, E 17.........Ark.

Pop. Place Index State

987 Newport, B 21.........Del.
795 Newport, I 7...........Ind.
30631 Newport, B 17.........Ky.
1400 Newport, (Newport Junction), K 12...........Me.
350*Newport, M 11.........Md.
500 Newport, Q 22.......Mich.
872 Newport, N 17.......Minn.
275 Newport, F 14.........Neb.
5304■Newport, N 8........N. H.
900 Newport, P 8.........N. J.
627 Newport, L 19.......N. Y.
480 Newport, J 20.......N. C.
150 Newport, I 6..........Ohio
600 Newport, N 18........Ohio
20 Newport, O 13........Okla.
2019 Newport, G 3............Ore.
1897 Newport, M 15..........Pa.
30532 Newport, L 20........R. I.
3575 Newport, N 21.......Tenn.
150 Newport, C 17..........Tex.
4902 Newport, B 16...........Vt.
200 Newport, N 4.............Va.
1174 Newport, E 24.......Wash.
.... New Portage, F 17....Ohio
4438 Newport Beach, O 16, R 5 Calif.
288 Newport Center (Center), B 15..........................Vt.
1400 Newport Jc. (Newport), K 12..........................Me.
100 New Portland, K 7.....Me.
37067 Newport News, P 21...Va.
920 New Port Richey, H 12.Fla.
500 Newportville, N 23.....Pa.
1645 New Prague, O 15...Minn.
14*New Prairie, L 7.....Minn.
798 New Preston, G 4....Conn.
392 New Providence (Borden), O 16...........................Ind.
236 New Providence, H 13.Iowa
2374 New Providence, E 16.N. J.
300*New Providence, P 19...Pa.
750 New Providence, K 9 Tenn.
254 New Raymer, C 18...Colo.
863 New Richland, Q 15..Minn.
368 New Richmond, H 9...Ind.
50*New Richmond, P 12 Mich.
1767 New Richmond, P 7...Ohio
2388 New Richmond, B 11..Wis.
264 New Riegel, F 11......Ohio
313 New Ringgold, L 20....Pa.
90*New River, C 14........Fla.
200 New River, L 17.....Tenn.
500 New River (New River Depot), O 4.................Va.
.... New River Jc., M 6...Ohio
2254 New Roads, K 13.........La.
58408 New Rochelle, G 6...N. Y.
45*New Rochester, D 10..Ohio
2017 New Rockford, J 17..N. D.
1007*New Rocky Comfort (Foreman), O 4.......Ark.
5*New Rome, J 16........Wis.
355 New Ross, I 11...........Ind.
150*New Rumley, I 19.....Ohio
180*New Russia, G 24....N. Y.
.... Newry, M 3................Me.
417 Newry, N 10...............Pa.
1000 Newry, C 4..........S. C.
257 New Salem, J 6...........Ill.
200 New Salem, K 19.......Ind.
110*New Salem, N 18.......Kan.
250 New Salem, D 9......Mass.
875 New Salem, N 9.....N. D.
200*New Salem, K 13.....Ohio
345 New Salem (York New Salem), P 17.............Pa.
900*New Salem. P 4...........Pa.
705*New Salem (Delmont) M 5.............................Pa.
321 New Salem, F 23.......Tex.
200 New Salisbury, P 14...Ind.
300*New Salsbury (Mulberry), O 7..........................Ohio
500*New Sarpy, N 17.........La.
150*New Scotland, O 23..N. Y.
60*News Ferry, Q 11.........Va.
1214 New Sharon, L 16.....Iowa
200 New Sharon, L 7.........Me.
1400*New Sheffield, L 2......Pa.
800 New Shoreham, P 24..R. I.
44*Newside, L 21..............Pa.
200 Newsite, H 19..............Ala.
4402 New Smyrna Beach, F 20 Fla.
300*Newsome, D 22.........Tex.
250*Newsoms, R 18..........Va.
326 New Springfield, F 21..Ohio
350*New Stanton, M 5.........Pa.
1473 New Straitsville, M 14.Ohio
600*New Suffolk, H 9....N. Y.
125*New Summerfield, G 22.Tex.
898 New Sweden, C 18.......Me.
15*Newt, I 14..................Ky.
1180*New Tazewell (Tazewell), L 20...........................Tenn.
222*New Thacker, P 3...W. Va.
616 Newton, N 20.............Ala.
514 Newton, N 7.................Ga.
2347 Newton, L 19...............Ill.
10462 Newton, K 14..........Iowa
11048 Newton, K 16..........Kan.
69873 Newton, F 18, N 2..Mass.
1800 Newton, K 17.........Miss.
125 Newton, Q 18..........N. H.
5533 Newton, C 12..........N. J.
5407 Newton, F 4...........N. C.
1400 Newton, I 25.............Tex.
549 Newton, B 11...........Utah
200*Newton, I 8...........W. Va.
50*Newton, P 15..............Wis.
.... Newton Center, F 18, N 2 (Pop incl. in Newton) Mass.
750 Newtonfalls, G 19....N. Y.
3120 Newton Falls, E 19...Ohio
339*Newton Grove, J 15..N. C.
395 Newton Hamilton, M 12 Pa.
.... Newton Highlands, F 18, O 2 (Pop. incl. in Newton).............Mass.
450*Newton Hook, Q 24..N. Y.
195 Newtonia, P 7.............Mo.
300 Newton Junction, Q 18 N. H.
.... Newton Lower Falls, F 18 N 1 (Pop. incl. in Newton).............Mass.
50*Newton Stewart, O 12..Ind.
166*Newtonsville, O 7.....Ohio
.... Newton Upper Falls, O 1 (Pop. incl. in Newton) Mass.
100*Newtonville, E 7........Ala.
155*Newtonville, Q 9.........Ind.
.... Newtonville, N 1.....Mass.
300*Newtonville, N 11....N. J.
500*Newtonville, N 23....N. Y.
603 Newtown, K 5........Conn.
293 Newtown, H 8............Ind.
285 Newtown, B 10............Mo.
22*Newtown (Peoli), H 17Ohio
1146*Newtown, O 7.........Ohio
2009 Newtown, N 24.............Pa.
60 Newtown, (Kirby) Q 3..Pa.
....*Newtown, O 3........W. Va.
300*Newtown, L 19............Va.

Pop. Place Index State

168*Newtown Square, P 22..Pa.
165 New Trenton, L 22....Ind.
237 New Tripoli, L 21.......Pa.
150 New Troy, Q 10.....Mich.
76*New Truxton, I 17.....Mo.
8743 New Ulm, P 11......Minn.
400 New Ulm, K 20.........Tex.
....*New Ulysses, see Ulysses Kan.
214 New Underwood (Underwood), J 5..........S. D.
52*New Upton, M 20.......Va.
197*New Verda, F 9...........La.
109*New Vernon, D 14....N. J.
229 New Vienna, F 22....Iowa
752 New Vienna, N 9.....Ohio
578 Newville, N 22...........Ala.
125*Newville, C 22............Ind.
24 Newville, E 17........N. D.
1758 Newville, O 14............Pa.
200*Newville, I 11......W. Va.
425 New Vineyard, K 7....Me.
410 New Virginia, N 11...Iowa
275 New Washington, O 18.Ind.
857 New Washington, F 12 Ohio
80* New Washington, J 9..Pa.
547 New Waterford, G 21..Ohio
250 New Waverly, F 14....Ind.
2184 New Waverly, J 22.....Tex.
75*New Wells, N 22.........Mo.
169 New Weston, I 5.......Ohio
518*New Willard, I 23......Tex.
1018 New Wilmington, I 2...Pa.
74*New Winchester, J 10..Ind.
517 New Windsor (Windsor), E 8.................................Ill.
529 New Windsor, D 10....Md.
2200*New Windsor, E 3...N. Y.
.... New Wood, J 10.........Wis.
368 New Woodstock, N 15.N. Y.
7454995 New York, I 5.....N. Y.
771 New York Mills, (New York), I 8...............Minn.
3628 New York Mills, L 17N. Y.
100*New Zion, H ...18...S. C.
299 Ney, D 6..................Ohio
590 Nezperce, H 6..........Idaho
26*Niagara, H 11..........N. C.
179 Niagara, H 21..........N. D.
2266 Niagara, O 8...........Wis.
78029 Niagara Falls, L 4...N. Y.
293 Niangua, N 11..............Mo.
1312 Niantic (East Lyme), M 20...........................Conn.
625 Niantic, I 14...............Ill.
58*Niantic, M 22...............Pa.
5 Niarada, F 3.............Mont.
75 Nibbe, K 17...............Mont.
200*Nicasio, C 14.........Calif.
160*Nice. F 4................Calif.
948 Niceville, N 6.............Fla.
942*Nichols Hills, H 12...Okla.
3192 Nicholasville, G 17.....Ky.
25*Nicholia, J 12.........Idaho
660 Nicholls, N 16.............Ga.
750 Nichols, O 7............Conn.
498 Nichols, I 15...............Fla.
.... Nichols, B 16................Ill.
357 Nichols, L 21..............Iowa
219 Nichols, O 9.................Mo.
10 Nichols, J 19............Mont.
541 Nichols, R 14...........N. Y.
292*Nichols, F 22...........S. C.
145*Nichols, N 14..............Wis.
212 Nicholson, E 12............Ga.
265 Nicholson, R 14.........Miss.
10 Nicholson, Q 21.......N. D.
1012 Nicholson, F 21............Pa.
250*Nicholsville, K 6.........Ala.
25 Nicholsville, P 8.........Ohio
250 Nicholville, D 20.......N. Y.
28*Nick, J 12....................Ky.
275 Nickbyrd, O 20..........Miss.
25*Nickel Mines, P 20.......Pa.
256 Nickelsville, E 6...........Va.
1052 Nickerson, K 13..........Kan.
75*Nickerson, I 19.........Minn.
159 Nickerson, J 22...........Neb.
100*Nickleville, H 5.............Pa.
45*Nicks Creek, M 18....Tenn.
212*Nicktown, L 8...............Pa.
177*Nickwall, F 21.........Mont.
67*Nicodemus, F 9...........Kan.
89*Nicolaus, G 7...........Calif.
80 Nicolin, L 16.................Me.
434*Nicolett, P 12..........Minn.
700*Nicoma Park (Nicoma), I 13...............................Okla.
34 Nicut, H 24..................Okla.
30*Nicut, H 8.............W. Va.
30 Nida, P 16....................Okla.
....*Niday, O 2....................Va.
105*Niederwald, K 17........Tex.
175*Nielsville, F 4..........Minn.
27*Nigh, I 23......................Ky.
50 Nighthawk, B 16.......Wash.
6 Nihill, J 14................Mont.
320 Nikep (Pekin), N 5......Md.
500 Niland, P 23..............Calif.
300 Nile, Q 7...................N. Y.
2500 Niles, E 22, I 6.......Calif.
40 Niles, H 17.................Fla.
2168*Niles, C 21....................Ill.
200 Niles, H 16.................Kan.
11328 Niles, R 11..............Mich.
.... Niles, G 16...............N. D.
16273 Niles, E 20...............Ohio
27 Niles, I 9...................Okla.
.... Niles Center, see Skokie.Ill.
.... Niles Jc., E 22...........Calif.
30 Niles Valley, E 14..........Pa.
325 Nilwood, K 11.................Ill.
1 Nimburg, J 21..............Neb.
217 Nimmons, B 21..............Ark.
....*Nimmons, B 4..........S. C.
12*Nimrod, H 4...............Mont.
31*Nimrod, I 15.................Tex.
30*Nimrod Hall, K 8...........Va.
.... Nina, M 12.....................La.
300*Ninaview, N 20..........Colo.
30*Nindes Store, I 18.........Va.
62 Ninemile, H 3..............Mont.
14*Nine Mile Falls, G 22 Wash.
95*Ninepoints, Q 20............Pa.
30*Nine Times, B 4.........S. C.
1453 Ninety Six, F 8.........S. C.
200 Ninevah, L 14...............Ind.
300 Nineveh, Q 17.............N. Y.
264 Nineveh, P 2...................Pa.
35*Nineveh, H 21...............Tex.
20*Nineveh, F 14..................Va.
50*Nineveh Jc., O 16......N. Y.
300 Ninnekah, L 10............Okla.
150 Niobe, R 2..................N. Y.
95 Niobe, E 7..................N. D.
629 Niobrara, E 18..............Neb.
300*Niota (East Fort Madison) G 5..Ill.
623 Niota, O 17..................Tenn.
241 Niotaze, O 20................Kan.
50*Nipinnawasee, J 12....Calif.
750 Nipomo, M 10.............Calif.
31*Nippa, G 22......................Ky.
16*Nipton, M 23..............Calif.
110*Nirvana, L 13.............Mich.
250 Nisbet, I 15......................Pa.
24*Nishnabotha, B 3...........Mo.
500*Niskayuna, N 23.......N. Y.

Pop. Place Index State

212 Nisland, H 3...............S. D.
150 Nisqually..................Wash.
63*Nisswa, J 12..............Minn.
276*Nisula, D 2................Mich.
.... Nitram, J 7.....................La.
2983 Nitro, K 5...............W. Va.
125*Nittany, K 12.................Pa.
25*Nitta Yuma, H 7..........Miss.
.... Niver Jc., P 7..................Pa.
.... Niver Shaft, P 8..............Pa.
50 Niverton, Q 7....................Pa.
600*Niverville, Q 24........N. Y.
....*Nivloc, K 10...............Nev.
175 Niwot, E 14................Colo.
370 Nixa, P 10........................Mo.
140*Nixburg, I 17.................Ala.
350 Nixon, F 5.......................Nev.
200*Nixon, G 17................N. J.
1835 Nixon, M 18.....................Tex.
30*Nixon Station, K 3..........Pa.
25*Nixonville, H 23..........S. C.
1161 Noank, M 23..............Conn.
31*Nobe, G 9.................W. Va.
855 Noble, M 19........................Ill.
....*Noble, H 17.....................Ind.
50*Noble, N 20....................Iowa
35*Noble, H 21........................Ky.
238 Noble, F 5..........................La.
35*Noble, Q 12......................Mo.
.... Noble, C 17 (Pop. incl. in Euclid)................................Ohio
536 Noble, K 13....................Okla.
....*Noble, N 22 (Pop. 1500 incl. in Abington)..........Pa.
90 Nobleboro, N 10...............Me.
600*Noblestown, M 3..............Pa.
5575 Noblesville, I 16............Ind.
100*Nobleton, G 14...............Fla.
1100 Nocatee, K 16.................Fla.
2605 Nocona, B 17..................Tex.
60*Noctor, G 21......................Ky.
270 Nodaway, O 7..................Iowa
70*Nodaway, D 4....................Mo.
200 Node, K 23....................Wyo.
515 Noel, R 6...........................Mo.
20*Noel, K 16...........................Va.
14*Noelette, D 3....................Tex.
5 Noel, K 24.........................Iowa
38*Noeton, L 20..................Tenn.
100 Nogal, K 15....................N. M.
5135 Nogales, P 17.................Ariz.
6*Nogo, F 10..........................Ark.
13 Nohle (Nohly), E 25.Mont.
13 Nohly (Nohle), E 25.Mont.
150 Nokesville, G 16..............Va.
250 Nokomis, O 8....................Ala.
79*Nokomis, K 13.................Fla.
2562 Nokomis, K 14....................Ill.
25*Nola, I 7............................Ark.
51*Nola (Prilliman), P 6......Va.
52 Nolan (Rand), I 7...........Nev.
50 Nolan, D 19....................N. M.
500*Nolan, F 12.....................Tex.
350*Nolan, O 2....................W. Va.
30*Noland, B 18....................Ark.
26*Noland, H 19.......................Ky.
30*Nolansburg, J 22................Ky.
157*Nolansville, H 17...........Tex.
250 Nolensville, N 11..........Tenn.
100*Nolin, H 13.........................Ky.
.... Nolin, C 18..........................Ore.
6*Noltings, N 13.....................Ill.
344 Noma, M 9..........................Fla.
277 Nome, N 21.....................N. D.
110 Nome, K 24.......................Tex.
48*Nomini Grove, K 19.........Va.
47 Non, M 18.........................Okla.
24*Nonchalanta, E 22............Ky.
20*Nonpareil, G 3..................Neb.
120*Nonquitt, N 20.............Mass.
100*Nook, M 13.........................Pa.
302 Nooksack, B 8................Wash.
520 Noonan, D 5..................N. D.
50*Nopal, M 18.......................Tex.
384*Nopeming, F 20.............Minn.
207 Nora, A 11............................Ill.
50*Nora, I 14..........................Ind.
39*Nora, J 16.............................Ky.
119 Nora, O 18.........................Neb.
27 Nora, O 24.......................S. D.
75*Nora, C 6..............................Va.
3 Noracres, A 4...................Minn.
.... Norala, B 8..........................Ala.
1198 Nora Springs, D 14.....Iowa
32*Norbeck, F 16.................S. D.
25 Norbert (Waltham), F 11 Mont.
1239 Norborne, F 9....................Mo.
440 Norcatur, D 7....................Kan.
1500*Norco, O 19...................Calif.
217 Norco (Sellers), N 17......La.
979 Norcross, E 8.....................Ga.
40 Norcross, H 14....................Me.
180*Norcross, K 5..................Minn.
.... Norcross, N 4........................Va.
130*Norden, G 8....................Calif.
48 Norden, F 12.....................Neb.
411 Nordheim, N 18.................Tex.
100 Nordland, F 7................Wash.
90*Nordman, B 4..................Idaho
50*Norene, N 12....................Tenn.
50 Norfield, N 9....................Miss.
25*Norfleet, J 17........................Ky.
304 Norfolk, B 13......................Ark.
1280 Norfolk, B 7....................Conn.
2294▲Norfolk, H 18..............Mass.
24 Norfolk, A 11....................Miss.
10490 Norfolk, H 20..................Neb.
1307 Norfolk, D 18................N. Y.
5 Norfolk, H 13.................N. D.
25 Norfolk, F 15....................Okla.
144332 Norfolk, P 21...................Va.
....*Norfolk Downs, G 20, P 5................................Mass.
162 Norge, L 10........................Okla.
129*Norge, N 20..........................Va.
8 Norheim, B 14..................Mont.
18*Noris, F 23...........................Ky.
250*Norland, C 6.........................Va.
400*Norlands (East Livermore), M 7..................................Me.
794 Norlina, C 15..................N. C.
200*Norma, N 7.....................N. J.
192 Norma, E 8......................N. D.
500*Norma, M 17..................Tenn.
.... Norma, E 12.......................Wis.
100*Normal, A 14.....................Ala.
6983 Normal, G 16......................Ill.
.... Normal, L 22......................Neb.
.... Normal Jc., G 16...............Ill.
200*Normalville, Q 4...............Pa.
512*Norman, K 7........................Ark.
125 Norman (Norman Station), M 13.........................Ind.
170 Norman (North Harwich), N 15.................................Mass.
98 Norman, N 16.......................Neb.
327*Norman, I 10.................N. C.
.... Norman, J 13.......................Ohio
11429Norman, J 12..................Okla.
.... Norman, I 7............................Pa.
25*Norman, F 10....................Wash.
150*Normandy, D 12...................Ill.
75*Normandy, F 15.....................Ky.
2500 Normandy, I 20....................Mo.
163 Normandy, P 12...............Tenn.
25*Normandy Beach, K 19 N. J.
535 Normangee, I 21..............Tex.

Pop. Place Index State

225 Normanna, O 18......Tex.
587 Norman Park, N 10.....Ga.
....*Norman Sta., see Norman, Ind.
122 Normantown, K 18......Ga.
7 Normantown, C 19.........Ill.
118*Normantown, H 9...W. Va.
....*Normoyle, L 16.........Tex.
2000*Noroton, Q 3..........Conn.
1600 Noroton Heights (Noroton Sta.), Q 3...................Conn.
695 Norphlet, P 11.............Ark.
1400 Norridgewock, L 9.......Me.
250 Norrie, K 12................Wis.
339 Norris, G 10....................Ill.
86*Norris (Harristown), O 14 Ind.
75 Norris, M 9................Mont.
177 Norris, C 4...................S. C.
90 Norris, M 10...............Tenn.
1250*Norris, M 18.............Tenn.
1295 Norris City, O 18...........Ill.
150*Norristown, J 19...........Ga.
80 Norristown, L 17............Ind.
38181Norristown, O 23...........Pa.
20*North, M 21.....................Ind.
733 North, I 13....................S. C.
500 North, M 21......................Va.
3000 North Abington, H 20 Mass.
22213 North Adams, C 3...Mass.
496 North Adams, Q 16..Mich.
175 North Alexandria (Bush Creek), M 13...............Tenn.
750 North Amherst, E 8..Mass.
310 North Amity, G 20...........Me.
24794 Northampton, F 8..Mass.
100 Northampton, K 22...N. Y.
9622 Northampton, I 22.........Pa.
7524■North Andover, B 19..Mass.
110*North Andover, F 21...Wis.
1200 North Anson, K 8...........Me.
1568*North Apollo, L 5............Pa.
9904*North Arlington, E 19.N. J.
2000*North Ashburnham, C 13 Mass.
100 North Ashford, B 21.Conn.
10359■North Attleboro, J 18 Mass.
2629 North Augusta, J 8....S. C.
772 North Aurora, C 19.........Ill.
73*North Avondale(Avondale), M 16.................................Colo.
100*North Baldwin, O 4.........Me.
2616 North Baltimore, E 9..Ohio
73*North Bancroft, H 18...Me.
319*North Bangor (Bangor), D 21...............................N. Y.
145*North Bass Island (Isle St. George), C 11.......Ohio
150*North Bay, L 16..........N. Y.
246 North Beach, K 15.........Md.
500 North Belgrade, M 9.....Me.
3022 North Belle Vernon, O 4.Pa.
495 North Bellingham, H 17 Mass.
1897*North Bellmore, I 7...N. Y.
1003 North Bend, J 21.........Neb.
679 North Bend, O 5...........Ohio
4262 North Bend, L 2.............Ore.
400 North Bend, H 13.............Pa.
646 North Bend, I 10.........Wash.
140*North Bend, F 16............Wis.
992 North Bennington, Q 5..Vt.
250*North Benton, F 19.......Ohio
39714■*North Bergen, E 20.N. J.
50*North Bergen, L 8.......N. Y.
1000 North Berwick, R 3.......Me.
200*North Bessemer, M 4....Pa.
2700 North Billerica, C 17 Mass.
200*North Bingham, F 12...Pa.
175 North Blenheim, P 21.N. Y.
50*North Bloomfield, F 9.Calif.
150*North Bloomfield, M 9 Ohio
300 North Bloomfield, D 19 Ohio
643*North Bonneville, Q 9 Wash.
182 Northboro, Q 5..............Iowa
1500 Northboro, F 15.......Mass.
180 Northboro (North Thetford), J 16...................Vt.
219*North Boston, N 5...N. Y.
55 North Bradford, J 13...Me.
15679*North Braddock, M 4..Pa.
119*North Bradley, L 17...Mich.
50*North Branch, K 8.........Iowa
75*Northbranch, C 13...Kan.
100 North Branch (Siebert), M 7.................................Md.
107 North Branch, E 12...Md.
724 North Branch, N 22..Mich.
762 North Branch, L 17..Minn.
56*North Branch Depot (North Branch), F 13 N. J.
200*North Branch, F 13...N. J.
150 North Branch, C 1...N. Y.
450 North Branford, L 12.Conn.
10242■Northbridge, H 14..Mass.
410 North Bridgton, N 3...Me.
197 North Bristol, D 20...Ohio
1265*Northbrook, C 21........Ill.
75* Northbrook, P 21........Pa.
2500 North Brookfield, G 12 Mass.
200*North Brookfield, N 17 N. Y.
121*North Brooklin, M 15...Me.
205 North Brooksville, M 15 Me.
40 North Buckfield, N 5...Me.
180*North Bucksport (Cedar Grove), L 14.............Me.
203*North Buena Vista, F 22 Iowa
.... North Buffalo Jc., M 4 N. Y.
35*North Calais, F 12.......Vt.
1572*North Caldwell, E 18..N. J.
250*North Caldwell (Caldwell), M 12.....................W. Va.
.... North Cambridge, E 19, L 3...............................Mass.
100 North Canton, G 11..Conn.
2988 North Canton, G 17..Ohio
8*North Cape May, R 11 N. J.
469 Northcarrollton (Carrollton) F 13.......................Miss.
360 North Carver, J 22....Mass.
180 North Castine, M 14.....Me.
2530*North Catasauqua, K 23Pa.
....*North Charleston, see Charleston North...S. C.
2674*North Charleroi, O 2.......Pa.
320 North Charlestown, N 6 N. H.
.... North Charlotte, H 6..N. C.
105*North Chatham, N 15.Mass.
65 North Chatham, H 18.N. H.
300*North Chatham, Q 24.N. Y.
....*North Chattanooga, Q 15 Tenn.
3000 North Chelmsford, C 16 Mass.
270 North Chesterville, L 7.Me.

Pop.	Place, Index	State
8465	North Chicago, A 21	Ill.
230	North Chichester, N 16	N. H.
350*	North Chili, L 8	N. Y.
1216	North Chillicothe, F 12	Ill.
200*	North Chittenango (Chittenango Station), L 15	N. Y.
601*	North City (Coello), O 15	Ill.
262	North Clarendon, L 8	Vt.
....	North Clinton, J 8	Mo.
70	North Clymer (Panama), Q 2	N. Y.
15	North Coalgate, N 17	Okla.
150*	North Cohassett, G 22, P 9	Mass.
350	North Cohocton, O 10	N. Y.
5231*	North College Hill, O 6	Ohio
1182	North Collins, O 4	N. Y.
67*	North Concord (Essex), E 20	Vt.
900	North Conway, I 18	N. H.
215	North Cornville, K 9	Me.
85*	Northcote, B 2	Minn.
48*	North Cove, F 1	N. C.
75	North Cove, L 2	Wash.
64*	Northcraft, Q 10	Pa.
....*	North Craftsbury, see Craftsbury Common	Vt.
....	North Creede, N 8	Colo.
700	North Creek, I 22	N. Y.
75*	North Creek, E 7	Ohio
....	North Cutler, L 23	Me.
26*	Northcutt, K 18	Mo.
137	Northdale, N 2	Colo.
14	Northdalles, Q 12	Wash.
84	North Danville, E 17	Vt.
1040	North Dartmouth, M 19	Mass.
386	North Deer Isle, N 15	Me.
81	North Derby, C 16	Vt.
265	North Dexter, J 11	Me.
1600	North Dighton, K 19	Mass.
256	North Dixmont, L 12	Me.
....	North Dover, see Bay Village	Ohio
....	North East, C 19	Md.
1328	North East, C 19	Md.
3704	North East, C 4	Pa.
....*	Northeast, M 10	Tenn.
43*	North East Carry, G 10	Me.
143*	North Eastham (Hastings), K 15	Mass.
625	Northeast Harbor, N 18	Me.
150	North East Jc., R 2	N. Y.
3000	North Easton, I 19	Mass.
50	North Eaton, R 19	Ohio
195	North Edgecomb, O 9	Me.
170*	North Egremont, G 1	Mass.
1300	North Emporia, Q 17	Va.
....	Northend, E 9	N. M.
865	North English, L 18	Iowa
166	North Enid, D 10	Okla.
40*	North Epping, P 18	N. H.
261*	Northern, H 22	Ky.
....	Northern Jc., N 12	Wis.
....	Northern Maine Jc., L 14	Me.
....	Northern Spy Mine, H 10	Utah
75	North Excello (Excello), M 6	Ohio
154*	North Evans, N 4	N. Y.
406	North Fairfield, E 13	Ohio
319	North Fair Haven, K 12	N. Y.
362	North Falmouth (Williams), M 23	Mass.
12	North Farmington, P 22	Mich.
....	North Fayston, F 12	Vt.
825	North Ferrisburg, G 6	Vt.
360	Northfield, G 8	Conn.
739*	Northfield, C 21	Ill.
20*	Northfield, J 17	Ky.
1975▲	Northfield, B 9	Mass.
4533	Northfield, O 16	Minn.
1543▲	Northfield, M 13	N. H.
2848	Northfield, P 15	N. J.
575	Northfield, D 17	Ohio
400	Northfield, B 12	Tex.
2129	Northfield, H 11	Vt.
150*	Northfield, G 15	Wis.
350	Northfield Falls, G 12	Vt.
2083	North Fond du Lac, N 17	Wis.
....	Northford (Clintonville), L 12	Conn.
550	Northford, L 12	Conn.
300*	North Fork, J 12	Calif.
20*	North Fork, J 11	Idaho
100*	North Fork (Marshall), D 19	Ky.
45	North Fork, B 17	Nev.
28*	North Fork, E 16	Va.
387	Northfork, Q 7	W. Va.
202	North Franklin (Lebanon), H 20	Conn.
547	North Freedom, J 18	Wis.
230	North Fryeburg, N 2	Me.
80*	North Garden, K 12	Va.
132	Northgate, C 7	N. D.
130	North Georgetown, G 20	Ohio
327	North Germantown, Q 23	N. Y.
1108	North Girard, D 2	Pa.
....	North Glenside, see North Hills	Pa.
150*	North Gorham, O 5	Me.
1150	North Grafton, G 15	Mass.
350	North Granby, B 12	Conn.
119*	North Granville, J 25	N. Y.
100	North Gray, O 6	Me.
275*	North Greece, K 8	N. Y.
50*	North Greenfield, I 10	Ohio
....	North Greenville, N 15	Mich.
....*	North Greenwood, see Greenwood	Miss.
2000	North Grosvenor Dale, B 24	Conn.
119*	Northgover, F 15	Ind.
900	North Guilford, L 13	Conn.
453	North Hackensack, D 20	N. J.
341*	North Hadley, E 7	Mass.
2761	North Haledon, D 19	N. J.
55*	North Hampton, F 11	Ill.
600	North Hampton, P 20	N. H.
383	North Hampton, K 8	Ohio
....	North Hanover, A 10	Ill.
300	North Hanover, H 21	Mass.
554▲*	North Harford (Harford), P 14	N. Y.
400*	North Harlowe, J 21	N. C.
216	North Hartland (Evarts), L 14	Vt.
170	North Harwich (Norman), M 13	Mass.
450	North Hatfield, E 7	Mass.
3502	North Haven, L 11	Conn.
200	North Haven, N 14	Me.
650	North Haverhill (Blackmount), I 10	N. H.
225	North Henderson, E 8	Ill.
250	North Hero. C 5	Vt.
2500*	North Hills (North Glenside), O 24	Pa.
....	North Hollywood, P 2 (Pop. incl. in Los Angeles)	Calif.
157*	North Holston, D 9	Va.
350*	North Hoosick, M 25	N. Y.
589*	North Hornell, Q 10	N. Y.
244▲	North Hudson, H 23	N. Y.
595	North Hudson, A 12	Wis.
315	North Hyde Park, D 12	Vt.
650	North Industry, G 18	Ohio
1153*	North Irwin, M 5	Pa.
400	North Islesboro, M 14	Me.
402	North Jackson, F 19	Ohio
250	North Java, N 7	N. Y.
500	North Jay, M 6	Me.
....	North Jefferson, I 14	Mo.
1408	North Judson, D 11	Ind.
....	North Jc., F 12	Ore.
2688	North Kansas City, G 6	Mo.
522	North Kemmerer (Frontier), N 3	Wyo.
500	North Kennebunk Port, Q 5	Me.
150*	North Kenova, R 13	Ohio
834	North Kingsville (Kingsville), B 20	Ohio
....	North La Crosse, F 17	Wis.
300	North Lake, N 19	Wis.
750*	North Lake Village, C 21	Ill.
105	Northland, F 6	Mich.
25*	Northland, L 14	Wis.
....	North Lansing, P 17	Mich.
1000	North Las Vegas, P 20	Nev.
450	North Lawrence, D 20	N. Y.
500	North Lawrence (Bowdil), F 17	Ohio
....*	North Leeds (Littleboro), M 7	Me.
2500	North Leominster, D 14	Mass.
720	North Lewisburg, J 9	Ohio
....	North Lexington, K 1	Mass.
978	North Liberty, B 12	Ind.
282	North Liberty, K 20	Iowa
350	North Lima, F 20	Ohio
56*	North Lincoln (Houstons), I 16	Me.
360	North Lisbon (Barrett), H 11	N. H.
21137	North Little Rock, I 13	Ark.
....	North Livermore, M 6	Me.
567	North Loup, J 16	Neb.
71*	North Lovell, N 3	Me.
282	North Lowell (Lowell), M 19	Wis.
....	North Los Angeles, see North Ridge	Calif.
400	North Lubec, K 24	Me.
452	North Lumberton, K 13	N. C.
....	North McAlester, K 19	Okla.
....	North Madison, L 14	Conn.
316	North Madison, N 19	Ind.
100	North Madison, B 19	Ohio
3170	North Manchester, E 15	Ind.
60	North Manitou Island, I 12	Mich.
3517*	North Mankato, P 12	Minn.
130	North Marshfield, H 22	Mass.
....*	North Matewan, O 3	W. Va.
75	North Mehoopany, F 20	Pa.
808	North Menominee, C 12	Wis.
....*	North Merchantville, L 10	N. J.
2000*	North Merrick, H 7	N. Y.
1973	North Miami, N 24	Fla.
393	North Miami, A 23	Okla.
871*	North Miami Beach, N 24	Fla.
376	North Middletown, F 18	Ky.
....	North Milwaukee, P 20	Wis.
450	North Monmouth, N 7	Me.
100	North Montpelier, F 14	Vt.
109*	Northmoor, F 5	Mo.
112*	North Morenci, R 18	Mich.
10	North Mountain, H 18	Pa.
100*	North Mountain, C 24	W. Va.
1694	North Muskegon, N 11	Mich.
75	North Newburg, L 13	Me.
263*	North New Castle, N 10	Me.
100*	North Newton (Bethel College), K 16	Kan.
300*	North Pearisburg (Bluff City), N 3	Va.
581*	North Newington (Newington Junction), E 13	Conn.
150*	North Newport (Northville) M 8	N. H.
570	North New Portland, K 7	Me.
300	North Newry, M 3	Me.
100	North Newtown, K 5	Conn.
180	North Norwich (Galena), N 17	N. Y.
3487	North Olmsted, D 16	Ohio
687	North Ogden, C 11	Utah
343	Northome, E 12	Minn.
100	North Orange, C 10	Mass.
1275	North Oxford, H 14	Mass.
150	North Parsonfield P 2	Me.
300*	North Pearisburg (Bluff City), N 3	Va.
5052*	North Pelham, G 6	N. Y.
200*	North Pembroke, H 21	Mass.
76*	North Penobscot, M 15	Me.
318*	North Perry, C 18	Ohio
220	North Pharsalia, O 16	N. Y.
139	North Pine Grove, H 7	Pa.
100*	North Pitcher, O 16	N. Y.
45*	North Plain, K 15	Conn.
10586	North Plainfield, F 16	N. J.
145	North Plains, C7	Ore.
12429	North Platte, K 10	Neb.
673	North Pleasanton, M 16	Tex.
200	North Pleasureville, E 16	Ky.
2000	North Plymouth, J 23	Mass.
80*	Northpoint, K 7	Pa.
237	North Point (Rommell), O 11	Pa.
300*	North Pomfret, K 13	Vt.
25*	North Pomona (Pomona), N 17	Calif.
3187	Northport, G 8	Ala.
85*	Northport, M 13	Me.
606	Northport, I 13	Mich.
150	Northport, I 3	Neb.
3093	Northport, G 8	N. Y.
2120*	Northport (East Northport), H 9	N. Y.
427	Northport, B 22	Wash.
200	Northport, M 14	Wis.
....	Northport Jc., G 7	N. Y.
....	North Portland Jc., C 7	Ore.
....*	North Port Point, I 13	Mich.
376	North Powder, F 21	Ore.
680	North Pownal, Q 5	Vt.
375	North Prairie, N 20	Wis.
12156■*	North Providence, D 8	R. I.
....*	North Quincy, F 19	Mass.
92	North Randall, D 18	Ohio
79	North Raymond, O 5	Me.
....▲	North Reading, D 19	Mass.
211*	North Redwood (Redwood), O 9	Minn.
....*	North Ridge, (North Los Angeles), Los Angeles, N 15, Q 4, (Pop. incl. in Los Angeles)	Calif.
125*	North Ridge, L 5	N. Y.
1500	North Ridgeville, D 15	Ohio
190*	North River, I 22	N. Y.
110*	North River (Mount Crawford), I 11	Va.
....	North River Jc., K 4	Wash.
40*	Northriver Mills, E 21	W. Va.
1036*	North Riverside, C 21	Ill.
2000*	North Roanoke, N 6	Va.
195*	North Robinson (Robinson), G 13	Ohio
175*	North Rochester (Hayes), N 19	N. H.
1600*	North Rochester, L 2	Pa.
134*	Northrop, Q 12	Minn.
750	North Rose, L 12	N. Y.
985*	North Roslyn, H 7	N. Y.
700*	North Roswell, E 7	Ga.
2559	North Royalton, Q 22	Ohio
50*	Northrup, K 19	Tex.
51*	North Rumford, M 4	Me.
3053*	North Sacramento, G 8	Calif.
3135	North Saint Paul, M 25	Minn.
511	North Salem, I 12	Ind.
45*	North Salem, C 11	Mo.
200	North Salem, Q 17	N. H.
150*	North Salem, E 7	N. Y.
100*	North Salem, J 17	Ohio
515	North Salt Lake, E 11	Utah
64	North Sandwich, K 15	N. H.
40*	North Sanford, Q 17	N. Y.
225*	North San Juan, F 8	Calif.
528	North Scituate, G 22	Mass.
850	North Scituate, E 10	R. I.
96*	North Sebago, O 4	Me.
162*	North Sedgwick, M 16	Me.
70	North Shapleigh, P 2	Me.
....*	North Sheldon, B 9	Vt.
325	North Shrewsbury, L 10	Vt.
....*	North Side, F 7	Ga.
56*	Northside, C 14	N. C.
....	North Sidell, L 20	La.
125	North Spadra, F 8	Ark.
102*	North Spring, P 5	W. Va.
3700	North Springfield (Ellet), F 17	Ohio
200	North Springfield (Springfield), D 2	Pa.
450	North Springfield, N 13	Vt.
....	North Stamford, P 2	Conn.
280	Northstar, N 16	Mich.
17	North Star, J 18	Neb.
200	North Star, I 6	Ohio
750	North Star (Tyre), M 2	Pa.
42	North Stephentown, O 24	N Y.
102	North Stockholm (Knapp), D 19	N. Y.
1236▲	North Stonington, K 24	Conn.
....	North Stoughton, H 19	Mass.
475	North Stratford, E 13	N. H.
600*	North Street (Evanshire), O 24	Mich.
250*	North Sudbury, F 17	Mass.
50*	North Sullivan, L 17	Me.
169	North Sutton, N 10	N. H.
2083*	North Syracuse, M 14	N. Y.
688	North Tazewell (Tazewell), C 10	Va.
8804*	North Tarrytown, F 6	N. Y.
800	North Terre Haute K 6	Ind.
180	North Thetford (Northboro), J 16	Vt.
2300	North Tiverton, H 22	R. I.
20254	North Tonawanda, K 5	N. Y.
250	North Towanda, E 17	Pa.
1077	North Troy, A 14	Vt.
296	North Truro (Moorland), J 15	Mass.
45	North Tunbridge, I 13	Vt.
150	North Turner, M 6	Me.
2740▲	Northumberland, F 14	N. H.
4469*	Northumberland, J 16	Pa.
34*	Northup, P 15	Ohio
1019	North Utica, (Utica), D 15	Ill.
500*	North Uvalde (Uvalde Jc.), M 14	Tex.
2500	North Uxbridge, H 15	Mass.
1159	Northvale, C 21	N. J.
575	North Vassalboro, M 10	Me.
3112	North Vernon, M 17	Ind.
98*	Northview, O 11	Mo.
31*	North View, Q 14	Va.
241	Northville, H 4	Conn.
3032	Northville, Q 21	Mich.
150*	Northville (North Newport) M 8	N. H.
1111	Northville, L 22	N. Y.
223	Northville, F 18	S. D.
37	North Wakefield (Mathews) L 19	N. H.
262*	North Waldoboro, N 11	Me.
2450	North Wales, O 23	Pa.
1425	North Walpole, O 6	N. H.
900	North Warren, E 7	Pa.
138*	North Washington, D 17	Iowa
136*	North Washington, K 4	Pa.
164	North Waterboro, P 3	Me.
130	North Waterford, N 3	Me.
....*	North Water Gap, see Minisink Hills	Pa.
75	North Wayne, M 7	Me.
300	North Weare, O 12	N. H.
343	North Webster, C 17	Ind.
....	North West Terminal, N 16	Minn.
38*	Northwest, R 22	Va.
211	North Westchester (Westchester), I 17	Conn.
....*	Northwestern, Q 22	Mich.
1750	North Westport, M 19	Mass.
3045	North Weymouth, Q 7	Mass.
436	North Whitefield, N 10	Me.
....*	North White Lake, see Kauneonga Lake	N. Y.
....	North White Plains, G 6	N. Y.
500*	Norwich, N 6	Va.
....	North Wilbraham, H 9	Mass.
1921	North Wildwood, R 12	N. J.
4478	North Wilkesboro, D 4	N. C.
160	North Williston (Williston, E 8	Vt.
472	North Wilmington, C 18	Mass.
300	North Windham, F 21	Conn.
325	North Windham, O 5	Me.
....	North Woburn, J 3	Mass.
....	North Woburn Jc., D 18	Mass.
6*	Northwood, G 3	Calif.
1724	Northwood, B 14	Iowa
300	Northwood, O 17	N. H.
1063	Northwood, I 22	N. D.
400	North Woodbury, I 7	Conn.
200*	Northwood Center, O 17	N. H.
300	Northwood Narrows, O 17	N. H.
90*	Northwood Ridge, O 17	N. H.
242	North Woodstock, A 22	Conn.
530	North Woodstock, I 12	N. H.
666▲	North Yarmouth (Dunns), O 6	Me.
2416	North York, P 17	Pa.
413	North Zulch, I 21	Tex.
10*	Norton, O 11	Ind.
2762	Norton, D 8	Kan.
2000	Norton, J 18	Mass.
525*	Norton (East Norton), J 18	Mass.
27*	Norton, G 10	Mo.
8	Norton, G 23	N. M.
....*	Norton, Q 5	N C.
150*	Norton, F 12	Tex.
300	Norton, A 20	Vt.
4006	Norton, D 5	Va.
500	Norton, G 14	W. Va.
28*	Nortonburg, M 16	Ind.
131*	Norton Hill, P 22	N. Y.
....	Norton Mills, see Norton	Vt.
43	Nortons, G 4	Ore.
79*	Nortonsville, J 12	Va.
50*	Nortonville, J 11	Ill.
562	Nortonville, E 23	Kan.
989	Nortonville, I 9	Ky.
150*	Nortonville, O 18	N. D.
160*	Norvell, Q 18	Mich
250*	Norvell, O 8	W. Va.
157*	Norvello, Q 13	Va.
....*	Norvelt, M 5	Pa.
3000*	Norwalk, Q 5	Calif.
39849	Norwalk, P 4	Conn.
377	Norwalk, L 12	Iowa
19*	Norwalk, K 12	Mich.
8211	Norwalk, E 13	Ohio
551	Norwalk, F 17	Wis.
80*	Norway, D 17	Ill.
407	Norway, J 19	Iowa
77*	Norway, E 15	Kan.
120*	Norway, E 10	Ind.
2446	Norway, N 4	Me.
3728	Norway, G 5	Mich.
125	Norway, M 3	Ore
488	Norway (Waynor), J 12	S. C.
20	Norway, H 16	Wis.
2446*	Norway Lake, N 4	Me.
1666▲	Norwell, H 21	Mass.
23652	Norwich, I 21	Conn.
60	Norwich, P 5	Iowa
411	Norwich, M 14	Kan.
8694	Norwich, O 17	N. Y.
50	Norwich, G 11	N. D.
177*	Norwich, K 16	Ohio
800	Norwich, K 15	Vt.
....	Norwichtown, I 21	Conn.
412	Norwood, M 4	Colo.
269	Norwood, G 16	Ga.
30	Norwood, K 6	Idaho
25	Norwood, E 8	Ill.
35*	Norwood, N 13	Iowa
200*	Norwood, J 14	La.
15383■	Norwood, G 19	Mass.
648	Norwood, N 13	Minn.
398	Norwood, O 13	Mo.
1512	Norwood, C 21	N. J.
1905	Norwood, D 18	N. Y.
1515	Norwood, H 8	N. C.
34010	Norwood, O 7	Ohio
3921	Norwood (Norwood Station), P 23	Pa.
1500	Norwood, F 15	R. I.
155	Norwood, L 11	Va.
....	Norwood Station, see Norwood	Pa.
150	Norwoodville, L 12	Iowa
863	Notasulga, J 19	Ala.
33	Noti, J 5	Ore.
10*	Notla, B 5	Tex.
65*	Notomine, K 6	W. Va.
200*	Nottawa, R 14	Mich.
20*	Nottingham, F 20	Ind.
100	Nottingham, O 18	N. H.
20	Nottingham, Q 20	Pa.
30*	Nottinghill, Q 12	Mo.
200	Nottoway, O 14	Va.
277	Notus, N 4	Idaho
24*	Nounan, Q 22	Idaho
265	Nova, F 14	Ohio
300	Novato, H 4	Calif.
207	Novelty, C 13	Mo.
100	Novelty, D 18	Ohio
10	Novelty, H 9	Wash.
200	Novi, P 21	Mich.
200*	Novice, G 14	Tex.
793	Novinger, B 12	Mo.
25*	Novum, H 14	Va.
3904	Nowata, C 19	Okla.
42	Nowlin, K 10	S. D.
10	No Wood, G 14	Wyo.
569	Noxapater, H 18	Miss.
1400	Noxen, G 19	Pa.
15	Noxie, A 19	Okla.
150	Noxon, E 1	Mont.
25*	Noxville, J 13	Tex.
18	Noyes, B 1	Minn.
500*	Nyota, E 14	Ala.
309*	Nuangola, I 20	Pa.
200*	Nubieber, C 9	Calif.
44*	Nuckols, H 10	Ky.
32*	Nuckols, M 13	Va.
361	Nucla, L 3	Colo.
30	Nuecestown, P 18	Tex.
350*	Nuevo, O 19	Calif.
50*	Nugent, E 14	Tex.
27*	Nulltown, K 20	Ind.
75*	Numa, J 7	Ind.
322	Numa, P 15	Iowa
15	Numa, B 12	Okla.
56*	Number Four, I 18	N. Y.
200	Numidia, K 18	Pa.
1500*	Nu Mine, L 5	Pa.
1077	Nunda, O 8	N. Y.
147	Nunda, J 23	S. D.
15	Nunda Jc., O 8	N. Y.
155	Nunez, J 18	Ga.
53*	Nunez, N 10	La.
300	Nunica, O 12	Mich.
190	Nunn, C 15	Colo.
520	Nunnelly, N 9	Tenn.
1022*	Nuremberg, J 19	Pa.
215*	Nuriva, P 6	W. Va.
28*	Nurseries, E 3	Va.
476	Nursery, N 19	Tex.
30*	Nutbush, P 13	Va.
21954	Nutley, E 19	N. J.
150	Nutrias, C 11	N. M.
100*	Nutrioso, G 23	Ariz.
20	Nutt, N 7	N. M.
43*	Nuttall, M 21	Va.
300	Nuttallburg (Nuttall), M 9	W. Va.
1803	Nutter Fort, E 12	W. Va.
155*	Nutterville, M 10	W. Va.
....*	Nutting Lake, D 18	Mass.
100*	Nuttsville, L 20	Va.
110*	Nutwell, H 14	Md.
30*	Nutwood, L 9	Ill.
500*	Nutwood (Fowler), D 21	Ohio
100	Nuyaka, H 18	Okla.
15	Nyack (Red Eagle), D 5	Mont.
5206	Nyack, F 5	N. Y.
68	Nyala, J 18	Nev.
32*	Nye, N 6	Kan.
20	Nye, M 13	Mont.
60	Nye, B 10	Wis.
150*	Nyesville, J 7	Ind.
70*	Nyesville, P 13	Pa.
....	Nymore, F 10	Minn.
1855	Nyssa, J 24	Ore.

O

Pop.	Place, Index	State
197	Oacoma, L 16	S. D.
54*	Oahe, I 13	S. D.
....*	Oak, D 5	Calif.
75*	Oak, E 15	Fla.
50*	Oak, Q 18	Ill.
96*	Oak (Thornhope), D 10	Ind.
177	Oak, O 18	Neb.
80*	Oakalla, J 17	Tex.
20*	Oakbeach, I 8	N. Y
1200	Oak Bluffs, O 24	Mass.
503	Oakboro, H 7	N. C.
30	Oak Center, P 20	Minn.
56*	Oak Center, N 17	Wis.
512	Oak City, E 19	N. C.
391	Oak City, J 9	Utah
1769	Oak Creek, D 9	Colo.
2592	Oakdale, I 9	Calif.
168	Oakdale, J 21	Conn.
175	Oakdale, O 13	Ill.
....*	Oakdale, K 20	Iowa
32*	Oakdale, H 20	Ky.
3933	Oakdale, J 9	La.
400	Oakdale, F 13	Mass.
561	Oakdale, H 18	Neb.
5	Oakdale, J 5	N. D.
1766	Oakdale, M 2	Pa.
900	Oakdale, N 17	Tenn.
70	Oakdale, H 16	Wis.
600*	Oakdale Station, H 8	N. Y.
75*	Oakes, C 4	N. Y.
1665	Oakes, Q 20	N. D.
590	Oakesdale, J 23	Wash.
127	Oakfield, M 9	Ga.
500	Oakfield, F 18	Me.
1876	Oakfield, L 7	N. Y.
310	Oakfield, D 20	Ohio
50*	Oakfield, O 5	Tenn.
655	Oakfield, M 17	Wis.
80*	Oakfield Center, O 14	Mich.
339	Oakford, I 11	Ill.
150*	Oakford (Fairfield), G 14	Ind.
1000*	Oakford (Neshaminy Falls), N 23	Pa.
825*	Oak Forest, D 21	Ill.
1500*	Oakglen, D 22	Ill.
50*	Oak Grove, P 5	Ala.
45*	Oakgrove, A 8	Ark.
19*	Oak Grove, K 9	Ky.
1654	Oak Grove, B 14	La.
150	Oak Grove, P 20	Mich.
680	Oak Grove, G 7	Mo.
1500*	Oak Grove, D 8	Ore.
12*	Oakgrove, K 16	Tenn.
219	Oak Grove, C 23	Tex.
225	Oak Hall (Oak Hall Station), K 13	Pa.
200*	Oak Hall, K 24	Va.
350	Oakham, F 12	Mass.
1925	Oak Harbor, C 11	Ohio
376	Oak Harbor, E 6	Wash.
159	Oakhill, L 11	Ala.
509*	Oak Hill, H 21	Fla.
10*	Oakhill, C 6	Ga.
100*	Oak Hill, F 11	Ill.
147	Oakhill, F 16	Kan.
....	Oak Hill, E 4	La.
....	Oakhill, K 12	Mich.
300*	Oak Hill, K 16	Mo.
161*	Oak Hill, O 22	N. Y.
1619	Oak Hill, P 13	Ohio
200	Oak Hill, P 24	Okla.
1200*	Oak Hill, L 3	Pa.
50*	Oak Hill (Wenonda), R 8	Va.
3213	Oak Hill, N 8	W. Va.
20*	Oakhurst, J 11	Calif.
900	Oakhurst, I 21	N. J.
200	Oakhurst, F 18	Okla.
750	Oakhurst, I 22	Tex.
....	Oak Lake, H 5	Minn.
75*	Oakland, A 11	Ark.
302163	Oakland, I 6, C 18	Calif.
518	Oakland, G 17	Fla.
1131	Oakland, J 20	Ill.
1317	Oakland, M 5	Iowa
....	Oakland, G 22	Kan.
221	Oakland, J 12	Ky.
45*	Oakland, A 10	La.
2666	Oakland, M 9	Me.
....*	Oakland (Glen Cove), N 12	Me.
1587	Oakland, O 1	Md.
30*	Oakland, P 12	Mich.
70*	Oakland, R 16	Minn.
516	Oakland, D 13	Miss.
58*	Oakland, M 12	Mo.
1380	Oakland, I 22	Neb.
932	Oakland, C 18	N. J.
184*	Oakland, Q 6	N. C.
311	Oakland, P 15	Okla.
367	Oakland, L 5	Ore.
964	Oakland, D 21	Pa.
500	Oakland, B 8	R. I.
251	Oakland, P 3	Tenn.
225	Oakland, L 19	Tex.
17*	Oakland, D 22	W. Va.
1600	Oakland Beach, H 16	R. I.
....*	Oakland City, F 7	Ga.
3068	Oakland City, P 7	Ind.
100*	Oakland Mills, O 20	Iowa
68*	Oakland Mills, L 14	Pa.
390	Oaklandon, I 16	Ind.
815*	Oakland Park, N 22	Fla.
....*	Oakland Recreation Camp, H 11	Calif.
13200*	Oak Lane, P 23	Pa.
3483	Oaklawn, C 21	Ill.
722	Oak Lawn, F 13	R. I.
200*	Oakley, H 6	Calif.
33	Oakley, J 22	Del.
813	Oakley, Q 13	Idaho
100*	Oakley, I 16	Ill.
1138	Oakley, G 5	Kan.
39*	Oakley, I 19	Ky.
31*	Oakley, P 13	Md.
270	Oakley, N 17	Mich.
50*	Oakley, K 9	Miss.
100*	Oakley (Oakley Depot), L 18	S. C.
127*	Oakley, L 15	Tenn.
305	Oakley, E 14	Utah
558	Oakley, O 3	Wyo.
100*	Oakley Depot (Oakley), L 18	S. C.
3869	Oaklyn, K 9	N. J.
897	Oakman, E 9	Ala.
225*	Oakman, C 5	Ga.
50	Oakman, M 16	Okla.
86*	Oak Mills, E 24	Kan.
6260	Oakmont, M 4	Pa.
125*	Oakmont, D 18	W. Va.
37*	Oaknolia, J 15	La.
....*	Oak Park, I 14	Fla.
280*	Oakpark, K 18	Ga.
66015	Oak Park, C 21	Ill.
1169*	Oak Park, P 22	Mich.
135*	Oak Park, L 14	Minn.
75*	Oak Park, Q 1	N. C.
35*	Oak Park, I 14	Va.
4*	Oak Point, B 4	Minn.
600	Oak Point, O 5	Wash.
373	Oak Ridge, B 12	La.
185	Oak Ridge, N 22	Mo.
251*	Oak Ridge, C 15	N. J.
400*	Oak Ridge, D 9	N. C.
520	Oakridge, K 8	Ore.
650	Oak Ridge, J 6	Pa.
90*	Oak Ridge, L 11	Va.
110	Oak Ridge Park, F 19	Mich.
....*	Oak Run, D 6	Calif.
29*	Oaks, K 19	Ky.
93	Oaks, E 23	Okla.
500	Oaks, O 22	Pa.
200*	Oaks Corners, M 11	N. Y.
90*	Oaksville, N 19	N. Y.
50*	Oak Terrace, M 21	Minn.
200	Oakton, K 4	Ky.
275*	Oakton, G 17	Va.
793	Oaktown, N 6	Ind.
170	Oak Vale, N 12	Miss.
....	Oak Vale, K 20	Mo.
100*	Oakvale (South Hammond), F 16	N. Y.
273	Oakvale, R 9	W. Va.
100	Oak Valley, N 20	Kan.
12*	Oakview (Tropic), O 14	Colo.
219	Oakville, G 5	Calif.
923	Oakville, I 8	Conn.
200	Oakville, H 19	Ind.
391	Oakville, N 22	Iowa
129*	Oakville (Red Oak), K 10	Ky.
536	Oakville, J 20	Mo.
115*	Oakville, O 14	Pa.
550*	Oakville (Forsythe), Q 1	Tenn.
150	Oakville, O 17	Tex.
39*	Oakville, M 11	Va.
418	Oakville, K 5	Wash.
207*	Oakwood, D 10	Ga.
555	Oakwood, H 21	Ill.
....	Oakwood, P 22	Mich.
1500	Oakwood, E 16	Mo.
70	Oakwood, F 23	N. D.
7652*	Oakwood, L 7	Ohio
466	Oakwood, E 7	Ohio
233	Oakwood, F 6	Okla.
1086	Oakwood, G 21	Tex.
300*	Oakwood, B 7	Va.
150*	Oakwood, P 21	Wis.
200*	Oakwoods, D 5	N. C.
52*	Oark, E 7	Ark.
50*	Oasis, I 16	Calif.
14*	Oasis, B 6	Ga.
27*	Oasis, R 10	Mo.
325	Oasis, J 8	Utah
22*	Oatlands, F 16	Va.
500	Oatman, G 3	Ariz.
100	Oats, F 17	S. C.
50*	Oatsville, P 6	Ind.
25*	Oatville, M 16	Kan.
35*	O'Bannon, F 14	Ky.
164▲	Obar, F 24	N. M.
50*	Obed, K 16	Ill.
75*	Obed, I 20	Ky.
170*	Obelisk, N 22	Pa.
170	Ober, C 12	Ind.
1878	Oberlin, D 6	Kan.
962	Oberlin, K 8	La.
15*	Oberlin, K 16	Mich.
4305	Oberlin, E 15	Ohio
215	Oberlin, Q 19	Okla.
564*	Oberlin, N 17	Pa.
106*	Obernburg, C 1	N. Y.
225	Oberon, H 17	N. D.
112	Obert, E 21	Neb.
771*	Obetz, K 11	Ohio
50	Obey City, M 15	Tenn.
400*	Obids, C 4	N. C.
1151	Obion, M 4	Tenn.
1547	Oblong, L 21	Ill.
896▲	O'Brien, C 11	Fla.
30*	O'Brien, R 4	Ore.
100	O'Brien, C 13	Tex.
400	O'Brien, I 8	Wash.
18*	Obrion, J 9	W. Va.
8986	Ocala, F 14	Fla.
24*	Ocala, I 17	Ky.
19*	Ocala, Q 4	Va.
833▲*	Ocate, D 17	N. M.
500*	Occidental, H 4	Calif.
213	Occoquan, H 17	Va.
300*	Occoquan (Woodbridge), G 17	Va.
15*	Occupacia, J 18	Va.
100	Ocean, M 5	Md.
250*	Oceana, P 23	Va.
100*	Oceana, O 6	W. Va.
28*	Ocean Bay Park, H 9	N. Y.
713	Ocean Beach. Q 18	Calif.
81*	Ocean Beach, H 9	N. Y.
211*	Ocean Bluff, H 22	Mass.
1052	Ocean City, N 25	Md.
4672	Ocean City, P 15	N. J.
75*	Ocean City, J 3	Wash.
242*	Oceangate, K 17	N. J.
650*	Ocean Grove, L 18	Mass.
3500	Ocean Grove, I 21	N. J.
650*	Oceanlake, G 4	Ore.
425	Oceano, M 9	Calif.
....*	Ocean Park, O 15 (Pop. incl. in Santa Monica)	Calif.
136*	Ocean Park, Q 5	Me.
250	Ocean Park, M 2	Wash.
15*	Ocean Point, O 10	Me.
3159	Oceanport, H 20	N. J.
4651	Oceanside, P 18	Calif.
9000*	Ocean Side, H 7	N. Y.
24*	Oceanside, D 4	Ore.
1881	Ocean Springs, R 20	Miss.
406	Ocean View, L 25	Del.
500	Ocean View, Q 13	N. J.
881	Ocean View, P 22	Va.
130	Oceanville, N 15	Me.
313	Oceanville, O 16	N. J.
102	Oceola, G 12	Ohio

Pop. Place Index State

333 Ochelata, C 19.....Okla.
100*Ocheltree, H 24.....Kan.
712 Ocheyedan, E 4.....Iowa
429 Ochlochnee (Ochlocknee), O 8.....Ga.
21 Ochoa, O 24.....N. M.
242*Ochopee, N 19.....Fla.
25*Ocie, Q 13.....Mo.
2124 Ocilla, M 13.....Ga.
220*Ocklawaha (Oklawaha), F 15.....Fla.
85*Ockley, G 11.....Ind.
702 Ocoee, G 17.....Fla.
135*Ocoee, G 16.....Tenn.
550 Oconee, I 15.....Ga.
278 Oconee, K 15.....Ill.
71 Oconee, I 19.....Neb.
4562 Oconomowoc, M 20.....Wis.
260 Oconto, K 13.....Neb.
5362 Oconto, P 12.....Wis.
1888 Oconto Falls, O 12.....Wis.
25 Oconto Jc., O 12.....Wis.
163*Ocononita, E 3.....Va.
157*Ocosta, K 3.....Wash.
30*Ocoya, F 17.....Ill.
10*Ocqueoc, M 13.....Mich.
600 Ocracoke, I 24.....N. C.
90*Ocran, L 21.....Va.
67 Ocra, M 9.....Ohio
500*Octagon, K 7.....Ala.
80 Octave, I 10.....Ariz.
151 Octavia, J 21.....Neb.
315 Octavia, N 24.....Okla.
Odair, H 18.....Wash.
600 Odanah, G 5.....Wis.
229 Odd, O 21.....W. Va.
53*Odd, P 8.....Ky.
20*Odds, J 21.....W. Va.
1350 Odebolt, H 6.....Iowa
102 Odell, D 4.....Ark.
927 Odell, E 17.....Ill.
200*Odell, O 9.....Ind.
404 Odell, O 21.....Neb.
34 Odell, Q 24.....Okla.
25 Odell, C 11.....Ore.
301 Odell, A 14.....Tex.
318 Odell, K-7.....W. Va.
6*Odell Lake, O 10.....Ore.
1147 Oden, P 13.....Tex.
250*Oden, J 6.....Ark.
97*Oden, G 15.....Mich.
Odense, O 11.....N. D.
175 Odenthal, N 9.....Pa.
400 Odenton, H 13.....Md.
347 Odenville, E 15.....Ala.
391 Odessa, D 21.....Del.
45 Odessa, H 13.....Fla.
316 Odessa, M 3.....Minn.
1881 Odessa, G 8.....Mo.
56 Odessa, M 14.....Neb.
424 Odessa, P 22.....N. Y.
37 Odessa, P 7.....N. D.
9573 Odessa, G 9.....Tex.
816 Odessa, I 19.....Wash.
21*Odessa, K 8.....W. Va.
79*Odessadale, H 5.....Ga.
37 Odetta, M 6.....Okla.
1849 Odin, M 15.....Ill.
198 Odin, Q 10.....Minn.
958 Odon, N 9.....Ind.
1187 O'Donnell, D 10.....Tex.
44*Odra, F 7.....La.
469 Odum, M 20.....Ga.
660 Oella, F 3.....Md.
212 Oelrichs, N 3.....S. D.
7801 Oelwein, F 19.....Iowa
125*Oenaville, H 18.....Tex.
35*Oermann, J 19.....Mo.
150*Ofahoma, I 14.....Miss.
2407 O'Fallon, J 3.....Mo.
618 O'Fallon, H 19.....Ill.
13*Offen, D 4.....N. C.
273 Offerle, L 9.....Kan.
483 Offerman, N 19.....Ga.
76*Officer, P 20.....Colo.
179*Offnutt, G 23.....Ky.
129 Ogallah, G 8.....Kan.
3159 Ogallala, K 7.....Neb.
125*Ogamaw, P 9.....Ark.
225 Ogden, O 5.....Ark.
431 Ogden, H 20.....Ill.
200 Ogden, J 18.....Ind.
1513 Ogden, I 10.....Iowa
494 Ogden (Ogdensburg), G 18.....Kan.
40*Ogden, B 12.....S. C.
43688 Ogden, D 11.....Utah
494*Ogdensburg (Ogden), Kan.
1165 Ogdensburg, B 14.....N. J.
16346 Ogdensburg, D 17.....N. Y.
327 Ogdensburg, F 15.....Pa.
207 Ogdensburg, L 14.....Wis.
50*Ogeechee, J 21.....Ga.
228 Ogema, J 5.....Minn.
250 Ogema, H 10.....Wis.
310*Ogemaw (Ogamaw), P 9.....Ark.
Ogilby, Q 24.....Calif.
438 Ogilvie, N 11.....Minn.
30*Ogilville, L 15.....Ind.
150 Oglala, N 5.....S. D.
50*Ogle, J 20.....Ky.
59*Oglesby, E 15.....Ga.
3938 Oglesby, J 15.....Ill.
74 Oglesby, C 19.....Miss.
390 Oglesby, H 18.....Tex.
1048 Oglethorpe, K 8.....Ga.
15*Ogontz, G 10.....Me.
Ogontz, N 22, (Pop. 500 incl. in Cheltenham).....Pa.
*Ogontz School, O 23 (Pop. 200 incl. in Abington).....Pa.
150*Ogletown (Felix), P 7.....Pa.
600 Ogunquit, R 4.....Me.
450*Ohatchee, E 17.....Ala.
78 Ohio (Ohio City), K 9.....Colo.
524 Ohio, D 13.....Ill.
25*Ohio, K 8.....Mo.
460*Ohio, K 19.....N. Y.
*Ohio City, K 8, see Ohio.....Colo.
870 Ohio City, G 6.....Ohio
*Ohio Falls, P 17.....Ind.
420 Ohiopyle, Q 5.....Pa.
326 Ohiowa, N 20.....Neb.
200*Ohley, M 6.....W. Va.
275 Ohlman, K 14.....Ill.
30 Ohlman, A 14.....Wyo.
135*Ohoopee, K 19.....Ga.
135*Ohop, K 4.....Wash.
38*Oil Center, I 17.....Calif.
500 Oilcenter, M 14.....Tex.
500 Oil City, J 13.....Ky.
10 Oil City, I 13.....La.
1030 Oil City, B 4.....Okla.
12 Oil City, N 20.....Okla.
20379 Oil City, G 4.....Pa.
4000*Oildale, G 17.....Calif.
50*Oilfield, K 20.....Ill.
350 Oilfields, K 16.....Calif.
400 Oil Hill, L 18.....Kan.
Oil Jc., M 13.....Calif.
42*Oilla, K 25.....Tex.
400*Oilmont, C 9.....Mont.
150*Oil Springs, G 22.....Ky.
1225 Oilton, F 16.....Okla.

500*Oilton, P 14.....Tex.
200*Oil Trough, E 16.....Ark.
42*Oilville, I 15.....Va.
1622 Ojai, N 13.....Calif.
9 Ojata, H 23.....N. D.
41*Ojibwa, F 8.....Wis.
70*Ojibway, O 20.....Mo.
50 Ojo, O 14.....Colo.
134*Ojo Caliente, D 14.....N. M.
50*Ojodel Padre, F 10.....N. M.
150*Ojo Feliz, D 17.....N. M.
100 Ojo Sarco, D 15.....N. M.
800 Ojus, N 24.....Fla.
40*O. K., I 17.....Ky.
50 Oka, J 13.....N. M.
31*Oka, I 8.....W. Va.
210 Okabena, Q 8.....Minn.
100 Okahumpka, G 15.....Fla.
1735 Okanogan, E 17.....Wash.
453 Okarche, H 10.....Okla.
31 Okaton, K 11.....S. D.
235*Okauchee, N 20.....Wis.
708 Okawville, N 13.....Ill.
*Okay, E 10.....Ark.
322 Okay, G 21.....Okla.
138 Okean, B 19.....Ark.
150 Okeana, N 5.....Ohio
50*Okee, K 19.....Wis.
10 Okee, K 19.....
1658 Okeechobee, K 21.....Fla.
163*Okeefe (Devon), N 2.....W. Va.
1079 Okeene, F 9.....Okla.
200*Okeetee (Switzerland), P 13.....S. C.
3811 Okemah, I 17.....Okla.
300 Okemos, O 17.....Mich.
100 Okesa, C 18.....Okla.
218 Oketo, C 18.....Kan.
75 Okfuskee, H 17.....Okla.
*Oklahoma (Rogers), I 20.....Okla.
204424 Oklahoma City, I 11.....Okla.
22 Oklarado, P 21.....Colo.
223 Oklaunion, B 15.....Tex.
220 Oklawaha (Ocklawaha), F 15.....Fla.
414 Oklee, K 6.....Minn.
16051 Okmulgee, H 18.....Okla.
271*Okoboji, B 6.....Iowa
42 Okobojo, H 12.....S. D.
525 Okolona, M 8.....Ark.
2117 Okolona, D 20.....Miss.
100*Okolona, D 7.....Ohio
51*Okonoko, D 21.....W. Va.
51*Okra, I 15.....Tex.
335 Okreek, N 13.....S. D.
233 Oktaha, H 20.....Okla.
837 Ola, H 9.....Ark.
34 Ola, M 5.....Idaho
10 Ola, L 16.....S. D.
300*Olaf, O 6.....Va.
200 Olalla, I 7.....Wash.
80 Olamon, J 5.....Me.
100*Olancha, K 16.....Calif.
326*Olanta, J 9.....Pa.
515 Olanta, H 18.....S. C.
528 Olar, L 12.....S. C.
705 Olathe, K 5.....Colo.
3797 Olathe, G 24.....Kan.
50*Olaton, H 11.....Ky.
36*Olberg, L 14.....Ariz.
15 Olcott, L 13.....Kan.
300 Olcott, K 5.....N. Y.
511 Olcott, L 5.....W. Va.
2000 Old Albuquerque, G 9.....N. M.
119*Old Appleton (Appleton), M 22.....Mo.
356*Old Brookville, H 7.....N. Y.
1020 Old Bridge, E 17.....N. J.
150 Old Chatham, P 24.....N. Y.
115*Old Church, L 18.....Va.
100*Old Concord, O 2.....Pa.
35*Old Dock, M 14.....N. C.
75*Olden, G 18.....Mo.
1026 Olden, R 15.....Tex.
*Oldenburg, L 11.....Ill.
533 Oldenburg, L 21.....Ind.
29*Oldenburg, N 6.....Miss.
50*Oldenburg, K 20.....Tex.
33*Old Faithful, A 3.....Wyo.
123*Old Field, H 9.....N. Y.
25*Old Fields, G 20.....W. Va.
840 Old Forge, I 19.....N. Y.
11892 Old Forge, H 21.....Pa.
774 Old Fort, O 9.....N. C.
158 Old Fort, E 16.....Ohio
85*Oldfort, Q 17.....Tenn.
100 Old Fort (Elkwater), I 14.....W. Va.
48*Oldframe, O 4.....Pa.
*Old Furnace (Furnace), F 11.....Mass.
100*Old Glory, D 13.....Tex.
2368 Old Greenwich (South Beach), R 2.....Conn.
35*Oldham, K 4.....Ky.
386 Oldham, J 22.....S. D.
50*Oldhams, J 19.....Va.
8000 Old Hickory, L 11.....Tenn.
100*Old Landing, G 20.....Ky.
600 Old Lyme (Lyme), M 18.....Conn.
Oldman, M 5.....N. J.
226 Old Marissa, O 12.....Ill.
416 Old Mines, L 19.....Mo.
100*Old Mission, J 14.....Mich.
272 Old Monroe, M 19.....Mo.
1120 Old Mystic, L 23.....Conn.
1650 Old Orchard Beach, Q 5.....Me.
250 Old Point (Ebenezer), B 12.....S. C.
Old Portage, E 17.....Ohio
113*Old Ripley, D 13.....Ill.
203 Olds, N 20.....Iowa
315 Oldsmar (Tampashores), I 12.....Fla.
*Old Station, A 18.....Calif.
609 Old Tappan, C 21.....N. J.
*Oldtown, Q 18 (Pop. incl. in San Diego).....Calif.
300 Old Town, D 11.....Fla.
240*Oldtown, E 22.....Ky.
7688 Old Town, K 15.....Me.
200*Oldtown, L 6.....Md.
50 Oldtown, Q 3.....Va.
500 Old Trap, D 23.....N. C.
297 Old Washington (Washington), J 17.....Ohio
1017*Old Westbury, H 7.....N. Y.
375 Oldwick, F 13.....N. J.
175*Old Zionsville, M 22.....Pa.
151*Olean, M 20.....Ind.
21506 Olean, R 6.....N. Y.
1506 Oleander, K 10.....Calif.
150*Olema, H 4.....Calif.
29*Olena, F 6.....Ill.
62 Olene, R 10.....Ore.
5 Olequa, N 5.....Wash.
25 Oleson, F 18.....Colo.
*Oleta, see Fiddletown.....Calif.
217 Oleum, A 18.....Calif.
21 Olex, D 15.....Ore.
720*Oley (Friedensburg), M 21.....Pa.

177*Oley Line (Limekin), M 21.....Pa.
39*Olga, J 15.....Pa.
11*Olga, O 22.....La.
100 Olga, D 20.....N. D.
5 Olga, C 6.....Wash.
707 Olin, I 22.....Iowa
50 Olin, E 6.....N. C.
449 Olinda, D 6.....Calif.
180 Olinda, D 6.....Calif.
250*Olinger, E 3.....Va.
48*Olio, H 6.....Ky.
100 Oliphant Furnace, Q 5.....Pa.
600 Olive, O 17.....Calif.
80*Olive, M 22.....Pa.
65*Olive, J 21.....N. M.
121 Olive, F 17.....Okla.
200 Olive Branch, R 14.....Ill.
441*Olive Branch, A 13.....Miss.
300 Olivebridge, B 4.....N. Y.
50*Oliveburg, I 7.....Pa.
1491 Olive Hill, E 21.....Ky.
146*Olivehill, Q 6.....Tenn.
211 Oliver, J 22.....Ga.
90*Oliver, J 21.....Ill.
60*Oliver, Q 3.....Ohio
22*Oliver (Riggs), D 22.....Ky.
1057*Oliver, P 4.....Pa.
201*Oliver, C 5.....Wis.
275*Oliverea, C 4.....N. Y.
125 Oliverian (E. Haverhill), I 10.....N. H.
855 Oliver Springs, N 17.....Tenn.
500*Olivers Mills, I 20.....Pa.
230 Olivet, L 21.....Mich.
50*Olivet, M 15.....Iowa
172 Olivet, I 21.....Kan.
604 Olivet, P 15.....Mich.
242 Olivet, N 21.....S. D.
987*Olivette, I 20.....Mo.
*Olive View, Q 4.....Calif.
17884 Olivia, N 9.....Minn.
325*Olivia, H 12.....N. C.
10*Olivia, N 20.....Tex.
120 Olivier, N 12.....La.
691 Olla, F 10.....La.
294 Ollie, N 18.....Iowa
30 Ollie, J 2.....S. D.
113 Ollie, I 25.....Mont.
*Ollie, I 23.....Tex.
300*Olmito, R 5.....Tex.
6 Olmitz, N 14.....Iowa
130*Olmitz, I 11.....Kan.
592 Olmstead, R 15.....Ill.
175*Olmstead, C 20.....Mont.
10 Olmstead, E 17.....N. D.
350*Olmstedville, G 23.....N. Y.
754 Olmsted Falls, D 15.....Ohio
7831 Olney, M 20.....Ill.
251 Olney (Hanston), K 8.....Kan.
36*Olney, I 8.....Md.
100*Olney, G 9.....Md.
74*Olney, G 17.....Mo.
100 Olney, C 3.....Mont.
112 Olney, N 17.....Okla.
75 Olney, A 4.....Ore.
3497 Olney, C 15.....Tex.
260 Olney Springs, M 18.....Colo.
Olneyville, E 14.....R. I.
331 Olpe, J 20.....Kan.
177 Olsburg, F 19.....Kan.
782 Olton, A 9.....Tex.
452 Olustee, L 13.....Fla.
570 Olustee, N 3.....Okla.
125*Olvey, B 10.....Ark.
100*Olympia, J 6.....Calif.
300 Olympia, F 20.....Ky.
13254 Olympia, K 5.....Wash.
101*Olympia Fields, C 21.....Ill.
20 Olney, D 4.....Mont.
130*Olyphant, P 16.....Ark.
9252 Olyphant, G 21.....Pa.
45*Olympic, M 13.....N. C.
200*Oma, M 11.....Miss.
21*Omage, D 11.....Ark.
146 Omaha (Cricket), A 9.....Ark.
211 Omaha, K 8.....Ga.
413 Omaha, P 19.....Ill.
*Omaha, H 22.....Ind.
223844 Omaha, K 24.....Neb.
623 Omaha, C 23.....Tex.
34*Omaha, C 6.....Va.
2918 Omak, E 17.....Wash.
19*Omar, H 15.....Ind.
1800 Omar, A 7.....W. Va.
25*Omarsville, I 17.....Ky.
65*Omega (Boswell), K 19.....Ala.
608 Omega, N 11.....Ga.
100*Omega, M 17.....Ind.
50*Omega, I 15.....Ind.
50*Omega, B 17.....Ky.
50*Omega, C 14.....La.
50*Omega, J 3.....N. M.
150 Omega, O 12.....Ohio
50*Omega, G 9.....Okla.
153*Omega, J 19.....Va.
950*Ome Gardens, L 7.....Ohio
123 Omemee, E 13.....N. D.
125 Omena, J 12.....Mich.
114*Omer, F 20.....Ky.
295 Omer, L 20.....Mich.
200 Omo Ranch, G 10.....Calif.
100*Omps, D 22.....W. Va.
1401 Omro, M 16.....Wis.
77 Ona, J 16.....Fla.
66*Ona, K 3.....W. Va.
741 Onaga, E 20.....Kan.
416 Onalaska, M 7.....Wash.
163*Onalaska, J 22.....Tex.
1200 Onalaska, M 7.....Wash.
1742 Onalaska, F 16.....Wis.
619 Onamia, K 14.....Minn.
1283 Onancock, L 23.....Va.
70 Onapa, I 21.....Okla.
1413 Onarga, G 20.....Ill.
185*Onativia (La Fayette), M 15.....N. Y.
3438 Onawa, I 2.....Iowa
91*Onawa, I 11.....Me.
250 Onaway, H 4.....Idaho
1449 Onaway, I 7.....Mich.
115 Onchiota, E 21.....N. Y.
33*Oneal, D 15.....Ark.
85*O'Neals, J 11.....Calif.
650 Oneco, J 21.....Conn.
200*Oneco, J 13.....Fla.
75*Oneco, A 12.....Ill.
295*Oneco, A 12.....
556 Oneida, E 10.....Ill.
84 Oneida, G 21.....Iowa
187 Oneida, D 21.....Kan.
300 Oneida, I 12.....Ky.
11234 Oneida, L 16.....N. Y.
150 Oneida, G 19.....Ohio
950*Oneida, K 19.....Pa.
1252 Oneida, L 17.....Tenn.
120 Oneida, H 4.....Wis.
556 Oneida Castle, M 16.....N. Y.
2 O'Neil, H 17.....Ore.
7532 O'Neill, F 22.....Neb.
340 Onekama, K 11.....Mich.
68*Onekama Jc., K 11.....Mich.
2376 Oneonta, E 15.....Ala.
11731 Oneonta, P 19.....N. Y.
50 Oneta, F 19.....Okla.

193 Ong, N 18.....Neb.
15*Onia, Q 11.....Ark.
42 Onia, C 12.....Ark.
597 Onida, H 13.....S. D.
400 Onley, L 24.....Va.
70 Only, N 8.....Tenn.
130*Onnalinda, N 9.....Pa.
34*Ono, D 5.....Calif.
37*Ono, O 11.....Ky.
170*Ono, N 18.....Pa.
220 Onondaga, P 16.....Mich.
325*Onondaga, M 15.....N. Y.
622*Onondaga Castle, M 14.....N. Y.
Onondaga Valley, M 14 (Pop. incl. in Syracuse).....N. Y.
500 Onoville, R 4.....N. Y.
1000 Onset, K 22.....Mass.
230 Onslow, I 22.....Iowa
225 Oremine (Mines), M 11.....Pa.
414 Onsted, O 18.....Mich.
14197 Ontario, O 17, Q 7.....Calif.
150*Ontario, A 19.....Ind.
90*Ontario, I 12.....Iowa
650 Ontario, L 10.....N. Y.
250*Ontario, G 13.....Ohio
3551 Ontario, J 24.....Ore.
86*Ontario, P 12.....Wis.
533 Ontario, M 15.....N. Y.
275*Ontario Center, L 10.....N. Y.
240*Ontarioville, B 19.....Ill.
100*Onton, H 9.....Ky.
2290 Ontonagon, A 24.....Mich.
10*Onville, H 16.....Va.
127 Onward, H 14.....Ind.
28*Onward, I 7.....Miss.
320 Onyx, I 8.....Ark.
125*Onyx, L 16.....Calif.
42*Oolite, G 12.....Ky.
1186 Oolitic, N 12.....Ind.
236 Oologah, D 19.....Okla.
524 Ooltewah, G 16.....Tenn.
742 Oostburg, P 17.....Wis.
25*Opal, J 5.....Ark.
30 Opal, G 6.....S. D.
78 Opal, O 3.....Wyo.
35 Opal City, H 12.....Ore.
497*Opa Locka, O 22.....Fla.
175 Opdyke, O 16.....Ill.
60 Opdyke, D 21.....Wash.
8487 Opelika, I 22.....Ala.
8980 Opelousas, K 11.....La.
120*Opequon, E 13.....Va.
100 Ophiem, E 9.....Ill.
344 Ophir, C 20.....Mont.
47*Ophelia, K 23.....Va.
2 Ophir, N 5.....Colo.
100*Ophir, F 21.....Ky.
300*Ophir, P 12.....Va.
100*Ophir, O 2.....Ore.
829 Ophir, G 10.....Utah
30 Opitz, K 11.....Ark.
225*Oplin, P 14.....Tex.
181*Opolis, N 25.....Kan.
3178 Opp, O 16.....Ala.
25 Oppermans (Opperman Mine), M 16.....Ohio
17 Opportunity, P 16.....Neb.
1500 Opportunity, G 24.....Wash.
160*Oppy, G 23.....Ky.
69 Optima, Q 6.....Okla.
194*Optimo, E 18.....N. M.
100*Optimus, C 13.....Ark.
912 Oquawka, F 6.....Ill.
260*Oquossoc, K 3.....Me.
155 Ora, D 12.....Ind.
225 Ora, M 15.....Miss.
375*Ora, D 8.....Va.
20 Ora, E 8.....Va.
200 Oracle, M 18.....Ariz.
2802 Oradell (Delford), C 20.....N. J.
18 Orafino, N 12.....Neb.
20 Oraibi, E 18.....Ariz.
75 Oral, M 3.....S. D.
140*Oralabor, K 12.....Iowa
140*Oramel, P 7.....N. Y.
1106 Oran, O 23.....Mo.
100*Oran, M 15.....N. Y.
210 Oran, D 16.....Tex.
7901 Orange, R 6.....Calif.
1200 Orange, N 7.....Conn.
30 Orange, C 2.....Fla.
175*Orange, K 20.....Ind.
5611*Orange, C 10.....Mass.
35717 Orange, E 18.....N. J.
Orange, O 17.....N. M.
492 Orange, P 25.....N. Y.
7472 Orange, K 25.....Tex.
50 Orange, H 14.....Vt.
1980 Orange, J 14.....Va.
58*Orange Beach, P 7.....Ala.
750 Orangeburg (Orangeburgh), N 13.....S. C.
10521 Orange, K 11.....
*Orange Center, see Vineland.....Fla.
489 Orange City, F 18.....Fla.
1920 Orange City, D 2.....Iowa
800*Orangefield, J 22.....Tex.
300*Orange Grove, R 22.....Miss.
906*Orange Grove, P 17.....Tex.
150*Orange Heights, D 14.....Fla.
200*Orange Lake, E 14.....Fla.
666 Orange Park, C 16.....Fla.
100 Orange Springs, E 15.....Fla.
407 Orangeville, A 12.....Ill.
265 Orangeville, O 11.....Ind.
434 Orangeville, D 21.....Ohio
652 Orangeville, J 15.....Utah
150 Oranville, F 13.....Ill.
43*Oraville, N 13.....Md.
729 Orbisonia, N 12.....Pa.
20 Orcas, D 6.....Wash.
865 Orchard, D 17.....Colo.
126*Orchard, O 6.....Idaho
495 Orchard, C 15.....Iowa
1115 Orchard, O 17.....Neb.
11*Orchard, P 10.....W. Va.
50*Orchardfarm (Orchard Farm), H 19.....Mo.
400*Orchard Hill, H 8.....Ga.
295*Orchard Lake, P 21.....Mich.
200*Orchard Mines, F 11.....Ill.
1304 Orchard Park (East Hamburg), N 5.....N. Y.
50*Orchard Place, B 21.....Ill.
75 Orchards, Q 7.....Wash.
75 Orchardville, N 17.....Ill.
32*Orchid, K 15.....Calif.
100*Orchid, O 11.....Ill.
75 Ord, L 18.....Neb.
2240 Ord, L 22.....Neb.
9*Ordean, C 17.....Mont.
400*Orderville, N 20.....Utah
49*Ordinary, N 20.....Va.
1150 Ordway, L 19.....Colo.
36 Ordway, D 19.....S. D.
75 Oreana, J 8.....Idaho
104*Oreana, I 6.....Ill.
68*Oreana, E 8.....Nev.
8 Oreapolis, K 24.....Neb.
40*Ore Bank, L 13.....Va.
300 Ore City, D 23.....Tex.
297*Orefield, K 21.....Pa.

2825 Oregon, B 14.....Ill.
18*Oregon, O 18.....Ind.
978 Oregon, C 4.....Mo.
1005 Oregon, K 21.....Wis.
6124 Oregon City, D 8.....Ore.
75*Oregon Hill, G 14.....Pa.
75*Oregon House, F 8.....Calif.
121*Oregonia, M 8.....Ohio
Ore Hill, see Mount Vernon Springs.....N. C.
103 Ore Hill, N 10.....Pa.
19*Ore Knob, C 4.....N. C.
25 Oreland, I 13.....Minn.
50 Oreland, O 15.....N. J.
900*Oreland, O 23.....Pa.
Oreland Jc., C 15.....N. J.
24 Orella, D 2.....Neb.
942*Orient, N 9.....Ill.
100 Orient, D 8.....Iowa
650*Orient, H 4.....Me.
175 Orient, L 11.....Ohio
1625*Orient, Q 4.....Pa.
250 Orient, G 17.....S. D.
*Orient, see Knox City.....Tex.
175*Orient, B 21.....Wash.
20 Orient, D 7.....Okla.
*Oriental, see Alder Springs.....Calif.
535 Oriental, I 21.....N. C.
Orient Heights, E 20.....Mass.
Orient Line Jc., D 16.....S. D.
127 Orillia, I 8.....Wash.
60 Orin, D 21.....Wash.
60 Orin, K 20.....Wyo.
225*Orinda, N 6.....Calif.
200 Oriole, P 20.....Md.
715 Orion, D 9.....Ill.
20*Orion, G 5.....Kan.
Orion, see Lake Orion.....Mich.
3 Orion, E 7.....Wis.
217 Oriska, M 21.....N. D.
1115 Oriskany, L 17.....N. Y.
126*Oriskany, J 6.....Va.
930 Oriskany Falls, M 17.....N. Y.
13*Oriva, C 17.....Wyo.
10*Orkney, H 22.....Ky.
105*Orkney Springs, G 11.....Va.
24*Orla, N 12.....Mo.
20 Orla, H 6.....Tex.
*Orlahwa, H 11.....Minn.
1366 Orland, E 5.....Calif.
1307 Orland, A 20.....Ind.
200 Orland, L 15.....Me.
36736 Orlando, Q 16.....Fla.
100*Orlando (Brush Creek), H 18.....
332 Orlando, E 12.....Okla.
190*Orlando, O 11.....W. Va.
631 Orland Park, C 20.....Ill.
56*Orlean, G 14.....Va.
140 Orleans, C 2.....Calif.
25*Orleans, J 10.....Ill.
1428 Orleans, Q 12.....Ind.
244*Orleans, B 6.....Iowa
850 Orleans, L 15.....Mass.
175*Orleans, N 14.....Mich.
50*Orleans, I 13.....Minn.
815 Orleans, O 14.....Neb.
150 Orleans, M 11.....N. Y.
1332 Orleans, C 16.....Vt.
250 Orleans Cross Roads (Orleans Roads), C 22.....W. Va.
515 Orlinda, K 11.....Tenn.
542*Orlovista, G 18.....Fla.
50*Orma, C 18.....W. Va.
50*Ormas, C 18.....Ind.
277 Orme, Q 13.....Tenn.
1914 Ormond, E 19.....Fla.
500*Ormond Beach, E 19.....Fla.
48*Ormonde, F 7.....Ill.
183*Ormsby, R 9.....Pa.
10 Ormsby, K 11.....Minn.
1602 Orofino, G 6.....Idaho
350*Oro Grande (Halleck), N 18.....Calif.
75 Orogrande, I 8.....Idaho
26*Orogrande, N 13.....N. M.
3000 Orondo, H 14.....Wash.
150 Orono, K 15.....Me.
110 Oronoco, P 19.....Minn.
593 Oronogo, O 6.....Mo.
1200*Orosi, K 13.....Calif.
80*Orovada, B 9.....Nev.
4421 Oroville, F 7.....Calif.
1206 Oroville, B 17.....Wash.
37 Orpha, J 20.....Wyo.
50*Orr, F 22.....Ky.
101 Orr, G 21.....Okla.
20*Orr, P 12.....Okla.
*Orr, D 5.....S. C.
666 Orrick, G 7.....Mo.
175 Orrin, H 14.....N. D.
100 Orrington, L 14.....Me.
459*Orrs Island, P 5.....Me.
294 Orrstown, O 13.....Pa.
250*Orrtanna, Q 14.....Pa.
173*Orrum, K 12.....N. C.
416 Orrville, K 10.....Ala.
4484 Orrville, G 16.....Ohio
417*Orsino, G 20.....Fla.
419 Ortega, K 16.....Fla.
60*Orth, D 15.....Tex.
1211 Orting, K 8.....Wash.
252 Ortiz, Q 11.....Colo.
184 Ortley, K 22.....S. D.
100*Orton, H 9.....Pa.
622 Ortonville, O 21.....Mich.
2469 Ortonville, M 3.....Minn.
15 Orum, J 23.....Neb.
217 Orvin, N 19.....Idaho
185 Orvisburg, P 15.....Miss.
280 Orviston, J 11.....Pa.
500 Orwell, J 15.....N. Y.
2182 Orwigsburg, L 20.....Pa.
475*Orwin, L 18.....Pa.
579 Orwell, C 19.....Ohio
100*Orwell, E 17.....Ohio
80 Orwell, J 5.....Vt.
4198 Osage, B 8.....Iowa
85*Osage, B 8.....Ill.
3196 Osage, I 6.....Iowa
110*Osage, H 6.....Minn.
78 Osage, O 4.....Okla.
628 Osage, E 17.....Okla.
100*Osage, H 13.....Tex.
225 Osage (Osage City), I 14.....Mo.

200 Osage, E 23.....Wyo.
500*Osage, C 13.....W. Va.
40*Osage Beach, K 11.....Mo.
2079 Osage City, I 21.....Kan.
225 Osage City (Osage), I 14.....Mo.
*Osage Hills (Meramee), I 20.....
122 Osage Jc., C 15.....Okla.
600 Osaka, D 4.....Va.
1483 Osakis, K 9.....Minn.
4415 Osawatomie, I 24.....Kan.
30*Osbernville, T 14.....Ill.
50*Osborn, P 15.....N. J.
85 Osborn, F 20.....Miss.
358 Osborn, D 6.....Mont.
1705 Osborn, K 8.....Ohio
45*Osborn (Adams Run), N 17.....S. C.
20*Osborne, E 20.....Iowa
1876 Osborne, F 11.....Kan.
18*Osborne (Townsend), K 12.....Md.
529*Osborne, L 3.....Pa.
500 Osborne, G 19.....Wash.
*Osborns Gap, C 5.....Va.
900 Osbornville, J 19.....N. J.
300 Osborn, E 6.....Idaho
50*Oscaloosa, I 22.....Ky.
65*Oscar, J 4.....Ky.
100*Oscar, K 13.....La.
21 Oscar, D 13.....Mont.
42 Oscar, Q 11.....Okla.
350*Osawana, F 5.....N. Y.
3226 Osceola, E 22.....Ark.
100 Osceola, F 19.....Fla.
498 Osceola, B 15.....Ind.
75*Osceola, E 12.....Ill.
3251*Osceola, N 11.....Iowa
12*Osceola, J 19.....La.
500*Osceola, B 3.....Mich.
1190 Osceola, L 8.....Mo.
1039 Osceola, K 19.....Neb.
90 Osceola, K 16.....N. Y.
568 Osceola, K 7.....Pa.
85*Osceola (Hancock), B 14.....S. C.
35 Osceola, I 21.....S. D.
500*Osceola, F 18.....Tex.
50*Osceola, W 14.....W. Va.
642 Osceola, A 10.....Wis.
2076 Osceola Mills, K 11.....Pa.
100 Osco, D 9.....Ill.
37*Osco, K 16.....Ky.
45 Oscoda, J 21.....Mich.
45 Oscuro, K 13.....N. M.
*Osdick, see Red Mountain.....Calif.
1198 Osgood, M 19.....Ind.
60*Osgood, C 8.....Iowa
183 Osgood, B 10.....Mo.
3 Osgood, N 24.....N. D.
179*Osgood, I 6.....Ohio
200 Osgood, H 7.....Pa.
3*Oshawa, H 11.....Minn.
910 Oshkosh, J 6.....Neb.
39089 Oshkosh, N 16.....Wis.
200*Oshoto, C 21.....Wyo.
200*Oshtemo, Q 12.....Mich.
25*Osie, J 9.....W. Va.
118*Osierfield, M 13.....Ga.
332 Osinda, E 12.....Okla.
1024 Oskaloosa, M 16.....Iowa
800 Oskaloosa, F 22.....Kan.
220 Oskaloosa, M 6.....Mo.
392 Oslo, I 11.....Minn.
48*Osman, H 16.....Ill.
796 Osmond, G 19.....Neb.
269 Osnabrock, E 20.....N. D.
65 Oso, E 9.....Wash.
100*Osprey, K 13.....Fla.
300 Osseo, R 16.....Mich.
738 Osseo, M 15.....Minn.
1105 Osseo, F 13.....Wis.
75*Ossette, C 21.....Mont.
784 Ossian, E 20.....Ind.
822 Ossian, O 19.....Iowa
100*Ossineke, J 21.....Mich.
15996 Ossining, F 6.....N. Y.
350 Ossipee, K 18.....N. H.
25 Ossipee, I 17.....Tenn.
347*Osteen, F 18.....Fla.
242 Osterburg, O 9.....Pa.
78*Osterdock, F 21.....Iowa
105*Osterhout (La Grange), G 20.....Pa.
800 Osterville, M 25, O 12.....Mass.
163*Ostrander, R 20.....Ohio
411 Ostrander, J 11.....Ohio
275 Ostrander, N 20.....Wash.
56*Ostrica, P 20.....La.
56 Oswald, J 25.....W. Va.
320*Oswald, H 15.....W. Va.
225 Oswalt, Q 12.....Okla.
175 Oswayo, E 11.....Pa.
750 Oswegatchie, G 18.....N. Y.
978 Oswego, C 18.....Ill.
125 Oswego, C 16.....Ind.
1913 Oswego, K 23.....Kan.
150 Oswego, E 21.....Mont.
22062 Oswego, K 17.....N. Y.
1726 Oswego, D 7.....Ore.
200 Oswego, G 16.....S. C.
769 Osyka, P 9.....Miss.
43*Otas, J 18.....Ky.
101 Ott, G 21.....Okla.
600 Oteen, O 6.....N. C.
100*Otego, D 13.....Kan.
580 Otego, F 17.....N. Y.
100*Otero, C 19.....N. M.
200*Otey, M 22.....Va.
80*Otey, O 5.....Va.
35*Otho, C 13.....N. C.
332 Othello, L 18.....Wash.
45*Othma, L 14.....
300 Otho, H 6.....Iowa
Otho, see Buckeye.....Ohio
498 Otis, E 21.....Colo.
175 Otis, B 9.....Ind.
150*Otis, J 20.....Iowa
419 Otis, I 10.....Kan.
16*Otis, H 8.....La.
1211 Otis, G 3.....Mass.
50 Otis, N 21.....N. M.
23 Otis, F 4.....Ore.
50 Otis, J 11.....Wis.
300 Otisco, O 18.....Ind.
100*Otisco, Q 16.....Minn.
185 Otisco Lake, M 14.....N. Y.
100*Otisco Valley, M 14.....N. Y.
500 Otisfield, O 4.....Me.
100 Otis Orchards, G 24.....Wash.
534 Otisville, M 20.....Mich.
889*Otisville, E 20.....N. Y.
410 Oto, H 3.....Iowa
200 Otoe, L 23.....Neb.
81*Otravio, F 10.....N. M.
3428 Otsego, P 15.....Mich.
150 Otsego, J 16.....Ohio
300*Otsego, P 6.....W. Va.
50*Otsego, L 19.....Wis.
50*Otsego Lake, J 18.....Mich.
118*Otselic, N 16.....N. Y.

Pop.	Place	Index	State
16*	Ott	A 14	Ark.
16005	Ottawa	D 15	Ill.
10193	Ottawa	H 23	Kan.
26*	Ottawa	I 18	Ky.
125	Ottawa	P 13	Minn.
2342	Ottawa	E 8	Ohio
....	Ottawa	B 24	Okla
35*	Ottawa	J 17	Pa.
300*	Ottawa	N 5	W. Va.
....*	Ottawa Beach	O 11	Mich.
1979	Ottawa Hills	B 9	Ohio
....	Ottawa Jc.	I 23	Kan.
250*	Ottawa Lake	R 21	Mich.
17*	Otter	M 21	Mont.
1963▲	Otter (Ivydale)	J 9	W. Va.
570	Otterbein	G 8	Ind.
600	Otter Creek	E 12	Fla.
13	Ottercreek	H 23	Iowa
159*	Otter Creek	M 17	Me.
15	Otter Creek	M 9	N. D.
....	Otter Creek Jc.	K 6	Ind.
515	Otter Lake	N 21	Mich.
100*	Otter Lake	L 18	N. Y.
11*	Otter Pond	J 8	Ky.
498	Otter River	D 12	Mass.
30*	Otter Rock	F 4	Ore.
254	Ottertail	I 7	Minn.
110*	Otterville	L 9	Ill.
430	Otterville	I 11	Mo.
219	Ottine	L 18	Tex.
5	Otto	E 20	Ill.
15*	Otto	O 18	Ind.
450	Otto	P 4	N. Y.
35*	Otto	Q 5	N. C.
200	Otto	H 19	Tex.
21*	Otto	I 8	W. Va.
300*	Otto	B 11	Wyo.
94*	Ottoman	L 21	Va.
152	Ottosen	E 9	Iowa
467	Ottoville	F 7	Ohio
900	Ottsville	M 23	Pa.
31570	Ottumwa	O 17	Iowa
10	Ottumwa	J 9	S. D.
....	Ottumwa Jc.	N 17	Iowa
250	Otway	J 22	N. C.
235	Otway	P 11	Ohio
125*	Otwell	E 18	Ark.
364	Otwell	P 8	Ind.
89*	Ouachita	N 10	Ark.
76*	Ouaquaga	Q 16	N. Y.
100	Oulu	E 6	Wis.
951	Ouray	M 6	Colo.
30	Ouray	H 22	Utah
113*	Ousley	P 12	Ga.
28*	Outing	I 13	Minn.
208	Outlook	B 23	Mont.
150	Outlook	N 15	Wash.
150	Outville	K 13	Ohio
....*	Outwood	J 9	Ky.
15*	Ova	G 21	Ky.
66*	Oval	C 3	N. C.
500	Oval	I 15	Pa.
250	Ovalo	F 13	Tex.
100	Ovando	H 6	Mont.
....*	Ovapa	K 8	W. Va.
100*	Overall	N 12	Tenn.
90*	Overall	G 13	Va.
10	Overbrook	J 23	Del.
575	Overbrook	H 22	Kan.
110	Overbrook	P 14	Okla.
500*	Overbrook Hills	N 22	Pa.
....	Overcup	G 17	Ark.
100*	Overgaard	F 20	Ariz.
200*	Overhills	H 13	N. C.
150	Overisel	P 12	Mich.
....	Overland Park Junction	G 15	Colo.
2934	Overland	I 20	Mo.
1500	Overland Park	G 24	Kan.
1212*	Overlea	F 14	Md.
125	Overly	F 13	N. D.
500*	Overpeck	M 6	Ohio
117▲	Overstreet	O 10	Fla.
250	Overton	F 14	Ala.
40	Overton	H 12	Mo.
491	Overton	M 14	Neb.
400	Overton	O 23	Nev.
63*	Overton	F 17	Pa.
2313	Overton	F 23	Tex.
467	Ovett	N 18	Miss.
687	Ovid	A 23	Colo.
135	Ovid	Q 22	Idaho
145*	Ovid	H 16	Ind.
1248	Ovid	N 17	Mich.
578	Ovid	N 12	N. Y.
....	Ovid Center, see Sheldrake Springs		N. Y.
1356	Oviedo	G 19	Fla.
19*	Ovil	J 9	Ky.
225	Ovina	L 17	Neb.
24	Ovington	F 3	Wash.
3*	Ovitt	H 14	Neb.
366	Owaneco	K 15	Ill.
105	Owanka	K 5	S. D.
117*	Owasa	G 14	Iowa
32*	Owasco	G 11	Ind.
150	Owasco	M 14	N. Y.
....*	Owasippe	N 11	Mich.
100*	Owassa	N 12	Ala.
371	Owasso	E 19	Okla.
8694	Owatonna	P 16	Minn.
5068	Owego	Q 14	N. Y.
25*	Owen	O 18	Ind.
....	Owen	A 19	Okla.
1083	Owen	H 12	Wis.
296	Owendale	L 22	Mich.
11	Owens	J 22	Del.
40	Owens	H 11	Ohio
23*	Owens	G 15	Tex.
25*	Owens	I 18	Va.
638	Owens	K 6	W. Va.
30245	Owensboro	G 10	Ky.
350	Owensburg	N 10	Ind.
250*	Owens Cross Roads	B 15	Ala.
325*	Owensdale	P 5	Pa.
....	Owensmouth, see Canoga Park		Calif.
10	Owensport	G 7	W. Va.
1188	Owensville	P 4	Ind.
1439	Owensville	J 16	Mo.
334	Owensville	O 8	Ohio
1190	Owenton	D 16	Ky.
27*	Owenton	K 18	Va.
69	Owenyo	J 16	Calif.
107*	Owings	M 14	Md.
400*	Owings	D 8	S. C.
27*	Owings	E 12	W. Va.
130	Owings Mills	E 12	Md.
948	Owingsville	F 19	Ky.
65	Owlhead	M 17	Ariz.
10*	Owls Bend	O 16	Mo.
200*	Owls Head	O 13	Me.
40*	Owls Head	E 22	N. Y.
14424	Owosso	O 19	Mich.
125*	Owsley	H 24	Ky.
25	Owyhee	A 16	Nev.
58*	Oxboro	N 16	Minn.
100*	Oxbow	E 16	Me.
200*	Oxbow	H 16	N. Y.
1393	Oxford	F 19	Ala.
225*	Oxford	B 14	Ark.
22	Oxford	P 6	Colo.
....	Oxford	K 8	Conn.
305	Oxford	F 15	Fla.
616	Oxford	F 9	Ga.
261	Oxford	Q 20	Idaho
863	Oxford	G 7	Ind.
542	Oxford	K 19	Iowa
1020	Oxford	N 16	Kan.
483	Oxford	N 5	Me.
136	Oxford (Welchville)	N 6	Me.
826	Oxford	K 17	Md.
2500	Oxford	H 13	Mass.
2144	Oxford	O 21	Mich.
3433	Oxford	C 15	Miss.
1141	Oxford	N 13	Neb.
1548▲	Oxford (Oxford Furnace)	E 10	N. J.
1713	Oxford	P 16	N. Y.
3991	Oxford	C 14	N. C.
2756	Oxford	M 5	Ohio
2723	Oxford	Q 20	Pa.
85*	Oxford	F 10	W. Va.
404	Oxford	J 17	Wis.
1548▲	Oxford Furnace (Oxford)	E 10	N. J.
705	Oxford Jc.	I 22	Iowa
....	Oxford Jc.	O 14	Neb.
200*	Oxford Mills	J 22	Iowa
103*	Oxley	D 11	Ark.
106	Oxly	R 19	Mo.
200	Oxmoor	G 12	Ala.
8519	Oxnard	O 13	Calif.
29*	Oxonia (Hitchcock)	O 14	Ind.
30*	Oxville	J 8	Ill.
104*	Oyens	E 3	Iowa
250*	Oyster	N 23	Va.
7500	Oyster Bay	H 7	N. Y.
466*	Oyster Bay Cove	H 7	N. Y.
....*	Oysterpoint	O 20	Va.
54	Oysterville (Winant)	G 3	Ore.
38	Oysterville	M 2	Wash.
133*	Ozan	O 6	Ark.
3601	Ozark	N 20	Ala.
1402	Ozark	F 6	Ark.
90	Ozark	Q 17	Ill.
42*	Ozark	J 15	Ky.
156*	Ozark	F 15	Mich.
961	Ozark	P 10	Mo.
75*	Ozark	K 19	Ohio
4	Ozark	H 22	Okla.
12*	Ozark	C 21	Tex.
60*	Ozark Beach	Q 11	Mo.
201	Ozawkie	F 23	Kan.
113*	Ozeana	K 19	Va.
20*	Ozette	F 1	Wash.
30*	Ozona	I 12	Fla.
1200	Ozona	I 11	Tex.
78*	Ozone	E 8	Ark.
200*	Ozone	N 16	Tenn.
....*	Ozone Park	H 6	N. Y.

P

Pop.	Place	Index	State
300*	Paavola	B 6	Mich.
150	Pablo	F 4	Mont.
426	Pace	E 7	Miss.
50*	Paces	Q 10	Va.
200*	Pachaug	G 22	Conn.
313	Pachuta	L 19	Miss.
20*	Pacific	G 10	Calif.
1687	Pacific	J 19	Mo.
357	Pacific	J 9	Wash.
....	Pacific Beach	Q 18	Calif.
436▲	Pacific Beach	J 1	Wash.
50	Pacific City	E 4	Ore.
6249	Pacific Grove	K 6	Calif.
558	Pacific Jc.	O 3	Iowa
....	Pacific Jc.	D 13	Mont.
....*	Pacific Palisades	N 15	Calif.
800*	Packanack Lake	C 18	N. J.
600*	Packard	K 19	Ky.
....	Packard	I 14	Me.
19	Packard	J 20	Wash.
65	Packer (Packerville)	G 23	Conn.
75*	Packerton (Packertown)	D 16	Ind.
590	Packerton	K 21	Pa.
500*	Packerton Junction	J 21	Pa.
65*	Packerville (Packer)	G 23	Conn.
194*	Packsville (Paxville)	H 17	S. C.
....*	Packsville	N 7	W. Va.
31	Packton	F 9	La.
200	Packwaukee	K 17	Wis.
....	Packwaukee Jc.	J 17	Wis.
256	Packwood	N 18	Iowa
....	Packwood	L 6	Wash.
....*	Pacoima	N 16 (Pop. incl. in Los Angeles)	Calif.
352	Pacolet	B 10	S. C.
2000*	Pacolet Mills	B 10	S. C.
30	Pactola	J 3	S. D.
129*	Pactolus	E 22	Ky.
369	Pactolus	F 19	N. C.
5*	Pad	I 8	W. Va.
25*	Paddock (Hillview)	J 6	Minn.
5	Paddy	Q 14	Mo.
194	Paden	B 23	Miss.
620	Paden	J 16	Okla.
....*	Padena	B 6	Ga.
2215	Paden City	C 9	W. Va.
21*	Paderborn	N 10	Ill.
180	Padroni	B 20	Colo.
45*	Padua	G 16	Ill.
33765	Paducah	J 5	Ky.
2677	Paducah	B 13	Tex.
50	Padus	M 10	Wis.
100*	Paeonian Springs	E 16	Va.
....*	Page	D 6	Idaho
....*	Page, see Page City		Kan.
335	Page	F 16	Neb.
428	Page	L 22	N. D.
422▲	Page	M 25	Okla.
25	Page (Redd)	N 19	Wash.
1200	Page	M 8	W. Va.
20*	Page Centre	P 6	Iowa
84*	Page City	G 4	Kan.
989	Pageland	C 16	S. C.
....*	Pages Mill, see Lake View		S. C.
700*	Pageton	R 7	W. Va.
7	Pagoda	D 7	Colo.
50	Pagosa Jc.	Q 8	Colo.
1591	Pagosa Springs	P 8	Colo.
515*	Paguate	G 5	N. M.
10	Paha	K 20	Wash.
4766	Pahokee	L 21	Fla.
70*	Paicines	K 8	Calif.
250	Paige	K 19	Tex.
300	Paincourtville	N 15	La.
....	Paine	H 9	Pa.
25	Paines	M 18	Mich.
2674	Painesdale	D 2	Mich.
12235	Painesville	B 18	Ohio
58	Paint Bank	M 5	Va.
325	Paint Cliff	K 17	Ky.
1700	Paint Creek	N 8	Pa.
2337	Painted Post	Q 11	N. Y.
300	Painter	L 23	Va.
25*	Painter	C 7	Wyo.
50	Paintersville	H 8	Calif.
28*	Paintfork	N 8	N. C.
18*	Paint Gap	N 9	N. C.
250	Paint Lick	H 18	Ky.
75	Painton	O 22	Mo.
282	Paint Rock	B 16	Ala.
120*	Paintrock	N 7	N. C.
390	Paint Rock	H 13	Tex.
2324	Paintsville	G 22	Ky.
18*	Pairs Store	Q 16	Va.
221	Paisaje	Q 11	Colo.
....	Paisano	J 6	Tex.
125*	Paisley	F 17	Fla.
237	Paisley	O 13	Ore.
25	Pajarito	G 10	N. M.
260	Pala	P 19	Calif.
....*	Palace	L 14	Mo.
2288	Palacious	N 21	Tex.
2222	Palatine	B 19	Ill.
585*	Palatine Bridge	N 21	N. Y.
7140	Palatka	D 17	Fla.
281	Palco	F 9	Kan.
300*	Palenville	Q 23	N. Y.
300	Palermo	F 7	Calif.
50	Palermo	M 10	Me.
178	Palermo	F 7	N. D.
25*	Palermo	M 4	W. Va.
345	Palestine	H 18	Ark.
1626	Palestine	L 22	Ill.
100*	Palestine	D 15	Ind.
200*	Palestine	J 6	Ohio
12144	Palestine	G 21	Tex.
310	Palestine	F 7	W. Va.
202*	Palisade	I 16	Minn.
799	Palisade	N 9	Neb.
120	Palisade	D 16	Nev.
1400*	Palisade	C 19	N. J.
855	Palisades	I 4	Colo.
400*	Palisades	E 5	N. Y.
300	Palisades	I 15	Wash.
....*	Palisades Park	Q 11	Mich.
8141	Palisades Park	D 21	N. J.
400*	Palito Blanco	P 17	Tex.
50*	Palliser, see Hodge		Calif.
150*	Pall Mall	L 16	Tenn.
125*	Palls	L 18	Va.
200*	Palm	M 22	Pa.
15*	Palm	O 13	Tex.
50	Palma	H 16	N. M.
300*	Palma Sola	J 13	Fla.
150*	Palm Bay (Tillman)	I 22	Fla.
3747	Palm Beach	L 24	Fla.
27*	Palm Beach Harbor	L 23	Fla.
100*	Palm City	Q 19	Calif.
95*	Palm City	K 23	Fla.
600	Palmdale	N 16	Calif.
100 *	Palmdale	L 18	Fla.
326	Palmer	K 14	Ill.
75*	Palmer	C 7	Ind.
305	Palmer	F 8	Iowa
182*	Palmer	E 17	Kan.
37*	Palmer	G 19	Ky.
9149■	Palmer	H 9	Mass.
650	Palmer	E 6	Mich.
110*	Palmer	L 17	Mo.
516	Palmer	K 17	Neb.
....*	Palmer	L 23	N. Y.
12	Palmer	D 9	Ore.
1228	Palmer	P 14	Tenn.
697*	Palmer	E 19	Tex.
55	Palmer	L 21	Va.
160	Palmer	J 9	Wash.
200*	Palmer	I 11	W. Va.
10	Palmer Jc.	D 21	Ore.
....	Palmer Jc.	I 9	Wash.
269	Palmer Lake	I 15	Colo.
1540*	Palmer Mine (Antram)	Q 4	Pa.
300	Palmers	E 14	Ala.
40*	Palmers	O 14	Md.
45*	Palmer Springs	Q 12	Va.
175*	Palmersville	L 5	Tenn.
7475	Palmerton	K 22	Pa.
....	Palmertown	K 21	Conn.
69	Palmerville	G 8	N. C.
3491	Palmetto	J 13	Fla.
1029	Palmetto	G 5	Ga.
444*	Palmetto	K 11	La.
500*	Palm Harbor (Sutherland)	I 12	Fla.
1218*	Palms	Q 2	Calif.
319	Palms	L 24	Mich.
3434*	Palm Springs	O 20	Calif.
54*	Palm Springs (White Water)	O 19	Calif.
40*	Palmyra	N 14	Ark.
824	Palmyra	K 10	Ill.
274	Palmyra	P 14	Ind.
45	Palmyra	K 11	Me.
300	Palmyra	R 19	Mich.
2285	Palmyra	D 16	Mo.
401	Palmyra	M 23	Neb.
5178	Palmyra	K 10	N. J.
2709	Palmyra	L 11	N. Y.
93*	Palmyra	D 18	N. C.
300	Palmyra (Diamond)	F 19	Ohio
5239	Palmyra	N 17	Pa.
100*	Palmyra	L 9	Tenn.
145	Palmyra	K 13	Va.
711	Palmyra	M 21	Wis.
250	Palo	P 19	Iowa
175	Palo	N 16	Mich.
16774	Palo Alto	F 20	Calif.
1934	Palo Alto	L 19	Pa.
27*	Palo Cedro	D 7	Calif.
25*	Paloduro	D 4	Tex.
140	Paloma	I 5	Ill.
14*	Palomar Mt.	P 19	Calif.
....	Palomas	L 7	Ariz.
27*	Palopinto	J 9	Mo.
482	Palo Pinto	E 16	Tex.
250*	Palos	F 11	Ala.
....*	Palos Heights	C 21	Ill.
596	Palos Park	C 20	Ill.
1028	Palouse	K 25	Wash.
500	Palo Verde	K 10	Ariz.
108▲	Palo Verde	P 22	Calif.
987*	Palos Verdes Estates	N 15	Calif.
164*	Paluxy	F 17	Tex.
5*	Palzo	P 15	Ill.
92*	Pamlico	I 21	N. C.
12895	Pampa	C 5	Tex.
28*	Pampa	M 20	Va.
555	Pamplico	G 20	S. C.
273	Pamplin	N 12	Va.
5966	Pana	K 15	Ill.
350	Panaca	K 23	Nev.
200 *	Panacea	C 5	Fla.
627	Panama	L 12	Ill.
255	Panama	K 4	Iowa
13*	Panama	F 21	Ky.
25	Panama	K 6	Mo.
174	Panama	M 23	Neb.
374	Panama	Q 2	N. Y.
70*	Panama (North Clymer)	Q 3	N. Y.
880	Panama	J 24	Okla.
11610	Panama City	O 9	Fla.
500*	Panama City Beach	N 9	Fla.
....*	Panamint Springs	K 16	Calif.
25	Panasoffkee	G 15	Fla.
75*	Panco	I 20	Ky.
100	Pancoast	K 8	W. Va.
112	Pancoastburg	M 11	Ohio
10*	Pandale	J 11	Tex.
35	Pando	H 10	Colo.
690	Pandora	F 8	Ohio
261	Pandora	M 17	Tex.
595	Pangburn	F 14	Ark.
1979	Panguitch	O 8	Utah
978	Panhandle	C 4	Tex.
35	Panic	J 7	Pa.
150*	Panna Maria	M 17	Tex.
150	Panola	H 4	Ala.
51*	Panola	F 15	Ill.
48*	Panola	G 18	Ky.
65	Panola	L 22	Okla.
1169	Panora	K 9	Iowa
200*	Pansey	O 22	Ala.
20*	Pansey	I 8	Pa.
57*	Pansey	G 18	W. Va.
25*	Pantano	O 18	Ariz.
294	Pantego	F 21	N. C.
28*	Panther	H 23	Pa.
300	Panther	Q 4	W. Va.
30*	Panther Burn	H 7	Miss.
30	Panton	H 5	Vt.
400	Paola	G 18	Fla.
3511	Paola	I 25	Kan.
11	Paola	D 5	Mont.
85	Paoli	C 22	Colo.
2218	Paoli	O 12	Ind.
423	Paoli	L 13	Okla.
2500	Paoli	P 22	Pa.
1117	Paonia	J 6	Colo.
50*	Papalote	O 18	Tex.
625*	Paperville (Modena)	P 21	Pa.
763	Papllion	K 23	Neb.
158*	Papineau	F 21	Ill.
200	Papoose	J 17	Okla.
10*	Parade	G 11	S. D.
300	Paradis	O 17	La.
75	Paradise	O 24	Ariz.
1250*	Paradise	E 7	Calif.
161	Paradise	G 11	Kan.
49*	Paradise	H 10	Ky.
300	Paradise	G 3	Mont.
15*	Paradise	B 23	Ore.
525	Paradise	P 20	Pa.
400	Paradise	D 17	Tex.
500	Paradise	D 12	Utah
33*	Paradise	J 4	W. Va.
3*	Paradise Inn	K 8	Wash.
400	Paradise Valley	B 11	Nev.
24	Paradox	L 2	Colo.
44*	Paradox	G 24	N. Y.
100	Paragon	L 3	Ala.
454	Paragon	K 11	Ind.
75*	Paragon	F 20	Ky.
365	Paragonah	O 7	Utah
7079	Paragould	C 20	Ark.
143	Paraloma	N 5	Ark.
22	Paralta	I 21	Iowa
3688*	Paramus	C 19	N. J.
250	Parchman	E 9	Miss.
934*	Parchment	Q 13	Mich.
604	Parco	O 14	Wyo.
....*	Parcoal	K 12	W. Va.
217*	Parcperdue	N 12	La.
19*	Pardee	H 5	Idaho
218	Pardee	D 5	Va.
1000*	Pardeesville	I 20	Pa.
1001	Pardeeville	K 18	Wis.
230	Pardoe	I 3	Pa.
50	Pardus	I 8	Pa.
30	Parent	L 13	Minn.
250	Parhams	G 12	La.
3430	Paris	G 7	Ark.
932	Paris	Q 22	Idaho
9281	Paris	J 22	Ill.
150	Paris (Paris Crossing)	N 18	Ind.
61*	Paris (Bunch)	P 16	Iowa
6697	Paris	E 18	Ky.
160	Paris	N 5	Me.
30*	Paris (Mt. Harmony)	M 14	Md.
150	Paris	M 13	Mich.
62*	Paris	C 16	Miss.
1473	Paris	F 14	Mo.
40	Paris	G 21	Mont.
85*	Paris	L 18	N. Y.
225	Paris	G 19	Ohio
6395	Paris	L 6	Tenn.
18678	Paris	C 21	Tex.
75*	Paris	F 14	Va.
1000	Parish (Parrish)	J 13	Fla.
109	Parish	K 20	Ga.
521	Parish	K 15	N. Y.
450	Parishville	D 20	N. Y.
17*	Paris Station	M 18	N. Y.
200*	Park (Buffalo Park)	G 6	Kan.
35*	Park	J 13	Ky.
40	Park	C 8	Wash.
354*	Park City (Glasgow Jc.)	J 14	Ky.
350	Park City	L 15	Mont.
3739	Park City	F 13	Utah
1000*	Park Crest	K 19	Pa.
278	Parkdale	R 16	Ark.
40	Parkdale	K 13	Colo.
125	Parkdale	D 10	Ore.
200	Parker	I 4	Ariz.
200	Parker	G 15	Colo.
245▲	Parker	N 9	Fla.
384	Parker	M 20	Idaho
26	Parker	Q 17	Ill.
786	Parker (Parker City)	H 20	Ind.
361	Parker	J 24	Kan.
112*	Parker	C 3	N. C.
30	Parker	M 17	Okla.
20	Parker	G 6	Ore.
1244	Parker	M 23	S. D.
5*	Parker	O 7	Tenn.
100*	Parker	I 16	Va.
125	Parker	M 13	Wash.
976*	Parker City (Parkers Landing)	I 5	Pa.
150*	Parker Dam	N 18, P 9	Calif.
375	Parker Ford	O 21	Pa.
257	Parkersburg	M 20	Ill.
50*	Parkersburg	I 10	Ind.
1260	Parkersburg	G 15	Iowa
105*	Parkersburg	J 15	N. C.
30103	Parkersburg	E 6	W. Va.
40	Parkersglen	G 24	Pa.
200*	Parkers Lake (Cumberland Falls)	J 17	Ky.
976	Parkers Landing (Parker City)	I 5	Pa.
781	Parkers Prairie	J 8	Minn.
150	Parkerton	J 18	Wyo.
235*	Parkertown	M 17	N. J.
105*	Parkerville	H 18	Kan.
2288	Parkesburg	P 21	Pa.
3252	Park Falls	H 8	Wis.
100	Parkfield	L 10	Calif.
300	Park Grove	E 20	Mont.
55*	Park Hall	P 15	Md.
300	Park Hill	G 23	Okla.
700*	Parkhill	M 8	Pa.
1615	Park Hills	C 17	Ky.
1412	Parkin	G 20	Ark.
....	Park Jc.	L 9	Wash.
20*	Parkland	G 12	Ill.
680*	Parkland	N 24	Pa.
750	Parkland	J 8	Wash.
....*	Park Lane	F 18	Va.
125	Parkman	J 11	Me.
300	Parkman	D 19	Ohio
260	Parkman	A 13	Wyo.
250*	Park Place	D 8	Ore.
370*	Park Place	J 19	Pa.
430	Park Place	L 22	Tex.
2643	Park Rapids	H 9	Minn.
77*	Park Rapids	D 22	Wash.
12063	Park Ridge	B 21	Ill.
2519	Park Ridge	C 20	N. J.
1408	Park River	F 21	N. D.
500	Parkrose	D 8	Ore.
30*	Parks (Maine)	D 13	Ariz.
50*	Parks	I 6	Ark.
150	Parks	O 7	Neb.
150*	Parks (Brogueville)	P 17	Pa.
500*	Parks	E 15	Tex.
1579*	Parkside	P 23	Pa.
701	Parksley	L 24	Va.
150	Park Springs	C 17	Tex.
1305	Parkston	M 20	S. D.
225	Parksville	H 16	Ky.
500	Parksville	C 2	N. Y.
168*	Parksville	I 7	S. C.
300	Parkton	B 13	Md.
441	Parkton	J 12	N. C.
25	Park Valley	B 4	Utah
500	Park View	C 10	N. M.
208*	Parkview	D 17	Ohio
....	Parkville	F 13	Conn.
85*	Parkville	I 18	Ill.
....*	Parkville	E 14	Md.
....*	Parkville	F 19	Minn.
671	Parkville	F 5	Mo.
15*	Parkway	K 8	Wash.
79	Parkwood	G 12	Ala.
125*	Parkwater	H 23	Wash.
....	Parler, see Santee		S. C.
35	Parlett	I 20	Ohio
776*	Parlier	K 10	Calif.
135	Parlin	K 9	Colo.
1500	Parlin	G 17	N. J.
35*	Parma	D 13	Ark.
1085	Parma	N 3	Idaho
575	Parma	Q 16	Mich.
1187	Parma	H 24, Q 22	Mo.
16365*	Parma	D 16	Ohio
1330*	Parma Heights	D 17	Ohio
417	Parmele	F 19	N. C.
245	Parmelee	N 10	S. D.
65*	Parmleysville	K 17	Ky.
6240	Parnassus	M 4	Pa.
71*	Parnassus	J 11	Va.
34*	Parnell	H 16	Ill.
263	Parnell	L 18	Iowa
12	Parnell	E 23	Kan.
32*	Parnell	J 16	Ky.
....	Parnell	O 14	Mich.
450	Parnell	A 6	Mo.
25*	Parnell	E 5	Tex.
315	Parole	I 14	Md.
62*	Paron	J 11	Ark.
1525	Parowan	O 6	Utah
124	Parr	D 8	Ind.
....*	Parr	E 12	S. C.
125*	Parran	L 14	Md.
870	Parrish	E 10	Ala.
1000*	Parrish (Parish)	J 13	Fla.
75	Parrish	O 16	Ill.
100	Parrish	K 10	Wis.
....	Parrish Jc.	K 10	Wis.
250	Parris Island	Q 15	S. C.
50	Parrot	H 19	Ky.
....	Parrot	J 10	Me.
337	Parrott	L 6	Ga.
99	Parrottsville	N 22	Tenn.
521*	Parryville	K 21	Pa.
75	Parshall	E 11	Colo.
570	Parshall	H 7	N. D.
50	Parshallville	P 20	Mich.
210	Parsippany	D 16	N. J.
10*	Parsley (Hale)	N 3	W. Va.
14294	Parsons	N 23	Kan.
....*	Parsons	H 20 (Pop. 5628 incl. in Wilkes-Barre)	Pa.
1079	Parsons	O 7	Tenn.
2077	Parsons	F 16	W. Va.
211	Parsonsburg	N 23	Md.
....	Parsonsfield	P 2	Me.
150*	Parsonville	D 4	N. C.
150*	Parthenon	C 9	Ark.
65*	Partlow	J 16	Va.
230	Partridge	K 14	Kan.
54*	Partridge	I 22	Ky.
50*	Parvin (Cressy)	G 19	Ky.
81864	Pasadena	O 16, Q 4	Calif.
205*	Pasadena	G 14	Md.
3436*	Pasadena	L 23	Tex.
16	Pasamonte	D 22	N. M.
5900	Pascagoula	R 22	Miss.
8	Paschal	J 6	Ga.
35*	Paschall (Merry Mount)	C 15	N. C.
34*	Pasche	H 13	Tex.
3913	Pasco	N 18	Wash.
1046	Pascoag	B 7	R. I.
345	Pascola	J 24	Mo.
45*	Paskenta	E 5	Calif.
3045	Paso Robles	L 9	Calif.
....*	Passaconoway	I 15	N. H.
200	Passadumkeag	L 15	Me.
398*	Pass-A-Grille Beach (Passagrille)	I 12	Fla.
75*	Passaic	J 6	Mo.
61394	Passaic	D 19	N. J.
2*	Passaic	B 16	Wyo.
63*	Passapatanzy	I 17	Va.
209	Patapsco	D 12	Md.
3338	Pass Christian	R 17	Miss.
30*	Passing	K 17	Va.
....	Passmore	J 10	Pa.
250	Passumpsic	F 18	Vt.
....*	Passyunk	P 23	Pa.
53*	Pastoria	L 24	Va.
200*	Pastura	H 17	N. M.
500	Patagonia	P 18	Ariz.
25	Pataha City	M 24	Wash.
209	Patapsco	D 12	Md.
824	Pataskala	K 13	Ohio
195	Patch Grove	F 20	Wis.
7181	Patchogue	H 9	N. Y.
484	Pateros	F 15	Wash.
139656	Paterson	D 19	N. J.
150	Paterson	O 16	Wash.
100	Patesville	G 11	Ky.
10*	Path (Warble)	M 14	Pa.
500	Pathfork	K 20	Ky.
150*	Patillo (Pattillo)	M 14	S. C.
240*	Patmos	P 7	Ark.
682	Patoka	M 15	Ill.
569	Patoka	P 5	Ind.
394	Paton	I 9	Iowa
500	Patoutville	N 12	La.
21*	Patricia	N 8	S. D.
40*	Patricia	E 10	Tex.
30*	Patrick	D 6	Ark.
32*	Patrick	F 23	Ky.
195*	Patrick	Q 1	N. C.
270*	Patrick	D 18	S. C.
500	Patricksburg	L 9	Ind.
60*	Patrick Springs (Shuff)	Q 5	Va.
257	Patriot	N 22	Ind.
100*	Patroon	G 24	Tex.
125	Patsburg	M 16	Ala.
38*	Patsey	G 19	Ky.
20	Patt	P 20	Colo.
225	Pattee (West Canaan)	L 10	N. H.
1250	Patten	G 16	Me.
500	Pattenburg	F 10	N. J.
....	Patten Jc.	G 16	Me.
284	Patterson (Jelks)	G 17	Ark.
1109	Patterson	I 8	Calif.
541	Patterson	N 19	Ga.
300*	Patterson	J 11	Idaho
201	Patterson (Wilmington)	J 8	Ill.
166*	Patterson	M 11	Iowa
1800	Patterson	O 14	La.
200*	Patterson	O 19	Mo.
600	Patterson	D 7	N. Y.
158*	Patterson	E 3	N. C.
198*	Patterson	G 9	Ohio
....	Patterson	K 22	Okla.
657*	Patterson Heights	L 2	Pa.
140	Pattersons Creek (Patterson)	C 20	W. Va.
108*	Patterson Springs	H 3	N. C.
200*	Pattersonville	M 22	N. Y.
24*	Pattersonville (Augusta)	G 19	Ohio
205*	Pattison	L 6	Miss.
200*	Pattison	K 21	Tex.
650	Patton	E 9	Ala.
4100	Patton	Q 10	Calif.
100*	Patton	N 21	Ill.
30*	Patton	F 11	Ind.
108*	Patton	N 21	Mo.
....	Patton	D 6	Ore.
3085	Patton	L 9	Pa.
1017	Pattonsburg	C 7	Mo.
83*	Pattonville	I 19	Mo.
200*	Pattonville	C 21	Tex.
200*	Patzau	C 5	Wis.
54*	Paul	N 11	Ala.
300*	Paul (Paul Spur)	P 22	Ariz.
606	Paul	Q 14	Idaho
40	Paul	M 24	Neb.
8*	Paulden	G 11	Ariz.
155	Paulding	L 8	Miss.
11	Paulding	K 23	Mo.
2044	Paulding	E 6	Ohio
200*	Paulette	G 21	Miss.
87*	Paulina	L 17	La.
25	Paulina	I 15	Ore.
10	Pauline	Q 17	Idaho
34*	Pauline	K 11	Ky.
119	Pauline	N 17	Neb.
39*	Pauline	C 9	S. C.
1230	Paullina	D 4	Iowa
7011	Paulsboro	L 7	N. J.
125*	Pauls Cross Roads	K 19	Va.
315	Paulsen (Wasioto)	K 20	Ky.
237*	Paul Smiths	D 21	N. Y.
300*	Paul Spur (Paul)	P 22	Ariz.
5104	Pauls Valley	M 12	Okla.
100	Paulton	P 16	Ill.
....	Paunina	M 10	Ore.
106*	Paupack	G 24	Pa.
100*	Pavia	N 9	Pa.
20	Pavilion	Q 14	Mich.
425	Pavilion	M 7	N. Y.
176	Pavilion	I 10	Wyo.
706	Pavo	O 10	Ga.
200*	Pavonia	G 13	Ohio
950*	Paw Creek (Thrift)	H 5	N. C.
5443	Pawhuska	C 16	Okla.
300	Pawlet	N 6	Vt.
300*	Pawleys Island (Waverly Mills)	J 21	S. C.
1446	Pawling	D 6	N. Y.
....	Pawn	I 4	Ore.
36*	Pawnee (Union)	D 20	Colo.
1006	Pawnee	J 13	Ill.
1647*	Pawnee (Pawnee City)	O 23	Neb.
2742	Pawnee	D 15	Okla.
1647	Pawnee City (Pawnee)	O 23	Neb.
388	Pawnee Rock	J 11	Kan.
75*	Pawnee Sta. (Anna)	L 25	Kan.
523	Pawpaw	C 15	Ill.
161*	Paw Paw	H 24	Ky.
1910	Paw Paw	Q 12	Mich.
25	Pawpaw	I 24	Okla.
990	Paw Paw	D 22	W. Va.
100*	Paw Paw Lake	Q 10	Mich.
75797	Pawtucket	D 15	R. I.
2000	Pawtuxet	F 17	R. I.
608	Pax	N 8	W. Va.
237	Paxico	G 20	Kan.
250*	Paxinos	J 16	Pa.
1707*	Paxtang	M 16	Pa.
25	Paxton	E 9	Calif.
50	Paxton	L 7	Fla.
3106	Paxton	G 19	Ill.
317	Paxton	M 7	Ind.
22*	Paxton	G 21	Ky.
250	Paxton	F 13	Mass.
8	Paxton	F 22	Mont.
551	Paxton	K 8	Neb.
....	Paxton	F 17	Ohio
10	Paxton	O 15	S. D.
119*	Paxton	G 24	Tex.
400	Paxtonville	K 15	Pa.
194*	Paxville (Packsville)	H 14	S. C.
3322	Payette	M 3	Idaho
55*	Payment	F 16	Mich.
10	Payne	P 3	Iowa
25*	Payne	G 19	Minn.
1003	Payne	F 5	Ohio
5	Payne	L 12	Okla.
....*	Payne Gap	I 22	Ky.
535*	Paynes (Payne)	I 10	Ga.
36*	Paynes Creek	E 6	Calif.
50*	Paynesville	N 19	Ind.
105*	Paynesville	B 23	Mich.
1317	Paynesville	M 10	Minn.
150	Paynesville	F 18	Mo.
28*	Paynesville	Q 4	W. Va.
53*	Payneville	F 12	Ky.
250	Payson	I 16	Ariz.
456	Payson	I 4	Ill.
96	Payson	I 14	Okla.
3591	Payson	H 12	Utah
57*	Paytes	I 16	Va.
35*	Payton	F 21	Ky
57*	Peabody	D 18	Ind.
1367	Peabody	K 17	Kan.
25*	Peabody	I 19	Ky.
21711	Peabody	D 20	Mass.
2000	Peace Dale	L 12	R. I.
45*	Peace Valley	Q 15	Mo.
150	Peach	G 20	Wash.
150	Peacham	F 16	Vt.
15	Peach Bottom	Q 19	Pa.
85*	Peachburg	K 20	Ala.
500	Peach Creek	N 4	W. Va.
27*	Peach Glen	P 15	Pa.
390	Peachland	I 8	N. C.
374	Peach Orchard	B 19	Ark.
49	Peach Orchard	F 23	Ky.
129	Peach Springs	F 7	Ariz.
125*	Peacock	L 7	Ala.
50 *	Peacock	L 13	Mich.
216	Peacock	D 12	Tex.
4	Peak (Alta)	M 21	N. D.
147*	Peak	F 12	S. C.
150*	Peake (Peaks Turnout)	L 17	Va.
27*	Peakland	O 17	Tenn.
125*	Peakville (Trout Brook)	R 19	N. Y.
....*	Peapack	E 14 (Pop. incl. in Peapack-Gladstone)	N. J.
1354	Peapack-Gladstone	E 14	N. J.

Pop.	Place	Index	State
18	*Peapatch	B 8	Va.
306	Pear	O 9	W. Va.
250	Pearce	O 22	Ariz.
217	Pearcy	K 8	Ark.
72	Pea Ridge	A 5	Ark.
160	*Pearblossom	N 15	Calif.
987	Pearisburg	N 3	Va.
539	Pearl	K 7	Ill.
20	*Pearl	K 18	Ky.
75	*Pearl (Chili)	I 16	Ohio
126	*Pearl	H 17	Tex.
40	Pearl	F 17	Wash.
500	*Pearland	L 22	Tex.
210	*Pearlbeach	O 25	Mich.
447	Pearl City	B 12	Ill.
130	Pearl Creek	M 7	N. Y.
318	Pearlington	R 15	Miss.
612	Pearl River	L 20	La.
3300	*Pearl River	G 5	N. Y.
....	*Pearly	B 7	Va.
54	*Pearman	H 12	Ky.
48	Pearre	C 1	Md.
3164	Pearsall	N 15	Tex.
75	*Pearson	F 13	Ark.
1057	Pearson	N 15	Ga.
40	*Pearson	O 16	Md.
164	*Pearson	K 12	Miss.
66	*Pearson	K 14	Okla.
50	Pearson	H 7	Wash.
125	Pearson	L 10	Wis.
35	Pearsonia	B 17	Okla.
45	*Pear Valley	H 15	Tex.
135	*Peary	N 21	Va.
126	Pease	L 14	Minn.
300	*Peasleeville	E 23	N. Y.
25	Peason	H 6	La.
220	*Peaster	D 17	Tex.
95	*Peavine	M 16	Tenn.
103	*Peay	N 16	Tenn.
150	*Pebble Beach	K 7	Calif.
36	*Pebworth	H 19	Ky.
96	*Pecan	Q 21	Miss.
409	*Pecan Gap	C 21	Tex.
50	*Pecan Island	O 10	La.
231	Pecan Point	F 22	Ark.
1302	Pecatonica	A 13	Ill.
165	Peck	G 5	Idaho
135	Peck	N 16	Kan.
381	Peck	M 24	Mich.
....	*Peck, see Ocala		Va.
30	Peckham	D 16	Colo.
120	Peckham	B 13	Okla.
61	*Pecks Mill	N 4	W. Va.
....	*Pecks Pond	H 23	Pa.
10	Pecksport	M 16	N. Y.
25	*Pecksridge	E 20	Ky.
8000	Peckville	G 21	Pa.
800	Peconic	F 11	N. Y.
1441	▲Pecos	F 15	N. M.
4855	Pecos	H 6	Tex.
206	Peculiar	I 6	Mo.
60	Pedee	G 5	Ore.
65	*Peden	C 4	N. C.
53	Pedernal	H 15	N. M.
50	*Pedigo	I 23	Tex.
200	*Pedlar Mills	M 10	Va.
200	Pedricktown	L 5	N. J.
150	Pedro	F 14	Fla.
30	*Pedro	Q 13	Ohio
14	Pedro	I 7	S. D.
....	*Pedro	K 19	Va.
57	*Pedro Valley	I 5, G 17	Calif.
150	Peebles	N 12	La.
1356	Peebles	P 11	Ohio
60	*Peebles	N 17	Wis.
150	Pee Dee	J 9	N. C.
31	Peedee (Pee Dee)	F 20	S. C.
12	*Peek	F 3	Okla.
17311	Peekskill	E 5	N. Y.
30	*Peeksville	H 7	Wis.
72	*Peel	A 10	Ark.
825	Pe-Ell	M 4	Wash.
....	*Peely	H 20 (Pop. 127 incl. in Hanover)	Pa.
103	*Peerless	C 21	Mont.
15	Peerless	I 16	Utah
113	*Peers	I 17	Mo.
207	Peetz	B 20	Colo.
272	Peever	D 23	S. D.
93	Peggs	F 22	Okla.
138	Pegram	R 23	Idaho
300	*Pegram	M 10	Tenn.
1208	*Peirce City (Pierce City)	P 7	Mo.
400	Pejepscot (Pejepscot Mills)	O 7	Me.
19407	Pekin	G 13	Ill.
386	Pekin	O 15	Ind.
50	*Pekin	N 18	Iowa
50	*Pekin	F 21	Ky.
320	Pekin (Nikep)	N 5	Md.
229	Pekin	I 19	N. D.
....	Pekin Jc.	F 14	Ill.
938	Pelahatchee	K 13	Miss.
46	*Pelan	B 4	Minn.
36	*Peletier	K 19	N. C.
450	*Pelham	G 13	Ala.
2579	Pelham	O 7	Ga.
400	Pelham	F 9	Mass.
150	Pelham	R 16	N. H.
1918	*Pelham	G 6	N. Y.
750	*Pelham	C 11	N. C.
330	Pelham	B 7	S. C.
165	*Pelham	P 13	Tenn.
150	Pelham	F 19	Tex.
5302	*Pelham Manor	F 6	N. Y.
310	Pelican	F 5	La.
....	Pelican	J 13	Ore.
60	Pelican Lake	L 23	Fla.
200	Pelican Lake (Pelican)	K 9	Wis.
1560	Pelican Rapids	I 5	Minn.
212	Pelion	I 12	S. C.
100	*Pelkie	E 4	Mich.
3638	Pella	M 15	Iowa
900	Pell City	F 16	Ala.
50	*Pell Lake	N 21	Wis.
....	Pells	H 24	N. Y.
562	Pellston	F 15	Mich.
116	*Pellville	G 11	Ky.
3712	Pelly	L 23	Tex.
95	*Pellyton	I 16	Ky.
40	Pelo (Bulah)	K 4	Ky.
12	*Pelsor	F 9	Ark.
19	Pelto	G 20	N. D.
80	*Pelzer	Q 7	Ind.
4000	Pelzer	C 6	S. C.
392	Pemaquid	O 10	Me.
28	*Pemaquid Beach	O 10	Me.
194	*Pemaquid Harbor	O 10	Me.
160	*Pemaquid Point	P 10	Me.
....	Pemberton	F 21	Mass.
129	Pemberton	Q 14	Minn.
906	Pemberton	K 13	N. J.
200	Pemberton	J 7	Ohio
28	*Pemberton	L 14	Va.
521	Pemberton	O 8	W. Va.
1036	Pemberville	D 10	Ohio
703	Pembina	C 23	N D.
238	Pembine Junction (Pembine)	O 9	Wis.
325	Pembroke	I 16	Fla.
1039	Pembroke	K 22	Ga.
570	Pembroke	K 9	Ky.
400	Pembroke	K 23	Me.
800	Pembroke	I 22	Mass.
50	Pembroke (East Pembroke)	O 15	N. H.
250	Pembroke	M 6	N. Y.
783	Pembroke	K 11	N. C.
800	Pembroke	N 4	Va.
1006	▲*Penablanca	F 11	N. M.
....	Penacook	N 13	N. H.
118	Penalosa	M 13	Kan.
4059	Pen Argyl	K 23	Pa.
600	Penasco	D 15	N. M.
25	*Penasse (American Point)	A 9	Minn.
110	*Penawawa	K 23	Wash.
3627	Penbrook	N 16	Pa.
125	*Pence	G 6	Ind.
1	*Pence	G 20	Ky.
400	Pence	H 5	Wis.
5	*Pencer	C 7	Minn.
100	*Pence Springs	O 10	W. Va.
35	*Pendennis	I 6	Kan.
1135	Pender	G 21	Neb.
....	Pender	C 17	N. C.
189	Pendergrass	E 11	Ga.
38	Pendleton	M 16	Ark.
....	Pendleton	K 18	Ga.
1681	Pendleton	I 17	Ind.
62	*Pendleton	D 15	Ky.
97	*Pendleton	H 17	Mo.
65	*Pendleton	C 19	N. C.
8847	Pendleton	C 19	Ore.
1278	Pendleton	C 5	S. C.
225	Pendleton	H 18	Tex.
50	*Pendletons	J 15	Va.
85	Pendroy	E 8	Mont.
240	*Penelope	G 19	Tex.
218	Penfield	F 13	Ga.
265	Penfield	H 20	Ill.
600	*Penfield	L 10	N. Y.
700	Penfield	I 9	Pa.
245	Pengilly	G 16	Minn.
50	*Pengra	J 7	Ore.
75	Penhook	P 8	Va.
31	Penick	G 16	Ky.
60	*Peniel	Q 14	Ohio
367	*Peniel	D 20	Tex.
573	Peninsula	E 17	Ohio
....	*Penistaja	E 10	N. M.
600	Penitas	Q 3	Tex.
30	*Penlan	L 12	Va.
125	*Penland	M 10	N. C.
136	*Penllyn	O 23	Pa.
....	*Penman	D 8	W. Va.
75	Pen Mar	R 13	Pa.
100	Penn	G 17	N. D.
180	Penn (McGlynn)	E 7	Ore.
1081	Penn	N 5	Pa.
....	*Penn, see Greenwood		Tex.
255	Pennellville	K 14	N. Y.
200	*Penngrove	G 4	Calif.
50	Penn Haven Jc.	J 21	Pa.
11	Penniman	N 20	Va.
130	*Pennington	K 6	Ala.
519	*Pennington	E 10	Minn.
1492	Pennington	H 12	N. J.
223	Pennington	H 22	Tex.
1990	Pennington (Pennington Gap)	E 4	Va.
....	Pennington	H 9	Wis.
89	*Penn Laird	H 11	Va.
219	Pennock	M 8	Minn.
201	Penn Run	L 7	Pa.
1738	Pennsboro	E 9	W. Va.
1548	*Pennsburg	M 22	Pa.
300	*Penns Creek	K 15	Pa.
150	*Pennsdale	H 16	Pa.
6488	Penns Grove	M 5	N. J.
1500	*Pennside	M 20	Pa.
150	*Penns Park	N 24	Pa.
412	*Pennsviile	M 5	N. J.
200	Pennsville	M 16	Ohio
632	Pennsville	O 5	Pa.
350	Pennsylvania Furnace	L 12	Pa.
....	Pennsylvania Jc.	J 13	Md.
1000	*Penn Valley	N 22	Pa.
598	Pennville	G 21	Ind.
35	*Penny	H 23	Ky.
370	Penny Farms	C 15	Fla.
5308	Penn Yan	O 11	N. Y.
17	Peno	J 25	Okla.
4	Peno	I 16	S. D.
700	Penobscot	M 15	Me.
102	*Penokee	F 8	Kan.
77	*Penola	K 17	Va.
1274	*Penowa	N 1	Pa.
10	Penrith	E 24	Wash.
92	*Penrod	I 10	Ky.
50	*Penrose	G 18	Ark.
90	*Penrose	K 15	Colo.
50	*Penrose	C 12	Ill.
30	*Penrose	Q 7	N. C.
300	Penryn	G 8	Calif.
165	*Penryn	N 18	Pa.
37449	Pensacola	N 2	Fla.
75	*Pensacola	N 9	N. C.
109	Pensacola	D 22	Okla.
100	Pensaukee	P 12	Wis.
17745	■Pensauken	K 9	N. J.
35	*Pensyl	J 18	Pa.
....	Pentland	M 13	Calif.
85	Pentoga	G 3	Mich.
50	*Penton	A 11	Miss.
100	*Pentress	C 13	W. Va.
820	Pentwater	M 10	Mich.
600	*Penwell	G 8	Tex.
125	Peoa	E 14	Utah
34	*Peoga	L 14	Ind.
72	*Peola Mills	I 13	Va.
4	Peola	N 23	Wash.
22	*Peoli (Newtown)	H 17	Ohio
150	*Peoples	H 19	Ky.
100	Peoples	N 12	La.
700	Peoria	K 12	Ariz.
105087	Peoria	G 12	Ill.
100	*Peoria	F 15	Ind.
65	*Peoria	L 15	Iowa
50	Peoria	I 24	Kan.
50	*Peoria	O 8	Miss.
52	*Peoria	D 2	N. C.
200	Peoria	I 10	Ohio
227	Peoria	A 24	Okla.
80	Peoria	H 6	Ore.
4376	Peoria Heights	F 12	Ill.
45	*Peosta	G 23	Iowa
1146	Peotone	D 21	Ill.
75	*Pepacton	Q 19	N. Y.
754	Pepin	C 14	Wis.
....	*Pepperell	I 22	Ala.
2500	Pepperell	C 15	Mass.
2000	Pepperell (East Pepperell)	C 15	Mass.
423	*Pepper Pike	D 17	Ohio
36	*Peppers	M 9	N. C.
585	*Pepperton	H 9	Ga.
45	*Peppertown	K 21	Ind.
265	Pepperwood	D 21	Calif.
515	Pequabuck (Terryville)	D 6	Conn.
20	*Pequaket	J 16	N. H.
251	Pequaming	D 3	Mich.
1200	*Pequannock	D 14	N. J.
50	Pequea	Q 19	Pa.
301	Pequot (Eileen)	E 18	Ill.
114	Pequot Lakes (Pequot)	I 12	Minn.
19	*Pera	M 10	Va.
573	Peralta	H 11	N. M.
68	*Percilla	G 22	Tex.
300	Percival	P 3	Iowa
958	Percy	O 13	Ill.
100	*Percy	L 14	Iowa
217	Percy	H 6	Miss.
60	Percy	E 15	N. H.
100	Percy	P 5	Pa.
13	Percy Jc.	E 7	Ind.
300	Perdido	P 8	Ala.
75	*Perdido Beach	P 7	Ala.
15	*Perdue	O 5	Va.
100	Perdue Hill	N 8	Ala.
16	*Perdueville	G 19	Ill.
76	Perham	C 17	Me.
1534	Perham	I 7	Minn.
34	*Perico	A 1	Tex.
20	*Perida	B 8	Wis.
55	*Perintown	N 7	Ohio
4121	Perkasie	M 23	Pa.
100	Perkins	G 8	Calif.
310	Perkins	I 20	Ga.
79	Perkins	C 2	Iowa
14	*Perkins	H 14	Me.
400	Perkins	G 8	Mich.
194	*Perkins	P 23	Mo.
79	*Perkins (Vinca)	F 14	Okla.
728	Perkins	G 14	Okla.
36	Perkins	P 20	S. D.
27	*Perkins	H 10	W. Va.
....	Perkins Mine	F 20	Minn.
275	Perkinston	Q 18	Miss.
200	*Perkinstown	H 11	Wis.
50	*Perkinsville	H 11	Ariz.
180	Perkinsville	H 16	Ind.
350	Perkinsville	O 9	N. Y.
24	*Perkinsville	E 3	N. C.
144	Perkinsville	M 13	Vt.
78	*Perkinsville	L 15	Va.
75	*Perkiomenville	N 22	Pa.
250	*Perks	Q 15	Ill.
15	*Perky	R 18	Fla.
270	Perla	K 11	Ark.
246	Perley	G 2	Minn.
30	Perma	G 3	Mont.
10	*Permon	K 19	Ky.
525	Pernell	N 12	Okla.
143	*Perote	L 19	Ala.
102	*Perrin	E 6	Mo.
475	Perrin	D 17	Tex.
300	*Perrin	N 21	Va.
1054	Perrine	O 23	Fla.
400	Perrineville	I 16	N. J.
385	Perrinton	N 17	Mich.
1011	Perris	O 18	Calif.
....	Perronville	G 7	Mich.
377	Perry	H 10	Ark.
2668	Perry	C 8	Fla.
1542	Perry	J 10	Ga.
456	Perry	J 7	Ill.
5977	Perry	J 10	Iowa
392	Perry	G 23	Kan.
170	*Perry	N 10	La.
500	Perry	K 24	Me.
541	Perry (South Hanover)	H 21	Mass.
879	Perry	O 19	Mich.
830	Perry	F 15	Mo.
4468	Perry	N 8	N. Y.
4	Perry	Q 22	N. D.
645	*Perry	C 18	Ohio
5045	Perry	E 13	Okla.
80	Perry	D 20	Ore.
141	Perry	I 12	S. C.
214	Perry	H 19	Tex.
383	Perry	C 11	Utah
10	*Perry	G 20	W. Va.
200	*Perry Center	N 8	N. Y.
100	*Perry City	P 12	N. Y.
128	Perrydale	F 5	Ore.
260	Perryman	D 17	Md.
1000	Perryopolis	O 4	Pa.
35	*Perry Park (Balls Landing)	D 16	Ky.
80	*Perry Point	C 18	Md.
96	*Perrysburg	E 14	Ind.
375	Perrysburg	P 4	N. Y.
3457	Perrysburg	C 10	Ohio
284	*Perrys Mills	C 24	N. Y
451	Perrysville	I 6	Ind.
728	Perrysville	H 14	Ohio
500	*Perrysville	L 3	Pa.
200	Perryton	J 14	Ohio
2325	Perryton	A 5	Tex.
150	*Perryville	I 11	Ala.
577	Perryville	H 10	Ark.
462	Perryville	G 16	Ky.
729	Perryville	C 18	Md.
3907	Perryville	M 22	Mo.
223	*Perryville (Blakeslee)	M 16	N. Y.
60	*Perryville (Lamartine)	H 19	Ohio
250	Perryville	O 7	Tenn.
....	Per Se	J 11	Pa.
21	*Pershing (Crater)	C 8	Colo.
305	Pershing (East Germantown)	J 21	Ind.
27	Pershing	E 13	Ind.
900	Pershing	M 14	Iowa
61	*Pershing	I 16	Mo.
16	Pershing	I 12	Ohio
46	Pershing	C 17	Okla.
1000	Pershing (Stauffer)	O 5	Pa.
395	Persia	K 4	Iowa
200	*Persia	L 22	Tenn.
110	*Persimmon Creek	Q 2	N. C.
50	*Persimon	K 14	Ky.
150	*Persinger	K 10	W. Va.
103	Personville	H 20	Tex.
50	*Perth	K 8	Ind.
300	Perth	O 15	Kan.
145	Perth	E 16	N. D.
41242	Perth Amboy	G 18	N. J.
420	Perthshire	D 6	Miss.
8983	Peru	E 15	Ill.
12432	Peru	E 15	Ind.
304	Peru	M 11	Iowa
487	Peru	O 20	Kan.
110	Peru	M 5	Me.
1024	Peru	N 24	Neb.
750	Peru	E 24	N. Y.
17	Peru	N 9	Vt.
110	*Peru	H 19	W. Va.
....	Peru Jc.	O 20	Kan.
27	*Perulack	M 13	Pa.
54	*Peruque	H 19	Mo.
119	Peruville (Peruton)	O 14	N. Y.
850	Pescadero	J 5	Calif.
500	Peshastin	H 14	Wash.
1947	Peshtigo	P 11	Wis.
367	Pesotum	I 18	Ill.
300	Petaca	C 13	N. M.
250	*Petal	N 18	Miss.
8034	Petaluma	H 4	Calif.
2521	Peterborough	Q 10	N. H.
300	*Peterman	M 10	Ala.
125	Peters	H 9	Calif.
175	*Peters	O 23	Fla.
20	Peters	O 15	N. D.
50	*Peters	K 21	Tex.
....	*Petersburg, see Englewood		Colo.
2586	Petersourg	I 11	Ill.
3075	Petersburg	O 8	Ind.
87	*Petersburg	G 21	Iowa
326	Petersburg	B 16	Ky.
789	Petersburg	Q 20	Mich.
657	Petersburg	I 18	Neb.
300	*Petersburg	R 11	N. J.
500	Petersburg	N 25	N. Y.
285	Petersburg	H 20	N. D.
500	Petersburg	F 21	Ohio
638	Petersburg	M 12	Pa.
....	Petersburg	O 19	Pa.
581	Petersburg	P 11	Tenn.
496	*Petersburg	B 10	Tex.
30631	Petersburg	O 17	Va.
1751	Petersburg	G 18	W. Va.
....	Petersburg Jc.	N 24	N. Y.
10	*Peters Creek	Q 19	Ill.
29	*Peters Creek	Q 5	Va.
194	Petersham	D 11	Mass.
35	*Peters Landing	O 7	Tenn.
200	Peterson	G 9	Ala.
47	*Peterson	E 21	Ind.
603	Peterson	D 5	Iowa
331	Peterson	Q 22	Minn.
56	Peterson	D 12	Utah
467	Peterstown	Q 10	W. Va.
65	*Petersville	L 16	Ind.
28	*Petersville	J 24	Iowa
104	*Petersville	D 21	Ky.
441	*Petersville (Conoquenessing)	J 3	Pa.
100	*Peterton	H 21	Kan.
6019	Petoskey	H 16	Mich.
7	Petrel	R 7	N. D.
258	*Petrey	L 16	Ala.
40	*Petries Corners	H 17	N. Y.
110	*Petroleum	F 20	Ind.
125	*Petroleum	K 12	Ky.
300	*Petroleum (Coles)	E 21	Ohio
200	*Petroleum	N 2	Tex.
110	*Petroleum	F 9	W. Va.
75	Petroleum Center	G 4	Pa.
50	*Petrolia	D 1	Calif.
100	*Petrolia	M 21	Ill.
95	Petrolia	L 22	Kan.
559	Petrolia	J 4	Pa.
597	Petrolia	B 16	Tex.
1300	Petros	M 17	Tenn.
62	*Petteway	I 20	Tex.
190	Pettibone	L 16	N. D.
210	Pettigrew	D 7	Ark.
307	Pettisville	C 7	Ohio
100	*Pettit (Avon)	G 6	Miss.
....	*Pettit	C 9	Tex.
210	*Pettus	J 14	Ark.
100	*Pettus	N 18	Tex.
150	Pettus	N 6	W. Va.
315	Petty	C 21	Tex.
311	*Pevely	K 19	Mo.
415	Pewamo	N 15	Mich.
1352	Pewaukee	N 20	Wis.
625	Pewee Valley	E 14	Ky.
123	Peyton	I 16	Colo.
25	*Peyton	M 7	Miss.
214	Peytona	M 5	W. Va.
8	*Peytonsburg	K 15	Ky.
65	*Pfafftown	D 8	N. C.
200	Pfeifer	H 10	Kan.
87	*Pfeiffer	D 15	Ark.
....	Pfeiffer Quarry	D 15	Ark.
500	Pflugerville	J 18	Tex.
75	Phair	D 19	Me.
27	*Phalanx	H 19	N. J.
100	Phalanx Station (Phalanx)	E 19	Ohio
500	Pharaoh	I 18	Okla.
40	Pharisburg	I 11	Ohio
4784	Pharr	Q 4	Tex.
351	Pheba	F 19	Miss.
65	*Phelan	N 18	Calif.
80	Phelan	K 18	Tex.
653	*Phelps	H 24	Ky.
195	*Phelps (Phelps City)	B 3	Mo.
1499	Phelps	M 11	N. Y.
75	Phelps	I 22	Tex.
500	Phelps	L 7	Wis.
195	*Phelps City (Phelps)	B 3	Mo.
....	Phelps Jc.	M 11	N. Y.
55	*Phenix	M 14	Ark.
10	*Phenix	F 20	Ind.
185	Phenix	N 8	Mo.
1668	Phenix	G 12	R. I.
340	*Phenix	P 11	Va.
15351	Phenix City	J 24	Ala.
....	Phoenix	C 4	Mich.
50	*Phil	I 16	Ky.
125	Philadelphia	I 9	Ill.
138	Philadelphia	J 16	Ind.
3711	Philadelphia	I 18	Miss.
166	Philadelphia	D 15	Mo.
722	Philadelphia	G 16	N. Y.
1931334	Philadelphia	P 24	Pa.
600	Philadelphia	O 18	Tenn.
50	*Philadelphia Rd	I 15	Ohio
75	*Philbrook	K 9	Minn.
533	Phil Campbell	C 8	Ala.
833	Philip	K 9	S. D.
530	Philipp	E 11	Miss.
1955	Philippi	F 14	W. Va.
1304	Philipsburg	J 5	Mont.
3963	Philipsburg	K 11	Pa.
734	Phillips	K 6	Me.
100	Phillips	E 16	Mont.
205	Phillips	L 17	Neb.
212	Phillips	N 18	Okla.
4000	*Phillips (Whittenburg)	B 4	Tex.
1915	Phillips	H 9	Wis.
170	▲Phillips	M 23	Wyo.
2109	Phillipsburg	D 9	Kan.
35	*Phillipsburg	H 15	Ky.
194	Phillipsburg	N 11	Mo.
18314	Phillipsburg	E 8	N. J.
504	Phillipsburg	K 7	Ohio
500	Phillipsdale	D 17	R. I.
155	*Phillipsport	D 4	N. Y.
50	*Phillipston (Filston)	K 13	La.
423	▲Phillipston	D 11	Mass.
187	Phillipston	J 4	Pa.
53	*Phillipstown	O 20	Ill.
154	*Phillippy	L 3	Tenn.
58	*Phillis	Q 13	Va.
1679	Philmont	P 24	N. Y.
400	*Philmont Club (Philmont)	N 23	Pa.
110	*Philo	F 3	Calif.
510	*Philo	I 19	Ill.
884	Philo (Taylorsville)	K 16	Ohio
58	*Philomath	F 14	Ga.
50	*Philomath	J 21	Ind.
856	Philomath	H 5	Ore.
172	*Philomont	F 15	Va.
45	*Philpot	G 10	Ky.
60	*Philpott	Q 7	Va.
150	Phippsburg	D 9	Colo.
132	Phippsburg	P 8	Me.
43	*Phlox	G 14	Ind.
250	Phlox	L 11	Wis.
....	Phoebe	N 11	Va.
3503	Phoebus	O 21	Va.
475	Phoenicia	R 21	N. Y.
65414	Phoenix	K 12	Ariz.
2875	*Phoenix	D 21	Ill.
106	*Phoenix	N 20	La.
515	Phoenix	D 14	Md.
....	Phoenix	C 4	Mich.
60	*Phoenix	J 9	Miss.
7	Phoenix	E 16	Neb.
1757	Phoenix	L 14	N. Y.
111	*Phoenix	M 16	N. C.
432	Phoenix	Q 7	Ore.
12282	Phoenixville	O 22	Pa.
6	Phon	G 20	Mont.
122	*Phoneton	K 7	Ohio
43	Phroso	E 6	Okla.
100	Piasa	L 10	Ill.
1000	Piave	N 20	Miss.
100	Picabo	O 13	Idaho
100	Picacho	M 15	Ariz.
419	▲Picacho	L 16	N. M.
....	Picardy	L 9	Minn.
5129	Picayune	R 14	Miss.
5848	Picher	A 23	Okla.
50	*Pickard	H 8	Ga.
85	Pickard	H 13	Ind.
18	Pickardville	K 12	N. D.
96	*Pickaway	P 11	W. Va.
60	*Pickens	N 17	Ark.
688	Pickens	I 12	Miss.
6	Pickens	O 23	Okla.
1637	Pickens	B 4	S. C.
475	Pickens	I 13	W. Va.
250	Pickensville	G 4	Ala.
210	*Pickerel	L 10	Wis.
5	Pickering	J 15	Iowa
300	Pickering	I 6	La.
315	Pickering	A 5	Mo.
384	Pickerington	K 13	Ohio
26	Pickert	K 21	N. D.
34	*Pickett	I 14	Ky.
175	*Pickett	M 16	Wis.
550	Pickford	F 18	Mich.
170	Pickrell	N 22	Neb.
500	Pickton	D 22	Tex.
102	Pickwick	Q 6	Tenn.
46	*Pickwick	D 16	Tex.
63	*Picnic	J 15	Ky.
28	Picnic Point	I 7	Wash.
2000	*Pico	Q 5	Calif.
50	*Picton	F 17	N. J.
537	Picture Rocks	H 17	Pa.
250	Pidcock	P 11	Ga.
50	*Pidcoke	H 17	Tex.
10	*Pie	O 3	W. Va.
4019	Piedmont	E 19	Ala.
9866	Piedmont	I 5	Calif.
38	*Piedmont	H 8	Ga.
200	*Piedmont	M 20	Kan.
1177	Piedmont	O 19	Mo.
55	Piedmont	L 8	Mont.
150	Piedmont	J 18	Ohio
151	Piedmont	H 11	Okla.
2500	Piedmont	C 6	S. C.
150	Piedmont	J 3	S. D.
50	Piedmont	F 4	Wash.
2677	Piedmont	D 19	W. Va.
30	Piedmont	Q 3	Wyo.
31	Piedra (Delpiedra)	J 13	Calif.
343	Pierce	C 16	Colo.
600	Pierce	I 15	Fla.
381	Pierce	G 7	Idaho
15	Pierce	D 22	Kan.
37	*Pierce	I 14	Ky.
1249	Pierce	G 19	Neb.
11	Pierce	P 4	N. D.
20	Pierce	I 20	Okla.
100	*Pierce (Pierce Station)	L 4	Tenn.
80	*Pierce	M 21	Tex.
500	Pierce	F 16	W. Va.
115	*Pierce Bridge (Bethlehem)	H 12	N. H.
10	*Pierceburg	L 21	Ill.
1208	Pierce City (Peirce City)	P 7	Mo.
750	Piercefield	F 20	N. Y.
100	*Pierce Station (Pierce)	P 7	Tenn.
895	Pierceton	D 16	Ind.
....	*Pierceville	B 7	Ga.
163	*Pierceville	L 20	Ind.
150	*Pierceville	L 5	Kan.
200	*Piercy	E 3	Calif.
200	Piermont	J 9	N. H.
1876	*Piermont	G 5	N. Y.
150	Pierpont	B 21	Ohio
362	Pierpont	D 20	S. D.
36	Pierport	K 12	Mich.
4322	Pierre	I 13	S. D.
154	Pierrepont Manor	I 15	N. Y.
300	Pierron	M 13	Ill.
541	Pierson	E 17	Fla.
150	Pierson (Pierson Station)	J 17	Ill.
531	Pierson	F 3	Iowa
147	*Pierson	N 15	Mich.
714	Pierz	K 12	Minn.
6	*Pie Town	J 4	N. M.
260	*Piffard	M 8	N. Y.
56	*Pigeon	H 23	Ky.
949	Pigeon	L 22	Mich.
15	*Pigeon (Frosts)	G 7	Pa.
26	*Pigeon	I 7	W. Va.
1306	Pigeon Cove	B 23	Mass.
651	▲*Pigeon Creek	M 14	Ala.
200	Pigeon Falls	E 14	Wis.
225	Pigeon Forge	N 20	Tenn.
65	*Pigeonroost	I 19	Ky.
2034	Piggott	A 21	Ark.
45	*Pike	F 9	Calif.
35	*Pike	C 7	Ga.
50	*Pike	K 6	Ill.
20	*Pike	H 12	Ind.
125	*Pike	F 19	Minn.
300	Pike	I 10	N. H.
307	Pike	O 7	N. Y.
50	Pike	Q 13	Okla.
32	*Pike	E 9	W. Va.
113	Pike	M 7	Ark.
100	*Pike Road	K 17	Ala.
400	*Pike Road	G 20	N. C.
40	*Pikes Peak	M 14	Ind.
....	Pikesville (Roslyn)	E 13	Md.
736	Piketon	O 12	Ohio
150	Pikeview	J 15	Colo.
65	*Pikeview (Dowagiac)	I 13	Ky.
50	*Pikeville	P 7	Ind.
4185	Pikeville	H 23	Ky.
425	Pikeville	G 16	N. C.
759	Pikeville	O 15	Tenn.
15	Pilchuck	E 9	Wash.
537	Pilger	H 20	Neb.
87	*Pilgrim	G 23	Ky.
	*Pilgrim	K 12	Mich.
20	*Pilgrim	L 18	Tex.
25	*Pilgrim Knob	B 7	Va.
27	*Pilkinton	M 15	Va.
348	Pillager	J 11	Minn.
79	Pillar Rock	N 3	Wash.
325	Pillow	L 16	Pa.
161	Pillsbury	L 21	N. D.
30	*Pilot	H 21	Ill.
60	*Pilot	G 20	Ky.
2	Pilot	H 21	N. D.
100	*Pilot	O 5	Va.
65	*Pilot Grove	P 20	Iowa
748	Pilot Grove	H 11	Mo.
40	*Pilot Hill	G 9	Calif.
62	*Pilot Knob	P 13	Ind.
462	Pilot Knob	M 19	Mo.
12	*Pilot Knob	J 24	N. Y.
282	Pilot Mound	I 10	Iowa
925	Pilot Mtn.	C 7	N. C.
1122	Pilot Point	C 19	Tex.
358	Pilot Rock	D 18	Ore.
200	*Pilottown	Q 22	La.
39	*Pilsen	J 17	Kan.
867	Pima	L 22	Ariz.
110	*Pimento	L 6	Ind.
150	*Pinch	K 6	W. Va.
555	Pinckard	N 20	Ala.
25	*Pinckney	H 21	Ark.
456	Pinckney	P 20	Mich.
3146	Pinckneyville	O 13	Ill.
50	*Pinckneyville	I 7	Ky.
100	*Pinckneyville	O 4	Miss.
1027	Pinconning	L 20	Mich.
200	Pindall	C 10	Ark.
220	Pine	I 15	Ariz.
60	*Pine (Pine Grove)	H 14	Colo.
35	Pine	O 8	Idaho
7	Pine	B 13	Ind.
200	*Pine	Q 17	Mo.
38	Pine	F 24	Ore.
70	Pine (Pine Station)	I 14	Pa.
125	*Pine	D 22	Tex.
455	*Pine Apple	L 11	Ala.
15	Pine Apple	L 11	Ala.
215	Pine Bank	Q 2	Pa.
100	Pine Barren	M 2	Fla.
163	*Pine Beach	J 17	N. J.
....	Pinebelt	K 10	Ala.
21290	Pine Bluff	L 14	Ark.
330	*Pinebluff	I 11	N. C.
771	Pine Bluffs	Q 24	Wyo.
500	*Pine Brook	D 15	N. J.
800	Pine Bush	D 4	N. Y.
564	*Pinecastle	G 17	Fla.
150	*Pine City	J 17	Ark.
1718	Pine City	K 17	Minn.
350	Pine City	R 12	N. Y.
100	Pine City	J 23	Wash.
26	*Pinecliffe	F 13	Colo.
255	*Pinecreek	B 6	Minn.
40	*Pine Crest	H 11	Calif.
192	Pinedale	I 20	Ariz.
518	Pinedale	J 12	Calif.
647	Pinedale	J 6	Wyo.
175	*Pine Forge (Pine Ironworks)	N 21	Pa.
112	*Pine Glen	K 12	Pa.
27	Pine Grove	L 20	Ala.
126	*Pine Grove	H 9	Calif.
60	*Pine Grove, (Pine)	H 14	Colo.
156	*Pine Grove	M 17	Ga.
136	*Pine Grove	F 18	Ky.
114	*Pine Grove	K 16	La.
2239	Pinegrove	M 18	Pa.
60	Pine Grove	O 14	Wis.
841	Pine Grove	D 11	W. Va.
25	Pine Grove Furnace	O 14	Pa.
395	Pine Grove Mills	K 12	Pa.
300	*Pinehaven	F 4	N. M.
400	*Pine Hall	C 8	N. C.
418	Pine Hill	L 8	Ala.
600	Pine Hill	H 18	Ky.
1537	*Pine Hill	L 10	N. J.
242	Pine Hill	Q 21	N. Y.
48	*Pinehill	P 8	Pa.
250	Pinehill	F 23	Tex.
474	Pinehurst	K 10	Ga.
125	*Pinehurst	D 6	Idaho
....	*Pinehurst	D 19	Mass.
1600	*Pinehurst	H 11	N. C.
70	*Pinehurst	K 22	Tex.
1200	*Pinehurst	G 9	Wash.
....	*Pine Ironworks, see Pine Forge		Pa.
1040	Pine Island	P 19	Minn.
180	*Pine Island	F 4	N. Y.
94	*Pineknob	N 7	W. Va.
....	*Pine Knot, see Big Bear Lake		Calif.
600	Pine Knot	K 17	Ky.
....	*Pinelake	B 10	Ind.
25	*Pineland	L 15	Fla.
47	*Pineland	O 13	S. C.
1800	Pineland	H 25	Tex.
100	Pine Level	K 17	Ala.
595	Pine Level	G 16	N. C.
691	*Pinellas Park	I 12	Fla.
118	*Pinelog	D 5	Ga.
400	Pine Meadow	D 10	Conn.
125	*Pinemount	C 10	Fla.
....	Pine Mountain	F 8	Ga.
100	*Pine Mountain	J 21	Ky.
....	*Pine Mountain Valley	I 4	Ga.
310	Pineola	D 2	N. C.
375	Pineora	K 23	Ga.
200	*Pine Orchard	N 12	Conn.
181	Pinepark	P 8	Ga.
800	Pine Plains	R 24	N. Y.
550	Pine Point	Q 5	Me.
64	*Pine Prairie	K 9	La.
38	*Pineridge	J 12	Calif.
100	*Pine Ridge	G 20	Ky.
50	*Pine Ridge	M 4	Miss.
4	*Pine Ridge	E 3	Neb.
15	*Pine Ridge	P 10	Ore.
618	Pine Ridge	O 5	S. D.
574	Pine River	I 11	Minn.
166	Pine River	L 15	Wis.
35	*Pinero	M 20	Va.
79	*Pine Station (Pine)	I 14	Pa.
37	Pinetop	I 20	Ariz.
43	*Pine Top	H 22	Ky.
713	Pinetops	F 17	N. C.
253	Pinetown	F 20	N. C.
14	*Pine Tree	D 19	Wyo.
300	Pinetta	B 9	Fla.
190	Pinetta	N 20	Va.
150	*Pine Valley	Q 19	Calif.
25	*Pine Valley	D 14	Miss.
27	*Pine Valley	L 10	N. J.
170	Pine Valley	Q 12	N. Y.
1700	Pine Valley	M 24	Okla.
60	Pine Valley	P 3	Utah
350	Pineview	L 11	Ga.
110	Pineview	K 16	Mont.
225	*Pineview	H 12	N. C.
26	*Pine View	H 16	Va.
303	Pine Village	G 7	Ind.
15	*Pineville	B 13	Ark.
3882	Pineville	K 20	Ky.
4297	Pineville	H 10	La.
524	Pineville	Q 6	Mo.
100	Pineville	F 20	Minn.
100	*Pineville	K 15	Miss.
70	*Pineville	Q 18	N. Y.
1144	Pineville	I 6	N. C.
278	*Pineville	N 24	Pa.
100	*Pineville	K 18	S. C.
769	Pineville	P 6	W. Va.
80	*Pinewood	F 9	Minn.
456	Pinewood	H 16	S. C.
200	Pinewood	N 8	Tenn.
....	Piney	G 25	Okla.
50	*Piney	D 11	W. Va.
25	*Piney Creek	B 4	N. C.
500	Piney Flats	L 24	Tenn.
1200	*Piney Fork	I 20	Ohio
60	*Piney Point	Q 15	Md.
....	*Piney River	L 11	Va.
....	Piney View	D 8	W. Va.
425	*Piney Woods	L 13	Miss.
53	Pingree	O 18	Idaho
167	Pingree	L 18	N. D.
130	*Pingree Grove	B 18	Ill.

Pop.	Place	Index	State
18	Piniele	M 24	Mont.
46	Pink	J 14	Okla.
307	*Pink Hill	I 17	N. C.
....	*Pinkney (So. Gastonia)	H 4	N. C.
54	Pinkney	Q 8	Tenn.
501	*Pinkstaff	M 22	Ill.
41	*Pinnacle	I 12	Ark.
52	*Pinnacle	D 8	Colo.
250	Pinnacle	C 7	N. C.
7	*Pinnacles	J 8	Calif.
40	Pinnebog	K 22	Mich.
11	*Pinoak	P 8	W. Va.
229	Pinola	L 12	Miss.
62	*Pinola	O 14	Pa.
934	Pinole	D 19	Calif.
16	Pinon	L 16	Colo.
151	▲Pinon	N 16	N. M.
210	Pinopolis	K 18	S. C.
150	Pinos Altos	M 3	N. M.
35	Pinoswells	I 15	N. M.
500	*Pinson (Mount Pinson)	E 14	Ala.
65	*Pinson (Pinsonfork)	H 24	Ky.
250	Pinson	O 5	Tenn.
65	*Pinsonfork (Pinson)	H 24	Ky.
100	Pintado	H 16	N. M.
300	*Pinto (Potomac)	M 5	Md.
4	Pinto	M 14	N. M.
5	*Pinto	Q 2	Utah
60	*Pintura	Q 4	Utah
400	Pioche	K 23	Nev.
129	*Pioneer	F 9	Iowa
513	Pioneer	H 21	Ky.
201	Pioneer	B 13	La.
....	*Pioneer	N 24	Minn.
10	Pioneer	J 6	Mont.
20	Pioneer	M 14	Nev.
686	Pioneer	C 6	Ohio
175	Pioneer	L 18	Tenn.
50	*Pioneer	I 15	Tex.
58	*Pioneerville	M 7	Idaho
15	*Piopolis	O 18	Ill.
29	*Pipecreek	K 16	Tex.
1000	Piper	H 11	Ala.
128	*Piper	F 24	Kan.
14	Piper	I 14	Mont.
663	Piper City	F 19	Ill.
650	*Pipers Gap	Q 3	Va.
200	*Pipersville	M 24	Pa.
200	*Pipestem	P 9	W. Va.
4682	Pipestone	Q 3	Minn.
40	*Pippapass	I 22	Ky.
258	Piqua	L 22	Kan.
53	*Piqua	D 19	Ky.
16049	Piqua	J 7	Ohio
....	*Pirates Cove	R 18	Fla.
30	*Pirkey	J 12	Va.
600	Pirtleville	P 23	Ariz.
800	Piru	N 14	Calif.
78	*Piscataway	K 11	Md.
21	*Piseco	J 20	N. Y.
242	Pisek	F 21	N. D.
300	*Pisgah	B 18	Ala.
48	*Pisgah	C 6	Ga.
30	*Pisgah	J 10	Ill.
397	Pisgah	J 3	Iowa
380	Pisgah	M 10	Md.
100	*Pisgah	G 9	N. C.
65	*Pisgah	C 15	W. Va.
775	*Pisgah Forest	Q 7	N. C.
1800	*Pismo (Pismo Beach)	M 9	Calif.
18	*Piso	H 23	Ky.
50	*Pistol River	O 2	Ore.
6310	Pitcairn	M 4	Pa.
105	*Pitcher	O 16	N. Y.
40	*Pitchfork	C 7	Wyo.
156	Pitkin	K 10	Colo.
300	Pitkin	J 7	La.
34	*Pitman	A 18	Ark.
5507	Pitman	M 8	N. J.
150	*Pitman	K 18	Pa.
305	Pitsburg	K 6	Ohio
7	Pitt	D 5	Calif.
18	Pitt	C 10	Minn.
1500	*Pittock	M 3	Pa.
100	*Pitts	E 18	Ark.
371	Pitts	L 11	Ga.
54	*Pitts	G 19	Ky.
510	Pittsboro	I 12	Ind.
276	Pittsboro	D 16	Miss.
826	Pittsboro	F 12	N. C.
9520	Pittsburg	A 23	Calif.
817	Pittsburg	P 16	Ill.
310	*Pittsburg (Durham)	B 2	Ga.
100	Pittsburg	F 10	Ind.
55	*Pittsburg	P 18	Iowa
17571	Pittsburg	N 24	Kan.
800	Pittsburg	I 18	Ky.
162	*Pittsburg	L 10	Mo.
600	Pittsburg	B 15	N. H.
....	*Pittsburg, see Farley		N. M.
689	Pittsburg	M 19	Okla.
2916	Pittsburg	D 23	Tex.
671659	Pittsburgh	M 3	Pa.
100	*Pittsburg Landing	Q 6	Tenn.
2284	Pittsfield	J 6	Ill.
2075	Pittsfield	L 11	Me.
49684	Pittsfield	E 2	Mass.
1300	Pittsfield	N 16	N. H.
150	Pittsfield	E 6	Pa.
125	Pittsfield	J 10	Vt.
8	Pittsfield Jct.	Q 21	Mich.
600	Pittsford	R 18	Mich.
1544	Pittsford	M 9	N. Y.
576	Pittsford	K 8	Vt.
403	Pittsford Mills	K 8	Vt.
50	Pittsgrove	N 8	N. J.
17828	Pittston	H 21	Pa.
165	Pittstown	F 10	N. J.
200	Pittsview	K 23	Ala.
436	Pittsville	N 23	Md.
84	*Pittsville	H 8	Mo.
69	*Pittsville	H 4	Pa.
556	Pittsville	I 14	Wis.
156	*Pittsville	C 7	Calif.
128	Pittwood	F 21	Ill.
40	Piute	M 15	Calif.
350	*Pixley	K 13	Calif.
100	*Place (Siler)	J 18	Ky.
100	Placedo	N 19	Tex.
1472	*Placentia	R 6	Calif.
75	Placer	P 5	Ore.
3064	Placerville	G 9	Calif.
46	Placerville	M 5	Colo.
146	Placerville	M 6	Idaho
110	*Placid	H 15	Tex.
200	Placitas	G 12	N. M.
35	*Plad	M 11	Mo.
....	Plain, see Forest, N. M.		
52	*Plain	H 13	Wash.
405	Plain	I 19	Wis.
1385	Plain City	J 10	Ohio
300	Plain City	D 11	Utah
1085	Plain Dealing	A 5	La.
2500	Plainfield	G 24	Conn.
182	*Plainfield	K 13	Ga.
1485	Plainfield	D 18	Ill.
1811	Plainfield	J 12	Ind.
362	Plainfield	E 16	Iowa
65	Plainfield	D 5	Mass.
125	Plainfield	L 7	N. H.
37469	Plainfield	F 16	N. J.
130	*Plainfield	J 16	Ohio
275	Plainfield	O 14	Pa.
521	Plainfield	G 14	Vt.
571	Plainfield	J 15	Wis.
50	Plaingrove	J 3	Pa.
528	Plains	L 6	Ga.
619	Plains (West Plains)	N 5	Kan.
624	Plains	G 3	Mont.
113	*Plains (Papakating)	C 13	N J.
15621	■*Plains	H 20	Pa.
125	Plains	D 8	Tex.
400	Plainsboro	H 13	N. J.
....	*Plainsville	H 20, (Pop. 216 incl. in Plains)	Pa.
704	Plainview	H 8	Ark.
33	*Plainview	F 14	Colo.
150	*Plainview	L 11	Ill.
36	Plainview	K 23	Iowa
1500	Plainview	P 20	Minn.
1411	Plainview	G 18	Neb.
....	Plainview	L 24	N. M.
....	Plainview	H 6	Ore.
13	Plainview	H 7	S. D.
8263	Plainview	A 10	Tex.
132	*Plain View	M 20	Va.
....	Plainview Jc.	Q 20	Minn.
6301	▲Plainville	G 11	Conn.
132	*Plainville	C 5	Ga.
249	Plainville	I 5	Ill.
619	Plainville	N 8	Ind.
1232	Plainville	F 10	Kan.
400	Plainville	H 17	Mass.
100	*Plainville	L 13	N. Y.
350	Plainville	N 5	Ohio
70	*Plainville	J 17	Wis.
2424	Plainwell	P 13	Mich.
217	Plaisted	B 15	Me.
700	Plaistow	Q 18	N. H.
18	Plana	D 19	S. D.
350	*Planada	I 10	Calif.
897	*Plandome	H 7	N. Y.
317	*Plandome Heights	H 7	N. Y.
694	Plankinton	L 19	S. D.
300	Plano	M 20	Idaho
1930	Plano	C 17	Ill.
209	Plano	P 14	Iowa
200	*Plano	N 9	Mo.
1582	Plano	D 19	Tex.
18	*Plant	H 12	Ark.
7491	Plant City	I 15	Fla.
400	Plantersville	I 12	Ala.
495	Plantersville	C 20	Miss.
80	*Plantersville	J 22	S. C.
362	*Plantersville	J 21	Tex.
3000	Plantsville	I 11	Conn.
5124	Plaquemine	M 14	La.
95	*Plaska	E 5	Tex.
50	*Plaster City	Q 22	Calif.
28	*Plasterco	E 8	Va.
281	Platea	E 2	Pa.
1500	*Plateau	P 5	Ala.
57	Plateau City	H 5	Colo.
30	*Platform	R 14	Ohio
25	*Platina	D 6	Calif.
100	Platner	E 21	Colo.
10	*Plato	F 20	Ill.
12	*Plato	J 17	Ky.
283	Plato	N 13	Minn.
200	*Plato	N 13	Mo.
50	*Plato	P 5	N. Y.
100	*Plato Center	C 18	Ill.
50	*Platt Clove	P 22	N. Y.
1017	Platte	M 18	S. D.
509	Platte Center	J 19	Neb.
675	Platte City	F 5	Mo.
230	*Platte City (Tracy)	F 5	Mo.
400	*Plattekill	R 21	N. Y.
410	Plattenville	N 15	La.
275	Platter	Q 16	Okla.
....	Platte River	J 22	Neb.
561	Platteville	D 15	Colo.
4762	Platteville	H 21	Wis.
20	*Plattin	K 19	Mo.
1915	Plattsburg	E 6	Mo.
16351	Plattsburg	D 24	N. Y.
125	*Plattsburg	K 10	Ohio
4268	Plattsmouth	L 24	Neb.
117	Plattsville	O 6	Conn.
250	*Plattville	D 18	Ill.
367	Plaucheville	J 11	La.
360	Plaza	H 8	N. D.
250	Plaza	I 23	Wash.
563	Pleasant City	K 17	Ohio
78	*Pleasant Corners (Jordan)	L 21	Pa.
1500	Pleasantdale	P 6	Me.
140	Pleasant Dale	M 21	Neb.
....	*Pleasant Dale	D 16	W. Va.
1000	Pleasant Gap	K 13	Pa.
300	*Pleasant Garden	E 10	N. C.
39	*Pleasant Green	H 11	Mo.
1066	*Pleasant Grove	G 6	Ala.
275	*Pleasant Grove (Redstripe)	D 13	Ark.
35	*Pleasant Grove	F 7	Calif.
7	*Pleasant Grove	Q 16	Ill.
30	*Pleasantgrove	O 21	Iowa
48	*Pleasantgrove	C 12	Miss.
500	Pleasant Grove (Culleoka)	O 10	Tenn.
1941	Pleasant Grove	G 12	Utah
79	*Pleasant Hall	P 13	Pa.
....	*Pleasant Hill	K 10	Ala.
200	Pleasant Hill	K 12	Ala.
706	Pleasant Hill	K 6	Ill.
737	Pleasant Hill	F 5	La.
48	*Pleasant Hill	A 13	Miss.
2118	Pleasant Hill	H 7	Mo.
100	*Pleasant Hill	C 17	N. C.
738	Pleasant Hill	J 6	Ohio
100	Pleasant Hill	R 24	Okla.
250	*Pleasant Hill	D 15	S. C.
178	Pleasant Hill	N 15	Tenn.
20	Pleasant Home	D 9	Ore.
200	Pleasant Hope	N 10	Mo.
2	*Pleasant Island	K 3	Me.
500	Pleasant Lake	B 22	Ind.
30	*Pleasant Lake	N 15	Mass.
87	Pleasant Lake	F 15	N. D.
39	*Pleasant Lane	H 8	S. C.
167	Pleasant Mills	E 23	Ind.
100	Pleasant Mound	M 14	Ill.
350	Pleasant Mount	F 22	Pa.
1278	Pleasanton	I 6	Calif.
180	Pleasanton	Q 12	Iowa
1227	Pleasanton	J 25	Kan.
235	Pleasanton	L 15	Neb.
2074	Pleasanton	M 16	Tex.
25	*Pleasant Plain	F 18	Ind.
171	*Pleasant Plain	N 19	Iowa
139	*Pleasant Plain	N 7	Ohio
156	*Pleasant Plains	F 5	Ark.
531	Pleasant Plains	I 11	Ill.
67	Pleasant Point	O 12	Me.
....	Pleasant Point	K 24	Me.
193	Pleasant Prairie	N 22	Wis.
....	Pleasant Ridge, see Ridge	H 5	Ala.
262	*Pleasant Ridge	P 22	Mich.
4500	Pleasant Ridge	N 5	Ohio
25	Pleasantridge	C 6	S. D.
160	*Pleasant Ridge	Q 23	Va.
124	*Pleasant Shade	L 13	Tenn.
600	Pleasant Unity	N 5	Pa.
320	Pleasant Valley	C 10	Conn.
200	Pleasant Valley	K 24	Iowa
32	*Pleasant Valley	F 19	Ky.
500	Pleasant Valley	Q 19	N. Y.
....	Pleasant Valley	C 5	N. Y.
30	*Pleasant Valley	J 16	Ohio
125	Pleasant Valley	F 13	Okla.
13	Pleasant Valley	G 22	Ore.
79	*Pleasant Valley	M 23	Pa.
315	Pleasant Valley	M 5	Pa.
150	*Pleasant Valley (Rockingham)	H 11	Va.
25	Pleasant Valley	B 6	Wash.
98	*Pleasant View	P 3	Colo.
200	*Pleasantview	H 7	Ill.
100	*Pleasant View	K 16	Ind.
517	Pleasant View	K 18	Ky.
40	*Pleasant View	L 8	Mo.
177	Pleasant View	L 10	Tenn.
310	Pleasant View	C 11	Utah
12	*Pleasantview	M 10	Va.
400	Pleasantville (Spurgeon)	P 7	Ind.
240	*Pleasantville	M 7	Ind.
895	Pleasantville	M 13	Iowa
50	*Pleasantville	C 16	Md.
11050	Pleasantville	O 13	N. J.
4454	Pleasantville	F 6	N. Y.
572	Pleasantville	L 14	Ohio
232	*Pleasantville	O 9	Pa.
689	Pleasantville	G 5	Pa.
125	*Pleasantville (Manatawny)	M 21	Pa.
110	*Pleasantville	O 8	Tenn.
50	Pleasure Ridge Park	F 13	Ky.
438	Pleasureville (South Pleasureville)	E 15	Ky.
350	*Pledger	N 21	Tex.
63	Plemons	B 4	Tex.
35	Plenty	I 21	Ariz.
1574	Plentywood	C 24	Mont.
300	*Plessis	H 15	N. Y.
150	Pletcher	I 13	Ala.
100	*Plevna	A 15	Ala.
73	*Plevna	F 15	Ind.
173	Plevna	K 13	Kan.
110	*Plevna	D 14	Mo.
291	Plevna	J 24	Mont.
92	*Pliny	I 5	W. Va.
280	Plover	E 8	Iowa
326	Plover	K 14	Wis.
20	*Plowville	N 20	Pa.
89	*Pluck (Stryker)	H 23	Tex.
175	Pluckemin	F 14	N. J.
100	*Plum.	K 20	Tex.
12	Pluma	I 2	S. D.
5405	▲*Plum Bayou	K 14	Ark.
142	*Plum Branch	H 7	S. C.
368	Plum City	B 13	Wis.
541	Plumerville	G 11	Ark.
200	*Plumfield	P 16	Ill.
399	Plummer	E 4	Idaho
312	Plummer	E 5	Minn.
....	Plummer Mine	H 6	Wis.
100	*Plummers Landing	E 20	Ky.
150	*Plumpoint	L 15	Md.
50	*Plum River	A 9	Ill.
750	*Plumsteadville	M 23	Pa.
110	*Plumtree	D 2	N. C.
40	*Plum Valley	Q 20	Colo.
469	Plumville	K 7	Pa.
300	*Plus	L 6	W. Va.
70	Plush	Q 15	Ore.
55	*Plutarch	G 21	Ky.
115	*Pluto	O 9	W. Va.
460	Plymouth	G 9	Calif.
500	Plymouth	G 9	Conn.
150	*Plymouth	G 17	Fla.
808	Plymouth	H 6	Ill.
5713	Plymouth	C 14	Ind.
427	Plymouth	C 14	Iowa
85	Plymouth	L 12	Me.
13100	■Plymouth	J 23	Mass.
5360	Plymouth	P 21	Mich.
434	Plymouth	N 21	Neb.
1800	Plymouth	K 12	N. H.
101	*Plymouth	O 16	N. Y.
2461	Plymouth	E 20	N. C.
1403	Plymouth	F 13	Ohio
15507	Plymouth	I 20	Pa.
292	Plymouth	B 10	Utah
10	Plymouth	L 11	Vt.
23	*Plymouth	N 16	Wash.
301	Plymouth	J 5	W. Va.
4170	Plymouth	O 17	Wis.
4	Plymouth Jc.	C 14	Iowa
300	*Plymouth Meeting	N 23	Pa.
62	*Plymouth Union	L 11	Vt.
300	Plymouth	J 21	Mass.
600	Poca	J 5	W. Va.
100	Pocahontas	E 9	Ala.
3028	Pocahontas	B 18	Ark.
750	Pocahontas	M 12	Ill.
1730	Pocahontas	F 8	Iowa
105	*Pocahontas	J 9	Miss.
119	*Pocahontas	N 22	Mo.
300	Pocahontas	Q 5	Tenn.
2623	Pocahontas	B 10, N 1	Va.
365	Pocasset	M 23	Mass.
300	Pocasset	J 10	Okla.
18133	Pocatello	P 19	Idaho
2739	Pocomoke (Pocomoke City)	Q 22	Md.
25	*Pocono Lake (Wagners)	I 23	Pa.
....	*Pocono Lake Preserve	I 23	Pa.
350	*Pocono Pines (Naomi Pines)	I 22	Pa.
195	*Pocono Summit (Pocono)	I 22	Pa.
50	*Pocopson	P 21	Pa.
52	*Pocotalago	E 13	Ga.
68	Poe	E 21	Ind.
....	Poe	O 17	Va.
125	*Poe	L 9	W. Va.
200	Poestenkill	N 24	N. Y.
22	*Poff	P 5	Va.
30	*Poindexter	K 14	Va.
30	*Point	B 10	La.
300	Point	D 21	Tex.
385	Point Arena	G 2	Calif.
30	*Pointe Aux Barques	L 23	Mich.
50	*Pointe Aux Pines	F 14	Mich.
164	*Pointblank	J 22	Tex.
108	*Point Cedar	L 8	Ark.
50	Point Chautauqua	Q 2	N. Y.
200	Point Clear	R 6	Ala.
....	Point Douglas	N 18	Minn.
515	Pointe a la Hache	O 20	La.
25	*Point Eastern	K 17	Va.
10	*Pointer	I 17	Ky.
....	Point Fermin	O 15, R 4	Calif.
210	Point Harbor	D 24	N. C.
....	*Point Independence	L 23	Mass.
82	Point Isabel	G 16	Ind.
....	Point Isabel, see Port Isabel		Tex.
117	*Point Loma	P 18	Calif.
50	*Point Lookout	P 3	Colo.
50	Point Lookout	Q 16	Md.
306	*Point Lookout	R 10	Mo.
60	*Point Lookout	I 7	N. Y.
2068	Point Marion	Q 4	Pa.
60	Point Mills	B 7	Mich.
....	Point of Pines	L 7	Mass.
370	Point of Rocks	F 7	Md.
40	Point of Rocks	O 9	Wyo.
5	*Point O'Woods	I 8	N. Y.
118	*Point Peninsula	G 15	N. Y.
16	*Point Peter	C 10	Ark.
100	*Point Peter	F 15	Ga.
....	*Point Place	C 10	Ohio
122	*Point Pleasant	E 14	La.
114	*Point Pleasant	R 23	Mo.
1500	*Point Pleasant	L 9	N. Y.
2082	Point Pleasant	J 20	N. J.
2059	Point Pleasant Beach	K 17	N. J.
75	*Point Pleasant	P 6	Ohio
325	*Point Pleasant	M 24	Pa.
3538	Point Pleasant	H 3	W. Va.
27	*Pointrest	L 22	Mo.
75	Point Reyes	H 3	Calif.
400	Point Reyes Station	H 4	Calif.
....	*Point Richmond (Ferry Point)	H 6	Calif.
281	Point Roberts	B 6	Wash.
60	*Point Rock	J 17	N. Y.
6	*Points	E 21	W. Va.
....	Point Terrace	J 4	Ore.
308	Pointville	K 14	N. J.
....	*Point Vivian	F 15	N. Y.
200	Point Washington	N 7	Fla.
596	▲Pojuaque	E 13	N. M.
225	Pokagon	R 11	Mich.
59	*Pokegama	J 18	Minn.
....	Pokegama	C 5	Wis.
600	Polacca	E 19	Ariz.
6	Poland	H 11	Ariz.
150	Poland	K 9	Ind.
150	Poland	N 5	Me.
....	Poland	M 24	Mich.
478	Poland	L 19	N. Y.
1240	Poland	F 20	Ohio
219	Poland (Poland Mines)	Q 3	Pa.
6	Poland Jc.	H 12	Ariz.
219	*Poland Mines (Poland)	Q 3	Pa.
1500	*Poland Spring (South Poland)	O 5	Me.
2	*Polar	D 12	Tex.
118	Polar	L 11	Wis.
25	Polaris	N 6	Mont.
12	Polebridge	C 4	Mont.
11	*Polemic	I 10	W. Va.
85	Poley	O 16	Ala.
50	*Polk	M 10	Mo.
493	Polk	K 19	Neb.
275	Polk	F 15	Ohio
3960	Polk	G 3	Pa.
58	*Polk	L 4	Tenn.
4	*Polkadotte	R 14	Ohio
195	*Polk City	H 16	Fla.
343	Polk City	K 12	Iowa
....	Polk City Jc.	J 12	Iowa
....	Polk Jc.	H 4	Pa.
521	Polkton	I 8	N. C.
175	*Polkville	K 14	Miss.
200	*Polkville	G 3	N. C.
339	Pollard	O 10	Ala.
169	Pollard	A 21	Ark.
153	Pollard	R 24	Okla.
100	Polley	G 11	Wis.
....	*Polleyton, see Verne		Ky.
300	*Pollock	D 6	Calif.
4	Pollock	J 5	Idaho
317	Pollock	G 10	La.
202	Pollock	B 11	Mo.
527	Pollock	B 13	S. D.
600	*Pollock	H 24	Tex.
408	Polloksville	I 19	N. C.
60	*Polly (Sandlick)	L 22	Ky.
2071	Polo	B 12	Ill.
590	Polo	E 7	Mo.
212	*Polonia	K 13	Wis.
25	*Polsgrove	E 16	Ky.
2156	Polson	F 4	Mont.
300	Polvadera	J 9	N. M.
250	*Polytechnic	K 16	Mont.
263	Pomaria	F 11	S. C.
300	*Pomerene	P 22	Ariz.
843	Pomeroy	G 8	Iowa
3581	Pomeroy	O 16	Ohio
600	Pomeroy	P 20	Pa.
1723	Pomeroy	M 23	Wash,
130	*Pompeys Pillar	K 16	Mont.
41	*Pomeroyton	F 20	Ky.
1500	Pomfret	C 23	Conn.
200	*Pomfret	M 11	Md.
100	Pomfret	K 13	Vt.
....	Pomfret Center	D 23	Conn.
13	*Pomins	G 9	Calif.
23539	Pomona	O 17, Q 7	Calif.
25	*Pomona (North Pomona)	N 17	Calif.
316	Pomona	E 17	Fla.
50	*Pomona	H 7	Ga.
500	*Pomona	Q 14	Ill.
485	Pomona	H 22	Kan.
275	Pomona	Q 15	Mo.
350	*Pomona	O 14	N. J.
300	*Pomona	F 5	N. Y.
1000	Pomona	D 9	N. C.
900	Pomona Mills	D 9	N. C.
600	Pomonkey	L 11	Md.
85	*Pomp	F 21	Ky.
4427	Pompano	M 24	Fla.
157	*Pompanoosuc	L 12	Vt.
150	Pompeii	N 16	Mich.
300	Pompey	M 15	N. Y.
130	Pompey's Pillar	L 17	Mont.
3189	Pompton Lakes	C 17	N. J.
1300	Pompton Plains	C 18	N. J.
194	*Ponca	C 8	Ark.
1003	Ponca	F 21	Neb.
16794	Ponca City	C 14	Okla.
382	Ponce de Leon	M 8	Fla.
190	Ponce de Leon	P 10	Mo.
50	*Ponce Park	F 20	Fla.
4001	Ponchatoula	L 17	La.
94	Poncha Jc. (Poncha Springs)	K 11	Colo.
94	*Poncha Springs (Poncha Jc)	K 11	Colo.
80	*Pond	M 13	Calif.
20	*Pond	P 4	Miss.
50	Pond	M 9	Tenn.
1019	Pondcreek	C 10	Okla.
150	Pond Eddy	D 2	N. Y.
36	Pond Eddy	G 25	Pa.
25	*Ponder	R 18	Mo.
201	*Ponder	D 19	Tex.
160	Ponderay	C 5	Idaho
100	*Ponderosa	E 10	N. M.
20	*Pondfork	Q 12	Mo.
216	*Pond Gap	L 8	W. Va.
300	Pondosa	C 7	Calif.
300	Pondosa	D 22	Ore.
....	Ponds	K 9	N. Y.
350	Pond Spring	B 2	Ga.
215	Pondsville	C 7	Md.
45	*Ponemah	F 7	Ill.
50	*Ponemah	E 10	Minn.
270	Poneto	F 20	Ind.
63	*Poniatowski	I 12	Wis.
....	Ponkapog	G 19	Mass.
....	Ponpon	N 16	S. C.
250	*Ponsford	H 6	Minn.
128	*Ponta	G 23	Tex.
500	*Ponte Vedra Beach	D 18	Fla.
9585	Pontiac	F 17	Ill.
66626	Pontiac	O 22	Mich.
27	*Pontiac	R 12	Mo.
1250	Pontiac	G 13	R. I.
165	*Pontoosuc	G 5	Ill.
1832	Pontotoc	C 18	Miss.
160	Pontotoc	N 15	Okla.
210	Pontotoc	I 15	Tex.
200	Pony	M 8	Mont.
75	Ponza	K 20	Ky.
....	*Ponzer	F 22	N. C.
18	*Pool	M 10	W. Va.
196	*Poole	H 8	Ky.
72	Poole	L 15	Neb.
736	Pooler	L 24	Ga.
204	Poolesville	G 8	Md.
180	Pooleville	N 12	Okla.
50	*Poolville	B 18	Miss.
261	Poolville	N 17	N. Y.
515	Poolville	D 17	Tex.
....	Poor Fork, see Cumberland		Ky.
300	*Pope	J 7	Ala.
248	Pope	C 12	Miss.
25	*Pope	O 7	Tenn.
200	Pope City	L 12	Ga.
199	Popejoy	F 13	Iowa
100	*Pope Mills	F 17	N. Y.
50	Popes Creek	N 11	Md.
180	*Pope Valley	G 5	Calif.
300	Popham Beach	P 9	Me.
....	Poplar	N 21	Idaho
....	Popular	E 21	Ky.
10	*Poplar	H 11	Minn.
1442	Poplar	E 23	Mont.
410	*Poplar	M 9	N. C.
462	Poplar	D 5	Wis.
11163	Poplar Bluff	Q 20	Mo.
325	Poplar Branch	C 24	N. C.
100	*Poplar Creek	F 15	Miss.
169	*Poplar Grove	K 18	Ark.
353	Poplar Grove	A 17	Ill.
27	*Poplar Hill	O 3	Va.
200	Poplar Plains	E 20	Ky.
109	*Poplar Ridge	M 13	N. Y.
....	*Poplars	K 14	Md.
50	*Poplarville	I 17	Ky.
1664	Poplarville	Q 15	Miss.
16	*Popple	F 14	Minn.
100	Poquetanuck	J 22	Conn.
600	Poquonock	C 14	Conn.
565	Poquonock Bridge	M 22	Conn.
400	Poquoson	O 21	Va.
10	Porcupine	O 7	S. D.
22	*Pores Knob	E 4	N. C.
15	Porphyry	R 8	Calif.
68	Port	J 4	Okla.
....	Portage	A 8	Ill.
700	Portage	C 1	Me.
4250	▲*Portage	Q 13	Mich.
30	Portage	F 10	Mont.
408	Portage	D 9	Ohio
4123	Portage	M 9	Pa.
342	Portage	A 10	Utah
75	Portage	H 9	Wash.
7016	Portage	J 18	Wis.
254	*Portage Des Sioux	H 19	Mo.
2107	Portageville	R 23	Mo.
460	Portageville	O 7	N. Y.
75	*Portal	O 24	Ariz.
556	*Portal	J 20	Ga.
....	Portal	K 23	Neb.
499	Portal	C 6	N. D.
5104	Portales	J 25	N. M.
2356	Port Allegany	E 11	Pa.
1898	Port Allen	L 14	La.
9409	Port Angeles	F 5	Wash.
495	Port Aransas	P 19	Tex.
46140	Port Arthur	K 25	Tex.
139	*Port Arthur	F 10	Wis.
517	Port Austin	K 23	Mich.
850	Port Barre	K 11	La.
150	Port Birmingham	F 12	Ala.
100	Port Blakely	H 7	Wash.
350	Port Bolivar	L 23	Tex.
861	Port Byron	D 9	Ill.
961	Port Byron	M 13	N. Y.
3279	Port Carbon	L 19	Pa.
23073	Port Chester	G 7	N. Y.
1700	Port Chicago (Bay Point)	A 22	Calif.
4505	Port Clinton	D 11	Ohio
407	Port Clinton	L 20	Pa.
425	Port Clyde	O 12	Me.
350	Port Colden	E 11	N. J.
593	Port Costa	A 19	Calif.
497	Port Crane	Q 16	N. Y.
883	Port Deposit	C 18	Md.
100	Port Discovery	F 16	Wash.
125	Port Eads	R 22	La.
1192	Port Edwards	J 14	Wis.
400	Port Elizabeth	P 10	N. J.
500	Porter	F 11	Ala.
1190	Porter	B 9	Ind.
883	▲Porter	P 2	Me.
250	Porter	O 4	Minn.
101	Porter	P 15	Ohio
562	Porter	G 20	Okla.
42	*Porter	I 7	Pa.
12	*Porter (Porters)	J 22	Tex.
387	▲Porter	K 5	Wash.
....	*Porter (Porters)	K 8	W. Va.
209	*Porters Corners	L 23	N. Y.
3116	Porterdale	G 9	Ga.
150	Porterfield (Center Belpre)	N 17	Ohio
100	*Porterfield	P 11	Wis.
25	Porters	C 21	Del.
50	Porters (Porters Sideling)	Q 16	Pa.
12	*Porters (Porter)	J 22	Tex.
200	*Portersburg	I 19	Ky.
160	*Porters Falls	D 10	W. Va.
32	*Porter Springs	C 9	Ga.
50	Porters Sideling (Porters)	Q 16	Pa.
115	Portersville	C 19	Ala.
125	*Portersville	O 9	Ind.
134	*Portersville (Emerson)	K 14	N. C.
80	*Portersville	L 14	Ohio
276	*Portersville	J 3	Pa.
40	*Portersville	K 4	W. Va.
6270	Porterville	K 13	Calif.
120	*Porterville	I 20	Miss.
95	*Porterville	O 5	N. Y.
150	Portersville	E 12	Utah
75	*Porterwood	G 15	W. Va.
1400	Port Ewen	R 23	N. Y.
1100	Port Fulton	P 17	Ind.
500	Port Gamble	G 7	Wash.
2748	Port Gibson	L 6	Miss.
350	*Port Gibson	M 11	N. Y.
83	*Port Haywood	N 21	Va.
1935	Port Henry	G 24	N. Y.
55	Porthill	A 5	Idaho
300	*Port Homer	I 20	Ohio
313	Port Hope	K 24	Mich.
65	*Port Hudson	J 14	La.
600	*Port Hueneme (Hueneme)	N 13	Calif.
32759	Port Huron	N 25	Mich.
393	Portia	C 18	Ark.
349	Portis	E 12	Kan.
1440	*Port Isabel (Point Isabel)	P 5	Tex.
3500	Port Jefferson	G 9	N. Y.
360	Port Jefferson	I 7	Ohio
1800	Port Jefferson Station	G 9	N. Y.
9749	Port Jervis	E 3	N. Y.
275	*Port Kennedy	N 22	Pa.
150	Port Kent	E 24	N. Y.
518	Portland	Q 16	Ark.
377	Portland	L 15	Colo.
2500	Portland	I 14	Conn.
200	*Portland	M 7	Fla.
158	*Portland	E 2	Ga.
6362	Portland	G 21	Ind.
50	Portland	D 14	Iowa
35	*Portland	N 16	Kan.
26	*Portland	I 15	Ky.
73643	Portland	P 6	Me.
2247	Portland	O 15	Mich.
200	Portland	I 15	Mo.
500	Portland	P 2	N. Y.
551	Portland	J 23	N. D.
300	*Portland	N 15	Ohio
305394	Portland	D 7	Ore.
427	Portland	K 23	Pa.
1212	Portland	K 12	Tenn.
300	Portland	P 19	Tex.
1	Portland Jc.	J 22	N. D.
60	*Portland Mills	J 10	Ind.
321	Portland Mills	H 8	Pa.
243	Portland Point	O 13	N. Y.
400	Portlandville	O 19	N. Y.
2069	Port Lavaca	N 20	Tex.
717	Port Leyden	J 18	N. Y.
200	Port Ludlow	G 9	Wash.
100	*Port Madison	H 6	Wash.
646	Port Matilda	K 11	Pa.
100	*Port Mayaca	K 23	Fla.
1500	Port Monmouth	G 20	N. J.
500	Port Morris	D 13	N. J.
300	Port Murray	E 11	N. J.
2487	Port Neches	K 25	Tex.
2100	Port Norris	P 10	N. J.
362	Port O'Connor	O 20	Tex.
2000	Portola	E 10	Calif.
662	Port Orange	F 19	Fla.
1566	Port Orchard	I 6	Wash.
755	Port Orford	O 2	Ore.
271	Port Penn	D 21	Del.
1031	*Port Perry	L 3	Pa.
150	Port Reading	F 18	N. J.
135	*Port Republic	M 14	Md.
402	Port Republic	N 15	N. J.
500	Port Republic	I 11	Va.
134	Port Richey	H 12	Fla.
420	*Port Richmond	M 19	Va.
179	*Port Royal	D 16	Ky.
744	Port Royal	M 14	Pa.
342	Port Royal	P 14	S. C.
60	*Port Royal	L 9	Tenn.
123	*Port Royal	K 17	Va.
2393	Port St. Joe	P 11	Fla.
204	Port Sanilac	N 25	Mich.
....	Port San Luis	M 9	Calif.
153	*Port Sewall	K 24	Fla.
320	Portsmouth	K 4	Iowa
75	*Portsmouth	H 21	Ky.
14821	Portsmouth	O 21	N. H.
50	*Portsmouth	I 23	N. C.
40466	Portsmouth	Q 11	Ohio
292	Portsmouth	I 20	R. I.
2500	Portsmouth	I 21	R. I.
50745	Portsmouth	P 21	Va.
162	Port Stanley	D 6	Wash.
50	*Port Sullivan	I 19	Tex.
550	*Port Sulphur	O 19	La.
1124	Port Tampa City	I 13	Fla.
110	*Port Tobacco	M 11	Md.
12	*Port Tobacco (Springhill)	L 12	Md.
4683	Port Townsend	F 6	Wash.
350	Port Trevorton	L 16	Pa.
1018	Portville	R 6	N. Y.
211	*Port Vincent	L 16	La.
3601	*Port Vue	L 3	Pa.
3000	Port Washington	H 6	N. Y.
493	Port Washington	I 18	Ohio
4046	Port Washington	P 18	Wis.
628	*Port Washington North	H 7	N. Y.
300	*Port Wentworth	L 24	Ga.
269	Port William	M 9	Ohio
1000	Port Wing	E 4	Wis.
502	Porum	I 22	Okla.
300	*Porvenir	K 4	Tex.
1386	*Posen	C 21	Ill.
239	Posen	I 20	Mich.
200	*Posen (Farwell)	K 16	Neb.
71	*Posey	L 13	Calif.
120	*Posey	M 13	Ill.
116	*Posey	O 8	W. Va.
948	Poseyville	Q 4	Ind.
125	*Poskin	C 10	Wis.
36	*Possession	E 7	Wash.
4	Post	I 14	Ore.
2046	Post	D 11	Tex.
....	Posta (La Posta)	P 5	Colo.
67	Post Creek	Q 12	N. Y.
....	Postell	I 11	Ga.
316	*Postell	Q 1	N. C.
42	*Postelle	J 18	Ark.
250	*Postelle, (Ducktown)	Q 18	Tenn.
843	Post Falls	D 3	Idaho
150	Post Mills	I 16	Vt.
52	Postoak	I 8	Mo.
112	*Postoak	D 16	Tex.
13	*Post Oak	J 16	Va.
118	*Postoak Point	K 20	Tex.
26	Poston (Sugar Creek)	N 15	Ohio
29	Poston	H 21	S. C.
....	*Postvale, see Marana		Ariz.
1194	Postville	D 20	Iowa
263	Potash	P 20	La.
4020	Poteau	K 24	Okla.
125	*Potecasi	C 19	N. C.
2315	Poteet	M 16	Tex.
509	Poth	M 17	Tex.
....	Potholes	Q 25	Calif.
800	Potlatch	F 4	Idaho
60	Potlatch	I 5	Wash.
646	Potomac (Marysville)	H 21	Ill.
300	*Potomac (Pinto)	M 5	Md.
22	Potomac	I 5	Mont.
100	*Potomac Beach	I 18	Va.
20	Potomac Manor	E 18	W. Va.
36	*Potomac Mills	J 19	Va.
....	Potomac Valley Jc.	C 5	Md.
2017	Potosi	L 18	Mo.
506	Potosi	G 22	Wis.
60	*Potrero	Q 19	Calif.
4821	Potsdam	D 18	N. Y.
229	*Potsdam (New Lebanon)	K 6	Ohio
150	Potter	J 4	Ark.
150	Potter	E 23	Kan.
110	*Potter (Potters)	F 23	Ky.
387	Potter	K 3	Neb.
176	Potter	O 15	Wis.
226	Potter Brook	E 13	Pa.
512	Potter Hill	M 5	R. I.
60	*Potter Hollow	O 23	N. Y.
330	Potter Place	M 11	N. H.
129	Pottersdale	J 9	Pa.

Pop.	Place	Index	State
339	Potters Mills	K 13	Pa.
110*	Pottersville	Q 14	Mo.
300	Pottersville	E 13	N. J.
329	Pottersville	I 23	N. Y.
512	Potter Valley	F 4	Calif.
200*	Potterville	J 8	Ga.
547	Potterville	P 17	Mich.
100*	Potterville	E 17	Pa.
....*	Potts	J 14	Nev.
....	Potts (Potsdam)	Q 9	N. D.
25	Potts	D 9	Wash.
342	Pottsboro	B 19	Tex.
394	Potts Camp	B 16	Miss.
26*	Potts Creek	M 6	Va.
190*	Potts Grove	I 17	Pa.
316	Pottstown	F 12	Ill.
20194	Pottstown	N 22	Pa.
....	Potts Valley Jc.	N 4	Va.
308	Pottsville	G 9	Ark.
24530	Pottsville	L 19	Pa.
176*	Pottsville	G 17	Tex.
487	Potwin	L 18	Kan.
300	Poughkeepsie	C 16	Ark.
40478	Poughkeepsie	C 6	N. Y.
150*	Poughquag	R 23	N. Y.
670	Poulan	M 10	Ga.
639	Poulsbo	H 7	Wash.
91*	Poulson	K 24	Va.
1333	Poultney	L 6	Vt.
218	Pound	C 5	Va.
310	Pound	O 11	Wis.
250*	Pounding Mill	C 9	Va.
170	Poway	P 19	Calif.
56*	Powcan	L 19	Va.
76	Powderhorn	L 8	Colo.
1000*	Powderly	F 13	Ala.
450	Powderly	I 10	Ky.
125*	Powderly	C 21	Tex.
60*	Powder Mills	I 13	Ky.
100	Powder River	I 15	Wyo.
431	Powder Springs	F 5	Ga.
100*	Powder Springs	M 20	Tenn.
25	Powderville	L 23	Mont.
20*	Powell	G 19	Ky.
17*	Powell	B 9	Miss.
60*	Powell	R 7	Mo.
100	Powell	O 20	Neb.
....	Powell	H 23	N. D.
300	Powell	J 11	Ohio
50*	Powell	P 15	Okla.
500	Powell	F 18	Pa.
75	Powell	K 9	S. D.
400	Powell (Powell Station)	M 18	Tenn.
521*	Powell	F 20	Tex.
81*	Powell	E 13	W. Va.
11*	Powell	H 6	Wis.
1948	Powell	B 9	Wyo.
400	Powell Butte	I 12	Ore.
100*	Powell's Point	D 24	N. C.
400	Powell Station (Powell)	M 18	Tenn.
267*	Powellsville	D 20	N. C.
20*	Powellton	G 6	Ill.
1300	Powellton	M 7	W. Va.
250*	Powellville	N 21	Md.
450*	Powelton (Retort)	J 10	Pa.
120	Power	F 9	Mont.
....	Power	O 23	N. D.
1532	Power	P 24	W. Va.
50*	Powers	G 21	Ind.
258	Powers	C 6	Mich.
....	Powers (Cunningham)	N 3	Ore.
15*	Powersburg	K 17	Ky.
79*	Powersite	Q 11	Mo.
464	Powers Lake	E 6	N. D.
175*	Powers Lake	O 22	Wis.
150*	Powersville	J 10	Ga.
294	Powersville	A 10	Mo.
500	Powhatan	F 11	Ala.
137	Powhatan	C 17	Ark.
300	Powhatan	F 7	La.
2054	Powhatan, (Powhatan Pt.)	K 20	Ohio
100	Powhatan	M 15	Va.
500	Powhatan	B 10	W. Va.
2054	Powhatan Point (Powhatan)	K 20	Ohio
184	Powhattan	D 21	Kan.
100	Pownal	O 6	Me.
350	Pownal	R 6	Vt.
500	Poyen	L 11	Ark.
870	Poynette	K 19	Wis.
50*	Poynor	R 18	Mo.
250*	Poynor	F 21	Tex.
85*	Poyntelle	E 22	Pa.
300	Poy Sippi	L 15	Wis.
264*	Pozo	M 11	Calif.
....	Pozo	K 14	Ariz.
900*	Praco	F 12	Ala.
23*	Prade Ranch	K 13	Tex.
251	Prado	Q 8	Calif.
30*	Prague	L 12	Ark.
385	Prague	K 21	Neb.
1422	Prague	I 15	Okla.
400	Praha	K 19	Tex.
185*	Prairie	K 9	Ala.
125	Prairie	N 7	Idaho
168*	Prairie	E 20	Miss.
....	Prairie, see Prairie City		Ore.
50	Prairie	D 8	Wash.
193*	Praireburg	H 21	Iowa
80*	Prairie Center	D 16	Ill.
574	Prairie City	G 9	Ill.
831	Prairie City	L 13	Iowa
647	Prairie City (Prairie)	H 19	Ore.
50	Prairie Creek	H 4	Ark.
175*	Prairie Creek	L 5	Ind.
4622	Prairie du Chien	F 20	Wis.
....*	Prairie du Pont	M 10	Ill.
576	Prairie du Rocher	O 10	Ill.
1001	Prairie du Sac	I 19	Wis.
16	Prairie Elk	F 21	Mont.
335	Prairie Farm	C 10	Wis.
887	Prairie Grove	C 4	Ark.
147*	Prairie Hill	E 12	Mo.
262*	Prairie Hill	H 20	Tex.
251	Prairie Home	H 12	Mo.
44	Prairie Home	L 22	Neb.
....	Prairie Jc.	H 8	N. D.
260	Prairie Lea	L 17	Tex.
250	Prairie Point	H 22	Miss.
312	Prairieton	K 5	Ind.
92*	Prairietown	L 11	Ill.
250*	Prairie View	G 7	Ark.
150	Prairie View	A 20	Ill.
205*	Prairie View	D 9	Kan.
10	Prairie View	K 21	Tex.
217	Prairieville	M 15	La.
150	Prairieville	P 14	Mich.
136*	Prairieville	E 20	Tex.
1030	Praise (Elkhorn City)	I 24	Ky.
40*	Prater	B 7	Va.
6591	Pratt	M 11	Kan.
32*	Pratt	Q 17	Minn.
417*	Pratt	L 7	W. Va.
....	Pratt City	F 13	Ala.
....	Pratt Jc.	L 10	Wis.
....	Pratts Jc.	E 14	Mass.
67	Pratts (Pratts Hollow)	M 16	N. Y.
42*	Pratts	I 13	Va.
635	Prattsburg	O 10	N. Y.
12*	Pratts Fork	N 16	Ohio
67*	Pratts Hollow (Pratts)	M 16	N. Y.
114*	Prattsville	L 11	Ark.
500	Prattsville	P 21	N. Y.
2664	Prattville	J 15	Ala.
192	Prattville	R 18	Mich.
60	Prattville Jc.	J 16	Ala.
60	Pratum	F 7	Ore.
3	Pray	M 11	Mont.
100*	Pray	H 14	Wis.
225	Preble	E 21	Ind.
150	Preble	N 14	N. Y.
25*	Preece	G 23	Ky.
100	Preemption	E 8	Ill.
75	Pregnall	L 16	S. C.
275	Premier	Q 6	W. Va.
1080	Premont	Q 17	Tex.
600	Prenter	M 7	W. Va.
20	Prentice	K 8	Ala.
87*	Prentice	J 9	Ill.
452	Prentice	H 10	Wis.
40*	Prentiss	I 11	Ky.
343	Prentiss	I 18	Me.
989	Prentiss	N 13	Miss.
100*	Prentiss	Q 5	N. C.
2	Prentiss	I 2	Okla.
6018	Prescott	H 11	Ariz.
3177	Prescott	N 8	Ark.
400	Prescott	N 8	Iowa
277	Prescott	K 25	Kan.
48	Prescott	E 10	Mass.
278	Prescott	K 20	Mich.
28*	Prescott	N 14	Mo.
210	Prescott	A 7	Ore.
324	Prescott	N 21	Wash.
857	Prescott	A 12	Wis.
150	Prescottville	J 8	Pa.
326	Presho	R 11	N. Y.
568	Presho	K 14	S. D.
52*	President	G 5	Pa.
1202	Presidio	L 4	Tex.
14*	Presley	B 10	Ga.
5456■	Presque Isle	D 19	Me.
45*	Presque Isle	H 19	Mich.
320*	Press	H 21	Ky.
160*	Pressmen's Home	L 22	Tenn.
2000*	Presston	L 3	Pa.
262*	Presto	M 3	Pa.
65*	Preston	G 4	Calif.
1000	Preston	I 23	Conn.
349	Preston	L 6	Ga.
4236	Preston	R 20	Idaho
50*	Preston	O 11	Ill.
....	Preston	K 6	Ind.
602	Preston	I 24	Iowa
328	Preston	L 12	Kan.
112*	Preston	E 19	Ky.
369	Preston	K 19	Md.
1447	Preston	R 21	Minn.
80*	Preston	H 20	Miss.
127*	Preston	L 10	Mo.
120	Preston	O 25	Neb.
25	Preston	C 19	N. M.
154	Preston	I 20	Nev.
75	Preston	O 17	N. Y.
250	Preston	H 19	Okla.
28*	Preston	Q 6	Va.
405	Preston	I 9	Wash.
150	Preston Hollow	P 21	N. Y.
50*	Preston Park	E 22	Pa.
2328	Prestonsburg	G 23	Ky.
296*	Prestonville	D 15	Ky.
175*	Prestwick	N 4	Ala.
5	Pretoria	M 7	Ga.
452	Pretty Prairie	L 14	Kan.
9	Pretty Rock	Q 8	N. D.
40*	Prevost	C 6	Wash.
25*	Prewitt	F 5	N. M.
....*	Pribble	M 21	Va.
150*	Price	G 19	Md.
3981*	Price (Ladue)	I 20	Mo.
47*	Price	C 9	N. C.
135	Price	M 11	N. D.
850*	Price	F 23	Tex.
5214	Price	I 17	Utah
2*	Price Creek	B 4	Colo.
250	Pricedale	O 10	Miss.
1100*	Pricedale (Somers)	N 4	Pa.
500	Price Hill	N 8	W. Va.
30*	Prices Fork	O 4	Va.
17*	Pricetown	I 16	Ky.
53*	Pricetown	O 9	Ohio
75*	Priceville	H 13	Ky.
6084	Prichard	Q 5	Ala.
30*	Prichard	D 7	Idaho
25*	Prichard	B 11	Miss.
200*	Prichard	L 1	W. Va.
200*	Priddy	H 16	Tex.
18*	Pride	K 15	La.
....	Pride	D 11	S. C.
....	Prides Crossing (Prides)	D 21	Mass.
1056	Priest River	C 4	Idaho
51*	Prillman (Nola)	P 6	Va.
34*	Prim	E 13	Ark.
....	Primero	P 15	Colo.
1081	Primghar	D 4	Iowa
14*	Primm	N 9	Tenn.
300*	Primos	P 23	Pa.
59*	Primrose	H 5	Ga.
65*	Primrose	P 20	Iowa
20*	Primrose	G 20	Ky.
176	Primrose	I 17	Neb.
200	Primrose	M 2	Pa.
647▲*	Primrose	K 20	Wis.
210*	Prince	N 8	W. Va.
200	Prince Frederick	M 14	Md.
35	Prince George	O 17	Va.
380	Princess	E 22	Ky.
942	Princess Anne	P 21	Md.
150	Princess Anne	Q 21	Va.
75*	Princeton	A 17	Ala.
238*	Princeton	M 11	Ark.
400	Princeton	F 6	Calif.
300	Princeton	O 23	Fla.
175	Princeton	F 4	Idaho
5224	Princeton	D 13	Ill.
7786	Princeton	P 4	Ind.
414	Princeton	K 25	Iowa
187	Princeton	I 23	Kan.
5389	Princeton	I 8	Ky.
60*	Princeton	C 6	La.
1000	Princeton	J 21	Me.
300	Princeton	E 13	Mass.
600	Princeton	F 7	Mich.
1865	Princeton	L 15	Minn.
1584	Princeton	C 9	Mo.
76	Princeton	M 22	Neb.
7719	Princeton	H 13	N. J.
512	Princeton	G 16	N. C.
12	Princeton	M 19	Ore.
167	Princeton	D 7	S. C.
564	Princeton	D 20	Tex.
7426	Princeton	Q 8	W. Va.
1247	Princeton	K 16	Wis.
700*	Princeton Depot (Princeton)	F 12	Mass.
75	Princeton Jc.	H 14	N. J.
996	Princeville	F 11	Ill.
818	Princeville	E 18	N. C.
300*	Princewick	O 8	W. Va.
130	Principio Furnace	C 18	Md.
125	Prindle	Q 8	Wash.
2358	Prineville	I 13	Ore.
....	Prineville Jc.	I 12	Ore.
2000*	Pringle	I 20	Pa.
273	Pringle	L 2	S. D.
42	Pringle	B 4	Tex.
100*	Prinsburg	N 9	Minn.
35*	Printer	H 22	Ky.
349	Prior Lake	O 15	Minn.
57*	Priors	E 2	Ga.
23*	Pripet	M 13	Me.
5*	Priscilla	D 16	Ill.
11*	Priscilla	F 8	Miss.
50*	Pritchardville	Q 14	S. C.
495	Pritchett	P 21	Colo.
250*	Pritchett	E 23	Tex.
36*	Proberta	E 5	Calif.
290*	Procious (Camp)	K 8	W. Va.
100*	Proctor	H 20	Ark.
75	Proctor	B 21	Colo.
20	Proctor	E 14	Fla.
25*	Proctor	G 18	Ill.
249	Proctor	H 20	Ky.
2468	Proctor (Proctorknott)	H 20	Minn.
100	Proctor	E 4	Mont.
218	Proctor	P 3	N. C.
300	Proctor	F 24	Okla.
227	Proctor	H 16	Pa.
200	Proctor	F 16	Tex.
2184	Proctor	K 8	Vt.
127	Proctor	B 10	W. Va.
2468*	Proctorknott (Proctor)	H 20	Minn.
643	Proctorsville	M 12	Vt.
209	Proctorville	L 12	N. C.
731	Proctorville	R 14	Ohio
112*	Proffit	J 13	Va.
500*	Progreso	P 4	Tex.
....*	Progress	I 20	Mo.
1550*	Progress	N 17	Pa.
35*	Progress	I 10	W. Va.
120	Progresso	I 13	N. M.
1500*	Project City	D 6	Calif.
37*	Prole	M 12	Iowa
150*	Promise	B 23	Ore.
30	Promise	E 12	S. D.
225	Promise City	P 13	Iowa
68	Promontory	C 8	Utah
202	Prompton	F 23	Pa.
1469	Prophetstown	D 11	Ill.
61*	Prosit	F 19	Minn.
45*	Prospect	E 9	Ala.
60	Prospect	J 10	Conn.
8*	Prospect	H 19	Ill.
31*	Prospect	E 14	Ky.
32	Prospect	M 14	Me.
285*	Prospect	L 17	N. Y.
915	Prospect	I 11	Ohio
125*	Prospect	Q 6	Ore.
547*	Prospect	J 4	Pa.
280*	Prospect (Prospect Station)	Q 10	Tenn.
109*	Prospect	D 16	Tex.
300*	Prospect	N 12	Va.
50*	Prospectdale	N 4	Va.
50	Prospect Ferry	M 14	Me.
200	Prospect Harbor	M 18	Me.
100*	Prospect Hill	D 12	N. C.
5714*	Prospect Park	D 19	N. J.
5100*	Prospect Park (Moores)	P 23	Pa.
160	Prospect Plains	H 15	N. J.
180*	Prospect Station (Prospect)	Q 10	Tenn.
250*	Prospectville	N 23	Pa.
85*	Prosper	R 22	Minn.
42	Prosper	M 24	N. D.
50	Prosper	M 2	Ore.
271	Prosper	D 19	Tex.
7*	Prosperine	M 12	Mo.
20*	Prosperity	B 9	Ark.
....*	Prosperity	I 12	Ky.
145	Prosperity	O 6	Mo.
175	Prosperity	O 2	Pa.
719	Prosperity	F 10	S. C.
311	Prosperity	N 8	W. Va.
99	Prosser	M 16	Neb.
....	Prosser	R 7	N. Y.
1719	Prosser	O 16	Wash.
846	Protection	O 9	Kan.
100	Protection	O 5	N. Y.
162*	Protem	Q 11	Mo.
290	Protivin	C 18	Iowa
8	Prouts Neck	Q 6	Me.
150*	Provemont (Lake Leelanau)	I 13	Mich.
300	Provencal	G 7	La.
70	Provence	P 14	Okla.
4397	Providence	H 8	Ky.
131	Providence	B 19	Md.
253504	Providence	E 15	R. I.
1110	Providence	B 12	Utah
40*	Providence Forge	N 18	Va.
20	Providence Jc.	Q 22	Va.
50*	Provident City	M 20	Tex.
50*	Province Lake	L 19	N. H.
3668■	Provincetown	J 13	Mass.
125*	Proving Ground	B 11	Ill.
....*	Proviso	C 21	Ill.
175	Provo	M 5	Ark.
50*	Provo	I 11	Ky.
20	Provo	N 1	S. D.
18071	Provo	G 12	Utah
40	Provolt	Q 5	Ore.
85*	Provost	M 14	Va.
100	Prowers	M 22	Colo.
600*	Pruden	L 20	Tenn.
62	Prudence	I 17	R. I.
525*	Prudence	N 8	W. Va.
100*	Prudenville	K 17	Mich.
....	Prue	E 17	Okla.
....*	Pruett	L 15	Ill.
30*	Pruitt	C 9	Ark.
....	Prunedale	B 20	Ore.
60*	Prunty	F 9	W. Va.
250	Pruntytown	E 14	W. Va.
500	Pryor	O 15	Colo.
150*	Pryor	M 16	Mont.
2501	Pryor	E 21	Okla.
....	Pryor	K 8	Ore.
230	Pryorsburg (Pryors)	K 5	Ky.
125*	Pryse	G 19	Ky.
32*	Public	I 17	Ky.
....	Puck	O 16	S. C.
150*	Puckett	L 13	Miss.
52162	Pueblo	L 16	Colo.
39*	Pueblo	K 17	Ky.
2200*	Puente	Q 6	Calif.
....	Puente	C 3	Tex.
....	Puertecito, see Field		N. M.
150	Puerto de Luna	H 19	N. M.
200	Puget Island	N 4	Wash.
142	Pughtown	N 24	W. Va.
90*	Pujol	O 11	Ill.
258	Pukwana	L 16	S. D.
34	Pulare	E 18	Okla.
241	Pulaski	K 20	Ga.
623	Pulaski	R 15	Ill.
100*	Pulaski	E 11	Ind.
400	Pulaski	P 17	Iowa
53*	Pulaski	I 17	Ky.
100	Pulaski (Wheelerton)	Q 16	Mich.
105	Pulaski	K 15	Miss.
1895	Pulaski	J 15	N. Y.
322	Pulaski	I 1	Pa.
5314	Pulaski	Q 10	Tenn.
8792	Pulaski	O 3	Va.
979	Pulaski	O 13	Wis.
200*	Pulcifer	N 12	Wis.
18*	Pulga	F 7	Calif.
25*	Pulleys Mill	P 15	Ill.
200*	Pullman	P 12	Mich.
4417	Pullman	L 24	Wash.
204	Pullman	F 9	W. Va.
150	Pulteney	O 11	N. Y.
257	Pultneyville	K 11	N. Y.
....*	Pumpkin Center	I 17	Ky.
24*	Pumpkin Chapel	I 16	Ky.
318	Puncheon	I 22	Ky.
610	Pungo	F 21	N. C.
120*	Pungo	Q 23	Va.
195	Pungoteague	L 23	Va.
1889	Punta Gorda	L 15	Fla.
12	Puntenney	G 11	Ariz.
9482	Punxsutawney	J 8	Pa.
75*	Puposky	E 10	Minn.
35	Purcell	C 16	Colo.
75*	Purcell	D 23	Kan.
204	Purcell	O 6	Mo.
3116	Purcell	L 12	Okla.
787	Purcellville	E 15	Va.
180*	Purchase	G 6	N. Y.
50*	Purchase Line	L 6	Pa.
303	Purdin	C 10	Mo.
262*	Purdon	F 20	Tex.
18	Purdum	H 12	Neb.
....*	Purdy	C 7	Ark.
28*	Purdy	O 13	Iowa
488	Purdy	Q 8	Mo.
60	Purdy	M 11	Okla.
100	Purdy	Q 16	Va.
65*	Purdy Creek	Q 10	N. Y.
235*	Purdy Station (Purdys)	E 6	N. Y.
44*	Purgitsville	E 20	W. Va.
500	Puritan	B 21	Mich.
200*	Puritan	M 9	Pa.
200*	Puritan (Puritan Mines)	O 3	W. Va.
50*	Purlear	D 4	N. C.
186*	Purling	P 23	N. Y.
56*	Purmela	H 17	Tex.
500*	Pursglove	C 14	W. Va.
1000	Purvis	O 16	Miss.
50*	Purvis	K 11	Mo.
45*	Purvis	J 11	N. C.
100*	Purvis (Buckham)	Q 20	Va.
368	Puryear	L 6	Tenn.
167*	Pushmataha	K 4	Ala.
202	Put-In-Bay	C 12	Ohio
150*	Putnam	K 6	Ala.
7775	Putnam	C 24	Conn.
125*	Putnam	K 6	Ga.
75	Putnam	E 13	Ill.
450*	Putnam (Putnam Station)	K 24	N. Y.
....*	Putnam	G 11	N. C.
142	Putnam	G 6	Okla.
487	Putnam	G 15	Tex.
50*	Putnam	D 7	Va.
104	Putnam Hall	D 15	Fla.
....	Putnam Jc.	E 6	N. Y.
450*	Putnam Station (Putnam)	K 24	N. Y.
145	Putnamville	K 10	Ind.
80*	Putney	M 7	Ga.
313*	Putney	J 21	Ky.
25	Putney	D 19	S. D.
296	Putney	P 13	Vt.
400	Putney	K 8	W. Va.
420*	Putneyville	L 5	Pa.
792	Puxico	P 21	Mo.
7889	Puyallup	J 8	Wash.
224	Pyatt	B 10	Ark.
89*	Pyatts	D 2	N. C.
15*	Pyatts	O 14	Ill.
150*	Pyland	D 19	Miss.
50*	Pylesville	B 16	Md.
201	Pyote	G 7	Tex.
....	Pyra	N 2	N. M.
47*	Pyramid	H 23	Ky.
13*	Pyramid	F 3	Nev.
600	Pyrites	E 18	N. Y.
100	Pyriton	G 19	Ala.
312	Pyrmont	L 6	Ohio
60*	Pyron	E 12	Tex.
28*	Pyrus	J 15	Ky.
120	Pysht	E 2	Wash.

Q

Pop.	Place	Index	State
25*	Quaid	G 12	La.
35*	Quail	I 17	Ky.
118*	Quail	E 6	Tex.
525*	Quakake	K 19	Pa.
22*	Quaker	L 18	Mo.
115*	Quaker (Mathers)	L 1	W. Va.
75	Quaker Bridge	R 4	N. Y.
634	Quaker City	K 18	Ohio
233	Quaker Hill	K 21	Conn.
275*	Quaker Hill	C 6	N. Y.
175*	Quaker Street	N 22	N. Y.
160	Quakertown	F 12	N. J.
5150	Quakertown	M 22	Pa.
22*	Quality	J 11	Ky.
50	Qualls	G 22	Okla.
85*	Quamba	K 17	Minn.
3767	Quanah	A 14	Tex.
200	Quantico	N 21	Md.
1139	Quantico	H 17	Va.
1054	Quapaw	A 24	Okla.
200	Quarai	H 12	N. M.
144	Quarry	I 15	Iowa
122*	Quarry	D 9	Va.
125*	Quarry	P 15	Wis.
....	Quarry Jc.	I 12	Conn.
60*	Quarryville	A 14	N. J.
1120	Quarryville	Q 19	Pa.
....	Quartz	K 10	Colo.
18	Quartzburg	M 5	Idaho
50*	Quartz Mountain	N 13	Ore.
60	Quartzsite	J 4	Ariz.
400	Quasqueton	G 19	Iowa
....*	Quay, see Winter Beach		Fla.
20	Quay	G 22	N. M.
104	Quay	E 15	Okla.
....	Quealy	N 3	Wyo.
150	Quealy	P 7	Wyo.
....	Quebec Jc.	G 14	N. H.
400	Quebeck	N 15	Tenn.
300	Quechee	K 14	Vt.
600*	Quecreek	O 7	Pa.
118*	Queen	N 10	Pa.
250	Queen Anne	I 18	Md.
646	Queen City	B 12	Mo.
321	Queen City	D 24	Tex.
26	Queen City Park	E 6	Vt.
20	Queen Creek	L 15	Ariz.
120	Queen Jc.	J 3	Pa.
12	Queens (Martin)	D 21	Ky.
90*	Queens	H 13	W. Va.
....*	Queensborough	C 5	La.
1297634*	Queens Boro, (part of New York City)	I 5	N. Y.
200*	Queen Shoals	K 8	W. Va.
140*	Queens Ridge	M 2	W. Va.
275	Queenstown	I 18	Md.
90*	Queenstown	J 5	Pa.
....*	Queens Village	H 6	N. Y.
50*	Queensville	M 17	Ind.
250	Quemado	I 4	N. M.
314	Quemado	N 12	Tex.
557	Quenemo	I 22	Kan.
200*	Quentin	N 6	Miss.
600*	Quentin	N 18	Pa.
250	Queponco (Newark)	O 24	Md.
56*	Quercus Grove	N 22	Ind.
900	Questa	C 15	N. M.
11	Quick	N 11	Neb.
103*	Quick	L 6	W. Va.
54*	Quick City	I 8	Mo.
67*	Quickle (Little Otter)	I 10	W. Va.
90*	Quicksand	G 21	Ky.
200*	Quicksburg	G 12	Va.
3*	Quietus	M 17	Mont.
300	Quihi	M 15	Tex.
400	Quilcene	G 6	Wash.
11*	Quill	C 7	Ga.
50*	Quillayute	F 2	Wash.
363	Quimby	F 4	Iowa
60	Quimby	C 16	Me.
46*	Quimby	P 13	Mich.
827*	Quinaby	F 8	Ore.
220	Quinault	I 3	Wash.
226*	Quinby	M 24	Va.
1800	Quincy	E 9	Calif.
3888	Quincy	B 4	Fla.
40469	Quincy	I 4	Ill.
300	Quincy	K 11	Ind.
125	Quincy	L 20	Kan.
252*	Quincy	D 21	Ky.
75810	Quincy	G 20	Mass.
1333	Quincy	R 16	Mich.
100*	Quincy	E 22	Miss.
90*	Quincy	L 9	Mo.
83*	Quincy	K 12	N. H.
536	Quincy	I 8	Ohio
303	Quincy	A 6	Ore.
400	Quincy	Q 14	Pa.
318	Quincy	J 16	Wash.
350	Quincy (Dickinson)	L 6	W. Va.
25	Quincy Jc.	E 9	Calif.
30	Quincy Jc.	K 5	Ill.
250*	Quindaro	F 25	Kan.
300	Quinebaug	A 23	Conn.
188	Quinlan	C 5	Okla.
677	Quinlan	D 20	Tex.
189	Quinn	K 7	S. D.
600	Quinnesec	G 5	Mich.
246	Quinney (Amalga)	B 11	Utah
500*	Quinnimont	M 8	W. Va.
34*	Quinque	J 13	Va.
481	Quinter	G 7	Kan.
150*	Quinton	F 11	Ala.
521*	Quinton	J 17	Ky.
500	Quinton	N 6	N. J.
1245	Quinton	K 21	Okla.
56*	Quinton	M 18	Va.
250	Quinwood	M 10	W. Va.
5	Quiring	E 10	Minn.
....	Quissett	N 22	Mass.
763	Quitaque	A 11	Tex.
393	Quitman	F 13	Ark.
4450	Quitman	P 11	Ga.
212*	Quitman	D 8	La.
1471	Quitman	L 20	Miss.
195*	Quitman	B 4	Mo.
1200	Quitman	D 22	Tex.
5*	Quitsna	E 20	N. C.
357	Qulin	R 21	Mo.
633	Quogue	H 11	N. Y.

R

Pop.	Place	Index	State
30	Raab	C 9	Ohio
700*	Rabbit Run	L 7	Va.
128*	Raber	F 16	Mich.
34*	Rabey	I 15	Minn.
5*	Raboin	G 12	Minn.
63*	Rabun	P 7	Ala.
90*	Raccoon	J 10	Ind.
35*	Raccoon	H 24	Ky.
750*	Raccoon (Joffre)	O 2	Pa.
40*	Raccoon Ford	H 14	Va.
....*	Raccourci, see Brownview		La.
1046	Raceland (Raceland Junction)	D 22	Ky.
500	Raceland	O 17	La.
7	Raceland Jc.	O 17	La.
1046*	Raceland Junction (Raceland)	D 22	Ky.
85*	Racepond	O 19	Ga.
20	Race Track	J 7	Mont.
30	Racetrack	C 21	Tex.
300*	Rachel	D 12	W. Va.
180	Racine	Q 19	Minn.
125*	Racine	P 6	Mo.
490	Racine	P 16	Ohio
357*	Racine (Homewood Junction)	L 2	Pa.
150*	Racine	L 6	W. Va.
67195	Racine	P 21	Wis.
....	Racine Jc.	P 21	Wis.
250*	Rackerby	F 8	Calif.
12*	Rackett	I 6	Neb.
350	Raco	F 17	Mich.
1*	Rada	E 21	W. Va.
200*	Radcliff	O 14	Ohio
631	Radcliffe	H 13	Iowa
....*	Radcliff	Q 14	Va.
43*	Raddle	P 13	Ill.
57*	Rader	M 23	Tenn.
152	Radersburg	K 9	Mont.
10*	Radford	J 15	Ill.
6990	Radford (East Radford)	O 4	Va.
13*	Radiant	J 14	Va.
....*	Radical	Q 9	Mo.
75*	Radical	C 4	N. C.
104*	Radio	F 4	Mont.
188	Radisson	F 8	Wis.
83	Radium	F 10	Colo.
85*	Radium	K 11	Kan.
48*	Radium	D 3	Minn.
....	Radium	N 17	S. C.
12*	Radium	Q 16	Va.
100*	Radium Springs (Ft. Selden)	N 9	N. M.
262*	Radley	M 25	Kan.
95*	Radnor	F 12	Ind.
100	Radnor (Meredith)	H 11	Ohio
650*	Radnor	O 23	Pa.
100*	Radnor	M 2	W. Va.
102	Radom	O 14	Ill.
....	Radum	E 23	Calif.
1621	Raeford	I 11	N. C.
85	Raeville	H 18	Neb.
163	Ragan	N 14	Neb.
120*	Ragersville	H 17	Ohio
4*	Ragged Mtn.	K 8	Colo.
1070	Ragland	E 17	Ala.
24	Ragland	O 3	W. Va.
75*	Raglesville	N 8	Ind.
50	Ragley	K 7	La.
8*	Rago	E 20	Colo.
200	Rago	N 14	Kan.
54*	Ragsdale	N 7	Ind.
187*	Rahns	O 22	Pa.
17498	Rahway	F 17	N. J.
472	Raiford	C 14	Fla.
4	Raiford	J 19	Okla.
279	Railroad (Shrewsbury Station)	Q 17	Pa.
219*	Rail Road Flat	H 10	Calif.
25*	Rainbow	J 5	Ore.
8*	Rainbow	F 17	Tex.
25	Rainbow	H 24	Utah
2	Rainbow Jc.	H 25	Utah
200*	Rainbow Lake	D 22	N. Y.
250*	Rainbow Springs	Q 4	N. C.
985	Rainelle	N 10	W. Va.
250*	Raines (Raine)	Q 1	Tenn.
1183	Rainier	A 7	Ore.
500	Rainier	K 7	Wash.
28*	Rains	G 21	S. C.
100	Rains	I 16	Utah
250	Rainsboro	N 10	Ohio
211*	Rainsburg	P 9	Pa.
100*	Rainsville	G 7	Ind.
100*	Rainsville	E 17	N. M.
58*	Rainswood	K 20	Va.
2	Rainy Butte	O 4	N. D.
....	Rainy Jc.	F 19	Minn.
100	Raisin (Raisin City)	K 11	Calif.
20	Raisin Center	R 19	Mich.
329	Rake	B 11	Iowa
147*	Raleigh	E 13	Fla.
94*	Raleigh	I 5	Ga.
483	Raleigh	P 18	Ill.
75*	Raleigh	J 19	Ind.
....	Raleigh	B 7	Iowa
644	Raleigh	L 15	Miss.
46897	Raleigh	F 14	N. C.
140	Raleigh	P 10	N. D.
287*	Raleigh	P 1	Tenn.
500*	Raleigh	O 8	W. Va.
1512	Ralls	C 10	Tex.
300*	Ralph	H 7	Ala.
60*	Ralph	F 5	Mich.
....	Ralph	I 5	Okla.
17	Ralph	C 4	S. D.
600	Ralphton	O 7	Pa.
202	Ralston	I 8	Iowa
834	Ralston	K 23	Neb.
250*	Ralston	D 14	N. J.
621	Ralston	D 15	Okla.
700	Ralston	G 16	Pa.
50	Ralston	K 21	Wash.
28	Ralston	B 9	Wyo.
....	Ralston Jc.	G 16	Pa.
150*	Ralstons Station (Ralston)	L 5	Tenn.
300*	Ramage	M 5	W. Va.
186	Ramah	I 17	Colo.
298	Ramah	G 3	N. M.
235*	Ramapo	F 5	N. Y.
500	Ramer	K 16	Ala.
157*	Ramer	Q 5	Tenn.
753	Ramey	K 10	Pa.
144*	Ramhurst	C 5	Ga.
115*	Ramirez	Q 16	Tex.
30*	Ramirito	R 16	Tex.
4*	Ramon	K 16	N. M.
1200	Ramona	P 19	Calif.
236	Ramona	I 17	Kan.
574	Ramona	D 18	Okla.
265	Ramona	J 23	S. D.
50	Ramos	O 15	La.
24*	Ramp	O 10	W. Va.
25*	Ramrod Key	R 19	Fla.
225*	Ramsay	L 19	La.
1300	Ramsay	C 3	Mich.
114*	Ramsay	B 21	Mont.
250*	Ramsaytown	M 9	N. C.
150	Ramsaytown	J 7	Pa.
56*	Ramsdell	D 6	Tex.
1220	Ramseur	F 10	N. C.
50	Ramsey	N 11	Ark.
881	Ramsey	L 16	Ill.
70*	Ramsey	P 14	Ind.
3566	Ramsey	C 19	N. J.
3	Ramsey	G 17	N. D.
100*	Ramsey	L 9	W. Va.
200*	Ranburne	F 20	Ala.
75	Ranchcreek	N 23	Mont.
800	Ranches of Taos	D 15	N. M.
189	Ranchester	A 14	Wyo.
400*	Rancho Santa Fe	P 19	Calif.
260	Rancocas	K 12	N. J.
100	Rand	D 11	Colo.
150*	Randado	R 16	Tex.
123*	Randalia	E 19	Iowa
605*	Randall (East Galesburg)	F 9	Ill.
250	Randall	H 12	Iowa
281	Randall	E 14	Kan.
362*	Randall	J 11	Minn.
99*	Randall	M 21	N. Y.
10*	Randall (Benson)	A 8	Wis.
50*	Randall Beach	P 22	Mich.
500*	Randallstown	E 12	Md.
100	Randallsville	N 16	N. Y.
160	Randle	M 9	Wash.
2032	Randleman	F 9	N. C.
172	Randles	O 22	Mo.
327	Randlett	P 7	Okla.
350	Randlett	G 22	Utah
120	Randolph	H 12	Ala.
27*	Randolph	L 14	Ariz.
35*	Randolph	H 16	Ill.
379	Randolph	O 4	Iowa
369	Randolph	E 18	Kan.
79*	Randolph	J 14	Ky.
50	Randolph	A 9	La.
200	Randolph	N 9	Me.
7634■	Randolph	H 19	Mass.
236*	Randolph	O 18	Minn.
239*	Randolph	D 17	Miss.
1094	Randolph	G 20	Neb.
75*	Randolph	G 16	N. H.
1321	Randolph	Q 4	N. Y.
450	Randolph	F 18	Ohio
115	Randolph	P 16	Okla.
52	Randolph	E 19	S. D.
275*	Randolph	C 20	Tex.
656	Randolph	B 15	Utah
1988	Randolph	I 11	Vt.
57*	Randolph	P 12	Va.
1146	Randolph	L 18	Wis.
150	Randolph Center	I 12	Vt.
1200*	Randolph Field	L 16	Tex.
613	Random Lake	P 18	Wis.
500	Randsburg	M 17	Calif.
120*	Range (Deer Range)	N 10	Ala.
70	Range	L 10	Ohio
53	Range	R 6	Okla.
40	Range	F 18	Ore.
866	Rangeley	K 4	Me.
8	Rangeley	H 13	N. D.
55	Rangely	E 3	Colo.
160*	Ranger	D 5	Ga.
4*	Ranger	Q 10	Ind.
55*	Ranger	R 2	N. C.
5*	Ranger	O 2	N. D.
4553	Ranger	E 16	Tex.
300*	Ranger	L 3	W. Va.
18*	Rangerville	R 5	Tex.
80*	Rangoon (Boulder)	F 14	W. Va.
228	Ranier	D 14	Minn.
781	Rankin	G 21	Ill.
38*	Rankin	J 16	Ky.
....	Rankin, see Reydon		Okla.
7470	Rankin	M 4	Pa.
90*	Rankin (Rankins Depot)	N 21	Tenn.
672	Rankin	H 9	Tex.
....*	Rankins Depot, see Rankin		Tenn.
41*	Ranlo	H 4	N. C.
2000*	Ranshaw (Brady)	J 16	Pa.
419	Ransom	E 16	Ill.
403	Ransom	I 8	Kan.

Pop. Place Index State
64*Ransom, H 24...Ky.
150 Ransom, R 16...Mich.
25 Ransom, Q 23...N. D.
150*Ransom, H 20...Pa.
750 Ransomville, K 4...N. Y.
77*Ransomville, G 21...N. C.
1171 Ranson, E 35...W. Va.
25 Ransons, M 12...Va.
2367 Rantoul, H 20...Ill.
164 Rantoul, I 23...Kan.
83 Rapatee, F 10...Ill.
175 Rapelje, K 14...Mont.
300*Raphine, K 9...Va.
100*Rapidan, P 13...Minn.
218 Rapidan, I 14...Va.
13844 Rapid City, J 3...S. D.
200 Rapid River, G 8...Mich.
275*Rapids City, D 9...Ill.
122*Rappahannock Academy, J 17...Va.
30*Rappsburg, Q 14...Ohio
200 Raquette Lake, I 20...N. Y.
306 Rarden, P 11...Ohio
170 Rardin, J 19...Ill.
250 Raritan, G 6...Ill.
4839 Raritan, F 14...N. J.
18*Rasar, O 19...Tenn.
150*Rash, A 17...Ala.
6 Rasmus, I 15...Mich.
20*Raspberry, E 10...Ark.
45*Rat, N 17...Mo.
337 Ratcliff, G 6...Ark.
320 Ratcliff, H 22...Tex.
100*Rathbone, Q 10...N. Y.
352 Rathbun, P 15...Iowa
2250 Rathburn (Soddy), P 15...Tenn.
511 Rathdrum, D 3...Idaho
200 Rathmel, I 8...Pa.
25 Ratio, L 18...Ark.
125*Ratliff, C 21...Miss.
7607 Raton, B 19...N. M.
47 Rattan, P 21...Okla.
50*Rattlesnake, I 14...Fla.
4 Rattlesnake, E 14...Mont.
40 Rattlesnake Buttes, N 16...Colo.
.... Rattlesnake Den, I 18...Wis.
125 Raub, F 6...Ind.
44 Raub, I 8...N. D.
350*Raubsville (Uhlersville), L 23...Pa.
27*Rauch, E 14...Minn.
150 Rauchtown, I 15...Pa.
30 Rauschs, L 20...Pa.
12 Rauville, F 23...S. D.
50 Ravalli, G 4...Mont.
75 Ravana (Ravanna), R 5...Ark.
177*Ravanna, A 9...Mo.
20*Raven, J 21...Ill.
73*Raven, H 22...Ky.
750*Raven, C 8...Va.
1810 Ravena, O 23...N. Y.
30*Ravencliff (McGraws), P 6...W. Va.
19*Ravendale, D 10...Calif.
240 Ravenden, B 17...Ark.
200*Ravenden Springs, B 17...Ark.
400 Ravenels, N 17...S. C.
1098 Ravenna, G 19...Ky.
451 Ravenna, N 12...Mich.
1429 Ravenna, L 15...Neb.
8538 Ravenna, E 18...Ohio
248 Ravenna, C 20...Tex.
300*Ravenrun, L 20...Pa.
626 Ravenscroft, N 15...Tenn.
109 Ravensdale, I 9...Wash.
175 Ravensford, O 5...N. C.
125 Ravenswood, O 15...Colo.
394*Ravenswood, J 14...Ind.
25*Ravenswood (Ravenwood), K 12...La.
1061 Ravenswood, G 5...W. Va.
125*Ravenwood, O 15...Colo.
336 Ravenwood, B 6...Mo.
424 Ravia, O 15...Okla.
83*Ravine, G 22...Miss.
550 Ravine (Lorberry Jc), M 19...Pa.
.... Ravinia, B 21...Ill.
155 Ravinia, N 19...S. D.
35 Rawhide, H 8...Nev.
125*Rawl, P 3...W. Va.
60*Rawles Springs, N 16...Miss.
2820▲Rawlings, N 5...Md.
100 Rawlings, P 15...Va.
50*Rawlingsville, O 19...Pa.
5531 Rawlins, N 14...Wyo.
18*Rawls, R 15...Ark.
72 Rawson, I 3...N. D.
441 Rawson, F 9...Ohio
1100 Ray, L 17...Ariz.
115 Ray, H 8...Ill.
203 Ray, A 22...Ind.
152 Ray, C 16...Minn.
579 Ray, F 4...N. D.
60*Ray, O 13...Ohio
30 Ray, G 22...Okla.
750*Ray (Clune), L 6...Pa.
.... Ray, B 19...Tex.
16*Rayborn, O 13...Mo.
550*Ray Brook, G 22...N. Y.
37*Rayburn, J 23...Tex.
638 Ray City, O 13...Ga.
16 Rayfield, I 15...Mont.
.... Ray Jc., L 17...Ariz.
681*Rayland, I 20...Ohio
200*Rayle, F 15...Ga.
110*Raymilton, H 3...Pa.
100 Raymond, J 11...Calif.
.... Raymond, Q 4...Calif.
200 Raymond, G 5...Ga.
160 Raymond, Q 23...Idaho
818 Raymond, K 13...Ill.
25*Raymond, K 20...Ind.
130*Raymond, G 18...Iowa
200*Raymond, J 13...Kan.
150 Raymond, O 5...Me.
487 Raymond, N 8...Minn.
641 Raymond, K 10...Miss.
70 Raymond, B 24...Mont.
199 Raymond, L 21...Neb.
900 Raymond, P 17...N. H.
250 Raymond (Raymonds), I 10...Ohio
49*Raymond, E 12...Pa.
206 Raymond, G 20...S. D
4045 Raymond, L 4...Wash.
100*Raymond City, J 5...W. Va.
128*Raymondville, O 15...Mo.
400 Raymondville, D 19...N. Y.
4050 Raymondville, Q 5...Tex.
207*Raymore, H 6...Mo.
4974 Rayne, M 10...La.
35 Raynesford, G 11...Mont.
800 Raynham, J 19...Mass.
75*Raynham, K 12...N. C.
1225*Raynham Center, K 20...Mass.
50 Rayo, I 11...N. M.
100*Rayo, J 15...Va.
....*Raysal, Q 5...W. Va.
40*Rays Crossing, K 17...Ind.
275 Raysville, J 18...Ind.
500*Raytown, H 6...Mo.
2412 Rayville, C 12...La.

Pop. Place Index State
242*Rayville, F 7...Mo.
147*Raywick, H 15...Ky.
150 Raywood, K 24...Tex.
75 Razorville, N 11...Me.
33*Rea, L 22...Idaho
128*Rea, C 5...Mo.
60*Rea, N 2...Pa.
400 Read, J 5...Colo.
145 Reader, N 9...Ark.
250*Reader, C 10...W. Va.
300 Readfield, M 8...Me.
....*Readfield Depot (Readfield) M 8...Me.
175*Readfield, M 15...Wis.
35*Reading, F 17...Ill.
302 Reading, I 20...Kan.
10866■*Reading, D 19...Mass.
1059 Reading, R 17...Mich.
115*Reading, Q 6...Minn.
6079 Reading, N 5...Ohio
110568 Reading, N 20...Pa.
171 Reading, L 12...Vt.
200*Reading Center, O 11...N. Y.
150 Readington, F 13...N. J.
150*Readland, R 17...Ark.
426 Readlyn, F 17...Iowa
140 Reads (Reads Landing), P 21...Minn.
667 Readsboro, R 8...Vt.
584 Readstown, F 18...Wis.
73*Readsville, H 15...Mo.
.... Readville, G 19...Mass.
19*Ready, H 12...Ky.
125*Readyville, N 12...Tenn.
168 Reagan, O 15...Okla.
75*Reagan, O 6...Tenn.
353 Reagan, H 20...Tex.
62*Reagan Wells, L 14...Tex.
500 Realitos, Q 16...Tex.
50*Reams, O 17...Va.
575*Reamstown, O 19...Pa.
27*Reamsville, D 11...Kan.
422 Reardan, G 21...Wash.
221 Reasnor, L 14...Iowa
50*Rea Valley, B 11...Ark.
120*Reaves, (Reeves) J 8...La.
308 Reaville, G 12...N. J.
342 Rebecca, L 11...Ga.
150 Rebel Creek, B 10...Nev.
275 Rebersburg, J 14...Pa.
65*Rebuck, L 17...Pa.
7*Recluse, B 17...Wyo.
400*Recovery, P 5...Ga.
1736 Rector, B 21...Ark.
26*Rector, N 15...Mo.
68*Rector, O 6...Pa.
15 Rector, M 4...W. Va.
135*Rectortown, F 15...Va.
6*Rectory, H 17...Va.
100*Redan, F 8...Ga.
10*Redart, M 22...Va.
500*Red Ash, C 8...Va.
10974 Red Bank, H 20...N. J.
96 Redbank, J 5...Pa.
....*Red Bank, Q 15...Tenn.
97*Red Banks, A 15...Miss.
1560 Red Bay, C 5...Ala.
125*Redbay, N 8...Fla.
180 Red Beach, J 23...Me.
75*Red Bird, K 16...Mo.
36 Redbird, E 17...Neb.
393 Redbird (Red Bird), G 20...Okla.
3824 Red Bluff, E 5...Calif.
900 Redboiling Springs, K 13...Tenn.
1302 Red Bud, O 11...Ill.
50*Redbud, J 21...Ky.
20*Redbush, G 22...Ky.
208 Redby, E 9...Minn.
35 Redcedar, C 13...Wis.
.... Red Clay, B 4...Ga.
715 Redcliff (Red Cliff), H 10...Colo.
1610 Red Cloud, O 16...Neb.
539 Red Creek, L 12...N. Y.
36*Redcreek, F 16...W. Va.
36*Red Cross (Redcross), K 13...La.
170*Red Cross (Red Cross Roads), L 16...Pa.
25 Redd (Page), N 19...Wash.
1500*Reddell, K 9...La.
25 Redden, N 19...Okla.
392 Reddick, E 14...Fla.
194 Reddick, E 18...Ill.
225*Reddies River, D 4...N. C.
8109 Redding, D 5...Calif.
500 Redding, M 5...Conn.
150 Redding (West Redding), M 4...Conn.
246 Redding, Q 9...Iowa
109*Redding, M 5...Me.
245 Redding Ridge, M 5...Conn.
15 Reddish, K 8...Ill.
500*Red Dragon (Blue Pennant), M 5...W. Va.
15 Red Eagle (Nyack), D 5...Mont.
45*Redelm, F 8...S. D.
10*Red Feather Lakes, B 13...Colo.
339 Redfield, K 13...Ark.
898 Redfield, K 10...Iowa
194 Redfield, L 24...Kan.
200 Redfield, J 16...N. Y.
90 Redfield, L 14...Ohio
2428 Redfield, G 18...S. D.
200*Red Fish, I 11...La.
.... Redford, P 21...Mich.
35*Redford, O 18...Mo.
600*Redford, C 23...N. Y.
397 Redford, L 5...Tex.
.... Red Fork, F 18...Okla.
25*Redfox, I 22...Ky.
857 Redgranite, L 16...Wis.
110*Red Gum (Junks), E 13...La.
....*Red Hill, J 3...N. M.
881 Red Hill, M 22...Pa.
40*Red Hill, K 12...Va.
1056*Red Hook, R 23...N. Y.
76*Redhouse, G 18...Ky.
16*Red House, B 9...Nev.
75 Red House, Q 5...N. Y.
100*Red House, O 11...Va.
210 Red House, J 4...W. Va.
18 Redig, E 3...S. D.
....*Redington, L 16...Ariz.
25 Redington, I 3...Neb.
.... Red Jacket, see Calumet, Mich.
1237 Red Jacket, P 3...W. Va.
1538 Redkey, G 21...Ind.
25 Redlake, E 9...Minn.
4 Redlake, J 24...N. M.
1530 Red Lake Falls, E 4...Minn.
.... Red Lake Falls Jc., E 4...Minn.
250 Redland, O 22...Fla.
150*Redland, F 24...Okla.
14324 Redlands, Q 9...Calif.
52*Redlawn, R 14...Va.
516 Red Level, N 14...Ala.
100*Red Lick, M 7...Miss.
25 Red Lion, B 22...Colo.
4891 Red Lion, P 18...Pa.
2950 Red Lodge, N 14...Mont.
270 Redmesa, Q 5...Colo.
226 Redmon, J 21...Ill.

Pop. Place Index State
1876 Redmond, I 12...Ore.
641 Redmond, K 11...Utah
530 Redmond, H 9...Wash.
36*Red Mound, F 18...Wis.
800*Red Mountain, N 20...Calif.
250*Red Oak, F 6...Ga.
95*Red Oak, A 12...Ill.
5763 Red Oak, O 6...Iowa
129*Red Oak (Oakville), J 11...Ky.
200*Red Oak, D 16...N. C.
484 Red Oak, L 22...Okla.
....*Red Oak (Cortez), G 21...Pa.
400*Red Oak, E 19...Tex.
37 Redoak, Q 12...Va.
116 Redondo, I 8...Wash.
13092 Redondo Beach, O 15, R 3...Calif.
12*Redore, F 19...Minn.
13 Redowl, H 6...S. D.
185 Redridge, C 2...Mich.
4 Redridge Jc., C 2...Mich.
50 Red River, C 16...N. M.
324 Red River, A 13...S. C.
....*Red River Hot Springs, H 7...Idaho
45 Red River Jc., E 8...Calif.
50 Redrock, M 16...Ariz.
19*Redrock, D 9...Ark.
125 Redrock, M 2...N. M.
395 Redrock, D 14...Okla.
95*Red Rock, E 9...Pa.
315 Red Rock, K 18...Tex.
54*Red Scaffold, G 9...S. D.
1559 Red Springs, J 11...N. C.
28*Red Springs, C 14...Tex.
37*Redstar, D 7...Ark.
600 Redstar, N 8...W. Va.
12*Redstone, H 8...Colo.
150 Redstone, C 23...Mont.
139*Redstone, I 18...N. H.
....*Redstripe, see Pleasant Grove...Ark.
60*Red Sulphur Springs, P 10...W. Va.
38*Redtop, J 16...Minn.
25*Redtop, N 10...Mo.
125 Redvale, L 4...Colo.
35*Redville, G 13...Wis.
2 Redwater, F 22...Mont.
319 Redwater, C 24...Tex.
9 Redwillow, O 11...Neb.
517*Redwine, F 21...Ky.
223 Redwing, N 14...Colo.
45*Redwing, I 12...Kan.
9962 Red Wing, O 19...Minn.
211*Redwood (North Redwood), O 8...Minn.
15*Redwood, J 7...Miss.
524 Redwood, F 16...N. Y.
47*Redwood, P 7...Va.
12453 Redwood City, I 5...Calif.
30*Redwood Estates, G 21...Calif.
3270 Redwood Falls, O 8...Minn.
.... Redwood Park, I 5, G 17, Calif.
30*Redwood Valley, F 3...Calif.
170*Reece, L 19...Kan.
105*Reed, G 9...Ky.
125 Reed, L 2...Okla.
102*Reed, I 5...Ore.
20 Reed (Dana), K 6...W. Va.
1845 Reed City, L 14...Mich.
263 Reeder, Q 4...N. D.
250*Reeders, I 23...Pa.
15 Reeding, G 11...Okla.
3170 Reedley, K 12...Calif.
158 Reedpoint, L 14...Mont.
35*Reeds, P 13...Ill.
162 Reeds, O 7...Mo.
3608 Reedsburg, J 18...Wis.
225 Reeds Ferry, Q 15...N. H.
56*Reeds Gap, M 13...Pa.
.... Reeds Lake (East Grand Rapids), O 13...Mich.
1421 Reedsport, K 3...Ore.
353 Reeds Spring, Q 9...Mo.
200 Reedsville, O 16...Ohio
1700*Reedsville, K 13...Pa.
324 Reedsville, D 15...W. Va.
729 Reedsville (Reedville), P 15...Wis.
1000*Reedurban, G 18...Ohio
89*Reedville (Finly), J 15...Ind.
50*Reedville, E 22...Ky.
200 Reedville, D 7...Ore.
500 Reedville, K 21...Va.
329 Reedy, H 7...W. Va.
45*Reedyville, I 11...Ky.
258 Ree Heights, I 16...S. D.
200 Reelsville, K 9...Ind.
118*Reeman, M 13...Mich.
569 Reese, M 20...Mich.
35*Reese, C 2...N. C.
34*Reese, F 22...Tex.
300*Reesedale, K 5...Pa.
50*Reese Mill, I 12...Ind.
407 Reeseville, M 19...Wis.
153 Reesville, M 9...Ohio
120 Reeves (Reaves), L 7...La.
175 Reevesville, Q 17...Ill.
217 Reevesville, K 15...S. C.
885 Reform, G 6...Ala.
....*Reform, J 10...Ark.
200*Reform, F 17...Miss.
27*Reform, F 14...Va.
160*Refton, P 19...Pa.
4077 Refugio, O 19...Tex.
50*Regal, D 14...Minn.
25 Regal, Q 2...N. C.
149 Regan, J 12...N. D.
.... Regan Jc., M 8...Pa.
261 Regent, P 6...N. D.
52*Regent, M 19...Va.
115 Reger, C 10...Mo.
217*Regina (Marrowbone), H 23...Ky.
13 Regina, F 17...Mont.
40 Regina, D 10...N. M.
32*Regina, L 21...Va.
30*Region, I 11...Ky.
321 Register, K 20...Ga.
12*Regnier, Q 1...Okla.
150*Rego, O 13...Ind.
56*Rehobeth, R 21...Md.
517*Rehoboth, K 9...Ala.
1247 Rehoboth (Rehoboth Beach), K 25...Del.
800 Rehoboth, K 18...Mass.
150*Rehoboth, F 3...N. M.
127 Rehoboth, L 15...Ohio
40*Rehoboth, P 13...Va.
1247 Rehoboth Beach (Rehoboth), K 25...Del.
38*Rehoboth Church, L 21...Va.
350 Rehrersburg, M 19...Pa.
25 Reichert, L 24...Okla.
39 Reibold, K 3...Pa.
67 Reichie (Glen), M 7...Mont.
.... Reichley, O 11...Pa.
.... Reids, J 8...La.
50*Reids Grove, M 18...Md.
805 Reidsville, L 19...Ga.
10387 Reidsville, C 10...N. C.
214 Reidville, B 8...S. C.
....*Reiff, F 4...Calif.
....*Reiffton, M 20...Pa.

Pop. Place Index State
100 Reiley Lake (Riley Lake), O 11...Ill.
250 Reiley (Rileys), J 14...La.
145 Reily, M 5...Ohio
25 Reimers, J 15...La.
1429 Reinbeck, H 16...Iowa
550*Reiner (Reinerton), K 19...Pa.
100 Reinersville, L 16...Ohio
216*Reinhardt, D 19...Tex.
400*Reinholds, N 19...Pa.
.... Reisor, C 4...La.
2000 Reisterstown, D 12...Md.
109*Reklaw, G 22...Tex.
2016 Relay, G 12...Md.
39*Relfs Bluff, N 14...Ark.
219 Reliance, K 15...S. D.
100*Reliance, P 17...Tenn.
62*Reliance, F 13...Va.
600 Reliance (Reliance Mine), O 8...Wyo.
.... Reliance Jc., O 7...Wyo.
86*Relief, F 21...Ky.
80*Relief, M 9...N. C.
....*Rella, K 20...Ky.
200*Rembert, G 16...S. C.
302 Rembrandt, E 6...Iowa
407 Remer, H 13...Minn.
30*Remerton, P 12...Ga.
869 Remington, F 8...Ind.
226 Remington, H 15...Va.
75*Remini (Rimini), G 16...S. C.
195*Remlap, E 14...Ala.
300*Remleys, L 18...S. C.
.... Remlig, H 25...Tex.
50*Remlik, M 20...Va.
15 Remmel, F 17...Ark.
17*Remo, L 21...Va.
15 Remote, N 4...Ore.
18*Removal (Guardian), J 11...W. Va.
1196 Remsen, E 3...Iowa
422 Remsen, K 18...N. Y.
400 Remsenburg, H 10...N. Y.
600 Remus, M 15...Mich.
15*Remy, L 17...La.
50*Rena Lara, C 8...Miss.
8 Renaraye, O 3...Colo.
188 Renault, O 10...Ill.
119*Rencona, F 16...N. M.
75*Rendalia, G 16...Ala.
387*Rendville, M 15...Ohio
200 Renfrew, K 4...Pa.
47*Renfroe, F 16...Ala.
....*Renfro Valley, I 18...Ky.
23*Renfrow, H 11...Ky.
115 Renfrow, A 11...Okla.
155 Renick, F 13...Mo.
388 Renick (Falling Spring), M 12...W. Va.
26*Renicks Valley, M 12...W. Va.
50 Renner, L 24...S. D.
109*Renner, D 19...Tex.
365*Rennerdale, M 3...Pa.
194 Rennert, J 12...N. C.
50*Renno, D 8...S. C.
53*Reno, P 7...Ga.
36*Reno, J 12...Idaho
209 Reno, L 13...Ill.
50*Reno, J 11...Ind.
21317 Reno, G 3...Nev.
139*Reno, M 17...Ohio
900 Reno, H 4...Pa.
2 Reno Jc., E 11...Calif.
19 Renova, L 8...Mont.
3784 Renovo, H 12...Pa.
300 Rensford, L 6...W. Va.
40*Renshaw (Dixon Springs), Q 17...Ill.
3214 Rensselaer, E 7...Ind.
51*Rensselaer, E 16...Mo.
10768 Rensselaer, O 24...N. Y.
265 Rensselaer Falls, E 18...N. Y.
300 Rensselaerville, O 22...N. Y.
120*Rentchler, N 11...Ill.
180 Rentiesville, I 21...Okla.
300 Renton, M 4...Pa.
4488 Renton, I 8...Wash.
50*Renton Jc., H 9...Wash.
319 Rentz, K 15...Ga.
1256 Renville, N 8...Minn.
470 Renwick, E 11...Iowa
113*Replete, K 12...W. Va.
30*Represa, G 8...Calif.
365 Repton, N 10...Ala.
47*Repton, H 7...Ky.
350*Republic, F 12...Ala.
376 Republic, C 15...Kan.
1250 Republic, E 5...Mich.
790 Republic, O 9...Mo.
546 Republic, E 12...Ohio
3000*Republic, P 4...Pa.
922 Republic, D 19...Wash.
....*Republic (Jochin), L 6...W. Va.
331 Republican City (Republican), O 14...Neb.
65*Republican Grove, Q 11...Va.
150 Requa, B 1...Calif.
20*Rerdell, G 14...Fla.
121*Resaca, C 4...Ga.
100*Rescue, G 9...Calif.
12 Rescue, J 21...Neb.
62*Rescue, Q 19...Va.
....*Reseda, O 15 (Pop. 5000 incl. in Los Angeles)...Calif.
172 Reserve, C 22...Kan.
2500 Reserve, M 17...La.
200 Reserve, C 24...Mont.
428▲Reserve, K 2...N. M.
82 Reserve, E 8...Wis.
.... Reservoir Switch, E 15...Mass.
....*Resort, see Mount Laguna...Calif.
18*Rest, M 22...Kan.
450*Retort (Powelton), K 11...Pa.
....*Retreat, I 13...La.
2000*Retreat, H 20...Pa.
700*Retsil, H 7...Wash.
300 Retsof, N 8...N. Y.
.... Retsof Jc., N 8...N. Y.
90*Retta, F 10...Ark.
.... Retta, B 12...Okla.
96*Retz, M 21...Va.
119 Reubens, G 4...Idaho
150*Reusens, N 10...Va.
12 Reva, D 4...S. D.
19*Reva, H 14...Va.
45*Revelo (Revilo), K 18...Ky.
26*Revenge, L 13...Ohio
34405 Revere, L 6...Mass.
197*Revere, P 8...Minn.
191*Revere, B 14...Mo.
25*Revere, M 7...N. C.
36 Revere, K 19...N. D.
102*Revere, N 23...Pa.
24 Revere, J 22...Wash.
28*Revere, H 10...W. Va.
19*Reverie, O 2...Tenn.
325 Revillo, F 24...S. D.
200*Revis, L 20...Va.
1350 Revloc, M 8...Pa.
300*Rew, D 9...Pa.
518*Reward, L 12...Calif.
267 Rewey, H 21...Wis.

Pop. Place Index State
225 Rex (Gilman), G 10...Colo.
101*Rex, F 7...Ga.
.... Rex, N 15...Iowa
60*Rex, I 13...Ky.
100*Rex, J 12...N. C.
50*Rex, E 5...Ore.
3437 Rexburg, N 20...Idaho
121*Rexburg, K 19...Va.
30 Rexfield, N 15...Iowa
244 Rexford, E 6...Kan.
200 Rexford, B 2...Mont.
500 Rexford, M 23...N. Y.
300*Rexford (Watauga Valley), M 24...Tenn.
500*Rexmont, N 18...Pa.
1025 Rexroat, P 13...Okla.
37*Rexrode, I 17...W. Va.
60*Rexton, D 21...Ky.
200 Rexton, F 15...Mich.
35*Rexville, C 6...Ind.
80*Rexville, M 20...Ind.
11*Rexville, F 21...Ky.
100 Rexville, Q 9...N. Y.
42 Reydel, L 16...Ark.
311*Reydon, (Rankin) H 2...Okla.
346 Reyno, A 19...Ark.
....*Reynolda, D 7...N. C.
275 Reynolds, H 8...Conn.
871 Reynolds, J 8...Ga.
75*Reynolds, P 5...Idaho
335 Reynolds, D 8...Ill.
408 Reynolds, E 9...Ind.
20*Reynolds (Reynolds Station), G 10...Ky.
300 Reynolds, N 17...Mo.
211 Reynolds, O 20...Neb.
315 Reynolds, I 23...N. D.
.... Reynolds, M 19...Okla.
....*Reynolds, see Saint Just Va.
275 Reynolds Bridge, H 8 Conn.
652 Reynoldsburg, K 13...Ohio
20*Reynolds Station (Reynolds), G 10...Ky.
25*Reynoldsville, Q 13...Ill.
3480 Reynoldsville, I 8...Pa.
200*Reynoldsville, F 12...W. Va.
283 Rhame, P 2...N. D.
58*Rhea, C 4...Ark.
20 Rhea, G 5...Okla.
150 Rhea Springs, O 16...Tenn.
260*Rheems, O 18...Pa.
227*Rheims, P 10...N. Y.
463 Rhine, L 13...Ga.
1697 Rhinebeck, R 23...N. Y.
500 Rhinecliff, R 23...N. Y.
75*Rhinehart, F 12...La.
204 Rhineland, I 16...Mo.
8501 Rhinelander, K 9...Wis.
78*Rhoadesville (La Fayette), J 14...Va.
300*Rhoda, O 15...La.
36*Rhodelia, F 12...Ky.
995*Rhodell, O 8...W. Va.
379 Rhodes (Edenville), J 14...Iowa
200 Rhodes, L 19...Mich.
56*Rhodesdale, M 18...Md.
163 Rhodes Point, R 18...Md.
930 Rhodhiss (Rhodhiss Junction), E 4...N. C.
50 Rhododendron, D 10...Ore.
340*Rhome, D 18...Tex.
1692*Rhone, I 20...Pa.
55 Rhonesboro, D 22...Tex.
25*Rhyse, M 16...Mo.
1770 Rialto, O 18...Calif.
45*Rialto, N 6...Ohio
20*Ribbon, J 16...Ky.
303▲Ribera, F 16...N. M.
110 Rib Falls, I 12...Wis.
1042 Rib Lake, I 10...Wis.
72*Ribolt, D 20...Ky.
75 Ricardo, I 19...N. M.
25 Ricardo, Q 18...Tex.
400 Riccars, O 5...Me.
....*Rice, see San Carlos...Ariz.
100 Rice, O 24...Calif.
10*Rice, O 13...Ill.
35*Rice, E 15...Kan.
15*Rice, E 22...Ky.
324 Rice, K 12...Minn.
489 Rice, F 20...Tex.
250*Rice, N 13...Va.
21 Rice, D 21...Wash.
364*Riceboro, L 22...Ga.
.... Ricedale, D 2...Mich.
5719 Rice Lake, D 9...Wis.
60*Rices, H 15...N. Y.
962 Rices Landing, P 3...Pa.
10*Rice Station, G 19...Ky.
8*Ricetown, H 20...Ky.
34*Riceville, P 11...Ind.
910 Riceville, B 16...Iowa
75*Riceville, G 22...Ky.
72*Riceville, F 4...Pa.
400 Riceville, P 17...Tenn.
....*Rich, see Rich Bar...Calif.
175*Rich, C 8...Miss.
1008 Richard City, Q 14...Tenn.
300 Richards, Q 23...Colo.
50*Richards, G 8...Iowa
246 Richards, L 6...Mo.
600*Richards, J 22...Tex.
.... Richards, I 12...Wyo.
30*Richardson, B 17...Ill.
163*Richardson, F 23...Ky.
720*Richardson, D 19...Tex.
3 Richardson, E 6...Wash.
50*Richardson, H 8...W. Va.
110*Richardson Grove (Hartsook), D 2...Calif.
5150 Richardson Park, B 21...Del.
72*Richardsville, I 12...Ky.
36*Richardsville, H 7...Pa.
24*Richardsville, I 14...Va.
682 Richardton, M 7...N. D.
50*Rich Bar (Rich), E 8...Calif.
310*Richboro, N 24...Pa.
564 Richburg, Q 7...N. Y.
183 Richburg, C 13...S. C.
215*Rich Creek, N 3...Va.
51*Richelieu, J 11...Ky.
.... Richey, K 22...Kan.
140 Richey, H 8...Miss.
362 Richey, F 23...Mont.
2000*Richeyville, N 2...Pa.
20*Richfield, D 6...Calif.
390 Richfield, P 12...Idaho
51*Richfield, I 6...Ill.
96 Richfield, N 1...Kan.
6750*Richfield, M 16...Minn.
55 Richfield, K 24...Neb.
266*Richfield, G 7...N. C.
300 Richfield, L 15...Pa.
3584 Richfield, L 10...Utah
225 Richfield, O 19...Wis.
300 Richfield Jc. (Cassville), M 18...N. Y.
1209 Richfield Springs, M 19...N. Y.
350 Richford, Q 14...N. Y.
1889 Richford, A 11...Vt.
300*Rich Fountain, J 15...Mo.
150*Richgrove, K 13...Calif.
1994 Rich Hill, K 6...Mo.
190*Richland (Vitis), H 13...Fla.
1497 Richland, K 5...Ga.
10*Richland, J 12...Ill.
50*Richland, K 19...Ind.

Pop. Place Index State
365 Richland, R 8...Ind.
614 Richland, N 19...Iowa
175 Richland, G 22...Kan.
327 Richland, P 12...Mich.
985 Richland, L 13...Mo.
160 Richland, J 20...Neb.
550 Richland, O 11...N. J.
150 Richland, J 24...N. M.
300 Richland, J 15...N. Y.
100 Richland, H 9...Ohio
10 Richland, O 13...Ohio
52 Richland, H 10...Okla.
254 Richland, G 23...Ore.
934 Richland, N 19...Pa.
75*Richland, C 4...S. C.
79 Richland, P 25...S. D.
369 Richland, G 20...Tex.
247 Richland, N 18...Wash.
4364 Richland Center, H 19...Wis.
688 Richlands, J 18...N. C.
2203 Richlands, C 8...Va.
65*Richlands, N 11...W. Va.
541 Richland Springs, H 15...Tex.
628 Richlandtown, M 23...Pa.
95*Richland Valley, C 19...Mont.
75*Richloam, G 14...Fla.
150 Richmond, K 11...Ala.
100 Richmond, O 4...Ark.
23642 Richmond, H 5, B 17...Calif.
559 Richmond, A 19...Ill.
....*Richmond, G 13...Ill.
35147 Richmond, J 23...Ind.
162*Richmond, L 20...Iowa
418 Richmond, I 23...Kan.
7335 Richmond, G 18...Ky.
1900 Richmond, N 8...Me.
500 Richmond, F 2...Mass.
1722 Richmond, O 23...Mich.
634 Richmond, L 11...Minn.
4240 Richmond, F 8...Mo.
125 Richmond, R 7...N. H.
174441 Richmond (part of New York City), I 5...N. Y.
458 Richmond, I 20...Ohio
34 Richmond, E 5...Okla.
84 Richmond, G 15...Ore.
110 Richmond (Richmond Furnace), P 12...Pa.
100*Richmond, (Alum Rock), I 6...Pa.
23 Richmond, D 18...S. D.
2026 Richmond, L 22...Tex.
1131 Richmond, B 12...Utah
692 Richmond, F 8...Vt.
193042 Richmond, M 17...Va.
28 Richmond, M 21...Wis.
780 Richmond Beach, H 8...Wash.
400*Richmondale (Richmond Dale), O 12...Ohio
190*Richmond Corner, N 8...Me.
400 Richmond Dale, Richmonddale, O 12...Ohio
110*Richmond Furnace (Richmond), P 12...Pa.
600*Richmond Highlands, H 8...Wash.
12802*Richmond Heights, I 20...Mo.
....*Richmond Hill H 6...N. Y.
.... Richmond Jc., J 23...Ind.
....*Richmond Point (Ferry Point), B 17...Calif.
598 Richmondville, O 20...N. Y.
100*Rich Mtn., J 4...Ark.
81*Rich Pond, J 11...Ky.
942 Rich Square, D 19...N. C.
48*Richtex, E 12...S. C.
107*Richton (Richton Park), C 21...Ill.
936 Richton, N 19...Miss.
107*Richton Park (Richton), C 21...Ill.
150*Richvale, F 7...Calif.
125*Richvalley, E 15...Ind.
15*Rich Valley, N 17...Minn.
600*Rich Valley, D 9...Va.
344 Richview, N 13...Ill.
300 Richville, M 20...Mich.
233 Richville, I 6...Minn.
274 Richville, F 17...N. Y.
52*Richville (Bigelow), D 17...N. Y.
75 Richville, G 17...Ohio
331 Richwood, L 10...Ga.
50*Richwood, H 6...Minn.
250*Richwood, M 8...N. J.
1628 Richwood, I 11...Ohio
5051 Richwood, L 11...W. Va.
100 Richwood, N 19...Wis.
160 Richwoods, K 18...Mo.
50 Rickardsville, F 22...Iowa
20*Ricker Mills (Rickers), E 16...Vt.
167*Ricketts, I 4...Iowa
176 Rickerall (Nesmith), F 5...Ore.
388 Rico, N 5...Colo.
12 Riddle, Q 6...Idaho
17*Riddle, P 13...Ind.
266 Riddle, C 23...N. C.
214 Riddle, N 5...Ore.
10*Riddlehill, J 12...Ill.
610*Riddlesburg, O 9...Pa.
.... Riddleton, N 6...N. J.
164*Riddleton, L 13...Tenn.
115*Riddleville, I 15...Ga.
....*Riders Mills (Riders), O 24...N. Y.
737 Riderwood, K 4...Ala.
400 Riderwood (Sherwood Station), E 14...Md.
207*Ridge, F 14...Colo.
58*Ridge, M 10...La.
192*Ridge, Q 14...Md.
.... Ridge, F 21...Minn.
35 Ridge, N 23...Mont.
20*Ridge, I 20...Tex.
33*Ridge, D 22...W. Va.
150 Ridgebury, L 3...Conn.
101*Ridgebury, E 3...N. Y.
100 Ridgecrest, O 9...N. C.
....*Ridgedale, Q 10...Mo.
890 Ridge Farm, I 22...Ill.
2050 Ridgefield, N 3...Conn.
104 Ridgefield, A 18...Ill.
5271 Ridgefield, D 20...N. J.
643 Ridgefield, P 7...Wash.
11277 Ridgefield Park, D 20...N. J.
233 Ridgeland, J 11...Miss.
1021 Ridgeland, P 13...S. C.
242 Ridgeland, D 11...Wis.
1907 Ridgeley, C 20...W. Va.
.... Ridgely, I 12...Ill.
920 Ridgely, I 19...Md.
1068 Ridgely, L 3...Tenn.
661 Ridge Spring, H 10...S. C.
351*Ridgetop, L 11...Tenn.
439 Ridgeview, E 15...Ind.
72*Ridgeview, F 10...S. D.
321*Ridgeview, M 5...W. Va.
260*Ridgeview Park, M 5...Pa.
150 Ridgeville, N 23...Ga.
52*Ridgeville, F 20...Ill.
1003 Ridgeville, H 22...Ind.
150*Ridgeville, D 12...N. C.
593 Ridgeville, L 16...S. C.
20*Ridgeville, E 19...W. Va.

Pop.	Place, Index	State
300	Ridgeville Corners, D 7	Ohio
323	Ridgeway, C 18	Iowa
300	Ridgeway, Q 19	Mich.
675	Ridgeway, B 8	Mo.
100	Ridgeway, C 15	N. C.
385	Ridgeway, H 9	Ohio
408	Ridgeway, E 14	S. C.
300*	Ridgeway, D 21	Tex.
422	Ridgeway, R 7	Va.
160*	Ridgeway, E 23	W. Va.
431	Ridgeway, H 20	Wis.
14948	Ridgewood, C 19	N. J.
354	Ridgway, M 6	Colo.
1167	Ridgway, P 19	Ill.
174*	Ridgeway, L 24	Mont.
6253	Ridgway, H 8	Pa.
3887	Ridley Park, Q 23	Pa.
2500	Ridlonville, L 5	Me.
169*	Ridott, A 13	Ill.
14	Riebeling, G 8	Mont.
4*	Riedel, E 14	Mont.
510	Riegelsville, F 8	N. J.
824	Riegelsville, L 23	Pa.
458	Rienzi, A 21	Miss.
433	Riesel, H 19	Tex.
44	Rieth, C 18	Ore.
10*	Riffie, M 18	Ill.
1373	Rifle, G 6	Colo.
....	Rift, C 9	Va.
10	Rift, R 5	W. Va.
349	Rifton, C 5	N. Y.
165	Riga, R 19	Mich.
....	Riga, G 12	N. D.
1978	Rigby, N 20	Idaho
1000*	Rigby, J 2	Pa.
4	Rigdon, G 16	Ind.
150*	Riggins, I 8	Idaho
22*	Riggs (Oliver), D 22	Ky.
44*	Riggston, J 8	Ill.
....	Riggsville, H 17	Mich.
25*	Riland, F 8	Colo.
287	Riley, K 7	Ind.
392	Riley, F 18	Kan.
200*	Riley, H 16	Ky.
207*	Riley, M 6	Me.
5	Riley, G 17	Minn.
37*	Riley (Rileys), J 20	Wis.
....*	Rileys (Reiley), J 14	La.
48*	Rileysburg, H 6	Ind.
250*	Rileyville, G 13	Va.
50	Rillito, N 16	Ariz.
834*	Rillton, N 4	Pa.
79*	Rimer (Rimerton), J 5	Pa.
1393	Rimersburg, J 5	Pa.
79*	Rimerton (Rimer), J 5	Pa.
35	Rimini, J 8	Mont.
75*	Rimini (Remini), I 16	S. C.
....	Rimroad, G 22	Mont.
25*	Rimrock, H 11	Ariz.
130	Rinard, M 18	Ill.
143	Rinard, H 9	Iowa
12*	Rinard Mills, M 19	Ohio
285	Rincon, K 24	Ga.
476	Rincon, N 9	N. M.
100	Rindge, R 10	N. H.
1000	Rindgemere (E. Rochester) N 19	N. H.
153	Riner, O 5	Va.
150*	Riney (Rineyville), G 13	Ky
36*	Ring, M 15	Wis.
100*	Ringdale, G 18	Pa.
882	Ringgold, B 3	Ga.
1006	Ringgold, D 6	La.
70	Ringgold, J 10	Neb.
49*	Ringgold, M 16	Ohio
100*	Ringgold, J 7	Pa.
415	Ringgold, B 17	Tex.
500*	Ringgold, R 9	Va.
85*	Ringle, K 12	Wis.
125	Ringling, K 11	Mont.
902	Ringling, P 11	Okla.
271*	Ringo, M 25	Kan.
303	Ringoes, G 11	N. J.
50	Ringold, P 23	Okla.
86*	Ringold, M 18	Wash.
150*	Ringos Mill, E 20	Ky.
508	Ringsted, C 9	Iowa
910	Ringtown, K 19	Pa.
200	Ringwood, A 18	Ill.
977	Ringwood (Ringwood Manor), B 18	N. J.
288	Ringwood, D 8	Okla.
....	Ringwood Jc., B 18	N. J.
977	Ringwood Manor (Ringwood), B 18	N. J.
50*	Rinnie, M 16	Tenn.
40	Rio, K 23	Fla.
188	Rio, E 9	Ill.
400	Rio, K 19	La.
6*	Rio, J 19	Miss.
24*	Rio, E 2	N. Y.
156*	Rio, F 21	W. Va.
696	Rio, K 18	Wis.
5	Rioblanco, F 5	Colo.
....	Rio Campo, see Northwood	Calif.
150*	Rio Creek, Q 13	Wis.
465*	Rio Dell, D 1	Calif.
50	Rio Frio, L 14	Tex.
375	Rio Grande, R 11	N. J.
204*	Rio Grande, P 14	Ohio
2283	Rio Grande City, Q 2	Tex.
804	Rio Hondo, Q 5	Tex.
8*	Riola, H 21	Ill.
500*	Rio Linda, G 8	Calif.
250*	Riomedina, L 16	Tex.
200*	Rion, D 12	S. C.
50*	Rionido, G 4	Calif.
197*	Rio Oso, F 7	Calif.
20	Riordan, G 14	Ariz.
100*	Rios (Santa Cruz), P 16	Tex.
1666	Rio Vista, H 6	Calif.
420	Riovista, F 18	Tex.
150	Riparia, L 22	Wash.
150*	Riparius (Riverside), I 23	N. Y.
200	Ripley, P 25	Calif.
173*	Ripley, I 8	Ill.
100	Ripley, K 11	Me.
2011	Ripley, A 18	Miss.
1200	Ripley, P 1	N. Y.
1623	Ripley, Q 9	Ohio
415	Ripley, F 14	Okla.
2784	Ripley, N 3	Tenn.
759	Ripley, H 5	W. Va.
113*	Riplinger, H 12	Wis.
1100	Ripon, I 8	Calif.
4566	Ripon, M 16	Wis.
421	Rippey, J 10	Iowa
300*	Ripplemead, N 3	Va.
75	Rippleton, M 16	N. Y.
250	Rippon, E 24	W. Va.
1000	Ripraps (Fox Hill), O 21	Va.
50	Ripton, I 8	Vt.
493*	Ririe, N 20	Idaho
429*	Risco, R 22, I 24	Mo.
2	Rising, G 11	N. D.
420	Rising City, K 20	Neb.
246	Rising Fawn, B 1	Ga.
1198	Rising Star, F 15	Tex.
1545	Rising Sun, M 22	Ind.
529	Rising Sun, B 18	Md.
645	Risingsun (Rising Sun), E 10	Ohio
184	Risley, O 12	N. J.
25*	Risner, H 22	Ky.
1005	Rison, M 13	Ark.
50*	Rison, M 10	Md.
200*	Rita, Q 17	La.
60*	Rita, I 20	Pa.
50*	Rita, N 4	W. Va.
42*	Ritchey (Ritchie), E 20	Ill.
152*	Ritchey, P 7	Mo.
70*	Ritchie, H 21	Ky.
50*	Ritner, K 17	Ky.
10	Ritter, F 18	Ore.
30*	Ritter, N 15	S. C.
110*	Ritter (Avondale), Q 5	W. Va.
2770	Rittman, F 16	Ohio
40*	Ritz, I 5	Ark.
1748	Ritzville, J 20	Wash.
83*	Riva (Riverview), H 14	Md.
....	Rivas, Q 6	Calif.
150*	River (Youngs), G 9	Calif.
39*	River, G 23	Ky.
16*	River, B 7	Minn.
400*	Rivera, Q 16	Calif.
97*	River Aux Vases, L 21	Mo.
1130	Riverbank, I 9	Calif.
60*	River Bend, H 17	Colo.
500	Riverdale, K 11	Calif.
207	Riverdale, F 7	Ga.
2865	Riverdale, D 21	Ill.
68	Riverdale, N 16	Kan.
2330	Riverdale, I 12	Md.
290	Riverdale, M 15	Mich.
121	Riverdale, M 15	Neb.
1110	Riverdale, C 14	N. J.
150	Riverdale, D 11	Utah
5287*	River Edge, C 19	N. J.
413	River Falls, N 14	Ala.
....	River Falls, A 6	S. C.
2806	River Falls, B 12	Wis.
9487	River Forest, C 21	Ill.
..	Rivergate, G 16	N. Y.
3301*	River Grove, C 21	Ill.
6000	Riverhead, G 10	N. Y.
....	River Hill, J 13	Miss.
7110	River Junction, B 2, M 12	Fla.
42	River Jc., L 21	Iowa
....	River Jc., Q 25	Minn.
....	River Jc., O 7	N. Y.
556	Rivermines, L 19	Mo.
....*	Rivermoor, H 21	Mass.
3000	River Point, G 12	R. I.
75	River Ridge, M 10	Ala.
17008	River Rouge, P 22	Mich.
135	Riverside, F 16	Ala.
34696	Riverside, Q 9	Calif.
3200	Riverside, R 2	Conn.
307	Riverside, O 9	Ga.
150	Riverside, O 18	Idaho
7935*	Riverside, C 21	Ill.
91*	Riverside, H 8	Ind.
633	Riverside, L 20	Iowa
18*	Riverside, H 20	Ky.
100*	Riverside, M 11	Md.
50	Riverside, M 9	Me.
350	Riverside, C 8	Mass.
....	Riverside, N 1	Mass.
75*	Riverside, Q 10	Mich.
....	Riverside, J 20	Mo.
4	Riverside, N 24	Nev.
7200	Riverside, J 10	N. J.
150*	Riverside (Riparius), I 23	N. Y.
643*	Riverside, Q 10	N. Y.
90*	River Side, C 3	N. C.
227*	Riverside (Harshman), L 7,	Ohio
35	Riverside, L 21	Ore.
501	Riverside (South Danville), J 17	Pa.
1600*	Riverside, M 16	Pa.
1750	Riverside, F 17	R. I.
28*	Riverside, C 14	S. C.
17	Riverside, L 20	S. D.
400*	Riverside, I 22	Tex.
190	Riverside, B 10	Utah
63*	Riverside, L 9	Va.
192	Riverside, D 16	Wash.
1043	Riverside, C 14	W. Va.
68	Riverside, Q 15	Wyo.
35	Riverside Jc., H 7	Miss.
4	Riverside Jc., R 5	N. Y.
100*	River Sioux, J 2	Iowa
40*	River Springs, O 14	Md.
250	Riverton, A 6	Ala.
212	Riverton, B 9	Conn.
1524	Riverton, I 13	Ill.
50*	Riverton, M 5	Ind.
543	Riverton, P 4	Iowa
236*	Riverton, D 22	Ky.
58*	Riverton, D 11	La.
141	Riverton, I 13	Minn.
390	Riverton, O 16	Neb.
2354	Riverton, K 10	N. J.
150	Riverton, M 2	Ore.
10*	Riverton, L 16	Tenn.
1025	Riverton, F 11	Utah
175	Riverton (West Berlin), G 12	Vt.
500	Riverton, F 14	Va.
121*	Riverton, I 17	W. Va.
2540	Riverton, I 11	Wyo.
....	Riverton Heights, H 9	Wash.
....	Riverton Jc., F 14	Va.
100*	Rivervale, E 19	Ark.
15	River Vale, N 13	Ind.
....	Rivervale, C 21	N. J.
150	River View, I 22	Ala.
150*	Riverview, I 14	Fla.
600	Riverview (Anson), K 8	Me.
*	Riverview, see Riva	Md.
804	Riverview, Q 22	Mich.
4	Riverview, E 14	Neb.
225*	Riverview, E 22	N. Y.
2000*	River View, O 21	Va.
211	Riverview, K 6	W. Va.
125	Riverville, M 11	Va.
130*	Rives, R 21	Mo.
481	Rives, L 4	Tenn.
....*	Rives Junction, Q 18	Mich.
1552	Rivesville, D 13	W. Va.
1981	Riviera, L 24	Fla.
500	Riviera, Q 18	Tex.
25	Rivulet, H 3	Mont.
36*	Rixeyville, H 14	Va.
518	Rixford, E 9	Pa.
300	Rixford, (East Highgate), B 9	Vt.
55	Rix Mills, K 16	Ohio
150*	Roach, C 13	Colo.
29*	Roach, L 11	Mo.
42*	Roach, K 2	W. Va.
....	Roach Creek, L 17	Tenn.
736	Roachdale, I 10	Ind.
140*	Rochdale, E 7	Miss.
....*	Road Fork, H 24	Ky.
46*	Roads, E 9	Mo.
200	Roads (Berlin Cross Roads) O 13	Ohio
220	Roadstown, O 6	N. J.
34*	Roane, F 20	Tex.
100*	Roanes, N 21	Va.
450	Roan Mtn., M 25	Tenn.
429	Roann, E 16	Ind.
4168	Roanoke, H 22	Ala.
1090	Roanoke, F 14	Ill.
808	Roanoke, E 19	Ind.
500	Roanoke, M 8	La.
75*	Roanoke, F 12	Mo.
485*	Roanoke, D 18	Tex.
69287	Roanoke, N 7	Va.
200*	Roanoke (Roanville), H 12	W. Va.
....	Roanoke Jc., I 22	Ala.
8545	Roanoke Rapids, C 17	N. C.
268*	Roans Prairie, I 21	Tex.
200*	Roanville (Roanoke), H 12	W. Va.
40	Roanwood, B 20	Mont.
255	Roaring Branch, G 16	Pa.
350*	Roaring Creek, K 18	Pa.
275*	Roaringfork, D 5	Va.
24*	Roaring Gap, B 5	N. C.
125*	Roaring River, D 5	N. C.
2724	Roaring Spring, N 10	Pa.
514	Roaring Springs, B 11	Tex.
100*	Roark, I 20	Ky.
45*	Roba, K 20	Ala.
342	Robards, G 9	Ky.
55*	Robat (Mt. Tabor), C 11	S. C.
21	Robb, E 23	Colo.
100*	Robbins, F 7	Calif.
1349	Robbins, D 21	Ill.
....	Robbins, C 24	Mich.
25*	Robbins, G 23	Okla.
50	Robbins, L 9	S. C.
600	Robbins, L 17	Tenn.
35	Robbins, K 8	Wis.
6018	Robbinsdale, N 16	Minn.
300	Robbinston, J 24	Me.
239*	Robbinsville, H 13	N. J.
399	Robbinsville, P 3	N. C.
150*	Robbs, Q 17	Ill.
125	Robe, F 9	Wash.
355	Robeline, F 6	La.
7000*	Roberdel (East Rockingham), J 10	N. C.
1407	Robersonville, E 18	N. C.
20	Roberta, M 19	Colo.
535	Roberta, I 9	Ga.
25*	Roberta, F 12	Ky.
15	Roberta, L 17	Tenn.
662	Robert Lee, G 12	Tex.
319	Roberts, N 19	Idaho
379	Roberts, G 19	Ill.
30*	Roberts, G 19	Md.
100*	Roberts, K 17	Miss.
200	Roberts, N 14	Mont.
50	Roberts, F 6	Ore.
10*	Roberts, I 13	Ore.
265	Roberts, B 12	Wis.
135*	Robertsburg, I 4	W. Va.
779	Robertsdale, Q 7	Ala.
1400	Robertsdale, O 11	Pa.
300	Robertson, I 20	Mo.
208▲	Robertson, Q 4	Wyo.
200	Robertstown, C 10	Ga.
135*	Robertsville, J 18	Mo.
300	Robertsville, G 19	Ohio
1570	Robesonia, N 19	Pa.
50	Robin, Q 19	Idaho
46	Robinette, G 24	Ore.
75*	Robinette, O 5	W. Va.
34*	Robinhood, O 9	Me.
205*	Robins, I 20	Iowa
500	Robins, K 17	Ohio
56*	Robinson, B 4	Ark.
128*	Robinson, G 14	Ga.
4311	Robinson, L 21	Ill.
30*	Robinson, H 20	Iowa
413	Robinson, D 22	Kan.
90*	Robinson, E 18	Ky.
160	Robinson, L 15	N. D.
195*	Robinson (North Robinson), G 12	Ohio
800*	Robinson, M 7	Pa.
100*	Robinson Creek, H 23	Ky.
215	Robinson, E 19	Me.
150	Robinsonville, A 10	Miss.
160*	Robjohn, K 5	Ala.
57*	Robley, L 19	Va.
25	Rob Roy, L 14	Ark.
200*	Rob Roy, H 7	Ind.
350*	Robson, C 5	La.
300*	Robson, L 8	W. Va.
6780	Robstown, P 18	Tex.
48*	Roby, J 13	Ill.
400	Roby, B 6	Ind.
50*	Roby, N 14	Mo.
904	Roby, E 12	Tex.
127	Roca, M 22	Neb.
1200	Rochdale, G 13	Mass.
100	Roche Harbor, D 5	Wash.
200	Rochelle, D 14	Fla.
1175	Rochelle, L 12	Ga.
4200	Rochelle, C 15	Ill.
1000	Rochelle, F 10	La.
515	Rochelle, H 14	Tex.
80*	Rochelle, I 14	Va.
5000	Rochelle Park, D 20	N. J.
396	Rocheport, H 12	Mo.
4*	Rochert, H 6	Minn.
464	Rochester, J 12	Ill.
3835	Rochester, D 14	Ind.
51	Rochester, K 22	Iowa
387	Rochester, I 11	Ky.
10	Rochester, L 21	Mass.
3759	Rochester, O 22	Mich.
26312	Rochester, Q 19	Minn.
90	Rochester, D 5	Mo.
12012	Rochester, N 19	N. H.
324975	Rochester, L 9	N. Y.
162*	Rochester, F 14	Ohio
7441	Rochester, L 2	Pa.
611	Rochester, D 13	Tex.
....	Rochester, see Moore	Utah
750	Rochester, J 10	Vt.
300	Rochester, L 6	Wash.
288	Rochester, O 21	Wis.
40	Rochester Jc., M 9	N. Y.
199*	Rochester Mills (Savan), K 7	Pa.
75	Rochford, J 2	S. D.
313▲*	Rociada, E 15	N. M.
200*	Rock, N 17	Kan.
300	Rock, K 22	Mass.
162*	Rock, G 9	Mich.
138*	Rock, K 19	Pa.
600	Rock, Q 8	W. Va.
25*	Rockawalking (Rock-a-walkin), N 21	Md.
3514	Rockaway, D 15	N. J.
300	Rockaway, C 4	Ore.
150*	Rockaway Beach, I 5	Calif.
194*	Rockaway Beach (Taneycono), Q 10	Mo.
....*	Rockaway Beach (Rockaway Park), H 6	N. Y.
....*	Rockaway Park, H 6	N. Y.
....*	Rockaway Point, H 5	N. Y.
75*	Rock Bluff, B 2, N 12	Fla.
247	Rockbridge, K 9	Ill.
50*	Rockbridge, J 14	Ky.
10*	Rockbridge, Q 13	Mo.
360	Rockbridge, M 13	Ohio
85*	Rockbridge, H 18	Wis.
52*	Rockbridge Alum Springs, K 8	Va.
100*	Rockbridge Baths, K 9	Va.
100*	Rock Camp, R 14	Ohio
89*	Rock Camp, Q 11	W. Va.
150	Rockcastle, G 10	Ala.
25*	Rock Castle, M 15	Va.
52*	Rock Castle, I 5	W. Va.
21*	Rockcastle Springs, J 18	Ky.
265	Rock Cave, H 12	W. Va.
134	Rock City, A 13	Ill.
200*	Rock City Falls, M 23	N. Y.
50*	Rockcliff, M 12	W. Va.
28*	Rock Creek, Q 12	Idaho
100	Rock Creek, F 22	Kan.
70	Rock Creek, K 17	Minn.
492*	Rock Creek, C 20	Ohio
210*	Rock Creek (Rockcreek Station), C 20	Ohio
50*	Rockcreek, D 14	Ore.
300*	Rock Creek, K 15	Tenn.
210	Rockcreek Station (Rock Creek), C 20	Ohio
157	Rock Crusher (Hasslers), G 14	Tex.
1532	Rockdale, D 19	Ill.
100*	Rockdale, L 20	Ind.
20*	Rockdale, E 17	Ky.
102*	Rockdale, P 17	N. Y.
150*	Rockdale, O 9	Tenn.
2136	Rockdale, J 19	Tex.
25	Rockdale, I 10	Wash.
136*	Rockdale, L 20	Wis.
....	Rockdale Jc., D 19	Ill.
125*	Rock Elm, C 13	Wis.
96	Rocker, K 7	Mont.
12	Rockerville, K 3	S. D.
1000	Rockfall, I 14	Conn.
4987	Rock Falls, C 12	Ill.
153*	Rock Falls, C 14	Iowa
300	Rockfield, F 12	Ind.
180*	Rockfield, J 11	Ky.
100*	Rockfield, O 19	Wis.
132*	Rockfish, J 12	N. C.
102*	Rockfish, L 11	Va.
394	Rockford, H 16	Ala.
84637	Rockford, A 15	Ill.
1054	Rockford, D 15	Iowa
1773	Rockford, N 12	Mich.
270	Rockford, M 14	Minn.
60	Rockford, N 22	Neb.
210	Rockford, C 6	N. C.
1066	Rockford, G 5	Ohio
20	Rockford, C 11	Ore.
950	Rockford, N 19	Tenn.
377	Rockford, I 24	Wash.
30*	Rockford Bay, D 4	Idaho
....	Rock Forge, C 14	W. Va.
125*	Rock Glen, N 7	N. Y.
250	Rock Glen, J 19	Pa.
130*	Rock Grove, A 13	Ill.
781	Rock Hall, G 17	Md.
220	Rockham, G 17	S. D.
131*	Rock Harbor, P 23	Fla.
70*	Rock Harbor, C 3	Mich.
25*	Rock Haven, F 13	Ky.
33*	Rock Hill, R 20	N. Y.
100	Rockhill, N 23	Pa.
15009	Rock Hill, B 13	S. C.
548*	Rock Hill Furnace, N 12	Pa.
25*	Rockholds (Rockhold), J 18	Ky.
15*	Rockhouse, B 7	Ark.
200*	Rockingham, M 18	Ga.
45	Rockingham, P 19	N. H.
3657	Rockingham, I 10	N. C.
325*	Rockingham, P 7	Pa.
....	Rockingham, O 13	Vt.
150*	Rockingham (Pleasant Valley), I 11	Va.
42775	Rock Island, D 8	Ill.
15	Rock Island, K 24	Okla.
90*	Rock Island, N 14	Tenn.
200	Rock Island, L 20	Tex.
130*	Rock Island, H 16	Wash.
348	Rocklake, D 17	N. D.
240	Rockland, A 21	Del.
277	Rockland, Q 17	Idaho
8899	Rockland, N 13	Me.
8087■	Rockland, H 21	Mass.
700	Rockland, B 24	Mich.
500	Rockland, R 20	N. Y.
210	Rockland, N 17	Ohio
25	Rockland, I 4	Pa.
216	Rockland, H 24	Tex.
171	Rockland, F 16	Wis.
580*	Rockland Lake, F 5	N. Y.
725	Rockledge, H 21	Fla.
125	Rockledge, J 16	Ga.
1773*	Rockledge, N 22	Pa.
....	Rockledge, Q 13	Tenn.
79*	Rockleigh, C 19	N. J.
....	Rock Lick, N 6	W. Va.
795	Rocklin, G 8	Calif.
60*	Rocklyn, P 21	Pa.
16	Rocklyn, H 20	Wash.
3764	Rockmart, E 3	Ga.
500	Rock Mills, H 22	Ala.
8*	Rock Mills, H 14	Va.
14*	Rockoak, F 20	W. Va.
500	Rock Point, O 12	Md.
250*	Rockport, F 3	Calif.
450	Rockport, J 6	Ill.
2421	Rockport, R 8	Ind.
501	Rockport, H 10	Ky.
1000	Rockport, N 13	Me.
3556■	Rockport, C 23	Mass.
100*	Rockport, M 11	Miss.
1406	Rockport, A 3	Mo.
1729	Rockport, P 19	Tex.
200	Rockport, D 10	Wash.
43*	Rockport, F 6	W. Va.
....	Rockport Jc., Q 8	Ind.
2556	Rock Rapids, B 2	Iowa
25*	Rockridge, Q 5	W. Va.
210	Rock Rift, Q 18	N. Y.
349	Rock River, O 18	Wyo.
75*	Rockroyal, Q 18	N. Y.
350*	Rock Run, D 20	Ala.
59*	Rock Run Station, D 20	Ala.
95*	Rocks, C 15	Md.
33*	Rocksdale, H 8	W. Va.
108*	Rock Spring (Canon), H 11	Ariz.
57*	Rock Spring, C 11	Ark.
125*	Rock Spring, B 2	Ga.
30	Rock Springs, I 20	Mont.
1339	Rocksprings, K 13	Tex.
9827	Rock Springs, P 8	Wyo.
65*	Rock Stream, O 12	N. Y.
50*	Rock Tavern, D 3	N. Y.
1156	Rockton, A 15	Ill.
200*	Rockton, I 9	Pa.
162	Rockton, E 12	S. C.
75*	Rockton, G 17	Wis.
575	Rockvale, L 14	Colo.
40*	Rockvale, G 11	Ky.
25	Rockvale, M 15	Mont.
250*	Rockvale, O 11	Tenn.
1507	Rock Valley, C 2	Iowa
150	Rockview, O 23	Mo.
35*	Rockview, P 6	W. Va.
200*	Rockville, M 7	Ala.
7572	Rockville, D 17	Conn.
2208	Rockville, J 7	Ind.
90*	Rockville, N 12	Me.
2047	Rockville, H 10	Md.
345*	Rockville, L 12	Minn.
336	Rockville, K 7	Mo.
233	Rockville, K 15	Neb.
54*	Rockville, M 24	Ore.
275	Rockville, K 5	R. I.
200	Rockville, Q 5	Utah
30*	Rockville, L 16	Va.
18613	Rockville Centre, I 7	N. Y.
1318	Rockwall, D 20	Tex.
779	Rockwell, D 14	Iowa
825	Rockwell, G 8	N. C.
2391	Rockwell City, G 8	Iowa
600	Rockwood, C 7	Ala.
100*	Rockwood, O 6	Colo.
246*	Rockwood, O 11	Ill.
350*	Rockwood (Kineo), H 9	Me.
1147	Rockwood, Q 22	Mich.
100	Rockwood, C 8	Ore.
1375	Rockwood, P 7	Pa.
3981	Rockwood, N 17	Tenn.
213*	Rockwood, H 14	Tex.
100	Rockwood, P 15	Wis.
50*	Rocky, J 4	Ark.
442	Rocky, K 6	Okla.
40	Rocky Bar, N 8	Idaho
200*	Rocky Bottom, B 4	S. C.
40*	Rocky Boy, C 12	Mont.
20*	Rockybranch, K 17	Ky.
284	Rocky Comfort, Q 7	Mo.
100*	Rocky Face, B 3	Ga.
3494	Rocky Ford, M 19	Colo.
320	Rocky Ford, J 21	Ga.
7*	Rockyford, M 5	S. D.
125	Rocky Gap, O 2	Va.
2000*	Rockygrove, H 4	Pa.
16*	Rockyhill, E 11	Ark.
1000	Rocky Hill (Rockyhill), G 14	Conn.
178*	Rockyhill, I 12	Ky.
404	Rocky Hill, H 14	N. J.
64*	Rocky Mount, H 5	Ga.
33*	Rocky Mount, B 5	La.
82*	Rocky Mount, J 12	Mo.
25568	Rocky Mount, E 16	N. C.
1366	Rockymount, P 7	Va.
395	Rocky Point, G 9	N. Y.
416	Rocky Point, L 17	N. C.
12	Rocky Point, J 13	Ore.
14*	Rocky Point, M 8	Va.
100*	Rockypoint, C 19	Wyo.
60	Rocky Ridge (Emmitsburg), C 8	Md.
275	Rockyridge (Rocky Ridge), D 11	Ohio
....	Rockyridge, O 11	Pa.
8291	Rockyriver, O 20	Ohio
111	Rocky River, O 14	Tenn.
1650	Roda, D 4	Va.
420	Rodanthe, F 25	N. C.
100	Rodarte, D 15	N. M.
25*	Rodden, A 9	Ill.
100*	Roddy, O 16	Tenn.
2500	Rodeo, A 18	Calif.
150	Rodeo, P 1	N. M.
100*	Roderfield, Q 5	W. Va.
40*	Roderick, G 4	Nev.
3700*	Rodessa, A 4	La.
26	Rodey, N 8	N. M.
14	Rodley, P 23	Colo.
170*	Rodman, D 9	Iowa
212	Rodman, I 15	N. Y.
900*	Rodman, C 13	S. C.
4	Rodna, I 22	Wash.
15*	Rodney, A 12	Ark.
131*	Rodney, H 3	Iowa
100	Rodney, L 13	Mich.
124	Rodney, M 5	Miss.
50*	Rodney, P 15	Ohio
86*	Roduco, C 20	N. C.
200*	Roe, J 16	Ark.
161*	Roe, I 22	N. C.
3300	Roebling, J 12	N. J.
250*	Roebuck, B 9	S. C.
100*	Roelofs, N 24	Pa.
32*	Roff, G 12	Ky.
705	Roff, N 15	Okla.
300*	Roganville, I 25	Tex.
3550	Rogers, A 5	Ark.
....	Rogers, I 19	Ga.
100*	Rogers (Oklahoma), G 20	Ky.
15*	Rogers, G 4	La.
274*	Rogers, M 15	Minn.
121	Rogers, J 21	Neb.
52	Rogers, J 24	N. M.
244	Rogers (Clintonville), E 24	N. Y.
174	Rogers, L 20	N. D.
300	Rogers, G 21	Ohio
911	Rogers, I 18	Tex.
14*	Rogers, O 5	Va.
42	Rogersburg, O 24	Wash.
3072	Rogers City, G 19	Mich.
100	Rogerson, Q 11	Idaho
....*	Rogers Rock (Baldwin), I 24	N. Y.
45*	Rogers Springs, Q 4	Tenn.
508	Rogersville, A 10	Ala.
430	Rogersville, O 11	Mo.
250	Rogersville, Q 2	Pa.
2018	Rogersville, L 22	Tenn.
110	Roggen, E 17	Colo.
180*	Rogillioville, J 13	La.
383	Rogue River, P 6	Ore.
500*	Rohnerville, D 2	Calif.
20*	Rohrer, J 10	Ill.
625*	Rohrerstown, O 19	Pa.
210*	Rohrersville, B 4	Md.
96*	Rohrersville (Trego), B 4	Md.
35	Rohrs, N 24	Neb.
90	Rohrsburg, I 18	Pa.
20	Rohrville, G 18	N. D.
142*	Rohwer, N 16	Ark.
38	Rokeby, M 21	Neb.
50*	Rokeby, I 18	Va.
40*	Rolan, K 16	Ky.
1025▲*	Roland, I 12	Ark.
20*	Roland, O 11	Ind.
791	Roland, I 12	Iowa
311	Roland, I 24	Okla.
....*	Roland Park, F 14	Md.
200	Rolapp, I 16	Utah
460	Rolette, E 14	N. D.
1122	Rolfe, E 9	Iowa
....	Rolfe Jc., R 14	Ark.
300	Roll, M 5	Ariz.
150	Roll (Dundee), F 19	Ind.
64*	Rolla, L 11	Ark.
284*	Rolla, O 2	Kan.
5141	Rolla, L 15	Mo.
1008	Rolla, D 15	N. D.
75*	Rolla (Verona), J 10	Va.
55*	Rollersville, D 11	Ohio
102*	Rollin, R 19	Mich.
530*	Rollingbay, H 7	Wash.
1320	Rolling Fork, H 7	Miss.
65*	Rolling Hill, O 11	Va.
500	Rolling Prairie, A 11	Ind.
66*	Rolling Prairie, M 18	Wis.
324	Rolling Stone, P 22	Minn.
15	Rollins, A 20	Ill.
14	Rollins, G 21	Minn.
107*	Rollins, E 5	Mont.
500	Rollinsford, N 20	N. H.
50*	Rollins Fork, J 18	Va.
53*	Rollinsville, F 13	Colo.
41*	Rollo, C 16	Ill.
10*	Rolston, C 6	Ga.
....*	Rolyat, see Stauffer	Ore.
1414	Roma, Q 2	Tex.
250	Roman, J 10	Va.
69*	Romance, G 13	Ark.
25*	Romance, Q 12	Mo.
18*	Romance, H 5	W. Va.
300	Romayor, J 23	Tex.
190*	Rombauer, P 20	Mo.
26282	Rome, D 2	Ga.
246*	Rome, F 12	Ill.
300*	Rome, R 12	Ind.
119*	Rome, O 20	Iowa
55*	Rome, G 10	Ky.
25	Rome, L 17	Me.
219	Rome, D 9	Miss.
58*	Rome, P 12	Mo.
34214	Rome, L 17	N. Y.
75	Rome, C 20	Ohio
169*	Rome (Stout), Q 11	Ohio
218	Rome, E 18	Pa.
315	Rome, M 13	Tenn.
159	Rome, M 20	Wis.
504	Rome City, B 18	Ind.
392	Romeo, P 11	Colo.
100*	Romeo, E 13	Fla.
170*	Romeo (Romeoville), D 20	Ill.
2637	Romeo, O 22	Mich.
100*	Romero (Romeroville), F 16	N. M.
100*	Romero, C 1	Tex.
100*	Romeroville (Romero), F 16	N. M.
24*	Romine, I 15	Ky.
300*	Rominger, D 2	N. C.
100	Rommell (North Point), O 11	Pa.
250	Romney, H 9	Ind.
2013	Romney, E 20	W. Va.
....	Romney Jc., E 20	W. Va.
353*	Romoland (Ethanac), O 20	Calif.
91*	Romona, L 9	Ind.
20	Romont, L 8	W. Va.
755*	Romulus, Q 22	Mich.
190	Romulus, N 12	N. Y.
58	Romulus, K 15	Okla.
496	Ronald, J 12	Wash.
1032	Ronan, G 4	Mont.
2265	Ronceverte, O 12	W. Va.
800	Ronco, Q 3	Pa.
379*	Ronda, D 5	N. C.
400	Ronda, L 7	W. Va.
201*	Rondo, I 19	Ark.
204	Rondout, B 20	Ill.
....	Rondout, R 23	N. Y.
200*	Roneys Point, Q 24	W. Va.
1500*	Ronkonkoma, H 9	N. Y.
169*	Ronks, P 19	Pa.
107*	Ronneby, L 14	Minn.
2557	Roodhouse, K 9	Ill.
27*	Rooney, E 22	Ky.
230	Roopville, G 3	Ga.
76*	Roosa Gap, R 20	N. Y.
....	Roosevelt, K 16	Ariz.
19*	Roosevelt, F 15	Ark.
60*	Roosevelt, C 14	La.
304	Roosevelt, B 9	Minn.
7000*	Roosevelt, I 7	N. Y.
744	Roosevelt, L 5	Okla.
62*	Roosevelt, J 13	Tex.
1264	Roosevelt, G 21	Utah
100	Roosevelt, Q 14	Wash.
....	Roosevelt Hot Springs, M 7	Utah
30*	Rooseveltown, C 20	N. Y.
....	Roots, H 16	N. Y.
200	Rootstown, F 18	Ohio
310	Rootstown (New Milford), F 18	Ohio
76	Roper, L 21	Kan.
716	Roper, E 21	N. C.
800*	Ropesville (Ropes), C 9	Tex.
90*	Roque Bluffs, L 21	Me.
64*	Rosa, J 12	La.
8	Rosa, B 7	N. M.
218*	Rosalia, L 19	Kan.
596	Rosalia, J 23	Wash.
250	Rosalie, H 22	Neb.
400*	Rosamond, N 14	Calif.
250	Rosamond, K 14	Ill.
205	Rosanky, K 18	Tex.
15	Rosario, C 6	Wash.
200	Rosati (Knobview), L 16	Mo.
131	Rosboro, L 7	Ark.
400	Rosburg, N 4	Wash.
94*	Rosbys Rock, B 11	W. Va.
....*	Roscoe, Q 4	Calif.
450	Roscoe, A 16	Ill.
56*	Roscoe, F 21	Ky.
171	Roscoe, L 10	Minn.
126*	Roscoe, L 8	Mo.
12	Roscoe, N 14	Mont.
10	Roscoe, K 8	Neb.
900	Roscoe, B 2, R 20	N. Y.
660	Roscoe, I 16	Ohio
1372	Roscoe, O 4	Pa.
608	Roscoe, D 16	S. D.
1166	Roscoe, E 12	Tex.
619	Roscommon, J 16	Mich.
26*	Rose, L 22	Kan.
210*	Rose, F 14	Neb.
400	Rose, L 12	N. Y.
40	Rose, E 22	Okla.
....	Rose, I 7	Pa.
....*	Roseann, B 7	Va.
25	Roseacres, C 9	Miss.
1775	Roseau, B 6	Minn.
32	Roseberry, K 6	Idaho
150	Roseboom, N 20	N. Y.
939	Roseboro, I 15	N. C.
200*	Rose Bud, G 14	Ark.
16*	Rosebud, R 18	Ill.
193	Rosebud, J 16	Mo.
250	Rosebud, K 20	Mont.
50	Rosebud, E 23	N. M.
120	Rosebud, N 11	S. D.
1842	Rosebud, I 19	Tex.
27*	Roseburg, I 13	Ky.
4924	Roseburg, M 5	Ore.
100*	Roseburgh, G 17	Ind.
400	Rosebush, L 15	Mich.
50*	Rose Center, P 22	Mich.
355	Rose City, J 18	Mich.
261	Rose Creek, R 18	Minn.
60*	Rosedale, E 4	Ark.
26*	Rosedale, L 9	Ill.
712	Rosedale, K 7	Ind.
418	Rosedale, L 13	La.
315	Rosedale, F 14	Md.
2063	Rosedale, E 6	Miss.
....*	Rosedale, H 6	N. Y.
112	Rosedale, L 13	Okla.
75*	Rosedale, P 21	Pa.
35*	Rosedale, M 18	Tenn.
200	Rosedale, I 7	Wash.
175*	Rosedale, I 10	W. Va.
150*	Rose Farm (Tropic), L 15	Ohio
125*	Rosefield, F 11	La.
43*	Rosefork, G 21	Ky.
50	Roseglen, I 8	N. D.
157	Rose Hill, L 19	Ill.
269	Rose Hill, M 17	Iowa
175*	Rose Hill, M 17	Kan.
125*	Rose Hill, G 16	Ky.
350	Rose Hill, K 19	Miss.
50*	Rose Hill, M 14	N. Y.
727	Rosehill, J 16	N. C.
....	Rosehill, F 16	S. C.
500*	Rose Hill, E 3	Va.
100	Roselake, D 5	Idaho
56*	Roseland, D 22	Ark.
75*	Roseland, I 22	Fla.
782	Roseland, B 13	Ind.
873	Roseland, J 17	La.
75*	Roseland, N 9	Minn.
187	Roseland, N 16	Neb.
1556	Roseland, D 17	N. J.
71*	Roseland, L 10	Va.
200	Roselawn, D 6	Ind.

Pop. Place Index State
63*Rose Lawn, M 12.....Wis.
694 Roselle, B 20...........Ill.
50*Roselle, N 20..........Mo.
13597 Roselle, F 18.........N. J.
9661 Roselle Park, F 18....N. J.
36 Rose Lodge, F 4.......Ore.
....*Rosemary, see Roanoke Rapids..............N. C.
5500*Rosemead, Q 4.......Calif.
75 Rosemont, N 17.......Neb.
61*Rosemont, G 10.......N. J.
2600*Rosemont, N 22..........Pa.
800 Rosemont, E 13....W. Va.
364 Rosemount, O 17....Minn.
3457 Rosenberg, L 21.......Tex.
30 Rosenburg, I 19......Neb.
300 Rosendale, C 5.........Mo.
671 Rosendale, R 22.......N. Y.
317 Rosendale, M 17........Wis.
800 Rosenhayn, O 8........N. J.
407*Rosepine, I 7.............La.
275 Rose Point, J 2.........Pa.
1778 Roseto, K 23...........Pa.
1000 Roseton, D 5..........N. Y.
130*Rosetta, E 8...........Ark.
113*Rosetta, O 4..........Miss.
72*Rosette, C 4...........Utah
359*Rose Valley...............Pa.
6653 Roseville, G 8.........Calif.
1061 Roseville, F 8............Ill.
9023 Roseville, P 23.......Mich.
1320 Roseville, L 15.......Ohio
133 Roseville(Rutland), E 16Pa.
265*Roseville, H 16..........Va.
35*Rosewood, D 4.......Minn.
200 Rosewood, J 8.........Ohio
50 Rosewood, E 22........Tex.
.... Rosewood, O 21........Wis.
362 Rosholt, B 24...........S. D.
523 Rosholt, K 13...........Wis.
1774 Rosiclare, Q 19...........Ill.
150 Rosie, E 16...............Ark.
50*Rosier, H 20...............Ga.
35*Rosiere, H 15..........N. Y.
33*Rosina, L 6..........W. Va.
48*Rosindale, L 14........N. C.
176*Rosine, H 11.............Ky.
27 Rosita, M 14...........Colo.
34*Roslin, M 16.........Tenn.
972 Roslyn, H 7.............N. Y.
....*Roslyn (Hillside), N 22 (Pop. 2,500 incl. in Abington)...............Pa.
253 Roslyn, D 21..........S. D.
1743 Roslyn, J 12.........Wash.
646*Roslyn Estates, H 7..N. Y.
....*Roslyn Heights, H 7..N. Y.
529 Rosman, Q 7............N. C.
.... Rosney, M 13..............Va.
.... Ross, see Deer Park, O 17 Ark.
1751 Ross, B 14.............Calif.
....*Ross, B 6..................Ind.
70*Ross, K 7.................Iowa
51*Ross, B 6................Minn.
150 Ross, G 6...............N. D.
400 Ross, N 5.................Ohio
51 Ross, G 18................Tex.
50 Ross, H 18..............Wyo.
37 Rossburg, I 15.........Minn.
50*Rossburg, O 7.........N. Y.
204 Rossburg, I 6...........Ohio
500*Roser, E 20..............Tex.
6000 Rossford, C 9...........Ohio
15 Ross Fork, H 13.......Mont.
.... Rossi, K 11...............Calif.
95 Rossie, D 6...............Iowa
706▲*Rossie, F 16..........N. Y.
1600 Rossiter, K 8.............Pa.
48*Rosslyn, G 19..............Ky.
432*Rosslyn (Rossyln Farms), L 3.......................Pa.
3000 Rosslyn, F 18..............Va.
175*Rossmore, O 4......W. Va.
475*Rossmoyne, N 5.......Ohio
100 Rosston, O 8..............Ark.
40*Rosston (Roston), I 13.Ind.
143 Rosston, B 2..........Okla.
200 Rosston, K 5..............Pa.
330 Rosston, C 18...........Tex.
3538 Rossville, B 2.............Ga.
1428 Rossville, H 22............Ill.
627 Rossville, G 11............Ind.
100*Rossville, C 21..........Iowa
601 Rossville, F 21..........Kan.
100*Rossville, P 16.............Pa.
190*Rossville, Q 3..........Tenn.
345 Rossville, M 16...........Tex.
.... Rossville Jc., H 21........Ill.
.... Roston, see Rosston....Ind.
300 Roswell, J 15..........Colo.
1622 Roswell, E 7...............Ga.
60 Roswell, N 3............Idaho
13482 Roswell, L 19.........N. M.
283 Roswell, I 18...........Ohio
96 Roswell, K 21..........S. D.
40*Rosy, E 12..............Minn.
2029 Rotan, D 12..............Tex.
47 Roth, D 12...............N. D.
250*Roth, B 7...................Va.
162*Rothbury, M 11.......Mich.
55 Rothiemay, J 14.....Mont.
415 Rothsay, I 4...........Minn.
812 Rothschild, J 12.........Wis.
800*Rothsville, O 19...........Pa.
30 Rothville, E 11...........Mo.
21 Rothwell, F 20.............Ky.
1000 Rotterdam Junction, M 22 N. Y.
45 Roubaix, J 2............S. D.
125*Roubidoux, N 14........Mo.
275 Rougemont, D 13.....N. C.
120*Rough and Ready, F 9.Calif.
30*Rough Run, G 18...W. Va.
800 Roulette, F 11.............Pa.
27*Round Butte, G 3...Mont.
75*Round Grove, C 11.......Ill.
325 Roundhead, H 9.........Ohio
75*Roundhill, I 11.............Ky.
337 Round Hill, E 15..........Va.
100*Round Knob, R 17........Ill.
252▲*Round Lake, M 11....Fla.
359 Round Lake, A 19..........Ill.
430 Round Lake, R 7.......Minn.
125*Roundlake, D 8.........Miss.
600*Round Lake, M 23....N. Y.
38 Round Mtn., D 20.......Ala.
117*Round Mtn., C 7.......Calif.
2 Round Mtn., J 4...........Me.
231 Round Mtn., I 12.........Nev.
15 Round Mtn., J 16.........Tex.
125*Round O, M 15..........S. C.
110*Round Oak, I 11...........Ga.
150 Round Pond, H 19.......Ark.
470 Round Pond, O 11.......Me.
75*Round Prairie, K 10..Minn.
1240 Round Rock, J 18.........Tex.
150*Round Spring, O 16......Mo.
23*Round Top, P 22.......N. Y.
60 Round Top, Q 14...........Pa.
120*Round Top, K 20..........Tex.
2644 Roundup, J 15.........Mont.
9 Round Valley, J 14......Neb.
250 Rouse, O 16...............Colo.
1846 Rouses Point, C 24....N. Y.
998 Rouseville, G 4..............Pa.
34*Rousseau, G 21..............Ky.
301*Rousseau, B 23..........Mich.
40*Routon, M 6..............Tenn.

Pop. Place Index State
60*Routt, C 8...........Colo.
950 Rouzerville, Q 13.......Pa.
150 Rover, I 8.............Ark.
26*Rover, Q 15............Mo.
316 Rowan (Rowen), F 12.Iowa
25*Rowanta, O 17..........Va.
1500 Rowayton, Q 4.......Conn.
25*Rowden, F 14...........Tex.
200 Rowe, B 5...........Mass.
30 Rowe, F 15..........N. M.
....*Rowe, B 7 ....Va.
65*Rowell, N 14............Ark.
5*Rowell, H 15..............Ill.
.... Rowen, see Rowan....Iowa
24*Rowena, J 16..............Ky.
80 Rowena, M 25.........S. D.
500 Rowena, G 13...........Tex.
2000*Rowes Run, O 4..........Pa.
402 Rowesville, K 14.......S. C.
300 Rowland, H 17............Ky.
7 Rowland, A 18...........Nev.
999 Rowland, L 12..........N. C.
3 Rowland, I 6.............Ore.
40*Rowland, O 14........Tenn.
75 Rowlands (Rowland), G 24.....................Pa.
170*Rowlandsville, B 17....Md.
1452 Rowlesburg, E 16...W. Va.
300*Rowlett, D 19...........Tex.
265 Rowletts, I 13............Ky.
233 Rowley, H 19...........Iowa
800 Rowley, B 20...........Mass.
200*Rowood (Clarkstown), N 9 Ariz.
32*Rowton, H 24.............Ky.
33*Rox, L 23..................Nev.
200 Roxabell, N 11.........Ohio
....*Roxalia, P 11.......W. Va.
160*Roxana, M 25.............Del.
1255 Roxana, L 11...............Ill.
75*Roxana, I 22..............Ky.
367*Roxana, F 12............Okla.
....*Roxana, C 4..............Tex.
4599 Roxboro, C 13..........N. C.
....*Roxboro, K 19.........Wash.
225 Roxbury, I 5...........Conn.
110*Roxbury, I 16...........Kan.
150 Roxbury, L 4...............Me.
475 Roxbury, P 20..........N. Y.
300*Roxbury, M 16..........Ohio
175 Roxbury, O 13...............Pa.
80 Roxbury, H 11...............Vt.
98*Roxbury, M 18...............Va.
385 Roxie, N 5.................Miss.
332 Roxobel, D 19...........N. C.
1200 Roxton, C 21...............Tex.
.... Roy, E 22.................Ark.
29*Roy, C 6.....................Ga.
70 Roy, Q 17.................Idaho
50*Roy, P 11.....................Mo.
175 Roy, G 15.................Mont.
1138 Roy, E 20..................N. M.
75 Roy, C 6......................Ore.
998 Roy, D 10....................Utah
261 Roy, K 7..................Wash.
110*Royal, J 9...................Ark.
120*Royal, H 20......................Ill.
426 Royal, D 5....................Iowa
.... Royal, K 16....................Mo.
193 Royal, G 18....................Neb.
600*Royal, H 21..................N. C.
.... Royal, M 12..................Okla.
865 Royal Center, E 11....Ind.
.... Royal Jc., P 6...............Me.
100 Royal Oak, K 17.........Md.
25087 Royal Oak, P 22....Mich.
795▲Royalston, B 10.......Mass.
350 Royalston (South Royalston), B 10...........Mass.
1772 Royalton, P 15................Ill.
75*Royalton, I 12............Ind.
209*Royalton, G 21..............Ky.
25 Royalton, Q 10.........Mich.
518 Royalton, K 12.........Minn.
100 Royalton, L 12...........Ohio
1201 Royalton, O 17................Pa.
70 Royalton, J 12...............Vt.
304 Royalton, L 14.............Wis.
600*Royalty, H 7................Tex.
.... Royce, C 24..............N. M.
110 Royer, M 10...................Pa.
3605 Royersford, O 22...........Pa.
100 Royerton, H 19...........Ind.
6 Royhl, I 23.................S. D.
46 Roy Jc., G 14............Mont.
....*Royrader, H 19...............Ky.
1190 Royse City, D 20.........Tex.
10 Royster, I 16...............Fla.
1549 Royston, D 14...............Ga.
205 Royston, E 12.............Tex.
40 Roza, L 14...............Wash.
206 Rozel, K 9...................Kan.
50 Rozet, D 20.................Wyo.
6*Ruark, L 20......................Va.
.... Ruarks, N 15................N. C.
195*Rubicon, N 19..............Wis.
140 Rubio, M 19...............Iowa
200*Ruble, O 18.....................Mo.
24 Rubottom, Q 12..........Okla.
....*Ruby, P 18...................Ariz.
300*Ruby, I 10......................La.
50*Ruby (Geren), E 11...Miss.
30 Ruby, M 8...............Mont.
25 Ruby, L 21...................Neb.
170 Ruby, B 5..................N. Y.
337 Ruby, C 17..................S. C.
20*Ruby, H 16....................Va.
40 Ruby, D 23...............Wash.
10*Rubys Inn, O 13..........Utah
95 Ruby Valley, E 19.....Nev.
17 Ruch, Q 6....................Ore.
90*Rucker, O 12..............Tenn.
50*Rucker, F 16..................Tex.
65*Ruckersville, E 18.........Ga.
550 Ruckersville, J 13............Va.
.... Ruckles (Dole), N 5.....Ore.
50*Ruckman, E 21......W. Va.
8*Rudd, B 8......................Ark.
410 Rudd, D 15.................Iowa
150 Ruddels Mill, E 18......Ky.
40*Ruddle, I 17...........W. Va.
50*Rudement, P 18..............Ill.
450 Rudolph, E 9..............Ohio
20 Rudolph, E 18............S. D.
115 Rudolph, J 14..............Wis.
89*Rudy, F 4........................Ark.
....*Rudy, see Salford...........Pa.
600 Rudyard, F 17.............Mich.
75*Rudyard, C 7...............Miss.
531 Rudyard, D 12...........Mont.
59*Rue, L 24........................Va.
20 Ruedi, H 9..................Colo.
131*Ruegg (Fort Bellefontaine), H 20.........................Mo.
60*Rueter, Q 11....................Md.
131 Rufe, P 22.....................Okla.
100 Ruff, J 19....................Wash.
450 Ruffin, C 11..................N. C.
443*Ruffin, M 14.................S. C.
500*Ruffs Dale, M 5...............Pa.
28*Rufus, E 3.....................N. C.
70 Rufus, C 13....................Ore.
135 Rugby, O 16..................Colo.
5*Rugby, B 9.........................Ga.
55*Rugby, L 16....................Ind.
2215 Rugby, F 15...............N. D.
275 Rugby, M 17.................Tenn.
200*Rugby, E 10........................Va.
5 Rugby Jc., N 19..........Wis.

Pop. Place Index State
150*Rugby Road (Elgin), L 17...............Tenn.
150*Ruggles (Rugless), D 21 Ky.
150*Rugless (Ruggles), D 21Ky.
530 Ruidosa, K 4..........Tex.
516▲*Ruidoso, L 15......N. M.
....*Ruin, F 21.................Ky.
124*Rule, B 8.................Ark.
1195 Rule, D 13.................Tex.
1378 Ruleville, E 9........Miss.
4 Rulison, G 5.............Colo.
808 Rulo, O 25..................Neb.
95*Ruma, O 10..................Ill.
160*Rumbley, P 19..............Md.
100*Rumely, F 8..............Mich.
8447■Rumford (Rumford Falls), M 4......................Me.
625 Rumford, D 17............R. I.
14 Rumford, N 2.............S. D.
30*Rumford, L 19..............Va.
150*Rumford Center, M 4..Me.
325 Rumford Corner, M 4..Me.
60 Rumford Jc., O 6......Me.
107 Rumford Point, M 4...Me.
28*Rumley, D 12..............Ark.
200*Rummel, P 7...................Pa.
100*Rummerfield, E 17......Pa.
365 Rumney, K 11............N. H.
210 Rumney Depot (Rumney), K 11......................N. H.
20 Rumsey, G 5...........Calif.
358*Rumsey, H 9................Ky.
2926 Rumson, H 21..............N. J.
31*Runa, L 10...........W. Va.
1001 Runge, N 18...............Tex.
388 Runnells, L 13...........Iowa
.... Run Jc., G 17..........Ohio
2835 Runnemede, L 9.......N. J.
18*Running Lake, B 18...Ark.
85*Running Springs, N 20. Calif.
25 Runningville (Badnation), L 13..S. D.
75 Running Water, P 20..S. D.
30*Running Water, A 10..Tex.
30*Runnymede, N 14....Kan.
....*Rupert, E 11..............Ark.
17*Rupert, J 8......................Ga.
3167 Rupert, Q 14..............Idaho
232 Rupert, N 6.....................Vt.
250 Rupert, N 11.............W. Va.
141 Ruppertown (Allens Creek), P 8...................Tenn.
55*Rural, L 7...................Ala.
32*Rural (Woods), H 21...Ind.
210 Rural, G 24.....................Ky.
65 Ruraldale, L 16..........Ohio
227 Ruralgrove, N 21........N. Y.
850 Rural Hall D 8..........N. C.
112 Rural Hill H 17..........Miss.
440 Rural Retreat P 1..........Va.
900 Rural Valley K 6..........Pa.
....*Ruse see Dukes........Mich.
100*Rush, C 11....................Ark.
200 Rush, J 17...................Colo.
275 Rush, E 22.......................Ky.
300*Rush, M 9...................N. Y.
95*Rush, E 19........................Pa.
.... Rush, I 15.....................S. C.
200*Rushcenter, J 10.........Kan.
1020 Rush City, L 17.........Minn.
1182 Rushford, Q 22..........Minn.
500 Rushford, P 7...........N. Y.
136*Rush Hill, G 15...........Mo.
41*Rushing, E 13..............Ark.
125 Rush Lake, M 16..........Wis.
105*Rushland, N 24................Pa.
200*Rushmere, O 20..............Va.
423 Rushmore, R 5...........Minn.
100*Rushmore, G 8............Ohio
300*Rush Run, I 20............Ohio
310*Rush Run, M 9........W. Va.
1422 Rush Springs, M 10...Okla.
560 Rushsylvania, I 9......Ohio
56 Rushton, I 22.............Miss.
200*Rush Tower, K 20........Mo.
200*Rushtown, P 12............Ohio
2480 Rushville, H 7...................Ill.
5960 Rushville, K 19...............Ind.
309 Rushville, E 4.....................Mo.
1125 Rushville, E 5..................Neb.
428 Rushville, N 11.............N. Y.
228 Rushville, L 14...............Ohio
76*Rushville, F 19....................Pa.
28*Rusk, N 10.........................Ind.
152*Rusk (Burch), C 6....N. C.
5699 Rusk, G 22........................Tex.
51*Rusk, D 12........................Wis.
600 Ruskin, I 13.....................Fla.
223 Ruskin, O 18....................Neb.
90 Ruskin, M 8....................Tenn.
65 Ruso, I 11.....................N. D.
100 Russell, O 4.......................Ala.
206*Russell, G 15...................Ark.
.... Russell, O 14..................Colo.
700*Russell, C 16.....................Fla.
126*Russell, E 10.........................Ga.
85*Russell, A 20.........................Ill.
642 Russell, O 14....................Iowa
4819 Russell, H 12.....................Kan.
1844 Russell, D 22........................Ky.
750 Russell, G 6.....................Mass.
464 Russell, P 5......................Minn.
75*Russell, J 21.....................Miss.
25 Russell, E 10.....................Mont.
500 Russell, F 18.....................N. Y.
70 Russell, E 11.....................N. D.
31*Russell, N 10......................Ohio
42 Russell (Blake), M 3..Okla.
500 Russell, E 7............................Pa.
150*Russell, H 21......................Tex.
775*Russell (Ft. Warren), Q 21..........................Wyo.
163*Russell City (De Young), G 8.........................Pa.
556*Russell Gardens, H 7.N. Y.
93*Russell Gulch, F 13...Colo.
554*Russels Point, H 9....Ohio
198 Russell Springs, H 4...Kan.
536*Russell Springs, J 16...Ky.
1500 Russellton, L 4...............Pa.
3510 Russellville, C 7...........Ala.
5927 Russellville, G 9...........Ark.
224 Russellville, M 23...........Ill.
380 Russellville, I 9...............Ind.
3983 Russellville, J 11.............Ky.
319 Russellville, J 13.............Mo.
452 Russellville, P 9...........Ohio
64 Russellville, K 21.....Okla.
400 Russellville, D 8.........Ore.
53*Russellville, K 18......S. C.
300 Russellville, M 21.....Tenn.
75*Russellville, M 9....W. Va.
50 Russett, P 15............Okla.
.... Russia, M 15..........N. M.
200 Russia, J 6..............Ohio
850 Russiaville, G 13..........Ind.
192*Russum, L 6.................Miss.
.... Rust, F 17..................Minn.
40*Rustad, H 3................Minn.
400 Rustburg, N 10...............Va.
7107 Ruston, C 9...................La.
739*Ruston, J 7.................Wash.
40*Rutan, P 2.......................Pa.
150*Rutersville, K 19..........Tex.
10*Ruth, D 3....................Calif.
60*Ruth, I 17.......................Ky.
100 Ruth, L 24...................Mich.

Pop. Place Index State
75*Ruth, N 10..........Miss.
2000 Ruth, H 20...............Nev.
318 Ruth, G 1..............N. C.
11*Ruth, I 13..................Va.
2 Ruthdale, B 19..........Okla.
110*Rutherford, K 21.......Ala.
319*Rutherford, G 5.......Calif.
15466 Rutherford, E 19....N. J.
771 Rutherford, M 4.....Tenn.
46*Rutherford, F 8.....W. Va.
330 Rutherford College, E 2 N. C.
615 Rutherford Heights (Rutherford), N 17...Pa.
2326 Rutherfordton, G 2...N. C.
80*Ruther Glen, K 17.......Va.
20*Rutheron, C 11.........N. M.
300*Ruthford, M 8...............Pa.
480 Ruthton, P 4..............Minn.
832 Ruthven, C 7...............Iowa
20*Ruthville, N 18.............Va.
462 Rutland, F 15..................Ill.
100*Rutland, C 13..............Ind.
255*Rutland, C 7................Iowa
1500 Rutland, E 13..............Mass.
305 Rutland, Q 22..............N. D.
562 Rutland, O 15..............Ohio
99 Rutland (Roseville), E 14 Pa.
250 Rutland, J 23.............S. D.
17082 Rutland, L 8...................Vt.
800*Rutland Heights, F 13 Mass.
289*Rutledge, M 15..............Ala.
550 Rutledge, F 11...............Ga.
161*Rutledge, J 18.............Minn.
249 Rutledge, B 14...............Mo.
796*Rutledge, P 23.................Pa.
518 Rutledge, M 20............Tenn.
.... Ruxton, N 21...............Colo.
341 Ryan, H 20....................Iowa
1115 Ryan, Q 10....................Okla.
53*Ryan, E 16........................Va.
4*Ryan, I 7....................W. Va.
225*Ryan, O 15...................Wyo.
85*Rydal, D 5.........................Ga.
22*Rydal, D 15.....................Kan.
....*Rydal, O 24 (Pop. 350 incl. in Abington)....Pa.
150*Ryde, G 8......................Calif.
118*Ryde, M 13............................Pa.
467 Ryder, I 9.......................N. D.
400 Ryderwood, M 5.......Wash.
40*Rye, O 14.........................Ark.
163 Rye, M 15........................Colo.
70*Rye, C 11...........................Ind.
1246▲Rye, P 21....................N. H.
9865 Rye, G 6..........................N. Y.
75 Rye, J 23..........................Tex.
125 Rye Beach, P 21.........N. H.
108*Rye Cove. E 5..................Va.
348 Ryegate, J 14..............Mont.
200 Ryegate, G 17.....................Vt.
....*Rye North Beach, P 21 N. H.
56 Rye Valley, H 23...........Ore.
100*Ryland, B 14....................Ala.
75*Ryland, D 21..................N. C.

S

106*Sabael, I 21..............N. Y.
12*Sabattis, G 19..........N. Y.
700 Sabattus, N 7...............Me.
100*Sabbathday Lake, O 5..Me.
16*Sabbath Day Point, I 24 N. Y.
409 Sabbath Resr, M 10....Pa.
2241 Sabetha, C 21.............Kan.
250 Sabillasville, B 8......Md.
210 Sabin, H 2..............Minn.
41*Sabina, H 16..................Ill.
1525 Sabina, M 9.................Ohio
1768 Sabinal, M 14...............Tex.
364 Sabine, K 25..................Tex.
300*Sabine, P 6.............W. Va.
300*Sabine Pass, K 25.........Tex.
200*Sabinoso, F 18...........N. M.
250 Sabinsville, E 13...............Pa.
32*Sabot, L 16......................Va.
1810 Sabraton (Sturgiss City), C 14........................W. Va.
771 Sabula, I 25...................Iowa
214*Sabula, N 18.....................Mo.
50 Sabula, I 9..........................Pa.
100*Sacandaga, L 22.........N. Y.
315 Sacaton, L 14................Ariz.
3165 Sac City, G 7.................Iowa
....*Sachem Head, L 10..Conn.
1962*Sacket Harbor, H 15.N. Y.
....*Sackett, J 22.....................Ky.
36*Sackett, F 8.........................Pa.
66 Saco, L 19.........................Ala.
8631 Saco, Q 5...........................Me.
.... Saco, Q 16......................Minn.
88*Saco, N 19..........................Mo.
452 Saco, D 18........................Mont.
105958 Sacramento, G 7...Calif.
20*Sacramento, O 18.............Ill.
379 Sacramento, H 9................Ky.
11 Sacramento, N 14........Neb.
10*Scaramento, M 15.....N. M.
168*Sacramento, K 19..............Pa.
752 Sacred Heart, N 7...Minn.
90 Sacred Heart, L 15...Okla.
25*Sacredwind, F 23..........Ky.
3 Sacton, H 6..................Iowa
650*Sacul, G 23.....................Tex.
163*Saddle (South Fork), B 15 Ark.
51 Saddle Mtn., L 7.......Okla.
816 Saddle River, C 19.....N. J.
....*Sadelestring, E 16....Wyo.
477 Sadieville, E 17..................Ky.
38*Sadler, H 12..........................Ky.
250 Sadler, C 19........................Tex.
100*Sadlersville (Sadlers), K 10.....................Tenn.
371 Sadorus, I 18......................Ill.
100*Sadsburyville, O 20..........Pa.
753*Saegerstown (Saegertown), F 3....................Pa.
121*Saegersville, L 21..............Pa.
.... Saegersville Quarries, L 21 Pa.
753 Saegertown (Saegerstown), F 3..................................Pa.
21*Safe, K 15..........................Mo.
263 Safe Harbor, P 18..............Pa.
694*Safety Harbor, I 12........Fla.
250*Saffaras, Q 10....................Ind.
24*Saffell, C 18.....................Ark.
300*Safford, J 11......................Ala.
2266 Safford, M 22..................Ariz.
210*Saffordville, J 19.............Kan.
790 Sagamore, L 24..........Mass.
1600 Sagamore, L 7...................Pa.
7*Sagamore Beach, L 24 Mass.
604*Sagamore Hills, E 17..Ohio
.... Saganing, L 20.............Mich.
300*Sagaponack, H 9.......N. Y.
48*Sage, C 15........................Ark.
107*Sage, O 20....................Calif.
50 Sage, O 2..........................Wyo.
17 Sageeyah, D 20.................Okla.
250 Sagerton, D 13.....................Tex.
....*Sagetown, see Gladstone.Ill.
2517 Sag Harbor, F 12....N. Y.

Pop. Place Index State
350 Saginaw, G 13...........Ala.
82794 Saginaw, N 20........Mich.
16 Saginaw, H 19.........Minn.
50*Saginaw, P 6...............Mo.
150 Saginaw, K 6...........Ore.
300 Saginaw, E 18...........Tex.
31 Sagle, C 5...............Idaho
.... Sago, F 21...................Ore.
52*Sago, P 7.......................Va.
74 Sago, H 13...............W. Va.
250 Sagola, F 4.................Mich.
316*Sagon, K 17......................Pa.
....*Sagon (Strong), K 17...Pa.
1219 Saguache, M 11...........Colo.
....*Sahara, J 14...............Mont.
200 Sahuarita, O 17..............Ariz.
15*Saidora, H 10..................Ill.
305 Sailor Springs, M 19....Ill.
600 Saint Agatha, B 17.......Me.
138 Saint Albans, K 11.......Me.
25*Saint Albans (Becker), J 17.........................Mo.
....*Saint Albans, H 6....N. Y.
8037 Saint Albans, C 7...........Vt.
3558 Saint Albans, K 5...W. Va.
241 Saint Albans Bay, C 7..Vt.
155*Saint Amant, M 15.......La.
....*Saint Amelia, see Hymel, La.
1000 Saint Andrew, N 9.......Fla.
25*Saint Andrews, Q 12.Tenn.
80*Saint Andrews, H 17..Wash.
19 Saint Ann, N 10...........Neb.
150 Saint Anna, O 16..........Wis.
1131 Saint Anne, E 21...............Ill.
934 Saint Ansgar, B 15......Iowa
2719 Saint Anthony, M 21..Idaho
150*Saint Anthony, P 9.....Ind.
211 Saint Anthony, I 14...Iowa
130 Saint Anthony, O 11..N. D.
110*Saint Aubert, I 15.........Mo.
80 Saint Augusta, L 12..Minn.
12090 Saint Augustine, D 18.Fla.
182 Saint Augustine, F 9...Ill.
100*Saint Benedict, D 10..Iowa
45*Saint Benedict, L 19.....La.
150*Saint Benedict, F 7.....Ore.
900 Saint Benedict, L 8........Pa.
85*Saint Bernard, D 13....Ala.
520 Saint Bernard, N 19.......La.
25 Saint Bernard, I 19.....Neb.
7387*Saint Bernard, O 6.....Ohio
600 Saint Bernice, J 5..........Ind.
300*Saint Bethlehem, L 9.Tenn.
72*Saint Bonaventure, Q 5 N. Y.
363 Saint Bonifacius, N 14 Minn.
310*Saint Bonifacius, M 8...Pa.
150*Saint Brides, Q 22..........Va.
200*Saint Catharine, G 15..Ky.
100*Saint Catharine (Saint Catherine), D 11....Mo.
200 Saint Catherine, G 15..Fla.
412 Saint Charles, K 17....Ark.
65*Saint Charles, G 4.........Ga.
429 Saint Charles, R 22..Idaho
5870 Saint Charles, C 18..........Ill.
331 Saint Charles, M 11...Iowa
536 Saint Charles, I 9..........Ky.
1300 Saint Charles, N 19..Mich.
1507 Saint Charles, Q 21..Minn.
10803 Saint Charles, H 19...Mo.
200*Saint Charles, I 6.........Pa.
63*Saint Charles, G 17...S. C.
100 Saint Charles, O 17...S. D.
482 Saint Charles, D 3.........Va.
155*Saint Clair (Lowndesboro), K 14...............................Ala.
160 Saint Clair, H 19..............Ga.
3471 Saint Clair, O 25.......Mich.
286 Saint Clair, Q 13.......Minn.
....*Saint Clair, N 17, M 24 Minn.
1410 Saint Clair, J 18..............Mo.
6809*Saint Clair, L 19...............Pa.
200 Saint Clair, L 22........Tenn.
25 Saint Clair, K 6..........Wash.
10405 St. Clair Shores, P 24.Mich.
160*Saint Clair Springs, E 16 Ala.
2797 Saint Clairsville, J 19..Ohio
114*Saint Clairsville, O 9....Pa.
56*Saint Clara, E 10...W. Va.
18*Saint Clere, F 20.......Kan.
2042 Saint Cloud, H 18.........Fla.
24173 Saint Cloud, L 12...Minn.
353 Saint Cloud, O 17..........Wis.
50*Saint Columbans, K 24 Neb.
50*Saint Croix, Q 11...........Ind.
1007 Saint Croix Falls, A 10.Wis.
150 Saint Croix Jc., J 23...Me.
350 Saint David, O 20.........Ariz.
859 Saint David, G 10..............Ill.
1400 Saint David, A 17..........Me.
1000*Saint Davids, P 23.........Pa.
32*Saint Davids Church, G 12..................................Va.
70*Saint Donatus, H 24..Iowa
893 Saint Edward, J 18.....Neb.
....*Sainte Charles Station, see Hahnville..............La.
2787 Sainte Genevieve, L 21.Mo.
175*Saint Elizabeth, K 13..Mo.
650*Saint Elmo, Q 4............Ala.
8 Saint Elmo, K 10..........Colo.
2290 Saint Elmo, L 16...............Ill.
293 Sainte Marie, L 20............Ill.
1369*Saint Ferdinand (Florissant), H 20.....................Mo.
350 Saint Florian, A 8..........Ala.
266 Saint Francis, A 21.......Ark.
1041 Saint Francis, D 2........Kan.
152*Saint Francis (Chicago), H 15....................................Ky.
1400 Saint Francis, B 14........Me.
150 Saint Francis, M 16..Minn.
273 Saint Francis, O 11...S. D.
500 Saint Francis, P 20........Wis.
1145 Saint Francisville, M 22. Ill.
821 Saint Francisville, J 13..La.
144*Saint Francisville, B 15.Mo.
500 Saint Francois, L 19.....Mo.
768 Saint Gabriel, M 15.........La.
468 Saint George, Q 19..........Ga.
203 Saint George, G 19.....Kan.
140 Saint George, O 12..........Me.
20*Saint George, O 12.........Mo.
.... Saint George, I 5.......N. Y.
1908 Saint George (Saint Georges), L 15..........S. C.
2434 Saint George, Q 2..........Utah
200*Saint George, F 16..W. Va.
50*Saint George Island, O 14 Md.
339 Saint Georges, C 21.......Del.
96*Saint Hedwig, L 16.........Tex.
125*Saint Helen, K 17........Mich.
1758 Saint Helena, G 5.......Calif.
92 Saint Helena, E 20.........Neb.
.... Saint Helena, P 16........S. C.
154*Saint Helens, G 20............Ky.
4304 Saint Helens, B 7.............Ore.
556 Saint Henry, I 5................Ohio
288 Saint Hilaire, E 4.........Minn.
50*Saint Huberts, F 23..N. Y.
100*Saint Huberts (Hubertus), O 19.......................................Wis.

Pop. Place Index State
2669 Saint Ignace, G 16...Mich.
768 Saint Ignatius, G 4..Mont.
160 Saint Inigoes, P 16....Md.
439 Saint Jacob, M 12.......Ill.
30 Saint Jacques, G 9...Mich.
317 Saint James, D 14......Ark.
102*Saint James, L 15.........Ill.
600 Saint James, N 16.........La.
85*Saint James (Lydia), B 4 Md.
300*Saint James, I 15.....Mich.
3400 Saint James, Q 10....Minn.
1812 Saint James, L 16.........Mo.
2000*Saint James, H 8.......N. Y.
90*Saint James City, L 16.Fla.
100*Saint James School, B 5 Md.
1010 Saint Jo, C 18..................Tex.
213 Saint Joe, C 11...............Ark.
150 Saint Joe, E 55..............Idaho
437 Saint Joe, C 22....................Ind.
10 Saint Joe, F 17...............N. D.
300 Saint John, Q 19........Idaho
314 Saint John (Saint Johns), O 14..................................Ill.
383 Saint John, C 6....................Ind.
1735 Saint John, K 11..............Kan.
28*Saint John, G 13...................Ky.
.... Saint John, B 14...................Me.
517 Saint John, D 15..............N. D.
125 Saint John, G 9..................Utah
526 Saint John, J 23...............Wash.
1300 Saint Johns, H 23.............Ariz.
314*Saint Johns (Saint John), O 14..................................Ill.
4422 Saint Johns, O 17............Mich.
220 Saint Johns, H 8...............Ohio
.... Saint Johns, C 7..................Ore.
75*Saint Johns, J 20....................Pa.
153*Saint Johnsburg, L 4..N. Y.
7437 Saint Johnsbury, E 18..Vt.
400 Saint Johnsbury Center (Centervale), E 18....Vt.
150 Saint Johnsbury East E 18..........................Vt.
20 Saint Johns Park, E 17.Fla.
2283 Saint Johnsville, M 20.N. Y.
.... Saint Joseph, H 14.........Fla.
810 Saint Joseph, H 20...............Ill.
60*Saint Joseph, G 10.............Ky.
1096 Saint Joseph, F 14...............La.
8963 Saint Joseph, Q 10.......Mich.
1055 Saint Joseph, L 12.....Minn.
75711 Saint Joseph, D 5...........Mo.
.... Saint Joseph, E 6..............Ore.
25*Saint Joseph, E 20................Pa.
200 Saint Joseph, Q 9...........Tenn.
....*Saint Josephs, C 2.......N. Y.
26*Saint Just (Reynolds), J 15 Va.
425 Saint Landry, J 10................La.
84*Saint Lawrence, M 8......Pa.
297 Saint Lawrence, I 17..S. D.
211*Saint Leo, H 14...............Fla.
125*Saint Leo, O 5...............Minn.
276 Saint Leon, L 22..................Ind.
92*Saint Leonard, M 14.......Md.
296 Saint Libory, N 12..............Ill.
142 Saint Libory, L 17..........Neb.
3039 Saint Louis, N 17.........Mich.
816048 Saint Louis, I 20........Mo.
326 Saint Louis, K 15.......Okla.
....*Saint Louis, see Zincville, Okla.
100 Saint Louis Crossing, L 16....................................Ind.
7737 Saint Louis Park, N 22 Minn.
298 Saint Louisville, J 14..Ohio
158*Saint Lucas, E 19.........Iowa
300*Saint Luce (Upper Frenchville), A 16.............Me.
40*Saint Lucie, J 22................Fla.
2234 Saint Maries, E 5.......Idaho
338 Saint Marks, C 5................Fla.
48*Saint Marks, H 5...............Ga.
.... Saint Marks Jc., B 5......Fla.
183*Saint Martin, L 11.....Minn.
130*Saint Martin, P 9...........Ohio
400 Saint Martins (Saint Martins Junction), O 21. Wis.
3501 Saint Martinville, M 12. Ky.
152*Saint Mary, H 15..................La.
100 Saint Mary (Smartville), N 23...............................Neb.
285 Saint Mary-of-the-Woods (St. Marys), K 5....Ind.
733 Saint Marys, P 22..............Ga.
84*Saint Marys, M 12.......Iowa
1132 Saint Marys (Saint Mary), F 20....................................Kan.
605 Saint Marys, L 21...........Mo.
5532 Saint Marys, H 7...........Ohio
7653 Saint Marys, H 9..................Pa.
2201 Saint Marys, E 8......W. Va.
65*Saint Marys City, O 14.Md.
750*Saint Marys College, I 6, B 21.................................Calif.
.... Saint Marys Jc., H 9...Pa.
8000 Saint Matthews, E 14...Ky.
2187 Saint Matthews, I 14..S. C.
83*Saint Maurice, F 8.............La.
900 Saint Meinrad, Q 10.......Ind.
389 Saint Michael, M 14.Minn.
48 Saint Michael, L 16.....Neb.
200*Saint Michael, H 16..N. D.
521*Saint Michael, N 8..........Pa.
400 Saint Michaels, E 24...Ariz.
1309 Saint Michaels, J 17.....Md.
243*Saint Michael Station (Albertville), M 14.Minn.
485 Saint Nazianz, O 16.......Wis.
191 Saint Olaf, E 21.............Iowa
90 Saint Omer, K 18................Ind.
150 Saint Onge, H 2..........S. D.
1308 Saint Paris, J 8..............Ohio
33*Saint Patrick, B 15...........Mo.
211 Saint Paul, D 7...................Ark.
695 Saint Paul, K 17...................Ind.
869 Saint Paul, M 23.............Kan.
27*Saint Paul, D 21.....................Ky.
287736 Saint Paul, N 17, N 24 Minn.
100*Saint Paul, I 18.................Mo.
1571 Saint Paul, K 17.............Neb.
183 Saint Paul, E 7..................Ore.
315 Saint Paul, I 16..............S. C.
108*Saint Paul, P 18................Tex.
746 Saint Paul, D 6......................Va.
1096*Saint Paul Park, N 17 Minn.
150*Saint Pauls, E 15.......Mont.
1923 Saint Pauls (Saint Paul), J 13................................N. C.
348 Saint Peter, L 16.....................Ill.
100 Saint Peter, F 7.....................Kan.
5870 Saint Peter, P 13..........Minn.
28 Saint Peter, G 9.............Mont.
305 Saint Peters, H 19.................Mo.
88 Saint Peters, O 21.......................Pa.
60812 Saint Petersburg, I 12.Fla.
510 Saint Petersburg, I 5...Pa.
30 Saint Phillips, H 25...Mont.
300 Saint Regis, G 2............Mont.
1080 Saint Regis Falls, D 20 N. Y.
300*Saint Remy, C 4, R 21 N. Y.
490 Saint Rose, N 18..................La.

Pop.	Place	Index	State
1000	Saint Simons Island	O 23	Ga.
50	*Saint Stephen (Saint Stephens)	E 11	Ohio
1185	Saint Stephen (Saint Stephens)	K 18	S. C.
72	*Saint Stephens	N 4	Ala.
247	Saint Stephens (Brockway)	L 12	Minn.
50	*Saint Stephens (Saint Stephen)	E 11	Ohio
....	*Saint Stephens	I 10	Wyo.
90	*Saint Stephens Church	L 19	Va.
150	Saint Tammany	L 19	La.
200	*Saint Thomas	J 13	Mo.
503	Saint Thomas	E 22	N. D.
410	Saint Thomas	P 12	Pa.
25	*Saint Vincent	G 7	Ky.
327	Saint Vincent	B 1	Minn.
....	Saint Vincent Jc.	B 1	Minn.
35	Saint Vrain	I 24	N. M.
10	Saint Vrains	E 15	Colo.
62	Saint Xavier	M 18	Mont.
700	*Salada Beach (Sharp Park)	I 5, F 17	Calif.
145	*Salado	E 15	Ark.
4	*Salado	G 4	Ore.
350	Salado	I 18	Tex.
9011	Salamanca	Q 5	N. Y.
191	Salamonia	G 22	Ind.
75	*Saldee (Copland)	H 21	Ky.
....	Salduro	E 2	Utah
329	Sale City	N 8	Ga.
600	Sale Creek	P 15	Tenn.
300	Salem	J 22	Ala.
574	Salem	A 14	Ark.
21	Salem	G 16	Colo.
300	Salem	J 19	Conn.
400	Salem	N 20	Idaho
7319	Salem	M 16	Ill.
3194	Salem	O 14	Ind.
457	Salem	O 20	Iowa
455	Salem	I 6	Ky.
80	*Salem	K 6	Me.
35	*Salem	L 19	Md.
41213	Salem	D 21	Mass.
180	*Salem	Q 20	Mich.
3151	Salem	M 16	Mo.
245	*Salem (Coffey)	C 8	Mo.
380	Salem	O 25	Neb.
1000	Salem	Q 17	N. H.
775	*Salem (Salem Depot)	Q 17	N. H.
8618	Salem	N 5	N. J.
91	Salem	M 8	N. M.
1034	Salem	L 25	N. Y.
12301	Salem	F 20	Ohio
30908	Salem	F 6	Ore.
115	*Salem	B 3	S. C.
1185	Salem	L 22	S. D.
21	*Salem	N 19	Tex.
659	Salem	H 12	Utah
5737	Salem	N 6	Va.
2571	Salem	E 11	W. Va.
350	Salem	O 22	Wis.
371	Salemburg	I 14	N. C.
75	Salem Center	B 20	Ind.
300	*Salem Center	F 6	N. Y.
75	*Salem Chapel (Dennis)	D 8	N. C.
775	Salem Depot (Salem)	Q 17	N. H.
328	*Salerno	K 23	Fla.
213	Salesville	K 18	Ohio
113	*Salesville	E 16	Tex.
83	*Salford (Rudy)	N 22	Pa.
150	*Salfordville	N 22	Pa.
600	*Salida	I 9	Calif.
4969	Salida	K 11	Colo.
21073	Salina	H 15	Kan.
....	*Salina	M 14	N. Y.
687	Salina	E 22	Okla.
500	Salina	M 5	Pa.
1616	Salina	K 11	Utah
11586	Salinas	J 7	Calif.
381	Saline	D 8	La.
1227	Saline	Q 20	Mich.
84	*Saline	A 9	Mo.
130	Saline City	L 8	Ind.
330	Salineno	O 2	Tex.
2018	Salineville	H 20	Ohio
1000	Salisbury	B 4	Conn.
13313	Salisbury	N 22	Md.
2000	Salisbury	A 21	Mass.
1759	Salisbury	F 11	Mo.
83	Salisbury	N 12	N. H.
92	*Salisbury	L 19	N. Y.
19037	Salisbury	F 7	N. C.
919	*Salisbury	Q 7	Pa.
400	Salisbury	I 6	Vt.
331	Salisbury Center	L 20	N. Y.
400	*Salisbury Mills	E 4	N. Y.
425	Salitpa	M 5	Ala.
392	Salix	H 1	Iowa
250	Salix	N 8	Pa.
200	*Salkum	M 8	Wash.
237	Salladasburg	H 15	Pa.
443	Salley	J 12	S. C.
287	Sallis	H 14	Miss.
2140	Sallisaw	I 24	Okla.
105	*Sallyards	L 20	Kan.
2439	Salmon	J 13	Idaho
48	*Salmon (Salmons)	K 12	Ky.
60	*Salmon	G 22	Tex.
500	Salmon Falls	N 20	N. H.
48	*Salmons (Salmon)	K 12	Ky.
75	*Salol	B 7	Minn.
50	*Saloma	I 15	Ky.
100	Salome	J 6	Ariz.
287	Salona	J 14	Pa.
116	*Salsbury Cove	M 17	Me.
....	Salsman	E 20	Okla.
19	Saltair	C 4	Ore.
42	*Saltair	F 11	Utah
22	*Saltaire	H 8	N. Y.
....	*Salt Creek, see Pueblo		Colo.
75	*Salt Creek	H 15	Wyo.
30	*Saltdale	M 13	Calif.
....	*Salter Path	J 21	N. C.
100	*Salters Depot (Salters)	J 19	S. C.
200	Saltese	G 1	Mont.
51	Saltfork, (Salt Fork)	C 12	Okla.
10	*Salt Gap	H 14	Tex.
35	*Salt Gum	J 19	Ky.
125	*Saltillo	O 14	Ind.
468	Saltillo	C 20	Miss.
150	Saltillo (Buckeye Cottage)	L 15	Ohio
433	Saltillo	M 12	Pa.
500	Saltillo	P 6	Tenn.
300	*Saltillo	D 22	Tex.
25	Salt Lake	I 2	N. M.
149934	Salt Lake City	E 11	Utah
498	Salt Lick	F 20	Ky.
347	Salt Mine (Avery Island)	N 11	La.
30	*Saltpetre (Saltpeter)	M 1	W. Va.
136	Salt Point	C 6	N. Y.
125	*Salt Rock	K 3	W. Va.
1097	Saltsburg	M 6	Pa.
....	Salt Springs	B 4	Okla.
100	*Salt Springville	N 19	N. Y.
29	Salt Sulphur Springs	P 11	W. Va.
2650	Saltville	D 9	Va.
539	Saluda	Q 8	N. C.
1516	Saluda	G 9	S. C.
200	Saluda	M 20	Va.
127	*Salunga	O 18	Pa.
84	*Salus	E 8	Ark.
64	*Saluvia	P 11	Pa.
....	Salva	G 7	Mich.
75	*Salvia	L 19	Va.
500	Salvisa	G 16	Ky.
100	*Salvisa (Bondville)	G 16	Ky.
....	*Salvo	F 24	N. C.
58	Salyer	C 2	Calif.
1254	Salyersville	G 22	Ky.
....	*Sam (Talbot)	N 22	Idaho
....	Sam	F 18	Wash.
75	*Samantha	G 8	Ala.
134	Samaria	R 19	Idaho
61	*Samaria	D 22	Ky.
200	*Samaria	R 21	Mich.
35	*Samaria	H 11	S. C.
136	*Sam Fordyce (La Joya)	P 4	Tex.
250	Sammonsville	M 21	N. Y.
150	*Sammylane	Q 9	Mo.
....	*Samnorwood	E 6	Tex.
600	Samoa	C 1	Calif.
25	Samos	P 24	Mo.
175	*Samos	L 20	Va.
300	*Samoset	J 14	Fla.
60	*Sample	G 12	Ky.
46	*Sample	M 18	Tex.
....	Sample Run	L 7	Pa.
500	*Sampsel	D 9	Mo.
22	Sampsel	R 3	Okla.
100	Sampson (Sampson City)	D 14	Fla.
....	*Sampson	J 21	Ky.
100	*Sampson City (Sampson)	D 14	Fla.
70	*Sampsons Wharf	K 21	Va.
25	*Sams	M 4	Colo.
2182	Samson	O 17	Ala.
50	*Samsonville	C 4, R 22	N. Y.
291	▲*Samsula	F 19	Fla.
50	Sams Valley	P 6	Ore.
....	Samuels	B 5	Idaho
150	*Samuels	G 14	Ky.
....	*Samville, see Bayshore		Fla.
123	San Acacia	I 9	N. M.
150	San Acacio	P 13	Colo.
1513	▲San Andreas	H 9	Calif.
25802	San Angelo	H 12	Tex.
5790	San Anselmo	B 14	Calif.
267	San Antonio (Lake Jovita)	H 14	Fla.
400	San Antonio	J 10	N. M.
253854	San Antonio	L 16	Tex.
50	*San Ardo	K 7	Calif.
500	*Sanatoga	N 22	Pa.
10	*Sanator	L 3	S. D.
....	*Sanatorium, see Spivak		Colo.
200	Sanatorium (State Sanatorium)	B 8	Md.
200	*Sanatorium	M 13	Miss.
57	*Sanatorium	I 12	N. C.
1475	Sanatorium	G 12	Tex.
1516	San Augustine	G 24	Tex.
80	*San Benito	K 9	Calif.
9501	San Benito	P 5	Tex.
43646	San Bernardino	O 18, Q 9	Calif.
120	*San Blas	N 9	Fla.
1344	Sanborn	C 4	Iowa
580	Sanborn	P 8	Minn.
....	Sanborn	O 7	Neb.
400	Sanborn	L 4	N. Y.
366	Sanborn	M 20	N. D.
100	Sanborn	G 6	Wis.
50	Sanbornton	M 13	N. H.
850	Sanbornville	L 19	N. H.
6519	San Bruno	I 5, E 16	Calif.
....	*San Buenaventura, see Ventura		Calif.
100	San Carlos (Rice)	K 18	Ariz.
3520	San Carlos	F 18	Calif.
....	Sanchez	Q 14	Tex.
479	San Clemente	O 17	Calif.
39	*Sanco	G 12	Tex.
201	*San Cristobal	C 15	N. M.
....	*Sand Beach, see Harbor Beach		Mich.
100	Sandberg	N 14	Calif.
16	*Sandbluff	P 20	Okla.
602	Sandborn	N 7	Ind.
175	*Sand Brook	G 11	N. J.
12	*Sandclift	K 16	Ky.
500	Sandcoulee	G 10	Mont.
25	Sand Creek	J 8	Ind.
100	*Sandcreek	R 19	Mich.
15	Sand Creek	F 22	Mont.
45	Sand Creek	B 10	Okla.
160	*Sand Creek	D 11	Wis.
621	*Sand Cut (Gouldsboro)	H 22	Pa.
150	San de Fuca	E 6	Wash.
20	Sandel	H 6	La.
56	*Sanders (Cheto)	G 24	Ariz.
35	Sanders	E 4	Idaho
278	Sanders	D 16	Ky.
50	Sanders	K 19	Mont.
100	*Sanderson	B 14	Fla.
2500	Sanderson	K 8	Tex.
80	*Sanderson	L 6	W. Va.
3566	Sandersville	I 15	Ga.
562	Sandersville	M 18	Miss.
....	*Sandford, see Paragould		Ark.
350	Sandford (Sanford)	K 5	Ind.
352	Sand Fork (Layopolis)	H 10	W. Va.
42	*Sandgap	H 19	Ky.
25	Sandgate	O 6	Vt.
....	*Sand Hill, see Redford		Mich.
500	Sand Hill	J 13	Miss.
125	*Sandhills	H 22	Mass.
....	Sandia	P 23	Calif.
....	Sandia	H 10	N. M.
250	Sandia	P 17	Tex.
80	*Sandia Park	G 11	N. M.
100	*Sandidges	M 10	Va.
203341	San Diego	Q 18	Calif.
2674	San Diego	P 17	Tex.
3500	*San Dimas	N 16, Q 5	Calif.
421	▲Sandisfield	H 3	Mass.
365	Sand Lake	N 13	Mich.
175	Sandlake	N 24	N. Y.
100	Sandlake	D 4	Ore.
60	*Sandlick	J 22	Ky.
....	Sandon	D 14	Ore.
1769	Sandoval	M 15	Ill.
817	▲*Sandoval	F 10	N. M.
100	Sandow	J 19	Tex.
220	Sandown	Q 17	N. H.
130	*Sand Patch	P 7	Pa.
4356	Sandpoint	C 5	Idaho
54	*Sand Prairie (Vincennes)	Q 20	Iowa
15	*Sand Ridge	H 8	W. Va.
45	*Sand Run (Sandrun)	H 13	W. Va.
12	Sand Run Jc.	F 17	W. Va.
130	Sands	F 7	Mich.
7	*Sands (Soham)	F 15	N. M.
....	Sands	E 10	Utah
628	*Sands Point	H 7	N. Y.
63	*Sand Springs	G 21	Iowa
58	*Sand Springs	I 18	Ky.
25	Sand Springs	H 18	Mont.
6137	Sand Springs	E 18	Okla.
750	*Sandston	M 17	Va.
1559	Sandstone	J 17	Minn.
300	Sandstone	O 9	W. Va.
40	Sandstown	K 15	Mich.
85	*Sandtown	D 15	Ark.
1512	Sandusky	N 24	Mich.
200	*Sandusky	P 5	N. Y.
24874	Sandusky	D 13	Ohio
2608	Sandwich	C 17	Ill.
900	Sandwich	L 24	Mass.
17	Sandwich	K 15	N. H.
473	Sandy	D 9	Ore.
11	*Sandy	J 16	Tex.
1487	Sandy	F 11	Utah
50	Sandy Creek	O 3	Me.
646	Sandy Creek	J 15	N. Y.
....	*Sandy Hill, see Hudson Falls		N. Y.
1743	Sandy Hook	K 6	Conn.
184	Sandy Hook (Martinsburg)	F 21	Ky.
200	*Sandy Hook	O 13	Miss.
67	*Sandyhook (Sandy Hook)	I 12	Mo.
50	*Sandy Hook	L 15	Va.
718	Sandy Lake	H 3	Pa.
18	*Sandy Level	P 9	Va.
225	Sandypoint	M 14	Me.
168	*Sandy Point	M 22	Tex.
....	*Sandy Point, see Westmoreland		Va.
300	Sandy Ridge	L 15	Ala.
100	Sandy Ridge	B 8	N. C.
410	*Sandy Ridge	K 12	Pa.
50	*Sandy River	Q 8	Va.
325	Sandy Run	J 20	Pa.
....	Sandy Run Jc.	O 10	Pa.
80	Sandy Spring	G 11	Md.
55	*Sandy Springs	D 5	S. C.
265	Sandyville	H 18	Ohio
150	Sandyville	H 6	W. Va.
550	San Elizario	G 1	Tex.
647	*San Felipe (Hagan Junction)	F 11	N. M.
305	San Felipe	K 21	Tex.
30	San Fernando	P 15	Ariz.
9094	San Fernando	N 15, P 3	Calif.
200	San Fidel	G 6	N. M.
200	Sanford	N 15	Ala.
736	Sanford	P 12	Colo.
....	*Sanford, see Topstone		Conn.
10217	Sanford	G 18	Fla.
45	*Sanford	K 10	Kan.
9500	Sanford	Q 3	Me.
150	Sanford	M 18	Mich.
200	Sanford	N 16	Miss.
4960	Sanford	G 12	N. C.
100	*Sanford	P 17	Tenn.
750	*Sanford	B 4	Tex.
80	*Sanford	K 24	Va.
3000	*Sanford & Springvale (Springvale)	Q 3	Me.
....	*Sanford Corners, see Calcium		N. Y.
634536	San Francisco	I 5, D 16	Calif.
11867	San Gabriel	Q 5	Calif.
110	*San Gabriel	I 19	Tex.
4017	Sanger	J 12	Calif.
75	Sanger	L 11	N. D.
1000	Sanger	C 18	Tex.
100	*Sanger	N 8	W. Va.
250	*Sangerfield	M 17	N. Y.
39	*San Geronimo	B 14, H 4	Calif.
825	Sangerville	J 11	Me.
75	San Gregorio	I 5	Calif.
165	*Sang Run	N 2	Md.
....	*San Haven	D 15	N. D.
100	*Sanibel	M 16	Fla.
75	*San Ignacio	H 17	N. M.
....	*Sanilac Center, see Sandusky		Mich.
500	*San Ildefons (Ildefonso)	F 13	N. M.
455	Sanish	H 6	N. D.
175	Sanitaria Springs	Q 16	N. Y.
....	Sanitarium Jc.	H 13	Ga.
1356	San Jacinto	O 19, R 11	Calif.
163	*San Joaquin	K 10	Calif.
200	San Jon	G 24	N. M.
68457	San Jose	I 6, G 23	Calif.
520	San Jose	H 12	Ill.
400	San Jose	F 15	N. M.
....	*San Jose, see Cobre		N. M.
....	*San Jose, see Terrell Wells		Tex.
678	San Juan (San Juan Bautista)	J 7	Calif.
2264	San Juan	P 4	Tex.
678	*San Juan Bautista (San Juan)	J 7	Calif.
1200	San Juan Capistrano	P 17	Calif.
7	*Sank	O 21	Mo.
942	*Sankertown	M 8	Pa.
14601	San Leandro	D 20	Calif.
63	*San Leon	L 23	Tex.
1000	San Lorenzo (Lorenzo)	D 20	Calif.
476	▲San Lorenzo	M 6	N. M.
75	San Lucas	K 8	Calif.
38	*San Luis	K 5	Ariz.
1000	San Luis	Q 13	Colo.
8881	San Luis Obispo	M 9	Calif.
75	*San Luis Rey	P 19	Calif.
400	San Marcial	K 9	N. M.
105	San Marcos	P 18	Calif.
6006	San Marcos	K 17	Tex.
8175	*San Marino	N 15, Q 4	Calif.
800	San Martin	J 7	Calif.
19403	San Mateo	E 18	Calif.
250	San Mateo	F 6	N. M.
....	San Mateo Jc.	D 17	Fla.
300	San Miguel	L 9	Calif.
300	San Miguel	O 10	N. M.
62	*Sano	J 16	Ky.
36	*Sanoma	G 7	W. Va.
250	*San Onofre	P 19	Calif.
489	San Pablo	B 17	Calif.
476	San Pablo	Q 13	Colo.
250	*San Patricio	K 16	N. M.
263	San Patricio	P 18	Tex.
....	San Pedro, R 4 (Pop. incl. in Los Angeles)		Calif.
....	*San Pedro, see Lopeno		Tex.
137	*San Perlita	O 5	Tex.
350	San Pierre	D 9	Ind.
328	San Quentin	B 15	Calif.
8573	San Rafael	H 5, B 15	Calif.
300	San Rafael	G 5	N. M.
200	*San Ramon	B 21, H 6	Calif.
2927	San Saba	H 15	Tex.
11	Sansarc	I 10	S. D.
200	*San Simeon	M 10	Calif.
700	San Simon	N 24	Ariz.
....	*Sansom, see North Uvalde		Tex.
5	*Sans Souci	O 25	Mich.
90	Santa	E 5	Idaho
31921	Santa Ana	O 16, R 6	Calif.
....	*Santa Anita	N 15, Q4	Calif.
1661	Santa Anna	G 14	Tex.
34958	Santa Barbara	N 12	Calif.
6650	Santa Clara	I 6, G 23	Calif.
250	Santa Clara	D 21	N. Y.
283	Santa Clara	Q 2	Utah
54	*Santa Claus	Q 9	Ind.
16896	Santa Cruz	J 6	Calif.
600	Santa Cruz	E 14	N. M.
....	Santa Cruz, see Rios		Tex.
86	*Santa Elena	O 3	Tex.
20	*Santa Fe	D 13	Fla.
116	*Santa Fe	F 15	Mo.
20325	Santa Fe	F 13	N. M.
215	Santa Fe	H 8	Ohio
40	Santa Fe	O 11	Okla.
250	*Santa Fe	O 10	Tenn.
2020	*Santa Fe Springs	N 15, Q 4	Calif.
700	Santa Margarita	M 9	Calif.
8522	Santa Maria	M 10	Calif.
250	*Santa Maria (Belandville)	M 3	Fla.
250	*Santa Maria	P 5	Tex.
53500	Santa Monica	O 15, Q 3	Calif.
....	Santa Monica	P 5	Tex.
....	Santander	Q 5	Tex.
8986	Santa Paula	N 13	Calif.
1297	Santaquin	H 12	Utah
1500	Santa Rita	M 5	N. M.
150	*Santa Rita Park	J 9	Calif.
....	Santa Rosa	N 14	Ariz.
12605	Santa Rosa	G 4	Calif.
250	Santa Rosa	N 7	Fla.
141	*Santa Rosa	D 6	Mo.
2310	Santa Rosa	H 19	N. M.
224	*Santa Rosa	Q 5	Tex.
124	*Santa Susana	N 13	Calif.
450	*Santa Ynez	N 11	Calif.
....	Santa Ysabel	Q 19	Calif.
400	*Santee	Q 19	Calif.
150	Santee	E 18	Neb.
55	*Santee (Parler)	J 14	S. C.
35	*Santeetlah (Millsaps)	P 3	N. C.
55	*Santiago	L 14	Minn.
524	Santo	E 16	Tex.
128	San Toy	M 15	Ohio
200	*Santuck (Santuc)	C 10	S. C.
165	Santuit	M 24	Mass.
200	San Ygnacio	N 1	Tex.
1368	San Ysidro	Q 19	Calif.
26	San Ysidro	F 10	N. M.
194	▲Sapello	E 16	N. M.
20	*Sapeloe	N 24	Ga.
70	Sapinero	K 7	Colo.
50	*Saponac	J 15	Me.
50	*Sapphire	Q 7	N. C.
130	*Sappho	F 3	Wash.
240	*Sappington	I 20	Mo.
....	Sappington	L 9	Mont.
12249	Sapulpa	F 18	Okla.
5	Sara	Q 7	Wash.
216	Saragosa	I 6	Tex.
300	*Saragossa	E 10	Ala.
28	*Sarah	B 9	Ga.
25	*Sarah	F 22	Ky.
150	*Sarah	B 11	Miss.
120	Sarah	N 21	Va.
150	Sarah Ann	O 4	W. Va.
140	*Sarah Furnace (Catfish)	I 6	Pa.
193	Sarahsville	L 17	Ohio
213	Saraland	P 5	Ala.
849	Saranac	O 15	Mich.
350	Saranac	D 23	N. Y.
500	*Saranac Inn (Upper Saranac)	F 1	N. Y.
7138	Saranac Lake	F 22	N. Y.
11141	Sarasota	J 13	Fla.
300	*Saratoga	C 16	Ala.
266	Saratoga	N 6	Ark.
2000	Saratoga	J 6	Calif.
349	Saratoga	H 22	Ind.
60	*Saratoga	B 17	Iowa
80	Saratoga	M 14	Miss.
292	*Saratoga	F 16	N. C.
1525	Saratoga	J 24	Tex.
810	Saratoga	P 15	Wyo.
13705	Saratoga Springs	L 23	N. Y.
100	Sarben	K 9	Neb.
1057	Sarcoxie	P 7	Mo.
135	Sardinia	M 17	Ind.
150	Sardinia	O 6	N. Y.
615	Sardinia	P 9	Ohio
49	*Sardinia	I 17	S. C.
667	Sardis	I 21	Ga.
208	*Sardis	D 19	Ky.
2022	Sardis	B 13	Miss.
40	Sardis	L 19	Ohio
46	Sardis	M 21	Okla.
419	Sardis	P 6	Tenn.
550	Sarepta	A 6	La.
150	*Sarepta	D 17	Miss.
138	*Sargeant	R 19	Minn.
200	Sargent	G 4	Ga.
847	Sargent	I 14	Neb.
15	*Sargent	N 22	Tex.
110	Sargents (Sargent)	L 10	Colo.
150	Sargentville	N 15	Me.
200	Sarita	N 4	Tex.
302	Sarles	D 17	N. D.
10	Saron	I 22	Tex.
150	Sarona	D 9	Wis.
124	Saronville	M 18	Neb.
....	*Sarpy	M 18	Mont.
532	Sartell	L 12	Minn.
27	*Sarton	P 11	W. Va.
....	Sartoria	L 14	Neb.
350	Sarver	L 4	Pa.
62	Sasabe	P 15	Ariz.
532	Sasakwa	L 16	Okla.
....	Sasco	M 15	Ariz.
225	Saspamco	M 17	Tex.
125	*Sassafras	I 22	Ky.
21	*Sassafras	M 20	Va.
168	*Sassamansville	N 22	Pa.
365	Sasser	M 7	Ga.
15	*Sasser	I 19	Ky.
345	Satanta	N 4	Kan.
152	*Satartia	I 9	Miss.
1200	Saticoy	N 13	Calif.
125	*Satin	H 19	Tex.
10	*Satolah	B 12	Ga.
300	Satsop	K 4	Wash.
114	*Satsuma	P 4	Ala.
125	Satsuma (Satsuma Heights)	D 16	Fla.
29	*Satsuma	L 16	La.
....	*Satsuma Heights, See Satsuma		Fla.
165	*Sattler	L 17	Tex.
30	*Sattley	F 10	Calif.
....	*Satuma, See Thornburg		Ark.
25	Satus	N 15	Wash.
300	Saucier	Q 18	Miss.
1500	*Saugatuck (Westport)	Q 5	Conn.
628	Saugatuck	P 11	Mich.
3916	Saugerties	Q 23	N. Y.
151	Saugus	N 15, P 2	Calif.
14825	■Saugus	E 20, K 5	Mass.
....	Saugus	I 22	Mont.
10	*Sauk	D 10	Wash.
3016	Sauk Center	L 9	Minn.
1325	Sauk City	J 19	Wis.
2981	Sauk Rapids	L 12	Minn.
431	Saukville	P 19	Wis.
175	*Saul	I 21	Ky.
....	*Saulsberry	E 22	Ky.
202	*Saulsbury	Q 4	Tenn.
100	*Saulston	G 16	N. C.
41	*Saulsville	P 7	W. Va.
15847	Sault Sainte Marie	E 18	Mich.
20	*Saum	E 11	Minn.
6	Saunders	N 25	N. D.
250	Saunderstown	K 14	R. I.
500	Saundersville	G 15	Mass.
341	Saunemin	F 18	Ill.
700	Sauquoit	M 18	N. Y.
3540	Sausalito	I 5, C 15	Calif.
75	*Sautee	C 10	Ga.
76	*Savage	K 16	Ky.
222	Savage	N 16	Minn.
40	*Savage	B 12	Miss.
400	Savage	F 24	Mont.
1100	Savage (Savage Factory)	G 12	Md.
32	Savageton	F 19	Wyo.
199	*Savan (Rochester Mills)	L 7	Pa.
4792	Savanna	B 10	Ill.
525	Savanna	L 19	Okla.
95996	Savannah	L 25	Ga.
2108	Savannah	C 5	Mo.
601	Savannah	M 12	N. Y.
358	Savannah	F 14	Ohio
1504	Savannah	P 6	Tenn.
644	*Savannah Beach (Tybee)	L 25	Ga
60	*Savedge	O 19	Va.
200	*Saverton	E 16	Mo.
29	Savery	R 13	Wyo.
653	Savona	P 10	N. Y.
125	Savona	K 6	Ohio
198	Savonburg	L 23	Kan.
50	*Savoy	C 5	Ark.
150	Savoy	I 19	Ill.
75	*Savoy	K 18	Ky.
190	Savoy	D 4	Mass.
....	*Savoy, see Irondale		Mo.
175	Savoy	D 16	Mont.
5	Savoy	I 1	S. D.
298	*Savoy	C 20	Tex.
30	*Savoyard	J 14	Ky.
121	Saw Pit	M 5	Colo.
....	*Sawtelle, see West Los Angeles		Calif.
239	Sawyer	N 12	Kan.
43	*Sawyer	K 18	Ky.
300	Sawyer	R 9	Mich.
180	*Sawyer	I 19	Minn.
....	Sawyer	M 19	Neb.
206	Sawyer	H 10	S. D.
175	Sawyer	Q 21	Okla.
100	Sawyers Bar	C 3	Calif.
82	*Sawyerville	I 8	Ala.
401	Sawyerville	L 11	Ill.
700	*Sawyerwood	E 17	Ohio
85	*Saxapahaw	E 11	N. C.
25	*Saxe	P 12	Va.
75	*Saxeville	K 16	Wis.
650	Saxis	K 24	Va.
110	*Saxman	J 14	Kan.
150	Saxman	L 11	W. Va.
225	*Saxon	O 7	W. Va.
900	Saxon	H 5	Wis.
524	*Saxonburg	K 4	Pa.
....	Saxonville	F 17	Mass.
....	Saxony	F 18	Ill.
150	Saxton	K 19	Ky.
1152	Saxton	O 10	Pa.
740	Saxtons River	O 13	Vt.
2332	▲Saybrook	M 18	Conn.
779	Saybrook	G 17	Ill.
150	Saybrook	B 19	Ohio
85	*Saybrook	E 7	Pa.
175	Saybrook Point	N 18	Conn.
35	*Sayle	M 22	Mont.
....	Sayler Park	O 5	Ohio
1416	Saylesville	C 16	R. I.
28	*Saylor	I 21	Ky.
50	Saylor	I 23	Okla.
250	*Saylorsburg	J 23	Pa.
140	*Sayner	K 7	Wis.
500	Sayre (Sayre Mines)	E 12	Ala.
75	*Sayre	L 15	Ohio
3037	Sayre	J 2	Okla.
7569	Sayre	D 18	Pa.
500	*Sayre Mines (Sayre)	E 12	Ala.
1000	*Sayreton	F 12	Ala.
8186	Sayreville	G 17	N. J.
4500	Sayville	H 9	N. Y.
50	Scales	E 19	Okla.
354	Scales Mound	A 9	Ill.
63	*Scalf	J 19	Ky.
1950	Scalp Level	N 8	Pa.
32	*Scaly	R 5	N. C.
737	Scammon	N 25	Kan.
614	Scandia	D 15	Kan.
100	Scandia (Copas)	M 18	Minn.
295	Scandinavia	L 14	Wis.
11	*Scanlon	C 8	Fla.
460	*Scanlon	I 18	Minn.
200	Scantic (East Windsor)	C 15	Conn.
336	Scappoose	C 7	Ore.
80	*Scarboro	I 20	Ga.
400	Scarboro (Scarboro Beach)	Q 5	Me.
500	*Scarborough	F 6	N. Y.
400	Scarboro Beach (Scarboro)	Q 5	Me.
950	Scarbro	N 8	W. Va.
125	*Scarlets Mill (White Bear)	N 21	Pa.
12966	Scarsdale	G 6	N. Y.
136	*Scarville	B 12	Iowa
310	*Scenery Hill	O 3	Pa.
349	Scenic	L 6	S. D.
50	Scenic	H 11	Wash.
50	*Schaal	N 6	Ark.
84	Schaberg	E 5	Ark.
900	*Schaefferstown	N 18	Pa.
75	Schafer	I 4	N. D.
250	Schaffer	G 7	Mich.
603	Schaghticoke	M 24	N. Y.
758	Schaller	G 5	Iowa
10	Schamber	L 11	S. D.
75	*Schamberville (Collinsville)	J 20	Miss.
75	*Schatz (Blossburg)	J 7	Mont.
1	Schaupps	K 15	Neb.
....	Schefield	N 5	N. D.
454	Schell City	L 7	Mo.
53	*Scheller	N 15	Ill.
328	Schellsburg	O 9	Pa.
84	Schellville (Shellville)	H 5, A 16	Calif.
87549	Schenectady	N 23	N. Y.
472	Schenevus	O 19	N. Y.
300	*Schenley	L 5	Pa.
998	Shererville	C 6	Ind.
13	*Scherr	F 18	W. Va.
315	*Schertz	L 17	Tex.
804	*Schiller Park	B 21	Ill.
100	*Schilling	D 6	Calif.
250	Schlater	F 10	Miss.
20	Schlegel	F 15	Okla.
....	*Schleisingerville, see Slinger		Wis.
628	Schleswig	H 5	Iowa
48	Schley	G 12	Minn.
20	*Schley	M 18	Ohio
270	*Schley	N 21	Va.
5	Schmidt	O 11	N. D.
400	Schnecksville	L 21	Pa.
283	Schneider	D 6	Ind.
125	Schnellville	P 10	Ind.
200	Schodak Landing	O 24	N. Y.
259	Schoenchen	H 10	Kan.
225	*Schoeneck	O 19	Pa.
1536	Schofield	J 12	Wis.
941	Schoharie	O 21	N. Y.
30	Schoharie Jc.	N 21	N. Y.
150	Scholle	I 11	N. M.
50	* Scholls	D 7	Ore.
....	Schoodic Stream Jc.	H 15	Me.
823	Schoolcraft	Q 13	Mich.
159	*Schooleys Mountain	D 14	N. J.
....	Schoolfield	R 9	Va.
8	Schoper	K 11	Ill.
12	Schrag	K 19	Wash.
836	Schram City	K 13	Ill.
158	Schriever	O 16	La.
54	*Schroeder	B 21	Minn.
36	*Schroeder	N 18	Tex.
650	Schroon Lake	H 23	N. Y.
1970	Schulenburg	L 19	Tex.
42	*Schuline	O 12	Ill.
500	Schulter	I 18	Okla.
54	*Schumm	G 5	Ohio
75	Schurz	I 6	Nev.
2808	Schuyler	J 21	Neb.
650	Schuyler	L 12	Va.
250	Schuyler Falls	D 24	N. Y.
20	Schuyler Jc.	L 23	N. Y.
1176	Schuyler Jc.	L 18	N. Y.
275	Schuyler Lake	N 19	N. Y.
1447	Schuylerville	L 24	N. Y.
6518	Schuylkill Haven	L 19	Pa.
483	*Schwenkville (Schwenksville)	N 22	Pa.
250	*Schwertner	J 18	Tex.
439	Science Hill	I 17	Ky.
480	Scio	Q 8	N. Y.
1181	Scio	I 19	Ohio
351	Scio	G 7	Ore.
156	Sciota	G 7	Ill.
200	*Sciota	C 24	N. Y.
200	*Sciota	J 23	Pa.
325	*Scioto Furnace	Q 13	Ohio
65	*Scioto Mills	A 12	Ill.
....	Sciotoville	Q 12	Ohio
150	Scipio	M 17	Ind.
76	*Scipio	K 19	Okla.
595	Scipio	J 10	Utah
100	*Scipio Center	M 13	N. Y.
48	Scipioville	N 13	N. Y.
147	Scircleville	H 13	Ind.
....	Scitico	B 16	Conn.
1000	Scituate	H 22	Mass.
235	*Scituate (Scituate Center)	G 22	Mass.
850	Scituate	F 10	R. I.
235	Scituate Center (Scituate)	G 22	Mass.
89	*Scobey	D 14	Miss.
1311	Scobey	C 22	Mont.
110	*Scofield	R 21	Mich.
259	Scofield	I 15	Utah
606	Scooba	I 22	Miss.
30	*Scopus	N 21	Mo.
63	Scotch Grove	I 22	Iowa
3500	Scotch Plains	F 16	N. J.
2200	Scotia	D 1	Calif.
30	*Scotia	L 17	Mo.
453	Scotia	J 16	Neb.
7960	Scotia	M 23	N. Y.
238	Scotia	N 12	S. C.
264	Scotia	F 24	Wash.
14	Scotia Jc.	J 16	Neb.
234	Scotland	F 11	Ark.
100	Scotland	G 21	Conn.
238	Scotland	L 15	Ga.
175	*Scotland (Scottland)	I 22	Ill.
110	Scotland	N 9	Ind.
1100	Scotland (Scotlandville)	L 14	La.
400	Scotland	J 20	Mass.
28	*Scotland	Q 16	Md.
400	Scotland	P 13	Pa.
1204	Scotland	N 21	S. D.
125	Scotland	C 16	Tex.
27	Scotland	O 19	Va.
....	*Scotland Beach	P 15	Md.
2559	Scotland Neck	D 18	N. C.
1100	*Scotlandville (Scotland)	L 14	La.
150	*Scotrun	I 23	Pa.
225	*Scott	J 13	Ark.
256	Scott	J 16	Ga.
407	Scott	M 11	La.
300	*Scott	E 7	Miss.
100	Scott	N 14	N. Y.
359	Scott	F 6	Ohio
24	Scott	J 9	Okla.
....	*Scott	I 10	W. Va.
15	*Scott (Scott Depot)	J 4	W. Va.
....	*Scott, see Batavia		Wis.
....	*Scott Bar	B 5	Calif.
1848	Scott City	I 5	Kan.
250	Scottdale	F 7	Ga.
6493	Scottdale	O 5	Pa.
15	*Scott Depot (Scott)	J 4	W. Va.
600	*Scott Haven	N 5	Pa.
650	*Scott Haven (Frank)	M 3	Pa.
50	Scott Lake	G 3	Mich.
175	Scottland (Scotland)	I 22	Ill.
64	*Scottown	R 14	Ohio
400	Scotts	Q 14	Mich.
18	*Scotts	E 5	N. C.
12057	Scottsbluff	H 2	Neb.
2834	Scottsboro	B 18	Ala.
2189	Scottsburg	O 16	Ind.
150	Scottsburg	O 9	N. Y.
100	Scottsburg	K 4	Ore.
239	Scottsburg	Q 11	Va.
1000	Scottsdale	K 13	Ariz.
320	Scotts Ferry	B 1	Fla.
49	*Scotts Hill	L 17	N. C.
235	*Scotts Hill	O 7	Tenn.
227	Scotts Mills	F 7	Ore.
41	Scottsmoor	G 20	Fla.
200	Scotts Sta. (Scott Sta.)	J 9	Ala.
207	*Scottsville	F 9	Ark.
187	*Scottsville	F 13	Kan.
1797	Scottsville	K 13	Ky.
925	*Scottsville	L 9	N. Y.
500	*Scottsville	E 24	Tex.
368	Scottsville	L 12	Va.

Pop.	Place Index	State
277	Scottville, J 10	Ill.
1162	Scottville, L 11	Mich.
32	*Scottville, B 3	N. C.
30	*Scoville, H 20	Ky.
60	*Scrabble, H 14	Va.
40	*Scranage, Q 7	Ala.
322	Scranton, F 7	Ark.
1014	Scranton, I 8	Iowa
500	Scranton, H 21	Kan.
127	*Scranton, F 20	Ky.
215	Scranton, G 22	N. C.
277	Scranton, Q 4	N. D.
140404	Scranton, H 21	Pa.
438	Scranton, H 19	S. C.
250	*Scranton, F 15	Tex.
31	Scraper, F 24	Okla.
664	Screven, N 20	Ga.
904	Scribner, I 22	Neb.
35	*Scroggins, D 22	Tex.
....	*Scrubgrass, see Kennerdell	Pa.
23	*Scruggs, P 7	Va.
14	*Scuddy, I 21	Ky.
66	Scullin, N 15	Okla.
275	Scullville, P 14	N. J.
300	*Scurry, E 20	Tex.
250	Scyrene, M 8	Ala.
150	Seabeck, H 6	Wash.
30	*Seaboard, N 4	Ala.
562	Seaboard, C 18	N. C.
50	Seaboard, C 8	Va.
125	*Seabold, H 7	Wash.
....	Seabreeze, E 19	Fla.
1000	Sea Breeze, L 9	N. Y.
779	Sea Bright (Seabright), H 21	N. J.
255	*Seabrook, I 12	Md.
1000	Seabrook, Q 20	N. H.
50	*Seabrook, P 14	S. C.
600	*Seabrook, K 22	Tex.
4416	*Sea Cliff, H 7	N. Y.
437	Seadrift, O 20	Tex.
40	*Seafield, F 9	Ind.
2804	Seaford, L 21	Del.
3100	Seaford, I 7	N. Y.
650	Seaford, O 21	Va.
148	*Seaforth, O 8	Minn.
30	*Seager, C 3, R 21	N. Y.
599	Sea Girt, J 20	N. J.
760	Seagoville, E 19	Tex.
3225	Seagraves, D 8	Tex.
316	*Seagrove, F 9	N. C.
300	*Seahurst, I 9	Wash.
91	*Sea Island Beach, N 22	Ga.
773	Sea Isle City, Q 13	N. J.
....	Sea Isle Jc., Q 13	N. J.
....	*Sealand, see Nahcotta	Wash.
1553	*Seal Beach, O 17, R 6	Calif.
600	*Seal Cove, N 17	Me.
289	Seale, K 23	Ala.
466	Sealevel, J 22	N. C.
319	Seal Harbor, N 17	Me.
150	*Seal Rock, H 4	Ore.
168	*Sealston, I 18	Va.
2500	Sealy, K 21	Tex.
100	*Sealy Springs, O 21	Ala.
100	Seama, G 7	N. M.
726	Seaman, P 10	Ohio
750	*Seanor, P 7	Pa.
100	Searchlight, Q 21	Nev.
3670	Searcy, G 15	Ark.
133	*Searight, M 16	Ala.
....	*Searing, I 3	N. D.
500	Searles, G 10	Ala.
....	Searles, L 17	Calif.
116	*Searles, P 10	Minn.
75	*Sears, L 19	Fla.
67	*Sears, L 14	Mich.
195	Searsboro, L 16	Iowa
542	▲Searsmont, M 12	Me.
1492	Searsport, M 14	Me.
2500	*Seaside, K 7	Calif.
2902	Seaside, A 4	Ore.
549	*Seaside Heights, K 17,	N. J.
653	Seaside Park, K 20	N. J.
271	Seaton, E 7	Ill.
18	*Seaton, L 15	Mo.
415	Seatonville, D 14	Ill.
1553	Seat Pleasant, J 12	Md.
368302	Seattle, H 8	Wash.
100	*Seattle Heights, F 10	Wash.
....	Seaver, H 16	Minn.
54	*Seavey, I 15	Minn.
112	*Seaview, N 23	Va.
400	Seaview, N 2	Wash.
100	Seaville, Q 14	N. J.
25	Sebago, O 3	Me.
265	Sebago Lake, P 4	Me.
125	*Sebasco Estates, O 8	Me.
425	Sebastian, I 22	Fla.
....	Sebastian, see Gabbard	Ky.
424	Sebastian, P 4	Tex.
1856	Sebastopol, H 4	Calif.
	Sebastopol, see Richmond,	Ind.
403	Sebastopol, J 16	Miss.
150	Sebec, I 12	Me.
100	*Sebec Lake, I 11	Me.
50	*Sebec Sta. (South Sebec), J 13	Me.
648	Sebeka, I 9	Minn.
1598	Sebewaing, M 21	Mich.
80	▲*Seboeis (Seboois), I 15	Me.
1085	▲Seboyeta, G 7	N. M.
1109	Sebree, H 9	Ky.
	*Sebree, See Vineyard	Tex.
27	*Sebrell, Q 18	Va.
3155	Sebring, J 18	Fla.
3902	Sebring, F 19	Ohio
427	*Secane, P 23	Pa.
9754	Secaucaus, E 20	N. J.
106	*Sechlerville, F 14	Wis.
722	Seco, I 23	Ky.
75	*Secondcreek, P 12	W. Va.
....	*Second Mesa, F 20	Ariz.
335	Secor, F 14	Ill.
344	Secretary, L 19	Md.
1800	Section, B 18	Ala.
200	Security, B 6	Md.
75	Security, J 22	Tex.
202	Sedalia, H 15	Colo.
150	Sedalia, G 12	Ind.
191	Sedalia, K 5	Ky.
20428	Sedalia, I 10	Mo.
25	*Sedalia, D 10	N. C.
278	Sedalia (Midway), L 10	Ohio
75	*Sedalia, D 10	S. C.
40	Sedan, Q 15	Iowa
1948	Sedan, O 20	Kan.
126	*Sedan, L 8	Minn.
11	Sedan, N 18	Neb.
55	Sedan, D 25	N. M.
100	*Sedgewickville, N 21	Mo.
152	Sedgwick, C 18	Ark.
373	Sedgwick, A 22	Colo.
738	Sedgwick, L 16	Kan.
699	Sedgwick, N 15	Me.
159	*Sedley, Q 19	Va.
116	*Sedona, E 13	Ariz.
2954	Sedro Woolley, D 8	Wash.
300	*Sedwick, E 14	Tex.
200	Seebert, M 13	W. Va.
....	Seek, K 20	Pa.
2000	Seekonk, L 17	Mass.
150	Seeley, Q 22	Calif.
87	*Seeley Lake, H 5	Mont.
20	*Seely, B 22	Wyo.
807	Seelyville, K 7	Ind.
600	Seelyville, F 23	Pa.
400	Seffner, I 14	Fla.
35	*Segal, I 12	Ky.
216	Segno, J 24	Tex.
200	Sego (Neslen), K 22	Utah
41	*Segovia, J 14	Tex.
200	Segreganset, K 19	Mass.
11	*Seguin, F 6	Kan.
7006	Seguin, L 17	Tex.
600	Segundo, Q 15	Colo.
50	*Seiad Valley, B 4	Calif.
249	Seibert, H 21	Colo.
50	*Seigler Springs, F 4	Calif.
629	Seiling, E 6	Okla.
45	Seisholtzville, M 22	Pa.
18	*Seitz, G 21	Ky.
208	Seitzland, Q 17	Pa.
50	*Seivern (Sievern), J 10	S. C.
28	*Sejita, Q 16	Tex.
150	Sekiu, E 2	Wash.
1130	Selah, L 14	Wash.
141	*Selby, H 6, B 21	Calif.
599	Selby, D 14	S. D.
150	Selbysport, L 1	Md.
882	Selbyville, M 24	Del.
150	*Selbyville, H 13	W. Va.
401	Selden, E 6	Kan.
55	*Selden, G 19	Me.
350	*Selden, H 8	N. Y.
108	*Selden, M 20	Va.
329	Selfridge, Q 11	N. D.
40	*Self, B 9	Ark.
500	Seligman, F 9	Ariz.
450	Seligman, R 8	Mo.
2877	Selinsgrove, K 16	Pa.
....	Selinsgrove Jc., K 16	Pa.
50	*Selkirk, I 3	Kan.
50	*Selkirk, K 19	Mich.
250	Selkirk, O 23	N. Y.
38	*Sellars, F 21	Ky.
415	Selleck, I 9	Wash.
150	*Sellers, K 16	Ala.
....	Sellers, see Norco,	La.
681	Sellers, F 21	S. C.
1121	Sellersburg, P 17	Ind.
2115	Sellersville, M 23	Pa.
40	*Sellman (Barnesville), G 9	Md.
400	Sells (Indian Oasis), O 13	Ariz.
19834	Selma, J 12	Ala.
133	*Selma, O 15	Ark.
3667	Selma, K 12	Calif.
424	Selma, H 20	Ind.
150	Selma, O 18	Iowa
36	Selma (Trilby), K 23	Kan.
150	Selma, F 10	La.
100	*Selma, N 4	Miss.
....	Selma, K 20	Mo.
2007	Selma, G 15	N. C.
150	Selma, L 9	Ohio
37	Selma, Q 4	Ore.
500	*Selma, L 6	Va.
200	Selman, B 3	Okla.
750	*Selman City, F 23	Tex.
957	Selmer, Q 5	Tenn.
....	*Selton, C 6	Va.
397	*Seltzer, L 19	Pa.
199	Selvin, Q 8	Ind.
81	*Selway, M 22	Mont.
180	*Selwyn, O 3	W. Va.
147	Selz, I 14	N. D.
350	*Seman, J 17	Ala.
291	Seminary, N 15	Miss.
....	*Seminary Hill, E 18	Tex.
150	Seminole, R 9	Ala.
11547	Seminole, J 15	Okla.
500	Seminole, J 6	Pa.
1761	Seminole, E 8	Tex.
34	*Semiway, H 9	Ky.
150	*Semmes, P 4	Ala.
36	*Semora, C 11	N. C.
130	*Sena, F 16	N. M.
1261	Senath, J 23	Mo.
1757	Senatobia, B 12	Miss.
82	*Seneca, E 9	Calif.
1235	Seneca (Crotty), D 17	Ill.
2015	Seneca, D 20	Kan.
40	*Seneca, G 9	Md.
75	*Seneca, R 19	Mich.
1091	Seneca, Q 6	Mo.
255	Seneca, H 10	Neb.
26	Seneca, C 25	N. M.
275	Seneca, I 18	Ore.
456	Seneca, H 5	Pa.
2155	Seneca, C 4	S. C.
243	Seneca, F 15	S. D.
300	Seneca, F 19	Wis.
250	*Seneca Castle, M 11	N. Y.
6452	Seneca Falls, M 12	N. Y.
802	Senecaville, K 17	Ohio
....	Seneschal, G 4	N. D.
150	Seney, F 12	Mich.
200	*Senia, D 2	N. C.
200	*Sennett, M 13	N. Y.
679	Senoia, G 6	Ga.
113	*Senora, L 21	Va.
78	Sentinel, L 8	Ariz.
30	*Sentinel, M 10	Mo.
1088	Sentinel, K 5	Okla.
256	Sentinel Butte, M 2	N. D.
44	Separ, O 3	N. M.
950	*Sepulveda, N 15, Q 4	Calif.
	*Seqiu, see Sekiu	Wash.
300	*Sequatchie, Q 14	Tenn.
676	Sequim, F 5	Wash.
100	*Sequoia National Park (Giant Forest), K 14	Calif.
82	*Serafina, F 16	N. M.
18	*Se Ree, G 12	Ky.
104	Serena, D 16	Ill.
....	*Serene, C 16	Colo.
126	*Sergeant, F 9	Pa.
587	Sergeant Bluff, G 1	Iowa
132	Sergeantsville, G 11	N. J.
75	*Sergent, I 23	Ky.
80	Serles, Q 4	Tenn.
158	Servia, E 17	Ind.
52	*Servia, J 10	W. Va.
145	*Service, L 4	Ala.
6	Service Creek, G 15	Ore.
35	*Servilla, Q 17	Tenn.
25	Servilleta, C 13	N. M.
2117	Sesser, O 15	Ill.
150	*Sessums, F 20	Miss.
2000	*Setauket, G 8	N. Y.
600	*Seth, M 6	W. Va.
135	*Seton, N 15, M 21	Minn.
42	*Settle, K 12	Ky.
....	*Settlement, see Shirley	Ark.
55	*Seven Fountains, G 12	Va.
555	*Seven Hills, D 17	Ohio
....	*Seven Islands, see Clayton Lake	Me.
549	Seven Mile, M 6	Ohio
114	*Seven Mile Ford, D 9	Va.
10	*Seven Oaks, N 18	Calif.
100	Sevenpoints, K 17	Pa.
170	Sevensprings, H 17	N. C.
25	*Seven Stars, P 15	Pa.
122	*Seventeen (Lock Seventeen) I 17	Ohio
154	*Seventy Six, K 16	Ky.
75	*Seventysix (Seventy-Six), M 22	Mo.
398	*Seven Valleys (Smyser), Q 17	Pa.
138	Severance, C 15	Colo.
266	Severance, D 23	Kan.
....	*Severance, H 24	N. Y.
200	*Severn, G 14	Md.
323	Severn, B 19	N. C.
210	Severn, N 21	Va.
300	*Severna Park, H 14	Md.
570	Severy, M 20	Kan.
166	*Sevier, F 1	N. C.
200	Sevier, M 9	Utah
1161	Sevierville, N 20	Tenn.
515	Seville, E 17	Fla.
245	*Seville, L 11	Ga.
850	Seville, F 16	Ohio
150	Sewal, Q 13	Iowa
1600	Sewanee, Q 13	Tenn.
175	Seward, A 13	Ill.
125	*Seward, K 12	Kan.
2826	Seward, L 20	Neb.
142	Seward, N 20	N. Y.
168	Seward, G 12	Okla.
845	Seward, M 7	Pa.
260	*Sewaren, G 18	N. J.
....	*Sewell, G 21	Ky.
550	Sewell, L 8	N. J.
....	*Sewell, see Brooksville	Okla
150	Sewell, M 9	W. Va.
75	*Sewellton, J 16	Ky.
....	*Sewell Valley, see East Rainelle	W. Va.
5614	Sewickley, M 3	Pa.
98	*Sexton, D 10	Iowa
97	*Sextons Creek, I 20	Ky.
150	*Sextonville, H 19	Wis.
50	Seymour, H 12	Ala.
6100	Seymour, L 9	Conn.
200	Seymour, H 18	Ill.
8620	Seymour, M 16	Ind.
1539	Seymour, P 14	Iowa
....	Seymour, D 15	Minn.
751	Seymour, O 12	Mo.
147	*Seymour, N 20	Tenn.
3328	Seymour, C 14	Tex.
1365	Seymour, N 14	Wis.
517	Seymourville, M 14	La.
50	Seyppel, I 21	Ark.
593	Shabbona, C 16	Ill.
75	Shackleford (Shackelford), G 10	Mo.
91	*Shacklefords, L 19	Va.
16	*Shacklet, I 16	Va.
39	*Shade, G 19	Ky.
60	*Shade, N 15	Ohio
156	*Shade Gap, N 12	Pa.
30	Shadehill, C 7	S. D.
150	*Shade Valley, N 12	Pa.
32	*Shadow, M 21	Va.
40	*Shadwell, J 13	Va.
57	*Shady, R 22, C 4	N. Y.
50	*Shady Bend, G 13	Kan.
100	*Shady Cove, Q 6	Ore.
159	Shady Dale, G 11	Ga.
170	*Shady Grove, L 18	Ala.
300	*Shady Grove, C 8	Fla.
220	Shady Grove, I 7	Ky.
300	*Shadygrove, Q 13	Pa.
310	Shadypoint (Shady Point), K 24	Okla.
80	*Shady Side, H 15	Md.
4048	Shadyside, K 20	Ohio
367	*Shady Spring. O 8	W. Va.
950	*Shady Valley, L 25	Tenn.
106	*Shafer, L 17	Minn.
16	Shaffton, K 25	Iowa
1200	*Shaft, K 19	Pa.
1258	Shafter, L 13	Calif.
50	Shafter, D 22	Nev.
300	*Shafter, K 5	Tex.
10	Shafter Lake, E 8	Tex.
250	Shaftsburg, O 18	Mich.
117	Shaftsbury, P 6	Vt.
23393	Shaker Heights, P 24	Ohio
2418	Shakopee, N 15, N 21	Minn.
25	Shale, M 12	Calif.
11185	■*Shaler, L 3	Pa.
350	Shallmar, O 3	Md.
381	Shallotte, N 15	N. C.
80	*Shallow Water (Shallow), I 5	Kan.
150	*Shallowater, C 10	Tex.
269	Shambaugh, P 6	Iowa
5	*Shambo, D 13	Mont.
18810	Shamokin, K 18	Pa.
764	*Shamokin Dam, K 16	Pa.
900	*Shamrock, D 10	Fla.
32	*Shamrock, H 15	Mo.
461	Shamrock, G 16	Okla.
117	*Shamrock (Shamrock Station), M 21	Pa.
3123	Shamrock, D 6	Tex.
....	Shamrock Jc., P 4	Pa.
117	*Shamrock Station (Shamrock), M 21	Pa.
10	*Shan, F 20	Minn.
500	Shandaken, Q 21	N. Y.
112	*Shandon, M 10	Calif.
250	Shandon, N 5	Ohio
....	Shaner, N 23	Kan.
453	Shanesville, H 17	Ohio
125	*Shanesville, N 21	Pa.
29	*Shanghai, L 19	Va.
46	*Shanghai, D 24	W. Va.
55	Shaniko, F 13	Ore.
36	*Shanks, E 21	W. Va.
324	*Shanksville, O 8	Pa.
375	Shannock, M 9	R. I.
42	Shannon, G 13	Ala.
1500	*Shannon, D 2	Ga.
561	Shannon, B 12	Ill.
31	*Shannon, E 23	Kan.
615	Shannon, D 20	Miss.
90	Shannon, K 12	N. C.
168	*Shannon, C 17	Tex.
288	Shannon City, O 9	Iowa
35	Shapleigh, Q 2	Me.
6	*Sharer, I 11	Ky.
27	*Sharkey, E 20	Ky.
500	Sharon, D 3	Conn.
282	Sharon, G 16	Ga.
749	Sharon, O 13	Kan.
50	*Sharon, C 16	Md.
1500	Sharon, H 18	Mass.
50	*Sharon, I 13	Miss.
371	Sharon, J 21	N. D.
150	Sharon, L 17	Ohio
226	Sharon, E 4	Okla.
25622	Sharon, I 1	Pa.
388	Sharon, B 11	S. C.
586	Sharon, M 5	Tenn.
140	Sharon, J 13	Vt.
25	Sharon, H 24	Wash.
300	Sharon, L 6	W. Va.
812	Sharon, M 22	Wis.
300	Sharon Center, F 16	Ohio
80	*Sharongrove, J 10	Ky.
4467	*Sharon Hill, P 23	Pa.
760	Sharon Springs, H 2	Kan.
433	Sharon Springs, N 20	N. Y.
300	Sharon Valley, C 3	Conn.
1157	Sharonville, N 7	Ohio
200	*Sharpes, H 21	Fla.
15	Sharples, C 9	Ohio
450	Sharples, N 5	W. Va.
700	*Sharp Park (Salada Beach), I 5, F 17	Calif.
150	Sharps, K 20	Va.
114	*Sharpsburg (Sharpsboro), G 5	Ga.
78	*Sharpsburg, J 14	Ill.
173	*Sharpsburg, P 8	Iowa
472	Sharpsburg, E 19	Ky.
834	Sharpsburg, D 6	Md.
345	Sharpsburg, E 16	N. C.
40	*Sharpsburg, N 15	Ohio
8202	Sharpsburg, M 3	Pa.
50	*Sharps Chapel, M 19	Tenn.
518	Sharpsville, G 14	Ind.
5129	Sharpsville, H 1	Pa.
653	Sharptown, M 21	Md.
232	Sharptown, M 6	N. J.
280	*Shartlesville, M 19	Pa.
750	*Shasta Dam, D 6	Calif.
100	Shattuc, M 14	Ill.
1275	Shattuck, E 2	Okla.
100	Shattuckville, C 7	Mass.
190	Shauck (Johnsville), H 13	Ohio
3	*Shaver Lake, J 12	Calif.
219	Shavertown, Q 19	N. Y.
823	*Shavertown, H 20	Pa.
50	Shaw, G 20	Colo.
75	*Shaw, M 23	Kan.
100	*Shaw, H 13	La.
1669	Shaw, F 7	Miss.
65	Shaw, F 7	Ore.
154	Shaw, D 18	W. Va.
28	*Shawanee (Waltersville), G 19	Ky.
250	Shawanee, K 20	Tenn.
84	*Shawanese, H 20	Pa.
1400	Shawangunk, R 21	N. Y.
5565	Shawano, M 13	Wis.
300	Shawboro, C 23	N. C.
186	*Shawhan, E 18	Ky.
106	*Shaw Island, D 6	Wash.
...	Shaw Jc., J 1	Pa.
1500	Shawmut, I 23	Ala.
175	*Shawmut, L 7	Ark.
200	Shawmut, L 10	Me.
100	Shawmut, J 14	Mont.
50	Shawmut, H 8	Pa.
50	Shawnee, H 13	Colo.
597	Shawnee, G 25	Kan.
1475	Shawnee, M 15	Ohio
22053	Shawnee, J 14	Okla.
50	Shawnee, K 21	Wyo.
200	*Shawnee on Delaware, J 23	Pa.
1963	Shawneetown, P 20	Ill.
128	*Shawneetown, N 23	Mo.
30	Shawneetown, Q 23	Okla.
500	*Shawomet, H 9	R. I.
....	*Shawsheen, see Pinehurst	Mass.
900	*Shawsheen Village (Shawsheen), C 19	Mass.
200	*Shawsville, O 5	Va.
50	*Shawver, N 9	W. Va.
150	*Shawver Mill, C 10	Va.
80	*Shawville, J 10	Pa.
15	*Shay, M 18	Ohio
28	Shay, Q 15	Okla.
14	Shea, O 21	Neb.
47	*Shea (Beechfork), L 18	Tenn.
138	*Sheakleyville, H 2	Pa.
....	*Shearer Valley, J 16	Ky.
4	*Sheaville, M 22	Ore.
40638	Sheboygan, P 17	Wis.
3395	Sheboygan Falls, P 17	Wis.
180	Shedd, H 6	Ore.
85	*Sheds (Sheds Corners), M 16	N. Y.
4	*Sheephorn, G 9	Colo.
300	Sheepranch, H 10	Calif.
85	Sheepscott, O 10	Me.
....	*Sheepshead Bay, I 5	N. Y.
....	Sheerin, B 3	Tex.
125	*Sheets, C 4	N. C.
50	Sheff, F 6	Ind.
7933	Sheffield, B 8	Ala.
....	Sheffield, G 7	Calif.
948	Sheffield, D 12	Ill.
1060	Sheffield, E 14	Iowa
1000	Sheffield, H 2	Mass.
60	*Sheffield, J 22	Mont.
733	*Sheffield, E 15	Ohio
2600	Sheffield, F 7	Pa.
10	Sheffield, I 20	S. D.
100	*Sheffield, I 9	Tex.
175	Sheffield, D 17	Vt.
5	Sheffield Jc., G 7	Pa.
1099	*Sheffield Lake, E 15	Ohio
56	Shekomeko, R 24	N. Y.
500	*Shelbiana (Shelby), H 23	Ky.
2107	Shelbina, E 14	Mo.
1606	Shelburn, L 6	Ind.
120	Shelburn, G 7	Ore.
1300	Shelburne, C 7	Mass.
62	*Shelburne, G 18	N. H.
500	Shelburne, F 6	Vt.
3300	Shelburne Falls, C 6	Mass.
750	Shelby, H 14	Ala.
400	Shelby, D 7	Ind.
627	Shelby, L 5	Iowa
500	Shelby (Shelbiana), H 23	Ky.
1367	Shelby, M 10	Mich.
1956	Shelby, D 8	Miss.
2538	Shelby, D 9	Mont.
627	Shelby, K 20	Neb.
14037	Shelby, H 3	N. C.
6643	Shelby, G 13	Ohio
28	*Shelby, I 13	Va.
100	*Shelby Gap, H 24	Ky.
35	*Shelbyville, C 16	Ark.
4092	Shelbyville, K 16	Ill.
10791	Shelbyville, K 16	Ind.
4392	Shelbyville, E 15	Ky.
161	*Shelbyville, P 11	Mich.
756	Shelbyville, D 14	Mo.
6537	Shelbyville, P 12	Tenn.
250	Shelbyville, G 25	Tex.
206	*Sheldahl, J 12	Iowa
1036	Sheldon, F 22	Ill.
3768	Sheldon, C 3	Iowa
463	Sheldon, M 6	Mo.
281	Sheldon, O 22	N. D.
125	*Sheldon, Q 14	S. C.
150	*Sheldon, K 22	Tex.
400	Sheldon, B 9	Vt.
199	*Sheldon, F 10	Wis.
55	Sheldon Junction (Fairgrounds), B 9	Vt.
380	Sheldon Springs, B 8	Vt.
317	Sheldonville, I 17	Mass.
....	*Sheldrake, see Sheldrake Springs	N. Y.
225	*Sheldrake Springs, N 12	N. Y.
29	*Shelfar, K 15	Va.
75	Shell, C 12	Wyo.
200	*Shell Beach, M 10	Calif.
75	*Shell Creek, M 24	Tenn.
1751	Shelley, O 19	Idaho
55	*Shellhorn, L 18	Ala.
35	*Shell Knob, D 8	Mo.
872	Shell Lake, D 8	Wis.
1063	Shellman, M 5	Ga.
20	Shellmound, Q 14	Tenn.
925	Shell Rock (Shellrock), F 16	Iowa
552	Shellsburg, I 19	Iowa
51	*Shelltown, P 20	Md.
84	*Shellville (Schellville), H 5, A 16	Calif.
344	Shelly, F 2	Minn.
125	*Shelly, M 23	Pa.
135	*Shelocta, L 7	Pa.
1073	▲*Shelter Island, H 9	N. Y.
100	*Shelter Island Heights, H 9	N. Y.
10971	Shelton, M 8	Conn.
600	*Shelton (Horseshoe), E 10	Fla.
983	Shelton, M 16	Neb.
110	*Shelton, E 13	S. C.
3707	Shelton, J 5	Wash.
6846	Shenandoah, P 5	Iowa
19790	Shenandoah, K 19	Pa.
1829	Shenandoah, H 12	Va.
3000	*Shenandoah Heights, K 19	Pa.
100	*Shenandoah Caverns, G 12	Va.
....	*Shenandoah Alum Springs, see Bird Haven	Pa.
250	Shenandoah Jc., E 25	W. Va.
157	Shenango, H 2	Pa.
10	Shepard, K 20	N. D.
100	*Shepards (Shepp), O 3	Tenn.
350	*Shepardsville, K 6	Ind.
852	Shepherd, M 17	Mich.
100	Shepherd, L 16	Mont.
109	*Shepherd (Chickamauga), Q 15	Tenn.
700	Shepherd, J 23	Tex.
90	*Shepherdstown, O 14	Pa.
945	Shepherdstown, D 25	W. Va.
762	Shepherdsville, F 14	Ky.
25	*Shepola, J 17	Ky.
100	*Shepp (Shepards), O 3	Tenn.
....	Sheppard, G 15	Wis.
41	*Sheppards, M 13	Va.
1040	*Sheppton, K 19	Pa.
....	Sherack, E 2	Minn.
95	*Sherard, C 8	Miss.
800	Sherborn, G 17	Mass.
1030	Sherburn, R 10	Minn.
150	*Sherburne, E 20	Ky.
200	*Sherburne, K 13	La.
1192	Sherburne, N 17	N. Y.
150	Sherburne Center (Killington), K 10	Vt.
1338	Sheridan, L 12	Ark.
198	*Sheridan, G 8	Calif.
442	Sheridan, D 17	Ill.
1720	Sheridan, H 14	Ind.
100	*Sheridan, I 7	Ky.
450	Sheridan, D 16	Me.
542	Sheridan, N 15	Mich.
377	Sheridan, A 6	Mo.
597	Sheridan, M 8	Mont.
6	Sheridan, H 16	Neb.
220	Sheridan, O 3	N. Y.
25	Sheridan, R 13	Ohio
1294	Sheridan, E 5	Ore.
200	*Sheridan, N 18	Pa.
218	*Sheridan, L 20	Tex.
25	Sheridan, L 3	W. Va.
115	*Sheridan, L 14	Wis.
10529	Sheridan, B 15	Wyo.
100	Sheridan Lake, K 23	Colo.
....	*Sherlock, see Nisqually	Wash.
477	▲Sherman, I 3	Conn.
500	*Sherman, J 20	Fla.
250	Sherman, I 12	Ill.
65	*Sherman (Sherman City), O 25	Kan.
115	Sherman, C 17	Ky.
183	*Sherman, G 17	Me.
370	Sherman (Sherman Sta.), G 16	Me.
449	Sherman, C 19	Miss.
200	*Sherman (Jedburg), I 19	Mo.
125	Sherman, M 6	N. M.
675	Sherman, Q 1	N. Y.
20	Sherman, D 6	Okla.
158	Sherman, L 25	S. D.
17156	Sherman, C 19	Tex.
35	*Sherman, G 5	W. Va.
65	*Sherman City (Sherman), O 25	Kan.
....	Sherman Jc., C 19	Tex.
1150	Sherman Mills, G 17	Me.
....	*Sherman Oaks, N 15, Q 4	Calif.
135	Shermans Dale, N 15	Pa.
370	*Sherman Station (Sherman), G 16	Me.
50	Shermansville, F 2	Pa.
415	Sherrard, D 8	Ill.
365	Sherrard, A 10	W. Va.
258	Sherrill, K 14	Ark.
204	*Sherrill, N 14	Mo.
2184	*Sherrill, L 17	N. Y.
41	*Sherrills Ford, F 4	N. C.
216	Sherritts, Q 14	Ohio
333	Sherrodsville, H 18	Ohio
80	Sherry, I 14	Wis.
90	*Sherry (Blenker), I 14	Wis.
75	*Sherwin (Sherwin Jc.), O 24	Kan.
75	*Sherwin Jc. (Sherwin), O 24	Kan.
29	*Sherwood, G 8	Iowa
60	Sherwood, K 16	Md.
281	Sherwood, R 15	Mich.
50	Sherwood, F 18	Minn.
300	*Sherwood, C 2	N. C.
390	Sherwood, D 9	N. D.
554	Sherwood, E 6	Ohio
100	Sherwood, O 24	Okla.
447	Sherwood, D 7	Ore.
1275	Sherwood, Q 13	Tenn.
339	Sherwood, H 11	Tex.
235	Sherwood, N 15	Wis.
....	*Sherwood Forest, H 14	Md.
....	*Sherwood Station, see Riderwood	Md.
226	*Shevlin, F 8	Minn.
642	*Shevlin, J 11	Ore.
431	Sheyenne, I 17	N. D.
342	Shickley, N 19	Neb.
2354	Shickshinny, I 19	Pa.
175	Shideler, H 19	Ind.
718	Shidler, B 16	Okla.
100	*Shields, G 14	Tex.
100	*Shields, I 6	Kan.
127	Shields, Q 10	N. D.
300	*Shields, M 3	Pa.
35	*Shields, L 24	Va.
4932	*Shillington, N 20	Pa.
420	*Shiloh, K 7	Ala.
127	Shiloh, F 13	Ark.
75	*Shiloh, H 21	Fla.
150	Shiloh, I 5	Ga.
409	Shiloh, M 11	Ill.
387	Shiloh, O 7	N. J.
500	Shiloh, C 23	N. C.
519	Shiloh, F 13	Ohio
75	*Shiloh, I 18	Va.
66	*Shimerville, M 22	Pa.
....	*Shinewell, P 24	Okla.
74	Shindler (Shindlar), M 24	S. D.
1520	Shiner, L 19	Tex.
....	*Shinewell, P 24	Okla.
119	*Shingle (Shingle Springs), G 9	Calif.
1106	Shinglehouse, E 11	Pa.
100	*Shingler, M 9	Ga.
119	*Shingle Springs (Shingle), G 9	Calif.
200	*Shingleton, F 10	Mich.
320	Shingletown, D 6	Calif.
27	*Shinhopple, R 19	N. Y.
100	*Shinnecock Hills, G 9	N. Y.
2817	Shinnston, E 13	W. Va.
190	*Shin Pond, F 15	Me.
90	*Shinrock, D 13	Ohio
592	Shiocton, N 14	Wis.
396	*Ship Bottom (Ship Bottom-Beach Arlington), K 17	N. J.
372	Shipman, L 10	Ill.
19	*Shipman, P 22	Miss.
300	*Shipman, L 11	Va.
19	Shippee, O 12	Neb.
5244	Shippensburg, P 13	Pa.
517	Shippenville, H 5	Pa.
441	Shippingport, L 1	Pa.
125	Shiprock, C 3	N. M.
286	Shipshewana, B 18	Ind.
777	Shiremanstown, N 16	Pa.
....	Shirkie, K 5	Ind.
140	*Shirland, A 14	Ill.
365	Shirley, E 12	Ark.
129	*Shirley, G 15	Ill.
952	Shirley, I 18	Ind.
236	▲*Shirley (Shirley Mills), I 10	Me.
2000	Shirley, D 15	Mass.
60	*Shirley, L 18	Mo.
50	*Shirley, J 22	Mont.
30	*Shirley, L 16	Tenn.
5	*Shirley, N 18	Va.
188	*Shirley, D 10	W. Va.
35	*Shirley, O 15	Wyo.
150	Shirley Center, D 15	Mass.
493	*Shirley City (Woodburn), D 22	Ind.
197	▲Shirley Mills (Shirley), I 10	Me.
242	Shirleysburg, N 12	Pa.
300	Shiro, J 21	Tex.
56	*Shive, G 17	Tex.
216	Shively, D 1	Calif.
1273	Shively, F 13	Ky.
35	*Shively, O 4	W. Va.
96	*Shivers, L 13	Miss.
26	*Shoal, I 21	Ky.
1031	Shoals, O 10	Ind.
125	*Shoals (Shoal), C 6	N. C.
55	*Shoals, L 1	W. Va.
50	Shoals Jct., E 6	S. C.
250	Shobonier, L 15	Ill.
47	*Shock, H 9	W. Va.
60	*Shockeysville, E 13	Va.
35	Shoemaker, E 18	N. M.
1081	*Shoemakersville, M 20	Pa.
19	*Shoffner, F 17	Ark.
55	*Shohola, H 23	Pa.
63	*Shohola Falls, H 24	Pa.
300	*Shokan, R 22	N. Y.
....	*Shokokon, see Carman	Ill.
72	Sholes, G 20	Neb.
113	*Shongaloo, A 6	La.
10	Shonkin, F 12	Mont.
....	Shonn, see Loyall	Ky.
19	*Shook, O 20	Mo.
10	*Shooks, E 10	Minn.
50	*Shoopman (Fidelity), K 17	Ky.
500	*Shooting Creek, R 3	N. C.
200	*Shop Spring, M 12	Tenn.
50	*Shopville, I 17	Ky.
....	*Shore Acres, G 22	Mass.
225	*Shoreham, Q 10	Mich.
25	*Shoreham, G 9	N. Y.
25	*Shoreham (East Shoreham), J 5	Vt.
77	Shoreham, I 5	Vt.
340	Shoreham Center, J 5	Vt.
....	*Shoreline, see Shorewood,	Wis.
150	*Shores, L 13	Va.
15184	Shorewood, P 20	Wis.
1064	*Shorewood Hills, K 20	Wis.
320	Short, H 25	Okla.
850	*Short Beach, K 11	Conn.
90	*Short Creek, F 6	Ariz.
60	*Short Creek, H 12	Ky.
150	*Short Creek, I 19	Ohio
220	Short Creek, P 24	W. Va.
530	Shorter (Shorters), J 18	Ala.
250	*Shorterville, N 22	Ala.
250	Short Falls, O 16	N. H.
355	*Short Hills, E 18	N. J.
319	Shortleaf, J 7	Ala.
27	*Shorts (Whalen), G 10	Ky.
150	*Shorts Creek, Q 3	Va.
1316	Shortsville, M 10	N. Y.
....	*Shortt Gap, B 8	Va.
53	*Shoshone, K 17	Calif.
1366	Shoshone, P 11	Idaho
2	*Shoshone, G 21	Nev.
226	Shoshoni, I 11	Wyo.
500	*Shouns, L 25	Tenn.
....	*Shoup, K 13	Idaho
1600	*Shousetown (Glenwillard), M 3	Pa.
75	*Shovel Lake, H 15	Minn.
131	*Showell, P 23	Md.
45	*Showers Pass, C 2	Calif.
450	Show Low, I 21	Ariz.
10	Showman, D 6	Md.
150	*Shrader (Stoffel), K 7	W. Va.
....	*Shraders, see Bishop	Va.
1113	Shreve, G 15	Ohio
98167	Shreveport, C 5	La.
....	Shreveport Jct., P 7	Ark.
200	Shreves Run, O 11	Pa.
315	Shrewder, M 2	Okla.
75	*Shrewsbury, H 12	Ky.
6000	Shrewsbury, G 14	Mass.
2182	*Shrewsbury, I 20	Mo.
1058	Shrewsbury, H 20	N. J.
720	Shrewsbury, Q 17	Pa.
25	Shrewsbury, L 10	Vt.
110	*Shrewsbury, L 7	W. Va.
279	*Shrewsbury Station (Railroad), Q 7	Pa.
50	*Shriver, N 14	Mont.
600	*Shrub Oak, F 6	N. Y.
404	Shubert, N 25	Neb.
756	Shubuta, M 20	Miss.
60	*Shuff (Patrick Springs), Q 5	Va.
400	*Shulerville, L 19	S. C.
1197	Shullsburg, I 22	Wis.
90	*Shulls Mills, C 2	N. C.
35	Shults, Q 24	Okla.
52	*Shumans, J 18	Pa.
28	*Shumansville, K 17	Va.
95	*Shumway, I 20	Ariz.
180	Shumway, K 17	Ill.
300	*Shungopavy, F 19	Ariz.
65	Shunk, G 17	Pa.
743	Shuqualak (Shuqulak), H 21	Miss.
250	Shushan, L 25	N. Y.
191	▲Shutesbury, E 9	Mass.
85	*Siam (Attica Jct.), F 12	Ohio
60	*Sias, L 3	W. Va.
265	Siasconset, R 15	Mass.
10	Siberia, N 21	Calif.
37	*Siberia, Q 11	Ind.

Pop.	Place Index	State
250	*Sibert, I 20	Ky.
374	Sibley, G 18	Ill.
2356	Sibley, B 4	Iowa
405	Sibley, C 6	La.
....	Sibley, Q 22 (Pop. incl. in Trenton)	Mich.
50	*Sibley, N 4	Miss.
200	Sibley, G 7	Mo.
90	Sicily, J 13	Ill.
400	Sicily Island, F 12	La.
409	Sicklerville (Sicklertown), M 10	N. J.
5	Sickles, J 8	Okla.
64	*Side Lake, E 17	Minn.
....	Sidell, K 15	Fla.
653	Sidell, I 21	Ill.
42	*Sidell, I 19	Ky.
500	*Sides (Alverda), L 6	Pa.
22	*Sideway, F 21	Ky.
300	*Sidman (Lovett), N 8	Pa.
300	Sidnaw, E 2	Mich.
153	Sidney, C 15	Ark.
100	Sidney, D 9	Colo.
657	Sidney, I 20	Ill.
194	Sidney, D 16	Ind.
1290	Sidney, P 4	Iowa
113	*Sidney, H 24	Ky.
600	Sidney, M 9	Me.
100	Sidney, N 15	Mich.
2978	Sidney, F 25	Mont.
3388	Sidney, K 4	Neb.
3022	Sidney, P 17	N. Y.
9790	Sidney, I 7	Ohio
122	*Sidney, G 16	Tex.
50	*Sidney (Coleman), L 2	W. Va.
351	Sidney Center (Maywood), P 18	N. Y.
180	*Sidon, G 14	Ark.
418	Sidon, G 11	Miss.
40	*Sidonia, L 5	Tenn.
30	Sieben, I 8	Mont.
100	Siebert (North Branch), M 6	Md.
284	Siegersville, L 21	Pa.
280	*Sieper, I 9	La.
4	*Sierra, E 9	Calif.
821	Sierra Blanca, H 3	Tex.
250	Sierra City, F 9	Calif.
4581	*Sierra Madre, N 15, Q 4	Calif.
133	Sierraville, F 10	Calif.
50	*Sievern (Seivern), J 10	S. C.
50	Sifton, Q 7	Wash.
281	Sigel, K 17	Ill.
450	*Sigel, I 7	Pa.
40	*Signal, G 20	Ohio
65	*Signal, J 6	Ore.
....	*Signal Hill, see Mountain View	Ark.
3184	*Signal Hill, N 15, Q 4	Calif.
1308	Signal Mountain, Q 15	Tenn.
84	Signet, F 14	Okla.
100	*Signpine, M 20	Va.
2355	Sigourney, M 18	Iowa
364	Sigurd, L 11	Utah
400	*Sikes, E 9	La.
7944	Sikeston, P 23	Mo.
350	Silas, M 4	Ala.
32	*Silas Creek, B 3	N. C.
50	Silcott, M 24	Wash.
64	*Siler, K 19	Ky.
100	*Siler (Place), J 19	Ky.
9	*Siler, D 13	Va.
2197	Siler City, F 11	N. C.
291	*Silerton, P 4	Tenn.
100	Silesia, M 15	Mont.
350	Siletz, G 4	Ore.
240	Silex, G 18	Mo.
....	*Silica, see Benton	Ark.
....	Silica, H 14	Colo.
10	*Silica, J 13	Kan.
250	Silica, C 9	Ohio
162	*Silica, H 15	W. Va.
....	Silo, Q 16	Okla.
105	Siloam, L 15	Colo.
318	Siloam, G 14	Ga.
30	*Siloam, I 5	Ill.
29	*Siloam, D 22	Ky.
150	Siloam, C 7	N. C.
2764	Siloam Springs, B 3	Ark.
54	*Siloam Springs, Q 14	Mo.
2525	Silsbee, J 25	Tex.
359	Silt, G 6	Colo.
16	Siltcoos, J 3	Ore.
1200	Siluria, G 13	Ala.
50	*Silva, O 20	Mo.
113	Silva, G 14	N. D.
24	*Silva, K 24	Va.
200	Silvana, F 8	Wash.
56	*Silver, K 7	Ark.
111	Silver, I 17	S. C.
5	*Silver, G 12	Tex.
200	*Silverado, O 17, R 6	Calif.
200	*Silver Bay, J 23	N. Y.
....	*Silver Beach, M 23	Mass.
56	Silverbell, N 15	Ariz.
92	Silverbow, K 7	Mont.
110	Silver City, P 3	Idaho
346	Silver City, N 4	Iowa
390	Silver City, H 9	Miss.
67	Silver City, H 3	Nev.
5044	Silver City, M 4	N. M.
84	Silver City, J 2	S. D.
160	Silver City, H 10	Utah
309	Silver Cliff, M 13	Colo.
250	Silver Creek, D 2	Ga.
65	*Silver Creek, M 13	Minn.
278	Silver Creek, N 12	Miss.
421	Silver Creek, K 19	Neb.
3067	Silver Creek, O 3	N. Y.
2453	*Silver Creek (New Philadelphia), K 19	Pa.
114	Silver Creek, M 7	Wash.
75	*Silvercross, N 4	Ala.
200	Silverdale, O 18	Kan.
200	*Silverdale, K 19	N. C.
293	Silverdale, N 23	Pa.
500	Silverdale, H 6	Wash.
....	*Silver Gate, M 11	Mont.
700	*Silver Grove (Stevens), C 18	Ky.
270	*Silverhill, Q 7	Ala.
75	*Silverhill, F 21	Ky.
169	*Silver Hill, C 11	W. Va.
109	*Silver Lake (Baker), M 20	Calif.
471	Silver Lake, D 16	Ind.
362	Silver Lake, G 21	Kan.
145	Silver Lake, I 22	Mass.
604	Silver Lake, N 12	Minn.
68	*Silver Lake, M 21	Mo.
225	Silver Lake (Madison), J 18	N. H.
....	Silver Lake, E 19	N. J.
50	Silver Lake, N 7	N. Y.
642	*Silver Lake, E 17	Ohio
....	Silver Lake, L 11, see Beal	Ore.
97	Silver Lake, N 12	Ore.
200	*Silver Lake, E 21	Tex.
25	*Silverlake, F 11	Utah
200	Silverlake, N 6	Wash.
50	Silver Lake, G 8	Wash.
365	Silverlake (Silver Lake), O 22	Wis.
....	Silver Lake Jc., N 7	N. Y.
....	Silver Lane, F 14	Conn.
20	Silverleaf, Q 20	N. D.
1000	Silver Mine, P 3	Conn.
148	*Silvermine, N 20	Mo.
15	Silvernails, R 24	N. Y.
122	Silverpeak, L 10	Nev.
....	Silver Peak, K 10	Nev.
139	Silver Plume, G 12	Colo.
200	*Silver Point, M 14	Tenn.
18	*Silver Run (Donohue), F 9	W. Va.
56	Silvers Mills, J 12	Me.
7500	Silver Spring, I 11	Md.
218	*Silver Spring (Bruckarts), O 19	Pa.
....	*Silver Springs, see Monte Ne	Ark.
100	Silver Springs, E 14	Fla.
12	Silver Springs, A 20	Miss.
766	Silver Springs, O 7	N. Y.
30	Silverstar, L 8	Mont.
146	Silverstreet (Silver Street), F 10	S. C.
1127	Silverton, N 6	Colo.
220	Silverton, J 19	N. J.
2907	Silverton, O 6	Ohio
2925	Silverton, F 7	Ore.
684	Silverton, A 11	Tex.
24	*Silverton, F 11	Wash.
67	*Silverton, H 5	W. Va.
3930	Silvertown, I 7	Ga.
56	*Silver Valley, G 14	Tex.
200	Silverwood, N 22	Mich.
10	Silver Zone, C 23	Nev.
3	*Silvies, J 18	Ore.
2990	Silvis, D 9	Ill.
35	Simcoe, H 11	N. D.
50	Simeon, E 10	Neb.
....	*Simeon, see Charlottesville	Va.
200	Simi, N 17	Calif.
421	Simla, I 17	Colo.
1215	Simmesport, J 12	La.
125	*Simmons, O 14	Mo.
150	*Simmons, O 17	Tex.
800	Simmons (Freeman), R 7	W. Va.
28	*Simms, G 9	La.
459	Simms, G 9	Mont.
172	*Simms, C 24	Tex.
40	*Simmsville, G 14	Ala.
25	*Simnasho, E 12	Ore.
7	*Simoda, I 17	W. Va.
14	*Simon, J 7	Nev.
40	Simon, P 5	W. Va.
50	*Simons, C 20	Ohio
125	*Simonson, K 20	Va.
77	*Simonsville, N 11	Vt.
49	*Simonton, L 22	Tex.
6	*Simpkins, Q 3	Va.
25	Simplicity, O 13	Va.
150	Simpson, F 19	Colo.
172	Simpson, Q 17	Ill.
235	Simpson, F 14	Kan.
47	*Simpson (Hampton), H 21	Ky.
30	*Simpson, I 7	La.
110	Simpson, Q 20	Minn.
14	Simpson, C 12	Mont.
150	Simpson, I 4	Nev.
298	*Simpson (Chicod), G 19	N. C.
52	Simpson, P 15	Okla.
....	Simpson, G 5	Ore.
5000	Simpson, F 22	Pa.
700	*Simpson (Cyclone), E 9	Pa.
250	Simpson, E 14	W. Va.
....	Simpsons, O 7	Me.
80	*Simpsons, P 5	Va.
220	*Simpsonville, E 15	Ky.
65	*Simpsonville, F 12	Md.
1298	Simpsonville, C 7	S. C.
200	*Simpson Yard (Grand Crossing), B 16	Fla.
39	*Sims, K 7	Ark.
69	*Sims (Hazel Creek), D 6	Calif.
358	Sims, N 17	Ill.
170	Sims, G 16	Ind.
173	*Sims (Simms), F 16	N. C.
98	Sims, N 9	N. D.
40	Sims, G 14	S. C.
500	Simsboro, C 8	La.
3941	▲Simsbury, D 12	Conn.
200	*Sims Chapel, N 4	Ala.
43	*Sinai, F 16	Ky.
182	Sinai, J 23	S. D.
18	*Sinclair, J 10	Ill.
13	*Sinclair, D 16	Me.
585	Sinclairville, P 3	N. Y.
1800	*Singac, D 18	N. J.
250	*Singer, K 6	La.
120	*Singers (Singer Glen) Glen, H 11	Va.
14	*Singerly, K 20	Va.
200	Singleton, I 21	Tex.
223	*Sinking Spring, O 10	Ohio
1861	Sinking Spring, N 20	Pa.
138	*Sinks Grove, P 11	W. Va.
500	Sinnamahoning (Sinnemahoning), H 11	Pa.
75	*Sinnickson, K 24	Va.
25	*Sinsabaugh (Acorn), Q 18	Mo.
247	*Sinsinawa, G 21	Wis.
3770	Sinton, P 18	Tex.
21	*Sioux, N 9	N. C.
1680	Sioux Center, D 2	Iowa
82364	Sioux City, G 1	Iowa
40832	Sioux Falls, M 24	S. D.
....	Sioux Falls Jc., K 24	S. D.
10	Sioux Pass, E 24	Mont.
1056	Sioux Rapids, E 6	Iowa
20	Sioux Valley Jc., I 24	S. D.
83	*Sipes Mill, P 11	Pa.
350	Sipe Springs, F 15	Tex.
300	*Sipesville, O 7	Pa.
900	Sipsey, E 11	Ala.
375	Siren, B 8	Wis.
105	*Sir Johns Run, C 23	W. Va.
32	*Sirocco, F 12	Ky.
30	Siskiyou, R 7	Ore.
2513	Sisseton, C 23	S. D.
....	*Sisson, see Mount Shasta	Calif.
140	*Sissonville, L 6	W. Va.
309	*Sister Bay, Q 12	Wis.
124	*Sisterdale, K 16	Tex.
150	*Sister Lakes, Q 11	Mich.
500	Sisters, I 11	Ore.
2702	Sistersville, D 9	W. Va.
44	*Sites, F 5	Calif.
80	*Sitka, B 16	Ark.
100	Sitka, O 9	Kan.
19	*Sitka, G 22	Ky.
100	*Sitkum, M 3	Ore.
79	*Sivells Bend, C 18	Tex.
....	Siverly, H 5	Pa.
317	*Six, R 5	W. Va.
48	Sixes, O 2	Ore.
3386	▲*Six Mile, H 11	Ala.
150	Six Lakes, N 15	Mich.
152	*Six Mile, B 5	S. C.
273	*Six Mile Run (Coaldale), O 10	Pa.
55	Sixprong, P 15	Wash.
43	Sixteen, K 11	Mont.
175	*Sizerock, I 21	Ky.
12	Skaar, K 1	N. D.
25	*Skaggs, F 22	Ky.
28	*Skagg Springs, G 4	Calif.
....	Skagit Jc., D 8	Wash.
....	Skagit Landing, D 8	Wash.
75	Skamania, Q 9	Wash.
250	Skamokawa, N 4	Wash.
100	*Skandia, F 7	Mich.
1949	Skaneateles, M 13	N. Y.
300	*Skaneateles Falls, M 14	N. Y.
120	Skaneateles Jc. (Hart Lot), M 13	N. Y.
315	Skanee, D 4	Mich.
2	*Skarda, C 14	N. M.
235	Skedee, D 15	Okla.
100	*Skeetrock, C 6	Va.
13	*Skeggs, B 8	Va.
10	*Skelly, C 2	Calif.
800	Skellytown, C 4	Tex.
50	*Skelton (Forksville), Q 13	Va.
650	*Skelton, O 8	W. Va.
100	*Skene, E 7	Miss.
1496	Skiatook, D 18	Okla.
22	Skibo, F 21	Minn.
64	*Skiddy, I 18	Kan.
498	Skidmore, B 4	Mo.
660	Skidmore, O 18	Tex.
50	*Skillman, G 11	Ky.
23	*Skillman, H 13	N. J.
11	*Skime, B 6	Minn.
18	*Skinner, L 5	Me.
200	Skinners Eddy, F 19	Pa.
400	*Skippack, N 22	Pa.
75	*Skippers (Trego), R 16	Va.
100	*Skipperville, N 20	Ala.
91	*Skipwith, Q 13	Va.
100	Skogmo, J 13	N. D.
7172	Skokie (Niles Center), B 21	Ill.
6681	Skowhegan, L 9	Me.
12	*Skull Creek, C 5	Colo.
80	Skull Valley, H 10	Ariz.
12	*Sky, H 21	Ky.
28	*Skyberg, P 18	Minn.
....	*Skyforest, M 20	Calif.
479	Skykomish, H 11	Wash.
212	*Skyland, O 7	N. C.
....	*Skyland, H 12	Va.
400	*Skyline, A 18	Ala.
25	*Skytop, I 23	Pa.
150	Skyway, H 4	Colo.
650	*Slab Fork, O 8	W. Va.
418	Slade, G 20	Ky.
120	*Slades Corners, O 22	Wis.
155	Slagle, I 7	La.
55	Slagle, O 5	W. Va.
62	*Slanesville, E 21	W. Va.
75	*Slant (Starnes), E 5	Va.
125	*Slat, K 16	Ky.
531	*▲Slate, E 16	Ala.
....	*Slate, B 7	Va.
296	*Slate, F 6	W. Va.
640	Slatedale, K 21	Pa.
100	*Slateford (Slateford Jc.), K 23	Pa.
200	*Slate Hill, D 4	N. Y.
87	*Slate Hill, Q 18	Pa.
91	*Slate Mills, H 14	Va.
30	Slater, B 7	Colo.
800	*Slater, L 16	Fla.
544	Slater, J 12	Iowa
3070	Slater, G 11	Mo.
....	Slater, H 8	Ohio
800	*Slater, B 6	S. C.
42	Slater, N 22	Wyo.
1539	Slatersville, A 11	R. I.
140	Slate Run, G 14	Pa.
125	Slaterville, D 11	Utah
210	Slaterville Springs, P 14	N. Y.
182	*Slate Spring, E 16	Miss.
4062	Slatington, K 21	Pa.
3587	Slaton, C 10	Tex.
26	*Slatyfork, L 13	W. Va.
306	Slaughter, K 14	La.
....	Slaughter, see Wintergreen	Va.
344	Slaughters (Slaughtersville), H 9	Ky.
32	*Slavans, K 18	Ky.
164	*Slayden, M 9	Tenn.
50	Slayden, L 18	Tex.
1587	Slayton, Q 6	Minn.
11	Slayton, J 15	Mont.
....	Sledge, I 4	Ala.
316	*Sledge, C 10	Miss.
101	*Sleeper, M 12	Mo.
300	Sleepy Creek, C 24	W. Va.
2923	Sleepy Eye, P 10	Minn.
16	*Sleith, I 10	W. Va.
....	*Slemp, I 21	Ky.
....	*Slemp, see Clinchfield	Va.
300	Slick, G 17	Okla.
50	*Slickford, J 16	Ky.
62	*Slick Rock, J 13	Ky.
1200	*Slickville, M 5	Pa.
2864	Slidell, M 20	La.
275	Slidell, C 18	Tex.
18	Sligo, B 17	Colo.
35	*Sligo, C 5	La.
70	Sligo, M 16	Mo.
948	Sligo, I 5	Pa.
....	Slim Buttes, D 4	S. D.
775	Slinger, O 19	Wis.
750	*Slingerlands, N 23	N. Y.
1269	Slippery Rock, I 3	Pa.
33	Sloan, H 6	Ind.
628	Sloan, H 2	Iowa
15	Sloan, G 4	Mont.
220	Sloan, P 20	Nev.
3836	*Sloan, O 5	N. Y.
....	*Sloan, H 22	Ky.
150	Sloans Valley, J 17	Ky.
209	*Sloansville, N 21	N. Y.
217	Sloat, E 9	Calif.
1771	*Slaotsburg, F 5	N. Y.
1041	Slocomb, O 20	Ala.
50	Slocum, N 12	Mich.
200	Slocum (Slocums), K 13	R. I.
160	*Slocum, G 21	Tex.
15	Sloss, H 9	Colo.
48	*Sloughhouse, G 8	Calif.
100	Slovaktown, J 15	Ark.
2800	Slovan, N 2	Pa.
125	*Slusher, K 20	Ky.
250	*Sly, C 3	N. C.
2235	Smackover, Q 11	Ark.
50	Small, M 19	Idaho
20	*Smallett, P 12	Mo.
....	*Smalley, see Martin	Ky.
140	*Small Point Beach, O 8	Me.
....	*Smallwood, C 2, R 20	N. Y.
320	Smarrs, H 9	Ga.
75	*Smartt (Smartts), O 13	Tenn.
84	*Smartville, F 8	Calif.
100	Smartville (Saint Mary), N 23	Neb.
....	*Smeadley, see Hartman	Ark.
1250	*Smeltertown, F 1	Tex.
200	*Smelterville, D 6	Idaho
....	Smeltz, B 19	Ore.
20	*Smethport, B 3	N. C.
1840	Smethport, E 10	Pa.
263	Smethport (East Smethport) E 10	Pa.
223	*Smicksburg, K 7	Pa.
....	Smilay, I 21	Ky.
27	*Smile, F 21	Ky.
515	Smiley, M 18	Tex.
19	*Smith, J 21	Ky.
14	*Smith, H 4	Nev.
100	*Smith, N 20	N. M.
40	*Smith (Smiths Turn Out), B 12	S. C.
222	Smithboro, L 13	Ill.
200	Smithboro, R 14	N. Y.
40	Smithboro, F 22	S. C.
300	Smithburg, E 10	W. Va.
1686	Smith Center, D 11	Kan.
20	*Smithdale, O 7	Miss.
550	*Smithdale, M 4	Pa.
2232	Smithers, L 7	W. Va.
359	Smithfield, G 9	Ill.
136	*Smithfield, E 15	Ky.
200	Smithfield, L 8	Me.
200	Smithfield, O 6	Mo.
158	Smithfield, M 13	Neb.
3678	Smithfield, G 15	N. C.
62	Smithfield (Weems), I 20	Ohio
1169	*Smithfield, I 20	Ohio
50	Smithfield, I 6	Ore.
996	Smithfield, Q 4	Pa.
200	Smithfield, C 12	R. I.
250	*Smithfield, E 18	Tex.
2461	Smithfield, B 12	Utah
1178	Smithfield, P 20	Va.
455	Smithfield, D 11	W. Va.
150	*Smithflat, G 9	Calif.
389	Smithland, H 3	Iowa
592	Smithland, I 6	Ky.
75	Smithland, D 24	Tex.
280	*Smith Hill, H 11	Ala.
800	*Smithmill, K 10	Pa.
150	*Smith Mills, G 8	Ky.
99	Smithonia, E 13	Ga.
59	*Smith Point, L 24	Tex.
300	Smith River, B 1	Calif.
500	*Smiths (Smiths Sta.), J 22	Ala.
102	*Smiths, F 9	Mass.
....	*Smiths, see Allenton	Mich.
70	*Smiths (Smiths Sta.), Q 16	Pa.
65	Smiths Basin, K 24	N. Y.
50	*Smithsboro, H 22	Ky.
619	Smithsburg, B 7	Md.
43	*Smiths Creek, E 21	Ky.
200	*Smiths Creek, O 25	Mich.
50	Smiths Ferry, L 6	Idaho
204	Smiths Ferry (Glasgow), L 1	Pa.
699	Smiths Grove, J 12	Ky.
225	Smithshire, F 7	Ill.
25	Smiths Lake, F 5	N. M.
....	*Smiths Landing, see Cementon	N. Y.
51	Smiths Mill, P 14	Minn.
42	*Smithsons Valley, L 17	Tex.
500	*Smiths Sta. (Smiths), J 22	Ala.
70	*Smiths Station (Smiths), Q 16	Pa.
40	*Smiths Turn Out (Smith), B 12	S. C.
261	Smithton, N 9	Ark.
448	Smithton, N 10	Ill.
404	Smithton, I 10	Mo.
737	*Smithton, N 5	Pa.
400	*Smith Town, K 18	Ky.
500	*Smithtown, (Atlantic), Q 20	N. H.
250	*Smithtown, G 9	N. Y.
1200	Smithtown Branch, G 9	N. Y.
126	Smith Valley, K 14	Ind.
250	Smithville, C 17	Ark.
619	Smithville, L 7	Ga.
350	Smithville, M 12	Ind.
402	Smithville, D 22	Miss.
772	Smithville, F 6	Mo.
171	Smithville, K 13	N. J.
150	Smithville, I 15	N. Y.
617	Smithville, G 16	Ohio
121	*Smithville (Weilersville), G 16	Ohio
290	Smithville, N 24	Okla.
24	Smithville, J 6	S. D.
919	Smithville, N 13	Tenn.
3100	Smithville, K 19	Tex.
250	*Smithville, F 8	W. Va.
200	Smithville Flats, P 16	N. Y.
63	Smithwick, N 3	S. D.
168	*Smoaks, M 14	S. C.
1500	*Smock, Q 4	Pa.
620	*Smoke Bend, M 15	La.
260	*Smoke Hole (Branch), H 17	W. Va.
114	*Smokeless, M 7	Pa.
25	Smokemont, O 5	N. C.
550	Smokerun, K 10	Pa.
125	*Smoketown, O 19	Pa.
210	*Smoky Jc., L 17	Tenn.
46	*Smoky Ordinary, Q 15	Va.
35	*Smoky Valley, E 21	Ky.
120	*Smolan, H 15	Kan.
15	*Smoot, N 11	W. Va.
300	Smoot, K 2	Wyo.
18	*Smoots, K 17	Va.
115	*Smullton, K 13	Pa.
78	*Smyer, M 7	Ala.
15	*Smyer, C 9	Tex.
55	*Smyrna, F 9	Ark.
1870	Smyrna, F 21	Del.
1440	Smyrna, F 6	Ga.
110	Smyrna, O 15	Mich.
5	Smyrna, O 18	Neb.
256	Smyrna, N 17	N. Y.
150	Smyrna, J 22	N. C.
133	*Smyrna, B 12	S. C.
493	Smyrna, N 11	Tenn.
20	Smyrna, K 17	Wash.
200	Smyrna Mills, F 18	Me.
398	Smyser (Seven Valleys), Q 17	Pa.
550	*Smyth (Balfour), P 8	N. C.
23	Snake River, M 19	Wash.
48	Snake River Jc., M 19	Wash.
15	*Snap, H 12	Ky.
727	Sneads, B 2, M 12	Fla.
125	*Sneads Ferry, K 18	N. C.
53	*Snedekerville (Snediker), E 17	Pa.
12	Sneed, O 13	Okla.
250	Sneedville, K 21	Tenn.
25	Sneffels, M 6	Colo.
7	*Snell, J 16	Va.
324	Snelling, I 10	Calif.
204	*Snellville, E 9	Ga.
45	*Snipe (Edmonds), M 22	Tex.
2794	Snohomish, G 9	Wash.
50	Snomac, K 16	Okla.
76	*Snook, J 20	Tex.
775	Snoqualmie, I 9	Wash.
....	Snoqualmie Falls, I 10	Wash.
225	Snover, N 23	Mich.
72	Snow, K 10	Ga.
44	*Snow, K 15	Ky.
18	Snow, L 4	N. D.
....	*Snow, N 21	Okla.
75	*Snowball, D 11	Ark.
500	*Snow Camp, E 11	N. C.
14	Snowden, E 25	Mont.
50	*Snowden, C 23	N. C.
30	*Snowden, M 10	Va.
250	Snowdoun, K 16	Ala.
659	Snowflake, H 21	Ariz.
24	*Snowflake, E 6	Va.
250	Snow Hill, L 12	Ala.
1926	Snow Hill, P 23	Md.
928	Snow Hill, G 17	N. C.
30	*Snow Hill, L 10	W. Va.
113	*Snow Lake, O 17	Ark.
4	Snowmass, H 8	Colo.
578	Snow Shoe, J 12	Pa.
800	*Snow Shoe (Clarence), K 12	Pa.
250	Snow Shoe Intersection (Wingate), J 12	Pa.
50	*Snowville, J 18	N. H.
195	Snowville, A 7	Utah
331	Snowville, P 4	Va.
100	*Snyder, Q 15	Ark.
300	Snyder, D 19	Colo.
129	Snyder (Dean Lake), E 10	Mo.
395	Snyder, I 21	Neb.
612	*Snyder, M 5	N. Y.
1278	Snyder, M 6	Okla.
3815	Snyder, E 11	Tex.
30	*Snyders, K 19	Pa.
200	*Snydersburg, I 6	Pa.
175	*Snydersville, I 23	Pa.
342	Snydertown, K 17	Pa.
50	Snyderville, K 8	Ohio
622	Soap Lake, I 17	Wash.
120	*Soap Lake (Grant Orchards), I 17	Wash.
257	*Sobieski, N 11	Wis.
25	Sobol, P 22	Okla.
1735	Social Circle, F 10	Ga.
687	Society Hill, D 18	S. C.
3012	Socorro, J 10	N. M.
600	Socorro, G 1	Tex.
35	*Sod, L 4	W. Va.
50	Soda, I 23	Tex.
....	*Soda Springs, F 9	Calif.
1087	Soda Springs, P 21	Idaho
99	Sodaville, H 7	Ore.
2250	Soddy (Rathburn), P 15	Tenn.
213	Sodom, I 22	N. Y.
....	*Sodus, see Pleasant Hill	La.
300	Sodus, Q 10	Mich.
1513	Sodus, L 11	N. Y.
300	Sodus Center, L 11	N. Y.
525	Sodus Point, K 11	N. Y.
75	*Soft Shell, I 22	Ky.
7	*Soham (Sands), F 15	N. M.
7	Solana, J 16	Minn.
259	*Solana Beach, Q 19	Calif.
40	Solano (Solana), E 21	N. M.
308	Soldier, I 3	Iowa
247	Soldier, E 21	Kan.
300	*Soldier, E 21	Ky.
450	Soldier, J 8	Pa.
106	Soldier Pond, B 15	Me.
....	*Soldiers Field, F 19, N 4	Mass.
778	Soldiers Grove, G 19	Wis.
....	*Soldiers Home, I 4	Ill.
....	*Soldiers Home, G 9	Ind.
....	Soldiers Home, see Wadsworth	Kan.
97	Soldier Summit, H 15	Utah
10	Sol Duc, F 3	Wash.
127	*Solebury, N 24	Pa.
861	Soledad, K 8	Calif.
200	Solen, P 11	N. D.
56	*Soles, M 21	Va.
86	*Solgohachia, G 11	Ark.
25	*Solo, O 14	Mo.
800	Solomon (Solomonsville), M 23	Ariz.
872	Solomon, H 16	Kan.
27	*Solomon Rapids, F 13	Kan.
266	Solomons, O 15	Md.
800	*Solomonsville (Solomon), M 23	Ariz.
515	Solon, K 20	Iowa
600	Solon, K 8	Me.
10	Solon, J 13	Mich.
40	*Solon, O 15	N. Y.
1508	Solon, D 18	Ohio
100	*Solon Mills, A 18	Ill.
392	Solon Springs, D 6	Wis.
218	Solsberry, M 10	Ind.
113	*Solsville, M 16	N. Y.
400	Solvang, N 11	Calif.
8201	Solvay, M 14	N. Y.
35	*Solway, G 13	Ky.
136	Solway, F 8	Minn.
....	*Sombrero Butte, L 16	Ariz.
	*Somerang, see Frenchglen,	Ore.
1170	*Somerdale, L 10	N. J.
250	Somerdale, H 18	Ohio
176	*Somerfield, P 7	Pa.
300	Somers, B 17	Conn.
213	Somers, G 9	Iowa
500	Somers, E 4	Mont.
100	*Somers, F 6	N. Y.
1100	*Somers (Pricedale), N 4	Pa.
....	*Somers, L 21	Va.
175	Somers, P 22	Wis.
600	Somerset, J 7	Colo.
189	Somerset, F 16	Ind.
6154	Somerset, J 17	Ky.
5873	■Somerset, L 19	Mass.
100	*Somerset, R 17	Mich.
2	Somerset, L 10	Neb.
150	Somerset, K 6	N. Y.
1352	Somerset, L 14	Ohio
5430	Somerset, P 7	Pa.
500	*Somerset, L 16	Tex.
115	*Somerset, J 14	Va.
476	Somerset, A 11	Wis.
300	*Somerset Center, R 17	Mich.
....	Somerset Jc., L 19	Mass.
1992	Somers Point, P 14	N. J.
800	Somersville, B 16	Conn.
6136	Somersworth, N 20	N. H.
1247	Somerton, M 1	Ariz.
200	Somerton, K 19	Ohio
17	*Somerton, P 24	Pa.
200	Somerville, C 13	Ala.
373	Somerville, P 6	Ind.
102177	Somerville, F 19, M 3	Mass.
8720	Somerville, F 14	N. J.
359	Somerville, M 5	Ohio
1570	Somerville, P 3	Tenn.
1621	Somerville, J 20	Tex.
18	*Somerville, G 15	Va.
50	*Somesbar, B 5	Calif.
308	*Somis, N 13	Calif.
610	Somonauk, C 17	Ill.
375	Sondheimer, C 14	La.
200	Sonestown, H 17	Pa.
150	Sonman, M 9	Pa.
12	*Sonnette, M 22	Mont.
30	*Sonoita, P 18	Ariz.
1158	Sonoma, A 16	Calif.
1500	Sonora, L 17	Ariz.
26	*Sonora, C 5	Ark.
2257	Sonora, H 10	Calif.
300	Sonora, H 13	Ky.
8	Sonora, Q 25	N. D.
231	Sonora, K 16	Ohio
2528	Sonora, J 12	Tex.
249	*Sontag, N 11	Miss.
48	*Sontag, P 7	Va.
500	Sonyea, N 8	N. Y.
32	Soo Jc., F 15	Mich.
....	Soo-Line Jc., M 24	Minn.
400	*Sopchoppy, C 4	Fla.
....	*Sopenah, see Vader	Wash.
481	Soper, Q 20	Okla.
1339	Soperton, K 16	Ga.
300	Soperton, M 10	Wis.
153	*Sophia, F 9	N. C.
1160	Sophia, O 8	W. Va.
45	*Sophie, E 21	Ky.
520	*Soppitt (Erico), I 4	Pa.
300	Sopris, Q 16	Colo.
1800	*Soquel, J 6	Calif.
840	Sorento, L 13	Ill.
13	*Sorrento (Hill), Q 19	Calif.
350	*Sorrento, G 16	Fla.
819	Sorrento, M 16	La.
100	*Sorrento, L 17	Me.
6	Sorum, D 4	S. D.
235	*Soso, M 17	Miss.
214	Soudan, I 19	Ark.
100	*Soudan, E 20	Minn.
40	*Soudan, Q 13	Va.
4	*Souder, Q 13	Mo.
227	*Soudersburg, O 19	Pa.
4036	Souderton, N 23	Pa.
....	Soules Mill, K 6	Me.
321	*Soulsbyville, H 11	Calif.
....	Sound, E 22	N. C.
....	*Sound Beach, see old Greenwich	Conn.
125	*Sound View, I 20	Conn.
259	Souris, D 12	N. D.
1504	Sourlake (Sour Lake), J 24	Tex.
43	*South, H 12	Ky.
....	*South Acton, Q 2	Me.
800	South Acton, E 17	Mass.
260	South Acworth, O 7	N. H.
40	South Albany, D 15	Vt.
117	Southam, G 19	N. D.
600	*South Altoona, M 10	Pa.
180	South Amana, K 18	Iowa
7802	South Amboy, G 18	N. J.
....	South Amherst, F 9	Mass.
847	South Amherst, D 14	Ohio
950	▲Southampton, G 6	Mass.
3818	Southampton, G 11	N. Y.
800	*Southampton, N 24	Pa.
62	*Southanna, K 14	Va.
50	*South Apalachin, Q 14	N. Y.
350	Southard, J 18	N. J.
500	Southard, F 8	Okla.
1000	*South Ardmore, P 23	Pa.
800	South Ashburnham, C 13	Mass.
170	*South Ashfield, D 6	Mass.
50	*South Athol, D 11	Mass.
5000	South Attleboro, J 17	Mass.
	South Auburn, see Auburn	Neb.
500	*South Baker, G 22	Ore.
....	*South Bancroft, G 18	Me.
1500	South Barre, E 11	Mass.
400	South Barre, G 13	Vt.
235	*South Bay, L 21	Fla.
....	South Bay Jct., N 5	Mass.
90	Southbeach, G 3	Ore.
....	*South Bellingham, C 8	Wash.
955	*South Belmar, I 18	N. J.
2825	South Beloit, A 15	Ill.
1	South Bend, M 16	Ark.
101268	South Bend, B 13	Ind.
100	South Bend, L 23	Neb.
100	*South Bend, K 6	Pa.
400	South Bend, D 15	Tex.
1771	South Bend, L 3	Wash.
91	*South Berlin, F 15	Mass.
35	South Berne, O 22	N. Y.
1800	South Berwick, R 3	Me.
500	*South Bethlehem, O 23	N. Y.
561	*South Bethlehem, I 6	Pa
238	South Bloomfield, L 11	Ohio
100	South Bloomingville, N 13	Ohio
159	South Boardman (Boardman), J 15	Mich.
175	South Bocagrande (South Boca Grande), L 14	Fla.
1500	Southboro, F 16	Mass.
....	South Boston, F 20, N 5,	Mass.
5252	South Boston, Q 11	Va.
1928	South Bound Brook, G 15,	N. J.
....	South Braintree, G 20, R 6,	Mass.
50	Southbranch, K 20	Mich.
75	South Branch, G 13	N. J.
31	*South Branch (French), D 21	W. Va.
....	South Brewer, L 14 (Pop. incl. in Bangor)	Me.
16825	■Southbridge, I 12	Mass.
146	South Bridgton, O 3	Me.
450	South Bristol, O 10	Me.
149	South Britain, J 6	Conn.
....	South Brooklyn, P 22	Ohio
300	South Brooksville, M 15,	Me.
5500	*South Brownsville, Q 4	Pa.
1100	Southbury, J 7	Conn.
200	*South Butler, L 11	N. Y.
300	*South Byfield, B 21	Mass.
255	*South Byron, M 7	N. Y.
104	*South Byron, N 17	Wis.
35	South Cabot, F 15	Vt.
50	*South Cairo, P 22	N. Y.
100	South Camp, H 17	Wyo.
100	*South Canaan, F 23	Pa.
4	*South Cape May, R 11	N. J.
324	*South Carbon (Carbon), M 7	W. Va.
296	*South Carrollton, I 10	Ky.
407	South Carver, K 22	Mass.
175	*South Casco, O 5	Me.
1198	South Charleston, L 9	Ohio
10377	South Charleston, K 5,	W. Va.
279	South Chatham, N 15	Mass.
....	*South Chatham, I 18	N. H.
550	South Chelmsford, D 17	Mass.
....	*South Chesterville, L 7	Me.
....	South Chicago, C 22	Ill.
1837	*South Chicago Heights, C 21	Ill.
256	South China, M 10	Me.
340	South Cle Elum, J 12	Wash.
....	*South Clermont, G 16	Fla.
250	South Clinchfield, D 7	Va.
1604	*South Coatesville, P 21	Pa.
364	South Coffeyville, A 20	Okla.
280	*South Colby, H 7	Wash.
500	South Colton, E 19	N. Y.
85	*South Columbia, J 19	N. Y.
....	*South Columbus, see Columbus	Ky.
2628	*South Connellsville, Q 4	Pa.
681	*South Corning, Q 10	N. Y.
900	South Coventry, F 19	Conn.
700	*South Covington, L 6	Va.
152	South Creek, H 21	N. C.
50	*South Cushing, O 12	Me.
160	*South Danbury (Converse), N 13	N. H.
76	*South Dansville, Q 10	N. Y.
110	South Danville, Q 18	N. H.
501	South Danville (Riverside), J 17	Pa.
1815	South Dartmouth, N 20	Mass.
643	South Dayton, P 3	N. Y.

Pop.	Place Index	State
1333	South Deerfield, D 7	Mass.
150*	South Deerfield, O 17	N. H.
150*	South Dennis, N 14	Mass.
228	South Dennis, Q 12	N. J.
140	South Dorset, N 7	Vt.
170*	South Dos Palos (Dos Palos) J 9	Calif.
....*	Southdown, I 22	Ky.
83*	South Durham, P 22	N. Y.
623	South Easton, I 19	Mass.
175	South Edmeston, N 18	N. Y.
....*	South Effingham, K 18	N.H.
400	South Egremont, H 1	Mass.
961	South Elgin, B 18	Ill.
....	South Eliot, see Eliot	Me.
288	South English, L 18	Iowa
1016*	South Enola, O 15	Pa.
375	Southern Cross, K 6	Mont.
2000*	Southern Hills (Carrmonte), L 7	Ohio
....	Southern Jc., D 7	Ill.
....	Southern Jc., N 13	Wis.
3225	Southern Pines, H 11	N. C.
700	South Essex, C 22	Mass.
6146	South Euclid, C 17	Ohio
....*	South Fairlee, see Ely	Vt.
1500	South Fallsburg (Fallsburgh), C 2	N. Y.
250*	Southfield, I 3	Mass.
500*	Southfields, E 3	N. Y.
....*	South Flatlands (Barren Island), I 5	N. Y.
510*	South Floral Park (Jamaica Square), H 7	N. Y.
262	Southford, K 7	Conn.
....*	Southfork, see Saddle	Ark.
125*	South Fork, D 2	Calif.
250	South Fork, O 9	Colo.
65*	South Fork (Arabia), H 17	Ky.
....*	Southfork, H 20	Ky.
40*	South Fork, R 14	Mo.
3023	South Fork, N 8	Pa.
2393	South Fort Mitchell, C 17	Ky.
2770*	South Fort Plain (Fort Plain), M 20	N. Y.
800*	South Fort Smith, G 4	Ark.
....*	South Framingham, see Framingham	Mass.
100	South Freeport, P 7	Me.
2050	South Fulton, L 4	Tenn.
600	South Gardiner (Lawrence Mills), N 9	Me.
....	South Gary B 7	Ind.
....*	South Gastonia (Pinkney), H 4	N. C.
26945	Southgate (South Gate), R 4	Calif.
40*	South Gate, K 20	Ind.
1841	Southgate, B 17	Ky.
108*	South Gibson, E 21	Pa.
163	South Gifford, D 12	Mo.
100*	South Gilboa, O 20	N. Y.
1500	South Glastonbury, G 15	Conn.
3081	South Glens Falls, K 24	N. Y.
150*	South Gouldsboro, M 18	Me.
210	South Greenfield, N 8	Mo.
2616*	South Greensburg, M 5	Pa.
....*	South Greenwood, F 8	S. C.
1175	South Groveland, B 19	Mass.
6856■	South Hadley, G 8	Mass.
....	South Hadley Falls, G 8	Mass.
1500	South Hamilton (Hamilton & Wenham), C 21	Mass.
100*	South Hammond (Oakvale), F 17	N. Y.
....	South Hampton, Q 19	N. H.
541	South Hanover (Perry), H 21	Mass.
....	South Hanson, see Hanson	Mass.
150	South Harpswell, P 7	Me.
115*	South Hartford, K 24	N. Y.
63*	South Hartwich, O 19	N. Y.
215	South Harwich, N 15	Mass.
405	South Haven, O 16	Kan.
4745	South Haven, P 11	Mich.
276	South Haven, M 12	Minn.
78	South Heart, M 4	N. D.
604	South Heights, L 2	Pa.
63	South Hero, D 5	Vt.
35*	South Hill, I 11	Ky.
1739	South Hill, Q 14	Va.
....*	South Hills, M 3	Pa.
1100	South Hingham, G 21	Mass.
225	South Hiram, P 2	Me.
2272*	South Holland, C 22	Ill.
475	South Hope, N 12	Me.
982*	South Houston (Dumont), K 22	Tex.
915	South Hutchinson, K 14	Kan.
5088	Southington, H 11	Conn.
125*	South Irvine, G 19	Ky.
....	South Jacksonville, C 17 (Pop. incl. in Jacksonville)	Fla.
797*	South Jacksonville, J 10	Ill.
295*	South Jamesport, H 9	N. Y.
205	South Jefferson, N 10	Me.
....	South Jc., D 24	N. Y.
10	South Jc., G 12	Ore.
110*	South Kent (Woodrow), G 3	Conn.
300	South Killingly, E 24	Conn.
325*	South Kinloch Park, I 20	Mo.
2000*	South Klamath, O 10	Ore.
112*	South Kortright, Q 19	N. Y.
225	South Lagrange, J 14	Me.
309*	South Laguna (Three Arches), O 17, R 6	Calif.
1200*	South Lakemont, M 10	Pa.
1000	South Lancaster (Thayer), E 15	Mass.
....*	Southland, see El Jobean	Fla.
280*	Southland, D 11	Tex.
921*	South Langhorne, N 24	Pa.
300	South Lansing, O 13	N. Y.
....	South Lawrence, B 18	Mass.
756*	South Lebanon, M 7	Ohio
400	South Lee, G 2	Mass.
100	South Lee, O 19	N. H.
75	South Levant, K 13	Me.
315	South Liberty, M 11	Me.
175*	South Lima, N 8	N. Y.
525*	South Lincoln (Lincoln), E 17	Mass.
235	South Lincoln, H 8	Vt.
....*	South Linton, see Linton	Ind.
127*	South Livonia, N 8	N. Y.
250	South Londonderry, O 10	Vt.
216	South Lubec, K 24	Me.
150*	South Lunenburg (Lunenburg), E 21	Vt.
350	South Lyme, M 20	Conn.
150	South Lynchburg, G 18	S. C.
170	South Lyndeboro, Q 12	N. H.
1017	South Lyon, P 21	Mich.
....*	South McAlester, see McAlester	Okla.
2299	South Manchester, E 16	Conn.
70	South Manitou, I 11	Mich.
433	South Mansfield, E 4	La.
100	South Marion, F 21	S. C.
300*	Southmayd (Southmayde), C 19	Tex.
600	South Meriden, J 12	Conn.
120*	South Merrimack, Q 13	N. H.
2408	South Miami, O 23	Fla.
200	South Middleboro, K 21	Mass.
135*	South Millbrook, C 6, R 23	N. Y.
300	South Milford, B 19	Ind.
479	South Mills, C 22	N. C.
11134	South Milwaukee, P 21	Wis.
....*	South Monrovia, see Monrovia	Calif.
500*	Southmont, F 8	N. C.
2146*	Southmont, M 8	Pa.
35	South Montesano, K 4	Wash.
126*	South Montrose, E 20	Pa.
....	Southmost, Q5	Tex.
55*	South Mound M 23	Kan.
200*	South Mountain, P 13	Pa.
1200	South Natick, G 17	Mass.
350	South New Berlin, O 17	N. Y.
145*	South Newbury, N 10	N. H.
114*	South Newbury (Conicut), H 17	Vt.
998*	South New Castle, J 2	Pa.
110*	South Newfane, Q 11	Vt.
....	South Norfolk, H 20	Neb.
8038	South Norfolk, Q 22	Va.
....	South Norwalk, Q 4 (Pop. incl. in Norwalk)	Conn.
....	South Norway, G 5	Mich.
2093*	South Nyack, F 5	N. Y.
....	South Oil City, H 5 (Pop. incl. in Oil City)	Pa.
1500	Southold, F 11	N. Y.
144*	South Olive, L 17	Ohio
....	South Omaha, K 24 (Pop. incl. in Omaha)	Neb.
13742	South Orange, E 18	N. J.
185*	South Orleans, M 15	Mass.
300	South Orrington (Mill Creek), L 14	Me.
365	South Otselic, O 16	N. Y.
....*	South Ozone Park, H 6	N. Y.
1961	South Paris, N 5	Me.
....	South Park, N 25	Minn.
....	South Park, Q 23 (Pop. incl.in Independence)	Ohio
14356	South Pasadena, O 16, Q 4	Calif.
50*	South Pass, Q 21	La.
50	South Pass City, L 9	Wyo.
64	South Peacham, F 16	Vt.
1044	South Pekin, G 12	Ill.
260	South Penobscot, M 15	Me.
200*	South Perry, M 13	Ohio
527*	South Philipsburg, K 12	Pa.
2285	South Pittsburg, Q 14	Tenn.
5379	South Plainfield, F 16	N. J.
125*	South Plains, B 11	Tex.
438*	South Pleasureville (Pleasureville), E 15	Ky.
25*	South Plymouth, O 17	N. Y.
605	South Point, R 13	Ohio
1500	South Poland (Poland Spring), O 5	Me.
150*	South Pomfret, K 13	Vt.
1480	Southport, P 6	Conn.
300	Southport (South Port), N 10	Fla.
549	Southport, J 14	Ind.
121*	Southport, O 10	Me.
....	Southport, R 12	N. Y.
1760	Southport, N 16	N. C.
15781	South Portland, P 6	Me.
500*	South Portsmouth, D 22	Ky.
....	South Portsmouth, K 20	R. I.
226	South Prairie, J 8	Wash.
918	South Range, D 2	Mich.
150	South Range, C 5	Wis.
370	South Rehoboth, L 18	Mass.
1018*	South Renovo, H 13	Pa.
....*	South Richmond, see Richmond	Ind.
41*	South Ripley, D 19	Ky.
10714	South River, G 17	N. J.
700	South Rockwood, Q 22	Mich.
350*	South Royalston (Royalston), C 11	Mass.
800	South Royalton, J 13	Vt.
231*	South Russell, D 18	Ohio
50*	South Rutland, H 16	N. Y.
346	South Ryegate, G 17	Vt.
....*	South Saint Joseph, E 5	Mo.
11844	South Saint Paul, N 25 N 17	Minn.
1000*	South Salem, F 6	N. Y.
185*	South Salem, N 11	Ohio
5701*	South Salt Lake, F 11	Utah
2708	South San Antonio, M 16	Tex.
....*	South Sandisfield, I 3	Mass.
100	South Sanford, Q 3	Me.
6629	South San Francisco, E 16 I 5	Calif.
450	South Schenectady, N 23	N. Y.
100*	South Schodack (Van Hoesen), N 24	N. Y.
132*	South Schroon, G 23	N. Y.
....	South Seabrook, Q 20	N. H.
400	South Seaville, Q 13	N. J.
50*	South Sebec (Sebec Sta.), J 13	Me.
510	South Shaftsbury, Q 6	Vt.
....*	South Shore, C 21	Ill.
65*	South Shore (Taylor), D 22	Ky.
296	South Shore, F 23	S. D.
210	Southside, G 4	N. C.
25*	Southside, I 4	W. Va.
4556	South Sioux City, F 22	Neb.
591	South Sioux Falls, M 24	S. D.
376	South Solon, L 9	Ohio
125	South Spencer, G 12	Mass.
214	South Standard, K 11	Ill.
200	South Sterling, H 23	Pa.
....*	South Stillwater, see Bayport	Minn.
73	South Strafford, J 14	Vt.
500	South Sudbury, F 17	Mass.
....	South Superior, C 4	Wis.
885	South Superior, O 8	Wyo.
255	South Sutton, N 10	N. H.
800*	South Swansea, L 19	Mass.
150	South Tamworth, K 16	N. H.
250	South Thomaston, O 12	Me.
445*	South Toms River (Sta.), K 18	N. J.
89*	Southton, L 16	Tex.
300	South Torrington, N 24	Wyo.
84*	South Tunnel, L 12	Tenn.
110*	South Union, J 11	Ky.
257	South Union, N 12	Me.
....	South Vallejo, A 19	Calif.
150*	South Valley, O 19	N. Y.
....	South Vernon (East Northfield), B 8	Mass.
420	South Vienna (Vienna), K 9	Ohio
500*	Southview, O 2	Pa.
225*	Southville, G 15	Mass.
506	South Vineland, O 10	N. J.
15	South Walden, E 15	Vt.
333*	South Wales, O 5	N. Y.
215	South Wallingford, M 8	Vt.
311*	South Walpole, H 18	Mass.
35	South Wanatah, C 9	Ind.
445	South Wareham, L 22	Mass.
150*	South Warren (Georges River), O 12	Me.
750*	South Washington, F 18	Va.
211	South Waterford, N 3	Me.
1212*	South Waverly, E 17	Pa.
331	South Wayne, I 22	Wis.
125	South Weare, P 12	N. H.
656	South Webster, P 13	Ohio
100	South Wellfleet, K 15	Mass.
300*	South Wenatchee, I 14	Wash.
....*	Southwest, I 11	D. C.
2000*	Southwest (Hecla), O 5	Pa.
525	South West City, R 5	Mo.
150*	South Westerlo, O 23	N. Y.
3002*	Southwest Greeneburg, M 5	Pa.
600	South West Harbor, N 17	Me.
150	Southwest Oswego, K 13	N. Y.
125	South Westport, N 20	Mass.
275	South Wethersfield (Spring Brook), G 14	Conn.
6500	South Weymouth, H 20	Mass.
1118	South Whitley, D 17	Ind.
35*	Southwick, H 3	Idaho
1400	Southwick, I 6	Mass.
6033	South Williamsport, I 15	Pa.
200	South Willington, D 19	Conn.
642	South Wilmington, E 18	Ill.
....	South Windham, G 20	Conn.
900	South Windham, P 5	Me.
107*	South Windham, O 11	Vt.
900	South Windsor (Wapping), E 15	Conn.
....	South Wolfeboro, L 17	N. H.
115*	South Woodbury, F 12	Vt.
100	South Woodstock, B 23	Conn.
290*	South Woodstock, L 12	Vt.
150*	South Worcester, O 19	N. Y.
....	South Worcester, G 14	Mass.
100*	Southworth, H 6	Wash.
645	South Yarmouth, N 13	Mass.
1338	South Zanesville, K 15	Ohio
70*	Souwilpa, L 4	Ala.
102*	Spades, M 20	Ind.
275*	Spadra, N 15, Q 4	Calif.
....	Spadra Jc., F 8	Ark.
20	Spafford, N 14	N. Y.
6	Spain, C 21	S. D.
155	Spalding, G 4	Idaho
200*	Spalding, H 6	Mich.
830	Spalding, I 17	Neb.
400	Spanaway, J 7	Wash.
203	Spangle, I 23	Wash.
3201	Spangler, L 8	Pa.
35*	Spanglin, F 21	Ky.
97*	Spangsville, M 20	Pa.
125*	Spanishburg, Q 8	W. Va.
4167	Spanish Fork, H 12	Utah
237*	Spanish Fort, N 19	La.
200*	Spanish Fort (Lucre), I 7	Miss.
350	Spanish Fort, B 17	Tex.
37*	Spann, J 16	Ky.
97*	Sparenberg, E 10	Tex.
25*	Spargursville, N 11	Ohio
960	Sparkill, G 5	N. Y.
840	Sparkman N 10	Ark.
....*	Sparkman, L 17	Fla.
695	Sparks, O 12	Ga.
75*	Sparks, D 23	Kan.
50*	Sparks, C 14	Md.
7	Sparks, D 12	Neb.
5318	Sparks, G 3	Nev.
339	Sparks, H 15	Okla.
110*	Sparks, L 10	W. Va.
3*	Sparks Hill, Q 19	Ill.
35*	Sparks Quarry (Burr), I 18	Ky.
130*	Sparksville, N 15	Ind.
60*	Sparksville, I 15	Ky.
509	Sparland, E 13	Ill.
150*	Sparr, E 15	Fla.
29*	Sparrow, F 16	Ky.
610	Sparrow Bush, E 2	N. Y.
....	Sparrows Point, F 15	Md.
1872	Sparta, H 14	Ga.
3664	Sparta, O 12	Ill.
500*	Sparta, C 16	Ky.
1945	Sparta, N 13	Mich.
237	Sparta, P 10	Mo.
1872	Sparta, C 14	N. J.
648	Sparta, B 5	N. C.
184*	Sparta, H 12	Ohio
25	Sparta, F 23	Ore.
2506	Sparta, N 15	Tenn.
46*	Sparta, K 17	Va.
5820	Sparta, G 16	Wis.
6	Sparta Jc., C 13	N. J.
....*	Sparta Military, see Camp McCoy	Wis.
318	Spartanburg, I 22	Ind.
32249	Spartanburg, B 8	S. C.
423	Spartansburg, E 5	Pa.
209	Spaulding, I 13	Ill.
25	Spaulding, B 19	Ill.
135	Spaulding, K 16	Okla.
255	Spavinaw, D 22	Okla.
100*	Speaks, M 19	Tex.
43*	Spear, D 2	N. C.
2139	Spearfish, I 2	S. D.
1105	Spearman, A 4	Tex.
603	Spearville, L 8	Kan.
16*	Spechts Ferry, G 23	Iowa
1022*	Specialville (Dixmoor), C 21	Ill.
278*	Speculator, I 20	N. Y.
800	Speed (Speeds), P 16	Ind.
111	Speed, E 9	Kan.
113*	Speed, H 12	Mo.
127*	Speed, E 18	N. C.
800*	Speeds (Speed), P 16	Ind.
1600*	Speedway, C 21	Ill.
2325	Speedway, J 14	Ind.
65*	Speedway, Q 9	W. Va.
86*	Speedwell, G 18	Ky.
36*	Speedwell, Q 6	N. C.
50	Speedwell, L 19	Tenn.
500	Speedwell, Q 2	Va.
....	Speedwell Jc., P 2	Va.
75	Speer, F 12	Ill.
50	Speer, P 20	Okla.
6	Speer, R 21	Wyo.
81	Speermoore, C 2	Okla.
852*	Speers (Belleveron), O 4	Pa.
81	Speers Ferry, E 5	Va.
25*	Speight, H 24	Ky.
300*	Speigner (Speigener), I 16	Ala.
300*	Spelter, F 12	W. Va.
116	Spencer, L 19	Idaho
2375	Spencer, L 9	Ind.
6599	Spencer, C 6	Iowa
37*	Spencer, A 11	La.
6641■	Spencer, G 12	Mass.
19*	Spencer, I 15	Mich.
635	Spencer, D 16	Neb.
615	Spencer, Q 13	N. Y.
3072	Spencer, F 7	N. C.
591	Spencer, E 15	Ohio
250	Spencer, I 12	Okla.
617	Spencer, L 22	S. D.
508	Spencer, O 14	Tenn.
75*	Spencer, R 6	Va.
2497	Spencer, H 7	W. Va.
506	Spencer, I 13	Wis.
1340	Spencerport, L 8	N. Y.
....*	Spencer Ridge, H 20	Ky.
300*	Spencertown, A 6, Q 24	N. Y.
300*	Spencerville, Q 24	N. Y.
310	Spencerville, C 21	Ind.
90*	Spencerville, G 9	Md.
1623	Spencerville, G 7	Ohio
50	Spencerville, P 22	Okla.
198*	Speonk, H 9	N. Y.
75*	Sperry, O 22	Iowa
570	Sperry, E 19	Okla.
....*	Sperry Springs, B 13	N. J.
800	Sperryville, H 13	Va.
1	Sphinx, N 11	Mont.
31*	Spice, M 14	W. Va.
....*	Spicer, C 11	Colo.
645	Spiceland, J 19	Ind.
480	Spicer, M 9	Minn.
130*	Spicewood, I 17	Tex.
587	Spickard (Spickardsville), B 9	Mo.
163*	Spider, H 22	Ky.
50*	Spies, H 10	N. C.
68*	Spiker (Speicher), E 16	Ind.
25	Spiker, I 23	Neb.
201	Spillertown, P 16	Ill.
....*	Spillman, J 14	La.
329	Spillville, C 18	Iowa
263	Spilman (Hallwood), G 4	W. Va.
3952	Spindale, H 1	N. C.
50	Spink, O 24	S. D.
245*	Spinnerstown, N 23	Pa.
20	Spion Kop, G 12	Mont.
100	Spirit, I 10	Wis.
60	Spirit Falls, I 10	Wis.
1006	Spirit Lake, C 3	Idaho
2161	Spirit Lake, B 6	Iowa
25*	Spirit Lake, O 9	Wash.
125	Spiritwood, M 19	N. D.
30*	Spiro, I 18	Ky.
1041	Spiro, J 24	Okla.
350*	Spivak, G 15	Colo.
181	Spivey, N 13	Kan.
150	Splashdam, B 6	Va.
150*	Splendora, J 22	Tex.
310*	Split Rock, M 14	N. Y.
6	Split Rock, K 13	Wyo.
269*	Spocari, K 7	Ala.
300	Spofford, Q 6	N. H.
319	Spofford, M 12	Tex.
20*	Spokane, P 10	Mo.
402	Spokane (Bristolville), D 19	Ohio
122001	Spokane, H 23	Wash.
48	Spokane Bridge, H 25	Wash.
25*	Spoke Plant, C 7	Ark.
4	Sponsler, M 8	Ind.
442	Spooner, C 11	Minn.
2639	Spooner, D 8	Wis.
184	Spoonerville, I 24	Mo.
77*	Spot, C 23	N. C.
1201	Spotswood, H 16	N. J.
61	Spotsylvania, J 16	Va.
10*	Spotted Horse, D 18	Wyo.
350	Spottsville, G 8	Ky.
4	Spottswood, H 18	S. D.
76*	Spottswood, K 10	Va.
46*	Spoutspring, G 19	Ky.
100*	Spout Spring, N 11	Va.
34*	Spraggs, Q 2	Pa.
75	Sprague, K 16	Ala.
121	Sprague, M 22	Neb.
641	Sprague, I 21	Wash.
550*	Sprague, O 8	W. Va.
72*	Sprague, I 17	Wis.
350	Sprague River, P 11	Ore.
116*	Spragueville, I 24	Iowa
150	Spragueville, G 17	N. Y.
220*	Sprakers, N 21	N. Y.
100*	Sprankle Mills, I 7	Pa.
25*	Spratt, K 15	Ohio
3000	Spray, B 9	N. C.
110	Spray, F 16	Ore.
50*	Spray Beach, K 17	N. J.
30*	Spread Eagle, M 9	Wis.
100	Spreckles, K 7	Calif.
81*	Sprigg, P 3	W. Va.
400	Spring, K 22	Tex.
500	Spring Arbor, Q 16	Mich.
157*	Spring Bay, F 13	Ill.
50*	Spring Beach, I 9	Wash.
466	Springboro, M 7	Ohio
570	Springboro, E 2	Pa.
40*	Spring Branch, L 16	Tex.
275*	Spring Brook (South Wethersfield), G 14	Conn.
131*	Springbrook, H 24	Iowa
210	Spring Brook, N 5	N. Y.
77	Spring Brook, G 3	N. D.
75*	Springbrook, D 6	Ore.
125	Springbrook, D 7	Wis.
1000	Spring Canyon, I 16	Utah
64*	Spring Church, L 5	Pa.
3022	Spring City, O 21	Pa.
1569	Spring City, O 16	Tenn.
839	Spring City, J 13	Utah
75*	Spring Creek, I 20	Ky.
100*	Springcreek, J 17	La.
17*	Spring Creek, M 14	Mo.
600*	Spring Creek, N 7	N. C.
37*	Spring Creek (Tank), E 21	Okla.
300	Spring Creek, E 5	Pa.
150	Springcreek, N 5	Tenn.
131	Spring Creek, D 14	Tex.
150	Springcreek, H 11	Va.
29*	Spring Creek, N 12	W. Va.
3319	Springdale, B 5	Ark.
4500	Springdale, Q 2	Conn.
....	Springdale, C 8	Fla.
50*	Springdale, D 20	Ky
75	Springdale, L 12	Mont.
5	Springdale, N 14	Nev.
4989	Springdale, M 4	Pa.
20	Springdale D 24	Tex.
209	Springdale; Q 5	Utah
227	Springdale, F 22	Wash.
500*	Spring Dale, N 8	W. Va.
301	Springer (Springerton), O 19	Ill.
1314	Springer, D 18	N. M.
325	Springer, O 14	Okla.
250	Springers (Pleasant Pt.), P 9	Tenn.
301	Springerton (Springer), O 19	Ill.
575	Springerville, I 24	Ariz.
....*	Springet, see Pleasureville	Pa.
100	Springfield, G 11	Ark.
1082	Springfield, O 22	Colo.
458	Springfield, K 24	Ga.
350	Springfield, O 17	Idaho
75503	Springfield, I 13	Ill.
1767	Springfield, G 15	Ky.
400	Springfield, L 17	La.
500	Springfield, I 18	Me.
149554	Springfield, H 8	Mass.
2361	Springfield, P 9	Minn.
61238	Springfield, O 10	Mo.
370	Springfield, K 23	Neb.
....	Springfield, N 6	N. H.
3600	Springfield, E 17	N. J.
50*	Springfield, C 4	N. C.
70662	Springfield, K 9	Ohio
3805	Springfield, J 6	Ore.
200*	Springfield (North Springfield), D 2	Pa.
50	Springfield, E 17	Pa.
4500*	Springfield, P 23	Pa.
786	Springfield J 12	S. C.
667	Springfield P 20	S. D.
6668	Springfield, L 10	Tenn.
5182	Springfield, N 13	Vt.
38*	Springfield, G 17	Va.
325*	Springfield, E 20	W. Va.
100	Springfield, N 22	Wis.
1188*	Springfield Bay, N 9	Fla.
285*	Springfield Center, N 19	N. Y.
....*	Springfield Gardens, H 6	N. Y.
....	Springfield Jc., J 6	Ore.
....	Spring Forest, see Willow Springs	Ill.
20*	Spring Gap, L 7	Md.
....*	Spring Gap, E 21	W. Va.
110*	Spring Garden, E 20	Ala.
120*	Spring Garden, E 9	Calif.
100	Spring Garden, O 16	Ill.
1100*	Spring Garden, M 5	Pa.
250*	Spring Glen, R 21	N. Y.
390	Spring Glen, L 17	Pa.
868	Spring Green, I 19	Wis.
209	Spring Grove, A 18	Ill.
967	Spring Grove, R 23	Minn.
1259	Spring Grove, Q 16	Pa.
40*	Spring Grove, O 19	Va.
2284▲	Spring Hill, P 4	Ala.
124*	Spring Hill, C 10	Ill.
28	Spring Hill, K 6	Ind.
146	Spring Hill, M 12	Iowa
489	Spring Hill, H 24	Kan.
2822	Springhill (Spring Hill), A 6	La.
12	Springhill (Port Tobacco), M 11	Md.
55*	Springhill, D 18	N. C.
121*	Spring Hill, J 9	Ohio
543	Spring Hill, O 10	Tenn.
2000	Spring Hill, K 5	W. Va.
1222	Spring Hope, E 15	N. C.
435*	Spring House, N 22	Pa.
250*	Springlake, C 17	Ky.
1329	Spring Lake, N 11	Mich.
42*	Spring Lake, F 14	Minn.
100	Spring Lake, L 17	Minn.
1650	Spring Lake (Spring Lake Beach), I 20	N. J.
50*	Springlake, B 9	Tex.
1076*	Spring Lake Heights, I 8	N. J.
80*	Spring Lick, H 11	Ky.
350*	Spring Mill (Wm. Penn), N 22	Pa.
620	Spring Mills, K 13	Pa.
400	Spring Mount, N 23	Pa.
600*	Spring Mountain, K 19	Pa.
175*	Springpark, M 15	Minn.
219	Spring Place, C 5	Ga.
189*	Springport, I 19	Ind.
502	Springport, Q 16	Mich.
48	Spring Ranch (Springranch), N 17	Neb.
35*	Spring Run, P 13	Pa.
162*	Springs, P 7	Pa.
162*	Springs, P 7	Pa.
28*	Springs (Craig Healing Springs), M 5	Va.
34*	Spring Sta., F 17	Ky.
67	Springston, D 4	Idaho
121*	Springton, Q 8	W. Va.
104	Springtown, B 4	Ark.
311	Springtown, F 9	N. J.
450*	Springtown, N 23	Pa.
500*	Springtown, E 17	Tex.
148*	Springvale, M 4	Ga.
3000	Springvale (Sanford & Springvale), Q 3	Me.
82*	Spring Vale, L 16	Minn.
36*	Spring Valley, C 4	Ark.
1000*	Spring Valley, Q 19	Calif.
5010	Spring Valley, E 13	Ill.
2133	Spring Valley, R 20	Minn.
4308	Spring Valley, F 5	N. Y.
468	Spring Valley, M 8	Ohio
105*	Spring Valley, N 23	Pa.
....	Spring Valley, N 22	S. D.
118*	Spring Valley, Q 2	Va.
16	Spring Valley, I 23	Wash.
973	Spring Valley, B 12	Wis.
347	Springview, E 13	Neb.
460	Springville, E 15	Ala.
....	Springville, K 14	Calif.
260	Springville, M 11	Ind.
608	Springville, I 21	Iowa
68	Springville, L 16	La.
200*	Springville, C 18	Miss.
2849	Springville, O 5	N. Y.
300	Springville, F 20	Pa.
150*	Springville, L 7	Tenn.
4796	Springville, G 13	Utah
500	Springwater, O 9	N. Y.
121*	Springwood, M 8	Va.
50*	Sprinkle, J 18	Tex.
62*	Sprott, I 11	Ala.
435	Sproul, N 10	Pa.
100	Sproul, L 5	W. Va.
50*	Spry, O 13	Utah
22	Spruce, I 20	Mich.
....	Spruce, F 19	Minn.
55*	Spruce, K 7	Mo.
6	Spruce, G 2	Wash.
12	Spruce, K 14	W. Va.
200	Spruce Creek, L 11	Pa.
100	Spruce Head, O 12	Me.
100*	Spruce Hill, M 14	Pa.
17	Sprucemont, E 20	Nev.
300	Spruce Pine, C 7	Ala.
1968	Spruce Pine, E 1	N. C.
57*	Spruceton, Q 22	N. Y.
31*	Sprule, J 19	Ky.
2136	Spur, C 12	Tex.
360	Spurgeon (Pleasantville), P 7	Ind.
....	Spurgeon, P 6	Mo.
40*	Spurgeon, D 5	N. C.
200*	Spurger, I 25	Tex.
56*	Spur Lake, J 3	N. M.
75*	Sprule, J 19	Ky.
125*	Spurlington, H 15	Ky.
20*	Spurlock, I 20	Ky.
50*	Spurlockville, M 3	W. Va.
15*	Spurrier, H 13	Ky.
35*	Spy Lake (Higgins Bay), I 21	N. Y.
35*	Spyrock, E 3	Calif.
....	Squannacook Jc., C 14	Mass.
....*	Squantum, F 20, N 5	Mass.
111	Squa Pan, D 17	Me.
85	Square Butte, G 12	Mont.
30*	Squaw Lake, F 14	Minn.
12*	Squawvalley, K 10	Calif.
....	Squaw Valley, Q 10	Ore.
12	Squib, I 17	Ky.
300*	Squire, Q 5	W. Va.
67*	Squires, Q 12	Mo.
77	Squirrel, M 22	Idaho
....	Squirrel Hill, M 3	Pa.
6*	Squirrel Island, P 9	Me.
500*	Staatsburg, C 5, R 23	N. Y.
13*	Stab, I 17	Ky.
7	Stacey, L 21	Mont.
50*	Stackhouse, N 7	N. C.
34*	Stacy, D 10	Calif.
138*	Stacy, L 18	Minn.
280	Stacy, J 22	N. C.
25	Stacy, H 14	Tex.
62*	Stacy (Matney), B 8	Va.
31*	Stacy Fork, G 21	Ky.
533	Stacyville, B 15	Iowa
170	Stacyville, G 16	Me.
....	Stacyville Jc., B 15	Iowa
11	Stady, D 2	N. D.
519	Stafford, F 4	Ala.
3401	Stafford Springs, B 18	Conn.
700	Stafford, B 19	Conn.
2011	Stafford, L 12	Kan.
30	Stafford, G 17	Neb.
400*	Stafford, M 7	N. Y.
163*	Stafford, L 18	Ohio
75	Stafford, H 4	Okla.
122*	Stafford, L 22	Tex.
60	Stafford, I 17	Va.
3401	Stafford Spgs. (Stafford), B 18	Conn.
50*	Stafford Spgs., L 18	Miss.
57*	Stafford Store, H 16	Va.
200*	Staffordsville, G 22	Ky.
50*	Staffordsville, N 4	Va.
500	Staffordville, B 18	Conn.
53*	Staffordville, K 17	N. J.
31*	Stage Jc., L 13	Va.
....	Stager, G 3	Mich.
....*	Stags Leap, A 18	Calif.
30	Stahl, B 11	Mo.
145*	Stahlstown, M 5	Pa.
400*	Stainville (Elijah), M 18	Tenn.
255*	Staley, F 10	N. C.
30*	Stalker, F 23	Pa.
250*	Stallo, I 18	Miss.
63*	Stals, D 14	Minn.
250*	Stalwart, F 16	Mich.
30*	Stambaugh, G 22	Ky.
2081	Stambaugh, F 2	Mich.
47938	Stamford, R 2	Conn.
260	Stamford, O 13	Neb.
1088	Stamford, P 20	N. Y.
30	Stamford, L 10	S. D.
4810	Stamford, D 13	Tex.
500	Stamford, R 7	Vt.
13	Stampede, D 5	N. D.
30*	Stampers, L 20	Va.
350	Stamping Ground, E 17	Ky.
16*	Stampley, M 5	Miss.
2405	Stamps, P 7	Ark.
500*	Stanaford, O 8	W. Va.
212	Stanardsville, I 13	Va.
1893	Stanberry, B 6	Mo.
124*	Stanchfield, K 14	Minn.
50*	Standard, F 20	Ariz.
600*	Standard, H 10	Calif.
334	Standard, E 14	Ill.
....	Standard, L 6	Ind.
250	Standard, F 10	La.
850*	Standard, M 5	Pa.
210*	Standard, L 6	W. Va.
250*	Standard, K 2	Wyo.
207*	Standard City, K 11	Ill.
200	Standardville, I 16	Utah
150	Standing Rock, H 22	Ala.
85	Standing Stone, F 18	Pa.
115*	Standish, D 10	Calif.
500	Standish, P 4	Me.
1692*	Standish, I 22	Mass.
981	Standish, L 20	Mich.
56*	Standish, F 9	Mo.
400*	Standish, D 23	N. Y.
115*	Stanfield, H 7	N. C.
241	Stanfield, C 18	Ore.
482	Stanford, G 14	Ill.
75*	Stanford, M 11	Ind.
1940	Stanford, H 17	Ky.
529	Stanford, H 12	Mont.
720	Stanford University, H 19	Calif.
200	Stanfordville, R 23	N. Y.
425	Stanhope, H 11	Iowa
1100	Stanhope, D 13	N. J.
94*	Stanislaus, H 10	Calif.
70	Stanley, M 10	Idaho
185*	Stanley, F 19	Iowa
200	Stanley, G 25	Kan.
200	Stanley, G 10	Ky.
....	Stanley, I 20	Mass.
190	Stanley, G 14	N. M.
200	Stanley, N 11	N. Y.
1036	Stanley, G 5	N. C.
1058	Stanley, G 6	N. D.
300	Stanley, N 20	Okla.
150*	Stanley, D 8	Ore.
150	Stanley, J 9	Pa.
317	Stanley, H 12	Va.
2021	Stanley, G 12	Wis.
750*	Stanleytown, Q 7	Va.
290	Stanton, I 12	Ala.
1000*	Stanton, R 6	Calif.
400	Stanton, B 21	Del.
571	Stanton, O 6	Iowa
625	Stanton, G 19	Ky.
908	Stanton, N 15	Mich.
250*	Stanton, N 5	Miss.
200	Stanton, K 17	Mo.
1526	Stanton, H 20	Neb.
164*	Stanton, G 11	N. J.
370	Stanton, K 10	N. D.
500*	Stanton, O 3	Tenn.
1245	Stanton F 10	Tex.
....	Stanton Jc., R 5	Calif.
595	Stantonsburg, G 16	N. C.
150	Stantonville, Q 6	Tenn.
569	Stanwood, J 22	Iowa
160	Stanwood, M 14	Mich.
100	Stanwood, G 16	Ohio
600	Stanwood, E 8	Wash.

Pop.	Place, Index	State
20	Staple, M 16	Ark.
234	Staplehurst, L 20	Neb.
2952	Staples, J 10	Minn.
250	Staples, L 17	Tex.
150*	Stapleton, P 7	Ala.
342	Stapleton, H 17	Ga.
399	Stapleton, J 11	Neb.
68*	Stapleton, M 11	Va.
225	Stapp, M 24	Okla.
410	Star, N 4	Idaho
350	Star, L 12	Miss.
5*	Star, G 16	Neb.
611	Star, G 9	N. C.
50	Star, J 23	Okla.
12	Star, K 7	Ore.
75	Star, H 16	Tex.
50*	Starboard, L 22	Me.
....	Starbuck, see Idledale	Colo.
972	Starbuck, L 7	Minn.
251	Starbuck, M 21	Wash.
1090	Star City, N 14	Ark.
550	Star City, E 11	Ind.
1175	Star City, C 14	W. Va.
500	Starford, L 8	Pa.
11*	Stargard, O 20	Wis.
75*	Starhill, J 15	La.
2000*	Star Junction, Q 4	Pa.
....	Stark, M 16	Iowa
160*	Stark, M 23	Kan.
10*	Stark, F 21	Ky.
1*	Stark, H 4	Mont.
53	Stark, E 15	N. H.
15	Stark, N 5	W. Va.
172*	Stark City, Q 6	Mo.
1480	Starke, D 14	Fla.
25*	Starkey, K 5	Idaho
100*	Starkey, O 12	N. Y.
100	Starkey, E 20	Ore.
600*	Starkey, O 6	Va.
....*	Starks (Farmington), C 5	Ark.
500*	Starks, L 5	La.
40	Starks, L 7	Me.
50*	Starks, K 9	Wis.
150	Starksboro, G 8	Vt.
945	Starkville, Q 16	Colo.
4900	Starkville, F 19	Miss.
250	Starkville, M 20	N. Y.
295	Starkweather, F 18	N. D.
75	Starlake, J 7	Wis.
35*	Starlight, F 23	Pa.
38*	Star Lime Works, J 7	Ky.
210	Starners, P 15	Pa.
75*	Starnes (Slant), E 5	Va.
250	Star Prairie, A 11	Wis.
10*	Starr, G 6	Pa.
349	Starr, E 5	S. C.
94*	Starrking, G 15	N. H.
184	Starrsville, G 9	Ga.
340	Starrucca, E 22	Pa.
59*	Start, C 12	La.
105*	Star Tannery, E 13	Va.
300	Startup, G 10	Wash.
34*	Star Valley, F 19	Wis.
....*	State, M 9	Pa.
....	State Capitol, I 12	Okla.
1033	State Center, I 14	Iowa
500*	State College, D 19	Ark.
300*	State College, G 19	Miss.
144*	State College, N 10	N. M.
6226	State College, K 12	Pa.
200	State Farm (Fiticut), J 21	Mass.
60*	State Farm, L 15	Va.
125	State Hospital, M 18	N. D
150	State Hospital (Winnebago), N 16	Wis.
4*	Stateline, G 9	Calif.
157*	State Line (State Line City), H 5	Ind.
....	State Line, O 5	Kan.
32*	State Line, L 4	Ky.
138	State Line, F 2	Mass.
....	State Line, I 20	Minn.
542	State Line, N 22	Miss.
60*	State Line, R 9	N. H.
50	State Line (Northville), Q 13	Pa.
200*	State Line, Q 13	Pa.
40*	State Line Jc., R 12	N. Y.
23*	Staten, H 8	W. Va.
....*	Staten Island, H 6	N. Y.
150	Statenville, P 15	Ga.
100*	State Road, D 6	N. C.
121*	Statesan, N 20	Wis.
300*	State Sanatorium, G 7	Ark.
200*	State Sanatorium (Sanitorium), B 8	Md.
5028	Statesboro, J 20	Ga.
200 *	Statesburg, G 16	S. C.
....*	State School, E 4	N. Y.
900	State Soldiers Home, D 13	Ohio
11440	Statesville, F 6	N. C.
250*	Statesville, M 12	Tenn.
605	Statham, E 11	Ga.
....*	Static, L 16	Tenn.
100*	Station Camp, G 19	Ky.
35*	Station Camp, L 12	Tenn.
36*	Statts Mills, H 5	W. Va.
50*	Stauffer, N 13	Calif.
12	Stauffer, L 15	Ore.
1000	Stauffer (Pershing), O 5	Pa.
4212	Staunton, L 11	Ill.
387	Staunton, K 8	Ind.
87	Staunton, M 10	Ohio
13337	Staunton, J 10	Va.
....	Stave, see Tipple	W. Va.
20*	Stay, H 20	Ky.
1085	Stayton, G 7	Ore.
35*	Stayton, L 9	Tenn.
8*	Stead, D 24	N. M.
200*	Steamboat, D 4	Nev.
385	Steamboat Rock, G 14	Iowa
1613	Steamboat Springs, C 9	Colo.
100	Steamburg, Q 4	N. Y.
50	Steamburg, F 1	Pa.
28*	Steaphead, B 2	Fla.
1200	Stearns, K 17	Ky.
30	Stearnsville, J 2	Wash.
230	Stecker, L 8	Okla.
200*	Stecoah, P 3	N. C.
356*	Stedman, I 14	N. C.
45*	Steedman, I 15	Mo.
210	Steedman, I 11	S. C.
100	Steeds, G 9	N. C.
50	Steel, J 20	Ohio
250*	Steele, E 16	Ala.
5	Steele, D 20	Ill.
1585	Steele, K 24	Mo.
721	Steele, N 14	N. D.
291	Steele City, O 21	Neb.
213*	Steeles Store, J 20	Tex.
78*	Steeles Tavern, K 10	Va.
1212	Steeleville, O 12	Ill.
406	Steelmanville, P 14	N. J.
....	Steelton, I 22	Ill.
13115	Steelton, N 16	Pa.
1013	Steelville, L 16	Mo.
40*	Steelville, P 20	Pa.
200*	Steen, R 4	Minn.
175*	Steens, F 22	Miss.
415	Steep Falls, P 4	Me.
18*	Steff, H 11	Ky.
100	Steffenville, D 15	Mo.
3369	Steger, D 22	Ill.
38	Stehekin, G 13	Wash.
832	Steilacoom, J 7	Wash.
4	Stein, N 23	Neb.
207	Steinauer, O 22	Neb.
60*	Steiner, F 18	Tex.
300	Steinhatchee, E 10	Fla.
225*	Steinman, C 6	Va.
100	Steins, O 1	N. M.
68*	Steinsburg, M 22	Pa.
100*	Steinsville, L 21	Pa.
10	Steirman, N 6	Idaho
225*	Stella, C 14	Ark.
34*	Stella, G 21	Ky.
221	Stella, Q 7	Mo.
396	Stella, N 24	Neb.
200*	Stella, Q 16	N. Y.
50*	Stella, J 19	N. C.
12	Stella, J 13	Okla.
16*	Stella, Q 6	Va.
17	Stella, N 5	Wash.
200*	Stella, Niagara, R 15	N. Y.
89*	Stellaville, H 18	Ga.
81*	Stelton, G 16	N. J.
218	Stem, D 13	N. C.
630	Stemmers Run, F 15	Md.
250	Stendal, P 8	Ind.
25*	Stennett, N 6	Iowa
150	Stephan, J 15	S. D.
673	Stephen, C 2	Minn.
....*	Stephen Creek, J 23	Tex.
998	Stephens, P 9	Ark.
116*	Stephens, F 13	Ga.
106*	Stephens, F 22	Ky.
100*	Stephensburg, H 13	Ky.
82*	Stephensburg, D 14	N. J.
600	Stephens City, E 13	Va.
218	Stephens Mills, P 9	N. Y.
....	Stephens Mine, F 20	Minn.
612	Stephenson, H 6	Mich.
....	Stephenson, O 5	Miss.
58*	Stephenson, E 14	Va.
151	Stephensport, F 12	Ky.
200	Stephensville, N 14	Wis.
250	Stephentown, O 24	N. Y.
205*	Stephentown Center, O 25	N. Y.
4768	Stephenville, F 16	Tex.
1200	Stepney Depot, M 6	Conn.
28*	Steprock, F 15	Ark.
415*	Steppville, D 12	Ala.
25	Stepstone, F 19	Ky.
60*	Steptoe, G 20	Nev.
172	Steptoe, K 23	Wash.
250	Sterley, B 11	Tex.
7411	Sterling, C 20	Colo.
590	Sterling, F 25	Conn.
124*	Sterling, N 23	Ga.
250*	Sterling, O 18	Idaho
1363	Sterling, C 12	Ill.
2215	Sterling, J 14	Kan.
500*	Sterling (Loring), E 14	Mass.
350	Sterling, K 18	Mich.
640	Sterling, N 22	Neb.
110	Sterling, N 13	N. D.
381	Sterling, F 16	Ohio
430	Sterling, M 9	Okla.
50	Sterling, H 23	Pa.
223	Sterling, J 12	Utah
250*	Sterling, F 16	Va.
....	Sterling, M 6	W. Va.
1000	Sterling City, G 11	Tex.
225	Sterling Forest, B 17	N. J.
50*	Sterling Forest, E 4	N. Y.
....	Sterling Jc., E 13	Mass.
430	Sterling Run, H 11	Pa.
15	Sterling Station, K 12	N. Y.
600	Sterlington, B 11	La.
150	Sterlington, F 4	N. Y.
125*	Sterlingville, G 16	N. Y.
250*	Sterrett, F 15	Ala.
10*	Sterretts Gap, N 15	Pa.
40*	Stet, F 8	Mo.
116*	Stetlersville, L 22	Pa.
125	Stetson, K 12	Me.
250	Stetsonville, H 11	Wis.
1825▲*	Stettin, J 12	Wis.
400	Steuben, M 19	Me.
105*	Steuben, F 14	Mich.
262	Steuben, G 20	Wis.
65	Steubenville, B 22	Ind.
38*	Steubenville, J 17	Ky.
37651	Steubenville, I 20	Ohio
359*	Steve, H 8	Ark.
700*	Stevens (Silver Grove), C 18	Ky.
275	Stevens, O 19	Pa.
30	Stevens, Q 25	S. D.
8*	Stevens, B 3	Tex.
85*	Stevensburg, I 15	Va.
30	Stevens Crossing, I 19	Ga.
793	Stevenson, A 18	Ala.
50*	Stevenson, N 5	Conn.
50*	Stevenson, G 21	Ky.
152*	Stevenson, E 13	Md.
226	Stevenson, F 17	Minn.
563	Stevenson, P 9	Wash.
15777	Stevens Point, K 14	Wis.
200*	Stevens Pottery, I 13	Ga.
400	Stevensville, I 16	Md.
382	Stevensville, Q 10	Mich.
703	Stevensville, J 4	Mont.
70	Stevensville, F 19	Pa.
86*	Stevensville, L 19	Va.
50*	Stevinson, I 9	Calif.
244	Steward, C 15	Ill.
....	Steward Jc., C 15	Ill.
659	Stewardson, K 16	Ill.
250	Stewart, H 8	Ala.
15	Stewart, G 6	Ind.
30*	Stewart, H 24	Ky.
636	Stewart, O 11	Minn.
241*	Stewart, F 14	Miss.
15*	Stewart, I 24	Mo.
412	Stewart, H 3	Nev.
25	Stewart, O 21	N. Y.
311	Stewart, N 16	Ohio
275	Stewart, L 8	Tenn.
....	Stewart, see Postville	Wis.
....	Stewart, N 23	Wyo.
10	Stewart, O 21	N. Y.
545*	Stewart Heights, K 22	Tex.
30*	Stewarts Point, A 15	Calif.
65	Stewartstown, C 14	N. H.
985	Stewartstown, Q 18	Pa.
250	Stewartsville, Q 3	Ind.
50	Stewartsville, D 17	Ky.
478	Stewartsville, D 6	Mo.
1100	Stewartsville, E 9	N. J.
325	Stewartsville, K 19	Ohio
1025	Stewartville, Q 19	Minn.
75*	Steyer, N 2	Md.
120	Stibnite, K 8	Idaho
11	Stickley, C 23	Mich.
2446*	Stickney, C 21	Ill.
5*	Stickney, L 14	Mo.
361	Stickney, M 19	S. D.
800*	Stickney, O 8	W. Va.
31*	Stidham, F 23	Ky.
103	Stidham, I 20	Okla.
1861	Stigler, J 22	Okla.
33*	Stiles, H 14	Ky.
....	Stiles, L 9	Minn.
200*	Stiles, Q 4	N. C.
16	Stiles, Q 24	N. D.
721*	Stiles, L 22	Pa.
161	Stiles, H 10	Tex.
75*	Stiles, O 12	Wis.
48*	Stilesboro, E 4	Ga.
75	Stiles Jc., O 12	Wis.
273	Stilesville, J 11	Ind.
11	Still, L 12	N. D.
17*	Stille, I 8	La.
333	Stillman Valley, B 14	Ill.
493	Stillmore, J 18	Ga.
32*	Stillmore, Q 17	Miss.
270	Still Pond, E 18	Md.
511	Still River, I 4	Conn.
323	Still River, D 14	Mass.
....	Stillman, F 9	Mich.
51*	Stillwater, G 20	Ky.
475	Stillwater, K 15	Me.
7013	Stillwater, N 18	Minn.
29	Stillwater, G 7	Nev.
200*	Stillwater, B 14	N. J.
971*	Stillwater, M 24	N. Y.
160	Stillwater, I 18	Ohio
10097	Stillwater, F 13	Okla.
200*	Stillwater, I 18	Pa.
200	Stillwater, C 13	R. I.
20	Stillwater, H 9	Wash
75	Stillwater Jc., L 7	Ohio
200*	Stillwell, J 24	Ga.
100	Stillwell, H 5	Ill.
229	Stillwell, B 12	Ind.
160*	Stilson, J 21	Ga.
100*	Stiltner, M 2	W. Va.
400	Stilwell, H 25	Kan.
1717	Stillwell, G 25	Okla.
....	Stimson, J 5	Wash.
337	Stinesville, L 10	Ind.
30*	Stingray Point, L 20	Va.
5	Stinnett, I 20	Ky.
635	Stinnett, B 4	Tex.
23*	Stinson, H 8	W. Va.
159*	Stinson Beach, I 4	Calif.
50	Stinson Lake, K 11	N. H.
30*	Stipek, G 23	Mont.
200	Stippville, N 24	Kan.
1400	Stirling, F 15	N. J.
450	Stirling City, E 7	Calif.
1000	Stirrat, O 4	W. Va.
135	Stirum, P 21	N. D.
25	Stissing, R 24	N. Y.
258	Stites, H 7	Idaho
....	Stithton, see Fort Knox	Ky.
350	Stittville, L 18	N. Y.
170	Stitzer, G 20	Wis.
26*	Stoakley, M 14	Md.
443	Stockbridge, G 8	Ga.
1500	Stockbridge, F 2	Mass.
852	Stockbridge, P 19	Mich.
150	Stockbridge, M 16	N. Y.
300	Stockbridge, J 10	Vt.
386	Stockbridge, O 16	Wis.
120*	Stockdale, F 18	Kan.
300	Stockdale, P 12	Ohio
907*	Stockdale, O 2	Pa.
926	Stockdale, M 17	Tex.
729	Stockertown, K 23	Pa.
500	Stockett, G 10	Mont.
197	Stockham, M 18	Neb.
1021	Stockholm, B 18	Me.
200	Stockholm, B 15	N. J.
114	Stockholm, F 24	S. D.
179	Stockholm, C 14	Wis.
171	Stockland, G 22	Ill.
30*	Stockley, K 22	Del.
100*	Stockman, G 24	Tex.
338	Stockport, O 19	Iowa
300*	Stockport, P 24	N. Y.
422	Stockport, M 16	Ohio
1100	Stockton, O 7	Ala.
54714	Stockton, H 8	Calif.
220	Stockton, O 14	Ga.
1440	Stockton, A 11	Ill.
134	Stockton, L 22	Iowa
1418	Stockton, E 9	Kan.
390*	Stockton (Stockton Springs), M 14	Me.
400	Stockton (Hursley), Q 23	Md.
180*	Stockton, P 23	Minn.
801	Stockton, M 8	Mo.
478	Stockton, H 10	N. J.
300	Stockton, P 2	N. Y.
86*	Stockton, N 6	Ohio
610*	Stockton, J 20	Pa.
163*	Stockton (Ben Stockton), L 16	Tenn.
332	Stockton, F 9	Utah
75*	Stockton (Burnt Chimneys), R 8	Va.
400*	Stockton Springs (Stockton), M 14	Me.
238	Stockville, N 11	Neb.
75*	Stockville, O 7	N. C.
513	Stockwell, H 10	Ind.
21	Stoddard, O 19	Neb.
218▲	Stoddard, P 9	N. H.
368	Stoddard, F 17	Wis.
18*	Stoddartsville, I 21	Pa.
150*	Stoffel, K 7	W. Va.
9	Stoil, L 13	Calif.
13*	Stokes, J 11	Miss.
216*	Stokes, F 19	N. C.
40*	Stokes, M 15	S. C.
32*	Stokes, Q 12	Wis.
1582▲*	Stokesbridge, F 17	S. C.
238	Stokesdale, D 9	N. C.
40	Stokesdale, F 15	Pa.
100	Stokesland, R 9	Va.
350*	Stollings, O 4	W. Va.
150	Stone, R 17	Idaho
996	Stone, H 24	Ky.
14*	Stone K 15	Ohio
313	Stonebluff, H 8	Ind.
155	Stonebluff, G 19	Okla.
1194	Stoneboro, H 3	Pa.
350	Stone Branch, M 4	W. Va.
112*	Stoneburg, C 17	Tex.
125*	Stone Church, K 24	Pa.
100	Stone City, L 15	Colo.
200	Stone City, I 21	Iowa
206*	Stone Cliff, N 9	W. Va.
100*	Stoneco, R 23	N. Y.
300*	Stonecoal, N 2	W. Va.
214*	Stone Creek, I 17	Ohio
524	Stonefort, Q 17	Ill.
1650	Stonega, D 4	Va.
100	Stoneham, C 19	Colo.
10765▲	Stoneham, E 19	Mass.
400	Stoneham, J 21	Tex.
383	Stoneharbor, R 13	N. J.
119*	Stonehenge, P 13	Pa.
25*	Stone Hill, M 16	Mo.
150	Stone Lake, D 8	Wis.
60*	Stoneham Lake, H 15	Ariz.
1408	Stone Mtn., F 8	Ga.
40*	Stone Mtn., N 8	Va.
636*	Stone Park, C 21	Ill.
50*	Stoner, P 3	Colo.
350*	Stone Ridge, R 22	N. Y.
50*	Stonersville, N 21	Pa.
165	Stoneville, G 6	Miss.
615	Stoneville, C 8	N. C.
9*	Stoneville, H 5	S. D.
84*	Stonewall, B 20	Ark.
200*	Stonewall, G 5	Ga.
300*	Stonewall, D 4	La.
2400	Stonewall, K 20	Miss.
261	Stonewall, I 21	N. C.
761	Stonewall, M 16	Okla.
96*	Stonewall, J 16	Tex.
65	Stonington, P 23	Colo.
1826	Stonington, M 24	Conn.
1103	Stonington, J 15	Ill.
20*	Stonington, D 22	Ky.
1000	Stonington, N 15	Me.
410	Stonington, G 9	Mich.
200*	Stony Bottom, K 15	W. Va.
819	Stony Brook, G 8	N. Y.
950	Stony Creek, N 13	Conn.
270*	Stony Creek, K 23	N. Y.
493	Stony Creek, P 17	Va.
750*	Stony Creek Mills, N 21	Pa.
75	Stonyford, F 5	Calif.
175*	Stony Fork, D 3	N. C.
38*	Stony Hill, J 16	Mo.
2700	Stony Point, F 5	N. Y.
1000	Stony Point, E 4	N. C.
33*	Stony Point, J 13	Va.
300	Stony Ridge, D 9	Ohio
95*	Stony Run, L 21	Pa.
23*	Stop, K 16	Ky.
115*	Storck, I 16	Va.
331	Storden, Q 7	Minn.
13	Storla, K 19	S. D.
5274	Storm Lake, F 6	Iowa
4*	Stormont, M 20	Va.
50*	Storms, N 11	Ohio
157*	Stormville, D 6	N. Y.
....*	Storrie, E 9	Calif.
200	Storrs, E 19	Conn.
....	Storrs, see Spring Canyon	Utah
28*	Story, J 7	Ark.
15	Story, L 12	Okla.
175	Story, C 15	Wyo.
1479	Story City, H 12	Iowa
102*	Stotesbury, L 6	Mo.
200*	Stotesbury, P 7	W. Va.
25*	Stotlers Cross Roads, D 23	W. Va.
268	Stotts City, O 8	Mo.
1079	Stottville, P 24	N. Y.
450*	Stouchsburg, M 19	Pa.
8632■	Stoughton, H 19	Mass.
4743	Stoughton, L 20	Wis.
....	Stoughton Jc., H 19	Mass.
135*	Stout, G 15	Iowa
169	Stout, Q 11	Ohio
244	Stoutland, L 12	Mo.
50*	Stouts Mills, H 10	W. Va.
179	Stoutsville, E 15	Mo.
509	Stoutsville, L 12	Ohio
200	Stovall, C 12	Ga.
415	Stovall, C 14	N. C.
41*	Stovall, E 9	La.
55*	Stovall, C 8	Miss.
125*	Stover, D 11	Miss.
584	Stover, J 11	Mo.
130*	Stow, N 2	Me.
700	Stow, E 16	Mass.
56*	Stow, Q 2	N. Y.
2500*	Stow, E 17	Ohio
12577■*	Stowe, L 3	Pa.
2000*	Stowe, N 22	Pa.
540	Stowe, E 11	Vt.
75*	Stowell, K 24	Tex.
....	Stowers, Q 7	N. D.
150	Stoy, L 21	Ill.
461	Stoystown, O 8	Pa.
1700*	Strabane, O 2	Pa.
150*	Strader (Tallmansville), H 13	W. Va.
175	Strafford, O 10	Mo.
500	Strafford, N 17	N. H.
300*	Strafford, O 21	Pa.
96	Strafford, J 14	Vt.
70*	Strahan, O 5	Iowa
160	Straight, G 9	Pa.
175	Straight Creek, K 20	Ky.
....	Straight Line Jc., Q 6	Ind.
170*	Straits, K 21	N. C.
57*	Straits Corner, Q 14	N. Y.
....	Straits Pond, P 9	Mass.
205	Strandburg, F 24	S. D.
43	Strandell, B 8	Wash.
180*	Strandquist, C 4	Minn.
110	Strang, N 19	Neb.
283	Strang, D 22	Okla.
135*	Strange Creek, J 9	W. Va.
....	Strasburg, H 13	Ala.
216	Strasburg, F 17	Colo.
435	Strasburg, K 17	Ill.
153*	Strasburg, I 7	Mo.
994	Strasburg, Q 14	N. D.
1297	Strasburg, H 17	Ohio
1048	Strasburg, P 19	Pa.
1968	Strasburg, F 13	Va.
125	Strasburg Jc., F 13	Va.
36	Strassel, C 6	Ore.
104*	Strata, K 16	Ala.
550	Stratford, K 11	Calif.
22580■	Stratford, O 8	Conn.
712	Stratford, H 11	Iowa
300	Stratford (Mapleton), E 14	N. H.
980	Stratford, L 10	N. J.
200*	Stratford, L 20	N. Y.
48*	Stratford, C 4	N. C.
80*	Stratford, I 12	Ohio
896	Stratford, L 14	Okla.
203	Stratford, E 19	S. D.
877	Stratford, A 3	Tex.
26*	Stratford, J 19	Va.
80	Stratford, I 18	Wash.
879	Stratford, I 13	Wis.
200	Stratham, P 20	N. H.
114*	Strathcona, C 5	Minn.
100	Strathmere, Q 14	N. J.
....*	Strathmoor, P 22	Mich.
1000*	Strathmore, L 13	Calif.
....	Strathmore, L 13	Va.
604	Strattanville (Strattonville), I 6	Pa.
623	Stratton, H 22	Colo.
....	Stratton, N 17	Ill.
601	Stratton, J 5	Me.
127*	Stratton, J 18	Miss.
630	Stratton, O 9	Neb.
597*	Stratton, H 20	Ohio
4	Stratton, D 12	S. D.
50*	Stratton, C 6	Va.
604	Strattonville (Strattanville), I 6	Pa.
40	Straubville, Q 21	N. D.
275	Straughn (Strawns), J 20	Ind.
100	Strauss, P 10	N. M.
339	Strausstown, M 19	Pa.
150*	Straven, G 12	Ala.
39*	Straw, I 12	Ky.
50	Straw, I 13	Mont.
110*	Strawberry, D 17	Ark.
25*	Strawberry, F 14	Ky.
50*	Strawberry, I 17	Ky.
125*	Strawberry, L 18	S. C.
400	Strawberry Plains, M 20	Tenn.
1223*	Strawberry Point, F20	Iowa
53*	Strawberry Ridge, I 17	Pa.
53*	Strawberry Valley, F 8	Calif.
199	Strawn, G 18	Ill.
187*	Strawn, J 21	Kan.
1107	Strawn, E 16	Tex.
14930	Streator, E 17	Ill.
4	Streator Jc., F 14	Ill.
35*	Street, C 16	Md.
647	Streeter, N 16	N. D.
85*	Streeter, I 14	Tex.
50*	Streeter, P 9	W. Va.
392	Streetman, G 20	Tex.
....	Streets, see Remlik	Va.
35	Strevell, R 16	Idaho
40*	Stribling, L 7	Tenn.
150	Strickland, M 7	Me.
17*	Strickland (Kalish), F 9	Wis.
49*	Strickler, D 4	Ark.
50*	Stricklett, D 21	Ky.
170*	Strieby, G 9	N. C.
300	Stringer, L 17	Miss.
150*	Stringtown, F 6	Miss.
718	Stringtown, N 18	Okla.
150*	Strobleton, H 6	Pa.
430	Stroh, B 20	Ind.
12	Strohm, C 16	Okla.
1127	Stromsburg, K 19	Neb.
156	Stronach, K 11	Mich.
4	Stroner, B 20	Wyo.
762	Strong, R 12	Ark.
848	Strong (Strong City), I 19	Kan.
500	Strong, L 6	Me.
118*	Strong, E 21	Miss.
....*	Strong (Sagon), K 17	Pa.
245	Strong City, H 2	Okla.
691	Stronghurst, F 6	Ill.
762	Strongs, F 16	Mich.
30*	Strongs Prairie, I 16	Wis.
100*	Strongstown, L 6	Pa.
2216	Strongsville, Q 21	Ohio
162	Strontia Springs, H 14	Colo.
50	Strool, D 5	S. D.
63*	Strother, E 12	S. C.
125	Stroud (Strouds) H 21	Ala.
1917	Stroud, G 16	Okla.
....*	Strouds, K 12	W. Va.
6186	Stroudsburg, J 23	Pa.
6404*	Stroudsburg (E. Stroudsburg), I 23	Pa.
....	Stroup, H 9	Pa.
134	Struble, E 2	Iowa
450	Strum, E 14	Wis.
128*	Strunk, K 17	Ky.
11739	Struthers, F 21	Ohio
29	Stryker, C 3	Mont.
929	Stryker, D 7	Ohio
89*	Stryker (Pluck), H 23	Tex.
300	Strykersville, N 6	N. Y.
15*	Stuart, B 16	Ark.
2438	Stuart, K 23	Fla.
1611	Stuart, L 9	Iowa
....	Stuart, K 7	Mont.
760	Stuart, F 15	Neb.
340	Stuart, L 18	Okla.
720	Stuart, Q 5	Va.
250	Stuarts Draft, K 10	Va.
46*	Stuckey, K 16	Ga.
310	Studa, N 1	Pa.
175	Studebaker, Q 5	Calif.
100*	Studley, F 7	Kan.
102*	Studley, L 18	Va.
30	Stukel, R 10	Ore.
19*	Stultz, O 14	Mo.
500*	Stump Creek (Cramer), I 7	Pa.
102*	Stumptown, H 9	W. Va.
250*	Stumpville, D 2	Calif.
300	Stumpy Point, F 24	N. C.
2227▲	Sturbridge, H 12	Mass.
....	Sturdivant, H 18	Ala.
103*	Sturdivant, P 22	Mo.
571	Sturgeon, G 13	Mo.
950*	Sturgeon, L 2	Pa.
5439	Sturgeon Bay, Q 12	Wis.
215	Sturgeon Lake, J 18	Minn.
....*	Sturgeonville, Q 15	Va.
54*	Sturges, D 9	Mo.
50*	Sturgills, B 3	N. C.
2321	Sturgis, H 7	Ky.
7214	Sturgis, R 14	Mich.
485	Sturgis, G 18	Miss.
3008	Sturgis, H 3	S. D.
....	Sturgiss City, see Sabraton	W. Va.
12	Sturgisson, C 15	W. Va.
110*	Sturkie, A 14	Ark.
5725*	Sturmerville, I 20	Pa.
803	Sturtevant (Corliss), P 22	Wis.
5628	Stuttgart, K 16	Ark.
78*	Stuttgart, D 9	Kan.
400	Stuyvesant, P 23	N. Y.
390	Stuyvesant Falls, P 24	N. Y.
200	Suamico (Big Suamico), O 13	Wis.
202*	Subiaco, G 7	Ark.
140	Sublett, Q 16	Idaho
84*	Sublett, G 21	Ky.
282	Sublette, D 14	Ill.
582	Sublette, N 5	Kan.
10*	Subletts, M 15	Va.
150*	Subligna, C 3	Ga.
250	Sublime, L 19	Tex.
280	Sublimity, F 7	Ore.
....*	Submarine Base (U.S. Submarine Base), I 21	Conn.
50*	Subtle, J 14	Ky.
100	Sucarnoochee, I 22	Miss.
618	Succasunna, D 14	N. J.
281	Success, A 19	Ark.
54*	Success, N 14	Mo.
18*	Success, F 14	Va.
27*	Suches, C 9	Ga.
974	Sudan, B 8	Tex.
300	Sudbury, E 16	Mass.
100	Sudbury, J 6	Vt.
27*	Sudith, F 20	Ky.
292	Sudlersville, G 19	Md.
165*	Sudley, H 15	Md.
350	Suedburg, M 18	Pa.
3768	Suffern, F 5	N. Y.
50	Suffield, Q 17	Colo.
1150	Suffield, B 14	Conn.
150	Suffield, F 18	Ohio
350	Suffolk, G 14	Mont.
11343	Suffolk, Q 20	Va.
697	Sugar (Sugar City), N 21	Idaho
50*	Sugar Bush, M 14	Wis.
300	Sugar Camp, J 11	Pa.
565	Sugar City, L 19	Colo.
1638	Sugar Creek, G 6	Mo.
836	Sugarcreek, H 17	Ohio
214	Sugar Grove, H 6	Ark.
200*	Sugar Grove, C 18	Ill.
39*	Sugar Grove, J 11	Ky.
215	Sugar Grove, C 2	N. C.
429	Sugar Grove, M 13	Ohio
440	Sugargrove, E 6	Pa.
250*	Sugar Grove, D 10	Va.
500*	Sugar Grove, J 17	W. Va.
599*	Sugar Hill, E 9	Ga.
500	Sugar Hill, H 11	N. H.
6*	Sugar Island, H 10	Me.
300	Sugarite, B 20	N. M.
2400	Sugar Land, L 22	Tex.
....	Sugarloaf, E 13	Colo.
115*	Sugar Loaf, E 4	N. Y.
500*	Sugarloaf (Gum Run), J 20	Pa.
2505	Sugar Notch, I 20	Pa.
80*	Sugar Ridge, D 9	Ohio
100	Sugar Run, F 19	Pa.
56*	Sugartown, J 7	La.
50	Sugar Tree, N 7	Tenn.
76*	Sugar Tree Ridge, O 9	Ohio
239	Sugar Valley, C 3	Ga.
20*	Sugar Valley, E 9	W. Va.
65	Sugarville, J 7	Utah
171	Sugden, P 10	Okla.
260	Suggsville, M 7	Ala.
52	Suggsville (Allen), M 7	Ala.
706	Suisun-Fairfield (Suisun City), A 21, H 6	Calif.
100*	Suit, Q 2	N. C.
125	Suiter, C 11, O 1	Va.
100	Sula, L 4	Mont.
1287	Sulligent, E 5	Ala.
32	Sullivan, G 15	Colo.
3101	Sullivan, J 17	Ill.
5077	Sullivan, M 6	Ind.
200*	Sullivan, H 7	Ky.
120	Sullivan, M 18	Me.
2517	Sullivan, K 17	Mo.
75	Sullivan, P 8	N. H.
267	Sullivan, F 15	Ohio
110*	Sullivan, O 8	W. Va.
286	Sullivan, M 20	Wis.
....*	Sullivan City, P 4	Tex.
402	Sully, L 15	Iowa
75*	Sully, H 15	W. Va.
27*	Sulphur, Q 12	Ind.
300	Sulphur, D 15	Ky.
3504	Sulphur, M 6	La.
36	Sulphur, D 7	Nev.
4970	Sulphur, N 14	Okla.
3	Sulphur, G 5	S. D.
150*	Sulphur Bluff, C 22	Tex.
80*	Sulphur City, C 5	Ark.
40	Sulphurdale, M 7	Utah
....	Sulphur Hill, see Geneva	Ind.
60*	Sulphur Lick, K 14	Ky.
281	Sulphur Rock, E 16	Ark.
435	Sulphur Springs, A 4	Ark.
235	Sulphur Springs (Hot Sulphur Springs), E 11	Colo.
3000	Sulphur Springs, I 12	Fla.
75*	Sulphur Springs, C 1	Ga.
292	Sulphur Springs, I 19	Ind.
50*	Sulphur Springs, F 6	Iowa
150	Sulphur Springs, J 20	Mo.
260	Sulphur Springs(Annapolis), G 12	Ohio
6742	Sulphur Springs, D 21	Tex.
80*	Sulphur Well, J 14	Ky.
961	Sultan, G 10	Wash.
200*	Sultana, K 13	Calif.
650	Sumas, B 8	Wash.
300*	Sumatra, C 2, O 12	Fla.
300	Sumatra, I 18	Mont.
75*	Sumerco, L 3	W. Va.
50*	Sumerduck, I 15	Va.
900*	Sumiton, E 10	Ala.
5	Summer Camp, B 21	Nev.
239*	Summerdale, Q 7	Ala.
600*	Summerdale, O 14	Pa.
150	Summerfield, J 11	Ala.
500	Summerfield, F 15	Fla.
283	Summerfield, M 12	Ill.
396	Summerfield, C 19	Kan.
200*	Summerfield, A 8	La.
167*	Summerfield, K 15	Mo.
595*	Summerfield, D 9	N. C.
372	Summerfield, L 18	Ohio
64*	Summerfield, L 23	Okla.
55*	Summerfield, E 2	Tex.
150	Summerfield, F 22	Tex.
200	Summerford, K 9	Ohio
150*	Summer Hill, J 6	Ill.
785*	Summerhill, M 8	Pa.
100	Summer Lake, L 13	Ore.
300	Summerland, N 12	Calif.
225*	Summerland, L 15	Miss.
36*	Summerlee, M 8	W. Va.
70*	Summers, C 3	Ark.
80	Summerset, L 12	Iowa
250	Summer Shade, J 14	Ky.
306	Summersville, O 15	Mo.
643	Summersville, L 10	W. Va.
958	Summerton, I 17	S. C.
148*	Summertown, I 18	Ga.
510	Summertown, P 9	Tenn.
1358	Summerville, C 2	Ga.
200*	Summerville, F 11	La.
80	Summerville, D 21	Ore.
1009	Summerville, I 6	Pa.
3023	Summerville, M 17	S. C.
85*	Summit, D 15	Ala.
198	Summit (Yellville), B 11	Ark.
125	Summit, N 17	Calif.
....	Summit, J 15	Colo.
1019*	Summit (Twin City) (Summit-Graymont), J 19	Ga.
7043*	Summit, C 21	Ill.
75*	Summit, G 13	Ky.
1254	Summit, O 9	Miss.
16165	Summit, E 17	N. J.
89	Summit, O 20	N. Y.
100	Summit, C 4	N. C.
1019	Summit and Graymont (Twin City), J 19	Ga.
300	Summit (Summit Sta.), K 13	Ohio
57*	Summit (Summithill), N 11	Ohio
....	Summit, H 21	Okla.
48	Summit, G 4	Ore.
150	Summit, H 7	R. I.
73*	Summit, H 11	S. C.
459	Summit, E 23	S. D.
146	Summit, O 6	Utah
91*	Summit (Walden Heights), E 16	Vt.
50*	Summit, J 17	Va.
1000*	Summit City (Toyon), D 6	Calif.
50*	Summit City, I 12	Mich.
5406*	Summit Hill, K 20	Pa.
75*	Summit Lake, L 10	Wis.
219	Summit Mills, Q 7	Pa.
125*	Summit Point, N 25	Utah
200	Summit Point, E 25	W. Va.
100*	Summit Sta. (Hammon), M 19	Pa.
991	Summitville, G 17	Ind.
300	Summitville, D 3	N. Y.
120*	Summitville, G 19	Ohio
250*	Summitville, O 13	Tenn.
194	Summum, H 9	Ill.
147	Sumner, E 11	Fla.
340	Sumner, M 10	Ga.
1070	Sumner, M 21	Ill.
1752	Sumner, E 18	Iowa
75*	Sumner, K 18	Ky.
63	Sumner, M 5	Me.
200	Sumner, M 15	Mich.
622	Sumner, D 10	Miss.
338	Sumner, E 10	Mo.
296	Sumner, L 14	Neb.
9*	Sumner, O 16	Ohio
80	Sumner, D 14	Okla.
50	Sumner, M 3	Ore.
200*	Sumner, B 21	Tex.
2140	Sumner, J 8	Wash.
300*	Sumneytown, N 22	Pa.
7	Sumpter, B 13	Okla.
420	Sumpter, G 20	Ore.
819	Sumrall, N 15	Miss.
200	Sumter, G 11	Ala.
100*	Sumter, L 8	Ga.
50*	Sumter, M 12	Minn.
15874	Sumter, H 17	S. C.

Pop.	Place	Index	State
....	Sumter Jc.	H 15	S. C.
150	Sumterville	I 4	Ala.
125	Sumterville (Sumpterville)	G 15	Fla.
250	Sun	K 19	La.
63	*Sun	K 16	Miss.
500	Sun	N 8	W. Va.
800	Sunapee	M 9	N. H.
100	*Sunapee (Weedell)	M 9	N. H.
11	Sunbeam	C 4	Colo.
30	*Sunbeam	L 12	Idaho
200	Sunbright	M 17	Tenn.
52	*Sunbright (Hortons Summit)	E 5	Va.
135	*Sunburg	M 8	Minn.
709	Sunburst	C 9	Mont.
60	*Sunbury	K 22	Iowa
225	Sunbury	C 21	N. C.
846	Sunbury	J 12	Ohio
15462	Sunbury	K 16	Pa.
85	*Sun City (Ross)	J 13	Fla.
305	*Sun City	N 11	Kan.
3000	Suncook	O 15	N. H.
238	*Suncrest	I 13	W. Va.
33	Sundale	P 14	Wash.
685	Sundance	C 22	Wyo.
21	*Sundell (Dorsey)	F 12	Mich.
400	*Sunderland	K 15	Md.
1000	Sunderland	E 8	Mass.
75	Sunderland	O 7	Vt.
26	*Sundown	B 3, R 20	N. Y.
90	*Sundown	C 9	Tex.
348	Sunfield	O 14	Mich.
45	*Sunfish	I 12	Ky.
100	*Sunflower	N 6	Ala.
630	Sunflower	F 9	Miss.
37	*Suniland (Fant City)	O 17	Tex.
....	*Sunkist	P 21	Okla.
....	*Sunland	N 15	Calif.
21	*Sunlight	N 11	W. Va.
352	Sunman	L 20	Ind.
50	*Sunmount	E 21	N. Y.
50	*Sunnybank	K 22	Va.
50	*Sunnybrook	K 16	Ky.
60	*Sunnyburn	Q 18	Pa.
24	*Sunnydale	H 11	Ky.
58	*Sunny Hill	J 17	La.
31	*Sunnylane	J 11	Ky.
100	*Sunnymead	O 21	Calif.
....	Sunnyside	Q 17	Ark.
123	Sunny Side	G 7	Ga.
4	Sunnyside	O 6	Idaho
26	Sunnyside	J 12	Ky.
210	*Sunny Side (Milesville)	N 4	Pa.
125	*Sunny Side	K 21	Tex.
424	Sunnyside	I 19	Utah
34	*Sunny Side	N 14	Va.
300	*Sunnyside	N 9	Fla.
2368	Sunnyside	N 15	Wash.
24	Sunnyside Jc.	N 14	Wash.
250	*Sunny South	L 8	Ala.
4373	Sunnyvale	H 22	Calif.
350	Sunol	F 24, I 6	Calif.
110	Sunol	K 4	Neb.
3	Sun Prairie	F 17	Mont.
1625	Sun Prairie	K 19	Wis.
1200	*Sunray (Altman)	B 3	Tex.
72	*Sunrise	D 18	Ky.
100	*Sunrise	L 18	Minn.
360	Sunrise	L 22	Wyo.
....	*Sunrise Beach	K 12	Mo.
2	*Sunrise Lodge	K 9	Wash.
59	Sun River	G 9	Mont.
100	Sunset	M 21	Ariz.
47	*Sunset	D 5	Ark.
19	Sunset	E 13	Colo.
50	Sunset	D 7	Idaho
630	Sunset	L 11	La.
150	Sunset	N 15	Me.
100	*Sunset	B 5	S. C.
665	Sunset	C 17	Tex.
276	Sunset	D 11	Utah
90	Sunset	J 23	Wash.
150	*Sunset Beach	P 16	Calif.
....	Sunset Heights	K 23	Tex.
72	*Sunset Hills (Wiehle)	F 17	Va.
....	*Sunshine	J 21	Ky.
200	*Sunshine	K 15	La.
160	*Sunshine	N 16	Me.
60	*Sunshine	C 7	Wyo.
35	Sunshine Valley	B 15	N. M.
63	*Sunside	P 22	N. Y.
16	Suntex	L 16	Ore.
....	Sunvale	J 19	Fla.
300	Sun Valley	N 12	Idaho
4000	Superior	K 16	Ariz.
205	Superior	F 14	Colo.
230	Superior	B 7	Iowa
350	Superior	G 3	Mont.
2650	Superior	O 18	Neb.
300	Superior	Q 13	Ohio
....	Superior	Q 14	Ohio
500	Superior	Q 6	W. Va.
35136	Superior	C 4	Wis.
1240	Superior	O 8	Wyo.
60	*Superior Station (Iron Mountain)		Mont.
75	Suplee	J 16	Ore.
25	Suplee	O 21	Pa.
250	*Supply	A 18	Ark.
110	*Supply	N 15	N. C.
414	Supply	C 3	Okla.
16	*Supply	J 18	Va.
691	Suquamish	H 7	Wash.
....	*Surber	M 7	Va.
100	Surf	N 9	Calif.
129	*Surf City	K 17	N. J.
295	*Surfside	O 22	Fla.
40	*Surginer	K 8	Ala.
250	Surgoinsville	L 22	Tenn.
437	Suring	N 12	Wis.
....	*Surosa	O 3	W. Va.
228	Surprise	K 20	Neb.
110	*Surprise	P 23	N. Y.
431	Surrency	M 19	Ga.
187	Surrey	G 20	N. D.
300	Surry	M 16	Me.
45	Surry	P 7	N. H.
254	Surry	O 19	Va.
4	Survey	G 7	Neb.
150	*Surveyor	I 10	Pa.
200	*Surveyor	O 7	W. Va.
500	Susan	N 21	Va.
80	*Susank	I 12	Kan.
600	Susanna (Yukon)	R 5	W. Va.
1575	Susanville	D 10	Calif.
109	Susanville	G 19	Ore.
25	*Susie	K 16	Ky.
20	*Suspension	K 20	Ala.
....	Suspension Bridge (Bridge)	L 4	N. Y.
2740	Susquehanna (Susquehanna Depot)	E 21	Pa.
1478	Sussex	A 14	N. J.
29	Sussex	P 18	Va.
548	Sussex	O 20	Wis.
18	Sussex	G 17	Wyo.
55	*Sutcliffe	D 3	Nev.
937	*Sutersville (Suters)	N 4	Pa.
....	Sutherland, see Palm Harbor		Fla.
875	Sutherland	D 5	Iowa
6	*Sutherland	I 22	Mont.
862	Sutherland	K 9	Neb.
....	Sutherland	J 8	Utah
61	*Sutherland	O 16	Va.
75	Sutherlands	C 3	N. C.
400	Sutherland Springs	M 17	Tex.
525	Sutherlin	L 5	Ore.
116	*Sutherlin	R 10	Va.
750	Sutter	F 7	Calif.
32	*Sutter	H 4	Ill.
1134	Sutter Creek	H 9	Calif.
256	*Suttle	I 10	Ala.
65	*Sutton	I 23	Ky.
....	Sutton	N 17	Me.
....	Sutton	H 14	Mass.
1403	Sutton	M 18	Neb.
200	Sutton	N 10	N. H.
150	Sutton	K 19	N. D.
125	Sutton	D 18	Vt.
1083	Sutton	I 10	W. Va.
470	Suttons Bay	I 13	Mich.
179	Suwanee	E 9	Ga.
35	*Suwanee (Correo)	H 8	N. M.
64	*Svea	N 9	Minn.
280	Svenson	A 5	Ore.
82	Svold	D 21	N. D.
34	*Swaim	A 17	Ala.
30	*Swain	D 8	Ark.
143	Swain	O 8	N. Y.
3575	Swainsboro	J 17	Ga.
312	Swainton	Q 12	N. J.
204	Swaledale	D 13	Iowa
64	*Swallowfield	E 16	Ky.
37	*Swallows	M 16	Colo.
75	*Swamp Branch	G 22	Ky.
200	*Swampers	E 12	La.
10761	■Swampscott	D 20, K 8	Mass.
100	*Swampton	G 21	Ky.
17	Swan (Dial)	B 7	Ga.
217	Swan	L 13	Iowa
23	*Swan	Q 11	Mo.
120	Swan Creek	G 8	Ill.
....	Swan Creek	C 17	Md.
350	Swandale	J 9	W. Va.
....	Swander, see Ink		Ohio
25	*Swanders	I 7	Ohio
100	Swanington	F 6	Ind.
50	Swan Lake	L 15	Ark.
12	Swanlake	Q 20	Idaho
50	*Swan Lake	J 19	Ky.
100	Swan Lake	E 10	Miss.
53	Swan Lake	F 4	Mont.
152	*Swan Lake	R 20	N. Y.
....	Swan Lake Jc.	Q 10	Ore.
2500	*Swannanoa	O 7	N. C.
271	Swanquarter	G 22	N. C.
93	Swan River	G 16	Minn.
454	Swansboro	K 19	N. C.
1156	Swansea	M 11	Ill.
1000	Swansea	L 18	Mass.
950	Swansea	I 12	S. C.
800	Swansea Center	L 18	Mass.
190	Swans Island	N 16	Me.
126	*Swanton	N 3	Md.
233	Swanton	N 21	Neb.
1594	Swanton	C 8	Ohio
1461	Swanton	B 7	Vt.
18	*Swan Valley	N 18	Idaho
60	Swanville	M 13	Me.
417	Swanville	K 10	Minn.
100	Swanwick	O 13	Ill.
150	Swanzey	Q 7	N. H.
....	Swanzy	F 7	Mich.
4061	Swarthmore	P 23	Pa.
175	*Swartout	N 15	Calif.
100	*Swartswood	B 14	N. J.
100	Swartswood Jc.	C 12	N. J.
200	*Swartwood	Q 13	N. Y.
500	Swartz	B 12	La.
1200	Swartz Creek	O 20	Mich.
....	Swastika, see Brilliant		N. M.
53	*Swastika	D 24	N. Y.
114	*Swatara	H 15	Minn.
104	*Swatara Station	M 16	Pa.
....	Swayne, see Dillon		Kan.
661	Swayzee	G 17	Ind.
735	Swea City	B 9	Iowa
51	*Swearingen	B 13	Tex.
100	*Sweatman	F 15	Miss.
175	*Swedeborg	L 13	Mo.
70	Swedeburg	K 22	Neb.
32	Swedehome	K 19	Neb.
1150	*Swedeland	N 22	Pa.
70	Sweden	C 18	Me.
28	*Sweden	P 12	Mo.
2268	Swedesboro	M 6	N. J.
75	*Swedesburg	N 20	Iowa
960	*Swedesburg	N 22	Pa.
110	*Sweeden	I 12	Ky.
800	Sweeny	M 22	Tex.
310	Sweet	M 5	Idaho
200	*Sweet Briar	M 10	Va.
50	Sweetbrier	N 10	N. D.
26	*Sweet Chalybeate	L 7	Va.
356	Sweetgrass	B 9	Mont.
48	Sweetgum	B 8	Ga.
36	*Sweet Hall	L 18	Va.
119	*Sweet Home	J 13	Ark.
1090	Sweet Home	H 7	Ore.
300	Sweet Home	M 19	Tex.
31	*Sweetland	L 3	W. Va.
125	Sweet Mine	I 16	Utah
784	Sweetser (Sweeters)	G 16	Ind.
1413	Sweet Springs	H 9	Mo.
250	Sweet Springs	P 13	W. Va.
226	Sweet Valley	H 19	Pa.
400	Sweet Water	K 7	Ala.
125	*Sweetwater	H 3	Idaho
120	*Sweet Water	H 11	Ill.
50	Sweetwater	L 14	Neb.
140	Sweetwater	I 2	Okla.
2593	Sweetwater	O 18	Tenn.
10367	Sweetwater	E 12	Tex.
12	Sweetwater	P 8	Wyo.
94	*Swenson	D 12	Tex.
800	Swepsonville	E 11	N. C.
150	*Swett	N 9	S. D.
56	Swift (Swifton)	J 24	Mo.
258	*Swift (Swifts)	M 16	Ohio
45	*Swift	G 24	Tex.
484	Swifton	D 17	Ark.
46	*Swifton (Swift)	J 25	Mo.
50	*Swiftown	G 10	Miss.
46	*Swift River	E 5	Mass.
42	*Swiftrun	H 11	Va.
....	*Swifts (Swift)	M 16	Ohio
68	Swiftwater	I 11	N. H.
150	Swiftwater	I 23	Pa.
13	*Swimley	E 14	Va.
20	*Swineford	K 16	Pa.
4	Swingley	L 12	Mont.
374	Swink	M 19	Colo.
116	Swink	P 22	Okla.
49	*Swinton	P 21	Mo.
93	*Swisher	K 20	Iowa
27	*Swiss	I 16	Mo.
110	*Swiss	N 8	N. C.
300	Swiss	L 8	W. Va.
50	Swisshome	I 4	Ore.
15919	Swissvale	M 4	Pa.
650	*Switchback (Lick Branch)	Q 7	W. Va.
405	Switz City	M 8	Ind.
300	Switzer	E 17	Ky.
120	*Switzer	C 8	S. C.
350	Switzer	O 4	W. Va.
20	*Switzerland (Moonlake)	N 18, P 9	Calif.
250	*Switzerland	C 16	Fla.
180	*Switzerland (Mount Mitchell)	M 9	N. C.
200	*Switzerland (Okeetee)	P 13	S. C.
80	*Swoope	J 10	Va.
200	*Swords	G 12	Ga.
200	Swords Creek	C 8	Va.
125	*Swormville	O 5	N. Y.
9234	Swoyersville	H 20	Pa.
200	*Sybertsville	J 20	Pa.
75	*Sybial	L 6	W. Va.
16	Sybrant	G 14	Neb.
631	Sycamore (Sycamore Mills)	G 16	Ala.
50	*Sycamore	F 6	Calif.
601	Sycamore	M 11	Ga.
4702	Sycamore	B 16	Ill.
71	Sycamore	G 16	Ind.
187	*Sycamore	O 21	Kan.
42	*Sycamore	Q 13	Mo.
816	Sycamore	F 11	Ohio
16	Sycamore	D 23	Okla.
63	*Sycamore	P 2	Pa.
324	*Sycamore	M 12	S. C.
70	*Sycamore	P 9	Va.
....	Sycamore Branch Jc.	O 2	W. Va.
36	*Sycamore Landing	N 7	Tenn.
....	Sycamore Mills, see Sycamore		Ala.
50	*Sycamore Valley	L 18	Ohio
350	*Sydney	I 14	Fla.
9	Sydney	N 18	N. D.
29	*Sydnorsville	P 7	Va.
2044	Sykes (Sykesville)	J 8	Pa.
35	*Sykes	M 13	Tenn.
273	Sykeston	K 16	N. D.
806	Sykesville	E 12	Md.
2044	Sykesville (Sykes)	J 8	Pa.
6269	Sylacauga	G 16	Ala.
150	*Sylamore (East Sylamore)	D 13	Ark.
1409	Sylva	P 6	N. C.
350	Sylvan	Q 12	Pa.
50	*Sylvan	K 8	Wash.
26	*Sylvan Beach (Wabaningo)	N 11	Mich.
450	*Sylvan Beach	L 16	N. Y.
540	Sylvan Grove	G 12	Kan.
75	*Sylvania	C 19	Ala.
2531	Sylvania	I 22	Ga.
65	Sylvania	I 7	Ind.
2199	Sylvania	B 9	Ohio
194	*Sylvania	E 17	Pa.
....	Sylvan Jc.	K 16	N. Y.
1041	Sylvan Lake	P 22	Mich.
215	Sylvarena	L 16	Miss.
125	*Sylvatus	Q 3	Va.
2191	Sylvester	M 10	Ga.
405	Sylvester	E 13	Tex.
477	Sylvia	K 12	Kan.
136	Sylvia	M 9	Tenn.
410	*Sylvia (East Beckley)	O 8	W. Va.
30	Sylvian	I 16	Okla.
....	*Symbol	I 18	Ky.
82	*Symerton	D 20	Ill.
150	*Symmes (Symmes Corners)	N 6	Ohio
130	*Symonds	E 7	Miss.
16	*Synarep	D 17	Wash.
1500	*Syosset	H 7	N. Y.
1346	Syracuse	C 16	Ind.
1226	Syracuse	K 2	Kan.
262	Syracuse	I 11	Mo.
982	Syracuse	M 23	Neb.
205967	Syracuse	M 15	N. Y.
676	Syracuse	O 16	Ohio
732	Syracuse	D 10	Utah
35	*Syria	I 13	Va.
30	*Syringa	L 20	Va.

T

Pop.	Place	Index	State
80	Tab	G 6	Ind.
26	*Tabb	N 20	Va.
3	Taber	O 18	Idaho
400	Taberg	K 17	N. Y.
100	Tabernacle	K 13	N. J.
100	*Tabernacle	N 21	Va.
150	Tabernash	E 12	Colo.
100	*Taberville	K 8	Mo.
211	Tabiona	G 17	Utah
8	Table	K 12	Neb.
480	Table Grove	H 8	Ill.
30	Tablemound	N 21	Kan.
62	Tabler	K 11	Okla.
562	Table Rock	O 24	Neb.
....	*Tablerock	F 2	N. C.
142	Tablerock	P 7	Ore.
45	*Table Rock	Q 15	Pa.
100	*Tablerock	O 9	W. Va.
30	Tabor	E 15	Colo.
11	*Tabor	H 15	Ill.
976	Tabor	O 4	Iowa
31	*Tabor	G 20	Ky.
109	*Tabor	D 2	Minn.
500	*Tabor (Mount Tabor)	D 15	N. J.
....	Tabor	G 17	Okla.
391	Tabor	O 21	S. D.
24	*Tabor	I 20	Tex.
1552	*Tabor City	M 13	N. C.
200	Taborton	N 25	N. Y.
47	*Tacketts Mill	E 16	Ky.
7	*Tacna	L 5	Ariz.
....	Tacoa	G 12	Ala.
14	*Tacoma	P 6	Colo.
....	Tacoma	E 13	Fla.
250	*Tacoma	K 19	Ohio
37	*Tacoma	F 24	Tex.
281	Tacoma	D 5	Va.
109408	Tacoma	J 7	Wash.
....	Tacoma Jc.	J 8	Wash.
14	Tacoma Park	D 19	S. D.
....	Tacon	P 5	Ala.
150	Taconic	A 4	Conn.
375	Taconite	G 16	Minn.
10	Taconite Jc.	G 15	Minn.
60	Tacony	K 18	Colo.
450	Tad	K 6	W. Va.
150	*Taff	C 20	Ala.
3205	Taft	M 12	Calif.
296	Taft	H 18	Fla.
30	*Taft	H 20	Ky.
260	Taft	N 17	La.
17	Taft	H 20	Minn.
5	Taft	G 1	Mont.
....	Taft	H 20	N. M.
2	Taft	J 24	N. D.
772	Taft	G 20	Okla.
350	Taft	F 4	Ore.
152	*Taft	Q 11	Tenn.
2686	Taft	Q 18	Tex.
46	Taft	L 21	Va.
141	*Tafton	G 23	Pa.
125	Taftsville	L 13	Vt.
3965	Taftville	H 22	Conn.
30	*Tague	I 9	W. Va.
140	Tagus	F 8	N. D.
54	*Tahawus	H 23	N. Y.
3027	Tahlequah	F 23	Okla
150	Tahoe (Lake Tahoe)	F 11	Calif.
10	*Tahoe Pines	F 9	Calif.
....	*Tahoe Valley	G 9	Calif.
200	*Tahoe Vista	F 9	Calif.
2129	Tahoka	D 10	Tex.
350	Taholah	I 1	Wash.
300	Tahona	J 24	Okla.
50	*Tahuya	I 6	Wash.
100	Taiban	I 22	N. M.
50	*Tailscreek	C 5	Ga.
75	*Taintor	L 15	Iowa
7	*Taiton	L 21	Tex.
60	Taits Gap	D 15	Ala.
200	Tajique	H 12	N. M.
14	Takilma	R 4	Ore.
....	Takoma (Takoma Park)	I 11	D. C.
8938	Takoma Park	I 11	Md.
188	Talala	C 19	Okla.
24	*Talbert	H 20	Ky.
101	*Talbot	G 6	Ind.
60	Talbot	G 6	Ore.
320	Talbott	M 21	Tenn.
50	Talbot Jc.	N 22	Idaho
1060	Talbotton	J 6	Ga.
912	Talco	C 22	Tex.
275	Talcott	P 10	W. Va.
300	Talcottville	E 16	Conn.
75	*Talcum	I 21	Ky.
381	Talent	Q 7	Ore.
1057	Talihina	M 23	Okla.
300	*Talisheek	K 19	La.
103	*Talking Rock	D 6	Ga.
14	*Talla Bena	C 15	La.
9298	Talladega	F 17	Ala.
150	Talladega Springs	H 15	Ala.
16240	Tallahassee	B 5	Fla.
175	Tallant	C 18	Okla.
2338	Tallapoosa	F 2	Ga.
154	Tallapoosa (Tallipoosa)	I 24, R 22	Mo.
1011	Tallassee	J 18	Ala.
....	*Tallassee	O 19	Tenn.
100	*Tallavast (Tallevast)	J 13	Fla.
55	*Tallega (Lone)	H 20	Ky.
40	*Tallega (Zold)	H 20	Ky.
500	*Tallieu	N 15	La.
154	*Tallipoosa (Tallapoosa)	I 24, R 22	Mo.
4	Tallmadge	E 22	Ill.
3452	Tallmadge	F 18	Ohio
100	*Tallman	K 9	Mich.
750	*Tallman (Tallmans)	F 5	N. Y.
150	*Tallmansville (Strader)	H 13	W. Va.
....	*Tall Timbers	O 14	Md.
604	Tallula	I 11	Ill.
26	*Tallula	I 6	Miss.
5712	Tallulah	C 14	La.
73	*Tallulah Falls	C 12	Ga.
175	*Tallulah Lodge	C 12	Ga.
6	*Tallulah Park	C 11	Calif.
350	*Talmage	G 4	Calif.
120	Talmage	O 10	Iowa
423	Talmage	M 24	Neb.
200	*Talmage	O 19	Pa.
160	Talmage	G 19	Utah
131	Talmo	D 10	Ga.
79	Talmo	D 15	Kan.
50	*Talmoon (Mack)	F 14	Minn.
533	Taloga	F 6	Okla.
35	*Talona	C 6	Ga.
50	Talpa	D 14	N. M.
254	Talpa	G 13	Tex.
52	*Talucah	B 14	Ala.
2832	Tama	J 16	Iowa
245	Tamaha	I 23	Okla.
70	*Tamalco	M 14	Ill.
12486	Tamaqua	K 20	Pa.
97	Tamarack	K 5	Idaho
300	Tamarack	D 7	Mich.
150	*Tamarack	I 16	Minn.
100	Tamarack	C 2	N. C.
79	*Tamarack	I 13	Pa.
951	Tamaroa	O 14	Ill.
300	*Tamassee	B 4	S. C.
125	*Tamburo	G 7	Miss.
....	*Tamiment	I 13	Pa.
500	*Tamina	K 22	Tex.
777	Tamms	R 14	Ill.
160	*Tamo	M 15	Ark.
131	Tamora	L 20	Neb.
108391	Tampa	I 13	Fla.
222	Tampa	I 17	Kan.
315	Tampashores (Oldsmar)	H 12	Fla.
727	Tampico	D 12	Ill.
75	Tampico	D 19	Mont.
250	Tampico (Hornsbyville)	N 20	Va.
90	Tamroy	N 8	W. Va.
750	Tams	P 7	W. Va.
300	Tamworth	K 16	N. H.
10	*Tamworth	M 13	Va.
11	*Tanbark	K 15	Ky.
	Taneycomo, see Rockaway Beach		Mo.
1208	Taneytown	B 10	Md.
128	*Taneyville	Q 11	Mo.
140	Tangent	H 6	Ore.
250	*Tangerine	G 17	Fla.
103	Tangier	I 7	Ind.
68	Tangier	D 3	Okla.
1020	*Tangier	L 22	Va.
319	Tangipahoa	J 17	La.
60	*Tanglewood	J 19	Tex.
75	*Tango	L 4	W. Va.
37	*Tank (Springcreek)	D 22	Okla.
48	*Tankersly	H 12	Tex.
26	*Tanksley	I 20	Ky.
500	*Tanner	B 12	Ala.
106	*Tanner	H 10	W. Va.
30	Tanners Falls	F 23	Pa.
640	Tannersville	Q 22	N. Y.
280	Tannersville	J 23	Pa.
45	*Tannersville	D 9	Va.
30	*Tannery	D 21	Ky.
108	Tansboro	M 12	N. J.
....	Tanwax Jc.	K 8	Wash.
151	Taopi	R 19	Minn.
965	Taos	D 15	N.M.
50	Taos Canyon	D 15	N.M.
65	Taos Jc.	D 14	N. M.
400	Tapicitoes	D 9	N.M.
35	*Taplin	O 4	W. Va.
783	Tappahannock	K 19	Va.
....	Tappan	N 25	Mich.
1200	*Tappan	G 5	N. Y.
120	*Tappan	I 18	Ohio
323	Tappen	M 15	N. D.
30	Tara	G 9	Iowa
7148	Tarboro	E 17	N. C.
9846	Tarentum	L 4	Pa.
69	*Tarheel (Tar Hill)	K 13	N. C.
1316	Tariffville	C 13	Conn.
250	Tarkiln	B 10	R. I.
2114	Tarkio	A 3	Mo.
50	Tarkio	H 3	Mont.
274	Tarlton	M 12	Ohio
98	Tarnov	J 20	Neb.
49	*Tarpley	L 15	Tex.
34	*Tarpon	C 6	Va.
....	Tarpon Jc.	I 13	Fla.
3402	Tarpon Springs	H 12	Fla.
6833	Tarrant	F 13	Ala.
14	*Tarrantine	H 8	Me.
350	Tarr (Tarrs)	O 5	Pa.
310	Tarrtown	K 5	Pa.
29	*Tarry	M 14	Ark.
10	Tarryall	I 13	Colo.
298	Tarrytown	K 16	Ga.
6874	Tarrytown	F 6	N. Y.
....	Tartar	E 5	Wis.
....	*Tarzana	N 15 (Pop. incl. in Los Angeles)	Calif.
46	*Tasco	F 7	Kan.
40	*Tascosa	C 3	Tex.
86	*Taskee Sta. (Taskee)	P 19	Mo.
125	*Tasley	L 24	Va.
13	*Tassajara Hot Springs	K 17	Calif.
350	*Tasso	Q 16	Tenn.
126	Taswell	P 12	Ind.
604	*Tatamy	K 23	Pa.
1548	Tate	D 6	Ga.
22	Tate	O 23	Neb.
....	*Tate, see Bean Station		Tenn.
500	*Tate Springs	M 20	Tenn.
375	Tatum	L 24	N. M.
181	*Tatum	D 20	S. C.
427	Tatum	E 23	Tex.
150	Tatums	N 12	Okla.
26	*Taulbee	G 21	Ky.
37395	Taunton	K 19	Mass.
207	*Taunton	O 5	Minn.
....	Taupa	M 8	Okla.
1119	Tavares	F 16	Fla.
40	*Tavener	L 21	Tex.
50	*Tavera	G 19	Wis.
91	*Tavernier	Q 23	Fla.
13	*Tavistock	L 10	N. J.
....	Tawas Beech	K 21	Mich.
1075	Tawas City	K 21	Mich.
50	Tawawa	J 8	Ohio
60	*Taxahaw	C 14	S. C.
100	Taycheedah	N 17	Wis.
400	Taylor	H 21	Ariz.
335	Taylor	R 8	Ark.
65	Taylor (South Shore)	D 22	Ky.
98	*Taylor (Nelson)	C 7	La.
30	Taylor	C 15	Md.
164	Taylor	C 15	Miss.
60	*Taylor	D 16	Mo.
349	Taylor	I 14	Neb.
56	Taylor (Taylor Springs)	D 20	N. M.
75	Taylor	O 15	N. Y.
251	Taylor	M 6	N. D.
12	Taylor	P 8	Okla.
9002	Taylor	H 21	Pa.
2500	Taylor (Taylors)	B 7	S. C.
7875	Taylor	J 18	Tex.
17	Taylor	J 14	Va.
250	Taylor	I 9	Wash.
314	Taylor	F 14	Wis.
100	Taylor Ridge	E 7	Ill.
2500	*Taylors (Taylor)	B 7	S. C.
20	Taylors Bridge	E 22	Del.
144	*Taylors Creek	L 22	Ga.
552	Taylors Falls	L 18	Minn.
500	Taylors Island	M 16	Md.
30	*Taylorsport	B 17	Ky.
624	Taylor Springs	L 13	Ill.
56	Taylor Springs (Taylor)	D 20	N. M.
350	Taylorstown	O 1	Pa.
80	*Taylorstown Sta. (Crothers)	O 2	Pa.
100	*Taylors Valley	E 9	Va.
275	Taylorsville	E 9	Calif.
926	Taylorsville	E 4	Ga.
265	Taylorsville	L 15	Ind.
921	Taylorsville	F 14	Ky.
40	Taylorsville	D 11	Md.
955	Taylorsville	M 16	Miss.
1122	Taylorsville	E 4	N. C.
884	*Taylorsville (Philo)	K 16	Ohio
59	*Taylortown	C 5	La.
8313	Taylorville	J 14	Ill.
80	*Taylorville	O 3	W. Va.
30	*Taylorville	O 10	Tenn.
80	*Tazewell	K 6	Ga.
800	Tazewell	L 20	Tenn.
1180	*Tazewell (New Tazewell)	L 20	Tenn.
1374	Tazewell (North Tazewell)	C 10	Va.
861	Tchula	G 11	Miss.
165	Tea	M 24	S. D.
....	*Teaberry	H 23	Ky.
228	*Teacheys	J 16	N. C.
50	*Teague	K 19	Ky.
3157	Teague	G 20	Tex.
13	*Teakean	G 6	Idaho
25275	■*Teaneck	C 19	N. J.
50	Teasdale	M 13	Utah
675	Teaticket	N 23	Mass.
50	*Teays	K 4	W. Va.
150	Tebbets	I 14	Mo.
....	*Tech	C 10	Tex.
....	*Teckla	D 19	Wyo.
600	Techny	B 21	Ill.
250	*Tecolotenos (Koogler)	F 18	N. M.
16	*Tecopa	K 16	Calif.
40	Tecumseh	D 20	Ala.
350	Tecumseh	G 22	Kan.
2921	Tecumseh	Q 19	Mich.
15	*Tecumseh	R 13	Mo.
2104	Tecumseh	N 23	Neb.
2042	Tecumseh	J 15	Okla.
....	Tecumseh Jc.	J 15	Okla.
24	*Tedders	J 19	Ky.
300	Tedrow	C 7	Ohio
42	*Teedee	M 24	Mont.
60	Teeds Grove	I 25	Iowa
150	Teegarden	C 12	Ind.
....	Teel, see Lorenzo		N. M.
....	*Teetersville	J 21	Ky.
86	*Tefft	D 9	Ind.
12	Tegarden	B 6	Okla.
42	*Teges	I 20	Ky.
1264	Tehachapi	M 14	Calif.
175	Tehama	E 6	Calif.
408	Tehuacana	G 20	Tex.
11	Teigen	H 15	Mont.
1925	Tekamah	I 23	Neb.
1383	Tekoa	J 24	Wash.
636	Tekonsha	Q 16	Mich.
20	Telbasta	I 22	Neb.
25	*Telegraph	J 14	Tex.
....	*Telegraph Creek	E 17	Mont.
350	*Telephone	C 20	Tex.
200	*Telferner (Telfener)	M 19	Tex.
423	*Telford	N 23	Pa.
1000	Telford	M 23	Tenn.
418	Tell	A 12	Tex.
5395	Tell City	R 10	Ind.
125	*Tellico	Q 4	N. C.
899	Tellico Plains	P 18	Tenn.
1337	Telluride	M 6	Colo.
150	*Telma	F 13	Wash.
56	Telocaset	E 21	Ore.
100	Telogia	B 3	Fla.
200	Temecula	P 18	Calif.
2906	Tempe	K 13	Ariz.
720	*Temperance	R 21	Mich.
100	Temperanceville	K 19	Ohio
224	Temperanceville	K 24	Va.
624	Temple	F 3	Ga.
32	*Temple	P 13	Ind.
29	*Temple	H 8	La.
120	Temple	L 6	Me.
102	Temple	L 16	Mich.
110	Temple	Q 11	N. H.
75	Temple	F 4	N. D.
1313	Temple	O 9	Okla.
1408	Temple	M 20	Pa.
15344	Temple	H 18	Tex.
3400	*Temple City	N 16	Calif.
50	*Temple Hill	R 18	Ill.
56	*Templeman Crossroads	J 19	Va.
215	*Temple Terrace	I 13	Fla.
450	*Templeton	L 9	Calif.
133	Templeton	G 8	Ind.
390	Templeton	J 7	Iowa
780	Templeton	D 12	Mass.
856	Templeton	K 5	Pa.
3	Templeton	J 18	S. D.
....	Templeton, see Sussex		Wis.
80	*Templeville	G 20	Md.
137	Temvik	P 13	N. D.
7413	Tenafly	D 21	N. J.
608	Tenaha	F 24	Tex.
275	Tenants Harbor	O 12	Me.
137	*Ten Brook	C 19	Ala.
20	Tendoy	K 14	Idaho
952	Tenino	K 6	Wash.
30	*Tenmile	M 6	Ore.
163	*Tenmile	P 2	Pa.
....	Ten Mile	N 18	S. C.
108	*Tenmile	H 13	W. Va.
....	*Ten Mile River	D 2	N. Y.
100	*Tennant	B 5	Calif.
109	*Tennant	L 5	Iowa
50	Tennemo	M 2	Tenn.
150	*Tennent	I 17	N. J.
243	Tennessee	H 7	Ill.
150	Tennessee City	M 8	Tenn.
125	*Tennessee Colony	G 21	Tex.
32	*Tennessee Pass	I 10	Colo.
290	*Tennessee Ridge	L 8	Tenn.
89	*Tenney	J 3	Minn.
175	Tennga	B 5	Ga.
50	Tennille	M 19	Ala.
1758	Tennille	I 15	Ga.
293	Tennyson	Q 8	Ind.
54	*Tennyson	F 13	Tex.
100	*Tensaw	O 7	Ala.
150	*Tensed	F 3	Idaho
345	Ten Sleep	E 14	Wyo.
83	*Tenso	C 6	Va.
239	Tenstrike (Tenstrike Center)	F 10	Minn.
109	Tercio	Q 15	Colo.
1000	Tererro	E 15	N. M.
25	*Teresita	E 16	Ky.
5	*Teresita (Terresita)	O 6	Mo.
15	Teresita	F 23	Okla.
500	*Terlingua	L 6	Tex.
245	Terlton	E 16	Okla.
....	*Terminal Island	N 15 (Pop. incl. in Los Angeles)	Calif.
21	*Termo	D 10	Calif.
1471	Terra Alta	D 16	W. Va.
250	*Terra Bella	L 13	Calif.
54	*Terrace	L 8	Minn.
1000	*Terrace	M 4	Pa.
979	▲Terra Ceia	J 12	Fla.
....	Terra Ceia Jct.	J 13	Fla.
858	*Terrace Park	N 5	Ohio
521	Terral	Q 10	Okla.
300	*Terraville	I 2	S. D.
75	Terrebonne	I 11	Ore.
75	Terre Haute	G 6	Ill.
62693	Terre Haute	K 7	Ind.
907	Terre Hill	O 20	Pa.
100	*Terrell	G 5	N. C.
124	*Terrell	L 4	Tenn.
10481	Terrell	E 20	Tex.
108	*Terrell Wells	L 16	Tex.
5	*Terresita (Teresita)	O 6	Mo.
30	*Terreton	N 19	Idaho
452	Terril	C 7	Iowa
20	*Terry	Q 11	Ind.
60	Terry	A 14	La.
401	Terry	L 10	Miss.
1012	Terry	I 22	Mont.
12	Terry	I 2	S. D.
180	*Terry	O 8	W. Va.
2250	Terryville	G 9	Conn.
515	*Terryville (Pequabuck)	D 6	Conn.
....	*Terryville	F 22	Ky.
250	*Terryville	H 9	N. Y.
402	Tescott	G 15	Kan.
62	*Tesla	I 10	W. Va.
10	*Tesnu	L 7	Tex.
....	*Tessville, see Lincolnwood		Ill.
100	Tesuque	F 13	N. M.
90	*Teterton	H 17	W. Va.
514	Teton	N 21	Idaho
250	Tetonia	N 23	Idaho
27	*Tetotum	I 18	Va.
46	*Tettington	N 18	Va.
806	Teutopolis	L 18	Ill.
6563	Tewksbury	C 18	Mass.
150	Texanna	I 21	Okla.
11821	Texarkana	P 5	Ark.
17019	Texarkana	C 24	Tex.
28840	Texarkana	(Tex. C 24)	Ark.-Tex.
....	Texas	E 8	Ala.
100	Texas	H 2	Ga.
100	*Texas	G 16	Ky.
1009	Texas	D 14	Md.
60	Texas City	P 19	Ill.
5748	Texas City	L 23	Tex.
20	Texas Creek	K 13	Colo.
....	Texas Jct.	Q 16	Okla.
577	Texhoma	R 4	Okla.
300	Texhoma	A 3	Tex.
34	Texico	N 16	Ill.
478	Texico	I 25	N. M.
....	Texla	J 25	Tex.
385	Texline	A 1	Tex.
337	Texola	J 1	Okla.
1200	*Texon	H 10	Tex.
300	Thacker	P 3	W. Va.
350	Thacker Mines	P 3	W. Va.
207	Thackerville	R 14	Okla.
200	Thackeray	O 18	Ill.
100	*Thackery	J 8	Ohio
28	Thaddeus	I 19	Ala.
60	*Thalia	B 14	Tex.
90	Thalmann	N 22	Ga.
....	Thamesville	J 22	Conn.
42	*Tharpe	K 7	Tenn.
1106	Thatcher	L 22	Ariz.
142	Thatcher	O 18	Colo.
32	Thatcher	Q 21	Idaho
125	Thatcher	B 9	Utah
19	Thatcher	D 7	Wash.
293	Thawville	G 19	Ill.
175	*Thaxton	C 17	Miss.
100	*Thaxton	N 8	Va.
789	Thayer	J 11	Ill.
185	Thayer	D 6	Ind.
157	Thayer	O 10	Iowa
461	Thayer	M 22	Kan.
1000	Thayer (South Lancaster)	E 15	Mass.

Pop. Place Index State
1692 Thayer, R 16........Mo.
135 Thayer, L 19........Neb.
207 Thayer, N 9........W. Va.
25 Thayer Jct., O 9........Wyo.
250 Thayne, J 2........Wyo.
30 Theadville, L 22........Miss.
520 Thealka, G 22........Ky.
27*Theall, N 9........La.
110 Theba, L 9........Ariz.
730 Thebes, R 13........Ill.
350 The Bridge (Jay), M 6..Me.
172*The Corner (Mt. Tremper) B 4........N. Y.
6266 The Dalles, C 12........Ore.
288 Thedford, H 11........Neb.
1040 The Falls (Ellsworth Falls) L 16........Me.
119*The Forks, I 8........Me.
64*The Glen, I 23........N. Y.
105*The Grove, H 18........Tex.
200*The Heights, K 17...Mich.
500*The Hollow (Pedigo), R 4........Va.
125*Theilman, P 21........Minn.
115 Thelma, C 17........N. C.
26*Thelma, K 14........Va.
.... Thenard, R 3........Calif.
100 Thendara, I 19........N. Y.
100*Theo, O 9........Ark.
500 Theodore, Q 4........Ala.
62*Theodosia, R 12........Mo.
418*Theological Seminary, G 18 Va.
300*The Plains, N 15........Ohio
372 The Plains, G 15........Va.
908 Theresa, G 16........N. Y.
418 Theresa, N 18........Wis.
58*Theresa (Marshville), N 18 Wis.
150*Theressa, D 15........Fla.
26*The Ridge, F 21........Ky.
91*Theriot, P 15........La.
.... Therma, see Eagle Nest, N. M.
300 Thermal, P 21........Calif.
2422 Thermopolis, G 10....Wyo.
179*The Rock, I 8........Ga.
30 Thetford (East Thetford), J 16........Vt.
100 Thetford, J 16........Vt.
200 Thetford Center, J 16...Vt.
212 The Weirs (Weirs), L 15 N. H.
5851 Thibodaux, O 16........La.
.... Thibodaux Jc., O 16....La.
255*Thicket, J 23........Tex.
60*Thida, E 16........Ark.
6019 Thief River Falls, D 4 Minn.
70*Thiel, L 12........Ark.
700*Thiells, F 5........N. Y.
645 Thiensville, P 19........Wis.
.... 30-Mile, E 15........Ore.
168 Thistle, H 13........Utah
38*Thivener, P 15........Ohio
29 Thoeny, C 19........Mont.
90*Thola, D 12........Ark.
.... Thomas, O 18........Idaho
25*Thomas, G 22........Ky.
168*Thomas, L 17........Md.
98 Thomas, O 21........Mich.
4*Thomas, D 24........N. M.
1220 Thomas, H 7........Okla.
150*Thomas, O 3........Pa.
32 Thomas (Cave), L 12..S. C.
75 Thomas, G 22........S. D.
195*Thomas, D 22........Tex.
.... Thomas, B 7........Va.
350 Thomas, I 8........Wash.
1449 Thomas, E 16........W. Va.
27*Thomasboro, J 21........Ga.
285 Thomasboro, H 19........Ill.
119*Thomas Hill, E 12........Mo.
.... Thomasson, A 20........Calif.
345 Thomaston, K 8........Ala.
3900 Thomaston, G 8........Conn.
6396 Thomaston, I 6........Ga.
15 Thomaston, C 10........Ind.
2200 Thomaston, O 12........Me.
1159*Thomaston, H 7........N. Y.
358 Thomaston, M 19........Tex.
100*Thomastown, H 14...Miss.
2000 Thomasville, L 7........Ala.
50 Thomasville, J 18........Ark.
12683 Thomasville, P 9........Ga.
12 Thomasville, K 12........Ill.
104*Thomasville, Q 16........Mo.
11041 Thomasville, E 8....N. C.
200 Thomasville, P 16........Pa.
50*Thomasville, L 9........Tenn.
206 Thompson, K 18........Ala.
400*Thompson, B 24........Conn.
664 Thompson, B 11........Iowa
244 Thompson, E 14........Mich.
75 Thompson, G 14........Mo.
35 Thompson, O 20........Neb.
276 Thompson, I 23........N. D.
150*Thompson, C 19........Ohio
339 Thompson, F 22........Pa.
90*Thompson (Thompsons), K 22........Utah
736 Thompson Falls, F 2.Mont.
120*Thompson Ridge, D 4.N.Y.
82*Thompsons (Thompsons Sta.), N 10........Tenn.
104*Thompsons, L 22........Tex.
90 Thompsons (Thompson), K 22........Utah
82 Thompsons Station, N 10 Tenn.
500 Thompsontown, M 15...Pa.
9643 Thompsonville, A 15 .Conn.
568 Thompsonville, P 17....Ill.
324 Thompsonville, J 10..Mich.
202*Thompsonville, D 3..N. Y.
3088 Thomson, G 18........Ga.
529 Thomson, B 10........Ill.
104*Thomson, I 20........Minn.
198*Thomson, K 24........N. Y.
300 Thonotosassa, I 14........Fla.
264 Thor, F 10........Iowa
95*Thor, I 16........Minn.
250 Thoreau, F 4........N. M.
.... Thorice, see Munuscong, Mich.
63*Thorn, E 17........Miss.
19*Thornburg, I 10........Ark.
35*Thornburg, E 4........Colo.
184 Thornburg, L 17........Iowa
.... Thornburg, P 23........Ohio
284*Thornburg, L 3........Pa.
21*Thornburg, J 16........Va.
500*Thorndale, P 21........Pa.
898 Thorndale, J 19........Tex.
429 Thorndike, L 11........Me.
1200 Thorndike, H 10........Mass.
5 Thorne, I 7........Nev.
45 Thorne, E 14........N. D.
31*Thorney, C 6........Ark.
50*Thornfield, Q 12........Mo.
150*Thorn Hill, M 20........Tenn.
30*Thornhill, J 15........Va.
96*Thornhope (Oak), D 10 Ind.
70 Thornhurst, I 21........Pa.
550 Thornton, N 12........Ark.
750*Thornton, H 8........Calif.
300 Thornton, N 20........Idaho
1101 Thornton, D 22........Ill.

Pop. Place Index State
398 Thornton, E 13........Iowa
110*Thornton, J 22........Ky.
40*Thornton, H 11........Miss.
100 Thornton, J 13........N. H.
150*Thornton, P 22........Pa.
4000 Thornton, E 14........R. I.
745 Thornton, H 20........Tex.
180 Thornton, J 24........Wash.
200*Thornton, E 14........W. Va.
19*Thornton, E 22........Wyo.
.... Thornton Jc., D 2........Pa.
1226 Thorntown, H 12........Ind.
411 Thornville, K 13........Ohio
33*Thornwell, N 8........La.
1500*Thornwood, G 6........N. Y.
177*Thornwood, J 15........W. Va.
320*Thorofare, L 8........N. J.
21*Thoroughfare, G 15........Va.
250 Thorp, J 13........Wash.
1052 Thorp (Thorpe) G 12..Wis.
500*Thorpe, Q 6........W. Va.
308 Thorp Spring, E 17........Tex.
772 Thorsby, H 13........Ala.
100*Thousand Island Park, F 15........N. Y.
750*Thousand Oaks, N 13.Calif.
100*Thousand Palms (Edom), P19, R9........Calif.
150*Thrall, L 20........Kan.
436*Thrall, J 18........Tex.
600*Thrasher, B 21........Miss.
450 Three Bridges, G 12..N. J.
16*Three Brothers, A 12..Ark.
31*Three Churches, E 20 W. Va.
65 Three Creek, R 9........Idaho
....*Threeforks, G 23........Ky.
876 Three Forks, L 9........Mont.
30 Three Forks, O 6........W. Va.
5 Three Lakes, G 9........Wash.
365 Three Lakes, L 8........Wis.
100*Threelinks, H 18........Ky.
....*Three Mile, D 2........N. C.
175*Three Mile, K 7........W. Va.
290*Three Mile Bay, G 14.N. Y.
1351 Three Oaks, R 9........Mich.
500*Three Point, K 21........Ky.
18*Threerivers, K 13........Calif.
1632 Three Rivers, G 9........Mass.
6710 Three Rivers, R 11........Mich.
50 Three Rivers, L 13........N. M.
1337 Three Rivers. O 17........Tex.
500 Three Sands, C 13........Okla.
427 Three Springs, O 12........Pa.
25*Three Square, L 15........Va.
82*Threeway, J 19........Va.
80*Threlkel, H 12........Ky.
950* Thrift (Paw Creek), H 5 N. C.
42*Thrift, B 15........Tex.
75 Thrifton, N 10........Ohio
40*Thrifty, G 15........Tex.
1133 Throckmorton, D 14...Tex.
7382 Throop, G 21........Pa.
886 Thunderbolt, L 25........Ga.
100 Thunder Hawk, B 8...S. D.
85*Thune, J 9........Neb.
500 Thurber, E 16........Tex.
147*Thurlow, K 20........Mont.
8 Thurman, G 20........Colo.
325 Thurman, P 4........Iowa
50 Thurman, J 23........N. Y.
113 Thurman (Centerville), P 14........Ohio
8*Thurman, F 20........Colo.
50*Thurmond, C 5........N. C.
339 Thurmond, N 9........W. Va.
1307 Thurmont, C 7........Md.
29*Thursday, F 9........W. Va.
221 Thurston, G 21........Neb.
424 Thurston, L 14........Ohio
56 Thurston, J 7........Ore.
100*Thyatira, B 14........Miss.
25 Ti, M 20........Okla.
36*Tiadaghton, F 14........Pa.
24 Tia Juana, Q 19........Calif.
47 Tiawah, E 20........Okla.
400 Tibbie, N 4........Ala.
100 Tibbie (Tibbee Sta.), F 21 Miss.
150*Tibitha, L 21........Va.
327 Tiburon, D 16........Calif.
550*Tice, L 17........Fla.
20 Tice, A 18........Vt.
46*Tichnor, L 17........Ark.
500 Tickfaw, K 17........La.
30 Ticknor, N 9........Ga.
3402 Ticonderoga, H 24...N. Y.
109*Ticonic, I 3........Iowa
70*Tidal, K 5........Pa.
.... Tidal Jc., J 6........Pa.
20 Tidedale, M 7........Pa.
103 Tidewater, F 12........Fla.
40 Tidewater, H 4........Ore.
58 Tidewater. K 20........Va.
953 Tidioute, F 6........Pa.
16*Tidwells J 20........Va.
100*Tiedtville C 20........Ill.
210*Tie Plant I 13........Ark.
60*Tie Plant, E 13........Miss.
65 Tiernan (Beck), I 3....Ore.
550 Tierra Amarilla, C 11 N. M.
204▲Tie Siding (Hermosa), R 19........Wyo.
350 Tieton, L 13........Wash.
138*Tiff, L 19........Mo.
25 Tiffany, Q 6........Colo.
100 Tiffany, L 21........Wis.
59*Tiff City, Q 5........Mo.
240*Tiffin, K 20........Iowa
89*Tiffin, L 8........Mo.
16102 Tiffin, F 11........Ohio
.... Tiffin, R 8........Okla.
30 Tiffin, E 16........Tex.
5228 Tifton, N 11........Ga.
600 Tigard, D 7........Ore.
....*Tiger, M 16........Ariz.
45*Tiger, G 12........Colo.
289*Tiger, B 12........Ga.
135 Tiger, C 23........Wash.
30 Tigerbay, I 16........Fla.
794 Tigerton, L 13........Wis.
105*Tigerville, A 7........S. C.
....*Tigiwon, G 9........Colo.
567 Tignall, F 16........Ga.
....*Tignor, K 17........Va.
90*Tigrett, N 3........Tenn.
75 Tilden, K 11........Ala.
1040 Tilden, O 12........Ill.
984 Tilden, H 18........Neb.
350 Tilden, O 16........Tex.
.... Tilden Jc., F 4........Minn.
81*Tilford, H 11........Ky.
36 Tilford, I 3........S. D.
700*Tilghman, J 18........Md.
50*Tiline, I 6........Ky.
2751 Tillamook, D 4........Ore.
.... Tillamook Gate, D 5...Ore.
229 Tillar, O 16........Ark.
140*Tillatoba, D 13........Miss.
125*Tilleda, M 12........Wis.
32 Tiller, N 6........Ore.
25 Tillery, D 18........N. C.
450*Tillicum, K 8........Wash.
.... Tillman, see Palm Bay .Fla.
119 Tillman, J 7........La.
50*Tillman, L 6........Miss.
.... Tillman, O 7........Okla.

Pop. Place Index State
398*Tillman, P 13........S. C.
400*Tillson, R 21........N. Y.
6*Tilly, E 10........Ark.
214*Tilly Foster, E 6........N. Y.
220*Tilton, G 18........Ark.
93*Tilton, C 4........Ga.
1486 Tilton, I 21........Ill.
18 Tilton, N 12........Miss.
1500 Tilton, M 13........N. H.
2360 Tiltonsville (Grover), J 20 ....Ohio
27*Timber, O 16........Mo.
75 Timber, C 6........Ore.
300*Timberlake (Helena), C 12........N. C.
512 Timber Lake, E 11...S. D.
50*Timberland, I 11........N. C.
200*Timberline Lodge, E 8.Ore.
175*Timber Ridge, L 9........Va.
252 Timberville, H 11........Va.
454*Timblin, J 7........Pa.
300*Timbo, D 13........Ark.
....*Timentwa, D 16........Wash.
52*Time Pike, J 16........Ill.
226 Timewell (Mound Station), I 7........Ill.
170*Timken, J 10........Kan.
70 Timmer, P 11........N. D.
1979 Timmonsville, G 18...S. C.
147 Timnath, C 15........Colo.
281 Timonium, D 14........Md.
80* Timothy, M 15........Tenn.
.... Timothy, see Newton..Wis.
80 Timpas, N 19........Colo.
1494 Timpson, F 24........Tex.
62*Tina, J 19........Ky.
274 Tina, E 9........Mo.
125*Tindall, C 9........Mo.
....*Tingle, H 5........N. M.
390 Tingley, O 10........Iowa
47*Tinicum, M 23........Pa.
39*Tinker, I 19........Ky.
1136 Tinley Park, D 20........Ill.
25 Tinmouth, M 7........Vt.
4 Tinney, N 7........Okla.
30 Tinnie, L 17........N. M.
200*Tinsley, K 19........Ky.
258 Tinsman, O 12........Ark.
200 Tintah, K 4........Minn.
....*Tinton, I 2........S. D.
500 Tintonfalls, H 19........N. J.
80*Tinus, I 16........La.
51*Tiny, C 7........Va.
300 Tioga, N 15........Colo.
126 Tioga, H 4........Ill.
12 Tioga, M 17........Iowa
1300 Tioga, H 10........La.
385 Tioga, F 5........N. D.
460 Tioga, E 15........Pa.
638 Tioga, C 19........Tex.
610 Tioga, K 11........W. Va.
15*Tioga, G 13........Wis.
200 Tioga Center, R 14...N. Y.
.... Tioga Jc., E 15........Pa.
1300 Tioga, I 9........La.
350 Tiona, F 7........Pa.
845 Tionesta, G 6........Pa.
300*Tionesta, B 9........Calif.
4*Tip, D 22........Okla.
225 Tipler, M 7........Wis.
140*Tiplersville, A 19........Miss.
2897 Tipp City, K 7........Ohio
300 Tippecanoe, D 14........Ind.
255 Tippencanoe, I 18........Ohio
.... Tippecanoe City, see Tipp City........Ohio
20 Tipperary (Barcamp), B 20........Ark.
.... Tipperary, N 14........Iowa
48*Tipperary, J 10........Wyo.
40*Tipple (Stave), P 6 .W. Va.
117*Tippo, D 11........Miss.
115 Tiprell (Arthur), L 20 Tenn.
800 Tipton, L 12........Calif.
5101 Tipton, H 15........Ind.
2518 Tipton, K 22........Iowa
248 Tipton, F 13........Kan.
150 Tipton, Q 18........Mich.
1219 Tipton, I 11........Mo.
1470 Tipton, N 5........Okla.
500 Tipton, L 10........Pa.
53*Tipton, P 2........Tenn.
35*Tipton, L 10........W. Va.
400*Tipton Hill, M 9........N. C.
1503 Tiptonville, L 3........Tenn.
....*Tip Top, G 21........Ky.
200*Tiptop, C 9........Va.
600*Tire Hill, P 7........Pa.
315 Tiro, F 13........Ohio
.... Tisbury, see Vineyard Haven........Mass.
200 Tisch Mills, P 15........Wis.
423 Tishomingo, B 23........Miss.
1951 Tishomingo, O 16........Okla.
920 Tiskilwa, E 13........Ill.
3 Titanic, F 24........Okla.
266 Titicus, N 3........Conn.
200 Titicut (State Farm), J 20........Mass.
574 Titonka, C 10........Iowa
125*Titus, J 17........Ala.
14*Titus, B 11........Ga.
2220 Titusville, G 20........Fla.
500 Titusville, H 11........N. J.
8126 Titusville, F 4........Pa.
3600 Tiverton, I 22........R. I.
621 Tiverton Four Corners, J 24........R. I.
30*Tivis, B 6........Va.
761 Tivoli, B 5, R 23........N. Y.
750*Tivoli, O 20........Tex.
49 Toadlena, D 2........N. M.
500 Toano, N 19........Va.
350*Toast, C 6........N. C.
100*Tobaccoport, K 8........Tenn.
59*Tobaccoville, D 7........N. C.
26*Tobaccoville, M 14........Va.
22*Tobar, C 18........Nev.
23 Tobe, P 19........Colo.
316 Tobias, N 20........Neb.
70*Tobins Harbor, C 4..Mich.
200*Tobinsport, R 11........Ind.
22*Tobique, H 11........Minn.
150*Toboso, J 13........Ohio
526 Tobyhanna, I 22........Pa.
5494 Toccoa, C 13........Ga.
150*Toccoa Falls, C 13........Ga.
332 Toccopola, O 17........Miss.
150 Tocsin, E 20........Ind.
15*Todd, I 17........Ky.
104 Todd (Elkland), C 3..N. C.
50*Todd, M 12........Pa.
150 Toddville, I 19........Iowa
350 Toddville, O 18........Md.
25*Toddville, H 23........S. C.
100*Toecane, M 9........N. C.
56*Toeterville, B 15........Iowa
75 Tofte, C 20........Minn.
105*Toga, M 12........Va.
5 Togo, Q 11........Iowa
3*Togo, E 14........Minn.
2350 Togus (Veterans Administration Home), N 9.Me.
2000 Tohatchie, E 2........N. M.
50*Tohickon, M 23........Pa.
250 Toimi, F 19........Minn.
450*Toivola, D 2........Mich.
410*Toivola, F 19........Minn.

Pop. Place Index State
89*Tokeland, L 3........Wash.
120 Tokio, M 6........Ark.
112 Tokio, H 18........N. D.
48*Tokio (Jonestown), G 6 Ohio
20*Tokio, D 8........Tex.
.... Tokio, see Wiggins........Tex.
50 Tolar, I 22........N. M.
320 Tolar, F 17........Tex.
225 Tolbert, A 14........Tex.
5 Tolchester Beach, F 18.Md.
195 Toledo, P 19........Ga.
852 Toledo, K 19........Ill.
2073 Toledo, J 16........Iowa
55 Toledo, I 19........Kan.
6*Toledo, Q 12........Mo.
23*Toledo, N 9........N. C.
282349 Toledo, C 10........Ohio
2288 Toledo, G 3........Ore.
523 Toledo, M 6........Wash.
10 Toledo Jc., G 13........Ohio
.... Toledo Terminal,........Ohio
600*Tolenas, H 6, B 22...Calif.
100*Toler, G 23........Ky.
121*Toliver, G 20........Ky.
10*Toliver, C 3........N. C.
50 Tolland, F 13........Colo.
165 Tolland, C 18........Conn.
50*Tolland, I 5........Mass.
325*Tollesboro, D 21........Ky.
1731 Tolleson, K 12........Ariz.
200 Tollette, N 6........Ark.
177 Tolley, E 8........N. D.
110*Toll Gate, E 9........W. Va.
70*Tollhouse, J 12........Calif.
250*Tollville, J 15........Ark.
172 Tolna, I 19........N. D.
56*Tolona, C 15........Mo.
876 Tolono, I 18........Ill.
150*Tolovana Park, B 5........Ore.
....*Tolson, O 14........Md.
171 Tolstoy, F 15........S. D.
460 Tolt, H 9........Wash.
25 Toltec, M 14........Ariz.
50 Toltec, O 15........Colo.
250 Tolu, H 7........Ky.
1433 Toluca, F 15........Ill.
20 Toluca, L 17........Mont.
200 Tom, R 25........Okla.
3817 Tomah, G 16........Wis.
75*Tomahawk, C 11........Ark.
35*Tomahawk, G 23........Ky.
24*Tomahawk, K 15........N. C.
3365 Tomahawk, J 10........Wis.
450 Tomales, H 5........Calif.
185*Tomato, C 23........Ark.
668*Tomball, K 22........Tex.
274 Tom Bean, C 20........Tex.
822 Tombstone, O 21........Ariz.
250 Tome, H 11........N. M.
1200 Tomkins Cove, F 5...N. Y.
.... Tom Nevers Head, R 16 Mass.
151*Tomnolen, F 16........Miss.
16*Tomotla, Q 3........N. C.
20*Tompkins Corners, E 6 N. Y.
1438 Tompkinsville, K 14....Ky.
225 Tompkinsville, O 12...Md.
219 Toms Brook, F 13........Va.
1500 Toms Creek, D 6........Va.
3290 Toms River, K 18....N. J.
445*Toms River Sta. (South Toms River), K 18.N. J.
3*Tonalea, E 13........Ariz.
643 Tonasket, C 17........Wash.
13008 Tonawanda, M 4....N. Y.
150*Toney, A 14........Ala.
35 Toneyfork, O 6........W. Va.
1 Tonga, H 11........Wash.
1114 Tonganoxie, G 23........Kan.
89*Tongs (Limeville), D 22 Ky.
150*Tongue River, M 17.Mont.
510 Tonica, E 15........Ill.
46*Tonieville, H 14........Ky.
3197 Tonkawa, C 13........Okla.
200 Tono, L 6........Wash.
50*Tonopah, K 12........Ariz.
2115 Tonopah, K 12........Nev.
189 Tontitown, B 5........Ark.
50*Tonto Basin, J 18........Ariz.
369 Tontogany, D 9........Ohio
186 Tony, G 10........Wis.
5001 Tooele, F 9........Utah
100*Tookland, B 7........Va.
593 Toomsboro, I 14........Ga.
350 Toomsuba, J 22........Miss.
305 Toone, P 4........Tenn.
84*Toonigh (Lebanon), E 6 Ga.
28*Top, I 18........Ore.
600*Topanga, O 15........Calif.
425*Topawa, N 14........Ariz.
80*Topaz, H 13........Calif.
50*Topaz, C 4........Mich.
25*Topaz, P 13........Mo.
82*Topeka, H 11........Ill.
496 Topeka, B 18........Ind.
67833 Topeka, G 21........Kan.
30 Topeka Jct., I 8........Ga.
46*Tophet, Q 10........W. Va.
121*Topinabee, G 16........Mich.
25*Topmost, H 22........Ky.
35*Topliff, G 10........Utah
19*Topnot, C 11........N. C.
55 Topock, H 3........Ariz.
50 Toponas, E 9........Colo.
3683 Toppenish, N 14........Wash.
50*Topping, M 21........Va.
225*Topsail, L 17........N. C.
1200 Topsfield, I 20........Me.
1150▲Topsfield, C 20........Mass.
1200 Topsham, O 8........Me.
165 Topsham, H 16........Vt.
100 Topstone (Sanford), M 4 Conn.
110*Topsy, C 20........N. C.
21*Topton, I 19........Ky.
250*Topton, Q 3........N. C.
1568 Topton, M 21........Pa.
263 Toquerville, Q 4........Utah
200*Torbert, J 13........La.
57*Torch, R 19........Mo.
100*Torch (Torch Hill), N 16 Ohio
143 Torchlight, F 23........Ky.
82*Toria, J 15........Ky.
100*Tornado, K 5........W. Va.
217*Tornillo, G 1........Tex.
350*Toro, H 5........La.
.... Toroda, B 19........Wash.
142*Toronto, J 23........Iowa
737 Toronto, L 21........Kan.
28*Toronto, L 12........Mo.
7426 Toronto, H 20........Ohio
362 Toronto, H 24........S. D.
75*Torpedo, F 6........Pa.
9950 Torrance, R 3........Calif.
48*Torrance, D 14........Miss.
5 Torrance, I 15........N. M.
500*Torrance, N 6........Pa.
200 Torras, I 12........La.
150*Torrent, G 20........Ky.
779▲Torreon, H 12........N. M.
32 Torres, Q 14........Colo.
231 Torrey, M 14........Utah
26988 Torrington, E 8....Conn.
2344 Torrington, M 24....Wyo.

Pop. Place Index State
....*Tortilla Flat, K 12....Ariz.
36*Toshes, P 9........Va.
200 Toston, K 10........Mont.
5130 Totowa, D 18........N. J.
.... Tottenville, J 4........N. Y.
41*Tottys, N 9........Tenn.
27*Totuskey, L 20........Va.
100*Totz, J 21........Ky.
250 Touchet, O 20........Wash.
38*Tougaloo, K 9........Miss.
450 Toughkenamon, Q 21...Pa.
73 Touhy, K 21........Neb.
500*Touisset, L 18........Mass.
1230 Toulon, E 11........Ill.
....*Toulouse, I 21........Ky.
15*Touristville, K 16........Ky.
20*Tousey, H 12........Ky.
37*Toutle, N 7........Wash.
933 Tovey (Humphrey), J 13 Ill.
39*Tow, I 16........Tex.
416*Towaco, D 14........N. J.
430 Towanda, G 16........Ill.
374 Towanda, L 17........Kan.
4154 Towanda, F 18........Pa.
50 Towaoc, P 2........Colo.
20*Tower, P 12........Ind.
200 Tower, H 18........Mich.
820 Tower, E 20........Minn.
215▲Tower, C 22........Wyo.
364 Tower City, M 22....N. D.
2221*Tower City, K 19........Pa.
3*Tower Falls, B 3........Wyo.
697 Tower Hill, K 15........Ill.
12 Tower Jc., E 20........Minn.
50*Towle (Baxter), N 18.Calif.
637 Town Creek, B 9........Ala.
175 Towner, K 24........Colo.
918 Towner, G 13........N. D.
250 Towners, D 6........N. Y.
75*Town Hill, I 19........Pa.
1175 Townley, E 9........Ala.
200 Town Line, M 5........N. Y.
.... Town of Temple. see Temple City........Calif.
216*Towns, L 15........Ga.
544 Townsend, E 21........Del.
450*Townsend, M 23........Ga.
1100 Townsend, C 15........Mass.
1309 Townsend, J 10........Mont.
378 Townsend, O 20........Tenn.
250 Townsend, O 23........Va.
409▲*Townsend, N 11........Wis.
500 Townsend Harbor, C 14 Mass.
90*Townsends Inlet, R 11 N. J.
18*Townshend (Osborne), J 12........Md.
210 Townshend, P 11........Vt.
221 Townsville, B 14........N. C.
294 Townville, F 4........Pa.
223 Townville, D 4........S. C.
2074 Towson, E 14........Md.
....*Toxaway, D 5........S. C.
300*Toxey, L 4........Ala.
464 Toyah, H 6........Tex.
30 Toyahvale, I 6........Tex.
1000*Toyon (Summit City), D 6........Calif.
165*Trabuco Canyon, P 17.Calif.
4056 Tracy, I 7........Calif.
120 Tracy, J 12........Conn.
375 Tracy, M 15........Iowa
130*Tracy, J 13........Ky.
3085 Tracy, P 6........Minn.
230*Tracy (Platte City), F 5 Mo.
100 Tracy, G 10........Mont.
100 Tracy, I 19........Tex.
2000 Tracy City, P 14........Tenn.
100*Tracys Landing, H 14..Md.
150 Tracyton, H 7........Wash.
100*Trade, D 12........Ala.
22*Trade, L 25........Tenn.
150 Trading Cove, J 21...Conn.
1493 Traer, I 16........Iowa
125*Traer, D 6........Kan.
500 Trafalgar (Liberty), K 14 Ind.
....*Traffic, N 15, M 22..Minn.
450 Trafford, E 13........Ala.
4017 Trafford, M 4........Pa.
120 Trail, E 6........Minn.
....*Trail, Q 13........Mo.
10 Trail, F 4........Okla.
28 Trail, P 7........Ore.
300 Trail City, D 11........S. D.
295 Trail Creek, B 9........Ind.
....*Trailcreek, D 4........Mont.
75*Trail Lake (Tralake), G 7........Miss.
.... Trail Ridge, B 13........Colo.
1716 Trainer, Q 22........Pa.
75*Tralake (Trail Lake), G 7........Miss.
100*Tralee, P 6........W. Va.
357*Tram, H 23........Ky.
75*Trammel, K 12........Ky.
150 Trammel, D 6........Va.
55 Trampas, D 14........N. M.
79*Tranquility, B 14........N. J.
165*Tranquillity (Tranquility), K 11........Calif.
.... Transfer, J 6........Ore.
160 Transfer, H 2........Pa.
150*Transit (East Amherst), N 5........N. Y.
50*Transylvania, B 14........La.
125*Traphill, C 5........N. C.
296 Trappe, K 18........Md.
497*Trappe, N 22........Pa.
....*Trappist, G 14........Ky.
226 Traskwood, K 11........Ark.
260*Trauger, N 5........Pa.
150*Traunik, F 9........Mich.
75 Travellers Rest, H 19...Ky.
1200 Travellers Rest, (Travelers Rest), B 6........S. C.
128*Traver, K 13........Calif.
14455 Traverse City, J 13..Mich.
....*Travis (Linoleumville), I 4........N. Y.
118*Travis, H 19........Tex.
309*Trawick, G 23........Tex.
14*Traxler, L 15........Miss.
3500*Trayser, P 2........Tenn.
73*Treadway, L 21........Tenn.
95 Treadwell, P 19........N. Y.
....*Treasure Island, F 11.N. J.
210 Treasureton, Q 21....Idaho
72*Treat, E 9........Ark.
25*Trebloc, E 19........Miss.
11*Trechado, H 4........N. M.
.... Tredegar, E 19........Ala.
568 Treece, O 25........Kan.
50*Trees, B 4........La.
....*Treetop, B 3........N. C.
96*Trego (Rohrersville), B 4........Md.
12 Trego, C 3........Mont.
75*Trego (Skippers), Q 16..Va.
200 Trego, D 8........Wis.
125 Treichlers (Treichler), K 22........Pa.
60 Treloar, I 17........Mo.
6 Tremain, O 24........Wyo.
500 Trementina, F 19....N. M.
935 Tremont, G 13........Ill.

Pop. Place Index State
112 Tremont, C 9........La.
40 Tremont, N 17........Me.
200 Tremont (West Wareham), L 22........Mass.
50*Tremont, C 22........Miss.
2314 Tremont, L 18........Pa.
50*Tremont, O 19........Tenn.
406 Tremont City, K 9....Ohio
1443 Tremonton, B 10........Utah
527 Trempealeau, E 16....Wis.
200 Trenary, F 8........Mich.
83*Trench, F 22........Ky.
26*Trenholm, M 15........Va.
25*Trent, G 20........Ky.
110 Trent, J 6........Ore.
240 Trent, K 24........S. D.
366 Trent, E 13........Tex.
126*Trent, P 5........W. Va.
165*Trenton, B 16........Ala.
773 Trenton, D 11........Fla.
570 Trenton, B 1........Ga.
1316 Trenton, M 12........Ill.
572 Trenton, K 9........Ky.
5284 Trenton, Q 22........Mich.
50 Trenton, K 15........Miss.
7046 Trenton, C 9........Mo.
920 Trenton, O 9........Neb.
124697 Trenton, I 13........N. J.
296 Trenton (Barneveld), K-17........N. Y.
431 Trenton, I 18........N. C.
80 Trenton, H 2........N. D.
777 Trenton, M 6........Ohio
408 Trenton, I 9........S. C.
3400 Trenton, N 4........Tenn.
634*Trenton, C 20........Tex.
553 Trenton, B 10........Utah
....*Trenton Jc., see West Trenton........N. J.
1500*Tresckow, J 21........Pa.
11*Tres Lagunas, J 4....N. M.
75 Tres Piedras, C 13...N. M.
330 Tres Pinos, J 8........Calif.
24*Tres Ritos, C 14........N. M.
2000*Treveskyn (Cuddy), L 3 Pa.
125*Trevett, O 9........Me.
57*Trevilians, (Trevilian) K 14........Va.
.... Trevino, C 14........Wis.
50*Trevlac, L 13........Ind.
184*Trevor, O 22........Wis.
2850 Trevorton, K 17........Pa.
400*Trevose, N 24........Pa.
85*Trexler, M 21........Pa.
380 Trexlertown, M 21........Pa.
219 Treynor, M 4........Iowa
527 Trezevant, M 5........Tenn.
359*Triadelphia, Q 24...W. Va.
75 Triana, B 13........Ala.
15*Triangle, Q 6........Idaho
250*Triangle, P 15........N. Y.
75*Triangle F Ranch (Bondurant), H 4........Wyo.
45*Triangle Ranch P.O., F 3 ....Mich.
40*Tribbett, G 7........Miss.
22*Tribbey, I 21........Ky.
150 Tribbey, K 14........Okla.
161*Tribble, I 4........W. Va.
800 Tribes Hill, M 21....N. Y.
607 Tribune, J 2........Kan.
20*Tribune, M 14........Mo.
75*Trickham, G 14........Tex.
290 Tridell, F 21........Utah
80*Trident, L 10........Mont.
125*Trigg, N 3........Va.
26*Trigo, J 11........Calif.
388 Trilby, H 14........Fla.
....*Trilby, see Selma........Kan.
.... Trilby, B 9........Ohio
200 Trilla, K 18........Ill.
150*Trimble, L 22........Ill.
85*Trimble, J 17........Ky.
126*Trimble, E 6........Mo.
686 Trimble, M 15........Ohio
763 Trimble, M 4........Tenn.
5*Trimble, I 8........Va.
775 Trimountain, D 2....Mich.
200 Trinchera (Trinchere), Q 18........Colo.
94 Trinidad, C 1........Calif.
13223 Trinidad, Q 16........Colo.
600*Trinidad, F 21........Tex.
210 Trinidad, J 16........Wash.
249 Trinity, B 11........Ala.
62*Trinity, D 20........Ky.
975 Trinity, E 9........N. C.
2217 Trinity, I 22........Tex.
6*Trinity Alps, D 3........Calif.
48*Trinity Center, D 3...Calif.
.... Trinity Place, N 4...Mass.
87*Trinity Springs, N 10..Ind.
432 Trinway, J 15........Ohio
148*Trio, J 20........S. C.
3800 Trion, C 2........Ga.
100*Triplet, E 21........Ky.
50*Triplet, Q 15........Va.
340 Triplett, E 10........Mo.
44*Triplett, C 2........N. C.
135*Triplett, H 7........W. Va.
1001 Tripoli, E 17........Iowa
200 Tripoli, I 9........Wis.
913 Tripp, N 20........S. D.
193*Tripp (Cassie), L 1..W. Va.
150*Triumph, O 13........Idaho
152 Triumph, D 15........Ill.
24*Triumph, P 20........La.
480 Triumph, Q 10........Minn.
75*Triunfo, N 13........Calif.
180 Trivoli, G 11........Ill.
60*Trixie, I 20........Ky.
200 Trojan, I 2........S. D.
166 Trommald, I 13........Minn.
775 Trona, L 18........Calif.
12 Tropic (Oakview), O 14 Colo.
514 Tropic, P 10........Utah
167 Trosky, Q 4........Minn.
150*Trosper, J 19........Ky.
950*Trotter, Q 4........Pa.
30 Trotters, K 1........N. D.
.... Trotters Point, B 9...Miss.
75*Trotville, C 21........N. C.
770 Trotwood, L 7........Ohio
....*Trough, see Pacolet Mills, S. C.
200*Trough Creek, N 11....Pa.
1526 Troup, F 22........Tex.
200 Troupsburg, R 9........N. Y.
202 Trousdale, L 10........Kan.
61 Trousdale, K 14........Okla.
.... Trout, Q 13........Idaho
850 Trout, F 10........La.
65*Trout, M 11........W. Va.
200*Trout Brook (Peakville), R 19........N. Y.
600 Trout Creek, E 1....Mich.
35 Trout Creek, F 1....Mont.
92*Trout Creek, Q 18....N. Y.
60 Trout Creek, I 2........Utah
211 Troutdale, C 8........Ore.
334 Trout Dale, E 10, Q 1..Va.
350 Trout Lake, F 16....Mich.
300 Troutlake, O 11........Wash.
50*Trout Lake, J 7........Wis.
566 Troutmans, F 6........N. C.
50 Trout River, C 21....N. Y.
175 Trout Run, H 15........Pa.

Pop.	Place	Index	State
....	*Troutville	G 10	Colo.
238	*Troutville	I 9	Pa.
500	Troutville	N 7	Va.
25	*Trowbridge	G 7	Calif.
55	*Trowbridge	K 16	Ill
75	*Trowbridge (Larew)	D 16	W. Va.
112	*Troxelville	K 15	Pa.
7055	Troy	M 18	Ala.
300	Troy	Q 20	Colo.
580	Troy	F 4	Idaho
1154	Troy	M 11	Ill.
599	Troy	Q 10	Ind.
110	Troy	P 18	Iowa
1049	Troy	D 23	Kan.
....	*Troy	J 15	La.
582	▲Troy	L 12	Me.
180	*Troy	P 22	Mich.
138	*Troy	C 19	Miss.
1493	Troy	H 18	Mo.
796	Troy	C 1	Mont.
1250	Troy	Q 8	N. H.
70304	Troy	N 24	N. Y.
1861	Troy	G 9	N. C.
9697	Troy	K 7	Ohio
150	Troy	O 15	Okla.
200	Troy	B 22	Ore.
1228	Troy	F 16	Pa.
224	Troy	G 7	S. C.
60	Troy	F 23	S. D.
513	Troy	L 4	Tenn.
650	Troy	H 18	Tex.
217	Troy	B 14	Vt.
39	*Troy	K 13	Va.
133	*Troy	G 10	W. Va.
130	Troy Center	N 21	Wis.
233	Troy Grove	D 15	Ill.
....	Troy Jc.	M 11	Ill.
200	*Troy Mills	I 20	Iowa
850	Truchas	E 14	N. M.
1000	Truckee	F 10	Calif.
231	*Trucksville	H 20	Pa.
50	Truckton	J 17	Colo.
600	*Trudeau	F 23	N. Y.
16	*True	P 9	W. Va.
21	*Truemans (Wellers)	G 7	Pa.
199	*Truesdail (Truesdale)	H 17	Mo.
135	*Truesdale	F 6	Iowa
50	*Truesdell	P 22	Wis.
5	*Truesville	E 17	Ky.
300	Trufant	N 14	Mich.
150	*Truhart	L 19	Va.
25	*Truitt	D 22	Ky.
353	▲*Trujillo (Vantanes)	F 18	N. M.
984	Truman	Q 11	Minn.
3381	Trumann (Truman)	E 20	Ark.
1130	Trumansburg	O 12	N. Y.
746	*Trumbauersville	M 23	Pa.
5294	▲Trumbull	N 7	Conn.
126	Trumbull	M 17	Neb.
100	*Trumbull	F 19	Tex.
353	Truro	N 11	Iowa
250	Truro	K 15	Mass.
7	Truro	E 9	N. D.
....	Truro	K 12	Ohio
475	Truscott	C 13	Tex.
1150	Trussville	F 14	Ala.
219	*Truthville	J 25	N. Y.
36	*Truxno	A 10	La.
200	Truxton	H 17	Mo.
250	Truxton	N 15	N. Y.
198	Tryon	J 10	Neb.
2043	Tryon	Q 9	N. C.
279	Tryon	G 14	Okla.
150	*Tryonville	F 4	Pa.
180	Tualatin	D 7	Ore.
500	Tubac	P 17	Ariz.
150	Tuba City	D 16	Ariz.
1100	Tucapau	B 8	S. C.
1000	Tuckahoe	P 13	N. J.
6563	Tuckahoe	G 6	N. Y.
26	*Tuckaseigee	Q 6	N. C.
250	Tucker	K 14	Ark.
400	Tucker	F 8	Ga.
90	Tucker	J 24	Okla.
75	*Tuckerdale	C 3	N. C.
88	*Tucker Hill	J 19	Va.
875	Tuckerman	E 17	Ark.
1320	Tuckerton	N 17	N. J.
....	Tuckertown	G 8	N. C.
36818	Tucson	N 17	Ariz.
6194	Tucumcari	G 22	N. M.
26	*Tudor	F 7	Calif.
75	Tuftonboro	K 17	N. H.
....	*Tufts College	L 3	Mass.
15	*Tugalo	C 13	Ga.
....	Tuggle	J 17	Tex.
....	Tujunga	Q 4 (Pop. incl. in Los Angeles)	Calif.
521	*Tukwila	I 9	Wash.
158	*Tula	C 16	Miss.
100	Tulalip	F 8	Wash.
8259	Tulare	K 13	Calif.
244	Tulare	H 18	S. D.
1446	Tularosa	M 13	N. M.
30	Tulasco	C 20	Nev.
785	*Tulelake (Tule Lake)	B 5	Calif.
162	*Tuleta	O 18	Tex.
113	*Tulga	D 22	Ky.
2055	Tulia	A 10	Tex.
180	*Tulip	M 11	Ark.
....	*Tulip (Fetner)	D 1	Ga.
20	*Tulip	P 10	Ohio
200	Tullahassee	G 21	Okla.
4549	Tullahoma	P 12	Tenn.
7	*Tullis	O 15	Wyo.
589	Tullos	F 10	La.
719	Tully	N 15	N. Y.
562	*Tullytown	O 25	Pa.
115	Tulot	E 20	Ark.
70	Tulpehocken	M 19	Pa.
142157	Tulsa	E 18	Okla.
150	*Tulsa, (La Barge)	M 3	Wyo.
100	*Tulsita	O 18	Tex.
50	Tumalo	I 11	Ore.
50	*Tumbling Shoals	E 14	Ark.
28	Tum Tum (Burnt Woods)	H 4	Ore.
100	Tumtum	G 22	Wash.
955	Tumwater	K 6	Wash.
33	*Tunas	M 11	Mo.
20	Tunbridge	F 14	N. D.
75	Tunbridge	I 13	Vt.
50	Tungsten	E 13	Colo.
86	*Tunica	J 13	Pa.
1322	Tunica	A 10	Miss.
156	*Tunis	C 20	N. C.
150	Tunis	J 20	Tex.
100	Tunis Mills	J 17	Md.
2161	Tunkhannock	G 20	Pa.
94	*Tunnel	Q 16	N. Y.
120	*Tunnel City	H 16	Wis.
255	Tunnel Hill	B 3	Ga.
200	*Tunnel Hill	Q 16	Ill.
50	*Tunnel Hill	G 14	Ky.
27	*Tunnel Hill	I 15	Ohio
625	Tunnel Hill	M 9	Pa.
100	*Tunnel Springs	M 10	Ala.
200	Tunnelton	N 13	Ind.
300	Tunnelton	M 6	Pa.
552	Tunnelton	E 15	W. Va.
35	*Tunstall	M 18	Va.
2000	Tuolumne	H 10	Calif.
....	*Tuolumne Meadows	I 11	Calif.
249	Tupelo	F 17	Ark.
8212	Tupelo	C 20	Miss.
450	Tupelo	M 17	Okla.
150	Tupelo	F 20	Tex.
....	*Tupelo, see Homeville		Va.
98	*Tupman	M 13	Calif.
5451	Tupper Lake	G 21	N. Y.
....	Tupper Lake Jc., see Tupper Lake		N. Y.
209	Tuppers Plains	O 16	Ohio
234	*Turbeville	H 18	S. C.
76	*Turbeville	Q 11	Va.
523	Turbotville	I 17	Pa.
146	Turin	G 5	Ga.
184	*Turin	I 3	Iowa
26	*Turin	H 20	Ky.
400	*Turin (McFarland)	F 7	Mich.
247	*Turin	J 17	N. Y.
50	*Turkey	B 11	Ark.
100	*Turkey	H 20	Ky.
188	*Turkey	I 15	N. C.
930	Turkey	A 12	Tex.
159	*Turkey City (Turkey)	I 5	Pa.
....	*Turkey, see Cleator		Ariz.
55	Turkey Creek	I 14	Fla.
81	*Turkey Creek	J 10	La.
17	Turkey Ford	C 24	Okla.
55	Turkey River	F 22	Iowa
22	*Turley	N 14	Mo.
....	Turley	C 6	N. M.
1200	Turley	E 18	Okla.
12	*Turley	L 18	Tenn.
4839	Turlock	I 9	Calif.
600	*Turn	H 6	N. M.
25	*Turnbull	P 4	Miss.
81	*Turner	K 18	Ark.
750	Turner	G 25	Kan.
350	Turner	N 6	Me.
1350	*Turner (Balnew)	D 14	Md.
159	Turner	L 20	Mich.
227	Turner	C 16	Mont.
414	Turner	F 7	Ore.
75	*Turner	Q 15	Va.
50	Turner	M 22	Wash.
....	Turner	J 7	W. Va.
150	*Turner Center	N 6	Me.
91	*Turners (Turners Station)	D15	Ky.
100	*Turnercrest	D 19	Wyo.
25	*Turners	O 10	Mo.
150	*Turnersburg	E 6	N. C.
6300	Turners Falls	C 8	Mass.
250	Turners Falls Jc.	D 8	Mass.
91	*Turners Sta. (Turners)	D 15	Ky.
....	*Turners Station, see Turner		Md.
796	*Turnersville	H 17	Tex.
75	*Turnerville	C 12	Ga.
200	*Turnerville	M 3	Wyo.
....	*Turney, see Prosit		Minn.
175	Turney	E 7	Mo.
200	*Turney	G 22	Tex.
70	*Turnpike (Hungerford)	Q 17	Pa.
200	Turnwood	R 20	N. Y.
594	Turon	L 13	Kan.
....	Turpentine	H 24	Tex.
100	Turpin	Q 7	Okla.
80	*Turpin (Venter)	L 18	Va.
515	Turrell	F 21	Ark.
15	*Turret	K 11	Colo.
89	*Turtle	N 16	Mo.
50	Turtle Bayou	K 24	Tex.
9805	Turtle Creek	M 4	Pa.
35	*Turtle Creek	M 5	W. Va.
....	Turtle Creek Jc.	M 6	Pa.
....	*Turtle Lake, see Marcell		Minn.
632	Turtle Lake	J 11	N. D.
616	Turtle Lake	C 10	Wis.
65	*Turtlepoint	E 10	Pa.
90	*Turtle River	F 10	Minn.
40	*Turtletown	Q 18	Tenn.
180	Turton	F 20	S. D.
20	Tusas	C 13	N. M.
27493	Tuscaloosa	G 8	Ala.
663	Tuscarawas	I 18	Ohio
69	*Tuscarora (Licksville)	D 8	Md.
75	Tuscarora	C 16	Nev.
180	*Tuscarora	O 8	N. Y.
900	*Tuscarora	K 20	Pa.
....	Tuscobia	D 9	Wis.
2838	Tuscola	I 19	Ill.
50	*Tuscola	F 23	Ky.
180	Tuscola	N 21	Mich.
150	*Tuscola	I 15	Miss.
600	Tuscola	F 13	Tex.
58	Tuscor	E 1	Mont.
210	Tusculum	J 23	Ga.
175	*Tusculum	M 22	Tenn.
5515	Tuscumbia	B 8	Ala.
269	Tuscumbia	K 13	Mo.
175	Tushka	O 18	Okla.
350	Tuskahoma	N 22	Okla.
18	*Tuskeegee	P 3	N. C.
3937	Tuskegee	J 20	Ala.
20	*Tuskegee	G 17	Okla.
375	Tuskegee Institute	J 20	Ala.
....	Tusler	J 22	Mont.
42	Tussy	N 12	Okla.
950	▲*Tusten	C 2, R 20	N. Y.
953	*Tustin	O 17, R 7	Calif.
253	Tustin	L 14	Mich.
55	*Tuthill	N 9	S. D.
79	*Tutor Key (Mingo)	G 22	Ky.
17	*Tuttle	P 10	Idaho
25	*Tuttle	J 19	Ky.
....	Tuttle	C 23	Nev.
357	Tuttle	L 14	N. D.
940	Tuttle	J 11	Okla.
665	Tutwiler	D 10	Miss.
44	*Tuweep	D 8	Ariz.
600	*Tuxedo	Q 8	N. C.
59	*Tuxedo	E 13	Tex.
525	*Tuxedo Park	B 21	Del.
2500	*Tuxedo Park (Tuxedo)	E 4	N. Y.
142	*Twain	E 10	Calif.
78	*Twain Harte	H 11	Calif.
217	Twelve Mile	E 13	Ind.
1200	*Twentynine Palms	M 20	Calif.
....	*Twentysix	F 20	Ky.
27	Twete	C 15	Mont.
1000	*Twila (Low)	K 21	Ky.
....	*Twilight, see Conway		Ark.
312	*Twilight	O 2	Pa.
3	Twilight	H 2	S. D.
25	Twin	E 3	Wash.
54	Twin Bluffs	H 19	Wis.
416	Twin Branch	Q 5	W. Va.
24	*Twin Bridges (Hebron)	P 13	Mo.
534	Twin Bridges	M 8	Mont.
121	Twin Brooks	E 24	S. D.
25	Twin Buttes	O 17	Ariz.
1019	*Twin City (Summit-Graymont)	N 13	Ga.
18	*Twin Creek	C 14	Ark.
11851	Twin Falls	Q 11	Idaho
....	*Twinfish	D 20	Wash.
189	Twining	L 20	Mich.
....	*Twining City (Randle Highlands)	I 11	D. C.
....	Twin Lake	O 3	Me.
125	*Twin Lake	N 11	Mich.
50	Twin Lakes	I 10	Colo.
....	*Twin Lakes	A 4	Conn.
....	*Twin Lakes	G 24	Pa.
150	*Twin Lakes	R 16	Minn.
409	Twin Lakes	N 22	Wis.
200	Twin Mountain	H 14	N.H.
480	Twin Peaks	Q 9	Calif.
80	Twin Rocks	C 4	Ore.
1541	*Twin Rocks	M 8	Pa.
800	Twinsburg	D 18	Ohio
100	*Twin Sisters	K 16	Tex.
300	*Twinton	L 15	Tenn.
844	Twin Valley	G 4	Minn.
477	Twisp	E 15	Wash.
12	*Twist	G 19	Ark.
95	*Twitty	D 6	Tex.
158	Two Buttes	O 23	Colo.
125	Twodot	J 12	Mont.
4046	Two Harbors	H 22	Minn.
100	Two Rivers	O 19	Wash.
10902	Two Rivers	Q 15	Wis.
....	Two Rivers Jc.	P 15	Wis.
27	*Two Rock	H 4	Calif.
21	*Twymans Mill	I 14	Va.
153	Tyaskin	O 20	Md.
....	*Tybee, see Savannah Beach		Ga.
100	Tye	F 13	Tex.
35	Tybo	J 16	Nev.
46	*Tyee	L 5	Ore.
200	Tye River	L 11	Va.
....	Tygart Jct.	F 14	W. Va.
64	*Tygarts Valley	D 22	Ky.
60	Tygh Valley	E 12	Ore.
12	Tyhee	P 18	Idaho
175	*Tyler	K 10	Ala.
26	*Tyler	F 14	Ark.
....	Tyler	D 12	Fla.
1005	Tyler	P 4	Minn.
150	Tyler	K 25	Mo.
6	*Tyler	H 14	Mont.
40	Tyler	P 25	N. D.
1536	Tyler	I 9	Pa.
28279	Tyler	F 22	Tex.
55	Tyler	I 22	Wash.
....	Tylerdale	O 2 (Pop. incl. in Washington)	Pa.
....	Tylerdale Jc.	O 2	Pa.
137	*Tyler Hill	F 23	Pa.
56	*Tylers	K 16	Va.
245	Tylersburg	H 6	Pa.
300	*Tylersburg (Leeper)	H 6	Pa.
350	*Tylersport	N 22	Pa.
255	*Tylersville	H 13	Pa.
30	Tylerton	R 19	Md.
1376	Tylertown	O 11	Miss.
110	*Tylerville (Goodspeeds)	K 16	Conn.
250	*Tynan	O 18	Tex.
1289	Tyndall	O 21	S. D.
318	Tyner	C 13	Ind.
121	*Tyner	H 19	Ky.
300	Tyner (Centre Hill)	D 21	N. C.
40	*Tyner	Q 15	Tenn.
1150	Tyngsboro	B 16	Mass.
250	*Tyngston (E. Wilton)	L 6	Me.
60	Typo	H 21	Ky.
60	*Tyre	N 23	Mich.
750	*Tyre (North Star)	M 2	Pa.
175	Tyringham	G 3	Mass.
160	*Tyro	N 15	Ark.
322	Tyro	O 21	Kan.
200	*Tyro	B 12	Miss.
75	*Tyro	L 11	Va.
50	Tyrola	L 16	Okla.
50	Tyrone (Yetta)	O 17	Colo.
118	Tyrone	G 6	Ga.
35	Tyrone	O 15	Iowa
190	Tyrone	F 16	Ky.
73	*Tyrone	O 15	Mo.
200	Tyrone	N 3	N. M.
75	*Tyrone	P 11	N. Y.
257	Tyrone	Q 6	Okla.
8845	Tyrone	L 11	Pa.
639	Tyronza	F 21	Ark.
....	Tyronza Jct.	F 20	Ark.
60	*Tyson (Morganville)	K 14	Ala.
79	*Tyson	M 11	Vt.
442	Ty Ty	N 10	Ga.

U

Pop.	Place	Index	State
597	Ubly	M 23	Mich.
50	Uceta	I 14	Fla.
449	Ucon	N 20	Idaho
24	Ucross	C 17	Wyo.
419	Udall	N 17	Kan.
78	*Udall	R 13	Mo.
137	Udell	P 16	Iowa
84	*Uebra	G 19	Mont.
253	Uehling	I 22	Neb.
33	*Uffington	C 14	W. Va.
107	*Uhlerstown	N 24	Pa.
350	*Uhlersville (Raubsville)	L 23	Pa.
6435	Uhrichsville	I 18	Ohio
264	Uintah	D 11	Utah
3731	Ukiah	F 3	Calif.
100	Ukiah	E 18	Ore.
105	*Ulah	F 9	N. C.
34	Ulan	K 19	Okla.
450	Uledi	P 4	Pa.
562	Ulen	G 4	Minn.
35	*Uler	I 8	W. Va.
375	*Uleta	O 22	Fla.
827	Ullin	Q 14	Ill.
146	*Ulm	J 16	Ark.
75	Ulm	G 9	Mont.
100	Ulm	B 16	Wyo.
85	*Ulman	K 13	Mo.
53	*Ulmer	H 7	Iowa
169	*Ulmers	M 12	S. C.
385	Ulster	E 18	Pa.
640	*Ulster Park	R 21	N. Y.
314	Ulvah	I 22	Ky.
11	Ulysses	J 13	Idaho
824	Ulysses	M 3	Kan.
35	*Ulysses	F 22	Ky.
429	Ulysses	K 20	Neb.
488	Ulysses (Lewisville)	E 13	Pa.
52	Umapine	B 20	Ore.
1149	Umatilla	F 17	Fla.
370	Umatilla	B 17	Ore.
30	*Umbarger	D 3	Tex.
74	*Umpire	L 5	Ark.
50	Umpqua	M 5	Ore.
16	*Una	E 11	Ark.
....	*Una	B 8	S. C.
1137	Unadilla	K 10	Ga.
223	Unadilla	M 23	Neb.
1079	Unadilla	P 18	N. Y.
200	*Unadilla Forks	O 19	N. Y.
36	*Unaka	Q 2	N. C.
170	Uncas	B 14	Okla.
989	*Uncasville	K 21	Conn.
....	Uncompahgre	L 6	Colo.
200	Underhill	E 9	Vt.
100	*Underhill	N 12	Wis.
100	*Underhill Center	E 9	Vt
325	*Underwood (Dogwood)	G 14	Ala.
250	*Underwood	O 17	Ind.
251	Underwood	L 4	Iowa
353	Underwood	J 6	Minn.
613	Underwood	K 10	N. D.
215	*Underwood	G 21	Pa.
214	*Underwood (New Underwood)	J 5	S. D.
200	Underwood	Q 10	Wash.
25	*Underwood	P 22	Wyo.
50	*Uneeda (Uneda)	M 5	W. Va.
10	Unger	Q 19	Okla.
210	Ungers Store	D 23	W. Va.
1500	Unicoi	M 24	Tenn.
45	Union	B 14	Ark.
36	Union (Pawnee)	D 19	Colo.
200	*Union (Julia)	K 4	Ga.
327	Union	B 17	Ill.
150	Union	P 6	Ind.
585	Union	H 14	Iowa
94	*Union	C 17	Ky.
740	*Union	N 16	La.
1200	Union	N 12	Me.
1543	Union	J 18	Miss.
2125	Union	J 18	Mo.
10	Union	G 22	Mont.
364	Union	L 24	Neb.
400	Union	M 19	N. H.
24730	■*Union (Unionbury)	E 17	N. J.
4000	Union	Q 15	N. Y.
40	Union	E 20	N. D.
280	Union	K 7	Ohio
587	Union (Union City)	I 10	Okla.
1398	Union	E 22	Ore.
8478	Union	C 10	S. C.
40	Union	M 17	Tex.
213	Union	F 11	Utah
175	Union	I 5	Wash.
346	Union	P 11	W. Va.
1893	Union Beach	G 19	N. J.
831	Union Bridge	C 10	Md.
24730	■Unionbury (Union)	E 17	N. J.
400	Union Center	Q 15	N. Y.
6	*Union Center	I 5	S. D.
190	Union Center	I 17	Wis.
125	*Union Church	M 7	Miss.
3500	Union City	J 9	Conn.
884	Union City	F 6	Ga.
3535	Union City	H 22	Ind.
40	*Union City	G 18	Ky.
1339	Union City	Q 15	Mich.
1497	*Union City	J 6	Ohio
5032	Union City		Ohio-Ind.
56173	Union City	E 20	N. J.
400	Union City (Union)	I 10	Okla.
3843	Union City	E 4	Pa.
7256	Union City	L 4	Tenn.
5	*Union Creek	P 7	Ore.
301	Uniondale	E 20	Ind.
1000	*Uniondale	H 7	N. Y.
348	Union Dale (Uniondale)	F 22	Pa.
600	*Union Deposit	N 17	Pa.
500	*Union Furnace	M 14	Ohio
976	Union Gap	M 14	Wash.
60	*Union Grove	C 15	Ala.
204	Union Grove	Q 20	N. Y.
100	*Union Grove	E 5	N. C.
973	Union Grove	O 21	Wis.
90	*Union Hall	P 7	Va.
150	*Unionhill	E 16	Ark.
75	*Union Hill	E 20	Ill.
125	*Union Hill	K 10	N. Y.
2	Union Jc.	E 21	Ore.
175	Union Level	Q 14	Va.
450	Union Mills	C 10	Ind.
225	Union Mills	B 11	Md.
175	*Union Mills	G 1	N. C.
118	*Union Mills	K 13	Va.
165	Union Mills	K 6	Wash.
225	*Union Pier	R 10	Mich.
1566	Union Point	F 14	Ga.
250	Unionport	I 20	Ohio
3107	Union Springs	K 19	Ala.
905	Union Springs	N 13	N. Y.
125	*Union Star	F 12	Ky.
411	Union Star	C 6	Mo.
1869	Uniontown	J 9	Ala.
130	Uniontown	E 4	Ark.
75	*Uniontown	Q 11	Ind.
277	Uniontown	L 24	Kan.
1327	Uniontown	G 8	Ky.
500	Uniontown	C 10	Md.
235	*Uniontown	M 22	Mo.
600	*Uniontown	G 18	Ohio
240	Uniontown (Fultonham)	K 15	Ohio
21819	Uniontown	P 4	Pa.
329	*Uniontown	M 16	Pa.
332	Uniontown	M 24	Wash.
13	Uniontown	C 11	W. Va.
111	*Union Valley	O 15	N. Y.
105	*Union Village	J 16	Vt.
2084	Unionville	F 11	Conn.
200	Unionville	R 17	Ill.
42	*Unionville	L 12	Ind.
253	Unionville	P 16	Iowa
140	*Unionville	L 19	Me.
156	Unionville	D 10	Md.
362	*Unionville	H 17	Mass.
500	Unionville	M 21	Mich.
2052	Unionville	A 11	Mo.
41	*Unionville	E 8	Nev.
387	Unionville	E 2	N. Y.
144	*Unionville	I 7	N. C.
480	*Unionville	B 19	Ohio
233	*Unionville (Unionville Center)	I 10	Ohio
321	*Unionville	L 2	Pa.
225	Unionville	P 21	Pa.
304	Unionville	K 12	Pa.
300	*Unionville	O 11	Tenn.
100	*Unionville	J 14	Va.
233	*Unionville Center (Unionville)	I 10	Ohio
220	*Uniopolis	H 8	Ohio
825	*United	N 5	Pa.
175	*United States Naval Ammunition Depot	J 7	Nev.
....	*United States Naval Training Station, see Naval Training Station—War College		R. I.
....	*United States Submarine Base (Submarine Base)	L 21	Conn.
310	*Unity	Q 13	Ill.
350	Unity	L 11	Me.
50	Unity	N 7	N. H.
700	*Unity	M 3	Pa.
286	Unity	H 12	Wis.
25	*Unityville	H 15	Pa.
95	Unityville	L 22	S. D.
603	Universal	K 5	Ind.
2000	*Universal	M 4	Pa.
....	*Universal City	N 15	Calif.
2000	*University	G 8	Ala.
....	*University	L 15	La.
15	*University	C 15	Miss.
7	*University	E 3	Nev.
30	University	E 12	N. C.
....	University	H 23	N. D.
....	University	K 12	Va.
32023	University City	I 20	Mo.
5981	*University Heights	D 16	Ohio
....	*University of Richmond	M 17	Va.
462	University Park	M 16	Iowa
....	*University Park	D 8	Ore.
14458	University Park	E 19	Tex.
....	*University Place	L 22 (Pop. incl. in Lincoln)	Neb.
11	*Uno	I 13	Va.
5	*Uno	P 5	W. Va.
7	*Unus	N 12	W. Va.
300	Upalco	G 19	Utah
50	*Upatoi	J 4	Ga.
53	*Upchurch	K 15	Ky.
243	Upham	F 12	N. D.
6316	Upland	Q 7	Calif.
900	Upland	G 18	Ind.
317	Upland	N 15	Neb.
2431	Upland	P 22	Pa.
5370	Upper Arlington	K 11	Ohio
500	*Upper Black Eddy	N 24	Pa.
90	*Upperco (Arcadia)	D 13	Md.
78	*Upper Dam	K 3	Me.
56883	■ Upper Darby	P 23	Pa.
510	Upper Fairmont	Q 20	Md.
300	Upper Falls	E 15	Md.
300	Upper Frenchville (Saint Luce)	A 16	Me.
25	*Upperglade	J 12	W. Va.
320	*Upper Gloucester	O 6	Me.
....	*Upper Hill	Q 20	Md.
250	*Upper Jay	F 23	N. Y.
500	Upper Lake	F 4	Calif.
700	*Upper Lehigh	I 20	Pa.
5	Upper Lehigh Jc.	J 21	Pa.
200	*Upper Lisle	Q 16	N. Y.
565	Upper Marlboro	J 13	Md.
20	*Upper Mattole	D 2	Calif.
2000	*Upper Mauch Chunk	J 21	Pa.
100	*Upper Middletown	P 4	Pa.
924	*Upper Nyack	F 5	N. Y.
510	Upper Saddle River	C 19	N. J.
....	*Upper St. Regis	D 21	N.Y.
3907	Upper Sandusky	G 11	Ohio
....	*Upper Saranac, see Saranac Inn		N. Y.
326	*Upper Strasburg	O 13	Pa.
80	*Upper Tract	I 17	W. Va.
406	*Upper Tygart	E 21	Ky.
270	Upperville	F 15	Va.
36	*Upper Zion	J 17	Va.
26	*Upright	K 19	Va.
347	Upsala	K 11	Minn.
100	*Upshaw	L 18	Va.
125	*Upson	H 6	Wis.
....	Upton	A 20	Ill.
30	Upton	R 2	Ind.
369	Upton	H 13	Ky.
140	*Upton	L 2	Me.
1500	Upton	H 16	Mass.
200	*Upton	N 14	Mo.
100	*Upton	E 3	N. C.
112	*Upton	E 17	Utah
545	Upton	E 22	Wyo.
35	Ural	C 2	Mont.
800	Urania	F 10	La.
119	*Urbain	O 16	Ill.
421	Urban	I 19	Ky.
142	*Urban	K 17	Pa.
26	*Urban	D 9	Wash.
175	*Urbana	Q 11	Ark.
14064	Urbana	H 19	Ill.
312	Urbana	E 16	Ind.
397	Urbana	H 19	Iowa
150	*Urbana	M 23	Kan.
375	*Urbana	M 11	Mo.
14	Urbana	M 19	N. D.
8335	Urbana	J 9	Ohio
185	*Urbana	J 23	Tex.
650	*Urbancrest	K 12	Ohio
1083	Urbandale	K 11	Iowa
93	*Urbanette	A 7	Ark.
482	Urbanna	L 20	Va.
75	*Uree	G 1	N. C.
25	Urey	K 8	Pa.
800	Uriah	N 8	Ala.
465	Urich	J 7	Mo.
164	*Urland (Cedar)	P 3	W. Va.
....	*Urlton, see Earlton		N. Y.
30	Ursa	I 4	Ill.
301	Ursina	Q 6	Pa.
....	Ursina Jc.	Q 6	Pa.
63	Ursine	K 23	Nev.
85	*Ursula	G 5	Ark.
250	*Ury	O 8	W. Va.
....	*Useppa Island	L 16	Fla.
150	*Ushers	M 23	N. Y.
221	Usk	E 24	Wash.
16	Usna	R 3	Okla.
15	*Usona	I 11	Calif.
200	*Usquepaugh	K 10	R. I.
....	*Usta	D 6	S. D.
200	Ustick	N 5	Idaho
....	Utah Railway Jc.	I 16	Utah
150	*Utahville	K 9	Pa.
30	*Ute	L 4	Colo.
581	Ute	I 4	Iowa
81	Ute Park	C 17	N. M.
1019	Utica (North Utica)	D 15	Ill.
325	Utica	P 17	Ind.
379	Utica	I 7	Kan.
300	Utica	H 10	Ky.
1022	*Utica	P 23	Mich.
179	Utica	Q 22	Minn.
818	Utica	L 8	Miss.
450	Utica	D 9	Mo.
62	*Utica	H 13	Mont.
539	Utica	L 20	Neb.
100518	Utica	L 18	N. Y.
1376	Utica	J 14	Ohio
90	Utica	Q 17	Okla.
216	Utica	G 4	Pa.
95	Utica	O 22	S. D.
65	*Utica Institute	L 9	Miss.
25	*Utility	G 11	La.
36	*Utley	K 18	Tex.
14	*Utleyville	Q 22	Colo.
500	Utopia	L 14	Tex.
....	Uva	M 21	Wyo.
20	*Uvada	G 20	Nev.
592	Uvalda	L 17	Ga.
6679	Uvalde	M 13	Tex.
150	Uvalde Jc. (North Uvalde)	M 13	Tex.
200	*Uwchland (Byers)	O 21	Pa.
6417	■*Uxbridge	I 15	Mass.
16	*Uz	I 22	Ky.
....	*Uzzell, see Carlisle		Ark.

V

Pop.	Place	Index	State
14	*Vacation	H 4	Calif.
1614	Vacaville	H 6	Calif.
....	Vaccaro	M 15	Calif.
115	Vacherie	N 16	La.
....	*Vade	G 10	Calif.
55	*Vade Mecum	C 8	N. C.
80	*Vaden	M 9	Ark.
479	Vader	M 5	Wash.
92	*Vadis	G 11	W. Va.
200	*Vadito	C 15	N. M.
225	*Vado	O 9	N. M.
18	*Vago	N 12	W. Va.
50	Vahki	L 13	Ariz.
601	Vaiden	G 14	Miss.
....	Vail	O 18	Ariz.
576	Vail	I 6	Iowa
85	*Vail (Vails)	D 11	N. J.
25	Vail	L 11	Pa.
125	*Vail	K 6	Wash.
200	Vails Gate	D 4	N. Y.
....	Vair	H 23	Tex.
1208	Valatie	P 24	N. Y.
25	*Valcour	D 24	N. Y.
98	*Valdasta	D 20	Tex.
580	Valders	P 16	Wis.
2615	Valdese	E 3	N. C.
250	Valdez	Q 16	Colo.
110	Valdez	C 15	N. M.
15595	Valdosta	P 12	Ga.
80	Vale (Fayette Junction)	C 5	Ark.
25	*Vale	E 21	Ky.
107	*Vale	G 4	N. C.
1083	Vale	J 23	Ore.
150	Vale	H 3	S. D.
93	*Vale	M 7	Tenn.
19	*Vale	M 12	W. Va.
100	*Valeda	O 23	Kan.
4	Valedon	N 2	N. M.
70	*Valeene	O 12	Ind.
350	Valencia	H 11	N. M.
296	Valencia	L 3	Pa.
110	Valentine	F 7	Ariz.
21	Valentine	H 16	Mont.
2188	Valentine	E 11	Neb.
499	*Valentine	I 5	Tex.
16	*Valentines	Q 15	Va.
310	*Valera	G 14	Tex.
79	*Valeria	K 14	Iowa
18	*Valeria	F 20	Ky.
200	Vale Summit	M 5	Md.
12	*Valhalla	K 9	Mo.
2200	*Valhalla	G 6	N. Y.
175	*Valhalla	Q 9	N. C.
100	*Valhermoso Springs	C 13	Ala.
930	Valier	O 15	Ill.
641	Valier	D 8	Mont.
500	Valier	J 7	Pa.
20	*Valjean (Dalesburg)	H 21	Ky.
160	*Vallecito	H 9	Calif.
800	*Vallecito	P 6	Colo.
275	Vallecitos	C 12	N. M.
200	*Valle Crucis	C 2	N. C.
20072	Vallejo	H 5	Calif.
64	*Valles Mines	J 19	Mo.
200	Valley City (Valley	J 7	Ill.
500	Valley	E 13	Ky.
107	*Valley	I 9	Miss.
985	Valley	J 23	Neb.
....	Valley	F 10	N. J.
15	*Valley	D 1	N. C.
275	Valley	E 22	Wash.
40	*Valley	E 21	W. Va.
80	*Valley	H 17	Wis.
80	Valley	E 6	Wyo.
1830	▲Valley Bend	I 14	W. Va.
200	Valley Center	P 19	Calif.
700	Valley Center	L 16	Kan.
139	*Valley Center	N 23	Mich.
18	*Valley Center	I 8	Va.
30	*Valley Chapel	G 11	W. Va.
5917	Valley City	M 21	N. D.
250	Valley City	E 16	Ohio
1000	*Valley Cottage	F 5	N. Y.
....	*Valley Creek	K 19	Tenn.
100	Valley Crossing	K 12	Ohio
1241	Valley Falls	F 22	Kan.
564	*Valley Falls	M 24	N. Y.
6	*Valley Falls	O 14	Ore.
5542	Valley Falls	C 17	R. I.
200	*Valley Ford	H 4	Calif.
250	Valleyford	H 24	Wash.
200	Valley Forge	O 22	Pa.
26	*Valleyfork	K 8	W. Va.
150	*Valley Grove	Q 24	W. Va.
439	Valley Head	B 20	Ala.
150	Valley Head	J 14	W. Va.
200	*Valley Home	I 9	Calif.
....	Valley Jc., see West Des Moines		Iowa
7	Valley Jc.	E 2	N. Y.
275	Valley Jc., (Zoarville)	H 18	Ohio
....	Valley Jc.	Q 16	Pa.
....	Valley Jc.	I 20	Tex.
45	Valley Jc.	H 16	Wis.
300	*Valley Lee	P 15	Md.
50	Valley Mills	J 13	Ind.
803	Valley Mills	G 18	Tex.
36	*Valleyoak	I 18	Ky.
26	*Valley Park	J 7	Miss.
2091	Valley Park	I 20	Mo.
41	*Valley Point	C 16	W. Va.
20	Valley Ranch	F 15	N. M.
115	*Valley Spring	I 15	Tex.
210	Valley Springs	B 10	Ark.
500	Valley Springs (Valley Spring)	H 9	Calif.
396	Valley Springs	L 25	S. D.
16679	Valley Stream	H 6	N. Y.
10	Valleytown	C 18	Mont.
200	Valley View	G 17	Ky.
11	Valleyview	H 14	Neb.
753	*Valley View	D 17	Ohio
1500	*Valley View	L 18	Pa.
700	Valley View	C 18	Tex.
103	*Valley Wells	O 14	Tex.
551	Valliant	Q 22	Okla.
160	*Vallicita	H 10	Calif.
486	Vallonia	N 14	Ind.
50	*Vallorso	Q 18	Colo.
750	Vallscreek (Hartwell)	R 6	W. Va.
591	Valmeyer	N 9	Ill.
20	Valmont	M 13	N. M.
110	Valmy	D 12	Nev.
125	*Valmora	E 17	N. M.
200	Valois	O 12	N. Y.
....	*Valona	M 23	Ga.
221	Valparaiso	N 5	Fla.
8736	Valparaiso	C 8	Ind.
403	Valparaiso	K 21	Neb.
100	*Valrico	I 14	Fla.
60	Valsetz	F 4	Ore.
300	Value (Brandon)	K 12	Miss.
300	*Valverda	J 13	La.
65	*Valyermo	N 16	Calif.
20	Vamoosa	L 16	Okla.
16	*Van	L 17	Ark.
85	*Van	I 22	Ky.
25	Van	C 9	Mont.
....	*Van	N 18	Ore.
50	*Van	H 5	Pa.
1500	Van	E 21	Tex.
300	*Van	M 5	W. Va.
7	Vanadium	M 5	Colo.
200	Vanadium (Hanover Junction)	M 4	N. M.
1650	*Van Alstyne	C 19	Tex.
125	Vananda	J 19	Mont.
90	*Vanatta	J 14	Ohio
5422	Van Buren	F 4	Ark.
825	Van Buren	F 18	Ind.
3300	Van Buren	B 19	Me.

Pop. Place Index State

458 Van Buren, P 18......Mo.
307 Vanburen (Van Buren), E 9......Ohio
32*Van Buren Furnace, F 12......Va.
....*Van Buren Point, Q 2.N. Y.
102*Vance, G 10......Ala.
115*Vance, C 10......Miss.
.... Vance, L 23......N. D.
125*Vance, K 14......S. C.
63*Vance, K 13......Tex.
700 Vanceboro, H 22......Me.
826 Vanceboro, H 19......N. C.
1184 Vanceburg, D 21......Ky.
.... Vance Jc., M 5......Colo.
98*Vancleave, R 21......Miss.
70 Van Cleve (Capron), I 15......Iowa
75*Vancleve (Calla), G 21..Ky.
25*Vancourt, H 12......Tex.
18788 Vancouver, Q 7......Wash.
....*Vancouver Barracks, Q 7......Wash.
5288 Vandalia, L 15......Ill.
360*Vandalia, R 12......Mich.
2672 Vandalia, F 16......Mo.
24 Vandalia, D 19......Mont.
378 Vandalia, K 7......Ohio
110 Vandalia, B 22......Tex.
436 Vandemere, H 21......N. C.
405 Vanderbilt, J 18......Mich.
1063*Vanderbilt, P 5......Pa.
250*Vanderbilt, M 20......Tex.
....*Vandercook, see Tilton..Ill.
65*Vandercook Lake, Q 17......Mich.
10725 Vandergrift, L 5......Pa.
75*Vanderlip (West Romney), E 20......W. Va.
100*Vanderpool, L 14......Tex.
30*Vanderpool, I 8......Va.
416 Vandervoort, K 4......Ark.
300*Vandiver, G 15......Ala.
970 Vandling, F 22......Pa.
291 Vanduser, P 23......Mo.
7000*Van Dyke, P 24......Mich.
52*Vandyke, B 8......Va.
200 Vandyne, N 16......Wis.
110*Vanetta, M 8......W. Va.
440 Van Etten, Q 13......N. Y.
30 Vang, D 20......N. D.
275 Van Hiseville, J 17....N. J.
100*Van Hoesen (South Schodack), N 24....N. Y.
329 Van Hook, H 7......N. D.
Van Horn, see Pine Grove......Ore.
1000 Van Horn, I 4......Tex.
22 Van Horn, D 10......Wash.
551 Van Horne, I 18......Iowa
117*Vanhornesville, J 19..N. Y.
600 Van Houten, C 18....N. M.
1723 Van Lear, G 22......Ky.
206 Vanleer (Van Leer), M 9......Tenn.
355 Vanlue, F 10......Ohio
436 Van Meter, L 11......Iowa
750*Van Meter, N 5......Pa.
50 Van Metre, J 11......S. D.
167*Vanna, D 14......Ga.
519 Vanndale, G 19......Ark.
18*Vannoy, C 4......N. C.
....*Van Nuys, O 15, Q 3 (Pop. incl. in Los Angeles).Calif.
81 Van Orin, D 13......Ill.
230 Van Ormer, L 9......Pa.
100 Vanoss, M 15......Okla.
875 Vanport, L 2......Pa.
56*Vansant, B 7......Va.
....*Vantanes, see Trujillo.N. M.
82 Van Tassell, K 24......Wyo.
275 Van Vleck, M 21......Tex.
150*Van Vleet, D 19......Miss.
500*Van Voorhis, O 3......Pa.
67*Vanvoorhis (Van Vorhis), C 13......W. Va.
20 Van Wagners, C 6....N. Y.
311*Van Wert, E 2......Ga.
383 Van Wert, O 11......Iowa
9227 Van Wert, F 6......Ohio
50 Van Wert, M 14......Pa.
*Vanwood, see Mead.W. Va.
....*Van Wyck, C 14......S. C.
64 Van Zandt, C 8......Wash.
19*Vanzant, G 11......Ky.
26*Vanzant, P 13......Mo.
626 Vardaman, E 17......Miss.
220 Varina, F 7......Iowa
500 Varina, G 13......N. C.
383 Varna, E 14......Ill.
169 Varna, P 14......N. Y.
315 Varnado, J 19......La.
150*Varnell, B 4......Ga.
5 Varner, M 15......Ark.
32*Varner, M 14......Kan.
75*Varney, H 23......Ky.
....*Varney, M 8......Mont.
11*Varney, P 4......W. Va.
917 Varnville, N 13......S. C.
250 Varysburg, N 6......N. Y.
861▲*Vasa, O 19......Minn.
200 Vashon, I 7......Wash.
40 Vashti, L 17......N. D.
135 Vashti, C 17......Tex.
.... Vasona, J 6......Calif.
75 Vasper, M 18......Tenn.
728 Vass, H 11......N. C.
100 Vassalboro, M 9......Me.
25*Vassar (Avon), F 4...Idaho
98*Vassar, H 22......Kan.
2154 Vassar, N 21......Mich.
700 Vaucluse, I 9......S. C.
50*Vaucluse, E 13......Va.
300 Vaughan, I 12......Miss.
218 Vaughan, C 16......N. C.
115*Vaughan, L 10......W. Va.
75 Vaughn, H 7......Ga.
25 Vaughn, J 10......Kan.
40 Vaughn, G 10......Mont.
1331 Vaughn, H 17......N. M.
300 Vaughn, I 6......Wash.
51*Vaughns Mill, G 19....Ky.
300 Vaughnsville, F 7......Ohio
123*Vaughtsville (Maymead), L 25......Tenn.
22*Vawter, K 12......Minn.
15 Vay, C 4......Idaho
108 Vayland, I 18......S. D.
31 Veach, H 24......Tex.
....*Vealmoor, F 10......Tex.
.... Veazie, K 15......Me.
486 Veblen, C 22......S. D.
1781 Veedersburg, H 7......Ind.
60*Vega, Q 19......N. Y.
34 Vega, K 17......S. D.
515 Vega, D 2......Tex.
57 Vega, J 7......Wash.
15*Vegan, H 13......W. Va.
*Vegas Verde, see North Las Vegas......Nev.
500 Veguita, I 10......N. M.
30*Vein Mtn., F 1......N. C.
600 Velarde, D 13......N. M.
755 Velasco, M 22......Tex.
....*Velma, D 14......Miss.
5 Velma, I 7......Neb.
120 Velma, N 11......Okla.
200 Velpen, P 8......Ind.
1017 Velva, H 11......N. D.

*Venable, see Carrboro.N. C.
100*Venado, G 3......Calif.
214 Venango, L 7......Neb.
300 Venango, F 3......Pa.
200*Venator, N 18......Ore.
50*Vendor, C 9......Ark.
174 Venedocia, G 6......Ohio
115*Venedy, N 12......Ill.
.... Veneer Jc., K 15....Mich.
200 Veneta, J 5......Ore.
512*Venetia (Anderson), N 3 Pa.
50*Venezia (Goodwin), I 11......Ariz.
35*Venia, B 7......Va.
.... Venice, Q 3 (Pop. incl. in Los Angeles)......Calif.
507 Venice, K 13......Fla.
5454 Venice, M 10......Ill.
300 Venice, Q 21......La.
250*Venice, D 13......Ohio
238 Venice, L 11......Utah
59*Venice Center, N 13..N. Y.
*Venice Hill, see Ivanhoe......Calif.
35*Venio, O 22......N. D.
.... Venter, see Turpin......Va.
29*Venters (Carmen), I 23.Ky.
7905 Ventnor, P 16......N. J.
210 Venton, P 20......Md.
36*Ventress, K 13......La.
....*Ventucopa, N 11......Calif.
13264 Ventura (San Buenaventura), N 13......Calif.
252 Ventura, D 12......Iowa
.... Ventura Jc., N 13....Calif.
257 Venturia, Q 16......N. D.
250*Venus, K 18......Fla.
3 Venus, F 17......Neb.
125*Venus, H 4......Pa.
321 Venus, E 18......Tex.
4 Veo, N 19......Iowa
98*Vera, L 15......Ill.
16*Vera, F 17......Mo.
.... Vera, Q 12......Ohio
208 Vera, D 19......Okla.
250*Vera, C 14......Tex.
50*Vera, N 12......Va.
142*Vera Cruz, F 20......Ind.
300*Vera Cruz, L 22......Pa.
35*Veradale, H 23......Wash.
18*Verba, L 18......Miss.
147 Verbank, C 6......N. Y.
88*Verbank Village, R 23, C 6......N. Y.
500 Verbena, I 14......Ala.
25 Verboort, D 6......Ore.
1500*Verda, J 21......Ky.
27*Verda, G 9......La.
108*Verdel, F 18......Neb.
575 Verden, K 9......Okla.
150 Verdery, F 7......S. C.
110 Verdi, P 3......Minn.
275 Verdi, G 2......Nev.
6*Verdi, E 5......Va.
556 Verdigre, F 18......Neb.
250 Verdigris, E 20......Okla.
397 Verdon, O 25......Neb.
65 Verdon, E 20......S. D.
26*Verdon, L 17......Va.
1500*Verdugo City, N 15...Calif.
116*Verdunville (Verdun), O 4......W. Va.
351 Vergas, I 6......Minn.
73 Verendrye, H 12......N. D.
324 Vergennes, P 14......Ill.
1662 Vergennes, G 5......Vt.
....*Verger, see Folsom......La.
39*Veribest, H 12......Tex.
24*Vermejo Park, C 18..N. M.
312 Vermilion, J 22......Ill.
1616 Vermilion, D 14......Ohio
184 Vermilion Grove, I 21...Ill.
300 Vermillion, D 20......Kan.
107*Vermillion, O 17......Minn.
3324 Vermillion, P 24......S. D.
945 Vermont, H 9......Ill.
564 Vermontville, P 15...Mich.
150*Vermontville, E 22...N. Y.
150*Verna, N 11......Miss.
1105▲Vernal, P 21......Miss.
2119 Vernal, F 23......Utah
210*Vernalis, I 8......Calif.
521 Verndale, I 9......Minn.
29*Verne (Polleyton), J 18.Ky.
50*Verner, O 4......W. Va.
200*Vernfield, N 22......Pa.
759 Vernon, E 5......Ala.
142 Vernon, I 22......Ariz.
850*Vernon, O 15, Q 3....Calif.
75 Vernon, E 23......Colo.
250 Vernon, E 16......Conn.
539 Vernon, M 9......Fla.
290 Vernon, M 15......Ill.
413 Vernon, M 18......Ind.
65*Vernon, L 22......Kan.
25*Vernon, K 15......Ky.
61*Vernon, D 9......La.
507 Vernon, O 19......Mich.
225 Vernon, A 15......N. J.
587 Vernon, L 17......N. Y.
175 Vernon, Q 13......Ohio
56 Vernon (Vernon Jc.), G 13......Ohio
420 Vernon, J 19......Okla.
75*Vernon, N 9......Tenn.
9277 Vernon, B 14......Tex.
210 Vernon, H 9......Utah
80 Vernon, R 12......Vt.
8*Vernon, I 10......W. Va.
355 Vernon Center, Q 12.Minn.
250*Vernon Center, L 17..N. Y.
75*Vernon Hill, Q 11......Va.
56*Vernon Jc. (Vernon), G 13......Ohio
1412 Vernonia, B 6......Ore.
3050 Vero Beach, J 22......Fla.
33*Verona, B 11......Ark.
75*Verona, G 7......Calif.
211 Verona, E 17......Ill.
156*Verona, C 17......Ky.
250*Verona, C 22......Mich.
526 Verona, D 20......Miss.
405 Verona, P 8......Mo.
41 Verona, E 13......Mont.
50 Verona, M 18......Neb.
8957 Verona, D 18......N. J.
192*Verona, L 17......N. Y.
100*Verona (Verona Sta), L 17......N. Y.
86*Verona, K 18......N. C.
201 Verona, P 20......N. D.
346 Verona, K 6......Ohio
4356 Verona, M 4......Pa.
75*Verona (Rolla), J 10....Va.
535 Verona, K 20......Wis.
100*Verona Station (Verona), L 17......N. Y.
1267*Verplanck, F 6......N. Y.
300*Versailles, H 22......Conn.
590 Versailles, I 7......Ill.
582 Versailles, M 20......Ind.
2548 Versailles, F 17......Ky.
1781 Versailles, J 11......Mo.
250 Versailles, O 4......N. Y.
1711 Versailles, I 6......Ohio
2401*Versailles, L 3......Pa.
140*Verse, I 19......Wyo.
65 Vershire, I 15......Vt.
53*Vertrees, G 13......Ky.

56 Veseleyville, F 22....N. D.
154*Veseli, P 16......Minn.
175*Vesper, G 13......Kan.
300 Vesper, I 14......Wis.
10*Vessie, L 15......Mo.
66*Vest, H 22......Ky.
334 Vesta, O 7......Minn.
125 Vesta, N 23......Neb.
80*Vesta, Q 5......Va.
50 Vesta, L 4......Wash.
500 Vestaburg, N 16......Mich.
1062*Vestaburg, O 3......Pa.
178*Vestal, Q 15......N. Y.
116*Vestal (Delmar), E 8...Va.
500 Vestal Center, R 15...N. Y.
31*Vester, I 15......Ky.
10 Vestry, Q 20......Miss.
75*Vests, Q 2......N. C.
375 Vesuvius, K 10......Va.
25 Vetal, N 10......S. D.
400*Veteran, N 23......Wyo.
.... Veterans Administration, see Wood......Wis.
.... Veterans Administration, Home, see Wadsworth......Kan.
.... Veterans Administration Home, see Togus....Me.
507*Veterans Administration Hospital, G 17......Ind.
....*Veterans Bureau Hospital, I 5......Calif.
1866*Veterans Home, G 5..Calif.
....*Veterans Home, see Bay Pines......Fla.
....*Veterans Hospital, G 8.Ala.
50*Veto, A 12......Ala.
1209 Vevay, N 21......Ind.
100 Veyo, P 2......Utah
941 Vian, I 23......Okla.
65*Vibbard, F 7......Mo.
29*Viboras, O 2......Tex.
659 Viborg, N 23......S. D.
150*Viburnum, M 18......Mo.
....*Vicars, see Vicker......Va.
175*Vicco, I 22......Ky.
14*Vicey, C 7......Va.
210 Vichy, K 15......Mo.
617 Vici, E 4......Okla.
50 Vick, Q 13......Ark.
325*Vick, I 11......La.
125*Vicker (Vicars), O 5....Va.
.... Vickers, C 10......Ohio
175*Vickery, D 12......Ohio
1000*Vickery, E 19......Tex.
250 Vickeryville, N 16....Mich.
180 Vicksburg, J 6......Ariz.
100 Vicksburg, M 7......Ind.
20*Vicksburg, I 6......Ky.
1774 Vicksburg, Q 13......Mich.
24460 Vicksburg, K 7......Miss.
210*Vicksburg, J 16......Pa.
225*Victor, H 8......Calif.
1784 Victor, J 14......Colo.
294 Victor, N 23......Idaho
763 Victor, K 17......Iowa
25*Victor, F 13......Kan.
350 Victor, J 4......Mont.
1111 Victor, M 10......N. Y.
6 Victor, L 24......Okla.
62 Victor, C 23......S. D.
100*Victor, L 8......W. Va.
446 Victoria, E 10......Ill.
884 Victoria, H 10......Kan.
57*Victoria, B 24......Mich.
276 Victoria, N 14......Minn.
19*Victoria, A 14......Miss.
162*Victoria, K 19......Mo.
260 Victoria, Q 14......Tenn.
11566 Victoria, N 19......Tex.
1555 Victoria, P 14......Va.
3000 Victorville, N 18......Calif.
50*Victory, I 19......Ky.
25 Victory, M 4......Okla.
104▲*Victory, E 20......Vt.
143*Victory, F 18......Wis.
520*Victory Mills (Victory), L 24......N. Y.
50*Vida, J 14......Ala.
10*Vida, L 15......Mo.
50 Vida, F 22......Mont.
79 Vida, I 8......Ore.
39*Vidal, N 20......Calif.
4109 Vidalia, K 18......Ga.
1318 Vidalia, G 13......La.
113*Vidauri, O 19......Tex.
25*Vidette, A 14......Ark.
160 Vidette, H 18......Ga.
400*Vidor, K 25......Tex.
.... Viele, Q 21......Iowa
2063 Vienna, L 10......Ga.
1173 Vienna, Q 16......Ill.
78 Vienna, O 16......Ind.
50 Vienna, B 9......La.
90 Vienna, M 7......Me.
385 Vienna, M 20......Md.
433 Vienna, K 14......Mo.
209 Vienna, D 11......N. J.
420*Vienna (South Vienna), K 9......Ohio
313 Vienna, H 22......S. D.
1237 Vienna, F 17......Va.
2338*Vienna, E 6......W. Va.
108*Viers, C 6......Va.
75*View, F 13......Tex.
85 Viewfield, J 5......S. D.
48*Viewtown, H 14......Va.
100 Vigo, N 13......Ohio
32*Vigo Park, E 3......Tex.
61*Vigus, I 19......Mo.
146 Viking, D 4......Minn.
129*Vilas, P 23......Colo.
45*Vilas, C 2......Fla.
47*Vilas, M 22......Kan.
50*Vilas, D 2......N. C.
91 Vilas, K 21......S. D.
50*Vildo, P 4......Tenn.
227 Villa, K 6......W. Va.
90*Village, Q 9......Ark.
....*Village O 15, Q 3....Calif.
....*Village, P 17......N. H.
158*Village, K 20......Va.
416 Village Mills, J 24......Tex.
150 Village Springs, E 14...Ala.
18*Villa Grande, G 3....Calif.
125 Villagrove (Villa Grove), L 12......Colo.
2072 Villa Grove, I 19......Ill.
....*Villa Maria, J 2......Pa.
125*Villamont, N 8......Va.
600*Villanova, P 23......Pa.
62*Villa Nova (Duck), J 9......W. Va.
600 Villanueva, G 16.....N. M.
7236*Villa Park, C 20......Ill.
106*Villa Park, I 18......N. J.
248 Villard, L 8......Minn.
1522 Villa Rica, F 4......Ga.
521 Villa Ridge, R 15......Ill.
165*Villa Ridge, J 18......Mo.
....*Villas, Q 12......N. J.
108*Villa Tasso (Bolton), N 6......Fla.
6 Villegreen, P 19......Colo.
3721 Ville Platte, K 10......La.
2011 Villisca, O 6......Iowa
259*Vilonia, H 13......Ark.
38*Vim, C 17......Colo.
82*Vim, O 3......N. D.

27*Vimville, K 21......Miss.
40*Vimy Ridge, J 11......Ark.
472 Vina, C 6......Ala.
300 Vina, E 6......Calif.
1900 Vinalhaven, O 15......Me.
18228 Vincennes, O 5......Ind.
54*Vincennes (Sand Prairie), Q 20......Iowa
1108 Vincent, G 15......Ala.
250 Vincent, G 21......Ark.
192 Vincent, H 10......Iowa
34*Vincent, H 20......Ky.
300 Vincent, N 17......Ohio
115*Vincent, F 11......Tex.
865 Vincentown, K 12....N. J.
79 Vinco (Perkins), F 14.Okla.
162*Vindex, N 3......Md.
25*Vine, H 19......Ky.
100*Vineburg, G 3......Calif.
30 Vinegar Bend, N 3.....Ala.
822 Vine Grove, G 13......Ky.
48 Vineland, L 16......Colo.
100 Vineland (Orange Center), H 17......Fla.
125*Vineland, K 19......Mo.
7914 Vineland, O 10......N. J.
55*Vineland, Q 15......Va.
125*Vinemont, D 12......Ala.
76*Vinemont, N 20......Pa.
258 Vineyard, J 18......Ark.
40*Vineyard, I 11......Ky.
50 Vineyard, D 17......Tex.
160 Vineyard, G 12......Utah
1500 Vineyard Haven, O 23Mass.
126*Vining, J 17......Iowa
188*Vining, D 17......Kan.
176 Vining, J 7......Minn.
18 Vining, B 9......Okla.
250*Vinings, E 6......Ga.
5685 Vinita, C 22......Okla.
60*Vinita, L 15......Va.
75*Vinland, H 23......Kan.
.... Vinland, G 6......Wash.
26*Vinnie, I 17......Ky.
188 Vinson, L 2......Okla.
310 Vintage, P 20......Pa.
75*Vinton, E 10......Calif.
4163 Vinton, I 18......Iowa
1787 Vinton, M 5......La.
387 Vinton, P 14......Ohio
141*Vinton, F 1......Tex.
3455 Vinton, N 7......Va.
161*Vinton, L 9......W. Va.
1516*Vintondale, M 8......Pa.
280 Viola, A 14......Ark.
123*Viola, D 7......Calif.
113*Viola, H 22......Del.
75 Viola, F 3......Idaho
743 Viola, E 8......Ill.
150 Viola, I 21......Iowa
131 Viola, N 15......Kan.
80*Viola (Corinne), F 13.Mich.
62*Viola, Q 20......Minn.
25*Viola, R 8......Mo.
40 Viola, E 8......Ore.
240*Viola, O 13......Tenn.
825 Viola, G 18......Wis.
33 Viola, M 4......Wyo.
57*Violet, O 20......La.
21 Violet, O 23......Neb.
25 Violet, P 18......Tex.
200*Violet Hill, C 14......Ark.
110*Viper, I 21......Ky.
3140 Virden, J 12......Ill.
206*Virden, P 2......N. M.
33 Virgelle, E 12......Mont.
500*Virgie, H 24......Ky.
99 Virgil, B 17......Ill.
494 Virgil, L 21......Kan.
75*Virgil, Q 21......Okla.
145 Virgil, I 19......S. D.
350*Virgilia, E 8......Calif.
358 Virgilina, R 11......Va.
143 Virgin, Q 5......Utah
10 Virgin, L 14......Wis.
250*Virginia, Q 20......Idaho
1418 Virginia, I 10......Ill.
12264 Virginia, F 19......Minn.
144 Virginia, N 22......Neb.
75 Virginia, O 24......W. Va.
2600 Virginia Beach, P 23....Va.
380 Virginia City, N 8...Mont.
488 Virginia City, H 3....Nev.
90 Virginia City, D 6......Va.
100 Virginia Dale, B 14...Colo.
.... Virginia Point, M 23...Tex.
150*Virginville, M 20......Pa.
50*Virginville, O 24....W. Va.
3549 Viroqua, F 18......Wis.
8904 Visalia, K 13......Calif.
129 Visalia, C 17......Ky.
3000*Vista, P 19......Calif.
100 Vista, L 9......Mo.
18*Vista, K 17......N. C.
15*Vistillas, O 14......Ore.
190 Vitis (Richland), H 14..Fla.
2460 Vivian, B 4......La.
4 Vivian, J 19......Okla.
200 Vivian, K 13......S. D.
3000 Vivian, Q 6......W. Va.
61*Vixen, N 9......N. C.
140 Vliets (Vleits), D 19...Kan.
100*Voca, H 14......Tex.
237 Volant, I 2......Pa.
40*Volborg, J 22......Mont.
150 Volcano, H 10......Calif.
9 Volcano (Hydrate), E 9......Colo.
50*Volcanoville, G 10....Calif.
417 Volga (Volga City), E 20......Iowa
632 Volga, I 23......S. D.
250 Volga, G 13......W. Va.
429*Volga City (Volga), E 20......Iowa
292 Volin, O 23......S. D.
48*Volland, H 20......Kan.
56*Volney, E 10......Va.
15 Volt, D 22......Mont.
62*Volta, J 9......Calif.
66 Voltage, M 19......Ore.
101 Voltaire, H 11......N. D.
200 Voluntown, I 24......Conn.
*Volusia, see National Gardens......Fla.
226 Vona, H 22......Colo.
*Vonnie, see Richards..Wyo.
400 Vonore, O 18......Tenn.
350*Von Ormy, M 16......Tex.
717 Voorheesville, O 23...N. Y.
75*Voorhies, G 17......Iowa
50*Vorden, G 8......Calif.
....*Voris, E 5......Mo.
83*Vortex, G 20......Ky.
300 Vosburg (Vossburg), L 19......Miss.
30 Voss, G 22......N. D.
57*Voss, G 14......Tex.
24*Votaw, K 24......Tex.
600*Voth, K 24......Tex.
75*Vowells Mill, G 7......La.
50*Vowinckel, H 6......Pa.
5*Vox, J 18......Ky.
666 Vredenburgh, M 9.....Ala.
*Vredenburgh Junction, see Hybart......Ala.
80 Vriesland, O 12......Mich.
40 Vroman, M 18......Colo.
1700 Vulcan, G 5......Mich.

29*Vulcan, M 19......Mo.
.... Vulcan, C 9......Ohio
69*Vulcan, P 3......W. Va.
4000*Vultee Field, N 15....Calif.
8*Vya, D 3......Nev.

W

3500 Waban, N 1......Mass.
26*Wabaningo (Sylvan Beach), N 11......Mich.
150*Wabash, K 19......Ark.
9653 Wabash, E 16......Ind.
75 Wabash, L 23......Neb.
75 Wabash, H 5......Ohio
2368 Wabasha, P 21......Minn.
248*Wabasso, I 22......Fla.
604 Wabasso, P 8......Minn.
90 Wabaunsee, G 20......Kan.
258 Wabbaseka, K 15......Ark.
25*Wabd, I 18......Ky.
5*Wabedo, G 12......Minn.
38 Wabek, H 8......N. D.
1200 Wabeno, M 10......Wis.
92 Wabuska, H 5......Nev.
125*Waccabuc (Lake Waccabuc), F 6....N. Y.
548 Wachapreague, L 24....Va.
125*Wacissa, C 6......Fla.
304 Waco, F 2......Ga.
226 Waco, G 18......Ky.
237 Waco, O 6......Mo.
203 Waco, L 19......Neb.
281*Waco, H 3......N. C.
55982 Waco, G 19......Tex.
25*Waconda Springs, F 13......Kan.
1315 Waconia, N 14......Minn.
130 Wacousta, O 17......Mich.
62*Waddams Grove, A 11..Ill.
50*Waddington, D 1......Calif.
671 Waddington, D 18....N. Y.
300*Waddy, F 16......Ky.
140*Wade, R 21......Miss.
380 Wade, H 13......N. C.
150 Wade, M 18......Ohio
200 Wade, Q 18......Okla.
377 Wadena, E 20......Iowa
2916 Wadena, I 8......Minn.
32*Wadesboro, L 17......La.
3587 Wadesboro, I 8......N. C.
.... Wadesboro Jc., J 8...N. C.
55*Wadestown, C 13...W. Va.
200 Wadesville, Q 3......Ind.
116*Wadesville, E 14......Va.
32*Wadeville, H 9......N. C.
200*Wadhams, F 24......N. Y.
*Wadhams Mills, see Wadhams......N. Y.
1000 Wading River, G 9...N. Y.
493 Wadley, H 20......Ala.
1133 Wadley, I 18......Ga.
80*Wadmalaw Island (Martins Point), N 19...S. C.
150 Wadsworth, I 15......Ala.
150*Wadsworth, A 20......Ill.
2300 Wadsworth (Veterans Administration Home), F 24......Kan.
200 Wadsworth, G 5......Nev.
14*Wadsworth, M 8......N. Y.
6495 Wadsworth, F 16......Ohio
200*Wadsworth, N 21......Tex.
.... Wadsworth Jc., M 9..N. Y.
1018 Waelder, L 18......Tex.
160*Wagar, N 5......Ala.
588 Wagener, I 11......S. C.
10*Wagersville, H 18......Ky.
14 Wages, D 23......Colo.
249 Waggoner, K 12......Ill.
75*Waggy, L 10......W. Va.
50 Wagner, D 17......Mont.
98*Wagner, L 14......Pa.
1319 Wagner, O 19......S. D.
150*Wagners (Pocono Lake), I 22......Pa.
28*Wago, K 15......Ky.
24 Wagoner, I 11......Ariz.
.... Wagoner, F 10......La.
30*Wagoner, C 3......N. C.
3535 Wagoner, F 21......Okla.
979 Wagon Mound, E 18.N. M.
7*Wagontire, N 18......Ore.
50*Wagontown, P 21......Pa.
35*Wagon Wheel Gap, O 8......Colo.
....*Wagon Works (Auburndale), C 9......Ohio
388 Wagram, J 11......N. C.
7 Waha, H 4......Idaho
60 Wahalak, H 21......Miss.
1500*Wahjamega, N 22....Mich.
20 Wahkiacus (Wahkiakus), P 12......Wash.
273 Wahkon, J 15......Minn.
.... Wahl, C 8......Wash.
4 Wahluke, L 17......Wash.
2648 Wahoo, K 22......Neb.
3747 Wahpeton, P 25......N. D.
25*Wahsatch (Wasatch), C 14......Utah
100*Waidsboro (Lanahan), P 7......Va.
410 Wainola, B 25......Mich.
157*Wainscott, G 11......N. Y.
185*Wainville, K 12.....W. Va.
45*Wainwright, I 14......Mo.
520 Wainwright, I 17......Ohio
162 Wainwright, H 20....Okla.
165*Waite, I 20......Me.
289*Waite Hill, C 18......Ohio
1427 Waite Park, L 12....Minn.
25*Waiteville, Q 12....W. Va.
4 Waitley, D 20......Colo.
20*Waitman, G 11......Ky.
936 Waitsburg, N 21......Wash.
675 Waitsfield, G 10......Vt.
.... Waits Jc., G 16......Fla.
210 Waits River, H 15......Vt.
1033 Wakarusa, B 15......Ind.
150*Wakarusa, G 21......Kan.
87*Waka, A 5......Tex.
86*Wake, M 21......Va.
1852 Wakeeney, G 8......Kan.
60*Wakefield, M 19......Ill.
513 Wakefield, F 17......Kan.
65*Wakefield, F 15......Ky.
27 Wakefield, J 13......La.
16223■Wakefield, D 19....Mass.
3591 Wakefield, B 22......Mich.
961 Wakefield, G 21......Neb.
50 Wakefield, L 19......N. H.
200*Wakefield, O 12......Ohio
4000 Wakefield, M 13......R. I.
104*Wakefield, I 23......Tex.
687 Wakefield, P 19......Va.
.... Wakefield Center, D 19......Mass.
.... Wakefield Jc., D 19...Mass.
1562 Wake Forest, E 15...N. C.
87 Wakelee, R 12......Mich.
522 Wakeman, E 14......Ohio
253 Wakenda, F 10......Mo.
40*Wakenva, C 6......Va.
444 Wakita, B 10......Okla.
451 Wakonda, O 23......S. D.
200 Wakpala, D 12......S. D.
320▲*Wakulla, C 5......Fla.

50*Wakulla, K 12......N. C.
985 Walbridge, C 10......Ohio
300 Walburg, I 18......Tex.
60 Walco, K 10......Ark.
122*Walcott, C 19......Ark.
440 Walcott, K 23......Iowa
375 Walcott, O 24......N. D.
46 Walcott, O 15......Wyo.
668 Walden, C 11......Colo.
200 Walden, I 10......Ga.
50*Walden, J 19......Ky.
4262 Walden, D 4......N. Y.
10 Walden, L 22......N. D.
30 Walden, E 16......Vt.
150*Waldenburg, E 19....Ark.
91*Walden Heights (Summit), E 16......Vt.
53*Waldheim, K 19......La.
1240 Waldo, P 8......Ark.
567 Waldo, D 14......Fla.
257 Waldo, G 11......Kan.
30*Waldo, H 22......Ky.
30 Waldo, M 13......Me.
50 Waldo, F 13......N. M.
341*Waldo, H 11......Ohio
.... Waldo, R 4......Ore.
324 Waldo, P 17......Wis.
1500 Waldoboro, N 11......Me.
700*Waldorf, L 12......Md.
240*Waldorf, Q 15......Minn.
630 Waldport, H 3......Ore.
75 Waldrip, H 14......Tex.
1298 Waldron, I 5......Ark.
600 Waldron, K 17......Ind.
163 Waldron, O 13......Kan.
424 Waldron, R 18......Mich.
235 Waldron, F 5......Mo.
36*Waldron, C 6......Wash.
110*Waldrop, K 15......Va.
20*Waldrup, L 18......Miss.
2475 Waldwick, C 19......N. J.
19*Wales, I 23......Ky.
400 Wales, N 7......Me.
367▲Wales, I 10......Mass.
50 Wales, G 22......Minn.
270 Wales, D 18......N. D.
124*Wales, P 10......Tenn.
223 Wales, I 13......Utah
170 Wales, N 20......Wis.
140*Wales Center, N 5...N. Y.
264 Waleska, D 6......Ga.
120*Walford, I 18......Iowa
2001 Walford (Bessemer), J 1.Pa.
93 Walhalla, L 11......Mich.
1138 Walhalla, D 21......N. D.
2820 Walhalla, C 3......S. C.
125*Walhonding, I 15....Ohio
39*Walker, I 11......Ariz.
50*Walker, H 15......Ark.
10*Walker, B 4......Calif.
30*Walker, I 15......Ill.
462 Walker, H 19......Iowa
110*Walker, H 10......Kan.
24*Walker, J 20......Ky.
424 Walker, L 16......La.
939 Walker, G 11......Minn.
265 Walker, L 7......Mo.
200*Walker, K 8......N. Y.
25 Walker, J 6......Ore.
15*Walker, C 10......S. D.
30*Walker, F 7......W. Va.
.... Walker, L 21......Wyo.
16*Walker Ford (Walkerford), M 10......Va.
60 Walkermine, E 9....Calif.
....*Walker Park, F 10....Ga.
....*Walkers, see Armada..Ark.
75*Walkers (Walker), M 19......Va.
150 Walker Springs, M 7...Ala.
731 Walkersville, D 8......Md.
205 Walkersville, H 12..W. Va.
1178 Walkerton, C 12......Ind.
90*Walkerton, L 19......Va.
410*Walkertown, D 8....N. C.
200*Walker Valley, R 21, C 4......N. Y.
250 Walkerville, M 11....Mich.
1880 Walkerville, K 7.....Mont.
2098*Wall, M 4......Pa.
500 Wall, K 7......S. D.
50*Wall, H 12......Tex.
60 Wallace, O 10......Ala.
117*Wallace, H 9......Calif.
3839 Wallace, E 7......Idaho
123*Wallace, I 7......Ind.
102*Wallace, G 2......Kan.
500*Wallace, M 17......La.
200*Wallace, H 7......Mich.
159*Wallace, E 5......Mo.
335 Wallace, L 9......Neb.
300 Wallace, P 9......N. Y.
1050 Wallace, J 16......N. C.
193 Wallace, F 22......S. D.
162 Wallace, E 7......Va.
650 Wallace, E 12......W. Va.
5 Wallace, Jc., K 10....Ind.
.... Wallace Jc., D 2......Pa.
....*Wallace Ridge, F 12....La.
386 Wallaceton, J 10......Pa.
1123▲Wallagrass, B 15......Me.
175 Walland, O 19......Tenn.
18109 Walla Walla, O 21..Wash.
19*Wallback, J 8......W. Va.
99*Wallburg, E 8......N. C.
1 Walle, I 24......N. D.
600*Walled Lake, P 22...Mich.
518 Waller, K 21......Tex.
200*Wallerville, B 19.....Miss.
92*Walling, O 14......Tenn.
11425 Wallingford, K 12...Conn.
233*Wallingford, B 8......Iowa
48*Wallingford, E 20......Ky.
1000*Wallingford, P 23......Pa.
700 Wallingford, M 8......Vt.
8981 Wallington, D 18......N. J.
150 Wallington, L 11.....N. Y.
903 Wallins Creek (Wallins), K 20......Ky.
1000 Wallis, L 21......Tex.
60 Wallis Run, H 16......Pa.
37*Wallisville, K 24......Tex.
800 Wallkill, D 4......N. Y.
762 Wall Lake, H 6......Iowa
14 Wallner, L 21......Pa.
90*Wallonia, J 8......Ky.
110*Walloon Lake, I 15...Mich.
110*Walloon Lake Station (Clarion), I 15.....Mich.
515 Wallopsburg (Beyer), K 7......Pa.
838 Wallowa, C 22......Ore.
25 Wallpack Center, B 11.N. J.
300*Walls, L 14......La.
150 Walls (Alpica), A 11..Miss.
39 Walls, K 23......Okla.
233 Wallsburg, G 14......Utah
518*Wallsend, K 20......Ky.
18*Wallula, F 24......Kan.
150 Wallula, O 18......Wash.
100*Wallum Lake, B 6....R. I.
211 Wallville, N 15......Md.
30 Wallville, M 12......Okla.
10*Walmsley, K 20......Va.
200*Walnut, D 8......Ark.
213*Walnut, O 15, Q 4....Calif.
961 Walnut, D 12......Ill.
.... Walnut, D 14......Ind.
902 Walnut, L 6......Iowa

Pop.	Place, Index	State
544	Walnut, M 24	Kan.
516	Walnut, A 19	Miss.
13	Walnut, F 17	Neb.
650*	Walnut, N 7	N. C.
150*	Walnut, M 14	Pa.
250*	Walnut Bottom (Greythorne), O 14	Pa.
1084	Walnut Cove, C 8	N. C.
1578	Walnut Creek, B 21	Calif.
150*	Walnut Creek, H 16	Ohio
206*	Walnut Grove, D 17	Ala.
60*	Walnut Grove, D 16	Ark.
631	Walnut Grove, H 7	Calif.
117*	Walnutgrove, F 10	Ga.
42*	Walnut Grove, G 8	Ill.
186*	Walnut Grove, I 18	Ky.
753	Walnut Grove, P 7	Minn.
653	Walnut Grove, J 16	Miss.
310	Walnut Grove, N 9	Mo.
175	Walnut Hill, R 7	Ark.
175	Walnut Hill, M 1	Fla.
160	Walnut Hill, N 15	Ill.
100	Walnut Hill, O 6	Me.
....*	Walnut Lake, see Pickens,	Ark.
1271	Walnutport, K 22	Pa.
2013	Walnut Ridge, C 18	Ark.
50*	Walnut Shade, Q 10	Mo.
50*	Walnut Springs, M 4	Ark.
723	Walnut Springs, F 18	Tex.
100*	Walpole, O 18	Ill.
120*	Walpole, O 10	Me.
7443■	Walpole, H 18	Mass.
475	Walpole, P 6	N. H.
5855	Walsenburg, O 15	Colo.
200	Walsens, O 15	Colo.
406	Walsh, P 23	Colo.
45*	Walsh, O 11	Ill.
21*	Walsh, D 22	Ky.
138*	Walsh, C 4	N. C.
130*	Walshville, K 12	Ill.
368	Walston, J 7	Pa.
198*	Walstonburg (Fieldsboro), G 17	N. C.
....*	Walter, see Hardin	Tex.
3373	Walterboro, N 15	S. C.
250*	Walterhill, N 12	Tenn.
536*	Walteria, O 15, Q 4	Calif.
45*	Walters, F 11	La.
46*	Walters (Whisp), D 21	Ark.
154*	Walters, R 13	Minn.
2238	Walters, O 8	Okla.
127*	Walters, Q 19	Va.
550*	Waltersburg, P 4	Pa.
28*	Waltersville (Shawanee), G 19	Ky.
400	Waltersville, K 7	Miss.
92	Walterville, J 7	Ore.
142	Walthall, F 17	Miss.
75	Walthall, N 17	Va.
40020	Waltham, F 18, M 1	Mass.
172	Waltham, Q 18	Minn.
25	Waltham (Norbert), G 11	Mont.
1204	Walthill, G 22	Neb.
300*	Walthourville, M 21	Ga.
218	Walthourville (Lambert), M 22	Ga.
20	Waltman, I 14	Wyo.
125*	Walton, J 22	Fla.
710	Walton, F 13	Ind.
217	Walton, K 16	Kan.
973	Walton, C 17	Ky.
150*	Walton (Essex), D 5	Mont.
75	Walton, L 22	Neb.
3697	Walton, Q 18	N. Y.
25	Walton, J 4	Ore.
10	Walton (Gaffney), E 13	Pa.
....	Walton, O 4	Va.
350	Walton, I 7	W. Va.
434	Waltonville, N 15	Ill.
205*	Waltreak, H 7	Ark.
23*	Waltz, E 21	Ky.
475	Waltz, Q 22	Mich.
....*	Waluga, see Lake Grove,	Ore.
50	Walum, K 20	N. D.
....	Walville, M 5	Wash.
10	Walworth, I 14	Neb.
500*	Walworth, L 10	N. Y.
875	Walworth, N 22	Wis.
1432	Wamac, N 14	Ill.
1767	Wamego, F 19	Kan.
400	Wamesit, C 18	Mass.
250	Wamic, E 11	Ore.
250*	Wampee, H 24	S. C.
282	Wampsville, L 16	N. Y.
1061	Wampum, K 2	Pa.
169	Wamsutter, O 12	Wyo.
130*	Wan, M 20	Va.
93*	Wana, C 13	W. Va.
150*	Wanakena, G 19	N. Y.
315	Wanamaker, J 15	Ind.
4	Wanamaker, M 10	S. D.
156*	Wanamakers (Wanamaker), L 21	Pa.
1600	Wanamie, I 20	Pa.
449	Wanamingo, P 18	Minn.
300*	Wananish, L 14	N. C.
3143	Wanaque (Wanaque-Midvale), C 17	N. J.
750	Wanatah, C 10	Ind.
300	Wanblee, L 9	S. D.
1000	Wanchese, E 25	N. C.
191*	Wanda, P 8	Minn.
125*	Wanderoos, B 10	Wis.
35	Wandin, L 8	Pa.
265	Wando, M 19	S. C.
18*	Wanego, J 8	W. Va.
25*	Waneta, H 19	Ky.
6*	Waneta, J 12	W. Va.
665	Wanette, L 14	Okla.
100	Wanilla, M 11	Miss.
56	Wann, K 23	Neb.
147	Wann, B 19	Okla.
50*	Wannaska, B 6	Minn.
....	Wannee, D 11	Fla.
1604*	Wanneta (Albion), E 2	Pa.
50*	Wannville (Wann), B 18	Ala.
68	Wanship, E 14	Utah
....	Wantage, A 15	N. J.
1284	Wantagh, I 7	N. Y.
4	Wanoga, K 11	Ore.
5225	Wapakoneta, H 7	Ohio
730	Wapanucka, O 16	Okla.
20	Wapato, D 6	Ore.
1483	Wapato, M 14	Wash.
496	Wapella, H 15	Ill.
1603	Wapello, N 22	Iowa
35	Wapinitia, F 12	Ore.
....*	Wapiti, C 7	Wyo.
150*	Wappapello, P 20	Mo.
986	Wapping, D 15	Conn.
900*	Wapping (South Windsor), E 15	Conn.
3427	Wappingers Falls, D 5	N. Y.
200	Wapwallopen, I 19	Pa.
336*	Waquoit, N 24	Mass.
1277	War, R 5	W. Va.
124	Warba, G 16	Minn.
....	Warbasse, see Hyper-Humus	N. J.
10*	Warble (Path), M 14	Pa.
25*	Warbranch, J 20	Ky.
25*	War Creek, G 20	Ky.
150*	Ward, J 4	Ala.
283*	Ward, I 14	Ark.
118*	Ward, E 13	Colo.
23*	Ward, B 5	Fla.
200*	Ward (Concordville), P 22	Pa.
204	Ward, H 10	S. C.
84	Ward, J 25	S. D.
160*	Ward, L 7	W. Va.
50*	Warda, K 19	Tex.
60	Wardell, F 21	Ark.
430	Wardell, I 24	Mo.
100*	Warden (Richland), C 12	La.
78	Warden, K 18	Wash.
195	Wardensville, G 21	W. Va.
432	Ward Hill, B 19	Mass.
861	Wardner, E 6	Idaho
....*	Wards, I 14	Ky.
75*	Wardsboro (East Jamaica), O 10	Vt.
125	Wardsboro, P 10	Vt.
58*	Ward Springs, K 10	Minn.
130*	Wardtown, M 23	Va.
217	Wardville, M 18	Okla.
75*	Ware, E 8	Iowa
32*	Ware, I 17	Ky.
7557■	Ware, G 10	Mass.
65	Ware (Acushnet), H 13	Mont.
219	Wareagle, B 6	Ark.
500	War Eagle, P 4	W. Va.
2600	Wareham, L 22	Mass.
10	Wareham, F 20	Neb.
1601	Warehouse Point, C 14	Conn.
500*	Ware Neck, N 21	Va.
240*	Waresboro, N 17	Ga.
4000	Ware Shoals, E 7	S. C.
511	Waretown, L 19	N. J.
296*	Warfield, G 23	Ky.
100*	Warfield, P 15	Va.
57*	Warford, P 9	W. Va.
80*	Warfordsburg, P 11	Pa.
269	Waring, K 15	Tex.
65	Warland, D 2	Mont.
314*	Warm Beach, G 8	Wash.
131*	Warminster, N 24	Pa.
36*	Warminster, L 11	Va.
....*	Warm Lake, L 7	Idaho
100*	Warm Springs, A 18	Ark.
59*	Warmsprings (Warm Springs), I 6	Calif.
608	Warm Springs, I 4	Ga.
1900	Warmsprings, K 7	Mont.
150	Warm Springs, G 12	Ore.
912	Warm Springs, J 7	Va.
100*	Warne, R 3	N. C.
750	Warner, N 11	N. H.
190	Warner, M 18	Ohio
391	Warner, I 21	Okla.
151	Warner, E 18	S. D.
....	Warner, F 9	Utah.
30*	Warner, L 20	Va.
600	Warners, L 14	N. Y.
34*	Warner Springs, P 20	Calif.
100	Warnerton, J 18	La.
20	Warnertown, I 22	Pa.
....	Warnertown Jc., I 22	Pa.
25	Warnerville, H 19	Neb.
300	Warnerville, O 21	N. Y.
56*	Warnock, D 22	Ky.
200*	Warnock, K 20	Ohio
2250	Warren, P 22	Ariz.
2516	Warren, O 13	Ark.
150	Warren, F 5	Conn.
50	Warren, J 7	Idaho
1119	Warren, A 11	Ill.
1388	Warren, F 18	Ind.
150*	Warren, J 19	Ky.
853	Warren, N 12	Me.
2200	Warren, G 11	Mass.
582	Warren, P 23	Mich.
1639	Warren, D 2	Minn.
50*	Warren, D 15	Mo.
15	Warren, N 15	Mont.
500	Warren, J 11	N. H.
200*	Warren, J 19	N. Y.
12	Warren, N 24	N. D.
42837	Warren, E 20	Ohio
75	Warren, M 5	Okla.
40	Warren, B 7	Ore.
14891	Warren, E 7	Pa.
8158■	Warren, G 19	R. I.
55*	Warren, P 3	Tenn.
300	Warren, I 24	Tex.
200	Warren, D 10	Utah
325	Warren, H 10	Vt.
56	Warren, L 12	Va.
*	Warren, see Bright	Wyo.
110*	Warren Center, E 17	Pa.
150	Warrendale, C 9	Ore.
500	Warrendale, L 3	Pa.
75	Warren Plains, C 16	N. C.
1200*	Warren Point, C 19	N. J.
275	Warrens (Warren), H 15	Wis.
49*	Warrens Bluff (Bluff), O 7	Tenn.
456	Warrensburg, I 15	Ill.
5868	Warrensburg, H 8	Mo.
2000	Warrensburg, J 23	N. Y.
150*	Warrensville, B 3	N. C.
2291▲	Warrensville, D 17	Ohio
221	Warrensville, H 16	Pa.
1175*	Warrensville Heights, D 17	Ohio
1284	Warrenton, G 16	Ga.
1254	Warrenton, H 17	Mo.
1147	Warrenton, C 16	N. C.
1365	Warrenton, A 4	Ore.
406	Warrenton, K 19	Tex.
1651	Warrenton, G 15	Va.
40*	Warrenville, D 23	Conn.
1000*	Warrenville, C 19	Ill.
300	Warrenville, J 9	S. C.
22*	Warrick, F 12	Mont.
1500	Warrington, N 2	Fla.
50	Warrington, I 17	Ind.
150*	Warrington, N 24	Pa.
1008	Warrior, E 13	Ala.
200*	Warriormine, Q 5	W. Va.
1339	Warrior Run, I 20	Pa.
220	Warriors Mark, L 11	Pa.
1309	Warroad, B 8	Minn.
335*	Warsaw, M 23	Ga.
1895	Warsaw, H 4	Ill.
6378	Warsaw, D 16	Ind.
880	Warsaw, C 16	Ky.
50*	Warsaw, P 16	Minn.
957	Warsaw, K 9	Mo.
3554	Warsaw, N 7	N. Y.
1483	Warsaw, I 16	N. C.
75	Warsaw, F 23	N. D.
455	Warsaw, I 15	Ohio
350	Warsaw, K 20	Va.
35	Warsaw Jc., I 15	Ohio
150*	Warshoal (Wolverine), H 21	Ky.
350	Wartburg, M 17	Tenn.
150	Warthen, H 15	Ga.
552	Wartrace, O 12	Tenn.
379*	Warwick, M 9	Ga.
200	Warwick, E 20	Md.
300	Warwick, C 9	Mass.
2534	Warwick, F 4	N. Y.
224	Warwick, I 18	N. D.
150	Warwick, F 17	Ohio
210	Warwick, H 14	Okla.
....	Warwick, see Warwick Neck	R. I.
28	Warwick, Q 12	Wash.
28757	Warwick Neck (Warwick), H 17	R. I.
25	Wasatch, F 12	Utah
25*	Wasatch (Wahsatch), C 14	Utah
4000	Wasco, L 13	Calif.
85*	Wasco, B 18	Ill.
303	Wasco, C 13	Ore.
100*	Wascott, D 5	Wis.
4270	Waseca, Q 15	Minn.
60	Wasepi, R 14	Mich.
937	Washburn, F 14	Ill.
72*	Washburn, G 17	Iowa
....*	Washburn, G 21	Kan.
2000	Washburn, C 18	Me.
300	Washburn, R 7	Mo.
901	Washburn, K 11	N. D.
200*	Washburn, M 20	Tenn.
67*	Washburn, D 4	Tex.
68*	Washburn, F 9	W. Va.
2363	Washburn, F 4	Wis.
432	Washington, N 7	Ark.
30	Washington, F 9	Calif.
1500*	Washington (Broderick), G 6	Calif.
1200	Washington, H 5	Conn.
425*	Washington (Washington Depot), H 5	Conn.
663091	Washington, J 11	D. C.
3537	Washington, F 16	Ga.
2456	Washington, F 13	Ill.
9312	Washington, O 7	Ind.
5227	Washington, M 20	Iowa
1598	Washington, D 17	Kan.
500	Washington, D 19	Ky.
1264	Washington, K 11	La.
100	Washington, N 11	Me.
150	Washington, F 4	Mass.
500	Washington, P 23	Mich.
200*	Washington, N 4	Miss.
6756	Washington, I 18	Mo.
84	Washington, J 24	Neb.
278▲	Washington, O 9	N. H.
4643	Washington, E 10	N. J.
8569	Washington, G 19	N. C.
297*	Washington (Old Washington), J 17	Ohio
359	Washington, K 12	Okla.
26166	Washington, O 2	Pa.
1000	Washington, H 11	R. I.
100	Washington, J 21	Tex.
507	Washington, Q 3	Utah
200	Washington, H 14	Vt.
245	Washington, G 14	Va.
48*	Washington, E 6	W. Va.
418*	Washington Boro (Washington Borough), O 18	Pa.
9402	Washington C. H., M 10	Ohio
40*	Washington College, M 23	Tenn.
300*	Washington Crossing, M 23	Pa.
425	Washington Depot (Washington), H 5	Conn.
160*	Washington Grove, G 10	Md.
750*	Washington Island (Detroit Harbor), Q 12	Wis.
....	Washington Jc., M 17	Me.
500*	Washington Mills, L 18	N. Y.
4523	Washington Park, M 10	Ill.
....*	Washingtons Birthplace, J 19	Va.
801*	Washingtonville, E 4	N. Y.
836	Washingtonville, F 20	Ohio
175*	Washingtonville, J 17	Pa.
44*	Washita, J 7	Ark.
147	Washita, K 8	Okla.
275	Washoe, N 14	Mont.
1267	Washougal, Q 8	Wash.
442	Washta, F 4	Iowa
285	Washtucna, L 20	Wash.
177	Washunga, B 15	Okla.
315	Wasioto (Paulsen), K 20	Ky.
28*	Waskish, D 11	Minn.
564	Waskom, E 24	Tex.
34*	Wasola, Q 12	Mo.
95*	Wason Flats, H 20	Mont.
350*	Wassaic, R 23, C 6	N. Y.
*	Wassaw, see Thunderbolt,	Ga.
300	Wasson, P 18	Ill.
153	Wasta, J 6	S. D.
487	Wataga, E 9	Ill.
65*	Watalula, E 6	Ark.
32*	Watauga, J 16	Ky.
133	Watauga, B 9	S. D.
400*	Watauga, L 24	Tenn.
300*	Watauga Valley, L 24	Tenn.
17*	Watch, J 19	Ky.
50	Watch Hill, O 3	R. I.
1158*	Watchung, G 14	N. J.
350	Waterboro, Q 3	Me.
99314	Waterbury, I 9	Conn.
30*	Waterbury, H 14	Md.
164	Waterbury, F 21	Neb.
3074	Waterbury, F 11	Vt.
510	Waterbury Center, F 11	Vt.
108*	Wateree, H 14	S. C.
60*	Waterfall, P 11	Pa.
30*	Waterfall, G 16	Va.
246*	Waterflow, C 4	N. M.
30	Waterford, N 20	Ala.
700*	Waterford, I 9	Calif.
100	Waterford, M 21	Conn.
50	Waterford, F 14	Ky.
100	Waterford, N 4	Me.
362*	Waterford, P 22	Mich.
300*	Waterford, A 15	Miss.
1500	Waterford (Waterford Works), M 12	N. J.
2903	Waterford, N 24	N. Y.
310	Waterford, M 17	Ohio
804	Waterford, E 4	Pa.
60	Waterford, F 20	Vt.
247	Waterford, E 16	Va.
786	Waterford, O 21	Wis.
1500	Waterford Works (Waterford), M 12	N. J.
31*	Watergap, G 23	Ky.
175	Water Gap (Minisink Hills), J 23	Pa.
29*	Waterlick (Water Lick), F 13	Va.
119*	Waterlily, C 24	N. C.
524	Waterloo, A 6	Ala.
500	Waterloo, O 9	Ark.
2361	Waterloo, N 10	Ill.
1257	Waterloo, B 21	Ind.
51743	Waterloo, G 17	Iowa
200	Waterloo (Patney), L 8	Mont.
381	Waterloo, K 23	Neb.
62*	Waterloo, N 13	N. H.
33	Waterloo, D 12	N. J.
4010	Waterloo, M 12	N. Y.
150*	Waterloo, Q 14	Ohio
15	Waterloo, H 12	Okla.
50	Waterloo, H 7	Ore.
150	Waterloo, E 8	S. C.
1474	Waterloo, L 20	Wis.
10*	Waterman, H 9	Calif.
579	Waterman, C 16	Ill.
13	Waterman, G 15	Ore.
521	Waterman, M 7	Pa.
50	Waterman, G 24	Tex.
815	Water Mill, G 11	N. Y.
300	Waterport, K 7	N. Y.
592	Water Proof, F 13	La.
45*	Waters, J 6	Ark.
80	Waters, J 17	Mich.
....	Waters Creek, Q 4	Ore.
176	Waterside, O 10	Pa.
600	Watersmeet, C 24	Mich.
150*	Water Street, L 11	Pa.
60	Watersville, E 11	Md.
....	Watersville Jc., E 10	Md.
3000	Watertown, H 8	Conn.
100	Watertown, C 12	Fla.
....	Watertown, D 9	Ill.
35427■	Watertown, M 2	Mass.
737	Watertown, N 13	Minn.
33385	Watertown, H 15	N. Y.
195	Watertown, M 17	Ohio
10617	Watertown, G 23	S. D.
908	Watertown, M 13	Tenn.
11301	Watertown, M 19	Wis.
....	Watertown Jc., H 15	N. Y.
....	Watertown Jc., G 23	S. D.
110*	Water Valley, L 3	Ala.
180*	Water Valley, B 17	Ark.
373	Water Valley, K 5	Ky.
3340	Water Vallly, D 14	Miss.
157*	Water Valley, H 12	Tex.
35*	Waterview, K 14	Ky.
80*	Waterview, N 21	Md.
250*	Water View, L 20	Va.
100*	Water Village, L 17	N. H.
....	Waterville, H 9	Conn.
253	Waterville, C 21	Iowa
717	Waterville, E 18	Kan.
16688	Waterville, M 10	Me.
....	Waterville, C 11	Mass.
1600	Waterville, P 15	Minn.
1489	Waterville, M 17	N. Y.
40*	Waterville, O 6	N. C.
961	Waterville, D 9	Ohio
130*	Waterville, H 15	Pa.
140	Waterville, C 11	Vt.
939	Waterville, H 15	Wash.
5*	Waterville Valley, J 14	N. H.
1193	Watervliet, Q 11	Mich.
16114	Watervliet, N 24	N. Y.
1073	Watford City, I 4	N. D.
214*	Watha, K 16	N. C.
860	Wathena, D 24	Kan.
75	Watkins, F 16	Colo.
110*	Watkins, J 18	Iowa
584	Watkins, M 11	Minn.
25*	Watkins, K 13	Mo.
....*	Watkins, F 21	Mont.
2913	Watkins Glen, P 12	N. Y.
558	Watkinsville, F 12	Ga.
25*	Watoga, L 14	W. Va.
2828	Watonga, G 8	Okla.
....	Watonga Jc., G 8	Okla.
100	Watova, C 20	Okla.
350	Watrous, E 17	N. M.
6	Watrous, P 7	N. D.
115*	Watrous (Gaines Jc.), F 13	Pa.
....	Watrousville, N 21	Mich.
3744	Watseka, F 21	Ill.
100	Watson (Mineral Springs), F 13	Ala.
236	Watson, N 17	Ark.
282	Watson, L 17	Ill.
100	Watson, P 17	Ind.
25*	Watson, L 16	La.
45*	Watson (Arnold), F 6	Mich.
290	Watson, N 6	Minn.
269	Watson, A 3	Mo.
28*	Watson, J 11	Mont.
200	Watson, N 25	Okla.
85*	Watson, M 22	Ore.
12	Watson, H 24	Utah
450	Watson, D 13	W. Va.
150*	Watsonia, I 6	Ala.
2282	Watsontown, I 16	Pa.
8937	Watsonville, J 6	Calif.
250	Watsonville Jc., J 6	Calif.
25	Wattenberg, E 15	Colo.
104*	Wattensaw, I 14	Ark.
150	Wattis, I 15	Utah
....	Wattis Jc., I 16	Utah
400	Watton, E 2	Mich.
60*	Watts, D 11	Ark.
307	Watts, F 24	Okla.
20	Watts, F 6	S. C.
1400	Watts (Watts Mills), D 8	S. C.
....*	Watts Bar Dam, O 16	Tenn.
36*	Wattsboro, P 14	Va.
290	Wattsburg, D 4	Pa.
180	Watts Flats, R 2	N. Y.
200*	Watts Mills (Watts), D 8	S. C.
600	Wattsville, F 16	Ala.
47	Wattsville, K 24	Va.
....	Watuppa, M 19	Mass.
882	Waubay, E 22	S. D.
130	Waubeek, I 20	Iowa
250	Waubeka, O 18	Wis.
438	Waubun, G 5	Minn.
160	Waucedah, G 6	Mich.
2710	Wauchula, J 16	Fla.
430	Waucoma, D 18	Iowa
639	Wauconda, A 19	Ill.
15	Wauconda, C 18	Wash.
50*	Waugh, K 17	Ala.
37*	Waugh, M 9	Va.
21	Wauhatchie, Q 15	Tenn.
118	Wauhillau, G 24	Okla.
250	Waukau, M 16	Wis.
473	Waukee, L 11	Iowa
200	Waukeenah, B 6	Fla.
34241	Waukegan, A 21	Ill.
18	Waukegan, J 22	Tex.
50*	Waukena, K 13	Calif.
19242	Waukesha, N 20	Wis.
397	Waukomis, E 10	Okla.
2972	Waukon, C 20	Iowa
75	Waukon, H 22	Wash.
33	Waukon Jc., C 21	Iowa
125*	Waumandee, D 15	Wis.
....	Waumbek Jc., G 14	N. H.
250	Wauna, A 6	Ore.
25	Wauna, I 7	Wash.
773	Waunakee, K 19	Wis.
75*	Wauneta, O 20	Kan.
770	Wauneta, N 8	Neb.
100	Wauneta, P 23	Wyo.
14*	Waunita Hot Springs, K 8	Colo.
3458	Waupaca, L 14	Wis.
27*	Waupeton, F 23	Iowa
6798	Waupun, M 17	Wis.
606	Wauregan, F 24	Conn.
2458	Waurika, P 10	Okla.
732	Wausa, F 19	Neb.
133	Wausau, M 10	Fla.
27268	Wausau, K 12	Wis.
....	Wausau Jc., K 12	Wis.
655	Wausaukee, O 10	Wis.
3016	Wauseon, C 8	Ohio
1180	Wautoma, K 16	Wis.
27769	Wauwatosa, P 20	Wis.
513	Wauzeka, F 20	Wis.
150	Wave, M 11	Ark.
150*	Waveland, H 7	Ark.
530	Waveland, I 9	Ind.
768	Waveland, R 16	Miss.
6000	Waverley, E 18, M 2	Mass.
331	Waverly, I 20	Ala.
40	Waverly, C 14	Colo.
250*	Waverly, I 17	Fla.
100*	Waverly, O 21	Ga.
1385	Waverly, J 10	Ill.
4156	Waverly, F 16	Iowa
566	Waverly, J 22	Kan.
323	Waverly, G 8	Ky.
350*	Waverly, C 14	La.
458	Waverly, N 13	Minn.
876	Waverly, G 9	Mo.
306	Waverly, L 22	Neb.
5450	Waverly, R 13	N. Y.
50*	Waverly, N 8	N. C.
1757	Waverly, O 12	Ohio
520*	Waverly, G 21	Pa.
50	Waverly, F 23	S. D.
1318	Waverly, M 8	Tenn.
1288	Waverly, O 18	Va.
131	Waverly, I 24	Wash.
285*	Waverly, E 7	W. Va.
569	Waverly Hall, I 4	Ga.
250*	Waverly Hills, E 14	Ky.
10	Waverly Jc., F 16	Iowa
....*	Waverly Mills, see Pawleys Island	S. C.
....*	Waves, F 24	N. C.
150*	Wawa, P 22	Pa.
230	Wawaka, C 18	Ind.
300	Wawarsing, C 3	N. Y.
100*	Wawasee, C 16	Ind.
25	Wawawai, L 24	Wash.
100*	Wawina, G 16	Minn.
25*	Wawona, I 11	Calif.
65	Wawpecong, F 15	Ind.
15*	Wax, H 12	Ky.
8655	Waxahachie, F 19	Tex.
50*	Waxhaw, E 7	Miss.
611	Waxhaw, J 6	N. C.
150*	Waxia, K 11	La.
29*	Waxpool, F 16	Va.
54*	Way, I 12	Miss.
96	Wayan, P 22	Idaho
16763	Waycross, O 18	Ga.
576	Wayland, N 20	Iowa
1950	Wayland, H 22	Ky.
921	Wayland, F 17	Mass.
1005	Wayland, P 13	Mich.
380	Wayland, B 16	Mo.
1795	Wayland, O 9	N. Y.
75*	Wayland, E 19	Ohio
250*	Wayland, E 15	Tex.
40*	Waymansville, M 15	Ind.
1095	Waymart, F 22	Pa.
25*	Wayne, K 7	Ala.
165*	Wayne, B 19	Ill.
102*	Wayne, D 15	Kan.
150	Wayne, M 7	Me.
4223	Wayne, Q 22	Mich.
45	Wayne, Q 8	Mo.
2719	Wayne, G 21	Neb.
500*	Wayne, C 17	N. J.
191*	Wayne, P 11	N. Y.
636	Wayne (Freeport), E 10	Ohio
401	Wayne, L 13	Okla.
5000	Wayne, O 22	Pa.
801	Wayne, L 2	W. Va.
581	Wayne City, N 17	Ill.
3793	Waynesboro, H 20	Ga.
1445	Waynesboro, M 21	Miss.
10231	Waynesboro, Q 13	Pa.
768	Waynesboro, P 8	Tenn.
7373	Waynesboro (Basic), J 11	Va.
500	Waynesburg, I 17	Ky.
1223	Waynesburg, H 18	Ohio
4891	Waynesburg, P 2	Pa.
592	Waynesfield, H 8	Ohio
275	Waynesville, N 21	Ga.
564	Waynesville, H 15	Ill.
468	Waynesville, L 13	Mo.
2940	Waynesville, P 6	N. C.
833*	Waynesville, M 8	Ohio
138	Waynesville (Corwin), M 8	Ohio
644*	Waynetown, I 9	Ind.
....	Waynmanville, I 7	Ga.
1584	Waynoka, C 6	Okla.
488*	Waynor (Norway), J 13	S. C.
100*	Ways, L 23	Ga.
125*	Wayside, H 11	Ga.
159*	Wayside, O 21	Kan.
40*	Wayside, N 12	Md.
750*	Wayside, G 6	Miss.
40	Wayside, D 3	Neb.
200	Wayside, I 20	N. J.
21	Wayside, B 19	Okla.
18*	Wayside, E 4	Tex.
....	Wayside, G 23	Wash.
26*	Wayside, P 11	W. Va.
150	Wayside, O 15	Wis.
14*	Wayton, D 9	Ark.
1473	Wayzata, M 21	Minn.
39*	Wealthia (Johnson), L 13	Va.
85	Weare, O 12	N. H.
208	Weatherby, D 7	Mo.
....	Weatherby, H 23	Ore.
2504	Weatherford, I 7	Okla.
5924	Weatherford, E 17	Tex.
2754	Weatherly, J 21	Pa.
32*	Weathers, C 7	Ark.
33	Weathers, M 20	Okla.
149*	Weathersby, L 13	Miss.
339	Weathersfield, M 14	Vt.
430	Weatogue, D 12	Conn.
439	Weaubleau, L 9	Mo.
400	Weaver, E 19	Ala.
134*	Weaver, P 20	Minn.
102	Weaver, E 18	N. D.
300*	Weaver, D 22	Tex.
75	Weaver, G 14	W. Va.
204*	Weaversford, B 3	N. C.
250*	Weavers Old Stand (Armbrust), N 5	Pa.
125*	Weavers Store, L 8	Tenn.
1200	Weaverville, D 4	Calif.
880	Weaverville, O 8	N. C.
379	Webb, N 22	Ala.
150*	Webb, O 22	Ariz.
40	Webb, G 3	Idaho
254	Webb, D 7	Iowa
606	Webb, D 10	Miss.
....	Webb (Marlboro Depot), Q 8	N. H.
20	Webb, G 5	Okla.
45*	Webb, Q 14	Tex.
35*	Webb, M 1	W. Va.
219	Webb City, F 6	Ark.
7033	Webb City, O 6	Mo.
352	Webb City, B 15	Okla.
104	Webber, D 14	Kan.
....*	Webber City, see Maud,	Okla.
486	Webbers Falls, I 22	Okla.
508	Webberville, P 19	Mich.
18	Webberville, K 18	Tex.
93*	Webb Lake, B 8	Wis.
....*	Webbs, see Ella Gap	Ga.
25*	Webbs, I 14	Ky.
36*	Webbs Cross Roads, I 16	Ky.
75	Webbville, F 22	Ky.
....	Weber Mine, E 14	Utah
33*	Weberstown, F 11	Ky.
100*	Webhannet, R 4	Me.
10*	Weblake, C 7	Wis.
454	Webster, G 15	Fla.
88*	Webster, G 5	Ill.
100	Webster, I 22	Ind.
165	Webster, L 18	Iowa
210	Webster, F 9	Kan.
115*	Webster, F 12	Ky.
13186■	Webster, I 13	Mass.
110*	Webster, P 16	Minn.
32	Webster, K 25	Mont.
27	Webster (Pleasant Valley), I 21	Neb.
1680	Webster, L 10	N. Y.
84*	Webster, P 5	N. C.
100	Webster, G 18	N. D.
212	Webster, J 6	Ohio
1800	Webster, O 4	Pa.
2173	Webster, E 21	S. D.
500	Webster, L 23	Tex.
1133	Webster, E 14	W. Va.
524	Webster, B 8	Wis.
6738	Webster City, G 11	Iowa
80*	Webster Crossing (Websters), N 9	N. Y.
18394	Webster Groves, I 20	Mo.
....	Webster Jc., G 13	Mass.
....	Webster Mills, I 13	Mass.
55*	Webster Mills, Q 11	Pa.
80*	Websters (Webster Crossing), N 9	N. Y.
1133	Webster Springs (Addison), J 12	W. Va.
15	Websterville, H 13	Vt.
261*	Weches, H 22	Tex.
300*	Wecoma, G 4	Ore.
25	Wecota, F 16	S. D.
50	Wedderburn, P 2	Ore.
500	Wedgefield, H 16	S. C.
60*	Wedgworth (Wedgeworth), I 7	Ala.
525	Wedowee, G 21	Ala.
202	Wedron, D 16	Ill.
5000	Weed, C 5	Calif.
35*	Weed, J 15	Ky.
80	Weed M 15	N. M.
5*	Weedman G 17	Ill.
38*	Weedonville I 18	Va.
1341	Weedsport, L 13	N. Y.
800	Weedville, I 10	Pa.
14363■	Weehawken, E 21	N. J.
20*	Weekapaug, L 10	R. I.
500	Weeks (Weeks Island), O 12	La.
20*	Weeks, H 5	Nev.
1578	Weeksbury, I 23	Ky.
....*	Weeks Island, see Weeks,	La.
75	Weeks Mills, M 10	Me.
110*	Weeksville, D 23	N. C.
62*	Weems (Smithfield), I 20	Ohio
250	Weems, L 21	Va.
1139	Weeping Water, L 23	Neb.
212	Weesatche, N 18	Tex.
149*	Wegdahl, N 7	Minn.
500*	Wehadkee, G 21	Ala.
40	Wehrum, M 8	Pa.
33*	Wehutty, Q 1	N. C.
350	Weidman, M 16	Mich.
102*	Weikert (Weiker), J 15	Pa.
121*	Weilersville (Smithville), G 16	Ohio
50*	Weimar (New England Mills), F 9	Calif.
1353	Weimar, L 19	Tex.
447	Weiner, E 18	Ark.
414	Weinert, D 14	Tex.
99*	Weingarten, L 20	Mo.
110	Weippe, G 7	Idaho
1038*	Weir (Weir City), N 25	Kan.
552	Weir, G 17	Miss.
240*	Weir, I 18	Tex.
....*	Weir, see Falling Rock,	W. Va.
1038	Weir City (Weir), N 25	Kan.
....	Weir Jc., K 19	Mass.
212*	Weirs (The Weirs), L 14	N. H.
303	Weirsdale, F 15	Fla.
9658	Weirton, N 24	W. Va.
....	Weirton Jc., N 24	W. Va.
75*	Weirwood (Wierwood), M 23	Va.
75*	Weisburg, L 22	Ind.
30*	Weisel, M 23	Pa.
3663	Weiser, L 3	Idaho
35*	Weiser Park, M 20	Pa.
100*	Weiss, K 15	La.
12	Weissert, J 14	Neb.
657	Weissport, K 21	Pa.
64*	Weitchpec, C 3	Calif.
10	Wekiwa, E 18	Okla.
457	Welaka, E 17	Fla.
50*	Wela Park, Q 6	Mo.
1000	Welborn, F 24	Kan.
36*	Welborn, I 17	Ky.
40*	Welbourne, O 23	Md.
....	Welby, F 15	Colo.
50	Welby, F 11	Utah
100*	Welch, O 19	Minn.
498	Welch, B 22	Okla.
17*	Welch, E 9	Tex.
6264	Welch, Q 6	W. Va.
75*	Welchburg, I 19	Ky.
40	Welches, E 9	Ore.
56*	Welchs Creek, H 12	Ky.
136	Welchville (Oxford) N 5	Me.
....	Welcome, I 14	Fla.
300*	Welcome, N 16	La.
15*	Welcome, M 11	Md.
630	Welcome, R 10	Minn.
150*	Welcome, E 8	N. C.
242*	Welcome, K 20	Tex.
18*	Welcome, I 18	Va.
175	Weld, L 5	Me.
162	Welda, J 23	Kan.
165	Weldon, F 17	Ark.
189*	Weldon, M 13	Calif.
521	Weldon, I 16	Ill.
250	Weldon, O 12	Iowa
10	Weldon, F 21	Mont.
2341	Weldon, C 18	N. C.
500	Weldon, H 22	Tex.
300	Weldona (Weldon), D 18	Colo.
100*	Weldon Springs, I 18	Mo.
1904	Weleetka, J 18	Okla.
25*	Welfare, K 16	Tex.
62*	Welge, P 12	Ill.
324	Wellborn, C 11	Fla.
500	Wellborn, J 20	Tex.
21	Wellers (Truemans), F 7	Pa.
357	Wellersburg, Q 8	Pa.
15127■	Wellesley, F 17	Mass.
....*	Wellesley Farms, F 18	Mass.
6000	Wellesley Hills, F 17	Mass.
890▲	Wellfleet, K 14	Mass.
111	Wellfleet, M 10	Neb.
454	Wellford, B 8	S. C.
85*	Wellford, K 20	Va.
50*	Wellford, J 7	W. Va.
30*	Wellhope, I 18	Ky.
80	Welling, G 23	Okla.
160	Wellington, E 18	Ala.
465	Wellington, C 15	Colo.
297	Wellington, G 21	Ill.
7246	Wellington, N 15	Kan.
35*	Wellington, F 20	Ky.
110	Wellington, K 10	Me.
656	Wellington, G 8	Mo.
75	Wellington, I 4	Nev.

Pop.	Place Index	State
2529	Wellington, E 15	Ohio
3308	Wellington, E 6	Tex.
674	Wellington, I 17	Utah
18*	Wellington, G 16	Va.
1129	Wellman, L 19	Iowa
50*	Wellman, D 9	Tex.
72	Wellpinit, G 21	Wash.
100*	Wells, G 15	Kan.
600	Wells, R 4	Me.
600*	Wells, M 21	Mich.
2217	Wells, Q 14	Minn.
12*	Wells, I 20	Neb.
830	Wells, C 20	Nev.
400*	Wells, K 21	N. Y.
....	Wells, M 7	Ohio
75*	Wells (Wellsdale), G 5	Ore.
696*	Wells, H 23	Tex.
250	Wells, M 6	Vt.
310	Wellsboro, B 11	Ind.
3665	Wellsboro, F 15	Pa.
60	Wellsboro Jc., F 15	Pa.
150	Wells Bridge, P 18	N. Y.
616	Wellsburg, G 15	Iowa
100	Wellsburg (Elmsgrove), C 19	Ky.
560	Wellsburg, R 12	N. Y.
125	Wellsburg, I 15	N. D.
415	Wellsburg (Lundys Lane), E 2	Pa.
6255	Wellsburg, O 24	W. Va.
50*	Wellscreek, O 7	Pa.
75	Wellsdale (Wells), G 5	Ore.
64*	Wellsford, M 11	Kan.
527	Wells River, H 17	Vt.
117*	Wells Tannery, O 11	Pa.
56*	Wellston, J 11	Ga.
50*	Wellston, J 10	Mich.
7400*	Welston, I 20	Mo.
5537	Wellston, O 14	Ohio
607	Wellston, H 14	Okla.
100*	Wells Store, G 9	Ky.
632	Wellsville, H 23	Kan.
1314	Wellsville, G 16	Mo.
5942	Wellsville, Q 8	N. Y.
7672	Wellsville, H 20	Ohio
271	Wellsville, P 16	Pa.
50*	Wellsville, O 19	Tenn.
1402	Wellsville, B 11	Utah
500	Wellton, M 4	Ariz.
25*	Wellville, O 15	Va.
36*	Well Water, M 12	Va.
....	Welon, M 4	Okla.
1822	Welsh, M 8	La.
100	Welshfield, D 18	Ohio
100*	Welton, J 24	Iowa
....	Welty, D 15	Colo.
100	Welty, H 17	Okla.
27*	Welview, H 13	Tex.
60*	Wemme, E 8	Ore.
150*	Wenasoga, A 21	Miss.
11620	Wenatchee, I 14	Wash.
50	Wendel, D 10	Calif.
800	Wendel, N 5	Pa.
180*	Wendel, E 14	W. Va.
72*	Wendelin, M 19	Ill.
1001	Wendell, P 11	Idaho
100	Wendell, D 9	Mass.
44*	Wendell (Wendell Depot), D 9	Mass.
273	Wendell, K 5	Minn.
100*	Wendell (Sunapee), N 8	N. H.
1132	Wendell, E 15	N. C.
44*	Wendell Depot (Wendell) D 9	Mass.
80	Wenden, J 7	Ariz.
800	Wendling, I 7	Ore.
....*	Wendover, I 20	Ky.
140	Wendover, E 1	Utah
80	Wendover, L 21	Wyo.
18	Wendte, J 12	S. D.
....*	Wengler, C 7	Calif.
1000	Wenham, C 20	Mass.
967	Wenona, E 15	Ill.
300	Wenona, P 19	Md.
....	Wenona Beach, M 20	Mich.
50	Wenona, F 21	N. C.
115	Wenonah, K 14	Ill.
1311	Wenonah, L 8	N. J.
350	Wenonah (Dott), Q 8	W. Va.
50*	Wenonda (Oak Hill), Q 9	Va.
5	Wentworth, P 24	Colo.
253	Wentworth, P 7	Mo.
100	Wentworth, J 11	N. H.
200	Wentworth, C 9	N. C.
303	Wentworth, K 23	S. D.
50*	Wentworth, D 5	Wis.
15*	Wentworth Location, D 18	N. H.
752	Wentzville, H 18	Mo.
65*	Weogufka, H 16	Ala.
210*	Weona, F 19	Ark.
150*	Weott, D 2	Calif.
....*	Wequetonsing, H 16	Mich.
137	Werner, K 6	N. D.
1160	Wernersville, N 19	Pa.
50	Wertz, M 11	Pa.
110*	Wesco, K 17	Mo.
500*	Wescosville, L 22	Pa.
143	Wescott (East Waterboro), Q 3	Me.
219	Weser, N 18	Tex.
205*	Weskan, G 2	Kan.
6883	Weslaco, Q 4	Tex.
116*	Wesley, D 6	Ark.
250	Wesley, J 18	Ga.
468	Wesley, D 10	Iowa
150*	Wesley, K 21	Me.
30	Wesley, N 19	Okla.
65*	Wesley, H 4	Pa.
125	Wesley, K 20	Tex.
25*	Wesleyan, P 10	Idaho
....	Wesley Jc., G 12	Ill.
113*	Wesleyville, E 21	Ky.
2918	Wesleyville, C 3	Pa.
15*	Wess, H 16	Ky.
18*	Wesser, P 4	N. C.
516	Wessington, I 18	S. D.
1352	Wessington Springs, J 18	S. D.
245	Wesson, R 10	Ark.
837	Wesson, M 10	Miss.
....*	West (West Hollywood), O 15 (Pop. incl. in Los Angeles)	Calif.
140	West, J 18	Iowa
402	West, G 14	Miss.
1979	West, G 19	Tex.
6*	West, C 11	W. Va.
535*	Westacres, P 22	Mich.
731	West Acton, D 16	Mass.
1169*	West Albany, N 23	N. Y.
5000*	West Albuquerque, G 10	N. M.
515	West Alburgh, A 5	Vt.
440*	West Alexander, O 1	Pa.
993	West Alexandria, L 6	Ohio
400*	West Aliance (Alliance), H 20	N. C.
2931	West Aliquippa, L 2	Pa.
36364	West Allis, O 20	Wis.
253	Westalton, H 20	Mo.
81*	West Alton, M 16	N. H.
80*	West Amboy, J 15	N. Y.
185*	West Andover (Gale), M 10	N. H.
125	West Andover, C 21	Ohio

Pop.	Place Index	State
250*	West Applegate (Applegate) G 9	Calif.
24*	West Appleton, N 12	Me.
250	West Arlington, O 6	Vt.
....	West Asheville, P 7	N. C.
100	West Athens, K 9	Me.
1200	West Auburn, H 14	Mass.
70*	West Augusta, I 10	Va.
1500*	West Babylon, H 9	N. Y.
949	West Baden, O 11	Ind.
....	West Bainbridge, P 6	Ga.
500	West Baldwin, O 3	Me.
200*	West Bangor, E 21	N. Y.
131	West Barnet, F 17	Vt.
2000	West Barrington, F 18	R. I.
....	West Bath, O 8	Me.
350	Westbay, N 8	Fla.
....*	West Beach, L 15	Md.
110	West Becket, G 3	Mass.
80*	West Bedford, I 15	Ohio
1000*	West Belmar, I 18	N. J.
737	West Bend, D 9	Iowa
100*	West Bend, F 19	Ky.
5452	West Bend, N 18	Wis.
85	West Berkshire, A 10	Vt.
162	West Berlin, (Carters), E 14	Mass.
200	West Berlin, L 10	N. J.
175	West Berlin (Riverton), G 12	Vt.
227	West Berne, O 22	N. Y.
200	West Bethel (Allens), M 2	Me.
1317	West Blocton, H 11	Ala.
350*	West Bloomfield, N 10	N.Y.
55*	West Bloomfield, L 15	Wis.
220	West Bolton, E 9	Vt.
250*	West Boothbay, O 10	Me.
5000	Westboro, G 15	Mass.
368	Westboro, A 3	Mo.
2000	Westboro (West Lebanon), L 7	N. H.
92	Westboro, N 9	Ohio
220	Westboro, H 10	Wis.
990	Westbourne, L 19	Tenn.
40	West Bowdoin, O 7	Me.
325	West Boxford, B 19	Mass.
2000	West Boylston, F 14	Mass.
719	West Branch, K 21	Iowa
1962	West Branch, K 18	Mich.
170*	West Brouch, L 17	N. Y.
560	West Brattleboro, Q 12	Vt.
240	West Brentwood, P 18	N. H.
2000	West Bridgewater, I 20	Mass.
1621*	West Bridgewater (Bridgewater), L 2	Pa.
92	West Bridgewater, L 11	Vt.
56*	West Brighton, (West New Brighton), I 4	N. Y.
40	Westbrook, K 10	Ala.
790	Westbrook, M 17	Conn.
11087	Westbrook, P 5	Me.
871	Westbrook, Q 7	Minn.
512	Westbrook, F 11	Tex.
128	West Brookfield, G 11	Mass.
50	West Brookfield, H 11	Vt.
67	West Brooklin, N 15	Me.
185	West Brooklyn, C 14	Ill.
260	West Brooksville, M 15	Me.
360*	Westbrookville, R 20	N. Y.
1844	West Brownsville, P 3	Pa.
316	West Burke, D 18	Vt.
1323	West Burlington, O 22	Iowa
200*	West Burlington, O 19	N. Y.
33*	Westbury, H 6	Minn.
4524	Westbury, H 7	N. Y.
363	West Butler, K 4	Ala.
400	West Buxton, P 4	Me.
369	Westby, B 25	Mont.
1438	Westby, G 17	Wis.
....	West Cairo, see Cairo	Ohio
3458*	West Caldwell, D 18	N. J.
400	West Camp, Q 23	N. Y.
150*	West Campton, J 13	N. H.
225	West Canaan (Pattee), L 9	N. H.
130*	West Candor, Q 14	N. Y.
934	West Cape May, R 11	N. J.
....	West Caribou, C 19	Me.
2176	West Carrollton, L 7	Ohio
1767*	West Carthage, H 15	N. Y.
....	West Chandler, K 13	Ariz.
300	West Charleston, B 18	Vt.
120*	West Chatham, N 15	Mass.
450	West Chazy, C 24	N. Y.
436*	West Chelmesford, C 17	Mass.
40*	West Cheshire (Cheshire), J 11	Conn.
211	Westchester (North Westchester), H 18	Conn.
621*	Westchester, C 21	Ill.
213	West Chester, M 19	Iowa
107	West Chester (Claryville), L 22	Mo.
....*	Westchester, I 5	N. Y.
300*	West Chester, M 6	Ohio
13289	West Chester, P 22	Pa.
75*	West Chesterfield, E 6	Mass.
125	West Chesterfield, O 5	N. H.
3355	West Chicago, C 19	Ill.
52	West Chop, O 23	Mass.
1017	West City, O 15	Ill.
600	West Claremont, N 6	N. H.
250*	West Clarkesville, Q 7	N. Y.
....	West Cleo, D 7	Okla.
429	Westcliffe, M 13	Colo.
100*	West Clifford, E 20	Pa.
250	West Clinton, J 5	Ind.
....	West Clinton, J 25	Iowa
....	West Collingswood, K 9	N. J.
1744*	West Columbia (New Brookland), H 12	S. C.
1573	West Columbia, M 22	Tex.
211	West Columbia, G 4	W. Va.
3500*	West Concord (Concord Junction), E 17	Mass.
744	West Concord, P 18	Minn.
2464*	West Conshohocken, N 22	Pa.
25*	West Copake, Q 24	N. Y.
50*	West Corinth, I 14	Vt.
226	West Cornwall, C 5	Conn.
....	Westcott, G 13	R. I.
1072*	West Covina, N 15	Calif.
....	West Coxsackie, P 23	N. Y.
....*	Westcreek, H 15	Colo.
500	West Creek, M 17	N. J.
50	West Cumbo, D 24	W. Va.
120*	West Cummington, D 5	Mass.
100	Westdale, I 20	Mass.
110*	Westdale, L 17	N. Y.
....	West Dana, J 5	Ind.
228	West Danby, P 13	N. Y.
200	West Danville (Farrington), E 16	Vt.
77*	West Davenport, Q 19	N. Y.
900	West Decatur (Blue Ball), J 10	Pa.
450	West Dennis, N 14	Mass.
....	West De Pere, O 14 (Pop. incl. in De Pere)	Wis.
4252	West Des Moines (Valley Jc.), K 12	Iowa
....	West Detroit, Q 23	Mich.
309	West Dover, C 15	Ohio
64*	West Dover, P 7	Vt.

Pop.	Place Index	State
200	West Dudley, I 12	Mass.
275	West Dummerston, Q 12	Vt.
....	West Dundee, Kane, see Dundee	Ill.
....	West Durham, E 12	N. C.
272	West Duxbury, I 22	Mass.
1159*	West Easton, K 23	Pa.
200*	West Eaton, M 16	N. Y.
180	West Eden, M 16	Me.
130	West Edmeston, N 18	N. Y.
175*	Westel, N 16	Tenn.
1297*	West Elizabeth, L 3	Pa.
223	West Elkton, M 5	Ohio
211	West Eminence, O 16	Mo.
250*	Westend, L 18	Calif.
....*	West End, J 15	Colo.
63	West End, P 17	Ill.
600	West End, H 11	N. C.
540	West Enfield, J 15	Me.
2700*	West Englewood, C 19	N. J.
200	West Enosburg, B 10	Vt.
200*	West Enterprise, L 20	Miss.
300	West Epping, P 18	N. H.
50	Westerheim, L 2	N. D.
200*	Westerlo (Chesterville), O 22	N. Y.
11199■	Westerly, N 3	R. I.
300	Westerly, M 7	W. Va.
437	Western, N 20	Neb.
240*	Western Grove, C 10	Ark.
200	Western Jc., M 12	Wis.
3565	Western Port, N 5	Md.
....	Western Jc., J 11	Ala.
4856	Western Springs, C 20	Ill.
250*	Westernville, K 18	N. Y.
213	Westervelt, J 16	Ill.
58	Westerville, J 14	Neb.
3146	Westerville, J 12	Ohio
100*	West Exeter, O 18	N. Y.
156	West Fairlee, I 16	Vt.
1820*	West Fairview, N 14	Pa.
16*	Westfall, H 14	Kan.
....	Westfall, H 2	Mont.
15	Westfall, J 22	Ore.
400	West Falls, N 5	N. Y.
57*	West Falls Church, F 17	Va.
150	West Falmouth, P 6	Me.
362	West Falmouth (Longview), M 23	Mass.
117*	West Fargo, M 24	N. D.
395	West Farmington (Westville), L 6	Me.
483*	West Farmington, D 19	Ohio
800*	West Fayetteville, P 13	Pa.
....	Westfield, I 14	Conn.
678	Westfield, K 20	Ill.
709	Westfield, I 14	Ind.
197	Westfield, E 1	Iowa
312	Westfield, D 19	Me.
18793	Westfield, H 6	Mass.
18458	Westfield, F 17	N. J.
3434	Westfield, P 1	N. Y.
150*	Westfield, C 7	N. C.
40	Westfield, Q 13	N. D.
1386	Westfield, E 13	Pa.
106*	Westfield, K 22	Tex.
200	Westfield, B 14	Vt.
851	Westfield, K 16	Wis.
80	West Finley, P 1	Pa.
500*	Westfir, J 5	Ore.
700*	Westford, C 23	Conn.
175*	Westford, N 20	N. Y.
51*	Westford, G 2	Pa.
75	Westford, D 8	Vt.
359	West Fork, D 5	Ark.
30	West Fork, P 11	Ind.
136*	West Fork, N 17	Mo.
6	West Fork, C 21	Mont.
30	West Fork (Dothan), O 5	Ore.
12383	West Frankfort, P 16	Ill.
250	West Franklin, L 17	Me.
150	West Freehold, I 18	N. J.
225*	West Friendship, E 12	Md.
225*	West Frostproof, I 17	Fla.
200	West Fulton, O 21	N. Y.
247	Westgate, E 18	Iowa
....	West Gilbert, P 4	W. Va.
68*	West Glover, C 15	Vt.
....	West Gonic, N 19	N. H.
50*	West Goshen, D 6	Conn.
140	West Gouldsboro, M 18	Me.
250*	West Graham (Hockman), B 10	Va.
300	West Granby, B 11	Conn.
100*	West Granville Corners, J 24	N. Y.
300	West Green, M 16	Ga.
100*	West Greene, H 6	Ala.
25	West Greenwich, G 14	R. I.
600	West Groton, C 15	Mass.
105*	West Grove, P 17	Iowa
1357	Westgrove, Q 21	Pa.
60	West Halifax, R 10	Vt.
300*	West Hamburg (Hamburg) M 20	Pa.
600	West Hamlin, K 3	W. Va.
....	West Hammond, see Calumet City, D 22	Ill.
146	West Hampstead (Hampstead), Q 17	N. H.
457	Westhampton, H 10	N. Y.
....*	Westhampton, M 17	Va.
969*	West Hampton Beach, H 10	N. Y.
700	West Hanover, H 21	Mass.
100	West Hanover, M 17	Pa.
311	West Harrison, L 23	Ind.
33776■	West Hartford, E 13	Conn.
200	West Hartford, K 14	Vt.
60*	West Hartland, D 13	Conn.
333	West Harwich, N 14	Mass.
200*	West Hatfield (Hatfield), F 7	Mass.
....	West Havana, H 10	Ill.
55*	Westhaven, K 12	Calif.
30021■	West Haven, (Allington), N 10	Conn.
500■	West Haven, Q 21	Va.
30	West Haven, K 4	Vt.
2533*	West Haverstraw, F 5	N. Y.
70*	West Hawley, C 5	Mass.
7523	West Hazleton, J 20	Pa.
4717	West Helena, K 19	Ark.
1000*	West Hempstead, H 7	N. Y.
200*	West Henrietta, L 9	N. Y.
565	West Hickory, G 5	Pa.
375	Westhoff, M 18	Tex.
....*	West Hollywood (West), O 15	Calif.
3526*	West Homestead, L 3	Pa.
460	Westhope, D 11	N. D.
150*	West Hopkinton, C 12	N. H.
315*	West Hurley, R 21	N. Y.
76*	West Hyannisport, N 12	Mass.
35	Westimber, C 5	Ore.
75*	West Independence, F 10	Ohio
170*	West Irvine, G 18	Ky.
883	West Jefferson, C 3	N. C.
1386	West Jefferson, K 10	Ohio
600	West Jonesport, M 21	Me.
1220	West Jordan, K 11	Utah
....	West Junction, A 12	Ill.
20	West Junction, N 12	Ohio
....	West Junction, Q 1	Tenn.

Pop.	Place Index	State
719	West Kennebunk, Q 4	Me.
80*	West Kill, Q 21	N. Y.
1000	West Kingston (Kingston), L 10	R. I.
1005*	West Kittanning, L 5	Pa.
6270	West Lafayette, G 10	Ind.
1152	West La Fayette, J 16	Ohio
50	Westlake, H 5	Idaho
20	Westlake, M 6	La.
3200	Westlake (Dover Center), C 15	Ohio
183	Westlake, J 3	Ore.
....	West Lake Wales, I 16	Fla.
800*	Westland, N 2	Pa.
85*	West Laurens, O 18	N. Y.
2080*	West Lawn (Intervilla), M 20	Pa.
581	West Lebanon, H 6	Ind.
200*	West Lebanon, Q 2	Me.
2000	West Lebanon (Westboro), L 7	N. H.
135*	West Lebanon (Adams Crossing), Q 24	N. Y.
110	West Lebanon, H 16	Ohio
105*	West Lebanon, L 6	Pa.
1123*	West Leechburg, M 5	Pa.
489*	West Leesport (Leesport), M 20	Pa.
326	West Leipsic, E 8	Ohio
1200	West Leisenring, P 4	Pa.
150*	Westley, I 8	Calif.
120*	West Leyden, B 7	Mass.
127*	West Leyden, J 17	N. Y
200	West Liberty, M 19	Ill.
1802	West Liberty, L 21	Iowa
573	West Liberty, F 21	Ky.
1228	West Liberty, J 9	Ohio
420	West Liberty, P 24	W. Va.
150	West Lima, H 18	Wis.
277	West Lincoln, L 21	Neb.
256	West Lincoln, H 8	Vt.
111	West Line, I 6	Mo.
250	Westline, F 8	Pa.
2165	West Linn, D 7	Ore.
2030	West Long Branch, I 20	N. J.
200	West Louisville, G 10	Ky.
300	West Lubec, K 24	Me.
....	West Lynn, E 20, K 6	Mass.
....	West McHenry (McHenry), A 18	Ill.
395	West Manchester, K 5	Ohio
565	West Mansfield, J 18	Mass.
739	West Mansfield, I 10	Ohio
....	West Marietta, M 17	Ohio
....*	West Marion, F 1	N. C.
225*	West Marion, F 21	S. C.
963*	West Mayfield, L 2	Pa.
45	West Mecca, D 20	Ohio
....	West Medford, L 3 (Pop. incl. in Medford)	Mass.
1625	West Medway (Woodside) H 16	Mass.
3369	West Memphis, H 21	Ark.
1126	West Middlesex, I 2	Pa.
200	West Middleton (Middletons), G 14	Ind.
300	West Middletown, M 6	Ohio
264*	West Middletown, N 1	Pa.
95	West Milan, E 16	N. H.
200*	West Milford, B 17	N. J.
389*	West Milford, F 12	W. Va.
75	West Millbrook (Millbrook) M 15	Mich.
237*	West Millbury, G 13	Mass.
197*	West Millgrove, E 10	Ohio
105	West Mills, L 7	Me.
1439	West Milton, K 6	Ohio
775	West Milton, J 16	Pa.
5010*	West Milwaukee, O 20	Wis.
486	West Mineral, N 24	Kan.
100	West Minot, N 5	Me.
2000*	Westminster, R 5	Calif.
534*	Westminster, F 15	Colo.
4692	Westminster, C 12	Md.
1600	Westminster, D 13	Mass.
150*	Westminster, G 8	Ohio
25	Westminster, C 3	Pa.
2014	Westminster, C 3	S. C.
290	Westminster, C 20	Tex.
270	Westminster, P 13	Vt.
....	Westminster Depot, D 13	Mass.
125	Westminster Station, P 14	Vt.
199	Westminster West, P 13	Vt.
12	Westmond, C 4	Idaho
618*	West Monessen (Lock No. 4), O 2	Pa.
6566	West Monroe, C 11	La.
42*	West Monroe, K 15	N. Y.
3044*	Westmont, C 20	Ill.
5000	Westmont, K 9	N. J.
3741	Westmont, N 8	Pa.
400	West Monterey, J 5	Pa.
2000*	Westmoore (Westmoor), I 20	Pa.
56	Westmore, I 24	Mont.
39	Westmore, C 18	Vt.
1010	Westmoreland (Westmorland), Q 22	Calif.
532	Westmoreland, F 20	Kan.
730	Westmoreland, P 6	N. H.
175*	Westmoreland (Westmoreland Depot), P 6	N. H.
400*	Westmoreland, L 17	N. Y.
426	Westmoreland, L 12	Tenn.
100*	Westmoreland, K 1	W. Va.
1200*	Westmoreland City, N 5	Pa.
1010	Westmorland (Westmoreland), Q 22	Calif.
300*	West Moshannon, J 8	Pa.
600	West Mystic, M 23	Conn.
1811	West Nanticoke, I 19	Pa.
56*	West New Brighton (West Brighton), I 4	N. Y.
1500	West Newbury, A 20	Mass.
100*	West Newbury, I 14	Vt.
300	West Newfield, P 2	Me.
250	West Newton, J 14	Ind.
....	West Newton, F 18, N 2 (Pop. incl. in Newton)	Mass.
2765	West Newton, O 4	Pa.
39439	West New York, E 20	N. J.
250	West Norfolk, P 21	Va.
76*	West Norwood, C 19	N. J.
80*	West Nottingham, O 17	N. H.
240*	West Nyack, F 5	N. Y.
400*	West Olive, O 12	Mich.
510	Weston, Q 15	Colo.
500	Weston, O 5	Conn.
173	Weston, L 6	Ga.
439	Weston, R 20	Idaho
287	Weston, G 17	Ill.
92*	Weston, M 4	Iowa
385	Weston, H 19	Me.
....*	Weston, F 18	Mass.
175	Weston, R 18	Mich.
1121	Weston, F 5	Mo.
371	Weston, K 21	Neb.
200	Weston, G 14	N. J.
859	Weston, D 7	Ohio
498	Weston, B 20	Ore.
140*	Weston, J 19	Pa.
300*	Weston, D 19	Tex.

Pop.	Place Index	State
200	Weston, N 10	Vt.
8268	Weston, G 12	W. Va.
100	Weston, C 12	Wis.
12	Weston, D 19	Wyo.
307*	West Oneonta, O 18	N. Y.
400	Westons (Westons Mills), R 6	N. Y.
25662	West Orange, E 18	N. J.
100*	West Ossipee (Mt. Whittier), J 10	N. H.
10*	West Outlet, H 9	Me.
200*	Westover, G 14	Ala.
13	Westover, K 14	La.
150*	Westover, Q 21	Md.
669	Westover, L 9	Pa.
5	Westover, L 12	S. D.
89*	Westover, C 15	Tex.
30*	Westover, N 18	Va.
1752	Westover, C 14	W. Va.
150	West Paducah (Maxon), I 5	Ky.
33693	West Palm Beach, L 24	Fla.
513	West Paris (Bates), M 4	Me.
700*	West Park, R 21	N. Y.
....	West Park, D 16	Ohio
3306	West Paterson, D 19	N. J.
1050	West Pawlet, M 5	Vt.
1124	West Peabody, D 20	Mass.
700	West Pembroke, K 23	Me.
275	West Peru, M 5	Me.
220	West Peterboro, Q 10	N. H.
200	Westphalia, N 7	Ind.
118*	Westphalia, K 5	Iowa
280	Westphalia, J 22	Kan.
386	Westphalia, O 16	Mich.
374	Westphalia, I 14	Mo.
....*	West Philadelphia, P 23	Pa.
....	West Pittsburg, A 23	Calif.
700	West Pittsburgh, J 2	Pa.
7943	West Pittston, H 20	Pa.
3*	Westplaines, B 20	Colo.
..*	West Plains, see Plains	Kan.
4026	West Plains, Q 15	Mo.
145*	West Point, G 15	Ark.
250*	Westpoint, H 9	Calif.
3591	West Point, I 3	Ga.
278	West Point, H 4	Ill.
300	Westpoint, G 9	Ind.
543	West Point, P 21	Iowa
992	West Point, F 13	Ky.
....	Westpoint, P 8	Me.
5627	West Point, F 20	Miss.
2510	Westpoint, I 21	Neb.
4530	West Point, E 5	N. Y.
....*	West Point, see Power Point	Ohio
274*	West Point, N 23	Pa.
450	Westpoint, Q 9	Tenn.
400	Westpoint, K 19	Tex.
1947	Westpoint, M 19	Va.
310	West Point Pleasant, J 20	N. J.
321*	West Poland, O 5	Me.
200	Westport, E 2	Calif.
8258▲	Westport, P 5	Conn.
1500	Westport (Saugatuck), P 5	Conn.
644	Westport, L 18	Ind.
75	Westport, D 15	Ky.
120*	Westport, M 19	Mass.
102*	Westport, L 7	Minn.
150	Westport, Q 7	N. H.
654	Westport, G 24	N. Y.
500	Westport, A 5	Ore.
125	Westport, H 12	Pa.
300	Westport, D 18	S. D.
150*	Westport, N 6	Tenn.
443	Westport, K 2	Wash.
....	West Portal, see Winter Park	Colo.
100*	West Portal, F 10	N. J.
30	West Port Arthur, K 25	Tex.
250*	Westport Factory, M 19	Mass.
221	Westport Point, N 20	Mass.
....	West Pownal, see Pownal	Me.
43*	West Prairie, F 18	Wis.
250*	West Prestonsburg, H 22	Ky.
7	West Quincy, D 16	Mo.
4907*	West Reading, M 20	Pa.
150	West Redding (Redding), M 4	Conn.
300	West Richfield, E 16	Ohio
90	West Ridge, E 21	Ark.
25*	West Ridge, I 19	Ill.
1000*	West Ridgway, G 8	Pa.
150	West Rindge, Q 10	N. H.
45*	West River, J 14	Md.
25	West Rockport, N 12	Me.
75*	West Romney (Vanderlip), E 21	W. Va.
....	West Roxbury, G 19, P 3	Mass.
150	West Rumney, K 11	N. H.
241	West Rupert, N 5	Vt.
145*	West Rush, M 9	N. Y.
149*	West Rushville, L 13	Ohio
50	West Rutland, F 12	Mass.
2500	West Rutland, L 8	Vt.
100*	West Rye, P 20	N. H.
100*	West Sacramento, G 7	Calif.
5733	West Saint Paul, N 24	Minn.
....	West Salamanca, Q 4	N. Y.
909	West Salem, N 20	Ill.
700	West Salem, F 15	Ohio
1490	West Salem, F 6	Ore.
1254	West Salem, F 17	Wis.
75	West Salisbury, Q 7	Pa.
600*	West Sand Lake, N 24	N. Y.
50	West Saugerties, A 4	N. Y.
1500*	West Sayville, G 8	N. Y.
483	West Scarboro, (Dunstan) Q 5	Me.
30*	West Seboois, J 15	Me.
200*	West Shokan, R 22	N. Y.
373	Westside, I 6	Iowa
15*	West Side, O 13	Ore.
....	West Side Jc., G 10	Mont.
200	West Simsbury, C 11	Conn.
250	West Sioux Falls, M 24	S. D.
2000*	West Slope, C 6	Ore.
675*	West Somerset, I 17	Ky.
....*	West Somerville, M 3	Mass.
150	West Sonora, K 6	Ohio
75	West Sound, C 6	Wash.
192*	West Southport, O 10	Me.
....*	West Spokane, H 22	Wash.
17135■	West Springfield, H 7	Mass.
100*	West Springfield, M 9	N. H.
250	West Springfield, D 1	Pa.
250	West Stafford, B 18	Conn.
60	West Stayton, G 7	Ore.
177*	West Stephentown, O 24	N. Y.
50*	West Sterling, E 13	Mass.
350	West Stewartstown, C 14	N. H.
500	West Stockbridge, F 2	Mass.
190	West Stockholm, D 19	N. Y.

Pop.	Place Index	State
380*	West Stoughton, H 19	Mass.
700	West Suffield, A 14	Conn.
612	West Sullivan, M 18	Me.
....*	West Summit, see New Province	N. J.
100	West Sumner, M 5	Me.
259*	West Sunbury, K 3	Pa.
600	West Swanzey, Q 7	N. H.
1324*	West Telford, N 22	Pa.
3729	West Terre Haute (Macksville), K 5	Ind.
170*	West Thornton, J 12	N. H.
100	West Tisbury, P 22	Mass.
135	West Topsham, H 15	Vt.
....	West Torrington, E 7	Conn.
175*	Westtown, D 3	N. Y.
150*	Westtown, P 22	Pa.
600	West Townsend, B 14	Mass.
180	West Townshend, P 11	Vt.
200	West Tremont, N 16	Me.
53*	West Trenton, I 12	N. J.
....	West Tulsa, F 19	Okla.
650	West Union, K 21	Ill.
2059	West Union, D 19	Iowa
78*	West Union, K 9	Minn.
53*	West Union, Q 9	N. Y.
1334	West Union, Q 10	Ohio
449	West Union, C 3	S. C.
1020	West Union, E 10	W. Va.
9221*	West University Place, K 22	Tex.
920	West Unity, C 6	Ohio
1190	West Upton, H 15	Mass.
470	West Valley, P 5	N. Y.
284*	West Van Lear, G 22	Ky.
110	West Vienna (Boles), Q 16	Ill.
27*	Westview, G 12	Ky.
407	Westview, E 16	Ohio
7215	West View, L 3	Pa.
28*	West View, M 14	Va.
700	Westville, M 8	Fla.
3446	Westville, I 22	Ill.
523	Westville, B 10	Ind.
395	Westville (West Farmington), L 6	Me.
400	Westville, Q 18	N. H.
3585	Westville, L 8	N. J.
180	Westville, J 9	Ohio
716	Westville, F 25	Okla.
190	Westville, I 8	Pa.
64*	Westville, E 15	S. C.
....	West Virginia Central Jc., D 19	W. Va.
265	West Virginia No. 2 (Wevaco), N 7	W. Va.
69*	West Wardsboro, P 7	Vt.
200	West Wareham (Tremont), K 22	Mass.
1736	West Warren, G 11	Mass.
18188■	West Warwick (Centerville), G 12	R. I.
75*	West Washington, N 11	Me.
40	Westwater, K 24	Utah
100	Westway, D 16	Conn.
250	West Weber, D 10	Utah
300*	West Webster, L 9	N. Y.
4992	Westwego, N 18	La.
150	West Whately, E 7	Mass.
250*	West Whiteland (Whitford Station), O 21	Pa.
146*	West Wildwood, Cape May, R 12	N. J.
77	West Willington, G 18	Conn.
162*	West Willow, O 19	Pa.
754	West Winfield, N 18	N. Y.
400	West Winfield, K 5	Pa.
5000	Westwood, D 9	Calif.
3000*	Westwood, E 22	Ky.
20*	Westwood, K 13	Md.
1400	Westwood, G 18, Q 1	Mass.
5388	Westwood, C 20	N. J.
....*	Westwood, O 6	Ohio
38*	West Wood, P 21	Pa.
25*	Westwood, M 18	Va.
25	West Woodburn, E 7	Ore.
....	Westwood Jc., D 9	Calif.
100	West Woodstock, B 22	Conn.
115*	West Woodstock, K 12	Vt.
....	West Wrentham, I 17	Mass.
....*	West Wrightstown, O 14	Wis.
2992*	West Wyoming, I 20	Pa.
100	West Yarmouth, N 13	Mass.
300	West Yellowstone, P 10	Mont.
316	West York, L 22	Ill.
5590	West York, P 17	Pa.
28	Weta, L 8	S. D.
32*	Wet Glaize, L 12	Mo.
9644▲	Wethersfield, F 14	Conn.
....	Wethersfield, see Kewanee	Ill.
311	Wetipquin, O 20	Md.
75	Wetmore, L 14	Colo.
425	Wetmore, E 21	Kan.
181*	Wetmore, E 13	Mich.
50*	Wetmore, E 8	Pa.
113*	Wetmore, Q 17	Tenn.
36*	Wetmore, L 16	Tex.
109	Wetonka, D 17	S. D.
2340	Wetumka, J 17	Okla.
3089	Wetumpka, J 16	Ala.
265	Wevaco (West Virginia No. 2), N 7	W. Va.
125	Wever, P 22	Iowa
161	Weverton, E 6	Md.
150	Wevertown, J 22	N. Y.
1022	Wewahitchka, C 1, O 11	Fla.
50*	Wewahotee, G 18	Fla.
75*	Wewanta, M 3	W. Va.
49	Wewela, O 14	S. D.
10315	Wewoka, K 16	Okla.
200*	Wexford, L 3	Pa.
19*	Weyanoke, J 13	La.
6*	Weyanoke, N 18	Va.
27*	Weyanoke (Lowe), Q 8	W. Va.
1175	Weyauwega, L 15	Wis.
49	Weybridge, H 6	Vt.
298	Weyerhauser, E 10	Wis.
262	Weyers Cave (Cave), I 11	Va.
23868■	Weymouth, G 20, R 7	Mass.
100	Weymouth, E 16	Ohio
....	Weymouth Heights, Q 6	Mass.
190*	Whalan, Q 22	Minn.
27*	Whalen (Shorts), G 11	Ky.
85*	Whaley, D 2	N. C.
400	Whaleyville (Whaleysville), N 24	Md.
450	Whaleyville, Q 20	Va.
150*	Whallonsburg, G 23	N. Y.
....	Wharf, L 15	Fla.
35	Wharncliffe, P 4	W. Va.
135*	Wharton, C 7	Ark.
3854	Wharton, D 14	N. J.
407	Wharton, G 10	Ohio
75	Wharton, G 12	Pa.
4386	Wharton, M 21	Tex.
100*	Wharton, M 5	W. Va
1339	What Cheer, M 17	Iowa

Pop.	Place	Index	State
300*	Whately	E 7	Mass.
309	Whatley	M 7	Ala.
141*	Wheat	N 17	Tenn.
174*	Wheat	D 11	W. Va.
70	Wheat Basin	L 14	Mont.
617	Wheatcroft	H 8	Ky.
439	Wheatfield	C 8	Ind.
19*	Wheatfield	F 13	Va.
496	Wheatland	G 8	Calif.
713	Wheatland	O 7	Ind.
535	Wheatland	J 23	Iowa
269	Wheatland	L 9	Mo.
196	Wheatland	M 23	N. D.
110	Wheatland	I 12	Okla.
1421	Wheatland	I 1	Pa.
2110	Wheatland	N 21	Wyo.
362	Wheatley (Wheetley)	I 11	Ark.
90*	Wheatley	D 16	Ky.
7389	Wheaton	C 19	Ill.
155	Wheaton	E 19	Kan.
1700	Wheaton	K 3	Minn.
393	Wheaton	Q 7	Mo.
500	Wheat Ridge	G 14	Colo.
250*	Wheat Road	N 13	N. J.
250*	Wheeler	B 10	Ala.
45*	Wheeler (Litteral)	C 5	Ark.
174	Wheeler	L 19	Ill.
251	Wheeler	B 8	Ind.
55*	Wheeler	D 2	Kan.
200*	Wheeler	J 19	Ky.
250	Wheeler	M 18	Mich.
170	Wheeler	B 21	Miss.
2400*	Wheeler	D 19	Mont.
5	Wheeler	H 16	Neb.
40*	Wheeler	O 10	N. Y.
259	Wheeler	C 4	Ore.
35	Wheeler	N 18	S. D.
848	Wheeler	C 6	Tex.
15	Wheeler	J 18	Wash.
40*	Wheeler	I 12	W. Va.
272*	Wheeler	C 11	Wis.
24*	Wheeler Ridge	M 13	Calif.
175*	Wheelersburg	G 21	Ky.
1500	Wheelersburg	Q 13	Ohio
29*	Wheelers Mill	I 13	Ky.
30*	Wheeler Springs	N 13	Calif.
100	Wheelerton (Pulaski)	Q 16	Mich.
60*	Wheelerton	Q 11	Tenn.
35*	Wheelerville	F 16	Pa.
2	Wheeless	R 1	Okla.
45*	Wheeling	B 14	Ark.
550	Wheeling	B 20	Ill.
450	Wheeling	D 10	Mo.
61099	Wheeling	Q 23	W. Va.
....	Wheeling Jc.	O 24	W. Va.
94	Wheelock	G 4	N. D.
....	Wheelock	Q 24	Ohio
218	Wheelock	I 20	Tex.
110	Wheelock	D 17	Vt.
2027	Wheelwright	H 23	Ky.
300	Wheelwright	F 11	Mass.
	*Wheetley, see Wheatley		Ark.
214*	Whelen Springs	N 9	Ark.
19*	Whetstone	K 15	Ky.
4	Whetstone	K 4	N. D.
80*	Whick	H 21	Ky.
533	Whigham	O 7	Ga.
57*	Whipholt	G 12	Minn.
2000	Whippany	D 16	N. J.
....*	Whipple	H 11	Ariz.
57*	Whipple	M 18	Ohio
160*	Whipple	N 8	W. Va.
200	Whippleville	D 21	N. Y.
30*	Whirlwind	O 4	W. Va.
46*	Whisp (Walters)	D 21	Ark.
....*	Whispering Pines	F 4	Calif.
4000	Whistler	P 5	Ala.
56*	Whitacre	E 13	Va.
....*	Whitaker	H 22	Ky.
2217*	Whitaker	M 4	Pa.
883	Whitakers	D 18	N. C.
35*	Whitby	N 7	W. Va.
10	Whitcomb	O 12	W. Va.
65	White	R 14	Ark.
474	White	D 5	Ga.
8	White	M 10	Neb.
200*	White	O 5	Pa.
233	White (Mooween)	L 6	Pa.
559	White	I 24	S. D.
204*	Whiteash	Q 16	Ill.
10	Whitebead	M 13	Okla.
858	White Bear Lake (White Bear)	M 17	Minn.
125*	White Bear (Scarlets Mill)	M 21	Pa.
100	White Bird	I 6	Idaho
522	White Bluff	M 11	Tenn.
600	White Bluffs	M 16	Wash.
51	White Butte	B 6	S. D.
1692	White Castle	M 14	La.
....	White City	J 23	Fla.
330	White City	L 11	Ill.
516	White City	H 19	Kan.
....*	White City	E 8	Tex.
....	White City	H 24	Tex.
45	Whiteclay (Dewing)	D 5	Neb.
75*	Whitecliffs	N 5	Ark.
59*	White Cloud	P 14	Ind.
16	White Cloud	O 4	Iowa
479	White Cloud	C 22	Kan.
811	White Cloud	M 13	Mich.
500	White Cottage	K 15	Ohio
200*	White Creek	L 25	N. Y.
110*	White Creek	J 17	Wis.
350	Whitedeer	J 16	Pa.
13	Whitedeer	C 8	S. D.
733	White Deer	C 4	Tex.
50	White Eagle	C 14	Okla.
350	White Earth	G 6	Minn.
272	White Earth	F 5	N. D.
....*	Whiteface	G 23	N. Y.
81*	Whiteface	C 8	Tex.
962▲	Whitefield	N 10	Me.
1000	Whitefield	G 13	N. H.
341	Whitefield	J 22	Okla.
2602	Whitefish	D 4	Mont.
9651	White Fish Bay	P 20	Wis.
150*	Whitefish Point	F 16	Mich.
200*	Whiteflat	B 11	Tex.
260	Whiteford	B 16	Md.
140*	White Gate	O 3	Va.
750*	White Hall	K 14	Ala.
75*	Whitehall	F 19	Ark.
599	White Hall	E 12	Ga.
3025	White Hall	K 8	Ill.
452	Whitehall	M 16	La.
225	White Hall	C 14	Md.
1407	Whitehall	M 10	Mich.
818	Whitehall	L 8	Mont.
4851	Whitehall	J 24	N. Y.
85*	White Hall	J 17	Pa.
600	Whitehall	N 14	S. C.
1035	Whitehall	F 14	Wis.
115*	Whitehaven	O 21	Md.
1528	White Haven	I 21	Pa.
50*	Whitehaven	P 2	Tenn.
35*	Whitehead	C 4	N. C.
350	White Heath	I 18	Ill.
200	White Hills	N 10	Calif.
60*	White Horn	M 22	Tenn.
250*	White Horse	B 8	Calif.
1800*	White Horse	H 13	N. J.
25	Whitehorse	B 6	Okla.
55	Whitehorse	E 10	S. D.
112*	White Horse Beach	J 23	Mass.
135*	Whitehouse	B 16	Fla.
200	Whitehouse	G 23	Ky.
115*	Whitehouse	F 11	N. J.
....	White House	R 6	N. Y.
718	White House	D 8	Ohio
239	Whitehouse	L 11	Tenn.
500*	Whitehouse	F 22	Tex.
5*	Whitehouse	M 18	Va.
1000	White House Station (White House)	F 12	N. J.
80*	White Lake	R 20	N. Y.
....*	White Lake	K 14	N. C.
496	White Lake	L 18	S. D.
548	White Lake	M 11	Wis.
403	Whiteland	K 15	Ind.
147	Whiteland	H 14	Tex.
225	Whitelaw	P 15	Wis.
78*	Whiteley (Garards Fort)	P 3	Pa.
300*	Whitemarsh	N 23	Pa.
50*	White Marsh	N 20	Va.
75*	White Mills	H 13	Ky.
650	White Mills	G 23	Pa.
....	White Mtn. Transfer	I 10	N. H.
25*	Whitener	C 6	Ark.
100	White Oak	L 22	Ala.
180*	White Oak	O 21	Ga.
121	White Oak	K 17	Ky.
136*	Whiteoak	J 23	Mo.
100*	White Oak	K 14	N. C.
75	Whiteoak	C 21	Okla.
125*	White Oak	E 13	S. C.
50	White Oaks	K 15	N. M.
20	White Owl	H 6	S. D.
45*	Whitepath	C 7	Ga.
1017	White Pigeon	R 13	Mich.
175	Whitepine	F 1	Mont.
46	Whitepine	H 15	Pa.
497	White Pine	M 21	Tenn.
36*	White Pine	H 9	W. Va.
160	White Pine Mine (White Pine)	B 23	Mich.
200*	White Pines	H 9	Calif.
364	White Plain (White Plains)	G 14	Ga.
382	White Plains	I 9	Ky.
150	White Plain	L 11	Md.
40327	White Plains	G 6	N. Y.
275	White Plains	C 6	N. C.
60*	White Plains	R 15	Va.
263	White Pond	J 11	S. C.
80	Whiteport	B 5, R 22	N. Y.
109*	Whitepost	G 24	Ky.
336	White Post	F 14	Va.
300	Whiteriver	J 21	Ariz.
562	White River	M 12	S. D.
2271	White River Jc.	K 15	Vt.
....	Whiterock	P 5	Me.
15	Whiterock	A 16	Nev.
400*	Whiterock	M 7	N. C.
141*	White Rock	G 12	S. C.
220	White Rock	B 24	S. D.
35*	White Rock (Hopson)	M 25	Tenn.
86	Whiterocks	F 21	Utah
18*	White Rose	H 15	Ky.
37*	White Run	H 11	Ky.
83*	Whites	H 18	Ky.
....	Whites	L 18	Okla.
20*	Whites	K 18	Va.
100	Whites (White)	K 5	Wash.
985	White Salmon (Bingen-White Salmon)	P 11	Wash.
....	Whitesand	N 13	Miss.
150*	Whitesbog	L 13	N. J.
500*	Whitesboro	R 11	N. J.
3532	Whitesboro	L 18	N. Y.
110	Whitesboro	M 23	Okla.
1560	Whitesboro	C 19	Tex.
341	Whitesburg	G 4	Ga.
1616	Whitesburg	I 22	Ky.
300	Whitesburg	M 21	Tenn.
....	Whites Corners	M 16	N. Y.
500*	Whites Creek	L 10	Tenn.
100*	Whites Creek (Cyrus)	L 1	W. Va.
350*	Whites Ferry (Hoban Heights)	G 20	Pa.
122*	Whiteside	G 17	Mo.
500	Whiteside	Q 14	Tenn.
185	Whiteson	E 6	Ore.
600	White Springs	B 11	Fla.
200*	Whitestone	C 6	Ga.
150*	White Stone	B 9	S. C.
200	White Stone	L 21	Va.
....*	Whitestone	H 6	N. Y.
429	Whitestown	I 12	Ind.
3*	White Sulphur Springs	H 5	Ga.
200	White Sulphur (Linwood)	L 23	Iowa
10*	White Sulphur Springs	G 10	La.
858	White Sulphur Springs	J 11	Mont.
400*	White Sulphur Springs	R 20	N. Y.
2093	White Sulphur Springs	O 13	W. Va.
75*	Whites Valley	E 23	Pa.
543	Whitesville	G 11	Ky.
132	Whitesville	C 5	Mo.
450	Whitesville	J 18	N. J.
650	Whitesville	R 8	N. Y.
942*	Whitesville	N 6	W. Va.
295	White Swan	N 12	Wash.
200	Whitetail	B 22	Mont.
50	White Tail	L 15	N. M.
42*	Whitethorn	O 4	Va.
100*	Whitetop	E 9	Va.
210*	White Valley (Coldbrook)	F 12	Mass.
58*	Whiteville	K 11	La.
3011	Whiteville	L 13	N. C.
796	Whiteville	P 4	Tenn.
23*	White Water (Palm Springs)	O 20	Calif.
125	Whitewater	I 4	Colo.
515	White Water	L 17	Kan.
175	Whitewater	O 22	Mo.
55*	White Water (Whitewater)	C 17	Mont.
75	Whitewater	N 5	N. M.
3689	Whitewater	M 21	Wis.
25*	Whitewood	I 15	Ky.
267	Whitewood	I 2	S. D.
64*	Whitewood	B 8	Va.
1537	Whitewright	C 20	Tex.
300	Whitfield	J 5	Ala.
300	Whitfield	K 11	Miss.
84*	Whitford	O 21	Pa.
250*	Whitford Station (West Whiteland)	O 21	Pa.
200*	Whitham	E 10	Mo.
10307	Whiting	B 6	Ind.
688	Whiting	I 2	Iowa
343	Whiting	E 22	Kan.
200	Whiting	L 23	Me.
100	Whiting	Q 24	Mo.
350	Whiting (Whitings)	K 17	N. J.
8	Whiting	J 6	Vt.
250	Whitingham	R 9	Vt.
1550*	Whitins (Linwood)	I 15	Mass.
7000	Whitinsville	H 14	Mass.
20	Whitlash	C 10	Mont.
1500	Whitley City (Whitley)	K 17	Ky.
40*	Whitleyville	L 14	Tenn.
150*	Whitlock	L 6	Tenn.
....*	Whitlocks Crossing	F 14	S. D.
40*	Whitlow	D 2	Calif.
....	Whitlow Jc.	Q 14	Ark.
7759■	Whitman	H 20	Mass.
150	Whitman	H 8	Neb.
125	Whitman	G 20	N. D.
....*	Whitman	I 22	Wyo.
200*	Whitmans (Whitman)	O 4	W. Va.
221	Whitmell	Q 8	Va.
265	Whitmer	H 16	W. Va.
3272	Whitmire	D 10	S. C.
44*	Whitmore	H 20	Ark.
110*	Whitmore	D 7	Calif.
575	Whitmore Lake	P 19	Mich.
300*	Whitnel	E 3	N. C.
150*	Whitney	E 16	Ala.
278	Whitney	R 21	Idaho
103*	Whitney	H 7	Mich.
154	Whitney	E 3	Neb.
129*	Whitney	P 21	Nev.
....	Whitney	G 8	N. C.
19	Whitney	G 20	Ore.
875	Whitney	N 6	Pa.
250*	Whitney	B 9	S. C.
824	Whitney	G 18	Tex.
115*	Whitney Crossings (Garwoods)	O 8	N. Y.
733	Whitney Point	P 15	N. Y.
190	Whitneyville	L 21	Me.
64	Whiton	O 23	Md.
500*	Whitsett	E 10	N. C.
560*	Whitsett (Whitsett Junction)	Q 4	Pa.
108*	Whitsett	N 17	Tex.
....	Whitson	H 20	Wis.
25	Whitstran	N 16	Wash.
527	Whitt	D 17	Tex.
300*	Whittaker	Q 20	Mich.
671	Whittemore	D 9	Iowa
420*	Whittemore	K 19	Mich.
227	Whitten	H 14	Iowa
4000*	Whittenburg (Phillips)	B 4	Tex.
....	Whittenton Jc.	J 18	Mass.
100*	Whitthorne	N 6	Tenn.
16115	Whittier	O 16, Q 5	Calif.
100*	Whittier	I 20	Iowa
287	Whittier	P 5	N. C.
300	Whittington	O 16	Ill.
100	Whittington	I 10	La.
16*	Whittle	J 16	Ky.
35*	Whittles Depot (Whittle)	P 9	Va.
100*	Whittlesey	F 15	Ohio
20*	Whittlesey	H 11	Wis.
2500	Whitwell	Q 14	Tenn.
100*	Whon	H 15	Tex.
....*	Whoopflarea	H 19	Ky.
65*	Whortonsville	I 21	N. C.
....	Whyte	F 23	Minn.
....*	Wianno	N 12	Mass.
625	Wibaux	H 25	Mont.
150*	Wiborg	K 18	Ky.
100*	Wichert	E 21	Ill.
114966	Wichita	M 16	Kan.
45112	Wichita Falls	B 16	Tex.
....*	Wichman	J 7	Nev.
57*	Wick	M 12	Iowa
50	Wick	C 20	Ohio
110*	Wick	D 9	W. Va.
80*	Wickatunk	H 18	N. J.
....	Wickboro	K 5	Pa.
995	Wickenburg	J 10	Ariz.
105	Wickersham	C 9	Wash.
121	Wickes	L 4	Ark.
85	Wickes	J 8	Mont.
....*	Wickett	H 7	Tex.
1065	Wickford	J 14	R. I.
100	Wickford Jc.	J 13	R. I.
200	Wickford Landing	J 14	R. I.
110*	Wickham	N 7	W. Va.
250*	Wickhaven	P 4	Pa.
14*	Wickliffe	P 12	Ind.
1039	Wickliffe	J 4	Ky.
27*	Wickliffe	K 14	La.
3155	Wickliffe	C 17	Ohio
200	Wicksburg	O 20	Ala.
165*	Wlcomico	M 12	Md.
121*	Wicomico	N 21	Va.
129*	Wicomico Church	L 21	Va.
1895	Wiconisco	M 17	Pa.
110	Wideman	B 14	Ark.
366*	Widemouth	P 8	W. Va.
1800	Widen	K 10	W. Va.
225*	Widener	H 19	Ark.
25	Wide Ruins	F 23	Ariz.
103*	Widewater	H 16	Va.
200*	Widnoon	L 5	Pa.
103	Widtsoe	O 11	Utah
91*	Wiehle (Sunset Hills)	F 17	Va.
10	Wier	M 12	Tenn.
1521	Wiergate	H 25	Tex.
75*	Wierwood (Weirwood)	M 23	Va.
75*	Wiggins	N 15	Ala.
275	Wiggins	D 17	Colo.
1141	Wiggins	P 18	Miss.
40*	Wiggins	O 15	S. C.
104*	Wightman	I 25	Tex.
54*	Wightman	P 13	Va.
885*	Wigton (Chester Hill)	J 9	Pa.
28*	Wikel	O 10	W. Va.
200*	Wikieup	H 6	Ariz.
66*	Wila	M 14	Pa.
25*	Wilark	B 6	Ore.
100*	Wilawana	E 17	Pa.
45*	Wilbar	D 4	N. C.
1355	Wilber	N 21	Neb.
324	Wilberforce	L 8	Ohio
54*	Wllbern	E 14	Ill.
40*	Wilbern	L 14	Ohio
40	Wilborn	I 8	Mont.
300	Wilbraham	H 9	Mass.
150*	Wilbur	K 21	Kan.
25*	Wilbur	F 23	Ky.
138	Wilbur	M 5	Ore.
1011	Wilbur	G 19	Wash.
200*	Wilbur	D 10	W. Va.
200*	Wilburn	F 13	Ark.
39*	Wilburn	P 13	Va.
113*	Wilbur Springs	G 5	Calif.
....	Wilburtha	I 12	N. J.
150*	Wilburton	O 1	Kan.
1925	Wilburton	L 22	Okla.
750*	Wilburton	J 18	Pa.
....	Wilby	P 20	Mo.
1200	Wilcoe	Q 6	W. Va.
....*	Wilcox (Gregville)	N 11	Ala.
53*	Wilcox	D 11	Fla.
98*	Wilcox	B 4	Mo.
310	Wilcox	N 15	Neb.
1000	Wilcox	G 9	Pa.
49	Wilcox	J 23	Wash.
236*	Wilda	H 8	La.
....	Wildcat	D 15	Colo.
100*	Wild Cat	I 19	Ky.
188	Wildcat	I 18	Okla.
125*	Wildcat	D 19	Wyo.
32*	Wildcat	H 10	W. Va.
100*	Wild Cherry	B 13	Ark.
....	Wild Dog	H 19	Ky.
507	Wilder	N 3	Idaho
51	Wilder (Wilders)	C 9	Ind.
70*	Wilder	H 24	Kan.
127*	Wilder	Q 9	Minn.
10*	Wilder	H 14	Mont.
500	Wilder	L 15	Tenn.
1125	Wilder	K 15	Vt.
400	Wilde	D 7	Va.
43*	Wilderness	Q 17	Mo.
20*	Wilderness	I 15	Va.
300*	Wildersville	N 6	Tenn.
12	Wilderville	P 4	Ore.
....	Wild Horse	J 21	Colo.
30*	Wildhorse	K 4	Idaho
75	Wildie	H 18	Ky.
51*	Wildomar	P 18	Calif.
105*	Wildorado	D 2	Tex.
45	Wild Rice	N 25	N. D.
472	Wildrose	E 4	N. D.
559	Wild Rose	K 15	Wis.
261	Wildsville	G 12	La.
1000*	Wildwood	D 2	Calif.
1346	Wildwood	F 15	Fla.
100*	Wildwood	B 1	Ga.
5150	Wildwood	R 12	N. J.
210	Wildwood	J 20	N. C.
150*	Wildwood	L 3	Pa.
5*	Wildwood	K 13	Va.
661	Wildwood Crest	R 12	N. J.
....	Wildwood Jc.	R 11	N. J.
....*	Wildyrie	H 13	Calif.
....	Wiles (Satterfield)	E 16	Tex.
413	Wiley	L 22	Colo.
16*	Wiley	C 12	Ga.
....	Wiley	M 13	Wash.
35*	Wiley Ford	D 19	W. Va.
200*	Wileyville	B 10	W. Va.
....	Wilfred	K 20	Ky.
50*	Wilgus	R 13	Ohio
40	Wilgus	K 8	Pa.
50*	Wilhelmina	I 22, R 20	Mo.
300*	Wilhoit (Dayhoit)	J 21	Ky.
30	Wilhoit	P 8	Ore.
54*	Wilhurst	G 21	Ky.
86236	Wilkes-Barre	I 21	Pa.
1309	Wilkesboro	D 4	N. C.
369	Wilkeson	J 9	Wash.
245	Wilkesville	O 14	Ohio
6	Wilkie	I 17	Tex.
500	Wilkins	P 15	S. C.
29853	Wilkinsburg	M 4	Pa.
....	Wilkinson	B 16	Ill.
336	Wilkinson	I 17	Ind.
63*	Wilkinson	G 11	Minn.
100*	Wilkinson	O 4	Miss.
550*	Wilkinson (Monitor)	O 4	W. Va.
780	Wilkinsonville	H 14	Mass.
25	Willa	O 7	N. D.
903	Willacooche	N 15	Ga.
75*	Willada (Lancaster)	K 22	Wash.
25*	Willailla	I 18	Ky.
1100	Willamette	E 8	Ore.
677	Willamina	E 5	Ore.
320	Willapa	L 4	Wash.
105	Willard	C 19	Colo.
106*	Willard	G 21	Kan.
165	Willard	E 22	Ky.
375*	Willard	O 9	Mo.
5	Willard	J 25	Mont.
462	Willard	H 13	N. M.
600*	Willard	N 12	N. Y.
100*	Willard	K 16	N. C.
4261	Willard	F 13	Ohio
541	Willard	C 11	Utah
100	Willard	P 10	Wash.
100*	Willard	G 12	Wis.
285	Willards	N 24	Md.
50	Willbridge	D 7	Ore.
....*	Willcockson, see Marble Falls		Ark.
884	Willcox	N 20	Ariz.
128*	Willcox Wharf	N 17	Va.
500*	Willernie	N 18	Minn.
250	Willet	P 15	N. Y.
....	Willett	I 7	Neb.
11	Willett	C 2	S. D.
265	Willette	L 13	Tenn.
300	Willetts	G 13	La.
11*	Willey House (Mount Carrigan)	J 16	N. H.
34*	Willhoit	Q 13	Mo.
2622	Williams	F 12	Ariz.
814	Williams	F 6	Calif.
300	Williams	N 10	Ind.
489	Williams	G 12	Iowa
30*	Williams	F 21	Ky.
362	Williams (North Falmouth)	M 23	Mass.
376*	Williams	B 10	Minn.
27	Williams	D 9	Mont.
16	Williams	O 20	Neb.
500	Williams	K 24	Okla.
20	Williams	Q 5	Ore.
4	Williams	Q 8	Pa.
218*	Williams	N 15	S. C.
717	Williams Bay	N 22	Wis.
97	Williamsburg	L 14	Colo.
250	Williamsburg	I 22	Ind.
1308	Williamsburg	K 18	Iowa
365	Williamsburg	I 22	Kan.
2331	Williamsburg	K 18	Ky.
120*	Williamsburg	M 18	Md.
1000	Williamsburg	E 6	Mass.
100	Williamsburg	J 14	Mich.
83*	Williamsburg	H 15	Mo.
1194	Williamsburg	O 8	Ohio
1898	Williamsburg	M 11	Pa.
3942	Williamsburg	N 20	Va.
177*	Williamsburg	M 12	W. Va.
470	Williamsfield	F 10	Ill.
100	Williamsfield	C 21	Ohio
600*	Williams Grove	O 15	Pa.
....*	Williams Mountain	M 5	W. Va.
217	Williamson	H 7	Ga.
412	Williamson	L 12	Ill.
10	Williamson	N 8	Iowa
616	Williamson	N 14	Iowa
1000	Williamson	K 11	N. Y.
250*	Williamson	P 13	Pa.
8366	Williamson	O 2	W. Va.
270*	Williamson School	P 22	Pa.
1222	Williamsport	H 7	Ind.
200	Williamsport	G 23	Ky.
1772	Williamsport	C 5	Md.
605	Williamsport	M 12	Ohio
44355	Williamsport	H 16	Pa.
112*	Williamsport	O 9	Tenn.
250*	Williams River	K 12	W. Va.
1704	Williamston	P 18	Mich.
3966	Williamston	E 19	N. C.
2509	Williamston	C 6	S. C.
75*	Williamstown	F 22	Kan.
1077	Williamstown	D 17	Ky.
3000	Williamstown	B 2	Mass.
158	Williamstown	B 15	Mo.
2000	Williamstown	M 10	N. J.
175	Williamstown	K 16	N. Y.
100*	Williamstown	F 10	Ohio
2769	Williamstown	M 17	Pa.
500	Williamstown	H 12	Vt.
1687	Williamstown	D 7	W. Va.
....	Williamstown Jc.	M 11	N. J.
649	Williamsville	I 12	Ill.
511	Williamsville	P 19	Mo.
3614*	Williamsville	M 5	N. Y.
44*	Williamsville	J 8	Va.
20*	Williams Wharf	M 21	Va.
192	Willie	L 21	Ga.
272	Williford	B 16	Ark.
....	Willimansett	H 8 (Pop. incl. in Holyoke)	Mass.
12101	Willimantic	F 20	Conn.
452	Willington	G 6	S. C.
160	Willis	D 22	Kan.
125	Willis	Q 20	Mich.
390	Willis	Q 15	Okla.
904	Willis	J 22	Tex.
300*	Willis	P 5	Va.
400*	Willis Branch	M 8	W. Va.
200*	Willisburg	F 15	Ky.
15*	Willis Creek	K 15	Ky.
890	Williston	E 13	Fla.
220	Williston	J 21	N. C.
5790	Williston	G 2	N. D.
300	Williston	C 11	Ohio
1107	Williston	K 11	S. C.
175*	Williston	P 3	Tenn.
198	Williston	E 7	Vt.
160	Williston (North Williston)	E 8	Vt.
5750	Williston Park	H 7	N. Y.
....	Willotta	A 20	Calif.
....	Willstown	P 21	Pa.
25	Willisville	P 8	Ark.
781	Willisville	O 12	Ill.
450	Willis Wharf	M 23	Va.
1625	Willits	F 3	Calif.
7623	Wilmar	M 9	Minn.
28*	Willmathsville	C 12	Mo.
300*	Willock	L 3	Pa.
50*	Willoughby	J 18	Miss.
4364	Willoughby	C 17	Ohio
105*	Willoughby (Kimball)	C 17	Vt.
300*	Willow	M 10	Ark.
50*	Willow	G 20	Ky.
....	Willow	Q 22	N. Y.
....	Willow	D 17	Ohio
248	Willow	K 3	Okla.
15*	Willow (Willow Island)	E 7	W. Va.
45*	Willow Bend	P 11	W. Va.
100	Willow Branch	I 17	Ind.
3000*	Willowbrook	O 15	Calif.
524	Willow City	E 13	N. D.
100*	Willow City	J 15	Tex.
140*	Willow Creek	D 2	Calif.
4*	Willow Creek	C 8	Colo.
....	Willow Creek	B 7	Ind.
350	Willow Creek	L 9	Mont.
25*	Willowcreek	M 22	Ore.
42*	Willowdale	N 13	Kan.
52*	Willowdale	H 11	Ore.
260	Willowemoc	R 20	N. Y.
4167*	Willow Glen	J 6	Calif.
12000	Willow Grove	O 24	Pa.
600*	Willow Grove	L 15	Tenn.
372	Willow Hill	L 20	Ill.
180*	Willow Hill	O 13	Pa.
50	Willow Island	L 12	Neb.
15*	Willow Island (Willow)	E 7	W. Va.
427	Willow Lake	H 21	S. D.
10	Willow Point	C 11	Nev.
300*	Willow Ranch	B 10	Calif.
314	Willow River	J 18	Minn.
2215	Willows	F 5	Calif.
25*	Willows	M 13	Md.
150*	Willows	L 7	Miss.
40*	Willows	E 9	Ore.
15*	Willow Shade	J 14	Ky.
125*	Willow Spring	E 14	N. C.
948*	Willow Springs (Spring Forest)	C 20	Ill.
1530	Willow Springs	P 14	Mo.
150*	Willow Springs	J 23	Tex.
2000*	Willow Springs (Greggton)	E 23	Tex.
250*	Willow Street	P 19	Pa.
200*	Willowton (Wills)	Q 9	W. Va.
43*	Willow Tree	G 19	Ky.
1000*	Willowvale	L 17	N. Y.
24	Willow View	K 13	Okla.
915*	Willowick	C 18	Ohio
....*	Willow Wood	R 14	Ohio
200*	Wills (Willowton)	Q 9	W. Va.
15*	Wills	E 5	Wis.
1100	Willsboro	F 24	N. Y.
100	Willseyville	P 14	N. Y.
513	Willshire	G 5	Ohio
5	Willson Landing	H 11	La.
200*	Wills Point	N 20	La.
1976	Wills Point	E 21	Tex.
....	Willton	C 4	Tex.
....	Wilma	C 2, O 12	Fla.
695	Wilmar	O 14	Ark.
....*	Wilmar	O 15 (Pop. incl. in San Gabriel)	Calif.
150	Wilmer	P 4	Ala.
300*	Wilmer	J 17	La.
263*	Wilmer	E 19	Tex.
5662	Wilmerding	N 4	Pa.
25	Wilmere	H 10	Pa.
17226	Wilmette	B 21	Ill.
....	Wilmington	Q 12	Ark.
....	Wilmington	P 15 (Pop. incl. in Los Angeles)	Calif.
112504	Wilmington	B 22	Del.
1921	Wilmington	E 20	Ill.
22	Wilmington	H 20	Kan.
3500	Wilmington	D 19	Mass.
300*	Wilmington	G 23	N. Y.
33407	Wilmington	M 17	N. C.
5971	Wilmington	N 9	Ohio
597	Wilmington	Q 9	Vt.
25*	Wilmington	K 13	Va.
....	Wilmington Jct.	C 18	Mass.
....	Wilmington Jct.	J 2	Pa.
361	Wilmont	Q 5	Minn.
212	Wilmore	O 10	Kan.
1228	Wilmore	G 17	Ky.
410	Wilmore	M 8	Pa.
70*	Wilmore	Q 4	W. Va.
625	Wilmot	R 15	Ark.
75*	Wilmot	N 18	Kan.
70	Wilmot	M 22	Mich.
145	Wilmot	M 11	N. H.
287	Wilmot	H 17	Ohio
628	Wilmot	D 23	S. D.
310	Wilmot	O 22	Wis.
203	Wilmot Flat	M 11	N. H.
100*	Wilpen	F 19	Minn.
800	Wilpen	N 7	Pa.
300	Wilsall	K 11	Mont.
348	Wilsey	I 19	Kan.
10*	Wilsie	I 10	W. Va.
1500	Wilson	E 22	Ark.
600	Wilson	E 14	Conn.
10	Wilson	O 4	Idaho
200*	Wilson	A 20	Ill.
1068	Wilson	H 13	Kan.
354	Wilson	J 14	La.
....*	Wilson	L 14	Md.
250	Wilson	G 7	Mich.
849	Wilson	K 5	N. Y.
19234	Wilson	F 17	N. C.
1700	Wilson	P 12	Okla.
3243	Wilson	N 3	Pa.
8217*	Wilson	K 23	Pa.
35	Wilson, (Wilson Mill)	I 18	S. C.
600*	Wilson	D 10	Tex.
23*	Wilson	E 17	W. Va.
188	Wilson	C 12	Wis.
50	Wilson	G 2	Wyo.
150	Wilsonburg	E 12	W. Va.
112*	Wilson Creek	P 7	Pa.
210	Wilsoncreek	I 18	Wash.
33*	Wilsondale	L 2	W. Va.
1000*	Wilson Dam	B 8	Ala.
....	Wilson Jc.	D 22	Ark.
130	Wilson Point	Q 4	Conn.
104*	Wilsons	O 15	Va.
50*	Wilsons Mills	K 2	Me.
436	Wilsons Mills	G 15	N. C.
749	Wilsonville	G 15	Ala.
300	Wilsonville	A 24	Conn.
902	Wilsonville	K 11	Ill.
382	Wilsonville	O 12	Neb.
110	Wilsonville	E 7	Ore.
422	Wilton	H 12	Ala.
319	Wilton	N 5	Ark.
10*	Wilton	H 8	Calif.
800	Wilton	O 4	Conn.
1146	Wilton (Wilton Junction)	L 22	Iowa
2500	Wilton	L 6	Me.
1100	Wilton (Dryden)	L 6	Me.
139*	Wilton	F 10	Minn.
1400	Wilton	Q 12	N. H.
250*	Wilton	K 23	N. Y.
851	Wilton	L 12	N. D.
2	Wilton	I 13	Ore.
150*	Wilton	L 20	Va.
486	Wilton	H 17	Wis.
1146	Wilton Jc. (Wilton)	L 22	Iowa
5	Wilwin	F 15	Mich.
250	Wily	M 12	Va.
20	Wilzetta	I 15	Okla.
557*	Wimauma	J 14	Fla.
124*	Wimberley	K 16	Tex.
357	Wimbledon	L 19	N. D.
20	Wimer	P 6	Ore.
45*	Win	G 22	Ky.
1835	Winamac	D 10	Ind.
54	Winant (Oysterville)	G 3	Ore.
109*	Winborn	A 17	Miss.
1285	Winburne	J 11	Pa.
....	Winchell	P 16	Colo.
100	Winchell	H 15	Tex.
6575■	Winchendon	B 11	Mass.
430	Winchendon Springs	B 12	Mass.
171	Winchester	N 16	Ark.
201*	Winchester	P 19	Calif.
52*	Winchester	K 9	Ga.
634	Winchester	H 4	Idaho
1651	Winchester	J 9	Ill.
5303	Winchester	H 21	Ind.
415	Winchester	F 23	Kan.
8594	Winchester	F 18	Ky.
15081■	Winchester	E 18, K 2	Mass.
359	Winchester	M 21	Miss.
900	Winchester	R 6	N. H.
....*	Winchester, see Winterset		Ohio
798	Winchester	P 10	Ohio
4	Winchester	A 6	Okla.
12	Winchester	M 5	Ore.
2760	Winchester	Q 12	Tenn.
410	Winchester	K 19	Tex.
12095	Winchester	E 14	Va.
39	Winchester	J 16	Wash.
78*	Winchester	J 6	Wis.
200	Winchester (Chatham)	F 11	Wyo.
275	Winchester Bay	K 3	Ore.
200	Winchester Center	C 7	Conn.
....	Winchester Highlands	K 3	Mass.
9057	Windber	O 8	Pa.
28*	Wind Cave	H 19	Ky.
81	Winde	G 8	Mich.
3974	Winder	E 11	Ga.
163*	Windermere	H 17	Fla.
835	Windfall	G 15	Ind.
1377	Windgap	K 23	Pa.
200	Windham	G 21	Conn.
115	Windham	H 12	Mont.
350	Windham (Windham Depot)	Q 16	N. H.
300	Windham	P 22	N. Y.
316	Windham	E 19	Ohio
30	Windham	D 19	Pa.
50	Windham	O 11	Vt.
100	Windham Center	P 5	Me.
350	Windham Depot (Windham)	Q 16	N. H.
250	Winding Gulf	O 8	W. Va.
196	Windom	J 14	Kan.
2807	Windom	Q 8	Minn.
300*	Windom	N 9	N. C.
290	Windom	C 21	Tex.
20*	Windom	P 6	W. Va.
250	Window Rock	G 24	Ariz.
200*	Wind Ridge	P 1	Pa.
50	Wind River	J 8	Wyo.
42	Windrock	M 18	Tenn.
500*	Windsor	H 4	Calif.
1811	Windsor	C 15	Colo.
6100	Windsor	D 14	Conn.
150	Windsor	D 14	Fla.
....*	Windsor, see New Windsor		Ill.
1005	Windsor	J 17	Ill.
23*	Windsor	I 16	Ky.
200*	Windsor (Windsorville)	N 10	Me.
100	Windsor	D 4	Mass.
2373	Windsor	I 9	Mo.
15	Windsor	M 6	N. H.
312	Windsor	I 14	N. J.
766	Windsor	R 16	N. Y.
1747	Windsor	E 20	N. C.
100	Windsor	M 17	N. D.
894▲	Windsor	C 19	Ohio
1108	Windsor	P 18	Pa.
151*	Windsor	J 11	S. C.
3402	Windsor	M 14	Vt.
411	Windsor	P 20	Va.
....*	Windsor (Windsor Heights)	O 24	W. Va.
210*	Windsor	K 19	Wis.
....	Windsor Beach	K 9	N. Y.
....*	Windsor Heights (Windsor)	O 24	W. Va.
....	Windsor Jc.	K 5	Ind.
4347▲	Windsor Locks	C 14	Conn.
150*	Windsor Shades (Boulevard)	M 19	Va.
300	Windsorville	C 15	Conn.
500*	Windthorst	C 16	Tex.
25*	Windy	J 16	Ky.
30*	Windy	G 6	W. Va.
300*	Windy Gap	D 4	N. C.
35*	Windyville	M 11	Mo.
180	Winegar	J 6	Wis.
14*	Winegars	K 17	Mich.
40*	Winesap	O 16	Tenn.

Pop.	Place, Index	State
80	Winesap, H 14	Wash.
115	Winesburg, H 16	Ohio
160	Winfall, D 22	N. C.
1662	Winfield, E 7	Ala.
31	Winfield, I 5	Ark.
567	Winfield, C 19	Ill.
933	Winfield, N 21	Iowa
9506	Winfield, N 18	Kan.
484	Winfield, H 18	Mo.
80*	Winfield (East Windfield), J 19	N. Y.
310	Winfield, K 16	Pa.
300	Winfield, L 17	Tenn.
500	Winfield, D 22	Tex.
318	Winfield, J 4	W. Va.
....	Winfield Jc. K 5	Pa.
....	Winford, J 4	Ky.
245	Winfred, K 22	S. D.
182*	Wing, H 8	Ark.
75*	Wing, F 18	Ill.
35*	Wing, M 9	N. C.
235	Wing, L 13	N. D.
380	Wingate, H 9	Ind.
800	Wingate, O 18	Md.
53*	Wingate, O 18	Miss.
541	Wingate, I 7	N. C.
200	Wingate (Snow Shoe Intersection), J 12	Pa.
300	Wingate, F 13	Tex.
500*	Wingdale, R 23	N. Y.
301	Winger, F 6	Minn.
52*	Wingett Run, M 17	Ohio
60*	Wingina, M 11	Va.
....	Wingo, A 16	Calif.
475	Wingo, K 5	Ky.
15	Wing Road, G 13	N. H.
79*	Winifred, D 19	Kan.
25*	Winifred, G 22	Ky.
300	Winifred, G 14	Mont.
400	Winifrede, L 6	W. Va.
129	Winigan, C 11	Mo.
1945	Wink, G 7	Tex.
10	Winkel, A 13	Ill.
524	Winkelman, L 18	Ariz.
103*	Winkle (East Danville), O 9	Ohio
8*	Winkler, E 18	Kan.
96*	Winkler, G 20	Tex.
63	Winlock, F 16	Ore.
861	Winlock, M 5	Wash.
100*	Winn, M 6	Ala.
250	Winn, I 17	Me.
150	Winn, M 14	Mich.
50*	Winnabow, M 16	N. C.
637	Winnebago, B 14	Ill.
1992	Winnebago, Q 12	Minn.
800	Winnebago, G 22	Neb.
150	Winnebago (State Hospital), N 16	Wis.
931	Winneconne, M 15	Wis.
25	Winnecook, L 11	Me.
270	Winnegance, O 8	Me.
2485	Winnemucca, C 10	Nev.
2426	Winner, M 14	S. D.
12430	Winnetka, A 21	Ill.
141	Winnetoon, F 18	Neb.
399	Winnett, H 16	Mont.
4512	Winnfield, F 9	La.
321	Winnie, K 24	Tex.
500	Winnipauk, P 4	Conn.
19*	Winnipeg, M 13	Mo.
....*	Winnpesaukee, K 15	N. H.
78*	Winnisquam, M 14	N. H.
2834	Winnsboro, E 12	La.
3181	Winnsboro, E 13	S. C.
2092	Winnsboro, D 22	Tex.
75*	Winokur, O 19	Ga.
30*	Winona, G 15	Ariz.
15	Winona, H 6	Idaho
125	Winona, C 12	Ind.
317	Winona, G 4	Kan.
125*	Winona, D 2	Mich.
22490	Winona, Q 23	Minn.
2532	Winona, F 14	Miss.
480	Winona, P 17	Mo.
4*	Winona, P 13	N. D.
185	Winona, G 19	Ohio
380*	Winona, L 17	Tenn.
600	Winona, E 22	Tex.
159	Winona, K 22	Wash.
800	Winona (Masters), M 9	W. Va.
743	Winona Lake, C 17	Ind.
6036	Winooski, E 6	Vt.
8	Winship, B 18	S. D.
451	Winside, G 20	Neb.
4577	Winslow, G 18	Ariz.
248	Winslow, D 5	Ark.
379	Winslow, A 12	Ill.
1382	Winslow, P 8	Ind.
3000	Winslow, M 10	Me.
130	Winslow, I 22	Neb.
300	Winslow, M 11	N. J.
500	Winslow, H 7	Wash.
....	Winslow Jc., M 12	N. J.
460*	Winslows Mills, O 11	Me.
9*	Winsper, M 18	Idaho
7674	Winsted, C 9	Conn.
660	Winsted, N 13	Minn.
65	Winston, H 15	Fla.
201*	Winston, F 4	Ga.
10*	Winston, G 19	Ky.
381	Winston, D 7	Mo.
100	Winston, J 9	Mont.
34	Winston (Fairview), K 7	N. M.
100*	Winston, I 14	Va.
79815	Winston-Salem, D 6	N. C.
169*	Winstonville (Chambers), E 7	Miss.
276	Winter, F 8	Wis.
31*	Winter Beach (Quay), I 23	Fla.
....	Winterburn, J 15	W. Va.
50*	Winterdale, F 23	Pa.
3060	Winter Garden, G 17	Fla.
....*	Wintergreen, see Cavallo	Ohio
28*	Wintergreen, K 11	Va.
600	Winter Harbor, M 18	Me.
11*	Winterhaven, Q 22	Calif.
6199	Winter Haven, I 16	Fla.
....*	Winter Haven, O 13	Tex.
....*	Winter Hill, F 19	Mass.
100*	Winter Park (West Portal), F 11	Colo.
4715	Winter Park, G 18	Fla.
100	Winterpock, N 16	Va.
900	Winterport, L 14	Me.
....	Winterport Ferry (Bucksport Center), L 14	Me.
623	Winterquarters, I 15	Utah
1133	Winters, G 6	Calif.
....	Winters, F 9	Mich.
2335	Winters, F 13	Tex.
12*	Wintersburg, K 9	Ariz.
3631	Winterset, M 10	Iowa
88	Winterest (Winchester), J 17	Ohio
265	Winterstown, Q 18	Pa.
300*	Winterton, R 20	N. Y.
503	Winterville, E 13	Ga.
410	Winterville, C 15	Me.
108*	Winterville, G 7	Miss.
848	Winterville, G 18	N. C.
336	Winthrop, N 4	Ark.
546	Winthrop, G 19	Iowa
2100	Winthrop, N 8	Me.
16768■	Winthrop, M 6	Mass.
1195	Winthrop, O 11	Minn.
....	Winthrop, E 4	Mo.
400	Winthrop, D 19	N. Y.
365	Winthrop, D 15	Wash.
....	Winthrop Beach, E 20, M 7	Mass.
785	Winthrop Harbor, A 20	Ill.
....	Winthrop Jc., E 6	Mich.
900	Winthrop Mine (National Mine), E 6	Mich.
375	Winton, J 9	Calif.
224	Winton, E 22	Minn.
733	Winton, C 20	N. C.
7989	Winton, G 22	Pa.
42	Winton, H 13	Wash.
150	Winton (Megeath), O 8	Wyo.
....*	Winton Place, C 16	Ohio
246*	Wiota, M 7	Iowa
25*	Wire Bridge, I 10	W. Va.
410*	Wireton (Anderson Rd.), M 2	Pa.
60*	Wirmingham, L 15	Tenn.
50*	Wirt, N 20	Ind.
111	Wirt, F 13	Minn.
650	Wirt, O 12	Okla.
100*	Wirtz, O 7	Va.
100*	Wisacky, G 17	S. C.
1200	Wiscasset, O 9	Me.
400*	Wiscoal, H 21	Ky.
....	Wisconsin Dam, J 10	Wis.
1762	Wisconsin Dells (Kilbourn), J 18	Wis.
....	Wisconsin Jc., L 9	Wis.
11416	Wisconsin Rapids, I 14	Wis.
700*	Wisconsin Veterans Home, L 14	Wis.
200	Wiscoy, O 7	N. Y.
52	Wisdom, J 14	Ky.
19*	Wisdom, K 9	Mo.
387	Wisdom, L 5	Mont.
265*	Wise, C 15	N. C.
1226	Wise (Gladeville), D 5	Va.
62*	Wiseman, B 15	Ark.
25*	Wisemantown, G 19	Ky.
100	Wise River, L 6	Mont.
73*	Wishart, N 9	Mo.
200	Wishaw, J 7	Pa.
1112	Wishek, P 16	N. D.
....	Wishkah, J 3	Wash.
25	Wishon, I 12	Calif.
300	Wishram, Q 12	Wash.
165	Wismer, N 24	Pa.
617	Wisner, E 12	La.
1256	Wisner, H 21	Neb.
763	Wister, K 24	Okla.
62*	Witch Creek, Q 20	Calif.
15	Witcher, H 12	Okla.
200*	Withams, K 24	Va.
275	Withamsville, O 7	Ohio
329	Withee, G 12	Wis.
1000*	Witherbee, G 24	N. Y.
....*	Witherbee, L 18	S. C.
75*	Withers (Mullins), H 18	Ky.
30*	Withers, G 9	W. Va.
214	Witherspoon, L 10	Ark.
47	Withrow, M 17	Minn.
60	Withrow, H 16	Wash.
250*	Witmer, O 19	Pa.
1490	Witt, L 14	Ill.
33*	Witt, G 19	Ky.
275	Witt, M 21	Tenn.
9	Witten, M 13	S. D.
84	Wittenberg, M 23	Mo.
20*	Wittenberg, R 22	N. Y.
900	Wittenberg, L 12	Wis.
....*	Wittensville, G 22	Ky.
12*	Witter, D 7	Ark.
30*	Witter Springs, F 4	Calif.
48*	Witting, L 19	Tex.
42*	Wittman (Nadaburg), I 10	Ariz.
67*	Wittman, J 17	Md.
27*	Witt Springs, G 19	Ky.
45*	Witt Springs, D 10	Ark.
114	Wiville, H 17	Ark.
200*	Wixom, P 22	Mich.
100*	Wizard Wells, C 17	Tex.
40	Woburn, L 14	Ill.
19751	Woburn, D 18, J 2	Mass.
19	Woburn, D 6	N. D.
305	Woden, C 11	Iowa
200*	Wooden, G 24	Tex.
39*	Wofford, K 18	Ky.
523	Wolbach, J 17	Neb.
280*	Wolco, C 16	Okla.
115	Wolcott, F 10	Colo.
80	Wolcott, H 10	Conn.
736	Wolcott, E 8	Ind.
225*	Wolcott, F 24	Kan.
1326	Wolcott, L 12	N. Y.
150	Wolcott, E 13	Vt.
612	Wolcottville, B 18	Ind.
20*	Wolf, F 8	Calif.
....	Wolf, K 4	Kan.
61*	Wolf, E 22	Ky.
....	Wolf, F 18	Minn.
75*	Wolf, I 17	Ohio
35	Wolf, B 14	Wyo.
34*	Wolf Bayou, E 14	Ark.
....	Wolf Butte, Q 5	N. D.
250	Wolf Coal, H 21	Ky.
58*	Wolf Creek, F 12	Ky.
110	Wolf Creek, H 9	Mont.
20*	Wolfcreek, M 16	Ohio
250	Wolfcreek, O 5	Ore.
25*	Wolf Creek, N 22	Tenn.
25*	Wolfcreek, O 11	W. Va.
50*	Wolfcreek, A 9	Wis.
550*	Wolfdale, N 2	Pa.
1750	Wolfeboro, L 17	N. H.
520	Wolfeboro Falls, L 17	N. H.
1339	Wolfe City, C 20	Tex.
220*	Wolfforth, B 10	Tex.
23*	Wolf Island, Q 24	Mo.
120	Wolf Lake, Q 13	Ill.
250	Wolflake, C 18	Ind.
257*	Wolf Lake, N 11	Mich.
20*	Wolf Mtn., Q 6	N. C.
206	Wolford, F 15	N. D.
1960	Wolf Point, E 22	Mont.
....*	Wolf River, L 16	Tenn.
450*	Wolf Run, H 20	Ohio
50*	Wolfrun (Leonard), E 7	Va.
96*	Wolfsburg, O 9	Pa.
45*	Wolfs Store, J 14	Pa.
65*	Wolf Summit, E 12	W. Va.
3000*	Wolftown, L 3	Pa.
25*	Wolfton, J 13	S. C.
65*	Wolftown, I 13	Va.
143*	Wolftrap, Q 11	Va.
....*	Wollaston, F 19	Mass.
12	Wolseth, F 10	N. D.
410	Wolsey, I 19	S. D.
150*	Wolverine (Warshoal), H 21	Ky.
300	Wolverine, I 17	Mich.
222*	Wolverton, I 2	Minn.
10	Womac, K 11	Ill.
60*	Womack, M 20	Mo.
150*	Womack Hill, L 5	Ala.
1450	Womelsdorf, N 19	Pa.
417*	Womelsdorf (Coalton), H 15	W. Va.
45*	Wonalancet, J 16	N. H.
15*	Wonder, G 23	Ky.
50	Wonder, Q 4	Ore.
793	Wonewoc, I 17	Wis.
25*	Wonnie, G 21	Ky.
173*	Wood, D 16	N. C.
1000*	Wood (Woodvale), O 11	Pa.
414	Wood, M 12	S. D.
....*	Wood, D 6	Va.
....*	Wood (Veterans Administration), (Pop. incl. in Milwaukee), O 23	Wis.
85*	Woodacre, H 4	Calif.
318	Woodard, E 20	N. C.
225*	Woodberry, O 11	Ark.
....*	Woodberry Forest, I 13	Va.
373	Woodbine, O 22	Ga.
102*	Woodbine, A 10	Ill.
1467	Woodbine, K 4	Iowa
212	Woodbine, H 18	Kan.
500*	Woodbine, J 19	Ky.
175*	Woodbine, D 11	Md.
2111	Woodbine, P 12	N. J.
90*	Woodbine, Q 18	Pa.
....*	Woodbine, M 10	Tenn.
50*	Woodbine, C 19	Tex.
68*	Woodbine, K 11	W. Va.
130*	Woodbluff, L 6	Ala.
500*	Woodbourne, C 3	N. Y.
239*	Woodbourne, N 25	Pa.
300*	Woodbridge, H 8	Calif.
450	Woodbridge, L 10	Conn.
27191■	Woodbridge, F 18	N. J.
400*	Woodbridge (Occoquan), H 17	Va.
471	Woodburn (Shirley City), D 22	Ind.
324	Woodburn, O 12	Iowa
306	Woodburn, J 12	Ky.
1982	Woodburn, E 7	Ore.
800	Woodbury, I 7	Conn.
865	Woodbury, I 6	Ga.
112*	Woodbury, I 11	Ky.
73	Woodbury, O 13	Mich.
8306	Woodbury, L 8	N. J.
307*	Woodbury, H 7	N. Y.
271	Woodbury, O 10	Pa.
663	Woodbury, N 12	Tenn.
250	Woodbury, E 14	Vt.
1137	Woodbury Heights, L 9	N. J.
200*	Woodcliff, J 21	Ga
1037	Woodcliff Lake, C 20	N. J.
119*	Woodcock, E 3	Pa.
148*	Woodcrest, R 10	Calif.
738*	Wooddale, C 19	Ill.
100	Woodford, O 13	Okla.
211*	Woodford, J 14	S. C.
65	Woodford, Q 7	Vt.
100*	Woodford, J 17	Va.
100	Woodford, J 22	Wis.
....	Woodfords, P 5	Me.
101*	Woodgate, L 17	N. Y.
....	Woodhaven, H 6	N. Y.
638	Woodhull, E 9	Ill.
339	Woodhull, R 10	N. Y.
300	Woodington, J 6	Ohio
425	Woodinville, G 9	Wash.
1146*	Woodlake, K 13	Calif.
436	Woodlake, O 7	Minn.
323	Wood Lake, F 12	Neb.
319*	Woodlake, H 23	Tex.
100*	Woodland, G 20	Ala.
6637	Woodland, G 6	Calif.
372	Woodland (Woodland Park) I 14	Colo.
489	Woodland, I 6	Ga.
140	Woodland, G 7	Idaho
334	Woodland, G 21	Ill.
88*	Woodland, I 16	La.
2017	Woodland, J 22	Me.
402	Woodland, P 15	Mich.
193*	Woodland, D 19	Miss.
25*	Woodland, D 16	Mo.
486	Woodland, C 19	N. C.
65*	Woodland (George), C 19	N. C.
1000	Woodland, J 10	Pa.
319	Woodland, B 22	Tex.
980	Woodland, P 6	Wash.
125*	Woodland, N 19	Wis.
35*	Woodland (Woodlands), B 10	W. Va.
200	Woodland Mills, L 4	Tenn.
372	Woodland Park (Woodland), I 15	Colo.
....	Woodlawn, F 13	Ala.
65*	Woodlawn (Johnson), E 17	Fla.
307	Woodlawn, N 16	Ill.
294*	Woodlawn, G 14	Ky.
270	Woodlawn, C 18	Md.
....*	Woodlawn, E 13	Md.
1920*	Woodlawn, M 4	N. Y.
....	Woodlawn, see Aliquippa	Pa.
....	Woodlawn, D 15, M 21	R. I.
35*	Woodlawn, L 9	Tenn.
265	Woodlawn, E 24	Tex.
58*	Woodlawn, Q 3	Va.
9*	Woodleaf, F 8	Calif.
250	Woodleaf, F 7	N. C.
310	Woodleigh, B 24	N. C.
....*	Woodlyn, P 23	Pa.
2861	Woodlynne, K 9	N. J.
150*	Woodman, H 24	Ky.
90*	Woodman, L 19	N. H.
108	Woodman, G 20	Wis.
400	Woodmen, J 15	Colo.
702*	Woodmere (Woodsburgh) H 7	N. Y.
748	Woodmont, N 9	Conn.
5739	Wood Ridge, D 19	N. J.
854	Woodridge, C 3	N. Y.
46*	Woodridge, K 13	Va.
8197	Woodriver, M 10	Ill.
829	Woodriver, L 16	Neb.
50	Wood River Jc., M 8	R. I.
140*	Woodrow, E 14	Ark.
12	Woodrow, E 20	Colo.
110*	Woodrow (South Kent), D 6	Conn.
14*	Woodrow, G 12	Ky.
75*	Woodrow, N 2	Pa.
225	Woodrow, J 8	Utah
180	Woodruff, H 21	Ariz.
140	Woodruff, C 10	Kan.
3508	Woodruff, C 9	S. C.
241	Woodruff, C 15	Utah
100*	Woodruff, B 11	W. Va.
650	Woodruff, J 8	Wis.
1434*	Woodruff Place, J 14	Ind.
619*	Wood Run (Elco), O 3	Pa.
....	Woods (Rural), H 21	Ind.
1	Woods, O 4	Kan.
100*	Woods, H 22	Ky.
5	Woods, N 23	N. D.
78	Woods, E 4	Ore.
10*	Woodsbend, F 21	Ky.
416	Woodsboro, C 9	Md.
1426	Woodsboro, O 19	Tex.
702*	Woodsburgh (Woodmere), H 7	N. Y.
211	Woods Cross, E 11	Utah
25*	Woods Cross Roads, M 20	Va.
100*	Woodsdale, C 12	N. C.
75	Woodsdale, M 7	Ohio
2442	Woodsfield, L 19	Ohio
600	Woods Hole, N 22	Mass.
189	Woodside, H 22	Del.
31*	Woodside, K 11	La.
1625*	Woodside (West Medway), H 17	Mass.
41	Woodside, J 4	Mont.
82	Woodside, N 23	Pa.
40	Woodside, J 19	Utah
314	Woodson, K 13	Ark.
266	Woodson, J 9	Ill.
100*	Woodson, B 6	Ore.
475	Woodson, D 15	Tex.
26	Woodson, L 10	Va.
220	Woodstock, G 11	Ala.
175	Woodstock, B 23	Conn.
389	Woodstock, E 6	Ga.
6123	Woodstock, A 17	Ill.
45*	Woodstock, I 18	Ky.
461	Woodstock, F 12	Md.
....*	Woodstock, see Cement City	Mich.
253	Woodstock, Q 4	Minn.
175	Woodstock, J 13	N. H.
300	Woodstock, B 4	N. Y.
263	Woodstock, J 10	Ohio
125	Woodstock, P 1	Tenn.
1325	Woodstock, L 13	Vt.
1546	Woodstock, F 12	Va.
100	Woodstock Valley, B 22	Conn.
286	Woodston, E 10	Kan.
2027	Woodstown, M 6	N. J.
1900	Woodsville, I 10	N. H.
1000*	Woodvale (Wood), M 11	Pa.
183*	Woodville, B 16	Ala.
60	Woodville, F 5	Conn.
200	Woodville, C 5	Fla.
458	Woodville, F 14	Ga.
....	Woodville, N 19	Idaho
75	Woodville, I 5	Ky.
79*	Woodville (Malcolm), L 14	Md.
200	Woodville, G 16	Mass.
60*	Woodville, M 13	Mich.
1433	Woodville, P 4	Miss.
20	Woodville, J 18	Neb.
112*	Woodville, I 14	N. Y.
426	Woodville, D 19	N. C.
1219	Woodville, D 11	Ohio
364	Woodville, Q 15	Okla.
4000*	Woodville, M 2	Pa.
50	Woodville, L 6	R. I.
1521	Woodville, I 24	Tex.
128*	Woodville, G 14	Va.
40*	Woodville, L 4	W. Va.
408	Woodville, C 12	Wis.
1500	Woodward, G 11	Ala.
895	Woodward, J 11	Iowa
5406	Woodward, D 3	Okla.
100	Woodward, K 14	Pa.
135	Woodward, D 13	S. C.
18*	Woodward, O 15	Tex.
300	Woodworth, I 9	La.
....*	Woodworth, H 4	Mont.
245	Woodworth, L 16	N. D.
100*	Woodworth, P 22	Wis.
23*	Woody, L 14	Calif.
15	Woody, K 8	Ill.
102	Woody Creek, H 8	Colo.
178*	Wooldridge, H 12	Mo.
200	Wooldridge, L 19	Tenn.
....	Wooley, L 17	Ariz.
130*	Woolford, M 17	Md.
375	Woolrich, I 14	Pa.
40*	Woolsey (Pitkin), D 5	Ark.
115*	Woolsey, G 7	Ga.
271	Woolstock, F 11	Iowa
19*	Woolum, E 11	Ark.
100*	Woollum, J 19	Ky.
189	Woolwich, O 9	Me.
50*	Woolwine, Q 5	Va.
49303	Woonsocket, A 13	R. I.
1050	Woonsocket, J 19	S. D.
....	Woonsocket Jc., I 16	Mass.
118	Wooster, G 12	Ark.
11543	Wooster, G 15	Ohio
100	Woosung, C 13	Ill.
....	Wooton, I 21	Ky.
20	Wootton, R 17	Colo.
....*	Wopowog, I 14	Conn.
193694	Worcester, G 13	Mass.
1000	Worcester, O 20	N. Y.
136*	Worcester (Center Point), O 23	Pa.
184	Worcester, F 13	Vt.
9	Worcester, I 9	Wis.
1264	Worden, L 11	Ill.
250	Worden, K 16	Mont.
65	Worden, R 9	Ore.
115	Worland, K 6	Mo.
2710	Worland, E 12	Wyo.
241	Worley, E 4	Idaho
15*	Worley, J 17	Ky.
32*	Worley, N 7	N. C.
1454*	Wormleysburg, N 14	Pa.
30	Worms, K 17	Neb.
522	Woronoco, H 5	Mass.
32*	Worry, E 2	N. C.
80*	Worsham, O 13	Va.
365	Wortendyke, C 19	N. J.
90	Worth, M 10	Ga.
702	Worth, C 21	Ill.
241	Worth, B 6	Mo.
305	Worth (Bear Wallow), Q 7	W. Va.
223*	Wortham, L 19	Mo.
1267	Wortham, G 20	Tex.
291	Worthing, M 24	S. D.
1729	Worthington, M 9	Ind.
326	Worthington, G 22	Iowa
918*	Worthington, D 22	Ky.
150	Worthington, E 5	Mass.
5918	Worthington, R 6	Minn.
220	Worthington, B 12	Mo.
1569	Worthington, J 11	Ohio
600*	Worthington, K 5	Pa.
507	Worthington, D 13	W. Va.
200*	Worthington (Worthington Springs), D 13	Fla.
90*	Worthley (East Peru), M 5	Me.
50*	Worthville, G 9	Ga.
333	Worthville, D 16	Ky.
313	Worthville, F 10	N. C.
105*	Worthville, J 7	Pa.
63	Wounded Knee, N 7	S. D.
208*	Woxall, N 22	Pa.
2061	Wray, E 23	Colo.
155	Wray, M 14	Ga.
150*	Wrayswood, F 12	Ga.
....	Wren, F 2	Iowa
277	Wren, G 5	Ohio
25	Wren (Wrens), G 5	Ore.
75*	Wren, O 11	Va.
40	Wrencoe, C 4	Idaho
1192	Wrens, H 18	Ga.
168	Wrenshall, I 19	Minn.
1000	Wrentham, I 17	Mass.
15*	Wright, L 14	Ark.
200*	Wright (Wrights), J 6	Calif.
125	Wright, M 16	Iowa
84*	Wright, L 8	Kan.
47*	Wright, N 9	La.
201*	Wright, I 17	Minn.
30*	Wright, E 7	Miss.
436	Wright (Wright City), H 18	Mo.
125*	Wright, K 25	N. Y.
7*	Wright, D 19	Wyo.
572	Wright City, P 23	Okla.
142	Wrights, K 9	Ill.
117*	Wrights, F 10	Pa.
103	Wrightsboro, M 18	Tex.
241	Wrightstown, J 14	N. J.
64*	Wrightstown, O 24	Pa.
718	Wrightstown, O 14	Wis.
317	Wrightsville, J 13	Ark.
1761	Wrightsville, I 16	Ga.
2120	Wrightsville, P 17	Pa.
252*	Wrightsville Beach, M 17	N. C.
23*	Wrightsville Sound, M 17	N. C.
300*	Wrightwood, M 17	Calif.
100	Wrigley, F 21	Ky.
733*	Wrigley, N 9	Tenn.
35*	Wriston, N 8	W. Va.
200	Wurtland, D 22	Ky.
487	Wurtsboro, D 3	N. Y.
517	Wyaconda, B 14	Mo.
706	Wyalusing, F 18	Pa.
103*	Wyalusing, F 21	Wis.
125*	Wyandanch, G 8	N. Y.
....*	Wyandotte, P 12	Ind.
30618	Wyandotte, Q 22	Mich.
142*	Wyandotte (Chambers), D 7	Miss.
348	Wyandotte, B 24	Okla.
868	Wyanet, D 13	Ill.
1100*	Wyano, M 4	Pa.
520	Wyanoka, H 22	Ark.
9*	Wyarno (Arno), B 14	Wyo.
150	Wyatt, B 14	Ind.
101	Wyatt, D 9	La.
417	Wyatt, P 24	Mo.
500*	Wyatt, D 12	W. Va.
60*	Wyatte, A 12	Miss.
212	Wybark, G 21	Okla.
500	Wyckoff, C 19	N. J.
200	Wyco, P 7	W. Va.
250*	Wycombe, N 24	Pa.
....	Wye, H 14	N. C.
107*	Wyebrooke, P 21	Pa.
125*	Wye Mills, I 18	Md.
....	Wyeth, K 13	Calif.
24	Wyeth, C 10	Ore.
100*	Wyett, F 21	Ky.
219	Wyeville, H 16	Wis.
521	Wykoff, R 20	Minn.
....	Wylam, F 12	Ala.
914	Wylie, D 19	Tex.
158*	Wylliesburg, Q 12	Va.
105*	Wyman, N 21	Iowa
50*	Wyman, M 14	Mich.
....	Wyman, F 20	Minn.
50*	Wyman Dam (Moscow), J 8	Me.
....*	Wymer, H 15	W. Va.
2457	Wymore, O 22	Neb.
200*	Wynantskill, N 24	N. Y.
1500*	Wyncote, N 22	Pa.
175*	Wyndale, E 7	Va.
499	Wyndmere, P 24	N. D.
2500*	Wyndmoor, N 22	Pa.
250	Wynnburg, L 3	Tenn.
3633	Wynne, G 19	Ark.
47	Wynne, Q 16	Md.
1000*	Wynnewood, N 22	Pa.
2318	Wynne Wood, M 13	Okla.
....*	Wynnton, J 4	Ga.
810	Wynona, C 17	Okla.
416	Wynot, E 20	Neb.
10	Wyo, E 6	Calif.
706	Wyocena, K 18	Wis.
....*	Wyola, D 5	Ark.
125	Wyola, N 18	Mont.
870	Wyoming, G 22	Del.
1360	Wyoming, E 11	Ill.
656	Wyoming, I 22	Iowa
2500*	Wyoming (Wyoming Park), O 14	Mich.
253	Wyoming, M 17	Minn.
6	Wyoming, M 24	Neb.
430	Wyoming, N 7	N. Y.
4466	Wyoming, N 7	Ohio
4728	Wyoming, H 20	Pa.
350	Wyoming, K 8	R. I.
3320	Wyomissing, N 20	Pa.
508*	Wyomissing Hills, M 20	Pa.
25*	Wysox, H 11	Ky.
100*	Wysox, E 18	Pa.
75	Wysocking, G 24	N. C.
4653	Wytheville, P 2	Va.
400*	Wytopitlock, H 18	Me.

X

Pop.	Place, Index	State
136*	Xena, G 20	Ky.
662	Xenia, M 17	Ill.
10633	Xenia, L 9	Ohio
28*	Xerxes, K 15	Ky.

Y

Pop.	Place, Index	State
40*	Yaak, B 1	Mont.
225	Yachats, H 3	Ore.
297	Yacolt, P 8	Wash.
72	Yadkin College, E 8	N. C.
200*	Yadkin Valley, E 3	N. C.
734	Yadkinville, D 6	N. C.
84	Yahola, G 20	Okla.
27221	Yakima, M 14	Wash.
30*	Yakt, B 4	Mont.
516	Yalaha, G 16	Fla.
58*	Yale, E 7	Ark.
50*	Yale (Granite), J 11	Colo.
176	Yale, L 20	Ill.
287	Yale, K 9	Iowa
200	Yale, M 25	Kan.
226*	Yale, F 20	Ky.
1489	Yale, N 23	Mich.
1407	Yale, E 15	Okla.
156	Yale, I 20	S. D.
....	Yale, O 2	Utah
75*	Yale, P 18	Va.
18	Yale, O 8	Wash.
1000	Yalesville, J 12	Conn.
143*	Yalmar (Yalmer), F 6	Mich.
200*	Yamacraw, K 18	Ky.
418	Yamhill, D 6	Ore.
426	Yampa, E 9	Colo.
23*	Yamsay, O 10	Ore.
600*	Yancey, J 21	Ky.
180*	Yancey, M 15	Tex.
64*	Yancey Mills, K 12	Va.
500	Yanceyville, C 11	N. C.
75*	Yancopin, N 17	Ark.
100*	Yancy Mills, M 15	Mo.
12	Yankee, B 20	N. M.
88*	Yankee Hill, E 7	Calif.
16*	Yankee Jims, F 9	Calif.
255*	Yankeetown, F 12	Fla.
150	Yankeetown, R 7	Ind.
6798	Yankton, O 22	S. D.
450	Yantic, I 21	Conn.
250*	Yantis, E 22	Tex.
300*	Yantley, K 3	Ala.
86*	Yantus, N 3	W. Va.
150	Yanush, M 21	Okla.
350	Yaphank, G 9	N. Y.
50	Yaquina, G 4	Ore.
310	Yarbo, M 4	Ala.
57*	Yarboro, J 21	Tex.
54*	Yard, G 21	Tex.
75*	Yardelle, C 9	Ark.
....	Yardley, H 24	Ky.
1459	Yardley, N 25	Pa.
89*	Yardley, H 22	Wash.
100	Yards (Flat Top Yard), N 1	Va.
800	Yardville, I 13	N. J.
177	Yarmouth, N 21	Iowa
1400	Yarmouth, P 6	Me.
1500	Yarmouth, M 13	Mass.
....	Yarmouth (Yarmouth Port) M 13	Mass.
....	Yarmouth Jc., P 6	Me.
54	Yarnaby, R 17	Okla.
66*	Yarnell, I 10	Ariz.
10	Yarnell, E 8	Wis.
25*	Yarrow, C 12	Mo.
100	Yates, F 12	Mo.
59	Yates, H 25	Mont.
41*	Yates, K 3	W. Va.
2067	Yatesboro, K 6	Pa.
2176	Yates Center, L 21	Kan.
576	Yates City, F 10	Ill.
240	Yatesville, I 8	Ga.
40*	Yatesville, F 23	Ky.
700*	Yatesville, I 20	Pa.
75*	Yava, H 9	Ariz.
210	Yawkey, N 4	W. Va.
7258	Yazoo City, I 10	Miss.
20	Yazoo Jc., I 10	Miss.
51*	Ydalpom, D 6	Calif.
70*	Yeaddis, I 21	Ky.
8524*	Yeadon, P 23	Pa.
82*	Yeager, I 23	Ky.
284*	Yeager, K 17	Okla.
1800	Yeagertown, L 14	Pa.
56	Yeaman, H 12	Ky.
....*	Yeatman (Natural Bridge), J 19	Mo.
....	Yeddo, I 8	Ind.
18	Yegen, L 16	Mont.
300*	Yellow Bluff, L 9	Ala.
27*	Yellowcreek, P 3	N. C.
3	Yellow Creek, H 21	Ohio
150*	Yellow Creek, O 10	Pa.
150*	Yellow House, M 21	Pa.
7	Yellow Jacket, O 3	Colo.
30*	Yellow Lake, B 8	Wis.
75*	Yellow Mountain, H 22	Ky.
100	Yellow Pine, N 3	Ala.
69*	Yellow Pine, L 7	Idaho
245	Yellow Pine, C 6	La.
32*	Yellowpine, H 25	Tex.
40*	Yellow Spring, F 21	W. Va.
200*	Yellow Springs, D 8	Md.
1640	Yellow Springs, L 9	Ohio.
200*	Yellowstone National Park, K 2	Wyo.
546	Yellville, B 11	Ark.
198*	Yellville (Summit), B 11	Ark.
378	Yelm, K 7	Wash.
81*	Yelvington, D 17	Fla.
100	Yelvington, G 10	Ky.
684	Yemassee, O 14	S. C.
160	Yeoman, F 11	Ind.
215*	Yerba, Q 6	W. Va.
....	Yerger, G 7	Miss.
964	Yerington, H 5	Nev.
175*	Yerkes, I 21	Ky.
162*	Yerkes, O 22	Pa.
500*	Yermo, M 19	Calif.
230	Yeso, I 19	N. M.
....	Yetta, see Tyrone	Colo.
200*	Yettem, K 13	Calif.
135*	Yetter, H 7	Iowa
20	Yewed, C 8	Okla
4733	Yoakum, M 19	Tex.
37	Yocemento, H 10	Kan.
70*	Yocum, F 20	Ky.
137	Yoder, J 17	Colo.
200	Yoder, E 20	Ind.
75	Yoder, L 14	Kan.
201	Yoder, N 23	Wyo.
528*	Yoe, P 17	Pa.
52*	Yokena, L 6	Miss.
....*	Yola, see Lake George	Minn.
....	Yolanda, D 15	Calif.
40	Yolande, G 10	Ala.
296	Yolo, G 7	Calif.
245	Yolyn, N 4	W. Va.
19*	Yoman, K 8	Wash.
277	Yoncalla, L 5	Ore.
....	Yonges, N 17	S. C.
250	Yonges Island, O 17	S. C.
730▲*	Yonkers (Younker), K 13	Ga.
142598	Yonkers, G 5	N. Y.
100	Yonkers, F 22	Okla.
1500*	Yorba Linda, O 17	Calif.
1783	York, J 4	Ala.
30	York, M 24	Ariz.
200*	York, K 22	Ill.
36*	York, D 21	Ky.
5383	York, L 19	Neb.
150*	York (York Center), M 8	N. Y.
325	York, G 15	N. D.
56712	York, P 17	Pa.
3495	York, B 12	S. C.
425	York Beach, R 4	Me.
150	*York Center (York), M 8	N. Y.
246	York Harbor, R 4	Me.
730	Yorkhaven, O 16	Pa.
336	Yorklyn, A 21	Del.
329	York New Salem (New Salem), P 17	Pa.
21*	Yorkshire, L 4	Iowa
300*	Yorkshire, P 5	N. Y.
134*	Yorkshire, I 6	Ohio
357	York Springs, P 15	Pa.
906	Yorktown, H 19	Ind.
197	Yorktown, P 6	Iowa
150*	Yorktown, N 7	N. J.
2081	Yorktown, M 18	Tex.
521	Yorktown, N 20	Va.
1500*	Yorktown Heights, F 6	N. Y.
1500	York Village, R 3	Me.
....*	Yorkville, F 3	Calif.
492	Yorkville, D 18	Ill.
85*	Yorkville, L 22	Ind.
....*	Yorkville, Q 13	Mich.
3311	Yorkville, L 18	N. Y.
1961*	Yorkville, J 20	Ohio
400	Yorkville, M 4	Tenn.
....*	Yosemite Lodge, I 12	Calif.
500*	Yosemite National Park, I 11	Calif.
155*	Yosemite, H 16	Ky.
36*	Yost (Belton), I 10	Ky.
172	Yost, A 4	Utah
27	Youghal, C 3	Colo.
240	Young, I 17	Ariz.
200	Young America, F 13	Ind.
406	Young America, N 13	Minn.
50*	Youngblood, L 17	Ala.
90*	Youngcane, B 9	Ga.
465*	Youngdale, H 13	Pa.
258	Young Harris, B 9	Ga.
10*	Youngs (River), G 9	Calif.
121*	Youngs, P 18	N. Y.
80*	Youngs Creek, O 12	Ind.
105*	Youngs Creek, K 19	Ky.
300	Youngstown, N 10	Fla.
80*	Youngstown, C 12	Mo.
799	Youngstown, K 4	N. Y.
167720	Youngstown, E 20	Ohio
547*	Youngstown, M 5	Pa.
647	Youngsville, M 11	La.
175	Youngsville, D 10	N. M.
250*	Youngsville, R 20	N. Y.

General Index of Cities in the U. S. Territories and Possessions

The location of each place on the map is indicated by the letter and figure reference.

MAP INDEX AND ABBREVIATIONS

Pop.	Place State	Index
.....	Hoopuloa, Haw.	O 20
71	Hope, Alaska	L 13
1051	Hormigueros, P. R.	F 3
.....	Hoya Mala, P. R.	D 4
.....	Hoyo Mulas, P. R.	C 17
.....	Hucares, P. R.	F 20
32	Hughes, Alaska	F 11
7624	Humacao, P. R	F 18
348	Hydaburg, Alaska	Q 24
72	Hyder, Alaska	P 25
8081	Iba, P. I.	E 9
22744	Ibajay, P. I.	I 14
1	Iditarod, Alaska	J 9
114	Igloo, Alaska	G 6
8178	Iguig, P. I.	B 13
.....	Ikatan, Alaska	R 4
31325	Ilagan, P. I.	C 14
28273	Iligan, P. I.	N 19
20959	Ilog, P. I.	L 16
90480	Iloilo, P. I.	K 15
3627	Impasugong, P. I.	N 21
23930	Inabanga, P. I.	L 19
.....	Inagauan, P. I.	L 6
11249	Indan, P. I.	G 16
.....	Indiera alta, P. R.	E 6
20348	Infanta, P. I.	F 13
.....	Ingenio, P. R.	B 14
18833	Initao, P. I.	N 19
.....	Innoko (Dishkacket), Alaska	I 9
10224	Inopacan, P. I.	K 21
.....	Inogbun, P. I	M 4
31228	Iriga, P. I.	G 17
.....	Irirun, P. I.	I 11
.....	Isabela, P. I.	P 14
3439	Isabela, P. R.	B 4
.....	Islote, P. R.	B 9
1625	Itbayat, P. I.	C 21
965	Ivana, P. I.	C 22
5007	Jabonga, P. I.	M 27
.....	Jacana, P. R.	G 12
15270	Jagna, P. I.	L 20
.....	Jagua, P. R.	G 8
.....	Jagual, P. R.	F 16
.....	Jagual, P. R.	G 16
.....	Jagua Pasto, P. R.	F 7
.....	Jaguey, P. R.	D 2
.....	Jagueyes, P. R.	E 15
.....	Jajomealto, P. R.	G 14
.....	Jajome bajo, P. R.	G 14
38678	Janiuay, P. I.	K 15
23970	Jaro, P. I.	J 20
.....	Jartin Pena, P. R.	C 15
.....	Jaucal, P. R.	H 12
1808	Jayuya, P. R.	E 9
.....	Jayuya abajo, P. R.	F 9
.....	Jayuya arriba, P. R.	E 10
12386	Jetafe, P. I.	L 19
24177	Jimenez, P. I.	N 18
.....	Jimenez, P. R.	D 19
.....	Jobos, P. R.	B 4
.....	Jobos, P. R.	H 14
12573	Jolo, P. I.	Q 12
4967	Jones, P. I.	H 14
.....	Jonesville, Alaska	K 13
23053	Jordán, P. I.	K 16
.....	Josefa, P. R.	I 14
.....	Joyuda, P. R.	G 2
3931	Juana Diaz, P. R.	G 10
.....	Juan Alonso, P. R.	E 4
.....	Juan Asencio, P. R.	D 15
.....	Juan Gonzales, P. R.	F 8
.....	Juan Martin, P. R.	D 20
.....	Juan Mina, C. Z.	F 19
.....	Juan Sanchez, P. R.	C 15
11961	Juban, P. I.	H 19
5009	Juncos, P. R.	E 17
5729	Juneau, Alaska	N 22
.....	Kaalualu, Haw.	P 21
.....	Kaanapal, Haw.	H 16
28847	Kabankalan, P. I.	L 16
31	Kaguyak, Alaska	P 11
.....	Kahana, Haw.	E 11
2251	Kahuku, Haw.	D 11
2193	Kahului, Haw.	H 17
381	Kailua, Haw.	M 20
419	Kake, Alaska	O 23
770	Kalaheo, Haw.	C 4
211	Kalapana, Haw	O 24
.....	Kalaupapa, Haw.	F 15
.....	Kalawao, Haw.	F 15
.....	Kalopa, Haw.	L 22
140	Kaltag, Alaska	H 9
.....	Kamalo, Haw.	G 16
445	Kamuela, Haw.	L 21
134	Kanatak, Alaska	P 9
2828	Kapaa, Haw.	B 5
.....	Kapapala, Haw.	O 22
483	Kapoho, Haw.	N 25
.....	Kapulena, Haw.	K 22
189	Karluk, Alaska	P 10
85	Kasaan, Alaska	P 24
26	Kashega, Alaska	B 25
44	Katalla, Alaska	L 16
.....	Kaumalapau, Haw.	H 15
722	Kaunakakai, Haw.	G 15
.....	Kaunalewa, Haw.	C 3
.....	Kaupo, Haw.	I 19
123	Kawaihae, Haw.	L 20
8491	Kawayan, P. I.	J 19
.....	Kawela Camp, Haw.	K 22
.....	Kayan, P. I.	C 11
.....	Kayapa, P. I.	D 11
373	Kealakekua, Haw.	N 20
758	Kealia, Haw.	B 5
106	Keanae, Haw.	H 19
.....	Keauhou, Haw.	O 23
.....	Keauhou, Haw.	N 20
.....	Keehia, Haw	L 22
.....	Keei, Haw.	N 20
24	Keewalik, Alaska	F 8
2536	Kekaha, Haw.	C 4
303	Kenai, Alaska	L 12
5	Kennecott, Alaska	K 17
454	Keokea, Haw.	H 17
.....	Keomuku, Haw.	H 16
4695	Ketchikan, Alaska	P 25
167	Kiana, Alaska	E 8
.....	Kihei, Haw.	H 17
.....	Kiholo, Haw.	M 20
548	Kilauea, Haw.	B 5
26	Killisnoo, Alaska	O 22
36	Kinak, Alaska	L 6
135	King Cove, Alaska	R 5
208	King Island, Alaska	G 5
.....	Kingshill, Virgin Is.	R 22
.....	Kipahulu, Haw.	I 19
98	Kivalina, Alaska	D 7
.....	Klangan, P. I.	C 12
455	Klawock, Alaska	P 24
.....	Kling, P. I.	Q 20
97	Klukwan, Alaska	M 21
864	Kodiak, Alaska	O 12
1255	Kohala, Haw.	K 20
47	Kokrines, Alaska	G 11
39647	Kolambugan, P. I.	N 19
1903	Koloa, Haw.	C 5
2218	Koronadal, P. I.	Q 21
35	Kotlik (Hamilton), Alaska	I 6
372	Kotzebue, Alaska	E 8
106	Koyukuk Station, Alaska	G 10
.....	Kukaiau, Haw.	L 22
408	Kukuihaele, Haw.	K 21
55	Kulukak, Alaska	N 8
.....	Kurtistown, Haw.	N 24
.....	Kvichak, Alaska	N 9
13228	Labo, P. I.	G 16
26122	La Carlota, P. I.	K 16
.....	Lagan, P. I.	B 7
18831	Lagonoy, P. I.	G 18
.....	Laguimanoc, P. I.	G 14
.....	Lagunas, P. R.	D 3
5217	Lahaina, Haw.	H 17
2294	Lajas, P. R.	G 3
.....	Lajas arriba, P. R.	H 5
.....	Lake Bay, Alaska	P 24
.....	Lalamilo, Haw.	L 20
12920	Lal-lo, P. I.	F 21
.....	La Muda, P. R.	D 15
3597	Lanai City, Haw.	H 15
.....	Lanes Landing, Alaska	G 6
7331	Lanuza, P. I.	M 23
42202	Laoag, P. I.	F 19
19783	Laoang, P. I.	I 21
.....	Lapa, P. R.	G 13
12974	La Paz, P. I.	K 21
.....	La Plata, P. R.	H 5
10652	Lapog, P. I.	B 11
4302	Lares, P. R.	D 6
7544	Larena, P. I.	M 18
278	Las Cascadas, C. Z.	H 18
391	Las Marias, P. R.	E 5
2055	Las Piedras, P. R.	F 18
.....	Las Vegas, P. R.	F 4
40	Latouche, Alaska	M 14
12617	Lauaan, P. I.	J 14
534	Laupahoehoe, Haw.	L 23
13806	Laur, P. I.	E 12
9502	Lavezares, P. I.	H 20
15153	Lazi, P. I.	M 18
41525	Legaspi, P. I.	H 17
.....	Leguisamo, P. R.	E 3
18870	Leyte, P. I.	J 20
15991	Lianga, P. I.	M 24
20253	Libacao, P. I.	J 14
6318	Libagon, P. I.	K 21
.....	Libertad, P. I.	N 24
7809	Libog, P. I.	H 18
4254	Lihue, Haw.	C 5
17242	Liloan, P. I.	K 19
13667	Liloan, P. I.	L 21
.....	Lima, P. R.	F 19
.....	Limon, P. R.	D 9
.....	Limon, P. R.	F 3
.....	Limon, P. R.	H 5
.....	Limones, P. R.	G 17
30270	Lingayen, P. I.	D 10
45175	Lipa, P. I.	G 12
.....	Lirios, P. R.	E 17
153	Livengood, Alaska	G 14
.....	Lizas, P. R.	H 17
.....	Llanadas, P. R.	B 4
.....	Llano, P. R.	G 7
.....	Llanos, P.R.	H 3
.....	Llanos, P. R.	G 12
.....	Llanos Costas, P. R.	H 2
.....	Llanos Tunas, P. R.	H 3
11570	Llorente, P. I.	J 23
.....	Lluveras, P. R.	H 7
8964	Lobo, P. I.	G 12
11073	Loboc, P. I.	L 19
2356	Loiza (new), P. R.	C 17
1454	Loiza (old), P. R.	B 18
.....	Lomas, P. R.	G 11
.....	Lomas, P. R.	D 18
.....	Lomas, P. R.	D 13
28	Long, Alaska	H 10
3942	Looc, P. I.	G 10
18538	Looc, P. I.	I 14
19501	López, P. I.	G 15
6782	Loreto, P. I.	N 23
.....	Loring, Alaska	P 25
317	Los Martires, P. I.	N 22
8963	Lubang, P. I.	G 10
.....	Lubuagan, P. I.	C 12
.....	Lubungan, P. I.	N 17
21253	Lucena, P. I.	G 13
.....	Lumbatan, P. I.	N 19
14710	Luna, P. I.	C 10
2013	Luquillo, P. R.	C 20
.....	Maalaea, Haw.	H 17
29242	Maasin, P. I.	L 20
10259	Mabini, P. I.	G 12
.....	Mabu, P. R.	F 18
.....	Macana, P. R.	G 8
.....	Macana, P. R.	G 7
.....	Machette, P. R.	I 14
.....	Machuchal, P. R.	G 5
.....	Machueloabajo, P. R.	G 9
.....	Machuelo arriba, P. R.	G 10
12212	Macrohon, P. I.	L 21
8604	Madridejos, P. I.	J 18
16634	Magalan, P. I.	E 11
15385	Magallanes, P. I.	H 19
.....	Magas, P. R.	G 7
.....	Magos, P. R.	D 5
11197	Magsingal, P. I.	B 10
.....	Maguayo, P. R.	C 13
.....	Magueyes, P. R.	G 9
147	Mahukona, Haw.	K 20
.....	Maizales, P. R.	E 19
.....	Majagual, C. Z.	B 10
15623	Makato, P. I.	I 15
903	Makawao, Haw.	H 18
1010	Makaweli, Haw.	C 4
.....	Makena, Haw.	I 17
10	Makushin, Alaska	B 24
.....	Mala, Haw.	H 16
10256	Malabang, P. I.	O 19
33443	Malasiqui, P. I.	E 10
18668	Malaybalay, P. I.	N 21
.....	Maleza alta, P. R.	B 2
.....	Malezas, P. R.	F 3
22238	Malitbog, P. I.	K 21
33376	Malolos, P. I.	F 12
.....	Malpaso, P. R.	D 2
7677	Maluko, P. I.	N 21
21291	Mambajao, P. I.	M 21
.....	Mambulao, P. I.	F 16
.....	Mamey, P. R.	C 3
.....	Mamey, P. R.	G 16
.....	Mameyes, P. R.	C 19
.....	Mameyes abajo, P. R.	D 10
.....	Mameyes arriba, P. R.	E 10
.....	Mameyes No. 2, P. R.	D 19
.....	Mamy, P. R.	D 15
.....	Mana, Haw.	C 3
.....	Mana, P. R.	E 12
3569	Manabo, P. I.	C 11
19904	Manapla, P. I.	K 17
6771	Manati, P. R.	B 16
11528	Manay, P. I.	O 24
17420	Mandaue, P. I.	K 18
.....	Manele Landing, Haw.	H 16
623492	Manila, P. I.	F 11
7080	Manito, P. I.	H 18
25935	Manjuyod, P. I.	L 17
6948	Mansalay, P. I.	I 12
.....	Maraquez Anon, P. R.	F 9
8602	Maria, P. I.	M 18
.....	Mariana, P. R.	G 18
.....	Marias, P. R.	C 3
.....	Marias, P. R.	D 3
13834	Maribojoc, P. I.	L 18
.....	Maricao, P. R.	C 12
1293	Maricao, P. R.	F 5
.....	Maricaoafuera, P. R.	F 4
.....	Marina, P. R.	E 2
.....	Mariquina, P. I.	F 12
	Marshall, see Fortuna Ledge, Alaska.	
.....	Marueno, P. R.	G 8
23340	Masbate, P. I.	I 18
6944	Masinloc, P. I.	E 9
16667	Matalom, P. I.	K 21
52	Matanuska, Alaska	K 13
10200	Mati, P. I.	P 24
4437	Matnog, P. I.	H 19
10122	Matnog, P. I.	K 19
.....	Maton abajo, P. R.	F 14
.....	Maton arriba, P. R.	G 14
14812	Mauban, P. I.	G 13
1255	Maunabo, P. R.	H 18
.....	Maunawai, Haw.	D 10
50376	Mayaguez, P. R.	F 3
.....	Mayaguez arriba, P. R.	E 3
	McCarthy, see Shushanna Junction, Alaska.	
138	McGrath, Alaska	I 10
18637	Medellin, P. I.	J 19
.....	Mediania Baja, P. R.	B 18
.....	Meehan, Alaska	H 14
26740	Mérida, P. I.	K 20
674	Metlakatla, Alaska	Q 25
16108	Meycauayan, P. I.	F 11
30180	Miagao, P. I.	K 15
30119	Milagros, P. I.	I 18
.....	Miller House, Alaska	G 15
15285	Minglanilla, P. I.	L 18
.....	Minillas, P. R.	C 14
.....	Minillas, P. R.	G 5
.....	Minto Road House, Alaska	H 13
.....	Miradero, P. R.	G 2
.....	Miradero, P. R.	E 2
.....	Miraflores, P. R.	D 9
80	Miraflores Locks, C. Z.	J 22
.....	Miramar, P. R.	B 15
.....	Mirasol, P. R.	E 5
36865	Misamis, P. I.	N 18
.....	Moaula, Haw.	O 22
3005	Moca, P. R.	C 3
12034	Mogpog, P. I.	G 13
8	Moira Sound, Alaska	Q 24
.....	Mokuleia, Haw.	E 10
.....	Monacillo, P. R.	C 15
7373	Mondragon, P. I.	I 20
.....	Monkayo, P. I.	N 23
6402	Montalban, P. I.	F 12
.....	Monte Grande, P. R.	G 2
20	Monte Lirio, C. Z.	E 11
.....	Monte Llano, P. R.	F 13
.....	Montes Llanos, P. R.	G 9
.....	Montones, P. R.	F 17
.....	Moose, Alaska	K 13
.....	Moose Creek, Alaska	K 13
.....	Moquawkie, Alaska	L 12
.....	Mora, P. R.	B 4
3301	Moron, P. I.	F 10
2157	Morovis, P. R.	D 11
.....	Morovis Norte, P. R.	D 11
22	Morzhovoi, Alaska	R 5
955	Mountainview, Haw.	N 23
11	Mount Hope, C. Z.	C 9
.....	Mulas, P. R.	G 16
.....	Mulitas, P. R.	E 15
48	Mumtrakmut, Alaska	M 7
18948	Murcia, P. I.	K 17
1038	Naalehu, Haw.	P 21
9756	Nabas, P. I.	I 14
26008	Naga, P. I.	K 18
22284	Naga (Nueva Caceres), P. I.	G 17
4185	Naguabo, P. R.	E 19
6872	Naguilian, P. I.	C 14
15987	Naguilian, P. I.	D 11
.....	Nahiku, Haw.	H 19
13813	Naic, P. I.	F 11
152	Naknek, Alaska	N 9
113	Napakiakamute, Alaska	K 7
103	Napoopoo, Haw.	N 20
.....	Naranjales, P. R.	E 5
.....	Naranjito, P. R.	C 7
1790	Naranjito, P. R.	D 13
.....	Naranjo, P. R.	D 3
.....	Naranjo, P. R.	E 14
.....	Naranjo, P. R.	F 6
.....	Naranjo, P. R.	D 3
.....	Naranjo, P. R.	D 19
22860	Narvacan, P. I.	C 10
18962	Naujan, P. I.	H 13
11657	Naval, P. I.	J 20
.....	Nawiliwili, Haw.	C 5
.....	Nelson, Alaska	L 15
231	Nenana, Alaska	H 13
132	Ninilchik, Alaska	M 12
77	Ninole, Haw.	L 23
.....	Niulii, Haw.	K 21
.....	Nizina, Alaska	K 17
336	Noatak, Alaska	D 7
1559	Nome, Alaska	G 6
82	Nondalton, Alaska	M 10
.....	Nonopapa, Haw.	C 1
211	Noorvik, Alaska	E 8
.....	Nualolo, Haw	B 3
	Nueva Caceres, see Naga, P. I.	
.....	Nuevo, P. R.	D 14
.....	Nuevo, P. R.	D 13
.....	Nugget, Alaska	G 6
204	Nulato, Alaska	H 9
41	Nushagak (Clarks Point), Alaska	N 8
23558	Oas, P. I.	H 17
16026	Odioñgan, P. I.	I 14
.....	Okagamut, Alaska	K 7
.....	Okoe, Haw.	P 20
.....	Olaa, Haw.	M 24
109	Old Harbor, Alaska	P 11
215	Olnes, Alaska	G 14
.....	Olowalu, Haw.	H 17
84	Ophir, Alaska	I 10
33814	Opon, P. I.	K 19
9662	Orani, P. I.	F 10
21181	Oras, P. I.	I 22
77349	Ormoc ,P. I.	J 20
1934	Orocovis, P. R.	E 12
21527	Oroquieta, P. I.	N 18
.....	Ortiz, P. R.	D 14
13473	Oslob, P. I.	L 17
20577	Otón, P. I.	K 15
253	Ouzinkee, Alaska	O 12
.....	Ovejas, P. R.	D 4
.....	Paauhau, Haw.	K 22
.....	Paauilo, Haw.	L 22
1651	Pahala, Haw.	O 22
1114	Pahoa, Haw.	N 24
.....	Pahoa Junction, Haw.	N 24
4272	Paia, Haw.	H 18
8	Paimiut, Alaska	J 8
.....	Pajaros, P. R.	C 14
.....	Pakala, Haw.	C 4
3109	Palanan, P. I.	C 15
19829	Palapag, P. I.	I 21
4405	Paluig, P. U.	E 9
.....	Palma Escrita, P. R.	E 5
.....	Palmar, P. R.	C 3
.....	Palmarejo, P. R.	D 12
.....	Palmarejo, P. R.	H 3
.....	Palmarito, P. R.	D 12
.....	Palmas, P. R.	H 13
.....	Palmas, P. R.	H 14
.....	Palmas Altas, P. R.	B 10
25471	Palo, P. I.	J 21
.....	Palo Hincado, P. R.	F 12
.....	Palomas, P. R.	E 14
29092	Palompón, P. I.	J 20
145	Palo Seco, C. Z.	L 23
797	Palo Seco, P. R.	B 14
.....	Palo Seco, P. R.	B 15
.....	Palo Seco, P. R.	G 17
3304	Paluan, P. I.	G 10
14714	Pambuhan, P. I.	I 21
7520	Pamplona, P. I.	E 20
7404	Pamplona, P. I.	G 16
15850	Panay, P. I.	J 16
19594	Pandan, P. I.	J 14
15075	Pandan, P. I.	G 19
3889	Pangil, P. I.	F 13
9735	Panglao, P. I.	L 18
19017	Paniqui, P. I.	E 11
14539	Panitan, P. I.	J 16
5655	Pantabangan, P. I.	D 12
11866	Paoay, P. I.	B 11
662	Papaaloa, Haw.	L 23
1566	Papaikou, Haw.	M 23
1448	Paraiso, C. Z.	I 20
.....	Parang, P. I.	O 20
.....	Parguera, P. R.	H 4
.....	Paris, P. R.	H 3
55161	Pasay, P. I.	F 12
27541	Pasig, P. I.	F 12
.....	Paso Palma, P. R.	F 8
28061	Passi, P. I.	J 15
.....	Pasto, P. R.	E 11
.....	Pasto, P. R.	G 7
.....	Pasto, P. R.	G 12
10065	Pasuquin, P. I.	E 19
2272	Patillas, P. R.	H 16
20015	Patnoñgon, P. I.	K 14
465	Pauwela, Haw.	H 18
.....	Peahi, Haw.	H 18
1938	Pearl City, Haw.	E 11
.....	Pearl Harbor Naval Station, Haw.	F 11
.....	Pedernales, P. R.	G 3
.....	Pedro Garcia, P. R.	F 11
752	Pedro Miguel, C. Z.	J 21
.....	Pelekunu, Haw.	G 16
.....	Pellejas, P. R.	F 11
.....	Pellejas, P. R.	E 7
.....	Peña Pobre, P. R.	E 18
9421	Peñaranda, P. I.	E 13
1462	Penuelas, P. R.	G 8
.....	Pepeekeo, Haw.	M 23
.....	Perchas, P. R.	D 12
.....	Perchas No. 1, P. R.	D 5
.....	Perchas No. 2, P. R.	E 5
92	Perryville, Alaska	Q 8
1323	Petersburg, Alaska	O 23
.....	Piedras, P. R.	G 14
.....	Piedra Gorda, P. R.	C 6
5793	Pilar, P. I.	B 11
20660	Pilar, P. I.	H 18
22269	Pilar, P. I.	J 16
.....	Piletas, P. R.	D 5
17950	Pili, P. I.	G 17
39	Pilot Station, Alaska	O 8
.....	Pinales, P. R.	D 3
16110	Pinamalayan, P. I.	H 12
.....	Piñas, P. R.	F 14
.....	Piñas, P. R.	C 13
10400	Pintuyan, P. I.	L 22
.....	Pirate Cove, Alaska	R 7
.....	Pitahaya, P. R.	H 15
.....	Pitahaya, P. R.	D 19
13997	Placer, P. I.	L 22
.....	Planas, P. R.	C 5
21908	Plaridel, P. I.	M 18
.....	Plata, P. R.	C 4
.....	Plata, P. R.	F 13
.....	Playa, P. R.	H 9
.....	Playa, P. R.	G 18
1007	Playa Fajardo, P. R.	D 20
.....	Playa Grande, P. R.	G 21
.....	Playa Grande, P. R.	E 2
9919	Pola, P. I.	H 13
65182	Ponce, P. R.	H 9
23242	Pontevedra, P. I.	J 16
20471	Pontevedra, P. I.	K 16
.....	Poohonu, Haw.	B 3
20	Poorman, Alaska	H 10
11522	Poro, P. I.	K 20
.....	Port Armstrong, Alaska	P 22
93	Port Graham, Alaska.	N 12
.....	Port Heiden, Alaska	P 8
.....	Portillo, P. R.	F 7
.....	Portugues, P. R.	G 8
21	Port Walter, Alaska	P 22
.....	Potala, P. R.	H 10
32970	Pototan, P. I.	K 16
.....	Pozas, P. R.	E 11
.....	Pozas, P. R.	D 4
.....	Prosperidad, P. I.	M 23
.....	Pueblo Viejo, P. R.	C 15
.....	Puerto de Tierra, P.R.	B 15
.....	Puerto Diablo, P. R.	F 24
.....	Puerto Ferro, P. R.	F 23
.....	Puerto Nuevo, P. R.	B 12
10723	Puerto Princesa, P. I.	L 7
.....	Puerto Real, P. R.	G 22
.....	Pugnado adentro, P.R.	C 11
52	Pukoo, Haw.	G 16
.....	Pulguillas, P. R.	F 12
.....	Punaluu, Haw.	P 22
.....	Puntas, P. R.	D 1
.....	Punta Santiago, P. R.	F 19
.....	Punta de Santiago, P.R.	F 19
4456	Puunene, Haw.	H 18
.....	Quadra, Alaska	Q 25
.....	Quebrada, P. R.	G 6
.....	Quebrada, P. R.	D 6
.....	Quebrada Arena, P.R.	G 16
.....	Quebrada arenas, P.R.	C 11
.....	Quebrada Arenas, P.R.	H 18
.....	Quebrada Arenas, P. R.	D 16
.....	Quebrada Arenas, P. R.	D 13
.....	Quebrada arriba, P. R.	G 16
.....	Quebrada Ceiba, P. R.	G 8
.....	Quebrada Cruz, P. R.	D 13
.....	Quebrada Farjardo, P. R.	D 20
.....	Quebrada Grande, P. R.	E 13
.....	Quebrada Grande, P. R.	D 17
.....	Quebrada Honda, P. R.	G 7
.....	Quebrada Infierno, P. R.	D 16
.....	Quebrada Limon, P. R.	G 8
.....	Quebrada Negrita, P. R.	D 16
.....	Quebradas, P. R.	G 7
.....	Quebrada Seca, P. R.	E 20
.....	Quebrada Vueltas, P. R.	D 21
.....	Quebradillas, P. R.	E 13
1945	Quebradillas, P. R.	B 5
.....	Quemado, P. R.	F 16
4444	Quezon, P. I.	G 14
224	Quinhagak, Alaska	M 7
.....	Rabanal, P. R.	F 14
11490	Ragay, P. I.	G 16
106	Rampart, Alaska	G 13
.....	Rancheras, P. R.	G 5
12018	Rapu-Rapu, P. I.	H 19
.....	Rayo, P. R.	G 5
.....	Real, P. R.	G 9
2231	Red Tank, C. Z.	J 21
.....	Retiro, P. R.	G 4
1678	Rincon, P. R.	D 1
.....	Rincon, P. R.	F 14
.....	Rincon, P. R.	G 5
.....	Rio, P. R.	D 15
.....	Rio, P. R.	E 18
.....	Rio Abajo, P. R.	C 12
.....	Rio Abajo, P. R.	E 19
.....	Rio abajo, P. R.	D 8
.....	Rio arriba, P. R.	D 8
.....	Rio Arriba, P. R.	D 19
.....	Rio arriba, P. R.	G 16
.....	Rio arriba Poniente, P.R.	C 10
.....	Rio arriba Saliente, P. R.	C 11
.....	Rio Blanco, P. R.	E 19
.....	Rio Canas, P. R.	E 16
.....	Rio Cañas, P. R.	E 5
.....	Rio Cañas Abajo, P.R.	H 11
.....	Rio Cañas arriba, P.R.	G 11
.....	Rio Grande, P. R.	C 1
2408	Rio Grande, P. R.	C 18
.....	Rio Hondo, P. R.	E 13
.....	Rio Hondo, P. R.	F 3
.....	Rio Jueyes, P. R.	H 13
.....	Rio Lajas, P. R.	C 13
19935	Rio Piedras, P. R.	C 16
.....	Rio Prieto, P. R.	F 7
.....	Rio Prieto, P. R.	E 6
.....	Rio Rosario, P. R.	G 3
5922	Rizal, P. I.	B 12
15938	Rizal, P. I.	E 12
.....	Robles, P. R.	C 4
.....	Rocha, P. R.	C 3
14309	Romblon, P. I.	I 15
.....	Roncador, P. R.	E 7
11950	Ronda, P. I.	L 18
.....	Rosario, P. R.	F 3
.....	Rosario alto, P. R.	F 4
.....	Rosario bajo, P. R.	F 4
.....	Rose Inlet, Alaska	Q 24
138	Ruby, Alaska	H 10
34	Russian Mission, Alaska	J 7
.....	Sabalos, P. R.	F 2
.....	Sabana, P. R.	B 13
.....	Sabana, P. R.	F 12
4783	Sabana Grande, P. R.	G 3
.....	Sabana Grande, P. R.	D 8
.....	Sabana Grande, P. R	G 5
.....	Sabana Hoyos, P. R.	C 9
.....	Sabana Llana, P. R.	C 16
.....	Sabana Yequa, P. R.	H 4
.....	Sabanetas, P. R.	G 10
.....	Sabanetas, P. R.	E 2
2851	Sablayan, P. I.	H 12
1844	Sabtang, P. I.	C 21
.....	Saco, P. R.	E 20
53662	Sagay, P. I.	K 18
9907	Sagay, P. I.	M 20
.....	Sagunto, P. I.	N 23
142	Saint Michael, Alaska	I 7
.....	Saint Thomas, see Charlotte Amalie, Virgin Is.	
135	Saint Timothys (Tanacross), Alaska	I 16
10778	Salay, P. I.	M 20
.....	Salchasket, Alaska	H 14
13237	Salcedo, P. I.	J 23
.....	Saliente, P. R.	B 11
3176	Sallinas, P. R.	H 12
.....	Saltillo, P. R.	F 8
.....	Salto, P. R.	C 4
.....	Salto abajo, P. R.	E 8
.....	Salto arriba, P. R.	E 7
.....	Saltos, P. R.	F 11
.....	San Anton, P. R.	C 16
6638	San Antonio, P. I.	F 9
.....	San Antonio, P. R.	B 6
47639	San Carlos, P. I.	D 10
69653	San Carlos, P. I.	K 18
9058	Sanchez Mira, P. I.	E 21
9975	San Dionisio, P. I.	D 22
99	Sand Point, Alaska	R 7
19362	San Fabian, P. I.	D 11
6556	San Felipe, P. I.	E 9
35661	San Fernando, P. I.	F 12
23318	San Fernando, P. I.	D 10
7585	San Fernando, P. I.	I 15
14657	San Fernando, P. I.	I 18
6446	San German, P. R.	G 4
16368	San Ildefonso, P. I.	E 12
.....	San Ildefonso, P. R.	G 12
12090	San Isidro, P. I.	E 11
.....	San Isidro, P. I.	J 19
23783	San Joaquin, P. I.	K 14
28545	San Jose, P. I.	E 12
12197	San José, P. I.	G 12
11716	San Jose, P. I.	I 12
382	San Jose de Buan, P. I.	I 21
29119	San Jose de Buenavista, P. I.	K 14
10941	San Juan, P. I.	C 10
8366	San Juan, P. I.	M 17
169247	San Juan, P. R.	B 15
5880	San Julian, P. I.	J 22
5181	San Lorenzo, P. R.	F 17
.....	San Lorenzo, P. R.	D 11
8406	San Marcelino, P. I.	F 10
.....	San Mateo, P. I.	M 23
26136	San Miguel, P. I.	E 12
9821	San Narciso, P. I.	E 9
5683	San Narciso, P. I.	G 16
13958	San Nicolás, P. I.	B 11
16088	San Nicolás, P. I.	D 11
46311	San Pablo, P. I.	G 13
4735	San Pascual, P. I.	H 16
.....	San Patricio, P. R.	F 9
.....	San Patricio, P. R.	C 15
13083	San Quintin, P. I.	D 11
21232	San Remigio, P. I.	J 18
10024	San Remigio, P. I.	K 14
.....	San Salvador, P. R.	F 15
4278	San Sebastian, P. R.	D 5
10174	Santa, P. I.	B 10
35709	Santa Bárbara, P. I.	K 16
.....	Santa Catalina, P. R.	G 12
12848	Santa Cruz, P. I.	C 10
2160	Santa Cruz, P. I.	D 12
11968	Santa Cruz, P. I.	E 9
17649	Santa Cruz, P. I.	F 13
24544	Santa Cruz, P. I.	G 14
33775	Santa Cruz, P. I.	O 25
.....	Santa Cruz, P. I.	P 22
.....	Santa Cruz, P. R.	D 17
7818	Santa Fé, P. I.	J 18
2348	Santa Isabel, P. R.	H 11
.....	Santa Isabel, P. R.	D 7
8999	Santa Luciá, P. I.	C 10
13204	Santa Mariá, P. I.	C 10
5794	Santa Mariá, P. I.	C 13
.....	Santana, P. R.	G 5
.....	Santana, P. R.	C 9
.....	Santana, P. R.	B 8
6507	Santander, P. I.	L 17
.....	Santa Olaya, P. R.	D 14
9947	Santa Rita, P. I.	J 21
.....	Santa Rita, P. R.	H 6
.....	Santa Rosa, P. I.	C 22
15069	Santa Rosa, P. I.	F 12
.....	Santa Rosa, P. R.	C 14
.....	Santa Rosa, P. R.	D 8
.....	Santa Rosa, P. R.	G 5
6017	Santiago, P. I.	C 10
34249	Santiago, P. I.	D 13
10976	Santo Domingo, P. I.	B 10
.....	Santo Domingo, P. R.	G 8
.....	Santoni, P. R.	C 1
10347	Santo Tomas, P. I.	D 11
.....	Santurce, P. R.	B 15
.....	San Vicente, P. R.	B 12
22422	Sara, P. I.	J 16
.....	Saug, P. I.	O 23
111	Saxman, Alaska	Q 25
.....	Schofield Barracks, Haw.	E 10
.....	Scow Bay, Alaska	O 23
.....	Sealevel, Alaska	P 25
239	Selawick, Alaska	E 9
410	Seldovia, Alaska	N 12
949	Seward, Alaska	M 13
92	Shageluk, Alaska	J 8
.....	Shakan, Alaska	P 23
128	Shaktolik, Alaska	H 8
.....	Shelton, Alaska	G 6
257	Shishmaref, Alaska	E 6
193	Shungnak, Alaska	E 10
49	Shushanna Jc. (McCarthy), Alaska	K 17
16951	Siaton, P. I.	M 16
22146	Sibalom, P. I.	K 14
21803	Sibonga, P. I.	L 18
.....	Sierra Alta, P. R.	G 6
.....	Sierra baja, P. R.	F 7
.....	Sigaboy, P. I.	P 23
10623	Sigma, P. I.	J 15
39571	Silay, P. I.	K 16
11743	Sinait, P. I.	B 10
7938	Sipocot, P. I.	G 16
15172	Siquijor, P. I.	M 17
5830	Siruma, P. I.	G 17
1987	Sitka, Alaska	O 22
634	Skaguay (Skagway), Alaska	M 21
	Skagway, see Skaguay, Alaska.	
.....	Skowl Arm, Alaska	Q 24
28396	Sogod, P. I.	K 21
17166	Solana, P. I.	B 13
17870	Solano, P. I.	D 12
106	Solomon, Alaska	G 6
9025	Solsona, P. I.	B 11
.....	Sonadora, P. R.	D 14
22097	Sorsogón, P. I.	H 19
.....	Steel Creek, Alaska	H 17
54	Stevens, Alaska	F 13
.....	Stillwater Jc., Alaska	L 17
.....	Strelna, Alaska	K 16
14510	Subic, P. I.	F 10
.....	Sugpon, P. I.	C 11
8003	Sulat, P. I.	I 22
226	Sulzer, Alaska	Q 24
.....	Sumidero, P. R.	E 15
66	Summit, C. Z.	I 20
78	Suntrana, Alaska	I 14
34255	Surigao, P. I.	L 22
12	Susitna, Alaska	K 13
.....	Susua alta, P. R.	G 6
.....	Susuabaja, P. R.	H 5
23004	Taal, P. I.	G 11
29989	Tabaco, P. I.	G 18
.....	Tabanuco, P. R.	F 5
20202	Tabogon, P. I.	K 18
31233	Tacloban, P. I.	J 21
5723	Taft, P. I.	I 22
15257	Tagbilaran, P. I.	L 18
12444	Tagoloan, P. I.	M 21
70	Takotna, Alaska	I 10
8126	Talakag, P. I.	N 20
3242	Talacogon, P. I.	M 22
26077	Talibon, P. I.	K 20
17474	Talisayan, P. I.	M 21
5500	Talisay, P. I.	G 16
136	Talkeetna, Alaska	K13
.....	Tallaboa, P. R.	H 8
.....	Tallaboa Alta, P. R.	G 8
.....	Tallares, P. R.	B 15
.....	Tamparan, P. I.	N 20
.....	Tanama, P. R.	C 8
170	Tanana, Alaska	G 12
	Tanacross, see St. Timothys, Alaska.	
26186	Tanauan, P. I.	G 12
22066	Tanauan, P. I.	J 21
13132	Tandag, P. I.	M 24
30991	Tanjay, P. I.	L 17
16329	Tanza, P. I.	F 12
17261	Tapas, P. I.	J 15
.....	Taral, Alaska	K 16
11589	Tarangnan, P. I.	I 20
55682	Tárlac, P. I.	E 11
75	Tatitlek, Alaska	L 15
12817	Tayasan, P. I.	L 16
4173	Taytay, P. I.	K 8
.....	Tejas, P. R.	G 17
.....	Tejas de las Piedras, P. R.	F 18
118	Teller, Alaska	F 5
188	Tenakee, Alaska	N 22
.....	Terranova, P. R.	B 5
.....	Tetuan, P. R.	E 9
66	Thane, Alaska	N 22
27148	Tiaong, P. I.	G 12
.....	Tibes, P. R.	G 9
10830	Tibiao, P. I.	J 14
.....	Tierras Nuevas Ponienta, P. R.	B 10
257	Tigara, Alaska	C 6
10921	Tinambac, P. I.	G 17
9788	Tinambacan, P. I.	I 20
121	Tin City, Alaska	F 5
1091	Toa Alta, P. R.	C 13
2015	Toa Baja, P. R.	B 13
.....	Tofty, Alaska	G 13
10	Togiak, Alaska	N 7
.....	Toita, P. R.	F 14
.....	Tokeen, Alaska	P 23
34436	Toledo, P. I.	K 18
15952	Tolong, P. I.	M 16
28	Tolovana, Alaska	H 13
.....	Tolstoi, Alaska	I 9
.....	Tomás de Castro, P. R.	E 16
.....	Toro Negro, P. R.	E 10
.....	Torrecillas alta, P. R.	B 17
.....	Torrecillas baja, P. R.	B 17
8983	Torrijos, P. I.	H 14
.....	Trento, P. I.	N 24
13	Treadwell, Alaska	N 22
.....	Tres Hermanos, P. R.	D 2

Pop.	Place State	Index	Pop.	Place State	Index	Pop.	Place State	Index	Pop.	Place State	Index	Pop.	Place State	Index	Pop.	Place State	Index
1014	Trujillo, Alto, P. R.	C 16	298	Unalaska, Alaska	R 2	....	Vega Redonda, P. R.	E 14	....	Vivi abajo, P. R.	E 8	....	Waikiki, Haw.	F 11	18462	Wright, P. I.	I 21
14228	Tuao, P. I.	B 13	....	Unangashik, Alaska	P 7	....	Vegas, P. R.	F 15	....	Vivi arriba, P. R.	E 8	7319	Wailuku, Haw.	H 17			
8344	Tubao, P. I.	D 10	152	Unga, Alaska	R 6	....	Vegas arriba, P. R.	F 8	36	Volcano House, Haw.	N 23	971	Waimanalo, Haw.	F 12	4542	Yabucoa, P. R.	G 17
21119	Tubigon, P. I.	L 19	....	Unibon, P. R.	D 12	....	Veruela, P. I.	N 23				1921	Waimea, Haw.	C 4	....	Yabucoa Playa, P. R.	G 19
45846	Tuburan, P. I.	K 18	11462	Unisan, P. I.	G 14	....	Victoria, P. R.	C 2	5420	Wahiawa, Haw.	E 11	....	Wainiha, Haw.	B 4	....	Yahuecas, P. R.	F 7
27616	Tuguegarao, P. I.	B 14	4430	Utuado, P. R.	E 8	2678	Vieques, P. R.	F 23	....	Waiakane, Haw.	G 14	341	Wainwright, Alaska	A 9	292	Yakutat, Alaska	M 19
88	Tuluksak, Alaska	K 7	1058	Uyugan, P. I.	O 22	11232	Viga, P. I.	G 19	....	Waiakea, Haw.	M 24	214	Waiohinu, Haw.	P 21	9985	Yauco, P. R.	G 6
14343	Tumauini, P. I.	C 14				20981	Vigan, P. I.	B 10	....	Waiakea Mill, Haw.	M 23	6906	Waipahu, Haw.	F 11	....	Yeguadilla occidental,	
....	Turabo, P. R.	E 15	....	Vacas, P. R.	F 11	16848	Villaba, P. I.	J 19	695	Waiakoa, Haw.	M 18	216	Waipio, Haw.	K 21		P. R.	O 7
136	Tyonek, Alaska	L 12	529	Valdez, Alaska	L 15	834	Villalba, P. R.	F 10	....	Waiakee, Haw.	D 11	193	Wales, Alaska	F 5	....	Yeguadilla oriental, P. R.	O 7
			13457	Valencia, P. I.	L 19	....	Villalba arriba, P. R.	F 10	2512	Waialua, Haw.	E 10	96	Wasilla, Alaska	K 13			
21456	Ubay, P. I.	L 20	....	Valenciano abajo, P. R.	F 17	13873	Villareal, P. I.	J 21	1078	Waianae, Haw.	E 10	....	Watertown, Haw.	F 11	131455	Zamboanga, P. I.	P 14
55	Ugasik, Alaska	O 9	14608	Valladolid, P. I.	K 16	18453	Villasis, P. I.	D 11	....	Waihee, Haw.	H 17	199	White Mountain, Alaska	G 7	10143	Zamboanguita, P. I.	M 17
....	Umnak, Alaska	B 24	3238	Vega Alta, P. R.	C 12	14153	Vintar, P. I.	A 11	....	Waikane, Haw.	E 11	53	Wiseman, Alaska	D 13	....	Zanja, P. R.	O 6
329	Unalakleet, Alaska	H 8	5409	Vega Baja, P. R.	C 11	19245	Virac, P. I.	G 19				1162	Wrangell, Alaska	O 24	....	Zarzal, P. R.	O 18

PRINCIPAL FOREIGN CITIES

Including Figures from the Latest Population Estimates

Page	Index	Name	Pop.
112	K 2	Aachen (Aix-la-Chapelle), Ger.	162774
108	I 23	Aberdeen, Scotland	167259
		Abo, see Turku, Fin.	
131	K 13	Addis Ababa, Eth.	129000
134	O 15	Adelaide, Australia.	31387
121	N 4	Aden, Aden	32490
123	F 11	Agra, India	284149
123	I 6	Ahmedabad, India	591267
		Aix-la-Chapelle, see Aachen, Ger.	
123	G 8	Ajmer, India	147258
127	I 12	Alep (Aleppo), Syr.	261605
130	C 3	Alexandria, Egypt	694000
129	B 16	Alger (Algiers), Alg.	264232
121	J 11	Alma-Ata, Sov. Un. Asia	230528
123	G 15	Allahabad, India	260630
111	F 13	Amiens, France	93773
125	M 16	Amman (Philadelphia), Transj.	15000
		Amoy, see Szeming, China.	
123	C 8	Amritsar, India	391010
114	C 4	Amsterdam, Neth.	781665
116	D 19	Andorra, Andorra	600
111	J 8	Angers, France	87988
127	D 7	Ankara (Angora), Turkey	157242
114	K 11	Anvers (Antwerp), Bel.	277929
120	D 13	Arkhangelsk, Sov. Un.	281091
131	A 9	Asmara, Eritrea	85000
120	N 19	Astrakhan, Sov. Un.	253655
101	N 7	Asuncion, Par.	100000
119	P 18	Athênai (Athens), Grc.	495490
112	P 8	Augsburg, Ger.	176575
97	N 19	Avellaneda, Arg.	399021
127	M 20	Baghdad, Iraq	500000
		Baía, see Salvador, Brazil	
109	J 22	Baile Atha Cliath (Dublin), Ireland	467691
120	Q 21	Baku, Sov. Un.	809347
133	J 3	Bandoeng, Neth. Ind.	167000
123	N 10	Bangalore, India	406760
122	P 4	Bangkok, Siam	681214
116	G 20	Barcelona, Spain	1081175
123	E 12	Bareilly, India	192688
113	J 20	Bari, Italy	164340
121	H 13	Barnaul, Sov. Un. Asia	148129
123	I 6	Baroda, India	153301
117	C 9	Basel, Switz.	200900
127	Q 24	Basra, Iraq	60000
133	J 3	Batavia, Neth. Ind.	600000
99	E 14	Belem (Para), Braz.	166662
109	D 23	Belfast, N. Ire.	415151
93	B 8	Belize, Brit. Hond.	17289
123	G 16	Benares, India	263100
119	J 14	Beograd (Belgrade), Yugo.	289272
131	J 24	Berbera, Br. Som.	20000
112	G 12	Berlin, Germany	4242501
117	H 9	Bern, Switz.	151200
127	M 10	Beyrouth (Beirut), Leb.	160716
112	D 16	Bialystok, Poland	105000
112	H 5	Bielefeld, Ger.	121031
116	C 13	Bilbao, Spain	195186
107	J 15	Birmingham, Eng.	1012700
112	I 3	Bochum, Ger.	314546
100	I 11	Bogota, Colombia	325658
113	E 9	Bologna, Italy	199000
107	G 12	Bolton, England	177253
123	K 6	Bombay, India	1489883
111	N 7	Bordeaux, France	258348
111	B 4	Boulogne sur Seine, Fr.	97379
107	N 14	Bournemouth, Eng.	116780
107	F 14	Bradford, England	300900
112	G 8	Braunschweig (Brunswick), Ger.	166800
128	L 12	Brazzaville, Fr. Eq. Afr.	17132
112	F 6	Bremen, Germany	323628
112	J 17	Breslau, Pol.	625198
107	N 19	Brighton, England	147427
134	K 24	Brisbane, Austl.	32829
107	L 12	Bristol, England	410870
118	G 9	Brno, Czech.	288000
		Brunswick, see Braunschweig, Ger.	
114	M 12	Bruxelles (Brussels), Bel.	194268
118	K 20	Bucuresti (Bucharest), Rom.	639789
112	R 21	Budapest, Hung.	1051804
97	N 19	Buenos Aires, Arg.	2567763
118	D 11	Bydgoszcz, Pol.	137000
116	O 8	Cadiz, Spain	87767
130	I 14	Cairo, Egypt	1311200
111	D 13	Calais, France	67568
123	I 22	Calcutta, India	2108891
115	L 16	Camaguey, Cuba	78458
99	N 19	Campos, Brazil	52677
134	P 20	Canberra, Austl.	12000
122	L 14	Canton, China	1145285
132	Q 7	Capetown, U. S. Afr.	352000
100	C 13	Caracas, Ven.	269030
107	L 10	Cardiff, Wales	223648
116	N 16	Cartagena, Spain	113468
129	E 5	Casablanca, Mor.	453000
113	O 16	Catania, Italy	199200
123	G 13	Cawnpore, India	487324
99	B 11	Cayenne, Fr. Gu.	11704
		Cernăuti, see Chernovitsy, Sov. Un.	
122	F 11	Changan (Sian), China	500000
122	K 18	Changchow, China	500000
121	B 21	Changchun (Hsinking), Manch.	415264
122	I 14	Changsha, China	607000
111	G 10	Chelyabinsk, Sov. Un. Asia	273127
112	K 11	Chemnitz, Ger.	350657
122	C 17	Chengte (Jehol), Manch.	650000
122	H 7	Chengtu, China	800000
122	G 19	Chinkiang, China	200000
120	M 2	Chernovitsy, Sov. Un.	111122
		Chisinau, see Kishinev, Sov. Un.	
120	K 23	Chkalovsk (Orenburg), Sov. Un.	172920
122	R 8	Cholon, Fr. In. Ch.	145050
135	M 12	Christchurch, N. Z.	101200
122	I 9	Chungking (Pahsien), China	635000
111	L 15	Clermont-Ferrand, Fr.	101128
118	I 17	Cluj, Hung	98550
132	R 13	Colombo, Ceylon	308000
97	P 2	Concepcion, Chile	85813
129	C 20	Constantine, Algeria	113777
		Constantinople, see Istanbul, Tur.	
		Copenhagen, see København, Den.	
109	P 11	Corcaigh (Cork), Ireland	80700
97	L 12	Cordoba, Argentina	339375
116	M 10	Cordoba, Spain	143296
107	J 15	Coventry, England	184700
107	L 19	Croydon, England	239960
123	H 23	Dacca, India	213218
121	J 19	Dairen, Manch.	481379
127	M 11	Damas (Damascus), Syr.	318922
112	C 19	Danzig, Pol.	238000
112	R 25	Debrecen, Hung.	119901
123	E 10	Delhi, India	521849
107	H 15	Derby, England	142406
131	I 21	Djibouti, Fr. Som.	15000
120	M 9	Dnepropetrovski (Ekaterinoslav), Sov. Un.	500662
112	I 4	Dortmund, Ger.	540875
112	J 13	Dresden, Ger.	642143
		Dublin, see Baile Atha Cliath, Ireland	
112	I 3	Duisburg, Ger.	440419
108	K 20	Dundee, Scotland	175933
132	L 21	Durban, U. S. Afr.	270000
112	J 3	Düsseldorf, Ger.	498600
107	B 23	Eastham, Eng.	146900
108	K 20	Edinburgh, Scot.	438998
112	J 9	Erfurt, Germany	140000
112	I 3	Essen, Germany	654461
122	L 14	Fatshan, China	400000
129	F 8	Fès (Fez), Mor.	179211
113	F 9	Firenze (Florence), Italy	285000
		Florence, see Firenze. It.	
		Foochow, see Minhow, China.	
99	F 22	Fortaleza (Ceará), Brazil	142453
112	L 5	Frankfurt-am-Main, Ger.	555071
110	J 23	Frederiksberg, Den.	109189
124	M 4	Fukuoka, Japan	323217
		Fusan, see Pusan, Kor.	
118	J 23	Galati, Rom.	102296
114	L 9	Gand (Ghent), Bel.	167084
112	I 3	Gelsenkirchen, Ger.	336227
117	N 2	Genève, Switz.	144000
113	E 4	Genova (Genoa), It.	347483
99	A 7	Georgetown, Br. Gu.	73171
		George Town, see Penang, Str. Setts.	
		Ghent, see Gand, Bel.	
112	I 2	Gladbach, Ger.	118000
108	N 15	Glasgow, Scotland	1088417
120	K 6	Gomel, Sov. Un.	144169
120	I 15	Gorki, Sov. Un.	644116
115	O 10	Göteborg, Sweden	262676
116	N 12	Granada, Spain	155405
118	I 8	Graz, Aus.	152706
107	G 19	Great Grimsby, Eng.	52463
107	L 20	Greenwich, Eng.	100879
114	C 22	Groningen, Neth.	115185
120	P 17	Grozni, Sov. Un.	172468
89	M 7	Guadalajara, Jal.	329235
93	G 4	Guatemala, Guat.	188042
102	D 3	Guayaquil, Ecuador	172948
114	F 12	Haarlem, Neth.	129126
95	H 6	Habana, Cuba	676376
112	I 4	Hagen, Germany	148300
124	H 12	Hakodate, Japan	203862
107	F 14	Halifax, England	98122
112	J 10	Halle, Ger.	209200
112	D 8	Hamburg, Ger.	1647000
85	M 10	Hamilton, Ont.	166337
122	H 19	Hangchow, China	506900
122	H 15	Hankow, China	778000
112	G 7	Hannover, Ger.	438922
122	M 8	Hanoi, Fr. In. Ch.	149000
122	H 15	Hanyang, China	400000
121	A 23	Harbin, Manch.	517127
		Havre, see Le Havre, Fr.	
112	N 5	Heidelberg, Ger.	84650
120	F 4	Helsinki (Helsingfors), Fin.	283598
126	H 16	Herat, Afg.	100000
124	L 8	Hiroshima, Japan	343968
123	I 21	Howrah, India	379292
		Hsinking, see Changchun, Manch.	
107	G 14	Huddersfield, Eng.	113467
122	O 9	Hué, Fr. In. Ch.	34000
107	F 18	Hull, England	313366
123	G 1	Hyderabad, India	96021
123	L 11	Hyderabad, India	739159
128	J 8	Ibadan and Suburbs, Nigeria	386907
123	I 9	Indore, India	203695
121	H 1	Irkutsk, Sov. Un. Asia	243380
126	I 7	Isfahân, Iran	204598
127	B 3	Istanbul (Constantinople), Tur.	793949
127	B 3	Istanbul and Suburbs, Tur.	1050000
120	H 13	Ivanovo, Sov. Un.	285069
120	H 20	Izhevsk, Sov. Un.	175740
127	F 1	Izmir (Smyrna), Tur.	184652
123	F 9	Jaipur, India	175810
		Jehol, see Chengte, Manch.	
125	N 10	Jerusalem, Palestine	125000
132	F 18	Johannesburg, U. S. Afr.	554000
123	I 13	Jubbulpore, India	178839
99	M 18	Juiz de Fora, Brazil	72254
123	D 9	Jukundur, India	71008
126	G 23	Kabul, Afg.	200000
124	Q 3	Kagoshima, Japan	190257
122	F 15	Kaifeng, China	223000
120	H 10	Kalinin, Sov. Un.	216131
124	J 15	Kanazawa, Japan	186297
123	G 1	Karachi, India	359490
112	O 4	Karlsruhe, Ger.	154902
		Kashgar, see Shufu, China	
112	I 6	Kassel (Cassel), Ger.	175000
123	F 18	Katmandu, Nepal	108800
120	I2	Kaunas (Kovno), Sov. Un.	152365
121	I 18	Kazan, Sov. Un.	401665
		Keijo, see Kyŏngsŏng, Kor.	
121	G 19	Khabarovsk, Sov. Un., Asia	199364
120	L 10	Kharkov, Sov. Un.	833432
128	H 19	Khartoum, A.E.Sud.	49741
112	C 8	Kiel, Germany	218000
120	L 6	Kiev, Sov. Un.	846293
94	J 8	Kingston, Jamaica	109056
122	B 23	Kirin, Manch.	138910
120	N 4	Kishinev, W. Sov. Un.	114445
124	M 12	Kobe, Japan	967234
110	J 23	København (Copenhagen), Den.	686343
		København and Suburbs, Den.	873044
112	J 3	Köln, Germany	756605
118	D 7	Königsberg, Pol.	315651
118	L 15	Kowloon, China	104000
118	F 13	Kraków, Pol.	255000
120	O 12	Krasnodar (Ekaterinodar), Sov. Un.	203946
112	I 2	Krefeld, Ger.	165300
121	G 14	Krasnoyarsk, Sov. Un., Asia	189999
120	M 8	Krivoi-rog, Sov. Un.	197621
123	R 2	Kuala Lumpur, Mal. St.	111800
120	J 19	Kuibyshev (Samara), Sov. Un.	390267
122	K 6	Kunming, China	150000
124	M 8	Kure, Japan	276085
122	C 13	Kweisu, China	200000
122	J 9	Kweiyang, China	100000
122	D 4	Kyŏngsŏng (Seoul), Kor.	935464
124	M 13	Kyoto, Japan	1089726
128	J 8	Lagos, Nigeria	126108
123	D 8	Lahore, India	671659
122	E 19	Laichou, China	100000
122	E 7	Lanchow, China	500000
98	H 4	La Paz, Bolivia	301000
97	N 20	La Plata, Arg.	125695
128	D 2	Las Palmas, Can. Is.	119595
117	K 4	Lausanne, Switz.	99900
107	F 15	Leeds, England	482789
		Leghorn, see Livorno, It.	
111	G 9	Le Havre (Havre), Fr.	164083
107	I 16	Leicester, England	239111
112	J 10	Leipzig, Germany	717000
120	F 7	Leningrad (Petrograd), Sov. Un.	3191304
128	L 12	Leopoldville, Bel. Cong.	35946
107	B 22	Leyton, England	128920
114	M 17	Liège, Belgium	165634
111	E 15	Lille, France	200575
102	L 8	Lima, Peru	533645
111	L 12	Limoges, France	95217
118	G 6	Linz, Aus.	108404
116	K 5	Lisboa (Lisbon), Port.	704669
107	G 10	Liverpool, England	856850
128	O 16	Livingstone, N. Rh.	5600
113	F 7	Livorno (Leghorn), It.	112400
118	E 12	Lódz, Poland	665000
107	L 19	London, England	4230200
107	L 19	London, Greater, England	8202818
128	M 11	Luanda, Angola	17947
112	D 8	Lübeck, Ger.	137700
123	F 14	Lucknow, India	387177
112	M 4	Ludwigshafen, Ger.	106000
114	R 20	Luxembourg, Lux.	57740
120	L 1	Lvov (Lwow), Sov. Un.	316177
111	L 19	Lyon, France	570622
122	L 15	Macau, China	74000
123	N 13	Madras, India	777481
116	I 12	Madrid, Spain	1088647
123	P 11	Madura, India	239144
112	H 9	Magdeburg, Ger.	306894
120	I 25	Magnitogorsk, Sov. Un.	145870
112	L 4	Mainz, Germany	142627
120	M 11	Makeevka, Sov. Un.	240145
116	O 11	Malaga, Spain	238085
115	Q 11	Malmö, Sweden	144482
93	K 11	Managua, Nic.	118900
107	G 13	Manchester, Eng.	758140
123	N 22	Mandalay, Burma	134950
112	M 5	Mannheim, Ger.	275162
100	C 6	Maracaibo, Ven.	135582
120	N 11	Mariupol, Sov. Un.	222427
129	I 4	Marrakech, Mor.	184400
111	P 20	Marseille, France	914232
132	K 18	Maseru, Bas.	2320
126	F 14	Mash-Had (Meshed), Iran	139300
127	L 4	Mecca, Sau. Ar.	70000
100	G 8	Medellín, Col.	143952
123	E 11	Meerut, India	169290
134	Q 19	Melbourne, Austl.	135048
113	N 17	Messina, Italy	114051
89	H 5	Mexico, Mex.	1464556
107	D 16	Middlesbrough, Eng.	138489
113	D 5	Milano, Italy	712844
122	J 19	Minhow (Foochow), China	322700
120	C 21	Minsk, W. Sov. Un.	238772
131	K 24	Mogadiscio, Som.	30000
120	F 10	Molotov, (Perm), Sov. Un., Asia	255196
101	P 19	Montevideo, Ur.	708233
87	P 15	Montreal, Quebec	903007
118	F 11	Moravská Ostrava, Czech.	125347
120	I 11	Moskva (Moscow), Sov. Un.	4137018
127	I 19	Mosul, Iraq	80000
122	B 20	Mukden, Manch.	863515
112	I 2	Mülheim, Ger.	131000
111	I 23	Mulhouse, France	96697
112	Q 9	München (Munich), Ger.	736000
112	H 4	Münster, Ger.	122210
116	M 16	Murcia, Spain	193731
123	O 9	Mysore, India	150540
124	N 2	Nagasaki, Japan	252630
124	M 15	Nagoya, Japan	1328084
123	J 12	Nagpur, India	301957
122	I 16	Nanchang, China	300000
111	H 22	Nancy, France	120578
122	G 18	Nanking, China	633500
122	J 18	Nanping (Yenping), China	200000
111	J 7	Nantes, France	195185
113	J 14	Napoli (Naples), It.	757251
107	C 15	Newcastle-on-Tyne, Eng.	283145
107	N 16	Newport, Eng.	11313
111	O 25	Nice, France	211916
127	K 8	Nicosia, Cyprus	23700
124	H 20	Niigata, Japan	150903
114	I 18	Nijmegen, Neth.	89534
122	H 20	Ningpo, China	213000
99	N 18	Niteroi, Brazil	125974
107	J 17	Northampton, Eng.	92314
107	I 23	Norwich, England	126207
107	H 16	Nottingham, Eng.	283030
121	H 12	Novo Sibirsk, Sov. Un. Asia	405589
112	N 9	Nürnberg, Ger.	410438
112	I 3	Oberhausen, Ger.	192300
118	I 25	Odessa, W. Sov. Un.	604223
124	L 10	Okayama, Japan	163552
107	G 13	Oldham, England	140309
128	H 18	Omdurman, A.E.Sud.	110436
121	G 11	Omsk, Sov. Un. Asia	280716
		Oporto, see Porto, Port.	
118	I 15	Oradea, Rom.	82355
129	D 12	Oran, Algeria	200671
		Orenburg, see Chkalovsk, Sov. Un. Asia.	
124	M 13	Osaka, Japan	3252340
115	M 9	Oslo, Norway	253124
112	G 5	Osnabrück, Ger.	94000
124	F 12	Otaru, Japan	164282
85	D 22	Ottawa, Ontario	154951
108	N 14	Paisley, Scot.	120268
113	N 13	Palermo, Italy	317735
115	J 21	Palma, Spain	114405
93	P 22	Panama, Panama	11893
		Para, see Belem, Braz.	
99	B 9	Paramaribo, N. Gu.	60723
111	H 14	Paris, France	2829746
123	G 18	Patna, India	159690
122	D 16	Peiping (Peking), China	1561027
119	P 18	Peiraievs, Grc.	284500
123	Q 1	Penang, Str. Setts.	148400
120	J 16	Penza, Sov. Un.	157145
		Perm, see Molotov, Sov. Un.	
		Pernambuco, see Recife, Brazil	
134	N 4	Perth, Australia	82290
123	B 5	Peshawar, India	130967
		Petrograd, see Leningrad, Sov. Un.	
122	F 13	Pingyangfu, China	173000
112	L 10	Plauen, Germany	113000
119	M 19	Plovdiv (Philippopolis), Bulgaria	100485
107	O 7	Plymouth, Eng.	208166
118	F 6	Plzeň, Czech.	114150
122	Q 7	Pnom Penh, Fr. In. Ch.	103000
123	K 6	Poona, India	258197
94	J 13	Port au Prince, Haiti	130000
116	G 5	Pôrto (Oporto), Port.	262790
99	Q 12	Porto Alegre, Braz.	262694
94	R 24	Port of Spain, Trin.	103155
130	C 22	Port Said, Egypt	121200
107	N 17	Portsmouth, Eng.	249288
118	D 10	Poznân (Posen), Pol.	269000
118	F 7	Praha (Prague), Czech.	945000
105	F 12	Preston, England	118839
132	F 18	Pretoria, U. S. Afr.	138000
89	I 6	Puebla, Mexico	138360
123	E 23	Punaka, Bhutan	5000
122	E 25	Pusan, Kor.	249734
87	K 21	Quebec, Quebec	150757
126	L 21	Quetta, Bal.	60272
102	B 5	Quito, Ecuador	165924
123	R 22	Rangoon, Burma	400415
123	B 6	Rawal Pindi, India	181169
107	L 17	Reading, Eng.	97153
99	H 25	Recife (Pernambuco), Brazil	327753
111	G 17	Reims, France	116687
111	I 6	Rennes, France	98538
126	D 5	Resht, Iran	121625
		Revel, see Tallinn, Sov. Un.	
120	H 3	Riga, Sov. Un.	385063
99	N 18	Rio de Janeiro, Brazil	1563787
113	I 11	Roma (Rome), It.	1062861
97	M 16	Rosario, Arg.	512872
112	C 10	Rostock, Ger.	93501
120	N 12	Rostov, Sov. Un.	510253
114	H 12	Rotterdam, Neth.	594948
111	E 15	Roubaix, France	107105
111	G 12	Rouen, France	122957
108	N 15	Rutherglen, Scot.	25157
112	N 2	Saarbrucken, Ger.	129085
122	Q 8	Saigon, Fr. In. Ch.	109000
111	M 19	Saint Etienne, Fr.	190236
79	K 25	Saint John's, Newf.	44000
124	M 13	Sakai, Japan	182147
128	O 18	Salisbury, S. Rh.	32974
		Salonika, see Thessalonikē, Grc.	
99	J 22	Salvador (Baía), Braz.	293278
121	J 10	Samarkand, Sov. Un. Asia	134346
95	K 13	Sancti Spiritus, Cuba	14164
93	N 14	San José, Costa Rica	74872
93	H 6	San Salvador, Sal.	103920
116	C 15	San Sebastian, Spain	103979
93	H 6	Santa Ana, Sal.	85130
128	F 2	Santa Cruz, Can. Is.	72358
97	L 16	Santa Fe, Arg.	147583
116	C 12	Santander, Spain	101793
97	M 4	Santiago, Chile	993207
95	O 21	Santiago de Cuba, Cuba	120577
99	N 15	Santos, Brazil	159648
99	N 15	São Paulo, Brazil	1253943
124	G 12	Sapporo, Japan	222827
119	K 11	Sarajevo, Yugo.	78182
120	K 17	Saratov, Sov. Un.	375860
114	M 12	Schaerbeek, Bel.	122790
123	L 11	Secunderabad, India	120801
133	J 4	Semarang, Neth. Ind.	217775
124	H 23	Sendai, Japan	223630
		Seoul, see Kyongsong, Kor.	
116	N 9	Sevilla, Spain	312123
114	H 11	's Gravenhage (The Hague), Neth.	482397
122	H 20	Shanghai, China	3703430
122	H 20	Shaohing, China	200000
122	H 13	Shasi, China	114000
107	G 15	Sheffield, England	517300
123	L 9	Sholāpur, India	212620
121	K 11	Shufu (Kashgar), China	80000
		Sian, see Changan, China.	
122	I 14	Siangtan, China	500000
120	O 8	Simferopol, Sov. Un.	142678
123	R 3	Singapore, Mal. St.	550000
120	I 7	Smolensk, Sov. Un.	156677
		Smyrna, see Izmir, Tur.	
121	K 11	Soche (Yarkand), China	70000
133	J 4	Soerabaja, Neth. Ind.	380863
119	L 17	Sofija (Sofia), Bul.	321094
122	H 20	Soochow, China	260000
118	F 12	Sosnowiec, Poland	116000
107	N 15	Southampton, Eng.	176025
107	L 22	Southend, Eng.	120093
107	C 15	South Shields, Eng.	113452
123	B 8	Srinagar, India	207787
120	M 16	Stalingrad (Tsaritsin), Sov. Un.	445476
120	M 11	Stalino, Sov. Un.	462395
118	C 7	Stettin, Pol.	270225
115	M 16	Stockholm, Swe.	543785
107	G 13	Stockport, Eng.	125505
107	H 13	Stoke on Trent, Eng.	276619
111	H 24	Strasbourg, France	193119
112	O 5	Stuttgart, Ger.	445000
119	I 13	Subotica, Yugo.	100058
98	K 9	Sucre, Bolivia	29857
122	I 7	Suifu, China	150000
107	C 15	Sunderland, Eng.	185870
123	I 6	Surat, India	171443
121	G 10	Sverdlovsk, Sov. Un. Asia	425544
107	L 8	Swansea, Wales	164825
122	K 17	Swatow, China	178600
134	O 22	Sydney, Austl.	138060
112	T 23	Szeged, Hungary	136438
122	K 18	Szeming (Amoy) China	234200
126	C 2	Tabriz, Iran	220000
120	N 12	Taganrog, Sov. Un.	188808
122	K 21	Taihoku, For.	340114
120	F 4	Tallinn (Revel), Sov. Un.	145565
128	O 24	Tananarive, Madag.	105258
121	J 10	Tashkent, Sov. Un. Asia	585005
120	Q 17	Tbilisi (Tiflis), Sov. Un.	519175
126	F 7	Tehran, Iran	360300
		The Hague, see 's Gravenhage, Neth.	
99	L 19	Theophilo-Ottoni, Brazil	12254
119	N 17	Thessalonikē (Salonika), Greece	265160
122	D 17	Tientsin, China	1209696
		Tiflis, see Tbilisi, Sov. Un.	
118	J 14	Timisoara, Rom.	91866
119	M 13	Tiranë, Albania	30806
124	M 20	Tokyo, Japan	6778804
121	G 13	Tomsk, Sov. Un. Asia	141215
123	D 2	Torino, It.	594698
85	L 12	Toronto, Ontario	667457
107	L 19	Tottenham, Eng.	157748
111	P 21	Toulon, France	150310
111	P 12	Toulouse, France	213220
111	J 11	Tours, France	83753
123	P 11	Trichinopoly, India	159566
113	D 13	Trieste, Italy	228583
129	E 12	Tripoli, Libya	86137
122	E 17	Tsinan, China	250000
122	E 19	Tsingtao, China	390000
97	H 10	Tucumán, Arg.	157480
120	J 11	Tula, Sov. Un.	272403
129	B 24	Tunis, Tunisia	202405
120	I 23	Ufa, Sov. Un.	245863
114	H 15	Utrecht, Neth.	160798
117	G 20	Vaduz, Liechtenstein	1405
116	J 17	Valencia, Spain	450756
116	F 11	Valladolid, Spain	116024
97	M 3	Valparaiso, Chile	209945
80	Q 12	Vancouver, B. C.	275353
113	D 11	Venezia (Venice), It.	162695
120	N 7	Vernoleninsk (Nikolaev), Sov. Un.	141400
113	D 8	Verona, Italy	113139
111	H 13	Versailles, France	73839
122	L 15	Victoria, HongKong	500000
		Vienna, see Wien, Aus.	
120	I 3	Vilnyus (Wilno), W. Sov. Un.	207000
121	I 20	Vladivostok, Sov. Un. Asia	206432
120	K 12	Voronezh, Sov. Un.	326836
120	M 12	Voroshilovgrad, Sov. Un.	213007
124	N 12	Wakayama, Japan	195203
107	I 14	Walsall, England	103102
107	L 20	Walthamstow, Eng.	132965
122	H 10	Wanhsien, China	208000
118	D 14	Warszawa (Warsaw), Pol.	1261000
122	E 18	Weihsien, China	100000
135	J 17	Wellington, N. Z.	120700
		Wenchow, see Yungkia, China.	
107	L 20	Westham, Eng.	276150
118	H 9	Wien (Vienna), Aus.	1843173
112	L 5	Wiesbaden, Ger.	159800
107	L 19	Willesden, Eng.	184410
		Wilno, see Vilnyus, Sov. Un.	
128	P 13	Windhoek, S. W. Afr.	10765
81	Q 16	Winnipeg, Man.	221960
107	I 13	Wolverhampton, Eng.	133190
107	L 20	Woolwich, Eng.	146944
122	H 15	Wuchang, China	610000
122	H 18	Wuhu, China	131000
112	I 13	Wuppertal, Ger.	408600
		Yarkand, see Soche, China.	
120	H 12	Yaroslavl, Sov. Un.	298065
		Yenping, see Nanping, China.	
120	R 16	Yerevan, Sov. Un.	200031
124	M 20	Yokohama, Japan	968091
124	N 17	Yokosuka, Japan	193358
107	F 16	York, England	84810
122	I 20	Yungkia (Wenchow), China	631300
119	J 8	Zagreb, Yugo.	185581
120	M 9	Zaporozhe, Sov. Un.	289188
116	G 16	Zaragoza, Sp.	233601
117	E 15	Zürich, Switz.	339200

GENERAL INDEX OF FOREIGN CITIES

Exclusive of the U. S. Territories and Possessions

An index of 30,000 foreign cities with the latest available population figures. The place-name is followed by the country wherein it is located and the index reference whereby it may be found on the map. (See Explanation of Index.)

MAP INDEX AND ABBREVIATIONS

Map Page	Country	Abbrev.
121	Aden	Aden
128	Anglo-Egyptian Sudan	A. E. Sud.
126	Afghanistan	Afg.
91	Aguascalientes	Agua.
119	Albania	Alb.
129	Algeria	Alg.
80	Alberta	Alta.
116	Andorra	And.
128	Angola	Ang.
97	Argentina	Arg.
118	Austria	Aus.
134	Australia	Austl.
10	Azores Is.	Az. Is.
94	Bahama Is.	Ba. Is.
90	Baja California	Baja Cal.
126	Baluchistan	Bal.
94	Barbados	Barb.
132	Basutoland	Bas.
80	British Columbia	B. C.
128	Bechuanaland	Bech.
114	Belgium	Bel.
128	Belgian Congo	Bel. Cong.
15	Bermuda Is.	Ber. Is.
123	Bhutan	Bhu.
133	British North Borneo	B. N. B.
98	Bolivia	Bol.
99	Brazil	Braz.
99	British Guiana	Br. Gu.
103	British Honduras	Br. Hond.
131	British Somaliland	Br. Som.
133	Brunei	Bru.
119	Bulgaria	Bul.
123	Burma	Bur.
128	Cameroons	Cam.
92	Campeche	Camp.
79	Canada	Can.
128	Canary Is.	Can. Is.
133	Celebes	Cel.
123	Ceylon	Cey.
92	Chiapas	Chia.
90	Chihuahua	Chih.
97	Chile	Chl.
122	China	Chn.
91	Coahuila	Coa.
100	Colombia	Col.
91	Colima	Colim.
111	Corsica	Cor.
93	Costa Rica	C. R.
95	Cuba	Cuba
94	Curaçao	Cur.
10	Cape Verde Is.	C. V. Is.
127	Cyprus	Cyp.
118	Czechoslovakia	Czech.
112	Danzig	Dan.
110	Denmark	Den.
92	Distrito Federal	D. F.
94	Dominica	Dom.
94	Dominican Republic	Dom. Rep.
90	Durango	Dur.
102	Ecuador	Ec.
130	Egypt	Eg.
107	England	Eng.
131	Eritrea	Erit.
131	Ethiopia	Eth.
110	The Faeroes	Faer.
96	Falkland Is.	Falk. Is.
135	Fiji Is.	Fiji Is.
120	Finland	Fin.
122	Formosa	For.
111	France	Fr.
128	French Equatorial Africa	Fr. Eq. Afr.
99	French Guiana	Fr. Gu.
122	French Indochina	Fr. In. Ch.
131	French Somaliland	Fr. Som.
128	French West Africa	Fr. W. Afr.
128	Gambia	Gam.
128	Gold Coast	G. C.
112	Germany	Ger.
116	Gibraltar	Gib.
119	Greece	Grc.
94	Grenada	Gren.
14	Greenland	Grnld.
94	Guadeloupe	Guad.
91	Guanajuato	Guan.
93	Guatemala	Guat.
91	Guerrero	Guer.
94	Haiti	Hai.
91	Hidalgo	Hid.
93	Honduras	Hond.
122	Hong Kong	Hong.
118	Hungary	Hung.
110	Iceland	Ice.
123	India	India
126	Iran	Iran
127	Iraq	Iraq
109	Ireland	Ire.
111	Italy	It.
91	Jalisco	Jal.
94	Jamaica	Jam.
124	Japan	Jap.
133	Java	Java
121	Karafuto	Kar.
128	Kenya	Kenya
122	Korea	Kor.
121	Kuwait	Kuw.
79	Labrador	Lab.
127	Lebanon	Leb.
94	Leeward Is.	Le. Is.
128	Liberia	Lib.
128	Libya	Libya
117	Liechtenstein	Liech.
114	Luxembourg	Lux.
82	Mackenzie	Mack.
128	Madagascar	Madag.
113	Malta	Mal.
122	Malay States	Mal. St.
81	Manitoba	Man.
122	Manchuria	Manch.
94	Martinique	Mart.
89	Mexico	Mex.
91	Michoacan	Michoa.
111	Monaco	Monaco
121	Mongolia	Mong.
129	Morocco	Mor.
92	Morelos	Morel.
128	Mozambique	Moz.
91	Nayarit	Nay.
83	New Brunswick	N. B.
133	New Caledonia	N. Cal.
123	Nepal	Nep.
114	Netherlands	Neth.
99	Netherlands Guiana	Neth. Gu.
133	Netherlands Indies	Neth. Ind.
79	Newfoundland	Newf.
133	New Guinea Ter.	N. Gui. Ter.
93	Nicaragua	Nic.
128	Nigeria	Nig.
109	Northern Ireland	N. Ire.
91	Nuevo Leon	N. L.
115	Norway	Nor.
128	Northern Rhodesia	N. Rh.
83	Nova Scotia	N.S.
128	Nyasaland	Nya.
135	New Zealand	N. Z.
92	Oaxaca	Oax.
121	Oman	Oman
85	Ontario	Ont.
125	Palestine	Pal.
93	Panama	Pan.
133	Papua Ter.	Pap. Ter.
101	Paraguay	Par.
83	Prince Edward Island	P. E. I.
102	Peru	Peru
118	Poland	Pol.
116	Portugal	Port.
128	Portuguese Guinea	Port. Gui.
92	Puebla	Pueb.
91	Quintana Roo	Q. R.
87	Quebec	Que.
91	Queretaro	Quer.
128	Rio de Oro	R. de O.
118	Romania	Rom.
93	Salvador	Sal.
133	Samoa	Sam.
133	Sarawak	Sar.
113	Sardinia	Sard.
81	Saskatchewan	Sask.
121	Saudi Arabia (Nejd)	Sau. Ar.
108	Scotland	Scot.
108	Shetland Islands	Shet. Is.
122	Siam	Siam
90	Sinaloa	Sin.
121	Sinkiang	Sink.
128	Sierra Leone	S. L.
91	San Luis Potosi	S. L. P.
113	San Marino	S. Mar.
131	Somaliland (It.)	Som.
90	Sonora	Son.
120	Soviet Union	Sovn. U.
121	Sov. Un. in Asia	Sov. Un. Asia
116	Spain	Sp.
128	Spanish Guinea	Sp. Gui.
129	Spanish Morocco	Sp. Mor.
128	Southern Rhodesia	S. Rh.
94	Santa Lucia	Sta. Luc.
94	St. Vincent	St. Vin.
133	Sumatra	Sum.
128	Southwest Africa	S. W. Afr.
132	Swaziland	Swaz.
115	Sweden	Swe.
117	Switzerland	Switz.
127	Syria	Syr.
92	Tabasco	Tab.
91	Tamaulipas	Tam.
128	Tanganyika	Tan.
135	Tasmania	Tas.
121	Tibet	Tib.
133	Timor	Tim.
92	Tlaxcala	Tlax.
125	Transjordan	Transj.
94	Trinidad	Trin.
121	Tannu Tuva	T. T.
129	Tunisia	Tun.
127	Turkey	Tur.
128	Uganda	Ug.
101	Uruguay	Ur.
132	Union of South Africa	U. S. Afr.
103	Venezuela	Ven.
92	Veracruz	Ver.
107	Wales	Wal.
94	West Indies	W. I.
118	Western Soviet Union	W. Sov. Un.
121	Yemen	Yem.
92	Yucatan	Yuc.
119	Yugoslavia	Yugo.
88	Yukon	Yuk.
91	Zacatecas	Zac.
128	Zanzibar	Zan.

A

Pop.	Place Country Index
2765	Aa (Lyngdal) Nor. N 5
10184	Aabenraa, Den., M 7
1254	Aabybro, (Denmark) D 9
162774	Aachen, (Aix-la-Chapelle) Germany, K 2
3254	Aadalen, Norway, L 8
3385	Aadorf, Switzerland, D 16
1202	Aadum, Den., I 4
3000	Aafjord, Norway, H 9
.....	Aaka, Palestine, G 9
1503	Aakirkeby, Denmark R 24
1812	Aal, Denmark, J 2
3500	Aal, Norway, L 7
345	Aalbaek, Denmark, B 13
48132	Aalborg, Denmark, D 10
12171	Aalen, Germany, O 7
	Aalesund, see Alesund
7562	Aalsmeer, Netherlands, G 14
442	Aalsö, Denmark, G 15
.....	Aalst, Netherlands, I 15
967	Aalst, Netherlands, J 17
11205	Aalten Netherlands, H 22
3749	Aamli, Norway, N 6
7300	Aamot, Norway, K 8
1673	Aanekoski, Fin., E 5
1612	Aarau, Switzerland, E 12
1609	Aarberg, Switzerland, G 8
2893	Aarburg, Switzerland, E 11
1606	Aardal, Norway, K 6
.....	Aardal, Norway N 6
2203	Aardenburg, Neth., K 7, Q1
95644	Aarhus, Denmark, H 12
163	Aarösund, Denmark, L 9
2152	Aars, Denmark, E 9
1067	Aarup, Denmark, L 10
2084	Aarwangen, Switz., F 10
3155	Aas, Norway, C 6
.....	Aaseral, Norway, N 5
358	Aasgaardstrand, Nor., E 4
5875	Aasnes, Norway, L 10
.....	Aasum, Denmark, L 13
.....	Aba, Egypt, P 10
.....	Abacaxis, Brazil, F 6
40100	Abadeh, Iran, K 7
.....	Abadiya, Egypt, O 22
.....	Abaete, Brazil, E 14
.....	Abaete, Brazil, L 16
.....	Abalua, Egypt, F 19
.....	Abaman, Brazil, F 4
5789	Abancay, Peru N 15
1050	Abapó, Bolivia, K 13
.....	Abarguh, Iran, K 8
.....	Abasabad Iran E 7
.....	Abashiri, Japan, F 14
929	Abasolo, Coa., D 11
349	Abasolo, Tam., H 19
.....	Abâyisha, Egypt, O 24
.....	Abazai, India, B 5
.....	Abbasa, Egypt, F 18
.....	Abbasabad, Iran, B 2
.....	Abbasabad, Iran, F 11
.....	Abbasabad, Iran, F 14
.....	Abbasabad, Iran, M 10
.....	Abbas yeh, Egypt, I 14
.....	Abbatia delle Tre Fontane, Italy, D 22
.....	Abbazia, Italy, D 14
19335	Abbeville, France, F 13
229	Abbey, Saskatchewan, O 4
.....	Abbeydorney, Ire., N 4
.....	Abbeyfeale, Ire., N 7
.....	Abbey Holme, Eng., D 10
.....	Abbeylara, Ire., H 16
.....	Abbeyleix, Ire., L 16
.....	Abbeyshrule, Ire., I 15
.....	Abbi Addi, Eth., D 9
.....	Abbin, Transjordan, J 16
.....	Abbotsbury, England, N 12
562	Abbotsford, B.C., P 5, Q 13
.....	Abbott, Argentina, O 19
10000	Abbottabad, India, B 7
.....	Abbotts, Australia, J 5
650	Abbottsford, Quebec, P 17
.....	Abdalabad, Iran, G 8
.....	Abdan, Afghanistan, E 22
.....	Abeche, Fr. Eq. Afr., I 14
75	Abee, Alberta, J 21
817	Abellin, Palestine, G 9
2256	Abensberg, Ger., O 10
45697	Abeokuta, Nigeria, I 8
.....	Abera, Eth., M 8
1155	Aberaeron, Wales, J 7
15370	Aberavon, Wales, L 8
.....	Abercorn, N. Rh., M 19
201	Abercorn, Quebec, R 18
235	Aberdalgie, Scotland, L 18
48751	Aberdare, Wales, K 9
231	Aberdeen, Sask., M 7
167259	Aberdeen, Scotland, I 23
2553	Aberdeen, U. S. Afr., O 13
1180	Aberdour, Scotland, G 23
1505	Aberfeldy, Scot., K 17
.....	Aberfeldy, U. S. Afr., I 19
1014	Aberfoyle, Scotland, L 14
2651	Abergele, Wales, H 9
.....	A Berka (Wells) Algeria, N 3
1094	Aberlady, Scotland, M 21
622	Abernethy, Scotland, H 17
1154	Abernethy, Scotland, L 19
.....	Aberporth, Wales, J 6
9474	Aberystwith, Wales, J 8
.....	Abi, Pal., E 13
.....	Abid, Iran, H 12
26143	Abidjan, Fr. W. Afr., J 5
.....	Abi Garm, Iran, J 12
.....	Ab-i-garm, Iran, N 14
.....	Abi Germek, Iran, I 3
.....	Ab-i-Khara, Iran, L 14
.....	Ab-i-Khurmeh, Alg., I 17
7240	Abingdon, England, L 16
21	Abington, Australia, E 19
.....	Abington, Scotland, O 17
.....	Abirevan, Afg., I 18
.....	Abnub, Egypt, L 18
	Abo, see Turku, Fin.
11205	Abomey, Fr. W. Afr., J 7
15777	Abony, Hung., I 13
.....	Abou Kemal, Iraq, L 16
1552	Aboyne, Scotland, I 21
.....	Abra Grande, Arg., H 12
.....	Abramo, Argentina, Q 13
.....	Abramova, Sov. Un., B 18
8881	Abrantes, Portugal, J 6
.....	Abra Pampa, Arg., E 10
.....	Albriachan, Scotland, H 14
2456	Abrud, Rom., I 17
.....	Abu Abta, Egypt, C 10
.....	Abuam, Morocco, J 8
.....	Abû Aqis, Egypt, Q 10
.....	Abû Donkach, Egypt, M 9
.....	Abu el Akbdar, Egypt, F 16
.....	Abû el Kaui, Egypt, F 10
.....	Abû-el-Mûtämûr, Egypt, D 5
.....	Aby el Nomros, Egypt, J 13
.....	Abufeda, Egypt, L 18
.....	Abu Ganchu, Egypt, L 9
.....	Abu Gandir, Egypt, M 9
1200	Abu Ghalib, Egypt, H 11
2961	Abû Gorg, Egypt, P 10
.....	Abû Hamad, A.E.Sud., H 19
812	Abu Hammâd, Egypt, F 17
.....	Abuit, Egypt, L 13
4069	Abû Kebir, Egypt, E 17
1493	Abû Kels, Egypt, F 11
.....	Abu Kir, Egypt, B 4
.....	Abu Kirkas, Egypt, K 17
1384	Abû Mâdi, Egypt, B 14
.....	Abuman, Brazil, H 1
.....	Abu Richah, Egypt, F 21
.....	Abu Ruba, Iraq, O 24
.....	Abu Sheqûq, Egypt, E 17
1940	Abu-Sir, Egypt, D 14
6000	Abusir, Egypt, M 13
.....	Abu Suwêr, Egypt, F 21
10770	Abû Tig, Egypt, M 19
.....	Abûxa, Egypt, L 10
2000	Abû Zabel, Egypt, H 15
.....	Acaciaville, N. S., N 9
5927	Acacio, Bolivia, J 8
.....	Acadieville, N. B., F10
13000	Acahay, Paraquay, O 7
1431	Acajutla, Salvador, H 5
17634	Acambaro, Guan., M 13
2171	Acanceh, Yuc., E 21
1085	Acandi, Colombia, E 5
2960	Acapetlahuaya, Guer., P 14
7196	Acaponeta, Nay., J 2
9993	Acapulco, Guer., R 15
.....	Acará, Brazil, E 14
.....	Acarahú, Brazil, E 21
.....	Acari, Peru, O 12
3969	Acarigua, Venezuela, E 9
215	Acatán, Nay., K 3
5591	Acatlan, Pueb., J 6
3385	Acatzingo, Pueb., I 7
5143	Acayucan, Ver., K 12
74937	Accra, Gold Coast, I 7
42973	Accrington, England, F 13
4000	Acebal, Argentina, M 16
800	Acevedo, Argentina, M 17
8600	Achacachi, Bolivia, H 3
.....	Achahoish, Scotland, M 10
.....	Achanalt, Scotland, G 12
2708	Achar, Uruguay, J 19
.....	Acharn, Scotland, K 16
1993	Achel, Belgium, K 17
.....	Achentee, Scotland, H 11
1371	Achéres, France, A 1
.....	Achill, Ire., G 4
.....	Achiltibuie, Scotland, E 11
12000	Achinsk, Sov. Un. Asia, G 13
545	Achiras, Argentina, M 11
5256	Achiri, Bolivia, I 3
2703	Achlat, Turkey, F 18
.....	Achnacarry, Scotland, J 12
.....	Achnasheen, Scot., G 12
.....	Achness, Scotland, D 15
3245	Achocallo, Bolivia, H 4
.....	Achonry, Ire., G 10
.....	Achray, Ontario, C 16
.....	Achriesgill, Scotland, D 12
22956	Acireale, Italy, O 17
.....	Acklam England, F 17
150	Aclare, Ire., G 9
285	Acme, Alberta, N 21
1351	Acobamba, Peru, L 10
1912	Acobamba, Peru, M 12
2120	Acomayo, Peru, N 16
1440	Acoria, Peru, M 11
1113	Acoyapo, Nicaragua, K 13
718	Acqua Santa, Italy, C 24
10848	Acquaviva, Italy, J 20
9904	Acqui, Italy, E 3
7893	Acre (Akka), Palestine, G 8
.....	Acreide, Italy, O 17
4346	Acri, Italy, L 19
70523	Acton, England, L 19
2063	Acton, Ontario, L 10
2363	Actonvale, Quebec, P 18
3284	Actopan, Hid., G 5
.....	Acuna, Arg., K 20
5907	Ada, G. C., J 7
	Adabasar, see Adapazari, Tur.
.....	Adadleh, Br. Som., I 16
	Adalia, see Antalya, Tur.
.....	Adâmiya, Egypt, P 23
4888	Adamstown, Austl., N 23
88119	Adana, Tur., H 10
972	Adanero, Spain, H 11
22839	Adapazari (Adabasar), Tur., C 5
.....	Adare, Ire., M 9
132	Adavale, Australia, J 19
.....	Addagalla, Eth., H 13
.....	Addington, England, D 22
129000	Addis Ababa, Eth., J 9
.....	Addis Alam, Eth., J 8
4347	Adegem, Belgium, R 1
.....	Adela, Eth., L 9
31387	Adelaide, Austl., O 15
316860	Adelaide (with suburbs), Australia, O 15
1080	Adelaide, U. S. Afr., O 15
.....	Adelaide River, Austl., B 12
2377	Adelboden, Switz., L 9
.....	Adelia, Algeria, C 15
819	Adelong, Australia, O 20
.....	Adelphi, B. C., O 15
.....	Adelschiwas, Tur., F 18
.....	Adelsö, Sweden, Q 19
3000	Ademuz, Spain, I 16
32490	Aden, Aden, N 4
2065	Adenau, Germany, K 2
20000	Aderkan, Iran, P 8
39637	Adernò, Italy, N 16
.....	Adghar, Algeria, L 13
10299	Adiaman, Tur., G 13
.....	Adi Caieh, Erit., B 9
2000	Adigrat, Eth., C 10
.....	Adiscia, Eth., E 8
5133	Adi ggri, Erit., B 8
.....	Adj Tamada, Algeria, R 15
6643	Adjud, Romania, I 21
180	Admiral, Sask., O 5
31640	Adoni, India, M 10
12450	Adra, Spain, O 13
13817	Adria, Italy, D 10
28	Adrian, Chih., K 19
	Adrianople, see Edirne, Tur.
.....	Adrigole, Ire., Q 4
5000	Adua, Eth., C 9
.....	Aduafil, Morocco, K 7
227	Advocate Harbour, N. S., K 12
	Aebeltoft, see Ebeltoft
5035	Aegina, Grc., P 18
.....	Aeito, I. E. A., G 20
.....	A. el Guerzim, Mor., L 1
7258	Aeltre, Belgium, Q 1
.....	Aernen, Switzerland, M 12
.....	Aerolito, Argentina, H 14
8755	Aerschot, Belgium, L 14
4521	Aer rycke, Belgium, L 5
603	Aesch, Switzerland, F 13
1288	Aéschi, Switzerland, D 9
.....	Af Abed, Erit, A 9
.....	Afata, Eth., K 6
.....	Afdam, Eth., I 10
2576	Affoltern, Switzerland, D 14
3125	Affoltern, Switz., E 14
7080	Affreville, Algeria, C 16
.....	Affua, Brazil, D 13
3000	Afgoi, I. S., R 17
.....	Aflfen, Morocco, I 4
.....	Aflkurahen, Morocco, K 2
1931	Aflou, Algeria, F 15
.....	Afranio, Braz., H 20
.....	Afvestäd, Sweden, M 14
2136	Afyon-Karahisar (Kara-(Hissar), Tur., F 4
.....	Agaba el Kebira, Eg., R 24
.....	Agadez, Fr. W. Afr., H 10
5730	Agadir, Morocco J 2
.....	Agalta, Honduras, F 11
.....	Agar, India, H 9
.....	Agartala India, H 25
501	Agassiz, B. C., O 6
9360	Agde, France, P 17
.....	Agdeh, Iran, J 8
27152	Agen, France, O 10
691	Agger, Denmark, E 2
.....	Aggersborg, Denmark, D 7
.....	Aggtelek, Hungary, A 19
.....	Aghada, Ire., Q 12
.....	Aghadowey, N. Ire., C 19
.....	Aghrad el Berkin, Algeria, J 21
321	Agincourt, Ontario, K 12
.....	Aglid, Egypt, Q 24
.....	Aglu, Morocco, K 2
816	Agno, Switzerland, P 17
5135	Agnone, Italy, I 15
.....	Agobel, Morocco, I 3
3056	Agordat, Erit., A 8
.....	Agori Khas, India, H 16
.....	Agosto, 25 de, Ur., O 18
284149	Agra, India, F 11
2925	Agrado Colombia, K 9
2716	Agramonte, Cuba, I 9
3000	Agreda, Spain, F 14
14562	Agrinion, Grc., O 15
2452	Agropoli, Italy, K 16
78	Agua Amarga, Chile, J 4
.....	Agua Azul, Chia., M 19
1540	Aguacaliente, Sin., R 19
2557	Aguacate, Cuba, H 7
.....	Agua Clara, Brazil, M 11
3780	Aguada, Cuba, I 10
7631	Aguadas, Colombia, H 8
2829	Aguadulce, Panama, Q 20
218	Aguairendal, Bolivia, N 12
1834	Agualeguas, N. L., E 16
132	Aguas Blancas, Chile, F 4
81124	Aguascalientes, Agua., K 9
86	Agua Verde, Chile, G 4
3503	Agudo, Spain, K 10
.....	Aguella, Fr. W. Afr., H 10
17078	Aguilas, Spain, N 15
2455	Aguililla, Michoa., O 8
.....	Aguire, Hond, F 12
.....	Agulu, Morocco, H 2
.....	Agurdi, Morocco, F 7
2564	Agyia, Grc., O 17
6000	Ahar, Iran, C 3
400	Ahascragh, Eth., J 11
1000	Ahaura, New Zealand, K 11
4927	Ahaus, Germany, H 3
82	Ahipara, N. Z., A 14
25000	Ahlen, Germany, H 4
.....	Ahmadi, Iran, O 11
42900	Ahmadnagar, India, K 8
10000	Ahmadpur, India, D 5
591267	Ahmedabad, India, I 6
.....	Ahnâsia-el-Medina, Eg., M 11
1000	Ahogill, N. Ire., C 21
.....	Ahouha, Algeria, Q 17
6453	Ahrweiler, Germany, K 3
.....	Ahuacatal, S. L. P., K 14
2946	Ahuacatlán, Nay., L 4
484	Ahuacatlán, Pueb., G 7
13505	Ahuachapán, Sal., H 5
807	Ahualulco, S. L. P., J 12
6275	Ahualulco, Jal., M 5
439	Ahuijullo, Jal., O 7
684	Ahun, France, L 13
1949	Ahus, Sweden, Q 12
.....	Ahwaz, Iran, K 4
3675	Aichach, Germany, P 9
.....	Aichiet, Erit., E 13
	Aidin, see Aydin, Tur.
7337	Aigachi, Bolivia, H 3
11011	Aigion, Greece, P 16
3938	Aigle, Switzerland, M 6
662	Aiguebelle, France, M 22
1687	Aigueperse, France, L 16
3878	Aiguesmortes, Fr., P 18
295	Aiguilles, Fr., N 23
37000	Aigun, Manch., H 18
1344	Aigurande, France, K 13
.....	Aihsien, China, N 11
1472	Aija, Peru, J 7
.....	Aijal, India, M 20
12000	Aikawa, Japan, G 19
.....	Ailbun, Palestine, G 11
474	Ailsa Craig, Ontario, N 5
.....	Aimé, Bolivia, C 6
900	Aimogasta, Argentina, I 8
.....	Ain Arik, Palestine, M 9
.....	Ainazi, Sov. Un., G 3
.....	Ain Baniou, Algeria, D 18
13968	Ain Beida, Algeria, C 21
5	Ain-ben-Khelil, Alg., G 12
.....	Ain Chair, Mor., H 10
.....	Ain Dalia, Sp. Mor., D 7
.....	Ain ed Duk, Palestine, M 11
.....	Ainegöl, Tur., D 4
.....	Ain el Arus, Transj., R 11
.....	Ain el Beida, Pal., R 11
.....	Ain el Feshkhah, Pal., N 11
.....	Ain el Ghuweir, Pal., N 11
5	Ain el Hadjadj, Alg., O 22
1819	Ain el Hadjar, Alg., E 13
.....	Ain el Hekr, Transj., M 15
.....	Ain el Helweh, Pal., J 12
.....	Ain el Jarud, Transj., P 13
.....	Ain el Kezbeh, Pal., N 7
.....	Ain el Mellaha, Pal., F 13
.....	Ain et Trabeh, Pal., O 11
.....	Ain Guetifa, Algeria, E 15
.....	Ain Guettar, Algeria, C 22
.....	Ain Hajlah, Palestine, M 12
.....	Ain Helweh, Palestine, J 12
.....	Ain Hemar, Transj., L 15
.....	Ain Jalud, Palestine, I 11
.....	Ain Jenneh, Transj., J 15
.....	Ain Jidy, Palestine, O 11
1735	Ain Karim, Palestine, M 9
.....	Ain Masa, Morocco, G 6
.....	Ain Melakou, Algeria, D 15
196	Ain Mokra, Algeria, B 21
.....	Ain Rubia, Transj., K 16
.....	Ain Sarah, Palestine, O 8
2907	Ain Sefra, Algeria, G 13
.....	Ain Sfissifa, Algeria, F 14
.....	Ain Shems, Palestine, N 7
	Aintab, see Gaziantep, Tur.
.....	Ain Taiba, Algeria, K 19
17478	Ain Temouchent, Alg., D11
.....	Ain Touta, Algeria, D 19
.....	Ain Tubaun, Pal., I 11
.....	Ain Yagout, Algeria, C 20
.....	Ain Zebub, Transj., Q 13
1920	Aipe, Colombia, J 9
5656	Aiquile, Bolivia, J 9
25954	Airdrie, Scotland, N 16
7619	Aire, France, E 14
3926	Aire, France, P 8
1767	Airolo, Switzerland, K 15
.....	Ait Duit, Morocco, I 3
.....	Aith, Shetland Is., B 5
.....	Aith, Shetland Is., C 3
.....	Ait Hamara, Morocco, G 8
.....	Ait Therho, Morocco, G 8
9478	Aiud, Rom., I 17
	Aivalik, see Ayvalik, Tur.
38332	Aix, France, P 21
3337	Aixe-sur-Vienne, Fr., L 11
	Aix-la-Chapelle, see Aachen, Ger.
1251	Aizenay, France, K 6
3346	Aizpute, Sov. Un., H 1
37146	Ajaccio, France, Q 2
.....	Ajaigarh, India, G 13
.....	Ajanta, India, J 8
5000	Ajigasawa, Japan, B 23, H12
500	Ajjeh, Palestine, J 9
.....	Ajlun, Transjordan, J 14
147258	Ajmer, India, G 8
.....	Ajo, Argentina, O 21
12000	Ajodhya, India, F 15
12500	Ajos, Paraguay, O 9
.....	Ajstrup, Denmark, D 11
8479	Ajtos, Bul., L 22
1966	Ajuchitlán, Guer., P 14
101	Ajuno, Michoa., N 11
4486	Akaa, Fin., E 3
.....	Akabli, Algeria, P 14
.....	Akalkot, India, L 9
1000	Akana, Japan, K 8
.....	Akanis, Tur., E 19
.....	Akanthou, Cyprus, K 8
.....	Akaogi, Japan, A 14
460	Akaroa, N. Z., M 13
2000	Akasaki, Japan, K 10
37244	Akashi, Japan, M 12
.....	Akassa, Nigeria, J 9
7000	Akbarpur, India, G 15
147	Akbaru, Palestine, G 12
.....	Akčar, Bul., K 17
.....	Akeha, Afghanistan, E 20
2500	Akershus, Norway, A 6
5400	Akhalkalki, Sov. Un., Q 16
13600	Akhaltsikh, Sov. Un., Q 15

Pop.	Place Country Index
.....	Akhisar, Tur., C 4
21192	Akhisar, Tur., E 2
.....	Akhtari, Sov. Un., N 11
24000	Akhmyn, Egypt, N 20
26995	Akhtirka, Sov. Un., L 9
.....	Akhtopol, Bul., L 23
5000	Aki, Japan, O 9
.....	Akimachi, Japan, L 8
.....	Akir, Palestine, M 6
51069	Akita, Japan, D 22
.....	Akka, Morocco, L 3
	Akka, see Acre, Pal.
	Akkerman, see Cetatea Albă, Rom.
572	Akkeshi, Japan, G 15
.....	Akkrum, Netherlands, D 19
35800	Akmolinsk, Sov. Un. Asia, H 11
.....	Ako, Japan, M 11
.....	Akoafim, Cam., K 12
.....	Akola, India, K 7
47632	Akola, India, J 10
.....	Akrabe, Palestine, J 10
1160	Akrabeh, Palestine, L 10
.....	Aksha, Sov. Un. Asia, H 16
7339	Akserai, Tur., F 9
10335	Akshehr, Tur., F 6
	Aksum see Axum, Eth.,
.....	Aktagh, India, A 11
.....	Akun, Iran, N 8
3000	Akune, Japan, P 3
4100	Akureyri, Iceland, B 21
37800	Akyab, Bur., N 20
.....	Akyâd el-Ghatowira, Eg., E 19
2836	Ala, Italy, C 8
.....	Alacam, Tur., B 10
5504	Alacranes, Cuba, I 8
.....	Aladja, Tur., D 9
.....	Aladjik, Tur., C 10
3456	Alaejos, Spain, G 10
.....	Alagoas, Brazil, H 24
13461	Alagôinhas, Brazil, I 22
6270	Alagon, Spain, F 15
316	Alaigne, France, P 13
.....	Alaiye (Alaya), Tur., I 6
9999	Alajuela, Costa Rica, N 14
.....	Alakhi, Transjordan, N 15
234	Alameda, Sask., R 11
.....	Alamerdasht, Iran, O 7
3008	Alamos, Son., K 14
.....	Alamos, Sp. Mor., D 8
.....	Alampur, India, M 11
.....	Alanas, Sweden, H 14
2628	Alange, Sp., K 8
506	Alanje, Panama, P 17
1073	Alaquines, S. L. P., K 16
1022	Alar del Rey, Spain, D 11
5925	Alaro, Spain, J 21
8375	Alashehr, Tur., F 2
28500	Alatir, Sov. Un., I 17
.....	Alatoz, Spain, K 15
4837	Alatri, Italy, I 13
12059	Alausi, Ecuador, D 5
11372	Alavus, Fin., E 4
5111	Alayor, Spain, I 23
.....	Al Azizya, Iraq, M 21
8904	Alba, Italy, E 3
.....	Albac, Rom., I 16
64222	Albacete, Spain, K 14
3144	Alba de Tormes, Sp., H 10
.....	Albaek, Denmark, G 12
12457	Alba-Iulia, Rom., I 17
426	Albanel, Quebec, D 19
4076	Albany, Australia, O 6
.....	Albany, P. E. I., H 14
1688	Albarracín, Spain, I 15
1048	Alberdi, Arg., I 10
846	Albergueria, Spain, H 8
7078	Alberique, Spain, K 16
1807	Alberni, B. C., Q 11
6720	Albert, France, F 14
300	Albert, N. B., J 12
721	Albert Mines, N. B., I 12
232	Alberton, Australia, Q 20
554	Alberton, P. E. I., F 14
2321	Albertville, Bel. Cong., M17
6103	Albertville, France, L 23
26	Albertville, Sask., K 8
649	Albeuve, Switz., K 7
30293	Albi, France, O 14
5435	Albion, Br. Gu., B 7
6365	Albistan, Tur., G 12
3310	Albocácer, Spain, I 17
1410	Albona, Italy, D 14
.....	Albue, Denmark, N 15
7420	Albufeira, Portugal, N 5
7989	Albunol, Spain, O 13
10015	Albuquerque la Roca, Sp., K 8
10543	Albury, Australia, P 20
500	Albury, New Zealand, N 9
713	Alca, Peru, O 15
8767	Alcacer do Sal, Port., L 5
3565	Alcalá, Bolivia, K 11
51855	Alcalá de Chisbert, Sp., I 18
20477	Alcalá de Guadaira, Sp., N9
18419	Alcalá de Henares, Sp., H13
3269	Alcalá de Jucár, Spain, K 15
9693	Alcala de los Gazules, Sp., P 9
26058	Alcala la Real, Spain, N 12
63051	Alcamo, Italy, N 12
1616	Alcañices, Spain, F 9
8935	Alcañiz, Spain, G 17
.....	Alcantara, Brazil, E 17
3954	Alcantara, Spain, J 7
10744	Alcantarilla, Spain, M 15
4879	Alcaraz, Spain, L 14
26141	Alcázar de San Juan, Sp., K 13
11000	Alcazarquivir, Sp. Mor., D 6
24518	Alcira, Spain, K 16
9029	Alcobaca, Brazil, L 21
.....	Alcobaca, Brazil, F 14
2661	Alcobaca, Portugal, J 5
445	Alcoléa del Pinar, Sp., G 14
4204	Alconchel, Spain, L 7
4541	Alcora, Spain, I 17
2417	Alcoutim, Portugal, N 6
45792	Alcôy, Spain, L 17
1422	Alcubierre, Spain, F 16
3305	Alcudia, Spain, I 22
2727	Aldama, Chih., G 19
1054	Aldama, Tam., J 19
.....	Aldansk, Sov. Un. Asia, E 18
.....	Aldbrough, England, F 19
890	Aldéa, Spain, H 8
1837	Aldeadávila, Spain, G 8
2480	Aldeburgh, England, J 25
9182	Aldeia Galega, Port., K 5
.....	Aldenham, England, A 19
127	Aldergrove, B. C., Q 13
34281	Aldershot, England, M 17
48	Aldersyde, Alberta, O 21
25000	Al Diwaniya, Iraq, O 21
.....	Alegre, Braz., M 10
16475	Alegrete, Brazil, Q 9
49	Alejandra, Argentina, J 17
	Aleksandrovsk, see Polyarnoye, Sov. Un.
51604	Aleksandrovskoe, Sov. Un., O 15
.....	Aleksandrya, W. Sov. Un., A 15
5384	Aleksinac, Yugo., K 15
.....	Aleksyeevka, Sov. Un., K 17
.....	Alem, Sweden, P 14
.....	Alemquer, Brazil, E 10
16688	Alençon, France, H 10
261605	Alep (Aleppo) Syria, I 12
298	Alert Bay, B. C. O 9
41385	Alès, France, O 18
43810	Alessandria, Italy, D 4
2913	Alessano, Italy, K 23
18373	Ålesund, Nor., J 5
870	Alexandra, N. Z., P 6
	Alexandrette, see Iskenderun, Tur
699400	Alexandria, Egypt, C 3
2175	Alexandria, Ontario, E 25
19387	Alexandria, Rom., K 20
.....	Alexandria, Scotland, M 14
336	Alexandria, U. S. Afr., Q 16
	Alexandropol, see Gymri, Sov. Un.
12013	Alexandroupolis (Dede Agach), Grc., N 21
.....	Alexandrov-Gai, Sov. Un., L 19
	Alexandrovsk, see Zaporozhe, Sov. Un.
.....	Alexis Creek, B. C., M 12
1000	Alfambra, Sp., H 15
1383	Alfambra, Sp., H 16
8186	Alfaro, Spain, E 15
7020	Alfeld, Germany, H 7
2227	Alford, Eng., H 20
1336	Alford, Scotland, H 21
30078	Alfortville, France, B 7
621	Alfred, Ontario, D 24
.....	Alfredton, N. Z., I 19
21232	Alfreton, England, H 15
.....	Alfta, Sweden, K 14
1179	Alfvestad, Sweden, P 12
15	Algarrobal, Chile, J 3
.....	Algarrobo, Argentina, Q 14
.....	Algarrobo, Cuba, L 16
.....	Algebuckina, Austl., K 14
25671	Algeciras, Spain, O 24
.....	Algeciras, Spain, P 9
17373	Algemesi, Spain, J 16
264232	Alger (Algiers), Alg., B 16
11799	Alghero, Italy, J 3
	Algiers, see Alger, Alg.
.....	Algorta, Uruguay, J 16
.....	Alguel, Morocco, I 3
1892	Alhama de Aragón, Sp., G 15
7591	Alhama de Granada, Sp., O 12
9597	Alhama de Murcia, Sp., M 15
25	Alhambra, Alberta, M 20
.....	Alhandra, Portugal, K 5
10681	Alhaurin-el-Grande, Spain, O 11
.....	Alhuampo, Argentina, H 14
.....	Alia, Palestine, F 10
.....	Aliabad, Iran, E 7
.....	Aliabad, Iran, G 7
.....	Aliabad, Iran, K 9
.....	Aliabad, Iran, N 11
.....	Aliabad, Iran, P 9
.....	Aliabad, Shahi, Iran, F 8
1043	Aliaga, Spain, H 16
.....	Alibag, India, K 6
96729	Alicante, Spain, L 17
1500	Alice, U.S. Afr., P 16
.....	Alice Arm, B. C., H 8
467	Alice Springs (Stuart), Austl., H 14
116	Alida, Sask., R 11
66963	Aligarh, India, F 11
4207	Alimena, Italy, N 14
8870	Alingsas, Sweden, O 10
.....	Alipore, India, I 21
7645	Aliwal North, U.S. Afr., M 16
360	Alix, Alberta, L 21
4160	Aljezur, Portugal, N 5
1985	Aljojuca, Pueb., I 7
.....	Alkali Lake, B. C., M 13
.....	Alkavare, Sweden, E 15
28294	Alkmaar, Neth., E 13
260630	Allahabad, India, G 15
.....	Allahabad, Iran, J 10
.....	Allair, India, L 12
382	Allan, Saskatchewan, N 7
928	Allanche, France, M 15
9403	Allariz, Spain, E 7
.....	Allata, Eth., M 9
.....	Alldans Kila, Afg., H 22
1213	Alle, Switzerland, D 7
.....	Allen, Argentina, Q 8
.....	Allenby, B. C., Q 15
.....	Allendale, England, C 13
1500	Allendale, Ont., I 11
5613	Allende, Coa., B 13
2105	Allende, Chih., J 20
329	Allenford, Ontario, H 7
43043	Allenstein, Pol., C 13
43838	Alleppey, India, P 9
.....	Allerslev, Denmark, M 20
.....	Alley, Jamaica, J 8
.....	Allianca, West Brazil, H 14
233	Alliance, Alberta, L 22
.....	Alligator Pond, Jamaica, J 7
2214	Allinge-Sandvig, Denmark, Q 23
1733	Alliston, Ontario, J 11
18244	Alloa, Scotland, M 17
.....	Allonby, England, D 10
825	Allora, Australia, K 23
5000	Allur, India, M 13
528	Alma, N B., J 11
207	Alma, Ontario, K 8
230528	Alma Ata, Sov. Un. Asia, J 11
11582	Almada, Portugal, K 4
12998	Almadén, Spain, K 11
8876	Almagro, Spain, K 12
10788	Almaguer, Colombia, L 6
16025	Almánsa, Spain, K 16
767	Almanza, Spain, D 10
.....	Almar, Afghanistan, F 19
1073	Almaraz, Spain, J 10
.....	Almas, Brazil, J 20
2265	Almaville, Quebec, L 18
2981	Almazan, Spain, G 14
8217	Almazora, Spain, I 17
.....	Almeirim, Brazil, E 11
32516	Almelo, Netherlands, F 23
2746	Almenar, Spain, F 14
21276	Almendralejo, Spain, K 8
.....	Almendricos, Spain, N 15
80180	Almeria, Spain, O 14
1566	Almirante, Pan., O 17
.....	Almis, Morocco, G 9
3682	Almkerk, Netherlands, I 14
4152	Almodóvar, Portugal, M 6
14633	Almodovar del Campo, Spain, K 11
8341	Almogia, Spain, O 11
2441	Almoloya, Méx., H 4
2543	Almonte, Ontario, E 20
8000	Almora, India, E 13
11110	Almuñecar, Spain, O 12
1303	Almuradiel, Spain, L 12
5760	Almyros, Grc., O 17
849	Alness, Scotland, G 15
6882	Alnwick, England, B 14
125	Alonsa, Manitoba, P 14
13968	Alora, Spain, O 10
12000	Alor-Star, N. F., Mal. St., N 19
37852	Alost, Belgium, L 10
.....	Alpachiri, Argentina, P 13
.....	Alpatacal, Argentina, M 9
3374	Alpera, Spain, K 15
17676	Alphen (Alfen), Neth., G13
2465	Alphen (Alfen), Neth., J 14
2555	Alpnachstad, Switz., H 13
4170	Alpujarra, Colombia, J 10
.....	Alpurussa, Brazil, E 5
687	Alqâm, Egypt, F 10
6360	Alquizar, Cuba, H 6
2000	Al Qunfidha, Sau. Ar., M 4
.....	Al Qurna, Iraq, P 24
.....	Alrö, Denmark, J 11
446	Als, Denmark, F 12
222	Alsask, Saskatchewan, N 3
2669	Alsásua, Spain, D 14
.....	Alsen, Sweden, I 12
5058	Alsfeld, Germany, K 6
439	Alslev, Denmark, N 20
.....	Alstahoug, Norway, F 11
.....	Alsted, Denmark, E 5
.....	Alstrup, Denmark, F 8
5000	Alta Gracia, Arg., L 12
3000	Altagracia, Venezuela, C 6
3491	Altagracia de Orituco, Venezuela, D 14
.....	Altaliva, Arg., K 15
.....	Alta Mira, Brazil, F 11
12	Altamira, Chile, G 4
490	Altamira, Dom. Rep., J 14
984	Altamira, Tam., J 20
.....	Altamirano, Arg., O 19
.....	Altamont, B. C., Q 15, O 3
.....	Altamullan, N. Ire., D 14
26877	Altamura, Italy, J 19
20000	Altan-Bulak, Mong., H 16
.....	Altaquer, Colombia, L 3
1109	Altar, Son., D 10
2972	Altare, Italy, E 3
.....	Altares, Cuba, P 22
100	Altario, Alberta, M 24
90	Altata, Sin., O 16
.....	Alta Vista, Argentina, P 14
4254	Altdorf, Switzerland, I 15
5827	Altea, Spain, L 17
16000	Altena, Germany, I 4
44000	Altenburg, Germany, J 10
.....	Altenkirchen, Ger., K 4
4470	Alter-do-Chão, Port., J 6
3680	Altkirch, France, I 24
.....	Altnabreac, Scotland, D 17
.....	Altnaharra, Scotland, D 14
.....	Alto Aripuanã, Brazil, G 5
4998	Alto Cedro, Cuba, N 21
.....	Alto del Fraile, Chile, H 3
.....	Alto de Sierra, Arg., L 7
.....	Alto dos Apiácas, Braz., H 7
.....	Alton, Australia, K 22
6172	Alton, England, M 17
510	Alton, Ontario, K 10
.....	Altona Germany, D 7
.....	Alto Pelado, Arg., N 10
11000	Altos, Paraguay, N 7
.....	Altötting, Ger., Q 11
.....	Alto Uruguay, Brazil, P 10
8394	Altstätten, Switz., E 20
9068	Altstetten, Switz., E 14
6000	Altun Köpri, Iraq., J 20
2000	Alula, Eth., F 24
4853	Alva, Scotland, M 17
.....	Alvar, Afghanistan, G 17,
5776	Alvarado, Ver., I 11
1500	Alvarez, Argentina, M 16
.....	Alvarez, Arg., M 16
.....	Alvarez Jonte, Arg., O 20
115	Alvaro Obregon (Mengel), Q. R., J 23
7439	Alvaro Obregon (Frontera) Tab., J 16
.....	Älvdalen, Swe., K 12
2307	Alvear, Argentina, J 22
450	Alveneu, Switzerland, J 21
541	Alvie, Scotland, I 16
699	Alvinston, Ontario, O 4
.....	Älvsby Swe., G 18
44760	Alwar, India, F 10
.....	Alwara, India, E 7
2629	Alyth, Scotland, K 19
7500	Alytus, W., Sov. Un., B 17
9148	Alzey, Germany, M 4
.....	Alzo, Italy, C 3
1011	Alzonne, France, P 14
.....	Amadia, Iraq, H 19
9032	Amagá, Colombia, H 8
181011	Amagasaki, Japan, M 13
6764	Amal, Sweden, N 11
3970	Amalfi, Italy, J 15
12365	Amalias, Grc., P 15
.....	Amaluza, Ecuador, F 3
681	Amance, France, I 21
956	Amandola, Italy, G 13
19000	Amanev, W. Sov. Un., H 24
	Amapa, see Montenegro, Braz.
	Amapala, Honduras, I 9
.....	Amar, Nig., J 11
16076	Amara, Iraq, O 23
	Amarante, Brazil, G 19
.....	Amarante, Portugal, G 6
.....	Amarapura, Bur., N 22
.....	Amarat, Iran, H 5
.....	Amarbet, Iran, G 12
	Amargoza, Brazil, J 21
1108	Amarillas, Cuba, I 10
.....	Amaro Leite, Brazil, J 14
	Amarracão, Brazil, E 20
.....	Amary, Brazil, G 2
.....	Amasra, Tur., B 7
11981	Amasya, Tur., C 11
649	Amatán, Chia., L 16
.....	Amateh, Transj., K 13
8400	Amatitlán, Guatemala, G 4
1319	Amatrice, Italy, H 12
6458	Amay, Belgium, N 16
.....	Ambaca, Ang., M 12
76326	Ambala, India, D 10
3167	Ambalema, Colombia, I 10
.....	Ambar, Peru, K 7
21147	Ambato, Ecuador, C 5
3330	Ambazac, France, L 13
.....	Ambela, India, B 6
27000	Amberg, Germany, N 10
3805	Ambérieu, France, L 21
7116	Ambert, France, M 17
.....	Ambir, Egypt, N 22
4208	Amble, England, B 15
2343	Ambleside, England, E 11
.....	Ambo, India, I 19
1243	Ambo, Peru, K 9
....	Amboina, Neth. Ind., I7
4483	Amboise, France, J 12
1108	Ambrieres, France, H 8
.....	Ambriz, Ang., M 11
.....	Ambrizette, Ang., M 11
24217	Ambur, India, N 12
1674	Amealco, Quer., M 14
13003	Ameca, Jal., M 5
2348	Amelia, Italy, H 11
29	Amelia, Sask., Q 4
.....	Amenabar, Argentina, N 14
1872	Amendolara, Italy, K 19
.....	América, Bolivia, C 3
2706	Amerongen, Neth., H 17
38551	Amersfoort, Neth., G 17
.....	Amesbury, England, M 14
.....	Amethyst, Alberta, O 22
.....	Amguid, Algeria, P 20
8620	Amherst, Nova Scotia, I 13
2853	Amherstburg, Ontario, R 1
.....	Ami, China, K 6
93773	Amiens, France, F 13
.....	Amigari, Ontario, O 13
100	Amisk, Alberta, L 23
2561	Amlwch, Wales, G 7
15000	Amman (Philadelphia), Transj., M 16
.....	Ammapet, India, O 11
1560	Ammi Moussa, Alg., D 14
.....	Amogson, India, J 13
850	Amoltepec, Oax., M 7
	Amonea, see Villa Thaumaturgo, W. Braz.
2835	Amos, Quebec, D 4
	Amoy, see Szeming, China
659	Amozoc, Pueb., I 7
8444	Amposta, Spain, H 18
.....	Amrabad, India, L 12
46832	Amraoti, India, J 10
6387	Amriswyl, Switz., C 19
391010	Amritsar, India, C 8
3000	Amrûs, Egypt, F 10
.....	Amshûl, Egypt, L 17
500	Amsoldingen, Switz., J 9
.....	Amsteg, Switz., J 15
.....	Amstelveen, Neth., G 14
781665	Amsterdam, Neth., C 4, F 14
150	Amsterdam, U.S. Afr., G 21
.....	Amtia, Nepal, F 20
.....	Amugersafin, Mor., H 7
20000	Amul, Iran, E 7
.....	Amulree, Scotland, K 17
.....	Amwas, Palestine, M 7
.....	Amzrou, Morocco, J 6
15000	Ana, Iraq, L 17
.....	Anab, Palestine, P 7
.....	Anadia, Brazil, H 24
105	Anahola, Hawaii, B 5
.....	Anajatuba, Brazil, F 18
10607	Anajaz, Brazil, E 13
20600	Anakapalle, India, L 16
.....	Anako, Eth., F 6
9200	Anand, India, I 6
7000	Anantapur, India, M 10
16565	Anapa, Sov Un., O 10
8204	Anapolis, Braz., K 14
8000	Anar, Iran, L 10
.....	Anarak, Iran, I 9
.....	Anardara, Afg., I 16
.....	Anascau, Ire., O 3
285	Anata, Palestine, M 10
.....	Añatuya, Argentina, I 14
511	Ancacato, Bolivia, J 7
375	Ancaster, Ontario, M 10
3492	Ancenis, France, J 7
.....	Anchow, China, D 16
472	Anco, Peru, M 12
2000	Ancober, Eth., I 10
1097	Ancón, Peru, L 8
66750	Ancona, Italy, F 13
9251	Ancoraimes, Bolivia, G 2
4078	Ancud, Chile, B 19
1328	Ancuya, Colombia, L 4
873	Ancy-le-Franc, France, I 17
6784	Andacollo, Chile, K 3
2309	Andahuaylas, Peru, M 14
.....	Andajes, Peru, K 8
.....	Andalgala, Argentina, I 10
2351	Andamarca, Bolivia, K 5
588	Andaray, Peru, P 15
535	Andeer, Switzerland, K 20
.....	Andelfingen, Switz., C 15
726	Andelot, France, I 20
.....	Andenäs, Norway, C 14
7543	Andenne, Belgium, N 15
2000	Anderaccia, Eth., L 5
1082	Andermatt, Switz., K 15
10111	Andernach, Germany, K 3
5991	Andes, Colombia, H 8
.....	Andijan, Iran, H 7
20000	Andkhui, Afghanistan, E 19
.....	Andoas, Ecuador, D 8
600	Andorra, Andorra, D 19
9692	Andover, England, M 15
342	Andover, N. B., F 4
6113	Andraix, Spain, J 21
.....	Andreas, England, E 7
55786	Andria, Italy, J 18
1831	Andrijevica, Yugo., L 13
.....	Androka, Madag., P 22
2069	Andros, Grc., P 20
24765	Andújar, Spain, M 11
1847	Anduze, France, O 18
1606	Anebta, Palestine, J 8
.....	Anekal, India, O 10
279	Aneroid, Sask, Q 6
.....	Anfast Beni Habbein, Egypt, L 13
8196	Angangueo, Michoa., N 14
.....	Ange, Sweden, J 14
.....	Angeles, Baja Cal., G 7
100	Angeline, Quebec, Q 17
8602	Angermünde, Ger., F 13
87988	Angers, France, J 8
294	Angers, Quebec, P 10
....	Angical, Brazil, I 17
.....	Angkor (ruins), Fr. In. Chn., P 6
165	Angliers, Quebec, H 1
100	Angmagssalik, Grnld, Q 4
3000	Angoche (António Enea), Moz., N 21
12398	Angol, Chile, Q 3
1000	Angolola, Eth., I 10
	Angora, see Ankara, Tur.
163	Angostura, Chile, H 4
160	Angostura, Chile, N 4
1704	Angostura, Colombia, G 8
38915	Angoulême, France, M 10
.....	Angra dos Reis, Brazil, N 17
.....	Angrui, Sp. Mor., D 7
.....	Angualasto, Argentina, K 5
3500	Anguhran, Iran, P 12
700	Angul, India, J 18
264	Angus, Ontario, I 10
25000	Anhai, China, K 18
1021	Anhee, Belgium, O 14
4336	Anhialo, Bul., L 23
.....	Ani, Japan, D 23
.....	Anin, Palestine, I 9
.....	Anina, Rom., J 15
585	Anizy le Chateau, Fr., G 16
3000	Anjanvei, India, L 6
18000	Anjar, India, H 3
.....	Anjar, Transjordan, K 14
13887	Anjeles, Chile, P 3
.....	Anjengo, India, Q 9
1585	Anjika, Japan, L 21
157242	Ankara (Angora), Tur., D 7
.....	Ankarsrum, Sweden, O 15
.....	Ankate, Eth., H 8
.....	Ankenes Norway,, D 15
	Anking, see Hwaining, China
16000	Anklam, Germany, D 12
10200	Ankleswar, India, I 6
	Ankober, see Ancober, Eth.
956	Anlier, Belgium, Q 18
.....	Anlu (Teian), China, H 14
.....	Anna, Sov. Un., K 13
20000	Annaberg, Germany, K 11
.....	Annacarriga, Ire., L 11
.....	Annacloy, N. Ire., E 24
.....	Annagassan, Ire., H 21
.....	Annaghdown, Ire., J 8
28000	An Najaf, Iraq, O 20
5000	Annaka, Japan, K 19
.....	Annalong, N., Ire., G 23
6302	Annan, Scotland, Q 19
12205	Annandale, Australia, I 16
782	Annapolis Royal, N. S., M 9
1466	Anna Regina, Br. Gu., A 6
.....	Annaszorg, N. Gu., B 9
.....	Annbank, Scotland, O 14
20289	Annecy, France, L 22
328	Annefors, Sweden, L 13
.....	Annestown, Ire., O 17
7200	Annigeri, India, M 8
.....	Anning, China, K 5
15427	Annonay, France, M 18
2000	Annotta, Jamaica, J 8
2459	Anolaima, Colombia, I 10
1826	Anori, Colombia, G 9
4400	Anping, For., L 20
12580	Ans, Belgium, M 17
23000	Ansbach, Germany, N 8
.....	Anse d'Ennery, Sta. Lucia, H 24
1240	Anseremme, Belgium, O 14
18284	Anshú, Kor., C 23
.....	Anshun, China, J 8
.....	Ansichow, China, C 2
100	Anson, Ontario, I 17
1542	Anta, Peru, M 16
2127	Antabamba, Peru, N 15
38520	Antakiya (Antioche), Tur., I 11
1000	Antalo, Eth., E 10
22993	Antalya (Adalia), Tur., H 5
	Antananarivo, see Tananarive, Madag.
37231	Antequera, Spain, O 11
421	Anthee, Belgium, O 13
.....	Anthony Lagoon Station, Australia, E 15
.....	Anthony's Well, Austl., H 14
26071	Antibes, France, O 25
2157	Antigonish, N. S., J 19
14067	Antigua, Guatemala, G 4
443	Antigua, Ver., H 10
375	Antiguo Morelos, Tam., J 17
842	Antilhue, Chile, R 3
1244	Antilla, Cuba, M 22
.....	Antillas, Argentina, H 11
	Antioche, see Antakiya, Tur.
3810	Antioquia, Colombia, G 8
133	Antler, Saskatchewan, R 11
49106	Antofagasta, Chile, F 3
4270	Antoing, Belgium, N 7
.....	Antolo, Arg., M 17
1491	Anton, Panama, Q 21
.....	Antonio Prado, Braz., P 12
.....	Anton Recio, Cuba, J 10
17645	Antony, France, C 4
2000	Antrim, N. Ire., D 21
4001	Antrodoco, Italy, H 12
220587	Antung, Manch., C 22
	Antwerp, see Anvers, Bel.
4000	An Uaimh (Navan), Ire., H 20
.....	Anundsjö, Sweden, I 16
.....	Anupgarh, India, E 6
8975	Anuradhapure, Cey., Q 13
277929	Anvers (Antwerp) Bel., K 11, Q 8
1504	Anyox, B. C., H 7
.....	Anyuan, China, K 16
10872	Anzaldo, Bolivia, I 8
504	Anzánigo, Spain, E 16
4843	Anzio, Italy, I 11
1394	Aoiz, Spain, D 15
77100	Aomori, Japan, H 12
12600	Aosta, Italy, C 1
.....	Aouguelmin, Morocco, L 1
.....	Aoulef, Algeria, O 14
.....	Å. Oussera, Algeria, D 16
3959	Āpam, Hid., H 6
.....	Aparicio, Argentina, Q 16
3614	Apaseo, Guan., M 13
.....	Apatahy, Brazil, E 11
.....	Apatin, Yugo., J 12
759	Apatzingán, Michoa., O 9
67080	Apeldoorn, Neth., G 19
3312	Apia, Colombia, I 7
3500	Apia, Samoa, K 20
....	Apiahy, Brazil, O 14
1427	Apipilulco, Guer., P 16
6768	Apizaco, Tlax., H 6
840	Aplao, Peru, P 15
.....	Apody, Brazil, G 23
223	Apohaqui, N. B., J 9
28000	Apolda, Germany, J 9
1886	Apolo, Bolivia, F 3
.....	Apora, Brazil, I 22
1300	Apostoles, Argentina, I 23
.....	Appelbo, Sweden, L 12
.....	Appelscha, Neth., D 20
4876	Appenzell, Switz., E 19
164	Appin, Ontario, O 5
6498	Appingedam, Neth., B 23
1618	Appleby, England, D 12
1033	Applecross, Scotland, H 9
.....	Appledore, England, M 7
807	Applegarth, Scotland, P 19
527	Apple Hill, Ontario, E 25
417	Apple River, N. S., K 11
580	Apples, Switz., K 3
.....	Appleton, Ontario, E 21
961	Approuague, Fr. Gu., B 12
8120	Apricena, It., I 17
.....	Aprilia, Italy, I 11
150	Apsley, Tasmania, D 7
6467	Apt, France, O 21
.....	A. Puisoye, Argentina, I 20
427	Apulco, Hid., G 6
.....	Apurema, Brazil, D 12
.....	Aputa, Japan, G 12
1500	Aqaba, Pal., (Turkey Map) R 9
	Aqsu, see Wensuh, Sink.
1041	Aquia, Peru, J 8
5929	Aquidauana, Brazil, M 9
38730	Aquila, Italy, H 13
599	Aquila, Switzerland, L 17
5000	Aquin, Haiti, J 12
520	Aquio, Bolivia, K 12
499	Aquismón, S. L. P., K 17
.....	Arababad, Iran, I 12
842	Arabate, Bolivia, K 10
6782	Arabkir, Tur., F 13
3591	Araca, Bolivia, I 5
50670	Aracajú, Brazil, I 23
4706	Aracataca, Colombia, C 12
17013	Araçatuba, Brazil, M 12
6803	Aracati, Brazil, F 23
7737	Aracena, Spain, M 8
77255	Arad, Romania, I 15
.....	Aradan, Iran, G 8
.....	Arafali, Erit., B 10
3031	Aragua de Barcelona, Venezuela, E 16
3234	Aragua de Maturin, Venezuela, D 18
16086	Araguary, Brazil, L 14
2500	Arai, Japan, N 16
.....	Arakaka, Br. Gu., A 5
.....	Arak el Menshiyeh, Pal., O 5
861	Aramberri, N. L., H 15
494	Arancay, Peru, J 8
9168	Aranda de Duero, Sp., F 12
7254	Arandas, Jal., L 9
.....	Arangjelovac, Yugo., K 14
5000	Arani, Bolivia, I 8
23646	Aranjũez, Spain, I 12
.....	Araouan, Fr. W. Afr., H 6
.....	Arapary, Braz., F 24
705	Arapata, Bolivia, H 5
1734	Arapey, Uruguay, G 16
599	Arapiles, Spain, H 9
.....	Arapua, Brazil, M 11
.....	Araquita, Venezuela, D 14
735	Ararah, Palestine, I 8
.....	Ararangua, Brazil, P 13
.....	Araras, Brazil, F 4
.....	Araras, Brazil, H 2
7345	Araras, Brazil, N 15
4914	Ararat, Australia, P 18
.....	Araria, India, F 21
.....	Araruama, Brazil, N 18
.....	Arash, Morocco, E 8
.....	Arassuahi, Brazil, K 19
.....	Arata, Argentina, O 12
500	Aratapu, N. Z., C 15
.....	Aratuhype, Braz., J 21
1071	Arauca, Colombia, G 18
.....	Araucaria, Brazil, O 13
2707	Aráuco, Chl., P 2
1775	Araure, Venezuela, E 9
10216	Araxá, Brazil, L 15
689	Arbaouat, Algeria, G 14
.....	Arba, Eth., J 11
1056	Arbelaez, Colombia, I 11
4000	Arbil (Erbil), Iraq, I 20
4772	Arboga, Sweden, M 10
8638	Arbon, Switz., C 19 42
.....	Arborfield, Sask., L 10
400	Arborg, Manitoba, O 16
1046	Arbra, Swe., K 14
17637	Arbroath, Scotland, K 28
13135	Arcachon, France, N 6
324	Arcadia, Nova Scotia, Q 8
.....	Arcadia Valley, Alberta, N 24
3223	Arcen, Netherlands, J 20
774	Arch, Switzerland, F 8
.....	Archag, Tur., F 19
8006	Archena, Spain, M 15
.....	Archibald, B. C., Q 17
2000	Archidona, Ecuador, B 8
10214	Archidona, Spain, O 11
2666	Arcis-sur-Aube, Fr., H 17
2126	Arco, Italy, C 8
563	Arcola, Sask., Q 11
257	Arcopongo, Bolivia, H 7
15748	Arcos de la Frontera, Spain, O 9
11000	Arcot, India, N 12
.....	Arctic Red River, Mack. E 3
16200	Arcueil, Fr., C 5
.....	Ardagh, Ire., I 15
.....	Ardagh, Ire., N 8
500	Ardara, Ire., D 11
.....	Ardardo, Som., M 19
.....	Ardatov, Sov. Un., I 14
.....	Ardatov, Sov. Un., I 16
.....	Ardcharnick, Scot., F 12
.....	Ardchattan, Scot., K 11
44808	Ardebil, Iran, C 4
1730	Ardee, Ire., H 20
.....	Ardekan, Iran, J 9
275	Arden, Manitoba, G 19
303	Arden, Man., Q 14
947	Ardentes, France, K 13
615	Ardetz, Switzerland, I 24
.....	Ardfert, Ire., N 4
.....	Ardfinnan, Ire., N 14
.....	Ardglass, N. Ire., F 25
10000	Ardistan, Iran, I 7
.....	Ardlussa, Scotland, M 9
.....	Ardmillan, N. Ire., E 24
.....	Ardmore, Ire., P 15
.....	Ardnacrosse, Scot., O 10
.....	Ardock, Australia, J 19
1320	Ardon, Spain, E 10
1240	Ardon, Switzerland, N 7
.....	Ardrahan, Ire., K 9
.....	Ardre, Sweden, O 17
1346	Ardres, France, E 13
.....	Ardrishaig, Scotland, M 10
13736	Ardrossan, Scotland, N 13
.....	Ards Beg., Ire., B 12
.....	Ardslavloch, Scotland, J 9
.....	Ardvourlie, Scotland, F 5
.....	Are, Sweden, I 11
.....	Areia, Brazil, G 24
.....	Areião, Brazil, F 14
150	Arelee, Sask., M 6
.....	Arenal, Argentina, G 11
132	Arenales, Argentina, N 16
10403	Arendal, (Arndal) Nor., N 6
4704	Arendo, Sp., E 14
5469	Arendonck, Belgium, K 15
.....	Arendskerke, Neth., J 9
.....	Arenillas, Cuba, L 17
.....	Arenillas, Ecuador, E 3
	Arensburg, see Kuressaàre, Est.
5475	Arênys de Mar, Spain, F 21
.....	Areopolis, Grc., Q 16
7000	Arequa, Paraguay, N 7
79185	Arequipa, Peru, P 17
1069	Arequito, Argentina, M 15
3580	Arévalo, Spain, G 11
19000	Arezzo, Italy, G 10
5156	Arganda, Spain, I 13
3114	Arganil, Portugal, I 6
.....	Argaon, India, J 10
89	Argeles de Bigorre, Fr., Q 9
2463	Argele Sur Mer, Fr., Q 16
3079	Argenta, Italy, E 10
7129	Argentan, France, H 10
1712	Argentat, France, M 13
59314	Argenteuil, France, A 3
5504	Argenton, France, K 12
687	Argentré, Fr., I 7
.....	Argesan, Afghanistan, K 21
.....	Arghana, Tur., F 15
2762	Arghana Maden, Tur., G 15
.....	Argibah, Iran, K 4
10504	Argos, Greece, P 17
8293	Argostolion, Greece, P 14
.....	Argun, Iran, G 4
8438	Ariano di Puglia, Italy, J 16
.....	Arias, Argentina, M 14
14064	Arica, Chile, B 3
.....	A. Rich, Algeria, E 17
1500	Arichat, N. S., J 22
.....	Arifiji, Algeria, H 19
.....	Arigna, Ire., G 12
.....	Arin, Morocco, I 2
.....	Arinakaig, Scotland, H 11
5924	Ario, Michoa., O 10
....	Arippu, India, Q 13
....	Arirmat el Gueumad, Morocco, H 2
.....	Arisaig, Scotland, H 9
346	Arista, S. L. P., J 13
6000	Arita, Japan, N 3
1433	Arizpe, Son., E 12
.....	Arjeplog, Sweden, F 16
10416	Arjona, Colombia, C 9
281091	Arkhangelsk, Sov. Un., D 13
5000	Arklow, Ire., L 22
406	Arkona, Ontario, N 4
.....	Arkösund, Sweden, N 15
1501	Arlanc, France, M 17
4332	Arlecdon, England D10
29465	Arles, France, P 19
1593	Arles, Fr., Q 15
3221	Arlesheim, Switz., D 10
11634	Arlon, Belgium, Q 18
...	Armadale, Scotland, C 16

Pop.	Place Country Index
.....	Armadale, Scotland, I 8
4554	Armadale, Scotland, M 18
544	Armadillo, S. L. P., K 13
7356	Armagh, N. Ire., F 20
410	Armagh, Quebec, L 23
.....	Armat Urika, Morocco, I 5
83677	Armavir, Sov. Un., O 14
5408	Armenia, Colombia, H 8
29673	Armenia, Colombia, I 8
22704	Armentières, France, E 15
6794	Armidale, Australia, M 22
.....	Armoy, N. Ire., B 21
1000	Armstrong, Arg., M 15
977	Armstrong, B. C., O 16
204	Arnager, Denmark, R 23
.....	Arnäs, Sweden, I 17
200	Arnaud, Manitoba, R 16
.....	Arnborg, Denmark, I 6
	Arndal, see Arendal, Nor.
5459	Arneiroz, Brazil, G 21
83999	Arnhem, Neth., H 19
.....	Arnisdale, Scotland, I 10
.....	Arniwala, India, D 7
14470	Arnold, England, H 16
3895	Arnprior, Ontario, D 20
22000	Arnstadt, Germany, K 9
205	Arnstein, Ont., C 10
1643	Aroa, Venezuela, C 10
6771	Aroche, Spain, M 8
.....	Aroegas, U.S. Afr., K 8
.....	Arolla, Switzerland, O 9
2418	Arolsen, Germany, I 6
6250	Aromaó Sicasica, Bolivia, I 5
4998	Arona, Italy, C 4
310	Aroostook Jc., N. B., E 4
3792	Arosa, Switz., I 20
1000	Arosa, Switzerland, I 20
.....	Arouca, Portugal, G 6
3578	Arpajon, France, H 13
.....	Arpalli, India, E 13
2647	Arpino, Italy, I 13
298	Arquata del Tronto, It., H 13
2260	Arquillos, Spain, M 13
2196	Arrabeh, Palestine, J 9
48922	Arrah, India, G 17
.....	Arraneh, Palestine, I 10
31488	Arras, France, E 15
938	Arreau, France, Q 10
.....	Arrecipal, Ecuador, J 20
48	Arrilalah, Australia, H 19
.....	Arrild, Denmark, M 5
3474	Arronches, Portugal, K 7
2585	Arrou, France, I 11
178	Arrowhead, B. C., O 17
.....	Arrowhenua, N. Z., N 10
.....	Arrowsmith, B. C., Q 11
230	Arrowtown, N. Z., O 5
205	Arrowwood, Alta., N 21
521	Arroyito, Argentina, L 13
.....	Arroyo Baru, Arg., L 19
.....	Arroyo Blanco, Cuba, N 21
8402	Arroyo del Puerco, Sp., J 8
991	Arroyo Grande, Ur., N 17
20000	Arroyos y Esteros, Par., N 8
.....	Arrozal, Brazil, F 7
2375	Arsiero, Italy, C 9
3100	Arsila, Sp. Mor., D 6
.....	Arsk, Sov. Un., I 19
.....	Arsuf, Palestine, K 6
7468	Arta, Greece, O 14
6005	Artá, Spain, J 22
.....	Artaki, Tur., C 2
.....	Artan, Sask., N 11
13084	Artemisa, Cuba, H 5
55165	Artemovsk, Sov. Un., M 11
5032	Arth, Switzerland, G 15
1883	Arthabaska, Quebec, N 20
937	Arthur, Ontario, K 8
.....	Arthurstown, Ire., O 19
16500	Artigas (San Eugenio), Uruguay, E 19
61	Artland, Sask., L 4
.....	Arum, Netherlands, C 17
.....	Arumateua, Brazil, F 14
2489	Arundel, England, N 16
.....	Arundel, U.S. Afr., M 14
.....	Aruppul Kottai, India, P11
.....	Arvagh, Ire., G 15
.....	Arvellos, Brazil, F 3
4530	Arvida, Que., F 21
862	Arvidsjaur, Sweden, G 17
7979	Arvika, Sweden, M 11
.....	Aryamun, Egypt, C 7
11000	Arzamas, Sov. Un., I 15
5160	Arzeu, Algeria, C 12
10396	Arzua, Spain, D 6
.....	Aš, see Asch, Ger.
872	Asaa, Denmark, D 13
.....	Asadabad, Iran, F 14
.....	Asalta, Egypt, O 24
31286	Asansol, India, H 20
.....	Asarne, Sweden, J 12
.....	Asaru, Iran, N 15
.....	Asbach, Germany, O 11
5711	Asbestos, Quebec, O 20
	Ascalon, see Askalan, Pal.
4784	Ascención, Bolivia, G 14
426	Ascension, N. L., H 15
2007	Asch, Belgium, I 7
36000	Aschaffenburg, Ger., M 6
28000	Aschersleben, Ger., I 9
2540	Ascó, Spain, G 18
18500	Ascoli Piceno, Italy, G 13
1626	Ascona, Switzerland, N 16
4000	Ascope, Peru, H 4
296	Ascotán, Chile, D 6
.....	Aseksem, Algeria, Q 19
1097	Asele, Sweden, H 15
1402	Asen, Sweden, K 12
.....	Asfûn, Egypt, P 23
7130	Ashburton, N. Z., N 11
5093	Ashby-de-la-Zouch, Eng. I 15
575	Ashcroft, B. C., O 14
	Ashdod, see Esdud, Pal.
.....	Asheda, Sweden, P 14
300	Ashern, Manitoba, O 15
15239	Ashford, England, M 22
.....	Ashford, Ire., I 7
.....	Ashford, Ire., N 8
43896	Ashikaga, Japan, K 20
.....	Ashio, Japan, K 20
5500	Ashiya, Japan, M 4
126580	Ashkhabad, Sov. Un. Asia, J 8
.....	Ashkirk, Scotland, O 21
.....	Ashment, Egypt, M 14
70	Ashmont, Alberta, J 22
.....	Ashmûn, Egypt, G 12
.....	Ashshi, Egypt, O 23
11400	Ashta, India, I 10
.....	Ashti, India, K 8
51573	Ashton, England, G 13
818	Asillo, Peru, O 19
.....	Asiret el Hatab, Pal., K 10
.....	Asirgarh, India, I 9
3960	Asisieh, Tur., E 5
.....	Askalan (Ascalon), Pal., N 3
461	Askar, Palestine, K 10
.....	Askeaton, Ire., M 8
7845	Asker, Norway, B 4
2102	Askersund, Sweden, N 13
2948	Askevold, Norway, K 3
.....	Askin, Sov. Un., H 23
.....	Askole, India, A 9
.....	Asmanjird, Iran, N 8
85000	Asmara, Erit., A 9
604	Asnaes, Denmark, J 18
71831	Asnières, France, A 4
2340	Asola. Italy, D 7
.....	Asosa, Eth., H 4
.....	Asp, Denmark, G 3
.....	Aspang, Ger., R 16
.....	Asparjan, Iran, K 7
5889	Aspasica, Colombia, E 13
3239	Aspatria, England, D 10
1693	Asperen, Netherlands, H 15
498	Aspres, Fr., N 21
214	Asquith, Sask., M 6
655	Assab, Erit., D 14
.....	Assale, Eth., C 11
.....	Assaye, India, J 9
10219	Assche, Belgium, L 10
394	Asselborn, Lux., P 20
17652	Assen, Netherlands, D 22
5479	Assenede, Belgium, Q 3
1559	Assens, Denmark, J 11
4842	Assens, Denmark, L 10
1202	Assesse, Belgium, O 15
.....	Assing, Denmark, I 5
1349	Assiniboia, Sask., Q 7
5353	Assisi, Italy, G 11
.....	Assissi, Neth. Guiana, C 10
.....	Assú, Brazil, G 23
769	Astafforť, France, O 10
.....	Astakos, Greece, P 14
20000	Asterabad, (Esterabad), Iran, E 9
25042	Asti, Italy, D 3
.....	Astica, Argentina, K 8
.....	Aston Manor, Eng., J 14
3000	Astor, India, A 8
14523	Astorga, Spain, E 9
1785	Astorp, Sweden, Q 11
253655	Astrakhan, Sov. Un., N 19
.....	Astray, Cuba, N 19
.....	Astros, Greece, M 9
2503	Astudillo, Spain, E 11
.....	Asturias, Argentina, O 15
.....	Asunción, Bolivia, C 4
.....	Asunción, Mex., H 3
100000	Asuncion, Paraquay, N 7
4041	Asunción, Venezuela, B 18
746	Asunta, Bolivia, H 6
16366	Aswân, Egypt, R 24
62400	Asyût, Egypt, L 18
.....	Atabet el Gisr, Egypt, F 23
.....	Atacames, Ecuador, A 3
.....	Atakpame, Fr. W. Afr., J 7
3318	Atalante, Greece, O 17
150	Ataliva, Argentina, K 15
4269	Ataques, Uruguay, G 20
4557	Atar, Fr. W. Afr., G 2
.....	Atashkardeh, Iran, J 13
.....	Atbasar, Sov. Un. Asia, H 11
3069	Ateca, Spain, G 15
1555	Atén, Bolivia, F 3
.....	Atens, Germany, D 5
3370	Atessa, Italy, H 15
2731	Atfî, Egypt, L 14
34900	Atgaon, India, J 8
10186	Ath, Belgium, N 9
.....	Athabaska, Alberta, I 20
.....	Athboy, Ire., I 18
910	Athenry, Ire., J 9
495490	Athénai (Athens), Grc., P 18
722	Athens, Ontario, H 21
301	Atherley, Ontario, H 12
.....	Athleague, Ire., I 12
.....	Athlit, Palestine, N 9
6617	Ath Luain (Athlone), Ire., J 13
.....	Athni, India, L 8
1050	Athol, N. Z., P 5
4858	Athos, Grc., N 19
3500	Athy, Ire., G 13
.....	Athy Moone, Ire., K 19
1685	Atienza, Spain, G 13
.....	Atilla, Bolivia, M 8
.....	Atina, See Pazar, Tur.
.....	A. Tindjoubart, Alg., P 17
10000	Atkarsk, Sov. Un., K 16
440	Atlin, B. C., B 5
17034	Atlixco, Pueb., I 6
.....	Atosanobori, Japan, F 14
9023	Atotonilco, Jal., M 9
2255	Atotonilco, Hid., G 6
5421	Atoyac, Jal., M 6
3372	Atoyac de Alvarez, Guer., A 3
.....	Atpadi, India, L 8
500	Atran, Sweden, P 11
.....	Atreucó, Argentina, P 13
3786	Atri, Italy, H 14
25000	Atsuta, Japan, M 15
.....	Attanagh, Ire., L 16
.....	Attara, Palestine, J 9
.....	Attara, Palestine, L 9
.....	Attarus, Transjordan, O 14
1097	Attert, Belgium, Q 18
889	Attigney, France, G 18
1656	Attil, Palestine, J 8
713	Attinghausen, Switz., I 15
.....	Attleborough, Eng., I 23
.....	Attock, India, B 6
.....	Attopeu, Fr. In. Ch., P 9
.....	Attymon, Ire., J 10
2367	Atures, Ven., K 12
3128	Atvidaberg, Sweden, O 14
236	Atwoods Brooks, N. S., R 9
10000	Atyrá, Par., N 7
2589	Atzalán, Ver., G 8
.....	Atzcapotzaltongo, Méx., H 11
.....	Auasc, Eth., J 10
13085	Aubagne, France, P 21
.....	Aubakhadleh, Br. Som., I15
3020	Aubel, Belgium, M 19
7378	Aubenas, France, N 18
55714	Aubervilliers, Fr., A 6
3820	Aubigny-sur-Nere, Fr., J 14
9387	Aubin, France, N 14
1559	Aubonne, Switzerland, L 3
.....	Auburn, Ire., I 14
125	Auburn, Nova Scotia, L 11
228	Auburn, Ontario, K 6
6324	Aubusson, France, L 13
12567	Auch, France, P 10
.....	Auchengray, Scotland, N 18
6624	Auchinleck, Scotland, O 15
.....	Auchmithie, Scotland, K 22
.....	Auchnagatt, Scotland, G 23
3098	Auchterarder, Scot., L 17
1459	Auchterless, Scot., G 22
106800	Auckland, N. Z., D 17
3128	Audegem, Belgium, R 6
6379	Audenarde, Belgium, M 8
1035	Audenge, France, N 7
4196	Audierne, France, H 1
1368	Audley, England, H 13
510	Augathella, Australia, J 20
.....	Augedal, Norway, E 3
.....	Augher, N. Ire., E 17
.....	Aughnacloy, N. Ire., E 18
.....	Aughrim, Ire., J 11
.....	Aughrim, Ire., L 22
.....	Augila (Oasis), Libya, F 15
176575	Augsburg, Germany, P 8
647	August, Switzerland, C 10
81	Augusta, Australia, O 4
17672	Augusta, Italy, O 17
982	Augustenborg, Den., N 10
12156	Augustów, Pol., H 22
.....	Aulam, Palestine, H 12
.....	Auldearn, Scotland, G 17
.....	Auldgirth, Scotland, P 18
.....	Auld's Ponds, Austl., D 13
2796	Aulendorf, Germany, Q 6
1730	Aulla, Italy, E 6
.....	Aultbea, Scotland, F 10
536	Aultsville, Ontario, F 23
6781	Aumale, Algeria, C 17
1842	Aumale, France, F 13
840	Aumont, France, N 16
925	Auneuil, Fr., G 13
29288	Aurangabad, India, J 8
.....	Auras, Cuba, M 20
7154	Auray, France, I 4
2319	Aure, Norway, I 7
6121	Aurich, Germany, D 4
17643	Aurillac, France, N 15
2732	Auronzo, Italy, B 11
.....	Aurora, Brazil, G 22
2726	Aurora, Ontario, J 12
78	Ausser Ferrera, Switz., K 20
.....	Aussim, Egypt, H 13
.....	Austin, Australia, K 5
264	Austin, Manitoba, Q 14
.....	Austral Downs Station, Australia, F 15
.....	Australia, Coa., E 9
1505	Auterive, France, P 12
395	Authier, Quebec, D 3
10723	Autlán, Jal., N 4
500	Autrey, Fr., J 20
14045	Autun, France, J 18
955	Auvermier, Switz., H 5
15000	Aux Cayes, Haiti, J 11
24282	Auxerre, France, I 16
5343	Auxonne, France, J 20
1183	Auzances, France, L 14
25000	Ava, Bur., N 22
.....	Availles, Fr., L 11
5387	Avallon, France, J 17
194	Avalos, Zac., G 11
1311	Avanzada, Chile, F 4
10533	Avaré, Brazil, N 14
.....	Avarik, Iran, G 3
210	Avegno, Switz., N 16
12735	Aveiro, Portugal, H 5
.....	Aveiros, Brazil, F 9
399021	Avellaneda, Arg., N 19
18300	Avellino, Italy, J 15
1606	Avenches, Switz., I 6
1355	Avenhorn, Neth., E 14
125	Avening, Ontario, I 10
9507	Avereest, Neth., E 21
22692	Aversa, Italy, J 14
5105	Avesnes, France, F 17
.....	Avia-Terai, Argentina, H 16
.....	Aviraya, Bolivia, J 6
59472	Avignon, France, O 20
20261	Avila, Ecuador, B 8
.....	Avila, Spain, H 11
18037	Avilés, Spain, C 9
1984	Aviz, Portugal, K 6
1049	Avning, Denmark, G 13
108	Avola, B. C., N 16
19702	Avola, Italy, O 17
.....	Avon-Downs, Austl., G 21
296	Avonlea, Sask., Q 8
418	Avonmore, Ontario, E 24
220	Avonport, N. S., L 13
6803	Avranches, France, H 7
.....	Awanui, N. Z., A 14
.....	Awaz, Iran, J 14
938	Awertah, Palestine, K 10
1193	Ax, Fr., Q 13
.....	Axalp, Switzerland, J 12
.....	Axalpan, Pueb., J 8
5826	Axel, Neth., N 9, Q 4
5000	Axum, Eth., C 9
7267	Ay, France, G 17
2481	Ayabaca, Peru, F 3
26633	Ayacucho, Arg., P 19
18275	Ayacucho, Peru, M 13
.....	Ayaguz (Sergiopol), Sov. Un., Asia, I 12
12136	Ayamonte, Spain, N 7
.....	Ayan, Sov. Un. Asia, F 19
1624	Ayapel, Colombia, E 9
.....	Ayas, Tur., I 10
.....	Ayash, Tur., I 9
5740	Ayata, Bolivia, G 3
11987	Aydin (Aidin), Tur., F 2
1117	Aye, Belgium, O 16
2046	Ayent, Switzerland, M 8
500	Ayer, Switzerland, N 9
2518	Ayerbe, Spain, E 16
465	Ayers Cliff, Quebec, R 19
.....	Aylen Lake, Ontario, D 16
13382	Aylesbury, England, K 17
122	Aylesbury, Sask., O 7
465	Aylesford, N. S., L 11
2476	Aylmer, Ontario, O 7
3115	Aylmer, Quebec, P 9
4690	Ayoayo, Bolivia, I 4
3426	Ayo el Chico, Jal., M 9
300	Ayoma, Bolivia, K 8
2912	Ayoquesco, Oax., M 9
6634	Ayora, Spain, K 16
40412	Ayr, Scotland, O 14
761	Ayr, Ontario, M 8
.....	Ayrão, Brazil, E 4
32	Ayton, Australia, D 20
462	Ayton, Ontario, J 7
1413	Ayton, Scotland, M 24
50000	Ayudhya, Siam, P 3
.....	Ayun Kussabon, Pal., O 5
3028	Ayutla, Jal., M 4
2794	Ayutla, Guer., R 17
13088	Ayvalik (Aivalik), Tur., D 1
3149	Aywaille, Belgium, N 17
.....	Azabet Abu Hagar, Eg., D 18
.....	Azabet Keleshi, Egypt, C 11
.....	Azaghar, Morocco, I 3
2619	Azángaro, Peru, O 19
194	Azapa, Chile, B 3
.....	Azapolskoe, Sov. Un., C 15
.....	Azazi, Egypt, E 19
.....	Azebiyeh et Tahta, Syr., C13
10351	Azemmour, Mor., G 4
.....	Azen, Ontario, R 24
.....	Aziar el Hammar, Mor., F 8
.....	Aziriyeh, Palestine, N 10
14768	Azogues, Ecuador, D 4
10500	Azov, Sov. Un., N 12
1593	Azrou, Morocco, G 8
5704	Azua, Dom. Rep., J 14
16577	Azuaga, Spain, L 9
.....	Azufrera, Peru, G 1
40000	Azul, Argentina, P 17
6141	Azurduy, Bolivia, L 12
1305	Azuzaqui, Bolivia, I 13

B

Pop.	Place Country Index
.....	Ba, Fiji Is., P 15
.....	Baadsfjord, Norway, A 24
5000	Baalbek, Syria, L 11
5892	Baar, Switzerland, F 15
3119	Baarle Nassau, Neth., J 14
12144	Baarn, Netherlands, G 16
.....	Baarse, Denmark, M 20
.....	Bab, Syria, I 12
6367	Baba, Ecuador, C 3
.....	Baba Ahmed, Iran, K 5
.....	Baba-Buruh, Tur., D 1
4781	Babadag, Romania, J 24
10000	Babahan, Iran, L 5
13169	Babahoyo, Ecuador, C 3
.....	Baba Kaless, Tur., D 1
.....	Babanna, Syria, J 11
.....	Bab Gebnan, Sp. Mor., D 8
.....	Babine, B. C., I 10
30000	Babol (Barfrush), Iran, E 8
26900	Babraich, India, F 15
1728	Baca, Yuc., E 22
.....	Bacabal, Brazil, G 8
28	Bacalar, Q. R., I 23
31264	Bacău, Romania, I 21
433	Bacavachi, Son., K 13
.....	Baccan, Nicaragua, H 14
5605	Baccarat, France, H 23
264	Baccaro, Nova Scotia, R 10
425	Bachimeto, Sin., O 16
.....	Back, Scotland, D 7
.....	Backergunge, India, I 24
10069	Backnang, Germany, O 6
.....	Baco, Eth., N 6
.....	Bacton, England, I 24
20606	Bacup, England, F 13
.....	Badaingarh, India, I 18
55869	Badajoz, Spain, K 8
48284	Badalona, Spain, G 21
.....	Bad Asia, Afg., H 22
.....	Badcall, Scotland, D 12
725	Baddeck, Nova Scotia, H 22
.....	Baddo, Baluchistan, Q 21
22217	Baden, Aus., H 8
31000	Baden, Germany, O 4
850	Baden, Ontario, L 8
10113	Baden, Switz., D 13
3493	Bad Gastein, Ger., S 11
.....	Badis (Velez), Sp. Mor., D 8
.....	Badjoum, Algeria, M 15
.....	Badkhor, Iran, E 13
.....	Badluchrach, Scotland, F 11
9900	Badnera, India, J 11
5000	Badnur, India, I 11
.....	Badueín, Som., L 20
.....	Badueñ, Som., M 14
9849	Badulla, Cey., R 14
.....	Badvel, India, M 13
434	Baekke, Denmark, K 6
407	Baelum, Denmark, E 11
24830	Baena, Spain, M 11
.....	Baepenay, Brazil, M 16
.....	Baetas, Brazil, G4
.....	Baeza, Ecuador, B 7
18136	Baeza, Spain, M 12
2739	Baflo, Netherlands, B 22
4000	Bafq, Iran, K 10
8182	Bafra, Tur., B 12
5000	Baft, Iran, N 11
2791	Bagadó, Colombia, H 7
.....	Bagalan, Afghanistan, E 22
18000	Bagalkot, India, L 8
31763	Bagé, Brazil, Q 10
1900	Bagenalstown, Ire., M 18
3000	Bagh, Baluchistan, M 22
.....	Baghan, Iran, N 7
500000	Baghdad, Iraq, M 20
19051	Bagheria, Italy, N 13
.....	Bagh-i-God, Iran, F 11
.....	Baghin, Iran, L 11
.....	Baglat, Egypt, O 17
.....	Bagli, India, I 9
8880	Bagnères de Bigorre, Fr., Q 10
3820	Bagnéres-de-Luchon, Fr., Q 10
3918	Bagnes, Switzerland, O 7
5414	Bagneux, France, C 5
646	Bagnkop, Denmark, O 13
28112	Bagnolet, France, B 7
4450	Bagnols-sur-Ceze, Fr., O 19
.....	Bagonei, Iran, N 7
3248	Bagotville, Que., F 22
.....	Bagtsche, Tur., J 13
223	Baguachica, Peru, G 5
.....	Bagual, Argentina, O 11
.....	Bagur, Egypt, G 12
.....	Bagusta, Eth., G 6
491	Bahabón, Spain, F 1 2
20943	Bahawalpur, India, E 5
72002	Bahia Blanca, Arg., Q 15
5000	Bahia de Caráquez, Ec., B 2
3498	Bahiahonda, Col., A 16
1402	Bahia Honda, Cuba, H 5
.....	Bahia Laura, Arg., D 23
.....	Bahia Negra, Par., E 6
.....	Bahrah, Afghanistan, F 24
.....	Bahramabad, Iran, F 6
.....	Bahûs, Brazil, L 10
.....	Baia, see Salvador, Braz.
1475	Baia-de-Aramă, Rom., J 16
13882	Baia Mare, Romania, H 17
.....	Baião, Brazil, E 14
.....	Baibiene, Argentina, J 19
10339	Baiburt, Tur., D 15
3000	Baidoa, Eth., K 23
3500	Baie Saint Paul, Que., I 23
126	Baie Verte, N. B., I 13
467691	Baile Atha Cliath (Dublin), Ire., J 21
10045	Bailén, Spain, M 12
13271	Bailesti, Rom., K 17
1200	Bailieborough, Ire., G 18
1818	Bailieborough, Ont., J 15
8545	Bailleul, France, E 14
350	Bailly, France, B 1
.....	Bainbridge, N. Ire., F 21
4215	Bain-de-Bretagne, Fr., I 6
1242	Bains-les-Bains, Fr., I 22
43	Baintree, Alberta, N 21
.....	Baira Mar, Brazil, R 11
3858	Bairnsdale, Australia, Q 20
.....	Baixa Grande, Brazil, I 21
27940	Baja, Hungary, I 11
.....	Bajada Colorado, Arg., R 6
.....	Bajina Bašta, Yugo., K 12
.....	Bajo Hondo, Arg., Q 15
.....	Bakalat, Egypt, G 20
2706	Bakel, Netherlands, J 18
118	Baker Brook, N. B., C 2
218	Baker Settlement, N. S., O 12
.....	Bakhchisarai, Sov Un., O 8
.....	Bakirköy (Makri), Tur., H 3
.....	Bakkeveen, Neth., C 20
809347	Baku, Sov. Un., Q 21
.....	Bakuh, Iran, J 14
.....	Bala, Afghanistan, K 20
404	Bala, Ontario, F 11
1395	Bala, Wales, H 9
.....	Bala Bayan, Iran, L 9
71	Balaclava, Australia, M 17
.....	Balad, Som., R 17
.....	Balag, Iran, R 14
6031	Balaguer, Spain, F 18
50000	Balakhany-Sabuntshi, Sov. Un., Q 21
.....	Balallan, Scotland, E 6
791	Balancán, Tab., K 18
.....	Balanda, Sov. Un., K 15
1000	Balao, Ecuador, D 3
276	Bala Park, Ontario, F 11
.....	Balapur, India, J 10
26846	Balashov, Sov. Un., K 15
11547	Balassagyarmat, Hung., H 12
21000	Balasore, India, I 20
105	Balbarrup, Australia, O 5
2300	Balbriggan, Ire., I 22
41701	Balcarce, Argentina, Q 19
397	Balcarres, Sask, P 10
1690	Balclutha, N. Z., Q 7
6651	Balcic, Bul., K 23
.....	Balde, Argentina, M 9
3171	Baldock, England, K 19
.....	Balerno, Scotland, M 19
.....	Balestrand, Norway, K 5
911	Balfate, Honduras, E 11
64	Balfés Creek, Austl., F 19
.....	Balfour, U.S. Afr., G 19
1200	Balfron, Scotland, M 15
.....	Baliâna, Egypt, N 21
.....	Balic, Cuba, O 17
26699	Balikesir (Balikesri), Tur., D 2
.....	Balintore, Scotland, G 16
.....	Balk, Netherlands, D 17
15000	Balkh, Afghanistan, E 20
.....	Balkis, Tur., H 5
.....	Balla, Ire., H 7
.....	Ballagh, Ire., M 13
1300	Ballaghaderreen, Ire., H 10
.....	Ballaghkeen, Ire., N 21
.....	Balla Maden, Tur., D 2
1076	Ballantrae, Scotland, P 12
211	Ballantyne's Cove, N. S., I 19
35683	Ballarat, Australia, P 18
.....	Ballasalla, England, E 6
1542	Ballater, Scotland, I 20
.....	Ballaugh, England, E 7
.....	Balle, Denmark, H 8
6162	Ballenstedt, Germany, I 9
897	Balleroy, France, G 8
2445	Ballerup, Denmark, J 22
1466	Ballestero, Spain, K 14
16400	Ballia, India, G 17
4500	Ballina, Ire., G 7
.....	Ballina, Ire., L 11
.....	Ballinafad, Ire., G 11
.....	Ballinagore, Ire., L 22
.....	Ballinakill, Ire., L 17
600	Ballinamore, Ire., G 14
.....	Ballinascarty, Ire., Q 8
4909	Ballinasloe, Ire., J 12
.....	Ballincollig, Ire., P 10
.....	Ballincreagh, Ire., N 18
.....	Ballindine, Ire., I 8
.....	Ballingarry, Ire., N 9
.....	Ballinlough, Ire., H 10
2000	Ballinrobe, Ire., I 7
.....	Ballintober, Ire., H 11
.....	Ballintoy, N. Ire., B 21
.....	Ballintra, Ire., E 13
.....	Ballinyoo, Australia, K 4
.....	Ballitore, Ire., K 19
.....	Ballivian, Bolivia, C 4
.....	Ballivor, Ire., I 18
.....	Balloch, Scotland, M 14
.....	Ballon, Ire., M 19
.....	Ballybay, Ire., G 18
.....	Ballybofey, Ire., D 14
.....	Ballyboy, Ire., I 13
.....	Ballybrack, Ire., J 22
.....	Ballybrophy, Ire., L 15
.....	Ballybunnion, Ire., M 4
.....	Ballycanew, Ire., M 22
1729	Ballycastle, N. Ire., B 21
.....	Ballycastle, Ire., F 6
.....	Ballyclare, N. Ire., D 22
.....	Ballyclare Jc., N. Ire., D 22
400	Ballyconnell, Ire., G 15
.....	Ballycottin, Ire., Q 13
.....	Ballyduff, Ire., O 13
.....	Ballyfarnan, Ire., G 12
.....	Ballygarrett, Ire., M 22
.....	Ballygawley, N. Ire., E 18
.....	Ballyglass, Ire., F 4
.....	Ballyglunin, Ire., I 9
.....	Ballygowan, N. Ire., E 24
.....	Ballyhack, Ire., O 18
.....	Ballyhaise, Ire., G 16
.....	Ballyhalbert, N. Ire., E 25
400	Ballyhaunis, Ire., H 9
.....	Ballyheige, Ire., N 4
.....	Ballyhornan, N. Ire., F 25
.....	Ballyjamesduff, Ire., H 17
.....	Ballykelly, N. Ire., C 18
.....	Ballylaan, Ire., L 6
.....	Ballylanders, Ire., N 11
.....	Ballyleakin, Ire., J 17
.....	Ballylidin, Ire., I 6
.....	Ballylongford, Ire., M 6
.....	Ballylooby, Ire., N 13
.....	Ballymacaw, Ire., O 18
.....	Ballymahon, Ire., I 14
800	Ballymartin, N. Ire., G 23
11381	Ballymena, N. Ire., C 21
.....	Ballymoe, Ire., I 10
2952	Ballymoney, N. Ire., B 20
.....	Ballymore, Ire., I 15
.....	Ballymore Eustace, Ire., K 20
1000	Ballymote, Ire., G 10
.....	Ballynacorra, Ire., P 12
.....	Ballynacourty, Ire., O 15
.....	Ballynahinch, N. Ire., E 23
.....	Ballynahinch, Ire., I 4
.....	Ballynamult, Ire., O 14
.....	Ballyneen, Ire., Q 8
.....	Ballyorgan, Ire., N 11
.....	Ballyporeen, Ire., O 13
.....	Ballyragget, Ire., L 16
.....	Ballyroney, N. Ire., F 22
.....	Ballysadare, Ire., F 10
2395	Ballyshannon, Ire., E 12
.....	Ballyvaghan, Ire., K 7
.....	Ballyvourney, Ire., P 7
.....	Ballywalter, N. Ire., D 25
.....	Ballywilliam, Ire., N 19
628	Balmaclellan, Scot., Q 16
.....	Balmaha, Scotland, M 14
.....	Balmakiel, Scotland, C 13
180	Balmoral, Manitoba, P 16
.....	Balmoral, N. B., A 7
7000	Balotra, India, G 5
619	Balquidder, Scotland, L 15
5570	Bals, Rom., K 18
234	Balsas, Guer., P 15
3642	Balsfjord, Norway, C 16
4123	Balsta, Sweden, P 19
.....	Balsthal, Switzerland, E 10
21400	Balta, W. Sov. Un., H 24
.....	Balta-Alba, Rom., J 22
2665	Baltanas, Spain, F 12
.....	Baltasound, Shetland Is., A 5
.....	Baltazar, Venezuela, N 12
30667	Balti, W. Sov. Un., H 22
	Baltic Port, see Baltiski Sov. Un.
1000	Baltimore, Ire., R 6
272	Baltimore, Ontario, J 15
1166	Baltiski (Baltic Port), Sov. Un., F 3
.....	Baluchan Chah, Iran, P 14
.....	Bam, Iran, E 13
10000	Bam, Iran, N 13
19952	Bamako, Fr. W. Afr., I 4
.....	Bamanhatti, India, I 9
593	Bambamarca, Peru, H 6
54000	Bamberg, Germany, M 8
.....	Bambuhy, Brazil, M 16
.....	Bamfield, B. C., R 11
.....	Bamha, Egypt, K 13
.....	Bamian, Afghanistan, G 21
.....	Bampton, England, K 15
1392	Bampton, England, M 9
.....	Bampur, Iran, P 15
.....	Banada, Ire., G 9
.....	Bañado de Rocha, Uruguay, H 20
1164	Banagher, Ire., K 13
1971	Banaguises, Cuba, I 10
.....	Banajun, China, G 4
1200	Banana, Angola, K 11
118	Banana, Australia, I 22
.....	Bananal, Brazil, F 15
.....	Bananal, Brazil, K 8
10259	Bananal, Brazil, N 17
.....	Bananeiras, Brazil, G 24
13347	Banbury, England, K 16
1690	Banchory, Scotland, I 22
7678	Banco, Colombia, E 12
1094	Bancroft, Ontario, F 16
22600	Banda, India, G 13
.....	Band Ali, Iran, L 5
8000	Bandar Abbas, Iran, P 11
19000	Bandar Abu Shehr (Bushire), Iran, N 6
6275	Bande, Spain, E 7
.....	Bandeira de Mello, Braz., J 20
.....	Bandera, Argentina, J 14
.....	Bandhogdrh, India, H 14
778	Bandholm, Denmark, N 18
.....	Bandiagara, Fr.W.Afr., H 6
4000	Band-i-kir, Iran, J 4
.....	Bandikui, India, F 9
66900	Bandjermasin, Neth. Ind., I 4
167000	Bandoeng, Neth. Ind., J 3
3100	Bandon, Ire., Q 9
.....	Bandundu, Bel. Cong., L 13
16000	Banes, Cuba, M 22
2200	Banff, Alberta, N 19
4136	Banff and Macduff, Scotland, G 22
406760	Bangalore, India, N 10
.....	Banganapalle, India, M 11
.....	Bangasso, Fr. Eq. Afr., J 15
681214	Bangkok, Siam., P 4
.....	Bangor, N. Ire., D 24
.....	Bangor, Ire., F 4
120	Bangor, Sask., P 11
10959	Bangor, Wales, H 8
.....	Bang Sapan Yai, Siam., Q 2
19353	Bangui, Fr. Eq. Afr., K 13
.....	Bania, Fr. Eq. Afr., K 12
.....	Bania de Acateno, Bol., E 14
.....	Banias, Syria, K 10
39478	Bani Suef, Egypt, M 13
22177	Banjaluka, Yugo., J 10
25066	Banjoewangi, Neth. Ind., J 4
1100	Banka, India, G 20
.....	Bankend, Scotland, O 17
.....	Bankfoot, Scotland, K 18
162	Bankhead, Alberta, N 19
175	Bannockburn, Ont., H 17
24768	Bannu, Ind., C 4
155	Banos, Chile, N 5
.....	Baños, Ecuador, C 5
5031	Baños de Cerrato, Sp., F 11
.....	Bansda, India, J 6
.....	Bansha, Ire., N 13
.....	Bansi, India, F 16
11321	Banská Bystrica, Czech., I 12
13292	Banská Stiavnica, Czech., G 12
5056	Bansko, Bul., M 18
.....	Banstead, England, D 21
7000	Banswara, India, H 7
.....	Banteer, Ire., P 9
3109	Bantry, Ire., Q 6
2500	Bantwal, India, N 8
.....	Banur, India, D 10
.....	Banzyville, Bel. Cong., K 14
.....	Bao Ha, Fr. In. Ch., L 7
8600	Bapatla, India, M 13
1907	Bapaume, France, F 15
.....	Baptista, Brazil, F 7
.....	Baqliyah, Egypt, D 13
689	Baquedano, Chile, F 4
.....	Bar, W. Sov. Un., G 21
.....	Bara naca, Colombia, I 20
.....	Barabhum, India, H 19
.....	Bar Abir, I. E. A., O 13
.....	Barão do Rio Blanco, Braz., H 23
346	Barachois, N. B., H 13
10395	Baracoa, Cuba, H 11
30456	Baradero, Argentina, M 14
8359	Barahona, Dom. Rep., J 14
657	Barahona, Spain, G 14
.....	Barakat, Egypt, B 10
.....	Bara Khel, Afghanistan, J 22
.....	Baraki, Iran, N 6
.....	Baramanni, Br. Gu., A 6
.....	Baramon, Egypt, C 15
.....	Baramula, India, B 7
5470	Baranoa, Colombia, C 10
.....	Baranówicze, see Baranovichi, Sov. Un.
22848	Baranovichi, W. Sov. Un., D 19
.....	Barao do Rio Blanco, Brazil, H 23
.....	Barash, Iran, F 15
.....	Barasha, W. Sov. Un., E 22
.....	Barasoli, Erit., D 13
.....	Barauta, Japan, G 12
.....	Barba, Spain, H 8
19466	Barbacena, Brazil, M 17
3739	Barbacoas, Colombia, L 3
3733	Barbacoas, Venezuela, E 13
9388	Barbastro, Spain, F 18
2269	Barberton, U.S. Afr., F 21
4231	Barbezieux, France, M 9
1740	Barbosa, Colombia, G 8
1369	Barbura, Palestine, H 13
2042	Barcaldine, Australia, H 20
12527	Barcellona, Italy, N 17
4315	Barcellos, Brazil, E 3
1081175	Barcelona, Spain, G 20
12370	Barcelona, Venezuela, D 17
1934	Barcelonnette, Fr., N 23
62221	Barcelos, Port., F 5
1855	Barco de Avila, Sp., I 12
6159	Barcs, Hungary, I 10
.....	Bardai, Fr. W. Afr., G 13
3500	Bardera, Som., R 15
7606	Bardijov, Czech., G 14
8000	Bardis, Egypt, N 21
.....	Bardi Shiraz, Iran, L 9
.....	Bardney, England, H 19
400	Bardo, Tunis, B 23
740	Bardon Vechia, Italy, D 1
.....	Bardu, Norway, C 16
.....	Bare, Cam., J 10
192688	Bareilly, India, E 12
.....	Barenburg, Germany, F 6
.....	Barentu, Erit., B 7
1102	Barfleur, France, F 7
.....	Barfrush, see Babol, Iran.
1147	Barga, Italy, F 7

Pop.	Place Country Index
.....	Bargal, Som., G 24
1867	Barge, Italy, E 1
780	Bargen, Switzerland, G 8
.....	Barhein, Egypt, E 16
.....	Barhi, India, H 18
.....	Barhill, Scotland, P 13
164340	Bari, Italy, J 20
2474	Barichara, Colombia, G 13
2000	Bariloche, Argentina, A 20
1615	Barinas, Venezuela, F 8
3187	Barinitas, Venezuela, F 7
5509	Bariry, Brazil, N 14
35716	Barisal, India, H 24
1988	Barjols, France, P 22
.....	Barkaker, Norway, E 3
.....	Barker, Argentina, P 18
255	Barkerville, B. C., L 14
51277	Barking, England, L 20
.....	Barking Side, Eng., B 24
1600	Barkly East, U.S. Afr., M17
1034	Barkly West, U.S. Afr., J 14
25500	Bârlad, Romania, I 22
16550	Bar-le-Duc, France, H 19
50055	Barletta, Italy, J 18
.....	Barloge, Ire., R 6
.....	Barlow, Yukon, L 7
	Barmen, see Wuppertal, Ger.
6000	Barmer, India, G 4
2491	Barmouth, Wales, I 8
.....	Barna, Ire., J 7
.....	Barnab, Ger., M 10
304	Barnaby River, N. B., E 10
.....	Barnacht, Egypt, J 13
3883	Barnard Castle, Eng., D 14
148129	Barnaul, Sov. Un. Asia. H 13
219	Barnes River Station, N. S. J 18
311	Barnesville, N. B., K 9
.....	Barnet, B. C., O 3
13757	Barneveld, Neth., G 17
469	Barneville, France, G 6
71522	Barnsley, England, G 15
14693	Barnstaple, England, M 8
.....	Barnstorf, Germany, F 5
150	Barnwell, Alberta, P 22
153301	Baroda, India, I 6
233	Barons, Alberta, P 22
.....	Bar Panjah, Afg., C 25
54176	Barquisimeto, Ven., D 9
4185	Barr, France, H 24
494	Barr, Scotland, P 13
.....	Barra, Brazil, I 18
.....	Barraca Concepción, Bolivia, C 6
9390	Barracão, Brazil, J 19
41800	Barrackpore, India, H 23
3206	Barra de Santa Lucia, Uruguay, P 18
.....	Barra de São João, Brazil, N 19
.....	Barra do Corda, Braz., G 17
.....	Barra do Maratonha, Brazil, F 20
.....	Barra do Rio de Contas, Brazil, J 21
.....	Barra do Rio dos Bugres, Brazil, J 8
.....	Barrage, Egypt, H 13
192	Barranca, Peru, F 8
.....	Barranca Bermeja, Ven., F 12
1542	Barrancas, Colombia, C 14
2083	Barrancas, Venezuela, F 20
.....	Barranco Branco, Braz., M 7
2660	Barranco de Loba, Col., E 11
.....	Barrancos, Portugal, L 7
150000	Barranquilla, Col., B 10
281	Barraza, Chile, K 3
227	Barre, France, O 17
.....	Barreiras, Brazil, I 17
.....	Barreirinhas, Brazil, E 19
10904	Barreiro, Portugal, K 4
6240	Barreiros, Brazil, H 25
522	Barrême, France, O 22
.....	Barrera, Cuba, G 7
17272	Barretos, Brazil, M 14
12308	Barrhead, Scotland, N 14
.....	Barri, Iran, E 2
9725	Barrie, Ontario, I 11
519	Barriefield, Ontario, I 20
.....	Barriere, B. C., N 15
277	Barrington, Australia, N 22
510	Barrington, N. S., R 9
73	Barrington, Quebec, R 15
.....	Barringun, Australia, L 19
.....	Barrisdale, Scotland, I 10
.....	Barro, Brazil, P 11
204	Barroteran, Coa., C 12
.....	Barrow, Argentina, Q 17
40	Barrow Creek, Austl., G 13
73490	Barrow in Furness, Eng., E 10
417	Barrydale, U.S. Afr., Q 10
1198	Barrys Bay, Ontario, D 17
1747	Barsingerhorn, Neth., E 14
.....	Bar's Corner, N. S., N 12
4313	Bar-sur-Aube, France, H 19
2742	Bar-sur-Seine. France, I 18
7181	Barth, Ger., C 11
1555	Bartica, Br. Gu., B 6
8681	Bartin, Tur., B 7
.....	Bartle. Cuba, M 18
.....	Bartolo, Baja Cal., I 4
6330	Barton, England, G 18
.....	Baru, Colombia, E 8
.....	Barûg, Egypt, M 19
.....	Baruk, Afghanistan, F 23
3779	Baruta, Venezuela, C 13
.....	Baruva, India, K 18
.....	Barvas, Sask., O 11
5876	Barvas, Scotland, D 6
1277	Barvaux, Belgium, O 17
.....	Barwa, India, H 17
6300	Barwani, India, I 8
.....	Basavilbaso, Arg., L 19
.....	Baschkoi, Tur., H 5
200900	Basel, Switz., C 9
494	Bashaw, Alberta, L 21
.....	Bashi, Iran, N 6
.....	Basht, Iran, L 6
13800	Basim, India, J 10
13862	Basingstoke, Eng., M 16
.....	Basiran, Iran, K 13
.....	Baskunchag, Sov. Un., M18
1000	Basman, Iran, O 14
.....	Basoko, Bel. Cong., K 16
60000	Basra, Iraq, Q 24
.....	Basra, Morocco, E 7
.....	Basring, Afg., K 17
.....	Bassac, Fr. In. Ch., O 8
582	Bassano, Alberta, N 22
10111	Bassano, Italy, C 10
45662	Bassein, India, K 6
13638	Basse Terre, Guadeloupe, B 22, L 23
9000	Basse Terre, St. Kitts, Wind Is., K 22
3211	Bassevelde Belgium, Q 3
325	Bass River, N. S., K 14
319	Bass River, N. B., G 11
2000	Bassus, Egypt, H 13
125	Basswood, Manitoba, P 13
.....	Basta, Shetland Is., A 4
649	Bastad, Sweden, P 11
3925	Bastelica, France, Q 3
22526	Basti, India, F 16
52208	Bastia, France, P 4
4085	Bastogne, Belgium, P 18
.....	Bastuträsk, Sweden, G 18
2019	Batabano, Cuba, I 7
33204	Batala, India, C 8
.....	Batalha, Brazil, F 19
.....	Batalha, Portugal. J 5
.....	Batalpashinsk, Sov. Un., O 4
6000	Batang, China, H 3
197	Bataques, Baja Cal., A 4
600000	Batavia, Neth. Ind., J 3
155	Bateman, Sask., Q 9
68801	Bath, England, L 12
421	Bath, N. B., G 4
303	Bath, Ontario, J 19
10097	Bathgate, Scotland, M 18
.....	Baths of Herod, Transjordan, O 13
.....	Bathurst, Argentina, P 15
10413	Bathurst, Australia, O 21
14370	Bathurst, Gam., I 1
3554	Bathurst, N. B., C 9
500	Bathurst, U.S. Afr., Q 17
.....	Bathurst Jc., N. B., C 10
.....	Batie, I. E. A., G 11
803	Batiscan, Quebec, L 19
.....	Batkak, Afg., E 19
34573	Batley, England, F 15
13565	Batna, Algeria, D 19
2109	Batopilas, Chih., K 16
.....	Batra, Egypt, C 15
5000	Batroun. Syria, L 10
15000	Battambang, Fr. In. Ch., P 5
.....	Battersea, Ont., H 20
11585	Batticaloa, Cey., Q 15
.....	Battipaglia, Italy, J 16
3490	Battle, England, M 21
.....	Battle Bridge, Ire., G 13
1317	Battleford, Sask., L 5
70807	Batumi, Sov. Un., Q 14
.....	Batunah, Iran, O 6
5320	Baturite, Braz., F 22
.....	Batyú, Hung., P 26
50000	Bauchi, Nig., I 10
5176	Baud, France, I 4
6961	Baudó, Colombia, H 5
2848	Baugé, France, J 9
.....	Baul, Venezuela, F 11
1123	Baulmes, Switzerland, I 4
2867	Bauma, Switzerland, E 16
3161	Baume-les-Dames, Fr., J 21
.....	Baunboy, Ire., M 18
2000	Baures, Bolivia, E 14
33067	Bauru, Brazil, N 13
41000	Bautzen, Germany, J 14
.....	Bavelse, Denmark, L 19
.....	Baxa, India, F 22
.....	Baxaft, Iran, J 5
214	Baxter Harbour, N. S., L 12
16161	Bayamo, Cuba, N 19
.....	Bayana, India, F 10
.....	Bayate, Cuba, N 21
.....	Bayaz, Iran, L 10
.....	Bayble, Scotland, E 8
321	Bay du Vin, N. B., E 11
7525	Bayeux, France, G 8
261	Bayfield, Nova Scotia, J 20
321	Bayfield, Ontario, L 5
6075	Bayona, Spain, E 5
31350	Bayonne, France, P 6
.....	Bayovar, Peru, G 1
37000	Bayreuth, Germany, M 9
327	Bay Saint Lawrence, N. S., E 23
.....	Bay Shore, N. B., L 8
235	Baysville, Ontario, F 13
20772	Baza, Spain. N 13
.....	Bazán, Argentina, J 9
29938	Bazargic, Bul., K 23
1168	Bazarjik, Tur., H 6
.....	Bazarjik, Tur., H 12
4410	Bazas, France, N 9
527	Beachburg, Ontario, C 19
229	Beachport, Australia, P 16
263	Beach Meadows, N.S., P 12
200	Beachport, Austl., P 16
.....	Beach Road, Ontario, M 11
500	Beachville, Ontario, N 8
806	Beaconsfield, Tas., C 6
20364	Beaconsfield, U.S. Afr., J 15
6204	Beafort West, U.S. Afr., O 12
.....	Beal, England, A 14
.....	Bealangeary, Ire., P 7
.....	Bealey, N. Z., L 11
.....	Beaminster, England, N 13
1309	Beamsville, Ontario, M 11
.....	Bear, Yukon, K 4
.....	Bearberry, Alberta. M 20
.....	Bearhaven, Ire., Q 3
211	Bear Point, N. S., R 9
1150	Bear River, N. S., N 9
1254	Beauceville, Que., N 23
1390	Beaudesert, Australia, K 23
15	Beaufield, Sask., N 4
697	Beaufort, France, K 20
7967	Beaufort West, U. S. Afr., O 12
3292	Beaugency, France, I 13
3550	Beauharnois, Quebec, Q 15
2346	Beaujeu, France, L 18
.....	Beaulieu, England, N 1
380	Beaulieu, Quebec, K 22
.....	Beauly, N. S., K 20
1000	Beauly, Scotland, G 14
1708	Beaumaris, Wales, H 8
309	Beaumesnil, France, H 11
1676	Beaumont, Belgium, O 11
259	Beaumont, France, F 6
.....	Beaumont, N. Z., P 7
5166	Beaumont-sur-Oise, Fr., G 13
11862	Beaune, France, J 19
3725	Beauport, Quebec, K 21
810	Beaupre, Quebec, J 22
1932	Beauraing, Belgium, P 15
224	Beaurivage, Quebec, M 21
1161	Beausejour, Man., Q 17
18738	Beauvais, France, G 14
268	Beaver Bank, N. S., M 15
.....	Beaver Crossing, Alta., I 23
275	Beaver Harbour, N. B., L 6
933	Beaverton, Ontario, I 12
28342	Beawar, India, G 7
.....	Beazley, Argentina, M 9
33074	Bebedouro, Brazil, M 14
8396	Beberibe, Brazil, F 22
1842	Becal, Camp., F 20
400	Becanchén, Yuc., G 22
272	Becancour, Quebec, M 18
6544	Beccles, England, J 24
7776	Becerrea, Spain, D 8
711	Bécherel, France, H 6
43834	Beckenham, England, L 20
3060	Beclean, Romania, H 18
7994	Bédarieux, France, P 15
.....	Bedda, Eth., E 10
.....	Beddington, England, D 21
59	Bedell, Ontario, F 22
305	Bedeque, P. E. I., H 14
311	Beder, Denmark, I 12
40573	Bedford, England, J 18
900	Bedford, N. S., N 14
1697	Bedford, Quebec, Q 17
912	Bedford, U.S. Afr., O 15
27315	Bedlington, England, C 15
.....	Bednodemiyanovsk, Sov. Un., J 14
.....	Bedourie, Australia, I 1
.....	Bedrashên, Egypt, J 14
283	Bedretto, Switzerland, L 14
152	Bedsted, Denmark, M 6
47812	Bedzin, Poland, F 12
1024	Beebe, Quebec, R 19
214	Beechwood, N. B., F 4
193	Beechy, Sask., O 6
4375	Beek, Netherlands, L 18
.....	Beekbergen, Neth., G 19
4572	Beelitz, Germany, H 11
.....	Beenbreek, U.S. Afr., J 8
752	Beenleigh, Australia, K 23
2498	Beeringen, Belgium, L 16
2959	Beersheba, Pal., Q 5
5192	Beeskaw, Germany, H 13
594	Beeton, Ontario, J 11
.....	Beetsterzwaag, Neth., C 19
2277	Bega, Australia, P 21
4555	Begard, France, H 3
.....	Behar, India, F 23
.....	Behbet, Egypt, K 13
1500	Behbit el-Hagar, Eg., D 14
.....	Behdadun, Iran, H 14
8184	Behesni, Tur., G 13
.....	Bêhnessa, Egypt, P 8
.....	Behût, Egypt, C 15
.....	Behwach, Egypt, G 11
5294	Beibazar, Tur., D 6
2023	Beieren, Norway, E 13
7773	Beilen, Netherlands, D 22
.....	Beilul, I. E. A., D 13
23694	Beira, Moz., O 19
	Beirut, see Beyrouth, Syr.
3100	Beisan, Palestine, I 12
.....	Beita, Palestine, K 10
.....	Beit Affeh, Palestine, N 4
.....	Beit Atab, Palestine, N 8
.....	Beit Aula, Palestine, O 7
.....	Beit Duros, Palestine, N 4
.....	Beit Edis, Transj., J 14
.....	Beit Ello, Palestine, L 8
766	Beit Fejjar, Palestine, N 9
5977	Beith, Scotland, N 14
996	Beit Hanina, Palestine, M 9
885	Beit Hanun, Palestine, O 3
446	Beitin, Palestine, M 10
2732	Beit Jala, Palestine, N 9
902	Beit Jenn, Palestine, G 11
1420	Beit Jibrin, Palestine, O 6
199	Beit Kad, Palestine, J 11
.....	Beit Lud, Palestine, K 9
1324	Beit Nabala, Palestine, L 7
.....	Beit Ras, Transj., I 15
.....	Beit Rima, Palestine, L 8
381	Beit Sira, Palestine, M 8
2006	Beitstad, Norway, H 10
.....	Beit Tamir, Palestine, N 10
606	Beit Tima, Palestine, N 4
147	Beit Ur el Foka, Pal., M 8
470	Beit Ur el Tahta, Pal., M 8
4294	Beius, Romania, D 4
13104	Beja, Portugal, L 6
.....	Beja, Tunis, B 23
.....	Bejaburi, Siam, P 2
.....	Bejan, Albania, C 4
12518	Bejar, Spain, H 9
8319	Bejucal, Cuba, H 6
.....	Bekal, India, O 8
28835	Békés, Hung., I 14
49295	Békéscsaba, Hung., I 14
4000	Bela, Baluchistan, Q 21
.....	Belad Sinjar, Iraq, I 18
.....	Belah, Palestine, J 8
.....	Belain Surdah, Pal., M 9
2499	Belalcázar, Colombia, H 8
9471	Belalcázar, Spain, L 10
.....	Belar, Baluchistan, R 17
.....	Belaugh, Ire., J 13
.....	Belaya Tser Kov, W. Sov. Un., F 24
.....	Belbeis, Egypt, G 16
3599	Belchite, Spain, G 16
.....	Belcoo, N. Ire., F 14
.....	Belcourt, Quebec, E 6
.....	Belder, Belgium, R 11
12900	Belebei, Sov. Un., I 22
.....	Belem, Brazil, G 19
7000	Belem, Portugal, K 4
166662	Belem (Para), Braz., E 14
7000	Belem, Port, K 4
2201	Belen, Argentina, I 8
197	Belén, Bolivia, M 11
5319	Belén, Colombia, H 13
.....	Belén, Panama, P 20
10000	Belen, Paraguay, K 7
1994	Belen, Uruguay, F 16
6465	Belen, Venezuela. D 12
.....	Belet Uen., Som., P 17
415151	Belfast, N. Ire., D 23
727	Belfast, U.S. Afr., F 20
.....	Belfodio, Eth., H 4
.....	Belford, England, B 14
45625	Belfort, France, I 23
125	Belfountain, Ont., K 10
13543	Belgard, Pol., C 9
42600	Belgaum, India, M 7
23000	Belgorod, Sov. Un., L 10
	Belgrade, see Beograd, Yugo.
180	Belgrave, Ontario, K 6
1000	Belgrove, N. Z., J 13
1514	Belhelvie, Scotland, H 23
.....	Beliffa, Egypt, M 12
726	Bélin, France, N 7
17289	Belize, Br. Hond., B 8
3880	Belkas, Egypt, C 15
.....	Bella, Brazil, I 1
3368	Bella, Italy, J 17
.....	Bella Brisco, Bolivia, C 7
3787	Bellac, France, L 11
986	Bellaco, Uruguay, K 15
.....	Bella Coola, B. C., M 9
.....	Bella Flor, Bolivia, C 4
.....	Bellaghy, N. Ire., D 20
.....	Bellalie, Australia, J 18
.....	Bellanamallard, N. Ire., E 15
.....	Bellananagh, Ire., G 16
.....	Bellangare, Ire., H 11
.....	Bellarena, N. Ire., B 18
47573	Bellary, India, M 10
1000	Bella Vista, Argentina, H 10
7000	Bella Vista, Argentina, I 18
.....	Bella Vista, Brazil, F 9
.....	Bella Vista, Brazil, K 14
5600	Bella Vista, Paraguay, I 9
140	Bellavista, Peru, G 5
	Bella Vista de Palma, see Clevelandia, Braz.
265	Belle Cote, N. S., G 21
130	Belledune River, N. B., B 9
.....	Belleek, N. Ire., E 13
.....	Belleek, Ontario, P 24
328	Bellefleur, N. B., D 4
866	Belle Fontaine, Bel., R 17
1126	Bellegarde, France, I 14
228	Belle Marche, N. S., F 22
1769	Belléme, France, H 10
1914	Bellerive, Tasmania, E 7
999	Belle River, Ontario, Q 2
2129	Belleville, France, L 19
1002	Belleville, N. S., Q 8
15710	Belleville, Ontario, I 17
219	Bell Ewart, Ontario. I 11
3359	Belley, France, L 21
.....	Bell Harbour, Ire., K 8
.....	Bellingham, Eng., C 13
10873	Bellinzona, Switz., N 17
128	Bellis, Alberta, J 22
327	Belliveau Cove, N. S., O 8
10500	Belluno, Italy, C 10
20000	Bell Ville, Argentina, M 14
10440	Belmez, Spain, L 10
325	Belmont, Manitoba, R 14
324	Belmont, Nova Scotia, K15
6413	Belmonte, Brazil, K 21
2698	Belmonte, Spain, J 14
219	Belmore, Ont., J 6
.....	Belmullet, Ire., F 3
2020	Beloeil Station, Que., P 16
179770	Belo Horizonte, Brazil, M 17
.....	Belomorsk, Sov. Un., D 10
3274	Belp, Switzerland, I 9
736	Belpech, France, P 13
13023	Belper, England, H 15
.....	Belturbet, Ire., G 16
902	Belvedere, Italy, L 18
1222	Belvés, France, N 11
3191	Belz, France, I 3
.....	Belz, W. Sov. Un., F 17
4269	Belzig, Germany, H 11
3614	Bembibre, Spain, D 9
6916	Bemmel, Neth., H 19
1543	Benabarre, Spain, E 17
.....	Ben Addrouk, Algeria, J 16
.....	Bena Dibele, Bel. Cong., L 15
.....	Bena Kamba, Bel. Cong., L 16
3965	Benalla, Australia, P 19
263100	Benares, India, G 16
.....	Benasque, Spain, E 18
.....	ben-Athman, Algeria, J 11
5796	Benavente, Spain, F 9
2741	Benavides, Spain, E 9
.....	Bendêla, Egypt, C 15
.....	Bender Cassim, Som., G 22
.....	Bender Ziade, Br. Som., H 21
125340	Bendigo, Australia, P 18
8307	Benešov, Czech., F 7
1328	Bénévent, France, L 12
30700	Benevento, Italy, J 15
33794	Bengasi (Berenice), Libya., E 14
.....	Ben Ghiada, Morocco, G 11
13423	Bengkoeloe, Neth. Ind., I 2
279	Bengough, Sask., R 8
5742	Benguela, Angola, N 12
18607	Benha, Egypt, G 13
1036	Beni Abbès, Alg., K 10
.....	Beni Affan, Egypt, M 13
.....	Beni Bekhit, Egypt, M 12
9598	Benicarlo, Spain, I 18
.....	Beni Harount, Egypt, M 13
1308	Beni Hassan, Egypt, K 18
.....	Beni Hodeir, Egypt, M 14
.....	Beni Mancour, Alg., C 18
.....	Beni Mazâr, Egypt, P 10
.....	Beni Meskin, Mor., G 5
.....	Beni Mohammed el Kofur, Egypt, Q 10
15000	Benin, Nigeria, J 9
1279	Beni Naim, Palestine, O 9
6036	Benisa, Spain, L 17
1196	Beni Selama, Egypt, G 10
.....	Beni Semguin, Mor., K 7
294	Benito, Man., N 12
.....	Benito, Sp. Gui., K 10
.....	Benjamin, Bolivia, D 10
.....	Benjamin Constant, Brazil, E 16
.....	Benjamin Constant, Brazil, G 21
.....	Benjamin Zorrilla, Arg., Q 11
.....	Benkendorf-Sosnovka, Sov. Un., J 13
.....	Bennettsbridge, Ire., M 17
100	Bennetts Junction, N. Z., M 12
.....	Bennington, England, H 20
.....	Ben Nur, Morocco, H 5
.....	Benoud, Algeria, H 13
.....	Bens, Honduras, E 14
10067	Bensheim, Germany, M 5
279	Bentley, Alberta, L 20
.....	Bentley, England, K 23
.....	Bento Goncalves, Brazil, P 11
82	Benton, N. B., I 4
.....	Bentota, Cey., R 13
235	Bény Bocage, France, H 8
.....	Beoaria. Algeria, D 22
.....	Beocinselo, Yugo., J 13
289272	Beograd (Belgrade), Yugo., J 14
.....	Ber, Br. Som., I 18
.....	Beragh, N. Ire., E 17
10403	Berat, Albania, N 13
.....	Berawa, Egypt, N 11
10000	Berber, Anglo-Egyptian Sudan, H 19
20000	Berbera, Br. Som., H 17
44486	Berchem. Belgium, K 12
439	Bercher, Switzerland, J 5
.....	Berchtesgaden, Ger., R 11
16433	Berck-sur-Mer, Fr., E 12
.....	Berda, Morocco, J 10
66306	Berdichev, W. Sov. Un., F 22
51664	Berdyansk. Sov. Un., N 10
.....	Berea, Bas., K 18
.....	Beregszasz, Hung., P 26
175	Berens River, Man., M 16,
13045	Berezhany, W. Sov. Un., G 18
.....	Berezina R., W. Sov. Un., B 21
.....	Berezino, W. Sov. Un., C 22
.....	Bereźno, W. Sov. Un., E 20
2000	Berezov, Sov. Un., Asia, E 11
.....	Berezovka, Sov Un., N 6
1176	Berg, Norway, C 15
.....	Berg, Sweden, J 13
13868	Bergama, Tur., E 1
21600	Bergamo, Italy, C 6
4633	Bergen, Germany, C 12
5259	Bergen, Neth., E 13
6522	Bergen, Neth., I 20
98546	Bergen, Norway, L 3
21168	Bergen op Zoom, Neth., J 11, P 8
17520	Bergerac, France, N 10
.....	Bergsjö, Sweden, K 15
3878	Bergues, France, D 14
.....	Bergum, Neth., C 19
650	Bergün, Switz., K 21
2996	Bergzabern, Germany, N 4
31500	Berhampore, India, H 21
37750	Berhampur, India, K 18
1700	Berimbâl, Egypt, B 8
.....	Berimbâl el Qâdima, Egypt, C 18
.....	Beris, Egypt, Q 17
.....	Berisal, Switz., M 12
.....	Berislav, Sov. Un., N 8
.....	Beristâin, Pueb., G 6
.....	Berizina, Algeria, G 15
.....	Berkaak, Norway, J 8
.....	Berkasieh, Palestine, N 6
.....	Berkeley, England, L 12
213	Berkeley, Ontario, I 8
2682	Berkhout, Neth., E 14
5958	Berkovica, Bul., L 17
1071	Berlevaag, Norway, A 23
4242501	Berlin, Germany, G 12,
.....	Berma, Egypt, E 11
1899	Bermejillo, Dur., L 23
.....	Bermejo, Argentina, L 8
1438	Bermejo, Bolivia, N 11
11739	Bermeo, Spain, C 14
1076	Bermillo de Sayago, Sp., G 9
151200	Bern, Switz., H 9
.....	Berna, Argentina, J 17
6528	Bernalda, Italy, K 19
12072	Bernau, Germany, G 12
7587	Bernay, France, G 10
38000	Bernburg, Ger., H 10
.....	Bernera, Scotland, H 10
1639	Bernierville, Que., N 20
2601	Bernissart, Belgium, N 8
.....	Bernkastel, Germany, L 2
	Beroun, see Beraun, Ger.
.....	Berozeh, Iran, E 2
.....	Berresof, Algeria, G 22
4041	Berrian, Algeria, G 17
.....	Berriedale, Scotland, E 18
762	Berrigan, Australia, O 19
3302	Berrouaghia, Algeria, C 16
.....	Berry Bank, U.S. Afr., L 13
250	Berry Mill, N. B., H 11
175	Berthier, Quebec, K 23
2631	Berthier, Quebec, N 16
17	Berthier Jc., Quebec, N 16
3566	Betrix, Belgium, Q 16
2116	Bervie, Scotland, J 23
962	Berwick, N. S., L 12
12299	Berwick-upon-Tweed, England, A 14
206	Berwyn, Alberta, G 17
.....	Berzeg, Algeria, F 17
65022	Besançon, France, J 22
.....	Beshbêsh, Egypt, C 13
.....	Beshir, Sp. Mor., D 11
.....	Beshshit, Palestine, M 5
.....	Besind, Iran, D 12
.....	Besiyûn, Egypt, D 10
.....	Bessbrook, N. Ire., F 21
822	Besse, France, P 22
.....	Bessemer, Ontario, F 17
.....	Bessemer Jc., Ont., F 16
.....	Besser, Denmark, I 14
533	Bessines, France, L 12
5124	Betanzos, Bolivia, K 9
10504	Betanzos, Spain, C 6
.....	Betet, Egypt, C 12
1200	Bethal, U.S. Afr., G 19
.....	Bethanie, Quebec, F 22
.....	Bethanie, S. W. Afr., P 13
325	Bethany, Ontario, J 14
.....	Bethany, U.S. Afr., K 15
6817	Bethlehem, Palestine, N 9
.....	Bethlehem. Palestine, H 9
10377	Bethlehem, U.S. Afr., I 18
19956	Bethune, France, E 15
210	Bethune, Sask., P 8
2858	Bettemburg, Lux., R 20
25800	Bettiah, India, F 17
.....	Bettingen, Lux., Q 19
.....	Bettobu, Japan, E 16
.....	Bettyhill, Scotland, D 15
4700	Betul, India, I 11
1310	Betulia, Colombia, G 7
2722	Betulia, Col., G 13
.....	Betûres, Egypt, D 5
400	Betz, France, G 15
80	Beulah, Manitoba, Q 12
100584	Beuthen, Pol., F 12
1207	Bevaix, Switzerland, H 5
2308	Bevensen, Germany, F 8
12964	Beveren, Belgium, K 11
249	Bevers, Switzerland, K 22
871	Beverley, Australia, N 5
14011	Beverley, England, F 18
3627	Beverloo, Belgium, L 16
9477	Beverwijk, Neth., F 12
174	Bevtoft, Denmark, L 6
4374	Bex, Switzerland, N 6
21229	Bexhill, England, N 21
32940	Bexley, England, C 24
.....	Bexley Heath, Eng., C 24
.....	Beypore, India, O 8
160716	Beyrouth (Beirut), Leb., M 10
2620	Beyshehr, Turk., G 6
7	Bezanson, Alberta, H 23
6880	Bezerros, Brazil, H 24
71527	Béziers, France, P 16
14310	Bezons, France, A 3
.....	Bezsonovka. Sov. Un., J 16
60427	Bezwada, India, L 14
.....	Bezzu, Morocco, H 6
.....	Bhadarwah, India, C 9
1900	Bhadrachalam, India, L 14
18500	Bhadrakh, India, J 20
83847	Bhagalpur, India, G 20
10700	Bhamo, Bur., M 23
30173	Bharatpur, India, F 10
22771	Bhatinda, India, D 8
75594	Bhavnagar, India, I 5
.....	Bhawana, India, C 6
18700	Bhera, India, C 6
7500	Bhilsa, India, H 11
.....	Bhind, India, F 11
5200	Bhind, India, G 12
17700	Bhir, India, K 9
35866	Bhiwani, India, E 9
.....	Bhogat, India, I 2
61037	Bhopal, India, H 10
.....	Bhor, India, K 6
.....	Bhuket (Puket), Siam, R 1
.....	Bhundesar, India, J 16
27989	Bhusawal, India, J 9
.....	Biahdjumand, Iran, F 11
.....	Biahmu, Egypt, L 11
17549	Biala Podlaska, Poland, D 16
.....	Biala, Pol., E 13
.....	Biala, Pol., F 12
105000	Bialystok, Poland, D 16
2568	Bianco, Italy, N 19
.....	Biaori, India, H 10
2000	Biar Darsen, Tun., G 25
20691	Biarritz, France, P 6
2812	Biasca, Switz., M 17
.....	Biasi, Nepal, E 14
.....	Bia Woraba, Eth., J 13
.....	Biba el-Kubra, Egypt, N 12
11099	Biberach, Germany, Q 6
4232	Biberist, Switz., F 9
3109	Bicester, England, K 16
210	Bickerdike. Alberta, K 18
7145	Bicske, Hungary, H 11
561	Bidache, France, P 7
.....	Bidar, India, K 10
8782	Bideford, England, M 7
.....	Bidersa, Eth., G 10
.....	Bidwây, Egypt, C 16
91	Biel, Switzerland, L 13
37861	Biel, Switz., G 8
121031	Bielefeld, Germany, H 5
22146	Biella, Italy, C 3
.....	Bielsk, Pol., D 16
22573	Bielsko, Poland, F 12
618	Bienfait, Sask., R 10
.....	Bienvenu, Fr. Gu., B 10
1138	Bière, Switzerland, K 2
2441	Biervliet, Neth., K 8
.....	Biesdorf, Ger., P 20
3384	Bietigheim, Ger., O 5
950	Bièvres, France, C 3
7480	Biga, Tur., C 1
237	Big Bras d'Or, N. S., G 23
.....	Big Cove, N. B., J 9
.....	Big Creek, B. C., N 12
1930	Biggar, Sask., M 5
2074	Biggar, Scotland, O 18
5844	Biggleswade, Eng., J 19
170	Bignasco, Switz., M 15
513	Big River, Sask., K 7
.....	Big Salmon, Yukon, O 10
.....	Big Stick Lake, Sask., P 4
.....	Biguassu, Brazil, P 13
.....	Biguatinga, Brazil, M 15
291	Big Valley, Alberta, M 21
8374	Bihac, Yugo., J 8
1308	Bihain, Belgium, O 18
45000	Bihar, India, G 19
80190	Biisk, Sov. Un., Asia, H 1
.....	Bijagarh, India, I 8
39747	Bijapur, India, L 8
.....	Bijapur, Nepal, F 20
5000	Bijar, Iran, F 3
5200	Bijawar, India, H 12
12367	Bijeljina, Yugo., K 12
3093	Bijelopolje, Yugo., L 13
...	Bijistan, Iran, H 13
.....	Bijni, India, F 24
23520	Bijnor, India, E 11
.....	Bikampur, India, F 5
85927	Bikaner, India, F 6
.....	Bikovo, Sov. Un., L 16
.....	Bilahaus, Iran, K 13
.....	Bilaspur, India, D 10
31374	Bilaspur, India, I 15
195186	Bilbao, Spain, C 13
4102	Bilecik (Biledjik), Tur., D 4
.....	Bilêda, Egypt, K 13
	Biledjik, see Bilecik, Tur.
.....	Bilen, Eth., K 16
.....	Bilgeki, Chn., B 3
.....	Bilgoraj, Poland, F 16
.....	Bilkot, Nepal, E 14
2546	Billerbeck, Germany, F 8
3588	Billom, France, L 16
4030	Bilsen, Belgium, L 17
31248	Bilston, England, I 14
.....	Biltâg, Egypt, D 11
10200	Bimlipatam, India, K 17
10000	Binah, Iran, D 2
.....	Binbân, Egypt, R 24
10550	Binche, Belgium, N 10
2728	Bindalen, Norway, G 11
.....	Bindâr el Gharbiya, Egypt, N 21
.....	Bindslev, Denmark, B 12
74400	Binh-dinh, French Indo-China, P 11
.....	Binh-Thuan, French Indo-China, Q 10
221	Binn, Switzerland, M 13
4000	Bint, Iran. Q 14
.....	Bir Abu Aruk, Egypt, E 23
.....	Birakan, Sov. Un., Asia, G 19
.....	Bir Bel Hadj, Algeria, H 21
.....	Birch, Ontario, H 10
137	Birch Grove, N. S., H 24
384	Birch Hills, Sask., L 8
1200	Birchip, Australia, O 18
85	Birch Island, B. C., N 15
200	Birch River, Man., M 12
.....	Birdhill, Ire., L 11
52	Birdsville, Australia, I 16
.....	Bireh, Palestine, M 9
9659	Birejik, Tur., H 13
.....	Bir el Hamalin (Wells), Algeria, N 9
.....	Bir en Nezla, Algeria, H 21
.....	Bir es Suk, Palestine, N 10
.....	Bir ez Zeit, Palestine, L 9
.....	Bir Gettar. Algeria, F 20
.....	Bir Hadjadj, Algeria, P 11
.....	Bir Hooker. Egypt, G 6
.....	Birin, Algeria, D 17
.....	Biris, Iran, O 9
25000	Birjand, Iran, J 13
.....	Bir Jiljulieh. Palestine, M12
2599	Birkenfeld, Germany, M 3
147946	Birkenhead, England, G 11
.....	Birket el Kateineh, Transjordan, Q 12
.....	Birket el Khulil, Pal., P 11
3000	Birket es Saba, Egypt, F 12
1012700	Birmingham, England, J 15
3391	Birr, Ire., K 13
.....	Birsay, Scotland, A 18
.....	Bir Selhub. Palestine, O 10
.....	Birsilpur, India, E 5
16700	Birsk, Eur. Sov. Un., I 22
.....	Birtebat, Egypt, P 9
646	Birtle, Man., P 12
.....	Bir Tuila. Tunisia, H 24
.....	Biržai, W. Sov. Un., A 18
.....	Bir Zouila (Wells), Tunisia, F 22
.....	Birzula, W. Sov. Un., H 24
2862	Bischofszell, Switz., D 18
.....	Biscia, Erit., A 7
300	Biscotasing, Ontario, Q 23
1131	Biscucuy. Venezuela, E 8
.....	Bishling, Afghanistan, I 19
20500	Bishnupur, India, H 20
12269	Bishop Auckland, Eng, D 15
1352	Bishops Castle. Eng., J 11
9509	Bishop Stortford, Eng., K 20
11231	Biskra, Algeria E 19
.....	Bisnulok, Siam, N 3
1000	Bissau, Portuguese Gui.. I 1
95	Bisserup, Denmark, L 18
.....	Bistan, Iran, J 11
13251	Bistrita, Rom., H 18
4023	Bitburg, Germany, L 2
.....	Bitchana, Eth., H 8
3486	Bitche, France, G 23
9050	Bitlis, Tur., F 17
32982	Bitolj, Yugo., N 15
26841	Bitonto, Italy, J 19
21000	Bitterfeld, Germany. I 10
4607	Bitti, Italy, K 5
1000	Bittir. Palestine, N 9
136	Bivio, Switz., L 21
4686	Bivona, Italy, O 13
10845	Bixot, Alg., C 20
.....	Biyâla, Egypt, C 14
42700	Bizana, U.S. Afr., M 20
.....	Bizcocho, Uruguay, L 15
23206	Bizerte, Tunisia, A 23
377	Bizot, Algeria, C 20
.....	Bjarko, Norway, C 14
.....	Bj. B. Areridj, Algeria, C 18
1060	Bjela, Bulgaria, K 20
.....	Bjeldaanes, Norway, F 13
.....	Bjelland, Norway, N 4
10279	Bjelovar, Yugo., J 9
.....	Bjergby, Denmark, B 11
1861	Bjerring, Denmark, G 9
12137	Björkö, Fin., F 6
	Björneborg, see Pori, Fin.
.....	Björnö, Sweden, I 16
2500	Björnör, Norway, H 9
.....	Björnsholm, Denmark, E 7
.....	Bjurholm, Sweden, H 17
1780	Blackall, Australia, I 19
.....	Black Bull, Ire., I 21

Pop.	Place Country Index
503	Bury, Quebec, P 21
.....	Burye, Eth., H 7
16708	Bury St. Edmunds, Eng. J 22
.....	Buséima, Libya, F 15
.....	Buseli, Egypt, B 7
.....	Bûsh, Egypt, M 13
.....	Bushey, England, A 18
	Bushire, see Bandar Abu Shehr, Iran.
.....	Bushmills, N. Ire., B 20
.....	Bushruye, Iran, H 12
.....	Busingen, Switz., B 15
.....	Busk, W. Sov., Un., F 18
937	Busot, Spain, L 17
1000	Busselton, Austl., O 4
898	Busserach, Switz., E 9
1821	Busseto, Italy, D 6
54	Bussigny, Switz., K 4
287	Busswil, Switz., G 8
6000	Bustam, Iran, E 10
595	Bustamante, Tam., I 15
2960	Bustamante, N. L., E 14
24507	Busto-Arisizio, Italy, C 4
24536	Busuluk, Sov. Un., J 21
8765	Buta, Bel. Cong., K 16
.....	Butedale, B. C., K 8
6909	Butera, Italy, O 14
3410	Bütswil, Switz., E 17
572	Butterworth, U.S. Afr., O 17
1122	Buttes, Switz., H 4
1600	Buttevant, Ire., O 10
28	Buttress, Sask., P 7
28089	Buturlinovka, Sov. Un., L 13
5285	Butzbach, Germany, K 5
5878	Bützow, Germany, D 10
.....	Buxar, India, G 17
.....	Buxburn, Scotland, I 23
3472	Buxtehude, Germany, E 7
15353	Buxton, England, H 14
.....	Buzabad, Iran, H 7
4349	Buzancais, France, K 12
36115	Buzău, Romania, J 21
.....	Buzias, Romania, J 15
.....	Buznabad, Iran, H 14
.....	Bwanamkubwa, N.Rh., N17
137000	Bydgoszcz, Pol., D 11
19600	Byelev, Sov. Un., J 10
7000	Byeli, Sov. Un., I 8
.....	Byelopole, Sov. Un., L 9
6000	Byelozersk, Sov. Un., G 11
.....	Byfield, England, J 16
.....	Bygaö, Nor., A 5
.....	Bygdea, Sweden, H 19
.....	Bygdö, Norway, A 5
2315	Bygland, Norway, N 6
.....	Bykle, Norway, M 5
281	Bylderup, Denmark, N 6
.....	Bynden, Ont., M 10
224	Byng, Ontario, O 11
725	Byng Inlet, Ontario, C 9
164	Byrock, Austl., M 20
7757	Byske, Sweden, G 1

C

Pop.	Place Country Index
6000	Caacupé, Paraguay, N 7
7000	Caaguazú, Paraguay, O 9
8000	Caapucú, Paraguay, P 7
26000	Caazapá, Paraguay, P 9
15656	Cabaiguan, Cuba, J 13
665	Caballococha, Peru, E 18
2278	Cabanaconde, Peru, O 16
1983	Cabañas, Cuba, H 5
342	Cabanillas, Peru, O 19
1867	Cabellos, Uruguay, F 17
.....	Cabeza de Buey, Arg., G 11
11762	Cabeza del Buëy, Sp., L 9
1181	Cabezas, Bolivia, J 13
3000	Cabhan (Cavan), Ire., G 16
1862	Cabildo, Chile, L 4
.....	Cabinda, Angola, M 11
.....	Cabo Alarcón, Arg., R 7
.....	Cabo Corrientes, Arg., Q 20
.....	Cabo de la Vela, Col., A 15
5759	Cabo Frio, Brazil, N 19
1404	Caborca, Son., D 9
.....	Caborys, Brazil, E 3
.....	Cabo Yubi, Rio de Oro, F 3
20779	Cabra, Spain, N 11
.....	Cabrejas, Spain, F 13
439	Cabri, Sask., P 5
942	Cabrillas, Spain, H 9
.....	Cabrobó, Brazil, H 21
.....	Cabruta, Venezuela, H 14
1271	Cabudare, Venezuela, D 10
1179	Cabure, Venezuela, B 9
.....	Caca, Czech., G 11
9116	Čačak, Yugo., K 13
267	Cacalotan, Sin., R 19
7677	Caçapava, Brazil, N 16
.....	Caçapava, Brazil, Q 10
1970	Cáceres, Col., F 9
39392	Cáceres, Spain, J 9
395	Cachache, Peru, H 6
.....	Cachari, Argentina, P 18
1004	Cache Bay, Ontario, A 10
.....	Cachendo, Peru, P 17
.....	Cacheuta, Arg., M 6
600	Cachi, Argentina, G 9
4865	Cachira, Colombia, F 13
.....	Cachiri, Colombia, F 13
10431	Cachoeira, Brazil, I 21
.....	Cachoeira, Brazil, G 22
.....	Cachoeira, Brazil, E 14
17498	Cachoeira, Brazil, Q 10
19208	Cachoeira do Itapemirim, Brazil, M 19
600	Cachuela Esperanza, Bolivia, B 8
4361	Cacocum, Cuba, N 20
.....	Cacota, Colombia, F 14
.....	Cadboll, Scotland, F 16
3895	Cadereyta, N. L., F 15
2960	Cadereyta, Quer., M 15
3013	Cadillac, France, N 9
196	Cadillac, Sask., Q 5
.....	Cadillal, Arg., H 10
87767	Cadiz, Spain, O 8
99	Cadogan, Alberta, L 23
61334	Caen, France, G 9
2326	Caerleon, England, L 11
35760	Caerphilly, Wales, L 10
346	Caesarea (Kaisarieh), Palestine, I 6
.....	Caetité, Brazil, J 19
1108	Cafayate, Argentina, H 9
81500	Cagliari, Italy, L 4
5029	Cagua, Venezuela, D 12
.....	Caguena, Bolivia, I 2
11308	Cahabón, Guatemala, E 5
.....	Caherconlish, Ire., M 11
.....	Cahermore, Ire., Q 2
1987	Cahersiveen, Ire., P 2
12667	Cahors, France, N 12
109	Cahuapanas, Peru, F 7
.....	Cahul, W. Sov. Un., I 23
2060	Caiazzo, It., J 14
19815	Caibarien, Cuba, I 13
2836	Caicara, Venezuela, D 18
1020	Caicara, Venezuela, H 14
.....	Caicó, Brazil, G 23
923	Cailloma, Peru, O 16
.....	Caimancito, Argentina, F11
1114	Caimanera, Cuba, O 23
317	Caimanes, Chile, L 4
2329	Caimito, Cuba, H 6
1138	Caina, Peru, K 9
521	Cainsville, Ontario, N 9
214	Caintown, Ontario, H 22
.....	Cairn Ryan, Scotland, Q 12
11993	Cairns, Austl., D 20
1311200	Cairo, Egypt, I 14
4838	Caislean An Bharraigh (Castlebar), Ire., H 7
.....	Caistor, England, G 19
7896	Caiza, Bolivia, L 9
2122	Caiza, Bolivia, M 13
1094	Cajacay, Peru, K 7
15553	Cajamarca, Peru, H 5
.....	Cajamarquilla, Peru, H 6
784	Cajarc, France, N 13
1645	Cajas, Bolivia, M 10
8294	Cajazeiras, Brazil, G 22
7551	Cajibio, Colombia, K 6
1348	Cajnica, Yugo., L 12
.....	Cajon, Argentina, J 12
.....	Cajurú, Brazil, M 15
.....	Cakovac, Yugo., I 8
686	Cala, U.S. Afr., N 17
.....	Calaares Senam, Tunisia, D 22
15000	Calabar, Nigeria, J 10
8131	Calabazar, Cuba, I 12
428	Calabogie, Ontario, E 19
3644	Calabozo, Venezuela, F 12
3964	Calacoto, Bolivia, I 3
.....	Cala d'Oliva, Italy, J 3
1519	Calaf, Spain, F 19
7831	Calafat, Romania, K 17
13199	Calahorra, Spain, E 14
67568	Calais, France, D 13
.....	Calama, Brazil, H 3
4967	Calama, Chile, E 5
800	Calamar, Colombia, L 14
6934	Calamar, Colombia, C 10
7063	Calamarca, Bolivia, H 4
2131	Calamocha, Spain, H 15
4152	Calanda, Spain, H 17
17890	Călărasi, Romania, K 22
.....	Călărasi-Targ, W. Sov. Un. H 23
7453	Calarca, Colombia, I 8
10342	Calasparra, Spain, L 15
.....	Calassim, Siam., O 6
445	Calatañazor, Spain, F 13
18419	Calatayud, Spain, G 15
3037	Calca, Peru, M 16
1544	Calcalotán, Sin., L 15
12592	Calceta, Ecuador, C 2
5769	Calcha, Bolivia, L 10
150	Calchaqui, Argentina, K 17
.....	Calcoene, Brazil, C 13
2108891	Calcutta, India, I 22
.....	Caldas, Colombia, J 6
6837	Caldas da Rainha, Port., J 5
.....	Caldenadas, Arg., M 10
226	Calder, Sask., O 11
1525	Caldera, Chile, H 3
235	Caldera, Panama, P 17
.....	Calderon, Arg., Q 15
6472	Caldono, Colombia, K 6
.....	Caledon, N. Ire., E 19
200	Caledon, Ontario, K 10
1498	Caledon, U.S. Afr., R 8
419	Caledon East, Ontario, K 10
865	Caledonia, N. S., O 11
1401	Caledonia, Ontario, N 10
214	Caledonia, P. E. I., H 17
2566	Calenzana, Cor., P 2
8426	Calera, Chile, M 4
2841	Calera, Zac., J 8
1371	Caleta Buena, Chile, C 3
.....	Caleta Coloso, Chile, F 3
.....	Caleufu, Arg., O 12
.....	Calf of Man, Eng., F 6
.....	Calfucurá, Arg., P 20
88904	Calgary, Alberta, N 20
.....	Calgary, Scotland, K 7
88366	Cali, Colombia, J 6
99273	Calicut, India, O 8
34	Caliento, Man., R 17
.....	California, Bolivia, C 6
3017	Calimaya, Mex., H 4
1638	Calimete, Cuba, I 10
.....	Calingapatam, India, K 17
.....	Calingasta, Argentina, L 6
6754	Calitri, Italy, J 17
1500	Calitzdorp, U.S. Afr., P 11
4199	Calkini, Camp., F 20
3552	Callac, France, H 3
1508	Callan, Ire., M 16
736	Callander, Ont., A 12
2423	Callander, Scotland, L 15
84438	Callao, Peru, L 8
5386	Callapa, Bolivia, I 4
243	Callayue, Peru, G 4
142	Calle Calle, Chile, R 3
.....	Callernish, Scotland, E 5
2681	Calloo, Belgium, Q 7
44	Calmali, Baja Cal., H 7
.....	Calmore, N. Ire., C 16
6582	Calmpthout, Belgium, P 9
2039	Calnali, Hid., E 6
3463	Calne, England, L 14
1679	Calotmul, Yuc., E 24
1046	Caloto, Colombia, K 7
5536	Caltabellotta, Italy, O 13
30845	Caltagirone, Italy, O 15
35200	Caltanissetta, Italy, O 14
705	Calumet, Quebec, P 13
2139	Calvi, Cor., P 2
2943	Calvillo, Agua., L 12
2000	Calvinia, U.S. Afr., N 8
5681	Calw, Germany, O 5
250	Cama, Switzerland, M 18
.....	Camacho, Bolivia, C 4
1127	Camacho, Bolivia, N 10
3053	Camaguán, Venezuela, G 12
78458	Camaguey, Cuba, L 16
12087	Camajuani, Cuba, I 12
.....	Camamú, Brazil, J 21
2253	Camaná, Peru, P 15
1095	Camarés, France, O 15
2000	Camargo, Bolivia, M 10
26	Camarones, Chile, B 4
1127	Camarones, Cuba, J 11
3215	Camata, Bolivia, G 3
3174	Camataqui, Bolivia, M 10
31877	Cambay, India, I 5
1500	Cambelltown, N. Z., Q 5
14157	Camborne, England, O 3
29655	Cambrai, France, F 15
236	Cambray, Ontario, I 13
66803	Cambridge, England, J 20
211	Cambridge, N. B., I 9
2330	Cambridge, N. Z., E 18
3342	Cambrils, Spain, G 19
27128	Cambuslang, Scotland, N 16
300	Camden, East, Ont., I 19
.....	Camedo, Switz., N 15
.....	Camet, Argentina, Q 20
.....	Cametá, Brazil, E 14
3146	Caminha, Portugal, F 5
.....	Caminiaga, Argentina, K 12
174	Camlachie, Ontario, N 4
.....	Cammin, Pol., C 8
7820	Camocim, Brazil, E 20
500	Camolin, Ire., M 21
222	Camooweal, Austl., F 16
.....	Camp, Afg., F 21
.....	Camp, Netherlands, E 13
556	Campagnac, France, N 16
2875	Campagnano, Italy, H 11
27944	Campana, Argentina, N 18
9440	Campanário, Spain, K 10
.....	Campbell, Argentina, K 16
639	Campbell, U.S. Afr., J 13
3018	Campbellford, Ont., I 16
900	Campbell's Bay, Que., P 8
219	Campbellsville, Ont., L 10
6748	Campbellton, N. B., A 7
6309	Campbelltown, Scot., G 16
847	Campbelltown, Tasmania, D 8
6757	Campbeltown, Scot., O 9
.....	Campden, Eng., K 14
23166	Campeche, Camp., G 20
6013	Campechuela, Cuba Q 18
44	Camper, Man., O 15
3029	Camperdown, Austl., Q 17
.....	Camperucho, Col., D 13
.....	Campestre, Brazil, J 19
.....	Campi, Italy, K 22
3520	Campiglia Marittima, Italy, G 7
7334	Campillos, Spain, N 10
.....	Campina, Brazil, F 3
17104	Câmpina, Romania, J 20
34023	Campina Grande, Brazil, G 24
79494	Campinas, Brazil, N 15
.....	Campione, Switz., P 17
.....	Campo, Spain, N 24
93	Campo, Switz., K 17
204	Campo, Switz., M 15
10915	Campo Alegre, Col., K 9
12118	Campobasso, Italy, I 15
7312	Campo Bello, Brazil, M 16
.....	Campo Cologno, Switzerland, N 24
.....	Campo Formoso, Brazil, I 21
23460	Campo Grande, Brazil, F 21
.....	Campo Largo, Brazil, I 17
.....	Campo Maior, Brazil, F 20
6179	Campo Maior, Portugal, K 7
.....	Campos, Brazil, I 22
52677	Campos, Brazil, N 19
357	Campo Santo, Arg., F 10
5326	Campos del Puerto, Sp., J 22
.....	Campos Novos de Paranapanema, Brazil, N 13
.....	Campos Salles, Brazil, G 21
13454	Câmpulung, Rom., J 19
7552	Câmpulungul-Moldov, Rom., H 19
2598	Camrose, Alberta, K 21
21000	Canada de Gomez, Argentina, M 16
.....	Canada Honda, Arg., L 7
.....	Canada Verde, Arg., N 12
11495	Çanakkale (Kale Sultaniye), Tur., C 1
.....	Canala, Italy, C 13
.....	Canaléjas, Argentina, O 9
.....	Canals, Arg., M 14
11006	Cananea, Son., C 12
11662	Cañar, Ecuador, D 4
212	Canard, Nova Scotia, L 13
.....	Canario, Cuba, M 18
1967	Cañasgerdas, Col., G 7
1046	Canatlán, Dur., O 21
1286	Cañaveras, Spain, I 14
12000	Canberra, Australia, P 20
6340	Cancale, France, H 6
.....	Cancha Labrada, Par., D 3
42	Canchas, Chile, G 4
222	Cancuc, Chia., M 16
301	Cancura, Chile, A 19
721	Candarave, Peru, P 19
1797	Candé, France, J 7
2072	Candela, Coa., D 13
7605	Candela, Italy, J 17
3000	Candelaria, Argentina, H 11
466	Candelaria, Arg., I 23
.....	Candelaria, Bolivia, D 3
1300	Candelaria, Col., J 7
2127	Candelaria, Cuba, I 5
380	Candelario, Arg., L 10
	Candia, see Erakleion, Grc.
	Canea, see Khania, Grc.
357	Canela, Chile, L 3
8000	Canelones, Uruguay, O 19
.....	Canelos, Ecuador, C 6
2695	Cañeta, Spain, I 15
3137	Cañete, Chile, Q 2
4 794	Cañete, Peru, M 9
157	Canfield Jc., Ontario, N 11
.....	Canford, B. C., P 14
.....	Canfunaro, Italy, D 14
902	Cangallo, Peru, M 13
.....	Cangan, Australia, G 5
15836	Cangas, Spain, E 5
9936	Cangas de Onis, Spain, C 10
23668	Cangas de Tinéo, Spain, C 8
.....	Cangó ó Bobi, Par., Q 9
.....	Canieül, Switz., K 20
.....	Canim, B. C., N 14
1365	Canisbay, Scotland, C 19
2923	Canjayar, Spain, O 14
700	Canmore, Alberta, N 19
34236	Cannanore, India, O 8
.....	Cannavieiras, Brazil, K 21
	Canne Ruins, see Qal'a Shargat, Iraq.
49032	Cannes, France, P 24
224	Cannes, Nova Scotia, J 22
663	Canneto, Italy, D 7
.....	Canning, India, I 22
827	Canning, N. S., L 12
763	Cannington, Ontario, I 13
34588	Cannock, England, I 14
.....	Cannor, B. C., P 5, Q 13
.....	Cannstatt, Germany, O 6
.....	Canoa, Ecuador, B 2
1146	Canoabo, Venezuela, C 11
1657	Canobbio, Italy, C 4
.....	Caño Colorado, Ven., D 19
.....	Canoinhas, Brazil, O 12
1508	Canonbie, Scotland, Q 21
1200	Canora, Sask., N 11
2412	Cansahcab, Yuc., E 22
1418	Canso, Nova Scotia, K 22
1584	Canta, Peru, L 9
1507	Cantaura, Venezuela, E 17
1924	Cantavieia, Sp., H 17
24450	Canterbury, Eng., L 23
398	Canterbury Station, New Brunswick, I 4
144	Canters, Switz., K 20
26000	Cantho, Fr. In. Ch., R 7
6237	Cantillana, Spain, N 9
.....	Cantin, Morocco, H 3
1145285	Canton, China, L 14
12	Canuck, Sask., R 5
13000	Canuelas, Argentina, N 19
.....	Canuman, Brazil, F 6
.....	Canutama, Brazil, G 2
232	Canwood, Sask., K 7
1073	Cany, France, F 11
.....	Canyon, Yukon, Q 9
.....	Capanema, Brazil, J 7
.....	Capannelle, Italy, D 25
.....	Capão Bonito, Brazil, N 14
3766	Capatarida, Venezuela, B 7
4582	Capaya, Venezuela, C 14
.....	Capayan, Arg., J 10
11961	Cap-de-la-Madeleine, Quebec, M 18
321	Cape Augnet, N. S., K 22
370	Cape Bald, N. B., H 13
17685	Cape Coast, Gold Coast, J 6
518	Cape Croker, Ontario, G 7
.....	Cape Foulwind, N. Z., K 10
114	Cape George, N. S., I 19
.....	Cape Jack, N. S., J 20
303	Capella, Austl., H 21
269	Cape Negro, N. S., R 10
365	Cape North, N. S., E 23
.....	Cape Scott, B. C., O 8
10934	Capesterre, Guadeloupe, B 23
7086	Capesterre (Marie Galante), Guadeloupe, C 24
130	Cape Tormentine, N. B., H 14
352000	Capetown, U.S.Afr., Q 7
20000	Cap Haitien, Haiti, H 13
22000	Capiatá, Paraguay, N 7
5620	Capinota, Bolivia, I 7
917	Capirato, Sin., N 16
.....	Capitan, Cuba, J 10
1193	Capitan Pastene, Chile, Q 3
8192	Capodistra, Italy, D 13
508	Capolago, Switzerland, P 17
.....	Cappaghwhite, Ire., M 12
.....	Cappamore, Ire., M 11
7544	Cappellen, Belgium, K 11
.....	Cappoquin, Ire., O 14
1641	Capreol, Ontario, R 24
870	Caprino, Italy, D 8
402	Cap Rouge, Quebec, L 21
3103	Caprycke, Belgium, Q 2
975	Cap Saint Ignace, Que., K 23
602	Cap Santé, Quebec, L 20
2419	Caqueza, Col., I 11
5959	Caquiaviri, Bolivia, I 3
14769	Caracal, Romania, K 18
266706	Carácas, Venezuela, C 13
3349	Caracato, Bolivia, I 5
195	Caracena, Spain, G 13
550	Caracenilla, Spain, I 14
1866	Carache, Venezuela, D 8
4871	Caracolla, Bolivia, I 6
11722	Caraguatay, Par., N 8
4341	Carahue, Chile, Q 3
.....	Carandasal, Brazil, L 8
9000	Caransebes, Romania, J 16
1765	Carapari, Bolivia, N 12
17000	Carapegua, Par., O 7
1657	Caraquet, N. B., B 11
.....	Cararigua, Venezuela, D 8
.....	Carasso, Switzerland, N 17
.....	Caratasca, Honduras, F 15
.....	Caratinga, Brazil, M 19
20645	Caravaca, Spain, M 14
7475	Caravaggio, Italy, D 6
1177	Caraveli, Peru, O 14
.....	Caravellas, Brazil, L 21
1100	Carayaó, Paraguay, N 9
18159	Carballo, Spain, C 6
931	Carberry, Manitoba, Q 14
.....	Carberry Jc., Man., Q 14
5095	Carbet, Martinique, F 24
409	Carbon, Alberta, N 21
68	Carbondale, Alberta, J 21
3450	Carbonear, Newf., K 25
2022	Carbonera, S. L. P., J 14
4664	Carboneras, Spain, O 15
1322	Carbonne, France, P 12
.....	Carbost, Scotland, H 7
.....	Carbury, Ire., J 18
17846	Carcagente, Spain, K 17
33441	Carcassonne, France, P 14
100	Carcross, Yukon, Q 10
37144	Cardeñas, Cuba, H 9
8478	Cárdenas, S. L. P., K 15
3082	Cárdenas, Tab., K 15
1700	Cardenete, Spain, J 15
223648	Cardiff, Wales, L 10
.....	Cardiff Jc., Alta., K 20
532	Cardigan, P. E. I., H 17
3309	Cardigan, Wales, J 6
1645	Cardinal, Ontario, G 23
.....	Cardón, Baja Cal., G 5
6474	Cardona, Spain, F 20
.....	Cardozo, Uruguay, J 19
14	Cardross, Sask., Q 7
1864	Cardston, Alberta, Q 21
.....	Cardwell Jc., Ontario, K 10
16085	Careii, Romania, H 16
.....	Carenero, Cuba, H 5
3656	Carentan, France, G 7
400	Cargill, Ontario, I 6
1257	Cargill, Scotland, K 19
4115	Carhaix, France, H 2
.....	Carhuamayo, Peru, K 9
7500	Carhue, Argentina, P 14
.....	Cariacica, Brazil, M 20
15163	Cariamanga, Ecuador, F 3
.....	Caribrod, Yugo., L 16
1096	Carichic, Chih., H 16
1878	Carignan, France, F 19
240	Carillon, Quebec, P 13
18224	Carinhanha, Brazil, J 18
12912	Carini, Italy, N 12
11847	Caripito, Ven., D 19
.....	Carlanstown, Ire., H 19
223	Carleton, N. S., P 8
4305	Carleton Place, Ont., F 21
600	Carlingford, Ire., G 22
57107	Carlisle, England, C 11
.....	Carlisle Fort, Ire., Q 12
7792	Carloforte, Italy, L 2
.....	Carlosama, Colombia, M 4
30287	Carlos Casares, Arg., O 16
	Carlow, see Ceatharloch, Ire.
.....	Carloway, Scotland, D 5
	Carlsbad, see Karlsbad, Ger.
	Carlsruhe, see Karlsruhe, Ger.
22336	Carlton, England, H 16
100	Carlton, Sask., L 7
10507	Carluke, Scotland, N 17
429	Carlyle, Sask., Q 11
.....	Carmacks, Yukon, N 8
3740	Carmagnola, Italy, E 2
1455	Carman, Man., R 15
229	Carmangay, Alberta, O 21
10310	Carmarthen, Wales, K 7
11129	Carmaux, France, O 14
.....	Carmelita Brazil, J 4
12000	Carmelo, Uruguay, N 15
.....	Cármen, Bolivia, C 4
439	Carmen, Chile, E 4
8228	Carmen, Colombia, D 10
9315	Carmen, Colombia, E 13
1122	Carmen, Colombia, J 10
7687	Carmen, Camp., J 17
.....	Carmen, Uruguay, L 19
.....	Carmen, Ver., K 13
.....	Carmen Alto, Bolivia, D 6
1095	Carmen Alto, Chile, E 4
11000	Carmen de Areco, Argentina, N 18
1127	Carmen de Cura, Venezuela, D 13
12638	Carmen del Paraná, Paraguay, R 9
.....	Carmensa, Argentina, O 8
.....	Carmo, Brazil, I 15
9470	Carmo do Fructal, Brazil, M 14
24876	Carmona, Spain, N 9
753	Carmyllie, Scotland, K 21
.....	Carn, N. Ire., C 18
.....	Carnach, Scotland, K 12
690	Carnamah, Australia, L 4
845	Carnarvon, Australia, I 3
2100	Carnarvon, U.S. Afr., M 11
8469	Carnarvon, Wales, H 7
736	Carnbee, Scotland, L 21
.....	Carncastle, N. Ire., C 23
800	Carndonagh, Ire., B 16
384	Carnduff, Sask., R 11
.....	Carneros, Coa., G 12
.....	Carnew, Ire., M 21
.....	Carney, Ire., F 10
3193	Carnforth, England, E 12
1514	Carnicerias, Col., K 8
.....	Carnish, Scotland, E 4
.....	Carnlough, N. Ire., C 22
908	Carnot, Algeria, C 15
5266	Carnot, Fr. Eq. Afr., J 12
4806	Carnoustie, Scotland, K 21
.....	Carnteel, N. Ire., E 18
.....	Carolina, Brazil, G 15
2049	Carolina, Colombia, G 8
.....	Carolina, Cuba, K 15
468	Carolina, U.S. Afr., F 21
164	Caron, Sask., P 7
8204	Carora, Venezuela, D 8
438	Carouge, Switz., K 5
8073	Carouge, Switz., N 1
526	Carp, Ontario, E 21
12632	Carpentras, France, O 20
11272	Carpi, Italy, E 8
5772	Carpino, Italy, I 18
.....	Carpinteria, Argentina, L 7
499	Carquefou, France, J 6
.....	Carracol, Brazil, N 15
23951	Carrara, Italy, F 6
222	Carrathool, Australia, O 19
.....	Carraweena, Australia, K17
3220	Carreno, Cuba, J 10
.....	Carr Glyn, Yukon, P 9
.....	Carrick, Ire., D 10
.....	Carrick, Ire., O 20
.....	Carrickart, Ire., B 14
4608	Carrickfergus, N. Ire., D 23
2000	Carrickmacross, Ire., G 19
1200	Carrick on the Shannon, Ire., G 13
5406	Carrick-on-Suir, Ire., N 16
4052	Carrieres-sur-Seine, Fr., A 2
.....	Carrig, Ire., P 5
.....	Carrigaholt, Ire., M 4
.....	Carrigaline, Ire., Q 11
.....	Carrigallen, Ire., G 15
.....	Carril, Spain, D 5
.....	Carrilobo, Argentina, L 13
3069	Carrion de los Condes, Spain, E 11
.....	Carrizal, Argentina, J 8
144	Carrizal Alto, Chile, I 3
271	Carrizal Bajo, Chile, I 3
167	Carrizalillo, Chile, H 4
107	Carroll, Manitoba, R 13
493	Carrouge, Switz., K 5
.....	Carrowkeel, Ire., B 17
86	Carruthers, Sask., L 4
135	Carseland, Alberta, O 21
.....	Carshalton, England, D 21
.....	Carskey, Scotland, P 9
1931	Carsoli, Italy, H 12
355	Carsphairn, Scotland, P 15
371	Carstairs, Alberta, N 20
2289	Carstairs, Scotland, N 17
73190	Cartagena, Colombia, C 9
113468	Cartagena, Spain, N 16
14750	Cartago, Colombia, I 8
9667	Cartago, Costa Rica, N 15
5545	Cartaxo, Portugal, J 5
6971	Cartaya, Spain, N 7
1940	Carterton, N. Z., J 18
465	Cartier, Ontario, R 23
.....	Cartmel, England, E 11
350	Cartwright, Manitoba, R 14
901	Carumas, Peru, P 19
15067	Carúpano, Venezuela, C 19
13	Carvel Station, Alberta, K20
.....	Carvoeiro, Brazil, E 4
85	Casabindo, Arg., E 9
2096	Casablanca, Chile, M 4
.....	Casa Blanca, Hond., E 11
463500	Casablanca, Mor., E 5
98	Casaccia, Switz., L 21
20543	Casale Monferrato, It., D 3
.....	Casares, Argentina, J 14
1827	Casas Grandes, Chih., D 15
3584	Casas Ibáñez, Sp., K 15
.....	Casas Viejas, Son., F 10
177	Cascade, B. C., Q 17
.....	Cascaes, Portugal, K 4
1538	Cascajal, Cuba, I 10
3702	Cascánte, Spain, F 15
.....	Cascota, Cuba, L 18
3503	Case Pilote, Martinique, G 24
.....	Caseros, Arg., M 19
.....	Casey, Argentina, P 15
2800	Cashel, Ire., M 14
1465	Casilda, Cuba, K 12
5287	Casino, Australia, L 23
.....	Casitas, Peru, E 2
10637	Cáslav, Czech., F 8
2676	Casma, Peru, J 6
9033	Caspe, Spain, G 17
1700	Cassel, France, E 14
	Cassel, see Kassel, Ger.
1021	Casselman, Ontario, E 24
.....	Cassidy, B. C., Q 12
36	Cassils, Alberta, O 22
.....	Cassinga, Ang., N 13
7002	Cassona, Italy, L 19
596	Castanet, France, P 12
4668	Castanheira, Portugal, K 4
1677	Castaño, Coa., D 11
.....	Castano Nuevo, Arg., K 5
207	Castasegna, Switz., M 20
2518	Castel Bolognese, Italy, E 10
.....	Castel del Pazzi, Italy, A 24
4192	Casteljaloux, France, N 9
.....	Castel la Cecchina, It., A 24
28340	Castellammare di Stabia, Italy, J 15
1918	Castellamonte, Italy, D 2
766	Castellane, France, O 23
723	Castelli, Argentina, O 20
19098	Castello, Brazil, F 20
46876	Castellon de la Plana, Sp., I 17
1913	Castellote, Spain, H 17
7891	Castelnaudary, Fr., P 14
1444	Castelnau de Médoc, Fr., M 8
9327	Castelo Branco, Port., I 7
7546	Castel-Sarrasin, Fr., O 12
2000	Casterton, Australia, Q 17
676	Castets, France, O 7
3990	Castiglione, Italy, D 7
284	Castilla, Chile, F 4
2260	Castilletes, Colombia, B 17
.....	Castillo (Ruinas), Q.R., F 25
142	Castillon, Fr., N 9
540	Castillon, Fr., Q 11
2703	Castillon-et-Capitourlan, France, N 9
	Castlebar, see Caislean An Bharraigh, Ire.
.....	Castlebay, Scotland, I 2
.....	Castlebellingham, Ire., G 21
.....	Castleblakeney, Ire., J 11
1553	Castleblayney, Ire., G 19
.....	Castlebridge, Ire., N 21
.....	Castlecomer, Ire., L 17
.....	Castleconer, Ire., F 8
.....	Castleconnell, Ire., M 10
.....	Castle Dawson, N. Ire., D 20
1000	Castlederg, N. Ire., D 15
.....	Castledermot, Ire., L 19
.....	Castle Donovan, Ire., Q 7
3008	Castle Douglas, Scot., Q 17
.....	Castlefinn, Ire., D 15
201	Castlegar, B. C., Q 17
.....	Castlegregory, Ire., O 2
.....	Castleisland, Ire., O 6
5221	Castlemaine, Australia, P19
200	Castlemaine, Ire., O 4
.....	Castlemarty, Ire., P 13
31	Castle Point, N. Z., J 19
.....	Castlepollard, Ire., H 16
1232	Castlereagh, Ire., F 7
.....	Castlereagh, Ire., H 11
462	Castleton, Ontario, J 16
1965	Castletown, Eng., E 6
.....	Castletown, Ire., D 12
.....	Castletown, Ire., G 7
.....	Castletown, Ire., J 16
.....	Castletown, Ire., Q 3
.....	Castletown, Ire., Q 8
.....	Castletown, Scotland, C 18
.....	Castletownroche, Ire., O 11
.....	Castletownsend, Ire., R 7
.....	Castlewarren, Ire., M 18
.....	Castlewellan, N. Ire., F 23
625	Castor, Alberta, L 22
29133	Castres, France, P 14
5281	Castricum, Neth., F 13
24000	Castries (Pt. Castries), Sta. Lucia, N 24
1258	Castries, Fr., P 18
5816	Castro, Brazil, O 13
85	Castro, Switz., L 17
17298	Castro del Rio, Spain, M 11
2131	Castrogeriz, Spain, E 11
26415	Castrogiovanni, Italy, O 15
7368	Castropol, Spain, C 8
2089	Castroreale, Italy, N 17
4958	Castro Verde, Portugal, M 6
8955	Castrovillari, Italy, L 18
872	Castrovirreina, Peru, M 11
9289	Castuera, Spain, K 9
8526	Catacaos, Peru, F 2
13817	Catacocha, Ecuador, E 3
.....	Catalao, Brazil, L 15
412	Catalina, Chile, G 4
215	Catalone, Nova Scotia, I 24
22200	Catamarca, Arg., I 10
.....	Catamarca, Bolivia, I 4
.....	Catamindi (In Disp. Ter.), Bolivia, M 13
199200	Catania, Italy, O 16
26900	Catanzaro, Italy, M 19
755	Catapilco, Chile, M 4
114	Cataract, Ontario, K 10
88	Catarina la Grande, Chia., N 15
5374	Catemaco, Ver., J 12
825	Cathcart, U.S. Afr., O 16
417	Catorce, S. L. P., I 12
.....	Catrilo, Arg., O 13
	Cattaro, see Kotor, Yugo.
.....	Catterline, Scotland, J 23
.....	Caudal, Cuba, K 6
7442	Caudete, Spain, L 16
2243	Caughnawaga, Quebec, Q15
6903	Caulonia, Italy, M 19
12987	Cauquenes, Chile, O 3
.....	Cauquira, Hond., F 15
3631	Caussade, France, O 13
95	Cavaignac, Algeria, C 14
11743	Cavaillon, France, O 20
.....	Cavalcante, Brazil, J 15
.....	Cavalcanti, Brazil, H 3
2027	Cavalese, Italy, C 9
	Cavalla, see Kavalla, Grc
	Cavan, see Cabhan, Ire.
79	Cavan, Ontario, I 14
3925	Cavari, Bolivia, I 6
6211	Cavarna, Bul., K 23
3971	Cavarzere, Italy, D 10
392	Cavasta, Argentina, L 17
.....	Cave, New Zealand, N 9
37	Cavell, Saskatchewan, M 5
75	Cavendish, Alberta, N 24
.....	Cavendish, P. E. I., G 15
204	Caviano, Switzerland, O 16
767	Cawdor, Scotland, G 16
487324	Cawnpore, India, G 13
.....	Cawood, England, F 16
.....	Cawsand, England, O 7
17409	Caxias, Braz., P 12
7254	Caxias, Brazil, F 18
.....	Caxias, West Brazil, F 15
11627	Cayambe, Ecuador, B 6
11704	Cayenne, Fr. Gu., B 11
133	Cayley, Alberta, O 21
1781	Cayma, Peru, P 17
.....	Cayo Venado, Chia., L 19
721	Cayuga, Ontario, N 10
10058	Cazalla de la Sierra, Sp., M 9
.....	Caza Pava, Arg., I 22
456	Cazaubon, France, O 9
2081	Cazéres, France, P 11
.....	Cazon, Argentina, O 18
13031	Cazorla, Spain, M 13
	Ceará, see Fortaleza, Braz.
.....	Ceará-Mirim, Brazil, G 25
6515	Ceatharloch (Carlow), Ire., L 19
1754	Ceballos, Cuba, K 15
.....	Cebollar, Arg., J 9
723	Cebollar, Chile, D 6
4347	Cebreros, Spain, H 11
4736	Ceccano, Italy, I 12
.....	Cecile Junction, Que., Q 14
3872	Cecina, Italy, G 7
5205	Ceclavin, Spain, I 8
1002	Cedar Dale, Ont., K 13
262	Cedar Grove, Ont., K 12
127	Cedar Springs, Ont., Q 4
.....	Cedarvale, B. C., I 8
6466	Cedéira, Spain, B 6
3472	Cedral, S. L. P., H 13
129	Cedrito, Coa., A 10
99	Cefalú, Italy, N 14
37344	Cegléd, Hung., I 12
17505	Ceglie Messapico, Italy, J 21
17316	Cehegin, Spain, M 15
.....	Cejolao, Argentina, I 14
7744	Celano, Italy, H 13
9834	Celanova, Spain, E 7
22766	Celaya, Guan. M 13
.....	Celbridge, Ire., J 20
4045	Celendin, Peru, H 6
515	Celestum, Yuc., E 20
392	Céligny, Switz., M 2
7602	Celje (Cilli), Yugo., I 7
6000	Celle, Germany, G 7
774	Celles, Fr., L 9
3200	Celorico, Portugal, H 7
.....	Cemmes, Wales, I 9
604	Centeno, Argentina, L 15
4942	Cento, Italy, E 9
21	Central, Chile, E 4

Pop.	Place Country Index
251	Central Butte, Saskatchewan, O 7
318	Central Greenwich, N. B., K 8
275	Centralia, Ontario, M 5
375	Centre Burlington, N. S., L 14
214	Centre Musquodoboit, N. S., L 16
301	Centreville, N. B., G 4
315	Centreville, N. S., L 12
400	Centreville, N. S., N 8
150	Centreville, Ont., I 19
.....	Cercal, Portugal, M 5
.....	Cercany, Ger., M 14
20	Cere, Chile, E 5
142	Cereal, Alberta, M 23
.....	Cereales, Arg., P 13
872	Ceres, Argentina, K 15
1155	Ceres, U.S. Afr., P 8
4918	Céret, France, Q 15
4503	Cerete, Colombia, E 8
36017	Cerignola, Italy, J 18
1186	Cérilly, France, K 15
916	Cerizay, France, K 8
.....	Cerknica, Yugo., J 6
.....	Cernăuti, see Chernovitsy, Sov. Un.
6459	Cernă-Vodă, Rom., K 23
2759	Cerralvo, N. L., E 16
.....	Cerre Morone, Arg., F 3
.....	Cerreto, Italy, E 7
3209	Cerreto, Italy, I 15
661	Cerrillos, Arg., G 10
.....	Cerrillos, Argentina, J 13
135	Cerrillos, Chile, I 4
235	Cerrillos, Chile, K 3
3422	Cerrito, Colombia, J 7
.....	Cerritos, Arg., E 5
6980	Cerritos, S. L. P., J 14
.....	Cerritos Bayos, Chile, E 5
1372	Cerro Azul, Peru, M 8
.....	Cerro Blanco, Arg., C 23
355	Cerro Blanco, Chile, I 4
.....	Cerro Chato, Ur., H 22
.....	Cerro Chato, Uruguay, L 21
.....	Cerro Colorado, Ur., M 20
.....	Cerro de las Cuentas, Uruguay, K 22
19187	Cerro de Pasco, Peru, K 9
2508	Cerro de San Antonio, Colombia, C 10
85	Cerro Gordo, Chile, D 4
.....	Cerro Negro, Arg., I 8
15	Cerro Negro, Chile, F 4
11	Cervatillo, Baja Cal., O 9
1237	Cervera, Spain, D 11
4239	Cervera, Spain, F 19
7101	Cervera del Rio Alhama, Spain, F 14
2357	Cervia, Italy, E 11
...	Cervo, Brazil, M 11
15943	Cesena, Italy, F 10
7692	Cesis, Sov. Un., H 3
14230	Ceská Lípa, Czech., F 7
43886	Ceské Budějovice, Czech., G 7
8589	Ceský Krumlov, Czech., G 7
33495	Cetatea Alba, W. Sov. Un., I 25
6367	Cetinje, Yugo., L 12
2382	Cetraro, Italy, L 18
	Cette, see Sète, Fr.
59115	Ceuta, Sp. Mor., C 8
371	Cevio, Switzerland, M 15
270	Ceylon, Sask., R 8
6348	Cezimbra, Portugal, L 4
1298	Chabanais, France, L 11
1015	Chabeuil, France, N 20
1656	Chablis, France, I 17
57347	Chacabuco, Arg., N 17
.....	Cha Calumba, Ang., M 14
.....	Chacance, Chile, E 4
510	Chacapa, Bolivia, G 4
568	Chacarilla, Bolivia, I 4
1541	Chacarilla, Chile, B 3
.....	Chacayán, Peru, K 9
.....	Chacchan, Peru, J 7
.....	Chacharan, India, E 4
.....	Chacras Arg., J 13
.....	Chadmal, Iran, E 13
.....	Chaga, Tur., C 6
.....	Chagai, Baluchistan, M 19
4742	Chagny, France, K 18
189	Chagres, Panama, O 21
1297	Chaguaramal, Ven., D 19
3774	Chaguaramas, Ven., E 14
.....	Chaguarurco, Ec., E 4
.....	Chahar Farakhi, Iran, K 14
.....	Chahar Gumbat, Iran, I 12
.....	Chahdausi, India, E 12
.....	Chahkambar, Iran, O 13
.....	Chahl Dakhtur, Afg. G 16
.....	Chahtalk, Iran, N 8
8700	Chaibasa, India, I 19
600	Chaillé-les-Marais, Fr., K 7
.....	Chainpur, Nepal, F 20
.....	Chajan, Argentina, M 11
.....	Chakansur, Afg., K 17
.....	Chakessar, India, B 6
.....	Chakilsumu, Chn., A 17
.....	Chal, Tur., G 4
721	Chala, Peru, O 13
674	Chalaco, Peru, F 3
803	Chalais, France, M 9
3490	Chalatenango, Sal., G 7
5659	Chalcatongo, Oax., P 16
6668	Chalchicomula, Pueb., I 8
3638	Chalchihuites, Zac., I 5
3208	Chalco, Méx., H 5
.....	Chalet of the Khedive, Egypt, F 23
2538	Chalgali, India, H 17
.....	Chalhuanca, Peru, N 14
274	Chalinga, Chile, L 4
.....	Chalingchow, China, J 14
112	Challabamba, Peru, M 16
.....	Challaco, Arg., Q 8
3502	Challacollo, Bolivia, J 5
.....	Challaguaya, Peru, Q 19
988	Challana, Bolivia, G 4
5609	Challans, France, K 6
4960	Challapata, Bolivia, K 6
.....	Chalman, Afg., G 19
3516	Chalonnes-sur-Loire, Fr., J 8
35530	Châlons-sur-Marne, Fr., G 18
32533	Châlon-sur-Saône, Fr., K 19
1516	Châlus, France, M 11
4766	Cham, Germany, N 11
.....	Cham, Iran, L 5
4407	Cham, Switz., F 14
.....	Chamaico, Arg., N 11
.....	Chaman, Bal., K 21
6000	Chamba, India, C 9
.....	Chambas, Cuba, J 14
114	Chamberlain, Sask., O 8
.....	Chamberlain, Ur., K 18
28073	Chambéry, France, M 21
456	Chambley, France, G 21
1185	Chambly Canton, Que., P 16
991	Chambon, Fr., L 14
1029	Chambord Jc., Que., F 19
.....	Chambrelien, Switz., H 5
100	Chamcook, N. B., L 5
.....	Chamdum Draya, China, H 3
.....	Chame, Panama, P 21
77	Chamela, Jal., N 3
770	Chamical, Argentina, K 9
6030	Chamizo, Uruguay, N 19
3811	Chamonix, France, L 23
1860	Chamoson, Switz., N 7
.....	Champa, India, I 16
.....	Champagne, Yukon, P 8
4423	Champagnole, France, K 21
.....	Champaran, India, F 18
1564	Champerico, Guat., G 2
792	Champery, Switz., N 5
27540	Champigny-sur-Marne, Fr. B 8
320	Champion, Alberta, O 21
556	Champlain, Quebec, M 18
1513	Champlitte, France, I 20
1569	Champotón, Camp., H 19
.....	Champur, Nep., F 20
.....	Chamuchina, Col., J 24
.....	Chamula, Chia., M 16
.....	Chamur, Turkey, E 18
3659	Chamusca, Port., J 6
	Chanak, see Kale Sultaniye, Tur.
.....	Chanar, Argentina, K 10
115	Chanar, Chile, J 3
2980	Chañaral, Chile, H 3
.....	Chanarcito, Chile, I 3
.....	Chancay, Peru, L 8
1931	Chanco, Chile, O 3
272	Chancy, Switz., N 1
28138	Chanda, India, J 12
.....	Chandaburi, Siam., P 4
26768	Chandausi, India, E 12
4100	Chanderi, India, H 11
32284	Chandernagore, India, H 21
.....	Chandid, Egypt, D 9
.....	Chandos, Australia, E 17
12600	Chandpur, India, E 11
.....	Chanduy, Ecuador, D 2
500000	Changan (Sian), China, F 11
.....	Changchow China, G 19
500000	Changchow, China., K 18
415264	Changchun (Hsinking), Manch., B 22
.....	Chang-hwa, China, M 10
.....	Changkiu, China, E 18
.....	Changkwan, Manch., A 24
.....	Changlang, India, B 11
.....	Changling, China, E 19
.....	Changlo China. E 18
.....	Chango, China, G 5
.....	Changpingchow, China, C16
.....	Changpinghsien, China, J 17
.....	Changpu, Manch., K 18
607000	Changsha, China, I 14
.....	Changteh, China, I 13
50000	Changte Ho, China, E 15
.....	Changwu, Manch., C 20
.....	Chanilao, Arg., O 13
.....	Channagiri, India, N 9
.....	Channerwick, Shetland Is., D 3
15127	Chantada, Spain, D 7
.....	Chantapilli, India, K 17
3667	Chantonnay, France, K 7
905	Chanzy, Algeria, E 12
.....	Chao, Peru, I 5
400000	Chaochow, China, E 15
.....	Chaochow, China, J 4
20000	Chaochowfu, China, K 17
.....	Chaohwa, China, G 9
30000	Chaotung, China, I 7
609	Chaource, France, I 17
35000	Chaoyang, Manch., C 19
.....	Chapadinha, Brazil, F 18
3142	Chapala, Jal., M 7
.....	Chapaleofú, Arg., P 18
4071	Chaparra, Cuba, M 20
26	Chaparra, Peru, O 13
5506	Chaparral, Col., J 9
471	Chapeau, Que., O 6
.....	Chapelizod, Ire., J 21
.....	Chapicuy, Uruguay, H 15
1525	Chapleau, Ontario, Q 22
165	Chaplin, Sask., P 6
.....	Chaplinka, Sov. Un., M 9
42400	Chapra, India, G 18
.....	Chapultepec Heights, Mex., N 1
1165	Chaqui, Bolivia, K 9
.....	Char, India, C 10
.....	Charadar, Argentina, I 17
4385	Charagua, Bolivia, K 13
.....	Charaks, Iran, I 15
2479	Charalá, Colombia, G 13
116	Charapaxi, Bolivia, H 6
.....	Charara, Paraguay, O 9
.....	Charata, Argentina, H 16
4096	Charazani, Bolivia, G 2
780	Charcana, Peru, O 14
6081	Charcas, S. L. P., I 12
4053	Chard, England, N 11
.....	Chardeh, Iran, H 11
1103	Chardonne, Switz., L 5
821	Charenton, Fr., K 15
21098	Charenton le Pont, Fr. B 6
655	Charette, Quebec, M 17
.....	Cha Rig, Iran, J 15
.....	Charkhari, India, G 12
.....	Charlbury, England, K 15
1150	Charlemagne, Quebec, O 16
.....	Charlemont, N. Ire., E 19
28069	Charleroi, Belgium, N 12
2789	Charlesbourg, Quebec, K 21
.....	Charleston, Australia, E 19
300	Charleston, N. Z., K 10
.....	Charlestown, Ire., G 9
1200	Charlestown, W. I., K 22
1255	Charlestown, Scotland, M 18
350	Charlestown, U.S. Afr., H 20
3205	Charleville, Australia, J 20
22708	Charleville, France, F 18
.....	Charlois, Neth., H 12
.....	Charlos Cove, N. S., K 21
195	Charlo Station, N. B., A 8
1123	Charlottenberg, Swe., M 11
353000	Charlottenburg, Germany, G 12, Q 15
.....	Charlottenlund, Den., J 23
14821	Charlottetown, P. E. I., H 16
.....	Charlotte Water, Australia, I 14
210	Charlton, Ontario, Q 24
1122	Charly, France, H 15
4332	Charmes, France, H 22
1244	Charmey, Switzerland, K 7
187	Charny, France, G 20
1017	Charny, France, I 15
2831	Charny, Que., L 21
2139	Charo, Michoa., N 12
3399	Charolles, France, K 18
1131	Chârost, France, K 13
6165	Charshamba, Tur., C 11
.....	Charshembe, (Tcha-Djuma), Tur., B 7
6978	Charters Towers, Australia, F 20
200	Chartierville, Quebec, Q 21
.....	Chartorisk, W. Sov. Un., E19
27071	Chârtres, France, H 13
.....	Chas, Argentina, O 19
28573	Chascomus, Arg., O 20
295	Chase, B. C., O 16
.....	Cha Shirmak, Iran, I 15
.....	Chashur, Iran, P 14
.....	Chasico, Argentina, Q 14
.....	Chasma, Iran, H 15
.....	Chasma Burg, Iran, L 12
.....	Chasma Shutaran, Iran, I 11
.....	Chastleton, Australia, J 17
217	Chaswood, N. S., L 16
7989	Châteaubriant, France, I 6
1680	Château-Chinon, Fr., J 17
3793	Chateau d'Oex, Switz., L 7
6558	Châteaudun, France, I 12
303	Châteaufort, France, C 1
6280	Château Gontier, Fr., I 8
1425	Chateauguay, Que., Q 15
894	Château la Vallière, Fr., J 10
3766	Châteaulin, France, H 2
3147	Châteaumeillant, Fr., K 14
504	Châteauneuf, France, H 6
1106	Château Renard, Fr., I 15
4097	Châteaurenault, Fr., J 11
680	Château Richer, Que., K 22
28578	Châteauroux, France, K 12
1808	Chateau Salins, Fr., H 22
8266	Château-Thierry, Fr., G 16
941	Château-Vilain, Fr., I 19
1176	Châteldon, France, L 16
15124	Chatelet, Belgium, O 12
18193	Chatelineau, Belgium, N12
17704	Châtellerault, France, K 11
2545	Chatel Saint Denis, Switzerland, K 6
2966	Chatenay-Malabry, Fr., C 4
846	Châtenois, France, H 21
42996	Chatham, England, L 21
4082	Chatham, N. B., E 10
17369	Chatham, Ontario, P 3
7488	Châtillon, France, C 5
1785	Chatillon, Italy, C 2
3416	Châtillon-sur-Indre, Fr., J 12
1845	Châtillon-sur-Loire, Fr., J 15
769	Châtillon-sur-Marne, Fr., G 17
4642	Châtillon-sur-Seine, Fr., I 19
10600	Chatra, India, H 18
.....	Chatria, Nepal, F 20
266	Chatsworth, Ont., I 7
.....	Chattargarh, India, E 6
.....	Chatteris, England, J 20
.....	Chau, I. E. A., J 7
.....	Chaudière, Quebec, L 21
.....	Chaudiere Jc., Quebec, L 21
.....	Chaudoc, Fr. In. Ch., Q 7
.....	Chaudri Turm, Afg., K 17
903	Chaulnes, France, F 15
18069	Chaumont, France, I 20
.....	Chaumun, India, F 8
9207	Chauny, France, F 15
.....	Chausa, India, G 17
979	Chaussin, France, J 20
.....	Chausy, W. Sov. Un., C 24
2383	Chauvigny, France, K 11
343	Chauvin, Alberta, L 24
.....	Chave Rio Velho, Brazil, M 11
.....	Chaves, Brazil, D 13
8842	Chaves, Portugal, F 7
10948	Chaville, France, C 3
576	Chavin de Pariarca, Peru, J 8
1222	Chavornay, Switz., J 4
.....	Chawani, Bech., P 15
5357	Chayanta, Bolivia, J 7
1426	Chayasa, Bolivia, M 11
1256	Chazuta, Peru, H 9
.....	Cheam, England, D 20
31549	Cheb, Czech., F 5
.....	Cheba, Tunisia, D 25
.....	Chebbi (Wells), Mor., I 9
.....	Cheberma, Algeria, N 25
1081	Checa, Spain, H 15
1280	Checacupe, Peru, N 17
.....	Checiny, Pol., F 13
.....	Cheddar, Ont., F 15
1555	Chef-Boutonne, France, L 9
132000	Chefoo, China, E 20
.....	Chegga, Algeria, E 19
.....	Chelaro, India, G 3
.....	Chelforo, Arg., Q 11
.....	Chellal, Algeria, D 18
848	Chellala, Algeria, D 15
29222	Chelm, Pol., E 17
12531	Chelmno, Pol., C 11
26537	Chelmsford, England, K 21
12	Chelmsford, Ontario, R 23
316	Chelsea, Nova Scotia, O 12
275	Chelsea, Quebec, P 10
.....	Chelsfield, England, D 24
49385	Cheltenham, England, K 13
210	Cheltenham, Ontario, K 10
5484	Chelva, Spain, J 16
273127	Chelyabinsk, Sov. Un., Asia, G 10
975	Chemainus, B.C., R 12
5500	Chembar, Sov. Un., K 15
350657	Chemnitz, Germany, K 11
	Chemulpo, see Jin-sen, Chosen.
.....	Chenan, China, L 8
.....	Chenbaret, Egypt, F 17
.....	Chenchou, China, J 14
.....	Chenchow, China, G 15
4861	Chendek, Tur., C 5
3362	Chêne, Switz., N 2
9920	Chenée, Belgium, N 18
569	Chéneville, Quebec, O 12
.....	Chenfan, China, D 7
.....	Chengan, China, I 10
.....	Chengchow, China, F 14
.....	Chenghsien, China, F 8
.....	Chengkiang, China, K 6
.....	Chengkow, China, G 11
.....	Chengpu, China, J 12
650000	Chengte (Jehol), Manch., C 17
.....	Chengting, China, D 15
800000	Chengtu, China, H 7
.....	Chennan, China, K 4
.....	Chenneni, Tunisia, F 24
.....	Chensiung, China, I 7
.....	Chenyuan, China, K 4
8214	Chepén, Peru, H 4
238	Chepes, Arg., L 9
1279	Chepo, Pan., O 22
4303	Chepstow, England, L 12
.....	Chera Punji, India, G 25
39105	Cherbourg, France, F 7
12650	Cherchel, Algeria, B 15
6000	Cheren, Erit., A 8
.....	Cherepa, Cuba J 11
21783	Cherepovets, Sov. Un., G 11
.....	Chereya, W. Sov. Un., B 22
120	Cherhill, Alberta, J 20
188	Cheria, Algeria, D 21
.....	Cherikov, W. Sov. Un., C 25
51693	Cherkasi, Sov. Un., L 7
3105	Chermük, Tur., G 14
67356	Chernigov, W. Sov. Un., E 25
.....	Cherni Yar, Sov. Un., M 17
.....	Chernobyl, W. Sov., Un., E 24
111122	Chernovitsy (Cernăuti), W. Sov. Un., G 20
.....	Cherra Punji, India, G 25
217	Cherry Valley, Ont., K 18
.....	Cherso, It., D 14
	Cherson, see Kherson, Sov. Un.
.....	Cherven, W. Sov. Un., C 21
360	Cheseaux, Switz., K 4
8809	Chesham, England, K 18
14651	Cheshunt, England, L 20
.....	Chesilton, England, N 12
1701	Chesley, Ontario, I 7
41438	Chester, England, H 11
1000	Chester, N. B., N 13
956	Chester Basin, N. S., N 13
61146	Chesterfield, Eng., H 15
16639	Chester-le-Street, Eng., D15
.....	Chesters, Scotland, O 22
26877	Chesterton, England, J 20
1067	Chesterville, Ontario, F 23
655	Cheticamp, N. S., F 21
425	Chevagnes, France, K 16
227	Cheverie, N. S., L 13
186	Chevilly, France, C 5
.....	Chevington, Eng., C 15
805	Chevron, Belgium, N 18
.....	Chewelik, Tur., F 15
1043	Chexbres, Switz., L 5
391	Cheyres, Switz., I 5
10000	Chhatarpur, India, G 13
9700	Chhindwara, India, I 12
.....	Chiab, Afg., D 23
.....	Chia Guz. Afg., J 17
.....	Chiamdo, China, G 2
8316	Chiantla, Guatemala, E 3
296	Chiapa, Chile, C 5
4919	Chiapa de Corzo, Chia., M 15
6765	Chiari, Italy, D 6
6141	Chiasso, Switz., Q 17
2556	Chiautla, Pueb., J 6
12501	Chiavari, Italy, E 5
3201	Chiavenna, Italy, C 5
49086	Chiba, Japan, M 21
20000	Chicacole, India, K 17
83	Chicalote, Agua., K 9
.....	Chicama, Peru, I 4
13911	Chichester, England, N 17
4226	Chichigalpa, Nic., J 10
2020	Chichimila, Yuc., F 24
.....	Chichinales, Arg., Q 9
.....	Chichoki, India, C 7
.....	Chicla, Peru, L 9
3144	Chiclana, Spain, L 13
12009	Chiclana de la Frontera, Spain, P 8
32646	Chiclayo, Peru, H 3
574	Chicomuselo, Chia., O 17
1546	Chicontepec, Ver., E 6
15974	Chicoutimi, Quebec, E 22
958	Chiculub, Yuc., E 21
25084	Chidambaram, India, O 12
.....	Chidmu, Egypt, M 10
74	Chiebul, Camp., I 19
.....	Chiehchow, China, F 12
443476	Chiengmai, Siam, M 2
.....	Chiengrai, Siam, M 3
22700	Chiéti, Italy, H 14
3220	Chietla, Pueb., J 6
4522	Chignahuapan, Pueb., G 7
219	Chignecto, N. S., J 13
.....	Chiguana, Bolivia, M 5
.....	Chigur Serai, Afg., G 24
.....	Chigwell, England, A 24
.....	Chihcheng, China, C 16
.....	Chihchow, China, H 17
40000	Chihfeng, Manch., B 18
.....	Chihilboorg, Afg., G 20
.....	Chihsien, China, F 15
56805	Chihuahua, Chih., H 18
1606	Chila, Pueb., K 6
6094	Chilapa, Guer., Q 17
.....	Chilas, India, A 7
6662	Chilaw, Cey, R 13
1341	Chilca, Peru, M 8
2220	Chilchota, Michoa., N 10
4000	Chilecito, Arg., J 8
.....	Chilekovo, Sov. Un., M 15
476	Chilete, Peru, H 5
.....	Chilia Nov̆a, W. Sov. Un., J24
.....	Chilianwala, India, C 7
473	Chillagoe, Australia, D 19
42817	Chillan, Chile, P 3
3675	Chilliwack, B. C., Q 13
.....	Chillundie, Australia, M 14
1838	Chilón, Bolivia, J 10
863	Chilón, Chia., L 17
8834	Chilpancingo, Guer., Q 16
.....	Chilpi, India, A 7
.....	Chim, India, D 11
1641	Chima, Colombia, D 9
3492	Chima, Colombia, G 12
961	Chimalapa (Sta. Maria), Oax., M 12
6264	Chimaltenango, Guat., F 4
434	Chimaltitán, Jal., K 6
.....	Chimán, Panama, P 23
.....	Chimay, Belgium, P 11
4108	Chimbarongo, Chile, N 4
.....	Chimberos, Chile, H 4
4243	Chimbote, Peru, J 5
74185	Chimkent, Sov. Un. Asia, J 10
.....	Chimpay, Arg., R 10
.....	Chimray, India, B 11
39	Chin, Alberta, P 22
.....	China, Afg., J 19
1500	China, N. L., F 16
3157	Chinacota, Col., F 14
2058	Chinameca, Ver., K 12
14967	Chinandega, Nic., J 10
12768	Chincha Alta, Peru, M 10
.....	Chinchao, Peru, J 9
1278	Chinchilla, Australia J 22
7616	Chinchilla de Monte Aragón, Spain, K 14
1218	Chinchiri, Bolivia, I 7
5074	Chinchon Spain, I 12
128541	Chinchow, Manch., C 19
.....	Chinchow, China, E 14
.....	Chinchuachen, China, F 14
2711	Chinde, Moz., O 20
.....	Chindon, Switz., F 7
.....	Chingleput, India, O 31
10000	Chinguetti, Fr. W. Afr., G3
.....	Chingurek, Afg., G 17
1228	Chinguri, Bolivia, J 9
25841	Chiniot, India, C 6
1104	Chinipas, Chih., J 15
200000	Chinkiang, China, G 19
48838	Chinnampo, Kor., D 23
.....	Chinnur, India, K 13
5751	Chinon, France, J 10
142	Chinook, Alberta, M 23
.....	Chintalnar, India, K 14
.....	Chinteche, Nyasaland, N 19
3953	Chinu, Colombia, D 9
20000	Chinwangtao, China, D 18
764	Chiny, Belgium, Q 16
22122	Chios, Greece, P 21
.....	Chipanchos, Chile, D 5
6095	Chipiona, Spain, O 8
.....	Chiplun, India, L 6
240	Chipman, Alberta, J 21
985	Chipman, N. B., H 9
8493	Chippenham, England, L 14
.....	Chipping, Eng., K 14
.....	Chipping Barnet, Eng. A 20
.....	Chipping Norton, Eng. K15
.....	Chique-Chique, Brazil. I 19
7350	Chiquimuilla, Guat., G 4
11832	Chiquimula, Guat., F 6
.....	Chiraghdan, Afg., H 19
.....	Chirak, Iran, Q 16
1237	Chirca, Bolivia, H 5
6000	Chirgalanta (Kobdo), Mong., I 14
3088	Chiriguaná, Col., D 12
90	Chirique Grande, Panama, O 18
.....	Chiru Maini, Afg., H 21
8350	Chiscas, Col., G 14
177	Chisholm, Alberta, I 19
38541	Chisimaio, Eth., K 23
.....	Chisinau, see Kishinev, W. Sov. Un.
.....	Chislehurst, England, D 24
17000	Chistopol, Sov. Un., I 19
.....	Chiswick, England, C 20
.....	Chita, Bolivia, L 6
1013	Chita, Col., H 14
102555	Chita, Sov. Un. Asia, H 16
1201	Chitaga, Col., G 14
.....	Chitaldroog, India, N 9
7600	Chitor, India, G 8
.....	Chitral, India, A 5
4790	Chitré, Panama, Q 21
.....	Chitrod, India, H 4
53156	Chittagong, India, I 25
.....	Chittagong, India, M 19
10000	Chittoor, India, N 12
.....	Chiusa (Klausen), It., B 9
1356	Chiusdino, Italy, G 8
2307	Chiusi, Italy, G 10
4843	Chiva, Spain, J 16
2027	Chivay, Peru, O 16
.....	Chivé, Bolivia D 3
52487	Chivilcoy, Argentina, N 17
2800	Chivril, Tur., F 4
.....	Chiza, Chile, B 4
.....	Chizu, Japan, L 11
172925	Chkalov (Orenburg), Sov. Un., K 23
.....	Chlumetz, Ger., L 15
.....	Chmielnik, Poland, F 14
.....	Choba, Eth., J 10
.....	Chochin, Sask., L 5
1472	Chocholá, Yuc., F 21
.....	Chochow, China, D 16
.....	Chocolatal, Brazil, H 2
1197	Choconta, Colombia, H 12
.....	Chodzieź, Poland, D 10
400	Choiseul, Sta. Lucia, I 24
27584	Choisy-le-Roi, France, C 7
1421	Choix, Sin., K 15
14255	Chojnice, Pol., C 10
.....	Chok, India, I 5
1236	Cholchol, Chile, Q 3
23385	Cholét, France, J 8
145000	Cholon, Fr. In. Ch., R 8
8424	Cholula, Pueb., I 6
5057	Choluteca, Hond., I 9
771	Chomérac, France, N 19
.....	Chonchintoc, Camp., H 21
20824	Chone, Ecuador, B 3
66958	Chongjin (Seishin), Kor., B25
11790	Chôngju, Korea E 24
.....	Chongos, Peru, L 11
42520	Chônju (Zenshū), Kor., E 24
.....	Chopda, India, I 8
.....	Chorak, Tur., I 7
.....	Choral, India, I 9
.....	Choranda, India, I 6
.....	Chorbat, India, A 10
.....	Chorestków, see Khorostkov, W. Sov. Un.
786	Choreti, Bolivia, L 12
30795	Chorley, England, G 12
3278	Choroni, Venezuela, C 12
6996	Chorrillos, Peru, L 8
25300	Choshi, Japan, M 22
4160	Chosica, Peru, L 9
495	Chos Malal, Argentina, P 5
.....	Chosmes, Argentina, M 9
.....	Chota, Peru, G 5
.....	Chotan, India, G 4
2705	Chota Udaipur India, I 7
1500	Choubar, Iran, R 15
.....	Choya, Argentina, I 11
9183	Christchurch, Eng., N 14
101200	Christchurch, N. Z., M 12
3000	Christiana, U.S. Afr., I 14
	Christiania, see Oslo, Nor.
289	Christian Island, Ont., G 10
97	Christianopel, Sweden, Q 14
	Christiansand, see Kristiansand, Nor.
	Christiansund, see Kristiansund, Nor.
13069	Christina, Brazil, N 16
.....	Christmas Island, N. S., I22
.....	Chrudim, Czech., F 8
70000	Chüanchow, China, J 12
.....	Chuanchowfu, China, K 18
.....	Chucheng, China, E 18
.....	Chüchow, China, F 18
.....	Chuchow, China, G 18
.....	Chuchow, China. I 14
.....	Chüchow, China, I 18
.....	Chuchow, China, I 19
253	Chudleigh, Tasmania, C 6
.....	Chudova, Sov. Un., G 7
.....	Chuho, Manch., A 24
.....	Chuhsung, Afg., J 19
.....	Chukloma, Sov. Un., G 14
.....	Chukmakchuk, Afg., I 21
482	Chullina, Bolivia, G 2
4312	Chuma, Bolivia, G 3
.....	Chumatien, China, G 15
552	Chumbicha, Argentina, J 9
.....	Chuña, Argentina, K 11
.....	Chunar, India, G 16
.....	Chunchi, Ecuador, D 4
16959	Chunchŏn, Kor., D 24
50000	Chungchow, China, H 10
635000	Chungking (Pahsien), China, I 9
.....	Chungmowhsien, Ch., F 15
.....	Chungtien, China, I 3
.....	Chungwei, China, E 8
4482	Chupaca, Peru, L 11
692	Chupan, Peru, J 9
2480	Chuquibamba, Peru, O 15
1191	Chuquibambilla, Peru, N 15
9715	Chuquicamata, Chile, E 5
15578	Chur, Switzerland, I 20
.....	Churani, Baluchistan, O 21
199	Churchbridge, Sask., O 11
.....	Church Hill, N. Ire., E 14
.....	Churchill, Manitoba, C 18
500	Church Point Station, N.S., O 8
1705	Church Stretton, Eng., I 12
.....	Churchtown, Ire., O 9
.....	Churchtown, Ire., O 22
.....	Churchtown, Ire., Q 13
.....	Churchtown, N. Ire., D 19
.....	Churqui, Argentina H 12
21965	Churu, India, E 8
2626	Churuguara, Ven., C 9
817	Churumuco, Michoa., O 10
706	Churwalden, Switz., I 20
301	Chutea Blondeau, Ont., D25
.....	Chute Lake, B. C., P 16
.....	Chwan-ping, China, G 11
13954	Ciechanów, Poland, D 14
29130	Ciego de Avila, Cuba, K 15
24708	Cienaga, Col., B 12
323	Ciénega de los Caballas, Dur., P 20
4970	Cienaga de Oro Caimito, Col., E 10
49452	Cienfuegos, Cuba, J 11
122	Cierfs, Switzerland, K 24
23499	Cieza, Spain, L 15
1742	Cifuentes, Cuba, I 12
5656	Cill Airne (Killarney), Ire., O 5
10046	Cill Choinnigh (Kilkenny), Ire., M 17
	Cilli, see Celje, Yugo.
.....	Cill Iurin, Ire., N 20
3288	Cill Mhantain (Wicklow), Ire., K 23
.....	Cinco Chanares, Arg., A 23
5191	Ciney, Belgium, O 15
5043	Cintalapa, Chia., M 14
.....	Cinto, Peru, Q 18
.....	Cintra, Argentina, L 14
5900	Cintra, Portugal, K 4
.....	Cipolleti, Argentina, Q 8
3356	Circasia, Colombia, I 8
319	Circuata, Bolivia, H 6
3371	Ciro, Italy, L 20
.....	Ciruelos, Chile, N 3
5423	Cisneros, Col., G 9
.....	Cisneros, Col., J 6
6798	Città di Castello, It., G 10
13494	Cittanova, Italy, N 18
1444	Cittanova, d'Istria, Italy D 13
3175	Citta Sant'Angelo, It., H 14
19789	Ciudad Bolivar (Bolivar), Venezuela, G 18
7705	Ciudad Camargo (Sta. Rosalia), Chih., I 20
1007	Ciudad Camargo, Tam., E 17
4558	Ciudad Chetumal (Pay Obispo), Q. R., I 25
5712	Ciudad del Maíz, S.L.P., J 16
10716	Ciudadela, Spain, I 22
6649	Ciudad González, Guan., K 12
1678	Ciudad Guerrero, Chih., H 16
2883	Ciudad Guerrero, Tam., D 16
22170	Ciudad Guzmán, Jal., N 5
48676	Ciudad Juárez, Chih., B 18
3321	Ciudad Manuel Doblado Guan., L 10
2099	Ciudad Mier, Tam., E 17
.....	Ciudad Obregon, Son., J 12
1413	Ciudad Ocampo, Tam., J 16
32931	Ciudad Real, Spain, K 12
12082	Ciudad Rodrigo, Spain, H 9
120385	Ciudad Trujillo (Santo Domingo), Dom. Rep., J 15
19087	Ciudad Victoria, Tam., I 17
4220	Cividale del Friuli, It., C 13
19659	Civitavecchia, Italy, H 10
2154	Civray, France, L 10
.....	Clabhach, Scotland, K 6
.....	Clachan, Scotland, N 10
2585	Clackmannan, Scot., M 17
15851	Clacton on Sea, Eng., K 23
100	Clair, N. B., D 2
31047	Clamart, France, C 4
4959	Clamecy, France, J 16
200	Clam Harbor, N. S., N 17
.....	Clandeboye, N. Ire., D 24
217	Clandeboye, Ontario, M 6
.....	Clane, Ire., J 19
1100	Clanwilliam, U.S. Afr., O 7
1590	Clara, Ire., J 15
.....	Claraz, Argentina, Q 18
1751	Clare, Australia, N 16
.....	Clare, England, K 21
.....	Clare, Ire., L 8
.....	Claregalway, Ire., J 8
526	Claremont, Ontario, J 12
1300	Claremorris, Ire., H 8
.....	Clarence, Bahama, E 10
201	Clarence, Ontario, D 23
400	Clarence Creek, Ont., D 23
294	Clarenceville, Que., R 16
.....	Clarens, Switz., L 6
1265	Claresholm, Alberta, P 21
.....	Clarinbridge, Ire., J 9
1266	Clarines, Venezuela, D 16
887	Clarkes Harbour, N. S., R 9
526	Clarksburg, Ontario, H 9
431	Clarksons, Ontario, L 11
898	Claro, Switz., N 17
.....	Clashmore, Ire., P 14
.....	Clashmore, Scotland, F 16
.....	Clashnessie, Scotland, E 11
.....	Claudy, N. Ire., C 17
39	Claverton, Austl., K 20
1370	Clavier, Belgium, N 16
8493	Clay Cross, England, H 15
.....	Clayoguot, B. C., Q 10
.....	Claythorpe, Eng., H 20
.....	Clayton, England, G 15
6582	Cleator Moor, Eng., D 10
3504	Cléguérec, France, H 3
.....	Clemente, Spain, J 14
321	Clementsport, N. S., N 9
531	Clementsvale, N. S., N 9
.....	Clenega de Flores, N. L., E 14
1406	Clermont, Australia, H 21
5540	Clermont, France, G 14
548	Clermont-en-Argonne, Fr., G 19
101128	Clermont-Ferrand, France, L 15
942	Clervalk, Lux., P 19
2273	Clés, Italy, C 8
7033	Clevedon, England, L 11
236	Cleveland, N. S., J 21
.....	Clevelandia (Belle Vista de Palma), Brazil, O 11
55692	Clichy, France, A 5
828	Clifden, Ire., I 3
.....	Cliffony, Ire., E 11
464	Clifford, Ontario, J 7
.....	Clifford, Wal., K 10
801	Clifton, Austl., K 20
.....	Clifton, England, D 12
.....	Clifton, N. Z., I 13
243	Climax, Sask., R 5
277	Clinton, B. C., O 14
360	Clinton, N. Z., Q 7
1896	Clinton, Ontario, L 6
651	Clive, N. Z., H 21
5000	Cliza, Bolivia, I 8
13	Cloan, Sask., L 5
.....	Clodomira, Argentina, I 12
.....	Clogh, Ire., L 17
.....	Clogh, N. Ire., C 21
.....	Cloghan, Ire., C 13
.....	Clogheen, Ire., O 13
.....	Clogher, Ire., G 3
.....	Clogher, N. Ire., E 17
.....	Cloghereen, Ire., P 6
.....	Cloghjordan, Ire., L 13
.....	Cloghran, Ire., I 22
.....	Cloghy, N. Ire., E 25
.....	Cloister, B. C., N 18
3098	Clonakilty, Ire., Q 8
.....	Clonamery, Ire., N 18
.....	Clonaslee, Ire., K 15
1584	Cloncurry, Australia, F 17
.....	Cloneen, Ire., N 15
.....	Clonegall, Ire., M 20
.....	Clonelly, N. Ire., E 14
2400	Clones, Ire., F 17
.....	Clonlyon, Ire., J 14
	Clonmel, see Cluain Meala, Ire.

Pop.	Place Country Index
.....	Clonmellon Ire., I 18
5000	Clontarf, Ire., J 22
.....	Clooncahir, Ire., H 14
.....	Cloondara, Ire., H 14
.....	Clooneen Beg, Ire., I 12
.....	Clo-oose, B. C., R 11
4996	Cloppenburg, Ger., F 5
1074	Closeburn, Scot., P 17
6100	Closepet, India, O 10
.....	Cloughton, England, E 18
651	Cloverdale, B.C., Q 13
1000	Cloyne, Ire., P 13
10200	Cluain Meala (Clonmel), Ire., N 15
.....	Cluffie, Sask., M 10
98550	Cluj, Rom., I 17
.....	Clun, England, J 11
.....	Clunie Inn, Scot., I 11
138	Cluny, Alberta, N 22
3549	Clusone, Italy, C 6
154	Clyde, B. C., I 20
.....	Clyde, N. Z., O 6
46963	Clydebank, Scot., M 14
317	Clyde River, N. S., R 10
.....	Clynnog, Wales, H 7
.....	Coachford, Ire., P 9
.....	Coagh, N. Ire., D 20
435	Coahuayutla, Guer., P 10
2485	Coalcomán, Michoa., O 7
.....	Coal Island, N. Ire., E 19
75	Coalspur, Alberta, L 18
.....	Coary, Brazil, F 3
3090	Coatán, Guat., E 2
43056	Coatbridge, Scotland, N 16
11459	Coatepec, Ver., H 8
4414	Coaticook, Quebec, R 20
11740	Coatzacoalcos (Puerto Mexico), Ver., K 13
1472	Coaza, Peru, N 19
2376	Cobalt, Ontario, Q 25
8001	Coban, Guatemala, E 5
1163	Cobar, Australia, M 19
316	Cobble Hill, B. C., R 12
656	Cobden, Ontario, D 19
6075	Cobh, Ire., P 12
	Coblence, see Koblenz, Ger.
621	Coboconk, Ontario, H 13
150	Cobos, Argentina, G 11
.....	Cobos, Ver., E 8
5973	Cobourg, Ontario, J 15
853	Cobram, Australia, O 19
.....	Cobre, Agua., K 10
.....	Coburn, Chile, O 4
.....	Coca, Ecuador, C 9
231	Cocagne, N. B., G 12
65952	Cocanada, India, L 15
60000	Cochabamba, Bolivia, I 7
.....	Cochas, Peru, K 7
3655	Cochem, Germany, L 3
22818	Cochin, India, P 9
298	Cochrane, Alberta, N 20
2844	Cochrane, Ontario, O 24
168	Cockburn, Australia, M 17
300	Cockburn Island, Ont., B 1
.....	Cockburnspath, Scot.,M 23
4789	Cockermouth, Eng., O 10
3080	Cócorit, Son., J 12
7706	Cocula, Jal., M 5
8483	Cocuy, Col., G 14
224	Coderre, Sask., P 7
.....	Codes, Nicaragua, K 12
.....	Codo, Brazil, F 18
800	Codrington, Barbuda, J 23
255	Coe Hill. Ontario, G 16
77	Coen, Australia, C 19
17404	Cognac, France, M 8
1139	Cogolludo, Spain, H 13
976	Cogoti, Chile, K 4
.....	Cogush, Ire., D 10
1686	Cohoni, Bolivia, H 5
.....	Cohundalun, Afg., J 20
839	Coihüe, Chile, P 3
1617	Coihueco, Chile, P 4
95198	Coimbatore, India, O 10
89407	Coimbra, Portugal, H 5
17348	Coin, Spain, O 10
1798	Coixtlahuaca, Oax., K 8
5371	Cojedes, Venezuela, D 10
3891	Cojocna, E. Hung., I 17
14912	Cojutepeque, Salvador, H 7
345	Colalao del Valle, Arg., H 9
994	Colborne, Ontario, J 16
3364	Colcha, Bol., J 7
960	Colcha, Bolivia, L 5
48607	Colchester, England, K 22
.....	Coldstream, England, B 13
.....	Coldstream, N. B., G 5
1922	Cold Stream, Scot., N 23
.....	Cole, England, M 12
222	Colebrook, Ontario, H 19
1870	Coleman, Alberta, P 20
150	Coleman, P. E. I., F 13
945	Coleraine, Austl., P 17
7785	Coleraine, N. Ire., B 19
.....	Coleraine, Quebec, O 21
2267	Colesberg, U.S. Afr., M 14
327	Coles Island N. B., I 9
.....	Colfin, Scotland, Q 12
845	Colico, Italy, C 5
889	Coligny, France, K 20
22455	Colima, Colim., O 6
.....	Coll, Scotland, D 7
315	Colla, Switzerland, O 18
539	Collana, Bolivia, H 4
1371	Colle Salvetti, Italy, F 7
3700	Collie, Australia., N 5
.....	Colliefields, Australia, N 5
.....	Collieston, Scot., H 24
450	Collilelfu, Chile, R 3
.....	Collingham, England, H 17
400	Collingwood, N. Z., I 12
6270	Collingwood, Ontario, H 9
432	Collingwood Corner, N. S., J 14
218	Collins Bay, Ontario, I 20
4057	Collipulli, Chile, Q 3
3460	Collo, Algeria, B 20
.....	Collon, Ire., H 21
565	Collonges, France, L 21
1359	Collonges, Switz., M 2
400	Collooney, Ire., F 11
.....	Colman, Argentina, O 18
49448	Colmar, France, I 23
351	Colmar, Luxembourg, Q 20
379	Colmars, France, O 23
.....	Colmena, Argentina, J 17
7951	Colmenar Viejo, Sp., H 12
.....	Colmi, Honduras, F 13
3106	Comillas, Sp., C 11
23790	Colne, England, F 13
.....	Colney Hatch, Eng., A 21
	Cologne, see Köln, Ger.
5129	Colomb Becher, Alg., I 10
61944	Colombes, France, A 4
660	Colombey, Fr., H 21
1239	Colombia, Col., J 10
308000	Colombo, Cey., R 13
.....	Colombres, Argentina, H 11
5226	Colomi, Bolivia, I 8
4000	Colón, Argentina, L 19
6400	Colón, Argentina, N 16
11833	Colón, Cuba, I 10
44393	Colón, Panama, O 21
4365	Colón, Venezuela, G 5
.....	Colonche, Ecuador, D 2
8500	Colonia, Uruguay, O 15
.....	Colonia Alvear, Arg., N 8
.....	Colonia Alvear Oeste, Argentina, N 8
.....	Colonia Brandzen, Arg., N 19
.....	Colonia Corrientos, Arg., Q 20
.....	Colonia Dora, Arg., J 14
1374	Colonia Guadalupe, Chih., C 18
.....	Colonia Guillermo Tell, Paraguay, P 11
.....	Colonia Las Heras, Arg., C 22
.....	Colonia Nacional, Paraguay, P 9
.....	Colonia Neuva Germania, Paraguay, K 8
.....	Colonia Penal, Par., I 7
.....	Colonia Risso, Par., I 6
.....	Colonia Sarmiento, Argentina, C 21
183	Colonsay, Sask., N 7
.....	Colorado, Honduras, E 9
.....	Colores, Cuba, M 16
597	Colotepec, Oax. O 8
5093	Colotlán, Jal., K 7
.....	Colpes, Argentina, I 9
8000	Colquechaca, Bolivia, J 8
.....	Colvend, Scot., Q 17
.....	Colvidale, Shetland Islands A 5
54	Colwell, Ontario, I 11
.....	Colwood, B. C., R 2
.....	Colyton, England, N 10
8697	Comacchio, Italy, E 10
2764	Comalcalco, Tab., J 15
.....	Comandante Salas, Argentina, N 8
5750	Comarapa, Bolivia, J 11
4758	Comayagua, Honduras,G 9
2112	Combarbala, Chile, L 4
.....	Comber, N. Ire., E 24
564	Comber, Ontario, Q 2
218	Combermere, Ontario, E 17
3707	Comblain-au-Pont, Bel., N 17
526	Comeauville, N. S., O 8
100	Comet, Australia, H 22
.....	Comieville, N. B., G 12
31365	Comilla, India, H 24
3106	Comillas, Spain, C 11
6080	Comines, Belgium, M 4
32166	Comiso, Italy, P 15
8683	Comitan, Chia.,N 17
10136	Commentry, Fr., L 14
6991	Commercy, France, H 20
40600	Como, Italy, C 5
416	Como, Quebec, P 14
.....	Comoapa, Nicaragua, J 12
4875	Comodoro Rivadavia, Argentina, C 22
6510	Comonfort, Guan., M 13
635	Comox, B. C., P 11
17852	Compiègne, France, G 15
2726	Compostela, Nay., L 3
182	Comps, France, O 23
425	Compton, Quebec, Q 20
.....	Comrat, W. Sov. Un., I 23
26	Comrey, Alberta, Q 24
1775	Comrie, Scotland, L 16
8866	Conakry, Fr. W. Afr., I 2
5995	Concarneau, France, I 2
19413	Conceicão, Brazil, G 14
.....	Conceicao da Barra, Brazil, L 21
16415	Conceicão do Arroio, Brazil, Q 12
.....	Conceicao do Coité, Brazil, I 21
6179	Conceicão do Norte, Brazil, I 15
.....	Conceicão do Serro, Brazil, L 18
4300	Concepcion, Arg., I 10
.....	Concepcion, Arg., I 20
775	Concepcion, Arg., I 20
5767	Concepcion, Bolivia, H 16
85813	Concepcion, Chile, P 2
1179	Concepción, Colombia, G 14
.....	Concepcion, Col., M 9
.....	Concepcion, Ecuador, A 4
325	Concepcion, Camp., J 21
2162	Concepcion, Panama, P 17
1384	Concepcion, Ven., C 5
847	Concepcion de la Sierra, Arg., I 23
9339	Concepción de la Vega, Dominican Republic,I 15
6028	Concepcion del Oro, Zac., G 11
	Concepcion del Uruguay, see Urugauy, Arg.
114	Concession, N. S., O 8
10	Conchi (Viejo), Chile, D 5
56	Conchi, Chile, E 6
61	Conchos, Chih., I 20
1939	Conchucos, Peru, I 6
704	Concise, Switzerland, I 4
36507	Concordia, Arg., L 20
404	Concordia, Honduras, G 11
2076	Concordia, Sin., Q 19
.....	Concordia, Nicaragua,I 11
.....	Concordia, U.S. Afr., K 7
.....	Conde, Brazil, I 23
592	Condé-en-Brie, Fr., H 16
512	Condega, Nicaragua, I 11
.....	Condé Mortrad, Fr., E 16
6708	Conde-sur-l'Escaut,France, E 16
.....	Condeúba, Brazil, J 19
2768	Condo, Bolivia, K 6
2572	Condobolin, Austl., N 20
6355	Condom, France, O 10
60	Conejos, Dur., L 22
746	Conesa, Argentina, P 20
301	Conestogo, Ontario, L 9
1009	Coneto, Dur., N 21
869	Conflans, France, G 21
2013	Confolens, France, L 11
.....	Cong, Ire., I 7
12885	Congleton, England, H 13
.....	Coniego, Cuba, I 2
6699	Conil, Spain, P 8
61376	Conjeevaram, India, O 13
6	Conklin, Alberta, H 22
.....	Connaugh, Ontario, E 23
.....	Connemarra, Australia,I 18
.....	Connor, U.S. Afr., P 15
78	Connors, N. B., D 1
.....	Cononaco, Ecuador, C 9
240	Conquest, Sask., N 6
7718	Conquista, Brazil, J 20
661	Consdorf, Lux., Q 21
531	Consecon, Ontario, J 17
2166	Conselve, Italy, D 10
12251	Consett, England, D 14
.....	Constable, U.S. Afr., P 9
.....	Constamana, Peru, H 11
.....	Constanca, W. Brazil, G 15
	Constance, see Konstanz, Ger.
60261	Constanta, Rom., K 24
113777	Constantine, Algeria, C 20
	Constantinople, see Istanbul, Turkey
14433	Constina, Sp., M 10
.....	Constitucion, Arg., M 17
7053	Constitucion, Chile, O 3
2388	Constitucion, Ur., G 16
8860	Consuegra, Spain, J 12
117	Consul, Sask., Q 3
3292	Conthey, Switz., N 8
8258	Contich, Belgium, R 8
.....	Contralmirante Cordero, Argentina, Q 8
.....	Contramaestre, Cuba, O 20
1041	Contrecoeur, Quebec, O 16
1547	Contres, France, J 12
1911	Contumaza, Peru, H 4
3210	Convencion, Col., E 13
.....	Conway, U.S. Afr., N 14
8769	Conway, Wal., H 8
586	Conzata, Bolivia, G 3
.....	Cooch, India, F 23
925	Cookeville, Ont., L 11
946	Cookshire, Quebec, Q 20
3685	Cookstown, N. Ire., D 19
600	Cookstown, Ontario, I 11
.....	Cookstown Junction, N. Ire., D 21
504	Cooktown, Australia, D 20
.....	Coolabara, Australia, I 19
.....	Coolaney, Ire., F 10
.....	Coolattin, Ire., L 21
200	Coole, Ire., H 16
650	Coolgardie, Australia, M 7
100	Coolgarra, Australia, E 19
.....	Coolie, Australia, I 19
.....	Coolooney, Ire., F 11
1969	Cooma, Australia, P 21
.....	Coomnahineha, Ire., P 2
2717	Coonamble, Australia,M 20
.....	Coondapoor, India, N 7
.....	Coongie, Australia, J 17
.....	Coons Mills, N. S., J 15
400	Coorbedar, Australia, L 5
4683	Cootamundra, Australia, O 20
1586	Cootehill, Ire., G 18
.....	Cop, Czech., H 18
.....	Copacabana, Argentina,I 8
.....	Copacabana, Bol., C 6
7735	Copacabana, Bol., H 2
1209	Copainala, Chia., L 15
715	Copala, Sin., Q 19
1183	Copalillo, Guer., P 17
.....	Copan (ruins), Hond., F 7
	Copenhagen, see København, Den.
.....	Copetonas, Arg., Q 17
15693	Copiapó, Chile, I 4
419	Coporaque, Peru, O 16
.....	Copper Creek, B. C., P 19
182	Copper Mountain, B. C., Q 15
546	Coppet, Switz., M 2
	Coptic Monastery, see Damyâne, Egypt
.....	Coquila, Oax., L 7
12300	Coquilhatville, Bel. Cong., K 14
2218	Coquimatlán, Colim., O 5
18863	Coquimbo, Chile, K 3
1539	Coquitlam, B. C., O 4
9446	Corabia, Romania, K 18
.....	Coraceros, Argentina, O 15
3671	Coracora, Peru, O 14
47930	Corato, Italy, J 19
431	Corban, Switz., E 9
11524	Corbeil, France, H 14
131	Corbetton, Ontario, J 9
253	Corbieres, Switz., J 7
1960	Corbigny, France, J 17
.....	Corbin, Alta., P 21
90	Corbin, B. C., P 20
.....	Corby, England, I 18
80700	Corcaigh (Cork), Ire.,P 11
1242	Corcelles, Switz., I 6
1578	Corcubion, Spain, D 5
844	Corculla, Peru, O 14
.....	Cordanan, Scot., J 12
1367	Cordes, France, O 13
3391375	Cordoba, Argentina, L 12
1548	Cordoba (Teton), Colombia, D 10
17816	Cordoba, Ver., I 8
143296	Cordoba, Spain, M 10
534	Còrdova, Peru, N 11
564	Cordova Mines, Ont., H 16
5748	Corella, Spain, F 15
.....	Corgarve, Ire., K 13
6423	Cori, Italy, I 12
3152	Còria, Spain, I 8
.....	Corieballie, Scotland, G 13
14552	Corigliano, It., L 19
1248	Corinaldo, Italy, F 12
4000	Coringa, India, L 15
186	Corinth, Ontario, O 7
1228	Corinto, Colombia, K 7
4876	Corinto, Nicaragua, J 9
800	Coripata, Bolivia, H 5
.....	Cork, Australia, H 18
	Cork, see Corcaigh, Ire.
14885	Corleone, Italy, N 13
110	Cormier Village, N. B.,H 13
523	Cormierville, N. B., G 12
1214	Cornaca, Bolivia, M 9
.....	Cornelia, U.S. Afr., H 19
.....	Cornesti, W. Sov. Un., H 22
.....	Corneto, Italy, H 10
123	Corn Hill, N. B., I 10
.....	Cornhill, Scotland, G 21
319	Cornus, France, O 16
14117	Cornwall, Ontario, F 25
18951	Coro, Venezuela, B 9
3000	Corocoro, Bolivia, I 3
1580	Coroico, Bolivia, H 5
2211	Coroma, Bolivia, K 7
619	Coromandel, N. Z., D 18
.....	Coromontibo, Fr. Gu., C 10
581	Coronation, Alberta, M 23
.....	Coronation, Mack, E 13
1725	Coronda, Argentina, L 16
14799	Coronel, Chile, P 2
.....	Coronel Alcerraca, A 4
748	Coronel Brandizen, Arg., N 19
.....	Coronel Martinez, Par., H4
27562	Coronel Súarez, Arg., P 15
2325	Corongo, Peru, I 6
2683	Coronie, N. Guiana, B 8
2757	Corowa, Austl., O 20
4519	Corozal, Colombia, D 9
.....	Corpach, Scotland, J 12
651	Corps, France, N 21
949	Corpus, Honduras, H 10
4629	Corque, Bolivia, J 5
.....	Corquin, Hond., G 7
.....	Corral, Son., J 12
.....	Corral de Lorca, Arg., N 9
3031	Corrales, Uruguay, H 21
.....	Corrales, Uruguay, L 22
.....	Corralillo, Cuba, H 10
3792	Corrall, Chile, R 2
3621	Correggio, Italy, E 8
.....	Corrente, Brazil, I 17
.....	Correntes, Brazil, M 9
.....	Correntina, Brazil, J 17
.....	Corribeg, Scotland, J 11
96405	Corrientes, Argentina, I 19
495	Corrofin, Ire., L 8
.....	Corry, Scotland, K 10
3793	Cortale, Italy, M 19
5267	Corte, France, P 3
4538	Cortemark, Belgium, L 5
777	Cortina, Italy, B 10
20151	Çorum, Tur., C 10
.....	Corumbá, Brazil, K 14
13345	Corumbá, Brazil, L 7
	Coruña, see La Coruña, Sp.
255	Corunna, Ontario, N 3
.....	Corwen, Wales, H 10
.....	Corzuela, Argentina, H 16
2118	Cosala, Sin., D 18
5417	Cosamaloapan, Ver., J 10
173	Cosapa, Bolivia, J 3
5266	Coscomatepec, Ver., I 8
24000	Cosenza, Italy, L 19
7035	Cosne, France, J 15
1500	Cosquin, Argentina, L 12
1100	Cossonay, Switz., K 3
.....	Costa Rica, Bolivia, C 3
.....	Costelloe, Ire., J 5
1187	Cotabambas, Peru, N 15
7494	Cotacachi, Ecuador, B 5
8136	Cotagaita, Bolivia, M 9
1354	Cotahuasi, Peru, O 15
385	Cotaxtla, Ver., I 9
.....	Coteau Jc., Que., Q 14
4204	Cotija, Michoa., N 8
3608	Cotoca, Bolivia, I 14
.....	Cotopaxi, Ecuador, B 5
1304	Cotorro, Cuba, H 7
8588	Cotrone, Italy, L 20
52089	Cottbus, Ger., I 13
416	Cottens, Switz., J 6
.....	Cottica, Neth. Guiana, C10
.....	Cottonwood, B. C., L 13
4590	Cotzal, Guatemala, E 4
1336	Cotzocon, Oax., L 10
5613	Couckelaere, Belgium, L 4
267	Coucy, France, G 16
1410	Couhe Varac, France, L 10
866	Couiza, France, Q 14
.....	Coulagh, Ire., Q 3
.....	Coulags, Scotland, H 11
637	Coulanges-sur-Yonne, Fr., J 16
6411	Coulommiers, France, H 16
2435	Coupar Angus, Scot., K 19
312	Couptrain, France, H 9
.....	Cour, Scotland, N 10
58638	Courbevoie, France, A 3
18071	Courcelles, Belgium, N 12
200	Courcelles, Quebec, O 22
1437	Courgenay Switz., D 7
1917	Courrendlin, Switz., E 8
1569	Courroux, Switz., E 8
4273	Coursan, France, P 16
10	Court, Saskatchewan, N 4
1185	Courtelary, Switz., F 7
704	Courtemaiche, Switz., D 6
1737	Courtenay, B. C., Q 11
1947	Courtenay, France, I 15
254	Courtepin, Switz., I 7
352	Courtland, Ontario, O 8
.....	Courtmacsherry, Ire., Q 9
.....	Courtown Harbour, Ire., M 22
38569	Courtrai, Belgium, M 6
325	Courtright, Ontario, O 3
4420	Court Saint Etienne, Belgium, N 12
1440	Courville, France, H 12
517	Coussey, France, H 20
6401	Coutances, France. G 6
3078	Couthuin, Belgium, N 15
5078	Coutras, France, M 9
200	Coutts, Alberta, Q 23
3116	Couvet, Switz., H 4
900	Covaleda, Spain, F 13
.....	Cove, Scotland, I 24
226	Covendo, Bolivia, G 6
184700	Coventry, England, J 15
.....	Cover, U.S. Afr., H 17
15640	Covilhã, Portugal, H 7
.....	Covunco Centro, Arg., Q 6
3452	Cowansville, Quebec, Q 17
12731	Cowdenbeath, Scot., M 19
10179	Cowes, England, N 16
.....	Cowley, Yukon, Q 10
.....	Cowpen, England, C 15
5056	Cowra, Australia, O 20
3800	Cox Bazar, India, I 25
.....	Coxen Hole, Hond., D 10
.....	Coxim, Brazil, L 9
485	Coyame, Chih., F 20
.....	Coyle, B. C., P 14
2366	Coylton, Scotland, O 14
.....	Coymbra, Austl., M 12
2396	Coyomeapan, Pueb., J 8
349	Coyotitán, Sin., P 18
.....	Coyra, Michoa., P 7
2084	Coyuca, Guer., P 13
1972	Coyuca de Benítez, Guer., R 14
602	Cozes, France, M 8
2211	C. Porvenir, Ur., J 16
	Cracow, see Kraków, Pol.
9268	Cradock, U.S. Afr., O 15
.....	Craig, Scotland, G 11
186	Craigmyle, Alberta, M 22
.....	Craignure, Scotland, K 9
90	Craigvale, Ontario, I 11
429	Craik, Saskatchewan, O 7
1596	Crail, Scotland, L 22
63063	Craiova, Romania, K 18
252	Cranbrook, Australia, O 5
2568	Cranbrook, B. C., Q 19
200	Crandall, Man., Q 13
.....	Cranford, Ire , B 14
418	Crapaud, P. E. I., H 15
.....	Cratheus, Brazil, F 21
.....	Crathie, Scotland, I 19
.....	Cratloe, Ire., M 9
10142	Crato, Brazil, G 21
.....	Craughwell, Ire., J 9
144	Craven, Sask., P 8
1572	Crawford, Scotland, O 18
572	Crawfordjohn, Scot., O 17
.....	Crawton, Scotland, J 23
.....	Creagh, Ire., R 6
1119	Crecy en Ponthieu, Fr., F 13
3490	Crediton, England, N 8
627	Crediton, Ontario, M 5
145	Creelman, Sask, Q 10
629	Creemore, Ontario, I 10
.....	Creeslough, Ire., B 13
.....	Creetown, Scotland, Q 15
.....	Cregg, Ire., K 7
11325	Crema, Italy, D 6
1643	Crémieu, France, L 20
42600	Cremona, Italy, D 6
615	Créon, France, N 8
5570	Crépy-en-Valois, Fr., G 15
.....	Crespo, Argentina, L 17
5250	Crest, France, N 20
.....	Cresta, Switz., L 20
1153	Creston, B. C., Q 19
1506	Creswick, Australia, P 18
11596	Creteil, France, C 7
11403	Crevillente, Spain, L 16
46061	Crewe, England, H 13
.....	Crianlarich, Scotland, L 13
1449	Criccieth, Wales, H 7
.....	Cricklade, England, L 14
6058	Crieff, Scotland, L 17
.....	Crinkill, Ire., K 14
1854	Cristo, Cuba, O 21
.....	Crixas, Brazil, K 13
.....	Crockenhill, England, D 24
.....	Croft, England, E 15
.....	Crofton, B. C., R 12
.....	Croghan, Ire., H 12
7919	Croissy, Fr., B 2
.....	Crolly, Ire., C 12
1232	Cromarty, Scotland, G 16
2887	Cromdale, Scotland, H 18
4177	Cromer, England, H 23
730	Cromwell, N. Z., O 6
114	Crooked River, Sask., L 10
.....	Crookhaven, Ire., R 4
600	Croom, Ire., N 9
100	Cross, Ire., P 14
.....	Crossakeel, Ire., H 18
.....	Crossdoney, Ire. G 16
409	Crossfield, Alberta, N 20
.....	Crossgar, N. Ire., E 24
.....	Crosshaven, Ire., Q 11
.....	Crossmaglen, N. Ire., G 20
1160	Crossmichael, Scot., Q 16
.....	Crossmolina, Ire., G 6
.....	Crossmount, Ire., P 6
272	Cross Roads, N. S., H 23
.....	Cross Roads Country Harbor, N. S., K 19
.....	Crotto, Argentina, P 17
.....	Crowie, England, G 17
1000	Crow's Nest, Austl., K 23
226	Croydon, Australia, E 18
.....	Croydon, B. C., L 15
239960	Croydon, Eng., L 19
7454	Crozen, France, H 1
226	Crucero, Peru, N 20
9043	Cruces, Cuba, J 11
2554	Cruden, Scotland, H 24
.....	Crumlin, N. Ire., D 22
.....	Crusheen, Ire., L 8
.....	Cruta, Hond., E 15
1114	Cruz, Argentina, M 15
16331	Cruz Alta, Brazil, P 10
2000	Cruz del Eje, Arg., K 11
11863	Cruzeiro, Brazil, N 16
.....	Cruzeiro do Sul, West Brazil, H 15
409	Cruzy, Fr., I 18
500	Crysler, Ontario, E 24
618	Crystal Beach, Ont., O 12
.....	Crystal Brook, Austl., N 15
26015	Csongrád, Hungary, I 13
4724	Csurgo, Hungary, I 9
1782	Cua, Venezuela, D 13
782	Cualac, Guer., P 18
12	Cuale, Jal., M 2
2374	Cuaró, Uruguay, F 18
2442	Cuatrocienegas, Coa., D 10
.....	Cuatro Companeros, Cuba, M 16
980	Cuauhtemoc, Chih., H 17
1880	Cuautepec, Guer., R 17
1582	Cuautitlán, Méx., H 5
6431	Cuautla, Morel., I 5
.....	Cuchivero, Venezuela,H 15
307	Cucho Ingenio, Bolivia, L 9
2114	Cuckfield, England, M 19
5384	Cucunubá, Colombia, H 11
37323	Cucuta, Colombia, F 14
7399	Cucutilla, Colombia, F 14
59057	Cuddalore, India, O 13
22602	Cuddapah, India, N 12
10630	Cudillero, Sp., C 9
598	Cudrefin, Switz., H 6
535	Cudworth, Sask., M 8
506	Cue, Australia, K 5
7514	Cuéllar, Sp., G 12
50392	Cuenca, Ecuador, D 4
24702	Cuenca, Sp., I 15
4072	Cueramaro, Guan., M 11
14421	Cuernavaca, Morel., I 4
10325	Cuesmes, Belgium, N 10
.....	Cueto, Cuba, N 21
1549	Cuetzalâde Progreso, Guer., P 15
7087	Cuetzalán, Pueb., G 8
.....	Cuevas, Spain, H 16
20403	Cuevas, Spain, N 14
2030	Cuevo, Bolivia, L 13
.....	Cuhimbe, Colombia, M 8
18940	Cuiabá, Braz., K 8
2193	Cuicatlan, Oax., K 8
.....	Cuidad Obregon, Son., J 12
.....	Cuil, Scotland, K 11
5586	Cuilapa, Guap., G 4
865	Cuisery, France, K 19
.....	Cuitzeo, Guan., M 11
3257	Cuitzeo, Michoa., M 12
100	Culdaff, Ire., B 17
9256	Culemborg, Neth., H 15
22025	Culiacán, Sin., O 17
.....	Culkein, Scotland, E 11
9502	Cullar de Baza, Spain,N 14
.....	Cullen, Ire., O 7
1814	Cullen, Scotland, G 21
15005	Cullera, Spain, K 17
.....	Cullerton, N. B., H 5
.....	Cullinan, U.S. Afr., F 19
.....	Culloville, N. Ire., G 20
1145	Cully, Switzerland, L 5
.....	Cullyhanna, N. Ire., F 20
.....	Culrain, Scotland, F 14
508	Culsamond, Scotland, H 21
726	Culta, Bolivia, K 8
.....	Cults, Scotland, H 21
.....	Cults, Scotland, I 23
.....	Cululli, I. E. A., C 11
100	Culverden, N. Z., L 13
25893	Cumaná, Venezuela, C 17
3144	Cumanacoa, Ven., D 18
2955	Cumanayagua, Cuba, J 11
6940	Cumarebo, Ven., B 9
885	Cumberland, B. C., Q 11
312	Cumberland, Ont., D 23
62	Cumberland House, Sask., K 11
6500	Cumbum, India, M 12
3417	Cumnock, Scotland, O 15
3001	Cumpas, Son., E 13
111	Cumuripa, Son, I 12
1203	Cunaco, Chile, N 4
.....	Cunagua, Cuba, J 16
.....	Cunany, Brazil, C 12
2639	Cunduacán, Tab., K 15
.....	Cuneira, Cuba, O 22
21600	Cuneo, Italy, E 2
.....	Cunha, Brazil, C 5
1676	Cunnamulla, Austl., K 20
.....	Cunningham, N. Ire., C 16
.....	Cunningsburgh, Shetland Is., C 3
.....	Cunuani, Brazil, C 5
399	Cupar, Sask., O 9
4596	Cupar, Scotland, L 20
.....	Cupica, Col., G 5
8235	Cuprija, Yugo, K 15
2374	Cuquio, Jal., L 7
.....	Cur, Ire., I 5
.....	Curacá, Brazil, H 21
5740	Curacuatin, Chile, Q 4
1504	Curahuara, Bolivia, J 4
.....	Curahuasi, Peru, M 15
3995	Curanilahue, Chile, P 2
1739	Curepto, Chile, O 3
.....	Curiche, Bol., K 17
21153	Curico, Chile, N 4
.....	Curie, Sask., P 7
2306	Curiepe, Venezuela, C 14
.....	Curimatahy, Brazil, L 17
101204	Curitiba, Brazil, O 13
.....	Curitybanos, Brazil, P 12
.....	Curle, Sask., P 8
.....	Curracloe, Ire., N 22
.....	Curracunya, Austl., K 19
12590	Curralinho, Brazil, F 19
12000	Curralinho, Brazil, K 13
.....	Curralinho, Brazil, L 17
255	Curran, Ontario, D 24
.....	Currawilla, Austl., I 18
104	Currie, Ont., M 8
104	Currie, Ont., N 8
6831	Curtea de Argés, Romania, J 19
.....	Curucay, Ven., I 19
3400	Curuguaty, Paraguay, M 10
.....	Curupachi, Braz.,G 7
.....	Cururupú, Brazil, E 17
10709	Curuzu Cuatia, Arg., J 20
8700	Curvello, Brazil, L 17
.....	Cushendall, N. Ire., B 22
.....	Cushendun, N. Ire., B 22
.....	Cushina, Ire., K 17
3017	Cusihuiriáchic, Chih., H 17
7672	Cusset, France, L 17
300	Cust, N. Z., M 12
.....	Cüstrin, Ger., G 14
299	Cut Knife, Sask., L 5
200	Cutler, Ont., A 3
5007	Cutro, Italy, M 20
65263	Cuttack, India, J 19
2479	Cutzamalá, Guer., P 13
20000	Cuxhaven, Germany, D 6
45158	Cuzco, Peru, M 16
1733	Cuzgun, Rom., K 23
139	Czar, Alberta, L 23
.....	Czarnkowo, Poland, D 9
	Czartorysk, see Chartorisk, Sov. Un.
136000	Czestochowa, Pol., F 12
.....	Czyżewo, Pol., D 15

D

Pop.	Place Country Index
100	Daaquam, Quebec, L 24
.....	Dabari, I. E. A., O 18
.....	Dabat, I. E. A., E 7
1827	Dabeida, Colombia, F 7
14000	Dabhoi, India, I 6
.....	Dabiya, Egypt, O 23
.....	Dabrowa, Poland, F 12
	Dabrowica, see Dombrovitsa, Sov. Un.
213218	Dacca, India, H 23
752	Dacknam, Belgium, R 5
.....	Dacross, Scot., G 16
.....	Dada-Nawa, Br. Gu., C 6
2000	Dadar, Baluchistan, M 22
.....	Dadi, Baluchistan, Q 18
3000	Dadu, India, F 1
108	Dafoe, Sask., N 9
.....	Dagabur, Eth., K 15
.....	Dagarita, Br. Som., G 15
.....	Dagenham, England, B 25
.....	Dagia, Morocco, F 7
.....	Dag-i-Farhad, Iran, O 14
1956	Dagmersellen, Switz., F 12
2173	Dagua, Colombia, J 6
.....	Dahan, Iran, Q 14
5000	Dahanu, India, J 5
.....	Dahlem, Germany, R 15
5136	Dahme, Germany, H 12
.....	Dahra, Egypt, B 18
19759	Daimiel, Spain, K 12
.....	Dainenji, Japan, I 16
.....	Dair, I. E. A., H 10
481379	Dairen, China, D 20
9000	Daishoji, Japan, J 15
6100	Dajal, India, E 4
103	Dajarra, Australia, G 17
76100	Dakar, Fr. W. Afr., H 1
.....	Dalan, Iran, P 10
.....	Dalantura, China, A 4
.....	Dalaouin, Tunisia, G 25
475	Dalarö, Sweden, R 23
5400	Dalat, Fr. In. Chn., Q 10
3011	Dalbeattie, Scotland, Q 17
2967	Dalby, Austl., K 22
.....	Dalby, Sweden, Q 11
.....	Dalbyneder, Denmark,F 12
.....	Dalcataig, Scotland, H 14
2000	Dalcross, Scotland, G 16
.....	Dale, Norway, K 4
.....	Dale, Shetland Is., B 3
28	Dalehurst, Alberta, K 17
3987	Dalen, Netherlands, E 23
1507	Dalence, Bolivia, J 6
.....	Dalfors, Sweden, K 13
7077	Dalfsen, Netherlands, F 20
.....	Dalhousie, Australia, J 15
4508	Dalhousie, N. B., A 8
.....	Dalhousie, Que., Q 13
135	Dalhousie Jc., N. B., A 7
.....	Dalhousie West, N.S.,M 10
9510	Dalias, Spain, O 13
.....	Daliburgh, Scotland, I 3
993	Daliet el Kurmul,Palestine, H 8
.....	Daliet er Ruhah, Pal., I 8
7854	Dalkeith, Scotland, M 20
4135	Dalkey, Ire., J 22
.....	Dallarossie, Scotland, H 16
.....	Dallas, Egypt, M 13
.....	Dalldorf, Germany, N 16
.....	Dalle, Germany, F 8
.....	Dalmacio Velez, Arg.,M 13
.....	Dalmally, Scotland, L 12
6151	Dalmellington, Scot., P 15
198	Dalmeny, Sask., M 7
3237	Dalmeny, Scot., M 19
286	Dalmose, Denmark, L 18
.....	Dalnacardoch, Scot., J 16
843	Dalry, Scotland, N 13
6827	Dalry, Scotland, P 16
570	Dalton, Scotland, Q 19
12303	Dalton in Furness, England, E 10
.....	Dalton Post, Yukon, Q 6
.....	Dalwhinnie, Scotland, J 15
.....	Daly Waters, Austl., D 13
.....	Dam, Neth Guiana, B 9
58700	Damanhur, Egypt, D 7
.....	Dâmanhûr el-Wahsh, Egypt, F 13
7000	Damao (Port.), India, J 6
.....	Damas, Egypt, E 14
318922	Damas (Damascus), Syr., M 11
.....	Dambacha, Eth., H 7
.....	Damban, Iran, P 13
.....	Dambulla, India, Q 14
.....	Damechli, Egypt, F 10
15000	Damghan, Iran, F 9
	Damietta, see Dumiât, Egypt
1302	Dammartin, France, G 14
5951	Damme, Germany, G 5
20728	Damoh, India, H 12
271	Damvant, Switz., E 6
997	Damville, France, H 11
.....	Damyâne (Coptic Monastery), Eg., B 15
75	Dana, Sask., M 8
138	Danby, Quebec, P 18
22565	Danda, Nepal, E 14
4270	Dandenong, Austl., Q 18
.....	Dandit, Egypt, F 14
.....	Dangan, Ire., P 13
548	Dange, France, K 10
.....	Dangila, Eth., G 7
.....	Danilov, Sov. Un., H 12
.....	Dankaz, Eth., E 7
.....	Dankov, Sov. Un., J 12
3209	Danli, Honduras, G 11

Pop.	Place Country Index
.....	Dannemora, Sweden, M 16
.....	Dannenberg, Germany, F 9
.....	Dantewara, India, K 14
.....	Dantock, Eng., M 9
1320	Danville, Quebec, O 19
238000	Danzig, Pol., C 11
.....	Daont, Eth., I 13
130	Dapp, Alberta, J 20
.....	Daqâdûs, Egypt, E 14
.....	Daqlet, Egypt, C 11
.....	Dar, Morocco, G 4
4000	Darab, Iran, N 9
10538	Dărăbani, Rom., H 21
.....	Darak, Iran, K 12
.....	Darak, Iran, K 13
.....	Daraksa, Egypt, C 17
.....	Darau, Egypt, R 24
.....	Darband, Bal., M 17
.....	Darband, Iran, E 11
60676	Darbhangah, India, G 19
.....	D'Arcy, B. C., O 13
33500	Dar es Salaam, Tan., M 21
2280	Dargaville, N. Z., C 15
.....	Dargazin, Iran, F 5
3286	Daridere, Bulgaria, M 20
24000	Darjeeling, India, F 21
.....	Darlac, Fr. Ind. Ch., Q 10
373	Darligen, Switz., J 10
1500	Darling, U.S. Afr., P 7
72093	Darlington, England, D 15
33	Darlington, Ontario, K 13
539	Darlington Point, Austl., O 20
90000	Darmstadt, Ger., M 5
3713	Daroca, Spain, G 15
.....	Daror, Eth., K 16
.....	Dar Ould Selemia, Mor., G 3
.....	Darowli, Afg., J 19
.....	Dar Pahan, Iran, P 12
.....	Darrangir, India, G 24
.....	Dar Shaui, Morocco, F 11
6709	Dartmouth, England, O 9
10847	Dartmouth, N. S., N 15
.....	Dar Uld Sidu, Mor., H 6
.....	Darut, Egypt, L 18
.....	Daruvar, Yugo., J 10
3232	Darvel, Scotland, O 15
42	Darwell, Alberta, K 20
.....	Darwin, Argentina, R 11
1500	Darwin, Australia, A 12
.....	Daryabad, India, F 14
.....	Darya Kahn, India, C 5
.....	Dasht, Iran, M 10
.....	Dashtab, Iran, N 11
.....	Dasht-i-Ber, Iran, N 11
.....	Dasht-i-kak, Iran, M 9
.....	Dashtût, Egypt, N 11
624	Dashwood, Ontario, M 5
.....	Dasjirdun, Iran, H 11
.....	Daspalla, India, J 18
.....	Dastgird, Iran, F 11
.....	Datha, India, J 5
24100	Datia, India, G 11
.....	Dattin, Iran, J 10
43226	Daugavpils, W. Sov. Un., A 19
.....	Daulatabad, India, J 7
.....	Daulatabad, Iran, G 4
17435	Daule, Ecuador, C 3
.....	Daun, Germany, L 2
.....	Dauntsey, Eng., L 14
4662	Dauphin, Manitoba, O 13
.....	Davbjerg, Denmark, G 7
.....	Davel, U.S. Afr., G 20
342	Daveluyville, Quebec, N 19
3608	Daventry, England, J 16
9222	David, Panama, P 17
456	Davidson, Sask, O 7
.....	Davik, Norway, K 4
.....	Daviot, Scotland, H 15
11167	Davos, Switzerland, I 22
.....	Dawadiya, Egypt, R 10
.....	Dawer, India, G 7
4578	Dawlish, England, N 9
1043	Dawson, Yukon, K 4
12663	Dax, France, O 7
5000	Daya, Algeria, E 12
.....	Dayentry, Eng., J 16
438	Daysland, Alberta, L 22
.....	Dayulgomba, China, H 2
5118	De Aar Junction, U.S. Afr., M 13
.....	Deacon, Honduras, E 13
13680	Deal, England, M 24
.....	de Añgeles, Zac., J 10
163	Dean, Nova Scotia, L 17
.....	Deán Funes, Arg., K 12
100	Dean Lake, Ontario, A 1
.....	Deanston, Scotland, L 16
4208	Deauville, France, G 9
6913	Debar, Yugo., M 14
.....	Debarech, Eth., D 8
184	Debden, Sask, K 7
1824	Debdu, Morocco, F 10
142	Debec, N. B., H 4
200	De Beaujeu, Que., Q 13
.....	Deblin, Poland, E 15
3000	Debra Birhan, Eth., I 10
.....	Debra Libanos, Eth., I 9
.....	Debra Mai, Eth., G 7
10000	Debra Marcos, Eth., H 7
3500	Debra Tabor, Eth., F 8
.....	Debra Wark, Eth., H 8
.....	Debra Zebit, Eth., F 9
119901	Debrecen, Hungary, H 14
602	Deburieh, Palestine, H 11
1620	Decimomannu, Italy, L 4
	Děčin, Czech, E 7
4384	Decize, France, K 16
.....	De Cocksdorp, Neth., C 14
	Dede Agach, see Alexandroupolis, Greece
.....	Deelfontein, U.S. Afr., M 13
436	Deep Brook, N. S., N 9
.....	Deerholme, B. C., Q 2
.....	Deerlake, Newf., L 23
.....	Deerness, Scotland, B 21
.....	Deery, Ire., G 5
.....	Deesa, India, H 5
.....	Defra, Egypt, E 12
.....	Degeberga, Sweden, Q 12
.....	Degerfors, Sweden, H 17
.....	Degerfors, Sweden, N 13
7843	Deggendorf, Germany, O11
.....	De Grey Station, Austl., F 6
.....	Dehak, Iran, I 6
.....	Dehbid, Iran, L 8
.....	Dehchah, Iran, M 9
.....	Dehgarda, Iran, K 7
.....	Deh-i-Baba, Afg., J 19
2000	Deh-i-Haji, Afg., K 20
.....	Deh-i-Mari, Iran, F 13
.....	Deh-i-Zawur, Afg., H 18
.....	Deh Khair, Iran, N 9
.....	Dehlur, Iran, I 6
40409	Dehra Dun, India, D 11
.....	Deh Shir, Iran, K 8
.....	Deier el Kamr, Syria, M 10
2236	Deil, Netherlands, H 16
.....	Deir Ammar, Palestine, L 8
916	Deir el Belah, Palestine, P 1
.....	Deir el Maaz, Transjordan, J 23
.....	Deir el Maksaba, Syria, B 11
.....	Deir esh Sheikh, Palestine, N 8
.....	Deir-ez-Zor, Syr., K-15
336	Deir Nakhkhas, Pal., N 7
.....	Deir Sineid, Palestine, O 2
15311	Dej, Romania, I 17
.....	De Kaag, Neth., G 12
.....	Dekarnes, Egypt, C 17
.....	Delaja, Iran, F 4
.....	Delatyn, W. Sov. Un., Q 18
326	Delaware, Ontario, N 6
308	Delburne, Alberta, M 21
.....	Deldoon, Algeria, M 13
6368	Delemont, Switz., E 8
.....	Delfshaven, Neth., I 11
50609	Delft, Neth., H 11
9481	Delfzijl, Neth., B 23
.....	Delga, Eth., H 10
.....	Delgany, Ire., K 23
.....	Delgo, A. E. Sud., G 18
521849	Delhi, India, E 10
2062	Delhi, Ontario, O 8
315	Delia, Alberta, M 22
.....	Delia, Cuba, K 15
.....	Dêlingat, Egypt, E 8
333	Delisle, Sask., N 6
14878	Delitzsch, Germany, I 10
.....	Delkam el-Atif, Egypt, Q 9
.....	Delli Abbas, Iraq, L 21
4374	Dellys, Algeria, B 17
138	Delmas, Sask., L 5
.....	Delmas, U.S. Afr., F 19
31284	Delmenhorst, Ger., F 5
773	Deloraine, Man., R 13
1550	Deloraine, Tasmania, C 6
333	Deloro, Ontario, H 17
.....	Delphi, Greece, P 16
32	Del Rio, Son., C 12
.....	Delsbo, Sweden, K 15
.....	Delta, Manitoba, Q 15
519	Delta, Ontario, H 21
958	Delting, Shetland Is., B 3
.....	Delvin, Ire., I 18
.....	Delvinë, Alb., N 13
3000	Delwa, India, E 7
150	Demaine, Sask., O 6
5000	Demavend, Iran, F 7
.....	Demene Krog, Ger., R 19
5948	Demirji, Tur., E 3
.....	Demirji, Tur., F 4
12783	Demmin, Germany, D 12
4330	Demnat, Mor., I 6
.....	Democracia, Ven., D 13
.....	Democracia, Ven., P 12
216	Demorestville, Ont., J 18
.....	Dénaa, Syria, N 11
26478	Denain, France, E 15
218	Denbigh, Ontario, F 17
7249	Denbigh, Wales, H 10
.....	Denderah, Egypt, N 23
	Dendermonde, see Termonde, Bel.
6195	Denekamp, Neth., F 24
.....	Denek-Maden, Tur., E 8
.....	Dengelbar, Eth., F 6
6096	Den Ham, Neth., F 22
14	Denhart, Alberta, O 23
95	Denholm, Sask., L 6
.....	Denholm, Scotland, O 22
12323	Denia, Spain, K 18
3192	Deniliquin, Australia, O 19
.....	Den Ilp, Neth., A 4
.....	Denison, Austl., L 3
17345	Denizli (Denizlu), Tur., G3
.....	Denjaya, Siam, N 3
.....	Denkhargen, Iran, C 2
700	Denmark, Australia, O 5
218	Denmark, N. S., J 16
.....	Denna, Palestine, I 12
9488	Denny, Scotland, M 16
224	Denver, Nova Scotia, K 19
207	Denzil, Sask., M 4
.....	Deogan, India, H 17
8800	Deogarh, India, H 20
5500	Deoli, India, G 8
5000	Deori, India, H 12
.....	De Overtoom, Neth., C 3
525	Depot Harbour, Ont., E 10
.....	Dêr, Egypt, P 23
27000	Dera Ghazi Khan, India, D 4
35100	Dera Ismail Khan, India, C 4
.....	Dêramês, Egypt, D 6
.....	Der Anba Beshoi, Egypt, H 6
.....	Dêr Baramûs, Egypt, H 6
31200	Derbent, Sov. Un., P 19
165	Derby, Australia, E 8
142406	Derby, England, H 15
.....	Derby, U.S. Afr., H 21
.....	Dêr Byâd, Egypt, N 13
115	Derby Junction, N.B., E 9
.....	Derdepoort, U.S. Afr., D 16
.....	Deregus, Afghanistan, E 21
.....	Dêr el Adra, Egypt, Q 9
6663	Derendah, Tur., F 12
.....	Dergachi, Sov. Un., L 10
.....	Deria Derre, Afg., I 19
1430	De Rijp, Neth., F 14
.....	Derkmore, Ire., F 10
736	Derland, Ontario, A 12
.....	Dêr Macarius, Egypt, H 8
11360	Derna, Libya, E 15
.....	Deroche, B. C., O 5
.....	Derra, Eth., H 9
.....	Derreen, Ire., Q 4
.....	Derrinkee, Ire., H 6
	Derry, see Londonderry, N. Ire.
.....	Derrybeg, Ire., B 12
500	Derrygonnelly, N. Ire., E 14
.....	Dershay, Egypt, E 8
.....	Dêr Suriâni, Egypt, H 6
2054	Derut, Egypt, C 8
.....	Dervazen, Afg., G 18
6651	Derventa, Yugo., J 10
.....	Dervock, N. Ire., B 20
693	Desaguadero, Bolivia, H 2
.....	Desamparados, Arg., L 7
608	Deschaillons, Quebec, L 19
770	Deschambault, Que., L 19
.....	Deschenes Mills, Que., P 10
.....	Descouse, N. S., J 22
.....	Descubridora, Dur., L 22
.....	Deseada, Chile, E 4
1261	Deseronto, Ontario, I 18
.....	Desford, England, I 16
2618	Deshaies, Guadeloupe, B 22
.....	Deshasha, Egypt, N 10
3200	Desmochados, Par., R 6
91423	Dessau, Germany, H 10
.....	Dessie, Eth., G 10
.....	Dessieh, Egypt, L 10
.....	Dessuk, Egypt, C 9
.....	Desunes, Egypt, C 6
.....	Desvio, Chile, F 4
.....	Desvio K. 392, Arg., I 17
.....	Desvio Km. 842, Arg., N 9
.....	Desvio Km. 815, Arg., N 9
.....	Desvio Km. 745, Arg., O 10
5119	Desvres, France, E 13
70	Detlor, Ontario, F 16
18000	Detmold, Ger., H 6
10316	Deurne, Neth., J 18
11264	Deutsch Eylau, Pol., C 12
.....	Deutsch-Wilmersdorf, Germany, Q 15
11000	Déva, Romania, J 16
3476	Deva, Spain, C 14
36227	Deventer, Neth., G 20
6058	Devizes, England, L 14
.....	Devondale, U.S. Afr., G 14
81700	Devonport, England, O 7
5153	Devonport, Tasmania, C 6
.....	Devrikjan, Tur., B 8
.....	Dewas, India, I 9
.....	Dewdney, B. C., O 5
966	De Wets Dorp, U.S. Afr., K 16
.....	De Wette, Yukon, Q 10
3375	De Wijk, Neth., E 21
75	De Winton, Alberta, O 20
117	Dewittville, Quebec, R 14
2490	Dewrek, Tur., B 6
54303	Dewsbury, England, G 15
.....	Deyhi Baiz, Afg., F 19
5157	Deynze, Belgium, L 7
.....	Dhandhuka, India, I 5
.....	Dhanera, India, H 5
18400	Dhar, India, I 8
6900	Dharampur, India, J 6
6800	Dharmavaram, India, M 11
.....	Dharur, India, K 9
41671	Dharwar, India, M 8
.....	Dhenkanal, India, J 18
.....	Dhiban, Transj., O 10
.....	Dhiban, Transj., O 14
.....	Dhirang Jong, India, F 25
.....	Dholera, India, I 5
15000	Dholka, India, I 5
.....	Dholpur, India, F 11
5000	Dhond, India, K 7
29302	Dhoraji, India, I 3
3700	Dhubri, India, F 23
39939	Dhulia, India, J 8
.....	Dhuneibeh, Syria, G 19
.....	Diabaig, Scotland, G 9
.....	Dia el Kom, Egypt, F 12
2260	Diamant, Martinique, G 24
9907	Diamantina, Brazil, L 18
.....	Diamantino, Brazil, J 8
2471	Diamond, Br. Gu., B 7
.....	Diamond Harbour, India, I 21
	Diarbekr, see Diyarbekir, Tur.
24100	Diatia, Ind., G 11
2000	Diaz, Argentina, L 16
.....	Díaz Ordaz, Oax., M 9
.....	Dibai, India, F 11
.....	Dibbela, Fr. W. Afr., H 12
.....	Dibi, Egypt, B 8
.....	Dibit, Som., N 21
.....	Dibo, Eth., G 8
9900	Dibrugarh, India, L 21
.....	Dibulla, Col., B 13
155	Dickinsons Landing, Ont., F 24
5808	Didam, Neth., H 20
.....	Didhav, Eth., E 12
892	Didsbury, Alberta, M 20
8217	Didymoteikhon, Grc., M 21
3304	Die, France, N 20
16756	Diégo-Suarez (Antsirane), Madag. N 25
3700	Diekirch, Luxembourg, Q 21
3411	Diemen, Neth., C 6
.....	Diemerbrug, Neth., D 6
.....	Diemerdam, Neth., D 8
1899	Diemtigen, Switz., J 9
5524	Diepenbeek, Belgium, L 17
6315	Diepenveen, Neth., G 20
25510	Dieppe, France, F 12
.....	Dieren, Netherlands, H 20
758	Diessbach, Switz., I 10
2325	Diessenhofen, Switz., B 16
8248	Diest, Belgium, L 15
6502	Dietikon, Switz., D 14
2388	Dieuze, France, G 22
1657	Digby, Nova Scotia, N 9
5202	Dignano, Italy, E 14
6737	Digne, France, O 23
6271	Digoin, France K 17
.....	Digranaes, Iceland, A 24
.....	Digsa, Erit., B 9
2700	Digwa, Egypt, G 13
96257	Dijon, France, J 19
.....	Dila, Afg., I 22
.....	Dilawar, India, E 5
.....	Dilbutan, Iran, F 3
.....	Diligent River, N. S., K 12
14021	Dili, Timor., J 7
.....	Dilling, Norway, E 5
10148	Dillingen, Ger., P 8
.....	Dillon, Eth., I 8
6000	Dilman, Iran, C 1
34	Diltz, Ontario, N 11
.....	Dimas, Cuba, I 2
1883	Dimboola, Austl., P 17
.....	Dimetoka, Tur., C 1
13400	Dinajpur, India, G 22
1084	Dinamita, Dur., M 23
10633	Dinan, France, H 6
6612	Dinant, Belgium, O 14
33699	Dinapur, India, G 18
43617	Dindigul, India, P 11
2732	Dineir, Tur., F 4
1786	Dingle, Ire., O 1
3879	Dingolfing, Germany, P 11
2763	Dingwall, Scotland, G 14
5067	Dinkelsbühl, Ger., O 7
.....	Dinnet, Scotland, I 20
.....	Dinshal, Egypt, D 8
215	Dinsmore, Sask., N 6
3448	Dinxperlo, Neth., H 22
.....	Diosig, Hung., H 16
.....	Dipalpur, India, I 8
.....	Dipkhur, Iran, Q 16
.....	Diplo, India, H 3
225	Dipper Harbour, N. B., L 7
90	Dipton, N. Z., Q 5
.....	Dir, India, A 6
.....	Diras, Egypt, D 14
30000	Dire Daua, I. E. A., I 12
8155	Diriamba, Nicaragua, K 11
2643	Dirksland, Neth., I 10
.....	Dirmil, Tur., H 4
.....	Disc, Syr., L 10
1768	Disentis, Switz., J 16
.....	Dishna, Egypt, O 23
.....	Dishu, Afg., L 18
.....	Diskerre, Iran, K 6
.....	Disna, W. Sov. Un., A 21
10501	Dison, Belgium, N 18
1338	Disraeli, Quebec, O 21
3422	Diss, England, J 23
.....	Ditrau, E. Hung., I 19
13206	Diu (Portuguese), India, J 4
.....	Divazza, Italy, C 14
4460	Dives-sur-Mer, France, G 9
.....	Div Hissar, Afg., G 19
.....	Divisoria, Argentina, L 7
.....	Divrigi, Tur., E 13
.....	Diwangiri, India, F 25
3234	Dixmude, Bel., L 4
385	Dixville, Quebec, R 20
42786	Diyarbekir (Diarbekr), Tur., G 15
.....	Diza, Tur., G 20
50000	Dizful, Iran, J 3
13773	Djakovica, Yugo., L 14
.....	Djakovo, Yugo., J 11
	Djanet, see Fort Charlet, Algeria
.....	Djanik, Tur., F 19
.....	Djarije, Iraq, L 17
.....	Djedeida, Tunisia, B 23
3739	Djelfa, Algeria, E 17
13	Djenien bov Rezg, Alg., H 12
.....	Djerdeb, Algeria, Q 23
15000	Djibouti, Fr. Som., F 14
.....	Djidiouia, Algeria, D 14
10725	Djidjelli (Jijelli), Alg., B 19
.....	Djilali, Algeria, D 14
.....	Djiring, Fr. In. Chn., Q 10
.....	Djisr-el-Choghour, Syr., J-11
.....	Djorfet Torba, Mor., I 10
.....	Djouni, Syr., L 10
.....	Djuanije, Iraq, L 18
.....	Djuro, Sweden, Q 25
6221	Djursholm, Sweden, Q 21
7300	Dmitriev, Sov. Un., K 9
	Dmitrievsk, see Makeevka, Sov. Un
.....	Dmitrov, Sov. Un., I 11
.....	Dmitrovsk, Sov. Un., K 9
500662	Dnepropetrovsk (Ekaterinoslav), Sov. Un., M 9
.....	Dno, Sov. Un., H 6
.....	Doab, Afg., F 21
.....	Doagh, N. Ire., D 22
.....	Doagh Beg, Ire., B 15
23000	Döbeln, Germany, J 12
.....	Doberan, Germany, C 10
.....	Doblas, Arg., P 13
4883	Doboj, Yugo., K 11
.....	Dobromil, W. Sov. Un., G 16
4683	Dobšiná, Czech., G 13
3165	Doctor Arroyo, N. L., I 14
.....	Dodoma, Tan., L 20
241	Dodsland, Sask., N 5
2038	Doel, Belgium, K 11
.....	Doega, Ire., G 3
4791	Doesburg, Neth., H 20
14330	Doetinchem, Neth., H 21
.....	Dog Creek, B. C., N 13
.....	Dog River Jc., Ont., P 18
.....	Dogumbezan, Iran, L 5
.....	Dojran, Yugo., M 16
.....	Dokara, Transj., I 14
5070	Dokkum, Neth., B 19
	Dokszyce, see Dokshitsy, Sov. Un.
	Dokshitsy, W. Sov. Un., B 21
4527	Dol, France, H 6
18066	Dôle France, J 20
.....	Doletabad, Iran, N 12
2261	Dolgelly, Wales, I 8
.....	Dolina, W. Sov. Un., G 17
1804	Dollar, Scotland, L 18
147	Dollard, Sask., Q 4
.....	Dolni Vakuf, Yugo., K 10
.....	Dolo, Eth., P 13
.....	Dolon-nor, China, B 16
27155	Dolores, Argentina, O 20
257	Dolores, Chile, C 4
1363	Dolores, Col., J 10
3026	Dolores, Col., K 6
422	Dolores, Guat., C 6
.....	Dolores, Hond., F 12
3203	Dolores, Spain, M 16
11500	Dolores, Uruguay, M 15
1649	Dolores, Ven., F 9
5915	Dolores Hidalgo, Guan., L 13
210	Dolphinton, Scotland, N 19
9074	Domazlice, Czech, F 5
8614	Dombóvár, Hungary, I 11
41681	Dombrovitsa, W. Sov. Un., E 20
1346	Domburg, Neth., J 7
.....	Domeh, Palestine, L 11
1423	Doméne, France, M 21
351	Domêvre, France, H 21
1517	Domeyko, Chile, F 5
3956	Domfront, France, H 9
.....	Dominguez, Cuba, M 19
3279	Dominion, N. S., H 24
.....	Dominion No. 6, N. S., H 25
.....	Dominion, Yukon, K 5
362	Dominion City, Man., R 16
573	Domme, France, N 12
.....	Domo, Eth., K 19
5804	Domodossola, Italy, C 3
903	Dompaire, France, H 21
10078	Dom Pedrito, Brazil, Q 9
.....	Don, Ontario, L 12
.....	Donado, Argentina, M 9
2213	Donaghadee, N. Ire., D 25
437	Donald, Ontario, F 14
.....	Donard, Ire., K 20
.....	Donato, Cuba, K 16
4821	Donauwörth, Ger., O 8
20931	Don Benito, Spain, K 9
63308	Doncaster, England, G 16
1214	Donegal, Ire., D 13
.....	Doneraile, Ire., O 10
.....	Donga, Australia, K 22
300	Dongarra, Australia, L 3
8488	Dongen, Neth., J 14
.....	Dong-hoi (Quang-binh), Fr. In. Chn., N 8
9000	Dongola, Anglo-Egyptian Sud., H 18
.....	Donkerbroek, Neth., D 21
.....	Donker Hoek, U. S. Afr., N 11
3060	Donnacona, Quebec, L 20
539	Donnaz, Italy, C 2
309	Donneloye, Switz., J 5
.....	Donoso, Pan., O 21
.....	Donoughmore, Ire., P 9
1093	Donzenac, France, M 12
1404	Donzy, France, J 15
289	Doodlakine, Austl., M 5
.....	Doogort, Ire., G 3
.....	Dookooma, Ire., G 3
621	Doon, Ontario, M 9
.....	Doonbeg, Ire, M 5
4351	Doornspijk, Neth., F 18
.....	Dopulun, Iran, J 5
.....	Doranda, India, H 18
10030	Dorchester, England, N 12
1237	Dorchester, N. B., I 12
521	Dorchester Sta., Ont., N 7
57059	Dordrecht, Neth., I 13
2052	Dordrecht, Union of South Africa, N 16
572	Dores, Scotland, H 15
.....	Dôres de Camaquan, Brazil, Q 12
5664	Doresdo Indayá, Brazil, L16
5388	Dorgali, Italy, K 5
224	Dorion, Ontario, P 19
.....	Dornegg, Italy, D 14
.....	Dornie, Scotland, H 10
2086	Dornoch, Scotland, F 16
6600	Dorogobuzh, Sov. Un., I 8
15373	Dorohoi, Rom., H 20
.....	Dorotea, Sweden, H 14
	Dorpat, see Tartu, Est.
.....	Dorrego, Argentina, Q 16
540875	Dortmund, Germany, I 4
1186	Dos Arroyos, Guer., R 15
.....	Dostabad, Iran, I 13
.....	Doti, Nepal, E 13
41598	Douai, France, E 15
27003	Douala, Cam., K 11
10536	Douarnenez, France, H 1
154	Doucet, Quebec, F 8
190	Doudeville, France, F 11
3185	Doué, France, J 8
6347	Douera, Algeria, B 16
21192	Douglas, England, E 7
154	Douglas, Manitoba, Q 13
1216	Douglas, U.S. Afr., J 13
212	Douglas Harbour, N. B., I 8
502	Douglastown, N. B., E 10
.....	Doui Menia, Algeria, O 10
.....	Douissa, Algeria, E 15
5699	Doullens, France, F 14
.....	Doumé, Cam., K 12
822	Doune, Scotland, L 16
.....	Doung, Iran, G 5
11890	Dour, Belgium, O 8
.....	Douro, W. Brazil, G 15
4697	Doussen, Algeria, E 18
613	Douvaine, France, K 22
1181	Douvres, France, G 9
41095	Dover, England, M 24
319	Dover, N. B., I 12
1463	Dovlen, Bul., M 19
2505	Dovre, Norway, J 8
.....	Dowally, Scotland, K 17
.....	Downderry, England, O 7
.....	Downe, England, D 23
2463	Downham Market, Eng., I 21
.....	Downhill, N. Ire., B 19
2993	Downpatrick, N. Ire., F 24
.....	Draa, Morocco, M 1
.....	Draaby, Denmark, J 20
.....	Drabble, Uruguay, M 16
1541	Dra el Mizan, Algeria, C 17
.....	Drăgănesti, Rom., K 20
6851	Dragasani, Rom., J 18
.....	Draghoender, U.S. Afr., K 10
2099	Dragör, Denmark, K 23
.....	Dragren, Neth., C 20
11418	Draguignan, France, P 23
.....	Draham, Tunisia, B 22
34000	Drama, Greece, M 18
25399	Drammen, Nor., M 8
42938	Drancy, France, A 7
20	Dranoel, Ontario, J 14
.....	Draperstown, N. Ire., D 19
504	Drayton, Ontario, K 8
.....	Drem, Scotland, M 21
642143	Dresden, Germany, J 13
1662	Dresden, Ontario, P 3
2584	Dreumel, Neth., I 17
12200	Dreux, France, H 12
.....	Drevsjo, Norway, K 10
.....	D. Ribeiro, Brazil, M 20
5598	Driebergen, Neth., H 16
3902	Driel, Neth., I 16
.....	Drimnin, Scotland, K 8
173	Drinkwater, Sask., P 8
4200	Drisa, W. Sov. Un., A 21
.....	Drishane Castle, Ire., O 8
27	Driver, Sask., N 4
2054	Dröbak, Norway, M 9
	Drogheda, see Droiehead Atha, Ire.
32622	Drogobych, W. Sov. Un. G 17
.....	Drochiczyn, Poland, D 16
.....	Drohiczyn, W. Sov. Un., D 18
	Drohobycz, see Drogobych, W. Sov. Un.
12716	Droiehead Atha (Drogheda), Ire., H 21
4553	Droitwich, England, J 13
.....	Dromara, N. Ire., E 22
.....	Dromard, Ire., F 10
.....	Dromcolliher, Ire., N 8
.....	Dromdaleague, Ire., Q 7
.....	Dromhair, Ire., F 12
.....	Dromina, Ire., N 9
.....	Dromineer, Ire., L 12
.....	Dromiskin, Ire., G 21
.....	Dromod, Ire., H 13
2400	Dromore, Ire., F 9
.....	Dromore, N. Ire., E 22
.....	Dromore, N. Ire., E 16
.....	Dromore, Scotland, Q 15
4530	Dronfield, England, G 15
.....	Drottningholm, Swe., Q 20
642	Droué, France, I 11
5000	Drug, India, D 4
679	Drulingen, France, G 23
.....	Drum, Ire., G 17
.....	Drum, Scotland, I 23
527	Drumbo, Ontario, M 8
.....	Drumcar, Ire., H 21
.....	Drumcliff, Ire., F 11
.....	Drumcondra, Ire., H 20
.....	Drumfin, Ire., G 11
2748	Drumheller, Alberta, N 22
.....	Drumhowna, Ire., H 16
.....	Drumkeeran, Ire., F 12
.....	Drumlish, Ire., H 14
.....	Drumlithie, Scotland, I 23
.....	Drummelzier, Scot., O 19
10555	Drummondville, Que., O 18
.....	Drummore Inns, Scot., R 13
.....	Drumnadrochit, Scot., H 14
.....	Drumquin, N. Ire., D 15
.....	Drumshabo, Ire., G 13
.....	Drumsna, Ire., G 13
1500	Drury, N. Z., D 17
5747	Druten, Neth., H 18
1641	Dryden, Ontario, O 16
.....	Drynoch, Scot., H 7
3743	Duaca, Ven., C 10
.....	Duanle, Eth., G 13
344	Duaringa, Australia, I 22
8344	Dubbo, Australia, N 20
.....	Dubbo Downs, Austl., I 16
.....	Dubbuk, Transjordan, L 15
.....	Dubdu, Morocco, F 9
.....	Dubil, Palestine, H 8
	Dublin, see Baile Atha Cliath, Ire.
362	Dublin, Ontario, L 6
1537	Dublineau, Algeria, D 13
12969	Dubno, W. Sov. Un., F 19
.....	Dubossari, W. Sov. Un., H 24
16400	Dubovka, Sov. Un., M 16
.....	Dubrovna, W. Sov. Un., B 24
18767	Dubrovnik, Yugo., L 10
.....	Duca Abruzzi, Som., R 17
.....	Ducamia, Ducambia, Erit., B 7
961	Ducey, France, H 7
551	Duck Lake, Sask., L 7
1407	Du Clair, France, G 11
.....	Dudeh, Iran, G 5
6474	Duderstadt, Germany, I 7
3259	Dudingen (Guin), Switz., I 7
.....	Dudinskoe, Sov. Un., Asia, D 13
59579	Dudley, England, J 13
.....	Dudo, Som., I 23
2245	Dudzeele, Belgium, K 6
10120	Duffel, Belgium, L 12
1454	Dufftown, Scotland, H 19
.....	Dugonti, Chn., A 9
.....	Duirat, Tunisia, G 24
.....	Duirinish, Scotland, H 6
440419	Duisburg (Duisburg-Hamborn), Germany. I 3
3773	Duitama, Col., H 13
3770	Duiven, Neth., H 20
.....	Duivendrecht, Neth., D 5
.....	Dujali, Iran, H 3
.....	Dujana, India, E 9
.....	Duk el Arba, Eth., F 6
.....	Dukhovshina, Sov. Un., I 8
.....	Duleek, Ire., I 21
.....	Dumagudiem, India, K 14
.....	Dumanitsch Assar, Tur., D 4
.....	Dumbarion, Scot., M 14
21546	Dumbarton, Scot., M 16
630	Dumbarton, N. B., K 5
10000	Dum Dum, India, I 22
19359	Dumfries, Scotland, Q 18
34812	Dumiât (Damietta), Eg., A 18
.....	Dumois, Cuba, M 22
	Dunaevtsy, W. Sov. Un., G21
11350	Dunaföldvár, Hungary, I 11
.....	Dunback, New Zealand, P 9
5062	Dunbar, Scot., M 22
.....	Dunbeath, Scot., E 18
136	Dunblane, Sask., O 6
2692	Dunblane, Scot., L 16
.....	Dunboyne, Ire., J 21
2189	Duncan, B. C., Q 2
.....	Duncannon, Ire., O 19
217	Dunchurch, Ont., D 11
.....	Duncormick, Ire., O 20
688	Dundalk, Ontario, J 9
13996	Dun Dealgan (Dundalk), Ire., G 21
175933	Dundee, Scotland, K 20
3783	Dundee, U.S. Afr., I 21
218	Dundela, Ontario, F 23
.....	Dundonnell, Ire., J 12
.....	Dundoo, Australia, K 19
.....	Dundrennan, Scot., R 16
.....	Dundrum, N. Ire., F 23
344	Dundurm, Sask., N 7
65200	Dunedin, N. Z., P 9
.....	Dunfanaghy, Ire., B 13
40918	Dunfermline, Scot., M 18
3830	Dungannon, N. Ire., E 19
328	Dungannon, Ont., K 5
.....	Dungarpur, India, H 7
4850	Dungarvan, Ire., O 15
100	Dungeness, England, N 23
.....	Dungiven, N. Ire., C 18
.....	Dunglow, Ire., C 11
.....	Dunkaga, Eth., I 11
585	Dunkeld, Australia, K 21
.....	Dunkeld, Scot., K 18
.....	Dunkerin, Ire., L 14
31017	Dunkerque (Dunkirk), Fr. D 14
	Dunkirk, see Dunkerque, Fr.
.....	Dunkur, Eth., F 5
35111	Dun Laoghaire, Ire., J 22
.....	Dunlavin, Ire., K 20
500	Dunleer, Ire., H 21
.....	Dunloy, N. Ire., C 20
1561	Dunmanway, Ire., Q 7
50	Dunmore, Alberta, O 24
.....	Dunmore, Ire., O 18
.....	Dunmore, Ire., I 9
12	Dunn, Alberta, L 23
.....	Dunnamanagh, N. Ire., C16
928	Dunnet, Scotland, C 18
.....	Dunnose, England, N 16
1987	Dunnottar, Scotland, I 23
4028	Dunnville, Ontario, O 11
865	Dunolly, Australia, P 18
260	Dunrea, Man., R 13
2704	Dunrossness, Shetland Is., D 3
2677	Duns, Scotland, N 23
.....	Dunseverick, N. Ire., B 20
.....	Dunshaughlin, Ire., I 20
8972	Dunstable, Eng., K 18
.....	Dunsyre, Scot., N 18
.....	Dunure, Scotland, O 13
189	Dunvegan, N. S., G 21
.....	Dunwick, England, J 24
.....	Dupeys Corner, N. B., H 13
15065	Dupnica, Bul., M 17
1072	Dupuy, Quebec, C 1
.....	Duque de Bragança, Ang M 13
.....	Dura, Palestine, O 8
.....	Duraghan, Tur., B 10
1000	Durán, Ecuador, D 3
33318	Durango, Dur., P 21
27000	Durazno, Uruguay, L 18
1242	Duraznos, Bolivia, K 10
	Durazzo, see Durrës Alb.
999	Durban, France, Q 15
270000	Durban, U.S. Afr., L 21
.....	Durdureh, Br. Som., H 21
39000	Düren, Germany, J 2
.....	Durgarayapatnam, India, N 13
.....	Durgu, India B 11
16223	Durham, England, D 15
1700	Durham, Ontario, I 8
401	Durham, Que., P 19
.....	Duria, Afg., J 18
.....	Durma, Afg., J 19
529	Durness, Scot., C 13
.....	Durnovskaya, Sov. Un., N 19
8739	Durrës, Albania, M 12
.....	Durrow, Ire., L 10
.....	Durrow, Ire., O 16
.....	Durrus, Ire., Q 5
.....	Durukhs, Iran, I 14
498600	Düsseldorf, Germany, J 3
.....	Dust-abad, Afg., J 16
.....	Dutaur, Arg., Q-15
.....	Duthil, Scotland, H 17
787	Dutton, Ontario, P 6
122	Duval, Sask., O 9
1494	Duvivier, Algeria, B 21
.....	Duz, Tunisia, F 23
	Duzdap, see Zahedan
.....	Dverberg, Norway, C 14
5000	Dwarka, India, I
2995	Dwingelo, Neth., D 21
.....	Dybvaag, Norway, N 7
1256	Dyce, Scotland, H 23
.....	Dyers, N. B., K 6
.....	Dyffryn, Wales, I 7
.....	Dyke, Scotland, G 17
278	Dyrholar, Iceland, D 21
.....	Dyrö, Norway, C 15
243	Dysart, Sask., O 9
.....	Dysart, Scotland, M 20
1314	Dzemul, Yuc., E 22
18000	Dzhalyal-Abad, Sov. Un. Asia, J 11
20000	Dzhulfa, Sov. Un., R 18
2055	Dzidzantún, Yuc., E 22
	Dzisna, see Disna, Sov. Un.
1398	Dzitas, Yuc., E 23
.....	Dzïua, Algeria, G 19

E

Pop.	Place Country Index
3791	Eaglehawk, Australia, P 19
.....	Eaidhouse, Scotland, N 18
.....	Ealing, England, B 19
.....	Ear Lake, Yukon, P 9
212	Earl Grey, Sask., O 8
745	Earlsferry, Scot., L 21
.....	Earlston, Scotland, N 22
.....	Earlton Jc., Ont., Q 24
319	Earltown, N. S., J 16
.....	Easington, England, G 20
.....	Easingwold, England, E 16
.....	Easkadale, Scot., J 8
.....	Easky, Ire., F 8
3501	East Angus, Quebec, P 20
57435	Eastbourne, England, N 21
1731	East Broughton, Que., N 22
.....	E. Burra, Shetland Is., C 3
625	East Chezzetcook, N. S., M 16
4595	East Cowes, Eng., N 16
5641	East Dereham, Eng., I 22

Pop.	Place Country Index
132	East Dover, Nova Scotia, N 14
542	Eastend, Sask., Q 4
264	Eastern Passage, N. S., N 15
7901	East Grinstead, Eng., M 20
146900	Eastham, Eng., B 23
.....	East Haven, Scotland, K 22
.....	East Highway, Eng., A 22
18333	Eastleigh, England, M 16
.....	Eastleigh, U.S. Afr., H 16
46631	East London, U.S. Afr., P18
.....	East Looe, England, O 6
205	East Margaree, N.S., G 21
.....	East Port Medway, N. S., P 12
619	East Pubnico, N. S., Q 9
21	Eastray, Quebec, Q 19
14228	East Retford, Eng., G 17
400	East Selkirk, Man., P 17
451	East Templeton, Que., P 10
7882	Eastview, Ont., D 22
.....	East Vlieland, Neth., C 15
14251	East Windsor, Ont., Q 1
292	Eatonia, Sask., O 4
.....	Ebbig, Egypt, E 10
31695	Ebbw Vale, England, K 10
.....	Ebdis, Palestine, N 4
1897	Ebeltoft (Aebeltoft), Den., H 14
.....	Ebenfurth, Ger., Q 17
6793	Eberbach, Germany, N5
.....	Ebersbach, Ger., J 14
31000	Eberswalde, Ger., F 13
12128	Ebingen, Germany, P 5
2758	Ebnat, Switz., F 18
9042	Eboli, Italy, J 16
.....	Ebshanna, Egypt, M 12
.....	Ebyar, Egypt, E 11
7319	Ecaussines d'Enghiem, Belgium, N 11
.....	Ecclefechan, Scotland, Q 19
44415	Eccles, England, G 13
1176	Echallens, Switz., J 4
133	Echarate, Peru, M 15
.....	Echerri, Eth., I 7
8923	Echt, Neth., K 19
1111	Echt, Scotland, I 22
3031	Echternach, Lux., Q 22
4411	Echuca, Australia, P 18
34895	Ecija, Spain, N 10
10150	Eckernförde, Ger., B 7
653	Eckford, Scot., O 23
135	Eckville, Alberta, M 20
3366	Ecommoy, France, I 10
179	Economy, N. S., K 14
264	Ecum Secum, N. S., M 19
261	Ecury sur Coole, Fr., H 18
.....	Ed, Eth., F 18
.....	Ed, Sweden, P 21
8191	Edam, Neth., F 15
179	Edam, Saskatchewan, L 5
132	Edberg, Alberta, L 21
.....	Edd, Erit., C 12
.....	Ed-Dahirira Egypt, C 17
.....	Ed Damieh, Transj., L 13
2441	Ed Dawaimch, Palestine, O 6
.....	Ed Deflaneh, Transj., J 22
.....	Ed Der, Egypt, N 11
.....	Ed Dêr, Egypt, O 11
200	Eddington, Australia, F 18
56	Eddys, Ontario, O 4
30604	Ede, Neth., H 18
.....	Edebäck, Sweden, M 12
150	Eden, Man., P 14
.....	Eden, N. Z., D 17
.....	Edenacarnan, Ire., B 14
.....	Edenburg, U.S. Afr., K 16
460	Edendale, N. Z., Q 5
2200	Edenderry, Ire., J 18
.....	Edeowie, Australia, M 16
.....	Eder, Morocco, G 3
.....	Ederny, N. Ire., E 15
13115	Edessa, Grc., N 16
.....	Edfina, Egypt, B 8
5800	Edfu, Egypt, Q 24
.....	Edgeworthstown, Ire., H 15
.....	Edgware, Eng., B 20
2266	Edh Dhaheriyeh, Palestine, P 7
.....	Edievale, New Zealand, P 6
438998	Edinburgh, Scot., M 20
.....	Edington, England, M 11
46447	Edirne (Adrianople), Tur., A 1
5751	Edku, Egypt, B 6
.....	Edmô, Egypt, R 9
93817	Edmonton, Alberta, K 20
77652	Edmonton, England, A 22
7096	Edmundston, N. B., C 3
.....	Edö, Nor., I 6
2028	Edolo, Italy, C 7
.....	Edouard, Fr. Guiana, C 11
12556	Edremid, Tur., D 1
1015	Edrom, Scot., N 23
.....	Edsberg, Sweden, Q 21
.....	Edvisan, Morocco, I 2
8800	Edwardesabad (Bannu), India, C 4
.....	Edzell, Scotland, J 21
13471	Eeckeren, Bel., Q 8
14672	Eecloo, Bel., K 8
.....	Eel Brook, Nova Scotia, Q 8
5500	Eernegham, Bel., L 4
.....	Effretikon, Switz., D 15
.....	Efremov, Sov. Un., J 11
.....	Egaña, Arg., P 18
1057	Eganville, Ontario, D 18
8438	Egéa de los Caballeros, Spain, E 16
30328	Eger, Hung., H 13
.....	Egerdir, Tur., G 5
.....	Egersa, Eth., K 11
3400	Egersund, Norway, N 4
2621	Eggiwil, Switz., I 11
1008	Eghezee, Bel., N 14
.....	Egin, Tur., E 13
.....	Egina, Australia, G 4
1363	Egletons, France, M 13
.....	Eglinton, N. Ire., C 17
1404	Eglisau, Switz., C 14
3060	Egmond aan Zee, Netherlands, F 12
500	Egmondville, Ont., L 6
.....	Egmont Bay, P. E. I., G 13
3097	Egnach, Switz., C 19
56340	Egorevsk, Sov. Un., I 12
110	Egremont, Alberta, J 21
6015	Egremont, England, E 9
.....	Egton, England, E 17
629	Egtved, Denmark, K 7
569	Eguzon, France, K 12
36	Eguzquiza, Arg., K 15
4845	Ehingen, Germany, P 6
8622	Eibergen, Neth., G 22
1248	Eich, Luxembourg, Q 20
8006	Eichstätt, Germany, O 8
510	Eid, Norway, J 4
6058	Eidskog, Norway, M 10
378	Eidsvold, Australia, J 22
10408	Eidsvold, Norway, L 10
200	Eigg, Scotland, J 7
3757	Eijsden, Neth., M 18
.....	Eiken, Norway, N 5
19000	Eilenburg, Germany, I 11
100458	Eindhoven, Neth., J 16
8028	Einsiedeln, Switz., G 16
1013	Eischen, Luxembourg, Q 19
45000	Eisenach, Germany, J 7
44800	Eisk (Yeisk), Sov. Un., N 11
25000	Eisleben, Germany, I 9
.....	Ejdrup, Denmark, E 8
.....	Ejerslev, Denmark, E 6
5500	Ejiri, Japan, M 18
.....	Ejsing, Denmark, G 5
4039	Ejutla de Crespo, Oax., M 9
	Ekaterinburg, see Sverdlovsk, Sov. Un.
.....	Ekaterinenskaya, Sov. Un., M 13
	Ekaterinenstadt, see Marxstadt, Sov. Un.
	Ekaterinodar, see Krasnodar, Sov. Un.
	Ekaterinoslav, see Dnepropetrovsk, Sov. Un
2211	Ekeberg, Norway, A 6
.....	Eker, Norway, M 8
.....	Ekerö, Sweden, Q 20
730	Eketahuna, N. Z., I 18
.....	Eklid, Iran, L 8
.....	Ekpedz, Yuc., F 23
.....	Ek Ram, Palestine, M 10
.....	Ekshärad, Sweden, L 12
6616	Eksjö, Sweden, O 13
.....	Ekwa el Hessa, Egypt, E 10
.....	El Abiod Si Cheikh, Algeria, G 14
12000	Elabuga, Sov. Un., I 20
464	El Achir, Algeria, C 18
.....	El Adâwi, Egypt, E 10
.....	El Adlieh, Egypt, B 18
.....	El Aduwa, Egypt, F 16
7507	El Affroun, Algeria, C 16
.....	El Afule, Palestine, I 10
.....	El Afweina, Br. Som., I 19
1155	El Akhmâs, Egypt, G 10
153	El Alamo, Baja Cal., B 2
.....	El Alia, Algeria, G 19
365	El Alto, Argentina, I 10
.....	El Ambek, Egypt, G 24
.....	El Ameireh, Transjordan, M 16
.....	El Amer, Algeria, O 13
.....	El Amri, Algeria, E 18
.....	Elan, Sov. Un., L 15
825	El Ancon, N. L., G 14
.....	Elands Vlei, U.S. Afr., O 8
.....	Elansa, Spain, E 21
13517	El Arahal, Spain, N 9
.....	El Araish, see Larache
.....	El Arefji, Tunisia, G 22
.....	El Aricha, Algeria, F 12
1146	El Arin, Egypt, E 18
.....	El Atf, Egypt, K 14
.....	El Atfa, Egypt, C 8
.....	El Atiat, Egypt, J 14
.....	El Attaf, Egypt, D 13
.....	El Attara, Egypt, R 24
.....	El Ayaicha, Tunisia, E 23
.....	El Ayat, Egypt, K 13
23178	Elaziz, Tur., F 14
.....	El Baa, Algeria, E 21
.....	El Baddala, Egypt, C 15
.....	El Bagaaieh, Egypt, D 17
7041	El Barco, Spain, E 8
.....	El Bardawil, Transj., M 15
.....	El Barnuqui, Egypt, D 7
.....	El Barûm, Egypt, E 18
13796	Elbasan, Albania, M 13
.....	El Basat-n, Egypt, I 14
.....	El Basqalûm, Egypt, O 10
.....	El Basra, Egypt, B 7
.....	El Bedâri, Egypt, M 19
.....	El Behay, Egypt, D 8
.....	El Bendariya, Egypt, E 11
.....	El Berâshiya, Egypt, C 17
	Elberfeld, see Wuppertal, Ger.
.....	El Berkemûn, Egypt, E 10
.....	El Betanun, Egypt, F 11
18379	Elbeuf, France, G 11
.....	El Beyda, Egypt, D 16
.....	El Bilamûn, Egypt, E 15
71000	Elbing, Pol., C 12
23	El Biodh, Algeria, M 19
.....	El Bireh, Transjordan, L 16
208	Elbow, Sask., O 7
.....	El Buha, Egypt, E 17
.....	El Bur, Som., O 19
2684	Elburg, Neth., F 18
3419	El-Burgo-de-Osma, Spain, F 13
.....	El Burro, Chih., H 22
3552	El Callao, Ven., H 21
.....	El Can, Dom. Rep., J 14
2432	El Carmen, Bolivia, F 14
.....	El Cayo, Gautemala, C 4
563	El Cerro, Bolivia, I 16
5460	El Cerro de Andévalo, Spain, M 8
.....	El Chacho, Argentina, K 10
4232	El Chaparro, Ven., F 16
46666	Elche, Spain, L 16
.....	El Chorafa, Egypt, J 14
.....	El Cobre, Cuba, O 21
1679	El Consejo, Ven., C 13
850	El Convento, Chile, M 3
22	El Coyote, Baja Cal., K 7
90	El Cuervo, Chih., E 20
.....	El Dab, Br. Som., J 18
3000	El Damer, A. E. Sud., H 19
.....	El Deir, Egypt, G 14
527	Elder Bank, N. S., M 16
.....	El Dia, Argentina, N 14
.....	El Dibber, I. E. A., N 21
.....	El Djem, Tunisia, D 24
.....	El Djemaa, Morocco, H 4
.....	Eldon, P. E. I., H 17
.....	Eldorado, Nicaragua, H 14
5171	Eldorado, Sin., O 17
38	Eldred, Sask., K 7
.....	Eldrom, Scotland, N 23
.....	El Duem, A. E. Sud., I 18
.....	El-Dukhêla, Egypt, C 2
.....	El Dur Elan, Br. Som., H 18
.....	El-Edwa, Egypt, L 11
.....	Elehu, Tur., C 14
2709	Elena, Bul., L 20
1677	El Escorial, Spain, H 11
50888	Elets (Yelets), Sov. Un., K 11
.....	Eleuthera, Bahamas, C 9
.....	El Fahmiya, Egypt, K 14
12000	El Fasher, Anglo-Egyptian Sudan, I 16
.....	El Feden, Transj., J 19
.....	El Fent, Egypt, O 11
.....	El Ferdan, Egypt, E 23
59829	El Ferrol, Sp., C 6
.....	Elfkarleby, Sweden, L 16
.....	El Fonduk, Palestine, K 9
178	El Forlón, Tam., I 17
.....	Elfrashe, Som., L 22
289	Elfros, Saskatchewan, N 9
.....	Elfsered, Sweden, P 11
.....	Elfsjö, Sweden, Q 21
3500	El Fuerte, Sin., L 15
.....	El Gamhûr, Egypt, O 10
.....	El Gemeliya, Egypt, C 19
1838	Elgg, Switz., D 16
.....	El Gharak, Egypt, M 9
.....	El Ghazâli, Egypt, E 19
.....	el-Giaghbub, Libya, F 15
362	Elgin, N. B., I 11
322	Elgin, Ontario, H 20
10192	Elgin, Scotland, G 19
218	Elginburg, Ont., I 20
18000	El Giza, Egypt, G 10
1455	El Goléa, Algeria, J 16
81	El Guerrah, Algeria, C 20
.....	El Guetariet (Wells), Algeria, G 21
.....	El Guettar, Algeria, E 15
.....	El Hacha, Ven., C 10
.....	El Hâchana, Algeria, L 18
.....	El Had, Sp. Mor., D 7
.....	El Haddem, Egypt, E 9
.....	El Hagar, Egypt, R 24
.....	El Hai, Egypt, K 14
.....	Elham, England, M 23
.....	El Hamid, Morocco, K 7
.....	El Hamma, Tunisia, F 23
.....	El Hammam, Algeria, D 16
.....	El Hamul, Egypt, B 13
.....	El Haram, Palestine, K 6
.....	El Harib, Algeria, L 6
.....	El Haritliyeh, Palestine, H 9
.....	El Hasa, Transj., P 10
1800	El Hawamdieh, Egypt, J 14
.....	El-Hebi (Medinet el-Gahil), Egypt, O 11
.....	El-Hêdûd, Egypt, C 11
.....	El Helf, Egypt, L 14
2957	El Helleh, Egypt, P 23
.....	El Herath, Transjordan, L 14
1701	El Higo, Ver., D 6
.....	El Hiyatim, Egypt, D 12
.....	El Howârta, Egypt, R 10
.....	Elhur, Eth., O 21
.....	El Husn, Transjordan, I 16
4956	Elias, Col., K 8
2723	El Ibrahimiya, Egypt, E 16
.....	Elie, Scotland, L 21
.....	Elim, U.S. Afr., R 8
250	Elisa, Argentina, L 19
16888	Elisabethville, Bel. Cong., N 17
	Elisavetgrad, see Kirovo, Sov. Un.
.....	Elista, Sov. Un., N 16
.....	Elizondo, Spain, D 15
.....	El Jaffariya, Egypt, F 12
.....	El Jaliba, Iraq, P 23
.....	El Jama, Morocco, H 7
.....	El Jib, Palestine, M 9
.....	El Jish, Palestine, F 11
.....	El Jorabado, Cuba, L 5
.....	El Juweilil, Syria, H 23
.....	El Kab, Egypt, P 24
.....	El Kalag, Egypt, H 15
.....	El Kantara, Algeria, D 19
.....	El Kantara, Egypt, E 23
.....	El Katrane, Transj., P 10
.....	El Kawadi, Egypt, H 12
.....	El Keneg, Algeria, P 16
.....	El Khanaqa, Egypt, H 15
.....	El Khatateba, Egypt, G 10
.....	El Kheil el Tessecra, Algeria, J 22
.....	El Khosous, Egypt, H 14
.....	El Khudra, Palestine, P 2
.....	El Khulil, see Hebron, Pal.
.....	El Kirâsh, Egypt, E 16
500	Elk Lake, Ontario, Q 24
230	Elko, B. C., Q 20
.....	El Kreider, Algeria, F 13
.....	El Krim, Morocco, G 4
36	Elkton, Alberta, M 20
.....	El Kubeibeh, Palestine, M 5
.....	El Kubeibeh, Palestine, O 6
.....	El Kula, Syria, D 13
.....	El Kuleikat, Palestine, O 4
.....	El Kunayisah, Egypt, D 11
.....	El Kustineh, Palestine, N 5
.....	El Lahûn, Egypt, M 12
.....	Ellendale, Ire., M 22
.....	Ellerdorf, Germany, C 7
.....	Ellerton, U.S. Afr., C 21
1872	Ellesmere, England, I 11
5058	Ellezelles, Belgium, M 8
.....	Ellhofen, Germany, R 7
26100	Ellichpur, India, J 10
257	Ellidshoj, Denmark, E 10
.....	Elliersville, P. E. I., F 14
767	Elliotdale, U.S. Afr., N 18
150	Elliston, Australia, N 14
1261	Ellon, Scotland, H 24
.....	Ellora, India, J 8
57342	Ellore, India, L 14
.....	El Lubban, Palestine, L 10
5653	Ellwangen, Germany, O 7
24	Ellwood, Ontario, E 22
892	Elm, Switz., H 18
.....	El Macta, Algeria, F 15
.....	El Mader, Morocco, H 10
.....	El Ma es Sifer, Algeria, N 11
.....	El Mahrug, Morocco, G 11
.....	El Maia, Algeria, G 15
.....	El Majdal, Pal., H 9
.....	El Makatlah, Egypt, L 12
.....	El Malaken, Egypt, E 18
4552	Elmaly, Tur., H 4
.....	El Manâgât el-Kabra, Egypt, E 20
1200	El Mandara, Egypt, B 4
1200	El Mandura, Egypt, C 9
72200	El Mansura, Egypt, D 15
.....	El Mansurah, Palestine, M 6
.....	El Marah, Palestine, I 7
.....	El-Marâzi, Egypt, M 14
.....	El Marâzik, Egypt, J 14
.....	El Mareighat, Transj., N 14
1528	El Masara, Egypt, I 14
.....	El Masara, Eg., L 18
.....	El Masgid, Egypt, L 14
1225	El Matanieh, Egypt, K 13
425	Elm Creek, Man., Q 15
.....	El Medall, Egypt, O 11
.....	El Megnûna, Egypt, C 17
.....	El Mejdel, Palestine, J 7
.....	El Mejdel, Palestine, N 3
.....	El Mekalis, Algeria, G 12
.....	El Meks, Egypt, C 2
.....	Elmelunde, Denmark, M 22
.....	El Menâir, Egypt, G 15
.....	El Menashi, Egypt, H 12
.....	El Mengob, Algeria, H 14
.....	El Mengoob, Morocco, H 11
.....	El Menshiya, Egypt, K 14
.....	El Menzala, Egypt, C 19
.....	El Menzeha el es Sohoud, Algeria, J 22
.....	El Merg, Egypt, H 15
.....	El Merhotta, Tunisia, G 23
.....	El Meridi, Algeria, C 22
.....	El Merkh, Algeria, J 23
.....	El Meruj, Syria, A 15
.....	El Meshed, Palestine, H 10
.....	El Mezareh, Transjordan, Q 12
.....	El Mezrah, Palestine, G 8
809	El Milia, Algeria, B 19
.....	El Milud (Wells), Alg., H 22
.....	El Minch, Palestine, O 2
34945	El Minya, Egypt, K 17
.....	El Minya, Eg., R 9
2012	Elmira, Ontario, L 8
110	Elmira, P. E. I., G 19
.....	El Mirr, Palestine, L 7
.....	El Misla, Alg., M 24
95	El Molino, Chile, B 4
.....	El Moro, Argentina, Q 19
.....	El Morro Argentina, M 10
425	Elmsdale, N. S., M 15
.....	Elmsdale, P. E. I., F 13
16000	Elmshorn, Germany, D 7
.....	El Mughair, Palestine, J 11
.....	El Mughar, Palestine, G 11
.....	El Mughar, Palestine, M 5
.....	El Mugheir, Palestine, L 11
.....	El Mugheiyan, Transjordan, I 16
.....	El Mugheiyir, Transjordan, I 19
.....	El Mugtáa (Moctar), Libya, E 14
.....	El Muntar, Palestine, N 11
924	Elmvale, Ontario, H 10
521	Elmwood, Ont., I 7
.....	El Nadour, Tunisia, E 24
800	El Negrito, Honduras, F 9
195	Elnora, Alberta, M 21
2500	Elnya, Sov. Un., J 8
88870	El Obeid, Anglo-Egyptian Sudan, I 18
.....	El Ogla, Algeria, G 22
1247	Elora, Ontario, L 9
.....	El Oudian, Tunis, F 22
12016	El Oued, Alg., G 20
.....	El Outaia, Algeria, D 19
2011	El Pájara, Col., B 15
4234	El Palmar, Ven., G 21
13239	El Pao, Ven., E 11
2948	El Pardo, Spain, H 12
.....	El Pedernal, Camp., K 20
.....	Elphin, Ire., H 12
.....	Elphin, Scotland, E 12
2458	El Pilar, Ven., C 19
.....	El Pino, Coa., B 7
326	El Plomo, Son., C 9
1905	El Porvenir, Chile, F 22
631	El Potrero, S. L. P., I 13
.....	El Progreso, Guat., E 5
.....	El Qala, Egypt, Q 24
.....	El Qasa, Egypt, Q 24
.....	El Qasâbi, Egypt, C 9
.....	El Qês, Egypt, P 10
.....	El Qitawiya, Egypt, F 17
	El Qsarel Kbir, see Alcazarquivir, Sp. Mor.
.....	El Qûni, Egypt, B 8
600	El Rastro, Ven., F 12
622	El Real, Pan., Q 25
26414	El Recreo, Ven., C 13
400	El Refresco, Chile, G 4
91	El Refugio, S. L. P., I 14
.....	El Resbalón, Chia., L 18
.....	El Retorno, Par., H 1
.....	El Rogue, Cuba, I 9
1949	El Ronquillo, Spain, M 9
4318	El Rosal, Col., L 6
523	El Rosario, Bolivia, O 7
1530	El Rosario, Ven., C 5
253	Elrose, Sask., O 5
.....	El Rubiat, Egypt, L 12
650	El Salto, Dur., P 20
.....	El Salto, Hid., G 4
.....	El Sawaleh, Egypt, F 18
.....	El Sebt, Morocco, H 3
1614	Elsenborn, Belgium, N 20
3320	Elsfleth, Germany, E 5
1923	El Sombrero, Ven., E 13
8727	Elst, Neth., H 18
4598	Elsterwerda, Germany, I 12
126	Elstow, Sask., N 7
.....	Elstree, England, A 19
.....	El Taiyibeh, Palestine, M 10
.....	El Tarf, Algeria, B 22
.....	Eltham, England, C 24
.....	El Tod, Egypt, E 8
.....	Elton, Sov. Un., M 17
318	El Transito, Chile, J 4
1000	El Triunto, Salvador, H 8
.....	El Uled, Sp. Mor., D 7
.....	El Valle, Col., G 5
.....	Elvanfoot, Scotland, O 18
11747	Elvas, Portugal, K 7
1367	El Verde, Sin., Q 19
11268	Elverum, Norway L 10
5086	El Viego, Nicaragua, J 10
.....	El Vigia, Ven., F 6
.....	Elvira, West Brazil, F 14
354	El Volcah, Chile, M 5
.....	El Wasta, Egypt, L 14
.....	El Wasta, Eg., L 19
7690	Ely, England, J 20
.....	El Yehudiyeh, Pal., L 6
.....	El Zahrieh, Egypt, E 10
.....	El Zawein, Egypt, H 14
.....	Embaba, Egypt, I 13
.....	Embarcacion, Arg., E 12
.....	Embinsk, Sov. Un. Asia, H 9
.....	Embo, Scot., F 16
5640	Emboscada, Par., N 7
464	Embro, Ontario, M 7
1826	Embrun, France, N 23
462	Embrun, Ontario, E 23
33000	Emden, Germany, E 4
1400	Emerald, Australia, H 21
155	Emerald Junction, Prince Edward Island, G 15
854	Emerson, Man., R 16
.....	Emily, Ire., N 11
1170	Emma, Argentina, O 17
1067	Emmaboda, Sweden, P 14
.....	Emmaus, U.S. Afr., J 15
40961	Emmen, Neth., D 24
.....	Emmenbrücke, Switz., G 13
13562	Emmerich, Germany, H 2
.....	Emo, Ire., K 17
551	Emo, Ontario, P 15
.....	Emorun, Ont., E 23
3985	Empalme, Son., I 11
.....	Empalme de Cañitas, Zac., I 8
.....	Emp. de Barajas, Zac., I 6
.....	Emp. de Libres, Pueb., H 7
6000	Emp. Escobedo, Guan., M 13
.....	Emp. Mazatlán, Sin., Q 18
2226	Empedrado, Argentina, I 19
537	Empedrado, Chile, O 3
8120	Empoli, Italy, F 8
341	Empress, Alberta, N 24
.....	Ems, Germany, K 4
1737	Ems, Switz., I 20
259	Emsdale, Ontario, D 12
15456	Emsdetten, Germany, G 4
534	Emu Park, Australia, H 23
.....	Emyvale, Ire., F 18
.....	En, Eth., K 15
.....	Enak, Transjordan, J 24
.....	Enanger, Sweden, K 15
2326	Enare, Fin., A 7
426	Encantada, Coa., F 12
5978	Encarnación, Jal., K 9
5295	Enciso, Col., G 14
.....	Encombe, B. C., J 11
3697	Encontrados, Ven., E 5
7511	Encrucijada, Cuba, I 12
.....	Encruzilhada, Brazil, K 20
538	Enderby, B. C., O 16
.....	Endingen, Switz. C 13
.....	Endor, Palestine, I 11
.....	Energia, Argentina, Q 18
.....	Enfidaville, Tunisia, C 24
67869	Enfield, Eng., L 20
272	Enfield, N. S., M 15
.....	Engbjerg, Denmark, F 2
243	Engcobo, U.S. Afr., N 18
2457	Engelberg, Switz., I 14
.....	Engelholm, Sweden, Q 11
73279	Engels (Pokrovsk), Sov. Un., K 17
.....	Engen, B. C., J 12
4832	Enghien, Belgium, M 9
158	Englefeld, Sask., M 9
1262	Englehart, Ontario, Q 24
.....	English Town, N. S., G 23
.....	Engoordina, Austl., I 14
5663	Enguera, Spain, K 16
.....	Engum, Denmark, J 9
225	Enilda, Alberta, H 18
8962	Enkhuizen, Neth., E 16
5986	Enköping, Sweden, M 15
80	Enlaugra, Quebec, R 18
3058	Enmore, Br. Gu., A 7
.....	En Naimeh, Transj., J 16
.....	En Nakhl, Egypt, Q 24
.....	En Nauifa, Egypt, E 18
.....	En Naurah, Palestine, H 11
2947	En Negêla, Egypt, E 10
.....	Ennery, Haiti, I 13
.....	Ennfield, Ire., J 19
	Ennis, see Inis, Ire.
5458	Enniscorthy, Ire., M 20
4847	Enniskillen, N. Ire., F 15
.....	Ennistimon, Ire., L 7
.....	Enotaevsk, Sov. Un., N 18
86766	Enschede, Neth., G 23
3042	Ensenada, Baja Cal., B 2
6261	Ensival, Belgium, N 19
5950	Entebbe, Uganda, K 18
.....	Enterprise, B. C., M 14
519	Enterprise, Ont., H 19
.....	Entfelden, Switz., E 12
2833	Entlebuch, Switz., H 12
2403	Entrambas-Aguas, Sp., C 12
35	Entrance, Alberta, K 17
930	Entraygues, France, N 15
.....	Entre Rios, Bolivia, M 12
10610	Entre Rios, Brazil, I 22
.....	Entre Rios, Brazil, M 17
470	Entrevaux, France, O 24
218	Entwistle, Alberta, K 19
807	Envermeu, France, F 12
4253	Envigado, Col., H 8
	Enzelli, see Pahlevi, Iran.
13371	Epe, Neth., F 19
20381	Epernay, France, G 17
1937	Epernon, France, H 13
1861	Epinac, Fr., J 18
4677	Epinac-les-Mines, Fr., J 18
27708	Epinal, France, I 22
14505	Epinay, France, A 5
.....	Epira, Br. Gu., B 7
.....	Episkopi, Cyprus, K 7
.....	Epping, England, A 24
27089	Epsom, England, L 19
630	Eptingen, Switz., D 11
.....	Eqfahss, Egypt, O 10
40900	Erakleion (Candia), Grc., R 20
21200	Erakulam, Ind., P 9
.....	Erale, Brazil, D 10
	Erbil, see Arbil, Iraq.
12096	Ercegnovi, Yugo., L 11
.....	Erco, Peru, F 2
4274	Erding, Germany, P 10
9544	Eregli, Tur., B 6
7476	Ereyli, Tur., H 9
140000	Erfurt, Germany, J 9
.....	Eriboll, Scotland, D 13
2500	Ericeira, Portugal, K 4
225	Erickson, Man., P 13
288	Erieau, Ontario, Q 4
.....	Erigave, Br. Som., H 19
290	Eriksdale, Man., P 15
499	Erin, Ont., K 10
212	Erindale, Ontario, L 11
3200	Erinpura, India, G 6
.....	Erinsboda, Sweden, P 13
32780	Erith, England, L 20
	Erivan, see Yerevan, Sov. Un.
.....	Erize, Argentina, P 14
705	Erlach, Switz., G 7
30000	Erlangen, Ger., M 8
2472	Erlenbach, Switz. E 15
1279	Erlenbach, Switz., J 9
14731	Ermelo, Neth., G 18
4546	Ermelo, U.S. Afr., G 20
6745	Ermenek, Tur., I 7
.....	Erment, Egypt, O 23
4845	Ernée, France, H 8
3409	Ernée, Fr., I 8
33672	Erode, India, O 11
50	Eromanga, Austl., J 18
2808	Erp, Neth., J 18
.....	Er Rahâma, Egypt, Q 24
.....	Er Rahamina, Egypt, B 18
2864	Er Rahel, Algeria, D 12
.....	Erreso, Denmark, K 9
1891	Errol, Scotland, L 19
22141	Ersekujvár (Nové Zámky), Czech, Q 20
.....	Erstavik, Sweden, R 22
3124	Erstfeld, Switz., I 15
1081	Ertingen, Switz., D 11
3658	Ertvelde, Belgium, R 3
939	Ervy, France, I 17
16104	Erzinjan, Tur., E 14
47706	Erzurum, Tur., D 16
.....	Esashi, Japan, E 13
12500	Esashi, Japan, G 12
28700	Esbjerg, Denmark, K 3
5716	Escada, Brazil, H 25
.....	Escalada, Argentina, K 17
343	Escalada, Spain, D 12
.....	Escalante, Argentina, C 22
2000	Escalhão, Portugal, G 7
.....	Escalón, Chih., K 21
1634	Escalona, Spain, I 11
2106	Escatrón, Spain, G 16
29369	Esch, Luxembourg, P 19
393	Esch, Luxembourg, R 19
.....	Eschede, Germany, F 8
.....	Eschenbach, Ger., M 10
1507	Eschenbach, Switz., G 13
.....	Eschershausen, Ger., H 7
3357	Escholzmatt, Switz., H 11
12748	Eschwege, Germany, J 7
33090	Eschweiler, Ger., J 2
6000	Escobar, Par., O 8
5214	Escoma, Bolivia, G 2
995	Escourt, U.S. Afr., K 20
.....	Escritos, Chile, B 3
5864	Escuinapa, Sin., R 19
6751	Escuintla, Guat., G 4
340	Escuminac, N.B., E 11
1955	Escuque, Ven., E 7
2566	Esdud (Ashdod), Palestine, N 4
.....	Eshershausen, Ger., I 8
857	Eshowe, U.S. Afr., J 22
.....	Esh Shehâbiya, Egypt, A13
.....	Esh Shêkh el Amiriya, Egypt, A 12
.....	Esh Shêkh el Maghrabi, Egypt, O 10
.....	Esh Shêkh Masûd, Egypt, P 9
.....	Esh Shobak, Egypt, J 14
.....	Eshua, Palestine, N 7
1000	Esk, Australia, K 23
378	Eskdalemuir, Scot., P 20
.....	Esker, Ire., J 17
10389	Eski-Dzumaja, Bul., L 21
.....	Eski-Foja, Tur., E 1
36801	Eskilstuna, Sweden, M 15
60747	Eskisehir (Eskishehr), Tur., D 5
.....	Esles, Cuba, I 10
6035	Eslöf, Sweden, Q 11
626	Esmeralda, Argentina, L 15
.....	Esmeralda, Par., H 1
.....	Esmeralda, Ven., O 15
13550	Esmeraldas, Ecuador, A 3
2347	Esmoraca, Bolivia, M 8
.....	Esn Shobek, Transj., Q 10
3645	Espalion, France, N 15
1551	Espanola, Ontario, A 5
.....	Espanola Jc., Ont., A 5
2067	Esparta, Costa Rica, N 14
300	Esperance, Austl., N 8
8000	Esperanza, Argentina, L 16
3524	Esperanza, Cuba, I 12
.....	Esperanza, Cuba, O 23
.....	Esperanza, Honduras, E 12
1408	Esperanza, Pueb., I 8
.....	Esperanza, Uruguay, J 15
6026	Espiel, Spain, L 10
5666	Espinal, Col., I 9
.....	Espinilho, Brazil, P 10
4360	Espino, Ven., F 15
3773	Espinosa de los Monteros Spain, D 12
4496	Espita, Yuc., E 23
.....	Espozende, Portugal, F 5
4005	Esquimalt, B. C., R 2
5000	Esquina, Argentina, K 18
1362	Esquipulas, Nicaragua, J 12
251	Esquiû, Argentina, J 11
50	Essa, Ontario, I 11
.....	Es Sabrigât, Egypt, F 10
.....	Es Saf, Egypt, K 14
.....	Es Saft, Egypt, D 13
.....	Es Salahat, Egypt, D 17
10000	Es Salt, Transjordan, L 14
.....	Es Samâini, Egypt, E 19
.....	Esschen, Bel., P 8
7440	Esschen-Frontiere, Bel., J12
.....	Es Sembellawen, Egypt, E 16
.....	Es Semua, Palestine, P 8
654461	Essen, Germany, I 3
.....	Essenbaek, Denmark, G 11
.....	Es-Serû, Egypt, C 17
1935	Essex, Ontario, Q 2
.....	Es-Siryaqûs, Egypt, H 14
41000	Esslingen, Germany, O 6
262	Essonville, Ontario, F 15
.....	Es Sûfên, Egypt, F 14
.....	Es-Sûfiya, Egypt, D 18
.....	Es Surariya, Egypt, Q 10
.....	Es Suwâf, Egypt, F 10
.....	Estacion Carrizal, Arg., J 9
.....	Estacion Casupa, Uruguay, N 20
.....	Estacion Nico Perez, Uruguay, M 21
.....	Estacion San Luis, Ur., N 16
.....	Estacion Toledo, Ur., O 19
.....	Estacion Villa Constitucion, Arg., M 17
.....	Estacion Zanjon, Arg., I 12
.....	Estanna, Egypt, G 13
1494	Estanzuela, Zac., L 6
1010	Estarca, Bolivia, M 9
4364	Estarreja, Portugal, H 5
2020	Estavayer le-lac, Switz., I 5
8874	Este, Italy, D 9
5587	Esteli, Nicaragua, I 11
7384	Estella, Spain, E 15
9534	Estepa, Spain, N 10
315	Estépar, Spain, E 12
11851	Estepona, Spain, P 10
	Esterabad, see Asterabad, Iran.
431	Esterhazy, Sask., P 11
570	Esternay, France, H 16
662	Esterri, Spain, E 19
2774	Estevan, Sask., R 10
.....	Estevao, Ven., Q 14
1134	Estinnes, Belgium, O 10
1498	Estissac, France, I 17
58	Estlin, Sask., P 8
13142	Eston, England, D 16
726	Eston, Sask., O 5
.....	Estrada, Cuba, N 21
8630	Estremoz, Portugal, K 7
.....	Estrupland, Den., F 13
100	Estuary, Sask., O 3
.....	Estvad, Denmark, G 6
.....	Es Zarqa, Egypt, C 17
	Eszék, see Osijek, Yugo.
17963	Esztergom, Hungary, H 11
.....	Etah, Greenland, K 2
8800	Etah, India, F 12
1034	Etalle, Belgium, Q 18
10067	Etampes, France, H 13
6534	Etaples, France, E 13
45400	Etawah, India, F 12
5139	Eten, Peru, H 3
.....	Ethea, Bolivia, C 6
269	Ethel, Ontario, K 7
300	Ethelbert, Man., O 12
2180	Etichove, Belgium, M 8
.....	Etla, Oax., L 9
2114	Etne, Norway, M 4
564	Eton, Austl., G 22
.....	Etrah, Egypt, M 10
1699	Etretat, France, F 10
.....	Etsa, Egypt, R 9
.....	Et Tabbin, Egypt, J 14
.....	Et Taiyiben, Palestine, K 7
.....	Et Taiyibeh, Transjordan, I 14
.....	Et-Tarya, Egypt, F 10
859	Et Tawila, Egypt, F 18
4058	Ettelbrück, Lux., Q 20
.....	Et Tell, Syria, G 13
.....	Etteridge, Scotland, I 16
.....	Et Tina, Egypt, O 23
.....	Et Tineh, Palestine, N 5
.....	Et Tireh, Palestine, H 7
.....	Et Tireh, Palestine, K 7
.....	Et Touadjer, Algeria, G 13
.....	Ettrick, N. Z., P 6
308	Ettrick, Scotland, O 20
.....	Etwab, Egypt, L 14
5641	Etzatlán, Jal., L 5
67	Etzikom, Alberta, P 23
5963	Eu, France, F 12
.....	Eucla, Austl., M 11
1220	Eudunda, Austl., O 16
12729	Eupen, Belgium, M 20
.....	Eureka, U.S. Afr., F 22
200	Eurelia, Austl., M 16
.....	Eurimbula, Austl., I 23
.....	Eurombah, Austl., J 22
14549	Euskirchen, Germany, K 2
200	Euston, Austl., O 18
7034	Eutin, Germany, C 8
.....	Eva Downs Station, Australia, E 14
.....	Evanton, Scotland, G 15

Pop. Place Country Index

1508 Evaux, France, L 14
.... Everdrup, Denmark, L 20
190 Everett, Ontario, I 10
8979 Everghem, Bel., L 8
.... Evesham, Australia, H 19
756 Evie and Rendall, Scot., A 19
843 Evilard, Switz., F 7
1232 Evolène, Switz., O 9
22061 Evora, Portugal, L 6
.... Evoramonte, Portugal, K 6
27700 Evpatoriya, Sov. Un., O 7
19315 Evreux, France, G 11
1475 Ewa, Hawaii, F 11
.... Ewano, Eth., L 9
.... Ewart, Ont., I 11
.... Ewarton, Jamaica, J 8
.... Ewell, England, D 20
.... Exaltación, Bolivia, C 6
.... Exaltación, Bolivia, E 9
60 Excel, Alberta, M 23
.... Excelsior, Ontario, O 4
2153 Exel, Belgium, K 16
66039 Exeter, England, N 9
1589 Exeter, Ontario, M 5
14584 Exmouth, Eng., N 9
126 Expanse, Sask., Q 7
.... Ex-Santa Cruz, see Liberdade, W. Brazil.
262 Exshaw, Alberta, N 20
.... Extrema, West Brazil, H15
6095 Eydtkuhnen, Ger., B 24
1733 Eye, England, J 23
161 Eyebrow, Sask., O 7
2321 Eyemouth, Scot., M 24
429 Eyzurande, France, M 14
1238 Eymet, France, N 10
3601 Eymoutiers, France, L 13
.... Eyre, Australia, M 9
13 Eyre, Sask., N 4
.... Eyrecourt, Ire., K 12
.... Eystrup, Ger., F 6
.... Ez Damru, Egypt, B 10
.... Ezraa, Syria, G 19
.... Ez Zib, Palestine, F 8

F

.... Faaberg, Norway, K 8
.... Faaborg, Denmark, K 4
4516 Faaborg, Denmark, M 12
490 Faarup, Denmark, F 10
8679 Fabriano, Italy, G 12
10607 Facatativa, Col., I 11
.... Fachow, China, L 12
.... Factory, Ire., H 20
.... Fada, Fr. Eq. Afr., H 15
.... Fada N'Gourma, Fr. W. Afr., I 7
.... Fadaei, see Gorgura, I.E.A.
.... Fademin, Egypt, H 9
22469 Faenza, Italy, E 10
7928 Fágáras, Rom., J 19
.... Fagasa, Morocco, D 8
1062 Faido, Switz., L 16
5000 Fai-fo (Quang-nam), Fr. In. Ch., O 10
107 Fairfield, U.S. Afr., R 9
100 Fairholme, Sask., K 6
800 Fairlie, N.Z., N 9
.... Fairlie, Scotland, N 13
.... Fairmont Springs, B.C., O 19
329 Fairview Sta., N. S., N 15
1750 Fairville, France, D 24
.... Faizabad, Afg., D 24
.... Faizabad, Iran, E 13
.... Faizabad, Iran, G 13
.... Fakenham, England, I 22
2015 Fakse, Denmark, L 21
1263 Fakse Ladeplads,Den.,L 21
.... Falaba, S. L., I 2
5667 Falaise, France, G 11
.... Falaun, Bur., M 20
.... Falciu, Romania, I 23
.... Falcon, Cuba, J 12
244 Falfala, Som., J 23
.... Falher, Alberta, H 17
4836 Falkenberg, Germany, I 12
5527 Falkenberg, Sweden, P 10
36000 Falkirk, Scotland, M 17
.... Falkner, Argentina, A 22
6736 Falköping, Sweden, O 12
.... Falla, Cuba, J 15
217 Fallbrook, Ontario, F 20
.... Fallison, Manitoba, K 14
1000 Falmouth, Antigua, K 23
13492 Falmouth, England, O 4
2136 Falmouth, Jamaica, I 7
285 Falmouth, N.S., M 13
3034 Falset, Spain, G 18
392 Falsterbo, Sweden, R 11
.... Falstone, England, C 13
14347 Fălticeni, Rom., H 20
13370 Falun, Sweden, L 14
1887 Famagusta, Cyprus, K 8
.... Fane, Norway, K 3
.... Fanoch, Iran, Q 14
.... Fâqûs, Egypt, E 18
.... Fara, Transjordan, J 13
4096 Farafangana, Madag., P 24
.... Farah, Afg., J 17
.... Faramanh, Fr. W. Afr., I 3
.... Farashbad, Iran, N 7
11575 Fareham, Eng., N 16
.... Fâres, Egypt, Q 24
5000 Fareskur, Egypt, B 18
87 Fargo, Ontario, Q 4
.... Faridkot, India, D 7
.... Faridpur, India, H 23
5577 Färila, Sweden, K 14
100 Farina, Austl., L 15
364 Farmerston, N. B., G 4
16359 Farnborough, Eng., D 24
4055 Farnham, Quebec, Q 16
.... Faro, Argentina, Q 16
.... Faro, Brazil, E 8
12925 Faro, Portugal, N 6
1769 Farr, Scotland, D 15
325 Farrellton, Quebec, O 9
4718 Farruco, Uruguay, K 21
51507 Farrukhabad, India, F 13
11277 Farsano, Italy, J 21
9800 Farshut, Egypt, Q 22
.... Farsis, Egypt, F 16
1042 Farsö, Denmark, E 7
1544 Farsta, Sweden, Q 23
6000 Farsund, Norway, N 4
.... Fashn, Egypt, G 16
505 Fasouten, Eth., H 4
.... Fasset, Quebec, P 12
.... Faster, Denmark, I 4
.... Fastov, W. Sov. Un., F 24
.... Fatahabad, India, J 23
.... Fatehganj, India, F 13
19300 Fatehpur, India, L 11
.... Fathiabad, Iran, R 8
.... Fatima Eri, Erit., B 11
400000 Fatshan, China, L 14
.... Fâu, Egypt, M 20
1900 Fauresmith, U.S. Afr., K 14
38 Faust, Alberta, H 18
34 Fawcett, Alberta, I 20
.... Faxina, Brazil, N 14

.... Faya, Fr. Eq. Afr., H 14
610 Fayence, France, P 23
.... Fayid, Egypt, Q 22
1788 Fayón, Spain, G 17
58200 Fayûm, Eg., L 11
8500 Fazilka, India, D 7
1492 Fearn, Scotland, F 16
.... Fearnmore, Scot., G 9
.... Featherston, N. Z., J 18
17263 Fécamp, France, F 10
13281 Fedala, Morocco, F 5
936 Federacion, Argentina, K 20
.... Fedorovskaya, Sov. Un.,
456 Fee-Fe, Switz., O 11
.... Feeny, N. Ire., C 13
4720 Fehmguzar, Afg., F 18
2696 Feira, Port., G 5
14222 Feira de Sant' Anna, Bra., E 19
11759 Felanitx, Spain, J 22
672 Felenne, Belgium, P 14
109 Flaxcombe, Sask., N 4
12037 Felixstowe, England, K 24
3114 Felletin, France, L 14
27041 Felling, England, C 15
905 Fels, Luxembourg, Q 21
729 Felsberg, Switz., L 20
383 Felsted, Denmark, M 8
6800 Feltre, Italy, C 10
.... Fenagh, Ire., G 14
431 Fénara, Morocco, F 6
3718 Fenaroa, Eth., D 9
1158 Fenelon Falls,Ontario,H 14
.... Fénérive, Madag., O 25
19000 Fenghwangcheng, Manch., C 21
.... Fengning, Manch., C 17
.... Fengsiang, China, F 10
.... Fengyang, China, G 17
500 Fensr, Ire. M 21
305 Fenton, Ontario, N 12
184 Fenwick, Sask., O 10
28656 Feodosiya, Sov. Un., O 9
.... Feolin Ferry, Scotland, N 8
.... Ferbane, Ire., J 14
1241 Ferdinandova, Bul., L 17
2215 Fère Champenoise, France, H 17
7776 Ferentino, Italy, I 13
2832 Fergus, Ontario, K 9
3841 Feria, Spain, L 8
.... Feriana, Tunisia, D 22
.... Ferkan, Algeria, E 21
14 Ferland, Sask., Q 6
7818 Fermo, Italy, G 13
3992 Fermoselle, Spain, G 9
.... Fermoy, see Manistir Fhear Muighe, Ire.
600 Fernández, Argentina, I 12
2307 Fernández, Peru, E 1
11436 Fernán Núñez, Spain, M 10
2545 Fernie, B. C., Q 20
.... Fernit, Morocco, J 2
.... Feron, Palestine, K 8
54351 Ferozepore, India, D 8
70415 Ferrara, Italy, E 9
5312 Ferreira, Portugal, L 6
8812 Ferrefafe, Peru, D 3
443 Ferrette, France, I 24
971 Ferrieres, France, I 15
.... Ferring, Denmark, F 2
.... Ferrona Junction, N.S,K17
.... Ferryden, Scotland, J 22
3164 Ferry Port on Craig (Tayport), Scotland, K 7
179211 Fès (Fez), Mor., E 6
15000 Fesa, Iran, G 11
9072 Festiniog, Wales, H 8
600 Festan, Rom., J 22
.... Fetesti, Rom., K 23
.... Fethard, Ire., N 15
.... Fethard, Ire., O 19
.... Fethiye, Tur., H 3
5282 Fetsund, Nor., M 9
525 Fettan, Switz., I 24
1087 Fettercairn, Scot., J 22
920 Feulen, Luxembourg, Q 20
4337 Feurs, France, L 18
1300 Fezâra, Egypt, C 7
549 Fiamignano, Italy, H 12
56797 Fianarantsoa,Madag.,O 23
2000 Ficce, Eth., J 9
.... Fiddown, Ire., N 17
407 Fideris, Switz., H 21
108 Fielding, Sask., M 6
3208 Fier, Alb., N 12
.... Fiesole, France, N 13
.... Figeholm, Sweden, O 15
8213 Figueira da Foz, Port., I 5
13192 Figueras, Spain, F 21
15000 Figuig, Morocco, H 12
1595 Filadelfia, Col., H 8
3580 Filandia, Col., I 8
3730 Filey, England, E 19
1917 Filipesti-de-Targ, Rom., H 20
.... Filipovskaya, Sov.Un.,M14
4632 Filipstad, Sweden, M 12
349 Filisur, Switz., J 21
169 Fillmore, Sask., Q 10
.... Filomeno Mara (Sta. Maria), Q R., G 23
.... Filonovskaya, Sov.Un.,L14
.... Filyas, Tur., B 7
5000 Fin, Iran, O 11
4570 Finale nell Emilia, It., E 9
397 Finch, Ontario, F 23
.... Finchley, England, B 21
.... Finderup, Denmark, G 7
.... Findhorn, Scotland, G 18
.... Findlay, Scotland, I 23
.... Fingvuidaishian, China, C5
481 Finhaut, Switz., O 9
.... Finnaas, Nor., M 3
.... Finnea, Ire., H 16
3245 Finsterwolde, Neth., C 16
.... Finstown, Scotland, B 19
.... Fintona, N. Ire., E 16
.... Fintown, Ire., C 12
736 Fintray, Scotland, H 23
4300 Fiorenzuola, It., D 6
6000 Firdaus (Tun), Iran, H 13
285000 Firenze (Florence), It., F 9
.... Firland, B. C., O 19
466 Firmat, Argentina, M 15
23154 Firozabad, India, F 11
12000 Firozpur Jhirka, India,F10
.... First South, N. S., O 13
.... Firuzkuh, Iran, F 8
.... Fisha es Sugra, Egypt,G 12
.... Fisherstreet, Ire., K 6
2963 Fishguard, Wales, K 5
150 Fiske, Sask., N 5
2109 Fismes, France, G 16
3178 Fitero, Spain, F 15
275 Fitzpatrick, Quebec, C 17
.... Fitz Roy, Argentina, Q 22

88 Fitzroy, Austl., E 8
157 Fitzroy, Ontario, D 20
52900 Fiume, Italy, D 14
.... Five Finger, Yukon, N 8
527 Five Fingers, N. S., C 5
624 Five Islands, N. S., K 13
.... Fivemiletown, N. Ire., E 16
.... Fivepenny Borve, Scot.,D7
.... Fives Lille, Argentina, K 17
.... Flyambiro, Eth., I 13
.... Fjaltring, Denmark, G 2
.... Fjeld, Norway, L 3
157 Fjellerup, Denmark, G 13
1502 Fjerritslev (Fjerreslev), Den., D 7
.... Flade, Denmark, C 13
.... Flagstone, B. C., Q 20
91 Flakkebjerg, Den., L 17
30 Flamboro, Ontario, M 14
.... Flamborough Head, Eng., J 19
.... Flatanger, Norway, H 9
.... Flateland, Norway, M 5
5757 Flawil, Switz., D 18
22983 Fleetwood, England, F 11
2259 Flekkefjord, Norway, N 4
5868 Flemalle-Haute, Bel., N 16
220 Fleming, Sask., Q 11
2031 Flen, Sweden, N 15
67000 Flensburg, Ger., B 7
.... Fleringe, Sweden, O 17
13022 Flers, France, H 8
431 Flesherton, Ontario, I 9
3583 Fleurance, France, O 11
3718 Fleurier, Switz., H 4
1229 Fleury-sur-Andelle,Fr.,G12
946 Flims, Switzerland, I 9
700 Flinders, Austl., N 14
7635 Flint, Wales, H 10
212 Flinton, Ontario, G 18
3655 Flisbeco, Belgium, M 8
139 Flöng, Denmark, B 21
.... Flora Argentina, L 14
1332 Florac, France, O 17
.... Flor de Oro, Argentina, J 18
317 Florence, Ontario, O 4
511 Florence, see Firenze, It.
152 Florenceville, N. B., G 4
4164 Florencia, Argentina, I 14
2974 Florencia, Bolivia, O 4
1892 Florencia, Col., L 9
.... Florennes, Belgium, O 13
.... Florenville, Belgium, Q 16
1716 Flores, Brazil, F 19
.... Flores, Brazil, H 22
3056 Flores, Brazil, J 15
2500 Flores, Guat., O 5
.... Floresta, Brazil, H 22
11704 Floriano, Brazil, G 18
.... Floriano Pixoto, West Brazil, J 23
25253 Florianopolis, Brazil, P 14
.... Florida, Argentina, J 17
829 Florida, Bolivia, B 8
8 Florida, Bolivia, J 13
7001 Florida, Col., L 5
1736 Florida, Cuba, L 16
12659 Florida, It., O 16
16000 Florida, Uruguay, N 19
10585 Florina, Greece, N 15
1411 Florö, Norway, K 3
1168 Flüelen, Switz., I 15
.... Flühen, Switz., D 9
1375 Flühli, Switz., H 12
4321 Flums, Switz., G 19
.... Flushing, see Vlissingen, Neth.
.... Fly, Denmark, G 6
.... Flyncher, Denmark, G 3
.... F. M. Parera, Arg., M 19
557 Foam Lake, Sask., N 10
4613 Foca, Yugo., L 11
32799 Focșani, Rom., J 22
.... Fochabers, Scotland, G 20
50000 Foggia, Italy, I 17
.... Foghill, Ire., F 7
6461 Foix, France, Q 13
5322 Fojnica, Yugo., K 10
.... Folby, Denmark, H 11
.... Foldalen, Norway, J 8
2745 Folden, Norway, E 13
.... Foldereid, Norway, G 11
256 Foleyer, Ontario, Q 23
1288 Foligno, Italy, G 11
35890 Folkestone, Eng., M 23
2415 Follonica, Italy, G 8
17381 Fomento, Cuba, J 12
13078 Fomeque, Col., I 12
1700 Fondo, It., B 8
.... Fondouk, Tunisia, C 23
14832 Fonsagrada, Spain, D 8
17075 Fontainebleau, Fr., H 14
.... Fonte Bôa, Braz., E 1
5943 Fontenay-aux-Roses, Fr., G 4
9423 Fontenay-le-Comte,Fr.,K 8
1000 Fonthill, Ontario, N 12
.... Fonti, Morocco, J 2
.... Foochow, see Minhow, China
.... Foots Cray, Eng., C 24
.... Fopingting, China, G 10
11491 Forbach, France, C 22
5355 Forbes, Australia, N 20
1904 Forcados, Nig., J 8
9574 Forchheim, Germany, M 8
5870 Ford (E. Windsor), Ontario Q 1
2690 Förde, Norway, K 4
1560 Fordham, England, J 21
426 Fordwich, Ont., K 7
264 Foremost, Alberta, P 23
5117 Forenza, Italy, J 18
1562 Forest, Ontario, N 4
150 Forester's Fall,Ontario,D19
89 Forfar, Ontario, G 21
11062 Forfar, Scotland, K 20
2000 Forg, Iran, O 9
100 Forgan, Sask., O 5
2013 Forges, France, G 12
152 Forget, Sask., R 10
204 Fork River, Man., O 13
4125 Forli, Italy, E 10
14764 Formby, England, C 11
7010 Formello, Italy, J 13
26000 Formerie, France, F 13
700 Formia, Italy, J 13
1432 Formosa, Argentina, H 19
.... Formosa, Brazil, K 15
.... Formosa, Denmark, G 15
360 Fornæss, Denmark, E 8
.... Forncett, England, I 23
1002 Fornovo di Taro, Italy, E 6
4698 Forres, Scotland, G 18
.... Forrest, Australia, Q 18
175 Forrest, Ontario, G 21
.... Forrodu, I. E. A., E 13
.... Fors, Sweden, I 15
61 Forsa, Sweden, K 15

.... Forsinain, Scotland, D 16
.... Forsinard, Scotland, D 16
7874 Forssa, Fin., F 3
38000 Forst, Germany, I 14
.... Fort, Egypt, A 15
.... Fort Ajrud, Egypt, I 23
31 Fort a la Corne, Sask., L 9
2000 Fort Aleksandrovsk, Sov. Un. Asia, I 8
.... Fortaleza, Bolivia, B 7
142453 Fortaleza, (Ceará), Brazil, F 22
.... Fort Antenne, Italy, A 22
25 Fort Appia, Italy, D 23
9777 Fort Archambault, Fr. Eq. Afr., J 13
.... Fort Ardeatina, Italy,D 21
2270 Fort Ashurada, Iran, E 9
18 Fort Assiniboine, Alberta, J 19
.... Fort Augustus, Scot., I 13
.... Fort Aurelia Antica, Italy, B 19
1039 Fort Beaufort, U. S. Afr., P 16
.... Fort Bowen, Austl., F 18
9832 Fort Braschi, Italy, B 19
3186 Fort Casilina, Italy, C 25
2061 Fort Charlet (Djanet), Alg., J 14
1072 Fort Coulonge, Quebec, O 7
.... Fort Crampel, Fr. Eq. Afr., J 13
3978 Fort Dauphin, Madag.,P 23
60685 Fort de France, Martinique, Q 24
326 Fort de Possel, Fr. Eq. Afr., J 14
59523 Fort Dras, India, B 9
36000 Fort du Mont Valerien, France, B 3
3139 Forte, Brazil, J 15
.... Forte de San Joaquim, Brazil, O 5
6566 Fort El Gemil, Egypt, B 21
3643 Fort Erie (Bridgeburg), Ont., N 13
467 Forteviot, Scotland, L 18
16998 Fort Flatters (Temassinim), Alg., M 21
5997 Fort Frances, Ont., P 13
412 Fort Fraser, B. C., J 11
155 Fort Hall, Kenya, K 21
5179 Fortierville, Quebec, M 19
3722 Fortin Aguilar, Arg., K 17
449 Fortin Guachalla, Par., I 1
.... Fortin Inca, Argentina, J 15
24605 Fortin Olmos, Arg., J 17
.... Fortin Uno, Arg., Q 11
9785 Fortin Wheeler, Par., I 5
1752 Fort Jameson, U. S. Afr., N 19
21558 Fort Johnston, Nyasaland, N 20
15272 Fort Lamy, Fr.Eq.Afr.,I12
503 Fort Langley, B. C., O 4
227 Fort Louisbourg, N. S., K 24
.... Fort Nadali, Afg., K 16
1048 Fort National, Algeria,B 18
12659 Fort Pampus, Neth., C 9
12 Fort Pitt, Sask., K 4
16000 Fort Prenestina, Italy, B 25
673 Fort Qu'Appelle, Sask., P 9
875 Fortrose, Scotland, G 16
500 Fort Saint John, B. C., G 14
.... Fort Saint Jullen, Egypt,
1044 Fort Sandeman, Bal., D 3
903 Fort Saskatchewan, Alberta, J 21
873 Fort Tiburtina, Italy, B 25
5483 Fort Trojani, Italy, C 19
2145 Fortuna, Argentina, O 11
30585 Fort Valcanuta, Italy, C 19
2527 Fort William, Ont., P 18
92659 Fort William, Scotland,J12
4735 Fortymile, Yukon, N 3
1169 Fossano, Italy, E 2
1102 Fosse, Belgium, O 19
3933 Fossombrone, Italy, F 12
354 Foster, Quebec, R 17
20432 Fougères, France, H 7
331 Fountainhall, Scot., N 21
903 Fourchu, N. S., J 24
300 Fouries Kolk, U.S.Afr.,L 11
565 Fournier, Ontario, O 24
300 Fours, France, K 17
6630 Fourteen Streams, U.S. Africa, I 14
133 Fovlum, Denmark, F 7
316 Fovsing, Denmark, F 3
7700 Fowchow, China, H 10
519 Fowey, England, O 5
.... Fox Creek, N. B., I 12
8107 Foxdale Mines, Eng., E 6
.... Foxford, Ire., G 8
316 Fox River, N. S., K 12
1510 Foxton, N. Z., I 18
427 Fox Valley, Sask., P 4
200 Foynes, Ire., L 6
.... Foza, Egypt, Q 24
9423 Foz, Spain, O 7
1000 Foz do Embira, West Brazil, G 14
4910 Foz do Iguassú, Brazil, O 10
.... Foz do Tarauscá, West Brazil, H 19
.... Foz do Tejo, West Brazil, H 19
9423 Fraai Plaats, U.S.Afr., K 13
1000 Fraga, Argentina, M 10
6817 Fraga, Spain, F 17
.... Fragueiro, Argentina, M 12
3922 Fraile Muerto, Uruguay,
3780 Fraile Pintado, Arg., F 11
13475 Frameries, Belgium, O 9
.... Framlev, Denmark, H 10
2007 Frampton, Quebec, H 23
21022 Franca, Brazil, M 15
80811 Franchetti, Algeria, E 13
1591 Francia, Uruguay, J 18
.... Francisco Madera, see Villa Francisco Madera, Coa.
8155 Francker, Neth., C 17
613 Frangy, France, M 19
204 Frank, Alberta, P 20
4125 Frankenberg, Ger., J 5
14764 Frankenberg, Ger., K 12
7010 Frankenthal, Ger., C 4
26000 Frankford, Ire., M 14
700 Frankford, Ontario, I 17
1432 Frankfort, U.S. Afr., L 18
555071 Frankfurt-am-Main, Ger., L 5
75000 Frankfurt-a. d.-Oder, Ger., G 14
.... Franklin, W. Brazil, G 14
175 Frankville, Ontario, G 21
.... Franö, Sweden, J 16
61 Franz, Ontario, P 21
.... Franzburg, Germany, C 11

10024 Frascati, Italy, I 11
123 Frasco, Switz., M 16
1200 Fraser River, U.S. Afr., N 10
10203 Fraserburgh, Scot., G 24
.... Fraserburgh Road, U. S. Afr., P 11
3227 Frasnes-lez Buissenal, Belgium, M 7
475 Frauenfeld, Switz., C 16
8750 Frauenkirchen, Ger., R 18
25 Fraxa, Ont., K 9
9500 Fray Bentos, Uruguay, L 14
.... Fray Marcos, Ur., N 20
1000 Frechilla, Spain, E 11
2270 Fredensborg, Den., J 22
20100 Fredericia, Den., K 10
10062 Fredericton, N. B., I 7
180 Fredericton Jc., New Brunswick, J 7
109189 Frederiksberg, Den., J 23
.... Frederiksdorp, Den., I 21
9882 Frederikshavn, Den., D 13
2061 Frederikssund, Den., J 21
3853 Frederiksvaerk, Den., I 20
.... Fredrika, Sweden, H 16
.... Fredrikshald, see Halden, Nor.
14101 Fredrikstad, Nor., N 9
263 Freelton, Ont., M 10
785 Freeport, N. S., O 7
326 Freeport, P. E. I., G 15
59523 Freetown, Sierra Leone,J 2
10806 Fregenal de la Sierra, Spain, L 8
36000 Freiberg, Ger., K 12
2135 Freiburg, Ger., D 6
99122 Freiburg, Ger., Q 3
2986 Freienwalde, Ger., E 15
1504 Freirina, Chile, I 3
17000 Freising, Germany, P 9
3643 Freistadt, Aus., G 7
9091 Fréjus, France, P 23
315 Frelighsburg, Quebec, R 17
16998 Fremantle, Australia, N 4
.... Frenchpark, Ire., H 11
412 French River, P. E. I., G 15
155 French Village, N. S., N 14
5179 Frenda, Algeria, D 14
.... Freshford, Ire., M 16
449 Fresnes, France, C 5
.... Fresnes Saint Mainés, France, J 21
24605 Fresnillo, Zac., I 8
9785 Freudenstadt, Ger., P 4
.... Freyung, Ger., P 12
1752 Frias, Argentina, J 11
21558 Fribourg, Switz., I 7
1287 Frick, Switz., D 12
11048 Friedberg, Germany, L 5
4190 Friedberg, Ger., P 8
11893 Friedek, Ger., M 20
.... Friedenau, Ger., R 16
.... Friedrichsfelde, Ger., Q 19
2786 Friedrichshafen, Ger., R 6
11289 Friockheim, Scotland, K 21
2615 Frisia, Argentina, N 14
3888 Fritzlar, Germany, J 6
.... Friuli, Italy, C 12
170 Frobisher, Sask., R 11
1748 Froid-Chapelle, Bel., P 12
10738 Frome, England, M 12
.... Fron, Norway, K 8
1044 Frontera, see Alvaro Obregon, Mex.
873 Fronteras, Son., C 13
5483 Frontignan, France, P 17
2145 Frosten, Norway, I 10
.... Frostviken, Sweden, H 12
.... Frunze, Sov. Un. Asia, J 11
4735 Frutigen, Switz., K 10
1169 Frutillar, Chile, A 19
.... Frydek, see Friedek, Ger.
.... Frydendal, Den., J 18
.... Fryksände, Sweden, M 11
10390 Fua, Egypt, H 10
.... Fua, Transjordan, I 15
2184 Fuchow, China, K 11
.... Fuchow, Manch., D 20
1800 Fuchow Ki, China, I 16
2786 Fudai, Japan, D 25
.... Fuencaliente, Spain, L 11
6630 Fuengirola, Spain, A 3
8316 Fuente del Maestre, Spain, L 8
15547 Fuente Ovejuna, Spain,L10
5994 Fuenterrabia, Spain, O 15
1228 Fuentes, Spain, J 15
3057 Fuentesaúco, Spain, G 9
10058 Fuentes de Andalucia, Sp., N 10
665 Fuerte Olimpo, Par., G 6
737 Fuglebjerg, Denmark, L 18
.... Fuglsev, Denmark, H 14
7066 Fujiyeda, Japan, N 17
2400 Fukaura, Japan, C 22
.... Fukiang, China, K 14
3684 Fukiang, China, F 8
19975 Fukien, Japan, K 17
44300 Fukuchiyama, Japan, L 12
44300 Fukui, Japan, K 6
38215 Fukui, Japan, N 4
323217 Fukuoka, Japan, M 4
45691 Fukushima, Japan, L 17
3200 Fukushima, Japan, A 23
38215 Fukushima, Japan, I 12
27000 Fukuyama, Japan, M 9
150 Fullarton, Ont., K 6
5339 Fullerton, England, M 15
888 Fumay, France, F 18
1407 Fumel, France, N 11
2007 Funabashi, Japan, P 22
10200 Funakawa, Japan, J 17
80811 Funchal, Madeira Is.,(Africa map) E 2
.... Fundão, Brazil, M 20
.... Fundukht, Iran, H 14
4847 Funes, Col., M 5
.... Fünfkirchen, see Pécs, Hung.
.... Funing, China, J 19
3434 Füquene, Col., H 11
.... Furbero, Ver., F 8
7599 Furnes (Veurne), Bel., L 3
2269 Furstenau, Ger., G 4
199 Fürstenberg, Ger., E 12
3793 Fürstenau, Switz., J 20
7310 Fürstenfeld, Ger., R 8
24000 Fürstenwalde, Ger., E 15
77875 Fürth, Germany, N 8
5850 Fürth, Germany, N 11
.... Furubetsu, Japan, E 16
6600 Furuning, China, J 19
5000 Furukawa, Japan, K 16
.... Furusund, Sweden, M 17
.... Fusan, see Pusan, Kor.

31538 Fushimi, Japan, M 13
118636 Fushun, Manch., C 21
133 Fusio, Switz., L 15
.... Füssen, Germany, R 8
6215 Futai, Japan, J 19
.... Futatsuya, Japan, I 16
4116 Futaye, Japan, O 2
5816 Fuyi, China, D 5
5816 Fuzesabony, Hungary,H 13
1397 Fyrendal, Denmark, L 17
3180 Fyvie, Scotland, H 22
5660 Fyzabad, India, F 15

G

.... Gabalah, Egypt, L 11
826 Gabares, Egypt, E 8
.... Gabarghar, India, C 4
215 Gabarouse, N. S., I 24
926 Gabarouse Lake, N. S., I 24
10000 Gabarret, France, O 9
657 Gabès, Tunisia, F 24
.... Gaboto, Argentina, A 16
.... Gaboury, Quebec, I 1
.... Gabrabad, Iran, H 6
13800 Gabrig, Iran, Q 13
1397 Gabrovo, Bul., L 20
1134 Gacé, France, H 10
1065 Gachalá, Col., I 12
4550 Gacheta, Col., I 12
.... Gacko, Yugo., L 11
.... Gada, Iran, L 4
.... Gadame, Eth., J 4
7000 Gadámes, Libya, E 11
8200 Gadarwara, India, I 12
170 Gadbjerg, Denmark, J 7
2382 Gadebusch, Ger., D 9
436 Gadmen, Switz., J 14
141 Gadsby, Alberta, L 22
10200 Gadwal, India, M 11
.... Gaerun, Denmark, O 13
6540 Gaesti, Rom., J 19
6393 Gaeta, Italy, J 13
4500 Gafsa, Tunisia, E 23
320 Gagetown, N.B., J 8
13253 Gagny, France, B 5
.... Gahlukul, Afg., D 23
7054 Gaillac, France, O 13
18285 Gaillimh (Galway), Ire., J 8
118 Gaiman, Argentina, B 23
60 Gainford, Alta., K 19
18654 Gainsborough, Eng., G 17
289 Gainsborough, Sask., R 11
2380 Gairloch, Scot., G 10
2610 Gais, Switz., E 20
.... Galadi, Eth., L 4
.... Galakhinskii, Sov. Un.,G20
1186 Galano, Fr. Som., G 13
.... Galan, Col., G 12
.... Galan, Eth., J 12
13478 Galashiels, Scot., O 21
322 Galata, N. Z., Z 21
102296 Galati, Rom., J 23
12512 Galatina, Italy, K 22
9718 Galatone, Italy, K 22
502 Galbally, Ire., N 12
1292 Galeana, N. L., G 15
.... Galera, Ecuador, A 3
.... Galeras, B. C., P 3
1163 Galich, Sov. Un., G 14
18 Galilee, Sask., Q 7
1163 Galisteo, Spain, I 9
38424 Galle, Ceylon, R 13
3000 Gallegos, Arg., E 22
146 Gallinazos, Chile, O 4
8019 Gallipoli, Italy, K 22
.... Gallipoli, see Gelibolu,Tur.
17 Gallivan, Sask., L 5
1975 Gällivare, Swe., E 18
437 Gällö, Sweden, J 14
6345 Galston, Scot., O 15
15346 Galt, Ontario, M 9
.... Galten, Norway, A 18
1957 Galvez, Arg., L 16
.... Galway, see Gaillimh, Ire.
.... Gamaches, France, F 12
1027 Gamay, Argentina, P 13
3000 Gambaga, G. C., I 6
.... Gambela Post, Eth., K 4
.... Gamboa, Cuba, N 19
.... Gamboola, Australia, D 18
.... Gameliera, Brazil, H 25
326 Gamla Karleby, see Kokkola, Fin.
.... Gamleby, Sweden, O 15
665 Gammel Skagen, Denmark, C 11
.... Gammelsogn, Den., H 2
.... Gampel, Switz., M 10
4044 Gamvik, Norway, A 22
65 Gananoque, Ontario, H21
.... Gananoque Jc.,Ontario,H21
167084 Gand (Ghent), Bel., L 9
.... Gandara, Argentina, O 9
.... Gandava, Bal., N 22
19975 Gandia, Spain, K 17
4381 Gandjabad, Iran, E 3
14334 Gangi, Italy, N 15
4300 Ganjam, India, K 18
.... Gannac, Fr. W. Afr., H 7
4558 Gannat, France, L 16
.... Gansur, Egypt, F 11
11717 Gao, Fr. W. Afr., H 7
.... Garabato, Argentina, J 17
.... Garabost, Scotland, D 5
31000 Garadi, Egypt, L 9
1249 Garag, India, M 8
.... Garagoa, Col., H 13
.... Garampi, Japan, H 7
16440 Garanhuns, Brazil, H 24
6473 Garches, France, B 3
2231 Garcia, N. L., F 14
.... Garcia, Iran, H 10
6460 Gardanne, France, P 21
8768 Gardelegen, Ger., F 10
.... Garden, Ont., R 21
264 Garden Hill, Ont., L 12
.... Gardenstown, Scot., G 22
.... Gardereen, Neth., C 18
.... Gardey, Argentina, P 18
3793 Gardo, Som., I 22
800 Garelochhead, Scot., M 14
.... Garfas, Egypt, Q 15
7074 Gargaliani, Greece, Q 15
.... Garha, India, I 3
150 Garibaldi, Argentina, L 15
25 Garin, Chile, H 4
5597 Garlasco, Italy, D 4
.... Garliestown, Scot., R 15

Pop.	Place	Country	Index
540	Garlin, France	P 8	
5275	Garmisch, Germany	R 8	
....	Garmsar, Iran	G 7	
105	Garneau Junction,Que.	L18	
....	Garnish, Newf.	K 25	
10276	Garoo, Iran	G 3	
5032	Garoua, Cam.	J 12	
....	Garrison, N. Ire.	E 13	
6008	Garrobillas, Spain	J 8	
....	Garrygualoch, Scot.	I 12	
....	Garstang, England	F 11	
....	Garthoy, Que.	O 21	
....	Garthok, China	H 3	
659	Gartly, Scotland	H 21	
....	Gartmore, Scotland	M 14	
....	Gartok, Tib.	M 12	
3548	Gartz, Germany	E 13	
....	Garuk, Baluchistan	M 21	
700	Garvagh, N. Ire.	C 19	
....	Garvald, Scotland	M 22	
....	Garvan, Scotland	J 11	
....	Garve, Scotland	G 13	
....	Garwa, India	H 17	
....	Garwolin, Poland	E 15	
....	Garza, Argentina	I 12	
548	Garza Valdez, Tam.	G 16	
4367	Garzon, Col.	K 9	
....	Gask, Iran	I 14	
....	Gaspar, Cuba	K 15	
3616	Gaspar Campos, Arg.	N 8	
....	Gasselte, Neth.	D 23	
4183	Gastouni, Greece	P 15	
4000	Gat, Libya	G 11	
....	Gatelo, Eth.	N 8	
3810	Gaucin, Spain	O 10	
21797	Gauhati, India	F 25, L 19	
....	Gaubazirgan, Iran	O 10	
....	Gausdal, Norway	K 8	
....	Gaviao, W. Brazil	F 24	
....	Gaviotas, Arg.	Q 13	
38868	Gävle, Sweden	L 15	
....	Gawan, India	H 19	
....	Gawilgarh, India	I 10	
1771	Gawler, Australia	O 16	
88005	Gaya, India	G 18	
970	Gayndah, Australia	J 23	
375	GaysRiver,NovaScotia	L15	
17069	Gaza, Pal.	O 2	
....	Gazar, Iran	I 14	
....	Gazdan, Baluchistan	R 18	
57200	Gaziantep (Aintab), Tur.	H 12	
....	Gdov, Sov Un.	G 5	
114000	Gdynia, Poland	B 11	
....	Geashills, Ire.	J 16	
3093	Gebize, Tur.	O 4	
....	Geddara, Morocco	F 10	
799	Gedinne, Belgium	P 14	
5772	Gediz, Tur.	E 3	
1153	Gedser, Denmark	O 20	
545	Gedsted, Denmark	F 8	
....	Geelan, Iran	Q 2	
16935	Geelong, Australia	O 18	
2660	Geertruidenberg,Neth.	I 14	
....	Geestemünde, Ger.	D 6	
2778	Geet Betz, Belgium	B 15	
....	Gehgan, Iran	N 14	
14349	Geislingen, Ger.	O 7	
2715	Geiveh, Tur.	C 5	
6205	Geldrop, Neth.	J 17	
....	Geledi, Eth.	N 16	
12404	Geleen, Neth.	J 17	
466	Gelligaer, Switz.	P 13	
6637	Gelibolu(Galipoli),Tur.	C1	
4749	Gelnhausen, Ger.	L 6	
....	Gelnica, see Gollnitz, Ger.		
336227	Gelsenkirchen, (Gelsenkirchen-Buer) Ger.	I 3	
5280	Gembloux, Belgium	N 12	
....	Gemerek, Tur.	E 11	
5720	Gemert, Neth.	J 13	
5910	Gemlik, Tur.	O 3	
5004	Gemona, Italy	O 12	
2374	Gemünden, Ger.	L 7	
915	Gençay, France	N 11	
28003	Genck, Belgium	L 17	
....	Gendrean, Quebec	K 2	
10190	Gendringen, Neth.	H 21	
3300	Genemuiden, Neth.	E 19	
1443	General Belgrano, Arg.	O 19	
935	General Bravo, N. L.	F 17	
....	General Capdevilla, Arg.	I 15	
2968	General Cepeda, Coa.	F 11	
25	General Lagos, Chile	A 4	
21069	General La Madrid, Arg.	P 16	
....	General Madariaga, Arg.	P 21	
....	General Obligado, Arg.	I 18	
2439	General Paz., Arg.	O 19	
....	General Paz., Arg.	I 20	
3896	General Saavedra, Bol.	I 18	
1727	General Terán, N. L.	F 15	
1453	General Trevino, N. L.	E 16	
....	Genesa, U.S. Afr.	G 13	
....	Geneva, U.S. Afr.	I 17	
144000	Geneva (Genève), Switz.	N 2	
....	Genichesk, Sov. Un.	N 9	
....	Genisdal, U. S. Afr.	M 6	
974	Genlis, France	J 20	
....	Gennefa, Eg.	H 23	
3272	Gennep, Neth.	I 19	
550	Gennes, France	J 19	
29360	Gennevilliers, France	A 5	
347483	Genova (Genoa), It.	E 4	
15823	Gentbrugge, Belgium	L 9	
9073	Genthin, Germany	G 10	
574	Genthod, Switz.	M 1	
489	Gentilly, Quebec	M 19	
62471	Gentofte, Denmark	J 22	
9070	George, U.S. Afr.	Q 12	
....	Georgemas, Scot.	D 13	
302	Georges, Switz.	K 2	
....	Georges River, N. S.	H 23	
154	Georgetown,Australia	E 19	
73171	George Town, Br. Gu.	A 7	
....	George Town, see Penang, Str. Setts.		
2562	Georgetown, Ontario	K 10	
769	Georgetown, P. E. I.	R 18	
600	Georgetown, St. Vincent	O 24	
272	Georgetown, Tasmania	E 7	
....	Georgetown Mills,B.C.	I 7	
22597	Georgievsk, Sov. Un.	O 15	
83000	Gera, Germany	K 10	
3932	Gerace, Italy	N 19	
100	Geraldine, Australia	K 4	
4984	Geraldton, Australia	E 21	
7577	Gerardmer, France	I 23	
....	Gerba, Eth.	I 10	
....	Gerdjanis, Tur.	D 14	
....	Gereis, Egypt	G 11	
4917	Gérgal, Spain	N 14	
....	Geriban (Gura Ali), Som.	L 21	
1098	Gerlev, Den.	K 17	
....	Gerlogubi, Eth.	L 16	
....	Germania, Arg.	N 15	
68129	Germiston, U.S. Afr.	F 18	
2806	Gerolzhofen, Ger.	M 7	
29632	Gerona, Spain	F 21	
854	Gerouville, Bel.	R 17	
136	Gerrard, B. C.	O 18	
....	Gerrild, Denmark	G 15	
1872	Gersau, Switz.	H 15	
2192	Gersié, Morocco	F 9	
....	Gersim, Algeria	L 11	
5354	Geryville, Alg.	F 14	
....	Gessing, Denmark	G 13	
337	Gessler, Arg.	L 16	
1714	Gesves, Bel.	N 15	
....	Getinge, Sweden	P 11	
9376	Geunen, Tur.	D 2	
1282	Geux, France	K 22	
6434	Geyer, Germany	K 11	
....	Geysdorp, U.S. Afr.	G 15	
....	Ghabah, Egypt	E 18	
7000	Ghadames, Libya	J 23	
....	Ghadir es Sultan, Transjordan	R 16	
12159	Ghardaia, Algeria	H 18	
....	Ghassoul, Algeria	G 14	
10200	Ghazal Transjordan	K 16	
....	Ghaziabad, India	E 10	
27498	Ghazian, Iran	G 17	
10000	Ghazni, Afg.	H 22	
15458	Ghedde, Baluchistan	N 20	
18545	Gheel, Belgium	K 14	
....	Ghent, see Gand, Bel.		
10942	Gheorgheni, E. Hung.	I 20	
6659	Gheris, Morocco	I 8	
....	Gherla, E. Hung.	I 17	
....	Ghetah, Egypt	G 16	
....	Ghimes-Faget, E. Hung.	I 20	
....	Ghink, Iran	I 13	
4228	Ghistelles, Belgium	K 5	
....	Ghourd, Fatima, Alg.	I 23	
....	Ghourd Rouba, Alg.	I 23	
....	Ghrardimaou,Tunisia	O 22	
50	Ghrebah, Sask.	L 6	
....	Ghubanie, Palestine	P 8	
10000	Ghuznigik, Afg.	E 22	
....	Ghuzzeh, see Gaza, Pal.		
9128	Giannitsa (Janica), Grc.	M 15	
9321	Giarre, Italy	N 17	
8045	Gibara, Cuba	K 21	
30	Gibbs, Sask.	P 8	
....	Gibeon, S. W. Afr.	P 13	
....	Gibelh, Br. Som.	I 15	
21372	Gibostad, Norway	O 15	
....	Gibson Lodge, B. C.	O 2	
....	Gidea, Sweden	I 17	
8194	Gien, France	I 15	
34000	Giessen, Ger.	K 5	
3488	Gieten, Neth.	D 23	
2260	Gieteloorn, Neth.	E 20	
409	Gif, France	D 2	
4454	Gifhorn, Germany	G 8	
172340	Gifu, Japan	L 15	
2068	Gigante, Col.	K 9	
911	Gigeo, Coa.	B 13	
....	Gigena, Arg.	M 12	
4000	Giggiga, Eth.	I 14	
2300	Gignac, France	P 17	
101341	Gijon, Spain	O 10	
....	Gilan, Iran	E 10	
246	Gilbert Cove, Nova Scotia	N 8	
25	Gilberton, Austl.	F 19	
804	Gilbert Plains, Man.	O 13	
4464	Gildeskaal, Norway	E 12	
....	Gildessa, Eth.	I 13	
1100	Gilford, N. Ire.	E 21	
....	Gilfors, Sweden	J 13	
....	Gilgit, India	A 8	
20	Gilgunnia, Australia	N 19	
....	Gilberga, Sweden	M 11	
1497	Gilleleje, Denmark	H 22	
....	Gillespies, N. Z.	M 7	
....	Gillies Point, N. S.	I 22	
60983	Gillingham, England	M 13	
....	Gillingham, England	L 21	
25301	Gilly, Belgium	N 12	
587	Gilly, Switz.	L 2	
....	Gilma, Tunisia	D 23	
7189	Gilze, Neth.	J 14	
953	Gimel, Switz.	K 2	
853	Gimli, Man.	P 16	
1806	Gimont, France	P 11	
....	Gims, Norway	D 12	
959	Ginestas, France	P 15	
1000	Gingin, Australia	M 4	
13117	Ginneken,Netherlands	J 13	
10746	Ginosa, Italy	K 19	
802	Giornico, Switz.	L 16	
621	Gira, Iran	R 4	
1986	Giraldo, Col.	G 7	
....	Girale, Som.	N 18	
....	Giram, Afg.	J 17	
22557	Girardot, Col.	I 10	
2038	Girardots, Col.	G 8	
13967	Giresun (Kérassunde) Tur.	C 13	
....	Girdu, Iran	K 9	
15000	Girga, Egypt	N 21	
23712	Girgenti, Italy	O 13	
21122	Giridih, India	H 19	
5000	Girishk, Afg.	K 19	
....	Girishk, Iran	R 13	
....	Giro, Australia	N 22	
....	Gir-oba, Tur.	G 2	
2134	Girón, Col.	G 13	
12224	Girón, Ecuador	E 4	
....	Giroull, Eth.	D 11	
6056	Girvan, Scotland	P 13	
93	Girvin, Sask.	O 7	
1986	Girza, Iran	P 9	
13900	Gisborne, N. Z.	G 23	
102	Giscome, B. C.	J 13	
....	Gisfa, Egypt	F 14	
....	Gishistindi, Sov. Un. Asia	O 19	
193	Gisikon, Switz.	G 14	
5564	Gisors, France	G 19	
3257	Gistel, Italy	H 15	
2386	Giswil, Switz.	I 12	
2611	Giubiasco, Switz.	N 15	
177	Giumaglio, Switz.	M 16	
....	Giumbo Eth.	K 23	
24503	Giurgiu, Romania	K 20	
1320	Give, Denmark	J 7	
6803	Givet, France	I 16	
14657	Givors, France	M 19	
1463	Givry, France	K 19	
....	Givskud, Eth.	J 6	
18714	Giza, Egypt	J 13	
25147	Glace Bay, N. S.	H 24	
70	Glacier, B. C.	N 17	
193529	Gladbach (Gladbach-Rheydt), Ger.	J 2	
3039	Gladich, Scot.	L 12	
....	Gladstone, Australia	I 23	
479	Gladstone, Australia	J 3	
1000	Gladstone, Australia	M 23	
669	Gladstone, Australia	M 16	
227	Glammis, Ontario	I 6	
9091	Glamoč, Yugo.	K 9	
....	Glandore, Ire.	R 7	
....	Glamire, Ire.	Q 11	
125	Glanworth, Ire.	O 11	
....	Glanworth, Ontario	O 6	
9091	Glaonaig, Scotland	N 10	
....	Glaris, Switz.	J 21	
5260	Glarus, Switz.	J 21	
....	Glascarnoch, Scot.	G 13	
1088417	Glasgow, Scotland	N 15	
153	Glaslough, Ire.	F 18	
....	Glaslyn, Saskatchewan	K 5	
....	Glassan, Ire.	I 14	
....	Glassdrummond, N. Ire.	F 23	
....	Glassel, Scotland	I 12	
771	Glasserton, Scot.	R 14	
200	Glassville, N. B.	G 5	
4515	Glastonbury, Eng.	M 11	
1909	Glattfelden, Switz.	O 14	
18000	Glatz, Pol.	D 9	
11300	Glauchau, Ger.	K 11	
11300	Glazov, Sov. Un.	G 20	
435	Gleichen, Alberta	N 21	
....	Gleisdorf, Ger.	S 16	
253	Glen Allen, Ontario	K 8	
34	Glenaman, Ontario	J 6	
20238	Glenarm, N. Ire.	C 23	
180	Glenavon, Sask.	Q 10	
....	Glenbarr, Scotland	O 9	
....	Glenboro, Man.	Q 14	
222	Glenbucket, Scotland	H 20	
50	Glenbush, Sask.	L 6	
....	Glencaple, Scotland	Q 18	
....	Glencassley, Scotland	E 13	
679	Glencoe, N. S.	J 22	
836	Glencoe, Ontario	O 5	
....	Glencoe, U. S. Afr.	E 20	
....	GlenColumbkille, Ire.	D10	
....	Glenealy, Ire.	K 22	
10409	Glenelg, Australia	O 16	
1690	Glenelg, Scotland	I 10	
200	Glenelg, Man.	F 14	
153	Glen Ewen, Sask.	R 11	
....	Glenfarn, Ire.	F 13	
....	Glenfinnan, Scotland	J 10	
....	Glengarriff, Ire.	Q 5	
....	Glengarrisdale, Scot.	M 9	
800	Glenham, N. Z.	Q 6	
....	Glenholme, N. S.	K 15	
5352	Glen Innes, Australia	L 22	
477	Glenisla, Scotland	J 19	
....	Glenlivet, Scotland	H 19	
2051	Glenluce, Scotland	Q 13	
....	Glenmuick, Scotland	E 13	
....	Glennagoul, Ire.	O 10	
....	Glennamaddy, Ire.	I 10	
270	Glenora, Tasmania	E 7	
....	Glenormiston, Austl.	H 16	
505	Glen Robertson, Ont.	E 25	
145	Glenside, Sask.	O 8	
....	Glenstrup, Denmark	F 10	
47	Glen Tay, Ontario	G 20	
....	Glenville, Ire.	P 11	
....	Glenwhilly, Scotland	Q 13	
....	Glesborg, Denmark	G 14	
....	Gletsch, Switz.	K 14	
891	Glimakra, Sweden	Q 12	
....	Glin, Ire.	M 7	
1339	Glis, Switz.	M 12	
27000	Gliwice, Pol.	E 9	
60983	Gloppen, Norway	J 5	
....	Gloria, Coa.	D 11	
....	Glorieta, Cuba	C 23	
....	Glossanter, Denmark	N 16	
19510	Glossop, England	G 14	
4192	Glostrup, Denmark	J 22	
....	Glotovsk, Sov. Un.	D 17	
52937	Gloucester, Eng.	L 21	
763	Gloucester Jc., N. B.	C 9	
6823	Glückstadt, Germany	D 7	
....	Glud, Denmark	J 11	
....	Glukhov, Sov. Un.	K 8	
687	Glurns, Italy	B 7	
....	Glush, W. Sov. Un.	D 22	
....	Glycerin, Brazil	H 24	
....	Glynn, N. Ire.	C 23	
21000	Gmünd, Germany	N 16	
5201	Gmünd, Germany	R 9	
7787	Gmunden, Aus.	H 6	
3647	Gnarp, Sweden	K 15	
....	Gnesen, see Gniezno, Pol.		
29924	Gniezno, Poland	D 10	
....	Go, India	D 13	
2300	Gôa, India	M 6	
....	Goaleh, Br. Som.	G 14	
6300	Goalpara, India	F 23	
5000	Goanikke, India	R 23	
....	Goarabee, Bal.	R 18	
....	Gobabis, S. W. Afr.	P 14	
4000	Gobo, Japan	O 12	
11761	Goch, Germany	H 2	
....	Gocoro, Hond.	E 1	
....	Godairi, India	K 17	
10400	Godalming, England	M 18	
....	Godar-i-Shah, Afg.	M 16	
....	Godda, India	G 19	
4557	Goddalir, Iceland	B 21	
....	Goderich, Ontario	K 5	
85	Godfrey, Ontario	H 19	
301	Godhavn, Greenland	N 4	
35110	Godhra, India	I 6	
....	Godigea, Eth.	N 7	
....	God-i-Namek, Iran	K 13	
1991	Godmanchester, Eng.	J 18	
150	Godoy, Argentina	M 17	
588	Godthaab, Greenland	O 5	
65	Godwan River, U.S. Afr.	F 21	
....	Goeree, Netherlands	I 12	
8969	Goes, Netherlands	J 9, P 5	
3896	Goes, France	F 18	
....	Goffs Harbour, Australia	M 24	
....	Gogawa, Japan	N 8	
....	Gogia, Eth.	E 7	
2900	Gogo, India	I 5	
....	Goha, Eth.	H 4	
15406	Goiânia, Brazil	K 14	
5991	Goiaz, Braz.	K 13	
....	Goico, Argentina	N 8	
5000	Gojo, Japan	N 13	
600	Gokak, India	L 8	
2900	Göksün, Tur.	G 11	
....	Gol, Eth.	G 9	
....	Gol, Norway	L 7	
2300	Gola Ghat, Nepal	E 14	
....	Golconda. India	L 11	
....	Goldau, Switzerland	G 15	
529	Goldboro, N. S.	L 20	
601	Golden, B. C.	N 18	
....	Golden, Ire.	N 13	
1453	Golden Fleece, Br. Gu.	A 6	
161	Golden Lake, Ont.	D 18	
782	Goldenville, N. S.	L 19	
....	Goldstream, B. C.	R 12	
3978	Gollnitz Slov.	O 24	
1700	Golondrina, Arg.	J 17	
1700	Golspie, Scot.	F 16	
6932	Golubac, Yugo.	K 15	
144149	Gomel, W. Sov. Un.	D 25	
1020	Gómez Farias, Tam.	I 17	
25526	Gómez Palacio, Dur.	M 23	
4669	Gommern, Germany	H 10	
12000	Gonaives, Haiti	I 12	
785	Goncelin, France	M 21	
15800	Gonda, India	F 15	
24573	Gondal, India	I 3	
3000	Gondar, Ire.	E 7	
....	Gondo, Switzerland	N 10	
1222	Gondrecourt, France	H 22	
2816	Goni, Uruguay	M 18	
3157	González, Col.	E 13	
....	González, Paraguay	Q 9	
....	González Chaves, Arg.	Q 17	
267	González Moreno, Arg.	O 13	
88	Good Hope, Mack.	G 5	
126	Good Narrows, N. S.	I 22	
5980	Goodwater, Sask.	R 9	
314	Goodwood, Ont.	J 12	
20238	Goole, England	F 17	
....	Goombalia, Austl.	L 19	
....	Goomsur, India	J 18	
....	Goona, India	H 10	
1700	Goondiwindi, Austl.	L 22	
3671	Goor, Netherlands	G 22	
....	Gooshkee, Bal.	N 19	
9700	Gooty, India	M 10	
22000	Gopalpur, India	K 18	
....	Göppingen, Ger.	O 6	
57985	Gorakhpur, India	F 16	
22000	Goransko, Yugo.	L 12	
2910	Gorbea, Chile	G 3	
....	Gorchs, Arg.	O 18	
4059	Gord, Iran	O 10	
1086	Gordola, Switz.	N 17	
20000	Gore, Eth.	E 5	
702	Gore Bay, Ontario	G 3	
4210	Gore Jc., N. Z.	Q 6	
....	Goresbridge, Ire.	M 18	
2291	Gorey, England	R 14	
....	Gorey, Ire.	M 22	
....	Gorgor, Peru	L 8	
....	Gorhi, Afg.	E 22	
13100	Gori, Sov. Un.	Q 16	
14034	Gorinchem, Neth.	I 15	
32800	Gorizia (Gorz), Italy	C 13	
7000	Gorki, Sov. Un.	J 8	
644116	Gorki (Nizhni Novgorod), Sov. Un.	I 15	
97	Görlev, Denmark	F 11	
92000	Görlitz, Germany	J 14	
62	Gorlitz, Sask.	O 11	
108693	Gorlovka, Sov. Un.	M 11	
....	Gornamaddin, Ire.	L 22	
....	Gorna, India	J 16	
9407	Gorna Dzumaja, Bul.	M 17	
8674	Gorni Orjechovica, Bul.	L 20	
12303	Gorodenka,W.Sov.Un.	G19	
....	Gorodishche, Sov. Un.	J 16	
....	Gorodnya,W.Sov.Un.	D 25	
....	Gorodok, W. Sov. Un.	B 23	
333	Goroke, Australia	P 17	
8000	Gorontalo, Oceania	D 19	
....	Gorredijk, Neth.	D 19	
576	Gorrie, Ont.	K 7	
7763	Gorssel, Neth.	G 21	
1500	Gort, Ire.	K 9	
....	Gort, N. Ire.	D 17	
4469	Görün, Tur.	F 12	
....	Gorz, see Gorizia, It.		
873	Göschenen, Switz.	J 15	
56769	Goshogawara, Japan	B 23	
22000	Goslar, Ger.	H 8	
37928	Gosport, England	N 16	
7847	Gossau, Switz.	D 18	
9585	Gosselies, Belgium	N 12	
6620	Gössnitz, Germany	K 11	
201	Gostivar, Yugo.	M 14	
....	Gostyn, Pol.	E 10	
....	Gostynin, Pol.	D 12	
46	Gota, Eth.	I 7	
262676	Göteborg, Sweden	O 10	
48000	Gotha, Germany	K 8	
78948	Gothem, Sweden	O 17	
47149	Göttingen, Germany	I 7	
236	Gottlieben, Switz.	B 18	
464	Gouarec, France	I 3	
29162	Gouda, Neth.	H 13	
1	Gouin, Algeria	D 15	
14849	Goulburn, Australia	O 21	
....	Goum, Eth.	F 12	
363	Goumbou, Fr. W. Afr.	H 4	
125	Goundam, Fr. W. Afr.	H 5	
4135	Gourdon, France	I 21	
1983	Gourin, France	I 2	
....	Gourlie, Colombia	I 23	
4617	Gournay, France	G 13	
331	Govan, Sask.	O 8	
89700	Govan, Scotland	N 15	
4651	Govena, Denmark	E 15	
643	Govero, France	O 8	
10461	Govero, Switz.	F 8	
31820	Goya, Argentina	J 18	
....	Goyania, Brazil	L 14	
1927	Goyaninha, Brazil	B 25	
....	Goyave, see Goiaz, Braz.		
11983	Graaf Reinet, U.S. Afr.	O13	
9279	Graafwater, U.S. Afr.	O 7	
1781	Graasten, Denmark	N 8	
4582	Gračanica, Yugo.	K 11	
1435	Gracay, France	J 17	
537	Gracefield, Quebec	N 9	
647	Grächen, Switz.	N 11	
1324	Gracias, Hond.	G 7	
....	Gracias a Dios, Hond.	F15	
8135	Gradačac, Yugo.	J 11	
4505	Gradefes, Spain	E 10	
1501	Gradisca, Italy	O 13	
5113	Grado, Italy	O 13	
857	Grafenau, Germany	H 21	
....	Grafenau, Germany	O 8	
648	Grafrath, Germany	R 9	
6411	Grafton, Australia	M 24	
38	Grafton, Ontario	H 17	
15406	Grahamstad, Bul.	M 17	
19768	Grahamstown, U. S. Afr.	P 16	
847	Graide, Belgium	P 14	
....	Graigue, Ire.	L 18	
....	Graiguenamanagh, Ire.	M 18	
2378	Granalote, Col.	F 14	
1633	Gramat, France	N 13	
23169	Gramichele, Italy	O 16	
12664	Grammont, Belgium	M 9	
4242	Gramsbergen, Neth.	E 22	
....	Gran, Norway	L 9	
2300	Gran, Iran	Q 12	
24843	Granada, Nicaragua	K 11	
155405	Granada, Spain	N 12	
819	Granadilla, Sp.	H 9	
....	Granard, Ire.	H 15	
14197	Granby, Quebec	Q 18	
336	Grancey, Fr.	I 19	
432	Grand-Anse, N. B.	B 11	
1735	Grand Bale, Quebec	F 22	
6932	Grand Bassam, French West Africa	J 5	
62	Grand Beach, Man.	P 17	
6992	Grand Bourg, Guad.	C 23	
767	Grandcour, Switz.	I 6	
....	Grande Anse, W. I.	B 24	
1724	Grande Prairie, Alberta	I 16	
1146	Grande Rivere,Martinique	F 24	
525	Grandes Piles, Que.	L 18	
427	Grand Etang, N. S.	F 21	
1806	Grand Falls, N. B.	E 4	
1259	Grand Forks, B. C.	R 17	
....	Grand Forks, see Bonanza, Yukon		
1267	Grand Halleux, Bel.	O 19	
172468	Grodno, W. Sov. Un.	P 17	
8608	Grand Mere, Quebec	L 15	
126	Grand Narrows, N. S.	I 22	
263	Grand Pré, N. S.	L 13	
....	Grand Rapids, Man.	L 14	
315	Grandrieu, France	N 17	
1659	Grandson, Switz.	I 4	
....	Grand Tracadie, Prince Edw. Island	G 16	
317	Grandval, Switz.	E 8	
622	Grand Valley, Ont.	K 9	
696	Grand View, Man.	O 12	
1525	Grandvilliers, France	G 13	
....	Grange, Ire.	E 10	
....	Grange, Ire.	H 13	
20682	Grangemouth, Scot.	M 17	
3454	Gränichen, Switz.	E 12	
....	Granito, Brazil	H 21	
....	Granja, Brazil	F 20	
....	Gran Laguna, Camp.	J 20	
4059	Granodillo, Spain	I 9	
....	Gransee, Germany	F 12	
....	Grant Desert, N. S.	H 16	
161	Grassy Lake, Alberta	P 23	
2302	Grave, Netherlands	I 18	
1130	Gravelbourg, Sask.	Q 8	
5448	Gravelines, France	D 13	
2122	Gravenhurst, Ont.	G 12	
35400	Gravesend, England	L 21	
10243	Gravina, Italy	J 19	
6649	Gray, France	J 21	
12	Grayburn, Sask.	O 7	
....	Grayford, England	O 25	
3920	Grayson, Sask.	P 11	
152776	Graz, Austria	A 18	
4298	Grazalema, Spain	O 9	
5916	Great Driffield, Eng.	F 18	
92463	Great Grimsby, Eng.	G 19	
....	Great Ilford, Eng.	B 23	
654	Great Marlow, Eng.	L 17	
355	Great Shemogue, N. B.	H 13	
....	Great Torrington, Eng.	M 7	
56769	Great Yarmouth, Eng.	I 25	
....	Grebbestad, Sweden	N 9	
3681	Greenbush, Sask.	J 6	
1477	Greencastle, Ire.	B 19	
....	Greencastle, Ire.	B 17	
171	Greencastle, N. Ire.	G 22	
11871	Greenfield, Ontario	E 24	
11195	Greenford, England	B 19	
201	Green Harbour, N. S.	Q 10	
42445	Greening, Quebec	F 12	
1348	Green Lake, Sask.	J 6	
1724	Greenlaw, Scot.	N 19	
78948	Greenock, Scot.	M 13	
800	Green River, New Brunswick	C 3	
140	Green Valley, Ontario	E 25	
....	Greenville, Liberia	J 5	
81	Greenwich, England	L 20	
363	Greenwich Park, Br. Gu.	A 7	
125	Greenwood, B. C.	Q 17	
1985	Greenwood, Ontario	J 12	
4651	Gregory Downs, Austl.	F16	
....	Greiba, Colombia	I 23	
25000	Greifenstein, Switz.	E 15	
25000	Greifswald, Ger.	C 12	
39000	Greiz, Germany	K 10	
....	Grein, Aus.	H 7	
8460	Grenaa, Denmark	G 15	
643	Grenade, France	O 8	
....	Grenchen, Switz.	E 8	
....	Grenchen, Switz.	F 8	
857	Grenfell, Sask.	P 10	
1238	Grenna, Sweden	O 13	
95806	Grenoble, France	M 21	
146	Grésy, Fr.	L 22	
2857	Gretna Green, Scotland	Q 20	
2089	Greven, Germany	H 4	
3747	Grevena, Greece	N 15	
2607	Grevenmacher, Lux.	Q 21	
....	Grey, Ont.	H 7	
1592	Grey Abbey, N. Ire.	L 20	
1180	Greytown, N. Z.	G 23	
....	Greytown, see San Juan del Norte, Nicaragua		
2700	Greytown, U.S. Afr.	K 21	
2637	Grez, Belgium	N 12	
139	Griffin, Sask.	Q 10	
648	Grignan, France	N 19	
....	Grigoriopol, W. Sov. Un.	H 24	
11310	Grimma, Germany	J 11	
4557	Grimmen, Germany	C 12	
2331	Grimsby, England	M 11	
2362	Grimstad, Norway	N 8	
....	Grimstrup, Den.	K 4	
3004	Grindelwald, Switz.	K 12	
2051	Grindrod, B. C.	O 16	
1592	Grindsted, Denmark	K 7	
....	Grisolles, France	O 12	
14206	Grisselhamn, Sweden	M 17	
255	Griswold, Man.	Q 13	
14206	Grivegnee, Belgium	M 18	
12942	Gródek, W. Sov. Un.	F 17	
49818	Grodno, W. Sov. Un.	O 17	
15578	Grodzisk, Poland	E 14	
2614	Groede, Neth.	K 7	
8090	Groesbeek, Neth.	I 19	
....	Gröjec, Pol.	E 14	
17519	Gronau, Germany	G 3	
....	Grönbae, Denmark	H 9	
....	Grong, Norway	H 11	
115185	Groningen, Neth.	C 22	
....	Groot Drink, U.S. Afr.	J 10	
7313	Grootegast, Neth.	C 20	
14300	Grootfontein, S. W. Africa	O 13	
....	Grorud, Norway	A 7	
550	Grosebay, Scotland	F 5	
11500	Grosseto, Italy	H 8	
....	Gross-Kanizsa, see Nagy-kanizsa, Hung.		
12911	Grossenhain, Ger.	J 12	
....	Grosse Scheideck, Switzerland	J 12	
550	Grosses Coques, N. S.	O 8	
550	Grosseto, Italy	H 8	
....	Grotli, Nor.	J 6	
347	Grouard, Alberta	H 18	
172468	Grozny, Sov. Un.	P 17	
50405	Grudziadz, Poland	C 12	
6479	Grue, Norway	L 10	
....	Gruinart, Scotland	N 7	
....	Grüm, Switz.	M 23	
12012	Grumo Appula, Italy	J 19	
....	Grundsunda, Sweden	J 17	
629	Gruñidora, Zac.	H 10	
294	Grupont, Belgium	P 16	
....	Gruver, Scotland	E 7	
1457	Gruyeres, Switz.	K 7	
3000	Gryazovets, Sov. Un.	G 12	
....	Grybów, Pol.	G 14	
....	Gstad, Switzerland	L 8	
762	Gsteig, Switz.	M 8	
1243	Guaca, Col.	J 7	
2516	Guacari, Col.	J 7	
6115	Guachucal, Col.	M 4	
....	Guacono, Col.	J 18	
329235	Guadalajara, Jal.	M 7	
23508	Guadalajara, Spain	H 13	
6931	Guadalcanal, Spain	L 9	
688	Guadalcázar, S. L. P.	J 14	
....	Guadales, Argentina	N 8	
659	Guadalupe, Bolivia	J 12	
759	Guadalupe, Bolivia	N 7	
1596	Guadalupe, Col.	K 9	
1044	Guadalupe, N. L.	E 14	
3969	Guadalupe, Zac.	J 9	
4078	Guadalupe, Peru	H 4	
3452	Guadalupe, Spain	J 10	
1840	Guadalupe de los Reyes, Sin.	J 8	
410	Guadalupo y Calvo, Chih.	L 17	
26023	Guadix, Spain	N 13	
1787	Guaitarilla, Col.	M 4	
....	Guajará Mirim, Bolivia	B 9	
....	Guajará Mirim, Brazil	I 5	
....	Guajaratuba, Brazil	F 3	
9334	Gualaceo, Ecuador	D 5	
397	Gualaco, Honduras	F 12	
13293	Gualán, Guatemala	F 6	
....	Gualaquiza, Ecuador	E 5	
3616	Gualdo Tadino, Italy	G 11	
....	Gualea, Ecuador	B 4	
12941	Gualeguay, Arg.	M 18	
24670	Gualeguaychú, Arg.	M 19	
2130	Guallala, Tunisia	P 25	
21999	Guamá, Venezuela	D 10	
20007	Guamal, Col.	J 13	
2517	Guamini, Arg.	P 14	
15968	Guamo, Col.	J 9	
....	Guamo, Col.	J 3	
....	Guamo, Cuba	N 19	
21999	Guanabacoa, Cuba	H 7	
3314	Guanagazapa, Guat.	H 5	
1754	Guanaceví, Dur.	M 19	
282	Guanaco, Chile	G 5	
23501	Guanajuato, Guan.	L 12	
5332	Guanape, Ven.	D 15	
3681	Guanipa Hill, Peru	I 4	
1477	Guaniito, Ven.	F 9	
1407	Guandacol, Arg.	J 4	
1409	Guane, Cuba	J 2	
....	Guanito, Cuba	L 19	
1724	Guano, Ecuador	C 5	
11871	Guano, Ecuador	O 17	
11195	Guantánamo, Cuba	O 23	
1348	Guapi, Col.	K 4	
1724	Guara, Cuba	H 7	
....	Guarabú, Brazil	O 14	
5000	Guanambá, Paraguay	O 7	
15606	Guaranda, Ecuador	C 4	
....	Guarapary, Brazil	O 14	
15654	Guaratinguetá, Brazil	N 16	
....	Guarda, Bolivia	D 6	
8158	Guarda, Portugal	H 7	
257	Guarda, Switz.	I 23	
9311	Guardia, Spain	E 5	
1801	Guardo, Spain	D 11	
1827	Guareiras, Cuba	I 10	
8835	Guarena, Spain	K 9	
9841	Guareñas, Ven.	C 13	
1173	Guasabas, Son.	F 14	
....	Guasimal, Cuba	M 13	
1598	Guasipati, Ven.	H 21	
....	Guaso, Cuba	O 23	
188042	Guatemala, Guatemala	G 4	
2103	Guateque, Col.	H 12	
2637	Guatimozin, Arg.	M 14	
....	Guatrache, Arg.	P 13	
3306	Guayabal, Cuba	N 17	
....	Guaviraví, Arg.	J 19	
3306	Guayabo, Ven.	F 9	
172948	Guayaquil, Ecuador	D 3	
8786	Guaymas, Son.	I 11	
2059	Guayos, Cuba	J 8	
580	Guazapares, Chih.	J 15	
6284	Gubbio, Italy	G 11	
....	Guasol-cúa, Par.	J 6	
44000	Gubden, Sov. Un.	P 19	
....	Guben, Pol.	E 7	
789	Gudhjem, Den.	Q 24	
....	Gudur, India	N 19	
2500	Gudur, India	N 13	
....	Gudvangen, Norway	K 5	
11164	Guebwiller, France	I 24	
....	Guedaidah, Egypt	H 23	
9390	Guelma, Algeria	B 21	
23273	Guelph, Ont.	L 9	

Pop.	Place Country Index
30	Guelph Junction, Ont., L 10
.....	Guemes, Argentina, F 11
932	Güemes, Tam., H 17
.....	Gueraco, Honduras, F 8
7984	Guéret, France, L 13
115	Guernsey, Sask., N 8
5475	Guerrara, Algeria, G 18
.....	Guerrara, Morocco, F 5
1029	Guerrero, Coa., B 14
1847	Guetaria, Spain, C 14
732	Guevea, Oax., M 11
.....	Guez el Aagam, Egypt, G 12
2611	Guggisberg, Switz., J 8
4935	Guglionesi, Italy, I 16
.....	Guhêna, Egypt, M 20
1938	Guichicovi, Oax., M 12
.....	Guichon, B. C., Q 13
705	Guido, Arg., P 20
.....	Guidonia, Italy, I 11
2039	Guildford, Australia, M 4
30753	Guildford, England, M 18
.....	Guilford, B. C., K 14
956	Guilestre, France, N 23
335	Guillon, France, J 17
.....	Guimarães, Brazil, E 17
70186	Guimarães, Portugal, F 6
.....	Guin, see Dudingen, Switz.
.....	Guinaze, Argentina, L 12
.....	Guinaze, Argentina, L 12
.....	Guineo, Col., M 7
22669	Güines, Cuba, H 7
8575	Guingamp, France, H 4
10824	Guira, Cuba, I 6
5283	Güiria, Venezuela, C 20
7097	Guise, France, F 16
58716	Gujranwala, India, C 7
25604	Gujrat, India, C 7
41083	Gulbarga, India, L 10
303	Gulev, Denmark, G 9
1723	Gulgong, Australia, N 21
.....	Gul Hoaz, Iran, I 15
.....	Gullewa, Australia, L 4
836	Gull Lake, Sask., P 5
.....	Gulnabad, Iran, J 7
2874	Gulpen, Neth., M 19
.....	Gulskogen, Norway, B 2
.....	Gulyai Pole, Sov. Un., N 10
.....	Gumbal, Colombia, M 4
19000	Gumbinnen, W. Sov. Un. B 15
.....	Gümenek, Tur., D 11
.....	Gummenen, Switz., H 8
18000	Gummersbach, Ger., J 4
3161	Gumusane, Tur., D 14
.....	Gunchu, Japan, N 8
.....	Gundabella, I. E. A., K 13
1255	Gundagai, Australia, O 21
.....	Gunderup, Denmark, E 11
.....	Gundutsu, Afg., I 16
.....	Gungaur, India, H 14
.....	Gunguane, Mongolia, A 14
.....	Gunmezah, Egypt, E 13
.....	Gunnarskog, Sweden, M 11
3591	Gunnedah, Australia, M 21
804	Günsberg, Switz., F 9
65179	Guntur, India, L 13
.....	Gunupur, India, K 17
5977	Günzburg, Germany, P 7
.....	Günzburg, Ger., Q 7
.....	Gura, Erit., B 9
5977	Gura-Humorului, Rom., H 20
.....	Gurais, India, B 8
.....	Gura Khan, Afg., H 18
32500	Gurev, Sov. Un. Asia, H 8
.....	Gurg, Iran, M 14
.....	Gurgab, Iran, I 4
.....	Gurgan, Iran, E 10
.....	Gurha, India, G 4
.....	Guri, Ven., H 19
.....	Gur-i-Sufaid, Afg., H 16
.....	Gurkha, Nepal, F 17
.....	Gurmab, Afg., J 19
.....	Gurmawuk, Afg., J 19
1700	Gurramkonda, India, N 12
.....	Gurupa, Brazil, E 12
.....	Gurupy-Mirim, Brazil, F 15
.....	Gus, Sov. Un., I 13
.....	Gushk, Iran, N 11
6483	Guspini, Italy, L-3
.....	Gustäfsberg, Sweden, Q 23
.....	Gustan, Iran, J 11
1000	Gustavia, West Indies, J 22
22464	Güstrow, Germany, D 10
.....	Gustung, Baluchistan, J 18
.....	Gusyatin, W. Sov. Un., G 20
24000	Gütersloh, Germany, H 5
66	Guthalungra, Austl., F 22
225	Guthrie, Scotland, J 21
2475	Gutierrez, Bolivia, K 13
.....	Gutihah, Transj., N 15
384	Guttannen, Switz., J 13
985	Güttingen, Switz., C 19
286	Guyancourt, France, C 1
995	Guysborough, N. S., K 20
326	Guysborough Intervale, N. S., K 20
4300	Gwadar, Baluchistan, R 17
21999	Gwalior, India, G 11
.....	Gwasht, Iran, O 16
3526	Gwelo, S. Rh., O 17
.....	Gwetter, Iran, R 16
.....	Gwydir, Wales, H 7
1102	Gy, France, J 21
.....	Gya, India, B 11
2487	Gyékényes, Hung., I 9
7749	Gympie, Austl., J 23
.....	Gymri (Alexandropol), see Leninakin, Sov. Un.
2129	Gyöhashi, Japan, M 5
50997	Györ, Hung., H 10
200	Gypsumville, Man., N 14
.....	Gysinge, Sweden, L 15
6899	Gythion, Greece, Q 17
25221	Gyula, Hung., I 14
6000	Gzhatsk, Sov. Un., I 9

H

Pop.	Place Country Index
7863	Haaksbergen, Neth., G 23
4235	Haapsalu, Sov. Un., G 23
725	Haarby, Denmark, L 11
129126	Haarlem, Neth., F 12
566	Haarlev, Denmark, L 22
.....	Haarslev, Denmark, K 11
.....	Haast, N. Z., N 6
676376	Habana, Cuba, H 6
1815	Habay la Neuve, Bel., Q 18
6231	Habelschwerdt, Ger., L 17
.....	Habiganj, India, G 24
677	Habkern, Switz., J 11
.....	Hachia, Japan, M 5
5047	Hachiman, Japan, L 16
3100	Hachimori, Japan, C 23
.....	Hachinohe, Japan, C 25
52906	Hachinohe, Japan, H 13
51866	Hachioji, Japan, M 20
898	Hachisaki, Japan, I 19
.....	Hacketstown, Ire., L 20
.....	Hadama, Eth., J 9
5682	Haddington, Scot., M 21
.....	Haddo, Ontario, G 23
.....	Hadele Gubo, Eth., F 12
7000	Hadera, Pal., J 6
16100	Haderslev (Hadersleben), Denmark, L 8
.....	Haditieh, Palestine, L 7
.....	Hadjikol, Tur., D 10
2952	Hadleigh, England, K 23
.....	Hadnall, England, I 12
2415	Hadsund, Denmark, F 11
2816	Haecht, Belgium, L 12
.....	Haeggedal, Norway, B 4
48649	Haeju, Kor., D 23
.....	Haestrup, Denmark, C 11
.....	Hafen, Baluchistan, R 19
342	Hafford, Sask., L 6
.....	Hafs, Egypt, D 6
.....	Hafsê-i-Kebir, Syr., I 13
.....	Haft Asail, Afg., H 22
.....	Haftawan, Iran, O 8
.....	Hafun, Som., H 24
.....	Hafverö, Sweden, J 13
148300	Hagen, Germany, I 4
.....	Hagenau, Germany, E 9
13	Hagenborg, B. C., M 9
1455	Hagersville, Ontario, N 10
.....	Häggenäs, Sweden, I 13
21000	Hagi, Japan, L 6
.....	Ha-giang, Fr. In. Ch., L 7
261	Hague, Sask., M 7
19514	Haguenau, France, G 24
.....	Hahi, Eth., N 16
.....	Haicheng, China, E 9
.....	Haicheng, Manch., C 20
.....	Haichow, China, F 18
.....	Haidarabad, Iran, N 8
.....	Haidar Pyamber, Iran, E 4
.....	Haidra, Tunisia, D 22
.....	Hai-duong, Fr. In. Ch., M 8
99000	Haifa, Palestine, H 7
.....	Haifung, China, L 16
20000	Hail, Sau. Ar., K 5
.....	Hailakandi, India, M 19
.....	Hailar, Manch., M 14
2268	Haileybury, Ont., Q 24
.....	Hailin, Manch., A 25
.....	Hailung, Manch., B 22
.....	Haining, China, H 20
80000	Haiphong, Fr. In. Ch., M 9
.....	Hait, Iran, Q 15
28861	Hajdubözörmény, Hungary, H 14
.....	Hajdunánás, Hung., H 14
.....	Hajduszaboszlo, Hung., H 14
.....	Hajiabad, Iran, I 9
.....	Hajiabad, Iran, P 11
21400	Hajipur, India, G 18
.....	Hajira, Algeria, H 19
.....	Hajki, Jap., N 2
.....	Hajrabad, Iran, G 13
.....	Haka, Bur., M 20
.....	Hakantorp, Sweden, N 11
22954	Hakata, Japan, M 4
.....	Hakiam, Iran, F 4
.....	Hakkasbyn, Sweden, E 19
203862	Hakodate, Japan, H 12, C 5
17308	Hal, Belgium, M 11
5000	Hala, India, G 1
3520	Halachó, Yuc., F 20
.....	Halaweh, Transjordan, J 13
48000	Halberstadt, Germany, H 9
.....	Hald, Denmark, F 11
10278	Halden (Fredrikshald), Nor., N 9
502	Haldenstein, Switz., I 20
2624	Halesworth, England, J 24
.....	Haleya, Br. Som., I 15
.....	Halfaya, Anglo-Egyptian Sudan, G 18
.....	Halfweg, Neth., F 13
975	Haliburton, Ont., F 14
98122	Halifax, England, F 14
70488	Halifax, N. S., N 15
.....	Halilah, Iran, N 6
1725	Halkirk, Scot., D 18
.....	Halladay, Alberta, N 22
.....	Hallatrow, Eng., M 12
2064	Halle, Ger., H 5
209200	Halle, Ger., J 10
.....	Hallencourt, France, E 13
.....	Hallestad, Sweden, N 14
.....	Hallia, India, G 15
.....	Hallsberg, Sweden, N 13
45	Halls Creek, Austl., E 10
.....	Hallstatt, Aus., H 6
.....	Hallum, Neth., C 18
23866	Halmstad, Sweden, P 11
1247	Hals, Den., D 12
.....	Halsen, Norway, G 1
60015	Hälsingborg, Sweden, Q 10
5878	Halstead, Eng., K 22
.....	Halsted, England, D 25
.....	Haltwhistle, England, C 12
2032	Ham, France, F 15
.....	Ham, Nepal, F 21
.....	Ham, Scotland, C 1
36000	Hama, Syria, K 11
2400	Hamada, Japan, K 7
103874	Hamadan, Iran, G 4
.....	Hamagavine, Afg., I 16
166346	Hamamatsu, Japan, N 17
2731	Hamameh, Palestine, N 3
.....	Hamân, Egypt, M 12
.....	Hamanaka, Japan, F 22
.....	Hamanaka, Japan, G 15
1300	Hamano, Japan, M 21
5965	Hamar, Norway, L 9
.....	Hamasaka, Japan, K 12
.....	Hama Tombetsu, Jap. E 13
3133	Hambantota, Cey., R 14
.....	Hamborn, Ger., see Duisburg, Ger.
1647000	Hamburg, Ger., D 8
9212	Hämeenlinna, Fin., F 4
.....	Hamelin Pool, Austl., J 3
28000	Hameln, Ger., H 6
61430	Hamhüng (Kankō), Kor., C 24
18973	Hamilton, Aust., N 22
5786	Hamilton, Austl., Q 17
17950	Hamilton, N. Z., E 18
166332	Hamilton, Ont., M 10
44204	Hamilton, Scot., N 16
3910	Hamina, Fin., F 5
524	Hamiota, Man., Q 13
.....	Hamirpur, India, G 13
.....	Hamitabad, Iran, G 14
52000	Hamm, Ger., I 4
3000	Hammamet, Tunisia, B 24
.....	Hamman Lif, Tunisia, B 24
.....	Hamman Meskoutine, Algeria, B 20
.....	Hammanskraal, U.S. Afr., F 18
.....	Hammar, Sweden, N 13
15016	Hamme, Belgium, L 10
334	Hammer, Denmark, I 8
.....	Hammerdal, Sweden, I 13
3646	Hammerfest, Norway, A 19
3215	Hammero, Norway, D 14
365	Hammershöj, Den., F 9
185	Hammond, Ont., D 23
150	Hammond Plains, N.S., M 14
217	Hammond Vale, N. B. J 10
180	Hampden, N. Z., O 9
260	Hampstead, Eng., B 21
231	Hampstead, N. B., L 8
650	Hampton, N. B., K 9
275	Hampton, Ont., J 14
1725	Hampton Court, British Guiana, A 6
.....	Hamra, Sweden, K 12
.....	Hamran, Egypt, N 22
.....	Hamza, Iraq, O 21
.....	Hanaka, Iran, M 12
1900	Hanamaki, Japan, E 24
40000	Hanau, Ger., L 5
1100	Hanawa, Japan, D 24
.....	Hanceville, Alta., M 13
.....	Hanchow, China, H 7
.....	Hanchung, China, G 9
5100	Handa, Japan, M 15
.....	Handeck, Switz., K 13
.....	Handia, India, I 10
.....	Handsworth, Sask., Q 10
.....	Hanee, Iran, E 1
506900	Hangchow, China, H 19
.....	Hanghei, Som., H 21
.....	Hangiya, Egypt, O 24
8151	Hangö (Hanko), Fin., F 3
1509	Hanimidi, Japan, I 22
.....	Haningo, Sweden, R 21
.....	Hanko, see Hangö, Fin.
778000	Hankow, China, H 15
800	Hanle, India, C 12
61600	Hanley, England, H 13
380	Hanley, Sask., N 7
1622	Hanna, Alberta, M 22
438922	Hannover, Germany, G 7
2381	Hannut, Belgium, M 15
149000	Hanoi, Fr. In. Ch., M 8
3290	Hanover, Ontario, J 7
1350	Hanover, U.S. Afr., M 14
15200	Hansi, India, E 9
661	Hansted, Denmark, D 4
907	Hantsport, N. S., L 13
1300	Hanumangarh, India, E 7
2600	Hanût, Egypt, E 13
.....	Hanwell, England, C 19
400000	Hanyang, China, H 15
.....	Hanyintung, China, G 11
.....	Hao, I. E. A., K 16
.....	H. Aouleggui, Algeria, M 18
2519	Haparanda, Sweden, F 21
929	Haquira, Peru, N 15
1675	Hara, Japan, M 18
50000	Harar, Eth., I 13
419	Harâra, Egypt, D 6
.....	Harbêt, Egypt, E 17
517127	Harbin, Manch., A 23
425	Harboöre, Denmark, F 2
.....	Harboard, Ontario, E 22
2250	Harbor Grace, Newf., K 25
112604	Harburg, Germany, E 7
275	Harcourt, N. B., G 10
.....	Harda, India, I 10
2494	Hardenberg, Neth., E 22
8613	Harderwijk, Neth., F 17
605	Harding, U.S. Afr., M 20
6655	Hardinxveld, Neth., I 14
457	Hardisty, Alberta, L 23
11200	Hardoi, India, F 13
33287	Hardwar, India, D 11
165	Hardwicke, New Brunswick, E 11
.....	Hardwood Ridge, New Brunswick, H 8
5080	Harfleur, France, G 10
17500	Hargeisa, British Somaliland, I 15
.....	Hargshamn, Sweden, L 17
12	Hargwen, Alberta, K 18
.....	Harihar, India, M 9
.....	Harim, Syria, I 11
.....	Haripur, India, B 6
.....	Harir, Afg., L 20
9066	Hârlău, Romania, H 21
10061	Harlebeke, Belgium, M 6
10443	Harlingen, Neth., C 16
7159	Harmanli, Bulgaria, M 21
.....	Harmon, Alberta, M 22
20	Harmony Jc., Prince Edward Island, G 18
227	Harmony Mills, N. S., O 11
.....	Harmony, N. S., L 12
444	Harndrup, Denmark, K 11
.....	Harnings Mills, Ont., I 9
11787	Härnösand, Swe., J 18
8539	Haro, Spain, E 13
.....	Haroldswick, Shetland Is., A 5
9300	Harpanahalli, India, M 9
.....	Harpanahalli, India, N 9
668	Harran, Tur., H 14
.....	Harraua, Eth., I 13
.....	Harre, Denmark, F 6
.....	Harring, Denmark, E 4
.....	Harrington, Quebec, O 13
237	Harris, Sask., N 6
4467	Harris, Scot., I 7
164	Harrisburg, Ontario, M 9
6756	Harrisburg, U.S. Afr. H 16
9208	Harrismith, U.S. Afr., I 19
161	Harrison Mills, B. C., O 5
1305	Harriston, Ontario, K 8
39785	Harrogate, England, F 15
1166	Harrow, Ontario, R 1
26378	Harrow on the Hill, England, H 18
427	Harrowsmith, Ont., I 20
4139	Hârsova, Romania, J 23
3771	Harstad, Norway, C 14
2762	Hartberg, Aus., H 8
.....	Hartland, England, M 6
847	Hartland, N. B., G 4
20545	Hartlepool, England, D 16
478	Hartney, Man., R 13
275	Hartsville, P. E. I., H 15
.....	Harunabad, Iran, G 2
.....	Harut, Syr., D 12
229	Harvey, N. B., J 6
394	Harvey, N. B., I 12
12700	Harwich, England, K 23
215	Harwood, Ontario, J 15
.....	Hasainah, Iran, P 9
.....	Hasanabad, Iran, L 7
.....	Hasan Kef., Tur., G 17
1335	Hasenkamps, Arg., L 18
5064	Haslev, Denmark, L 20
.....	Hassaina, Egypt, D 16
.....	Hassan, India, N 9
.....	Hassan-Kala, Tur., D 17
.....	Hassâya, Egypt, Q 24
25840	Hasselt, Belgium, L 16
2294	Hasselt, Neth., E 18
.....	Hassetchê, Syria, I 16
.....	Hassian Taiebin, Alg., Q 14
.....	Hassi Berghaoui, Alg., I 17
.....	Hassi Insokki, Alg., M 17
.....	Hassi Messeguem (Wells), Alg., H 19
.....	Hassing, Denmark, E 3
3238	Hassleholm, Swe., Q 12
65199	Hastings, Eng., N 22
13650	Hastings, N. Z., H 21
754	Hastings, Ont., I 16
.....	Hasvik, Norway, A 18
368	Hatate, Japan, E 23
3401	Hateg, Romania, J 16
.....	Hatha, Bur., M 23
.....	Hatherleigh, England, N 7
37900	Hathras, India, F 11
.....	Ha-tinh, Fr. In. Chn., N 8
7547	Hato, Col., B 8
5800	Hatta, India, H 13
.....	Hatta, India, K 10
4410	Hattem, Neth., F 19
110	Hatton, Sask., P 3
.....	Hatuey, Cuba, I 11
1496	Hatuey, Cuba, M 17
15369	Hatvan, Hungary, H 12
17217	Haugesund, Nor., M 3
.....	Haus, Nor., L 4
293	Hauss onvillers, Alg., B 17
532	Hauts Geneveys, Switz., G 5
.....	Hauzien, Eth., C 10
.....	Havana, see Habana, Cuba
4264	Havant, England, N 17
803	Havdrup, Denmark, K 21
1631	Havelange, Belgium, O 16
5413	Havelberg, Ger., F 10
326	Havelock, N. B., I 10
143	Havelock, N. Z., I 15
260	Havelock, N. Z., Q 7
1113	Havelock, Ont., H 16
6113	Haverfordwest, Wales, K 5
3827	Haverhill, England, J 21
.....	Haverigg, England, E 10
.....	Havering, England, B 25
569	Havndal, Denmark, F 12
.....	Havningberg, Nor., A 24
.....	Havre, see Le Havre, Fr.
365	Havre Boucher, N. S., J 20
.....	Hawara, Transjordan, I 16
175	Hawarden, Sask., N 7
.....	Hawera, N. Z., H 16
18214	Hawick, Scot., O 21
.....	Hawk, Ont., Q 21
466	Hawker, Australia, M 16
6263	Hawkesbury, Ont., G 25
210	Hawkestone, Ont., H 11
.....	Hawkshead, England, E 11
.....	Hawkswood, N. Z., L 14
.....	Hawston, U.S. Afr., R 8
.....	Hawt, Siam., N 2
309	Hawtrey, Ont., N 8
3156	Hay, Australia, O 19
1500	Hay, Wales, K 10
915	Hayle, England, O 3
.....	Haynes, B. C., Q 16
.....	Hay River, Mack., P 13
216	Hays River, N. S., H 21
.....	Hayward Jc., B. C., Q 2
.....	Hazar Durukht, Afg., I 19
20977	Hazaribagh, India, H 18
.....	Hazar Juft, Afg., K 18
14859	Hazebrouck, Fr., E 14
.....	Hazel Dell, Sask., N 10
288	Hazel Grove, P.E.I., G 15
300	Hazel Hill, N.S., K 22
455	Hazelton, B. C., I 9
1743	Hazenmore, Sask., Q 6
.....	Hazrat Imam, Afg., D 22
.....	Hazro, Tur., G 16
.....	H. Babbah, Algeria, D 16
.....	Headford, Ire., I 8
.....	Headford, Ire., P 6
214	Headingley, Man., Q 15
264	Head of Chezzetcook, N S., N 16
624	Head of Millstream, N. B., I 9
321	Head of Saint Margarets Bay, N.S., N 13
22386	Heanor, England, H 16
995	Hearst, Ontario, O 22
.....	Heast, Scotland, I 9
31	Heath, Alberta, K 23
.....	Heath, Bolivia, D 3
285	Heatherton, N. S., J 19
24125	Hebburn, England, C 15
835	Hebertville Station P. O., Quebec, E 21
528	Hebron, N. S., Q 8
.....	Hebron, Newf., H 20
17532	Hebron (El Khulil), Pal., O 8
2926	Hecelchakan, Camp., G 20
5109	Hechingen, Ger., P 5
.....	Hede, Sweden, J 12
3800	Hedemora, Sweden, L 14
772	Hedensted, Denmark, J 9
.....	Hedesunda, Sweden, L 15
.....	Hedgehope, N. Z., Q 5
624	Hedley, B. C., Q 15
1509	Hedon, England, F 19
3900	Hedrum, Norway, F 1
8565	Heerde, Neth., F 19
.....	Heerenveen, Neth., D 19
46885	Heerlen, Neth., J 18
.....	Heibak, Afg., E 22
10646	Heide, Ger., C 6
84650	Heidelberg, Ger., N 5
5828	Heidelberg, U.S. Afr., G 18
3300	Heidelberg, U.S. Afr., Q 10
3079	Heiden, Switz., D 20
21000	Heidenheim, Ger., O 7
26366	Heijthuijsen, Neth., K 19
1200	Heilbron, U.S. Afr., H 18
60300	Heilbronn, Ger., N 6
8641	Heiligenstadt, Ger., I 7
.....	Heinersdorf, Ger., O 18
2721	Heino, Neth., F 20
.....	Heis, Br. Som., G 19
140	Heisler, Alberta, L 22
.....	Heituwo, China, C 16
943	Hejls, Denmark, K 8
311	Hejnsvig, Denmark, J 5
1109	Helchteren, Belgium, L 17
6088	Helden, Netherlands, K 19
29339	Helder, Netherlands, D 13
1120	Helechosa, Spain, J 10
.....	Helen's Bay, N. Ire., D 24
8893	Helensburgh, Scot., N 13
1018	Helensville, N. Z., D 16
.....	Helgenaes, Den., H 12
.....	Helif, Tur., H 16
13723	Hellendoorn, Neth., F 22
.....	Hellerup, Denmark, J 23
.....	Hellesjö, Sweden, J 14
.....	Hellevad, Denmark, C 11
2161	Hellevoetsluis, Neth., I 11
.....	Helligsö, Denmark, F 3
25643	Hellin, Spain, L 15
25410	Helmond, Neth., J 18
.....	Helmsdale, Scot., E 17
.....	Helmsley, Eng., E 16
18000	Helmstedt, Ger., H 9
.....	Helmur, Ont., E 10
.....	Helpmakaar, U.S. Afr., J 21
.....	Helsingfors, see Helsinki, Fin.
15841	Helsingör, Denmark, I 22
283598	Helsinki (Helsingfors), Finland, F 4
2544	Helston, England, O 3
.....	Helstrup, Denmark, G 10
2131	Helvoirt, Neth., I 16
.....	Helwan, Egypt, J 14
.....	Helwan Baths, Egypt, J 14
.....	Hem, Denmark, F 6
.....	Hem, Denmark, F 11
40	Hemaruka, Alta., M 23
.....	Hemmed, Denmark, G 14
128	Hemmet, Denmark, I 3
368	Hemmingford, Que., R 15
429	Hemmishofen, Switz., B 16
3372	Hemnes, Norway, F 12
475	Hemse, Sweden, P 17
.....	Hemsedal, Norway, L 7
.....	Hemyock, England, N 10
56014	Hendon, England, B 20
.....	Hengchow, China, J 14
34328	Hengelo, Neth., F 23
4645	Hengelo, Neth., H 21
.....	Hengtaoholze, Manch., A 24
99	Henne, Denmark, J 2
268	Henniez, Switz., J 6
.....	Henry Py, Argentina, I 20
429	Henryville, Quebec, R 16
665	Hensall, Ontario, M 5
25100	Henzada, Bur., O 22
290	Hepworth, Ont., H 7
100000	Herat, Afg., H 16
875	Herbert, Sask., P 6
869	Herberton, Australia, E 20
755	Herbillon, Algeria, B 21
.....	Herb Lake, Man., J 13
3368	Herck-la-Ville, Bel., L 15
10331	Heredia, Costa Rica, N 14
.....	Heredra Marsh, Col., C 10
24159	Hereford, England, K 11
8989	Herencia, Spain, J 12
.....	Herend, Iran, J 7
7274	Herent, Belgium, L 13
12086	Herenthals, Belgium, K 13
37000	Herford, Ger., H 5
2048	Hergiswil, Switz., J 10
.....	Herguela, Tunisia, C 24
5552	Hericourt, France, I 22
1572	Herinnes-les-Pecq, Bel., M 7
250	Heriot, N. Z., P 6
13601	Herisau, Switz., E 19
.....	Herlufsholm, Den., L 19
356	Hermance, Switz., M 2
22	Hermannsburg, Austl., H 12
.....	Hermannstadt, see Nagyszeben, Rom.
443	Hermeton sur Meuse, Bel., O 13
18830	Hermosillo, Son., G 11
21156	Hermupolis, Greece, P 20
.....	Hernandaris, Arg., K 17
98600	Herne, Ger., I 3
11244	Herne Bay, England, L 23
10866	Herning, Den., H 5
11461	Hernösand, Sweden, J 16
1111	Heron, Belgium, M 15
.....	Herpele, Italy, D 14
1466	Herradura, Cuba, I 4
.....	Herrera, Cuba, M 21
5101	Herrera del Duque, Spain, K 10
1664	Herreras, N. L., E 16
345	Herring Cove, Nova Scotia, N 15
.....	Herris, Iran, D 4
.....	Herrljunga, Sweden, O 11
137	Herschel, Sask., N 5
1500	Herschel, U.S. Afr., M 17
6021	Herseaux, Belgium, M 6
11269	Hersfeld, Ger., K 7
24832	Herstal, Belgium, M 17
8368	Herta, Romania, G 20
.....	Herta, W. Sov. Un., H 20
11376	Hertford, England, K 20
.....	Herval, Brazil, R 10
4071	Herve, Belgium, M 19
651	Herznach, Switz., D 12
3191	Herzogenbuchsee, Switz., F 10
2511	Hesdin, France, E 13
3058	Hespeler, Ontario, L 9
.....	Het Loo, Neth., G 19
.....	Het Schouw, Neth., B 6
561	Hettlingen, Switz., C 15
17672	Hetton-le-Hole, Eng., D 15
428	Heurne, Belgium, O 16
1900	Heusden, Neth., I 15
.....	Hevir, Iran, C 4
8888	Hexham, England, C 13
.....	Hex River, U.S. Afr., Q 8
5812	Heyst, Belgium, K 6
9184	Heyst op den Berg, Bel., L 13
.....	H Parez, Algeria, O 16
.....	Hianzan, Bur., M 21
.....	Hiaoyi, China, G 11
8000	Hiaty, Par., O 8
.....	Hiayang, Chn., E 20
.....	Hi Bel Hairane, Alg., I 20
.....	Hi Ben. Algeria, I 18
.....	Hi Bottine, Algeria, I 21
.....	Hibou Khenissa, Alg., I 19
.....	Hi Bou Tali (Wells), Alg., J 15
214	Hickson, Ontario, M 7
.....	Hida, Japan, N 5
1323	Hidalgo, Tam., H 16
402	Hidalgo, Chile, N 3
.....	Hi Djemel (Wells), Alg., J 18
.....	Hi Einonanau, Alg., J 13
.....	Hi el Aicha (Wells), Algeria, I 18
.....	Hi el Biodh (Wells), Algeria, I 20
.....	Hi el Hadjad, Algeria, N 19
.....	Hi el Hadjadj (Wells), Algeria, I 18
.....	Hi el Hadjar (Wells), Algeria I 19
.....	Hi el Heida, Algeria, L 12
.....	Hi el Mongar, Algeria, N 16
.....	Hierepetra, Greece, R 21
.....	Highams, Australia, H 3
311	Highgate, Ontario, P 4
400	High Prairie, Alberta, H 18
1430	High River, Alberta, O 21
254	Higueritas, Chile, K 3
2045	Higuerote, Ven., C 14
3144	Higuey, Dom. Rep., J 16
.....	Hihya, Eg., E 16
.....	Hii, Japan, O 11
.....	Hi Inhal, Algeria, K 15
.....	Hi In Ifel, Algeria, K 18
3853	Hijar, Spain, G 16
.....	Hiji, Japan, N 6
2800	Hikata, Japan, N 12
3300	Hikida, Japan, N 11
18400	Hikone, Japan, L 16
.....	Hilario Ascasubi, Arg., R 14
225	Hilda, Alberta, O 24
6212	Hildburghausen, Ger., L 8
62000	Hildesheim, Germany, H 7
35000	Hilla, Iraq, N 20
.....	Hille, Sweden, L 15
10821	Hillegom, Neth., G 13
6822	Hillerød, Denmark, I 22
.....	Hillesö, Norway, B 16
.....	Hillested, Norway, D 2
.....	Hillested, Denmark, N 18
.....	Hillhead, N. Ire., F 22
.....	Hilli, India, G 22
913	Hillsborough, N. Ire., I 12
.....	Hillsborough, N. Ire., E 22
930	Hillsborough, N. B., I 12
525	Hillsburgh, Ontario, K 9
456	Hillsdale, Ontario, H 11
.....	Hillswick, Shetland Is., B 2
200	Hilltown, N. Ire., F 22
.....	Hilton, Man., I 14
3517	Hilvarenbeek, Neth., J 15
66627	Hilversum, Neth., G 15
.....	Hi Mamoura (Wells), Algeria, I 13
.....	Himarë, Albania, N 13
104259	Himeji, Japan, M 12
10600	Himi, Japan, I 15
.....	Hi Mokhanza, Algeria, J 20
.....	Hi Mouileh Matallah, Algeria, L 19
1600	Hinagu, Japan, P 3
16030	Hinckley, England, I 16
.....	Hindaken, Iran, K 13
.....	Hindaun, India, F 10
1014	Hindelbank, Switz., G 9
986	Hindeloopen, Neth., D 16
2147	Hinderwell, England, D 17
.....	Hindiyah, Iraq, L 5
.....	Hindol, India, J 18
200	Hinds, N. Z., N 10
.....	Hingan, China, G 11
22601	Hinganghat, India, J 12
60000	Hinghwa, China, J 19
17300	Hingoli, India, J 10
.....	Hini, Tur., F 15
.....	Hinojo, Argentina, P 18
14844	Hinojosa del Duque, Spain, L 10
112	Hinterrhein, Switz., K 18
.....	Hinter-Wäggithal Switz., G 17
.....	Hintsy, W. Sov. Un., G 23
3153	Hinwil, Switz., E 16
.....	HiOudjen (Wells), Alg., J 14
.....	Hirado, Japan, M 2
.....	Hiraj, Japan, O 10
.....	Hirasawa, Japan, E 22
1700	Hirasawa, Japan, L 18
.....	Hi Redjel Imrad, Alg., R 14
.....	Hirono, Japan, J 23
43338	Hirosaki, Japan, C 23
343968	Hiroshima, Japan, L 8
11403	Hirson, France, F 17
25179	Hissar, India, E 9
10000	Hissar, Iran, E 2
.....	Hissar, Iran, F 5
.....	Hissar, Iran, L 5
5000	Hit, Iraq, M 18
.....	Hi Tamesguida (Wells), Algeria, J 19
13535	Hitchin, England, K 19
.....	Hi Tirechoumine, Alg., Q 15
3200	Hitoyoshi, Japan, P 4
.....	Hitterdal, Norway, M 7
1500	Hiwasa, Japan, O 11
1800	Hiyama, Japan, J 18
515	Hizmeh, Palestine, M 10
748	Hjallerup, Denmark, D 12
400	Hjardarholt, Iceland, B 19
.....	Hjardemaal, Den., D 5
.....	Hjelmeland, Norway, M 4
.....	Hjerkin, Norway, J 8
524	Hjerm, Den., G 4
841	Hjerming, Den., G 9
428	Hjerting, Den., K 3
2758	Hjo, Sweden, N 12
11126	Hjörring, Denmark, B 10
.....	Hjortdal, Denmark, D 8
.....	Hjortshöj, Denmark, H 12
.....	Hkamti, Bur., L 22
.....	Hlaingdet, Bur., N 22
.....	Ho, Denmark, K 2
.....	Hoadley, Alberta, L 20
.....	Hoaz Safed, Iran, I 10
61500	Hobart with suburbs, Tasmania, E 7
95	Hobbema, Alberta, L 21
2987	Hobo, Col., K 9
32877	Hoboken, Belgium, K 8
6425	Hobro, Denmark, F 9
1558	Hocaba, Yuc., E 22
3424	Hochdorf, Switz., F 13
.....	Hochih, China, K 10
.....	Hochow, China, H 9
238	Höckstetten, Switz., H 10
8751	Hockenheim, Ger., N 5
1651	Hoctún, Yuc., E 22
40000	Hodeida, Yemen, N 4
185	Hodgson, Manitoba, O 14
60176	Hódmezövásárhely, Hungary, I 13
14882	Hodonin, Czech., G 9
.....	Hodsager, Denmark, H 6
.....	Hoed, Denmark, H 15
3574	Hoesselt, Belgium, M 17
43000	Hof, Germany, L 10
.....	Hofengchow, China, H 12
149	Hofsos, Iceland, A 21
30000	Hofuf, Sau. Ar., L 6
5609	Höganäs, Sweden, Q 10
.....	Högdal, Sweden, J 12
.....	Högdal, Sweden, N 9
700	Hogi, Japan, K 11
.....	Högsby, Sweden, P 14
.....	Hohensalza, see Inowroclaw, Pol.
.....	Hohen-Schönhausen, Germany, O 20
.....	Hohsien, China, K 13
20000	Hoihow, China, M 12
.....	Hoisanabad, Iran, J 14
.....	Höjer, Den., M 4
.....	Höjerup, Denmark, L 23
508	Höjsley, Denmark, F 7
.....	Hokianga, Den., F 7
.....	Hokianga, New Zealand, B 14
.....	Hokienfu, China, D 16
.....	Hoking, China, J 4
2730	Hokitika, N. Z., L 9
1400	Hokoda, Japan, L 22
.....	Hokow, Fr. In., Ch., L 7
6111	Holbeach, England, I 20
12473	Holbaek, Denmark, F 12
.....	Holberg, B. C., O 8
263	Holdfast, Sask., O 8
.....	Holdic, Argentina, C 22
1017	Hole, Norway, N 4
231	Hole, Norway, D 6
35865	Holguin, Cuba, M 20
.....	Holijsloot, Neth., B 8
.....	Holland, Ont., H 7
.....	Hollum, Neth., B 17
.....	Hollymount, Ire., I 8
.....	Hollywood, Ire., K 20
361	Holme, Denmark, H 12
.....	Holmedal, Swe., M 10
.....	Holme Lacy, England, K 12
1961	Holmestrand, Norway, M 8
200	Holmfield, Man., R 13
445	Holmsbu, Nor., D 4
.....	Holmsho, Norway, M 8
.....	Holmstrup, Den., K 18
.....	Holmsund, Sweden, I 17
.....	Holmudde, Sweden, O 18
10015	Holstebro, Denmark, G 4
1014	Holsted, Denmark, K 5
376	Holstein, Ontario, J 8
.....	Holsteinborg, Den., L 17
1403	Holsworthy, England, N 7
.....	Holt, England, H 22
3603	Holt, Norway, N 6
.....	Holt, Wales, H 11
.....	Holtaalen, Norway, J 10
3938	Holten, Neth., G 21
.....	Holtsljunga, Sweden, O 11
.....	Holwan, Iran, L 1
.....	Holwerd, Neth., B 18
.....	Holycross, Ire., M 14
10707	Holyhead, Wales, G 6
.....	Holy Mount, Ire., F 13
3423	Holywell, Wales, H 10
.....	Holywood, N. Ire., D 23
12192	Holzminden, Germany, H 6
12312	Homberg, Germany, J 6
4785	Hombourg, France, G 24
.....	Hommelvik, Norway, I 9
1069	Hompre, Belgium, P 18
4000	Homs, Libya, E 12
5000	Homs, Syr., K 11
1756	Homún, Yuc., F 22

Pop.	Place Country Index
.....	Honanfu (Loyang), China, F 14
.....	Honavalli, India, N 9
6900	Honawar, India, N 7
12424	Honda, Col., H 10
3173	Hönefoss, Norway, L 8
1320	Hongu, Japan, O 13
3008	Honiton, England, N 10
7100	Honjo, Japan, E 22
1775	Hooge, Neth., I 13
2294	Hoogeloon, Neth., J 16
15331	Hoogeveen, Neth., E 22
11219	Hoogezand, Neth., C 23
.....	Hooghalen, Neth., D 22
30000	Hooghly, India, H 21
4269	Hooglede, Belgium, L 5
2904	Hoogstraeten, Bel., J 14
.....	Hook, England, D 19
.....	Hookee, Baluchistan, R 20
2699	Hook of Holland, Netherlands, H 10
.....	Hoopstad, U.S. Afr., I 15
.....	Hoorn, Netherlands, B 16
12026	Hoorn, Netherlands, E 15
36	Hoosier, Sask., N 4
.....	Hootalinqua, Yukon, O 10
2884	Hopa, Tur., B 16
515	Hope, B. C., Q 14
.....	Hopedale, Newf., I 21
218	Hopefield, P. E.I., I 17
437	Hopefield, U.S. Afr., P 7
.....	Hopeman, Scotland, G 18
31	Hopetoun, Austl., O 7
750	Hopetown, U.S. Afr., K 13
336	Hopewell, N. S., K 17
327	Hopwell Cape, N. B., I 12
718	Hopewell Hill, N. B., J 12
.....	Hopinghsien, China, K 16
529	Hoptrup, Denmark, L 8
12	Horburg, Alberta, M 19
325	Hörby, Denmark, C 12
875	Horconcitos, Pan., P 18
.....	Horcones, Arg., C 11
34575	Hörde, Germany, I 4
440	Hördum, Denmark, E 4
.....	Horg, Norway, I 9
9372	Horgen, Switz., F 15
.....	Hörken, Sweden, M 13
.....	Horn, Switzerland, D 20
7208	Hornachos, Spain, L 9
1024	Hornbaek, Denmark, H 22
135	Hornby, Ontario, L 10
3496	Horncastle, Eng., H 19
.....	Horne, Denmark, B 10
.....	Horne, Denmark, J 3
.....	Horne, Denmark, M 11
.....	Hornefors, Sweden, I 18
1548	Hornindal, Norway, J 5
517	Hornos, Coa., F 8
4450	Hornsea, England, F 19
95524	Hornsey, England, B 21
12029	Hornu, Belgium, N 8
	Horodenka, see Gorodenka, Sov. Un.
800	Horoizum, Japan, G 14
6000	Horqueta, Paraguay, J 8
.....	Horquilla, Argentina, I 17
.....	Horsefly, B. C., M 14
.....	Horsens, Denmark, D 11
28300	Horsens, Denmark, J 9
.....	Horsey, England, I 24
5273	Horsham, Austl., P 18
13579	Horsham, England, M 19
1579	Hörsholm, Denmark, I 22
432	Horslunde, Denmark, N 16
7131	Horst, Neth., J 19
10797	Horten, Norway, M 8
.....	Hortensia, Argentina, O 16
515	Hörve, Denmark, J 17
13500	Hoshangabad, India, I 11
25925	Hoshiarpur, India, D 9
.....	Hosh Isa, Egypt, D 6
632	Hosingen, Lux., P 20
.....	Hoskot, India, N 11
81	Hosmer, B. C., P 20
3500	Hososhima, Japan, P 5
.....	Hosp, Switzerland, K 13
.....	Hosp, Switzerland, K 15
.....	Hosp, Switzerland, Q 7
277	Hospenthal, Switz., K 15
21673	Hospet, India, M 9
.....	Hospice, Switz., N 12
.....	Hospicio, Chile, B 3
700	Hospital, Ire., N 11
1970	Hostotipaquillo, Jal., L 5
.....	Hostrup, Denmark, K 3
.....	Hotagen, Sweden, H 12
50000	Hotien (Khotan), Sink., K 12
	Hotin, see Khotin, W. Sov. Un.
.....	Hötting, Ger., S 9
1963	Houdan, France, H 12
7592	Houdeng, Belgium, N 10
19078	Houeilles, France, O 9
1318	Houffalize, Belgium, P 18
15153	Houilles, France, A 3
.....	Houmar, Sp. Mor., D 6
.....	Houmt Souk, Tunisia, E 25
.....	Hounslow, England, C 19
.....	Houston, B. C., J 10
1219	Houyet, Belgium, O 14
474	Hov, Denmark, I 12
.....	Hov, Denmark, M 15
.....	Hov, Norway, L 8
.....	Hove, Denmark, F 2
54994	Hove, England, N 19
.....	Hoven, Denmark, J 4
.....	Hövik, Norway, A 4
83	Hövlbjerg, Denmark, G 10
962	Howard, Australia, J 24
630	Howick, N. Z., D 17
484	Howick, Quebec, Q 15
.....	Howland, Ont., G 14
200	Howley, Australia, B 12
.....	Howmore, Scotland, H 3
174	Hownam, Scotland, O 22
379292	Howrah, India, I 21
4032	Howth, Ire., J 23
7212	Höxter, Germany, H 6
2477	Hoya, Germany, F 6
15215	Hoyland, England, G 15
.....	Hoyün, China, K 15
17818	Hradec Králové, Czech., F 8
13359	Hrubieszów, Poland, E 17
.....	Hsingcheng, Manch., C 19
	Hsinking, see Changchun, Manch.
.....	Hsüchow, China, F 15
.....	Huaca, Ecuador, A 6
614	Huacaraje, Bolivia, E 13
.....	Huacaya, Bolivia, M 13
510	Huacaybamba, Peru, J 8
1574	Huachacalla, Bolivia, J 4
.....	Huachana, Argentina, H 13
13320	Huacho, Peru, K 7
.....	Huachos, Peru, M 11
723	Huacrachuco, Peru, I 8
4549	Huajuapan de León, Oax., K 7
1690	Hualahuises, N. L., G 15
1010	Hualane, Chile, N 3
.....	Hualcan Uco, Peru, J 7
1173	Hualgayoc, Peru, H 5
1490	Huallanca, Peru, J 8
2324	Huamachuco, Peru, H 6
.....	Huamantanga, Peru, L 8
7287	Huamantla, Tlax., H 7
757	Huambos, Peru, G 4
2049	Huamelula, Oax., N 11
1757	Huamuxtitlán, Guer., P 18
.....	Huanacache, Arg., L 7
1155	Huanay. Bol., G 4
600	Huancabamba, Peru, F 4
722	Huancane, Bolivia, J 6
2236	Huancané, Peru, O 20
72	Huancano, Peru, M 10
1500	Huancarama, Peru, N 14
8139	Huancavelica, Peru, M 11
28679	Huancayo, Peru, L 11
8000	Huanchaca, Bolivia, L 7
500	Huanchaco, Peru, I 4
811	Huandoval, Peru, I 6
2475	Huango, Michoa., N 11
4439	Huanta, Peru, M 12
122	Huantajaya, Chile, C 3
12877	Huanuco, Peru, J 9
.....	Huanuluan, Arg., B 21
1677	Huanuni, Bolivia, J 6
4690	Huaqui, Bolivia, H 3
1794	Huara, Chile C 4
.....	Huaral, Peru, L 8
12099	Huarás, Peru, J 7
1407	Huari, Bolivia, K 6
1924	Huari, Peru, J 7
.....	Huariaca, Peru, K 9
6129	Huarina, Bolivia, H 3
428	Huarmaca, Peru, G 4
.....	Huarmey, Peru, J 6
.....	Huascan, Peru, L 8
1537	Huasco, Chile, I 3
5643	Huatabampo, Son., K 13
6349	Huatusco, Ver., N 17
5779	Huauchinango. Pueb., G 7
521	Huautla, Guer., Q 14
2158	Huautla, Hid., E 5
9589	Huautla Jiménez, Oax., K 9
1568	Huaxolotitlán, Oax., N 7
629	Huayco, Bolivia, M 11
1246	Huaylas, Peru, I 6
811	Huayllate, Peru, N 15
606	Huayopata, Peru, M 15
718	Huaytará, Peru, N 11
426	Hubbards, N. S., N 13
855	Huberdeau, Quebec, N 13
.....	Hubert, B. C., J 9
89982	Hubli, India, M 8
60000	Huchow, China, H 19
17338	Hucknall Torkard, Eng., H 17
113467	Huddersfield, Eng., G 14
787	Huddinge, Sweden, R 21
.....	Huderup, Denmark, G 5
7321	Hudiksvall, Sweden, K 15
.....	Hudin, Br. Som., J 20
731	Hudson, Quebec, P 14
547	Hudson Bay Jc., Sask., L 11
.....	Hudson Hope, B. C., G 14
34000	Hué, Fr. In. Ch., O 9
5469	Huedin, E. Rom., I 16
2642	Huehuetán, Chia., P 17
9513	Huehuetenango, Guat., E 3
1356	Huehuetla, Hid., F 7
205	Huehuetlán, S. L. P., L 17
3914	Huejotzingo, Pueb., I 6
1855	Huejucar, Jal., J 7
2843	Huejutla, Hid., E 6
1248	Huelgoat, France, H 2
7739	Huelma, Spain, N 12
56427	Huelva, Spain, N 7
216	Huentelauquén, Chile, L 3
13030	Huércal-Overa, Spain, N 14
.....	Huergo, Argentina, P 14
865	Huesa, Spain, G 16
17730	Huesca, Spain, E 17
11451	Huéscar, Spain, M 14
5607	Huetamo de Núñez, Michoa., O 13
2779	Huete, Spain, I 14
1116	Hueypoxtla, Méx., G 5
.....	Huftadrum, Iran, J 15
1823	Hughenden, Australia, G 19
.....	Huguesburg, Neth. Gu., B 9
1839	Huichapan, Hid., F 4
500	Huigra, Ecuador, D 4
.....	Huiltepec, Oax., M 8
2496	Huimanguillo, Tab., K 15
1301	Huimilpan, Quer., M 14
.....	Huinca Renancó, Arg., N 12
.....	Huisduinen, Neth., D 13
5271	Huissen, Neth., H 19
2092	Huitzo, Oax., L 9
3759	Huitzuco, Guer., P 16
6828	Huixtla, Chia., P 16
7692	Huizen, Neth., G 16
.....	Huj, Palestine, O 4
50000	Hukow, China, I 17
1927	Hulhal, Palestine, O 8
.....	Hulilan, Iran, H 3
313366	Hull, England, F 18
32947	Hull, Quebec, P 10
.....	Hulle, I. E. A., L 7
3924	Hulst, Neth., K 10, Q 6
1929	Hultsfred, Sweden, O 14
526	Humahuaca, Arg., E 10
1138	Humansdorp, U.S. Afr., Q 14
44	Humapalca, Chile, A 4
358	Humay, Peru, N 10
.....	Humaytá, Brazil, G 3
2963	Humberstone, Ont., O 12
1745	Humboldt, Sask., M 8
477	Humlebaek, Denmark, I 23
478	Humlum, Denmark, F 4
.....	Hummarah, Syria, C 16
.....	Hummenne, Slov., N 25
6680	Humocaro Bajo, Ven., D 8
330	Humphrey, N. B., H 12
38000	Hunchun, Manch., B 25
.....	Hundstrup, Den., D 5
.....	Hune, Denmark, C 9
5000	Huneodoara, Romania, J 16
2483	Hünfeld, Germany, K 7
80	Hungerford, Australia, K 18
17898	Hunghae, Kor., C 23
.....	Hung-Hea, Fr. In. Ch., L 7
.....	Hunin, Palestine, E 12
.....	Hunker, Yukon, K 5
.....	Hunmanby, Eng., E 18
3131	Hunstanton, England, H 21
180	Hunter River, P. E. I., G 15
640	Hunterville, N. Z., H 18
179	Huntingdon, B. C., P 5
4108	Huntingdon, Eng., J 19
1952	Huntingdon, Que., R 14
386	Huntley, Ont., E 21
2090	Huntly, N. Z., E 18
4579	Huntly, Scot., G 21
135	Hunts Point, N. S., P 11
2770	Huntsville, Ontario, E 12
4719	Hunucmá, Yuc., E 21
.....	Hunyüan, China, D 14
.....	Hunza, India, A 8
.....	Hunzari, Afg., I 20
.....	Hurlford, Scotland, O 14
.....	Huron, Ont., K 6
.....	Hursley, England, M 16
.....	Hurso, Eth., I 12
.....	Hurum, Norway, C 4
.....	Husainabad, Iran, M 7
.....	Husby, Denmark, H 2
.....	Husby, Denmark, L 10
807	Husby, Sweden, L 14
15953	Husi, Romania, I 22
.....	Husiatyn, see Gusyatin, Sov. Un.
8156	Huskvarna, Sweden, O 12
.....	Hussan Gelan, Afg., J 18
116	Hussar, Alberta, N 22
.....	Husseinabad, Iran, J 8
9962	Husum, Germany, B 6
	Huszt, see Khust, W. Sov. Un.
.....	Hutados, Col., E 8
.....	Hutchinson, U.S. Afr., N 12
.....	Hutshiku, Yukon, N 7
4127	Huttwil, Switz., G 11
1076	Hüttwilen, Switz., C 16
14261	Huy, Belgium, N 16
.....	Huyamampa, Arg., I 12
299	Hvalps, Denmark, F 7
676	Hvalso, Denmark, K 19
.....	Hvetlanda, Sweden, O 13
767	Hvidbjerg, Denmark, F 4
119	Hvidding, Denmark, L 4
.....	Hvilsager, Denmark, G 12
262	Hvitsten, Norway, C 5
.....	Hwachow, China, F 11
.....	Hwaianfu, China, G 18
40000	Hwaining (Anking), China, H 17
.....	Hwaiyüan, China, E 11
30000	Hwangchow, China, H 15
6000	Hwangshihkang, Chn., H 16
.....	Hwangyen, Chn., I 20
.....	Hwanhsien, Chn., E 10
.....	Hwayüan, China, H 15
.....	Hweichang, China J 16
.....	Hweichow, Chn., H 18
.....	Hweilichow, China, J 5
.....	Hwochow, China, E 13
32066	Hyde, England, G 13
200	Hyde, N. Z., P 8
302	Hyde Park Jc., Ont., N 6
96021	Hyderabad, India, G 1
739159	Hyderabad, India, L 11
3547	Hydra, Greece, P 18
22967	Hyères, France, P 22
.....	Hygum, Denmark, L 6
.....	Hyllebjerg, Denmark, E 7
.....	Hyllested, Den., H 15
388	Hyllinge, Denmark, J 20
.....	Hynish, Scotland, K 4
8397	Hythe, England, M 23
9394	Hyvinkaa, Fin., F 4

I

Pop.	Place Country Index
104640	Iasi, Rom., H 22
.....	Iat, Iran, J 9
386907	Ibadan and Suburbs, Nigeria, J 8
27448	Ibagué, Col., I 9
13798	Ibarra, Ecuador, B 6
.....	Ibbenbüren, Germany, G 4
.....	Ibdar, Transjordan, H 15
.....	Iberg, Switz., G 16
3454	Iberville, Quebec, Q 16
.....	Ibi, Nig., J 10
.....	Ibitimi, Paraguay, O 8
5377	Ibitinga, Brazil, M 14
9644	Ibiza, Sp., K 20
.....	Ibn Ibrak, Palestine, L 6
4541	Ibo, Moz., N 22
1100	Ibshan, Egypt, C 13
.....	Ibshwai, Egypt, L 9
21437	Ica, Peru, N 11
.....	Icano, Argentina, J 10
.....	Icatú, Brazil, E 18
	Icel, see Mersin, Tur.
.....	Ich, Alg., H 12
112000	Ichang, China, H 13
.....	Ichang Hun, China, J 14
5064	Iche (Silifke), Tur., I 8
.....	Ichibo, Japan, L 15
1200	Ichiku, Japan, Q 2
2000	Ichinohe, Japan, D 24
2000	Ichinomiya, Japan, L 15
42229	Ichinomiya, Japan, M 21
.....	Ichinoseki, Japan, F 24
2158	Ichoca, Bolivia, I 6
708	Ichocán, Peru, H 6
.....	Ichohapuram, India, K 18
.....	Ichow, China, F 18
5302	Ichteghem, Belgium, L 4
167	Ichuña, Peru, P 19
2326	Icla, Bolivia, K 11
.....	Ida, Morocco, L 2
.....	Ida (Nitif), Morocco, K 5
.....	Idabo, Eth., I 9
3845	Idanha-a-Nova, Port., I 7
.....	Idar, India, H 6
.....	Ideles, Algeria, R 20
1300	Idhna, Palestine, O 7
.....	Idiru, China, D 2
.....	Idlib, Syria, J 11
.....	Idom, Denmark, G 3
5041	Idria, Italy, C 14
.....	Iduagor, Morocco, I 2
.....	Idutywa U.S. Afr., O 18
15759	Iesi, It., F 12
.....	Ifag, Eth., F 7
.....	Ifenik, Algeria, P 21
24	Iffley, Austl., F 18
300	Ifni, Morocco, K 1
.....	Ifras, Morocco, I 2
.....	Iftoa, I. E. A., J 11
.....	Igarapava, Brazil, M 14
.....	Igarapé-Miry, Brazil, E 14
.....	Igatpuri, India, J 7
.....	Igdir, Iran, B 3
11651	Iglesias, Italy, L 3
.....	Igli, Algeria, J 10
.....	Igli, Morocco, J 4
.....	Ignacio, Cuba, L 17
1607	Ignacio Allende, Dur., O 22
851	Ignaly, France, O 15
12756	Iguala, Guer., P 16
15603	Igualada, Spain, F 19
.....	Iguape, Brazil, O 14
.....	Iguarassú, Brazil, H 25
.....	Iguassu, Brazil, N 18
7456	Iguatú, Brazil, G 22
.....	Iguembe, Bolivia, L 12
18000	Iida, Japan, H 17
13500	Iida, Japan, L 17
555	I'Isle, Fr., J 17
1514	Ijlst, Neth., D 17
.....	Ijmuiden, Neth., F 12
.....	Ijseir, Palestine, E 13
5837	Ijsselmonde, Neth., H 12
2840	Ijsselmuiden, Neth., E 18
4849	Ijsselstein, Neth., H 14
2935	Ijzendijke, Neth., Q 2
3070	Ikaalinen, Fin., E 3
1607	Ikast, Den., H 7
880	Iksal, Palestine, H 10
2918	Ikuno, Japan, L 12
1559	Ilabaya, Bolivia, G 3
350	Ilderton, Ontario, N 6
.....	Ilebo, Bel. Cong., L 14
10950	Iletsk, Sov. Un., K 23
.....	Iletskii Gorodek, Sov. Un., K 21
131046	Ilford, England, L 20
9174	Ilfracombe, England, M 7
11616	Ilhavo, Portugal, H 5
15707	Ilhéos, Brazil, J 22
.....	Iliang, China, K 6
.....	Ilidja, Tur., D 16
.....	Iligh, Morocco, K 2
42253	Iliisk, Sov. Un. Asia, J 11
.....	Ilinskaya, Sov. Un., O 13
32809	Ilkeston, England, H 16
.....	Ilkhan, Iran, B 3
6085	Illapel, Chile, L 3
771	Illecas, Uruguay, M 21
1853	Illescas, Spain, I 12
.....	Illig, Som., K 23
.....	Illimani, Bolivia, C 5
3724	Illnau, Switz., D 16
.....	Ilmola, Fin., E 3
.....	Ilo, Nigeria, I 8
1043	Ilo, Peru, Q 17
.....	Ilom, Guatemala, E 3
47590	Ilorin, Nigeria, J 8
2263	Ilpendam, Netherlands, A 6
.....	Ilża, Pol., E 14
900	Imabetsu, Japan, B 23
2412	Imaidzunti, Japan, F 24
.....	Imaja, Transjordan, I 16
7000	Imari, Japan, M 3
.....	Imaruhy, Brazil, P 13
.....	Imbabo, I. E. A., I 7
43730	Imbari, Japan, M 8
.....	Imbituba, Brazil, P 13
.....	Imgrad, Morocco, I 2
.....	Imi, Eth., M 13
1300	Imi, Japan, M 6
.....	Imias, Cuba, O 24
.....	Imilac, Chile, F 5
.....	Imi Ougadir, Morocco, L 3
.....	Immensee, Switz., G 14
5614	Immenstadt, Germany, R 7
	Imoharu, see Imbari, Japan
15497	Imola, Italy, E 9
.....	Imotski, Yugo., L 9
9900	Impendhle, U. S. Afr., L 19
.....	Imperial, Chile, Q 3
320	Imperial, Sask., O 8
1036	Imperoyal, N. S., N 15
85804	Imphal (Manipur), India, L 19
.....	Imterhadjen, Algeria, R 20
.....	Ina, Japan, K 3
.....	Ina, Japan, L 17
.....	Inangahua Jc., N. Z., K 11
4000	Inatori, Japan, N 19
12176	Inca, Spain, J 21
3965	Inch, Scotland, Q 12
.....	Inchigeelagh, Ire., P 7
.....	Inchnadamph, Scot., E 12
102473	Inchon (Jinsen), Kor., D 24
507	Inchture, Scot., K 19
.....	Indal, Sweden, J 15
.....	Indarab, Afg., F 23
851	Inde, Dur., M 20
2114	Independencia, Bolivia, I 7
.....	Independencia, Brazil, G 21
116	Independencia, Chia., N 18
.....	Inderöen, Norway, H 10
.....	Indiana, Brazil, N 12
225	Indian Harbour, N. S., N 14
1349	Indian Head, Sask., P 9
.....	Indian River, Yukon, K 3
203695	Indore, India, I 9
.....	Indslev, Denmark, K 10
.....	Indviken, Norway, K 5
5085	Inebolu, Tur., A 8
.....	Ine-göl, Tur., F 3
9953	Infantes, Spain, K 13
.....	Infiesto, Spain, C 10
.....	Ingarö, Sweden, Q 23
.....	Ingavi, Bolivia, H 4
7637	Ingelmunster, Bel., M 5
.....	Ingeniero Luiggi, Arg., O 12
5782	Ingersoll, Ontario, N 7
.....	Inghar, Algeria, O 15
.....	Ingledoun, Australia, H 17
631	Inglewood, Austl., L 22
1280	Inglewood, N. Z., G 16
428	Inglewood, Ontario, K 10
.....	Ingoie, India, R 19
29000	Ingolstadt, Germany, O 9
360	Ingonish, N. S., F 23
1955	Ingreő Taoeri, Bol., L 12
10563	Inhambane, Moz., P 19
5093	Inis (Ennis), Ire., L 8
.....	Inishannon, Ire., Q 10
.....	Inishcrone, Ire., F 8
.....	Inishkeen, Ire., G 20
.....	Inistioge, Ire., N 18
3869	Injesu, Tur., F 10
326	Inkerman, Ontario, F 23
.....	Inlalen, Algeria, N 20
8	Inmaculada, Son., E 10
336	Innerkip, Ont., M 7
3747	Innerleithen, Scotland, N 20
1069	Innertkirchen, Switz., J 13
.....	Innerwick, Scot., K 15
684	Innerwick, Scotland, M 23
.....	Innichen, Italy, B 11
.....	Innien, Germany, C 7
1223	Innisfail, Alberta, M 20
253	Innisfree, Alberta, K 22
215	Innisville, Ontario, F 20
61072	Innsbruck, Aus., H 3
.....	Inongo, Bel. Cong., L 14
30862	Inowroclaw, Pol., D 11
2000	Inquisivi, Bol., I 6
2091	Ins, Switzerland, H 7
29	Insalah, Algeria, O 15
.....	Insch, Scotland, H 22
1249	Insh, Scotland, I 16
.....	Inshas, Egypt, G 15
.....	Insjön, Sweden, L 13
40000	Insterburg, W. Sov. Un., B 15
3732	Interlaken, Switz., J 11
.....	Intiyaco, Argentina, J 17
893	Intragna, Switz., N 15
.....	Inver, Ire., D 12
.....	Inver, Scotland, F 16
.....	Inver, Scotland, K 18
.....	Inverallochy, Scot., G 24
.....	Inveramsay, Scot., H 22
.....	Inveran, Scotland, F 14
989	Inveraray, Scotland, L 12
773	Inverarity, Scotland, K 21
.....	Inverarnan, Scotland, L 13
.....	Invercannich, Scot., H 13
22600	Invercargill, N. Z., Q 5
.....	Invercauld, Scotland, K 18
.....	Inverchaolain, Scot., M 12
5305	Inverell, Australia, L 22
.....	Invergarry, Scotland, I 13
.....	Invergowrie, Scot., K 20
.....	Inverie, Scotland, I 11
.....	Inverinate, Scot., H 10
1206	Inverkeillor, Scot., K 22
4968	Inverkeithing, Scot., M 19
640	Inverkeithny, Scot., G 21
207	Invermay, Sask., N 10
.....	Invermoriston, Scot., H 15
157	Inverness, B. C., M 21
2975	Inverness, N. S., J 7
212	Inverness, Quebec, H 21
22582	Inverness, Scotland, H 15
.....	Inverness Jc., N. S., J 21
.....	Inveroran, Scot., K 13
.....	Inversanda, Scot., J 11
.....	Invershiel, Scotland, H 10
.....	Invershin, Scotland, F 14
.....	Inversnaid, Scotland, L 13
.....	Inverugie, Scot., G 24
4415	Inverurie, Scotland, H 22
48	Inwood, Ontario, O 4
.....	In Yagguin, Algeria, L 21
5887	Inza, Col., K 7
.....	Inza, Sov. Un., J 17
.....	Inzelman Tikhsin (Wells), Alg., Q 21
20800	Ioannina, Grc., O 14
77	Iona. Ontario, O 6
.....	Ioshkar-Ola, Sov. Un., H 17
493	Ipahuaza, Bolivia, N 13
6428	Ipala, Guat., G 6
7452	Ipameri, Brazil, L 14
8343	Ipiales. Col., M 4
.....	Ipoh, Fed. Malay States, O 20
22498	Ipswich, Australia, K 23
87557	Ipswich, England, K 23
5042	Ipú, Brazil, F 21
.....	Ipueiras, Brazil, F 20
38094	Iquique, Chile, C 3
34231	Iquitos, Peru, E 13
.....	Iracema, West Brazil, K 22
666	Iracoubo, Fr. Guiana, B 11
.....	Iraj, Iran, I 9
.....	Iraola, Argentina, P 16
2917	Irapa, Ven., C 20
32377	Irapuato, Guan., M 11
.....	Irara, Brazil, I 22
.....	Iraty, Brazil, O 12
.....	Irbid, Palestine, H 12
2500	Irbid, Transjordan, I 15
.....	Iredame, Som., H 22
21335	Iri, Kor., E 24
965	Iridere, Bul., M 20
671	Irigoyen, Arg., L 16
1000	Iriki, Japan, Q 2
39	Irimbo, Michoa., N 14
99	Iriona, Honduras, D 13
326	Irish Cove, N. S., I 22
213	Irishtown, N. B., H 12
243380	Irkutsk, Sov. Un. Asia, H 15
84	Irolo, Hid., G 6
227	Iron Mines, N. S., I 21
310	Ironside, Quebec, P 10
956	Iroquois, Ontario, G 23
1302	Iroquois Falls, Ont., P 24
172	Irricana, Alberta, N 21
14368	Irún, Spain, C 15
700	Irupana, Bolivia, H 6
.....	Irupana ó Peña de Guarayo, Bolivia, D 6
240	Irvine, Alberta, O 24
8318	Irvine, Scotland, O 14
147	Irvine Bank, Austl., E 19
.....	Irvinestown, N. Ire., E 15
528	Isaac's Harbor, N. S., L 20
1000	Isaba, Spain, D 16
2842	Isabela, Cuba, H 12
4342	Isaccea, Rom., J 23
.....	Isajab, Baluchistan, Q 18
.....	Isakhel, India, C 5
1107	Iscayachi, Bolivia, M 10
.....	Isca Yacu, Arg., H 11
	Ischl, Aus., H 6
.....	Iscia Baidoa, Som., Q 15
7985	Iscuande, Col., K 4
14738	Iseghem, Belgium, L 6
482	Iseltwald, Switz., J 12
.....	Isenhagen, Ger., F 8
538	Isenthal, Switz., I 15
32000	Iserlohn, Germany, I 4
7469	Isernia, Italy, I 14
204598	Isfahán, Iran, I 7
.....	Isgeder, Morocco, K 1
.....	Is Heer, Netherlands, J 8
11506	Ishim, Sov. Un. Asia, G 11
.....	Ishimachi, Japan, K 22
9000	Ishioka, Japan, L 21
.....	Ishitoritani, Japan, E 24
.....	Ishkashim, Afg., E 25
15000	Ishmomaki, Japan, G 24
1832	Isigny, France, G 7
2038	Isili, Italy, L 4
248	Isis, Australia, J 23
323	Isisford, Austl., I 19
19277	Iskenderun (Alexandrette), Tur., I 11
10698	Iskilip, Tur., C 9
9567	Isla Cristina, Spain, N 7
9400	Islamabad, India, B 8
4884	Isla Mala, Uruguay, N 18
.....	Islamgarh, India, E 4
.....	Islamkot, India, H 3
.....	Islanderabad, Iran, K 9
.....	Island Falls Jc., Ont., O 23
2000	Isla Ombú Paraguay, Q 6
.....	Isla Sacá, Paraguay, Q 9
2490	Isla Sarandi, Uruguay, F 17
.....	Isla Verde, Argentina, M 14
132	Islay, Alberta, K 23
205	Isle aux Coudres, Que., I 23
425	Isle Maligne, Que., E 20
.....	Isle of Whitehorn, Scot., R 15
.....	Isleworth, England, C 19
.....	Islikon, Switz., C 16
2500	Islington, Ont., L 11
26123	Ismail, W. Sov. Un., J 24
.....	Ismailabad, Iran, M 11
15507	Ismailia, Egypt, F 22
2645	Ismaning, Germany, Q 9
.....	Isment, Egypt, N 12
.....	Ismil, Tur., G 7
.....	Isna, Egypt, P 23
.....	Isnak, Iran, H 12
5932	Isola, Italy, D 13
708	Isone, Switz., O 17
18433	Isparta, Tur., G 5
1198	Ispir, Tur., D 16
.....	Issehoved, Den., I 13
550	Issigeac, France, N 10
6037	Issoire, France, M 16
11684	Issoudun, France, J 13
1989	Is-sur-Tille, France, J 19
44091	Issy-les-Moulineaux, Fr., B 4
.....	Istaka, Iran, P 15
793949	Istanbul (Constantinople), Tur., B 3
1050000	Istanbul and Suburbs, Tur., B 3
.....	Istanoz, Tur., H 4
1601	Istmina, Col., I 6
5547	Istres, France, P 19
30252	Itá, Paraguay, N 7
.....	Itabaianinha, Brazil, I 23
8185	Itabayanna, Brazil, G 24
.....	Itaberaba, Brazil, I 20
.....	Itabo, Cuba, H 10
15868	Itabuna (Tabocas), Brazil, J 21
.....	Itacoatiara, Brazil, F 7
10000	Itacurubi del Rosario, Paraguay, M 8
.....	Itaituba, Brazil, F 9
13367	Itajahy, Brazil, P 14
14940	Itajubá, Brazil, N 16
.....	Itala, Som., R 18
5761	Italaque, Bolivia, G 2
.....	Italo, Argentina, N 13
.....	Itambé, Brazil, G 25
9000	Itapé, Paraguay, O 8
.....	Itapebi, Uruguay, G 16
.....	Itapecerica, Brazil, M 16
6792	Itaperuna, Brazil, M 19
13007	Itapetininga, Brazil, N 14
.....	Itapipoca, Brazil, F 21
7975	Itapira, Brazil, N 15
.....	Itaporanga, Brazil, I 23
.....	Itaporanga, Brazil, N 13
.....	Itapura, Brazil, M 12
.....	Itaquy, Brazil, P 8
5150	Itarare, Brazil, N 13
.....	Itarsi, India, I 11
613	Itati, Argentina, I 20
5244	Itatuba, Brazil, G 3
9000	Itaugua, Paraguay, N 7
1231	Iteghem, Belgium, R 11
.....	Itfu, Egypt, N 20
3265	Ithake, Grc., P 14
.....	Itima, Algeria, E 15
5300	Itoigawa, Japan, I 18
5309	Itri, Italy, J 13
2854	Ituango, Col., G 8
.....	Ituassú, Brazil, J 20
406	Ituna, Sask., O 10
619	Itundujía. Oax., M 7
.....	Itung, Manch., B 22
.....	Iturbe, Argentina, E 20
.....	Iturbide, Camp., H 21
457	Iturbide, S. L. P., J 13
1705	Iturbide, Tab., J 16
.....	Ituverava, Brazil, M 14
21000	Itzehoe, Germany, D 7
164	Ivanhoe, Australia, N 19
.....	Ivanjica, Yugo., L 13
.....	Ivankov, W. Sov. Un., E 24
285069	Ivanovo Sov. Un., H 13
.....	Iveran, Scot., F 14
.....	Ivershin, Scot., F 14
948	Ivo, Bolivia, L 13
.....	Ivohibe, Madag., P 23
188	Ivón, Bolivia, C 7
5614	Ivrea, Italy, D 2
44859	Ivry-sur-Seine, France, B 5
3000	Iwafune, Japan, G 21
10000	Iwakuni, Japan, M 7
1200	Iwamatsu, Japan, O 7
2000	Iwanai, Japan, F 12
.....	Iwanchow, China, D 18
5000	Iwanuma, Japan, H 23
.....	Iwatate, Japan, C 22
5800	Iwatsuki, Japan, L 20
2472	Ixcaquixtla, Pueb., J 7
1395	Ixhuata, Oax., N 13
.....	Ixhuatlan, Ver., F 7
826	Ixiamas, Bolivia, E 4
2080	Ixmiquilpan, Hid., F 5
7069	Ixtépexi, Oax., L 9
2845	Ixtián, Michoa., M 9
1301	Ixtlahuaca, Mex., H 4
5780	Ixtlan del Río, Nay., L 4
1648	Izabal, Guat., E 7
7709	Izalco, Salvador, H 6
5552	Izamal, Yuc., E 22
.....	Izashiki, Japan, R 3
412	Izcuchaca. Peru, M 11
175740	Izhevsk, Sov. Un., H 20
184652	Izmir (Smyrna), Tur., F 1
.....	Izmit, Tur., C 4
6391	Iznalloz, Spain, N 12
3749	Izozog, Bolivia, K 14
7500	Izúcar de Matamoros, Pueb., J 6
7562	Izughara, Japan, K 2
5000	Izumozaki, Japan, H 19
5200	Izushi, Japan, K 12
13000	Izyum, Sov. Un., L 10

J

Pop.	Place Country Index
33855	Jablonec, Czech., F 8
1166	Jacala, Hid., E 5
960	Jachal, Argentina, K 6
.....	Jackson, N. Z., L 10
120	Jackson's Point. Ont., I 12
10000	Jacmel, Haiti, J 13
10800	Jacobabad, India, E 2
.....	Jacobina, Brazil, I 20
.....	Jacobsberg, Sweden, Q 20
763	Jacobsdal, U. S. Afr., K 14
5750	Jacona, Michoa., N 9
526	Jacquet River, N. B., A 9
.....	Jacury, Brazil, E 12
.....	Jacy Paraná, Brazil, H 2
510	Jaén, Peru, G 5
54631	Jaén, Spain, M 12
.....	Jaevnaker, Norway, L 9
6000	Jafarabad, India, J 4
.....	Jafarabad, Iran, J 11
71000	Jaffa, Palestine, L 5
45708	Jaffna, Cey., P 13
189	Jaffray, B. C., Q 20
.....	Jaflabad, Iran, E 13
.....	Jagdalik, Afg., G 23
.....	Jagdalpur, India, K 15
4087	Jagersfontein, U. S. Afr., K 14
.....	Jagua, Col., K 8
10747	Jaguarão, Brazil, R 10
.....	Jaguaribe-Mirim, Brazil, G 22
2857	Jagueyal, Cuba, K 15
2629	Jaguey Grande, Cuba, I 9
.....	Jahanabad, India, G 18
.....	Jahital, India, A 8
.....	Jaicós, Brazil, G 20
.....	Jaidar, Iran, I 3
.....	Jaintiapur, India, G 25
175810	Jaipur, India, F 9
7000	Jaisalmer, India, F 4
7515	Jajce, Yugo., K 10
.....	Jajpur, India, J 20
.....	Jaju, India, F 11
.....	Jakhau, India, H 2
.....	Jalaca, Bolivia, M 5
3000	Jalalabad, Afg., G 24
7696	Jalapa, Guat., F 5
.....	Jalapa, Nicaragua, H 12
3081	Jalapa, Oax., N 11
1114	Jalapa, Tab., K 16
39530	Jalapa, Ver., H 9
8200	Jalaun, India, G 12
.....	Jale, I. E. A., J 8
.....	Jalelo, I. E. A., G 14
.....	Jaleswar, India, I 20
34375	Jalgaon, India, J 8
.....	Jalkot, India, A 7
22408	Jalna, India, J 9
.....	Jalor, India, G 6
2374	Jalpa de Méndez, Tab., K 15
9700	Jalpaiguri, India, F 22
1389	Jalpan, Quer., L 16
.....	Jalrez, Afghanistan, G 22
4451	Jaltipan, Ver., K 12
145	Jalud, Palestine, L 10
.....	Jalzan, Iran, K 5
.....	Jam, Iran, O 7
.....	Jama, Ecuador, B 2
1350	Jamaica, Cuba, O 23
.....	Jamaike, Neth. Gu., C 10
30346	Jamalpur, India, G 19
23077	Jamalpur, India, G 23
.....	Jamarj, Afg., C 24
.....	Jamba el Hammam, Morocco, F 8
4933	Jambaló, Col., K 7
.....	Jamberai, India, B 5
7968	Jambes, Belgium, N 14
27400	Jambol, Bul., L 21
1393	Jamestown, Australia, N 16
.....	Jamestown, Ire., G 13
.....	Jamestown, Scot., M 14
.....	Jamha, Transjordan, I 15
2129	Jamiltepec, Oax., N 7
64300	Jamkhandi, India, L 8
38613	Jammu, India, C 8
50000	Jamnagar, India, I 3
.....	Jamner, India, J 8
.....	Jamrood, Afg., I 22
.....	Jamui, India, G 19
1718	Jamundi, Col., J 6
.....	Janakpur, India, H 15

Pop. Place Country Index
..... Jandinga, Cuba, M 21
..... Jangas, Peru, J 7
..... Janghyn, Tur., D 10
Janica, see Giannitsa, Grc.
..... Janitca, Greece, E 8
1600 Janjira, India, K 6
..... Jan Jumeh, Afg., E 19
..... Jankoi, Sov. Un., O 8
..... Janów, Poland, D 16
..... Janów, Poland, F 16
181 Jansen, Sask., N 8
1355 Jansenville, U. S. Afr., P 14
5961 Januaria, Brazil, K 17
1137 Janville, France, I 13
4103 Janzé, France, I 7
..... Jaochow, China, I 17
..... Jaoz, Afg., H 18
..... Japaratuba, Brazil, I 23
521 Jaqui, Peru, O 12
..... Jaragua, Brazil, K 13
2024 Jaraicejo, Spain, J 9
5325 Jaral, Guan., M 12
2158 Jarandilla, Spain, I 10
15000 Jardim, Brazil, G 21
..... Jardin, Col., H 8
..... Jarlsberg, Nor., E 3
3880 Jarnac, France, L 9
..... Jarocin, Pol., E 10
..... Jaronu, Cuba, K 17
22330 Jaroslaw, Poland, F 16
..... Jarrillas, Argentina, M 9
56 Jarrow, Alberta, K 22
32018 Jarrow, Eng., C 15
..... Jarsughat, Tur., H 10
591 Jarvis, Ontario, O 10
1600 Jashpurnagar, India, I 17
Jasina, see Körosmezö, Hung.
..... Jask, Iran, Q 12
850 Jasper, Alberta, L 17
..... Jasrasar, India, F 7
..... Jasrota, India, C 9
..... Jassa, Brazil, C 12
Jassy, see Iasi, Rom.
..... Jaszapati, Hung., H 13
..... Jászárokszállás, Hung., R 22
29874 Jászbereny, Hung., H 13
..... Jaszuny, W. Sov. Un., B 18
..... Jatahy, Brazil, L 12
..... Jath, India, L 8
7409 Jatibonico, Cuba, K 14
14148 Játiva, Spain, K 17
15796 Jatoba do Tacaratu, Brazil, H 22
1406 Jauche, Belgium, M 14
..... Jauco, Cuba, O 25
8000 Jauf, Sau. Ar., J 4
8276 Jauja, Peru, L 11
1275 Jaumave, Tam., I 16
745 Jaun, Switzerland, K 8
..... Java, Sask., P 5
6136 Jávea, Spain, K 18
..... Jawad, India, H 8
..... Jawhar, India, J 6
..... Jaxmorian, Iran, P 13
3413 Jayanca, Peru, G 3
..... Jaygah, Afg., K 20
..... Jaygarh, India, L 6
..... Jaytena, Brazil, F 4
679 Jazpampa, Chile, C 3
..... Jeba, Palestine, H 7
1372 Jeba, Palestine, J 10
..... Jeba, Palestine, M 10
..... Jeba, Palestine, N 8
..... Jebata, Palestine, H 9
..... Jebba, Nig., J 8
..... Jebda, Sp. Mor., D 9
..... Jeb Hadireh, Syria, F 12
..... Jebin, Transjordan, K 15
337 Jebjerg, Denmark, F 6
4110 Jedburgh, Scot., O 22
..... Jeddore Oyster Pond, N. S. M 16
..... Jedireh, Palestine, M 9
12835 Jedrzejów, Poland, F 13
..... Jedway, B. C., L 5
..... Jeeramungup, Austl., N 6
..... Jefferu, Iran, I 11
..... Jegerup, Denmark, L 7
..... Jehellama, Tunisia, D 24
..... Jehlam, India, C 7
Jehol, see Chengte, Manch.
327 Jeida, Palestine, H 9
5656 Jekabpils, W. Sov. Un., A 19
..... Jelamel, Palestine, J 7
..... Jelbon, Palestine, J 11
33048 Jelgava, W. Sov. Un., A 17
1009 Jellina, Denmark, J 8
..... Jelok Anson, Fed. Mal. States, P 20
..... Jelsa, Norway, M 4
..... Jelstrup, Denmark, C 9
..... Jelul, Transjordan, N 15
..... Jemala, Transjordan, K 15
14573 Jemappes, Belgium, N 9
2209 Jemelle, Belgium, O 16
3711 Jemeppe, Belgium, N 13
13725 Jemeppe, Belgium, N 17
125 Jemseg, N. B., I 8
57000 Jena, Germany, K 9
6774 Jenesano, Col., H 12
..... Jengidsha, Iran, E 3
..... Jenhwai, China, I 8
..... Jenin, Transjordan, I 14
2696 Jenin, Palestine, J 10
27 Jenner, Alberta, N 23
799 Jeparit, Australia, O 17
13403 Jequié, Brazil, J 21
..... Jerablus, Tur., H 13
..... Jerahi (Wells), Alg., F 21
2512 Jerécuaro, Guan., M 14
..... Jereh, Iran, M 7
12000 Jeremie, Haiti, I 11
8834 Jeremoabo, Braz., H 22
7813 Jerez, Zac., J 7
89525 Jerez de la Frontera, Sp., O 9
16154 Jerez de los Caballeros, Spain, L 8
..... Jerfsö, Sweden, K 14
430 Jericho, Australia, H 20
1029 Jericho, Palestine, M 12
18949 Jerico, Col., H 8
4922 Jerico, Col., H 14
700 Jerilderie, Austl., O 19
..... Jerm, Afg., E 24
..... Jernved, Den., K 5
..... Jeronimo, Oax., M 12
..... Jerruck, India, G 1
263 Jerseyville, Ontario, M 10
..... Jersie, Denmark, K 21
..... Jerslev, Denmark, C 11
125000 Jerusalem, Palestine, N 10
..... Jesmond, B. C., N 13
4745 Jesselton, B. N. B., G 5
..... Jessica, B. C., Q 14
8300 Jessore, India, H 22
..... Jesuitas, Par., D 4
1401 Jesús, Peru, H 5
2308 Jesus de Machaca, Bol., H 3
..... Jesus Maria, Arg., K 11
15294 Jesus Maria, Col., H 11
10000 Jesús y Trinidad, Paraguay, R 10
22973 Jetpur, India, I 3
..... Jetsmark, Denmark, D 9
21307 Jette, Belgium, M 11
6042 Jever, Germany, D 5

Pop. Place Country Index
..... Jeypore, India, K 16
..... Jezazi, Transjordan, K 15
..... Jezierna, W. Sov. Un., F 19
..... Jezire-Ibn-Omar, Tur., H 17
Jeznas, W. Sov. Un., B 17
3400 Jhabua, India, I 7
8000 Jhalrapatan, India, H 9
36035 Jhang-Maghiana, India, D 6
66432 Jhánsi, India, G 11
2540 Jhow, Baluchistan, Q 20
..... Jibacoa, Cuba, H 7
..... Jibaro, Cuba, K 14
..... Jibbari, Baluchistan, O 20
..... Jibia, Palestine, L 9
..... Jicaco, Nicaragua, H 11
1886 Jicayan, Oax., N 7
11034 Jičín, Czech., F 8
25000 Jidda, Sau. Ar., L 4
13995 Jiguani, Cuba, O 20
31031 Jihlava, Czech., G 8
Jijelli, see Djidjelli.
6942 Jijona, Spain, L 16
..... Jiliulich, Palestine, M 12
..... Jiljilia, Palestine, L 9
..... Jiljulieh, Palestine, K 7
460 Jilotán, Jal., O 7
1650 Jilotepec, Méx., G 4
10123 Jimena de la Frontera, Spain, P 10
5175 Jiménez, Chih., J 20
1171 Jiménez, Coa., A 13
897 Jimzu, Palestine, M 7
8000 Jind, India, E 9
..... Jindaran, Iran, O 13
10472 Jindřichův Hradec, Czech., G 7
4820 Jinotega, Nicaragua, I 12
9107 Jinotepe, Nicaragua, K 11
22097 Jipijapa, Ecuador, C 2
7560 Jiquilpan, Michoa., M 8
..... Jisr el Allan, Syria, G 16
..... Jizanabad, Iran, F 13
..... J. M. Balmaceda, Chile, G 4
73234 João Pessoa (Parahiba), Braz., G 25
..... Joazeiro, Brazil, H 21
1715 Jobabo, Cuba, M 18
..... Jockmock, Sweden, F 17
..... Jocoli, Argentina, M 7
1915 Jocon, Honduras, F 1
14385 Jocotan, Guatemala, F 6
..... Jocotan, Salvador, G 7
..... Jocote, Nicaragua, H 11
4409 Jocotepec, Jal., M 6
12315 Jódar, Spain, M 13
94736 Jodhpur, India, G 6
..... Jodiya, India, I 3
4265 Jodoigne, Belgium, M 14
5283 Joensuu, Finland, E 7
2336 Joesuu, Sov. Un., G 5
16 Joffre, Alberta, L 21
..... Joga Pana, Afg., I 22
1109 Joggin Mines, N. S., J 12
554000 Johannesburg, U. S. Afr., F 18
5169 Johannisburg, Ger., D 24
12837 Johnstone, Scot., N 14
400 Johnstown, Ire., J 19
..... Johnstown, Ire., L 15
15312 Johore Bharo, Malay States, R 3
6610 Joigny, France, I 16
16883 Joinville, Brazil, O 13
13425 Joinville, France, B 7
3808 Joinville, France, H 20
2984 Jojutla, Morel., J 5
3500 Jolburi, Thai., P 3
12749 Joliette, Quebec, N 16
..... Jolostotitlán, Jal., L 9
Joníškis, W. Sov. Un., A 16
30918 Jönköping, Sweden, O 12
13769 Jonquiére, Quebec, E 21
1332 Jonuta, Tab., K 17
3041 Jonzac, France, M 8
291 Jordan, Ontario, M 12
632 Jordan Falls, N. S., Q 10
2900 Jorhat, India, L 21
..... Jorn, Iran, J 4
946 Jörn, Sweden, G 18
162 Josefina, Arg., L 15
..... José Joaquin Perez, Chl., G 4
..... Joseni, E. Hung., I 19
1915 Josselin, France, I 4
956 Jostedal, Norway, K 5
..... Joure, Netherlands, D 18
1274 Jouy-en-Josas, France, C 2
13324 Jovellanos, Cuba, H 9
..... Jovita, Argentina, N 12
..... Jowai, India, G 25
14349 Joyabajo, Guat., F 4
1425 J. Suárez, Ur., O 19
..... Juancho, Argentina, P 21
..... Juan E. Barra, Arg., Q 17
2118 Juanjui, Peru, H 8
25778 Juarez, Arg., P 18
..... Juarez, S. L. P., K 13
..... Jubbett es Safa, Syria, E 19
178839 Jubbulpore, India, I 13
..... Jubilee, Argentina, L 19
1256 Júcaro, Cuba, K 14
2546 Juchipila, Zac., L 7
14541 Juchitán, Oax., N 12
2275 Juchitlán, Jal., M 5
..... Juchow, China, F 14
..... Juckasjärvi, Sweden, D 18
6196 Jucuapa Sal., H 8
19 Judah, Alberta, G 17
..... Juddangi, India, L 15
6787 Judenburg, Ger., S 14
324 Judique, N. S., I 20
797 Juelsminde, Denmark, J 10
..... Jufna, Palestine, M 9
3299 Juigalpa, Nicaragua, K 13
509 Juile, Ver., K 12
72254 Juiz de Fora, Brazil, M 18
17840 Jujuy, Argentina, F 10
71008 Jukundur, India, D 9
..... Julamerk, Tur., G 19
..... Julduk, Afg., J 21
..... Juleijil, Palestine, K 10
7002 Juliaca, Peru, O 19
8585 Jülich, Germany, J 2
1030 Julimes, Chih., H 20
..... Julis, Palestine, N 4
898 Jumeaux, France, M 16
30183 Jumet, Belgium, N 12
21165 Jumilla, Spain, L 15
..... Jumla, Nepal, E 15
39890 Junagad, India, I 3
3639 Junchara, Bolivia, M 10
167 Jundah, Australia, I 18
29891 Jundiahy, Brazil, N 15
4213 Junee, Australia, O 20
..... Jungtseh, China, F 14
38 Juniata, Sask., M 6
528 Junin, Arg., M 7
55854 Junin, Argentina, N 16
361 Junin, Chile, C 3
12329 Junin, Col., I 11
3058 Junin, Peru, K 10
127 Junin de los Andes, Arg., R 5
..... Juning, China, G 15
46 Junkins, Alberta, K 19
9 Junor, Sask., K 6
..... Junosuando, Sweden, E 19
..... Junsele, Sweden, I 15

Pop. Place Country Index
..... Juntas de San Antonio, Argentina, E 11
..... Juquery, Brazil, N 16
300 Juquilá, Oax., N 8
1628 Jurado, Col., F 5
Jurbarkas, W. Sov. Un., B 16
..... Juruena, Brazil, J 6
..... Jurupary, Western Brazil, H 14
2194 Jussey, France, I 21
9085 Jussiape, Brazil, J 19
653 Jussy, Switz., N 2
2431 Justlahuaca, Oax., L 6
..... Justo Duract, Arg., N 11
8110 Jüterbog, Germany, H 12
7157 Jutiapa, Guat., G 5
3836 Juticalpa, Honduras, G 12
..... Juwain, Asia, K 16
..... Juwun, Iran, O 8
349 Juzbado, Spain, G 9
..... Juzgado, Coa., A 10
8124 Jyväskylä, Finland, E 5

K

..... Kaaden, Ger., L 12
..... Kaafjord, Norway, B 19
..... Kaapmuiden, U. S. Afr., F 22
..... Kaarvik, Norway, B 16
Kabakovsk, see Serov, Sov. Un.
..... Kabalo, Bel. Cong., M 16
..... Kabango, Angola, L 14
..... Kabbaah, Palestine, G 12
..... Kabelvaag, Norway, D 13
..... Kabinda, Bel. Cong., L 16
..... Kabrit, Egypt, C 8
..... Kabuda, Iran, I 14
200000 Kabul, Afg., G 23
365 Kabul, Palestine, G 9
..... Kachek, China, M 12
3300 Kada, Japan, O 13
..... Kades, Palestine, F 12
..... Kadi-Kai, Tur., B 3
..... Kadikoi, Tur., E 7
2473 Kadina, Australia, N 15
2400 Kadnikov, Sov. Un., G 13
3200 Kado, Japan, D 23
7000 Kadom, Sov. Un., J 14
..... Kaduna, Nig., I 9
3900 Kadur, India, N 9
..... Kadzand, Neth., P 1
5219 Kaëdi, Fr. W. Afr., H 2
13500 Kaeryŏng, Korea, B 25
56595 Kaesŏng, Korea, D 24
..... Kafla Kingi, A. E. Sud., J 16
..... Kafku, Iran, N 11
700 Kafr Abû-Ghâlib, Egypt, B 16
..... Kafr Abu-Homs, Egypt, C 6
..... Kafr Abu Sad, Egypt, B 17
..... Kafr Amar, Egypt, K 13
..... Kafr Bûlin, Egypt, E 9
..... Kafr Chokn, Egypt, F 14
..... Kafr Dâwud, Egypt, G 6
..... Kafr Dawud, Egypt, G 10
439 Kafr Defriya, Egypt, D 11
..... Kafr Duar, Egypt, C 5
3780 Kafr el Battikh, Egypt, B 18
..... Kafr el Gerâyida, Egypt, C 14
..... Kafr el Gharbi, Egypt, C 12
..... Kafr el-Ghêti, Egypt, D 4
..... Kafr el Manazlah, Egypt, B 17
..... Kafr el Sharki, Egypt, C 13
..... Kafr esh Shekh, Egypt, C 11
..... Kafr esh Shemûti, Egypt, B 15
..... Kafr ez Zaiyat, Egypt, E 11
..... Kafr Hûrin, Egypt, F 13
..... Kafr Lizwâui, Egypt, B 16
..... Kafr Mukfût, Egypt, L 11
..... Kafr Sakr, Egypt, E 17
259 Kafr Sebtâs, Egypt, E 12
..... Kafr Ziada, Egypt, E 9
..... Kagan, India, B 7
..... Kagbeni, Nepal, E 17
66853 Kagi, For., K 20
190257 Kagoshima, Japan, Q 3
..... Kahama, Tan., L 19
..... Kahan, Bal., M 23
..... Kahbune, Egypt, E 19
..... Kahlen-Berge, Ger., O 16
..... Kahlilabad, Iran, G 13
..... Kai, Egypt, M 12
1610 Kaiapoi, N. Z., M 12
..... Kaichow, China, J 9
223000 Kaifeng, China, F 15
..... Kaigorodskoe, Sov. Un., F 20
..... Kaigul, Afg., G 25
..... Kaiho, Manch., B 25
..... Kaihsien, China, H 10
500 Kaihu, N. Z., B 15
..... Kaihwa, China, K 7
..... Kaiisu, Japan, N 3
669 Kaikoura, N. Z., L 14
6442 Kailaria, Greece, N 15
..... Kaindy, India, A 9
..... Kainsk, Sov. Un. Asia, G 12
..... Kaintira, India, J 17
..... Kaiping, China, D 18
..... Kair, Iran, R 15
10400 Kaira, India, I 5
21532 Kairouan, Tunisia, C 24
..... Kairovo, Sov. Un., H 23
Kaisarieh, see Kayseri, Tur.
Kaisarieh, see Caesarea, Pal.
61000 Kaiserslautern, Ger., N 14
350 Kaiserstuhl, Switz., C 4
1280 Kaitangata, N. Z., Q 7
15800 Kaithal, India, E 9
700 Kaitoke, N. Z., J 17
..... Kaja, Tur., H 3
7700 Kajaani, Finland, D 6
..... Kajiado, Kenya, L 20
3500 Kajikazawa, Japan, M 18
2500 Kajiki, Japan, Q 3
401 Kakabeka Falls, Ont., P 18
..... Kakamas, U. S. Afr., J 9
..... Kakegawa, Japan, N 17
..... Kakhk, Iran, H 13
Käkisalmi, see Kexholm, Sov. Un.
1601 Kakon, Palestine, J 7
..... Kala Agha, Iran, L 10
..... Kalaa Tessaout, Mor. H 6
..... Kálábágh, India, C 5
2695 Kalabaka, Greece, O 15
..... Kalach, Sov. Un., L 13
..... Kalach, Sov. Un., M 15
5000 Kaladgi, India, L 8
..... Kala Fath, Afg., L 16
..... Kalah-i-Kah, Afg., J 16
..... Kala Husen Khan, Iran, J 11
..... Kalai Bikui, Iran, O 9
..... Kala-i-Maidan, Iran, F 13
..... Kala-i-Reis, Iran, I 3
..... Kalai-Yar-Muhammed, Afg., I 18
..... Kala Kalsang, Iran, G 15
..... Kalakata, Afg., J 21

Pop. Place Country Index
..... Kalala, Eth., H 9
..... Kalalabad, Iran, J 13
..... Kalam, India, A 6
28955 Kalamai, Greece, Q 16
..... Kalamshah, Egypt, M 11
..... Kalan Chah, Iran, G 12
..... Kalandarabad, Iran, F 14
..... Kala Nuvi, Iran, K 11
..... Kalanzao, Iran, P 14
12000 Kalat, Baluchistan, N 21
..... Kalat Blat, Transj., M 17
..... Kalat el Hosn, Transj., L 10
15000 Kalat-i-Ghilzai, Afg., J 21
..... Kalau, Ger., I 13
1790 Kalavryta, Greece, P 16
..... Kalbe, Germany, H 10
3520 Kalecik (Kalejik), Tur., D 8
..... Kaleh Nau, Afg., G 17
28 Kaleida, Man., R 15
Kalejik, see Kalecik, Tur.
Kale Sultaniye, see Çanak Kale, Tur.
..... Kalewa, Bur., M 21
..... Kalga, Iran, K 5
..... Kalgalaksha, Sov. Un., C 10
60000 Kalgan, China, C 15
9088 Kalgoorlie, Austl., M 7
..... Kalimeh, Iran, N 6
216131 Kalinin (Tver), Sov. Un., H 10
69728 Kalininsk (Petrozavodsk), Sov. Un., F 9
..... Kalinjar, India, G 13
..... Kalinovskaya, Sov. Un., P 17
55125 Kalisz, Poland, E 11
..... Kalk, Germany, J 3
..... Kalkfontein, S. W. Afr., Q 14
2803 Kalkilich, Palestine, K 7
..... Kall, Sweden, I 12
288 Kallehave, Denmark, M 21
19801 Kalmar, Sweden, P 15
..... Kalmar, Sweden, P 18
..... Kalmars, Iran, I 11
..... Kalö, Denmark, H 13
11877 Kalocsa, Hungary, I 11
..... Kalomo, N. Rh., O 16
..... Kalpi, India, G 12
1343 Kalpitiya, Cey., Q 12
..... Kalu, India, E 7
89484 Kaluga, Sov. Un., J 10
6926 Kalundborg, Den., J 16
12131 Kalush, W. Sov. Un., G 18
Kalusz, see Kalush, Sov. Un.
..... Kaluszyn, Poland, D 15
Kalvarija, W. Sov. Un., C 16
Kalvarija, W. Sov. Un., A 15
14280 Kalutturai, Cey., R 13
..... Kalvar, Iran, K 5
..... Kalvslund, Denmark, L 5
26291 Kalyan, India, K 6
..... Kalyazin, Sov. Un., H 11
..... Kal Zohak, Iran, D 3
..... Kama, Ont., P 19
..... Kamaishi, Japan, F 25
..... Kamard, Afg., F 21
2531 Kamberg, Ger., L 5
..... Kambove, Bel. Cong., M 17
..... Kamchouch, Egypt, G 11
3100 Kameda, Japan, E 22
..... Kameh, Iran, H 13
..... Kamenkashirski, W. Sov. Un., E 18
32041 Kamenets-Podolsk, W. Sov. Un., G 20
Kamenka, W. Sov. Un., H 23
50897 Kamensk, Sov. Un., M 13
11169 Kamenz, Ger., J 13
4900 Kameoka, Japan, L 13
..... Kames, Scotland, N 11
5414 Kameyama, Japan, M 14
..... Kamezan, Iran, G 5
..... Kamieniec Litewski, W. Sov. Un., D 17
Kamien Koszyrski, see Kamen Kashirski, Sov. Un.
27 Kamileroy, Austl., F 17
1200 Kamimura, Japan, L 17
..... Kamioka, Japan, K 22
..... Kamionka-Strumilowa, W. Sov. Un., F 18
..... Kamion Kawoloska, W. Sov. Un., F 17
25467 Kamishin, Sov. Un., L 16
5959 Kamloops, B. C., O 15
19 Kamloops Jc., B. C., O 15
Kammin, see Cammin, Ger.
520 Kamo, N. Z., B 16
1000 Kamori, Japan, M 15
470 Kamouraska, Quebec, H 25
19838 Kampen, Neth., F 19
..... Kampot, Fr. In. Ch., R 6
1792 Kamsack, Sask., O 11
..... Kan, Bur., M 21
12000 Kanagawa, Japan, M 20
..... Kanajee, Baluchistan, P 21
..... Kanal, W. Sov. Un., D 20
..... Kanarak, India, J 19
20360 Kanauj, India, F 13
186297 Kanazawa, Japan, J 15
..... Kanchow, China, D 5
20000 Kanchow, China, J 15
60000 Kandahar, Afg., K 20
..... Kandahar, India, K 10
101 Kandahar, Sask., N 9
..... Kanda Kanda, Bel. Cong., M 15
12400 Kandalaksha, Sov. Un., B 9
819 Kandersteg, Switz., L 10
..... Kandestederne, Den., A 12
2469 Kandra, Tur., B 5
7600 Kandukur, India, M 13
37147 Kandy, Cey., R 14
..... Kanegasaki, Japan, F 24
..... Kanem, China, N 10
..... Kanetsu, Japan, J 15
..... Kanev, Sov. Un., L 6
..... Kanevskaya, Sov. Un., N 12
..... Kanghri, Tur., C 8
4700 Kangra, India, C 9
20000 Kangting, China, H 6
..... Kani, Afg., M 19
..... Kani, Bur., M 21
..... Kanigiri, India, M 13
..... Kanita, Japan, B 24
9852 Kankan, Fr. W. Afr., I 3
3900 Kanker, India, J 14
400 Kannir, Palestine, I 8
5000 Kano, Japan, L 15
89462 Kano, Nigeria, I 10
148 Kanowna, Australia, L 7
..... Kanoya, Japan, R 3
12882 Kansk, Sov. Un. Asia, G 14
..... Kan Tang, Siam., R 1
..... Kantenville, Sask., R 7
..... Kantir, Egypt, E 19
..... Kantse, China, G 4
1630 Kanturk, Ire., O 8
7000 Kanuma, Japan, K 21
..... Kaoan, China, I 15
44300 Kaolack, Fr. W. Afr., I 1
..... Kaomi, China, E 18
..... Kaotai, China, D 5

Pop. Place Country Index
..... Kaou, China, H 4
..... Kaoyihsien, China, E 15
..... Kapa, Bur., P 24
..... Kapalu, India, A 10
..... Kapciamiestis, W. Sov. Un., C 17
32688 Kaposvár, Hungary, I 10
..... Kappel, Denmark, N 16
..... Kappel, Germany, D 6
1969 Kappel, Switz., E 18
..... Kappelshamn, Swe., O 17
15600 Karachey, Sov. Un., J 9
359490 Karachi, India, G 1
3500 Karad, India, L 7
..... Karaften, Iran, E 2
..... Karaganda, Sov. Un., Asia, I 11
Kara-Hissar, see Afyon-Karahisar, Tur.
6200 Karaim, Egypt, F 18
..... Karaj, Iran, F 6
..... Karaketchela, Tur., D 8
..... Kara Kilissa, Tur., D 18
..... Karamea, N. Z., J 11
4869 Kara Punar, Tur., G 8
885 Karasjok, Norway, C 21
3000 Karasuyama, Japan, K 21
..... Karat, Iran, H 15
..... Karata, I. E. A., F 7
8000 Karatsu, Japan, M 3
23500 Karauli, India, G 10
35000 Karbala, Iraq, N 20
..... Karbas-ab, Iran, H 11
448 Karböle, Sweden, K 13
..... Karby, Den., E 4
24269 Karcag, Hungary, H 14
13883 Karditsa, Greece, O 16
..... Kare, Afg., G 22
..... Karema, Tan., M 18
..... Karera, India, G 7
..... Karesvando, Sweden, D 19
..... Karez, Iran, G 15
..... Kargil, India, B 9
3000 Kargopol, Sov. Un., F 12
19363 Karikal, India, P 13
..... Karil, Iran, I 12
..... Karim, Iran, N 8
..... Karimât, Egypt, L 1
..... Karin, Afg., I 22
..... Karin, Br. Som., G 17
2206 Karis, Fin., F 3
642 Karise, Den., L 22
2000 Kariwano, Japan, E 23
..... Kariz Zameh, Iran, F 14
3000 Karjat, India, K 6
..... Karlebotten, Norway, A 23
..... Karleby, Denmark, N 21
..... Karl Gustaf, Sweden, F 20
..... Karl Johansväern, Nor., D 4
21208 Karlovac, Yugo., J 8
..... Karlovci-Sremski, Yugo., J 13
7189 Karlovo, Bulgaria, L 19
24029 Karlovy Vary, Czech., F 5
..... Karlsborg, Sweden, N 12
..... Karlshafen, Ger., I 6
7487 Karlshamn, Sweden, Q 13
..... Karlshorst, Ger., Q 20
25492 Karlskrona, Swe., Q 14
..... Karlslunde, Denmark, K 22
154902 Karlsruhe, Ger., O 4
27081 Karlstad, Sweden, M 12
Karlstadt, see Karlovac, Yugo.
13 Karluk, Sask., R 4
..... Karmala, India, K 8
2000 Karnak, Egypt, O 23
..... Karnak, Egypt, P 24
25371 Karnal, India, E 10
8970 Karnobat, Bulgaria, L 22
..... Karonga, Nyasaland, M 19
2576 Karpenisian, Greece, O 15
..... Karraree, Baluchistan, R 21
18059 Kars, Tur., C 18
..... Kartchoo, Afg., F 21
..... Kartuzy, Pol., C 11
9183 Karumai, Japan, C 25
23 Karumba, Austl., E 18
..... Karup, Denmark, C 12
442 Karup, Denmark, G 7
..... Karvasaras, Greece, O 15
..... Karvaselka, Fin., B 6
..... Karwan, Iran, R 14
16800 Karwar, India, M 7
305 Karyai, Grc., N 19
1866 Karystos, Greece, P 19
..... Karytaina, Greece, M 7
..... Karzok, India, C 11
..... Kasama, N. Rh., M 18
..... Kasaragod, India, O 7
..... Kasassin, Eg., F 19
..... Kasauli, India, D 10
3300 Kaseda, Japan, Q 2
..... Kash, Afg., K 17
40000 Kashan, Iran, H 7
Kashgar, see Shufu, Sink.
7500 Kashin, Sov. Un., H 11
..... Kash-i-Nakbud, Afg., K19
60000 Kashing, China, H 20
8500 Kashiwazaki, Japan, I 19
..... Kasil, Transj., J 21
15000 Kasimov, Sov. Un., I 13
Kaskinen, see Kaskö, Fin.
1718 Kaskö (Kaskinen), Fin., E 2
468 Kaslo, B. C., P 18
7228 Kasmark, Slov., N 23
..... Kasongo, Bel. Cong., L 17
..... Kasrak, Iran, P 11
..... Kasr Baghdad, Egypt, E 11
..... Kasr ber Rchid, Mor., G 5
..... Kasrin, Tunisia, D 22
..... Kasrkand, Iran, Q 15
..... Kasr Mediouna, Mor., F 5
..... Kasr Mudenin, Tunisia, F 24
16468 Kassaba, Tur., F 2
..... Kassaba, Tur., I 4
51183 Kassala, Anglo-Egyptian Sudan, H 20
175000 Kassel (Cassel), Ger., I 6
13791 Kastamonu, Tur., B 9
..... Kastel, Germany, L 5
10308 Kastoria, Greece, N 15
3726 Kastro, Grc., N 20
Kastro, see Rhodes, Tur.
5300 Kasukabe, Japan, L 20
46815 Kasur, India, D 8
..... Kaswig, Ger., H 11
..... Kataehi, Afg., I 18
700 Katakura, Japan, L 21
..... Katangi, India, I 13
10138 Katerini, Grc., N 16
2900 Katha, Bur., M 22
178 Katherine, Austl., C 13
..... Kathi, India, I 7
..... Kathu, U. S. Afr., I 12
621 Katikati, N. Z., E 19
..... Katkop, U. S. Afr., L 9
108800 Katmandu, Nepal, F 18
133000 Katowice, Poland, F 11
..... Katrah, Palestine, M 5
7805 Katrineholm, Sweden, N14
..... Katru, Iran, N 9
8000 Katsena, Nigeria, J 10
..... Katsina, Nig., I 9
1400 Katsuura, Japan, P 13
..... Kattewara, Bal., R 21
..... Katwa, India, H 21

Pop. Place Country Index
15752 Katwijk aan Zee, Neth., G 11
1969 Kaub, Germany, L 4
9160 Kaufbeuren, Ger., Q 8
..... Kaukab, Palestine, G 10
..... Kaukabah, Palestine, N 4
400 Kaukapakapa, N. Z., D 16
..... Kau-Kebir, Egypt, M 20
..... Kaulas, India, K 10
152365 Kaunas (Kovno), W. Sov. Un., B 17
873 Kautokeino, Norway, C 19
..... Kavadar, Yugo., M 16
8208 Kavajë, Alb., M 12
..... Kavak, Tur., C 11
8600 Kavali, India, M 13
54980 Kavalla, Greece, N 19
..... Kavar, Iran, M 7
234 Kaw, Fr. Guiana, B 12
..... Kawachi, Japan, B 24
34204 Kawagoe, Japan, L 20
2200 Kawaguchi, Japan, I 20
..... Kawaharada, Japan, H 19
385 Kawakawa, N. Z., B 16
..... Kawâmil el-Qadima, Egypt, N 21
5300 Kawanoe, Japan, N 9
11200 Kawanoji, Japan, M 9
..... Kawardha, India, I 14
..... Kawend, Iran, E 4
..... Kayakulam, India, Q 9
12233 Kayes, Fr. W. Africa, H 3
..... Kaying, China, K 16
52397 Kayseri (Kaisarieh), Tur., F 10
6800 Kazalinsk, Sov. Un. Asia, I 9
401665 Kazan, Sov. Un., I 18
11780 Kazanlik, Bulgaria, L 20
Kazatin, W. Sov. Un. F 23
7000 Kazerun, Iran, M 6
..... Kazimbazar, Iran, D 5
..... Kazis, Switz., J 20
203 Kazubazua, Quebec, O 9
1400 Keady, N. Ire., F 19
..... Keale, Ire., O 8
..... Kealkill, Ire., Q 6
342 Kearney, Ontario, D 12
503 Keban-Maden, Tur., F 14
..... Kebili, Tunisia, F 23
79505 Kecskemst, Hung., I 12
552 Kedgwick, N. B., B 5
65 Keefers, B. C., P 14
..... Keel, Ire., G 3
60 Keeler, Sask., P 7
Keelung, see Kiirun, Formosa.
418 Keene, Ontario, I 15
3752 Keetmanshoop, S. W. Afr., P 13
22000 Keffi, Nigeria, J 9
..... Kefr Abil, Transj., J 14
1374 Kefr Ana, Palestine, L 6
..... Kefr Anan, Palestine, G 11
..... Kefrein, Palestine, I 8
..... Kefr Jaiz, Transj., I 15
785 Kefr Kara, Palestine, I 8
1175 Kefr Kenna, Palestine, H 11
..... Kefr Kud, Palestine, J 10
..... Kefr Lakif, Palestine, K 8
..... Kefr Menda, Pal., H 10
..... Kefr Misre, Palestine, H 11
..... Kefr Najib, Transj., K 16
..... Kefr Saba, Palestine, K 7
870 Kefr Yasif, Palestine, G 9
9467 Kehl, Germany, O 4
..... Kehsi Mansam, Bur., N 24
40440 Keighley, England, F 14
Keijo, see Kyŏngsŏng, Kor.
..... Keiss, Scotland, D 19
6082 Keith, Scotland, G 20
..... Keithley Creek, B. C., L 14
300 Kekerangu, N. Z., K 15
..... Kekri, India, G 8
..... Kelabiya, Egypt, P 23
..... Kelekova, Iran, E 2
..... Kelend, Afg., I 16
80 Kelfield, Sask., M 5
3954 Kelheim, Germany, O 10
..... Kelibia, Tunisia, B 25
1990 Kelkit, Tur., D 14
348 Kelliher, Sask., O 9
..... Kellmünz, Germany, Q 7
2400 Kells, Ire., H 18
2198 Kells, Ire., P 2
..... Kells, N. Ire., C 21
5118 Kelowna, B. C., P 16
70 Kelsey, Alberta, L 21
1200 Kelso, N. Z., Q 6
4279 Kelso, Scotland, N 23
..... Kelty, Scotland, M 19
..... Kelvedon Hatch, Eng., A 25
7000 Kelve Mahim, India, J 5
615 Kelvington, Sask., M 10
225 Kelwood, Manitoba, P 14
12500 Kem, Sov. Un., D 10
1590 Kemakh, Tur., E 14
..... Kemanai, Japan, D 24
..... Kemarat, Thai., O 7
..... Kemboma, Fr. Eq. Afr., K 11
..... Kemer, Tur., I 5
..... Kemer, Tur., D 1
..... Kemerovo, Sov. Un., Asia, H 13
4535 Kemijärvi, Fin., C 6
1468 Kemnay, Scotland, H 22
4824 Kempsey, Australia, M 23
26097 Kempten, Germany, R 7
..... Kemptville, N. S., P 9
1214 Kemptville, Ontario, F 22
..... Kenadsa, Morocco, I 10
239 Kenaston, Sask., N 7
..... Kenda, India, I 15
15575 Kendal, England, E 12
139 Kendal, Sask., Q 9
147 Kendal, Sask., P 9
..... Kendal, U. S. Afr., F 19
15200 Kendrapara, India, J 20
5000 Kengawar, Iran, G 3
13000 Kenghung, China, L 4
..... Kengis, Sweden, E 20
..... Keng-tung, Bur., N 25
484 Kenhart, U. S. Afr., K 10
1200 Kenmare, Ire., P 5
231 Kenmore, Ontario, E 23
961 Kenmore, Scotland, K 16
237 Kennedy, Sask., Q 11
274 Kennetcook Cor., N. S., L 14
7745 Kenora, Ontario, O 15
767 Kensington, P. E. I., G 15
..... Kentani, U. S. Afr., O 18
100 Kent Junction, N. B., G 10
..... Kentra, Scotland, J 9
3928 Kentville, N. S., L 12
..... Keonjhar, India, I 19
..... Kepno, Poland, E 11
..... Kerak, Palestine, H 13
3000 Kerak, Transj., Q 13
2463 Kerang, Australia, O 18
Kêrassunde, see Giresun, Tur.
104471 Kerch, Sov. Un., O 10
7087 Kerdassa, Egypt, I 13
..... Kerei, Iran, D 11
549 Keremeos, B. C., Q 15
Keren, see Cheren, I. E. A.
..... Kerensk, Sov. Un., J 14
800 Kerker, Iran, B 2
36766 Kerkrade, Neth., L 19

Pop.	Place Country Index
.....	Kerkur, Palestine, J 7
32221	Kerkyra, Grc., O 13
59500	Kerman, Iran, L 11
88622	Kermanshah, Iran, G 2
.....	Kermanshahan, Iran, K 10
.....	Kermata, Morocco, F 9
2962	Kerns, Switzerland, I 13
.....	Kerpe, Tur., B 5
.....	Kerr Lake, Ontario, Q 24
650	Kerrobert, Sask., M 4
.....	Kerrykeel, Ire., B 15
3171	Kerteminde, Denmark, K 14
1638	Kerzers, Switz., H 7
5200	Kesennuma, Japan, F 24
.....	Kesh, N. Ire., E 14
.....	Kesla, Palestine, M 7
3580	Kessel, Belgium, K 13
11917	Kessel-Loo, Belgium, L 13
.....	Kessera, Tunisia, C 23
.....	Kessock, Scotland, G 15
509	Kesswil, Switz., C 19
.....	Kestel, Tur., H 4
3833	Kesteren, Neth., H 17
.....	Keston, England, D 23
4635	Keswick, England, D 10
10664	Keszthely, Hung., I 10
.....	Ketchuk, Iran, J 3
31220	Kettering, England, J 17
.....	Kettla Ness, Shet. Is., C 3
3079	Ketzin, Germany, G 11
3820	Kexholm (Käkisalmi), Sov. Un., F 7
.....	Key Harbour, Ont., C 8
62	Key Junction, Ont., C 8
7228	Kezmarok, Czech., G 14
.....	Kgetloa, U. S. Afr., F 13
199364	Khabarovsk, Sov. Un. Asia G 19
519	Kh. Abu Felah, Palestine, L 10
6000	Khaf, Iran, H 15
13700	Khairabad, India, F 14
.....	Khairabad, Iran, J 3
.....	Khairabad, Iran, M 8
.....	Khairigarh, India, E 13
.....	Khairigarh, India. I 14
.....	Khairpur, India, E 5
7300	Khairpur, India, F 2
.....	Khajwana, India, F 7
.....	Khaledabad, Iran, H 7
.....	Khalgali, Baluchistan, O 20
.....	Khalghati, India, M 7
17297	Khalkis, Greece, P 18
.....	Khamaung, India, N 19
23462	Khámgaon, India, J 9
.....	Knamir, Iran, J 13
.....	Khamir, Iran, P 10
.....	Khammamett, India, L 13
.....	Khan, Iran, O 12
.....	Khana Abasa, Chn., B 15
20000	Khanagin, Iraq., L 21
34622	Khandwa, India, I 9
.....	Khanewal, India, D 5
.....	Khan ez Zeit, Transj., M 17
.....	Khanguet el Hadid, Algeria, P 19
.....	Khanh-hoa, French Indo-China, Q 11
25484	Khania (Canea), Grc., R 19
.....	Khaniadhana, India, G 11
.....	Khan-i-Katum, Iran, M 12
.....	Khan-i-marbut, Iran, O 9
.....	Khanagin, Iraq, L 21
7500	Khanpur, India, E 4
.....	Khantaisk, Sov. Un. Asia, E 13
.....	Khar, Iran, I 13
.....	Kharaba, Egypt, B 4
.....	Kharabilinskoe, Sov. Un., N 18
.....	Kharaghoda, India, H 5
1500	Kharan, Baluchistan, N 19
.....	Kharaobo, Chn., B 8
.....	Kharar, India, D 10
.....	Kharas, Palestine, N 8
.....	Kharda, India, K 8
.....	Kharga, Egypt, P 17
833432	Kharkov, Sov. Un., L 10
.....	Kharmang, India, B 9
.....	Kharmanzil, Iran, N 14
.....	Kharput, Tur., F 14
.....	Kh. Armitta, Palestine, P 2
2000	Kharsawan, India, I 19
49741	Khartoum, Anglo-Egyptian Sudan, H 19
.....	Kharwah, India, G 2
.....	Khasav Yurt. Sov. Un., P 18
26622	Khaskovo, Bulgaria, M 20
.....	Khatanga, Sov. Un., Asia, D 14
.....	Khayara, Syria, E 19
.....	Kh. Budekhan, Syria, B 13
.....	Khed, India, L 6
97	Khedive, Sask, Q 8
.....	Kh el Ahmar, Palestine I 12
.....	Kh el Lahm, Palestine, O 6
	Khem-Belder, see Kyzyl, Tannu Tuva.
.....	Khen, Afg., F 23
5774	Khenchela, Algeria, D 21
.....	Kherdu, Iran, G 4
6200	Kheri, India, F 14
.....	Kheri, India, I 9
97186	Kherson, Sov. Un., N 7
.....	Khewa, Egypt, P 24
.....	Kh. Ilasa, Palestine, M 8
.....	Khipro, India, G 3
.....	Khir, Iran, M 8
.....	Khisht, Iran, M 6
.....	Khist, Iran, I 13
23700	Khiva, Sov. Un. Asia, J 9
.....	Kh. Kaaun, Palestine, J 12
.....	Kh. Kefr Thilth, Palestine, K 8
.....	Khlot, Sp. Mor., D 7
	Khmelnik, W. Sov. Un., F 22
.....	Khobbeizeh, Palestine, I 8
.....	Kohbr, China, C 14
	Khodorkov, W. Sov. Un., F 23
.....	Khodrahim, Iran, J 5
25000	Khoi, Iran, B 1
	Khoiniki, W. Sov. Un., D 24
.....	Khojá Saleh, Afg., D 20
.....	Kholan, Sov. Un., L 11
24000	Kholm, Sov. Un., H 7
.....	Kholmogorskaya, Sov. Un., D 13
.....	Kholmogory, Sov. Un., D 13
.....	Kholt, Chn., A 7
.....	Khong, Fr. In. Ch., P 8
16000	Khonsar, Iran, I 5
.....	Khooshk, Afg., F 20
.....	Khora, I. E. A., J 10
.....	Khoremderreh, Iran, E 4
.....	Khoringher, China, C 13
8390	Khorol, Sov. Un., L 9
	Khorostkov, W. Sov. Un., G20
.....	Khorramabad, Iran, H 3
21900	Khorramshahr (Mohammerah, Iran, L 3
.....	Khosro, Iran, C 2
	Khotan, see Hotien, Chn.
15287	Khotin, W Sov. Un., G 19

Pop.	Place Country Index
.....	Khozâm, Eg., O 23
.....	Khozat, Tur., E 14
.....	Khubbis, Iran, K 12
.....	Khuim, India, D 13
10400	Khulna, India, H 23
.....	Khumain, Iran, H 5
.....	Kh. Umm Jerrar, Palestine, P 2
.....	Khungcha, Bur., N 20
6000	Khur, Iran, H 9
.....	Khurda, India, J 19
.....	Khur-i-Sarhang, Iran, I 14
27400	Khurja, India, F 11
2000	Khurramabad, Iran, E 6
.....	Khusab, India, C 6
.....	Khushalgarh, India, B 5
.....	Khuspas, Afg., J 17
.....	Khusrin, Iran, O 14
.....	Khusru Khan, Afg., H 18
17897	Khust, W. Sov. Un., G 17
20000	Khvalinsk, Sov. Un., K 18
.....	Khwaja Do Chahan, Iran, K 15
.....	Kh. Yerzeh, Palestine, K 11
.....	Khynabad, Iran, G 13
.....	Kiachow, China, D 12
.....	Kiaichow, China, G 8
1500	Kiama, Austl., O 22
.....	Kiamika, Quebec, M 11
.....	Kianfu, China, J 15
.....	Kiangchow, China, F 13
.....	Kiangchow, China, J 6
.....	Kiangpei, China, I 9
35000	Kiaochow, China, E 19
.....	Kiaokia, China, J 6
.....	Kiating, China, H 7
479	Kibaek, Denmark, I 5
694	Kibbiah, Palestine, L 8
.....	Kiberg, Norway, A 24
.....	Kičevo, Yugo., M 14
.....	Kichal, Iran, P 10
.....	Kichow, China, E 12
.....	Kichownan, China, E 16
.....	Kichowpei, China, C 17
.....	Kidal, Fr. W. Afr., H 8
.....	Kidd, B. C., K 14
28914	Kidderminster, Eng., J 13
.....	Kidmang, India, B 11
.....	Kido, Japan, L 14
.....	Kidre, Iran, F 5
.....	Kidri, Iran, H 13
3161	Kidwelly, Wales, K 7
.....	Kiehsiu, China, E 13
218000	Kiel, Germany, C 8
58397	Kielce, Pol., F 14
.....	Kieldrecht, Belgium, Q 6
.....	Kienchangfu, China, I 17
.....	Kienchowpeih, China, G 8
.....	Kienchwan, China, J 3
4500	Kienning, China, J 18
.....	Kiensi, China, J 8
.....	Kienthal, Switz., K 10
.....	Kienyang Fu, China, J 18
455	Kiesen, Switz., I 9
846293	Kiev, W. Sov. Un., E 25
.....	Kiffa, Fr. W. Afr., H 3
.....	Kifri, Iraq, K 21
.....	Kigoma, Tan., L 18
87400	Kiirun (Keelung), For., K 21
.....	Kikwit, Bel. Congo, L 13
829	Kil, Sweden, M 11
.....	Kila Barbar, Bal., J 22
.....	Kilafors, Sweden, K 14
.....	Kilag-i-ab, Iran, M 15
.....	Kila-i-Muila, Afg., H 16
.....	Kila Jhan, Afg., L 18
.....	Kila Najil, Afg., F 24
.....	Kilar, India, C 9
.....	Kilbeggan, Ire., J 16
.....	Kilbennan, Ire., I 8
.....	Kilberry, Ire., K 18
.....	Kilberry, Scotland, N 9
8193	Kilbirnie, Scot., N 13
.....	Kilbrittain, Ire., Q 9
.....	Kilcalmonell, Scot., N 9
.....	Kilcar, Ire., D 10
4007	Kilchberg, Switz., E 15
.....	Kilchean, Scotland, J 8
.....	Kilchenichbeg, Scot., K 4
.....	Kilchiaran, Scotland, N 6
.....	Kilchrenan. Scotland, L 11
.....	Kilchu, Kor., C 25
.....	Kilchu, India, B 10
.....	Kilcock, Ire., J 20
131	Kilconnell, Ire., J 11
300	Kilcoole, Ire., K 23
.....	Kilcrea, Ire., P 9
1380	Kildalton, Scotland N 8
1753	Kildare, Ire., K 19
501	Kildare, Quebec, N 15
.....	Kildavnet, Ire., H 3
1454	Kildonan, Scotland, E 17
.....	Kildorrery, Ire., O 11
.....	Kilfenora, Ire., K 7
1489	Kilfinan, Scotland, M 11
.....	Kilfinichen, Scotland, L 8
.....	Kilfinnane, Ire., N 11
.....	Kilgarvan, Ire., P 6
.....	Kilglass, Ire., F 8
.....	Kilimatinde, Tan., L 19
.....	Kilimli, Tur., B 6
24620	Kilis, Tur., I 12
.....	Kilissakend, Iran, B 1
1700	Kilkee, Ire., M 5
.....	Kilkeel, N. Ire., G 23
.....	Kilkelly, Ire., H 9
	Kilkenny, see Cill Cainnig. Ire.
.....	Kilkenzie, Scotland, O 9
.....	Kilkhampton, Eng., N 6
501	Kilkivin, Australia, J 23
.....	Kill, Ire., J 20
.....	Killabeg, Ire., J 7
.....	Killadysert, Ire., M7
.....	Killagan, N. Ire., C 21
600	Killala, Ire., F 7
1000	Killaloe, Ire., L 11
618	Killaloe, Ontario, D 17
628	Killaly, Sask., P 11
347	Killam, Alberta, L 22
825	Killarney, Australia, L 23
	Killarney, see Cill Airne, Ire.
.....	Killarney, Ont., B 6
.....	Killashandra, Ire., G 15
.....	Killbride, Scotland, I 3
.....	Killconnell, Ire., J 11
.....	Killcullen, Ire., K 19
.....	Killean, Scotland, N 9
908	Killearn, Scotland, M 15
.....	Killelu, I. E. A., H 12
.....	Killen, N. Ire., D 15
.....	Killenagh, Ire., M 22
.....	Killenaule, Ire., M 15
.....	Killichonan, Scotland, K 15
.....	Killimor, Ire., K 12
1414	Killin, Scotland, K 15
.....	Killiney, Ire., J 22
.....	Killinny, Ire., K 8
.....	Killorglin, Ire., O 4
.....	Killough, N. Ire., F 24
.....	Killoughter, Ire., K 23
.....	Killucan, Ire., I 17
.....	Killundine, Scotland, K 8
.....	Killure, Ire., J 12
.....	Killybegs, Ire., D 11
.....	Killylea, N. Ire., E 19
.....	Killyleagh, N. Ire., E 24

Pop.	Place Country Index
.....	Kilmacdaugh, Ire., K 9
.....	Kilmacow, Ire., N 17
.....	Kilmacrenan, Ire., C 14
.....	Kilmacthomas, Ire., O 16
.....	Kilmainham, Ire., H 19
.....	Kilmalkedar, Ire., O 1
1200	Kilmallock, Ire., N 10
36393	Kilmarnock, Scot., O 14
.....	Kilmartin, Scotland, L 10
4396	Kilmaurs, Scot., N 14
.....	Kilmeadan, Ire., O 17
.....	Kilmelford, Scotland, L 10
.....	Kilmessan, Ire., I 20
213	Kilmodan, Scotland, M 11
2894	Kilmonivaig, Scot., J 12
1300	Kilmore, Australia, P 19
.....	Kilmore, Ire., O 20
.....	Kilmore, Scotland, L 10
.....	Kilmory, Scotland, O 11
.....	Kilmote, Scotland, E 17
705	Kilmuir, Scotland, G 16
.....	Kilmaurry, Ire., L 6
.....	Kilnaleck, Ire., H 16
.....	Kilninian, Scotland, K 7
.....	Kilninver, Scotland, L 10
.....	Kilnsea, England, G 20
.....	Kilo, Bel. Cong., K 18
.....	Kilometer 52, Arg., Q 14
.....	Kilometer 579, Arg., I 13
.....	Kilometer 213, Arg., J 17
.....	Kiloran, Scotland, M 7
.....	Kilquane, Ire., O 10
800	Kilrea, N. Ire., C 20
.....	Kilroot, N. Ire., C 24
3393	Kilrush, Ire., M 6
10047	Kilsyth, Scotland, M 16
900	Kiltamagh, Ire., H 8
.....	Kiltegan, Ire., L 20
.....	Kiltoom, Ire., I 13
.....	Kiltormer, Ire., J 12
300	Kiltyclogher, Ire., F 13
.....	Kilwa, Tan., M 21
8531	Kilwinning, Scotland, N 13
.....	Kilworth, Ire., O 12
383	Kimba, Australia, N 14
19	Kimball, Alberta, Q 22
2000	Kimberley, B. C., P 19
38941	Kimberley, U. S. Afr., J 14
.....	Kimmura, Japan, K 3
.....	Kimry, Sov. Un., H 11
24	Kimsquit, B. C., L 9
.....	Kinawley, N. Ire., F 15
.....	Kinbrace Station, Scot., D 16
216	Kinburn, Ontario, E 21
259	Kincaid, Sask., Q 6
2507	Kincardine, Ontario, I 5
962	Kincardine, Scotland, F 14
1847	Kincardine O'Neil, Scot., I 21
990	Kincolith, B. C., I 7
990	Kindersley, Sask., N 5
5903	Kindu, Bel. Cong., L 16
.....	Kinel Cherkaskaya, U. S. S R., J 20
75378	Kineshma, Sov. Un., H 14
.....	Kineton, England, J 15
300	King, Ontario, K 11
.....	Kingchow, China, E 16
.....	Kingchow, China, H 13
.....	Kingchow, China, F 10
.....	Kingcome Inlet B. C., O 10
.....	King Edward, Scot., G 22
.....	Kingissep, Sov. Un., G 6
54	Kingman, Alberta, K 21
294	Kingoldrum, Scot., K 20
2978	Kingsbridge, Eng., O 8
246	Kingsburg, Nova Scotia, O 13
164	Kingsbury, Quebec, P 19
326	Kingscote, Australia, O 15
900	Kingscourt, Ire., H 19
84	Kingscourt Junction, Ontario, N 4
20580	King's Lynn, Eng., I 21
400	Kingsport, N. B., L 13
500	Kingston, Australia, P 16
109056	Kingston, Jamaica, J 8
526	Kingston, N. B., K 8
40	Kingston, N. Z., P 5
500	Kingston, N. S., L 11
30126	Kingston, Ontario, I 20
.....	Kingston, Scotland, G 19
.....	Kingston Jc., Ontario, I 20
.....	Kingston Mills, Ont., I 20
39052	Kingston-upon-Thames, Eng., L 19
3900	Kingstown, St. Vincent, O 24
2317	Kingsville, Ontario, R 2
.....	Kingswilliamstown, Ire., O 7
1742	Kington, England, J 11
.....	Kingtung, China, K 4
.....	Kingtzekwan, China, G 13
1067	Kingussie, Scotland, I 16
9532	King Williams Town, Union of South Africa, P 17
.....	Kingyang, China, E 10
.....	Kingyüan, China, K 10
.....	Kinhwafu, China, I 19
564	Kinistino, Sask., L 8
.....	Kinitty, Ire., K 14
100	Kinloch, N. Z., O 4
181	Kinloch, Scotland, D 14
.....	Kinlochailort, Scot., J 10
.....	Kinlochewe, Scot., G 11
.....	Kinlochhourn, Scot., I 11
.....	Kinlochmoidart, Scot., J 9
.....	Kinloch Rannoch, Scot., J 15
778	Kinloss, Scotland, G 18
.....	Kinlough, Ire., E 12
525	Kinmount, Ontario, G 14
2759	Kinna, Sweden, O 11
.....	Kinnared, Sweden, P 11
.....	Kinneff, Scotland, J 23
.....	Kinnegad, Ire., I 18
663	Kinnethmont, Scot., H 21
3200	Kinomoto, Japan, O 13
70	Kinross, P. E. I., H 17
2991	Kinross, Scotland, L 18
4000	Kinsale, Ire., Q 10
.....	Kinta, China, C 4
376	Kintail, Scotland, H 11
.....	Kintampo, G. C., J 6
2202	Kintore, Scotland H 23
.....	Kinvarra, Ire., K 8
.....	Kioraiseki, Japan, L 18
.....	Kioshan, China, G 15
.....	Kiosu, Japan, M 15
79	Kipawa, Quebec, K 2
470	Kipling, Sask., Q 10
293	Kippel, Switz., L 10
1356	Kippen, Scotland, M 15
.....	Kir, Iran, N 7
.....	Kirateh, Syria, G 19
5617	Kirchberg, Switz., D 17
2488	Kirchberg, Switz., G 9
2657	Kirchhain, Germany, J 6
.....	Kircubbin, N. Ire., E 25
6526	Kirdzali, Bul., M 20
.....	Kirensk, Sov. Un. Asia, G 15
.....	Kirili, Tur., G 6
4300	Kirilov, Sov. Un., G 11
138910	Kirin, Manch., B 23
.....	Kirit, Br. Som., J 18
52906	Kiriu, Japan, K 20
9811	Kirk Agach, Tur., E 2

Pop.	Place Country Index
560	Kirkbean, Scotland, Q 18
1370	Kirkby Lonsdale, Eng., E 12
.....	Kirkby Moorside, Eng., E 17
46019	Kirkcaldy, Scot., M 20
1388	Kirkcolm, Scotland, Q 12
3962	Kirkconnel, Scot., O 16
3188	Kirkcudbright, Scot., R 16
.....	Kirkeby, Den., M 13
60	Kirkella, Man., Q 12
.....	Kirkerup, Den., J 21
430	Kirkfield, Ontario, H 13
1155	Kirkhill, Scotland, H 14
1004	Kirkinner, Scotland, R 14
17308	Kirkintilloch, Scot., M 15
.....	Kirkjuvogur, Iceland, C 18
20200	Kirkland Lake, Ont., Q 24
20891	Kirklareli (Kirk-Kilisse), Tur., A 2
1554	Kirkmaiden, Scotland, R 12
.....	Kirkmichael, Eng., E 6
762	Kirkmichael, Scot., J 18
1575	Kirkmichael, Scot, P 14
1802	Kirkoswald, Scotland, P 13
.....	Kirkpatrick, Scot., Q 19
236	Kirkton, Ontario, M 6
25000	Kirkuk, Iraq, J 20
3517	Kirkwall, Scotland, B 20
	Kirmasti, see Mustafakemalpasa, Tur.
143181	Kirov (Vyatka), Sov. Un., G 18
84000	Kirovabad (Gandzha), Sov. Un., Q 18
90600	Kirovo (Zinovevsk), Sov. Un., M 7
.....	Kirovsk, Sov. Un., B 9
4755	Kirriemuir, Scotland, K 20
26051	Kirsanov, Sov. Un., K 14
14052	Kirshehr, Tur., E 9
.....	Kirtomy, Scotland, C 15
.....	Kirton, Eng., G 18
.....	Kiruna, Swe., D 16
5600	Kisarazu, Japan, M 20
4073	Kisbér, Hungary, H 11
271	Kisbey, Sask., Q 10
.....	Kishanganj, India, F 21
.....	Kishani, Afg., J 22
12700	Kishengarh, India, F 4
114445	Kishinev, W. Sov. Un., H 23
35102	Kishiwada, Japan, M 12
.....	Kishlauk, Afg., H 17
.....	Kishm, Afg., E 23
4000	Kishm, Iran, P 11
.....	Kishtwar, India, B 9
38204	Kiskunfélegyháza, Hung., I 12
28804	Kiskunhalas, Hung., I 12
51289	Kislovodsk, Sov. Un., P 15
67819	Kispest, Hung., H 12
.....	Kispiox, B. C., H 9
.....	Kisra, Palestine, G 10
.....	Kissingen, Germany, L 7
.....	Kistrand. Norway, A 20
14531	Kisújszállás, Hungary, H 14
2450	Kisumu, Kenya, K 20
.....	Kita, Fr. W. Afr., I 3
.....	Kitai, Sink., J 13
.....	Kitchberg, Switz., E 15
35657	Kitchener, Ontario, L 8
.....	Kitchu, India, B 10
.....	Kitimat, B. C., J 8
234	Kitscoty, Alberta, K 23
.....	Kitsuki, Japan, N 6
.....	Kittigazuit, Mack., B 4
.....	Kittyclogher, Ire., F 13
.....	Kituta, N. Rh., M 18
.....	Kitwanga, B. C., I 9
10272	Kitzingen, Germany, M 7
80200	Kiukiang, China, I 16
.....	Kiungchow, China, H 7
46000	Kiungchow, Chn., M 12
.....	Kiwar, India, C 11
.....	Kiz, Iran, I 6
4025	Kizil-Agač, Bul., L 21
.....	Kizilalan, Iran, E 9
.....	Kizil Bulak, Afg., G 16
17100	Kizlyar, Sov. Un., P 18
8500	Kizuki, Japan, K 9
.....	Kjelvik, Norway, A 21
.....	Kjöllefjord, Norway, A 22
4241	Kladanj, Yugo., K 11
20671	Kladno, Czech., F 7
29909	Klagenfurt, Aus., I 6
40000	Klaipéda, W. Sov. Un., B 14
.....	Klampenborg, Den., J 23
.....	Klarup, Denmark, D 11
14088	Klatovy, Czech., G 5
	Klausen, see Chiusa, Italy
	Klausenberg, see Cluj, Hung.
852	Kleber, Algeria, C 12
251	Kleinburg, Ontario, K 11
.....	Kleinen, Germany, D 9
1155	Kleinlützel, Switz., D 8
.....	Klejtrup, Den., F 9
8953	Klerksdorp, U. S. Afr., G 16
.....	Kleszczele, Pol., D 16
20288	Kleve, Germany, H 2
499	Klim, Denmark, D 7
.....	Kliman, Scot., M 12
5000	Klin, Sov. Un., I 10
1351	Klingnau, Switz., C 13
198	Klinte, Denmark, K 12
.....	Klintehamn, Sweden, P 17
22229	Klintsi, Sov. Un., K 7
.....	Klipplaat, U. S. Afr., P 14
.....	Klip River, U. S. Afr., G 18
558	Klitmöller, Denmark, D 4
8960	Ključ, Yugo., K 9
.....	Klofsjö, Sweden, J 12
15141	Klosterneuberg, Aus., H 9
2578	Klosters, Switz., I 22
.....	Kloten, Sweden, M 13
1828	Kloten, Switz., D 15
4286	Klötze, Germany, G 9
.....	Kloven, Norway, C 15
.....	Kluane. Yukon, P 5
4843	Klundert, Neth., I 12
.....	Kmuskh, Afg., G 17
5942	Knaresborough, Eng., F 15
.....	Knebel, Denmark, H 13
.....	Knesebeck, Germany, F 8
1836	Knighton, Wales, J 11
.....	Knight's Town, Ire., P 1
1500	Knin, Yugo., K 8
.....	Knock, Scotland, E 7
.....	Knock, Scotland, I 9
1334	Knockando, Scotland, G 19
.....	Knockcroghery, Ire., I 13
6906	Knocke, Belgium, K 6
.....	Knock of Kincardine, Scotland, H 17
.....	Knocktopher, Ire., N 17
646	Knonau, Switzerland, F 14
972	Knowlton, Quebec, Q 18
.....	Knudshoved, Den., L 15
.....	Knyaginin, Sov. Un., I 16
1700	Knysna, U. S. Afr., Q 12
.....	Kobbo, I. E. A., F 10
967234	Kobe, Japan, M 12
686343	København (Copenhagen), Den., J 23

Pop.	Place Country Index
873044	København and Suburbs, Den., J 23
65300	Koblenz, Germany, K 3
	Kobryn, see Kobrin, W. Sov. Un.
10101	Kobrin, W. Sov. Un., D 17
.....	Kobt, Egypt O 24
.....	Kobuk, Iran, P 18
29038	Koburg, Germany, L 8
.....	Kočane, Yugo., M 16
3079	Kočevje, Yugo., J 7
.....	Koche, B. C., Q 17
2259	Kochel, Germany, R 9
106644	Kochi, Japan, O 9
.....	Kochow, China, L 12
.....	Kod, India, M 8
.....	Kodal, Norway, E 1
.....	Kodarabad, Iran, O 11
.....	Kodinar, India, J 3
69	Kodok, Anglo-Egyptian Sudan, J 18
.....	Kodzar, Baluchistan, O 21
1968	Koedijk, Neth., E 13
7171	Koepang, Neth. In., J 6
10858	Koesfeld, Germany, H 3
10684	Koetaradja, Neth. Ind., G 1
6885	Koevorden, Neth., E 23
3287	Koffiefontein, U. S. Afr., K 14
.....	Kofr, Iran, E 12
102419	Kofu, Japan, L 18
8700	Koga, Japan, L 20
6097	Köge, Denmark, K 21
.....	Kohafa, Egypt, L 11
22700	Kohat, India, B 5
.....	Kohek, Baluchistan, Q 17
.....	Kohima, India, L 21
.....	Kohiri, Iran, P 15
2066	Kohlfurt, Pol., E 8
.....	Kohlu, Bal., L 23
.....	Koida, Sov. Un., C 14
83878	Koil-Aigarh, India, F 11
.....	Koilkonda, India, L 11
	Koindanovo, W. Sov Un., C 20
.....	Köinge, Sweden, P 10
.....	Kojak, Iran, D 10
84665	Kokand, Sov. Un. Asia, J 10
.....	Kokassan, Iran, E 5
.....	Kok Fara, I. E. A., H 10
.....	Kokkilai, Cey., Q 14
6457	Kokkola (Gamla Karleby), Fin., D 4
.....	Kokonga, N. Z., O 8
178604	Kokura, Japan, M 4
.....	Kola, Sov. Un., D 11
.....	Köla, Sweden, M 10
600	Kola, Sov. Un., A 9
.....	Kolahira, India, I 17
.....	Kolan, China, D 13
85103	Kolar Gold Fields, India, N 11
.....	Kolaras, India, G 10
33000	Kolberg, Pol., C 9
4000	Kolbuszowa, Pol., F 15
22400	Kolding, Denmark, K 8
.....	Kole, Bel. Cong., L 15
69860	Kolhapur, India, L 7
18509	Kolín, Czech., F 8
608	Kolind, Denmark, G 14
.....	Kolki, W. Sov. Un., E 19
.....	Kollegal, India, O 10
.....	Kollur, India, N 7
756605	Köln, Germany, J 3
2600	Kologriv, Sov. Un., G 15
.....	Kololo, I. E. A. L 13
75139	Kolomna, Sov. Un., I 12
	Kolomyja, see Kolomyya, Sov. Un.
33385	Kolomyya, W. Sov. Un., G 19
.....	Kolosana, Egypt, Q 9
	Kolozsvár, see Cluj., Rom.
.....	Kolpni, Sov. Un., K 10
.....	Kolvereid, Norway, G 10
35000	Kom, Iran, N 10
.....	Kom Abu Khelad, Egypt, M 12
.....	Kôm Abû Râdi, Egypt, L 13
21137	Komárno, Czech., H 11
	Komarno, W. Sov. Un., F 17
.....	Komati Poort, U. S. Afr., F 22
.....	Komatsu, Japan, H 21
12800	Komatsu, Japan, J 15
4000	Komatsushima, Japan, N 11
.....	Kôm-el-Ahmar, Egypt, O 10
.....	Kôm-el-Akhdar, Egypt, D 6
.....	Kom-el-Magaber, Egypt, D 4
.....	Kom-el-Nur, Egypt, E 14
.....	Komenotsu, Japan, P 3
.....	Kôm-er-Resrâs, Egypt, Q 24
.....	Kom-et-Tawil, Egypt, C 13
416	Komgha, U. S. Afr., O 17
.....	Kom Hamad, Egypt, E 9
.....	Komi, Japan, C 13
.....	Kom Kabru, Egypt, C 8
.....	Kom Mastara, Egypt, B 10
201	Komoka, Ontario, N 6
.....	Kom Ombo, Egypt, R 24
3000	Komoro, Japan, K 18
.....	Komotau, Ger., L 12
30136	Komotēnē, Grc., M 20
.....	Kompong-cham, French Indo-China, P 7
....	Komsomol'sk, Sov. Un. Asia, G 19
.....	Kondinin, Australia, N 5
.....	Köng, Denmark, L 11
.....	Köng, Denmark, M 19
2184	Kong, Fr. W. Afr., J 5
32000	Kongmoon, China, L 14
.....	Kongolo, Bel. Cong., L 17
7287	Kongsberg, Norway, M 8
2003	Kongsvinger, Norway, L 10
.....	Kongun, Iran, O 7
	Konia, see Konya. Tur.
315651	Königsberg, W. Sov. Un., B 13
5967	Königsberg, Ger., F 14
.....	Königshofen, Ger., L 7
.....	Königshofen, Ger., N 6
	Königshütte, see Krolewska Huta, Pol.
3740	Königstein, Ger., K 13
10390	Konin, Poland, D 11
10987	Köniz, Switz., H 8
2497	Konjica, Yugo., K 10
.....	Konolfingen, Switz., I 10
6000	Konosu, Japan, L 20
38800	Konotop, Sov. Un., K 8
.....	Konsar, Iran, M 9
11102	Konskie, Poland, E 13
	Konstantinograd, see Krasnograd, Sov. Un.
	Konstantinov, W. Sov. Un., F 21
32950	Konstanz, Ger., Q 5
.....	Kontcha, Cam., J 11
.....	Kontoum, Fr. In. Ch., P 9
.....	Konus, Tur., E 17
56581	Konya (Konia), Tur., G 7
4095	Koog, Neth., C 13

Pop.	Place Country Index
4095	Koog an den Zaan, Neth., A 1
.....	Koolai, Bal., R 17
	Koomisheh, see Shahriza, Iran
.....	Koor, Baluchistan, N 20
.....	Koorba, Iran, G 3
.....	Kooringa, Australia, N 16
.....	Kootwijk, Neth., G 18
.....	Köpenick, Germany, G 12
1691	Kopervik, Norway, M 3
6395	Köping, Sweden, M 14
	Kopychintsy, W. Sov. Un., G 20
1000	Koppa, India, N 8
.....	Koppang, Norway, K 9
9472	Koprivnica, Yugo., I 9
	Kopyczynce, see Kopychintsy, Sov. Un.
	Korat, see Nagor Rajasima
.....	Korba, India, I 16
22787	Korçë (Koritza), Alb., N 14
.....	Korea, India, H 16
.....	Koreb, Eth., G 9
.....	Korenovskaya, Sov. Un., O 12
	Korets, W. Sov. Un., F 21
4978	Korhogo, Fr. W. Afr., I 5
.....	Koriabo, Br. Gu., A 6
51364	Korijama, Japan, I 22
9944	Korinthos, Grc., P 17
.....	Koro, Fr. W. Afr., J 4
10615	Körösmezö, W. Sov. Un., P 29
.....	Korosten, W. Sov. Un., E 22
	Korostishev, W. Sov. Un., F 23
.....	Korpilombolo, Swe., E 20
9728	Korsör, Denmark, L 16
.....	Korsun, Sov. Un., J 17
2600	Korumburra, Austl., Q 19
	Korzec, see Korets, Sov. Un.
10275	Koscian, Pol., D 9
.....	Koscierzyna, Pol., C 11
.....	Kosha, A. E. Sud., G 8
.....	Kosha, Eth., M 7
.....	Koshan, Iran, P 16
12400	Koshu, Kor., I 21
70232	Košice, Czech., G 14
30000	Köslin, Pol., C 9
.....	Koslu, Tur., B 6
.....	Kosowo, see Kossovo, Sov. Un.
	Kossovo, W. Sov. Un., D 18
535	Kossukavak, Bul., M 20
2034	Kostajnica, Yugo., J 9
	Kostelec, Czech., F 9
.....	Kosti, A. E. Sud., I 19
121205	Kostroma, Sov. Un., H 13
12000	Kota Bharu, Malay States, P 3
5000	Kot Adu, India, D 4
14843	Kota Bharu, N. F. Mal. St., N 22
37876	Kotah, India, G 9
.....	Kotal Loweitan, Afg., F 20
3076	Kotel, Bulgaria, L 21
.....	Kotelnich, Sov. Un., G 17
.....	Kot Imamgarh, India, F 2
18502	Kotka, Finland, F 5
.....	Kotkina, Sov. Un., B 17
.....	Kotlas, Sov. Un., F 16
.....	Kotli, India, B 8
2500	Kotomari, Japan, B 23
5011	Kotor (Cattaro), Yugo., L 11
.....	Kotra, Bal., N 22
.....	Kotra, India, H 6
8000	Kotri, India, G 1
2515	Kotsch-hissar, Tur., F 8
	Kottbus, see Cottbus
.....	Kouandé, Fr. W. Afr., I 7
619	Kouchibouguac, N. B., F 11
.....	Kouklia, Cyprus, K 7
.....	Koulikoro, Fr. W. Afr., I 4
1200	Koura, Japan, N 18
658	Kourou, Fr. Guiana, B 11
7873	Kouroussa, Fr. W. Afr., I 3
.....	Koury, Fr. W. Afr., I 5
.....	Kousseri, Fr. Eq. Afr., I 12
6300	Kouvola, Fin., F 5
27650	Kovel, W. Sov. Un., E 18
.....	Kovnac, Iran, J 4
	Kovno, see Kaunas, Sov. Un.
67163	Kovrov, Sov. Un., I 13
	Kowel, see Kovel, W. Sov. Un.
.....	Kowlbyan, Afg., F 19
104000	Kowloon, China, L 15
.....	Kowpangtze, Manch., C20
7600	Kowshu, Kor., H 20
50225	Kozhva, Sov. Un., O 20
12702	Koziani, Grc., N 15
.....	Kozienice, Pol., E 15
	Kozlov, see Michurinsk, Sov. Un.
5000	Kozmodemiansk, Sov. Un., H 17
3200	Kraakstad, Norway, C 7
.....	Krabble, Argentina, P 16
.....	Krabi, Siam., Q 1
.....	Kra Bin, Siam., P 4
.....	Kragelund, Denmark, H 8
195	Kragernaes, Den., N 17
4329	Kragerö, Norway, N 7
27249	Kragujevac, Yugo., K 14
.....	Krailsheim, Germany, N 7
255000	Kraków, Pol., F 13
.....	Kralfallah, Algeria, E 14
	Králiky, Czech., F 9
.....	Kraljevo, Yugo., K 14
.....	Kranganur, India, P 9
4214	Kranidion, Grc., P 17
4191	Kranj, Yugo., I 6
.....	Krantzkop, U. S. Afr., J 21
.....	Krapina, Yugo., I 8
.....	Krasilov, W. Sov. Un., F 21
4485	Kraslava, Sov. Un., I 4
.....	Krasnenka, Sov. Un., G 8
11615	Krasnik, Poland, E 15
5700	Krasnii Kut, Sov. Un., L 17
.....	Krasnii Yar, Sov. Un., L 16
.....	Krasnii Yar, Sov. Un., N 19
700	Krasnoborsk, Sov. Un., F 15
.....	Krasnobaki, Sov. Un., H 16
203946	Krasnodar (Ekaterinodar), Sov. Un., O 12
.....	Krasnoe, Sov. Un. Asia, D 16
.....	Krasnograd (Konstantinograd), Sov. Un., M 9
12000	Krasnogvardeisk (Trotsk). Sov. Un., G 7
.....	Krasnoslobodsk, Sov. Un. J 15
29600	Krasnovodsk, Sov. Un. Asia, J 7
189999	Krasnoyarsk, Sov. Un. Asia, G 14
10435	Krasnystaw, Pol., E 16
1000	Kratie, Fr. In. Ch., Q 8
.....	Kratovo, Yugo., M 16
1844	Krauchthal, Switz., H 9
165300	Krefeld (Krefeld-Uerdingen), Ger., I 2
89553	Kremenchug, Sov. Un., M 8

Pop.	Place	Country	Index
19997	Kremenets, W. Sov. Un.,		F 19
2768	Kremmen, Germany,		F 11
14587	Krems, Ger.,		F 16
18583	Kremsier (Kroměříž), Ger.,		N 18
....	Kreuz, Germany,		F 16
12264	Kreuzburg, Ger.,		J 19
8641	Kreuzlingen, Switz.,		C 18
26000	Kreuznach, Germany,		M 4
1844	Kribi, Cam.,		K 10
....	Krichev, Sov. Un.,		J 7
643	Kriegstetten, Switz.,		F 9
7418	Kriens, Switz.,		H 13
....	Krimskaya, Sov. Un.,		O 11
23500	Krishnagar, India,		H 22
18700	Kristiansand, Nor.,		N 5
690	Kristiansfeld, Den.		S
117	Kristianso, Denmark,		Q 25
13515	Kristianstad, Swe.,		Q 12
14028	Kristiansund, Nor.,		I 6
....	Kristiina, see Kristinestad, Fin.		
12434	Kristinehamn, Swe.,		N 12
3450	Kristinestad (Kristiina), Fin.,		E 3
13629	Kriva Palanka, Yugo.,		M 16
....	Krivitz, Ger.,		E 10
197621	Krivoi-rog, Sov. Un.,		M 8
7032	Krizevci, Yugo.,		I 9
....	Krnov, see Jägerndorf, Ger.		
....	Krolevets, Sov. Un.,		K 8
80734	Krolewska Huta, Pol.,		F 12
....	Kroměříž, see Kremsier, Ger.		
6244	Kromolów, Pol.,		F 12
66	Kronach, Ger.,		L 9
....	Kronau, Sask.,		P 9
....	Kronborg, Denmark,		I 23
43800	Kronstad, Sov. Un.,		F 6
....	Kronstadt, see Brasov, Rom.		
13629	Kroonstad, U. S.Afr.,		I 17
31586	Kropotkin, Sov. Un.,		O 13
12125	Krosno, Poland,		F 15
12969	Krotoszyn, Pol.,		E 10
3096	Krotovka, Sov. Un.,		J 20
5473	Kroub, Algeria,		C 20
....	Krško, Yugo.,		I 8
4027	Kruë, Albania,		M 13
54814	Krugersdorp, U. S. Afr.,		F 17
....	Kruidfontein, U. S.Afr.,		P 11
4014	Kruiningen, Neth.,		J 9
8589	Krumau (Cesky Krumlov), Sov. Un.		
3474	Krumbach, Germany,		P 7
11	Krupp, Sask.,		P 4
11054	Krusevac, Yugo.,		L 15
134	Krydor, Sask.,		L 6
....	Krzemienice,seeKremenets, Sov. Un.		
....	Ksab, Morocco,		E 16
1819	Ksar el Hiran, Alg.,		F 16
....	Ksar el Kebir, Algeria,		O 15
....	Ksar el Maghzen, Mor.,		G 9
....	Ksar Guerara, Algeria,		F 16
....	Ksar Smeïdi, Fr. W. Afr.,		G 6
....	Ksar Tinrharhit, Alg.,		M 11
4111	Kuala Lipis, Fed. Mal. St.,		O 22
111800	Kuala Lumpur, Fed. Mal. St.,		P 21
13970	Kuala Trengganu, N. F. Mal. St.,		O 23
....	Kuantan, Fed. Mal. St.,		P 23
14500	Kuba, Sov. Un.,		Q 20
....	Kubalan, Palestine,		L 11
8641	Kuban, Sov. Un.,		O 13
....	Kubatieh, Palestine,		J 10
....	Kubokawa, Japan,		O 8
....	Kučevo, Yugo.,		K 15
16500	Kuchan, Iran,		E 13
....	Kucheng, see Kitai, Sink.		
25000	Kuching, Sarawak,		H 4
600	Kuchitagi, Japan,		K 8
....	Kudabandan, Bal.,		P 19
....	Kudo, Japan,		G 12
....	Kuekini, Camp.,		F 20
7129	Kufstein, Ger.,		R 10
8100	Kuga, Japan,		M 7
....	Kugia Parin, Afg.,		D 25
....	Kuhfelde, Germany,		F 9
390267	Kuibyshev (Samara), Sov. Un.,		J 19
3003	Kuivaniemi, Fin.,		C 5
1700	Kuji, Japan,		D 25
20000	Kukawa, Nig.,		I 12
....	Kuki, Japan,		L 8
8613	Kula, Turkey,		F 3
....	Kulat Balud, Transj.,		O 17
....	Kulat Bustra, Syria,		E 14
....	Kulat el Kurein, Palestine,		F 9
7200	Kulat Zerka, Transj.,		L 18
....	Kuldiga, Sov. Un.,		H 1
....	Kuldja, see Ningyüan, China		
....	Kuleh, Palestine,		L 7
....	Kulena, Sov. Un.,		O 9
....	Kulenborg, see Culemborg, Neth.		
11874	Kulmbach, Ger.,		L 9
....	Kulonieh, Palestine,		M 9
....	Kulnusweh, Palestine,		K 7
....	Kum, see Qum, Iran		
....	Kumabad, Iran,		L 11
....	Kumagawa, Japan,		J 23
....	Kumagaya, Japan,		L 20
210038	Kumamoto, Japan,		O 4
16949	Kumanovo, Yugo.,		M 15
460	Kumara, N. Z.,		L 10
....	Kumarskaya, Sov.Un.Asia,		G 18
44627	Kumasi, G. C.,		J 6
....	Kumata, Japan,		O 5
62317	Kumbakonam, India,		H 22
....	Kumban, Iran,		J 6
195	Kumbazeh, Palestine,		I 8
....	Kumein, Transj.,		I 14
....	Kumukh, Sov. Un.,		Q 19
....	Kumta, India,		M 7
....	Kunana, U. S. Afr.,		G 15
....	Kunar, Afg.,		G 25
....	Kunchow, China,		G 13
....	Kunda, Sov. Un.,		F 5
....	Kundian, Jc., India,		O 5
....	Kundi Shor, Bal.,		R 18
20000	Kunduz, Afg.		E 22
....	Kuneitra, Syria,		M 10
50000	Kungchang, China,		F 8
2017	Kungsbacka, Sweden,		O 10
....	Kunkels, Switz.,		I 19
150000	Kunming (Yünnanfu), China,		K 6
42850	Kunun, Cho.,		E 24
....	Kunudj, Iran,		O 12
13515	Kunyang, China,		K 6
42857	Kunsan, Chosen,		I 21
24341	Kuopio, Finland,		E 6
7800	Kupyansk, Sov. Un.,		L 11
301	Kur, Palestine,		K 8
30114	Kurashiki, Japan,		M 10
....	Kurauchinuma, Japan,		O 25
....	Kurayoshi, Jap.,		K 10
276085	Kure, Japan,		M 8
3700	Kure, Japan,		O 8
....	Kureim, Syria,		O 14
....	Kureiyat, Transj.,		O 14
3467	Kuressaare (Arensburg), Est.,		G 2
53224	Kurgan, Sov.Un.Asia,		G 10
....	Kurghuree, Bal.,		R 19
....	Kuriet Jit, Palestine,		K 9
....	Kuripapanga, N. Z.,		G 20
....	Kurki Tagrish, Afg.,		K 18
....	Kurkur, Egypt,		R 21
....	Kurno, I. E. A.,		J 6
35314	Kurnool, India,		M 11
125	Kuroki, Sask.,		N 10
300	Kurow, N. Z.,		O 8
119072	Kuruk, Sov. Un.,		K 10
....	Kuruk, Iran,		C 1
....	Kursumlija, Yugo.,		L 15
....	Kurum, Iran,		L 10
24500	Kuruman, U. S. Afr.,		H 12
83008	Kurume, Japan,		N 4
....	Kürün, see Keelung, Taiwan.		
10467	Kurunegala, Cey.,		Q 13
....	Kuryet and Enah, Palestine,		N 8
10585	Kus, Egypt,		Q 24
5294	Kush Adasi, Tur.,		E 4
....	Kushchevska, Sov. Un.,		N 12
3000	Kushi, Japan,		R 2
2619	Kushimoto, Japan,		P 12
....	Kushimura, Japan,		N 7
51584	Kushiro, Japan,		G 14
....	Kushkak, Iran,		M 8
....	Kushkub, Iran,		L 8
....	Kushva, Sov. Un.,		Q 24
....	Kusi-ib, Afg.,		K 20
6087	Kuskkizard, Iran,		K 7
707	Kusrah, Palestine,		L 11
4403	Küssnacht, Switz.,		G 14
35200	Kustanai, Sov. Un.Asia,		G 10
....	Kustendje, see Constanta, Rom.		
....	Kusu, Iran,		N 9
....	Kusumoto, Japan,		O 6
17266	Kutaia, Tur.,		E 4
81479	Kutaisi, Sov. Un.,		Q 15
....	Kut-al-Hai, Iraq,		N 22
....	Kut-al-Imara, Iraq,		N 22
....	Kutat Umm Bagheb, Pal.,		Q 11
....	Kutien, China,		J 18
....	Kutna Hora, see Kuttenberg, Ger.		
23451	Kutno, Pol.,		D 2
....	Kutraneh, Transj.,		Q 16
....	Kutru, India,		K 14
13900	Kütsing, China,		J 7
....	Kuttenberg, Ger.,		M 15
....	Kuty, W. Sov. Un.		H 19
14634	Kuusamo, Fin.,		C 7
20000	Kuwana, Japan,		M 15
30000	Kuweit, Kuweit,		K 6
....	Kuya, Sov. Un.,		J 8
....	Kuyüan, China,		F 9
....	Kuyishu, Manch.,		A 23
....	Kuzan, Palestine,		K 10
....	Kuzaniyeh, Syria,		D 11
3500	Kuze, Japan,		L 10
30300	Kuznetsk, Sov. Un.,		J 17
....	Kuznetsk, see Stalinsk.		
....	Kuznica, Pol.,		C 17
....	Kuzoncan, Sov. Up.,		O 11
....	Kvaedjord, Norway,		C 14
1223	Kvalsund, Norway,		A 20
....	Kvänangen, Norway,		B 18
....	Kvelle, Norway,		F 1
....	Kvernaes, Norway,		I 6
2956	Kvinesdal, Norway,		N 5
....	Kvindherred, Norway,		L 4
....	Kvong, Denmark,		J 3
....	Kwadshak, Bal.,		P 20
....	Kwancheng, Manch.,		C 18
....	Kwang Binh, see Dong Hoi, Fr. In. Ch.		
....	Kwanghengtze,seeChang-chun, Chn.		
....	Kwangan China,		H 9
....	Kwangchow, China,		G 15
....	Kwangchow, China,		M 12
....	Kwangpingfu, China,		E 15
....	Kwangshun, China,		J 9
....	Kwangsichow, China,		K 6
....	Kwangsinfu, China,		I 18
....	Kwangtechow, Chn.,		H 19
....	Kwarenko, Tai.,		G 7
....	Kwei Chenyüan, China,		J 10
....	Kweichow, China,		H 11
....	Kweichow, Chn.,		H 12
200000	Kweisu, China,		C 13
....	Kweite, China,		L 9
100000	Kweiteh, China,		E 5
....	Kweiteh, China,		F 16
100000	Kweiyang, China,		J 9
12000	Kweiyang, China,		J 13
....	Kwohwa, China,		L 9
....	Kyabra, Australia,		J 18
....	Kyaukse, Bur.,		N 22
....	Kyelakin, Scot.,		N 9
1672	Kyelakin, Scot.,		D 12
3790	Kymi, Greece,		O 18
....	Kyndby, Denmark,		J 19
935464	Kyŏngsŏng (Seoul), Kor.,		D 24
1089726	Kyoto, Japan,		M 13
4443	Kyparissia, Greece,		Q 15
1986	Kyperia, Cyprus,		J 8
907	Kythera, Grc.,		R 17
....	Kyuquot, B. C.,		F 4
15403	Kyustendil, Bulgaria,		M 16
6000	Kyzyl (Khem-Belder), Tannu Tuva,		H 14
30000	Kzyl Orda, Sov. Un. Asia,		I 10

L

Pop.	Place	Country	Index
....	La Aguada, Cuba,		M 20
4237	La Amunia de Doña Godina, Spain,		G 15
....	Laasby, Denmark,		H 10
276	Laax, Switzerland,		I 9
512	La Baie, Quebec,		N 18
10000	La Banda, Arg.,		I 12
6425	La Bañeza, Spain,		E 9
13427	LaBarca, Jal.,		M 9
....	Labardin, Arg.,		P 19
....	Labasheeda, Ire.,		M 7
1156	L'Abbaye, Switz.,		J 2
9100	Labé, Fr. W. Afr.,		I 2
....	Labtana, Spain,		C 10
28831	Labinskaya, Sov. Un.,		O 13
4500	La Bisbal, Spain,		F 21
14	La Bomba, Baja Cal.,		B 4
1329	Laboulaye, Arg.,		N 13
74	Labrar, Chile,		J 3
....	Labrea, Brazil,		G 2
1000	La Brea, Honduras,		H 9
483	La Brède, France,		N 8
195	La Broquerie, Man.,		R 17
600	L'Acadie, Quebec,		Q 16
3876	La Calle, Algeria,		B 22
....	La Calle, Chile,		F 4
....	La Calle, Tunisia,		B 22
1002	La Canourgue, France,		N 16
651	La Carlota, Arg.,		M 13
14875	La Carolina, Spain,		L 12
1163	La Catalina, Cuba,		H 7
550	Lac aux Sables, Que.,		K 19
75	Lac Beauport, Quebec,		K 21
790	Lac du Bonnet, Man.,		P 17
11293	La Ceiba, Honduras,		E 10
1397	La Ceiba, Ven.,		E 6
784	la Celle, Fr.,		B 2
....	La Cesira, Arg.,		M 14
4776	La Charité, France,		J 15
1287	La Chartre-sur-le Loir, France,		I 10
1508	la Chataigneraie, Fr.,		K 8
3880	La Châtre, France,		K 13
35473	La Chaux de Fonds, Switz.,		K 19
3070	Lachen, Switz.,		F 16
48	La Chéze, France,		I 4
3325	La Chiffa, Algeria,		C 16
19898	Lachine, Quebec,		P 15
....	La Chorrera, Col.,		N 13
200	La Chorrera, Panama,		P 21
4345	La Chorrera, Panama,		P 21
5310	Lachute, Quebec,		P 13
12425	La Ciotat, France,		P 21
517	Lac la Biche, Alberta,		I 22
1631	La Clayette, France,		L 18
585	La Clarita, Cuba,		L 16
1314	Lacfield, Ont.,		I 15
585	Lakefield, Que.,		L 24
874	Lacolle, Quebec,		R 16
1603	Lacombe, Alberta,		L 21
....	La Conception, Que.,		N 13
1253	La Concordia, Chia.,		N 16
1985	Laconi, Italy,		K 4
104220	La Coruña, Spain,		C 20
2021	La Cruz, Arg.,		J 21
420	La Cruz, Chih.,		J 20
....	La Cruz, Col.,		F 9
2614	La Cruz, Col.,		F 13
11107	La Cruz, Col.,		L 6
....	La Cruz, Uruguay,		N 19
273	Lac Saguay, Que.,		L 11
....	La Cumbre, Arg.,		K 12
5493	Ladismith, U. S. Afr.,		Q 10
1002	Ladner, B. C.,		P 3
1610	Lado, A. E. Sud.,		J 18
1834	La Dorada, Col.,		H 10
....	La Dorida, Arg.,		M 8
....	La Dormida, Arg.,		M 8
....	Ladreborg, Denmark,		K 20
....	La Dulce, Arg.,		Q 18
4749	Ladybrand, U. S.Afr.,		J 17
273	Lady Frere, U. S. Afr.,		N 17
1500	Lady Grey, U. S. Afr.,		J 18
1706	Ladysmith, B. C.,		Q 12
9701	Ladysmith, U. S. Afr.,		J 20
....	Lae, N. Gui. Ter.,		J 11
31800	Laeken, Bel.,		L 11
2000	Laerdalsören, Norway,		K 6
32	La Escala, Spain,		E 22
1427	La Escmeralda, Coa.,		B 12
6	La Esperanza, Cuba,		I 3
1252	La Esperanza, Hond.,		G 8
27240	La Estrada, Spain,		D 6
....	La Falda, Arg.,		K 12
1833	la Fère, France,		F 16
586	La Ferté, Fr.,		I 20
4494	La Ferté Bernard, Fr.,		I 8
3518	La Ferté Saint Aubin, France,		I 14
4710	La Ferté sur Jouarre, Fr.,		H 16
10115	La Flèche, France,		I 10
483	La Fleche, Sask.,		Q 6
1527	La Fregeneda, Spain,		G 8
....	La Fria, Ven.,		G 5
....	Laga, Nepal,		D 14
....	Lagão, Brazil,		I 19
23167	la Garenne, France,		A 3
418	Lagarpampa, Bolivia,		J 10
....	Lagarto, Brazil,		I 23
....	Lages, Brazil,		G 24
....	Lages, Brazil,		P 12
621	Lagg, Scotland,		I 13
3142	Laggan, Scotland,		I 13
678	Laggan, Scot.,		I 15
330	Laggan, Scotland,		N 7
....	Laggavoulin, Scot.,		N 7
10347	Laghouat, Algeria,		F 16
3668	La Gineta, Spain,		K 14
12	La Glace, Alberta,		H 22
1131	La Gleize, Belgium,		N 19
1331	La Gloria, Col.,		E 12
....	La Gloria, Tam.,		G 19
1672	Lagnieu, France,		L 20
6936	Lagny, France,		H 15
9888	Lagôa, Portugal,		N 5
....	Lagôa Rica, Brazil,		M 10
....	Lagôa Vermelha, Brazil,		P 11
....	Lago Grande, Brazil,		G 14
....	La Gomera, Guatemala,		G 3
12490	Lagos de Moreno, Jal.,		L 10
126108	Lagos, Nigeria,		J 8
9443	Lagos, Portugal,		N 5
6000	La Goulette, Tunisia,		B 24
12116	La Grande Combe, Fr.,		K 24
4142	La Granja (San Ildefonso o la Granja), Spain,		H 11
2838	La Grita, Cuba,		J 3
....	La Grita, Ven.,		J 3
10103	La Gulla, Ven.,		O 13
3099	La Guampita, Arg.,		J 17
....	La Guerche-de-Bretagne, France,		I 7
3221	La Guerche-sur-l'Aubois France,		K 15
....	Laguna, Brazil,		P 13
....	Laguna de Mayrán, Coa.,		F 9
669	Lagunas, Chile,		D 5
1333	Lagunilla, S. L. P.,		K 16
9413	Lagunillas, Bolivia,		K 13
391	Lagunillas Guer.,		P 10
1405	Lagunillas Ven.,		C 6
6850	Lagunillas, Ven.,		F 6
....	Lahaiwa, Egypt,		N 20
835	Lahara, India,		I 18
....	Laharpur, India,		H 5
503	La Have, N. S.,		Q 12
211	La Have Island, N. S.,		P 13
1270	La Haye du Puits, Fr.,		G 7
214	La Hechicera, Baja Cal.,		A 4
357	La Higuera, Chile,		J 3
7000	Lahijan, Iran,		D 6
4795	Lahinch, Ire.,		L 6
....	Lahnstein, Germany,		L 4
2886	Laholm, Sweden,		P 11
671659	Lahore, India,		D 8
14075	Lahr, Germany,		P 3
10989	Lahti, Fin.,		F 4
4	La Huaca, Peru,		C 1
....	La Hullera, Arg.,		M 7
....	La Joya, Bolivia,		I 5
....	La Joya, Peru,		F 16
613	La Julia, Cuba,		H 8
3867	Laichou, China,		E 19
....	Laicheng, China,		I 11
5727	Laigle, France,		H 10
998	Laignes, France,		I 18
1265	Laingsburg, U. S. Afr.,		P 10
284	Laird, Sask.,		L 7
1065	Laird Post, B. C.,		B 9
3500	Laishev, Sov. Un.,		I 18
7109	Laja, Bolivia,		H 4
5252	Lajas, Cuba,		J 11
961	La Joya, Bolivia,		I 5
264	La Junta, Chih.,		H 17
....	La Junta, Michoa.,		N 14
550	Lake Ainslie, N. S.,		H 21
200	Lake Ainslie, South Side, N. S.,		H 21
264	Lake Ainslie, West Side, N. S.,		H 21
295	Lake Cowichan, B. C.,		Q 1
262	Lake Etchemin, Que.,		M 23
1945	Lakefield, Ont.,		I 15
585	Lake George, N. S.,		M 12
7414	Lake Frontier, Que.,		L 24
1334	Lake Grace, Australia,		N 6
240	Lake Lenore, Sask.,		M 8
31	Lake Nash Station, Australia,		G 15
....	Lakeport, Ontario,		I 16
225	Lakevale, Nova Scotia,		I 19
211	Lake Verde, P. E. I.,		H 17
195	Lakeville, Ire.,		G 16
....	Lake Weedon, Quebec,		O 21
....	Lakh, Baluchistan,		M 22
....	Lakhpat, India,		H 2
....	Lakki, India,		C 4
....	Lakra, Baluchistan,		O 20
390	La Laguna, Arg.,		M 13
....	Labenque, France,		N 12
1610	Lalehzar, Iran,		M 11
1834	La Libertad, Guat.,		O 5
6	La Lima, Cuba,		M 22
....	La Lima, Honduras,		E 12
....	Lalin, Manch.,		A 23
38188	La Linea, Spain,		N 24
7000	Lalitpur, India,		H 11
....	Lalla Fathma, Mor.,		H 3
....	Lalla Marnia, Algeria,		E 11
3339	La Loma, Bolivia,		M 11
1798	La Loupe, France,		H 11
24351	La Louviere, Belgium,		N 11
....	Lalpura, Afg.,		G 25
....	Lam, Ger.,		O 11
....	La Macta, Algeria,		C 13
....	La Madrid, Arg.,		I 11
....	La Madrid, Arg.,		F 16
1476	Lamadrid, Coa.,		D 10
2324	La Malbaie, Quebec,		M 24
....	La Manga, Nicaragua,		K 13
1003	Lamarche, France,		I 21
....	La Maroma, Arg.,		O 10
5625	Lamas, Peru,		G 8
3712	La Mastre, France,		M 18
4708	Lamballe, France,		I 5
825	Lambate, Bolivia,		H 5
6846	Lambayeque, Peru,		H 3
525	Lambeth, Ontario,		O 6
578	Lambton, England,		I 15
581	Lambton, Quebec,		O 22
1476	Lamego, Portugal,		G 6
16251	Lamentin, Martinique,		G 22
392	Lameque, N. B.,		H 12
831	La Merced, Peru,		H 11
14205	Lamia, Greece,		O 16
392	Lamington, Scotland,		O 18
....	La Mochis, Sin.,		M 14
438	Lamont, Alberta,		J 21
2347	Lamorlciere, Alg.,		E 12
45	La Mothe Achard, Fr.,		K 6
....	La Motte du Caire, France,		O 20
2619	Lampa, Peru,		O 19
3639	Lampazos, N. L.,		D 14
1742	Lampeter, Wales,		J 8
199	Lamphun, Sask.,		R 10
....	Lamu, Kenya,		L 22
2253	Lamud, Peru,		G 6
....	La Mulata, Cuba,		M 4
....	Lanakan, Belgium,		M 17
....	Lanark, Ontario,		H 20
9133	Lanark, Scot.,		N 17
43896	Lancaster, England,		F 12
684	Lancaster, Ontario,		E 25
153	Lancer, Sask.,		O 4
500000	Lanchow, China,		E 7
10076	Lanciano, Italy,		H 5
15000	Landau, Germany,		N 4
....	Landau, India,		D 11
4113	Landeck, Aus.,		H 2
3508	Landen, Belgium,		M 15
7424	Landerneau, France,		H 2
1567	Landeron, Sw.,		G 6
....	Landguard Point, Eng.,		K 24
4	Landi, Afg.,		L 18
198	Landis, Sask.,		M 5
....	Landivisiau, France,		H 1
3546	Landrecies, France,		F 17
504	Landrienne, Quebec,		K 16
46000	Landsberg, Pol.,		D 8
7728	Landsberg, Germany,		Q 8
32000	Landshut, Germany,		P 10
18534	Landskrona, Sweden,		Q 11
3363	Landsmeer, Neth.,		A 5
314	Lang, Sask.,		Q 9
1721	Langaa, Denmark,		G 10
493	Langaa, Denmark,		L 14
....	Langar, Iran,		O 15
95	Langdon, Alberta,		N 21
4267	Langeac, France,		M 17
3450	Langeais, France,		J 10
300	L'Ange Gardien, Que.,		K 22
7891	Langen, Germany,		M 5
835	Langenbruck, Switz.,		E 10
....	Langenburg, Sask.,		P 11
11969	Langensalza, Germany,		J 8
2796	Langenschwalbach, Ger.,		L 4
7232	Langenthal, Switz.,		F 10
....	Langes, Nor.,		O 13
1910	Langesund, Norway,		N 8
318	Langham, Sask.,		M 6
4795	Langhemarck, Bel.,		M 4
2770	Langholm, Scot.,		P 20
....	Langholt, Iceland,		C 21
....	Langley Port., B. C.,		P 4
....	Langnja, China,		I 4
3867	Langogne, France,		N 17
3450	Langon, France,		N 9
7868	Langres, France,		I 19
175	Langruth, Manitoba,		P 15
8000	Lang-son, Fr. In.Ch.,		L 9
....	Langsum, Siam.,		R 1
1	Langtjern, Sweden,		H 15
....	Langton Herring, Eng.,		N 12
2646	Langwies, Switz.,		I 21
323	Langwies, Switz.,		I 21
359	Lanigan, Sask.,		N 8
3527	Lannilis, France,		H 1
6274	Lannion, France,		G 2
86	La Noria, Chile,		O 4
475	Landsdowne, Ont.,		H 21
301	L'Anse à Giles, Que.,		J 23
613	Lanslebourg, France,		M 23
3458	Lanusei, Italy,		K 5
2039	Lanzo, Italy,		D 2
2023	La Opela, Dur.,		M 22
....	Lao-Kay, Fr. In. Ch.,		L 7
60	La Orilla, Michoa.,		P 9
20254	Laon, France,		F 16
262	Lapa, Brazil,		O 13
262	La Palca, Bolivia,		J 10
1945	La Palisse, France,		L 17
26	La Palma, Arg.,		A 9
1103	La Palma, Pan.,		P 24
7414	La Palma, Spain,		H 8
156	La Pampa, Chile,		J 4
204	La Pastora, S. L. P.,		K 15
10000	La Para, Arg.,		K 18
....	La Para, Arg.,		M 8
301000	La Paz, Bolivia,		H 4
508	La Paz, Chile,		R 3
3598	La Paz, Honduras,		G 9
10401	La Paz, Baja Cal.,		P 12
2776	La Paz, Nicaragua,		J 10
7919	La Paz, Uruguay,		O 16
1014	La Penca, Arg.,		N 11
216	La Perade, Quebec,		L 19
....	Lapidinskaya, Sov. Un.,		E 19
12369	La Piedad, Michoa.,		M 10
1627	Lapierre House, Yukon,		E 8
....	La Pinte, Bel.,		L 8
4860	La Plaine, Quebec,		O 15
256378	La Plata, Arg.,		N 20
1897	La Plata, Col.,		E 5
391	Lapleau, France,		M 14
6676	La Pola de Gordón, Spain,		D 9
3881	Lappeenranta, Fin.,		F 6
3955	Lappi, Fin.,		D 3
....	Lappo, Fin.,		D 4
2936	Lapprairie, Quebec,		O 15
....	LaPrida, Arg.,		I 11
814	Laprida, Arg.,		P 16
10147	La Puebla, Spain,		J 22
7008	La Puebloe Monteban, Spain,		J 11
....	La Puerta, Arg.,		K 13
....	La Puerto de San Jose, Arg.,		I 8
328	La Punta, Arg.,		I 11
515	La Purisima, Baja Cal.,		L 9
....	Lâpusul, E. Rom.,		H 17
....	Lagey, Pol.,		D 16
1093	La Quebrada, Ven.,		E 7
2000	La Quemada, Jal.,		L 5
7000	La Quiaca, Arg.,		E 10
....	Lar, Iran,		O 9
....	La Rabida, Spain,		N 7
....	Laracor, Ire.,		X 22
962	Laragne, France,		N 21
32010	Larache (El Araish), Sp. Mor.,		D 6
....	La Raie, St. Lucia,		H 24
....	La Ramada, Arg.,		H 11
831	La Merced, Peru,		H 11
....	Larangeiras, Brazil,		I 23
....	Laranjal, Brazil,		F 7
1023	Laraos, Peru,		G 6
488	Larder, Scotland,		M 17
....	Lardeau, B. C.,		O 24
45	Lardenne, Algeria,		O 15
255	Lavarande, Algeria,		O 15
5704	Laredo, Spain,		C 13
6206	Laredo, Spain,		C 13
572	La Reforma, Coa.,		C 9
658	La Reine, Quebec,		O 1
3695	La Réole, France,		N 10
121	Laret, Switz.,		I 21
1293	Largentiere, France,		N 23
41	L'Argentiere, France,		N 23
2299	Largo, Scotland,		L 20
8740	Largs, Scotland,		N 13
....	La Rica, Arg.,		O 18
4966	Larino, Italy,		I 16
12536	La Rioja, Arg.,		J 9
24125	Larissa, Greece,		O 16
14500	Larkana, India,		F 2
....	Larkhall, Scotland,		N 16
5	Larkollen, Norway,		N 5
9765	Larnaca, Cyprus,		K 8
8036	Larne, N. Ire.,		C 23
3609	La Robla, Spain,		D 9
1928	La Roche, Belgium,		N 19
1076	La Roche, Switz.,		J 7
2143	Rochefoucauld, Fr.,		L 10
47737	La Rochelle, France,		L 8
14538	La Roche-sur-Yon, Fr.,		L 8
11602	La Roda, Spain,		K 13
5110	La Roda de Andalucia, Sp.		
1259	La Sagne, Switz.,		G 5
7	La Salada, Baja Cal.,		O 10
87	La Salette, Ont.,		O 9
102	La Salle, Man.,		Q 16
988	Las Anod, Br. Som.,		K 20
2167	La Sarre, Quebec,		O 2
398	Las Bombas, Chile,		H 4
....	Las Bonitas, Ven.,		G 15
1032	Las Cabras, Chile,		N 4
3500	Las Canas,Costa Rica,		M 13
....	Las Casetas, Spain,		F 16
....	Las Casuarinas, Arg.,		L 7
....	Las Catitas, Arg.,		M 8
....	Las Cejas, Arg.,		H 11
22	Las Cruces, Tam.,		I 17
....	Las Dones, Chile,		E 4
....	La Dureh, Br. Som.,		H 18
1672	La Senia, Algeria,		D 12
21742	La Serena, Chl.,		K 3
2881	Las Esperanzas, Coa.,		C 12
33316	Las Flores, Argentina,		O 18
....	Lash, Afg.,		K 16
358	Lashburn, Sask.,		K 4
....	Lashio, Bur.,		M 23
....	Las Juntas, Michoa.,		P 8
....	Lask, Poland,		E 12
....	Las Khoreh, Br. Som.,		G 20
4205	la Souterraine, France,		L 13
514	Las Palmas, Arg.,		H 19
119595	Las Palmas, Can. Is.,		D 2
663	Las Palmas, Panama,		Q 19
....	Las Palmeras, Arg.,		K 16
1094	Las Pemas, Arg.,		K 12
1829	Las Plumas, Arg.,		B 22
2127	Las Rosas, Arg.,		L 15
....	L'Assomption, Que.,		O 16
....	Las Tablas, Panama,		Q 21
....	Last Chance, Yukon,		K 4
....	Las Toscas, Uruguay,		O 20
3670	Las Vegas, Ver.,		H 8
20357	Lqtacunga, Ecuador,		C 5
1712	Las Suze, Perou,		I 9
345	Las Vacas, Coa.,		A 12
....	Las Varillas, Arg.,		L 14
....	Las Vientos, Chile,		F 4
408	La Torre, Chile,		K 3
4275	La Tour-de-Peilz, Switz.,		I 5
3435	La Tour du Pin, Fr.,		M 20
3351	La Tremblade, Fr.,		L 6
4303	La Trinidad, Col.,		H 16
1740	La Trinidad, Col.,		H 16
20000	Lattaquié, Syr.,		J 10
7919	La Tuque, Quebec,		L 17
2819	Lauda, Ger.,		M 6
216	Lauderback, Man.,		R 13
1214	Lauder, Scotland,		N 21
628	Laufen, Switz.,		B 15
2560	Laufen, Switz.,		D 5
1463	Laufenburg, Switz.,		C 12
4860	Lauffen, Germany,		N 5
....	Lauzharne, Wal.,		K 6
11884	Laun, Ger.,		M 13
4071	Launceston, Eng.,		N 6
27532	Launceston, Tasmania,		C 7
7234	La Union, Bolivia,		C 3
7289	La Union, Chile,		K 4
5	La Union, Col.,		J 9
2626	La Union, Col.,		J 5
892	La Union, Guer.,		P 10
....	La Union, Jal.,		L 10
....	La Union, Peru,		J 8
5969	La Union, Salvador,		I 9
10079	La Union, Spain,		H 8
5080	La Unión, Ven.,		G 12
1329	Laupen, Switz.,		H 8
5743	Laupheim, Germany,		P 7
44	Laura, Australia,		D 19
654	Laura, Australia,		N 15
88	Laura, Sask.,		N 6
1942	La Urbana, Ven.,		I 13
113	Laurel, Quebec,		O 13
....	Laureles, Paraguay,		R 7
1772	Laureles, Uruguay,		Q 20
1713	Laurenckirk, Scot.,		J 22
5189	Lauria, Italy,		K 18
....	Lauriers Roses, Alg.,		D 13
99900	Lausanne, Switz.,		K 4
4730	Lauterbach, Ger.,		K 6
1678	Lauterbourg, France,		O 5
2890	Lauterbrunnen, Switz.,		K 11
585	Lautrec, France,		P 14
5892	Lauwe, Bel.,		M 6
27792	Laval, France,		I 8
399	La Valette, France,		M 10
4000	Lavalle, Arg.,		J 18
398	Lavanham, England,		J 22
1335	Lavertezzo, Switz.,		N 16
121	Laverton, Australia,		K 7
690	Lavey, Switz.,		N 6
8554	La Victoria, Ven.,		D 12
212	Lavin, Switz.,		I 23
26	Lavinia, Man.,		Q 13
7300	La Virgen, Nicaragua,		L 12
1	La Virgen, Portugal,		I 5
4032	La Voulte-sur-Rhone, Fr.,		N 19
178	Lavoy, Alberta,		K 22
1263	Lavras, Brazil,		G 22
11350	Lavras, Brazil,		M 16
6393	Lavrion, Grc.,		P 19
3000	Lawa, India,		G 5
....	Lawley, U. S. Afr.,		Q 7
650	Lawrence Jc., N. Z.,		Q 7
589	Lawrencetown, N. S.,		M 10
....	Laxa, Sweden,		N 13
....	Laxey, England,		E 7
....	Laxford Br., Scot.,		D 12
....	Laxsjö, Sweden,		I 13
131	Layo, Peru,		N 17
564	La Yunta, Spain,		H 15
3866	Lazcano, Ur.		
....	Lazo, Arg.,		M 10
....	Leadburn, Scotland,		N 19
650	Leader, Sask.,		O 4
589	Leadgate, England,		D 14
....	Leadhills, Scotland,		O 17

Pop.	Place Country Index
1500	Leales, Argentina, H 10
29662	Leamington, Eng., J 15
5858	Leamington, Ont., R 2
.....	Leap, Ire., R 7
6183	Leaside, Ontario, K 12
251	Leask, Sask., L 7
2179	Leau, Belgium, M 15
16700	Lebedin, Sov. Un., L 9
.....	Lebedyan, Sov. Un., K 12
.....	Lebesby, Norway, A 22
19343	Le Blanc, France, K 11
6555	Le Bourget, France, A 7
.....	Le Brassus, Switz., K 2
1372	Lebrija, Col., G 13
14536	Lebrija, Spain, O 9
3827	Lebu, Chile, P 2
3077	Lebus, Germany, G 13
8747	Le Cateau, France, F 16
40000	Lecce, Italy, K 22
12702	Lecco, Italy, C 5
4874	Le Chesnay, France, B 2
1258	Le Chesne, France, G 18
29417	Le Creusot, France, K 18
4040	Lectoure, France, O 11
19258	Leçzno, Pol., E 16
3283	Ledbury, England, K 12
7330	Lede, Belgium, L 9
13359	Ledeberg, Belgium, L 9
2743	Ledesma, Arg., F 11
2860	Ledesma, Spain, G 9
.....	Ledingen, Norway, D 13
.....	Ledmore, Scotland, E 12
876	Leduc, Alberta, K 20
482789	Leeds, England, F 15
425	Leeds Village, Que., M 21
18556	Leek, England, H 14
7881	Leek, Neth., C 21
.....	Leeman, Alta., K 19
.....	Leenane, Ire., I 5
1805	Leende, Neth., K 17
12232	Leer, Germany, E 4
9032	Leerdam, Neth., H 15
650	Leeston, N. Z., M 12
48482	Leeuwarden, Neth., C 18
.....	Leeuwdoorns, U. S. Afr., H 15
9091	Leeuw Saint Pierre, Belgium, M 10
210	Lefaivre, Ontario, C 24
.....	Lefka, Cyprus, K 7
.....	Lefkoniko, Cyprus, K 8
325	Lefroy, Ontario, I 11
462	Legal, Alberta, J 20
5211	Leganés, Spain, I 12
	Leghorn, see Livorno, It.
3662	Legnago, Italy, D 9
.....	Legoniel, N. Ire., D 23
8624	Le Gosier, Guadeloupe, B 23
.....	Legya, Bur., N 23
3500	Leh, India, B 11
164083	Le Havre (Havre), Fr., G 9
.....	Lehe, Germany, D 5
613	Lehman, Arg., K 15
265	Le Horps, France, H 9
10735	Lehrte, Germany, G 7
7000	Leiah, India, D 4
239111	Leicester, England, I 16
.....	Leichhardt's Bar, Australia, C 14
70860	Leiden, Netherlands, G 12
45313	Leigh, England, G 12
.....	Leigh Creek, Australia, L 16
.....	Leighlinbridge, Ire., L 18
1505	Leignon, Belgium, O 15
.....	Leila, Tunisia, E 23
15	Leilehua Jc., Hawaii, E 11
.....	Leimebamba, Peru, H 6
2159	Leinefelde, Germany, I 8
.....	Leipo, China, I 7
717000	Leipzig, Germany, J 10
62570	Leiria, Portugal, I 5
7808	Leisnig, Germany, J 11
602	Leissigen, Switz., J 10
4184	Leiston, England, J 24
216	Leitche's Creek, N.S., H 23
100	Leitche Creek, N. S., H 23
80488	Leith, Scotland, M 20
500	Leithbhearr (Lifford), Ire., C 15
.....	Leitrim, Ire., K 11
.....	Leixoes, Portugal, G 5
.....	Lejjun, Transjordan, Q 15
2472	Lekanger, Norway, J 4
.....	Le Kef, Tunisia, C 22
4317	Lekkerkerk, Neth., H 13
1401	Leksand, Sweden, L 13
2962	Leksviken, Norway, I 9
.....	Lelie Fontaine, U. S. Afr., L 7
.....	L'Elivaz, Switz., L 7
12075	Le Locle, Switzerland, G 5
1837	Le Luc, France, P 23
3343	Le Lude, France, I 9
366	Lem, Denmark, F 5
84525	Le Mans, France, I 10
5607	Lembecq-lez-Hal, Bel., M 10
	Lemberg, see Lvov., Sov. Un.
705	Lembeye, France, P 9
795	Le Merlerault, Fr., H 10
.....	Lemförde, Ger., G 5
.....	Lemmer, Neth., D 18
.....	Lemming, Denmark, H 9
3203	Le Monastier, Fr., N 18
600	Le Monétier, Fr., M 23
459	Le Montet-aux-Moines, France, K 15
4574	Lemvig, Denmark, F 3
15532	Lena, Spain, C 9
1199	Lencloitre, France, K 10
14217	Lencóes, Brazil, I 19
15177	Lencóes, Brazil, N 14
.....	Lendalfoot, Scotland, P 12
13181	Lengerich, Germany, G 4
2396	Lengnau, Switz., H 10
67707	Leninakin (Gymri), Sov. Un., Q 16
3191304	Leningrad (Petrograd), Sov. Un., F 7
.....	Lenin, W. Sov. Un., D 21
81980	Leninsk, Sov. Un., M 16
1731	Lenk, Switz., L 9
16100	Lenkoran, Sov. Un., R 20
.....	Lennoxtown, Scot., M 15
2150	Lennoxville, Que., Q 20
172	Lenore, Man. Q 12
32730	Lens, France, E 14
23942	Lentini, Italy, O 16
.....	Lenvik, Nor., C 16
.....	Lenya, Bur., R 24
346	Lenz, Switz., J 20
4115	Lenzburg, Switz., E 13
11438	Leoben, Aus., H 7
.....	Leogane, Haiti, J 12
5707	Leominster, England, J 11
.....	Leon, Argentina, F 10
74155	León, Guan., L 10
30573	León, Nicaragua, J 10
44755	León, Spain, D 10
121	Leona Vicario (Sta. Maria), Q. R., E 25
1574	Leonessa, Italy, H 12
21830	Leonforte, Italy, O 15
2906	Leonidion, Greece, Q 17
.....	Leopoldina, Brazil, J 12
7393	Leopoldina, Brazil, M 18
.....	Leopoldini, Brazil, C 5
35946	Leopoldville, Bel. Cong., L 12
6438	Leova, W. Sov. Un., I 23
3206	Le Palais, France, J 3
.....	Lepanto, Greece, P 16
2755	Le Pecq, France, A 1
.....	Lepel, W. Sov. Un., B 21
1941	L'Epiphanie, Quebec, O 15
.....	Le Pont, Switzerland, J 2
.....	Lepreau, N. B., L 7
.....	Lepsha, Sov. Un., E 12
20288	Le Puy, France, M 17
4110	Lequeitio, Spain, C 14
.....	Lequeitio, Cuba, I 11
13014	Le Raincy, France, A 8
.....	Lerbjerg, Denmark, G 11
10601	Lercara, Italy, N 13
9349	Lerdo, Dur., M 23
1938	Lerida, Col., I 9
41464	Lérida, Spain, F 18
1097	Lerma, Camp., G 20
1315	Lerma, Méx., H 4
2331	Lerma, Spain, F 12
.....	Lervik, Norway, M 3
6506	Lerwick, Shetland Is., C 4
5396	Les Andelys, France, G 13
.....	Les Attafs, Algeria, C 15
1151	Les Bois, Switz., F 6
367	Les Cabannes, France, Q 13
.....	Les Eboulements, Que., I 24
.....	Le Sentier, Switz., K 2
.....	Le Sepey, Switz., M 6
962	Les Essarts, France, K 7
.....	Leshë, Albania, M 12
2931	Lesje, Norway, J 7
17615	Leskovac, Yugo., L 15
126	Leslie, Sask., N 9
3983	Leslie, Scotland, L 19
19500	Les Lilas, France, B 7
194	Les Loges, France, C 2
805	Les Mées, France, O 22
3419	Lesparre, France, M 7
500	Les Pieux, France, G 6
.....	Les Pins, Algeria, E 12
.....	Les Plans, Switz., N 7
.....	Les Ponts, Switz., H 5
13660	Les Sables d'Olonne, France, K 5
10380	Lessines, Belgium, M 9
271	Lestock, Sask., O 9
463	Les Trembles, Algeria, D 13
1281	Les Vans, France, N 18
1266	Les Verrieres, Switz., H 3
16506	Leszno, Poland, E 9
318	L'Etete, N. B., L 6
14612	Lethbridge, Alberta, P 22
721	Le Thiel, France, I 11
	Letichev, W. Sov. Un., G 21
.....	Leticia, Col., R 19
5719	Le Tréport, France, F 12
.....	Letterfrack, Ire., I 3
.....	Letterfinlay, Scotland, I 13
2200	Letterkenny, Ire., C 14
...	Letters, Scotland, F 12
1963	Leuk, Switz., M 10
525	Leukerbad, Switz., M 10
5865	Leuze, Belgium, N 8
12552	Leva (Levice), Hung., P 20
12585	Levadeia, Greece, P 17
65186	Levallois-Perret, Fr., A 5
1607	Levanger, Norway, I 10
7411	Leven, Scotland, L 20
512	Levens France O 24
540	le Verdon, Fr., M 7
375	Levet, France, K 14
4546	Levico, Italy, C 9
4274	Le Vigan, France, O 17
2820	Levin, N. Z., I 18
11991	Levis, Quebec, K 22
5086	Levkas, Greece, O 14
8935	Levoča, Czech., G 14
.....	Levuka, Fiji Is., P 18
10785	Lewes, England, N 20
.....	Lewis, Yukon, Q 10
.....	Lewisham, Eng., C 22
.....	Leydsdorp, U. S. Afr., D 21
.....	Leyland, Alta., L 17
128920	Leyton, England, B 22
.....	Lézajsk, Poland, F 16
1827	Lezama, Ven., D 14
7152	Lezignan, France, P 15
1779	Lezoux, France, L 16
50000	Lhasa, Tibet, M 14
.....	Lian, Norway, B 6
30000	Liangchow, China, D 7
.....	Liaochow, China, E 14
38638	Liaoyang, Manch., C 21
.....	Liard, Mackenzie, Q 7
.....	Libano, Argentina, P 16
.....	Libenge, Bel. Cong., K 14
.....	Liberdade (Ex Santa Cruz), W. Brazil, H 16
38525	Liberec, Czech., E 8
3492	Liberia, Costa Rica, M 12
5609	Libertad, Uruguay, O 18
4624	Libertad, Venezuela, E 11
2055	Libertad, Ven., F 9
.....	Libertad de Orituco, Venezuela, E 14
178	Liberty, Sask., O 8
1137	Libin, Belgium, P 16
25600	Libode, U. S. Afr., N 19
6608	Liborina, Colombia, G 8
19103	Libourne, France, N 9
1528	Libramont, Belgium, P 17
.....	Libres, Argentina, J 21
1530	Libres, Pueb., H 7
4605	Libreville, Fr. Eq. Afr., K 10
24963	Licata, Italy, O 14
8508	Lichfield, England, I 14
.....	Lichow, China, I 13
.....	Lichtenau, Germany, J 7
2081	Lichtenberg, Ger., P 20
5811	Lichtenburg, U. S. Afr., F 15
5358	Lichtenfels, Germany, L 9
1663	Lichtensteig, Switz., E 18
6242	Lichtervelde, Belgium, L 6
19490	Lida, W. Sov. Un., C 18
833	Liddes, Switz., P 7
9296	Lidköping, Sweden, N 11
2519	Liebenwalden, Ger., F 12
.....	Liebig, Uruguay, L 15
165634	Liége, Belgium, M 17
76000	Liegnitz, Pol., E 9
.....	Lienhwa, China, J 15
.....	Lienkong, China, J 19
6197	Lienz, Aus., H 4
57098	Liepaja, W. Sov. Un., A 14
.....	Lier, Norway, B 2
1600	Lierne, Norway, H 12
3266	Lierneux, Belgium, O 18
27700	Lierre, Belgium, K 12
6705	Liestal, Switz., D 10
	Lifford, see Leithbhearr, Ire.
1885	Ligniéres, France, K 14
2045	Ligny, Belgium, N 13
4837	Ligua, Chile, L 4
460	Liguata, Bolivia, G 4
1367	Ligueil, France, J 11
1903	Liica, Bol., K 4
.....	Likiang, China, J 4
.....	Likhvin, Sov. Un., J 10
.....	Lild, Denmark, D 6
.....	Liling, China, I 14
200575	Lille, France, E 15
.....	Lille Elvedalen, Nor., J 9
5436	Lillehammer, Nor., K 9
1198	Lillesand, Nor., N 6
.....	Lillherrdal, Sweden, K 12
1467	Lillo, Belgium, Q 8
.....	Llong, China, L 15
2500	Lima, Paraguay, L 9
533645	Lima, Peru, L 8
3836	Limache, Chile, M 3
.....	Limahualda, Chile, L 3
.....	Limanowa, Pol., F 13
13302	Limasol, Cyprus, K 7
.....	Limavady, N. Ire., C 18
.....	Limbdi, India, I 5
4330	Limburg, Belgium, N 19
11552	Limburg, Ger., K 4
30000	Limchow, China, L 11
	Limerick, see Luimneach, Ire.
296	Limerick, Sask., Q 7
.....	Limerick Jc., Ire., N 12
189	Lime Ridge, Quebec, P 20
.....	Limoeiro, Brazil, H 23
12601	Limoeiro, Brazil, H 24
95217	Limoges, France, L 12
9760	Limôn, Costa Rica, N 16
1059	Limon, Honduras, D 12
.....	Limon, Peru, F 7
2398	Limonar, Cuba, H 8
.....	Limoquije, Bolivia, G 10
7639	Limoux, France, Q 14
18000	Limpio, Paraguay, N 7
.....	Linanfu, China, K 6
17108	Linares, Chile, O 4
9810	Linares, N. L., G 16
47562	Linâres, Spain, M 12
.....	Linchong, China, F 17
.....	Linchow, China, K 13
45835	Lincoln, Argentina, N 15
66246	Lincoln, England, H 18
502	Lincoln, N. Z., M 12
.....	Lindass, Norway, K 4
13582	Lindau, Germany, R 6
.....	Lindelse, Denmark, N 14
.....	Linden, Germany, G 7
3242	Lindesberg, Sweden, M 13
.....	Lindholm, Germany, B 6
3818	Lindi, Tanganyika, M 21
1150	Lindley, U. S. Afr., I 18
8403	Lindsay, Ontario, I 14
200	Lingan, N. S., G 24
.....	Lingchow, China, D 9
9000	Lingeh, Iran, Q 9
10898	Lingen, Germany, G 4
.....	Lingfe, India, C 11
.....	Linghed, Sweden, L 14
.....	Ling Shan, China, L 11
8293	Linguaglossa, Italy, N 17
695	Linière, Quebec, N 23
25000	Linkiang, China, I 16
29845	Linköping, Sweden, N 14
7157	Linlithgow, Scotland, M 18
.....	Linn of Dee, Scot., I 18
.....	Linpingchow, China, K 15
.....	Linsell, Sweden, J 12
831	Lintgen, Luxembourg, Q 20
1756	Linththal, Switz., H 17
168	Lintlaw, Sask., N 10
59	Linton, Quebec, J 19
.....	Linton, Scotland, N 19
375	Lintrathen, Scot., K 19
911	Lintsi, Greece, P 15
.....	Lintsingchow, China, E 16
217	Linwood, N. S., J 20
495	Linwood, Ont., L 8
.....	Linying, China, G 15
108404	Linz, Aus., G 6
368	Lions Head, Ont., F 7
66625	Lipetsk, Sov. Un., K 12
.....	Liping, China, J 11
.....	Lipki, Sov. Un., L 15
10415	Lipno,
	Lipnyazhka, W. Sov. Un., G 25
19000	Lippstadt, Ger., I 5
353	Lipton, Sask., O 9
75	Lircai, Chile, O 3
2012	Lircay, Peru, M 12
9557	Liria, Spain, J 16
.....	Lisbellaw, N. Ire., F 15
704669	Lisboa (Lisbon), Portugal, K 5
12388	Lisburn, N. Ire., E 22
.....	Liscannor, Ire., L 6
.....	Liscarroll, Ire., O 9
.....	Liscasey, Ire., L 7
536	Liscomb, N. S., L 19
.....	Lisdoonvarna, Ire., K 7
.....	Lisemore, Ire., O 13
.....	Lisheen, Ire., O 7
.....	Lishtar Sara, Iran, L 5
15362	Lisieux, France, G 10
4266	Liskeard, England, O 6
.....	Liski, Sov. Un., L 12
.....	Liskovo, Sov. Un., I 16
216	Lisle, Ontario, I 10
776	L'Isle, Switzerland, K 3
4243	L'Isle Adam, Fr., G 14
847	L'Isle-Jourdain, Fr., L 11
3560	L'Isle Jourdain, Fr., P 11
1946	L'Isle Rousse, Cor., P 2
699	L'Islet, Quebec, J 24
.....	Lislevane, Ire., Q 9
.....	Lisma, Sweden, R 22
11762	Lismore, Austl., L 24
.....	Lisnaskea, N. Ire., F 16
7763	Lisse, Neth., G 13
2394	Lisseweghe, Belgium, K 5
3400	Listowel, Ire., N 6
3013	Listowel, Ontario, K 7
.....	Lit, Sweden, I 13
.....	Litang, China, H 4
5272	Litera, Sp., F 18
22000	Lithgow, Austl., N 22
18509	Litoměřice, Czech., F 7
275	Little Bras d'Or, N. S., H 23
261	Little Britain, Ont., I 13
36	Little Brook Station, N. S., O 8
1069	Little Current, Ont., B 5
327	Little Dover, N. S., K 22
10181	Littlehampton, Eng., N 18
.....	Little Harbor, Bahamas, A 8
364	Little River, N. S., O 8
.....	Little Salmon, Yukon, N 9
.....	Little Scheideck, Switzerland, K 12
.....	Liüanchow, China, H 17
.....	Liuchow, China, K 11
.....	Liupa, China, G 10
1791	Livarôt, France, H 10
856850	Liverpool, England, G 1
3170	Liverpool, N. S., P 12
4105	Livilivi, Bolivia, M 10
5154	Livingston, Guatemala, E 7
.....	Livingston, Yukon, P 11
5600	Livingstone, N. Rh., O 16
20600	Livni, Sov. Un., K 11
.....	Livno, Yugo., K 9
112400	Livorno (Leghorn), It., F 7
.....	Livramento, Brazil, E 8
27048	Livramento, Brazil, K 8
21366	Livry-Gargan, France, A 8
.....	Liwale, Tan., M 21
.....	Lixnaw, Ire., N 5
.....	Liz, Iran, I 3
59768	Ljubljana, Yugo., I 6
3019	Ljungby, Sweden, P 12
.....	Ljusa, Sweden, F 19
.....	Ljusdal, Sweden, K 14
5604	Ljusne, Sweden, K 15
.....	Llabaya, Peru, Q 19
3505	Llai Llai, Chile, M 4
1212	Llama, Peru, H 4
.....	Llanbedr, Wales, I 8
13677	Llandudno, England, G 8
38393	Llanelly, Wales, K 7
.....	Llanerchymedd, Wales, G 7
20421	Llanes, Spain, C 11
1449	Llanfyllin, Wales, I 10
2937	Llangollen, Wales, H 10
2356	Llanidloes, Wales, J 9
.....	Llanilar, Wales, J 8
745	Llanguera, Bolivia, J 5
.....	Llanrhaiadr-yn-Mochnant, Wal., I 10
.....	Llanrhystid, Wales, J 7
2366	Llanrwst, Wales, H 8
1464	Llanz. Switz., J 18
609	Llera, Tam., I 17
8217	Llerena, Spain, L 9
1903	Llica, Bolivia, K 4
300	Llico, Chile, N 3
572	Lloydminster, Alta., K 23
1052	Lloydminster, Sask., K 4
9790	Llummayor, Spain, J 21
.....	Lluta, Chile, B 3
10000	Loango, Fr. Eq. Afr., L 11
12653	Löbau, Ger., J 14
3535	Lobbes, Belgium, O 11
.....	Lobburi, Siam., O 3
3200	Lobenstein, Germany, L 9
29456	Loberia, Argentina, Q 19
.....	Lobestadl, Norway, C 15
.....	Lobinstown, Ire., H 20
3373	Lobito, Ang., N 12
30754	Lobos, Argentina, O 18
6588	Locarno, Switz., N 16
220	Lochaber, N. S., K 19
.....	Lochaline, Scotland, K 9
.....	Lochalsh, Scotland, H 10
2004	Lochbroom, Scot., F 12
.....	Lochbuy, Scotland, L 9
967	Lochcarron, Scot., H 10
21	Lochearn, Alberta, M 20
.....	Lochearnhead, Scot., L 15
5673	Lochem, Netherlands, G 21
4754	Loches, France, J 12
11879	Loch Garman (Wexford), Ire., N 21
939	Lochgilphead, Scot., M 10
.....	Lochgoilhead, Scot., L 12
.....	Lochinver, Scotland, E 11
.....	Lochlaggan, Scot., I 14
275	Loch Lomond, N. S., I 23
.....	Lochluichart, Scot., G 13
2460	Lochmaben, Scot., P 18
.....	Loch Ranza, Scot., N 11
.....	Loch Tay, Scot., K 15
.....	Lochwan, China, F 11
.....	Lockeport, B. C., L 5
1084	Lockeport, N. S., Q 11
2344	Lockerbie, Scot., P 19
1751	Locmine, France, I 4
634	Locumba, Peru, Q 18
.....	Lodbjerg, Denmark, E 3
.....	Lodeinoe Pole, Sov. Un., F 9
6629	Lodeve, France, O 16
.....	Lodhran, India, E 5
668	Lodi, Algeria, C 16
21661	Lodi, Italy, D 5
.....	Lödingen, Norway, D 14
3797	Lodosa, Spain, E 15
665000	Lódz, Poland, E 12
1352	Loenen, Neth., G 19
.....	Loeries Fontein, U. S. Afr., M 8
.....	Löfanger, Sweden, H 19
262	Loganville, N. S., J 16
.....	Log Cabin, B. C., B 4
435	Loggieville, N. B., E 10
1452	Logierait, Scotland, K 17
46182	Logroño, Spain, E 14
6033	Logrosán, Spain, J 10
2734	Lögstör, Denmark, E 8
222	Lögten, Denmark, H 12
1718	Lögumkloster, Denmark, M 6
609	Lohals, Denmark, M 15
.....	Loharu, India, E 9
.....	Lohee, Baluchistan, P 21
380	Lohn, Switz., B 15
5900	Lohr, Germany, L 6
20776	Loja, Ecuador, E 4
23998	Loja, Spain, N 12
24267	Lokeren, Belgium, L 9
1441	Lökken, Denmark, C 9
6000	Lokoja, Nigeria, J 9
120	Lolligna, Switz., L 17
2438	Lom, Norway, K 7
.....	Lo Mantang, Nepal, E 17
47	Lomas, Son., C 11
.....	Lomas, Peru, O 12
200	Lombardy, Ontario, G 21
719	Lombez, France, P 11
.....	Lombillo, Cuba, K 17
10400	Lomé, Fr. W. Afr., J 7
.....	Lomela, Bel. Cong., L 15
.....	Lomitas, Bolivia, I 5
9791	Lommel, Belgium, K 16
129	Lomond, Alberta, O 22
14475	Lom-Palanka, Bul., K 17
25065	Lomza, Poland, D 15
3100	Lonar, India, J 9
.....	Lönborg, Denmark, I 3
6449	Londerzeel, Bel., L 11
225	Londesborough, Ont., K 5
4230200	London, Eng., L 19
8202818	London, Greater, England, L 19
78264	London, Ontario, N 6
45159	Londonderry, N. Ire., I 8
178	Londonderry Station, N.S., K 15
1112	Longarone, Italy, C 10
1561	Longavi, Chile, O 4
649	Longburn, N. Z., I 18
22339	Long Eaton, Eng., I 16
305	Longeau, France, I 20
	Longford, see Longphor, Ire.
400	Longford, Ontario, H 12
1100	Longford, Tasmania, C 7
260	Longformacus, Scot., N 22
2329	Longjumeau, France, D 4
231	Longlac, Ontario, O 20
105	Longobucco, Italy, L 19
3800	Longphor (Longford), Ire., H 14
100	Long Point, N. S., I 20
3274	Longreach, Australia, H 19
2321	Longside, Scot., G 24
2902	Long Sutton, Eng., I 20
.....	Longton, England, H 13
.....	Longtown, England, C 11
510	Longueville, France, F 11
.....	Longworth, B. C., K 14
14811	Longwy, France, F 20
4804	Lonigo, Italy, D 9
31135	Lonneker, Neth., G 24
14101	Lons-le-Saunier, Fr., K 21
357	Lönstrup, Denmark, B 9
1343	Loo, Belgium, L 3
12	Looma, Alberta, K 21
65	Loon, Ont., M 9
10254	Loon op Zand, Neth., I 15
.....	Loosduinen, Neth., H 10
1644	Lopik, Neth., H 14
.....	Loping, China, I 17
.....	Loping, China, K 7
3442	Loppersum, Neth., B 23
11465	Lora del Rió, Spain, M 9
69639	Lorca, Spain, M 15
153	Loreburn, Sask., O 7
10262	Lorena, Brazil, N 16
.....	Lorenz, Brazil, C 12
524	Loreto, Argentina, I 12
1649	Loreto, Bolivia, F 10
.....	Loreto, Brazil, G 17
.....	Loreto, Col., R 19
.....	Loreto, Ecuador, B 8
732	Loreto, Baja Cal., L 10
2564	Loretteville, Quebec, K 21
6146	Lorica, Col., D 8
45817	Lorient, France, I 2
1118	L'Orignal, Ontario, C 25
546	Loring, Ontario, C 10
3168	Loriol, France, N 19
.....	Lorne, Ontario, I 5
.....	Lorne, Yukon, Q 10
62	Lorneville, Jc., Ont., H 13
.....	Loros, Chile, I 4
18000	Lörrach, Germany, R 3
.....	Lorraine, Alberta, L 22
.....	Lorrha, Ire., K 12
.....	Lort, Iran, I 2
.....	Los, Sweden, K 13
1070	Los Aldamas, N. L., E 16
.....	Los Amoros, Arg., I 17
12409	Los Andes, Chile, M 4
.....	Los Angeles, Bolivia, D 6
20979	Los Angeles, Chl., P 3
.....	Los Animas, Chile, H 4
1056	Los Arroyos, Cuba, I 2
6739	Los Barrios, Spain, N 23
.....	Los Callejones, Arg., N 15
3846	Los Guayos, Ven., D 11
.....	Los Indios, Cuba, K 5
.....	Los Menucos, Arg., A 22
15449	Losoncz (Lučenec), Czech., P 22
2612	Los Palacios, Cuba, I 4
.....	Los Palos, Cuba, I 8
.....	Los Portales, Tam., F 21
159	Los Pozos, Chile, H 4
5452	Los Reyes, Michoa., N 9
1953	Los Santos, Panama, Q 21
8214	Los Santos de Maimona, Spain, L 8
2158	Los Sauces, Chile, Q 3
14762	Losser, Neth., G 24
3914	Lossiemouth, Scot., G 19
395	Lostallo, Switz., M 18
11101	Los Teques, Ven., C 13
.....	Los Toldos, Arg., N 16
.....	Los Toros, Chia., Q 17
1325	Lostwithiel, Eng., O 5
1305	Los Vilos, Chile, L 3
5069	Los Yébenes, Spain, J 12
31087	Lota, Chile, P 2
343	Loth, Scotland, E 17
.....	Lotingchow, China, L 13
203	Lotus, Ontario, J 14
40000	Louang-prabang, Fr. In. Ch., M 5
5433	Loudeac, France, H 4
5252	Loudun, France, K 9
26945	Loughborough, Eng., I 16
195	Lougheed, Alberta, L 22
.....	Lough Eske, Ire., D 13
.....	Loughgall, N. Ire., E 20
.....	Loughmoe, Ire., L 14
2799	Loughrea, Ire., K 10
.....	Loughshinny, Ire., I 22
.....	Loughton, England, A 23
4144	Louhans, France, K 20
.....	Louisburg, Ire., H 4
1012	Louisburg, N. S., I 24
.....	Louis Creek, B. C., O 15
227	Louisdale, N. S., J 21
3542	Louiseville, Quebec, M 17
16709	Loulé, Portugal, N 6
.....	Louny, Czech, F 6
11529	Lourdes, France, P 9
47390	Lourenço Marques, Moz., P 18
3000	Lourical, Portugal, I 5
8752	Lourmel, Algeria, D 12
1000	Louth, Austl., L 19
9678	Louth, England, G 19
.....	Louth, Ire., G 20
40028	Louvain, Belgium, M 13
1157	Louveciennes, Fr., B 2
10357	Louviers, France, G 11
3360	Louvigné du Desert, Fr., H 8
.....	Louvis, Coa., A 10
314	Löve, Denmark, K 17
9111	Loveč, Bulgaria, L 19
.....	Loventuel, Arg., O 11
4245	Lovere, Italy, C 6
156	Loverna, Sask., N 3
154	Lovett, Alberta, L 18
.....	Lovns, Den., F 7
.....	Lovrana, Italy, D 14
.....	Lövsta, Swe., Q 20
850	Lower Argyle, N. S., Q 9
200	Lower Caraquet, N.B., B 11
318	Lower Concession, N. S., O 8
305	Lower East Pubnico, Nova Scotia, R 9
.....	Lower Laberge, Yukon, O 9
165	Lower La Have, N.S., O 13
101	Lower Montague, P. E. I., H 18
518	Lower Prince William, N. B., I 6
527	Lower Sackville, N. S., N 15
264	Lower Sandy Point, N.S., Q 10
185	Lower Selmah, N.S., K 15
267	Lower Ship Harbour, N. S., M 17
216	Lower Ship Harbour East, N. S., M 17
195	Lower West Pubnico, N.S., R 9
520	Lower Wood Harbour, N. S., R 9
394	Lowerz, Switz., G 15
41768	Lowestoft, England, I 25
17613	Lowicz, Poland, E 13
.....	Lowther, N. Z., P 5
71	Loyalist, Alberta, M 23
6276	Loznica, Yugo., K 12
17947	Luanda, Ang., M 11
25200	Luarca, Spain, C 9
.....	Lubaanum (ruins), Guat., D 7
.....	Lubaczów, Pol., F 16
.....	Lubartów, Pol., E 16
7574	Lübben, Ger., H 13
137700	Lübeck, Ger., D 8
120000	Lublin, Poland, E 16
21308	Lubni, Sov. Un., L 8
.....	Lucan, Ire., J 21
631	Lucan, Ont., M 6
.....	Lucan Crossing, Ontario, M 5
54500	Lucca, Italy, F 7
1417	Lucea, Jamaica, J 7
4100	Lucena, Spain, I 17
32687	Lucena, Spain, N 11
4251	Lucena del Cid, Sp., I 17
630	Luc-en-Diois, Fr., N 21
	Lučenec, Czech., H 12
1429	Lucens, Switz., J 5
15939	Lucera, Italy, I 16
	Lucerne, see Luzern, Switz.
.....	Luchow, China, I 8
3055	Lüchow, Germany, F 9
.....	Lüchow, China, G 17
722	Luchsingen, Switz., H 17
.....	Lucila, Arg., K 16
.....	Lucio V. Mansilla, Arg., K 17
	Luck, see Lutsk, W. Sov. Un.
4550	Luckau, Germany, H 12
26000	Luckenwalde, Ger., H 12
387177	Lucknow, India, F 14
867	Lucknow, Ontario, J 6
268	Lucky Lake, Sask., O 6
581	Lucma, Peru, H 5
6462	Luçon, France, K 7
11249	Ludd, Palestine, M 6
.....	Ludenscheid, Ger., J 4
3272	Luderitz (Angra Pequena) S. W. Afr., P 12
66098	Ludhiana, India, D 9
5642	Ludlow, England, J 11
161	Ludlow, N. B., G 8
5050	Ludvika, Sweden, M 13
32000	Ludwigsburg, Ger., O 6
106000	Ludwigshafen, Ger., M 4
7179	Ludwigslust, Ger., E 9
5559	Ludza, Sov. Un., H 5
.....	Luebo, Bel. Cong., L 15
2403	Lüfjenburg, Ger., C 8
5700	Luga, Sov. Un., G 6
15269	Lugano, Switz., P 17
	Lugansk, see Voroshilovgrad, Sov. Un.
2887	Lugareño, Cuba, L 18
3500	Lugh, Som, P 14
10467	Lugo, Italy, E 10
42805	Lugo, Spain, D 7
25000	Lugoj, Rom., J 14
....	Lugones, Arg., I 13
.....	Luib, Scotland, K 14
.....	Luichow, China, M 11
39448	Luimneach (Limerick), Ire., M 10
.....	Luirbest, Scotland, E 7
.....	Luis Son., K 14
.....	Luisa, Ecuador, C 5
1259	Luján, Argentina, L 10
.....	Luján, Argentina, M 7
32610	Luján, Argentina, N 18
.....	Lukh, Baluchistan, Q 21
.....	Lukkeir, Baluchistan, R 17
6924	Lukovit, Bulgaria, L 18
13971	Lukow, Poland, E 16
.....	Luku, China, I 5
.....	Luku, Eth., K 12
11334	Lulea, Sweden, G 19
.....	Lumb, Argentina, Q 16
.....	Lumbreras, Argentina, G 11
	Lumbushski, see Medveshya Gora, Sov. Un.
625	Lumby, B. C., P 16
.....	Lumby, Denmark, K 12
830	Lumphanan, Scot., I 21
530	Lumsden, N. Z., P 5
449	Lumsden, Sask., P 8
.....	Luna, India, H 3
757	Lunahuaná, Peru., M 10
.....	Lunal, Belgium, M 13
.....	Lunan, China, K 6
1190	Lunas, France, P 16
9000	Lunawada, India, H 7
.....	Lund, India, D 4
24512	Lund, Sweden, Q 11
.....	Lundby, Denmark, E 8
.....	Lunde, Denmark, J 3
2702	Lunde, Norway, N 4
250	Lundeborg, Den., M 14
977	Lunderskov., Den., K 7
.....	Lundö, Den., F 7
.....	Lundum, Denmark, I 10
178	Lundur, Iceland, C 19
31000	Lüneburg, Germany, E 8
.....	Lunen, Ger., I 4
2856	Lunenburg, N. S., O 13
230	Lunenburg, Ontario, F 24
23665	Luneville, France, H 22
.....	Lungan, China, G 7
.....	Lungchow, Chn., F 9
20000	Lungchow, China, L 9
1730	Lungern, Switz., I 13
.....	Lungkula Mongolia, A 18
.....	Lungling, China, K 3
3448	Lungro, Italy, L 18
.....	Lungyenchow, China, K 17
.....	Luninets, W. Sov. Un., D 20
.....	Luniniec, see Luninets, Sov. Un.
.....	Luossanavare, Sweden, D 17
.....	Lupei, Manch., A 19
.....	Lupeni, Romania, J 17
.....	Lupungu, Bel. Cong., L 15
.....	Luqsor (Luxor), Eg., O 23
25000	Luque, Paraguay, N 7
.....	Lur, Afghanistan, J 18
2802	Lurcy Lévy, France, K 16
6291	Lure, France, I 22
12553	Lurgan, N. Ire., E 21
2141	Lurin, Peru, L 8
.....	Lurio, Moz., N 21
.....	Luro, Argentina, P 15
.....	Luro, Arg., R 14
4568	Lusaka, N. Rhod., N 17
5610	Lusambo, Bel. Cong., L 16
400	Luscar, Alberta, L 17
370	Luseland, Sask., M 4
143760	Lushun (Riojun) (Port Arthur) Manch., D 20
1274	Lusignan, France, K 10
772	Lusigny, France, I 18
.....	Lusk, Ire., I 22
988	Lussac-les-Châteaux, France, K 11
.....	Lussanvira, Brazil, M 12
4060	Lussin Piccolo, Italy, E 15
1204	Lustin, Belgium, O 14
.....	Lutesville, N. B., H 11
1721	Luthern, Switzerland, G 11
.....	Lutien, China, J 6
68526	Luton, England, K 18
2588	Lutry, Switz., L 4
.....	Lutschinen, Switz., K 11
35700	Lutsh, W. Sov. Un., F 19
.....	Lutzel, Switz., D 8
3744	Lützelflüh, Switz., H 10
57740	Luxembourg, Lux., R 20
5488	Luxeuil, France, I 22
403	Luxey, France, O 8
	Luxor, see Luqsor, Eg.
600	Luzech, France, N 12
74700	Luzern (Lucerne), Switz., G 13
1549	Luzy, Fr., K 17
316177	Lvov, W. Sov. Un., F 17
	Lwōw, see Lvov, W. Sov. Un.
.....	Lyari, Baluchistan, Q 21
.....	Lybster, Scotland, D 19
84	Lyby, Denmark, F 6
15000	Lyck, Pol., C 15
.....	Lycksele, Sweden, H 16
2778	Lydd, England, M 23
3845	Lydenburg, U. S. Afr., E 20
.....	Lydney, England, K 12

Pop. Place Country Index
..... Lydum, Denmark, J 3
162 Lyleton, Man., R 12
2620 Lyme Regis, England, N 11
5157 Lymington, England, M 14
176 Lyndedoch, Ont., O 8
24 Lyndhurst, Australia, F 20
305 Lyndhurst, Ontario, H 21
..... Lyngaa, Denmark, H 11
..... Lyngby, Denmark, E 11
8724 Lyngby, Denmark, J 23
2765 Lyngdal (Aa), Norway, N 5
253 Lynge, Denmark, L 18
5712 Lyngen, Norway, B 17
..... Lyngor, Norway, N 7
..... Lyn Junction, Ont., H 22
..... Lynton, Australia, K 3
2012 Lynton, England, M 8
570622 Lyon, France, L 19
255 Lyon's Brook, N. S., J 17
..... Lysaker, Norway, A 5
5866 Lysekil, Sweden, N 9
..... Lysgaard, Denmark, G 8
3457 Lyss, Switzerland, D 8
805 Lyster, Quebec, M 20
25760 Lytham, England, F 11
3110 Lyttleton, N. Z., M 13
501 Lytton, B. C., P 14
3000 Lyubim, Sov. Un., G 13

M

..... Maabo, Neth. Gu., B 9
..... Maad, Palestine, I 13
..... Maadiya, Egypt, O 5
..... Maalla, Eg., P 23
..... Maalselven, Norway, C 16
..... Maam, Ire., I 5
2000 Maan, Transj., Q 10
..... Maanet el Noman, Syr., J 11
3568 Maarttensdijk, Neth., G 15
..... Maas, Som., O 18
1817 Maasbracht, Neth., K 19
13226 Maasbree, Neth., J 19
..... Maasö, Norway, A 20
10026 Maassluis, Neth., H 11
60533 Maastricht, Neth., M 18
3928 Mablethorpe, England, G 20
636 Mabou, N. S., H 20
427 Mabou Harbour, N.S., H 20
..... Mabrouk, Fr. W. Afr., H 6
810 McAdam Jc., N. B., J 5
1330 Macagua, Cuba, I 10
9719 Macaíbe, Brazil, N 19
3500 Macalle, I. E. A., D 10
..... Macao, Brazil, F 24
..... Macapá, Brazil, D 12
510 Macaracas, Panama, Q 20
607 Macari, Peru, N 18
1500 Macas, Ecuador, D 6
74000 Macau, China, L 15
160 McAuley, Man., Q 12
307 McBride, B. C., K 15
500 Maccan, N. S., J 13
34902 Macclesfield, England, H 13
..... McClintock, Yukon, Q 10
325 McCreary, Man., P 13
..... McCreary Jc., Man., P 13
..... McDames Creek, B. C., C 8
318 Mac Dougalls, N. B., H 12
31 Mac Dowall, Sask., L 7
85949 Maceio, Brazil, H 25
13200 Macerata, Italy, G 13
700 Macetown, N. Z., O 5
..... Macfinn, N. Ire., B 20
35 McGivney Jc., N. B., G 7
264 McGregor, Ontario, Q 1
500 MacGregor, Man., Q 14
..... McGuire, B. C., F 13
6318 Macha, Bolivia, J 8
3486 Machaca, Bolivia, I 7
..... Machacamarca, Bolivia, J 6
420 Machadodorp, Union of South Africa, F 21
..... Machagai, Arg., H 17
7730 Machala, Ecuador, E 3
600 Machalilla, Ecuador, C 1
..... Machaquila, Guat., D 6
..... Macheri, India, F 9
..... Machingen, Switz., G 7
4734 Machiques, Ven., D 4
..... Machurucuto, Ven., D 15
1892 Machynlleth, Wales, I 8
..... Macia, Argentina, L 15
5000 Maciel, Paraguay, P 9
5524 Măcin, Romania, J 23
10665 Mackay, Australia, G 22
..... McKay, Alta., F 21
..... Mackies, Ont., F 18
502 Macklin, Sask., M 4
132 McKinlay, Australia, G 17
..... McKinnon, B. C., O 14
150 McKinnons Harbour, N.S., I 22
150 McLean, Sask., P 9
1600 Maclean, Australia, L 24
7675 Maclear, U. S. Afr., M 18
650 McLennan, Alberta, H 17
1912 Macleod, Alberta, P 21
..... Macmerry, Scotland, M 21
..... Macmine Jc., Ire., N 20
..... McMorran, Sask., N 5
12 McMunn, Man., Q 18
200 McMurray, Alberta, F 22
214 Mac Nutt, Sask., O 11
..... Maco, Bolivia, D 6
3923 Macomer, Italy, K 3
..... Macomir, Scotland, J 12
18496 Macon, France, K 19
129 Macoun, Sask., R 10
..... McPherson, Mackenzie, D 2
..... Macrae, Yukon, Q 9
2385 Macroom, Ire., P 8
475 Mac-Tier, Ontario, F 11
1475 Macuspana, Tab., K 16
1666 Macuto, Ven., C 13
..... Madahpura, India, G 20
..... Madan, Iran, E 13
272 Madang, New Guinea Ter., I 11
376 Madawaska, Ontario, D 15
..... Maddagiri, India, N 10
..... Madebing, U. S. Afr., G 12
..... Madha, India, K 8
..... Madhepur, India, G 19
6800 Madhupur, India, H 20
..... Madibi, U. S. Afr., F 15
..... Madiuna, Morocco, F 4
1162 Madoc, Ontario, H 17
49 Madoc Jc., Ont., I 17
..... Madracea, Algeria, D 20
777481 Madras, India, N 13
1088647 Madrid, Spain, I 12
3172 Madrigal de las Altos Torres, Spain, G 10
2911 Madruga, Cuba, H 7
..... Madum, Denmark, H 3
239144 Madura, India, P 11
84925 Maebashi, Japan, K 19
5675 Maeseyck, Belgium, K 18
5080 Maevatansna, Madag., O 24
..... Mafarkin, Tur., G 16
4666 Mafeking, U. S. Afr., F 15
..... Mafeteng, U. S. Afr., K 17
..... Mafsula, Iran, D 4
769 Magadino, Switz., O 16
..... Magallanes, see Punta Arenas, Chl.

Pop. Place Country Index
..... Magalo, Eth., M 11
..... Magara (Wells), Algeria, M 7
..... Magarabomba, Cuba, K 16
..... Magas, Iran, E 10
3500 Magdala, Eth., G 9
25507 Magdalena, Arg., N 20
2000 Magdalena, Bolivia, E 12
1126 Magdalena, Honduras, H 8
7831 Magdalena, Son., D 11
16057 Magdalena del Mar, Peru, L 8
306894 Magdeburg, Ger., H 9
237 Magenta, Algeria, E 12
7600 Magenta, Italy, D 4
325 Maggia, Switz., N 16
..... Maghâgha, Egypt, O 10
1000 Maghera, N. Ire., C 19
..... Maghera, Ire., D 10
..... Magherafelt, N. Ire., D 20
..... Maghery, Ire., C 11
..... Magi, I. E. A., M 5
..... Magilligan, N. Ire., B 18
244 Magiscatzin, Tam., J 18
4196 Maglai, Yugo., K 11
..... Maglebysteens, Denmark, L 22
9848 Maglie, Italy, K 23
..... Magnabon, Cuba, M 19
213 Magnetawan, Ontario, D 11
145870 Magnitogorsk, Sov. Un., I 25
32 Magnolia, Alberta, K 19
9034 Magog, Quebec, Q 19
..... Magra, Iran, F 11
1207 Magrath, Alberta, P 22
..... Maguires Bridge, N. Ire., F 16
6500 Magwe, Bur., N 21
..... Magyarovar, Hung., H 10
..... Magyléta, Hung., R 25
..... Mahaddei, Som., R 17
..... Mahadera Miriam, I. E. A., F 8
..... Mahagi, Bel. Cong., K 18
7029 Mahaicony, Br. Gu., A 7
51900 Mahalla el Kobra (Mehallet Kebir), Egypt, D 13
..... Mahalu, Iran, M 7
..... Mahares, Tunisia, E 24
3238 Mahates, Col., C 10
5000 Mahdia, Tun., C 25
1500 Mahdiya, Egypt, F 16
14092 Mahé, India, O 8
..... Mahenge, Tan., M 20
..... Mahfud, I. E. A., I 10
700 Mahia, N. Z., G 23
..... Mahmehabad, Iran, D 12
..... Mahmudabad, Iran, D 14
..... Mahmudabad, Iran, N 12
10100 Mahoba, India, G 13
..... Mahomadabad, Iran, J15
17459 Mahón, Spain, I 24
1025 Mahone Bay, N. S., O 13
..... Mahsameh, Egypt, F 20
..... Mahun, Iran, L 12
..... Mahur, India, J 11
..... Mai, Eth., F 12
..... Maianet Kalha, Egypt, N 11
..... Mai Atal, Erit., A 9
..... Maibut, Iran, J 9
..... Maidan-i-Naftun, Iran, J 4
17520 Maidenhead, Eng., L 17
42259 Maidstone, England, M 21
230 Maidstone, Ont., Q 2
416 Maidstone, Sask., L 4
..... Maiduguri, Nig., I 12
1425 Maienfeld, Switz., H 20
..... Maigun, Iran, K 14
6800 Maihar, India, H 14
..... Maikaba, Eth., O 7
67302 Maikop, Sov. Un., O 13
..... Maiman, Iran, N 7
25000 Maimana, Afg., F 19
..... Maimera, Arg., F 10
215 Mainadieu, N. S., H 25
..... Maingkwan, Bur., L 23
..... Mainpuri, India, F 12
..... Maintenon, France, H 12
3192 Maintirano, Madag., O 23
142627 Mainz, Germany, L 4
..... Maioro, N. Z., D 17
45000 Maipu, Argentina, M 6
2356 Maipu, Argentina, P 20
..... Maipure, Colombia, H 24
23 Mair, Sask., Q 11
1976 Mairanai, Bolivia, J 12
..... Mairang, India, M 20
..... Maisach, Germany, Q 8
2000 Maisaka, Japan, H 16
24341 Maison Carree, Alg., B 17
31012 Maisons-Alfort, France, C 7
13573 Maisons Laffitte, France, A2
..... Mait, Br. Som., G 19
12329 Maitland, Australia, N 22
600 Maitland, N. S., K 15
134 Maitland, Ontario, G 22
..... Maitland Bridge, N. S., N10
8300 Maizuru, Japan, L 13
2575 Majagua, Cuba, K 14
1752 Majagual, Col., E 11
..... Majanal, Iran, K 12
..... Majarad, Iran, H 10
6226 Majdal, Pal., G 12
..... Majdanpek, Yugo., K 15
..... Majetie, Eth., H 10
161 Majona, Zac., H 11
135 Major, Sask., M 4
22444 Majunga, Madag., N 24
..... Makabana, Fr. Eq. Afr. L 11
..... Makalle, Argentina, H 18
1106 Makamik, Quebec, D 22
11685 Makarska, Yugo., L 9
88500 Makasser, Neth. Ind., I 5
..... Makatal, Iran, H 6
240145 Makeevka (Dmitrievsk), Sov. Un., M 11
..... Maketu, N. Z., E 20
86847 Makhach-Kala(Petrovsk), Sov. Un., P 19
..... Makin, India, C 4
132 Makinak, Man., O 13
..... Makival, see Maquival, Moz.
..... Makkaur, Nor., A 24
35814 Makó, Hungary, I 13
..... Makoulek, U. S. Afr., A 22
..... Maków, Poland, D 14
..... Maków, Poland, F 13
..... Makrai, India, F 13
..... Makri, see Bakirköy, Tur.
..... Maku, Iran, A 1
..... Makum, India, L 22
1500 Mala, Peru, M 9
874 Mal Abrigo, Argentina, J 17
..... Mal Abrigo, Uruguay, N 17
..... Malacatepec, Méx., H 3
45000 Malacca, (Sts. Setts.) Malay States, Q 22
5210 Malaga, Col., G 14
238085 Málaga, Spain, O 11
..... Malagas, U. S. Afr., R 10
9883 Malagón, Spain, K 12
..... Malagueno, Arg., L 12
..... Malahide, Ire., I 22
..... Malakal, A. E. Sud., I 18
..... Malakwa, B. C., O 11
..... Malangen, Norway, C 16

Pop. Place Country Index
3817 Malanje, Ang., M 13
1116 Malans, Switz., H 20
36520 Malatia, Tur., J 13
..... Malatiya, Egypt, O 11
..... Malaträsk, Sweden, G 16
..... Malazgirt, Tur., E 18
..... Malbran, Argentina, J 14
6772 Malchin, Germany, D 11
4075 Malchow, Germany, N 19
10709 Maldeghem, Bel., K 7
6559 Maldon, England, K 22
8000 Maldonado, Uruguay, P 21
26 Maleb, Alberta, Q 23
32462 Malegaon, India, J 7
1870 Malesherbes, France, I 14
1623 Malestroit, France, I 5
..... Maletas, Sweden, P 14
3507 Male Tirnovo, Bul., M 23
..... Mal-Gazol, Iran, L 15
3924 Malgrat, Spain, F 21
1038 Malhah, Palestine, N 9
..... Malik Obdar, Iran, Q 13
..... Malilla, Sweden, O 14
..... Malin, Ire., B 16
..... Malin Beg, Ire., D 9
60438 Malines (Mechlin), Belgium, L 12
392 Malix, Switz., I 20
..... Malka, Transj., H 14
..... Malkaid, India, L 10
..... Malkangiri, India, K 15
13000 Malkapur, India, J 9
..... Malkinia Dl., Pol., D 15
2940 Mallama, Col., M 4
..... Mallaranny, Ire., G 4
..... Mallersdorf, Germany, O 10
428 Mallorytown, Ontario, H 22
4542 Mallow, Ire., O 10
679 Mallwyd, Wales, I 9
4300 Malmberget, Sweden, E 18
5275 Malmedy, Belgium, N 20
2334 Malmesbury, Eng., L 13
4085 Malmesbury, U. S. Afr., Q 7
3500 Malmizh, Sov. Un., H 19
144482 Malmö, Sweden, Q 11
..... Maloja, Switz., L 21
3188 Malonne, Belgium, N 13
7098 Malpica de Bergantiños, Spain, C 5
..... Malpur, India, H 6
..... Malsach, Ger., Q 8
..... Malstatt-Burbach, Ger., N 2
3850 Malters, Switz., G 13
4418 Malton, England, E 17
..... Malung, China, J 6
..... Malung, Sweden, L 12
1285 Malvaglia, Switz., L 17
15632 Malvern, England, K 13
177 Malvern, Ontario, K 12
207 Mamaia, Rom., K 24
..... Mamanguape, Brazil, G 25
253 Mamantel, Camp., J 19
1655 Mamara, Peru, N 15
4600 Mamers, France, H 10
299 Mamiña, Chile, C 5
..... Mammern, Switz., C 17
..... Mamoré, Bolivia, I 11
..... Mamorely, Bolivia, C 6
..... Mamoura, Morocco, E 6
1873 Mana, Fr. Guiana, B 10
19060 Manacor, Spain, J 22
..... Manado, see Menado, Neth. Ind.
87620 Managua, Nicaragua, K 11
..... Manahrit, Egypt, E 16
690 Manaia, N. Z., H 15
..... Manajanabo, Cuba, J 12
..... Manakau, N. Z., I 17
17284 Mananjary, Madag., O 24
300 Manantiales, Arg., O 10
9000 Manantoddy, India, O 9
67866 Manáus (Manaos), Brazil, E 5
..... Manaquiry, Brazil, F 5
1322 Manare, Col., H 15
..... Manaraqa, Egypt, K 13
5426 Manati, Col., O 10
..... Manati, Cuba, L 19
9581 Mancha Real, Spain, M 12
758140 Manchester, Eng., G 13
..... Manchouli, Manch., H 17
..... Mand, Baluchistan, Q 16
3591 Mandal, Norway, O 5
1400 Mandali, Iraq, L 21
134950 Mandalay, Bur., N 22
..... Manderville, Que., M 16
..... Mandi, India, C 10
..... Mandjulik, Tur., E 12
5400 Mandla, India, I 15
..... Mandleshwar, India, I 8
..... Mandra, India, B 7
20936 Mandsaur, India, H 8
13686 Manduria, Italy, K 21
25342 Mandvi, India, J 2
..... Mandvi, India, J 6
13275 Manfredonia, Italy, I 18
3400 Mangaldoi, India, F 25
2776 Mangalia, Romania, K 24
24 Mangalore, Australia, J 20
66756 Mangalore, India, N 8
..... Mangaonesco, Chile, I 3
..... Mangani, Italy, A 24
423 Mangas, Peru, K 8
345 Mangaweka, N. Z., H 19
..... Mangawhai, N. Z., C 16
4503 Manger, Norway, L 3
1000 Manglaratto, Ecuador, C 1
..... Mangonui, N. Z., A 14
12000 Mangrol, India, J 3
4986 Mangualde, Portugal, H 6
6340 Manguito, Cuba, I 10
1915 Mangulile, Honduras, F 10
..... Mania, Egypt, E 9
3823 Maniago, Italy, C 11
..... Manian, Iran, F 4
..... Manias, Tur., D 2
..... Manicoré, Brazil, G 4
14 Manigotagon Man., O 17
..... Manikganj, India, H 23
..... Manikgarh, India, K 12
..... Manikpur, India, I 25
225 Manilla, Ontario, I 13
..... Manipur, see Imphal, India.
..... Maniquiau, Western Brazil, I 24
37641 Manisa, Tur., D 2
4125 Manistir Fhear Muighe (Fermoy), Ire., O 12
706 Manitowaning, Ont., C 5
2320 Maniwaki, Quebec, M 9
..... Maniwaki Jc., Que., P 10
51025 Manizales, Col., H 9
..... Mankabâd, Egypt, L 18
..... Mankera, India, D 5
..... Mankheri, India, H 17
..... Mankova-Kalitvenskaya, Sov. Un., M 13
..... Mankur, India, H 21
1870 Manle, Bur., M 22
..... Manlin, Chi., B 19
7100 Manmad, India, J 7
4084 Mannar, Cey., Q 13
155 Manners Sutton, N. B., J 6
275162 Mannheim, Ger., M 5
396 Mannville, Alta., K 22
..... Manoel Cardoso, Brazil, G8
211 Manor, Sask., Q 11
2600 Manor Hamilton, Ire., F 12

Pop. Place Country Index
475 Manotick, Ont., E 22
36381 Manresa, Spain, F 20
..... Mansaraz, Portugal, L 7
2329 Mansavillagra, Ur., M 20
464 Manseau, Que., M 19
46075 Mansfield, England, H 16
..... Manshieh, Egypt, M 11
..... Mansilla, Argentina, M 18
1501 Mansilla de las Mulas, Spain, E 10
14248 Manta, Ecuador, C 1
9944 Mantes-sur-Seine, Fr., G 13
..... Mantgum, Neth., C 18
39600 Mantova (Mantua), It., D 8
1169 Mantua, Cuba, J 2
..... Mantua, see Mantova, It.
..... Manua, Iran, F 8
..... Manujan, Iran, P 12
..... Manulla, Ire., H 7
396 Manville, Alberta, K 22
200 Manyberries, Alberta, P 24
18451 Manzanares, Spain, K 13
35730 Manzanillo, Cuba, O 18
6831 Manzanillo, Colim., O 4
..... Manziri, W. Sov. Un., I 24
..... Mao, Fr. Eq. Afr., I 12
1000 Mapastepec, Chia., P 16
..... Mapien, China, I 6
3854 Mapimi, Dur., M 22
1796 Mapiri, Bolivia, G 3
385 Maple, Ontario, K 11
1085 Maple Creek, Sask., P 4
58 Maplewood, N. S., N 12
..... Maquassi, U. S. Afr., H 15
..... Maquinchao, Arg., B 21
..... Maquival (Makival), Moz., O 20
..... Mara, B. C., O 16
919 Mara, Peru, N 16
30 Marabastad, U.S. Afr., C 19
135582 Maracaibo, Ven., C 6
..... Maracanã, Brazil, E 15
32992 Maracay, Ven., D 12
..... Marâgha, Egypt, M 20
1500 Maragha, Iran, D 2
..... Maragogy, Brazil, H 25
2241 Maragua, Bolivia, K 8
4000 Maraisburg, U. S. Afr., N 15
..... Marand, Iran, C 2
..... Maranguape, Brazil, F 22
..... Maranhao, see São Luiz, Braz.
3707 Marans, France, L 7
..... Maraoachita, Brazil, C 5
..... Marapanim, Brazil, E 15
27836 Maras, Tur., H 12
..... Marâshda, Egypt, O 23
..... Maratahuna, Brazil, E 16
1492 Maratea, Italy, K 18
38 Marathon, Australia, G 18
2023 Marathon, Greece, P 18
3900 Maravatio, Michoa., N 14
..... Marayes, Argentina, L 8
1121 Marbach, Switz., D 20
1420 Marbach, Switz., I 11
8982 Marbella, Spain, P 10
83 Marble Bar, Australia, G 6
200 Marble Mtn., N. S., I 21
26000 Marburg, Germany, K 5
..... Marburg, see Maribor, Yugo.
716 Marca, Peru, K 7
385 Marcapata, Peru, M 17
257 Marcelin, Sask., L 7
8939 March, England, I 20
39 Marchagee, Australia, M 4
3829 Marche, Belgium, O 17
19859 Marchena, Spain, N 10
22952 Marchienne au Pont, Belgium, O 11
560 Marchigüe, Chile, N 3
5087 Marchin, Belgium, N 16
1938 Marcigny, France, L 17
554 Marcillat, France, L 15
21907 Marcinelle, Belgium, O 12
..... Marcos, Jal., L 5
2000 Marcos Paz, Arg., N 19
801 Marcourt, Bel., O 17
50000 Mar del Plata, Arg., Q 20
..... Mar del Plata Sud., Arg., Q 20
22249 Mardin, Tur., H 16
..... Mareigny, Fr., L 18
429 Mareil, France, B 1
4082 Marennes, France, L 7
..... Mareth, Tunisia, F 24
7801 Margao (Port), India, M 7
536 Margaree Harbour, Nova Scotia, G 21
328 Margaretsville, N. S., L 11
141 Margarita, Arg., J 17
2046 Margarita, Col., D 11
31312 Margate, England, L 24
5936 Marggrabowa, Ger., C 24
1329 Marguerittes, France, O 18
..... Marhametabad, Iran, D 2
425 Marhoun, Algeria, E 12
1134 Mariager, Denmark, F 11
..... Mariampole, W. Sov. Un., B 16
114743 Marianao, Cuba, H 6
5262 Marianna, Braz., M 18
7177 Mariánske Lazne, Czech., F 5
..... Mariastein, Switz., D 9
2101 Mariazell, Aus., I 8
4606 Maribo, Denmark, N 18
33149 Maribor, Yugo., I 8
27100 Marico, U. S. Afr., F 16
..... Marico West, U. S. Afr., F 16
1362 Mariefred, Sweden, M 15
..... Marie Joseph, N. S., M 19
2309 Mariel, Cuba, H 6
1353 Mariembourg, Bel., P 12
7127 Marienberg, Germany, K 12
24000 Marienburg, Pol., C 12
..... Marienthal, Ger., R 19
6143 Mariestad, Sweden, N 12
2394 Marieville, Quebec, P 16
..... Marifjären, Norway, K 5
502 Marigny, France, G 7
..... Marigot, Haiti, J 13
1494 Mariguitar, Ven., C 18
..... Marikana, U. S. Afr., F 17
5261 Marin, Martinique, N 24
16294 Marin, Spain, D 2
3591 Marinilla, Col., G 9
..... Marino, N. Ire., D 23
8555 Marino, Italy, I 11
..... Marion Bridge, N. S., H 24
262 Marion Downs, Austl., H17
..... Maripaondre, N. Gu., B 9
5533 Maripi, Col., H 11
3817 Mariquita, Col., H 10
222427 Mariupol, Sov. Un., N 11
..... Marka, Eth., D 11
..... Marka, Morocco, I 9
..... Markapur, India, M 12
..... Markaryd, Sweden, P 12
870 Markdale, Ont., I 8
4966 Markelo, Neth., G 21
9312 Market Harborough, England, J 17
..... Markethill, N. Ire., F 20
2048 Market Rasen, Eng., G 18
1204 Markham, Ontario, K 12

Pop. Place Country Index
128 Markinch, Sask., O 9
8477 Markinch, Scot., L 20
..... Markovo, Sov. Un., L 12
15000 Marksshtadt (Ekaterinenstadt), Sov. Un., K 18
410 Marlbank, Ont., I 18
150 Marlboro, Alberta, K 18
..... Marlborough, Br. Gu., A 6
2327 Marle, France, F 16
1519 Marly, France, B 1
..... Marmagao, India, M 6
9555 Marmande, France, N 10
..... Marmaras, see Mermeris, Tur.
5949 Marmolejo, Spain, M 11
1106 Marmora, Ontario, H 17
750 Marnay, France, J 21
430 Marnes, France, B 3
..... Maroa, Ven., O 12
..... Marol, India, B 9
4055 Maromme, France, G 12
13677 Maroua, Cam., I 12
..... Márquez, Chih., G 20
96 Marquis, Sask., P 7
3693 Marquise, France, E 12
1805 Marradi, Italy, F 9
184400 Marrakech, Morocco, I 4
243 Marree, Austl., L 16
264 Marriot Cove, N. S., N 13
1382 Marroquin, Col., H 14
..... Marsa, Tunisia, B 24
30788 Marsala, Italy, N 11
914232 Marseille, France, P 20
884 Marsens, Switz., J 6
94 Marshall, Sask., K 4
..... Marshfield, P. E. I., H 16
2171 Marstal, Denmark, N 13
..... Marsuria, Morocco, F 5
..... Martaban, Bur., P 23
..... Martham, England, I 24
5060 Marti, Cuba, M 18
3229 Martigne-Ferchaud, Fr., I 6
2761 Martigny-Ville, Switz., O 6
8876 Martigues, France, P 19
24355 Martina Franca, Italy, J 21
..... Martins, Brazil, G 23
..... Martins River, N. S., N 13
369 Martintown, Ont., E 24
973 Martinano, Italy, L 19
2830 Marton, N. Z., H 18
4295 Martorell, Spain, G 19
27131 Martos, Spain, M 11
..... Maru, India, B 9
..... Marucha, Argentina, O 15
..... Maruchak, Afg., F 17
28842 Marugame, Japan, M 10
6344 Marum, Neth., C 20
1152 Marvão, Port., J 7
3888 Marvejols, France, N 16
..... Marwar Jc., India, G 6
..... Marwick, Scotland, A 18
12000 Maryborough, Austl., J 24
6000 Maryborough, Austl., P 18
924 Maryculter, Scot., I 23
333 Maryfield, Sask., Q 11
..... Maryhill, Scotland, M 15
1163 Marykirk, Scotland, J 22
10182 Maryport, England, D 10
104 Marysville, B. C., P 19
1651 Marysville, N. B., I 7
..... Marzahn, Germany, O 20
32411 Masan, Kor., F 25
..... Masasi, Tan., M 21
19827 Masaya, Nicaragua, K 11
31449 Mascara, Alg., D 13
..... Mascasin, Arg., L 9
4507 Mascota, Jal., M 3
..... Maseltrangen, Switz., F 17
2320 Maseru, Bas., K 18
..... Masgirt, Tur., E 15
1995 Masham, Eng., E 15
..... Mashâyikh, Egypt, P 24
139300 Mash-Had (Meshed), Iran, F 14
600 Mashike, Japan, F 13
..... Mashita, Transj., N 17
..... Mashiz, Iran, M 11
..... Mashor, Iran, L 4
..... Mashtul-es-Suk, Eg. G 15
1742 Masisea, Peru, I 12
674 Maskinonge, Quebec, N 17
..... Maskotu, Iran, P 14
10000 Masqat (Muscat), Oman, M 7
18400 Massa, Italy, F 6
10380 Massafra, Italy, J 20
6023 Massa Marittima, It., G 8
20480 Massâua, Erit., A 9
425 Massett, B. C., J 5
752 Massey, Ontario, A 4
1386 Massiac, France, M 16
..... Massid, Egypt, F 17
..... Massinga, Moz., P 19
263 Mass Town, N. S., K 15
1802 Massy, France, C 4
9480 Masterton, N. Z., J 18
..... Mastian, Iran, K 15
..... Mastuj, India, A 6
..... Mastung, Bal., M 21
..... Masuda, Japan, L 7
42100 Masulipatam, India, L 14
..... Matacora, Brazil, F 14
6548 Matadi, Bel. Cong., L 12
..... Matador, Sask., O 5
8506 Matagalpa, Nicaragua, I 12
..... Matagua, Cuba, J 12
1385 Matahuasi, Peru, L 11
3072 Matai, Egypt, O 10
10415 Matale, Cey., R 14
691 Matalele, U. S. Afr., L 19
..... Matam, Fr. W. Afr., H 2
7961 Matamoros, Tam., F 20
..... Matâna, Egypt, P 23
126 Matancilla, Chile, L 4
..... Matanuco, Baja Cal., A 2
10206 Matanzas, Col., F 14
864 Matanzas, Chile, N 3
49591 Matanzas, Cuba, H 8
..... Matapy, Brazil, D 12
8274 Mataquescuintla, Guat., G 5
..... Matará, Argentina, I 13
18893 Matara, Cey., R 14
861 Matará, Peru, M 15
..... Matarba, Morocco, G 20
..... Matarie, Egypt, H 14
29920 Mataró, Spain, F 21
315 Matatlán, Jal., L 7
1530 Mataura, N. Z., Q 6
..... Matawa, New Zealand, F 22
..... Matbul, Egypt, D 12
16365 Matehuala, S. L. P., I 13
..... Mater Tunisia, B 23
20200 Matera, Italy, J 19
1640 Matha, France, L 9
..... Mathew Town, Bahamas, G 11
..... Matiari, India, G 2
..... Matjes Kloof, U. S. Afr., O 11
..... Matjestfontein, U. S. Afr., P 9
7500 Matlalapa, Pueb., J 9
..... Matmar, Egypt, M 19
..... Matmara, Algeria, G 20
..... Mato, Peru, J 6
205 Matsqui, B. C., P 5
44496 Matsue, Japan, K 9
72141 Matsumoto, Japan, K 18

Pop. Place Country Index
..... Matsuna, Japan, M 19
117534 Matsuyama, Japan, N 8
13000 Matsuzaka, Japan, N 14
723 Matt, Switz., H 18
15000 Matta de São João, Brazil, J 22
1971 Mattawa, Ontario, A 14
..... Mattmar, Sweden, I 12
..... Mattmark, Switz., O 11
..... Matto Grosso, Brazil, J 6
..... Mattozinhos, Port., G 5
..... Matûbis, Egypt, B 8
1746 Matucana, Peru, L 9
10705 Maturin, Ven., D 19
..... Matushiro, Japan, J 18
..... Mau, India, G 12
..... Mau, India, G 14
21354 Mau, India, G 17
..... Mau, India, I 13
24221 Maubeuge, France, E 16
1878 Maubourguet, Fr., P 9
2484 Mauchline, Scot., O 15
..... Maud, Scotland, G 23
608 Mauensee, Switz., F 12
..... Maués, Brazil, F 7
925 Maulde, Belgium, N 7
4316 Mauléon Licharre, Fr., P 7
1585 Maullin, Chile, B 19
..... Mauná, Braz., E 14
..... Maura, Japan, N 21
3312 Mauriac, France, M 14
1000 Mauriceville, N. Z., I 18
4178 Maurik, Neth., H 17
3749 Mauron, France, I 5
1507 Maurs, France, N 14
..... Mavilette, N. S., P 8
77 Mawer, Sask., P 7
3911 Maxcanú, Yuc., F 20
5416 Maximo Gomez, Cuba, H 9
769 Maxville, Ontario, E 24
..... Maxwelltown Scot., Q 18
..... Mayabe, Cuba, M 21
1161 Mayajigua, Cuba, J 14
..... Mayar, Iran, J 7
3300 Mayari, Cuba, N 22
..... Mayat, Morocco, H 5
27100 Mayavaram, India, O 13
6180 Maybole, Scotland, O 13
14287 Mayen, Germany, L 3
8751 Mayenne, France, H 9
217 Mayerthorpe, Alberta, J 19
205 Maymont, Sask., L 6
700 Maynooth, Ire., J 20
310 Maynooth, Ont., E 16
..... Mayo, Ire., H 7
..... Mayol, Arg., Q 17
..... Mayo Landing, Yukon, L 9
25 Maytown, Australia, D 19
..... Maza, Argentina, P 13
32200 Mazagan, Morocco, E 5
1422 Mazamitla, Jal., N 7
..... Mazán, Argentina, J 9
1595 Mazapil, Zac., G 11
..... Mazara, Iran, K 9
11569 Mazarrón, Spain, N 15
15113 Mazatenango, Guat., G 3
32132 Mazatlán, Sin., R 18
..... Mazeikiai, Sov. Un., H 2
..... Mazer, Algeria, D 18
330 Maziéres, Fr., K 9
..... Mazinan, Iran, F 11
903 Mazingen, Switz., C 17
..... Mazlikiai, W. Sov. Un., A 15
..... Mazowieck, Poland, G 16
20285 Mazzara del Valle, It., O 11
18165 Mazzarino, Italy, O 15
1550 Mbabane, Swaz., G 22
6000 Mbocayaty, Paraguay, O 9
6000 Mbuyapey, Paraguay, P 8
..... Mdaourouch, Algeria, C 22
..... Mdoukal, Algeria, D 18
971 Meadow Lake, Sask., J 5
219 Meadowvale, Ontario, L 11
2662 Meaford, Ontario, H 8
150 Meaghers Grant, N.S., M 16
..... Meanook, Alberta, I 21
14169 Meaux, France, H 14
..... Mebruk, Algeria, L 13
..... Mecapalapa, Pueb., F 7
70000 Mecca, Sau. Ar., L 4
2676 Mechelen, Belgium, L 17
2615 Mecheria, Algeria, F 13
..... Mechlin, see Malines, Bel.
..... Mechoacane, Arg., Q 19
900 Medak, India, K 11
77000 Médan, Neth. Ind., H 1
..... Medanos, Arg., O 14
16431 Medea, Algeria, C 16
143952 Medellín, Col., G 8
1112 Medellín, Ver., I 10
3649 Medemblik, Neth., E 15
..... Meder, Erit., B 11
6389 Medgidia, Rom., K 23
..... Media Luna, Cuba, O 18
..... Mediano, Spain, E 17
15000 Medias, Rom., I 18
10571 Medicine Hat, Alberta, O 24
2752 Medina, Col., I 13
30000 Medina, Sau. Ar., L 4
845 Medinaceli, Spain, F 14
13154 Medina del Campo, Sp., G 11
2097 Medina de Pomar, Sp., D 13
4791 Medina de Rioseco, Sp., F 11
1264 Medinas, Arg., I 10
12486 Medina-Sidonia, Sp., P 9
..... Medinet el Gahil (El-Hebi), Egypt, O 11
22 Medonte, Ont., H 11
..... Medrano, Arg., M 7
..... Meduhar, Morocco, E 9
..... Medûm, Egypt, L 14
..... Medvezhya Gora, Sov. Un., E 10
..... Medvin, W. Sov. Un., F 25
..... Medzhibozh, W. Sov. Un., F 21
4400 Meean Meer, India, D 8
1086 Meekatharra, Austl., J 5
25000 Meerane, Germany, K 10
1989 Meerle, Belgium, I 3
..... Meersburg, Germany, R 6
5291 Meerssen, Neth., M 18
169290 Meerut, India, E 11
..... Mega, Eth., P 8
2373 Megalopolis, Greece, P 16
2070 Megantic, Quebec, P 22
10441 Megara, Greece, P 18
6578 Megarin, Algeria, G 20
1531 Meggen, Switz., G 14
4000 Mehallet-Damenne, Egypt, D 16
..... Mehallet el Kebir, see Mahalla el Kobra, Egypt.
..... Mehallet Kêt, Egypt, D 6
3600 Mehallet-Menûf, Egypt, E 11
..... Mehallet Musa, Egypt, C 11
..... Mehallet Ruh, Egypt, E 12
1500 Mehallet Sa, Egypt, D 10
4800 Mehallet Ziyâd, Egypt, D 14
402 Meham, Norway, A 23
..... Mehdia, Morocco, E 5
..... Mehidpur, India, H 8
..... Mehmandost, Iran, F 9

Pop.	Place Country Index
5337	Méhun-sur-Yèvre, Fr., J 14
.....	Meiden, Switz., N 10
.....	Meiden, Switz., J 15
.....	Meigle, Scotland, K 20
7200	Meiktila, Bur., N 22
4238	Meilen, Switz., E 15
.....	Meilmanj, Afg., G 18
20000	Meiningen, Ger., K 8
3078	Meiringen, Switz., J 13
154	Meiron, Palestine, G 11
.....	Meis, Palestine, F 12
46000	Meissen, Germany, J 12
.....	Mejdel esh Shems, Syria E 15
.....	Mejdel Yaba, Palestine, L 7
.....	Mejez el Bab, Tunisia, B 23
142	Mejia, Peru, P 16
1056	Mejillones, Chile, E 3
.....	Mejorana, Cuba, O 22
.....	Mekalia, Algeria, D 13
.....	Mekkam Si Brahim, Algeria, J 13
113900	Meknes, Morocco, F 7
.....	Mekong, Siam., P 3
135048	Melbourne (with suburbs), Austl., Q 19
326	Melbourne, Ont., O 5
340	Melbourne, Quebec, P 19
.....	Melchthal, Switz., I 13
.....	Meldalen, Norway, I 8
.....	Melegob, Tur., F 9
.....	Meleitig, Egypt, F 12
.....	Melekes, Sov. Un., J 19
.....	Melen, Sweden, I 11
2608	Melena, Cuba, H 7
.....	Melendes, Peru, F 7
.....	Melenki, Sov. Un., I 13
.....	Melfjord, Norway A 19
2005	Melfort, Sask., L 9
.....	Melgaço, Brazil, E 12
.....	Melgaço, Brazil, K 9
1259	Melgar, Col., I 10
2614	Melgar de Fernamental, Spain, E 12
.....	Melghat, India, I 10
.....	Melhakde, Eth., C 13
2801	Melhus, Nor., I 9
707	Melide, Switz., P 17
76902	Melilla, Sp. Mor., D 10
9316	Melipilla, Chile, M 4
1495	Melito Porto Salvo, Italy, N 18
75735	Melitopol, Sov. Un., N 9
.....	Melitsch, Tur., B 11
.....	Mellaha, Egypt, C 3
.....	Mellansel, Sweden, I 17
29000	Mellawi, Eg., K 18
6556	Melle, Belgium, R 4
.....	Melle, Eth., H 13
2151	Melle, France, L 9
1577	Mellerud, Sweden, N 10
1048	Mellier, Belgium, Q 17
1556	Mellingen, Switz., D 13
.....	Mellouneche, Tunisia, D 25
.....	Melness, Scotland, D 14
.....	Melnik, Bul., M 17
.....	Mělnik, Czech., F 7
11549	Mélnik, Ger., L 14
23000	Mélo, Uruguay, J 23
.....	Melouprey, Fr. In. Ch., P 7
.....	Melrose, N. B., H 14
4518	Melrose, Scotland, O 21
.....	Melstadur, Iceland, B 20
.....	Meltegat el Ouidane, Algeria, J 12
10437	Melton Mowbray, Eng., I 17
16356	Melun, France, H 15
.....	Melvaig, Scotland, F 9
.....	Melvern Square, N.S., M 11
400	Melvich, Scotland, D 16
32	Melville, Ont., K 10
4011	Melville, Sask., P 10
.....	Memba, Moz., N 21
.....	Membidj, Syr., I 13
	Memel, see Klaipědec, Sov. Un.
14049	Memmingen, Ger., Q 7
510	Memramcook, N. B., I 12
28400	Menado, Neth. Ind., H 7
.....	Menâka, Fr. W. Afr., H 8
.....	Mendah, Transj., I 13
6056	Mende, France, N 17
639	Mendelin, Tur., G 1
639	Méndez, Tam., G 18
100429	Mendoza, Arg., M 7
3953	Mendrisio, Switz., P 17
13377	Menemen, Tur., E 1
.....	Menéndez, Uruguay, J 18
3107	Menerville, Algeria, B 17
.....	Menezla, Algeria, F 13
10170	Menfi, Italy, O 12
.....	Mengcheng, China, G 17
	Mengel, see Alvaro Obregon, Q. R.
.....	Menglien, China, L 3
.....	Mengting, China, K 3
193000	Mengtsz, China, K 6
.....	Menhir, Transj., O 15
19723	Menin, Belgium, M 5
509	Menindie, Australia, M 18
19	Menisino, Man., R 17
.....	Menlough, Ire., J 8
612	Menmuir, Scotland, J 21
.....	Menock, Scotland, P 17
.....	Menocucho, Peru, I 5
.....	Menshiya, Egypt, N 21
21703	Menton, France, O 25
.....	Menuf, Egypt, G 11
.....	Menzel, Tunisia, C 24
7542	Menzelinsk, Sov. Un., I 21
1500	Menzies, Australia, L 6
.....	Menzies Bay, B. C., P 10
3096	Meoqui, Chih., H 20
224	Meota, Sask., L 5
12133	Meppel, Neth., E 20
5621	Meppen, Germany, F 4
4230	Mequinenza, Spain, G 18
3165	Mer, France, I 13
.....	Mera, Ecuador, C 6
.....	Meraker, Norway, I 10
.....	Meramer, Morocco, H 3
19185	Merano, Italy, B 8
2025	Merauke, Neth. Ind., J 10
.....	Merbat, Oman, M 5
3288	Mercadal, Spain, I 23
7597	Mercaderes, Col., L 5
.....	Mercara, India, O 8
11315	Mercedes, Argentina, J 20
47719	Mercedes, Arg., N 18
30000	Mercedes, Uruguay, L 15
98	Merceditas, Chile, I 4
350	Mercer, N. Z., D 17
3056	Merckem, Belgium, L 4
.....	Mercural, Ven., F 18
5014	Mercurea-Ciucului, Rom., I 20
.....	Merda, Palestine, L 9
.....	Merdibba, Eth., E 5
.....	Mere, England, M 13
.....	Meregh, Som., Q 20
872	Méréville, France, H 13
.....	Mergawar, Iran, D 1
.....	Mergen, Manchuria, H 18
.....	Mergo, Morocco, E 8
20405	Mergui, Bur., Q 24
98852	Mérida, Yuc., E 21
25501	Mérida, Spain, K 8
14544	Mérida, Ven., F 6
604	Merishausen, Switz., B 15
.....	Merligen, Switz., J 10
2066	Mermeris (Marmaras), Tur., H 2
.....	Meroin, Australia, L 5
794	Merrickville Ontario, F 21
940	Merritt, B. C., P 15
2993	Merritton, Ontario, N 12
1099	Mersch, Luxembourg, Q 20
29000	Merseburg, Ger., J 10
.....	Mersel Abiod, Mor., G 6
30007	Mersin (Icel), Tur., H 9
4400	Merta, India, F 7
.....	Methven, Scot., L 18
71099	Merthyr-Tydfil, Wales, K 9
4547	Mértola, Portugal, M 6
.....	Mertoutek Algeria, R 18
30600	Merv, Sov Un. Asia, K 9
6675	Merville, France, E 14
196	Mervin, Sask., K 5
27174	Merxem, Bel., K 12
379	Mery, Fr., G 14
.....	Merza, I. E. A., F 10
13058	Merzifon, Tur., C 10
7500	Merzig, France, G 22
10259	Merzig, Ger., N 2
593	Meschers, France, M 7
.....	Meselieh, Palestine, J 10
2049	Mesemvrija, Bul., L 23
337	Mesha, Palestine, L 8
	Meshed, see Mash-Had, Iran.
.....	Meshêkh, Egypt, N 21
.....	Meshia, Morocco, I 5
.....	Meshia Zerzu, Sp. Mor., E 10
.....	Meshla, Egypt, E 10
.....	Meshoor, Iran, B 1
391	Mesinge, Denmark, K 14
.....	Mesir, Egypt, D 12
1130	Meskiana, Algeria, D 21
.....	Meskuiciai, W. Sov. Un., A 16
1044	Meslay, Fr., I 8
629	Mesnil, Fr., A 2
1100	Mesocco, Switz., L 18
9270	Mesolongion, Greece, P 15
.....	Messad, Algeria, F 17
2211	Messancy, Bel., R 18
6725	Messene, Greece, Q 16
114051	Messina, Italy, N 17
350	Messina Mine, U. S. Afr., A 20
2255	Messkirch Ger., Q 5
.....	Mestre, Italy, D 10
414	Mesvres, France, K 18
1469	Metabetchouan, Que., F 19
1600	Metan, Arg., G 11
10561	Metapa, Nicaragua, I 11
825	Meteghan, N. S., P 8
....	Meteghan Centre, N.S., P 8
436	Meteghan River, N.S. O 8
277	Meteghan Station, N. S., O 8
....	Metekki, Algeria, H 20
1481	Methlick, Scotland, H 23
1991	Methone, Greece, Q 15
771	Methven, N. Z., M 11
1670	Methven, Scotland, K 18
.....	Metileo, Arg., O 13
.....	Metkovich, Yugo., L 10
.....	Metlili, Algeria, H 17
.....	Metslawier, Neth., B 19
2156	Metsovon, Grc., O 15
3158	Mettet, Belgium, O 13
.....	Mettupalaiyam, India, O 9
83119	Metz, France, G 21
1368	Metztitlán, Hid., F 5
20870	Meudon, France, B 4
.....	Mevagh, Ire., B 14
.....	Mex, Egypt, Q 17
15856	Mexborough, Eng., G 16
18785	Mexicali, Baja Cal., A 4
1464556	México, Méx. D. F., H 5
1526	Mexquitic, Jal., J 6
1988	Mexticacán, Jal., L 8
.....	Meyadine, Syr., K 16
.....	Meyer, Cuba, K 11
.....	Meyerton, U. S. Afr., G 18
3611	Meymac, France, M 13
259	Meyronne, Sask., Q 6
.....	Mezeirib, Syria, N 10
2000	Mezen, Sov. Un., C 14
	Mezha River, W. Sov. Un.
1322	Mezidon, France, G 9
10214	Mézières, France, F 18
515	Mézières, Switz., K 5
1598	Mézin, France, O 10
7482	Mezöhegyes, Hung., I 13
27645	Mezötúr, Hungary, I 13
.....	Mezquite, Coa., E 9
4557	Mezzolombardo, Italy, C 8
7631	Mglin, Sov. Un., J 8
.....	Mhangursta, Scotland, E 4
29800	Mhow, India, I 9
4180	Miahuatlán, Oax., N 9
2902	Miahuatlán, Pueb., J 8
8302	Miajadas, Spain, K 9
248	Mialqui, Chile, K 4
356	Miami, Man., R 15
7000	Mianeh, Iran, D 3
6000	Miani, India, I 2
.....	Mianrud, Afg., J 16
770	Michel, B. C., P 20
224	Michelet, Algeria, B 18
70202	Michurinsk (Kozlov), Sov. Un., K 13
400	Micksburg, Ont., D 18
2271	Midale, Sask., R 10
.....	Mid Clyth, Scot., D 19
18389	Middelburg, Neth., J 7
5778	Middelburg, U. S. Afr., F 19
7480	Middelfart, Denmark, K 10
4424	Middelharnis, Neth., I 10
3001	Middelkerke, Belgium, K 3
5371	Middleburg, U. S. Afr., N 14
.....	Middleham, England, E 14
.....	Middlemarch, N. Z., P 8
219	Middleport, Ont., N 10
105	Middle Sackville, N.B., I 13
138489	Middlesbrough, Eng., D 16
.....	Middle Southampton, N B., I 5
618	Middle Stewiacke, Nova Scotia, L 16
29189	Middleton, England, G 13
3200	Middleton, Ire., P 12
1172	Middleton, N. S., M 11
304	Midgic Station, N.B., I 13
1500	Midhurst, England, M 17
.....	Midieh, Palestine, M 7
6800	Midland, Ont., G 10
3200	Midleton, Ire., P 12
.....	Midnapore, India, I 20
3918	Midyat, Tur., H 17
5400	Midzusawa, Japan, F 24
.....	Miechów, Poland, F 13
.....	Miedzychód, Poland, D 9
16837	Miedzyczec, Poland, E 16
.....	Miélan, France, P 10
.....	Mielegiany, W. Sov. Un., B 19
6310	Mienchow, China, H 7
.....	Mienning, China, I 6
.....	Mienning, China, K 3
.....	Mienyang, China, H 14
.....	Mier, U. S. Afr., G 9
5007	Mierlo, Neth., J 18
607	Mier y Noriega, N. L., I 14
6310	Miguelturra, Spain, K 12
5000	Migues, Uruguay, O 20
3203	Mihailena, Rom., G 20
.....	Miharu, Japan, I 22
.....	Mihr, Iran, F 12
4594	Mijdrecht, Neth., G 14
.....	Mikawa, Japan, J 15
9000	Mikhailov, Sov. Un., J 12
10018	Mikkeli, Fin., E 6
7785	Mikulov, Czech., G 9
.....	Mikuriya, Japan, K 10
8011	Mila, Algeria, C 20
.....	Milagird, Iran. I 5
16389	Milagro, Ecuador, D 3
.....	Milam, India, D 13
10031	Milana, Alg., C 15
712844	Milano, Italy, D 5
7346	Milas, Tur., G 2
211	Milden, Sask., N 6
.....	Mildenhall, England, J 21
771	Mildmay, Ontario, J 7
6617	Mildura, Australia, O 17
10935	Mile End, Quebec, P 15
618	Milford, N. B., K 8
181	Milford, N. S., L 15
267	Milford, Ontario, K 18
10116	Milford, Wales, K 5
13521	Miliana, Algeria, C 15
12489	Militello, Italy, O 16
335	Milk River, Alberta, Q 23
3739	Mill, Neth., I 18
1998	Millas, France, Q 15
16190	Millau, France, O 15
419	Millbank, Ontario, L 7
.....	Mill Bay, B. C., I 7
663	Millbrook Jc., Ontario, J 14
.....	Millchester, Austl., F 20
231	Mill Cove, N. S., N 13
710	Mille Roches, Ont., F 24
419	Millerton, N. B., E 9
325	Millet, Alberta, K 21
.....	Millford, Ire., B 14
78	Millicent, Alberta, O 23
1574	Millicent, Australia, Q 16
.....	Mill Isle, N. Ire., D 25
426	Millstream, N. B., I 10
.....	Millstreet, Ire., O 8
216	Millsville, N. S., J 17
.....	Millton, Scotland, H 14
.....	Milltown, Ire., G 16
.....	Milltown, Ire., I 8
.....	Milltown, Ire., O 4
1876	Milltown, N. B., L 5
.....	Milltown, N. Ire., C 23
.....	Milltown, Scotland, N 8
1300	Milltown Malbay, Ire., L 6
1896	Milluhuaya, Bolivia, H 5
458	Millview, P. E. I., H 17
210	Mill Village, N. S., P 12
128	Millville, N. B., H 5
.....	Milmil, I. E. A., L 23
93	Milnet, Ontario, Q 23
5056	Milngavie, Scotland, M 15
.....	Milnthorpe, England, E 12
98	Milon, Fr., C 1
102	Milparinka, Australia, L 17
4395	Miltenberg, Germany, M 6
544	Miltepec, Oax., M 13
1550	Milton, N. Z., Q 8
1142	Milton, N. S., P 11
1955	Milton, Ontario, L 10
1015	Milverton, Ontario, L 7
8070	Mimico, Ontario, L 11
.....	Mimitsu, Japan, P 5
310	Mimizan, France, O 6
.....	Mimsina, Morocco, K 7
824	Mina, N. L., E 13
.....	Minab, Baluchistan, Q 17
11000	Minab, Iran, P 12
502	Minaca, Chih., H 16
.....	Minard, Ire., O 2
1526	Minas, Cuba, L 17
32000	Minas, Uruguay, N 21
9060	Minas de Río Tinto, Spain, M 8
.....	Minas Novas, Brazil, K 19
170	Minas Nueves, Son., J 14
.....	Minas Nuevas, Chih., J 19
341	Minas Prietas, Son., G 11
25	Minas Viejas, N. L., D 14
18539	Minatitlán, Ver., K 13
.....	Minato, Japan, C 25
10000	Minato, Japan, L 22
2948	Minaya, Spain, K 14
.....	Minbu, India, N 21
129	Minburn, Alberta, K 22
.....	Minchow, China, F 7
4902	Mindelheim, Ger., Q 7
28000	Minden, Germany, G 6
550	Minden, Ontario, G 14
6315	Minehead, England, M 9
.....	Mineiros, Brazil, L 12
20000	Mineral del Oró, Méx., G 3
.....	Minerales, Arg., C 22
1509	Mineral Ocampo, Chih., H 15
2500	Mineyama, Japan, K 13
332	Mingenew, Australia, L 4
.....	Mingin, Bur., M 21
.....	Mingkiang, China, G 15
.....	Mingkwang, China, G 18
3049	Minglanilla, Spain, J 15
700	Minhla, Bur., O 22
322700	Minhow (Foochow), J 19
.....	Miniet, Egypt, C 8
325	Miniota, Man., Q 12
410	Minitonas, Man., N 12
.....	Miniya Asiya, Egypt, D 8
.....	Minlow, Scotland, G 24
1629	Minnedosa, Man., Q 13
.....	Minneri, Cey., Q 14
1144	Minnigaff, Scot., Q 14
.....	Minshat, Egypt, M 11
238772	Minsk, W. Sov. Un., C 21
13132	Minsk Mazowiecki, Pol., D 15
179	Minto, Man., R 13
910	Minto, N. B., H 8
.....	Minto Bridge, Yukon, L 9
.....	Minu, Iran, R 16
21443	Minusinsk, Sov. Un. Asia, H 14
.....	Minyet el-Qamb, Egypt, F 15
1068	Miquihuana, Tam., I 15
8930	Mira, Portugual, H 5
2422	Mira, Spain, J 15
.....	Mirabad, Iran H 4
200	Mira Cut, N. S., H 24
.....	Mirador, Brazil, G 17
2000	Miraflores, Arg., J 10
2066	Miraflores, Col., H 13
490	Mira Flores, Baja Cal., Q 12
.....	Mira Flores, W. Brazil, I 19
5000	Miragoane, Haiti, J 12
26465	Miraj, India, L 7
860	Miramar, Argentina, Q 20
.....	Miramar, Pan., O 22
.....	Miranda, Brazil, M 8
15116	Miranda de Ebro, Spain, E 13
4425	Miranda do Corvo, Port., I 6
1053	Miranda-do-Douro, Portugal, F 9
1828	Mirande, France, P 10
2049	Mirandela, Port, F 8
4424	Mirandola, Italy, E 8
356	Mirani, Australia, G 21
2468	Mirano, Italy, D 10
.....	Mirazard Iran, O 10
.....	Mir Daud Sarai, Afg., H 16
.....	Mirebalais, Haiti, J 13
857	Mirebeau, France, J 20
5508	Mirecourt, France, H 21
3341	Mirepoix, France, Q 13
.....	Mirgorod, Sov. Un. L 8
.....	Miriam, Afg., G 24
.....	Mirletombille, Bolivia, D 5
.....	Mirpur, India, E 3
2500	Mirpur, India, G 2
570	Mirror, Alberta, L 21
.....	Mir Wali, Ind a, A 7
61184	Mirzapur, India, G 15
.....	Misahohe, Fr. W. Afr., J 7
4000	Misaki, Japan, N 20
300	Misaki, Japan, P 7
3484	Miscantla, Ver., G 9
4000	Mishima, Japan, M 19
.....	Mishkin, Iran, E 5
.....	Mishqal el-Qadi, Egypt, F 16
.....	Mishta, Egypt, M 19
11548	Misilmeri, Italy, N 13
.....	Miskara, Iran, B 1
.....	Miskeh, Palestine, K 7
62208	Miskolc, Hung., H 13
1957	Mission, B. C., Q 13
.....	Mission, Man., O 15
.....	Missis, Tur., H 10
1292	Mistassini, Quebec, D 19
148	Mistatim, Sask., L 10
9951	Mistek, Czech., F 11
4907	Mistelbach, Aus., G 9
12055	Mistretta, Italy, N 15
800	Misumi, Japan, O 3
4000	Misurata, Libya, E 13
.....	Mit Abu el Hares, Egypt, D 14
.....	Mit Abû Ghâlib, Egypt, B 17
6100	Mitajiri, Japan, M 6
1532	Mitare, Ven., B 8
.....	Mit Asseim, Egypt, G 13
4100	Mit Bedr Halawa, Egypt, E 14
.....	Mit Bera, Egypt, F 13
.....	Mitcham, Eng., D 21
1200	Mitchell, Australia, J 21
1777	Mitchell, Ontario, L 6
2300	Mitchelstown, Ire., O 12
1700	Mit Demsês, Egypt, E 14
.....	Mit el-Nasarah, Egypt, C 17
.....	Mit es Sûdân, Egypt, E 12
.....	Mit Fadalah, Egypt, E 15
.....	Mit Fâres, Egypt, D 17
11200	Mit Ghamr, Egypt, E 14
1250	Mit Halfa, Egypt, H 14
.....	Mithankot, India, E 4
1500	Mit Hawai, Egypt, E 13
1400	Mit Heml, Egypt, G 16
2000	Mithi, India, H 3
.....	Mit Kenana, Egypt, G 14
2298	Mitla, Oax., M 9
50647	Mito, Japan, K 22
11848	Mitrovica, Yugo., J 13
.....	Mitrovica, Yugo., L 14
.....	Mit Sehil, Egypt, G 15
.....	Mitsumata, Japan, J 19
20000	Mittweida, Ger., J 11
.....	Mitu, Col., M 19
.....	Mituas, Col., J 22
.....	Mit Yazid, Egypt, F 14
693	Mixtepec, Oax., N 8
1200	Mixtepec, Oax., N 10
4700	Miyako, Japan, E 25
30421	Miyakonojo, Japan, Q 4
1800	Miyanaka, Japan, L 22
1800	Miyano-ura, Japan, A 13
8400	Miyatsu, Japan, K 13
54596	Miyazaki, Japan, Q 5
.....	Miyoshi, Japan, L 8
.....	Miz Ali, Iran, Q 15
6488	Mizil, Rom., J 21
2000	Mizque, Bolivia, J 9
.....	Mjesing, Denmark, H 10
5911	Mjölby. Sweden, N 13
	Mladá Boleslav, Czech., F 7
19584	Mlawa, Poland, D 13
1356	Mo, Norway, F 12
.....	Moabit, Ger., P 16
779	Moama, Australia, P 19
.....	Moana, N. Z., G 20
.....	Moate, Ire., J 14
.....	Möborg, Denmark, G 3
6063	Moca, Dominican Rep., J 14
11775	Mocajuba, Brazil, E 14
6898	Moçambique, Moz., N 22
5000	Mocha, Yem., N 4
217	Mochelle, N. S., M 10
.....	Mochrum, Scotland, R 14
8000	Mochudi, Bech., P 16
.....	Möckmühl, Ger., N 6
1206	Mocoa, Col., L 7
6250	Mocomoco, Bolivia, G 2
.....	Mocoreta, Arg., K 20
2387	Mocorito, Sin., M 16
2188	Moctezuma, Son., F 13
2017	Moctezuma, S. L. P., J 12
3616	Modane, France, M 23
.....	Modderfontein, Union of South Africa, L 12
51320	Modena, Italy, E 8
55817	Modica, Italy, P 16
.....	Modlin, Poland, D 14
18736	Mödling, Aus., H 9
.....	Modum, Norway, A 1
.....	Modzba, Algeria, E 13
.....	Moeira, Brazil, D 3
6002	Moerbeke, Belgium, R 5
.....	Mofa, Eth., G 11
2522	Moffat, Scot., P 19
30000	Mogadiscio, Som., R 17
21400	Mogador, Mor., E 5
.....	Mogadouro, Port., G 8
19000	Mogaira, Morocco, F 7
.....	Mogar, Eth., K 8
18800	Mogaung, Bur., L 23
700	Mogeely, Ire., P 13
335	Moggio, Italy, C 12
.....	Moghnin, Egypt, F 10
22992	Mogilev, W. Sov. Un., G 22
99440	Mogilev, W. Sov. Un., C 23
.....	Mogilno, Poland, D 11
.....	Mogna, Arg., K 7
.....	Mogok, Bur., M 22
.....	Mogor, Afg., G 17
6800	Mograr Foukani, Alg., H 13
.....	Mograr Tatani, Alg., H 13
8028	Moguer, Spain, N 8
.....	Mogy das Cruzes, Brazil, N 16
17228	Mohács, Hung., I 11
.....	Mohaka, N. Z., G 21
.....	Mohaleshoek, Bas., L 17
.....	Mohammerah, see Khorramshahr, Iran.
.....	Moheda, Sweden. P 13
.....	Mohill, Ire., H 14
.....	Moholm, Sweden, N 12
.....	Mohovano, Coa., D 6
1178	Mohoza, Bolivia, I 6
.....	Mohpani, India, I 12
.....	Mohsinabad, Iran, G 15
4817	Moinesti, Rom., I 21
.....	Moira, N. Ire., E 21
.....	Moisaküla, Sov. Un., G 4
486	Moisdon, Fr., J 7
600	Moises Ville, Arg., K 15
7435	Moissac, France, O 11
4906	Mojácar, Spain, O 15
.....	Mojarh, India, E 5
138997	Moji, Japan, M 5
1514	Mojo, Bolivia, N 9
3117	Mojocoya, Bolivia, K 11
.....	Mojon Vado de Chizos, Coa., A 7
955	Mojos, Bolivia, F 2
1531	Mojotoro, Bolivia, K 10
.....	Mojú, Brazil E 14
.....	Mokai, N. Z., F 19
.....	Mokameh, India, G 19
100	Mokihinui, N. Z., J 11
.....	Mokoange, Bel. Cong., J 14
.....	Mokoia, N. Z., H 16
.....	Mokopon, Bech., P 15
62457	Mokpo, Korea, F 24
.....	Mokroc, W. Sov. Un., D 21
.....	Mokus, Tur., G 18
.....	Moland, Norway, M 6
5133	Mold, Wales, H 10
3222	Molde, Norway, J 6
3000	Mole St. Nicholas, Haiti, H 12
45407	Molfetta, Italy, J 19
.....	Moliko, Eth., O 15
2866	Mölin, Switz. C 11
5117	Molina, Chile, N 4
.....	Molina, Cuba, L 16
2338	Molina de Aragan, Sp., H 14
3205	Molinero, Bolivia, J 9
.....	Molino, Baja Cal., F 5
520	Molinos, Arg., G 9
132	Molinis, Switz., K 21
4628	Moliterno, Italy, K 18
.....	Molkwerum, Neth., D 16
15203	Moll, Belgium, K 15
250	Molle, Chile, K 3
12628	Mollendo, Peru, P 16
2111	Molles, Uruguay, K 18
2097	Mollis, Switz., G 18
.....	Molodechno, W. Sov. Un., C 20
.....	Molodeczno, see Molodechno, Sov. Un.
1400	Molong, Austl., N 20
255196	Molotov (Perm), Sov. Un., G 23
98	Molson, Man., Q 17
1080	Molteno, U. S. Afr., N 16
968	Momax, Zac., K 6
18800	Mombasa, Kenya, L 21
.....	Mombetsu, Japan, F 14
.....	Momein, China, J 2
2047	Momignies, Belgium, P 10
.....	Momostenango, Guatemala, F 3
6694	Mompos, Col., D 11
.....	Mon, Sweden, N 10
2020	Monaco, Monaco, O 25
4300	Monaghan, Ire., F 18
.....	Monar Lodge, Scot., H 12
.....	Monasterevan, Ire., K 18
226	Monastery, N. S., J 20
8000	Monastir, Tunisia, C 25
.....	Monastyrishche, W. Sov. Un., G 24
.....	Monastyrishche, W. Sov. Un., B 25
.....	Moncão, Brazil, F 17
8960	Monceau sur Sambre, Belgium, N 11
8143	Monchique, Port., N 5
7181	Monclova, Coa., D 11
1036	Moncoutant, France, K 8
22763	Moncton, N.B., H 12
9153	Mondoñedo, Spain, C 7
1443	Mondoubleau, France, I 11
3605	Mondovi, Algeria, B 21
5813	Mondovi, Italy, E 2
.....	Mone, Bur., N 24
.....	Monemvasia, Greece, Q 17
6948	Monesterio, Spain, L 8
539	Monestier de Clermont, France, M 21
.....	Monet, Quebec, F 11
.....	Moneygall, Ire., L 13
.....	Moneymore, N. Ire., D 19
9659	Monfalcone, Italy, C 13
13200	Monfalût, Egypt, L 18
21264	Monforte de Lemos, Spain, D 7
.....	Mongalla, A. E. Sud., J 18
52863	Monghyr, India, G 19
.....	Mongu Lealui, N. Rh., N 15
3921	Monifieth, Scotland, K 21
1059	Monikie, Scotland, K 21
2419	Moniquira, Col., H 12
.....	Monisât, Egypt, P 24
.....	Monitaco, Ven., G 17
82	Monitor, Alberta, M 23
.....	Monivea, Ire., J 9
.....	Monje, Argentina, L 16
.....	Monkira, Australia, I 17
.....	Monkstown, Ire., Q 11
4731	Monmouth, Eng., K 12
2482	Monnickendam, Netherlands, F 15
14884	Monopoli, Italy, J 20
.....	Monor, Hung., R 22
9933	Monovar, Spain, L 16
2654	Monreal-del-Campo, Sp., H 15
16486	Monreale Italy, N 13
10000	Monrovia, Lib., J 3
2111	Monroy, Spain, J 8
27719	Mons, Belgium, N 10
10472	Monster, Neth. H 10
1624	Monsteras. Sweden, P 15
952	Mont, Belgium, O 18
4148	Montabaur, Germany, K 4
144	Montagrier, France, M 10
769	Montague, P. E. I., H 17
1729	Montague, U. S. Afr., Q 9
.....	Montague Jc., P.E.I., H 17
4515	Montaigu, Belgium, L 14
1635	Montaigu, France, J 7
1124	Montaigut, France, L 15
2272	Montalbán, Spain, H 16
2446	Montalbán, Ven., D 11
1314	Montalbo, Spain, J 14
.....	Montalegre, Port., F 7
1000	Montalvão, Portugal, J 7
1542	Montana, Switz., M 9
5056	Montanchez, Spain, K 9
12859	Montargis, France, I 14
.....	Montastruc, Fr., P 12
29981	Montauban, France, O 12
4193	Montbard, France, I 18
749	Montbazon, France, J 11
12767	Montbeliard, France, I 23
4707	Montblanch Spain, G 19
539	Montbovon, Switz., L 6
575	Montbozon, France, J 22
7645	Montbrison, France, M 17
180	Montcalm, Quebec, O 15
656	Montcuq, France, N 12
11854	Mont de Marsan, Fr., O 7
4706	Montdidier, France, F 14
1687	Monte, Arg., O 19
4367	Monteagudo, Bolivia, K 12
91	Monte Aguilla, Chile, P 3
.....	Monte Alegre, Brazil, E 10
.....	Monte Alegre, Brazil, L 14
.....	Monte Alto, Brazil, J 18
60	Monte Amargo, Chile, H 3
.....	Monte Carmello, Brazil, L 15
2500	Monte Caseros, Arg., K 20
.....	Monte Coman, Arg., N 8
8614	Montecristi, Ecuador, C 2
.....	Monte Cristo, Bolivia, B 6
1318	Montecristo, Tab., K 18
2728	Montefiascone, Italy, H 10
13246	Montefrio, Spain, N 12
10552	Montegneé, Belgium, M 17
11547	Montego Bay, Jamaica, I 7
9392	Monteleone, Italy, M 18
13696	Montelimar, France, N 20
5544	Montemorelos, N. L., F 15
9479	Montemor-o-Novo, Portugal, K 6
2491	Montemór-o-Velho, Port. H 5
1523	Montendre, France, M 9
.....	Montenegro (Amapa), Brazil, C 12
7180	Montenegro, Brazil, Q 11
899	Montenotte, Algeria, C 14
.....	Montepa, Col., N 9
781	Monte Patria, Chile, K 4
.....	Montepascali, Italy, G 8
.....	Monte Poterillo, Cuba, K 12
2772	Montepulciano, Italy, G 9
9314	Montereau-fout-Yonne, Fr. H 16
12804	Monteria, Col., E 8
.....	Monterico, Guatemala, H 4
2537	Monteros, Arg., H 10
186092	Monterrey, N. L., F 14
6203	Monterrey, Spain, F 7
....	Montes, Bolivia, M 13
18203	Monte Sant' Angelo, Italy, I 18
.....	Monte Santo, Brazil, I 21
13972	Montes Claros, Braz., K 18
1973	Montessen, France, A 2
5005	Montevarchi, Italy, F 9
1701	Monte Verde, Oax., M 7
708233	Montevideo, Uruguay, P 19
1387	Montfort, France, I 6
418	Montfort, France, O 7
225	Montfort, Quebec, O 13
26164	Montgomery, India, D 6
918	Montgomery, Wales, I 10
3621	Monthermé, France, F 18
4880	Monthey, Switz., N 6
384	Monthois, France, G 18
1923	Montignal, Fr., M 12
25350	Montignies-sur-Sambre, Belgium, O 12
549	Montigny, Fr., I 19
769	Montijo, Pan., Q 20
11113	Montijo, Spain, K 8
22527	Montilla, Spain, N 11
6490	Montivilliers, France, F 9
.....	Montjoie, Germany, K 2
2661	Mont Laurier, Quebec, L 11
359	Mont-Louis, France, Q 14
42515	Montluçon, France, K 14
4585	Montmagny, Quebec, K 23
290	Montmartre, Sask., Q 10
1686	Montmédy, France, G 19
603	Montmelian, France M 22
1884	Montmirail, France, H 16
718	Montmoreau, France, M 10
4766	Montmorillon, France, K 12
3860	Montoir-de-Bretagne. Fr., J 5
14980	Montoro, Spain, M 11
90787	Montpellier, France, P 17
300	Montpellier, Quebec, O 11
563	Montpezat, Fr., O 12
1699	Montpont, Fr., M 10
903007	Montreal, Quebec, P 15
.....	Montreal Lake, Sask., J 8
2246	Montrejeau, France, P 10
2823	Montreuil, France, E 13
1962	Montreuil-Bellay, Fr., J 9
71803	Montreuil sous Bois, Fr., B 7
2222	Montreux, Switz., L 6
835	Montrevel, France, K 20
59	Montrose, P. E. I., E 14
11889	Montrose, Scotland, J 22
33260	Montrouge, France, B 5
17754	Mont St. Amand, Bel., R 4
592	Montsalvy, France, N 14
10843	Mont-sur-Marchienne, Bel., O 12
1138	Montsurs, France, I 8
.....	Monveda, Bel. Cong., K 15
.....	Monwel, India, I 4
6000	Mon-ywa, Bur., M 22
37388	Monza, Italy, C 5
514	Monzon, Peru, J 9
4077	Monzón, Spain, F 17
.....	Mookut, Afg., I 21
6	Moon Hill, Sask., L 6
1321	Moonta Australia, O 15
.....	Moore, Ire., J 13
362	Moorefield, Ont., K 8
182	Moores Mills, N. B., K 5
264	Mooretown, Ontario, O 3
1400	Mooroopna, Austl., P 19
4410	Moorseele, Belgium, M 5
.....	Moorwinstow, Eng., M 6
718	Moose Creek, Ont., E 24
.....	Moosehorn, Man., O 15
20753	Moose Jaw, Sask., P 8
.....	Moose Lake, Man., K 12
.....	Moose Range, Sask., L 10
433	Moose River Gold Mines, N. S., L 17
1088	Moosomin, Sask. Q 11
250	Moosonee, Ont., M 24
.....	Mopea, Moz., O 20
3718	Moquegua, Peru, Q 18
10052	Mora, Spain, J 12
.....	Mora, Sweden, L 13
4995	Morachata, Bolivia, I 7
142414	Moradabad, India, E 12
3940	Mora de Ebra, Spain, G 18
2745	Mora de Rubielos, Sp., I 16
7255	Moral de Calatrava Sp., K 13
3979	Morales, Col., E 12
27	Moran, N. B., E 8
.....	Morar, India, G 11
.....	Morat, Switz., H 7
14536	Moratalla, Spain, L 15
125347	Moravská Ostrava, Czech., F 11
428	Morawhanna, Br. Gu., A 6
2325	Moraya Bolivia, M 9
546	Mörbylanga, Sweden, P 15
1954	Morcenx, France, O 7
499	Morcote, Switz., P 17
.....	Mordale, Eth., H 13
.....	Morden, Eng., D 20
.....	Morden N. S., L 11
719	Morebattle, Scot., O 23
24586	Morecambe Eng., E 11
4355	Moree, Australia, L 22

Pop.	Place Country Index
341	Morel, Switz, M 12
44304	Morelia, Michoa., N 12
5037	Morella, Spain, H 17
195	Morelos, Chih., K 16
1882	Morelos, Coa., B 13
1174	Morelos, Pueb., I 8
1668	Moreno, Arg., N 19
1238	Moreno, Col., H 13
2361	Moret, Fr., H 15
.....	Moreton, Austl., B 19
176	Morewood, Ont., E 23
5126	Morez, France, K 22
473	Morgan, Australia, N 16
5068	Morges, Switz., K 3
2800	Mori, Japan, G 12
1000	Mori, Japan, N 5
.....	Mori, Iran, J 5
580	Morinville, Alberta, K 20
62255	Morioka, Japan, E 24
.....	Mork, Norway, K 7
435	Mörke, Denmark, G 13
14073	Morlaix, France, H 2
101	Morley, Alberta, N 20
23397	Morley, England, F 15
.....	Morlunda, Sweden, O 9
.....	Mornington, Ire., H 22
.....	Mornshausen Ger., K 5
.....	Moroch, W. Sov. Un., D 21
1522	Morococha, Peru, L 9
5589	Morogoro, Tan., M 21
.....	Morokwen, U. S. Afr., G 13
10418	Moroleon, Guan., M 12
3158	Moromoro, Bolivia, J 12
17023	Moron, Cuba, J 15
1112	Morón, Spain, G 14
14200	Morón, Spain, O 10
3284	Morondava, Madag., O 23
26575	Morónde la Frontera, Sp., O 10
55857	Mororan, Japan, G 12
.....	Moroturo, Ven., C 9
7390	Morpeth, England, C 15
.....	Morretes, Brazil, O 14
216	Morrin, Alberta, M 21
.....	Morrinhos, Brazil, L 14
2000	Morrinsville, N. Z., E 18
953	Morris, Man., R 16
1575	Morrisburg, Ontario, F 24
210	Morriston, Ontario, L 10
125	Morristown, N. S., M 12
1000	Morro, Ecuador, D 2
.....	Morro do Chapeo, Brazil, I 20
3909	Morropon, Peru, F 3
1783	Mörschwil, Switz., D 19
373	Morse, Sask., P 6
31000	Morshansk, Sov. Un., J 14
.....	Morsill, Sweden, I 12
.....	Morsot, Algeria, D 22
.....	Mörswil, Switz., D 19
3366	Mortagne, France, H 11
1307	Mortain, France, H 8
4084	Morteau, France, J 22
.....	Mortimer, England, L 16
238	Mortlach, Sask., P 7
.....	Mortlake, England, C 20
115	Morton, Ont., H 21
.....	Moruga, Trinidad, R 24
179	Moruya, Australia, P 21
255	Morven, Australia, J 20
10000	Morvi, India, I 4
.....	Mosambi, West. Brazil, F 18
4641	Mosbach, Ger., N 6
.....	Mosbjerg, Den., B 12
1390	Moscar, Bolivia, J 8
	Moscow, see Moskva, Sov. Un.
263	Mosers River, N. S., M 18
2150	Mosgiel Jc., N. Z., P 8
.....	Moshi, Tanganyika, L 20
.....	Mosita, U. S. Afr., G 14
1986	Mosjöen, Norway, F 12
.....	Moskenäsö, Norway, D 12
4137018	Moskva (Moscow), Sov. Un., I 11
2285	Mosnang, Switz., E 17
1486	Mosquera, Col., I 11
4529	Mosquitos, Uruguay, O 20
8259	Moss, Norway, M 9
10578	Mossamedes, Angola, N 11
606	Mossbank, Sask., Q 7
.....	Mossburn, N. Z., P 4
7220	Mossel Bay, U. S. Afr., Q 11
13643	Mossoró, Brazil, F 23
.....	Mosspaul, Scotland, P 21
28211	Most, Czech., F 6
38555	Mostaganem, Alg., C 13
20292	Mostar, Yugo., L 10
.....	Mosty, W. Sov. Un., C 18
80000	Mosul, Iraq, I 19
.....	Mota, Eth., G 8
1238	Mota del Marqués, Spain, F 10
5985	Motala, Sweden, N 13
3506	Motatan, Ven., E 7
.....	Mothecombe, Eng., O 7
64708	Motherwell, Scot., N 16
1016	Môtiers, Switz., O 4
.....	Motiton, U. S. Afr., H 13
20495	Motril, Spain, O 12
.....	Mottingham, Eng., C 23
1730	Motueka, N. Z., J 13
5384	Motul, Yuc., E 22
4396	Motupe, Peru, G 4
.....	Motykaly, Pol., D 17
.....	Mouinoah, Algeria, J 14
372	Moulamein, Australia, O 18
2775	Moulin, Scotland, J 17
22225	Moulins, France, K 16
61301	Moulmein, Bur., P 23
.....	Moulsey, England, D 19
38381	Mountain Ash, Wales, L 9
416	Mountain Park, Alta., L 18
667	Mount Albert, Ont., J 12
224	Mount Ayliff, U. S. Afr., M 19
200	Mount Bellew, Ire., I 11
550	Mount Brydges, Ont., O 5
.....	Mount Cashel, Ire., J 4
.....	Mountcharles, Ire., D 12
.....	Mount Douglas Station, Australia, G 21
.....	Mount Fletcher, U.S. Afr. M 18
1890	Mount Forest, Ont., J 8
.....	Mount Frere, U. S. Afr., M 18
5542	Mount Gambier, Australia, Q 16
211	Mount Hanly, N. S., L 10
3300	Mount Isa, Austl., F 17
414	Mount Magnet, Australia, K 5
2275	Mountmellick, Ire., K 16
3262	Mount Morgan, Australia, I 22
.....	Mount Nugent, Ire., H 17
432	Mount Perry, Australia, J 23
218	Mount Pleasant, Ont., I 14
472	Mount Pleasant, Ont., N 9
1700	Mountrath, Ire., K 15
.....	Mount Saint Amand, Belgium, R 4
.....	Mountshannon, Ire., L 11
340	Mount Stewart, P.E.I., G 17
1833	Moura, Brazil, E 4
6971	Moura, Portugal, L 7
.....	Mouras, Argentina, O 15
31835	Mouscron, Belgium, M 6
.....	Mousehole, England, P 2
.....	Moussoro, Fr. Eq. Afr., I 13
696	Mouthe, France, K 22
215	Mouth of Keswick, N. B., H 6
4703	Moutier (Münster), Switz, E 8
2002	Moûtiers, France, M 23
.....	Mov, Denmark, E 12
1500	Moville, Ire., B 17
.....	Mowchow, China, G 7
500	Moy, N. Ire., E 19
.....	Moy, Scotland, H 16
.....	Moy, Scotland, J 14
.....	Moya, Peru, M 11
2294	Moyá, Spain, F 20
1605	Moya, Spain, I 15
1494	Moyahua, Zac., L 7
.....	Moyale, Kenya, K 21
.....	Moyamba, S. L., J 2
.....	Moyascragh, Ire., J 2
.....	Moycullen Ire., J 7
.....	Moyeni, Bas., L 17
175	Moyie, B. C., Q 19
.....	Moynalty, Ire., H 19
.....	Moyne Abbey, Ire., F 7
7500	Moyobamba, Peru, G 8
.....	Moyoro, Japan, G 14
700	Moyos, Chia., L 16
.....	Moyvally, Ire., J 18
11039	Mozdok, Sov. Un., P 16
574	Mozet, Belgium, N 14
.....	Mozhaisk, Sov. Un., I 10
10800	Mozir, W. Sov. Un., D 23
.....	M-Peng, Siam, M 2
35400	Mquanduli, U. S. Afr., N 18
3085	Mraier, Algeria, F 19
798	Msila, Algeria, C 18
.....	Mstislavl, W. Sov. Un., B 25
.....	Mtâl, Morocco, G 4
.....	Mtsensk, Sov. Un., J 10
.....	Muadamiyeh, Syria, D 19
.....	Muana, Brazil, E 14
.....	Mubarakpur, India, D 6
.....	Mubarikan, Iran, G 5
.....	Mubasher, Egypt, E 16
.....	Muchalld Palestine, J 6
.....	Muchalls, Scotland, I 23
145	Muchanes, Bolivia, G 5
2685	Mucuchies, Ven., F 7
.....	Mucury, Braz., L 20
.....	Mud, Iran, J 1
5030	Mudanya, Tur., C 3
561	Muddy Creek, P. E. I., G 14
3000	Mudgal, India, M 9
3993	Mudgee, Australia, N 21
.....	Mudki, India, D 8
.....	Mudurlu, Tur., C 6
117	Muenster, Sask., M 8
.....	Muff, Ire., B 16
200	Muff, Ire., C 17
622	Muggio, Switzerland, P 17
.....	Mughan, Iran, P 8
7061	Mugia, Spain, C 5
.....	Mugla, Tur., H 2
6061	Mühldorf, Ger., Q 11
3900	Mühlhausen, Ger., J 8
6506	Mühlheim, Ger., J 3
2786	Muiden, Neth., G 15
400	Muikaichi, Japan, L 7
4500	Muileann Cearr (Mullingar), Ire., I 16
20	Muir, Manitoba, Q 14
.....	Muirapinina, Brazil, E 5
4358	Muirkirk, Scotland, O 16
.....	Mujeidil, Syria, G 21
	Mukačevo, see Munkács, Hung.
25000	Mukalla, Aden, N 5
863515	Mukden, Manch., B 21
201	Mukeibeleh, Palestine, I 10
.....	Mukes, Transjordan, I 14
.....	Mukher, India, K 10
361	Mukhmas, Palestine, M 10
.....	Muktinath, Nepal, E 17
14312	Mula, Spain, N 17
.....	Mul Adam, Algeria, F 18
150	Mulatos, Son., H 14
.....	Mulben, Scotland, G 20
6829	Mulchén, Chile, P 3
.....	Mulebbis, Palestine, L 6
1026	Mulegé, Baja Cal., K 9
3056	Muleros, Dur., P 22
1057	Mulgrave, N. S., J 20
131000	Mülheim, Ger., I 2
96697	Mulhouse, France, I 23
3000	Mulki, India, N 7
.....	Mullagh, Ire., H 18
.....	Mullagh, Ire., I 6
.....	Mullaghmore, Ire., E 11
1480	Mullaittivu, Cey., Q 14
818	Mullewa, Australia, L 4
3724	Müllheim, Germany, Q 3
1416	Müllheim, Switz., C 17
.....	Mullinahone, Ire., M 16
.....	Mullinavat, Ire., N 17
.....	Mullingar, see Muileann Cearr, Ire.
7	Mullingar, Sask., L 6
.....	Mullion, England, P 3
2590	Müllrose, Germany, H 13
.....	Mulock, Ontario, R 25
4000	Multai, India, I 11
142768	Multan, India, D 5
.....	Multyfarnham, Ire., I 16
.....	Mulvin, N. Ire., D 15
.....	Mumbles, Wales, L 8
2371	Mümliswil, Switz., E 10
3484	Muna, Yuc., F 21
736000	München (Munich), Ger., Q 9
2266	Münchenbuchsee, Switz., H 9
.....	Münchwilen, Switz., D 17
756	Mundare, Alberta, K 21
11983	Münden, Germany, I 7
.....	Mundesley, England, I 24
.....	Mundo Novo, Brazil, I 20
.....	Muni, India, H 15
.....	Munich, see München, Ger.
26123	Munkáchevo, W. Sov. Un., G 16
.....	Munkács, see Munkáchevo, W. Sov. Un.
377	Munkebo, Denmark, K 13
4262	Munkfors, Sweden, M 12
.....	Muñoz, Arg., P 16
.....	Munsa, Egypt, G 11
3995	Münsingen, Switz., I 9
139	Munson, Alberta, M 21
4641	Munster, France, I 24
1400	Munster, Germany, F 7
122210	Münster, Germany, H 4
	Münster, see Moutier, Switz.
1185	Münster, Switz., F 13
664	Münster, Switz., J 25
482	Münster, Switz., L 13
.....	Muong-sing, Fr. In. Ch., L 3
923	Muonionalusta, Swe., D 19
2286	Muota, Switz., H 16
1932	Muquiyauyo, Peru, L 11
10800	Murakami, Japan, G 21
7200	Muramatsu, Japan, H 20
2401	Murat, France, M 15
2721	Muravera, Italy, L 5
.....	Murca, Portugal, F 5
193731	Murcia, Spain, M 16
.....	Murcielago, Honduras, G 11
1130	Murei, Japan, J 18
3482	Muret, France, P 12
.....	Murg, Switz., G 18
.....	Murga, Cuba, I 9
.....	Murghab, Iran, L 8
.....	Murgoo, Australia, K 4
.....	Murgos, Egypt, D 9
3123	Muri, Switz., E 13
3928	Muri, Switz., H 9
2960	Murias de Parêdes, Sp. D 8
.....	Murillo, Bolivia, C 4
1003	Murillo, Spain, E 16
1494	Murindo, Col., G 6
.....	Murity, Brazil, G 4
.....	Murjek, Sweden, F 18
.....	Mürlenbach, Germany, L 2
117054	Murmansk, Sov. Un., A 9
22607	Murom, Sov. Un., I 14
10475	Muros, Spain, D 5
.....	Muroyeh, Iran, L 11
71	Murra Murra, Austl., K 20
3651	Murray Bridge, Australia, O 16
431	Murray Harbour, Prince Edward Island, I 18
662	Murray Harbour, North, P. E. I., H 18
1271	Murraysburg, Union of South Africa, N 13
16000	Murree, India, B 7
.....	Mürren, Switz., K 11
.....	Murrisk, Ire., H 5
.....	Murrow, England, I 20
2851	Murrumburrah, Australia, O 20
4400	Mursan, India, F 11
15200	Murshidabad, India, H 21
.....	Murtazapur, India, J 10
.....	Murtinho, Brazil, M 9
	Murú, see Villa Seabra, W. Brazil.
859	Muruata, Bolivia, H 5
.....	Murud, India, K 6
21959	Murwara, India, H 13
3895	Murwillumbah, Austl., L 24
7000	Murzuch, Libya., F 12
7762	Mürzzuschlag, Aus., H 8
.....	Musa, Afg., J 22
.....	Musaiyib, Iraq, M 20
4277	Mush, Tur., F 17
.....	Muskiiman, India, J 8
	Muskat, see Masqat, Oman
4850	Muskau, Germany., I 14
.....	Muskoka Wharf, Ont., G 12
201	Musquash, N. B., L 8
845	Musquodoboit Harbour, N S., M 16
16996	Musselburgh, Scot., M 20
2203	Mussidan, France, M 10
.....	Mussooree, India, D 11
1112	Mussy, Fr., I 18
.....	Mustafakemalpasa (Kirmasti), Tur., D 3
.....	Musters, Arg., A 22
.....	Muth, India, C 11
1212	Muthill, Scotland, L 17
.....	Mutshtahir, Egypt, G 14
4000	Muttaburra, Austl., H 19
5022	Muttenz, Switz., C 10
60590	Muttra, India, F 10
.....	Mutum, Brazil, H 2
.....	Mutum, Brazil, M 11
18000	Muya, Japan, N 11
647	Muy Muy, Nicaragua, J 12
.....	Muzaffarabad, India, B 6
.....	Muzaffargarh, India, D 5
35347	Muzaffarnagar, India, E 11
43700	Muzaffarpur, India, G 18
3264	Muzo, Col., H 11
5186	Múzquiz, Coa., C 11
4278	Mwanza, Tan., L 19
.....	Myaing, Bur., M 22
220	Myalla, Tasmania, B 4
.....	Myanaung, Bur., O 21
1100	Mychaung, Bur., N 20
.....	Mydan, Afg., H 20
.....	Myedu, Bur., M 22
.....	Mygdal, Denmark, B 11
.....	Myglind, Denmark, B 13
25457	Myingyan, Bur., N 22
.....	Myitkyina, Bur., L 23
9330	Myjava, Czech., G 10
.....	Mykland, Norway, N 6
.....	Mylvina, Sov. Un., E 20
30480	Mymensingh, India, G 24
124	Myrtle, Ont., J 13
150540	Mysore, India, O 9
10000	Mytho, Fr. In. Ch., R 8
.....	Mytikas, Greece, O 14
33000	Mytilini, Grc., O 22
.....	Mziwa, Morocco, J 5

N

Pop.	Place Country Index
.....	Naaf, India, I 25
11747	Naaldwijk, Neth., H 11
25	Naama, Algeria, G 13
1000	Naaneh, Palestine, M 6
5664	Naarden, Neth., G 15
6000	Nabaro, Egypt, C 14
.....	Nabend, Iran, P 7
7000	Nabeul, Tunisia, B 25
10000	Nabha, India, D 9
17171	Nablus, (Shechem), Palestine, K 10
.....	Nabón, Ecuador, E 4
.....	Nabresina, Italy, C 13
.....	Nabtit, Egypt, G 15
2109	Nacaome, Honduras, H 9
.....	Na-cham, Fr. In. Chn., L 9
13532	Náchod, Czech., F 9
.....	Nácori, Son., G 12
5196	Nacozari, Son., D 13
.....	Nacuñan, Arg., N 8
.....	Nadali, Afg., K 18
.....	Naden Harbour, B. C., J 5
.....	Nadhia, Iran, K 12
34584	Nadiad, India, I 6
.....	Nadik, Iran, L 10
11785	Nădlac, Rom., I 14
.....	Nadvornaya, W. Sov. Un., P 18
.....	Nadwórna, see Nadvornaya, Sov. Un.
.....	Naes, Norway, L 8
2423	Naes, Norway, L 7
.....	Naesbjerg, Denmark, J 4
.....	Naesborg, Denmark, D 8
11301	Naestved, Denmark, L 20
2953	Näfels, Switz., G 17
.....	Naga, Japan, N 20
800	Nagahama, Japan, L 14
1000	Nagakubo, Japan, K 18
73912	Nagano, Japan, J 18
57866	Nagaoka, Japan, I 19
700	Nagar, India, N 8
.....	Nagar, India, K 14
.....	Nagar, India, C 10
252630	Nagasaki, Japan, N 2
1200	Nagasaki, Japan, I 20
1600	Nagase, Japan, K 11
3500	Nagashima, Japan, N 14
6000	Nagasu, Japan, N 3
.....	Nagasu, Japan, N 5
13000	Nagaur, India, F 7
4910	Nag Hamâdi, Eg., O 22
.....	Nagore, India, P 13
599165	Nagor Rajasima (Korat), Siam, O 5
1328084	Nagoya, Japan, M 15
301957	Nagpur, India, J 12
.....	Nagyboeskó, Hung., P 28
30936	Nagykanizsa, Hung., I 9
28584	Nagykoros, Hung., I 12
60537	Naha, Japan, E 12
.....	Nahan, India, D 10
.....	Nahap, U. S. Afr., L 7
.....	Naharind, Iran, G 4
.....	Nahuel Mapa, Arg., N 10
.....	Nahuel Ruca, Arg., P 20
.....	Nai, Egypt, H 14
4500	Naiband, Iran, J 12
359	Naica, Chih., I 19
279	Naicam, Sask., M 9
.....	Naico, Arg., P 12
3950	Naila, Germany, L 9
.....	Nain, Newf., I 20
5000	Nain, Iran, I 8
7600	Naini Tal, India, E 12
78	Nairn, Ontario, A 6
5282	Nairn, Scotland, G 17
200	Nairn Center, Ont., A 6
13	Nairns Falls, Que., H 24
20400	Nairobi, Kenya, L 20
670	Najac, France, O 13
2541	Nájera, Spain, E 14
28473	Najibabad, India, E 11
.....	Najin (Rashin), Kor., B 25
3500	Nakamiti, Eth., J 6
.....	Nakamura, Japan, G 21
3300	Nakamura, Japan, I 23
500	Nakamura, Japan, L 12
1200	Nakamura, Japan, O 8
2300	Nakatsugawa, Japan, L 17
1300	Nakayama, Japan, J 19
55438	Nakhichevan, Sov. Un., R 18
8800	Nakhichevan, Sov. Un., N 13
.....	Nakiloo, Iran, P 8
485	Nakina, Ontario, O 20
10303	Naklo, Poland, D 10
5100	Nako, Japan, L 6
.....	Nakon Panom, Siam., N 7
14742	Nakskov, Denmark, N 16
700	Nakusp, B. C., P 19
.....	Nal, Bal., O 20
.....	Naldrug, India, L 9
5900	Nalgonda, India, L 12
940	Nallıhan, Tur., D 6
.....	Namakkal, India, O 11
77351	Namangan, Sov. Un., Asia, J 10
34000	Nam-dinh, Fr. In. Ch., M 8
8900	Namdo, Sweden, R 25
.....	Namerakawa, Japan, J 17
1762	Namiquipa, Chih., G 16
.....	Namosi, Fiji Islands, Q 16
3637	Namsos, Norway, H 10
.....	Namu, B. C., M 8
30389	Namur, Belgium, N 13
312	Namur, Quebec, O 12
.....	Namyung, China, K 15
6635	Nanaimo, B. C., Q 12
21258	Nanam (Ranan) Kor., B 25
.....	Nanaufu, China, J 15
9000	Nanao, Japan, I 16
300000	Nanchang China, I 16
.....	Nanchwan, China, I 9
120578	Nancy, France, H 22
26992	Nander, India, K 10
6300	Nandgaon, India, J 14
.....	Nanfeng, China, J 17
978	Nangaroinza, Bolivia, M 13
3065	Nangis, France, H 15
6000	Nanjangud, India, O 9
.....	Nankangfu, China, I 16
726711	Nanking, China, G 18
153	Nannine, Austl., J 5
	Nanning, see Yungning, China.
200000	Nanping (Yenping), China, J 18
46065	Nanterre, France, B 3
195185	Nantes, France, J 7
151	Nanticoke, Ontario, O 10
718	Nanton, Alberta, O 21
2377	Nantua, France, L 21
7132	Nantwich, England, H 12
13190	Nant-y-glo, Wales, K 10
.....	Nanyang, China, G 14
.....	Naoetsu, Japan, I 18
1600	Naokata, Japan, M 4
10250	Naousa, Grc., N 16
3405	Napanee, Ontario, I 19
16650	Napier, New Zealand, H 21
2500	Napierville, Quebec, Q 16
255	Napinka, Man., R 12
	Naples, see Napoli It.
.....	Napo, Ecuador, C 8
757251	Napoli (Naples), It., J 14
.....	Napu, China, I 3
52781	Nara, Japan, M 13
2400	Narai, Japan, K 17
.....	Narakadu, India, Q 12
.....	Naran, Ire., D 11
.....	Narania, Arg., O 18
4000	Naranjal, Ecuador, D 3
.....	Naranjito, Col., K 9
.....	Naranjito, Ecuador, D 3
34189	Narayanganj, India, H 23
1046	Narberth, Wales, K 6
30047	Narbonne, France, P 16
.....	Narcaba, Erit., B 6
.....	Nardin, Iran, E 11
14810	Nardò, Italy, K 22
.....	Naré, Argentina, K 17
.....	Narek, Iran, L 6
.....	Narin, Afg., E 23
.....	Narkhan, Iran, F 13
21905	Narnaul, India, F 8
3545	Narni, Italy, H 11
18765	Naro, Italy, O 14
.....	Narö, Norway, H 10
.....	Närpes, Fin., E 3
2911	Narrabri, Austl., M 22
7155	Narracoorte, Austl., P 16
4119	Narrandera, Austl., O 19
2500	Narrogin, Austl., N 5
.....	Narsat, Afg., F 25
.....	Narseid, Tur., H 13
8800	Narsinghgarh, India, H 10
11000	Narsinghpur, India, I 12
.....	Naruto, Japan, M 21
24970	Narva, Sov. Un., G 6
162	Narvaez, Bolivia, M 11
9995	Narvik, Norway, D 15
	Narwa, see Narva, Sov. Un.
5000	Narwar, India, G 11
.....	Narym, Sov. Un., Asia, G12
.....	Nas, Sweden, L 13
.....	Nasa, see Nas Na Riogh, Ire.
3300	Näsäud, Rom., H 18
.....	Näshult, Sweden, P 13
240	Nashwaaksis, N. B., I 7
.....	Našice, Yugo, J 11
48703	Nasik, India, J 7
.....	Nasir, A. E. Sudan, J 19
.....	Nasir, Transj., J 23
20200	Nasirabad, India, G 8
40000	Nasiriye, Iraq, P 22
3288	Nas Na Riogh (Nasa), Ire., J 20
.....	Nasrabad, Iran, H 7
.....	Nasratabad, Iran, M 14
29391	Nassau, Bahama Is., C 8
.....	Nassau, Neth. Guiana, B 9
1099	Nässeby, Norway, A 23
.....	Nass Harbour, B. C., I 7
9113	Nässjo, Sweden, O 13
1000	Nassogne, Belgium, P 17
847	Natá, Pan., P 20
4066	Natagaima, Col., J 9
51896	Natal, Brazil, G 25
680	Natal, B. C., P 20
.....	Natap, S. W. Africa, C 2
2875	Naters, Switz., M 12
.....	Nathana, India, D 9
.....	Natividad, Bolivia, D 6
.....	Natividade, Brazil, I 15
.....	Nätra, Sweden, I 16
.....	Nattavaara Sweden, E 18
2300	Naua, Egypt, H 14
872	Naucelle, France, O 14
.....	Naudpishan, Iran, H 14
9583	Nauen, Germany, G 11
165	Naughton, Ontario, A 7
31000	Naumburg, Ger., J 10
.....	Naumiestis, W. Sov. Un., B 15
	Naumiestis, W. Sov. Un., B16
689	Nauta, Peru, F 13
1140	Nautla, Ver., G 9
1822	Nava, Coa., B 13
5221	Nava del Rey, Spain, G 10
1327	Navas, Cuba, I 9
4630	Navalcarnero, Spain, I 11
6831	Navalmoral de la Mata, Spain, J 10
2116	Navarro, Argentina, N 18
8386	Navia, Spain, C 8
.....	Navia, Arg., N 10
11009	Navojoa, Son., J 13
7163	Navplion, Grc., P 17
.....	Navr., Denmark, G 4
24397	Navsari, India, J 6
.....	Navua, Fiji Islands, Q 16
23300	Nawabganj, India, G 22
.....	Nawabshah, India, G 1
.....	Nawakot, India, E 5
5584	Nawalapitiya, Cey., R 14
.....	Nawalgarh, India, F 8
.....	Nawibandar, India, I 2
2160	Naxos, Greece, Q 20
3521	Nay, France, P 9
.....	Naya Dumka, India, H 20
386	Nazacara, Bolivia, H 3
1359	Nazarena, Bolivia, M 9
.....	Nazaret, Bolivia, C 7
4746	Nazareth, Belgium, L 7
.....	Nazareth, Brazil, D 8
5471	Nazareth, Brazil, G 25
13482	Nazareth, Brazil, J 22
8719	Nazareth, Palestine, H 10
.....	Nazareth, Peru, F 5
2125	Nazas, Dur., N 22
.....	Nazca, Peru, N 12
12005	Nazilli, Tur., F 2
.....	Nazla, Egypt, C 17
2100	Nazlet-Abit, Egypt, R 10
.....	N'Djole, Fr. Eq. Afr., K 11
.....	Neale, Ire., I 7
.....	Neapolis, Greece, Q 17
33322	Neath, Wales, L 8
2120	Neba, Japan, M 17
.....	Nébeck, Syria., I 12
.....	Neber, Tunisia, C 22
.....	Nebo, Palestine, M 8
.....	Neby Hud, Transjordan, K 16
.....	Neby Musa, Palestine, N 11
.....	Neby Sebelen, Palestine, F 11
.....	Nechi, Col., F 10
40527	Necochea, Arg., Q 19
.....	Necum Teuch, N. S., M 19
.....	Nedd, Scotland, E 11
.....	Neder Kalix, Sweden, F 19
.....	Neder Lulea, Sweden, G 19
5825	Nedroma, Algeria, E 11
5433	Neede, Neth., G 22
2292	Neepawa, Man., P 14
1309	Neerlinter, Belgium, M 14
752	Neerwinden, Bel., M 15
.....	Nees, Denmark, G 3
.....	Nefisha, Egypt, F 22
.....	Nefta, Tunisia, F 22
48527	Negapatam, India, P 13
25297	Negombo, Cey., R 13
.....	Negotin, Yugo., K 16
6218	Negotin, Yugo., K 17
7725	Negréira, Spain, D 5
.....	Negrine, Algeria, E 21
7078	Negritos, Peru, F 1
.....	Negro Quemado, Arg., N 8
.....	Neh, Iran, K 14
.....	Nehavend, Iran, F 5
.....	Nehhalin, Palestine, N 8
185	Neidpath, Sask., P 6
373	Neils Harbour, N. S., E 23
.....	Nein, Palestine, I 11
36000	Neisse, Pol., F 10
15096	Neiva, Col., K 9
305	Nejed, Palestine, O 4
.....	Nekhla, Egypt, D 10
.....	Nekmard, India, G 21
.....	Nekmaria, Algeria, C 13
.....	Nekor, Sp. Mor., D 9
.....	Nekrach, Egypt, E 9
2819	Neksö, Den., M 17
45895	Nellore, India, N 13
5912	Nelson, B. C., Q 18
38306	Nelson, England, F 13
380	Nelson, N. B., E 20
11400	Nelson, N. Z., J 14
.....	Nelson Jc., N. B., E 10
116	Nelspruit, U. S. Afr., F 21
.....	Néma, Fr. W. Afr., H 4
10657	Nemecky Brod, Czech., F 8
1420	Nemocon, Col., I 11
7073	Nemours, Algeria, D 11
3728	Nemours, France, I 15
5200	Nemuro, Japan, F 15
4800	Nenagh, Ire., L 12
3046	Nendaz, Switz., N 8
4968	Nentón, Guatemala, E 3
11000	Nepalganj, India, F 15
626	Nepeña, Peru, J 6
54	Neptune, Sask., R 9
.....	Neqâda, Egypt, O 23
5827	Nérac, France, O 10
11200	Nerchinsk, Sov. Un., Asia H 17
3000	Nerekhta, Sov. Un., H 13
103	Nerepis Station, N.B., K 7
	Neris (Viliyi) River, W. Sov. Un.
7224	Nerja, Spain, O 12
5012	Nerpio, Spain, M 14
.....	Nerschiki, Tur., F 16
.....	Nes, Netherlands, B 18
.....	Nes, Sov. Un., C 14
.....	Nesha Damira, Egypt, O 15
.....	Neshanî, Iran, I 8
.....	Neshart, Egypt, D 10
3081	Nesne, Norway, F 12
1832	Nesting, Shetland Is., B 4
5674	Neston, England, G 11
.....	Nesvizh, W. Sov. Un., O 20
133	Netherhill, Sask., N 4
.....	Nethy Bridge, Scot., H 17
2239	Netstal, Switz., G 17
.....	Netzeband, Ger., F 11
900	Neu, Japan, K 10
13675	Neubrandenburg, Ger., D12
7564	Neuburg, Germany, P 9
22775	Neuchâtel, Switz., H 6
420	Neudorf, Sask., P 10
2354	Neuenegg, Switz., I 8
.....	Neuenhaus, Germany, F 3
.....	Neufahrn, Germany, P 10
2377	Neufchâteau, Bel., Q 17
4059	Neufchâteau, France, H 20
406	Neufchâtel, Fr., G 17
4128	Neufchâtel, France, F 12
10864	Neuhaldensleben, Ger., G 9
4173	Neuhaus, Ger., D 6
.....	Neu Hoben, Ger., O 19
768	Neuilly l'Eveque, Fr., I 20
10415	Neuilly-sur-Marne, Fr., B 8
53491	Neuilly-sur-Seine, Fr., B 4
.....	Neümarkt, Aus., I 6
7766	Neumarkt, Germany, N 9
.....	Neumarkt, Ger., P 11
.....	Neumarkt, Italy, C 9
40000	Neumünster, Ger., C 7
1173	Neunkirch, Switz., B 14
.....	Neunkirchen, Ger., N 3
.....	Neunstetten, Ger., N 7
3622	Neuötting, Germany, Q 11
	Neu-Pest, see Ujpest, Hung.
2342	Neuquén, Arg., Q 8
20000	Neuruppin, Ger., F 11
.....	Neu Saint Johann, Switz., F 18
55800	Neuss, Germany, I 2
7660	Neustadt, Germany, K 10
.....	Neustadt, Germany, L 7
.....	Neustadt, Germany, L 9
17000	Neustadt, Germany, N 4
2391	Neustadt, Germany, N 8
.....	Neustadt, Germany, Q 4
455	Neustadt, Ontario, J 7
16000	Neustettin, Pol., C 10
19400	Neustrelitz, Ger., E 12
2860	Neuteich, Danzig, C 20
1452	Neutla, Guan., L 13
11919	Neu Ulm, Germany, P 7
2531	Neuveville, Switz., G 7
2338	Neuville, France, L 19
2887	Neuville, France, K 14
1162	Neuville-aux-Bois, France, I 13
21000	Neuwied, Ger., K 3
10058	Neuzen (Terneuzen), Neth. K 9
10000	Nevel, W. Sov. Un., A 23
3058	Nevele, Belgium, L 8
.....	Never, Sov. Un., Asia, G 18
33699	Nevers, France, I 18
.....	Nevesinje, Yugo., L 11
165	Neville, Sask., Q 5
1500	Nevin, Wales, H 7
84	Nevis, Alberta, L 21
7190	Nevrokop, Bulgaria, M18
13454	Nevsehir, Tur., F 9
.....	New Aberdeen, N. S., H 23
.....	New Agatha, U.S. Afr., C20
.....	New Albany, N. S., M 11
.....	Newalpur, Nepal, F 17
10525	New Amsterdam, British Guiana, B 7
18055	Newark, England, H 17
.....	New Barnet, England, A 21
.....	Newbawn, Ire., N 19
6904	Newbiggin, Eng., C 15
.....	New Birmingham, Ire., M 15
.....	Newbliss, Ire., F 17
332	Newboro, Ont., H 20
2250	Newbridge, Ire., K 19
.....	Newburg, N. B., H 5
471	Newburgh, Ont., I 19
.....	Newburgh, Scotland H 24
2152	Newburgh, Scotland, L 19
13336	Newbury, England, L 16
285	Newbury, Ont., O 5
165	New Campbellton, N. S., G 23
13657	Newcastle, Austl., N 22
1765	Newcastle, N. Ire., F 23
2687	Newcastle, Ire., N 8
3781	Newcastle, N. B., E 9
742	Newcastle, Ont., K 14
4274	Newcastle, U. S. Afr., I 20
762	Newcastle Emlyn, Wales, J 6
283145	Newcastle-on-Tyne, Eng., C 15
.....	New Castleton, Scot., P 21
23246	Newcastle under Lyme, England, H 13
93	Newcastle Waters, Austl., E 13
.....	New Dailly, Scot., P 13
353	Newdale, Man., Q 13
3666	New Deer, Scot., G 23
64855	New Delhi, India, E 10
105	New Denmark, N. B., E 4
.....	Newent, England, K 12
307	New Galloway, Scot., Q 16
.....	New Galloway Station, Scotland, Q 16
995	New Germany, N. S., N 12
9210	New Glasgow, N. S., J 17
1402	New Hamburg, Ont., M 8
.....	New Harbour West, N. S., L 20
6790	Newhaven, England, N 20
167	Newington, Ont., F 24
.....	Newinn, Ire., M 14
267	New Jerusalem, N. B., J 8
.....	Newlands, B. C., J 13
3019	New Liskeard, Ont., Q 24
258	New Lowell, Ont., I 10
423	New Luce, Scotland, Q 13
2113	New Machar, Scot., H 23
18868	Newmarket, England, J 21
.....	New Market, Ire., L 8
1000	Newmarket, Ire., O 8
4026	Newmarket, Ont., J 12
.....	Newmill, Scotland, G 20
225	New Mills, N. B., A 8
.....	Newmilns, Scotland, O 15
1035	Newnham, England, K 12
190	New Norcia, Austl., M 5
2190	New Norfolk, Tasmania, E7
.....	New Passage, Eng., L 12
.....	New Pitsligo, Scot., G 23
17550	New Plymouth, N. Z., G 15
3439	Newport, England, I 13
89198	Newport, England, L 13
11313	Newport, England, N 16

Pop. Place Country Index

1000 Newport, Ire., H 6
..... Newport, Ire., M 11
300 Newport, N. S., M 14
3275 Newport, Scotland, K 20
..... Newport, Wales, K 6
..... Newport Landing, N. S., L 14
5958 Newquay, England, O 4
1112 New Quay, Wales, J 7
..... New Radnor, Wales, J 10
1786 New Romney, Eng., M 23
5055 New Ross, Ire., N 19
11963 Newry, N. Ire., F 21
..... New Shoreham, Eng., N 19
..... New Southampton, N. B., I 5
..... Newstead, Austl., H 22
..... New Taochow, China, F 7
..... Newton, England, B 15
212 Newton, Ontario, L 7
15003 Newton Abbot, Eng., N 9
..... Newtonmore, Scot., I 16
1914 Newton Stewart, Scot., Q 14
..... New Town, N. B., I 10
..... Newtown, Ire., C 15
..... Newtown, Ire., K 13
..... Newtown, Tasmania, E 7
5152 Newtown, Wales, J 10
9587 Newtownards, N. Ire., D 24
..... Newtownbarry, Ire., M 20
500 Newtown Butler, N. Ire., F 16
..... Newtown Crommelin, N. Ire., C 21
..... Newtown Forbes, Ire., H 14
..... Newtown Hamilton, N. Ire., F 20
350 Newtownmountkennedy, Ire., K 23
..... Newtown Stewart, N. Ire., D 16
831 Newtyle, Scotland, K 20
21967 New Westminster, B. C., Q 13
909 Nexon France, M 11
264 Nexpa, Guer., R 16
29116 Nezhin (Nyezhin), Sov. Un., K 7
..... Nezla, Algeria, I 19
..... Nezla Smira, Morocco, H 4
..... Nezlet esh-Shêkh Hasan, Egypt, Q 10
8430 Ngaoundéré, Cam., J 12
300 Ngapara, N. Z., O 9
..... Nggeleni, U. S. Afr., N 19
..... Nguigmi, Fr. W. Afr., I 11
..... Ngusa, Alg., H 19
..... Ngwedaung, Bur., O 23
..... Nha-trang, Fr. In. Ch., Q 11
1926 Nhill, Austl., P 17
20589 Niagara Falls, Ont., N 13
1541 Niagara on the Lake, Ontario, M 13
..... Niamey, Fr. W. Afr., I 8
..... Niangara, Bel. Cong., K 18
1989 Nibe, Denmark, D 9
8000 Nicaragua, Nicaragua, L 11
15511 Nicastro, Italy, M 19
211916 Nice, France, O 25
..... Nichol, B. C., K 12
..... Nickleton, Ontario, R 23
153 Nicola, B. C., P 15
3751 Nicolet, Quebec, M 18
23700 Nicosia, Cyprus, K 8
12519 Nicosia, Italy, N 15
4598 Nicotera, Italy, M 18
4215 Nicoya, Costa Rica, N 12
350 Nictaux Falls, N. S., M 11
..... Nictheroy, see Niteroi, Braz.
..... Nidaros, see Trondheim, Nor.
2570 Nidau, Switz., G 8
2448 Nieblo, Spain, N 7
715 Niederglatt, Switz., D 15
240 Niederried, Switz., J 11
..... Nieder-Schönhausen, Germany, N 17
..... Niederstetten, Ger., N 7
673 Niederweningen, Switz., D 14
933 Niederwil, Switz., E 11
10307 Niel, Belgium, L 11
10416 Nienburg, Germany, F 6
647 Niepos, Peru, H 4
..... Nieswiez, see Nesvizh, W. Sov. Un.
4856 Nieuport, Belgium, K 3
..... Nieuw Amsterdam, Neth. Gu., B 9
2586 Nieuwendam, Neth., B 5
..... Nieuwjaars Fontein, U. S. Afr., O 12
3570 Nieuwleusen, Neth., E 21
824 Nieuwpoort, Neth., H 14
..... Nieves, Cuba, H 8
3129 Nieves, Zac., H 8
9463 Nigde, Tur., G 9
725 Nigg, Scot., G 16
680 Nightcaps, N. Z., Q 4
8000 Nihommatsu, Japan, I 22
150903 Niigata, Japan, H 20
..... Niimi, Japan, L 10
..... Nijar, Iran, C 4
10107 Nijar, Spain, O 14
9687 Nijkerk, Neth., G 17
89534 Nijmegen, Neth., I 18
3500 Nikko, Japan, J 20
167108 Nikolaev (Vernoleninsk), Sov. Un., N 7
20000 Nikolaevsk, Sov. Un. Asia, F 20
..... Nikolaevsk, see Pugachev, Sov. Un.
..... Nikolaistad, see Vassa, Fin.
..... Nikolsk, Sov. Un., G 15
..... Nikolsk Ussuriisk, see Voroshilov, Sov. Un., Asia.
4936 Nikopol, Bulgaria, K 19
..... Nikpei, Iran, E 4
6647 Niksar, Tur., C 12
4164 Nikšić, Yugo., L 12
..... Nilgiri, India, I 20
..... Nili, Algeria, G 16
..... Nim, Denmark, I 9
..... Nimach, India, H 8
93758 Nimes, France, O 18
..... Nimlabagh, Afg., G 23
..... Nimra, Egypt, D 12
..... Nimule, A. E. Sud., K 19
314 Nine Mile River, N. S., L 15
30000 Ningan, Manch., A 25
..... Ningchow, China, F 10
..... Ningchow, China, K 6
..... Ninghiafu, China, D 9
..... Ningkiang, China, G 9
..... Ningkwo, China, H 18
..... Ningling, China, E 9
..... Ningming, China, L 9
213000 Ningpo, China, H 20
..... Ningtu, China, J 16
..... Ningyüan, China, C 4
30000 Ningyüan (Kuldja), Sink., J 12
..... Ningyüan, China, I 6
..... Ninh-binh, Fr. In. Ch., M 8
10355 Ninove, Belgium, M 9
..... Nioac, Brazil, M 9

Pop. Place Country Index

..... Nioro, Fr. W. Afr., H 3
27830 Niort, France, K 9
..... Nipani, India, L 7
1344 Nipawin, Sask., L 10
650 Nipigon, Ontario, P 19
77 Nipissing, Ontario, B 11
..... Nipissing Jc., Ont., A 12
3434 Niquero, Cuba, O 17
2636 Nirazaki, Japan, L 18
..... Niriz, Iran, M 9
..... Nirmal, India, K 11
35384 Niš, Yugo., L 15
16329 Niscemi, Italy, O 15
20000 Nishapur, Iran, F 13
1932 Nishikata, Japan, P 2
111792 Nishinomiya, Japan, M 12
..... Nisibin, see Nuseybin, Tur.
1852 Nismes, Belgium, P 12
..... Nisse, Sweden, P 17
1865 Nissedal, Norway, M 6
125974 Niteroi (Nictheroy), Braz., N 18
12 Niton, Alberta, K 19
21259 Nitra, Czech., H 11
306 Nivaa, Denmark, I 23
12794 Nivelles, Belgium, N 11
5000 Nizampatam, India, M 14
..... Nizhne Kolymsk, Sov. Un. Asia, B 18
12283 Nizhneudinsk, Sov. Un. Asia, G 15
..... Nizhnii Chirskaya, Sov. Un., M 15
..... Nizhne Kamchatsk, Sov. Un. Asia, D 21
..... Nizhnii Novgorod, see Gorki, Sov. Un.
..... Nizhnii Pesha, Sov. Un., C 16
159864 Nizhi Tagil, Sov. Un., G 24
..... Njurunda, Sweden, J 15
..... Noagarh, India, J 15
..... N-O-Aker, Norway, A 6
6500 Noakhali, Ind., H 24
3368 Noalinco, Ver., D 14
..... Nobaran, Iran, G 5
..... Nobber, Ire., H 19
..... Nobcoka, Japan, P 5
577 Nobel, Ontario, E 10
..... Nobel, W. Sov. Un., E 19
216 Nobleton, Ontario, K 15
..... Noccundra, Australia, K 18
13727 Nocera dei Pagani, It., J 15
2251 Nocera Tirinese, It., M 18
1061 Nocera Umbra, Italy, G 12
4470 Nochistlan, Zac., L 8
464 Nochixtlan, Oax., L 8
..... Noda, Japan, J 25
..... Nodoa, China, M 11
..... Noel, N. S., K 14
..... Noêra, Egypt, M 12
..... Noerdange, Lux., Q 19
13867 Nogales, Son., C 11
1165 Nogaro, France, N 9
7218 Nogent-le-Rotrou, Fr., H 12
2000 Nogent-sur-Marne, Fr., B 8
3611 Nogent-sur-Seine, Fr., H 16
..... Noggara, Eth., D 6
..... Nogorekhana, Iran, K 12
7250 Nogoyá, Arg., L 17
4700 Nohar, India, E 8
815 Noirétable, France, L 17
..... Noirmont, Switz., I 8
1600 Noirmont, Switz., F 6
3254 Noirmoutier, France, J 4
2337 Noisy-le-Grand, Fr., B 8
663 Noisy-le-Roi, France, B 1
22332 Noisy-le-Sec, France, B 7
1200 Nojiri, Japan, N 14
421 Nokomis, Sask., O 8
8333 Nola, Italy, J 15
..... Nolev, Denmark, I 12
4800 Nolinsk, Sov. Un., H 18
..... Nom, China, A 2
..... Nombre de Dios, Cuba, I 3
1785 Nombre de Dios, Dur., P 22
533 Nominingue, Quebec, M 12
1361 Nonancourt, France, H 12
6000 Nong Khay, Siam., N 5
..... Nonno, Eth., J 7
..... Nonoava, Chih., J 13
3112 Nontron, France, M 11
509 Nonza, Cor., P 3
..... Noondera, Australia, M 10
..... Noondroo, Bal., Q 20
..... Noongal, Australia, K 4
10130 Noordwijk-aan Zee, Neth., G 12
994 Nopala, Hid., F 4
2631 Nora, Sweden, M 13
737 Noradjuha, Australia, P 17
2246 Noranda, Que., F 2
1030 Norberg, Sweden, M 14
1056 Norborg, Denmark, M 9
588 Nordby, Denmark, I 13
..... Nordby, Denmark, K 3
..... Nordalen, Norway, J 6
10999 Norden, Germany, D 4
37000 Nordhausen, Germany, I 8
..... Nordingrä, Sweden, J 16
..... Nordkyn Sandfjord, Nor., A 22
8589 Nördlingen, Germany, O 8
489 Nordmaling, Sweden, I 17
..... Nordreisen, Norway, B 18
5098 Norg, Netherlands, C 21
269 Norham, Ontario, J 16
..... Nörholm, Denmark, D 10
657 Noria La Sin., Q 18
1330 Noria de Angeles, Zac., J 11
..... Norley, Australia, K 19
..... Norman, Mack., I 7
..... Normanby, England, E 17
1200 Normanton, Austl., E 18
105 Nörop, Den., J 7
306 Norquay, Sask., N 11
..... Norquin, Arg., P 5
..... Nörre Bork., Den., I 2
..... Nörre Felding, Den., G 4
..... Nörre Lyndelse, Denmark, L 12
546 Nörre Nebel, Denmark, J 2
..... Nörre Omme, Denmark, H 5
6913 Nörresundby, Den., D 11
67727 Norrköping, Sweden, N 14
..... Norrsunda, Sweden, P 21
..... Norrsundet, Sweden, L 15
4875 Norrtälje, Sweden, M 17
378 Norseman, Austl., M 8
..... Norsholm, Sweden, N 14
2014 Norsjö, Sweden, G 17
4787 Northallerton, Eng., E 15
5000 Northam, Austl., M 5
689 Northampton, Austl., K 3
92314 Northampton, Eng., J 17
506 North Augusta, Ont., G 22
4745 North Battleford, Sask., L 6
15599 North Bay, Ontario, A 12
261 North Bend, B. C., P 14
4083 North Berwick, Scot., M 21
207 North Brookfield, N.S., O 11
..... North Cray, Eng., C 24

Pop. Place Country Index

264 Northeast Harbour, N. S., R 10
200 Northeast Margaree., N.S., G 21
9424 Northeim, Germany, I 7
..... North Erradale, Scot., F 9
527 North Esk Boom, N.B., E 9
..... North Fairford, Man., O 14
27 Northgate, Sask., R 11
410 North Gower, Ont., F 22
..... North Ham, Quebec, O 20
472 North Hatley, Que., Q 19
776 North Head, New Brunswick, M 6
..... North Junction, Man., O 13
..... North Junction, Ont., N 8
175 North Lancaster, Ont., E 25
..... Northleach, Eng., K 14
1343 Northmavine, Shetland Is., B 2
..... Northolt, England, B 18
600 Northpine, Austl., K 23
263 North Port, Ont., J 18
145 North Portal, Sask., R 10
..... North Pubnico, Nova Scotia, Q 9
..... North Queensferry, Scotland, M 19
337 North River, N. S., K 16
215 North Rustico, P.E.I., G 16
..... North Somercotes, England, G 20
..... North Star, B. C., Q 19
6836 North Sydney, N. S., H 23
118 North Transcona, Man., Q 16
519 North Tryon, P. E. I., H 15
8914 North Vancouver, B. C., Q 12
..... North Wakefield, Que., O 9
4137 North Walsham, Eng., I 24
..... Northwest Harbour, N. S., R 10
18200 Northwich, Eng., L 17
..... North Wootton, Eng., I 21
682 Norton, N. B., J 9
321 Norval, Ontario, L 10
1039 Norway Bay, Quebec, P 8
..... Norway House, Man., K 15
126207 Norwich, England, I 23
1268 Norwich, Ontario, N 8
..... Norwich Jc., Ont., N 8
..... Norwood, England, C 21
762 Norwood, Ontario, I 16
10161 Noshiro, Japan, D 22
..... Nosovka, Sov. Un., L 7
3261 Nossa Senhora Apparecida, Brazil, G 13
..... Nossa Senhora do Dôres, Brazil, I 23
..... Notitu, China, K 9
17443 Noto, Italy, P 16
426 Notre Dame, N. B., H 21
335 Notre Dame, Quebec, K 19
..... Notre Dame de la Dore, Que., D 18
405 Notre Dame de Lourdes, Man., R 14
275 Notre Dame du Portage, Que., H 25
805 Notre Dame du Rosaire, Que., K 23
..... Nottam, India, P 11
512 Nottawa, Ontario, H 9
283030 Nottingham, Eng., H 16
1114 Nottwil, Switzerland, G 12
10708 Nouméa, New Caledonia, M 15
..... Nouvelle Anvers, Bel. Cong., K 14
..... Nova Cruz, Brazil, G 25
16388 Nova Friburgo, Brazil, N18
4546 Nova Lisboa, Ang., N 13
221 Novar, Ont., D 12
44564 Novara, Italy, D 4
2000 Nova Safala, Moz., O 19
9871 Nova Zagora, Bul., L 21
11994 Nove da, Spain, L 16
..... Nové Zamky, Czech., H 11
..... Novgorod, Sov. Un., G 7
38000 Novgorod Syeversk, Sov. Un., K 8
..... Novigrad, Yugo., K 7
13969 Novi Ligure, Italy, E 4
1326 Noville, Belgium, P 18
347 Novion Porcien, Fr., G 18
4270 Novi-Pazar, Bulgaria, K 22
10364 Novipazar, Yugo., L 14
63966 Novi Sad, Yugo., J 13
4700 Novita, Col., I 6
..... Növling, Denmark, E 11
..... Novo-Alexandrovskoe, Sov. Un., O 14
..... Novo Bayazet, Sov. Un., R 17
81286 Novocherkassk, Sov. Un., N 13
6367 Novogrodok, W. Sov. Un., C 19
13248 Novo Mariinsk, Sov. Un. Asia, B 19
4045 Novo Mesto, Yugo., J 7
4000 Novo Redondo, Ang., L 12
95280 Novorossiisk, Sov. Un., O 11
405589 Novo-Sibirsk, Sov. Un. Asia, H 12
..... Novo Sokolniki, W. Sov. Un., A 23
..... Novotorzhskaya, Sov. Un., H 10
25000 Novoukrainsk, Sov. Un., M 6
..... Novouzensk, Sov. Un., L 18
21505 Novozibkov, Sov. Un., K 7
..... Novy Dvar, W. Sov. Un., D 17
13785 Nový Jičín, Czech., G 11
..... Nowe Miasto, Po., E 14
11000 Nowgong, India, F 25
..... Nowogródek, see Novogrodok, Sov. Un.
..... Noworadomsk, Pol., E 12
2978 Nowra, Australia, O 21
..... Nowy Dwor, see Novy Dvar, Sov. Un.
30278 Nowy Sacz, Poland, G 14
10406 Nowy Targ, Poland, G 13
..... Nowy Tomysl, Pol., D 9
..... Nowy Troki, W. Sov. Un., D 18
10687 Noya, Spain, D 5
174 Noyant, France, J 9
..... Noyant Jc., Que., R 16
6483 Noyon, France, G 15
420 Nozeroy, France, K 21
..... Nqamaqwe, U. S. Afr., O 18
..... N. Sridharmaraj, Thai., R 1
357 Nuba, Palestine, O 8
..... Nub Tarif, Egypt, E 15
..... Nudeibeh, Transj., J 23
..... Nueimeh, Syria, H 18
..... Nueva Colonia, Bol., D 4
..... Nueva Gallia, Arg., O 11
1184 Nueva Gerona, Cuba, K 6
6643 Nueva Imperial, Chl., Q 3

Pop. Place Country Index

4191 Nueva Palmira, Ur., M 14
6151 Nueva Rosita, Coa., C 12
399 Nueva Zelandia, Tab., K 15
57424 Nueve de Julio, Arg., O 16
12029 Nuevitas, Cuba, K 18
..... Nuevo Berlin, Ur., K 15
28774 Nuevo Laredo, Tam., C 16
..... Nuevo Morelos, Tam., J 17
..... Nuhf, Palestine, G 10
3233 Nuits-Saint-Georges, Fr., J 19
..... Nukanome, Japan, H 22
26300 Nukha, Sov. Un., Q 19
..... Nukhaila, Morocco, G 6
6374 Nules, Spain, J 17
49 Nullagine, Austl., G 6
..... Nullukh, Afg., J 18
4732 Numada, Japan, J 20
4162 Numansdorp, Neth., I 12
44026 Numazu, Japan, M 19
3058 Nunchia, Col., H 15
46305 Nuneaton, England, J 15
3268 Nunen, Neth., J 17
..... Nungamarra, Austl., I 5
..... Nunspeet, Neth., F 18
..... Nuolen, Switz., F 16
7494 Nuoro, Italy, K 5
..... Nurabad, Iran, L 6
..... Nurabad, Iran, O 12
1000 Nurmes, Fin., D 7
410438 Nürnberg, Germany, N 9
5000 Nurpur, India, C 9
..... Nurpur, India, D 4
..... Nusa-el-Ghait, Egypt, D 14
2851 Nuseybin (Nisibin), Tur., H 16
..... Nush-ki, Baluchistan, M 20
..... Nut Mountain, Sask., N 10
7823 Nuwara Eliya, Cey., R 14
..... Ny, Sweden, L 11
..... Nyandoma, Sov. Un., F 12
9740 Nyborg, Denmark, L 15
..... Nyborg, Norway, A 23
4011 Nybro, Sweden, P 14
..... Nyezhin, see Nezhin, Sov. Un.
..... Nyhem, Sweden, J 14
52776 Nyiregyháza, Hung., H 15
..... Nykirke, Norway, D 3
4058 Nyköbing, Denmark, I 18
13919 Nyköbing, Denmark, N 20
7982 Nyköbing, Denmark, E 5
11953 Nyköping, Sweden, N 15
608 Nyland, Sweden, J 16
575 Nylstroom, U. S. Afr., D 18
160 Nymagee, Austl., N 20
11890 Nymburk, Czech., F 7
1500 Nyngan, Austl., M 20
5119 Nyon, Switz., L 2
3157 Nyons, France, N 20
..... Nýřany, Czech., F 5
321 Nyrup, Den., K 12
..... Nysätra, Sweden, H 19
..... Nystad, see Uusikaupunki, Fin.
1716 Nysted, Denmark, O 19
..... Nyukhatskoe, Sov. Un., D 16
..... Nyukhotskoe, Sov. Un., D 10

O

130 Oadweina, Br. Som., I 16
150 Oak Bay, N. B., K 5
264 Oakburn, Man., P 12
3191 Oakham, England, I 17
464 Oak Lake, Man., Q 12
..... Oakland, Man., Q 15
214 Oakland, Ontario, N 9
211 Oak Point, N. B., K 11
..... Oakura, N. Z., Q 15
175 Oakville, Man., Q 15
4115 Oakville, Ontario, M 11
282 Oakwood, Ont., I 14
7600 Oamaru, N. Z., O 9
..... O. Amizour, Algeria, B 19
29306 Oaxaca, Oax., L 9
81 Oba, Ontario, P 21
9700 Obama, Japan, L 13
..... Oban, Sask., M 5
5759 Oban, Scotland, K 10
2400 Obata, Japan, A 24
..... Obbe, Scotland, F 4
2500 Obbia, Som., N 21
..... Obdorsk, see Sale Khard, Sov. Un.
..... Obeh, Afg., H 17
2281 Obenammergau, Ger., R 8
967 Oberglatt, Switz., D 14
192300 Oberhausen, Ger., I 3
1155 Oberhofen, Switz., J 10
..... Obernburg, Ger., M 6
569 Oberried, Switz., J 11
701 Obersaxen, Switz., J 18
..... Ober Schönweide, Ger., R20
10712 Oberstein, Ger., M 3
221 Oberwald, Switz., K 14
5000 Obi, Japan, Q 4
..... Obidos, Brazil, E 9
4125 Obidos, Portugal, J 5
1032 Obispos, Ven., F 8
500 Obok, Fr. Somaliland, F 14
11900 Oboyan, Sov. Un., K 10
..... Obrenovac, Yugo., K 13
393 Ocampo, Arg., I 18
..... Ocampo, Coa., D 9
9937 Ocaña, Col., F 17
9953 Ocaña, Spain, I 12
1000 Ocean Falls, B. C., M 9
..... Ochandio, Arg., Q 18
..... Ochi, Neth. Guiana, C 10
302 Ochre River, Man., O 13
3713 Ochsenfurt, Ger., M 7
..... Ockelbo, Sweden, L 15
6000 Ocna-Sibiului, Rom., J 17
7255 Ocnele-Mari, Rom., J 18
144 Ocobamba, Peru, M 14
..... Ocoña, Peru, P 15
513 Ocongate, Peru, N 17
1554 Ocós, Guatemala, G 2
3028 Ocotal, Nicaragua, H 11
..... Ocotepec, Oax., M 9
14209 Ocotlán, Jal., M 8
3059 Ocotlán, Oax., M 9
202 Ocourt, Switzerland, E 7
420 Ocoyo, Peru, N 12
..... Ocozingo, Chia., M 17
4178 Ocozocuautla, Chia., M 15
6175 Ocumare del Tuy, Ven. D 13
1073 Ocuri, Bolivia, J 8
..... Odaka, Japan, I 23
3000 Odaki, Japan, N 21
..... Odalen, Norway, L 10
..... Odalla, I. E. A., K 11
7165 Odate, Japan, D 23
15000 Odawara, Japan, M 19
..... Odda, Norway, L 5
4628 Odder, Denmark, I 11
103 Oddesund, Denmark, F 4
..... Oddur, Som., P 4
4162 Odemira, Portugal, M 5
..... Ödemish, Tur., F 2
76119 Odense, Denmark, L 13
1195 Ödeshog, Sweden, O 13

Pop. Place Country Index

724 Odessa, Ontario, I 19
207 Odessa, Sask., Q 9
604223 Odessa, W. Sov. Un., I 25
5915 Odobesti, Rom., I 21
20000 Odomari, Sov. Un., Asia, K 24
12304 Odoorn, Neth., D 23
9000 Odorhei, Rom., I 19
..... Odsted, Denmark, J 8
..... Ödum, Denmark, G 12
..... Odune, Col., J 18
..... Oebisfelde, Germany, G 9
4891 Oedelem, Bel., K 6
..... Oeguchi, Japan, N 5
6251 Oeiras, Portugal, K 4
..... O el Atchen, Algeria, Q 11
17000 Oelsnitz, Germany, L 10
1804 Oensingen, Switz., E 10
..... Oetling, Arg., I 17
..... Oeynhausen, Ger., G 5
..... Offen, Germany, F 7
82000 Offenbach, Germany, L 5
..... Offerdal, Sweden, I 12
1058 Offranville, France, F 11
..... Ofi, Eth., J 11
753 Oficina Valparaiso, Chile, F4
..... Ofoten, Norway, D 14
..... Ofvansjö, Sweden, L 15
..... Öfver Kalix, Sweden, F 20
..... Öfver Lulea, Sweden, F 19
..... Öfverum, Sweden, O 14
21 Ogden, Alberta, N 21
330 Ogema, Sask., Q 8
3800 Ogi, Japan, H 19
..... Ogilvie, Arg., J 17
..... Ogilvie, Yukon, L 4
836 Oginaga, Chih., F 21
..... Oglat bou el Adam (Wells), Algeria, L 9
..... Oglat Tinejiouk (Wells), Algeria, L 9
1326 Ogne, Norway, N 3
8000 Ogulin, Yugo., J 7
..... Ohadar, Iran, Q 14
1390 Ohaeawai, N. Z., G 18
..... Ohama, Japan, M 13
..... Ohanet, Alg., L 23
..... Ohasma, Afg., J 21
..... Ohat, Algeria, Q 19
53 Ohaton, Alberta, K 21
500 Ohau, N. Z., I 17
1043 Ohey, Belgium, N 15
..... Ohio, Nova Scotia, J 19
7280 Ohrdruf, Germany, K 8
9776 Ohrid, Yugo., M 14
..... Ohuki, N. Z., D 19
1500 Oi, Japan, M 17
1034 Oiba, Col., H 12
..... Oieren, Norway, M 9
1141 Oignies, Belgium, P 12
190 Oil City, Ontario, O 4
458 Oil Springs, Ontario, O 4
11700 Oirat-Tura (Ulala), Sov. Un., Asia, H 13
4645 Oirschot, Neth., J 16
1024 Oisemont, France, F 13
..... Oishi, Japan, H 19
5702 Oisterwijk, Neth., J 16
57294 Oita, Japan, N 5
..... Oja, Sweden, P 17
..... Ojeda, Argentina, O 18
..... Ojeda, Chile, D 4
1939 Ojen, Spain, O 10
..... Ojer, Norway, K 9
3131 Ojitlan, Oax., K 9
..... Ojitos, Chih., D 15
8500 Ojiya, Japan, J 19
3783 Ojocaliente, Zac., J 9
634 Ojo Caliente, S. L. P., K 13
540 Ojo de Agua, Arg., J 13
1828 Ojo de Agua, Cuba, J 11
609 Ojuelos, Jal., K 10
800 Okaihau, N. Z., B 15
..... Okanagan Lodge, British Columbia, P 16
..... Okawa, Japan, D 23
..... Okawa, Japan, E 25
163552 Okayama, Japan, L 10
65507 Okazaki, Japan, M 16
..... Okbiyen, Egypt, C 20
3352 Okehampton, England, N 8
..... Okhotsk, Sov. Un. Asia, E 19
791 Okotoks, Alberta, O 21
..... Okpo, Bur., O 21
..... Oksnes, Norway, C 13
..... Okura, Japan, I 21
..... Okura, N. Z., N 5
49333 Olavarria, Arg., P 17
..... Old Barns, N. S., K 15
..... Old Bastar, India, K 15
35918 Oldbury, England, J 13
900 Oldcastle, Ire., H 17
3380 Old Deer, Scotland, G 23
..... Old Dorak, Iran, K 4
8407 Oldebroek, Neth., F 19
2918 Oldenburg, Ger., B 7
66951 Oldenburg, Ger., E 5
10021 Oldenzaal, Neth., F 23
..... Oldesloe, Germany, D 8
140309 Oldham, England, G 13
..... Old Luce, see Glenluce, Scot.
1589 Old Meldrum, Scot., H 23
1337 Olds, Alberta, M 20
..... Old Taochow, China, F 7
..... Oldtown, Ire., L 22
..... Oldtown, Ire., I 21
..... Old Upsala, Sweden, M 16
305 O'Leary, P. E. I., F 13
2600 Olekminsk, Sov. Un. Asia, F 17
..... Olemskoe, Sov. Un., D 15
..... Olents, Sov. Un., F 8
1661 Olgod, Den., J 4
..... Olgopol, W. Sov. Un., G 24
11050 Olhão, Port., N 6
..... Olifants River, U. S. Afr., N 7
1800 Oliva, Arg., L 13
18407 Oliva, Spain, K 17
..... Olivares, Paraguay, N 7
45437 Oliveira, Brazil, M 17
12492 Olivenza, Spain, K 6
203 Oliver, B. C., Q 16
781 Olivone, Switz., K 17
806 Ollaechea, Peru, N 18
..... Ollerton, England, H 17
3961 Ollon, Switz., M 6
..... Olmedo, Ecuador, C 2
3046 Olmedo, Spain, G 11
1312 Olmeto, Cor., Q 2
2163 Olmos, Peru, G 3
..... Olney, England, J 17
65989 Olomouc, Czech., G 10
2000 Olonets, Sov. Un., F 8
10202 Oloron Saint Marie, France, P 8
14333 Olot, Spain, E 20
..... Olpas, Argentina, K 10
6498 Olpe, Germany, J 4
..... Öls, Germany, J 18
..... Olshanka, W. Sov. Un. G 25
5613 Olst, Neth., F 20
..... Ölsted, Denmark, J 9
405 Olta, Arg., K 9

Pop. Place Country Index

13555 Olten, Switz., E 11
10396 Oltenita, Rom., K 21
..... Oltingen, Switz., H 8
427 Olympia, Grc. P 15
..... Oma, Japan, A 24
..... Oma, Japan, H 12
..... Oma, Sov. Un., C 16
..... Om Agar, Erit., C 6
4836 Omagh, N. Ire., D 16
..... Omai, British Guiana, B 6
..... Omaja, Cuba, M 19
..... Omarama, N. Z., O 8
593 Omate, Peru, P 18
110436 Omdurman, Anglo-Egyptian Sudan, H 18
3500 Ome, Japan, L 19
..... Omeath, Ire., G 21
..... Omei, China, H 7
..... Omemee Jc., Ont., I 14
1840 Omereque, Bolivia, J 10
4162 Ometepec, Guer., R 19
..... Ominato, Japan, B 25
..... Ominato, Japan, H 12
7879 Ommen, Neth., F 21
632 Omoa, Honduras, E 8
1000 Omori, Japan, K 8
..... Omorkot, India, J 15
..... Omoto, Japan, E 25
280716 Omsk, Sov. Un. Asia, G 11
..... Omura, Austl., L 18
10000 Omura, Japan, N 3
1344 Oña, Spain, D 13
..... Onahama, Japan, J 23
..... Onaping, Ont., R 23
7304 Onda, Spain, I 17
..... Onderstedoorns, Union of South Africa, L 10
2700 Onega, Sov. Un., D 11
..... Oneglia, Italy, F 3
11500 Onehunga, N. Z., D 17
..... O'Neil, Scotland, I 21
10000 Ongole, India, M 13
320 Ongoy, Peru, M 14
..... Onich, Scotland, J 11
65 Onion Lake, Sask., J 4
..... Onitsha, Nig., J 9
2300 Ono, Japan, K 15
29084 Onomichi, Japan, M 9
3054 Onoto, Ven., E 16
409 Onsbjerg, Denmark, I 13
..... Onslev, Denmark, N 20
156 Onslow, Australia, H 3
5000 Onso, Norway, E 7
13564 Ontenjente, Spain, K 16
2000 Onuki, Japan, O 2
..... Onuma, Japan, G 22
100 Oodnadatta, Austl., J 14
..... Ookiep, U. S. Afr., K 6
..... Oola, Ire., M 12
3224 Ooltgensplaat, Neth., I 11
6662 Oostcamp, Belgium, K 6
..... Oosterend, Neth., B 16
15107 Oosterhout, Neth., I 14
1821 Oostmalle, Bel., K 13
3636 Oostzaan, Neth., A 4
24616 Ootacamund, India, O 9
1542 Ootmarsum, Neth., F 23
..... Oparino, Sov. Un., F 17
..... Opatów, Poland, F 14
36083 Opava, Czech., F 11
4250 Opdal, Norway, J 8
..... Opdal, Norway, I 5
300 Ophir, N. Z., O 7
684 Ophir, Scotland, B 19
1990 Opichen, Yuc., F 21
..... Opien, China, I 6
5658 Opochka, W Sov. Un., A 21
1315 Opoco, Bolivia, K 7
..... Opoczno, Pol., E 13
556 Opodepe, Son., E 11
..... Opole, Pol., E 15
584 Opont, Belgium, P 15
..... Oporto, see Pôrto, Port.
..... Opoteca, Honduras, G 9
1510 Opotiki, N. Z., F 22
..... Oppegaard, Norway, B 6
44000 Oppeln, Pol., J 17
3929 Oppenheim, Ger., M 4
..... Ops, Ontario, I 13
700 Opua, N. Z., B 15
1020 Opunake, N. Z., G 15
1737 Oputo, Son., E 13
7134 Opwyck, Belgium, L 10
..... Orabela, Hond., E 15
82355 Oradea, Rom., I 15
..... O. Rahmoun, Alg., C 21
200671 Oran, Algeria, D 12
970 Orán, Argentina, E 11
9634 Orange, Austl., N 21
11956 Orange, France, O 20
..... Orange River, U. S. Afr., K 13
2692 Orangeville, Ont., J 10
2718 Orange Walk, Br. Hond., A7
3208 Oranienbaum, Ger., I 11
14689 Oranienburg, Ger., F 12
..... Oranmore, Ire., J 8
1300 Orari, N. Z., N 10
7500 Orăstie, Romania, J 17
9046 Oravita, Rom., J 15
474 Orbaek, Denmark, L 14
3199 Orbe, Switz., J 4
3965 Orbetello, Italy, H 8
..... Orbo, Spain, D 11
1660 Orbost, Austl., Q 20
..... Orbynus, Sweden, L 16
4979 Orchanie, Bul., L 18
..... Orchha, India, G 9
..... Orcopampa, Peru, O 16
10195 Ordenes, Spain, C 6
..... Ording, Denmark, F 5
..... Ordóñez, Arg., M 14
8209 Ordu, Tur., C 13
127172 Ordzhonikidze (Vladikavkaz), Sov. Un., P 16
..... Ore, Norway, I 6
..... Orealla, Br. Guiana, B 7
45663 Örebro, Sweden, M 13
1201 Öregrund, Sweden, L 17
304 Örehoved, Denmark, M 19
..... Orekhovka, Sov. Un., O 15
20844 Orekhovo-Zuevo, Sov. Un., I 12
110567 Orel, Sov. Un., K 10
4184 Orellana, Spain. K 10
..... Orenburg, see Chkalov, Sov. Un.
174 Orendain, Jal., L 6
..... Orense, Argentina, Q 18
28397 Orense, Spain, E 7
702 Orepuki, N. Z., Q 4
..... Orfani, Greece, N 18
..... Orford Ness, Eng., J 24
1073 Organja, Spain, E 18
3154 Orgaz, Spain, J 12
911 Orgon France, O 20
14805 Orhei, W. Sov. Un., H 23
9730 Oria, Italy, K 21
1031 Oriental, Pueb., H 7
..... Oriente, Chile, F 4
43619 Orihuela, Spain, M 16
..... Oril, Western Brazil, F 18
9798 Orillia, Ontario, H 12
1722 Orinoca, Bolivia, K 6
4427 Oriolo, Italy, K 19

Pop. Place Country Index

9833 Oristano, Italy, K 3
47982 Orizaba, Ver., I 8
6058 Orjechovo, Bul., K 18
3000 Orkedal, Norway, I 8
210 Orland, Ont., J 16
..... Orlandet, Norway, I 8
73155 Orléans, France, I 13
325 Orleans, Ont., D 23
9020 Orleansville, Algeria, C 15
12556 Orlikon, Switz., E 15
3300 Orlov, Sov. Un., G 18
..... Orlov-Gai, Sov. Un., L 18
..... Orlovsk, Sov. Un., J 25
1020 Orly, France, C 6
143 Ormesson, France, A 5
..... Ormevalla, Sweden, O 10
2032 Ormiston, Scotland, M 20
..... Ormsby Jc., Ontario, G 17
17121 Ormskirk, England, G 11
887 Ormstown, Quebec, R 14
..... Ornaes, Norway, L 7
2405 Ornans, France, J 22
5032 Örnsköldsvik, Sweden, I 17
..... Orocue, Col., I 17
..... Orocue, Col., L 13
..... Orohesa, Spain, I 10
275 Oromocto, N. B., I 7
596 Oron, Switzerland, K 5
836 Orono, Ontario, J 14
3370 Oropesa, Spain, I 10
914 Oropesa, Sp., I 17
2222 Orosei, Italy, K 5
14492 Oroya, Peru, L 10
..... Orre, Denmark, H 5
..... Orre, Norway, N 3
..... Orreslev, Denmark, I 10
..... Orsa, Sweden, L 13
6189 Orsara, Italy, J 16
1685 Orsera, Italy, D 13
22011 Orsha, W. Sov. Un., B 23
2214 Orsières, Switz., O 7
65799 Orsk, Sov. Un. Asia, K 25
..... Orskog, Norway, J 5
..... Orsleykloste, Denmark, F 7
8528 Orsova, Romania, J 16
..... Orsten, Norway, J 5
2101 Orta-koi, Bulgaria, M 21
..... Ortaköy, Tur., G 9
2243 Ortega, Col., J 9
10344 Ortelsburg, Pol., C 14
5952 Orthez, France, P 8
22152 Ortigueira, Spain, B 7
1579 Ortiz, Ven., E 12
..... Orton, England, D 12
..... Orton, Scotland, G 19
8124 Ortona, Italy, H 15
..... Orträsk, Sweden, H 17
..... Oruden, Scotland, H 24
1969 Oruiki, Japan, L 22
..... Orum, Denmark, D 11
50000 Oruro, Bolivia, J 6
7137 Orvieto, Italy, H 10
325 Orwell, Ontario, O 7
104 Orwell Cove, P. E. I., H 17
..... Oryekhovka, Sov. Un., J 20
67 Osage, Sask., Q 9
3252340 Osaka, Japan, M 13
3026 Osaki, Japan, I 19
..... Osawa, Japan, C 23
..... Osawe, Japan, K 21
..... Osborne Bay Jc., B. C., P 2
10439 Oschatz, Germany, J 11
13489 Oschersleben, Ger., H 9
..... Osdorp, Neth., C 1
..... Osgoode, Ont., F 22
28813 Oshawa, Ontario, J 13
..... Osh el Ghurab, Palestine, M 12
..... Oshian, Afg., I 22
..... Oshmûn Janna, Egypt, D 17
..... Oshuc, Chia., M 17
..... Osi, Norway, N 5
40339 Osijek, Yugo., J 11
6603 Osimo, Italy, G 13
..... Oskarsborg, Norway, C 5
8674 Oskarshamn, Sweden, P 15
200 Osler, Sask., M 7
253124 Oslo, Norway, M 9
..... Oslos, Denmark, D 6
1805 Osma, Spain, G 13
..... Osmanabad, Iran, H 2
..... Osmanje, Tur., H 1
4213 Osmanjik, Tur., C 9
94000 Osnabrück, Germany, G 5
506 Osogna Switz., M 17
25075 Osorno, Chile, A 19
..... Osowiec, Poland, C 16
2641 Ospiño, Ven., E 9
14601 Oss, Neth., I 17
..... Osseby-Garn, Sweden, P 22
3230 Ossendrecht, Neth., J 11
..... Ossidinge, Nig., J 10
..... Ostashkov, Sov. Un., H 8
524 Ostbirk, Denmark, I 9
..... Ostein, Switz., N 12
49261 Ostend, Belgium, K 4
..... Ostend, Germany, R 20
5400 Oster, W. Sov. Un., E 25
..... Österaker, Sweden, P 23
..... Osterburg, Germany, F 10
..... Österby, Denmark, C 16
..... Östergarn, Sweden, O 17
2250 Osterholz, Germany, E 6
124 Österild, Denmark, D 5
..... Ostermundigen, Switz., H 9
..... Ostermyra, Fin., D 3
17000 Osterode, Pol., C 13
..... Öster Ryd, Sweden, P 22
..... Öster Skerninge, Den., M 12
14138 Östersund, Sweden, I 13
1078 Östhammar, Sweden, L 16
..... Ostia, Italy, I 11
..... Ostra Torp, Sweden, R 11
12975 Ostrog, W. Sov. Un., F 20
22990 Ostrogozhsk, Sov. Un., L 12
13488 Ostroleka, Poland, G 15
3127 Ostrov, Romania, I 20
6300 Ostrov, Sov. Un., H 5
..... Ostrów, Poland, D 15
17611 Ostrów, Poland, E 11
22215 Ostrowiec, Pol., E 14
209 Ostula, Michoa., O 6
19298 Ostuni, Italy, J 21
24228 Osuna, Spain, N 10
9754 Oswestry, England, I 11
12187 Oswiecim, Pol., F 12
5500 Ota, Japan, K 22
1800 Ota, Japan, M 22
1200 Otani, Japan, H 17
..... Otarama, N. Z., M 11
164282 Otaru, Japan, F 12
10708 Otavalo, Ecuador, B 5
..... Otavi, S. W. Afr., O 13
..... Othello, B. C., Q 14
122 Otis, N. B., I 5
..... Otley, Alberta, K 19
..... Otočac, Yugo., J 7
675 Otorohanga, N. Z., F 18
2729 Otranto, Italy, K 23
..... Otsu, Japan, G 14
34380 Otsu, Japan, M 14
154951 Ottawa, Ontario, D 22
..... Ottawa Jc., Ontario, E 22
..... Ottenby, Sweden, Q 15

..... Otterbacken, Sweden, N 12
..... Otterburn, England, C 13
177 Otterburne, Man., R 16
..... Otterlo, Neth., G 18
..... Otterswick, Shetland Is., B 4
1179 Otterup, Denmark, K 12
610 Otterville, Ontario, N 8
3713 Ottery, England, N 10
3623 Ottignies, Belgium, M 13
364 Ottone, Italy, E 5
..... Ottweiler, France, N 3
..... Otuako, N. Z., B 14
2237 Otumba, Méx., G 5
..... Otumpa, Argentina, H 14
3534 Otuzco, Peru, I 5
..... Otwâni, Egypt, P 24
13012 Ouagadougou, Fr. W. Afr., I 6
..... Ouahigouya, Fr. W. Afr., I 6
..... Oualata, Fr. W. Afr., H 5
5524 Ouargla, Alg., H 19
..... Ouchy, Switz., L 4
3664 Oudorp, Neth., I 9
5730 Oudenbosch, Neth., J 12
..... Ouderef, Tunisia, E 24
3814 Ouderkerk, Neth., D 4
..... Oudesluis, Neth., E 14
3130 Oudewater, Neth., H 14
19976 Oudjda, Alg., E 11
13225 Oudtshoorn, U. S. Afr., Q 11
..... Oued Riou, Alg., C 14
..... Oued Sly, Alg., C 15
4131 Oued Zenati, Algeria, C 21
..... Ouesso, Fr. Eq. Afr., K 12
19230 Ouezzane, Mor., E 7
900 Oughterard, Ire., J 6
19763 Ougrée, Belgium, N 17
..... Ouhe, Honduras, E 14
11700 Ouidah, Fr. W. Afr., J 7
..... Oulad Mellouk, Mor., G 9
..... Oulart, Ire., M 21
..... Ouled Jellal, Algeria, E 19
..... Ouloual, Algeria, F 19
24924 Oulu (Uleaborg), Finland, C 5
..... Oum el Bouaghi, Alg., C 21
4500 Ourem, Portugal, J 5
..... Ouricury, Brazil, G 21
4565 Ourique, Portugal, M 5
..... Ourlana, Algeria, F 20
8928 Ouro Preto, Brazil, M 18
..... Oussekr, Algeria, E 14
331 Outarville, France, I 13
..... Outjo, S. W. Afr., O 13
712 Outlook, Sask., N 6
..... Outre Rhone, Switz., N 6
..... Ouyen, Australia, O 17
14807 Ovalle, Chile, K 3
10482 Ovar, Portugal, G 5
3371 Ovejas, Col., D 10
..... Overaas, Norway, J 7
6326 Overath, Germany, J 3
..... Overhallen, Norway, H 10
13 Overland, Sask., R 9
..... Overton, Ontario, I 19
5300 Ovidiopol, W. Sov. Un., I 25
82548 Oviedo, Spain, C 9
..... Oviken, Sweden, I 13
..... Ovrebygden, Norway, C 17
6100 Ovruch, W. Sov. Un., E 22
..... Ovsted, Denmark, I 10
233 Ovtrup, Denmark, J 3
557 Owaka, N. Z., Q 7
5500 Owashi, Japan, O 14
14002 Owen Sound, Ontario, H 7
..... Owen Spring, Austl., H 13
..... Owerri, Nig., J 9
..... Owl Creek, B. C., P 13
216 Owl's Head Harbour, N.S., H 17
465 Oxbow, Sask., R 11
..... Oxby, Denmark, K 2
3197 Oxelösund, Sweden, N 15
80540 Oxford, England, K 16
1297 Oxford, N. S., J 14
919 Oxford, N. Z., M 2
127 Oxford Jc., N. S., J 14
302 Oxford Mills, Ontario, F 22
5050 Oxkutzcab, Yuc., F 22
43 Oxley, Austl., O 19
..... Oxton, Scotland, N 21
..... Oxwich, Wales, L 7
326 Oyen, Alberta, M 24
..... Oykell, Scotland, F 13
630 Oyne, Scotland, H 22
1316 Oyolo, Peru, O 14
80 Oyster Bed Bridge, P. E. I., G 16
8733 Ozieri, Italy, J 4
..... Ozolotepec, Oax., N 9
14979 Ozorków, Poland, E 12
2601 Ozu, Japan, N 7
1408 Ozuluama, Ver., D 7

P

..... Paardeburg, U. S. Afr., J 15
18580 Paarl, U. S. Afr., Q 7
..... Paauwpan, U. S. Afr., L 14
45614 Pabjanice, Poland, E 12
951 Pacarán, Peru, M 10
..... Pacaraos, Peru, K 8
6615 Pacasmayo, Peru, H 4
16756 Pacatuba, Brazil, F 22
1390 Paccha, Bolivia, K 10
1214 Pachas, Peru, J 8
303 Pachia, Chile, A 3
13858 Pachino, Italy, P 16
825 Pachiza, Peru, H 8
..... Pachmul, Q. R., H 24
..... Pachow, China, G 9
53354 Pachuca, Hid., G 6
63 Pacific, B. C., I 8
..... Pacific Jc., N. B., H 11
654 Pacllón, Peru, K 8
13714 Pacora, Col., H 8
1778 Pacy-sur-Eure, Fr., G 12
..... Padam, India, B 10
..... Padana, India, I 3
52600 Padang, Neth. Ind., H 2
..... Padaung, Bur., O 21
570 Padcaya, Bolivia, N 11
24674 Paddington, Austl., M 19
150 Paddockwood, Sask., K 8
35000 Paderborn, Ger., I 5
..... Padiham, Eng., F 13
7485 Padilla, Bolivia, K 11
83086 Padova (Padua), It., D 10
8189 Padrón, Spain, D 5
1929 Padstow, England, N 4
..... Padua, see Padova, It.
3791 Padula, Italy, K 17
2260 Paeroa, N. Z., E 19
..... Pagancillo, Argentina, J 7
..... Pagham, England, N 18
..... Pagistin, Iran, R 14
1971 Paglieta, Italy, H 15
37511 Pahlevi (Enzeli), Iran, D 5
..... Pahsien, see Chungking, China.
..... Paible, Scotland, G 2
2857 Paicol, Col., K 8
2980 Paide, Sov. Un., G 4
18405 Paignton, England, O 9
720 Paihuano, Chile, K 4

2980 Paillaco, Chile, R 3
2392 Paimboeuf, Fr., J 5
2802 Paimpol, France, G 4
1461 Paine, Chile, N 4
62 Painsec Jc., New Brunswick, H 12
1006 Paipa, Col., H 13
120268 Paisley, Scotland, N 14
709 Paisley, Ontario, I 6
7177 Paita, Peru, F 1
10900 Paithan, India, K 8
..... Pajala, Sweden, E 20
..... Pajalta, Argentina, A 23
..... Pajan, Ecuador, C 2
669 Pajarito, Col., H 14
..... Pajeczno, Pol., E 12
..... Pajembango, Oceania, H 2
..... Pajûralis, W. Sov. Un., B 15
..... Pakala, India, N 12
..... Pakan, Iran, J 7
..... Pakchan, Bur., R 24
550 Pakenham, Ontario, E 20
35000 Pakhoi, China, L 11
..... Pakiay, Fr. In. Ch., N 4
..... Paknampo, Siam., O 3
23115 Pakokku, Bur., N 22
6500 Pakpattan, India, D 6
..... Pakrac, Yugo., J 10
11817 Paks, Hungary, I 11
..... Pak-san, Fr. In. Ch., N 6
..... Pak-sé, Fr. In. Ch., O 8
..... Paksha, China, L 13
591 Palacios, Arg., K 15
7905 Pala Frugell, Spain, F 21
4555 Palaiseau, France, D 4
..... Palamau, India, H 17
..... Palambla, Peru, G 3
5037 Palamós, Spain, F 21
..... Palanga, W. Sov. Un., A 14
20347 Palanpur, India, H 5
..... Palas, India, A 7
14653 Palazzolo Acreide, It., O 16
110000 Palembang, Neth. Ind., I 2
34283 Palencia, Spain, E 11
..... Palenque, Ecuador, C 3
433 Palenque, Chia., L 17
1983 Palermo, Col., K 9
317735 Palermo, Italy, N 13
..... Palestina, Chile, F 4
..... Palestina, Bolivia, O 5
6208 Palestrina, Italy, I 12
6818 Palestro, Algeria, B 17
552 Palézieux, Switzerland, K 5
49064 Palghat, India, P 9
..... Palhoca, Brazil, P 13
..... Pali, India, G 6
..... Palingun, Iran, O 10
12800 Palitana, India, I 5
1404 Palizada, Camp., J 17
711 Palizada, Méx., H 3
10400 Palkonda, India, K 17
3778 Pallanza, Italy, C 4
..... Pallas, Ire., I 14
..... Pallas Green, Ire., M 11
..... Pallaskenry, Ire., M 9
..... Palma, Brazil, F 20
..... Palma, Brazil, J 15
..... Palma, S. L. P., K 16
114405 Palma, Spain, J 21
..... Palma Alta, Cuba, L 6
15042 Palma del Rio, Spain, M 10
3545 Palmanova, Italy, C 12
496 Palmar, Bolivia, J 13
2361 Palmarito, Cuba, O 21
1474 Palmarito, Ven., H 8
..... Palmas, Brazil, O 11
..... Palma Sola, Ven., C 10
15743 Palma Soriano, Cuba, O 21
..... Palmeira, Brazil, P 10
5529 Palmeira dos Indios, Brazil, H 23
..... Palmeiras, Braz., K 14
..... Palmeiras, Brazil, O 13
13920 Palmela, Portugal, K 5
47 Palmer, Sask., Q 7
790 Palmerston, N. Z., P 9
1418 Palmerston, Ont., K 8
23600 Palmerston North, New Zealand, I 18
..... Palmerstown, Ire., F 7
..... Palmerville, Austl., D 19
..... Palmillas, Cuba, I 10
697 Palmillas, Tam., I 16
..... Palmira, Bolivia, O 4
21235 Palmira, Col., J 7
5865 Palmira, Cuba, J 11
..... Palmira, Ecuador, D 5
..... Palmitas, Uruguay, L 16
2082 Palmito, Col., D 9
2000 Palmyre, Syr., L 13
..... Palnatz, Tur., E 18
..... Palomas, Uruguay, G 16
5797 Palomino, Col., B 13
..... Palomitas, Arg., G 11
..... Paloncha, India, L 14
3907 Palos, Cuba, I 8
1922 Palos de la Frontera, Spain, N 8
..... Palo Seco, Cuba, M 18
2171 Palpa, Peru, L 8
8000 Palpa, Peru, N 11
642 Palqui, Chile, K 4
3703 Palu, Tur., F 15
..... Pambitya, India, Q 13
13164 Pamiers, France, P 12
..... Pampa, Uruguay, J 19
1920 Pampa Aullagas, Bol., K 6
..... Pampa Blanca, Arg., F 10
3389 Pampa Grande, Bol., J 12
1738 Pampa Grande, Bol., M 10
..... Pampas, Peru, H 5
1622 Pampas, Peru, L 11
469 Pampas Grande, Peru, J 6
2062 Pampatar, Ven., B 18
..... Pampa Vieja, Arg., K 6
506 Pampelonne, France, O 14
..... Pampita, Arg., M 8
14207 Pamplona, Col., F 14
61188 Pamplona, Spain, D 15
..... Pampoen-Poort, U. S. Afr., M 12
..... Pamzal, India, B 12
..... Pan Bur., N 24
597 Panabá, Yuc., E 23
9582 Panagiurišlite, Bul., L 18
111893 Panama, Panama, P 22, K 24
..... Panapie, Neth. Gu., C 10
954 Panao, Peru, J 10
5422 Panaquire, Venezuela, D 14
..... Pancajche, Guatemala, E 5
22113 Pančevo, Yugo., J 14
..... Panchun, India, F 6
6910 Panciu, Rom., I 21
..... Pandaria, India, I 15
..... Pan de Azucar, Chile, H 3
3409 Pan de Azúcar, Ur., P 21
10981 Pauderma, Tur., C 2
28600 Pandharpur, India, L 8
9600 Pando, Uruguay, O 19
..... Panemunis, W. Sov. Un., A 18
22000 Panevezys, W. Sov. Un., A 17
..... Pangal, India, L 11
..... Pangtzula, China, I 3
67 Panguipulli, Chile, R 4

3590 Panindicuaro, Michoa., M 10
32915 Panipat, India, E 10
76 Panix, Switz., I 18
..... Panjab, Afg., G 18
10000 Panjim, India, M 6
..... Pankow, Germany, N 18
13300 Panna, India, H 13
15200 Panruti, India, O 13
..... Pantanaw, Bur., P 21
37716 Pantin, France, A 7
..... Panuco, Coa., D 12
1389 Pánuco, Sin., Q 19
5942 Pánuco, Ver., C 6
963 Panuco de Cronado, Dur., O 22
3544 Panzós, Guatemala, E 5
2153 Pao, Ven., F 16
..... Paokan, China, G 13
..... Paoking, China, J 13
9328 Paola, Italy, L 18
..... Paoning, China, H 9
..... Paoshan (Yungchang), China, J 3
..... Paotch, China, D 12
80000 Paotingfu, China, D 16
..... Paotowchen, China, C 12
21352 Pápa, Hungary, H 10
..... Papadil, Scot., I 7
6835 Papantla, Ver., F 8
..... Papatowai, N. Z., Q 7
8456 Papeete, Society Is., L 25
9444 Papenburg, Ger., E 4
..... Papile, W. Sov. Un., A 16
1023 Papineauville, Quebec, P 12
101 Paposo, Chile, G 3
..... Pappenheim, Ger., O 8
674 Papudo, Chile, M 3
..... Papun, Bur., O 23
..... Paquetteville, Que., R 21
44259 Pará, Brazil, M 17
..... Para, see Belem, Braz.
5330 Paracanjuba, Brazil, K 14
..... Paracatú, Brazil, K 15
7265 Paracin, Yugo., K 15
..... Paracurú, Brazil, F 22
..... Parada Ayur, Arg., K 20
..... Parada Leis, Arg., I 23
8828 Paradas, Spain, N 10
198 Paradise, N. S., M 10
..... Paradiso House, Ire., M 8
..... Parag, Iran, R 15
..... Paragua, Ven., I 19
8000 Paraguari, Par., O 7
..... Parahyba, see João Pessoa
1675 Paraíso, Chiap., M 13
164 Paraje Seco, Dur., K 19
..... Parakou, Fr. W. Afr., I 8
60723 Paramaribo, Neth. Guiana, B 9
..... Paramonga, Peru, K 7
74854 Paraná, Arg., L 17
..... Paraná, Cuba, N 21
..... Paranacito, Arg., M 18
13027 Paranagua, Brazil, O 14
1572 Paranagaricutiro, Michoa., N 9
..... Paraopeba, Brazil, L 16
..... Parapet, B. C., P 18
4448 Parapiti Grande, Bol., L 13
..... Pararin, Peru, K 7
..... Paraty, Brazil, O 14
..... Paravur, India, P 9
6469 Paray-le-Monial, Fr., K 17
11857 Parchim, Germany, E 10
428 Parcoy, Peru, I 7
..... Parczew, Poland, E 16
429 Pardilla, Spain, G 12
..... Pardo, Arg., O 18
..... Pardo, Ecuador, D 7
28841 Pardubice, Czech., F 8
..... Paredes, Cuba, K 18
558 Paredón, Coa., F 12
25 Paredones, Baja Cal., A 5
..... Parenda, India, K 8
502 Parent, Quebec, G 13
637 Parentis-en-Born, Fr., N 7
1471 Parenzo, Italy, D 13
..... Parga, Greece, O 14
..... Pari, Iran, H 5
5965 Paria, Bol., I 6
1792 Pariaguán, Ven., F 16
3663 Parijs, U. S. Afr., G 17
..... Parintins, Brazil, E 8
2829746 Paris, France, H 14
4637 Paris, Ontario, M 9
..... Paris, Yukon, K 5
973 Parita, Panama, Q 20
..... Pariz, Iran, M 10
..... Parkar, India, H 4
101 Parkbeg, Sask., P 7
..... Parkdale, Ontario, L 12
5846 Parkes, Austl., N 20
104 Park Head, Ont., H 7
1030 Park Hill, Ont., N 5
..... Parkmore, Ire., B 22
..... Parkside, Sask., L 8
112 Parksville Jc., B. C., Q 11
..... Parlakot, India, K 14
69200 Parma, Italy, E 7
..... Parnaguá, Brazil, H 18
22571 Parnahyba, Brazil, F 20
..... Parnahyba, Brazil, N 15
20660 Pärnu (Pernau), Sov. Un., G 3
..... Paro, Bhutan, F 22
182 Parobamba, Peru, I 7
..... Paroei, Taiwan, L 20
..... Paromovskoe, Sov. Un., D 19
..... Parpa, Iran, M 9
68 Parpan, Switz., J 20
10225 Parral, Chile, O 3
24231 Parral (Hidalgo del Parral), Chih., K 19
..... Parral Jc., Chih., J 20
18076 Parramatta, Austl., O 21
15555 Parras, Coa., F 10
..... Parravicini, Arg., P 20
207 Parronal, Chile, N 3
1971 Parrsboro, N. S., K 13
72 Parry, Sask., Q 8
5765 Parry Sound, Ont., E 10
..... Parsberg, Ger., N 9
..... Partabgarh, India, G 15
9800 Partabgarh, India, H 8
..... Partabpur, India, H 16
..... Partabpur, India, J 13
6830 Parthenay, France, K 8
..... Partick, Scotland, N 15
20805 Partinico, Italy, N 12
548 Parton, Scotland, Q 16
..... Partridge, Alta., P 22
2085 Paruro, Peru, N 16
..... Parvar, Baluchistan, P 19
..... Parvatipur, India, G 22
..... Parwan, Afg., F 23
..... Pascani, Rom., H 21
13750 Pascualitos, Baja Cal., A 4
89 Pasewalk, Ger., E 13
18 Pashley, Alberta, O 24
3022 Pašmakli, Bul., M 19
..... Paso del Cerro, Ur., H 20
1411 Paso del Macho, Ver., I 9
2294 Paso de Sotos, Jal., K 8
..... Paso Real, Cuba, I 4

..... Paso Real, Hond., E 12
46 Pasqua, Sask., P 8
..... Passage, Ire., O 18
..... Passagem Franca, Brazil, G 18
3024 Passage West, Ire., P 11
25000 Passau, Germany, P 12
280 Passekeag, N. B., J 9
17585 Passo Fundo, Brazil, P 11
12980 Passos, Brazil, M 15
..... Pastour, Arg., N 15
27564 Pasto, Col., M 5
..... Pastos Bons, Brazil, G 18
..... Pasvalys, W. Sov. Un., A 17
1230 Pata, Bolivia, F 2
..... Patab, Iran, Q 14
..... Patac-amaya, Bol., I 2
..... Patacamaya, Bol., I 4
7748 Pátacuaro, Michoa., N 11
32000 Patan, India, H 5
..... Patana, India, E 10
28300 Patani, India, P 2
..... Pataudi, India, E 10
1310 Patay, France, I 13
214 Patay, Peru, I 7
1480 Patea, N. Z., H 16
31436 Paterno, Italy, O 16
5000 Pathankot, India, C 9
..... Pathri, India, K 9
..... Pati, India, I 8
1224 Patia, Col., L 5
55129 Patiala, India, D 9
600 Patience, Alberta, K 20
175706 Patna, India, G 18
..... Patna, India, J 16
..... Patna, Scotland, O 14
..... Patquia, Arg., K 9
73300 Patrai (Patras), Grc., P 15
..... Patras, see Patrai, Grc.
..... Patria, Col., F 7
..... Patricia Bay, B. C., Q 2
..... Patricios, Argentina, O 16
..... Patrie, Que., Q 21
1500 Patrimonio, Brazil, G 19
..... Patrocinio, Brazil, G 20
6159 Patrocinio, Brazil, L 15
..... Patsobolong, Mongolia, C 11
10000 Pattani, Thai., Q 15
4786 Patti, Italy, N 16
..... Pattikonda, India, M 10
..... Patuca, Honduras, E 14
..... Paturages, Belgium, O 9
40451 Pau, France, P 8
1173 Paucarbamba, Peru, L 12
1382 Paucartambo, Peru, K 9
4650 Pauillac, France, M 7
..... Pauk, Bur., N 21
1218 Paulhaguet, France, M 16
12887 Paulista, Braz., H 20
2561 Paurito, Bolivia, J 4
..... Pausania, It., J 14
11490 Paute, Ecuador, D 5
1480 Pauza, Peru, N 10
..... Pavagada, India, N 10
547 Pavarandocito, Colo., F 7
4811 Pavas, Colombia, J 7
35724 Pavia, Italy, D 5
..... Pavilion, B. C., O 14
41000 Pavlograd, Sov. Un., M 10
..... Pavlovo, Sov. Un., I 14
16357 Pavlovskaya, Sov. Un., N 12
..... Pavlovskii Polsad, see Orekhovo-Zuevo, Sov. Un.
..... Pavoloch, W. Sov. Un., F23
..... Payas, Tur., I 11
..... Payenjungko, China, E 6
4974 Payerne, Switz., I 6
183 Paynton, Sask., L 5
..... Payogasta, Arg., G 9
..... Payo Obispo, see Ciudad Chetumal, Q. R.
46000 Paysandu, Uruguay, J 15
1849 Pazar (Atina), Tur., C 16
..... P. de Maciel, Ur., M 18
873 Peace River, Alberta, G 17
477 Peachland, B. C., Q 15
305 Peake Station, P. E. I., G 17
65 Peak Hill, Australia, J 5
1200 Pearston, U. S. Afr., O 14
..... Peazens, Neth., B 20
13194 Peč, Yugo., L 14
..... Pecanha, Brazil, L 19
212 Peccia, Switz., L 15
64391 Pécs, Hungary, I 11
731 Pedasi, Panama, R 21
656 Pedaso, Italy, G 13
389 Peddie, U. S. Afr., P 17
..... Pedernal, Arg., L 6
..... Pedernales, Arg., O 17
..... Pedernales, Ecuador, B 3
..... Pedernales, Ven., G 7
625 Pedersborg, Denmark, K 18
..... Pedra Branca, Brazil, G 21
..... Pedraza, Ven., G 7
601 Pedregal, Chile, K 4
..... Pedregal, Honduras, I 9
309 Pedregal, Panama, Q 17
1855 Pedregal, Ven., B 8
..... Pedreiras, Brazil, F 18
4508 Pedreiras, Brazil, N 15
1043 Pedricena, Dur., N 22
..... Pedro Affonso, Brazil, H 15
..... Pedro Antonio Santos (Sta. Cruz Chico), Q. R., I 24
4405 Pedrogão Grande, Portugal, I 6
4500 Pedro Gonzalez, Par., R 5
..... Pedro Montt, Chile, H 4
703 Pedroso, Spain, G 10
6402 Peebles, Scotland, N 20
34 Peebles, Sask, Q 10
3304 Peel, England, E 6
130 Peel, N. B., G 4
134 Peel, Ont., K 10
3847 Peer, Belgium, K 17
175 Peferlaw, Ontario, I 12
2667 Pegnitz, Ger., M 9
21712 Pegu, Bur., O 22
..... Peguahó, Argentina, I 19
..... Pehčevo, Yugo., M 17
58148 Pehuajo, Argentina, O 15
185 Pehuen, Chile, P 2
18000 Peine, Germany, G 7
..... Peint, India, J 6
1561027 Peiping (Peking), Chn. D 16
284500 Peiraievs, Grc., P 18
4853 Peixe, Brazil, I 14
..... Pekan, Malay States, Q 3
..... Peking, see Peiping, China.
2170 Pelechuco, Bolivia, F 2
6520 Pelhrimov, Czech., G 8
..... Pelicura, Argentina, Q 14
..... Pella, U. S. Afr., K 7
211 Pelletier Mills, N. B., D 1
217 Pelluhue, Chile, O 3
311 Pelly, Sask., N 11
86 Pelly, Yukon, M 6
62714 Pelotas, Brazil, Q 11
..... Pelton, Ontario, Q 1
..... Pemba, N. Rh., N 17

..... Pemberton, B. C., P 13
..... Pemberton, Eng., G 12
..... Pembrey, Wales, K 7
11159 Pembroke, Ontario, C 18
12008 Pembroke, Wales, L 5
..... Pembroke Shore, N. S., Q 8
..... Pemez, Iran, G 3
1703 Pemuco, Chile, P 3
5770 Penafiel, Portugal, G 6
4367 Peñafiel, Spain, F 12
3425 Penamacor, Portugal, I 8
148400 Penang (GeorgeTown), Sts. Setts, O 19
4027 Peñaranda, Spain, H 11
17710 Penarth, Wales, L 10
5903 Peñas, Bolivia, H 3
3286 Peñas de San Pedro, Spain, L 15
..... Pendembu, S. L., J 3
200 Pendra, India, I 15
4521 Penetanguishene, Ont., G 10
..... Pengan, China, H 9
5466 Peniche, Portugal, J 4
5198 Penicuik, Scot., N 19
..... Peninsula, Bolivia, C 5
2975 Peñiscola, Spain, I 18
2733 Penjamillo, Michoa., M 10
8795 Pénjamo, Guan., M 11
764 Pennabilli, Italy, F 10
..... Pennan, Scotland, G 23
233 Pennant, Sask., P 5
32566 Pennapolis, Brazil, M 13
312 Penne, Fr., N 11
4199 Penne, Italy, H 14
598 Pennfield, N. B., L 6
304 Penobsquis, N. B., J 10
1456 Penol, Col., G 9
1000 Penola, Austl., P 17
2418 Penonomé, Panama, P 21
783 Penpont, Scotland, P 17
9065 Penrith, England, D 12
3414 Penryn, England, O 4
272 Pense, Sask., P 8
2936 Pensilvania, Col., H 9
..... Pentecostes, Brazil, F 22
174 Pentland, Austl., G 20
..... Peñuelas, Agua., K 9
157145 Penza, Sov. Un., J 16
11342 Penzance, England, O 3
897 Peotillos, S. L. P., J 13
..... Peperga, Neth., D 19
3139 Pepinster, Belgium, N 19
3823 Peralta, Spain, E 15
..... Percas, Argentina, I 13
..... Percy H. Scott, Arg., A 23
..... Percyville, Austl., F 19
295 Perdue, Sask., M 6
..... Perehinsko, W. Sov.Un., G 18
30762 Pereira, Col., I 8
..... Pereiro, Brazil, G 22
5300 Perekop, Sov. Un., N 8
4411 Perelló, Spain, H 18
70367 Pergamino, Arg., N 17
2708 Pergola, Italy, F 12
301 Peribonca, Quebec, D 19
772 Perico del Carmen, Arg., F 10
210 Perico de San Antonio, Argentina, F 10
1158 Pericos, Sin., N 16
32 Perigord, Sask., M 10
37615 Périgueux, France, M 11
831 Perkins, Quebec, P 10
..... Perlas, Nic., J 15
10250 Perleberg, Ger., F 10
..... Perm, see Molotov, Sov. Un.
..... Pernambuco, see Recife, Braz.
4314 Péronne, France, F 15
4348 Perote, Ver., H 8
..... Perpetuo Socorro, Bol., B 6
72207 Perpignan, France, Q 16
17738 Perregaux, Algeria, D 13
..... Perret, Fr., A 15
281 Perreux, France, L 18
..... Persepolis (ruins), Iran, M 7
..... Pertegrel, Tur., C 16
2108 Pertek, Turkey, F 14
82290 Perth, Australia, N 4
406 Perth, N. B., F 4
4458 Perth, Ontario, F 21
..... Perth, Ont., L 7
34807 Perth, Scotland, L 18
5030 Pertuis, France, O 21
..... Peru, Argentina, P 13
24133 Perugia, Italy, H 11
7927 Peruwelz, Bel., N 8
39200 Pervomaisk (Olviopol) Sov. Un., M 6
2679 Perwez, Belgium, N 13
..... Peryaslavl Zalyeski, Sov. Un., H 12
18506 Pesaro, Italy, F 12
5254 Pescado, Bolivia, K 11
..... Pescadores Is., For., P19
5543 Pescara, Italy, H 14
741 Pesé, Panama, Q 20
130967 Peshawar, India, B 5
..... Peski, Sov. Un., L 14
9212 Pespire, Honduras, H 9
8519 Pesqueira, Brazil, D 13
10706 Pessac, France, N 7
7160 Peštera, Bul., M 18
834 Petalcingo, Chia., L 17
700 Petane, N. Z., G 21
4077 Petare, Venezuela, C 13
2531 Petatlán, Guer., Q 11
25350 Peterboro, Ontario, I 15
3059 Peterborough, Austl., N 16
22445 Peterborough, Eng., I 19
15285 Peterhead, Scotland, G 25
..... Petersham, England, C 19
36 Petersville, N. B., J 7
..... Pethah Tiqva, Pal., L 6
5936 Petilia-Policastro, It., L 20
7160 Petit Bourg, Guadeloupe, B 23
876 Petitcodiac, N. B., I 10
352 Petit de Grat Bridge, N. S., J 22
350 Petite Riviere Bridge, Nova Scotia, O 12
260 Petit Etang, N. S., F 21
10000 Petit Goave, Haiti, J 12
523 Petit Rocher, N. B., B 9
2761 Petlalcingo, Pueb., K 7
5104 Peto, Yuc., G 22
11050 Petone, N. Z., J 17
1098 Petorca, Chile, L 4
..... Petrerillos, Hond., F 8
10100 Petric, Bul., M 17
5537 Petrinja, Yugo., J 9
..... Petrograd, see Leningrad, Sov. Un.
2801 Petrolia, Ont., N 4
..... Petrolia Jc., Ontario, O 4
..... Petrolina, Brazil, H 20
91678 Petropavlovsk, Sov. Un. Asia, G 11
1000 Petropavlovsk Kamchatski, Sov. Un. Asia, D 21

Pop.	Place Country Index
14465	Petrosani, Rom., J 17
.....	Petrosita, Rom., J 20
4347	Petrovac, Yugo., K 9
13000	Petrovsk, Sov. Un., J 23
	Petrovsk, see Makhach Kala, Sov. Un.
	Petrozavodsk, see Kalininsk
.....	Petrusburg, U. S. Afr., J 15
345	Petten, Neth., E 13
.....	Pettigoe, Ire., E 14
.....	Pevensey, England, N 21
663	Peyrolles, France, P 21
548	Peyruis, France, O 22
7327	Pézenas, France, P 16
4518	Pfaffenhofon, Ger., P 9
1746	Pfaffers, Switz., H 20
3824	Pfäffikon, Switz., E 16
.....	Pfaffikon, Switz., F 16
3539	Pfarrkirchen, Ger., P 11
1344	Pfin, Switz., C 17
79000	Pforzheim, Ger., O 5
.....	Pfreimd, Germany, N 10
1382	Pfyn, Switz., C 17
.....	Phagwara, India, D 9
13900	Phalodi, India, F 5
.....	Phalsund, India, F 5
10000	Phaltan, India, K 7
.....	Phan-rang, Fr. In. Ch., Q 11
.....	Phan-thiet, Fr. In. China, Q 10
.....	Pharis, N. Ire., B 21
3223	Pharsala, Grc., O 16
	Philadelphia, see Amman, Transj.
9293	Philiatra, Greece, Q 15
66112	Philippeville, Algeria, B 20
1255	Philippeville, Belgium, O 12
1174	Philippine, Neth., Q 3
2000	Philippolis, U.South Africa, L 15
	Philippopolis, see Plovdiv, Bulgaria,
.....	Phillipstown, Ire., J 16
754	Phillipstown, U. S. Afr., L 14
200	Phillipsville, Ontario, G 21
38	Phippen, Sask., M 5
.....	Phuljhar, India, J 16
.....	Phulpur, India, G 15
.....	Phu-yen, Fr. In. China, P 11
43277	Piacenza, Italy, D 6
1077	Piana, Cor., Q 2
.....	Pianco, Brazil, G 23
497	Piangil, Australia, O 18
.....	Piatra, Romania, K 18
26511	Piatra-Neamt, Rom., I 21
27479	Piazza d'Armi, Italy, B 21
1075	Pica, Chile, C 4
404	Pich, Camp., H 20
.....	Pichanal, Argentina, E 11
598	Pichigua, Peru, N 17
650	Pichilemu, Chile, N 3
.....	Pichi Mahuida, Arg., Q 12
95	Pickardville, Alberta, J 20
3668	Pickering, England, E 17
615	Pickering, Ontario, K 13
.....	Pico, Argentina, O 13
.....	Picos, Brazil, G 18
.....	Picos, Brazil, G 20
.....	Picton, England, E 16
3901	Picton, Ontario, J 18
1390	Picton, N. Z., J 15
3069	Pictou, N. S., J 17
226	Pictou Landing, N. S., J 17
6974	Piedecuesta, Col., G 13
4326	Piedimonte, Italy, I 15
350	Piedmont, Quebec, O 14
5490	Piedrabuena, Spain, K 11
.....	Piedra de Afilar, Ur., P 20
.....	Piedra del Aguila, Arg., R 6
2798	Piedrahita, Spain, H 10
15878	Piedras Negras, Coa., B 13
.....	Piedra Sola, Ur., I 19
1083	Piedrecitas, Cuba, K 15
2800	Pieksämäki, Fin., E 5
100	Pienaar's River, U.S. Afr., E 18
.....	Pieres, Argentina, Q 19
798	Pierré Buffiére, France, M 12
329	Pierrefitte, Fr., H 20
11645	Pierrefitte-sur-Seine, Fr., A 5
1302	Pierreville, Quebec, N 17
219	Pierson, Man., R 12
12046	Piešťany, Czech., G 10
47421	Pietermaritzburg, U.S.Afr., K 21
9131	Pietersburg, U. S. Afr., O 19
5209	Pietrasanta, Italy, F 7
.....	Piet Retief, U. S. Afr., H 21
714	Pieve di Cadore, Italy, B 11
.....	Pigeon, Guadeloupe, B 22
.....	Pigue, Argentina, P 15
2501	Pihuamo, Jal., N 7
1652	Pijijiapan, Chia., O 15
.....	Pik, Iran, G 6
.....	Pikwitonei, Man., H 16
3111	Pila, Argentina, O 19
.....	Pilão Arcado, Brazil, I 19
25766	Pilar, Argentina, L 12
1064	Pilar, Argentina, L 16
.....	Pilar, Brazil, G 25
.....	Pilar, Brazil, J 13
6694	Pilares de Nacozari, Son., D 13
.....	Pilbarra, Australia, G 4
.....	Piles Junction, Que., M 18
36892	Pilibhit, India, E 13
.....	Pilica, Poland, F 13
.....	Pillahuinco, Arg., Q 16
.....	Pilling, England, F 11
.....	Pillinger, Tasmania, D 4
.....	Pilltown, Ire., N 17
.....	Pilon, Cuba, P 18
.....	Pimenta Bueno, Brazil, I 5
.....	Pimenteiro, Brazil, J 5
.....	Pin, China, L 10
2489	Pina, Spain, G 16
26241	Pinar del Rio, Cuba, I 3
1767	Pinas, Oax., O 10
.....	Pinas, Peru, E 3
994	Pincher Creek, Alta., P 21
.....	Pinches, Peru, D 8
.....	Pinchow Sung, China, E 17
.....	Pinchwan, China, J 5
.....	Pinczów, Poland, F 14
.....	Pindapoy, Argentina, I 23
60	Pindar, Australia, K 4
15000	Pind Dadan Khan, India, C 6
115	Pine Creek, Austl., B 13
1000	Pinega, Sov. Un., D 14
96	Pinehill, Australia, I 20
153	Pine River, Man., N 12
13736	Pinerolo, Italy, D 1
429	Pinette, P. E. I., I 16
839	Piney, France, H 18
.....	Pingangchow, China, E 14
.....	Pingchüan, Manch., C 18
766	Pingelly, Australia, N 5
.....	Pingkiang, China, I 14
10000	Pingliang, China, F 9
.....	Pinglo, China, K 12
.....	Pingtu, China, E 19
444	Pinguente, Italy, D 14
173000	Pingyangfu, China, F 13
.....	Pingyüan, China, J 8
8159	Pinheiro, Brazil, E 17
2660	Pinhel, Portugal, H 7
.....	Pinhsiang Ki, China, I 15
1205	Pinillo, Col., D 11
562	Pinjarra, Australia, N 5
10743	Pinneberg, Germany, D 7
.....	Pinner, England, B 18
4092	Pinola (Los Rosas), Chia., N 17
2861	Pinón, Col., C 10
3014	Pinos, Zac., J 11
3249	Pinotepa Nacional, Oax., N 6
31913	Pinsk, W. Sov. Un., D 19
349	Pintados, Chile, C 4
.....	Pinto, Argentina, J 14
1005	Pinto, Argentina, N 15
1382	Pinto, Chile, P 3
19759	Piombino, Italy, G 7
110	Piopolis, Que., P 22
51281	Piotrków, Poland, E 13
6135	Piperno, Italy, I 12
238	Pipestone, Man., R 12
.....	Pipinas, Arg., O 20
3309	Pipriac, France, I 5
965	Piquetberg, U. S. Afr., P 7
.....	Piquillan, Argentina, L 13
.....	Piracuruca, Brazil, F 20
	Piraeus, see Peiraievs, Grc.
.....	Pirajú, Brazil, N 13
.....	Piran, Argentina, P 20
.....	Piranhas, Brazil, H 23
5587	Pirano, Italy, D 13
.....	Pirapo, Paraguay, Q 9
7513	Pirapora, Brazil, K 17
.....	Piratu, Brazil, C 3
10000	Pirayú, Paraguay, O 7
3260	Pirdop, Bulgaria, L 18
9000	Piribebuy, Paraguay, N 8
2357	Piritu, Ven., D 16
1066	Piritu, Ven., E 9
47200	Pirmasens, Ger., N 3
32000	Pirna, Germany, K 13
11238	Pirot, Yugo., L 16
8545	Piryatin, Sov. Un., L 7
51774	Pisa, Italy, F 7
1105	Pisac, Peru, M 17
528	Pisagua, Chile, C 3
.....	Pisciadella, Switz., L 23
1260	Pisciotta, Italy, K 16
14609	Pisco, Peru, N 9
16973	Pisek, Czech., G 6
.....	Pishin, Baluchistan, L 21
.....	Pisi, Baluchistan, N 18
3271	Pisino, Italy, D 14
242	Pisquid, P. E. I., G 17
600	Pissos, France, O 7
9287	Pisticci, Italy, K 19
29967	Pistoia, Italy, F 8
567	Pisva, Col., H 14
3135	Pitalito, Col., L 8
5309	Pitantora, Bolivia, J 9
.....	Pitcaple, Scotland, H 22
3102	Pitea, Sweden, G 19
19630	Pitesti, Romania, J 19
5995	Pithiviers, France, I 14
1287	Pitiquito, Son., D 9
.....	Pitlawar, India, H 8
1000	Pitlochry, Scotland, J 17
.....	Pitraga, Sov. Un., G 2
5193	Pitrufquén, Chile, Q 3
2600	Pitschen, Ger., J 19
.....	Pitsunda, Sov. Un., P 13
1644	Pittenween, Scotland, L 21
.....	Pitts Town, Bahamas, E 11
1600	Pittsworth, Australia, K 22
9410	Piuma, Brazil, M 20
23583	Piumhy, Brazil, M 16
20000	Piura, Peru, F 2
3135	Pivijay, Col., C 11
.....	Pixuna, Western Brazil, G 23
.....	Piyang, China, G 14
.....	Pizarro, Cuba, H 9
7312	Pizzo, Italy, M 19
140	Pjedsted, Denmark, K 9
20375	Placetas, Cuba, J 13
.....	Placilla, Chile, C 3
724	Placilla, Chile, H 4
1361	Plaffeien, Switz., J 8
129	Plainby, Australia, I 22
217	Plainfield, Ontario, I 18
550	Plaisance, Quebec, P 11
788	Plaka, Grc., Q 19
.....	Plan, Spain, E 18
1294	Plancoet, France, H 5
.....	Planta, Chih., J 20
.....	Plantage, Germany, R 19
600	Plantagenet, Ontario, D 24
16255	Plasencia, Spain, I 9
881	Plaster Rock, N. B., E 5
5814	Plato, Col., D 11
119	Plato, Sask., O 5
.....	Platrand, U. S. Afr., H 19
.....	Platta, Switz., J 16
.....	Platte, Switz., K 11
5798	Plattling, Germany, O 11
721	Plattsville, Ontario, M 8
.....	Platz, Switz., J 19
113000	Plauen, Germany, L 10
.....	Playa Chica, Peru, L 7
87	Playas, Coa., C 8
400	Playas del Morro, Ec., D 2
.....	Playa Tical, Guat., C 6
.....	Plchi Ciego, Arg., M 8
327	Pleasant Bay, N. S., E 22
241	Pleasant Harbour, N. S., M 17
.....	Pleasant River, N. S., O 11
2972	Plélan-le-Grand, Fr., I 6
236	Plélan le Petit, France, H 5
1800	Plencia, Spain, C 13
7784	Plenita, Rom., K 17
178	Plenty, Sask., N 5
3522	Plessisville, Quebec, N 20
.....	Plettenberg, Germany, J 4
30200	Pléven, Bulgaria, L 19
6189	Plevlje, Yugo., L 12
219	Plevna, Ontario, F 18
32777	Plock, Pol., D 13
.....	Ploegsteert, Belgium, M 4
5436	Ploermel, France, I 5
76873	Ploesti, Romania, J 20
	Plomari, see Potamos, Grc.
1591	Plombieres, Fr., I 22
3955	Plön, Germany, C 8
10393	Plonsk, Poland, D 13
.....	Plottier, Argentina, Q 8
201	Plouagat, France, H 4
2525	Plouaret, France, H 2
3946	Ploudalmézeau, Fr., H 1
3866	Plouescat, France, G 1
100485	Plovdiv (Philippopolis), Bulgaria, M 19
440	Plum Coulee, Man., R 15
5434	Pluvigner, France, I 4
208166	Plymouth, England, O 7
1900	Plymouth, Montserrat, K 23
226	Plymouth, N. S., Q 8
114150	Plzeň, Czech., F 6
103000	Pnom Penh, Fr. In. Ch., Q 7
	Poběživice, see Ronspera, Ger.
.....	Pocahontas, Alberta, L 17
888	Pocanche, Bolivia, H 7
.....	Pochinki, Sov. Un., J 16
2404	Pochutla, Oax., O 9
311	Pocillas, Chile, O 3
2640	Pocklington, England, F 17
.....	Pocoata, Bolivia, J 8
2645	Pocona, Bolivia, I 9
147	Poconchile, Chile, B 3
.....	Poconé, Brazil, K 8
3238	Pocpo, Bolivia, J 9
.....	Podanur, India, P 10
.....	Podea, Nic., I 11
1330	Podensac, France, N 8
.....	Podgazhe, W. Sov. Un., G 19
10651	Podgorica, Yugo., L 12
	Podhajce, see Podgazhe, Sov. Un.
.....	Podili, India, M 13
	Podolinec, Czech., G 14
72422	Podolsk, Sov. Un., I 11
.....	Podor, Fr. W. Afr., H 1
.....	Podosinovskaya, Sov. Un., F 16
.....	Pogau, Ger., J 10
	Pogodina, W. Sov. Un., B 24
.....	Poi, India, C 12
226	Point Cross, Nova Scotia, F 21
236	Point du Chene, N.B., H 12
43551	Pointe a Pitre, Guad., L 24
1083	Pointe au Pic, Quebec, H 24
365	Pointe Bleue, Que., E 19
.....	Pointe du Boise, Man., P 18
650	Pointe du Lac, Que., M 18
1811	Pointe du Macouba, Martinique, F 24
9494	Pointe Noire, Guadeloupe, B 22
1363	Point Edward, Ont., N 3
322	Point Fortune, Que., P 13
.....	Point Max, Paraguay, J 7
.....	Point Michaud, N. S., J 23
.....	Pointzpass, N. Ire., F 21
.....	Poirierville, N. S., J 22
44235	Poitiers, France, K 10
6628	Pojo, Bolivia, I 10
.....	Pokemouche Jc., N.B., B12
7100	Pokharan, India, F 5
.....	Pokhra, Nepal, E 17
	Pokrovsk, see Engels, Sov. Un.
.....	Pokrovski, Sov. Un., G 12
.....	Pokrovskoe, Sov. Un., M 10
36047	Pola, Italy, E 13
27210	Pola de Siero, Sp., C 10
57	Polapi, Chile, D 6
.....	Polbain, Scotland, E 11
34	Polboxol, Camp., J 19
.....	Polegate, England, N 20
2403	Polesella, Italy, E 10
.....	Policastro, Italy, K 17
3687	Poligny, France, K 20
7256	Polikhnitos, Grc., O 21
9323	Polistena, Italy, M 18
3938	Polla, Italy, K 17
8984	Pollensa, Spain, I 21
42	Pollockville, Alberta, N 23
.....	Polmak, Norway, B 23
.....	Polmont, Scotland, M 18
	Polonnoe, W. Sov. Un., F 21
.....	Poloski, Scotland, J 18
1091	Polotitlan, Méx., G 4
25826	Polotsk, W. Sov. Un., A 22
.....	Polruan, England, O 6
130305	Poltava, Sov. Un., L 9
365	Poltimore, Quebec, O 10
619	Polulos, Bolivia, N 7
8600	Polur, India, O 12
160	Polwarth, Scotland, N 23
.....	Polyarnoye (Alekandrovsk), Sov. Un., A 9
1551	Pomarance, Italy G 8
.....	Pombal, Brazil, E 12
.....	Pombal, Brazil, G 23
7336	Pombal, Portugal, I 5
.....	Pomeroy, N. Ire., D 18
.....	Ponce, Cuba, H 9
53101	Pondichéry, India, O 13
13008	Ponferrada, Spain, E 9
.....	Ponnani, India, P 8
3000	Ponneri, India, N 13
.....	Ponoi, Sov. Un., C 13
1306	Ponoka, Alberta, L 21
4427	Pons, France, M 8
1759	Pons, Spain, F 19
.....	Ponta d'Areia, Brazil, L 21
29864	Ponta Grossa, Brazil, O 12
12646	Pont a Mousson, Fr., G 21
.....	Ponta Porá, Brazil, N 9
11984	Pontarlier, France, J 22
5953	Pont-Audemer, Fr., G 10
1666	Pont Aven, France, I 2
4613	Pontchâteau, France, J 6
2587	Pont-Croix, France, I 1
.....	Ponte, Switz., K 22
530	Ponteba, Algeria, C 15
1598	Pontebba, Italy, B 12
.....	Ponte Bottero, Italy, D 22
4781	Pontecorvo, Italy, I 13
.....	Ponte de Lima, Port., F 6
.....	Ponte de Pedra, Brazil, J 8
8642	Pontedera, Italy, F 7
6705	Ponte de Sor, Port., J 6
19053	Pontefract, England, G 16
545	Ponteix, Sask., Q 6
11950	Ponte Nova, Brazil, M 18
36968	Pontevedra, Spain, E 6
.....	Pontheirville, Bel. Cong., K 16
45440	Pontianak, Neth. Ind., H 4
.....	Pontina, Italy, I 12
.....	Ponti Torre Quinto, Italy, A 22
9440	Pontivy, France, I 3
6724	Pont l'Abbé, France, I 1
2818	Pont L'Eveque, Fr., G 10
.....	Pont Llanio, Wales, J 8
11709	Pontoise, France, G 13
2958	Pontorson, France, H 7
3589	Pontremoli, Italy, E 6
958	Pontresina, Switz., L 22
.....	Pontrilas, England, K 11
1865	Pont Rouge, Que., L 20
4409	Pont Saint Esprit, Fr., O 18
264	Pontypool, Ontario, J 14
42737	Pontypridd, Wales, L 10
.....	Ponupo, Cuba, O 22
57258	Poole, England, N 14
.....	Poolewe, Scotland, F 10
258197	Poona, India, K 6
127	Pooncarie, Austl., N 17
4725	Poopo, Bolivia, J 6
18292	Popayán, Col., K 7
11554	Poperinghe, Belgium, M 3
.....	Popova, Sov. Un., B 22
2998	Popovo, Bulgaria, K 21
1280	Poppel, Belgium, J 15
1195	Poppi, Italy, F 10
.....	Poragarh, India, K 15
.....	Porangahau, N. Z., I 20
33383	Porbandar, India, I 2
1679	Porco, Bolivia, K 8
12677	Porcuna, Spain, M 11
12247	Pordenone, Italy, C 11
982	Pore, Col., H 15
	Porechie, W. Sov. Un., A 24
18395	Pori (Björneborg), Finland, E 2
5600	Porkhov, Sov. Un., H 6
9621	Porlamar, Ven., C 18
2352	Poroma, Bolivia, J 9
4593	Poros, Greece, P 18
113	Porquis Jc., Ont., P 24
5818	Porrentruy (Pruntrut), Switz., D 7
.....	Porretta, Italy, F 8
9021	Porsgrunn, Norway, N 7
.....	Portachuelo, Bolivia, C 7
6543	Portachuelo, Bolivia, I 13
.....	Portacloy, Ire., F 4
29850	Port Adelaide, Austl., O 16
11727	Portadown, Ire., E 21
.....	Portaferry, Ire., E 25
.....	Portage des Roches, Que., F 21
361	Portage du Fort, Que., P 7
7187	Portage la Prairie, Manitoba, Q 15
4584	Port Alberni, B. C., Q 11
.....	Port Albert, N. Z., C 16
26200	Portalegre, Portugal, J 7
3243	Port Alfred, Quebec, F 22
2928	Port Alfred, U. S. Afr., P 16
300	Port Alice, B. C., O 8
6272	Port Antonio, Jamaica, J 9
212	Portapique, N. S., K 14
.....	Port Appin, Scot., K 10
1951	Portarlington, Ire., K 17
	Port Arthur, see Lushun, Manch.
24426	Port Arthur, Ontario, P 18
.....	Port Askaig, Scotland, N 8
3270	Port Augusta, Austl., M 15
130000	Port au Prince, Haiti, J 13
.....	Port-aux-Basques, Newf., L 23
.....	Port Ballintrae, N.Ire., B 20
82	Port Bickerton, N. S., L 20
.....	Port Blair, Nicobar Is., R 20
3475	Portbou, Spain, E 21
717	Port Burwell, Ontario, P 7
509	Port Carling, Ontario, F 11
.....	Port Carlisle, Eng., C 10
	Port Castries, see Castries.
.....	Port Charlotte, Scot., N 6
.....	Portchladhach (Portlaw), Ire., N 17
6913	Port Colborne, Ont., O 12
1524	Port Coquitlam, B. C., O 4
.....	Port Cornwallis, India, Q 20
2160	Port Credit, Ontario, L 11
1723	Port Dalhousie, Ont., M 12
.....	Port de Marciel, Ur., M 18
10000	Port de Paix, Haiti, H 12
.....	Port Dickson, Fed. Malay States, Q 21
.....	Port Dinorwi, Wales, H 7
162	Port Douglas, Austl., D 20
1968	Port Dover, Ontario, O 9
645	Port Dufferin, N.S., M 18
17107	Port du Moule, Guadeloupe, L 24
.....	Portel, Brazil, E 13
600	Port Elgin, N. B., H 14
1395	Port Elgin, Ontario, H 6
118000	Port Elizabeth, U. S. Afr., Q 15
1000	Port Ellen, Scotland, O 7
442	Port Elliot, Austl., P 16
217	Port Elmsley, Ont., G 21
4193	Porte Maggiore, It., E 10
.....	Port Epworth, Mack., F 15
.....	Port Erin, England, E 6
.....	Porter Landing, B. C., C 7
1497	Porterville, U. S. Afr., P 8
.....	Portessie, Scotland, G 20
.....	Port Essington, B. C., J 7
.....	Porteynon, Wales, L 7
2000	Port Fairy, Austl., Q 17
217	Port Felix, N. S., K 21
120	Port George, N. S., L 10
19616	Port Glasgow, Scot., M 13
.....	Portglenone, N. Ire., C 20
.....	Port Gower, Scotland, E 17
465	Port Greville, N. S., K 12
.....	Port Grosvenor, U. S. Afr., N 20
278	Port Haney, B. C., O 4
.....	Port Harcourt, Nig., J 9
129	Port Hardy, B. C., O 9
.....	Port Harvey, B.C., O 10
401	Port Hastings, N. S., J 21
1031	Port Hawkesbury, Nova Scotia, J 21
218	Port Hedland, Austl., F 5
.....	Port Herald, Nyasaland, O 19
536	Port Hillford, N. S., L 19
.....	Porthleven, England, P 3
647	Port Hood, N. S., I 20
4723	Port Hope, Ont., K 15
.....	Port Isaac, England, N 5
3908	Portishead, England, L 11
216	Port Joli, N. S., Q 11
1619	Portknockie, Scot., G 20
6647	Port Lairge (Waterford), Ire., O 18
357	Port Lambton, Ont., O 3
2370	Portland, Australia, Q 17
270	Portland, Ontario, G 21
	Portland, see Dyrholar, Ice.
12018	Portland Isle, Eng., N 12
223	Port la Tour, N. S., R 10
	Portlaw, see Portchladhach. Ire.
3360	Port Leighise, Ire., K 17
3006	Port Lincoln, Austl., O 15
.....	Port Logan, Scotland, R 12
319	Port Lorne, N. S., M 10
3511	Port Louis, France, I 2
7292	Port Louis, Gaudeloupe, L 24
30761	Port Lyautey, Mor., F 6
973	Port McNicoll, Ont., G 11
1727	Port Macquarie, Austl., M 23
3986	Portmadoc, Wales, H 8
.....	Portmagee, Ire., P 1
4193	Porte Maggiore, It., E 10
120	Port Maitland, Ont., O 11
571	Port Maitland, N. S., P 8
517	Port Mann, B. C., O 4
2481	Port Maria, Jamaica, J 8
1181	Port Marly, France, B 1
.....	Portmarnock, Ire., J 22
1512	Port Moody, B. C., Q 13
.....	Port Morant, Jamaica, J 9
2075	Port Moresby, Papua Ter., J 11
785	Port Morien, Nova Scotia, H 25
.....	Portnahaven, Scotland, N 6
.....	Port Nelson, Man., F 19
992	Portneuf, Quebec, L 19
2126	Port Nolloth, U. S. Afr., K 5
13700	Port Novo, India, O 13
262790	Pôrto (Oporto), Port., G 5
.....	Porto Acre, Western Brazil, J 23
.....	Porto Alegre, Brazil, F 19
.....	Porto Alegre, Brazil, G 3
2956	Porto Alegre, Brazil, I 18
262694	Porto Alegre, Brazil, Q 12
1500	Porto Alexandre, Ang. N 11
1633	Porto Amelia, Moz., N 22
733	Portobelo, Pan., O 21
.....	Porto Casado, Paraguy, I 6
.....	Porto de Moz, Brazil, E 11
.....	Porto de Pedras, Brazil, H 25
.....	Porto Esperança, Brazil, L 7
103155	Port of Spain, Trinidad, R 24
.....	Porto Grande, Brazil, D 12
4502	Portogruaro, Italy, C 11
.....	Porto Lagos, Grc., M 20
.....	Porto Maurizio, It., F 2
.....	Porto Murtinho, Brazil, M 7
.....	Portonaccio, Italy, B 24
.....	Portonaccio Station, It., B 23
.....	Porto Nacional, Brazil, I 14
27000	Porto Novo, Fr. W. Africa, J 7
.....	Porto Tibiricá, Brazil, M 11
4704	Portotorres, Italy, J 3
1932	Porto Vecchio, Cor., R 3
4743	Porto Vecchio, Fr., R 3
.....	Porto Velho, Brazil, H 2
.....	Porto Vesme, Italy, L 3
.....	Porto Victoria, Brazil, E 11
13998	Portoviejo, Ecuador, C 2
1800	Portpatrick, Scot., Q 12
1245	Port Perry, Ontario, J 13
11677	Port Pirie, Australia, N 15
.....	Port Progress, B. C., O 9
.....	Portraine, Ire., I 22
3000	Port Ree, Scotland, H 7
523	Port Robinson, Ont., N 12
.....	Port Roper, Australia, C 14
661	Port Rowan, Ont., P 8
2100	Portrush, N. Ire., B 19
121200	Port Said, Egypt, C 22
1010	Port Sainte Marie, Fr., O 10
200	Port Saint Johns, U. S.Afr., N 19
.....	Port Saint Mary, Eng., E 6
.....	Portsalon, Ire., B 15
406	Port Shepstone, U. S. Afr., M 21
.....	Port Simpson, B. C., I 7
.....	Portskerry, Scotland, C 16
.....	Port Smith, Mack., D 16
2400	Portsmouth, Dominica, D 23
249288	Portsmouth, Eng., N 17
3128	Portsmouth, Ont., I 20
1651	Portsoy, Scotland, G 21
1177	Port Stanley, Ont., P 6
.....	Port Stewart, N. Ire., B 19
19135	Port Sudan, A. E. Sud., G 20
.....	Port Swettenham, Fed. Malay States, P 20
127	Port Sydney, Ontario, E 12
.....	Port Tewfik, Egypt, I 24
1888	Portugalete, Bolivia, M 8
10612	Portugalete, Spain, C 13
631	Portuguese Cove, N.S., N 15
1000	Portumna, Ire., K 12
.....	Port Vladimir, Sov. Un., A 9
.....	Port Wade, N. S., N 9
.....	Port Weld, Fed. Mal. St., O 19
217	Port Weller, Ontario, M 12
.....	Port Wemyss, Scot., N 6
.....	Port Whitby, Ontario, K13
.....	Port William, Scot., R 14
612	Port Williams, N. S., L 12
.....	Porus, Jamaica, J 8
	Porvoo, see Borga, Fin.
20000	Posadas, Arg., I 22
7350	Posadas, Spain, M 10
3717	Poschiavo, Switz., M 23
	Posen, see Poznán, Pol.
.....	Posi, China, K 6
600	Posorja, Ecuador, D 2
.....	Posse, Brazil, J 16
14625	Pössneck, Germany, K 9
.....	Post Aleksandrovski, Sov. Un. Asia, F 20
.....	Post Konstantinovski, Sov. Un. Asia, G 20
1614	Postrer Valle, Bolivia, J 13
1315	Pōtam, Son., J 11
6481	Potamos (Plomari), Grc., O 22
19099	Potchefstroom, Union of South Africa, G 16
.....	Potemkinskaya, Sov. Un., M 15
13895	Potenza, Italy, J 18
1139	Potes, Spain, D 11
400	Potgietersrust, U. S. Afr., D 19
16200	Poti, Sov. Un., Q 14
247	Poto, Peru, N 20
2294	Potobamba, Bolivia, K 9
40000	Potosi, Bolivia, K 8
2319	Potrerillo, Cuba, J 11
.....	Potrerillos, Chile, J-4
882	Potrerillos, Honduras, F 8
1471	Potrerillos, Tam., G 15
.....	Potrero, Nic., J 12
70000	Potsdam, Germany, G 12
2762	Pouancé, France, I 7
901	Pougues, Fr., J 15
3014	Pouillon, France, P 7
2012	Pouilly, France, J 15
.....	Poulamond, N S., J 22
11741	Pouso Alegre, Brazil, I 7
.....	Povenets, Sov. Un., E 10
12362	Povoa de Varzim, Port., F5
775	Powassan, Ontario, B 12
.....	Powellinna Pool, Australia, H 5
3000	Powell River, B. C., P 11
.....	Powells Creek, Australia, E 13
.....	Poxim, Brazil, H 24
14055	Pozarevac, Yugo., K 14
7110	Pozega, Yugo., J 11
269000	Poznán (Posen), Pol., D10
1577	Pozo Almonte, Chile, C 4
16702	Pozoblanco, Spain, L 10
.....	Pozo del Buey, Par., D 4
.....	Pozo del Molle, Arg., L 14
.....	Pozo Hondo, Arg., H 11
.....	Pozo Noriega, Son., F 10
2938	Pozos, Guan., L 14
2677	Pozuelo de Alarcón, Spain, H 12
132	Pozuzo, Peru, J 10
3511	Pradera, Col., J 7
4170	Prades, France, Q 14
.....	Prado, Brazil, K 21
1028	Prado, Col., J 10
1442	Praestö, Denmark, M 21
	Prague, see Praha, Czech.
.....	Praga, Poland, D 14
945000	Praha (Prague), Czech., F 7
.....	Prai, Malay States, R 14
21000	Praia, Cape Verde Is., L 2
.....	Praid, Rom., I 19
.....	Prainha, Brazil, O 15
75	Prairie River, Sask., L 10
.....	Praskoveya, Sov. Un., O 16
.....	Prata, Brazil, L 14
19926	Prato, Italy, F 8
317	Prato, Switz., L 15
4799	Pratteln, Switz., D 10
441	Prauthoy, France, I 20
11208	Právia, Spain, C 9
985	Precheur, Martinique, F 24
1392	Pregonero, Ven., G 5
19000	Preigo de Córdoba, Sp., N 11
554	Prelate, Sask., O 4
1157	Prémery, France, J 16
22000	Prenzlau, Germany, E 13
22362	Prérov, Czech., G 10
3223	Prescott, Ontario, G 23
.....	Presidente Epitacio, Braz., M 11
.....	Presidente Penna, Brazil, M 13
21870	Prešov, Czech., G 14
	Pressburg, see Bratislava, Czech.
1102	Presteigne, Wales, J 11
523	Prestholar, Iceland, A 23
3472	Presto, Bolivia, K 11
118839	Preston, England, F 12
6704	Preston, Ont., M 9
5986	Prestonpans, Scot., M 20
85	Pretil, Tam., I 18
138000	Pretoria, U. S. Afr., F 18
8659	Preveza, Greece, O 14
.....	Pribalkhash, Sov. Un., Asia, I 11
10468	Příbram, Czech., F 6
250	Priceville, Ont., I 8
.....	Prichard, B. C., O 15
25181	Priego, Spain, N 11
6700	Prieska, U. S. Afr., K 11
6623	Prijedor, Yugo., J 9
21405	Prilep, Yugo., M 15
28615	Priluki, Sov. Un., L 7
123	Primate, Sask., M 4
46	Prince, Sask., L 5
.....	Prince Albert, Ont., J 13
1778	Prince Albert, U. S. Afr., P 11
12508	Prince Albert, Sask., L 8
2027	Prince George, B. C., K 13
6714	Prince Rupert, B. C., J 7
1855	Princeton, B. C., Q 15
452	Princeton, Ont., M 8
1140	Princeville, Quebec, N 20
250	Prince William, N. B., I 5
25908	Pringles, Arg., Q 16
11103	Prinsenhage, Neth., J 13
16948	Priština, Yugo., L 14
8328	Pritzwalk, Ger., E 10
6681	Privas, France, N 18
18952	Prizren, Yugo., M 14
9592	Prizzi, Italy, N 13
1683	Prjeslav, Bul., L 21
210	Procter, B. C., P 18
4657	Proença-a-Nova, Port., I 6
.....	Progreso, Cuba, H 9
11990	Progreso, Yuc., E 21
1980	Progreso, Coa., C 12
314	Progresso, Arg., K 16
.....	Prokhladnaya, Sov. Un., P 16
6030	Prokuplje, Yugo., L 15
26900	Prome, Bur., O 22
10414	Propria, Brazil, I 23
31990	Proskurov, W. Sov. Un., F 21
55	Prospect., N. S., N 14
33487	Prostêjov, Czech., G 10
.....	Proteccion, Hond., G 9
7569	Provadija, Bul., L 22
.....	Providence, Mack., O 12
320	Providence Bay, Ont., C 4
.....	Providencia, Méx., H 3
8845	Provins, France, H 15
518	Provost, Alberta, L 23
5506	Prozor, Yugo., K 10
2840	Prum, Ger., L 2
	Pruntrut, see Porrentruy, Switzerland,
.....	Pruźany, see Pruzhany, Sov. Un.
.....	Pruzhany, W. Sov. Un., D 18
.....	Przasnysz, Poland, D 14
51379	Przemysl, Poland, F 16
.....	Przeworsk, Poland, F 16
59898	Pskov, Sov. Un., H 5
722	Pua, Chl., Q 3
27758	Puan, Arg., P 14
402	Pubnico, N. S., Q 9
2368	Pucalpa, Peru, I 11
3506	Pucará, Bolivia, J 12
651	Pucará, Peru, O 19
8488	Pucarani, Bolivia, H 3
.....	Puchow, China, F 15
.....	Puchow, China, F 12
.....	Puck, Poland, B 11
1720	Pucon, Chile, R 4
2507	Pudlein, Slov., N 23
.....	Pudozh, Sov. Un., F 10
26900	Pudukkotai, India, P 12
138360	Puebla, Pueb., I 6
1028	Puebla de Sanabria, Sp., E 8
5746	Puebla de Trives, Sp., E 8
.....	Pueblo, Yukon, P 9
.....	Pueblo Brugo, Arg., L 17
1540	Pueblo Hundido, Chile, H 4
.....	Pueblo Nuevo, Col., I 21
6039	Pueblo Nuevo, Ven., A 8
.....	Pueblo Nuevo del Mar, Spain, J 17
8302	Pueblo Solis, Uruguay, O 20
1867	Pueblo Viejo, Col., B 12
11089	Puebloviejo, Col., H 13
2158	Pueblo Viejo, Ver., C 7
.....	Puente de Ixtla, Morel., J 4
1760	Puente del Arzobispo, Spain, J 10
.....	Puerh, China, K 4
5199	Puers, Belgium, R 7
.....	Puerta de Golpe, Cuba, I 4
1000	Puerto Acosta, Bol., G 2
294	Puerto Angel, Oax., O 9
99	Puerto Arista, Chia., O 14
3328	Puerto Armuelles, Pan., Q 16
2603	Puerto Barrios, Guat., E 7
381	Puerto Bermejo, Arg., H 19
.....	Puerto Bermudez, Peru, K 11
4511	Puerto Berrio, Col., G 10
1000	Puerto Bolivar, Ec., E 3
20571	Puerto Cabello, Ven., C11
.....	Puerto Casado, Par., I 6
.....	Puerto Castilla, Hond., D11
.....	Puerto Cesar, Col., E 7
4896	Puerto Colombia, Col., B 10
7019	Puerto Cortez, Hond., E 8
.....	Puerto de la Selva de Mar, Spain, E 21
.....	Puerto de Lobos, Son., E 8
.....	Puerto del Sauce, Ur., O 16
.....	Puerto de Manta, Ec., C 1
10	Puerto de Maruata, Michoa., P 7
.....	Puerto de San Juan, Camp., H 21

Pop.	Place Country Index
.....	Puerto de Santa Cruz, Spain, J 10
29197	Puerto de Santa Maria, Spain, O 8
1500	Puerto Deseado, Arg., D 23
276	Puerto Dominguez, Chile, Q 3
.....	Puerto Escondido, Camp., I 19
.....	Puerto Goya, Arg., J 18
.....	Puerto La Paloma, Ur. O 23
.....	Puerto Libertad, Son., E 8
.....	Puerto Limon, Col., M 7
24676	Puertollano, Spain, L 11
.....	Puerto Loyalo, Arg., E 22
1200	Puerto Madryn, Arg., B 23
.....	Puerto Magdalena, Baja Cal., O 9
1000	Puerto Maldonado, Peru, M 20
.....	Puerto Max, Par., J 7
8273	Puerto México, Ver., K 13
.....	Puerto Militar, Arg., Q 15
21360	Puerto Montt, Chile, B 19
28	Puerto Morelos, Yuc., E 25
.....	Puerto Nuevo, Arg., J 18
1161	Puerto Nutrias, Ven., G 9
	Puerto Pacheco, see Bahia Negra, Par., E 6
8187	Puerto Padre, Cuba, L 20
.....	Puerto Penasco, Son., C 7
.....	Puerto Piracuacito, Argentina, I 18
.....	Puerto Piraoua, Arg., I 18
2000	Puerto Pizarro, Peru, E 2
11891	Puerto Plata, Dom. Rep., H 14
14854	Puerto Real, Spain, O 9
.....	Puerto Rico, Bolivia, C 5
838	Puerto Ruiz, Arg., M 18
2200	Puerto Santa Cruz, Argentina, D 22
.....	Puerto Santos, Col., F 13
.....	Puertos Pinasco, Par., J 6
2000	Puerto Sûarez (In. Disp. Ter.), Bol., K 23
2738	Puerto Vallarta, Jal., M 2
4146	Puerto Varas, Chile, B 19
.....	Puerto Villamizar, Colombia, E 15
2055	Puerto Wilches, Col., F 12
.....	Puesto del Marquez, Argentina, E 10
24431	Pugachev (Nikolaevsk), Sov. Un., K 18
1034	Puget-Théniers, Fr., O 24
726	Pugwash, N. S., I 15
175	Pugwash Jc., N. S., I 15
163	Puhl, Iran, E 7
2508	Puigcerdá, Spain, E 19
945	Puina, Bolivia, F 2
9138	Pujili, Ec., C 5
225	Pujols, France, N 9
.....	Pukearuhe, N. Z., G 16
168	Pukeuri Jc., N. Z., O 10
.....	Pukow, China, G 18
4000	Pulacayo, Bolivia, L 7
73191	Pulantien, Kwantung, D 21
5400	Pulicat, India, N 13
828	Pullo, Peru, O 13
.....	Pulteneytown, Scot., D 19
15510	Pultusk, Poland, D 14
628	Pülümer, Turkey, E 15
.....	Puna, Arg., I 14
.....	Puna, Bol., L 10
600	Puna, Ec., D 3
2979	Punacachi, Bol., J 7
5000	Punaka, Bhutan, E 23
8000	Punata, Bolivia, I 8
8200	Punch, India, B 7
5000	Pundi, India, K 18
.....	Pundri, India, E 10
.....	Pungal, India, E 6
4087	Pungarabato, Guer., P 13
.....	Punjoor, Baluchistan, N 22
252	Punnichy, Sask., O 9
15999	Puno, Peru, O 19
.....	Punta Alta, Chile, D 5
29883	Punta Arenas(Magallanes), Chl., E 21
.....	Punta Blanco, Cuba, I 4
2579	Punta Brava, Cuba, H 6
.....	Punta de Diaz, Chile, I 4
926	Punta Gorda, Br. Hond., D 7
230	Punta Negra, Chile, I 4
8265	Puntarenas, Costa Rica, N 13
1978	Pupiales, Col., M 5
.....	Puquina, Peru, P 18
6183	Puquio, Peru, N 13
415	Puquios, Chile, H 4
3843	Purace, Col., K 7
2993	Purchéna, Spain, N 14
7153	Purépero, Michoa., N 10
39700	Puri, India, J 19
4196	Purificacion, Col., J 10
.....	Purificación, Jal., N 4
.....	Puriri, N. Z., D 19
.....	Puriscal, Costa Rica, N 14
6077	Purisima, Col., D 8
648	Purisima, Dur., P 20
.....	Purley, England, D 21
.....	Purmamarca Tumbaya, Arg., F 10
6117	Purmerend, Neth., F 14
.....	Pursat, Fr. In. Ch., Q 6
8643	Puruándiro, Michoa., N 10
25974	Purulia, India, H 19
.....	Purwadeh, Iran, I 12
5100	Pusad, India, J 10
249734	Pusan, Korea, E 25
.....	Pusht-i-Radan, Iran, I 10
.....	Pustozersk, Sov. Un., B 18
3355	Putaendo, Chile, M 4
406	Putanges, France, H 9
43286	Puteaux, France, B 3
2713	Putla, Oax., M 7
.....	Putney, Eng., C 20
.....	Puttaisong, Siam., O 5
6905	Puttalam, Cey., Q 13
7317	Putten, Neth., G 18
.....	Pu-Vieng, Thai., N 5
.....	Pweto, Bel. Cong., M 17
3599	Pwllheli, Wales, I 7
.....	Pyapon, Bur., P 22
62875	Pyatigorsk, Sov. Un., O 14
.....	Pyaungbyin, Bur., M 22
.....	Pyckon, Bur., N 22
2315	Pylos, Grc., Q 15
285965	Pyŏngyang (Heijo), Kor., D 23
12055	Pyrenopolis, Brazil, K 14
964	Pyrgos, Greece, P 15
184	Pyrgos, Greece, Q 16
.....	Pyrmont, Germany, H 6
.....	Pyu, Bur., O 22

Q

Pop.	Place Country Index
.....	Qaha, Egypt, H 13
5000	Qain, Iran, I 14
.....	Qal 'a Shargat (Canne Ruins), Iraq, J 19
.....	Qalibshu, Egypt, B 14
.....	Qalin, Egypt, D 10
8600	Qalyub, Egypt, H 13
.....	Qamula, Egypt, O 23
2225	Qara Qês Egypt, D 8
	Qara Shahr, see Yenki, Chn.
18176	Qaregnon, Belgium, N 9
60000	Qazvin, Iran, F 5
27523	Qena, Egypt, N 23
.....	Qermila, Egypt, R 24
.....	Qishlaq, Iran, G 7
.....	Qorashiyan, Egypt, E 1
.....	Qotûr Demât, Egypt, D 13
.....	Quackenbrück, Ger., F 51
28	Quaco, N. B., K 9
.....	Quaggas Poort, U. S. Afr., H 19
503	Quambatook, Austl., O 18
.....	Quang-ngai, Fr.In.Ch., O 10
.....	Quang-tri, Fr. In. Ch., O 9
584	Qu'Appelle, Sask., P 9
7794	Quarahy, Brazil, Q 8
.....	Quarries, Ontario, Q 1
220	Quarryville, N. B., F 9
.....	Quatá, Brazil, N 12
.....	Quatsino, B. C., O 8
150757	Quebec, Quebec, K 21
.....	Quebracho, Uru., I 15
228	Quebrachos, Arg., J 13
27000	Quedlinburg, Ger., I 9
2941	Queenborough, Eng., L 22
190	Queensboro, Ont., H 17
2000	Queenscliff, Austl., Q 18
1264	Queenstown, Br. Gu., A 7
	Queenstown, see Cobh, Ire
920	Queenstown, N. Z., O 5
3693	Queenstown, Tasmania, D 4
18254	Queens Town, U. S. Afr., N 16
.....	Queimadas, Brazil, I 21
9288	Quelimane, Moz., O 20
670	Quelite, S. L. P., J 13
.....	Queluz, Brazil, M 17
8414	Quema do de Guines, Cuba, I 11
.....	Quemu Quemu, Arg., O 13
33563	Queretaro, Quer., M 14
436	Querigut, France, Q 14
.....	Querocottilla, Peru, F 2
11309	Quesada, Spain, M 13
.....	Quesna, Egypt, F 13
653	Quesnel, B. C., L 13
4206	Questembert, France, I 5
125	Quetena, Bolivia, N 6
.....	Quetrequen, Arg., N 12
60272	Quetta, Baluchistan, L 21
1416	Quetzaltepec, Oax., M 10
85	Queule, Chl., R 3
2837	Quevaucamps, Bel., N 8
36162	Quezaltenango, Guat., F 3
8253	Quezaltepeque, Guat., G 6
1108	Quiatoni, Oax., M 10
5278	Quibdo, Col., H 6
3556	Quiberon, France, I 3
3147	Quibor, Ven., D 9
379	Quicacha, Peru, O 13
12100	Quiche, Guat., F 3
.....	Quiebra Vara, Ven., C 11
19000	Quiindy, Par., P 7
95	Quila, Sin., O 17
208	Quilca, Peru, P 16
1325	Quiliacas, Bol., K 6
303	Quilimari, Chile, L 3
507	Quilino, Arg., K 12
201	Quillabamba, Peru, M 15
13969	Quillacollo, Bolivia, I 7
229	Quillagua, Chile, D 4
3464	Quillan, France, Q 14
2730	Quillaquilla, Bolivia, K 9
.....	Quille, Sweden, N 9
264	Quillen, Chile, Q 3
350	Quill Lake, Sask., N 9
154	Quillo, Peru, J 6
15700	Quillon, India, Q 9
17232	Quillota, Chile, M 4
548	Quilpie, Austl., J 19
1746	Quime, Bolivia, I 6
.....	Quimili, Arg., I 14
18297	Quimper, France, I 1
8969	Quimperlé, France, I 3
.....	Quin, Ire., L 9
327	Quinan, N. S., Q 9
84	Quindalup, Austl., O 4
1396	Quines, Arg., L 10
.....	Qui-nhon, Fr. In. Ch., P 11
9498	Quintanar de la Orden, Spain, J 13
598	Quintero, Tam., J 17
2300	Quintin, France, H 4
2792	Quinto, Spain, G 17
1331	Quinto, Switz., L 16
.....	Quintos, Port., M 6
6000	Quiquió, Paraguay, P 8
3034	Quirihue, Chile, O 3
2700	Quirindi, Austl., M 22
2236	Quiroga, Bolivia, J 9
8380	Quiroga, Spain, E 7
.....	Quiroz, Arg., J 11
.....	Quisiro, Ven., C 6
.....	Quissaman, Brazil, N 19
165924	Quito, Ecuador, B 5
2194	Quivican, Cuba, H 6
40385	Quixeramobim, Brazil, F 22
52637	Qum, Iran, G 6
33700	Qumbu, U. S. Afr., M 18
	Qumisheh, see Shahriza, Iran.
1000	Quorn, Austl., M 15
.....	Qurna, Iraq., P 24
.....	Qusiya, Egypt, L 17
793	Quyon, Quebec, P 8

R

Pop.	Place Country Index
	Raab, see Györ, Hung.
.....	Raade, Norway, E 7
4637	Raahe, Fin., D 5
9124	Raalte, Neth., F 21
.....	Raastad, Norway, F 3
.....	Raasted, Denmark, G 10
415	Raba, Palestine, J 11
3858	Rabastens, France, O 13
122106	Rabat, Mor., E 6
1716	Rabaul, N. Gui. Ter., I 12
.....	Rabbania, Egypt, M 19
12474	Rabinal, Guat., F 4
11832	Racalmuto, Italy, O 14
7165	Racconigi, Italy, E 2
.....	Rachgoun, Algeria, D 11
172	Racine, Quebec, P 19
.....	Raekwick, Scot., B 18
.....	Rada, Sweden, M 11
.....	Radarchaneh, Iran, O 12
16808	Rădăuti, Rom., H 20
16000	Radeberg, Ger., J 13
.....	Radford, Yukon, K 4
902	Radicofani, Italy, G 10
349	Radisson, Sask., M 6
3500	Radkan, Iran, E 9
.....	Radkersburg, Aus., I 8
7026	Radolfzell, Ger., R 5
78063	Radom, Poland, E 14
952	Radomir, Bulgaria, L 17
1500	Radomisl, W. Sov. Un., E 23
.....	Radul, W. Sov. Un., D 24
	Radviliskis, W. Sov. Un., A 18
813	Radville, Sask., R 9
.....	Radymno, Pol., F 16
.....	Radziechow, Poland, M 19
.....	Radzivilov, W. Sov. Un., F 16
	Radziwillow, see Radzivilov, Sov. Un.
.....	Radzymin, Poland, D 14
.....	Rae, Mack., M 13
15900	Rae Bareli, India, G 14
20000	Rafaela, Arg., L 15
.....	Rafala, Mor., H 6
202	Rafat, Palestine, M 9
438	Rafidia, Palestine, K 10
1569	Rafz, Switz., C 15
2159	Ragaz, Switz., H 20
.....	Raghdadije, Iraq, L 18
.....	Raghugarh, India, H 10
350	Raglan, N. Z., E 17
.....	Ragunda, Sweden, J 14
33072	Ragusa, Italy, O 16
	Ragusa, see Dubrovnik, Yugo.
.....	Rahbur, Iran, N 11
.....	Raheen, Ire., I 10
.....	Raheita, Erit., E 14
8893	Raho, Hung., P 29
.....	Rahuri, India, K 8
25000	Raichur, India, M 10
6800	Raigarh, India, I 16
5000	Raigarh, India, J 15
76	Rainham, Ontario, O 10
1205	Rainy River, Ont., P 15
45390	Raipur, India, J 15
.....	Rais, Iran O 8
.....	Rajaburi, Siam., P 2
63526	Rajahmundry, India, L 15
.....	Rajam, India, K 17
3900	Rajanpur, India, E 4
.....	Rajaori, India, B 7
5200	Rajapur, India, L 6
11000	Rajgarh, India, F 8
5400	Rajgarh, India, H 9
47485	Rajkot, India, I 4
.....	Rajmahal, India, G 21
.....	Rajpipla, India, I 7
.....	Rajuri, India, K 10
759	Rakaia, N. Z., M 11
.....	Rakka, Syria, J 14
4383	Rakkestad, Norway, M 9
.....	Raknet el Haleb, Alg., I 14
.....	Rakov, W. Sov. Un., C 20
	Raków, see Rakov, Sov. Un.
12418	Rakvere, Sov. Un., G 5
.....	Raley, Alberta, Q 22
46	Ralph, Sask., Q 9
.....	Rama, I. E. A., E 10
690	Rama, Nic., K 14
201	Rama, Sask., N 10
.....	Ramadi, Iraq, M 19
324	Ramadilla, Chile, I 5
161	Ramadilla, Chile, P 2
4287	Ramallah, Pal., M 9
1661	Ramallo, Arg., M 17
.....	Ramapatnam, India, M 13
.....	Ramasig, Scot., H 5
5767	Rambervillers, Fr., H 22
.....	Ramblon, Arg., L 7
6720	Rambouillet, Fr., H 13
.....	Ramdurg, India, M 8
.....	Rameh, Palestine, G 11
.....	Ramelton, Ire., C 15
.....	Rämen, Sweden, M 12
390	Ramerupt, France, H 18
5000	Rameswaram, India, Q 12
.....	Ramgarh, India, H 18
5000	Ramgarh, India, I 14
.....	Ramgarhati, India, M 19
.....	Ramgir, India, K 12
.....	Ram Hormuz, Iran, K 5
.....	Ramikhet, India, E 12
320	Ramin, Palestine, K 9
.....	Ramirez, Hond., E 10
7963	Ramiriqui, Col., H 12
.....	Ramkola, India, H 16
10417	Ramle, Pal., M 6
.....	Ramleh, Egypt, C 3
.....	Ramlet el Angab, Egypt, G 11
.....	Ramlöse, Denmark, I 21
.....	Rammas, Swe., M 14
309	Ramme, Denmark, G 3
14500	Ramnad, India, Q 12
.....	Ramnagar, India, E 12
4400	Ramnagar, India, G 22
5000	Ramnagar, India, I 14
.....	Ramnes, Norway, E 3
14830	Râmnicu Sărat, Rom., J 21
15162	Râmnicu-Vâlcea, Rom., J 18
.....	Ramon M. Castro, Argentina, Q 7
362	Ramore, Ontario, P 24
1551	Ramos Arizpe, Coa., F 12
751	Ramos, S. L. P., J 10
3500	Ramoutsa, Bech., P 16
.....	Rampa, India, L 15
5000	Rampur, India, D 10
73156	Rampur, India, E 12
.....	Rampur, India, J 17
23400	Rampur Beauleah, India, H 22
.....	Ramree, Bur., O 21
.....	Ramsele, Sweden, I 14
1260	Ramsen, Switz., B 16
5180	Ramsey, England, E 7
.....	Ramsey, England, J 19
33597	Ramsgate, Eng., L 24
.....	Ramsjö, Sweden, J 14
.....	Ramtch, Iran, Q 13
8700	Ramtek, India, I 12
8500	Ranaghat, India, H 22
31018	Rancagua, Chile, N 4
1507	Rance, Belgium, P 11
.....	Rancheria, Baja Cal., J 5
50517	Ranchi, India, H 18
1751	Rancho Veloz, Cuba, H 11
3789	Ranchuelo, Cuba, J 11
.....	Randalstown, N. Ire., D 21
1010	Randan, France, L 16
15929	Randazzo, Italy, N 16
30254	Randers, Denmark, G 10
8790	Randon, Alg., B 21
.....	Ranea, Sweden, F 19
.....	Ranenburg, Sov. Un., J 12
.....	Rangi, India, J 13
2200	Rangiora, N. Z., M 12
400415	Rangoon, Bur., P 22
20749	Rangpur, India, G 22
.....	Raniganj, India, G 21
15000	Raniganj, India, H 20
.....	Ranipur, India, F 2
2036	Ranis, Germany, K 9
2015	Ransdorp, Neth., F 15
.....	Raphoe, Ire., C 15
.....	Rapid Falls, N. S., P 11
4715	Rapperschwil, Switz., F 16
.....	Raqaba, Egypt, R 24
.....	Raristan, Iran, P 10
.....	Rarnish, Scot., E 7
700	Raron, Switz., M 11
.....	Ras Arubah, Bal., R 19
7500	Raseiniai, W. Sov. Un., B16
.....	Ras el Ain, Mor., F 11
.....	Ras-êl-Esch, Egypt, C 22
.....	Ras-el-Khalig, Egypt, C 17
.....	Ras el Ma, Algeria, E 12
.....	Ras el Ma, Algeria, K 12
.....	Rasharkin, N. Ire., C 20
22758	Rashîd (Rosetta), Eg., B 7
.....	Rashin, Kor., B 25
.....	Raška, Yugo., L 14
.....	Raskelf, Eng., E 16
.....	Ras Malan, Bal., R 20
.....	Rasnavolotskaya, Sov. Un., B 9
.....	Rasta, Iran, G 6
14003	Rastatt, Ger., O 4
.....	Ras Tolob, Alg., E 21
.....	Rasul, Transjordan, J 14
.....	Rasulgar, Iran, F 8
.....	Ratan, Sweden, H 18
.....	Rätan, Sweden, J 13
11700	Ratangarh, India, F 8
5400	Ratanpur, India, I 15
.....	Rathangan, Ire., J 18
.....	Rathcormack, Ire., O 12
.....	Rathdowney, Ire., L 15
.....	Rathdrum, Ire., L 22
.....	Rathduff, Ire., P 10
28000	Rathenow, Ger., G 11
.....	Rathfryland, N. Ire., F 22
1550	Rathkeale, Ire., M 8
.....	Rathlackan, Ire., F 7
.....	Rathmore, Ire., O 7
.....	Rathmullen, Ire., B 15
.....	Rathnew, Ire., K 23
.....	Rathowen, Ire., I 15
.....	Rathsherry, N. Ire., C 21
.....	Rathvilly, Ire., L 20
245	Rathwell, Man., R 15
50000	Ratibor, Pol., F 11
28000	Ratlam, India, H 8
23906	Ratnagiri, India, L 6
8497	Ratnapura, Cey., R 14
.....	Ratra, Ire., H 11
.....	Rattenberg, Aus., H 3
702	Rättvik, Sweden, L 13
4555	Ratzeburg, Ger., D 8
3500	Rauch, Arg., P 18
.....	Raukin, Ont., D 18
.....	Rauland, Norway, M 6
9002	Rauma, Finland, E 2
600	Ravenglass, Eng., E 10
23063	Ravenna, Italy, E 10
18000	Ravensburg, Ger., R 6
2339	Ravenstein, Neth., I 17
.....	Ravenswood, Austl., F 21
14	Ravine Bank, Sask., K 9
.....	Ravnkilde, Denmark, F 10
72	Ravnstrup, Denmark, G 7
.....	Rawa, Eth., L 13
.....	Rawa, Poland, E 13
.....	Rawâfa, Egypt, O 23
181169	Rawalpindi, India, B 6
.....	Rawanduz, Iraq, I 20
	Rawa Ruska, see Rawa Russkaya, Sov. Un.
11146	Rawa Russkaya, W. Sov. Un., F 17
.....	Rawdon, N. S., L 14
1235	Rawdon, Quebec, N 15
315	Rawene, N. Z., B 14
11827	Rawicz, Pol., E 10
18570	Rawmarsh, Eng., G 16
1459	Rawson, Arg., B 23
.....	Rawson, Arg., N 17
28575	Rawtenstall, Eng., F 13
.....	Raya, India, C 8
5000	Rayachoti, India, N 12
.....	Rayadrug, India, M 10
.....	Rayagudda, India, K 16
.....	Rayaina, Eg., M 20
2089	Raymond, Alberta, P 22
266	Raymore, Sask., O 9
1553	Rayón, S. L. P., K 16
.....	Rayong, Siam, P 4
	Razdelnaya, W. Sov. Un., H 25
14588	Razgrad, Bulgaria, K 21
97153	Reading, Eng., L 17
150	Readlyn, Sask., Q 7
.....	Real, Braz., D 4
50	Real del Castillo, Baja Cal., A 2
5000	Realejo, Nicaragua, J 10
.....	Realicó, Arg., N 12
1676	Reálmont, France, O 14
223	Realp, Switz., K 14
.....	Rear of Ball Creek, N. S., H 23
190	Reata, Coa., E 12
.....	Reawick, Shetland Is., C 3
719	Reay, Scotland, C 17
.....	Rebaya, Algeria, G 21
.....	Reboledo, Uruguay, N 20
.....	Recalde, Arg., P 16
.....	Recess, Ire., I 5
327753	Recife (Pernambuco), Brazil, H 25
87000	Recklinghausen, Ger., I 3
835	Recodo, Sin., Q 18
2131	Reconquista, Arg., J 18
493	Recreo, Arg., J 11
1572	Recuay, Peru, J 7
.....	Redange, Lux., Q 19
20159	Redcar, England, D 17
.....	Red Castle, Ire., B 17
1111	Redcliff, Alberta, O 24
300	Redcross, Ire., L 22
2924	Red Deer, Alberta, M 20
19280	Redditch, England, J 14
.....	Redem, Mor., E 7
.....	Redempcão, Brazil, I 9
.....	Redêsiya, Egypt, Q 24
.....	Red Hill, Ire., G 11
219	Rednorsville, Ont., J 18
5309	Redon, France, I 5
16927	Redondela, Spain, E 6
.....	Redondo, Baja Cal., A 2
6875	Redondo, Portugal, K 6
.....	Red Pass, B. C., L 16
211	Red Rapids, N. B., F 5
9904	Redruth, England, O 4
.....	Redstone, B. C., M 12
592	Redu, Belgium, P 15
218	Reducción, Arg., M 12
195	Redvers, Sask., R 11
.....	Redwan, Tur., G 17
.....	Reedham, Eng., I 24
.....	Reeds Well, Austl., O 17
1525	Reefton, N. Z., K 11
.....	Reepham, Eng., I 23
32	Reford, Sask., M 5
.....	Refsund, Sweden, J 13
.....	Refteled, Sweden, P 12
.....	Regeneracão, Brazil, G 19
81000	Regensberg, Ger., O 10
408	Regensberg, Switz., D 14
40118	Reggio, It., E 8
93606	Reggio Calabria It., N, 18
10000	Reghin, Rom., I 18
58245	Regina, Sask., P 9
243	Regina Beach, Sask., P 8
.....	Registro do Araguayu, Brazil, K 12
23037	Regla, Cuba, H 6
.....	Regoa, Portugal, G 7
.....	Regûm el Khel, Egypt, G 20
6195	Rehau, Ger., L 10
.....	Reh-Berge, Ger., O 16
.....	Rehoboth, Pal., M 5
9000	Rehoboth, S. W. Afr., P 13
.....	Rehovoth, Pal., R 3
5000	Rehti, India, H 12
32000	Reichenbach, Ger., K 10
2397	Reichenbach, Switz., K 10
1117	Reichenburg, Switz., F 17
.....	Reichenhall, Ger., R 11
.....	Reid, Aus., G 6
2273	Reiden, Switz., F 11
.....	Reiff, Scot., E 10
30830	Reigate, Eng., M 19
116687	Reims, France, G 17
4379	Reinach, Switz., F 13
.....	Reinickendorf, Ger., G 12
8481	Reinosa, Spain, D 11
.....	Reish, Iran, J 6
1200	Reitz, U. S. Afr., I 18
.....	Rejaf, A. E. Sud., J 18
15380	Relizane, Algeria, D 14
.....	Remanso, Brazil, H 19
.....	Remanso, Western Brazil, H 15
1162	Remedios, Col., G 10
10485	Remedios, Cuba, I 13
886	Remedios, Panama, Q 18
1683	Remich, Luxembourg, R 21
9629	Remiremont, France, I 23
.....	Remo, B. C., J 8
4461	Remolino, Col., C 11
.....	Remontnaya, Sov. Un., N 15
1165	Remoulins, France, O 19
101200	Remscheid, Ger., J 3
.....	Remtheh, Transjordan, I 17
.....	Remus, Switz., I 25
2224	Renaico, Chile, P 3
24085	Renaix, Belgium, M 7
1111	Renault, Algeria, C 14
241	Renca, Arg., M 11
2359	Rendalen, Norway, K 9
18000	Rendsburg, Ger., C 7
216	Renforth, N. B., K 8
.....	Renfrevy, Scot., N 14
5511	Renfrew, Ont., D 19
6730	Rengo, Chile, N 4
.....	Reni, India, E 8
.....	Reni, W. Sov. Un., J 23
18522	Renkum, Neth., H 18
2176	Renmark, Austl., N 16
98538	Rennes, France, I 6
98	Rennie, Man., Q 18
12	Reno, Alberta, H 17
80	Renown, Sask., N 8
.....	Repecho, Ur., O 21
.....	Reposte, Chia., N 20
.....	Republiek, Neth. Gu., B 10
.....	Reqôa, Port., G 6
19422	Requeña, Spain, J 15
.....	Resan, Yugo., N 14
.....	Resele, Sweden, I 15
.....	Resen, Denmark, G 4
.....	Resen, Denmark, G 7
1527	Reserve Mines, N. S., H 24
.....	Reshiat, I. E. A., O 5
.....	Reshida, Mor., F 10
121625	Resht, Iran, D 5
35000	Resistencia, Arg., I 18
20008	Resita, Romania, J 15
.....	Resolana, Arg., N 7
.....	Resolution, Sask., O 15
420	Reston, Man., R 12
.....	Reston Jc., Scot., N 23
7284	Retalhuleu, Guat., G 2
.....	Retamosa, Ur., M 22
5940	Rethel, France, G 17
3823	Rethy, Bel., K 15
8675	Rethymnon, Grc., R 19
.....	Reti, Ind., E 3
2505	Retiro, Col., K 8
518	Reumen, Chile, R 3
32285	Réus, Spain, G 19
32000	Reutlingen, Ger., P 6
	Revel, see Tallinn, Sov. Un.
2106	Revelstoke, B. C., O 17
170	Revenue, Sask., M 5
1912	Revigny, Fr., H 19
25000	Rewa, India, H 14
.....	Rewan, New Zealand, K 10
24800	Rewari, India, F 10
603	Rexton, N. B., F 11
.....	Reyes, Argentina, F 10
1805	Reyes, Bolivia, F 5
34231	Reykjavik, Iceland, C 18
4846	Reynosa, Tam., E 18
.....	Rezabad, Iran, L 7
49800	Rezaieh (Urmia), Iran, D 1
.....	Rezeh, Iran, G 9
12680	Rezekne, W. Sov. Un., A 20
.....	Rhadhanpur, India, H 4
.....	Rhayader Gwy, Wales, J 9
601	Rhäzüns, Switz., I 19
4849	Rheda, Germany, H 5
23225	Rheden, Neth., H 19
468	Rhein, Sask., O 11
2091	Rheinau, Switz., C 15
31000	Rheine, Germany, G 4
3831	Rheinfelden, Switz., C 10
7457	Rhenen, Neth., H 17
.....	Rhiconich, Scotland, D 12
.....	Rhine Falls, Switz., B 15
.....	Rhinow, Germany, F 11
6672	Rhodes, Belgium, M 12
	Rhodes, see Rodi.
141344	Rhondda, Wales., L 9
.....	Rhoscolyn, Wales, H 6
.....	Rhossilly, Wales, L 8
.....	Rhunahaorine, Scot., N 9
.....	Rhykjahlid, Iceland, B 23
13489	Rhyl, Wales, G 9
.....	Riabad, Iran, E 11
.....	Riachão, Brazil, G 16
15311	Riacho de Sant' Anna, Brazil, J 18
1766	Riaño, Spain, D 10
1178	Rians, France, P 21
1764	Riaza, Spain, G 13
9567	Ribadéo, Sp., C 8
8228	Ribadesella, Spain, C 10
5895	Ribe, Denmark, L 5
47795	Ribeirão Preto, Brazil, M 14
3800	Riberac, France, M 10
4500	Riberalta, Bolivia, B 7
4527	Ribnitz, Germany, C 11
.....	Ricaurte, Ecuador, B 3
.....	Riccarton Jc., Scotland, P 21
7673	Riccia, Italy, I 16
154	Richardville, Que., N 21
1828	Richelieu, France, K 10
1201	Richibucto, N. B., F 11
.....	Richibucto Village, N. B., F 12
.....	Richill, N. Ire., E 20
.....	Richisau, Switz., G 17
906	Richmond, Austl., G 18
4769	Richmond, England, E 15
37791	Richmond, England, L 19
1140	Richmond, N. Z., J 13
457	Richmond, Ont., E 22
3082	Richmond, Que., P 19
97	Richmond, Sask., P 3
384	Richmond, U. S. Afr., L 20
1500	Richmond, U. S. Afr., M 13
318	Richmond Corner, N. B., H 4
4617	Richterswil, Switz., F 16
.....	Ricken, Switz. E 17
.....	Rickham, Eng., O 8
.....	Riddarhyttan, Swe., M 14
986	Riddes, Switz., N 7
251	Ridgedale, Sask., L 9
1944	Ridgetown, Ont., Q 5
838	Ridgeway, Ontario, O 13
6806	Ried, Ger., Q 12
771	Ried, Switz., L 10
6353	Riehen, Switz., C 10
26000	Riesa, Germany, J 12
16697	Riesi, Italy, O 14
.....	Rietavas, W. Sov. Un., B 15
.....	Riet Fontein, U. S. Afr., G9
10052	Rieti, Italy, H 12
.....	Riet Vlei, U. S. Afr., O 11
.....	Riffel, Switz., P 10
385063	Riga, W. Sov. Un., A 17
.....	Rigan, Iran, N 13
1099	Rigaud, Quebec, P 13
.....	Rigird, Iran, H 6
9700	Riihimäki, Fin., F 4
.....	Rijen, Neth., J 14
4346	Rijnsburg, Neth., G 12
8647	Rijssen, Neth., F 22
.....	Rikenbach, Switz., D 17
.....	Rima, Bur., K 23
.....	Rimah, Transjordan, J 25
	Rimav Sobota, Hung., P 22
410	Rimbey, Alberta, L 20
.....	Rimbo, Sweden, M 17
21306	Rimini, Italy, F 11
.....	Rimsö, Denmark, G 15
233	Rincón, Coa., D 6
148	Rincón, Guan., L 12
150	Rinconada, Arg., E 9
2571	Rincón de Romos, Agua., K 9
.....	Rind, Denmark, H 6
1863	Ringe, Denmark, L 13
4516	Ringebu, Norway, K 8
.....	Ringgive, Denmark, J 7
3995	Ringköbing, Den., H 3
12237	Ringsaker, Norway, L 9
6148	Ringsted, Den., K 19
.....	Ringville, Ire., O 15
.....	Ringwood, Eng., N 14
212	Ringwood, Ontario, K 12
.....	Rinsumageest, Neth., C 19
5478	Rinteln, Ger., G 6
27459	Riobamba, Ecuador, C 5
1168	Rio Blanco, Chile, M 5
20	Rio Blanco, Ver., I 10
.....	Rio Bonito, Brazil, L 11
.....	Rio Bonito, Brazil, P 12
6611	Rio Branco, Brazil, P 10
.....	Rio Branco, W. Brazil, J 22
6110	Rio Caribe, Ven., C 19
.....	Rio Cauto Cuba, N 19
.....	Rio Chico, Arg., D 22
1916	Rio Chico, Ven., D 14
.....	Rio Colorado, Arg., Q 13
89600	Rio Cuarto, Arg., M 12
1563787	Rio de Janeiro, Brazil, N 18
1638	Rio de Oro, Col., E 13
1506	Rio Feo, Cuba, J 3
.....	Rio Formoso, Brazil, H 25
382	Rio Grande, Bolivia, M 6
50330	Rio Grande, Braz., Q 11
5111	Rio Grande, Zac., H 7
.....	Rio Guadalquivir, Sp., O 8
5651	Rio hacha, Colombia, B 14
11042	Riom, France, L15
.....	Rio Molato, Bolivia, K 6
.....	Rio Negro, Argentina, Q 9
5436	Rio Negro, Brazil, O 13
1831	Rionegro, Col., F 13
.....	Rionegro, Col., L 25
.....	Rio Negro, Ur., K 18
10331	Rionero, Italy, J 17
2244	Riópar, Spain, L 14
.....	Rio Pardo, Braz., K 19
.....	Rio Pardo, Brazil, M 10
.....	Rio Pardo, Brazil, M 19
6538	Rio Pardo, Brazil, Q 11
.....	Rio Piedras, Arg., G 11
8804	Rio Salado, Algeria, D 12
.....	Rio Seco, Cuba, O 23
1718	Riosucio, Col., F 6
5801	Riosucio, Col., H 8
.....	Rio Verde, Brazil, L 12
8503	Rio Verde, S. L. P., K 15
.....	Ripley, England, F 15
13415	Ripley, England, H 15
391	Ripley, Ont., J 5
6991	Ripoll, Spain, E 20
8576	Ripon, England, E 15
447	Ripon, Quebec, O 11
128	Ripur, Iceland, B 20
.....	Riri, Nepal, F 16
809	Risbäck, Sweden, H 14
1078	Riscle, France, P 9
.....	Rishin, Iran, G 9
.....	Rishon, Pal., L 5
3076	Risör, Norway, N 7
.....	Rissen, Norway, I 9
4355	Riva, Italy, C 8
1150	Riva, Switz., P 17
150	Rivadavia, Arg., F 13
435	Rivadavia, Chile, K 4
6698	Rivas, Nicaragua, L 12
.....	Rivas, Uruguay, I 15
14707	Rive-de-Gier, France, M 18
.....	River, Ont., R 22
.....	Rivera, Arg., P 14
17000	Rivera, Ur., F 21
.....	Riverchapel, Ire., M 22
140	River Denys, N. S., I 21
1025	River Hebert, N. S., J 13
252	Riverhurst, Sask., O 6
627	River John, N. S., J 16
100	River Philip, N. S., J 14
262	Riverport, N. S., O 13
802	Rivers, Manitoba, Q 13
.....	Riversdale, N. Z., Q 5
4160	Riversdale, U. S. Afr., Q 10
230	Riverside, N. B., J 12
.....	Riverside, N. S., L 14
.....	Rivers Inlet, B. C., N 9
181	Riverton, Manitoba, O 16
900	Riverton, N. Z., Q 4
3280	Rives, France, M 20
5103	Rivesaltes, France, Q 16
801	Riviere a Pierre Jc., Que., K 19
8713	Riviere du Loup, Que., G 25
672	Riviere Ouelle, Que., I 24
7411	Rivoli, Italy, D 2
.....	Rixdorf, Ger., Q 18
30000	Riyadh, Sau. Ar., L 5
3000	Riz, Iran, O 7
.....	Rizab, Iran, J 10
14717	Rize, Tur., C 15
.....	Rizokarpaso, Cyprus, J 9
.....	Rizqat, Egypt, P 23
.....	R. J. Neild, Arg., O 16
.....	Rlpin, Poland, G 12
2674	Róa, Spain, F 12
.....	Roade, England, J 17
.....	Roag, Scotland, H 6
40502	Roanne, France, L 17
755	Roatan, Hond., D 11
.....	Robat, Afghanistan, E 22
.....	Robat, Afg., M 18
.....	Robat, Iran, L 9
.....	Robat Abdullah Kha, Afg., E 19
.....	Robat-i-Sangi, Afg., H 16
.....	Robat-i-Shan Bal., Iran, H 15
.....	Robat Karim, Iran., F 6
282	Robechies, Belgium, P 11
7000	Robert, Martinique, F 24
.....	Roberton, Scot., O 18
.....	Roberts, Arg., N 15

Pop.	Place Country Index
.....	Robertsbridge, Eng., M 21
576	Robertson, Quebec, N 21
4945	Robertson, U. S. Afr., Q 8
.....	Robertsport, Lib., J 2
.....	Robertstown, Ire., J 19
1199	Robertville, Algeria, B 20
3220	Roberval, Quebec, E 19
.....	Robichand, N. B., H 13
.....	Robin Hood's Bay, Eng., E 18
52	Robinson, Alberta, J 19
.....	Robinson, Yukon, Q 10
765	Roblin, Man., O 12
302	Roblindale, Ont., I 18
93	Robsart, Sask., Q 4
14125	Rocafuerte, Ecuador, C 2
404	Rocanville, Sask., P 11
2783	Roccapalumba, Italy, N 13
2690	Roccastrada, Italy, G 8
6277	Roccella, Italy, M 19
.....	Roch, Wales, K 4
25000	Rocha, Uruguay, O 23
90278	Rochdale, England, G 13
4048	Rochechouart, France, L 12
3505	Rochefort, Belgium, O 16
29482	Rochefort France, L 8
550	Rochefort, Switz., H 5
24	Rochester, Alberta, I 20
.....	Rochester, England, B 13
31196	Rochester, England, L 21
6240	Rochlitz, Germany, J 11
.....	Rockcorry, Ire., G 18
177	Rock Creek, B. C., Q 16
29369	Rockhampton, Austl., H 23
156	Rockingham, Austl., N 4
364	Rockingham Station, Nova Scotia, N 15
1395	Rock Island, Que., R 19
.....	Rock Lake, Ontario, R 22
2040	Rockland, Ontario, D 23
.....	Rocklin, N. S., K 17
231	Rockport, Ontario, I 21
.....	Rockstone, Br. Gu., B 6
221	Rockville, N. S., Q 8
631	Rockwood, Ontario, L 10
201	Rockyford, Alberta, N 21
203	Rocquencourt, France, B 2
2442	Rocroi, France, F 18
.....	Roda, Egypt, K 18
.....	Roda, Egypt, L 12
.....	Roda, Germany, K 10
678	Roda, Spain, G 19
3408	Rodas, Cuba, J 10
3108	Rödby, Denmark, O 18
.....	Roddam, Scot., G 25
.....	Rödding, Denmark, F 5
.....	Rödding, Denmark, G 9
1488	Rödding, Denmark, L 6
.....	Rödeby, Sweden, Q 14
1111	Rödekro, Denmark, M 8
5210	Roden, Neth., C 21
975	Rodeo, Dur., N 21
16195	Rodez, France, O 15
27466	Rodi, Italy, I 18
20000	Rodi (Rhodes), Rhodes (Turkey Map) I 2
675	Rödkaersbro, Den., G 8
.....	Rodna-Veche, Rom., H 18
702	Rodney, Ontario, P 5
	Rodosto, see Tekirdagi, Tur.
2310	Rodrigo, Cuba, I 11
9017	Rodriguez, Uruguay, O 18
.....	Rodriguez Clara, Ver., K 11
642	Rödvig, Denmark, L 22
154	Roebourne, Austl., G 4
.....	Roelse, Denmark, H 13
16599	Roermond, Neth., K 20
9103	Rogachev, W. Sov. Un., C 23
732	Rogart, Scotland, F 15
10019	Rogatica, Yugo., K 12
.....	Rögen Sjelle, Den., H 10
.....	Rogers, B. C., N 17
705	Rogersville, N. B., F 10
3702	Rogliano, Italy, L 19
623	Rohan, France, I 4
.....	Rohatyn, W. Sov. Un., G 18
8800	Rohi, India, F 2
.....	Rohtak, India, E 10
1264	Roisel, France, F 15
.....	Rokbet en Naga, Alg., E 21
5483	Roken, Norway, B 3
.....	Rokitno, W. Sov. Un., E 21
503	Roland, Man., R 15
.....	Rold, Denmark, E 10
.....	Röldal, Nor., M 5
3183	Roldanillo, Col., I 7
2163	Rolle, Switz., L 3
130	Rolleston, Australia, I 21
.....	Rolling Dam, N. B., K 5
3369	Roma, Australia, J 21
1062861	Roma (Rome), It., I 11
.....	Roma, Sweden, O 17
28948	Roman, Romania, I 21
6102	Romanshorn, Switz., C 19
18957	Romans-sur-Isere, France, M 20
	Rome, see Roma, It.
30	Romero, Chl., J 4
.....	Romford, Eng., B 25
14073	Romilly-sur-Seine, France, H 15
25749	Romni, Sov. Un., L 8
2251	Romont, Switzerland, J 6
8001	Romorantin, France, J 13
4863	Romsey, England, M 15
.....	Rönbjerg, Denmark, F 5
5726	Ronciglione, Italy, H 10
26170	Ronda, Spain, O 10
.....	Roni, India, E 8
10537	Rönne, Denmark, R 23
5774	Ronneby, Sweden, Q 13
.....	Rönninge, Denmark, L 13
.....	Roode School, Neth., B 22
17200	Roorkee, India, E 11
22053	Roosendaal, Neth., J 12
.....	Roosky, Ire., H 13
.....	Roossenekal, U. S. Afr., E 20
.....	Ropczyce, Poland, F 15
1005	Roquefort, France, O 8
1412	Roquemaure, France, O 19
.....	Rörbek, Denmark, F 9
.....	Rörby, Denmark, K 16
10972	Rorschach, Switz., D 20
340	Rörvig, Denmark, I 19
.....	Rosales, Arg., N 13
1168	Rosales (Santa Cruz Rosales), Chih., H 19
1532	Rosales, Coa., B 13
1162	Rosa Morada, Nay., K 2
.....	Rosamuk, Afg., H 16
512872	Rosario, Arg., M 16
372	Rosario, Baja Cal., E 3
.....	Rosario, Brazil, E 18
.....	Rosario, Brazil, J 8
6782	Rosario, Brazil, Q 9
6864	Rosario, Coa., D 9
2442	Rosario, Col., F 15
347	Rosario, Dur., K 19
8323	Rosario, Sin., R 19
8500	Rosario, Uruguay, O 16
568	Rosario de la Frontera, Argentina, G 11
689	Rosario de Lerma, Arg., G 10
.....	Rosas, Argentina, O 18
2669	Rosas, Spain, E 21

Pop.	Place Country Index
.....	Rosbercon, Ire., N 18
4318	Roscoff, France, G 2
1900	Ros Comain, Ire., I 12
3061	Roscrea, Ire., I 14
.....	Rosdaul, Ire., I 11
10000	Roseau (Charlottetown), Dominica, D 23, M 24
150	Rosebery, B. C., P 18
.....	Rosegreen, Ire., N 14
1267	Rosehearty, Scotland, G 23
.....	Rosehell, Scotland, F 14
.....	Roseires, A. E. Sud., I 19
.....	Rose Lake, B. C., J 10
110	Rosemary, Alberta, N 22
217	Rosemont, Ontario, J 10
.....	Rosendo Márquez, Pueb., I 7
191	Rosenfeld, Man., R 16
18000	Rosenheim, Ger., Q 10
.....	Rosenlaui, Switz., J 13
1819	Rosenthal, Ger., N 17
1470	Rosetown, Sask., N 5
	Rosetta, see Raschid, Egypt
.....	Rose Valley, P. E. I., H 15
.....	Roshanawan, Iran, H 13
.....	Rosh Pinna, Pal., G 13
477	Rosignol, Br. Gu., B 7
812	Rosillas, Bolivia, N 10
11118	Rosiori-de-Vede, Rom., K 19
14149	Roskilde, Denmark, J 20
.....	Roslagskulla, Sweden, P 24
25992	Roslavl, Sov. Un., J 7
770	Roslev, Denmark, F 6
4833	Rosmalen, Neth., I 17
2100	Rosmaninhal, Port., I 7
.....	Rosmead Jc., U. S. Afr., N 14
14477	Rosny-sous-Bois, France, B 8
2438	Rosporden, France, I 2
4738	Ross, England, K 12
460	Ross, N. Z., L 9
130	Rossa, Switz., M 18
10787	Rossano, Italy, L 19
443	Rossburn, Man., P 12
550	Ross Carbery, Ire., R 8
266	Rosseau, Ontario, E 11
.....	Rosses, Ire., F 10
18	Ross Jc., Sask., N 11
3657	Rossland, B. C., Q 17
.....	Rosslare, Ire., O 22
.....	Rosslea, N. Ire., F 17
.....	Rossnowlagh, Ire., E 12
.....	Rossön, Sweden, I 14
.....	Rossosh, Sov. Un., L 12
.....	Rossow, Germany, F 11
.....	Rostak, Iran, N 9
1149	Rosthern, Sask., L 7
93501	Rostock, Ger., C 10
20864	Rostov, Sov. Un., H 12
510253	Rostov, Sov. Un., N 12
2456	Rostrenen, France, H 3
.....	Rostrevor, N. Ire., G 22
10958	Rota, Spain, O 8
.....	Rotebro, Sweden, P 21
5078	Rotenburg, Ger., E 7
5581	Roth, Ger., N 8
1255	Rothbury, England, C 14
313	Rothenback, Switz., I 10
.....	Röthenburg, Ger., J 14
8828	Rothenburg, Ger., N 7
5078	Rothenthurm, Switz., G 15
69689	Rotherham, England, G 16
1854	Rothes, Scotland, G 19
521	Rothesay, N. B., K 8
9346	Rothesay, Scotland, N 12
926	Rothiemay, Scotland, G 21
218	Rothsay, Ontario, K 8
4516	Rothwell, England, J 17
.....	Rotkreuz, Switz., G 14
6540	Rotorua, N. Z., F 20
3096	Rotselaer, Belgium, L 13
594948	Rotterdam, Neth., H 12
10556	Rottweil, Ger., P 4
107105	Roubaix, France, E 15
122957	Rouen, France, G 12
956	Rougemon, France, J 22
429	Rougemont, Que., P 17
1145	Rougemont, Switz., L 7
5060	Rouiba, Algeria, B 17
812	Rouillac, France, L 9
.....	Rouissat, Algeria, H 19
1835	Roujan, France, P 16
.....	Roukecha, I. E. A., J 11
27690	Roulers (Rousselaere), Bel. L 5
139	Roum, Denmark, F 9
125	Round Hill, N. S., M 10
.....	Roundstone, Ire., J 3
.....	Roundtown, Ire., J 22
	Rousselaere, see Roulers, Bel.
407	Roussillon, Fr., M 19
326	Routhier, Ont., D 24
756	Routville, U. S. Afr., L 16
8808	Rouyn, Que., F 2
6600	Rovaniemi, Fin., C 6
.....	Rovenki, Sov. Un., L 12
11836	Roveredo, Italy, C 8
106	Roveredo, Switz., N 18
9453	Rovigno, Italy, D 13
13191	Rovigo, Italy, D 10
40788	Rovno, W. Sov. Un., F 20
.....	Rovnoe, Sov. Un., M 6
219	Rowena, Ontario, F 23
115	Rowley, Alberta, M 21
	Rowne, see Rovno, Sov. Un.
430	Roxborough, Austl., G 16
.....	Roxburgh, N. Z., P 4
698	Roxburgh, Scot., O 22
795	Roxton Falls, Quebec, P 18
.....	Royal, India, C 12
52	Royalty Jc., P. E. I., G 16
11328	Royan, France, M 7
.....	Roycroft, Alberta, H 16
5309	Roye, Fr., F 14
.....	Roza-i-bagh, Afg., H 16
.....	Rozaj, Yugo., L 13
6670	Rožňava, Czech., G 14
	Roznava, see Rozsnyo, Hung.
.....	Ruan, Ire., L 8
.....	Rubanovka, Sov. Un., N 9
4437	Rubio, Ven., H 4
.....	Rucanello, Arg., O 17
.....	Rudabkina, W. Sov. Un., D 22
.....	Rudarpur, India, F 1
.....	Rudbar, Afg., L 17
5224	Ruddervoorde, Bel., L 6
.....	Rudenz, Switz., I 13
4390	Rüdesheim, Germany, L 4
4129	Rudköbing, Den., N 14
.....	Rudok, Tib., L 12
16000	Rudolstadt, Ger., K 9
2807	Rue, France, E 13
443	Rue, Switz., J 5
2421	Rüeggisberg, Switz., I 9
24924	Rueil, France, B 3
3194	Ruffec, France, L 9
600	Rufino, Arg., N 14
23824	Rugby, England, J 16
8484	Ruhla, Germany, J 7
3067	Ruhland, Germany, I 13
.....	Ruhrort, Germany, I 2
4461	Ruinen, Neth., E 21
2815	Ruinerwold, Neth., E 21

Pop.	Place Country Index
390	Ruines, France, N 16
468	Ruis, Switz., J 18
.....	Ruislip, England, B 18
.....	Ruivaes, Port., F 6
.....	Rujm el Meseih, Transjordan, N 14
.....	Rujm Taihin, Transjordan, M 16
.....	Rujum el Al, Transjordan, P 16
.....	Rujum Rishan, Transjordan, Q 16
.....	Rukanpur, India, E 5
.....	Rum, Iran, I 14
.....	Ruma, Yugo., J 13
.....	Rumeish, Palestine, F 10
4639	Rumelange, Lux.
2013	Rumes, Belgium, N 6
516	Rumigny, France, F 17
4116	Rumilly, France, L 22
548	Rummaneh, Palestine, H 10
.....	Rummelsburg, Ger., Q 19
6728	Rummelsburg, Pol., C 10
703	Rummon, Palestine, M 10
90	Rumsey, Alberta, M 21
18158	Runcorn, England, G 12
231	Rungis, France, C 5
561	Rurrenabaque, Bol., F 4
.....	Rurumoppe, Japan, F 13
80	Rusagornis, N. B., I 7
1654	Rush, Ire., I 22
.....	Rushkar, Iran, G 14
125	Rush Lake, Sask., P 6
.....	Rushyland, N. Ire., C 16
50300	Russe, Bul., K 20
783	Russell, Man., P 12
385	Russell, N. Z., K 16
750	Russell, Ont., E 23
825	Russell, Ontario, E 23
180	Russell, Tasmania, E 6
3500	Russellkonda, India, J 18
164	Russo, Switz., N 15
6104	Rustenburg, U. S. Afr., F 17
205	Rustico, P. E. I., G 16
.....	Rustringen, Ger., D 5
4278	Ruswil, Switz., G 12
25157	Rutherglen, Scotland, N 15
2912	Ruthin, Wales, H 10
1316	Rüti, Switz., E 20
5678	Rüti, Switz., F 16
.....	Rüti, Switz., J 13
.....	Rutli, Switz., H 15
3848	Ruurlo, Neth., G 21
.....	Ružomberok, Czech., G 12
1293	Ry, Denmark, J 19
.....	Ryazan, Sov. Un., J 12
95358	Ryazan, Sov. Un., J 12
13000	Ryazhsk, Sov. Un., J 13
139011	Rybinsk, Sov. Un., H 12
.....	Ryde, Denmark, G 5
10519	Ryde, England, N 16
3947	Rye, England, M 22
.....	Ryechitsa, W. Sov. Un., D 24
.....	Ryehill, Ire., J 10
.....	Rygge, Norway, E 6
.....	Rylach, N. Ire., D 16
323	Ryley, Alberta, K 22
.....	Rymanów, Poland, G 15
	Ryojun, see Lushun, Manch.
485	Ryomgaard, Den., G 13
.....	Rypin, Pol., D 12
452	Ryslinge, Den., L 13
27499	Rzeszów, Poland, F 15
54081	Rzhev, Sov. Un., I 9

S

Pop.	Place Country Index
.....	Saadana, Tunisia, G 22
19000	Saalfeld, Germany, K 9
4706	Saanen, Switz., L 8
.....	Saanicht on Bay, B. C., Q 2
129085	Saarbrücken, Ger., N 2
32000	Saarlouis, Ger., N 2
.....	Saatwinkel, Germany, O 15
21616	Saavedra, Arg., P 15
12563	Sabac, Yugo., I 13
47831	Sabadell, Spain, F 20
.....	Sabahiya, Egypt, P 23
6000	Sabalgarh, India, G 10
1649	Sabalo, Cuba, J 3
.....	Sabán, Q. R., G 23
.....	Sabana, Col., J 18
.....	Sabana, Honduras, F 10
3090	Sabana de Mendoza, Venezuela, E 7
11432	Sabanalarga, Col., C 10
1803	Sabanaso, Cuba, M 19
513	Sabancuy, Camp., I 19
2391	Sabanilla, Cuba, O 25
.....	Sabanja, Tur., C 5
7684	Sabara, Brazil, M 17
.....	Sabaria, Cuba, N 25
.....	Sabaudia, Italy, J 12
.....	Sabderat, Erit., A 13
.....	Sabha, Transjordan, J 22
6825	Sabinas, Coa., C 12
6912	Sabinas Hidalgo, N. L., E 14
20000	Sabiyah, Sau. Ar., M 4
.....	Sablah, Iran, L 3
137	Sable River, N. S., Q 11
5611	Sablé-sur-Sarthe, France, I 9
.....	Sablistar, Iran, M 12
12181	Saboya, Col., H 11
.....	Sabra, Sweden, J 16
843	Sabres, France, O 7
.....	Sabriya, Tunisia, F 23
.....	Sabugal, Portugal, H 7
.....	Säby, Sweden, O 13
.....	Sabzawar Sebzar, Afg., I 17
18000	Sacaba, Bolivia, I 8
18037	Sacaba, Bolivia, I 8
10972	Sacaca, Bolivia, J 7
.....	Sachelid, Rom., H 15
.....	Sachkheri, Sov. Un., P 15
2018	Sachseln, Switz., I 13
.....	Sacki, Japan, O 6
2489	Sackville, N. B., I 13
289	Saclay, France, C 2
.....	Sacramento, Brazil, K 9
.....	Sacramento, Brazil, M 15
1073	Sacramento, Coa., D 10
1036	Sacramento, Coa., E 11
1000	Sacramento, Dur., M 23
.....	Sacré Coeur de Marie, Quebec, N 22
11579	Sa da Bandeira (Lubango), Ang., N 12
.....	Sadaka, Egypt, D 17
.....	Sadat, Iran, K 6
.....	Sadeh, Transjordan, J 22
.....	Sadfe, Egypt, M 19
5000	Sadiya, India, K 22
3400	Sadowara, Japan, Q 5
1600	Sadras, India, O 13
2525	Saeby, Denmark, C 13
.....	Saeby, Denmark, K 17
.....	Saedder, Denmark, K 20
.....	Saeding, Denmark, I 3
5000	Säel Hagar, Egypt, D 10
.....	Saenz, Argentina, Q 14
.....	Safaris, Iran, F 3
.....	Safe, Pal., N 8
9446	Safed, Palestine, G 12
3322	Saffelacre, Belgium, R 4
.....	Saffelaere, Belgium, L 9

Pop.	Place Country Index
35574	Safi, Morocco, E 5
.....	Safidab, Iran, H 7
1306	Safiriyeh, Palestine, L 6
9899	Safru, Morocco, F 8
2039	Säfsjö, Sweden, O 13
.....	Säfsjöström, Sweden, P 14
.....	Saft el Muluk, Egypt, D 8
.....	Saft Zarik, Egypt, E 15
.....	Safur, Egypt, E 15
.....	Safvar, Sweden, H 18
.....	Saga, Bur., N 23
46178	Saga, Japan, N 3
1600	Saga, Japan, O 8
.....	Sagaing, Bur., N 22
18000	Sagan, Pol., E 8
5400	Saganoseki, Japan, N 6
.....	Sagar, India, L 9
.....	Sagar, India, N 7
.....	Sagaye, Japan, G 22
.....	Sagres, Port., N 4
1725	Sagua de Tanamo, Cuba, N 23
15539	Sagua la Grande, Cuba, I 12
20	Saguenay Power Jc., Que., F 20
20253	Sagunto, Spain, J 17
6500	Sagzabad, Iran, F 5
.....	Sagzi, Iran, I 7
4308	Sahagun, Col., D 9
2855	Sahagun, Spain, E 11
78655	Saháranpur, India, D 10
.....	Sahem el Kefarat, Transjordan, H 15
.....	Sahibganj, India, G 21
.....	Sahiwal, India, C 6
.....	Sahlabad, Iran, J 14
.....	Sahraght, Egypt, F 14
2665	Sahuaripa, Son., G 14
10465	Sahuayo, Michoa., M 8
.....	Sahwet el Kamh, Syr., I 20
.....	Saiburi, Thai., Q 16
13809	Saida, Algeria, E 13
13500	Saida (Sidon), Syr., M 10
.....	Saidabad, Iran, K 7
.....	Said Khan, Afg., J 21
.....	Saighan, Afg., G 21
1356	Saignelégier, Switz., F 6
350	Saignes, France, M 14
.....	Saigo, Japan, I 10
100000	Saigon, Fr. In. Ch., Q 8
5600	Saijo, Japan, N 9
1127	Saillans, France, N 20
578	Saillon, Switz., N 7
1465	Sain Alto, Zac., I 7
.....	Sain Kala, Iran, E 2
1275	Sains, France, F 16
6181	Saint Affrique, Fr., O 15
445	Saint Agapit, Quebec, L 21
2724	Saint Aignan, Fr., J 11
555	Saint Aime, Quebec, O 17
616	Saint Alban, Quebec, L 19
28625	Saint Albans, Eng., K 19
697	Saint Albert, Alberta, K 20
462	Saint Albert, Quebec, N 19
300	Saint Alexandre de Kamouraska, Que., H 25
1790	Saint Alexis, Quebec, F 22
490	Saint Alexis des Monts, Quebec, M 16
.....	Saint Alphonse, Que., N 15
14720	Saint Amand, Fr., E 15
615	Saint Amand, France, I 11
8858	Saint Amand-Mont-Rond, France, K 14
482	Saint Amant de Boixe, France, L 10
3558	Saint Ambroix, Fr., O 18
1432	Saint Amour, Fr., K 20
1284	Saint André, France, H 12
451	Saint André, France, O 23
444	Saint André, Quebec, O 25
3974	Saint Andre de Cubzac, France, M 9
.....	Saint Andrew, Barbados, O 25
1167	Saint Andrews, N. B., L 5
250	Saint Andrews, N. Z., N 10
8269	Saint Andrews, Scot., L 21
230	Saint Andrews West, Ont., F 24
150	Saint Ann, N. S., H 22
2614	Saint Annaland, Neth., J 10
.....	Saint Anne Mills, Que., J 22
2090	Saint Ann's Bay, Jamaica, J 8
510	Saint Anselme, Que., L 22
304	Saint Anthony, N. B., G 12
950	Saint Antoine, Que., O 16
.....	Saint Antonien, Switz., H22
593	Saint Apollinaire, Que., L 21
.....	Saint Arnaud, Austl., P 18
3053	Saint Astier, France, M 10
131	Saint Auban, Fr., O 23
78	Saint Aubin, France, D 2
1162	Saint Aubin, Switz., H 5
929	Saint Aubin du Cormier France, I 7
.....	Saint Aurelie, Que., N 24
8295	Saint Austell, England, O 5
750	Saint Barnabe Nord., Que., M 17
1050	Saint Basile, Quebec, L 20
703	Saint Bazile le Grand, Quebec, P 16
.....	Saint Beatrix, Que., N 15
553	Saint Benin d'Azy, France K 16
355	Saint Benoit, Quebec, P 14
232	Saint Bernard, N. S., O 8
.....	Saint Bernardino, Switzerland, L 18
1606	Saint Blaise, Switz., H 6
385	Saint Blin, France, H 20
530	Saint Bonaventure, Que., O 18
563	Saint Boniface de Shawinigan, Quebec, L 17
842	Saint Bonnet, France, N 22
952	Saint Boswells, Scot., O 21
354	Saint Brais, Switz., E 7
31640	Saint Brieuc, France, H 4
150	Saint Brieux, Sask., M 8
426	Saint Bruno, Que., M 22
.....	Saint Buryan, Eng., P 2
3333	Saint Calais, France, I 11
400	Saint Camille, Quebec, M24
1307	Saint Casimir, Que., L 19
30275	Saint Catherines, Ont., M 12
357	Saint Celestin, Que., N 19
382	Saint Cergue, Switz., L 1
1209	Saint Cesaire, Que., Q 17
213	Saint Charles, Man., Q 15
673	Saint Charles Jc., Que., L 22
1809	Saint Chely d' Apcher, France, N 16
2550	Saint Chinian, France, P 15
656	Saint Chrysostome, Que., R 15
877	Saint Ciers-du-Taillon, Fr., M 8
148	Saint Clair, France, G 8
537	Saint Clair Jc., Ont., C 6
13436	Saint Claude, France, K 21
301	Saint Claude, Man., R 15
.....	Saint Clears, Wales, K 6

Pop.	Place Country Index
362	Saint Clements, Ont., L 8
3089	Saint Cloud, Algeria, D 12
16341	Saint Cloud, France, B 3
.....	Saint Columb Major, England, N 4
.....	Saint Combs, Scot., G 24
610	Saint Côme, Que., M 15
475	Saint Constant, Que., Q 15
1309	Saint Cyprien, France, N 11
300	Saint Cyriac, Que., F 21
725	Saint Cyrille, Quebec, O 18
7339	Saint Cyr-l'Ecole, Fr., B 1
1173	Saint Cyrus, Scotland, J 23
.....	Saint Damien, Quebec, L 23
204	Saint Davids, Ontario, M13
.....	Saint Davids, Wales, K 4
734	Saint Denis, Belgium, N 13
78401	Saint Denis, Fr., G 14
10608	Saint Denis-du-Sig, Alg., D 13
19695	Saint Die, France, H 23
18292	Saint Dizier, France, H 19
7944	Saint Dogmells, Wales, J 6
258	Sainte Agathe de Lotbiniere, Quebec, M 21
3357	Sainte Agathe des Monts, Quebec, N 13
125	Sainte Agnes, Quebec, R 13
15249	Sainte Anne, Guadeloupe, B 23
108	Sainte Anne, Ont., D 25
1781	Sainte Anne de Beaupre, Quebec, J 22
1102	Sainte Anne de la Pocatière, Quebec, I 24
.....	Sainte Anne de Prescott, Ont., D 25
305	Sainte Anne des Chenes, Man., Q 17
2359	Sainte Barbe du Tlelat, Alg., D 12
765	Sainte Cecile de Whitten, Quebec, P 22
6343	Sainte Croix, Switz., I 3
552	Sainte Euphémie, Quebec, L 23
3155	Sainte Foy la Grande, France, N 10
255	Sainte Helene, Quebec, H 25
300	Sainte Julie, Quebec, M 20
.....	Sainte Eleanor's, Prince Edward Island, G 14
450	Sainte Madeleine, Que., P 17
.....	Sainte Marie, Guadeloupe, B 23
1735	Sainte Marie, Que., M 22
2384	Sainte Maure, France, J 11
4617	Sainte Menehould, Fr., G 18
596	Sainte Mère Eglise, Fr., G 7
256	Sainte Monique, Quebec, N 18
470	Sainte Ephrem de Tring, Quebec, N 22
.....	Sainte Rosalie, Que., P 17
501	Sainte Rose de Watford, Quebec, M 23
359	Sainte Rose du Lac (Saint Rose), Manitoba, O 14
775	Sainte Scholastique, Quebec, P 14
20592	Saintes, France, L 8
904	Sainte Thecle, Quebec, K18
4661	Sainte Therese, Quebec, P 15
.....	Saint Etienne, Belgium, N 12
190236	Saint Etienne, Fr., M 19
755	Saint Eugene, Ont., D 5
1564	Saint Eustache, Que., P 15
654	Saint Evariste, Que., O 23
1655	Saint Fargeau, Fr., I 15
1607	Saint Felicien, Que., E 18
841	Saint Fergus, Scot., G 24
.....	Saintfield, N. Ire., E 24
.....	Saint Fillans, Scot., L 16
463	Saint Flavien, Quebec, L 21
896	Saint Florent, Cor., P 3
2884	Saint Florentin, Fr., I 17
5201	Saint Flour, France, M 15
6252	Saint Francois, Guad., B 24
673	Saint Francois du Lac, Quebec, N 17
1530	Saint Gabriel, Quebec, M 16
64020	Saint Gallen (Saint Gall), Switz., D 19
6516	Saint Gaudens, Fr., P 11
2458	Saint Gaultier, Fr., K 13
696	Saint Gedeon, Que., E 20
12	Saint Genevieve, Manitoba, Q 17
609	Saint Genis, France, M 8
550	Saint Grégoire, Que., O 17
19095	Saint George, Grenada, P 17
206	Saint George, Man., P 17
1169	Saint George, N. B., L 6
.....	Saint George, Ont., M 9
1940	Saint George East, Quebec, N 23
813	Saint Georges, France, J 8
1024	Saint Georges, Newf., L 23
6484	Saint Georges sur Meuse, Belgium, N 16
.....	Saint Germain, Quebec, O 18
21996	Saint Germaine-en-laye, France, H 13
681	Saint Germain les Belles, France, M 12
398	Saint Gervais, Fr., L 23
975	Saint Gervais, Quebec, L 22
1369	Saint Gilles-sur-Vie, Fr., K 5
.....	Saint Gilles-Waes, Belgium, K 10
6178	Saint Girons, France, Q 12
.....	Saint Goar, Ger., L 4
550	Saint Grégoire, Que., M 18
907	Saint Guillaume, Que., O 17
.....	Saint Helens, Eng., D 14
106793	Saint Helens, Eng., G 12
773	Saint Hilaire, Fr., P 14
.....	Saint Hilaire, N. B., D 2
701	Saint Hilaire, Que., P 17
.....	Saint Hilaire Church, New Brunswick, C 2
907	Saint Hippolyte, Fr., J 23
3221	Saint Hubert, Bel., P 17
452	Saint Hugues, Que., O 17
17798	Saint Hyacinthe, Que., F 17
7011	Saint Imier, Switz., F 6
21978	Saint Ingbert, Ger., G 23
250	Saint Irenée, Que., H 24
326	Saint Isidore, N. B., C 11
474	Saint Isidore, Que., L 22
.....	Saint Isidore, Quebec, Q 15
425	Saint Isidore de Prescott, Ont., D 24
2664	Saint Ives, England, J 19
6687	Saint Ives, England, O 3
.....	Saint Jacob, Switz., C 10
.....	Saint Jacobi, Neth., C 18
514	Saint Jacobs, Ont., L 28
550	Saint Jacques, N. B., C 3
1634	Saint Jacques, Que., O 15
.....	Saint Jean Chrysostome Levis, Quebec, L 22
6745	Saint Jeand' Angely, Fr., L 9

Pop.	Place Country Index
1266	Saint Jean de Losne, Fr., J19
4146	Saint Jean de Maurienne, France, M 23
4710	Saint Jean-de-Monts, Fr., K 5
525	Saint Jean d'Orleans, Que., K 22
1143	Saint Jean Pied de Port, France, P 7
995	Saint Jean Port Joli, Quebec, J 24
11286	Saint Jerome, Quebec, O 14
51741	Saint John, N. B., K 8
10000	Saint Johns, Antigua, Le. Is., K 23
44000	Saint John's, Newf., K 25
11256	Saint Johns, Quebec, Q 16
.....	Saint Johnstown, Ire., C 15
268	Saint Joseph, Algeria, B 21
.....	Saint Joseph, Dominica, D23
206	Saint Joseph, N. B., I 12
1024	Saint Joseph, Quebec, M 22
2028	Saint Joseph, Trinidad, R 24
6449	Saint Joseph d'Alma, Quebec, E 20
.....	Saint Joseph du Moine, N. S., G 21
1059	Saint Jovite, Quebec, N 13
612	Saint Jude, Quebec, O 17
804	Saint Julien, France, L 22
525	Saint Julien L'Ars, Fr., K 10
10123	Saint Junien, Fr., L 12
4356	Saint Just, Eng., O 2
650	Saint Justin, Que., M 16
22	Saint Kilda, Alberta, Q 23
.....	Saint Kol. Bialowiéza, W. Sov. Un., D 17
6320	Saint Lambert, Quebec, P 16
3200	Saint Laurent, Belgium, K 8
1921	Saint Laurent, Fr. Gu., B10
279	Saint Laurent, Man., P 16
.....	Saint Lawrence, Austl., H 22
1577	Saint Leger, Bel., R 18
859	Saint Leonard, Switz., N 8
5990	Saint Léonard-de-Noblat, Fr., L 13
610	Saint Leonard Jc., Que., N18
.....	Saint Leonardo, Sp., F 13
.....	Saint Leonards, Eng., N 22
862	Saint Leonards Station, N. B., D 4
1342	Saint Lin, Quebec, O 15
20	Saint Lin Jc., Que., P 15
497	Saint Lizier, Fr., Q 11
10985	Saint Lô, France, G 8
30817	Saint Louis, Fr. W. Afr., H1
7829	Saint Louis, (Marie Galante), Guadeloupe, C 23
209	Saint Louis, P. E. I., E 13
135	Saint Louis, Sask., L 8
588	Saint Loup, France, K 9
2920	Saint Loup-sur-Semouse, France, I 22
5518	Saint Maixent, Fr., K 8
490	Saint Malachie, Que., M 23
12864	Saint Malo, France, H 5
222	Saint Malo, Quebec, Q 21
21257	Saint Mandé, France, B 7
12000	Saint Marc, Haiti, I 12
3764	Saint Marcellin, Fr., M 21
.....	Saint Margaret's Hope, Scotland, B 20
171	Saint Maria, Switz., K 16
9469	Saint Marie-aux-Mines, Fr., H 23
.....	Saint Marks, U. S. Afr., N 17
.....	Saint Martin, Man., N 14
91	Saint Martin, Switz., J 18
1368	Saint Martin de Re, Fr., L 7
375	Saint Martine, Que., Q 15
87	Saint Martine Jc., Que., P 15
610	Saint Martins N. B., K 10
.....	Saint Mary, Eng., N 9
1311	Saint Mary, Quebec, M 22
.....	Saint Mary Cray, Eng., D 2
3635	Saint Marys, Ont., M 6
.....	Saint Mary's, Scot., B 20
1100	Saint Mary's, Tasmania, C 9
2571	Saint Maurice, Switz., N 6
57164	Saint Maur-les Fosses, France, B 8
.....	Saint Mawes, Eng., O 4
2601	Saint Meen, France, I 5
900	Saint Michel des Saints, Quebec, L 14
4581	Saint Mihiel, France, H 21
3823	Saint Moritz, Switz., L 22
43281	Saint Nazaire, France, J 4
4314	Saint Neots, England, J 19
41527	Saint Nicolas, Belgium, K 11
8552	Saint Nicolas, Bel., N 17
774	Saint Nicolas de Rédon, France, I 5
5342	Saint Nicolas du Port, France, H 22
1201	Saint Niklaus, Switz., N 11
400	Saint Norbert, Quebec, N 16
17815	Saint Omer, France, E 13
250	Saint Onesime, Quebec, I 25
51106	Saint Ouen-sur-Seine, France, A 5
600	Saint Ours, Quebec, O 17
1254	Saint Pacome, Que., I 25
1373	Saint Palais, France, P 7
950	Saint Pamphile, Que., K 25
918	Saint Pardoux la Rivière, France, M 11
1265	Saint Pascal, Quebec, I 25
.....	Saint Patrickswell, Ire., M 9
1018	Saint Paul, Alta., J 22
1989	Saint Paul de Fenouillet, Fr., Q 14
752	Saint Paulin, Que., M 17
.....	Saint Paul Junction, Alta., K 21
.....	Saint Paul of Chester, Que., N 20
641	Saint Paul's, N. B., G 11
1049	Saint Pé, France, P 9
2595	Saint Péray, France, N 19
1032	Saint Peters, N. S., J 22
	Saint Petersburg, see Leningrad, Sov. Un.
.....	Saint Peters Jc., N. S., J 21
700	Saint Philippe de Néri, Quebec, I 25
1009	Saint Pie, Quebec, P 17
599	Saint Pierre, Bel., Q 17
11947	Saint Pierre, France, L 6
3090	Saint Pierre, Martinique, M 24
311	Saint Pierre, Quebec, K 23
.....	Saint Pierre, Switz., P 7
982	Saint Pierre Eglise, Fr., F 7
2206	Saint Pierre-le-Montier, France, K 15
12422	Saint Pol, France, E 14
3137	Saint Pons, France, P 15
1344	Saint Prex, Switz., L 3
441	Saint Prime, Quebec, E 18
425	Saint Prosper, Que., L 18

Pop.	Place Country Index
49448	Saint Quentin, France, F 15
922	Saint Quentin, N. B., C 5
2157	Saint Raymond, Que., K 20
1431	Saint Remi, Que., Q 15
354	Saint Remi d'Amherst, Quebec, N 12
429	Saint Remy, France, D 1
.....	Saint Roch des Aulnaies Quebec, J 24
275	Saint Rosalie, Que., P 17
1450	Saint Sauveur, Bel., M 7
528	Saint Savin, France, M 9
779	Saint Sebastien de Beauce, Quebec, O 22
475	Saint Seine, France, J 19
739	Saint Sermin, France, O 15
12693	Saint Servan, France, H 5
1400	Saint Sever, France, H 7
2166	Saint Sever, France, O 8
858	Saint Simeon, Quebec, H 25
3306	Saint Stephen, N. B., L 5
1056	Saint Sulpice, Switz., H 4
952	Saint Symphorien, Fr., N 8
.....	Saint Theophile, Que., O 23
17132	Saint Thomas, Ont., O 6
.....	Saint Thomas Mt. India, N 13
2385	Saint Tite, Quebec, L 18
700	Saint Tite des Caps, Que., J 22
16494	Saint Trond, Bel., M 16
4324	Saint Tropez, France, P 23
344	Saint Ubalde, Que., L 19
.....	Saint Urbain, Quebec, I 23
207	Saint Urban, Switz., F 11
1144	Saint Ursanne, Switz., E 7
2608	Saint Valery en-Caux, France, F 10
3071	Saint Valery-sur-Somme, France, F 12
3967	Saint Vallier, France, M 20
587	Saint Vaury, France, L 13
.....	Saint Veit, Aus., I 6
.....	Saint Vigeans, Scot., K 22
880	Saint Vincent de Tyrosse, France, P 6
2459	Saint Vith, Belgium, O 20
79	Saint Vivien, France, M 7
447	Saint Walburg, Sask., K 5
297	Saint Wenceslas, Que., N 19
8706	Saint Wendel, Ger., M 2
365	Saint Williams, Ont., O 9
7307	Saint Yrieix-la-Perche, France, M 12
.....	Saint Zenon, Que., L 15
7900	Saipur, India, H 15
2022	Saipurú, Bolivia, K 14
.....	Sairus su, Mon., J 16
227	Sajama, Bolivia, J 3
.....	Saka, Egypt, D 11
1400	Sakai, Japan, J 15
182147	Sakai, Japan, M 13
22000	Sakata, Japan, F 22
5272	Sakawa, Japan, N 8
.....	Sakhir, Afg., I 17
.....	Sakib, Transjordan, K 15
.....	Sakiet Mikki, Egypt, I 13
.....	Sakinohama, Japan, O 10
22300	Sakti, India, I 16
5600	Sakura, Japan, M 21
1700	Sakurai, Japan, M 4
8022	Sala, Sweden, M 15
1112	Saladas, Argentina, I 19
35951	Saladillo, Argentina, O 18
.....	Salado, Argentina, I 8
41	Salado, Chile, H 3
.....	Salakia, Tunisia, D 25
13548	Salamá, Guat., F 5
2819	Salamanca, Chile, L 4
11985	Salamanca, Guan., M 12
1092	Salamanca, Peru, O 15
71872	Salamanca, Spain, H 9
270	Salamaua, N. Gui. Ter., J 11
.....	Salami, Iran, H 14
.....	Salâmib, Egypt, B 13
6183	Salamina, Col., H 8
7757	Salamis, Grc., P 18
.....	Salangen, Norway, C 15
840	Salás, Peru, G 3
810	Salás, Spain, E 19
.....	Salatu, China, B 10
3403	Salaverry, Peru, I 5
326	Salavina, Argentina, J 13
3017	Salazar, Col., F 14
3467	Salbris, France, J 13
348	Salcabamba, Peru, L 12
2383	Salcombe, Eng., O 8
.....	Saldaña, Spain, E 11
3693	Saldus, Sov. Un., H 2
4262	Sale, Australia, Q 20
44350	Salé, Mor., F 5
1000	Sale Khard (Obdorsk), Sov. Un. Asia, E 11
129702	Salem, India, O 11
270	Salem, Ontario, K 9
10648	Salemi, Italy, N 12
.....	Salena, Nepal, E 15
1560	Salernes, France, P 22
34125	Salerno, Italy, J 15
2092	Salgar, Col., H 7
15213	Salgótarján, Hung., Q 22
.....	Salgueiro, Brazil, H 22
.....	Salian, Iran, G 6
5193	Salies, France, P 7
.....	Salihiye, Egypt, E 20
9127	Salihli, Tur., F 2
423	Salim, Palestine, K 11
.....	Salimkasr, Iran, J 13
5393	Salina Cruz, Oax., N 11
4629	Salinas, Bol., K 5
685	Salinas, Bolivia, N 11
.....	Salinas, Brazil, E 15
.....	Salinas, Brazil, K 19
6589	Salinas, Ecuador, B 6
3847	Salinas, S. L. P., J 11
.....	Salinas, Peru, K 7
.....	Salinas de Anána, Sp., D 12
6962	Salinas de Yocalla, Bol., K 8
342	Salinita, Chile, G 4
4721	Salins, France, J 21
26456	Salisbury, England, M 14
321	Salisbury, N. B., I 11
32974	Salisbury, S. Rh., O 18
397	Salitral, Peru, F 3
1300	Salladillo, Arg., M 14
563	Salles-Curan, France, O 15
.....	Sallins, Ire., J 20
.....	Salliquelo, Arg., P 14
.....	Salmant, Egypt, G 15
.....	Salmat, Afg., H 17
14206	Salmi, Fin., F 8
300	Salmo, B. C., Q 18
836	Salmon Arm., B. C., O 16
265	Salmon River, N. S., P 8
1900	Salo, Fin., F 3
4340	Salo, Italy, D 7
.....	Salobra, Brazil, M 8
13193	Salon-de-Provence, France, P 20
	Salonika, see Thessalonikē, Grc.
15488	Salonta, Rom., I 15
35357	Salta, Arg., G 10
3603	Saltash, England, O 7
457	Saltcoats, Sask., O 11
10173	Saltcoats, Scot., O 13
.....	Saltdal, Norway, E 13
218	Saltford, Ontario, K 5
.....	Salt Hill, Ire., J 8
49658	Saltillo, Coa., F 12
.....	Saltness, Scot., C 19
26787	Salto, Arg., N 17
518	Salto, Chia., L 16
4600	Salto, Uruguay, H 16
.....	Saltrou, Haiti, J 13
3225	Saltsjöbad, Sweden, Q 23
417	Salt Springs, N. S., J 17
1759	Saltum, Denmark, C 9
.....	Salumbar, India, H 7
9786	Saluzzo, Italy, E 2
293278	Salvador, (Baia), Braz., J 22
141	Salvador, Sask., M 4
1021	Salvan, Switz., O 6
4473	Salvaterra de Magos, Portugal, K 5
8341	Salvatierra, Guan., M 13
1511	Salvatierra, Spain, D 14
9871	Salvatierra, Spain, E 6
63231	Salzburg, Aus., H 5
16000	Salzwedel, Germany, F 9
4329	Samaca, Col., H 12
1761	Samaden, Switz., K 22
.....	Samadun, Egypt, G 11
5064	Samaipata, Bolivia, J 12
.....	Samanco, Peru, J 5
3195	Samaniego, Col., L 4
.....	Samara, Iraq, L 20
	Samara, see Kuibyshev, Sov. Un.
11800	Samarinda, Neth. Ind., H 5
134346	Samarkand, Sov. Un. Asia, J 10
.....	Samata, Egypt, N 23
.....	Samava, Iraq, P 21
12900	Sambalpur, India, I 17
10900	Sambhar, India, F 8
22111	Sambor, W. Sov. Un., G 16
.....	Sambro, N. S., O 15
2131	Samer, France, E 12
.....	Samhopa, China, K 17
2644	Samhûd, Egypt, O 21
.....	Sami, Baluchistan, Q 18
.....	Samma, Transjordan, I 15
20000	Samnan, Iran, F 8
386	Samnaun, Switz., H 25
10260	Samokov, Bulgaria, L 17
.....	Sampacho, Arg., M 12
3677	Sampués, Col., D 9
.....	Samrah, Palestine, H 13
3500	Samre, I. E. A., D 9
7400	Samshui, China, L 14
36917	Samsun, Tur., B 11
.....	Samua, Transjordan, I 14
.....	Samuda Songrâm, Siam, P 3
.....	Samuhi, Arg., I 17
1589	Saña, Peru, H 3
20000	Sana, Yem., N 4
.....	Sanabu, Egypt, L 17
180	San Agustin, Arg., L 12
.....	San Agustin, Arg., Q 19
468	San Agustin, Bol. M 5
1538	San Agustin, Col., L 8
1746	San Andrés, Chih., H 18
1959	San Andres, Col., D 9
2262	San Andres, Col., G 14
10154	San Andrés Tuxtla, Ver., J 12
.....	San Andros, Col., D 9
.....	San Antonio, Arg., A 23
405	San Antonio, Arg., I 20
.....	San Antonio, Arg., J 11
3033	San Antonio, Arg., N 18
55	San Antonio, Baja Cal., Q 12
.....	San Antonio, Brazil, E 11
.....	San Antonio, Camp., J 21
	San Antonio, see Cuauhtemoc, Chih.
175	San Antonio, Chile, I 4
11859	San Antonio, Chile, M 3
2117	San Antonio, Col., B 14
3167	San Antonio, Costa Rica, N 14
.....	San Antonio, Par., D 3
1696	San Antonio, S. L. P., K 17
3960	San Antonio, Ur., H 16
2919	San Antonio, Ur., O 19
1536	San Antonio, Ven., C 13
3218	San Antonio, Ven., H 6
5377	San Antonio-Abad, Spain, K 19
.....	San Antonio del Aiquã, Uruguay, N 22
.....	San Antonio del Curaray, Ecuador, C 8
196	San Antonio de Lipez, Bolivia, N 3
14456	San Antonio de los Banos, Cuba, H 6
.....	San Antonio de los Cobres, Argentina, F 9
.....	San Antonio del Sur, Cuba, O 24
290	San Antonio de Obligado, Argentina, I 18
6552	Sanarate, Guat., F 5
1895	Sanare, Ven., D 9
819	San Bartolo, Dur., O 23
311	San Bartolo, Hid., F 6
161	San Bartolo, S. L. P., J 15
3414	San Bartolomé, Chia., N 16
.....	San Bartolomé, Peru, L 8
.....	San Bartolo Naucalpan, Mex., M 1
4051	San Bautista, Ur., O 19
6103	San Benito, Bolivia, I 8
1134	San Benito, Col., E 10
497	San Benito, Sin., M 16
245	San Benito, Chia., Q 17
20673	San Bernardo, Chile, M 4
918	San Bernardo, Dur., L 19
1801	San Blas, Sin., L 14
1380	San Blas, Nay., K 2
375	San Borja, Bol., G 5
750	San Buenaventura, Bol., F 4
2890	San Buenaventura, Chih., E 16
3038	San Buenaventura, Coa. D 11
1983	San Buono, Italy, I 15
256	San Carlos, Arg., G 9
.....	San Carlos, Arg., M 6
2682	San Carlos, Bolivia, I 12
495	San Carlos, Chih., G 22
9411	San Carlos Chile, O 3
1410	San Carlos, Coa., A 12
1495	San Carlos, Col., E 8
1441	San Carlos, Nic., L 13
.....	San Carlos, Pan., P 21
309	San Carlos, Peru, G 6
1028	San Carlos, Tam., G 17
10700	San Carlos, Ur., P 21
.....	San Carlos, Ven., B 6
3650	San Carlos, Ven., D 10
.....	San Carlos, Ven., Q 13
7176	San Carlos de la Rapita, Spain, H 18
240	San Carlos Minas, Argentina, K 11
.....	San Cayetano, Cuba, I 3
2337	Sancerre, France, J 15
.....	Sancha, China, F 9
33	Sanchez, Chih., I 16
3592	Sanchez, Dom. Rep., I 15
.....	Sanchor, India, G 5
.....	Sanchursk, Sov. Un., H 17
1749	San Clemente, Chile, O 4
635	San Cosme, Argentina, I 19
2000	San Cosme, Par., R 8
955	San Cristobal, Arg., K 16
1386	San Cristobal, Bol., M 6
1873	San Cristobal, Cuba, I 5
.....	San Cristobal, Hond., F 13
31447	San Cristóbal, Ven., H 5
11768	San Cristobal Las Casas, Chia., M 16
14164	Sancti Spiritus, Cuba, K 13
.....	Sand, Iran, N 6
.....	Sand, Norway, M 4
.....	Sandager, Denmark, L 10
.....	Sandahur, Egypt, G 16
13826	Sandakan, B. N. B., G 5
.....	Sandawa, Egypt, H 14
284	Sandby, Denmark, N 16
.....	Sande, Norway, C 2
5921	Sandefjord, Nor., N 8
314	Sandfield, Ont., C 5
.....	Sandfjord, Nor., A 22
18327	Sandgate, Austl., K 24
.....	Sandhead Inn, Scot., R 12
.....	Sandhorn, Nor., E 12
1482	Sandia, Peru, N 19
.....	San Diego, Arg., J 19
343	San Diego, Bol., M 12
1090	San Diego, Ven., C 11
2897	San Diego, Ven., G 16
1603	San Diego de la Unión, Guan., L 13
.....	San Diego del Valle, Cuba I 12
16800	Sandila, India, F 13
2967	Sandnes, Norway, N 3
.....	Sandness, Shetland Is., B 2
.....	Sandoa, Bel Cong., M 15
.....	Sandomierz, Poland, F 15
.....	Sandominic, Rom., I 20
94	Sandon, B. C., P 18
5535	San Dona, Italy, D 11
.....	San Donnino, Italy, E 6
3000	Sandoway, Bur., O 21
6167	Sandown, England, O 16
178	Sand Point, Ontario, D 20
148	Sandstone, Austl., K 6
.....	Sandträsk, Sweden, F 18
.....	Sandur, India, M 9
.....	Sandviken, Nor., A 4
10715	Sandwich, Ont., Q 1
.....	Sandwick, Scot., E 7
.....	Sandwick, Shetland Is., A 3
.....	Sandwick, Shetland Is., D 3
.....	Sandy Cove, N.S., N 8
7036	Sandykly, Tur., F 4
532	Sandy Point, N. S., Q 10
.....	San Enrique Arg., O 17
15000	San Estanislao, Par., M 9
554	San Esteban, British Honduras, A 8
325	San Esteban, Hond., F 12
	San Eugenio, see Artigas, Uruguay.
4406	San Felio de Llobregat, Spain, G 20
.....	San Felipe, Baja Cal., C 5
15	San Felipe, Camp., K 21
13168	San Felipe, Chile, M 4
2086	San Felipe, Cuba, I 7
.....	San Felipe, Hond., G 13
11067	San Felipe, Ven., C 10
7583	San Feliu de Guixols, Sp., F 21
876	San Felix, Panama, Q 18
979	San Felix, Ven., G 20
48817	San Fernando, Arg., N 18
1200	San Fernando, Baja Cal., E 4
2838	San Fernando, Chia., M 15
14419	San Fernando, Chile, N 4
2686	San Fernando, Col., D 11
1634	San Fernando, Cuba, J 11
.....	San Fernando, Cuba, J 15
26953	San Fernando, Spain, P 8
1472	San Fernando, Tam., G 19
18621	San Fernando, Trinidad, R 24
8751	San Fernando de Apure, Ven., G 12
809	San Fernando de Atobapo, Ven., M 12
30000	San Francisco, Arg., L 15
1598	San Francisco, Arg., M 10
.....	San Francisco, Chih., H 16
459	San Francisco, Col., L 7
706	San Francisco, Panama, Q 19
19	San Francisco, Son., D 8
1142	San Francisco, Zac., J 9
.....	San Francisco Botes, Q. R., K 23
.....	San Francisco de Cara, Ven., D 13
12015	San Francisco del Rincón, Guan., L 10
10397	San Francisco de Macoris, Dom. Rep., I 15
4273	San Francisco de Tiznados, Ven., E 12
9093	San Fratello, Italy, N 15
	San Fructuoso, see Tacuarembo, Uruguay.
.....	Sanga, Sweden, Q 20
.....	Sangabad, Iran, N 14
7847	San Gabriel, Ecuador, A 6
.....	Sangachal, Sov. Un., Q 21
3725	San Gavino, Italy, L 3
11937	Sangerhausen, Ger., I 9
.....	Sang-gird, Iran, F 13
.....	Sanghast, Iran, F 14
.....	Sanghos, Iran, E 12
7811	San Gil, Col., G 13
.....	San Gines de la Jara, Spain, N 16
.....	Sangir, Iran, E 9
23496	Sangjin, Kor., C 25
.....	Sanglech, Afg., E 24
29818	Sangli, India, L 7
.....	Sang Nishanda, Afg., H 21
.....	Sangod, India, G 9
738	San Gregorio, Arg., N 15
6004	San Gregorio, Ur., J 20
.....	Sangrelaya, Hond., D 13
3608	Sangüesa, Spain, E 16
.....	San Guillermo, Arg., K 15
1313	Sanguinetto, Italy, D 9
.....	San Gustavo, Arg., K 18
5000	Sanhat, India, H 16
.....	Sanhur, Egypt, D 8
.....	San Ignacio, Arg., P 19
2265	San Ignacio, Bolivia, F 9
777	San Ignacio, Bolivia, H 17
3464	San Ignacio, Bolivia, I 12
1131	San Ignacio, Chih., C 18
9331	San Ignacio, Par., Q 7
1635	San Ignacio, Sin., P 18
38595	San Isidro, Arg., N 19
.....	San Isidro, S. L. P., H 13
.....	San Jacinto, Arg., P 17
7005	San Jacinto, Col., D 10
4646	San Jacinto, Uruguay, O 19
955	San Javier, Arg., K 17
383	San Javier, Bolivia, F 10
2435	San Javier, Bolivia, H 15
5183	San Javier, Chile, O 3
3366	San Jeronimo de Juárez, Guer., Q 13
13115	Sanji, Japan, L 20
9000	Sanjo, Japan, H 20
656	San Joaquin, Bolivia, E 11
5000	San Joaquin, Paraguay, N 9
1815	San Joaquin, Ven., D 12
1895	San Jorge, Nicaragua, L 12
3000	San José, Argentina, H 9
.....	San José, Arg., K 11
.....	San José, Bolivia, D 8
3514	San José, Bolivia, I 17
300	San José, Chih., D 18
.....	San José, Colombia, K 4
.....	San José, Colombia, K 23
4873	San José, Colombia, L 3
74872	San José, Costa Rica, N 14
7947	San José, Cuba, H 7
1356	San José, Cuba, I 10
2644	San José, Guatemala, H 4
1392	San José, Honduras, F 7
.....	San Jóse, Méx., G 3
6500	San José, Par., O 8
30000	San José, Uruguay, O 18
.....	San José, Ven., K 19
965	San José de Gracia, Sin., L 16
94	San José de las Rusias, Tam., I 19
2638	San José del Cabo, Baja Cal., R 13
1516	San José de Mariquina, Chile, R 3
.....	San José de Sisa, Peru, H 8
1986	San José de Tiznados, Venezuela, E 12
1006	San José de Uchupiamonas, Bolivia, F 4
.....	San Juan, Arg., I 18
35236	San Juan, Arg., L 7
.....	San Juan, Bolivia, J 19
2222	San Juan, Bolivia, M 10
.....	San Juan, Chile, G 4
1400	San Juan, Coa., C 6
13099	San Juan, Col., D 10
12000	San Juan, Bautista Misiones, Paraguay, Q 6
700	San Juan de Allende, Coa., B 13
2235	San Juan de Cesar, Colombia, C 14
191	San Juan de Dios, Guatemala, C 5
2767	San Juan de Guadalupe, Dur., O 24
2137	San Juan de la Vega, Guan., M 13
3814	San Juan del Mezquital, Zac., H 7
571	San Juan del Norte, Nicaragua, L 15
5792	San Juan de los Lagos, Jal., L 9
.....	San Juan de los Morris, Venez., D 12
2427	San Juan del Pirai, Bolivia, L 12
535	San Juan del Potrero, Bolivia, J 11
1966	San Juan del Rio, Dur., N 22
6694	San Juan del Rio, Quer., M 15
1261	San Juan del Sur, Nicaragua, L 12
803	San Juan de Sabinas, Coa., C 12
2310	San Juan Evangelista, Ver., K 12
2400	San Juanico, Baja Cal., L 10
2562	San Juan Ixcoy, Guat., E 3
821	San Justo, Arg., K 17
.....	Sankaridrug, India, O 11
.....	Sankt Goar, Ger., L 4
.....	Sankt Ingbert, Ger., N 3
.....	Sankt Johann, Ger., N 2
36247	Sankt Pölten, Aus. H 8
7306	Sankt Veit, Ger., T 13
.....	Sankt Wendel, Ger., N 3
.....	San Leandro, Cuba, O 21
325	San Leo, Italy, F 10
.....	San Lorenzo, Bolivia, C 6
.....	San Lorenzo, Bol., E 9
1128	San Lorenzo, Bolivia, M 11
17	San Lorenzo, Camp., J 17
163	San Lorenzo, Chile, K 4
.....	San Lorenzo, Italy, B 23
5500	San Lorenzo, Par., Q 11
32848	Sanlúcar de Barrameda, Spain, O 8
820	Sanlúcar de Guadiana, Spain, N 7
10555	San Lucas, Bolivia, L 10
82	San Lucas, Dur., R 22
.....	San Luis, Arg., E 13
1200	San Luis, Arg., I 19
28741	San Luis, Arg., M 10
1845	San Luis, Col., H 9
7389	San Luis, Cuba, J 3
10819	San Luis, Cuba, O 21
.....	San Luis, Guat., G 2
4574	San Luis, Ven., B 9
1702	San Luis Canete, Peru, M 9
5562	San Luis de la Paz, Guan., L 13
1177	San Luis del Cordero, Dur., M 22
872	San Luis de Lozada, Nay., K 4
.....	San Luis de Shuaro, Peru. K 11
77161	San Luis Potosi, S.L.P., K 12
4557	Sanluri, Italy, L 4
219	San Marcial, Son., H 12
170	San Marcos, Chile, K 3
653	San Marcos, Coa., F 8
6029	San Marcos, Guat., F 2
2855	San Marcos, Guer., R 16
344	San Marcos, Pueb., H 7
2000	San Marino, San Marino, F 11
.....	San Martin, Arg., B 21
.....	San Martin, Arg., J 10
.....	San Martin, Arg., J 21
85000	San Martin, Arg., M 7
600	San Martin, Arg., M 10
.....	San Martin, Arg., R 5
.....	San Martin, Chile, D 6
1634	San Martin, Col., E 12
1276	San Martin, Col., J 12
4185	San Martin, Jal., M 5
2313	San Martin, S. L. P., L 18
4426	San Martín-de-Val de Iglesias, Spain, I 11
1243	San Mateo, Peru, L 9
3638	San Mateo, Spain, H 17
2071	San Mateo, Ven., C 12
1204	San Mateo, Ven., D 17
5376	San Mateolxtatan, Guat., D 3
189	San Matias, Bol., H 22
.....	San Matias, Cuba, H 7
777	San Michele, Italy, C 8
284	San Miguel, Arg., I 20
.....	San Miguel, Bol., C 3
2479	San Miguel, Bol., H 17
4586	San Miguel, Cuba, H 7
.....	San Miguel, Cuba, L 18
8215	San Miguel. Ecuador, C 4
8085	San Miguel, Ecuador, C 5
9030	San Miguel, Guan., L 13
3264	San Miguel, Guat., F 4
4495	San Miguel, Jal., L 9
5000	San Miguel, Paraguay, P 7
706	San Miguel, Peru, M 13
18930	San Miguel, Salvador, H 8
.....	San Miguel Cozumel, Q. R., F 25
114	San Miguel de Hauchi, Bolivia, G 6
4096	San Miguel del Mezquital, Zac., H 7
2976	San Miguel el Grande, Oax., L 7
550	San Miguelito, Nicaragua, L 13
5000	San Nepomuceno, Par., P 8
309	San Nicolao, Cor., P 4
50493	San Nicolas, Arg., M 17
3254	San Nicolas, Cuba, I 7
3600	Sannohe, Japan, C 24
11757	Sannois, France, A 4
.....	Sannox, Scot., N 11
14262	Sanok, Poland, G 15
2937	San Onofre, Col., D 9
.....	San Onofrio, Italy, A 20
.....	San Pablo, Arg., H 10
.....	San Pablo, Bolivia, C 7
205	San Pablo, Bolivia, M 7
1349	San Pablo, Col., M 4
5533	San Pablo, Méx., G 3
810	San Pablo Balleza, Chih., K 18
.....	San Paolo, Italy, C 21
539	San Pedro, Arg., I 11
40415	San Pedro, Arg., M 18
.....	San Pedro, Bolivia, C 4
.....	San Pedro, Bolivia, F 10
.....	San Pedro, Bol., J 8
.....	San Pedro, Br. Hond., A 8
24	San Pedro, Camp., I 16
100	San Pedro, Chih., D 16
57	San Pedro, Chile, D 6
648	San Pedro, Chile, G 4
92	San Pedro, Chile, H 4
	San Pedro, see Villa Francisco Madera, Coa.
.....	San Pedro, Col., J 7
833	San Pedro, Dur., L 19
20392	San Pedro, Honduras, E 8
.....	San Pedro, Honduras, H 10
.....	San Pedro, Jal., M 7
.....	San Pedro, N. L., F 14
.....	San Pedro. Peru, C 10
.....	San Pedro, Peru, H 6
300	San Pedro, Sin., O 16
300	San Pedro Atacama, Chile, E 6
.....	San Pedro de Jujuy, Argentina, F 11
886	San Pedro del Gallo, Dur., M 22
5286	San Pedro de Lloc, Peru, H 4
20000	San Pedro del Paraná, Paraguay, Q 9
19147	San Pedro de Macoris, Dom. Rep., J 16
3259	San Pedro de Pinatar, Spain, M 16
.....	San Pedro do Sul, Portugal, H 6
816	San Pedro el Alto, Oax., N 9
456	San Pedro Ocampo, Zac., G 11
1684	San Pelayo, Col., D 8
.....	San Pietro, Italy, D 14
3346	Sanquhar, Scotland, P 16
223	San Quintin, Baja Cal., D 3
47153	San Rafael, Arg., N 7
1455	San Rafael, Bolivia, I 18
.....	San Rafael, Par., N 8
.....	San Rafael, Ven., K 19
1737	San Rafael del Sur, Nic., K 10
1770	San Rafael de Mojan, Venezuela, B 5
.....	San Ramón, Arg., I 12
612	San Ramón, Bol., F 6
1275	San Ramón, Peru, K 11
6000	San Ramón, Ur., N 19
19456	San Remo, Italy, F 2
.....	San Roque, Bolivia, B 6
12371	San Roque, Spain, N 24
3315	San Rosenda, Chile, P 3
223	San Salvador, Arg., L 19
.....	San Salvador, Par., J 7
103920	San Salvador, Salvador, H 6
103979	San Sebastian, Spain, C 15
.....	San Sebastiano, Italy, C 23
.....	San Sepé, Braz., Q 10
33237	San Severo, Italy, I 17
40000	Sansing, Manch., H 19
.....	Sanskimost, Yugo., J 9
.....	Santa, Egypt, E 13
.....	Santa, Italy, C 13
.....	Santa Agnese, Italy, B 23
280	Santa Ana, Argentina, I 23
1891	Santa Ana, Bol., E 8
124	Santa Ana, Bol., G 5
985	Santa Ana, Bol., H 18
.....	Santa Ana, Bol., J 21
2105	Santa Ana, Bolivia, M 11
6245	Santa Ana, Col., D 11
1439	Santa Ana, Costa Rica, N 14
11470	Santa Ana, Ecuador, C 2
433	Santa Ana, Hond., G 10
3500	Santa Ana, Peru, M 15
46343	Santa Ana, Sal., H 6
266	Santa Ana, S. L. P., K 13
.....	Santa Ana, Ur., F 16
1709	Santa Ana, Ven., B 18
6524	Santa Ana de Calacala, Bolivia, I 7
.....	Santa Barbara, Brazil, M 18
13902	Santa Bárbara, Chih., K 19
3120	Santa Barbara, Col., H 8
.....	Santa Barbara, Cuba, K 5
2762	Santa Barbara, Hond,, F 8
10353	Santa Barbara, Ven., F 5
.....	Santa Barbara, Ven., I 21
1656	Santa Bárbara de Samaná, Dom. Rep., J 15
1033	Santa Catalina, Col., C 9
.....	Santa Catalina, Ur., M 16
140	Santa Catarina, Baja Cal., F 4
1095	Santa Catarina, N. L., F 14
188	Santa Catarina, S. L. P., K 16
517	Santa Clara, Chile, P 3
27925	Santa Clara, Cuba, I 12
.....	Santa Clara, Michoa., N 11
.....	Santa Clara, Par., P 8
.....	Santa Clara, Ur., K 22
4710	Santa Coloma, Spain, F 20
.....	Santa Corazón, Bol., J 21
1200	Santa Cruz, Arg., I 10
32800	Santa Cruz, Bolivia, I 13
.....	Santa Cruz, Brazil, G 24
.....	Santa Cruz, Brazil, K 14
3555	Santa Cruz, Brazil, K 21
9602	Santa Cruz, Brazil, Q 11
72358	Santa Cruz, Canary Is., F 2
2132	Santa Cruz, Chile, N 4
5151	Santa Cruz, Costa Rica, N 12
1767	Santa Cruz, Ven., F 5
	Santa Cruz Chico, see Pedro Antonio Santos, Q. R.
2258	Santa Cruz de Bravo, Q. R., H 24
5947	Santa Cruz de la Zarza, Spain, J 12
6265	Santa Cruz del Norte, Cuba, H 7
2196	Santa Cruz del Sur, Cuba, N 16
8790	Santa Cruz de Mudela, Spain, L 13
1015	Santa Cruz de Valle Ameno, Bolivia, F 3
750	Santa Cruz de Yojoa, Hond., F 8
.....	Santa Elena, Arg., K 18
3082	Santa Elena, Bolivia, L 11
12731	Santa Elena, Ecuador, D 1
6045	Santa Eulalia, Chih., H 19
4777	Santa Eulalia, Spain, K 20
147583	Santa Fé, Argentina, L 16
1101	Santa Fé, Chile, D 4
1092	Santa Fé, Chile, P 3
1693	Santa Fé, Cuba, K 6
.....	Santa Fé, Michoa., N 11
7951	Santa Fe, Spain, N 12
.....	Santa Helena, Brazil, G 1
1967	Santa Inéz Ahuatempan, Pueb., J 7
.....	Santa Isabel, Arg., N 15
703	Santa Isabel, Bolivia, M 8
608	Santa Isabel, Chile, E 4
1464	Santa Isabel, Chih., H 18
8345	Santa Isabel, Sp. Gui., K 10
81	Santa Isabel, Tam., F 18
.....	Santa Justina, Arg., I 14
6721	Santa Librada, Col., K 8
.....	Santa Lucia, Arg., J 17
304	Santa Lucia, Arg., J 19
688	Santa Lucia, Chile, C 4
2239	Santa Lucia, Cuba, M 18
1183	Santa Lucia, Cuba, M 21
88	Santa Lucia, Peru, O 12
1591	Santa Lucrecia, Ver., L 12
1655	Santa Luisa, Chile, G 4
.....	Santa Luzia, Brazil, K 15
.....	Santa Maria, Arg., H 9
1023	Santa Mariá, Brazil, E 4
.....	Santa Maria, Brazil, J 17
.....	Santa Maria, Honduras, E 12
.....	Santa Maria, Par., Q 7
	Santa Maria, see Filomeno Mara, Q. R.
	Santa Maria, see Leona Vicario, Q. R.
171	Santa Maria, Switz., K 25
.....	Santa Maria, Ven., E 6
.....	Santa Maria, Western Brazil, F 15
1206	Santa Maria de Ipire, Ven., F 16
1022	Santa Maria del Oro, Dur., L 20
1432	Santa Maria del Oro, Nay., L 4
1868	Santa Maria de los Angeles, Jal., J 6
2759	Santa Maria del Rio, S.L. P., K 13
.....	Santa Maria de Taguatinga, Brazil, I 16
874	Santa Maria la Real de Nieva, Sp., G 11
1630	Santa Maria Ocotlán, Dur., R 21
.....	Santamarina, Arg., Q 18
25113	Santa Marta, Col., B 12
4421	Santander, Col., K 7
101793	Santander, Spain, C 12
1354	Santander Jiménez, Tam., H 18
.....	Sant'Anna, Brazil, E 7
27048	Sant'Anna do Livramento, Brazil, Q 9
.....	Sant'Anna do Paranahyba, Brazil, M 12
.....	Sant'Anna dos Brejos, Brazil, J 18
.....	Sant'Anna dos Ferros, Brazil, L 18
3429	Santa Olalla del Cala, Sp., M 9
.....	Santa Philomena, Brazil, H 16
7666	Santarem, Brazil, E 10
.....	Santarém, Brazil, J 21
12106	Santarem, Portugal, J 5
15502	Santa Rita do Rio Pretto, Brazil, I 17
868	Santa Rosa, Arg., L 11
915	Santa Rosa, Arg., L 13
.....	Santa Rosa, Bolivia, B 5
2676	Santa Rosa, Bolivia, I 12
.....	Santa Rosa, Br. Gu., A 6
385	Santa Rosa, Chile, C 3
5502	Santa Rosa, Col., J 10
1248	Santa Rosa, Col., L 7
7184	Santa Rosa, Ecuador, C 9
3738	Santa Rosa, Guat., G 5
6018	Santa Rosa, Hond., F 7
6500	Santa Rosa, Par., Q 8
.....	Santa Rosa, Peru, N 18
5414	Santa Rosa, Ur., E 16
4881	Santa Rosa, Ur., O 19
1578	Santa Rosa, Ven., E 17
21018	Santa Rosa de Cabal, Colombia, I 8
2196	Santa Rosa de Cueva, Bolivia, L 13
5500	Santa Rosa de Toay, Argentina, P 12
6175	Santa Rosalia, Baja Cal., J 9
	Santa Rosalia, see Ciudad Camargo, Chih.
.....	Santa Rosalia, Ven., G 8
23755	Santa Tecla, Salvador, H 6
404	Santa Teresa, Arg., M 16
.....	Santa Teresa, Nay., J 4
2787	Santa Teresa, Ven., D 13
1567	Santa Teresa di Galiura, Italy, J 4
.....	Santa Thereza, Brazil, M 20
.....	Santa Ursula, Mex., R 2
.....	Santa Victoria, Arg., M 13
5788	Santa Victoria do Palmat, Brazil, R 10
401	San Telmo, Baja Cal., C 2
3585	Santhia, Italy, D 3
1668	Santhoven, Belgium, Q 10
64414	Santiago, Argentina, I 12
688	Santiago, Baja Cal., J 8

Pop. Place Country Index

1525 Santiago, Bolivia, J 20
993207 Santiago, Chile, M 4
52943 Santiago, Dominican Republic, I 14
..... Santiago, Hond., E 8
4253 Santiago, Panama, Q 20
7000 Santiago, Par., Q 8
49191 Santiago, Spain, D 6
3915 Santiago de Chuco, Peru, I 6
120577 Santiago de Cuba, Cuba, O 21
8306 Santiago de Haute, Bolivia, H 3
9385 Santiago de la Vegas, Cuba, H 6
3875 Santiago dè Machaca, Bolivia, I 2
7322 Santiago Ixcuintla, Nay., K 2
3036 Santiago Papasquiaro, Dur., N 20
7602 Santibanez, Bolivia, I 7
325 San Tiburcio, Zac., H 11
24992 Santipur, India, H 21
8678 Santisteban del Puerto, Spain, L 13
..... Santo Alto, Chile, K 4
11051 Santo Amaro, Brazil, J 22
7923 Santo Angelo, Brazil, P 10
..... San Antonio, Brazil, E 11
..... Santo Antonio, Brazil, J 3
..... Santo Antonio da Gloria, Brazil, H 22
..... Santo Antonio de Balsas, Brazil, H 16
..... Santo Antonio dos Patos, Brazil, L 16
879 Santo Corazón, Bolivia, J 21
..... Santo Domingo, Arg., P 20
20 Santo Domingo, Baja Cal., M 9
2263 Santo Domingo, Col., G 9
3244 Santo Domingo, Cuba, I 11
Santo Domingo, see Ciudad Trujillo, Dom. Rep.
..... Santo Domingo de la Calzada, Spain, E 13
..... Santo Domingo de los Colorades, Ecuador, B 4
..... Santo Ignacio, Braz., C 4
11136 Santoña, Spain, C 13
127 Santo Tomás, Baja Cal., B 3
159648 Santos, Brazil, N 15
3079 Santo Tomas, Col., C 10
..... Santo Tomas, Guat., E 7
877 Santo Tomas, Peru, N 16
3899 Santo Tomé, Arg., J 22
..... San Toribio, Guat., C 6
9000 Santuao, China, J 19
682 Sanur, Palestine, J 10
1053 San Urbano, Arg., M 15
2682 San Vicente, Arg., N 19
..... San Vicente, Baja Cal., C 2
355 San Vicente, Bolivia, M 8
2602 San Vicente, Col., G 12
5261 San Vicente, Col., I 7
13158 San Vicente, Salvador, H 7
10693 San Vicénte de Alcantara, Spain, J 8
3896 San Vincente de Castillos, Ur., N 23
2202 San Vincénte de la Barquera, Spain, C 11
3915 San Vito, Italy, C 12
..... Sanway, Oceania, H 6
5733 San Zenon, Col., D 11
..... São Benedicto, Brazil, F 20
..... São Bento, Brazil, E 17
..... São Bento, Brazil, O 13
..... São Bento da Amontada, Brazil, E 21
7932 São Bernardo, Brazil, F 19
..... São Bernardo das Russas, Brazil, F 22
8774 São Borja, Brazil, P 8
..... São Braz, Brazil, H 23
..... São Caetano de Olivelas, Brazil, E 15
24763 São Carlos, Brazil, H 2
..... São Carlos do Pinhal, Brazil, M 14
..... São Domingos, Brazil, J 16
..... São Domingos de Boa Vista, Brazil, E 15
..... São Felippe, W. Brazil, H 19
6560 São Felix, Brazil, J 21
..... São Francisco, Brazil, G 19
..... São Francisco, Brazil, K 16
10280 São Francisco, Brazil, O 14
12461 São Gabriel, Brazil, Q 9
8621 São Goncalo, Brazil, G 24
..... São Jeronymo, Brazil, Q 11
..... São João, Brazil, G 14
1999 São João, Portugal, G 7
..... São João Baptista, Brazil, L 18
..... São João de Barra, Brazil, M 19
..... São João de Camaquan, Brazil, Q 11
22912 São João d'el-Rey, Brazil, M 17
..... São João de Paraguassu, Brazil, J 20
..... São João do Piauhy, Brazil, H 19
..... São João do Triumpho, Brazil, O 12
..... São Joaquim da Costa da Serra, Brazil, P 12
..... São Joaquin, W. Brazil, D 25
..... São José, Brazil, G 17
..... São José da Boa Vista, Brazil, N 13
4727 São José do Duro, Brazil, I 16
..... São José do Egypto, Brazil, G 23
..... São José do Mipibú, Brazil, G 25
..... São José do Norte, Brazil, R 11
..... São José dos Mattoes, Brazil, G 18
..... São José do Tocantins, Brazil, J 14
14003 São Leopoldo, Brazil, Q 12
..... São Lourenco, Brazil, K 9
7443 São Lourenco, Brazil, Q 11
59476 São Luiz (Maranhao), Brazil, E 18
..... São Luiz de Caceres, Brazil, K 7
..... São Luiz do Quitunde, Brazil, H 24
6162 São Luiz Gonzaga, Brazil, P 9
..... São Luiz Gonzaga, Brazil, F 17
..... São Maria, W. Braz., I 21
1000 São Martinho, Portugal, J 4
..... São Matheus, Brazil, G 21
..... São Matheus, Brazil, L 20
..... São Miguel, Brazil, G 22
..... São Miguel, Brazil, J 21
..... São Miguel dos Guanhães, Brazil, L 18
1253943 São Paulo, Brazil, N 15
São Paulo de Luanda, see Luanda, Ang.
..... São Paulo de Olivenca, Western Brazil, E 20
..... São Pedro, Brazil, F 5
..... São Pedro, Western Brazil, K 20
..... São Pedro de Uberabinha, Brazil, L 14
..... São Pedro do Turvo, Brazil, N 13
..... São Raymundo Nonato, Brazil, H 19
..... São Thiago de Cacem, Portugal, L 5
..... São Vicente, Brazil, Q 9
..... São Vicente do Araguaya, Brazil, G 15
..... São Vicente Ferrer, Brazil, E 17
3115 Sapiranqui, Bolivia, I 4
1459 Sapiranqui, Bolivia, M 13
6447 Sappemeer, Neth., C 23
..... Sapperton, B. C., O 3
222827 Sapporo, Japan, G 12
6000 Sapucay, Par., O 8
..... Sapushan, China, J 6
..... Saqiet-Musa, Egypt, K 17
Saragossa, see Zaragoza, Sp.
7890 Saraguro, Ecuador, E 4
..... Sarah, Arg., N 13
..... Saraiva, Brazil, F 9
78182 Sarajevo, Yugo., K 11
316 Sarampiuni, Bolivia, G 3
..... Sarandë, Albania, O 13
5600 Sarandi del Yi, Ur., L 20
5000 Sarandi Grande, Ur., M 19
5200 Sarangarh, India, I 16
6300 Sarangpur, India, H 9
12000 Saransk, Sov. Un., J 16
3121 Sarapuhy, Brazil, N 14
..... Sarat, India, J 6
375860 Saratov, Sov. Un., K 17
..... Saravane, Fr. In. Ch., O 8
..... Sarawa, Egypt, H 12
..... Sarayacu, Ecuador, C 7
..... Sarbaz, Iran, Q 16
..... Sarclet, Scotland, D 19
..... Sardahan, Iran, I 7
..... Sardão, Portugal, M 5
..... Sardeh, Iran, J 13
..... Sardinal, Costa Rica, M 12
452 Sardis, B. C., P 5
..... Sardu, Iran, M 12
421 Sargans, Switz., G 19
..... Sarhit, Iran, Q 15
..... Sarhibeh, Transjordan, K 15
10000 Sari, Iran, E 8
..... Sar-i-bagh, Afg., F 22
..... Sarih, Transjordan, I 16
3836 Sariñena, Spain, F 17
1590 Sarishaban, Grc., M 19
..... Sarkun, Iran, R 15
6497 Sarlat, France, N 12
..... Sarmani, Eth., H 13
..... Sarmiento, Arg., K 12
..... Sarna, Sweden, K 11
..... Sar Naran, Iran, O 14
5282 Sarnen, Switz., I 13
18734 Sarnia, Ontario, N 3
1760 Sarnico, Italy, C 5
..... Sarny, W. Sov. Un., E 20
12559 Saronno, Italy, C 5
12401 Sarpsborg, Norway, M 9
3715 Sarralbe, France, G 22
6485 Sarrebourg, France, H 22
Sarrebruck, see Saarbrücken, Ger.
14371 Sarreguemines, Fr., G 22
15167 Sarria, Spain, D 7
531 Sarrola, Cor., Q 2
5097 Sarstedt, Germany, G 7
6445 Sarthe, France, K 2
17354 Sartrouville, France, A 3
..... Saru, Japan, G 13
..... Sarvasiddni, India, L 16
..... Sarymsakly, Tur., F 11
..... Sarywan, Iran, D 12
6642 Sasaima, Col., I 10
23644 Sasaram, India, G 17
5000 Sasayama, Japan, L 12
205989 Sasebo, Japan, M 2
..... Sasi, W. Sov. Un., H 22
900 Sasiki, Japan, P 3
..... Saskolskoe, Sov. Un., M 18
43027 Saskatoon, Sask., M 7
..... Sasovo, Sov. Un., J 14
335 Sassa, Italy, H 12
..... Sassabaneh, I. E. A., K 15
35862 Sassari, Italy, J 3
3982 Sassnitz, Germany, B 12
3904 Sassuolo, Italy, E 8
615 Sastre, Arg., L 15
2934 Sas van Gent, Neth., K 9
2934 Sas van Gent, Neth., Q 9
..... Satalana, India, G 6
..... Satar, India, I 10
26500 Satara, India, I 7
2176 Säter, Sweden, L 14
..... Sätila, Sweden, O 10
18431 Sátoraljaújhely, Hungary H 14
5000 Sattur, India, P 11
51074 Satu-Mare, Rom., H 16
..... Saturna, B. C., Q 3
6935 Sauce, Ur., O 19
140 Sauceda, Coa., F 11
1005 Saucelle, Spain, G 8
2426 Saucillo, Chih., I 20
..... Saudades, Western Brazil, F 16
..... Saude, Norway, M 4
..... Saude, Norway, M 7
..... Saugeen, Ont., I 8
..... Saugeen, Ont., I 9
38517 Saugor, India, H 12
443 Saujil, Arg., I 9
2963 Saujon, France, L 8
..... Saul, N. Ire., E 24
3114 Saulieu, France, J 18
225 Saulnierville, N. S., O 8
711 Sault, France, O 20
25794 Sault Sainte Marie, Ont., R 21
516 Saulx, France, I 22
..... Saumar, Iran, H 1
16532 Saumur, France, J 9
145 Saunders, Alberta, M 19
..... Sautaoho, Chn., C 10
1483 Sauve, France, O 17
759 Sauveterre, France, P 7
..... Sauwerd, Neth., B 22
9443 Sava, Italy, K 21
3442 Savanna la Mar, Jamaica J 7
..... Savantvadi, India, M 6
..... Savanur, India, M 8
7000 Savé, Iran, G 6
4212 Savelli, Italy, L 20
3223 Savenay, France, J 6
4738 Săveni, Rom., H 21
3227 Saverdun, France, P 12
7916 Saverne, France, H 24
10046 Savigliano, Italy, E 2
976 Savigny, Switz., K 5
2705 Savigny-sur-Braye, Fr., I 11
..... Savilla, Cuba, O 22
566 Savines, France, N 23
210 Savona, B. C., O 15
51832 Savona, Italy, E 3
..... Savran, W. Sov. Un., G 25
..... Saw, Bur., N 21
..... Sawalem, Egypt, C 17
10000 Sawara, Japan, M 22
621 Sawyerville, Quebec, Q 21
1821 Saxon, Switz., O 7
..... Saxony, U. S. Afr., P 13
807 Saya, Bolivia, H 6
1229 Sayán, Peru, K 8
..... Sayula, Chia., L 15
9340 Sayula, Jal., N 6
..... Sbeitla, Tunisia, D 23
6697 Scaer, France, I 2
511 Scanfs, Switz., K 23
2561 Scanno, Italy, I 14
..... Scansano, Italy, I 9
475 Scarboro, Ont., K 12
..... Scarboro Jc., Ont., K 12
41791 Scarborough, Eng., E 18
833 Scarborough, Tobago (W. I.), Q 25
..... Scariff, Ire., L 10
..... Scarl, Switz., J 25
..... Scarnish, Scot., K 5
89 Scarth, Man., Q 12
..... Scatsta, Shetland Is., B 3
6995 Sceaux, France, C 4
162 Sceptre, Sask., O 4
..... Schachen, Switz., I 16
122790 Schaerbeek, Bel., M 12
34100 Schaffhausen, Switz., B 15
3732 Schagen, Neth., E 14
..... Schallasaig, Scot., M 7
1079 Schangnau, Switz., I 11
2025 Schanis, Switz., F 17
..... Scharleyschia, Tur., E 11
3222 Scharmbeck, Ger., E 6
..... Scheinfeld, Ger., M 7
..... Scheinige Platte, Switzerland, J 11
..... Schellidere, Tur., I 8
2692 Schellebelle, Belgium, R 5
..... Schellingwoude, Neth., B 6
2052 Scherzingen, Switz., C 18
61038 Schiedam, Neth., H 12
755 Schiermonnikoog, Netherlands, B 20
1960 Schiers, Switz., H 21
2015 Schiltach, Ger., P 5
912 Schinznach, Switz., D 12
10648 Schio, Italy, C 9
647 Schleins, Switz., I 25
1589 Schleitheim, Switz., B 14
6120 Schleiz, Ger., K 10
19000 Schleswig, Ger., B 7
4318 Schleusingen, Ger., K 8
..... Schlieben, Ger., I 12
3202 Schlüchtern, Ger., L 6
4000 Schlusselfeld, Ger., M 8
1461 Schmitten, Switz., I 8
9189 Schneeberg, Ger., K 11
41000 Schneidemühl, Pol., D 40
618 Schnottwil, Switz., G 8
1870 Schöftland, Switz., E 12
..... Schohchow, China, D 13
..... Schöllang, Germany, R 7
480 Schomberg, Ont., J 11
2606 Schönberg, Ger., D 10
35100 Schönebeck, Ger., H 10
3307 Schöngau, Germany, R 8
..... Schönhausen, Ger., O 19
..... Schönholz, Ger., O 16
..... Schönsea, Ger., N 10
2048 Schoondijke, Neth., K 7
4537 Schoonhoven, Neth., H 13
12713 Schooten, Belgium, Q 9
985 Schreiber, Ont., P 19
3947 Schrobenhausen, Ger., P 9
..... Schuders, Switz., H 21
150 Schuler, Alberta, O 24
..... Schull, Ire., R 5
1357 Schuls, Switz., I 24
2140 Schüpfen, Switz., G 8
3592 Schüpfheim, Switz., H 12
3962 Schwaan, Ger., D 10
11782 Schwabach, Ger., N 8
3762 Schwabmünchen, Ger., Q 8
2968 Schwanden, Switz., H 18
8633 Schwandorf, Ger., N 10
..... Schwarzseebad, Switz., J 8
8930 Schwedt, Ger., F 13
5394 Schweidnitz, Pol., F 9
39000 Schweinfurt, Ger., L 7
52000 Schwerin, Ger., D 9
6690 Schwerin, Pol., D 8
20 Schwitzer, Manitoba, R 13
8246 Schwyz, Switz., H 15
20052 Sciacca, Italy, D 10
..... Sciaradda, Eth., L 6
20661 Scicli, Italy, P 16
4499 Scilla, Italy, N 18
1656 Sclayn, Belgium, N 15
..... Scormont, Bel., P 11
265 Scotch Village, N. S., L 14
100 Scotia, Ont., M 13
429 Scotland, Ontario, N 9
..... Scotscalder, Scot., D 18
120 Scotsguard, Sask., Q 5
..... Scotstown, Ire., F 17
1273 Scotstown, Quebec, P 21
258 Scott, Sask., M 6
500 Scott Junction, Que., M 22
268 Scott's Bay, Nova Scotia, K 13
1175 Scottsdale, Tasmania, C 8
218 Scoudouc, New Brunswick, H 12
..... Scourie, Scot., D 12
..... Scrabby, Ire., H 15
..... Scroggie Creek, Yukon, L 4
Scutari, see Shkodër, Alb.
329 Seabright, Nova Scotia, N 14
6570 Seaford, Eng., N 20
1668 Seaforth, Ont., L 6
19394 Seaham Harbour, Eng., D 16
..... Seah Khana, Afg., I 17
909 Sea Lake, Australia, O 18
..... Searut, Afg., I 16
1139 Sebaco, Nic., I 11
..... Sebbah, Morocco, F 6
..... Sebbeh, Palestine, P 11
1159 Sebdou, Algeria, E 12
9213 Sebes, Rom., I 17
..... Sebezh, W. Sov. Un., A 21
..... Sebia, Mor., F 8
..... Sebka Gurara, Algeria, L 12
..... Sebkha d'Amadghor, Algeria, R 22
..... Sebkha Sidiel Hani, Tunisia, D 24
11848 Sebnitz, Ger., J 13
549 Sebringville, Ont., L 7
..... Sebt, Mor., J 4
..... Sebustieh, Palestine, K 9
18000 Sebzewar, Iran, F 12
300 Sechelt, B. C., O 2
3826 Sechura, Peru, G 2
109 Seclantas, Arg., G 9
120801 Secunderabad, India, L 11
..... Sedan, Australia, F 17
..... Sedan, Australia, I 18
18908 Sedan, France, F 19
618 Sedano, Spain, D 12
..... Seddon, N. Z., K 15
450 Sedéron, France, O 21
..... Sedia, Morocco, E 11
171 Sedley, Sask., Q 9
..... Sedrun, Switz., J 16
..... Sedura, W. Sov. Un., A 17
5644 Seebach, Switz., D 15
445 Seedorf, Switz., I 15
2853 Seehausen, Ger., F 10
..... Seeheim, S. W. Afr., P 13
653 Seelisburg, Switz., H 15
2972 Seelow, Germany, G 13
310 Seely's Bay, Ontario, H 21
..... Seem, Denmark, L 5
1285 Seengen, Switz., E 13
4292 Sees, France, H 9
329 Seesen, Germany, H 7
811 Seewen, Switz., D 10
..... Seewen, Switz., G 15
..... Seffle, Sweden, N 11
4000 Seffurieh, Palestine, H 10
537 Sefton, N. Z., M 12
..... Segauli, India, F 18
..... Segeberg, Ger., D 8
2582 Seghill, Eng., C 15
814 Segonzac, France, M 9
6487 Ségou, Fr. W. Afr., I 4
1973 Segovia, Col., F 10
24977 Segovia, Spain, H 11
4806 Segré, France, I 8
3191 Segura de la Sierra, Sp., L 14
..... Segurola, Argentina, P 20
..... Sehdeh, Iran, I 14
5000 Sehkoha, Iran, K 16
..... Sehore, India, H 10
5200 Sehwan, India, F 1
817 Seiches, Fr., J 9
..... Seida, Norway, A 23
4408 Seidi Schehir, Tur., G 6
3564 Seilles, Belgium, N 15
..... Seirijai, W. Sov. Un., C 17
..... Sejerslev, Denmark, E 5
..... Sejling, Denmark, H 9
..... Sejlstrup, Denmark, C 10
..... Seki, Japan, L 16
..... Sekida, Japan, J 22
5000 Sekiyado, Japan, L 21
1500 Sekiyama, Japan, J 18
22256 Sekondi, G. C., J 6
2278 Sel, Norway, K 8
2096 Selamûn, Egypt, E 10
4229 Selbu, Norway, I 10
10064 Selby, England, F 16
..... Selby, Ontario, I 18
..... Selde, Denmark, E 6
281 S. el Debba, Tun., F 25
10959 Selestat, France, H 23
..... Selfit, Palestine, L 9
..... Selim, Transjordan, J 14
..... Selindi, Turkey, I 7
2878 Seljord, Norway, M 6
4915 Selkirk, Man., P 16
426 Selkirk, Ontario, O 10
7075 Selkirk, Scotland, O 21
..... Selkirk, Yukon, M 6
114 Sellwood, Ontario, Q 23
141 Selmah, Nova Scotia, K 15
912 Selongey, France, J 19
1500 Selsey Hill, England, N 17
1620 Seltz, France, G 25
..... Selva, Argentina, J 15
1000 Selwyn, N. Z., M 12
..... Selwyn, Yukon, M 5
2068 Selzach, Switz., F 9
8060 Selzaete, Bel., K 9
223000 Semarang, Neth. Ind., J 4
3800 Semenov, Sov. Un., H 15
..... Semenovka, Sov. Un., N 10
2800 Semenud, Egypt, D 14
..... Semenovka, Sov. Un., K 7
..... Semiostrovskoe, Sov. Un., B 11
109779 Semipalatinsk, Sov. Un. Asia, H 12
..... Semira, Morocco, H 4
..... Semiram, Iran, K 6
..... Semkharat, Egypt, C 9
..... Semlay, Egypt, G 12
..... Semmeh, Transj., I 19
..... Semnajan, Iran, F 3
1241 Sempach, Switz., G 13
..... Sempre, Cuba, O 23
858 Semsales, Switz., K 6
3042 Sémur-en-Auxois, Fr., J 18
..... Sena, Bolivia, C 5
3710 Senado, Cuba, K 17
..... Senafa, Egypt, E 15
..... Senafe, Erit., B 9
..... Senbat, Egypt, L 10
223630 Sendai, Japan, H 23
..... Send Bast, Egypt, E 14
2436 Sendenhorst, Ger., H 4
..... Sendiun, Egypt, H 13
..... Seneca, Ontario, N 10
481 Senecu, Chih., B 18
1560 Senekal, U. S. Afr., J 17
18000 Senftenberg, Ger., I 13
..... Sengilei, Sov. Un. Asia, J 18
..... Senhaga, Morocco, K 5
..... Senhûr, Egypt, L 10
10175 Senigallia, Italy, F 12
..... Senillosa, Argentina, Q 8
4931 Senise, Italy, K 19
3072 Senj, Yugo., J 7
..... Senkara, Transj., J 15
129 Senlac, Sask., L 4
6673 Senlis, France, G 14
..... Senna Madureira, Western Brazil, J 21
8000 Sennar, Anglo-Egyp. Sudan, I 11
1124 Sennecey le Grand, Fr., K 19
..... Senno, W. Sov. Un., B 23
2789 Sennwald, Switz., F 20
17465 Sens, France, I 16
2683 Sensenti, Hond., G 7
3278 Sensuntepeque, Sal., H 7
32044 Senta, Yugo., J 13
..... Sento Sé, Brazil, H 20
..... Senuris, Egypt, L 11
3178 Seo de Urgel, Spain, E 19
11900 Seoni, India, I 12
935464 Seoul (Kyöngsöng), Kor., D 23
2589 Sepino, Italy, I 15
1729 Sepúlveda, Spain, G 12
710 Sequeros, Spain, H 9
..... Serafimovich (Ust Medyveditsa), Sov. Un., L 15
4254 Serai-K., Tur., F 3
45310 Seraing, Belgium, N 17
49600 Serampore, India, I 21
..... Serapeum, Egypt, E 23
20893 Serdobal, Sov. Un., E 7
..... Sereba, Eth., D 11
..... Serebryakovsk, Sov. Un., O 18
..... Serenje, N. Rh., N 18
..... Serenli, Som., R 13
..... Seresek, Tur., F 10
1700 Sergach, Sov. Un., I 16
21563 Sergievsk, Sov. Un., J 20
..... Sergiopol, see Ayaguz Sov. Un. Asia.
..... Serimbai, Egypt, C 8
8600 Seringapatam, India, O 9
..... Serneus, Switz., I 22
627 Serodino, Arg., M 16
..... Serouenoul, Algeria, R 22
64719 Serov (Kabakovsk), Sov. Un., F 24
25000 Serowe, Bech., A 17
6889 Serpa, Port., M 7
90766 Serpukhov, Sov. Un., I 11
6243 Serracapriola, Italy, I 16
29640 Serrai, Grc., M 18
..... Serrano, Argentina, N 13
..... Serrawr, Iran, Q 12
818 Serres, France, N 21
..... Serrezuela, Arg., K 10
970 Serrières, France, M 19
..... Serro, Brazil, L 18
..... Sersena, Egypt, L 12
..... Serup, Den., H 8
3250 Servia, Grc., N 16
4027 Sesquile, Col., I 12
8346 Sesto Fiorentine, Italy F 8
..... Seta, W. Sov. Un., B 17
..... Setanai, Japan, G 12
37321 Sète, France, P 17
10388 Sete Lagôas, Brazil, L 17
31736 Setif, Algeria, C 19
..... Setil, Algeria, E 19
37304 Seto, Japan, N 2
23866 Settat, Morocco, G 5
..... Sette Cama, Fr. Eq. Afr., L 10
2500 Settle, England, E 13
..... Setubal, Port., K 5
37074 Setubal, Port., L 5
1882 Seurre, France, J 20
..... Sevaroho, Bolivia, K 6
111946 Sevastopol, Sov. Un., O 7
184 Sevel, Denmark, G 5
2042 Sevelen, Switz., G 20
2862 Sevenum, Neth., J 19
15137 Severek, Tur., G 14
..... Severin, Chile, G 4
..... Severn, Ontario, G 12
333 Severn Bridge, Ontario, G 12
..... Sevilla, Col., C 12
312123 Sevilla, Spain, N 9
9335 Sevlijevo, Bulgaria, L 19
..... Sevogle, N. B., P 15
15457 Sevres, France, B 3
325 Sexsmith, Alberta, J 15
..... Seyafa, Egypt, G 13
2593 Seybo, Dom. Rep., J 15
298 Seyches, France, N 10
2340 Seyé, Yuc., E 22
151 Seymore, U. S. Afr., O 16
2505 Seymour, Australia, P 19
848 Seyssel, France, L 21
5158 Sezanne, France, H 16
6683 Sezze, Italy, I 12
10933 Sfântul-Gheorghe, Rom., I 20
39969 Sfax, Tunisia, D 25
..... Sfissifa, Algeria, H 12
..... Sfissifa, Morocco, H 11
482397 's Gravenhage (The Hague), Neth., H 11
6500 's Gravenzande, Neth., H 10
..... Shabbâs Amir, Egypt, C 10
..... Shabbas el Milh, Egypt, C 9
..... Shader, Scot., D 6
2366 Shaftesbury, England, M 13
..... Shagab, Egypt, P 23
..... Shah, Iran, O 2
20000 Shahabad, India, D 9
5000 Shahabad, India, G 10
..... Shahabad, Iran, D 12
..... Shahabadan, Iran, H 7
..... Shahabadshar, Iran, D 6
9000 Shahapur, India, K 6
..... Shahaziz Kahn, Afg., K 18
5000 Shahbandar, India, H 1
..... Shahbaz, Iran, D 11
..... Shahbund, Afg., J 18
..... Shahgarh, India, F 3
..... Shahgarh, India, H 12
72616 Shahjahanpur, India, F 13
..... Shahkir, Iran, O 9
..... Shah Murza, Afg., K 18
..... Shah Mushed, Afg., G 18
..... Shahor, Manch., B 24
6000 Shahpur (Dilman), Ind., C 1
..... Shahpur, India, C 6
..... Shahpura, India, H 14
..... Shahrabad, Iran, I 7
..... Shahristanak, Iran, F 6
4000 Shahriza (Qumisheh), Iran, J 7
..... Shahrjird, Iran, H 6
15100 Shahrud, Iran, E 10
..... Shahsien, China, J 18
..... Shakbetsu, Japan, G 14
289 Shakespeare, Ontario, M 7
..... Shakhnan, Sov. Un. Asia, K 13
155081 Shakhty, Sov. Un., N 13
304 Shallow Lake, Ontario, H 7
..... Shalshalamûn, Egypt, G 15
..... Shalûf et Terraba, Egypt, H 11
..... Shamalan, Afg., K 18
..... Shambe, A. E. Sud., J 18
..... Shamil, Iran, P 11
..... Shamirabad, Iran, F 8
..... Shamiran, Iran, G 5
..... Shamsabad, Iran, J 6
8400 Shamsabad, Iran, K 8
..... Shamu, Afg., F 24
..... Shanagolden, Ire., M 7
..... Shanawan, Egypt, F 12
..... Shane Ali Rezah, Iran, J 12
3703430 Shanghai, China, H 20
..... Shangketu, China, B 16
..... Shangnan, China, G 12
..... Shangsze, China, L 10
..... Shangyu, China, J 15
..... Shaniya, Egypt, O 22
5071 Shanklin, England, N 16
920 Shannon, N. Z., I 18
..... Shannonbridge, Ire., J 13
..... Shannon Harbor, Ire., J 13
258 Shannonville, Ont., I 18
200000 Shaohing, China, H 20
..... Shaowu, China, J 17
1227 Shap, England, D 12
..... Shapur, Iran, M 6
..... Shar, Afg., H 23
..... Sharabas, Egypt, C 17
..... Sharâra, Egypt, K 18
..... Sharâwna, Egypt, P 24
500 Sharbot Lake, Ont., G 20
..... Sharef, Algeria, L 14
..... Shari, Japan, F 15
..... Sharifkhaneh, Iran, C 2
..... Sharôna, Egypt, P 10
..... Sharretalai, India, P 9
..... Shashush, Iran, D 11
114000 Shasi, China, H 13
..... Shastana, Afg., H 21
..... Shatra, Iraq., O 22
1603 Shaunavon, Sask., Q 5
Shavli, see Siauliai, Sov. Un.
..... Shawa, Afg., G 24
..... Shawbost, Scot., D 6
628 Shawbridge, Que., O 14
20325 Shawinigan Falls, Que., L 17
892 Shawville, Quebec, P 8
..... Shebeka, Tunisia, E 22
..... Sheblenga, Egypt, G 14
Shechem, see Nablus, Pal.
310 Shedden, Ontario, O 6
2147 Shediac, N. B., H 12
..... Shediac Road, N. B., H 11
154 Sheenboro, Que., N 6
3873 's Heer Arenskerke, Neth., P 4
79 Sheerness, Alberta, M 22
16721 Sheerness, England, L 22
681 Sheet Harbour, N. S., M 17
2790 Shefa Amr, Palestine, H 9
705 Shefawa Qurûn, Egypt, D 11
517300 Sheffield, England, G 15
725 Sheffield, N. B., I 8
1500 Sheffield, N. Z., M 11
..... Shefford, England, K 19
..... Shegalqil, Egypt, L 18
270 Sheho, Sask., N 10
7000 Shehr-i-Babek, Iran, L 10
..... Shehri Ibrahim, Bal., P 19
..... Shehri Mirdat, Bal., P 19
..... Shehri Moorcheh, Afg., J 20
..... Shehur Khoj, Afg., H 18
..... Sheigra, Scot., D 12
..... Sheikh Muannis, Palestine, L 6
..... Shêkh Abû Nûr, Eg., N 12
..... Shêkh Ali, Eg., R 24
..... Shêkh Batami, Eg., R 24
..... Shêkh Fadl, Eg., P 10
..... Shêkh Herdi, Eg., M 20
1605 Shelburne, N. S., Q 10
1005 Shelburne, Ontario, J 10
12690 Sheldon, England, D 12
..... Shellborough, Austl., F 5
489 Shellbrook, Sask., L 7
91 Shellmouth, Man., P 12
..... Shell River, Sask., K 6
20000 Shemakha, Sov. Un., Q 20
..... Shemisseh, Syria, C 14
..... Shenacadie, N. S., H 22
..... Shenchow, China, F 12
..... Shenchowfu, China, I 12
12936 Shendi, A. E. Sud., H 19
..... Shenhûr, Egypt, O 24
..... Shenkursk, Sov. Un., E 14
..... Shenley, England, A 20
..... Sheopur, India, G 10
90 Shepard, Alberta, M 21
4108 Shepton-Mallet, Eng., M 12
..... Sheptovka, W. Sov. Un., F 21
..... Sheramin, Iran, D 2
6542 Sherborne, England, M 13
523 Sherbrooke, N. S., L 19
35965 Sherbrooke, Quebec, Q 20
..... Shercock, Ire., G 18
..... Shergarh, India, G 9
..... Shergarh, India, H 18
..... Sherkston, Ontario, O 12
..... Sherpur, India, G 23
..... Sherq Selin, Egypt, M 19
..... Sherrack, Morocco, E 10
200 Sherrington, Quebec, R 16
..... Sher Saffa, Afg., G 20
5000 Sher Shah, India, D 5
41969 's Hertogenbosch, Neth., I 16
..... Shesh Burjeh, Afg., H 21
..... Shevar, Iran, P 8
..... Shiba, Tunisia, D 22
13000 Shibata, Japan, H 21
..... Shibberagu, Afg., E 19
..... Shibetoro, Japan, E 16
2710 Shibin el-Kanâter, Egypt, G 14
24604 Shibin-El-Kom, Egypt, F 12
3500 Shibushi, Japan, R 4
5000 Shichinohe, Japan, C 24
..... Shidzukawa, Japan, G 24
..... Shielday, Scot., G 10
14000 Shigatse, Tib., M 13
..... Shihchu, China, H 10
..... Shihnan, China, F 15
..... Shihnan, China, H 11
..... Shihping, China, K 5
..... Shihtao, China, E 21
..... Shihtsien, China, J 10
62505 Shikarpur, India, E 1
10800 Shikohabad, India, F 12
..... Shild, Iran, J 5
200 Shillelagh, Ire., L 20
21300 Shillong, India, G 25, L 19
19000 Shimabara, Japan, O 3
8600 Shimada, Japan, N 17
55664 Shimizu, Japan, M 18
1500 Shimoda, Japan, L 16
5000 Shimoda, Japan, N 18
..... Shimodate, Jap., K 21
20661 Shimoga, India, N 8
..... Shimonita, Japan, K 19
196022 Shimonoseki, Japan, M 5
..... Shin, Egypt, D 11
..... Shinchao, Mong., D 10
..... Shinchi, Japan, H 23
..... Shinchuan, China, G 11
..... Shinemecas Bridge, N. S., I 14
10000 Shingu, Japan, O 13
11000 Shinjo, Japan, F 22
..... Shino, Iran, D 1
..... Shinraq, Egypt, E 13
..... Shinrone, Ire., K 13
2500 Shiokoshi, Japan, F 22
..... Shiotori, Japan, K 16
7655 Ship Harbour, N. S., M 17
30243 Shipley, England, F 14
575 Shippigan, N. B., B 12
1010 Shippigan Island, N. B., B 12
..... Shipu, China, F 21
..... Shiraghian, Iran, I 7
5000 Shirahama, Japan, N 20
5300 Shirahi, Japan, K 20
9600 Shirakawa, Japan, J 22
..... Shirasawa, Japan, C 23
129023 Shiraz, Iran, M 7
25473 Shirbin, Egypt, C 16
..... Shirghist, Iran, H 11
..... Shiriuchi, Japan, A 23
9000 Shirpur, India, I 8
..... Shirsabad, Iran, H 13
..... Shirwan, Iran, D 12
5000 Shishawen, Sp. Mor., D 8
..... Shishikai, Japan, O 10
568 Shisonaccia, Cor., Q 3
..... Shiuchow, China, K 14
..... Shiudengomba, China, H 2
..... Shiuhing, China, L 14
..... Shiurian, Iran, Q 15
1500 Shizukuishi, Japan, E 24
212198 Shizuoka, Japan, N 18
..... Shklov, W. Sov. Un., B 23
29209 Shkodër, Alb., M 12
..... Shlüsselburg, Sov. Un., G 8

Pop.	Place Country Index
.....	Shmargendorp, Ger., Q 15
22096	Shmerinka, W. Sov. Un., G 22
.....	Sh. Miskin, Syria, H 18
.....	Shoa Ghimirra, I. E. A., M 5
.....	Shoal Bay, B. C., O 10
737	Shoal Lake, Man., P 13
2500	Shobara, Japan, L 9
.....	Shokshi, Sov. Un., F 10
212620	Sholāpur, India, L 9
.....	Shomyo, Japan, L 6
.....	Shopford, Eng., C 12
.....	Shorabak, Afg., J 18
.....	Shoreham, Eng., D 25
.....	Shore Line Junction, New Brunswick, L 5
200	Shoruk, Afg., H 16
9640	Shoshu, Kor., I 22
.....	Showa, Egypt, D 15
.....	Showyang, China, E 14
.....	Shpola, Sov. Un., M 6
32370	Shrewsbury, England, I 11
.....	Shrigonda, India, K 7
.....	Shrule, Ire., I 8
7000	Shubra, Egypt, H 14
.....	Shubra Hechun, Egypt, F 14
.....	Shubrâ Hur, Egypt, D 15
2423	Shubra Khêt, Egypt, D 9
207	Shufeh, Palestine, K 8
80000	Shufu (Kashgar), Sink., K 11
.....	Shuha, Egypt, D 16
.....	Shuiskoe, Sov. Un., G 13
5900	Shujabad, India, D 5
.....	Shukur, Iran, H 15
.....	Shul, Iran, I 6
.....	Shumbah, Iran, N 6
.....	Shunan, China, H 18
.....	Shunking, Chn., H 9
.....	Shunning, China, K 4
.....	Shuntehfu, China, E 15
.....	Shurab, Iran, F 13
.....	Shurab, Iran, I 15
.....	Shurgaz, Iran, N 14
.....	Shurifabad, Iran, F 14
40000	Shusha, Sov. Un., R 18
18000	Shushtar, Iran, J 4
.....	Shutta, Palestine, I 11
.....	Shuweikeh, Palestine, J 8
57950	Shuya, Sov. Un., H 13
.....	Shwebo, Bur., M 22
.....	Shwegyin, Bur., O 23
.....	Siadehan, Iran, F 5
.....	Siah Kala, Iran, H 14
85093	Sialkot, India, C 8
	Sian, see Changan, China.
.....	Siang, China, K 11
500000	Siangtan, China, I 14
40000	Siangyan, China, G 13
.....	Siaohocheng, China, F 9
.....	Siaokan, China, H 15
.....	Siaokiakang, China, H 15
5328	Siatista, Greece, N 15
27000	Siauliai (Shavli), W. Sov. Un. A 16
.....	Siay, Iran, D 12
.....	Sibambe, Ecuador, D 5
.....	Sibate, Col., I 11
134	Sibaya, Chile, C 5
96	Sibbald, Alberta, M 24
37284	Sibenik, Yugo., K 8
.....	Sibicia, Algeria, L 7
48013	Sibiu, Rom., J 18
1156	Sibret, Bel., P 18
5700	Sibsagar, India, L 21
184	Sicamous, B. C., O 16
2200	Sicaya, Bolivia, I 7
2700	Sicaya, Peru, L 11
.....	Sichow, China, E 12
.....	Sichwan, China, G 13
7036	Sicuani, Peru, N 17
.....	Sid, Yugo., J 12
.....	Sidaro Kastron, Grc., M 18
.....	Sidcup, England, C 24
.....	Sidek, Iraq, H 20
6349	Siderokastron, Grc., Q 15
.....	Sidi Ali Boo Daud, Morocco, E 9
.....	Sidi Amur, Mor., J 4
.....	Sidi Bader, Algeria, B 22
52966	Sidi-bel-Abbes, Alg., D 12
.....	Sidi el Arbi, Alg., I 16
.....	Sidi Gaber, Egypt, C 3
1723	Sidi Gasi, Tur., E 5
.....	Sidi Ibrahim, Mor., G 3
.....	Sidi Kasem, Mor., F 7
.....	Sidi Khelil, Alg., F 19
1339	Sidi Merouan, Algeria, C 19
.....	Sidi Mokhtar, Mor., I 3
.....	Sidi Nich, Tun., E 23
.....	Sidi Rached, Alg., G 19
.....	Sidi Taieb, Mor., J 10
979	Sidney, B. C., R 12
.....	Sidney Inlet, B. C., Q 9
	Sidon, see Saida, Syr.
36927	Siedlce, Poland, D 15
20000	Siegburg, Ger., J 3
32000	Siegen, Germany, J 4
.....	Siemreap, Fr. In. Ch., P 6
31817	Siena, Italy, G 9
	Sieniawaka, see Sinyavka, Sov. Un.
0537	Sieradz, Poland, E 11
1111	Sierek, France, G 21
10051	Sierpc, Poland, D 13
334	Sierra Gorda, Chile, E 5
1096	Sierra Mojada, Coa., D 6
22	Sierra Prieta, Son., C 8
5023	Sierre, Switz., M 9
.....	Siflah, Iran, P 10
.....	Siflaq, Egypt, N 20
202	Sifton, Man., O 13
.....	Sifton Jc., Man., O 13
.....	Sigdal, Norway, M 8
3159	Sigean, France, Q 15
27646	Sighet, Rom., H 17
13096	Sighisoara, Rom., I 19
5282	Sigmaringen, Ger., Q 6
16700	Signakh, Sov. Un., Q 18
2655	Signau, Switz., H 10
3447	Sigriswil, Switz., J 10
1031	Sigtuna, Sweden, M 16
4013	Sigüenza, Spain, G 13
6016	Siguiri, Fr., W. Afr., I 3
393	Sihochac, Camp., H 20
.....	Sihuatlan, Jal., N 4
.....	Siirt, Tur., G 17
22300	Sikar, India, F 8
11200	Sikasso, Fr. W. Afr., I 5
5523	Siklós, Hungary, J 11
.....	Siku, China, F 7
2594	Silacayoapan, Oax., L 7
.....	Silanen, China, H 11
13880	Silao, Guan., L 11
2092	Silenen, Switzerland, I 15
954	Silenrieux, Belgium, O 12
.....	Sil Garhi, Nepal, E 14
17415	Silistra, Bul., K 22
12073	Silkeborg, Den., H 9
17473	Sillein, Czech., N 20
2770	Sillé le Guillaume, Fr., H 9
.....	Sillerud, Sweden, M 10
1618	Silly, Belgium, N 9
525	Sils, Switz., J 20
343	Sils, Switz., L 21
.....	Silung, China, K 8
406	Silvaplana, Switz., L 22
.....	Silver Center, Ont., Q 24
.....	Silvermines, Ire., L 12
131	Silverton, Australia, M 17
4400	Silves, Brazil, E 6
9577	Silves, Portugal, N 5
2203	Silvia, Col., K 7
.....	Silwa, Egypt, Q 24
.....	Sily, Palestine, I 9
1422	Simacota, Col., G 12
5131	Simav, Tur., E 3
.....	Simbach, Ger., Q 11
	Simbirsk, see Ulyanovsk, Sov. Un.
.....	Simbold, Arg., I 12
6037	Simcoe, Ontario, O 9
.....	Simcoe Jc., Ont., O 9
67	Simested, Denmark, F 9
142678	Simferopol, Sov. Un., O 8
.....	Simikot, Nepal, D 14
3034	Simiti, Col., E 12
37000	Simla, India, D 10
7496	Simleul-Silvaniei, Rom., H 16
3108	Simmern, Ger., L 3
1664	Simojovel, Chia., L 16
3722	Simola, Fin., F 6
5398	Simonstown, U. S. Afr., R 7
370	Simplon, Switz., N 12
.....	Simpson, Mack, N 9
206	Simpson, Sask., N 8
2505	Simrishamn, Swed., Q 12
.....	Simsim, Palestine, O 3
3906	Sinaia, Rom., J 20
1666	Sinaloa, Sin., M 15
.....	Sinantien, China, G 15
.....	Sinbo, Bur., M 23
8287	Sincé, Col., D 10
11014	Sincelejo, Col., D 9
.....	Sincheng Ho, China, F 15
.....	Sinchow Sha, China, D 14
.....	Sinclair, Man., R 12
1336	Sindal, Denmark, B 11
.....	Sindbjerg, Denmark, J 8
.....	Sindhnur, India, M 9
.....	Sindhulia, Nepal, F 19
.....	Sindri, India, G 5
.....	Sindyûn, Egypt, C 8
.....	Sinera, Egypt, L 10
5613	Sines, Portugal, M 5
.....	Singa, A. E. Sud., I 19
550000	Singapore, (Sts. Setts.) Mal. St., R 24
.....	Singapur, India, J 16
179	Singhampton, Ont., I 9
3668	Singleton, Australia, N 22
.....	Singpur, India, H 16
.....	Singshan, China, H 12
.....	Singyifu, China, K 8
.....	Sinhwa, China, J 12
.....	Siningfu, China, E 6
3539	Siniscola, Italy, J 5
.....	Sinj, Yugo., K 9
.....	Sinjil, Palestine, L 10
.....	Sinmin, Manch., B 20
.....	Sinnak, Mack., C 2
1451	Sinnamary, Fr. Gu., B 11
.....	Sinoia S. Rh., O 18
5006	Sinop, Tur., B 10
.....	Sins, Switz., F 14
.....	Sinsiang, China, F 14
.....	Sinsin, Iran, H 6
.....	Sinsing, China, K 5
334	Sintaluta, Sask., P 10
51347	Sinuiju, Kor., C 22
.....	Sinyang, China, G 15
.....	Sinyavka, W. Sov. Un., D 20
3150	Siófok, Hung., I 11
7960	Sion (Sitten), Switz., N 8
.....	Sion Mills, N. Ire., D 15
1756	Sioux Lookout, Ont., O 16
9310	Sipesipe, Bolivia, I 7
.....	Siping, China, G 15
5600	Sipri, India, D 10
1078	Siqueros, Sin., Q 18
1515	Siquisique, Ven., C 9
4000	Sira, India, N 10
40401	Siracusa(Syracuse),It.,O 17
.....	Sir Bahir, Palestine, N 10
63	Sirdar, B. C., Q 18
10024	Siret, Romania, H 20
5300	Sirhind, India, D 9
.....	Siri, Eth., K 10
4000	Siri, India, N 10
.....	Sirian, Iran, H 13
.....	Sirik, Iran, Q 12
681	Sirin, Palestine, H 12
15000	Sir-i-pul, Afg., F 20
494	Siris, Palestine, J 10
7225	Sirnach, Switz., D 17
.....	Sirohi, India, G 6
.....	Siroki, Baluchistan, R 16
2800	Sironcha, India, K 13
.....	Sironj, India, H 10
.....	Sirpur, India, K 12
15800	Sirsa, India, E 8
10800	Sirs el Layyan, Eg., G 12
.....	Sirsi, India, M 7
.....	Sirte, Libya, E 13
.....	Sirur, India, K 7
.....	Siryan, Iran, L 8
.....	Sirz Samuel, Austl., K 7
.....	Sis, Tur., H 10
10910	Sisak, Yugo., J 9
112	Sisal, Yuc., E 20
315	Sisikon, Switz., H 15
.....	Sisophon, Fr. In. Ch., P 5
3051	Sissach, Switz., D 11
1323	Sissonne, France, G 17
3354	Sisteron, France, O 22
.....	Sita, China, G 3
.....	Sita, Sov. Un., H 5
.....	Sitabaldi, India, J 12
.....	Si Taieb, Mor., J 10
.....	Sitaman, India, H 8
21600	Sitapur, India, F 14
.....	Site of Fort Confidence, Mack., G 11
.....	Site of Ft. Enterprise, Mackenzie, J 15
.....	Site of Fort Frances, Yuk. O 18
.....	Site of Fort Franklin, Mack., I 8
.....	Site of Fort Reliance, Mack., M 18
.....	Sitia, Grc., R 22
2632	Sitiecito, Cuba, H 11
4630	Sitionuevo, Col., C 11
3776	Sitjes, Spain, G 20
.....	Sitlaha, India, G 14
.....	Sits, Egypt, N 11
14570	Sittard, Neth., L 19
	Sitten, see Sion, Switz.
.....	Sittona, Erit., C 7
.....	Sivakasi, India, Q 11
41247	Sivas, Tur., E 12
6119	Sivri-hissar, Tur., E 6
1655	Sivry, Belgium, O 11
.....	Siwan, India, G 17
.....	Sixmilebridge, Ire., M 9
.....	Sixmilecross, N. Ire., E 17
77679	Sizran, Sov. Un., J 18
.....	Själevad, Sweden, I 15
3534	Sjenice, Yugo., L 13
188	Sjörring, Denmark, E 4
.....	Skaanevik, Norway, M 4
1384	Skaerbaek, Denmark, L 5
.....	Skaerum, Denmark, C 12
.....	Skaerup, Denmark, K 8
4048	Skagen, Denmark, A 13
.....	Skaill, Scotland, B 18
675	Skais, Denmark, F 8
.....	Skala, W. Sov. Un., G 20
682	Skals, Den., F 7
.....	Skalstugan, Sweden, I 11
4085	Skanderborg, Den., I 11
.....	Skannerup, Denmark, H 9
6770	Skara, Sweden, N 11
.....	Skardo, India, A 9
.....	Skarrild, Denmark, I 5
.....	Skaw, Scot., I 23
.....	Skedsmo, Norway, M 9
.....	Skee, Sweden, N 9
.....	Skeena City, B. C., J 7
9121	Skegness, Eng., H 20
.....	Skelbo, Scot., F 16
2226	Skeldon, Br. Gu., B 8
5203	Skellefteå, Sweden, G 19
2860	Skelskör, Denmark, L 17
.....	Skelton, Honduras, F 14
625	Skelund, Denmark, E 12
1310	Skene, Scotland, I 23
2985	Skern, Denmark, I 3
2134	Skerries, Ire., L 22
.....	Ski, Norway, B 6
3208	Skibbereen, Ire., R 6
.....	Skidegate, B. C., K 5
15605	Skien, Norway, M 8
20191	Skierniewice, Pol., E 13
38	Skiff, Alberta, P 23
.....	Skinnerup, Denmark, D 4
12434	Skipton, England, F 14
9644	Skive, Denmark, F 6
.....	Skivum, Denmark, E 9
.....	Skjellerup, Denmark, F 10
.....	Skjerstad, Norway, E 13
.....	Skjoldnaes, Denmark, N11
.....	Skod, Denmark, H 10
.....	Skodborg, Den., K 6
2794	Skog, Sweden, K 15
.....	Skon, Sweden, J 15
.....	Skopin, Sov. Un., J 12
64807	Skoplje, Yugo., M 14
.....	Skoppum, Norway, E 3
.....	Skorodnoe, Sov. Un., K 10
1151	Skörping, Den., E 10
.....	Skorup, Denmark, H 10
10838	Skövde (Sköfde), Swe., N 12
13219	Skradin, Yugo., K 8
1205	Skudesneshavn, Nor., M 3
	Skutari, see Usküdar, Tur.
28084	Skvira, W. Sov. Un., F 24
.....	Slagan, Scotland, F 10
744	Slains, Scot., H 24
.....	Slane, Ire., H 20
1090	Slangerup, Denmark, I 21
.....	Slang River, U. S. Afr., M 17
6274	Slânic, Romania, J 20
11010	Slatina, Romania, K 18
.....	Slatina, Yugo., J 10
54	Slave Lake, Alberta, H 19
.....	Slavgorod, Sov. Un. Asia, H 11
.....	Slavkov, Czech., G 9
75542	Slavyansk, Sov. Un., M 11
7024	Sleaford, England, H 18
.....	Sledmere, England, E 18
5139	Sleen, Neth., E 23
5489	Sleydinge, Bel., K 8
.....	Slidre, Nor., K 7
13157	Sliedrecht, Neth., I 13
12496	Sligeach (Sligo), Ire., F 11
.....	Sligichan, Scot., H 8
30100	Sliven, Bul., L 21
.....	Slobodskoi, Sov. Un., G 18
7605	Slobozia, Rom., J 22
.....	Slobozia, Rom., K 19
183	Slocan City, B. C., P 18
13461	Slochteren, Neth., C 23
.....	Sloependen, Norway, A 4
16284	Slonim, W. Sov. Un., D 18
.....	Sloten, Neth., C 2
735	Sloten, Neth., D 17
.....	Sloten, Neth., G 13
.....	Sloterdijk, Neth., B 3
33530	Slough, Eng., L 18
1309	Slovensky Gradec, Yugo. I 7
3127	Sluis, Neth., K 7
.....	Slunj, Yugo., J 8
15000	Slutsk, W. Sov. Un., C 20
6307	Smederevo, Yugo., K 14
84354	Smethwick, Eng., J 14
6597	Smilde, Neth., D 22
.....	Smirisari, Scot., J 9
300	Smith, Alberta, H 19
...	Smithborough, Ire., F 17
759	Smithers, B. C., I 9
215	Smithfield, Ontario, J 17
600	Smithfield, U. S. Afr., L 16
7159	Smiths Falls, Ont., G 21
720	Smithville, Ont., N 11
.....	Smokovec, Czech., G 13
430	Smoky Lake, Alberta, J 21
156677	Smolensk, W. Sov. Un., B 25
22985	Smyela, Sov. Un., M 7
	Smyrna, see Izmir, Tur.
2385	Snaasen, Norway, H 11
14860	Sneek, Neth., D 18
.....	Sneem, Ire., P 3
.....	Sneissa, Algeria, O 9
.....	Snevaldj, Iran, D 12
.....	Snfendou, Algeria, B 20
	Sniatyn, see Snyatyn, Sov. Un.
.....	Snizort, Scotland, G 7
	Snovidovichi, W. Sov. Un., E 21
179	Snowflake, Man., R 14
.....	Snurla, India, B 10
10915	Snyatyn, W. Sov. Un., G 19
2006	Soacha, Col., I 11
2272	Soata, Col., H 14
.....	Soatata, Col., F 6
302	Soazza, Switz., M 18
.....	Sobakino, Sov. Un., K 12
.....	Sobat, Anglo-Egyptian Sudan, I 18
.....	Söborg, Denmark, H 22
13625	Sobral, Brazil, F 21
.....	Söby, Denmark, G 12
.....	Söby, Denmark, H 10
.....	Söby, Denmark, N 12
10822	Sochaczew, Poland, D 13
70000	Soche(Yarkand),Sink.,K11
13300	Sochi, Sov. Un., P 12
1295	Socoltenango, Chia., N 17
7891	Socorro, Col., G 13
.....	Socna, Libya, F 13
1500	Socota, Eth., E 9
.....	Soc-trang, Fr. In. Ch., R 8
.....	Soda Creek, B. C., M 13
5548	Sodankyla, Fin., B 6
.....	Söderfors, Sweden, L 15
11643	Söderhamn, Sweden, K 15
2868	Söderköping, Sweden, N 14
14371	Södertälge, Sweden, N 16
.....	Sodisdale, Scotland, K 6
.....	Södra Möckelby, Sweden, P 15
85	Södring, Denmark, F 12
356000	Soerabaja, Neth. Ind., J 4
22000	Soest, Germany, I 5
321094	Sofija (Sofia), Bul., L 17
.....	Sofisk, Sov. Un. Asia, F 20
5216	Sogamoso, Col., H 13
.....	Sogndal, Norway, K 5
.....	Sogndal, Norway, N 4
1270	Sögüd, Tur., Asia, D 4
.....	Soh, Iran, I 6
7400	Sohagpur, India, H 14
.....	Sohran, Iran, O 12
10599	Soignies, Belgium, N 10
18705	Soissons, France, G 16
12135	Sokal, Poland, F 18
.....	Soke, Tur., G 1
.....	Soknedal, Norway, J 10
.....	Sokólka, Pol., C 16
.....	Sokolo, Fr. W. Afr., H 5
.....	Sokolów, Poland, D 15
8000	Sokoto, Nigeria, I 9
2197	Sokurai, Japan, N 13
.....	Sol, Egypt, L 14
.....	Sola, Arg., L 18
.....	Sola, Cuba, K 17
2376	Sola de la Vega, Oax., N 8
.....	Solam, Palestine, I 10
10971	Solana, Spain, K 13
.....	Solanet, Arg., P 19
.....	Solano, Ven., Q 13
.....	Solari, Arg., J 19
17	Soldadito, Tam., F 19
4088	Soldado, Col., B 15
300	Soledad, Arg., K 16
11500	Soledad, Col., C 10
.....	Soledad, Col., F 8
.....	Soledad, Ec., D 2
30	Soledad, Baja Cal., N 9
4250	Soledad, Ver., I 10
2486	Soledad, Ven., G 18
.....	Soledade, Brazil, P 11
.....	Soligalich, Sov. Un., G 14
488	Solignac-sur-Loire,Fr.,N 17
140200	Solingen, Ger., I 3
2500	Solís, Mêx., G 3
.....	Sollas, Scotland, G 3
.....	Solledad, Bol., I 5
2735	Solleftea, Sweden, I 15
10586	Sóller, Spain, J 21
2666	Sollies-Pont, Fr., P 22
.....	Solna, Sweden, Q 21
9800	Solola, Guatemala, F 3
21700	Solothurn, Switz., F 9
2689	Solsona, Spain, E 19
5723	Soltau, Germany, F 7
.....	Solun, Manch., A 19
3943	Sölvesborg, Sweden, Q 13
1700	Solvichegodsk,Sov.Un.,F16
3655	Soma, Tur., E 2
32256	Sombor, Yugo, J 12
421	Sombra, Ontario, O 3
5628	Sombrerete, Zac., I 6
4117	Someren, Neth., J 18
5774	Somerghem, Bel., L 7
245	Somerset, N. S., L 11
6034	Somerset East, U. S. Africa, P 15
.....	Somersham, Eng., J 19
5558	Somiedo, Spain, D 9
39	Somkeli, U. S. Africa, I 23
7474	Sömmerda, Germany, J 9
483	Sommersted, Den., L 8
3130	Sommiéres, France, O 17
.....	Somotillo, Honduras, I 10
347	Sompuis, France, H 18
1574	Somvix, Switz., J 17
593	Son, Norway, D 5
1411	Soná, Panama, Q 19
.....	Sonachan, Scotland, L 12
596	Sonaguera, Hond., E 11
.....	Sonala, India, J 10
1223	Sonceboz, Switz., F 7
12100	Sönderborg, Den., N 10
259	Sönder Broby, Den., L 12
.....	Sönder Felding, Den., I 5
.....	Sönderholm, Den., D 9
93	Sönder Mern, Den., M 20
.....	Sönder Nisum, Den., G 2
498	Sönder Omme, Den., I 6
488	Sönderse, Den., K 12
9978	Sondershausen, Ger., I 8
.....	Sönderup, Denmark, E 9
378	Sönder Vium, Den., J 3
6349	Sondrio, Italy, C 6
.....	Sonepat, India, E 10
.....	Song-cau, Fr. In. Ch., P 11
.....	Songea, Tan., M 20
.....	Songkhla (Singora), Siam, Q 15
11797	Songuldak, Tur., B 6
.....	Sonkovo, Sov. Un., H 11
.....	Sonmeanee, Bal., R 21
20000	Sonneberg, Germany, L 9
2000	Sonobe, Japan, L 13
4700	Sonoki, Japan, N 3
321	Sonora, N. S., L 19
8984	Sonsón, Col., H 9
20553	Sonsonate, Salvador, H 6
.....	Sontshi, Chn. A 12
	Soochow, see Wuhsien, China.
521	Sooke, B. C., R 2
.....	Soormasing, Bal., N 21
2431	Sopachui, Bolivia, K 11
3334	Sophades, Gr., O 16
.....	Soping, China, C 13
2680	Soplavientos, Col., C 10
35887	Sopron, Hung., H 9
1600	Sorab, India, M 8
2466	Sorasora, Bolivia, J 6
2000	Sorata, Bolivia, G 3
6063	Sorbas, Spain, O 14
1096	Sorbie, Scotland, R 14
532	Sore, France, O 8
12251	Sorel, Quebec, N 17
416	Sorell, Tasmania, E 8
13054	Soria, Spain, F 14
6306	Soriano, Uruguay, L 14
2854	Sorö, Denmark, K 18
14661	Soroca, W. Sov. Un., H 22
.....	Sörreisen, Norway, C 16
.....	Sorsele, Sweden, G 15
1109	Sort, Spain, E 19
	Sortavala, see Serdobal, Sov. Un.
364	Soruco, Chile, K 3
.....	Sorunda, Sweden, N 16
3747	Sós, Spain, E 16
.....	Sosa, Argentina, L 17
.....	Sosa, Paraguay, P 8
.....	Sosnitsa, Sov. Un., K 7
116000	Sosnowiec, Poland, F 12
17232	Sosonate, Sal., H 6
.....	Soto, Argentina, K 11
353	Soto la Marina, Tam., H 19
1098	Sotomayor, Bolivia, K 10
5462	Sottegam, Bel., M 9
2645	Sotuta, Yuc., F 22
266	Soubey, Switz., E 6
.....	Souch Bulak, Iran, E 2
4500	Soueïda, Syria, N 11
.....	Souerah Kedima, Mor., H 2
2480	Soufriere, Sta. Lucia, H 24
2501	Souillac, France, N 13
528	Souilly, France, G 19
14370	Souk-Ahras, Algeria, B 22
.....	Souk-el Arba, Tunisia, B 23
.....	Soukhné, Syria, K 14
.....	Souk Tleta, Mor., G 4
7279	Souphlion, Grc., M 21
	Sour, see Tyr, Syr.
.....	Soure, Brazil, I 22
.....	Soure, Brazil, E 14
7843	Soure, Portugal, I 5
1346	Souris, Man., Q 13
1114	Souris, P. E. I., G 18
.....	Sourlies, Scotland, I 10
25324	Sousse, Tunisia, C 24
3773	Soustons, France, O 7
176025	Southampton, Eng., N 15
.....	Southampton, N. B., H 5
177	Southampton, N. S., J 13
1600	Southampton, Ont., H 6
234	South Bay, N. B., L 8
430	Southbridge, N. Zeal.,M 12
234	South Brookfield, N. S.,O11
525	Southdean, Scotland, O 22
930	South Devon, N. B., I 7
120093	Southend, England, L 22
640	Southend, Scotland, P 9
615	Southern Cross, Austl., M 6
.....	Southerness, Scot., Q 18
.....	South Erradale, Scot., G 9
287	Southey, Sask., O 9
263	South Farmington, N. S., M 11
332	South Indian, Ont., E 23
317	South Ingonish, N. S., F 23
18	South Jc., Man., R 18
201	South Maitland, N. S.,L 15
2831	South Molton, Eng., M 8
300	South Mountain, Ont., F 23
367	South Ohio, N. S., P 8
.....	South Penticton, B. C.,Q 16
5000	South Porcupine, Ont.,P 23
4218	Southport, Australia, L 24
78927	Southport, England, G 11
838	South River, Ont., C 12
113452	South Shields, Eng., C 15
212	South Slocan, B. C., Q 17
194	South Wellington, B. C., P1
2753	Southwold, England, J 25
2623	Souvigny, France, K 15
.....	Souza, Brazil, G 22
.....	Souzel, Brazil, E 12
.....	Sovata, Rom., I 19
127	Sovereign, Sask., N 6
.....	Sovietskaia Gavan, Sou. Un. Asia, G 20
.....	Sovrana, Switz., L 20
.....	Sowar, Afg., H 16
1082	Soy, Belgium, O 17
.....	Soya, Japan, E 13
495	Soyhieres, Switz., E 8
3304	Sozopol, Bul., L 23
.....	Sozoranga, Ecuador, F 3
8163	Spa, Belgium, N 19
.....	Spa, Ire., N 4
	Spalato, see Split, Yugo.
12592	Spalding, England, I 19
.....	Spandau, Germany, G 12
.....	Spanga, Sweden, Q 21
219	Spanish, Ontario, A 4
212	Spanish Mills, Ont., B 3
12007	Spanish Town, Jamaica, J 8
.....	Sparbu, Norway, H 10
5682	Spartē, Greece, Q 16
.....	Spasklepiki, Sov. Un., I 13
.....	Spaskoe, Sov. Un., G 16
.....	Spean Bridge, Scot., J 12
135	Spedden, Alberta, J 22
31	Speddington, Sask., M 10
145	Speers, Sask., L 6
1500	Speightstown, Barbados, O 25
.....	Spence, Ontario, D 11
417	Spencerville, Ont., G 22
425	Spences Bridge, B. C., P 14
16361	Spennymoor, Eng., D 15
.....	Spey Bridge, Scotland, I 16
26000	Speyer (Spires), Ger., N 4
76061	Spezia La, Italy, F 6
407	Spahkia, Grc., R 19
.....	Spiddle, Ire., J 6
4967	Spiez, Switz., J 10
.....	Spillimachene, B. C., O 18
10731	Spinazzola, Italy, J, 18
497	Spincourt, France, G 20
276	Spirit River, Alberta, H 16
11206	Spisská Nová Ves, Czech., G 13
.....	Spital of Glenshee, Scotland, J 18
4899	Spittal, Aus., I 5
.....	Spittal, England, A 14
43808	Split (Spalato), Yugo, L 9
326	Splügen, Switz., K 19
224	Spodsbjerg, Denmark, N 15
9618	Spoleto, Italy, H 11
559	Spontin, Belgium, O 14
.....	Spörring, Denmark, H 12
200	Spragge, Ontario, A 3
48	Sprague, Man., R 18
.....	Spreeuwfontein, U. S. Afr., P 11
12669	Spremberg, Ger., I 13
3775	Sprimont, Belgium, N 18
1500	Springbok, U. S. Afr., K 6
200	Springbrook, Ont., I 17
.....	Springburn, N. Z., M 10
321	Springfield, N. B., H 6
724	Springfield, N. B., J 9
200	Springfield, N. Z., M 11
214	Springfield, N. S., N 11
451	Springfield, Ont., O 7
1000	Springfontein, U. S. Afr., L 15
225	Springford, Ont., N 8
218	Springhaven, N. S., Q 9
.....	Spring Hill, N. B., I 6
7170	Springhill, N. S., J 13
260	Spring Hill, Quebec, P 22
190	Spring Hill Jc., N. S., J 13
632	Springlands, Br. Gu., B 8
181	Springside, Sask., O 10
712	Springsure, Austl., I 21
.....	Spring Valley, I. F. S., I 19
118	Spring Valley, Sask., Q 8
375	Springville, N. S., K 17
147	Springwater, Sask., M 5
218	Sprucedale, Ont., D 12
138	Spruce Lake, Sask., K 5
214	Spry Bay, N. S., M 18
133	Spy Hill, Sask., P 11
1872	Spynie, Scotland, G 19
551	Squamish, B. C., P 12
2738	Squillace, Italy, M 19
.....	Srbobran, Yugo., J. 13
7980	Srebrenica, Yugo, K 12
.....	Sredne Kolymsk, Sov. Un. Asia, C 18
.....	Srednyaya, Sov. Un., K 11
.....	Srem, Poland, D 10
.....	Sretensk, Sov. Un., G 17
207787	Srinagar, India, B 8
.....	Srinagar, India, D 12
.....	Srivardhan, India, K 6
.....	Sroda, Poland, D 10
1970	Stabio, Switz., Q 17
4396	Stabroeck, Belgium, K 12
.....	Staby, Denmark, H 2
.....	Stad, Switz., G 19
14842	Stade, Ger., D 7
4969	Staden, Belgium, L 5
.....	Stadil, Denmark, H 2
.....	Stadskanaal, Neth., D 24
8140	Stadthagen, Ger., G 6
.....	Stadtsteinach, Ger., L 9
4754	Stäfa, Switz., F 16
.....	Staffelstein, Ger., M 8
29485	Stafford, Eng., I 13
200	Stafford, N. Z., L 9
.....	Stair, Palestine, O 9
797	Stalden, Switz., N 11
82540	Stalinabad, Sov. Un. Asia, K 10
445476	Stalingrad (Tsaritsin), Sov. Un., M 16
462395	Stalino, Sov. Un., M 11
169538	Stalinsk (Kuznetsk), Sov. Un. Asia, H 13
.....	Ställdalen, Sweden, M 13
24823	Stalybridge, Eng., G 14
9881	Stamford, England, I 18
500	Stamford, Ont., N 13
.....	Stamford Bridge, Eng., F 17
.....	Stammheim, Switz., C 16
.....	Stampa, Switz., M 20
.....	Stamullin, Ire., I 22
.....	Stanbridge, Que., R 17
218	Standard, Alberta, M 23
5596	Standerton, U.S.Afr., G 19
.....	Stanford, U. S.Afr., R 8
.....	Stange, Norway, L 9
.....	Stangvik, Norway, I 7
1746	Stanhope, Eng., D 14
22100	Stanimaka, Bul., M 19
60256	Stanislav, W. Sov. Un., G 18
	Stanislawów, see Stanislav, Sov. Un.
284	Stanley, N. B., G 6
.....	Stanley, Scotland, K 18
100	Stanley Bridge, P.E.I., G15
.....	Stanley Junction, N. B., H7
13179	Stanleyville, Bel. Cong., K 16
211	Stanleyville, Ontario, G 20
98	Stammore, Alberta, M 23
.....	Stanmore, Eng., A 19
.....	Stannstad, Switz., H 13
2921	Stans, Switz., H 14
845	Stanstead, Quebec, R 20
2158	Stanthorpe, Austl., L 23
6574	Staphorst, Neth., E 21
.....	Stapleton, England, L 12
.....	Stara Khasa Yurt, Sov.Un., P 18
20196	Stara Oskol, Sov. Un., K 11
22487	Staraya Russa, Sov. Un., H7
29857	Stâra Zagora, Bul., L 20
231	Starbuck, Man., Q 16
591	Star City, Sask., L 9
2741	Stargard, Ger., E 12
35000	Stargard, Pol., C 8
5400	Staritsa, Sov. Un., H 9
.....	Starobino, W. Sov. Un., D 21
13000	Starobyelsk, Sov Un., M 12
.....	Starodub, Sov. Un., K 8
.....	Starogrod, Poland, C 11
.....	Stary Bykhov, W. So. Un., C 23
.....	Sta. Sejed, Pal., N 6
16000	Stassfurt, Ger. H 9
8500	Staszów, Poland F 14
.....	Station, Denmark, F 11
.....	Station, Egypt, H 15
2045	Staufen, Ger., Q 3
46780	Stavanger, Norway, M 3
.....	Staveley, Eng., H 16
273	Stavely, Alberta, O 21
3683	Stavenhagen, Ger., D 11
.....	Stavnshoved, Denmark, F 15
962	Stavoren, Neth., D 16
.....	Stavropol, Sov. Un., J 19
	Stavropol, see Voroshilovsk, Sov. Un.
4747	Stawell, Austl., P 17
1078	Stayner, Ont., I 10
3139	Steckborn, Switz., B 17
279	Steele, B. C., P 19
9322	Steenbergen, Neth., I 10
3882	Steenderen, Neth., G 20
7202	Steenwijk, Neth., E 20
6803	Steenwijkerwold, Neth., D 20
136	Steep Creek, Sask., L 8
.....	Steep Rock Junction, Manitoba, O 15
.....	Steffisburg, Switz., I 10
2549	Stege, Den., M 21
2101	Stegen, Norway, D 13
.....	Steglitz, Ger., R 15
.....	Stegman, Arg., Q 15
2088	Stein, Switz., B 16
501	Stein, Switz., F 18
	Steinamanger, see Szombathely, Hung.
.....	Steinkopf, U. S. Afr., K 6
8635	Stekene, Bel., K 10
264	Stella, Ont., J 19
5351	Stellarton, N. S., J 17
8782	Stellenbosch, U. S. Afr., Q 8
3026	Stenay, France, G 20
392	Stenbjerg, Denmark, E 3
30000	Stendal, Germany, G 10
506	Stenderup, Denmark, K 9
234	Stenen, Sask., N 11
.....	Stenild, Denmark, F 9
2701	Stenkjer, Nor., H 10
.....	Stenmagle, Denmark, K 18
.....	Stensele, Sweden, G 15
756	Stenstorp, Sweden, O 12
.....	Stepan, W. Sov. Un., E 20
25336	Sterlitamak, Sov. Un., J 23
12767	Sternberk, Czech., F 10
	Sterzing, see Vipiteno, It.
270225	Stettin, Pol., C 7
1295	Stettler, Alberta, L 21
5476	Stevenage, England, K 19
541	Stevensville, Ont., N 13
950	Steveston, B. C., Q 12
27	Steveville, Alta., N 23
446	Stewart, B. C., G 7
3700	Stewarton, Scot., N 14
.....	Stewart River, Yukon, L 4
100	Stewartstown, N. Ire., E 19
321	Stewarttown, Ont., L 10
2250	Steynsburg, U.S. Afr., M 15
22512	Steyr, Aus., G 7
703	Steytlerville, U. S. Afr., P 13
.....	Stige, Denmark, K 13
6660	Stigliano, Italy, K 18
310	Stilli Switz. D 13
12080	Stip, Yugo, M. 16
437	Stirling, Alberta, P 22
526	Stirling, N. Z., Q 7
990	Stirling, Ont., I 17
22897	Stirling, Scotland, M 16
4979	Stitten, Algeria, F 14
214	Stittville, Ont., E 21
.....	Stjördal, Norway, I 9
.....	Stobin, W. Sov. Un., D 20
.....	Stockbridge, Eng., M 15
11347	Stockerau, Aus., H 9
543785	Stockholm, Swe., M 16
125505	Stockport, Eng., G 13
67724	Stockton on Tees, Eng., D 16
1305	Stod, Norway, H 10
.....	Stöde, Sweden, J 15
.....	Stoer, Scotland, E 11
804	Stoke, N. Z., J 14
.....	Stoke-Canon, Eng., N 9
276619	Stoke on Trent, Eng., H 13
.....	Stokesley, Eng., E 16
.....	Stokke, Norway, F 3
4157	Stolac, Yugo, L 10
.....	Stolbtsy, W. Sov. Un., C 20

Pop.	Place, Country, Index
18000	Stolburg, Ger., J 2
.....	Stolin, Poland, I 22
44000	Stolp, Pol., C 10
	Stolpce, see Stolbtsy, Sov. Un.
.....	Stolzenau, Ger., G 6
5952	Stone, England, I 13
.....	Stonefield, Ire., F 4
532	Stoneham, Que., K 21
4185	Stonehaven, Scot., I 23
107	Stonehenge, Austl., I 19
3704	Stonehouse, Scot., N 16
.....	Stonetown, Ire., I 10
1020	Stonewall, Man., Q 16
877	Stoney Creek, Ont., M 11
205	Stony Mountain, Man., P 16
566	Stony Plain, Alberta, K 20
.....	Stora, Syria, B 15
2442	Storehedinge, Den., L 22
.....	Storelvedalen, Nor., K 9
.....	Store Magleby, Den., K 23
1927	Stören, Norway, I 9
.....	Storisjör, Iceland, C 21
3459	Storkow, Ger., H 13
.....	Störlien, Sweden, I 10
.....	Stormberg Jc., U. S. Afr., M 16
.....	Stormont, Ont., F 24
3771	Stornoway, Scotland, E 7
9204	Storojnet, W. Sov. Un., H 19
.....	Storvik, Sweden, L 15
1243	Stouffville Jc., Ont., J 12
302	Stoughton, Sask., Q 10
5949	Stourport, England, J 13
295	Stovby, Denmark, J 10
747	Stövring, Denmark, E 10
.....	Stövring, Denmark, G 11
1280	Stow, Scotland, N 21
4296	Stowmarket, Eng., J 23
1266	Stow on the Wold, Eng., K 14
5107	Strabane, N. Ire., C 16
546	Strachan, Scot., I 22
499	Strachur, Scot., L 12
.....	Stradbally, Ire., K 17
.....	Stradbally, Ire., O 16
.....	Stradone, Ire., G 17
275	Straffordville, Ont. O 8
429	Strahan, Tasmania, D 4
1080	Straiton, Scotland, P 14
9786	Strakonice, Czech., G 6
.....	Stralau, Germany, Q 18
42000	Stralsund, Ger., C 12
.....	Strancally Castle, Ire., O 14
3161	Strand, Norway, M 4
.....	Stranden, Norway, J 5
.....	Strandhill, Ire., F 11
.....	Strangford, N. Ire., E 25
.....	Strangway Springs, Australia, L 14
.....	Stranortar, Ire., D 14
6490	Stranraer, Scot., Q 12
193119	Strasbourg, France, H 24
442	Strasbourg, Sask., O 8
1600	Strassfurt, Germany, H 9
6284	Straszbrug, Ger., E 12
.....	Stratfieldsay, Eng., L 16
3900	Stratford, N. Z., G 16
17038	Stratford, Ont., M 7
11616	Stratford-upon-Avon, England, J 16
.....	Strathan, Scot., I 11
.....	Strathaven, Scot., N 15
1161	Strathblane, Scot., M 15
250	Strathclair, Man., P 13
133	Strathcona, Ont., I 19
179	Strathachlan, Scot., M 11
560	Strathmore, Alta., N 21
.....	Strathnaver, B. C., K 13
.....	Strathpeffer, Scot., G 14
3016	Strathroy, Ont., N 5
.....	Strathy, Scotland, C 16
.....	Strathyre, Scot., L 15
.....	Stratton, Eng., N 6
24000	Straubing, Ger., O 11
.....	Streamstown, Ire., J 15
.....	Streatham, Eng., C 21
.....	Street, Ire., H 16
709	Streetsville, Ont., L 11
7999	Strehaia, Rom. K 17
3611	Strehla, Ger., J 12
.....	Stretton, Eng., I 11
.....	Strib Stovby, Den., K 10
2024	Strichen, Scot., G 23
4623	Strijen, Neth., I 12
.....	Strö, Denmark, I 21
2341	Strobel, Arg., L 17
.....	Stroeder, Arg., A 24
.....	Strokestown, Ire., H 13
233	Strome, Alberta, L 22
.....	Strome Ferry, Scot., H 10
.....	Strömmen, Norway, A 7
2116	Stromness, Scot., B 18
3073	Strömstad, Sweden, N 9
.....	Strond, Iceland, C 19
.....	Strone, Scotland, H 14
94	Strongfield, Sask., O 7
3312	Strongoli, Italy, L 20
.....	Strontian, Scotland, K 10
8360	Stroud, England, K 13
227	Stroud, Ontario, I 11
.....	Struan, Scot., J 16
5463	Struer, Denmark, G 4
.....	Struga, Yugo, M 14
9586	Strumica, Yugo, M 16
.....	Struy, Scotland, H 13
30682	Stry, W. Sov. Un., G 17
460	Strydenburg, U. S. Afr., L13
	Stryj, see Stry, W. Sov. Un.
400	Stuarts Town, U. S. Afr., L 20
2145	Stubbeköbing, Den., N 20
93	Studholme Jc., N. Z., O 10
.....	Stung-treng, Fr. In. Ch., P 8
4538	Sturgeon Falls, Ont., R 24
15	Sturgeon Landing, Sask., J7
11	Sturgeon River, Sask., K 7
346	Sturgis, Sask., N 11
.....	Sturgis Jc., Sask., N 11
905	Stutterheim, U. S. Afr., O17
445000	Stuttgart, Ger., O 5
2727	Stylis, Grc., O 17
.....	Suâdi, Egypt, R 10
.....	Suafiresh Shemaliyeh, Palestine, N 5
1573	Suaita, Col., H 12
4759	Suakin, Anglo-Egyptian Sudan, H 20
.....	Suakin, Morocco, E 9
2604	Suances, Spain, C 12
.....	Suanhwa, China, C 15
1099	Suaqui, Son. G 13
824	Suaruro, Bolivia, M 12
.....	Suayan, Iran, I 13
.....	Subathu, India, D 10
.....	Subeit, Morocco, G 4
7183	Subiaco, Italy, I 12
100058	Subotica, Yugo., I 13
.....	Subz, Afg., L 18
17101	Suceava, Romania, H 2
.....	Suchan, Sov. Un. Asia, I 20
830	Suches, Bolivia, F 2
2565	Suchiapa, Chia., M 15
.....	Suchow, China, C 4
.....	Süchow, China, G 17
50000	Süchow, China, F 17
29857	Sucre, Bolivia, K 9
2485	Sucre, Col., E 11
.....	Sucuriû, Brazil, H 18
7007	Sudbury, England, K 22
32203	Sudbury, Ont., R 23
.....	Sudshi, Chn., B 8
19890	Sueca, Spain, K 17
.....	Suenia, Morocco, H 5
35547	Suez, Egypt, I 24
91	Suffield, Alberta, O 23
.....	Suffuh, Afg., L 18
.....	Sufian, Iran, C 2
120000	Sugash Shuyukh, Iraq, P 23
.....	Sugny, Belgium, Q 14
22000	Sûhâg, Egypt, N 20
16000	Suhl, Germany, K 8
2671	Suhr, Switz., E 12
.....	Suichow, China, G 14
.....	Suiping, China, G 15
2480	Suippes, France, G 18
.....	Suitechow, China, E 12
.....	Suiyangh, China, I 9
10000	Suiyuan, China, C 13
9700	Sujangarh, India, F 8
6780	Sukagawa, Japan, I 22
.....	Sukand, Iran, J 10
.....	Suk el Arba, Morocco, E 7
.....	Sukhinichi, Sov. Un., J 9
.....	Sukhir, Afg., I 19
.....	Sukhnin, Palestine, G 10
21537	Sukhumi, Sov. Un., P 13
.....	Suk Telata, Mor., E 8
2000	Sukumo, Japan, P 7
436	Sulaco, Honduras, F 9
15000	Sulaimaniya, Iraq, J 21
.....	Suldrup, Denmark, E 9
.....	Suledal, Norway, M 4
1839	Sulen, Norway, K 3
2778	Sulgen, Switz., C 18
	Sulimov, see Batalpashinsk, Sov. Un.
5924	Sulina, Rom., J 25
22344	Sullana, Peru, F 2
.....	Sulphur, Yukon, K 4
148	Sulsted, Denmark, D 11
.....	Sultanabad, Iran, G 13
55000	Sultanabad, Iran, H 5
.....	Sultanabad, Iran, N 11
.....	Sultaniyah, Iran, E 4
1600	Sultanpur, India, C 10
9600	Sultanpur, India, G 15
2016	Sultepec, Méx., I 3
5822	Sulzbach, Ger., N 9
.....	Sumad, Transjordan, J 21
.....	Sumdbland, Arg., O 14
.....	Sumdero, Cuba, I 3
26600	Sumen, Bul., L 22
.....	Sumesar, Nepal, F 17
63883	Sumi, Sov. Un., L 9
5422	Sumiswald, Switz., G 10
.....	Summeil, Palestine, L 5
.....	Summerhill, Ire., I 19
900	Summerland, B. C., Q 16
5034	Summerside, P. E. I., G 14
200	Summerstown, Ont., F 25
313	Summerville, N. S., L 13
.....	Sumnal, India, A 12
9000	Sumoto, Japan, N 12
15707	Sumperk, Czech., F 9
.....	Sunchow, China, L 11
.....	Sundalsoren, Nor., J 7
.....	Sundby, Denmark, E 5
.....	Sunder, India, B 9
185870	Sunderland, Eng., C 15
749	Sunderland, Ontario, I 13
100	Sundre, Alta., M 20
.....	Sundre, Sweden, P 17
45	Sundridge, Ont., C 12
308	Sunds, Denmark, H 6
18006	Sundsvall, Sweden, J 15
.....	Sungki, China, I 18
.....	Sungkiangfu, China, H 20
.....	Sungming, China, J 6
.....	Sungpan, China, G 7
5249	Sungurlû, Tur., D 9
.....	Sunhwa, China, E 6
.....	Sunning, China, L 14
1368	Sunny Brae, N. B., H 12
241	Sunnybrae, N. S., K 18
.....	Suojärvi, Fin., E 8
.....	Supanburi, Thai., O 3
3100	Supaul, India, G 20
2181	Supe, Peru, K 7
32	Superior Junction, Ontario, O 17
.....	Surafend, Palestine, L 6
.....	Surag, Iran, R 13
.....	Suran, Iran, P 16
.....	Suran, Pal., M 7
.....	Surar, I. E. A., L 11
.....	Surashtra Dhani, Thai., R 1
500	Surat, Austl., K 22
171443	Surat, India, I 6
4555	Suratá, Col., F 14
.....	Surbiton, England, D 19
.....	Sürenberg, Switz., I 12
.....	Surendalen, Norway, I 7
32018	Suresnes, Fr., B 4
.....	Suretka, Pan., O 16
3550	Surgeres, France, L 7
.....	Surgut, Sov. Un. Asia, F 12
3049	Suri, Bolivia, H 6
1265	Surif, Palestine, N 8
.....	Surindra, Thai., O 5
3203	Sürmene, Tur., C 15
3475	Sursee, Switz., F 12
.....	Sur-Sung, Afg., H 19
.....	Suru, India, B 9
1199	Surumi, Bolivia, J 8
255	Süs, Switz., J 23
3089	Susa, Italy, D 1
16104	Sušak, Yugo., J 6
4700	Susaki, Japan, O 8
3500	Susami, Japan, O 12
.....	Sushevo, Sov. Un., H 6
	Sušice, see Schüttenhofen, Ger.
3027	Sussex, N. B., J 10
888	Sutherland, Sask., M 7
800	Sutherland, U. S. Afr., O 9
.....	Suthri, India, H 2
2654	Sutri, Italy, H 10
3718	Sutsutsu, Japan, G 12
.....	Sutton, England, D 21
1051	Sutton, Ontario, I 12
1118	Sutton, Quebec, R 18
2837	Sutton Bridge, Eng., I 20
25151	Sutton-in-Ashfield, Eng., H 16
.....	Sutton on Sea, Eng., G 20
8394	Suva, Fiji Is., Q 17
21539	Suwalki, Poland, C 16
468	Suxy, Belgium, Q 16
744	Suyo, Peru, F 2
.....	Suyung, China, I 8
132	Svabensverk, Sweden, L 14
1271	Svaneke, Denmark, Q 25
2157	Svansten, Sweden, E 20
5021	Svärdsjo, Sweden, L 14
.....	Svärholt, Norway, A 21
.....	Svatsum, Norway, K 8
.....	Svedala, Sweden, Q 11
.....	Sveen, Norway, M 3
.....	Sveg, Sweden, J 13
1162	Svelvik, Norway, C 3
14392	Svendborg, Denmark, M 13
.....	Svenljunga, Sweden, O 11
636	Svenstrup, Denmark, E 10
425544	Sverdlovsk, Sov. Un. Asia G 10
.....	Sverero, Sov. Un. Asia, D 13
4583	Svilajnac, Yugo., K 14
8364	Svilengrad, Bul., M 21
691	Svinninge, Denmark, J 17
.....	Svinör, Norway, O 5
.....	Svisloch, W. Sov. Un., D 17
12067	Svistov, Bulgaria, K 20
10441	Svitavy, Czech., F 9
.....	Sviyazhsk, Sov. Un., I 18
2749	Svolvär, Norway, D 13
.....	Svyentsyany, W. Sov. Un., B 19
2783	Swaffham, Eng., I 22
.....	Swainbost, Scot., D 7
2814	Swakopmund, S. W. Afr., P 12
4083	Swalmen, Neth., K 20
114	Swalwell, Alberta, N 21
6276	Swanage, Eng., N 14
3560	Swan Hill, Austl., O 18
.....	Swanlinbar, Ire., F 14
1129	Swan River, Man., M 12
164825	Swansea, Wales, L 8
42	Swanson, Sask., N 6
890	Swastika, Ont., Q 24
178600	Swatow, China, K 17
.....	Swatragh, N. Ire., C 19
401	Sweetsburg, Quebec, Q 18
3784	Swellendam, U. S. Afr., Q 9
6053	Swevezeele, Belgium, L 6
	Swieciany, see Svyentsyany, Sov. Un.
.....	Swiecie, Pol., C 11
.....	Swift Creek, B. C., L 16
5594	Swift Current, Sask., P 5
62407	Swindon, Eng., L 14
.....	Swineford, Ire., G 8
.....	Swineshead, Eng., H 19
13820	Swinton, Eng., G 16
.....	Switzers, N. Z., P 6
	Swizlocz, see Svisloch, Sov. Un.
.....	Swords, Ire., I 22
614	Sydenham, Ont., H 20
138060	Sydney, Australia, O 22
28305	Sydney, N. S., H 24
8198	Sydney Mines, N. S., Q 23
710	Sydpröven, Grnld., Q 6
.....	Sydvaranger, Norway, B 24
.....	Syevsk, Sov. Un., K 9
2848	Syke, Ger., F 6
4500	Syktyvkar (Ust Sisolsk), Sov. Un., E 18
21435	Sylhet, India, G 25
.....	Sylhet, India, L 19
150	Sylvania, Sask., M 9
805	Sylvan Lake, Alta., M 20
580	Symington, Scot., O 18
3050	Syngem, Belgium, L 7
	Syracuse, see Siracusa, It.
.....	Syston, Eng., I 17
.....	Syudan, Afg., G 21
	Szabadka, see Subotica, Yugo.
.....	Szamotuly, Poland, D 9
25490	Szarvas, Hungary, I 13
	Szatmárnemeti, see Satu-Mare, Rom.
.....	Szczuczyn, Pol., C 15
.....	Szecheng, China, K 8
.....	Szechow, China, G 18
.....	Szechow, China, J 11
136438	Szeged, Hungary, I 13
40731	Székesfehérvár, Hung., H 11
14025	Szekszárd, Hung., I 11
20000	Szemao, Chn., L 4
234200	Szeming (Amoy), China, K 18
.....	Szenan, China, I 20
.....	Szengenfu, China, L 10
32885	Szentes, Hungary, I 13
.....	Szepingkai, Manch., B 21
.....	Szeshui Ho, China, F 14
31437	Szigetvár, Hung., I 10
38730	Szolnok, Hung., I 13
.....	Szolvya, Hung., O 27
35756	Szombathely, Hung., H 9
.....	Szomolnok, Hung., O 23

T

Pop.	Place, Country, Index
1438	Taarbaek, Denmark, J 23
673	Taarnby, Denmark, J 23
509	Taars, Denmark, C 11
6988	Tabacundo, Ecuador, B 5
2266	Tabalosos, Peru, G 8
.....	Tabankulu, U. S. Afr., M 19
10000	Tabapy, Par., O 7
.....	Tabarca, Tunisia, B 22
.....	Tabas Kuchak, Iran, K 12
.....	Tabatinga, W. Brazil, F 19
6000	Tabbas, Iran, I 12
.....	Tabelkosa, Algeria, K 13
1331	Taber, Alberta, P 22
11411	Tabérnes, Spain, K 17
577	Tabia, Algeria, E 12
1447	Tablas, Bolivia, I 8
	Tabocas, see Itabuna, Braz.
14251	Tábor, Czech., N 14
7943	Tabora, Tan., L 19
.....	Tabossi, Arg., L 17
.....	Tabou, Fr. W. Afr., J 4
.....	Tabriaa, Morocco, F 10
220000	Tabriz, Iran, C 2
.....	Tabsor, Palestine, K 6
.....	Tabucintac, N. B., D 11
.....	Tabul, China, C 15
1258	Täby, Sweden, P 22
420	Taca, Bolivia, H 5
1089	Tacacoma, Bolivia, G 3
4471	Tacambaro de Codallos, Michoa., O 11
.....	Tacanas, Arg., H 11
1621	Tacaquira, Bol., L 10
1157	Tacarigua, Venez., C 14
110866	Tacgu, Kor., E 25
.....	Tachin, Siam, P 3
3329	Tachkoi, Tur., B 8
7051	Tachov, Czech., F 5
16776	Tacna, Chile, A 3
11378	Tacna, Peru, Q 19
2667	Taco Taco, Cuba, I 5
1394	Tacotalpa, Tab., K 16
24000	Tacuarembo (San Fructuoso) Urug., H 19
.....	Tacubaya, Méx. D.F., H 5
.....	Tacurupucú, Par., N 11
.....	Tadafal, Mor., I 7
.....	Tadami, Japan, I 20
14	Tadanac, B. C., Q 17
.....	Tadcaster, England, F 16
.....	Taddart, Algeria, E 21
120	Tademit, Algeria, E 17
732	Tadgemout, Algeria, F 16
.....	Tadjentourt, Algeria, N 22
.....	Tadjerouma, Alg., G 16
3000	Tadjoura, Fr. Som., F 14
1263	Tado, Col., H 7
6200	Tadotsu, Japan, M 10
766	Tadoussac, Que., F 25
.....	Tadwan, Tur., F 17
.....	Taebring, Denmark, E 4
16400	Taejŏn, Kor., E 24
6303	Tafalla, Spain, E 15
.....	Tafelfelt, Mor., F 6
1443	Tafers, Switz., I 7
.....	Tafersit, Sp. Mor., E 9
.....	Tafessach, Algeria, Q 22
.....	Tafetti, Italy, A 24
188808	Taganrog, Sov. Un., N 12
.....	Tagasago, Japan, M 12
.....	Taga Zong, Bhutan, F 23
.....	Taghmon, Ire., N 20
.....	Tagish, Yukon, Q 11
.....	Tagmout, Morocco, K 3
.....	Tagnaout, Morocco, E 6
2000	Tago, Japan, N 18
.....	Taguin, Algeria, E 15
.....	Tahantas, Algeria, L 14
4000	Taha Yub, Egypt, H 14
538	Tahdzibichén, Yuc., F 23
.....	Tahilla, Ire., P 4
.....	Tahirbegg, Afg., F 18
.....	Tahiri, Iran, O 7
12520	Tahoua, Fr. W. Afr., H 9
.....	Tahrud, Iran, G 9
.....	Tahta, Egypt, M 19
711	Tahua, Bolivia, L 5
.....	Tâhu el Amûdên, Egypt, R 9
.....	Taichow, China, I 20
51572	Taichu, For., K 20
.....	Taiebah, Egypt, E 7
340114	Taihoku, For., K 21
.....	Taikung, China, J 10
	Taikyū, see Tacgu, Korea
2176	Tain, Scotland, F 16
112142	Tainan, For., L 20
21111	Taiping, China, H 18
.....	Taiping, Mal. St., R 15
.....	Taipling, China, L 9
5800	Taira, Japan, J 23
.....	Taiserbo, Libya, F 15
.....	Taito, For., K 21
.....	Taitunsze, Chn., C 10
	Taiyuan, see Yangku, China.
3300	Taiza, Japan, K 13
1500	Tajima, Japan, I 21
5000	Tajimi, Japan, L 16
.....	Tajrish, Iran, F 7
9300	Tajumulco, Guat., F 2
.....	Taka, Japan, L 10
.....	Takachi, Japan, G 14
700	Takahagi, Japan, K 22
.....	Takahara, Japan, J 21
5300	Takahashi, Japan, L 10
430	Takaka, N. Z., I 13
111207	Takamatsu, Japan, M10
4300	Takanabe, Japan, P 5
76380	Takao, For., L 20
51760	Takaoka, Japan, J 16
6400	Takaoka, Japan, O 9
59923	Takasaki, Japan, K 19
2700	Takase, Japan, N 4
30934	Takata, Japan, I 18
4000	Takato, Japan, L 17
800	Takatsu, Japan, L 7
13600	Takayama, Japan, K 16
.....	Takdicht, Morocco, J 5
2200	Takeda, Japan, L 12
.....	Takefu, Japan, K 14
.....	Takeo, Fr. In. Ch., R 7
.....	Takeshiki, Japan, K 2
.....	Takhfikhan, Afg., D 20
.....	Takhling, China, L 13
.....	Takht, Iran, P 11
.....	Takoradi, G. C., K 6
.....	Takot, India, B 6
.....	Takriets, Algeria, B 18
.....	Taku, China, D 17
.....	Takuw-pa, Thai., R 1
.....	Takwan, China, I 7
.....	Tala, Algeria, M 14
86	Tala, Chile, A 3
9653	Tala, Egypt, F 11
.....	Tala, Egypt, N 11
.....	Tala, Tunisia, D 23
9086	Tala, Uruguay, O 20
5194	Talaberaó Puna, Bol., K 9
.....	Talachi, China, E 8
.....	Talakan, Afg., G 23
2500	Talamba, India, D 5
2746	Talamone, Italy, H 8
.....	Talamuyuna, Arg., J 9
.....	Talanfu, China, E 17
.....	Talang, China, K 5
1503	Talapampa, Bolivia, L 7
.....	Talar, Baluchistan, R 18
12985	Talara, Peru, F 1
.....	Talat ed Dumm, Palestine, M 11
18631	Talavera de la Reina, Spain, I 11
50464	Talca, Chile, O 4
.....	Talca, Oax., L 10
35774	Talcahuano, Chile, P 2
.....	Talcher, India, J 18
.....	Taldora, Australia, F 18
.....	Taleta, Eth., J 11
23000	Tali, China, J 4
.....	Talia, Australia, N 14
.....	Talikhan, Afg., E 23
8232	Talina, Bolivia, M 8
.....	Talisker, Scot., H 6
.....	Taliwar, Iran, E 11
5200	Talkha, Egypt, D 15
.....	Talladale, Scotland, G 10
.....	Tallahint, Morocco, K 2
482	Tallard, France, N 22
145565	Tallinn (Revel), Sov. Un., F 4
.....	Tallow, Ire., O 13
56	Talmage, Sask., Q 9
1116	Talmont, France, K 6
.....	Talmún, S. L. P., K 18
.....	Talnoe, W. Sov. Un., G 25
2849	Talpa, Jal., M 3
4077	Talsi, Sov. Un., G 2
5659	Taltal, Chile, G 3
2659	Talvik, Norway, B 19
445	Tama, Argentina, K 9
.....	Tama, Egypt, M 19
.....	Tamagawa, Japan, H 21
1043	Tamalameque, Col., E 12
1644	Tamames, Spain, H 9
.....	Tamanart, Morocco, L 3
.....	Tamangueyu, Arg., Q 19
3463	Tamara, Col., H 15
.....	Tamarin, Neth. Gu., B 10
42444	Tamási, Hungary, I 11
23207	Tamatave, Madag., O 24
.....	Tamatea, N. Z., C 16
3619	Tamazula, Jal., N 7
798	Tamazula, Sin., N 15
880	Tamazula, Dur., N 17
1439	Tamazulapan, Oax., K 7
4538	Tamazunchale, S.L.P., L 18
.....	Tamberias, Arg., L 6
.....	Tambillo, Ec., B 5
500	Tambo, Austl., I 20
630	Tambo, Chile, K 4
1323	Tambo, Col., K 6
1481	Tambo, Col., L 5
1462	Tambo, Peru, M 13
1033	Tambobamba, Peru, N 15
1000	Tambo de Mora, Peru, M 9
.....	Tambores, Uruguay, I 19
17321	Tamboril, Brazil, F 21
121285	Tambov, Sov. Un., K 13
.....	Tambul el Kubra, Egypt, E 14
.....	Tamdegost, Morocco, I 4
.....	Tamdelt, Algeria, M 8
.....	Tamdjart, Algeria, P 21
1154	Tame, Col., G 15
.....	Tamentit, Algeria, N 13
.....	Tamerna, Algeria, F 20
.....	Tamerza, Tunisia, E 22
3950	Tamesis, Col., H 8
.....	Tamessinet, Algeria, M 11
.....	Tamezred, Tunisia, F 24
.....	Tamgrut, Morocco, K 7
1571	Tamiahua, Ver., E 8
.....	Tamingfu, China, E 15
624	Tamins, Switz., I 19
13262	Tamise, Belgium, R 7
.....	Tamluk, India, I 21
	Tammerfors, see Tampere, Fin.
.....	Tamnugalt, Morocco, J 6
59200	Tampere, Fin., E 3
82475	Tampico, Tam., C 7
1009	Tampico el Alto, Ver., C 7
.....	Tamrurat, Morocco, J 3
2992	Tamsweg, Aus., H 6
.....	Tamuh, Egypt, J 14
9913	Tamworth, Austl., M 22
581	Tamworth, Ontario, H 19
.....	Tamza, Algeria, D 20
.....	Tan, China, M 11
.....	Tana, Chile, C 4
3200	Tanabe, Japan, B 25
6300	Tanabe, Japan, O 12
105258	Tananarive, Madag., O 24
.....	Tancacha, Arg., L 12
1323	Tancanhúitz, S. L. P., K 17
.....	Tanchon, Kor., C 24
2164	Tancítaro, Michoa., O 9
787	Tancoco, Ver., E 7
410	Tancook Island, N. S., N 13
.....	Tancuayalab, S. L. P., K 18
.....	Tanda, Egypt, K 17
.....	Tandawanna, Austl., K 22
.....	Tanderagee, N. Ire., E 21
.....	Tanderup, Denmark, L 10
.....	Tandi, India, C 10
52647	Tandil, Arg., P 18
.....	Tanemoi, Japan, F 16
.....	Tanesimet, Morocco, G 10
.....	Tang, Iran, Q 15
7500	Tanga, Tanganyika, L 21
3569	Tangancícuaro, Michoa., N 9
.....	Tangar, China, E 5
13123	Tangermünde, Ger., G 10
60000	Tangier, Morocco, D 7
352	Tangier, N. S., M 17
.....	Tangku, China, D 17
.....	Tanha, Brazil, G 21
1200	Taniai, Japan, L 15
66889	Tanjore, India, P 12
4400	Tank, India, C 4
1193	Tanlajas, S. L. P., K 17
.....	Tannas, Egypt, H 13
826	Tannay, France, J 16
.....	Tannuk, Palestine, I 9
1900	Tano, Japan, O 10
.....	Tano, Japan, Q 4
.....	Tanor, India, G 21
.....	Tanot, India, F 4
.....	Tanout, Algeria, O 24
20	Tanque, Coa., B 6
1138	Tanquián, S. L. P., K 18
.....	Tanquinco, Guat., E 6
.....	Tansa, Egypt, N 12
.....	Tansetta, Morocco, J 7
.....	Tansoor, Morocco, E 8
23759	Tansui, For., K 21
94421	Tanta, Egypt, E 12
118	Tantallon, Sask., P 11
334	Tantima, Ver., E 7
3574	Tantoyuca, Ver., E 6
750	Tantûra, Palestine, I 7
.....	Tanub, Egypt, F 10
.....	Tanûf, Egypt, L 17
.....	Tanum, Sweden, N 9
.....	Taochow, China, J 13
.....	Taoeri, Bolivia, L 12
.....	Taokow, China, F 15
3466	Taormina, Italy, N 17
.....	Taoulala, Algeria, F 15
.....	Taourirt, Algeria, P 14
1769	Taourirt, Morocco, I 7
.....	Taourirt Kebira, Alg., R 19
.....	Taourirt Sghira, Alg., Q 18
3704	Tapa, Sov. Un., G 4
7693	Tapacari, Bolivia, I 7
15187	Tapachula, Chia., Q 17
1926	Tapalpa, Jal., M 6
1317	Tapalque, Arg., O 17
.....	Taplong, Nepal, F 20
7055	Tapolca, Hung., I 10
5681	Taquara do Mundo Novo, Brazil, Q 12
.....	Taquaralsinho, Brazil, H 7
.....	Tara, N. Ire., E 25
495	Tara, Ontario, H 7
.....	Tara, Sov. Un. Asia, G 12
.....	Tarabad, Iran, M 10
	Tarabolous, see Tripoli, Syr.
9162	Tarabuco, Bolivia, K 10
439	Taraco, Peru, O 19
1063	Tarairi, Bolivia, M 13
.....	Tara Klu, Tur., C 5
.....	Taramsa, Egypt, O 23
6779	Tarancón, Spain, I 13
89534	Taranto, Italy, K 21
.....	Tarapaca, Col., Q 20
9249	Tarapoto, Peru, G 8
.....	Tarapur, India, J 5
11474	Tarare, France, L 18
.....	Tarariras, Uruguay, O 16
4870	Tarascon, France, O 19
1834	Tarascon, France, Q 12
.....	Tarashcha, W. Sov. Un., F 25
347	Tarasp, Switz., I 24
3500	Tarata, Bolivia, I 8
1678	Tarata, Chile, A 3
.....	Tarauacá, West Brazil, I 18
.....	Tarawera, N. Z., G 20
11237	Tarazona, Spain, F 15
890	Tarbat, Scotland, F 17
600	Tarbert, Ire., M 6
.....	Tarbert, Scot., F 5
.....	Tarbert, Scot., M 9
.....	Tarbert, Scot., N 10
34749	Tarbes, France, P 10
1905	Tarcento, Italy, C 12
1921	Tardientá, Spain, F 16
.....	Tärendö, Sweden, E 19
265	Taretan, Michoa., O 10
.....	Tarfside, Scot., J 21
.....	Targa, Morocco, D 7
15424	Târgoviste, Romania, J 20
5074	Targu-Frumos, Rom., H 21
12944	Târgu-Jiu, Rom., J 17
12592	Targul-Ocna, Rom., I 21
5000	Targul-Săcuesc, Rom., I 20
38116	Târgu-Mures, Rom., I 18
9127	Târgu-Neamt, Rom., H 20
.....	Tarhgan, Iran, J 6
14815	Tarifa, Spain, P 9
.....	Tarij, Iran, H 12
27000	Tarija, Bolivia, M 11
3165	Tarimoro, Guan., M 13
.....	Taringla, Hond., G 9
947	Tarkastad, U. S. Afr., N 15
671	Tarkwa, G. C., J 6
310	Tarm, Denmark, I 4
7876	Tarma, Peru, L 10
.....	Tärna, Sweden, G 13
9000	Târnava-Sân-Martin, Rom., I 18
35831	Tarnopol, W. Sov. Un., F19
45235	Tarnów, Poland, F 14
15773	Tarnowskie Gory, Pol., F 12
.....	Taroa, Col., A 17
438	Taroom, Austl., J 22
2452	Tarporley, Eng., H 12
35648	Tarragona, Spain, G 19
45081	Tarrasa, Spain, F 20
24382	Tarsus, Tur., H 9
2641	Tartaş, France, O 8
3150	Tartous, Syr., K 10
59000	Tartu, Sov. Un., G 5
8793	Tarudant, Mor., J 3
.....	Tarumaville, Br. Gu., C 7
3700	Tarumidzu, Japan, Q 3
4082	Tarvita, Bolivia, L 11
349	Täsch, Switz., O 10
636	Taschereau, Que., D 3
.....	Tasgaon, India, L 7
11631	Tashinchiao, Manch., C 20
585005	Tashkent, Sov. Un. Asia, J 10
10000	Tash-Kurgan, Afg., E 21
.....	Tasht, Iran, M 8
.....	Tasjö, Swe., H 14
.....	Tasremost, Mor., I 5
.....	Tasseiya, Syria, C 19
.....	Tassgong, Bhutan, F 24
.....	Tassiting, India, F 21
.....	Tatah, Mor., F 6
980	Tatamagouche, N.S., J 15
.....	Tatar-Bunar, W. Sov. Un., I 25
24200	Tatar Pazardjik, Bul., M 18
.....	Tatekawa, Japan, N 9
5300	Tateoka, Japan, G 22
.....	Tati, Bech., O 17
.....	Tating, China, J 8
	Tatsienfu, see Kangting, China.
900	Tatsuno, Japan, L 11
10800	Tatta, India, G 1
.....	Tattershall, England, H 19
28492	Tatung, China, D 14
.....	Taufers, Italy, B 10
.....	Taug, Iraq, K 20
.....	Tauisk, Sov. Un. Asia, D 19
2755	Taule, France, H 2
2760	Taumarunui, N. Z., G 18
22800	Taungs, U. S. Afr., H 14
.....	Taungup, Bur., O 21
25177	Taunton, England, M 10
700	Taupo, N. Z., G 19
2000	Taura, Ec., D 3
.....	Taurage, W. Sov. Un., B 15
3910	Tauranga, N. Z., E 19
9074	Taus (Domazlice), Ger., N11
6214	Táuste, Spain, F 16
.....	Tavanasa, Switz., J 18
3356	Tavannes, Switz., F 7
12762	Tavira, Portugal, N 6
.....	Tavisk, Afg., J 16
1066	Tavistock, Ont., M 7
.....	Tavolato, Italy, C 24
29018	Tavoy, Bur., Q 24
.....	Tawfikiyah, Egypt, E 10
.....	Tawila, Egypt, C 15
1179	Tayabamba, Peru, I 8
1081	Tayahua, Zac., K 7
.....	Tayeh, China, H 15
.....	Taylorton, Sask., R 10
.....	Tay-ninh, Fr. In. Ch., Q 8
	Tayport, see Ferry Port on Craig, Scot.
21800	Taza, Morocco, E 9
.....	Tazerut, Morocco, I 4
519175	Tbilisi (Tiflis), Sov. Un., Q 17
	Tcha-Djuma, see Charshemba, Tur.
.....	Tchemmich, Sp. Mor., D 6
16251	Tczew, Pol., C 12
2690	Teabo, Yuc., F 22
3843	Teano, Italy, J 14
2023	Teapa, Tab., L 16
2450	Te Aroha, N. Z., E 19
.....	Teatree Well, Austl., G 13
900	Te Aute, N. Z., H 21
.....	Tebalbalet (Wells), Algeria, N 21
.....	Tebay, England, E 12
8163	Tebessa, Algeria, D 21
.....	Tebourba, Tunisia, B 24
.....	Tebulba, Tunisia, C 25
3143	Tecamachalco, Pueb., I 7
493	Tecate, Baja Cal., A 2
2769	Tecoh, Yuc., F 21
.....	Tecojate, Guat., G 3
387	Tecolutla, Ver., F 8
1727	Tecoman, Colim., O 5
715	Tecomavaca, Oax., K 8
2010	Tecomaxtlahuaca, Oax., L 6
9219	Tecpam, Guatemala, F 4
3636	Tecpan de Galeana, Guer., Q 13
7460	Técsö, Hung., P 28
6456	Tecuala, Nay., J 2
128	Tecuanapa, Guer., R 18
17259	Tecuci, Rom., I 22
2412	Tecumseh, Ontario, Q 1
.....	Teddington, England, C 19
.....	Tedjida, Algeria, Q 24
.....	Tedjidkan, Algeria, M 24
.....	Tedmama, Algeria, E 15
.....	Tedsi, Morocco, J 3
.....	Teelin, Ire., D 10
.....	Teeranearagh, Ire., P 1
819	Teeswater, Ont., J 6
700	Teetulpa, Austl., M 17
.....	Teffé, Brazil, F 2
.....	Tegel, Germany, N 15
10553	Tegelen, Neth., K 20
2366	Teggiano, Italy, K 17
47223	Tegucigalpa, Hond., G 10
.....	Tehan, China, I 16
55000	Tehchow, China, E 16
.....	Teh el Barud, Egypt, E 8
540087	Tehran, Iran, F 7
16278	Tehuacan, Pueb., J 8
9252	Tehuantepec, Oax., N 11
2238	Tehuitzingo, Pueb., J 6
146	Teiasir, Palestine, J 11
10019	Teignmouth, Eng., N 9
1880	Teirshiha, Palestine, F 10
.....	Tejedor, Argentina, O 14
6116	Tejutla, Guat., F 2
.....	Tekaf-Baluri, Iran, L 5
.....	Tekart, Morocco, E 7
6061	Tekax, Yuc., G 22
.....	Tekbalet, Algeria, D 11
	Tekfur Dagh, see Tekirdagi, Tur.

Pop.	Place Country Index
20354	Tekirdagi (Rodosto), Tur. C 2
2267	Tekit, Yuc., F 22
2620	Te Kuiti, N. Z., F 17
.....	Telaritos, Arg., J 10
13000	Telav, Sov. Un., Q 17
140000	Tel Aviv, Pal., L 5
2530	Telbâna, Egypt, D 16
	Telechany, see Telekhany, Sov. Un.
.....	Telegraph Creek, B. C., D 7
.....	Telekhany, W. Sov. Un., D 19
.....	Tel el-Amarna, Egypt, L 18
.....	Tel el-Kufara, Egypt, Q 10
.....	Telén, Argentina, O 11
5000	Tel Kiaf, Iraq, I 19
197	Telkwa, B. C., I 9
.....	Tell Abu Hureireh, Palestine, P 3
.....	Tell Asur, Palestine, L 10
.....	Tell Atrum, Transj., K 15
.....	Tell Damieh, Transj., L 13
.....	Tell Deir Alla, Transj., K 13
.....	Tell el Husn, Transj., J 13
.....	Tellel Kebir, Egypt, F 18
.....	Tellel Mazar, Palestine, K12
.....	Tell es Safi, Palestine, N 6
.....	Tell et Truny, Palestine, M 11
.....	Téllez, Hid., G 5
.....	Tell Ghariyeh, Transj., J 23
.....	Tell Ghassul, Transj., M 13
.....	Tell Hammam, Transj., M 14
.....	Tell Juhflje, Transj., I 15
.....	Tell Kalah, Syr., K 11
.....	Tello, Arg., L 9
.....	Tell Zaraa, Transj., I 14
25177	Teloekbetoeng, Neth. Ind., I 3
5140	Teloloapan, Guer., P 15
.....	Tel Rak, Egypt, E 18
6200	Telsiai, W. Sov. Un., A 15
.....	Telt, Egypt, O 10
.....	Tel Tenis, Egypt, C 22
.....	Teluk Anson, Mal. St., Q 2
7260	Temacin, Algeria, G 20
.....	Temamsan, Morocco, D 9
.....	Temapache, Ver., E 7
761	Temascaltepec, Méx., I 3
	Temassinin, see Fort Flatters, Alg.
2690	Temax, Yuc., E 22
1456	Tembladera, Peru, H 4
3617	Tembleque, Spain, J 13
.....	Temesuin Hadaja, Mor., E 9
	Temesvár, see Timisioara, Rom.
12	Temjabiche, Baja Cal., N 11
5700	Temnikov, Sov. Un., J 15
3823	Temora, Austl., O 20
2363	Temosachic, Chih., G 16
.....	Tempelhof, Ger., R 17
1800	Templemore, Ire., L 14
.....	Templetouhy, Ire., L 14
3353	Templeuve, Belgium, N 6
7539	Templin, Germany, F 12
.....	Tempo, N. Ire., E 16
.....	Temran, Tur., E 15
42035	Temuco, Chile, Q 3
772	Ten, Col., H 15
.....	Tena, Ecuador, C 8
2098	Tenabo, Camp., G 20
3382	Tenamaxtlan, Jal., M 5
6644	Tenancingo, Méx., I 4
5462	Tenango, Méx., I 4
1572	Tenango, Hid., F 6
.....	Tenbury, England, J 12
4108	Tenby, Wales, L 6
3863	Tence, France, M 18
3550	Tendo, Japan, G 22
262	Tenejapa, Chia., M 16
1810	Tenerife, Col., D 11
6998	Tenez, Alg., C 15
.....	Tengchow, China, G 13
.....	Tengchow, China, E 19
.....	Tengchwan, China, J 4
.....	Tenientre, Arg., Q 14
3078	Teniet el Haad, Alg., D 15
27338	Tenkasi, India, Q 10
31	Tennant Creek, Austl., F 14
1440	Tennäs, Sweden, J 11
1090	Tenneville, Belgium, P 17
1733	Tenosique, Tab., L 18
6698	Tensa, Col., I 12
3473	Tenterden, England, M 22
2700	Tenterfield, Austl., L 23
7909	Teocaltiche, Jal., L 8
3896	Teocelo, Ver., H 8
1180	Teococuilco, Oax., L 9
600	Teodolina, Arg., N 15
1784	Teopisca, Chia., M 16
1422	Teotepec, Oax., N 8
2288	Teotihuacán, Méx., H 5
2112	Teotitlán, Oax., J 8
.....	Tepa, Hid., G 6
5894	Tepatitlan, Jal., L 8
2992	Tepeaca, Pueb., I 7
2432	Tepecoacuilco, Guer., P 16
1606	Tepehuanes, Dur., N 19
1770	Tepelmeme, Oax., K 8
706	Tepetongo, Zac., J 7
785	Tepetzintla, Ver., E 7
17547	Tepic, Nay., K 3
30911	Teplice-Sanov, Czech., F 6
1171	Teposcolula, Oax., L 7
4576	Tequila, Jal., L 6
.....	Tequisquiapan, Guer., M 15
775	Tequixtepec, Oax., K 7
267	Tequizquiapan, Guan., L 13
3833	Ter Aar, Neth., G 13
5400	Teradomari, Japan, H 19
.....	Terai, Iran, Q 12
9865	Teramo, Italy, H 13
2200	Terang, Austl., Q 17
.....	Ter Apel, Neth., D 24
1771	Terbalu, Tur., F 1
.....	Terborg, Neth., H 21
1396	Terebinto, Bolivia, I 13
.....	Terenga, Sov. Un., J 18
.....	Terenos, Brazil, M 9
35254	Teresina, Braz., F 19
.....	Terespol, Pol., D 17
4329	Terheiden, Neth., I 13
.....	Teri, India, B 5
24900	Termez, Sov. Un. Asia, K 10
18307	Termini Imerese, It., N 14
5324	Termoli, Italy, I 16
.....	Termonbarry, Ire., H 13
.....	Termoncarragh, Ire., F 3
9997	Termonde (Dendermonde), Belgium, L 10
.....	Termonfeckin, Ire., H 22
3469	Ternath, Belgium, M 10
8200	Terneuzen, Neth., K 9
	Terneuzen see Neuzen, Neth.
26775	Terni, Italy, H 11
.....	Terontola, Italy, G 10
355	Terrace, B. C., I 8
9780	Terracina, Italy, J 2
3570	Terrasson, France, M 12
2209	Terrebonne, Quebec, O 15
.....	Térrero, Hond., F 11
.....	Terryglass, Ire., K 12
.....	Tersa, Egypt, I 13
.....	Terschelling, Neth., B 15
.....	Terslev, Den., L 20
.....	Terter, Sov. Un., R 19
16172	Teruel, Spain, I 16
9845	Tešanj, Yugo, K 11
.....	Tesfrut, Mor., G 8
7200	Teshio, Japan, E 13
25804	Tesin, Czech., F 11
.....	Tesl n, Yukon, Q 13
.....	Tessaoua, Fr. W. Afr., I 10
142	Tessala, Alg., D 12
6398	Tessenderloo, Bel., L 15
.....	Testour, Tunisia, B 23
.....	Tetaff, Algeria, O 13
2237	Tetbury, England, L 13
2756	Tete, Moz., N 19
263	Tete a Gauche River, N.B., C 9
208	Tetecala, Morel., I 4
2259	Teteringen, Neth., J 14
7228	Teterow, Germany, D 11
3878	Teteven, Bulgaria, L 18
.....	Teton, see Cordoba, Col.
16372	Tetovo, Yugo, M 14
.....	Tetrina, Sov. Un., C 11
48347	Tetuán, Sp. Mor., D 8
4800	Tetyushi, Sov. Un., I 18
4326	Teufen, Switz., E 19
3782	Teulada, Italy, M 3
578	Teulon, Man., P 16
632	Teustepe, Nicaragua, J 12
541	Tewantin, Austl., K 24
4352	Tewkesbury, England, K 13
5437	Texcoco, Méx., H 5
.....	Texupilco, Méx., I 3
8386	Teziutlán, Pueb., G 8
5207	Tezontepec, Hid., G 5
.....	Tha Aleda, Bur., M 22
1134	Thaba Nchu, U. S. Afr., J 17
.....	Thal, India, B 4
.....	Thaldat, India, A 12
8061	Thalwil, Switz., E 15
3019	Thame, England, K 17
4220	Thames, N. Z., D 18
521	Thamesford, Ont., N 7
828	Thamesville, Ont., P 4
21816	Thana, India, B 5
16000	Thana, India, K 6
6100	Thaneswar, India, D 10
7500	Thanh-hoa, Fr. Indo China, M 8
6623	Thann, France, I 23
.....	Thann, Germany, Q 10
700	Thargomindah, Austl., K 19
.....	Tharsis, Spain, M 7
.....	Thaungdut, Bur., M 21
12900	Thayetmyo, Bur., O 21
2063	Thayngen, Switz., B 15
7113	Thebes, Greece, P 17
.....	Theddlethorpe, Eng., G 20
623	Thedford, Ontario, M 4
.....	The Falls, N. S., J 16
	The Hague, see 's Gravenhage, Neth.
.....	Thekhek, Fr. In. Ch., N 7
37	Thelma, Alta., P 24
.....	The Mound, Scot., F 16
.....	The Naze (Lindesnäs), Norway, O 4
335	Theodore, Sask., O 10
	Theodosiya, see Feodosiya, Sov. Un.
12254	Theophilo-Ottoni, Brazil, L 19
3181	The Pas, Man., K 12
.....	The Rag, Ire., M 13
	Theresiopel, see Subotica, Yugo.
	Therezina, see Teresina, Braz.
.....	Thesa, Morocco, E 9
1316	Thessalon, Ontario, R 22
265160	Thessaloniké (Salonika) Grc., N 17
4097	Thetford, Eng., J 22
12716	Thetford Mines, Que., N 21
5137	Theux, Belgium, N 18
1076	Thevenard, Austl., M 13
5787	Thiais, France, C 6
.....	Thicket Portage, Man., I 15
1568	Thielen, Belgium, K 14
11611	Thielt, Belgium, L 6
8103	Thiene, Italy, C 9
16383	Thiers, France, L 16
13356	Thiès, Fr. W. Afr., H 1
.....	Thio, Erit., B 12
18934	Thionville, France, G 21
3000	Thirsk, Eng., E 16
8047	Thisted, Denmark, D 5
.....	Thistle Creek, Yukon, L 4
3285	Thiviers, France, M 11
3143	Tholen, Neth., J 10
1000	Thomastown, Ire., M 18
.....	Thomazina, Brazil, N 13
120	Thomson, N. S., J 14
11291	Thonon-les-Bains, France, K 23
541	Thorburn, N. S., J 18
1677	Thorn, Neth., K 19
	Thorn, see Torun, Pol.
.....	Thornbury, Eng., L 12
130	Thornbury, N. Z., Q 4
838	Thornbury, Ont., M 9
305	Thorndale, Ont., N 7
.....	Thorne, Eng., G 17
800	Thornhill, Scot., P 17
.....	Thornton, Ont., I 11
.....	Thornton, Scot., L 20
5305	Thorold, Ont., N 12
.....	Thorrill, Ont., K 12
.....	Thorrisdale, Scot., D 15
3200	Thorshavn, Den., E 24
.....	Thorshöfn, Iceland, A 24
8181	Thouars, France, J 9
11074	Thourout, Bel., L 5
706	Three Hills, Alberta, M 21
32	Throne, Alberta, M 23
1773	Thuillies, Bel., O 11
6620	Thuin, Belgium, O 11
16428	Thun, Switz., J 10
.....	Thunderhill Junction, Manitoba, M 12
4500	Thurles, Ire., M 14
.....	Thurlow, B. C., O 10
1292	Thurso, Quebec, P 11
4095	Thurso, Scot., C 18
1292	Thusis, Switz., J 20
107	Thylungra, Austl., J 19
567	Thyregod, Den., I 7
2162	Tiabaya, Peru, P 17
5440	Tiaguanaco, Bolivia, H 3
.....	Tiallalin, Mor., H 9
18158	Tiangua, Brazil, F 20
1202	Tianguistengo, Hid., F 6
23622	Tiaret, Algeria, D 15
.....	Tiaret, Tunisia, I 24
.....	Tiba, Egypt, F 15
24555	Tibagy, Brazil, O 12
10759	Tibaná, Colombia, H 12
.....	Tibati, Cam., J 11
.....	Tiberius, see Tubariya, Pal.
.....	Tibnah, Palestine, N 7
.....	Tibneh, Palestine, L 8
.....	Tibneh, Transj., M 10
.....	Tibrikot, Nepal, E 15
.....	Tiburon, Haiti, J 11
.....	Tical, Guat., B 17
130	Tichborne, Ont., G 19
42	Tichfield, Sask., O 6
.....	Tichma, Algeria, O 11
.....	Ticint, Morocco, K 5
173	Ticuamar, Chile, B 4
1137	Ticucha, Bolivia, L 12
9034	Ticul, Yuc., F 21
165	Tidehead, N. B., A 7
.....	Tidewater, B. C., Q 2
316	Tidnish, N. S., I 14
235	Tiefenkastel, Switz., J 21
46282	Tiehling, Manch., B 21
12370	Tiel, Neth., H 16
.....	Tienchen, China, C 15
1209696	Tientsin, China, D 17
802	Tiermas, Spain, E 16
1156	Tierra Blanca, Guan., L 14
7255	Tierra Blanca, Ver., J 10
1977	Tierra Nueva, S. L. P., K 13
.....	Tiffin, Cuba, K 18
	Tiflis, see Tbilisi, Sov. Un.
31698	Tighina, Sov. Un., N 5
.....	Tigili, Sov. Un. Asia, D 20
435	Tignish, P. E. I., E 14
.....	Tihodaït, Algeria, Q 21
.....	Tihon, Iran, N 12
1412	Tihuatlan, Ver., F 7
50000	Tihwa (Urumchi), Sink., J 13
16486	Tijuana (Zaragoza), Baja Cal., A 1
.....	Tijucas, Brazil, P 13
6600	Tikhvin, Sov. Un., G 9
.....	Tikrit, Morocco, J 6
.....	Tikrit, Iraq., K 19
348	Tilama, Chile, L 4
87297	Tilburg, Neth., J 15
2155	Tilbury, Ontario, Q 3
525	Tilcara, Argentina, F 10
.....	Tilghemt, Algeria, G 16
.....	Tillberga, Sweden, M 15
193	Tilley, Alberta, O 23
316	Tilley, N. B., E 4
.....	Tillin, Morocco, D 2
4002	Tillsonburg, Ont., O 8
.....	Tillsonburg Jc., Ont., O 8
.....	Tilmas el Mra, Alg., N 19
.....	Tilrum, Norway, G 11
57286	Tilsit, W. Sov. Un., B 15
458	Tiltil, Chile, M 4
364	Tim, Denmark, H 3
.....	Timahoe, Ire., L 17
2713	Timana, Colombia, K 8
17800	Timaru, N. Z., N 10
2138	Timbio, Col., K 6
4356	Timbiqui, Col., K 4
.....	Timbo, Fr. W. Afr., I 2
267	Timboon, Australia, Q 18
	Timbuctu, see Tombouctou, Fr. W. Afr.
3642	Time, Norway, N 3
4828	Timimoun, Algeria, L 13
.....	Timiskaming Jc., Quebec, K 1
91866	Timisoara, Rom., J 14
.....	Timker, Sp. Mor., D 10
28790	Timmins, Ont., P 23
.....	Timoleague, Ire., Q 9
.....	Timote, Argentina, O 15
.....	Timring, Denmark, H 4
1070	Timusi, Bolivia, G 3
.....	Tin, Norway, L 7
1126	Tinaco, Ven., D 11
.....	Tinahely, Ire., L 21
3787	Tinaquillo, Ven., D 11
.....	Tinazrat, Algeria, M 13
.....	Tindivanam, India, O 13
1000	Tindouf, Alg., M 4
21338	Tineo, Spain, C 9
.....	Tingchow, China, D 15
.....	Tingchow, China, J 17
.....	Tingfan, China, J 9
1111	Tinglev, Denmark, N 7
.....	Tingnan, China, K 15
.....	Tingo Maria, Peru, J 10
.....	Tingsas, Sweden, P 13
.....	Tingstade, Sweden, O 17
.....	Tingsted, Denmark, N 20
2756	Tinguindin, Michoa., N 9
9989	Tinguipaya, Bol., K 8
.....	Tingyüanting, China, G 10
.....	Tingyüanying (Wang Ye fu), Chn., D 8
57078	Tinnevelly, India, Q 10
3000	Tinogasta, Arg., I 8
2485	Tinos, Grc., P 20
.....	Tinpak, China, L 13
1653	Tinta, Peru, N 17
.....	Tintazart, Morocco, K 4
3968	Tintin, Bolivia, J 9
.....	Tintina, Arg., H 14
180	Tintinara, Austl., O 17
.....	Tinylkoum, Alg., Q 25
392	Tinzen, Switz., K 21
.....	Tio, Eth., E 12
5384	Tiobraid Arann (Tipperary), Ire., N 12
35792	Tipton, England, I 13
847	Tipuani, Bolivia, G 4
1488	Tira, Egypt, C 14
.....	Tiradentes, Brazil, M 17
30806	Tiranë, Albania, M 13
4056	Tirano, Italy, C 7
.....	Tirapata, Peru, O 19
7132	Tiraque, Bolivia, I 8
.....	Tiraque, Bol., I 10
31600	Tiraspol, W. Sov. Un., H 24
15228	Tirat, Alg., D 15
3985	Tirebolu, Tur., C 14
20662	Tirlemont, Belgium, M 14
12802	Tirnovo, Bulgaria, L 20
.....	Tiro General, S. L. P., I 12
.....	Tirserum, Sweden, O 14
.....	Tirstrup, Denmark, G 18
.....	Tirúa, Chile, Q 2
25500	Tiruchendur, India, Q 11
18700	Tirupatur, India, P 11
27769	Tiruvannamalai, India, O 12
1237	Tisdale, Sask., L 9
.....	Tise, Denmark, F 7
.....	Tismoulin, Alg., F 13
.....	Tissemsi, Algeria, D 15
.....	Tistrup, Den., J 4
591	Tisvildeleje, Denmark, I 21
.....	Titao, China, F 7
1700	Tittmoning, Ger., Q 11
9611	Tiverton, Eng., N 9
650	Tiverton, N. S., O 8
265	Tiverton, Ont., I 5
14502	Tivoli, Italy, I 17
.....	Tivourvourt, Fr. W. Afr., H 1
2309	Tixkokob, Yuc., E 22
6130	Tixtla, Guer., Q 16
3048	Tizapán, Jal., M 7
3379	Tizauljak (Výlok), Hung., P 26
.....	Tizi, Algeria, D 13
6687	Tizimin, Yuc., E 24
3673	Tizi Ouzou, Algeria, B 17
352	Tjaereborg, Den., K 3
.....	Tjele, Denmark, G 9
.....	Tjölling, Norway, G 2
5463	Tlacotalpan, Ver., J 11
5297	Tlacolula, Oax., M 9
244	Tlacolula, Ver., H 8
1217	Tlacotepec, Pueb., I 7
2212	Tlahualilo (de Zaragosa), Dur., L 23
4889	Tlajomulco, Jal., M 6
1768	Tlalchapa, Guer., P 14
1674	Tlalixcoyan, Ver., I 10
3216	Tlalnepantla, Méx., H 5
5385	Tlalpujahua, Michoa., N 14
.....	Tlaltenango, Zac., K 6
798	Tlaltizapan, Morel., I 5
3320	Tlapa, Guer., Q 18
2876	Tlapacoyan, Ver., G 8
1013	Tlancualpican, Pueb., J 5
.....	Tlaring, U. S. Afr., H 13
374	Tlatlaya, Méx., J 3
8270	Tlaxcala, Tlax., H 6
2182	Tlaxco, Tlax., H 6
8701	Tlaxiaco, Oax., L 7
1154	Tlayacapan, Morel., I 5
.....	Tlelis, Algeria, D 12
26384	Tlemçen, Alg., E 12
.....	Toanan, Manch., A 20
1227	Toay, Arg., P 12
.....	Toba, Arg., J 17
4600	Toba, Japan, N 15
13110	Tobarra, Spain, L 15
5000	Tobati, Paraguay, N 8
.....	Tober, Ire., F 13
.....	Tobercurry, Ire., G 9
.....	Tobermore, N. Ire., D 19
771	Tobermory, Scot., K 9
.....	Tobin Mills, Quebec, J 22
.....	Toblach, Italy, B 10
.....	Tobo, I. E. A., L 9
14798	Tobolsk, Sov. Un. Asia, G 11
.....	Toca da Onca, Brazil, J 21
3727	Tocaima, Col., I 10
22400	Tochigi, Japan, K 21
1696	Tocla, Bolivia, L 10
6556	Toco, Bolivia, I 8
547	Tocomechi, Bolivia, I 14
15516	Tocopilla, Chile, E 4
.....	Tocra, Libya, E 14
2645	Tocuyo, Ven., D 8
3457	Todi, Italy, H 11
22223	Todmorden, Eng., G 14
.....	Todmorden, Ont., K 12
192	Todos Los Santos, Colombia, G 18
.....	Todos Santos, Bolivia, D 6
1253	Todos Santos, Baja Cal., Q 12
551	Tofield, Alta., K 21
.....	Tofnis, Egypt, P 23
2800	Togane, Japan, M 21
.....	Togi, Japan, I 16
.....	Tognuf, Erit., A 7
250	Togo, Sask., O 11
.....	Toi, Japan, G 12
.....	Toirim, Chn., A 10
270	Tojo, Bolivia, M 10
.....	Tokaanu, N. Z., G 19
5069	Tokaj, Hungary, H 14
.....	Tokanui, N. Z., Q 6
4000	Tokar, A. E. Sud., H 20
21261	Tokat, Tur., D 11
.....	Tokatsukutsu, Taiwan, K 20
.....	Tokéterebes (Trebišov), Hung., O 25
663	Tokomaru, N. Z., I 18
.....	Tokoto, China, C 12
.....	Tokuda, Japan, J 22
119581	Tokushima, Japan, N 11
11500	Tokuyama, Japan, M 6
6778804	Tokyo, Japan, M 20
530	Tolé, Panama, Q 19
1661	Toledo, Bolivia, J 5
162	Toledo, Chile, H 4
300	Toledo, Ont., G 21
34592	Toledo, Spain, I 11
5189	Tolentino, Italy, G 12
.....	Tolentino, S. L. P., J 13
4132	Tolfa, Italy, H 10
.....	Tolgen, Norway, J 9
.....	Toli, Eth., J 8
3082	Tolimán, Quer., L 15
.....	Tollerton, England, F 16
3521	Tolmezzo, Italy, C 12
.....	Tolombon, Arg., H 9
13583	Tolosa, Spain, D 15
.....	Tolsta, Scotland, D 8
.....	Tolstrup, Denmark, C 10
1014	Toltén, Chile, R 3
.....	Tolti, India, A 9
5804	Tolú, Col., D 9
3875	Tolú, Viejo, Col., D 9
43429	Toluca, Méx., H 4
.....	Tölz, Ger., R 9
.....	Tom, Norway, E 6
6012	Tomabe, Bolivia, L 7
.....	Tomakomai, Japan, G 13
.....	Tomamai, Japan, F 13
.....	Toman Agha, Afg., G 16
9730	Tomar, Port., J 5
.....	Tomara, Morocco, F 6
.....	Tomari, Japan, B 25
.....	Tomari, Japan, F 15
.....	Tomarrazón, Col., B 14
.....	Tomasiri, Peru, Q 18
38065	Tomaszów Mazowiecki, Poland, E 13
10433	Tomaszów, Pol., F 17
10	Tomate, Baja Cal., P 11
798	Tomatlán, Jal., M 2
1514	Tomayapo, Bolivia, M 10
5495	Tombouctou (Timbuctu), Fr. W. Afr., H 6
.....	Tomdown, Scot., I 12
28982	Tomelloso, Spain, K 13
705	Tomepampa, Peru, O 15
.....	Tomgrancy, Ire., L 10
.....	Tomia, Egypt, K 12
600	Tomintoul, Scot., H 19
.....	Tomioka, Japan, J 23
3100	Tomioka, Japan, O 2
1300	Tomiya, Japan, G 23
827	Tommerup, Denmark, L 11
409	Tompkins, Sask., P 4
.....	Tompkinsville, N. S., K 20
141215	Tomsk, Sov. Un. Asia, G 13
.....	Tomter, Norway, C 7
.....	Tonala, Ver., K 13
6379	Tonalá, Chia., N 14
2605	Tonalá, Jal., M 7
2130	Tonalá, Oax., K 7
.....	Tonatins, W. Brazil, D 22
33870	Tonbridge Wells, Eng., M 21
5728	Tönder, Denmark, M 5
.....	Tondi, India, P 12
216	Toney Mills, N. S., J 17
669	Tongland, Scotland, Q 16
356	Tongoi, Chile, K 3
11525	Tongres, Belgium, M 16
1184	Tongue, Scotland, D 14
298	Tonichi, Son., H 13
33900	Tonk, India, G 9
4495	Tonnay-Charente, Fr., L 8
6746	Tonneins, France, O 10
4463	Tonnerre, France, I 17
3577	Tönning, Germany, C 6
.....	Tono, Japan, E 24
370	Tonosi, Pan., R 20
11980	Tönsberg, Norway, E 3, M 8
531	Toodyay, Australia, M 4
.....	Toome, Ire., D 20
.....	Toompine, Australia, J 19
.....	Toomyvara, Ire., L 13
.....	Toorkubar, Bal., P 21
.....	Tooting, England, C 21
26423	Toowoomba, Austl., K 22
.....	Top Camp, Austl., I 4
910	Topia, Dur., N 18
.....	Topkia, Nepal, F 21
.....	Topley, B. C., J 10
.....	Toplita-Romana, Rom., 119
.....	Topolja, Yugo., J 12
538	Topolobampo, Sin., M 14
.....	Toprak-Kale, Tur., D 18
.....	Torão, Brazil, H 17
437	Torato, Peru, P 18
.....	Torbalü, Tur., D 5
.....	Torbay, N. S., L 21
110	Torbrook, N. S., M 11
218	Torbrook Mines, N. S., M 11
3579	Tordesillas, Spain, G 10
12616	Torgau, Germany, I 11
4487	Toribio, Col., K 7
1672	Torigni, Fr., G 8
2216	Torin, Son., J 12
594698	Torino, It., D 2
.....	Torla, Spain, E 17
.....	Torne, Sweden, P 13
.....	Torning, Denmark, H 8
2307	Tornio, Fin., C 5
4433	Toro, Colombia, I 7
8346	Toro, Spain, F 10
3781	Torocari, Bolivia, J 8
4475	Torondoy, Ven., F 6
667457	Toronto, Ontario, L 12
6253	Toropalca, Bolivia, L 9
.....	Toropets, W. Sov. Un., A 24
.....	Torp, Sweden, J 14
.....	Torpshammar, Sweden, J 15
46165	Torquay, England, O 9
200	Torquay, Sask., R 9
.....	Torr, N. Ire., B 22
3424	Torreblanca, Spain, I 18
1230	Torrecilla en Cameros, Spain, F 14
2181	Tôrre de Moncorvo, Portugal, G 8
5118	Torrejoncillo, Spain, I 9
2367	Torrelaguna, Spain, H 13
19315	Torrelavega, Spain, C 11
12138	Torre Maggiore, Italy, I 16
.....	Torrent, Arg., J 22
75796	Torreon, Coa., F 7
9541	Torre-Pacheco, Spain, M 16
2026	Torre Pellice, Italy, E 1
.....	Torres, Brazil, Q 13
.....	Torres, Son., G 11
.....	Torre Schiari, Italy, B 24
12387	Torres Novas, Port., J 6
.....	Torres Vedras, Port., J 4
9274	Torrevieja de la Mata, Spain, M 17
.....	Torridon, Scotland, G 10
3666	Torrijos de los Olivares, Spain, I 11
.....	Torrin, Scotland, I 8
841	Törring, Denmark, I 8
104	Torrowangee, Austl., M 18
7384	Torrox, Spain, O 12
.....	Torsaker, Sweden, L 15
.....	Torsas, Sweden, Q 14
97	Torslev, Denmark, D 8
2038	Tortoli, Italy, K 5
10391	Tortona, Italy, D 4
38269	Tortosa, Spain, H 18
492	Tortugas, Arg., M 15
.....	Torum, Denmark, F 6
54280	Torun, Pol., D 11
108	Torup, Denmark, D 7
.....	Torup, Denmark, E 11
.....	Torup, Sweden, P 11
12700	Torzhok, Sov. Un., H 9
.....	Toscaig, Scotland, H 9
.....	Toscanella, Italy, H 10
.....	Tosno, Sov. Un., G 7
.....	Töss, Switzerland, D 15
10048	Tossia, Tur., C 9
15264	Totana, Spain, M 15
.....	Totatiche, Jal., K 6
.....	Totma, Sov. Un., G 14
4525	Totnes, Eng., O 8
5623	Totonicapan, Guat., F 3
2231	Totora, Bolivia, I 4
7470	Totora, Bolivia, I 9
.....	Totora, Peru, Q 19
.....	Totoral, Argentina, K 8
.....	Totoral, Uruguay, I 18
.....	Totoralejos, Arg., J 11
15	Totoralillo, Chile, J 3
157748	Tottenham, Eng., L 19
561	Tottenham, Ont., J 10
.....	Torteridge, England, A 20
37189	Tottori, Japan, K 11
.....	Toucheng, China, C 13
12108	Touggourt, Alg., G 20
.....	Toujan, Tunisia, F 24
13267	Toul, France, H 21
150310	Toulon, France, P 21
1137	Toulon-sur-Arroux, Fr., K 17
213220	Toulouse, France, P 12
.....	Touma, Tunisia, B 23
23223	Toungoo, Bur., O 22
206	Tounin, Algeria, C 13
6900	Tourane, Fr. In. Ch., O 10
78393	Tourcoing, France, E 15
	Tour de Peilz, see la Tour-de-Peilz, Switz.
35898	Tournai, Bel., N 7
2001	Toúrnan, France, H 15
931	Tournay, France, P 10
5043	Tournon, France, M 19
51031	Tournus, France, K 19
.....	Touros, Brazil, F 25
83753	Tours, France, J 11
.....	Tourvilles, Quebec, O 18
52	Toussus, Fr., C 2
.....	Touws River, U. S. Afr., P 8
3639	Tovar, Ven., G 5
.....	Towcester, England, K 17
25876	Townsville, Australia, F 20
.....	Towshan, China, L 14
3803	Towyn, Wales, I 8
.....	Toyaco, Honduras, F 12
.....	Toyahara, Japan, J 21
127859	Toyama, Japan, J 17
.....	Toyohara, Kar., G 21
142716	Toyohashi, Japan, M 16
6300	Toyooka, Japan, K 12
6000	Toyoura, Japan, L 5
.....	Tozeur, Tunisia, F 22
32749	Trabzon (Trebizond), Tur., C 15
760	Tracadie, N. B., C 11
225	Tracadie, N. S., J 20
1383	Trachselwald, Switz., H 10
10285	Traighli (Tralee), Ire., O 4
8828	Traiguen, Chile, Q 3
9392	Trail, B. C., Q 18
	Tralee, see Traighli, Ire.
12343	Trälleborg, Swe., R 11
3584	Tramelon, Switz., F 7
1900	Tramore, Ire., O 17
211	Tramping Lake, Sask., M 5
.....	Tranas, Arg., H 10
2514	Trancoso, Brazil, K 21
2898	Trancoso, Port., G 7
805	Tranebjerg, Den., J 14
407	Tranekaer, Den., M 15
33223	Trani, Italy, J 19
5000	Tranquebar, India, P 13
.....	Tranqueira, Brazil, H 18
4973	Tranqueras, Uruguay, G 20
5495	Transcona, Man., Q 17
.....	Trantlebeg, Scot., D 16
.....	Tranum, Denmark, D 8
55532	Trapani, Italy, N 11
.....	Trapiará, Western Brazil, H 14
3116	Trapichillo, Guat., E 2
551	Traquair, Scot., O 20
.....	Traria, Algeria, E 13
117	Trasquila, Tlax., H 6
9028	Traunstein, Ger., R 11
75	Travers, Alberta, O 22
70	Traverse, P. E. I., H 14
1853	Travers, Switz., H 4
6334	Travnik, Yugo., K 10
92	Traynor, Sask., M 5
3556	Trebbin, Germany, H 12
13295	Třebic, Czech., G 9
6241	Trebinje, Yugo. L 11
	Trebizond, see Trabzon, Tur.
	Trebon, see Wittingau, Ger.
8006	Trecate, Italy, D 4
23195	Tredegar, Eng., K 10
.....	Tregaron, Wales, J 8
3019	Tréguier, France, G 3
.....	Trehorningsjö, Swe., I 17
18500	Treinta y Tres, Ur., L 23
3500	Trelew, Arg., B 23
306	Trelex, Switz., L 2
	Trembovaya, W. Sov. Un., G 19
	Trembowla, see Trembovaya, Sov. Un.
2115	Tremp, Spain, E 18
11796	Trenčín, Czech., G 11
30567	Trenque Lauquen, Arg., O 14
31146	Trento, Italy, C 8
8323	Trenton, Ont., J 17
2699	Trenton, N. S., J 17
.....	Trenton Jc., Ont., J 17
4335	Treptow, Germany, D 12
.....	Treptow, Germany, Q 19
.....	Tres Algarrobos, Arg., O 14
.....	Tres Arboles, Uruguay, J 18
46000	Tres Arroyos, Arg., Q 17
150	Tres Cruces, Chile, J 3
.....	Tres Lomas, Arg., O 14
.....	Tres Palos, Peru, I 6
.....	Tres Picos, Arg., Q 15
.....	Tres Portenas, Arg., M
61	Tres Puntas, Chile, I 4
791	Tres Valles, Ver., J 10
2965	Trets, France, P 21
.....	Tretten, Norway, K 9
5620	Treuenbrietzen, Ger., H 11
242	Trévés, France, O 16
	Treves, see Trier, Ger.
962	Trevi, Italy, G 11
.....	Trevino, Spain, D 13
29840	Treviso, Italy, D 10
2361	Trévoux, France, L 19
4181	Treysa, Germany, J 6
82	Tribune, Sask., R 9
6838	Tricarico, Italy, J 18
159566	Trichinopoly, India, P 11
45658	Trichur, India, P 9
.....	Trida, Austl., N 19
76700	Trier (Treves), Ger., M 2
228583	Trieste, Italy, D 13
3126	Trigal, Bolivia, J 12
1251	Trikeri, Grc., O 17
18682	Trikkala, Greece, O 15
.....	Trillick, N. Ire., E 15
926	Trillo, Spain, H 14
1500	Trim, Ire., I 19
.....	Trincheras, Chih., G 21
10160	Trincomalee, Cey., Q 14
4364	Tring, England, H 18
.....	Tring Junction, Que., M 22
7481	Trinidad, Bolivia, F 10
241	Trinidad, Chile, N 3
15453	Trinidad, Cuba, K 12
1745	Trinidad, Honduras, F 7
132	Trinidad, Son., H 14
15700	Trinidad, Ur., M 18
.....	Trinitaria, Chia., N 17
7622	Trinité, Martinique, F 24
8482	Trino, Italy, D 3
655	Trins, Switz., I 19
86137	Tripoli, Libya, E 12
35000	Tripoli (Tarabolous), Syr. L 10
14397	Tripolis, Greece, P 16
.....	Triumpho, Brazil, H 22
889	Triunfo, Baja Cal., P 12
96016	Trndrum, India, Q 10
2271	Trn, Bulgaria, L 16
23971	Trnava, Czech., G 10
480	Trochu, Alberta, M 21
614	Troense, Denmark, M 13
1966	Trogen, Switz., D 20
5830	Troia, Italy, I 17
10795	Troina, Italy, N 15
12000	Troiskoe, Sov. Un. Asia, F 11
42007	Trois Rivieres, Quebec, M 18
.....	Trois Saumons, Que., J 24
41900	Troitsk, Sov. Un. Asia, G 10
.....	Troitskoe-Pechorskoe, Sov. Un., D 21
.....	Troizkii-Verchotoimskii, Sov. Un., E 15
3926	Trojan, Bul., L 19
369	Trolhede, Denmark, I 4
15018	Trollhättan, Sweden, N 10
10359	Tromsö, Norway, B 16
5736	Tronchiennes, Bel., L 7
.....	Trondenes, Norway, C 14
54135	Trondheim (Nidaros), Norway, I 9
5323	Tropea, Italy, M 18
800	Trosa, Sweden, N 16
	Trotsk, see Krasnogvardeisk, Sov. Un.
.....	Troup Junction, B.C., Q 18
376	Trout Creek, Ont., C 12
.....	Trout Lake, B. C., O 17
345	Trovolhue, Chile, Q 2
12011	Trowbridge, Eng., M 13
57961	Troyes, France, I 17
110	Truax, Sask., Q 8
1423	Trubschachen, Switz., H 11
4514	Trujillo, Hond., D 11
38961	Trujillo, Peru, I 5
13753	Trujillo, Spain, J 9

Pop. *Place* *Country* *Index*
12688 Trujillo, Ven., E 7
1259 Truns, Switz., J 17
11074 Truro, England, O 4
10272 Truro, N. S., K 16
..... Truskava, W. Sov. Un., B 17
598 Trustrup, Denmark, G 15
15923 Trutnov, Czech., F 9
518 Tryon, P. E. I., H 15
Tryskiai, W. Sov. Un., A 15
601 Tsagezi, Grc., O 17
..... Tsaochowfu, China, F 16
..... Tsarev, Sov. Un., M 16
Tsaritsin, see Stalingrad, Sov. Un.
30881 Tsarskoe-Selo, Sov. Un., G 8
..... Tsau, Bech., O 15
..... Tsehchow, China, F 14
..... Tsengshinhsien, China, L15
..... Tsharschamba, Tur., C 6
..... Tshilongo, Bel. Cong., M 16
250000 Tsinan, China, E 17
..... Tsingchowfu, China, E 18
..... Tsingchow Hun, China, J 11
..... Tsinghu, China, J 17
..... Tsingkiangpu, Chn., F 18
..... Tsinglo, China, D 13
..... Tsingshuiho, China, D 13
350000 Tsingtao, China, E 19
..... Tsingyün, China, K 14
..... Tsining, China, F 17
30000 Tsitsihar, Manch., H 18
..... Tsolo, U. S. Afr., N 18
..... Tsomo, U. S. Afr., O 17
56088 Tsu, Japan, M 14
10295 Tsuchiura, Japan, L 21
9274 Tsuchizaki, Japan, D 22
..... Tsuhata, Japan, J 16
..... Tsukawa, Japan, H 21
..... Tsumeb, S. W. Afr., O 13
..... Tsumis, U. S. Afr., C 5
..... Tsunagi, Japan, H 21
..... Tsuno, Japan, P 5
40000 Tsunyi, China, I 9
20461 Tsurucka, Japan, F 21
11621 Tsuruga, Japan, K 14
..... Tsurusaki, Japan, N 6
5959 Tsuwano, Japan, L 7
34159 Tsuyama, Japan, L 10
..... Tsuyung, China, K 5
4180 Tuam, Ire., I 9
260 Tuamarina, N. Z., J 15
34400 Tuapse, Sov. Un., P 12
6992 Tubarão, Brazil, P 13
8633 Tubariya (Tiberius), Pal., H 12
3449 Tubas, Palestine, J 11
..... Tubber, Ire., K 9
8951 Tubbergen, Neth., F 23
28686 Tübingen, Germany, P 5
2053 Tucacas, Ven., C 11
2152 Tucacas Lagoon, Colombia, A 17
..... Tucano, Brazil, I 22
..... Tucavaca, Bol., J 18
1236 Tuchan, France, Q 15
..... Tuchola, Pol., C 11
1372 Tucta Pari, Bolivia, L 10
..... Tucule, Eth., D 9
157480 Tucumán, Argentina, H 10
1449 Tucume, Peru, G 3
328 Tucumilla, Bolivia, M 10
1972 Tucupido, Ven., E 15
3408 Tucupita, Ven., F 21
..... Tucura, Colombia, F 8
..... Tûd, Egypt, P 23
3171 Tudela, Spain, F 11
13134 Tudela, Spain, F 15
..... Tudse, Denmark, J 18
..... Tueileh, Transj., I 17
..... Tuen, Australia, K 20
518 Tuffé, France, I 10
..... Tuffuh, Palestine, O 8
..... Tug, Eth., M 12
..... Tuggur, Morocco, G 9
..... Tughar, India, B 11
717 Tuito, Jal., M 2
..... Tukab, Iran, I 12
..... Tukaghat, Afg., H 20
..... Tukh, Egypt, G 13
..... Tûkh el-Qarmus, Egypt, F 17
7653 Tukums, W. Sov. Un., A 16
..... Tukuyu, Tan., M 19
1858 Tula, Hid., G 4
3629 Tula de Tamaulipas, Tam., I 15
272403 Tula, Sov. Un., J 11
4900 Tulach Mhor (Tullamore), Ire., J 16
296 Tulahuen, Chile, K 4
12552 Tulancingo, Hid., G 6
..... Tulantongo, Oax., L 8
..... Tulbagh, U. S. Afr., P 8
12828 Tulcan, Ec., A 6
20108 Tulcea, Romania, J 24
..... Tulchin, W. Sov. Un., G 23
10447 Tulear, Madag., P 22
..... Tulia, Egypt, H 12
..... Tuliapur, India, K 9
..... Tulit, Morocco, I 6
..... Tuljapur, India, K 9
4815 Tul Karm, Palestine, K 8
..... Tulkhba, Afg., K 17
600 Tulla, Ire., L 9
Tullamore, see Tulach Mhor, Ire.
15021 Tulle, France, M 13
4594 Tullins, France, M 20
1616 Tullow, Ire., L 19
..... Tullyallen, Ire., H 21
..... Tulsk, Ire., H 12
..... Tulu, I. E. A., L 12
12017 Tulua, Colombia, J 7
204 Tulum, Q. R, F 25
9671 Tumaco, Col., L 2
64 Tumbaya, Arg., F 10
6355 Tumbes, Peru, E 2
..... Tumbut, Afg., J 19
2729 Tumeremo, Ven., H 22
9900 Tumkur, India, N 10
..... Tumlong, India, F 22
..... Tummel Bridge, Scot., J 16
..... Tummo, Libya, G 12
994 Tumupasa, Bolivia, E 4
568 Tumusla, Bolivia, L 9
..... Tuna, Sweden, O 14
..... Tunas de Zaza, Cuba, K 13
16332 Tunbridge, Eng., M 21
..... Tune, Denmark, J 21
..... Tungchang, China, E 16
..... Tungchow, China, D 16
..... Tungchow, China, G 20
..... Tungchow, China, F 11
..... Tungchwan, China, H 8
..... Tungchwan Yun, China, J 6
..... Tungi, Afg., H 20
..... Tungjen, China, J 11
..... Tungkwan, China, F 12
..... Tunglan, China, K 9

Pop. *Place* *Country* *Index*
..... Tungliaochen, Manch., B 19
..... Tungping, China, F 16
..... Tungtse, China, I 9
..... Tunguskoie, Sov. Un. Asia, F 13
7700 Tuni, India, L 16
3474 Tunia, Col., K 6
202405 Tunis, Tunisia, B 24
16597 Tunja, Col., H 12
..... Tunstall, England, H 13
..... Tunuyán, Afg., M 6
..... Tupambae, Ur., K 22
4000 Tupiza, Bolivia, M 8
..... Tuppeh Yarkhan, Afg., J 18
200 Tupperville, N. S., M 10
4324 Tuquerres, Col., M 4
..... Tura, Egypt, I 14
..... Tura, India, G 23
..... Turbachthal, Switz., L 8
8977 Turbaco, Col., C 9
5000 Turbat-i Haidari, Iran, G 14
..... Turbat-i-Shekh Jam, Iran, G 15
2324 Turbenthal, Switz., D 16
..... Turbina, Ont., A 6
1097 Turbo, Col., E 7
..... Turchal, Tur., D 11
1267 Turco, Bolivia, J 4
20057 Turda, Romania, I 17
..... Tureby, Denmark, L 21
..... Turek, Poland, E 11
..... Turgai, Sov. Un. Asia, H 10
1436 Turgi, Switz., D 13
21676 Turgutlu, Tur., D 12
599 Turicato, Michoa., O 11
121 Turin, Alta., P 22
Turin, see Torino, It.
..... Turiscatio, Michoa., P 9
10145 Turka, W. Sov. Un., G 16
21787 Turkestan, Sov. Un. Asia., J 10
..... Turki, Sov. Un., K 15
67722 Turky (Abo), Fin., F 3
26792 Turnhout, Bel., K 14
10153 Turnu-Măgurele, Rom., K 19
20872 Turnu Severin, Rom., K 16
..... Turov, Sov. Un., K 4
..... Turovo, Sov. Un., K 11
3944 Turriff, Scot., G 22
2433 Tursi, Italy, K 19
275 Turtleford, Sask., K 5
709 Turtmann, Switz., M 10
11179 Turtucaia, Bul., K 21
3488 Turúchipa, Bolivia, K 10
..... Turukhansk, Sov. Un. Asia, E 13
..... Turup, Denmark, L 10
..... Tury-Assú, Brazil, E 17
663 Tuschen, Br. Gu., A 7
..... Tushihkow, Manch., C 16
..... Tusnad, Rom., I 20
..... Tussûm, Egypt, F 23
..... Tutbury Eng., I 15
60395 Tuticorin, India, Q 11
..... Tutoya, Brazil, E 19
17000 Tuttlingen, Ger., Q 5
..... Tuweiyil Abu Jerwal, Palestine, P 5
721 Tuxcacuesco, Jal., N 5
105 Tuxford, Sask., P 7
13381 Tuxpan, Ver., E 8
6278 Tuxpan, Jal., N 7
10315 Tuxpan, Nay., K 2
2683 Tuxtepec, Oax., K 10
..... Tuxtla, Ver., J 11
2448 Tuxtla, Chico, Chia., P 17
15883 Tuxtla Gutierrez, Chia., M 15
13500 Túy, Spain, E 5
..... Tuyen-quang, Fr. In. Ch., L 8
..... Tuyün, China, J 10
..... Tuz Khurmatli, Iraq, K 20
16711 Tuzla, Yugo., K 11
..... Tuzly, Iran, F 4
..... Tved, Denmark, H 12
1141 Tvedestrand, Nor., N 7
Tver, see Kalinin, Sov. Un.
307 Tvingstrup, Denmark, I 11
111 Tvis, Denmark, G 5
790 Twann, Switz., G 7
1343 Tweed, Ont., H 18
..... Tweedmouth, Eng. A 14
177 Tweedsmuir, Scot., O 18
9573 25 de Mayo, Arg., O 17
..... Twickenham, Eng., C 19
3217 Twillingate, Newf., J 24
..... Twin City Jc., Ont., P 18
..... Two Rivers, N. S., J 12
720 Twynholm, Scot., Q 16
331 Tyborön, Denmark, F 2
..... Tynagh, Ire., K 11
..... Tynan, N. Ire., F 19
..... Tynda, Sov. Un. Asia, G 18
64913 Tynemouth (N. Shields), Eng., C 15
..... Tyne Valley, P. E. I., G 14
4500 Tyr (Sour), Syr., M 10
..... Tyrellspass, Ire., J 16
..... Tyresö, Sweden, R 23
2195 Tyrie, Scot., G 23
..... Tyrma, Sov. Un. Asia, G 19
7158 Tyrnavos, Greece, O 16
162 Tyrone, Ont., J 14
509 Tyrsted, Denmark, J 10
2852 Tysfjord, Norway, D 14
4408 Tysnes, Norway, L 3
..... Tystrup, Denmark, L 18
75537 Tyumen, Sov. Un. Asia, G 10
130 Tyvan, Sask., Q 9
..... Tzchotien, China, E 18
..... Tzechow, China, H 8
..... Tzechow Chi, China, E 15

U

..... Uajda, Algeria, M 13
..... Ualdia, Eth., F 10
..... Ualual, Eth., L 17
..... Uanda, Australia, G 19
..... Uanle, Som., R 17
..... Uapixanas, Bracil, C 5
..... Uarandab, Eth., L 15
..... Uarof, Eth., J 19
..... Uarsceich, Som., R 17
..... Uaruf, Eth., H 13
..... Uaxactum(ruins), Guat., B 5
113 Uayamen, Camp., H 20
7499 Ubala, Col., I 12
2682 Ubate, Col., H 11
5192 Ubbergen, Neth., I 19
145 Ubby, Denmark, K 17
31093 Ubeda, Spain, M 13
33786 Uberaba, Brazil, L 14
5207 Uberlingen, Ger., Q 6
485 Ubinas, Peru, P 18
..... Ubinzal, Brazil, E 16
..... Ubiriba, Brazil, F 8
745307 Ubol, Siam., O 7
14700 Ubombo, U. S. Afr., I 22
7599 Ubrique, Spain, O 10

Pop. *Place* *Country* *Index*
50225 Uccle, Belgium, M 11
7600 Uch, India, E 4
1700 Uchinoura, Japan, R 3
430 Uchire, Ven., D 15
6500 Uckermünde, Ger., D 13
3557 Uckfield, Eng., M 20
1239 Uclés, Spain, J 13
951 Uco, Peru, J 8
44035 Udaipur, India, H 7
..... Udale, Scotland, G 15
205 Udby, Denmark, F 12
..... Udby, Denmark, J 19
15104 Uddevalla, Sweden, N 10
..... Uddington, Scotland, O 17
7643 Uden, Neth., I 17
..... Udepur, India, I 19
6000 Udgir, India, K 10
52691 Udine, Italy, C 12
8000 Udipi, India, N 7
12 Udney, Ont., H 12
1474 Udny, Scotland, H 23
3914 Udo, Japan, O 4
..... Udskoi Ostrog, Sov. Un. Asia, F 19
35133 Ueda, Japan, K 18
..... Uelzen, Germany, F 8
..... Uema, Eth., H 12
15000 Ueno, Japan, M 14
245863 Ufa, Sov. Un., I 23
..... Ufran, Algeria, M 13
..... Ugadale, Scot., O 10
3650 Ugento, Italy, K 22
355 Uggelhuse, Denmark, G 12
..... Uggerlöse, Denmark, K 18
800 Ugie, U. S. Afr., N 18
3080 Ugijar, Spain, O 13
Uhersky Brod, Czech., G 10
..... Uhnow, W. Sov. Un., F 17
3363 Uig, Scotland, E 4
4000 Uig, Scotland, G 7
..... Uitdam, Neth., A 9
20584 Uitenhage, U. S. Afr., Q 15
3778 Uitgeest, Neth., F 13
4474 Uithuizen, Neth., B 22
..... Uitkijki, U. S. Afr., O 11
..... Ujgan, Iran, K 15
1700 Ujiie, Japan, K 21
..... Ujiji, Tanganyika, L 18
53779 Ujjain, India, H 9
Ujvidék, see Novi Sad, Yugo.
12000 Ukmerge, W. Sov. Un., B 18
..... Ulad Sidi Seian, Mor., H 10
Ulala, see Oirot Tura, Sov. Un. Asia.
70000 Ulan Bator Khoto (Urga), Mong., H 16
129417 Ulan Ude (Verkneudinsk), Sov. Un. Asia, H 16
285 Ulapes, Argentina, L 10
..... Ulasch, Tur., E 12
..... Ulbjerg, Denmark, F 8
3748 Ulčinj, Yugo., M 12
6782 Uldecona, Spain, H 18
701 Uldum, Denmark, J 8
Uleaborg, see Oulu, Fin.
..... Uled Raffa, Africa, M 11
..... Ulefos, Norway, M 7
941 Ulflingen, Lux., O 20
..... Ulg, Scot., E 4
4000 Uliassutai, Mong., I 14
..... Ulla, W. Sov. Un., B 22
1800 Ulladulla, Australia, O 22
800 Ullapool, Scot., F 12
..... Ullard, Ire., M 19
346 Ullaulla, Bolivia, F 2
..... Ullensaker, Nor., M 8
..... Ullensvang, Norway, L 5
229 Ullerslev, Denmark, L 14
4406 Ulloma, Bolivia, I 3
62590 Ulm, Germany, P 7
..... Ulnaes, Norway, L 7
4138 Ulricehamn, Sweden, O 11
..... Ulrichen, Switz., L-13
3798 Ulrum, Neth., B 21
..... Ulsta, Shetland Is., B 4
139 Ulsted, Denmark, D 12
501 Ulstrup, Denmark, E 8
..... Ulun, Hond., F 13
10121 Ulverston, Eng., E 11
1934 Ulverstone, Tasmania, C 5
1742 Ulvik, Norway, L 5
102106 Ulyanovsk (Simbirsk), Sov. Un., J 18
..... Umach, Algeria, E 19
471 Umachiri, Peru, O 18
5320 Umala, Bolivia, I 4
40600 Uman, W. Sov. Un., G 25
3120 Umán, Yuc., E 21
20201 Umanskaya, Sov. Un., N 12
3000 Umarkot, India, G 3
..... Umburanas, Brazil, H 20
..... Um Dribina, Mor., J 9
11138 Umea, Sweden, I 18
..... Umeria, India, H 13
..... Um Hakim, Egypt, D 9
..... Umm Dinâr, Egypt, H 12
..... Umm el Qusur, Egypt, L 18
..... Umm el Walud, Transjordan, N 15
..... Ummern, Germany, G 8
..... Umm es Surab, Transj., J 19
94 Umm et Tut, Palestine, I 7
..... Umm Junieh, Palestine, H 13
..... Umm Nabari, A. E. Sud., G 18
5530 Umtata, U. S. Afr., N 18
37200 Umzimkulu, U. S. Afr., L 19
2262 Umzinto, U. S. Afr., L 21
..... Una, Brazil, K 21
13100 Unao, India, G 13
..... Unapool, Scot., E 12
..... Unare, Ven., D 16
..... Uncia, Bol., J 6
..... Undersaker, Sweden, I 11
..... Understed, Denmark, C 13
5927 Ungarisch Brod, Ger., G 10
Ungvâr, see Užhgorod, Sov. Un.
..... União, Brazil, F 19
..... União, Brazil, F 23
6191 União, Brazil, H 24
..... União da Victoria, Brazil, O 12
5443 Unieh, Tur., C 12
..... Uniket, Mongolia, A 16
..... Union, Argentina, O 10
6560 Union, Chile, A 19
..... Union, Col., P 16
212 Union, Ont., O 6
1500 Union, Paraguay, N 9
14 Unión, Son., G 11
13533 Union, Ur., P 19
487 Union Bay, B. C., Q 11
1400 Uniondale, U. S. Afr., Q 12
6743 Union de Reyes, Cuba, H 8
4083 Unión de Tula, Jal., M 4
..... Unionhall, Ire., R 7
4070 Unión Hidalgo, Oax., N 12
682 Unity, Sask., M 4
40999 Unley, Austl., O 16
..... Unquillo, Arg., K 12
..... Unter Egeri, Switz., G 15
1972 Unterhallau, Switz., B 14

Pop. *Place* *Country* *Index*
1572 Unterkulm, Switz., E 12
3102 Unterseen, Switz., J 11
..... Unzha, Sov. Un., H 15
12000 Uotsu, Japan, I 17
3794 Upata, Ven., G 20
6345 Upington, U. S. Afr., I 10
212 Upper Blackville, N. B., F 9
231 Upper Cape, N. B., H 14
264 Upper Dorchester, N. B., I 12
273 Upper Falmouth, N. S., M 13
227 Upper Gagetown, N. B., I 8
118 Upper Kennetcook, N. S., L 14
..... Upper Laberge, Yukon, P 9
220 Upper Middleboro, N. S., I 15
1542 Upper Musquodoboit, N.S., L 17
213 Upper Newport, N. S., L 14
371 Upper Rawdon, N. S., L 15
225 Upper Sackville, N. B., I 13
260 Upper Stewiache, N. S., L 16
..... Upperud, Sweden, N 10
5292 Uppingham, Eng., I 17
35212 Uppsala, Sweden, M 16
..... Uprara, India, I 16
69 Uptergrove, Ont., H 12
..... Upton, Ire., Q 10
735 Upton, Quebec, P 18
..... Uraca, Peru, P 15
..... Uraca, Ven., G 5
1505 Uracoa, Ven., F 20
..... Urado, Japan, O 9
..... Uragawa, Japan, G 19
..... Urakawa, Japan, G 13
..... Uralka, Sov. Un., J 23
66201 Uralsk, Sov. Un. Asia, G8
..... Urandangie, Austl., G 16
2000 Urasa, Japan, I 19
6415 Urawa, Japan, L 20
..... Urbakh, Sov. Un., K 17
..... Urbana, Austl., H 18
5231 Urbino, Italy, F 11
2096 Urcos, Peru, N 16
..... Urdinarrain, Arg., M 19
26 Uren, Sask., P 6
2857 Ures, Son., F 12
35266 Urfa, Tur., H 14
..... Urfahr, Ger., P 13
4501 Urgub, Tur. F 9
..... Uri, Honduras, F 9
..... Uri, Switz., J 15
..... Uribe, Col., J 11
..... Uribia, Col., A 16
..... Uriburu, Arg., P 13
2860 Urica, Ven., D 17
270 Urif, Palestine, K 9
..... Urikon, Switz., F 16
344 Urique, Chih., J 16
5421 Urlati, Rom., J 21
..... Urling, B. C., K 14
..... Urlingford, Ireland, M 15
Urmia, see Rezaieh, Iran.
..... Urmirjo, Bolivia, J 6
..... Urnäsch, Switz., E 19
..... Urnen, Switz., G 17
..... Urosozoro, Sov. Un., E 9
1473 Urquhart, Scotland, G 19
4032 Urr, Scotland, Q 17
..... Ursel, Belgium, R 1
433 Urtas, Palestine, N 9
20162 Uruapan, Michoa., N 10
..... Urubamba, Peru, M 16
1128 Urubichá, Bolivia, G 15
..... Urubú, Brazil, J 18
..... Urucaguy, Brazil, F 9
4348 Urucara, Brazil, E 7
..... Urucaro, Brazil, E 7
23394 Uruguay (Concepcion del Uruguay), Arg., L 19
21774 Uruguayana, Brazil, Q 8
Urumchi, see Tihwa, Sink.
..... Urundel, Arg., F 11
..... Urupá, Brazil, I 4
..... Urus Martan, Sov.Un., P 17
..... Uryupinskaya, Sov. Un., L 14
4423 Urzhum, Sov. Un., H 18
8705 Urziceni, Romania, J 21
..... Usetsu, Japan, H 17
16882 Ushak, Tur., F 3
..... Ushibuka, Japan, P 2
1246 Ushuaia, Arg., F 23
2430 Usila, Oax., K 9
..... Usk, B. C., I 8
1315 Usk, England, K 11
Uskub, see Skoplje, Yugo.
54848 Usküdar (Skutari), Tur., B 3
9800 Usmañ, Sov. Un., K 12
..... Usnujan, Iran, G 5
..... Uspallata, Arg., M 6
..... Uss, Iraq, L 18
6120 Ussel, France, M 14
1957 Usseröd, Denmark, I 22
877 Ustarits, France, P 6
9663 Uster, Switz., E 16
45663 Ustí, Czech., F 6
18100 Ust Kamenogorsk, Sov.Un., Asia, I 12
..... Ust Kyakhta, Sov. Un., Asia, H 16
..... Ust Maisk, Sov. Un. Asia, E 18
..... Ust Olensk, Sov. Un., Asia, C 15
..... Ust-Tsylma, Sov. Un., C 18
..... Ust Ukhta, Sov., Un., D19
..... Ust Ussa, Sov. Un., C 20
..... Ust-Vazhskii, Sov. Un., E14
..... Ust Vilyuisk, Sov. Un., Asia, E 17
..... Ust Yansk, Sov. Un., Asia, B 17
11000 Ustyug Velikii, Sov. Un., F 16
5100 Ustyuzhna, Sov. Un., G 10
11400 Usuki, Japan, O 6
8622 Usulután, Salvador, I 8
..... Usumbura, Bel. Cong., L 18
..... Utaradit, Siam., N 3
..... Utena, W. Sov. Un., B 18
..... Utiarity, Brazil, J 7
12411 Utiel, Spain, J 15
..... Utracan, Arg., P 12
160798 Utrecht, Neth., H 15
1848 Utrecht, U.S. Afr., I 21
30440 Utrera, Spain, N 9
81380 Utsunomiya, Japan, K 21
..... Uttad, Morocco, G 8
316 Utterson, Ont., E 12
688 Uttwil, Switz., C 19
..... Uuksu, Fin., F 8
4063 Uusikaupunki (Nystad), Fin., E 2
..... Uvarovo, Sov. Un., K 14
..... Uvira, Bel. Cong., L 17
44281 Uwajima, Japan, O 7
1406 Uxbridge, Ont., J 12
5000 Uyuni, Bolivia, L 7
695 Uzel, France, H 4
2900 Uzerche, France, M 12
4456 Uzês, France, O 18
26669 Užhgorvd, W. Sov. Un., G 15

Pop. *Place* *Country* *Index*
7481 Uzice, Yugo., K 13
..... Uziua, Morocco, K 4
2412 Uznach, Switz., F 17

V

3144 Vaage, Norway, K 8
..... Vaaler, Norway, D 7, L 10
805 Vaalse, Den., N 19
29200 Vaasa (Nikolaistad), Finland, D 3
..... Vaassen, Neth., G 19
21098 Vác, Hung., H 12
6422 Vacas, Bolivia, I 9
..... Vaccaria, Brazil, P 12
..... Vacchereccia, Italy, A 20
..... Vaddö, Sweden, M 17
2050 Vadsö, Norway, A 24
2922 Vadstena, Sweden, N 13
..... Vadum, Denmark, D 10
1405 Vaduz, Liechtenstein, G 20
6736 Vaerdalen, Norway, I 10
1411 Vaggeryd, Sweden, O 12
463 Valangin, Switz., H 6
11 Valbrand, Sask., K 7
6523 Valburg, Neth., H 18
..... Valchetta, Italy, D 21
360 Valcourt, Quebec, P 19
7404 Valcov, W. Sov. Un., J25
3500 Valdai, Sov. Un., H 8
750 Val David, Quebec, N 14
2579 Valdemarsvik, Sweden, O15
30409 Valdepeñas, Spain, K 13
3076 Valderrobres, Spain, H 17
1017 Valdestillas, Spain, G 11
34496 Valdivia, Chile, R 3
6454 Valdiva, Col., F 8
10709 Valenca, Brazil, N 17
2952 Valenca, Portugal, E 6
2874 Valencay, France, J 12
36582 Valence, France, N 20
572 Valence, France, O 10
..... Valencia, Col., C 13
450756 Valencia, Spain, J 17
53938 Valencia, Ven., D 11
12024 Valencia de Alcántara, Spain, J 8
2527 Valencia de Don Juan, Spain, E 10
42564 Valenciennes, France, E 16
4227 Vălenii-de-Munte, Rom., J 20
..... Valentines, Uruguay, L 21
7071 Valenza, Italy, D 4
6000 Valenzuela, Paraguay, O 8
10553 Valera, Ven., E 7
11055 Valjevo, Yugo, K 13
11999 Valka, Sov. Un., G 4
6350 Valkenswaard, Neth., K 16
6402 Valladolid, Yuc., F 23
116024 Valladolid, Spain, F 11
1767 Valldemusa, Spain, J 21
..... Valle, Norway, M 5
60614 Vallecas, Spain, I 12
4870 Valle de la Pascua, Venezuela, E 15
904 Valle de Olivos, Chih., J 18
12278 Valle de Santiago, Guan., M 12
..... Valle Edén, Uruguay, H 19
724 Valle Fertil, Arg., K 8
6000 Vallegrande, Bolivia, J 12
1067 Valle Nacional, Oax., K 10
8472 Vallenar, Chile, J 4
..... Vallentuna, Sweden, P 22
6842 Valles, S. L. P., K 17
23855 Valletta, Malta, Q 15
17052 Valleyfield, Que., Q 14
998 Valley Jc., Quebec, M 22
..... Vallo, Norway, E 4
150 Vallöby, Denmark, K 22
2765 Vallo della Lucania, Italy, K 17
4134 Vallorbe, Switz., J 3
10866 Valls, Spain, G 19
306 Val Marie, Sask., R 5
3486 Valmaseda, Spain, C 13
8368 Valmiera, Sov. Un., H 4
1182 Valmy, Algeria, D 13
5033 Valognes, France, G 7
Valona, see Vlonë, Alb.
1300 Valoria la Buena, Sp., F 11
..... Valparaiso, Bolivia, B 7
209945 Valparaiso, Chile, M 3
2546 Valparaiso, Zac., I 6
4737 Valreas, France, N 20
..... Valsam Platz, Switz., K 18
..... Valtos, Scot., E 6
7500 Valuiki, Sov. Un., L 11
..... Valverde, Spain, I 8
2343 Valverde de Júcar, Spain, J 14
8887 Valverde del Camino, Spain, M 8
2017 Vamdrup, Denmark, K 8
9362 Van, Tur. F 19
..... Vananda, B. C., Q 11
275353 Vancouver, B. C., Q 12
235 Vandel, Denmark, J 6
350 Vanderhoof, B. C., J 12
1377 Vanegas, S. L. P., H 12
..... Vaneja, Eth., F 9
120 Vanessas, Ont., N 9
626 Vang, Denmark, D 4
..... Vang, Norway, K 7
259 Vanguard, Sask., Q 6
1414 Vankleek Hill, Ont., D 25
..... Vännäs, Sweden, H 17
22413 Vannes, France, I 4
..... Van Nivel, Par., F 2
6000 Van Rhyns Dorp, U.S. Afr., N 7
..... Vanse, Norway, N 4
70 Vantage, Sask., Q 7
19450 Vanves, France, B 4
..... Van Wyks Vlei, U. S. Afr., L 10
2451 Varallo, Italy, C 3
13645 Varazdin, Yugo, I 9
8561 Varberg, Sweden, P 10
..... Varcan Vakuf, Yugo, K 9
6514 Varde, Denmark, J 3
3587 Vardö, Norway, A 24
8622 Varel, Germany, E 5
533 Varen, Switz., M 9
..... Varéna, W. Sov. Un., C 17
550 Varennes, Fr., G 19
808 Varennes, Quebec, P 16
3276 Varennes-sur-Allier, Fr., K 16
17570 Varese, Italy, C 4
..... Vargem Grande, Brazil, F 18
..... Varhaug, Norway, N 3
1160 Varilhes, France, Q 12
..... Varilla, Chile, F 4
72200 Varna, Bul., L 23
4054 Värnamo, Swe., P 12
1500 Varnavin, Sov. Un., H 15
Varniai, W. Sov. Un., A 15
22793 Varnsdorf, Czech., E 7
..... Värö, Sweden, P 10
302 Vars, Ontario, E 23
..... Värtan, Sweden, Q 22
1173 Varzy, France, J 16
..... Vasby, Sweden, P 21
..... Vascău, Romania, I 16
5976 Váscăuti, W. Sov. Un., G19
..... Vashak, Baluchistan, O 19

Pop. *Place* *Country* *Index*
..... Vashki, Sov. Un., F 11
1311 Vasiliko, Bul., L 23
21333 Vasilkov, W. Sov. Un., F24
15388 Vaslui, Rom., I 22
77 Vassar, Man., R 17
30378 Västeras, Sweden, M 15
12611 Västervik, Swe., O 15
8622 Vasto, Italy, H 15
8636 Vathy, Greece, P 23
9878 Vatra Dornei, Romania, H 19
..... Vättis, Switzerland, H 20
404 Vaubecourt, France, H 19
10841 Vauclin, Martinique, G 25
3141 Vaucouleurs, France, H 20
506 Vaudreuil, Quebec, Q 14
323 Vauhalland, France, C 3
..... Vaul, Scotland, K 5
813 Vaulruz, Switz., K 6
4015 Vauvert, France, P 18
64 Vauxhall, Alberta, O 22
..... Vavenby, B. C., N 15
2975 Vaxholm, Sweden, M 17
9699 Växjö, Swe., P 13
..... Vayalpad, India, N 11
720 Vayrac, France, N 13
..... Veblungsnaes, Norway, J 6
5497 Vechta, Germany, F 5
1059 Vedbaek, Denmark, J 22
..... Vedersö, Denmark, H 2
2478 Vedrin, Belgium, N 14
..... Vedslet, Denmark, I 11
13348 Veendam, Neth., C 23
7882 Veenendaal, Neth., H 17
..... Veenwouden, Netherlands, C 19
970 Veere, Neth., J 8
5074 Vefsen, Norway, F 12
709 Vega de Alatorre, Ver., G 9
734 Vegas de Itata, Chile, O 2
..... Vegerlöse, Denmark, O 20
4360 Vegesack, Germany, E 6
7513 Veghel, Neth., I 17
1696 Vegreville, Alberta, K 22
..... Vegreville Junction, Alberta, K 22
1922 Veguitas, Cuba, O 19
..... Vejby, Denmark, F 5
3111 Vejen, Denmark, K 6
10110 Vejer de la Frontera, Spain, N 21
..... Vejerslev, Denmark, G 10
23400 Vejle, Denmark, J 8
..... Vejrum, Denmark, G 9
..... Vela, Argentina, P 18
..... Velachha, India, I 6
1929 Velada, Spain, I 11
1432 Velaines, Belgium, M 7
2179 Velardeña, Dur., N 23
..... Velasco, Cuba, K 16
..... Velasco, Cuba, M 20
13440 Veles, Yugo., M 15
2996 Velez, Col., H 12
Velez, see Badis, Morocco
3599 Velez de Benaudalla, Spain, O 12
28894 Vélez Málaga, Spain, O 11
10517 Velez Rubio, Spain, M 14
1544 Velfjorden, Norway, G 11
28011 Veliká Kikinda, Yugo., J 13
..... Velikaya, Sov. Un., G 18
20771 Velikie Luki, Sov. Un., H 6
32831 Veliky Beckerek Yugo., J13
2991 Veliky Berezny, Hung., N 26
250 Velille, Peru, N 16
..... Velivona, W. Sov. Un., B16
12000 Velizh, W. Sov. Un., A 24
275 Vélizy, France, C 3
..... Vellberg, Germany, O 7
..... Velling, Denmark, I 2
57265 Vellore, India, N 12
41260 Velsen, Netherlands, F 13
2000 Velsk, Sov. Un., F 13
7382 Velten, Ger., G 12
..... Vemmelev, Denmark, L 17
..... Vemmetofte, Den., L 22
1670 Venaco, France, Q 3
2003 Venado, S. L. P., J 12
853 Venado Tuerto, Arg., M 13
3558 Venafro, Italy, I 14
..... Venancio, Arg., Q 14
..... Vena Park, Austl., E 18
4192 Vence, France, O 24
1835 Vendeuvre, Fr., I 18
9301 Vendôme, France, I 12
4456 Vendrell, Spain, G 19
8942 Venersborg, Sweden, N 10
..... Venev, Sov. Un., J 11
162695 Venezia (Venice), It., D 11
20158 Vengurla, India, M 6
7 Venice, Alberta, I 22
Venice, see Venezia, It.
..... Venjan, Sweden, L 12
24287 Venlo, Neth., J 20
8891 Venosa, Italy, J 18
12381 Venray, Neth., J 19
563 Ventersburg, U. S. Africa, I 17
3197 Ventila, Bolivia, I 7
5112 Ventnor, Eng., N 16
212 Ventnor, Ontario, G 23
17253 Ventspils (Windau), Sov. Un., G 1
450 Vera, Arg., J 17
6888 Vera, Spain, N 15
71720 Veracruz, Ver., I 10
..... Veramin, Iran, G 7
21114 Veraval, India, J 3
4507 Verbicaro, Italy, L 18
25680 Vercelli, Italy, D 3
906 Verchères, Quebec, O 16
10084 Verden, Ger., F 6
1081 Verdun-sur-Doubs, France, K 19
19460 Verdun-sur-Meuse, France, G 20
1037 Vereda Nueva, Cuba, H 6
..... Vergara, Uruguay, K 24
1431 Vergato, Italy, E 8
329 Vergeletto, Switz., N 15
298 Verigin, Sask., N 11
8137 Verin, Spain, F 7
..... Verkhne Kolymsk, Sov. Un. Asia, C 18
..... Verkhnii Chirskaya, Sov. Un., M 15
..... Verkhoyansk, Sov. Un. Asia, D 17
1361 Vermenton, France, I 17
1408 Vermilion, Alberta, K 23
122 Verna, Italy, F 10
956 Vernayaz, Switz., O 6
900 Verner, Ont., A 10
4662 Verneuil, France, H 11
2896 Vernier, Switz., N 1
..... Verninge, Denmark, L 12
Vernoleninsk, see Nikolaev, Sov. Un.
5209 Vernon, B. C., P 16
10621 Vernon, France, G 12
110 Vernon, P. E. I., H 16
259 Verny, France, G 21
113139 Verona, Italy, D 8
263 Verona, Ontario, H 19
14589 Verria, Greece, N 16
1493 Verrieres, Fr., C 4
73839 Versailles, France, H 13

Pop.	Place Country Index
.....	West Leichhardt, Austl., F16
590	Westlock, Alberta, J 20
.....	West Looe, England, O 6
728	West Lorne, Ontario, P 5
264	Westmeath, Ont., C 19
362	West Monkton, Ont., L 7
336	West New Annan, N.S., J 15
168	West Newdy Quoddy, Nova Scotia, M 18
.....	Weston, N. S., L 11
5740	Weston, Ontario, K 11
28555	Weston super Mare, England, L 11
3892	Westport, Ire., H 6
4240	Westport, N. Z., K 10
510	Westport, N. S., O 7
726	Westport, Ont., G 20
.....	Westport Quay, Ire., H 5
75	West River, N. S., J 17
305	West River Station, Nova Scotia, K 17
421	Westruther, Scot., N 23
350	West Shefford, Que., Q 18
.....	West Toronto, Ont., K 12
4115	Westville, N. S., J 17
.....	West Wickham, Eng., D 22
2318	Wetaskiwin, Alberta, K 21
.....	Wetherby, England, F 15
.....	Wetlands, Australia, H 18
.....	Wetter, Germany, J 5
17857	Wetteren, Belgium, L 9, R 4
6875	Wetzikon, Switz., E 16
17000	Wetzlar, Germany, K 5
10668	Wevelghem, Belgium, M 5
	Wexford, see Loch Garman, Ire.
6179	Weyburn, Sask., Q 9
980	Weymouth, N. S., O 8
21982	Weymouth and Melcombe Regis, England, N 13
.....	Whakataki, N. Z., I 19
.....	Whaletown, B. C., P 11
7600	Whangarei, N. Z., B 16
200	Whangaroa, N. Z., A 15
.....	Wharanui, N. Z., K 15
785	Wheatley, Ont., R 3
.....	Whetstone, Eng., B 21
2240	Whitburn, Scot., N 18
11441	Whitby, England, E 18
5904	Whitby, Ont., K 13
.....	Whitby Jc., Ont., K 13
6016	Whitchurch, Eng., H 12
.....	White Abbey, N. Ire., D 23
100	White Bear, Sask., O 5
.....	Whitechurch, Eng., M 16
179	Whitechurch, Ont., J 6
.....	White Cliffs, N. Z., M 11
115	White Court, Alberta, J 19
21142	Whitehaven, Eng., D 9
151	White Head, N. S., L 21
.....	Whitehills, Scot., G 21
1796	Whithorn, Scot., R 14
541	Whitehorse, Yukon, P 9
.....	Whitehouse, N. Ire., D 23
.....	Whitehouse, Scot., N 10
227	Whitelaw, Alberta, H 17
302	Whitemouth, Man., Q 17
402	White River, Ont., P 21
264	Whitevale, Ontario, K 12
689	Whitewood, Sask., P 11
100	Whitney, N. B., E 9
300	Whitney, Ont., D 15
648	Whitney Pier, N. S., H 24
.....	Whittington, Eng., H 15
300	Whonnock, B. C., O 4
421	Whycocomagh, N. S., I 21
1749	Wiarton, Ont., G 7
10383	Wick, Scot., D 19
.....	Wickford, Eng., L 21
262	Wickham, N. B., J 8
	Wicklow, see Cill Mhantain, Ire.
.....	Widewall, Scot., B 20
40608	Widnes, Eng., G 12
	Widze, see Vidzy, Sov. Un.
4924	Wiedenbrück, Ger., H 5
.....	Wiedhafen, Tan., M 20
13220	Wielén, Poland, D 9
.....	Wieliczka, Poland, F 13
.....	Wielun, Poland, E 11
1843173	Wien (Vienna), Aus., H 9
36751	Wiener Neustadt, Aus., H 9
10807	Wierden, Neth., F 22
159800	Wiesbaden, Ger., L 5
189	Wiesen, Switz., J 21
85357	Wigan, England, G 12
.....	Wigan, Yukon, Q 10
3521	Wigton, Eng., D 11
1531	Wigtown, Scot., Q 14
5746	Wijchen, Neth., I 18
4874	Wijhe, Neth., F 20
5084	Wijk-aan-Zee en Duin, Netherlands, F 12
3285	Wijk bij Duurstede, Netherlands, H 15
754	Wikwemikong, Ont., C 5
7523	Wil, Switz., D 17
750	Wil, Switz., H 9
623	Wilcannia, Austl., M 18
247	Wilcox, Sask., Q 9
10058	Wildervank, Neth., C 23
3018	Wildeshausen, Ger., F 5
1075	Wildhaus, Switz., F 19
.....	Wildungen, Ger., J 6
	Wileika, see Vileika, Sov. Un.
77000	Wilhelmshaven, Ger., D 5
.....	Wilkesport, Ontario, O 3
1222	Wilkie, Sask., M 5
.....	Wilkinstown, Ire., H 19
13587	Willebroeck, Bel., R 8
2113	Willemstad, Neth., I 11
25848	Willemstad, Curaçao, P 16
21147	Willenhall, Eng., I 13
184410	Willesden, Eng., L 19
.....	Williams, Ontario, K 10
.....	Williamsburgh, Austl., N 5
214	Williamsford, Ontario, I 7
621	Williams Lake, B. C., M 13
732	Williamstown, Ontario, E 25
3037	Willisau, Switz., G 12
120	Willowbrook, Sask., O 10
454	Willowbunch, Sask., R 7
2031	Willowmore, U.S. Afr., P 12
.....	Willowvale, U. S. Afr., O 18
.....	Wilmersdorf, Ger., Q 15
500	Wilmington, Austl., M 15
9760	Wilmslow, Eng., G 13
	Wilno, see Vilnyus, W. Sov. Un.
2213	Wilsnack, Ger., F 10
....	Wilsontown, Scot., N 18
2193	Wilton, Eng., M 14
263	Wilton, Ontario, I 19
1326	Wiltz, Luxembourg, P 19
59520	Wimbledon, Eng., L 19
1428	Wimmis, Switz., J 10
.....	Winagami, Alberta, H 18
2500	Winburg, U. S. Afr., J 17
.....	Winchelsea, Eng., M 22
22969	Winchester, Eng., M 16
549	Winchester, N. Z., N 10
427	Winchester Springs, Ont., F 23
	Windau, see Ventspils, Sov. Un.
.....	Windermere, B. C., O 19
5701	Windermere, England, E 11
20300	Windhoek, S. W. Afr., P 13
20115	Windsor, Eng., L 18
3436	Windsor, N. S., M 13
105311	Windsor, Ontario, Q 1
.....	Windsor Junction, New Zealand, O 9
134	Windsor Junction, Nova Scotia, M 15
3368	Windsor Mills, Quebec, P 20
.....	Windsuach, Ger., N 8
160	Windthorst, Sask., Q 10
.....	Windygates, Man., R 15
.....	Wine Harbor, N. S., L 19
1328	Winenne, Belgium, P 14
2030	Wingham, Ont., K 6
.....	Winifreda, Arg., O 12
2391	Winigen, Switz., G 10
1665	Winkel, Neth., E 13
.....	Winlaw, B. C., Q 18
125	Winnifred, Alberta, P 23
221960	Winnipeg, Man., Q 16
911	Winnipegosis, Man., N 13
655	Winona, Ontario, M 11
13343	Winschoten, Neth., C 24
4718	Winsen, Germany, E 8
.....	Winsford, England, H 1
60	Winter, Sask., L 4
483	Wintersingen, Switz., D 11
17944	Winterswijk, Neth., H 23
53944	Winterthur, Switz., D 16
1958	Winterton, England, G 18
.....	Winterton, U. S. Afr., J 19
1400	Winton, Australia, H 18
880	Winton, N. Z., Q 5
2809	Wiranschehir, Tur., H 15
3911	Wirksworth, Eng., H 15
11316	Wisbech, Eng., I 20
.....	Wish, Egypt, D 14
25300	Wishaw, Scot., N 16
.....	Wish-el-Hager, Egypt, D 14
.....	Wismar, Br. Gu., B 7
26000	Wismar, Germany, D 9
3698	Wissekerke, Neth., J 8
5332	Wissembourg, France, G 25
8263	Witbank, U. S. Afr., F 19
4367	Witham, England, K 22
4251	Withernsea, England, F 20
.....	Withington, Eng., G 13
.....	Witmarsum, Neth., C 16
.....	Witney, England, K 15
.....	Witpoort, U. S. Afr., F 20
72600	Witten, Germany, I 4
24000	Wittenberg, Germany, H 11
27000	Wittenberge, Ger., F 10
4838	Wittingau, Ger., O 14
6346	Wittlich, Germany, L 2
7564	Wittstock, Germany, E 11
1262	Wiveliscombe, Eng., M 11
56277	Wloclawek, Poland, D 12
.....	Wlodawa, Poland, E 17
	Wlodzimierz, see Valdimir Volynsk, W. Sov. Un.
.....	Wloszczowa, Poland, E 13
.....	Wobo, Eth., H 6
.....	Woburn, Quebec, Q 22
4633	Wodnan, Ger., N 13
4010	Woensdrecht, Neth., J 11
.....	Woensel, Neth., J 17
7316	Woerden, Neth., H 14
1907	Wognum, Neth., E 15
5851	Wohlen, Switz., E 13
2774	Wohlen, Switz., H 8
.....	Wokha, India, L 21
.....	Wolborough, Eng., O 9
6	Wolf Creek, Alberta, K 18
32	Wolfe, Sask., M 5
602	Wolfe Island, Ont., I 20
20000	Wolfenbüttel, Ger., H 8
1329	Wolfenschiessen, Switzerland, H 14
6165	Wolfsberg, Ger., T 14
1944	Wolfville, N. S., L 13,
7198	Wolgast, Ger., C 13
2769	Wolhusen, Switz., G 12
	Wolkowysk, see Volkovish, Sov. Un.
18500	Wollongong, Australia, O 22
13400	Wolmaransstadt, Union of South Africa, H 15
4240	Wolmirstedt, Ger., H 9
.....	Wolozyn, W. Sov. Un., C 20
.....	Wolpa, Poland, F 19
838	Wolseley, Sask., P 10
.....	Wolszlyn, Pol., D 9
.....	Wolvega, Neth., D 19
.....	Wolvehoek, Un. of S. Afr., H 18
133190	Wolverhampton, Eng., I 13
4148	Wolverthem, Belgium, L 11
12870	Wolverton, England, K 17
18365	Wombwell, Eng., G 16
.....	Wonderfontein, Union of South Africa, F 20
64029	Wŏnsan (Genzan), Korea, D 24
13	Wood Bay, Man., R 14
4734	Woodbridge, England, J 23
1054	Woodbridge, Ont., K 11
.....	Woodford, Eng., B 24
300	Woodford, Ire., K 11
.....	Woodford Wells, Eng., A 23
54190	Woodgreen, Eng., L 19
.....	Woodhaven, Scot., K 20
.....	Woodin, Cuba, K 16
.....	Wood Island, P. E. I., I 17
.....	Woodlawn, Ire., J 11
65	Woodlawn, Ont., D 21
119	Wood Mountain, Sask., R 7
184	Woodridge, Man., R 17
197	Woodrow, Sask., Q 6
235	Woodslee, Ont., Q 2
.....	Woodslee, Ont., O 2
3593	Woodstock, N. B., H 4
12461	Woodstock, Ont., N 7
1050	Woodville, N. Z., I 19
394	Woodville, Ontario, I 13
.....	Woodwick, Scot., A 19
.....	Wooler, Eng., B 14
.....	Woolford Station, Alta., Q 22
146944	Woolwich, England, L 20
.....	Wooroorooka, Australia, L 20
.....	Woosung, China, H 20
4506	Worb, Switz., H 9
.....	Worbarrow, Eng., N 13
50497	Worcester, Eng., J 13
12515	Worcester, U. S. Afr., Q 8
24691	Workington, Eng., D 9
26286	Worksop, England, H 16
4038	Workum, Neth., D 16
49000	Worms, Ger., M 4
.....	Wörth, Germany, M 6
46230	Worthing, England, N 19
3087	Woudenberg, Neth., H 16
2038	Woudrichem, Neth., I 15
4989	Wouw, Neth., J 11
.....	Wragby, Eng., G 18
75	Wrentham, Alberta, P 22
18567	Wrexham, Wales, H 11
7282	Wriezen, Ger., F 13
.....	Wrigley, Mack., L 7
425	Wroxeter, Ont., J 7
140	Wroxton, Sask., O 11
.....	Września, Poland, D 10
.....	Wubai, Afg., L 20
610000	Wuchang, China, H 15
90000	Wuchow, China, K 13
.....	Wudd, Baluchistan, O 21
4846	Wuestwezel, Belgium, J 13
.....	Wugai, Afg., H 22
260000	Wuhsien (Soochow), China, H 20
131000	Wuhu, China, H 18
.....	Wukang, China, J 12
.....	Wulakai, Manch., A 23
6100	Wun, India, J 12
1900	Wuntho, Bur., M 22
408600	Wuppertal (Barmen-Elberfeld), Ger., J 3
101000	Würzburg, Ger., M 7
19000	Wurzen, Ger., J 11
.....	Wuting, China, J 5
964	Wyalong, Australia, N 20
201	Wyandra, Australia, J 19
.....	Wyke Regis, Eng., N 12
.....	Wylye, England, M 14
100	Wyman, Quebec, P 8
165	Wymark, Sask., P 5
.....	Wymondham, Eng., I 23
390	Wyndham, Australia, C 10
6970	Wynghene, Bel., L 6
.....	Wynndel, B. C., Q 19
1080	Wynyard, Sask., N 9
523	Wyoming, Ontario, N 4
.....	Wysock, W. Sov. Un., E 20
10768	Wyzków, Pol., D 15

X

Pop.	Place Country Index
.....	Xaltepec, Oax., L 8
33712	Xanthe, Greece, M 20
.....	Xapury, West. Brazil, K 21
.....	Xavier, Cuba, O 21
66	Xbonil, Camp., I 20
3320	Xerokhorion, Grc., O 17
2342	Xicoténcatl, Tam., I 17
1679	Xilita, S. L. P., K 17
186	Xkalak, Q. R., J 24
.....	Xkanha, Q. R., H 22

Y

Pop.	Place Country Index
102	Yaamba, Australia, H 22
334	Yaapeet, Austl., O 17
.....	Yabaros, Son., K 13
1733	Yabid, Palestine, J 9
.....	Yabroco, Peru, Q 19
1100	Yabuki, Japan, J 22
.....	Yachow, China, H 6
2296	Yaco, Bolivia, I 5
2446	Yacuiba, Bolivia, N 12
.....	Yadgir, India, L 10
615	Yafa, Pal., H 10
.....	Yaftai, Afg., D 24
8699	Yaguachi, Ecuador, D 3
8796	Yaguajay, Cuba, J 13
1730	Yaguara, Col., K 9
1176	Yaguaramas, Cuba, J 10
1459	Yaguaraparo, Ven., C 19
18000	Yaguarón, Par., O 7
1389	Yaguarú, Bolivia, G 15
.....	Yah-fufa, Syria, A 18
165	Yahk, B. C., Q 19
4013	Yahualica, Jal., L 8
.....	Yahudiyah, Egypt, E 8
.....	Yaita, Japan, J 20
1117	Yajalón, Chia., L 17
700	Yakata, Japan, L 12
.....	Yakdan, Afg., E 20
.....	Yakoba, Nigeria, I 10
.....	Yakuk, Palestine, G 12
23000	Yakutsk, Sov. Un. Asia, E 17
3407	Yalalac, Oax., L 10
.....	Yalama, Sov. Un., Q 20
200	Yalgoo, Austl., K 5
.....	Yalo, Palestine, M 8
2635	Yalova, Tur., C 3
30000	Yalta, Sov. Un., O 8
831	Yamachiche, Que., M 17
28000	Yamada, Japan, E 25
3600	Yamada, Japan, N 15
63423	Yamagata, Japan, H 22
2829	Yamagawa, Japan, R 3
31322	Yamaguchi, Japan, L 6
1100	Yamasaki, Japan, P 3
.....	Yamashiro, Japan, J 15
.....	Yamashita, Japan, H 23
.....	Yamchow, China, L 10
8700	Yamethin, Bur., N 22
5427	Yamparaez, Bolivia, K 10
19000	Yanagawa, Japan, N 4
1384	Yanaoca, Peru, N 17
5711	Yanaon, India, L 15
4586	Yangchow, China, G 19
.....	Yangkao, China, C 14
50000	Yangku (Taiyuan), China, E 14
.....	Yangshan, China, K 13
758	Yani, Bolivia, G 3
.....	Yannarie, Austl., H 3
	Yannina, see Ioannina, Grc.
71	Yanun, Palestine, K 11
.....	Yaochan, China, J 4
6451	Yaoundé, Cam., K 11
.....	Yapaunla, Nic., I 14
.....	Yar, Sov. Un. Asia, C 17
1325	Yara, Cuba, O 19
84	Yaraka, Austl., I 19
.....	Yaransk, Sov. Un., H 17
430	Yaras, Peru, Q 18
.....	Yarda, Fr. Eq. Afr., H 14
4800	Yarensk, Sov. Un., E 17
5495	Yaritagua, Ven., D 10
	Yarkand, see Soche, Sink.
370	Yarker, Ont., I 19
7790	Yarmouth, N. S., Q 8
298065	Yaroslavl, Sov. Un., H 12
.....	Yarpuz, Tur., G 12
.....	Yarpuz, Tur., H 11
1908	Yarrawonga, Austl., P 19
.....	Yarrocurracoo, Austl., H 15
459	Yarrow, Scot., O 20
.....	Yartsevo, Sov. Un., I 8
8693	Yarumal, Col., G 8
.....	Yasin, India, A 7
2200	Yass, Austl., O 21
172	Yasuf, Palestine, L 10
1284	Yasur, Palestine, N 5
.....	Yat, Fr. W. Afr., G 12
68	Yata, Bolivia, B 9
2700	Yatabe, Japan, M 22
5100	Yataity, Par., O 9
.....	Yate, Eng., L 12
10100	Yatsushiro, Japan, O 4
.....	Yatton, Australia, H 22
.....	Yauca, Peru, O 12
821	Yauli, Peru, L 10
1487	Yauri, Peru, O 17
1058	Yauyos, Peru, M 10
.....	Yavita, Ven., O 12
261309	Yawata, Jap., M 5
4300	Yawatahama, Japan, N 7
.....	Yayus, Transjordan, L 16
.....	Yazdikhast, Iran, K 7
.....	Yazghulam, Afg., C 24
.....	Yazudzuka, Japan, I 19
5265	Ybbs, Ger., Q 14
182	Ydby, Denmark, F 3
1791	Yebnah, Palestine, M 5
22371	Yecla, Spain, L 16
.....	Yeeda, Australia, E 8
	Yeisk, see Eisk, Sov. Un.
	Yelets, see Elets, Sov. Un.
.....	Yelgandel, India, K 12
423	Yellow Grass, Sask., Q 9
.....	Yelvertoft, Austl., F 16
.....	Yemtsa, Sov. Un., E 12
.....	Yenan, China, E 11
.....	Yenbai, Fr. In. Ch., L 7
3000	Yenbo, Sau. Ar., K 4
.....	Yencheng, China, G 14
.....	Yenchow, China, I 19
60000	Yenchow, China, F 17
3296	Yendi, G. C., I 7
2057	Yenikhan, Tur., D 11
6511	Yenishehr, Tur., C 1
.....	Yenki (Qara Shahr), Sink., J 13
.....	Yenking, China, C 16
	Yenping, see Nanping, China.
.....	Yeomans, Sask., Q 9
19078	Yeovil, England, M 12
.....	Yerangöme, Tur., G 3
429	Yerbas Buenas, Chile, I 4
200031	Yerevan, Sov. Un., R 16
978	Yerka, Palestine, G 9
.....	Yershov, Sov. Un., K 18
132	Yeruá, Arg., L 19
9997	Yeste, Spain, L 14
100	Yetman, Austl., L 22
3801	Yeu, France, K 5
.....	Yeungchun, China, L 13
.....	Yeungkong, China, L 13
.....	Yey, Bur., P 23
55100	Yezd, Iran, K 9
...	Yezon, Bur., N 22
8000	Yhacanguazú, Par., P 8
3231	Yhú, Paraguay, N 9
.....	Yichow, China, D 16
.....	Yihsien, China, F 17
.....	Yingchow, China, G 16
165918	Yingkow (Newchwang), Manch., C 20
.....	Yingtak, China, K 14
.....	Yining, China, I 15
.....	Yipang, China, L 4
102	Ymir, B. C., Q 18
5000	Yochow, China, I 14
.....	Yocoro, Honduras, E 11
.....	Yocoroso, Q. R., J 22
.....	Yoeman, Sask., Q 9
5442	Yoita, Japan, I 19
51811	Yokkaichi, Japan, M 15
.....	Yokobori, Japan, F 23
968091	Yokohama, Japan, M 20
1900	Yokosuka, Japan, N 17
193358	Yokosuka, Japan, M 20
800	Yokota, Japan, K 9
8100	Yokote, Japan, E 23
20000	Yola, Nigeria, J 11
.....	Yomah, Afg., E 24
33632	Yonago, Japan, K 10
44731	Yonezawa, Japan, H 22
25	Yonker, Sask., L 4
573	Yorito, Hond., F 10
1600	York, Austl., M 5
84810	York, England, F 16
.....	York Factory, Man., F 20
.....	York River, Ontario, F 16
5577	Yorkton, Sask., O 11
1353	Yoro, Hond., F 10
3800	Yoshida, Japan, L 8
5900	Yoshida, Japan, O 7
3000	Yoshiwara, Japan, M 18
.....	Yosii, Jap., N 4
644	Yotaú, Bolivia, H 15
240	Youbou, B. C., R 11
4011	Young, Austl., O 21
340	Young, Sask., N 7
316	Youngs Cove, N. B., I 9
188	Youngstown, Alberta, M 23
13661	Yozgat, Tur., D 9
15338	Ypres, Belgium, M 4
6777	Yssingeaux, France, M 18
11444	Ystad, Sweden, R 12
.....	Ystrad-y-Iodwg (Rhondda) Wales, L 10
.....	Ytter, Sweden, J 12
.....	Yüanchow Hun, Chn., J 11
.....	Yüanchow Ki, China, I 15
.....	Yüankiang, China, K 5
9500	Yuasa, Japan, N 12
.....	Yubetsu, Japan, F 14
.....	Yuchsi, China, I 6
.....	Yühchow, China, G 14
.....	Yüki, China, J 18
.....	Yulglun Agatch, Iran, E 3
..	Yulin, China, D 11
2099	Yumbel, Chile, P 3
2471	Yumbo, Col., J 6
.....	Yumen, China, C 3
1100	Yumura, Japan, K 11
.....	Yünchow, China, K 4
.....	Yungan, China, J 17
3671	Yungay, Chile, P 4
	Yungchang, see Paoshan, China.
.....	Yungchowfu, China, J 13
.....	Yungchun, China, K 18
.....	Yungkang, China, L 10
631300	Yungkia (Wenchow), China, I 20
.....	Yungning, China, E 12
.....	Yungning, China, I 4
.....	Yungning, China, J 8
.....	Yungning, China, K 11
73000	Yungning (Nanning), China, L 10
.....	Yungpeh, China, J 4
.....	Yungpingfu, China, D 18
.....	Yungshun, China, I 11
.....	Yungsui, China, I 11
.....	Yungting, China, I 12
.....	Yünho, China, I 19
.....	Yunlung, China, J 3
	Yünnanfu, see Kunming, China
.....	Yunsi, Iran, G 13
.....	Yünsiao, China, K 17
.....	Yuntah, Syria, C 16
30000	Yünyang, China, G 12
3682	Yura, Bolivia, L 8
.....	Yura, Peru, P 16
8956	Yurécuaro, Michoa., M 9
5918	Yurimaguas, Peru, G 9
1500	Yushima, Japan, K 12
803	Yusuf, Algeria, B 22
.....	Yutta, Palestine, P 8
12000	Yuty, Par., Q 9
.....	Yütze, China, E 14
.....	Yuyang, China, I 11
6600	Yuzawa, Japan, F 23
	Yuzovka, see Stalino, Sov. Un.
9743	Yverdon, Switz., I 4
7134	Yvetot, France, F 11
1087	Yvonand, Switz., I 5

Z

Pop.	Place Country Index
.....	Zaacha, Algeria, E 19
5646	Zaachila, Oax., M 9
3575	Zaamslag, Neth., K 9
3575	Zaamslag, Neth., R 9
33183	Zaandam, Neth., F 14, A 2
.....	Zabore, Sov. Un., G 10
.....	Zabul, Iran, K 16
.....	Zabunabad, Iran, F 11
15191	Zacapa, Guat., F 6
7942	Zacapoaxtla, Pueb., G 7
21846	Zacatecas, Zac., J 9
10822	Zacatecoluca, Salvador, H 7
7942	Zacoalco, Jal., M 6
3001	Zacualpan, Méx., I 4
2707	Zacualtipan, Hid., F 6
.....	Zafar, Egypt, D 17
5218	Zafaranboli, Tur., B 7
.....	Zaffra, Alg., E 16
8545	Zafra, Spain, L 8
.....	Zagantuguruk, Chn., A 12
.....	Zagorsk, Sov. Un., I 11
.....	Zaghouan, Tunisia, B 24
185581	Zagreb, Yugo., J 8
.....	Zagubica, Yugo., K 15
.....	Zaguda, Iran, F 11
.....	Zahari, Iran, H 12
.....	Zahedan (Duzdab), Iran, M 15
13000	Zahle, Syria, M 10
13000	Zahlen, Syria, A 16
.....	Zahmekan, Iran, O 12
.....	Zaidabad, Iran, M 10
.....	Zaidi, Iran, M 6
10602	Zaječar, Yugo., K 16
.....	Zakariya, Palestine, N 7
.....	Za Kerzaz, Alg., L 11
.....	Zakho, Iraq., H 18
17703	Zakopane, Poland, G 13
.....	Zak River, U. S. Afr., M 9
11609	Zakynthos, Grc., P 14
13100	Zalaegerszeg, Hung., I 9
8497	Zalamea de la Serena, Spain, L 9
8500	Zalau, Rom., H 17
.....	Zalee, Afg., I 21
4099	Zaltbommel, Neth., I 16
5000	Zamborondon, Ecuador, D 3
2702	Zambrano, Col., D 10
15488	Zamora, Michoa., M 9
32388	Zamora, Spain, F 9
24273	Zamość, Poland, F 16
.....	Zana, Algeria, D 19
2282	Zanatepec, Oax., N 13
.....	Zancudos, Col., K 19
7788	Zandvoort, Neth., F 12
.....	Zân el Hager, Egypt, D 19
.....	Zangaran, Sp. Mor., E 10
.....	Zangi Chah, Iran, G 12
.....	Zangin, Iran, Q 14
.....	Zangla, India, B 10
.....	Zanja Honda, Ur., E 17
.....	Zanna, Iran, H 2
45276	Zanzibar, Zanzibar, M 21
.....	Zapala, Arg., Q 7
.....	Zapata, Arg., M 6
4617	Zapatoca, Col., G 13
606	Zapatosa, Col., I 14
2751	Zapicán, Ur., M 21
525	Zapiga, Chile, C 4
2592	Zapopan, Jal., L 6
289188	Zaporozhe (Aleksandrovsk), Sov. Un., M 9
.....	Zapote, Mex., P 14
1569	Zapotitlán, Pueb., J 8
2869	Zapotlanejo, Jal., M 7
57000	Zaqaziq, Eg., F 16
11990	Zara (It.), Yugo., K 7
5947	Zara, Tur., E 13
.....	Zaragoza, Coa., C 7
1052	Zaragoza, Col., F 10
4246	Zaragoza, Coa., B 12
1041	Zaragoza, N. L., H 15
238601	Zaragoza, Sp., G 16
	Zaragoza, see Tijuana, Baja Cal.
.....	Zaraisk, Sov. Un., J 12
.....	Zarand, Iran, L 11
.....	Zarasai, W. Sov. Un., A 19
.....	Zárat, Tunisia, F 24
42993	Zarate, Arg., N 18
3871	Zaraza, Ven., E 16
.....	Zaria, Nig., I 9
.....	Zarin, Iran, I 9
13657	Zaruma, Ecuador E 3
1738	Zarumilla, Peru, E 2
4221	Zarzal, Col., I 7
3740	Zarza la Mayor, Spain, I 7
.....	Zarzaou, Alg., Q 23
18061	Zarzis, Tunisia, F 25
.....	Zatec, Czech., F 6
600	Zautla, Pueb., H 7
...	Zawayda, Egypt, O 23
32713	Zawiercie, Pol., F 12
.....	Zawiet Sakr, Egypt, D 5
.....	Zâwiya, Egypt, L 14
1312	Zaza del Medio, Cuba, K 13
2994	Zazárida, Ven., B 7
.....	Zbaraz, W. Sov. Un., F 19
22904	Zdunskawola, W. Sov. Un., E 12
515	Zealand, N. B., H 6
172	Zealandia, Sask., N 6
.....	Zebbacha, Alg., G 16
.....	Zebda, Transj., I 13
.....	Zebda, Transj., I 15
.....	Zebeda, Syria, M 11
.....	Zebuk, Afg., E 25
2877	Zedelghem, Bel., L 5
.....	Zeebrugge, Belgium, K 5
1600	Zeehan, Tasmania, C 4
1215	Zeerust, U. S. Afr., E 15
1500	Zeilah, Br. Somaliland, G 15
1087	Zeita, Palestine, J 8
.....	Zeitün, Tur., G 12
35000	Zeitz, Ger., J 10
15094	Zele, Belgium, L 10
5651	Zelhem, Neth., H 21
1463	Zell, Switz., G 11
.....	Zella, Libya, F 13
3349	Zellam, Aus., H 4
.....	Zelwan, Sp. Mor., D 10
.....	Zemio, Fr. Eq. Afr., J 16
.....	Zemlet el Harcha, Alg., I 22
28083	Zeman, Yugo., J 13
.....	Zenataia, Mor., J 8
9090	Zenica, Yugo., K 10
147	Zenina, Alg., E 16
10200	Zenjan, Iran, E 4
.....	Zenkelun, Eg., F 15
.....	Zenkov, Sov. Un., L 8
	Zenta, see Senta, Yugo.
1829	Zenzontepec, Oax., N 7
7196	Zepče, Yugo., K 11
154	Zephyr, Ont., J 12
.....	Zer, Palestine, H 12
20000	Zerbst, Ger., H 10
727	Zerin, Palestine, I 10
982	Zermatt, Switz., P 10
.....	Zernukah, Palestine, M 5
.....	Zersin, Tunisia, F 23
.....	Zervreila, Switz., K 18
.....	Zêtûn, Egypt, M 13
6033	Zevenaar, Neth., H 20
8904	Zevenbergen, Neth., J 12
26646	Zgierz, Poland, E 12
.....	Zhigansk, Sov. Un. Asia, D 16
95090	Zhitomir, W. Sov. Un. F 22
.....	Zhizdra, Sov. Un., J 9
905	Ziefen, Switz., D 10
6864	Zierikzee, Neth., I 9
2514	Ziesar, Ger., G 11
13700	Zifte, Egypt, E 14
.....	Zik, Baluchistan, Q 19
.....	Zikhron, Pal., I 7
15168	Zile, Tur., D 11
	Zilina, Czech., G 12
266	Zillis, Switz., K 20
1598	Zimapán, Hid., F 4
.....	Zimara, Tur., E 13
4358	Zimatlán, Oax., P 17
10933	Zimnicea, Rom., K 20
.....	Zimus, Iran, B 2
3548	Zinacantepec, Pueb., J 8
.....	Zinal, Switz., O 10
2608	Zinapécuaro, Michoa., N 13
10356	Zinder, Fr. W. Africa, I 10
.....	Zinnêga, Egypt, R 10
	Zinovevsk, see Kirovo, Sov. Un
3981	Zipaquira, Col., I 11
.....	Zirab, Iran, F 8
1080	Zirándaro, Guer., P 12
.....	Ziru, Iran, N 6
.....	Zisad, Iran, R 16
.....	Zistersdorf, Ger., P 17
11434	Zitacuaro, Michoa., N 14
2467	Zitlala Guer., Q 17
40000	Zittau, Ger., J 14
1188	Zizers, Switz., H 20
.....	Zlaté Moravce, Czech., H 11
.....	Zlatopol, Sov. Un., M 6
	Zloczów, see Zolochev, Sov. Un.
25832	Znojmo, Czech., G 9
.....	Zobbenitz, Ger., G 9
1428	Zoersel, Bel., K 13
5524	Zofingen, Switz., E 12
.....	Zólkiew, W. Sov. Un., F 17
2367	Zollikofen, Switz., H 9
13265	Zolochev, W. Sov. Un., F 18
.....	Zolotonosha, Sov. Un., L 7
107813	Zomba, Nyasaland, N 20
	Zombor, see Sombor, Yugo.
3045	Zongo, Bolivia, H 4
1174	Zongolica, Ver., J 8
5224	Zonhoven, Bel., L 16
2232	Zonnebeke, Bel., M 4
27500	Zoppot, Danzig, B 19
.....	Zorbatiya, Iraq, M 22
1593	Zorritos, Peru, E 2
4924	Zossen, Ger., H 12
.....	Zouarin, Tunisia, C 23
.....	Zouiret, Alg., L 24
.....	Zoutkamp, Neth., B 21
.....	Zoutpan, U. S. Afr., B 19
7456	Zschopau, Ger., K 12
.....	Zuart, Switz., I 24
.....	Zubair, Iraq, Q 24
.....	Zubiaurre, Arg., Q 16
.....	Zubien, Transjordan, J 15
.....	Zuchu, Iran, L 7
3667	Zuera, Spain, F 16
11124	Zug, Switz., F 14
3370	Zuidhorn, Neth., C 21
4243	Zuidlaren, Neth., C 23
8200	Zújar, Spain, N 13
5905	Zulueta, Cuba, J 13
5583	Zumpango, Méx., M 15
3333	Zumpango del Rio, Guer., Q 16
6585	Zundert, Neth., J 13
.....	Zungeru, Nig., I 9
.....	Zupaniac, Yugo., K 9
.....	Zurabad, Iran, F 15
.....	Zur ab Raked, Egypt, D 17
552	Zurich, Ont., L 5
339200	Zürich, Switz., E 15
.....	Zurrah Oboh, Afg., K 20
.....	Zurumatá, Brazil, D 8
1850	Zurzach, Switz., C 13
19732	Zutphen, Neth., G 20
967	Zuz, Switz., K 22
.....	Zvanka, Sov. Un., F 8
11217	Zvolen, Czech., G 12
3487	Zvornik, Yugo., K 12
.....	Zvyagel, W. Sov. Un., E 21
12200	Zwart Kop, U. S. Afr. L 10
.....	Zwartruggens, U. S. Afr., F 16
3606	Zwartsluis, Neth., E 19
.....	Zwei Lütshinen, Switz., K 11
15783	Zweibrücken, Ger., N 3
2383	Zweisimmen, Switz., K 8
87000	Zwickau, Ger., K 11
.....	Zwing, Switz., J 15
132	Zwischbergen, Switz., N 12
40560	Zwolle, Neth., F 20
.....	Zywiec, Pol., F 12

Physical Features of the World

MAP INDEX AND ABBREVIATIONS

Map Page	Country	Abbrev.
121	Aden	Aden
119	Aegean Is.	Aeg. Is.
126	Afghanistan	Afg.
128	Africa	Afr.
91	Aguascalientes	Agua.
23	Alabama	Ala.
74	Alaska	Alsk.
119	Albania	Alb.
80	Alberta	Alta.
129	Algeria	Alg.
116	Andorra	And.
128	Anglo-Egyptian Sudan	A. E. Sud.
128	Angola	Ang.
136	Antarctica	Ant.
136	Arctic Regions	Arc. Reg.
97	Argentina	Arg.
24	Arizona	Ariz.
25	Arkansas	Ark.
121	Asia	Asia
134	Australia	Austl.
10	Azores Is.	Az. Is.
94	Bahama Is.	Ba. Is.
90	Baja California	Baja Cal.
126	Baluchistan	Bal.
94	Barbados	Barb.
132	Basutoland	Bas.
80	British Columbia	B. C.
128	Bechuanaland	Bech.
114	Belgium	Bel.
128	Belgian Congo	Bel. Cong.
15	Bermuda Is.	Ber. Is.
123	Bhutan	Bhu.
133	British North Borneo	B. N. B.
98	Bolivia	Bol.
99	Brazil	Braz.
99	British Guiana	Br. Gu.
103	British Honduras	Br. Hond.
131	British Somaliland	Br. Som.
133	Brunei	Bru.
119	Bulgaria	Bul.
123	Burma	Bur.
26	California	Calif.
128	Cameroons	Cam.
92	Campeche	Camp.
79	Canada	Can.
128	Canary Is.	Can. Is.
133	Celebes	Cel.
93	Central America	Cen. Am.
123	Ceylon	Cey.
92	Chiapas	Chia.
90	Chihuahua	Chih.
97	Chile	Chl.
122	China	Chn.
91	Coahuila	Coa.
100	Colombia	Col.
91	Colima	Colim.
28	Colorado	Colo.
29	Connecticut	Conn.
111	Corsica	Cor.
93	Costa Rica	C. R.
95	Cuba	Cuba
94	Curaçao	Cur.
10	Cape Verde Is.	C. V. Is.
127	Cyprus	Cyp.
75	Canal Zone	C. Z.
118	Czechoslovakia	Czec.
40	Delaware	Del.
110	Denmark	Den.
92	Distrito Federal	D. F.
94	Dominica	Dom.
94	Dominican Republic	Dom. Rep.
90	Durango	Dur.
102	Ecuador	Ec.
130	Egypt	Eg.
107	England	Eng.
131	Eritrea	Erit.
131	Ethiopia	Eth.
104	Europe	Eur.
110	The Faeroes	Faer.
96	Falkland Is.	Falk. Is.
135	Fiji Is.	Fiji Is.
120	Finland	Fin.
30	Florida	Fla.
122	Formosa	For.
111	France	Fr.
128	French Equatorial Africa	Fr. Eq. Afr.
99	French Guiana	Fr. Gu.
122	French Indochina	Fr. In. Ch.
131	French Somaliland	Fr. Som.
128	French West Africa	Fr. W. Afr.
128	Gambia	Gam.
31	Georgia	Ga.
128	Gold Coast	G. C.
112	Germany	Ger.
116	Gibraltar	Gib.
119	Greece	Grc.
14	Greenland	Grnld.
94	Grenada	Gren.
94	Guadeloupe	Guad.
91	Guanajuato	Guan.
93	Guatemala	Guat.
91	Guerrero	Guer.
94	Haiti	Hai.
76	Hawaii	Haw.
92	Hidalgo	Hid.
93	Honduras	Hond.
122	Hong Kong	Hong.
118	Hungary	Hung.
110	Iceland	Ice.
35	Iowa	Ia.
32	Idaho	Ida.
128	Ifni	Ifni
33	Illinois	Ill.
34	Indiana	Ind.
123	India	India
126	Iran	Iran
127	Iraq	Iraq
109	Ireland	Ire.
113	Italy	It.
91	Jalisco	Jal.
94	Jamaica	Jam.
124	Japan	Jap.
133	Java	Java
36	Kansas	Kan.
128	Kenya	Kenya
122	Korea	Kor.
121	Kuwait	Kuw.
37	Kentucky	Ky.
38	Louisiana	La.
79	Labrador	Lab.
94	Leeward Is.	Le. Is.
128	Liberia	Lib.
128	Libya	Libya
117	Liechtenstein	Liech.
114	Luxembourg	Lux.
82	Mackenzie	Mack.
128	Madagascar	Madag.
113	Malta	Mal.
122	Malay States	Mal. St.
81	Manitoba	Man.
121	Manchuria	Manch.
94	Martinique	Mart.
41	Massachusetts	Mass.
40	Maryland	Md.
39	Maine	Me.
92	Mexico	Mex.
42	Michigan	Mich.
91	Michoacan	Michoa.
43	Minnesota	Minn.
44	Mississippi	Miss.
45	Missouri	Mo.
111	Monaco	Monaco
121	Mongolia	Mong.
46	Montana	Mont.
129	Morocco	Mor.
92	Morelos	Morel.
128	Mozambique	Moz.
14	North America	N. A.
91	Nayarit	Nay.
83	New Brunswick	N. B.
54	North Carolina	N. C.
133	New Caledonia	N. Cal.
55	North Dakota	N. D.
47	Nebraska	Neb.
123	Nepal	Nep.
114	Netherlands	Neth.
133	Netherlands Borneo	Neth. Bor.
99	Netherlands Guiana	Neth. Gu.
133	Netherlands Indies	Neth. Ind.
48	Nevada	Nev.
79	Newfoundland	Newf.
133	New Guinea Ter.	N. Gui. Ter.
49	New Hampshire	N. H.
93	Nicaragua	Nic.
128	Nigeria	Nig.
109	Northern Ireland	N. Ire.
50	New Jersey	N. J.
91	Nuevo Leon	N. L.
51	New Mexico	N. M.
115	Norway	Nor.
128	Northern Rhodesia	N. Rh.
83	Nova Scotia	N. S.
52	New York	N. Y.
128	Nyasaland	Nya.
135	New Zealand	N. Z.
92	Oaxaca	Oax.
133	Oceania	Ocea.
56	Ohio	Ohio
58	Oklahoma	Okla.
121	Oman	Oman
85	Ontario	Ont.
59	Oregon	Ore.
60	Pennsylvania	Pa.
125	Palestine	Pal.
93	Panama	Pan.
133	Papua Ter.	Pap. Ter.
101	Paraguay	Par.
83	Prince Edward I.	P. E. I.
102	Peru	Peru
77	Philippine Is.	P. I.
118	Poland	Pol.
116	Portugal	Port.
128	Portuguese Guinea	Port. Gui.
78	Puerto Rico	P. R.
92	Puebla	Pueb.
92	Quintana Roo	Q. R.
87	Quebec	Que.
91	Queretaro	Quer.
128	Rio de Oro	R. de O.
62	Rhode Island	R. I.
118	Romania	Rom.
96	South America	S. A.
93	Salvador	Sal.
133	Samoa	Sam.
133	Sarawak	Sar.
113	Sardinia	Sard.
81	Saskatchewan	Sask.
121	Saudi Arabia (Nejd)	Sau. Ar.
63	South Carolina	S. C.
108	Scotland	Scot.
64	South Dakota	S. D.
108	Shetland Islands	Shet. Is.
122	Siam	Siam
90	Sinaloa	Sin.
121	Sinkiang	Sink.
128	Sierra Leone	S. L.
91	San Luis Potosi	S. L. P.
113	San Marino	S. Mar.
90	Sonora	Son.
120	Soviet Union	Sov. Un.
121	Soviet Union in Asia	Sov. Un. Asia
116	Spain	Sp.
129	Spanish Guinea	Sp. Gui.
129	Spanish Morocco	Sp. Mor.
128	Southern Rhodesia	S. Rh.
94	Santa Lucia	Sta. Luc.
94	St. Vincent	St. Vin.
133	Sumatra	Sum.
128	Southwest Africa	S.W. Afr.
132	Swaziland	Swaz.
115	Sweden	Swe.
117	Switzerland	Switz.
127	Syria	Syr.
92	Tabasco	Tab.
91	Tamaulipas	Tam.
128	Tanganyika	Tan.
121	Tannu Tuva	T. T.
135	Tasmania	Tas.
37	Tennessee	Tenn.
66	Texas	Tex.
121	Tibet	Tib.
133	Timor	Tim.
92	Tlaxcala	Tlax.
125	Transjordan	Transj.
94	Trinidad	Trin.
129	Tunisia	Tun.
127	Turkey	Tur.
128	Uganda	Ug.
14	United States	U. S.
101	Uruguay	Ur.
132	Union of South Africa	U. S. Afr.
65	Utah	Utah
69	Virginia	Va.
103	Venezuela	Ven.
92	Veracruz	Ver.
68	Vermont	Vt.
107	Wales	Wal.
70	Washington	Wash.
94	West Indies	W. I.
72	Wisconsin	Wis.
10	World	World
71	West Virginia	W. Va.
73	Wyoming	Wyo.
121	Yemen	Yem.
92	Yucatan	Yuc.
119	Yugoslavia	Yugo.
88	Yukon	Yuk.
91	Zacatecas	Zac.
128	Zanzibar	Zan.

ISLANDS

Index	Name	Location
A 8	Abaco, Great	W. I.
G 2	Achill	Ire.
F 11	Acklin	W. I.
C 21	Adah	Alaska
I 11	Admiralty	Ocea.
Q 23	Aegean	Aeg. Is.
N 12	Aerö	Den.
O 11	Afognak	Alaska
D 11	Agrigan	Ocea.
L 18	Ahvenanmaa (Åland), Fin.	Swe.
G 15	Ailinglap	Ocea.
F 16	Ailuk	Ocea.
L 23	Aitutaki	Ocea.
R 3	Akutan	Alaska
F 14	Alabat	P. I.
E 11	Alamangan	Ocea.
	Åland, see Ahvenanmaa	
Q 13	Alboran	Sp.
M 23	Aldabra (Br.)	Africa
Q 13	Alderney	Eng.
B 21	Aleutian	Alaska
O 22	Alexander Archipelago	Alaska
K 17	Alexa Reef	Ocea.
K 19	Alofa	Ocea.
J 7	Alor	Ocea.
C 13	Amamio	Jap.
I 7	Ambon	Ocea.
L 15	Ambryn	Ocea.
C 20	Amchitka	Alaska
B 18	Ameland	Neth.
C 22	Amlia	Alaska
Q 21	Amorgos	Grc.
Q 13	Ana Capa	Calif.
E 11	Anatahan	Ocea.
H 11	Anchorite	Ocea.
Q 20	Andaman	India
K 22	Andrew	N. S.
P 20	Andros	Grc.
C 7	Andros	W. I.
M 16	Aneityum	Ocea.
F 7	Angel de la Guarda	Baja Cal.
G 6	Anglesey	Wal.
G 9	Angour	Ocea.
J 22	Anguilla	W. I.
E 18	Anholt	Den.
J 12	Anna Maria Key	Fla.
K 8	Annobon (Sp.)	Africa
K 23	Anticosti	Can.
H 3	Antilles, Greater	W. I.
P 18	Antilles, Lesser	W. I.
L 20	Antiope Reef	Ocea.
K 16	Anuda	Ocea.
H 16	Apaiang	Ocea.
H 17	Apamama	Ocea.
H 3	Apostle	Wis.
R 6	Appledore	Me.
L 15	Arag	Ocea.
K 4	Aran	Ire.
C 11	Aran	N. Ire.
G 16	Arno Atoll	Ocea.
I 18	Arorai (Hurd)	Ocea.
J 9	Aru	Ocea.
M 2	Ascension	Africa
J 3	Asinara	It.
L 15	Astrolabe Reef	Ocea.
D 11	Asuncion	Ocea.
M 19	Ata	Ocea.
J 20	Atafu	Ocea.
M 23	Atiu	Ocea.
C 22	Atka	Alaska
B 18	Attu	Alaska
G 16	Aurh	Ocea.
L 13	Avon	Ocea.
G 20	Awo	Jap.
J 2	Axel Heiberg	N. Am.
H 18	Azores	World
E 21	Babuyan	P. I.
D 15	Baffin	Can.
L 10	Bahama	W. I.
A 7	Bahama, Great	W. I.
Q 5	Bahrein	Iran
A 6	Bailie	Mack.
C 10	Baily	Ocea.
N 18	Baker	Me.
H 19	Baker	Ocea.
N 2	Balabac	P. I.
J 21	Balearic	Sp.
J 5	Bali	Ocea.
K 17	Balmoral Reef	Ocea.
L 14	Bampton Reefs	Ocea.
I 16	Banaba	Ocea.
I 12	Bananal	Braz.
N 2	Bancalan	P. I.
I 3	Banka	Ocea.
B 7	Banks	Can.
K 15	Banks	Ocea.
J 18	Bantayan	P. I.
G 9	Baobeltaob	Ocea.
O 25	Barbados	W. I.
J 23	Barbuda	W. I.
I 13	Barca	P. R.
I 6	Bardsey	Wal.
N 20	Baronga	India
I 2	Barra	Scot.
N 17	Barren	Md.
P 14	Basilan	P. I.
B 12	Bass, Middle	Ohio
B 12	Bass, North	Ohio
C 12	Bass, South	Ohio
C 21	Batan	P. I.
G 19	Batan	P. I.
A 11	Bathurst	Can.
K 8	Bathurst	Ocea.
J 14	Bauro	Ocea.
D 11	Bay	Cen. Am.
Q 3	Bear	Ire.
G 14	Beaver	Mich.
J 15	Belcher	Can.
K 23	Bellingshausen	Ocea.
J 3	Belle-Ile	Fr.
K 13	Bellona	Ocea.
H 3	Benbecula	Scot.
I 11	Berberia	P. R.
E 14	Berens	Mack.
J 4	Berlengas	Port.
Q 15	Bermuda	N. Am.
F 3	Bernera	Scot.
L 21	Beveridge Reef	Ocea.
F 16	Bikar Atoll	Ocea.
F 15	Bikini	Ocea.
I 3	Billiton	Ocea.
P 13	Bird	La.
O 24	Biscayne Key	Fla.
I 11	Bismarck Archipelago	Ocea.
P 13	Blakistone	Md.
I 8	Blanquilla	Ver.
R 11	Block	R. I.
I 6	Boeton	Ocea.
L 19	Bohol	P. I.
L 24	Bora Bora	Ocea.
D 3	Borkum	Ger.
H 4	Borneo	Ocea.
Q 23	Bornholm	Den.
C 8	Borodino	Ocea.
J 13	Bougainville	Ocea.
L 11	Bougainville Reef	Ocea.
L 8	Brač	Yugo.
C 4	Bressay	Shet. Is.
P 22	Breton	La.
O 8	Brewster	Mass.
H 7	British Isles	Europe
J 15	Brougham Shoal	Ocea.
R 18	Brush	La.
M 21	Buffon Reef	Ocea.
N 3	Bugsuk	P. I.
I 13	Buka	Ocea.
M 20	Bulls	S. C.
H 16	Burias	P. I.
I 7	Buru	Ocea.
I 10	Bushanga	P. I.
I 6	Buton	Ocea.
B 14	Bylot	Can.
M 14	Caballones, Cayo de	Cuba
L 12	Cagayan	P. I.
O 6	Cagayan Sulu	P. I.
F 13	Caicos	W. I.
R 17	Caillou	La.
I 8	Calamian Group	P. I.
A 14	Camaguin	P. I.
F 7	Camano	Wash.
K 19	Camotes	P. I.
M 6	Campobello	N. B.
F 2	Canary	Africa
R 20	Candia (Crete)	Grc.
I 7	Canna	Scot.
K 7	Cantiles, Cayo	Cuba
I 20	Canton	Ocea.
F 21	Cape Breton	N. S.
N 14	Capel Bank	Ocea.
M 20	Capers	S. C.
J 18	Cape Verde	World
G 6	Capraia	It.
K 15	Capri	It.
L 10	Carmen	Baja Cal.
G 12	Caroline	Ocea.
J 25	Caroline Atoll	Ocea.
I 19	Carondelet Reef	Ocea.
H 9	Carteret Reef	Ocea.
R 18	Cat	Miss.
C 10	Cat	W. I.
G 19	Catanduanes	P. I.
M 13	Cato	Ocea.
L 14	Cayo Costa	Fla.
K 18	Cebu	P. I.
H 4	Cedros	Baja Cal.
I 6	Celebes	Ocea.
P 14	Cephalonia (Kephallenia)	Grc.
I 8	Ceram	Ocea.
P 12	Cerralvo	Baja Cal.
R 14	Ceylon	India
Q 12	Channel	Eng.
P 24	Chappaquiddick	Mass.
O 9	Charles	Conn.
E 14	Cherso	It.
L 13	Chesterfield	Ocea.
B 19	Chiloe	Chl.
O 21	Chios	Grc.
B 22	Chishima (Kuril)	Asia
J 13	Choiseul	Ocea.
B 19	Chonos Archipelago	Chl.
G 9	Christian	Ont.
H 23	Christmas	Ocea.
J 3	Christmas	Ocea.
B 23	Chuginadak	Alaska
H 10	Cinco Leguas, Cayos	Cuba
H 3	Clare	Ire.
R 6	Clear	Ire.
C 11	Clerk	Mack.
Q 5	Cockenoe	Conn.
C 18	Cocne	Ven.
K 1	Cocos (Keeling)	Ocea.
R 18	Coiba	Pan.
K 6	Coll	Scot.
L 7	Colonsay	Scot.
C 21	Commander	Sov. Un., Asia
M 22	Comoro (Fr.)	Africa
K 16	Conanicut	R. I.
I 5	Coney	N. Y.
Q 18	Contreras	Pan.
M 17	Conway Reef	Ocea.
L 22	Cook	Ocea.
O 13	Corfu (Kerkyra)	Grc.
L 11	Coringa	Ocea.
A 9	Corker Cay	Br. Hond.
L 20	Cormorant Rock	R. I.
J 16	Corn, Great	Nic.
J 16	Corn, Little	Nic.
A 1	Coronados	Baja Cal.
P 23	Coronation	Alaska
F 11	Corregidor	P. I.
Q 3	Corsica	Fr.
M 24	Cosmoledo	Africa
R 20	Crete (Candia)	Grc.
I 1	Crocker	N. Am.
O 10	Crooked	Fla.
L 23	Cross	Me.
J 13	Cuba	Cuba
C 17	Cubagua	Ven.
L 24	Culebra	C. Z.
D 24	Culebra	P. R.
I 9	Culion	P. I.
P 24	Cumberland	Ga.
P 16	Curacao	W. I.
B 19	Cure	Ocea.
O 19	Curtis	Ocea.
H 3	Cutch	India
O 20	Cuttyhunk	Mass.
J 10	Cuyo	P. I.
Q 20	Cyclades	Grc.
K 8	Cyprus	Tur.
I 11	Dampier	Ocea.
G 4	Dampier Archipelago	Austl.
J 22	Danger	Ocea.
N 7	Deer	Me.
M 6	Deer	N. B.
J 12	D'Entrecasteaux	Ocea.
R 16	Derniere, Isle	La.
N 4	Derre	Ocea.
E 20	Desolation	Chl.
B 12	Devon	Can.
K 23	Dinagat	P. I.
N 4	Dirk Hartog	Ocea.
R 16	Dodecanese	Europ.
D 23	Dominica	W. I.
F 20	Drummond	Mich.
Q 12	Dry Tortugas	Fla.
N 18	Duck	Me.
R 6	Duck	Me.
J 15	Duff (Wilson Gr.)	Ocea.
K 6	Dugiotok	Yugo.
K 9	Dumaran	P. I.
F 13	Dunkin Reef	Ocea.
I 10	Durour	Ocea.
Q 1	Dursey	Ire.
I 6	East Indies	Ocea.
L 22	East	R. I.
L 19	Eastern Group	Ocea.
H 17	Eastern Neck	Md.
B 21	East Frisian	Neth.
H 16	Ebon	Ocea.
L 15	Efate	Ocea.
J 8	Eigg	Scot.
H 7	Elba	It.
C 9	Eleuthera	W. I.
O 22	Elizabeth	Mass.
O 14	Elizabeth Reef	Ocea.
K 2	Ellesmere	N. Am.
B 2	Ellice	Mack.
J 18	Ellice	Ocea.
O 23	Elliotts Key	Fla.
I 20	Enderbury	Ocea.
G 11	Enderby	Ocea.
B 21	Engelschinan Plaat	Neth.
F 14	Eniwetok (Brown) Atoll	Ocea.
L 15	Epi	Ocea.

ISLANDS—Continued

Index	*Name*	*Location*
P 24	Ernest Legouve Reef	Ocea.
L 16	Erromanga	Ocea.
O 19	Escudo de Veraguas	Pan.
O 12	Espíritu Santo	Baja Cal.
L 15	Espiritu Santo	Ocea.
M 19	Eua	Ocea.
D 10	Euphrosyne (Sail Rock)	Ocea.
M 23	Fabert	Ocea.
E 23	Faeroes, The	Den.
J 20	Fakaofu	Ocea.
Q 12	Falkland	S. Am.
O 16	Falkner	Conn.
N 20	Falster	Den.
H 23	Fanning	Ocea.
K 3	Fanö	Den.
L 20	Fanualai	Ocea.
G 11	Faraulep	Ocea.
A 15	Farne	Eng.
B 9	Fehmarn	Ger.
L 23	Fenua Ura	Ocea.
L 18	Fernando Noronha	World
K 10	Fernando Po. (Sp.)	Africa
O 23	Ferrol	La.
A 6	Fetlar	Shet. Is.
F 10	Feys	Ocea.
K 19	Field Bank	Ocea.
L 17	Fiji	Ocea.
I 24	Fillippo Reef	Ocea.
I 8	Fire	N. Y.
E 12	Fishers	N. Y.
L 25	Flamenco	C. Z.
K 24	Flint	Ocea.
J 6	Flores	Ocea.
Q 21	Florida Keys	Fla.
O 19	Folly	S. C.
K 20	Formentera	Sp.
K 19	Fortuna	Ocea.
C 1	Foula	Shet. Is.
L 23	Foulness	Eng.
G 14	Fox	N. Y.
H 13	Fragoso, Cayos	Cuba
A 24	Franz Josef Land	World
M 12	Frederick Reef	Ocea.
J 9	Fred Hendrik	Ocea.
C 21	French Frigate Shoal	Ocea.
D 4	Frisian, East	Ger.
H 8	Fro	Nor.
J 18	Funafuti	Ocea.
Q 11	Furneaux Group	Ocea.
L 12	Fyn	Den.
Q 2	Galapagos	Ec.
A 10	Galeta	C. Z.
A 22	Galita	Tun.
F 11	Galvez Bank	Ocea.
K 15	Gana	Ocea.
G 14	Garden	Mich.
G 12	Gardiners	N. Y.
N 7	Gardner	Haw.
I 12	Gardner	Ocea.
I 19	Gardner	Ocea.
D 25	Gharbs	Tun.
N 9	Gigha	Scot.
H 8	Giglio	It.
H 16	Gilbert	Ocea.
I 2	Glénans, Iles de	Fr.
C 17	Goat	Calif.
L 18	Goat	R. I.
I 10	Goeree	Neth.
N 1	Goto	Jap.
O 17	Gottland	Swe.
F 17	Goulburn	Mack.
J 17	Gould	R. I.
J 14	Gower	Ocea.
P 15	Gozo	It.
R 19	Grand	La.
E 10	Grand	Mich.
R 17	Grand	Miss.
I 4	Grand Cayman	W. I.
M 14	Grande, Cayo	Cuba
N 6	Grand Manan	N. B.
Q 20	Grande Terre	La.
E 7	Granite	Mich.
H 3	Great Natuna	Ocea.
N 13	Great Sandy	Ocea.
O 3	Greenland	N. Am.
P 24	Grenada	W. I.
G 14	Grenadier	N. Y.
F 11	Grimes	Ocea.
M 20	Griswold	Conn.
K 9	Groote Eylandt	Ocea.
A 24	Guadeloupe	W. I.
F 11	Guam	Ocea.
C 12	Guanaja	Hond.
Q 12	Guernsey	Eng.
E 11	Guguan	Ocea.
I 15	Guillermo, Cayo	Cuba
G 13	Gull	Mich.
N 12	Hainan	Chn.
G 12	Hall	Ocea.
H 7	Halmahera (Jilolo)	Ocea.
N 23	Handeleur	La.
L 20	Hapai Group	Ocea.
M 21	Harans Reef	Ocea.
F 15	Hart	Md.
N 15	Haut, Isle au	Me.
O 18	Havre Rock	Ocea.
M 22	Hawaii	Hawaii
D 23	Hawaiian	Ocea.
N 22	Haymet Rocks	Ocea.
G 2	Hebrides	Scot.
C 5	Helgoland	Ger.
E 15	Hepburn	Mack.
Q 13	Herm	Eng.
I 11	Hermit	Ocea.
A 8	Heron	N. B.
A 6	Herschel	Yuk.
L 23	Hervey	Ocea.
R 19	Hichijo	Jap.
G 13	High	Mich.
J 13	Hispaniola	W. I.
I 7	Hitteren	Nor.
G 14	Hog	Mich.
H 19	Hog	R. I.
F 13	Hokkaido (Yezo)	Jap.
A 14	Holy	Eng.
G 6	Holyhead	Wal.
L 15	Hongkong	Chn.
K 16	Honshu	Jap.
A 3	Hooper	Mack.
I 17	Hope	R. I.
R 21	Horn	Miss.
K 18	Horne	Ocea.
H 19	Howland	Ocea.
B 18	Hoy	Scot.
L 24	Huaheine	Ocea.
I 20	Hull	Ocea.
M 16	Hunter	Ocea.
F 9	Hunter Reef	Ocea.
P 15	Hunting	S. C.

ISLANDS—Continued

Index	*Name*	*Location*
L 14	Huon	Ocea.
I 18	Hurd (Aurorai)	Ocea.
L 9	Hvar	Yugo.
P 23	Hyéres, Isle d'	Fr.
G 11	Ianthe Shoal	Ocea.
D 6	Ibayat	Ocea.
G 16	Ibbetson	Ocea.
B 21	Iceland	Den.
G 11	Ifalik	Ocea.
G 12	Inagua, Great	W. I.
H 14	Indiana Reef	Ocea.
K 13	Indispensable Reefs	Ocea.
H 2	Inishbofin	Ire.
H 3	Inishturk	Ire.
L 6	Iona	Scot.
O 13	Ionian	Grc.
H 5	Ireland	Eur.
E 6	Isle of Man	Eng.
K 6	Isle of Pines	Cuba
M 15	Isle of Pines	Ocea.
O 16	Isle of Wight	Eng.
G 10	Iuripik	Ocea.
K 19	Iviza	Sp.
O 19	Izu	Jap.
G 15	Jabwat	Ocea.
G 16	Jaluit	Ocea.
J 7	Jamaica	W. I.
L 16	James	Md.
C 20	Jan Mayen	World
I 9	Jappen	Ocea.
K 8	Jardines Bank	Cuba
H 23	Jarvis	Ocea.
J 4	Java	Ocea.
O 23	Jekyl	Ga.
E 24	Jerba	Tun.
R 13	Jersey	Eng.
H 7	Jilolo (Halmahera)	Ocea.
O 18	Johns	S. C.
E 21	Johnston	Ocea.
Q 12	Jolo	P. I.
K 24	Jupiter	Fla.
L 16	Kajak	Alaska
G 9	Kajangle	Ocea.
C 21	Kanaga	Alaska
L 18	Kandavu	Ocea.
P 9	Kangaroo	Ocea.
H 13	Kapingamarangi (Greenwich)	Ocea.
M 5	Karagu	Iran.
H 7	Karakelang	Ocea.
R 23	Karpathos (Scarpanto)	Aeg. Is.
C 5	Kauai	Haw.
D 22	Kaula	Ocea.
L 25	Kaukura	Ocea.
K 1	Keeling (Cocos)	Ocea.
I 8	Kei	Ocea.
C 13	Kelleys	Ohio
M 13	Kenn	Ocea.
I 16	Kent	Md.
P 14	Kephallēnia (Cephalonia)	Grc.
P 25	Kerguelen	World
N 13	Kerkyra (Corfu)	Grc.
O 18	Kermadec	Ocea.
M 5	Kharaj	Iran
O 18	Kiawah	S. C.
Q 11	King	Ocea.
G 22	Kingman Shoal	Ocea.
D 11	King William	Can.
P 10	Kishm	Iran.
P 11	Kodiak	Alaska
A 15	Kolguev	Sov. Un.
L 9	Korčula	Yugo.
G 9	Korror	Ocea.
P 2	Koshiki	Jap.
J 6	Krk	Yugo.
D 19	Krusenstern Rock	Ocea.
H 17	Kuria	Ocea.
O 7	Kuria Muria	Asia
B 22	Kuril (Chishima)	Asia
G 14	Kusaie (Ualah)	Ocea.
G 15	Kwadjelinn	Ocea.
N 4	Kyushu	Jap.
N 15	Laberinto de Doce Leguas	Cuba
G 5	Labuan	Ocea.
O 5	Laccadive	India
Q 17	Ladrones	Pan.
C 15	Laesö	Den.
G 19	Lagosta	It.
I 22	Lambay	Ire.
G 11	Lamotrek	Ocea.
H 15	Lanai	Haw.
D 8	Langdale	Ocea.
N 14	Langeland	Den.
B 2	Langley	Mack.
K 8	Largo, Cayo	Cuba
P 23	Largo, Key	Fla.
A 12	Largo Remo	C. Z.
E 14	Lawford	Mack.
M 5	Laysan	Haw.
K 22	Leeward	W. I.
N 20	Lemnos	Grc.
O 21	Lesbos (Mytilini)	Grc.
O 19	L'Esperance Rock	Ocea.
L 19	Lette	Ocea.
J 4	Lettermullan	Ire.
N 10	Levanzo	It.
O 14	Levkas	Grc.
L 18	Levuka	Ocea.
K 21	Leyte	P. I.
G 15	Lib	Ocea.
M 15	Lifu	Ocea.
L 12	Lihou Reef	Ocea.
F 15	Likieb	Ocea.
H 3	Lingga Archipelago	Ocea.
M 15	Lipari	It.
M 3	Lisianski	Haw.
D 14	Liston	Mack.
I 8	Lobos, I. de	Ver.
C 13	Lofoton	Nor.
N 17	Lolland	Den.
J 6	Lomblen	Ocea.
J 5	Lombok	Ocea.
G 8	Long	N. Y.
E 10	Long	W. I.
C 12	Lopez	C. Z.
D 6	Lopez	Wash.
O 14	Lord Howe	Ocea.
H 8	Lord North	Ocea.
N 23	L'Orne Bank	Ocea.
K 13	Louisiade Archipelago	Ocea.
M 15	Loyalty	Ocea.
G 10	Lubang	P. I.
G 13	Luknnor	Ocea.
G 16	Lukunor	Ocea.
M 6	Lundy	Eng.
E 14	Lussin	It.
E 11	Luzon	P. I.
B 16	Lyakhov	Sov. Un., Asia
I 19	McKean	Ocea.

ISLANDS—Continued

Index	*Name*	*Location*
O 19	Macauley	Ocea.
M 25	Machias	Me.
G 17	Mackinac	Mich.
O 23	Madagascar	Africa
E 3	Madeira	Africa
G 4	Madeline	Wis.
J 4	Madura	Ocea.
K 15	Maewo	Ocea.
C 20	Magdalen	Mar. Prov.
H 16	Maiana	Ocea.
L 25	Maitea	Ocea.
J 21	Majorca	Sp.
G 16	Majuro	Ocea.
L 25	Makatea	Ocea.
H 17	Makin (Taritari)	Ocea.
J 14	Malaita	Ocea.
I 23	Malden	Ocea.
K 25	Maldive	World
L 15	Malekula	Ocea.
G 16	Maloelab	Ocea.
Q 15	Malta	It.
M 23	Mangaia	Ocea.
I 7	Mangola	Ocea.
H 5	Manhattan	N. Y.
K 22	Manihiki	Ocea.
G 3	Manitou	Wis.
C 3	Manitoulin	Ont.
P 15	Mantinicus Rock	Me.
K 21	Manua	Ocea.
H 9	Mapia	Ocea.
C 12	Maraca	Braz.
H 17	Maraki	Ocea.
E 16	Marcet	Mack.
M 15	Mare	Ocea.
B 17	Margarita	Ven.
M 24	Maria (Hull)	Ocea.
L 3	Maria Augustina Bank	Ocea.
E 11	Mariana (Marianne)	Ocea.
P 24	Maria Theresa Reef	Ocea.
C 24	Marie Galante	W. I.
G 14	Marinduque	P. I.
L 12	Marion Reef	Ocea.
N 10	Marittimo	It.
F 15	Marken	Neth.
C 20	Maro Reef	Ocea.
J 13	Marova	Ocea.
L 11	Marquesas	World
P 12	Marsh	La.
G 16	Marshall	Ocea.
P 23	Marthas Vineyard	Mass.
G 23	Martinique	W. I.
I 17	Masbate	P. I.
O 20	Matagorda	Tex.
K 25	Matahiva	Ocea.
J 15	Matema Group	Ocea.
M 16	Matthew	Ocea.
D 11	Maug	Ocea.
H 18	Maui	Haw.
M 23	Mauki	Ocea.
M 24	Mauritius	World
F 12	Mayaguana	W. I.
J 8	Maytiquid	P. I.
H 8	Meangis	Ocea.
E 11	Medinilla	Ocea.
J 18	Meek Shoal	Ocea.
G 16	Mejit	Ocea.
C 19	Melbourne	Mack.
L 13	Mellish Reef	Ocea.
B 9	Melville	Can.
K 8	Melville	Ocea.
R 23	Mergui Archipelago	India
O 13	Metinic	Me.
K 5	Mi	Jap.
D 19	Miao Tao	Chn.
O 14	Middleton Reef	Ocea.
L 1	Midway	Haw.
G 16	Mili Atoll	Ocea.
F 15	Miller	Md.
Q 14	Milton Head	S. C.
P 19	Mindanao	P. I.
H 11	Mindoro	P. I.
M 18	Minerva Reefs	Ocea.
I 23	Minorca	Sp.
L 24	Miquelon	Can.
A 12	Miscou	N. B.
I 8	Misoöl	Ocea.
M 23	Mitiero	Ocea.
P 19	Miyake	Jap.
L 10	Mljet	Yugo.
J 7	Moa	Ocea.
N 21	Möen	Den.
G 14	Mokil	Ocea.
F 15	Molokai	Haw.
Q 2	Mona	P. R.
P 12	Monhegan	Me.
J 13	Mono	Ocea.
O 16	Monomoy	Mass.
L 14	Montague	Alaska
M 22	Moose Park	Me.
L 23	Mopeha	Ocea.
H 8	Morotai	Ocea.
E 5	Mors	Den.
M 17	Mount Desert	Me.
O 17	Mount Desert Rock	Me.
J 7	Muck	Scot.
I 10	Muertos, Caja de	P. R.
L 24	Murea	Ocea.
R 12	Muskeget	Mass.
P 19	Mustang	Tex.
P 21	Mykoni	Grc.
O 21	Mytilini (Lesbos)	Grc.
I 10	Naka	Jap.
G 12	Namoi	Ocea.
G 12	Namoluk	Ocea.
G 15	Namorik	Ocea.
G 15	Namu	Ocea.
M 20	Namuka Group	Ocea.
J 17	Nanomana	Ocea.
I 17	Nanomea	Ocea.
R 14	Nantucket	Mass.
L 24	Naos	C. Z.
K 22	Nassau	Ocea.
H 15	Nauru	Ocea.
F 22	Navarin	Arg.
P 21	Naxos (Naxia)	Grc.
K 15	Ndeni	Ocea.
O 9	Necker	Haw.
F 6	Negros	Ocea.
N 25	Neilson Rock	Ocea.
I 6	Netherland Indies	Ocea.
M 23	New	Ocea.
O 1	New Amsterdam	World
J 12	New Britain	Ocea.
M 15	New Caledonia	Ocea.
K 24	Newfoundland	Can.
I 10	New Guinea (Papua)	Ocea.
I 12	New Hanover	Ocea.
L 15	New Hebrides	Ocea.
I 12	New Ireland	Ocea.

ISLANDS—Continued

Index	*Name*	*Location*
B 16	New Siberian	Asia
Q 17	New Zealand	Ocea.
G 13	Ngatik	Ocea.
G 9	Ngoli	Ocea.
P 21	Nicaria	Grc.
B 6	Nicholson	Mack.
Q 18	Nicobar	India
O 10	Nihoa	Haw.
C 1	Niihau	Haw.
G 11	Nile Shoal	Ocea.
I 9	Nishino	Jap.
I 13	Nissan	Ocea.
L 19	Niuafou	Ocea.
L 20	Niuatobutabu	Ocea.
L 21	Niue	Ocea.
I 18	Niutao	Ocea.
K 5	Noirmoutier, I. de	Fr.
H 17	Nonuti	Ocea.
O 15	Norfolk	Ocea.
N 23	North	La.
Q 17	North	Ocea.
O 18	Northern Sporades	Grc.
H 13	North Fox	Mich.
I 12	North Manitou	Mich.
M 13	Northwest Bellona Reef	Ocea.
C 11	Novaya Zemlya	Asia
J 18	Nui	Ocea.
F 23	Nuima	Ven.
J 18	Nukufetan	Ocea.
J 18	Nukulailai	Ocea.
I 18	Nukunaui	Ocea.
J 20	Nukunono	Ocea.
H 13	Nukuoro	Ocea.
K 4	Nunivak	Alaska
J 18	Nurakita	Ocea.
E 11	Oahu	Haw.
I 7	Obi Major	Ocea.
C 10	Ogasawara	Ocea.
I 10	Oki	Jap.
L 6	Oléron, Ile d'	Fr.
G 12	Olol	Ocea.
O 16	Olutanga	P. I.
I 14	Ongtong Java (Lord Howe)	Ocea.
I 17	Onoatoa	Ocea.
M 18	Ono i Laa	Ocea.
G 13	Oraluk	Ocea.
C 6	Orcas	Wash.
B 19	Orkney	Scot.
K 11	Osprey Reef	Ocea.
M 25	Ossabaw	Ga.
H 2	Outer	Wis.
F 3	Pabray	Scot.
O 6	Padre	Tex.
K 7	Pag	Yugo.
E 11	Pagan	Ocea.
I 1	Pagi	Ocea.
L 6	Palawan	P. I.
J 11	Palmarola	It.
L 22	Palmerston	Ocea.
G 22	Palmyra	Ocea.
D 21	Palominos	P. R.
J 15	Panay	P. I.
P 11	Pangutarang Group	P. I.
L 21	Panoan	P. I.
J 7	Pantar	Ocea.
O 10	Pantelleria	It.
I 10	Papua (New Guinea)	Ocea.
D 9	Parece Vela	Ocea.
E 9	Parry	Ont.
B 10	Parry Group	Ocea.
H 17	Patience	R. I.
O 13	Paxos	Grc.
G 9	Pelew	Ocea.
I 6	Peling	Ocea.
M 19	Pelorus Reef	Ocea.
L 21	Pemba	Africa
O 21	Penikese	Mass.
K 25	Perico	C. Z.
P 22	Perlas	Cen. Am.
H 17	Peru	Ocea.
R 22	Petit Bois	Miss.
M 20	Petit Manan	Me.
L 15	Petrie Reef	Ocea.
O 15	Philip	Ocea.
F 12	Philippine	P. I.
I 20	Phoenix	Ocea.
H 6	Pianosa	It.
G 11	Pikelot	Ocea.
L 15	Pine	Fla.
E 20	Pineros	P. R.
G 14	Pingelap	Ocea.
O 21	Plum	Conn.
B 22	Plum	Mass.
E 14	Polillo	P. I.
A 19	Pomona	Scot.
G 13	Ponape	Ocea.
J 12	Ponza	It.
E 16	Pooles	Md.
N 12	Portland	Eng.
I 23	Portsmouth	N. C.
O 1	Pribilof	Alaska
H 16	Prince Edward	P. E. I.
C 10	Prince of Wales	Can.
H 3	Prince Patrick	N. Am.
L 8	Princess Royal	B. C.
K 9	Principe (Port)	Africa
I 17	Prudence	R. I.
E 10	Puerto Rico	P. R.
G 8	Pulo Anna	Ocea.
H 8	Pulu Mariere	Ocea.
G 11	Pulusuk	Ocea.
D 3	Puná	Ec.
K 4	Queen Charlotte	B. C.
H 8	Raasay	Scot.
J 6	Rab	Yugo.
P 13	Rabbit	La.
M 21	Raccoon Key	S. C.
L 24	Raiatea	Ocea.
J 22	Rakahanga	Ocea.
G 15	Ralik Chain	Ocea.
K 3	Ramsey	Wal.
O 19	Raoul	Ocea.
M 23	Rarotonga	Ocea.
C 20	Rat	Alaska
G 17	Ratak Chain	Ocea.
A 21	Rathlin	N. Ire.
C 8	Raza	Ocea.
K 6	Ré, Ile de	Fr.
P 6	Recherche Archipelago	Ocea.
E 18	Rene Reef	Ocea.
K 13	Rennell	Ocea.
Q 25	Rhodes	Aeg. Is.
B 3	Richards	Mack.
M 24	Rimitara	Ocea.
E 18	Rional Reef	Ocea.
M 25	Rodrigues	World
J 16	Romano, Cayo	Cuba
M 3	Römö	Den
G 9	Rona	Scot.

ISLANDS—Continued

Index	*Name*	*Location*
B 20	Ronaldshay, South	Scot.
F 15	Rongelap Atoll	Ocea.
F 15	Rongerik Atoll	Ocea.
B 10	Rosario	Ocea.
K 7	Rosario, Cayo	Cuba
K 21	Rose	Ocea.
K 13	Rossel	Ocea.
E 11	Rota	Ocea.
K 6	Rotti	Ocea.
A 22	Rottum	Neth.
K 17	Rotumah	Ocea.
L 5	Rowley Shoals	Ocea.
A 2	Royal	Mich.
C 13	Rügen	Ger.
I 7	Rum	Scot.
M 24	Rurutu	Ocea.
D 11	Ryukyu	Jap.
I 13	Sable	Ocea.
G 19	Sado	Jap.
J 12	St. Aignan	Ocea.
C 10	St. Alessandro	Ocea.
I 18	St. Andrews	Nic.
M 13	St. Bellona Reefs	Ocea.
P 12	St. Catherine	Md.
M 25	St. Catherines	Ga.
K 22	St. Christopher	W. I.
Q 22	St. Croix (U. S.)	Vir. Is.
Q 15	St. Georges	Md.
N 5	St. Helena	Africa
I 13	St. John	Ocea.
J 23	St. John	(U. S.) Vir. Is.
E 19	St. Jonas	Sov. Un., Asia
N 14	St. Joseph	Ont.
O 19	St. Joseph	Tex.
H 4	St. Lawrence	Alaska
H 23	St. Lucia	W. I.
H 10	St. Martin	Mich.
F 11	St. Martins Keys	Fla.
J 1	St. Matthew	Alaska
I 12	St. Matthias	Ocea.
H 3	St. Natuna	Ocea.
O 1	St. Paul	World
K 18	St. Paul Rocks	World
N 24	St. Simons	Ga.
J 20	St. Thomas	(U. S.) Vir. Is.
E 11	Saipan	Ocea.
F 20	Sakhalin	Sov. Un., Asia
B 11	Salut	Fr. Gu.
Q 13	Samales Group	P. I.
I 20	Samar	P. I.
K 20	Samoa	Ocea.
P 22	Samos	Grc.
N 21	Samothraki	Grc.
J 13	Samsö	Den.
C 10	San Augustino	Ocea.
Q 14	San Clemente	Calif.
O 24	Sands Key	Fla.
Q 19	Sandwich Group	World
H 7	Sangihe	Ocea.
M 15	Sanibel	Fla.
N 11	San José	Baja Cal.
C 5	San Juan	Wash.
O 9	San Miguel	Calif.
R 5	Sannak	Alaska
P 13	San Nicolas	Calif.
D 11	San Salvador	W. I.
P 13	Santa Barbara	Calif.
P 15	Santa Catalina	Calif.
M 11	Santa Catalina	Baja Cal.
O 12	Santa Cruz	Calif.
K 15	Santa Cruz	Ocea.
E 20	Santa Ines	Chl.
L 15	Santa Maria, Cayo	Cuba
O 10	Santa Rosa	Calif.
N 4	Santa Rosa	Fla.
F 11	Santa Rosa Reef	Ocea.
K 9	São Thomé (Port.)	Africa
N 24	Sapelo	Ga.
G 23	Sarah Anne	Ocea.
G 7	Sarangani	Ocea.
K 13	Sarasota Key	Fla.
K 3	Sardinia	It.
E 11	Sarigan	Ocea.
Q 13	Sark	Eng.
J 24	Saseno	It.
G 11	Satawal	Ocea.
K 20	Savaii	Ocea.
J 18	Savava	(U. S.) Vir. Is.
K 6	Savu	Ocea.
H 9	Saxegaard	Ocea.
R 23	Scarpanto (Karpathos)	Aeg. Is.
H 25	Scatari	N. S.
B 19	Schiermonnikoog	Neth.
E 18	Schjetman Reef	Ocea.
E 18	Schokland	Neth.
H 9	Schouten	Ocea.
I 9	Schouwen	Neth.
P 1	Scilly	Eng.
C 23	Seguam	Alaska
A 19	Seiland	Nor.
I 1	Seins, I. de	Fr.
I 16	Sejerö	Den.
Q 9	Semidi	Alaska
I 12	Semirara	P. I.
C 20	Semisopochnoi	Alaska
G 13	Seniavina	Ocea.
N 10	Sete Quedas	Braz.
L 24	Seychelles	World
E 19	Shantar	Sov. Un., Asia
R 5	Sheffield	Conn.
F 11	Shelter	N. Y.
L 23	Sheppey	Eng.
C 3	Shetland	Scot.
F 7	Shiant	Scot.
N 9	Shikoku	Jap.
R 19	Ship	Miss.
B 13	Shippigan	N. B.
O 12	Shuyak	Alaska
L 24	Siargao	P. I.
I 1	Siberet	Ocea.
H 15	Sibuyan	P. I.
B 21	Simons Zand	Neth.
R 24	Singapore	India
M 18	Siguijor	P. I.
K 18	Sjaelland	Den.
R 6	Skerkin	Ire.
K 4	Skomer	Wal.
H 7	Skye	Scot.
O 19	Skyros	Grc.
I 9	Sleat	Scot.
O 24	Smith	Va.
Q 18	Smiths	Md.
L 24	Society	Ocea.
J 24	Socotra	World
I 7	Soela	Ocea.
J 5	Soembawa	Ocea.
J 14	Solomon	Ocea.
C 11	Somerset	Can.
G 8	Sonserol	Ocea.

ISLANDS—Continued

Index	Name	Location
G 10	Sorol	Ocea.
G 11	Sotavento, Cayo	Cuba
R 16	South	Ocea.
G 14	Southampton	Can.
H 13	South Fox	Mich.
O 18	South Georgia	World
I 12	South Manitou	Mich.
P 18	South Marsh	Md.
Q 17	South Orkneys	World
R 16	South Shetlands	Ocea.
	South Victoria Land	S. Pol. Reg.
I 12	Squally	Ocea.
N 13	Squid Ledge	R. I.
L 14	Stanley	Ocea.
J 23	Starbuck	Ocea.
F 24	Staten	Arg.
I 4	Staten	N. Y.
J 14	Stewart	Ocea.
G 3	Stockton	Wis.
H 13	Stony	N. Y.
O 19	Strati	Grc.
Q 14	Strivali	Grc.
M 18	Stromboli	It.
H 7	Stuart	Alaska
E 18	Sugar	Mich.
C 10	Sulphur	Ocea.
G 6	Sulu Archipelago	Ocea.
I 2	Sumatra	Ocea.
J 6	Sumba	Ocea.
H 10	Summer	Mich.
E 10	Summer	Scot.
J 3	Sunda	Ocea.
K 22	Suvarov	Ocea.
A 22	Svalbard	World
A 14	Sverdrup	World
K 20	Swains	Ocea.
N 16	Swans	Me.
I 20	Sydney	Ocea.
I 14	Tablas	P. I.
L 24	Tabuaimanu	Ocea.
K 12	Tagula	Ocea.
L 24	Tahaa	Ocea.
L 25	Tahiti	Ocea.
G 7	Taiwan	Jap.
M 23	Takutea	Ocea.
H 7	Talaur	Ocea.
I 7	Taliabu	Ocea.
I 17	Tamana	Ocea.
C 21	Tanaga	Alaska
L 16	Tanna	Ocea.
E 15	Taongi	Ocea.
I 17	Taputeuea	Ocea.
F 4	Taransay	Scot.
H 17	Tarawa	Ocea.
H 17	Taritari (Makin)	Ocea.
I 14	Tasman	Ocea.
R 11	Tasmania	Ocea.
K 9	Tawitawi	P. I.
M 16	Taylors	Md.
O 19	Ten Thousand	Fla.
B 16	Terschelling	Neth.
B 19	Testigos	Ven.
C 13	Texel	Neth.
N 19	Thasos	Grc.
O 13	Thimble	Conn.
F 14	Thousand	N. Y.
K 10	Thursday	Ocea.
G 8	Tiburón	Son.
H 18	Ticao	P. I.
I 10	Tiger	Ocea.
K 25	Tikehau	Ocea.
K 16	Tilghman	Md.
R 18	Timbalier	La.
J 7	Timor	Ocea.
J 8	Timor Laut	Ocea.
F 16	Tinaga	P. I.
E 11	Tinian	Ocea.
J 9	Tinkers	Mass.
K 5	Tiree	Scot.
Q 24	Tobago	W. I.
L 19	Tofoa	Ocea.
L 20	Tonga	Ocea.
J 23	Tongareva	Ocea.
M 19	Tongatabu	Ocea.
K 15	Torres	Ocea.
M 23	Tortola	C. Z.
B 16	Tortuga	Ven.
B 12	Tory	N. Ire.
L 18	Totoya	Ocea.
D 16	Treasure	Calif.
L 12	Tregrosse	Ocea.
R 24	Trinidad	W. I.
Q 10	Trinity	Alaska
J 12	Trobriand	Ocea.
G 12	Truk (Hogolu)	Ocea.
K 2	Tsu	Jap.
M 11	Tuamotu Archipelago	World
M 25	Tubuai	Ocea.
M 24	Tubuai (Austral.)	Ocea.
R 13	Tuckernuck	Mass.
K 15	Tueopia	Ocea.
F 14	Turks	W. I.
B 9	Turneffe	Br. Hond.
K 19	Tuscarora Bank	Ocea.
K 20	Tutuila	Ocea.
C 20	Two Brothers Reef	Ocea.
K 19	Uea	Ocea.
G 3	Uist, North	Scot.
H 3	Uist, South	Scot.
F 14	Ujelang	Ocea.
Q 1	Uji	Jap.
F 10	Uluthi (Mackenzie)	Ocea.
B 24	Umnak	Alaska
B 24	Unalaska	Alaska
R 4	Unimak	Alaska
J 20	Union Group	Ocea.
A 5	Unst	Shet. Is.
K 20	Upolu	Ocea.
D 11	Uracas	Ocea.
E 17	Urk	Neth.
C 13	Usedom	Ger.
H 1	Ushant	Fr.
M 13	Ustica	It.
F 16	Utirik Atoll	Ocea.
D 10	Utila	Hond.
K 15	Utupua	Ocea.
M 15	Uvea	Ocea.
J 18	Vaitupu	Ocea.
Q 10	Vancouver	B. C.
P 1	Valentia	Ire.
K 15	Vanikoro	Ocea.
K 15	Vanua Lava	Ocea.
L 18	Vanua Levu	Ocea.
L 19	Vatanua	Ocea.
L 19	Vatoa	Ocea.
L 20	Vavan	Ocea.
F 10	Vegen	Nor.
J 13	Vella Lavella	Ocea.
L 22	Venado	C. Z.
G 11	Verde, Cayo	Cuba
D 9	Victoria	Can.
F 22	Vieques	P. R.
G 10	Vigten	Nor.
N 14	Vinal Haven	Me.
R 17	Vine	La.
H 13	Virazon, Cayos	Cuba
J 21	Virgin	W. I.
O 24	Virginia Key	Fla.
L 8	Vis	Yugo.
I 12	Vischer	Ocea.
L 17	Vitti Levu	Ocea.
C 14	Vlieland	Neth.
C 10	Volcano	Ocea.
J 24	Vostok	Ocea.
O 24	Wachusett Reef	Ocea.
D 15	Wake	Ocea.
J 7	Walcheren	Neth.
E 10	Walney	Eng.
M 16	Walpole	Ocea.
G 22	Washington	Ocea.
R 10	Washington	Wis.
M 22	Wass	Me.
L 10	Wellesley	Ocea.
D 19	Wellington	Chl.
F 15	Wells	N. Y.
K 9	Wessel	Ocea.
L 22	West	R. I.
	West Antarctica	S. Pol. Reg.
A 22	West Spitsbergen	World
G 11	West Faiu	Ocea.
C 15	West Frisian	Neth.
J 7	Wetar	Ocea.
C 12	White	Sov. Un., Asia
D 14	Wieringen	Neth.
	Wilkes Land	S. Pol. Reg.
L 12	Willis	Ocea.
J 15	Wilson Group (Duff)	Ocea.
P 24	Windward	W. I.
G 10	Wolea	Ocea.
F 22	Wollaston	Arg.
C 13	Wollin	Ger.
N 19	Wolverene Bank	Ocea.
J 12	Woodlark	Ocea.
F 16	Wotje	Ocea.
F 15	Wottho	Ocea.
C 1	Wrangel	N. Am.
A 18	Wrangell	Sov. Un., Asia
M 13	Wreck Reef	Ocea.
D 6	Y'Ami	Ocea.
N 21	Yakobi	Alaska
F 9	Yap	Ocea.
B 3	Yell	Shet. Is.
D 16	Yerba Buena	Calif.
K 5	Yeu, Ile d'	Fr.
F 13	Yezo (Hokkaido)	Jap.
J 14	Ysabel	Ohio
P 14	Zante	Grc.
L 22	Zanzibar	Africa
D 12	Zora	C. Z.

CAPES, HEADS, POINTS

Index	Name	Location
A 3	Agujereada, Pt.	P. R.
R 9	Agulhas	U. S. Afr.
C 18	Alexander	Mack.
I 7	Anamur	Tur.
E 3	Angamos, Pt.	Chl.
F 21	Arenas, Pt.	P. R.
K 6	Arnauti	Cyp.
E 11	Au Sable, Pt.	Mich.
A 7	Bathurst	Mack.
N 21	Beachy Head	Eng.
J 13	Beata	Dom. Rep.
L 9	Big Sable Pt.	Mich.
K 2	Blaavands Huk	Den.
A 23	Blanc	Tun.
G 1	Blanco	Afr.
C 23	Blanco	Arg.
B 11	Bloody Foreland	N. Ire.
A 11	Bojeador	P. I.
A 24	Bon	Tun.
B 20	Boujaroun	Alg.
A 11	Burlus	Eg.
J 8	Cabull Pt.	P. I.
J 1	Cajon, Punta	Cuba
G 10	Calavite	P. I.
R 7	Cambodia Pt.	Fr. In. Chn.
G 21	Canaveral	Fla.
O 22	Carnsore Pt.	Ire.
B 12	Cassipore	Braz.
D 25	Catoche	Yuc.
O 23	Charles	Va.
C 14	Chelyuskin	Sov. Un., Asia
C 18	Churchill	Man.
J 14	Cod	Mass.
M 18	Cornfield Pt.	Conn.
Q 10	Comorin	India
Q 20	Corrientes	Arg.
H 5	Corrientes	Col.
O 17	Cruz	Cuba
F 11	Diamond Head	Haw.
N 15	Daio	Jap.
N 2	Disappointment	Wash.
C 19	Duncansbay Head	Scot.
O 1	Dunmore Head	Ire.
L 18	Easton Pt.	R. I.
I 17	Engaño	Dom. Rep.
A 14	Engaño	P. I.
I 4	Eugenia, Punta	Baja Cal.
R 12	Falso	Baja Cal.
N 16	Fear	N. C.
E 18	Flamborough Head	Eng.
D 1	Flattery	Wash.
O 11	Frio	Afr.
N 19	Frio	Braz.
A 2	Galera	Ec.
O 25	Galeta, Punta	Cuba
H 21	Gilbjerg Hoved	Den.
R 7	Good Hope	U. S. Afr.
F 15	Gracias a Dios	Nic.
D 12	Gris Nez	Fr.
I 25	Guardafui	Afr.
F 6	Hague, de la	Fr.
M 16	Hammonasset Pt.	Conn.
J 25	Henlopen	Del.
P 23	Henry	Va.
R 10	Horn	S. Am.
M 22	Inubol	Jap.
N 14	Judith, Pt.	R. I.
C 1	Jiguero, Pt.	P. R.
Q 21	Kalae, Pt.	Haw.
H 19	Kauiki Head	Haw.
B 6	Kellett	Can.
C 6	Keweenaw Pt.	Mich.
F 24	Kinnaird Head	Scot.
N 24	Kumukahi	Haw.
O 2	Lands End	Eng.
B 6	Lisburne	Alaska

CAPES, HEADS, POINTS—Continued

Index	Name	Location
K 22	Lookout	N. C.
D 21	Lopatka	Sov. Un., Asia
K 10	Lopez	Afr.
A 11	Mairaira Pt.	P. I.
R 21	Mala Pt.	Pan.
A 15	Malin Head	N. Ire.
R 19	Mariato Pt.	Pan.
Q 16	Matapan	Grc.
R 3	Mizen Head	Ire.
G 1	Monze	India
A 20	Navarin	Sov. Un., Asia
K 23	Naze, The	Eng.
O 4	Naze, The	Nor.
P 21	Negrais	India
A 21	North	Nor.
L 24	North Foreland	Eng.
D 14	North Pt.	P. E. I.
B 20	Olyutorsk	Sov. Un., Asia
A 24	Oma	Jap.
B 7	Ortegal	Sp.
M 16	Palos, de	Sp.
F 1	Parina Pt.	Peru
P 17	Passero	It.
P 7	Pine Creek Pt.	Conn.
L 24	Pointe Aux Barques	Mich.
E 5	Prince of Wales	Alaska
O 21	Rasa Pt.	Arg.
H 22	Ras Bir	Fr. Som.
M 7	Ras el Hadd	Asia
K 4	Roca, de	Port.
J 4	Romanzof	Alaska
R 9	Sable	N. S.
K 3	St. Davids Head	Wal.
R 14	St. Frances	U. S. Afr.
P 22	Ste. Marie	Madag.
K 17	St. Martin	Sp.
N 4	St. Vincent	Port.
O 21	San Antonio	Arg.
P 10	San Blas	Fla.
F 23	San Diego	Arg.
C 20	San Juan	P. R.
B 12	San Juan de Guia	Col.
R 3	Satano	Jap.
P 12	Shionomi	Jap.
A 14	Skaw, The	Den.
C 7	Spartel	Mor.
G 19	Spurn Head	Eng.
P 8	Stratford Pt.	Conn.
H 7	Tell es Semak	Pal.
J 10	Tiburon	Hai.
D 10	Tres Forcas	Mor.
J 20	Upolu Pt.	Haw.
P 11	Varela	Fr. In. Chn.
L 23	Warren Pt.	R. I.
O 3	Watch Hill Pt.	R. I.
D 16	Whitefish Pt.	Mich.
K 23	Wicklow Head	Ire.
C 12	Wrath	Scot.

MOUNTAINS AND DESERTS

Index	Name	Location
O 23	Abajo	Utah
N 13	Abarim	Pal.
K 6	Abraham	Me.
E 6	Absaroka Range	Wyo.
F 9	Abuna Yobel	Eth.
L 6	Aconcagua (22,834 ft.)	Arg.
G 16	Adams	N. H.
N 11	Adams (12,307 ft.)	Wash.
N 9	Adams Head	Utah
R 13	Adams Peak	India
G 21	Adirondack	N. Y.
K 18	Adula Group	Switz.
B 20	Agathla Peak	Ariz.
M 7	Aguila	Ariz.
N 10	Ajo	Ariz.
D 6	Akarai	Braz.
C 6	Ala	Tur.
D 12	Ala Dagh	Iran
E 10	Alaji	Erit.
J 12	Alaska Range	Alaska
K 22	Albula Group	Switz.
J 13	Alder, Ben	Scot.
O 10	Aleutian Range	Alaska
R 7	Algauer Alps	Ger.
Q 22	Alhambra Peak	Utah
L 13	Alice	Utah
F 16	Alkali Desert	Nev.
H 21	Allegheny	U. S.
M 9	Alps	Eur.
O 12	Alvarez	Ariz.
J 5	Alvo	It.
J 10	Amambahy	Par.
F 4	Amne Machin Range	Chn.
E 16	Amour	Alg.
F 11	Ampamento	Cen. Am.
A 19	Anadyr	Sov. Un.
G 1	Anareesh	Iran
H 9	Anderson Peak	Ida.
K 9	Andes	S. Am.
J 19	Angus, Braes of	Scot.
P 1	Animas Range	N. M.
O 23	Ankaratra	Madag.
M 11	Antelope	Ore.
K 4	Antelope	Utah
L 10	Antelope Hills	Wyo.
C 21	Antelope Peak	N. M.
O 3	Antelope Range	Utah
B 18	Anti-Lebanon	Pal.
B 6	Antisana	Ec.
F 11	Anti Taurus	Tur.
P 4	Antuco	Arg.
K 18	Apache	Ariz.
P 22	Apo	P. I.
N 15	Appalachian	N. Am.
F 9	Appenines	It.
F 11	Applehouse Hill	R. I.
N 8	Aqua Dulce	Ariz.
I 19	Arabian Desert	Eg.
D 20	Ararat (Vol., extinct, 16,916 ft.)	Tur.
F 19	Ardennes	Fr.
H 9	Arening Mawr	Wal.
E 15	Armine, Ben	Scot.
N 21	Arrow Canon	Nev.
G 21	Asahi	Jap.
J 11	Asbestos	U. S. Afr.
M 5	Ascotan	Bol.
M 13	Ascutney	Vt.
I 5	Ashnar	Iran
O 5	Aso Peak	Jap.
Q 8	Aspen	Wyo.
O 4	Aspiring (9,975 ft.)	N. Z.
F 6	Atacama Desert	Chl.
J 5	Atlas	Mor.
Q 20	Australian Alps	Austl.
N 14	Auvergne	Fr.
C 4	Aymanon	P. R.
L 20	Aymores	Braz.

MOUNTAINS AND DESERTS—Continued

Index	Name	Location
H 5	Azufre (Copiapó)	Chl.
I 10	Babine Range	B. C.
O 14	Baboquivari	Ariz.
J 11	Bachelor Butte	Ore.
O 1	Backbone	Md.
E 11	Badger	Ore.
H 15	Badger	Wash.
Q 16	Badger Peak	Ida.
H 19	Bad Land Cliffs	Utah
D 9	Baird	Alaska
H 3	Baird	Wyo.
C 10	Baker (10,750 ft.)	Wash.
G 14	Bakharz	Iran.
B 17	Bald	Conn.
D 6	Bald	Ida.
G 8	Bald	Ida.
M 8	Bald	N. C.
F 23	Bald	Ore.
J 3	Bald	Wyo.
F 17	Bald Cap Dome	N. H.
H 6	Bald Hill	R. I.
P 5	Baldi	Ore.
B 19	Bald Peak	Calif.
J 22	Baldy	Ariz.
M 9	Baldy	Utah
A 7	Ball	Conn.
I 19	Ball	Okla.
I 22	Bandai	Jap.
B 6	Bangs	Ariz.
A 2	Bannock Peak	Wyo.
C 5	Bare	Ore.
G 16	Barkut	Afg.
C 5	Barrack	Conn.
J 12	Barrier	Mack.
J 22	Battock	Scot.
F 1	Bayan Kara Range	Chn.
F 3	Bayantukmu	Chn.
N 3	Bear	Me.
J 8	Bear	N. M.
J 13	Bear Creek Butte	Ore.
B 16	Bearfort	N. J.
Q 1	Beaver Dam	Utah
M 4	Beaver Lake	Utah
M 23	Bebnina Group	Switz.
M 16	Belted Range	Nev.
L 14	Ben Lomond	Scot.
J 12	Ben Nevis	Scot.
L 13	Ben Vorlich	Scot.
E 3	Berkshire	Mass.
L 14	Bernese Alps	Switz.
I 9	Berwyn	Wales
J 12	Beseck	Conn.
L 22	Big Bend	Ida.
E 3	Big Black	Va.
J 6	Bigelow	Me.
N 22	Big Hole	Ida.
J 8	Big Horn	Ariz.
C 13	Big Horn	Wyo.
M 4	Big Savage	Md.
C 9	Bigstone	Va.
I 17	Bihar	Rom.
P 19	Billings	Yuk.
G 12	Bill Williams	Ariz.
O 19	Binaca	P. I.
M 17	Birch Butte	Ida.
G 8	Birdtail Divide	Mont.
J 3	Bitter Root Range	Mont.
H 19	Black	Afg.
F 3	Black	Ariz.
G 19	Black	Calif.
K 11	Black	Eng.
H 16	Black	N. H.
H 16	Black	N. H.
F 8	Black	Utah
P 9	Black Butte	Wyo.
L 19	Black Crater	Calif.
O 21	Blackfoot	Ida.
P 12	Black Hills	Ore.
I 2	Black Hills	S. D.
C 24	Black Hills	Wyo.
I 4	Black Peak	Ariz.
R 16	Black Pine	Ida.
L 5	Black Range	N. M.
M 8	Black Rock	Ore.
C 6	Black Rock Desert	Nev.
L 7	Black Rock (Vol.)	Utah
G 17	Blacktail	Utah
E 16	Blounts	Ala.
O 21	Blue	Austl.
K 22	Blue	Okla.
E 19	Blue	Ore.
L 19	Blue	Pa.
O 23	Blue	Wash.
R 4	Blue Hill Range	Mass.
F 2	Blue Ridge	Ariz.
D 7	Blue Ridge	Md.
D 4	Blue Ridge	N. C.
A 5	Blue Ridge	S. C.
I 22	Blue Ridge	U. S.
K 10	Blue Ridge	Va.
N 11	Bohemian Forest	Ger.
G 9	Bohemian Moravian Highlands	Czech.
N 7	Bokkeveld	U. S. Afr.
C 18	Bonaparte	Wash.
N 4	Bone	Ore.
J 23	Book Cliffs	Utah
D 17	Bou Kahil	Alg.
N 11	Boulder	Ida.
P 23	Boulder Canon	Nev.-Ariz.
E 16	Box	Conn.
I 12	Bradshaw	Ariz.
C 12	Brazos Peak	N. M.
K 9	Brecan Beacons	Wales
M 15	Breckinridge	Calif.
Q 3	Bridger Butte	Wyo.
I 10	Broken Top	Ore.
O 9	Bromley	Vt.
D 12	Brooks Range	Alaska
J 22	Brown (Roan) Cliffs	Utah
H 24	Brushy	Okla.
E 20	Buck	N. Y.
D 15	Buck	Wash.
H 9	Buckhorn	Utah
I 6	Buckskin	Ariz.
G 8	Bulgar Dagh	Tur.
G 4	Burgess	Yuk.
N 4	Burro, Big	N. M.
G 5	Bushnell	Conn.
F 19	Butte	Nev.
M 10	Caaguazú	Par.
M 8	Caballo	N. M.
B 6	Cabinet	Ida.-Mont.
L 14	Cactus Range	Nev.
J 9	Cambrian	Wales
J 11	Cameroon	Afr.
P 18	Campbell Range	Yuk.
B 5	Canaan	Calif.
H 3	Cannibal	Ore.

MOUNTAINS AND DESERTS—Continued

Index	Name	Location
D 10	Cantabrian	Sp.
G 5	Carbuncle Hill	R. I.
F 17	Caribes	P. R.
K 14	Cariboo Range	B. C.
O 23	Caribou Range	Ida.
H 8	Carmel	Pal.
B 11	Carnic Alps	It.
G 16	Carpathians	Eur.
J 11	Carr	N. H.
O 4	Carrantuohill	Ire.
H 14	Carrigain	N. H.
B 23	Carrizo	Ariz.
H 17	Carter Dome	N. H.
M 14	Casa Grande	Ariz.
D 12	Cascade	N. Am.
J 17	Casper Range	Wyo.
B 7	Cassiar	B. C.
L 4	Castle Dome	Ariz.
M 23	Castle Peak	Calif.
B 13	Castle Peak	Wash.
J 21	Castle Rock	Ore.
B 5	Castor Peak	Wyo.
B 14	Cathedral Peak	Wash.
C 5	Cathedral Peak	Wyo.
P 22	Catskill	N. Y.
P 17	Caucasus	Sov. Un.
B 6	Cayambe (19,023 ft.)	Ec.
G 13	Cayey	P. R.
F 8	Cebolleta	N. M.
H 6	Cebolleta	N. M.
L 22	Cedar	Ore.
F 6	Cedar	Utah
Q 19	Cedar Butte	Ida.
B 10	Cedar Peak	Calif.
J 23	Cedar Range	Nev.
D 9	Cejita Blanca	N. M.
J 10	Cerro de los Pinos	N. M.
H 14	Cerro de San Felipe	Sp.
F 2	Cerro Diablo	Tex.
O 16	Cevennes, Les	Fr.
P 7	Chachanuen	Arg.
J 9	Chaffee	Vt.
B 24	Chang-Pai-Shan	Chn.
L 22	Chappar	Bal.
O 17	Charleston Peak	Nev.
G 7	Chasseral	Switz.
B 3	Chattooga Ridge	S. C.
F 13	Chelan Range	Wash.
H 4	Chemehuevis	Ariz.
J 15	Chestnut	Conn.
C 12	Cheviot Hills	Eng.
C 4	Chimborazo (20,702 ft.)	Ec.
J 18	Chimney Rock	Utah
K 4	Chinati	Tex.
F 22	Chiokai	Jap.
N 24	Chiricahua	Ariz.
O 24	Chiricahua Peak	Ariz.
M 6	Chisos	Tex.
C 5	Chittenden	Wyo.
L 3	Chocolate	Ariz.
P 24	Chocolate	Calif.
J 16	Chocorua	N. H.
M 9	Choroloque	Bol.
K 15	Chugach	Alaska
F 2	Chuncho Cabana	Bol.
D 2	Chusca	N. M.
K 5	Cienega	Tex.
M 13	Cimarron	Ariz.
G 9	Clachain, Ben	Scot.
Q 8	Clastenbury	Vt.
P 19	Clay Hills	Utah
K 17	Clear Creek	Wyo.
K 12	Cleman	Wash.
E 8	Clinch	Va.
G 23	Clinton	N. Y.
D 9	Coast Range	N. Am.
D 7	Coeur d'Alene	Ida.
N 16	Comeragh	Ire.
J 2	Confusion Range	Utah
K 14	Congoon Hill	R. I.
H 8	Continental Divide	U. S.
J 16	Continental Divide	Pan.
M 19	Cook	Alaska
M 8	Cook (12,349 ft.)	N. Z.
N 6	Cooks Range	N. M.
I 21	Cool	Afg.
H 5	Copiapo (Azufre) (19,947)	Chl.
M 5	Copper	Ariz.
C 15	Copperas	N. J.
L 6	Corazones	Tex.
L 12	Cordoba	Arg.
E 19	Cornudo Hills	N. M.
D 12	Corozal	P. R.
E 21	Corson	Utah
E 15	Cortez	Nev.
I 9	Coseguina (Vol.)	Nic.
K 18	Coso Valley Desert	Calif.
C 6	Cotopaxi (19,498 ft.)	Ec.
F 7	Cottonwood Cliffs	Ariz.
L 13	Cotswold Hills	Eng.
K 15	Coyote Peak	Calif.
P 10	Crater	Wash.
E 7	Crater	Wyo.
D 8	Crater Peak	Calif.
O 9	Crater Peak	Ore.
C 15	Crawford	Utah
L 5	Cricket	Utah
N 23	Cuchillas De Toar	Cuba
D 4	Cumberland	Va.
D 11	Cumbrian	Eng.
Q 16	Curupira	Ven.
C 11	Custer Ridge	Wash.
L 7	Cuzco	Bol.
M 6	Dahna (Roba el Khali) Desert	Asia
K 4	Dalthorp	Mack.
F 6	Damon	Wyo.
H 13	Dana	Calif.
O 24	Darien	Cen. Am.
J 12	Dasht i Lut Desert	Iran
I 6	Datil	N. M.
J 5	Davis	Tex.
N 7	Dawson	Yuk.
E 17	Deadman	Utah
F 12	Dearg, Ben	Scot.
K 19	Death Valley Desert	Calif.
H 21	Debenet	Fr. Som.
H 1	Deep Creek	Utah
H 4	Delaware	Tex.
F 7	Demavend	Iran
O 10	Dent Blanche	Switz.
N 7	Dent De Morcles	Switz.
N 6	Dent du Midi	Switz.
P 7	Derrynasaggart	Ire.
C 12	Derryveagh	Ire.
H 10	Desatoya	Nev.
N 19	Desert Range	Nev.
J 5	Detroit	Utah
E 16	Dhaulagiri	India

Physical Features of the World

MOUNTAINS AND DESERTS—Continued

Index	Name	Location
L 4	Diablo Range	N. M.
F 17	Diamond	Nev.
L 8	Diamond Peak	Ore.
L 9	Dinaric Alps	Yugo.
G 11	Dipilto	Cen. Am.
A 9	Disaster Peak	Nev.
M 24	Diuata	P. I.
C 5	Doane	Wyo.
C 9	Dolomite Alps	It.
B 7	Dome	Calif.
E 12	Dome Peak	Wash.
J 3	Dome Rock	Ariz.
N 7	Dorset	Vt.
N 23	Dos Cabezas	Ariz.
B 9	Double Head	Calif.
M 13	Douglas	Mont.
J 8	Dovre (Fjeld)	Nor.
M 23	Downs, North	Eng.
M 18	Downs, South	Eng.
N 21	Dragoon	Ariz.
D 21	Drakensbergen	U. S. Afr.
K 19	Drakesberg	U. S. Afr.
J 15	Drum	Alaska
G 15	Duchak	Iran
H 4	Dugway	Utah
O 4	Dutchmans Butte	Ore.
N 9	Dutton	Utah
C 10	Eagle Peak	Calif.
K 7	Eagle Tail	Ariz.
P 11	Eastern Ghats	Asia
C 15	Echo Cliffs	Ariz.
N 2	Edson Butte	Ore.
G 15	Egmont	N. Z.
P 14	Elbrus (18,468 ft.)	Sov. Un.
E 6	El Burz	Iran
G 14	El Cuervo Butte	N. M.
Q 22	Eldorado Range	Nev.
N 10	Electric Peak	Mont.
K 19	Elgon	Ug.
C 6	El Huerfano	N. M.
E 17	Elizabeth Peak	Utah
G 6	El Juf Desert	Fr. W. Afr.
H 8	Elk	Colo.
I 10	Elk	Ida.
P 16	Elk	Wyo.
Q 18	Elkhorn	Ida.
J 21	Elles	Br. Som.
J 22	Elmes	Br. Som.
N 12	Elonga	Ang.
G 4	Elwund	Iran
J 21	Ely Range	Nev.
N 12	Emigrant Peak	Mont.
R 3	Emily	Ore.
D 7	Emma	Ariz.
E 19	Emmons Peak	Utah
M 7	Emory	Tex.
O 19	Empire	Ariz.
K 23	Engadine	Switz.
N 6	Eolus	Vt.
O 6	Equinox	Vt.
E 9	Erjias	Tur.
L 12	Erz Gebirge	Ger.
C 3	Escalante Hills	Colo.
F 7	Espiritu Santo	Cen. Am.
N 7	Essex	Wyo.
O 16	Etna (Vol., active, 10,741 ft.)	It.
O 15	Euchre Butte	Ore.
E 19	Everest (29,141 ft.)	India
I 1	Everett	Mass.
K 7	Excelsior	Nev.
L 16	Fahute Peak	Calif.
M 20	Fairweather (15,399 ft.)	Alaska
D 22	Fanny	Ore.
L 14	Ferris	Wyo.
M 10	Fichte Gebirge	Ger.
E 5	Field	Tas.
G 2	Finlay	Tex.
M 12	Fish Lake	Utah
I 3	Fish Spring	Utah
F 5	Flathead Range	Mont.
O 7	Florida	N. M.
F 10	Floyd	Ariz.
I 12	Flume	N. H.
J 12	Foraker	Alaska
M 23	Fountain Peak	Calif.
K 15	Four Peaks	Ariz.
C 4	Fox	Nev.
L 8	Fra Cristobal Range	N. M.
I 8	Franklin	Mack.
D 9	Fredonyer	Calif.
D 9	Fredonyer Peak	Calif.
K 21	Freezeout	Ore.
M 16	Freezeout	Wyo.
K 6	Fremont Butte	Wyo.
O 11	Fuego	Ore.
M 18	Fuji (12,461 ft.)	Jap.
K 6	Galdhopigen	Nor.
M 12	Galena Peak	Ida.
K 21	Galeta	C. Z.
M 20	Galiuro	Ariz.
M 11	Gallatin Range	Mont.
I 7	Gallinas	N. M.
D 10	Gallinas Peak	N. M.
N 13	Galty	Ire.
C 22	Gammori	Jap.
D 24	Ganju	Jap.
K 20	Ganti	Afg.
M 19	Gap Bald	Okla.
F 7	Garfield Peak	Wyo.
H 6	Gargish	Iran
H 12	Garnet	N. H.
M 6	Gausta	Nor.
J 7	Gelkie	Wyo.
K 6	Gennargentu	It.
G 23	Giant	N. Y.
F 18	Gibson Peak	Nev.
I 8	Gibsons Desert	Austl.
L 22	Gila	Ariz.
M 4	Gila	Ariz.
L 9	Gila Bend	Ariz.
E 19	Gilbert Peak	Utah
L 13	Gilead	Pal.
F 12	Glacier Peak	Wash.
B 7	Glass	Calif.
J 7	Glass	Texas
O 11	Glebe	Vt.
J 12	Glee Hills	Eng.
N 11	Glenlyon Range	Yuk.
K 7	Glitteruni	Nor.
S 11	Glockner, Gr.	Ger.
L 9	Goat	Ida.
J 17	Gobi Desert	Asia
K 19	Golden Gate	Nev.
I 20	Gold Hill	C. Z.
G 3	Gold Hill	Utah
O 16	Gold Range	Br .Col.
F 13	Golon	Cen. Am.
Q 13	Goose Creek	Ida.

MOUNTAINS AND DESERTS—Continued

Index	Name	Location
F 11	Gore Range	Colo.
D 21	Goshute	Nev.
I 7	Gospel	Ida.
K 16	Grampian	Scot.
A 6	Gran Desierto Desert	Son.
D 5	Grand Wash Cliffs	Ariz.
L 13	Granite	Wyo.
L 19	Granite Peak	Calif.
D 4	Granite Peak	Nev.
D 4	Granite Range	Nev.
O 22	Gran Piedra	Cuba
I 19	Grant Range	Nev.
M 12	Grape Vine	Nev.
G 10	Grave	Ida.
E 4	Gravel Peak	Wyo.
L 9	Grayhound	Ida.
J 17	Graylock Butte	Ore.
N 15	Grays Butte	Ore.
H 14	Great Altai	Asia
H 20	Great Dividing Range	Austl.
H 18	Great Khingan	Asia
E 11	Great North	Va.
H 20	Great North	W. Va.
Q 7	Great St. Bernard	Switz.
G 10	Great Salt Desert	Iran
F 4	Great Salt Lake Desert	Utah
G 9	Great Sandy Desert	Austl.
O 4	Great Smoky	N. C.
K 9	Great Victoria Desert	Austl.
P 11	Great Zwartberg	U. S. Afr.
I 11	Gredos	Sp.
A 4	Green	Ore.
E 10	Green	Vt.
L 12	Green	Wyo.
I 23	Greens Peak	Ariz.
C 3	Greylock	Mass.
H 3	Gros Ventre Range	Wyo.
B 2	Grouse Creek	Utah
N 9	Growler	Ariz.
N 18	Guadalupe	N. M.
G 4	Guadalupe	Tex.
F 4	Guadalupe Peak	Tex.
D 6	Guarione	P. R.
F 7	Guaybana	P. R.
A 10	Gusharbrum	India
G 22	Gwas	Jap.
M 12	Gypsum Hills	N. M.
F 22	Hajikak	Afg.
P 4	Haku	Jap.
K 15	Hakusan	Jap.
H 12	Halcon	P. I.
K 9	Haldane	Yuk.
H 19	Haleakala Crater	Haw.
J 7	Hamilton	Calif.
K 14	Hampton Butte	Ore.
D 4	Hancock	Wyo.
B 7	Hansels	Utah
J 6	Harcuvar	Ariz.
D 7	Harkness Peak	Calif.
J 7	Harquahala	Ariz.
I 8	Harz	Ger.
P 3	Hatchet	N. Mex.
N 4	Hawk	Me.
P 1	Hawkins Peak	Utah
E 24	Hayachine	Jap.
E 16	Hayden Peak	Utah
A 7	Haystack	Conn.
Q 9	Haystack	Vt.
K 17	Haystack	Wyo.
F 2	Hay Stack Butte	S. D.
E 14	Hazar Maziid	Iran.
B 8	Heart	Wyo.
F 14	Heber	Utah
C 20	Hekla	Ice.
N 17	Henry	Utah
K 11	Herjehognen	Swe.
I 13	Higby	Conn.
K 23	Highland Range	Nev.
H 17	Hight	N. H.
G 12	Highwood	Mont.
L 13	Hilgard	Utah
M 22	Hilonghilong	P. I.
D 13	Himalaya	India
H 9	Himmelbjerg	Den.
E 23	Hindu Kush	Afg.
I 14	Hitchcock	N. H.
I 3	Hoback	Wyo.
B 7	Hoffman	Calif.
C 5	Hog	Utah
G 7	Hogback	Vt.
Q 10	Hogback	Vt.
M 9	Holly	Utah
O 18	Holmes	Utah
D 10	Hood (11,537 ft.)	Ore.
B 5	Hoodoo Peak	Wyo.
J 8	Hooker	Wyo.
N 1	Hooppole Ridge	Md.
E 4	Hoosac	Mass.
H 21	Hope	R. I.
N 10	Horn, The	Mack.
I 15	Hot Creek	Nev.
E 9	Hotham Peak	Alaska
E 5	Howland	Conn.
E 15	Hoyt Peak	Utah
P 20	Huachuca Peak	Ariz.
G 6	Hualpai Peak	Ariz.
I 13	Huapi	Cen. Am.
J 7	Huascan (22,051 ft.)	Peru
Q 4	Hubbard	Yuk.
D 12	Hubbardston	Mass.
D 21	Huckleberry	Wash.
B 6	Hudson Bay Divide	Mont.
O 13	Hueco	N. M.
F 2	Hueco	Tex.
E 8	Humboldt Range	Nev.
B 4	Humbug	Ore.
F 13	Humphreys Peak	Ariz.
M 3	Hunsrück	Ger.
P 4	Ichibusa	Jap.
J 2	Ida	Mor.
G 5	Igidi Desert	Afr.
H 21	Iide	Jap.
H 22	Imataca	Ven.
C 16	Independence	Nev.
F 6	Indian (Thar) Desert	India
N 2	Indian Peak	Utah
F 19	Ingalls	N. H.
P 9	Ingram	Yuk.
H 2	Iron	Mont.
M 17	Iron	Ore.
P 3	Iron	Utah
C 23	Iwaki	Jap.
I 6	Ixtaccihuatl	Pueb.
M 21	Jack Fork	Okla.
E 12	Jagatai	Iran.
L 18	Jagerndorf	Ger.
N 12	Jamal Bariz	Iran.
B 13	Jay Peak	Vt.
B 21	Jebel Muarra	Pal.

MOUNTAINS AND DESERTS—Continued

Index	Name	Location
G 9	Jefferson	Ore.
E 10	Jemez	N. M.
D 10	Jenny Jump	N. J.
J 15	Jicarilla	N. M.
B 1	Jilan	Iran.
K 4	Jorat	Switz.
K 7	Jotun	Nor.
E 12	Juan Gonzalez (Toa)	P. R.
Q 11	Jubilee	Yuk.
B 14	Julian Alps	It.
J 7	Julian Alps Kapela	Yugo.
K 11	Jungfrau (13,671 ft.)	Switz.
F 9	Juniper	Ariz.
I 21	Juniper	Ore.
N 15	Juniper	Ore.
M 12	Jupar	Iran
K 21	Jura	Fr.
C 11	Jydskeaas	Den.
P 15	Kalahari Desert	Bech.
M 21	Kaldash	Eth.
L 7	Kamala	Iran
I 14	Kancamacus	N. H.
E 21	Kanehanjanga	India
F 4	Karaghan	Iran
A 9	Karakoram	India
J 8	Kara Kum Desert	Sov. Un., Asia
G 14	Katahdin	Me.
B 4	Kawaikini Peak	Haw.
K 16	Kawich Range	Nev.
P 16	Kazbek	Sov. Un.
D 16	Kebnekaisse	Swe.
N 10	Kefez	Iran
L 9	Kelateh	Iran
M 19	Kellog	Ariz.
C 8	Kelly	Alaska
F 13	Kendrick Peak	Ariz.
K 21	Kenya	Afr.
C 20	Kettle River Range	Wash.
D 24	Keum-Kang	Kor.
J 8	Kho	Iran
M 24	Kiamichi	Okla.
N 23	Kilauea	Haw.
L 20	Kilimanjaro (19,324 ft.)	Afr.
K 4	Killdeer	N. D.
K 10	Killington Peak	Vt.
I 15	Kimball	Alaska
I 3	King	Yuk.
L 21	Kingston Range	Calif.
Q 3	Kirishima	Jap.
Q 22	Kirthar Range	Bal.
C 11	Kittatinny	N. J.
H 13	Kjolen	Swe.
D 15	Klibreck, Ben	Scot.
O 13	Knockmealdown	Ire.
K 5	Kofa	Ariz.
K 5	Koma	Eth.
J 20	Komanago	Jap.
G 13	Ksour	Alg.
G 8	Kua-I-Gugird	Iran
N 5	Kuju	Jap.
L 22	Kukahuala	Haw.
N 22	Kulani	Haw.
D 9	Kultus	Wash.
E 5	Kumiva Peak	Nev.
E 2	Kunlun	Chn.
E 2	Kurtak	Iran
K 20	Kwaja Amran	Afg.
D 3	La Cadena	P. R.
G 5	La Giganta	Mex.
E 6	Lakeside	Utah
R 11	Laki Peak	Ore.
E 17	La Motte Peak	Utah
I 16	Langdon	N. H.
M 7	Lange Berg	U. S. Afr.
R 5	Lanin	Arg.
L 20	Laramie	Wyo.
K 12	La Sal	Peru
F 16	Las Cruces	P. R.
D 8	Lassen (Vol., 10,453 ft.)	Calif.
O 20	Las Vegas	Nev.
P 10	Laurier	Yuk.
L 11	Lebanon	Leb.
E 21	Leidy Peak	Utah
K 15	Lemhi Range	Ida.
M 18	Lemmon	Ariz.
E 23	Lena	Utah
M 15	Lepontine Alps	Switz.
O 16	Les Cevennes	Fr.
N 7	Leucite Hills	Wyo.
F 16	Libyan Desert	Afr.
E 5	Licancaur	Chl.
J 4	Limbara	It.
L 2	Linas	It.
I 13	Lincoln	N. H.
G 8	Lincoln	Vt.
O 24	Linnaeus	Utah
N 7	Lipez	Bol.
H 11	Little Belt	Mont.
G 11	Little Carpat's	Czech.
K 6	Little Horn	Ariz.
L 16	Little Lost River	Ida.
E 15	Little Rocky	Mont.
P 10	Little Zwartsberg	U. S. Afr.
P 3	Lizard Head	Eng.
M 15	Ljuboten (8,235 ft.)	Yugo.
Q 5	Llaima	Arg.
F 6	Llullaillaco	Arg.
D 8	Logan	Ariz.
J 8	Logan	Ida.
O 19	Logan (19,850 ft.)	Yuk.
F 12	Lone Peak	Utah
C 20	Lookout	Ala.
E 11	Lookout	Ore.
M 16	Lost River	Ida.
P 4	Lowe	Calif.
M 10	Ludlow	Vt.
K 13	Lui, Ben	Scot.
C 23	Lukachukai	Ariz.
E 18	Luquillos	P. R.
H 13	Lyell	Calif.
P 11	McClintock Peak	Yuk.
M 15	McDonalds Peak	Wyo.
I 7	McDowell	Utah
J 12	McKinley (20,300 ft.)	Alaska
I 18	Macdhui Cairntoul, Ben	Scot.
G 23	MacIntire	N. Y.
K 3	Mackenzie	Mack.
M 9	MacMillan	Yuk.
G 16	Madison	N. H.
E 17	Madison Butte	Ore.
N 10	Madison Range	Mont.
K 8	Magdalena	N. M.
L 11	Maglič	Yugo.
F 21	Magpie Peak	Ore.
K 12	Mahagasha	Eth.
M 23	Mahogany	Ore.
N 6	Maipo	Arg.
M 16	Malik Siah	Afg.
L 17	Malik Teznan	Afg.

MOUNTAINS AND DESERTS—Continued

Index	Name	Location
H 2	Manisht	Iran
D 10	Mansfield	Vt.
L 11	Maracaju	Par.
L 11	Maricopa	Ariz.
N 24	Maritime Alps	Fr.
N 10	Markham	Vt.
I 16	Marra	A. E. Sud.
E 22	Marsh Peak	Utah
L 12	Marvine	Utah
H 4	Marys Peak	Ore.
N 17	Matindang	P. I.
P 10	Matterhorn (14,780 ft.)	Switz.
G 20	Matumbala	N. Y.
L 22	Mauna Kea (Vol., 13,784 ft.)	Haw.
N 21	Mauna Loa (Vol., 13,680 ft.)	Haw.
J 8	Maxie	Me.
I 15	Mazatzal	Ariz.
H 19	Meader	N. H.
M 3	Meadow	Md.
M 22	Meadow Valley	Nev.
B 12	Medicine	Wyo.
B 11	Medicine Bow Range	Colo.-Wyo.
-----	Melbourne	S. Pol. Reg.
M 11	Mendip	Eng.
L 18	Mescal	Ariz.
G 15	Meshomasic	Conn.
Q 11	Michie	Yuk.
I 9	Middle Sister	Ore.
M 6	Mineral	Utah
D 11	Miseno	Iran
F 9	Misery	R. I.
F 11	Misoco	Cen. Am.
F 5	Mission Range	Mont.
P 18	Misti (Vol., 19,166 ft.)	Peru
K 20	Mitchell	U. S.
H 3	Mohave	Ariz.
M 7	Mohawk	Ariz.
E 5	Mohawk	Conn.
M 17	Mojave Desert	Calif.
N 21	Mokuaweoweo	Haw.
J 11	Momotombo	Cen. Am.
I 15	Monagh Lea	Scot.
I 15	Monitor Range	Nev.
M 10	Monroe Peak	Utah
L 23	Mont Blanc (15,781 ft.)	Fr.
M 23	Mont Cenis	Fr.
K 10	Monte Cristo	Nev.
P 11	Monte Rosa	Switz.
J 10	Montes de Toledo	Sp.
N 25	Monument Peak	Calif.
I 7	Moosalamoo	Vt.
E 3	Moose Creek	Ida.
M 7	Moosehorn	Vt.
P 10	Morati	Par.
E 13	More Assynt, Ben	Scot.
G 18	Moriah	N. H.
D 23	Moriyoshi	Jap.
G 15	Mormon	Ariz.
M 23	Mormon Range	Nev.
O 12	Moro	Switz.
I 7	Mosquito	Me.
M 4	Muggins	Ariz.
P 22	Mule	Ariz.
N 7	Mullaghareirk	Ire.
D 21	Murchison Range	U. S. Afr.
G 24	Muskrat	Okla.
O 10	Nagles	Ire.
H 5	Nahoni Range	Yuk.
D 13	Nanda Devi	India
A 8	Nanga Parbat	India
D 3	Nan Shan Range	Chn.
Q 17	Navajo	Utah
O 6	Needle	Colo.
L 19	Needle Peak	Calif.
K 5	Nefud Desert	Asia
J 19	Negoi (8,320 ft.)	Rom.
L 2	Negro	Md.
G 5	Nephin Beg	Ire.
M 23	New England Range	Austl.
G 11	New Pass Range	Nev.
O 10	Nieuwveld Range	U. S. Afr.
M 16	Nikalo	Afr.
B 8	North Promontory	Utah
I 11	North Sister	Ore.
E 12	North Star	Wash.
R 9	North Tirolese Alps	Ger.
E 23	Norway	N. Y.
F 14	Nowy Sacz	Pol.
G 18	Nubian Desert	Afr.
D 11	Observation Peak	Calif.
F 9	Olallie Butte	Ore.
G 3	Olympic	Wash.
N 16	Olympus	Grc.
G 3	Olympus	Wash.
B 4	Onion Peak	Ore.
M 21	Orange Cliffs	Utah
J 22	Ord	Ariz.
F 6	Ore	Czech.
J 18	Orenge	Jap.
N 11	Organ	N. M.
D 16	Orion	Sp.
N 17	Orizaba (Vol.)	Mex.
P 16	Oro Blanco	Ariz.
K 15	Orohai	Ariz.
C 8	Ortler	It.
D 16	Orulgan	Sov. Un., Asia
K 11	Oscuro	N. M.
K 16	Ou	Jap.
J 7	Ouachita	Ark.
E 14	Oval	Wash.
G 9	Owl Creek	Wyo.
K 15	Ozarks	U. S.
M 20	Pacaraima	Ven.
K 21	Pahroc Range	Nev.
L 13	Pahsimeroi	Ida.
M 15	Pahute Mesa	Nev.
E 16	Painted Desert	Ariz.
L 6	Palomas	Ariz.
J 10	Pamirs	Asia
K 18	Panamint Range	Calif.
I 19	Pancake Range	Nev.
J 6	Parecis Chapadão	Braz.
C 2	Parima	Braz.
O 17	Parima	Ven.
C 9	Park Range	Colo.
J 18	Parnassus	Conn.
O 7	Parowan Range	Utah
J 15	Passaconaway	N. H.
L 21	Patkai	India
J 16	Paugus	N. H.
L 9	Pavan	Utah
F 6	Peacock	Ariz.
F 6	Peacock Peak	Ariz.
M 25	Peale	Utah
H 14	Pedernal, Hills of	N. M.
O 24	Pedregosa	Ariz.

MOUNTAINS AND DESERTS—Continued

Index	Name	Location
M 24	Pelee (Vol.)	W. I.
O 14	Pelly Range	Yuk.
M 25	Peloncillo	Ariz.
I 11	Pemigewasset	N. H.
L 10	Pencoso	Arg.
O 17	Pennell	Utah
O 10	Pennine Alps	Switz.
F 12	Pennine Chain	Eng.
G 3	Penones	P. R.
P 22	Pequop	Nev.
E 3	Perija	Ven.
E 16	Peters Butte	Ore.
H 7	Peterson Butte	Ore.
E 18	Pic de Nethou	Sp.
K 10	Pico Peak	Vt.
E 10	Pija	Cen. Am.
J 14	Pike's Peak (14,109 ft.)	Colo.
P 15	Pillar Butte	Ida.
J 9	Pilot	Nev.
J 12	Pilot Butte	Ore.
H 7	Pilot Knob	Ida.
J 10	Pilot Peak	Nev.
D 2	Pilot Range	Utah
M 22	Pinalino	Ariz.
O 15	Pindus	Grc.
H 22	Pine	N. Y.
O 25	Pine	Okla.
B 6	Pine	Va.
A 7	Pine Forest Range	Nev.
Q 3	Pine Valley	Utah
F 19	Piney Buttes	Mont.
D 6	Pinnacle	Wyo.
L 4	Pinos Altos Range	N. M.
K 19	Pinto Peak	Calif.
N 19	Pintwater Range	Nev.
A 8	Pisgah	Conn.
P 7	Pisgah	N. C.
J 12	Pisgue	Conn.
L 16	Placidus Butte	Ore.
J 4	Plomosa	Ariz.
A 15	Pochuck	N. J.
N 16	Popocatepetl (Vol., 15,927 ft.)	Mex.
J 3	Popocatepetl	Ore.
E 15	Porcupine Ridge	Utah
F 9	Pot	Ida.
L 25	Poteau	Okla.
K 8	Potosi	Bol.
M 4	Potts	Va.
M 10	Pozo Redondo	Ariz.
I 12	Profile	N. H.
F 4	Prospect	Conn.
M 22	Providence	Calif.
G 13	Provo Peak	Utah
J 5	Puertacitas	Tex.
G 22	Pugman	Afg.
R 12	Pulpit	Vt.
I 2	Pushti	Iran
P 20	Putnam	Ida.
M 20	Puu Hualalai	Haw.
O 21	Puu o Keokeo	Haw.
K 20	Pyramid Peak	Calif.
J 15	Pyramid Peak	Ida.
L 14	Pyramid Peak	Wyo.
N 7	Purenees	Eur.
E 7	Quaker Peak	Ida.
M 7	Quartz	Ore.
E 23	Quartz	Utah
-----	Queen Maud's Range	Ant.
N 12	Quijotoa	Ariz.
O 14	Quinlan	Ariz.
K 18	Quinn Canon	Nev.
H 2	Quitman	Tex.
B 19	Raccoon	Ala.
B 4	Raft River	Utah
K 10	Rainier	Wash.
L 6	Rainy Mtn. Range	Okla.
D 8	Ras Dashan	Eth.
H 21	Rattlesnake	Okla.
K 14	Rattlesnake	Wyo.
I 14	Rattlesnake Hill	N. M.
I 7	Rawhide	Ariz.
K 15	Red Butte	S. D.
M 2	Red Buttes	Utah
C 20	Redwood	Calif.
L 16	Reveille Range	Nev.
K 20	Rhaetian Alps	Switz.
G 22	Rhatiron Chain	Switz.
M 19	Rhodope	Bul.
P 9	Rice Hill	Vt.
C 7	Richardson	Yuk.
K 16	Riesen Gebirge	Ger.
A 4	Riga	Conn.
O 8	Riley	N. M.
J 2	Risoux	Switz.
D 2	Ritter	Chn.
J 22	Roan (Brown) Cliffs	Utah
F 15	Roberts	Nev.
G 21	Rock Creek Butte	Ore.
-----	Rockefeller	Ant.
J 3	Rocky	Can.
F 6	Rocky	Mont.
H 7	Rocky	U. S.
E 13	Rogans Seat	Eng.
N 8	Roggeveld	U. S. Afr.
O 2	Rouge River	Ore.
O 8	Rokkeveld Range	U. S. Afr.
F 2	Roman	Iran
J 4	Roman Nose	Ore.
K 23	Rose Peak	Ariz.
M 19	Rosebud	Mont.
L 6	Rosillos	Tex.
N 15	Roskruge	Ariz.
J 5	Rothhaar Gebirge	Ger.
L 20	Rotten Peak	Calif.
G 18	Royce	N. H.
E 18	Ruby	Nev.
K 17	Ruwenzori Range	Afr.
-----	Sabine	S. Pol. Reg.
H 18	Sable	N. H.
L 14	Sacaton	Ariz.
N 15	Sacramento	N. M.
B 5	Saddle	Ore.
M 21	Saddle	Ore.
K 15	Saddle	Wash.
B 5	Saddle	Wyo.
F 23	Saddleback	N. Y.
G 18	Safd	Afg.
N 15	Safid	Iran
C 11	Sagir	Iran
M 14	Sagra	Sp.
G 11	Sahara Desert	Afr.
M 16	Sain Dak	Bal.
L 17	St. Elias	Alaska
N 9	St. Helens	Wash.
J 4	Sajama (Vol., 21,390 ft.)	Bol.
L 11	Salinas Peak	N. M.
L 11	Salmon River	Ida.
P 2	Salomons Peak	Utah

MOUNTAINS AND DESERTS—Continued

Index	*Name*	*Location*
E 7	Salt Desert	Tur.
L 12	Salt River	Ariz.
J 2	Salt River Range	Wyo.
Q 8	Saluda	N. C.
L 9	Sambe	Jap.
M 11	San Andres Range	N. M.
J 12	San Antonio	Nev.
O 20	San Bernardino	Calif.
O 22	San Blas	Cen. Am.
G 11	Sandia	N. M.
R 7	San Diego Peak	Calif.
M 11	Sand Tank	Ariz.
K 8	Sandy Desert	Iran
M 11	San Felipe	Arg.
J 1	San Francisco Range	N. M.
P 6	San Gabriel	Calif.
C 6	Sangay	Ec.
M 13	Sangre de Cristo	Colo.
P 21	San Jacinto	Calif.
I 14	San Joaquin	Calif.
N 6	San Jose	Arg.
O 8	San Juan	Colo.
R 7	San Juan Hill	Calif.
G 6	San Mateo	N. M.
M 4	San Miguel	Colo.
J 12	San Pitch	Utah
K 23	Sans-Bois	Okla.
R 8	Santa Ana	Calif.
N 18	Santa Catalina	Ariz.
E 5	Santa Cruz	Cen. Am.
G 9	Santa Maria	Ariz.
B 13	Santa Marta	Col.
Q 2	Santa Monica	Calif.
O 18	Santa Rita	Ariz.
N 14	Santa Rosa	Ariz.
B 11	Santa Rosa	Nev.
L 20	Santa Teresa	Arg.
L 20	Santa Teresa	Ariz.
L 7	Santiago	Tex.
F 18	Santis	Switz.
L 3	Sapajo	Bol.
O 6	Sapaleri	Bol.
N 18	Sarawani	Bal.
E 15	Sarjektjakko	Swe.
H 6	Sarmiento (Vol.)	Arg.
M 10	Sauceda	Ariz.
C 4	Savalan	Per.
I 10	Sawatch	Colo.
M 3	Sawtooth Peak	Utah
B 13	Sayles Hill	R. I.
E 10	Scafell	Eng.
C 6	Scappoose	Ore.
F 16	Scarper Peak	Calif.
R 16	Schneeberg	Ger.
L 6	Scott	Ore.
Q 4	Seattle	Yuk.
C 5	Sedgwick	Yuk.
M 15	Seminoe	Wyo.
L 18	Sentinel Peak	Calif.
F 23	Sentinel Range	N. Y.
J 4	Seven Devils	Ida.
L 3	Severa	It.
G 21	Seward	N. Y.
O 11	Shamil	Iran
C 6	Shasta	Calif.
M 4	Sheep	Ariz.
Q 18	Sheep	Wyo.
J 9	Sheepeater	Ida.
N 20	Sheep Range	Nev.
D 2	Sheikh Iva	Iran
G 22	Shell Creek	Nev.
H 10	Shenandoah	Va.
D 3	Sheridan	Wyo.
J 20	Shirane	Jap.
M 16	Shirley	Wyo.
I 11	Shoshone	Nev.
N 16	Shoshone	Nev.
L 9	Shrewsbury Peak	Vt.
H 9	Siabod	Wales
C 10	Shuksan	Wash.
F 13	Siah Kuh	Iran
H 7	Sierra de Estrella	Port.
H 9	Sierra de Gava	Sp.
H 16	Sierra de Gudar	Sp.
F 5	Sierra de las Mina	Cen. Am.
N 22	Sierra del Cristal	Cuba
F 14	Sierra del Moncayo	Sp.
I 4	Sierra de los Organos	Cuba
N 24	Sierra de Purial	Cuba
M 14	Sierra de Tilaran	Cen. Am.
O 10	Sierra de Tolox	Sp.
G 12	Sierra Guadarrama	Sp.
N 16	Sierra Madre	Calif.
Q 21	Sierra Madre	Mex.
Q 14	Sierra Madre	Wyo.
O 14	Sierra Madre del Sur	Mex.
E 7	Sierra Madre Occidental	Mex.
O 18	Sierra Maestra	Cuba
L 10	Sierra Morena	Sp.
E 22	Sierra Negra	N. M.
D 14	Sierra Nevada	N. Am.
O 13	Sierra Nevada	Sp.
O 16	Sierrita	Ariz.
P 9	Sifton	Yuk.
G 20	Sikhota Alin	Sov. Un., Asia
M 9	Silver	Ida.
L 12	Silvermine	Ire.
L 10	Silver Peak	Nev.
I 23	Silvretta	Switz.
N 12	Simcoe	Wash.
J 22	Simmonsville Hill	R. I.
Q 18	Simpson Range	Yuk.
H 12	Sischu	Alaska
B 2	Siskiyou	Calif.
O 6	Skeleton	Ore.
D 11	Skiddaw	Eng.
N 16	Skull	Nev.
Q 9	Slap Spring Peak	Utah
O 4	Slieve Mish	Ire.
O 4	Slim Butte	S. D.
D 12	Smoke Creek Desert	Calif.
D 4	Smoke Creek Desert	Nev.
I 12	Smoky	Nev.
J 7	Snaehatten	Nor.
H 23	Snake Range	Nev.
H 2	Snake River Range	Wyo.
H 9	Snowdon	Wales
H 14	Snowy	Mont.
G 11	Snowy Peak	Ida.
B 17	Soapstone	Conn.
O 15	Solimana	Peru
H 12	Sonora Peak	Calif.
G 3	Sorata	Bol.
M 8	Southern Alps	N. Z.
J 9	South Sister	Ore.
G 14	Spanish Fork Peak	Utah
C 14	Sparta	N. J.
N 10	Sphinx	Mont.
F 24	Split	Utah

MOUNTAINS AND DESERTS—Continued

Index	*Name*	*Location*
N 18	Spotted Range	Nev.
P 19	Spring	Nev.
P 6	Spruce Peak	Vt.
N 5	Stacks	Ire.
J 12	Stadjan	Swe.
E 18	Stanovoi	Asia
P 19	Steens	Ore.
O 1	Steins Peak Range	N. M.
G 8	Stillwater	Nev.
C 2	Stone	N. C.
O 9	Stratton	Vt.
I 18	Strawberry	Ore.
L 7	Stripe Peak	P. I.
I 12	Stuart	Wash.
K 16	Sudets	Ger.
F 8	Sugar Loaf	Md.
F 10	Sulaco	Cen. Am.
K 24	Sulaiman Range	Bal.
F 16	Sulphur Spring	Nev.
G 3	Sungur	Iran
K 16	Superstition	Ariz.
E 2	Survey Peak	Wyo.
P 6	Swabian Jura	Ger.
O 4	Swett Peak	Utah
O 23	Swisshelm	Ariz.
P 19	Syniop	P. I.
J 5	Syrian Desert	Asia
L 7	Tabernacle Butte	Wyo.
P 7	Table	Wyo.
N 9	Tabor	Vt.
J 17	Tachin Shan	Chn.
E 2	Taconic	Mass.
O 22	Tahohait	Alg.
K 12	Takla Makan Desert	Asia
O 16	Talamanca	Cen. Am.
G 18	Talladega	Ala.
D 5	Tanian	Iran
L 6	Tank	Ariz.
N 19	Tanque Verde	Ariz.
K 17	Tateyama	Jap.
S 11	Tauern, Hohe	Ger.
S 13	Tauern, Niedere	Ger.
L 5	Taunus	Ger.
G 7	Taurus	Tur.
J 13	Tecumseh	N. H.
P 19	Tehuantereo	Mex.
K 18	Telescope Peak	Calif.
P 19	Tent Peak	Yuk.
F 15	Terrace	N. H.
C 5	Terrace	Utah
L 12	Terral	Utah
E 6	Terri	Switz.
N 11	Terrible	Vt.
-----	Terror	Ant.
G 2	Teton Pass	Wyo.
F 2	Teton Range	Wyo.
G 4	Teutoburger Wald	Ger.
F 6	Thar (Indian) Desert	India
D 2	The Alps	It.
H 10	The Crags	Ida.
I 5	Thomas Range	Utah
F 14	Thompson Peak	N. M.
H 17	Thorn	N. H.
I 11	Three Creek Butte	Ore.
K 9	Thunder	Ida.
E 8	Thunder Butte	S. D.
I 12	Tian Shan	Asia
G 13	Tibesti	Afr.
J 4	Tierra Vieja	Tex.
C 16	Tiffany	Wash.
K 5	Tigonankiveine	Mack.
C 17	Timan	Sov. Un.
B 8	Timber	Calif.
M 15	Timber	Nev.
L 18	Timpahute Range	Nev.
H 17	Tin	N. H.
N 4	Tinajas Atlas	Ariz.
N 6	Tinguiririca	Arg.
F 4	Tipton	Ariz.
F 18	Tirband-Turkestan	Afg.
E 12	Toa (Juan Gonzalez)	P. R.
D 23	Toand Range	Nev.
M 9	Tobacco Root	Mont.
H 9	Toby	Conn.
N 5	Todos Santos	Bol.
P 15	Tolad	Iran
F 6	Tom	Conn.
G 7	Tom Range	Mass.
C 18	Tomuzkhaya R., Sov. Un.	Asia
H 14	Toquema Range	Nev.
J 5	Toro	Arg.
L 17	Tortilla	Ariz.
M 17	Tortillita Range	Ariz.
K 5	Tortolas	Arg.
F 14	Touila	Alg.
I 12	Toyabe	Nev.
J 18	Transylvanian Alps	Rom.
I 12	Trapper Peak	Ida.
E 15	Truchas Peaks	N. M.
L 2	Trigo	Ariz.
C 8	Trumbull	Ariz.
F 8	Tsinchow	Chn.
F 10	Tsin Ling Shan	Chn.
K 22	Tuckers Knob	Okla.
N 16	Tucson	Ariz.
G 22	Tucumcari Peak	N. M.
K 3	Tularosa Range	N. M.
N 6	Tule Desert	Ariz.
P 16	Tumacacori	Ariz.
D 9	Tumuc-Humac	Braz.
M 6	Tupungato	Arg.
D 17	Turimquiri	Ven.
E 18	Turkey	N. M.
D 13	Turtle	N. D.
N 15	Turtle	S. D.
N 8	Tushar	Utah
P 19	Tutupaca (Vol.)	Peru
L 12	Twin Peak	Ida.
N 14	Twin Peaks	Utah
D 12	Tygh Hills	Ore.
L 8	Ubina	Bol.
E 17	Uintah	Utah
Q 2	Unaka	N. C.
P 19	Unaka	Tenn.
N 3	Unzen Peak	Jap.
D 21	Ural	Eur.
E 4	Urayoan (Yacueca)	P. R.
K 3	Urticu	It.
F 23	Ute Creek	N. M.
H 8	Valdai Hills	Sov. Un.
M 22	Vanderwhacker	N. Y.
I 4	Van Horn	Tex.
K 8	Velebit	Yugo.
D 17	Verkhoyansk	Sov. Un., Asia
B 14	Vermillion Cliffs	Ariz.
Q 10	Vermillion Cliffs	Utah
J 15	Vesuvius (Vol., 4,300 ft.)	It.
L 5	Victoria Peak	P. I.
J 10	Vinegar Hill	Ida.

MOUNTAINS AND DESERTS—Continued

Index	*Name*	*Location*
C 5	Virgin	Ariz.
F 3	Virginia	Nev.
K 6	Vogel Klip	U. S. Afr.
K 6	Vogels Gebirge	Ger.
I 22	Vosges	Fr.
J 9	Vulture	Ariz.
L 25	Waas	Utah
K 3	Wagner	Wyo.
L 3	Wah Wah	Utah
E 8	Walker	Va.
I 6	Walker River	Nev.
E 23	Wallowa	Ore.
C 10	Warren Peak	Calif.
F 14	Wasatch	Utah
B 3	Washburn	Wyo.
H 16	Washington	N. H.
I 22	Watch Tower Peak	Ida.
F 15	Waumbeck	N. H.
A 15	Wawayanda	N. J.
I 10	Weaver	Ariz.
H 8	Weaver Hills	R. I.
H 12	Wenatchee	Wash.
P 10	Western Ghats	Asia
O 15	West Spanish Peak (13,623 ft.)	Colo.
N 14	Wet	Colo.
J 13	Wetterhorn (12,166 ft.)	Switz.
E 24	Wheeler	Utah
H 23	Wheeler Peak	Nev.
O 20	Whetstone	Ariz.
G 19	White	Afg.
J 23	White	Ariz.
H 12	White	Calif.
G 16	White	N. H.
Q 12	White	Yuk.
P 5	White Butte	Utah
G 11	White Carpathians	Czech.
K 11	White Clay Butte	S. D.
C 3	Whitefish	Mont.
P 10	White Hill	Vt.
E 10	Whitehorse	Wash.
H 18	White Pine	Nev.
H 18	White Pine Peak	Nev.
N 6	White Rock	Ore.
O 20	Whitestone	Ariz.
K 11	White Tank	Ariz.
K 15	Whitney (14,495 ft.)	Calif.
L 7	Wichita	Okla.
J 11	Wickenburg	Ariz.
K 21	Wicklow	Ire.
E 3	Wildcat Peak	Wyo.
I 23	Wildhorse	Okla.
O 25	Williams	Okla.
C 7	Williams Fork	Colo.
P 5	Wilson	Calif.
B 24	Wilson	Ore.
L 2	Winding Ridge	Md.
M 23	Winding Stair	Okla.
H 6	Wind River Range	Wyo.
B 16	Windy Peak	Wash.
C 9	Winnemucca Peak	Nev.
O 23	Wisshelm	Ariz.
G 17	Witwaters Berg	U. S. Afr.
N 19	Wolf	Mont.
E 8	Wood	Wyo.
K 16	Wrangell	Alaska
G 17	Yablonovoi	Sov. Un., Asia
E 4	Yacueca (Urayoan)	P. R.
L 15	Yakima Ridge	Wash.
N 11	Yamsey	Ore.
L 18	Yatsugatake	Jap.
B 24	Yatsukota	Jap.
H 12	Yeluc	Cen. Am.
J 15	Young Peak	Utah
M 3	Yuma Desert	Ariz.
I 18	Yung Ling	Chn.
N 15	Yuoca	Nev.
D 18	Zab	Alg.
B 20	Zoutpansberg	U. S. Afr.
R 8	Zugspitze	Ger.
G 4	Zuni Buttes	N. M.

RIVERS, CREEKS, CANALS AND BAYOUS

F 10	Aar	Switz.
H 8	Abbal	Eth.
B 5	Abuna	Bol.
E 14	Acará	Braz.
N 11	Acaray	Par.
K 20	Acre (Aquiri)	W. Braz.
C 8	Adige	It.
O 7	Adour	Fr.
H 13	Affric	Scot.
H 12	Afrin	Tur.
C 18	Agattu	Alaska
E 10	Aguan	Hond.
O 24	Agusan	P. I.
F 15	Aisne	Fr.
M 8	Alabama	Ala.
L 5	Alamito Cr.	Tex.
K 6	Alamosa	N. M.
N 13	Alapaha	Ga.
E 12	Alatna	Alaska
M 15	Albany	Can.
E 18	Aldan	Sov. Un., Asia
D 6	Alene	Ida.
H 13	Alkali Cr.	Wyo.
C 12	Allagash	Me.
C 22	Alle	Ger.
J 5	Allegheny	Pa.
F 6	Aller	Ger.
F 23	Alligator	N. C.
O 5	Alloway Cr.	N. J.
M 18	Altamaha	Ga.
F 18	Altar	Alg.
D 12	Amazon	Braz.
N 19	Ambleve	Bel.
L 16	Amite	La.
I 10	Ammonoosuc	N. H.
P 9	Amper	Ger.
G 17	Amur	Asia
B 19	Anadyr	Sov. Un., Asia
B 6	Anderson	Mack.
N 6	Androscoggin	Me.
G 15	Angara	Sov. Un., Asia
B 23	Angerapp	Ger.
I 15	Angerman	Swe.
D 7	Angora	Tur.
P 5	Animas	Colo.
K 15	Anna	Va.
P 19	Annan	Scot.
O 12	Apalachicola	Fla.
N 18	Apaporis	Col.
N 17	Apishapa	Colo.
Q 6	Applegate	Ore.
M 14	Appomattox	Va.
D 21	Appoquinimink Cr.	Del.
G 12	Apure	Ven.

RIVERS, CREEKS, CANALS AND BAYOUS—Continued

Index	*Name*	*Location*
L 14	Apurimao	Peru
K 7	Aquidaban	Par.
K 20	Aquiri (Acre)	W. Braz.
D 12	Araguary	Braz.
H 13	Araguaya	Braz.
I 9	Arauca	Ven.
J 17	Arbuckle Cr.	Fla.
B 6	Arenal, Rio	C. Z.
J 19	Arges	Rom.
P 12	Ariege	Fr.
F 22	Arikaree	Colo.
H 17	Ariporo	Col.
L 14	Arkansas	U. S.
F 8	Arno	It.
H 17	Aro	Ven.
E 5	Arosa	Port.
N 15	Ashepoo	S. C.
D 17	Ashuapmouchouan	Que.
P 7	Ashuelot	N. H.
N 24	Asotin Cr.	Wash.
N 5	Aspetuck	Conn.
L 2	Assaka	Mor.
Q 14	Assiniboine	Man.
H 20	Atbara	Afr.
K 12	Atchafayala	La.
K 7	Athabaska	Can.
M 9	Atoyac	Oax.
G 6	Atrato	Col.
I 11	Attawapiskat	Ont.
O 9	Atuel	Arg.
H 17	Aube	Fr.
K 18	Au Sable	Mich.
F 23	Ausable	N. Y.
J 14	Avon	Eng.
L 13	Avon	N. S.
J 10	Bad	S. D.
H 12	Badwater	Wyo.
L 8	Baegna	Nor.
F 18	Baghmati	India
E 8	Bailey Br.	Me.
K 14	Bajo Urubamba	Peru
J 10	Bakers	N. H.
K 11	Bald Eagle Cr.	Pa.
K 4	Balsas	Guer.
O 13	Bampur	Iran.
G 21	Banana	Fla.
Q 8	Bandon	Ire.
P 10	Banister	Va.
C 19	Bann	N. Ire.
F 23	Baptism	Minn.
I 18	Baraboo	Wis.
I 11	Barron	Ky.
L 19	Barrow	Ire.
C 15	Barter	Alaska
N 15	Bartholomew Bayou	Ark.
I 16	Bartsch	Ger.
N 5	Bassett Cr.	Ala.
K 17	Bates Cr.	Wyo.
J 19	Batiscan	Que.
M 14	Batsto	N. J.
E 13	Bavispe	Son.
D 14	Bayamon	P. R.
L 12	Bean Blossom Cr.	Ind.
F 8	Bear	Calif.
B 6	Bear Cr.	Ala.
M 2	Bear Cr.	Kan.
B 23	Bear Cr.	Miss.
P 21	Bear Cr.	N. D.
M 8	Bear Cr.	S. D.
E 9	Bear Cr.	Va.
O 22	Bear Cr.	Wyo.
I 22	Beaver	Alta.
D 16	Beaver	Minn.
H 18	Beaver	N. Y.
H 6	Beaver	Sask.
C 17	Beaver Br.	Me.
F 14	Beaver Cr.	Alaska
F 19	Beaver Cr.	Colo.
G 4	Beaver Cr.	N. D.
N 9	Beaver Cr.	Okla.
I 15	Beaver Cr.	Ore.
J 10	Beaver Cr.	Wyo.
I 20	Beaverdam Cr.	Ga.
N 7	Beaverhead	Mont.
B 7	Belize	Br. Hond.
F 7	Bell	Yukon
E 20	Belle Fourche	Wyo.
C 7	Beni	Bol.
J 3	Bennet Cr.	N. D.
Q 9	Bennett Cr.	N. Y.
J 9	Benue	Nig.
M 17	Berens	Man.
F 13	Bermejo	Arg.
E 14	Bheri	Nep.
L 9	Bhima	India
I 9	Big	R. I.
Q 3	Big Cr.	Ind.
D 12	Big. Cr.	La.
B 7	Big Cr.	Mo.
A 21	Big. Cr.	Okla.
P 13	Big Beaver Cr.	N. D.
K 7	Big Black	Miss.
C 9	Big Black	Me.
E 18	Big Black Cr.	S. C.
I 5	Big Blackfoot	Mont.
E 18	Big Blue	Kan.
B 3	Big Blue Cr.	Tex.
B 22	Big Cabin Cr.	Okla.
E 16	Big Canoe Cr.	Ala.
J 15	Big Coulee Cr.	Mont.
I 14	Big Fishing Cr.	Pa.
M 5	Big Hole	Mont.
N 17	Big Horn	Mont.
M 14	Big Lost	Ida.
D 15	Big Machias Str.	Me.
C 23	Big Muddy Cr.	Mont.
L 11	Big Niangua	Mo.
L 13	Big Salkehatchie	S. C.
H 7	Big Sandy	Ariz.
L 1	Big Sandy	W. Va.
J 21	Big Sandy Cr.	Colo.
M 7	Big Sandy Cr.	Wyo.
D 24	Big Sheep Cr.	Ore.
J 23	Big Sioux	S. D.
C 16	Big Spring Cr.	Ala.
G 9	Big Sun Flower	Miss.
D 13	Big Wateree Cr.	S. C.
O 12	Big Wood	Ida.
E 17	Bijou Cr.	Colo.
Q 18	Biloxi	Miss.
F 15	Birch Cr.	Alaska
D 18	Bird Cr.	Okla.
J 8	Birdwood Cr.	Neb.
J 4	Bitter Root	Mont.
K 22	Black	Ariz.
C 17	Black	Ark.
C 14	Black	B. C.
G 12	Black	La.
H 18	Black	Mich.

RIVERS, CREEKS, CANALS AND BAYOUS—Continued

Index	*Name*	*Location*
P 19	Black	Mo.
I 17	Black	N. Y.
J 19	Black	S. C.
L 11	Black	Vt.
F 15	Black	Wis.
P 18	Black Cr.	Miss.
B 9	Black Cr.	Vt.
E 23	Black Cr.	W. Va.
D 12	Black Bear Cr.	Okla.
E 21	Blackbird Cr.	Del.
A 11	Blackbird Cr.	Mo.
L 10	Black Pine Cr.	S. D.
Q 5	Blacks Cr.	Mass.
K 17	Black Squirrel Cr.	Colo.
G 14	Blackstone	Mass.
B 15	Blackstone	R. I.
I 6	Blackstone	Yukon
H 8	Black Warrior	Ala.
H 18	Blackwater	Ire.
O 9	Blackwater	Ire.
N 18	Blackwater	Md.
H 8	Black Water	Mo.
N 13	Blackwater	N. H.
O 19	Blackwater	Va.
G 9	Blanchard	Ohio
K 13	Blover	Wis.
K 25	Blue	Ariz.
F 11	Blue	Colo.
J 18	Blue	Ind.
I 5	Blue	Neb.
O 17	Blue	Okla.
D 9	Blue Earth	Ia.
J 14	Bluefields	Nic.
I 19	Blue Nile	Afr.
Q 9	Bluestone	W. Va.
M 17	Blue Water Cr.	N. M.
N 8	Bluff Cr.	Kan.
A 13	Boeuf	La.
G 2	Bogachiel	Wash.
D 19	Bohemia	Md.
N 5	Boise	Ida.
N 7	Boise, North Fk.	Ida.
O 8	Boise, South Fk.	Ida.
O 18	Bone Hill Cr.	N. D.
J 22	Bonita Cr.	Ariz.
L 23	Bonita Cr.	Ariz.
K 15	Bonito	N. M.
F 10	Boone	Ia.
G 24	Boquet	N. Y.
F 17	Bosque	Tex.
J 8	Boulder	Mont.
M 12	Boulder	Mont.
D 12	Boundary Cr.	N. D.
E 20	Bow Cr.	Neb.
E 13	Bowstring	Minn.
E 16	Boxelder Cr.	Colo.
J 5	Box Elder Cr.	S. D.
K 4	Boyer	Ia.
I 18	Boyne	Ire.
I 17	Brahmani	India
M 14	Brahmaputra	Asia
D 4	Branco	Braz.
M 13	Brandford	Conn.
J 21	Brazos	Tex.
H 19	Brier Cr.	Ga.
E 13	Broad	Ga.
B 15	Broad	Md.
E 11	Broad	S. C.
Q 14	Broad	S. C.
K 6	Broye	Switz.
P 7	Bruneau	Ida.
A 17	Buck Cr.	Okla.
E 13	Buck Cr.	Ore.
H 13	Buckhannon	W. Va.
H 3	Buffalo	Minn.
N 8	Buffalo	Tenn.
D 13	Buffalo	Wis.
B 3	Buffalo Cr.	Okla.
E 21	Buffalo Cr.	Wyo.
C 11	Buffalo	Ark.
D 16	Bug	Cen. Eur.
C 3	Bull Cr.	S. D.
N 2	Bullier Cr.	N. D.
F 16	Bull Run	Va.
J 21	Bully Cr.	Ore.
D 11	Burnshirt	Mass.
H 22	Burnt	Ore.
G 13	Burntwood	Man.
H 8	Burro Cr.	Ariz.
F 7	Butte Cr.	Ore.
B 17	Butter Cr.	Ore.
J 22	Buzău	Rom.
D 16	Bynum Cr.	Md.
J 15	Cabriel	Sp.
E 21	Cacapon	W. Va.
O 9	Cache Cr.	Okla.
O 13	Caddo Cr.	Okla.
B 13	Cagayan	P. I.
I 11	Cahaba	Ala.
K 10	Cajones	Oax.
G 13	Calamus	Neb.
F 2	Calawah	Wash.
L 8	Calcasieu	La.
J 9	Calfpasture	Va.
L 15	Caloosahatchee	Fla.
O 10	Camas Cr.	Ida.
E 18	Camas Cr.	Ore.
K 14	Campine (Kempen) Canal	Bel.
J 19	Canada Cr.	N. Y.
F 20	Canadian	N. Mex.
K 10	Canadian	U. S.
E 12	Canche	Fr.
J 19	Candelaria	Camp.
B 18	Caney	Okla.
Q 9	Canisteo	N. Y.
Q 9	Cannonball	N. D.
L 23	Canoochee	Ga.
I 11	Capanaparo	Ven.
L 23	Cape Cod Canal	Mass.
K 13	Cape Fear	N. C.
D 5	Caquéta (Yapurá)	S. Am.
I 23	Cardenas	C. Z.
G 10	Cariahy	Braz.
H 19	Caroni	Ven.
I 19	Carrizo Cr.	Ariz.
L 10	Carrot	Sask.
H 4	Carson	Nev.
D 12	Cascade	Wash.
P 13	Casiquiare	Ven.
J 17	Casper Cr.	Wyo.
K 17	Catacoma Cr.	Ala.
Q 17	Catahoula Cr.	Miss.
F 4	Catatumbo	Ven.
I 5	Catawba	N. C.
M 7	Catawba Cr.	Va.
P 23	Catskill Cr.	N. Y.
Q 13	Cat-tail Cr.	N. D.
P 5	Cattaraugus Cr.	N. Y.
F 10	Cauca	Col.

RIVERS, CREEKS, CANALS AND BAYOUS—Continued

Index	*Name*	*Location*
I 16	Caura	Ven.
N 20	Cauto	Cuba
O 10	Cauvery	India
E 10	Cebolla	N. M.
M 23	Cebollati	Ur.
H 18	Cedar	Ia.
K 20	Cedar	Ia.
H 15	Cedar	Neb.
Q 6	Cedar	N. D.
I 10	Cedar	Wash.
I 22	Cedar Cr.	Del.
G 17	Cedar Cr.	Neb.
D 13	Cesar	Col.
E 3	Chaco	N. M.
N 12	Chacon Cr.	Tex.
P 19	Chacuaco Cr.	Colo.
E 3	Chadron Cr.	Neb.
D 6	Chagres	C. Z.
O 25	Chagrin	Ohio
D 4	Chajul	Guat.
G 9	Chambal	India
I 9	Chap aré	Bol.
L 8	Charente	Fr.
D 12	Chariton	Mo.
N 3	Charles	Mass.
G 16	Charlie	Alaska
G 14	Chatanika	Alaska
F 5	Chattahoochee	Ga.
B 2	Chattooga	S. C.
M 22	Chaudiere	Que.
E 16	Cheat	W. Va.
I 12	Chedotlothna	Alaska
K 5	Chehalis	Wash.
B 14	Cheliff	Alg.
C 7	Chenab	India
P 16	Chenango	N. Y.
C 8	Chepachet	R. I.
L 11	Cherry	W. Va.
J 18	Cherry Cr.	Ariz.
G 8	Cherry Cr.	S. D.
F 18	Chester	Md.
Q 3	Chetco	Ore.
H 18	Chevalon Cr.	Ariz.
C 15	Chewack Cr.	Wash.
I 8	Cheyenne	S. D.
C 20	Chicago Drainage Canal	Ill.
M 19	Chicamacamico Cr.	Md.
M 18	Chickahominy	Va.
M 21	Chickasawhay	Miss.
D 21	Chico	Arg.
H 8	Chicopee	Mass.
K 10	Chilatchie Cr.	Ala.
B 11	Chimmenticook Br.	Me.
I 10	Chimore	Bol.
L 21	Chindwin	India
C 22	Chinle Cr.	Ariz.
G 10	Chino Cr.	Ariz.
M 17	Chippewa	Mich.
L 6	Chippewa	Minn.
D 13	Chippewa	Wis.
E 11	Chirgua	Ven.
J 17	Chisana	Alaska
H 12	Chitanana	Alaska
J 14	Chivapuri	Ven.
N 21	Choctawhatchee	Ala.
M 8	Choctawhatchee	Fla.
H 10	Choluteca	Hond.
I 19	Choptank	Md.
N 20	Choteau Cr.	S. D.
D 21	Chowan	N. C.
J 10	Christian Cr.	Va.
B 22	Chubut	Arg.
O 22	Chugwater Cr.	Wyo.
E 16	Churchill	Man.
L 10	Chuzitna	Alaska
I 9	Cienaga de Zapata	Cuba
N 3	Cimarron	Kan.
C 5	Cimarron	Okla.
L 11	Cinti	Bol.
M 10	Cispus	Wash.
F 9	Clackamas	Ore.
B 8	Clam	Wis.
I 8	Clare	Ire.
H 6	Clarion	Pa.
M 17	Clark Cr.	Pa.
H 17	Clear Cr.	Ariz.
C 16	Clear Cr.	Wyo.
P 19	Clear Boggy Cr.	Okla.
F 8	Clearwater, North Pk.	Ida.
L 20	Clinch	Tenn.
E 5	Clinch	Va.
G 20	Cloquet	Minn.
L 23	Clover Cr.	Nev.
M 13	Clyde	Scot.
K 19	Coal Cr.	Okla.
M 19	Cocheco	N. H.
L 9	Cochetopa Cr.	Colo.
B 11	Cochrane	Sask.
B 11	Coco Solo	C. Z.
E 2	Codajaz	Braz.
P 7	Cohansey Cr.	N. J.
P 10	Cohocton	N. Y.
E 10	Cojedes	Ven.
B 11	Coldwater	Miss.
Q 10	Colorado	Arg.
H 7	Colorado	N. M.
I 16	Colorado	Tex.
K 4	Colorado	U. S.
C 4	Columbia	U. S.
C 12	Colville	Alaska
D 21	Colville	Wash.
J 7	Comanche Cr.	Tex.
O 15	Combahee	S. C.
E 2	Commission Cr.	Okla.
J 11	Conant Cr.	Wyo.
D 8	Concepción, Rio de la	Son.
F 19	Conchas	N. M.
H 20	Conchos	Chih.
G 18	Conchos	Tam.
D 18	Concord	Mass.
O 13	Conecuh	Ala.
M 7	Conemaugh	Pa.
E 7	Conewango Cr.	Pa.
H 13	Congaree	S. C.
G 12	Congaree Cr.	S. C.
K 15	Congo	Afr.
G 14	Connecticut (U. S.)	Conn.
J 20	Cooli	C. Z.
J 10	Coon	Ia.
L 18	Cooper	S. C.
I 15	Coosa	Ala.
N 12	Coosawhatchie	S. C.
L 16	Copper	Alaska
E 5	Copper Cr.	Va.
G 13	Coppermine	Mack.
M 2	Coquille	Ore.
P 17	Corinth Canal	Grc.
E 10	Corrientes	Peru
B 15	Costilla Cr.	N. M.

RIVERS, CREEKS, CANALS AND BAYOUS—Continued

Index	*Name*	*Location*
G 9	Cosumnes	Calif.
P 7	Cottonwood	Minn.
E 11	Cottonwood Cr.	Wyo.
J 3	Cottonwood Cr.	Wyo.
K 6	Coulonge	Que.
B 7	Courantyne	Gui.
G 16	Cowhouse Cr.	Tex.
N 7	Cowlitz	Wash.
K 16	Crab Cr.	Wash.
D 17	Crazy Woman Cr.	Wyo.
H 17	Croche	Que.
D 17	Crocodile	U. S. Afr.
I 13	Crooked	Ore.
H 7	Crooked Cr.	Ill.
M 6	Crooked Cr.	Kan.
F 7	Crooked Cr.	Mo.
F 15	Crooked Cr.	Mont.
B 17	Crow Cr.	Colo.
J 16	Crow Cr.	S. D.
I 10	Crow Wing	Minn.
E 18	Cuareim	Ur.
M 13	Cuarto	Arg.
I 14	Cuchivero	Ven.
H 15	Cuculaia	Nic.
G 19	Cuervo Cr.	N. M.
G 17	Cuivre	Mo.
N 17	Culiacán	Sin.
J 16	Cumberland	Ky.
L 9	Cumberland	Tenn.
H 8	Cumberland Canal	Md.
D 8	Cumina	Braz.
I 10	Cunaviche	Ven.
J 3	Cupsuptic	Me.
N 16	Current	Mo.
J 24	Curundu	C. Z.
D 9	Cut Bank Cr.	N. D.
I 24	Cuyuni	Ven.
A 7	Cypress Cr.	Ala.
H 18	Czeremosz	Pol.-Rom.
F 13	Dall	Alaska
B 7	Dan	N. C.
R 10	Dan	Va.
N 16	Danube	Eur.
P 9	Dargabind	Iran
N 18	Darling	Austl.
I 8	Date Cr.	Ariz.
C 3	Daule	Ec.
G 8	Dearborn	Mont.
H 11	Dee	Eng.
I 20	Dee	Scot.
F 11	Deep Cr.	N. D.
O 7	Deep Red	Okla.
C 20	Deer	N. Y.
C 16	Deer Cr.	Md.
I 7	Deer Cr.	Miss.
O 2	Deer Cr.	N. D.
C 6	Deerfield	Mass.
Q 8	Deerfield	Vt.
I 3	Deerhorn Cr.	Minn.
H 10	Delaware	(U. S.) N. J.
G 5	Delaware Cr.	Tex.
D 9	Delije-Irmak	Tur.
I 15	Delta	Alaska
R 22	Delta of the Mississippi	La.
D 14	Delta of the Nile	Eg.
E 21	De Reest	Neth.
F 16	Derwent	Eng.
K 10	Deschutes	Ore.
L 7	Deschutes	Wash.
C 22	Deseado	Arg.
J 11	Des Moines	Ia.
E 9	Desolation Brook	Me.
G 2	Des Quinze	Que.
Q 23	Detroit	Mich.
K 11	Devils	Tex.
N 14	Devott	Alb.
C 17	Diamond	N. H.
C 21	Diep	Neth.
D 18	Dinnebito Wash	Ariz.
M 25	Dirickson Cr.	Del.
H 9	Dismal, North Branch	Neb.
L 16	Dneister	Eur.
K 17	Dnepr	Eur.
E 6	Dog Cr.	Kan.
D 20	Dog Cr.	Okla.
P 10	Dogtooth Cr.	N. D.
O 3	Dolores	Colo.
L 25	Dolores	Utah
H 20	Don	Scot.
M 13	Don	Sov. Un.
C 2	Dora Baltca	It.
N 10	Dordogne	Fr.
K 20	Dori	Afg.
F 6	Doubs	Switz.
F 3	Douglas Cr.	Colo.
J 8	Douglas Cr.	N. D.
G 5	Douro	Sp.
L 5	Draa, Wad	Mor.
I 10	Drava	Yugo.
L 15	Driftwood	Ind.
J 12	Drina	Yugo.
K 3	Dry Piney Cr.	Wyo.
M 6	Dry Wood Cr.	Mo.
F 16	Duchesne	Utah
N 8	Duck	Tenn.
F 22	Duck Cr.	Nev.
J 13	Dulce	Arg.
M 5	Dumoine	Que.
D 9	Duncans Cr.	S. C.
F 7	Dungarvon	N. B.
B 13	Dunkard Cr.	W. Va.
F 4	Dunlap	Neb.
O 21	Durance	Fr.
E 14	Dvina	Sov. Un.
E 15	Eagle Cr.	Nebr.
C 7	Eagle Chief Cr.	Okla.
L 17	Earn	Scot.
N 15	East	Conn.
M 6	East Nishnabotna	Ia.
F 12	Eau Claire	Wis.
G 15	Ebro	Sp.
D 12	Eden	Eng.
K 13	Edisto	S. C.
D 3	Eel	Calif.
E 14	Eel	Ind.
J 10	Eel	Ind.
G 16	Eem	Neth.
K 18	Eight Mile	Conn.
I 11	Elbe	Ger.
G 13	Elbe-Oder Canal	Ger.
Q 17	Eleven Point	Mo.
A 11	Elk	Ala.
H 8	Elk	Wis.
J 7	Elk	W. Va.
J 4	Elk Cr.	Okla.
J 5	Elk Cr.	S. D.
H 19	Elkhorn	Neb.
F 4	Elkhorn Cr.	Wyo.
K 22	Elm	N. D.

RIVERS, CREEKS, CANALS AND BAYOUS—Continued

Index	*Name*	*Location*
F 4	Elwha	Wash.
L 21	Embarrass	Ill.
F 4	Ems	Ger.
L 11	Engaños	Col.
K 18	English	Ia.
H 18	Enitachopko Cr.	Ala.
R 14	Enns	Ger.
C 8	Enoree	S. C.
G 14	Entiat	Wash.
E 12	Ephraim Cr.	Okla.
L 5	Erie Canal	N. Y.
O 14	Escalante	Utah
M 2	Escambia	Fla.
F 7	Escanaba	Mich.
R 22	Escatawpa	Miss.
J 19	Esk	Scot.
F 9	Esla	Sp.
A 3	Esmeraldas	Ec.
C 7	Essequibo	Gui.
B 9	Etsch	It.
J 5	Euphrates	Asia
G 12	Eure	Fr.
D 6	Ewers Cr.	Okla.
C 15	Fabius	Mo.
F 12	Farmington	Conn.
N 6	Feale	Ire.
L 19	Felix	N. M.
E 13	Feno Ho	Chn.
E 19	Fenton	Conn.
M 8	Fergus	Ire.
F 7	Feuther	Calif.
F 11	Finlay	B. C.
D 13	Finn	N. Ire.
Q 6	Fish	Ala.
K 13	Fish Cr.	Mont.
J 16	Fish Cr.	N. Y.
D 2	Fisher	Mont.
Q 12	Fishhole Cr.	Ore.
D 16	Fishing Cr.	N. C.
C 13	Fishing Cr.	S. C.
C 10	Fishing Cr.	W. Va.
F 10	Flambeau	Wis.
M 9	Flat Cr.	Ala.
G 3	Flathead	Mont.
B 15	Flint	Ala.
I 7	Flint	Ga.
G 17	Floodwood	Minn.
F 2	Floyd	Ia.
M 3	Fontenelle Cr.	Wyo.
G 22	Forest	N. D.
C 10	Forest Cr.	S. C.
M 16	Forth	Scot.
C 12	Fort Nelson	B. C.
L 5	Four Mile Cr.	Ohio
C 16	Foyle	N. Ire.
L 4	Frazer	Can.
M 15	Fremont	Utah
B 9	French	Ont.
D 4	French Cr.	Pa.
N 21	French Broad	Tenn.
N 15	Frio	Tex.
J 7	Fulda	Ger.
J 15	Gakona	Alaska
M 10	Gallatin	Mont.
F 18	Gallinas	N. M.
E 16	Gandak	Nep.
G 21	Ganges	India
H 4	Garden Cr.	N. D.
O 10	Garonne	Fr.
L 14	Gasconade	Mo.
L 10	Gatineau	Que.
L 9	Gauley	W. Va.
E 3	Gediz	Tur.
P 7	Genesee	N. Y.
K 17	Georges Cr.	Wyo.
G 11	German	Va.
O 10	Gers	Fr.
P 2	Ghuzzeh, Wady	Pal.
I 13	Giguela	Sp.
C 12	Gihon	Vt.
L 10	Gila	Ariz.
N 12	Gilbert Swamp	Md.
M 8	Gironde	Fr.
G 9	Gisasa	Alaska
J 7	Glane	Switz.
K 9	Glommen	Nor.
K 12	Godavari	India
F 16	Gogra	India
I 21	Goose	N. D.
E 9	Gooseberry Cr.	Wyo.
O 10	Göta	Swe.
Q 11	Grand	Ia.
O 11	Grand	Mich.
C 7	Grand	Mo.
C 8	Grand	S. D.
F 17	Grand Canal	Chn.
D 10	Grand Canyon of the Colorado	Ariz.
H 13	Grande	Bol.
L 12	Grande	Braz.
E 5	Grande de Anasco	P. R.
C 8	Grande de Arecibo	P. R.
M 16	Grande	Chia.
I 15	Grande	Nic.
C 21	Grande Ronde	Ore.
G 21	Grant	Wis.
G 15	Grass	Man.
F 18	Grass	N. Y.
F 9	Grass Cr.	Wyo.
J 6	Gravel	Mack.
I 8	Great Bear	Mack.
N 13	Great Egg	N. J.
H 9	Green	Ky.
L 3	Green	N. D.
I 6	Green	U. S.
I 10	Green	Wash.
N 12	Greenbrier	W. Va.
D 9	Greybull	Wyo.
J 3	Greys	Wyo.
J 15	Grijalva	Chia.-Tab.
J 6	Grinsted	Den.
M 12	Groen	U. S. Afr.
G 4	Gros Ventre	Wyo.
B 2	Grouse Cr.	Utah
R 24	Grove Cr.	W. Va.
N 9	Guadalquivir	Sp.
K 7	Guadiana	Sp.-Port.
K 22	Guainia	Col.
E 15	Guamá	Braz.
G 10	Guanaparo	Ven.
F 12	Guanape	Hond.
F 9	Guanarito	Ven.
I 15	Guaniamo	Ven.
K 4	Guapi	Col.
G 10	Guaporé	S. Am.
F 13	Guárico	Ven.
H 8	Guaritico	Ven.
K 16	Guaviare	Col.
I 8	Guden	Den.

RIVERS, CREEKS, CANALS AND BAYOUS—Continued

Index	*Name*	*Location*
C 2	Guenen	Tur.
D 16	Guere	Ven.
F 14	Gumti	India
K 13	Gum Swamp	Ga.
K 6	Gunnison	Colo.
E 16	Gurupy	Braz.
M 3	Guyandot	W. Va.
D 16	Halladale	Scot.
D 21	Hallail	Alg.
L 13	Hammonasset	Conn.
G 13	Han Kiang	Chn.
I 16	Harud	Afg.
J 10	Hassayampa Cr.	Ariz.
D 7	Hat Cr.	Calif.
O 2	Hat Cr.	S. D.
O 2	Hatchie	Tenn.
H 16	Hatchet Cr.	Ala.
D 10	Havasu Cr.	Ariz.
G 11	Havel	Ger.
P 13	Hay	Mack.
G 19	Hayes	Man.
G 14	Hazel	Va.
N 8	Heart	N. D.
E 2	Heath	Bol.
L 17	Helmand	Afg.
D 11	Hennepin Canal	Ill.
L 12	Hess	Yuk.
O 4	Hesy, Wady el	Pal.
K 20	Hill Cr.	N. D.
P 16	Hiwassee	Tenn.
F 11	Hogatza	Alaska
G 2	Hoh	Wash.
E 8	Holston	Va.
N 11	Homathko	B. C.
D 17	Homing Cr.	Okla.
O 4	Homochitto	Miss.
L 19	Hondo	N. M.
K 14	Honey Cr.	Pa.
N 12	Horn	Mack.
L 6	Horse Cr.	Ala.
E 19	Horse Cr.	Wyo.
J 4	Horse Cr.	Wyo.
P 22	Horse Cr.	Wyo.
D 9	Horton	Mack.
E 19	Horyn	Pol.
L 7	Housatonic	Conn.
J 10	Howard Cr.	Tex.
H 9	Huallaga	Peru
G 4	Huancabamba	Peru
H 5	Hubbards	Mass.
K 5	Hubbardton	Vt.
P 24	Hudson	N. Y.
N 15	Huerfano	Colo.
F 8	Hughes	W. Va.
G 18	Humber	Eng.
C 18	Humboldt	Nev.
D 8	Humboldt	Nev.
J 3	Humptulips	Wash.
K 9	Hungshui Kiang	Chn.
L 14	Hunting Cr.	Md.
F 13	Huron	Ohio
E 12	Hwang-Ho	Chn.
E 6	Iatuman	Braz.
K 14	Ibar	Yugo.
N 11	Ica	Peru
D 6	Ica (Putumayo)	S. Am.
B 11	Ikpikpuk	Alaska
J 11	Ili	Sov. Un., Asia
J 8	Illinois	Ill.
F 23	Illinois	Okla.
Q 3	Illinois	Ore.
D 17	Illinois & Michigan Canal	Ill.
F 9	Illinois Bayou	Ark.
D 25	Imnaha	Ore.
L 24	Indian	Del.
H 21	Indian	Fla.
I 21	Indian	N. Y.
N 10	Indian Cr.	Ga.
Q 7	Indian Cr.	Mo.
K 15	Indian Field Cr.	S. C.
C 17	Indigirka	Sov. Un., Asia
L 14	Indio	Nic.
J 15	Indravito	India
J 11	Indre	Fr.
F 2	Indus	India
N 7	Ingulets	Sov. Un.
K 21	Inirida	Col.
I 9	Innoko	Alaska
D 22	Inyankara Cr.	Wyo.
E 12	Iowa	Ia.
C 20	Ipswich	Mass.
O 10	Iquassú	Braz.
F 20	Iroquois	Ill.
E 7	Iroquois	Ind.-Ill.
N 21	Irrawaddy	Bur.
G 11	Irtysh	Sov. Un., Asia
O 14	Irvine	Scot.
M 22	Isère	Fr.
H 10	Ishim	Sov. Un., Asia
L 6	Ishkar, Wady	Pal.
K 18	Isker	Bul.
F 7	Iskut	B. C.
K 19	Isla	Scot.
F 14	Israel	N. H.
F 18	Itapicuru	Braz.
D 11	Itonomas	Bol.
O 14	Jahret	Alg.
I 15	James	N. D.
J 20	James	S. D.
M 15	James	Va.
E 7	Jamundá	Braz.
K 20	Jantra	Bul.
G 14	Jaquirana (Javary)	W. Braz.
I 3	Jaru	Braz.
D 11	Jary	Braz.
E 4	Jauapery	Braz.
F 17	Jedi	Alg.
C 6	Jehlam	India
N 10	Jenil	Sp.
B 7	Jennings	B. C.
G 11	Jihun	Tur.
K 16	Jind Zu	Jap.
J 18	Jiu	Rom.
E 12	John	Alaska
G 16	John Day	Ore.
D 17	Johnson Cr.	Ore.
I 15	Jonk	India
R 15	Jordan	Miss.
K 12	Jordan	Pal.
K 11	Joselah, Wady	Pal.
K 22	Juba	Afr.
J 15	Jucar	Sp.
G 13	Judith	Mont.
G 13	Jumna	India
G 10	Jump	Wis.
N 12	Juniata	Pa.
F 9	Jurua	S. Am.
G 20	Jutahy	W. Braz.
M 18	Jutate	Chia.

RIVERS, CREEKS, CANALS AND BAYOUS—Continued

Index	*Name*	*Location*
C 16	Kaibito Cr.	Ariz.
Q 15	Kair	Iran
H 9	Kaiyuh	Alaska
P 12	Kalamazoo	Mich.
O 7	Kalamo	Wash.
E 13	Kali	India
G 10	Kal Mura	Iran
C 10	Kanab Cr.	Ariz.-Utah
I 4	Kanawha	Alaska
M 7	Kanektok	Alaska
E 21	Kankakee	Ill.
J 16	Kan Kiang	Chn.
G 18	Kansas (Kaw)	Kan.
F 12	Kanuti	Alaska
K 3	Karun	Iran
L 13	Kasai	Afr.
H 19	Kasai	India
J 17	Kash Rud	Afg.
J 6	Kashunuk	Alaska
M 14	Kaskaskia	Ill.
G 9	Kateel	Alaska
G 18	Kaw (Kansas)	Kan.
M 4	Keg Cr.	Ia.
C 12	Kelkia	Tur.
B 12	Kelley Cr.	Nev.
E 20	Keltma	Sov. Un.
K 14	Kempen (Campine) Canal	Bel.
Q 3	Kenmare	Ire.
N 8	Kennebec	Me.
J 9	Kennebecasts	N. B.
E 16	Kentucky	Ky.
P 13	Kerak, Wady	Transj.
F 12	Kerima	Alg.
I 2	Kerkhah	Iran
L 15	Kern	Calif.
H 17	Kerulen	Asia
J 18	Kettle	Minn.
H 12	Kettle Cr.	Pa.
N 14	Keya Paha	S. D.
D 15	Khatanga	Sov. Un., Asia
L 14	Khoper	Sov. Un.
N 20	Kiamichi	Okla.
G 19	Kickapoo	Wis.
N 19	Kieger Cr.	Ore.
C 7	Kiel Canal	Ger.
L 7	Kinchafoonee Cr.	Ga.
G 9	Kingfisher Cr.	Okla.
J 13	Kings	Calif.
B 1	Kiowa Cr.	Okla.
J 20	Kissimmee	Fla.
L 11	Kistna	India
C 8	Kizil-Irmak	Tur.
D 4	Kizil Uzun	Iran
B 2	Klamath	Calif.
R 9	Klamath	Ore.
L 11	Klar	Swe.
O 11	Klickitat	Wash.
N 10	Klinaklini	B. C.
O 3	Kluane	Yuk.
L 14	Knapp Cr.	W. Va.
L 6	Knife	N. D.
K 14	Knik	Alaska
E 9	Kobuk	Alaska
K 21	Köge	Den.
H 10	Kokadjo	Me.
C 18	Kolyma	Sov. Un., Asia
F 22	Komati	Swaz.
C 2	Kootenay	Mont.
G 13	Kostroma	Sov. Un.
G 8	Koyuk	Alaska
G 10	Koyukuk	Alaska
N 13	Kubango	Afr.
L 5	Kugulik	Alaska
D 19	Kuinder (Tjonger) Canal	Neth.
C 8	Kukpowruk	Alaska
C 7	Kukpuk	Alaska
J 8	Kulpa	Yugo.
O 17	Kuma	Sov. Un.
N 13	Kunene	Afr.
I 10	Kungan Kiang	Chn.
Q 19	Kura	Sov. Un.
K 4	Kurdistan	Iran
H 11	Kuruman	U. S. Afr.
J 16	Kush Ruduk	Afg.
K 7	Kuskokwim	Alaska
M 13	Kwango	Afr.
K 12	Kwei Kiang	Chn.
L 7	Laagen	Nor.
L 4	La Barge Cr.	Wyo.
O 3	Lac Qui Parle	Minn.
K 12	La Creuse	Fr.
I 3	Ladder Cr.	Kan.
Q 18	Lafourche, Bayou	La.
E 22	Lagan	N. Ire.
K 5	Lahn	Ger.
A 5	Lamar	Wyo.
D 7	Lamoille	Vt.
K 12	Lansing	Yuk.
N 19	Laramie	Wyo.
L 7	Las Animas Cr.	N. M.
L 20	Laughery Cr.	Ind.
M 19	Lavaca	Tex.
J 2	Lawrence Cr.	Neb.
O 18	Leaf	Miss.
N 3	Lebos Cr.	Okla.
P 9	Lee	Ire.
E 3	Lee Cr.	Ark.
P 8	Lech	Ger.
F 22	Leipsic	Del.
H 14	Lek	Neth.
K 15	Lemhi	Ida.
I 5	Lemon Fair	Vt.
I 16	Lemonweir	Wis.
G 5	Lempa	Sal.
E 17	Lena	Asia
G 17	Leon	Tex.
M 8	Lewes	Yuk.
O 7	Lewis	Wash.
G 7	Lewis Cr.	Vt.
H 5	Liard	Can.
O 8	Liard	Mack.
D 10	Lick Cr.	Va.
D 18	Licking	Ky.
O 10	Lievre	Que.
J 19	Liffey	Ire
K 12	Lim	Yugo
K 2	Limari	Chl
B 13	Limestone Cr.	Ala
D 8	Limfjorden	Den.
P 17	Limpopo	Afr.
L 19	Lincoln Cr.	Neb.
E 18	Line Cr.	Miss.
D 9	Linganore Cr.	Md.
G 17	Lipa	Col.
H 5	Lippe	Ger.
O 7	Little	Ala.
F 16	Little	Ga.
O 12	Little	Ga.
B 5	Little	Ia.

RIVERS, CREEKS, CANALS AND BAYOUS—Continued

Index	*Name*	*Location*
O 22	Little	Okla.
E 9	Little	S. C.
F 3	Little Bitter Root	Mont.
O 19	Little Blue	Neb.
P 15	Little Buffalo	Mack.
G 22	Little Cabin Cr.	Okla.
C 16	Little Cedar	Ia.
E 15	Little Colorado	Ariz.
K 11	Little Deschutes	Ore.
G 8	Little Kanawha	W. Va.
O 9	Little Miami	Ohio
L 2	Little Missouri	N. D.
F 14	Little Red	Ark.
L 14	Little Salkehatchie	S. C.
D 24	Little Sheep Cr.	Ore.
I 3	Little Sioux	Ia.
C 20	Little Sitkin	Alaska
F 21	Little Tallapoosa	Ala.
M 19	Little Wabash	Ill.
H 5	Little Westfield	Mass.
O 13	Little Wood	Ida.
I 12	Ljungan	Swe.
J 14	Ljusne	Swe.
I 14	Llano	Tex.
E 7	Lockhart	Mack.
Q 22	Lodge Pole Cr.	Wyo.
F 20	Logan Cr.	Neb.
H 16	Lögde	Swe.
E 6	Lögstor Bredning	Den.
J 9	Loire	Fr.
L 16	Lomami	Bel. Cong.
G 18	Long Cr.	Ore.
G 6	Long Cane Cr.	S. C.
B 1	Longs Cr.	Tex.
N 4	Los Almos Cr.	Tex.
P 6	Los Pinos	Colo.
O 9	Lost	Ind.
N 13	Lot	Fr.
K 18	Loup	Neb.
P 10	Louse Cr.	N. D.
H 7	Lovat	Sov. Un.
G 16	Loyalsock Cr.	Pa.
N 9	Ludwigs Canal	Ger.
F 5	Luxapallila Cr.	Ala.
C 17	Lwan Ho	Chn.
G 18	Lynches	S. C.
M 6	Lys	Bel.
I 7	McKenzie	Ore.
L 14	Macaya	Col.
K 20	Machias	Me.
F 5	Mackenzie	Can.
F 15	Mackinaw	Ill.
M 10	Macmillan	Yuk.
B 14	Macon Bayou	La.
K 10	Macoupin Cr.	Ill.
J 13	Mad	N. H.
G 9	Mad	Vt.
B 18	Madawaska	Me.
E 18	Madawaska	Ont.
F 10	Madeira	S. Am.
E 4	Madidi	Bol.
N 9	Madison	Mont.
C 5	Madre de Dios	Bol.
K 6	Magaguadavic	N. B.
B 18	Magalakuin	U. S. Afr.
C 13	Magat	P. I.
B 10	Magdalena	Col.
C 9	Magnetawan	Ont.
K 3	Magpie Cr.	N. D.
M 9	Maigue	Ire.
M 8	Main	Ger.
K 5	Maitland	Ont.
K 22	Malheur	Ore.
E 9	Mamoré	Bol.
F 14	Manapira	Ven.
I 19	Manasquan	N. J.
J 14	Manatee	Fla.
G 12	Manchester Canal	Eng.
K 14	Manistee	Mich.
G 12	Manistique	Mich.
F 24	Manitou	Minn.
J 7	Manitowish	Wis.
L 9	Mantaro	Peru
P 10	Manumuskin Cr.	N. J.
N 22	Maple	N. D.
E 7	Mapurea	Braz.
H 22	Maquoketa	Ia.
K 13	Marais Cr.	Mo.
G 5	Marañon	Peru
C 13	Marble Canyon	Ariz.
B 7	Mareb	Erit.
D 8	Marias	Mont.
E 9	Maricuru	Braz.
M 20	Maritza	Bul.
L 6	Marmiton	Mo.
G 17	Marne	Fr.
B 10	Maroni	Gui.
F 2	Marsh	Minn.
K 19	Marshyhope Cr.	Md.
L 12	Martre, R. la	Mack.
B 19	Marys	Nev.
H 19	Masambi	C. Z.
L 9	Mascoma	N. H.
P 17	Mashkel	Iran
J 16	Matta	Va.
K 15	Mattagami	Ont.
L 21	Mattapoisett	Mass.
L 18	Mattaponi	Va.
H 17	Mattawamkeag	Me.
K 15	Mattawin	Que.
L 11	Mattawoman Cr.	Md.
E 6	Maumee	Ohio
O 9	Maurice	N. J.
I 8	Mayenne	Fr.
I 14	Mayo	Son.
B 5	Mazaruni	Br. Gu.
J 16	M'bomu	Afr.
B 10	Meade	Alaska
L 9	Meadow	W. Va.
J 12	Mechum	Va.
C 9	Medicine Cr.	Mo.
K 13	Medicine Cr.	S. D.
N 16	Medicine Bow	Wyo.
L 15	Medvyeditsa	Sov. Un.
K 14	Meguiden	Alg.
P 13	Meherrin	Va.
N 2	Mei Ping	Thai.
N 7	Mekong	Thai.
G 11	Melozitna	Alaska
A 24	Memel	Ger.
O 3	Menam	Thai.
F 2	Menderes	Tur.
H 6	Menominee	Mich.-Wis.
K 17	Meramec	Mo.
J 17	Merevari	Ven.
M 13	Merrimack	N. H.
G 12	Mersey	Eng.
H 19	Meta	Col.
D 14	Methow	Wash.

RIVERS, CREEKS, CANALS AND BAYOUS—Continued

Index	*Name*	*Location*
H 11	Metolius	Ore.
M 5	Mettawee	Vt.
K 9	Meuse	Eur.
O 12	Mexcala	Mex.
D 15	Mezen	Sov. Un.
K 14	Miakka	Fla.
L 7	Miami	Ohio
H 7	Miami Canal	Ohio
L 10	Middle	Ia.
D 3	Middle	Minn.
Q 10	Middle Fork	Ind.
F 7	Miguel Cr.	N. M.
N 15	Miguel Cr.	Tex.
D 16	Milk	Mont.
D 8	Mill	Mass.
E 7	Mill Cr.	Calif.
I 11	Mill Cr.	Ind.
D 4	Mill Cr.	Ia.
C 10	Millers	Mass.
C 13	Mina	Alg.
P 20	Mindanao	P. I.
F 5	Minho	Port.
N 6	Minnesota	Minn.
F 9	Miramichi	N. B.
I 22	Mispillion Cr.	Del.
B 13	Missisquoi	Vt.
H 20	Mississinewa	Ind.
I 15	Mississippi	U. S.
E 11	Missouri	U. S.
K 6	Mixteco	Oax.
K 23	Mizpah Cr.	Mont.
P 5	Mobile	Ala.
E 5	Moctezuma	Hid.
D 15	Mohawk	N. H.
M 19	Mohawk	N. Y.
N 18	Mojave	Calif.
H 9	Mokelumne	Calif.
F 11	Molopo	U. S. Afr.
R 3	Monongahela	Pa.
C 14	Monongahela	W. Va.
O 24	Montezuma Cr.	Utah
I 18	Moorefield	W. Va.
E 20	Moose	Vt.
C 6	Moose	Wis.
E 14	Mooseleuk	Me.
E 19	Mora	N. M.
K 13	Morava	Yugo.
J 13	Moreau	Mo.
E 6	Moreau	S. D.
D 6	Morona	Peru
K 7	Mosby Cr.	Ore.
H 21	Moselle	Fr.
C 14	Moshassuck	R. I.
F 10	Moswansicut	R. I.
F 6	Motagua	Guat.
G 8	Moy	Ire.
D 3	Mud	Calif.
K 3	Mud	W. Va.
O 11	Mud Cr.	Okla.
K 10	Muddlety Cr.	W. Va.
L 16	Muddy	Utah
H 9	Muddy Br.	Md.
L 19	Muddy Cr.	Ill.
E 3	Muddy Cr.	N. D.
P 3	Muddy Cr.	Wyo.
O 19	Muddy Boggy Cr.	Okla.
E 10	Mulawai	Mor.
J 12	Mulberry	Ala.
E 6	Mulberry	Ark.
E 4	Mulberry Cr.	Tex.
J 11	Mulde	Ger.
A 8	Mule Cr.	Okla.
L 13	Mullica	N. J.
O 5	Mun	Thai.
O 17	Murray	Austl.
N 14	Muscatatuck	Ind.
O 8	Muscatatuck, East Fk.	Ind.
E 10	Musconetcong	N. J.
L 15	Muskegon	Mich.
L 16	Muskingum	Ohio
I 12	Muskrat Cr.	Wyo.
J 16	Musselshell	Mont.
K 5	Mustinka	Minn.
L 23	Mystic	Conn.
L 4	Mystic	Mass.
N 10	Naab	Ger.
P 8	Nabend	Iran
J 17	Nabesna	Alaska
K 12	Naches	Wash.
D 13	Nacozari	Son.
J 7	Nahr Iskanderaneh	Pal.
O 5	Nam	Thai.
H 11	Namsen	Nor.
L 5	Nan Hu	Fr. In. Chn.
M 20	Nanticoke	Md.
D 13	Napo	Peru
H 12	Narbada	India
L 10	Narenta	Yugo.
C 14	Narew	Pol.
B 19	Narocz	Pol.
G 6	Nashwaak	N. B.
H 8	Nass	B. C.
E 21	Natchaug	Conn.
F 8	Naugatuck	Conn.
D 15	Naver	Scot.
B 16	Navajo Cr.	Ariz.
I 24	Neches	Tex.
F 10	Nechi	Col.
N 15	Neck	Conn.
O 6	Neckar	Ger.
R 11	Negro	Arg.
E 14	Negro	Bol.
D 13	Negro	Hond.
D 11	Negro	S. Am.
J 19	Negro	Ur.
B 5	Nehalem	Ore.
G 17	Nelson	Man.
N 15	Nemozine Cr.	Va.
L 13	Nenagh	Ire.
J 21	Neosho (Grand)	Kan.
E 21	Neosho (Grand)	Okla.
R 3	Neponsel	Mass.
E 5	Nestucca	Ore.
Q 7	Neuquen	Arg.
I 20	Neuse	N. C.
C 3	New	Fla.
L 3	Niagara	N. Y.
N 13	Niagara	Ont.
L 19	Niantic	Conn.
C 19	Niemen	Pol.
I 8	Niger	Afr.
F 18	Nile	Afr.
E 12	Niobrara	Neb.
C 9	Nipisiguit	N. B.
M 4	Nishnabotna	Ia.
N 4	Nisling	Yuk.
K 7	Nisqually	Wash.
P 17	Nith	Scot.
P 19	Nitra	Ger.

RIVERS, CREEKS, CANALS AND BAYOUS—Continued

Index	*Name*	*Location*
D 9	Noatak	Alaska
P 6	Nodaway	Ia.
M 22	Nolichucky	Tenn.
B 10	Nooksack	Wash.
K 18	Noorder Canal	Neth.
M 17	Nore	Ire.
F 8	North	Ala.
H 21	North	Mass.
J 15	North Anna	Va.
F 9	North Loup	Neb.
L 22	North Platte	Wyo.
G 8	North Santiam	Ore.
J 3	North Saskatchewan	Sask.
E 13	Norwood Cr.	Wyo.
E 9	Nossob	U. S. Afr.
L 3	Nottaway	Ont.
P 16	Nottoway	Va.
C 16	Notwani	U. S. Afr.
O 15	Nueces	Tex.
M 9	Nushagak	Alaska
L 6	Nusrah, Wady	Pal.
C 21	Nuthegan	Vt.
L 13	Oak Cr.	S. D.
J 11	Oakmulgee Cr.	Ala.
D 11	Ob	Asia
E 9	Obigo	Sp.
M 3	Obion	Tenn.
G 17	Occoquan Cr.	Va.
Q 7	Ochlockonee	Ga.
C 7	Ocilla	Fla.
H 9	Ocmulgee	Ga.
I 15	Oconee	Ga.
F 13	Oder	Ger.
J 21	Ogeechee	Ga.
I 5	Ogilvie	Yuk.
J 17	Ohio	U. S.
I 15	Ohio Canal	Ohio
F 14	Oise	Fr.
I 12	Oka	Sov. Un.
D 16	Okanogan	Wash.
M 13	Okatoma Cr.	Miss.
L 4	Okatuppa Cr.	Ala.
H 13	Okobojo Cr.	S. D.
B 19	Oldtown Cr.	Miss.
D 16	Olenek	Sov. Un., Asia
D 20	Olijants	U. S. Afr.
O 2	Olmos Cr.	Tex.
L 17	Olustee Cr.	Ala.
J 6	Omme	Den.
C 19	Omolon	Sov. Un., Asia
E 12	Onega	Sov. Un.
E 23	Oranje Canal	Neth.
K 5	Orange	U. S. Afr.
J 11	Orentes	Syr.
C 8	Orinoco	S. Am.
F 13	Orituco	Ven.
I 8	Orka	Nor.
G 9	Orne	Fr.
C 7	Orton	Bol.
K 12	Osage	Mo.
F 17	Oswegatchie	N. Y.
M 16	Oswego	N. J.
K 14	Oswego	N. Y.
L 11	Ottauguechee	Vt.
B 17	Ottawa	Ont.
C 12	Otter	Mass.
N 5	Otter	Nor.
J 18	Otter	Rom.
O 9	Otter	Va.
N 11	Otter Cr.	Utah
H 5	Otter Cr.	Vt.
J 4	Otter Tail	Minn.
B 11	Ouachita	La.
J 8	Ouchita	Ark.
J 16	Owens	Calif.
Q 4	Owyhee	Ida.
M 22	Owyhee	Ore.
J 9	Oxus	Sov. Un., Asia
C 11	Oyapock	Braz.-Fr. Gui.
F 13	Oykell	Scot.
J 11	Pachitea	Peru
E 4	Pacific Cr.	Wyo.
L 11	Painted Woods	N. D.
K 11	Pak Ho	Chn.
H 12	Palacios	Bol.
B 4	Paladuro Cr.	Tex.
N 3	Palo Blanco Cr.	Tex.
L 7	Palomaso	N. M.
K 22	Palouse	Wash.
H 20	Pamlico	N. C.
L 17	Pamunkey	Va.
G 12	Panama Canal	C. Z.
O 8	Pangwitch Cr.	Utah
E 8	Panora	It.
F 7	Pantepec, R. de	Ver.
D 5	Pánuco	S. L. P.
E 11	Pao	Ven.
J 11	Papaloapan	Ver.
D 14	Para	Braz.
J 19	Paragua	Ven.
I 13	Paraguay	S. Am.
L 12	Paraná	S. Am.
G 12	Paraopeba	Braz.
K 14	Parapeti	Bol.
K 20	Pardo	Braz.
F 20	Park	N. D.
H 17	Parnahyba	Braz.
H 12	Parsnip	B. C.
D 10	Parú	Braz.
Q 21	Pascagoula	Miss.
C 5	Pasion, Rio de la	Guat.
J 16	Passadumkeag	Me.
E 17	Passaic	N. J.
F 18	Passumpsic	Vt.
E 8	Pastaza	Peru
G 13	Patapsco	Md.
L 3	Patia	Col.
P 5	Patoka	Ind.
M 15	Patsaliga Cr.	Ala.
E 19	Patterson Cr.	W. Va.
F 13	Patuca	Hond.
I 14	Patuxent	Md.
E 6	Pauté	Ec.
M 6	Pawcatuck	R. I.
F 10	Pawtuxet	R. I.
M 7	Payette	Ida.
N 18	Pea	Ala.
F 17	Peace	Alta.
M 12	Pearl	Miss.
B 12	Pease	Tex.
F 14	Pecan Bayou	Tex.
A 13	Pecatonica	Ill.
B 18	Pechora	Sov. Un.
N 9	Pecos	U. S.
J 15	Pedernales	Tex.
D 20	Pee Dee	S. C.
F 22	Pee Dee Little	S. C.
G 11	Peel	Yuk.

RIVERS, CREEKS, CANALS AND BAYOUS—Continued

Index	*Name*	*Location*
D 12	Peene	Ger.
K 11	Pe Kiang	Chn.
K 12	Pelahatchee Cr.	Miss.
M 11	Pelly	Yuk.
E 24	Pend Oreille	Wash.-Idaho
N 16	Pěneios	Grc.
M 15	Penitentia	C. R.
J 14	Penn Cr.	Pa.
M 11	Penner	India
G 13	Penobscot	Me.
J 7	Pepan Kiang	Chn.
M 1	Perdido	Fla.
M 10	Peribonka	Que.
P 9	Periyax	India
D 16	Persante	Ger.
E 5	Persimmon Cr.	Okla.
H 13	Pescara	It.
N 10	Peshtigo	Wis.
G 14	Pesqueria	Mex.
B 15	Petawawa	Ont.
E 16	Phillips Brook	N. H.
L 19	Piankatank	Va.
F 5	Piceance Cr.	Colo.
P 7	Piedra	Colo.
C 8	Pierce Cr.	Ariz.
L 7	Pierre Bayou	Miss.
P 7	Pig	Va.
Q 6	Pigeon	Ind.
M 17	Pigeon	Man.
M 14	Pigeon Cr.	Ala.
M 14	Pilcomayo	Bol.
H 19	Pine	Wis.
M 8	Pine	Wis.
F 14	Pine Cr.	Pa.
L 11	Pine Barren Cr.	Ala.
D 15	Pinega	Sov. Un.
E 9	Piney Cr.	Ark.
N 16	Pingue Canal	Cuba
N 17	Pinon Cr.	N. M.
K 16	Pintlalla Cr.	Ala.
K 17	Pipestem Cr.	N. D.
I 13	Piray	Bol.
J 9	Piscataquis	Me.
O 13	Piscataquog	N. H.
F 10	Pisuerga	Sp.
C 7	Pit	Calif.
C 8	Pitmegea	Alaska
G 2	Piura	Peru
M 13	Plata	S. Am.
L 12	Platte	Neb.
G 21	Platte	Wis.
H 13	Pleasant	Me.
F 12	Plum Cr.	Neb.
D 7	Po	It.
D 12	Pocasset	R. I.
J 6	Pocatalico	W. Va.
P 23	Pocomoke	Md.
H 16	Pocotaligo	S. C.
I 12	Poison Cr.	Wyo.
E 19	Polacca Wash	Ariz.
F 19	Polecat Cr.	Okla.
M 5	Pomme de Terre	Minn.
L 10	Pomme de Terre	Mo.
J 6	Pomperaug	Conn.
D 14	Ponca Cr.	Neb.
B 17	Pond Cr.	Okla.
M 18	Poplar	Man.
E 16	Porcupine	Alaska
C 3	Porcupine	Can.
D 20	Porcupine Cr.	Mont.
P 12	Porcupine Cr.	N. D.
H 7	Portland Canal	B. C.
P 19	Port Neuf	Ida.
F 10	Portuguesa	Ven.
G 12	Potenia	It.
P 14	Potomac	Md.
H 15	Potowomut	R. I.
M 22	Powder	Mont.
F 22	Powder	Ore.
L 19	Powell	Tenn.
F 16	Prairie	Minn.
H 16	Prairie	Minn.
J 10	Prairie	Wis.
J 13	Pranbito	India
B 23	Pregel	Ger.
A 3	Priest	Ida.
H 15	Prinzapolca	Nic.
K 5	Pripyat	Sov. Un.
F 16	Providence	R. I.
I 23	Prut	Rom.-W. Sov. Un.
C 14	Pueblo	N. M.
D 13	Puerco	Ariz.
O 21	Pulangi	P. I.
I 2	Pumpkin Cr.	Neb.
G 21	Pungo	N. C.
N 19	Purgatoire	Colo.
E 4	Pursak	Tur.
F 9	Purûs	S. Am.
D 6	Putumayo (Içá)	S. Am.
K 8	Puyallup	Wash.
H 8	Quartzville Cr.	Ore.
K 11	Queens	R. I.
L 14	Quesnel	B. C.
I 2	Quinalt	Wash.
H 11	Quinebaug	Mass.
B 10	Quinn	Nev.
H 10	Rabá	Hung.
E 6	Rabbit Cr.	S. D.
A 3	Rabbit Ear Cr.	Tex.
B 11	Rainy	Minn.
K 12	Rancocas Cr.	N. J.
C 10	Rapid	Minn.
H 14	Rapidan	Va.
I 15	Rappahannock	Va.
E 19	Raquette	N. Y.
G 19	Raritan	N. J.
E 16	Rat	Alaska
L 23	Rawhide Cr.	Wyo.
D 18	Rayado Cr.	N. M.
M 11	Red	U. S.
D 12	Red, of the North	U. S.
P 18	Red Cr.	Miss.
C 15	Red Cedar	Ia.
E 15	Red Horse Wash	Ariz.
E 6	Red Lake	Minn.
P 7	Red Rock Cr.	Mont.
D 12	Red Rock Cr.	Okla.
G 22	Red Water	Mont.
D 23	Red Willow Cr.	Colo.
O 8	Redwood	Minn.
P 3	Reed Cr.	Va.
C 6	Reedy	S. C.
H 7	Reedy Cr.	W. Va.
H 10	Reindeer	Sask.
O 15	Republican	Neb.
B 5	Restigouche	N. B.
D 13	Reuss	Switz.
L 9	Rhine	Eur.
N 19	Rhône	Fr.

RIVERS, CREEKS CANALS AND BAYOUS—Continued

Index	*Name*	*Location*
I 10	Rib	Wis.
H 6	Rind	Den.
E 14	Rio de la Plata	P. R.
L 14	Rio del Fuerte	Sin.
O 8	Rio Grande	U. S.
G 8	Rio Puerco	N. Mex.
K 13	Rivanna	Va.
D 18	Roanoke	N. C.
P 10	Roanoke	Va.
B 22	Roaring Brook	Vt.
C 16	Rock	Ala.
D 10	Rock	Ill.
C 2	Rock	Ia.
L 21	Rock	Wis.
M 6	Rock Cr.	Fla.
J 5	Rock Cr.	Mont.
C 14	Rock Cr.	Nev.
A 7	Rock Cr.	Okla.
O 12	Rock Cr.	S. D.
K 11	Rockfish	Va.
P 2	Rogue	Ore.
G 4	Roosevelt	Braz.
B 5	Roseau	Minn.
K 20	Rosebud Cr.	Mont.
L 12	Rouge	Que.
P 6	Roughty	Ire.
M 20	Rovuma	Afr.
I 5	Ruhr	Ger.
K 16	Ruidoso Cr.	N. M.
N 20	Rule Cr.	Colo.
K 14	Rum	Minn.
M 11	Rush Cr.	Okla.
G 3	Russian	Calif.
J 10	Saale	Ger.
J 7	Saane	Switz.
K 14	Sabari	India
O 18	Sabi	Afr.
F 4	Sabine	La.
M 8	Sac	Mo.
K 22	Sacandaga	N. Y.
F 5	Sacramento	Calif.
G 4	Sacramento Wash	Ariz.
L 5	Sado	Port.
C 12	Sage Cr.	Mont.
M 10	Saguache Cr.	Colo.
F 23	Saguenay	Que.
O 25	St. Clair	Mich.
I 21	St. Croix	Me.
A 11	St. Croix	Wis.
C 20	St. Francis	Ark.
N 20	St. Francis	Mo.
E 6	St. Joe	Ida.
B 13	St. John	Me.
E 4	St. John	N. B.
C 16	St. Johns	Fla.
A 13	St. Joseph	Ind.
Q 15	St. Joseph	Mich.
D 5	St. Joseph	Ohio
D 21	St. Joseph of Maumee	Ind.
N 20	St. Lawrence	Can.
N 25	St. Martin	Md.
P 20	St. Marys	Ga.
E 21	St. Marys	Ind.
F 18	St. Marys	Mich.
E 19	St. Marys Falls Canal	Mich.
J 17	St. Maurice	Que.
C 5	Sakaria	Tur.
G 22	Sakata	Jap.
J 21	Sakonnet	R. I.
P 14	Salado Cr.	Tex.
N 20	Salado	Cuba
D 15	Salado	N. L.
F 18	Salamonie	Ind.
G 15	Salcha	Alaska
N 5	Salem Cr.	N. J.
C 15	Saleratus Cr.	Utah
K 8	Salinas	Calif.
M 13	Saline	Ark.
F 7	Saline	Kan.
H 23	Sallisaw Cr.	Okla.
I 16	Salmon	Conn.
I 5	Salmon	Ida.
G 9	Salmon	N. B.
J 15	Salmon	N. Y.
O 10	Salmon	Wash.
L 10	Salmon, Middle Fk.	Ida.
F 15	Salmon Br.	Conn.
H 7	Salmon Trout Cr.	Mont.
K 14	Salt	Ariz.
D 13	Salt	Mo.
D 13	Salt, Middle Fk.	Mo.
H 12	Salt Cr.	Ill.
L 14	Salt Cr.	Okla.
D 6	Saluda	S. C.
P 11	Saludo	Arg.
N 24	Salween	Bur.
Q 24	Sambu	Pan.
K 20	Sampit Cr.	S. C.
C 10	Sams Cr.	Md.
E 15	San	Pol.
L 8	San Antonio	Calif.
N 17	San Antonio	Tex.
J 18	Sand	Minn.
M 17	Sand Cr.	Ind.
C 17	Sand Cr.	Ore.
F 3	Sandhill	Minn.
F 11	Sandusky	Ohio
F 3	Sandy Cr.	N. D.
P 21	San Felipe	Calif.
K 25	San Francisco	Ariz.-N. M.
K 7	San Francisco Cr.	Tex.
H 10	Sangamon	Ill.
J 9	San Joaquin	Calif.
F 8	San Jorge	Col.
L 15	San Juan	Cen. Am.
I 6	San Juan	Col.
B 3	San Juan	N. M.
Q 18	San Juan	Utah
O 17	San Lorenzo	Sin.
H 14	San Miguel	Bol.
L 5	San Miguel	Colo.
B 18	San Pablo Cr.	Calif.
M 19	San Pedro	Ariz.
E 11	San Pedro	Bol.
L 16	San Pedro, Rio de	Cuba
E 19	Sanpoil	Wash.
K 18	San Rafael	Utah
I 12	San Saba	Tex.
G 25	San Simon Cr.	Ariz.
R 7	Santa Ana	Calif.
P 3	Santa Clara	Utah
D 21	Santa Cruz	Arg.
M 15	Santa Cruz	Ariz.
M 12	Santa Maria	Calif.
N 11	Santa Ynez	Calif.
J 8	Santee	S. C.
E 8	Santiago	Hond.
K 9	Santo Domingo	Oax.
J 19	São Francisco	Braz.

RIVERS, CREEKS, CANALS AND BAYOUS—Continued

Index	Name	Location
L 19	Saône	Fr.
E 5	Sappa Cr.	Kan.
E 22	Saranac	N. Y.
H 11	Sari Su	Sov. Un., Asia
I 8	Sarthe	Fr.
E 19	Sassafras	Md.
M 10	Saskatchewan	Can.
N 18	Satilla	Ga.
O 14	Satus Cr.	Wash.
M 5	Saugatuck	Conn.
J 5	Saugus	Mass.
L 10	Sauk	Minn.
D 10	Sauk	Wash.
J 11	Sava	Yugo.
D 4	Savannah	S. C.
F 8	Sazava	Czech.
C 15	Scantic	Conn.
C 17	Scarham Cr.	Ala.
O 8	Scheldt	Bel.
P 21	Schoharie Cr.	N. Y.
H 23	Schroon	N. Y.
N 21	Schuylkill	Pa.
O 12	Scioto	Ohio
C 16	Seal	Man.
E 7	Sebu	Mor.
G 9	Secure	Bol.
G 14	Segovia	Cen. Am.
G 12	Seine	Fr.
O 8	Sekong	Fr. In. Chn.
E 9	Selawik	Alaska
H 15	Selenga	Asia
H 8	Selway	Idaho
M 13	Semen	Alb.
L 13	Seneca	N. Y.
H 2	Senegal	Afr.
N 14	Sepulga	Ala.
I 20	Sereth	Rom.
L 12	Severn	Eng.
H 14	Severn	Md.
F 9	Severn	Ont.
K 6	Sevier	Utah
H 19	Shamattawa	Man.
J 13	Shannon	Ire.
E 15	Sheenjek	Alaska
H 7	Shell Cr.	N. D.
E 15	Shell Rock	Ia.
G 12	Shenandoah	Va.
M 13	Sherman Cr.	Pa.
C 6	Sheslay	B. C.
I 15	Sheyenne	N. D.
N 19	Shiawassee	Mich.
K 11	Shields	Mont.
I 20	Shinano	Jap.
K 16	Shira	Jap.
A 9	Shoal Cr.	Ala.
D 8	Shoal Cr.	Mo.
C 8	Shoshone	Wyo.
J 13	Siang Kiang	Chn.
H 14	Sicsionas	Nic.
K 4	Sieg	Ger.
K 15	Silero	India
O 17	Silver Cr.	Ind.
L 17	Silver Cr.	Ore.
O 4	Silver Mine	Conn.
J 18	Silvies	Ore.
I 16	Simonette	Alta.
G 11	Sinah	India
I 11	Sinaruco	Ven.
J 10	Sinaruguito	Ven.
L 12	Sipapo	Ven.
F 8	Sipsey	Ala.
J 14	Siquia	Nic.
M 11	Sisquoc	Calif.
O 23	Sittang	India
J 5	Siuslaw	Ore.
N 16	Sixaola	Pan.
D 9	Skagit	Wash.
F 9	Skeena	B. C.
J 7	Skeena	B. C.
E 11	Skeleton Cr.	Okla.
G 16	Skellefteå	Swe.
I 4	Skjerne	Den.
Q 2	Skull Cr.	N. D.
D 15	Skuna	Miss.
K 14	Skunk	Ia.
G 10	Skykomish	Wash.
M 21	Slaney	Ire.
N 4	Slate Cr.	Wyo.
C 21	Slave	Alta.
D 20	Smilde Canal	Neth.
K 4	Smiths	Ore.
I 17	Smoky, Little	Alta.
H 6	Smoky Hill	Kan.
E 21	Smyrna	Del.
B 5	Snake, Little	Colo.
H 3	Snake	Ida.
K 16	Snake	Minn.
F 7	Snake	Neb.
F 3	Snake, So. Fk.	Wyo.
J 9	Snake Cr.	N. D.
H 11	Snoqualmie	Wash.
C 6	Sohan	India
I 4	Soldier	Ia.
D 9	Solimões	S. Am.
F 10	Solomon	Kan.
F 14	Somme	Fr.
G 13	Son	India
M 7	Song Ca	Fr. In. Chn.
F 12	Sonora, Rio de	Son.
H 17	Soto la Marina	Tam.
Q 11	Souhegan	N. H.
F 9	Souris	N. Dak.
J 15	South	N. C.
H 12	South Concho Cr.	Tex.
K 9	South Coon	Ia.
H 10	South Platte	U. S.
L 4	South Platte	Neb.
D 23	Spavinaw Cr.	Okla.
F 16	Spencer Cr.	Mo.
H 18	Spey	Scot.
G 21	Spokane	Wash.
F 23	Spokane, Little	Wash.
E 11	Spoon Cr.	Ill.
P 10	Sprague	Ore.
G 13	Spree	Ger.
B 16	Spring	Ark.
O 7	Spring	Mo.
P 4	Spring Cr.	Ga.
N 8	Spring Cr.	Neb.
B 22	Spring Cr.	Nev.
E 22	Spring Cr.	Okla.
H 7	Spring Cr.	W. Va.
F 4	Spring Cr	Wyo.
D 23	Stads Canal	Neth.
H 10	Stanislaus	Calif.
M 15	Starvation Cr.	Utah
D 9	Steinhatchee	Fla.
H 7	Stevens Cr.	S. C.
L 5	Stewart	Yuk.

RIVERS, CREEKS, CANALS AND BAYOUS—Continued

Index	Name	Location
L 16	Stewiacke	N. S.
F 6	Stikine	B. C.
E 18	Stokhod	Pol.
C 17	Stolpe	Ger.
B 14	Stony Br.	Conn.
F 5	Stony Cr.	Calif.
H 15	Stony Cr.	N. Y.
G 3	Stony Cr.	N. D.
F 14	Stony Tunguska	Sov. Un., Asia
G 5	Stor	Den.
E 16	Stora-Lulea	Swe.
O 6	Stow Cr.	N. J.
G 17	Strawberry	Utah
L 12	Strong	Miss.
D 16	Strule	N. Ire.
P 14	Struma	Eur.
G 16	Stryi	Pol.
E 2	Sturgeon	Mich.
G 12	Suarez	Col.
I 11	Suck	Ire.
D 22	Suez Canal	Eg.
R 7	Sugar Cr.	Mo.
E 17	Sugar Cr.	Pa.
M 14	Suir	Ire.
F 14	Sukhona	Sov. Un.
G 5	Sulphur Cr.	S. D.
O 15	Suncook	N. H.
G 7	Sungpan Ho	Chn.
M 6	Surar, Wady es	Pal.
H 6	Suripa	Ven.
C 17	Susie Cr.	Nev.
J 13	Susitna	Alaska
E 18	Susquehanna	Pa.
D 2	Susurla-chai	Tur.
D 7	Sutlej	India
E 11	Suwanee	Fla.
P 17	Suwanee	Ga.
O 8	Swains Cr.	Utah
K 14	Swamp Cr.	Ala.
M 10	Sweet Briar Cr.	N. D.
K 13	Sweet Grass Cr.	Mont.
L 11	Sweetwater	Wyo.
J 16	Swift	N. H.
G 16	Szamos	Rom.
B 20	Tabor Cr.	Nev.
D 10	Tabusintac	N. B.
J 6	Tagus	Port.
C 3	Tahuamanu	Bol.
G 6	Ta Kiang	Chn.
C 5	Taku	B. C.
J 13	Talkeetna	Alaska
N 18	Tallahalla Cr.	Miss.
C 14	Tallahatchie	Miss.
L 19	Tallahoma Cr.	Miss.
I 19	Tallapoosa	Ala.
O 16	Taltson	Mack.
D 12	Tamarac	Minn.
F 6	Tamega	Port.
J 17	Tames	Tam.
I 14	Tanana	Alaska
N 24	Tao	Cuba
F 13	Tapajoz	S. Am.
F 18	Tar	N. C.
K 12	Tara	Yugo.
F 11	Taracue	Col.
J 12	Tarim	Asia
O 13	Tarn	Fr.
H 6	Ta tu Ho	Chn.
K 19	Taunton	Mass.
K 17	Tay	Scot.
F 6	Tchaneta	Mack.
Q 6	Tebicuary	Par.
D 15	Tees	Eng.
F 17	Telegraph Cr.	Mont.
M 12	Tempisque	C. R.
K 16	Tennessee	U. S.
M 17	Tenryugawa	Jap.
D 14	Tensas	La.
P 6	Tensaw	Ala.
H 4	Tensift	Mor.
E 1	Terra Blanca Cr.	Tex.
P 11	Teslin	Yuk.
C 9	Tetagouche	N. B.
E 7	Teton	Mont.
F 14	Teuco	Arg.
K 21	Thames	Conn.
L 22	Thames	Eng.
H 13	Theiss (Tisza)	Hung.
K 21	Thelon	Mack.
D 5	Thief	Minn.
I 5	Thirteenmile Cr.	W. Va.
O 6	Thirty Mile Cr.	N. D.
E 5	Thomas Cr.	Calif.
O 14	Thompson	B. C.
N 19	Thompson Cr.	Miss.
F 9	Thornapple	Wis.
B 20	Thousand Cr.	Nev.
E 7	Thunder Butte Cr.	S. D.
F 20	Tibbee	Miss.
H 11	Tiber	It.
D 4	Ticino	It.
L 16	Ticino	Switz.
L 12	Tieton	Wash.
C 8	Tiger	S. C.
D 9	Tigre	Peru
O 18	Tigre Canal	Cen. Am.
H 18	Tigris	Iraq
F 18	Tiljimga	India
C 10	Tilly	Mass.
P 6	Timber Cr.	N. D.
D 15	Tioga	Pa.
E 10	Tippecanoe	Ind.
R 23	Tisza (Theiss)	Hung.
D 19	Tjonger (Kuinder) Canal	Neth.
F 5	Tobique	N. B.
G 10	Tobol	Sov. Un., Asia
G 15	Tocantins	Braz.
C 9	Tocuyo	Ven.
M 7	Togiak	Alaska
F 12	Tokmasu	Tur.
J 9	Tomahawk	Wis.
I 22	Tomah Cr.	Me.
K 8	Tomassino	Que.
I 5	Tombigbee	Ala.
L 5	Tonawanda	N. Y.
M 20	Tongue	Mont.
D 21	Tongue	N. D.
I 16	Tonto Cr.	Ariz.
N 13	Toppenish Cr.	Wash.
E 18	Torneå	Fin.-Swe.
L 7	Tornillo Cr.	Tex.
C 7	Totagatic	Wis.
N 22	Touchet	Wash.
D 15	Touil	Alg.
N 7	Toutle	Wash.
F 16	Towanda Cr.	Pa.
H 6	Toyah Cr.	Tex.
C 5	Traders Cr.	Okla.
M 18	Transquaking Cr.	Md.

RIVERS, CREEKS, CANALS AND BAYOUS—Continued

Index	Name	Location
D 5	Trask	Ore.
E 15	Trempealeau	Wis.
G 17	Trent	Eng.
C 3	Trinity	Calif.
G 21	Trinity	Tex.
D 8	Trombetas	Braz.
G 8	Trout Cr.	Ariz.
G 3	Truckee	Nev.
M 22	Tucannon	Wash.
P 12	Tuckahoe	N. J.
C 13	Tugaloo	Ga.
E 2	Tule Cr.	Tex.
H 12	Tuma	Nic.
E 2	Tumbes	Peru
M 10	Tungabhadra	India
E 14	Tunguska, Lower	Sov. Un.
F 14	Tunguska, Upper	Sov. Un.
J 10	Tuolumne	Calif.
F 6	Tupinabaranas	Braz.
E 17	Turiya	Pol.
D 20	Turkey	Ia.
E 10	Turkey Cr.	Okla.
H 8	Turkey Cr.	S. C.
F 16	Turo	Bol.
H 22	Turtle	N. D.
K 11	Turtle Cr.	N. D.
G 18	Turtle Cr.	S. D.
A 13	Tweed	Eng.
N 23	Tweed	Scot.
K 1	Twelvepole Cr.	W. Va.
H 4	Twin Butte Cr.	Kan.
E 14	Twisp	Wash.
N 22	Two Butte Cr.	Colo.
B 20	Tyende Cr.	Ariz.
F 14	Tygart	W. Va.
H 10	Tymochtee	Ohio
C 14	Tyne	Eng.
M 22	Tyne	Scot.
E 21	Tyronza	Ark.
I 13	Tzu Kiang	Chn.
K 13	Ubangi	Afr.
H 10	Ucayali	Peru
K 23	Uchee Cr.	Ala.
K 16	Uele	Bel. Cong.
C 17	Umatilla	Ore.
K 4	Umpqua	Ore.
M 7	Umpqua, North	Ore.
N 6	Umpqua, South	Ore.
J 8	Una	Yugo.
P 17	Unadilla	N. Y.
K 6	Uncompahgre	Colo.
H 9	Ungalik	Alaska
K 17	Union	Me.
L 23	Union Flat Cr.	Wash.
J 4	Upatore Cr.	Ga.
I 3	Upia	Col.
B 19	Upper Iowa	Ia.
B 7	Upsalquitch	N. B.
L 21	Ural	Sov. Un.
E 15	Ure	Eng.
J 16	Urique	Chih.
G 15	Urubicha	Bol.
M 13	Uruguay	S. Am.
G 5	Utubamba	Peru
I 15	Vaal	U. S. Afr.
P 11	Vaigai	India
F 11	Valderaduey	Sp.
M 15	Vardar	Grc.
E 11	Varta	Pol.-Ger.
D 16	Vashka	Sov. Un.
G 14	Vaspuc	Nic.
M 18	Vaupés	Col.
E 21	Vecht	Neth.
P 20	Vegas Wash	Nev.
L 14	Ventuari	Ven.
I 14	Verde	Ariz.
F 18	Verde	Bol.
N 7	Verde	Oax.
D 4	Verde	S. L. P.
C 20	Verdigris	Okla.
B 17	Vermejo	N. M.
F 16	Vermilion	Ill.
N 11	Vermilion	La.
D 18	Vermilion	Minn.
L 12	Vester Dal	Swe.
H 15	Vetluga	Sov. Un.
I 18	Vichada	Col.
J 10	Vienne	Fr.
E 16	Vilyui	Sov. Un., Asia
N 13	Viosé	Alb.
O 23	Virgin	Nev.
Q 3	Virgin	Utah
N 15	Vistrits	Grc.
C 11	Vistula	Pol.
K 18	Volga	Sov. Un.
J 9	Vrbas	Yugo.
G 18	Vyatka	Sov. Un.
E 17	Vychegda	Sov. Un.
E 18	Vym	Sov. Un.
G 8	Wabash	Ind.
E 18	Wabiskaw	Alta.
K 22	Waccamaw	S. C.
M 15	Wading	N. J.
J 21	Wahoo Cr.	Neb.
H 17	Waits	Vt.
P 13	Walnut Bayou	Okla.
K 12	Walnut Cr.	Okla.
L 20	Wambraw Cr.	S. C.
B 17	Wanaque	N. J.
I 15	Wapiti	Alta.
F 18	Wapsipinicon	Ia.
J 11	Wardha	India
L 12	Washita	Okla.
G 14	Wassataquoik Str.	Me.
E 11	Waterbury	Vt.
D 14	Wateree	S. C.
Q 12	Watonwan	Minn.
F 13	Webster Brook	Me.
F 11	Wei Ho	Chn.
M 4	Weiser	Ida.
A 9	Welden	Mo.
I 19	Welland	Eng.
N 12	Welland Canal	Ont.
H 13	Wenatchee	Wash.
I 22	Wensum	Eng.
I 5	Werra	Ger.
F 6	Weser	Ger.
N 14	West	Conn.
O 7	West Cache Cr.	Okla.
D 4	Westfield	Mass.
F 12	West Fork	W. Va.
M 20	Westport	Mass.
Q 7	Weymouth Fore	Mass.
A 12	Wheeling Cr.	W. Va.-Pa.
J 21	White	Ariz.
K 16	White	Ark.
O 6	White	Ind.
J 20	White	Nev.
M 6	White	S. D.

RIVERS, CREEKS, CANALS AND BAYOUS—Continued

Index	Name	Location
L 15	White	U. S.
J 9	White	Vt.
N 2	White	Yuk.
G 5	White Earth	N. D.
Q 19	Whitegrass Cr.	Okla.
K 20	Whitewater	Ind.
J 4	White Woman Cr.	Kan.
B 14	Wichita	Tex.
N 21	Wicomico	Md.
O 12	Wicomico	Md.
F 11	Wigger	Switz.
N 12	Wild Horse Cr.	Okla.
C 18	Wild Horse Cr.	Wyo.
P 23	Wild Rice	N. D.
H 6	Willamette	Ore.
J 19	Willems Canal	Neth.
I 5	Williams	Ariz.
N 13	Williams	Vt.
K 12	Williams	W. Va.
D 18	Willimantic	Conn.
H 14	Willow	Minn.
F 19	Willow Cr.	Mont.
I 22	Willow Cr.	Ore.
C 5	Wilson	Ore.
P 9	Wind	Wash.
H 7	Wind	Wyo.
H 10	Wind	Yuk.
P 17	Winnipeg	Man.
F 8	Winooski	Vt.
H 20	Wisconsin	Wis.
H 18	Witham	Eng.
F 13	Withlacoochee	Fla.
Q 18	Wolf	Miss.
Q 2	Wolf	Tenn.
M 13	Wolf	Wis.
A 14	Wolf Cr.	Nev.
G 16	Wolf Cr.	S. D.
A 5	Wolf Cr.	Tex.
J 7	Wood	R. I.
A 13	Wyaconda Cr.	Mo.
J 4	Wynooche	Wash.
H 10	Xingú	Braz.
B 1	Yaak	Mont.
G 8	Yadkin	N. C.
J 13	Yakima	Wash.
E 15	Yalobusha	Miss.
C 23	Yalu	Cho.
C 2	Yampa	Colo.
C 16	Yana	Sov. Un., Asia
H 10	Yangtse Kiang	Chn.
I 20	Yantic	Conn.
H 12	Yapacani	Bol.
D 5	Yapurá (Caquéta)	S. Am.
H 13	Yaqui	Son.
F 14	Yaquirana	Peru
M 11	Yari	Col.
L 15	Yavero	Peru
J 9	Yaxartes	Sov. Un., Asia
J 8	Yazoo	Miss.
M 4	Yellow	Fla.
B 8	Yellow	Wis.
I 15	Yellow	Wis.
A 22	Yellow Cr.	Miss.
D 10	Yellow Cr.	Mo.
J 18	Yellowstone	Mont.
D 13	Yenesei	Asia
C 11	Yeshil Irmak	Tur.
L 18	Yi	Ur.
C 13	Yocona	Miss.
H 16	Yonne	Fr.
N 19	York	Va.
R 5	Youghiogheny	Pa.
F 14	Youngs Cr.	Mo.
K 8	Ypane	Par.
J 6	Yukon	Alaska
I 20	Zab, Little	Iraq.
M 10	Zak	U. S. Afr.
O 18	Zambesi	Afr.
K 13	Zaza	Cuba
N 12	Zekiak Swamp	Md.
G 17	Zequerir	Alg.
K 15	Zerka, Wady	Transj.
P 21	Zumbro	Minn.
G 23	Zuni	Ariz.

LAKES, PONDS, RESERVOIRS

Index	Name	Location
J 17	Abamgamook	Me.
M 8	Abaya	Eth.
P 15	Abert	Ore.
I 18	Abhebad	Fr. Som.
D 1	Abitibi	Que.
C 3	Abullonia	Tur.
N 16	Adams	B. C.
I 20	Addie	N. D.
P 9	Agency	Ore.
H 21	Ainslie	N. S.
O 7	Aishihik	Yuk.
F 6	Akshehr	Tur.
I 12	Ala	Sov. Un., Asia
H 20	Alamogordo	N. Mex.
K 18	Albert	Afr.
K 16	Alcova Reservoir	Wyo.
K 12	Alikameg	Man.
N 15	Alkali	Ore.
E 10	Allagash	Me.
G 13	Allen	Ire.
F 22	Alligator	N. C.
Q 20	Alvord	Ore.
F 20	Amabelish	Que.
J 11	Amisk	Sask.
Q 9	Ammer	Ger.
Q 2	Apalachia Reservoir	N. C.
G 16	Apopka	Fla.
I 9	Aral	Asia
D 13	Arary	Braz.
I 17	Arbuckle	Fla.
M 14	Archambault	Que.
I 12	Arkaia	Scot.
I 21	Arre	Den.
Q 17	Arrow, Lower & Upper	B. C.
L 18	Artillery	Mack.
E 10	Ashanggi	Erit.
D 3	Ashley	Mont.
C 14	Askitichi	Que.
P 13	Asnen	Swe.
Q 9	Aspen	Ore.
E 13	Assiwanan	Que.
B 6	Athabaska	Sask.
B 5	Atlin	B. C.
H 7	Attean	Me.
K 15	Attikonak	Que.
L 11	Awe	Scot.
D 16	Aylen	Ont.
J 18	Aylmer	Mack.
O 5	Babcocks Pond	R. I.
I 9	Babine	B. C.
K 16	Backs	Mack.
J 13	Bagrash kul	Asia

LAKES, PONDS, RESERVOIRS—Continued

Index	Name	Location
F 13	Baheiret el Huleh	Pal.
H 16	Baikal	Asia
T 19	Balaton	Hung.
I 11	Balkhash	Asia
K 3	Balls Pond	Conn.
B 10	Balsam	Wis.
N 18	Bangweulu	Afr.
F 7	Bantam	Conn.
K 11	Barbers Pond	R. I.
D 16	Bark	Ont.
M 22	Barlow	Mack.
I 19	Bashahegan	Me.
D 11	Bass	Ind.
D 7	Bass	Wis.
E 13	Bays	Ont.
K 14	Bear	B. C.
B 14	Bear	Utah
A 13	Beau	Me.
O 15	Beaver	N. D.
H 18	Beaver	N. Y.
M 18	Beaver	Wis.
O 9	Becharof	Alaska
H 19	Beechey	Mack.
D 23	Belfast	N. Ire.
J 13	Bellville Pond	R. I.
F 9	Bemidji	Minn.
L 14	Benjamin	Ore.
P 3	Benton	Minn.
G 6	Beyshehr Göl	Tur.
E 8	Bezitcho	Mack.
G 7	Bienne	Switz.
C 22	Big	Ark.
J 20	Big	Me.
K 7	Big Payette	Ida.
H 13	Big Rice	Minn.
L 2	Big Stone	Minn.
G 20	Big Tupper	N. Y.
J 24	Billings	Conn.
M 11	Birch	Mack.
J 3	Birch	Que.
L 8	Birket Qarun	Eg.
J 19	Bisby Chain	N. Y.
B 16	Bistcho	Alta.
C 5	Bistineau	La.
L 14	Biwa	Jap.
H 18	Black	Mich.
E 16	Black	N. Y.
M 7	Black	Que.
B 14	Black	Wash.
E 10	Blackduck	Minn.
B 21	Black Pond	Conn.
K 9	Blackwater	Mack.
N 12	Blackwater Reservoir	N. H.
C 7	Blue Ridge	Ga.
G 13	Boderg	Ire.
F 9	Bois, des	Mack.
P 12	Bolmen	Swe.
K 6	Bomosee	Vt.
G 17	Bonaparte	N. Y.
J 8	Boon Pond	R. I.
M 20	Borgne	La.
H 18	Bostonnais	Que.
G 16	Bottle	Ont.
H 8	Bouchette	Que.
F 19	Bouchette	Que.
C 10	Boulder	N. M.
J 7	Boulder	Wyo.
L 22	Bourget, du	Fr.
B 4	Bowman	Mont.
N 22	Boyd	Mack.
H 9	Bracciano	It.
I 24	Brant	N. Y.
I 22	Bras D'Or	N. S.
H 8	Brassua	Me.
F 16	Brevoort	Mich.
H 19	Brewster Pond	Conn.
C 17	Bridgeport	Tex.
K 11	Brienz	Switz.
G 7	Bristol Pond	Vt.
G 15	Brownwood	Tex.
E 18	Brule	Ont.
B 10	Brulos	Eg.
I 15	Buchanan Reservoir	Tex.
B 16	Buck	N. H.
M 13	Buena Vista	Calif.
P 13	Buffalo	Mack.
K 17	Buffalo	Wis.
H 8	Bull	Wyo.
P 20	Buluan	P. I.
F 4	Burdur Göl	Tur.
C 13	Burnt	Ont.
H 17	Burt	Mich.
H 18	Butler,	Fla.
L 8	Butternut	Wis.
H 17	Buyer nor	Asia
F 11	Byelo	Sov. Un.
E 24	Caddo	Tex.
R 16	Caillou	La.
F 23	Calaveras Reservoir	Calif.
N 7	Calcasieu	La.
L 19	Campbell	Mack.
L 15	Camsell	Mack.
E 4	Canadohta	Pa.
N 10	Canandaigua	N. Y.
J 9	Candle	Sask.
M 15	Canim	B. C.
G 6	Canoe	Sask.
K 16	Caousagaouta	Que.
E 15	Caratasca Lagoon	Hond.
O 18	Caribou	Man.
G 11	Caribou	Me.
E 13	Carl Blackwell	Okla.
H 10	Carr Pond	R. I.
O 6	Carrie Lauquen	Arg.
H 6	Carson	Nev.
D 15	Caspian Pond	Vt.
G 11	Cass	Minn.
G 11	Catahoula	La.
A 13	Catawba Reservoir	S. C.
J 19	Catfish	N. C.
K 22	Cathance	Me.
K 10	Catherine	Ark.
G 22	Catlin	N. Y.
F 9	Caucomgomoc	Me.
O 12	Cayuga	N. Y.
K 13	Cedar	Man.
M 10	Cedar	Minn.
B 14	Cedar	Ont.
I 12	Chad	Africa
F 11	Chamberlain	Me.
N 7	Chamo	Eth.
D 5	Champlain	Vt.-N. Y.
D 11	Chander	Alaska
G 17	Chao Hu	Chn.
M 11	Chapala	Mex.
N 5	Chapman Pond	R. I.
I 14	Charlevoix	Mich.
M 17	Charlotte	N. S.
D 22	Chateaugay, Lower	N. Y.

LAKES, PONDS, RESERVOIRS—Continued

Index	Name	Location
D 23	Chateaugay, Upper	N. Y.
R 3	Chatuge Reservoir	N. C.
I 13	Chaubunagungamaug	Mass.
Q 2	Chautauqua	N. Y.
D 23	Chazy	N. Y.
F 14	Chelan	Wash.
D 10	Chemquassabamticook	Me.
E 13	Chergui, Chott ech	Alg.
M 20	Cherokee Reservoir	Tenn.
C 23	Cherokees, Lake of the	Okla.
K 10	Cheslatta	B. C.
F 11	Chesuncook	Me.
P 16	Chickamauga Reservoir	Tenn.
Q 10	Chiemsee	Ger.
N 12	Chilko	B. C.
F 8	Chippewa	Wis.
G 21	Chiputneticook	Me.
O 18	Chiriqui Lagoon	Pan.
J 7	Christina	Minn.
K 9	Christina	Wyo.
M 13	Christmas	Ore.
G 6	Christopherson	Que.
G 15	Chudskoe	Eur.
E 12	Churchill	Me.
G 6	Churchill	Sask.
B 8	Clam	Wis.
L 11	Clark	Alaska
F 4	Clear	Calif.
C 13	Clear	Ia.
H 9	Clear	Ore.
J 15	Clear	Que.
L 15	Clearwater	B. C.
I 12	Cle Elum	Wash.
J 20	Clinton Colden	Mack.
D 4	Coeur d'Alene	Ida.
K 4	Coipasa	Bol.
I 22	Cold	Alta.
F 8	Colville	Mack.
I 21	Colville	Wash.
C 5	Como	It.
F 21	Conchas Reservoir	N. M.
C 16	Conconully	Wash.
N 8	Conesus	N. Y.
I 6	Congamond Pond	Mass.
G 7	Conn	Ire.
F 2	Conneaut	Pa.
B 16	Connecticut	N. H.
C 19	Constance	Switz.
H 15	Contwoyto	Mack.
O 19	Cooper	Wyo.
J 12	Cormorant	Man.
H 5	Cormorant	Minn.
C 9	Coronados, Lagunas	Tex.
O 16	Corpus Christi	Tex.
I 8	Corrib	Ire
M 23	Cow Creek	Ore.
I 18	Crab	Wash.
P 15	Crab Orchard	Ill.
G 19	Cranberry	N. Y.
N 9	Crater	Ore.
E 8	Cree	Sask.
E 17	Crescent	Fla.
L 9	Crescent	Ore.
F 3	Crescent	Wash.
L 15	Croche	Que.
B 20	Crooked	Ind.
B 17	Cross	Me.
Q 15	Crump	Ore.
J 10	Crystal	Mich.
C 17	Crystal	Vt.
I 13	Culate, la	Que.
K 10	Cultus	Ore.
J 11	Cumberland	Sask.
D 9	Cunningham	Tex
C 19	Curlew	Wash.
H 18	Cypress	Fla.
H 17	Dalai nor	Asia
K 14	Dale Hollow Reservoir	Ky.-Tenn.
D 19	Dallas	Tex.
O 13	Dauphin	Man.
K 10	Davis	Ore.
C 9	Deadwood	B. C.
C 8	Dease	B. C.
J 5	Deep Pond	R. I.
E 15	Deer	Minn.
E 22	Deer	Wash.
K 15	Delsbo	Swe.
D 9	Depot	Me.
I 10	Deschambault	Sask.
O 16	Deskenatlata	Mack.
H 17	Devils	N. D.
F 4	Devils	Ore.
J 12	Dexter Pond	Me.
Q 6	Dezadeash	Yuk.
M 8	Diamond	Ore.
C 16	Diamond Pond	N. H.
F 2	Dichey	Wash.
C 7	Dickens	Ia.
H 7	Dinwoody	Wyo.
F 12	Dismal	Mack.
F 22	Djerib, Chott	Tun.
B 12	Doda	Que.
D 11	Doe	Ont.
Q 13	Dog	Ore.
M 16	Dojransko	Yugo.
P 14	Doon	Scot.
N 21	Douglas Reservoir	Tenn.
Q 20	Dry	Nev.
C 22	Dry Wood	S. D.
B 6	Duck	Mont.
P 6	Duck	Utah
E 17	Dummer Ponds	N. H.
J 5	Dumoine	Que.
O 18	Duncan	B. C.
J 8	Dunmore	Vt.
E 2	Duparquet	Que.
D 9	Eagle	Calif.
B 16	Eagle	Me.
E 11	Eagle	Me.
J 6	Eagle	Miss.
C 11	Eagle	Ont.
G 15	Eagle	Ont.
L 7	Eagle	Wis.
D 17	Eagle Mtn.	Tex.
D 13	Eask	N. Ire.
K 11	East	Ore.
C 10	East Branch Reservoir	Conn.
M 20	Eckelson	N. D.
C 6	Edku	Eg.
K 18	Edward	Afr.
I 19	Edward	Que.
F 5	Egerdir Göl	Tur.
H 23	El Djeneyen	Tun.
K 8	Elephant Butte Reservoir	N. M.
R 9	Elsinore	Calif.
C 10	El Vado	N. Mex.
F 3	Emma Matilda	Wyo.

LAKES, PONDS, RESERVOIRS—Continued

Index	Name	Location
A 7	Enare	Fin.
I 14	Endless	Me.
I 16	Ennel	Ire.
G 20	Erie	U. S.
E 14	Erne	N. Ire.
F 15	Erne, Upper	N. Ire.
G 10	Eskwahani	Que.
I 22	Esrom	Den.
D 15	Etawney	Man.
L 8	Ethel	Yuk.
H 3	Expanse	Que.
K 15	Eyre	Austl.
K 12	Fabre	Mack.
B 8	Fairfield Pond	Vt.
I 17	Fairlee Pond	Vt.
O 10	Fairy	N. S.
G 12	Fannich	Scot.
P 4	Fantana Reservoir	N. C.
M 11	Fawn	Mack.
J 8	Fence	Wis.
C 14	Fish	Me.
M 9	Fish	Ore.
L 12	Fish	Utah
L 3	Fish	Wyo.
E 10	Fishing	B. C.
P 16	Flagstaff	Ore.
J 5	Flagstaff Pond	Me.
H 16	Flamand	Que.
H 7	Flambeau Reservoir	Wis.
F 4	Flathead	Mont.
N 19	Fort Loudon Reservoir	Tenn.
C 3	Fort Supply Reservoir	Okla.
F 9	Foster	Sask.
A 19	Fox	Ill.
M 17	Fox	Wis.
B 17	Foyle	Ire.
O 17	Frances	Yuk.
C 15	Francis	N. H.
J 10	Francois	B. C.
E 19	Franklin	Nev.
E 20	Franklin D. Roosevelt	Wash.
I 6	Fremont	Wyo.
F 6	Frobisher	Sask.
I 19	Fulton Chain	N. Y.
G 13	Galilee	Pal.
G 11	Gara	Ire.
D 8	Garda	It.
I 19	Gardner	Conn.
K 23	Gardner	Me.
H 3	Garfield	Mass.
I 12	Garry	Scot.
F 22	Garson	Alta.
H 7	Gatun	C. Z.
H 7	Gaud-i-Zirreh	Afg.
L 4	Geneva	Switz.
N 22	Geneva	Wis.
H 18	Gentry	Fla.
E 19	George	Mich.
I 24	George	N. Y.
L 2	George	Vt.
E 16	George	Fla.
C 12	Georgiaville Pond	R. I.
F 12	Gharbi, Chott el	Alg.
A 6	Gladys	B. C.
B 13	Glazier	Me.
I 18	Gods	Man.
D 17	Golden	Ont.
B 10	Goose	Calif.
R 14	Goose	Ore.
L 9	Goose Pond	N. H.
M 18	Goose Reservoir	S. C.
H 15	Gown	Ire.
L 17	Graham	Me.
N 8	Grand	La.
O 13	Grand	La.
F 14	Grand	Me.
G 20	Grand	Me.
J 19	Grand	Me.
I 20	Grand	Mich.
I 8	Grand	N. B.
H 21	Grand	Que.
K 11	Grandin	Mack.
E 15	Grand Lake Seboeis	Me.
G 12	Granville	Man.
I 16	Gras	Mack.
M 9	Greasy	Mack.
J 19	Great	N. C.
A 21	Great Averill Pond	Vt.
H 10	Great Bear	Mack.
G 23	Great Bitter	Eg.
M 8	Great Pond	Me.
D 7	Great Salt	Utah
N 15	Great Slave	Mack.
J 22	Great South Pond	Mass.
F 17	Great West Loon	Ont.
M 10	Green	Minn.
M 17	Green	Wis.
E 15	Greifen	Switz.
F 10	Greenwood	S. C.
E 8	Grindstone	Wis.
E 5	Grouard	Mack.
I 12	Grouard	Mack.
R 17	Guano	Ore.
I 11	Gull	Minn.
B 16	Guzmán, Laguna	Chih.
Q 14	Hales Bar Reservoir	Tenn.
E 14	Haliburton	Ont.
E 13	Hallwyl	Switz.
K 9	Hamilton	Ark.
K 15	Hamun-I-Helmand	Iran
J 12	Hardisty	Mack.
M 18	Harney	Ore.
N 6	Harrison	B. C.
H 18	Hart	Fla.
Q 16	Hart	Ore.
D 16	Hay	Alta.
D 5	Hayden	Ida.
K 9	Hayden	Me.
D 4	Heart	Wyo.
O 9	Hebgen Reservoir	Mont.
N 9	Hemlock	N. Y.
K 21	Henrys	Ida.
R 8	Heron	Minn.
G 17	Herrington	Ky.
A 8	Herring Pond	R. I.
Q 2	Hiwassee Reservoir	N. C.
L 19	Hicpochee	Fla.
K 15	Higgins	Mich.
C 8	Highland	Conn.
M 9	Highland	Mack.
F 7	Hinesburg Pond	Vt.
M 14	Hjelmar	Swe.
H 5	Holeb Pond	Me.
M 9	Holland	Nor.
D 10	Honey	Calif.
C 14	Hopatcong	N. J.
F 15	Horn Afvan	Swe.
B 10	Horse	N. M.
K 6	Hortonia	Vt.

LAKES, PONDS, RESERVOIRS—Continued

Index	Name	Location
I 12	Hottaw	Mack.
K 17	Houghton	Mich.
J 20	Hubbard	Mich.
F 7	Humboldt Sink	Nev.
F 18	Hungtze Hu	Chn.
J 15	Hunter	Mack.
F 19	Huron	U. S.
I 18	Hutchincha	Fla.
M 10	Iliamna	Alaska
G 7	Ilmen	Sov. Un.
H 7	Ilopango	Sal.
B 9	Imandra	Sov. Un.
F 10	Indian	Mich.
I 21	Indian	N. Y.
H 8	Indian	Ohio
E 14	Indian, Southern	Man.
E 11	Inver	Scot.
F 17	Irvin	N. D.
I 12	Isabella	Mack.
K 18	Island	Man.
E 15	Island	N. D.
B 20	Island Pond	Vt.
C 4	Isnik	Tur.
J 11	Issyk kul	Sov. Un., Asia
J 18	Istokpoga	Fla.
G 8	Itasca	Minn.
E 6	Izabal	Cen. Am.
I 18	Jackson, L.	Fla.
J 19	Jackson	Fla.
B 21	James	Ind.
P 18	James	Wyo.
J 9	James Pond	R. I.
F 3	Jenny	Wyo.
F 13	Jessie	Minn.
I 20	Jessie	N. D.
E 16	Joes Pond	Vt.
I 16	Jordan	Ala.
E 11	Joseph	Ont.
K 9	Junin	Peru
I 18	Junior	Me.
N 20	Juniper	Ore.
I 12	Kachess	Wash.
E 13	Kahweambelewagamot	Ont.
I 9	Kakebonga	Que.
H 12	Kall-sjön	Swe.
G 9	Kamachigama	Que.
D 16	Kaminiskeg	Ont.
G 22	Kampeska	S. D.
N 9	Kandiyohi	Minn.
H 7	Kanikwanika	Que.
F 18	Kaoyu Hu	Chn.
F 10	Kapitachuan	Que.
J 14	Kara nor	Asia
O 23	Kasba	Mack.
G 15	Kathawachaga	Mack.
C 14	Kazanjerri	Man.
D 7	Keck Pond	R. I.
B 14	Kemp	Tex.
J 4	Kennebago	Me.
F 20	Kenogami	Que.
E 11	Kenozero	Sov. Un.
N 7	Kentucky Reservoir	Tenn.
O 11	Keuka	N. Y.
H 20	Khanka	Asia
F 5	Kiemawisk	Que.
P 5	Killarney	Ire.
D 5	Killingly Pond	R. I.
F 3	Kinojevis	Que.
B 4	Kintla	Mont.
K 19	Kioga	Ug.
J 1	Kipawa	Que.
J 14	Kiskitto	Man.
J 14	Kiskittogisu	Man.
I 18	Kissimmee	Fla.
H 12	Kississing	Man.
Q 9	Klamath, Upper	Ore.
O 4	Kluane	Yuk.
H 11	Kokadjo	Me.
K 15	Koko nor	Asia
G 14	Kolind Sund	Den.
P 19	Kootenay	B. C.
M 20	Koshkonong	Wis.
H 15	Kossogol	Asia
G 12	Kubenskoe	Sov. Un.
Q 8	Kusawa	Yuk.
F 11	Lacha	Sov. Un.
D 20	Lac La Croix	Minn.
L 11	Lac la Martre	Mack.
K 6	Lac Vieux Desert	Wis.
F 8	Ladoga	Sov. Un.
I 13	Laggan	Scot.
P 15	Lago Maggiore	Switz.
E 5	La Motte	Que.
N 19	Lanao	P. I.
J 10	Lava	Ore.
H 15	Lay	Ala
B 18	Leba	Ger.
G 5	Lee	Miss.
G 11	Leech	Minn.
D 8	Lektsha	Sov. Un.
M 9	Lenore	Sask.
H 17	Lenore	Wash.
K 14	Leopold II	Bel. Cong.
H 18	Lesser Slave	Alta.
K 13	Leven	Scot.
D 3	Lewis	Wyo.
I 6	Lida	Minn.
O 12	Lillooet	B. C.
N 15	Liman, Gr.	Sov. Un.
K 11	Linnhe, Loch	Scot.
E 3	Little Bitter Root	Mont.
O 6	Little Salt	Utah
K 14	Little Squam	N. H.
G 20	Little Tupper	N. Y.
O 6	Llancanelo	Arg.
J 13	Lob nor	Asia
G 10	Lobster	Me.
D 14	Lock Raven Reservoir	Md.
C 4	Logging	Mont.
M 14	Lomond	Scot.
A 18	Long	Me.
D 11	Long	Me.
O 4	Long	Me.
I 21	Long	Mich.
I 12	Long	Minn.
E 15	Long	N. D.
N 14	Long	N. D.
H 21	Long	N. Y.
K 14	Long	Que.
D 8	Long	Wis.
G 7	Long Meadow Pond	Conn.
K 20	Long Pond	Mass.
H 7	Long Pond	Me.
J 18	Long Pond	N. H.
D 16	Long Pond	Vt.
F 10	Loon	Me.
F 22	Loon	Wash.
C 11	Lower	Calif.
P 16	Lower Campbell	Ore.

LAKES, PONDS, RESERVOIRS—Continued

Index	Name	Location
F 17	Lower Crystal Springs Reservoir	Calif.
E 9	Lower Red	Minn.
L 3	Lower Richardson	Me.
H 14	Lucerne	Switz.
P 17	Lugano	Switz.
G 13	Luichart	Scot.
P 9	Lure	N. C.
K 7	McConaugh	Neb.
C 5	McDonald	Mont.
M 20	McMillan	N. Mex.
J 6	McNeil	Wash.
D 15	Machias, Big	Me.
K 16	Mackay	Mack.
O 6	Madre	Tex.
G 20	Madre, Laguna	Tam.
E 14	Madu See	Ger.
I 5	Magaguadavic	N. B.
C 4	Maggiore	It.
M 15	Mahood	B. C.
D 20	Maidstone	Vt.
L 22	Mainit	P. I.
G 14	Malgamaj	Swe.
N 11	Malgeak	N. S.
M 19	Malheur	Ore.
J 11	Managua	Cen. Am.
C 2	Manias	Tur.
F 13	Manistique	Mich.
L 4	Manito	Sask.
O 15	Manitoba	Man.
O 20	Manns	Ore.
I 14	Manuan	Que.
F 6	Manuel	Mack.
D 6	Maracaibo	Ven.
K 14	Mar Chiquita	Arg.
A 13	Marcia	N. J.
C 3	Mareotis	Eg.
K 16	Margaret	Mack.
F 24	Marguerite	Que.
I 18	Marion, L.	Fla.
G 10	Marion	Ore.
L 23	Markham	Mack.
Q 10	Marsh	Yuk.
G 15	Mary	Ariz.
L 8	Mascoma	N. H.
I 12	Mashamengoos	Que.
A 20	Mashapaug	Conn.
A 12	Mashipacong Pond	N. J.
M 24	Mashpee Pond	Mass.
I 6	Mask	Ire.
M 12	Maskinonge	Que.
I 6	Mason	Wash.
K 14	Matawin	Que.
K 9	Matsue	Jap.
G 22	Mattamuskeet	N. C.
G 8	Mattawamkeag	Me.
E 8	Maunior	Mack.
M 17	Maurepas	La.
D 13	Maxinkuckee	Ind.
K 10	Mayo	Yuk.
L 24	Mayran, Laguna de	Coa.
E 21	Meacham	N. Y.
O 23	Mead	Nev.
J 21	Meddybemps	Me.
D 24	Medicine	Mont.
E 20	Melrhir, Shott	Alg.
J 21	Melville	Ont.
E 11	Melvin	Ire.
A 16	Memphremagog	Vt.
K 20	Mendota	Wis.
C 20	Menzala	Eg.
D 15	Merced	Calif.
E 19	Merouan, Shott	Alg.
F 13	Meshanticut	R. I.
C 10	Metcalf Pond	Vt.
B 6	Miccosukee	Fla.
F 17	Michigan	U. S.
B 11	Middle Alkali	Calif.
J 14	Mille Lacs	Minn.
E 13	Millinocket	Me.
G 14	Millinocket	Me.
D 16	Millsfield Pond	N. H.
J 8	Miltona	Minn.
N 11	Mink	Mack.
N 21	Minnetonka	Minn.
L 7	Minnewaska	Minn.
L 9	Miosen	Nor.
I 23	Mira	N. S.
J 20	Miraflores	C. Z.
K 24	Mirim	Ur.
G 14	Mississauga	Ont.
L 8	Mistassini	Ont.
I 15	Mitchell	Ala.
H 14	Moberly	B. C.
L 18	Molasses Pond	Me.
D 23	Moncouche	Que.
H 12	Mono	Calif.
B 12	Monomonac	Mass.
J 8	Montreal	Sask.
K 10	Moose	Me.
J 13	Moose	Man.
G 9	Moosehead	Me.
G 7	Moose Lake Reservoir	Wis.
D 14	Mooseleuk	Me.
K 3	Mooselookneguntic	Me.
K 19	Mopang Pond	Me.
H 6	Morat	Switz.
J 16	Moses	Wash.
D 12	Mud	Calif.
M 19	Mud	Ida.
B 17	Mud	Me.
E 4	Mud	Nev.
H 5	Mud Pond	Me.
H 17	Mullet	Mich.
E 12	Munsungan	Me.
E 11	Müritz See	Ger.
P 14	Murray	Okla.
H 22	Murray	Que.
N 9	Muskegon	Mich.
F 11	Muskoka	Ont.
D 12	Musquacook	Me.
M 17	Mweru	Africa
L 2	Mystic	Mass.
G 12	Nahmakanta	Me.
J 4	Nahwatel	Wash.
N 9	Nakmek	Alaska
F 7	Namakagon	Wis.
B 20	Narocz	Pol.
H 12	Nasworthy	Tex.
D 20	Neagh	N. Ire.
E 8	Nellie	Que.
H 13	Nemiscachi	Que.
E 10	Nepaug Reservoir	Conn.
I 13	Ness	Scot.
E 16	Netsalik	Can.
I 5	Neuchatel	Switz.
K 3	Neversink Pond	Conn.
I 6	New Fork	Wyo.
L 12	Newfound	N. H.

LAKES, PONDS, RESERVOIRS—Continued

Index	Name	Location
O 15	Ngami	Bech.
L 13	Nicaragua	Cen. Am.
J 17	Nicatous	Me.
E 18	Nicolet	Mich.
H 9	Nimrod Reservoir	Ark.
N 8	Ninigret Pond	R. I.
K 10	Nipigon	Ont.
A 11	Nipissing	Ont.
J 19	Nippenicket Pond	Mass.
M 8	Niriz	Iran.
E 8	Niwelin	Mack.
M 12	Nominingue	Que.
J 21	Nonguit Pond	R. I.
A 13	Norfolk	Ark.
E 15	North Indian	Man.
K 7	North Twin	Wis.
B 20	Norton Pond	Vt.
M 9	Norway	Minn.
B 9	Nottely Reservoir	Ga.
E 21	Noxontown Pond	Del.
H 4	Noyes Pond	Mass.
N 19	Nyasa	Africa
F 6	Obaska	Que.
A 13	Obatogamau	Que.
L 9	Odell	Ore.
M 14	Ohridsko	Yugo.
P 15	Okanagan	B. C.
K 20	Okeechobee	Fla.
E 17	Omak	Wash.
C 22	Onatchiway	Que.
I 11	Onawa	Me.
F 9	Onega	Sov. Un.
L 15	Oneida	N. Y.
D 12	Onkammis	Que.
E 2	Onota	Mass.
F 21	Ontario	U. S.
K 10	Ootsa	B. C.
H 7	Opekwan	Que.
C 15	Opeongo	Ont.
E 14	Orange	Fla.
K 11	Ordway	N. D.
J 6	Oromocto	N. B.
Q 14	Orta	Switz.
K 8	Osakis	Minn.
A 17	Osoyoos	Wash.
K 18	Ossipee	N. H.
N 19	Otsego	N. Y.
M 4	Ottawa	Que.
I 6	Otter Tail	Minn.
G 15	Oughter	Ire.
N 13	Owasco	N. Y.
I 16	Owel	Ire.
K 17	Owens	Calif.
M 10	Owikano	B. C.
L 23	Owyhee Reservoir	Ore.
I 16	Oxford	Man.
K 11	Ozarks	Mo.
F 1	Ozette	Wash.
I 23	Pachaug Pond	Conn.
H 22	Palfrey	Me.
B 16	Palmer	Wash.
B 22	Pamouscachiou	Que.
B 12	Pang-ong	India
O 7	Panguitch	Utah
H 23	Paradox	N. Y.
J 1	Parmachene	Me.
D 10	Paskagama	Que.
M 10	Pasquiset Pond	R. I.
L 14	Pathfinder Reservoir	Wyo.
Q 11	Patos Lagoon	Braz.
I 17	Paul	Mack.
K 11	Paulina	Ore.
E 9	Payne	Que.
B 11	Pecan	Miss.
I 6	Pelican	Minn.
I 12	Pelican	Minn.
N 17	Pelly	Yuk.
C 5	Pend Oreille	Ida.
G 7	Penobscot	Me.
O 20	Pepin	Minn.
L 10	Pere Marquette	Mich.
G 5	Peter Pond	Sask.
F 15	Pey Lagoon	Bol.
F 22	Phelps	N. C.
G 14	Pigeon	Ont.
A 7	Pinage	Ont.
I 7	Pine	Minn.
K 18	Pinopolis Reservoir	S. C.
I 15	Pipestone	Man.
A 23	Pipmuakan	Que.
K 10	Piscatongue	Que.
J 20	Piseco	N. Y.
F 22	Placid	N. Y.
F 9	Plantagenet	Minn.
J 12	Pleasant	Ariz.
J 21	Pleasant	N. Y.
P 11	Pleasant Pond	N. H.
I 7	Plonge, Lac la	Sask.
H 16	Pocotopaug	Conn.
H 22	Poinsett	S. D.
I 15	Point	Mack.
M 13	Point Judith Pond	R. I.
M 18	Pontchartrain	La.
D 2	Pontoosuc	Mass.
J 5	Poopo	Bol.
J 19	Porcumpus	Me.
C 15	Portage	Me.
D 4	Portage	Mich.
M 23	Poschiavo, L. di	Switz.
J 21	Powder	N. M.
J 9	Pownan	Que.
I 17	Poyang Hu	Chn.
M 15	Poygan	Wis.
M 14	Prespa	Yugo.
J 6	Presque Isle	Wis.
C 13	Pretty Boy Reservoir	Md.
B 4	Priest	Ida.
M 14	Prosperous	Mack.
L 17	Puckaway	Wis.
K 15	Pushaw	Me.
B 8	Puskitamika	Que.
F 1	Pymatuning	Pa.
E 12	Pyramid	Calif.
F 4	Pyramid	Nev.
E 11	Quabbin Reservoir	Mass.
G 12	Quabog Pond	Mass.
I 7	Quasepaug Pond	Conn.
L 15	Quesnel	B. C.
K 23	Quicksand Pond	R. I.
P 12	Quiet	Yuk.
N 9	Quill	Sask.
I 3	Quinalt	Wash.
G 14	Quinsigamond	Mass.
O 6	Quonochontaug Pond	R. I.
G 11	Ragged	Me.
B 14	Rainy	Minn.
K 4	Rangeley	Me.
J 14	Rannoch	Scot.
I 8	Rapides, L. des	Que.

LAKES, PONDS, RESERVOIRS—Continued

Index	Name	Location
I 20	Raquette	N. Y.
D 9	Red	Minn.
L 16	Red	S. D.
C 6	Red Bluff Reservoir	Tex.
L 12	Red Deer	Man.
P 8	Red Rock	Mont.
I 13	Ree	Ire.
L 3	Reelfort	Tenn.
E 11	Reindeer	Sask.
B 9	Reservoir	Okla.
L 20	Reservoir	Colo.
D 9	Rica, Laguna	Tex.
G 7	Rice	Minn.
I 15	Rice	Minn.
I 15	Rice	Ont.
H 19	Richard	Ariz.
F 21	Rideau	Ont.
G 12	Ripogenus	Me.
L 15	Rocher, L. du	Mack.
J 23	Rock	Wash.
F 6	Rogagua	Bol.
G 15	Rogers	Ariz.
H 20	Rognon	Que.
E 8	Rogoaguado	Bol.
L 18	Rogers	Conn.
G 18	Rohrville	N. D.
I 9	Ronge, Lac la	Sask.
J 17	Roosevelt	Ariz.
F 6	Rorey	Mack.
B 6	Roseau	Minn.
E 11	Rosseau	Ont.
B 16	Round	N. H.
Q 9	Round	Ore.
E 19	Ruby	Nev.
K 20	Rudolf	Afr.
I 7	Rush	Minn.
C 18	Rush	N. D.
G 9	Russell Pond	Me.
O 4	Sabine	La.
K 25	Sabine	Tex.
E 23	Saheen	Wash.
M 5	St. Catharine	Vt.
P 24	St. Clair	Mich.
E 20	St. Francis	Ark.
B 15	St. Froid	Me.
E 19	St. John	Que.
F 8	St. John Pond	Me.
H 6	St. Marys	Ohio
C 6	St. Marys, Lower	Mont.
C 5	St. Marys, Upper	Mont.
N 17	St. Peter	Que.
J 10	Ste. Therese	Mack.
B 17	Salem Pond	Vt.
D 8	Saline	La.
G 9	Salt	Tex.
K 7	Salt	Utah
O 18	Salvador	La.
L 9	Sana	Wis.
I 5	San Andrés o' de Petén	Guat.
L 20	San Carlos Reservoir	Ariz.
B 18	San Pablo Reservoir	Calif.
C 18	Sand Point	Minn.
H 16	Sandy	Minn.
G 22	Sanford	N. Y.
B 17	Santa Maria, Laguna de	Chih.
J 16	Santee Reservoir	S. C.
P 3	Santeetlah	N. C.
N 21	Santiaguillo, Laguna	Dur.
M 23	Saratoga	N. Y.
B 14	Sardis Reservoir	Miss.
I 13	Sarnen	Switz.
I 17	Sauvage, Lac du	Mack.
N 20	Savannah	Md.
E 8	Schaffers	Tex.
H 16	Schlawaer	Ger.
I 13	Schoodix	Me.
M 8	School House Pond	R. I.
I 23	Schroon	N. Y.
D 9	Schweriner See	Ger.
I 13	Scugog	Ont.
O 4	Sebago	Me.
K 12	Sebasticook	Me.
I 11	Sebec	Me.
I 14	Seboois	Me.
G 8	Seboomook	Me.
P 20	Sebu	P. I.
B 17	Second	N. H.
E 9	Seg	Sov. Un.
C 4	Selidgi	Mack.
P 22	Selwyn	Mack.
N 14	Seminoe Reservoir	Wyo.
F 12	Sempach	Switz.
O 12	Seneca	N. Y.
J 3	Seul, Lac	Ont.
K 4	Sevier	Utah
I 19	Seymour	Vt.
D 7	Shabogama	Que.
L 9	Shala	Eth.
C 6	Shasta Reservoir	Calif.
N 12	Shawano	Wis.
M 11	Sheepscot Pond	Me.
F 7	Shelburne Pond	Vt.
D 8	Shell	Wis.
C 17	Shenipsit Pond	Conn.
M 12	Sherbrooke	N. S.
K 12	Sherman Pond	R. I.
P 6	Shetek	Minn.
E 14	Shin	Scot.
C 2	Shoshone	Wyo.
C 8	Shoshone Reservoir	Wyo.
O 16	Shuswap	B. C.
F 7	Sifton	Que.
K 13	Siljan	Swe.
J 3	Siltcoos	Ore.
I 22	Silver	Mass.
A 14	Silver	Nev.
K 17	Silver	N. H.
N 13	Silver	Ore.
M 17	Silver	Ore.
K 17	Silvies Reservoir	Ore.
H 12	Simcoe	Ont.
E 12	Simmons Reservoir	R. I.
N 11	Simon	Que.
D 8	Simpson	Mack.
M 14	Skaneateles	N. Y.
E 11	Skeleton	Ont.
C 16	Smet, L. de	Wyo.
N 6	Smith	N. C.
H 10	Snaasen	Nor.
J 14	Snare	Mack.
B 14	Sneech Pond	R. I.
E 23	Snowbank	Minn.
E 15	Snow Shoe	Me.
G 7	Soghlah Göl	Tur.
F 13	Sourdnahunk	Me.
L 14	Spectacle	B. C.
L 18	Spectacle Pond	Me.
I 6	Spencer Pond	Me.
D 23	Spirding	Ger.
A 6	Spirit	Ia.
N 8	Spirit	Wash.
K 3	Spot Pond	Mass.
F 13	Spring	N. D.
I 13	Springfield	Ill.
K 14	Squam	N. H.
D 18	Squapan	Me.
B 17	Square	Me.
J 8	Squirrel	Wis.
H 23	Staffords Pond	R. I.
I 6	Star	Minn.
O 6	Stefanie	Eth.
G 6	Steinhude	Ger.
P 16	Stone Corral	Ore.
C 12	Stony	Ont.
H 16	Stony	Ont.
F 15	Storafven	Swe.
F 5	Storm	Ia.
I 12	Storsjö	Swe.
G 14	Stor-Uman	Swe.
E 24	Strangford	N. Ire.
H 13	Stromsvotn	Swe.
J 12	Stuart	B. C.
H 19	Stump	N. D.
F 18	Success Pond	N. H.
Q 7	Sucker Pond	Vt.
F 16	Sudbury Reservoir	Mass.
O 14	Summer	Ore.
L 9	Summit	Ore.
M 9	Sunapee	N. H.
D 17	Superior	U. S.
M 13	Swan	Me.
P 12	Swan	Minn.
J 6	Swan	Utah
K 10	Tache	Mack.
H 10	Tacla	B. C.
A 5	Tagish	B. C.
J 4	Tahkenitch	Ore.
F 11	Tahoe	Calif.
D 10	Tahoka	Tex.
H 19	Tai Hu	Chn.
D 7	Tamiahua, L. de	Ver.
F 7	Tana	Eth.
Q 10	Taneycomo	Mo.
L 17	Tanganyika	Africa
G 16	Tasha Ho	Chn.
F 19	Tasung Hu	Chn.
M 11	Tatla	B. C.
K 15	Tay	Scot.
N 14	Tegeler	Ger.
N 20	Tencent	Ore.
L 14	Tengri nor	Asia
H 11	Tenmile	Minn.
A 6	Teslin	B. C.
F 16	Tesseyuakjuak	Can.
K 10	Tetachuck	B. C.
N 5	Texcoco	Mex.
B 19	Texoma	Tex.
Q 16	Texoma	Okla.
Q 18	Thekulthili	Mack.
C 6	Thief	Minn.
I 22	Thompson	S. D.
M 13	Thorn	Ore.
K 10	Thun	Switz.
F 10	Thutage	B. C.
G 11	Tigri, Chott	Mor.
L 8	Tikchik	Alaska
Q 25	Timiskaming	Ont.
C 17	Tippecanoe	Ind.
H 7	Titicaca	S. Am.
F 9	Tjele Lang	Den.
F 17	Tohopekaligo	Fla.
J 8	Tomahawk	Wis.
K 9	Tomassino	Que.
P 5	Tonle Sap (Great Lake)	Fr. In. Chn.
I 15	Torch	Mich.
D 17	Tornea Träsk	Swe.
M 18	Trafford	Fla.
G 9	Trasimeno	It.
K 2	Traverse	Minn.
J 16	Travis	Tex.
F 17	Trench	Que.
G 18	Trout	B. C.
P 9	Trout	Mack.
E 19	Trout	Minn.
J 7	Trout	Wis.
E 20	Trout Pond	N. Y.
P 16	Tsu	Mack.
M 12	Tuckers Pond	R. I.
H 19	Tule	Wash.
Q 20	Tumtum	Ore.
H 13	Tung Ting	Chn.
F 9	Turtle	Minn.
J 11	Turtle	N. D.
L 13	Tustumena	Alaska
G 7	Tuya	B. C.
E 8	Tuz	Tur.
A 4	Twin	Conn.
E 20	Twin	Wash.
E 4	Two Ocean	Wyo.
E 14	Tygard Reservoir	W. Va.
L 11	Tzacha	B. C.
H 14	Ubsa nor	Asia
D 18	Umbagog	N. H.
E 16	Umcolcus	Me.
L 11	Unity Pond	Me.
B 10	Upper	Calif.
D 22	Upper Chateaugay	N. Y.
F 17	Upper Crystal Springs Reservoir	Calif.
Q 9	Upper Klamath	Ore.
D 10	Upper Red	Minn.
K 2	Upper Richardson	Me.
D 20	San Leandro Reservoir	Calif.
F 21	Upper Saranac	N. Y.
C 1	Urmia	Iran
G 12	Utah	Utah
G 18	Utikuma	Alta.
E 18	Van	Tur.
E 19	Vermilion	Minn.
I 16	Vermillion	Que.
K 19	Victoria	Africa
H 6	Victoria	Que.
H 10	Vigo	Sov. Un.
E 11	Vodlo	Sov. Un.
F 12	Vozhe	Sov. Un.
I 14	Wabaskout	Que.
G 19	Wabiskaw	Alta.
L 15	Waccamaw	N. C.
G 18	Waco	Tex.
K 9	Waldo	Ore.
G 18	Walen-See	Switz.
I 15	Walker	Man.
I 6	Walker	Nev.
H 16	Walloon	Mich.
D 23	Wallowa	Ore.
K 16	Walmsley	Mack.
B 17	Wanaque Reservoir	N. J.
E 18	Wangumbaug	Conn.
I 9	Wapawekka	Sask.
P 20	Wappapello Reservoir	Mo.
F 4	Waremaug	Conn.
K 19	Warm Springs Reservoir	Ore.
G 16	Warwick Pond	R. I.
I 8	Washeka	Que.
H 20	Washington	Fla.
H 6	Washington	Miss.
H 8	Washington	Wash.
A 8	Waswanipi	Que.
N 7	Watchaug Pond	R. I.
F 11	Waterbury Dam Reservoir	Vt.
E 14	Wateree Reservoir	S. C.
N 6	Waterville	N. C.
O 16	Watts Barr Reservoir	Tenn.
M 19	Watuppa Pond	Mass.
L 5	Webbs Pond	Me.
K 19	Wee Tee	S. C.
G 13	Wenatchee	Wash.
N 11	Wener	Swe.
L 18	Wentworth	N. H.
J 6	West Battle	Minn.
C 9	Wetetnagami	Que.
O 12	Wetter	Swe.
C 8	Whatcom	Wash.
O 19	Wheatland Reservoir	Wyo.
N 19	Wheatland Reservoir No. 3	Wyo.
O 9	White	La.
N 10	White	Mass.
E 20	White	Ont.
G 6	White Earth	Minn.
H 12	Whitefish	Minn.
D 10	Whites Pond	Me.
C 13	White Trout	Ont.
R 13	Whitewater	Man.
H 14	Whitins Pond	Mass.
R 7	Whitman Pond	Mass.
O 22	Wholdaia	Mack.
G 11	Wickabog Pond	Mass.
C 18	Willoughby	Vt.
I 6	Willow	Wyo.
I 20	Wilmington	Fla.
I 10	Wilson Pond	Me.
E 22	Wind	Minn.
H 20	Winder, L.	Fla.
H 16	Windigo	Que.
N 16	Winnebago	Wis.
F 4	Winnemucca	Nev.
L 16	Winnipesaukee	N. H.
F 12	Winnibigoshish	Minn.
M 16	Winnipeg	Man.
M 13	Winnipegosis	Man.
C 18	Wolf	Ind.
C 10	Wollaston	Sask.
H 12	Women	Minn.
B 4	Wononskopomuc	Conn.
H 6	Wood Pond	Me.
A 10	Woods, Lake of the	Minn.-Ont.
L 11	Worden Pond	R. I.
D 10	Wotilmata	Que.
F 11	Wrightville Reservoir	Vt.
Q 9	Würm	Ger.
I 18	Wyagamack	Que.
G 18	Wytopitlock	Me.
K 10	Yawcoo Pond	R. I.
K 5	Yawcoog Pond	R. I.
C 8	Yellow	Wis.
C 4	Yellowstone	Wyo.
F 8	Yojoa	Hond.
O 6	Ypao, Lagoon	Par.
H 12	Zaisan nor	Sov. Un., Asia
L 13	Zilling tso	Asia
G 14	Zug	Switz.
E 15	Zürich	Switz.
K 9	Zwai	Eth.

OTHER HYDROGRAPHIC FEATURES (Bays, Channels, Fjords, Gulfs, Harbors, Oceans, Seas, Sounds, Straits, etc.)

Index	Name	Location
M 9	Aabenraa Fjord	Den.
B 13	Aalbaek Bay	Den.
B 5	Abu Kir Bay	Eg.
G 8	Acre Bay	Pal.
H 5	Adalia Gulf	Tur.
O 5	Aden Gulf	Asia
D 1	Adramyti Gulf	Tur.
G 16	Adriatic Sea	It.
O 20	Aegean Sea	Grc.
P 18	Aegina Gulf	Grc.
I 17	Alalakeiki Channel	Haw.
M 16	Alaska Gulf	Alaska
D 21	Albemarle Sound	N. C.
J 19	Alenuihaha Channel	Haw.
H 10	Alexandrette Gulf	Tur.
P 14	Almeria Gulf	Sp.
H 3	Alsea Bay	Oreg.
N 24	Altamaha Sound	Ga.
D 7	Amatigue Gulf	Cen. Am.
A 20	Anadyr Gulf	Asia
P 25	Anchor Bay	Mich.
L 1	Ancon de Sardinas Bay	Col.
P 9	Aniakchak Bay	Alaska
B 22	Annisquam Harbor	Mass.
B 24	Aomori Bay	Jap.
D 6	Apalachee Bay	Fla.
D 2	Apalachicola Bay	Fla.
O 8	Arabian Sea	Asia
J 9	Arafura Sea	Ocea.
P 19	Aransas Bay	Tex.
P 14	Arcadia Gulf	Grc.
B 5	Arctic Sea	World
Q 18	Argolis Gulf	Grc.
N 3	Ariake Sea	Jap.
R 4	Ariakeno Bay	Jap.
O 14	Arta Gulf	Grc.
J 3	Asinara Gulf	Sard.
Q 14	Atchafalaya Bay	La.
I 17	Atlantic, N. Ocean	World
N 19	Atlantic, S. Ocean	World
M 15	Atsuta Bay	Jap.
H 16	Auau Channel	Haw.
E 11	Authie Bay	Fr.
L 23	Azanian Sea	Africa
N 10	Azov Sea	Sov. Un.
O 4	Bab-el Mandeb Strait	Asia
E 21	Babuyan Channel	P. I.
B 16	Baffin Bay	Can.
N 5	Baffins Bay	Tex.
H 13	Baltic Sea	Europe
I 7	Banda Sea	Ocea.
M 2	Banderas Bay	Jal.
M 22	Banes Bay	Cuba
O 19	Bannow Bay	Ire.
P 19	Barataria Bay	La.
A 22	Barents Sea	World
E 3	Bark Bay	Wis.
L 19	Barnegat Bay	N. J.
M 12	Barnstable Harbor	Mass.
J 3	Barra, Passage of	Scot.
R 10	Barrington Bay	N. S.
B 11	Barrow Strait	Can.
J 6	Batabano Gulf	Cuba
C 9	Bear River Bay	Utah
	Beaufort Sea	Arc.
J 23	Belle Strait	Can.
	Bellinghausen Sea	Ant.
P 13	Bengal Bay	Asia
A 3	Bering Sea	N. Am.
G 5	Bering Strait	Alaska
P 13	Bernard Bay	La.
G 9	Big Bay	Mich.
G 13	Big Sandy Bay	N. Y.
R 20	Biloxi Bay	Miss.
M 9	Biscay Bay	Europe
O 23	Biscayne Bay	Fla.
L 3	Björne Fjord	Nor.
N 18	Black Sea	Europe
G 2	Blacksod Bay	Ire.
N 12	Blanca Bay	S. Am.
P 9	Block Island Sound	R. I.
I 4	Bonifacio Strait	Sard.
D 12	Boothia Gulf	Can.
H 2	Boqueron Bay	P. R.
B 4	Bosporus Strait	Tur.
M 6	Boston Bay	Mass.
I 19	Bothnia Gulf	Swe.
C 10	Boylagh Bay	Ire.
N 2	Brandon Bay	Ire.
B 18	Breida Fjord	Ice.
P 22	Breton Sound	La.
N 8	Bridgeport Harbor	Conn.
O 6	Bristol Bay	Alaska
M 7	Bristol Channel	Eng.
I 7	Broa Bay	Cuba
E 7	Broad Bay	Scot.
M 3	Bukke Fjord	Nor.
M 21	Bulls Bay	S. C.
O 6	Bungo Strait	Jap.
O 11	Bute, Sound of	Scot.
C 17	Button Bay	Man.
N 22	Buzzards Bay	Mass.
H 5	Cabanas Bay	Cuba
P 8	Cadiz Bay	Sp.
O 7	Cadiz Gulf	Sp.
M 5	Cagliari Gulf	Sard.
R 15	Caillou Bay	La.
E 3	California Gulf	Mex.
J 5	Cambay Gulf	India
M 20	Campeche Bay	Mex.
Q 20	Candia Sea	Grc.
K 21	Canso Strait	N. S.
L 12	Cape Cod Bay	Mass.
H 9	Cardenas Bay	Cuba
J 6	Cardigan Bay	Wales
J 15	Caribbean Sea	World
L 7	Carmarthen Bay	Eng.
H 6	Carnarvons Bay	Wales
C 16	Carpentaria Gulf	Austl.
P 8	Casco Bay	Me.
M 23	Caspian Sea	Europe
N 13	Castellamare Gulf	It.
I 22	Cedar Bay	N. C.
H 6	Celebes Sea	Ocea.
R 17	Cerigo Channel	Grc.
L 22	Chaleur Bay	Can.
R 19	Champagne Bay	La.
O 2	Chanco Bay	Chl.
N 22	Chandeleur Sound	La.
L 20	Chaparra Bay	Cuba
Q 17	Charco Azul	Cen. Am.
N 19	Charleston Harbor	S. C.
P 23	Chatham Strait	Alaska
H 14	Chaumont Bay	N. Y.
K 20	Chedabucto Bay	N. S.
I 22	Chesapeake Bay	U. S.
B 15	Cheshskaya Bay	Sov. Un.
K 12	Chignecto Bay	N. S.
D 18	Chihli Gulf	Chn.
P 24	Chincoteague Bay	Md.
J 25	Chincoteague Bay	Va.
Q 18	Chiriqui Gulf	Cen. Am.
J 4	Choco Bay	Col.
N 6	Choctawhatchee Bay	Fla.
K 10	Cienfuegos Bay	Cuba
H 4	Clew Bay	Ire.
K 14	Cobequid Bay	N. S.
K 9	Cochinos Bay	Cuba
G 8	Colpoys Bay	Ont.
O 20	Combermere Bay	India
P 2	Concepcion Bay	Chl.
L 16	Controller Bay	Alaska
F 21	Cook Bay	Chl.
L 12	Cook Inlet Bay	Alaska
Q 19	Copana Bay	Tex.
L 13	Coral Sea	Ocea.
B 19	Corcovado Gulf	Chl.
J 22	Core Sound	N. C.
P 17	Corinth Gulf	Grc.
O 15	Coronado Bay	Cen. Am.
D 16	Coronation Gulf	Mack.
P 19	Corpus Christi Bay	Tex.
P 19	Cote Blanche Bay	La.
E 24	Croatan Sound	N. C.
I 8	Cuillin Sound	Scot.
M 12	Culebra Bay	Cen. Am.
E 17	Cumberland Sound	Can.
P 24	Cumberland Sound	Ga.
C 24	Currituck Sound	N. C.
I 2	Cutch Gulf	India
B 12	Danzig Bay	Pol.
B 1	Dardanelles	Tur.
D 6	Darien Gulf	Col.
B 9	Darnley Bay	Mack.
P 23	Davao Gulf	P. I.
D 19	Davis Strait	Can.
L 12	Dawson Bay	Man.
D 8	Deadmans Bay	Fla.
O 11	Dead Sea	Pal.
M 9	Dean Channel	B. C.
P 19	Delagoa Bay	Africa
H 23	Delaware Bay	U. S.
D 17	Denmark Strait	World
P 1	Dingle Bay	Ire.
C 13	Dolphin and Union Str.	Mack.
E 11	Donegal Bay	Ire.
O 5	Dorchester Bay	Mass.
H 1	Douarnenez, Bay de	Fr.
N 23	Dover Strait	Eng.
H 22	Drogheda Bay	Ire.
M 20	Dry Bay	Alaska
J 22	Dublin Bay	Ire.
P 16	Dulce Gulf	Cen. Am.
G 21	Dundalk Bay	Ire.
F 23	Dundrum Bay	N. Ire.
O 16	Dungarvon Bay	Ire.
I 23	Duxbury Bay	Mass.
D 12	Dvina Gulf	Sov. Un.
L 20	East China Sea	Asia
F 13	Egmont Bay	P. E. I.
K 7	English Channel	Eur.
L 14	Escambia Bay	Fla.
M 8	Estero Bay	Calif.
M 16	Estero Bay	Fla.
D 9	Exuma Sound	W. I.
P 16	Fehmarn Sound	Den.
K 3	Fens Fjord	Nor.
F 14	Finland Gulf	Europe
N 9	Flensburg Fjord	Den.
Q 19	Florida Bay	Fla.
D 3	Florida Strait	W. I.
I 8	Fonseca Gulf	Cen. Am.
K 19	Formosa Strait	Chn.
F 14	Foxe Channel	Can.
B 8	Franklin Bay	Mack.
M 18	Frenchmans Bay	Me.
G 19	Frobisher Bay	Can.
M 9	Fundy, Bay of	N. S.
J 19	Funing Bay	Chn.
I 24	Gabarus Bay	N. S.
E 24	Gabes Gulf	Tun.
G 13	Galilee Sea	Pal.
L 23	Galveston Bay	Tex.
K 6	Galway Bay	Ire.
F 11	Gardiners Bay	N. Y.
L 14	Gasparilla Pass Channel	Fla.
R 6	Gasque Bay	Ala.
F 4	Genoa Gulf	It.
E 7	Georgian Bay	Ont.
E 20	Georgia Bay	Ga.
Q 12	Georgia Strait	B. C.
P 9	Gibraltar Strait	Sp.
E 7	Good Hope Bay	Alaska
D 22	Grande Bay	Arg.
L 24	Grand Manan Channel	Me.
I 14	Grand Traverse Bay	Mich.
K 3	Grays Harbor Bay	Wash.
P 20	Great Bay	N. H.
N 17	Great Bay	N. J.
O 11	Great Australian Bight (G)	Austl.
G 10	Great Peconic Bay	N. Y.
I 8	Great South Bay	N. Y.
P 12	Green Bay	Wis.
B 20	Greenland Sea	World
H 15	Greenwich Bay	R. I.
N 17	Guacanayabo Gulf	Cuba
J 1	Guadiana Bay	Cuba
P 23	Guantanamo Bay	Cuba
D 2	Guayaquil Gulf	Ec.
K 7	Guinea Gulf	Africa
N 19	Hagion Oros Gulf	Grc.
M 10	Hainan Strait	Fr. In. Ch.
F 15	Half Moon Bay	Calif.
R 19	Hammond Bay	Mich.
H 19	Hangchow Bay	Chn.
I 17	Hannah Bay	Ont.
L 4	Hardanger Fjord	Nor.
M 11	Harima Sea	Jap.
D 5	Haro Strait	Wash.
L 5	Hecate Strait	B. C.
I 13	Hillsboro Bay	Fla.
H 16	Hillsboro Bay	P. E. I.
A 16	Honda Bay	Col.
H 4	Honda Bay	Cuba
D 9	Honduras Gulf	Cen. Am.
L 16	Honghai Bay	Chn.
K 4	Hooper Bay	Alaska
I 12	Horsens Fjord	Den.
I 14	Hudson Bay	Can.
G 17	Hudson Strait	Can.
O 18	Illana Bay	P. I.
L 1	Indian Ocean	World
I 11	Indian Pass Channel	Fla.
M 6	Inland Sea	Jap.
Q 12	Ionian Sea	Europe
F 6	Irish Sea	Eng.
Q 4	Isanotski Strait	Alaska
I 19	Ise Fjord	Den.
G 16	James Bay	Ont.
C 7	Jammer Bay	Den.
I 21	Japan Sea	Asia
I 4	Java Sea	Ocea.
J 16	Jiguey Bay	Cuba
I 7	Jiquilisco Bay	Cen. Am.
E 3	Juan de Fuca Strait	Wash.
M 9	Jura, Sound of	Scot.
N 12	Kachemak Bay	Alaska
Q 3	Kagoshima Bay	Jap.
F 13	Kaiwi Channel	Haw.
P 15	Kalmar Sound	Swe.
G 15	Kalohi Channel	Haw.
H 12	Kalvö Bay	Den.
D 12	Kara Sea	Asia
N 7	Karkinitskii Gulf	Sov. Un.
N 18	Kassandra Gulf	Grc.
H 11	Kattegat Gulf	Europe
D 7	Kauai Channel	Haw.
B 2	Kaulakahi Channel	Haw.
D 4	Keweenaw Bay	Mich.
E 20	Kiaochow Bay	Chn.
B 8	Kiel Bay	Ger.
F 7	Killala Bay	Ire.
O 11	Kit Channel	Jap.
E 4	Kogatuk Bay	Que.
K 22	Köge Bay	Den.
A 10	Kola Bay	Sov. Un.
Q 5	Kompong Som Bay	Fr. In. Ch.
D 21	Korea Bay	Kor.
F 25	Korea Strait	Kor.
G 2	Kos Gulf	Tur.
E 6	Kotzebue Sound	Alaska
E 12	Kouchibouguac Bay	N. B.
O 18	Kuma Gulf	Sov. Un.
M 6	Kuskokwim Bay	Alaska
Q 17	Laconia Gulf	Grc.
C 14	Laesö Channel	Den.
P 10	Laholm Bay	Swe.
B 13	Lancaster Sound	Can.
C 15	Laptev (Nordenskiöld) Sea	Asia
B 20	Lauwers Zee	Neth.
A 22	Laxefjord	Nor.
K 13	Lemon Bay	Fla.
C 19	Liaotung Gulf	Chn.
O 9	Ligurian Sea	Europe
C 8	Limon Bay	Canal Zone
Q 17	Lions Gulf	Fr.

Physical Features of the World

OTHER HYDROGRAPHIC FEATURES
(Bays, Channels, Fjords, Gulfs, Harbors, Oceans, Seas, Sounds, Straits, etc.)—Continued

Index	Name	Location
L 5	Liscannor Bay	Ire.
G 6	Little Minch Strait	Scot.
H 14	Little Traverse Bay	Mich.
G 9	Long Island Sound	N. Y.
C 9	Lübeck Bay	Ger.
R 13	Luce Bay	Scot.
N 11	Lyme Bay	Eng.
B 17	Lyngen Fjord	Nor.
D 17	McLelan Strait	Que.
C 10	McClintock Channel	Can.
B 8	McClure Strait	Can.
E 10	McSwynes Bay	Ire.
M 20	Macajalar Bay	P. I.
B 2	Mackenzie Bay	Mack.
G 16	Mackinac Strait	Mich.
O 9	Magdalena Bay	Mex.
E 22	Magellan Strait	Arg.
N 13	Mahone Bay	N. S.
G 2	Makri Gulf	Tur.
B 15	Malangenfjord	Nor.
D 5	Malletts Bay	Vt.
F 15	Malpeque Bay	P. E. I.
R 11	Manar Gulf	India
K 19	Manati Bay	Cuba
I 18	Manfredonia Gulf	It.
F 12	Manila Bay	P. I.
B 16	Manitou Sound	Minn.
E 18	Marcos, South Bay	Braz.
F 13	Mariager Fjord	Den.
P 16	Marmora Sea	Europe
P 23	Martaban Gulf	India
E 21	Massachusetts Bay	Mass.
N 20	Matagorda Bay	Tex.
G 9	Matanzas Bay	Cuba
D 18	Matanzas Inlet	Fla.
B 24	Matias Gulf	Arg.
E 2	Mayaguez Bay	P. R.
R 13	Mediterranean Sea	Europe
B 9	Melville Sound	Can.
Q 16	Messenia Gulf	Grc.
N 18	Messina Strait	It.
I 14	Mexico Bay	N. Y.
H 21	Mexico Gulf	Mex.
C 13	Mezen Gulf	Sov. Un.
L 12	Minas Channel	N. S.
M 19	Mindanao Sea	P. I.
D 11	Miramichi Bay	N. B.
R 20	Mississippi Sound	Miss.
A 7	Missisquoi Bay	Vt.
R 5	Mobile Bay	Ala.
O 15	Monica Bay	Calif.
J 6	Monterey Bay	Calif.
R 19	Montijo Gulf	Cen. Am.
F 10	Morecambe Bay	Eng.
F 2	Moreno Bay	Chl.
P 16	Moro Gulf	P. I.
D 8	Morrosquillo Gulf	Col.
O 19	Mosquitos, Gulf de Los	Cen. Am.
H 21	Mount Hope Bay	R. I.
O 21	Mozambique Channel	Afr.
E 1	Mukkaw Bay	Wash.
K 9	Mull, Sound of	Scot.
P 25	Muskeget Channel	Mass.
G 4	Nabuga Bay	Col.
N 1	Nahant Bay	Mass.
K 7	Nahant Bay	Mass.
I 17	Nanao Bay	Jap.
O 13	Nantucket Sound	Mass.
J 14	Naples Bay	It.
J 17	Narragansett Bay	R. I.
C 3	Nehalem Bay	Ore.
E 19	Nelson Strait	Chl.
E 3	Nestucca Bay	Ore.
D 3	Netarts Bay	Ore.
N 11	New Haven Harbor	Conn.
G 20	New York Lower Bay	N. J.
O 13	Nicoya Gulf	Cen. Am.
M 22	Nipe Bay	Cuba
B 10	Nipisiguit Bay	N. B.
G 2	Nissum Fjord	Den.
N 16	North Channel	Ont.
O 10	North Channel	Scot.
E 8	North Minch Strait	Scot.
E 9	North Sea	Europe
K 4	North Sound	Ire.
G 14	Northumberland Strait	N. S.
H 7	Norton Bay	Alaska
H 6	Norton Sound	Alaska
H 9	Nottawasaga Bay	Ont.
K 19	Nuevitas Bay	Cuba
J 14	Ocoa Bay	Dom. Rep.
E 20	Okhotsk Sea	Asia
F 9	Old Bahama Channel	W. I.
I 13	Old Tampa Bay	Fla.
M 7	Oman Gulf	Asia
N 2	Omura Gulf	Jap.
D 11	Onega Gulf	Sov. Un.
K 20	Onslow Bay	N. C.
I 23	Ore Sound	Den.
K 2	Oristano Gulf	It.
Q 11	Ormuz Strait	Iran
K 6	Orosei Gulf	It.
M 12	Osaka Bay	Jap.
N 11	Osaka Strait	Jap.
L 25	Ossabaw Sound	Ga.
K 24	Otranto Strait	It.
P 14	Outer Santa Barbara Ch.	Calif.
G 8	Owen Sound	Ont.
B 12	Oyapock Bay	Fr. Gu.
I 8	Pacific, N. Ocean	World
N 11	Pacific, S. Ocean	World
G 17	Pailolo Channel	Haw.
P 13	Palk Strait	India
G 10	Paluan Bay	P. I.
H 23	Pamlico Sound	N. C.
P 22	Panama Bay	Cen. Am.
Q 23	Panama Gulf	Cen. Am.
O 15	Paranagua Bay	Braz.
C 21	Paria Gulf	Ven.
Q 21	Parita Gulf	Cen. Am.
E 9	Parry Sound	Ont.
F 15	Patras Gulf	Grc.
F 11	Pearl Harbor	Haw.
A 19	Pechora Bay	Sov. Un.
E 11	Pelly Bay	Can.
C 19	Peñas Gulf	Chl.
N 14	Penobscot Bay	Me.
N 1	Perdido Bay	Fla.
E 8	Philippine Sea	Ocea.
L 7	Persian Gulf	Asia
P 9	Petachalco, Bay de	Mex.
M 15	Pleasant Bay	Mass.
O 7	Plymouth Sound	Eng.
K 23	Pocomoke Sound	Va.
K 17	Policastro Gulf	It.
P 19	Ponce de Leon Bay	Fla.
N 25	Poponesset Bay	Mass.
A 21	Porsangerfjord	Nor.
Q 15	Port Royal Sound	S. C.
L 22	Praesto Bay	Den.
L 15	Prince William Sound	Alaska
H 8	Puget Sound	Wash.
K 6	Quarnero Gulf	It.
N 8	Queen Charlotte Sound	B. C.
P 6	Quincy Bay	Mass.
J 23	Raleigh Bay	N. C.
F 12	Randers Fjord	Den.
G 19	Raritan Bay	N. J.
G 21	Red Sea	Africa
K 25	Rehoboth Bay	Del.
N 19	Rendina Gulf	Grc.
M 16	Resurrection Bay	Alaska
H 12	Rincon Bay	P. R.
H 14	Riga Gulf	Europe
M 16	Rockery Bay	Fla.
F 12	Romsdal Fjord	Nor.
I 5	Ross Sea	Ant.
J 7	Rum, Sound of	Scot.
H 14	Sacket Harbor	N. Y.
N 19	Sagami Sea	Jap.
L 22	Saginaw Bay	Mich.
F 18	Saglek Bay	Que.
C 6	St. Albans Bay	Vt.
O 24	St. Andrew Sound	Ga.
G 23	St. Ann Bay	N. S.
H 4	St. Brieuc Bay	Fr.
M 25	St. Catherines Sound	Ga.
I 20	St. George Bay	N. S.
I 6	St. Georges Channel	Eur.
D 3	St. Georges Sound	Fla.
P 17	St. Helena Sound	S. C.
P 11	St. Josephs Bay	Fla.
D 23	St. Lawrence Bay	N. S.
L 22	St. Lawrence Gulf	Can.
R 17	St. Louis Bay	Miss.
J 23	St. Lucie Sound	Fla.
N 14	St. Margaret Bay	N. S.
O 8	St. Mary Bay	N. S.
H 6	St. Michel Bay	Fr.
I 2	Salada Bay	Chl.
J 16	Salerno Gulf	It.
M 11	Salinas Bay	Cen. Am.
O 21	Salisbury Sound	Alaska
N 17	Salonika Gulf	Grc.
P 22	Salton Sea	Calif.
I 15	Samana Bay	Dom. Rep.
I 20	Samar Sea	P. I.
G 11	Sams Bay	Fla.
O 20	San Antonio Bay	Tex.
H 19	San Bernardino Strait	P. I.
P 11	San Blas Bay	Fla.
N 23	San Blas Gulf	Cen. Am.
Q 18	San Diego Bay	Calif.
D 12	Sandusky Bay	Ohio
E 17	San Francisco Bay	Calif.
C 23	San Jorge Gulf	Arg.
H 19	San Jorge Gulf	Sp.
M 9	San Luis Obispo Bay	Calif.
Q 23	San Miguel Gulf	Cen. Am.
A 16	San Pablo Bay	Calif.
R 4	San Pedro Bay	Calif.
P 15	San Pedro Channel	Calif.
O 11	Santa Barbara Channel	Calif.
P 16	Santa Catalina Gulf	Calif.
O 12	Santa Cruz Channel	Calif.
D 1	Santa Elena Bay	Ec.
N 25	Santa Lucia Channel	W. I.
C 6	Santarem Channel	W. I.
M 24	Sapelo Sound	Ga.
C 1	Saros Gulf	Tur.
H 5	Sebastián Vizcaino Bay	Mex.
G 1	Sechura Bay	Peru
I 17	Sejerö Bay	Den.
H 24	Sendai Bay	Jap.
G 12	Shediak Bay	N. B.
P 10	Shelikof Strait	Alaska
Q 4	Siam Gulf	Siam
H 15	Sibuyan Sea	P. I.
F 3	Siletz Bay	Ore.
G 10	Skagerrak Gulf	Europe
I 11	Sleeping Bear Bay	Mich.
F 9	Sligo Bay	Ire.
D 17	Sloter Sea	Neth.
D 1	Smyrna Gulf	Tur.
K 11	Sodus Bay	N. Y.
K 5	Sogne Fjord	Nor.
E 10	South Bay	Mich.
G 17	South Channel	Mich.
P 9	South China Sea	Asia
G 8	Southtown Bay	N. Y.
G 20	Soya Strait	Asia
O 15	Spencer Gulf	Austl.
M 20	Squillace Gulf	It.
G 15	Sturgeon Bay	Mich.
A 21	Suisun Bay	Calif.
N 9	Sulu Sea	P. I.
M 21	Surigao Sea	P. I.
N 18	Suruga Bay	Jap.
I 14	Suttons Bay	Mich.
N 11	Taganrog Gulf	Sov. Un.
N 19	Taiwan Strait	Asia
J 12	Tampa Bay	Fla.
Q 19	Tangier Sound	Md.
A 12	Tannis Bay	Den.
L 17	Tanon Strait	P. I.
K 20	Taranto Gulf	It.
F 20	Tatar Strait	Asia
K 21	Tawas Bay	Mich.
Q 19	Tehuantepec Gulf	Mex.
R 17	Terrebonne Bay	La.
I 6	The Hebrides Gulf	Scot.
F 20	The Narrows Strait	N. J.
N 15	The Solent Strait	Eng.
E 5	Thisted Gulf	Den.
I 22	Thunder Bay	Mich.
C 3	Tillamook Bay	Ore.
R 18	Timbalie Bay	La.
K 7	Timor Sea	Ocea.
D 18	Tjcuke Sea	Neth.
N 7	Togiak Bay	Alaska
M 20	Tokyo Bay	Jap.
M 9	Tonkin Gulf	Fr. In. Ch.
O 9	Toso Bay	Jap.
N 16	Tottomi Bay	Jap.
I 17	Toyama Bay	Jap.
N 3	Tralee Bay	Ire.
I 7	Tremadoc Bay	Wal.
C 13	Trieste Gulf	It.
I 9	Trondheim Fjord	Nor.
H 22	Tsugaru Strait	Asia
L 3	Tsushima Strait	Jap.
A 24	Tunis Gulf	Tun.
D 17	Tury-Assú Bay	Braz.
K 11	Tyrrhenian Sea	It.
P 12	Ugak Bay	Alaska
E 14	Ungava Bay	Que.
E 20	Upper Bay	N. J.
E 6	Uraba Gulf	Col.
H 15	Uri Bay	Switz.
A 24	Varanger Fjord	Nor.
J 10	Vejle Fjord	Den.
B 7	Venezuela Gulf	Ven.
D 11	Venice Gulf	It.
O 11	Vermilion Bay	La.
D 12	Vestfjord	Nor.
E 23	Vieques Sound	P. R.
O 22	Vineyard Sound	Mass.
J 18	Visayan Sea	P. I.
E 10	Waccassassee Bay	Fla.
K 14	Wakasá Bay	Jap.
B 1	Walvis Bay	U. S. Afr.
	Weddell Sea	Ant.
K 15	Wellfleet Harbor	Mass.
I 19	Wenchow Bay	Chn.
E 16	Whitefish Bay	Mich.
R 12	Whitefish Bay	Wis.
C 16	White Sea	Europe
P 20	Whitewater Bay	Fla.
R 15	Wigtown Bay	Scot.
L 2	Willapa Bay	Wash.
K 3	Winchester Bay	Ore.
H 11	Windward Channel	W. I.
E 11	Winyah Bay	S. C.
E 11	Withlacoochee Bay	Fla.
M 18	Yakutat Bay	Alaska
G 4	Yaquina Bay	Ore.
P 3	Yatsushiro Bay	Jap.
J 19	Yellow Sea	Asia
P 15	Youghal Bay	Ire.

Altitudes of Selected World Cities

Key to Abbreviations Used Below

A. E. Sud	Anglo-Egyptian Sudan	Del	Delaware	Ind	Indiana
Afg	Afghanistan	Den	Denmark	Ire	Ireland
Ala	Alabama	Eng	England	Kan	Kansas
Arg	Argentina	Eth	Ethiopia	Ky	Kentucky
Ariz	Arizona	Fla	Florida	La	Louisiana
Austl	Australia	Fr. Eq. Afr	French Equatorial Africa	Leb	Lebanon
Aus	Austria	Fr. Gu	French Guiana	Lux	Luxembourg
Bel. Cong	Belgian Congo	Fr. In. Ch	French Indochina	Madag	Madagascar
Br. Gu	British Guiana	Fr. Som	French Somaliland	Mal. St	Malay States
Br. Som	British Somaliland	Ga	Georgia	Manch	Manchuria
Calif	California	Ger	Germany	Md	Maryland
Colo	Colorado	Gt. Brit	Great Britain	Mass	Massachusetts
Conn	Connecticut	Guat	Guatemala	Mich	Michigan
Czech	Czechoslovakia	Ill	Illinois	Minn	Minnesota
D. C.	District of Columbia				

Abbr.	Meaning	Abbr.	Meaning
Mo	Missouri	Som	Somaliland
N. Car	North Carolina	Sov. Un	Soviet Union
Neth	Netherlands	S. W. Afr	Southwest Africa
Neth. Ind	Netherlands Indies	Switz	Switzerland
Newf	Newfoundland	Tenn	Tennessee
N. J	New Jersey	Ur	Uruguay
N. Mex	New Mexico	U. S.	United States
N. Y	New York	U. S. Afr	Union of South Africa
N. Z	New Zealand	Va	Virginia
Okla	Oklahoma	Ven	Venezuela
Ore	Oregon	Wash	Washington
Pa	Pennsylvania	Wis	Wisconsin
Par	Paraguay	Wyo	Wyoming
R. I.	Rhode Island	Yugo	Yugoslavia

Name	Feet
A	
Aachen (Aix-la-Chapelle), Ger.	580
Aberdeen, Scotland	25
Addis Ababa, Eth.	9850
Adelaide, Australia	35
Aden, Aden	50
Agra, India	650
Aguascalientes, Mex.	6280
Ahmedabad, India	260
Aix-la-Chapelle, see Aachen, Ger.	
Ajmer, India	1685
Akron (Ohio), U. S.	875
Albany (N. Y.), U. S.	20
Albuquerque (N. Mex.), U. S.	4950
Alep (Aleppo), Syria	1400
Alexandria, Egypt	25
Alger (Algiers), Algeria	200
Allahabad, India	315
Amman (Philadelphia), Transjordan	2400
Amoy, China	50
Amritsar, India	740
Amsterdam, Neth.	40
Andorra la Vieja, Andorra	3425
Angers, France	75
Ankara (Angora), Turkey	2250
Anking, China	540
Anvers (Antwerp), Belgium	30
Asheville (N. Car.), U. S.	1985
Astrakhan, Sov. Un.	-50
Asuncion, Par.	253
Athēnai (Athens), Greece	300
Atlanta (Ga.), U. S.	1050
Augsburg, Ger.	1340
B	
Baghdad, Iraq	125
Bala, see Salvador, Brazil	
Baile Atha Cliath (Dublin), Ire.	30
Baku, Sov. Un.	115
Baltimore (Md.), U. S.	20
Bangalore, India	3100
Bangkok, Siam	40
Barcelona, Spain	25
Bari, Italy	30
Basel, Switz.	685
Batavia, Neth. Ind.	25
Beirut, see Beyrouth, Leb.	
Belem (Para), Brazil	25
Belfast, N. Ireland	6
Belgrade, see Beograd, Yugo.	
Belize, Brit. Honduras	15
Benares, India	255
Beograd (Belgrade), Yugo.	2270
Berbera, Br. Som.	50
Berlin, Germany	115
Bern, Switz.	1788
Beyrouth (Beirut), Leb.	25
Bilbao, Spain	100
Birmingham, Eng.	400
Birmingham (Ala.), U. S.	600
Blackburn, Eng.	650
Bochum, Ger.	325
Bogota, Colombia	8630
Bologna, Italy	165
Bolton, England	480
Bombay, India	25
Bordeaux, France	40
Boston (Mass.), U. S.	21
Bournemouth, Eng.	25
Bradford, England	635
Braunschweig (Brunswick), Ger.	236
Brazzaville, Fr. Eq. Afr.	1055
Bremen, Germany	75
Breslau, Pol.	390
Bridgeport (Conn.), U. S.	10
Brighton, England	160
Brisbane, Austl.	25
Bristol, England	190
Brno, Czech	745
Brunswick, see Braunschweig, Ger.	
Bruxelles (Brussels), Belgium	190
Bucuresti (Bucharest), Romania	276
Budapest, Hungary	450
Buenos Aires, Arg.	45
Buffalo (N. Y.), U. S.	585
Bydgoszcz, Poland	320
C	
Cairo, Egypt	300
Calcutta, India	85
Cambridge (Mass.), U. S.	30
Camden (N. J.), U. S.	30
Campinas, Brazil	2220
Campos, Brazil	69
Canberra, Austl.	2000
Canton, China	50
Canton (Ohio), U. S.	1030
Capetown, U. S. Afr.	25
Carácas, Ven.	3164
Cardiff, Gt. Brit.	75
Cartagena, Spain	25
Catania, Italy	75
Cawnpore, India	400
Cayenne, Fr. Gu.	25
Cernăuti, see Chernovitsy, Sov. Un.	
Cerro de Pasco, Peru	14385
Changchow, China	250
Changsha, China	450
Chattanooga (Tenn.), U. S.	675
Chemnitz, Ger.	950
Chengte (Jehol), Manch.	1630
Chengtu, China	2700
Chernovitsy, Sov. Un.	1040
Chicago (Ill.), U. S.	595
Chihuahua, Mex.	4635
Chisinau, see Kishinev Sov. Un.	
Chita, Sov. Un.	2300
Cholon, Fr. In. Ch.	100
Christchurch, N. Z.	100
Chungking, China	1120
Cincinnati (Ohio), U. S.	550
Clermont-Ferrand, France	383
Cleveland (Ohio), U. S.	580
Cochabamba, Bolivia	8435
Cody (Wyo.), U. S.	4980
Colombo, Ceylon (India)	50
Columbus (Ohio), U. S.	780
Constantine, Algeria	2170
Constantinople, see Istanbul, Turkey.	
Copenhagen, see Köbenhavn, Den.	
Cordoba, Argentina	1240
Coventry, England	325
Croydon, England	5
Cuyaba, Brazil	771
Cuzco, Peru	11440
D	
Dacca, India	70
Dairen, Manch.	80
Dallas (Texas), U. S.	435
Damas (Damascus), Syria	2250
Danzig, Pol.	25
Darjeeling, India	6982
Dayton (Ohio), U. S.	745
Delhi, India	770
Denver (Colo.), U. S.	5280
Derby, England	85
Des Moines (Iowa), U. S.	805
Detroit (Mich.), U. S.	585
Djibouti, Fr. Som.	25
Dnepropetrovsk (Ekaterinoslav), Sov. Un.	210
Dortmund, Ger.	285
Dresden, Ger.	402
Dublin, see Baile Atha Cliath, Ire.	
Duluth (Minn.), U. S.	610
Dundee, Scotland	30
Durango, Mex.	6207
Durban, U. S. Afr.	25
Düsseldorf, Ger.	128
E	
Eastham, Eng.	245
Edinburgh, Scotland	195
Ekaterinodar, see Krasnodar, Sov. Un.	
Elizabeth (N. J.), U. S.	21
El Paso (Texas), U. S.	3695
Erfurt, Germany	650
Erie (Pa.), U. S.	671
Essen, Germany	334
Evansville (Ind.), U. S.	385
F	
Fairbanks, Alaska	512
Fall River (Mass.), U. S.	40
Fatshan, China	50
Fés (Fez), Morocco	1020
Firenze (Florence), Italy	165
Flagstaff (Ariz.), U. S.	6890
Flint (Mich.), U. S.	715
Florence, see Firenze, Italy.	
Foochow, China	35
Fortaleza (Ceará), Brazil	25
Fort Wayne (Ind.), U. S.	790
Fort Worth (Texas), U. S.	620
Frankfurt-am-Main, Ger.	300
Fukuoka, Japan	60
Fusan, see Pusan, Korea	
G	
Garmisch-Partenkirchen, Ger.	2330
Gartok, Tibet	14240
Gary (Ind.), U. S.	590
Genève, Switz.	400
Genova (Genoa), Italy	25
Georgetown, Br. Gu.	25
Glasgow, Scotland	300
Gorki, Sov. Un.	163
Göteborg, Sweden	30
Granada, Spain	2195
Grand Rapids (Mich.), U. S.	610
Graz, Aus.	1170
Greenwich, Eng.	235
Grenoble, Fr.	770
Groningen, Neth.	130
Guadalajara, Mexico	5051
Guatemala, Guat.	4850
Guayaquil, Ecuador	30
H	
Habana, Cuba	30
Hagen, Germany	325
Haiphong, Fr. In. Ch.	25
Hakodate, Japan	50
Halle, Ger.	330
Hamburg, Ger.	75
Hamilton, Canada	306
Hangchow, China	25
Hankow, China	150
Hannover, Ger.	190
Hanoi, Fr. In. Ch.	200
Hanover (Pa.), U. S.	600
Hanyang, China	150
Harbin, Manchuria	530
Hartford (Conn.), U. S.	40
Havre, see Le Havre, France.	
Helsinki (Helsingfors), Finland	25
Hiroshima, Japan	75
Hong Kong (Island Colony), China	25
Honolulu, Hawaii	25
Hot Springs (Ark.), U. S.	607
Houston (Texas), U. S.	40
Huddersfield, Eng.	330
Hull, England	25
Hyderabad, India	1740
I	
Indianapolis (Ind.), U. S.	710
Innsbrück, Austria	2900
Iquitos, Peru	350
Irkutsk, Sov. Un.	1600
Istanbul (Constantinople), Turkey	30
Izmir (Smyrna), Turkey	35
J	
Jacksonville (Fla.), U. S.	20
Jaichan, Tibet	15870
Jaipur, India	1600
Jersey City (N. J.), U. S.	20
Jerusalem, Palestine	2500
Johannesburg, U. S. Afr.	5689
Jubbulpore, India	1500
K	
Kabul, Afg.	7280
Kagoshima, Japan	35
Kaifeng, China	670
Kalgan, China	2550
Kansas City (Kan.), U. S.	750
Kansas City (Mo.), U. S.	750
Karachi, India	25
Karlsruhe, Ger.	360
Kassel (Cassel), Ger.	500
Katmandu, Nepal	4223
Kaunas, Sov. Un.	255
Kazañ, Sov. Un.	125
Keijo, see Kyöngsöng, Korea	
Khabarovsk, Sov. Un.	310
Kharkov, Sov. Un.	350
Khartoum, A. E. Sud.	1252
Kiel, Germany	50
Kiev, Sov. Un.	1000
Kingston, Jamaica	25
Kishinev, Sov. Un.	130
Knoxville (Tenn.), U. S.	890
Kobe, Japan	50
Köbenhavn (Copenhagen), Den.	25
Köln, Germany	118
Königsberg, Sov. Un.	70
Kraków, Poland	800
Krasnodar (Ekaterinodar), Sov. Un.	85
Krasnoyarsk, Sov. Un.	430
Kuibishev (Samara), Sov. Un.	570
Kumamoto, Japan	25
Kunming, China	6080
Kure, Japan	275
Kyöngsöng, (Keijo) Korea	250
Kyoto, Japan	360
L	
Lagos, Nigeria	2
Lahore, India	706
Lanchow, China	7040
La Paz, Bolivia	12200
La Plata, Arg.	40
Leadville (Colo.), U. S.	10190
Leeds, England	245
Le Havre (Havre), France	95
Leicester, England	245
Leipzig, Germany	350
Leningrad (Petrograd), Sov. Un.	25
Leopoldville, Bel. Cong.	1045
Leyton, England	240
Lhasa, Tibet	11800
Lille, France	120
Lima, Peru	501
Linz, Aus.	805
Lisboa (Lisbon), Portugal	285
Liverpool, England	130
Livorno (Leghorn), Italy	10
Lodz, Poland	905
London, England	245
Long Beach (Calif.), U. S.	35
Los Angeles (Calif.), U. S.	340
Louisville (Ky.), U. S.	450
Lowell (Mass.), U. S.	100
Luanda, Angola	35
Lübeck, Ger.	30
Lucknow, India	425
Ludwigshafen, Ger.	308
Luxembourg, Lux.	1200
Luzern, Switz.	1450
Lvov (Lwów), Sov. Un.	1020
Lynn (Mass.), U. S.	25
Lyon, France	770
M	
Madras, India	30
Madrid, Spain	2150
Madura, India	445
Magdeburg, Ger.	177
Mainz, Germany	269
Malaga, Spain	25
Malmö, Sweden	30
Managua, Nicaragua	150
Manaus, Braz.	30
Manchester, Eng.	275
Manila, Philippine Is.	25
Mannheim, Ger.	312
Maracaibo, Ven.	30
Marrakech, Morocco	1600
Marseille, France	30
Medellin, Colombia	4880
Meerut, India	720
Melbourne, Austl.	30
Memphis (Tenn.), U. S.	275
Mérida, Mexico	30
Mérida, Ven.	5415
Messina, Italy	25
Mexico, Mexico	7349
Miami (Fla.), U. S.	10
Middlesbrough, Eng.	30
Milano, Italy	400
Milwaukee (Wis.), U. S.	635
Minneapolis (Minn.), U. S.	815
Minsk, Sov. Un.	640
Mogadiscio, Som.	25
Monterrey, Mex.	1624
Montevideo, Ur.	30
Montreal, Canada	63
Moskva (Moscow), Sov. Un.	625
Mosul, Iraq	800
Mukden, Manch.	560
München (Munich), Ger.	1700
Münster, Ger.	203
Muzaffarnagar, India	790
N	
Nagasaki, Japan	200
Nagoya, Japan	50
Nagpur, India	1125
Nancy, France	225
Nanking, China	640
Nantes, France	100
Napoli (Naples), Italy	25
Nashville (Tenn.), U. S.	450
Newark (N. J.), U. S.	55
New Bedford (Mass.), U. S.	15
Newcastle, Austl.	20
Newcastle-on-Tyne, Eng.	195
New Haven (Conn.), U. S.	40
New Orleans (La.), U. S.	5
New York (N. Y.), U. S.	55
Nice, France	94
Niigata, Japan	50
Norfolk (Va.), U. S.	10
Northampton, Eng.	235
Norwich, England	30
Nottingham, Eng.	235
Novo-Sibirsk, Sov. Un.	400
Nürnberg, Ger.	1150
O	
Oakland (Calif.), U. S.	25
Oberhausen, Ger.	121
Odessa, Sov. Un.	35
Okayama, Japan	200
Oklahoma City (Okla.), U. S.	1195
Oldham, England	450
Omaha (Neb.), U. S.	1040
Omdurman, A. E. Sud.	400
Omsk, Sov. Un.	285
Oporto, see Pôrto, Portugal.	
Oran, Algeria	35
Orizaba, Mex.	4028
Oruro, Bolivia	12122
Osaka, Japan	50
Oslo, Norway	40
Osnabrück, Ger.	210
Otaru, Japan	275
Ottawa, Canada	214
Ouray (Colo.), U. S.	7710
P	
Palermo, Italy	25
Panama, Panama	40
Pará, see Belem, Brazil.	
Paramaribo, Neth. Guiana	20
Paris, France	300
Paterson (N. J.), U. S.	135
Patna, India	170
Peiping (Peking), China	600
Peiraievs, Greece	30
Peoria (Ill.), U. S.	470
Pernambuco, see Recife, Brazil.	
Perth, Australia	25
Petropavlovsk, Sov. Un.	313
Philadelphia (Pa.), U. S.	100
Phoenix (Ariz.), U. S.	1090
Pittsburgh (Pa.), U. S.	745
Plauen, Germany	1335
Plymouth, Eng.	25
Plzeň, Czech	990
Poona, India	1700
Port au Prince, Haiti	25
Portland (Ore.), U. S.	75
Pôrto (Oporto), Portugal	25
Port of Spain, Trinidad	25
Port Said, Egypt	30
Portsmouth, Eng.	25
Potosi, Bolivia	13600
Poznán (Posen), Poland	175
Praha (Prague), Czech	575
Pretoria, U. S. Afr.	4472
Providence (R. I.), U. S.	80
Puebla, Mexico	7150
Puno, Peru	12648
Pusan, Korea	25
Q	
Quebec, Canada	150
Quito, Ecuador	9300
R	
Rangoon, Burma	100
Rawal Pindi, India	1726
Reading (Pa.), U. S.	265
Recife (Pernambuco), Brazil	10
Regensburg, Ger.	1075
Reims, France	300
Reno (Nevada), U. S.	4490
Richmond (Va.), U. S.	20
Riga, Sov. Un.	35
Rio de Janeiro, Brazil	30
Rochester (N. Y.), U. S.	515
Roma (Rome), Italy	95
Rosario, Arg.	65
Rostov, Sov. Un.	100
Rotterdam, Neth.	25
Roubaix, France	100
Rouen, France	90
S	
Saarbrucken, Ger.	625
Saint Etienne, France	1800
Saint John's, Newf.	100
Saint Louis (Mo.), U. S.	455
Saint Moritz, Switz.	6037
Saint Paul (Minn.), U. S.	780
Sakai, Japan	100
Salisbury, S. Rhodesia	4700
Salonika, see Thessalonikē, Greece.	
Salt Lake City (Utah), U. S.	4390
Salvador (Baia), Brazil	200
Samarkand, Sov. Un.	2160
San Antonio (Texas), U. S.	650
San Diego (Calif.), U. S.	20
San Francisco (Calif.), U. S.	65
San José, Costa Rica	3868
San Juan, Puerto Rico	20
San Salvador, Salvador	2178
Santa Fe (N. Mex.), U. S.	6950
Santiago, Chile	1800
Santo Amaro, Brazil	25
Santos, Brazil	40
São Paulo, Brazil	2700
São Paulo de Luanda, see Luanda, Angola.	
Sapporo, Japan	250
Saranac Lake (N. Y.), U. S.	1575
Saratov, Sov. Un.	200
Scranton (Pa.), U. S.	725
Seattle (Wash.), U. S.	10
Sendai, Japan	250
Sevilla, Spain	30
's Gravenhage (The Hague), Neth.	25
Shanghai, China	300
Sheffield, England	325
Sholapur, India	1435
Sian, China	1120
Siangtan, China	640
Simla, India	6944
Singapore, Mal. St.	25
Siningfu, China	8000
Smyrna, see Izmir, Turkey.	
Soerabaja, Neth. Ind.	25
Sofija (Sofia), Bulgaria	1700
Somerville (Mass.), U. S.	15
Soochow, China	150
Sosnowiec, Poland	1000
Southampton, Eng.	40
South Bend (Ind.), U. S.	710
South Shields, Eng.	25
Spokane (Wash.), U. S.	1890
Springfield (Mass.), U. S.	85
Srinagar, India	5130
Stalingrad (Tsaritsin), Sov. Un.	75
Stettin, Pol.	50
Stockholm, Sweden	35
Stockport, Eng.	235
Stoke on Trent, Eng.	515
Strasbourg, France	450
Stuttgart, Ger.	710
Sucre, Bolivia	8900
Suifu, China	1300
Sunderland, Eng.	25
Sun Valley (Idaho), U. S.	6000
Surat, India	100
Sverdlovsk, Sov. Un.	860
Swansea, Wales	25
Sydney, Austl.	25
Syracuse (N. Y.), U. S.	400
T	
Tabriz, Iran	4500
Tacoma (Wash.), U. S.	110
Taihoku, Formosa	275
Tallinn, Sov. Un.	25
Tampa (Fla.), U. S.	15
Tananarive, Madag.	4200
Tashkent, Sov. Un.	750
Tbilisi, Sov. Un.	1450
Tegucigalpa, Hond.	3500
Tehran, Iran	4000
The Hague, see 's Gravenhage, Neth.	
Thessalonike (Salonika), Greece	25
Tientsin, China	40
Tirana, Albania	1500
Tokyo, Japan	30
Toledo (Ohio), U. S.	585
Tombouctou, Fr. W. Afr.	770
Tomsk, Sov. Un.	303
Toronto, Canada	254
Tottenham, Eng.	270
Toulouse, France	490
Tours, France	165
Trenton (N. J.), U. S.	35
Trichinopoly, India	240
Trieste, Italy	30
Tripoli, Libya	25
Tsaritsin, see Stalingrad, Sov. Un.	
Tucson (Ariz.), U. S.	2390
Tucumán, Arg.	1500
Tulsa (Okla.), U. S.	804
Tunis, Tunisia	30
U	
Ulan-Bator-Khoto. Tannu Tuva	4160
Utica (N. Y.), U. S.	415
V	
Valencia, Spain	30
Valparaiso, Chile	25
Vancouver, Canada	38
Venezia (Venice), Italy	25
Verona, Italy	194
Versailles, France	460
Victoria, Hong Kong	25
Vienna, see Wien, Austria	
Vilnyus (Wilno), Sov. Un.	500
Vladivostok, Sov. Un.	100
W	
Wakayama, Japan	60
Walsall, England	460
Walthamstow, England	270
Warszawa (Warsaw), Poland	240
Washington (D. C.), U. S.	25
Wellington, N. Z.	25
Westham, Eng.	270
Wichita (Kan.), U. S.	1290
Wien (Vienna), Austria	550
Wiesbaden, Ger.	470
Willesden, Eng.	235
Wilmington (Del.), U. S.	135
Wilno, see Vilnyus, Sov. Un.	
Winnipeg, Canada	773
Woolwich, Eng.	225
Worcester (Mass.), U. S.	475
Wuchang, China	150
Wuppertal, Ger.	1100
Y	
Yakutsk, Sov. Un.	210
Yokohama, Japan	110
Yokosuka, Japan	50
Yonkers (N. Y.), U. S.	10
Youngstown (Ohio), U. S.	840
Z	
Zacatecas, Mex.	8010
Zagreb, Yugo.	430
Zaragoza, Spain	30
Zürich, Switz.	1360
Zwickau, Ger.	855

PRINCIPAL LAKES, OCEANS, AND SEAS OF THE WORLD AND THEIR AREAS

Lake Location	Area Sq. Miles	Lake Location	Area Sq. Miles	Lake Location	Area Sq. Miles	Lake Location	Area Sq. Miles	Lake Location	Area Sq. Miles
Aral, L., Soviet Union	26,166	Caribbean Sea, W. Indies	750,000	Hudson Bay, N. America	472,000	Michigan, L., United States	22,400	Superior, L., U. S.-Canada	31,810
Arctic O.	5,541,000	Caspian Sea, Asia	169,383	Huron, L., U. S.-Canada	23,010	Nicaragua, L., Nicaragua	2,975	Tanganyika, L., Africa	12,355
Athabaska, L., Canada	2,842	Chad, L., Africa	10,400	Indian O.	28,357,000	North Sea, Europe	221,000	Titicaca, L., Peru-Bolivia	3,261
Atlantic O.	31,529,000	East China Sea, Asia	480,000	Japan Sea, Asia	405,000	Nyasa, L., Africa	10,231	Torrens, L., Australia	2,400
Baikal, L., Soviet Union	13,197	Erie, L., U. S.-Canada	9,940	Koko-Nor(L.),Tibet–China	2,300	Okhotsk Sea, Asia	582,000	Van, L., Turkey	2,500
Balkhash, L., Soviet Union	7,115	Eyre, L., Australia	3,700	Ladoga, L., Soviet Union	7,000	Onega, L., Soviet Union	3,800	Vänern (L.), Sweden	2,150
Baltic Sea, Europe	158,000	Gairdner, L., Australia	3,000	Leopold II,L.,Belgian Congo	1,700	Ontario, L., U. S.-Canada	7,540	Victoria, L., Africa	26,828
Bangweulu, L., N. Rhodesia	2,000	Great Bear L., Canada	14,000	Manitoba, L., Canada	1,817	Pacific O.	63,985,000	Winnipeg, L., Canada	9,400
Bering Sea, N. Pacific	878,000	Great Salt L., United States	2,560	Mediterranean Sea, Eur.	1,145,000	Red Sea, Africa–Asia	178,000	Winnipegosis, L., Canada	2,085
Black Sea	168,500	Great Slave L., Canada	7,100	Mexico, G. of, N. America	700,000	Rudolf, L., Kenya	3,500	Yellow Sea, Asia	480,000

PRINCIPAL ISLANDS OF THE WORLD AND THEIR AREAS

Island Location	Area Sq. Miles	Island Location	Area Sq. Miles	Island Location	Area Sq. Miles	Island Location	Area Sq. Miles	Island Location	Area Sq. Miles
Baffin, Arctic Region	231,000	Greenland, Arctic Region	837,620	Mindanao, Phil. Is.	36,906	Novaya Zemlya, Arctic Region	35,150	Somerset, Arctic Region	12,000
Banks, Arctic Region	25,000	Hainan, South China Sea	13,000	Mindoro, Phil. Is.	3,794	Palawan, Phil. Is.	4,500	South (N. Zeal.), South Pacific O.	58,092
Borneo, Oceania	282,416	Hawaii, Pacific O.	4,015	Negros, Phil. Is.	4,903	Panay, Phil. Is.	4,448	Southampton, Hudson Bay	17,800
Celebes, Oceania	72,966	Hispaniola, West Indies	29,536	New Britain, Oceania	10,000	Prince Edward, Arctic Region	2,184	Sumatra, Oceania	164,165
Ceylon, Indian Ocean	25,332	Hokkaido, Japan	30,000	New Caledonia, South Pacific O.	8,458	Prince of Wales, Arctic Region	15,000	Taiwan (Formosa), China Sea	13,836
Corsica, Mediterranean Sea	3,367	Honshu, Japan	87,500	Newfoundland, North Atlantic O.	42,734	Puerto Rico, West Indies	3,435	Tasmania, Australia	26,215
Crete, Mediterranean Sea	3,330	Iceland, Arctic Region	39,709	New Guinea (Papua), Oceania	342,232	Samar, Phil. Is.	5,124	Timor, Oceania	13,094
Cuba, West Indies	44,164	Ireland, North Atlantic O.	31,829	New Ireland, Oceania	3,000	Sardinia, Mediterranean Sea	9,299	Vancouver, Canada	12,468
Cyprus, Mediterranean Sea	3,584	Jamaica, West Indies	4,450	North Island (N. Zeal.), South Pacific O.	44,281	Sicily, Mediterranean Sea	9,935	Victoria, Arctic Region	60,000
Devon, Arctic Region	24,000	Java, Oceania	50,745					West Spitzbergen, Arctic Region	15,260
Ellesmere, Arctic Region	41,000	Karafuto, Sov. Un.	29,100					Wrangel, Arctic Region	1,806
Great Britain, North Atlantic O.	88,745	Luzon, Phil. Is.	40,814						
		Madagascar, Indian Ocean	228,707						
		Melville, Arctic Region	20,000						

PRINCIPAL MOUNTAINS OF THE WORLD AND THEIR HEIGHTS

Mountain Location	Height in Feet	Mountain Location	Height in Feet	Mountain Location	Height in Feet	Mountain Location	Height in Feet	Mountain Location	Height in Feet
Aconcagua, Argentina	22,834	Citlaltepetl, Mexico	17,360	Huanacuni, Bolivia	19,829	Mauna Kea, Hawaii	13,784	San Francisco, Arizona,U.S.	12,611
Albaron, France	12,014	Colima, Mexico	13,572	Huascaran, Peru	22,188	Mauna Loa, Hawaii	13,680	Sangay, Ecuador	17,465
Albert Edward, Papua	13,222	Colorados, Argentina-Chile	19,846	Hubbard, Canada	14,950	Mercedario, Arg.-Chile	21,884	San Jose, Argentina-Chile	20,067
Albert Markham,Antarctica	10,459	Condori, Peru	18,045	Huelacalloc, Bolivia	19,082	Misti, Peru	19,166	Sarmiento, Chile	20,670
Alestschhorn, Switzerland	13,803	Condoriri, Bolivia	20,043	Huila, Colombia	18,701	Mont Blanc, Italy	15,780	Semeru, Java	12,060
Altar, Ecuador	17,730	Cook, New Zealand	12,349	Illampu. Bolivia	21,276	Monte Rosa, Italy-Switz.	15,217	Shasta, California, U. S.	14,161
Ampato, Peru	21,702	Copiapo, Chile	19,947	Illimani. Bolivia	21,282	Mustagh Ata, Turkestan	24,357	Socompa, Argentina-Chile	19,787
Ancohuma, Bolivia	21,490	Coropuna, Peru	22,802	Incahuasu, Argentina-Chile	21,720	Nanga Parbat, India	26,629	Steele, Canada	16,439
Antisana, Ecuador	18,885	Cotopaxi, Ecuador	19,498	Ixtaccihuatl, Mexico	17,338	Nauhcampatepen, Mexico	18,415	Taapaca, Bolivia	19,079
Apo, Philippine Islands	9,610	Cuzco (Ausangate), Peru	20,187	Juncal, Argentina-Chile	19,965	Niitakayama, Taiwan	12,959	Tacora, Peru	19,521
Ararat, Turkey	16,916	Del Acay, Argentina	20,801	Jungfrau, Switzerland	13,671	Ojos del Salado, Arg–Chile	22,573	Tengri Khan, Soviet Union	23,622
Arjias Dagh, Turkey	12,566	Demavend, Iran	18,605	Kanchanjanga, India	28,146	Ollague, Bolivia–Chile	19,259	Tocorpuri Bolivia-Chile	22,163
Aux Sources, Basutoland	10,761	Dos Conos, Argentina	22,507	Kaufmann, Soviet Union	23,386	Orizaba, Mexico	18,541	Tolima, Colombia	18,433
Bear, Alaska	14,850	Dykh-tau, Soviet Union	17,054	Kazbek, Soviet Union	16,546	Payachata, Bolivia	20,768	Toluca, Mexico	15,448
Blackburn, Alaska	16,140	Elbert, Colorado, U. S.	14,431	Kenya, Africa	17,044	Pelée, Martinique	5,200	Tortolas, de las, Chile	20,018
Blanc, France-Italy	15,781	Elbrus, Soviet Union	18,468	Kilimanjaro, Africa	19,324	Pichu Pichu, Peru	18,373	Tres Cruces, Chile	21,720
Blanca, Colorado, U. S.	14,390	Erebus, Antarctica	13,300	King, Canada	16,971	Pikes, Colorado, U. S.	14,109	Turpungato, Chile	21,490
Bona, Canada	16,422	Etna, Sicily	10,755	Klyuchevskaya, Soviet Un.	16,125	Pili, Chile	19,850	Ushba, Soviet Union	15,409
Bonete, Argentina	21,031	Everest, Nepal	29,141	Koshtan-tau, Soviet Union	17,096	Pissis, Argentina	22,245	Vancouver, Canada	15,700
Borah, Idaho, U. S.	12,655	Fairweather,Alaska-Canada	15,399	La Plata, Colorado, U. S.	14,342	Popocatepetl, Mexico	17,840	Veladero, Argentina	20,735
Byelukha, Soviet Union	14,890	Falso Azufre, Arg.-Chile	22,277	Lassen, California, U. S.	10,453	Porongos, Argentina-Chile	20,512	Vesuvius, Italy	4,012
Caca Aca, Bolivia	20,329	Foraker, Alaska	17,000	Lincacabur, Chile–Bolivia	19,456	Pular, Chile	20,342	Vilcanota, Peru	17,998
Cachi, Argentina	21,326	Forel, Greenland	11,286	Llullaillaco, Arg.-Chile	22,015	Quincy Adams, Alaska	15,560	Weisshorn, Switzerland	14,804
Carstensz, Papua	16,404	Fremont, Wyoming, U. S.	13,785	Logan, Canada	19,850	Rainier, Washington, U. S.	14,408	Wheeler, Nevada, U. S.	13,058
Cayambe, Ecuador	19,023	Fujiyama, Japan	12,395	Lucania, Canada	17,150	Ras Dashan, Ethiopia	14,960	White, Calif. U. S.	14,242
Ceachuca, Bolivia	19,407	Godwin Austen, India	28,251	McKinley, Alaska	20,300	Ruwenzori, Belgian Congo	16,798	Whitney, California, U. S.	14,496
Charles Louis, Papua	18,000	Grand Teton, Wyo. U. S.	13,747	Maipo, Argentina-Chile	17,459	St. Elias, Alaska–Canada	18,008	Wilhelmina, Papua	15,584
Chimborazo, Ecuador	20,702	Hekla, Iceland	5,105	Matterhorn, Switz.-Italy	14,780	Sajama, Bolivia	21,390	Wood, Canada	15,880
Cincel, Bolivia	20,102	Hood, Oregon, U. S.	11,253			Sanford, Alaska	16,210	Wrangell, Alaska	14,005

PRINCIPAL RIVERS OF THE WORLD AND THEIR LENGTHS

River Location	Length in Miles	River Location	Length in Miles	River Location	Length in Miles	River Location	Length in Miles	River Location	Length in Miles
Albany, North America	610	Don, Europe	1,100	Magdalena, South America	950	Parnahyba, South America	850	Tagus, Europe	550
Amazon, South America	3,900	Donets, Europe	650	Marañon, South America	1,000	Peace, North America	1,050	Tapajos, South America	1,150
Amur, Asia	2,900	Dubawnt, North America	575	Mekong, Asia	2,600	Pechora, Europe	1,000	Tennessee, North America	652
Araguaya, South America	1,550	Dvina, Europe	1,100	Meuse, Europe	575	Pilcomayo, South America	1,000	Theiss, Europe	800
Arkansas, North America	1,460	Elbe, Europe	700	Mississippi, North America	2,470	Plata-Paraguay, S. America	2,300	Tocantins, South America	1,000
Athabaska, North America	750	Euphrates, Asia	1,700	Mississippi-Missouri, N. A.	3,988	Purus, South America	1,500	Ucayali, South America	1,100
Backs, North America	600	Fraser, North America	700	Missouri, North America	2,475	Putumayo, South America	900	Ural, Europe	1,400
Brahmaputra, Asia	1,800	Ganges, Asia	1,455	Nelson, North America	1,660	Red, North America	1,018	Uruguay, South America	1,100
Branco, South America	580	Gila, North America	630	Niemen, Europe	550	Rhine, Europe	700	Vistula, Europe	630
Brazos, North America	870	Green, North America	730	Niger, Africa	2,600	Rhone, Europe	500	Volga, Europe	2,300
Canadian, North America	906	Hwang, Asia	2,700	Nile, Africa	4,000	Rio Grande, North America	1,800	Vyatka, Europe	680
Churchill, North America	1,000	Indus, Asia	2,000	North Platte, N. America	618	Rio Negro, South America	1,400	White, North America	690
Colorado, North America	1,300	Jurua, South America	1,200	Ob, Asia	3,200	Roosevelt, South America	950	Xingu, South America	1,300
Columbia, North America	1,214	Kama, Europe	1,115	Oder, Europe	550	St. Lawrence, North America	2,150	Yangtze, Asia	3,100
Congo, Africa	2,900	Lena, Asia	2,860	Ohio, North America	981	Salado, South America	1,000	Yapura, South America	1,200
Cumberland, North America	687	Liard, North America	550	Oka, Europe	914	São Francisco,South America	1,800	Yellowstone, North America	671
Danube, Europe	1,725	Loire, Europe	650	Orinoco, South America	1,600	Saskatchewan,North America	1,205	Yenisei, Asia	2,800
Dnieper, Europe	1,400	Mackenzie, North America	2,500	Ottawa, North America	690	Sava, Europe	550	Yukon, North America	1,800
Dniester, Europe	800	Madeira, South America	1,200	Paraná, South America	2,450	Snake, North America	1,038	Zambezi, Africa	1,600

Largest World Cities
Arranged According to Population

1.	New York, U. S. (Greater New York—11,690,520)	7,454,995
2.	Tokyo, Japan	6,778,804
3.	Berlin, Germany	4,242,501
4.	London, England (Greater London—8,202,818)	4,230,200
5.	Moskva, Soviet Union	4,137,018
6.	Shanghai, China	3,703,430
7.	Chicago, U. S.	3,396,808
8.	Osaka, Japan	3,252,340
9.	Leningrad, Soviet Union	3,191,304
10.	Paris, France	2,829,746
11.	Buenos Aires, Argentina	2,567,763
12.	Calcutta, India	2,108,891
13.	Philadelphia, U. S.	1,931,334
14.	Wien, Austria	1,843,173
15.	Hamburg, Germany	1,647,000
16.	Detroit, U. S.	1,623,452
17.	Rio de Janeiro, Brazil	1,563,787
18.	Peiping, China	1,561,027
19.	Los Angeles, U. S.	1,504,277
20.	Bombay, India	1,489,883
21.	México D. F., Mexico	1,464,556
22.	Nagoya, Japan	1,328,084
23.	Cairo, Egypt	1,311,200
24.	Sydney, Australia	1,267,350
25.	Warszawa, Poland	1,261,000
26.	SaõPaulo, Brazil	1,253,943
27.	Tientsin, China	1,209,696
28.	Canton, China	1,145,285
29.	Kyoto, Japan	1,089,726
30.	Madrid, Spain	1,088,647
31.	Glasgow, Scotland	1,088,417
32.	Barcelona, Spain	1,081,175
33.	Roma, Italy	1,062,861
34.	Budapest, Hungary	1,051,804
35.	Melbourne, Australia	1,016,500
36.	Birmingham, England	1,012,700
37.	Santiago, Chile	993,207
38.	Yokohama, Japan	968,091
39.	Kobe, Japan	967,234
40.	Praha, Czechoslovakia	945,000
41.	Kyŏngsŏng (Seoul), Korea	935,464
42.	Marseille, France	914,232
43.	Montreal, Canada	903,007
44.	Cleveland, U. S.	878,336
45.	Mukden, Manchuria	863,515
46.	Baltimore, U. S.	859,100
47.	Liverpool, England	856,850
48.	Kiev, Soviet Union	846,293
49.	Kharkov, Soviet Union	833,432
50.	St. Louis, U. S.	816,048

Notable Bridges

Name	*River, Bay, etc.*	*Location*	*Type*	*Channel Span, ft.*	*Total Length, ft.*
Ambassador	Detroit R.	Mich.–Ont.	Suspension	1,850	3,640
Austerlitz	Seine R.	Paris, Fr.	Arch		459
Bear Mountain	Hudson R.	New York	Suspension	1,632	2,257
Brooklyn	East R.	New York	Suspension	1,595	5,990
Bulwayo	Sabi R.	S. Rhodesia	Girder		1,080
Britannia	Menai Str.	Wales	Girder	459	1,500
Cairo	Ohio R.	Ill.–Ky.	Simple Truss	523	20,461
Carquinez	Carquinez Str.	Calif.	Cantilever	1,100	4,482
Central R. R. of N. J.	Newark Bay	N. Y.–N. J.	Cantilever	660	7,411
Charleston	Cooper R.	S. Car.	Cantilever	1,050	15,840
Cologne	Rhine R.	Germany	Suspension		605
Coos Bay	Coos Bay	Oregon	Cantilever	793	5,337
Delaware River	Delaware R.	Pa.–N. J.	Suspension	1,750	4,500
De Waal River	De Waal R.	Neth.			2,994
Düsseldorf	Rhine R.	Germany	Arch		595
Forth	Firth of Forth	Scotland	Cantilever	1,710	8,098
Gandy	Old Tampa Bay	Florida	Double bascule		13,200
George Washington	Hudson R.	N. Y.–N. J.	Suspension	3,500	5,600
Golden Gate	San Francisco Bay	Calif.	Suspension		8,940
Hell Gate	East R.	New York	Arch	977	18,000
Ia.–Ill. Memorial	Mississippi R.	Ia.–Ill.	Suspension	1,480	5,552
Ironton	Ohio R.	Ohio	Cantilever	705	2,526
Khabarovsk	Amur R.	Sov. Un.			7,593
Kill Van Kull	Kill Van Kull	N. Y.–N. J.	Steel Arch	1,675	7,040
Little Belt	Little Belt Str.	Denmark			3,960
London	Thames R.	London, Eng.	Arch	152	1,005
Louisville–Jeffersonville	Ohio R.	Ind.–Ky.	Girder	538	9,358
Lower Zambezi	Lower Zambezi R.	Mozambique	Girder		12,064
Manhattan	East R.	New York	Suspension	1,470	6,855
McKinley	Mississippi R.	St. Louis, Mo.	Girder	1,500	3,700
Memphis	Mississippi R.	Arkansas-Tenn.	Cantilever	790	9,240
Menai	Menai Str.	Wales	Suspension	580	1,150
Metropolis	Ohio R.	Ill.–Ky.	Girder	720	5,592
Mirabeau	Seine R.	Paris, Fr.	Cantilever		306
M. K. T.	Missouri R.	Boonville, Mo.	Lift Span		1,638
Montreal Harbor	St. Lawrence R.	Canada	Cantilever	1,097	11,220
Municipal (St. Louis)	Mississippi R.	Mo.–Ill.	Simple Truss	668	18,258
Newport News-James R.	James R.	Va.	Vertical Lift		25,271
New Orleans (Huey Long)	Mississippi R.	Louisiana	Cantilever	440	3,525
Peace	Niagara R.	New York	Simple Truss	360	4,150
Pensacola	Pensacola Bay, Sta. Rosa Sd.	Florida	Arch		21,120
Ponchartrain	Lake Ponchartrain	Louisiana	Arch		26,400
Poughkeepsie	Hudson R.	New York	Suspension	1,500	4,072
Puente Cuscatlan	Lempa R.	Salvador	Suspension	820	1,350
Quebec	St. Lawrence R.	Canada	Cantilever	1,800	3,741
Queensboro	East R.	New York	Cantilever	1,182	7,440
Rainbow	Niagara R.	N. Y.–Can.	Arch	950	
Saint John's	Willamette	Oregon	Suspension	1,207	
San Francisco–Oakland	San Francisco Bay	Calif.	Suspension	2,310	22,720
Storström	Masned Sund	Denmark	Girder		10,530
Sydney	Sydney Harbor	Australia	Steel Arch	1,650	3,770
Tay Viaduct	Tay R.	Scotland	Girder	245	10,780
Thousand Islands	St. Lawrence R.	N. Y.–Can.	Suspension	800 & 750	36,960
Tower	Thames R.	London, Eng.	Suspension-bascule		940
Traneberg		Stockholm, Swe.	Concrete		600
Tri-Boro	Harlem R., Hell Gate, Little Hell Gate, Randalls & Wards Is.	New York	Suspension	2,900	17,500
Victoria Falls	Zambezi R.	U. S. Africa	Arch	500	
Williamsburg	East R.	New York	Suspension	1,600	7,308

Principal Ship Canals

Name	*Location*	*Year Completed*	*Length Miles*	*Depth Feet*	*Width Feet*
Amsterdam	(Neth.)	1876	16½	23	88
Baltic-White Sea	(Sov. Un.)	1933	152		
Beaumont-Port Arthur	(U. S.)	1926	48	30	250
Cape Cod	(U. S.)	1914	8	25	150
Corinth	(Greece)	1893	4	26¼	72
Elbe and Trave	(Ger.)	1900	41	10	72
Göta	(Sweden)	1832	115	10	47
Kiel	(Ger.)	1895	61	45	150
Kronstadt-Leningrad	(Sov. Un.)	1890	16	20½	220
Manchester	(Eng.)	1894	35½	26	120
New Orleans Industrial	(U. S.)	1921	6	30	150
Panama	Canal Zone	1914	50½	45	300
Princess Juliana	(Neth.)	1935	20	16	52
Sault Ste. Marie	(U. S.)	1855	1.6	22	100
Sault Ste. Marie	(Canada)	1895	1.11	20¼	142
Suez	(Egypt)	1869	100	30	147
Welland	(Canada)	1932	27½	25	200

Tallest Structures

Structure	*Location*	*Height in Feet*
A. I. U. Citadel (Bldg.)	Columbus, U. S.	555
American Furniture Mart Bldg.	Chicago, U. S.	474
Amiens Cathedral	Amiens, France	384
Baltimore Trust Bldg.	Baltimore, U. S.	500
Bank Bldg.	New York, U. S.	513
Bankers Trust Bldg.	New York, U. S.	539
Bank of Manhattan Bldg.	New York, U. S.	838
Board of Trade Bldg.	Chicago, U. S.	610
Book Tower (Bldg.)	Detroit, U. S.	473
Capitol Dome	Washington, D. C., U. S.	288
Carbide and Carbon Bldg.	Chicago, U. S.	502
Carew Tower (Bldg.)	Cincinnati, U. S.	574
Carlyle Bldg.	New York, U. S.	570
Chanin Bldg.	New York, U. S.	680
Chase National Bank Bldg.	New York, U. S.	513
Chrysler Bldg.	New York, U. S.	1,046
City Bank Farmers Trust Bldg.	New York, U. S.	686
City Hall Tower (Bldg.)	Philadelphia, U. S.	548
Cologne Cathedral	Köln (Cologne), Ger.	512
Consolidated Gas Bldg.	New York, U. S.	514
Continental Bank Bldg.	New York, U. S.	558
Daily News Bldg.	New York, U. S.	500
Eiffel Tower	Paris, France	985
Empire State Bldg.	New York, U. S.	1,248
Equitable Trust Bldg.	New York, U. S.	550
Fidelity National Bank Bldg.	Kansas City, U. S.	475
Field Estate Bldg.	Chicago, U. S.	535
Five Hundred Fifth Ave. Bldg.	New York, U. S.	697
Florence Cathedral	Firenze (Florence), It.	387
Foreman National Bank Bldg.	Chicago, U. S.	479
Foshay Bldg.	Minneapolis, U. S.	496
General Electric Bldg.	New York, U. S.	570
Gulf Bldg.	Pittsburgh, U. S.	584
Irving Trust Bldg.	New York, U. S.	627
K. C. Power and Light Bldg.	Kansas City, U. S.	475
Kopper's Bldg.	Pittsburgh, U. S.	447
La Salle-Wacker Bldg.	Chicago, U. S.	491
Lincoln Bldg.	New York, U. S.	638
Mather Tower (Bldg.)	Chicago, U. S.	519
Medinah Bldg.	Chicago, U. S.	475
Metropolitan Life Bldg.	New York, U. S.	700
Milan Cathedral	Milano (Milan), It.	360
Morrison Hotel Bldg.	Chicago, U. S.	526
Municipal Bldg.	New York, U. S.	580
Navarre Bldg.	New York, U. S.	513
Nelson Towers (Bldg.)	New York, U. S.	525
New York Central Bldg.	New York, U. S.	560
New York Life Bldg.	New York, U. S.	610
One North La Salle Bldg.	Chicago, U. S.	530
Palmolive	Chicago, U. S.	468
Penobscot Bldg.	Detroit, U. S.	557
Pisa, Leaning Tower of	Pisa, Italy	179
Pittsfield Bldg.	Chicago, U. S.	556
Pure Oil Bldg.	Chicago, U. S.	523
Pyramid of Cheops	Egypt	450
R. C. A. Bldg.	New York, U. S.	850
Ritz Tower (Bldg.)	New York, U. S.	540
Rouen Cathedral	Rouen, France	465
St. Paul's Cathedral	London, Eng.	365
St. Peter's Church	Roma, Italy	432
St. Stephen's Cathedral	Wien (Vienna), Ger.	470
Salisbury Cathedral	Salisbury, Eng.	404
Saving Fund Bldg.	Philadelphia, U. S.	475
Sherry-Netherlands Bldg.	New York, U. S.	620
Singer Bldg.	New York, U. S.	612
Sixty Wall Tower	New York, U. S.	950
Smith Tower (Bldg.)	Seattle, U. S.	500
Statue of Liberty	New York, U. S.	301
Strasbourg Cathedral	Strasbourg, Fr.	465
Ten East 40th Bldg.	New York, U. S.	620
Terminal Tower (Bldg.)	Cleveland, U. S.	708
Transportation Bldg.	New York, U. S.	542
Travelers Tower (Bldg.)	Hartford, U. S.	527
Tribune Tower	Chicago, U. S.	462
Twenty North Wacker Drive Bldg.	Chicago, U. S.	555
Twenty Two East 40th Bldg.	New York, U. S.	503
Ulm Cathedral	Ulm, Ger.	530
Union Central Bldg.	Cincinnati, U. S.	500
Union Trust Bldg.	Detroit, U. S.	482
U. S. Court House	New York, U. S.	579
Waldorf-Astoria Bldg.	New York, U. S.	626
Washington Monument	Washington, D. C., U. S.	555
Williamsburgh Savings Bank Bldg.	New York, U. S.	512
Woolworth Bldg.	New York, U. S	792

Principal Waterfalls

Name	*Location*	*Height in Feet*
Angel	Venezuela	3,000
Aughrabies	Union of South Africa	450
Bridal Veil	Calif., United States	620
Chamberlain	British Guiana	310
Chirombo	Northern Rhodesia	880
Fairy	Wash., United States	700
Gastein, Lower	(Austria) Ger.	280
Gavarnie	France	1,385
Gersoppa	India	830
Giessbach	Switzerland	980
Gollinger	(Austria) Ger.	203
Grand	Labrador	315
Granite	Wash., United States	350
Guayra	Brazil-Paraguay	375
Handeck	Switzerland	240
Handöl	Sweden	148
Harspränget	Sweden	240
Herval Cascades	Brazil	400
Iguassu	Argentina-Brazil	210
Illilouette	Calif., United States	370
Kaieteur	British Guiana	822
Kalambo	Northern Rhodesia	740
Krimmler	(Austria) Ger.	1,246
Kukenaam	British Guiana	2,000
Maletsunyane	Basutoland	650
Maradalsfos	Norway	640
Marina	British Guiana	495
Minnehaha	Minn., United States	50
Missouri	Mont., United States	90
Montmorenci	Que., Canada	265
Multnomah	Ore., United States	850
Murchison	Uganda	120
Narada	Wash., United States	168
Nevada	Calif., United States	594
Niagara	United States-Canada	167
Panlo Affonso	Brazil	266
Pissevache	Switzerland	215
Reichenbach	Switzerland	300
Ribbon	Calif., United States	1,612
Rjukanfos	Norway	490
Roraima	British Guiana	2,000
Schaffhausen	Switzerland	100
Seven Falls	Colo., United States	266
Shoshone	Idaho, United States	200
Silver Strand	Calif., United States	1,170
Skjaeggedalsfos	Norway	533
Skykjedalsfos	Norway	650
Sluiskin	Wash., United States	300
Snoqualmie	Wash., United States	270
Splendor-of-Sun	Japan	350
Staubbach	Switzerland	980
Stirling	New Zealand	510
Stora Sjöfallet	Sweden	130
Sutherland	New Zealand	1,904
Takkakaw	Brit. Col., Canada	1,300
Taughannock	N. Y., United States	215
Tequendama	Colombia	480
Terni	Italy	650
Tower	Wyo., United States	132
Trümmelbach	Switzerland	950
Tugela	Union of South Africa	1,800
Twin	Idaho, United States	180
Vernal	Calif., United States	317
Vettifos	Norway	850
Victoria	Southern Rhodesia	343
Virginia	N. W. Ter., Canada	315
Vöringsfos	Norway	471
Yellowstone, Lower	Mont., United States	310
Yellowstone, Upper	Mont., United States	110
Yosemite, Lower	Calif., United States	320
Yosemite, Middle	Calif., United States	626
Yosemite, Upper	Calif., United States	1,430

Seven Wonders of the Ancient World

The name, Seven Wonders of the Ancient World, is said to have been applied by Antipater of Sidon to a selection of man-made works of art in about the 2nd century B.C. Later lists were, of course, recorded by other critics, most of them being in more or less agreement as to the greatest masterpieces of our early civilization.

The Seven Wonders include 1—The Pyramids of Egypt. 2—The Hanging Gardens of Babylon. 3—The Statue of Jupiter at Olympia. 4—The Temple of Diana at Ephesus. 5—The Mausoleum at Halicarnassus. 6—The Colossus at Rhodes. 7—The Pharos of Alexandria.

The Pyramids

The Pyramids of Egypt were constructed during the period from the 4th to the 12th Dynasty (previous to 3000 years B.C.), to serve as tombs for the great. They have a polygonal base and triangular sides meeting in an apex, and were constructed of rough-hewn stone blocks held together with a small amount of mortar. Inside the pyramids and usually below the ground level was built the sepulchral room, reached in every case by a passage from the north. The entrance was carefully sealed and in many cases the passages were blocked with sealed partitions to give the impression that there were no rooms beyond.

The largest of Egypt's many pyramids is the Great Pyramid at Gizeh which covers 13 acres of ground and is about 450 feet in height. It served as a tomb for Cheops (or Khufu) and contained several exceedingly well-hidden passages.

Hanging Gardens of Babylon

These great gardens were constructed under Nebuchadnezzar, King of Babylon, at about 600 B.C. and consisted of a garden of trees and flowers, built on a series of arches about 75 feet high. They were in the form of a square and covered about 4 acres. Water for their irrigation was raised from the Euphrates.

Statue of Jupiter (Zeus) at Olympia

The statue of Jupiter (Zeus) at Olympia was made by the Greek sculptor Phidias about 430 B.C. It was a colossal figure inlaid with ivory, and draperies of beaten gold. In the 5th century A.D. it was carried to Constantinople where it was destroyed by fire in 476 A.D.

Temple of Diana (Artemis) at Ephesus

This beautiful temple was located at Ephesus, a vanished Ionian city situated on the west coast of Asia Minor a few miles south of Izmir (Smyrna). The structure was built about 400 B.C. of marble with over a hundred great columns 60 feet high, and covered nearly two acres. In about 350 B.C. it was destroyed by fire.

The Mausoleum at Halicarnassus

The tomb of Mausolus, the ruler of Caria, was erected to his memory by his wife Artemesia about 350 B.C. at Halicarnassus on the east side of the Aegean Sea. It was constructed of marble and greenstone, exquisitely carved and decorated, and around its base were numerous groups of statues. On a pedestal within the building stood a great statue of Mausolus, and the walls surrounding it were covered with beautiful friezes depicting the outstanding historical events of his reign. An earthquake is supposed to have destroyed the Mausoleum.

The Colossus of Rhodes

The Colossus of Rhodes was a huge bronze statue of the sun-god Helios made at Rodi (Rhodes) by the sculptor Chares. While its exact location is not certain, the colossal figure is supposed to have straddled the entrance to the harbor, ships passing between its legs. It required 12 years to construct and stood about 110 feet high. An earthquake about 225 B.C. is said to have destroyed it.

The Pharos at Alexandria

The great lighthouse and observation tower of Alexandria was built during the reigns of the first and second Ptolemys, being completed about 250 B.C. It stood on the island of Pharos in the harbor of Alexandria, and was connected with the mainland by a long causeway. The structure was about 400 feet high, built of marble, and it is said to have cost nearly a million dollars. It was destroyed by an earthquake in the fourteenth century.

Seven Scientific Wonders of the World

The Seven Scientific Wonders of the World were named a few years ago by a group of outstanding scientists and engineers, each of whom made an individual selection. Not only were the ingenuity and perseverance surrounding the discovery of each considered, but the social effects as well. The list includes: 1—Telegraph and telephone. 2—Wireless telegraphy and radio. 3—The airplane. 4—X-Ray. 5—Radium. 6—Anesthesia, antiseptics, and antitoxins. 7—Spectroscopy.

Telegraph and Telephone

The basic principles of telegraphy and telephony were evolved in the early part of the eighteenth century when physicists discovered the conductivity of electric current. Years of experimenting followed, during which time such devices as pith ball, spark, electrolytic, electromagnetic needle, and other devices were tried, the last named instrument made by Joseph Henry in 1831 being the most practicable.

In 1831, Samuel F. B. Morse began a series of experiments that resulted in the establishment of a telegraph line between Washington, D. C., and Baltimore. The first message was sent on May 24, 1844.

The telephone was invented by Alexander Graham Bell in 1876 who described the device in his patent application as an "improvement in telegraphy."

Wireless Telegraph and Radio

The wireless transmission of sound waves had its beginning in 1865 when J. C. Maxwell of England wrote an article on the "Dynamical Theory of the Electromagnetic Field." In the latter eighties Heinrich R. Hertz, a German physicist, carried on a series of experiments, based on Maxwell's Theory, which resulted in the discovery of Hertzian Waves.

Subsequent studies by other physicists on measuring, sending, receiving, and controlling Hertzian waves culminated in G. Marconi's establishment of wireless communication between England and Newfoundland in 1901.

The Airplane

Man's attempt to fly is so old that its origin is lost in ancient legends. The first trials of heavier-than-air craft were confined to models, one of the earliest being George Cayley's in 1706. Others by Henson (1842), Stringfellow (1848 and 1868), and Langley (1896) contributed to a knowledge of design, while glider experiments by Lilienthal and Chanute taught the basic principles of aerodynamics.

Early in the twentieth century Wilbur and Orville Wright began to experiment with gliders. In 1903 they added a light motor to their glider, and on December 17th of the same year, Orville Wright made the first flight.

X-Ray

X-rays or Röntgen rays were discovered in 1895 by William K. Röntgen, a German physicist. He discovered in his experiments that certain radiations in the general spectrum of electromagnetic waves occurred after ultra-violet rays, and that these radiations had the power to pass through many opaque bodies. Not only were these rays visible, but it was possible to obtain an impression of them on a photographic plate after they had passed through a substance. Naturally the value of this discovery, particularly to the field of medicine, can hardly be measured.

Radium

Radium is a metallic chemical element which is present in pitchblende, a uranium mineral. It was first obtained by Pierre and Mme. Curie and G. Bémont in 1898 after years of research. They called it radium on account of the intensity of its radioactive emanations. Due to the action of radium on other elements its value has become securely established, particularly in therapeutics.

Anesthesia, Antiseptics, and Antitoxins

A knowledge of the anesthetizing effects of certain chemicals dates back to Sir Humphrey Davy who, in 1800, discovered the anesthetic principles of "laughing gas." Following that, Faraday (1818), Godman (1822), Jackson (1833), Wood (1834), and Bache (1834) showed that the inhalation of ether vapor had similar effects. However, the discoveries were simply regarded as interesting phenomena. In March, 1842, Dr. Crawford W. Long performed an operation at Jefferson, Georgia, using ether as an anesthetic—the first painless operation in history.

The use of antiseptics as a means of preventing bacterial infection was an outgrowth of the work of Louis Pasteur. They were first employed in surgery in 1865 by Lord Lister, the eminent English physician.

Antitoxins, the formation of antibodies in the system by introducing toxins into it, were discovered in the latter part of the nineteenth century. Many diseases, from which the death-rate was formerly 60 to 70 per cent, have been almost completely eradicated through antitoxins. They are truly a great boon to mankind.

Spectroscopy

Spectroscopy or spectrum analysis had its origin in the works of Gustav R. Kirchhoff and Robert W. von Bunsen, German scientists, in 1859. Under the basic law that each chemical element has its own characteristic spectrum, instruments called spectroscopes have been so perfected that the spectrum is the key not only to chemical composition, but also to the physical condition under which the radiation is excited.

Seven Natural Wonders of the World

Carlsbad Caverns National Park, New Mexico

In the rugged foothills of the Guadalupe Mountains, in picturesque semi-desert country scarred by arroyos and ragged canyons, is the gaping mouth of the largest system of underground caverns known to man.

Most spectacular feature of the Caverns is the Big Room, upon whose floor parties of visitors are of no more consequence than a line of ants marching through a warehouse. It is nearly 4,000 feet long and 625 feet wide, with a ceiling at places 300 feet above the floor.

The ceiling has disappeared under billions of stalactites ranging from needle-like spines to enormous masses whose weight and length cannot be estimated. The floor is lost in formations of infinite variety of size and shape. There are complicated coralline encrustations, branched and delicate—smooth mounds of flowstone 200 feet across supporting carved and fluted domes 60 or 70 feet high—jeweled splash-cups—ghostlike stream poles. The Big Room is but the largest of many chambers and corridors in the Caverns whose myriad beauties and wide variety of formations make it not only the largest but the most interesting of underground wonders. It is ingeniously lighted throughout.

A View in Carlsbad Caverns

Crater Lake National Park, Oregon

Crater Lake National Park, in the heart of the Cascade Range of southern Oregon, is a treasure box of incomparable scenery where visitors long to linger. Breath-taking when first viewed, awe inspiring when its immensity is realized, mystifying in its strange silence, unique in its unbelievably blue color, Crater Lake is truly a wonder of the world.

Geologists tell us that ages ago a volcano, which they call Mount Mazama, raised its cone to 14,000 feet where Crater Lake now rests. Alternate periods of eruption were interspersed with years of inaction, during which glaciers formed on the peak and nosed down the mountain sides, gouging out U-shaped valleys and depositing layers of smoothed boulders. Then something happened to destroy the top of Mount Mazama; either a stupendous eruption blew it off, or the molten lava within subsided and the whole cone collapsed, leaving a yawning crater

Crater Lake, Oregon

several thousand feet deep, whose rim is 8,000 feet above sea level. Falling snow and rain have filled the abysmal depression to a depth of 2,000 feet, forming Crater Lake. Circular in shape, it is surrounded by an unbroken wall of delicately tinted lava cliffs rising abruptly from the water's edge to from 500 to 2,000 feet.

Grand Canyon, Arizona

Human experience knows nothing with which to compare this deepest, widest, mightiest of canyons. That it is from 4 to 18 miles wide from rim to rim—that it is over a mile deep from the northern rim—that its coloring includes every tint imaginable—these are cold statistics. To describe it is impossible. One comes upon it suddenly, without warning. The mingled surprise and awe with which he first beholds the sublimity of its templed depths and the bewildering glory of its gorgeous coloring, the emotions aroused by its inexplicable mystery and utter silence —these are as unforgettable as they are indescribable.

The plateau into which the river has cut is built up of layer upon layer of nearly horizontal beds of varicolored sandstone, shale, and limestone. The Colorado and its tributaries have made, not an empty, straight-sided canyon, but one whose walls descend in seried steps and slopes, with sizable canyons cut back into them. At the

bottom, within an "inner gorge" 1,000 feet deep, flows the muddy river, some 300 feet wide and 30 feet deep, still hard at work deepening and widening the canyon.

Rainbow Natural Bridge National Monument, Utah

Rainbow Natural Bridge is not only the largest known natural bridge in the world, but it is unique in that it has not only a symmetrical arch below, but presents a curved surface above, thus roughly imitating the arch of a rainbow. The dimensions are 309 feet in the clear from the bottom of the canyon and 278 feet from pier to pier. If placed in Washington it would arch over the dome of the capitol with room to spare. Of salmon pink sandstone, its proportions are so nearly perfect that it dwarfs all human architecture of the sort.

The Redwood Trees, California

Fringing the Pacific coast from south of San Francisco to just over the Oregon line, and extending inland 10 to 30 miles to include the western slopes of the Coast Range, is the Redwood Empire, home of the stately redwood tree (*Sequoia sempervirens* or Sequoia immortal), renowned alike for the great age and size it attains, and for the magnificence of the groves in which it grows. It is said that redwoods 3,000 years old have been felled, while growing specimens of 1,200 summers are known to science. Most of those cut have been 400 to 800 years old, in which time they have attained heights of from 200 to 340 feet, with diameters of up to 28 feet, though the average is nearer 15 feet.

Beneath these towering giants of the plant world man walks as an ant at the foot of a geranium. From the deep shade of a ferngrown floor the huge, red brown, fluted trunks shoot straight up to 75 or 100 feet before branching out in a leafy fullness through which shafts of sunlight penetrate like great golden spears.

Sheathed in rough, tough bark from 6 to over 12 inches thick, redwoods are seldom destroyed or even seriously damaged by the intense heat of the furious forest fires which occasionally consume less hardy trees beside them. Within, the wood is reddish grey, close-grained, and soft, easily split and worked. It resists decay and dispels insects.

The redwoods are cousins of the Big Trees or Sequoias (*Sequoia gigantea*), found on the western slopes of the higher, drier Sierra Nevada Range to the east. These two species, now natives of California, are the sole survivors of a genus of huge trees once common to the entire northern hemisphere.

Many of the finest stands of redwoods are preserved in public parks and monuments, of which Muir Woods National Monument just north of San Francisco is one of the most beautiful and accessible. Other lovely groves border U. S. Highway 101 as it traverses the Redwood Empire from San Francisco to Oregon.

Redwoods—the Oldest Living Things

Victoria Falls, Rhodesia

This mighty waterfall, discovered by Dr. Livingstone in 1855, is situated on the Zambezi River, which forms part of the boundary between Northern and Southern Rhodesia.

A peculiarity about these wonderful falls is that the general level of the country is the same above and below the cataracts, the water disappearing into a great fissure or cañon, whose steep sides, 343 feet high, are at right angles to the course of the river. The cleft in the plain is, in some places, less than 400 feet. The actual falls, though over a mile from end to end, are much broken by islands and rocks, so that their edge appears more rounded than is actually the case. A heavy cloud of mist rises constantly from the base of the falls, while their roar may be heard at a distance of many miles.

Yellowstone National Park, Wyoming

Yellowstone National Park, located in northwestern Wyoming and encroaching slightly on Montana and Idaho, was established in 1872. It has an area of about 3,438 square miles and is essentially a broad, elevated, volcanic plateau flanked by high mountain ranges.

Nearly the entire park is remarkable for its hot water phenomena, geysers, colored hot springs, and mud volcanoes. Its geysers are celebrated the world over, because, for size, power, and variety of action, as well as number, the region has no competitor. New Zealand, which ranks second, and Iceland, where the word "geyser" originated, possess the only other geyser basins of prominence, but both together do not offer the visitor what he may see in 2 or 3 days in Yellowstone. Indeed, the spectacle is one of extraordinary novelty. There are few spots in the world where one is so strongly possessed by emotions of wonder and mystery. The visitor is powerfully impressed by a sense of nearness to nature's secret laboratories. Practically the entire region is volcanic. Not only the surrounding mountains but the great interior plain are made of material once ejected, as ash and lava, from depths far below the surface. Positive evidence of Yellowstone's volcanic origin is apparent to all in the black glass of Obsidian Cliff, the whorled and contorted breccias along the road near the top of Mount Washburn, and the brilliantly colored decomposed lava walls of the Grand Canyon. For a long time the chief public interest in Yellowstone centered around its spouting geysers and similar uncanny wonders of a dying volcanic region. Now that good roads and trails have made this great wilderness accessible, its beautiful forests, troutfilled lakes and streams, and its wild animal population attract as many visitors as do the volcanic wonders.

Its mountain scenery is magnificent and Yellowstone Gorge and Falls rank second only to the Grand Canyon in Arizona.

Fossil forests are located over extensive areas in the northern part of the park. The two most prominent areas are in the newly acquired region on the northwest, known as the "Gallatin Petrified Forests," and in the northeast, known as the "Yellowstone-Lamar River Petrified Forests."

The park is also one of the largest and most successful game refuges in the country, elk, antelope, mountain sheep, moose, bison, deer, and bear abounding in large numbers.

Looking Across the Grand Canyon

GEOGRAPHICAL NAMES IN OCCASIONAL USE

A

Aa. Dutch and Danish name for a rivulet or river.

Abyssinia. Former name for Ethiopia.

Acadia. Old French colonial territory now forming Eastern Maine, the Canadian Maritime Provinces, and the Gaspé Peninsula of Quebec. Sometimes confined to Nova Scotia.

Achaia. Ancient name sometimes applied to Greece.

Açores. Portuguese name for the Azores Is.

Afrique Equatoriale Française. French name for French Equatorial Africa.

Afrique Occidental Française. French name for French West Africa.

Agassiz, Lake. Name applied to an ancient (Quarternary) lake occupying the Red River basin of the north.

Alaouites. One-time name of Latakia, one of the former states of Syria.

Albion. Ancient name of Britain. Now used only poetically.

Alexandra Land. A vast region of Australia, in Northern Territory.

Algérie. French name for Algeria.

Allemagne. French name for Germany.

Alp. Name in the Aryan languages sometimes applied to a hill.

Alsace-Lorraine. Region in northeastern France comprising the present departments of Bas-Rhin, Haut-Rhin, and Moselle.

Anatolia. Old name of Asia Minor; now limited to Turkish portion.

Anglia. Name applied to the original home of the Anglians in northwestern Germany.

Antilles. Collective name for West India Islands. Comprises Greater Antilles (Cuba, Jamaica, Puerto Rico, and Hispaniola), and Lesser Antilles (Leeward, Windward, Virgin, etc.).

Antipodes. Name occasionally applied to New Zealand on account of its geographical location being diametrically opposite to the British Isles.

Aragon. A name formerly applied to a kingdom in northern Spain.

Armenia. Name applied to a former country of Western Asia which is now occupied by the Soviet Union and Turkey.

Arroyo. Spanish term for the channel of an intermittent stream.

Atlantis. Name for the legendary continent west of Europe which is said to have disappeared.

Asia Minor. A geographical name for the peninsula in western Asia, now part of Turkey. It is bounded on the north by the Black Sea, on the west by the Aegean Sea, and on the south by the Mediterranean Sea.

Assyria. Ancient Asiatic empire centered at Nineveh in upper Tigris valley. Included modern Palestine, Syria, Lebanon, Iraq, and parts of Armenia and Iran.

B

Babylonia. Ancient Asiatic empire centered at Babylon in Euphrates valley. Included modern Iraq, Syria, Lebanon and Palestine.

Bad. German term for bathing or watering place.

Bad Lands. Name applied to the rough, arid regions of western United States. The largest areas are in the western Dakotas and central Wyoming.

Bahia. Spanish name for a bay.

Baie. French term for a bay.

Balkan States. Countries of the Balkan Peninsula (Romania, Bulgaria, Yugoslavia, Albania, Greece, and European Turkey).

Baltic States. Estonia, Latvia, and Lithuania—republics from 1919 to 1940 when they became part of the Soviet Union.

Banat. Name occasionally applied to the region in Central Europe which is bounded by the Transylvanian Alps and by the Thiess, Danube, and Maros rivers.

Bank. A sub-oceanic elevation rising to within 600 feet of the surface.

Barbary. Old name of coast countries of Northern Africa west of Egypt (now Morocco, Algeria, Tunisia, and Libya).

Barren Grounds. Name applied to the treeless tundra regions of northern North America.

Basque Country. Region on Bay of Biscay, now Spanish Provinces of Vizcaya, Guipúzcoa, and Alava, and French Department of Basses-Pyrénées.

Bayern. German name for Bavaria.

Bayou. Term used in the United States for a lake or intermittent stream formed in an abandoned river channel. It also refers to one of the half closed channels of a river delta.

Belgie, Belgique. Belgian names for Belgium.

Belgisch Congo. Flemish name for Belgian Congo.

Ben. A Gaelic word signifying a mountain in Scotland and a hill or rocky promontory in Ireland.

Bessarabia. Name referring to the region between the Prut and Dniester rivers. Part of Romania from 1919 to 1940 when it was annexed by the Soviet Union.

Big Muddy. Popular name for the Missouri River.

Black Belt. A term sometimes applied to a belt or region in the United States in which the percentage of colored population is greatest.

Black Earth Region. Name sometimes applied to the fertile, black-soil portion of the European Soviet Union.

Bois. French name for a wood.

Bosnia. Name applied to a former Austro-Hungarian country south of the Sava River. Now part of Yugoslavia.

Brasil. Brazilian name for Brazil.

Britannia. Ancient name of Britain.

British America. Name ordinarily restricted to Canada and Newfoundland.

British Central Africa. Old name of Nyasaland Protectorate.

British East Africa. Old name of Kenya Colony.

British South Africa. Old name of Southern Rhodesia.

Brittany. Northwesternmost peninsula of France. Now in Departments of Finistère, Côtes-du-Nord, Morbihan, Ille-et-Vilaine, and Loire Inférieure. Included towns of St. Malo, Brest, Lorient, and Rennes.

Bucht. German name for a bay.

Burgundy. Old province of east-central France, in basins of Rhône, Seine, and Loire. Now Departments of Côte-d'Or, Saône-et-Loire, Yonne, and parts of Ain and Aube. Towns, Dijon, Macon, Autun, Auxerre, Chalon-sur-Saône, etc.

Butte. Term used in the United States for a lone hill rising with precipitous cliffs or steep slopes.

Byzantine. Name referring to the Byzantine or Eastern Roman Empire which included Syria, Asia Minor, Egypt, Greece, Macedonia, Crete, Bulgaria, and Turkey. It was founded in 395 A. D. Capital was at Byzantium, now called Istanbul (Constantinople).

C

Cabo. Spanish and Portuguese term for a cape.

Caledonia. Ancient name for Scotland north of Firths of Clyde and Forth. Now poetically applied to all Scotland.

Campos. Brazilian name for plains.

Canada East. Old name for Province of Quebec.

Canada West. Old name for Province of Ontario.

Cañon. Spanish-American term for a mountain gorge.

Cap. French term for a cape.

Capo. Italian term for a cape.

Caribbees. The Lesser Antilles.

Carniola. Former Austrian crownland Krain, now divided between Italy and Yugoslavia.

Carthage. An ancient city in northern Africa near Tunis, founded by the Phoenicians. It was destroyed by the Romans in 146 B. C.

Castile. Name designating a former kingdom occupying the central portion of Spain.

Cathay. A name applied to China during the Middle Ages.

Catinga. Brazilian term for an extensive, brushy woodland.

Caucasia. General name for territory in southeastern Soviet Union, between Black and Caspian seas, traversed by Caucasus Mountains.

Cayo. Spanish name for a rock, shoal, or islet.

C. C. C. P. Russian abbreviation for the Soviet Union. Transliteration reads "Soyuz Socialisticheskikh Sovetskikh Respublik."

Central America. Name applied to that portion of North America south of Mexico.

Cerro. Spanish term for a hill or highland which is in general craggy.

Československo. Bohemian name for Bohemia-Slovakia, applied to Czechoslovakia.

Chaldea. Ancient empire established in the valleys of the Tigris and Euphrates rivers.

Champagne. Name referring to old French province centered around the city of Troyes.

Chang. Chinese name for a village, borough, or market.

Chemins de Fer. French term for railroads.

Cilicia. Old division of southeastern Asia Minor on Mediterranean; now in Turkish Province (Vilayet) of Adana.

Circassia. Former district in old Russian Province of Kuban, on Black Sea.

Cisleithania. Old name for Austria, the river Leitha forming part of boundary with Hungary. Besides Austria proper, it included dart of Galicia, and Bukovina.

Citta. Italian name for a city.

Ciudad. Spanish term for a city or town.

Columbia. Poetical name for the United States, given in honor of Columbus.

Congo Belge. Belgian name for Belgian Congo.

Cordilleras. A name sometimes applied to the mountain system of western North and South America. Spanish term for a mountain range.

Corea. Old name for Chosen.

Costa. Italian and Spanish term for coast.

Côte. French name for coast or escarpment.

Côte des Somalis. French name for French Somaliland (Somali Coast).

Côte d'Ivoire. French name for Ivory Coast.

Coulee. American term applied to a low lava ridge, a wash, or an arroyo.

Crimea. A peninsula in the Black Sea, part of the Soviet Union.

Croatia. Former Hungarian division, now part of Yugoslavia.

D

Dalmatia. Division of former Austria-Hungary.

Danish West Indies. Former Danish Colony, now the U. S. Virgin Is.

Danmark. Danish name for Denmark.

Dansk-Vestindiske Öer or **Dansk Vestindien.** Danish names for Danish West Indies.

Dark Continent. Name popularly applied to Africa.

Death Valley. Name referring to the low desert in Inyo County, California.

Desht. Persian term for a plain.

Desierto. Spanish name for a desert.

Deutsches Reich. German name indicating German Empire.

Deutsch Ostafrica. German name for German East Africa.

Deutschösterreich. German name for German Austria.

Deutsch Sudwestafrica. German name for former German Southwest Africa.

Diserto. Italian name for a desert.

Divide. American term for a water-parting or height of land between two watersheds.

Dixie. Popular term for U. S. southern states.

Dodecanese Is. Name sometimes applied to the southeastern Aegean Islands, belonging to Italy.

Down. Old English name for a hill or mound.

Dra, Draa. Arabian term used in northern Africa to indicate a chain of hills or dunes.

Drift. Dutch name for a current.

Dutch West Indies. Name sometimes applied to the Dutch islands in the West Indies such as Curaçao, Aruba, Bonaire, etc., lying just north of South America.

E

Eastern Archipelago. Name for the Malay Archipelago.

Eastern Townships. Counties of Quebec lying south of the St. Lawrence and north of New Hampshire, Vermont, and New York.

East Indies. Collective name now commonly restricted to the British and Dutch island groups in Malay Archipelago.

Eesti. Estonian term meaning "Estonian."

Egypte. Local name for Egypt.

Eire. Official name for Ireland.

Eisenbahn. German term for railway.

El Salvador. Official name for Salvador.

Emerald Isle. A popular name for Ireland.

Entente. General name for a voluntary league or alliance (offensive, defensive, or both) of nations, such as the Dual Alliance of France and Russia, formed in the nineties to preserve the balance of power as an offset to the Triple Alliance of Germany, Austria, and Italy.

Epirus. A country of ancient Greece, now included in southern Albania and northwestern Greece.

Erg. Arabian term for a dune or a land of dunes.

Erin. Popular name for Ireland.

España. Spanish name for Spain.

Est. French name for east.

Estrecho. Spanish term for a strait.

Établissements de l'Inde. French name for French Settlements in India.

Établissements de l'Oceanie. French name for French Oceania.

Étang. French name for a lagoon, pond, or small lake.

État. French name for a state.

Ethiopia. Ancient name for countries in Africa south of Egypt; later restricted to the Empire of Ethiopia (Abyssinia).

Etruria. Name applied to an ancient country of northern Italy.

Eupen. Former German town and district, 50 miles west of Köln, now part of Belgium.

Everglades. A name referring to the swampy region in southeastern Florida.

F

Far East. Collective name for Asiatic countries east of Iran, and including the Philippines, Malaysia, and Oceania. Same as "Orient."

Far Eastern Republic. Territory on the eastern coast of Asia, part of the Soviet Union.

Farther India. Old name for Peninsula of Indochina.

Fertile Crescent. Ancient name for the lands along the east end of the Mediterranean including the valleys of the Tigris and Euphrates rivers.

Filipinas. Spanish name for the Philippine Islands.

Fjord. Danish and Norwegian term for a firth or long narrow inlet.

Française. French term for "French."

Freie Stadt. German words meaning "free city."

French America. Name applied to French islands of St. Pierre and Miquelon off southern coast of Newfoundland.

French Coast. Name applied to west coast of Newfoundland, on which French had exclusive fishing rights; long disputed by British and largely extinguished by treaty in 1904.

Fu. Chinese name for a prefecture, a town of the second order, or a district capital.

Fürstentum. German term meaning principality.

G

Galicia. District of former Austro-Hungarian Empire, north of Carpathian Mountains; western part known as "Austrian Poland." Now largely included in Poland.

Gaul. Historical name for that part of Europe which includes France, Belgium and parts of Germany, Netherlands, and Switzerland. The Roman name was Gallia.

Gebirge. German name for a mountain range.

Geul, Gol, or Göl. Turkish names for a lake.

Ghat. Indian term for a mountain pass.

Giant's Causeway. A basaltic formation on the north coast of Ireland.

Golf. German name for a gulf.

Golfe. French name for a gulf.

Golfo. The Italian, Spanish, and Portuguese name for a gulf.

Granada. Name designating a former Moorish kingdom in southern Spain, centered around the present city of Granada.

Grand Banks. Name applied to the shoals southeast of Newfoundland which are noted as a fishing ground.

Great American Desert. Old name for Great Salt Lake Desert in Utah, west of Great Salt Lake.

Great Basin. Plateau between Wasatch Mountains of Utah and the Sierra Nevadas of California. Comprises western Utah, almost all Nevada, and part of southeastern California.

Great Britain. Name referring to England, Wales, and Scotland.

Great Lakes. Collective name for Lakes Superior, Michigan, Huron, St. Clair, Erie, and Ontario.

Great Plains. Name for vast region between Rocky Mountains on west, and Appalachian and Laurentian systems on east, extending from Arctic Ocean to Gulf of Mexico.

Great South Land. Name sometimes applied to continent of Australia.

Guinea. Collective name for all lands on west coast of Africa between Senegal and the Southwest Africa Protectorate of the Union of South Africa.

Guinée. French name for Guinea.

Guyane. French word for Guiana.

H

Haf. Swedish name for a sea or an ocean.

Hai. Chinese term for a sea; also occasionally applied to a lake.

Hammada. Arabic term for a high, dry plateau.

Hanse Towns (Hanseatic League). Confederacy of some 90 European cities in Middle Ages, to protect commerce against raids of the Norse vikings. Hamburg, Lübeck, and Bremen still called Hanseatic cities.

Haute-Volta. French name for Upper Volta.

Haut Senegal-Niger. French name for Upper Senegal and Niger.

Hav. Danish and Norwegian name for a sea or an ocean.

Hellas. Ancient name of Greece.

Helvetia. The Latin name for Switzerland.

Hercegovina. An old duchy south of Bosnia which now forms part of Yugoslavia.

Hibernia. Ancient name of Ireland.

Ho. Chinese name for a river—any river.

Hoek. Dutch name for a cape or headland.

Holland. A name sometimes applied to the Netherlands.

Holy Land. A familiar term for Palestine.

Holy Roman Empire. Name sometimes applied to the German Roman Empire of the 12th and 13th centuries.

Horn. German term for a peak. Also English name for an elongated peninsula.

Hrvatska. The Serb-Croatian term for Croatia.

Hu. Chinese name for a lake.

Hudson Bay Territory. Vast area of North America granted by charter of King Charles II to Hudson's Bay Company, 1670. Company's territorial rights sold to Canada, 1869. Included Northern Ontario and Quebec, Manitoba, Saskatchewan, Alberta, Yukon Territory, and Northwest Territories.

I

Iberia. Ancient name of Spanish Peninsula of Europe.

Ile. French name for an island.

Ilha. Portuguese term for an island.

Illyria. Ancient country on east coast of Adriatic Sea. Now divided between Yugoslavia and Italy.

Inde. French name for India.

Indian Territory. Old name of region north of Texas set apart as abode for tribal Indians. Included greater part of Oklahoma and parts of Kansas and Nebraska.

Indochina. Old name for southeastern peninsula of Asia; now generally restricted to Siam and French Indochina.

Indo-Chine. French name for Indochina.

Inkeri. Local term for North Ingermanland, now part of Soviet Union.

Inland Empire. Name for the Western white pine lumber region of the great interior basin of the Columbia river. Comprises northern Idaho, western Montana, and eastern Washington and Oregon.

Insel. German name for an island.

Ionia. Old name of country on west coast of Asia Minor. Now in Izmir territory. Contained cities of Ephesus and Izmir (Smyrna).

Iran. Official name of Persia. Also applied to great plateau stretching east and west between the Tigris and Indus rivers, and north from the Arabian to the Caspian seas, including Iran, Afghanistan, and Baluchistan.

Irmak. Turkish name for a river.

Isla. Spanish name for an island.

Istmo. Italian and Spanish term for an isthmus.

Italia. Italian name for Italy.

J

Jebel. Arabian term for a mountain.

K

Kaap. Dutch name for a cape.

Karolinen. German name for the Caroline Islands.

Kiang. Chinese name for a large river.

Kiauchau or Kiautschou. Formerly a leased possession of Germany in China. Now known as Kiaochow.

Kionga. Formerly a portion of German East Africa. Now part of Mozambique.

Klondike. Name sometimes used to indicate the Canadian-Alaskan gold fields.

Kol. Term used in eastern Turkey to indicate a valley or ravine. Sometimes applied to a foothill.

Kraal. Dutch term applied to a collection of native huts.

Ksar. Arabic term for a village.

Kyo. Japanese name for a town or capital.

Kum. See Qum.

Küste. German name for coast.

L

Lac. French term for a lake.

Lago. Italian word for a lake.

Laguna. Spanish and Italian term for a lake or lagoon.

Lake District. Picturesque, lake-studded mountain region in northwestern England, in Cumberland, Westmoreland, and Lancashire.

Land of Little Sticks. Name often applied to the treeless plains of northern North America.

Land of the Midnight Sun. Norway.

Lapland. Name applied to a region in northern Europe which is inhabited by Lapps. Not an administrative district.

Latin America. Name embracing all of the Western Hemisphere south of the United States, including Mexico, West Indies (except Puerto Rico), Central America, and South America.

Lattaquie. French name for Latakia.

Laurentian Lakes. Name applied to the lakes of the glacial period which covered the area occupied by and adjacent to the Great Lakes of the present time.

Leeward Islands. Name confusingly applied to various West India Island groups—generally with a reference to direction of the prevailing trade winds from the east, "Leeward" meaning "to the west," in contradistinction to "Windward" ("to the east").

Left Bank. See "Right Bank."

Levant. Name derived from Latin "levare" (to raise), meaning "the rising" or "the east." Formerly applied to coast lands around eastern end of Mediterranean (Greece, Turkey, Asia Minor, Syria, Lebanon, Palestine, and Egypt); now also includes Cyprus, all Asia Minor, Iran, Iraq, and Arabia.

Libia. Italian name for Libya.

Lietuva. Lithuanian name for Lithuania.

Little America. Admiral Byrd's base in Antarctica. 79° S. lat. 62° 30′ W. long. (approx.).

Little Entente. Defensive alliance of Yugoslavia, Czechoslovakia, and Romania organized to oppose territorial ambitions of Hungary after the Great War.

Little Russia. Region in southwestern Sov. Un. comprising Governments of Kharkov, Kiev, Poltava, and Chernigov, peopled by Slavs akin to Ruthenians of Czechoslovakia.

Llanos. Name applied to the sandy, treeless plains of the Orinoco valley in northern South America.

Loch. Name used in Ireland and Scotland for a lake or an arm of the sea.

Lombardy. Old division of Northern Italy on Swiss border, now a Department comprising Provinces of Bergamo, Brescia, Como, Cremona, Mantova, Milano, Pavia, and Sondrio. Contains Lakes Maggiore, Como, and Garda. Chief city, Milano (Milan).

Louisiana Territory. Name given to the region in the United States acquired by the Louisiana Purchase.

Low Countries. A name popularly applied to the Netherlands.

Lower Canada. Old name for Province of Quebec.

Lusitania. Ancient Roman province comprising chiefly modern Portugal.

M

Macedonia. Ancient Kingdom north of Greece, around head of Gulf of Salonika, between Illyria on west and Thrace on east. Capital, Pella; chief port, Thessalonike (Salonika). Now mainly included in Greece, partly in Yugoslovia, and Bulgaria.

Magyarország. Hungarian name for Hungary.

Malacca. Old name sometimes applied to Malay Peninsula.

Malmedy. Former German town and district, 50 miles west of Köln, now part of Belgium.

Mar. Spanish and Portuguese term for a sea.

Marianen. German name for the Mariana Islands.

Maritime Provinces. Canadian Provinces of Prince Edward Island, Nova Scotia, and New Brunswick.

Marruecos. Spanish name for Morocco.

Mason and Dixon Line. Boundary between Pennsylvania and Maryland. The dividing line (in part) between the North and South in the American Civil War.

Matta, The. Brazilian name for the jungles of the upper Amazon valley.

Mauretania. Ancient name of northwesternmost part of Africa, embracing modern Morocco and part of Algeria. Distinguished from Mauritania, a French protectorate on west coast of Africa, north of Senegal, merging into the Sahara on the east.

Meer. German name for a sea or an ocean.

Melanesia. Name applied to that division of the Pacific Islands which includes the Bismarck Archipelago, Solomon, New Hebrides, Loyalty, Santa Cruz, New Caledonia, Fiji, and several smaller groups of islands.

Mer. French term for a sea.

Mesa. Spanish name for the flat surface on the top of a hill or a mountain.

Mesopotamia. Former Turkish territory, now known as Iraq.

Micronesia. Name applied to that division of the Pacific Islands lying north of Melanesia. It embraces the Mariana, Palau, Caroline, Marshall, and Gilbert groups.

Moçambique. Portuguese name for Mozambique.

Moldavia. Former principality in southeastern Europe, now part of Romania and the Soviet Union.

Mont. French term for a hill or mount.

Montagna. Italian term for a range of mountains.

Montagne. French term for a mountain.

Monte. Italian, Portuguese, and Spanish name for a mountain.

Moyen Congo. French name for Middle Congo, a division of French Equatorial Africa.

Muscovy. Name referring to ancient Russia.

Muskeg. Term used in the United States and Canada for a bog or marsh.

N

Naes. Danish and Norwegian name for a cape.

Nahr. Turkish name for a river or perennial stream.

Navigator's Islands. Old name of Samoa.

Near East. Collective name covering the Balkan States, the countries of the Levant, Malta, and all the Mediterranean coast lands of Africa west to and including Morocco.

Nederland. Dutch name for the Netherlands.

Nederlandsch-Indie. Dutch name for Netherlands Indies.

Nejd. Former name for the region of central Arabia, now known as Saudi Arabia.

New Amsterdam. Old name of New York City under Dutch régime.

New France. Old name now used only in historical reference to the French colonies in North America yielded to the British in 1763 after the capture of Quebec.

New Ontario. Popular term for part of Canadian Province of Ontario north of the Great Lakes, lying between boundaries of Quebec and Manitoba, and extending north to Albany river.

Nez. French name for a cape or point.

Nippon. Old name of Japanese Empire, sometimes restricted to Hondo, the principal island.

Nor. The Mongolian and Tibetan name for a lake.

Nord. French, German, and Scandinavian term for north.

Norge. Norwegian name for Norway.

Normandy. Ancient province of France, on English Channel. Capital, Rouen. Included lower Seine Valley, and coast towns of Dieppe, Havre, and Cherbourg. Now constitutes Departments of Seine-Inférieure, Eure, Calvados, Manche, and Orne.

Norte. Spanish and Italian word for north.

North Ingermanland. Former state of Russia near the Finnish border, now part of the Soviet Union.

Northwestern Territory. Old name of Hudson Bay Territory.

Northwest Territories. Former name of a vast region including all Canada between British Columbia (and Alaska) on the west, and the Labrador coast strip on the east, except the Maritime Provinces and those parts of Ontario and Quebec tributary to the Great Lakes and the St. Lawrence River. Name now restricted to the most northerly parts of the Dominion, now composing the Districts of Keewatin, Mackenzie, and Franklin.

Northwest Territory. Old name of region extending from Ohio River to the Great Lakes, and from border of Pennsylvania to the Mississippi River, ceded by England to the United States at the close of the Revolution, 1783.

North Woods. Name popularly used to designate the forest regions of northern Michigan, Wisconsin, and Minnesota.

Nouvelle Caledonie. French name for New Caledonia.

Nouvelles Hebrides. French name for New Hebrides.

Nyanza or Nyasa. Bantu term for a lake.

O

Ö or Ø. Scandinavian term for an island.

Oberschlesien. German name for Upper Silesia.

Occident. General name for Western Europe and the New World. Used in contradistinction to "Orient"—more particularly with reference to the characteristic social, political, and religious ideals underlying their respective developments.

Odde. Danish and Norwegian term for a point or tongue of land.

Old Mexico. Term sometimes used to designate the Republic of Mexico.

Oltre Giuba. Italian name for Jubaland, now part of Italian Somaliland.

Oost. Dutch name for east.

Oranje Vrij Staat. Boer name for Orange Free State.

Oregon Country. Name for the region in northwestern U. S., the status of which was settled by the Treaty of 1846.

Orient. Same as the "Far East."

Ost. German name for east.

Öst. Danish and Norwegian name for east.

Österreich. German name for Austria.

Ottoman Empire. Name sometimes applied to the old Turkish Empire.

Ouest. French name for west.

P

Painted Desert. A name sometimes given to the plateau region of Arizona.

Palatinate. Name applied to several political districts (Upper, Lower, Rhenish) in old German Empire, now included in Bavaria, Baden, Hesse, and Prussia. Principal towns, Heidelberg and Mannheim.

Pampas. Name referring to the extensive plains of Argentina.

Pan-American Union. Name applied to the union formed by the republics in North and South America for the purpose of better mutual understanding and more friendly commercial, political, and social intercourse.

Panhandle. Name applied to a strip of territory prominently projecting from the main body of a State or Territory—for example, the northern extension of Texas, the western extension of Oklahoma, the northern extension of Idaho, the southeastern extension of Alaska, and the northern strip of West Virginia between the Ohio River and the Pennsylvania border.

Parthia. An ancient name referring to the region southeast of the Caspian Sea.

Pas. French term for a channel.

Patagonia. Name applied to a region in southern South America.

Peloponnesus. Name applied to that part of Greece which lies south of the Corinthian Isthmus.

Persia. Former name for Iran.

Phoenicia. An ancient country embracing an area between the Mediterranean and Lebanon.

Pic. French name for a peak.

Pico. Portuguese and Spanish name for a peak.

Piedmont. Name applied to any foothill region, such as the Piedmont division in Northern Italy, merging into the Alps; and the Piedmont section of Virginia, off the eastern slopes of the Blue Ridge Mountains.

Pillars of Hercules. Name for the two promontories on the Strait of Gibraltar.

Polynesia. Name often applied to all the islands in the central and western Pacific Ocean, but properly restricted to the eastern division of these islands. Includes the Hawaiian, Phoenix, Society, Marquesas, Samoa, Tuamotu, and numerous smaller groups.

Prairie Provinces. Collective name for Canadian Provinces of Manitoba, Saskatchewan, and Alberta.

Preussen. German name for Prussia, a division of Germany.

Pueblo. Spanish term for a town or village.

Puerto. Spanish name for a port.

Punta. Italian and Spanish name for a point.

Q

Qum (Kum). Turkish term for a desert.

R

Ras. Arabian name for a cape or headland.

Red River Settlement. Old name of territory originally constituting the Canadian Province of Manitoba.

Regno d'Italia. Italian name for Kingdom of Italy.

Republique Libanaise. French name for the Republic of Lebanon.

Ria. Spanish term for the mouth of a river.

Rift. An elongated fissure or depression produced by faulting of the earth's surface.

Right Bank. Term used to indicate location alongside a waterway as one faces downstream, not upstream. Left bank is on opposite side. E.g., St. Louis, Mo., is on right bank of Mississippi River; Quebec, on left bank of St. Lawrence.

Rio. Italian, Portuguese, and Spanish term for a river

Riviera. Popular name for a narrow coastal strip of French and Italian territory around head of Gulf of Genoa, extending from Cannes (France) to Spezia (Italy). Includes cities of Nice and Genova (Genoa), and many resorts (Monte Carlo, Mentone, San Remo, etc.). Name also applied to part of the Ticino valley in Switzerland.

Riviére. French name for a river.

Roof of the World. Name popularly applied to the high plateau of Tibet.

Ruhr. Name applied to the industrial section surrounding the Ruhr River valley in Germany.

Rumelia. Old name loosely used at one time to indicate all the Balkan States north of Greece; at another, European Turkey; at still another, restricted to southeastern part of Balkan Peninsula (ancient Thrace) now constituting European Turkey and part of Greece and Bulgaria.

Rupert's Land. Name formerly applied to Hudson Bay Territory.

Ruthenia. Old name loosely used to include former Austrian Provinces of Galicia and Bukovina and parts of Hungary and Southwestern Russia, peopled by a branch of the Slavic race, the Russniaks or Red Russians. Now largely included in the Soviet Union.

S

Saar Basin. Name designating the industrial section centered in the Saar River valley in Germany.

Saargebiet. German name for the Saar.

Sachsen. German name for Saxony.

Sahara Español. Spanish name for Spanish Sahara.

Sahara Occidental. Spanish name for Western Sahara.

St. Petersburg. Name of the former Russian capital. Name changed to Petrograd, September 1, 1914; changed to Leningrad, March, 1924; capital removed to Moskva (Moscow), March 14, 1918.

Saki. Japanese name for a cape or promontory.

Sandwich Islands. Former name of Hawaii.

Saorstát Éireann. Irish name for Irish Free State.

Sardegna. Italian name for Sardinia.

Sargasso Sea. An elliptical ocean area northeast of West Indies, extending from about 40° to 75° W. long., and from 20° to 35° N. lat., and laden with drifting weeds, chiefly gulfweed (Sargassum).

Sarre. French name for the Saar.

Savannah. Spanish name for a meadow or treeless area.

Savoy. Name applied to a former division of the Kingdom of Sardinia. Now popularly employed to designate southeastern France.

Scandinavia. Collective name including Norway, Sweden, and Denmark.

Sebka. Arabic name for a marsh or saltpan.

See. German name for a lake or sea.

Selva. Portuguese and Spanish word for a wood or forest.

Serb-Croat-Slovene Kingdom. Former name for Yugoslavia.

Serbia. Name of a former kingdom of Europe; now part of Yugoslavia.

Serra. Italian and Portuguese term for a mountain range.

Shahr. Persian term for a town.

Shima. Japanese term for an island.

Shire. English term for a land division or county.

Shott. Arabian name for a salt pan, a large river, or an extensive area of salt water.

Shqypnië, Shqyptare, Shqiptare, Shqipnia, Shquipenia. Albanian variants for Albania.

S. H. S. Kingdom. Abbreviation for name of Serb-Croat (Hrvatska)-Slovene Kingdom or Yugoslavia.

Siberia. A name given to the Asiatic portion of the Russian Empire, now part of the Soviet Union.

Sicilia. Italian name for Sicily.

Sierra. Spanish term for a rugged mountain range.

Silvas. Name applied to the forest regions of the Amazon Valley in South America.

Sjö. Swedish name for a sea.

Slesvig. Formerly a portion of Schleswig-Holstein. Following the World War a plebiscite was held and territory became part of Denmark.

Sö. Danish and Norwegian name for a sea.

Somalia Italiana. Italian name for Italian Somaliland.

Soudan Français. French name for French Sudan.

Southern Ocean. Name formerly applied to ocean waters south of 40° S. lat. to Antartic Circle.

South Sea. Name formerly applied to the Pacific Ocean, especially the South Pacific.

Spanish Main. Name formerly applied to the southern portion of the Caribbean Sea and the contiguous coast of South America.

Spitze. German name for the summit or top of a mountain.

S. S. S. R. Abbreviation of Soyuz Socialistitcheskikh Sovietskikh Republik.

Stadt. German name for a city.

Steppe. Russian term for a vast treeless plain or prairie.

Stretto. Italian term for a strait.

Succession States. Collective name for the countries of Europe now sharing the territory of the former Austro-Hungarian Empire—namely, former Austria, Hungary, Italy, Poland, former Czechoslovakia, Romania, and Yugoslavia.

Sud. French and Spanish term for south.

Süd. German term for south.

Suidafrika. Boer name for South Africa, referring to the Union of South Africa.

Suidwes Afrika. Boer name for Southwest Africa.

Suomi. Finnish name for Finland.

Sverige. Swedish name for Sweden.

Swabia. Ancient country which included parts of southeastern Germany, Alsace, and eastern Switzerland.

Syd. Danish and Norwegian term for south.

T

Terra del Fuego. Name meaning Fireland, used to indicate a region in southern Patagonia.

Territorios Españoles del Golfo de Guinea. Spanish term indicating Spanish territories on the Gulf of Guinea.

Thal. German name for a valley or dale.

Thessaly. A district in northern Greece, formerly part of Turkey. One of the chief cities is Larissa.

Thule. Ancient name for the most northern part of the habitable world. Believed to have been Norway, Iceland, or one of the Shetland Islands.

Tor. A Celtic term for a tower-like rock.

Toscano. Italian name for Tuscany.

Thrace. Ancient name originally applied to entire Balkan Peninsula north of Greece; in Roman times, to that part of north Greece east of Macedonia and south of the Balkans, including the present southern Bulgaria, northeastern Greece, and European Turkey.

Transleithania. Old name of Hungarian portion of Austro-Hungarian Empire, the river Leitha forming part of the boundary between Austria and Hungary. Now divided between Hungary, Romania (Transylvania), and Yugoslavia (Croatia, Slovania, and part of Dalmatia).

Transylvania. Formerly a principality and part of Austria-Hungary. Since 1919 it was a part of Romania, but in 1940 a large portion was ceded to Hungary.

Trough. English term for a sub-oceanic elongated and wide depression.

Tso. Tibetan name for a lake.

Tundras. Russian name applied to the marshy, treeless plains of northern Europe, Asia, and North America.

Tunisie. French name for Tunisia.

Türkiye. Turkish name for Turkey.

Two Sicilies. A former kingdom in Italy composed of Sicilia (Sicily) and Napoli (Naples).

U

Ultramar. Spanish term meaning beyond the sea.

Unie van Suid Afrika. Boer term for the Union of South Africa.

United Kingdom. The name includes England, Wales, Scotland, and Northern Ireland.

Upper Canada. Old name for Province of Ontario.

V

Valle. Italian, Portuguese, and Spanish term for a valley.

Vallée. French term for a valley.

Van Diemen's Land. Former name of Tasmania.

Veld. Dutch name for an open plain.

Vest. Scandinavian term for west.

Villar. Spanish name for a village or hamlet.

Ville. French name for a city or town.

Vinland. Name given the northeastern coast of North America by the Norsemen.

W

Wad or Wady. Arabian term for a river valley, generally of an intermittent stream.

Watershed. A divide or water-parting. Also applied to the drainage area of a stream.

Wenden. Former portion of Russia, now part of Latvia.

Western Reserve. Early name for a region of the United States reserved by Connecticut near Lake Erie; now part of Ohio.

West Griqualand. Former division of Cape of Good Hope, now part of the Union of South Africa.

Windward Islands. Name confusingly applied to various West India Island groups, to distinguish them from the more westerly Leeward Islands (see Leeward Islands).

Woest. Dutch term for a desert.

Wüste. German term for a desert.

Y

Yama. Japanese name for a mountain.

Z

Zee. Dutch term for a sea.

Zuid Afrikaansche Republik. Boer name for South African Republic.

Zuidwest Afrika. Boer name for Southwest Africa.

Zululand. Former native kingdom in northeastern South Africa, now part of the Union of South Africa.

VOYAGES OF DISCOVERY AND EXPLORATION

Name	Place of Birth	Year	Region Explored
		B. C.	
King Necho	Egypt	600	At Necho's orders a Phoenician expedition is said to have sailed around Africa.
Hanno	Carthage	500	Visited northwestern coast of Africa.
Himilco	Phoenician	500	Visited southwestern coast of Europe.
Scylax of Caryanda	Caria	500	Explored coast of Asia west of the Indus River.
Alexander the Great	Macedonia	334–23	Explored and conquered Iran, Palestine, and Egypt; entered India.
Nearchus	Macedonia	325	Visited coast of Asia between Indus and Euphrates rivers.
Pytheas	Greece	315	Visited western coast of Europe. Sailed around England.
Eudoxus of Cyzicus	Greece	130	Explored Arabian Sea and visited western coast of Africa.
Gaius Julius Caesar	Rome	62–49	Conquered and explored western Europe and Britain.
		A. D.	
Gnaeus Julius Agricola	Rome	80–86	Explored and conquered various sections of England and Wales.
Erik the Red	Norse	982	Voyaged to southern Greenland.
Bjarni Heriulfsson	Norse	986	Crossed Atlantic Ocean to Greenland and northeastern coast of North America.
Leif Eriksen	Norse	1001	Reached what is now Newfoundland, Labrador, Nova Scotia, and New England.
Benjamin of Tudela	Navarre	1150	Visited the Near East, Iran, and penetrated to the frontier of China
William of Rubruquis	Netherlands	1248–52	Visited southeastern Europe and Turkestan.
Marco Polo	Venice	1271–95	Traveled through Iran, central Asia, China, returning by junks to Iran.
Ibn Battuta	Arabia	1325–55	Traveled through Asia Minor, central Asia, and northern Africa.
Jehan de Mandeville	England	1340	Visited the Near East, Arabia, India, and northeastern Africa.
Gil Eannes	Portugal	1434	Sailed along northwestern coast of Africa. Rounded Cape Bogador.
Diogo Cam	Cão	1482–86	Discovered the mouth of the Congo River and explored mid-western coast of Africa.
Bartholomeu Diaz de Novaes	Portugal	1488	Visited western coast of Africa; rounded Cape of Good Hope.
Christopher Columbus	Italy	1492–1502	Made four voyages across the Atlantic, visiting the West Indies and South America.
John Cabot	Italy	1497–98	Explored coasts of eastern North America and southern Greenland for England.
Vasco da Gama	Portugal	1497–99	Sailed from Portugal, around Cape of Good Hope to India and back.
Amerigo Vespucci	Italy	1497–1503	Explored northern coast of South America.
Sebastian Cabot	Italy	1497–1529	First sailed with his father, John Cabot. Later explored Paraguay and Paraná rivers in South America.
Alonso de Ojeda	Italy	1499	Explored coast of Venezuela.
Vicente Yañez Pinzon	Spain	1499–1500	Crossed the Atlantic and reached the South American coast below Cape St. Augustine. Discovered the mouth of the Amazon River.
Pedro Alvarez Cabral	Portugal	1500	Crossed the Atlantic to Brazil, South America, and from there proceeded to Cape of Good Hope and Ceylon.
Gaspar Corte-Real	Portugal	1500–01	Explored northeastern coast of North America.
Ludovico di Varthema	Italy	1502–10	Traveled from Europe to Egypt; thence to Near East and southern Asia.
Juan Ponce de Leon	Spain	1513	Explored in Florida, U. S.
Vasco Nuñez de Balboa	Spain	1513–14	Crossed Panama and discovered the Pacific Ocean.
Ferdinand Magellan	Portugal	1519–22	Circumnavigated the earth. Visited the eastern coast of South America, the Philippine Islands, and the East Indies.
Hernando Cortés	Spain	1519–27	Visited and conquered Mexico and Central America.
Gil Gonzalez Davila	Spain	1522–23	Explored Nicaragua.
Francisco Pizarro	Spain	1523–41	Explored western South America and conquered Peru.
Giovanni da Verrazano	France	1524	Discovered New York Bay and Hudson River; explored east coast of North America northward to Newfoundland.
Diego de Almagro	Spain	1525–30	Explored in Peru, Bolivia, and Chile. Crossed the Atacama Desert.
Alvarez Nuñez Cabeza de Vaca	Spain	1527–37	Visited southern coast of North America and crossed Mexico.
Jacques Cartier	France	1534–37	Explored Gulf of St. Lawrence and ascended to Quebec.
Gonzalo Jiminez de Quesada	Spain	1536–37	Explored interior of Colombia.
Francisco de Ulloa	Spain	1539	Visited coasts of California and Mexico.
Hernando de Soto	Spain	1539–42	Explored southeastern United States and the lower Mississippi Valley.
Francisco Vasquez de Coronado	Spain	1540–42	Explored what is now Arizona, New Mexico, southern California, and northwestern Mexico.
Pedro de Valdivia	Spain	1540–54	Explored and founded Chile.
Francisco de Orellana	Spain	1541–42	Crossed the Andes between Guayaquil, Ecuador, and the headwaters of the Amazon, descended that stream and went northwest along the South American coast.
Sir Martin Frobisher	England	1576–78	Crossed the Atlantic to southern Greenland, thence to Frobisher Bay. Discovered Hudson Straits
Sir Francis Drake	England	1577–80	Circumnavigated the earth.
John Davis	England	1585–96	Explored the Arctic islands of North America and the Antarctic region south of South America.
Jan Huyghen van Linschoten	Netherlands	1594–95	Explored the European Arctic regions.
William Barents	Netherlands	1594–97	Discovered Svalbard, Barents Sea, and Novaya Zemlya.
Sir Walter Raleigh	England	1595	Explored the Orinoco River and Guiana.
Pedro Fernandez de Quiros	Spain	1595–1606	Discovered New Hebrides Island.
Sebastian Vizcaino	Spain	1602–03	Visited coast of California.
Samuel de Champlain	France	1603–15	Explored and mapped eastern Canada.
John Smith	England	1605–09	Visited eastern coast of U. S. and explored Virginia.
Luis Vaes de Torres	Spain	1606	Visited the northern East Indies and the Philippine Islands. Traversed Torres Strait.
Henry Hudson	England	1607–10	Visited Svalbard and Novaya Zemlya. Explored New York Bay and the lower Hudson River and later went to Hudson Bay.
William Baffin	England	1615–16	Sought Northwest Passage and discovered Baffin Bay.
Willem Cornelis Schouten and Jacob Lemaire	Netherlands	1615–17	First to sail around Cape Horn. Visited the East Indies.
Dirk Hartog	Netherlands	1616	Visited west coast of Australia.
Jean Nicolet	France	1634	Journeyed from Lake Huron to the mouth of the Mississippi River.
Abel Janszoon Tasman	Netherlands	1642–44	Discovered Tasmania and explored South Pacific region. First to circumnavigate Australia.
Pierre Radisson	France	1658–62	Traveled extensively in the region of the Great Lakes.
René Robert Cavelier LaSalle	France	1669–87	Explored the Great Lakes region and the lower Mississippi River Valley.
Jacques Marquette and Louis Joliet	France	1673	Explored the upper Mississippi River valley.
William Dampier	England	1699–1711	Explored the coast of Australia and the South Sea Islands.
Vitus Bering	Denmark	1725–41	Explored northeastern Asia and discovered Bering Strait, proving that Asia and North America were not connected.
Louis Antoine de Bougainville	France	1766–69	Sailed around the world and discovered and named many South Pacific islands.
Samuel Hearne	England	1769–72	Explored Arctic region of North America.
Captain James Cook	England	1769–79	Circumnavigated the globe. Explored the region around the Society Islands, New Zealand, Australia, Hawaiian Islands, and other portions of the Pacific, as far north as Alaska.
Juan Perez	Spain	1774	Visited the west coasts of the U. S. and Canada.
Felix de Azara	Spain	1781	Surveyed the Paraguay and Paraná river systems.
Jean-François de Galaup La Pérouse	France	1785–88	Crossed the Pacific Ocean and surveyed the Asiatic coast to Kamchatka; visited Alaska.
Sir Alexander Mackenzie	Scotland	1785–93	Explored northern Canada and visited its Pacific Coast.
Captain Robert Gray	United States	1788–92	Discovered Gray's Harbor and explored the Columbia River.
George Vancouver	England	1791–95	Explored the Australian coast, South Sea Islands, and the northwestern coast of North America.
Matthew Flinders	England	1794–1803	Surveyed southern coast of Australia.
Mungo Park	Scotland	1795–97	Explored part of the Niger River valley.

Voyages of Discovery and Exploration

Name	Place of Birth	Year	Region Explored
Baron Friedrich Heinrich Alexander von Humboldt	Germany	1799–1829	Extensive expeditions into upper sections of Orinoco River. Went up the Magdalena River to Equador and Peru. Crossed Russia and Siberia.
Meriwether Lewis and William Clark	United States	1803–06	Headed expedition in the U. S. from St. Louis to the Pacific Coast and back, covering 8,000 miles of unexplored territory.
Zebulon Montgomery Pike	United States	1805–07	Explored the upper main branch of the Mississippi River and southwestern U. S.
René Auguste Caillié	France	1816–28	Visited the Niger River region and went to Tombouktou, then crossed northern Africa to Fès.
William Edward Parry	England	1818–27	Made extensive explorations of American Arctic islands.
Sir John Ross	England	1818–33	Made several expeditions to the Arctic regions.
Sir James Clark Ross	England	1818–43	Made several voyages to the Arctic and Antarctic regions. Located the North Magnetic Pole.
Fabian G. von Bellinghausen	Russia	1819–21	Circled the Antarctic Ocean, discovering Peter I. Island and Alexander I. Land.
Sir John Franklin	England	1819–47	Made several voyages to the northern coast of North America and Arctic islands.
Hugh Clapperton and Dixon Denham	England	1822–27	Explored the Sahara Desert region south of Tunisia.
James Weddell	England	1823	Explored the Weddell Sea.
Richard Lemon Lander	England	1825–31	Explored the Niger River country in Africa.
Charles Sturt	England	1828–45	Explored the Darling River region in Australia.
John Biscoe	England	1830–32	Discovered Graham Land and Enderby Land.
Robert Fitzroy	England	1830–36	Explored the southern coast of South America. Fixed the longitude of many secondary meridians for navigational purposes.
John Charles Frémont	United States	1838–53	Surveyed and mapped the central Rocky Mountain region.
John Balleny	England	1839–40	Sailed into Antarctic Ocean and discovered Balleny Islands.
Edward John Eyre	England	1839–41	Explored Australia; discovered Lake Torrens.
David Livingstone	Scotland	1841–73	Explored south-central Africa, including Zambezi River valley.
F. W. L. Leichhardt	Germany	1844–48	Explored Queensland, Australia.
Heinrich Barth	Germany	1847–54	Explored the Near East and northern and central Africa.
R. M'Clure	Ireland	1850–53	Explored north Canadian islands.
Richard Francis Burton	England	1854–58	Made a survey into the interior of Africa and discovered lakes Victoria, Tanganyika, and Nyasa.
John Hanning Speke	England	1854–60	Surveyed and explored in central Africa.
Paul Belloni du Chaillu	France	1855–65	Made extensive explorations in West Africa.
John M'Douall Stuart	Scotland	1858–62	Explored central Australia and crossed the continent from south to north.
Robert O'Hara Burke and William Gorman Wills	Ireland	1860–61	Crossed Australia from south to north.
James Augustus Grant	Scotland	1860–63	Explored the upper Nile region with J. H. Speke.
Charles Hall	United States	1860–71	Explored the north Canadian islands.
Sir Samuel White Baker	England	1861–65	Explored the upper Nile Valley.
Georg August Schweinfurth	Germany	1863–88	Explored in north-central Africa and Arabia.
Baron Ferdinand P. W. von Richthofen	Germany	1868–72	Traced network of routes over southern and central China.
John Wesley Powell	United States	1867–71	Systematically explored the Colorado River and regions of the Southwest.
Gustav Nachtigal	Germany	1870–74	Explored in the eastern Sahara region and the western Nile Valley.
Nils Adolf Erik Nordenskiöld	Finland	1870–79	Explored Arctic regions and made first voyage around the northern coast of Eurasia.
Nikolai Mikhailovich Prjeválsky	Russia	1870–88	Carried on extensive scientific explorations in Tibet and the Gobi region.
P. Egerton Warburton	England	1873	Crossed Australia from Alice Springs to Roeburn on the west coast.
Verney Lovett Cameron	England	1873–88	Was the first European to cross equatorial Africa. Also explored in the Euphrates River valley.
Henry Morton Stanley	Wales	1874–89	Explored southern and central portions of Africa; developed Congo route from the Atlantic side. Found David Livingstone.
Ernest Giles	England	1875–83	First to cross the central Australian desert.
Emin Pasha (Eduard Schnitzer)	Germany	1875–90	Traveled in east-central Africa.
A. W. Greely	United States	1881–84	Explored northern portion of Greenland.
Sven Anders Hedin	Sweden	1885—	Traveled extensively in central Asia.
Francis Edward Younghusband	England	1886—	Traveled extensively in central Asia.
Admiral Robert E. Peary	United States	1886–1909	Explored in the Arctic and discovered the North Pole in 1909.
Fridtjof Nansen	Norway	1893–96	Explored North Polar region. Drifted across the Arctic Ocean in the "Fram."
Aurel Stein	England	1899—	Made extensive explorations in central Asia, western China, and Iran.
Duke of the Abruzzi	Italy	1900–09	Led expedition to Fridtjof Nansen Land. Also explored mountains of Africa and Asia.
Captain Robert Falcon Scott	England	1900–12	Made extensive surveys in the Ross Sea area and other Antarctic regions. Reached the South Pole in 1912, one month after Amundsen.
Otto Nordenskjöld	Sweden	1901–03	Led expedition to Antarctic regions
Roald Amundsen	Norway	1903–28	Carried on extensive explorations in the North Polar region—navigated through the Northwest Passage. Discovered the South Pole in 1911.
Ludvig Mylius-Erichsen	Denmark	1906–07	Mapped northern coast of Greenland.
Sir Ernest Shackleton	England	1908–17	Made extensive Antarctic explorations and located the South Magnetic Pole. Sailed through the Antarctic Ocean.
Hudson Stuck	England	1913—	Ascended Mt. McKinley, Alaska.
Donald B. Macmillan	United States	1913—	Made several expeditions to the Canadian Arctic islands.
Theodore Roosevelt	United States	1913–14	Explored a portion of the southern Amazon River valley.
Vilhjalmur Stefansson	Canada	1913–18	Carried on studies and explorations of north Arctic islands.
Dr. Roy Chapman Andrews	United States	1916—	Conducted a series of expeditions in the Gobi Desert and other Mongolian territory.
Lincoln Ellsworth	United States	1925—	Flew across the North Pole with Amundsen in the "Norge." Later made aerial surveys of the Antarctic continent.
Admiral Richard E. Byrd	United States	1926—	Flew over the North Pole with Floyd Bennett as pilot. Headed expeditions in Antarctica.
Sir Hubert Wilkins	England	1928—	Explored by air the Arctic regions, passing over the Polar Sea. Also made Antarctic aerial surveys.
Bertram Thomas	England	1930–31	Crossed the Great Arabian Desert on camel.
Frank S. Smythe	England	1931—	Climbed Mt. Kamet in the Himalaya Mountains.
H. St. John Philby	England	1932—	Discovered the ancient city of Wabar in the Rub al Khali desert of Arabia.

WORLD AGRICULTURAL PRODUCTION

Country	Wheat (bushels)	Corn (bushels)	Oats (bushels)	Rye (bushels)	Rice (bushels)	Potatoes (bushels)	Sugar (short tons)	Tobacco (pounds)	Cotton (bales)	Crude Rubber (metric tons)
Argentina	271,173,000	411,394,000	37,168,000	16,948,000	2,792,000	43,357,000	566,000	40,990,000	235,200	
Australia	91,592,000	7,057,000	19,443,000	a	2,592,000	10,084,000	930,614	4,750,000	13,600	
Belgium	7,900,000		49,895,000	13,755,000		112,105,000	286,598	10,529,000		
Brazil	6,731,000	233,576,000		a	73,594,000	a	1,425,094	190,894,000	2,463,700	12,000
British Isles	83,250,000		180,694,000	a		307,464,000	683,426	a		
Bulgaria	61,839,000	42,124,000	9,370,000	8,582,000	936,000	a	41,887	110,230,000	46,100	
Canada	551,390,000	6,956,000	404,309,000	13,994,000		70,097,000	112,735	60,296,000		
Chile	29,825,000	3,015,000	5,867,000	360,000	a	15,320,000	a	16,967,000		
China	700,000,000	242,809,000	a	a	2,252,000,000	a	400,000	941,034,000	2,354,000	
Colombia		a			a	a	47,040	a	17,900	
Cuba					a	a	2,726,000	56,130,000	a	
Denmark	6,980,000		62,694,000	9,645,000		51,440,000	270,064	a		
France	273,470,000	17,701,000	284,215,000	31,933,000	a	636,194,000	386,000	74,076,000		
Germany	246,257,000	a	472,455,000	372,221,000		2,411,088,000	3,782,000	96,231,000		
Greece	32,938,000	11,614,000	10,518,000	2,278,000		a	a	107,818,000	76,700	
Hungary	75,965,000	116,686,000	29,922,000	30,234,000		126,446,000	198,414	36,376,000		
India	402,603,000	74,960,000		a	1,633,091,000	a	5,560,369	1,094,240,000	4,841,000	12,000
Italy	268,226,000	135,071,000	39,318,000	5,998,000	41,185,000	113,000,000	611,776	92,814,000	69,200	
Japan	66,134,000	3,303,000	14,135,000	a	549,968,000	a	176,657	180,799,000	1,200	
Malay States						27,765,000				549,000
Mexico	13,337,000	66,158,000	a		5,222,000	a	330,400	50,706,000	288,000	
Netherlands	15,304,000		30,950,000	23,760,000		112,081,000	316,085	a		
Netherlands Indies						32,629,000			9,700	545,000
New Zealand	8,400,000	404,000	3,512,000	a		a	a	2,832,000		
Norway	2,530,000		10,946,000	215,000		41,482,000	a	a		
Paraguay					a	a	13,730	17,154,000	46,100	
Peru	3,858,000	a			4,762,000	a	504,000	a	382,900	
Poland	83,407,000	a	198,415,000	300,382,000		1,269,777,000	601,670	32,209,000		
Romania	89,295,000	200,800,000	31,349,000	6,791,000		51,405,000	201,000	35,715,000	8,500	
Soviet Union	1,520,169,000	105,900,000	1,170,505,000	881,289,000	a	1,738,138,000	2,910,000	a	3,000,000	
Spain	105,742,000	33,199,000	32,973,000	16,152,000	13,472,000	146,000,000	209,614	a	7,700	
Sweden	15,869,000		71,759,000	11,205,000		82,294,000	330,690	847,000		
Switzerland	6,063,000	150,000	3,582,000	1,287,000		32,341,000	16,534	2,734,000		
Union of South Africa	16,163,000	85,861,000	7,354,000	a		a	571,200	31,450,000	1,700	
Uruguay	7,055,000	6,023,000	1,240,000	a	980,000	a	a	1,113,000		
Yugoslavia	69,327,000	172,438,000	19,835,000	8,311,000	150,000	70,179,000	126,764	45,856,000	6,900	
United States	816,698,000	2,449,200,000	1,235,628,000	40,601,000	52,754,000	397,722,000	2,220,000	1,451,966,000	12,566,000	
Other Countries	117,510,000	627,601,000	137,949,000	149,059,000	2,506,108,000	121,986,000	8,157,649	843,244,000	3,793,900	189,000
World Total	6,067,000,000	5,054,000,000	4,576,000,000	*1,945,000,000	7,200,000,000	7,960,000,000	34,714,000	5,630,000,000	30,230,000	1,411,000

*Excluding China.   a Figures not available.

WORLD MINERAL PRODUCTION

Country	Gold (fine ounces)	Silver (fine ounces)	Iron Ore (metric tons)	Petroleum (barrels)	Tin (long tons)	Lead (metric tons)	Copper (metric tons)	Zinc (metric tons)	Coal (metric tons)	Bauxite (metric tons)
Argentina	12,249	3,242,200		20,486,000	1,600	14,000		17,700	72,363	17,461	
Australia	1,628,777	14,955,905	2,617,039		3,500	275,000	81,460	185,700	29,847	1,000
Belgium			180,920			82,000				
Bolivia		5,626,380			110,000	37,923		14		20,000
Brazil	318,935	24,694	255,548							
British Isles	2,428	70,818	12,049,531		1,800	10,000	37	50,440	236,700	
Bulgaria	200	13,000	20,115				320			
Burma	1,209	6,175,000		7,979,000	5,500	77,220	3,600			
Canada	5,322,857	23,815,715		8,955,000		172,880	317,000	159,338	15,923	
Chile	341,000	1,515,563	1,749,840				337,021			
Colombia	631,900	260,310		26,067,000						
France	87,354	565,000	33,137,000	496,000		42,000	600	60,262	51,000	700,000
Germany	8,650	7,010,000	15,375,208	4,544,000		181,440	66,000	212,285	464,000	20,000
Greece		335,000								50,000
Hungary	5,079	46,632				147	336		10,625	700,000
India	289,000	22,745	3,116,087			38,102	1,000	33,566	28,214	15,000
Italy	5,016	812,481				10,200		33,566		530,000
Japan	836,000	10,100,000		2,639,000	1,700	10,200	104,000	45,500	41,912	
Malay States	36,174	3,500	1,873,875		85,384					63,787
Netherlands								20,534	13,058	
Netherlands Indies	81,183	618,026		60,830,000	44,447		94			274,345
Peru	288,167	18,450,250		13,427,000		37,072	33,584			
Poland		62,244								
Romania	130,760	500,204		43,231,000		5,100				40,000
Soviet Union	5,236,000	8,022,000	26,529,700	212,909,000		55,000	144,000	65,000	132,888	300,000
Spain	a	600,000	2,900,000		110	27,000	30,000	11,340		
Sweden	197,995	1,122,865	13,787,202				9,610			
Switzerland	1,447									
Union of South Africa	14,047,000	1,292,000	638,757			11	17,963		17,176	
Uruguay	1,762									
Venezuela	146,792			184,761,000						
Yugoslavia	33,662	2,293,634				10,652	42,951	6,025		150,000
United States	4,862,979	68,286,535	74,878,718	1,351,847,000	44	468,675	922,369	630,740	403,229	445,958
Other Countries	7,007,855	118,261,549	25,890,470	279,734,000	50,692	303,501	528,341	225,907	87,967	2,016,910
World Total	41,560,000	275,654,000	215,000,000	2,149,378,000	231,700	1,810,000	2,658,000	1,800,000	1,550,000	4,627,000

Descriptive Facts About the U. S. States

State	Topography	Soil	Climate Average Temperature, Average Annual Rainfall	Principal Agricultural Products	Principal Mineral Products	Principal Forest and Fisheries Products	Principal Manufactures
Alabama	Mountainous in the north and northeast. Southward the land gradually slopes to sea level.	North—red clays and dark loams; central—lime and marls; south—sandy.	South tempered by Gulf of Mexico; north by mountains. Temp.: Jan. 50°; July 80°. Rainfall: 62 in.	Cotton, corn, peanuts, vegetables, sweet potatoes, fruits, tobacco, nuts.	Coal and coke, iron, clay, cement, stone, bauxite, graphite, lime.	Yellow pine and southern hardwood lumber. Gum naval stores.	Cotton goods, lumber and wood products, iron and steel products, fertilizers, machinery, cottonseed products, clothing.
Arizona	South—high plains with scattered mountains Plateaus and rough mountains in north.	Sandy and gravelly loams. Valleys fertile.	Dry and clear. Temp. Jan. 50°; July 90°. Rainfall: 7.9 in.	Grains, hay, cotton, potatoes, citrus fruits, dates, olives, livestock.	Copper, gold, silver, lead, zinc, gypsum, stone, mercury, tungsten, antimony, molybdenum.	Western yellow pine.	Lumber and wood products, refined metals, flour and grist, chemicals, cottonseed products, packed meat.
Arkansas	Mountainous toward northwest. River valley in east and central.	Silty loams and clays in valleys. Uplands and mountains—heavy loams.	Decidedly mild. Temp. Jan. 41°; July 81°. Rainfall: 49.9 in.	Cotton, rice, grains, fruits, general farm crops.	Petroleum, natural gas and gasoline, coal, bauxite, manganese, mercury, stone, zinc.	Yellow pine, white oak, hickory, walnut, and ash.	Machinery, lumber and wood products, refined metals, refined petroleum, beverages, cottonseed products.
California	Traversed by two parallel mountain systems with valley between.	Clays, sands, and sandy loams. Lava and volcanic ash in north.	Mild along Pacific. Hot and dry in interior. Temp. Jan. 56°; July 63°. Rainfall: 22.3 in.	Citrus and other fruits, nuts, grains, sugar beets, flaxseed, rice, olives, vegetables, nursery products, poultry, dairy products.	Crude oil, gold, platinum, mercury, borax, magnesite, cement, chromite, copper, natural gas, tungsten, antimony, gypsum, potash.	Sequoias, Douglas and white fir, oak, cedar, pine. Deep-sea fisheries.	Lumber and wood products, packed meat, canned foods, refined metals, refined sugar, motion pictures, aircraft, motor vehicles, refined petroleum.
Colorado	East—Great Plains. West—Colorado Plateau of the Rockies with high mountains.	Detritus soils in east Sandy loams along rivers. Sandy and gravelly loams on bench lands.	Great daily and annual range of temperature. Temp. Jan. 29°; July 72°. Rainfall: 14 in.	Grains, sugar beets, hay, fruits, potatoes, livestock.	Gold, silver, coal, lead, zinc, copper, natural gas, tungsten, molybdenum, uranium, vanadium.	Yellow and lodge-pole pine, spruce, hemlock, cedar, poplar, cottonwood.	Refined sugar, packed meat, foundry products, refined metals, flour, lumber, machinery.
Connecticut	Rolling mountains, with small valleys. Low coastal plateau. Connecticut Valley in central part.	Lower slopes chiefly glacial till; level portions are loamy.	Healthful and varied. Temp. Jan. 27°; July 72°. Rainfall: 47.2 in.	Corn, hay, tobacco, vegetables, fruits and nuts, nursery products, dairy products, poultry.	Stone, clay products, sand and gravel, lime.	Cod, flounders, menhaden, lobsters, oysters.	Textiles, firearms, hardware, clocks and watches, pottery, cutlery, tools, woolen goods, rubber goods, brass products.
Delaware	North—rugged and hilly. South—great plain with meandering rivers.	Soils of north are very fertile; fine clays toward south.	Very mild, with abundance of rainfall. Temp. Jan. 33°; July 77°. Rainfall: 43.2 in.	Grains, forage, fruits, berries, vegetables, poultry and dairy products.	Clays, stone, sand and gravel.	Oysters, sturgeon, and deep sea fish.	Leather, paper and pulp, boats, textiles, clothing, chemicals, iron and steel products, machinery.
Florida	Low and flat, with high central ridge. Sand reefs and islands along coast. Swamp area in southeast.	Deep mucky soils in south. Sands and sandy loams in north.	Mild and equable, almost sub tropical. Temp. Jan. 69°; July 84°. Rainfall: 38.7 in.	Citrus and other fruits, tobacco, vegetables, peanuts, sugar cane.	Phosphate rock, Fuller's earth, cement, stone and gravel, lime.	Yellow pine and cypress. Gum naval stores. Mullet, shad, red snapper, mackerel, oysters, sponges.	Tobacco products, fertilizers, lumber and wood products, canned foods, paper.
Georgia	Piedmont section across north-central. Northwest and north are mountains. Coastal Plain toward southeast.	Red loams and clays in east; sandy and silty loams in west. Heavy soils along coast.	Varies considerably, with hot summers. Humidity high on coast. Temp. Jan. 42°; July 78°. Rainfall: 49.4 in.	Cotton, grains, sweet potatoes, peanuts, fruits and nuts, tobacco, mules.	Iron, manganese, bauxite, barite, lime, stone, clays, cement, Fullers earth, graphite, mica.	Yellow pine, cypress, oak, yellow poplar. Gum naval stores.	Textiles, cottonseed products, tobacco products, fertilizers, lumber and wood products, foundry products.
Idaho	Southwest—plateau plains bounded by mountains. East—Rocky Mountains.	Range from fine silty loams on plateaus to rocky and mineral soils in mountains.	Great extremes. Temp. Jan. 29°; July 73°. Rainfall: 12.7 in.	Hay and forage, wheat, vegetables, sugar beets, fruit, potatoes, livestock, dairy products.	Lead and zinc, gold, silver, copper, phosphate rock, antimony, tungsten, stone, mercury.	White pine, larch, cedar, white fir, yellow pine.	Lumber and wood products, flour and grist, refined sugar, metal products.
Illinois	Broad plain, undulating and ridged in north. Hilly in extreme south.	Brown and silty loams, with alluvial soils in stream channels. Soils in general are rich.	Great extremes; tempered by Lake Michigan in north. Temp. Jan. 24°; July 73°. Rainfall: 33.3 in.	Soybeans, grains, hay and forage, vegetables, nursery products, fruit, livestock, dairy products.	Coal and coke, petroleum, natural gas, zinc, lead, stone, cement, fluorspar, Fuller's earth.	Sycamore, walnut, tupelo, yellow poplar, pine, cedar, oak, ash, elm, maple, hickory, sweet gum.	Packed meat, processed food, transportation equipment, chemicals, machinery, metal products, printing and publishing, clothing.
Indiana	Undulating to rolling prairie. Sand hills in north; rocky in south. Well drained.	Drift deposits; peat and muck southeast of Lake; loess in lower portion.	Unusually equable. Temp. Jan. 28°; July 76°. Rainfall: 41.5 in.	Grains, soybeans, hay and forage, vegetables, tobacco, fruit, livestock.	Coal and coke, petroleum, gas, Portland cement, building stone, clays.	Oak, walnut, and other hardwoods.	Packed meat, refined petroleum, automobiles, glass, machinery, steel products, chemicals, electrical goods.
Iowa	Lies in prairie table-land of Mississippi. Undulating to rolling.	Deep, fertile, well supplied with organic matter.	Great extremes of heat and cold; dry winter and wet summer. Temp. Jan. 18°; July 75°. Rainfall: 34 in.	Corn and other grains, hay, vegetables, flaxseed, soybeans, nursery products, livestock, dairy products, poultry.	Coal, cement, clays, gypsum, limestone, sandstone.		Packed meat, corn products, flour and grist mill products, machinery, laundry equipment.
Kansas	Undulating plain, rising toward west, interspersed with rugged hills and ridges.	Dark rich loams.	Great extremes of heat and cold, with dry atmosphere. Temp. Jan. 30°; July 79°. Rainfall: 30.6 in.	Wheat and other grains, hay and forage, sorghum, flaxseed, fruits, livestock, dairy products.	Petroleum, natural gas and gasoline, coal, lead, zinc, limestone, salt, cement, clay.		Packed meat, flour and grist mill products, refined petroleum, iron and steel products, chemicals, clothing.
Kentucky	West—fairly level. Central—undulating. East—mountainous and rough.	Range from fine silty loams to heavy and stony loams; extremely fertile.	Mild and even. Temp. Jan. 34°; July 79°. Rainfall: 44.3 in.	Corn and other grains, hay, tobacco, potatoes, livestock.	Coal, petroleum, natural gas and gasoline, clays, zinc, lead, fluorspar, stone.	Oak, maple, beech, walnut, ash, pine, cedar.	Flour, tobacco products, distilled liquors, packed meat, refined petroleum, chemicals, iron and steel products.
Louisiana	Uplands in north; alluvial and swamp regions along river and coast.	Fine, sandy and silty loams, with clays in Coastal Plain.	Semi tropical and equable. Temp. Jan. 53°; July 81°. Rainfall: 57.4 in.	Cotton, sugar cane, rice, corn, forage crops, sweet potatoes, fruits, livestock.	Petroleum, natural gas, gasoline, salt, sulfur, cement, sand and gravel, stone.	Longleaf pine, cypress, oak, poplar, red gum, tupelo, ash, hickory. Shrimps, oysters.	Refined sugar, lumber and wood products, refined petroleum, cottonseed products, paper and pulp, chemicals.
Maine	Rugged, dissected by numerous stream valleys. Coast fringed with promontories and rocky islands.	Mostly glacial drift. Along rivers soil is very productive.	Summers pleasant but winters very cold. Temp. Jan. 22°; July 68°. Rainfall: 42.5 in.	Potatoes, hay and forage, fruits, grains, vegetables, dairy products.	Granite, limestone, clay, slate, cement, sand and gravel, feldspar.	Pulpwood. Herring, lobster, clams, cod, haddock, salmon, smelt, mackerel.	Paper and pulp, lumber and wood products, textiles, machinery, boots and shoes, canned foods.
Maryland	Eastern and southern—low, level plain; central and north—hilly; western—mountainous.	Range from clays to sands and sandy loans.	East and south—winters mild and summers hot; west—winters cold and summers cool. Temp. Jan. 33°; July 77°. Rainfall: 43.2 in.	Fruits, vegetables, grains and field crops, tobacco, dairy products, poultry.	Coal, building stone, sand and gravel, cement, clay products, potash, lime.	Yellow pine, cypress, spruce, white pine, hemlock, beech, maple, cedar, red gum. Oysters, shad, bass, perch.	Clothing, textiles, tinware, iron and steel products, tobacco products, packed meat, canned foods, fertilizers, chemicals.
Massachusetts	Low coast plain; east and west—highlands; central—Connecticut Valley.	Finely textured along streams; sandy and gravelly in uplands.	Along coast climate is mild, but in highlands winters are long and severe. Temp. Jan. 27°; July 71°. Rainfall: 43.4 in.	Truck garden products, grains, cranberries, tobacco, dairy products.	Stone, sand and gravel, lime, clay products.	Cod, haddock, mackerel, halibut, lobster, shell fish.	Boots and shoes, textiles, hardware, machinery, food products, tools, chemicals, rubber products, paper, leather.
Michigan	Upper—undulating, rugged in west, swampy in north. Lower—generally rolling.	Sandy loams to dark clays in Lower Peninsula. Upper—thin in northwest; other portions rich.	Lower Peninsula tempered by Great Lakes; cold and uniform in Upper. Temp. Jan. 24°; July 72°. Rainfall: 32.2 in.	Grains, apples, peaches, small fruits, hay and forage, potatoes, vegetables, sugar beets, maple sugar.	Iron, copper, cement, limestone, petroleum and gas, magnesium, gypsum, bromine, manganese, lime, salt, coal, coke.	Jackpine, aspen, hardwoods. Whitefish, perch, smelt.	Automobiles and parts, lumber, furniture, food products, foundry and machine-shop products, drugs, aircraft, paper, electrical goods.
Minnesota	Rolling prairies in southern and central portion; worn down mountain range in north.	Silty loams in unglaciated portion; red clays and clay loams near Lakes; Red River Valley—black clay loams; north—sand and gravel.	Severe winter cold modified by dryness. Temp. Jan. 12°; July 72°. Rainfall: 28.7 in.	Wheat, corn, and other grains, hay and forage, potatoes, flax, vegetables, nursery products, fruits and nuts, livestock, dairy products.	Iron ore, manganese, stone, sand, gravel, clay.	White pine, spruce, birch, larch, cottonwood, balsam. Lake trout, whitefish, herring.	Flour, lumber and wood products, packed meat, machinery, chemicals, iron and steel products, foundry products.
Mississippi	Rolling to hilly, sloping gently to south and west. Much lies in Yazoo-Mississippi Delta.	Alluvial and silty loams in Delta; sands, sandy loams, silty loams, and heavy clays in remainder.	Mild and equable in south, extremes increasing toward north. Temp. Jan. 47°; July 80°. Rainfall: 53.7 in.	Cotton, corn, sweet potatoes, vegetables, hay and forage, fruits and nuts, peanuts.	Clay, petroleum, natural gas, gravel, glass sand.	Yellow pine, oak, red gum, cottonwood, cypress, poplar, hickory, ash. Gum naval stores. Oysters, shrimps.	Cottonseed products, lumber and wood products, canned fish, textiles, stone, clay, and glass products, beverages, clothing.
Missouri	South and southwest—Ozark uplift; southeast—low, swampy; northwest—prairie land.	North—silty, with brown and yellow loams; Ozarks—stony; Bottoms—loess deposits.	Considerable variation, due to altitude. Temp. Jan. 31°; July 79°. Rainfall: 37.2 in.	Grains, soybeans, hay and forage, vegetables, fruits, nuts, cotton, hogs, beef and dairy cattle, horses, sheep, mules.	Lead, zinc, coal, iron, cement, mineral paints, clays, stone, lime.	Oak, yellow pine, gum, tupelo, elm, cottonwood, walnut, sycamore, cypress.	Packed meat, boots and shoes, flour and grist mill products, drugs, chemicals, malt liquors, clothing, tobacco, metal products.
Montana	Rockies cover western third; remainder consists of plateaus and undulating plains.	Mountain valleys contain dark-colored silts and gravelly loams.	Dry and healthful. Temp. Jan. 20°; July 67°. Rainfall: 12.8 in.	Sheep, cattle, horses, swine, hay and forage, wheat and other grains, fruits, vegetables, flax, potatoes, sugar beets, wool.	Copper, silver, gold, zinc, platinum, gypsum, coal, petroleum, lead, manganese, tungsten, natural gas.	White pine, larch, cedar, yellow pine, Douglas fir, spruce, lodgepole pine, balsam, hemlock.	Refined and smelted copper, lumber, flour, refined sugar, packed meat, refined petroleum.
Nebraska	Undulating to rolling, sloping gradually to east. Low sand hills in north-central; buttes and foothills in west.	Fertile silty loams, with rich, black, vegetable top soil. Grazing lands in sandy region.	Severe winters and warm summers; dry climate. Temp. Jan. 20°; July 76°. Rainfall: 30.7 in.	Corn, barley, and other grains, potatoes, vegetables, sugar beets, apples, livestock, dairy products.	Clay products, cement, pumice stone, gravel, sand.		Packed meat and poultry, drugs, flour, machinery, metal products.

266

Descriptive Facts about the U. S. States

State	Topography	Soil	Climate Average Temperature, Average Annual Rainfall	Principal Agricultural Products	Principal Mineral Products	Principal Forest and Fisheries Products	Principal Manufactures
Nevada	Great elevated table-land, bounded on west and east by mountain ranges.	Sand and gravel loams prevail, with clay in lake basins, and alkaline sands in southern deserts.	Excessively dry and great daily and annual range in temperature. Temp. Jan. 29°; July 72°. Rainfall: 8.4 in.	Hay and forage, grains, truck garden, fruits, livestock, dairy products.	Gold, silver, lead, zinc, copper, stone, mercury, antimony, tungsten, borax, gypsum, graphite.	Small stands of pine.	Refined copper and other metals, cut stone, packed meat, planing mill products.
New Hampshire	Surface broken by mountain ridges, culminating in White Mountains in north.	Rough and rocky in uplands; deep alluvial deposits in bottomlands.	Considerable variation between sections: winters in general severe and summers cool. Temp. Jan. 21°; July 69°. Rainfall: 40.1 in.	Vegetables, fruits, hay, corn, oats, dairy products.	Granite and other stone, mica, clay products, sand and gravel, feldspar.	Spruce, pine, hemlock, birch, balsam.	Textiles, boots and shoes, lumber and wood products, clay and stone products, machinery, paper.
New Jersey	Southern half—low coastal plain; northwest—rugged; inland—highlands.	Red loams and clays in northwest; shales, limestone, and trap rock in highlands.	Tempered by ocean along coast; extremes in higher altitudes. Temp. Jan. 32°; July 72°. Rainfall: 40.8 in.	Potatoes, vegetables, grains, cranberries, fruits, hay, dairy products, market gardening.	Building stone, clay products, sand and gravel, iron ore, lime, zinc ore.	Oysters, clams, trout, seabass, cod, bluefish.	Refined petroleum, textiles, plastics, machinery, tobacco products, chemicals, jewelry, pottery, refined metals.
New Mexico	Plateau region in north and northwest, broken by Rockies; table-land, arid, toward southeast.	Range from sandy and gravelly material to heavy loams in river valleys.	Dry atmosphere, making extremes less severe. Temp. Jan. 28°; July 69°. Rainfall: 14.5 in.	Hay and forage, grains, vegetables, fruits, nuts, broom corn, sorghum, livestock.	Coal, copper, gold, silver, zinc, lead, petroleum, natural gas, manganese ore, potash.	Western yellow pine, spruce, red fir, ash, scrub oak, cedar, cottonwood, sycamore, walnut.	Refined ores, cottonseed products, lumber.
New York	Rolling plateau, culminating in east in Catskills and north in Adirondacks.	Stony and shale loams in uplands; clays and sandy loams in valleys and gentler slopes.	Frequent hot and cold waves cause variability. Summer in north pleasant. Temp. Jan. 30°; July 74°. Rainfall: 44.6 in.	Hay and forage, potatoes, vegetables, grains, nursery products, maple syrup, fruits, dairy products, poultry.	Clays, iron ore, salt, petroleum, natural gas, cement, graphite gypsum, slate, talc, zinc, aluminum, coke.	Spruce, balsam, hemlock, white pine, maple, birch.	Clothing, printing and publishing, textiles, tobacco products, packed meat, iron and steel products, machine shop products, footwear.
North Carolina	Coastal Plain in eastern third; Piedmont section in central; Appalachians in extreme west.	Silty and sandy loams along coast; gray or yellow sandy soils in Piedmonts; clays in mountains.	Varies with altitude; subtropical in south. Temp. Jan. 40°; July 79°. Rainfall: 49.2 in.	Cotton, grains, tobacco, vegetables, peanuts, sweet potatoes, fruits, swine, cattle, mules, horses.	Mica, silver, gold, copper, talc, stone, clay products, bromine, sand and gravel, aluminum.	Pine, oak, spruce, hemlock, chestnut, yellow poplar, cedar, tupelo, basswood. Shad, oysters, mullet, alewives, clams, black bass.	Textiles, clothing, hosiery, tobacco products, lumber and wood products, fertilizers, furniture.
North Dakota	East—low, level plain. Central—glaciated plateau. West—residual prairies.	Dark clays and clay loams in Red River Valley. Remainder fine to stony loams.	Uniform over entire state, extremes mitigated by dry atmosphere. Temp. Jan. 7°; July 70°. Rainfall: 17.6 in.	Wheat, rye, and other grains, hay and forage, vegetables, flaxseed, dairy products, poultry.	Coal and lignite, building stone, natural gas, clays, sand and gravel.		Flour and grist mill products, tanned leather, packed meat, concrete products.
Ohio	Undulating, rising from plain in northwest to Plateau in northeast.	Range from silty loams to dark, mucky soils, interspersed with sandy and stony soils.	Modified in north by Lake Erie; generally uniform. Temp. Jan. 32°; July 78°. Rainfall: 38.3 in.	Grains, vegetables, tobacco, maple syrup, fruits, nursery products, soybeans, livestock, poultry	Coal and coke, petroleum, natural gas, stone, cement, lime, salt, clays.	White oak, walnut, beech, maple, yellow poplar, elm, ash, hickory, basswood, sycamore. Lake fisheries.	Iron and steel products, refined petroleum, rubber products, machinery, chemicals, tobacco products, transportation equipment, pottery.
Oklahoma	East is mountainous, succeeded to west by rolling prairies and high plains. In extreme north, west, and south are rugged mountains.	Clay, sandy, and gravelly loams.	Warm and dry, with very hot summers. Temp. Jan. 35°; July 80°. Rainfall: 31.7 in.	Wheat and other grains, forage, broom corn, sorghum, cotton, peanuts, pecans, fruits, livestock, poultry, dairy products.	Petroleum, natural gas and gasoline, zinc, lead, coal, clays, gypsum.	Pine, cottonwood, elm, walnut, hickory, cedar, tupelo, oak, ash.	Refined petroleum, flour and grist mill products, refined metals.
Oregon	Bisected by Cascade Range and Coast Range, between which is the Willamette River Valley.	Fine loams and clays in east. Lava and volcanic ash in southwest. Alluvial deposits on coast.	Humid, mild, and uniform along coast; great ranges toward east. Temp. Jan. 39°; July 66°. Rainfall: 45.1 in.	Grains, flax, hay and forage, fruits, nuts, vegetables, hops, horses, cattle, sheep, swine.	Gold, silver, copper, cement, chromite, stone, platinum, mercury, sand and gravel.	Western yellow pine, spruce, hemlock, cedar, larch, fir. Salmon, sturgeon, halibut, oysters, cod, smelt, herring, carp.	Lumber and wood products, paper, flour, canned foods, woolen goods, clothing, iron and steel products.
Pennsylvania	Five regions—Atlantic Coastal Plain; Piedmont district; Appalachian Mountains; Allegheny Plateau; Glacial Plain along Lake Erie.	Clays, clay loams, sandy loams, silts, and stony mixtures.	Southeast—mild and equable; central—extremes; northwest—uniform. Temp. Jan. 32°; July 76°. Rainfall: 41.2 in.	Grains hay, vegetables, fruits, nuts, potatoes, maple sugar, tobacco, livestock, nursery products.	Coal and coke, oil, natural gas, iron, building stone, slate, glass-sand, cement, lime.	Oak, chestnut, and other northern hardwoods.	Blast furnace products, iron and steel products, glass, textiles, refined petroleum, tobacco products, electrical equipment, transportation equipment.
Rhode Island	Composed of 3 divisions: Narragansett Basin, glaciated highlands and Block Island.	Silty, sandy, and gravelly loams in east; uplands, coarse and stony soils.	Generally mild, with small range. Temp. Jan. 31°; July 68°. Rainfall: 44.4 in.	Dairy products, poultry, truck farm products, nursery stock.	Building stone, clays, lime, sand and gravel.	Lobster, mackerel, herring, bluefish, scup.	Textiles, jewelry, refined gold and silver, machinery, iron and steel products, rubber products, woolens.
South Carolina	Coastal Plain occupies three-fifths of state; remainder Blue Ridge Mountains and Piedmont Plateau.	Coast soils are alluvial; fine sands and loams inland; sandy surface soil in Piedmonts	Tempered by ocean; subtropical in character. Temp. Jan. 49°; July 81°. Rainfall: 52.1 in.	Cotton, grains, tobacco, vegetables, hay and forage, fruits.	Stone, clays, mica, gold, silver, sand and gravel.	Pine, hardwoods. Gum naval stores. Shad, sea bass, oysters, clams, shrimp, terrapin, mullet, jewfish, channel bass.	Cotton and rayon goods, textiles, lumber and wood products, cottonseed products, fertilizers, paper, canned foods.
South Dakota	High level plateau, with Bad Lands in the southwest, followed by Black Hills region.	Prairie regions—brown and yellow silt and loams; west—sandy loams and clays.	Summers hot and winters long and cold, but dry. Temp. Jan. 14°; July 75°. Rainfall: 16.6 in.	Wheat, rye, barley and other grains, flaxseed, vegetables, livestock, dairy products, poultry.	Gold, silver, stone, cement mica, tin, natural gas, sand and gravel.	Yellow pine, spruce.	Flour and grist mill products, packed meat, wood products, stone, clay, and glass products.
Tennessee	West—Low Gulf Coastal plain; central—Highland Rim and Limestone Basin; east—Cumberland Plateau and Appalachians.	Heavy loams and clays along rivers; silty and clay loams in central; stony soils in mountains.	Very agreeable climate. Temp. Jan. 38°; July 79°. Rainfall: 48.5 in.	Grains, cotton, hay and forage, vegetables, tobacco, fruits, nuts, dairy products.	Coal, copper, iron ore, phosphate rock, zinc, petroleum, silver, gold, lead, manganese, stone, cement, clays, aluminum.	Oak, gum, yellow poplar, pine, hemlock, chestnut, cypress, ash, hickory, elm, maple.	Wood products, flour, textiles, hosiery, footwear, iron and steel products, chemicals, tobacco products, clothing, refined metals.
Texas	Western part is mountainous, prairie region in central part; low in Gulf portion.	Range from fine silty loams to sands, sandy loams and gravels.	Warm and moist along the coast; hot and dry toward north and west. Temp. Jan. 53°; July 83°. Rainfall: 47.1 in.	Cotton, grains, peanuts, hay and forage, vegetables, broom corn, sorghum, rice, citrus and other fruits, nuts, cattle, goats, sheep, mules, wool.	Petroleum, natural gas, gasoline, helium, asphalt, sulfur, cement, clays, sand and gravel, stone, lime, Fuller's earth, coal, mercury, silver, copper.	Yellow pine, oak, sweet gum, cypress, hickory, ash. Oysters, shrimps, squeteague, red snapper, redfish.	Refined petroleum, cottonseed products, flour, packed meat, lumber and wood products, oil-field machinery.
Utah	East—plateau broken by deep valleys; west—great level desert plain. Wasatch Mountains in central part.	East—sandy and gravelly loams; poor, sandy to desert land in west; alluvial deposits in plateau region.	Great diversity due to high altitudes and deep valleys. Temp. Jan. 29°; July 76°. Rainfall: 16.0 in.	Hay and forage, grains, sugar beets, potatoes, fruits, sheep and other livestock, dairy products.	Silver, coal, copper, gold, lead, zinc, uranium, vanadium, asphalt, clays, gypsum, lime, molybdenum, natural gas, stone	Yellow pine.	Refined and smelted metals, refined sugar, packed meat, flour, petroleum and coal products, iron and steel products.
Vermont	Plateau-upland, dissected by Green Mountains, Tacoma Range, and Granitic Mountains	Formed by glacial drift, largely clays, sand, and gravel.	Winters long and severe; summers cool. Temp. Jan. 16°; July 68°. Rainfall: 31.6 in.	Hay and forage, vegetables, grains, nursery products, maple syrup, fruits, farm animals, dairy products.	Building and monumental stone, slate, talc, asbestos, lime.	Spruce, hemlock, white pine, hardwoods.	Marble and stone products, lumber products, machine tools, textiles, paper, clothing.
Virginia	Coastal Plain merges west into Piedmont Plateau, followed by Blue Ridge Mountains and Great Limestone valley.	Soils vary from clays, loams, and sand in lowlands to sandstones and shales in mountains.	Equable along coast, diminishing inland. Temp. Jan. 40°; July 78°. Rainfall: 49.5 in.	Grains, vegetables, tobacco, hay and forage, peanuts, fruits, nuts, livestock.	Coal, stone, iron, slate, gypsum, gold, lead, bauxite, zinc, manganese, mica, clay products, lime, sand and gravel, stone, mineral waters.	Yellow pine, oak, chestnut, gum, hemlock, hickory, walnut, cypress, poplar, cedar. Oysters, menhaden, shad, clams, crabs, squeteague, alewives.	Lumber and wood products, tobacco products, paper, furniture, textiles, fertilizers, clothing, machinery.
Washington	Cascade Mountains in middle, with Coast Range on west undulating in the east.	Glacial till in north; fine loams and clays in east; alluvial deposits along coast.	Equable along coast, becoming more extreme in mountains. Temp. Jan. 39°; July 64°. Rainfall: 36.5 in.	Wheat and other grains, hay and forage, vegetables, hops, fruits, livestock, dairy products	Coal, gold, silver, copper, lead, zinc, lime, clays, building stone, iron, cement, sand and gravel, tungsten, aluminum.	Fir, yellow and white pine, hemlock, spruce, larch, cedar. Salmon, halibut, shad, cod, mackerel, herring, oysters, shrimps.	Lumber and wood products, flour, canned fish and fruit, packed meat, paper and pulp, tinware.
West Virginia	Greater portion in Allegheny Plateau; east—limestone valleys.	Fertile alluvial soils in Valley; clay and sand loams in Plateau.	Considerable variations due to altitude. Temp. Jan. 31°; July 76°. Rainfall: 40.2 in.	Grains, hay and forage, vegetables, fruits, nuts, tobacco, cattle.	Coal and coke, petroleum, natural gas and gasoline, iron, stone, salt, clays, lime, sand and gravel.	Oak, chestnut, hemlock, maple, yellow poplar, spruce, beech, basswood, birch, hickory, ash, walnut.	Lumber and wood products, glass and glass products, iron and steel products, pottery, chemicals, metal products.
Wisconsin	Southwest—rough and dissected; remainder rolling to level glaciated plateau.	Glacial till in northern portion; silty loams in south and along lakes.	Long, cold winters and short, warm summers. Temp. Jan. 20°; July 70°. Rainfall: 31.4 in.	Grains, hay, vegetables, tobacco, peas, potatoes, cranberries, fruits, dairy products.	Iron, zinc, lead, clays, paint minerals, stone, lime, sand and gravel, cement.	Hemlock, white pine, spruce, cedar, maple, beech, birch, basswood, elm. Whitefish, lake trout, smelt.	Lumber and wood products, canned foods, packed meat, motor vehicles, leather, heavy machinery, malt liquors, paper.
Wyoming	Elevated plateau, traversed north-south by Rocky Mountains.	Alluvial deposits from mountain streams.	Great daily and annual ranges. Temp. Jan. 26°; July 67°. Rainfall: 13.6 in.	Sheep, cattle, horses, grains, potatoes, sugar beets, hay and forage, dairy products, wool.	Petroleum, coal, natural gas and gasoline, clay, gold, iron, silver, stone, gypsum.	Lodgepole pine, Western yellow and white pine, spruce, hemlock.	Lumber and wood products, stone, clay, and glass products, packed meats, refined petroleum.

Interesting and Historical Facts of each State of the United States

State	Capital	Nickname	First Permanent Settlement	When Settled	By Whom Settled	Admitted As a Territory	Admitted As a State
Alabama	Montgomery	Cotton	Mobile Bay	1702	French	March 8, 1817	Dec. 14, 1819
Arizona	Phoenix	Sunset	Tucson	1692	Spaniards	Feb. 24, 1863	Feb. 14, 1912
Arkansas	Little Rock	Bear	Arkansas Post	1685	French	July 4, 1819	June 15, 1836
California	Sacramento	Golden	San Diego	1769	Spaniards		Sept. 9, 1850
Colorado	Denver	Centennial	Denver	1858	Americans	Feb. 28, 1861	Aug. 1, 1876
Connecticut*	Hartford	Nutmeg	Windsor	1633	Puritans		Jan. 9, 1788
Delaware*	Dover	Blue Hen	Cape Henlopen	1627	Swedes		Dec. 7, 1787
Dist. of Columbia	Washington			1660	English	July 16, 1790	†March 3, 1791
Florida	Tallahassee	Peninsula	St. Augustine	1565	Spaniards	March 30, 1822	March 3, 1845
Georgia*	Atlanta	Cracker	Savannah	1733	English		Jan. 2, 1788
Idaho	Boise	Gem	Franklin	1860	Americans	March 3, 1863	July 3, 1890
Illinois	Springfield	Sucker	Cahokia	1699	French	March 1, 1809	Dec. 3, 1818
Indiana	Indianapolis	Hoosier	Vincennes	1732	French	May 7, 1800	Dec. 11, 1816
Iowa	Des Moines	Hawkeye	Dubuque	1788	French	July 3, 1838	Dec. 28, 1846
Kansas	Topeka	Sunflower	Fort Leavenworth	1827	Americans	May 30, 1854	Jan. 29, 1861
Kentucky	Frankfort	Blue Grass	Harrodsburg	1774	Americans		June 1, 1792
Louisiana	Baton Rouge	Pelican	Ft. Iberville	1699	French	March 3, 1805	April 30, 1812
Maine	Augusta	Pine Tree	Saco	1630	English		March 15, 1820
Maryland*	Annapolis	Old Line	Kent Island	1631	English		April 28, 1788
Massachusetts*	Boston	Bay	Plymouth	1620	Pilgrims		Feb. 6, 1788
Michigan	Lansing	Wolverine	Sault Ste. Marie	1668	French	June 30, 1805	Jan. 26, 1837
Minnesota	St. Paul	Gopher	Grand Portage	1731	French	March 3, 1849	May 11, 1858
Mississippi	Jackson	Bayou	Biloxi Bay	1699	French	April 7, 1798	Dec. 10, 1817
Missouri	Jefferson City	Show Me	Ste. Genevieve	1735	French	June 4, 1812	Aug. 10, 1821
Montana	Helena	Stub Toe	Big Horn River	1807	Americans	May 26, 1864	Nov. 8, 1889
Nebraska	Lincoln	Cornhusker	Bellevue	1805	Americans	May 30, 1854	March 1, 1867
Nevada	Carson City	Silver	Carson River (Genoa)	1849	Americans	March 2, 1861	Oct. 31, 1864
New Hampshire*	Concord	Granite	Rye	1623	Puritans		June 21, 1788
New Jersey*	Trenton	Jersey Blue	Bergen	1617	Swedes		Dec. 18, 1787
New Mexico	Santa Fe	Cactus	Santa Fe	1609	Spaniards	Dec. 13, 1850	Jan. 6, 1912
New York*	Albany	Empire	Manhattan Isl.	1613	Dutch		July 26, 1788
North Carolina*	Raleigh	Old North	Albemarle	1660	English		Nov. 21, 1789
North Dakota	Bismarck	Flickertail	Fort Clark	1808	Americans	March 2, 1861	Nov. 2, 1889
Ohio	Columbus	Buckeye	Marietta	1788	Americans	May 7, 1800	March 1, 1803
Oklahoma	Oklahoma City	Sooner	Salina	1796	French	May 2, 1890	Nov. 16, 1907
Oregon	Salem	Beaver	Astoria	1811	Americans	Aug. 14, 1848	Feb. 14, 1859
Pennsylvania*	Harrisburg	Keystone	Delaware River	1625	Swedes		Dec. 12, 1787
Rhode Island*	Providence	Little Rhody	Providence	1636	English		May 29, 1790
South Carolina*	Columbia	Palmetto	Ashley River	1670	English		May 23, 1788
South Dakota	Pierre	Sunshine	Bad River	1817	Americans	March 2, 1861	Nov. 2, 1889
Tennessee	Nashville	Big Bend	Fort Loudon	1756	English		June 1, 1796
Texas	Austin	Lone Star	Ysleta	1682	Spanish		Dec. 29, 1845
Utah	Salt Lake City	Deseret	Salt Lake City	1847	Americans	Sept. 9, 1850	Jan. 4, 1896
Vermont*	Montpelier	Green Mountain	Fort Dummer	1724	English		March 4, 1791
Virginia*	Richmond	Old Dominion	Jamestown	1607	English		June 25, 1788
Washington	Olympia	Evergreen	Tumwater	1845	Americans	March 2, 1853	Nov. 11, 1889
West Virginia	Charleston	Panhandle	Bunker Hill	1726	English		June 20, 1863
Wisconsin	Madison	Badger	Green Bay	1669	French	July 3, 1836	May 29, 1848
Wyoming	Cheyenne	Equality	Fort Laramie	1834	Americans	July 25, 1868	July 10, 1890

†District.　　*One of the Thirteen Original States.

Interesting and Historical Facts of Each State of the United States

STATE	MOTTO	FLOWER	Extreme Length N & S (Miles)	Extreme Width E & W (Miles)	ALTITUDE (Feet) Highest	Lowest	TEMPERATURE Jan. Mean	July Mean	Max. Annual	Min. Annual	Annual Rainfall Inches
Alabama	Here We Rest	Goldenrod	330	200	2,407	sea level	50	80	102	-1	62.0
Arizona	Ditat Deus	Saguero Cactus	390	335	12,611	100	50	90	119	12	7.9
Arkansas	Regnat Populus	Apple Blossom	240	275	2,800	55	41	81	106	-12	49.9
California	Eureka	Golden Poppy	800	375	14,495	b 276	56	63	101	-29	22.3
Colorado	Nil Sine Numine	Columbine	270	380	14,420	3,350	29	72	105	-29	14.0
Connecticut	Qui Transtulit Sustinet	Mountain Laurel	75	90	2,355	sea level	27	72	100	-14	47.2
Delaware	Liberty and Independence	Peach Blossom	95	35	440	sea level	33	77	105	-7	43.2
Dist. of Columbia	Justitia Omnibus	American Beauty Rose	15	15	420	sea level	33	77	106	-15	43.5
Florida	In God We Trust	Orange Blossom	460	400	325	sea level	69	84	100	41	38.7
Georgia	Wisdom, Justice, Moderation	Cherokee Rose	315	250	4,784	sea level	42	78	100	-8	49.4
Idaho	Esto Perpetua	Syringa	490	305	12,078	720	29	73	111	-28	12.7
Illinois	State Sovereignty—National Union	Violet	380	205	1,241	279	24	72	103	-23	33.3
Indiana	Our Liberties We Prize, and Our Rights We Will Maintain	Zinnia	265	160	1,240	316	28	76	106	-25	41.5
Iowa		Wild Rose	205	310	1,600	477	18	75	106	-32	34.0
Kansas	Ad Astra per Aspera	Sunflower	205	410	4,135	700	30	79	107	-22	30.6
Kentucky	United We Stand, Divided We Fall	Goldenrod	175	350	4,150	257	34	79	107	-20	44.3
Louisiana	Union, Justice and Confidence	Magnolia	275	300	400	sea level	53	81	102	7	57.4
Maine	Dirigo	Pine Cone and Tassel	310	210	5,268	sea level	22	68	103	-21	42.5
Maryland	Scuto Bonae Voluntatis Tuae Coronasti Nos	Blackeyed Susan	120	200	3,340	sea level	33	77	105	-7	43.2
Massachusetts	Ense Petit Placidam Sub Libertate Quietem	Mayflower	110	190	3,491	sea level	27	71	104	-14	43.4
Michigan	Si Quaeris Peninsulam Amoenam Circumspice	Apple Blossom	400	310	2,023	572	24	72	104	-24	32.2
Minnesota	L'Etoile du Nord	Moccasin Flower	400	350	1,920	602	12	72	104	-41	28.7
Mississippi	Virtute et Armis	Magnolia	340	180	780	sea level	47	80	101	-1	53.7
Missouri	Salus Populi Suprema Lex Esto	Hawthorn	280	300	1,800	230	31	79	107	-22	37.2
Montana	Oro y Plata	Bitter Root	315	570	12,850	1800	20	67	103	-42	12.8
Nebraska	Equality Before the Law	Goldenrod	210	415	5,340	825	20	76	110	-32	30.7
Nevada	All For Our Country	Sagebrush	485	315	13,145	470	29	72	104	-28	8.4
New Hampshire		Purple Lilac	185	90	6,288	sea level	21	69	102	-35	40.1
New Jersey	Liberty and Prosperity	Violet	166	70	1,805	sea level	32	72	104	-7	40.8
New Mexico	Crescit Eundo	Yucca	390	350	13,306	2,876	28	69	97	-13	14.5
New York	Excelsior	Rose	310	330	5,344	sea level	30	74	102	-13	44.6
North Carolina	Esse Quam Videri		200	520	6,711	sea level	40	79	102	-5	49.2
North Dakota	Liberty and Union, Now and Forever, One and Inseparable	Wild Prairie Rose	210	360	3,468	790	7	70	107	-45	17.6
Ohio	Imperium in Imperio	Scarlet Carnation	230	205	1,550	425	32	78	105	-17	38.3
Oklahoma	Labor Omnia Vincit	Redbud	210	460	4,800	300	35	80	108	-17	31.7
Oregon	Alis Volat Propriis	Oregon Grape	290	375	11,245	sea level	39	66	102	-2	45.1
Pennsylvania	Virtue, Liberty, and Independence	Mountain Laurel	180	310	3,213	sea level	32	76	106	-6	41.2
Rhode Island	Hope	Violet	50	35	812	sea level	31	68	92	-6	44.4
South Carolina	Dum Spiro, Spero	Jessamine	215	285	3,548	sea level	49	81	104	7	52.1
South Dakota	Under God the People Rule	Pasque Flower	240	360	7,242	962	14	75	110	-40	16.6
Tennessee	Agriculture, Commerce	Iris	120	430	7,025	182	38	79	104	-13	48.5
Texas	Friendship	Bluebonnet	710	760	8,700	sea level	53	83	99	8	47.1
Utah	Industry	Sego Lily	345	275	13,498	2,000	29	76	102	-20	16.0
Vermont	Freedom and Unity	Red Clover	155	90	4,393	95	16	68	100	-28	31.6
Virginia	Sic Semper Tyrannis	Dogwood	205	425	5,720	sea level	40	78	105	2	49.5
Washington	Alki	Rhododendron	230	340	14,408	sea level	39	64	96	11	36.5
West Virginia	Montani Semper Liberi	Rhododendron	200	225	4,860	240	31	76	106	-27	40.2
Wisconsin	Forward	Violet	300	290	1,940	581	20	70	102	-25	31.4
Wyoming	Cedant Arma Togae	Indian Paintbrush	275	365	13,785	3,100	16	67	100	-38	13.6
United States	E Pluribus Unum		1,600	2,780	14,495	b 276					

b Below sea level.   — Below zero.

2

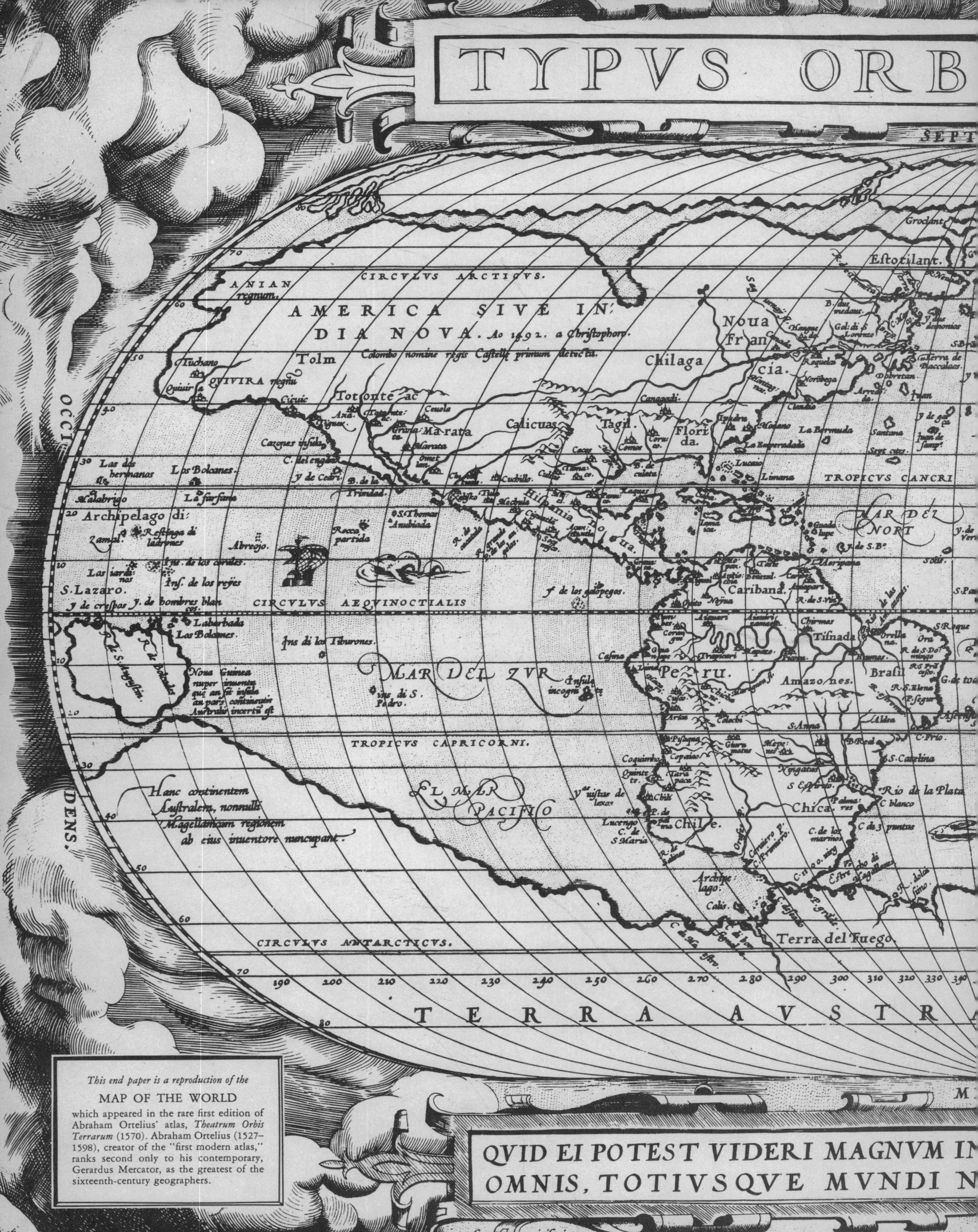

TYPVS ORB

SEPT

CIRCVLVS ARCTICVS.

ANIAN regnum.

AMERICA SIVE INDIA NOVA. Ao 1492. a Christophoro.

Colombo nomine regis Castellæ primum detecta.

Groclant.

Estotilant.

Noua Fran cia.

Chilaga

Tuchano — Tolm
Quiuir la — QVIVIRA regnu
Cicuic — Totonte ac
Cazones insulæ — Grana Marata
C. del engaño — Marata
y de Cedri — Calicuas — Tagil — Flori da.
Malabrigo — La sal sanaa
Archipelago di — B. de la Trinidad.
Zamal — R. restinga di ladrones
Abreojo. — Rocca partida
Ins. de los corales — S. Thomas Anubiada
Las iardi nas — Ins. de los reyes
S. Lazaro. — y de hombres blan cos.
y de crespos — Labarbada — Las Boloanes.
Ins di los Tiburones
Noua Guinea nuper inuenta quæ an sit insula an pars continentis Australis incertū est — MAR DEL ZVR — Ins di S. Pedro. — Insulæ incognitæ

TROPICVS CANCRI

MAR DEL NORT

Caribana.

Peru.

Amazones.

Brasil.

CIRCVLVS AEQVINOCTIALIS

f de los galapegos

TROPICVS CAPRICORNI.

EL MAR PACIFICO

Hanc continentem Australem, nonnulli Magellanicam regionem ab eius inuentore nuncupant.

Coquimbo
Chile.
Chica.

Rio de la Plata

CIRCVLVS ANTARCTICVS.

Archie lago.

Terra del Fuego

OCCI DENS.

190 200 210 220 230 240 250 260 270 280 290 300 310 320 330 34

80

TERRA AVSTR

This end paper is a reproduction of the

MAP OF THE WORLD

which appeared in the rare first edition of Abraham Ortelius' atlas, *Theatrum Orbis Terrarum* (1570). Abraham Ortelius (1527–1598), creator of the "first modern atlas," ranks second only to his contemporary, Gerardus Mercator, as the greatest of the sixteenth-century geographers.

QVID EI POTEST VIDERI MAGNVM I
OMNIS, TOTIVSQVE MVNDI N

Cum priuilegio.